October 21–25, 2013
Barcelona, Spain

Association for
Computing Machinery

Advancing Computing as a Science & Profession

MM'13 Vol. 2 of 2

Proceedings of the
2013 ACM Multimedia Conference

Sponsored by:

ACM SIGMM

Supported by:

FXPAL, HUAWEI, technicolor, YAHOO! LABS, Google, Springer, Microsoft Research, facebook, Telefonica, IBM Research, NSF, University of Trento, Universitat Pompeu Fabra, Inria, and MEDIA MIXER

Association for
Computing Machinery

Advancing Computing as a Science & Profession

The Association for Computing Machinery
2 Penn Plaza, Suite 701
New York, New York 10121-0701

ISBN: 978-1-4503-2404-5 (Digital)

ISBN: 978-1-4503-2692-6 (Print)

Additional copies may be ordered prepaid from:

ACM Order Department
PO Box 30777
New York, NY 10087-0777, USA

Phone: 1-800-342-6626 (USA and Canada)
+1-212-626-0500 (Global)
Fax: +1-212-944-1318
E-mail: acmhelp@acm.org
Hours of Operation: 8:30 am – 4:30 pm ET

Printed in the USA

Message from the General Chairs

We are delighted to welcome you to the 21st ACM International Conference on Multimedia, ACM Multimedia 2013, which will be held from October 21th to October 25th, 2013 in Barcelona, Spain.

Barcelona was founded on the Mediterranean coast, between two rivers, over 2,000 years ago. Since then, it has been the traditional gateway to Spain. Through it entered Romans, Arabs and Christians, as well as the many diverse cultures, which came to enrich its heritage. The traces of this history and diversity can be followed as you walk through the city; through its Gothic Quarter, built on the Roman ruins; through its art-nouveau Eixample district, presided over by Gaudí's exuberant architecture, which at the same time reveals an ordered and rational urban layout. This diversity and harmony are also apparent in the character of the people of Barcelona, who are enterprising and hard-working, enjoy life and, in particular, have great civic pride and are lovers of culture.

These "multimedia" characteristics have made Barcelona into a first-class tourist destination and the ideal setting for meetings and congresses. This open, welcoming city, which shed its skin and opened up to the sea in order to host the 1992 Olympic Games, has since then focused its energies on another major global project: the 2004 Forum of Cultures. This event, the renewed expression of Barcelona's vocation to be an international benchmark for meetings and dialogue, has made it possible to complete the city's seafront, and improve significantly its range of services in the field of congresses, hotels and catering and culture. In a nutshell, Barcelona is the perfect venue for ACM Multimedia and we hope you will enjoy Barcelona as much as its inhabitants do it every single day!

ACM Multimedia is the premier conference and worldwide event bringing together multimedia experts and practitioners across academia and industry. The central feature of the conference, which continues this year as in every year since its inception, is the outstanding Technical Program. This year's conference features both oral and poster presentations covering all aspects of the multimedia field chosen through a highly selective review process.

In addition to the Technical Program, this year's conference features a diverse range of activities including Panels, Demonstrations, and Tutorials. Additionally, a wide array of Workshops brings focus on new topics for investigation. The conference features also special sessions on Brave New Ideas, a Grand Challenge contest and Open Source Software Competition and includes a Doctoral Symposium for mentoring graduate students. Finally, the conference provides a rich Multimedia Art Exhibition to stimulate artists and researchers alike to meet and discover the frontiers of multimedia artistic communication!

Innovations for this Year's Conference:

In attempt to continuously improve ACM Multimedia and ensure its vibrant role for the multimedia community, we have made a number of enhancements for this year's conference:

- The Technical Program Committee defined twelve Technical Areas for major focus for this year's conference, including introducing new Technical Areas for Music & Audio and Crowdsourcing to reflect their growing interest and promise. We have also changed the names of some traditional Technical Areas and provided extensive description of each area to help the authors choosing the most appropriate Technical Area for their manuscripts.

- We have introduced a new role in the organization of the conference: the author's advocate. His explicit role was to listen to the authors, and to help them if reviews are clearly below average quality. The authors could request the mediation of the author's advocate after the reviews have been sent to them and they had to clearly justify the reasons why such mediation is needed (the reviews or the meta-review were below average quality). The task of the advocate was to investigate carefully the matter and to request additional review or reexamination of the decision of the particular manuscript. This year, the author's advocate was Pablo Cesar, CWI, The Netherlands.
- We have decided to keep a couple of plenary sessions which will bring singular focus to conference activities: keynotes, Multimedia Grand Challenge competition, Best Paper session, Technical Achievement Award and Best PhD Award sessions. The other technical sessions are held in parallel to allow pursuit of more specialized interests at the conference. We have limited the number of parallel sessions to no more than 3 to minimize the risk of having overlapping interests.
- Workshops and Tutorials are held on separate days from the main conference in order to reduce conflict with the regular Technical Program.
- The Multimedia Art Exhibition features both invited and selected artists. It will be open for the duration of the conference in the satellite venue located in the center of the city.
- Following the last two years' precedent, Tutorials are made free for all participants.
- Recognizing that students are the lifeblood of our next generation of multimedia thinkers, this year's Student Travel Grant is greatly expanded.

We hope these innovations make for a special conference this year.

We greatly acknowledge those who have contributed to the success of ACM Multimedia 2013. We thank the many paper authors and proposal contributors for the various technical and program components. We thank the large number of volunteers, including the Organizing Committee members and Technical Program Committee members who worked very hard to create this year's outstanding conference. Every aspect of the conference was also aided by local committee members and by the hard work of Grupo Pacifico, to whom we are very grateful. We thank also ACM staff and Sheridan Communications for their constant support.

Finally, we thank our many supporters who generously supported ACM Multimedia 2013. They include FXPAL, HUAWEI, YAHOO! LABS, Technicolor, MediaMixer, Microsoft Research, Facebook, IBM Research, Telefonica, Google, and INRIA. Other generous support was kindly provided by SIGMM, Springer, and NSF.

ACM Multimedia 2013 General Chairs

Alejandro Jaimes
Yahoo Labs, Spain

Nicu Sebe
University of Trento, Italy

Nozha Boujemaa
INRIA, France

Message from the Technical Program Chairs

Benvinguts a Barcelona! We are excited to introduce the Technical Program of the *ACM International Conference on Multimedia 2013*. This year, we built upon the guidelines from previous editions of the conference and introduced several new procedures and policies with the goal of improving the quality of the review process, the feedback provided to the authors, and the overall diversity of the technical program.

As in the last couple of years, the conference review process was structured with a two-tier Technical Program Committee. Following a discussion process that involved the General Chairs and the Program Chairs, we revised and expanded the list of areas from last year's conference and defined 12 areas for 2013 to bring topic diversity and growth to the conference: Art, Entertainment and Culture; Authoring and Collaboration; Crowdsourcing; Media Transport and Delivery; Mobile and Multi-Device; Multimedia Analysis; Multimedia HCI; Music and Audio; Search, Browsing, and Discovery; Security and Forensics; Social Media and Presence; and Systems and Middleware.

The Technical Program Committee was first created by appointing Area Chairs (ACs). A total of 29 colleagues agreed to serve in this role. Each Area was represented by two ACs, with exception of two Areas (Multimedia Analysis and Search, Browsing, and Discovery) whose scope has traditionally attracted the largest proportion of papers and so required further coordination. The added topic diversity brought an increase in gender diversity to the ACs, which increased from approximately 12% in previous years to 22% for 2013. We also made a conscious effort to bring new talent and excellence into the community and to better represent emerging trends in the field. For this we appointed many young and well recognized ACs who served in this role for the first time. For each junior AC, we co-appointed a senior researcher as their co-AC to aid in their shepherding. In a second step, the Area Chairs were responsible for appointing the TPC members (reviewers) for their coordinated areas. This was a large effort to grow the TPC base for the conference as well as ensure proper expertise was represented in each area. We coupled this with a hard goal of limiting the number of submissions assigned to each TPC member for review. For example, two years ago, the average number of papers assigned to a reviewer was 9 with over 38% of the approximately 225 TPC members receiving 10 or more papers to review. With our design, we had a total of 398 reviewers receiving an average of 4.13 papers per reviewer. While we were unable to keep a hard ceiling limitation, only 2.51% of the TPC received 10 or more papers to review—all TPC members who had agreed to serve in more than one area. The Area Chairs were in charge of assigning all papers for review, and each submission was reviewed double-blind by three TPC members. Reviews and reviewer assignments of papers co-authored by Area Chairs, Program Chairs, and General Chairs were handled by Program Chairs who had no conflicts of interest for each specific case.

Another novelty introduced in the reviewing process was to set the paper submission deadline to a significantly earlier date than previous years, in order to allocate more time for reviews, rebuttals, discussions, and final decisions. Despite the reduced time given to authors, the response to the Call for Papers was enthusiastic with a total of 235 long papers and 278 short papers going through review.

The authors of long papers were asked to write a rebuttal after receiving the reviews. A new element in the reviewing process was the introduction of the Author's Advocate figure, created to provide authors with an independent channel to express concerns about the quality of the reviews for their papers, and to raise a flag about these reviews. All cases were brought to the attention to the corresponding Area Chair. After evaluating each case reported to him (16 reviews out of 761 long paper reviews), the Author's Advocate recommended in 5 cases that new reviews were generated and added to the discussion. The reviewers had a period for on-line discussion of reviews and rebuttals, after which the Area Chairs drafted a meta-review for each paper.

Decisions on long and short papers were made at the TPC meeting held at the University of Amsterdam on June 11, 2013. The meeting was physically attended by one of the General Chairs, three of the Program Chairs, the Author's Advocate, and 86% of the ACs. Many of the ACs who were unable to attend were tele-present online for discussions. On the first half day of the TPC meeting, the Area Chairs worked in breakout sessions to discuss the papers that were weak accepts and weak rejects, with the exception of conflict of interest papers which were handled out of band as previously mentioned. In the second half of the first day, the ACs met in a plenary session where they reviewed the clear accepts and defended the decisions on the borderline papers based on the papers themselves, reviews, meta-reviews, on-line discussions, and authors' rebuttal comments. In many cases, an emergency reviewer was added if there was clear intersection with a related submission area. If a paper had any conflict of interest during the plenary session with an Area, Program, or General Chair, they were excused from the room. On June 12, 2013, the Program Chairs finalized the process and conference program in a separate meeting—arranging the sessions by thematic narratives and not by submission area to promote cross-area conversations during the conference itself.

The review process resulted in an overall acceptance rate of 20.0% for long papers and 27.7% for short papers. All accepted long papers were shepherded by the Area Chairs themselves or by qualified TPC members who were in charge of verifying that the revised papers adequately addressed concerns raised by the reviewers and changes promised by authors in their rebuttals. This step ensured that all of the accepted papers are of the highest quality possible. In addition, four papers with high review scores were nominated at the TPC meeting as candidates for the Best Paper Award. Each nominated paper had to be successfully championed and defended by the ACs from that area. The winner will be announced at the Conference Banquet.

The Technical Program of ACM Multimedia would not have been possible without the research of the MM community of authors and the commitment of all the members of the TPC. It is now our turn to sincerely thank all of them for their participation, rigorous work, and engagement.

We hope you enjoy the program!

David A. Shamma
Program Co-Chair
Yahoo Labs, USA

Marcel Worring
Program Co-Chair
Univ. of Amsterdam
The Netherlands

Roger Zimmermann
Program Co-Chair
Nat. Univ. of Singapore
Singapore

Daniel Gatica-Perez
Program Co-Chair
Idiap and EPFL
Switzerland

Pablo Cesar
Author's Advocate
CWI
The Netherlands

Table of Contents

Session Order 7: Brave New Topics: Social and Cognitive Aspects

Session Order 8: Action and Event Recognition

Session Order 9: Streaming and Synchronization

Session Order 10: Keynote Address

Session Chair: Nozha Boujemaa *(INRIA)*

Session Order 11: Multimedia Grand Challenge

Session Chairs: Yiannis Kompatsiaris *(CERTH)*
Neil O'Hare *(Yahoo!)*

Session Order 12: Demos

Session Chairs: Xavier Anguera *(Telefonica)*
Yi Yang *(CMU)*

Volume 2

Session Order 13: Posters 2

Session Order 14: Security and Forensics

Session Chair: Rita Cucchiara *(University of Modena and Reggio Emilia)*

Session Order 15: Open Source Software

Session Chairs: Yiannis Patras *(Queen Maqry, University of London)*
Andrea Vedaldi *(University of Oxford)*

MM 2013 Conference Organization

General Chairs: Alejandro (Alex) Jaimes *(Yahoo Labs, Spain)*
Nicu Sebe *(University of Trento, Italy)*
Nozha Boujemaa *(INRIA, France)*

Program Chairs: Daniel Gatica-Perez *(IDIAP & EPFL, Switzerland)*
David A. Shamma *(Yahoo Labs, USA)*
Marcel Worring *(University of Amsterdam, The Netherlands)*
Roger Zimmermann *(National University of Singapore, Singapore)*

Author's Advocate: Pablo Cesar *(CWI, The Netherlands)*

Multimedia Grand Challenge Chair: Yiannis Kompatsiaris *(CERTH, Greece)*
Neil O'Hare *(Yahoo Labs, Spain)*

Interactive Arts Chairs: Antonio Camurri *(University of Genova, Italy)*
Marc Cavazza *(University of Teesside, UK)*

Local Arrangements Chair: Mari-Carmen *Marcos (University Pompeu Fabra, Spain)*

Sponsorship Chairs: Ricardo Baeza-Yates *(Yahoo Labs, Spain)*
Bernard Merialdo *(Eurecom, France)*

Panel Chairs: Yong Rui *(Microsoft, China)*
Winston Hsu *(National Tawain University, Taiwan)*
Michael Lew *(University of Leiden, The Netherlands)*

Brave New Ideas Chairs: Jiebo Luo *(University of Rochester, USA)*
Shuicheng Yan *(National University of Singapore, Singapore)*

Doctorial Symposium Chairs: Hayley *Hung (Technical University of Delft, The Netherlands)*
Marco Cristani *(University of Verona, Italy)*

Open Source Software Competition Chairs: Ioannis (Yiannis) Patras *(Queen Mary, University of London, UK)*
Andrea Vedaldi *(Oxford University, UK)*

Tutorial Chairs: Kiyoharu Aizawa *(University of Tokyo, Japan)*
Lexing Xie *(Australian National University, Australia)*

Workshop Chairs: Maja Pantic *(Imperial College, UK)*
Vladimir Pavlovic *(Rutgers University, USA)*

Student Travel Grants Chairs: Ramanathan Subramanian *(ADSC, Singapore)*
Jasper Uijlings *(University of Trento, Italy)*

Publicity Chairs: Marco Bertini *(University of Florence, Italy)*
Ichiro Ide *(Nagoya University, Japan)*

Technical Demo Chairs: Yi Yang *(Carnegie Mellon University, USA)*
Xavier Anguera *(Telefonica Research, Spain)*

Proceedings Chairs: Bogdan Ionescu *(University Politehnica of Bucharest, Romania)*
Qi Tian *(University of Texas San Antonio, USA)*

Web & Social Media Chair: Michele Trevisol *(Yahoo Labs, Spain)*

History Preservation Chairs: Selcuk Candan *(Arizona State University, USA)*
Noboru Babaguchi *(Osaka University, Japan)*

MM 2013 Area Chairs

Frank Bentley *(Yahoo! Research, USA)*
Antonio Camurri *(University of Genova, Italy)*
Marc Cavazza *(University of Teesside, UK)*
Munmun De Choudhury *(Microsoft Research, USA)*
Matthew Cooper *(FXPAL, USA)*
Rita Cucchiara *(University of Modena, Italy)*
Pascal Frossard *(EPFL, Switzerland)*
Mohamed Hefeeda *(Simon Fraser University, Canada)*
Winston Hsu *(NTU, Taiwan)*
Jochen Huber *(MIT, USA)*
Dhiraj Joshi *(FXPAL, USA)*
Aisling Kelliher *(CMU, USA)*
Lyndon Kennedy *(Yahoo! Research, USA)*
Hyoung Joong Kim *(Korea University, Korea)*
Martha Larson *(TU Delft, The Netherlands)*
Cynthia Liem *(TU Delft, The Netherlands)*
Rainer Lienhart *(University of Augsburg, Germany)*
Tao Mei *(Microsoft Research Asia, China)*
Max Mühlhäuser *(TU Darmstadt, Germany)*
Wei Tsang Ooi *(NUS, Singapore)*
Bryan Pardo *(Northwestern Ubiversity, USA)*
Alan Smeaton *(Dublin City University, Ireland)*
Raphael Troncy *(EURECOM, France)*
Wanmin Wu *(Ricoh, USA)*
Shuicheng Yan *(NUS, Singapore)*
Zheng-Jun Zha *(NUS, Singapore)*
Lei Zhang *(Tsinghua University, China)*
Michael Zink *(University of Massachusetts, Amherst, USA)*
Roelof van Zwol *(Netflix, USA)*

MM 2013 Technical Program Committee

Maha Abdallah *(University of Paris 6, France)*
Dewan Ahmed *(University of Ottawa, Canada)*
Luca Maria Aiello *(Yahoo! Research, Spain)*
Kevin Almeroth *(University of California, Santa Barbara, USA)*
Maria Teresa Andrade *(University of Porto, Portugal)*
Oya Aran *(IDIAP, Switzerland)*
Grenville Armitage *(Swinburne University of Technology, Australia)*
Olivier Aubert *(University Claude Bernard Lyon, France)*
Yannis Avrithis *(National Technical University of Athens, Greece)*
Brian Bailey *(University of Illinois, USA)*
Santosh Basapur *(Motorola Mobility Inc., USA)*
Christian Bauckhage *(University of Bonn, Germany)*
Ali Begen *(Cisco Systems, Inc., USA)*
Frank Bentley *(Motorola Labs, USA)*
Nadia Berthouze *(University College London, UK)*
Vijay Bharadwaj
Giulia Boato *(University of Trento, Italy)*
Susanne Boll *(Universität Oldenburg, Germany)*
Jan Borchers *(RWTH Aachen, Informatik 10, Germany)*
Laszlo Böszörmenyi *(University Klagenfurt, Austria)*
Alessandro Bozzon *(Delft University of Technology, The Netherlands)*
Francois Bremond *(INRIA, France)*
Dick C.A. Bulterman *(CWI, The Netherlands)*
Christoph Busch *(CAST-Forum, Germany)*
Daragh Byrne *(Arizona State University, USA)*
Rui Cai *(Microsoft Research Asia, China)*
Simone Calderara *(University of Modena, Italy)*
Liangliang Cao *(IBM Watson Research Center, USA)*
Axel Carlier *(University of Toulouse, France)*
Mark Cartwright *(Northwestern University, USA)*
Federico Casalegno *(MIT, USA)*
Marc Cavazza *(University of Teesside, UK)*
Pablo Cesar *(CWI, The Netherlands)*
Teresa Chambel *(University of Lisbon, Portugal)*
Antoni Chan *(City University of Hong Kong, Hong Kong)*
Gary Chan *(The Hong Kong University of Science and Technology, Hong Kong)*
Surendar Chandra *(Backup Recovery Systems, EMC, USA)*
Edward Chang *(Google Research, USA)*
Shi-Fu Chang *(Columbia University, USA)*
Vincent Charvillat *(University of Toulouse, France)*
Berlin Chen *(National Taiwan Normal University, Taiwan)*
Chang Wen Chen *(State University of New York at Buffalo, USA)*
Francine Chen *(FXPAL, USA)*
Huizhong Chen *(Stanford University, USA)*
Kuan-Ta Chen *(Academia Sinica, Taiwan)*
Songqing Chen *(George Mason University, USA)*
Tim Cheng *(Univ. of California, USA)*
Elaine Chew *(Queen Mary, University of London, UK)*
Liang-Tien Chia *(Nanyang Technological University, Singapore)*
Konstantinos Chorianopoulos *(Ionian University, Greece)*
Wei-Ta Chu *(National Chung Cheng University, Taiwan)*
Ching-Hua Chuan *(University of North Florida, USA)*
Yung-Yu Chuang *(National Taiwan University, Taiwan)*
Mark Claypool *(WPI, USA)*
Karin Coninx *(Hasselt University - EDM, Belgium)*
Matthew Cooper *(FX Palo Alto Lab, Inc., USA)*
Marco Cristani *(Università degli Studi di Verona, Italy)*
Rita Cucchiara *(University of Modena and Reggio Emilia, Italy)*
Walid Dabbous *(INRIA, France)*
Elizabeth M. Daly *(IBM Research, Ireland)*
Madirakshi Das *(Eastman Kodak Company, USA)*

Ritendra Datta *(Google, USA)*
Sushovan De *(Arizona State University, USA)*
Munmun De Choudhury *(Microsoft Research, USA)*
Giorgio De Michelis *(Univrsity of Milano - Bicocca, Italy)*
Giovanni De Poli *(University of Padova, Italy)*
Arjen de Vries *(CWI, The Netherlands)*
Alberto Del Bimbo *(Universita degli Studi di Firenze, Italy)*
David Demirdjian *(Toyota Research Institute, USA)*
Luigi Di Stefano *(University of Bologna, Italy)*
Christian Dittmar *(Fraunhofer IDMT, Germany)*
Ming Dong *(Wayne State University, USA)*
Tiziana D'Orazio *(ISSIA CNR, Italy)*
Lingyu Duan *(Peking University, China)*
Zhiyao Duan *(University of Rochester, USA)*
Isao Echizen *(Tokyo Institute of Technology, Japan)*
Alexander Eichhorn *(Simula, Norway)*
Dan Ellis *(Columbia University, USA)*
Aiman Erbad *(Qatar University, Qatar)*
Slim Essid *(Telecom ParisTech, France)*
Georg Essl *(University of Michigan, USA)*
Sebastian Ewert *(Queen Mary University, London, UK)*
Jianping Fan *(UNCC, USA)*
Morwaread Farbood *(New York University, USA)*
Sidney Fels *(University of British Columbia, Canada)*
Jiashi Feng *(National University of Singapore, Singapore)*
Wu-Chang Feng *(Portland State University, USA)*
Wu-Chi Feng *(Portland State University, USA)*
Rogerio Feris *(IBM T.J. Watson Research Center, USA)*
Rebecca Fiebrink *(Princeton University, USA)*
Frederic Fol Leymarie *(University of London, UK)*
Federico Fontana *(Universita degli Studi di Udine, Italy)*
Piero Fraternali *(Politecnico di Milano, Italy)*
Jason Freeman *(Georgia Institute of Technology, USA)*
Gerald Friedland *(International Computer Science Institute, USA)*
Pascal Frossard *(EPFL, Switzerland)*
Yun Fu *(Northeastern University, USA)*
Takuya Fujishima *(Yamaha Corp., Japan)*
Andrew Gallagher *(Cornell University, USA)*
Huiji Gao *(Arizona State University, USA)*
Lluis Garcia Pueyo *(Google, USA)*
Ravi Garg *(UMD, USA)*
Daniel Gatica-Perez *(Idiap and EPFL, Switzerland)*
Weina Ge *(GE Global Research, USA)*
David Geerts *(IBBT / K.U.Leuven, Belgium)*
Bo Geng *(Peking University, China)*
Andreas Girgensohn *(FX Palo Alto Laboratory, USA)*
Jordi Gonzalez *(Universitat Autònoma de Barcelona, France)*
Masataka Goto *(National Institute of Advanced Industrial Science and Technology (AIST), Japan)*
Valerie Gouet-Brunet *(IGN - Laboratoire MATIS, France)*
Fabien Gouyon *(INESC Porto, Portugal)*
Costantino Grana *(University of Modena and Reggio Emilia, Italy)*
Guillaume Gravier *(CNRS, IRISA, France)*
Carsten Griwodz *(University of Oslo, Norway)*
Peter Grosche *(Huawei European Research Center, Germany)*
Yang Guo *(Bell Labs, Alcatel-Lucent, USA)*
Michael Gurevich *(University of Michigan, USA)*
Aristotelis Hadjakos *(TU Darmstadt, Germany)*
Thomas Haenselmann *(Saarland Univerity, Germany)*
Pål Halvorsen *(University of Oslo & Simula, Norway)*
Raouf Hamzaoui *(De Montfort University, UK)*
Jinyu Han *(Northwestern University, USA)*
Mei Han *(Google Inc, USA)*
Alan Hanjalic *(Delft University of Technology, The Netherlands)*
Tatsuya Harada *(The University of Tokyo, Japan)*
Gunnar Harboe *(Motorola, Switzerland)*
Melanie Hartmann *(AGT International, Germany)*
Alex Hauptmann *(Carnegie Mellon University, USA)*
Jiyin He *(CWI, The Netherlands)*
Junfeng He *(Columbia University, USA)*

Mohamed Hefeeda *(Simon Fraser University, Canada)*
Hermann Hellwagner *(University of Klagenfurt, Austria)*
Tristan Henderson *(University of St Andrews, UK)*
Niels Henze *(University of Stuttgart, Germany)*
Jason Hockman *(McGill University, Canada)*
Steven C. H. Hoi *(Nanyang Technological University, Singapore)*
Lars Erik Holmquist *(Yahoo! Labs, USA)*
Henry Holtzman *(MIT Media Lab, USA)*
Richang Hong *(Hefei University of Technology, China)*
Cheng-Hsin Hsu *(National Tsing Hua University, Taiwan)*
Winston Hsu *(University of Taiwan, Taiwan)*
Ke Hu *(Kuzer Co., USA)*
Yuheng Hu *(Arizona State University, USA)*
Gang Hua *(Nokia Research Center Hollywood, USA)*
Xian-Sheng Hua *(Microsoft Research Asia, USA)*
Polly Huang *(NTU, EE, Taiwan)*
Jochen Huber *(SUTD & MIT Media Lab, Singapore & USA)*
Wolfgang Huerst *(Utrecht University, The Netherlands)*
Benoit Huet *(Eurecom, France)*
Hayley Hung *(Delft University of Technology, The Netherlands)*
Ichiro Ide *(Nagoya University, Japan)*
Christian Jacquemin *(LIMSI-CNRS, France)*
Giulio Jacucci *(Helsinki Institute for Information Technology, Finland)*
Sina Jafarpour *(Yahoo! Research, USA)*
Vidit Jain *(Yahoo! Labs, USA)*
Frankie James *(General Motors Research, USA)*
S. Jamin *(University of Michigan, Ann Arbor, USA)*
Rongrong Ji *(Columbia University, USA)*
Shen Jialie *(Singapore Management University, Singapore)*
Wei Jiang
Yu-Gang Jiang *(Fudan University, China)*
Ajita John *(Avaya Labs, USA)*
Alexis Joly *(INRIA, France)*
Gareth Jones *(Dublin City University, Ireland)*
Dhiraj Joshi *(FX Palo Alto Lab, Inc., USA)*
Chris Joslin *(Carleton University, Canada)*
Oskar Juhlin *(Interactive Institute, Sweden)*
Yannis Kalantidis *(National Technical University of Athens, Greece)*
Ton Kalker *(DTS, inc, USA)*
Mohan Kankanhalli *(National University of Singapore, Singapore)*
Ian Kegel *(BT Innovate, UK)*
John Kender *(Columbia University, USA)*
Lyndon Kennedy *(Yahoo! Research, USA)*
Hyoung Joong Kim *(Korea University, Republic of Korea)*
Gudrun Klinker *(Technische Universität München, Germany)*
Ben Knapp *(Virginia Tech, USA)*
Stephan Kopf *(Mannheim University, Germany)*
Pavel Korshunov *(École Polytechnique Fédérale de Lausanne, Switzerland)*
Adarsh Kowdle *(Cornell University, USA)*
Wessel Kraaij *(Radboud University Nijmegen, The Netherlands)*
Mritunjay Kumar
Shang-Hong Lai *(National Tsing Hua University, Taiwan)*
Rodrigo Laiola Guimaraes *(CWI, The Netherlands)*
Paul Lamere *(The Echo Nest, USA)*
Oswald Lanz *(FBK-irst, Italy)*
Martha Larson *(Delft University of Technology, The Netherlands)*
Rynson Lau *(City University of Hong Kong, Hong Kong)*
Matt Lease *(University of Texas at Austin, USA)*
Hyowon Lee *(Singapore University of Technology and Design, Singapore)*
Jin Ha Lee *(University of Washington, USA)*
Marc Leman *(Universiteit Gent, Belgium)*
Mark Levy
Baochun Li *(University of Toronto, Canada)*
Congcong Li *(Google, USA)*
Jia Li *(Yahoo! Research, USA)*
Jia Li *(The Pennsylvania State University, USA)*

Kang Li *(UGA, USA)*
Xirong Li *(Renmin University of China, China)*
Xuelong Li *(University of London, China)*
Zhiwei Li *(Microsoft Research Asia, China)*
Zhu Li *(Hong Kong Polytechnic University, USA)*
Chunyuan Liao *(FXPAL Palo Alto, USA)*
Cynthia Liem *(Delft University of Technology, The Netherlands)*
Rainer Lienhart *(Universitt Augsburg, Germany)*
Yu-Ru Lin *(Harvard/Northeastern Universities, USA)*
Dong Liu *(Columbia University, USA)*
Jiangchuan Liu *(Simon Fraser University, Canada)*
Qiong Liu *(FX Palo Alto Laboratory, USA)*
Wei Liu
Yong Liu *(Polytechnic Institute of NYU, USA)*
Zhu Liu *(AT&T, USA)*
Antoine Liutkus *(Grenoble Institute of Technology, France)*
Alexander Loui *(Eastman Kodak Labs, USA)*
Lie Lu
Yijuan Lu *(Texas State University, USA)*
Jiebo Luo *(University of Rochester, USA)*
Mathias Lux *(University of Klagenfurt, Austria)*
Nazanin Magharei
Erik Mannens *(Ghent University, Belgium)*
Ketan Mayer-Patel *(UNC, USA)*
Stephen McKenna *(University of Dundee, UK)*
Andrew McPherson *(Queen Mary, University of London, UK)*
Tao Mei *(Microsoft Research Asia, China)*
Bernard Merialdo *(EURECOM, France)*
Florian Metze *(Carnegie Mellon University, USA)*
Vasileios Mezaris *(Centre for Research and Technology Hellas, Greece)*
Christian Micheloni *(University of Udine, Italy)*
Krystian Mikolajczyk *(University of Surrey, UK)*
David R. Millen
Max Muehlhaeuser *(Technische Universitaet Darmstadt, Germany)*
Meinard Mueller
Philippe Mulhem *(LIG-CNRS, France)*
Vittorio Murino *(University of Verona, Italy)*
Phivos Mylonas *(National Technical University of Athens, Greece)*
Frank Nack *(University of Amsterdam, The Netherlands)*
Klara Nahrstedt *(University of Illinois, Urbana-Champaign, USA)*
Alok Nandi *(Architempo, Belgium)*
Arun Narayanan
Paolo Nesi *(University of Florence, DSI, Italy)*
Shawn Newsam *(University of California, Merced, USA)*
Chong-Wah Ngo *(City University of Hong Kong, Hong Kong)*
Eric Nichols *(Indiana University, USA)*
Laurence Nigay *(LIG- University of Grenoble, France)*
Naoko Nitta *(Osaka University, Japan)*
Lyndon Nixon *(STI International, Austria)*
Jasminko Novak *(European Institute for Participatory Media, Germany)*
Noel E. O Connor *(Dublin City University, Ireland)*
Jauvane Oliveira *(LNCC/MCT, Brazil)*
Nuria Oliver *(Telefonica Research, Spain)*
Wei Tsang Ooi *(National University of Singapore, Singapore)*
Vincent Oria *(NJIT, USA)*
Nicola Orio *(University of Padova, Italy)*
Max Ott *(NICTA, Australia)*
Daniel Overholt *(University of California, Santa Barbara, Denmark)*
Wei Pan *(MIT, USA)*
Minwoo Park *(Eastman Kodak Company, USA)*
Geoffroy Peeters *(Ircam, France)*
Catherine Pelachaud *(CNRS Telecom ParisTech, France)*
Nils Peters *(University of California, Berkeley, USA)*
Julien Pettre
Dinh Phung *(Deakin University, Australia)*
Massimo Piccardi *(University of Technology, Sydney, Australia)*
Maria Da Graça Pimentel *(Universidade de Sao Paulo, Brazil)*
Hamed Pirsiavash

Stefan Podlipnig *(University of Innsbruck, Austria)*
Fatih Porikli *(MERL, USA)*
Balakrishnan Prabhakaran *(University of Texas at Dallas, USA)*
Yannick Prié *(LINA - University of Nantes, France)*
Mu Qiao
Nicholas Race *(Lancaster University, UK)*
Zafar Rafii
Nitendra Rajput *(IBM Research, India Research Lab, India)*
Sanjay Rao *(Purdue University, USA)*
Nikhil Rasiwasia *(University of California San Diego, USA)*
Carlo Regazzoni *(University of Genova, Italy)*
Paolo Remagnino *(Kingstone University, UK)*
Mikel Rodriguez *(INRIA, France)*
Michael Rohs *(University of Hannover, Germany)*
Enrico Rukzio *(Ulm University, Germany)*
Lloyd Rutledge *(Open Universiteit Nederland, The Netherlands)*
Harald Sack *(Hasso-Plattner-Institut, Universität Potsdam, Germany)*
Alireza Sahami *(University of Stuttgart, Germany)*
Jitao Sang *(Chinese Academy of Science, China)*
Maria Luisa Sapino *(Universita degli Studi di Torino, Italy)*
Nabil Sarhan *(Wayne State University, USA)*
Shin'Ichi Satoh *(National Institute of Informatics, Japan)*
Markus Schedl *(Johannes Kepler University, Austria)*
Ansgar Scherp *(University of Koblenz-Landau, Germany)*
Klaus Schoeffmann *(Klagenfurt University, Austria)*
Bjoern Schuller *(Technical University Munich, Germany)*
Nicu Sebe *(University of Trento, Italy)*
Doree Seligmann *(Avaya Labs Research, USA)*
Subhabrata Sen *(AT&T Research, USA)*
Joan Serrà *(Spanish National Research Council, Spain)*
Nikitas Sgouros *(University of Piraeus, Greece)*
David A. Shamma *(Yahoo! Research, USA)*
Caifeng Shan *(Philips Research, The Netherlands)*
Heng Tao Shen *(University of Queensland, Australia)*
Shu Shi
Shervin Shirmohammadi *(University of Ottawa, Canada)*
Börkur Sigurbjörnsson
Vivek Singh *(Massachusetts Institute of Technology, USA)*
Malcolm Slaney *(Yahoo! Research, USA)*
Paris Smaragdis *(University of Illinois, Urbana-Champaign, USA)*
Arnold W. M. Smeulders *(University of Amsterdam, The Netherlands)*
John Smith *(IBM T.J. Watson Research Center, USA)*
Cees Snoek *(University of Amsterdam, The Netherlands)*
Mohammad Soleymani *(Imperial College London, UK)*
Ryan Spicer *(Arizona State University, USA)*
Jürgen Steimle *(MIT Media Lab, USA)*
Eckehard Steinbach *(TU München, Germany)*
Ralf Steinmetz *(TU Darmstadt, Germany)*
Hari Sundaram *(Arizona State University, USA)*
Marco Tagliasacchi *(Politecnico di Milano, Italy)*
Kartik Talamadupula *(Arizona State University, USA)*
John Tang *(Microsoft Research, USA)*
David Temperley *(University of Rochester, USA)*
Jelena Tesic *(Mayachitra, USA)*
Qi Tian *(The University of Texas at San Antonio, USA)*
Christian Timmerer *(Klagenfurt University, Austria)*
Steve Tjoa
Dian Tjondronegoro *(Queensland University of Technology, Australia)*
Giorgos Tolias *(National Technical University of Athens, Greece)*
Naoko Tosa *(Kyoto University, Japan)*
Raphael Troncy *(EURECOM, France)*
Joe Tullio *(Google, USA)*
George Tzanetakis *(University of Victoria, Canada)*
Yoshitaka Ushiku *(the University of Tokyo, Japan)*
Leon Van Noorden *(IPEM, University of Ghent, Belgium)*
Roelof van Zwol *(Netflix, USA)*

Nuno Vasconcelos *(UCSD, USA)*

Nalini Venkatasubramanian *(University of California Irvine, USA)*

Ruben Verborgh *(Ghent University, Belgium)*

Roberto Vezzani *(Università degli Studi di Modena e Reggio Emilia, Italy)*

Marie-Luce Viaud *(Institut National de Audiovisuel, France)*

Changhu Wang *(Microsoft Research Asia, China)*

Feng Wang *(The University of Mississippi, USA)*

Hua Wang *(Colorado School of Mines, USA)*

James Wang *(The Pennsylvania State University, USA)*

Jingdong Wang *(Microsoft Research Asia, China)*

Ju-Chiang Wang *(National Taiwan University, Taiwan)*

Jun Wang *(Columbia University, USA)*

Meng Wang *(AKiiRA Media Systems Inc., Singapore)*

Xin-Jing Wang *(Microsoft Research Asia, China)*

Ye Wang *(National University of Singapore, Singapore)*

Andrew M. Webb *(Texas A&M University, USA)*

Michael Weber *(University of Ulm, Germany)*

Robert Wechsler *(MotionComposer, Germany)*

Joerg Widmer *(Institute IMDEA Networks, Spain)*

Lynn Wilcox *(FX Palo Alto Laboratory, USA)*

Marcel Worring *(University of Amsterdam, The Netherlands)*

Fei Wu *(Zhejiang University, China)*

Wanmin Wu *(Ricoh, USA)*

Xiao Wu

Jiangjian Xiao

Lexing Xie *(Australian National University, Australia)*

Lingxi Xie *(Tsinghua University, China)*

Xing Xie *(Microsoft Research Asia, China)*

Changsheng Xu *(Institute of Automation, Chinese Academy of Sciences, China)*

Shuicheng Yan *(National University of Singapore, Singapore)*

Jianchao Yang

Jie Yang *(Carnegie Mellon University, USA)*

Linjun Yang *(Microsoft Research Asia, China)*

Ming Yang *(NEC laboratories America, USA)*

Xin Yang *(University of California, Santa Barbara, USA)*

Yi Yang *(Carnegie Mellon University, USA)*

Yi-Hsuan Yang *(Academia Sinica, Taiwan)*

Woon Seung Yeo *(KAIST, Republic of Korea)*

Jude Yew *(National University of Singapore, Singapore)*

Jie Yu

Meng Yu *(University of California, Irvine, USA)*

Xinnan Yu

Junsong Yuan *(Nanyang Technological University, Singapore)*

Eric Zavesky *(AT&T Research, USA)*

Zheng-Jun Zha *(National University of Singapore, Singapore)*

Jian Zhang

Lei Zhang *(Microsoft Research Asia, China)*

Zhengyou Zhang *(Microsoft, USA)*

Yan-Tao Zheng *(National University of Singapore, Singapore)*

Zhigang Zhu

Roger Zimmermann *(National University of Singapore, Singapore)*

Michael Zink *(University of Massachusetts, USA)*

Goranka Zoric *(Mobile Life @ Interactive Institute, Sweden)*

MM 2013 Brave New Topics Program Committee

Kiyoharu Aizawa *(The University of Tokyo, Japan)*
Dick Bulterman *(CWI, Netherlands)*
K. Selcuk Candan *(Arizona State University, USA)*
Tat-Seng Chua *(National University of Singapore, Singapore)*
Jianping Fan *(UNCC, USA)*
Alan Hanjalic *(Delft University of Technology, The Netherlands)*
Qingmin Huang *(Chinese Academy of Sciences, China)*
Benoit Huet *(Eurecom, France)*
Jiebo Luo *(University of Rochester, USA)*
Tao Mei *(Microsoft Research Asia, China)*
Chong-Wah Ngo *(City University of Hong Kong, China)*
Mubarak Shah *(UCF, USA)*
Cees Snoek *(University of Amsterdam, The Netherlands)*
Hari Sundaram *(Arizona State University, USA)*
Qi Tian *(The University of Texas at San Antonio, USA)*
Shuicheng Yan *(National University of Singapore, Singapore)*
Zhenjun Zha *(Chinese Academy of Sciences, China)*

MM 2013 Doctoral Program Committee

Valerie G Brunet *(CNAM, France)*
Antonio Camurri *(University of Genoa, Italy)*
Surendar Chandra *(FXPAL Inc., USA)*
Elaine Chew *(Queen Mary University of London, UK)*
Isao Echizen *(National Institute of Informatics, Japan)*
Alexander Eichhorn *(Simula Research Laboratory, Norway)*
Federico Fontana *(University of Udine, Italy)*
Gerald Friedland *(ICSI Berkeley, USA)*
Thomas Haenselmann *(University of Mannheim, Germany)*
Benoit Huet *(EURECOM, France)*
Ichiro Ide *(Nagoya University, Japan)*
Christian Jacquemin *(LIMSI-CNRS, France)*
David R Millen *(IBM Research and the Center for Social Software, USA)*
Klara Nahrstedt *(University of Illinois at Urbana-Champaign, USA)*
Vincent Oria *(NJIT, USA)*
Maria L Sapino *(University of Turin, Italy)*
Shin'ichi Satoh *(National Institute of Informatics, Japan)*
Caifeng Shan *(Philips, The Netherlands)*
Arnold Smeulders *(CWI and University of Amsterdam, The Netherlands)*
George Tzanetakis *(University of Victoria, Canada)*
Ye Wang *(National University of Singapore, Singapore)*

MM 2013 Technical Demo Program Committee

Xavier Anguer Miro *(Telefonica Research Lab, Spain)*
Liangliang Cao *(IBM Research, USA)*
Lixin Duan *(SAP Research, Singapore)*
Yahong Han *(Tianjin University, China)*
Lu Jiang *(Carnegie Mellon University, USA)*
Florian Metze *(Carnegie Mellon University, USA)*
Zhigang Ma *(University of Trento, Italy)*
Chunhua Shen *(The University of Adelaide, Australia)*
Cees Snoek *(University of Amsterdam, The Netherlands)*
Wei Tong *(Carnegie Mellon University, USA)*
Jinhui Tang *(Nanjing University of Science and Technology, China)*
Jasper Uijlings *(University of Trento, Italy)*
Sen Wang *(The University of Queensland, Australia)*
Fei Wu *(Zhejiang University, China)*
Lexing Xie *(Australian National University, Australia)*
Yi Yang *(Carnegie Mellon University, USA)*
Shoou-I Yu *(Carnegie Mellon University, USA)*
Zheng-Jun Zha *(National University of Singapore, Singapore)*
Luming Zhang *(National University of Singapore, Singapore)*

MM 2013 Additional Reviewers

Marco Bertini
Niamh Caprani
Zhiyong Cheng
Patrick Chiu
Kevin Collins
Matthew Fong
Kenneth Funes
Stephen Gilroy
Siqiong He
Michiel Hildebrand
Yu Huang
Adarsh Kowdle
Sven Kratz
Martha Larson
Christoph Lassner
Bin Li
Liangyue Li
Wen Li
Yuncheng Li
Zhonghua Li
Taoran Lu
Xiguo Ma
Alvaro Marcos
Gregor Miller
Minwoo Park
Fabian Richter
Christian Ries
Stefan Romberg
Julian Seifert
Xianbiao Shu
Gaurav Srivastava
Jichao Sun
Yichen Tang
Emrah Tasli
Lam Tran
Nalini Venkatasubramanian
Dayong Wang
Jialei Wang
Jing Wang
Ju-Chiang Wang
Xinxi Wang
Zhaowen Wang
Julie Williamson
Christian Winkler
Pengcheng Wu
Meng Xu
Quanzeng You
Xiangqian Yu
Jianbo Yuan
Dian Zhang
Yu Zhang
Zhenxing Zhang
Peilin Zhao
Jinfeng Zhuang

ACM Multimedia 2013 Sponsors & Supporters

Sponsor

SIGMM

Corporate Supporters

FX PAL

HUAWEI

technicolor

YAHOO! LABS

Google™

Springer
science+business media

Microsoft®
Research

orporate
upporters
continued)

facebook

Telefónica

Telefónica
Investigación y Desarrollo

IBM Research

---

nstitutional
upporters

NSF

UNIVERSITY
OF TRENTO - Italy

upf. Universitat
Pompeu Fabra
Barcelona

Inria

---

roject
upporter

MEDIA
MIXER

Organizing Committee

General Chairs
Kien Hua (Univ. of Central Florida)
Yong Rui (Microsoft Research)
Ralf Steinmetz (Technische Univ. Darmstadt)

Program Chairs
Alan Hanjalic (Delft Univ. of Technology)
Apostol Natsev (Google)
Wenwu Zhu (Tsinghua Univ.)

High-Risk-High-Return Papers Chairs
Abdulmotaleb El Saddik (Univ. of Ottawa)
Rainer Lienhart (Univ. of Augsburg)
Balakrishnan Prabhakaran (Univ. of Texas at Dallas)

Panel Chairs
Wolfgang Klas (Univ. of Vienna)
Chang Wen Chen (Univ. of Buffalo)

Multimedia Grand Challenge Chairs
Changsheng Xu (Chinese Academy of Sciences)
Cha Zhang (Microsoft Research)

Technical Demo Chairs
Shu-Ching Chen (Florida Int. Univ.)
Stefan Göbel (Technische Univ. Darmstadt)
Carsten Griwodz (Univ. of Oslo)

Workshop Chairs
Andreas Mauthe (Univ. of Lancaster)
Max Mühlhäuser (Technische Univ. Darmstadt)
Hari Sundaram (Arizona State Univ.)

Tutorial Chairs
Hermann Hellwagner (Univ. of Klagenfurt)
Wei Tsang Ooi (National Univ. of Singapore)

Interactive Art Exhibit Chair
Andrea Cavallaro (Queen Mary Univ. of London)

Industrial Panel Chairs
Borko Furht (Florida Atlantic Univ.)
Ivica Rimac (Bell Labs/Alcatel Lucent)

Doctorial Symposium Chairs
Laszlo Böszörmenyi (Univ. of Klagenfurt)
Christian Breitender (Technical Univ. of Vienna)
Oge Marques (Florida Atlantic Univ.)

Focus Area Multimedia Security and Privacy Chair
Gerald Friedland (Int. Computer Science Inst., Berkeley)

Proceedings Chairs
Ying Cai (Iowa State Univ.)
Wallapak Tanavapong (Iowa State Univ.)

Local Arrangements Chairs
Mainak Chatterjee (Univ. of Central Florida)
Marshall Tappen (Univ. of Central Florida)
Cliff Zou (Univ. of Central Florida)

Travel Grant Chairs
Danzhou Liu (Symantec)
JungHwan Oh (Univ. of North Texas)

Sponsorship Chair
Mark Liao (Academia Sinica, Taipeh)

Finance and Registration Chairs
Tai Do (Microsoft)
Ning Jiang (Institute for Systems Biology)
Ming Li (California State Univ.)

Publicity and Social Media Chair
Grace Ngai (Hong Kong Polytechnic Univ.)

Web Chair
Alex Aved (U.S. Air Force)

History Preservation Chairs
Duc Tran (Univ. of Massachusetts in Boston)
Roy Villafane (Andrews Univ.)

SIGMM Chair
Shih-Fu Chang (Columbia Univ.)

SIGMM Records EiC
Carsten Griwodz (Univ. of Oslo)

SIGMM Director of Conferences
Nicu Sebe (Univ. of Trento)

About ACM Multimedia 2014

Since the founding of ACM SIGMM in 1993, ACM Multimedia has been the worldwide premier conference and a key world event to display scientific achievements and innovative industrial products in the multimedia field. At ACM Multimedia 2014, we will celebrate its twenty-second iteration with an extensive program consisting of technical sessions covering all aspects of the multimedia field in forms of oral and poster presentations, tutorials, panels, exhibits, demonstrations and workshops, bringing into focus the principal subjects of investigation, competitions of research teams on challenging problems, and also an interactive art program stimulating artists and computer scientists to meet and discover together the frontiers of artistic communication. Details and updates will be published on the conference's website: www.acmmm.org/2014

Call for Contributions

ACM Multimedia 2014 solicits submissions of contributions for the following programs (partial list, please visit the website for details):

- Full papers & Short papers
- High-risk-high-return papers
- Interactive art exhibition
- Open source software competition
- Multimedia grand challenge competition
- Tutorials
- Panels
- Doctoral symposium
- Technical demonstrations
- Workshops

Important Dates

The dates for submissions to the abovementioned contribution categories and other key dates will be provided on the conference's website. Please check the website frequently for the latest news and updates.

Conference Location – Orlando, Florida

Orlando, nicknamed "The City Beautiful," is also considered the theme park capital of the world. In addition to world-renowned tourist attractions and the most beautiful beaches in the U.S., Orlando is unique in its mix of academia and industry. It is nationally recognized for innovation in the areas of digital media, aerospace, microelectronics, nanotechnology, optics, photonics, and sustainable energy, and it also hosts the University of Central Florida, which is one of the largest and fastest growing universities in the country.

Association for Computing Machinery

SIGMM
Special Interest Group on Multimedia

Classifying Tag Relevance with Relevant Positive and Negative Examples

Xirong Li[1] and Cees G. M. Snoek[2]
[1]Key Lab of Data Engineering and Knowledge Engineering, Renmin University of China, China
[2]Intelligent Systems Lab Amsterdam, University of Amsterdam, the Netherlands
xirong@ruc.edu.cn, cgmsnoek@uva.nl

ABSTRACT

Image tag relevance estimation aims to automatically determine what people label about images is factually present in the pictorial content. Different from previous works, which either use only positive examples of a given tag or use positive and random negative examples, we argue the importance of *relevant positive* and *relevant negative* examples for tag relevance estimation. We propose a system that selects positive and negative examples, deemed most relevant with respect to the given tag from crowd-annotated images. While applying models for many tags could be cumbersome, our system trains efficient ensembles of Support Vector Machines per tag, enabling fast classification. Experiments on two benchmark sets show that the proposed system compares favorably against five present day methods. Given extracted visual features, for each image our system can process up to 3,787 tags per second. The new system is both effective and efficient for tag relevance estimation.

Categories and Subject Descriptors

I.4.8 [**Image Processing and Computer Vision**]: Scene Analysis—*Object recognition*

Keywords

Image tag relevance, relevant examples, fast classification

1. INTRODUCTION

We consider the problem of estimating the relevance of a user-provided image tag, as exemplified in Fig. 1. Although all the three images are labeled with the tag 'sheep', only image (a) is genuinely a picture of sheep. Since image (b) is clearly dissimilar to a typical scene wherein a sheep is present, using a few positive examples of sheep as a reference for visual similarity will help separate (a) and (b), as is commonly done in the literature, *e.g.*, [3,5,6,8,10]. However, as image (a) and image (c) are similar in terms of their visual appearance as well, using the positive examples alone is limited for distinguishing between the two images. To resolve the issue, negative examples, which are visually close to the positives, have to be taken into account. Exploiting both positives and negatives with respect to a specific tag, as we propose, is important for tag relevance estimation.

Figure 1: Examples of user-labeled images. Although all the three images are labeled with the tag 'sheep', only image (a) is truly a picture of sheep. While a few positive examples with respect to the tag will help separate (a) and (b), negative examples which are visually close to the positives are required to distinguish (a) from (c).

There are good efforts on selecting relevant positives [12] and relevant negatives [7] from crowd-annotated images in the context of visual categorization. However, what positive and negative examples to use for tag relevance estimation remains open. In fact, per-tag modeling has been challenged by [6], due to its quest for many well labeled training examples and the inefficiency in applying models for many tags. Recently, Chen *et al.* [3] propose to train Support Vector Machines per tag, and they adopt the linear kernel for reasons of efficiency. In their work, user-labeled images are directly used as positive examples, while negative examples are obtained by random sampling. Hence, the impact of relevant positives and relevant negatives on tag relevance estimation remains unclear.

In this paper we propose a *classification system* for tag relevance that takes into account both relevant positive and relevant negative examples. We build on the rich heritage from tag relevance estimation for positive example selection [6,12]. We draw inspiration from recent advancements in visual categorization for negative example selection [7] and their efficient classification [7,9]. Using the system we perform an empirical study to assess the value of relevant positive and negative examples for tag relevance estimation.

2. CLASSIFYING TAG RELEVANCE

Our goal is to build effective tag relevance estimators per tag, by exploiting the large amounts of crowd-annotated images on the Internet. For learning from large data, combin-

MM'13, October 21–25, 2013, Barcelona, Spain.

ACM 978-1-4503-2404-5/13/10 ...$15.00.
http://dx.doi.org/10.1145/2502081.2502129.

ing many classifiers built on small subsets of the data is a promising approach [2]. We thus follow this ensemble learning approach. To make our discussion more formal, we use ω to denote a tag of interest. Let x be an image. Its content-based representation is a d-dimensional feature vector. We refer to an image and its feature vector interchangeably, using $x(i)$ to indicate the i-th dimension of the vector. Let $G(x)$ be a tag relevance estimator for ω. We express $G(x)$ as an ensemble of T meta classifiers:

$$G(x) = \frac{1}{T}\sum_{t=1}^{T} g_t(x), \tag{1}$$

where $g_t(x)$ indicates the decision function of a meta classifier. We instantiate the meta classifiers using SVMs, for its well recognized performance on two-class learning:

$$g_t(x) = b_t + \sum_{j=1}^{n_t} \alpha_{t,j} \cdot y_{t,j} \cdot \mathcal{K}(x, x_{t,j}), \tag{2}$$

where b_t is the intercept, n_t the number of support vectors, $\alpha_{t,j}$ the positive coefficient of support vector $x_{t,j}$, $y_{t,j} \in \{1, -1\}$ a class label of $x_{t,j}$ with respect to ω, and $\mathcal{K}$ a kernel function.

Obtaining optimal $g_t(x)$ requires proper positive and negative training data. The relevance of negative examples with respect to ω depends on positive examples of the tag. In that regard, we first describe how to select relevant positive examples in Section 2.1, and then depict negative example selection in Section 2.2. While the selected positives and negatives lead to an effective ensemble of SVMs, the computational complexity of $G(x)$ is proportional to the size of the ensemble. We describe in Section 2.3 acceleration techniques which will make the complexity independent of the ensemble size. The proposed system is illustrated in Fig. 2.

2.1 Selecting Relevant Positive Examples

We choose to combine two state-of-the-art methods: semantic field [12] and neighbor voting [6]. As the two methods exploit textual and visual information respectively, they are orthogonal to each other. Combining them makes sense.

Given a specific tag ω, the semantic field method determines the positiveness of an image in light of the averaged semantic similarity between ω and the tags assigned to that image [12]. The semantic similarity between two tags is computed by combining the Flickr context similarity and the WordNet Wu-Palmer similarity. The Flickr similarity is based on the Normalized Google Distance, but with tag statistics acquired from Flickr image collections instead of Google indexed web pages. The WordNet similarity exploits path length in WordNet hierarchy to infer tag relatedness.

The neighbor voting method determines the positiveness of an image with respect to ω by exploiting tagging redundancies among multiple users [6]. The method retrieves k nearest neighbors from a large set of user-labeled images by content-based search. The number of neighbors labeled with ω is used as the positiveness score.

From the above discussion we see that the output scores of the two methods are of different scales. Hence, we use CombSUM with rank-based score normalization, a robust choice for multimedia fusion. Given images labeled with ω, we sort the images in descending order by their scores, and preserve the top l ranked results as relevant positives.

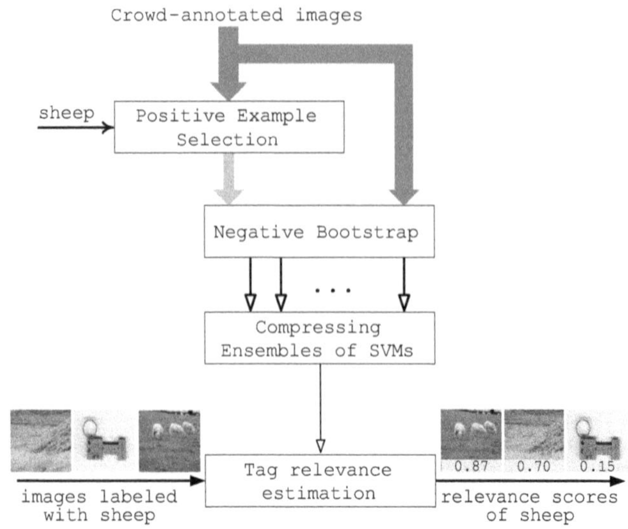

Figure 2: The proposed classification system for image tag relevance estimation. For each given tag, the system automatically selects a set of relevant positive examples from crowd-annotated images. Subsequently, relevant negative examples are selected via Negative Bootstrap [7], yielding an ensemble of SVMs. By compressing the ensemble to make the test complexity independent of the ensemble size, the system is both effective and efficient.

2.2 Selecting Relevant Negative Examples

While negative examples can be easily acquired by random sampling, see [3], such random negatives are inadequate for attacking challenging cases, like image (c) shown in Fig. 1. To separate (a) and (c), one might want to manually add positive examples of tags which resembles visual context of 'sheep', say 'grass' or 'hill'. However, the relevance of a negative example depends on the underlying visual features and classifiers, and is not necessarily consistent with what an observer may expect. It is thus difficult to specify relevant negatives by hand-crafted rules. In order to automatically select relevant negatives, we extend the Negative Bootstrap algorithm [7] to the tag relevance estimation problem. Different from [7] that departs from a few expert-labeled examples, we use purely crow-annotated examples.

Given the l positives selected in Section 2.1, Negative Bootstrap finds relevant negatives in an iterative manner. In the first iteration an initial classifier $g_1(x)$ is derived from the positives and l random negatives. In the t-th iteration, the algorithm randomly samples m examples to form a candidate set, and uses the ensemble of $t-1$ classifiers previously obtained to classify each candidate element. The top l most misclassified elements are selected and used together with the positives to derive a new meta classifier $g_t(x)$. Negative Bootstrap with T iterations produces an ensemble of T meta classifiers, which will be the tag relevance estimator for ω.

2.3 Compressing Ensembles of SVMs

As noted earlier, despite the effectiveness of ensemble learning, the intensive computation associated with applying all meta classifiers puts the practical use of per-tag modeling into question. To overcome the difficulty, we study how to accelerate ensembles of SVMs. In particular, we consider linear SVMs (used in [3], but they do not consider ensembles), and histogram intersection kernel SVMs (HIKSVMs) for which there are works on fast classification of a single classifier [9] and an ensemble [7].

For linear SVMs, we sum over the i-th dimension of support vectors of the meta classifiers, i.e.,

$$C_i = \sum_{t=1}^{T}\sum_{j=1}^{n_t} \alpha_{t,j} \cdot y_{t,j} \cdot x_{t,j}(i). \qquad (3)$$

Combining Eq. (2) and Eq. (3), we can rewrite $G(x)$ as

$$\frac{1}{T}(b_0 + \sum_{i=1}^{d} x(i) \cdot C_i), \qquad (4)$$

where $b_0 = \sum_{t=1}^{T} b_t$. As both C_i and b_0 are constant with respect to x, computing Eq. (4) has an order of $O(d)$ only.

For HIKSVMs, the nonlinear kernel does not allow us to compress each dimension using Eq. (3). Instead, we follow [7], constructing the decision function per dimension as

$$H_i(z) = \sum_{t=1}^{T}\sum_{j=1}^{n_t} \alpha_{t,j} \cdot y_{t,j} \cdot \min(z, x_{t,j}(i)), \qquad (5)$$

where z is a variable. The paper [7] shows that for any z, there exists a specific pair of ordered points $z_{i,r}$ and $z_{i,r+1}$ such that $H_i(z)$ can be computed by linear interpolation on $H_i(z_{i,r})$ and $H_i(z_{i,r+1})$. Further, by uniformly quantizing the value range of each dimension into q segments, and having $H_i(z)$ of the $q+1$ points precomputed, computing Eq. (1) boils down to doing a linear interpolation operation for each dimension, followed by summing over $d+1$ values. Hence, the time complexity of executing the compressed ensemble of HIKSVMs is now reduced to $O(d)$ also.

In sum, for a given tag, the proposed system automatically selects relevant positive and relevant negative examples from crowd-annotated images with no need of extra manual annotation. Such relevant examples result in ensembles of classifiers with better discrimination ability than their counterparts derived from random examples. Compressing the ensembles ensures fast classification, with a time complexity independent of the number of meta classifiers and the number of support vectors.

3. EMPIRICAL STUDY

3.1 Experimental Setup

Training data. To collect crowd-annotated images for training, we use over 25,000 WordNet tags as queries to uniformly sample Flickr images uploaded between 2005 and 2010. After removing batch-tagged images and those failed to extract visual features, we obtain 964,849 images.

Two test sets. We use two public test sets: Social20 [6] and NUSWIDE [4]. The Social20 set[1] consists of 19,971 Flickr images, with ground truth available for 20 tags corresponding to visual objects and scenes such as 'airplane', 'sheep', and 'street'. The NUSWIDE test set[2] contains 103,688 Flickr images, with ground truth available for 81 tags covering a range of objects, scenes, and events. The training and test sets were collected independently (data statistics shown in Table 1).

Table 1: The training set and the two test sets.

	Training	Social20 [6]	NUSWIDE [4]
No. images	964,849	19,971	103,688
No. users	145,029	10,972	32,415
No. test tags	N.A.	20	81

Evaluation criteria. For each test tag, we sort images labeled with this tag in descending order by their relevance scores, and compute Average Precision on the entire ranked list. For overall comparison, we report mean Average Precision (mAP).

We extract a 1,024-dimensional bag of visual codes feature, by quantizing densely sampled SIFT descriptors [11]. For each test tag, we empirically preserve the top 500 ranked examples from the training set as its relevant positives. We then seek relevant negatives by running negative bootstrap with 10 iterations. Meta classifiers are trained using LIBSVM [1] with its default cost parameter because the positive and negative examples are perfectly balanced.

Baselines. We compare with the following five present day methods: tag position [10], tag ranking [8], neighbor voting [6], semantic field [12], and linear SVMs [3]. For a fair comparison, all methods use the same training data.

3.2 Experiments

Experiment 1. The Impact of Relevant Examples. In order to justify the need of relevant examples, we compare the following four strategies: 1) random positives with random negatives; 2) relevant positives with random negatives; 3) random positives with relevant negatives, and 4) relevant positives with relevant negatives. For a fair comparison, whenever applicable we will make the four strategies share the same input and parameters.

As shown in Table 2, for both linear SVMs and HIKSVMs, relevant positives in combination with relevant negatives perform best. Substituting relevant positives for random positives is useful, improving mAP of HIKSVMs from 0.781 to 0.794 on Social20 and from 0.624 to 0.633 on NUSWIDE. Since the relevance of negative examples depends on positive examples, unreliable positives could confuse negative bootstrap. Consequently, we observe that given random positives, substituting relevant negatives for random negatives is useless in general. We conclude from the results that both relevant positives and relevant negatives are important for tag relevance estimation, and they have to be used together.

Experiment 2. Efficiency Analysis. Having visual features extracted, running the compressed ensemble of HIKSVMs for a given tag costs merely 0.264 millisecond per image, on average, on our machine with 2.4 GHz multi-core cpu and 24 GB memory. The corresponding number for linear SVMs is 0.221 millisecond. This means, for each image, the proposed system (with fast ensembles of HIKSVMs) can process 3,787 tags per second. Noticing that the averaged number of distinct user tags per image is around 6 [6], our per-tag modeling approach is practical.

Experiment 3. Comparison with Present Day Methods. As shown in Table 3, the proposed system compares favorably over all five baselines. Compared to the best baseline, *i.e.*,

[1]`mediamill.nl`

[2]`http://lms.comp.nus.edu.sg/research/NUS-WIDE.htm`. While the NUSWIDE test set originally contains 107,859 images, 4171 images are no longer available on Flickr.

Table 2: **The impact of relevant examples on tag relevance estimation. Combining relevant positive examples (RelPos) and relevant negative examples (RelNeg) works best.**

SVMs	RelPos	RelNeg	Social20	NUSWIDE
Linear	No	No	0.680	0.572
	Yes	No	0.694	0.582
	No	Yes	0.667	0.569
	Yes	**Yes**	**0.734**	**0.604**
Histogram intersection kernel	No	No	0.781	0.624
	Yes	No	0.794	0.633
	No	Yes	0.781	0.636
	Yes	**Yes**	**0.817**	**0.655**

Table 3: **Comparing different methods for tag relevance estimation on the two test sets.**

Method	Social20	NUSWIDE
tag position [10]	0.565	0.560
tag ranking [8]	0.643	0.575
neighbor voting [6]	0.772	0.617
semantic field [12]	0.647	0.577
linear SVMs [3]	0.680	0.572
This work	**0.817**	**0.655**

Figure 3: The top 5 results of 'sheep' sorted by tag relevance scores produced by different estimators.

neighbor voting which scores an mAP of 0.772 on Social20 and 0.617 on NUSWIDE, our system reaches an mAP of 0.817 and 0.655 on the two test sets. Concerning the choice of SVMs, HIKSVMs clearly outperform linear SVMs. In addition, since the positive selection method presented in Section 2.1 can also be used for tag relevance estimation, we compare that method, and find that our system beats it as well. Fig. 3 shows a qualitative result. These results justify the effectiveness of the proposed system for tag relevance estimation.

4. CONCLUSIONS

This paper presents a per-tag classification approach to image tag relevance estimation. We build a system which exploits both relevant positive and relevant negative examples with respect to individual tags. Experiments on two benchmark sets support the following conclusions. As the main contribution of this work, we empirically show that relevant positives and relevant negatives are important for constructing effective tag relevance estimators, and such relevant examples can be automatically selected from crowd-annotated images with no need of extra manual annotation. We find that relevant positives and relevant negatives have to be used simultaneously. Replacing relevant positives (or negatives) by random positives (or negatives) would yield sub-optimal performance. Concerning the choices of classifiers, histogram intersection kernel SVMs (HIKSVMs) are superior to linear SVMs. Equipped with ensembles of HIKSVMs trained on relevant positives and relevant negatives, the system beats five present day methods. Moreover, with fast classification of the ensembles, our system can process up to 3,787 tags per second. The effectiveness and efficiency make the proposed tag relevance estimation system promising for real-world deployment.

Acknowledgements. This research was supported by the Basic Research funds in Renmin University of China from the central government (No. 13XNLF05), the Dutch national program COMMIT, and the STW STORY project.

5. REFERENCES

[1] C.-C. Chang and C.-J. Lin. LIBSVM: A library for support vector machines. *TIST*, 2011.

[2] N. Chawla, L. Hall, K. Bowyer, and W. Kegelmeyer. Learning ensembles from bites: A scalable and accurate approach. *JMLR*, 2004.

[3] L. Chen, D. Xu, I. Tsang, and J. Luo. Tag-based web photo retrieval improved by batch mode re-tagging. In *CVPR*, 2010.

[4] T.-S. Chua, J. Tang, R. Hong, H. Li, Z. Luo, and Y.-T. Zheng. NUS-WIDE: A real-world web image database from National University of Singapore. In *CIVR*, 2009.

[5] Y. Gao, M. Wang, Z.-J. Zha, J. Shen, X. Li, and X. Wu. Visual-textual joint relevance learning for tag-based social image search. *TIP*, 2013.

[6] X. Li, C. Snoek, and M. Worring. Learning social tag relevance by neighbor voting. *TMM*, 2009.

[7] X. Li, C. Snoek, M. Worring, D. Koelma, and A. Smeulders. Bootstrapping visual categorization with relevant negatives. *TMM*, 2013.

[8] D. Liu, X.-S. Hua, L. Yang, M. Wang, and H.-J. Zhang. Tag ranking. In *WWW*, 2009.

[9] S. Maji, A. Berg, and J. Malik. Classification using intersection kernel support vector machines is efficient. In *CVPR*, 2008.

[10] A. Sun, S. Bhowmick, K. Nguyen, and G. Bai. Tag-based social image retrieval: An empirical evaluation. *JASIST*, 2011.

[11] K. van de Sande, T. Gevers, and C. Snoek. Evaluating color descriptors for object and scene recognition. *TPAMI*, 2010.

[12] S. Zhu, Y.-G. Jiang, and C.-W. Ngo. Sampling and ontologically pooling web images for visual concept learning. *TMM*, 2012.

Non-Rigid Target Tracking based on 'Flow-Cut' in Pair-Wise Frames with online Hough Forests

Tao Zhuo, Yanning Zhang and Peng Zhang
School of Computer Science
Northwestern Polytechnical University, China
zhuotao@mail.nwpu.edu.cn
ynzhang@nwpu.edu.cn
zh0036ng@nwpu.edu.cn

Wei Huang
School of Information Engineering
Nanchang University, China
huangwei@ncu.edu.cn

Hichem Sahli
Dept. of Electronics and Information Processing (ETRO)
Vrije Universiteit Brussel, Belgium
hsahli@etro.vub.ac.be

ABSTRACT

In conventional online learning based tracking studies, fixed-shape appearance modeling is often incorporated for training samples generation, as it is simple and convenient to be applied. However, for more general non-rigid and articulated object, this strategy may regard some background areas as foreground, which is likely to deteriorate the learning process. Recently published works utilize more than one patches to represent non-rigid object with foreground object segmentation, but most of these segmentation for target representation are performed only in single frame manner. Since the motion information between the consecutive frames was not considered by these approaches, when the backgrounds are similar to the target, accurate segmentation is hard to be achieved.

In this work, we propose a novel model for non-rigid object segmentation by incorporating consecutive gradients flow between pair-wise frames into a Gibbs energy function. With help from motion information, the irregular target areas can be segmented more accurately during precise boundary convergence. The proposed segmentation model is incorporated into a semi-supervised online tracking framework for training samples generation. We test the proposed tracking on challenging videos involving heavy intrinsic variations and occlusions. As a result, the experiments demonstrate a significant improvement in tracking accuracy and robustness in comparison with other state-of-art tracking works.

Categories and Subject Descriptors

I.4 [**Image Processing and Computer Vision**]: Segmentation; I.4.8 [**Scene Analysis**]: Tracking

Keywords

Segmentation, Online Learning, Tracking, Hough Forests

1. INTRODUCTION

Realistic target is hard to track because of its frequent appearance changes, especially for the non-rigid target, challenges mainly come from the intrinsic changes such as rotation, distortion and scaling. To effectively adapt to the appearance changes of target, online learning based tracking approaches have become more attractive and many of them have obtained impressive performance.

A majority of the published online tracking works utilize regular geometry shapes such as bounding-box or ellipse to represent the target. These fixed-shape based tracking methods can track the targets of rigid shape such as vehicle or human head robustly, but they often fail in tracking the non-rigid targets with good accuracy, especially when targets have intrinsic changes or part occlusions. To overcome this limitation, Kwon *et. al.* proposed an articulated object tracking approach by using a pre-defined bounding-box collection to represent different parts of the target [10]. With adaptive Basin Hopping Monte-Carlo Sampling (BHMC), Kwon's approach can automatically update the dynamic target appearance changes and geometry relations over time.

However, such pre-defined parts representation influences the generic application for this method, especially when the target is composed by several objects, e.g. motor rider, which is hard to be described by discrete rectangles. Thus, using continuous contour to smoothly estimate target's contour/shape would provide higher accuracy for target presentation. Sun *et. al.* proposed a supervised level set model (SLSM) for tracking [13] in order to obtain more precise convergence to the target during tracking. With the specific knowledge of target region and edge cues, the contour curve can converge to the candidate area with maximum likelihood in a Bayesian manner. Recently, a HT based approach revived attraction in handling the problem of fixed-shape limitations. Barinova *et. al.* proposed a probabilistic framework for multiple object instances detection by using Hough transforms [1]. And the major interest of this research inspired by the work of Godec *et. al.*[7]. In Godec's *HT* tracker, the 'GrabCut' segmentation [12] is incorporated with Hough Forest learning framework for non-rigid target tracking. By using the back-projection to support tracking in online domain, the *HT* tracker beyond many state-of-art work based on fix-shape. However, heavily relying on the discrimination of color Gaussian kernels makes the segmentation result unexpectedly, especially when intrinsic changes happen in the uniform color background containing obvious edges.

In this study, we propose a 'Flow-Cut' model to achieve more accurately guided segmentation for online learning based tracking. Compared with the roughly guided segmentation in [7], the proposed model is able to segment the target more precisely with the help of motion information between pair-wise frames. The segmented target areas can provide more precise samples for online classifier training. To effectively describe the appearance of non-rigid object, we utilize the Random Forests to construct an online *tracking* framework in Hough transformation domain, which is more accurate than the fixed rectangle domain for target appearance updating during tracking. The proposed tracking shows more robust in many challenge scenes including rotation, intrinsic compression/stretching, aspect ratio changes, etc.

The organization of the paper is as follows: Section 2 introduces the proposed model for target segmentation and section 3 briefly presents our online learning tracking framework. Section 4 shows experiment results and discussion and section 5 gives the conclusion of this paper.

2. FOREGROUND SEGMENTATION FOR LEARNING SAMPLES GENERATION

A crucial issue for most of online tracking-by-detection approaches[8] is learning samples updating strategy. For the fixed-shape based approaches, the main challenge is: the correctness of generated samples for online learning is hard to be guaranteed due to the noise in coarse data by the annotated rectangle. The purpose of the proposed segmentation model is to separate the foreground from the background with fine-smooth contour. The accurately separated foreground can provide higher quality samples for online learning. The segmented region are consisted of two parts: positive samples which are within the segmented foreground areas; negative ones which are in the background. During initialization, the occupied areas by target are positive while the other positions inside the maximum-object-sized bounding-box are background.

2.1 Proposed Model for Smooth-Fine Segmentation

In the spatial temporal domain, suppose a gray level image sequence is $\mathcal{I} = \{I_1, ..., I_t\}$. For each image I_t, let the image lattice to be $\mathbf{p}(x, y, t)$, its pixel values are composed by a N-size array of $\mathbf{I} = \{I(\mathbf{p}_1), I(\mathbf{p}_2), ..., I(\mathbf{p}_N)\}$. Let α to represent an array of 'opacity' values $\{\alpha_1, ..., \alpha_N\}$ for each pixel of one video frame, for binary segmentation $\alpha \in \{0,1\}$, with 0 for the background and 1 for target, but generally, $0 \leq \alpha \leq 1$. Suppose there are parameters $\underline{\theta} = \{h(I;\alpha), \alpha = 0,1\}$ representing the image foreground and background grey-level distributions, and consist of histograms assembled directly from labeled pixels from the respective the regions of foreground and background. Hence, the target segmentation in one frame is to infer the unknown opacity variables α from the given image data $\mathbf{I}$ and the model $\underline{\theta}$. For gray-level image, the e_φ can be defined as:

$$e_\varphi(\alpha, h, \mathbf{I}) = \sum_{i \in N} -\log h(I(\mathbf{p}_i); \alpha_i) \qquad (1)$$

For the segmentation of consecutive pair-wise frames, we assume as [5] that the gray values of target in consecutive frames do not have substantial changes over time. Thus, its final segmentation also needs to consider the contour smoothness caused by motion, which can be estimated by a Gibbs likely energy function as:

$$e(\alpha, h, \mathbf{I}) = \Big[e_\varphi(\alpha, h, \mathbf{I})\Big] + \Big[e_\phi(\alpha, \mathbf{I}) \oplus e_\psi(u, v, \mathbf{I})\Big] \qquad (2)$$

In equation 2, e_φ represents the opacity distribution α to the pixel data $\mathbf{p}$ by the given normalized histogram model h. The boundary smoothness of target segmentation is described by the smoothness energy function consisting of two parts: e_ϕ represents the coherence in the boundary regions of similar gray-levels within one image spatial domain, while e_ψ is used to describe the piecewise smoothness of the flow field caused by the motion of two consecutive frames. The operator $\oplus$ is the interleaved optimization process for two energy functions e_ϕ and e_ψ due to the shared parameters. For the pixels $I(\mathbf{p})$ in the boundary neighborhood region C of target, its smoothness function can be written as:

$$e_\phi(\alpha, \mathbf{I}) = \gamma \cdot \sum_{\mathbf{p}_i, \mathbf{p}_j \in C} \frac{\exp(-\beta(\mathbf{I}(\mathbf{p}_i) - \mathbf{I}(\mathbf{p}_j))^2)}{s(\mathbf{I}(\mathbf{p}_i), \mathbf{I}(\mathbf{p}_j))}, \quad \text{where } \alpha_i \neq \alpha_j \qquad (3)$$

β and γ are the regularization parameters that control the smoothness at different levels and $s(\cdot)$ is the Euclidean distance of neighboring pixels. Usually to obtain a satisfactory result, we define the pixels to be neighbors if they are adjacent either horizontally/vertically or diagonally, which is an 8-direction connectivity. The factor β is used to switch equation 3 appropriately between low and high contrast and the value has been suggested by Boykov *et. al.* in [3] for effective smoothness tendency relieving. The detailed optimization of γ can be found in [2].

Since we consider pair-wise consecutive frames to discover the coherence of the target motion at one time. We also assume that, the displacement flow field $\mathbf{w} = (u(\mathbf{p}), v(\mathbf{p}), 1))$ within the boundary neighborhood region C is constant [5]. For any possible location (x,y) in boundary neighborhood regions of motion, calculating the $\mathbf{w}$ can be achieved by only estimating the best increment $d\mathbf{w}(d\mathbf{w} = (du, dv))$.

Let $I_z(\mathbf{p}) = I(\mathbf{p} + \mathbf{w}) - I(\mathbf{p})$, $I_x(\mathbf{p}) = \frac{\partial}{\partial x} I(\mathbf{p} + \mathbf{w})$ and $I_y(\mathbf{p}) = \frac{\partial}{\partial y} I(\mathbf{p} + \mathbf{w})$. By using the first-order Taylor expansion on $I_z(\mathbf{p}) = I(\mathbf{p} + \mathbf{w}) - I(\mathbf{p})$:

$$I(\mathbf{p} + \mathbf{w}) - I(\mathbf{p}) \approx I_z(\mathbf{p}) + I_x(\mathbf{p}) du(\mathbf{p}) + I_y(\mathbf{p}) dv(\mathbf{p}) \qquad (4)$$

We vectorize u,v,du,dv into U, V, dU, dV, and let $\mathbf{I}_x = diag(I_x)$ and $\mathbf{I}_y = diag(I_y)$ are the diagonal matrices of the diagonals images I_x and I_y. If we set $\delta_\mathbf{p}$ is a column vector only containing value '1' at location $\mathbf{p}$ such as $\delta_\mathbf{p} I_z = I_z(\mathbf{p})$, $\mathbf{D}_x$ and $\mathbf{D}_y$ are the matrices of derivative filters ($\mathbf{D}_x U = u * [0, -1, 1]$) in x- and y- directions [11]. the optical flow in the continuous domain can be re-written in discrete manner as:

$$e_\psi(u, v, \mathbf{I}) = \sum f(\mathcal{A}) + \rho \cdot g(\mathcal{B}) \qquad (5)$$

Here, we use the following definition for more concisely representation.

$$\mathcal{A} = (\delta_\mathbf{p}^T (I_z + \mathbf{I}_x dU + \mathbf{I}_y dV))^2$$
$$\mathcal{B} = (\delta_\mathbf{p}^T \mathbf{D}_x (U + dU))^2 + (\delta_\mathbf{p}^T \mathbf{D}_y (U + dU))^2 + (\delta_\mathbf{p}^T \mathbf{D}_x (V + dV))^2 + (\delta_\mathbf{p}^T \mathbf{D}_y (V + dV))^2 \qquad (6)$$

2.2 Energy Minimization for Contour Convergence

To accurately separate the target from the image, the cutting curve requires converging to the target boundary smoothly by using energy minimization process, as shown in Algorithm 1. If we define two matrices $\Psi' = diag[f'(\mathcal{A})]$, $\Phi' = diag[g'(\mathcal{B})]$ and generalized Laplacian filter $\mathbf{L} = \mathbf{D}_x^T \Phi' \mathbf{D}_x + \mathbf{D}_y^T \Phi' \mathbf{D}_y$, the linear equation for dU,dV update would be:

$$\begin{bmatrix} \Psi' \mathbf{I}_x^2 + \rho \mathbf{L} & \Psi' \mathbf{I}_x \mathbf{I}_y \\ \Psi' \mathbf{I}_x \mathbf{I}_y & \Psi' \mathbf{I}_y^2 + \rho \mathbf{L} \end{bmatrix} \begin{bmatrix} dU \\ dV \end{bmatrix} = - \begin{bmatrix} \Psi' \mathbf{I}_x \mathbf{I}_x I_z + \rho \mathbf{L} U \\ \Psi' \mathbf{I}_y \mathbf{I}_x I_z + \rho \mathbf{L} U \end{bmatrix} \quad (7)$$

Algorithm 1 Target segmentation process

Require: pair-wise consecutive frames of I_{t-1}, I_t
Ensure: segmented target region
  set $dU = 0, dV = 0$
  set $\alpha = 0$ for background, $\alpha = 1$ for foreground
  while $\Delta(dU) > \epsilon$ and $\Delta(dV) > \epsilon$ **do**
    while $\Delta(k_i) > \epsilon$ **do**
      associate GMM components with pixels $\mathbf{p}$ in foreground
      compute $k_i = \arg\min[-\log(\pi \cdot \mathbf{G})]$
      learn parameters h from $\mathbf{I}$ using obtained $\mathbf{k}$
    end while
    estimate dU, dV
    compute Ψ', Φ' by dU, dV
    update dU, dV using (7)
    compute $\min[\min \mathbb{E}(\alpha, h, \mathbf{I})]$
  end while
  Border matting using [12]

The proposed segmentation can make the target contour adaptive to the geometry variation of different non-rigid objects. To estimate the center $\mathbf{o}$ of the target, we calculate the center of mass O_m for the segmented foreground areas and employ ϵ as a shift for fine-adjustment as $\mathbf{o} = O_m \pm \epsilon$. We keep the bounding-box during sampling because this can be regarded as remedy for segmentation failure. This strategy is verified to work as a bounding-box based tracking to update the classifiers effectively since the intrinsic and extrinsic occlusion of target is hard to be recognized most of the time. For the online learning framework, the Random Forests based Hough voting is well known for its capability of dealing with bad samples labeling and noise. In the following section, we introduce Random Forests framework for online tracking.

3. ONLINE TRACKING BY LEARNING

In our tracking framework, the Hough voting based classification is used in an online learning domain. Hence, it requires the proposed tracking to model foreground probabilities and voting maps within each leaf node online. To obtain the candidate foreground areas more accurately, the proposed segmentation is able to guarantee lower noise than using fixed-shape region. The segmented target areas are used to extract the 16×16 patches randomly as the Hough Forests positive samples, while the same size patches coming from the background act as the negative ones. All the training data are split in a tree structure by assigning each leaf node a set of positive samples. For all the positive samples $\mathcal{S}$ ended in a leaf node $\mathcal{L}$, the distribution of Hough voting in this node for position $\mathbf{x}$ can be approximated by a sum of Dirac measures $\delta_\mathbf{d}$ according to the samples' offset vectors $\mathbf{d}$ for a single $\mathcal{T} \in \{\mathcal{T}_i\}_{i=1}^M$.

$$p(E(\mathbf{o})|\mathcal{L}(\mathbf{x});\mathcal{T}) \propto \sum_{\mathcal{S}(\mathbf{x})} p[l=1|\mathcal{L}(\mathbf{x});\mathcal{T}] \cdot \delta_\mathbf{d}(\mathbf{x}-\mathbf{o}) \quad (8)$$

For the entire Hough Forest, the forest-based estimation can use the mean of the probabilities coming from all the different trees:

$$p(E(\mathbf{o})|\mathcal{L}(\mathbf{x});\{\mathcal{T}_i\}_{i=1}^M) \propto \sum_{\mathcal{T}_i}^{\mathcal{T}_M} \sum_{\mathcal{S}(\mathbf{x})} p[l=1|\mathcal{L}(\mathbf{x});\mathcal{T}_i] \cdot \delta_\mathbf{d}(\mathbf{x}-\mathbf{o}) \quad (9)$$

This classification calculates the Hough image patch and obtains a collection of its maxima locations with values as the classification hypotheses [4][9].

4. EXPERIMENT AND DISCUSSION

In our experiment, the proposed tracking is initialized with the bounding box surrounding the target object in two consecutive frames, then the flow-cut model will automatically generate an accurate target contour and tracking starts from the 3rd frame. We assume that the target appearance does not change drastically in consecutive frames, hence the whole tracking process would not be sensitive to this initialization. The tracking performance was tested on the benchmark video sequences [6] containing both rigid and non-rigid objects with challenge intrinsic deformation and occlusion.

We compared the proposed tracking with popular state-of-art tracking approaches including *HT*[7], *BHMC*[10], *TLD*[8] tracker and *CT*[14]. Due to the page limitation, we select two typical trackers for presentation, which are shown in Figure. 1. The comparison shows that the proposed tracker can track different non-rigid objects more accurately than non-rigid tracker *HT* [7] and bounding-box tracker *TLD* [8] when different targets change their appearances greatly during tracking. For the tracking failure of *TLD*, the background areas in the bounding-box might be recognized as the target and are used for classifier learning and updating. For the inaccurate tracking by *HT*, since the *HT* tracker utilize the detection points of target to guide the 'GrabCut' segmentation, unfortunately, such guidance is hard to be accurately always without motion information between frames for a long time. Comparatively, the proposed tracking can obtain satisfactory results on most of the testing videos.

Table 1: Tracking of different objects: percentage of correctly tracked frames until failure

Sequence	*FlowCut*	*HT*	*BHMC*	*TLD*	*CT*
Sylvester(1345)	100	86	90	89	75
Girl(502)	86	17	8	84	78
Tiger1(354)	17	17	7	65	78
Mountain-bike(228)	100	100	70	26	19
Motocross1(164)	100	62	5	16	12
Motocross2(23)	100	100	30	82	73
Cliff-dive1(76)	100	100	100	100	75
Cliff-dive2(69)	88	82	26	21	50
Volleyball(500)	44	32	50	25	58
Diving(231)	26	26	100	26	22
Average	76.1	62.2	48.6	53.4	54.0

To show the robustness comparison between different trackers, we employed the percentage of the successfully tracked frames of all frames in each testing video as the measurement, which was also used by other works [8][7][14]. The comparison results are shown in Table. 1, and the numbers in the bracket of column 1 are the total number of the frames of each video. In some testing videos containing rigid objects such as 'Girl', the *TLD* and is more robust than *CT*,

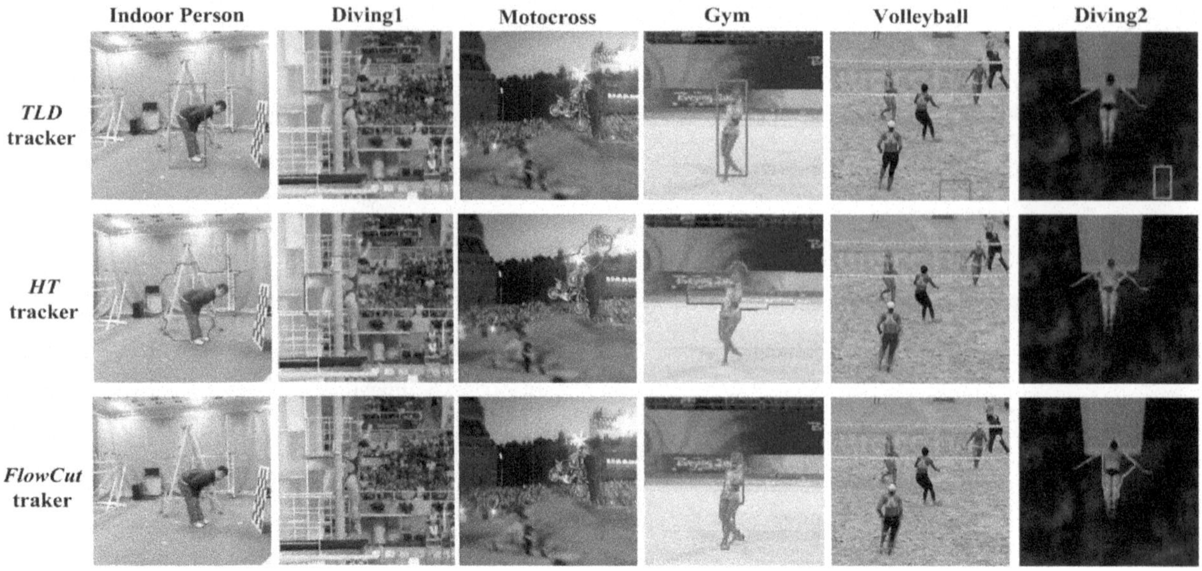

Figure 1: Non-rigid target tracking comparison between the proposed tracking and other state-of-art works on other challenge testing videos

BHMC and *HT* since the framework of *TLD* utilizes the motion trajectory estimation/calibration to re-initialize the tracker when it begins to drift from the target. While the proposed tracking can track both the rigid and non-rigid objects more robustly as shown in the table. For the difference shown in Table. 1 and [7], it is caused by the instable performance of the *HT* tracker on some testing videos such as 'Cliff-div2' and 'Motocross1'. The main reason of the this problem is that the randomly feature extraction used in [7] is not stable enough, which may lead to detection failure when the segmentation is rough. During our experiment, we run *HT* tracker 20 times and use the average as the final value. The average running speed for the proposed tracking is 1.5-2.5fps without any code optimization.

5. CONCLUSION

In this paper, we presented a non-rigid target tracking method based on object segmentation with online learning. By incorporating the gradients flow into a 'Gibbs' energy function, the irregular target areas can be extracted more accurately than using single frame for segmentation. Compared with fixed-shape based tracking approaches, more precise segmentation leads to more accurate samples generation for online learning. Experiments on challenging videos have demonstrated the accuracy and robustness improvement in tracking different non-rigid targets when compared with other state-of-art tracking works.

Although the proposed tracking strategy can handle the presented problems well, for other more challenging problems in the tracking studies, such as long-term heavy occlusion, abrupt motion of the target, etc, there is still room for improvement. Those problems will be tackled in our future studies.

6. ACKNOWLEDGEMENT

This research is supported by Research Fund for the Doctoral Program of Higher Education of China (No:20126102120055) and National Natural Science Foundation of China (No:61231016 & No:61272288).

7. REFERENCES

[1] O. Barinova, V. Lempitsky, and P. Kohli. On detection of multiple object instances using hough transforms. *IEEE CVPR*, 2010.

[2] A. Blake, C. Rother, M. Brown, P. Perez, and P. Torr. Interactive image segmentation using an adaptive gmmrf model. *ECCV*, 2004.

[3] Y. Boykov and M. Jolly. Interactive graph cuts for optimal boundary and region segmentation of objects in n-d images. *IEEE ICCV*, 2001.

[4] L. Breiman. Random forests. *Machine Learning*, 2001.

[5] A. Bruhn, J.Weickert, and C. Schnağorr. Lucas/kanade meets horn/schunk: combining local and global optical flow methods. *Internatial Journal of Computer Vision*, 6(3):211–231, 2005.

[6] M. Godec. Hough-based tracking of non-rigid objects. `http://lrs.icg.tugraz.at/research/houghtrack/`.

[7] M. Godec, P. Roth, and H. Bischof. Hough-based tracking of non-rigid objects. *IEEE ICCV*, 2011.

[8] Z. Kalal, K. Mikolajczyk, and J. Matas. Tracking learning detection. *IEEE T-PAMI*, 6(1):1409–1422, 2010.

[9] P. Kontschieder, S. Bulo, H. Bischof, and M. Pelillo. Structured class-labels in random forests for semantic image labelling. *IEEE ICCV*, 2011.

[10] J. Kwon and K. Lee. Tracking of a non-rigid object via patch based dynamic appearance modeling and adaptive basin hopping monte carlo sampling. *IEEE CVPR*, 2009.

[11] C. Liu. Beyond pixels: Exploring new representations and applications for motion analysis. *Doctoral Thesis, Massachusetts Institute of Technology*, May 2009.

[12] C. Rother, V. Kolmogorov, and A. Blake. Grabcut: Interactive foreground extraction using iterated graph cuts. *ACM SIGGRAPH*, pages 309–314, 2004.

[13] X. Sun, H. Yao, and S. Zhang. A novel supervised level set method for non-rigid object tracking. *IEEE CVPR*, 2011.

[14] K. Zhang, L. Zhang, and M. Yang. Real-time compressive tracking. *ECCV*, pages 864–877, 2012.

Object Coding on the Semantic Graph for Scene Classification

Jingjing Chen [1], Yahong Han [1,3], Xiaochun Cao [1,2], Qi Tian [4]

[1] School of Computer Science and Technology, Tianjin University, China
[2] State Key Laboratory of Information Security, Chinese Academy of Sciences
[3] Tianjin Key Laboratory of Cognitive Computing and Application
[4] Department of Computer Science, University of Texas at San Antonio
chenjingjing.tju@gmail.com, yahong@tju.edu.cn,
caoxiaochun@iie.ac.cn, qitian @cs.utsa.edu

ABSTRACT

In the scene classification, a scene can be considered as a set of object cliques. Objects inside each clique have semantic correlations with each other, while two objects from different cliques are relatively independent. To utilize these correlations for better recognition performance, we propose a new method - Object Coding on the Semantic Graph to address the scene classification problem. We first exploit prior knowledge by making statistics on a large number of labeled images and calculating the dependency degree between objects. Then, a graph is built to model the semantic correlations between objects. This semantic graph captures semantics by treating the objects as vertices and the objects affinities as the weights of edges. By encoding this semantic knowledge into the semantic graph, object coding is conducted to automatically select a set of object cliques that have strongly semantic correlations to represent a specific scene. The experimental results show that the Object Coding on semantic graph can improve the classification accuracy.

Categories and Subject Descriptors

I.5.2 [**Pattern Recognition**]: Design Methodology—*Classifier design and evaluation*; I.2.10 [**Artificial Intelligence**]: Vision and Scene Understanding—*Representations, data structures, and transforms*

Keywords

scene classification; object coding; semantic graph

1. INTRODUCTION

Scene classification is a challenging task in the field of high-level visual recognition. One major reason is the discrepancy between image representations and the high-level semantics, which is widely known as semantic gap. In the past years, many efforts have been made to narrow the semantic gap, such as developing more sophisticated models [6][13], generating intermediate representations by making statistics on robust low level descriptors [15], or proposing structure sparsity methods to select the discriminative features by incorporating semantic information[2][14][3]. Although the above mentioned methods are demonstrated to improve the recognition accuracy, as they are based on low-level descriptors and ignore the high-level semantics (correlation between semantic concepts), the performances are constrained. Recently, a lot of method have been proposed to introducing high-level semantics[8][7] [1][5]. For example, [5] models the joint relationship between the low-level events in a graph where each low-level event is consider a node and whenever there is a correlation between two low-level events the graph has an edge between the corresponding nodes. And then learn a discriminative model of complex event in the video by using latent SVM formulation. This method is proved to perform well in complex event recognition by exploring semantics correlations between low-level events. [7] proposes object bank method, which uses objects as attribute and represents the image in high-level. Then a regularized logistic regression is utilized to learn and classify complex scenes. However, this method ignores the semantic correlations between objects. If these semantic correlations are taken into account, we can further narrow down the mantic gap and achieve better classification accuracy.

In this paper, we propose a model of object coding on the semantic graph to induce a process of supervised feature selection for scene classification. In our method, images are present in object-level and a semantic graph is built to introduce the semantic correlations among objects. In the graph, each object is regarded as vertex and the semantic correlation between objects is considered as the weight of the edge. Selecting object cliques for the representation of a specific scene in fact a process of selecting a path of from the semantic graph. The flowchart of object coding on the semantic graph is shown in Figure 1. If the weight between two objects is small, then these two objects will be picked out in low cost, which means semantic correlations between the linked objects are strong. Selecting these two semantically related objects for the classification of a specific is more interpretable than selecting each object separately and therefore the performance of scene classification will be improved.

MM'13, October 21-25, 2013, Barcelona, Spain.

2. SCENE CLASSIFICATION VIA OBJECT CODING

The motivation of our method is that a scene is composed of object cliques in which the objects have semantic correlations. It is helpful to select appropriate object cliques to represent a specific scene. We obtain the representation of a scene by the regression model regularized by the object coding penalty. As it contains ad-

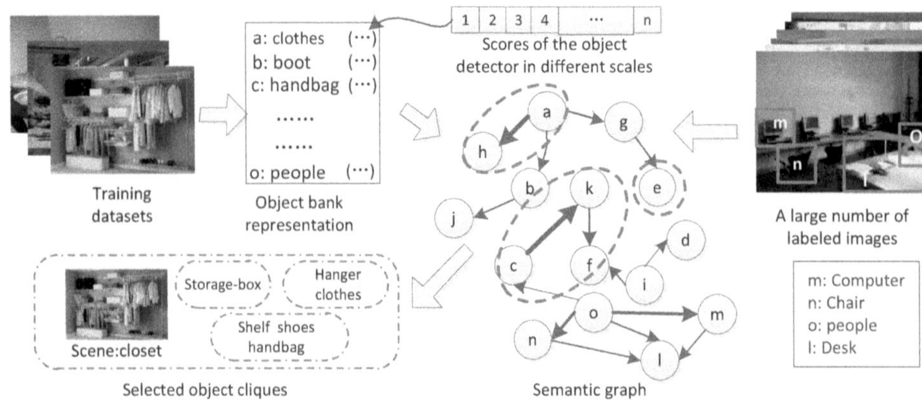

Figure 1: Flowchart of the object coding on the semantic graph. Step. 1: Make statistics on large numbers of images to obtain semantic correlations between objects, and build a graph to model the semantic correlations. The thicker the edge is the stronger correlations are between the objects. Step. 2: For training dataset, extract object bank representations (a, b, c... stand for objects). Step. 3: Use the graph to guide for object cliques selection for a specific scene.

ditional semantic information, our method can help to pick out the object cliques that represent the meaning of a scene as much as possible. Let $\mathbb{X} = [X_1^T, X_2^T, ..., X_N^T] \in \mathbb{R}^{N \times J_r}$, an $N \times J_r$ matrix, imply the representation of N images which are obtained by J object detectors; Where r is the dimension of the vector representation of an object. Suppose we detect the object in three-level scale pyramids and spatial pyramids, respectively, then the object is represented as a vector, whose dimension is $3 \times (1+4+16)$. Actually, an object vector can be seen as a group of features. Let $\mathbb{Y} = [y_1, y_2, ..., y_N] \in \{0,1\}^N$ denote the binary classification labels of N samples. A classifier is a function $h_\beta : \mathbb{R}^{J_r} \to \{0,1\}$ defined as $h_\beta(X) \triangleq argmax_{y \in \{0,1\}} X\beta$, where $\beta = (\beta_1, \beta_2, ...\beta_{J_r}) \in \mathbb{R}^{J_r}$ is a vector of parameters to be estimated. This leads to the following learning problem: $min_{\beta \in \mathbb{R}^{J_r}} \lambda\Omega(\beta) + \frac{1}{m}\sum_{i=1}^{m} L(\beta; X_i, y_i)$, where $L(\beta; X, y)$ is a non-negative, convex loss, m is the number of training images, $\Omega(\beta)$ is a regularizer. And λ is the regularization coefficient, whose value can be determined by the cross validation. In our method, $\Omega(\beta)$ is defined to be the object coding regularizer, whose goal is to introduce the prior semantic information among objects.

2.1 Object Coding on the Semantic Graph

Object Coding is formulated to be a process of object clique selection on the predefined semantic graph, which is modeled to incorporate semantic correlations among objects. The semantic correlations are considered as prior knowledge, which is obtained by making statistics on a large number of images and calculating the dependency degree between objects appearing in images. In our method, we make statistics on the a subset of the labeled images of MIT-indoor and use θ-coordinate [4] to obtain the second-order relationship between objects.

$$\theta_{12} = log\frac{p_{11}p_{00}}{p_{01}p_{10}}, \tag{1}$$

where θ_{12} is used to measure the dependency degree between objects, e.g. A and B. p_{11} is the probability that A and B occur simultaneously in one image, p_{00} is the probability that both A and B do not co-occur, p_{10} is the probability that only A occurs, and p_{01} is the probability that only B occurs. We obtain them by calculating the joint distribution between the objects. The advantages of using the θ-coordinate is that it is independent of certain database. Then semantic graph is built to model the semantic correlations between objects. We first consider the features of an object as an entity. And this entity is indeed an object. Then the objects are considered as vertices, and the relationship between objects are considered as an edge. The weights of edges are defined as following:

$$w_{i,j} = \begin{cases} \infty, & \theta_{i,j} \leqslant T, \quad (2) \\ 1/\theta_{i,j}, & \theta_{i,j} > T. \quad (2') \end{cases}$$

where T is a threshold: if $\theta_{i,j} > T$, object i and object j are linked by one edge. In the semantic graph, the weight $w_{i,j}$ is the cost of picking the couples. The lower the weights are, the stronger correlations are between the objects. Thus it costs less to pick the couples with high correlations out. Then we remove the cycle in the semantic graph and define a unified direction of each edge. In this way, we convert the graph to directed acyclic graph whose goal is to simplify the solution of our model. Figure 2 shows an semantic DAG. (In figure 2, the start node s and end node t will be explained in the following section). Note that an object is represented as a vector of responding scores in different scales. Coding an object is indeed to code these scores. Thus, for each object, we link these scores in cascade with unified low weight for simplicity, as shown in Figure 2. If we choose the object, the features in it are all included in low cost. The advantage of constructing such a semantic graph to guide for object selection is that: i. the selection of a sets of semantically meaningful objects might be more interpretable than the selection of isolated one. ii. such a graph enrich semantic information by introducing prior knowledge.

2.2 Formulation of Object Coding

In this section, we will concentrate on how to formulate object coding penalties $\Omega(\beta)$ on the semantic DAG $G = (V, E)$ to induce an automatic way of selecting a set of object cliques for the specific scene. And this is in fact a process of selecting a small number of connected subgraphs from the DAG. To map the problem to network flow optimization, we enrich the original directed acyclic graph by introducing a source node s and a sink node t. And in the new graph $G' = (V', E')$: $V' \triangleq V \bigcup \{s, t\}$, $E' \triangleq E \bigcup \{(s, v) : v \in V\} \bigcup \{(u, t) : u \in V\}$. Node s, t are linked to every object, as shown in Figure 2. The weights between source node s and other nodes are denoted as γ. γ encourages selecting features in a long path. Let's assume a cost configuration $[c_{uv}]_{(u,v) \in E'}$, and set of flows $\mathcal{F}$ on G'. The object selection problem is equivalent to looking for the value f_{uv} of a flow on every arc (u,v) of the graph. The cost $[c_{uv}]$ is the exactly the weight of the edge between u and

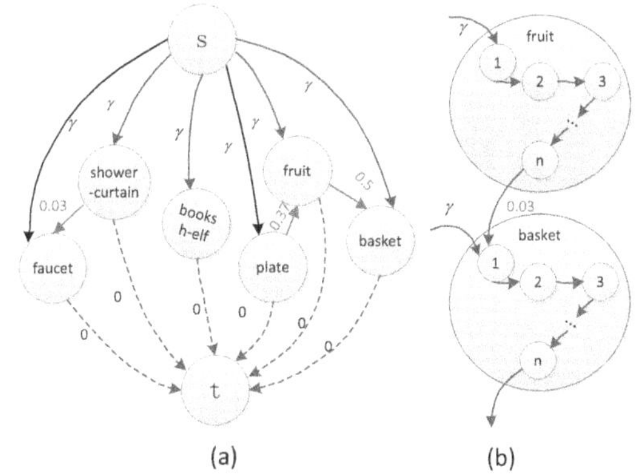

Figure 2: Object graph G' with a source s and sink t. In G', the object is considered as a subgraph where every feature of the object sit. (a), The objects are firstly considered as vertices, and the correlations between objects are considered as weighted edges. The weights are obtained according to the semantic correlation between objects. (b), Subgraphs of objects fruit and basket. Vertex {1, 2, 3,... n} stand for detector's scores of object in different scales. Selecting object cliques for the scene is equivalent to selecting paths in G'.

v. Denote $s_j(f) \triangleq \sum_{u \in V':(u,j) \in E'} f_{uj}$ as the cost on the amount of flow going through a vertex j in $V = 1, 2...J_r$. It is easy to equivalently replace a vertex with a capacity/cost to two vertices linked by an arc carries the capacity/cost in the network. Thus we can apply minimum cost flow to solve this problem. $\Omega_(\beta)$ can be rewritten as following:

$$\Omega_(\beta) = \min_{f \in \mathcal{F}} \{ \sum_{(u,v) \in E'} f_{uv} c_{uv} s.t s_j(f) \geq |\beta_j|, \forall j \in \{1, ..., J_r\}\}, \quad (3)$$

where $\mathcal{F}$ is the set of flows on G'. This is exactly a minimum cost flow problem with some lower-capacity constraints which can be computed in strong polynomial time. To make use of proximal gradient method to solve regularized problem, we first compute the proximal operators of $\Omega_(\beta)$.

$$f^* \in arg \min_{f \in \mathcal{F}} \{ \sum_{(u,v) \in E'} f_{uv} c_{uc} + \sum_{j=1}^{J_r} \frac{1}{2} \max(|\mathbf{u}_j| - s_j(f), 0)^2 \} \quad (4)$$

where $\mathbf{u}$ is in $\mathbb{R}$, and $\mathcal{F}$ is the set of flows on G'. This is a minimum cost flow problem with piecewise quadratic costs, which can be computed in polynomial time. Denote by $\mathbf{w}^* \triangleq Prox_\Omega[\mathbf{u}]$, and for all j in $V = 1, .., p, \mathbf{w}^* = sign(\mathbf{u}_j) min(|\mathbf{u}_j|, s_j(f^*))$[10]. The minimum cost flow problems can be solved with a worst-case complexity of $O\big((|V| log|V|)(|E| + |V| log|V|)\big)$ operations. And in practical terms, the complexity of network flows is often much better [10]. So our equation can be solved efficiently.

3. EXPERIMENTAL RESULTS

3.1 Dataset

We conduct experiments on two dataset: MIT-indoor [11] and UIUC-event[9]. For each dataset, we use the object bank features provided by [8]. We remove the scores obtained by the detectors whose corresponding objects are not contained in the datasets. Then we extract $130 \times 3 \times (1+4+16)$ dimension of features from the the original 44604 dimensional visual features of object bank, and build a graph to model the semantic correlations between objects according to the θ value between objects. In the experiments, we use mean accuracy to evaluate the classification performance.

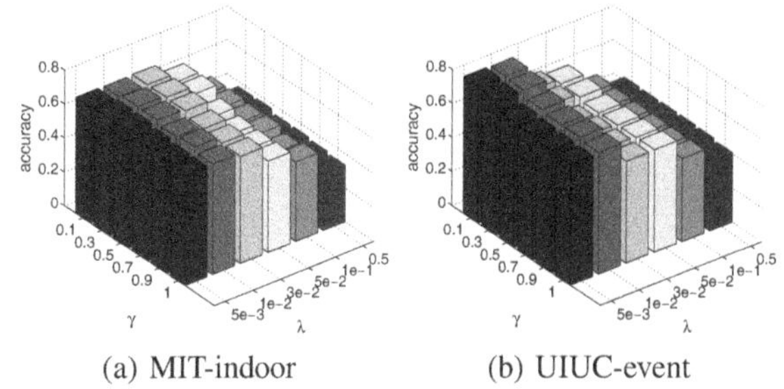

Figure 3: Parameters tuning of the datasets. The respective range of λ and γ are {5e-3, 1e-2, 5e-2, 1e-1, 3e-1, 0.5} and {0.1, 0.3, 0.5, 0.7, 0.9, 1}

A brief introduction of the datasets is as follows. **MIT-indoor**: The database contains 68 Indoor categories, such as artstudio, bar, bedroom, bookstore, classroom, gry, etc. and a total of 15620 images. The number of images varies across categories, but there are at least 100 images per category. **UIUC-event**: This database contains 1579 sports scenes images which is categorized into 8 classes, including badminton, bocce, croquet, polo, rock climbing, rowing, sailing, and snow boarding. Each class contains about 100-200 images.

3.2 Parameter setting

In the experiments, three parameters need to set: threshold T, regularization coefficient λ, and start weight γ. The threshold T is set to 2.0 which is a empirical value. It is important to notice that we set the stop weight as 0 in our experiment to ensure the path can be terminated at any object in a low cost. Then we tune the other two parameters λ and γ for each data set. In this experiment, we use cross validation on the training dataset to trim the value of this two parameters. The ranges of λ and γ for MIT-indoor and UIUC-event datasets are {5e-3, 1e-2, 5e-2, 1e-1, 3e-1, 0.5} and {0.1, 0.3, 0.5, 0.7, 0.9, 1}. To efficiently tune the parameters for MIT indoor dataset, we randomly randomly select 10 class of scenes to tune the parameter. The parameter tuning results are shown in Figure 4. The best performance on MIT-indoor and UIUC-event was obtained when when $\lambda = 0.01$, $\gamma = 0.3$ and $\lambda = 0.005$, $\gamma = 0.1$ respectively. In the following, we fix the value of λ and γ to be the values with which the best performance is obtained.

3.3 Results and analysis

The time complexity of our method is $O(n^2 logn + n^2 (logn)^2)$, where n is the dimension of features. We first explore the object selection results of our method. Table 1 presents object cliques selection results for sample scenes, (the objects with quite small coefficient ($< 1e-4$) are not listed in the table) and Figure 4 shows the corresponding sampled scenes. Because the detectors are not accurate enough to make sure the validity of the detecting results, the object cliques selected by our method are not good as ideally. For example, as is shown in Table 1, pen is included in the object cliques set to represent the buffet. Another important reason is the limited number of detectors used in object bank. However, it should be notice that our method can select object cliques which have high discriminative power. And these high discriminative object cliques are selected with high coefficient. Our method is particular suitable for classifying complex scenes, which contain several objects. Then we discuss the classification performance of our method. In order to investigate the performance of object coding on the semantic graph method, we compare our classification accuracy with the state-of-the-art methods on MIT-indoor and Event datasets. For the

Scene	Sel. O. cliq.	coefficient	Scene	Sel. O. cliq.	coefficient
Bowl.	pool ball	0.290	Closet	Suit	0.057
	pool table	0.234		Attire	0.032
	mirror	0.061		Shelf	0.084
	box	0.010		Handbag	0.011
	bottle	0.049		Hanger	0.054
	people	0.082		Shoes	0.016
buffet	plate	0.085		knife	0.013
	fruit	0.057		mug	0.009
	vase	0.022		blanket	0.002
	pen	0.012		wall	0.011

Table 1: Object cliques selection results for sample scenes. Take the bowling for example, object coding on the Semantic Graph selects the cliques < pool ball, pool table>, <mirror>, <box>, <bottle>, <people> for representation. And the objects in the clique < pool ball, pool table> get the highest coefficients.

Figure 4: Sample scenes corresponding to Table 1

MIT-indoor dataset, 60 images in each class are chosen for training and 40 for testing. For the UIUC-event Scene dataset, 50 randomly drawn images from each scene classes are used for training and 30 for testing. Figure 5 summarizes the average performance of multi-way classification results. We compare our method against baseline([11] of MIT-indoor, [9] of Event), ScSPM [13], Objectbank-SVM [8], Objectbank-LR [7] and Object bank linear regression with Lasso regularization [12]. For Objectbank-SVM [8], the dimension of the vector representing an image in our experiment is the same as our method; In [13], features are generated on the three-level spatial pyramid; For object bank representation with linear regression [7] whose regularizer is $\Omega(\beta) \triangleq \lambda_1||\beta||_{1,2} + \lambda_2||\beta||_1$, we also tune the parameters to achieve a better performance. By our method, the accuracy of classification results on UIUC-event achieves 80.7%, while object bank with SVM classifier is 70%; [7] is 76.1%; ScSPM is 78%; Linear regression Lasso in object bank obtains 76.4%. In MIT-indoor dataset, the accuracy of our method is 33.1%, which improves 18.2% than object bank-SVM and 6% than ScSPM. Based on the above experimental results, it is obvious that our method achieve the highest accuracy. The stronger predict power of the models trained with our method demonstrate that it is able to select object cliques to describe as much semantic information of the scene as possible.

4. CONCLUSIONS

In this paper, we propose an object coding on semantic graph method for scene classification. The method is formulated on a semantic graph which is built to model the semantic correlation between objects. By introducing much richer semantic information, our method induces selecting objects in the sets of path over this semantic graph. Objects in the same path constitute an object clique, which is more interpretable than single object. Experiments results show that our method can select discriminative and semantically meaningful object cliques for a specific scene. Comparing to other method, our method achieves a better classification accuracy.

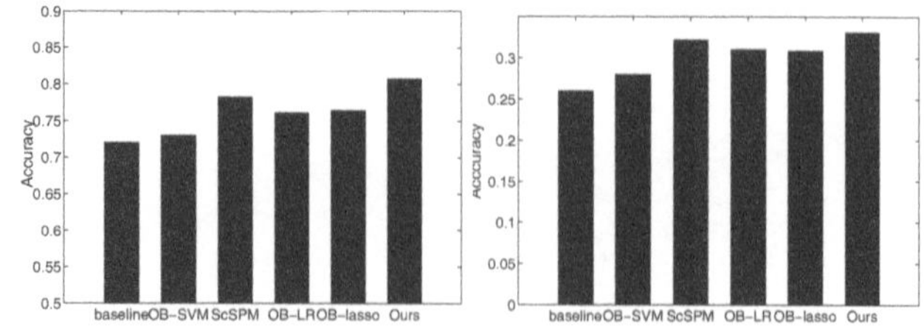

(a) UIUC-event (b) MIT-Indoor

Figure 5: Comparison of classification performance of different Methods(Baseline vs. Object bank-SVM vs. ScSPM-SVM vs. Object bank-LR vs. Object bank-lasso vs. Object Coding) on UIUC-event and MIT-Indoor datasets.

5. ACKNOWLEDGEMENT

This work was supported by National Program on Key Basic Research Project (2013CB329305), NSFC(61003200, 61202166, 61222210), National High-tech R&D Program of China (2012AA 011503) and 100 Talents Programme of The Chinese Academy of Sciences, and was supported in part to Dr. Qi Tian by ARO grant W911BF-12-1-0057, NSF IIS 1052851, Faculty Research Awards by Google, FXPAL, NEC Laboratories of America, and 2012 UTSA START-R Research Award respectively.

6. REFERENCES

[1] Y. Han, F. Wu, X. Lu, Q. Tian, Y. Zhuang, and J. Luo. Correlated attribute transfer with multi-task graph-guided fusion. In *ACM MM*, 2012.

[2] Y. Han, F. Wu, D. Tao, J. Shao, Y. Zhuang, and J. Jiang. Sparse unsupervised dimensionality reduction for multiple view data. *IEEE Transactions on Circuits and Systems for Video Technology*, 22(10):1485–1496, 2012.

[3] Y. Han, F. Wu, Q. Tian, and Y. Zhuang. Image annotation by input-output structural grouping sparsity. *IEEE Transactions on Image Processing*, 21(6):3066–3079, 2012.

[4] Y. Hou, L. He, X. Zhao, and D. Song. Pure high-order word dependence mining via information geometry. *Advances in Information Retrieval Theory, ICTIR 2011*, 6931:64–76, 2011.

[5] H. Izadinia and M. Shah. Recognizing complex events using large margin joint low-level event model. In *ECCV*, 2012.

[6] S. Lazebnik, C. Schmid, and J. Ponce. Beyond bags of features: Spatial pyramid matching for recognizing natural scene categories. In *CVPR*, pages 2169–2178, 2006.

[7] L. Li, H. Su, E.P.Xing, and F. Li. Oobject bank: A high-level image representation for scene classification and semantic feature sparsification. In *NIPS*, 2010.

[8] L. Li, H. Su, Y. Lim, and F. Li. Object as attributes for scene classification. In *ECCV*, 2010.

[9] L.-J. Li and L. Fei-Fei. What, where and who? classifying event by scene and object recognition. In *ICCV*, pages 1–8, 2007.

[10] J. Mairal and B. Yu. Supervised feature selection in graphs with path coding penalties and network flows. *CoRR*, 2012.

[11] A. Quattoni and A. Torralba. Recognizing indoor sceces. In *CVPR*, pages 413–420, 2009.

[12] R. Tibshiran. Regression shrinkage and selection via the lasso. *Journal of the Royal Statistical Society: Series B (Statistical Methodology)*, 58(1):267–288, 1996.

[13] J. Yang, K. Yu, Y. Gong, and T. Huang. Linear spatial pyramid matching using sparse coding for image classification. In *CVPR*, pages 1794–1801, 2009.

[14] Y. Yang, Y. Zhuang, F. Wu, and Y. Pan. Harmonizing hierarchical manifolds for multimedia document semantics understanding and cross-media retrieval. *IEEE Transactions on Multimedia*, 10(3):437–446, 2008.

[15] J. Zhang, M. Marszalek, S. Lazebnik, and C. Schmid. Local features and kernels for classification of texture and object categories: A comprehensive study. *IJCV*, 73(2):213–238, June 2007.

Beyond Bag of Words: Image Representation in Sub-semantic Space

Chunjie Zhang[1], Shuhui Wang[2], Chao Liang[3], Jing Liu[4], Qingming Huang[1,2], Haojie Li[5], Qi Tian[6]

[1]School of Computer and Control Engineering, University of Chinese Academy of Sciences, 100049, Beijing, China
[2]Key Lab of Intell. Info. Process, Institute of Computing Technology, Chinese Academy of Sciences, Beijing, 100190, China
[3]National Engineering Research Center for Multimedia Software, School of Computer, Wuhan University, 430072, Wuhan, China
[4]National Laboratory of Pattern Recognition, Institute of Automation, Chinese Academy of Sciences, Beijing, China
[5]School of Software, Dalian University of Technology, Liaoning, China
[6]Department of Computer Sciences, University of Texas at San Antonio, TX, 78249, U.S.A

{cjzhang, shwang, qmhuang}@jdl.ac.cn, cliang@whu.edu.cn, jliu@nlpr.ia.ac.cn, hjli@dlut.edu.cn, qitian@cs.utsa.edu

ABSTRACT

Due to the semantic gap, the low-level features are not able to semantically represent images well. Besides, traditional semantic related image representation may not be able to cope with large inter class variations and are not very robust to noise. To solve these problems, in this paper, we propose a novel image representation method in the sub-semantic space. First, examplar classifiers are trained by separating each training image from the others and serve as the weak semantic similarity measurement. Then a graph is constructed by combining the visual similarity and weak semantic similarity of these training images. We partition this graph into visually and semantically similar sub-sets. Each sub-set of images are then used to train classifiers in order to separate this sub-set from the others. The learned sub-set classifiers are then used to construct a sub-semantic space based representation of images. This sub-semantic space is not only more semantically meaningful but also more reliable and resistant to noise. Finally, we make categorization of images using this sub-semantic space based representation on several public datasets to demonstrate the effectiveness of the proposed method.

Categories and Subject Descriptors

I.2.10 [**Artificial Intelligence**]: Vision and Scene Understanding—*representation, data structures, and transforms*; I.4.10 [**Image Processing and Computer Vision**]: Image Representation—*statistical*

Keywords

Object categorization, sub-semantic space, examplar classifier, sparse coding.

MM '13, October 21 - 25 2013, Barcelona, Spain
Copyright 2013 ACM 978-1-4503-2404-5/13/10 ...$15.00.
http://dx.doi.org/10.1145/2502081.2502132.

1. INTRODUCTION

The local feature based image representation is widely used by researchers recently. Local features are first extracted either by detection or dense sampling. k-means clustering or sparse coding is then used to generate the codebook and encode these local features. Images are finally represented by bag-of-visual-words (BoW) representation. The BoW model has been proven effective by many researchers [1-5]. However, the visual words have no explicit semantic correspondence with human perception which hinders the discriminative power of the BoW model.

To alleviate this problem, a lot of works have been done. On one hand, more discriminative and powerful features are proposed [2-5]. These well designed features capture more information and are more robust to outliers than traditional BoW model. For example, the spatial pyramid matching (SPM) is proposed by Lazebnik *et al.* [2] and is widely used since its introduction. With the fast development of computational power, the explore of more powerful features will be a hot topic in the future.

On the other hand, the use of semantic related representation is also widely studied. Semantic space based image representation is more interpretable than using local features directly for humans. These semantic spaces can be generated by latent space learning [6-8], using the training images [9-10] or generic object classifiers [11]. However, the learning of effective and robust semantic space is very hard due to the well-known semantic gap. Besides, the semantic space is often learned using all the training images of the same class. However, objects may pose large inter class variations which makes it very difficult to learn reliable classifiers for robust semantic representation. For example, the frontal view and the side view of a car are quite different. To alleviate this problem, the use of attribute is introduced [12-15] which helps to improve the image representation effectiveness. However, the attributes have to be pre-defined. Besides, choosing the proper attributes requires experience and extensive human labor which limits its scalability for large scale applications.

Recently, the use of examplar image for object detection [16] and categorization [17] become popular. The use of examplar classifier takes the advantage of semantic space based image representation and is also more efficient and easy to train than traditional methods [6-11]. Although proven effective, not all of the examplar classifiers are equally useful for image representation. It would be more effective if we can choose some discriminative examplar classifiers instead of use all of them. Besides, images of the same class often exhibit large inter class variations which means the semantic meaning of examplar classifiers may not be so semantic meaningful for efficient image representation.

To solve the problems mentioned above, in this paper, we go one step further byond the bag of words based image representation and propose to represent images in sub-semantic space. First, we train exampler classifier for each training image which serves as the weak semantic similarity measurement. A visual and semantic similarity graph is constructed by combing the visual similarity and weak semantic similarity of training images. We then partition this graph to get sub-sets of images which are visually and semantically similar. Each sub-set of images are used to construct a sub-semantic space representation of images. This is achieved by learning SVM classifiers which separate one sub-set of images from the others. Since we use a sub-set of images for representation, this semantic space is named as sub-semantic space. This sub-semantic space based image representation is not only more semantically meaningful than examplar based representation but also more resistant to noise than traditional semantic space based image representation. Finally, to demonstrate the effectiveness of the proposed image representation method, we conduct object categorization experiments on two public datasets.

2. SUB-SEMANTIC SPACE BASED IMAGE REPRESENTATION

In this section, we give the details of the proposed sub-semantic space based image representation method. We use the sparse coding with locality constraints [18] and max pooling technique as the raw image representation. For each training image, visual similarity along with examplar classifier based weak semantic representation are used to construct a visual-semantic similarity graph. This graph is then partitioned to get sub-class partitions of training images. These sub-class partitioned images are trained to get the final sub-semantic representation of images by separating each sub-class from the rest sub-classes.

2.1 Examplar classifier based weak semantic similarity

We use the semantic space technique to represent images. We try to learn a set of exemplar classifiers for each of the training images. Each exemplar classifier is trained with the corresponding training image and all the other images of different classes which exhibits weak semantic meanings. Since this is much easier than classifying the full-class images, we can use simpler classifiers such as linear SVM. This weak semantic information is then used to measure the weak semantic similarity of images.

Formally, let $X = [x_1, ..., x_N] \in \mathbb{R}^{D \times N}$ be the set of D-dimensional BoW representation of N images, where $x_i \in \mathbb{R}^{D \times 1}, i = 1, ..., N$. These images are of K classes and let $Y = (y_1, ..., y_N) \in \{1, ..., K\}^N$ denote the corresponding image labels. For each training image $x_i, i = 1, 2, ..., N$, we try to learn the optimal parameters (w_i, b_i) to separate x_i from all the other images of different classes by the largest possible margin, where $w_i \in \mathbb{R}^{D \times 1}$. This is achieved by solving the following optimization problem for all i as:

$$min_{w_i, b_i} \parallel w_i \parallel^2 + C \times \ell(w_i^T x_i + b_i) + \sum_{j=1}^{N} \ell(-w_i^T x_j - b_i) \quad (1)$$

$$\forall y_j \neq y_i$$

Where C is the weighting parameter which controls the relative importance of x_i. We use the hinge loss as our loss function which has the form of:

$$\ell(x) = max(0, 1 - x) \quad (2)$$

Libsvm is used to train each exemplar classifier and we can use it for weak semantic image representation. For a given image x, we predict its semantic meanings for each exemplar classifier and use the output of these classifiers as the weak semantic representation $h \in \mathbb{R}^{N \times 1}$, where $h_i = w_i^T x + b_i, i = 1, 2, ..., N$. The spatial pyramid matching (SPM) with three pyramid levels ($L = 0, 1, 2$) is also used to combine the spatial information and scale changes of this weak semantic representation.

The weak semantic similarity $s_{wss}(i, j)$ between image i and j is then defined as:

$$s_{wss}(i, j) = exp^{\|h_i - h_j\|^2 / \sigma_1} \quad (3)$$

where σ_1 is the parameter which controls the relative influence of weak semantic similarity.

2.2 Visual-semantic graph construction and partition

Similarly, we can define the visual similarity $s_{vs}(i, j)$ between image i and j as:

$$s_{vs}(i, j) = exp^{\|x_i - x_j\|^2 / \sigma_2} \quad (4)$$

where σ_2 is the parameter which controls the relative influence of visual similarity.

We propose to use a visual-semantic graph to model the visual similarity as well as the weak semantic similarity of images. The nodes correspond to the training images while the edges correspond to the visual-semantic similarity which is defined as the sum of visual similarity and weak semantic similarity

$$w(i, j) = \alpha s_{wss}(i, j) + (1 - \alpha) s_{vs} \qquad y_i == y_j \quad (5)$$

α is a balancing parameter which controls the relative importance of visual similarity and weak semantic similarity. Not that only images of the same class are considered. Let W be the graph matrix with $W = (w_{i,j})_{i,j=1,...,n}$ and D

be the corresponding diagonal degree matrix with its diagonal elements as $d_i = \sum_{j=1}^{n} w_{i,j}$. The corresponding graph Laplacian matrix is then defined as:

$$L = D - W \tag{6}$$

We adopt the spectral clustering technique to group the visual-semantic similarity graph into M sub-sets for each image class. This is achieved by finding the first M eigenvalues (ordered increasingly) and corresponding eigenvectors of L [22]. After these sub-sets of images are obtained, we can use them to construct the sub-semantic representation of images.

2.3 Sub-semantic space based image representation

Let $X = [X_1, ..., X_{MK}]$ be the partitioned training images with X_k is the k-th subset. We propose to train linear SVM classifiers to separate each subset of images with the others and use the output of these learned classifiers for sub-semantic space representation. This image representation not only takes advantage of the semantic based representation, but also is more reliable and robust to noise than examplar based weak semantic representation [17]. This is because we can get ride of some confusing training samples during the graph partition process. This makes the final image representation more semantically meaningful. In fact, the traditional semantic space based image representation [9-10] and examplar based method [17] can be viewed as special cases of the proposed sub-semantic space method. If we set α to 0 and M to 1, the sub-semantic space based image representation will degenerate to the traditional semantic space method. If we set α to 1 and M to the number of training images per class, the proposed sub-semantic space method will degenerate to the examplar based method.

We choose to conduct object categorization experiments to demonstrate the effectiveness of the proposed sub-semantic space based image representation method. We follow the one-versus-all strategy as [17] did and learn K binary SVM classifiers to predict the categories of images.

3. EXPERIMENTS

We evaluate the proposed sub-semantic space based image representation method for categorization on two public datasets: the Scene-15 dataset [2] and the Caltech-256 dataset [19] as [17] did for fair comparison. We follow the same experimental setup and densely extract SIFT descriptors on overlapping 16×16 pixels with an overlap of 6 pixels. Sparse coding [3] with locality constraint [18] is used to encode local features as it has been proven more effective than k-means clustering method. Max pooling is then used to extract image representation which is used for training exemplar classifiers. The codebook size is set to 1,024 for the two datasets.

3.1 Scene-15 dataset

The Scene-15 dataset has 15 categories (bedroom, CALsuburb, coast, forest, highway, industrial, insidecity, kitchen, livingroom, mountain, opencountry, PARoffice, store, street, tallbuilding) with a total of 4,485 images and ranges from natural scenes to man-made environments. Each class of the Scene-15 dataset has 200 to 400 images. The average image size is 300×250 pixels. For fair comparison, we randomly choose 100 training images per category and use the rest images for testing, as did in [2, 3, 17]. We repeat this process for 6 times. We report our final results by the mean and standard deviation of the average of per-class classification rates.

Table 1: Performance comparison on the Scene-15 dataset. (ScSPM: Sparse coding along with spatial pyramid matching; KSPM: Spatial pyramid matching and kernel SVM classifier; LSS: Low-dimensional semantic spaces with weak supervision; OB: Object Bank; KCSPM: Kernel codebook and spatial pyramid matching; WSR-EC: Weak semantic representation with examplar classifier; S^3R: the proposed sub-semantic space representation.

Algorithm	Performance
KSPM [3]	76.73 ± 0.65
ScSPM [3]	80.28 ± 0.93
KSPM [2]	81.40 ± 0.50
LSS [9]	72.20 ± 0.20
OB [11]	80.9
KCSPM [20]	76.70 ± 0.40
WSR-EC(k-means) [17]	77.82 ± 0.63
WSR-EC(sparse coding) [17]	81.54 ± 0.59
S^3R (k-means)	78.35 ± 0.64
S^3R (sparse coding)	**82.86 ± 0.75**

We give the performance comparison of the proposed method with [2, 3, 9, 11, 17, 20] in Table 1. KCSPM [20] tried to alleviate the information loss during hard assignment of visual words and used soft assignment instead. We give the results of the proposed method using k-means clustering and sparse coding for local feature encoding respectively. We can see from Table 1 that the proposed method achieves good performance which clearly demonstrates the effectiveness of the proposed method. The use of sub-semantic based image representation makes the S^3R not only more semantically meaningful than examplar classifier based method but also helps to get ride of some noisy examplar image which may hinder the final performance. The use of sparse coding helps improve the performance over k-means clustering based method.

On analysis of the detailed categorization performance, we found that the relative improvement of S^3R over WSR-EC is on the indoor classes. We believe this is because the outdoor classes are relatively easy and has smaller inter class variations compared with indoor classes. It is sufficient to use examplar classifier based method while still obtaining good performance for the outdoor class.

3.2 Caltech-256 dataset

The Caltech-256 dataset contains 256 categories of 29,780 images with high intra-class variability and object location variability. Each class of the Caltech-256 dataset has at least 80 images. We follow the experimental setting as [3, 17] did and randomly choose 15, 30 and 45 images per class for training and use the rest of images for testing.

We give the performance comparison of the proposed method with other methods [3, 17-22] in Table 2. Classemes [21] used weakly trained object classifiers for object categorization while the NBNN [22] method worked directly on local features without local feature quantization. We can see

Table 2: Performance comparison on the Caltech-256 dataset. (Classemes: Classification with weakly trained object classifiers based descriptor; NBNN: Naive-Bayes Nearest-Neighbor; LLC: Locality-constrained linear coding.)

Algorithm	15 training	30 training	45 training
KSPM [3]	23.34 ± 0.42	29.51 ± 0.52	–
ScSPM [3]	27.73 ± 0.51	34.02 ± 0.35	37.46 ± 0.55
Classemes [21]	–	36.00	–
OB [11]	–	39.00	–
NBNN(1 Desc)[22]	30.45	38.18	–
KSPM [19]	–	34.10	–
LLC [18]	34.36	41.19	45.31
KCSPM [20]	–	27.17 ± 0.46	–
WSR-EC [17]	35.28 ± 0.65	42.01 ± 0.47	45.82 ± 0.54
S^3R	**37.18 ± 0.52**	**42.87 ± 0.54**	**46.06 ± 0.48**

from table 2 that S^3R performs better than WSR-EC which demonstrates the effectiveness of using sub-semantic space for image representation. Besides, S^3R also outperforms the OB method which leverages the internet resources for semantic image representation. Since images of the Caltech-256 dataset have larger inter class variations than the Scene 15 dataset, more sub-semantic classes are needed in order to get better object categorization performance.

In our future work, we will study how to select the proper sub-semantic space with sparsity constraints [23, 24].

4. ACKNOWLEDGEMENT

This work is supported in part by National Basic Research Program of China (973 Program): 2012CB316400; the President Fund of UCAS; the Open Project Program of the National Laboratory of Pattern Recognition (NLPR); China Postdoctoral Science Foundation: 2012M520434, 2013T60156, 2013M530350, 2013M530739; National Natural Science Foundation of China: 61025011, 61272329; This work is supported in part to Dr. Qi Tian by ARO grant W911BF-12-1-0057, NSF IIS 1052851, Faculty Research Awards by Google, FXPAL, and NEC Laboratories of America and 2012 UTSA START-R Research Award respectively. This work is supported in part by NSFC 61128007.

5. REFERENCES

[1] J. Sivic and A. Zisserman. "Video Google: A text retrieval approach to object matching in videos. *ICCV*, pages 1470-1477, 2003.

[2] S. Lazebnik, C. Schmid, J. Ponce, Beyond bags of features: Spatial pyramid matching for recognizing natural scene categories, *CVPR*, 2006, pp. 2169-2178.

[3] J. Yang, K. Yu, Y. Gong, and T. Huang, Linear spatial pyramid matching using sparse coding for image classification, *CVPR*, June 2009, pages 1794-1801.

[4] C. Zhang, J. Liu, Q. Tian, C. Xu, H. Lu and S. Ma, Image classification by non-negative sparse coding, low-rank and sparse decomposition, *CVPR*, 2011, pages 1673-1680.

[5] P. F. Felzenszwalb, R. B. Girschick, D. McCallester, D. Ramanan, Object detection with discriminatively trained part based models, IEEE *Transactions on Pattern Analysis and Machine Intelligence*, 32(9) (2010) 1627-1645.

[6] Thomas Hofmann, Probabilistic latent semantic analysis, *UAI*, Sweden, 1999, pages 289–296.

[7] D. Blei, A. Ng, M. Jordan, Latent Dirichlet Allocation, *Joruanl of Machine Learning Research*, 3(1) (2003) 993-1022.

[8] A. Oliva, A. Torralba, A. Guerin-Dugue, J. Herault, Global semantic classification of scenes using power spectrum templates, *CIR*, UK, 1999.

[9] N. Rasiwasia, N. Vasconcelos, Scene classification with low-dimensional semantic spaces and weak supervision, *CVPR*, USA, 2008, pages 1-6.

[10] A. Hauptmann, Rong. Yan, W. Lin, M. Christel, H. Wactlar, Can high-level concepts fill the semantic gap in video retrieval? A case study with broadcast news, IEEE *Transactions on Multimedia*, 9(5) (2007) 958-966.

[11] L. Li, H. Su, E. Xing, F. Li, ObjectBank: A high-level image representation for scene classification & semantic feature sparsification, *NIPS*, 2010, pages 1-9.

[12] A. Farhadi, I. Endres, D. Hoiem, D. Forsyth, Describing objects by their attributes, *CVPR*, USA, 2009, pages 1778-1785.

[13] C. Lampert, H. Nickisch, S. Harmeling, Learning to detect unseen object classes by between-class attribute transfer, *CVPR*, USA, 2009, pages 951-958.

[14] D. Parikh, K. Grauman, Interactively building a discriminative vocabulary of nameable attributes, *CVPR*, USA, 2011, pages 1681-1688.

[15] D. Parikh, K. Grauman, Relative attributes. *ICCV*, Spain, 2011, pages 1-8.

[16] T. Malisiewicz, A. Gupta, A. Efros, Ensemble of exemplar-SVMs for object detection and beyond, *ICCV*, Spain, 2011, pages 89-96.

[17] C. Zhang, J. Liu, Q. Tian, C. Liang, and Q. Huang, Beyond visual features: A weak semantic image representation using exemplar classifier for classification, *Neurocomputing*, 2012.

[18] J. Wang, J. Yang, K. Yu, F. Lv, T. Huang, Y. Gong, Locality-constrained linear coding for image classification, *CVPR*, USA, 2010, pages 3360-3367.

[19] G. Griffin, A. Holub, P. Perona, Caltech-256 object category dataset, Technical report, CalTech, 2007.

[20] J. C. Gemert, C.J. Veenman, A. Smeulders, J. Geusebroek, Visual word ambiguity, IEEE *Transactions on Pattern Analysis and Machine Intelligence*, 32(7), 2010, pages 1271-1283.

[21] L. Torresani, M. Szummer, A. Fitzgibbon, Efficient object category recognition using classesmes. *ECCV*, Greece, 2010, pages 776-789.

[22] O. Boiman, E. Shechtman, M. Irani, In defense of nearest-neighbor based image classification, *CVPR*, USA, 2008, pages 1-8.

[23] C. Zhang, J. Liu, Q. Tian, Y. Han, H. Lu, S. Ma, A Boosting Sparsity-Constrained Bilinear Model for Object Recognition, *IEEE Multimedia*, 2012, 19(2):58-68.

[24] C. Zhang, J. Liu, Q. Tian, C. Liang, Q. Huang, Image Classification Using Harr-like Transformation of Local Features with Coding Residuals, *Signal Processing*, 2012, 93(8):2111-2118.

Speaking Swiss: Languages and Venues in Foursquare

Darshan Santani
Idiap Research Institute
EPFL, Lausanne, Switzerland
dsantani@idiap.ch

Daniel Gatica-Perez
Idiap Research Institute
EPFL, Lausanne, Switzerland
gatica@idiap.ch

ABSTRACT

Due to increasing globalization, urban societies are becoming more multicultural. The availability of large-scale digital mobility traces e.g. from tweets or checkins provides an opportunity to explore multiculturalism that until recently could only be addressed using survey-based methods. In this paper we examine a basic facet of multiculturalism through the lens of language use across multiple cities in Switzerland. Using data obtained from Foursquare over 330 days, we present a descriptive analysis of linguistic differences and similarities across five urban agglomerations in a multicultural, western European country.

Categories and Subject Descriptors

H.4 [**Information Systems Applications**]: Miscellaneous

Keywords

Multilingualism, Foursquare, Linguistic Geography

1. INTRODUCTION

Urbanization is increasing at a faster pace than ever. For the first time in human civilization, a majority of the world's population lives in urban areas. Rural and transnational populations migrate towards cities in search for better opportunities and livelihood. As a result of these trends, it becomes relevant to understand its impact on urban societies, and especially on multiculturalism. Human mobility has been studied extensively in various disciplines. The availability of large-scale digital mobility traces e.g. from *tweets* or *checkins* is providing a new alternative to examine questions that until recently could only be addressed using survey-based research.

It is well established that multiculturalism and diversity promote innovation and creativity [8]. Previous studies have found correlations between the diversity of individuals' social connections and the economic prosperity of their respective communities. In this paper, we are interested in studying a basic facet of multiculturalism using data obtained from Foursquare. Our long-term goal is to investigate the feasibility of LBSN data to facilitate understanding of multicultural trends in cities. One such thread of inquiry could examine communication patterns amongst different ethnic communities and investigate heterogeneity of public places.

In many countries, multiculturalism is expressed directly through language use, both by the local population and migrant communities. In this paper, we take a first step towards characterizing cities through the lens of language used by Foursquare users. Our objective is to characterize basic patterns of multilingualism in cities at a country level. For our analysis, we have chosen Switzerland, that has a well-known geographic diversity of languages and where Foursquare is reasonably popular. Multilingual countries like Switzerland are facing cultural shifts. Swiss media have recently reported that "the language debate is reaching new heights in Switzerland with French and Italian speakers uneasy about the progressive abandonment of their languages by the German-speaking community in favor of English" [3].

This paper addresses three research goals. First, we characterize Swiss cities by their language distribution using place comments. Users, in addition to checking into given places or venues, also leave comments about the place. Comments usually serve the purpose of providing relevant feedback to the Foursquare community. One could potentially extend this research using reviews obtained from local directory services like Yelp or TripAdvisor. Our second objective is to compare these basic patterns of geographically grounded language usage with traditional demographic data sources, so as to assess the adequacy of Foursquare data. And last but not least, to extract basic content trends via topic models. Topic modeling represents a family of statistical methods to discover main themes (or topics) in an unstructured collection of documents [6].

Recent work has proposed a multi-level generative model to infer regional variations of latent topics using geotagged tweets [9]. In [5] the authors have presented a spatio-temporal topic model to discover topics in urban neighborhoods. Using checkin tweets obtained from Foursquare, the paper characterized the topics' spatial coverage and temporal evolution. A study similar to ours was conducted in parallel, to explore linguistic trends across geography in multilingual regions using Twitter [11]. Our research differs from these related work on two specific grounds. First, to capture cultural and linguistic idiosyncrasies better, we have focused our analysis on place metadata as opposed to checkin tweets. Second, the textual content of our dataset span 53 different

MM'13, October 21–25, 2013, Barcelona, Spain.

ACM 978-1-4503-2404-5/13/10 ...$15.00.
http://dx.doi.org/10.1145/2502081.2502133.

Figure 1: Map showing the spatial distribution of languages used for comments in our data. Each dot denotes a comment, with color depicting its language with red being EN, green is DE, blue is FR and black is IT. Language border is visible across different language-speaking cantons.

languages as opposed to merely English, which is mostly the case in prior literature.

2. DATASET AND PREPROCESSING

2.1 Swiss Checkin Dataset

To guide our analysis, we have collected a place-level dataset (F) for Foursquare venues in Switzerland. We have gathered information from 8,846 users who have visited 26,034 places over a period of 330 days, starting from December 19, 2011. The place-level data includes information on the total number of checked in users, place comments, place category, etc.

We have focused our data collection to be within Switzerland. Geographically, Switzerland is located at the intersection of three major European countries: Germany, Italy and France. As a result, it has found itself at the confluence of linguistic and cultural influences by neighboring countries. It has four national languages: German, French, Italian and Romansh. As per 2000 population census, of all native residents, 63.7% speak German, 20.4% speak French, 6.5% speak Italian, 0.5% speak Romansh, while the remaining 9% speak other languages [4]. Furthermore, it is interesting to note that Switzerland has delineated regions (so called *language borders*, see Figure 1) where one language dominates over the rest. Being a federal republic of 26 cantons, 17 cantons are officially German-speaking, 4 French-speaking, 1 Italian-speaking, with 3 cantons officially declared as bilingual (German, French), while one canton is trilingual (German, Romansh, Italian).

2.2 Comments Dataset

In Foursquare, users are allowed to leave comments (or tips) to visited places. Comments usually serve the purpose of providing feedback to friends and other users. Given that our focus is to analyze user comments, we filter our original dataset F to keep all places where users have left at least one comment (dataset C). As a result of filtering, we are left with 9,010 places with 21,780 comments from 8,748 users in 53 automatically identified different languages, ranging from English to French to Slovak to Zulu. To identify the language used in comments, we have used an off-the-shelf language detection tool [10], which is pre-trained on 97 different languages, but excluding Romansh. (The list of identified languages likely contains false positives.) We perform the language detection at the comment level. Table 1 lists the proportion for the top 4 languages in our comments dataset. Figure 1 shows the comments by its language on the Switzerland map.

Language Used	% of Total Comments	% of Users
English (EN)	58.22	61.28
German (DE)	21.91	20.52
French (FR)	10.68	9.28
Italian (IT)	3.41	3.64

Table 1: Top Languages used for Comments Dataset C

2.3 Comments Translation

Instead of creating a polylingual model (due to the presence of multiple languages), we pursued our analysis in one language. For translation and topic modeling, we have ignored all comments which are not EN, DE, FR or IT. We have chosen English as our base language, and all comments in other languages were translated to English. We have used Systran Home Translator [1] for FR to EN translation, and Linguatec Personal Translator [2] for DE,IT to EN translations.

2.4 Venues as Documents

We treat all comments for each venue as a single text document. In the comment dataset C, more than 88% of places have less than 5 comments, while the average word count for a comment stands at 10.69, which implies that the majority of places have cumulative word count of roughly 50. Given such skewness in comment and word distribution, we define the analysis dataset (A) as a subset of dataset C, where all places having a cumulative word count of comments less than δ are filtered. We have set the value of $\delta = 100$. We also follow the standard text processing pipeline which includes tokenization, lower casing, including words and number only and (English) stopword removal.

3. ANALYSIS

3.1 Users and Languages

We begin our analysis by examining users' dominant language, where dominant language for a user is defined as the one used most often while expressing recommendations on Foursquare. Table 1 highlights the proportion of users who use EN, DE, FR, or IT as their dominant language. Interestingly, the majority of users employ English, while the rest of the language trends follow the official census statistics in terms of ranking (Section 2). In other words, the most common spoken language in Switzerland (German) correctly matches the second most popular language in Foursquare, and the same trend applies to the other top Swiss languages.

The dominance of English in a non-English native speaking country can be explained by multiple factors. First, a significant proportion of Foursquare users might be tourists, some of whom might use English to express themselves. Second, Switzerland is an attractive destination to a significant migrant population (both skilled and non-skilled) who do not speak a Swiss national language and use English as *lingua franca*, including international students and profession-

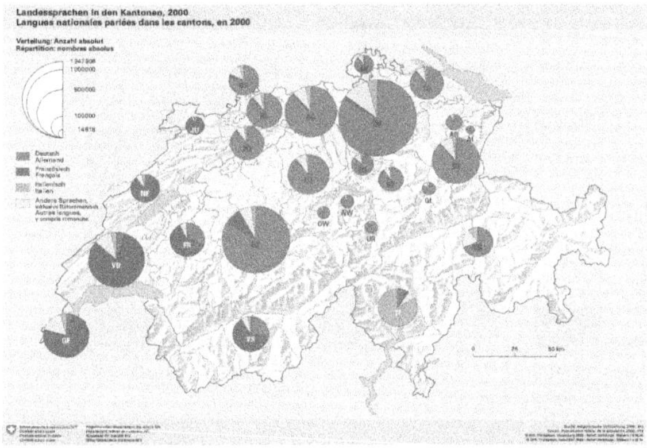

Figure 2: Relative popularity of national languages (DE,FR,IT) across all cantons in Switzerland as per 2000 census [4]. For example, in Ticino, IT is the most popular national language followed by DE, and then FR.

Languages Used	1	2	3	4
% of Users	81.0%	14.77%	3.05%	0.83%
% of Places	72.0%	21.71%	5.00%	0.98%
Language Pairs	EN-DE	EN-FR	EN-IT	DE-FR
% of Bilingual Users	42.57%	18.89%	8.36%	1.32%

Table 2: Users Multilingualism Characteristics

als (so called *expats*). The growing emergence of English is in fact one of the current sources of multicultural tensions in Switzerland [3]. Third, young Swiss natives often speak English and might use it (at least partially) to interact with non-Swiss friends and contacts.

To gain further insight into this matter, we analyze the breadth of language use.Table 2 lists the proportion of users who speak multiple languages on Foursquare. 81% of users adopt one primary language, but we also observe a compelling fraction of users (more than 18%) who use more than one language. These results clearly indicate multilingualism. We further examine the language pairs used by bilingual users. As shown in Table 2, out of 1,292 bi-lingual users, about half of them use a combination of EN and DE, while almost 19% use EN with FR, and 8% use EN-IT pairs. We also observe that more than 15% of bilingual users employ EN in combination with a language other than DE, FR or IT. This indicates that the third factor highlighted above occurs in practice. To validate first and second factors, one could develop a method to identify tourists vs. locals by studying the level of Foursquare activity across space and time, which is the subject of future work.

3.2 Venues and Languages

Now we turn our attention towards understanding the spatial distribution of language use across five cantons (or states) in Switzerland. Of 26 cantons we have chosen Zurich, Geneva, Bern, Vaud and Ticino for our current analysis. The key reasons for selecting them include the presence of cultural and linguistic diversity, in addition to high penetration of Foursquare in these cantons. It is important to note that each canton respectively contains a major urban agglomeration within it. Furthermore, Zurich and Geneva can be considered international cities with substantial expatriate population, while Bern and Lausanne (Vaud) are more local cities with a predominant local resident population.

Canton	EN	DE	FR	IT
Zurich (DE)	4215 (63.20%)	1912 (28.67%)	84 (1.26%)	114 (1.71%)
Geneva (FR)	2429 (71.74%)	37 (1.09%)	654 (19.31%)	61 (1.80%)
Bern (DE)	1091 (53.74%)	735 (36.21%)	58 (2.86%)	38 (1.87%)
Vaud (FR)	1117 (49.06%)	27 (1.19%)	947 (41.59%)	44 (1.93%)
Ticino (IT)	451 (50.79%)	54 (6.08%)	18 (2.02%)	319 (35.92%)

Table 3: Language use across cantons. For each canton, the total number of comments per language is shown along with their percentages (shown in brackets). The official language for each canton is shown in brackets.

Table 3 lists the languages used for commenting in venues across these 5 cantons. Following the analysis in Section 3.1, it is not surprising to find English topping the charts across all regions. More significantly, we observe that the official cantonal language (as per census, see the pie-charts in Figure 2) matches the second most popular language in that canton amongst Foursquare users. For example, Zurich is predominantly a German canton, and we observe German to be the second most popular language amongst Zürchers. This trend is equally observable amongst all other cantons. Furthermore, we highlight that the relative rankings of secondary spoken languages in different cantons (e.g, French or Italian in Zurich) as per the national census, matche with our results in Table 3. Another relevant pattern is that global cities (Zurich and Geneva) have a large proportion of English usage (63-71%) in comparison to more local cities (49-53%). This is specially interesting because it might respond to a different combination of the factors discussed earlier (tourists, migrants, and locals.)

3.3 Topical Analysis

In previous sections, we have explored users' multilingualism and places' spatial distribution of language use across Switzerland. In this section, we examine what users are talking about specifically in these places. We are interested in extracting basic place themes and explore similarities and differences (if any) between places across different regions. Please be reminded that topic analysis is performed on analysis dataset A, which does not take into account the canton differentiation made in the previous section.

To discover topics from user comments, we treat each place as a single document as described in Section 2.4 and apply Latent Dirichlet Allocation (LDA) model [7]. After experimenting with different values for the number of topics and given the document set size (348) and vocabulary count (7,361 tokens after preprocessing), we set the number of topics to be 10. Table 4 lists five key discovered topics along with their most frequent words. Based on manual in-

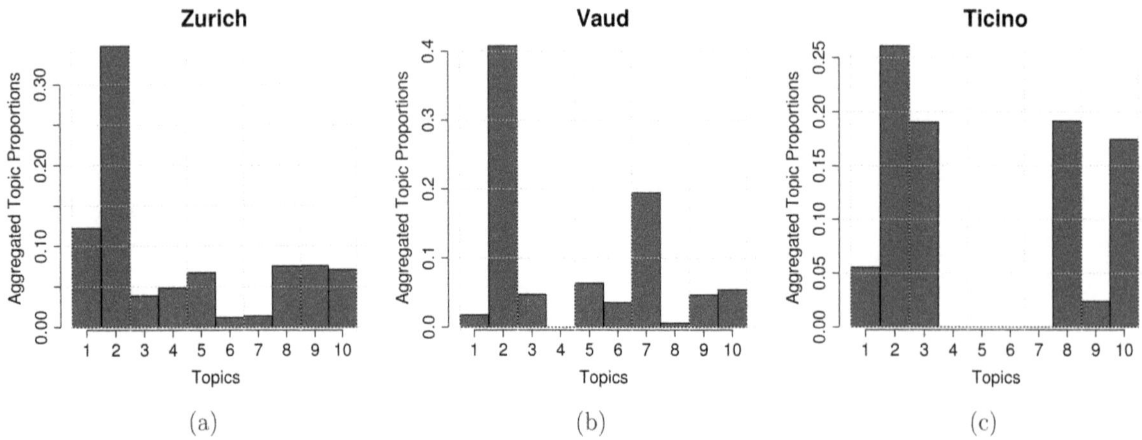

Figure 3: Aggregate Topic Proportions for all places in a) Zurich b) Vaud and c) Ticino

T1: airport train swiss ticket hour don't zurich security class chf wi-fi area long buy shop switzerland shopping expensive open trains
T2: excellent beer delicious restaurant geneva eat don't wine super terrace brunch day price people drink small zurich drinks order perfect
T3: pizza italian pizzas pasta pie tiramisu shopping pretty terrible restaurant chocolate vis al store bernerhof made special gnocchi manor luxemburgerli
T7: burger burgers de drink forget fries chips kind generous dont cheese owners backpacker hostel pub guinness romandie big live hamburgers
T8: valid actions rosti salad st price season compared sausage bratwurst veal unzumutbar goods backyard sauber delivery o'clock noise mixed frying

Table 4: Topics discovered for Analysis (A) dataset, along with top 20 frequent words. Out of 10 topics, only topics 1, 2, 3, 7, 8 are shown.

spection, discovered topics conforms to our understanding of Foursquare, in particular in its ability to uncover keywords associated with daily rhythms of city life.

We inspect the spatial distribution of topics to understand topical peculiarities of cantons. For all places belonging to a canton, we aggregate place-topic probabilities for a given topic. Figure 3 shows normalized topic proportions for all topics across 3 cantons. (Other cantons are omitted due to space constraints.) We observe that Topic 2, being a generic topic, is predominant across all cantons. Topic 1 (*transport*) plays a bigger role in Zurich, which is the major transport hub in the country, while topic 7 (*fast food*) in canton Vaud is prominent possibly due to a large student community. For Ticino, being an Italian canton, topic 3 (*italian cuisine*) and topic 8 (*swiss-german food*) are dominant. Ticino is known to be a destination for Swiss Germans. These analyses suggest that the spatial distribution of topics can capture multicultural idiosyncrasies of a city.

4. CONCLUSIONS

In this paper we studied linguistic patterns in Switzerland, using place metadata collected from Foursquare. We found clear evidence of multilingualism. English is the dominant language amongst the majority of Foursquare users, and global cities show a larger proportion of English usage in comparison to more local cities. Another finding is that the relative rankings of secondary languages in different cantons (e.g, French in German-speaking Bern) as per national census data match Foursquare's trends. While obviously Foursquare users do not represent a fair sample of the Swiss population, our findings suggest the potential of Foursquare to complement census data to monitor cultural trends in urban settings. We believe that these results can be equally appealing to other contemporary multicultural nations.

5. ACKNOWLEDGMENTS

We thank Andrei Popescu-Beli (Idiap) for discussions and Thomas Meyer (Idiap) for his assistance in translation. This work was funded by the SNSF through the HAI project.

6. REFERENCES

[1] http://www.systran.co.uk/.
[2] http://www.linguatec.net/.
[3] English challenges multilingual Switzerland. http://bit.ly/LlzaJt. [Online; accessed May, 2013].
[4] Swiss Federal Statistical Office (SFSO), Swiss Statistics Web site. http://bit.ly/VRH1rA. [Online; accessed May, 2013].
[5] S. Bauer et al. Talking Places: Modelling and Analysing Linguistic Content in Foursquare. In *IEEE International Conference on Social Computing*, 2012.
[6] D. Blei. Probabilistic topic models. *Communications of the ACM*, 55(4):77–84, 2012.
[7] D. Blei, A. Ng, and M. Jordan. Latent dirichlet allocation. *JMLR*, 3:993–1022, 2003.
[8] N. Eagle, M. Macy, and R. Claxton. Network diversity and economic development. *Science*, 2010.
[9] J. Eisenstein et al. A latent variable model for geographic lexical variation. In *EMNLP*, 2010.
[10] M. Lui and T. Baldwin. langid. py: An off-the-shelf language identification tool. In *ACL*, 2012.
[11] D. Mocanu et al. The Twitter of Babel: Mapping World Languages through Microblogging Platforms. *PloS one*, 2013.

What are the Distance Metrics for Local Features?

Zhendong Mao[1,2], Yongdong Zhang[2], Qi Tian[3]
[1]University of Chinese Academy of Sciences
[2]Institute of Computing Technology,Chinese Academy Of Sciences
[3]University of Texas at San Antonio
{maozhendong,zhyd}@ict.ac.cn, qitian@cs.utsa.edu

ABSTRACT

Previous research has found that the distance metric for similarity estimation is determined by the underlying data noise distribution. The well known Euclidean(L2) and Manhattan (L1) metrics are then justified when the additive noise are Gaussian and Exponential, respectively. However, finding a suitable distance metric for local features is still a challenge when the underlying noise distribution is unknown and could be neither Gaussian nor Exponential. To address this issue, we introduce a modeling framework for arbitrary noise distributions and propose a generalized distance metric for local features based on this framework. We prove that the proposed distance is equivalent to the L1 or the L2 distance when the noise is Gaussian or Exponential. Furthermore, we justify the Hamming metric when the noise meets the given conditions. In that case, the proposed distance is a linear mapping of the Hamming distance. The proposed metric has been extensively tested on a benchmark data set with five state-of-the-art local features: SIFT, SURF, BRIEF, ORB and BRISK. Experiments show that our framework better models the real noise distributions and that more robust results can be obtained by using the proposed distance metric.

Categories and Subject Descriptors

H.3.3 [**Information Search and Retrieval**]: Information filtering, Retrieval models, Search process, Selection process; I.4.7 [**Feature Measurement**]: Feature representation

Keywords

distance metric, local feature, noise distribution

1. INTRODUCTION

L2 and L1 metrics are frequently used in matching traditional local features such as SIFT[4], SURF[1], while Hamming metric is frequently used in matching binary local features such as BRIEF [2], ORB [6], and BRISK [3]. However, the connection between the three metrics and the prevalent local features has not been fully studied yet.

Sebe et al [7] is one of the first (if not first) efforts to relate distance metric to noise distribution from a maximum likelihood perspective. In [7], they justified that Gaussian, Exponential, and Cauchy distributions result in L2, L1, and Cauchy metrics, respectively. The common assumption is that the real noise distribution should fit either the Gaussian or the Exponential. But for local features (especially binary local features), Gaussian or Exponential assumption is often invalid. This arises the question: whether we could find a more accurate noise model for both traditional and binary local features? whether we could find a generalized distance metric which incorporates L1, L2 and Hamming metrics as the special cases?

To address this issue, we develop a noise modeling framework and a generalized distance metric for local features. When given a local feature, we first model its noise distribution using our framework, and then determine our distance metric. Our main contributions are:

- A framework for modeling arbitrary noise distributions is presented and a generalized distance metric for local features based on this framework is proposed.
- L1, L2 and Hamming distance are proved as special cases of the proposed distance. Specially, necessary conditions of using Hamming metric are specified and thus we give theoretical support for the use of Hamming metric in binary feature matching.
- Theoretical lower bound of distance threshold used in feature matching is justified as the product of feature dimension and noise entropy.

To validate our framework, we compute the real noise distributions of SIFT and SURF and apply different models to fit them. We also illustrate the efficiency of our distance metric by comparing it with traditional distance metrics on benchmark image set.

MM'13, October 21–25, 2013, Barcelona, Spain.
Copyright 2013 ACM 978-1-4503-2404-5/13/10 ...$15.00.
http://dx.doi.org/10.1145/2502081.2502134.

2. NOISE MODELING FRAMEWORK AND FEATURE DISTANCE METRIC

Maximum Likelihood theory allows us to relate a data distribution to a distance metric. Suppose there are two subsets of D features from the database A: $X \subset A, Y \subset A$ which according to the ground truth are matching: $X \equiv Y$. This can be presented in detail:

$$x_i = y_i + d_i, i = 1, ..., D \tag{1}$$

where d_i is the noise which represented by the difference between corresponding features x_i and y_i. In this context, the similarity probability between X and Y can be defined:

$$P(X,Y) = \prod_{i=1}^{D} p(d_i) \quad (2)$$

where function p is the probability density of the noise, and $p(d_i)$ describes the similarity between x_i and y_i. According to (2) we have to find the probability density function of the noise that maximizes the similarity probability. This is the maximum likelihood estimator for X, given Y.

Taking the negative logarithm of (2) we find that we have to minimize the expression:

$$\sum_{i=1}^{D} \rho(d_i), \quad \rho(d_i) = -\log(p(d_i)) \quad (3)$$

Expression (3) is the metric which maximizes the similarity probability [7].

According to (3), which measure to use can be determined if the underlying noise distribution is known or well estimated. Sebe [7] focus on modeling the noise by continuous probability distributions and then determined by the probability density function which distance measure to use. However, in many applications, finding a suitable continuous probability distribution for the feature noise is an even more difficult problem. Instead, we found that the real distribution could be approximated by a multinomial distribution sampled from it and the accuracy of the approximation could be adjusted by sampling density. Therefore, we propose a framework to model the noise by multinomial distribution and a generalized distance metric based on this framework.

2.1 Distance Metric for Local Features

Without loss of generality, we suppose a local feature has N elements (N dimensions) and each element is stored in m bits. The special case $m = \infty$ denotes that the elements of features are stored in an unlimited space and thus the noise distributions of features are continuous. The distribution of the noise d_i is a joint distribution of each dimension:

$$p(d_i) = p(d_{i0}, d_{i1}, ..., d_{iN}) \quad (4)$$

where d_{ij} is the noise of j-th dimension. Since d_{ij} is represented by the difference between two corresponding elements and each element is stored in m bits, we can define (we suppose the noise of each dimension is independent and is identically distributed, which is the most common case):

$$\Pr(d_{ij} = c) = P_c, \quad (c \in [1-2^m, 2^m-1], \quad j = 1, ..., N) \quad (5)$$

Obviously, d_{ij} is multinomial distributed. Then $p(d_i)$ representing the probability of the noise $d_i (d_i = [d_{i0}, d_{i1}, ..., d_{iN}])$ can be written as:

$$p(d_i) = \prod_{c=1-2^m}^{2^m-1} P_c^{k_c} \quad (6)$$

where

$$k_c = \sum_{j=1}^{N} \delta_c(d_{ij}), \quad \delta_c(d_{ij}) = \begin{cases} 1 & if \quad d_{ij} = c \\ 0 & otherwise \end{cases} \quad (7)$$

k_c represents the number of d_{ij} that equals to c. So we have:

$$\sum_{c=1-2^m}^{2^m-1} k_c = N \quad (8)$$

Our distance metric between two local features x and y is defined as the negative logarithm of (6):

$$T_m(x,y) = \sum_{c=1-2^m}^{2^m-1} -k_c \log(P_c) \quad (9)$$

When the noise is distributed as Gaussian or double Exponential ($m = \infty$ is underlying):

$$P_c \sim e^{-c^2} \quad or \quad P_c \sim e^{-|c|} \quad (10)$$

our distance is equivalent to L2 or L1 distance.

$$T_m(x,y) = \sum_{c=-\infty}^{+\infty} k_c \cdot c^2 \quad or \quad T_m(x,y) = \sum_{c=-\infty}^{+\infty} k_c \cdot |c| \quad (11)$$

Therefore, L1 and L2 distance are special cases of the proposed distance. It is also worth mentioning that arbitrary continuous distributions of noise could be discretized by sampling and then result in a distance metric by using (9). Besides, quantization could be applied to noise for reducing the computation cost.

2.2 Distance Metric for Binary Local Features

By introducing (8) into (9) and let $m = 1$, we get the distance metric for binary local features:

$$T(x,y) = \log(\frac{P_0}{P_{-1}})k_{-1} + \log(\frac{P_0}{P_1})k_1 - N \log P_0 \quad (12)$$

Since the noises of binary features are intrinsically multinomial distributed (all possible values of element noise are -1, 0, and 1), (12) is the theoretical distance metric for binary local features according to Maximum Likelihood theory. To investigate the relationship between Hamming distance and the proposed distance, We define two conditions C1 and C2 as follows:

$$C1 : P_{-1} < P_0, P_1 < P_0 \qquad C2 : P_{-1} = P_1$$

If these two conditions are met, we can rewrite the proposed distance as:

$$T(x,y) = h \cdot (k_{-1} + k_1) + t \quad (13)$$

where

$$h = \log(\frac{P_0}{P_{-1}}), h > 0, t = -N \log(P_0) \quad (14)$$

As we all know, Hamming distance can be defined as:

$$H = k_{-1} + k_1 \quad (15)$$

One can note that when condition $C1$ and $C2$ are satisfied, Hamming distance is a strictly positive linear mapping of the proposed distance. In this case, Hamming metric is the theoretical distance metric. In case that $C1$ is satisfied but $C2$ is not strictly satisfied, Hamming metric is still a suitable distance metric. If $C1$ is not met, Hamming distance is opposite to the similarity of features. On that condition, Hamming distance should not be used to match features .

2.3 Distance Threshold

In section 2.2, the distance between two corresponding local features x and y is given by (9). Let x_i and y_i represent the i-th elements of x and y, respectively. Let $E(c)$ denotes the event $x_i - y_i = c, i = 1, ...N$. Note that k_c is the number of times $E(c)$ occurs and P_c is the probability of $E(c)$'s occurrence. According to Borel's law of large numbers:

$$\frac{k_c}{N} \rightarrow P_c \quad as \quad N \rightarrow \infty \tag{16}$$

By introducing (16) into (9) :

$$T_m(x, y) \rightarrow u(m) \quad as \quad N \rightarrow \infty, \tag{17}$$

where

$$u(m) = -N \cdot \sum_c P_c \log(P_c) \tag{18}$$

(17) demonstrates that the proposed distance of two corresponding features converges in probability to $u(m)$, which is the product of feature dimension and noise entropy. For most local features, dimension N is very large (SIFT and SURF have 128 dimensions, binary features have even more), which means the proposed distances of corresponding features are very close to $u(m)$. If the distance threshold used in feature matching is larger than $u(m)$, most correct matches would be excluded. Therefore, $u(m)$ is the theoretical lower bound of distance threshold when using the proposed distance metric. Since we have demonstrated that L2, L1 and Hamming distance are special cases of the proposed distance, $u(m)$ is also the theoretical lower bound of distance threshold when using these distance metrics.

Based on analysis above, we further develop our distance metric as:

$$T'_m(x, y) = T_m(x, y) - u(m) \tag{19}$$

3. EXPERIMENT AND ANALYSIS

The proposed distance metric has been extensively tested on five well-known local features: SIFT, SURF, BRIEF, ORB and BRISK. For each feature, we inspect how proposed distance metric performs comparing to several traditional distance metrics such as L1, L2 and Hamming metrics. Besides, Gaussian, Exponential and our models are applied to fit the noise distributions of SIFT and SURF to evaluate our modeling framework.

3.1 Experimental setup

Data set: The testing environment is the benchmark image set proposed by Mikolajczyk et al [5]. The image set consists of 8 categories. Each category contains a sequence of six images exhibiting an increasing amount of transformation. We find that the latter images in each category contain larger transformation, which is too hard for some

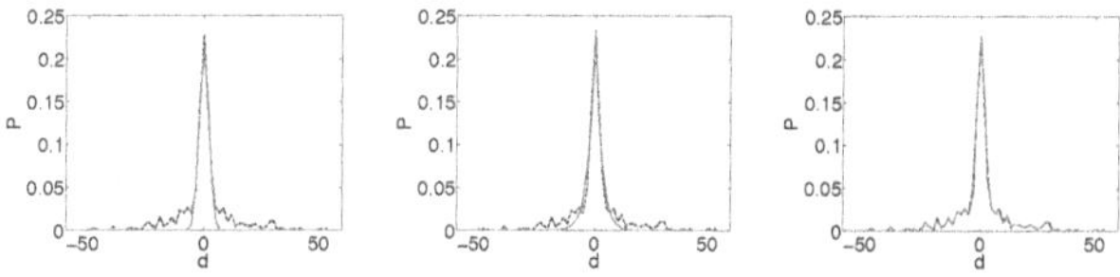

(a) Gaussian (b) Exponential (c) Multinomial

Figure 1: Real noise distribution of SIFT on training set modeled by three distributions. The dashed black line represents the real noise distribution and the solid red line represents the estimation. (R-square score representing goodness of fit is: (a) 0.94 ; (b) 0.96 ; (c) 0.99).

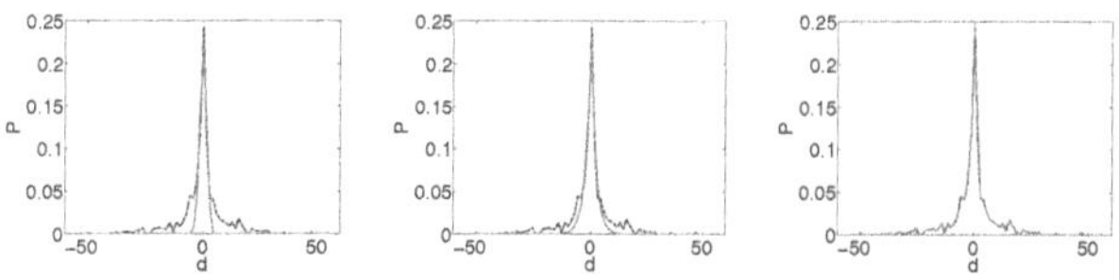

(a) Gaussian (b) Exponential (c) Multinomial

Figure 2: Real noise distribution of SURF on training set modeled by three distributions. The dashed black line represents the real noise distribution and the solid red line represents the estimation. (R-square score representing goodness of fit is: (a) 0.87 ; (b) 0.92 ; (c) 0.99).

features. Therefore, only the first three images are picked from each category. The first image and the second image in each category are selected as training set for computing real noise distribution, while the first image and the third image in each category are selected as test set for matching.

Matching strategy: Following [5], two features A and B are matched if B is the nearest neighbor to A and if the distance ratio between the first and the second nearest neighbor is below a threshold: $\|A - B\|/\|A - C\| < t$, where B is the first and C is the second nearest neighbor to A. For SIFT and SURF , we set $t = 0.8$. For binary features, we set $t = 0.95$.

All detectors and descriptors are implemented using public OpenCV source code with default parameters.

3.2 Distance Metric for SIFT and SURF

We consider the following steps to evaluate the modeling framework and the proposed distance metric:

Step1: Compute SIFT and SURF features and find correct matches from the training set. Normalize all features into a fixed range(from -60 to 60).

Step2: Compute the noise distribution from the differences between corresponding elements of matched features.

Step3: Quantize the noises by round-off (-60 to 60, 121bins), hence get a multinomial distribution.

Step4: Fit the Exponential, the Gaussian, and the multinomial distributions to the real distribution. Compare each of the model distribution M to the real noise distribution R using R-square (Coefficient of determination):

$$R\text{-square} = \frac{\sum_i (R_i - M_i)^2}{\sum_i (R_i - \bar{R})^2} \tag{20}$$

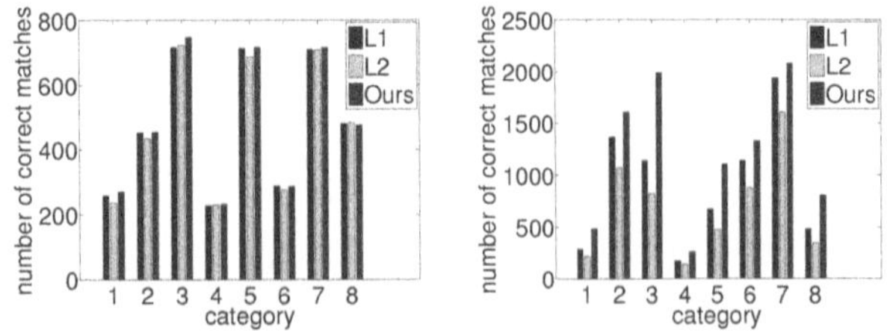

(a) SIFT (b) SURF

Figure 3: Performance of distance metrics on local features.

Table 1: Real noise distribution of binary features on training set

Categories	$p(d=-1)$	$p(d=0)$	$p(d=1)$
BRIEF	6.12%	87.77%	6.11%
ORB	6.10%	87.44%	6.46%
BRISK	5.24%	89.53%	5.23%

Step5: Apply the corresponding distance metric of each model distribution on test set (L1, L2 and our distance metric). Compare the matching performance.

In Figure 1 and 2 we have the matchings of the real noise distributions of SIFT and SURF considering the three distributions. The quantitative results of the estimation accuracy are also given by R-square score in Figure 1 and 2. One could notice that our framework is more effective to find a better model for the real noise distribution.

Figure 3 shows the matching results of SIFT and SURF when different distance metrics are used. The vertical scale of these two figures records the number of correct matches which represents matching performance. From the Figure 3 we can find that the proposed distance metric performs the best. For SIFT, the performances of the three distance metric have no big difference. The reason is that the R-square score of the three distributions modeling SIFT noise are very close. For SURF, the R-square score of the multinomial distribution is much higher than the other distributions. As a result, the proposed distance metric performs much better than L1 and L2 distance metrics. As a conclusion, the matching performance is in the same order of the R-square score, which means finding a better distance metric can be understood as establishing a better model for the real noise distribution. This conclusion is in accordance with the theory described in the Section 2.

3.3 Distance Metric for Binary Features

The real noise distributions of BRIEF, ORB, and BRISK are also computed based on the training set. These are given in table 1. We can see that for all three binary features, the condition C1 is satisfied ($P_{-1} < P_0, P_1 < P_0$) and the condition C2 is approximately satisfied ($P_{-1} \approx P_1$). According to the theory described in section 2.3, Hamming distance metric is then an approximate positive linear mapping of the theoretical distance on these features. Therefore, we give theoretical support for using Hamming distance metric on BRIEF, ORB, and BRISK. Furthermore, we also illustrate a framework to test whether Hamming metric should be used for matching a new binary feature.

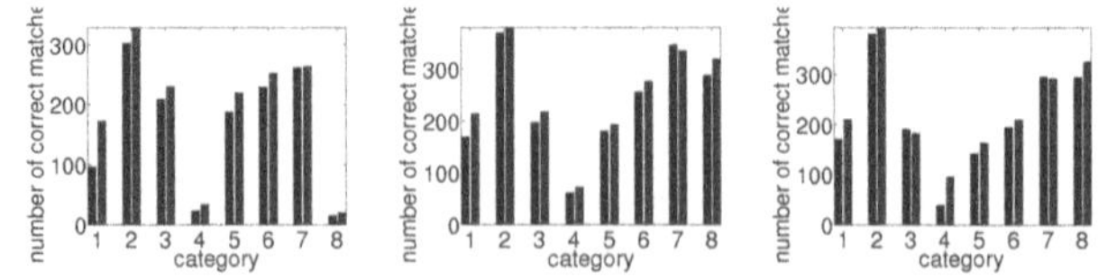

(a) BRIEF (b) ORB (c) BRISK

Figure 4: Performance of distance metrics on binary local features. Blue bars represent performance of Hamming metric and Red bars represent performance of ours.

The comparison results of our metric and Hamming metric on test set are given in Figure 4. We can see that our metric outperforms Hamming metric on all three features. The reason is that our metric can better reflect the real noise model on this data set. In addition, the experimental results illustrate that Hamming metric is also an effective distance metric for these three binary features.

4. CONCLUSION

In this paper, we propose a generalized distance metric for local features according to Maximum Likelihood theory. The proposed metric is based on a framework which approximates the feature noise distribution by multinomial distribution. Prevalent traditional distances such as L1, L2 and Hamming distance are justified as the special cases of the generalized distance.

We investigate the noise distributions of state-of-the-art local features. Our modeling framework is identified to be very effective to model their noise distributions. We also compare the matching performances of our distance metric and prevalent traditional ones. In all the experiments, better results are obtained based on our distance metric.

5. ACKNOWLEDGMENTS

This work is supported by National Nature Science Foundation of China (61273247, 61271428), National Key Technology Research and Development Program of China (2012BAH-39B02). This work was supported in part to Dr. Qi Tian by ARO grant W911BF-12-1-0057, NSF IIS 1052851, Faculty Research Awards by Google, FXPAL, and NEC Laboratories of America, and 2012 UTSA START-R Research Award respectively. This work was supported in part by NSFC 61128007.

6. REFERENCES

[1] H. Bay, T. Tuytelaars, and L. Van Gool. Surf: Speeded up robust features. In *ECCV*, 2006.
[2] M. Calonder, V. Lepetit, and et al. Brief: Binary robust independent elementary features. In *ECCV*, 2010.
[3] S. Leutenegger, M. Chli, and R. Siegwart. Brisk: Binary robust invariant scalable keypoints. In *ICCV*, 2011.
[4] D. Lowe. Distinctive image features from scale-invariant keypoints. *IJCV*, 2004.
[5] K. Mikolajczyk and C. Schmid. A performance evaluation of local descriptors. *PAMI*, 2005.
[6] E. Rublee, V. Rabaud, and et al. Orb: an efficient alternative to sift or surf. In *ICCV*, 2011.
[7] N. Sebe, M. Lew, and D. Huijsmans. Toward improved ranking metrics. *PAMI*, 2000.

Salient Object Detection in Videos by Optimal Spatio-Temporal Path Discovery

Ye Luo and Junsong Yuan
School of Electrical and Electronic Engineering
Nanyang Technological University
luoy0009@e.ntu.edu.sg, jsyuan@ntu.edu.sg

ABSTRACT

Many consumer videos focus on and follow salient objects in a scene. Detecting such salient objects is thus of great interests to video analytics and search. Instead of detecting salient object in individual frames separately, we propose to detect and track salient object simultaneously by finding a spatio-temporal path of the highest saliency density in the video. As salient video objects usually appear in consecutive frames, leveraging the motion coherence of videos can detect salient object more robustly. Without any prior knowledge of the salient objects, our method can automatically detect the salient objects of different shapes and sizes, and is able to handle noisy saliency maps and moving cameras. Experimental results on two public datasets demonstrate the effectiveness of the proposed method on salient video object detection.

Categories and Subject Descriptors

I.4 [**Image Processing and Computer Vision**]: Miscellaneous;; I.2.11 [**Vision and Scene Understanding**]: Metrics—*motion, video analysis*

Keywords

Optimal path discovery, Salient object detection, Temporal coherence

1. INTRODUCTION

Despite extensive studies of visual saliency, accurate salient object detection remains a challenging problem. First of all, without any prior knowledge of the salient objects (e.g. location, size, category, shape), it is very difficult to detect them reliably in an unsupervised way. Furthermore, even with a reasonable saliency map, it is not a trivial problem to accurately locate and crop the salient object as the obtained saliency map could be noisy due to the distractions from the cluttered background. Last but not the least, detecting saliency object in videos brings extra challenges as we need to consider both appearance and motion cues to find the saliency objects.

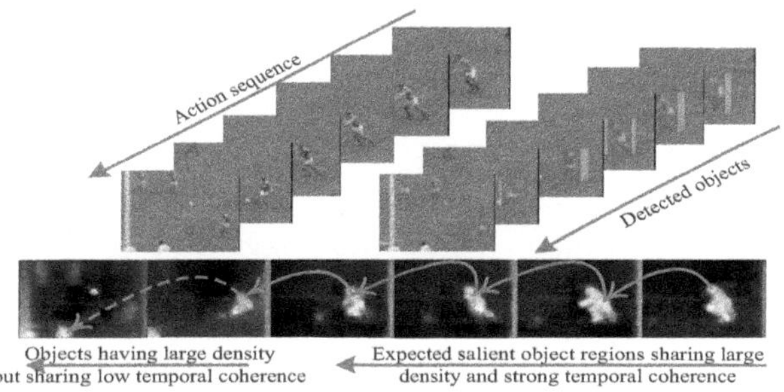

Figure 1: The main idea of our method. Salient objects in a video (regions with yellow masks) can be detected by discovering a salient path which has the maximum accumulated saliency density. By adding the temporal coherence constraints to the most dense regions, our method can accurately detect the salient objects (regions with blue masks).

We propose a novel method to discover salient objects in a video clip. Given a video clip, we first estimate the visual saliency map of each frame using both appearance and motion cues. We then assign a saliency density score to each pixel based on a local spatial window. Given the saliency density map $M(x, y, t)$, where x, y, t indicate the spatial and temporal location of a pixel and $M(x, y, t)$ is its saliency density, our salient object detection is formulated as a spatio-temporal salient path discovery problem in $M(x, y, t)$. Each spatio-temporal path connects local pixels across different frames, and is evaluated by the accumulated score of all local scores as well as the smoothness of the object trajectory based on the optical flow. Assuming the path of the highest accumulated saliency score corresponds to the salient object trajectory, our formulation has two advantages. First, as the discovered path smoothly connects pixels across frames, it naturally detects and tracks the salient object in the video. Second, the path can well handle noisy saliency map in individual frames as only the accumulated score matters.

To find the optimal path of maximum accumulated score, a dynamic programming algorithm is proposed. Our solution is similar to the optimal path discovery (OPD) [11] which localizes objects by maximizing accumulated classification scores across frames. However, there are two differences. First of all, our saliency map contains all positive scores, thus is our formulation is not performed on a discriminative score map as OPD requires. Second, we take the motion coherence between neighboring video frames into consideration and define the edges between pixels in neighboring frames to model their motion smoothness. This can

MM'13, October 21–25, 2013, Barcelona, Spain.

Figure 2: Sample results of video saliency detection: original frames (the first row), context aware saliency map (the second row), motion saliency map (the third row) and our fused results (the fourth row).

help track the salient object more robustly. We briefly explain the idea of our method in Fig. 1. A referee who breaks into the view will be detected as the salient object if we use the saliency map alone. On the contrary, the football player can be consistently tracked as the salient object if we detect it in the video. Extensive experiments on hundreds of videos from two public datasets demonstrate the effectiveness of the proposed method on salient video object detections.

2. RELATED WORK

Salient object detection in videos has been broadly explored [2]. In order to automatically segment objects from videos, a Markov Random Field model with estimated saliency as priors is used for salient object segmentation [3]. However, the computation complexity is relatively high. An efficient and unsupervised method has been proposed to detect salient video objects by finding maximum saliency density regions [7]. However, it ignores the temporal correlations among the salient object regions. Liu et al. proposed to train a Conditional Random Field (CRF) model and then use the model to detect the salient objects [6]. Benefited from the training, they may achieve better performance but lost the generality to handle real data as an unsupervised method does.

Saliency based object tracking is also closely related to our work. Instead of tracking a specific object, saliency based object tracking aims to track objects which are salient in a video [5, 12, 8, 1]. Similar to traditional tracking methods, salient objects are first detected by the trained CRF model and then tracked by the Particle Filters [12]. Mahadevan et al. proposed to track salient objects by first learning discriminative features to describe foreground objects in previous frame and then detecting the salient objects by the responses of the learned features in current frame [8]. As a further improvement of the aforementioned two methods, the descriptors of the background and the objects are first learned and particle filters are used for tracking in [1]. Different from them, our method targets to first detect and then locate the salient objects in every frame in an unsupervised way.

3. THE PROPOSED METHOD

3.1 Video Saliency Estimation

To obtain the visual saliency map for every frame, we simply combine image saliency S_I and motion contrast S_M to obtain the video saliency map M for each frame as Eq.1 shows:

$$M = N(S_M) + N(S_I), \tag{1}$$

where $N()$ is the min-max normalization operator. This equation is also plausible as both saliency clues (i.e. the static image saliency and the motion contrast) are equally important.

We adopt S_I from [4] as the image saliency of our video saliency estimation since context is considered important to salient object detection in videos. Besides the image saliency, our motion saliency is calculated as the motion contrast, which is obtained via removing the camera motion from the estimated motion vectors. After projecting the estimated motion vectors V and the global motion G into x and y axes as V_x and V_y, G_x and G_y, respectively, we remove the global motion from the estimated motion vector and obtain the local motion of objects or the motion contrast saliency as:

$$S_M = \sqrt{(V_x - G_x)^2 + (V_y - G_y)^2}. \tag{2}$$

The sample results of our video saliency maps are shown in Fig. 2. As can be seen, our results well balance the static saliency and the motion saliency, while neither of them can provide better saliency estimation results individually.

3.2 Salient Path Discovery Model

Given a sequence of saliency maps $M = \{M_1, \cdots, M_T\}$ where T is the number of frames in a video, our goal is to detect and locate salient objects by selecting their a salient spatio-temporal path that can track the salient object in the video. Denote a spatio-temporal position by (u, t) ($u = (x, y)$, $x \in [1, w]$ and $y \in [1, h]$), a 2D sliding window by W which is centered at (u, t), and its shape is decided by the height h_0 and the aspect ratio r_0. Suppose the area of the window and the summed saliency within the window are $S(W)$ and $M(W)$, respectively, the saliency density of W can be calculated as: $d(u, t) = \frac{M(W)}{S(W)}$.

We assume that the salient object should correspond to a location of high salient density $d(u, t)$ and windows with high saliency density can be the candidates of the salient objects. By connecting suitable candidate windows in a video, a spatio-temporal path denoted by p can be obtained and the accumulative score of all nodes along the path shows the evidence of the occurrences of salient object.

More formally, the salient video object detection problem, becomes to find the optimal path p^* with the maximum accumulated saliency density:

$$p^* = argmax_{p \in path(\mathcal{G})}(D(p)), \tag{3}$$

where $D(p) = \sum_{u,t} d(u, t)$ is the summed saliency density along a path p which starts from the start location (x_s, y_s, t_s) to the end location (x_e, y_e, t_d) and $path(\mathcal{G})$ is a set of all possible paths, where each path is a smooth spatio-temporal trajectory of arbitrary length.

Solving the above objective function implies to capture the occurrences of salient objects. However, the density $d(u, t)$ in each frame is obtained independently and no motion coherence is considered into $d(u,t)$ and $d(v,\text{t-1})$, where $v = (x', y')$ is one of the 9-neighbors[1] of u in frame t-1. To discriminate the windows located at different positions, a subscript of W is used, such as W_u and W_v. In order to incorporate the motion coherence, we calculate a weight for each pair of neighboring locations u and v in two neighboring frames $w_{u,t}(v,\text{t-1}) = \frac{Op(W_u, W_v)}{S(W_u)}$, where the numerator is the number of pixel points which are in the window W_u but mapped into the window W_v after the optical flow estimation. The large value of the ratio means that more pixels in W_u are from W_v and the higher similarity between W_u and W_v. For each pixel u in frame t, we connect it to its neighbors v in frame t-1, and the weight of the edge is $w_{u,t}(v, t-1) \in [0,1]$. Thus, by adding a motion constraint between the saliency density maps, we can update our objective function $D(p)$ in Eq. 4 as:

$$D(p) = \sum_{u,t} w_{u,t}(v, t-1) \times d(u,t). \tag{4}$$

In both Eq. 3 and Eq. 4, we use windows W of fixed size. To track salient object of varying sizes, we extend Eq. 3 into a multiple window detection with different sizes and aspect ratios, such that the salient object can be cropped by the adjustment of the window scales. We start the detection at a large scale and decrease it gradually to avoid the detection stopping at a small window with large density. The parameters such as the number of scales and the steps to change the height and the aspect ratio are empirically set during the experiments. A dynamic programming algorithm to solve our salient object location problem is proposed and illustrated in Alg. 1, which is similar in spirit to the optimal path discovery (OPD) proposed in [12]. After back tracing the recorded positions in P, a global optimal salient path to detect salient objects in a video is obtained.

Algorithm 1: Salient Path Discovery Algorithm

Data: Saliency maps M; the estimated optical flow V;
Result: $P(u,t)$: the best path record for tracing back;
$A(u,t)$: the accumulated scores of $P(u,t)$ leads to (u,t);
l^*: the ending location of the best path;
A^*: the accumulated scores of the best path;
begin
  Set $A(u,1) = d(u,1), \forall u$; $p = null, \forall(u,t)$;
  $A^* = -\infty$; $l^* = null$;
  for $t \leftarrow 2$ **to** T **do**
    for $u \in [1 \cdots w] \times [1 \cdots h]$ **do**
      Calculate $w_{u,t}(v, t-1)$;
      $v' \leftarrow argmax_{v \in N(u)} A(v, t-1) \times w_{u,t}(v, t-1)$;
      $A(u,t) \leftarrow A(v', t-1) + d(u,t) \times w_{u,t}(v, t-1)$;
      $P(u,t) \leftarrow (v', t-1)$;
      if $A(u,t) \leq A^*$ **then**
        $A^* \leftarrow A(u,t)$;
        $l^* \leftarrow (u,t)$;

4. EXPERIMENTS AND ANALYSIS

4.1 Experimental Setup

Datasets: We conduct experiments on two datasets: *UCF-Sport* [10] and *Ten-Video-Clips* [3]. The UCF-Sport dataset consists of 150 video sequences of 10 different action classes. Each video clip features one action performed by one or several people, which are the salient objects. The ground truth of each salient object is labeled by a bounding box. Ten-Video-Clips dataset contains 10 short video clips of 5 to 10 seconds each. Every video clip focuses on one major object in the natural scene. The ground truths are provided as segmented object masks. For fair comparisons, the minimum bounding box which includes the segmented object is used for evaluation.

Evaluation Metrics: Given the ground truth S_g which is the mask of the salient object and the detected salient object region S_d, we evaluate the performance of our method based on F-measure:

$$\text{F-measure} = \frac{(1+\alpha) \times \text{precision} \times \text{recall}}{\alpha \times \text{precision} + \text{recall}}, \tag{5}$$

where precision $= \frac{\|S_g \cap S_d\|}{\|S_d\|}$, recall $= \frac{\|S_g \cap S_d\|}{\|S_g\|}$ and α is a positive constant. We take $\alpha = 0.3$ as suggested in [6]. For a video clip, F-measure is calculated in each frame, and then averaged as the overall measurement for the video.

4.2 Experimental Results

Since [6] is a supervised method and there is no quantitative results provided in [3], for fair comparisons, we only compare our method with OPD [11] and MSD [7], both of which can detect salient object in videos. Since OPD is only for discriminative maps, we first find a threshold for each saliency map by Otsu [9], and then OPD is performed on the saliency map after subtracting the threshold. The same parameters are used in both our method and OPD. However, different from OPT, we take the motion coherence into consideration when finding the salient path. For MSD, we use the parameters which get the best performance as [7] did.

The detection results on two video clips are shown in Fig. 3. Based on the same saliency map and the same parameters for the initial scale and the aspect ratio, OPD takes more background regions as the salient object compared to our results in the third row. This is probably because each saliency map is thresholded independently and motion coherence among detected regions is not considered. Similarly, MSD locates the salient object for each frame and the decision is made only based on the saliency density in the individual frame. Thus only the most salient objects have been detected (e.g. the person nearby the football player who is kicking). It is also worth mentioning that our method is able to detect multiple salient video objects. We can perform our method on the remained saliency maps by wiping the previously detected object regions out to detect the salient video objects one by one. Fig. 4 depicts the quantitative results for three different methods on videos from UCF-Sport and Ten-Video-Clips datasets. Our method improves the F-measure to 77.33% comparing to 70.23% for OPD and 68.58% for MSD on action videos of kicking. The poor performance for the 6_{th} video in kicking videos is mainly caused by the noisy video saliency estimation results. In order to evaluate

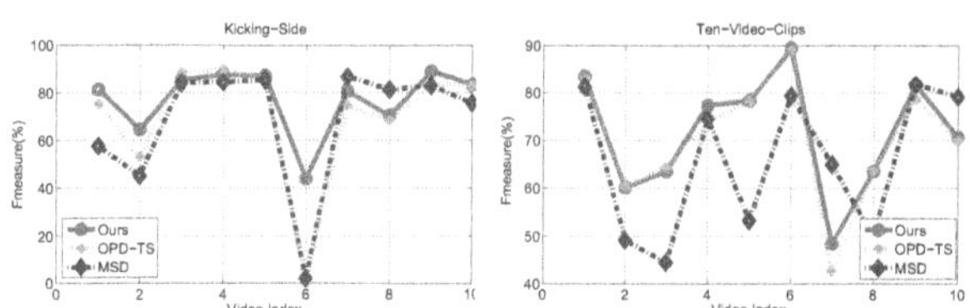

Figure 4: F-measure evaluations of our method (the red line), MSD (the blue line) and OPD (the green line).

[1]The 9-neighbors are the same position as u and its 8-neighbors in frame t-1.

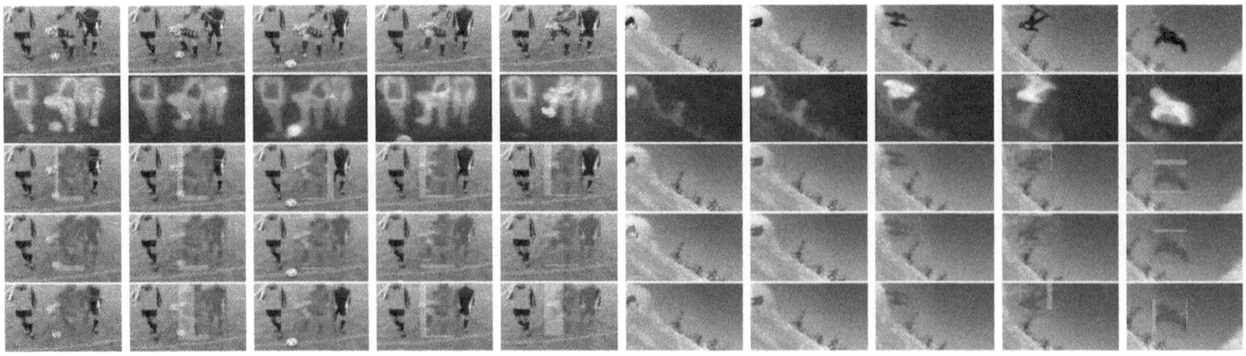

Figure 3: Sample results by our method (third row), OPD (fourth row) and MSD (last row). The blue masks indicate the detected results while the orange ones are the ground truths. Without considering the motion coherence, OPD missed the small salient object (i.e. the people who is skating) and MSD wrongly detect other football player as the salient object).

Table 1: Averaged F-measure (%) ± Standard Deviation for our method by a single-scale window and multi-scale windows on 'Swing-Side Angle' videos.

	F-measure	Std. Dev.
Multi-scale	46.46	0.17
Single-scale	40.73	0.16

the performance of our method on handling deformable object detection, we test on "'Swing-Side Angle"' videos where the athlete has articulated body movements as shown in Fig. 5. As the salient object keeps changing its shapes and sizes across frames, we use multi-scale window to capture it. Comparing with using windows of fixed size, the performance is improved by using multi-scale windows, as shown in Table 1.

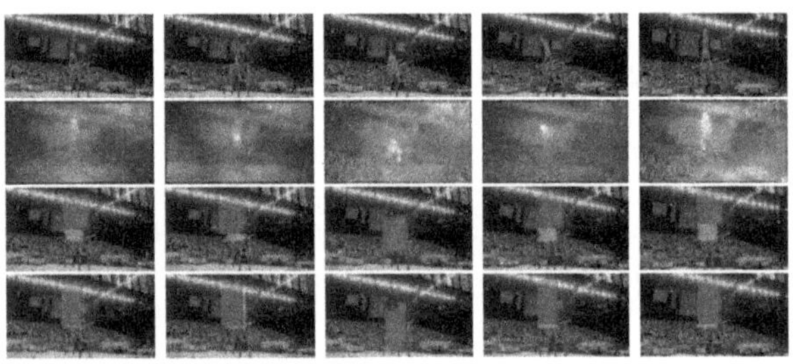

Figure 5: Performance comparisons by using fixed size window (third row) and windows with multiple scales (fourth row). The blue masks are the detection results while the orange ones are the ground truths.

More detection results for horse-riding, swing-side-angle, running and skate-board-front videos are provided in Table 2. Without any prior knowledge of the salient object, the person performing actions in a complex scene can be captured by our salient object discovery method.

Table 2: Averaged F-measure (%) ± Standard Deviation for four types of action videos.

	Ride	Swing	Run	Skate
Ours	65.19±0.22	49.62±0.42	55.49±0.34	43.37±0.36
OPD[11]	63.92±0.21	44.23±0.38	54.46±0.24	42.68±0.35
MSD[7]	38.63±0.18	39.17±0.37	52.19±0.34	42.96±0.35

5. CONCLUSION

We formulate video salient object detection as an optimal salient path discovery problem and propose a dynamic programming algorithm to solve it efficiently. By adding the constraint of motion coherence in salient path discovery, our method obtains superior performance compared to two state-of-the-art methods. Moreover, without any prior knowledge of the salient objects, our method can automatically detect various salient objects across different scales and aspect ratios. Extensive experiments on two public dataset demonstrate the effectiveness of our approach.

6. ACKNOWLEDGMENTS

This work is supported in part by the Nanyang Assistant Professorship SUG M4080134.

7. REFERENCES

[1] A. Borji, S. Frintrop, D. N. Sihite, and L. Itti. Adaptive object tracking by learning background context. In *CVPR Workshops'12*, pages 23–30, 2012.

[2] A. Borji, D. N. Sihite, and L. Itti. Salient object detection: A benchmark. In *ECCV*, volume 7573, pages 414–429, 2012.

[3] K. Fukuchi, K. Miyazato, A. Kimura, S. Takagi, and J. Yamato. Saliency-based video segmentation with graph cuts and sequentially updated priors. In *ICME*, pages 638–641, 2009.

[4] S. Goferman, L. Zelnik-Manor, and A. Tal. Context-aware saliency detection. In *CVPR*, 2010.

[5] G. Hua, C. Zhang, Z. Liu, Z. Zhang, and Y. Shan. Efficient scale-space spatiotemporal saliency tracking for distortion-free video retargeting. In *ACCV'09*, pages 182–192, 2009.

[6] T. Liu, N. Zheng, W. Ding, and Z. Yuan. Video attention: Learning to detect a salient object sequence. In *ICPR*, pages 1–4, 2008.

[7] Y. Luo, J. Yuan, P. Xue, and Q. Tian. Saliency density maximization for efficient visual objects discovery. *TCSVT*, 21(12):1822 -1834, 2011.

[8] V. Mahadevan and N. Vasconcelos. Saliency-based discriminant tracking. In *CVPR*, pages 1007–1013, 2009.

[9] N. Otsu. A threshold selection method from gray-level histograms. *IEEE Transactions on Systems, Man and Cybernetics*, 9:62–66, 1979.

[10] M. D. Rodriguez, J. Ahmed, and M. Shah. Action MACH a spatio-temporal Maximum Average Correlation Height filter for action recognition. In *CVPR*, pages 1–8, 2008.

[11] D. Tran and J. Yuan. Optimal spatio-temporal path discovery for video event detection. In *CVPR*, 2011.

[12] G. Zhang, Z. Yuan, N. Zheng, X. Sheng, and T. Liu. Visual saliency based object tracking. In *ACCV*, pages 193–203, 2009.

Multiview Semi-Supervised Ranking for Automatic Image Annotation

Ali Fakeri-Tabrizi* Massih-Reza Amini† Patrick Gallinari*

*Université Pierre et Marie Curie
Laboratoire d'Informatique de Paris 6
4, place jussieu
75252 Paris, France
First.Last@lip6.fr

†Université Joseph Fourier
Laboratoire d'Informatique de Grenoble
Centre Equation 4
38041 Grenoble, France
Massih-Reza.Amini@imag.fr

ABSTRACT

Most photo sharing sites give their users the opportunity to manually label images. The labels collected that way are usually very incomplete due to the size of the image collections: most images are not labeled according to all the categories they belong to, and, conversely, many class have relatively few representative examples. Automated image systems that can deal with small amounts of labeled examples and unbalanced classes are thus necessary to better organize and annotate images. In this work, we propose a multiview semi-supervised bipartite ranking model which allows to leverage the information contained in unlabeled sets of images in order to improve the prediction performance, using multiple descriptions, or views of images. For each topic class, our approach first learns as many view-specific rankers as available views using the labeled data only. These rankers are then improved iteratively by adding pseudo-labeled pairs of examples on which all view-specific rankers agree over the ranking of examples within these pairs. We report on experiments carried out on the NUS-WIDE dataset, which show that the multiview ranking process improves predictive performances when a small number of labeled examples is available specially for unbalanced classes. We show also that our approach achieves significant improvements over a state-of-the art semi-supervised multiview classification model.

Categories and Subject Descriptors

I.2 [**Artificial intelligence**]: Learning; I.4 [**Image processing and computer vision**]: General—*Image processing software*

General Terms

Theory, Algorithms, Experimentation

Keywords

Multiview semi-supervised ranking, Image Annotation

1. INTRODUCTION

Image annotation is the task of assigning labels to images. Each label describes an entity, a content or even a part of a given information contained in an image. In some photo sharing sites, users have the opportunity to manually assign labels to images; these labels are further used to browse or search the image collection. Labeling a huge collection of images is usually a difficult and a time consuming task, and the automatisation of image annotation has motivated the development of many different methods in the past years.

The intrinsic properties of image collections that have to be considered when developing automatic annotation tools are (a) in many categories, there are generally a very limited number of labeled examples, together with a very large number of additional unlabeled images, (b) images are naturally represented by several distinct features sets, or *views*, such as RGB color histograms or *textual* features; such as the bag-of-words representation of the surrounding texts of images, and, (c) classes are imbalanced such that the number of examples in one class could be very few, or in the opposite dominates the other classes. Recently, multi-view semi-supervised learning techniques for classification have been developed to address this kind of problem [11]. Some approaches use the labeled data to train several view-specific classifiers, and rely on the intuition that these predictors should have similar predictions on the unlabeled set in order to assign pseudo-labels to these examples and to train new view-specific classifiers using the initial labeled training set and the newly pseudo-labeled unlabeled examples [1].

In this work we propose a new multiview bi-partite ranking framework for this task. Our approach to semi-supervised multiview ranking follows the same intuition than before. Given V score functions $(h_1, \dots, h_V)$ independently trained on each view, we define a notion of global agreement between them as the expectation, over random pairs of images $(\mathbf{x}, \mathbf{x}')$, that two score functions $(h_v, h_{v'})$ predict the same relative ordering. We hence describe a learning process in which view-specific ranking functions should achieve high ranking performance on the labeled training set, while minimizing a disagreement measure between each other on the unlabeled dataset. The overall motivation of using a bi-partite ranking framework rather than classification one here, is that it has recently been shown that in the supervised case, the associated classifier of a ranking function can better handle class imbalancements [5]. Our experimental results show that our approach achieves significant improvements over a state-of-the art semi-supervised multiview classification model.

2. SEMI-SUPERVISED MULTIVIEW RANKING FOR IMAGE ANNOTATIONS

We suppose that we have n labeled examples $\mathcal{Z} = (\mathbf{x}^i, y^i)_{i=1}^n$ composed of pairs of (observation,target), where $y^i \in \{-1, 1\}$ is the relevance associated to the observation x^i. In a semi-supervised learning setting we also assume to have access to a set of unlabeled examples $\mathcal{U} = \{(\mathbf{x}^{n+i}) | i = 1, \ldots, m\}$. In the single view setting, the aim of learning is to find a scoring function h, so that relevant observations (i.e. those with $y = +1$) are assigned higher scores than irrelevant ones, and the ranking criterion to be optimized to achieve this goal is usually the Area Under the ROC Curve (AUC).

In the multiview setting, an observation (e.g. an image described by different feature sets), $\mathbf{x} = (x_1, ..., x_V)$ is represented in several vector spaces, $\mathcal{X}_v, v \in \{1 \ldots V\}$, such that each vector x_v (an image descriptor) can be used to build a predictor. Following the framework of [9] for multiview classification or regression, we can define the objective of multiview ranking as jointly learning *view-specific* scoring functions $h_v : \mathcal{X}_v \to \mathbb{R}$ (in our case, h_v only considers the v-th descriptor of images) so that their average risk is small, where the joint learning of these view-specific predictors consists in constraining them to agree with each other (i.e. have similar predictions). In this framework, the agreement between predictors is measured without knowing the labels of the observations, and therefore it can be estimated and optimized from the pool of unlabeled data. Since constraining the view-specific predictors to have a low disagreement reduces the function space, we can expect better generalization guarantees using semi-supervised multiview learning than using supervised learning.

A measure of disagreement, D, between two scoring functions h_v and $h_{v'}$ can be defines as the probability, over any two random observations, that they do not predict the same ordering:

$$D(h_v, h_{v'}) = \mathbb{P}\big((h_v(X) - h_v(X'))(h_{v'}(X) - h_{v'}(X')) \leq 0\big)$$

which can be estimated on the *unlabeled* data set U by $\widehat{D}_U(h_v, h_{v'})$ defined as :

$$\frac{1}{m(m-1)} \sum_{i \neq j} \mathbb{1}_{(h_v(x_v^{n+i}) - h_v(x_v^{n+j})) \times (h_{v'}(x_v^{n+i}) - h_{v'}(x_v^{n+j})) \leq 0}$$

Where, $\mathbb{1}_.$ is the indicator function. This notion of disagreement and its empirical counterpart can then be extended to more than two views by taking the average disagreement between scoring functions for any pair of views:

$$\widehat{D}_U(h_1, \ldots, h_V) = \frac{2}{V(V-1)} \sum_{v < v'} \widehat{D}_U(h_v, h_{v'}) \ . \qquad (1)$$

To avoid the costly computation of the disagreement at each iteration for all unlabeled data, we consider an estimation to use the pairs sampled at the current iteration. Our semi-supervised multiview process follows existing iterative pseudo-labeling methods for classification, but it has two properties which reduce the overall time and space complexity to $\tilde{O}(n + m)$. The first one is a reduction from the pseudo-labeled pairs to bipartite ranking in order to use efficient learning to rank algorithms. The second one is a random sampling of pairs at each iteration rather than considering all possible pairs of unlabeled examples.

Following iterative pseudo-labeling methods for classification (here, applied to pairs of inputs) we form unlabeled pairs of examples and decide whether or not they contain information that should be added to the training set based on a measure of confidence of the pseudo-label. We hence select only the pairs for which all the view-specific rankers agree on the relative ordering. This requirement of unanimity may be too restrictive when there are many views, but we observed that it works very well in practice.

Algorithm 1: Semi-supervised Multiview Ranking

Input:
▷ supervised bipartite ranking algorithm: $\mathcal{A}$;
▷ size of the random pairs sample: S;
▷ labeled $\mathcal{Z}$, and unlabeled $\mathcal{U}$ multiview training data;
Initialize:
for each view, train $h_v^{(0)}$ on Z with $\mathcal{A}$.
$t \leftarrow 0$;
repeat
  for $s = 1..S$ **do**
    $(i, j) = \text{sample}(\{(k, \ell) \in \{1, ..., m\}^2, k \neq \ell\})$
    if $\forall v, h_v^{(t)}(x_v^{n+i}) > h_v^{(t)}(x_v^{n+j})$ **then**
      $Z \leftarrow Z \cup \{(x^{n+i}, +1), (x^{n+j}, -1)\}$
    else if $\forall v, h_v^{(t)}(x_v^{n+i}) < h_v^{(t)}(x_v^{n+j})$ **then**
      $Z \leftarrow Z \cup \{(x^{n+i}, -1), (x^{n+j}, +1)\}$
    end if
  end for
  $t \leftarrow t + 1$;
  for each view, train $h_v^{(t)}$ on Z with $\mathcal{A}$;
until $\hat{D}_U(h_1^{(t)}, ..., h_V^{(t)}) \geq \hat{D}_U(h_1^{(t-1)}, ..., h_V^{(t-1)})$
Output: $\forall v \in \{1, .., V\}, h_v^{(t)}$;

3. ALGORITHM

The pseudo-code of our proposed approach is given in Algorithm 1. In an initialization step, each view-specific ranker is trained independently on the labeled training set. Then, the algorithm iteratively re-trains one ranker per view on increasing training sets composed of the initial labeled examples, and additional pseudo-labeled examples. The iterative procedure is repeated until the disagreement does not decrease after re-training.

Considering our notion of empirical disagreement Eq. (1), it is then natural to define a notion of pseudo-labeling on *pairs* of unlabeled observations: a pair $(\mathbf{x}^{n+i}, \mathbf{x}^{n+j})$ would be labeled $+1$ if the various view-rankers agree on, and -1 if they agree on the inverse relative ordering. After pseudo-labeling, we would then obtain a training set with pseudo-pairwise preferences (instead of pseudo labels in $\{-1, 1\}$). From a computational point of view, however, this procedure would be extremely costly for two reasons. First, it would require a pass over all pairs of unlabeled inputs at each round. Since there are about m^2 pairs, this is too large by an order of magnitude. Secondly, the pairs of unlabeled inputs selected to be added in the training set do not have the structure of a proper bipartite ranking. The underlying supervised learning algorithm should then be an algorithm that can deal with arbitrary pairwise preferences, which have $\Omega(\ell^2)$ space and time complexity (ℓ is the number of objects in the training set). By contrast, efficient algorithms for bipartite ranking like SVM^{multi} [6] run in time $\tilde{O}(\ell)$ and require $O(\ell)$ space.

4. EXPERIMENTS AND RESULTS

In this work, we use the NUS-WIDE-LITE image collection which is a subset of the original image collection NUS-WIDE provided by the National University of Singapour [4]. This smaller dataset is composed of 28,807 images for training and 28,808 images for testing. The images in these two sets belong to one or more of 81 classes. This collection provides six visual features already extracted. Three of them are color based features: 1) a color histogram, 2) a color auto-correlogram and 3) block-wise color moments. Using the texture-base technique, two other feature types have been extracted: 4) an edge direction histogram and 5) a wavelet texture. The last set of visual features in this collection is 6) a bag of visual words, obtained by using the SIFT method [7]. All these features are included in the dataset distribution and are based on the visual content. In addition, we extracted a new set of features, based on textual data. We extracted these textual feature automatically from user tags associated to each image, and we took into account a bag-of-words representation with a tf.idf term weighting after filtering out rare words [8]. In [2], it has been shown that the more views are independent the more we can expect higher generalization performance. Therefore, in order to enhance the independence between different feature sets, we concatenate features within the same classes of visual descriptors resulting in four different views ($V = 4$): 1) concatenation of color-based features, 2) concatenation of texture-based features, 3): the bag of visual words and 4): textual feature. Each set of these 4 new features is considered as a *view* in our multiview approach.

To simulate a semi-supervised learning scenario, we divide the training data into two subsets: a subset will be used as the *labeled set* in which we consider that the labels are known; for the remaining training images, the labels are hidden and this subset will be used as the *unlabeled set*. The split is performed randomly, and each experiment is repeated 50 times, over 50 different subsamplings of the training data. We tried four different size for the *labeled set*: 50, 100, 200, 1000 (Resp. 28757, 28707, 28607, 27807 for *unlabeled set*); In each split, the proportions of the class are kept similar to what was observed in the training data set (stratified sampling). The test collection is left unchanged, and all reported results apply to this test collection.

To study the behavior of our model in presence of class imbalancement, we focus on 22 classes of NUS-WIDE-LITE upon which 7 classes have a positive percentage rate greater than 15% and 15 other classes are highly imbalanced having less than 15% positive examples.

In our experiments, we compared our multi view ranking strategy with 4 other strategies: three supervised learning baselines which consists in two ranking and one classification models and one semi-supervised multiview classification model proposed in [1].

- **Supervised Ranking.** A supervised view-specific bipartite ranking model trained on each view separately (`R_SUP`). Reported results for for `R_SUP` are the average results of each of the view-specific rankers.
- **Classification.** Supervised view-specific SVMs trained on each view separately (denoted as `C_SUP`). Results for `C_SUP` correspond to the average performance of the view-specific classifiers which are optimized over the F_1 measure [6].
- **Concatenation.** A supervised Ranking SVM working on the concatenation of all of the views (`R_Concat`).
- **Semi-supervised multiview classification learning.** The semi-supervised multiview classification algorithm (`C_SemSUP`) proposed in [1]. As baseline classifiers, we use SVM optimized over the F_1 measure in order to be less affected by the imbalance effects [6].
- **Semi-supervised multiview ranking learning.** Our approach (`R_SemSUP`). At test time, we sum the scores of all views-specific rankers and rerank the scores according to the the summed scores.

In all of our experiments, we used linear kernels and we set the regularization parameter of $\mathtt{SVM}^{multi}$, C, to 1. We also tried to find the parameter C by cross-validation but for small labeled training sets, we considered, this strategy leads easily to overfitting. The performance is reported in terms of Accuracy and AUC of the view-specific scoring functions over the four views mentioned above and different classes.

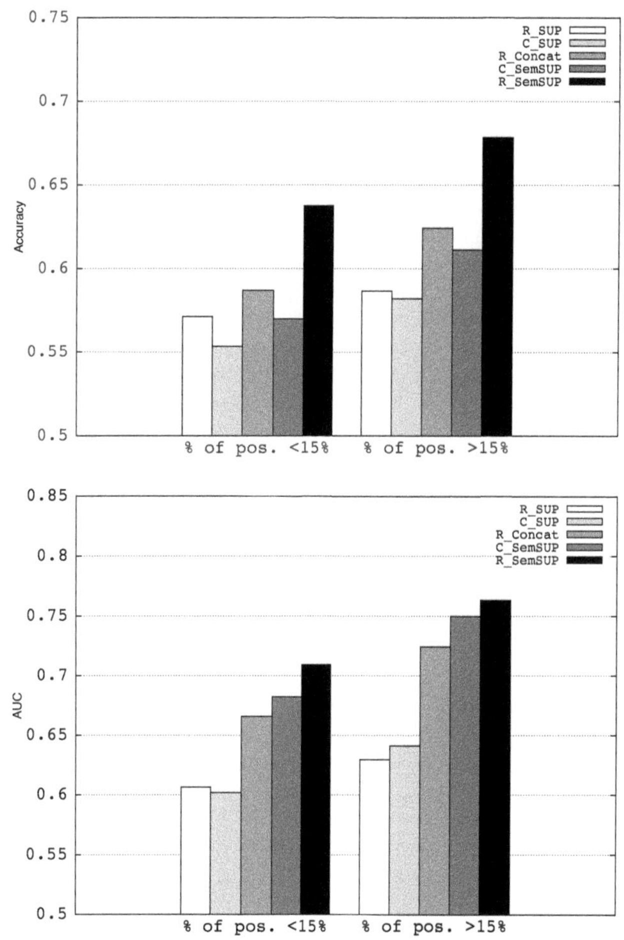

Figure 1: Accuracy (top) and AUC (bottom) performance of all models for 50 labeled examples and two cases where the percentage of positive class is below (left in each figure) and above (right in each figure) 15%.

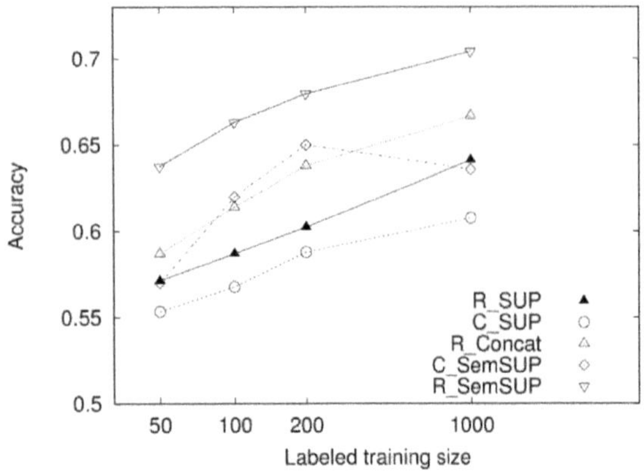

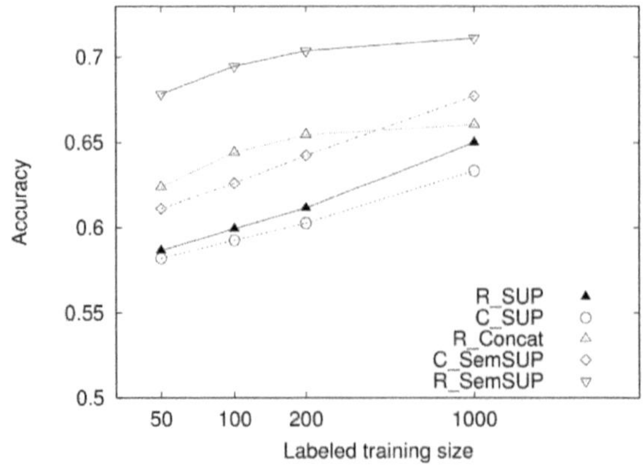

Figure 2: Accuracy of different strategies with respect to four different labeled training size and when the percentage of positive class is below (left) and above (right) 15%, on the NUS-WIDE-LITE dataset. Performance are averaged over 22 classes and 50 random splits.

The histograms in figure 1 illustrate the average of Accuracy and AUC measures over all classes for different strategies. We separated the performance for the cases where the percentage of positives was below or above 15%, in order to see the impact of this imbalancement over the classification and ranking strategies. We see that `R_SemSUP` clearly outperforms the three supervised baselines `R_SUP`, `C_SUP` and `R_Concat`, as well as the semi-supervised classification strategy `C_SemSUP`, specially when the imbalancement is more pronounced. These results also suggest that supervised bi-partite ranking over the concatenation of all of the views may sometimes outperform a semi-supervised multi-view classification strategy which optimizes a F_1 value.

Figure 2, shows the accuracy performance of five strategies with respect to different labaeled training size and when the percentage of positive class is below and above 15%. These results are averaged over 50 random labeled/unlabeled splits of the training data and all the classes. From these results, we see that when the percentage of the positive class is below 15%, `C_SemSUP` overcomes in some extent the class imbalancement, one the case where the number of labeled examples increase, but not always, while `R_SemSUP` is not so affected by class imbalancement and that for every number of labeled examples we considered in our experiments.

5. CONCLUSION

In this paper, we proposed a mutiview semi-supervised ranking algorithm for image annotation task in the general case where images are naturally described with heterogeneous visual feature sets, as well as multimodal (visual/text) feature representations, and where classes are mostly imbalanced. The proposed algorithm takes advantage of the existing different views of examples in order to overcome the lack of labeled examples by reducing the disagreement of different view-specific rankers on the unlabaled training set. Experiments conducted on the NUS-WIDE dataset show that our strategy can better tackle the class imbalancement problem than a state-of-the-art multiview semi-supervised classification method, in the most interesting case where the number of labeled training examples is low. Finally, the approach is generic in the sense that it can be applied to many other multi-modal image applications [3, 10].

6. REFERENCES

[1] M. R. Amini, N. Usunier, and C. Goutte. Learning from multiple partially observed views - an application to multilingual text categorization. In *Neural Information Processing Systems (NIPS)*, pages 28–36, 2009.

[2] A. Blum and T. M. Mitchell. Combining labeled and unlabeled data with co-training. In *Conference on Learning Theory (COLT)*, pages 92–100, 1998.

[3] X. Cai, F. Nie, H. Huang, and F. Kamangar. Heterogeneous image feature integration via multi-modal spectral clustering. In *CVPR*, 2011.

[4] T. S. Chua, J. Tang, R. Hong, H. Li, Z. Luo, and Z. Zheng. Nus-wide: A real-world web image database from national university of singapore. In *Conference On Image And Video Retrieva (CIVR)*, 2009.

[5] A. Fakeri-Tabrizi, S. Tollari, N. Usunier, and P. Gallinari. Improving image annotation in imbalanced classification problems with ranking svm. In *CLEF*, pages 291–294, 2010.

[6] T. Joachims. A support vector method for multivariate measures. In *International Conference on Machine Learning (ICML)*, 2005.

[7] D. G. Lowe. Object recognition from local scale-invariant features. In *International Conference on Computer Visio (ICCV)*, pages 1150–1157, 1999.

[8] G. Salton. *Introduction to modern information retrieval.* McGraw-Hill, 1986.

[9] K. Sridharan and S. M. Kakade. An information theoretic framework for multiview learning. In *COLT*, pages 403–414, 2008.

[10] H. Wang, F. Nie, H. Huang, S. L. Risacher, A. J. Saykin, and L. Shen. Identifying disease sensitive and quantitative trait-relevant biomarkers from multidimensional heterogeneous imaging genetics data via sparse multimodal multitask learning. *Bioinformatics*, 2012.

[11] X. Zhang, J. Cheng, C. Xu, H. Lu, and S. Ma. Multi-view multi-label active learning for image classiffication. In *ICME*, pages 258–261, 2009.

How Do We Deep-Link? Leveraging User-Contributed Time-Links for Non-Linear Video Access

Raynor Vliegendhart, Babak Loni, Martha Larson, and Alan Hanjalic
Multimedia Information Retrieval Lab, Delft University of Technology, Delft, The Netherlands
{r.vliegendhart, b.loni, m.a.larson, a.hanjalic}@tudelft.nl

ABSTRACT

This paper studies a new way of accessing videos in a non-linear fashion. Existing non-linear access methods allow users to jump into videos at points that depict specific visual concepts or that are likely to elicit affective reactions. We believe that deep-link comments, which occur unprompted on social video sharing platforms, offer a new opportunity beyond existing methods. With deep-link comments, viewers express themselves about a particular moment in a video by including a time-code. Deep-link comments are special because they reflect viewer perceptions of noteworthiness, that include, but extend beyond depicted conceptual content and induced affective reactions. Based on deep-link comments collected from YouTube, we develop a Viewer Expressive Reaction Variety (VERV) taxonomy that captures how viewers deep-link. We validate the taxonomy with a user study on a crowdsourcing platform and discuss how it extends conventional relevance criteria. We carry out experiments which show that deep-link comments can be automatically filtered and sorted into VERV categories.

Categories and Subject Descriptors:
H.3 [Information Storage and Retrieval]: H.3.3 Information Search and Retrieval—*Search process*

Keywords: comments; deep-links; non-linear video access; video retrieval; relevance criteria; YouTube

1. INTRODUCTION

Current mainstream social video sharing platforms retrieve full videos. Results consisting of time-links to particular points in videos are relatively unknown. Viewers consume video results by watching linearly from the beginning or scrubbing through the video in search of interesting moments. There are, however, two readily available sources of evidence indicating that time-code level access, or finer granularity in general, is important for users. First, we find that, in the area of textual information, conventional search engines include links to parts of webpages in their search results. By extension, we surmise that search results including links to parts of videos would also be helpful for users. Second, simply observing social interactions on video sites such as YouTube reveals a phenomenon called *deep-linking*: people explicitly referring to specific video moments in their comments by mentioning the corresponding time-codes. We build upon this phenomenon and make use of this source of user-contributed deep-link comments to enable a new innovative form of non-linear video access.

Figure 1: User deep-link comments provide time-code-level access to videos. These examples depict viewers' expressions of surprise.

Figure 1 depicts our vision of a future retrieval system that uses deep-link comments to offer time-code-level access to videos. Technically speaking, a deep-link is a time-code that points to a particular moment in the video and, like a hyperlink in a webpage, can be clicked to jump to the target. Deep-links comments occur in the wild on the YouTube platform as no special actions are required to create deep-links. Simply including a textual representation of the time-code using one of two formats in a comment, i.e., "0m00s" or "0:00", will result in a deep-link. A deep-link comment retrieval system, as envisioned in Figure 1, would index deep-link comments, i.e., comments containing at least one deep-link, in order to provide deep-links as jump-in points to its users. Users enter a topical query, here, 'cats at play' and also gives an indication of the type of deep-link comments they are interested in, here, comments expressing 'surprise'.

The special interest of deep-link comments for non-linear video access is that they provide users with a new perspective on moments in the video. Currently, techniques that automatically select time points are based on two relevance criteria, i.e., reasons that users would find the time points relevant. The first of these takes the "Depicted Visual Content" perspective on moments in videos. These approaches

MM'13, October 21–25, 2013, Barcelona, Spain.
Copyright 2013 ACM 978-1-4503-2404-5/13/10
http://dx.doi.org/10.1145/2502081.2502137 ...$15.00.

provide users with moments in video that are relevant because they depict certain objects and scenes. In other words, they carry out visual concept detection [12]. The second relevance criterion takes the "Viewer Affective Reaction" perspective. These approaches provide users with moments in a video at which they, as viewers, are likely to experience certain emotional responses [5]. They make use of highlight detection approaches, for example, algorithms that analyze the roar of the crowd to predict emotional response peaks during sports videos [11].

The perspective offered by deep-link comments goes above and beyond these relevance criteria because deep-links mark points in the video that users perceive to be worthy of remark. In other words, it is not enough for a moment to depict a concept or evoke an emotion, the moment must also be interesting enough to trigger viewers to express a response. We call this response "Viewer Expressive Reaction" (VER). The exact reasons triggering the response are complex and involve many dependencies, e.g., context and personal taste. For this reason, we do not focus on the exact nature of the trigger, but on the *type* of reaction that is triggered, or the "Viewer Expressive Reaction Variety" (VERV). As is explained in detail in this paper, viewers' reactions include, but also extend beyond, references to depicted content or expressions of affective reaction.

2. RELATED WORK

Non-linear video access: Non-linear access to video content has been extensively studied before. Its importance is evidenced by a variety of methods that have been developed to enable non-linear access. Work by Hanjalic et al. [4] focused on automatically grouping shots together into logical story units based on temporal visual consistency amongst the shots. For retrieving video shots based on what is being depicted, many different visual concept detectors have been developed [12]. Analysis of audience response within a video has been used to detect highlights for specific genres of videos, such as sitcoms [3] and soccer matches [11]. Other studies proposed approaches to find interesting points in a video by capturing playback behaviour [2, 13]. None of the researched methods, however, considers the notion of noteworthiness or investigate reactions that are explicitly expressed by the viewer.

User comments and video access: Comments have been used and proved useful for various information retrieval tasks [9]. A priori, our motivation to investigate deep-link comments as a source of a new relevance criterion is the literature on user-contributed comments. This insight is expressed by [9], which characterizes what users want to find in comments as "some kind of 'surprise'". We aim to extend this insight from conventional comments to deep-link comments. One of the few, if not the only, studies on time-linked video comments is [15]. This work describes a system that uses comments to retrieve scenes. The comments studied were created in a laboratory setting on a limited number of videos. This system needs explicit interval annotation and cannot benefit from casual user generated comments containing time-codes.

The closest study to our work is [8] in which the authors propose a classification scheme for YouTube comments. The proposed scheme consists of a large number of categories, some quite similar to each other. The authors, however, do not use their scheme for automatic classification. Our taxonomy is different from existing studies of types of comments, because it is specific to deep-link comments, which are associated with specific time-points in social videos.

3. ANALYSIS OF DEEP-LINK COMMENTS

3.1 Video Deep-Link Comments Dataset

This paper uses a dataset of 1,707 YouTube videos, which comprise 33% of all English-language YouTube videos in the publicly available MSRA-MM dataset [7]. The videos were selected because they had both "survived" from the dataset release (June 2009) to the time or our crawl of the comments and metadata (October 2012) and had also accumulated at least one deep-link comment by that time.

For each video, we randomly sampled three deep-link comments from all the deep-link comments associated with it. We used a large crowdsourcing study (Section 3.2) to collect annotations for the deep-links resulting in a total set of 3,359 deeplink comments. Our sampling procedure was chosen to yield a deep-link comment set of a size large enough to be representative, but not so large as to prevent carrying out a crowdsourcing experiment. The videos were distributed over the following YouTube categories: *music* (454), *entertainment* (388), *comedy* (214), *film* (178), *people* (115), *sports* (96), *autos* (48), *news* (36), *animals* (22), *travel* (18), *howto* (14), *games* (8), *tech* (8), *education* (4), and *shows* (3).

Finally, we note that the MSRA-MM dataset was created to contain relatively popular videos, which means that the average that we measured (50 deep-link comments per video) is probably not entirely typical of online video in general. However, we find that on average 4.4% of the comments posted to any video in our set contain deep-links, confirming that deep-linking in comments is a well-established practice.

3.2 Analyzing How Users Deep-Link

Our analysis of how users deep-link focuses on the creation of a taxonomy of deep-link comment classes. Our taxonomy is different from existing studies of types of comments because it is specific to deep-link comments, which are associated with specific time-points in social videos.

Deep-link Comment Taxonomy: In order to be able to base our taxonomy on a large number of deep-link comments, we carry out a crowdsourcing experiment to elicit input on the types of deep-links in existence. Crowdsourcing-based elicitation makes it possible to review more data than we could exclusively by hand and also gather input of a large number of different human judges. It has been successfully applied to collect user perceptions of multimedia, e.g., in [14] it was used to create classes of user-perceived multimedia similarity.

For our crowsourcing experiments, we make use of Amazon Mechanical Turk (AMT, www.mturk.com), a large commercial crowdsourcing platform. The AMT microtask (i.e., HIT) that we used for the elicitation crowdsourcing experiment was titled "Why watch this video moment? Give reasons for which people create video time-links." In this HIT, workers were presented with a video and three deep-link comments. They were told that the comments had been written by a viewer of the video and were asked to watch the video around the time-link and provide a description of the reason for which they thing that the person posted the comment. Quality control took two forms on this HIT: First,

Table 1: VERV taxonomy of comment types

VERV class	ID	Description
Yeah! I love it.	love	Personal, positive reaction to linked time-point
Booo. I hate it!	hate	Personal, negative reaction to linked time-point
Here's what's here	here	Describing or providing neutral information
Whoops!	whoops	Reacting to a mistake or blooper
Whoa! / Wow!	wow	Reacting to something uncommon that is surprising and impressive
What?	what	Asking for information

we gave a very explicit statement concerning the quality required for the HIT, which specified that the workers must provide 2–4 sentences. Second, we inspected the answers by hand and eliminated those that were grammatically not reasonable well formed. Note that with this HIT, we aimed to *discover* reasons why people deep-link to videos and not to calculate the relative frequencies of the different reasons. We selected three comments from each of 33 videos to use for the elicitation HIT. Examples of reasons provided by workers are: "this comment is mentioning the technical errors in the movie [...]" (comment: *at 2:15 Zac has his mike on the stand when he clearly took it off earlier[...]*), "He must have liked the pics of Jennifer Aniston, [...]" (comment: *luv the pic 1:38 thru 1:40 nice video*) and "He was curious about the song title. [...]" (comment: *what the name of this song there is from 0:37 to 0:44[...]*). We applied a card sorting process [10] that involved manually inspecting the reasons given for the reaction of the person posting the comment and grouping the comments according to the type of reason.

In the end, we arrived at a taxonomy of six classes that characterize the reactions expressed in comments, depicted in Table 1. We refer to the classes as Viewer Expressive Reaction Varieties (VERVs). For each class of comment we chose an expression, formulated in colloquial language, that captured the spirit of all the comments in the class, which is given in the left column of Table 1.

Taxonomy Validation and Annotation: We carry out a second crowdsourcing experiment that has two purposes. First, it validates the taxonomy in Table 1 by checking that human judges are able to reliably judge the VERV of deep-link comments. The validation provides evidence that the VERV taxonomy serves to explain how users deep-link, i.e., that it covers most of the possible types of reaction. Second, it allows us to generate ground truth annotations for our data set, which we use to understand the distribution of VERV deep-link comments over videos and also as the basis for our deep-link comment classification experiments.

The AMT HIT used for validation and annotation was titled "Watch short snippets of YouTube videos (and support research on video search engines)" and presented workers with a video and three selected comments for the video. They were asked to read the comments and watch the video around the time-link, and then, for each comment, answer a series of questions. First, we asked the workers to verify whether or not the deep-link comment contained an actual deep-link and an actual Viewer Expressive Reaction. This question allowed us to distinguish advertisements and also comments that contained a string of digits and a colon that did not designate a timecode. In these cases, YouTube mistakenly makes a hyperlink from the string. Most of this cases involve scripture verses, such as "Isaiah 11:6". Then, we presented the workers with a list of VERVs and asked them to pick the one that best corresponded to the spirit of the comment. In addition to these questions, other questions were asked that had the goal of collecting additional information about the comments not treated in this paper and also for checking the consistency of workers' answers for the purposes of quality control.

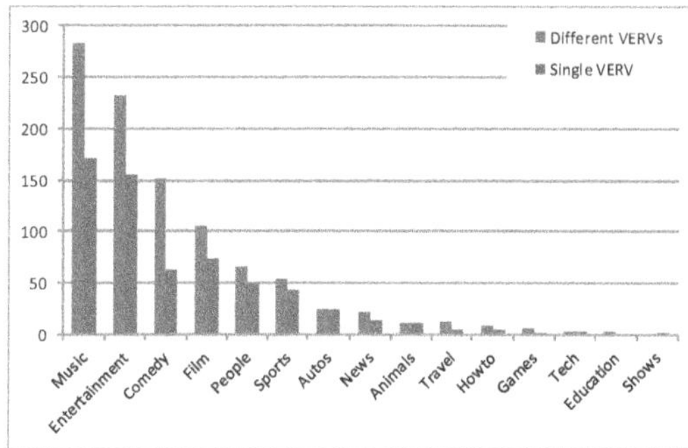

Figure 2: Number of videos that have different types of comments vs. those that have a single type.

Most comments were annotated by five workers, but a few were by less, since some workers failed the quality control for these comments. After removing low quality work, we arrived at a total of 3,359 annotated deep-link comments. The ground truth was then formed by majority vote. We only used deep-link comments for which workers reached an agreement in our classification experiments (Section 4): 2,842 comments (84.6%) for the first experiment (VER/non-VER, Table 2) and 2,140 comments (63.7%) for the second experiment (VERV-class, Table 3). Note that the number of instances used in the second experiment is substantially lower. This is due to the fact that workers only were asked to assign a comment to a VERV-class if the comment truly contained a Viewer Expressive Reaction in the first place.

We carried out an investigation to determine if certain videos have an attraction for certain kinds of deep-link comments. Figure 2 compares, for each YouTube category, videos whose sampled deep-link comments belong to a single VERV class versus those whose VERV comments belong to multiple VERV classes. As illustrated in this figure, the number of videos with different VERV comments is always larger than the number of videos with the same VERV comments for all categories. The figure also reveals that the VERV of one comment associated with a video is not a reliable predictor for the VERV of the other comments. We therefore anticipate that features derived from the comments themselves rather than from the video will be most helpful in automatically classifying the VERV class of comments (Section 4).

4. CLASSIFYING DEEP-LINK COMMENTS

In order to effectively use deepink comments, we build a classifier to filter and sort deep-link comments. Note that our interest in comment classification for deep-link retrieval is motivated by the finding of [9] that formulating queries for retrieving comments directly is not a simple task for users.

Classification approach and experimental setup: In this study we adopt a linear SVM classifier. Several features from comments are extracted and combined. Simple text

Table 2: WFM of VER/non-VER classifier

	Dev set	Test set
Unigrams	0.92	0.89
Baseline	0.85	0.84

Table 3: WFM of VERV classifier

	Dev set	Test set
Unigrams	0.44	0.45
Baseline	0.20	0.23

features such as unigrams and bigrams have been proved to be useful for short text classification such as YouTube comments [6]. We use unigrams as features, since they outperformed mixtures of unigrams and bigrams in exploratory experimentation on the development set. Exploratory experimentation also revealed that, as anticipated by the discussion of the distribution in Figure 2, that the Video ID does not contribute to classification performance. We restricted our main experiments to unigrams only and implemented our classifier using LibSVM [1].

We performed two experiments for comment classification. First, we filtered out comments that are not a VER comment, i.e., VER versus non-VER classification, and second, we classified comments into the VERV categories which are listed in Table 1. The comments in our dataset are divided into 60% training set, 20% development set and 20% independent test set.

VER/non-VER classification: Table 2 compares the performance of the VER/non-VER classifier to a baseline classifier using the weighted F-measure (WFM) scores. The baseline classifier assigns all comments to the largest class. Table 2 also lists the results on the independent test set.

VERV-class classification: For the VERV-class classification experiment, we used the same set of features. The WFM scores of the VERV classifier on both development and test set is listed in Table 3 and the confusion matrix of this classifier is shown in Table 4.

The VERV classification confusion matrix in Table 4 reveals that there are many samples for which the classifier assigns a different label compared to human annotators. The largest portion of confusion occurs between the `here` and `love` classes. For example, the comment *0:16-0:22 is sooo funny lol* is labeled as `here` by the majority of human annotators, but the classifier assigns it the label `love` instead. Evidently, human annotators do not always find "funniness" a personal opinion, but some see it as rather merely neutral information about a point in the video. Further exploration of our dataset reveals that there is less agreement in cases where a comment clearly has multiple interpretations or contains multiple sentences.

Table 4: VERV classifier confusion matrix (dev set)

T\E	love	hate	here	whoops	wow	what
love	138	0	18	0	1	1
hate	9	0	2	0	0	0
here	108	0	54	0	2	2
whoops	9	0	4	0	0	0
wow	42	0	17	0	3	0
what	53	1	9	0	1	61

5. CONCLUSION

This paper has presented a study of deep-link comments that opens up the possibility of a new relevance criterion for non-linear video access. The study resulted in a Viewer Expressive Reaction Variety (VERV) taxonomy that captures how viewers deep-link.

The main contributions of this paper are twofold: an analysis of deep-linking in social video collections and a demonstration that deep-link comments are useful for non-linear video access, i.e., in the deep-link retrieval system that we envision (cf. Figure 1). Our future work will concentrate on developing such a retrieval system. The system will allow users to formulate a topical keyword query and filter the returned results with respect to a VERV-class. We will investigate the ability of VERV-classes to compensate for known-problems of query formulation for comments and to satisfy user needs for non-linear video acces.

6. ACKNOWLEDGMENTS

The research leading to these results has received funding from the European Commission's 7th Framework Programme under grant agreement N° 287704 (CUbRIK).

7. REFERENCES

[1] C.-C. Chang and C.-J. Lin. LIBSVM: A library for support vector machines. *ACM Trans. Intell. Syst. Technol.*, 2(3):27:1–27:27, May 2011.

[2] K. Chorianopoulos, I. Leftheriotis, and C. Gkonela. SocialSkip: pragmatic understanding within web video. In *EuroITV'11*, pages 25–28. ACM, 2011.

[3] G. Friedland, L. Gottlieb, and A. Janin. Using artistic markers and speaker identification for narrative-theme navigation of Seinfeld episodes. In *IEEE ISM'09*, pages 511–516, December 2009.

[4] A. Hanjalic, R. Lagendijk, and J. Biemond. Automated high-level movie segmentation for advanced video-retrieval systems. *IEEE Trans. Circuits Syst. Video Technol.*, 9(4):580–588, June 1999.

[5] A. Hanjalic and L.-Q. Xu. Affective video content representation and modeling. *IEEE Trans. Multimedia*, 7(1):143–154, 2005.

[6] C.-F. Hsu, E. Khabiri, and J. Caverlee. Ranking comments on the social web. In *IEEE CSE'09*, volume 4, 2009.

[7] H. Li, M. Wang, and X.-S. Hua. MSRA-MM 2.0: A large-scale web multimedia dataset. In *IEEE ICDMW'09*, pages 164–169, December 2009.

[8] A. Madden, I. Ruthven, and D. McMenemy. A classification scheme for content analyses of YouTube video comments. *J Doc*, 2013. In press.

[9] M. Potthast, B. Stein, F. Loose, and S. Becker. Information retrieval in the commentsphere. *ACM Trans Intell Syst Technol*, 3(4):68:1–68:21, Sept. 2012.

[10] G. Rugg and P. McGeorge. The sorting techniques: a tutorial paper on card sorts, picture sorts and item sorts. *Expert Syst*, 14(2):80–93, 1997.

[11] E. Smits and A. Hanjalic. A system concept for socially enriched access to soccer video collections. *IEEE Multimedia*, 17:26–35, 2010.

[12] C. G. M. Snoek and M. Worring. Concept-based video retrieval. *Found Trends Inf Retr*, 2(4):215–322, Apr. 2009.

[13] R. Vliegendhart, M. Larson, and A. Hanjalic. LikeLines: collecting timecode-level feedback for web videos through user interactions. In *ACM MM'12*, pages 1271–1272. ACM, 2012.

[14] R. Vliegendhart, M. Larson, and J. Pouwelse. Discovering user perceptions of semantic similarity in near-duplicate multimedia files. In *CrowdSearch 2012*, pages 54–58, 2012.

[15] S. Wakamiya, D. Kitayama, and K. Sumiya. Scene extraction system for video clips using attached comment interval and pointing region. *Multimed Tools Appl*, 54(1):7–25, 2011.

Compact Bag-of-words Visual Representation for Effective Linear Classif cation

Xiaodan Zhuang, Shuang Wu, Pradeep Natarajan
Speech, Language and Multimedia Business Unit
Raytheon BBN Technologies
Cambridge, MA, USA
xzhuang@bbn.com, swu@bbn.com, pradeepn@bbn.com

ABSTRACT

Bag-of-words approaches have been shown to achieve state-of-the-art performance in large-scale multimedia event detection [4]. However, the commonly used histogram representation of bag-of-words requires large codebook sizes and expensive nonlinear kernel based classifiers for optimal performance. To address these two issues, we present a two-part generative model for compact visual representation, based on the *i-vector* approach recently proposed for speech and audio modeling [3]. First, we use a Gaussian mixture model (GMM) to model the joint distribution of local descriptors. Second, we use a low-dimensional factor representation that constrains the GMM parameters to a subspace that preserves most of the information. We further extend this method to incorporate overlapping spatial regions, forming a highly compact visual representation that achieves superior performance with fast linear classifiers. We evaluate the method on a large video dataset used in the TRECVID 2011 MED evaluation. With linear classifiers, the proposed representation, with one-tenth of the storage footprint, outperforms soft quantization histograms used in the top performing TRECVID 2011 MED systems.

Categories and Subject Descriptors

I.2 [**Computing methodologies**]: ARTIFICIAL INTELLIGENCE

Keywords

bag of words, linear classifier, generative model

1. INTRODUCTION

Bag-of-words approaches describe media data by a set of low-level visual features, and have shown promise in large scale visual recognition [15, 6]. In particular, the soft quantization histogram [15] first assigns each descriptor to a predefined set of codewords with a soft weight, and then pools the weights to construct a codeword histogram. It has been successfully used for both audio and visual pattern recognition problems [15]. Having a large number of codewords is generally required for optimal performance. Furthermore, the histogram does not work well with linear classifiers.

Previous works that reduce the number of codewords include the GMM supervector [16] and the Fisher Vector [13]. For large-scale datasets, however, the final representations are usually of even higher dimensionalities than the histograms (often beyond tens of thousands), leading to high computational cost in downstream processing.

This work presents a compact bag-of-words visual representation based on a two-part generative model, that extends recent work on audio modeling [3, 17]. In this model, the first part is a Gaussian Mixture Model (GMM) that generates the local descriptors. The second part, characterizing a low-dimensional factor, constrains the GMM parameters to a subspace where the most of the variation across videos is preserved. This low-dimensional factor forms a compact and robust vector representation. Considering the overlapping spatial regions, we train a region-independent model, apply the model to local descriptors in each region and take the union of the estimated factors from all the regions as the final representation.

Multimedia Event detection performances on the 2011 TRECVID MED dataset demonstrate the efficacy of the presented method in linear classifiers, which outperforms soft quantization histograms with much larger dimensionality.

2. SOFT QUANTIZATION HISTOGRAMS

In the bag-of-words approach, a video clip is represented as a set of local descriptors $X = \{x_i | i \in \{1 \cdots N\}\}$, such as the SIFT visual descriptors extracted on a dense pixel grid. To achieve better spatial resolution, we leverage multiple overlapping spatial regions and take the union of the bag-of-words representations over each of the regions. In this work, we use the same eight regions as defined in the Spatial Pyramid Matching [9]. In Sections 2 and 3, we omit the region subscripts for notation brevity when this is not confusing.

One commonly used bag-of-words approach to compare the two distributions parameterizes them as two histograms. A finite set of codewords $\{c_k | k \in \{1 \ldots K\}\}$ are identified through clustering. Within each clip, the *coding* step assigns each local descriptor to one or multiple codewords, denoted by the operator f. The "pooling" step produces a numerical representation for each codeword according to descriptors assigned to that codeword, denoted by the operator g. In the *pooling* step, multiple image regions ($m = 1 \ldots M$) are

MM'13, October 21–25, 2013, Barcelona, Spain.

http://dx.doi.org/10.1145/2502081.2502138.

processed separately and the union of the output is taken as the final representation.

$$[\alpha_{i,1} \cdots \alpha_{i,K}] = f(x_i) \quad i = 1..N_m \tag{1}$$

$$h_{m,k} = g(\{\alpha_{i,k}\}_{i \in N_m}) \quad k = 1, ..., K \tag{2}$$

where N_m is the number of local descriptiors in region m.

Soft quantization [15], as a coding strategy, distributes a local descriptor x_i to a codeword c_k in the following way,

$$\alpha_{i,k} = \frac{\exp\left(-\beta ||x_i - c_k||^2\right)}{\sum_{j=1}^{K} \exp\left(-\beta ||x_i - c_j||^2\right)} \tag{3}$$

where β controls the smoothness of the soft assignment. Further, average pooling takes the average of the $\alpha_{i,k}$'s among all i to obtain the final value for the kth bin in the histogram for region m: $h_{m,k} = \frac{1}{N}\sum_{i=1}^{N_m} \alpha_{i,k}$. These values for each region are normalized so they sum up to one. The union constructs the final soft quantization histogram: $[h_{m,k}, m = 1, \ldots, M, k = 1, \ldots, K]$.

For large datasets with significant variance, histograms typically require a large set of codewords, as a richer selection of codewords increases the representation capability. Even with the improvements such as soft quantization, most top performing systems in high-level event detection on unconstrained video use thousands of codewords [2, 8, 10, 14]. Furthermore, these histograms are usually found to provide good performance only with nonlinear classifiers, such as χ^2 SVMs, which are more expensive than linear classifiers.

3. COMPACT VISUAL REPRESENTATION

3.1 Two-part generative model

An ideal bag-of-words representation should have the capability to represent the highly variant distributions of local visual descriptors. It should be robustly estimated from the limited observations extracted from each video clip. Further, we prefer the representation to be compact for efficient storage and access. Finally, a representation that works well with linear classifiers is desirable.

We leverage a two-part generative model for the bag of patch descriptors within each video, illustrated in Figure 1. For each region in a particular video, the patch descriptors are generated by a unique Gaussian Mixture Model (GMM). Further, the parameters of these GMMs are generated as the summation of a "global mean component" and a region-specific component characterized by a low-dimensional factor w. w serves as a compact and robust representation for the region. The union of the w's from the M regions constitute the final representation for the video.

GMMs meet the requirement of high representation capability as they can approximate any distribution with increased number of mixtures. For robustness, a shared GMM, referred to as the Universal Background Model (UBM), is first trained using randomly selected local descriptors across different training videos, characterized by the F dimensional mean vectors μ_k^0, the mixture weights ω_k, and the covariance matrices Σ_k ($k \in \{1 \ldots K\}$). We only change the mean vectors to differentiate the video-specifc region-specific bag of local descriptors. When this is done by adapting the mean vectors of the UBM based on the observed local descriptors, it has been shown [1] that the KL divergence between two such GMMs, $g \in \{a, b\}$, can be bound by a distance measure $D(a||b) \approx \frac{1}{2}\sum_{k=1}^{K} \omega_k (\mu_k^a - \mu_k^b)' \Sigma_k^{-1} (\mu_k^a - \mu_k^b)$, with the

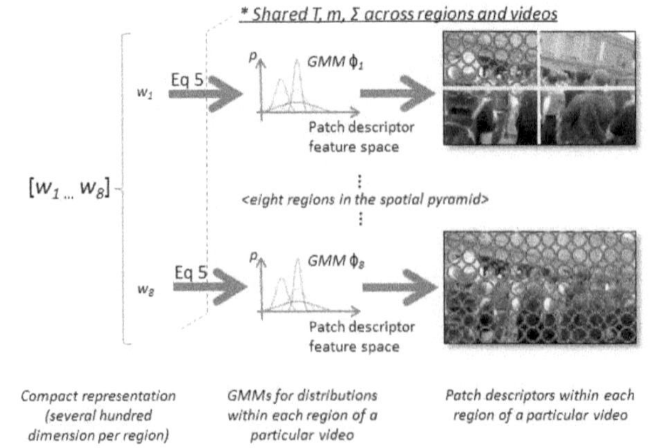

Figure 1: Proposed generative model for bag-of-words

corresponding kernel function being the dot product of

$$\phi(g) = [\sqrt{\frac{\omega_1}{2}}\Sigma_1^{-\frac{1}{2}}\mu_1^g; \cdots; \sqrt{\frac{\omega_K}{2}}\Sigma_K^{-\frac{1}{2}}\mu_K^g], g \in \{a, b\}. \tag{4}$$

In recent speaker verification literature [3], the "i-vector" is proposed to confine the FK dimensional ϕ in Equation 4 into a single "total variability" subspace $\mathbf{T}$ shown in Equation 5:

$$\phi = m + \mathbf{T}w, \tag{5}$$

where m is the global mean component of ϕ, calculated according to Equation 4 and the mean vectors of the UBM. The total variance matrix $\mathbf{T}_{KF \times R}$ can be viewed as a projection matrix from the high-dimensional space for ϕ to the low-dimensional subspace of the factor w. Let w observe a standard normal distribution $N(0; I)$, then ϕ observes $N(m, \mathbf{TT}')$. The R dimensional factor w is referred to as the i-vector, as it has a dimensionality between those of the local descriptors and ϕ.

We adopt the i-vector approach to model the GMMs for bags of local visual descriptors. We estimate a region-independent $\mathbf{T}$ on all the local descriptors using unlabeled clips that covers a wide range of different target events as well as background data. $\mathbf{T}$ is estimated in the same way as the eigenvoice matrix in the speaker verification literature [7], except that each clip carries a unique label in replacement of the speaker label. Details of the EM algorithm can be found in [7]. We highlight the following two steps in each iteration:

First, the posterior of factor w is estimated,

$$P(w|X, \mathbf{\Sigma}, \mathbf{T}) \sim N(l^{-1}(X)\mathbf{T}'\mathbf{\Sigma}^{-1}\mathbf{S}_X(X), l^{-1}(X)), \tag{6}$$

- $\mathbf{S}_X(X)$ is the concatenation of the centered first-order statistics on the K mixtures;
- $\mathbf{\Sigma}$ is the block diagonal matrices for $\Sigma_1 \ldots \Sigma_K$;
- $l(X) = I_{R \times R} + \mathbf{T}'\mathbf{\Sigma}^{-1}\mathbf{N}(X)\mathbf{T}$, where $\mathbf{N}(X)$ is a block diagonal matrix of the zeroth-order statistics of the mixtures $N_1(X)I_{F \times F}, ...N_K(X)I_{F \times F}$.

Second, the total variance matrix $\mathbf{T}$ is updated using linear regression with w being the explanatory variable.

Given Σ and $\mathbf{T}$, the factor w for a region is estimated as,

$$\begin{aligned}\hat{w} &= l^{-1}(X)\mathbf{T}'\mathbf{\Sigma}^{-1}\mathbf{S}_X(X) \\ &= \left(I_{R\times R} + \sum_{k=1}^{K} \mathbf{B}N_k(X)\right)^{-1} \mathbf{C}\mathbf{S}_X(X). \quad (7)\end{aligned}$$

$\mathbf{B}$ and $\mathbf{C}$ are $R\times R$ and $R\times KF$ matrices fixed after training.

Note that changing w only changes the video and region specific GMM within a constrained GMM parameter subspace, in contrast to the Maximum A Posteriori estimation [16]. The factor w serves as the vector representation, whose dimensionality is determined by the width R of matrix $\mathbf{T}$.

With the multiple overlapping spatial regions considered for the visual representation, the factor w is estimated for each overlapping spatial region separately, and the union of these factors serve as the proposed representation for the video clip. No annotation is needed either in estimating $\mathbf{T}$ and $\mathbf{\Sigma}$, or in estimating w for each region and clip.

3.2 Related work on visual representation

The GMM has been used for bag-of-words visual representation in other ways. The Fisher Vector approach [12] characerizes each video using the normalized derivatives with regard to the GMM parameters. The GMM supervector method uses the ϕ in Equation 4 on each video [16].

Both approaches use reduced number of codewords, compared to the histogram. However, both lead to very high dimensionality in the final representation, usually on the order of tens of thousands, though effective lossy compression methods at the cost of minor performance drop exist [12]. For the 128-dimensional SIFT descriptor and a UBM with 512 mixtures, the GMM supervector representation is of 65536 dimensions. Its significant storage footprint hinders its applicability in large-scale problems. Similar issues exist with the Fisher Vector approach. Both can have even higher dimensionalities if the higher-order statistics are considered.

While the GMM supervector ϕ appears in the construction of the proposed generative model in Section 3.1, our approach fundamentally differs from the former [16]. First, our representation uses a generative process to constrain GMM parameters adapted to the bag of descriptors, while the GMM supervector directly performs the adaptation according to Maximum A Posteriori criterion. Second, our representation uses the low-dimensional factor w of this generative process in Equation 5, while the GMM supervector method uses the high-dimensional ϕ. Third, we do not first estimate GMM supervectors and then estimate dimensionality reduction projection. Instead, the low-dimensional w is jointly updated with the total variability matrix T according to the EM algorithm in Section 3.1.

4. EXPERIMENTS

4.1 Dataset and setup

We tested our approach on the TRECVID 2011 MED dataset of ~45000 videos [11]. The dataset contains ten complex events in Table 1, along with a large collection of diverse background video instances.

We carried out multimedia event detection experiments using either audio or visual information, according to the official evaluation protocol. A binary linear classifier [5] is trained for each event. The SVM hyperparameters are estimated through cross-validation grid search within the training set, for each representation separately. We combine the two modalities using a fusion approach averaging the SVM output scores. No region partitioning is performed for the audio descriptors.

Event	Description	# Training	# Evaluation
E006	birthday party	182	186
E007	changing a vehicle tire	112	111
E008	flash mob gathering	174	132
E009	getting a vehicle unstuck	128	95
E010	grooming an animal	137	87
E011	making a sandwich	125	140
E012	parade	157	231
E013	parkour	113	104
E014	repairing an appliance	130	78
E015	sewing project	129	81
NULL	(background)	11695	30576
Total		13081	31821

Table 1: TRECVID 2011 MED dataset statistics

4.2 Local descriptors

We extract the standard 128-dimension SIFT descriptors against dense pixel grids for every 50th frame in each video. We also extract 45-dimension mel-frequency cepstral coefficients (MFCCs) audio descriptors by computing the energy and 14 Mel-warped cepstral coefficients for overlapping frames with 10ms steps in the frequency band of 80-6000 Hz, together with their first and second order derivatives across temporally adjacent frames.

4.3 Visual representations

We evaluate the proposed visual representation with and without the eight overlapping spatial regions, as well as the audio representation. For the SIFT-based visual representation, a 500 dimensional vector is extracted for each overlapping spatial region, using a region-independent total variance matrix and a UBM with 512 Gaussians. As the baseline, the soft quantization histograms have 5000 dimensions for each region, as optimized for the MED task in the 2011 TRECVID Evaluation. The audio representation has 400 and 5000 dimensions for the proposed representation and the baseline histogram respectively. The codebook sizes K, the dimensionalities of the proposed representation R are chosen empirically using train/dev partitions within the "Training" partition in Table 1. It is noteworthy that the baseline soft quantization histogram approach has shown competitive performance to GMM supervector and Fisher vector [4], though the comparison is not strict.

4.4 Results

We compare the multimedia event detection performances using the soft quantization histogram and the proposed representation. According to the Area Under the Curve (AUC) measures in Table 2, the proposed representation (denoted as "IVEC") outperforms the soft quantization histogram (denoted as "Hist"). We also reduced the dimensionality of "Hist" by Principal Component Analysis (PCA) for comparison. The use of the overlapping spatial regions (denoted as "+SPM") improves the performance for both "IVEC" and "Hist". Fusing audio and visual information results in additional improvement (denoted as "AV Hist" and "AV IVEC").

The linear SVM training times are 7 mins for the visual "IVEC" (500×8 dimension) and 4 hrs 57 mins for the soft-quantization histograms (5000×8 dimension) on the same training data. We did not further investigate the GMM

Table 2: Classification performances with different representations, across ten events in Table 1.

AUC	Dim	Mean	E006	E007	E008	E009	E010	E011	E012	E013	E014	E015
MFCC Hist	5,000	0.801	0.852	0.683	0.865	0.836	0.718	0.719	0.838	0.810	**0.898**	0.792
MFCC Hist (PCA)	1,000	0.790	0.851	0.679	0.864	0.835	0.714	0.719	0.836	0.807	0.897	0.790
MFCC Hist (PCA)	400	0.501	0.489	0.502	0.492	0.507	0.507	0.509	0.498	0.497	0.511	0.497
MFCC IVEC	**400**	**0.844**	**0.889**	**0.782**	**0.905**	**0.866**	**0.826**	**0.737**	**0.873**	**0.877**	0.890	**0.799**
SIFT Hist	5,000	0.844	0.785	0.854	0.926	0.905	0.802	0.797	0.886	0.830	0.854	0.805
SIFT Hist (PCA)	1000	0.843	0.783	0.853	0.925	0.904	0.801	0.795	0.885	0.827	0.853	0.803
SIFT Hist (PCA)	500	0.841	0.780	0.850	0.923	0.902	0.798	0.792	0.883	0.822	0.852	0.804
SIFT IVEC	**500**	**0.894**	**0.879**	**0.880**	**0.966**	**0.919**	**0.842**	**0.877**	**0.952**	**0.913**	**0.896**	**0.813**
SIFT Hist+SPM	40,000	0.860	0.811	0.876	0.945	**0.914**	0.820	0.809	0.905	0.852	0.860	0.811
SIFT IVEC+SPM	**4,000**	**0.910**	**0.912**	**0.905**	**0.972**	0.912	**0.873**	**0.885**	**0.955**	**0.936**	**0.912**	**0.841**
AV Hist	45,000	0.877	0.888	0.838	0.952	**0.921**	0.824	0.807	0.910	0.876	0.918	0.836
AV IVEC	**4,400**	**0.913**	**0.919**	**0.894**	**0.975**	0.914	**0.897**	**0.864**	**0.932**	**0.949**	**0.938**	**0.844**

supervectors or the Fisher Vectors as they would have been extremely large at about $65000 \times 8 = 520,000$ dimensions or more, according to Section 3.2.

5. CONCLUSION AND DISCUSSION

In large-scale multimedia event detection, bag-of-words approaches have been shown to achieve state-of-the-art performance. However, the common bag-of-words histograms require large codeword sets, and the representation does not perform well with efficient linear classifiers.

In this work, we present a compact bag-of-words visual representation, with only a few hundred dimensions for each region. The joint distribution of local visual descriptors within each overlapping spatial region is generated by a two-part generative model. The first part approximates the distribution using a Gaussian mixture model. The second part generates the parameters of the GMMs in a constrained space, corresponding to a low-dimensional factor. The union of factors from the different overlapping spatial regions form a highly compact yet informative representation that achieves superior performance in linear classifiers.

Experiments using the TRECVID 2011 multimedia event detection (MED) benchmark video dataset show that the proposed representation, with one-tenth of the storage footprint, outperforms the bag-of-words soft quantization histograms commonly used in the state-of-the-art systems in the 2011 TRECVID MED Evaluation.

6. ACKNOWLEDGMENT

This work is supported by the Intelligence Advanced Research Projects Activity (IARPA) via the Department of Interior National Business Center contract number D11PC20071. The U.S. Government is authorized to reproduce and distribute reprints for Governmental purposes notwithstanding any copyright annotation thereon. The views and conclusions contained herein are those of the authors and should not be interpreted as necessarily representing the official policies or endorsements, either expressed or implied , of IARPA, DoI/NBC, or the U.S. Government.

7. REFERENCES

[1] W. Campbell, D. Sturim, and D. Reynolds. Support vector machines using GMM supervectors for speaker verification. *Signal Processing Letters, IEEE*, 13(5):308 – 311, May 2006.

[2] L. Cao, S.-F. Chang, N. Codella, C. Cotton, D. Ellis, L. Gong, M. Hill, G. Hua, J. Kender, M. Merler, Y. Mu, A. Natsev, and J. R. Smith. IBM Research and Columbia University TrecVid-2011 Multimedia Event Detection (MED) System. In *Proceedings of NIST TrecVid Workshop*, MD, 2011.

[3] N. Dehak, P. Kenny, R. Dehak, P. Dumouchel, and P. Ouellet. Front-end factor analysis for speaker verification. *Audio, Speech, and Language Processing, IEEE Transactions on*, 19(4):788 –798, May 2011.

[4] B. A. et. al. 2011 TRECVID Workshop Multimedia Event Detection Task. www-nlpir.nist.gov/projects/tvpubs/tv11.slides/tv11.med.slides.pdf, 2012.

[5] R.-E. Fan, K.-W. Chang, C.-J. Hsieh, X.-R. Wang, and C.-J. Lin. LIBLINEAR: A library for large linear classification. *Journal of Machine Learning Research*, 9:1871–1874, 2008.

[6] Y.-G. Jiang, S. Bhattacharya, S.-F. Chang, and M. Shah. High-level event recognition in unconstrained videos. *International Journal of Multimedia Information Retrieval*, pages 1–29, 2012.

[7] P. Kenny, G. Boulianne, and P. Dumouchel. Eigenvoice modeling with sparse training data. *Speech and Audio Processing, IEEE Transactions on*, 13(3):345 – 354, May 2005.

[8] B. L., Y. SI, L. ZZ, O. A., J. Q., L. B., G. M., B. S., M. F., and H. A. Informedia@TRECVID 2011. In *Proceedings of NIST TrecVid Workshop*, MD, United States, 2011.

[9] S. Lazebnik, C. Schmid, and J. Ponce. Beyond bags of features: Spatial pyramid matching for recognizing natural scene categories. In *Computer Vision and Pattern Recognition, 2006 IEEE Computer Society Conference on*, volume 2, pages 2169 – 2178, 2006.

[10] P. Natarajan, P. Natarajan, V. Manohar, S. Wu, S. Tsakalidis, S. N. Vitaladevuni, X. Zhuang, R. Prasad, G. Ye, D. Liu, I.-H. Jhuo, S.-F. Chang, H. Izadinia, I. Saleemi, M. Shah, B. White, T. Yeh, and L. Davis. BBN VISER TRECVID 2011 Multimedia Event Detection System. In *Proceedings of NIST TrecVid 2011 Workshop*, Gaithersburg, MD., Dec. 2011.

[11] P. Over, G. Awad, M. Michel, J. Fiscus, W. Kraaij, A. F. Smeaton, and G. QuÃl'enot. TrecVid 2011 – An Overview of the Goals, Tasks, Data, Evaluation Mechanisms and Metrics. In *Proceedings of TRECVID 2011*. NIST, USA, 2011.

[12] F. Perronnin, Y. Liu, J. SÃÍÂćnchez, and H. Poirier. Large-scale image retrieval with compressed Fisher vectors. In *CVPR*, pages 3384–3391. IEEE, 2010.

[13] F. Perronnin, J. Sánchez, and T. Mensink. Improving the Fisher kernel for large-scale image classification. In *Proceedings of the 11th European Conference on Computer vision: Part IV*, ECCV'10, pages 143–156, Berlin, Heidelberg, 2010. Springer-Verlag.

[14] C. G. M. Snoek, K. E. A. van de Sande, X. Li, M. Mazloom, Y.-G. Jiang, D. C. Koelma, and A. W. M. Smeulders. The MediaMill TrecVid 2011 Semantic Video Search Engine. In *Proceedings of NIST TrecVid Workshop*, MD, United States, 2011.

[15] J. C. van Gemert, C. J. Veenman, A. W. M. Smeulders, and J. M. Geusebroek. Visual word ambiguity. *IEEE Transactions on Pattern Analysis and Machine Intelligence*, 32(7):1271–1283, 2010.

[16] X. Zhou, X. Zhuang, S. Yan, S.-F. Chang, M. Hasegawa-Johnson, and T. S. Huang. SIFT-Bag kernel for video event analysis. In *Proceedings of the 16th ACM International Conference on Multimedia*, MM '08, pages 229–238, New York, NY, USA, 2008. ACM.

[17] X. Zhuang, S. Tsakalidis, S. Wu, P. Natarajan, R. Prasad, and P. Natarajan. Compact audio representation for event detection in consumer media. In *Proc. Interspeech*, Oregon, USA, 2012.

Large-scale Web Video Shot Ranking Based on Visual Features and Tag Co-occurrence

Do Hang Nga Keiji Yanai
Department of Informatics, The University of Electro-Communications
Chofu, Tokyo 182-8585 JAPAN
{dohang,yanai}@mm.cs.uec.ac.jp

ABSTRACT

In this paper, we propose a novel ranking method, VisualTextualRank, which extends [1] and [2]. Our method is based on random walk over bipartite graph to integrate visual information of video shots and tag information of Web videos effectively. Note that instead of treating the textual information as an additional feature for shot ranking, we explore the mutual reinforcement between shots and textual information of their corresponding videos to improve shot ranking. We apply our proposed method to the system of extracting automatically relevant video shots of specific actions from Web videos [3]. Based on our experimental results, we demonstrate that our ranking method can improve the performance of video shot retrieval.

Categories and Subject Descriptors

H.4 [**Information Systems Applications**]: Miscellaneous

Keywords

Web Video, Ranking, Bipartite Graph

1. INTRODUCTION AND RELATED WORKS

Given an action keyword such as "running" or "watching television" provided by a user, an online video search engine is supposed to rank the Web videos in its database according to their relevance to the query and then return the most relevant ones at the top. Howerver, in general, the relevant videos account for only a small portion of the videos retrieved by conventional video search engines. Moreover, even relevant videos may contain many unrelated video shots since Web videos belong to UGC (User Generated Content) and are created for various purposes. Here, a video shot is a part of a video which refers to a set of consecutive frames representing a specific scene. Video shot retrieval for specific actions must encounter many difficulties including computation cost, noise, diversity of keywords as well as human actions and so on.

In case of image retrieval, the popular Google Image search engine adopts a ranking method called VisualRank [1] which exploits the visual link structure between images. According to VisualRank, images found to share the most visual characteristics with the group at large shall be determined as the most relevant ones and brought to the top of search results. VisualRank was applied in our previous works [3, 4]. With VisualRank, we succeeded in retrieving relevant video shots for many action categories. However, the problem is that, by applying VisualRank, solely visual relationships between shots are explored, thus we obtained at the top only video shots which have similar appearances. This causes the loss of variety in the results. Especially, in some cases, most of those top ranked video shots do not correspond to the given action keywords even though they are visually related.

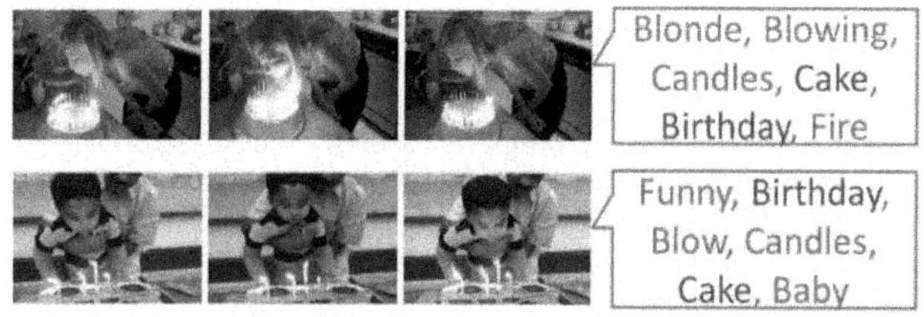

Figure 1: An example of Web video retrieval result. This figure shows two video shots together with tag lists of their videos which are retrieved by YouTube with "blow candle" keyword. We can see that some relevant words such as "birthday" and "cake" are tagged to both videos. Thus we can presume that these two video shots are semantically related to each other and relevant to "blow candle" even though they are not visually similar.

Since human actions are too diverse, their corresponding video shots are not always visually similar even if they are semantically related. The change in camera view or the way how people perform the action may cause visual differences. Our intuition is that, two video shots which belong to two videos tagged with related keywords may represent the same action even if they do not hold the same visual features (See Fig.1). Hence, shot ranking should additionally consider tag information. Besides, tags are supposed to be more efficiently adopted if their relevance is evaluated considering not only their intra-relationships but also their correlation with video shots. For example, if we find that a video shot is important, or in other words, related to the given action keyword, so that the tags of the video have high chance to be important as well. And vice versa, if a tag was found as being relevant to the keyword, it is highly probable that the videos annotated with it are also relevant.

As efforts on tag ranking considering their relevance, Yang et al. [5] proposed a method to evaluate tag relevance scores

MM'13, October 21–25, 2013, Barcelona, Spain.

ACM 978-1-4503-2404-5/13/10 ...$15.00.
http://dx.doi.org/10.1145/2502081.2502139.

of all tags based on tag co-occurrence statistics. Dong et al. [6] proposed a method to measure tag relevance scores by combining the probabilistic relevance score estimation and random-walk based refinement. Especially, Liu et al. [2] presented a Web video topic discovery and tracking method via bipartite graph which represents the correlation between videos and their tags. Actually, our idea is inspired by their work. However, the objective as well as the methodology of their work are different from ours. While they tried to find relevant videos of a topic, we aim to detect relevant video shots of a specific action. In terms of methodology, they used only textual information, while we use both textual and visual features.

In this paper, we propose a novel ranking method, VisualTextualRank, which extends [1] and [2]. Our method is based on a random walk over bipartite graph to integrate visual information of video shots and tag information of Web videos effectively. Note that instead of treating the textual information as an additional feature for shot ranking, we explore the mutual reinforcement between shots and textual information of their corresponding videos to improve shot ranking. We apply our proposed method to the system of extracting automatically relevant video shots of specific actions from Web videos [3]. Based on our experimental results, we demonstrate that our ranking method can improve the performance of video shot retrieval. Our contribution is a co-analysis of visual links among video shots along with textual link between videos and their tags and its application to the learning of semantic similarities of video shots.

The reminder of this paper is organized as follows: In the next section we shall introduce our proposed method. In Section 3, we describe how we apply it to the system of video shot extraction. We present conducted experiments and show their results in Section 4. Conclusion and further discussion are presented in Section 5.

2. PROPOSED METHOD

The basic idea of VisualTextualRank (abbreviated as VTR) is that, the relevant tags are used to annotate relevant videos; the relevant video shots are from videos annotated with relevant tags and visually similar to each other. Thus VTR co-ranks tags and video shots so that at each iterative ranking step, ranks of shots are refined using their visual similarities as well as their relevance with corresponding tags, and then, ranks of tags are updated based on their relevance with video shots in conjunction with refined ranking positions of video shots. Figure 2 sketches the idea of VTR.

VTR is an extension of VisualRank [1] with idea motivated by [2]. In [2], tags and videos are also co-ranked using their correlation to refine their relevance with a specific topic. However, unlike our work, in [2], relevance of the whole video, not every scene in it, is evaluated and visual features of videos are totally ignored. On the other hand, VisualRank exploits only a visual linkage between images and does not take textual information into account. In VisualRank, the ranking position of the image which looks similar to many images with high ranking position becomes higher after iterative processing. Our proposed VTR employs both visual and textual features of Web videos to explore the mutual reinforcement across video shots and tags.

The proposed co-ranking method can be represented by following iterative processes:

$$\mathbf{RS_k} = \alpha \times SM^* \times SC^* \times \mathbf{RT_k} + (\mathbf{1}-\alpha)\ \mathbf{p} \quad (1)$$

$$\mathbf{RT_{k+1}} = (SC')^* \times \mathbf{RS_k} \quad (2)$$

RS and RT are vectors which represent rank positions of shots and tags, respectively. Let the number of shots be n_s and the number of tags be n_t, the dimension of RS will be $n_s \times 1$ and the dimension of RT will be $n_t \times 1$. SM refers to shot-shot similarity matrix where $SM_{i,j}$ means visual similarity score between shot i and shot j; SM^* is its column-normalized matrix with size as $n_s \times n_s$. SC represents shot-tag similarity matrix where $SC_{i,k}$ measures textual relevance score between the video of shot i and tag k; SC^* is its $n_s \times n_t$ column-normalized matrix. SC' refers to the transposed matrix of SC which represents tag-shot similarity matrix and SC'^* is its column-normalized matrix. Note that since the textual features, here refer to tag co-occurrence, are considered as being noisier than content-based features,we rank video shots first and use their refined ranking positions to update ranks of tags.

RT is initially defined as a uniform vector. At each ranking step, after ranking positions of video shots are updated based on their visual similarities and their correlation with tags following Eq.1, video shots cast their votes for tags through Eq.2. Thus relevant shots will cast important votes for tags which are strongly connected with them. And then at the next iterative step, those tags again help boost ranking positions for video shots which are tight linked with them. Gradually, video shots and tags with few important votes will go to the bottom.

Following VisualRank, we also introduce damping factor α and damping vector p into shot ranking. Damping factor α has been found empirically as holding minor impact on global ordering in ranking results [1, 3]. $\alpha \geq 0.8$ is often chosen for practice. Damping vector p can be a uniform vector or a nonuniform vector. For example, we can use a nonuniform damping vector as in [4] to bias shots which are visually related to relevant images during ranking computation.

3. APPLICATION AND IMPLEMENTATION DETAILS

We apply our proposed ranking method to our system of automatically extracting from tagged Web videos video shots corresponding to specific actions proposed in [3]. Our system consists of two main steps: video ranking and shot ranking. At the shot ranking step, in [3] we applied VisualRank to rank shots from top ranked videos. In this paper, we adopt our ranking method to this step to compare the effectiveness of our method and VisualRank.

The implementation details are described as follows. At first, we collect video IDs and tags for at most 1000 Web videos of search results of the action keyword via YouTube API. Tags here refer to words in retrieved values for "keyword" and "title" fields. The co-occurrence frequencies among tags are then exploited to build a tag database which provides us tag co-occurence based inter- and intra-relationships between tags and videos. Note that while in [3], this tag database is only adopted to measure relevance between videos and the action keyword, here it is also employed to calculate relevance between videos and tags.

In video ranking, videos are ranked in the descending order of their tag relevance scores with the given keyword. Tag relevance score of a video V to a word t is calculated by the following equation.

$$Sc_t(V) = \frac{1}{|\mathcal{T}|} \sum_{t_i \in \mathcal{T}} \log_2 F(t, t_i) \quad (3)$$

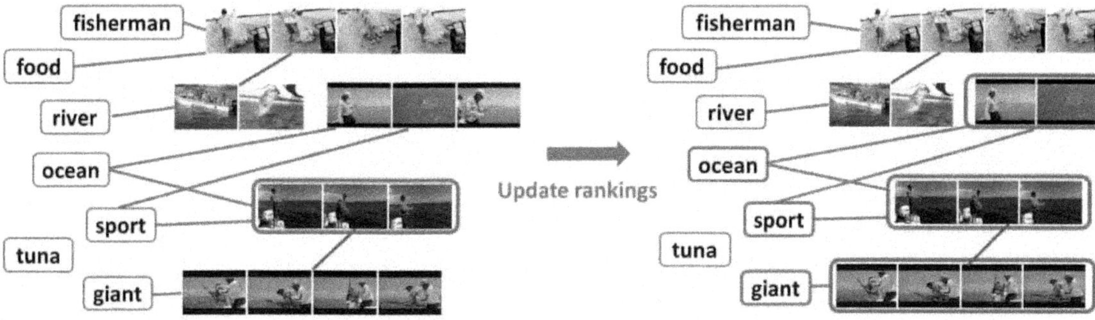

Figure 2: Illustration of VisualTextualRank by an example of "catch fish" action. Blue links represent relevance between video shots and tags. Purple links refer to visual relationships between shots. Objects marked with red bounding box are considered as being important. Assume that at first we found one important shots as shown at the left of this figure. It will cast its vote for shots and tags which are strongly linked with it. And then at the next step of ranking process, those shots and tags again cast their votes for objects which are tight connected with them. Finally, we can obtain relevant objects of "catch fish" as seen at the left of this figure.

Table 1: Experimental results. VR and VTR refer to performance of video shot retrieval system adopting VisualRank and proposed VisualTextualRank respectively.

Action	VR	VTR
soccer+dribble	100	100
fold+origami	96	99
crochet+hat	95	97
arrange+flower	94	96
paint+picture	88	87
boxing	86	84
jump+parachute	82	63
jump+trampoline	82	92
do+exercise	79	61
do+aerobics	78	79
do+yoga	77	70
surf+wave	75	73
shoot+arrow	73	81
massage+leg	72	78
fix+tire	67	77
batting	66	61
basketball+dribble	64	87
blow-dry+hair	64	59
knit+sweater	64	68
ride+bicycle	62	70
curl+bicep	58	59
shoot+ball	58	58
tie+shoelace	57	73
laugh	50	54
dive+sea	49	41
harvest+rice	49	46
ski	49	60
iron+clothes	47	48
twist+crunch	47	32
dance+flamenco	45	53
dance+hiphop	43	68
eat+ramen	42	47
dance+tango	41	41
play+trumpet	41	59
AVG. (1-34)	**65.9**	**68.3**

Action	VR	VTR
play+drum	40	45
skate	37	42
swim+crawl	36	49
cut+hair	35	42
run+marathon	35	43
count+money	33	58
paint+wall	33	32
shoot+football	33	29
draw+eyebrows	32	32
fieldhockey+dribble	32	68
hit+golfball	32	70
lunge	32	27
play+piano	32	34
row+boat	32	23
sing	32	65
chat+friend	31	52
clean+floor	31	38
cut+onion	31	24
shave+mustache	31	30
pick+lock	30	28
plaster+wall	30	55
blow+candle	29	44
wash+face	29	24
walking+street	29	46
brush+teeth	28	27
catch+fish	28	59
drive+car	28	40
plant+flower	28	24
play+guitar	28	41
lift+weight	27	51
raise+leg	27	40
hang+wallpaper	26	46
jump+rope	26	49
AVG. (35-67)	**31.0**	**41.7**

Action	VR	VTR
climb+tree	24	24
ride+horse	24	15
roll+makizushi	24	36
sew+button	24	46
fry+tempura	23	12
slap+face	20	45
read+book	19	21
squat	19	34
row+dumbell	16	30
wash+clothes	15	29
wash+dishes	15	39
comb+hair	14	26
drink+coffee	14	16
swim+breaststroke	13	18
cry	12	12
eat+sushi	12	23
serve+teniss	11	27
tie+necktie	11	28
boil+egg	9	11
head+ball	9	16
swim+backstroke	9	9
take+medicine	8	7
serve+volleyball	7	40
swim+butterfly	7	9
bake+bread	6	8
cook+rice	6	11
grill+fish	5	13
jog	5	6
slice+apple	5	16
peel+apple	5	14
bowl+ball	4	4
smile	4	6
kiss	2	3
AVG. (68-100)	**12.2**	**19.8**
AVG. (ALL)	**36.6**	**43.5**

$F(t, t_i)$ is the number of videos tagged with both word t and word t_i so it represents the co-occurrence frequency of t and t_i. $\mathcal{T}$ is a set of the words other than t which are tagged to V and frequently co-appear with t. The maximum size of $\mathcal{T}$ is set to 10. As the result of the video ranking step, the videos tagged with many words which have high co-occurence frequency with the action keyword will be ranked to the top.

Only the top ranked videos are selected to be downloaded and used since they are considered as being more related to the action keywords than the remains. These videos are then segmented into video shots based on their RGB histograms. Finally, shot rankings are iteratively calculated by applying our proposed method, VisualTextualRank.

To calculate ranking positions of shots in VisualTextualRank, we must construct shot-shot similarity matrix SM and shot-tag similarity matrix SC as shown in Eq.1. The similarity between two shots is calculated by histogram section of their bags of spatio-temporal features. We use the same method of spatio-temporal feature extraction described in [3]. Relevance of a video to a tag is measured in the similar way as represented in Eq.3 using the tag database constructed in advance. Note that here shots are obtained by segmenting selected videos but filtered according to their length and tags are tags of selected videos but filtered based on their occurrence frequencies. We select only shots which last longer than one second and shorter than one minute. To avoid using personal tags, we choose tags which appear at least five times over selected videos.

Damping factor is set to 0.8 and damping vector is defined following the best results obtained in [3]. That means damping vector here is a nonuniform vector derived from tag relevance of the videos to the keyword as follows.

$$p_i = \begin{cases} 1/k & (i \le k) \\ 0 & (i > k) \end{cases} \tag{4}$$

As shown above, damping vector is defined by giving uniform bias values to the elements corresponding to the top k shots regarding tag relevance of their videos to the keyword. k equals 1000 in our experiments.

4. EXPERIMENTS

We conduct experiments on our human action database described in [3]. This database consists of 100 action categories. Each category has 2000 video shots on average. Precision is defined as the percentage of relevant video shots in the top ranked 100 shots (Prec@100). We consider action with precision higher than 40% as "succeeded action", action with precision lower than or equal to 40% but higher than 25% as "acceptable action" and the remain as "failed action". The results reported in [3] are: 34 succeeded, 33 acceptable, 34 failed. We want to compare the performance of our video shot retrival system proposed in [3] adopting VisualRank and VisualTextualRank proposed in this paper. Experimental results are shown in Table 1.

Experimental results demonstrate that by adopting our proposed ranking method, more relevant shots are brought to the top. In terms of overall performance, VTR improves the average precision by approximately 7%. Fig.3 shows

Figure 3: Relevant shots among top ranked 15 shots. Bounded by blue boxes and red boxes are respectively results obtained by applying VisualRank and our proposed VisualTexutualRank. The results show that our ranking method helps to boost more relevant shot to the top.

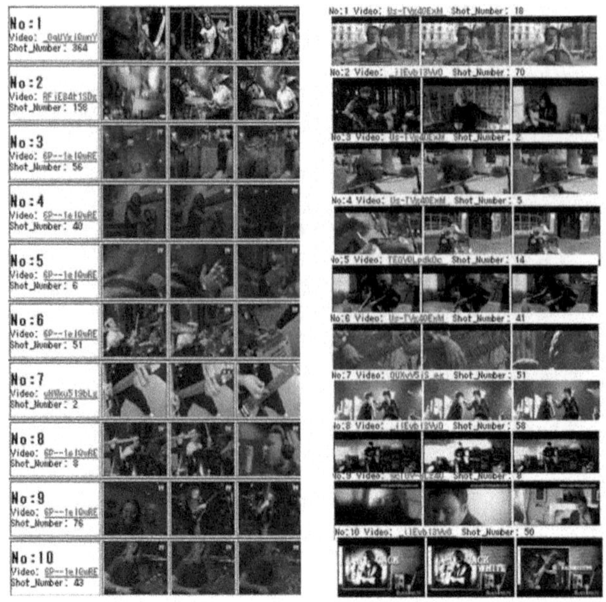

Figure 4: Diversity of results obtained by video shot retrieval system with VisualRank (right) and with VisualTextualRank (left). The category here is "play+guitar". In the original framework [3], more than half of top 10 shots are from the same video with ID "6P–1elQwRE" since they are visually similar. On the other hand, applying VisualTextualRank can select relevant shots from different videos since it regards not only visual similarities but also textual similarities of the shots.

some examples of detected relevant shots by applying VisualRank and our VisualTextualRank.

Table 1 shows that VTR enhances video shot retrieval system on most of categories. Especially, precision is boosted greatly in cases such as "hit+golfball", "dance+hiphop", "plaster+wall", "blow+candle", "jump+rope", "catch+fish", "play+guitar", "wash+dishes" and "slap+face". The acceptable group is the most significantly improved. By applying proposed VTR, the number of succeeded actions increases from 34 to 51 and the number of failed ones decrease from 34 to 23.

Not only precision, VTR also improves the performance of the shot retrieval system in the sense that it increases the variety of final results. Since VisualRank employs only visual features, visually similar elements are often ranked to the top. On the other hand, VTR additionally exploits the correlation between videos and tags so that not only visually similar video shots but also video shots having strong textual links with relevant shots also have chances to be ranked high as well (See Fig.4).

5. CONCLUSION

In this paper, we propose a novel graph based ranking method, VisualTextualRank, which performs co-ranking of video shots and tags employing both visual links between video shots along with textual links between videos and their tags. We apply VTR to the system of extracting automatically relevant video shots for specific human actions. The effectiveness of proposed VTR was validated by experimental results.

As for future work, we intend to improve our VTR by introducing more visual information such as appearance of objects. Most of human actions are associated with particular objects. For example, in general, "eat" scenes include "tableware" or in scenes of "type" action, "keyboard" is supposed to be seen. Hence we expect that by applying human-object interaction models proposed by [7] or [8], our VTR can achieve better performance.

6. REFERENCES

[1] Y. Jing and S. Baluja, "Visualrank: Applying pagerank to large-scale image search," *IEEE Transactions on Pattern Analysis and Machine Intelligence*, vol. 30, no. 11, pp. 1870–1890, 2008.

[2] L. Liu, L. Sun, Y. Rui, Y. Shi, and S. Yang, "Web video topic discovery and tracking via bipartite graph reinforcement model," in *Proc. of the ACM International World Wide Web Conference*, pp. 1009–1018, 2008.

[3] D. H. Nga and K. Yanai, "Automatic construction of an action video shot database using web videos," in *Proc. of IEEE International Conference on Computer Vision*, 2011.

[4] D. H. Nga and K. Yanai, "Automatic collection of web video shots corresponding to specific actions using web images," in *Proc. of CVPR Workshop on Large-Scale Video Search and Mining (LSVSM)*, 2012.

[5] Q. Yang, X. Chen, and G. Wang, "Web 2.0 dictionary," in *Proc. of ACM International Conference on Image and Video Retrieval*, pp. 591–600, 2008.

[6] J. Deng, W. Dong, R. Socher, J. Li, K. Li, and L. Fei-Fei, "Imagenet: A large-scale hierarchical image database," in *Proc. of IEEE Computer Vision and Pattern Recognition*, 6 2009.

[7] B. Yao and L. Fei-Fei, "Modeling mutual context of object and human pose in human-object interaction activities," in *Proc. of IEEE Computer Vision and Pattern Recognition*, pp. 17–24, 2010.

[8] A. Gupta, A. Kembhavi, and L.S. Davis, "Observing human-object interactions: Using spatial and functional compatibility for recognition," *IEEE Transactions on Pattern Analysis and Machine Intelligence*, vol. 31, no. 10, pp. 1775–1789, 2009.

Locality Preserving Verification for Image Search

Shanmin Pang[1], Jianru Xue[1], Nanning Zheng[1], Qi Tian[2]
Institute of Artificial Intelligence and Robotics, Xi'an Jiaotong University[1]
Dept. of Computer Science, University of Texas at San Antonio, Texas, TX 78249[2]
pangshanminn@sina.com, jrxue@xjtu.edu.cn, nnzheng@aiar.xjtu.edu.cn, qitian@cs.utsa.edu

ABSTRACT

Establishing correct correspondences between two images has a wide range of applications, such as 2D and 3D registration, structure from motion, and image retrieval. In this paper, we propose a new matching method based on spatial constraints. The proposed method has linear time complexity, and is efficient when applying it to image retrieval. The main assumption behind our method is that, the local geometric structure among a feature point and its neighbors, is not easily affected by both geometric and photometric transformations, and thus should be preserved in their corresponding images. We model this local geometric structure by linear coefficients that reconstruct the point from its neighbors. The method is flexible, as it can not only estimate the number of correct matches between two images efficiently, but also determine the correctness of each match accurately. Furthermore, it is simple and easy to be implemented. When applying the proposed method on reranking images in an image search engine, it outperforms the-state-of-the-art techniques.

Categories and Subject Descriptors

H.3.3 [**Information Storage and Retrieval**]: Information Search and Retrieval—*Selection process*

Keywords

Image retrieval, linear time complexity, local geometric structure, re-ranking

1. INTRODUCTION

Image retrieval, with its goal of searching similar images of a query image from a large corpus of images, has achieved a great improvement in recent years. Many state-of-the-art retrieval systems use the bag-of-words (BoW) model, in which each image is represented as histograms of visual words. Due to its efficiency and memory saving, BoW representation of an image makes it possible to query from millions or even billions of images. However, BoW has a limitation that the retrieval accuracy is often low since this representation discards spatial information of images. Thus, large-scale image retrieval typically adds a *post-processing* step after the *searching* step. Specifically, in the *searching* step, similar images are retrieved from the large database based on the BoW representation, and an initial ranking is generated. The *post-processing* step then refines the initial ranking, and provides a more precise ranking of the retrieved images. This step is linear in the number of images to match, hence its speed is crucial.

Post-processing is usually accomplished by spatial verification. Spatial verification is important in improving the accuracy of matching and re-ranking. It first considers the spatial configurations of features, and then filters out mismatches produced by clustering features with different semantics into the same visual word, and finally achieves the goal of re-ranking images.

The existing spatial verification methods can be roughly divided into two categories: the local methods and the global methods. The methods in [5, 9] belong to the first category. A weak geometric constraint, which requires that neighboring matches in the query image lie in a surrounding area in the retrieved image, is used in [9]. A similar idea appears in [5], in which the inverted file stores scale and orientation of local features, and groups of matches need to agree with their relative scale. Examples of the second category include [7, 10, 11]. In [11], the geometric context among local features is encoded into binary maps, and geometrically inconsistent matches are removed by analyzing those coding maps. Based on the assumption that two images are related by a homography, FSM [7] estimates a global transformation between the query image and a database image by LO-RANSAC [4, 6]. An advantage of FSM is that it enumerates all hypotheses by exploiting shape information in the Hessian affine regions, and therefore removes the randomness of RANSAC. Unfortunately, FSM is quadratic in the number of matches. HPM [10] is a relaxed spatial matching method, and has linear time complexity. However, it can not determine the correctness of a match accurately.

In this paper, we propose a new spatial verification method by exploiting the local linear geometric structure in images. The proposed method can find correct correspondences accurately and efficiently. The assumption of our method is that: the local geometric structure among a feature point and its neighbors is not easily affected by complex transformations (for example, shape deformations). Thus this structure should be preserved after photometric and geo-

MM'13, October 21–25, 2013, Barcelona, Spain.

ACM 978-1-4503-2404-5/13/10 ...$15.00.
http://dx.doi.org/10.1145/2502081.2502140.

metric transformations. We model this structure by linear coefficients that reconstruct each point from its neighbors.

2. FAST SPATIAL MATCHING METHOD

In this section, we first present our spatial matching method (Line 1-8, algorithm 1), and then present two ways to identify the correct matches. *The fast implementation* (Line 9-10, algorithm 1) estimates the number of correct matches efficiently, and *the accurate implementation* (Line 11-12, algorithm 1) filters out mismatches exactly.

2.1 Spatial Matching by Reconstruction

In image search, an image is represented by a set of local features, where each local feature is described by a descriptor, position, scale and orientation, etc. Let us suppose that there are N tentative matches between images I_1 and I_2, where a match means the corresponding descriptors are quantified to a same visual word in the BoW model. For convenience, we use a set P to store these N tentative matches, and simply use $x_i \leftrightarrow y_i$ to denote the ith ($i = 1, \cdots, N$) match, where $x_i = (u_i, v_i)^T$ and $y_i = (u_i', v_i')^T$ are locations of this match in I_1 and I_2, respectively.

For x_i, we find its K ($K \geq 2$) nearest neighbors $x_{i1}, \cdots, x_{iK}$ in image I_1, where $ij \in \{1, \cdots, N\}$ and $j = 1, \cdots, K$. x_i and its neighbors thus formulate a local geometric structure. This local geometric structure can be described by linear coefficients that reconstruct x_i from $x_{i1}, \cdots, x_{iK}$. That is,

$$x_i = \sum_{j=1}^{K} w_{ij} x_{ij}, \tag{1}$$

where w_{ij} is a coefficient, and can be obtained by solving the following least-square problem:

$$\begin{aligned} \min \| x_i - \sum_{j=1}^{K} w_{ij} x_{ij} \|_2^2, \\ s.t. \sum_{j=1}^{K} w_{ij} = 1. \end{aligned} \tag{2}$$

It should be noted that Eq.(1) reflects the relative location relationship among x_i and x_{ij} ($j = 1, \cdots, K$). According to [8], the local geometric structure described by Eq.(1) is invariant to similarity transformation. Similarly, we can describe the relative location relationship between y_i and y_{ij} ($j = 1, \cdots, K$) by

$$y_i = \sum_{j=1}^{K} w_{ij}' y_{ij}, \tag{3}$$

where y_{ij} is the location of a feature point in I_2 and it corresponds to x_{ij}.

Based on that x_{ij} ($j = 1, \cdots, K$) are neighbors of x_i, and similarity invariance of Eq.(1), we can conclude that if $x_i \leftrightarrow y_i$, $x_{ij} \leftrightarrow y_{ij}$ are all correct matches, then w_{ij} and w_{ij}' should be nearly same, or at least

$$\| w_i - w_i' \|_1 < \epsilon, \tag{4}$$

where $w_i = (w_{i1}, \cdots, w_{iK})^T$, $w_i' = (w_{i1}', \cdots, w_{iK}')^T$, and $\epsilon > 0$ is a preset threshold. By analogy, if Eq.(4) holds, we can also safely think $x_i \leftrightarrow y_i$, $x_{ij} \leftrightarrow y_{ij}$ are all correct; otherwise, at least one match is false, though we do not know which match is incorrect.

We repeat the above process until each feature point x_i ($i = 1, \cdots, N$) is processed. After processing all x_i, the matches that satisfy Eq.(4) are collected, and constitute a subset Q of correct matches. It is easy to know that there are both positive and negative matches in set $P - Q$. The remaining of our problem is then to identify the correctness of each match in $P - Q$. We provide two ways for solving this problem in Section 2.2 and Section 2.3.

Algorithm 1 The proposed spatial matching method

Input:
the set of N tentative matches, P
Output:
the number of correct matches M, or the set of correct matches Q
Initialization:
initialize Q to be an empty set, and let $L = 0$

```
1: for i = 1 : N do
2:     Find K nearest neighbors x_i1, ..., x_iK of x_i;
3:     Reconstruct x_i and y_i by Eq.(1) and Eq.(3), respectively;
4:     if Eq.(4) holds then
5:         Q = Q ∪ {x_i ↔ y_i, x_i1 ↔ y_i1, ..., x_iK ↔ y_iK};
6:         L = L + 1.
7:     end if
8: end for
9: if the fast implementation then
10:    Compute M by Eq.(6);
11: else if the accurate implementation then
12:    Determine the correctness of each match in P − Q by Eq.(10), and update Q.
13: end if
```

2.2 The Fast Implementation

Our first method is a coarse approach, and only estimates the number of correct matches between I_1 and I_2. Assume that M out of N matches are correct, and there are L columns between W and W' satisfying Eq.(4), where $W = (w_1, \cdots, w_N)$ and $W' = (w_1', \cdots, w_N')$. Thus, by maximum likelihood estimation, we can get

$$(M/N)^{K+1} = L/N. \tag{5}$$

This means M is approximately equal to

$$M = N \times (L/N)^{1/(K+1)}. \tag{6}$$

Though this method does not explicitly determine which match is correct, we will see it is effective for purpose of geometric verification (Section 3). Moreover, this method has $O(N)$ complexity, so it is efficient and suitable for *post-processing* in large-scale image retrieval.

2.3 The Accurate Implementation

The second method estimates the correctness of each match accurately. As aforementioned, if I_1 and I_2 are similar, some matches satisfying Eq.(4) have been collected. Without loss of generality, we assume these matches are $x_l \leftrightarrow y_l (l = 1, \cdots, n)$. Consequently, the relationship between I_1 and I_2 can be characterized by these n correct matches. In fact, a correct match $x_l \leftrightarrow y_l$ means there exists a vector-valued function f [1] which maps point x_l to point y_l, i.e.,

$$f(x_l) = y_l, \quad l = 1, \cdots, n. \tag{7}$$

In order to achieve accuracy and robustness to noise, we use the method proposed in [3] to estimate f. That is, we solve the following minimization problem

$$\min_{f \in \mathcal{H}} \{ \frac{1}{n} \sum_{l=1}^{n} \|y_l - f(x_l)\|_2^2 + \lambda \|f\|_{\mathcal{H}}^2 \}, \tag{8}$$

[1] If the photographed scene is a plane, then f is a homography matrix that we are familiar with.

(a) (b) (c)

Figure 1: Two examples of the proposed method and FSM. (a) There are 134 tentative matches obtained by the BoW model in two similar images (top). There are 42 mismatches obtained by BoW in two unrelated images (bottom). (b) Only 40 correct matches in top image pair are found by 5-dof FSM, and many correct matches are missed. In bottom image pair, 3 matches are wrongly determined to be correct by 5-dof FSM. (c) 99 correct matches consisting with human's perception are found by the proposed method in top image pair, and no correct matches are found in bottom image pair. *Note:* for visibility, only 50 randomly selected matches are presented in top left and top right image pairs.

where $\lambda > 0$ is a regularization parameter, $\mathcal{H}$ is a reproducing kernel Hilbert space (RKHS), and $\|\cdot\|^2_{\mathcal{H}}$ denotes the norm in the RKHS $\mathcal{H}$. The solution of Eq.(8) is given by [3]

$$f(x) = \sum_{l=1}^{n} \gamma(x, x_l)c_l, \; with \; (\Gamma + \lambda n I_{2n\times 2n})C = Y, \quad (9)$$

where $\gamma(x, x_l)$ is a kernel matrix with size 2×2, and $c_l \in \mathbb{R}^{2\times 1}$ is the corresponding coefficient. Γ is a $n \times n$ block matrix, and the (i, j)-th block is $\gamma(x_i, x_j)$. $C = (c_1^T, c_2^T, \cdots, c_n^T)^T$ and $Y = (y_1^T, y_2^T, \cdots, y_n^T)^T$ are $2n$ dimensional vectors.

For efficiency, we choose $\gamma(x_i, x_j) = e^{-\beta\|x_i - x_j\|^2} I_{2\times 2}$ (where $\beta > 0$ is a scalar parameter), one of the most simplest kernel matrices, as our choice for solving Eq.(9). Thus, the coefficient matrix $\Gamma + \lambda n I_{2n\times 2n}$ is positive definite. Furthermore, to solve linear system in Eq.(9), the low rank matrix approximation strategy in [1] is used. This means we can obtain f with linear time complexity.

After getting f, we determine the correctness of each match $x_i \leftrightarrow y_i$ in $P - Q$ by

$$\xi_i = \|y_i - f(x_i)\|_2^2, \quad i = n + 1, \cdots, N. \quad (10)$$

If $|\xi_i|^2 < \tau$(where $\tau > 0$ is a scalar parameter), $x_i \leftrightarrow y_i$ is thought to be a true match, and put it in set Q; otherwise, it is considered to be false.

The proposed fast spatial matching method is summarized in algorithm 1.

3. EXPERIMENTS AND RESULTS

Datasets. We apply the proposed method to perform re-ranking in an image retrieval engine, and test it on two publicly available image retrieval datasets: *Oxford 5K datset* [7] and *Flicker 1M dataset* [5]. To test the performance of the proposed method on large-scale image retrieval, we add *Flicker 1M dataset* as distractors to the *Oxford 5K datset.* To better compare our method with others, we use the descriptors provided by [7, 5] on the dataset web pages.

Evaluation criteria. We measure the performance of the proposed method via *mean Average Precision*(mAP), and evaluate it against two state-of-the-art methods: Fast Spatial Matching (FSM) [7] and Hough Pyramid Matching (HPM) [10]. In image retrieval, the standard *tf-idf* weighting scheme [2] is often used to distinguish different matched features. However, from experimental results, we find this scheme has little effect in improving retrieval results. For example, on the *Oxford 5K datset*, simply counting the number of matched features yields the mAP 0.611; using tf-idf weighting scheme only increases it to 0.618. This observation is also described in [11]. For this reason, we calculate the similarity between two images by counting the number of matches with L_2 normalization.

Parameters initialization: To demonstrate the performance of the proposed method, four sizes ($200K$, $500K$, $750K$, $1M$) of vocabulary are tested. In our experiments, we set $\epsilon = 0.5$, $\beta = 0.1$, $\lambda = 3$ and $\tau = 0.1$ in algorithm 1 through this paper. When re-ranking top 800 images on *Oxford 5K datset*, the mAP of *the fast implementation* is 0.725, 0.708, 0.714 with $K = 2$, 3, 4, respectively. $K = 2$ gives the best results and is used in our report results.

3.1 Results

We compare our method with 5-dof FSM (In [7], the author implements 3-dof, 4-dof and 5-dof transformations, and 5-dof affine transformation is the best of them.) on the three factors: speed, memory usage and retrieval accuracy.

Speed: Our method has linear time complexity, while FSM is quadratic in the number of N. From our experiments, we find *the fast implementation*(TFI) is about 5 times faster than FSM in matching image pairs, and the speed up of *the accurate implementation*(TAI) over FSM is about 3 times.

Memory usage: In the inverted file, our method only stores image ID and the location of each feature. However, FSM and HPM need additional memory to store the scale and angle of each feature point. This means our method can save a couple of bytes per indexed feature compared with FSM and HPM.

Table 1: Comparison results of our method and FSM on the *Oxford* $5K$ *dataset.* (a) Results of using a $200K$ visual vocabulary(no re-ranking $= 0.472$). (b) Results of using a $500K$ visual vocabulary(no re-ranking $= 0.518$). (c) Results of using a $750K$ visual vocabulary(no re-ranking $= 0.532$). (d) Results of using a $1M$ visual vocabulary(no re-ranking $= 0.611$).

Method/Re-rank N	100	200	400	800
FSM(5dof)	0.513	0.528	0.544	0.560
TFI	**0.518**	**0.533**	**0.553**	**0.579**
TAI	0.511	0.527	0.546	0.574

(a)

Method/Re-rank N	100	200	400	800
FSM(5dof)	0.549	0.562	0.578	0.593
TFI	0.558	0.579	0.602	0.629
TAI	**0.560**	**0.582**	**0.606**	**0.633**

(b)

Method/Re-rank N	100	200	400	800
FSM(5dof)	0.577	0.589	0.600	0.613
TFI	**0.584**	**0.603**	**0.624**	**0.668**
TAI	0.582	0.599	0.618	0.659

(c)

Method/Re-rank N	100	200	400	800
FSM(5dof)	0.648	0.657	0.660	0.664
TFI	**0.650**	**0.670**	**0.689**	**0.725**
TAI	0.647	0.666	0.683	0.716

(d)

Retrieval accuracy: Varying the number of re-ranked images, we measure mAP for FSM and our method. We report the comparison results on Oxford 5K dataset and Flicker 1M dataset, separately.

Two examples of the proposed method and FSM are shown in Fig 1. From this figure, it can be observed that our approach is more accurate than FSM in removing mismatches. Table 1 compares mAP of our approach with FSM under different vocabulary sizes on the *Oxford 5K dataset.* It clearly shows that both TFI and TAI have superior performance to FSM. Compared with FSM, when re-ranking top 800 images with a $1M$ visual vocabulary, TAI increases the mAP from 0.664 to 0.725, an 9% improvement can be obtained. There are also clear improvements with vocabulary sizes of $750K$, $500K$ and $200K$. It should be noted that our method is much faster than FSM.

Our best score (0.725) outperforms the best score (0.692, reported in [10]) achieved by HPM, though the latter re-ranking $1K$ images and its specific codebook.

Table 2 shows the retrieval accuracy when adding Flicker 1M images as distractors. Experimental results in table 2 clearly show that both TAI and TFI outperform FSM, too.

In theory, TAI should be better than TFI. However, to our surprise, TFI has a similar (even better) performance with TAI(see tables 1 and 2). We think this may be caused by the choice of matrix γ in TAI and we will investigate it as our future work.

4. CONCLUSIONS

In this paper, by exploiting the local geometric structure, we propose an efficient and effective spatial verification method to boost the performance of image search. The proposed method is simple and easy to be implemented. From theoretical analysis and experimental results, one can know that the proposed method has three major advantages over FSM: 1) It has linear complexity and is faster than FSM, since FSM is quadratic in the number of correspondences; 2) It does not need the constraint that two corresponding images are related by a homography [2], while this constraint is required by FSM; 3) It is more accurate than FSM and uses less memory than FSM.

Table 2: Comparison results of our method and FSM on the *Oxford* $5K$ *dataset* with Flicker $1M$ images as distractors. The vocabulary size is $1M$, and the mAP with no re-ranking images is $= 0.389$.

Method/Re-rank N	100	200	400	800
FSM(5dof)	0.435	0.446	0.455	0.462
TFI	**0.452**	**0.469**	**0.486**	**0.503**
TAI	0.449	0.466	0.477	0.491

5. ACKNOWLEDGEMENTS

This work was supported by National Basic Research Program of China (973 Program) under Grant No. 2012CB316400, and the National Natural Science Foundation of China (NSFC) projects 61273252 and 90920301. This work was supported in part to Dr. Qi Tian by ARO grant W911BF-12-1-0057, NSF IIS 1052851, Faculty Research Awards by Google, FX-PAL, and NEC Laboratories of America, and 2012 UTSA START-R Research Award respectively. This work was supported in part by NSFC 61128007.

6. REFERENCES

[1] X. S. Andriy Myronenko. Point set registration: Coherent point drift. *IEEE TPAMI*, 32(12):2262–2275, Dec. 2010.

[2] R. Baeza-Yates and B. Ribeiro-Neto. *Modern information retrieval.* ACM press, New York, 1999.

[3] L. Baldassarre, L. Rosasco, A. Barla, and A. Verri. Vector field learning via spectral filtering. In *ECML*, pages 56–71, 2010.

[4] O. Chum, J. Matas, and Š. Obdržálek. Enhancing RANSAC by generalized model optimization. In *ACCV*, pages 812–817, 2004.

[5] H. Jégou, M. Douze, and C. Schmid. Hamming embedding and weak geometric consistency for large scale image search. In *ECCV*, pages 304–317, 2008.

[6] K. Lebeda, J. Matas, and O. Chum. Fixing the locally optimized ransac. In *BMVC*, pages 1–11, 2012.

[7] J. Philbin, O. Chum, M. Isard, J. Sivic, and A. Zisserman. Object retrieval with large vocabularies and fast spatial matching. In *CVPR*, pages 1–8, 2007.

[8] S. Roweis and L. Saul. Nonlinear dimensionality reduction by locally linear embedding. *Science*, 290(5500):2323–2326, 2000.

[9] J. Sivic and A. Zisserman. Video google: A text retrieval approach to object matching in videos. In *ICCV*, pages 1470–1477, 2003.

[10] G. Tolias and Y. Avrithis. Speeded-up, relaxed spatial matching. In *ICCV*, pages 1653–1660, 2011.

[11] W. Zhou, Y. Lu, H. Li, Y. Song, and Q. Tian. Spatial coding for large scale partial-duplicate web image search. In *ACM Multimedia*, pages 511–520, 2010.

[2]This means the photographed scene lies in a plane.

Undo The Codebook Bias by Linear Transformation for Visual Applications

Chunjie Zhang[1], Yifan Zhang[2], Shuhui Wang[3], Junbiao Pang[4], Chao Liang[5], Qingming Huang[1,3], Qi Tian[6]

[1]School of Computer and Control Engineering, University of Chinese Academy of Sciences, 100049, Beijing, China
[2]National Laboratory of Pattern Recognition, Institute of Automation, Chinese Academy of Sciences, Beijing, China
[3]Key Lab of Intell. Info. Process, Institute of Computing Technology, Chinese Academy of Sciences, Beijing, 100190, China
[4]College of Computer Science and Technology, Beijing University of Technology, 100124, China
[5]National Engineering Research Center for Multimedia Software, School of Computer, Wuhan University, 430072, Wuhan, China
[6]Department of Computer Sciences, University of Texas at San Antonio, TX, 78249, U.S.A

{cjzhang, shwang, qmhuang}@jdl.ac.cn, yfzhang@nlpr.ia.ac.cn, junbiao_pang@bjut.edu.cn, cliang@whu.edu.cn, qitian@cs.utsa.edu

ABSTRACT

The bag of visual words model (BoW) and its variants have demonstrate their effectiveness for visual applications and have been widely used by researchers. The BoW model first extracts local features and generates the corresponding codebook, the elements of a codebook are viewed as visual words. The local features within each image are then encoded to get the final histogram representation. However, the codebook is dataset dependent and has to be generated for each image dataset. This costs a lot of computational time and weakens the generalization power of the BoW model. To solve these problems, in this paper, we propose to undo the dataset bias by codebook linear transformation. To represent every points within the local feature space using Euclidean distance, the number of bases should be no less than the space dimensions. Hence, each codebook can be viewed as a linear transformation of these bases. In this way, we can transform the pre-learned codebooks for a new dataset. However, not all of the visual words are equally important for the new dataset, it would be more effective if we can make some selection using sparsity constraints and choose the most discriminative visual words for transformation. We propose an alternative optimization algorithm to jointly search for the optimal linear transformation matrixes and the encoding parameters. Image classification experimental results on several image datasets show the effectiveness of the proposed method.

MM '13, October 21 - 25 2013, Barcelona, Spain

http://dx.doi.org/10.1145/2502081.2502141.

Categories and Subject Descriptors

I.2.10 [**Artificial Intelligence**]: Vision and Scene Understanding—*representation, data structures, and transforms*

Keywords

codebook bias, linear transformation, sparsity

1. INTRODUCTION

The bag of visual words model (BoW)[1] plays a very important role for visual applications (*e.g.* image classification, retrieval and segmentation). Basically, the BoW model can be divided into four components: local feature extraction, codebook generation, local feature encoding and histogram based image representation. It has been widely used on various datasets [2-8] with encouraging visual application results. To consider the spatial information, spatial pyramid matching (SPM)[4] and its variants are also widely used by researchers.

Although proven effective, there is one problem with the BoW model and its variants. The codebook has to be learned for each image dataset separately and the performances of directly using codebooks generated by other datasets are less competitive than using the codebook generated with the corresponding dataset. This is because the state-of-the-art image datasets are collected for particular purposes[9]. To overcome this problem, a lot of works [10-23] have been done. Khosla *et al.* [10] tried to undo the dataset bias by jointly learning the bias vectors and visual words' weights in a discriminative manner. An online domain adaption of cascade classifiers is proposed by Jain and Miller [11]. Kulis *et al.* [12] proposed an asymmetric kernel transformation based object categorization method. The dataset shift problem is systematically analyzed by Candela *et al.* [13]. Zhang *et al.* [14] proposed a non-negative sparse coding based image classification approach. Gopalan *et al.* [15] took an unsupervised approach to adapt the object categorization problem while Zhang *et al.* [16] used a bilinear model for recognition. Saenko *et al.* [17] tried to adapt object model of a particular visual domain to new domain by minimizing the effect of

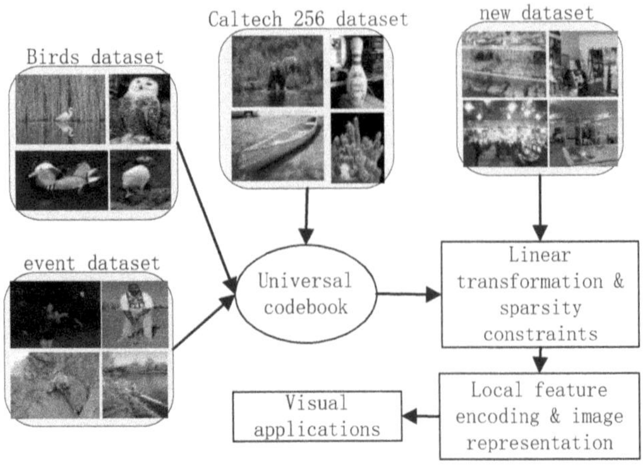

Figure 1: Flowchart of the proposed linear codebook transformation for visual application method.

feature distribution discrepancy While Zhang *et al.* [18] adopt the weak semantic representation. A heterogeneous transfer learning algorithm is proposed by Zhu *et al.* [19] for image classification with good performance. Zhang *et al.* [20] used harr-like transformation of local features. To cope with the lack of training images, Wang *et al.* [21] proposed a dyadic knowledge transfer approach for cross-domain classifications.

All of these methods demonstrate the usefulness of considering the dataset bias for visual applications. However, most of these methods ignore the codebook bias problem with different datasets and only try to adapt the pre-learned classifiers instead. In fact, if we take a close look at the four components of the BoW model, we can find that the codebook is the only component which varies from datasets. The other three components of the BoW model have not such dataset dependence. For example, dense SIFT feature is used for local feature extraction, sparse coding or nearest neighbor assignment is used for local feature encoding and images are represented by visual word histogram. Hence, if we can cope with the codebook bias problem, we will be able to make the BoW model less dataset dependent and improve the performance of visual applications using the BoW representation.

To solve the codebook bias problem, in this paper, we propose a novel linear transformation based codebook adaption method. For the local feature space, the number of bases should be no less than the space dimensions. Hence, we try to view each codebook as a linear transformation of these bases. In this way, we can linearly transform the pre-learned codebooks for a new dataset. However, not all of the visual words are equally important, it is more effective if we can choose the most discriminative visual words for transformation. We use the popular sparsity constraints in this paper for visual word selection. Besides, we also propose an alternative optimization algorithm to jointly search for the optimal linear transformation matrixes and the encoding parameters. To test the effectiveness of the proposed method, we conduct image classification experiments on several image datasets. The results show the effectiveness of codebook transformation for undoing the dataset bias. Figure 1 shows the flowchart of the proposed method.

The rest of this paper is organized as follows. In Section 2 we give the details of the proposed linear codebook transform method for undoing the codebook bias. The experimental results are given in Section 3. Finally, we conclude in Section 4.

2. LINEAR CODEBOOK TRANSFORMATION FOR VISUAL APPLICATIONS

In this section, we will give the details of the proposed linear codebook transform method to undo the codebook bias and apply it to image classification problems.

2.1 Undo the dataset bias by linear codebook transformation

For the local feature space, the number of bases should be no less than the space dimensions. Suppose we have a set of bases $B = [b_1, b_2, ..., b_Q] \in \mathbb{R}^{P \times Q}$ which can completely represent each local feature in this space. P is the dimension of local feature space and Q is the number of bases with $Q > P$. Let $D_1 = [d_1^1, d_1^2, ..., d_1^M] \in \mathbb{R}^{P \times M}$ be a codebook generated using a particular dataset where M is the number of visual words. Since each visual word in codebook D_1 can be viewed as a point in the local feature space, each element of D_1 can be linearly represented by B as:

$$d_1^i = a_1^1 b_1 + a_1^2 b_2 + ... + a_1^Q b_Q, \forall i = 1, ..., Q \quad (1)$$

This can be rewritten in a matrix form as:

$$D_1 = A_1 B \quad (2)$$

with A_1 is the corresponding linear transformation matrix. In this way, we can generate a codebook D_1 by linearly combine the bases of local feature space. This can also be written as:

$$B = A_1^+ D_1 \quad (3)$$

Where A_1^+ is the psedoinverse of matrix A_1. Similarly, we can generate a codebook D_2 as:

$$D_2 = A_2 B = A_2 A_1^+ D_1 \quad (4)$$

Let $A = A_2 A_1^+$, Eq.4 can be rewritten as:

$$D_2 = A D_1 \quad (5)$$

Suppose we have learnt the codebook D_1 for dataset 1, to generate the codebook D_2 for dataset 2, all we need to do is to find the corresponding transformation matrix A. If the transformation matrix A has been learnt, we can use the corresponding codebook D_2 for local feature encoding. We use the sparse coding technique [24] in this paper as it has been shown very effective for encoding local features. Let $x \in \mathbb{R}^{P \times 1}$ be the local feature to be encoded, α is the corresponding sparse coding parameter with λ is the parameter which controls the sparsity of α as:

$$min_{\alpha, D_2} \| x - \alpha^T D_2 \|^2 + \lambda \| \alpha \|_1 \quad (6)$$

This can be optimized over α and A as:

$$min_{\alpha, A} \| x - \alpha^T A D_1 \|^2 + \lambda \| \alpha \|_1 \quad (7)$$

This problem can be solved efficiently by alternatively optimizing over α / A while keeping the other fixed. When α is fixed, Eq.7 equals to solving the following optimization problem as:

$$min_A \| x - \alpha^T A D_1 \|^2 \quad (8)$$

When A is fixed, Eq.7 equals to solving the following optimization problem as:

$$min_{\alpha} \parallel x - \alpha^T AD_1 \parallel^2 + \lambda \parallel \alpha \parallel_1 \quad (9)$$

Since D_1 is pre-learned and fixed, let $D = AD_1$, Eq.9 can be rewritten as:

$$min_{\alpha} \parallel x - \alpha^T D \parallel^2 + \lambda \parallel \alpha \parallel_1 \quad (10)$$

Eq.8 and Eq.10 can be effectively optimized by the feature-sign search algorithm and the Lagrange dual algorithm proposed in [24]. In this way, we can transform the codebook D_1 generated using dataset 1 to dataset 2 accordingly. However, the transformation of only one codebook is often too weak, especially when the two image datasets are quite different. It would be more effective if we can transform a number of codebooks for an unseen dataset.

Formally, suppose we have M pre-learned codebooks generated using the corresponding image datasets. To encode local feature x, the optimization problem can be written similarly as:

$$min_{\alpha_i, A_i, i=1,2,...,M} \parallel x - \sum_{i=1}^{M} \alpha_i^T A_i D_i \parallel^2 + \lambda_i \sum_{i=1}^{M} \parallel \alpha_i \parallel_1 \quad (11)$$

Where λ_i is the sparsity constraint parameter for the $i-th$ dataset, α_i is the corresponding encoding parameter. Let $\beta = [\alpha_1; \alpha_2; ...; \alpha_M]$, $E = [D_1; D_2; ...; D_M]$ and $C = diagA_1, A_2, ..., A_M$, Eq.11 can be rewritten as:

$$min_{\beta, C} \parallel x - \beta^T CE \parallel^2 + \lambda \parallel \beta \parallel_1 \quad (12)$$

This problem can be solved similarly as Eq.7 by alternatively optimizing over β and C.

2.2 Max pooling based image representation for visual applications

After learning the corresponding linear transformation matrix C, we can use it to encode local features by fixing C. We encode each local feature individually. We follow the popular max pooling scheme [14, 16, 18, 20, 22, 23, 25] to extract information from local features for image representation. The max pooling is proven effective when combined with sparse coding for image representation. Besides, to combine the spatial information of local features, we adopt the spatial pyramid matching (SPM) technique [4]. We use the first three pyramids as $2^L \times 2^L, L = 0, 1, 2$.

To test the effectiveness of the proposed linear codebook transformation method for undoing the dataset bias, we conduct image classification performances. This is achieved by training a set of classifiers. We use the one-vs-all linear SVM classifier.

3. EXPERIMENTS

To evaluate the effectiveness of the proposed linear codebook transformation method, we conduct image classification performance on several public image datasets: the Bird dataset[2], the Butterfly dataset[3], the Scene-15 dataset[4], the Event dataset[5], the Indoor dataset[6], the Corel-5K dataset[7] and the Caltech-256 dataset[8]. We densely extract SIFT features of size 16×16 pixels with an overlap of 6 pixels. For the seven datasets, we randomly choose 50, 16, 100, 70, 80, 50 and 30 images per class for the corresponding image dataset. This process is repeated for five times to get reliable results. The codebook size for each dataset is set to 1,024. We use the classification rate as the performance measurement method.

We give the performance comparison of the proposed linear codebook transfer for undoing the dataset bias algorithm on the seven image datasets in Table 1. The horizontal row indicates the dataset that the codebook is generated while the vertical column indicates the dataset that the classification is performed. We also give the performance of the proposed linear codebook transfer algorithm on the corresponding vertical column by transfering the codebook generated by the other six datasets.

We can see from Table 1 that the codebook generated by one particular image dataset achieves the best classification performance on the corresponding dataset. This is because of the manual selection of images for particular purposes [9]. However, we can see from Table 1 that we can achieve better results by transfering the codebooks instead of directly using the codebooks generated by other datasets. In fact, the codebook generated by the corresponding image dataset is the upper performance bound of the proposed codebook transfer algorithm.

Besides, the relative improvement of the proposed codebook transfer algorithm varies over image datasets. For example, the proposed method achieves equal performance on the Butterfly and Corel-5K datasets while performs 3/2 percent less on the Caltech-256/Indoor dataset compared with the codebook generated by the corresponding datasets. We believe this is because the difficulties of these datasets are different. The Caltech-256 dataset and the Indoor dataset are more difficult to classify that the Corel-5K dataset and the Butterfly dataset. This is not only because of the increased number of image classes but also because of the large intra and inter class variations.

On analyzing the details of the classification performance, we can have two conclusions. First, Compared with the codebook generated by the corresponding dataset, the use of other datasets generated codebooks perform better on similar image classes than on dissimilar image classes. For example, the Scene-15 dataset can be roughly divided into the indoor class and the outdoor class. When using the Indoor dataset generated codebook for classification, the performances are comparable or a little less that the Scene-15 generated codebook on the indoor class (*e.g.* kitchen, livingroom, store). However, for the outdoor class (e.g. highway/mountain decreases by 4/3 percent respectively). Fortunately, the proposed codebook transfer method can alleviate this problem by transfer the elements of datasets with similar image classes for better image representation. We can achieve comparable classification rates by codebook transformation (*e.g.* the Scene-15 dataset and the Corel-5K dataset). These results prove the effectiveness of transfering codebook for undoing the dataset bias and improve the classification performance.

4. CONCLUSION

In this paper, we proposed a novel linear codebook transformation method to undo the codebook bias. This is achieved by linearly transform the pre-learned codebooks for new visual applications. We also impose sparisity constraints for discriminative visual words transformation. An alternative optimization algorithm is proposed to jointly learn the optimal transformation matrix and encoding parameters. Experimental results on seven public datasets prove the effectiveness of the proposed method.

5. ACKNOWLEDGEMENT

This work is supported in part by National Basic Research Program of China (973 Program): 2012CB316400; the President Fund of UCAS; the Open Project Program of the National Laboratory of Pattern Recognition (NLPR); China Postdoctoral Science Founda-

Table 1: Mean classification rates on the seven image datasets: the Bird dataset, the Butterfly dataset, the Scene-15 dataset, the Event dataset, the Indoor dataset, the Corel-5K dataset and the Caltech-256 dataset. The horizontal row indicates the dataset that the codebook is generated while the vertical column indicates the dataset that the classification is performed. We also give the performance of the proposed linear codebook transfer algorithm by transfering the codebook generated by the other six datasets on the corresponding vertical column.

datasets	Bird	Butterfly	Scene-15	Event	Indoor	Corel-5K	Caltech-256
Bird	**0.83± 0.07**	0.72 ± 0.09	0.78 ± 0.06	0.79 ± 0.07	0.39 ± 0.08	0.61 ± 0.04	0.29 ± 0.06
Butterfly	0.75 ± 0.08	**0.72± 0.08**	0.77 ± 0.06	0.78 ± 0.07	0.38 ± 0.06	0.60 ± 0.04	0.29 ± 0.05
Scene-15	0.72 ± 0.06	0.69 ± 0.08	**0.79± 0.05**	0.78 ± 0.08	0.40 ± 0.07	0.62 ± 0.05	0.28 ± 0.06
Event	0.73 ± 0.06	0.73 ± 0.07	0.74 ± 0.07	**0.81± 0.07**	0.41 ± 0.07	0.61 ± 0.03	0.31 ± 0.06
Indoor	0.70 ± 0.08	0.72 ± 1.01	0.77 ± 0.05	0.79 ± 0.08	**0.43± 0.06**	0.62 ± 0.04	0.32 ± 0.07
Corel-5K	0.72 ± 0.09	0.70 ± 0.09	0.76 ± 0.06	0.78 ± 0.08	0.39 ± 0.08	**0.67± 0.05**	0.31 ± 0.05
Caltech-256	0.71 ± 0.08	0.71 ± 0.08	0.75 ± 0.05	0.79 ± 0.09	0.40 ± 0.05	0.64 ± 0.04	**0.38± 0.06**
codebook transfer	**0.81± 0.07**	**0.72± 0.08**	**0.78± 0.05**	**0.80± 0.08**	**0.41± 0.07**	**0.67± 0.04**	**0.35± 0.06**

tion: 2012M520434, 2013T60156, 2013M530350, 2013M530739; National Natural Science Foundation of China: 61025011, 61202325, 61202234; Beijing Municipal Natural Science Foundation of China No.4132010. This work is supported in part to Dr. Qi Tian by ARO grant W911BF-12-1-0057, NSF IIS 1052851, Faculty Research Awards by Google, FXPAL, and NEC Laboratories of America and 2012 UTSA START-R Research Award respectively. This work is supported in part by NSFC 61128007.

6. REFERENCES

[1] J. Sivic and A. Zisserman, Video google: A text retrieval approach to object matching in videos, *ICCV*, pp.1470-1477, UK, 2003.

[2] S. Lazebnik, C. Schmid, and J. Ponce, A maximum entropy framework for part-based texture and object recognition, *ICCV*, pp.832-838, China, 2005.

[3] S. Lazebnik, C. Schmid, and J. Ponce, Semi-local affine parts for object recognition, *BMVC*, pp. 959-968, 2004.

[4] S. Lazebnik, C. Schmid, and J. Ponce, Beyond bags of features: Spatial pyramid matching for recognizing natural scene categories, *CVPR*, pp.2169-2178, USA, 2006.

[5] L. Li, and Li Fei-Fei, What, where and who? Classifying event by scene and object recognition, *ICCV*, pp.1-8, 2007.

[6] A. Quattoni and A. Torralba, Recognizing indoor scenes, *CVPR*, pp.413-420, USA, 2009.

[7] G. Liu, Z. Li, L. Zhang, and Y. Xu, Image retrieval based on micro-structure descriptor, *Pattern Recognition*, 44(9):2123-2133, 2011.

[8] G. Griffin, A. Holub, and P. Perona, Caltech-256 object category dataset, Technical Report, CalTech, 2007.

[9] A. Torralba and A. Efros, Unbiased look at dataset bias, *CVPR*, pp.1521-1528, USA, 2011.

[10] A. Khosla, T. Zhou, T. Malisiewicz, A. Efros, and A. Torralba, Undoing the damage of dataset bias, *ECCV*, pp.158-171, 2012.

[11] V. Jain and E. Miller, Online domain adaption of a pre-trained cascade of classifiers, *CVPR*, pp.577-584, USA, 2011.

[12] B. Kulis, K. Saenko, and T. Darrell, What you saw is not what you get: Domain adaptation using asymmetric kernel transforms, *CVPR*, pp.1785-1792, USA, 2011.

[13] J. Candela, M. Sugiyama, A. Schwaighofer, and N. Lawrence, *Dataset shift in machine learning*, MIT Press, 2009.

[14] C. Zhang, J. Liu, Q. Tian, C. Xu, H. Lu and S. Ma, Image classification by non-negative sparse coding, low-rank and sparse decomposition, *CVPR*, 2011, pages 1673-1680.

[15] R. Gopalan, R. Li, and R. Chellappa, Domain adaptation for object recognition: An unsupervised approach, *ICCV*, pp.999-1006, 2011.

[16] C. Zhang, J. Liu, Q. Tian, Y. Han, H. Lu, S. Ma, A Boosting Sparsity-Constrained Bilinear Model for Object Recognition, *IEEE Multimedia*, 2012, 19(2):58-68.

[17] K. Saenko, B. Kulis, M. Fritz, and T. Darrell, Adapting visual category models to new domains, *ECCV*, pp.213-226, 2010.

[18] C. Zhang, J. Liu, Q. Tian, C. Liang, Q. Huang, Beyond Visual Features: A Weak Semantic Image Representation Using Exemplar Classifiers for Classification, *Neurocomputing*, DOI:10.1016/j.neucom.2012.07.056.

[19] Y. Zhu, Y. Chen, Z. Lu, S. Pan, G. Xue, Y. Yu and Q. Yang, Heterogeneous transfer learning for image classification, *AAAI*, USA, 2011.

[20] C. Zhang, J. Liu, Q. Tian, C. Liang, Q. Huang, Image Classification Using Harr-like Transformation of Local Features with Coding Residuals, *Signal Processing*, 2012, 93(8):2111-2118.

[21] H. Wang, F. Nie, H. Huang, and C. Ding, Dyadic transfer learning for cross-domain image classification, *ICCV*, pp.551-556, 2011.

[22] C. Zhang, S. Wang, Q. Huang, J. Liu, C. Liang, Q. Tian, Image Classification Using Spatial Pyramid Robust Sparse Coding, *Pattern Recognition letters*, 34(9):1046-1052.

[23] C. Zhang, S. Wang, Q. Huang, C. Liang, J. Liu, Q. Tian, Laplacian affine sparse coding with tilt and orientation consistency for image classification, *Journal of Visual Communication and Image Representation*, 24(7), pp.786-793, 2013.

[24] H. Lee, A. Battle, R. Raina, and A. Ng, Efficient sparse coding algorithms, *NIPS*, 2007.

[25] C. Zhang, J. Liu, J. Wang, Q. Tian, C. Xu, H. Lu, S. Ma, Image Classification Using Spatial Pyramid Coding and Visual Word Reweighting, *ACCV* 2010, pp. 239-249.

GLocal Structural Feature Selection with Sparsity for Multimedia Data Understanding

Yan Yan
DISI, University of Trento, Italy
yan@disi.unitn.it

Zhongwen Xu
CS, Zhejiang University, China
zhongwen19901215@gmail.com

Gaowen Liu
DISI, University of Trento, Italy
gaowen.liu@unitn.it

Zhigang Ma
DISI, University of Trento, Italy
ma@disi.unitn.it

Nicu Sebe
DISI, University of Trento, Italy
sebe@disi.unitn.it

ABSTRACT

The selection of discriminative features is an important and effective technique for many multimedia tasks. Using irrelevant features in classification or clustering tasks could deteriorate the performance. Thus, designing efficient feature selection algorithms to remove the irrelevant features is a possible way to improve the classification or clustering performance. With the successful usage of sparse models in image and video classification and understanding, imposing structural sparsity in *feature selection* has been widely investigated during the past years. Motivated by the merit of sparse models, we propose a novel feature selection method using a sparse model in this paper. Different from the state of the art, our method is built upon $\ell_{2,p}$-norm and simultaneously considers both the global and local (GLocal) structures of data distribution. Our method is more flexible in selecting the discriminating features as it is able to control the degree of sparseness. Moreover, considering both global and local structures of data distribution makes our feature selection process more effective. An efficient algorithm is proposed to solve the $\ell_{2,p}$-norm sparsity optimization problem in this paper. Experimental results performed on real-world image and video datasets show the effectiveness of our feature selection method compared to several state-of-the-art methods.

Categories and Subject Descriptors

H.3.1 [**Information Storage and Retrieval**]: Content Analysis and Indexing; I.2.10 [**Vision and Scene Understanding**]: Video analysis

Keywords

Global and Local, Feature Selection, $\ell_{2,p}$-norm, Image and Video Classification

MM'13, October 21–25, 2013, Barcelona, Spain.
Copyright 2013 ACM 978-1-4503-2404-5/13/10 ...$15.00..

1. INTRODUCTION

In the past years, there have been many feature selection methods proposed in the multimedia and computer vision research community. The classical Fisher Score [1] feature selection method evaluates the relevance of features according to the label distribution of the data points. Recently, the sparsity representation model has been successfully used. The sparse model in feature selection has also been widely investigated. Nie *et al.* [6] leverage a joint $\ell_{2,1}$-norm minimization on both loss function and regularization for feature selection. Yang *et al.* [12] have proposed a $\ell_{2,1}$-norm regularized feature selection method for unsupervised learning considering the manifold structure of data representation. The intuition for this type of approaches is that many real-world data are often sparse which means feature selection can be achieved by searching the sparse representation of the data.

Sparse models for feature selection have proved to be effective but most existing methods have two limitations. On one hand, the widely used ℓ_1-norm and $\ell_{2,1}$-norm are not flexible enough to control the sparseness of feature representation. Hence, useful features could be neglected or noisy features could be selected. In other words, they may not find out the optimal subset of the original features. On the other hand, many of these methods only consider global information of the data representation but ignore the local structure of data distribution which also has significantly useful information for selecting more discriminating features. To address these issues, in this paper we propose a novel and robust feature selection method by employing a $\ell_{2,p}$-norm based sparse model which considers both global and local data structures. We name our method GLocal Structural feature selection with Sparsity (GLSS). Instead of using the traditional ℓ_1-norm or $\ell_{2,1}$-norm, we propose to exploit the $\ell_{2,p}$-norm based sparse model. Since we can adjust the value of p in our framework, our algorithm is more flexible to control the sparseness of the feature representation, thus resulting in a better subset of the original feature set. To use the information of both global and local data structure, we build two regression models in a joint framework: one for all the data points and one for the local neighboring data points. Fig.1 illustrates the overview of our feature selection method. All training and test samples are represented by feature vectors. Our GLSS method considers global and local information with sparsity. Then the selected features are fed into a classifier to do image or video classification.

The main contributions of our work are as follows:

- GLSS utilizes the $\ell_{2,p}$-norm based sparse model for feature selection. This model is more capable of selecting discriminative features by adjusting the value of p;
- GLSS is built upon both global and local data structures. Exploring the GLocal information helps boosting the efficacy of feature selection.

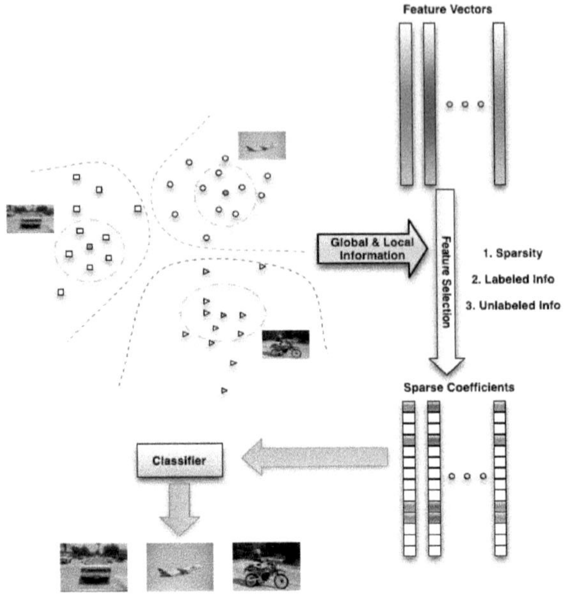

Figure 1: Our GLocal Structural feature selection with Sparsity (GLSS) Framework.

2. PROBLEM FORMULATION

The low-level features of images incorporate different information, either globally or locally. Intuitively, effective analysis on both levels would boost the feature selection efficacy. Therefore, we first explore the local data structure to help select discriminating features from the original representation. We build a local set $\mathcal{N}_i$ for each datum x_i. $\mathcal{N}_i = \{x_i, x_{i1}, ..., x_{ik-1}\}$ consisting of x_i and its $k-1$ nearest neighbors. For each local set, a local prediction function f_i is defined to correlate the data within the set with their predicted labels and we can obtain f_i through the following objective function:

$$\sum_{x_k \in \mathcal{N}_i} \ell\left(f_i(x_k), q_k\right) + \alpha \Omega(f_i) \tag{1}$$

where $\ell(\cdot)$ is the loss function and $\Omega(\cdot)$ is the regularizer. $x_k \in \mathcal{N}_i$ and q_k is the predicted label for x_k. α is a regularization parameter.

Globally, we also define a prediction function f to correlate all the n data points with their predicted labels as follows:

$$\sum_{i=1}^{n} \ell\left(f(x_i), q_i\right) + \gamma \Omega(f) \tag{2}$$

where q_i is the predicted label for x_i and γ is a regularization parameter.

Suppose the feature dimension is d and there are c classes. We apply linear regression model and obtain $f_i(x) = W_i^T x + b_i$ and $f(x) = W^T x + b$, where $W_i \in \mathbb{R}^{d\times c}$ and $W \in \mathbb{R}^{d\times c}$ are two projection matrices, b_i and b are bias terms in linear regression. We aim to leverage both the global and local information. Let local data set $X_i = [x_i, x_{i1}, ..., x_{ik-1}] \in \mathbb{R}^{d\times k}$ and local predicted label set $Q_i = [q_i, q_{i1}, ..., q_{ik-1}]^T \in \mathbb{R}^{k\times c}$, global data set $X = [x_1, x_2, ..., x_n] \in \mathbb{R}^{d\times n}$, global predicted label set $Q = [q_1, q_2, ..., q_n]^T \in \mathbb{R}^{n\times c}$. Hence, we propose the following joint framework:

$$\min_{W, W_i, Q, Q_i, b, b_i} \sum_{i=1}^{n} \left(\left\|X_i^T W_i + 1_k b_i^T - Q_i\right\|_F^2 + \alpha \|W_i\|_F^2\right) + \beta\left(\left\|X^T W + 1_n b^T - Q\right\|_F^2 + \alpha \|W\|_{2,p}\right) \tag{3}$$

where $1_k \in \mathbb{R}^k$ and $1_n \in \mathbb{R}^n$ are two vectors with all ones, $(\cdot)^T$ is the transpose operator, β is a parameter and $\|\cdot\|_F$ is the Frobenius norm of matrix. As the global projection matrix W is used for feature selection, a sophisticated regularizer is needed to make W able to reflect the importance of different features. The sparse models are used to make some of the feature coefficients shrink to zeros. As a result, W can be regarded as the combination coefficients for the most discriminative features to achieve feature selection. Specifically, we propose to minimize $\|W\|_{2,p} = \left(\sum_{i=1}^{d} (\sum_{j=1}^{c} |W_{ij}|)^{\frac{p}{2}}\right)^{\frac{1}{p}}$ to achieve the goal. $\|\cdot\|_{2,p}$ denotes the $\ell_{2,p}$-norm $(0 < p < 2)$. p is used to control the degree of sparseness. The lower p is, the more sparse is W or in other words, more rows of W would shrink to zeros. A merit of using $\ell_{2,p}$-norm, compared to using $\ell_{2,1}$-norm or ℓ_1-norm, is that we can adjust the value of p to search for the optimal subset from the original features.

Next, we build up the connection between the predicted labels $Q \in \mathbb{R}^{n\times c}$ and the ground truth labels $Y \in \mathbb{R}^{n\times c}$. Q is supposed to be consistent with Y and we propose to minimize $Tr\left((Q-Y)^T U (Q-Y)\right)$ inspired by [14, 10, 9]. U is a diagonal matrix whose diagonal element $U_{ii} = \infty$ if x_i is labeled and $U_{ii} = 1$ otherwise. To this end, we propose the following objective function for feature selection based on both local and global data structure:

$$\min_{W, W_i, Q, Q_i, b, b_i} \sum_{i=1}^{n} \left(\left\|X_i^T W_i + 1_k b_i^T - Q_i\right\|_F^2 + \alpha \|W_i\|_F^2\right) + \beta\left(\left\|X^T W + 1_n b^T - Q\right\|_F^2 + \alpha \|W\|_{2,p}\right) + Tr\left((Q-Y)^T U (Q-Y)\right) \tag{4}$$

3. OPTIMIZATION

In this section, we present our solution for Eqn. (4). Since it involves the $\ell_{2,p}$-norm which is non-smooth and cannot be solved in a closed form, we adopt alternating minimization algorithm to optimize the objective with respect to b_i, W_i, b, Q_i, Q and W respectively in five steps as follows:

Step 1, Fix W_i, b, Q_i, Q, W, Optimize b_i. By setting the derivative of Eqn. (4) *w.r.t.* b_i to zero, we have:

$$b_i = \frac{1}{k}(Q_i^T 1_k - W_i^T X_i 1_k)$$

Step 2, Fix b_i, b, Q_i, Q, W, Optimize W_i. By setting the derivative of Eqn. (4) *w.r.t.* W_i to zero, we have:

$$W_i = (X_i H_k X_i^T + \alpha I)^{-1} X_i H_k Q_i$$

where $I \in \mathbb{R}^{d \times d}$ is an identity matrix and $H_k = I - \frac{1}{k} 1_k 1_k^T$ is a locally centering matrix.

Step 3, Fix b_i, W_i, Q_i, Q, W, Optimize b. By setting derivative of Eqn. (4) *w.r.t.* b to zero, we have:

$$b = \frac{1}{n}(Q^T 1_n - W^T X 1_n)$$

Step 4, Fix b_i, W_i, b, W, Optimize Q_i and Q. Denote $G_i = H_k - H_k X_i^T (X_i H_k X_i^T + \alpha I)^{-1} X_i H_k$ and define a selection matrix $S \in \{0,1\}^{n \times k}$, where $S^{ij} = 1$ if x_i is the jth element in $\mathcal{N}_i$ and $S^{ij} = 0$, otherwise [13]. Consequently, $Q_i = S^T Q$ and we can obtain:

$$\sum_{i=1}^{n} Tr(Q_i^T G_i Q_i) = Tr\left(Q^T (\sum_{i=1}^{n} S G_i S^T) Q\right) = Tr(Q^T L_l Q)$$

where $L_l = \sum_{i=1}^{n} S G_i S^T$ reflects the exploration of local data structure. In this way, Q_i absorbed by Q which means we only need to optimize Q. Then Eqn. (4) becomes:

$$\min_{Q} Tr(Q^T L_l Q) + \beta \left\| X^T W + 1_n b^T - Q \right\|_F^2 + Tr\left((Q - Y)^T U (Q - Y)\right)$$

By setting the derivative *w.r.t.* Q to zero, we have:

$$Q = (L_l + \beta H + U)^{-1} (UY + \beta H X^T W).$$

where $H = I - \frac{1}{n} 1_n 1_n^T$ is the global centering matrix.

Step 5, Fix b_i, W_i, Q_i, Q, b, Optimize W. Denoting $W = [w^1, ..., w^d]^T$, we define a diagonal matrix D with its diagonal elements $D^{ii} = \frac{1}{\frac{2}{p}\|w^i\|_2^{2-p}}$. The objective is then equivalent to:

$$\min_{W} \left\| X^T W + 1_n b^T - Q \right\|_F^2 + \alpha Tr(W^T D W)$$

By setting the derivative *w.r.t.* W to zero, we obtain:

$$W = (A + \alpha \beta D)^{-1} B$$

where $A = XH\left(\beta I - \beta^2 (L_l + U + \beta H)^{-1}\right) H X^T$ and $B = \beta X H (L_l + U + \beta H)^{-1} U Y$.

According to the optimization, we propose Algorithm 1 to solve the objective function of Eqn. (4).

4. EXPERIMENTS

In this section, we conduct extensive experiments to evaluate the performance of our feature selection method. We also compare our method with other state-of-the-art feature selection methods.

Algorithm 1: The algorithm for GLocal Structural feature selection with Sparsity (GLSS).

Input:
The training data $X \in \mathbb{R}^{d \times n}$;
The training data labels $Y \in \mathbb{R}^{n \times c}$;
Parameters α, β and p.
Output:
Optimized $W \in \mathbb{R}^{d \times c}$.
1: Construct X_i for each datum;
2: Compute U;
3: Compute H_k, H;
4: Compute the selection matrix S;
5: Let $G_i = H_k - H_k X_i^T (X_i H_k X_i^T + \alpha I)^{-1} X_i H_k$;
6: Construct L_l as $L_l = \sum_{i=1}^{n} S G_i S^T$;
7: Set $t = 0$, initialize $W_t \in \mathbb{R}^{d \times c}$ randomly;
8: Compute $A = XH\left(\beta I - \beta^2 (L_l + U + \beta H)^{-1}\right) H X^T$;
9: Compute $B = \beta X H (L_l + U + \beta H)^{-1} U Y$;
10: **repeat**
Compute $W_t = [w_t^1, ..., w_t^d]^T$;
Compute the diagonal matrix D_t as:
$$D_t = \begin{bmatrix} \frac{1}{\frac{2}{p}\|w^1\|_2^{2-p}} & & \\ & \cdots & \\ & & \frac{1}{\frac{2}{p}\|w^d\|_2^{2-p}} \end{bmatrix};$$
Update W_{t+1} as: $W_{t+1} = (A + \alpha \beta D_t)^{-1} B$;
$t = t + 1$.
until *Convergence*;
11: Return W.

4.1 Datasets and Comparison Methods

The datasets and the low level features that we used in the experiments are listed in Table 1. We compare our GLSS with six different methods: Baseline (**No Feature Selection**), Fisher Score feature selection (**F-score**) [1], Feature selection with Joint $\ell_{2,1}$-norm minimization (**FSNM**) [6], Subspace Sparsity Collaborated feature selection (**SSC**) [5], Minimum-Redundancy-Maximum-Relevance feature selection (**MRMR**) [7], Fast Correlation Based Filter feature selection (**FCBF**) [4].

Table 1: Dataset Description

Dataset	Size	Features	# of Classes
COREL-50 [2]	5000	36-d color/egde/wavelet Histogram	50
Kodak [11]	3590	144-d Color Correlogram	22
HumanEva [8]	10000	168-d Joint Relative	10
MIR FLICKR [3]	25000	512-d GIST	38

4.2 Experimental Setup

In our experiments, each feature selection algorithm is first used to select features. Then the classifier is applied based on the selected features. The parameters α and β in Eqn. (4) are tuned from {0.01, 1, 100}. The parameter p is tuned from {0.05, 0.5, 1}. We tune the regularization parameters for other compared algorithms similarly. For all the algorithms in our experiments, the number of selected features is set as {40, 80, 120} for Kodak and HumanEva dataset, {150, 250, 350} for the MIR FLICKR dataset and {10, 20, 30} for the COREL-50 dataset. The local neighbor set is fixed as 5 in all experiments. The original dataset is randomly partitioned into 3 subsets. Of the 3 subsets, a single subset is retained as the test data and the remaining 2 subsets are used as training data. We use 3-fold cross validation in all the experiments and report the average results with standard deviation.

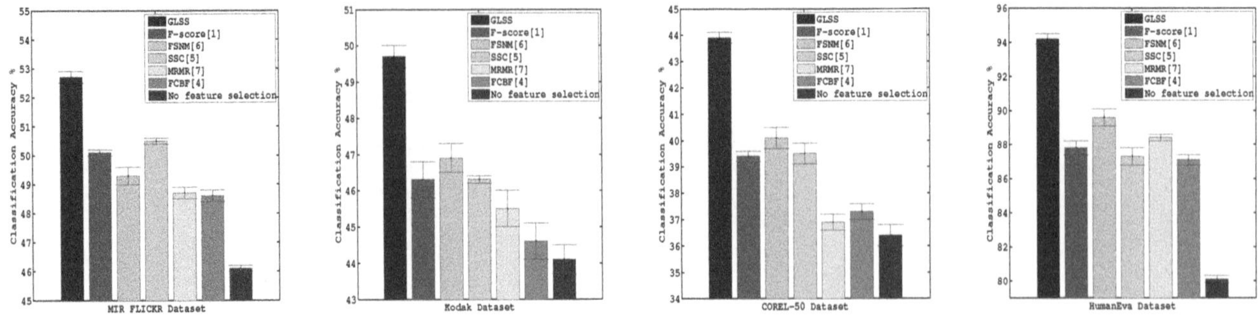

Figure 2: Classification Accuracy Comparision (MAP±Standard Deviation) when 10% training samples are labeled on MIR FLICKR, Kodak, COREL-50, HumanEva dataset respectively.

4.3 Results

Fig.2 shows the KNN (N = 5) classification results using different methods based on different datasets when 10% of the training samples are labeled. Our GLSS outperforms other methods on all four datasets. 3%, 3%, 4%, 5% more accuracy has been achieved on MIR FLICKR, Kodak, COREL-50, HumanEva datasets respectively over the second best feature selection method. 6%, 6%, 8%, 14% more accuracy has been achieved respectively when compared to the baseline (i.e., not using feature selection). The results demonstrate the advantage of our GLSS method. GLSS could control the feature sparsity level through $\ell_{2,p}$-norm and considers both global and local structures of data distribution which are both critical in classification tasks. Therefore, GLSS has shown better performance than all other feature selection methods which do not consider these important factors.

To understand KNN classifier effect for our proposed GLSS feature selection method. We evaluate different neighborhood parameter N for KNN classifiers (10% of the training samples are labeled). Table 2 shows the classification accuracy (GLSS method accuracy/No feature selection accuracy) on several datasets. Multi-label classifier is adopted when it is necessary. We can see from Table 2 that the largest performance gain is acchieved when N = 5 compared with simply classifying without any feature selection method tested on four different datasets.

Table 2: KNN Classifier Effect

GLSS/No-FS	N = 3	N = 5	N = 7
COREL-50[2]	43.1%/36.3%	43.9%/36.7%	43.7%/36.0%
Kodak[11]	47.7%/44.7%	49.3%/45.7%	47.5%/44.3%
HumanEva[8]	92.7%/79.8%	94.2%/80.1%	93.2%/79.1%
MIR FLICKR[3]	51.3%/45.1%	52.7%/46.1%	51.8%/45.0%

5. CONCLUSIONS

In this paper, we have proposed a novel feature selection method for different multimedia applications. By using the $\ell_{2,p}$-norm based sparse model, our method is able to jointly select features across all data points and has more flexibility in choosing the discriminating subset from the original features. Meanwhile, by considering both the global and local structures of data distribution, the feature selection can be boosted as the two structures are both critical in classification tasks. Experimental results performed on real-world image and video datasets show the efficacy of our feature selection method compared to several state-of-the-art feature selection methods.

6. REFERENCES

[1] R. Duda, P. Hart, and D. Stork. *Pattern Classification*. John Wiley & Sons, New York, 2 edition, 2001.

[2] S. C. Hoi, R. Jin, J. Zhu, and M. R. Lyu. Semi-supervised svm batch mode active learning for image retrieval. In *CVPR*, 2008.

[3] M. J. Huiskes and M. S. Lew. The mir flickr retrieval evaluation. In *ACM MIR*, 2008.

[4] H. Liu and L. Yu. Feature selection for high - dimensional data: A fast correlation-based filter solution. In *ICML*, 2003.

[5] Z. Ma, F. Nie, Y. Yang, J. Uijlings, and N. Sebe. Web image annotation via subspace-sparsity collaborated feature selection. *IEEE Transactions on Multimedia*, 14(4):1021–1030, 2012.

[6] F. Nie, H. Huang, X. Cai, and C. Ding. Efficient and robust feature selection via joint $l_{2,1}$-norms minimization. In *NIPS*, 2010.

[7] H. Peng, F. Long, and C. Ding. Feature selection based on mutual information: Criteria of max-dependency, max-relevance, and min-redundancy. *IEEE PAMI*, 27(8):1226–1238, 2005.

[8] L. Sigal, A. Balan, and M. J. Black. HumanEva: Synchronized video and motion capture dataset and baseline algorithm for evaluation of articulated human motion. In *IJCV, Vol. 87 (1-2)*, 2010.

[9] Y. Yan, G. Liu, E. Ricci, and N. Sebe. Multi-task linear discriminant analysis for multi-view action recognition. In *ICIP*, 2013.

[10] Y. Yan, R. Subramanian, O. Lanz, and N. Sebe. Active transfer learning for multi-view head-pose classification. In *ICPR*, 2012.

[11] A. Yanagawa, A. C. Loui, J. Luo, S.-F. Chang, D. Ellis, W. Jiang, L. Kennedy, and K. Lee. Kodak consumer video benckmark data set: concept definition and annotation. In *Columbia University ADVENT Technical Report 246-2008-4, Sep*, 2008.

[12] Y. Yang, H. Shen, Z. Ma, Z. Huang, and Z. Xiaofang. $l_{2,1}$-norm regularized discriminative feature selection for unsupervised learning. In *IJCAI*, 2011.

[13] Y. Yang, D. Xu, F. Nie, J. Luo, and Y. Zhuang. Ranking with local regression and global alignment for cross media retrieval. In *ACM MM*, 2009.

[14] X. Zhu, Z. Ghahramani, and J. Lafferty. Semi-supervised learning using gaussian fields and harmonic functions. In *ICML*, 2003.

Score-Informed Audio Decomposition and Applications

Jonathan Driedger
International Audio Laboratories Erlangen*
jonathan.driedger@audiolabs-erlangen.de

Harald Grohganz
Bonn University
grohganz@cs.uni-bonn.de

Thomas Prätzlich
International Audio Laboratories Erlangen
thomas.praetzlich@audiolabs-erlangen.de

Sebastian Ewert
Queen Mary University of London
sebastian.ewert@eecs.qmul.ac.uk

Meinard Müller
International Audio Laboratories Erlangen
meinard.mueller@audiolabs-erlangen.de

ABSTRACT

The separation of different sound sources from polyphonic music recordings constitutes a complex task since one has to account for different musical and acoustical aspects. In the last years, various score-informed procedures have been suggested where musical cues such as pitch, timing, and track information are used to support the source separation process. In this paper, we discuss a framework for decomposing a given music recording into note-wise audio events which serve as elementary building blocks. In particular, we introduce an interface that employs the additional score information to provide a natural way for a user to interact with these audio events. By simply selecting arbitrary note groups within the score a user can access, modify, or analyze corresponding events in a given audio recording. In this way, our framework not only opens up new ways for audio editing applications, but also serves as a valuable tool for evaluating and better understanding the results of source separation algorithms.

Categories and Subject Descriptors

H.4 [**Information Interfaces and Presentation**]: Sound and Music Computing

Keywords

Score-informed processing, source separation, audio editing, alignment, music synchronization

1. INTRODUCTION

In recent years, the task of separating a mixture of superimposed sound sources into its constituent components has been a central research topic in the field of digital signal processing. In speech, for example, these components could be the individual conversations of simultaneously speaking persons ("Cocktail party scenario", see [1]). In the context of music, the sources might correspond to the main melody, a bassline, a drum track or another instrument track [5, 6, 13, 14]. To guide the source separation process in such a scenario, it has become a common strategy to provide the algorithm with additional information. Such information can, for example, be given in the form of user-specified annotations [2], or by a musical score. In *score-informed* procedures the explicit timing, pitch and instrument information encoded by the score is utilized to guide and support the source separation processes.

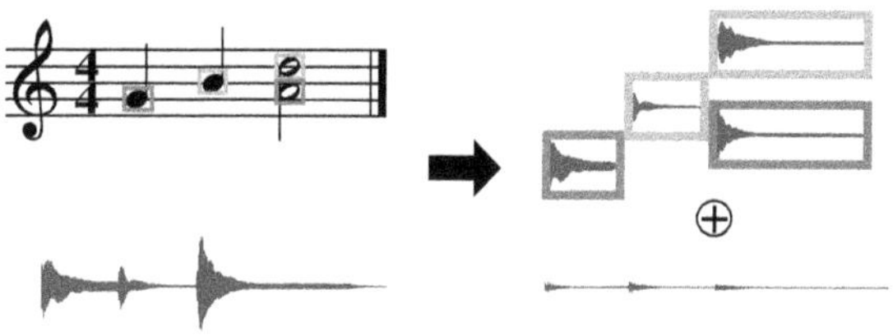

Figure 1: Score-informed decomposition of a given audio recording into note-wise audio events and a residual signal.

Most current score-informed approaches are designed for extracting individual instruments as specified by the score, see [8, 10, 17]. In this paper, we go beyond this scenario by introducing a framework for decomposing a music recording into elementary building blocks or sound events. More precisely, a musical score can be considered as a composition of elementary events given by the individual musical notes. These notes have some explicit musical meaning (in terms of pitch, onset time, and duration) and are directly intelligible by a human. The core idea of this contribution is to decompose a given music recording into a set of note-wise audio events, where each audio event is directly associated with a note in the musical score, see Figure 1. Based on this decomposition, we introduce an intuitive interface that allows a user to directly access the audio recording in a note-wise fashion, which opens up explicit ways of editing and manipulating audio material. Such an interface also provides novel possibilities to better understand the quality achieved by the underlying source separation algorithm. For example, subtracting all note-wise audio events from the original recording yields a *residual signal* which can be interpreted as the part of the recording that was not captured by the source separation process (for example because it was not reflected by the given

*The International Audio Laboratories Erlangen are a joint institution of the Friedrich-Alexander-Universität Erlangen-Nürnberg (FAU) and Fraunhofer - Institut für Integrierte Schaltungen (IIS).

MM'13, October 21–25, 2013, Barcelona, Spain.
Copyright 2013 ACM 978-1-4503-2404-5/13/10 ...$15.00.
http://dx.doi.org/10.1145/2502081.2502143.

musical score). Analyzing this residual can then reveal parts in the original recording where the source separation algorithm typically fails or where data inconsistencies occur.

The remainder of this contribution is structured as follows. In Section 2 we summarize a recent score-informed source separation algorithm used in our experiments. Furthermore, we show how to derive the note-wise decomposition of the audio recording and discuss some manipulation strategies. In Section 3, we present a prototype of a user interface for intuitive score-based audio editing and analysis. Finally, in Section 4, we close this paper with conclusions and future work.

2. AUDIO DECOMPOSITION

In the last years, techniques based on non-negative matrix factorization (NMF) have been applied to decompose a magnitude spectrogram into a set of template (column) vectors and activation (row) vectors [15]. To better control this factorization, additional score information has been used to constrain NMF and to yield a musically more meaningful decomposition [7]. In this section, we summarize the score-informed procedure as introduced in [3] (Section 2.1) and then describe how to decompose a given audio recording x into note-wise audio events x_m, $m \in [1 : M]$, where M is the number of note events specified in the score, and a residual signal r such that $x = \sum_m x_m + r$ (Section 2.2).

2.1 Constrained NMF-based Source Separation

Given a matrix $V \in \mathbb{R}_{\geq 0}^{S\times T}$, the goal of classical NMF is to derive two matrices $W \in \mathbb{R}_{\geq 0}^{S\times K}$ and $H \in \mathbb{R}_{\geq 0}^{K\times T}$, such that the distance, typically a modified Kullback-Leibler divergence, between V and WH is minimized [12]. In the context of source separation, given an audio recording x with spectrogram X, the goal is to factor the magnitude spectrogram $V := |X|$ into a matrix W of *template vectors* (every column corresponding to the prototype spectrum of a certain tone) and a matrix H of *activations* (every row encoding when and how loud a corresponding tone is played). In standard NMF the matrices W and H are derived by iteratively updating two randomly initialized matrices using multiplicative update rules. However, the result of this process is often not musically meaningful as discussed for example in [3].

To overcome this issue, [3] proposed a score-informed approach, where the score information is used to initialize both matrices W and H to guide the NMF update process in a musically meaningful direction. More precisely, having the score of the audio recording at hand in form of a MIDI file, high-resolution synchronization techniques are used to temporally align the MIDI events with the audio recording [4, 11]. Each of the M note events of the synchronized MIDI file yields information about the pitch, the onset time and the duration of a corresponding audio event that should occur in the recording according to the score. For each occurring pitch in the MIDI file, a harmonic template (column of the matrix W), which encodes the rough harmonic structure of the pitch, is initialized. This template is defined to have non-zero entries at frequency bins that are related to the fundamental frequency and the overtones of the given pitch and zero entries otherwise. Similarly, the activation matrix H is initialized by the specified onset times and note durations obtained from the synchronization procedure. For later use, we link the initialization of H with the corresponding synchronized MIDI events as follows. A binary constraint matrix $C_m \in \mathbb{R}^{K\times T}$ is constructed for each $m \in [1 : M]$, where C_m is 1 at entries that correspond to the pitch and temporal position of the mth MIDI event and 0 otherwise. Each C_m therefore constitutes

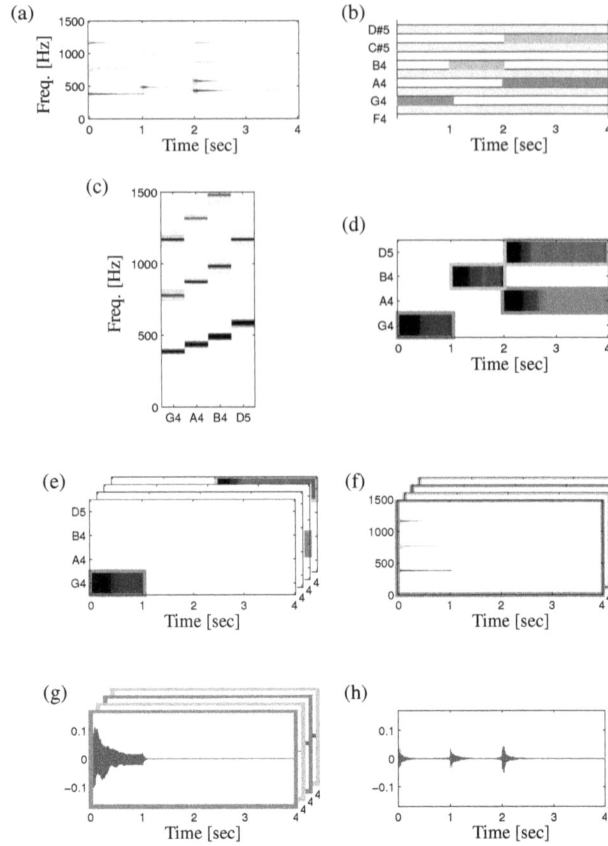

Figure 2: (a) Magnitude spectrogram V. (b) Synchronized MIDI note events. (c) Template matrix W learned by NMF. (d) Activation matrix H learned by NMF. (e) Note-wise activation matrices H_m. (f) Note-wise spectrograms X_m. (g) Note-wise audio events x_m. (h) Residual signal r.

a link between specific entries in H and a MIDI note event. The union (OR-sum) of all C_m is then used as initialization of H. At this point, the crucial observation is that the multiplicative NMF update rules can only change the non-zero entries. Therefore, applying NMF to the initialized matrices W and H yields a decomposition, where the relations expressed by the C_m between MIDI note events and entries in the activation matrix H are preserved, see Figure 2a-d. The result after the NMF-learning procedure can be seen as a refinement of the initially constrained harmonic template and activation matrices.

2.2 Note-Based Audio Decomposition

Let W and H denote the template and activation matrices after applying the NMF learning procedure. We now use the note-wise constraints given by the matrices C_m, $m \in [1 : M]$, to derive the note-wise audio events x_m. To this end, we first compute a note-wise activation matrix $H_m := H \odot C_m$, where the operator $\odot$ denotes the point-wise multiplication. Afterwards, we derive a spectral mask $M_m := (WH_m) \oslash (\sum_m WH_m + \epsilon)$, where $\oslash$ is understood as point-wise division and ϵ is a small positive constant to avoid a potential division by zero. The mask M_m can be interpreted as a weighting matrix that reflects the contribution of the mth note event to the original spectrogram X. Finally, we compute the note-wise spectrogram $X_m := X \odot M_m$ and apply the inverse short-time Fourier transform to obtain the audio event x_m, see Figure 2e-h. The audio events x_m represent a decomposition of the original signal x (the music recording) according to the note events specified by the given musical score. Obviously, this decomposition becomes problematic in the case that the recorded performance deviates from the musical score. More generally, synchronization inaccuracies, i. e. deviations in the alignment of the MIDI events and their expected realization in the music recording, may lead to local errors in the decomposition. Furthermore, simplifying model assumptions (such as the assumption that the partials' relative energy distribution is independent of the loudness), deviations in the expected tuning, or additional sound components caused by resonance or reverberation may cause artifacts in the decomposition. Therefore, we also compute a residual signal $r = x - \sum_m x_m$. The signal r holds a lot of valuable information since it does not only give a deeper insight into the source separation process, but it may also reveal inconsistencies between the musical score and the audio recording. Therefore, it is a natural idea to analyze r in more detail. In the next section we present an interface that supports such an analysis by enabling the user to study the decomposition and the residual signal more thoroughly.

3. APPLICATIONS

In this section, we show how the decomposition of an audio recording can be utilized as a basis for various applications. To this end, we developed a user interface (Section 3.1) which offers a user-friendly access to such a decomposition[1]. Furthermore, we show how this interface can be used for intuitive audio editing (Section 3.2) and the analysis of the underlying source separation procedure by investigating the residual signal r (Section 3.3).

3.1 User Interface

Besides standard audio player functionalities, our interface comes with a set of additional tools related to the score-informed audio decomposition introduced in the previous section. In its current state, our interface provides a piano roll representation of the musical score. While playing back the audio recording, the synchronized MIDI events are displayed and allow a user to directly access every single corresponding note-wise audio event, see Figure 3. Additionally, the interface also provides a set of plugins that can be used to manipulate, analyze and visualize the note-wise audio events. Some plugins included in our interface are discussed next. In general our Matlab-based framework is not restricted to these use cases and is flexible enough to support a wide range of further applications.

3.2 Audio Editing

Our interface provides easy-to-use possibilities for manipulating the audio recording in a musically informed manner. For example dragging a MIDI event in the piano roll representation and dropping it at a different position is an intuitive way of changing the onset time (horizontal displacement) and the pitch (vertical displacement) of a note. Having the note-wise audio decomposition at hand, we are able to transfer the same manipulations to the audio recording. If the user wishes to displace a note with respect to time and pitch, the corresponding audio event is first subtracted from the original recording and a suitably time- and pitch-shifted version (using a standard pitch shifting procedure such as [16]) of the event is added afterwards. We keep track of all the applied manipulations such that it is possible to manipulate a previously edited note again. By using similar strategies it is also possible to

[1]A demo of the proposed interface can be found at `http://www.audiolabs-erlangen.de/resources/2013-ACMMM-AudioDecomp/`.

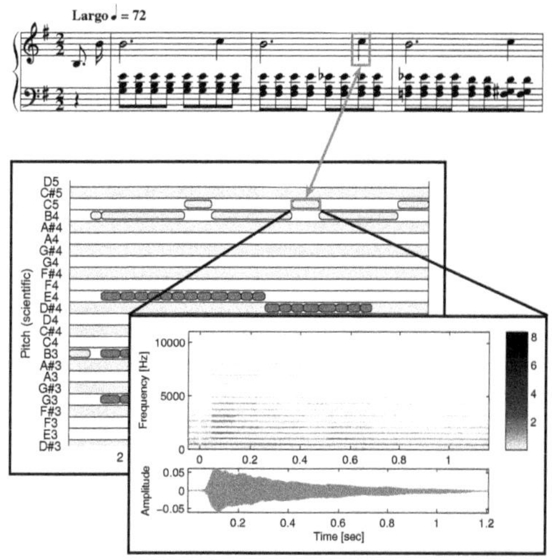

Figure 3: Top: Score of the first three measures of Op. 28 No. 4 by Frédéric Chopin. Bottom: Our user interface showing the corresponding part in an audio recording of the piece. Each note-wise audio event can be accessed separately.

change the duration or the volume level of notes, to remove notes completely from the audio recording, or to add additional notes by copying and manipulating existing ones.

3.3 Source Separation Analysis

Analyzing the decomposition of a music recording, and especially the residual signal r offers novel possibilities to investigate the behavior of the underlying source separation algorithm. Positions in the original audio recording where r shows high energy indicate passages where the source separation procedure could not assign all of the recording's energy to the note-wise audio events. To analyze such positions, our interface has been equipped with a plugin that plots the color-coded short-time energy of r in the background of the standard visualization, see Figure 4. This way, one can directly observe temporal relations between bursts of energy in r and the synchronized MIDI note events.

As an illustrative example how this tool can be used, we consider a short excerpt of Chopin's Prelude Op. 28 No. 4 as shown in Figure 4. Often a musical score does not completely describe what is actually played by the performing musician. An example for this are ornamental notes which are not reflected directly by the score (see, e.g., the pink boxes in Figure 4). Such deviations typically lead to local misalignments between the MIDI events and the audio recording. Even worse, additionally played notes that are not contained in the MIDI file may neither have an appropriate template vector in W, nor entries in the activation matrix H. It is therefore impossible for the score-informed source separation procedure to properly capture these notes. As Figure 4 shows, the residual r can reveal such inconsistencies between the notated score and the performance.

Local energy peaks in the residual are commonly aligned with note onsets (see the green and orange boxes in Figure 4). While smaller peaks, like shown in the lower green box, commonly emerge from oversimplifications in the musical model of the source separation algorithm (the derived template vectors in W can often not describe the sound of an onset accurately), more massive bursts of energy often arise from slightly misaligned MIDI events (e.g., the two bass notes marked in orange are played slightly earlier than they are encoded in our synchronized MIDI file).

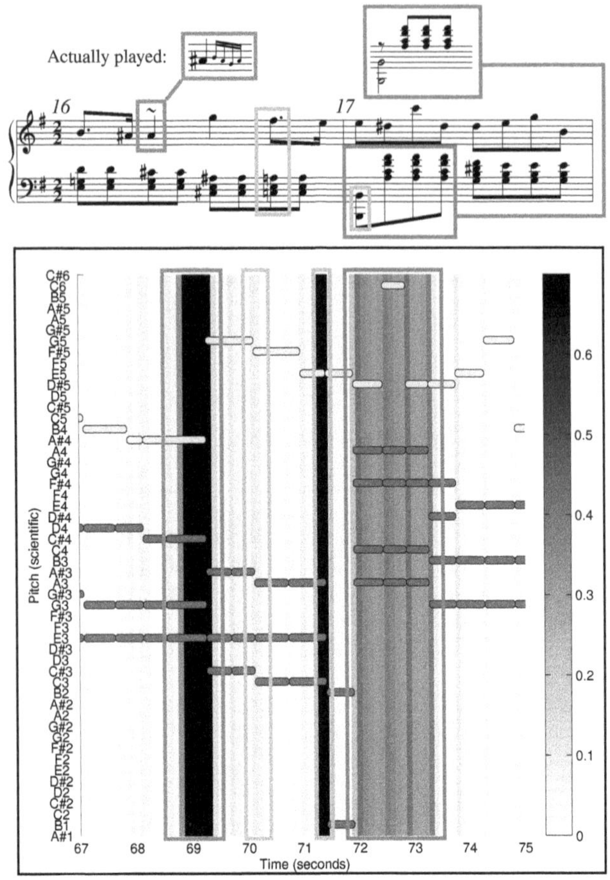

Figure 4: Top: Score of measures 16 and 17 of Op. 28 No. 4 by Frédéric Chopin. Bottom: Our user interface showing the corresponding part in an audio recording of the piece. The short-time energy of the residual signal r is visualized in a color-coded format in the background.

Another aspect that can not be captured appropriately by the used source-separation procedure are acoustical phenomena like resonance or reverberation (see the red boxes in Figure 4). At the beginning of measure 17, the performing musician holds the pedal of the piano and all played notes are therefore sustained until the pedal is released again in the middle of the same measure. Furthermore, the pressed pedal allows all strings of the piano to resonate with the actually played notes, thus creating an even more complex sound mixture. This information is not reflected in the audio decomposition and a large amount of energy migrates to the residual in the source separation process.

4. CONCLUSION AND FUTURE WORK

In this paper we presented a framework that allows for decomposing a given audio recording into score-based, and therefore musically meaningful audio events. Furthermore, we showed how this decomposition can be used for audio editing and analysis purposes. As discussed in Section 3.3, the residual signal r provides valuable information about deviations between a performance and a corresponding score as well as about misalignments of the MIDI events with the audio recording. As for future work, building a classifier that can automatically distinguish between different kinds of error sources may not only be beneficial for the source separation procedure itself, but could also aid in performance analysis applications or in improving alignment techniques. A further challenge is to investigate to which extend our decomposition may serve as an instance of object-oriented sound representation with applications to parametric audio coding and interactive remixing, see [9].

5. REFERENCES

[1] C. E. Cherry. Some experiments on the recognition of speech, with one and with two ears. *Journal of the Acoustic Society of America (JASA)*, 24:975–979, 1953.

[2] J.-L. Durrieu and J.-P. Thiran. Musical audio source separation based on user-selected f0 track. In LVA/ICA, pages 438–445, 2012.

[3] S. Ewert and M. Müller. Using score-informed constraints for NMF-based source separation. In *Proc. of the IEEE Intern. Conference on Acoustics, Speech, and Signal Processing (ICASSP)*, pages 129–132, Kyoto, Japan, 2012.

[4] S. Ewert, M. Müller, and P. Grosche. High resolution audio synchronization using chroma onset features. In *Proc. of the IEEE Intern. Conference on Acoustics, Speech, and Signal Processing (ICASSP)*, pages 1869–1872, Taipei, Taiwan, 2009.

[5] O. Gillet and G. Richard. Transcription and separation of drum signals from polyphonic music. *IEEE Transactions on Audio, Speech and Language Processing*, 16(3):529–540, 2008.

[6] M. Goto. A robust predominant-F0 estimation method for real-time detection of melody and bass lines in CD recordings. In *IEEE Intern. Conference on Acoustics, Speech, and Signal Processing ICASSP*, volume 2, pages 757–760, 2000.

[7] R. Hennequin, R. Badeau, and B. David. Time-dependent parametric and harmonic templates in non-negative matrix factorization. In *Proc. of the Intern. Conference on Digital Audio Effects (DAFx)*, pages 246–253, Graz, Austria, 2010.

[8] R. Hennequin, B. David, and R. Badeau. Score informed audio source separation using a parametric model of non-negative spectrogram. In *Proc. of the IEEE Intern. Conference on Acoustics, Speech and Signal Processing (ICASSP)*, pages 45–48, Prague, Czech Republic, 2011.

[9] J. Herre and L. Terentiv. Parametric coding of audio objects: Technology, performance and opportunities. In *Proc. of the Audio Engineering Society Conference (AES)*, Ilmenau, Germany, 2011.

[10] K. Itoyama, M. Goto, K. Komatani, T. Ogata, and H. G. Okuno. Instrument equalizer for query-by-example retrieval: Improving sound source separation based on integrated harmonic and inharmonic models. In *Proc. of the Intern. Conference for Music Information Retrieval (ISMIR)*, pages 133–138, Philadelphia, USA, 2008.

[11] C. Joder, S. Essid, and G. Richard. A conditional random field framework for robust and scalable audio-to-score matching. *IEEE Transactions on Audio, Speech, and Language Processing*, 19(8):2385–2397, 2011.

[12] D. D. Lee and H. S. Seung. Algorithms for non-negative matrix factorization. In *Proc. of the Neural Information Processing Systems (NIPS)*, pages 556–562, Denver, CO, USA, 2000.

[13] M. Müller, D. P. W. Ellis, A. Klapuri, and G. Richard. Signal processing for music analysis. *IEEE Journal on Selected Topics in Signal Processing*, 5(6):1088–1110, 2011.

[14] M. Ryynänen and A. P. Klapuri. Automatic transcription of melody, bass line, and chords in polyphonic music. *Computer Music Journal*, 32(3):72–86, 2008.

[15] P. Smaragdis. Non-negative matrix factor deconvolution; extraction of multiple sound sources from monophonic inputs. In *Proc. of the Intern. Conference on Independent Component Analysis and Blind Signal Separation (Lecture Notes in Computer Science 31959*, pages 494–499, Grenada, Spain, 2004.

[16] W. Verhelst and M. Roelands. An overlap-add technique based on waveform similarity (wsola) for high quality time-scale modification of speech. In *Proc. of the IEEE Intern. Conference on Acoustics, Speech, and Signal Processing (ICASSP)*, Minneapolis, USA, 1993.

[17] J. Woodruff, B. Pardo, and R. B. Dannenberg. Remixing stereo music with score-informed source separation. In *Proc. of the Intern. Conference on Music Information Retrieval (ISMIR)*, pages 314–319, 2006.

Background Subtraction via Coherent Trajectory Decomposition

Zhixiang Ren, Liang-Tien Chia and Deepu Rajan
School of Computer Engineering, Nanyang Technological University, Singapore
{renz0002,asltchia,asdrajan}@ntu.edu.sg

Shenghua Gao
Advanced Digital Sciences Center, Singapore
shenghua.gao@adsc.com.sg

ABSTRACT

Background subtraction, the task to detect moving objects in a scene, is an important step in video analysis. In this paper, we propose an efficient background subtraction method based on coherent trajectory decomposition. We assume that the trajectories from background lie in a low-rank subspace, and foreground trajectories are sparse outliers in this background subspace. Meanwhile, the Markov Random Field (MRF) is used to encode the spatial coherency and trajectory consistency. With the low-rank decomposition and the MRF, our method can better handle videos with moving camera and obtain coherent foreground. Experimental results on a video dataset show our method achieves very competitive performance.

Categories and Subject Descriptors

I.4.8 [**Image Processing and Computer Vision**]: Scene Analysis

Keywords

background subtraction, trajectory, low-rank, sparse

1. INTRODUCTION

Background subtraction, the task to detect moving objects in a scene, plays an important role in many video analysis tasks such as video surveillance, vehicle/robot navigation, etc. In the literature, many algorithms have been proposed for background subtraction. Among them, a typical and intuitive category [4][16] is to first build a background model with a manually labeled frame, and then compare the incoming frames with it. The areas varying from the estimated background model are detected as the moving objects/foreground. However, these models have two drawbacks which limit their applicability: (1) They are semi-supervised and require a training phase to learn the initial background model. (2) Their performance suffers due to large camera motion. For videos taken by moving camera, the background has severe motion which makes it hard to comply with the background model estimated from history frames. In general, it is infeasible for these methods to automatically deal with videos with large camera motion.

Recently, the effectiveness of Robust Principal Component Analysis (RPCA) has resulted in some automated background subtraction methods [13]. Most of these methods assume the vectorized image frames can be decomposed into a low-rank matrix representing the background, and a sparse matrix indicating the foreground objects. To enforce the spatial connectivity of the foreground pixels, block-sparse constraint is considered in decomposition process [5][6]. These methods achieve promising results on videos with static camera and illumination variance. However, they still suffer due to camera motion which makes the background no longer low-rank. To alleviate this problem, [15] and [9] use 2D parametric transforms to align vectorized video frames so that the background is still low-rank. However, for videos with large camera motion, the background has changed significantly. Thus these methods may fail to align vectorized video frames. As stated in [15], it performs poorly on the videos with large camera motion, such as "cars1", "cars9" and "cars10" sequences in Fig. 3(c). In addition, it is not easy for these methods to encode the long-term temporal consistency due to the lack of correspondence between two nonadjacent frames and the extremely high computational complexity. For this reason, Cui et al. [3] propose to use trajectory matrix as input and decompose it to a low-rank matrix (background) and group sparse matrix (foreground). Although [3] preserves temporal consistency by enforcing the pixels belonging to the same trajectory to have similar labels, it cannot model spatial connectivity in their framework, which is another important attribute for foreground objects.

Motion segmentation [1][14][12] is another feasible solution for background subtraction under large camera motions. Since the foreground will move differently from the background, we can separate them according to their motion patterns. These methods usually first derive the affinity matrix by measuring the similarity between trajectories, and then use some clustering techniques (e.g. spectral clustering) to get the segmentation results. However, most of these methods are sensitive to non-Gaussian noises.

In this paper, we present a novel algorithm to automatically detect moving objects with spatial and temporal consistency by motion decomposition. By leveraging large displacement optical flow [2], we use trajectories as the input

MM'13, October 21–25, 2013, Barcelona, Spain.

http://dx.doi.org/10.1145/2502081.2502144.

and decompose them into background and foreground. We assume that the trajectories from background lie in a low-rank subspace, and foreground trajectories are sparse outliers in this background subspace. Meanwhile, the trajectories belonging to the same moving object should be similar and spatially close. Therefore, we use the Markov Random Fields (MRFs) to simultaneously model the sparsity and trajectory coherency of foreground.

Compared to previous work, our model offers the following advantages: 1) Due to the trajectory representation, the proposed method can not only handle videos with large camera motion, but also preserve temporal consistency by considering the trajectory as a whole. 2) We incorporate spatial connectivity and trajectory similarity in the framework, thus our method can detect moving objects with spatial coherence.

2. TRAJECTORY DECOMPOSITION

2.1 Problem Formulation

In our framework, we first use the dense point tracker [2] to get trajectories of P tracked points through F image frames. The trajectory of the ith point can be represented by a vector $M_i = [x_{1i}, y_{1i}, x_{2i}, y_{2i}, ..., x_{Fi}, y_{Fi}]^T \in \mathbb{R}^{2F\times 1}$, where x and y denote the $2D$ coordinates in each frame. We define a $2F \times P$ matrix $\mathbf{M} = [M_1, \ldots, M_P]$ to represent the collected P trajectories. Note that some trajectories obtained by the dense point tracker [2] may be incomplete. We complete the missing entries of such trajectories by a sparse reconstruction method proposed in [8]. After we get the complete motion trajectory matrix $\mathbf{M}$, we aim to estimate the background trajectory matrix $\mathbf{B} \in \mathbb{R}^{2F\times P}$ as well as the foreground support $S \in \mathbb{R}^{P\times 1}$:

$$S_i = \begin{cases} 1, & \text{if the } i\text{th trajectory is foreground} \\ 0, & \text{if the } i\text{th trajectory is background.} \end{cases} \quad (1)$$

Background Constraint As indicated in [8][11], the trajectories of background from a single rigid motion will lie in a low-rank subspace. Specifically, under the assumption of orthographic projection, the subspace is spanned by three basis trajectories [11], i.e. the rank is 3. Therefore, some methods [10][3] impose a specific rank constraint on the background trajectory matrix $\mathbf{B}$. We follow them to require the rank of the background trajectory matrix $\mathbf{B}$ to be:

$$rank(\mathbf{B}) = 3. \quad (2)$$

It can be seen from the experiments that, such constraint achieves satisfactory performance for most of sequences.

Foreground Constraint The foreground is usually assumed to occupy a small portion of the scene, so sparsity [13] or group sparsity [3][5] is commonly used to constrain the foreground matrix. In our model, we also require the foreground support to be sparse. Moreover, the foreground trajectories belonging to the same object should occupy a contiguous spatial region. Thus, we model the binary states of entries in foreground support S by a MRF framework [7]. Our task is to infer a binary vector $S = [S_1, \ldots, S_P]^T$ so that $S_i = 1$ or 0 indicates whether the ith trajectory belongs to foreground or not. We state the problem as the minimization of the following energy function:

$$E(S) = \sum_i S_i + \gamma \sum_{i,j} W_{ij}(S_i - S_j)^2, \quad (3)$$

where the first term (unary term) is to penalize a high proportion of foreground trajectories. The second term (smooth term) encourages similar and proximate trajectories to have similar labelings. γ is the parameter controlling the strength of mutual interaction between trajectories. The affinity matrix $\mathbf{W}$ is defined as

$$W_{ij} = exp(-d^2(i,j)), \quad (4)$$

where $d^2(i,j)$ is the distance between the ith trajectory and jth trajectory. We use the pair-wise distance definition in [1], which measures difference between trajectories as the maximum difference of their motion over time:

$$d^2(i,j) = \max_t d_t^2(i,j) \quad (5)$$

where the distance between two trajectories at a particular instant t is calculated as:

$$d_t^2(i,j) = d_{sp}(i,j)\frac{(u_t^i - u_t^j)^2 + (v_t^i - v_t^j)^2}{5\sigma_t^2}. \quad (6)$$

$d_{sp}(i,j)$ is the average spatial Euclidean distance of ith trajectory and jth trajectory in 5 frames. u_t and v_t are the aggregated optical flows over 5 frames. σ_t denotes the normalization parameter. Note that such definition not only preserves the motion consistency between two trajectories over time, but also maintains the spatial coherency by taking the spatial distance of two trajectories into account.

Objective Formulation We combine the above two constraints together and get the following objective function:

$$\min_{B,S} \frac{1}{2}\sum_{S_i=0} \|M_i - B_i\|_F^2 + \beta\sum_i S_i + \gamma\sum_{i,j} W_{ij}(S_i - S_j)^2$$
$$s.t. \quad rank(\mathbf{B}) = 3, \quad S_i \in \{0,1\} \quad (7)$$

where B_i is the ith column of the background matrix $\mathbf{B}$. The weight factors β and γ are the trade-off parameters. The first term in Eq. (7) requires that the estimated background trajectories should be close to the original corresponding trajectories. The second and third terms are from the foreground energy function. The former expresses the sparsity of foreground and the latter preserves the motion consistency and spatial coherency.

By rewriting Eq. (7), we can get the matrix form:

$$\min_{B,S} \frac{1}{2}\|(\mathbf{M} - \mathbf{B})(\mathbf{I} - \text{diag}(S))\|_F^2 + \beta\|S\|_1 + \gamma S^T \mathbf{L} S$$
$$s.t. \quad rank(\mathbf{B}) = 3, \quad S_i \in \{0,1\} \quad (8)$$

where diag(S) denotes a $P \times P$ diagonal matrix with S as the diagonal elements and $\mathbf{I}$ is the identity matrix. $\mathbf{L}$ is the Laplacian matrix defined as $\mathbf{L} = \mathbf{D} - \mathbf{W}$ and $\mathbf{D}$ is a diagonal matrix with the definition $D_{ii} = \sum_j W_{ij}$. Note that S is a binary vector, so $\|S\|_0 = \|S\|_1$.

(a) 4th (b) 5th (c) 6th (d) Final

Figure 1: The intermediate results of our iteration process on "cars3". Green/red points denote foreground/background. Please enlarge for a better view.

2.2 Objective Optimization

The objective function defined in Eq. (8) is non-convex because of the low-rank constraint. Moreover, it contains both continuous and discrete variables which make simultaneous optimization extremely difficult. So, we adopt an alternating algorithm to efficiently optimize $\mathbf{B}$ and S. The optimization process can be divided into two steps: B-step and S-step with unknown $\mathbf{B}$ or S. We initialize $\mathbf{B}$ to be $\mathbf{M}$ and S to be a zero vector.

B-step Given the estimated $\hat{S}$, the objective function with respect to B can be rewritten as:

$$\min_{B} \|\mathbf{M}(\mathbf{I} - \operatorname{diag}(\hat{S})) + \mathbf{B}\operatorname{diag}(\hat{S}) - \mathbf{B}\|_F^2$$
$$s.t. \quad rank(\mathbf{B}) = 3 \tag{9}$$

The optimal $\mathbf{B}$ can be iteratively derived via the Singular Value Decomposition (SVD). Particularly, we iteratively update $\mathbf{B}$ by applying the SVD to $\mathbf{M}(\mathbf{I} - \operatorname{diag}(\hat{S})) + \mathbf{B}^k \operatorname{diag}(\hat{S})$, and then use three left/right-singular vectors with the largest singular values to reconstruct $\mathbf{B}^{k+1}$.

S-step Given the estimated $\hat{\mathbf{B}}$, the objective function (Eq. (8)) with respect to S can be rewritten as follows:

$$\min_{S} \sum_i (\beta - \frac{1}{2}\|M_i - \hat{B}_i\|_F^2) S_i + \gamma S^T \mathbf{L} S + C$$
$$s.t. \quad S_i \in \{0, 1\}, \tag{10}$$

where $C = \frac{1}{2}\sum_i \|M_i - \hat{B}_i\|_F^2$ is a constant. The above energy function has the standard form [7] and can be solved by using graph cuts [7].

We iteratively employ these two steps until the algorithm converges to a local minimum[1]. Fig. 1 shows some intermediate results of the iteration process on the video "cars3". We can see that foreground regions are gradually detected in the iteration process. After we get the labels of the tracked points, it is quite straightforward to obtain a pixel level segmentation based on color or edge information.

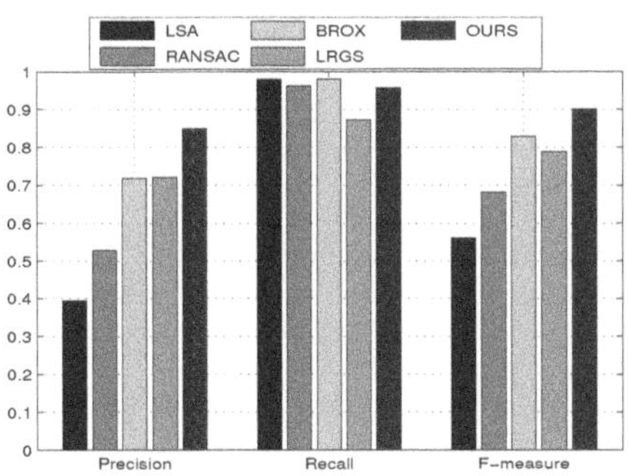

Figure 2: Quantitative comparison.

3. EXPERIMENTS

We quantitatively evaluate our background subtraction model on the Berkeley motion segmentation dataset[2], with pixel-accurate annotation of moving objects. This dataset contains 26 videos, in which 12 of the sequences (10 car and 2 people sequences) are taken from the Hopkins 155 dataset [12]. Since these videos are annotated for motion segmentation instead of background subtraction, we follow [3] to treat all the moving objects as foreground and the rest as background.

We evaluate the results of different models using Precision and Recall, which are defined as:

$$Precision = \frac{TP}{TP + FP}, \quad Recall = \frac{TP}{TP + FN} \tag{11}$$

where TP is the number of trajectories with support value 1 and falling into the foreground regions, and FP is the number of trajectories with support value 1 but falling into the background regions. FN is the number of trajectories with support value 0 but falling into the foreground regions. We also define F-measure as follows:

$$F - measure = \frac{2 \times Precision \times Recall}{Precision + Recall}. \tag{12}$$

We compare the proposed method with four state-of-the-art algorithms including: (1) Local Subspace Affinity (LSA) [14], (2) RANSAC [12], (3) Long term analysis of point trajectories (BROX) [1][3] and (4) Background subtraction method using Low-Rank and Group Sparsity constraints (LRGS) [3]. LSA and RANSAC are downloaded from website[4]. We implement the LRGS method. Since LSA and RANSAC require the number of segments in advance, we give them the correct number. We generate the trajectories by using the dense point tracker [2], in which the sampling parameter is set to 8. Except the BROX method, all other methods require the trajectories to have full length. So we use a sparse reconstruction strategy [8] to complete the incomplete trajectories. However, this strategy will fail in some sequences due to insufficient complete trajectories. For this reason, we only conduct experiments on the 12 sequences from Hopkins 155 dataset. For LSA, RANDSAC and BROX methods, following [3], we take the segment with the largest trajectory number as the background and the rest as the foreground. Please note that the DECOLOR method proposed in [15] is based on pixel labeling, not trajectory labeling. So we do not compare our method with it. We only show some visual results of it in the third column of Fig. 3.

For the proposed method, there exists two parameters: β and γ, which affect the performance. The parameter β controls the sparsity of the foreground support. As seen from Eq. (10), if $\frac{1}{2}\|M_i - \hat{B}_i\|_F^2 > \beta$, $\hat{S}_i$ is more likely to be 1. Hence the choice of β depends on the proportion of foreground which is unknown in advance. Thus we start our algorithm with a relatively large $\beta = max_i\|M_i - \hat{B}_i^0\|_F^2$, where $\hat{B}_i^0$ is the estimation of B_i in the first iteration. We then reduce β by a factor 0.5 after each iteration until it reaches the low boundary (set to be 0.001). By using this conservative manner, the foreground can be gradually detected along with the decrease of β (see Fig. 1). In our experiments, γ is empirically set to be 2β. To be fair, we tune parameters for all the compared methods to get the highest F-measure.

Fig. 2 shows the Precision, Recall and F-measure of all compared methods. It can be seen that most of methods can

[1]The convergence of B-step and S-step has been proved by SVD and [7] respectively, so the algorithm must converge to a local minimum.

[2]http://lmb.informatik.uni-freiburg.de/resources/datasets/

[3]http://lmb.informatik.uni-freiburg.de/resources/binaries/

[4]http://www.vision.jhu.edu/code/

(a) Frame (b) GT (c) DECOLOR [15] (d) LSA [14] (e) RANSAC [12] (f) BROX [1] (g) LRGS [3] (h) OURS

Figure 3: Results of the compared methods. Green/red points denote foreground/background. From top to bottom, the sequences are cars1, cars9, cars10 and people2. Please enlarge for a better view.

achieve a high Recall but a relatively low Precision. In contrast, the proposed method achieves much better Precision and comparable Recall. Overall, our method outperforms all the other methods in terms of F-measure.

In Fig. 3, we show some results of the compared methods. All these sequences are captured by a moving camera, especially for the "cars9" and "cars10", in which the background is a 3D scene with a large depth and the camera moves a lot. Due to large camera motion in "cars1" and "cars10", [15] works poorly on these sequences (Fig. 3(c)). For the difficult sequence "cars9", [15] even fails to detect the moving objects. As seen, with the help of trajectory representation, the proposed method can segment foreground from background in these sequences. Therefore, instead of raw pixels, it is desirable to use trajectories for background subtraction on sequences with large camera motion. Both our method and LRGS [3] have a specific rank constraint to model background. However, LRGS only requires the points belonging to the same trajectory to have similar labeling, it still misclassifies some trajectories, such as the small car are partially missed in "cars1". Thank to the spatial coherency and trajectory consistency, the proposed method significantly outperforms all the compared methods on the two difficult sequences "cars9" and "cars10". LSA [14] and RANSAC [12] detect a lot of background points as foreground. BROX [1] works better than LSA and RANSAC on "cars10", but still worse than our method. We show some video results of our method in the supplementary materials.

4. CONCLUSION

In this paper, we propose an efficient approach to automatically perform background subtraction based on a trajectory decomposition framework. We leverage the fact that trajectories from a single rigid motion will lie in a low-rank subspace to estimate background motion and detect outliers as foreground. We incorporate spatial connectivity and trajectories similarity into decomposition process by using MRF model. In this manner, the proposed method can detect moving objects with spatial and temporal consistency. Extensive experiments illustrate the effectiveness of our method.

5. REFERENCES

[1] T. Brox and J. Malik. Object segmentation by long term analysis of point trajectories. In *ECCV*, 2010.

[2] T. Brox and J. Malik. Large displacement optical flow: Descriptor matching in variational motion estimation. *PAMI*, 33(3), 2011.

[3] X. Cui, J. Huang, S. Zhang, and D. Metaxas. Background subtraction using group sparsity and low rank constraint. In *ECCV*, 2012.

[4] A. M. Elgammal, D. Harwood, and L. S. Davis. Non-parametric model for background subtraction. In *ECCV*, 2000.

[5] Z. Gao, L.-F. Cheong, and M. Shan. Block-sparse rpca for consistent foreground detection. In *ECCV*, 2012.

[6] C. Guyon, T. Bouwmans, and E.-H. Zahzah. Foreground detection based on low-rank and block-sparse matrix decomposition. In *ICIP*, 2012.

[7] V. Kolmogorov and R. Zabih. What energy functions can be minimized via graph cuts? *PAMI*, 26(2), 2004.

[8] S. Rao, R. Tron, R. Vidal, and Y. Ma. Motion segmentation in the presence of outlying, incomplete, or corrupted trajectories. *PAMI*, 32(10), 2010.

[9] Z. Ren, L.-T. Chia, and D. Rajan. Video saliency detection with robust temporal alignment and local-global spatial contrast. In *ICMR*, 2012.

[10] Y. Sheikh, O. Javed, and T. Kanade. Background subtraction for freely moving cameras. In *ICCV*, 2009.

[11] C. Tomasi and T. Kanade. Shape and motion from image streams under orthography: a factorization method. *IJCV*, 9(2), 1992.

[12] R. Tron and R. Vidal. A benchmark for the comparison of 3-d motion segmentation algorithms. In *CVPR*, 2007.

[13] J. Wright, A. Ganesh, S. Rao, Y. Peng, and Y. Ma. Robust principal component analysis: Exact recovery of corrupted low-rank matrices via convex optimization. In *NIPS*, 2009.

[14] J. Yan and M. Pollefeys. A general framework for motion segmentation: Independent, articulated, rigid, non-rigid, degenerate and non-degenerate. In *ECCV*, 2006.

[15] X. Zhou, C. Yang, and W. Yu. Moving object detection by detecting contiguous outliers in the low-rank representation. *PAMI*, in press, 2012.

[16] Z. Zivkovic. Improved adaptive gaussian mixture model for background subtraction. In *ICPR*, 2004.

Motion Matters: A Novel Framework for Compressing Surveillance Videos

Xiaojie Guo[1] Siyuan Li[2] Xiaochun Cao[1]
[1]State Key Laboratory Of Information Security, IIE, CAS, Beijing 100093, China
[2]School of Computer Science and Technology, Tianjin University, Tianjin 300072, China
xj.max.guo@gmail.com siyuan@tju.edu.cn caoxiaochun@iie.ac.cn

ABSTRACT

Currently, video surveillance plays a very important role in the fields of public safety and security. For storing the videos that usually contain extremely long sequences, it requires huge space. Video compression techniques can be used to release the storage load to some extent, such as H.264/AVC. However, the existing codecs are not sufficiently effective and efficient for encoding surveillance videos as they do not specifically consider the characteristic of surveillance videos, *i.e.* the background of surveillance video has intensive redundancy. This paper introduces a novel framework for compressing such videos. We first train a background dictionary based on a small number of observed frames. With the trained background dictionary, we then separate every frame into the background and motion (foreground), and store the compressed motion together with the reconstruction coefficient of the background corresponding to the background dictionary. The decoding is carried out on the encoded frame in an inverse procedure. The experimental results on extensive surveillance videos demonstrate that our proposed method significantly reduces the size of videos while gains much higher PSNR compared to the state of the art codecs.

Categories and Subject Descriptors

H [**Information Systems**]:
Information Storage and Retrieval

Keywords

Video Compression, Video Surveillance, Motion

1. INTRODUCTION

Video compression has a long history. Many compression standards have been developed, like H.120, H.261, MPEG-1, H.263 [6] and H.264/AVC [4] [7], the primary goal of which is to reduce the file size meanwhile preserve the quality as much as possible. There are two kinds of compression, *i.e.* lossless and lossy. Lossless compression aims to compress the original file with none lose of the information. In practice, this kind of compression is not attractive because the size of a compressed file is often the same as it was before compression. Lossy compression typically significantly reduces the file size but with some information lost. However, by exploiting temporal and spatial redundancy, the compression can reduce a relatively large size before affecting visual experience. So lossy compression is more suitable and popular for a wide spectrum of applications.

Although the existing codecs are with relatively high performance in the compression of general videos, they are still not sufficiently efficient for encoding surveillance videos. Since they do not specifically consider the characteristic of surveillance videos, *i.e.* the background of surveillance video has intensive redundancy. In addition, the foreground (motion) appearing in the surveillance video is of more importance than the background. In other words, from a perspective of surveillance, the foreground or to say the motion matters more than the background. To exploit the strong temporal redundancy of surveillance video, Chen *et al.* [2] propose to apply low rank and sparse decomposition, in which the frames of surveillance video are separated into the low rank component and the residual. This method, as reported, outperforms the state of the arts in terms of PSNR up to 3dB, but it has two disadvantages that can not be ignored: 1) processing frames in a batch mode is not so appropriate to the task of surveillance video compression, since frames are desired to be processed immediately as they come in, and 2) a single video is split into two videos, which is kind of inconvenient and cumbersome, and probably hurts the saving of file sizes.

In this paper, we propose a novel framework for compressing surveillance videos. To reduce the redundancy in videos, we try to train a background dictionary based on several observed frames. With the trained background dictionary, every frame is separated into the background and motion (foreground). The compressed motion and the reconstruction coefficient of background that corresponds to the background dictionary are stored as the compressed frame. Such a scheme encodes the frames in an individual mode, and avoids generating multiple videos for the original. The decoding is simply carried out on the encoded frame in a reversed procedure.

The rest of the paper is organized as follows. First, we describe our method in Sec. 2. Next, to show the performance of the proposed framework, Sec. 3 presents experimental results on both simulated data and extensive real videos. Finally, the conclusion is drawn in Sec. 4.

MM'13, October 21–25, 2013, Barcelona, Spain.
Copyright 2013 ACM 978-1-4503-2404-5/13/10 ...$15.00.
http://dx.doi.org/10.1145/2502081.2502145.

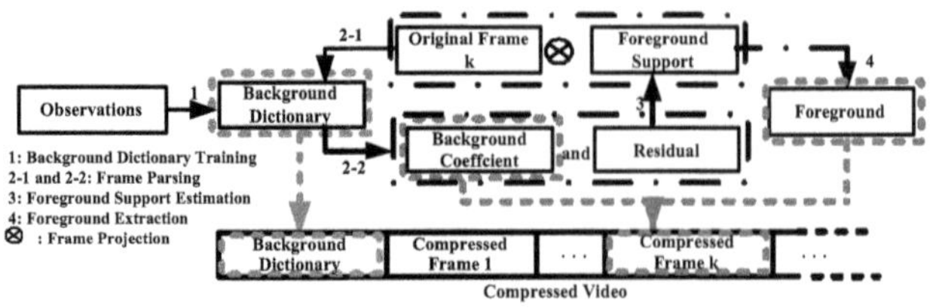

(a) Framework of our surveillance video encoding scheme

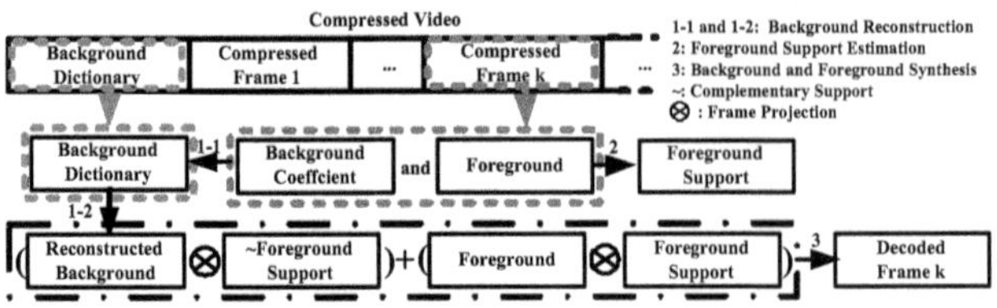

(b) Framework of our surveillance video decoding scheme

Figure 1: Overview of our proposed surveillance video compression method. The steps from foreground to compressed frame in (a) and from compressed frame to foreground in (b) can be processed by any codec. In this work, we adopt H.264/AVC.

2. OUR METHOD

In this section, we detail our surveillance video compression framework including two main components, *i.e.* video encoding and decoding, and background dictionary training. The framework of our proposed method is shown in Fig. 1.

2.1 Video encoding and decoding

Suppose we already have a well-trained background dictionary $\boldsymbol{U}$. (Latter, we will discuss how to effectively and efficiently train the background dictionary.) Given a frame $\boldsymbol{f}$, we first propose to parse the frame into foreground and background, with the assumption that the background $\boldsymbol{b}$ of the frame $\boldsymbol{f}$ can be represented by a linear combination of the items in $\boldsymbol{U}$, *i.e.* $\boldsymbol{f} = \boldsymbol{Ux} + \boldsymbol{m}$. So the problem can be naturally formulated as:

$$\min \|\boldsymbol{m}\|_0 \quad \text{s.t.} \quad \boldsymbol{f} = \boldsymbol{Ux} + \boldsymbol{m}, \tag{1}$$

where $\|\cdot\|_0$ denotes the ℓ^0 norm, and $\boldsymbol{m}$ represents the foreground. Due to the non-convexity of ℓ^0 norm, we employ ℓ^1 norm as the surrogate of ℓ^0 norm to make the problem tractable. The problem thus becomes convex and solvable with the formulation:

$$\min \|\boldsymbol{m}\|_1 \quad \text{s.t.} \quad \boldsymbol{f} = \boldsymbol{Ux} + \boldsymbol{m}. \tag{2}$$

To solve the problem (2), now the formulation (2) can be easily cast in the Augmented Lagrangian Multiplier (ALM) shape as follows:

$$\begin{aligned} \mathcal{L}_\mu(\boldsymbol{x}, \boldsymbol{m}, \boldsymbol{y}) = \|\boldsymbol{m}\|_1 + \frac{\mu}{2}\|\boldsymbol{f} - \boldsymbol{Ux} - \boldsymbol{m}\|_2^2 \\ + < \boldsymbol{y}, \boldsymbol{f} - \boldsymbol{Ux} - \boldsymbol{m} >, \end{aligned} \tag{3}$$

where $\boldsymbol{y}$ is the Lagrangian Multiplier vector. With help of the Alternating Direction Minimizing (ADM) strategy [8], we have the iteration, like:

$$\begin{aligned} \boldsymbol{x}_{k+1} &= \boldsymbol{U}^\dagger(\boldsymbol{f} + \boldsymbol{y}_k \mu_k^{-1} - \boldsymbol{m}_k), \\ \boldsymbol{m}_{k+1} &= \mathcal{S}_{\mu_k^{-1}}[\boldsymbol{f} - \boldsymbol{Ux}_{k+1} + \mu_k^{-1}\boldsymbol{y}_k], \\ \boldsymbol{y}_{k+1} &= \boldsymbol{y}_k + \mu_k(\boldsymbol{f} - \boldsymbol{Ux}_{k+1} - \boldsymbol{m}_{k+1}), \\ \mu_{k+1} &= \rho\mu_k, \end{aligned} \tag{4}$$

where $\boldsymbol{U}^\dagger$ stands for the Moore-Penrose pseudoinverse of $\boldsymbol{U}$, $\mu_k > 0$ is monotonously increased and ρ is a constant larger than 1. $\mathcal{S}_\varepsilon(\cdot)$ is the shrinkage operator: $\mathcal{S}_\varepsilon(x) = \text{sgn}(x)\max(|x| - \varepsilon, 0)$. The extension of the shrinkage operator to vectors is applying it element-wise. The algorithm terminates when $\|\boldsymbol{f} - \boldsymbol{Ux}_k - \boldsymbol{m}_k\|_F \leq \delta\|\boldsymbol{f}\|_F$ with $\delta = 10^{-7}$ or the maximal number of iterations is reached.

As $\boldsymbol{m}$ is the difference between $\boldsymbol{f}$ and $\boldsymbol{Ux}$, it has arbitrary value in $[-255, 255]$. To obtain the intrinsic foreground, we estimate the support of foreground Ω, *i.e.* $\mathcal{P}_\Omega(\boldsymbol{f})$ represents the foreground, while $\mathcal{P}_{\Omega^\perp}(\boldsymbol{f})$ the background. The operator $\mathcal{P}_\Omega(\cdot)$ denotes the orthogonal projection of a matrix onto the linear space of matrices supported by Ω, and $\Omega^\perp$ is the complementary support of Ω. To estimate Ω, we assume the distribution of the values in $\boldsymbol{m}$ satisfies the Gaussian distribution (η, σ). Note that, the frame does not contain any motions and noises if the values of the elements in $\boldsymbol{m}$ are all very close to zero. Therefore, we have $t = \max(\eta + \sigma, \beta)$ (in our experiences, $\beta = 0.1$ works practically well). Then the estimation of Ω is done via: if $|\boldsymbol{m}_i| < t$, $\Omega_i = 1$; $\Omega_i = 0$ otherwise. To further improve the estimation, we run morphological closing on the support estimated above to recall possible missing foregrounds.

The encoding of the frame thus can focus on the foreground $\mathcal{P}_\Omega(\boldsymbol{f})$ and the coefficient $\boldsymbol{x}$ corresponding to the background dictionary $\boldsymbol{U}$. The encoding is only performed on the foreground, which would be very efficient by using existing block-based codecs[1], since most of blocks in $\boldsymbol{w} = \mathcal{P}_\Omega(\boldsymbol{f})$ are flat. We then encode $\boldsymbol{w}$ together with $\boldsymbol{x}$, instead of processing both the background and the foreground separately which is inconvenient and cumbersome in both encoding and decoding. Please notice that the background dictionary can be either embraced in the beginning of the video or stored independently. The space cost by the background dictionary is nearly negligible, because surveillance videos usually contain extremely long sequences.

Decoding is the inverse procedure of encoding. We first decode the foreground of the frame $\hat{\boldsymbol{w}}$ and the coefficient $\boldsymbol{x}$, then extract the support of foreground. The extraction is efficiently accomplished by: if the pixel p_i has value larger than a predefined threshold τ, then $\hat{\Omega}_i = 1$, otherwise $\hat{\Omega}_i = 0$. Finally, the frame $\hat{\boldsymbol{f}}$ is recovered by:

$$\hat{\boldsymbol{f}} = \mathcal{P}_{\hat{\Omega}}(\hat{\boldsymbol{w}}) + \mathcal{P}_{\hat{\Omega}^\perp}(\boldsymbol{Ux}). \tag{5}$$

2.2 Background Dictionary Training

Suppose that we are given n observations of a surveillance video, then stack the observations as columns of a matrix $\boldsymbol{O} \in \mathbb{R}^{m \times n}$, where m is the pixel amount of every single frame. As expected, we want to learn background dictionary $\boldsymbol{U}$ from $\boldsymbol{O}$. As $\boldsymbol{O}$ contains not only the background but also the foreground, *i.e.* $\boldsymbol{O} = \boldsymbol{U} + \boldsymbol{M}$, where $\boldsymbol{U}$ stands for the background matrix and $\boldsymbol{M}$ represents foreground matrix, we have to separate $\boldsymbol{U}$ from $\boldsymbol{M}$. Due to the stationary background and the correlation between frames, $\boldsymbol{U}$ has low rank. And the foreground $\boldsymbol{M}$ represents, for example, cars and pedestrians that usually occupy only a fraction of the image pixels and hence can be treated as sparse error. Both $\boldsymbol{U}$ and $\boldsymbol{M}$ can be of arbitrary magnitude.

[1]Any codec can be chosen to do the job. In our experiments, we use H.264/AVC as our codec, an example software of which can be found at `http://iphome.hhi.de/suehring/tml/download/`.

Figure 2: First and Third Rows: Sample polluted images (Pollution rate, Noise variance). From left to right: $(0.1, 0.1)$, $(0.2, 0.2)$, $(0.3, 0.3)$, $(0.4, 0.4)$ **and** $(0.5, 0.5)$, **and** $(0.6, 0.6)$, $(0.7, 0.7)$, $(0.8, 0.8)$, $(0.9, 0.9)$ **and** $(1.0, 1.0)$, **respectively. Second and Fourth Rows: Corresponding backgrounds recovered by using 20 polluted images shown in the upper rows.**

Therefore, the problem can be written as:

$$\min \operatorname{rank}(\boldsymbol{U}) + \lambda\|\boldsymbol{M}\|_0 \quad \text{s.t.} \quad \boldsymbol{O} = \boldsymbol{U} + \boldsymbol{M}. \tag{6}$$

The optimization problem above is investigated and solved by Robust PCA [1] with some convex relaxations such as replacing ℓ^0 norm by ℓ^1 norm. And several speeding up algorithms [3] have also been developed. A more general formulation for the problem is written as:

$$\min \|\boldsymbol{O} - \boldsymbol{U} - \boldsymbol{M}\|_F^2 \quad \text{s.t.} \quad \operatorname{rank}(\boldsymbol{U}) \leq r, \quad \|\boldsymbol{M}\|_0 \leq k, \tag{7}$$

where $\|\cdot\|_F$ denotes Frobenius norm. The solution of this formulation is proposed by [10] named GoDec.

The main difference of (7) compared to (6) is to consider the dense small noise existing in the observations, say $\boldsymbol{O} = \boldsymbol{U} + \boldsymbol{M} + \boldsymbol{N}$, where $\boldsymbol{N}$ stands for dense small noise. Actually, for the background dictionary training problem, our concern is the low rank term, so the noise is not necessary to be considered individually. Applications on computer vision tasks, like [9] and [5], have proven the robust performance of RPCA. In our experiments, as a result, we adopt RPCA as our solution[2] for training background dictionary $\boldsymbol{U}$.

3. EXPERIMENTAL RESULTS

In this section, we demonstrate the performance of our proposed method on both simulated data and real data. Without explicit clarification, all the parameters are fixed through our experiments. τ for decoding is set to be 7, and 20 observed frames are used to train the background dictionary. The parameters of the RPCA code are set as default, and all the codecs appear in the experiments are with dynamic bit-rate to obtain optimal results.

There is no doubt that the dictionary trained using more frames is very likely to have better quality. However, due to the size of background coefficient depending on the size of background dictionary, we have to balance the quality of the dictionary and the file size after compressing. Although the performance of RPCA has been theoretically reported in [1], we still want to show its ability by fixing the number of trained frames 20 while varying the pollution rate and the noise variance level to see the quantitative results of background dictionary training. Note that RPCA is not specially limited by the spatial distribution and the type of errors. We synthetically perturb varying proportions of the template image by, without loss of generality, uniformly distributed Gaussian white noise of different variances. The task is to recover the template (background) from the polluted images (synthesized data). As can be seen from Fig. 2, the recovery gives perfect backgrounds using 20 images from $(0.1, 0.1)$ up to $(0.4, 0.4)$. Even the result of $(0.5, 0.5)$ is visually pleasing and acceptable. Therefore, we employ 20 frames to train the dictionary for the rest experiments on real data. Furthermore, the results shown in Fig. 3 are the evidence of the robustness to global illumination changes of our proposed background reconstruction strategy. Figure 4 gives an example result of foreground extraction. Due to the robustness of our support estimation method, the foreground can be accurately extracted according to the residual between the original and its reconstructed background.

To quantitatively show the overall performance of the proposed compression framework, we compare it with the traditional H.264/AVC method on surveillance videos[3]. Please notice that, due to the limited space of paper, we only show the results of 10 videos, which covers as many scenes (cases) as possible. The 10 videos include BackDoor (number of frame: 2000, resolution: 320×240), BusStation (1250, 360×240), Highway (1700, 320×240), Office (2050, 360×240), Pedestrians (1099, 360×240), TramStop (3200, 432×288), Sofa (2750, 320×240), Mv2_016 (8294, 480×320), Browse4 (1142, 384×288) and Fight_OneManDown (962, 384×288).

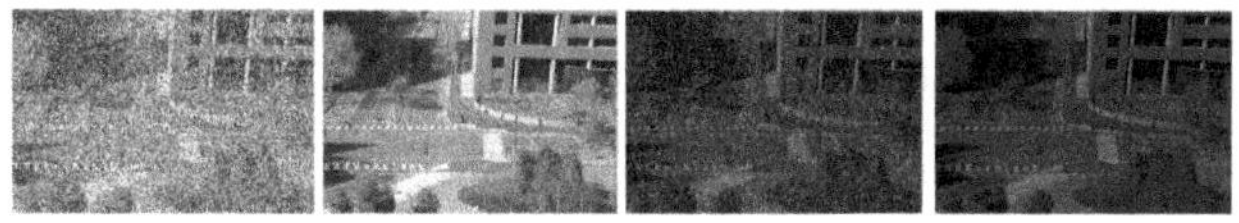

Figure 3: Illustration of the robustness to pollution and global illumination changes of the background reconstruction scheme. First and Third: the perturbed frames by 70% **Gaussian white noise of variance** 1.0 **and illumination preserved, and** 30% **Gaussian white noise of variance** 1.0 **and** 40% **illumination decreased, respectively. Second and Fourth: the corresponding recovered backgrounds, respectively.**

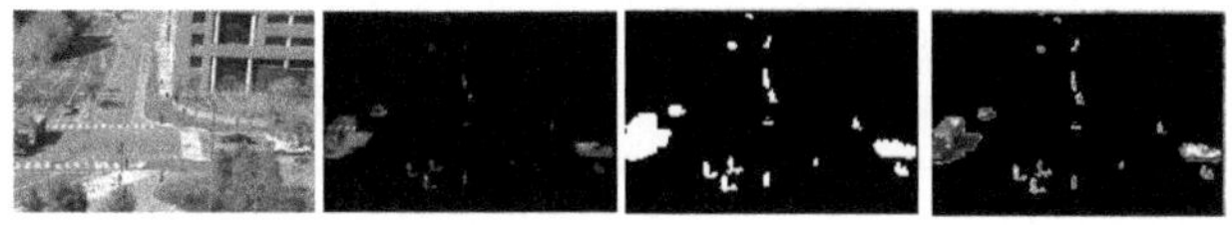

Figure 4: Example of our foreground extraction method. From left to right: the original, the residual between the original and its reconstructed background, the estimated foreground support, and the extracted foreground.

[2]The code can be downloaded from `http://perception.csl.illinois.edu/matrix-rank/sample_code.html`.

[3]The videos can be downloaded from `http://www.ee.cuhk.edu.hk/~xgwang/MITtraffic.html`, `http://www.changedetection.net/`

Table 1: Performance Comparison in terms of file size of compressed videos and PSNR

	BackDoor		BusStation		Highway		Office		Pedestrians	
	Size	PSNR	Size	PSNR	Size	PSNR	Size	PSNR	Size	PSNR
H.264/AVC	3.24MB	39.4dB	2.16MB	39.3dB	4.76MB	38.7dB	3.21MB	40.7dB	1.81MB	40.3dB
Our Method	2.15MB	78.3dB	1.93MB	77.59dB	2.18MB	78.4dB	1.27MB	77.8dB	1.07MB	81.0dB

	TramStop		Sofa		Mv2_016		Browse4		Fight_OneManDown	
	Size	PSNR	Size	PSNR	Size	PSNR	Size	PSNR	Size	PSNR
H.264/AVC	10.90MB	39.3dB	2.51MB	41.3dB	16.20MB	41.4dB	2.10MB	40.5dB	1.86MB	40.4dB
Our Method	6.45MB	77.4dB	1.40MB	84.4dB	9.81MB	75.2dB	377KB	80.1dB	597KB	79.6dB

We adopt two metrics, including: 1) file size of compressed video and 2) PSNR, to accomplish the comparison.

In implementation, we do not store every background reconstruction coefficient, since we observe that the background is very unlikely to change fast in surveillance videos. Therefore, we record the background reconstruction coefficient only when the current reconstructed background has sufficient difference with the latest recorded one. This can be easily done by introducing a flag to indicate whether the background is replaced. The compression benefits from this strategy to further reduce the size.

It is shown in Table 1 that our method significantly outperforms the H.264/AVC in terms of both file size of compressed video and PSNR. As can be seen from the results, all the PSNRs obtained by our method are approximately doubled of those obtained by the traditional H.264/AVC codec. This is because, in surveillance videos, the changes between frames are mainly from motions. Our method is exactly motivated by this observation and thus focuses on the motions. Note that the PSNR of alternative method [2], as reported, gains an increase of at most 3dB compared to H.264, which is significantly smaller than ours.

As for the file sizes, due to the redundancy of background, most space of compressed videos is taken by the motions. Therefore, the size of compressed videos depends on how many motions appear in the videos. As backgrounds in surveillance videos have intensive redundancy, they can be well reconstructed according to the well-trained background dictionaries by storing corresponding reconstruction coefficients, which is the origin of size reduction. Although the saving of space by our method shown in Table 1 varies in a relatively large range, we still can find that our method cuts about 40% space on average, compared to H.264/AVC. Specially, for the video Browse4, even more than 80% of space cost is reduced. The experimental results on real data confirm that motion matters in surveillance videos.

4. CONCLUSION

Usually, motions are the main changes and backgrounds have massive redundancy in surveillance videos. The traditional codecs do not fully utilize such redundancy. In this paper, we have introduced a novel framework for compressing surveillance videos based on the observation above, which recovers the backgrounds from a trained background dictionary in a reconstruction way, and pays more attention on the motions. The proposed method can process immediately as frames came in. The experiments have verified the efficacy of the proposed method, and demonstrated that our method significantly outperforms H.264/AVC codec in terms of both file size and PSNR for surveillance videos.

Acknowledgment

This work was supported by National Basic Research Program of China (2013CB329305), National High-tech R&D Program of China (2013AA01A601), National Natural Science Foundation of China (No. 61003200), and 100 Talents Programme of The Chinese Academy of Sciences.

5. REFERENCES

[1] E. Candès, X. Li, Y. Ma, and J. Wright. Robust principal component analysis? *Journal of ACM*, 58(3):1–37, 2011.

[2] C. Chen, J. Cai, W. Lin, and G. Shi. Surveillance video coding via low-rank and sparse decomposition. In *ACM Multimedia*, pages 713–716, 2012.

[3] Z. Lin, M. Chen, L. Wu, and Y. Ma. The augmented lagrange multiplier method for exact recovery of corrupted low-rank matrices. Technical Report UILU-ENG-09-2215, UIUC Technical Report, 2009.

[4] J. Ostermann, J. Bormans, P. List, D. Marpe, M. Narroschke, F. Pereira, T. Stockhammer, and T. Wedi. Video coding with h.264/avc: tools, performance, and complexity. *IEEE Circuits and Systems Magazine*, 4(1):7–28, 2004.

[5] Y. Peng, A. Ganesh, J. Wright, W. Xu, and Y. Ma. Rasl: Robust alignment by sparse and low-rank decomposition for linearly correlated images. *IEEE Trans. on PAMI*, 34(11):2233–2246, 2012.

[6] K. Rijkse. H.263: video coding for low-bit-rate communication. *IEEE Commun. Mag.*, 34(12):42–45, 1996.

[7] T. Wiegand, G. Sullivan, G. Bjøntegaard, and A. Luthra. Overview of the h.264/avc video coding standard. *IEEE Trans. Circuits Syst. Video Technol.*, 13(7):560–576, 2003.

[8] X. Yuan and J. Yang. Sparse and low-rank matrix decomposition via alternating direction methods. *Pacific Journal of Optimization*. Preprint.

[9] Z. Zhang, A. Ganesh, X. Liang, and Y.Ma. Tilt: Transform invariant low-rank textures. *IJCV*, 99(1):1–24, 2012.

[10] T. Zhou and D. Tao. Godec: Randomized low-rank & sparse matrix decomposition in noisy case. In *ICML*, pages 33–40, 2011.

Spatialized Audio Multiparty Teleconferencing with Commodity Miniature Microphone Array *

Viet Anh Nguyen[1], Shengkui Zhao[1], Tien Dung Vu[1], Douglas L. Jones[2], Minh N. Do[2]
[1]Advanced Digital Sciences Center, Singapore
[2]University of Illinois at Urbana-Champaign, IL, USA
{vanguyen,shengkui.zhao,johan.vu}@adsc.com.sg, {dl-jones,minhdo}@illinois.edu

ABSTRACT

This paper presents a Spatialized Audio Multiparty Teleconferencing (SAMT) system with a radically new communication experience for group teleconferencing. The system includes our recently developed 3D audio technologies: 3D sound source localization (SSL) and 3D audio capture and reproduction using a low-cost and compact design microphone array. In essence, the SAMT system offers 3D audio capture capability and spatial audio perception with multiple participants at a site, which still falls short in teleconferencing solutions. In addition to being able to identify and automatically track the active speaker, the system allows more compelling visual presentation for effective communication. Requiring only a low-cost microphone array and a consumer depth camera, the proposed system runs reliably and comfortably in real time on a commodity laptop or desktop PC. With such a minimal deployment requirement, we present a variety of user experiences created by SAMT.

Categories and Subject Descriptors

H.5.1 [**Multimedia Information Systems**]: Video; I.4.9 [**Image Processing and Computer Vision**]: Applications

Keywords

Video conferencing; 3D sound localization; 3D spatialized audio

1. INTRODUCTION

Virtual meetings have become increasingly popular these years, thanks to the proliferation of advanced networks and media technologies. They offer a good alternative to face-to-face meeting to save time and financial cost. For effective communication, virtual meetings require a high quality teleconferencing solution with a realistic and rich media presentation.

Last few decades have witnessed tremendous efforts in teleconferencing to realize truthful visual display and natural interaction of remote participants. For example, high-end teleconferencing products such as Cisco TelePresence [1] are designed to create a lifelike meeting perception with a proprietary installation and high-cost setup. Recently, Lu *et al.* [7] developed a more practical video conferencing system with a commodity setup that allows merging two or more remote participants into the same virtual space for natural and integrated interactions. However, existing video conferencing approaches typically provide a single audio stream from each site. The use of a single audio stream tends to impoverish the communication experience, especially in group meetings. For instance, without spatialized audio perception it is difficult to quickly determine the speaker among multiple participants.

To address above issues, a few high-end systems [1, 2] attempted to mimic a 3D sound field by rendering the sound of each participant from a certain speaker location. They generally assume a single participant at each site, which is not the case in group teleconferencing. Recently, Microsoft RoundTable [9] has been developed to automatically track and provide a close-up of the active speaker in a multiple participant setting. However, the system requires a non-trivial setup with a specific stand-alone circular microphone array and multiple cameras while not supporting 3D audio capture and reproduction. Meanwhile, traditional video conferencing systems such as Skype also do not offer any sound spatialization due to the hardware and complexity concerns.

Motivated by these challenges and more, we present in this paper a Spatialized Audio Multiparty Teleconferencing (SAMT) system based on a low-cost and compact setup (e.g., a miniature microphone array and a consumer depth camera). The system targets group teleconferencing scenarios to provide a radically new communication experience. Specifically, based on our developed miniature microphone array designed in the world's smallest size, the system offers 3D audio capture and reproduction with multiple participants at a site, a rare feature in teleconferencing. Leveraging on our recently developed 3D sound source localization (SSL), the SAMT system can also identify and automatically track the active speaker with the help of visual cues. This allows more intuitive visual presentation for effective communication experience.

Taking a holistic system design and optimization approach, this paper addresses the challenges in the key components of the SAMT system including 3D sound localization, 3D audio capture and reproduction, visual tracking, and immersive video composition. As an end result, the system performs two-way group teleconferencing in real time with a spatialized audio experience and intuitive visual presentation on a commodity laptop or desktop PC.

1.1 Related Work

As discussed in the introduction, the existing high-end teleconferencing systems [1, 2] essentially simulate spatialized audio by rendering the sound of remote participants from specific locations

*This study is supported by the research grant for the Human Sixth Sense Programme at the Advanced Digital Sciences Center from Singapore's Agency for Science, Technology and Research (A*STAR).

MM'13, October 21–25, 2013, Barcelona, Spain.
Copyright 2013 ACM 978-1-4503-2404-5/13/10 ...$15.00.
http://dx.doi.org/10.1145/2502081.2502146.

rather than creating a truly 3D immersive audio. This is usually done with a number of permanently installed loudspeakers, which limit their wide applications in daily practice. Meanwhile, several systems with spatialized audio [5] typically assume one participant at each station and do not offer 3D audio capture; therefore, they are in effective in group teleconferencing. In order to have a better intelligibility and an easier comprehension in such scenarios, several attempts were explored by utilizing the SSL and visual information to automatically detect and track the active speaker. They often require a multiple and large spatially separated microphone setup [3, 4, 8] or a specific stand-alone microphone array device (e.g., Microsoft RoundTable [9]). These setups are still bulky and not very portable compared to the microphone array in our system that is ranked as the world's smallest size for the 3D SSL. Given the size of our microphone array, it can be easily integrated within an audio/visual device upon commercialization.

2. SAMT SYSTEM

The SAMT system supports two-way group video conferencing with an immersive audio experience and intuitive visual presentation. The system uses our developed low-cost miniature microphone array for 3D binaural audio capture and reproduction and a color-plus-depth camera (e.g., Asus Xtion depth camera) for video capture as shown in Fig. 1. We leverage on our in-house communication platform to compress and transmit the processed audio visual signals from each site in real time. The simplified data flows and major components of a SAMT client, the main focus of this paper, are illustrated in Fig. 2. The 3D SSL together with the user tracking using the depth sensor allow automatically detecting and tracking the active speaker for a better communication experience.

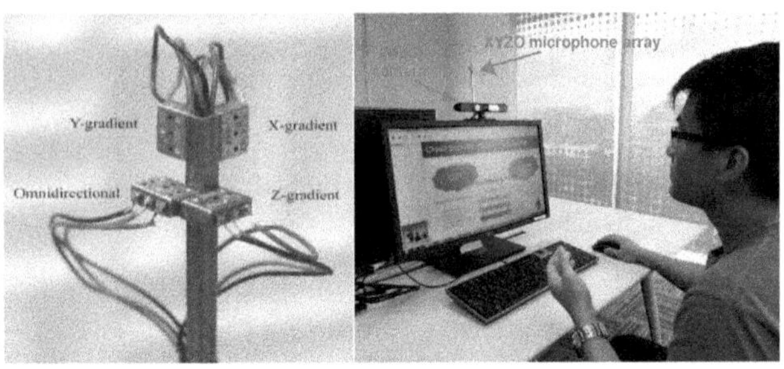

Figure 1: System setup with miniature microphone array enlarged (left).

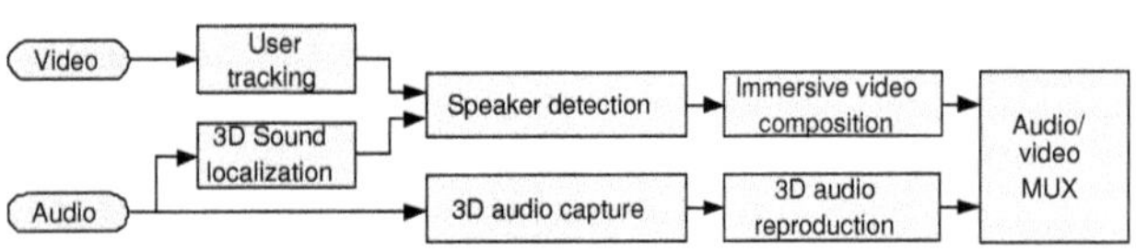

Figure 2: Block diagram and data flows of a SAMT client.

2.1 3D Sound Localization

Unlike the conventional SSL systems requiring a large spatially separated microphone array [3, 4], the novelty of our 3D SSL technology comes from a successful use of a significantly compact hardware design. Four collocated miniature microphones are constructed in the approximation of the acoustic vector sensors (AVS) as shown in Fig. 1, which is our newly built microphone array and it is successfully applied to beamformer in [6]. This AVS array consists of three orthogonally mounted acoustic particle velocity gradient microphones X, Y, and Z and one omni-directional acoustic pressure microphone O, which is referred to as the XYZO array. The use of gradient microphones over traditional pure pressure microphones is to exploit more available acoustic information including the amplitude as well as the time difference compared to only the time difference as used in pure pressure microphone arrays. As a result, the XYZO array offers better performance in a much smaller size. In this work, we first time deploy the XYZO array for the 3D SSL problem. To utilize the XYZO array for the 3D SSL, an offline calibration process is performed once to obtain the steering vectors of the array, which is the impulse response of the array in the 3D (vertical $180^\circ \times$ horizontal 360°) space. The proposed online 3D sound localization module consists of the sound capturing interface, the target sound detection and more importantly the direction of arrival (DOA) estimation. The DOA estimation is implemented as a 3D search on the formulated spatial spectrum of the complete frequency range.

The overall workflow of the DOA estimation is shown in Fig. 3. The multichannel input received at the XYZO array is processed by the DOA estimation as follows. The multichannel input is first segmented by a rectangular window, which has a size of 15360 signal samples. Each segment of signal data is termed as a frame. There is one frame for each microphone in the XYZO array, which is equally split into 30 blocks of 512 samples. A Hamming window and a fast Fourier transform (FFT) are applied to each block of 512 samples for converting the data into the frequency domain. For each frequency bin, the covariance matrix is average estimated based on the 30 blocks of data. To estimate the narrowband spectrum for each frequency bin, the inverse of the covariance matrix is calculated and multiplied by the steering vector. The obtained narrowband spectrums are summed across all the frequency bins to give a combined spectrum. The DOA output representing by the horizontal and vertical angles of the sound source is then found by searching the peak along the combined spectrum, which corresponds to the 3D spatial space $\Phi \in [0^\circ, 180^\circ] \times [0^\circ, 360^\circ]$. Mathematically, the DOA estimation is represented as

$$\hat{\theta}_s = \arg\max_{\theta \in \Phi} \sum_{w} f\left(\hat{R}_X(w, \theta)\right) \tag{1}$$

where $\hat{\theta}_s$ denotes the estimated DOA of the sound source, $f(\cdot)$ is a function of a narrowband directional spatial spectra. In this work, we successfully compute this function by using the frequency-domain minimum variance beamformer [6], which has been shown to be robust to background noise. $\hat{R}_X(w, \theta)$ is the covariance matrix of the input vector and it is estimated by the sample-averaging approach.

Generally, the DOA estimation complexity is intensive and increases with a finer search resolution. Currently, without source code optimization, we can achieve a real-time CPU implementation of the 3D SSL with the resolution of 5°, which allows accurate identification of the active speaker in our field trials as shown later. It should also be noted that with the highly parallel computational structure, a real-time 3D SSL with a finer resolution can be obtained with only an additional GPU that may benefit in a complex meeting setup with a large number of participants. To justify, we realize a GPU implementation of 3D SSL using CUDA programming by parallelizing each 3D search direction and each time-frequency bin using independently different thread blocks. For run-time simulation, the GPU implementation achieved 501X and 130X speedup compared to a single-thread and multi-thread CPU implementation with the resolution of 1°, as shown in Table 1, respectively.

Table 1: 3D SSL runtime comparison in msec.

CPU		GPU	Speedup	
Single	Multi-thread		Single	Multi-thread
7367	1919	14.71	501	130

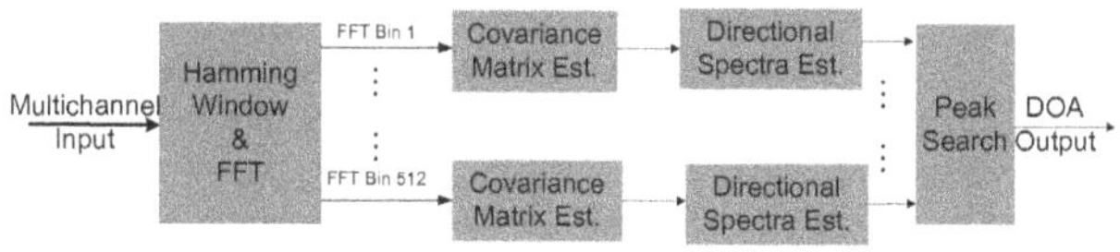

Figure 3: Workflow of the DOA estimation.

2.2 3D Capture and Reproduction

The key contribution of the proposed 3D audio capture and reproduction approach is to utilize a compact design microphone array, which is different from the existing approaches. Our approach requires a one-time offline process to determine the optimal time-invariant filter coefficients. These coefficients will be used to convert the B-format signal captured from the XYZO microphone array into the binaural signal for 3D sound playback. In the proposed system, the optimal coefficients are estimated in the frequency domain using the minimum mean squared error (MMSE) approach.

In concise, the signals received at the left and right ears are the convolutions of the head related impulse response (HRIR) and the incident plane waves. In the frequency domain, these signals can be modeled as a linear combination of the head related transfer functions (HRTFs) and the incident plane waves, in which the HRTFs are mapped to the incident directions of the plane waves. The number of directions is chosen according to the number of angles considered in the spatial space. The HRTF used for each direction is independent of the number of sound sources. At each frequency bin in the frequency domain, the signal received at each ear, $Y(w)$, can be approximated using a gain vector on an array output vector

$$\hat{Y}(w) = \mathbf{g}^H(w)X(w) \tag{2}$$

where $\mathbf{g}^H(w)$ is the gain vector and $X(w)$ is the signal received from the XYZO microphone array in the frequency domain. The optimal gain vector can be obtained by solving the MMSE problem as

$$\hat{\mathbf{g}}(w) = \arg\min_{\mathbf{g}^H(w)} E\left[\left|Y(w) - \mathbf{g}^H(w)X(w)\right|^2\right] \tag{3}$$

It should be noted that the gain vectors are estimated separately for the left and right ears. In the current implementation, the frequency-domain signals are obtained using a 512-point FFT. As a result, we have 512 gain vectors for each ear signal; each vector contains four elements corresponding to four-channel outputs of the XYZO array. These optimal gain vectors are computed in an offline manner for the real-time system. The optimal time-invariant filter coefficients for each channel are obtained through inverse FFT.

In a real-time system, the online process consists of signal acquisition, signal segmentation and mapping using the optimal filters, and 3D binaural playback. The sound inputs received at the four microphones are first segmented separately by a rectangular window, which has a size of 512 samples. Each segment of data samples is shifted to a frame with a size of 1024 samples. The convolutions of the filtering are performed in the frequency domain using a 1535-point FFT with zeros padding method. The results of convolutions from each channel are summed to give a combined output for the binaural playback. Since the complexity of the online process mostly involves convolutions, the 3D audio reproduction can perform comfortably in real time on a commodity desktop/laptop.

2.3 Active Speaker Detection

In the SAMT system, the output of the 3D SSL will be used together with the user tracking information obtained through a depth sensor to identify an active speaker. We utilize the OpenNI SDK for depth sensor to track multiple participants in the same physical room at one site and obtain their corresponding visual contents in real time. Specifically, each participant is associated with a user ID,

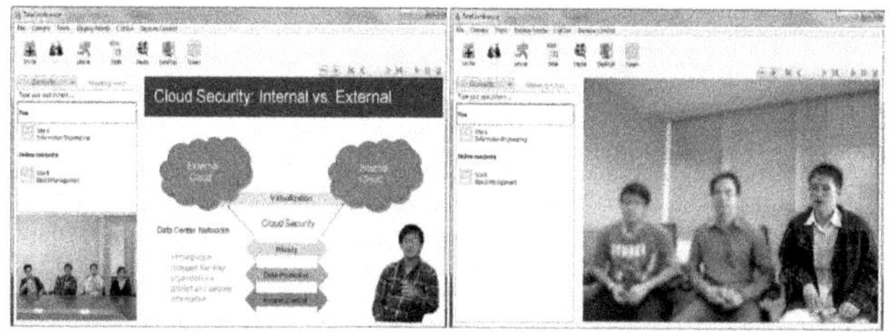

Figure 4: Active speaker detection with intuitive visual presentation. Left: Presentation mode with the immersive composition of the current speaker into the shared slides. Right: Discussion mode with the focusing effect on the speaker.

which can be used to extract useful information (e.g., user's center of mass and joints' 3D positions relative to the camera coordinate, 2D user's image coordinates and user's color segmentation). Thus, the video region of the current speaker can be extracted through his user ID induced by mapping the detected sound source angles from the 3D SSL to the depth sensor's user tracking 3D positions. By fusing cues from different sensors, it also prevents a wrong 3D SSL detection result, if any, when it loses track due to the room noise. Meanwhile, the knowledge of a sound source also helps to retrieve a lost tracking when a participant happens to move out of the scene and return. For more compelling user experience, the active speaker is segmented and immersively composited for various intuitive presentations (see Fig. 4 and Section 3). Although the user's segmentation can be obtained by simply thresholding the depth information, the quality is generally unsatisfactory with significantly misclassified boundary pixels. To improve the performance, we probabilistically fuse different cues together with spatial and temporal priors of the color sensor as well as the important depth information to build non-parametric probability models of the background and foreground for more accurate segmentation.

3. EXPERIMENTS

This section first evaluates the performances of the key modules and then presents the overall user experience study.

3D Sound Localization. We evaluated the performance of the proposed 3D SSL with various noise and reverberation levels. Different reverberations were obtained by convolving varying clean speech signals with the measured impulse response of different lengths corresponding to different reverberation times. The tested reverberation lengths were 0msec, 100msec, 200msec, and 300msec. To get different noise levels, an additive white Gaussian noise was added to the resulted signals. The tested noise levels measured by SNR are 10dB, 20dB, and 30dB. Six testing directions of sound sources were randomly selected from the 3D space for all the conditions.

For 20 testing realizations, the mean localization results over the total realizations and the mean standard deviations over the total tested directions are illustrated in Fig. 5. It is observed that the proposed approach provided the estimated mean azimuth and elevation angles within a small range of the target positions for all the tested conditions. In addition, the mean standard deviations are less than 1° for the reverberation time RT60=0msec and less than 6° when the SNR decreases to 10dB and the reverberation time RT60 increases to 300msec. The results also show that the proposed DOA method offers considerable robustness to additive noise, but it tends to degrade the performance in reverberant conditions. The overall results indicate that the localization accuracy of the XYZO array is within 6° error in a relatively noisy and reverberant meeting room.

3D Binaural Audio Reproduction. To evaluate the 3D audio reproduction accuracy of the proposed system, psychological

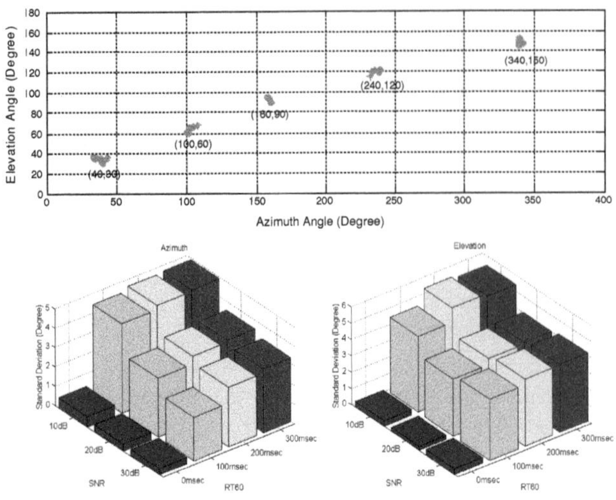

Figure 5: The DOA estimation results. Top: Mean values. The values in the brackets are the tested sound source angles. Bottom: Mean standard deviations.

subjective tests were carried out. There were five subjects involved in the evaluation. The assessment criterion is the ability to localize audio sources. In the experiment, the tested audio sources were recorded as follows: for $0°$ elevation angle there were 24 positions recorded for the azimuth angles varying from $0°$ to $360°$ with $15°$ interval, and for $0°$ azimuth angle there were 24 positions recorded for the elevation angles varying from $-90°$ to $90°$. The azimuth localization and elevation localization were tested separately. During each test, the subject was required to hear the processed audio signals and point to the direction of the audio source. A score of accuracy over 24 positions was obtained by comparing to the original directions of the audio sources. Table 2 shows the average scores over all the subjects for different reproduction resolutions as $1°$, $15°$, $30°$, and $45°$. The results show the effectiveness of the proposed system, in which the average scores over all the subjects were 20 for 24 azimuth positions and 10 for 24 elevation positions. It is observed that the sound localization for the azimuth positions, which is a more important factor in our system, was better than that for the elevation positions.

Table 2: Subject SSL scores for various resolutions.

	Azimuth				Elevation			
	$1°$	$15°$	$30°$	$45°$	$1°$	$15°$	$30°$	$45°$
Score	20	20	12	8	10	9	5	2

Active Speaker Detection. A real-life experiment was conducted to evaluate the performance of the active speaker detection and his/her video extraction. We invited up to six participants to join a group meeting. They were placed in the same room and each took turns to speak. The simulation results show that the 3D SSL module could detect the angle of a speaker with the accuracy of $6°$ in real time. Together with the user tracking information obtained through a depth sensor, this always led to an accurate active speaker identification and his/her correct video content extraction. It is worth mentioning that the speaker video distractingly switched too often whenever there was a noise sound source within a short period. To eliminate this undesired effect, we used a threshold to verify the 3D SSL new detection output. The system only switches to the new speaker video when a consistent detection output is presented within a certain period.

User Experience. We have deployed our system for field trials in group teleconferencing scenarios. For intuitive visual presentation, we implemented two modes: 1) *Presentation mode*: the active speaker is segmented and immersively merged with the shared contents, 2) *Discussion mode*: without any shared contents, the entire remote room is displayed with the active speaker in focus and the blurring effect for other participants (see Fig. 4). We conducted user experience surveys and collected some initial useful feedbacks. Generally, users liked the speaker detection and immersive visual composition features in the presentation mode. They felt the quality of the meeting was more effective with the ease to keep track of both the slide contents and the speaker video at the same time. They commented that the engagement of the active speaker with the shared contents also led to a more effective presentation and discussion. The survey results also show that the 3D audio reproduction feature was more useful in the discussion mode than the presentation mode. In the presentation mode, the main focus was usually on the shared contents and the current speaker. Therefore, users commented that they did not strongly perceive and pay much attention to the spatialized audio. In fact, as the speaker appeared at the corner of the shared slides, spatialized audio might even have undesired effects. Thus, 3D audio reproduction was turned off in this mode. In the discussion mode, immersive audio assisted users to quickly identify who is talking and perceive the direct conversation flow. However, it is worth mentioning that users were not fully satisfied with the focusing/blurring effect in the discussion mode. They felt that it hindered them to see the expressions and reactions of other participants to understand the meeting dynamics.

4. CONCLUSION

In this paper, we have presented the complete realization of a Spatialized Audio Multiparty Teleconferencing (SAMT) system to overcome the impoverished communication experience in the existing group teleconferencing systems. The proposed system was designed based on a truly commodity hardware (e.g., a compact microphone array and a consumer depth camera) and computing setup. We addressed the challenges in the key components of the proposed SAMT system including 3D sound capture and reproduction, 3D SSL, and intuitive visual presentation to maximize the overall system performance and user experience. Our future plan is to further improve the current system and its related key technology to ultimately make the system practical and accessible to massive users. For this purpose, we also plan to conduct a more extensive evaluation of user experience.

5. REFERENCES

[1] Cisco TelePresence. http://cisco.com/telepresence.

[2] Polycom TelePresence. http://www.polycom.com.

[3] R. Cutler *et al.* Distributed meetings: Ameeting capture and broadcasting system. In *Proc. ACM MM*, 2002.

[4] J. H. Dibiase. A high-accuracy, low-latency technique for talker localization in reverberation environment using microphone arrays. In *Ph.D. dissertation, Brown Univ., Providence*, 2001.

[5] K. Inkpen *et al.* Exploring spatialized audio and video for distributed conversations. In *Proc. ACM MM*, 2010.

[6] D. Jones *et al.* Beamformer performance with acoustic vector sensors in air. *J. Acoust. Soc. Am.*, 2006.

[7] J. Lu *et al.* CuteChat: A lightweight tele-immersive video chat system. In *Proc. of ACM Multimedia*, 2011.

[8] H. Wang and P. Chu. Voice source localization for automatic camera pointing system in videoconferencing. In *Proc. ICASSP*, 1997.

[9] C. Zhang *et al.* Maximum likelihood sound source localization and beamforming for directional microphone arrays in distributed meetings. *Trans. Multimedia*, 2008.

Learning Articulated Body Models for People Re-identification

Davide Baltieri, Roberto Vezzani, Rita Cucchiara
University of Modena and Reggio Emilia
Via Vignolese 905, 41125 Modena - Italy
{davide.baltieri, roberto.vezzani, rita.cucchiara}@unimore.it

ABSTRACT

People re-identification is a challenging problem in surveillance and forensics and it aims at associating multiple instances of the same person which have been acquired from different points of view and after a temporal gap. Image-based appearance features are usually adopted but, in addition to their intrinsically low discriminability, they are subject to perspective and view-point issues. We propose to completely change the approach by mapping local descriptors extracted from RGB-D sensors on a 3D body model for creating a view-independent signature. An original bone-wise color descriptor is generated and reduced with PCA to compute the person signature. The virtual bone set used to map appearance features is learned using a recursive splitting approach. Finally, people matching for re-identification is performed using the Relaxed Pairwise Metric Learning, which simultaneously provides feature reduction and weighting. Experiments on a specific dataset created with the Microsoft Kinect sensor and the OpenNi libraries prove the advantages of the proposed technique with respect to state of the art methods based on 2D or non-articulated 3D body models.

Categories and Subject Descriptors

I.5.4 [**Pattern Recognition**]: Applications—*Computer Vision*

General Terms

Algorithms,Experimentation

Keywords

People re-identification, Microsoft Kinect, RGB-D sensors

1. INTRODUCTION

People re-identification is a challenging task extremely useful for video surveillance or forensics. It aims at discovering multiple instances of the same person captured from different points of view or after a significant temporal gap. However, differently from biometric techniques, re-identification trusts on appearance information only and thus it is mainly based on the color, texture and shape of people clothing [4]. Features such as color and texture histograms have been deeply tested and applied rather than shape and geometrical properties, leading to an intrinsically low discriminability of the computed signatures.

To solve this problem, 2D models and, recently, non-articulated 3D models of the human body have been introduced. Differently from motion capture or action analysis approaches, the models are not required to be extremely precise but fast. However, a model-based localization provides more coherent and representative descriptions and allows a correct comparison of corresponding body parts. Problems due to occlusions and segmentation errors can also be minimized.

In this work we made a step forward by proposing a new original 3D approach to re-identification based on articulated body models. A 3D model is adopted to map appearance descriptors to skeleton bones (See Fig. 1). The color, depth and skeleton streams produced with the Microsoft Kinect sensor [11] and the OpenNi libraries are exploited as input. The skeleton is further refined using a learning approach in order to generate a "bone" set. The obtained signature is strictly related to the real body structure, thus it also allows an attribute based description, which could be useful is some applications [8]. In addition, a learned metric is adopted which simultaneously acts as feature selection and body part weighting.

2. RELATED WORKS

Simplified *2D models* are the most commonly used in people re-identification. Among the others, in surveillance and forensics the *cylindrical* shape and the *legs-torso-head* structure are the most widely adopted. By modeling a person as a cylindrical shape (or more generally as a solid of revolution) the horizontal variations of the people appearance are neglected, supposing that the color or texture distribution along the vertical axis is the only important

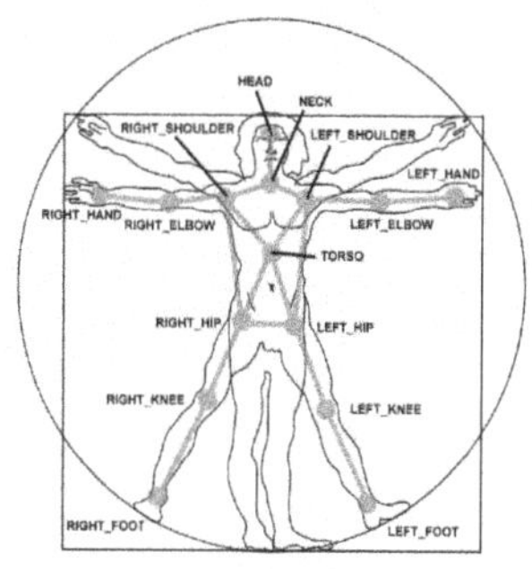

Figure 1: Vitruvian body model with superimposed the joints and bones used in the proposed system

MM'13, October 21–25, 2013, Barcelona, Spain.

ACM 978-1-4503-2404-5/13/10 ...$15.00.
http://dx.doi.org/10.1145/2502081.2502147.

data. For example, in [3] the person mask is divided into ten horizontal stripes (ideally corresponding to legs, torso, and head) and the mean color of each stripe is stored as representative feature. Weber *et al* adopted a part based detector to separately segment a personâĂŹs upper and lower clothing regions [13]. Similarly, Farenzena *et al* [5] compute the cut points from profile histograms. Moreover, they operate a further split in two of the torso and legs parts using a symmetry based algorithm.

Very recently, simplified *3D models* have been proposed to improve the feature localization. For example, a non-articulated 3D model called Sarc3D [1] has been proposed to map color appearance features on a vertex based model. The main drawback of Sarc3D is the lack of articulation. The rigid container requires a corresponding rigid posture of the person, while it will fail on people in sitting or bending positions. Articulated motion capture has been addressed in the past on color images [10, 9] and, more recently, using depth images [11, 12], but never applied to re-identification. Recently, the introduction of low cost range sensors like the Microsoft Kinect opened new solutions to surveillance and forensics research fields, included the re-identification task. Soft-biometry features can be extracted from the tracked skeleton stream and used to generate a person profile. For example, in [2] a set of ratios of joint distances is used as person signature. However, the intrinsic noise on the estimation of the joint positions do not allow to reach very high performance.

3. BONE FEATURE SET AND SIGNATURE

In order to provide a spatial location to each appearance feature, pixels of the color image need to be connected to a bone of the person. To this aim, OpenNi is exploited to find a set of human joints (see the red dots in Figure 1). Then these joints are linked together to build a simple human skeleton (see Figure 1). Let be $\Psi = \{\psi_1, \ldots, \psi_{15}\}$ the set of 15 joints, where each of the elements ψ_i corresponds to the 3D position of the joint. Based on Ψ, the corresponding "bone" set $\mathcal{B} \subset \Psi \times \Psi$ is obtained as the set of edges of the joint graph (see Figure 1). Each bone $b_i \in \mathcal{B}$ is defined using the 3D coordinates of the two extremities: $b_i = (\psi_r, \psi_s)$. Let $N = |\mathcal{B}|$ be the number of bones, 18 in our skeleton model.

Given the point cloud $\mathcal{W} = \{(x_1, c_1) \ldots (x_W, c_W)\}$, where x_j and c_j are the position and the color of each point respectively, a point-to-bone assignment is provided using a min-distance criteria and the subsets $\mathcal{W}_i$ of points connect to the i-th bone b_i are obtained as follows:

$$\mathcal{W}_i = \{(x_j, c_j) \in \mathcal{W} | i = \phi(x_j)\}, j = 1 \ldots W \quad (1)$$

where ϕ is the function returning the index of the closest bone:

$$\phi(x_j) = \arg\min_{i=1 \ldots N} d(x_j, b_i) \quad (2)$$

The pixel-to-bone distance $d(x_j, b_i)$ is the common point-to-segment Euclidean distance.

After the pixel-to-bone assignment, the signature of the person is composed by the set of color histograms computed for each bone:

$$\mathbf{H}^p = \{H_1^p, \ldots, H_N^p\}. \quad (3)$$

where H_i^p is the color histogram for the bone b_i of the p-th person. In the experiments reported in the paper, H_i^p are RGB color histograms with a 8 bin quantization for each channel, normalized to sum up to 1. If the person model is obtained as integration of multiple views, the histograms are computed using all the image points assigned to the same bone. A visual example of the pixel-to-bone assignment is reported in Figure 2(b).

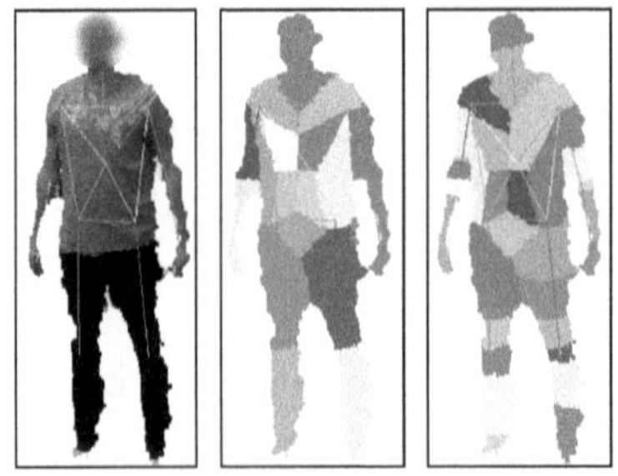

(a) (b) (c)

Figure 2: Point cloud to bone assignment. a) the skeleton, b) the point assignment using the default bone set and c) after automatic fragmentation.

4. DISTANCE METRIC

The distance between two person signatures $\mathbf{H}^i$ and $\mathbf{H}^j$ can be computed as the sum of distances between each corresponding couple of histograms:

$$d(\mathbf{H}^i, \mathbf{H}^j) = \sum_{n=1}^{N} \alpha_n \cdot d(H_n^i, H_n^j), \quad (4)$$

where $d(H_n^i, H_n^j)$ is the Mahalanobis distance between H_n^i and H_n^j. However, the distance function of Eq. 4 requires the estimation of the bones weights α_n. Moreover, the dimensionality of the signature $\mathbf{H}^p$ computed for each person as in equation Eq. 3 is too high, leading to problems on its storage and matching. Using the defined skeleton model composed by 18 bones and using 512 bins for each histogram, the final signature is composed by 9216 elements. Each signature is thus processed with a PCA step, which simultaneously reduce the dimensionality and filter the intrinsic noise. The person signature obtained from $\mathbf{H}^p$ becomes a 96 dimensional feature vector $x_p = x(\mathbf{H}^p)$. The PCA subspace has been learned on the training set and it is kept fixed for all the experiments, in order to obtain comparable signatures.

Instead of using Eq. 4, the metric scheme we adopted to compare person signatures is inspired from the one presented in [7], called Relaxed Pairwise Metric Learning (RPML), that has proved to be a highly efficient and effective metric learning approach. RPML aims at computing a pseudo-metric M, which, similarly to the Mahalanobis distance, provides a dissimilarity score of two feature vectors x_i and x_j:

$$\begin{aligned} d_M(\mathbf{H}^i, \mathbf{H}^j) &\doteq d_M(x_i, x_j) \\ &= (x_i - x_j)^\top M (x_i - x_j) = \\ &= \| L(x_i - x_j) \|^2 \end{aligned} \quad (5)$$

where $M = L^\top L$.

In order to exploit the discriminative information of the data during the metric learning, the person re-identification problem is redefined as a two-class problem: firstly, samples from the data space are converted to the label agnostic difference space. Secondly, the original class labels are discarded and the sample are rearranged into the *similar* and *different* classes $\mathcal{S}$ and $\mathcal{D}$ (i.e., if two signatures belong to the same person, their difference is labeled as $\mathcal{S}$, otherwise as $\mathcal{D}$).

Starting from the following objective function:

$$\mathcal{L}(L) = \frac{1}{|\mathcal{S}|}\sum_{(i,j)\in\mathcal{S}}||L(x_i - x_j)||^2 - \frac{1}{|\mathcal{D}|}\sum_{(i,j)\in\mathcal{D}}||L(x_i - x_j)||^2 \quad (6)$$

the problem of finding the best M can then be defined as

$$\begin{aligned} \arg\min \quad & \mathcal{L}(M) \\ \text{subject to} \quad & M \succeq 0, \\ & L\Sigma_S L^\top = L\Sigma_D L^\top = I \end{aligned} \quad (7)$$

where

$$\mathcal{L}(M) = tr(M(\Sigma_S - \Sigma_D)) \quad (8)$$

and

$$\Sigma_S = \frac{1}{|\mathcal{S}|}\sum_{(i,j)\in\mathcal{S}} (x_i - x_j)(x_i - x_j)^\top \quad (9)$$

$$\Sigma_D = \frac{1}{|\mathcal{D}|}\sum_{(i,j)\in\mathcal{D}} (x_i - x_j)(x_i - x_j)^\top \quad (10)$$

By relaxing the positivity constraint $M \succeq 0$, the problem can be simplified into finding M such that

$$tr(M(\Sigma_S - \Sigma_D)) = 0 \quad (11)$$

A bounded approximation for M ca be found as $M = (\Sigma_S{}^{-1} - \Sigma_D{}^{-1})$.

5. AUTOMATIC BONE FRAGMENTATION

The bone set $\mathcal{B}$ defined using the fifteen joints from OpenNi is not optimized for people re-identification. The main drawbacks are related to the different lengths of the bones and the semantic differences between bones and appearance regions. To this aim, an automatic bone fragmentation step has been introduced in order to generate a set of bones $\mathcal{B}^*$ more suitable for re-identification tasks. Our goal is to find the skeleton partitioning which maximizes the re-identification score (see Section 6). The size of the corresponding search space is too high for an exhaustive global maximum selection. An iterative procedure inspired to the Cuckoo search approach [14] has been implemented.

The set $\mathcal{B}^*$ is iteratively derived from $\mathcal{B}$ replacing one of the existing bones with the couple of sub-bones obtained after a split. A split $S = (b_i, \alpha)$ is represented by the index of the selected bone b_i and the split position $\alpha \in [0, 1]$. At each iteration, a set of candidates $\{S^k\}$ is randomly generated by selecting both the bone index and the split point α using a fast uniform distributed generator. The best split is then selected maximizing the re-identification score on a training set of samples. The iterative algorithm is stopped when the re-identification performance are not increased by adding an additional split. The final bone set created using our training set and the corresponding pixel-to-bone assignment are depicted in Figure 2(c) and is composed by 38 elements.

6. EXPERIMENTAL EVALUATION

In order to evaluate the proposed method we created a new dataset using Microsoft Kinect to extract depth information and relative point cloud. The dataset contains various images of 40 people in different poses and orientations, for a total of 450 shots and relative skeleton and point clouds. Half of the images were used for metric learning and as training set for the bone fragmentation learning, while the remaining 225 shots as testing. Some sample images from the dataset are reported in Figure 3.

Figure 3: Sample images and corresponding point clouds with the estimated skeletons from the Kinect dataset

As well-established in re-identification and recognition tasks, for each testing item we ranked the training gallery elements using the distance metric defined in the previous sections. The summarized performance results are reported using the the Cumulative Matching Characteristic (CMC) curve [6]. In order to evaluate the contribution of the bone fragmentation algorithm described in Section 5 and the metric learning defined in Section 4 we firstly performed an internal comparison. The results obtained using the base system (i.e., using the OpenNi bone set and the distance function of Eq. 4 with uniform weights) and with the integration of the two learning steps are reported in Figure 5(a). The curves have been obtained averaging 50 experiments with different training and the testing sets (randomly selected). As highlighted by the graph, the learned metric strongly improves the re-identification performance.

We also compared our method with two state of the art algorithms, namely SDALF [5] and Sarc3D [1]. SDALF is a purely two dimensional method. It consists in the extraction of features that model three complementary aspects of the human appearance: the overall chromatic content (using weighted HSV histograms), the spatial arrangement of colors into stable regions (Maximally Stable Color Regions), and the presence of recurrent local motifs with high entropy. All these features are derived from different body parts, and opportunely weighted by exploiting symmetry and asymmetry perceptual principles (each appearance image is segmented into legs/torso/head using simple heuristics). The online code has been adopted and applied to the RGB images after the removal of the background by means of the depth stream. Sarc3D, instead, is a 3D method based on a non-articulated model. HSV histograms are extracted from patches of the foreground appearance image projected on a 3D surface. The tests have been carried out using our re-implementation of the method, exploiting the vertex model available online. The head and feet positions from the skeleton stream have been adopted as reference to align the model on the images. Results of the three methods are reported in Figure 5(b). The proposed method outperforms both the Sarc3D and the SDALF approaches. It requires an off-line training in order to learn the metric (which takes on average 4 seconds) and the best splits of the skeleton (195 minutes on average). The creation of a person model requires less than 10 ms (9.74ms for the computation of the point cloud by OpenNi and 0.47ms for the computation of the histograms), the matching score computation takes on average 2.11ms. All tests were performed on an Intel Core i5 running at 2.66 GHz. Some sample results of the three methods on the new dataset are shown in Figure 4, as can be seen our method is much more resilient to pose changes, unlike SDALF and Sarc3D which assume people in a vertical standing position.

7. CONCLUSIONS

We proposed a new and effective solution for the re-identification of people. Differently from currently available proposals, we exploited an articulated 3D body model to spatially localize the identifying patterns and colors on virtual bones. The articulated body model allows to create a invariant signature for each mon-

Figure 4: Sample results ot the three tested methods on our dataset

itored person despite postures and view-points. Two learning algorithms have been introduced to create an optimized bone set for re-identification purposes and a specific metric learning, respectively. Experimental results on a Microsoft Kinect dataset prove the improvement obtained using articulated models instead of fixed containers (e.g., Sarc3D [1]) or 2D body models (e.g., SDALF [5]).

8. REFERENCES

[1] D. Baltieri, R. Vezzani, and R. Cucchiara. Sarc3d: a new 3d body model for people tracking and re-identification. In *Proc. of IEEE Int. Conf. on Image Analysis and Processing*, pages 197–206, Ravenna, Italy, Sept. 2011.

[2] I. B. Barbosa, M. Cristani, A. D. Bue, L. Bazzani, and V. Murino. Re-identification with rgb-d sensors. In *ECCV Workshops (1)*, volume 7583 of *LNCS*, pages 433–442. Springer, 2012.

[3] N. Bird, O. Masoud, N. Papanikolopoulos, and A. Isaacs. Detection of Loitering Individuals in Public Transportation Areas. *IEEE Trans. on Intelligent Transportation Systems*, 6(2):167–177, June 2005.

[4] G. Doretto, T. Sebastian, P. H. Tu, and J. Rittscher. Appearance-based person reidentification in camera networks: problem overview and current approaches. *J. Ambient Intelligence and Humanized Computing*, 2(2):127–151, 2011.

[5] M. Farenzena, L. Bazzani, A. Perina, V. Murino, and M. Cristani. Person re-identification by symmetry-driven accumulation of local features. In *Proc. of CVPR*, pages 2360–2367, June 2010.

[6] D. Gray, S. Brennan, and H. Tao. Evaluating Appearance Models for Recognition, Reacquisition, and Tracking. In *Proc. of 10th IEEE Int. Workshop on PETS*, 2007.

[7] M. Hirzer, P. Roth, M. KÃűstinger, and H. Bischof. Relaxed pairwise learned metric for person re-identification. In *ECCV 2012*, volume 7577 of *LNCS*, pages 780–793. Springer Berlin Heidelberg, 2012.

[8] R. Layne, T. M. Hospedales, and S. Gong. Towards person identification and re-identification with attributes. In *ECCV Workshops (1)*, volume 7583 of *LNCS*, pages 402–412. Springer, 2012.

[9] G. Pons-Moll, L. Leal-Taixé, T. Truong, and B. Rosenhahn. Efficient and robust shape matching for model based human motion capture. In *Proc. of ICPR*, DAGM'11, pages 416–425, Berlin, Heidelberg, 2011. Springer-Verlag.

[10] M. Salzmann and R. Urtasun. Combining discriminative and generative methods for 3d deformable surface and articulated pose reconstruction. In *Proc. of CVPR*, pages 647 –654, june 2010.

[11] J. Shotton, A. Fitzgibbon, M. Cook, T. Sharp, M. Finocchio, R. Moore, A. Kipman, and A. Blake. Real-time human pose recognition in parts from single depth images. In *Proc. of CVPR*, pages 1297 –1304, june 2011.

[12] J. Taylor, J. Shotton, T. Sharp, and A. W. Fitzgibbon. The vitruvian manifold: Inferring dense correspondences for one-shot human pose estimation. In *Proc. of CVPR*, pages 103–110, 2012.

[13] M. Weber, M. BÃd'uml, and R. Stiefelhagen. Part-based Clothing Segmentation for Person Retrieval. In *IEEE International Conference on Advanced Video and Signal-Based Surveillance (AVSS)*, page 6, Aug. 2011.

[14] X.-S. Yang and S. Deb. Engineering optimisation by cuckoo search. *Int. J. Mathematical Modelling and Numerical Optimisation*, 1:330–343, 2010.

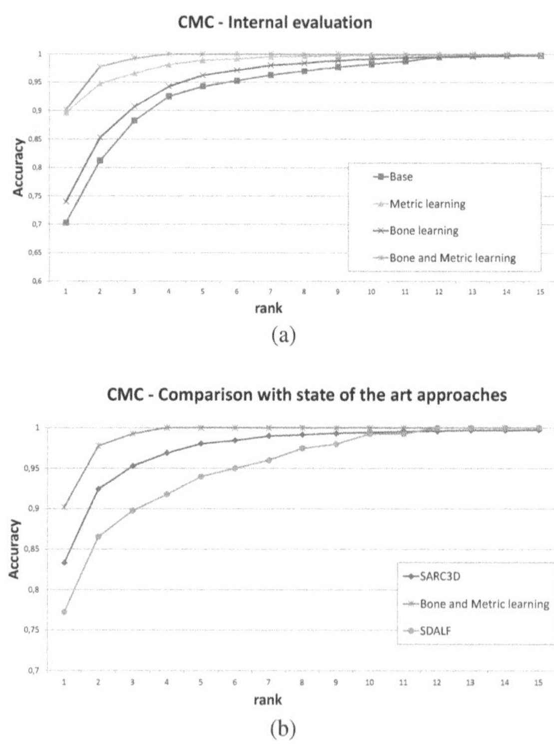

Figure 5: CMC of the method on the Kinect dataset, showing a) the contribution of the metric and bone fragmentation learning and b) the improvement on two state of the art techniques

Facial Landmark Localization based on Hierarchical Pose Regression with Cascaded Random Ferns

Zhanpeng Zhang[1,2] Wei Zhang[1] Jianzhuang Liu[1,2,3] Xiaoou Tang[1,2]
[1]Shenzhen Key Lab of Computer Vision and Pattern Recognition,
Shenzhen Institutes of Advanced Technology, Chinese Academy of Sciences, China
[2]Department of Information Engineering, The Chinese University of Hong Kong, China
[3]Media Lab, Huawei Technologies Co. Ltd., China
{zp.zhang, zhangwei}@siat.ac.cn, liu.jianzhuang@huawei.com, xtang@ie.cuhk.edu.hk

ABSTRACT

The main challenge of facial landmark localization in real-world application is that the large changes of head pose and facial expressions cause substantial image appearance variations. To avoid high dimensional regression in the 3D and 2D facial pose spaces simultaneously, we propose a hierarchical pose regression approach, estimating the head rotation, facial components and landmarks hierarchically. The regression process works in a unified cascaded fern framework. We present generalized gradient boosted ferns (GBFs) for the regression framework, which give better performance than traditional ferns. The framework also achieves real time performance. We verify our method on the latest benchmark datasets. The results show that it outperforms state-of-the-art methods in both accuracy and speed.

Categories and Subject Descriptors

I.4.9 [**Image Processing and Computer Vision**]: Applications

Keywords

facial landmark localization; pose regression; random fern

1. INTRODUCTION

Facial landmark localization is a key step in many human-computer interaction systems. Many recent algorithms locate facial landmarks by optimization or regression. Optimization based approaches, such as AAM [3], usually solve this problem by fitting a parametric model to the input face. Specifically, AAM contains the statistical information of the shape and texture of the faces in the training set. The algorithm finds the model parameters which minimize the difference between the input face and synthesized model, based on gradient descent optimization. But these approaches have difficulty with generalization and may not work well on unseen instances. Meanwhile, the optimization process may fall into local optimal. Differently, regression based approaches aim to learn the mapping between the image appearance and the targets [4, 2]. Due to the high computational efficiency, random fern regression has been used in this area recently. In [5], a cascaded fern approach is proposed for 2D pose regression. Also, [2] employs cascaded ferns for face alignment. In both cases, each fern needs pose-indexed features which satisfy a weak invariant assumption [5]. These features are ideal for 2D pose estimation with 2D data in an image. However, when dealing with 3D pose, we cannot define such features. So the performance of these approaches may drop when dealing with faces with large rotations. Meanwhile, computing the pose-indexed feature in every cascaded fern adds additional cost.

To overcome these problems, we propose a unified cascaded fern regression framework to locate the facial landmarks. Usually, a fern is fed with pixel-comparison-based features. In this paper, we generalize the use of ferns by employing patch-comparison-based features, to increase the discriminative power of our regression framework. Besides, the algorithms works in a hierarchical way. Fig. 1 shows the overview of our approach. There are three levels in the hierarchical pose regression: the head rotation, face components, and facial landmarks. For simplicity, we often refer the parameters of these three levels together as facial pose. In each level, we estimate the pose using generalized Gradient Boosted Ferns (GBFs). Specifically, with the head rotation estimated in the top level, we obtain the conditional probability over the whole view space. Then we estimate the rest pose parameters with the view-based GBFs in level 2 and level 3. The motivation for our hierarchical structure is that joint regression in the entire pose space is too difficult. We can reduce the image appearance variations in each level gradually. Meanwhile, reducing the regression dimension also makes the learning process easier.

In the experiments, we evaluate the performance of our approach with the latest challenging datasets [4, 11], which contain outdoor faces with various pose, expression, and illumination. The experiments show that our approach generates high quality results with real time performance.

MM'13, October 21–25, 2013, Barcelona, Spain.

ACM 978-1-4503-2404-5/13/10 ...$15.00.
http://dx.doi.org/10.1145/2502081.2502148.

2. BOOSTED REGRESSION WITH COMPARISON-BASED FEATURES

Comparison-based features are ideal for real time applications as they can be computed very fast. Traditional random ferns work with pixel-comparison-based features, which can work well within limited target space. However, for images

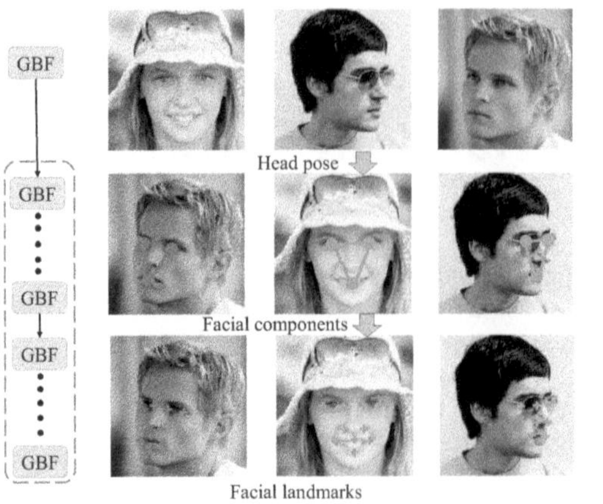

Figure 1: Overview of our hierarchical pose regression approach, which is based on a unified framework with sequential groups of generalized gradient boosted ferns (GBFs). The conditional view-based GBFs are enclosed by the red rectangle on the left.

with large appearance variations, these features are too weak and lower the convergence rate. So we extend the use of ferns and use patch-comparison-based features. These generalized ferns work with comparison-based features of different scales in different levels of our hierarchical regression.

Given input data $\{x_i \in \mathbb{R}^F\}_1^N$ in an F-dimensional feature space with the regression target $\{y_i \in \mathbb{R}^S\}_1^N$, a fern takes an input feature vector $q_i \in \mathbb{R}^M (M < F, q_i$ is a subset of $x_i)$ and outputs prediction $y_i \in \mathbb{R}^S$. It contains a threshold for each dimension of q_i, assigning every input vector to one of the 2^M bins. The M-dimensional input features and thresholds are selected randomly in the training process. The output of a bin is the mean of the predictions y of the training samples that fall into the bin.

We introduce random fern to the gradient boosting framework [8]. Our goal is to train a function $F(x)$ that maps a feature vector x to target y, while minimizing the expected value of the loss function $\Psi(y, F(x))$. $F(x)$ is the sum of weak regression functions, $F(x) = \sum_{t=1}^{T} \alpha f(q^t; \theta^t)$, where α is a learning rate. $f(q^t; \theta^t)$ is the regression function of a fern, with q^t and θ^t as the selected features and thresholds.

A greedy stage-wise approach is employed in the training process. At each stage t, we find a weak regressor $f(q^t; \theta^t)$ that maximally decreases the loss function:

$$\{q^t, \theta^t\} = \arg\min_{q,\theta} \sum_{i=1}^{N} \Psi(y_i, F_{t-1}(x_i) + f(q_i; \theta)). \quad (1)$$

A steepest descent step is then applied for the minimization problem of (1). However, it is infeasible to apply gradient descent on q and θ as a fern represents a piecewise-constant function. Instead, at each stage t, we compute the "pseudo-residuals" by $\tilde{y}_i = -\left[\frac{\partial \Psi(y_i - F(x_i))}{\partial F(x_i)}\right]_{F(x)=F_{t-1}(x)}$.

We use the least-squares for loss function $\Psi(y, F(x))$ and then $\tilde{y}_i = y_i - F_{t-1}(x_i)$. So we have

$$\{q^t, \theta^t\} = \arg\min_{q,\theta} \sum_{i=1}^{N} \|\tilde{y}_i - f(q_i; \theta)\|^2. \quad (2)$$

The pseudocode of the training process is as Algorithm 1.

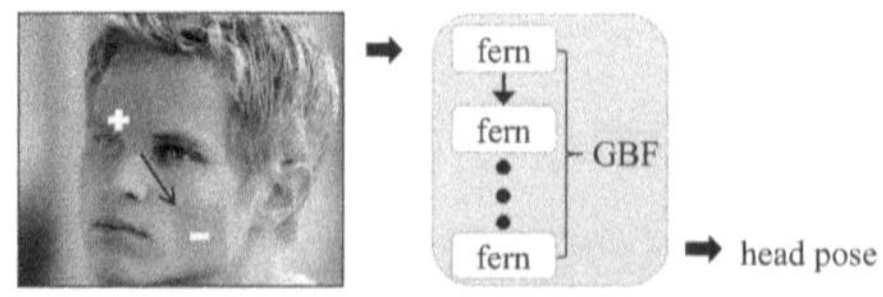

Figure 2: Patch-comparison-based features used in the GBF regression to estimate the head pose.

Algorithm 1 Gradient Boosted Fern Regression

Given the training samples $\{x_i \in \mathbb{R}^F\}_1^N$ with target values $\{y_i \in \mathbb{R}^S\}_1^N$.
$F_0(x) = \text{mean}\{y_i\}_1^N$.
for $t = 1$ to T **do**
  Randomly select a set of M-dimensional features $\{q^r\}_{r=1}^R$ from the F-dimensional input features, and a set of corresponding thresholds $\{\theta^r\}_{r=1}^R$.
  $\{q^t, \theta^t\} = \arg\min_{q^r,\theta^r} \sum_{i=1}^N \|\tilde{y}_i - f(q_i^r; \theta^r)\|^2$, where $\tilde{y}_i = y_i - F_{t-1}(x_i)$.
  $F_t(x) = F_{t-1}(x) + \alpha f(q^t; \theta^t)$
end for

3. HIERARCHICAL POSE REGRESSION

3.1 Head pose level

We estimate the 3D head rotation with a GBF. Each training sample contains a face roughly localized by a face detector and annotated with head rotation values ω. In the training process of GBF, we randomly generate a pool of simple patch-comparison-based features:

$$v(\gamma, I) = \frac{1}{|Q_1|} \sum_{p \in Q_1} I(p) - \frac{1}{|Q_2|} \sum_{p \in Q_2} I(p), \quad (3)$$

where $\gamma = \{Q_1, Q_2\}$ with Q_1 and Q_2 being the squares within the image I. This feature can be efficiently computed with integral images. After the GBF training process, we store γ, the threshold and the predictions of the bins for every fern. In testing, as there are just some comparison and look-up operations for a fern, the head pose regression can run extremely fast. The process is illustrated in Fig. 2.

With the estimated head rotation ω', we can compute the conditional probabilities over the 3D view space and estimate the 2D facial pose with conditional view-based GBFs. Here we discretize the space of ω into disjoint sets $\{\Phi_i\}$. The Gaussian Kernel is employed to estimate the distance $d(\omega', \Phi_i)$ between ω' and Φ_i, so $d(\omega', \Phi_i) = \frac{1}{2\pi\sigma^2} \exp(-\|\omega' - \omega_i\|^2/2\sigma^2)$, where ω_i is the centroid of Φ_i, and σ is the bandwidth parameter ($\sigma = 5$ in implementation). To estimate the 2D facial pose u, we have

$$u = \sum_{\Omega_i} u(i) P(\omega'|\Omega_i) = \sum_{\Omega_i} u(i) \frac{d(\omega', \Phi_i)}{\Sigma_{\Omega_i} d(\omega', \Phi_i)}, \quad (4)$$

where $u(i)$ is the 2D pose estimated by the GBFs in the Φ_i view space. The estimation algorithm is presented in Sections 3.2 and 3.3.

3.2 Facial component level

The 2D facial pose is estimated in view-based model. Here we further sperate the pose into the component level and landmark level (i.e., $u = \{u_c, u_l\}$), to reduce the regression difficulty. Then we solve this problem with our hierarchical

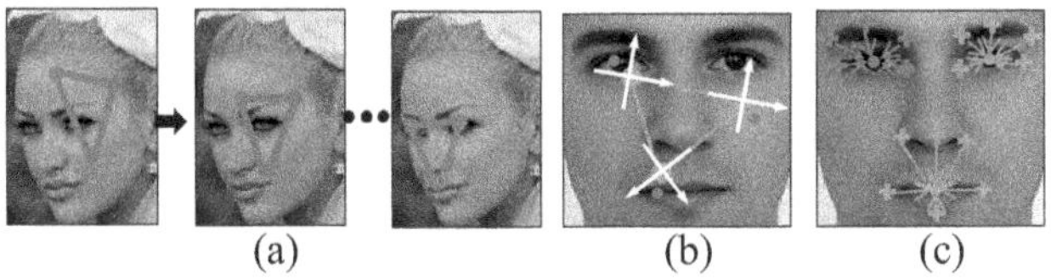

Figure 3: (a) Cascaded GBF regression. (b) Red pixel pairs indexed by the homogeneous coordinates (white crosses) of current estimated components. (c) A hierarchical configuration for the facial components and landmarks. A landmark (the cross) is described by a displacement vector (the arrow) from it to its parent component.

approach. The regression process firstly works on a component level, estimating the locations of facial parts (e.g., eyes, nose, mouth).

We use cascaded GBFs $(G^1, G^2, ..., G^K)$ in this level. Given the input image I and initial pose u_c^0, each GBF estimates the pose increment Δu_c and update the pose, as shown in Fig. 3(a). For each GBF, the features are related to the image I and the current pose (called *pose-indexed features* [5]). So we have

$$u_c^k = u_c^{k-1} + G^k(I, u_c^{k-1}),\ k = 1, 2, ...K. \quad (5)$$

Given an object, the value of pose-indexed features should only depends on the difference between the input pose and the ground truth pose. Here, for the pose-indexed feature, we simply use the intensity difference of two pixels, which are indexed by pose, not the image coordinates. Such feature is extremely easy to compute. We can define an associated homography matrix for each facial component and express the pixel in the homogeneous coordinates, as illustrated in Fig. 3(b). We use a hierarchical structure to manage the components. The rotation of the homography matrix is defined by the displacement between the child and parent components.

We take a greedy approach to train the cascaded GBFs sequentially. Firstly, we take the mean pose of the training samples as the initial pose. In every stage, we randomly generate a pool of pose-indexed features, and then train a GBF as Algorithm 1, which minimizes the current residual. Afterwards, current poses are updated by this GBF. The training process stops if it reaches the maximum stage or the residual is unable to reduce.

3.3 Facial landmark level

Cascaded GBFs are also used in this stage. A hierarchical configuration for the facial components and landmarks is defined, as illustrated in Fig. 3(c). We assign a parent component to each landmark based on the spatial distribution. A landmark is described by a displacement vector from it to its parent component, so we need to estimate the displacement via the cascaded GBF regression.

The training process for the cascaded GBFs in this level is similar to that of the upper one. The only difference is that the pose-indexed features are sampled within a smaller area. This is to reduce the effect of nonrigid deformation and to capture features in a more detailed level.

For the initial pose in testing, we use the the mean displacement vectors in the training samples, and the facial component locations estimated by the upper level as constraints. The test instances go through the cascaded GBFs and we obtain the 2D facial pose $u(i)$ in a view space Φ_i. Then the final locations for the landmarks are computed by Equation (4).

Table 1: Mean and standard deviation of the errors for the 3D head rotation estimation.

Method	GBF	SVR
Pitch error	$8.60° \pm 8.56°$	$14.96° \pm 11.34°$
Yaw error	$6.77° \pm 6.69°$	$10.05° \pm 7.99°$
Roll error	$4.75° \pm 5.68°$	$6.89° \pm 6.87°$

4. EXPERIMENTS AND EVALUATIONS

4.1 Head pose regression

We use the Biwi Kinect Head Pose Database [7] to verify the head pose regression. The head rotation range in the database is between $\pm 75°$ for yaw, $\pm 60°$ for pitch, and $\pm 50°$ for roll. We roughly crop the faces in RGB images and then rescale them to 150×150 pixels for our experiment.

The main parameters of a GBF are the numbers T of stages, the dimension F of features generated for training, the fern depth M, learning rate α and the R feature subsets from which we select the best in each stage. Here we set $T = 5000, F = 10000, M = 5, \alpha = 0.05$ and $R = 20$.

Estimation accuracy. We perform a 4-fold cross validation on the dataset and compare the GBF regression with the support vector regression (SVR), which is a popular technique for head pose regression [1]. In the experiment, SVR is fed with the same features as GBF. The results in Table 1 show that the GBF regression outperforms SVR.

Running time performance. The GBF regression runs on an Intel Pentium 3.2GHz CPU with C++ implementation. It is extremely fast, taking only 0.55ms for an image.

4.2 2D facial pose regression

The dataset published most recently in [4] is used to verify the proposed algorithm. It contains 13,233 faces taken from the LFW database [9]. Different from earlier datasets like [10], this dataset contains outdoor faces with large variations in pose and illumination. The faces in this dataset are annotated with the locations of 10 facial landmarks (like the ones in Fig. 5a). As our algorithm also needs the locations of eyes and mouth for the facial component level, the eyes' locations are set as the mean of the eyes' corners, and the mouth location as the mean of the mouth's corners. We crop the faces with a face detection algorithm and then rescale the images to 150×150 pixels. The faces in this dataset are split into 5 subsets manually, based on the yaw angle of the head. We use this information for head pose regression by labeling them with real world angles $\omega \in \{-60, -30, 0, 30, 60\}$.

For the head pose regression, we use the same parameters as Section 4.1. As for the 2D facial pose regression, we use 20 GBFs in both level 2 and level 3. In each GBF, we set $T = 500, F = 256, M = 5$, and $R = 5$. Five view-based-GBF models are trained according to the yaw angles.

We perform a 10-fold cross validation on the dataset. Similar to most previous works, the localization error is normalized by inter-ocular distance. Table 2 presents the results of our method and two state-of-the-art ones [6, 4], showing that our method outperforms both methods at most of the landmarks. Besides, our method is much faster than the two competitors. The method in [6] cannot achieve real time performance and the method in [4] is reported to consume about 100ms for the accuracy listed in Table 2, while ours takes only about 30ms on a similar desktop computer.

Table 2: **Mean errors ($\times 10^{-2}$) of the landmark localization by three methods.**

Method	[6]	[4]	Ours
left eye left	16.21	6.82	5.78
left eye right	10.70	5.65	5.32
right eye left	9.37	5.67	5.40
right eye right	11.16	7.36	5.75
mouth left	10.76	7.38	7.13
mouth right	15.14	7.80	7.30
nose strip left	10.85	5.92	6.69
nose strip right	12.08	7.05	6.71
upper outer lip	-	6.40	6.69
lower outer lip	-	9.53	8.52

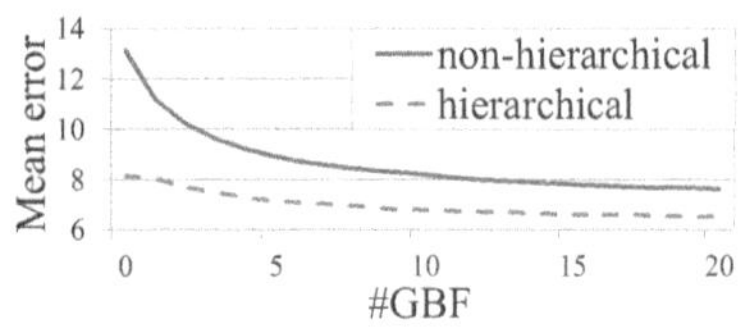

Figure 4: Convergence of the localization errors ($\times 10^{-2}$) by hierarchical and non-hierarchical approaches.

To further demonstrate the effectiveness of the proposed hierarchical approach, we compare it with non-hierarchical pose regression, which skips the first 2 levels and estimate the landmarks directly. The mean errors of the two approaches in the facial landmark level are shown in Fig. 4. For the hierarchical approach, the initial error is much less and we obtain better results. Fig. 4 also demonstrates the convergence of the algorithm. The mean errors decrease gradually, converge with around 20 GBFs and does not overfit. It shows that we do not need to carefully tune the number of GBF for the algorithm.

Fig. 5 presents some results of our algorithm on the test images and AFLW dataset [11]. It shows that the algorithm can deal with appearance variations caused by head rotations, facial expressions and partial occlusions.

5. CONCLUSIONS

In this paper, we split the facial pose into three different levels and propose a real time hierarchical pose regression approach for facial landmark localization. The experiments show that the algorithm runs faster and obtains higher accuracy than the state-of-the-art algorithms. Besides, we propose a unified cascaded fern regression framework based on generalized gradient boosted ferns. The discriminative power, computation efficiency and convergence are demonstrated in the tests.

6. ACKNOWLEDGEMENTS

This work was supported by grants from Natural Science Foundation of China (61201443, 61070148), Science, Industry, Trade, and Information Technology Commission of Shenzhen Municipality, China (JC201005270378A), and Guangdong Innovative Research Team Program (No. 201001 D0104648280).

7. REFERENCES

[1] C. BenAbdelkader. Robust head pose estimation using supervised manifold learning. In *ECCV*, 2010.

Figure 5: Some results on the LFW(a) and AFLW(b) dataset.

[2] X. Cao, Y. Wei, F. Wen, and J. Sun. Face alignment by explicit shape regression. In *CVPR*, 2012.

[3] T. Cootes, G. Edwards, and C. Taylor. Active appearance models. *IEEE TPAMI*, 23(6):681–685, 2001.

[4] M. Dantone, J. Gall, G. Fanelli, and L. Van Gool. Real-time facial feature detection using conditional regression forests. In *CVPR*, 2012.

[5] P. Dollar, P. Welinder, and P. Perona. Cascaded pose regression. In *CVPR*, 2010.

[6] M. Everingham, J. Sivic, and A. Zisserman. Hello! my name is... buffy-automatic naming of characters in tv video. In *BMVC*, 2006.

[7] G. Fanelli, M. Dantone, J. Gall, A. Fossati, and L. Gool. Random forests for real time 3d face analysis. *IJCV*, 101:437–458, 2013.

[8] J. H. Friedman. Greedy function approximation: A gradient boosting machine. *Annals of Statistics*, 29:1189–1232, 2000.

[9] G. B. Huang, M. Ramesh, T. Berg, and E. Learned-Miller. Labeled faces in the wild: A database for studying face recognition in unconstrained environments. Technical Report 07-49, University of Massachusetts, Amherst, 2007.

[10] O. Jesorsky, K. J. Kirchberg, and R. Frischholz. Robust face detection using the hausdorff distance. In *the Third International Conference on Audio- and Video-Based Biometric Person Authentication*, 2001.

[11] M. Kostinger, P. Wohlhart, P. Roth, and H. Bischof. Annotated facial landmarks in the wild: A large-scale, real-world database for facial landmark localization. In *ICCV Workshops*, 2011.

Image Context Discovery from Socially Curated Contents

Akisato Kimura*, Katsuhiko Ishiguro, Makoto Yamada
Communication Science Labs, NTT Corporation
Keihanna Science City, Japan

Alejandro Marcos Alvarez†
Systems and Modeling Research Unit, University of Liege, Liege, Belgium

Kaori Kataoka, Kazuhiko Murasaki
Media Inteligence Labs, NTT Corporation
Yokosuka, Kanagawa, Japan

ABSTRACT

This paper proposes a novel method of discovering a set of image *contents* sharing a specific *context* (attributes or implicit meaning) with the help of image collections obtained from social curation platforms. Socially curated contents are promising to analyze various kinds of multimedia information, since they are manually filtered and organized based on specific individual preferences, interests or perspectives. Our proposed method fully exploits the process of social curation: (1) How image contents are manually grouped together by users, and (2) how image contents are distributed in the platform. Our method reveals the fact that image contents with a specific context are naturally grouped together and every image content includes really various contexts that cannot necessarily be verbalized by texts.

Categories and Subject Descriptors

J.3.1 [**Human-centered computing**]: Collaborative and social computing—*Collaborative and social computing theory, concept and paradigms*

Keywords

Social curation, contexts, graph clustering, classification

1. INTRODUCTION

One of the ultimate goals in the field of computer vision and pattern recognition is to learn the structure of our visual world with the help of large amount of real data such as images, videos and texts. This problem is known to be challenging but fundamentally important. High performance comparable with humans seems to be extremely difficult to achieve due to variations in appearances, especially when dealing with contexts that are often difficult to verbalize.

*The corresponding author. E-mail: akisato@ieee.org

†He contributed to this work during his internship at NTT CS Labs.

MM'13, October 21–25, 2013, Barcelona, Spain.

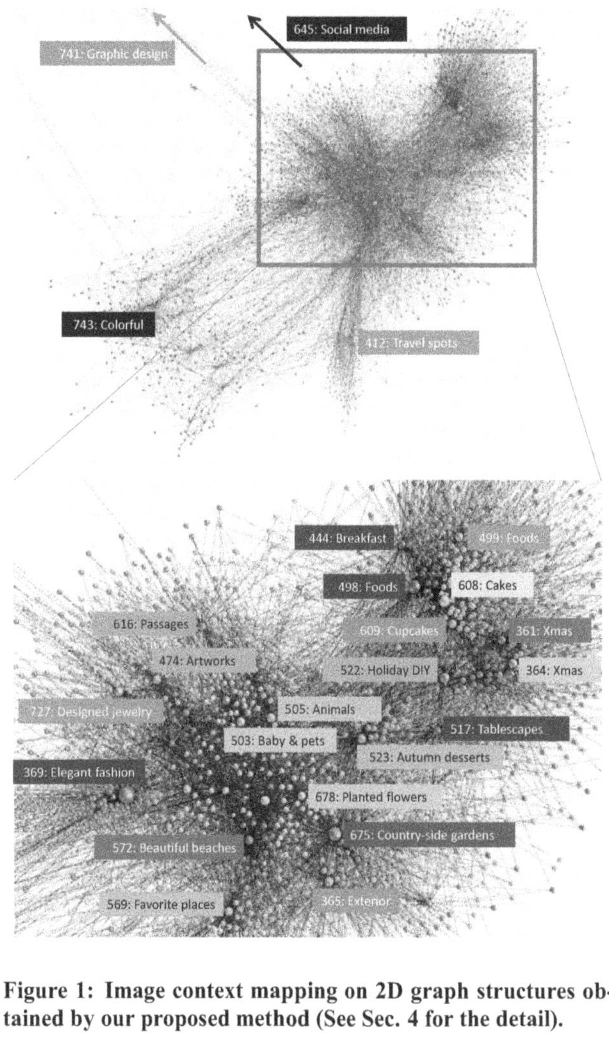

Figure 1: Image context mapping on 2D graph structures obtained by our proposed method (See Sec. 4 for the detail).

This background would direct researchers to the use of social network services (SNSs) as a promising resource, since they contain huge amount of side information useful for understanding contexts of image contents. Such side information includes user profiles, geo locations and user networks. The major interest of the current SNS developers and users are rapidly shifting from conventional text-based (micro)blogs such as Twitter and Facebook to multimedia contents such as Flickr, Snapchat, MySpace and Tumblr. However, the ability to analyze and exploit these unorganized multimedia data still remain inadequate, even with state-of-the-art media processing techniques.

This paper focuses on another emerging trend called *social curation*, a human-in-the-loop alternative to automatic algorithms for social media analysis [15]. Social curation can be defined as a spontaneous human process of remixing social media contents for the purpose of further consumption. What characterizes social curation is definitely the *manual efforts* involved in organizing social media contents, which indicates that curated contents are information sources potentially richer than automatic summaries generated by algorithms. Also, curated contents would provide latent perspectives and contexts that are not explicitly presented in the original resources. Following this trend, several studies have tried to examine and exploit social curation data [7, 9].

The main claim in this paper is that social curation data has a great potential as corpora to discover, visualize and retrieve contexts of image contents. In particular, this paper focuses on Pinterest, one of the most emerging social curation platforms dealing with image contentsPinterest has favorable and unique characteristics for mining image contexts.

(1) Focused contexts: There are so many groups (called *"boards"* in Pinterest) of image contents that are all manually collected, selected and maintained, so that board contributors and consumers can easily and quickly find images they want [10]. Therefore, most of the images on a specific board share the same context board contributors keep in mind.

(2) Content-centric networks: Contents and boards form networks in Pinterest, whereas users and user groups are the basis in conventional SNSs. Users may have several boards, follow boards of other users, collect contents from these following boards, and put them on their own boards. As a result, contents are distributed from boards to boards, which constitutes a diffusion network. This is very different from other SNSs that constitute user-centric networks in nature.

The above two characteristics readily imply that two boards sharing a lot of image contents often share some specific context. Our method makes the full use of this insight, which enables us to reveal various kinds of contexts engraved in every image content. When doing this, content diffusion takes an important role: Groups of boards sharing specific contexts can be discovered from content diffusion as shown in Figure 1, even though we know nothing about visual contents of images (See Sec. 4 in detail). With the additional use of image content information, we can further augment the benefits to unseen images, which enables us to visualize image contexts more clearly and to build a simple context-aware image-to-image retrieval [12].

2. RELATED WORK

Finding and understanding image contexts is quite a difficult task since it has not been well formulated yet, although several stimulating attempts have been executed so far (collaborative filtering with graphical models [5, 6], indexing representative images [19] and predicting importance of images [3]).

Meanwhile, image content analysis powered by social network information has become a hot topic in recent years, since a huge amount of side information such as associated texts, geo-tags and underlying user networks is freely available. A typical resource for this purpose is Flickr, the most famous image sharing platform. Images taken from Flickr have been broadly utilized in various researches such as preference recommendation [22, 18], community detection [13] and learning to rank for images [17]. In particular, Qi et al. [14] presented a method of embedding both content similarities and content-tag links in SNSs. Recently, other types of

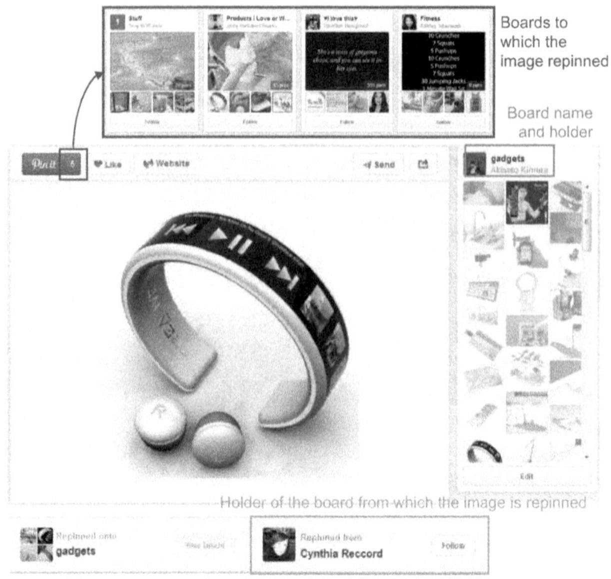

Figure 2: Example of pinned image (See http://pinterest.com/pin/221662231390591260/).

SNSs have also been utilized for content recommendation with the help of content diffusion [1] and image annotation [20].

Our major contribution against the above researches is to focus on the utilization of social curation data for image context discovery, rather than usual social networks.

Social curation services have grown in popularity in recent years [15], however, few academic researches have been performed so far (see [11]). Hall and Zarro [8, 21] investigated the potential of Pinterest as a social curation platform from a sociological aspect. Duh et al. [7] first analyzed several characteristics of data collections taken from social curation services. Ishiguro et al. [9] estimated view counts of image contents as an indicator of their interestingness with the help of socially curated collections of microblogs.

To the best of our knowledge, our work is the first trial to explore image contexts from social curation data.

3. DEPICTING CONTENT DIFFUSION

3.1 Corpus Analysis

First we briefly describe the structure of Pinterest. An example of a pinned image is depicted in Figure 2. Every user has several boards and can *"pin"* (verb, meaning link and publish) an image to a specific *"board"* (a group of pinned images). Two major ways to pin an image are served in Pinterest: (1) Pin an image, namely upload a link to the image and publish it on her own board, and (2) *"repin"* an image, namely create a new link to an existing pin to her own board, quite similar to a retweet in Twitter. Typical users try to associate every board to a specific context comprising objects, scenes, feelings, events etc., so that they and their followers can easily find images they want [10]. The process of pinning shown above is indeed a sort of social curation.

We collected pinned images from Pinterest. The list of collected pins can be seen in the supplemental material (pinIdList.txt). The number of pins is 1063832, including 142385 original pins and 921447 repins, the number of unique images is 776860, and the total number of boards is 188818. As shown in Figure 2, every pin contains several useful information, such as (1) the pinned board

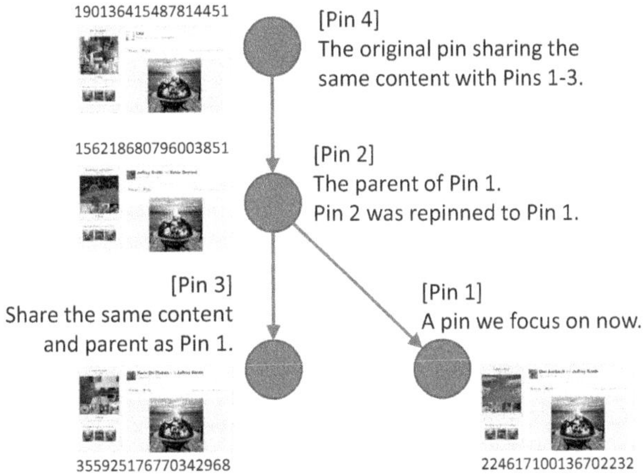

Figure 3: A simple example of pin diffusion graph

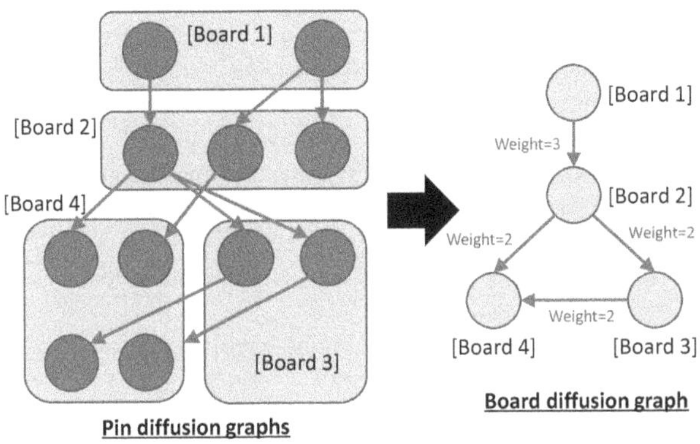

Figure 4: A simple example of board diffusion graph

name (red), (2) the board name and holder from which the image is repinned (blue), the original pinner and pinned board (green), and (4) the name of boards to which the pin is repinned (purple).

3.2 Building a Board Diffusion Network

This section describes a procedure for building image content diffusion graphs from the collected data. We illustrate one simple example in Figures 3 and 4. This structure takes an important role in revealing image contexts.

Let us focus on Pin 1 shown in Figure 3. From the collected data, Pin 2 can be identified as the parent of (the pin that was repinned to) Pin 1. Here, we create two nodes (pin nodes) of Pins 1 & 2 and one directed edge (a pin edge) from Pin 2 to Pin 1. The pin edge represents a route of content diffusion. In a similar manner, the route of diffusion related to Pin 1 can be identified. This results in yielding a tree-structured directed graph as shown in Figure 3, which we call a *pin diffusion graph*. Investigating all the pins in this way, a lot of pin diffusion graphs can be obtained.

Note that every board can be expressed as a disjoint set of pins. Thus, an induced graph can be created from those pin diffusion graphs by integrating all the pin nodes in the same board into a new single node (a board node), as shown in Figure 4. Through this procedure, pin edges are also integrated into a new single edge (a board edge) with weight the same as the number of pin edges. We call this induced graph a *board diffusion graph*.

Table 1: Board names in major 10 clusters

1	christmas-cookies-and-desserts, cooooookies, natural-christmas, salads-salads, recipes, christmas-cuisine
2	holidays-christmas-decor-new-year, christmas-joy, cards-and-printables, vintage-illustrations, crafting-christmas
3	christmas-trees, christmas-decor, interior-exterior-design, holiday-seasonal-decorating-ideas, white-christmas
4	favorite-crafts, gift-wrap, christmas-ideas, gifts-to-go, christmas-quilts-crafts, snowmen-and-santa-claus
5	fashion-style, leggings-tights-and-socks, red-black, colored-redwinesspectrum, the-clothes-i-wish-i-owned
6	dresses-let-s-play-dress-up, classy-and-elegant, gorgeous-fashion, fall-winder-2012-trends, 2012-2013-high-fashion
7	silver-black-glitter-sparkles, sparkle-and-shine, silver-chrome-and-shine, bling, my-imaginary-closet
8	book-covers, just-kids-other-books, covers-we-love, book-cover-inspirations, judge-books-by-their-covers
9	type-i-like, packaging-and-identity, logos-and-icons, magazines, packaging, books-worth-reading, typography
10	preschool, homeschool-ideas, auntie-jenna-s-board-of-kid-crafts, creative-spaces, fun-for-kids, toy-lust-wish-list

We created a board diffusion graph from the collection and derive a 2-D node allocation with a standard spring model for visualization. The number of board nodes is 188818, and the number of board edges is 319591. The obtained graph with GML format can be seen in the supplemental material (boardDiffusionGraph.gml).

4. DISCOVERING IMAGE CONTEXTS

Once a board diffusion graph is obtained, groups of image contents sharing a specific context can be discovered without any help of image content information. Let us remember that boards sharing a lot of pinned image contents would share some specific context, as described in Sec. 1. From this viewpoint, finding board groups sharing similar contexts can be formulated by a problem of finding an optimal set of clusters that maximizes modularity. We adopt Louvain method [4, 16], one of the standard and scalable techniques for modularity-based graph clustering. However, its direct application to a board diffusion graph often yields several huge clusters due to the nature of board diffusion graphs, which makes it difficult to analyze the results. To mitigate the problem, our method performs adaptive hierarchical clustering: clusters with a number of nodes larger than a threshold are separated again into sub-clusters. This produces clusters with moderate sizes.

A part of the clustering result is shown in Table 1 that contains major 10 clusters and several board names as their members. The entire clustering result can be seen in the supplemental material (clusteringResultsHierarchical.csv). The result indicates that board names of every cluster implicitly describe a specific context of the cluster. It also indicates that hierarchical clustering effectively produces a layered structure of contexts. For example, abstract contexts related to Christmas (clusters 1-4) are separated into more specific contexts such as Christmas dinners (cluster 1), decorations (cluster 2), Christmas trees (cluster 3) and gifts (cluster 4).

A visualization of a board diffusion graph according to the clustering result with Gephi [2] can be seen in Figure 1 (Page 1), where the size of each node reflects its degree and nodes sharing the same color belong to the same cluster. The colored graph with GML format is in the supplemental material (clusteredBoardDiffusionGraph.gml). For simplicity, we selected only the clusters with more than 1000 nodes and more than 2 degrees in this visualization. This visualization implies that (1) every cluster has a specific context, (2) similar contexts (ex. cakes and foods, gardens and exterior) are

Table 2: **Classification accuracy (in %) averaged over 10 runs. Column: Type of features. Row: Type of classifiers.**

		User	Board	Cluster
Linear regression		87.09	98.94	97.36
kNN	$k = 1$	85.46	98.70	97.13
	$k = 5$	88.08	98.88	97.64
	$k = 10$	88.78	98.84	97.62

close to each other and (3) contexts that tend to appear together (ex. holiday DIY, cakes and Xmas) are also close to each other.

5. PRELIMINARY VALIDATIONS

This section validates our hypothesis that every board in a specific board cluster share a similar context, which would indicate the utility of image contexts founded by our method as a corpus of context-aware image retrieval.

The task in the validation is image classification according to the following setup: We selected about 380,000 pins and associated 200,000 unique images with 10 classes (architecture, fashion, cupcake, animals, chocolate, flowers, blue, sea, Christmas and green) from the whole collection shown in Sec. 3. Class label for each image was determined by the names of boards the image belongs to.

We utilized three types of features for classification: user, board and cluster features. (1) User feature $\boldsymbol{x}_i^u$ (192 dim.): If user j pinned or repinned image i, then the j-th element is set to 1, otherwise 0. (2) Board feature $\boldsymbol{x}_i^b$ (963 dim.): If image i was pinned to board l, then the l-th element is set to 1, otherwise 0. (3) Board cluster feature $\boldsymbol{x}_i^c$ (570 dim.): The m-th element is given by $n_{i,m}/n_i$, where $n_{i,m}$ is the number of times image i is (re)pinned to a board contained in cluster m, and n_i is the sum of $n_{i,m}$ over all m. Note that single image might be pinned or repinned to multiple boards by multiple users. From the above setup, board features should yield the highest classification performance (but not necessarily 100%).

The classification was performed with linear regression and k-NNs. The features were compared based on the classification accuracy averaged over 10 runs, where each run randomly selected 150,000 images for learning and 50,000 images for testing.

Table 2 summarizes the classification performance for three feature types (user, board and board cluster) and four classifiers (linear regression and k-NNs with $k = 1, 5, 10$). The table indicates that cluster features achieved performance comparable to board features and significantly higher than naive user features for all the classifiers. We observe that board clusters discovered by our method appropriately captured image contexts.

6. CONCLUDING REMARKS

This paper presented that social curation data has a great potential as corpora to discover, visualize and retrieve various kinds of contexts engraved in image contents. Especially, we revealed image contexts from a million image collection with the full use of the nature of a social curation platform and a content-centric network. Although we have exploited Pinterest as corpora in this paper, our method does not rely on any specific platforms if they have a structure with content diffusion and context-specific grouping.

Until then, we did not matter image contents. We have enjoyed the benefits of content diffusion on a social curation platform to reveal image contexts. However, our method shown in this paper considered only pinned images, which implies that any other images have been still out of focus. With the use of another method we have developed [12], we take the content into account to augment the benefits to much broader areas.

Since the image collection we have utilized was clean and well-organized and it had several favorable characteristics, fundamental techniques with well-designed features were sufficient for our purpose. However, we should develop more sophisticated techniques for further improvements.

Acknowledgments

We would like to thank Dr. Junji Yamato and Mr. Koh Takeuchi of NTT Communication Science Labs for their fruitful discussions.

7. REFERENCES

[1] Baluja et al. Video suggestion and discovery for YouTube: Taking random walks through the view graph. In *Proc. WWW*, 2008.

[2] Bastian et al. Gephi: An open source software for exploring and manipulating networks. In *Proc. ICWSM*, 2009.

[3] Berg et al. Understanding and predicting importance in images. In Proc. *CVPR*, 2012.

[4] Blondel et al. Fast unfolding of communities in large networks. *Journal of Statistical Mechanics*, 2008.

[5] Boutemedjet et al. A graphical model for context-aware visual content recommendation. *IEEE Trans. MM*, 2008.

[6] De Pessemier et al. Context aware recommendations for user-generated content on a social network site. In *Proc. EuroTV*, 2009.

[7] Duh et al. Creating stories: Social curation of Twitter messages. In *Proc. ICWSM*, 2012.

[8] C. Hall et al. Social curation on the website Pinterest.com. In *Proc. ASIST*, 2012.

[9] Ishiguro et al. Towards automatic image understanding and mining via social curation. In *Proc. ICDM*, 2012.

[10] Jess Swiderski. *Pinterest for Business*. Que, 2012.

[11] Kimura. Social curation as corpora for large-scale multimedia content analysis. presented in *ICMR*, http://bit.ly/ICMR2013Curation, 2013.

[12] Marcos Alvarez et al. Exploiting socially-generated side information to improve dimensionality reduction. In *Proc. IWSAM*, 2013.

[13] Negoescu et al. Modeling Flickr communities through probabilistic topic-based analysis. *IEEE Trans. MM*, 2010.

[14] Qi et al. Exploring context and content links in social media: A latent space method. *IEEE Trans. PAMI*, 2012.

[15] Rosenbaum. Why content curation is here to stay. http://on.mash.to/ZAayZo, 2010.

[16] Shiokawa et al. Fast algorithm for modularity-based graph clustering. In *Proc. AAAI*, 2013.

[17] Trevisiol et al. Image ranking based on user browsing behavior. In *Proc. SIGIR*, 2012.

[18] Wang et al. Recommending Flickr groups with social topic model. *Information Retrieval*, 2012.

[19] Wang et al. Towards indexing representative images on the Web. In *Proc. ACMMM*, 2012.

[20] Xu et al. Towards annotating media contents through social diffusion analysis. In *Proc. ICDM*, 2012.

[21] Zarro et al. Wedding dresses and wanted criminals: Pinterest.com as an infrastructure for repository building. In *Proc. ICWSM*, 2013.

[22] Zheng et al. Flickr group recommendation based on tensor decomposition. In *Proc. SIGIR*, 2010.

Moment Feature Based Forensic Detection of Resampled Digital Images

Lu Li
IAIR, Xi'an Jiaotong University
lilu.acrobat@gmail.com

Jianru Xue
IAIR, Xi'an Jiaotong University
jrxue@mail.xjtu.edu.cn

Zhiqiang Tian
IAIR, Xi'an Jiaotong University
tianzq@gmail.com

Nanning Zheng
IAIR, Xi'an Jiaotong University
nnzheng@aiar.xjtu.edu.cn

ABSTRACT

Forensic detection of resampled digital images has become an important technology among many others to establish the integrity of digital visual content. This paper proposes a moment feature based method to detect resampled digital images. Rather than concentrating on the positions of characteristic resampling peaks, we utilize a moment feature to exploit the periodic interpolation characteristics in the frequency domain. Not only the positions of resampling peaks but also the amplitude distribution is taken into consideration. With the extracted moment feature, a trained SVM classifier is used to detect resampled digital images. Extensive experimental results show the validity and efficiency of the proposed method.

Categories and Subject Descriptors

I.4.m [**Image Processing**]: Miscellaneous

Keywords

Digital Forensic, Resampling Detection, Moment Feature

1. INTRODUCTION

It is easier to make digital image forgeries than ever before in the history. With the sophisticated image editing software, even a beginner can make a forged digital image in less than ten minutes. The fact that seeing is not believing puts an urgent demand for the techniques of image forensic detection. It also motivates recent intense research on digital image forensic tools [12] that can assess the authenticity of digital images without access to source images or source devices, which is called passive-blind image forensics.

Although digital forgeries may leave no visual clues of having been manipulated with image editing operations, they will alter underlying patterns of pixels which compose the digital image. Several methods have been developed to detect digital forgeries, such as cloning [2, 5], splicing [6, 8], and recompression [1, 14]. Facing the fact that resampling operations are involved in most of the digital image forgeries, the detection of resampled images [3, 4, 9, 10, 11, 13] has become an important kind of approaches in the field of passive-blind image forensics.

In this paper, we propose a moment feature based method to detect resampled images. The moment feature is defined to exploit the periodic interpolation characteristics in the frequency domain. Not only the positions of resampling peaks but also the amplitude distribution is taken into consideration. With the extracted moment feature, a trained SVM classifier is used to realize the resampling detection. The resulted method not only provides a new way for the resampling detection based image forensic tools to extend their usage, but also improves the performance of previous methods.

The rest of the paper is organized as follows: Section 2 provides a brief overview of prior work; Section 3 introduces the resampling operation and our moment feature based detection method. The performance of the proposed method is presented in Section 4. Finally, Section 5 concludes this paper.

MM'13, October 21–25, 2013, Barcelona, Spain.

ACM 978-1-4503-2404-5/13/10 ...$15.00.
http://dx.doi.org/10.1145/2502081.2502150.

2. RELATED WORK

In practice, interpolation is an essential step of resampling. Hence, the characteristics which are induced by interpolation are often used to detect the resampling operation. Specifically, due to the interpolation, a spatial periodic interpixel correlation pattern is introduced into the resampled images and is presented as peaks in the frequency domain.

Popescu and Farid [11] indicated that the trace of interpolation can be regarded as a characteristic to detect resampling. The method in [11] estimates the correlation pattern induced by interpolation with an expectation-maximization algorithm (EM) and realizes the resampling detection through Fourier analysis. Mahdian and Saic [10] proposed an automatic method which searches for the traces of periodic properties contained in the derivatives of the resampled image. Rather than using the EM algorithm, Kirchner [9] employed a linear filter to achieve the resampling detection. In [9], the linear filter with preset coefficients is utilized to approximate the correlation between pixels. Dalgaard et al. [3] and Vazquez-Padin et al. [13] exploited the underlying cyclostationarity of communication signals.

They focused on the study of prefilters used in the detection to improve the estimation accuracy of the resampling rate.

Most of the previous methods concentrate on the positions of characteristic resampling peaks. However, the positions of resampling peaks alone cannot reveal the particular resampling rate. Sometimes, images with different resampling rates may have the same periodicity. Hence, it is impossible to distinguish the resampling rate merely according to the positions of resampling peaks. On the other hand, without taking the periodic interpolation characteristics into consideration, Feng et al. [4] proposed a normalized energy density-based method for resampling detection which mainly describes the changes of energy density distribution of resampled images in the frequency domain. The method in [4] is capable of solving the ambiguity in determining the resampling rate.

3. DETECTION OF RESAMPLED IMAGES

The periodic inter-pixel correlation pattern introduced by the resampling is shown as peaks in the frequency domain of the resampled image. Based on this observation, we exploit the correlation pattern by using a moment feature. Then we train a SVM classifier based on the moment feature. We finally use this SVM classifier to detect the resampling.

3.1 Resampling Operation

Generally, scaling is an indispensable manipulation in making a forged image. However, it does not leave any visual clues of manipulations. In this paper, we focus on the detection of resampling employed by the scaling operation. The geometric transformation that equals to the resampling is implemented with two steps, mapping and interpolation. A mapping of integer target coordinates $\mathcal{X} = (X_1, X_2)$ to real-valued source coordinates $\boldsymbol{x} = (x_1, x_2)$ is the first step. The mapping operation can be defined as:

$$\boldsymbol{x} = A^{-1}\mathcal{X} \quad (1)$$

where A is a 2×2 transformation matrix. Then, an interpolation operation is employed to smooth, which can be written as:

$$i(A^{-1}\mathcal{X}) = \sum_{N \in \mathbb{Z}^2} h(A^{-1}\mathcal{X} - N)i(N) \quad (2)$$

where i denotes the intensity of the original image, and h is the interpolation kernel. In this paper, only scaling is taken into consideration, Equation (2) reduces to:

$$i(\frac{1}{s}\mathcal{X}) = \sum_{N \in \mathbb{Z}^2} h(\frac{1}{s}\mathcal{X} - N)i(N) \quad (3)$$

where s denotes the resampling rate. As a part of resampling, the interpolation introduces a spatial periodic inter-pixel correlation pattern.

3.2 Moment Feature

A periodic inter-pixel correlation pattern is introduced into the resampled images. As testified in [9, 11], the correlation between adjacent pixels can be described with a linear model, which is given by:

$$I(X_1, X_2) = \sum_{m,n=-K}^{K} t_{m,n} I(X_1+m, X_2+n) + \varphi(X_1, X_2) \quad (4)$$

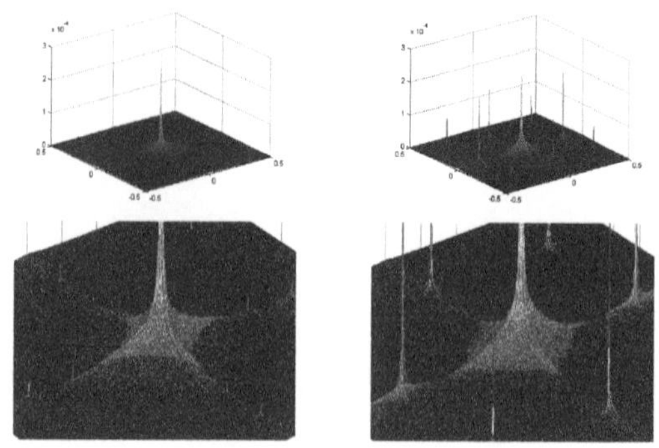

Figure 1: The amplitude distributions of the absolute residual maps of images in different resampling rates. The first row shows the average amplitude distributions of absolute residual maps calculated from 1000 images for 80% (left) and 150% (right) resampling. The corresponding magnified versions are shown on the second row.

where I denotes the intensity of the resampled image, and $t_{m,n}$ is the coefficient of linear predictor. φ denotes the residual. The degree of linear dependence is measured by the absolute value of the residual. In this paper, we apply a highpass filter H to the image's intensity channel. The highpass filter H is defined as:

$$H = \begin{bmatrix} 1 & 1 & 1 \\ 1 & -8 & 1 \\ 1 & 1 & 1 \end{bmatrix} \quad (5)$$

The absolute value of the filtered image is calculated to obtain the absolute residual map. The periodic inter-pixel correlation pattern is implied in the absolute residual map. Due to the periodic pattern, peaks will present in the frequency domain of the absolute residual map, as shown in Figure 1.

Let $r(x, y)$ denote the absolute residual map. By applying 2D-DFT to $r(x, y)$, we obtain $R(u, v)$, where (u, v) denotes the frequency. The range of frequency (u, v) is then normalized. As mentioned in Section 2, the positions of resampling peaks alone cannot reveal the particular resampling rate. Both the positions and amplitude distribution of these peaks change according to the resampling rate, as shown in Figure 1.

To fully exploit the characteristics of peaks shown in the frequency domain of the absolute residual map, we define a moment feature P. Let Ω denote the area of feature extraction with two given parameters ω and Δ. As shown in Figure 2, Ω is defined as:

$$\Omega = \{(u, v) | \omega < D_{u,v} \leq \omega + \Delta\} \quad (6)$$

where ω is the parameter for feature extraction, and Δ denotes the step size of ω. $D_{u,v}$ is the Chebyshev distance from the frequency (u, v) to $(0, 0)$, which is defined as:

$$D_{u,v} = max(|u|, |v|) \quad (7)$$

The moment feature P is then defined as:

$$P(\omega) = \sum_{(u,v) \in \Omega} \frac{1}{500} \frac{|R(u, v)|}{E_d} D_{u,v}, \quad 0 \leq \omega \leq 0.5 - \Delta \quad (8)$$

where $|R(u, v)|$ denotes the amplitude of the Fourier coefficient at the frequency (u, v). R denotes the absolute residual

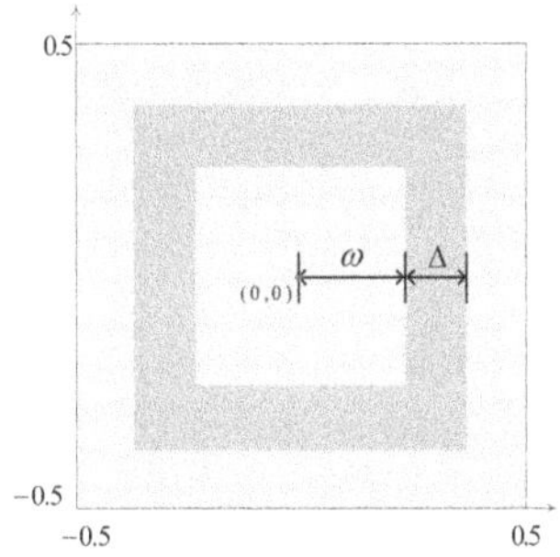

Figure 2: The representation of feature selection area Ω with two given parameters ω and Δ. Area Ω is marked as orange. The red dot indicates the frequency (0,0).

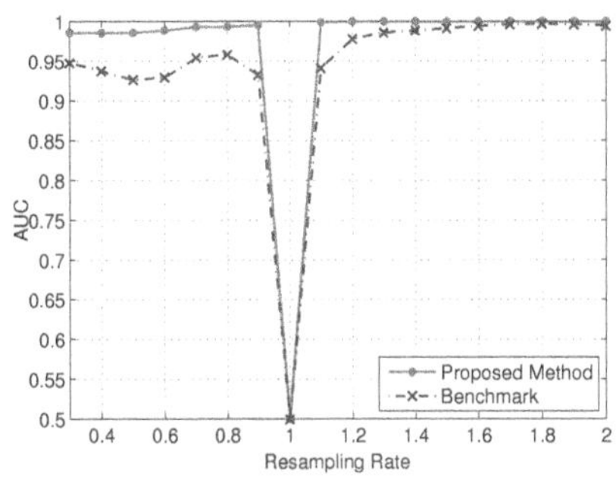

Figure 3: The resampling detection results of the proposed method and the approach in [4]. The area under the ROC curve (AUC) is employed to evaluate the performance of detection. The performance of the proposed method is demonstrated with a solid line. The method in [4] is used as a benchmark and its performance is demonstrated with a dashed line.

map after Fourier transform. E_d is given as the average amplitude of all the elements of R except the DC value.

With the parameter ω ranging from 0 to 0.475 in steps of 0.025, a 20-D feature vector is extracted from the frequency domain of the absolute residual map. Δ is set to 0.025. Both the positions of resampling peaks and the amplitude distribution are involved in the 20-D feature vector. Finally, a trained SVM classifier is used to detect resampled images with the moment feature vectors.

4. EXPERIMENTAL RESULTS

We collected 1490 raw images from the Dresden Image Database [7]. These images are resampled with the resampling rate ranging from 0.3 to 2 in steps of 0.1 using Bicubic interpolation method. Anti-aliasing is also applied to these images, which makes the experiments closer to the real situation. Then, the images are cropped to 512×512, so that only the central parts are preserved. Finally, 26820 images are obtained in such way to form test data set.

In the proposed method, a trained SVM classifier is used to detect resampling. The extracted 20-D feature vectors are used as the inputs of the SVM classifier. Radial basis

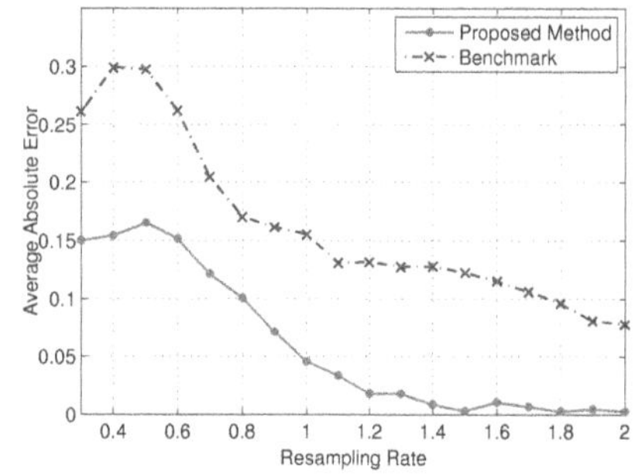

Figure 4: The results of resampling rate determination. The average absolute error is employed to evaluate the performance of detection. The performance of the proposed method is demonstrated with a solid line. The method in [4] is used as a benchmark and its performance is demonstrated with a dashed line.

function (RBF) is used as the SVM kernel. The parameters of RBF, C and γ, are selected as 10 and 0.05 according to grid searching.

The method in [4], which is capable of determining the resampling rate without additional restrictions and uses the SVM classifier to detect resampling, is used as a benchmark.

4.1 Detection of Resampling

First, these test images are respectively classified by the proposed method and the approach in [4] as resampled (labeled as positive) or not. We apply the feature extraction to these images and then detect the trace of resampling. For each resampling rate, a SVM classifier is trained by using the training set.

In the experiment, the images are divided into two groups. Half of the images are used as ground truth for training, and the other half are used for testing. The experiment is repeated 500 times with a different set of images at each time. Then ROC curves of the test sets are obtained with the experimental results. The area under the ROC curve (AUC) is employed to evaluate the performance of the resampling detection. In Figure 3, the curves of average AUC show the results of comparison between the proposed method and the method in [4]. It shows that the detection performance degrades with decreasing resampling rate in downsampled images. Nevertheless, for the proposed method, the average AUC is larger than 0.98 in each resampling rate. Either in upsampling or downsampling, the proposed method presents a better performance.

Then, we apply the proposed method and the approach in [4] to determinate the resampling rate. The resampling rate determination is based on a one-versus-one strategy. A series of SVM classifiers are trained between every pair of classes which have different resampling rates. The test sample is classified by each of the SVM classifiers, and the vote for the assigned class is increased by one vote. Finally, the resampling rate with most votes is the result.

In the experiment, the images are divided into two groups. Half of the images are used as ground truth for training, and the other half are used for testing. The trial is repeated

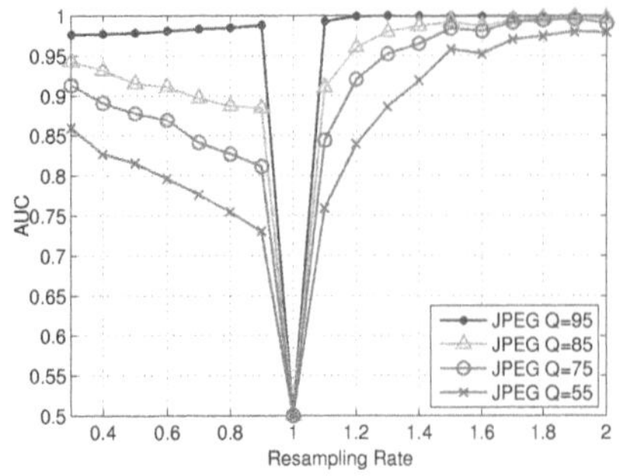

Figure 5: The resampling detection results in different compression qualities. The area under the ROC curve (AUC) is employed to evaluate the performance of detection.

500 times with a different set of images at each time. The average absolute error is used to evaluate the performance on resampling rate determination. As shown in Figure 4, the average absolute error of the proposed method is less than 0.18 in each resampling rate. For upsampled images, the results are much more reliable. When the resampling rate is 1.8, the average absolute error is even 0.0027. The proposed method not only presents a better performance in different resampling rates, but also suggests a reasonable accuracy for images with the resampling rate as small as 0.3.

4.2 Detection After JPEG Compression

Furthermore, to show the robustness, we test our method on the compressed images. The resampled images used in Section 4.1 are compressed in the compression quality factor 95, 85, 75, and 55, respectively. In the test, the images are divided into two groups. Half of the images are used as ground truth for training, and the other half are used for testing. The experiment is repeated 500 times with a different set of images at each time. Then ROC curves of the test sets are obtained with the experimental results. In Figure 5, the curves of average AUC show the results of resampling detection in different compression qualities. The performance of detection gradually decreases with the descent of the compression quality. Though the JPEG compression has an adverse influence on the detection, with the compression quality of 55, which is rarely utilized, the proposed method still access a average AUC over 0.73 in each resampling rate.

5. CONCLUSIONS

We propose a moment feature based method for resampling detection. Rather than concentrating on the positions of characteristic resampling peaks, we utilize the moment feature to fully exploit the resampling characteristics presented in the frequency domain of the absolute residual map. The detection is finally accomplished with a SVM classifier. The resulted method not only provides a new way for these resampling detection based image forensic tools to extend their usage, but also improves the performance of previous methods. Experimental results on a large set of images show the validity and efficiency of the proposed method.

6. ACKNOWLEDGEMENT

This work was supported by the National Basic Research Program of China (973 Program) under Grant No.2012CB316400, the National Natural Science Foundation of China (NSFC) Nos. 61273252, 61075007, and 90920301.

7. REFERENCES

[1] S. Battiato and G. Messina. Digital forgery estimation into dct domain: a critical analysis. In *Proceedings of the First ACM workshop on Multimedia in forensics*, pages 37–42, 2009.

[2] S. Bayram, H. T. Sencar, and N. Memon. An efficient and robust method for detecting copy-move forgery. In *IEEE International Conference on Acoustics, Speech and Signal Processing (ICASSP)*, pages 1053–1056, 2009.

[3] N. Dalgaard, C. Mosquera, and F. Pérez-González. On the role of differentiation for resampling detection. In *2010 17th IEEE International Conference on Image Processing (ICIP)*, pages 1753–1756, 2010.

[4] X. Feng, I. J. Cox, and G. Doërr. Normalized energy density-based forensic detection of resampled images. *IEEE Transactions on Multimedia*, 14(3):536–545, 2012.

[5] A. J. Fridrich, B. D. Soukal, and A. J. Lukáš. Detection of copy-move forgery in digital images. In *Proceedings of Digital Forensic Research Workshop*, 2003.

[6] A. C. Gallagher and T. Chen. Image authentication by detecting traces of demosaicing. In *IEEE Computer Society Conference on Computer Vision and Pattern Recognition Workshops(CVPRW)*, pages 1–8, 2008.

[7] T. Gloe and R. Böhme. The dresden image database for benchmarking digital image forensics. *Journal of Digital Forensic Practice*, 3(2-4):150–159, 2010.

[8] Y.-F. Hsu and S.-F. Chang. Camera response functions for image forensics: an automatic algorithm for splicing detection. *IEEE Transactions on Information Forensics and Security*, 5(4):816–825, 2010.

[9] M. Kirchner. Fast and reliable resampling detection by spectral analysis of fixed linear predictor residue. In *Proceedings of the 10th ACM workshop on Multimedia and security*, pages 11–20, 2008.

[10] B. Mahdian and S. Saic. Blind authentication using periodic properties of interpolation. *IEEE Transactions on Information Forensics and Security*, 3(3):529–538, 2008.

[11] A. C. Popescu and H. Farid. Exposing digital forgeries by detecting traces of resampling. *IEEE Transactions on Signal Processing*, 53(2):758–767, 2005.

[12] J. A. Redi, W. Taktak, and J.-L. Dugelay. Digital image forensics: a booklet for beginners. *Multimedia Tools and Applications*, 51(1):133–162, 2011.

[13] D. Vazquez-Padin and F. Perez-Gonzalez. Prefilter design for forensic resampling estimation. In *IEEE International Workshop on Information Forensics and Security (WIFS)*, pages 1–6, 2011.

[14] F. Zach, C. Riess, and E. Angelopoulou. Automated image forgery detection through classification of jpeg ghosts. *Pattern Recognition*, pages 185–194, 2012.

Towards Precise POI Localization with Social Media

Adrian Popescu
CEA, LIST,
Vision & Content Engineering Laboratory
Gif-sur-Yvette, France
adrian.popescu@cea.fr

Aymen Shabou
CEA, LIST,
Vision & Content Engineering Laboratory
Gif-sur-Yvette, France
aymen.shabou@gmail.com

ABSTRACT

Points of interest (POIs) are a core component of geographical databases and of location based services. POI acquisition was performed by domain experts but associated costs and access difficulties in many regions of the world reduce the coverage of manually built geographical databases. With the availability of large geotagged multimedia datasets on the Web, a sustained research effort was dedicated to automatic POI discovery and characterization. However, in spite of its practical importance, POI localization was only marginally addressed. To compute POI coordinates an assumption was made that the more data were available, the more precise the localization will be. Here we shift the focus of the process from data quantity to data quality. Given a set of geotagged Flickr photos associated to a POI, close-up classification is used to trigger a spatial clustering process. To evaluate the newly introduced method against different other localization schemes, we create an accurate ground truth. We show that significant localization error reductions are obtained compared to a coordinate averaging approach and to a X-Means clustering scheme.

Categories and Subject Descriptors

H.3.1 [**Content Analysis and Indexing**]

General Terms

Algorithms, Experimentation

Keywords

geographic information extraction, POI localization, Flickr

1. INTRODUCTION

The success of geographically enabled applications, such as location based services (LBS), mapping interfaces or navigation systems), is highly dependent on the coverage and quality of the points of interest (POIs) present in geographic databases. POI were classically added to databases by a large number of domain experts who visited physical locations or browsed existing resources [7]. The resulting databases are accurate but their constitution and update have a significant cost. Large geotagged multimedia datasets are a by-product of the success of social media and they were exploited in a number of geographic information extraction tasks. Representative works that leverage user-generate content for POI mining include [8], [2], [7] and are focused on the extraction of POI names, categories and/or popularity. Curiously, while POI localization imprecision drastically limits the practical utility of automatically extracted POIs in LBS, it was only marginally considered in existing works. We improve POI localization through an appropriate combination of text and image analysis. Text is used to retrieve the initial set of images associated to a POI and visual information is then exploited to filter the initial set. Our key hypotheses are that not all items are equally important for deriving POI location and that the best approximations of true POI locations are given by spatially dense and socially diverse data subsets. To test these hypotheses, we perform close-far image classification and introduce a simple but efficient spatial clustering algorithm seeded with POI close-up photos. By doing so, we add a qualitative aspect to the localization process and shift its focus from quantitative approaches that prevail in existing work. The evaluation of the approach is done using a Flickr dataset.

The evaluation of POI localization algorithms is a difficult task due to the non-existence of standardized datasets [7]. It is usually performed against POI coordinates from manually created databases, such as Geonames[1]. A close inspection of the coordinates provided by Geonames shows that no coherent rules are followed when placing the POIs and that a more accurate ground truth is needed. We create such a ground truth through manual inspection of Google Maps.

In addition to coordinates, we also estimate a POI radius that can be used as a proxy for an acceptable localization error. Experiments carried on this new dataset show that significant improvements are obtained through the use of multimedia processing.

2. RELATED WORK

To our knowledge, existing works explored the use of multimedia data to geotag individual documents but multimedia geotagging was not tested for POIs. This section discusses relevant prior work in geographic information extraction, with focus on geotagged multimedia datasets, and in

[1]http://geonames.org

MM'13, October 21–25, 2013, Barcelona, Spain.
Copyright 2013 ACM 978-1-4503-2404-5/13/10$15.00..
http://dx.doi.org/10.1145/2502081.2502151.

image classification. Rattenbury and al. [8] pioneered the use of Flickr data to extract POI name, popularity and location using spatial burst detection. In a follow-up, Kennedy and Naaman [5] focused on using multimedia clustering to produce representative and diversified visual representation of POIs. One of their key findings is that socially representative clusters (i.e. including a large number of users) are more relevant than the others. Rae and al. [7] exploited Web search snippets to scale-up POI discovery. These works focus on POI properties such as name, category or popularity and give only limited attention to POI location. A simple coordinate averaging procedure was introduced in [8] and statistical location models were used in [7]. Typical location errors are in the hundreds of meters range (290 m in [7]), an imprecision that is too big for direct use of automatically extracted POIs in LBS.
Given its high applicative value, individual document localization received a lot of attention. Hays and Efros [4] proposed an algorithm that predicts the location of an image based on global visual descriptors. With this simple visual method, the reported precision is in the range of hundreds of kilometers. Crandall and al. [2], analyzed a 30 million geotagged image dataset using image local features (SIFTs) and textual features to estimate image location. In a simple classification setting (10 possible locations), a combination of visual and textual features achieves approximately 70% accuracy and textual features clearly outperform visual ones when exploited alone. Textual location modeling was proposed in [9] using an adaptation of language models. Image localization within 1 km from the true coordinates is successful in 14.1% of the cases. While interesting, these performances are not sufficient to localize POIs accurately.

Image depth estimation using wavelet based image indexing was introduced in Torralba and Oliva [11]. They used the scene structure to derive the absolute mean depth of the image. The problem we tackle here is somewhat similar although, given the high variability of images available on social media, we do not set out to estimate the absolute depth but rather to rank images associated to a POI in the close-far spectrum. Also relevant is indoor-outdoor classification [10], which became a standard classifier in scene understanding. However, given the similarity of inside/outside close-ups and the fact that there are no indoor photos for POIs that cannot be visited on the inside, we don't consider indoor-outdoor classification.

3. POI LOCALIZATION

The problem we address here can be formulated as: *"given a set of geotagged images associated to a POI, leverage their metadata, textual annotations and/or visual content to automatically predict the best possible POI location."*
When deriving POI location from geotagged photo datasets available on social media, there are three main types of problems that lead to inaccurate results: (1) Photos are usually placed at the point where they were taken and this point is often distant from the true POI location; (2) Geotagging errors may occur, especially when the process is manual because users often do not place the photos exactly where they were taken; (3) Given that there is no control of user generated content, only a fraction of the photos tagged with a POI name actually depict it. For instance, bulk upload was identified to have a negative effect on POI extraction [7].
We tackle the first difficulty directly by using a photo ranking based on their probability to be close-ups. The second and the third problems are indirectly tackled by the introduction of spatial clustering algorithms that favor regions that have a high density of close-up photos and that are socially diversified. Different text-based and multimedia POI localization methods were tested. The most representative of them are described in the next two subsections, along with textual and visual close-far classifiers.

3.1 Text-based POI localization

3.1.1 Text-based close-up ranking

Here we exploit textual cues to determine if a photo is a close-up. We retain 48,815 geotagged photo annotations that are taken from less than 50 meters and more than 300 meters w.r.t. the coordinates of a POI in order to form *textual close* and *textual far* classes. The distance thresholds for the two classes were empirically chosen after testing different combinations. We compute each word's *textual close* probability by dividing its *textual close* count by its total count. The photos associated to a POI are ranked using the dot product similarity between each photo's tags and title and the representation of *textual close*. Preliminary tests showed that the best results are obtained when the first 40% of the ranked photos list are retained.

3.1.2 Text-based POI localization methods

We test the following text localization methods:
* *Simple Avg* - baseline method introduced in [8]. It computes the coordinates from by averaging the coordinates of all the images available for a POI. For this type of method to work well, photos should be evenly distributed in all directions around the POI. Such a condition is seldom met because of the physical configuration of POIs and of the fact some POI parts arouse more interest than others.
* *No Bulk* - method that uses the same averaging procedure as *Simple Average* but is applied after bulk removal (i.e. removal of images uploaded by an user that have the same coordinates and the same set of tags).
* *Txt Close* - method that exploits the text-based close-up ranking. The POI location is computed by retaining only those images that were considered to be close-ups. No bulk removal is performed.
* *Txt Close Iter* - method that combines *No Bulk* to produce an initial average location and textual close-up ranking. The initial location is used to seed a second iteration that considers only a percentage of the photos that are closest to the initial location (*neigh*(%)) and that belong to *textual close*. Supplementary iterations do not improve results.

3.2 Multimedia POI localization

3.2.1 Visual close-up classifer

Given the wide variety of available images, we build a learning base that contains 2000 diversified examples for each of the *visual close* and *visual far* classes. The visual classifier is built on top of a bag of visual words representation of images. Dense SIFTs are extracted and clustered using K-means to build a codebook of size 128. Then SIFTs are encoded over the obtained codebook by locality soft coding and aggregated using the max-pooling scheme. We use a spatial pyramid matching (1 + 2x2 + 3x3) to add global spatial contextual information to the final signature, which is obtained through the concatenation of individual signatures. *Visual close* and *visual far* classes are learned with a linear SVM which is then used to classify test images. Scores vary between 1 (close) and 0 (far). The learning set was split in half to test performances of the approach and we obtained 84% correct classifications. To further improve accuracy, only images whose close-up score is above 0.6 were retained for experiments. We illustrate classification results for the Eiffel Tower (fig. 1). There is a strong concentration of close-ups around the Eiffel Tower's true coordinates. Inversely, long-distance depictions of the Eiffel Tower are concentrated in areas that offer a good panoramic view, such as the Trocadero, Champs de Mars and Bir-Hakeim Bridge.

3.2.2 Multimedia POI localization methods

We test the following multimedia localization methods:
* *Vis Close* - Method that is similar to *Txt Close* but exploits *visual close* class instead of *textual close*.
* *Vis Close Iter* - Method that is similar to *Txt Close Iter* but exploits *visual close* class instead of *textual close*.
* *Density Clustering* - method that retrieves dense regions in a POI's spatial footprint. As illustrated in 1 the intuition that supports this approach is that regions that include a lot of close-up photos uploaded by a large number of users are likely to be close to the real POI location. First, bulk removal is applied and and photos are ranked with *visual close* to select close-ups. Second, the top k photos from the *visual close* class are used as seeds and clusters are obtained by retaining all close-ups within a radius *rad* of the seed. Finally, clusters are ranked based on the number of distinct users that contributed to them. Ties are broken using by favoring clusters that contain larger numbers of *visual close* images. The final POI coordinates are computed by averaging the coordinates of images from the top ranked cluster.

The cluster ranking based on the number of contributors exploits an insight from [5], who show that user frequency based landmark clustering outperforms term based clustering due to the negative influence of bulk upload. Our algorithm is related to OPTICS [1], the main difference being that we introduce a global radius to cluster points instead of a maximum local radius that is used to retain new points.
* *Spatial X-Means* - X-Means [6] is an extension of K-Means that estimates the optimal number of clusters automatically for a dataset. The Weka 3 implementation of the X-Means [3] is used here to assess the performances of standard clustering algorithms in a POI localization task. The results of *Vis Close Iter* are used as input for *Spatial X-Means* and the centroid of the largest cluster is predicted as POI location.

4. EVALUATION

We first present a new POI localization ground truth, then describe the test dataset used and discuss localization results obtained with the methods presented in section 3.

4.1 POI Localization Ground Truth Creation

Precise POI localization is a difficult task since in involves mapping POIs that have dimensions in the range of tens or hundreds of meters to point-based representations. A close inspection of Geonames shows that the proposed POI locations are not consistently attributed. Coordinates are often placed at the center of the POI but also in other parts of the area covered by it or even outside the POI area. To create a precise ground truth, we have selected 1200 POIs that are represented by at least 250 images in Flickr, are situated in various regions of the world, correspond to different geographic categories and have a variable spatial extent. We inspected Google Maps to determine the coordinates of the center of the POI. It was possible to precisely find the point-based location and the radius for 704 POIs that are used in further experiments. The radius was estimated only for shapes that allow such an estimation (rectangular, circles, square, etc.). It is used as a proxy for the acceptable localization error if we consider as acceptable all localizations that fall within the POI area. The average Geonames localization error is 18.2 m and 84.8% of Geonames POIs are placed within the surface covered by the POI. There is no publicly available accurate ground truth for evaluating POI localization and we release the one created here[2].

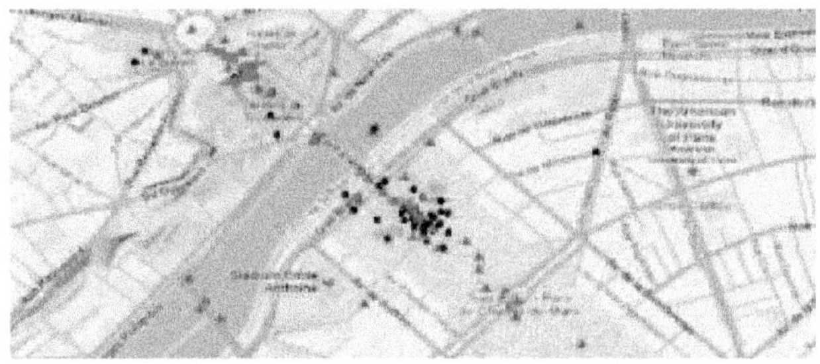

Figure 1: Close/far classification results - circles/triangles Eiffel Tower (centered).

4.2 Test Dataset

Using the Flickr API, we downloaded 250 images and associated metadata (tags, titles, geotags) for each POI represented in the ground truth. For each POI, textual annotations were ranked with respect to their similarity to *textual close*. Similarly, images were indexed and classified based on their similarity to *visual close*. To facilitate reproducibility, the raw textual annotations and image URLs of the test dataset are distributed with the ground truth.

4.3 Evaluation Results

We first test the influence of the number of available images on POI localization error and present results obtained using *Simple Avg* with 10 to 250 images, with a step of 10 in fig. 2. The number of available photos has an important effect up to 50 available photos and the performance improvement is weaker beyond. For instance, the average

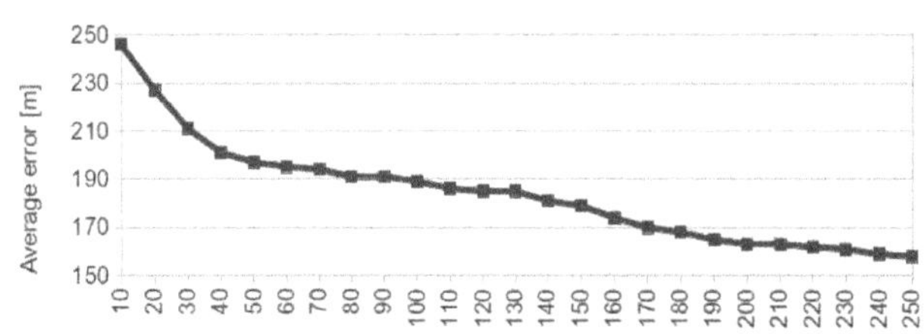

Figure 2: Evolution of the average localization error with the number of available images for *Simple Avg*.

[2]http://comupedia.org/poiLocation/

error is 163 m for 200 photos and 158 for 250. These results show the limits of purely quantitative POI localization methods and support the introduction of qualitative methods to improve performances.
The POI localization methods described in section 3 were applied to the test dataset and results are presented in table 1. We performed a grid search for parameter optimization and obtained the best performances with: $neigh = 60\%$ for *Txt Close Iter*, *Vis Close Iter* and *Density Clustering*; $k =$ 10 seeds for *Density Clustering*; $rad = 100$ m for *Density Clustering*; $x_{min} = 3$ and $x_{max} = 10$ for *Spatial X-Means*. The smallest localization error is obtained with *Density Clustering* (average error - 65.6 m, 10.5 m standard deviation), followed by *Vis Close Iter* (77.1 m, 11.9 m) and *Spatial X-Means* (78.1 m, 12.3 m). A t-test indicates that the difference between *Density Clustering* and the other methods is statistically significant at $p < 0.01$.

These results show that that multimedia POI localization outperforms all text based localization and that *Density Clustering*, seeded with the visual close-ups, is better than *Spatial X-Means*, a standard clustering and than *Vis Close Iter*, an iterative global localization procedure. The worst results are obtained with *Simple Avg*, the baseline method. Bulk removal, the use of *textual close* and of *visual close* cues bring a small improvement compared to *Simple Avg*. A larger improvement is obtained for *Txt Close Iter* and *Vis Close Iter*, the two global ranking methods. The comparison of similar text and visual localization methods indicates that visual cues have a more important effect than textual cues. Results for the percentage of automatic locations situated inside the POI area show similar performances to average error. *Density Clustering* places the largest number of POIs within their area.

The performances of *Density Clustering* are globally better than those of the other methods tested. However, there are configurations in which this method fails. For example, if the photos are evenly distributed around the true coordinates but are all taken from a certain distance (for instance, when the POI is not physically accessible), averaging methods have better performances. Another problematic case is that when the densest cluster of close-ups is away from the true coordinates and photos that are closer to these coordinates are discarded. Here the problem can be caused either by irrelevant POI tagging and/or by a small number of users that contribute to the POI representation. Yet another problematic case is that of elongated POIs, such as bridges for which it is difficult to compute accurate coordinates using density based methods. However, computing coordinates for elongated objects is problematic for all methods since it is rare that these objects' photos are evenly distributed around their central point.

Table 1: POI localization errors with different methods. Avg. err. is the average error expressed in meters. St. dev. is the standard deviation in meters. Inside is the percentage of localizations that fall within the surface covered by the POI

Method Name	Avg. err.[m]	St. dev[m]	Inside[%]
Simple Avg	158	21.7	43.7
No Bulk	151.2	19.4	39.9
Txt Close	151	19.1	39.8
Txt Close Iter	89.7	13.7	64.1
Vis Close	140.7	18.8	46
Vis Close Iter	77.1	11.9	72.2
Density Clust.	**65.6**	**10.5**	**76.7**
Spatial X-Means	78.1	12.3	71.2

5. CONCLUSIONS

We presented different methods for automatic POI localization and showed that significant improvements are obtained compared to a coordinate averaging approach [8]). *Density Clustering* equally outperforms *Spatial X-Means*, a standard clustering algorithm, a result that supports the importance of an appropriate seeding in the POI localization process. Also, visual cues are more important in the localization process than textual cues. Even if the best automatic results still lag behind manual POI coordinates assignment, the gap was reduced. The average error difference compared to manual POI geotagging remains consequent (65.6 m for *Density Clustering* vs. 18.23 m for Geonames). However, the percentage of POI localizations that lie inside the POI area is comparable (76.7% for *Density Clustering* and 84.9% for Geonames). The last measure is more important in practice since it allows one to correctly indicate POI locations on a map and to use them for LBS services, such as tourist guiding. To facilitate result reproducibility, we share the ground truth along with the dataset used in the experimental section.
Future work will focus on a dynamic tuning of *Density Clustering* in function of the POI characteristics (POI footprint proportion of close-ups, etc.). Here we considered all photos tagged with the POI name, regardless of the relevance of the annotation, and this choice might hurt overall performances. Consequently, another line of work will concern the use of image reranking to remove potentially irrelevant clusters.

6. REFERENCES

[1] M. Ankerst and al. Optics: ordering points to identify the clustering structure. In *SIGMOD 1999*.

[2] D. J. Crandall and al. Mapping the world's photos. In *WWW2009*, pages 761–770, 2009.

[3] M. Hall and al. The weka data mining software: an update. *SIGKDD Explor. Newsl.*, 11(1):10–18, 2009.

[4] J. Hays and A. A. Efros. im2gps: estimating geographic information from a single image. In *CVPR 2008*.

[5] L. S. Kennedy and M. Naaman. Generating diverse and representative image search results for landmarks. In *WWW 2008*.

[6] D. Pelleg and A. Moore. X-means: Extending k-means with efficient estimation of the number of clusters. In *ICML 2000*.

[7] A. Rae and al. Mining the web for points of interest. In *SIGIR 2012*.

[8] T. Rattenbury and al. Towards automatic extraction of event and place semantics from flickr tags. In *SIGIR 2007*, pages 103–110, 2007.

[9] P. Serdyukov and al. Placing flickr photos on a map. In *SIGIR 2009*, pages 484–491, 2009.

[10] M. Szummer and R. W. Picard. Indoor-outdoor image classification. In *CAIVD 1998*.

[11] A. Torralba and A. Oliva. Depth estimation from image structure. *IEEE PAMI*, 24(9):1226–1238, 2002.

Sim-Min-Hash

An efficient matching technique for linking large image collections

Wan-Lei Zhao
INRIA, Rennes

Hervé Jégou
INRIA, Rennes

Guillaume Gravier
CNRS/IRISA, Rennes

ABSTRACT

One of the most successful method to link all similar images within a large collection is min-Hash, which is a way to significantly speed-up the comparison of images when the underlying image representation is bag-of-words. However, the quantization step of min-Hash introduces important information loss. In this paper, we propose a generalization of min-Hash, called Sim-min-Hash, to compare sets of real-valued vectors. We demonstrate the effectiveness of our approach when combined with the Hamming embedding similarity. Experiments on large-scale popular benchmarks demonstrate that Sim-min-Hash is more accurate and faster than min-Hash for similar image search. Linking a collection of one million images described by 2 billion local descriptors is done in 7 minutes on a single core machine.

Categories and Subject Descriptors: I.4.7 Image processing and computer vision Feature Measurement
Keywords: Image linking/search, large-scale, min-Hash

1. INTRODUCTION

In the last decade, we have witnessed the explosion of multimedia contents in Internet. Professional and user-generated multimedia data proliferate over TV channels and Internet, in particular on social networks. There exist a significant proportion of the images (near-)duplicate or visually related content. A recent survey in [16] estimates that 22% of images have near-duplicates in a collection of two billion web images, and 8% are near-duplicate to more than ten images.

This raises the scientific challenge of linking all images within a large collection, to facilitate copyright enforcement, smart navigation, and more generally the analysis and organization of the multimedia databases by adding hyper-links among images/videos [6, 10]. In addition, a graph connecting relevant visual content is useful to improve the quality of traditional content-based image search methods. For instance, the graph is a pre-requisite for search techniques based on reciprocal nearest neighbors [8, 12] or database augmentation techniques [1].

MM'13, October 21 - 25 2013, Barcelona, Spain

http://dx.doi.org/10.1145/2502081.2502152.

This paper considers this cross-matching problem for large image collections. The solutions [4, 14, 15, 3] that have been proposed to overcome the underlying quadratic complexity can be grouped into two categories, depending on whether the features they adopt are global or local. The global approaches are the most efficient. For instance, the method presented in [15] maps global feature vectors to binary hash codes. Images are grouped as near-duplicates once their binary codes are identical or similar. As other approaches based on global descriptors, this approach is efficient but only able to connect very similar images.

The methods based on local features are the most precise. Thanks to the introduction of BoVW based retrieval framework, one can find the results associated with a query image in a fraction of second [9, 7, 12]. However, in the cross-matching problem, all the images of one collection have to be submitted in turn. A very simple local approach [14] circumvents the problem by using a very small number of descriptors per image. This reduces the constant factor significantly, but results in poor linking quality, as shown in our experiments. One of the most successful approach to this problem is the min-Hash technique, which was first introduced in image retrieval for fast matching [4, 5]. It incorporates geometrical verification in the construction process to remove outliers [3] and links all images that are spatially related. In essence, this method computes a similarity measure which aims at approximating the Jaccard similarity between bag-of-words. As a result, it provides an excellent trade-off between linking efficiency and quality. However, as now shown in many papers (*e.g.*, [7]), the bag of words introduces large amount of quantization errors and has been outperformed in content-based image retrieval.

This paper introduces an extension of min-Hash, called Sim-min-Hash (SMH), to compare sets of real-valued vectors. It drastically improves the comparison metric between images while being very efficient for the retrieval and linking problems. This is achieved by adding to the original sketches extra information, in particular in the form of binary codes. The underlying motivation is to exploit the similarity measurements between vectors, in the spirit of Hamming Embedding technique [7] in the bag-of-word context. It is then applied in the context of min-Hash for the purpose of image link discovery. As a result, our method drastically decreases the number of false collisions between hash codes and improve the precision. In addition, unlike traditional min-Hash, it is possible to keep all the matches in the main memory for a million-sized image collection, as will be demonstrated by our experiments in Section 4.

2. BACKGROUND: MIN-HASH

This section briefly introduces the basics of min-Hash [2], as first introduced in the general context of efficiently estimating the Jaccard measure between sets. We then explain how it was used for the purpose of image comparison.

Let's first consider the space $\mathcal{O}$ of possible objects. For instance, this space could be the set of English words. The space $\mathcal{O}$ is assumed discrete but not necessarily finite. The similarity between two objects o_1 and o_2 is binary: They are identical or different, which is denoted by the Kronecker operator: $\delta(\mathsf{o}_1, \mathsf{o}_2) = 1$ *iff* $\mathsf{o}_1 = \mathsf{o}_2$, otherwise 0.

A document $\mathcal{X} \subset \mathcal{O}$ is a set of objects. Various similarity measures exist to assess the resemblance of two documents $\mathcal{X}$ and $\mathcal{Y}$. We consider the Jaccard similarity coefficient, which normalizes the number of objects by the number of distinct objects in the two sets:

$$J(\mathcal{X}, \mathcal{Y}) = \frac{|\mathcal{X} \cap \mathcal{Y}|}{|\mathcal{X} \cup \mathcal{Y}|}. \tag{1}$$

This similarity equals 0 when there is no object in common, and to 1 *iff* the sets are identical. In practice, this similarity measure is costly. The objective of min-Hash is to estimate the Jaccard coefficient in a probabilistic manner to speed-up the comparison. For this reason, it is seen as a kind of Locality-Sensitive-Hashing technique for sets.

Min-Hash proceeds as follows. First, we define a set of M hash functions π_j, $j = 1 \ldots \mathsf{M}$. Each function $\pi_j : \mathcal{O} \rightarrow \mathbb{N}$ maps any possible object to an integer: $\mathsf{o} \mapsto \pi_j(\mathsf{o})$. Then, for any set $\mathcal{X} \subset \mathcal{O}$, we compute a set of M distinct hash keys $\sigma_j(\mathcal{X})$ as

$$\sigma_j(\mathcal{X}) = \min_{\mathsf{o} \in \mathcal{X}} \pi_j(\mathsf{o}). \tag{2}$$

The concatenation of these keys gives a vector of integers $\boldsymbol{\sigma}(\mathcal{X}) = [\sigma_1(\mathcal{X}), \ldots, \sigma_{\mathsf{M}}(\mathcal{X})]$, which is the min-Hash representation of the set $\mathcal{X}$.

The key property exploited by min-Hash is the following. For any key $\sigma_j(.)$ and two documents $\mathcal{X}$ and $\mathcal{Y}$, we have

$$\mathbb{P}\left(\sigma_j(\mathcal{X}) = \sigma_j(\mathcal{Y})\right) = J(\mathcal{X}, \mathcal{Y}). \tag{3}$$

Since the expectation of $\delta(\sigma_j(\mathcal{X}), \sigma_j(\mathcal{Y}))$ equals the probability $\mathbb{P}\left(\sigma_j(\mathcal{X}) = \sigma_j(\mathcal{Y})\right)$, and assuming that the hash functions are independently drawn, min-Hash estimates the Jaccard coefficient by a similarity $\mathsf{s}_{\mathsf{mh}}(.,.)$ as

$$J(\mathcal{X}, \mathcal{Y}) \approx \mathsf{s}_{\mathsf{mh}}(\mathcal{X}, \mathcal{Y}) = \frac{1}{\mathsf{M}} \sum_{j=1}^{\mathsf{M}} \delta(\sigma_j(\mathcal{X}), \sigma_j(\mathcal{Y})), \tag{4}$$

where the variance of the approximation linearly depends on M^{-1}. One key ($\mathsf{M} = 1$) is not sufficient because the result is binary. A reasonable approximation for the estimated similarity s_{mh} is typically obtained with a few hundreds keys, depending on the statistical property of subsets of $\mathcal{O}$.

Sketches. The comparison can be sped-up by compounding several hash keys into one [4], which is called *sketch*. This reduces the false positive rate since it is equivalent to requiring the co-occurrence of multiple objects. For instance, by compounding two keys into one, min-Hash identifies matching pairs of objects. Note that the use of sketches also reduces the probability of observing the true matches. A good compromise is to combine two hash keys into one, *i.e.*, to focus on the pairs of objects [3].

Image comparison with min-Hash. min-Hash is particularly adapted to the case of binary BoVW [13], where a visual vocabulary comprising k visual words is used to produce a binary vector that represents the image. The ith component equals 1 if at least one SIFT descriptor is assigned to the ith visual word, otherwise 0.

Min-Hash is straightforwardly applied by considering all visual words as objects. The functions σ_j are defined as independent random permutations of the set $[1 \ldots \mathsf{k}]$. We consider specifically the case of sketches where a code is produced from a pair of hash keys as

$$\sigma'_j(\mathcal{X}) = (\sigma_{2j}(\mathcal{X}) - 1) \times \mathsf{k} + \sigma_{2j-1}(\mathcal{X}), \tag{5}$$

in which case the sketch $\sigma'_j(\mathcal{X}) \in [1...\mathsf{k}^2]$. An image is then described by the min-Hash vector re-defined as $\boldsymbol{\sigma} = [s'_1(\mathcal{X}), \ldots, s'_{\mathsf{M}'}(\mathcal{X})]$, where $\mathsf{M}' = \mathsf{M}/2$ denotes the number of sketches. Two vectors are compared with Eqn. 4. This is efficiently done by storing the images, based on their sketches, in look-up tables or inverted files. For details, the reader may refer to [3].

The computational advantage of min-Hash over binary BoVW is that the intersection is carried out via pairwise comparison of sketch vectors. This is cheaper than performing the bag-of-words comparison for two reasons. Firstly, the number of sketches M' is smaller than the number of non-zero components. Secondly, considering sketches made from pairs of features (*i.e.*, co-occurrences), the space of possible values is significantly larger than the number of visual words. Therefore with min-Hash, comparing vectors which are significantly more sparse than binary BoVW, is a key factor for efficient comparison [9].

3. SIM-MIN-HASH

This section first introduces our Sim-min-Hash framework for matching set of real-valued vectors. It then focuses on the particular case of using Hamming Embedding as a similarity measurement, before a discussion on implementation details.

Sim-min-Hash: The principle. We are interested in using a similarity between vectors that is no longer binary, unlike for the objects considered in regular min-Hash. Therefore, we consider a similarity measure $m : \mathcal{O} \times \mathcal{O} \rightarrow \mathbb{R}+$ assigning a real value $m(\mathsf{x}, \mathsf{y})$ to any pair of objects. We are specifically interested in similarity measures of the form

$$\begin{cases} m(\mathsf{x}, \mathsf{y}) = 0 & \text{if } q(\mathsf{x}) \neq q(\mathsf{y}) \\ m(\mathsf{x}, \mathsf{y}) = \Omega(\mathsf{x}, \mathsf{y}) & \text{if } q(\mathsf{x}) = q(\mathsf{y}) \end{cases}, \tag{6}$$

where $q(.)$ is a hashing function, for instance a quantizer assigning a visual word to a vector. Such similarities are interesting for computational purpose, as only vectors assigned to the same quantization index are compared. Note that the constant function $\Omega(.,.) = 1$ amounts to performing a binary comparison between objects. This shows that the regular min-Hash is a particular case of our method.

The Sim-min-Hash method proceeds as follows.

1. The functions π_j are defined by applying a random permutation to the quantization indexes.
2. For each hash function π_j, we compute the hash key as in Eqn. 2. However, we also keep track of the object (*i.e.*, the vector) for which the minimum is obtained, which is denoted by $\mathsf{c}_j(\mathcal{X})$. Note that we assume that this object is unique, *i.e.*, only one vector of $\mathcal{X}$ is assigned to the same index. Since it is not the case for local descriptors, we select one based on a rule. In our case, we simply keep the one that appears first when enumerating the set $\mathcal{X}$.

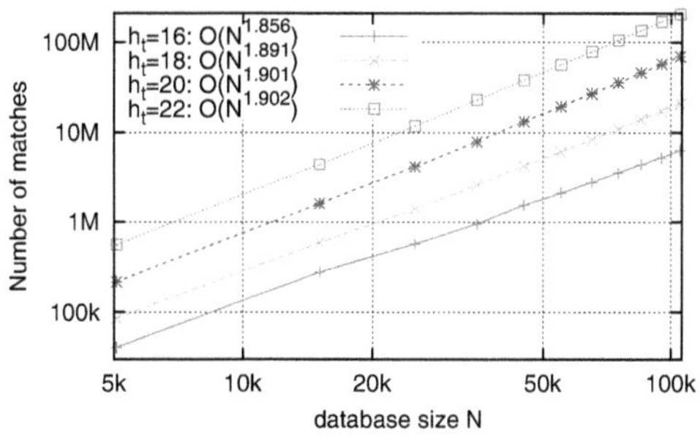

Figure 1: Number of collected matches sketches for varying image set size and of threshold h_t ($M = 768$). The complexity is empirically estimated for all h_t.

The similarity from Eqn. 4 is then modified to integrate the measurement between vectors, as

$$s_{smh}(\mathcal{X}, \mathcal{Y}) = \frac{1}{M} \sum_{j=1}^{M} \Omega(c_j(\mathcal{X}), c_j(\mathcal{Y})). \quad (7)$$

The sketch extension mentioned in Section 2 is also naturally integrated in this framework, as explained below.

SMH with Hamming Embedding (HE). HE [7] is an effective extension of BoVW to better compare images based on their local features. Compared to BoVW, a binary signature $b(x)$ is computed per feature x, which is then represented by a tuple $(q(x), b(x))$. The advantage of using a binary code is that the feature is compact in memory: The binary code length is typically 64 bits (8 bytes). HE formally computes the similarity between two images as

$$s_{he}(\mathcal{X}, \mathcal{Y}) = \frac{1}{\alpha_{\mathcal{X}} \alpha_{\mathcal{Y}}} \sum_{x \in \mathcal{X}} \sum_{y \in \mathcal{Y}} w\left(h\left(b(x), b(y)\right)\right) \times \delta(q(x), q(y)), \quad (8)$$

where $\alpha_{\mathcal{X}}$ and $\alpha_{\mathcal{Y}}$ are normalization factors and $h(.,.)$ measures Hamming distance between $b(x)$ and $b(y)$. The scalar function $w(.)$ gives a weight to the Hamming distance between the bit-vectors $b(x)$ and $b(y)$. The lower is the distance, the stronger is the weight, which equals 0 above a certain threshold h_t. We adopt the entropy weighting scheme [7].

The Sim-min-Hash framework naturally applies to HE: Eqn. 7 is simply used with

$$\Omega(c_j(\mathcal{X}), c_j(\mathcal{Y})) = w\left(h\left(b(c_j(\mathcal{X})), b(c_j(\mathcal{Y}))\right)\right). \quad (9)$$

In the case of sketches obtained from multiple hash keys, $\Omega(c_j(\mathcal{X}), c_j(\mathcal{Y})) = 0$ if (a) one of the quantization indices is different or if (b) one of the Hamming distances is above the threshold h_t. If none of these conditions is satisfied, the weight is obtained by summing the different weights (in Eqn. 9) associated with the Hamming distances. In the rest of the paper, a sketch is obtained from two hash keys.

Implementation details. Similar to HE, the Sim-min-Hash representation takes a set of tuples (key, two binary codes) as input. The main difference is that the set of tuples is of fixed size, *i.e.*, M'. An inverted file is constructed for each of the M' sketches. The lists are accessed with the keys (which are obtained with Eqn. 5). Each element in the list contains an image id and two binary codes. Note that there is exactly one such entry per image in each inverted file. The search is conducted similarly as in HE. The difference is that SMH queries M' sketches separately in M' inverted files.

Table 1: Retrieval Performance on University of Kentucky (4×Recall@top4) and Oxford5k (mAP), Oxford105k (mAP) Datasets. k=32k.

Method	UKB	Oxford5k	Oxford105k	AVG. time*
BoVW	2.97	33.8	20.3	72 ms
HE [7]	**3.59**	**66.1**	**62.0**	46 ms
mHash [3]	2.37	19.1	13.8	26 ms
SMH	2.70	32.5	22.0	1.2 ms
Miner [14]	1.74	1.1	1.1	1.2 ms

*: the average time cost is measured on Oxford105k.

In the cross-matching scenario, the matched sketches are kept in a long buffer to improve the memory access efficiency (better use of cache with sequential access). This is possible if the number of matches does not explode with the size of dataset, which is possible with our technique even for million-sized collection. For the regular min-Hash, BoVW or HE, the total number of matches becomes rapidly prohibitive as the database grows. This strategy improves the speed by more than one order of magnitude compared to updating an array cumulating image scores.

The threshold h_t is one of the two parameters (along with M) that affects the quality and efficiency of the HE Sim-min-Hash. Its impact is analyzed in Fig. 1, where we plot the total number of matches collected when performing the full cross-matching of a large collection, namely the Oxford105k benchmark [11]. The figure shows that the number of matches grows quadratically for larger thresholds. This has an undesirable impact on both the memory and the efficiency. Lower thresholds reduce the burden of processing the matches and suppress the fast growth of memory consumption. In the rest of the paper, we adopt $h_t = 18$ as a compromise between quality and memory/speed complexity.

4. EXPERIMENTS

This section compares Sim-min-Hash with HE with the regular min-Hash [3]. We also compare with the conventional BoVW and HE [7] approaches, and with the recent *Miner* technique [14], which focuses on image linking in large collections. The Miner uses fewer features (10 per image) and a smaller vocabulary size (k=1024), on purpose. For all other algorithms, we used the same input SIFT descriptors and visual vocabulary (k=32k) learned on an independent dataset. The standard choices are adopted for BoVW and HE [7], except that we use the RootSIFT [1] variant. $M' = 768$ sketches are used for both min-Hash and SMH. We focus on the quality of the initial links provided by these algorithms, which is the most costly operation. Note that techniques such as spatial verification or query expansion are complementary and shown effective with min-Hash [3].

Datasets and evaluation protocol. We have used public benchmarks, namely the Oxford5k-105k [11] (up to 105k images) and UKB benchmarks [9] (10k images). The evaluation is carried out considering two scenarios:

1. A regular image search task;
2. The discovery task to detect visually related images.

For image search, we adopt the standard evaluation protocol associated with each benchmark: mean average precision (mAP) is employed for Oxford datasets and the average number of images ranked in first 4 positions is used for UKB. For discovery, the systems must attribute a score to all possible links in the collection. The pairwise connections between

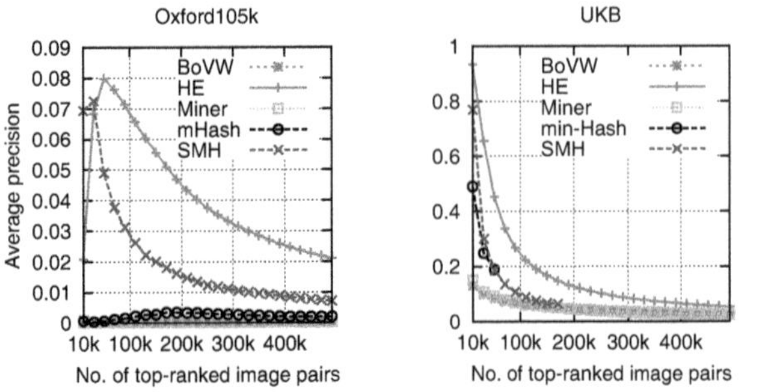

Figure 2: Link discovery: average precision against the number of selected links.

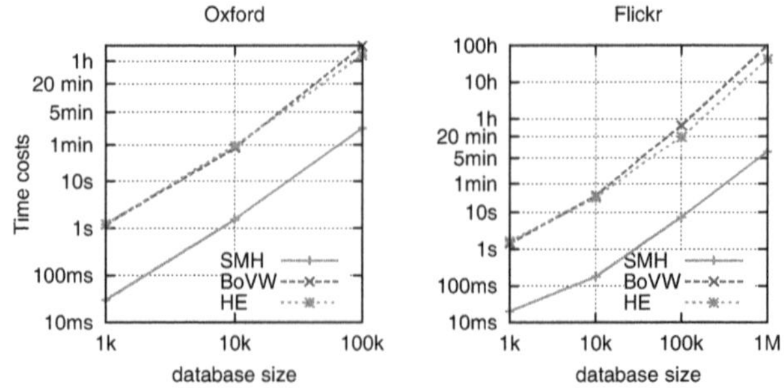

Figure 3: Timings for linking an image collection.

images from image groups are treated as the ground-truth. The precision curves are drawn by checking the percentage of true-positive connections at each truncating point. Note that the precision on Oxford105k is low, partly because many true-positive pairs are out of the ground-truth coverage [3]. All the experiments have been pulled out on single core (2.8GHz).

Image retrieval scenario. Table 1 shows that the performance of SMH is consistently better than that of conventional min-Hash. It is also much faster by limiting the number of random memory accesses. Note however that SMH uses more memory (+16 bytes/sketch) to store the binary vectors. The SMH's performance is close to BoVW for this task, but it is 60 times faster. As expected, HE performs the best, but is much slower than SMH and requires more memory because the number of features is larger than the number of sketches. The Miner technique is not adapted to this retrieval task: It is very efficient but gives poor results.

Link discovery scenario. Figure 2 reveals a consistent behavior of the algorithms over two datasets. Both Miner and BoVW achieve poor performances because the absolute scores are not reliable. In contrast, the Jaccard measure estimated by min-Hash is more consistent across queries. This explains the better behavior of min-Hash over BoVW for discovery compared to the search task, since search only considers the relative scores for a given query.

The best methods are clearly those using a non-binary similarity between local descriptors, namely HE and our SMH method. In this discovery task, SMH significantly outperforms BOW and min-Hash. SMH is especially interesting for this task because it is the most discriminative approach in the set of efficient approaches (mHash and Miner).

Complexity and timings. All the algorithms considered here are *theoretically* quadratic in the number of images. Figure 3 reports the cost, for varying subset sizes and excluding the description cost, of finding all the links from the Oxford105k dataset and from a larger dataset comprising one million Flickr images and described by a total of approximately 2 billion descriptors. The timings have been measured on a single core of the same machine. The code has a similar degree of optimization for all techniques.

As one can see, SMH is between one and two orders of magnitude faster than BoVW and HE. With the same query time, it processes a set at least one order of magnitude larger than these techniques.

5. CONCLUSION

Sim-min-Hash is an efficient and effective way to compare sets of vectors, which improves the original min-Hash technique for comparing set of vectors. It is well adapted to linking images in large collections, thanks to its higher efficiency over regular search techniques: Linking the images of a million-sized image collection is fulfilled in about 7 minutes on a single processor core.

Acknowledgements. This work was done within the Quaero project, funded by Oseo, French agency for innovation.

6. REFERENCES

[1] R. Arandjelović and A. Zisserman. Three things everyone should know to improve object retrieval. In *CVPR*, 2012.

[2] A. Z. Broder. On the resemblance and containment of documents. In *Proc. Compression and Complexity of Sequences*, 1997.

[3] O. Chum and J. Matas. Large-scale discovery of spatially related images. *PAMI*, Feb. 2010.

[4] O. Chum, J. Philbin, M. Isard, and A. Zisserman. Scalable near identical image and shot detection. In *CIVR*, 2007.

[5] O. Chum, J. Philbin, and A. Zisserman. Near duplicate image detection: min-hash and tf-idf weighting. In *BMVC*, 2008.

[6] K. Heath, N. Gelfand, M. Ovsjanikov, M. Aanjaneya, and L. J. Guibas. Image webs: Computing and exploiting connectivity in image collections. In *CVPR*, 2010.

[7] H. Jégou, M. Douze, C. Schmid. Improving bag-of-features for large scale image search. *IJCV*, May 2010.

[8] H. Jégou, C. Schmid, H. Harzallah, and J. Verbeek. Accurate image search using the contextual dissimilarity measure. *PAMI*, Jan. 2010.

[9] D. Nistér and H. Stewénius. Scalable recognition with a vocabulary tree. In *CVPR*, 2006.

[10] L. Pang, W. Zhang, H.-K. Tan, and C.-W. Ngo. Video hyperlinking: libraries and tools for threading and visualizing large video collection. In *ACMMM*, 2012.

[11] J. Philbin, O. Chum, M. Isard, J. Sivic, and A. Zisserman. Object retrieval with large vocabularies and fast spatial matching. In *CVPR*, 2007.

[12] D. Qin, S. Gammeter, L. Bossard, T. Quack, and L. van Gool. Hello neighbor: Accurate object retrieval with k-reciprocal nearest neighbors. In *CVPR*, 2011.

[13] J. Sivic and A. Zisserman. Video Google: A text retrieval approach to object matching in videos. In *ICCV*, 2003.

[14] W. Voravuthikunchai, B. Crémilleux, and F. Jurie. Findging groups of duplicate images in very large datasets. In *BMVC*, 2012.

[15] B. Wang, Z. Li, M. Li, and W.-Y. Ma. Large-scale duplicate detection for web image search. In *ICME*, 2006.

[16] X.-J. Wang, L. Zhang, M. Liu, and W.-Y. Ma. ARISTA: image search to annotation on billions of web photos. In *CVPR*, 2010.

Recognizing the Royals - Leveraging Computerized Face Recognition for Identifying Subjects in Ancient Artworks

Ramya Srinivasan, Amit Roy-Chowdhury
Department of Electrical Engineering
University of California, Riverside

Conrad Rudolph, Jeanette Kohl*
Department of Art History
University of California, Riverside

ABSTRACT

We present a work that explores the feasibility of automated face recognition technologies for analyzing identities in works of portraiture, and in the process provide additional evidence to settle some long-standing questions in art history. Works of portrait art bear the mark of visual interpretation of the artist. Moreover, the number of samples available to model these effects is often limited. From a set of portraiture of the Renaissance and Baroque periods, where the identities of subjects are known, we derive appropriate features that are based on domain knowledge of artistic renderings, and learn and validate statistical models for the distribution of the match and non-match scores, which we refer to as portrait feature space (PFS). Thereafter, we use this PFS on a number of cases that have been "open questions" to art historians. They are usually in the form of validating two portraits as belonging to the same person. Using statistical hypothesis tests on the PFS, we provide quantitative measures of similarity for each of these questions. It is, to the best of our knowledge, the first study that applies automated face recognition technologies to the analysis of portraits of multiple subjects in various forms - paintings, death masks, sculptures.

Categories and Subject Descriptors

I.4.9 [**Image Processing and Computer Vision**]: Applications

Keywords

Face recognition; Portrait art; Feature selection

1. INTRODUCTION

Portraits have had a long history encompassing a wide range of art works from ancient sculptures to modern day paintings. Most premodern and early modern portraiture were depictions of people important in their own worlds – from kings and queens to other prominent aristocrats in the society. However, a large number of portraits from before the nineteenth century have lost identities of their subjects through the fortunes of time.

Analysis of faces in portraits can offer significant insights into the personality, social standing, profession and age of the subject they represent. However, this is not a simple task since a portrait can be "subject to social and artistic conventions that construct the sitter as a type of their time" [9], thus resulting in large uncertainty about their identities. Art historians have some lingering ambiguities (based on resemblance of facial features) with respect to certain pairs of portraits whose identities are unknown. Face recognition technologies can be very valuable in providing a quantifiable measure of similarity and an independent source of evidence that can help resolve these long-standing questions.

Challenges: Face recognition in artworks has challenges apart from typical ones such as variations in pose, illumination and facial expression. Some are described below.

1) Choice of features: The chosen features should best justify artists' renditions and possess high discriminating power. Although there has been some preliminary work on this for paintings in general [3], there is little to no work on understanding how to model the style in face portraiture across artists. This leads to interesting questions in machine learning on combinations of various algorithms that are pertinent to the present scenario.

2) Lack of sufficient training data: Many existing face recognition methods assume that extensive training data is available. This is rarely the case here since we are asked to identify similarity between two faces drawn by different artists without having a variety of training examples for these artists. This is due to the difficulty in acquisition of such images from musuems owing to their limited availability, cost and established authenticity. Merely pulling images off the internet would lack scientific integrity. Further, we need to logically choose a set of related images that are relevant to art historians and adhering to specific period styles.

Overview: Figure 1 illustrates the procedure adopted in our work. Artists' renditions are examined to arrive at relevant features for analysis (Sec 2.1) - these being local features (LF) and anthropometric distances (AD). For the pairs of images with *known* identities, we compute LF and AD similarity. Similarly, set of non-match scores are obtained from instances that are known to not match (Sec 2.2). Using Fischer linear discriminant analysis, scores from LF and

*This work was partially supported by an award from the National Endowment for the Humanities, Award No: HD-51735-13.

MM'13, October 21–25, 2013, Barcelona, Spain.
Copyright 2013 ACM 978-1-4503-2404-5/13/10 ...$15.00.
http://dx.doi.org/10.1145/2502081.2502153 .

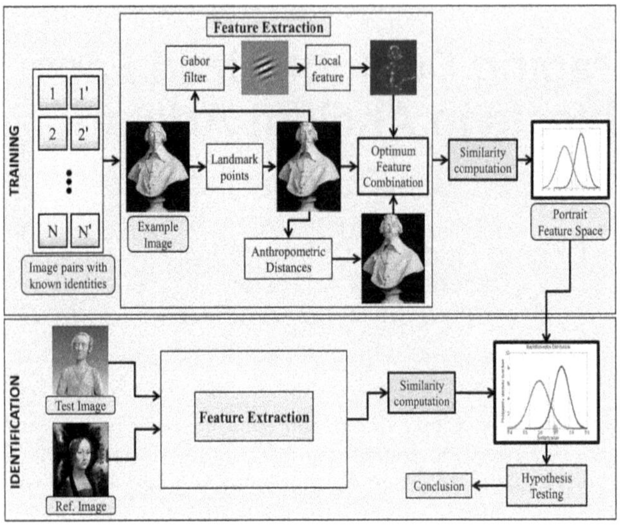

Figure 1: Overview of the Methodology

AD are fused in a way so as to maximize the variance between classes (match/non-match) while maintaining a small variance within each class. Thereafter, using RANSAC algorithm, we fit probability density functions (PDF) to the match and non-match scores and prune outliers to obtain distributions of match and non-match scores (Sec 2.3). We call these learned distributions as Portrait Feature Space (PFS),which is then validated on known instances. For identification purposes, the position of the similarity score between test and reference image in the PFS is used to arrive at conclusions using statistical hypothesis tests (Sec 3).

Contributions: The following are the main contributions of the work :

1. Based on domain knowledge of artists' styles, we identify relevant features that possess high discriminating power.
2. Using statistical pattern recognition tools, we learn and validate PFS from instances with known subjects.
3. We show how unknown subjects can be compared against a reference image using hypothesis testing on the learned distributions.

Related work: Face recognition can be categorized under the broad heading of biometric identification [2]. A survey of still and video based face recognition research is provided in [11]. The vast majority of face recognition techniques have been employed in surveillance and entertainment applications.

Analysis of paintings using sophisticated computer vision tools has gained popularity in recent years [6]. A recent work has explored application of computer based facial image analysis in artworks [7]. The proposed approach used a statistical method for 3D face shape estimation to qualitatively evaluate similarity. While [7] focussed on validating one subject against 4 candidates, our problem is broader. We discriminate between multiple subjects (both genders) across many art-forms/artists taking into account artistic conventions of those times to learn PFS and analyze test cases with respect to PFS. Also, for the present analysis, shape information was found to be less discriminative when compared to other features such as AD and LF. This can be partly attributed to the evidence that artists often focused on LF and took some liberties with shape [9]. This is further substantiated by the use of local features in matching forensic sketches (an art-form) to human faces in works such as [12].

Description of the Dataset: We were provided 34 pairs of images where the identities of the subjects were known. A part of these images was used to learn the PFS and the rest was used to validate it. We were also provided 11 pairs of reference and test images wherein we had to find whether the subject depicted in test image(whose identity is unknown)is same as that depicted in reference image (whose identity is known).The art works consisted of death masks, paintings and sculptures of several aristocrats. A sample representation is provided in Figure 2. The images were carefully vetted for authencity and relevance to a particular artistic style.

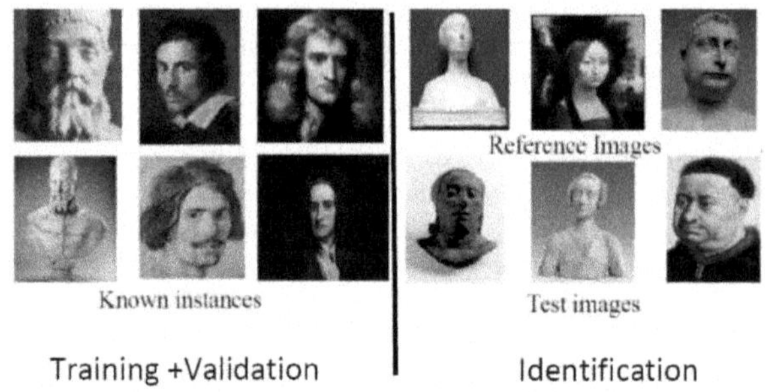

Figure 2: Sample representation of dataset—Columns 1-3 denote images used to learn and validate PFS while columns 4-6 denote images used in testing.

2. LEARNING PORTRAIT FEATURE SPACE

2.1 Feature Selection

Understanding artists' styles: Prominent facial features of a subject are retained in art works of the same subject by various artists [9]. Evidence regarding preserving certain salient body proportions (also known as anthropometric distances) in art works can be obtained from [8]. The importance of these distances is evident in various cultures starting from the ancient Egyptian era to the more recent Renaissance era.

Choice of Features: We find the following aspects emphasized by various artists particularly useful for analysis.

1. Local Features: These include features such as eye corners, nose tip, etc. which are specific to a person. One of the most well-known approaches to analyze local facial features is by Elastic Bunch Graph Matching [10] where faces are represented as image graphs based on fiducial points on the face (e.g., eyes, nose) extracted using Gabor filters. Gabor wavelets are very robust and biologically relevant since they mimic the behavior of visual cortex. This method is useful in extracting the features which artists emphasize.

2. Anthropometric Distances: These include salient distances such as width of forehead etc. We leverage upon methods that have provided normative models of facial measurements with the degree of deviation [1].

2.2 Feature Extraction

Each of the features mentioned above is extracted from the portrait images, the details of which, we explain below.

1. Local features: A set of 22 fiducial points is used to represent each face. These include forehead tips (left, right), forehead center, chin bottom, eye corners (right, left of each eye), iris (left, right), cheekbones (left, right), nose top, nose bottom, mouth corners (left, right), chin ear corners (left, right), points on temple (left, right), and points on chin (left, right). The precise location of these points is determined by registering a generic mesh on the face and finding the corresponding points between them.

Gabor jets are evaluated at each of these fiducial points. A jet describes a small patch of grey values in an image around the fiducial points described above. It is based on convolution of the image with Gabor wavelets corresponding to 5 frequencies and 8 orientations.

We evaluate similarities between jets across corresponding fiducial points n in two faces as described in [10]. LF similarity score between two portraits is evaluated as the average of jet similarities over all fiducial points N.

Anthropometric Distances: All images are normalized with respect to scale and orientation. A set of 11 salient anthropometric distances, represented as a vector, characterizes each face. These distances include distance between iris, between forehead center and chin bottom, between forehead tips, between nose top and bottom, between chin ear cornors, between mouth corners, between cheekbones, between points on chin, between forehead center and nose bottom, between points on temples and width of nose. The similarity between two AD vectors is evaluated by converting the distance into a similarity measure as $s_{AD}(m,n) = e^{-\beta * d}$, where d is the 2D Euclidean distance between the AD vectors $\vec{m}$, $\vec{n}$, and β is a co-efficient that is chosen suitably to obtain a discriminative dynamic range of values. In our experiements, we set β to be 5.

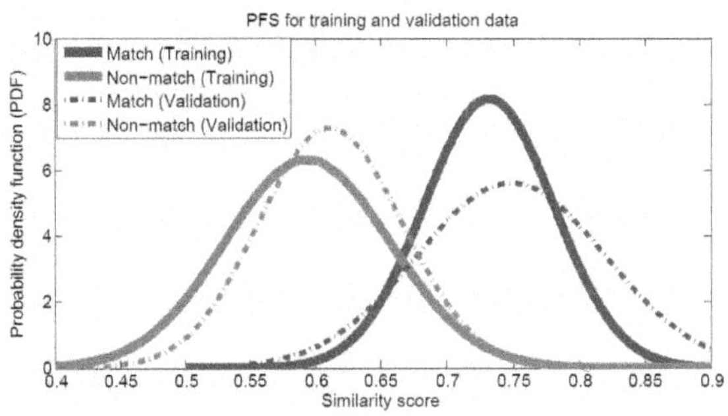

Figure 3: PFS depicting distribution of match and non-match scores. For training, match distribution was $G(.73, .048)$ **and for non-match was** $G(.59, .063)$**. The validation curves for match was** $G(.75, .055)$ **and** $G(.61, .071)$ **for non-match.** $G(\mu, \sigma)$ **denotes Gaussian distribution with mean** μ **and standard deviation** σ**.**

2.3 PFS Learning Framework

A set of portrait pairs authenticated to be of the same subject by our collaborators in art history are used as *training examples* to learn PFS and the remaining is used to validate it. We fuse scores obtained from LF and AD features of these images in a way such that the resulting distribution of match and non match scores are as peaked and disjoint as possible so as to enable efficient decision making in identification cases. Towards this, we employ the following methodology.

1. We consider a convex combination of the scores from the two measures LF and AD as $\lambda * s_{LF} + (1-\lambda) * s_{AD}$, λ being varied from 0 to 1 in steps of 0.1.
2. For every λ, we evaluate the mean and standard deviation of match and non-match scores using the RANSAC algorithm [4] to prune outliers.
3. At each λ, we evaluate the Fisher linear discriminant function, $J = \frac{S_b}{S_w}$, where S_b is between class variance and S_w is within class variance. We choose that value of $\lambda = \lambda_{opt}$ that gives the maximum value of J.
4. The distributions of match and non-match scores, with λ_{opt} obtained in Step 3, for the combined (LF and AD) feature set are modelled as Gaussians distributions with means and standard deviations estimated from Step 2.

Validation of learned PFS: We perform two-fold cross validation on the set of images, i.e., we divide the set of instances into two groups F_1 and F_2. In fold 1, we learn the PFS from F_1 and validate on F_2. In fold 2, we learn PFS from F_2 and validate on F_1. μ and σ of match and non-match scores from two folds are averaged to obtain the resulting curves shown in Fig 3. It is to be noted that these curves are dependent on the data under consideration.

3. IDENTIFICATION EXPERIMENTS

Our collaborators in art history provided us 11 paradigms wherein we were required to verify whether subjects in two potraits were the same or not. These were (1) sculptural portrait of Sforza against a death mask by Laurana, (2) Sforza painitng against a death mask by Laurana, (3) portrait of a lady at the window against Lady with Primroses attributed to Verrocchio, (4) bust of a young woman attributed to Verrocchio against a de' Benci painting by Da Vinci, (5) bust of Strozzi by Fiesole against a painting by Campin, (6a,6b,6c) uncertain painted portrait compared to a drawing, photograph and painting of Mary Queen of Scotts, (7a,7b) uncertain painted portrait compared to painted portraits of James Scott by Kneller and Wissing, and (8a) uncertain photographic portrait compared to painting of Constanze Mozart by Lange.

3.1 Identification Framework

Given the learned PFS, the question now is to verify an unknown test image against a reference image. Towards this, we employ hypothesis testing.

Hypothesis Testing: This is a method for testing a claim or hypothesis about a parameter in a population [5]. Below, we summarize it with respect to the learned PFS in arriving at the conclusion for a match.

1. Null hypothesis claims that the match distribution accounts for the test's similarity score (with reference) better than non-match distribution. The alternate hypothesis is that non-match distribution models the score better.
2. We set level of significance α (test's probability of incorrectly rejecting the null hypothesis) as 0.05, as per common pratice in such problems.
3. We compute the test statistic using one independent non-directional z test [5], which determines the number of standard deviations the similarity score deviates from the mean similarity score of the learned distributions.
4. We compute p values which are the probabilities of obtaining a test statistic at least as extreme as the one that was actually observed, assuming that the null hypothesis is true. If $p \leq \alpha$, we reject the null hypothesis.

Identity Verification: In order to examine the validity

Reference		Distractors		Conclusion
Match	Non-match	Match	Non-match	
$p > \alpha$	$p \leq \alpha$	$p \leq \alpha$	$p > \alpha$	Match
$p \leq \alpha$	$p > \alpha$	$p < \alpha$	$p \geq \alpha$	Non Match
$p > \alpha$	$p > \alpha$	NA	NA	No decision
$p < \alpha$	$p < \alpha$	NA	NA	No decision
$p > \alpha$	$p \leq \alpha$	$p > \alpha$	$p \leq \alpha$	No decision
$p \leq \alpha$	$p > \alpha$	$p \leq \alpha$	$p > \alpha$	No decision

Table 1: Various possibilities for p values of test with reference and distractors. Different colors indicate different reasons (as explained in text) for reaching the corresponding conclusion. NA: Not applicable

of the chosen approach, we consider similarity scores of the test image with artworks known to depict different persons other than the one depicted in reference image. We call these images as distractors. Depending on availability, we choose similar works by the same artist (artist of reference image) as distractors. If a test image indeed represents the same subject as in the reference image, not only should its score with the reference image be modeled through match distribution, but also its scores with distractor faces should be modeled by non-match distribution.

3.2 Analysis Scenarios

We computed similarity scores of test cases with corresponding reference image and with 10 distractors. Table 1 lists various hypothesis test scenarios that can arise [5] and the corresponsing conclusions that one can infer. Match and non-match cases are straight forward to infer from Table 1. In cases where both match and non-match distributions are likely to account for the test data in the same way, it can be said that the learned PFS cannot accurately describe the test data (black rows in Table 1). If either match or non-match distribution is more likely to account for both test as well as distractors (magenta rows in Table 1), it can be inferred that the chosen features do not possess sufficient discriminating power to prune outliers. Thus in these scenarios, it is not possible to reach any conclusion.

3.3 Case Studies of Test Images

Table 2 lists the various p values for the identification attempts. The following are the main categories of conclusions that can be inferred.

Match: Since p values satisfy conditions in blue row of Table 2, cases 1, 2, 3 and 8a are more likely modeled by match distribution.

Non match: Since case 4 satisfies conditions in red row of Table 2, it is more likely modeled by non-match distribution.

No conclusion: For cases 5, 6a, 6b and 7a both match/non-match distributions were accountable for the test scores obtained, and for cases 7b and 6c, distractors caused confusion.

4. CONCLUSIONS

We presented a work that explores the feasibility of computer based face recognition in identifying works of portriature. We provided experimental results validating the proposed approach. We also analysed the identification attempts against the backdrop of known hypotheses. We believe that these results can serve as a source of complementary evidence to the art historians. Future work will analyze larger datasets and model artistic styles.

Test	R_m	R_{nm}	D_m	D_{nm}	Conclusion
1	.485	.05	.05	.34	Match
2	.298	.002	.04	.15	Match
3	.764	.015	.04	.56	Match
4	.038	.562	.03	.5	Non-match
5	.322	.1552	.03	.55	No Decision
6a	.267	.187	.04	.4	No Decision
6b	.275	.18	.41	.3	No Decision
6c	.45	.05	.21	.02	No Decision
7a	.144	.28	.03	.5	No Decision
7b	.352	.05	.44	.03	No Decision
8a	.187	.3	.05	.56	Match

Table 2: p values for test cases. R_m and D_m denote p values of reference and distractor images with respect to match while R_{nm} and D_{nm} denote p values of reference and distractor images with respect to non-match distribution.

5. REFERENCES

[1] L. Farkas. International anthropometric study of facial morphology in various ethnic groups/races. *The Journal of Craniofacial Surgery*, 16(4):615–646, 2005.

[2] A. K. Jain, A. Ross, and K. Nandakumar. Introduction to biometrics: A textbook. *Springer Publishers ISBN: 978-0-387-77325-4*, 2011.

[3] J. Li, L. Yao, and J. Wang. Rhythmic brushstrokes distinguish Van Gogh from his contemporaries: Findings via automated brushstrokes extraction. *IEEE Trans. Patt. Anal. Mach. Intell.*, 34(6):159–176, 2012.

[4] M.Fischler and R. Bolles. Random sample consensus: A paradigm for model fitting with applications to image analysis and automated cartography. *Comm. of the ACM*, 24(6):381–395, 1981.

[5] J. Shao. Mathematical statistics. *Springer New York,ISBN-13: 9781441929785, 2nd Edition*, 2012.

[6] D. Stork. Computer vision and computer graphic analysis of paintings and drawings: An introduction to the literature. *Proc. Comp Anal. Images. Patt.*, 2009.

[7] C. Tyler, W. Smith, and D. Stork. In search of Leonardo : Computer based facial image analysis of renaissance artworks for identifying Leornado as subject. *Human Vision and Electronic Imaging*, 2012.

[8] F. Vegter and J. Hage. Clinical anthropometry and canons of the face in historical perspective. *History of Facial Anthropometry*, 106(5):1090–1096, 2005.

[9] S. West. Portriature. *Oxford University Press*, 2004.

[10] L. Wiskott, J. Fellous, N. Kruger, and C. Malsburg. Face recognition by elastic graph bunch graph matching. *IEEE Trans. Patt.Anal. Mach. Intell.*, 7:775–779, 1997.

[11] W.Zhao and R. Chellappa. Face processing: Advanced modeling and methods. *Academic Press*, 2006.

[12] L. Zhifeng and A.K.Jain. Matching forensic sketches to mug shot photos. *Patt. Anal. Mach. Intell.*, 33(3):639–646, 2011.

CollARt: a Tool for Creating 3D Photo Collages Using Mobile Augmented Reality

Asier Marzo
Public University of Navarre
Pamplona, Spain
asier.marzo@unavarra.es

Oscar Ardaiz
Public University of Navarre
Pamplona, Spain
oscar.ardaiz@unavarra.es

ABSTRACT

A collage is an artistic composition made by assembling different parts to create a new whole. This procedure can be applied for assembling tridimensional objects. In this paper we present CollARt, a Mobile Augmented Reality application which permits to create 3D photo collages. Virtual pieces are textured with pictures taken with the camera and can be blended with real objects. A preliminary user study (N=12) revealed that participants were able to create interesting works of art. The evaluation also suggested that the possibility of itinerantly mixing virtual pieces with the real world increases creativity.

Categories and Subject Descriptors

H.5.m [**Information Interfaces and Presentation**]: Misc

Keywords

Collages; mobile; augmented reality; creativity

1. INTRODUCTION

The collage technique consists in sticking together different pieces. This technique has been used by some famous artists such as Pablo Picasso and Marcel Duchamp. Nowadays it is properly established and used by both art professional and amateurs. Collages are composed of pieces from other works of art, pictures, newspaper clips or bits of colored papers. All of these elements are glued on a canvas forming a shallow creation. Nonetheless, pieces may be glued tilted or perpendicularly in order to create a tridimensional work. In the same way, stacking clippings of pictures gives some depth to collages. Extending this idea, some collages are made with physical objects or mock-ups; however, their assemblage is more difficult.

Digital technologies can be used for reducing required technical level to execute certain creative activities or to increase the effectiveness and quality of creations. Technology lowers barriers or gives new possibilities to artistic creations. It makes very interesting the idea of creating digital counterparts of traditional artistic techniques. For instance, Pottery [16] permits to mold and decorate different kinds of virtual pots, vases or jugs. Digital adaptations may not have the same haptic response as the real activity. Nevertheless, they are endowed with additional features. Options such as undo, redo and quick preview of outcomes improve exploration. Additionally, collaboration with other users and sharing through social networks are common features of present applications. Exploration, collaboration and open interchange are essential for creativity support tools [17].

Augmented reality is a visualization technique which overlaps virtual content over the real world [1]. Advances made in the recent years permit to implement this technique in handheld multi-touch devices.

We have developed CollARt, a Mobile Augmented Reality (MAR) application for creating 3D photo collages. A paper marker is used for determining the device position. The paper is the canvas in the real and in the virtual world. Therefore, the application provides intuitive navigation and placement of new pieces for the user. Furthermore, mobile platforms are widely available and support an itinerant way of creating works of art.

2. RELATED WORK

A number of applications allow the users to create collages automatically. For instance, CollageMachine [11] assembles images fetched from the Internet based on the preferences and interests of the user. Similarly, StainedGlass [7] extracts frames from a video and creates a digest of it in form of a photo composition. Setting a target illustration an algorithm can place a set of images in an empty canvas trying to fit the shapes, colors and textures of the target picture [9]. In the same way as Arcimboldo did in his paintings. The same principle can be applied for assembling a set of tridimensional objects to conform a target 3D volume [6]. PhotoPieces is a mobile application [15] in which the users create photo collages filling with pictures a template made of different regions. Templates are chosen from a library or made by segmenting a photo.

Augmented Reality has been used for painting virtually over the surface of real objects using a head mounted display (HMD) and an electronic pencil [8]. Different textures can be used for the stroke as well as solid colors or patterns captured from the real world. In addition, virtual objects with premade textures can be attached to the real entities. A field study conducted with a similar system in an architecture school [10] revealed several benefits derived from its tangibility; however a projector was used instead of a HMD. Additionally, the system permitted to attach different virtual objects to tangible markers improving the configurability [2]. Small planar markers or panoramic views can be augmented with virtual objects [12] and shared with other users. That system is composed of a mobile augmented reality application and a server which stores the creations. ColAR [5] recognizes the outlines of a picture from a set of predefined ones. It can reproduce a 3D animation using the real filling that the users painted as textures for the objects. ARPaint [13] can augment a picture permitting to trace strokes on the plane which contains it.

Our work differs from previous ones as CollARt is a multi-touch mobile augmented reality application which merges virtual objects with real objects. Furthermore, it permits to create tridimensional photo collages naturally and its workflow encourages exploration.

MM'13, October 21–25, 2013, Barcelona, Spain.

http://dx.doi.org/10.1145/2502081.2502154

3. COLLART

CollARt is a mobile application which allows the user to create 3D compositions. Using augmented reality, virtual objects can be blended with the real world. Pieces are textured with pictures taken with the camera (Figure 1). When the paper marker is detected by the application it shows the live feedback of the camera and the virtual pieces overlapped with it. By touching the screen the menu icons toggle visible, permitting to undo, redo, clear, select or add a new piece.

Pressing the add icon makes the camera view to come out for taking a picture. Afterwards the placement options permit you to rotate, scale, adjust the texture or select between different shapes for the current piece (Figure 2). Planar pieces such as squares, circles or rectangles as well as tridimensional volumes, namely cubes, spheres or pyramids are available. For the rotation mode we used the interaction technique defined in [14]. The position and rotation of the piece relative to the device will remain constant. Additionally, one finger can be used to perform an Arcball rotation in view space, and two fingers to rotate or change the depth of the object across the view axis. Adjusting the texture allows the user to modify the part of the previously taken picture which is mapped to the current piece.

Whenever the marker is detected by the camera and placing mode is active, the tick button appears. Pressing it will place a piece on the current position. As a result, the marker is only needed to place pieces or to observe the ongoing creation. Pressing the finish button will return to the main menu. By pressing the select icon the application switches to select mode. In this mode a crosshair is shown, permitting to select any object for modifying it.

Figure 1. Tridimensional pieces textured with pictures taken with the camera.

Figure 2. Placing one piece using the interface as seen by a user on the mobile device screen.

Virtual objects are blended with real objects. Therefore, the real pieces occlude and clip virtual objects (Figure 3). Visual recognition in real time of the world objects would require a considerable time of processing or to paint them with markers. Consequently, several premade scenes were created, defining virtual replicates of the real objects.

CollARt has been implemented using C++, OpenGL and GLSL. The target platform is iOS and the library Vuforia [17] has been used for tracking the marker.

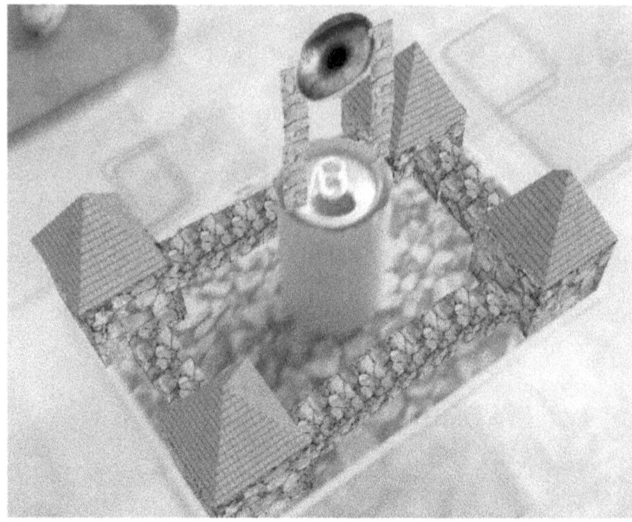

Figure 3. A creation which blends virtual pieces with a real canister.

4. USER EVALUATION

A preliminary evaluation was conducted with 12 people (3 women and 9 men), aged between 18 and 43 (M=27.75, SD=7.08). Participants had heterogeneous professions and computer experience in some cases. Two users were left-handed. Four of the participants had formal artistic education and two of them worked as professional artists.

The main purpose of the evaluation was to check if blending virtual elements with real objects and itinerant creations are interesting properties to the users. As a general objective we tried to determine whether users were able to create original collages with artistic value. Additionally, we aimed to detect usability problems and annotate interesting behaviors of the users. Searching for more concrete uses of the tools was another goal of the study.

Participants performed the evaluation individually and without time constraints. At the beginning they had to complete the training activity. In it, users were asked to place four cubes at each corner of the canvas and two squares perpendicularly between them on the middle. The purpose was to teach the users how to use the basic functions of the application. Accordingly, they were assisted during it.

Four tasks were designed: table, vertical, cylinder and on the move. In the table and vertical tasks the users had to create a collage having no restriction on shapes, pictures or time. In the table task the canvas rested horizontally on a table whereas in the vertical task it was stuck to a wall, this simple orientation change may affect usability and creations. The cylinder task consisted of placing a real canister in the middle of the canvas. The real cylinder clipped and hid virtual pieces influencing the collage as it was another existing piece. In the on the move task, using indoor and outdoor pictures was mandatory.

Users were split randomly into two groups. The first group performed the training activity followed by the table and vertical tasks. The second group did the training activity and subsequently the cylinder and the on the move tasks. Therefore, group 2 was more focused on exclusive features of the application such as blending virtual pieces with reality and on the move use.

Figure 4. Various collages made by the participants.

Afterwards, all the participants filled in a questionnaire for measuring the system usability (SUS) [3] and a series of question for determining CollARt's value as a creativity support tool (CSI) [4]. Both SUS and CSI range from 0 to 100, the higher the value the more usable or creativity supportive. In addition, they had to score the ease and originality of each task using a one to five Likert scale. Various open questions were answered by the users, namely: what aspects have been more interesting?, what difficulties have arisen using the tool?, in what places or context would you use the tool? and can you devise a game to be played with the tool?. T-tests were used for comparing both CSI and SUS scores between the first group and second group. One-way-ANOVA was used for the Ease and Originality scores between the tasks as each participant performed only two of them.

The average CSI score reported by the participants was 71.66 (SD=7.52) for the group 1 and 73.88 (SD=7.57) for the group 2. The score is higher in the group 2; however, there was not a significant difference between the groups ($t(10) = -0.50$, $p > 0.05$). The average SUS of the questionnaires was 72.08 (SD=11.77) for the group 1 and 80.83 (SD=15.46) for the group 2. The score is higher in the group 2. Nonetheless, there was not a significant difference between the groups ($t(9) = -1.10$, $p > 0.05$).

The easiness of completing each task was 4.08 (SD=1.24) for the training, 4.16 (SD=0.40) for the table task, 4.16 (SD=0.75) for the vertical task, 4.16(SD=1.16) for the cylinder and 4.33 (SD=0.81) for the on the move task; there was no significant difference between the four tasks ($F_{3,20} = 0.06$, $p > 0.05$). The perceived originality of the creation for each task was 2.25 (SD=1.05) for the training, 3.5 (SD=1.37) for the table task, 3.66 (SD=1.36) for the vertical task, 3.83 (SD=0.98) for the cylinder and 4.33 (SD=1.03) for the on the move task; there was no significant difference between the four tasks ($F_{3,20}= 0.43$, $p > 0.05$).

Mean time to perform the evaluation was approximately half an hour. Users spent in average 10 minutes per task. Creations represented buildings, creatures or abstract shapes (Figure 4). The training period lasted five minutes in average and all users managed to work with the application. Nevertheless, one user created collages without sense of space as pieces were placed randomly. In the same way five users did not use all the features, specifically they did not scale pieces or adjusted the textures. All of the participants took more than one picture and expressed to enjoy the activity. Furthermore, six of them asked if the application was available for later use.

5. DISCUSSION

Features such as mixing virtual content with the real world and on the move creations seem to provide better support for creativity than other features of the application as the group 2 obtained higher scores. Nonetheless, the difference was not significant and since the evaluation was preliminary, CSI results were not weighted. SUS scores were higher in the second group. The reason is that the real cylinder intersects the virtual objects. Therefore, it provides a better perception of the position and orientation of the ongoing piece placement. According to the questionnaires, placing the objects and perceiving their true position was the most difficult aspect of using the application.

During the on the move task the marker was smaller, consequently the users did not need to be so far from it. In that task they did not have to connect anything with the cylinder. Those may be the reasons of why they reported the task as the easiest one to perform. The training was slightly more difficult as it required placement of objects with a certain layout. Owing to the fact that placing objects is the most problematic aspect, future improvements will add snap to grid or vertex features. Another possibility would be to add physic simulation or shadows to the collage pieces. Professional 3D software may give more precise results; however, the time required for teaching the users to perform the same tasks is more elevated.

Originality was higher for the on the move task. Probably the users had more objects to photograph. The cylinder task was not the most original. Apparently the cylinder shape conditioned the placement of the pieces. All the users agreed that the most interesting aspect was to take pictures and apply them to tridimensional objects using a quick workflow. Several of them pointed out that integrating virtual objects with the cylinder was interesting. Furthermore, one said that it would be interesting to do it with famous buildings or paintings.

Suggested games could be grouped as map editors, interactive simulations or replacement of images in traditional board games. Map editors for platform games, Minecraft (Figure 5) or Sims' homes and interactive simulations such as Rude-Goldberg machines or Jenga using the pieces. CollARt could be used for playing Pictionary or Taboo but using tridimensional collages instead of pictures. Two users attached the marker to some part of their body and used it for playing (Figure 6). General improvements recommended were to add multiplayer support or the ability to share creations on Facebook.

Figure 5. A user tried to replicate a Minecraft landscape.

Figure 6. This user made a skull and performed Hamlet.

6. CONCLUSION

CollARt is a mobile augmented reality application which permits to create tridimensional photo collages. It can be used itinerantly to create works of art that blend virtual objects with real world elements. These features increase the creativity support index of the tool. New techniques for improving the tridimensional placement of objects should be evaluated. Nonetheless, users generally used the application properly, enjoyed it and created interesting works of art.

7. ACKNOWLEDGEMENTS

This work has been partially funded by the Government of Navarra through a research grant.

8. REFERENCES

[1] Azuma, R., Baillot, Y., Behringer, R., Feiner, S., Julier, S. and MacIntyre, B. Recent advances in augmented reality. Computer Graphics and Applications, vol. 21, no. 6, pp. 34-47. 2001.

[2] Binder, T., De Michelis, G., Gervautz, M., Jacucci, G., Matkovic, K., Psik, T. and Wagner, I. Supporting configurability in a mixed-media environment for design students. Personal and Ubiquitous Computing, vol. 8, no. 5, pp. 310-325. 2004.

[3] Brooke, J. SUS: A 'quick and dirty' usability scale. Usability Evaluation in Industry 189. Taylor and Francis. 1996.

[4] Carroll, E. A., Latulipe C., Fung, R. and Terry, M. Creativity Factor Evaluation: Towards a Standardized Survey Metric for Creativity Support. Creativity & Cognition Berkeley, pp. 127-136. 2009.

[5] Clark, A. and Dunser, A. An interactive augmented reality coloring book. 3D User Interfaces (3DUI), pp. 7-10. 2012.

[6] Gal, R., Sorkine, O., Popa, T., Sheffer, A. and Cohen-Or, D. 3D collage: expressive non-realistic modeling. Non-photorealistic animation and rendering, pp. 7-14. 2007.

[7] Girgensohn, A. and Chiu, P. Stained glass photo collages. IEEE International Conference on Image Processing, vol.2, pp. 871-874. 2003.

[8] Grasset, R., Boissieux, L., Gascuel, J.D. and Schmalstieg, D. Interactive mediated reality. Australasian conference on User interface, vol. 40, pp. 21-29. 2005.

[9] Huang, H., Zhang, L. and Zhang, H. Arcimboldo-like collage using internet images. ACM Transactions on Graphics, vol. 30, no. 6, p. 155. 2011.

[10] Jacucci, G., Oulasvirta, A., Salovaara, A., Psik, T. and Wagner, I. Augmented reality painting and collage: evaluating tangible interaction in a field study. Human-Computer Interaction-INTERACT, pp. 43-56. 2005.

[11] Kerne, A. Collage Machine: Temporality and Indeterminacy in Media Browsing via Interface Ecology. SIGCHI Extended Abstracts, vol. 2. 1997.

[12] Langlotz, T., Mooslechner, S., Zollmann, S., Degendorfer, C., Reitmayr, G. and Schmalstieg, D. Sketching up the world: in situ authoring for mobile augmented reality. Personal and Ubiquitous Computing, pp. 1-8. 2011.

[13] Lee, S., Jung, J., Hong, J., Ryu, J.B. and Yang, H. AR Paint: A Fusion System of a Paint Tool and AR. Entertainment Computing, pp. 122-129. 2012.

[14] Marzo, A., Bossavit, B. and Ardaiz, O. Interacting with multi-touch handheld devices in augmented reality spaces: effects of marker and screen size. Interacción Persona-Ordenador, p. 8. 2012.

[15] Marzo, A. and Ardaiz, O. A Smart Phone Tool to Create Photo Collages, Procedia Computer Science, vol. 15, pp. 159-162. 2012.

[16] Pottery. 2010. http://www.idreams.pl/Pottery/

[17] Qualcomm. Vuforia. https://www.vuforia.com/

[18] Shneiderman, B., Fischer, G., Czerwinski, M., Resnick, M., Myers, B. and 13 others. Creativity Support Tools: Report from a U.S. National Science Foundation Sponsored Workshop. Int. J. of Human–Computer Interaction vol. 20, no. 2, pp. 61-77. 2006

Spatio-Temporal Fisher Vector Coding for Surveillance Event Detection

Qiang Chen[‡+], Yang Cai[†], Lisa Brown[‡], Ankur Datta[‡], Quanfu Fan[‡], Rogerio Feris[‡]
Shuicheng Yan[+], Alex Hauptmann[†], Sharath Pankanti[‡]
National University of Singpore[+], IBM Research[‡], Carnegie Mellon University[†]
{chenqiang,eleyans}@nus.edu.sg, {caiyang,alex+}@cs.cmu.edu,
{lisabr, ankurd, qfan, rsferis,sharat}@us.ibm.com

ABSTRACT

We present a generic event detection system evaluated in the Surveillance Event Detection (SED) task of TRECVID 2012. We investigate a statistical approach with spatio-temporal features applied to seven event classes, which were defined by the SED task. This approach is based on local spatio-temporal descriptors, called MoSIFT and generated by pair-wise video frames. A Gaussian Mixture Model(GMM) is learned to model the distribution of the low level features. Then for each sliding window, the Fisher vector encoding [12] is used to generate the sample representation. The model is learnt using a Linear SVM for each event. The main novelty of our system is the introduction of Fisher vector encoding into video event detection. Fisher vector encoding has demonstrated great success in image classification. The key idea is to model the low level visual features as a Gaussian Mixture Model and to generate an intermediate vector representation for bag of features. FV encoding uses higher order statistics in place of histograms in the standard BoW. FV has several good properties: (a) it can naturally separate the video specific information from the noisy local features and (b) we can use a linear model for this representation. We build an efficient implementation for FV encoding which can attain a 10 times speed-up over real-time. We also take advantage of non-trivial object localization techniques to feed into the video event detection, e.g. multi-scale detection and non-maximum suppression. This approach outperformed the results of all other teams submissions in TRECVID SED 2012 on four of the seven event types.

Categories and Subject Descriptors

H.4 [**Information Systems Applications**]: Miscellaneous; D.2.8 [**Software Engineering**]: Metrics—*complexity measures, performance measures*

Keywords

Video Event Detection, Feature Coding, System

MM'13, October 21–25, 2013, Barcelona, Spain.

http://–enter the whole DOI string from rightsreview form confirmation.

1. INTRODUCTION

Recognizing human actions is of central importance in a variety of real-world application domains, such as intelligent video surveillance. However, accurate recognition of human actions is a challenging task due to cluttered backgrounds, occlusions, and viewpoint changes. Therefore, most approaches make simplifying assumptions, such as small changes to scale and viewpoint, in order to make the approach tractable. However, such assumptions rarely hold in practice in real-world environments, such as airports, banks, supermarkets, where intelligent video surveillance is becoming ubiquitous. Thus, there is a need to develop accurate surveillance event detection algorithms for real-world environments.

A lot of schemes have been proposed for the human action recognition, among them, methods based on feature descriptors around local interest points are now widely used in object recognition. However, most of the work [13, 14, 15, 16] can't be applied to real world application as their experimental set-up is relatively simple and clear, and in most of the conditions, very few people are performing any semantically complex action at all. Even the same type of actions may exhibit enormous variations due to cluttered background, different viewpoints and many other factors in unconstrained real-world environment as demonstrated in TREC Video Retrieval Evaluation (TRECVID) [20] [1]. To our knowledge, TRECVID has made the largest effort to bridge the research efforts and the challenges in real-world conditions by providing an extensive 144-hour surveillance video dataset recorded in London Gatwick Airport from i-LIDS Multiple Camera Tracking Scenario data [2]. In this dataset, the cameras are fixed, but the scenes are very complex, and there are a lot of people walking through on the scenes. In TRECVID 2012 Evaluation, there are 7 required events such as "CellToEar", "Embrace", "ObjectPut", "Pointing" "peopleMeet", "PeopleSplitUp" and "PersonRuns".

Most of the previous work focus on the two parts of the video action recognition: (1) the low level local feature design. Recently, spatio-temporal local features [13, 14, 15, 16, 17] have been used for motion recognition in video. The key to the success of part-based methods is that the interest points are distinctive and descriptive. Therefore, interest point detection algorithms play an important role in a part-based approach. and (2) robust classifier learning algorithm. Due to the complex nature of this problem, researchers seek non-linear or partition-based classifier, e.g. the kernel meth-

[1] `http://www-nlpir.nist.gov/projects/trecvid/`
[2] `http://www.ilids.co.uk`

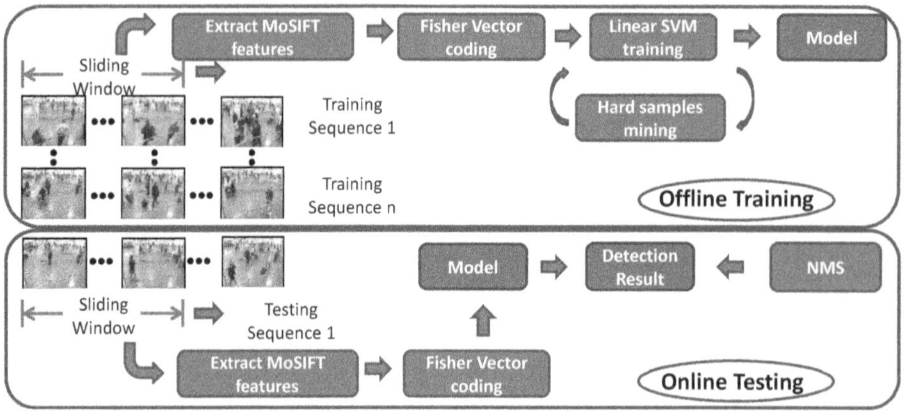

Figure 1: the illustration of the proposed system. At the offline training stage, the system represents the training video sequences as the Fisher vectors. Linear SVM and iterative hard samples mining are used. At the online testing, sliding window approach is adopted with NMS for the obtained raw detection result.

ods [5] or random forest [19] and cascade SVM [18]. In this work, we are mostly interested in two key problems of the real system: (1) how to generate the robust middle-level representation from the spatio-temporal features and (2) the efficient classifier learning. We present a generic event detection system evaluated in the SED task of TRECVID 2012. The retrospective system uses MoSIFT [17] as low level feature, Fisher Vector encoding [12] to represent samples generated by sliding window approach and linear SVM for event classification. We report our result on TRECVID 2012 dataset and our system achieves the state-of-the-art performance.

2. FISHER VECTOR ENCODING FOR SURVEILLANCE EVENT DETECTION

2.1 Framework

The framework of our surveillance event detection system is illustrated in Figure 1. During the offline training stage, we select a set of positive samples, corresponding to short video segments of a particular event specified in the ground truth annotation, and a set of negative samples, corresponding to video chunks randomly extracted from pieces of the video not containing the event of interest. For each video segment, we extract low-level features based on Motion SIFT (MOSIFT) descriptors [17], which combine information from local SIFT points and optical flow. We then obtain a more powerful mid-level representation of the video segments by applying Fisher Vector encoding (FV) [12] over MOSIFT features. Fisher vector encoding has demonstrated great success in the PASCAL VOC [2] and Image Net challenges [7] for image classification. We provide more details about this encoding technique in the next section. Finally, we use Linear SVM [1, 6] to learn the model, in conjunction with hard example mining.

During the testing stage, we use a sliding window approach for event detection. In particular, we consider multiple temporal window scales, and select the scale with the best score. We also apply non-maximum suppression to exclude multiple detections at a certain time slot.

2.2 Fisher Vector Encoding

Suppose we have a probability density function $u_\lambda(x)$ which models a generative process in feature space. Let $X = \{x_1, \cdots, x_N\}$ be the set of N local features extracted from a video segment. Then the video segment can be described by the gradient vector of log likelihood with respect to the model parameters λ:

$$G_\lambda^X = \frac{1}{N}\nabla_\lambda \log u_\lambda(X). \tag{1}$$

A natural kernel on these gradients is $K(X,Y) = G_\lambda^{X'} F_\lambda^{-1} G_\lambda^Y$ where F_λ is the Fisher information matrix of u_λ: $F_\lambda = E_{x\sim u_\lambda}[\nabla_\lambda \log u_\lambda(x) \nabla_\lambda \log u_\lambda(x)']$. As F_λ is symmetric and positive definite, it can be decomposed as $F_\lambda = L'_\lambda L_\lambda$, and the kernel $K(X,Y)$ can be expressed as a dot-product between normalized vectors $\mathcal{G}_\lambda^X = L_\lambda G_\lambda^X$ called Fisher vectors. We stress that learning a kernel classifier using the Fisher kernel is equivalent to learning a linear classier on the Fisher vectors $\mathcal{G}_\lambda^X$. As been recognized widely, linear classifiers offer significant advantages in terms of efficiency both for training and testing.

Fisher Vector encoding utilizes a Gaussian mixture model (GMM), $u_\lambda(x) = \sum_{k=1}^K \pi_k u_k(x)$ trained on local features of a large image set using Maximum Likelihood (ML) estimation. The parameters of the trained GMM are denoted as $\lambda = \{\pi_k, \mu_k, \Sigma_k, k = 1, \cdots, K\}$, where $\{\pi, \mu, \Sigma\}$ are the prior probability, mean vector and diagonal covariance matrix of the Gaussian mixture respectively. This GMM is used for description of low level features. Then for a set of low level features $X = \{x_1, \cdots, x_N\}$ extracted from a video segment y, the soft assignments of the descriptor x_i to the kth Gaussian component γ_{ik} is computed by:

$$\gamma_{ik} = \frac{\pi_k u_k(x_i)}{\sum_{k=1}^K \pi_k u_k(x_i)} \tag{2}$$

And the Fisher vector (FV) for X is denoted as $\phi(X) = \{\mathcal{G}_{\mu_1}^X, \mathcal{G}_{\sigma_1}^X, \cdots, \mathcal{G}_{\mu_K}^X, \mathcal{G}_{\sigma_K}^X\}$ where $\mathcal{G}_{\mu_k}$ and $\mathcal{G}_{\sigma_k}$ is defined as:

$$\mathcal{G}_{\mu_k}^X = \sum_{i=1}^N \frac{1}{N\sqrt{\pi_k}}\gamma_{ik}\frac{x_i - \mu_k}{\sigma_k}, \tag{3}$$

$$\mathcal{G}_{\sigma_k}^X = \sum_{i=1}^N \frac{1}{N\sqrt{2\pi_k}}\gamma_{ik}[\frac{(x_i-\mu_k)^2}{\sigma_k^2} - 1], \tag{4}$$

in which σ_k is the square root of the diagonal values of Σ_k. The FV has several good properties: (a) Fisher Vector encoding is not limited to computing visual word occurrences. It also encodes the distribution information of the feature points, which will perform more stable when encoding a single feature point. (b) it can naturally separate the video specific information from the noisy local features. (c) we can use a linear model for this representation. We have built an efficient implementation for FV which can reach the speed of 10 times faster than real time.

Power Normalization and L2 Normalization: It is easy to observe that as the number of Gaussians increases, Fisher vectors become sparser, and the distribution of features in a given dimension becomes more peaky around zero. This issue is addressed by a combination of power normalization and l2 normalization for each Fisher vector descriptor. Suppose z is one dimension of the fisher vector ϕ, the power normalization is defined as $f(z) = sign(z)|z|^{\alpha}$ where $0 \leq \alpha \leq 1$ is a parameter of the normalization and we choose $\alpha = 0.5$ in all the experiments. Subsequently, the Fisher vectors are $l2$ normalized.

2.3 Efficient Implementation

Compared with standard Bag-of-Words (BoW), Fisher vector encoding offers significant advantages in terms of computational cost. For BoW [4], the computation mainly comes from the Vector Quantization(VQ) step which has the complexity of $\mathcal{O}(NDM)$ where N is the number of local features, D is the dimensionality of local feature and M is the codebook size. For FV, the cost has two parts: (1) the GMM assignment calculation γ_{ik} which has complexity of $\mathcal{O}(NDK)$ where K is the GMM model size, and (2) the FV calculation which often takes much less time than the first part (usually $\leq 1\%$). Then we can see that since we usually use a much smaller number of Gaussians for FV (usually 128 or 256) than the number of visual words for BoW (usually a few thousands), the computation for FV is highly efficient compared to standard BoW. Our experiments show that our implementation can produce the FV 10 times faster than real time excluding the local feature extraction cost.

2.4 Multiscale Detection and Non-maximum Suppression

We need to search over different temporal scales and different step sizes to locate the exact event shot in the video sequence. However, we note that the temporal length of ground truth events can vary significantly. For example, the maximum length of PersonRuns event in the Dev dataset is 1000 frames while the minimal length is 10 frames – such diversity of event duration brings a huge search space causing the computation cost to be too high. Instead of an exhaustive search, we select three scales which are closest to the average duration of each event and accept the scale with best performance.

Non-maximum suppression (NMS) is widely used in many computer vision tasks, e.g. edge detection or object detection. For the SED task, we perform NMS by setting all scores in the current neighborhood that are lower than the maximum value in that neighborhood to zero (or lowest value). The current score of the sliding window is then compared to this maximum value. If lower it is set to zero otherwise the value is unchanged.As a result, we supress multiple detections for a single event.

3. EXPERIMENTS

3.1 Experimental Setting

We tested the effectiveness of our approach on 7 events defined in the TRECVED SED dataset, i.e. "CellToEar", "Embrace", "ObjectPut", "Pointing" "peopleMeet", "PeopleSplitUp" and "PersonRuns". The dataset was collected in a busy airport environment using 5 cameras as shown in Figure 2. In addition to high-level activity, other challenges of this data set include camera view changes, large variances in events (i.e. PeopleMeet), and small objects (i.e. CellToEar), to name a few. The training data (also called development set) consists of 100 hours of video and the evaluation set has an additional 50 hours of data. The annotations of the development set (temporal extents and event labels) are made available to the participants. In our experiments, we partitioned the development set into two equal part for validation.

Figure 2: **Typical video shot for TRECVID dataset. Top-left and top-right are "Pointing" event. Bottom-left is "CellToEar" event. Bottom-right is "PersonRuns" event.**

We use Fisher Vector encoding to represent video events, and build linear event detector both for efficiency and performance. We first extracted MoSIFT descriptors on each frame. Each MoSIFT feature is further reduced to 80 dimensions by PCA. We then trained a GMM model with 256 codebooks, which leads to a Fish Vector of length of $2 \times 80 \times 256 = 40960$. We also performed hard samples mining on the training set to make the detectors more generalized. More specifically, we tested the learned model on the training data and set the negative samples with high confidence as hard samples. Finally, we performed 2-fold cross validation to determine the detection threshold. Ideally an exhaustive search over temporal space would be needed for test. However such a method is prohibitively costly, and could result in imbalanced output with different scales. Thus we only performed event detection at three window sizes (i.e. 30, 60 and 120 frames), with the best performance taken as the final output. We follow the TRECVID evaluation rule. The performance of the detection results is evaluated by the actual Detection Cost Rate (DCR) and minimum DCR. DCR is a linear combination of the two errors: Missed Detections (MD) and False Alarms (FA) [3], and reflects a tradeoff between these two error types. A lower DCR indicates a better performance.

3.2 Evaluation on Development Set

We split the development set into half for training and half for testing. Only the results on Camera 3 (1/5 of the overall data, roughly 20 hours of data) are reported here since Camera 3 has the most frequent events. The results on other cameras are consistent with those of camera 3 according to our experiments. We primarily compared our proposed FV-based approach against the popularly used BoW method in

[3]http://www.itl.nist.gov/iad/mig/tests/trecvid/2012/doc/SED12-EvalPlan-v03.html

Table 1: The minimum DCR comparison on the development dataset.

	FV_30	FV_60	FV_60_noNMS	FV_120	BoW_60	FV_best
CellToEar	**1.0001**	1.0005	1.0005	1.0005	1.0005	1.0001
Embrace	0.9632	**0.9358**	0.9902	0.9702	0.9913	0.9358
ObjectPut	0.9999	**0.9993**	1.005	1.005	1.0005	0.9993
PeopleMeet	0.9012	**0.8866**	1.005	0.9125	0.9988	0.8866
PeopleSplitUp	1.005	**0.9913**	1.005	1.005	1.0005	0.9913
PersonRuns	**0.6324**	0.6555	0.7995	0.6812	0.9957	0.6324
Pointing	**0.9824**	0.9991	0.9972	0.9991	1.0005	0.9824

Table 2: The actual DCR and minimum DCR comparison between FV primary run, BoW2011 and the others' best 2012. Please note the test video data of 2012 is different with 2011s'.

		FV		*Other's Best 2012*	
	Ranking	ActDCR	MinDCR	ActDCR	MinDCR
CellToEar	1	**1.0007**	1.0003	1.0040	0.9814
Embrace	1	**0.8000**	0.7794	0.8247	0.8240
ObjectPut	2	1.0040	0.9994	**0.9983**	0.9983
PeopleMeet	3	1.0361	0.9490	**0.9799**	0.9777
PeopleSplitUp	1	**0.8433**	0.7882	0.9843	0.9787
PersonRuns	1	**0.8346**	0.7872	0.9702	0.9623
Pointing	3	1.0175	0.9921	**0.9813**	0.9770

event detection. Table 1 lists the minimum DCR results under different settings. Here FV_n and FV_n_noNMS are our proposed approaches with and without NMS using a sliding window of size n while FV_best is the best performance out of the three tested window sizes of 30, 60 and 120 frames. BoW_60 is an implementation of BoW [4] with non-linear Chi-Square SVM using a sliding window size of 60 frames. From Table 1, we can conclude that (1) our FV-based approach outperforms BoW by a large margin on 4 events; (2) NMS contributes significantly to the overall performance improvement; and (3) multi-scale tuning helps further for some events (i.e. PersonRuns and Pointing).

3.3 Comparison with the State-of-the-art

We also compared our results on the evaluation set against the other teams' best results from 2012's TRECVID SED evaluation in Table 2. Our system performance leads the others' best performances in four events out of seven events in 2012 challenge, i.e. PersonRuns, PeopleSplitUp, Embrace and PeopleMeet. It again demonstrated the success of our system, especially the advantages of the sophisticated feature encoding method. We have also observed that our results on 4 events (for example, CellToEar) are still close to random (with DCR close to 1). Those events are often with small duration and trivial movement. We plan to seek localized methods,e.g., human detection and tracking, to tackle these more challenging events in the future.

4. CONCLUSION

In this work, we propose Fisher vector coding for surveillance event detection. With this powerful representation, we achieve an efficient solution and state-of-the art accuracy. The multi-scale detection and non-maximum suppression have been shown to be effective for event detection. We would like to incorporate other object localization methods into our BoW framework to further tackle those difficult tasks.

Acknowledgement

This work is supported by the CSIDM Project No.CSIDM-200803 partially funded by a grant from the National Research Foundation (NRF) administered by the Media Development Authority (MDA) of Singapore.

5. REFERENCES

[1] C. J. C. Burges. A tutorial on support vector machines for pattern recognition. *Data Min. Knowl. Discov.*

[2] Everingham, M. and Van Gool, L. and Williams, C. K. I. and Winn, J. and Zisserman, A. The Pascal Visual Object Classes (VOC) Challenge. IJCV. 2010.

[3] S. Lazebnik, C. Schmid, and J. Ponce. Beyond Bags of Features: Spatial Pyramid Matching for Recognizing Natural Scene Categories. In *CVPR*.2006

[4] F.-F. Li and P. Perona. A bayesian hierarchical model for learning natural scene categories. In *CVPR*.2006

[5] B. Schölkopf, R. Herbrich, and A. Smola. A generalized representer theorem. *Computational Learning Theory*, 2001.

[6] Hsieh, C.J., Chang, K.W., Lin, C.J., Keerthi, S.S., Sundararajan, S.: A dual coordinate descent method for large-scale linear svm. In: ICML. (2008).

[7] J. Deng, W. Dong, R. Socher, L.-J. Li, K. Li and L. Fei-Fei,: ImageNet: A Large-Scale Hierarchical Image Database. In: CVPR. (2009).

[8] Chatfield, K., Lempitsky, V., Vedaldi, A.: The devil is in the details: an evaluation of recent feature encoding methods. In: BMVC. (2011)

[9] Zhou, X., Yu, K., Zhang, T.: Image classification using super-vector coding of local image descriptors. In: ECCV. (2010)

[10] Yang, J., Yu, K., Gong, Y.: Linear spatial pyramid matching using sparse coding for image classification. In: CVPR. (2009)

[11] Wang, J., Yang, J., Yu, K., Lv, F., Huang, T.: Locality-constrained linear coding for image classification. In: CVPR. (2010)

[12] Florent Perronnin, J.S., Mensink, T.: Improving the Fisher Kernel for Large-Scale Image Classification. In: ECCV. (2010)

[13] I. Laptev, T. Lindeberg. Space-time interest points. In: ICCV. (2003)

[14] Schuldt, C. Laptev, B. I. Caputo Recognizing human actions: a local SVM approach. In: ICPR. (2004)

[15] S.-F. Wong, R. Cipolla Extracting spatiotemporal interest points using global information. In: ICCV. (2007)

[16] G. Willems, T. Tuytelaars, L. V. Gool. An efficient dense and scale-invariant spatio-temporal interest point detector. In: ECCV. (2008)

[17] Ming-yu Chen, Alex Hauptmann MoSIFT: Reocgnizing Human Actions in Surveillance Videos. CMU-CS-09-161, Carnegie Mellon University, 2009

[18] L. Zhang , L. Jiang , L. Bao, S. Takahashi, Y. Li, A. Hauptmann CMU-Informedia @ TRECVID 2011 Surveillance Event Detection. In NIST TRECVID workshop, (2011)

[19] Andy Liaw, Matthew Wiener Classification and Regression by Random Forest. R News. (2002)

[20] A. F. Smeaton, P. Over, W. Kraaij Evaluation campaigns and TRECVID. In: MIR. (2006)

Efficient Image and Tag Co-Ranking: A Bregman Divergence Optimization Method

Lin Wu, Yang Wang and John Shepherd
School of Computer Science and Engineering
The University of New South Wales
Sydney, Australia
{linw,wangy,jas}@cse.unsw.edu.au

ABSTRACT

Ranking on image search has attracted considerable attentions. Many graph-based algorithms have been proposed to solve this problem. Despite their remarkable success, these approaches are restricted to their separated image networks. To improve the ranking performance, one effective strategy is to work beyond the separated image graph by leveraging fruitful information from manual semantic labeling (i.e., tags) associated with images, which leads to the technique of co-ranking images and tags, a representative method that aims to explore the reinforcing relationship between image and tag graphs. The idea of co-ranking is implemented by adopting the paradigm of random walks. However, there are two problems hidden in co-ranking remained to be open: the high computational complexity and the problem of out-of-sample. To address the challenges above, in this paper, we cast the co-ranking process into a Bregman divergence optimization framework under which we transform the original random walk into an equivalent optimal kernel matrix learning problem. Enhanced by this new formulation, we derive a novel extension to achieve a better performance for both in-sample and out-of-sample cases. Extensive experiments are conducted to demonstrate the effectiveness and efficiency of our approach.

Categories and Subject Descriptors

H.3.3 [**Information Storage and Retrieval**]: [Information search and retrieval]

Keywords

Co-Ranking; Bregman Divergence; Out-of-Sample

1. INTRODUCTION

The explosion of online community-contributed multimedia data results in great focus on image retrieval. Most of social media sharing websites like Flickr allow users to upload personal images and annotate content with descriptive keywords called tags. Many ranking algorithms specialized to images on such social media repositories have been proposed to help organize the shared media data [4] or to facilitate the image ranking process [7]. However, these methods mainly focus on centrality measures on image content and the evaluations of the relative importance of images have been carried out independently, which ignores the rich information from tags, and annotations, etc. Similarly, the well-studied treatments on tag recommendation [4] and tag ranking [10] are conducted solely on the tag graph. To leverage the useful metadata including tags, and images vice versa, ranking algorithms should consider the reinforcing dependency between images and tags, which is beneficial to further improving ranking results. To this end, in this paper, we study a problem of great interest, that is, how to effectively and efficiently handle dual-relational data over two graphs, which can be named as the Co-Ranking problem (CoR).

The main idea of CoR is to explore the mutually reinforcing relationship between image and tag graphs by constructing a combined graph connecting the two graphs together. Then random walks are performed to rank the data with respect to the intrinsic geometric structure revealed by a large amount of data. CoR assigns each data point a relative ranking score by collectively leveraging the ranking information from both the image graph and tag graphs. Some works have witnessed the feasibility of CoR on a variety of data types [17, 14].

One of the main drawbacks of CoR is its high computational complexity. Given a query, CoR constructs two affinity graphs and propagates the ranking scores over the combined graph, yielding to a complexity of $O(n^3)$, where n is the size of samples in the database. Such a high cost is prohibited in large-sized databases. Another limitation of CoR comes from the case of out-of-sample. Normally, if an in-sample query is issued, CoR can use off-line pre-computation to reduce the computational cost. However, if the query is out of the database, the expensive ranking score propagation step needs to be performed in the on-line stage, which is referred to be the out-of-sample problem [1].

In this paper, we reformulate the idea of random walks into a Bregman divergence optimization fashion, which provides us a novel perspective towards the co-ranking algorithm. That is, the optimal co-ranking function can be modeled by learning an optimal kernel matrix under the Bregman divergence matrix based metric. Moveover, an efficient and effective extension is induced to figure out the challenges of high computational cost and out-of-sample case.

MM'13, October 21–25, 2013, Barcelona, Spain.

http://dx.doi.org/10.1145/2502081.2502156 .

We may summarize the main contributions of this paper as follows: (i) We formulate the CoR algorithm as a Bregman divergence optimization problem. (ii) With the new formulation, we have a novel understanding of CoR's aim, that is, to learn an optimal kernel matrix, which allows a novel extension to combat the challenges of high computational cost as well as out-of-sample problem.

2. PRELIMINARIES

2.1 The Co-Ranking Algorithm

Given the well-constructed image graph G_M and tag graph G_T, the co-ranking paradigm is coupled with two random walks over G_M and G_T. Consider the transition matrix $\mathbf{Q}$ derived from G_M, and $r_k(i)$ denotes the relevance score of image v_i with respect to the query image at iteration k. The ranking score can be obtained from the unique solution as the random walk converges:

$$\mathbf{r}_\pi = (1-\rho)(\mathbf{I}-\rho\hat{\mathbf{Q}})^{-1}\mathbf{c} \quad (1)$$

where $\mathbf{c}$ is the initial ranking vector, $\mathbf{Q}$ is changed to be the ergodic $\hat{\mathbf{Q}}$ and ρ denotes the damping factor [2].

Similarly, given the transition matrix $\mathbf{Z}$ (with random walk matrix $\hat{\mathbf{Z}}$) induced by the tag graph G_T, the random walks over G_T converge to another stationary probability distribution:

$$\mathbf{f}_\pi = (1-\rho)(\mathbf{I}-\rho\hat{\mathbf{Z}})^{-1}\bar{\mathbf{c}} \quad (2)$$

where $\bar{\mathbf{c}}$ denotes the initial relevance scores of a tag.

The random walk over the combined graph is presented in terms of a random surfer who is capable of jumping over images and their tags as well. Thus, in the process of coupling two random walks, a probability distribution will have the form ($\mathbf{r}_\pi$,$\mathbf{f}_\pi$) [17], satisfying $\| \mathbf{r}_\pi \|_1 + \| \mathbf{f}_\pi \|_1 = 1$.

2.2 The Bregman Matrix Divergence

Let $\phi : \Lambda \to \mathbb{R}$ be a real-valued strictly convex function defined over a convex set Λ. The Bregman divergence [3] with respect to ϕ is defined as

$$D_\phi(\mathbf{x},\mathbf{x}_0) = \phi(\mathbf{x}) - \phi(\mathbf{x}_0) - (\mathbf{x}-\mathbf{x}_0)^T \nabla\phi(\mathbf{x}_0).$$

Intuitively, the Bregman divergence is used to measure the closeness of two vectors. For example, if $\phi(\mathbf{x}) = \mathbf{x}^T\mathbf{x}$ then the corresponding Bregman divergence turns out to be the squared Euclidean distance: $D_\phi(\mathbf{x},\mathbf{x}_0) = \| \mathbf{x}-\mathbf{x}_0 \|^2$. We can naturally extend this definition to convex functions defined over matrices [8]. In this case, given a strictly convex, continuously differentiable function $\phi(\mathbf{X})$, the Bregman matrix divergence is defined to be

$$D_\phi(\mathbf{X},\mathbf{X}_0) = \phi(\mathbf{X}) - \phi(\mathbf{X}_0) - tr((\nabla\phi(\mathbf{X}_0))^T(\mathbf{X}-\mathbf{X}_0))$$

where $tr(\mathbf{X}_0)$ denotes the trace of matrix $\mathbf{X}_0$. Examples include $\phi(\mathbf{X}) = \| \mathbf{X} \|_F^2$, which leads to the squared Frobenius norm $\| \mathbf{X}-\mathbf{X}_0 \|_F^2$.

In this paper, we specialize on the log-determinant function $\phi(\mathbf{X}) = -\log det\mathbf{X}$, which can be expressed as the Burg entropy of the eigenvalues, i.e., $\phi(\mathbf{X}) = -\sum_i log\lambda_i$. The resulting matrix divergence becomes

$$\mathbb{D}(\mathbf{X},\mathbf{X}_0) = tr(\mathbf{X}\mathbf{X}_0^{-1}) - \log det(\mathbf{X}\mathbf{X}_0^{-1}) - n \quad (3)$$

which we call the Log-Determinant divergence [8].

3. BREGMAN DIVERGENCE DERIVED RANDOM WALKS

In the following, we will derive the random walks from a Bregman divergence optimization framework. By virtue of the new derivation, some extensions can be naturally derived to combat the aforementioned challenges.

Consider the convergent solution in Eq.(1), we can rewrite it as follows:

$$\mathbf{r}_\pi^* = (\mathbf{I}-\rho\hat{\mathbf{Q}})^{-1}\mathbf{c} = \mathbf{K}\mathbf{c}. \quad (4)$$

We omit the scaling factor 1-ρ as it does not influence the solutions. Let $\mathbf{T} = [\mathbf{t}_1, \mathbf{t}_2, \ldots, \mathbf{t}_n] \in \mathbb{R}^{m\times n}$ be the data representation in a new tag feature space of the data samples. In particular, we define $\mathbf{t}_i = \Phi(\mathbf{v}_i)$, for $i = 1, \ldots, n$, where Φ is a transformation function of the original image vector to the new tag feature space. Specifically, we introduce a canonical representation $[\widetilde{t}_1, \widetilde{t}_2, \ldots, \widetilde{t}_m]$ for $\mathbf{t}_i$, which is composed of the 0-1 indication of the tag feature basis. Specifically, we have

$$\mathbf{t}_i(j) = \begin{cases} 1, & \text{if } p(\mathbf{v}_i|\widetilde{t}_j) \geq \varepsilon; \\ 0, & \text{otherwise.} \end{cases} \quad (5)$$

Intuitively, we project each image into a tag feature space using a binary representation, which indicates to which extent the image is associated with basis tags.

We define the matrix $\mathbf{K}$ as

$$\mathbf{K} = \mathbf{T}^T\mathbf{T}, \quad (6)$$

which is a positive semi-definite matrix. Then, we present our primary theorem over the new derivation on random walks as follows.

THEOREM 1. *The matrix $\mathbf{K}$ in the convergence formulation (Eq. (4)) is the solution of the following optimization problem:*

$$\min_{\mathbf{K}} \mathbb{D}(\mathbf{K},\mathbf{I})$$
$$s.t. \sum_{i,j} \| \tfrac{1}{d(v_i)}\mathbf{t}_i - \tfrac{1}{d(v_j)}\mathbf{t}_j \|^2 q_{ij} \leq \epsilon, \ \mathbf{K} \succeq 0,$$

where ϵ is a smoothness parameter constraining similar images having close distance in the new space.

PROOF. The optimization problem seeks a $\mathbf{K}$ closest to the identity matrix measured by the Log-Determinant divergence with a regularization on normalized graph Laplacian smoothness, which can be written as a matrix form [16]:

$$\sum_{i,j} \| \frac{1}{\sqrt{d(v_i)}}\mathbf{t}_i - \frac{1}{\sqrt{d(v_j)}}\mathbf{t}_j \|^2 q_{ij} = tr(\mathbf{T}\mathbf{L}\mathbf{T}^T),$$

where $\mathbf{L} = \mathbf{I} - \hat{\mathbf{Q}}$ is the normalized graph Laplacian.

Replacing the objective function with Eq.(3) and introducing the Lagrange multiplier, the minimizing optimization problem can reformulated as follows:

$$\begin{aligned} &\min_{\mathbf{K}} \mathbb{D}(\mathbf{K},\mathbf{I}) \quad (7) \\ &= \min_{\mathbf{K}\succeq 0} tr(\mathbf{K}\mathbf{I}^{-1}) - \log det(\mathbf{K}) + \eta tr(\mathbf{T}\mathbf{L}\mathbf{T}^T) \\ &= \min_{\mathbf{K}\succeq 0} tr(\mathbf{K}\mathbf{I}) + \eta tr(\mathbf{T}^T\mathbf{T}\mathbf{L}) - \log det(\mathbf{K}) \\ &= \min_{\mathbf{K}\succeq 0} tr(\mathbf{K}\mathbf{E}) - \log det(\mathbf{K}), \end{aligned}$$

where $\mathbf{E} = \mathbf{I} + \eta\mathbf{L}$ is a positive-definite matrix and η is the Lagrange multiplier. The optimal solution $\mathbf{K}^*$ of the above optimization problem is $\mathbf{K}^* = \mathbf{E}^{-1} = (\mathbf{I} + \eta\mathbf{L})^{-1}$ [6]. Recall that $\mathbf{E} = \mathbf{I} + \eta\mathbf{L} = (1+\eta)(\mathbf{I} - \frac{\eta}{(1+\eta)}\hat{\mathbf{Q}})$, then we have $\mathbf{K}^* = (\mathbf{I} - \beta\hat{\mathbf{Q}})$, where $\beta = \frac{\eta}{(1+\eta)}$. We use $\mathbf{K}_M^*$ for the sake of distinguish. □

Similarly, we can derive another new extension from the perspective of Bregman divergence metric for the random walks over the tag graph, which is summarized in the following theorem. We define $\mathbf{K}_T$ as $\mathbf{K}_T = \mathbf{C}^T\mathbf{C}$, where $\mathbf{C} = [\mathbf{c}_1, \ldots, \mathbf{c}_n] \in \mathbb{R}^{m \times n}$ is the representation that transforms the tag samples to a new feature space. Likewise, we rewrite the Eq.(2) as follows:

$$\mathbf{f}_\pi^* = (\mathbf{I} - \rho\hat{\mathbf{Z}})^{-1}\bar{\mathbf{c}} = \mathbf{K}_T\bar{\mathbf{c}}. \quad (8)$$

THEOREM 2. *The matrix $\mathbf{K}_T$ in the convergence formulation (Eq. (8)) is the solution of the following optimization problem:*

$$\min_{\mathbf{K}_T} \mathbb{D}(\mathbf{K}_T, \mathbf{I})$$
$$s.t. \sum_{i,j} \| \frac{1}{\sqrt{D_{ii}}}\mathbf{c}_i - \frac{1}{\sqrt{D_{jj}}}\mathbf{c}_j \|^2 z_{ij} \le \epsilon,\ \mathbf{K}_T \succeq 0,$$

Likewise, we have the optimal matrix $\mathbf{K}_T^*$, which is exactly equal to the matrix $\mathbf{K}_T$ in Eq. (8).

3.1 Efficient Co-Ranking Algorithm

In the perspective of Bregman divergence, the random walk essentially learns an optimal matrix $\mathbf{K}$ close to the identity matrix under certain constraints. However, we still need to inverse a $n \times n$ matrix $\mathbf{I} + \eta\mathbf{L}$, which has the complexity of $O(n^3)$. In the following, we derive an efficient extension of co-ranking algorithm. Suppose the mapping of $\mathbf{t}_i = \Phi(\mathbf{v}_i)$ is linear, i.e., $\mathbf{T} = \mathbf{P}^T\mathbf{V}$, where $\mathbf{P}$ is a $k \times m$ matrix, then we have

$$\begin{aligned} & tr(\mathbf{K}\mathbf{I}^{-1}) - \log det(\mathbf{K}) + \eta tr(\mathbf{T}\mathbf{L}\mathbf{T}^T) \quad (9) \\ &= tr(\mathbf{V}^T\mathbf{P}\mathbf{P}^T\mathbf{V}) - \log det(\mathbf{V}^T\mathbf{P}\mathbf{P}^T\mathbf{V}) + \eta tr(\mathbf{P}^T\mathbf{V}\mathbf{L}\mathbf{V}^T\mathbf{P}) \\ &= tr(\mathbf{H}\mathbf{V}\mathbf{V}^T) - \log det(\mathbf{V}\mathbf{V}^T) - \log det(\mathbf{H}) + \eta tr(\mathbf{H}\mathbf{V}\mathbf{L}\mathbf{V}^T), \end{aligned}$$

where $\mathbf{H} = \mathbf{P}\mathbf{P}^T \succeq 0$.

As a result, the optimization problem Eq. (7) becomes

$$\min_{\mathbf{H} \succeq 0} tr(\mathbf{H}(\underbrace{\mathbf{V}\mathbf{V}^T + \eta\mathbf{V}\mathbf{L}\mathbf{V}^T}_{k \times k})) - \log det(\mathbf{H}), \quad (10)$$

where $\mathbf{H}$ is a $k \times k$ matrix. To get the optimal matrix $\mathbf{H}$, we only need to inverse a matrix with size $k \times k$, which remains unchanged as the size of database (n) grows. That is, if $k \ll n$, the computational complexity of matrix inversion is reduced dramatically. Thereby, we optimize a small matrix $\mathbf{H}$ to estimate the optimal matrix $\mathbf{K}_T^*$ or $\mathbf{K}_M^*$. Then, the complexity is reduced from $O(n^3)$ to $O(m^3) + O(n^2)$.

In fact, the computation of optimal matrix $\mathbf{H}$ learns a distance metric:

$$d_{\mathbf{H}}^2 = \| \mathbf{P}^T\mathbf{v}_i - \mathbf{P}^T\mathbf{v}_j \|^2 = (\mathbf{v}_i - \mathbf{v}_j)^T\mathbf{H}(\mathbf{v}_i - \mathbf{v}_j). \quad (11)$$

With the learned distance metric $\mathbf{H}$, $\mathbf{K}_M^*$ can be computed by $\mathbf{K}_M^* = \mathbf{T}^T\mathbf{T} = \mathbf{V}^T\mathbf{H}\mathbf{V}$. Hence, each element of the $\mathbf{K}_M^*$ can be calculated by

$$\mathbf{K}_M^*[ij] = \exp(-d_{\mathbf{H}}^2(\mathbf{v}_i, \mathbf{v}_j)/2\sigma^2) \quad (12)$$

Therefore, similar to Eq.(4), the ranking on image graph can use $\mathbf{K}_M^*$ to compute ranking scores:

$$\mathbf{r}_\pi^* = \mathbf{K}_M^*\mathbf{c} \quad (13)$$

3.2 Out-of-Sample Extension

Given a sample query out of the database, e.g., a new image query, we only need to compute a new column of the matrix $\mathbf{K}_M^*$, which avoids the update over the entire matrix. Assume that $\hat{\mathbf{V}} = [\mathbf{V}, \mathbf{v}_u] \in \mathbb{R}^{k \times (n+1)}$ is the new data matrix with the new sample $\mathbf{v}_u$, then we have the new optimal matrix $\hat{\mathbf{K}}_M^* \in \mathbb{R}^{(n+1)\times(n+1)}$:

$$\hat{\mathbf{K}}_M^* = \begin{pmatrix} \mathbf{K}_M^* & \mathbf{k}_{nu} \\ \mathbf{k}_{nu} & 1 \end{pmatrix} \quad (14)$$

Compared with traditional ranking algorithms based on random walks, which need $O(n^3)$ to propagate the ranking score, our approach updates the matrix $\mathbf{K}_M^*$ with the complexity of $O(n)$.

4. EXPERIMENTS

In this section, we conduct experimental studies over the task of contented-based image retrieval (CBIR) to show the effectiveness and efficiency of our approach.

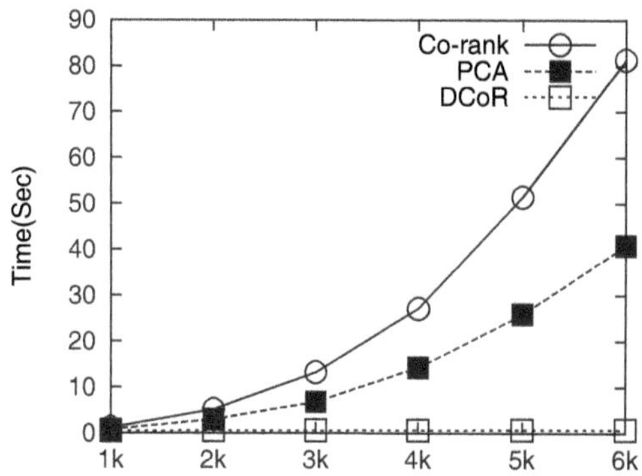

Figure 1: Time complexity. We report the running time performances of the three algorithms by ranging the size of sample from 1k to 6k. This experiment is performed over the benchmark of Caltech101 database.

4.1 Experimental Setup

Databases. All experiments are conducted on two real-world image databases: COREL and Caltech101. COREL is a widely used database for CBIR, which contains 7,000 images categorized into 70 classes [15, 5]. The Caltech101 database contains about 9,000 images divided into 101 categories with 90 averaged images per category [1].

Baselines. We implemented the following algorithms as baselines.

- PCA: PCA is the most popular linearly dimensional reduction method [13]. We set the reduced dimensionality to be 40 in our experiments.
- CoR: Co-Ranking is the simple paradigm using combined random walks to do image and tag ranking [14].
- DCoR: the efficient extension on co-ranking made in this paper by using the Bregman divergence principle.

[1] $http://www.vision.caltech.edu/Image_Datasets/Caltech101$

Image Features. We extract three features from each image: Grid color moment, wavelet texture [9] and local binary pattern [12]. Thereby, a 260-dimensional vector is formed to describe images.

Evaluation Metrics. Three evaluation metrics are considered: the Precision at top $\mathcal{K}$ ($\mathcal{P}@\mathcal{K}$), NDCG@$\mathcal{K}$ and Mean Average Precision (MAP) [11]. We present the definitions of NDCG@$\mathcal{K}$ and MAP in the follows:

$$NDCG@\mathcal{K} = Z_n \sum_{j=1}^{\mathcal{K}} \frac{2^{r(j)} - 1}{\log_2(j+1)}, \tag{15}$$

where $r(j)$ is the relevance score of the jth returned item and Z_n is a normalization constant.

MAP, as defined in [11] is:

$$MAP(Q) = \frac{1}{|Q|} \sum_{j=1}^{|Q|} \frac{1}{m_j} \sum_{k=1}^{m_j} Precision(R_{jk}) \tag{16}$$

where Q is a set of queries, q_j is one query from Q with m_j relevant items $\{i_1, \ldots, i_{m_j}\}$, and R_{jk} is the set of ranked items for q_j until i_k is reached.

4.2 Performance Evaluations

Table 1: Results on COREL and Caltech101 data sets over $\mathcal{P}@\mathcal{K}$, NDCG@$\mathcal{K}$ and MAP.

	COREL			Caltech101		
Metric	PCA	CoR	DCoR	PCA	CoR	DCoR
$\mathcal{P}$@10	40.57%	42.99%	**44.77%**	34.54%	34.94%	**38.65%**
$\mathcal{P}$@20	34.46%	37.55%	**38.35%**	29.83%	30.87%	**35.79%**
$\mathcal{P}$@30	31.83%	**34.67%**	34.05%	29.83%	30.88%	**33.73%**
NDCG@10	42.49%	45.09%	**47.51%**	35.43%	36.31%	**40.37%**
NDCG@20	38.12%	41.02%	**41.98%**	33.15%	36.07%	**37.67%**
NDCG@30	34.47%	38.20%	**38.27%**	31.81%	32.84%	**36.05%**
MAP	32.38%	**36.71%**	35.47%	31.07%	35.22%	**36.56%**

Ranking evaluations. As shown in Table 1, in terms of COREL database, as the image features are discriminative, the baselines of PCA and CoR perform reasonably well by simply using the Euclidean distance. Our approach only loses slightly to the best performance shown by CoR.

For the Caltech101 database, the method of PCA doesn't show good performance, partially due to the large number of categories and complex content in images. Also, the approach of CoR is unable to show promising results because the graphs used in CoR are based on the Euclidean distance, which cannot capture the true metrics between images. In contrast, our method constantly shows superior results over baselines by the virtue of distance metric learning.

Time complexity. We show running time complexity in Fig.1. It can be seen that CoR needs high computational cost and it is hard to be applied on the application of large-scaled databases. Although PCA reduces the running time to some degree, the cost of its computation is still not low enough to make it applicable on large-sized data sets. In contrast, our approach is more efficient as the size of database increases.

5. CONCLUSIONS

In this paper, we present a new perspective of random walks, which learns an optimal kernel matrix implemented by the Bregman matrix divergence metric. This novel formulation allows us to derive an efficient extension over the co-ranking algorithm as well as an effective strategy for the case of out-of-sample. The two extensions reduce the computational complexity dramatically. Extensive experiments are conducted to show the superiority of our approach.

6. REFERENCES

[1] Y. Bengio, J. Paiement, P. Vincent, O. Delalleau, N. L. Roux, and M. Ouimet. Out-of-sample extensions for lle, isomap, mds, eigenmaps and spectral clustering. In *NIPS*, pages 177–184, 2004.

[2] P. Berkhin. A survey on pagerank computing. *Internet Mathematics*, 2(1):73–120, 2005.

[3] L. Bregman. The relaxation method of finding the common point of convex sets and its application to the solution of problems in convex programming. *USSR computational mathematics and mathematical physics*, 7(3):200–217, 1967.

[4] Z. Guan, J. Bu, Q. Mei, C. Chen, and C. Wang. Personalized tag recommendation using graph-based ranking on multi-type interrelated objects. In *SIGIR*, 2009.

[5] X. He, D. Cai, and J. Han. Learning a maximum margin subspace for image retrieval. *IEEE Transactions on Knowledge and Data Engineering*, 20(2):189–201, 2007.

[6] S. C. H. Hoi, W. Liu, and S.-F. Chang. Semi-supervised distance learning for collaborative image retrieval and clustering. *ACM Transactions on multimedia computing, communications and applications*, 6(3), 2010.

[7] Y. Jing and S. Baluja. Pagerank for product image search. In *WWW*, 2008.

[8] B. Kulis, M. Sustik, and I. Dhillon. Learing low-rank kernel matrices. In *ICML*, 2006.

[9] M. Lades, J. Vorbruggen, J. Buhmann, J. Lange, C. von der Malsburg, R. Wurtz, and W. Konen. Distortion invariant object recognition in the dynamic link architecture. *IEEE Transactions on Computers*, 42(3):300–311, 1993.

[10] D. Liu, X.-S. Hua, L. Yang, M. Wang, and H.-J. Zhang. Tag ranking. In *WWW*, pages 351–360, 2009.

[11] C. Manning, P. Raghavan, and H. Schutze. *Introduction to information retrieval.* Cambridge University Press, Cambridge, 2008.

[12] T. Ojala, M. Pietikainen, and D. Harwood. A comparative study of texture measures with classification based on featured distributions. *Pattern recognition*, 29(1):51–59, 1996.

[13] J. Shlens. A tutorial on principal component analysis. Technical report, Measurement, 2005.

[14] L. Wu, Y. Wang, and J. Shepherd. Co-ranking images and tags via random walks on a heterogeneous graph. In *Multimedia Modeling*, 2013.

[15] B. Xu, J. Bu, C. Chen, D. Cai, X. He, W. Liu, and J. Luo. Efficient manifold ranking for image retrieval. In *SIGIR*, pages 525–534, 2011.

[16] D. Zhou, O. Bousquet, T. N. Lal, J. Weston, and B. Schölkopf. Learning with local and global consistency. In *NIPS*, 2003.

[17] D. Zhou, S. A. Orshanskiy, H. Zha, and C. L. Giles. Co-ranking authors and documents in a heterogeneous network. In *ICDM*, pages 739–744, 2007.

Real-Time Privacy-Preserving Moving Object Detection in the Cloud

Kuan-Yu Chu
National Taiwan University
chuwfuny@gmail.com

Yin-Hsi Kuo
National Taiwan University
kuonini@gmail.com

Winston H. Hsu
National Taiwan University
winston@csie.ntu.edu.tw

ABSTRACT

With the advance of cloud computing, growing applications have been migrating to the cloud for its robustness and scalability. However, sending raw data to the cloud-based service providers will generally risk our privacy; especially for cloud-based surveillance system, where privacy is one of the major concerns as continuously recording daily life. Thus, privacy-preserving intelligent analytics are in dire needs. In this preliminary research, we investigate real-time privacy-preserving moving object detection in the encrypted cloud-based surveillance videos. Moving object detection is one of the core techniques and can further enable other applications (e.g., object tracking, action recognition, etc.). One possible approach is using homomorphic encryption which provides corresponding operations between unencrypted and encrypted data. However, homomorphic encryption is impractical in real case because of formidable computations and bulky storage consumption. In this paper, we propose an efficient and secure encryption framework, which entails real-time analytics (e.g., moving object detection) in encrypted video streams. Experiments confirm that the proposed method can achieve similar accuracy as detection on original raw frames.

Categories and Subject Descriptors

K.4.4 [**Electronic Commerce**]: Security

Keywords

Privacy-preserving surveillance; Real-time detection

1. INTRODUCTION

Surveillance system has been widely used in our daily life, including roads, airports, and buildings. Although surveillance system can help us find the suspects, it somehow also invades our privacy at the same time. This subject has been addressed over years. Traditionally, surveillance systems are settled in the public space, and data are put in their own storage, so privacy is not a big issue. However, with the advance of cloud computing, computation and data are migrating to the cloud, and privacy becomes important. Although cloud computing has privacy issues, it has lots of benefits. When data is stored on the cloud, users do not need to worry about losing them, and data can be accessed everywhere. Because of these benefits, cloud-based surveillance rapidly emerges. One might enjoy the surveillance service simply via installing an IP (Internet Protocol) camera at his location. Under this setting, the computation and communication of the client (IP camera) should be as less as possible. Also, all the content recorded by the camera should be protected (encrypted) and stored in the cloud, including background. Besides, the encrypted data should be able to be decrypted for watch at users' needs. However, we still hope to entail intelligent analytic services (e.g., moving object detection, event detection, etc.) on the encrypted video streams.

MM'13, October 21–25, 2013, Barcelona, Spain.
Copyright 2013 ACM 978-1-4503-2404-5/13/10 ...$15.00.
http://dx.doi.org/10.1145/2502081.2502157.

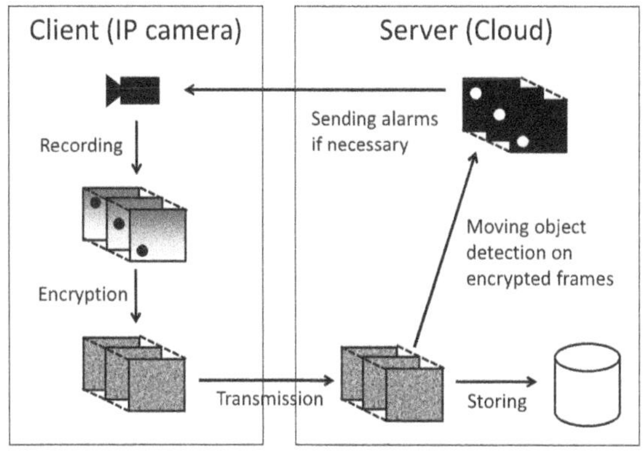

Figure 1: Our system architecture. Moving object detection operates directly in encryption domain without additional communication overhead.

Keith B. Frikken *et al.* proposed a complex secure protocol to check whether invaders are legal based on *oblivious transfer* [1]. However, it needs lots of communication between the client and server, and thus inefficient in the real application. In [4], Maneesh Upmanyu *et al.* proposed an efficient encryption method that can trace objects in encryption domain. Their main idea is to separate the data into multiple pieces, send them to isolated clouds (providers) to compute, and then combine them back by using *Chinese Remainder Theorem.* Its security is based on that every cloud only knows part of information. Although it is much faster than previous method, it is still impractical to find isolated clouds, belonging to different providers, to perform the same operations. Practically, the surveillance system is more likely to be provided by only one provider. Our setting is similar to [2]. They use Paillier cryptosystem, which is one of the most used homomorphic encryption systems, to fulfill detection in the encryption domain. However, comparison in encryption domain by using Paillier cryptosystem is quite slow. It needs more than 30 seconds to determine whether one face belongs to a 280-people database [2].

Compared with that, we propose an efficient encryption method that moving object detection can be performed directly on the encrypted frames in real time. Besides, it only

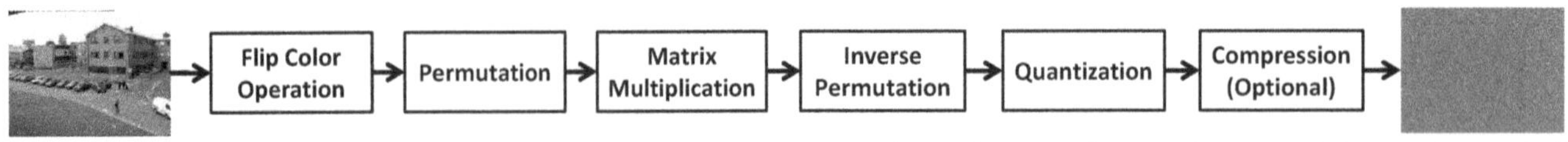

Figure 2: Our encryption flow. This encryption flow is conducted on each raw frame. Private keys of all steps should remain unchanged across all frames in one surveillance period. If keys are changed, about 100 frames (<1 minute) are needed for training a new background model.

needs one cloud to participate. You can see the demo video on youtube[1]. Figure 1 illustrates the architecture of our proposed system. First, video is recorded through the camera, and is separated into raw frames for further encryption. Then, the proposed efficient encryption method (Section 2.2) is performed on each raw frame. After encryption, the encrypted frames are sent to the server (cloud). Server will do two things when it received encrypted frames. First, it will store encrypted frames into the storage. Second, it will do foreground (moving object) detection directly on encrypted frames. Then, the contours of the objects[2] will be detected as shown in Figure 1. Server will send an alarm if some moving objects are detected in P (e.g., 10) continuous frames.

2. MECHANISM

To provide a real-time moving object detection system on encrypted frames, we first introduce the traditional detection method on raw frames in Section 2.1. Then, an efficient encryption method which allows using the same detection method on encrypted frames is proposed in Section 2.2. We further discuss the reason why the same detection method can be applied in encryption domain in Section 2.3. Finally, the way of decrypting encrypted frames is illustrated in Section 2.4.

2.1 Detection method on raw frames

Nowadays, most researchers adopt adaptive background model because it is hard to manually initialize non-adaptive model [3]. In this paper, we use the method proposed by Chris Stauffer *et al.* [3], where every pixel is modelled by K Gaussian distributions. The probability of observing a new value X_t at time t of one pixel is modelled by the mixture of K Gaussian distributions on that pixel.

$$P(X_t) = \sum_{i=1}^{K} w_{i,t} \times \eta(X_t, \mu_{i,t}, \Sigma_{i,t}),$$

where K is the number of Gaussian distributions, $w_{i,t}$, $\mu_{i,t}$ and $\Sigma_{i,t}$ are estimated weight, mean value and covariance matrix of the i_{th} Gaussian in the mixture at time t respectively. η is a Gaussian probability density function. In order to compute efficiently, $\Sigma_{i,t}$ is assumed to be diagonal.

Every time a new pixel value X_t comes, it is checked against the existing K Gaussian distributions until a match is found. Followed by the setting in [3], a match is defined as a pixel value within 2.5 standard deviations of a distribution. Weights of the distributions will be adjusted as follows

$$w_{k,t} = (1-\alpha)w_{k,t-1} + \alpha(M_{k,t}),$$

where α is the learning rate and $M_{k,t}$ is 1 for the matched distribution and 0 for the remaining distributions. Besides, the mean value μ and variance σ of the matched distribution will be changed according to the learning rate α. If no one matches the new pixel value, the K_{th} distribution will be replaced with a distribution with the current value as its mean value, an initially high variance, and low prior weight. Gaussian distributions are sorted by the ratios of w/σ. Only the top B distributions defined by the threshold T are treated as background.

$$B = argmin_b(\sum_{k=1}^{b} w_k > T)$$

After detecting all foreground pixels, they use connected components algorithm to filter out noise. If the connected components of one foreground region is less than a threshold T_c, it is treated as noises and is simply deleted.

2.2 Encryption method

To enable detection on encrypted frames, our proposed encryption flow is depicted in Figure 2. When one color image frame comes, it will first be converted into a gray-level image[3]. Then, the gray-level image is passed through *flip color operation*, *permutation*, *matrix multiplication*, *inverse permutation*, *quantization* and finally *compression* to become the corresponding encrypted frame. The purpose and details of each step will be described next.

2.2.1 Flip color operation

For every pixel, our flip color function f_c will perform

$$f_c\ (I(x,y), key(x,y)) = \begin{cases} I(x,y) & if\ key(x,y) = 0 \\ 255 - I(x,y) & if\ key(x,y) = 1 \end{cases}$$

where $I(x,y)$ represents the intensity of the gray-level image at position (x,y), and $key(x,y)$ is the corresponding private key. After passing this function, no matter what original value the pixel is, the output expected value is always 255/2. That will make the final encrypted image become a flat noise image as shown in Figure 2 and thus hard to crack.

2.2.2 Permutation, matrix multiplication and inverse permutation

Figure 3 describes the details of these three steps. They are the cores of our encryption system. First, the pixels of an image are permuted, so that originally non-neighbor pixels will probably become neighbors like Figure 3(a). Then, each N-by-N pixel array is treated as a block. Every block is multiplied by a different randomly-generated N-by-N private encryption matrix (e.g., M_1, M_2) as Figure 3(b). Finally, the inverse permutation function is used to permute the pixels back to their original positions as Figure 3(c). These operations are the same as randomly choosing N pixels as a group, summing them by different weights, and then filling the computed values back to the positions. After do-

[1]http://youtu.be/24pyL0eWUfM

[2]Contours can be further used for a lot of other applications, such as object recognition, action recognition, etc.

[3]For a color image, we can encrypt RGB channels separately. One channel is used here for simplicity.

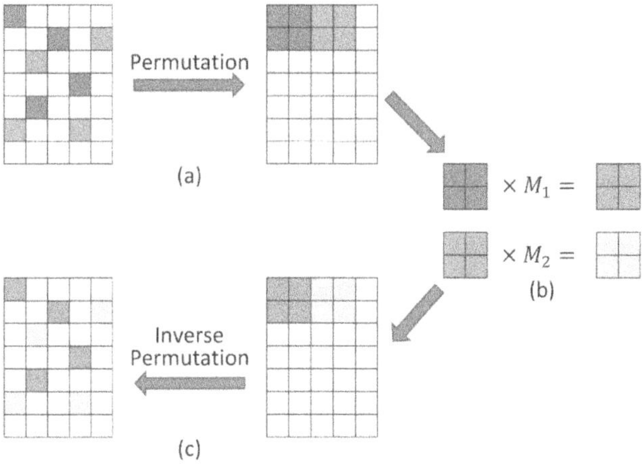

Figure 3: Core operations of our encryption system. (a) Permutation will make non-neighbor pixels become neighbors like red pixels in this figure. (b) Then, each N-by-N block is multiplied by a randomly-generated N-by-N matrix ($N = 2$ as a demonstration). (c) Finally, pixels are permuted back to their original positions.

ing these operations, we can make sure that

$$I_{enc}(x, y) = w_1 \times I_{ori}(x, y) + \sum_{i=2}^{N} w_i \times I_{ori}(x_i, y_i),$$

where I_{ori} and I_{enc} represent the values before and after these three operations, and $w_1, \ldots, w_N$ represent the weights in the encryption matrix. It shows that the encrypted value is always related to the original value at the same position. Thus, the geometric positions are reserved after encryption. Besides, in order to avoid one weight overwhelming others, every element in the encryption matrix is forced in the range 1 to 2. Empirically, to make sure the inverse matrix is computable, the absolute value of the determinant of the encryption matrix should be larger than one.

2.2.3 Quantization and compression

Previous operations are all linear. To make this system more secure and reduce the communication cost, here we introduce *quantization* and *compression*, which are both nonliner. After previous operations, the encrypted value (I_{enc}) will be in the range between 0 and 255×2N since each element in the encryption matrix is restricted. *Quantization* step is to make the range become 0 to 255. That is, $\lfloor I_{enc}/2N \rfloor$. Preliminarily, *compression* is optional and initially introduced by JPEG format.

2.3 Detection on encryption domain

As described in Section 2.1, every pixel is assumed to be represented by a mixture of Gaussian distributions on raw frames. In this section, we will show that even after encryption, every pixel still can be represented by a mixture of Gaussian distributions, and thus, the detection method in [3] can be directly applied on the encrypted frames.

For *flip color operation*, if the key is 0, Gaussian distributions remain unchanged. If the key is 1, for one distribution $\eta(X, \mu, \Sigma)$, only the mean of the distribution will change to $255 - \mu$, and become another Gaussian distribution $\eta(X, 255 - \mu, \Sigma)$. *Permutation* and *inverse permutation* will not have any impact because every pixel have its own Gaussian distributions. Furthermore, based on the Gaussian property (i.e., the sum of Gaussian variables is also a Gaussian), we can make sure that after *matrix multiplication*, every pixel still can be represented by a Gaussian. *Quantization* only has a few impact on modelling as Gaussian because we choose a small N in real application. *Compression* has strong influence since our encrypted frames are quite like noise pattern (e.g., the rightmost image in Figure 2), and thus hard to compress. The influences of the last two operations will be discussed in Section 3. Note that the private keys, including keys for *flip color operation*, *permutation* and *matrix multiplication*, should be the same across all frames in one surveillance period. Otherwise, the discussions above will not hold. If keys are changed, about 100 frames are needed for training a new background model.

One might ask how can we guarantee that one point detected on the raw frame also detected on the encrypted frame. We cannot always guarantee that because the value of every encrypted pixel is composed by N components. If two or more components change simultaneously with different directions, they might cancel out the change. Fortunately, this is not a frequent event. Besides, for one detected object in raw frames, it is often with certain pixels in size because connected components less than T_c are treated as noise. Thus, some undetected points in encryption domain will not affect the final object detection results. Another issue is whether undetected pixels in raw frames will become detected in encrypted frames. It happens quite frequently because one pixel in the raw frame will influence N pixels in the encrypted frame. However, because the other $N - 1$ pixels are randomly chosen, the noise will spread evenly on the encrypted frame, and hard to form a connected components more then T_c. Then, they will be filtered out, and the detection result will not change too much.

2.4 Decryption from encrypted frames

When client receives an alarm, user might want to see what really happened in that period. Thus, our encrypted frames should be able to be decrypted. To decrypt the frames, inverse operations are performed in reverse order of Figure 2 as follows. First, an encrypted frame is read from BMP (or JPG) source, and is multiplied by 2N. Then, *permutation*, inverse matrix multiplication, *inverse permutation*, and *flip color operation* are performed subsequently.

3. EXPERIMENTS

We do the experiments on two different datasets. One is PETS 2001 dataset. It contains 3064 training frames and 2688 testing frames. The other is IPPR 2006 dataset. It only contains 300 testing frames without training frames. In order to initialize our model properly, we choose 10 frames without people and duplicate them to 200 frames as training frames. Empirically, we set $K = 3$, learning rate $\alpha = 0.01$, background threshold $T = 0.6$, connected components threshold $T_c = 75$, and the width of one block matrix $N = 4$.

In this paper, because we only do foreground detection without tracking, evaluations are not based on each object. Instead, we evaluate the correctness on each frame. For every detected foreground object, a smallest bounding box will be found. One correct detection is defined as

$$\frac{R_d \cap R_g}{R_d \cup R_g} > 0.5,$$

where R_d and R_g represent the regions inside the bounding boxes of one detected frame and the corresponding ground truth frame respectively.

Table 1: **Detection performances on two datasets.**

Quality	PETS dataset (%)		IPPR dataset (%)	
	Precision	Recall	Precision	Recall
Raw frames [3]	80.02	79.22	94.98	93.64
No quantization	83.58	82.47	91.79	90.81
BMP	83.77	82.44	91.76	90.46
JPG100	83.58	82.28	91.40	90.11
JPG99	**83.62**	**82.36**	**93.19**	**91.87**
JPG98	83.01	81.85	90.32	89.05
JPG97	82.04	80.96	91.43	90.46
JPG96	80.44	79.26	92.09	90.46

Detection performances of different encryption qualities are shown in Table 1. This detection method performs better on encrypted frames than raw frames in PETS dataset because of the light change at the corner at the end of the video. As we randomly choose N points as a group in encryption, the degree of light change will become smaller after *matrix multiplication* and *quantization*. Thus, it can tolerate more light change. For IPPR dataset, because of no severe light change, the performance slightly degrades reasonably. The performance gap between "No quantization" and "BMP" shows the influence of *quantization*, which is not severe as stated in Section 2.3. For *compression*, if we do not want to lose too much performance, JPG99 is recommended.

The other important factor is the quality of the decrypted frames. The decrypted results from different quality sources and corresponding PSNR (Peak Signal-to-Noise Ratio) values are shown in Figure 4. The wall of the building starts appearing visible noises from quality 98 (JPG98). From PSNR values, we can find that more compression will lead worse decryption quality.

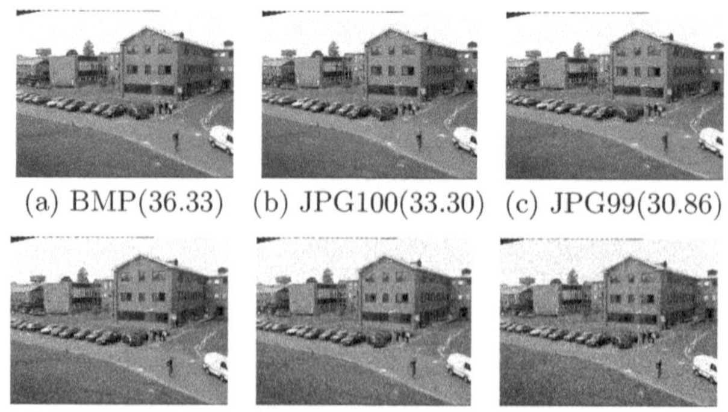

(a) BMP(36.33) (b) JPG100(33.30) (c) JPG99(30.86)

(d) JPG98(27.02) (e) JPG97(24.09) (f) JPG96(21.90)

Figure 4: Decrypted frames from different quality sources. From JPG98, the wall of the building starts appearing visible noises. The values inside parentheses are corresponding PSNR values.

4. SECURITY ANALYSIS

In this section, two widely used security attack models are conducted. *Ciphertext only attack* is discussed in Section 4.1 and *known plaintext attack* is discussed in Section 4.2.

4.1 Ciphertext only attack

In *ciphertext only attack* model, opponents only can access the encrypted frames. Because opponents do not have any raw frame, it is impossible to find inverse matrix for decryption, and thus no way to crack the system.

4.2 Known plaintext attack

In *known plaintext attack* model, opponents know a number of pairs of raw frames and their corresponding encrypted frames. Besides, they also have the right to access all encrypted frames. Thus, this attack is more severe than previous one (*ciphertext only attack*).

If one can correctly find the private keys for *flip color operation* and *permutation*, he can derive the image before *matrix multiplication* and the corresponding image after *matrix multiplication* and *quantization* from each pair. Then, approximate inverse matrix can be derived by minimizing the total decryption error for all pairs.

Fortunately, the robustness of our system is not only based on the encryption matrix. It is also based on the difficulty of finding the permutation function. However, one might think he can find the permutation function by analyzing correlations between pixels. In our preliminary experiments, 4 pixels are treated as a group. Thus, if one pixel value is changed (unchanged) in encrypted frames, other three pixel values in the same group are likely to be changed (unchanged).

To show our system can tolerate this analysis, we do the correlation analysis on randomly chosen 8000 pixels on all frames of PETS dataset, including training and testing frames. For every pixel, top 3 most related pixels are found, and considered as one *guessed group*. Then, the correctness is verified on each *guessed group*. The correct rate for the 1st, 2nd and 3rd related pixels in one *guessed group* are 0.82, 0.52, and 0.21 respectively. When the 3rd one is correct, the others are always correct. Thus, adversary has 0.21 probability to find one right grouping. In one 768×576 frame, there are 110,592 ($768 \times 576/4$) groups needed to be correctly found. Thus, it is hard to find the permutation function.

5. CONCLUSIONS AND FUTURE WORKS

In this paper, we propose an efficient encryption method that allows doing detection directly on encrypted frames. Our detection method does not need any other communication between client and server except data transmission. Unlike traditional homomorphic encryption, which needs lots of communication overhead when doing comparison. Because of this, our proposed method is much faster than homomorphic encryption method. Besides, moving objects can be detected correctly with less performance degradation. Although the encryption-friendly compression method for our work is still under development, the data needed to be transmitted is already much smaller than Paillier cryptosystem. In Paillier cryptosystem, it needs 1024 bits to represent one pixel in encryption domain, while we only need 8 bits. Besides, compression on temporal domain might be possible and can be done in the future. For the quality of decrypted images, the issue might be solved by some techniques like super-resolution in the future.

6. REFERENCES

[1] K. B. Frikken and M. J. Atallah. Privacy preserving electronic surveillance. In *WPES*, pages 45–52, 2003.

[2] H. Sohn, K. N. Plataniotis, and Y. M. Ro. Privacy-preserving watch list screening in video surveillance system. In *PCM (1)*, pages 622–632, 2010.

[3] C. Stauffer and W. E. L. Grimson. Adaptive background mixture models for real-time tracking. In *CVPR*, pages 2246–2252, 1999.

[4] M. Upmanyu, A. M. Namboodiri, K. Srinathan, and C. V. Jawahar. Efficient privacy preserving video surveillance. In *ICCV*, pages 1639–1646, 2009.

With One Look: Robust Face Recognition Using Single Sample Per Person

De-An Huang
Research Center for Information Technology Innovation, Academia Sinica, Taipei, Taiwan
andrew800619@gmail.com

Yu-Chiang Frank Wang
Research Center for Information Technology Innovation, Academia Sinica, Taipei, Taiwan
ycwang@citi.sinica.edu.tw

ABSTRACT

In this paper, we address the problem of robust face recognition using single sample per person. Given only *one* training image per subject of interest, our proposed method is able to recognize query images with illumination or expression changes, or even the corrupted ones due to occlusion. In order to model the above intra-class variations, we advocate the use of external data (i.e., images of subjects *not* of interest) for learning an exemplar-based dictionary. This dictionary provides auxiliary yet representative information for handling intra-class variation, while the gallery set containing one training image per class preserves separation between different subjects for recognition purposes. Our experiments on two face datasets confirm the effectiveness and robustness of our approach, which is shown to outperform state-of-the-art sparse representation based methods.

Categories and Subject Descriptors

I.4.9 [**Image Processing & computer vision**]: Applications; I.5.4 [**Pattern Recognition**]: Applications—*Computer Vision*; H.3.3 [**Information Storage & Retrieval**]: Information Search & Retrieval

General Terms

Algorithms, Experimentation, Performance

Keywords

Face recognition, sparse representation, low-rank matrix decomposition, affinity propagation

1. INTRODUCTION

Recognizing faces in real-world scenarios not only requires one to deal with illumination or expression changes, the face images to be recognized might also be corrupted due to occlusion or disguise. Solving the above task is typically known as *robust face recognition* [10]. Although very promising performance has been reported in recent works like [10, 2], their requirement of collecting a large number of training data might not be practical. If a sufficient amount of training face images cannot be obtained for modeling intra and inter-class variations, one cannot expect satisfactory recognition performance. For real-world face recognition, one might have only *one* training image for each subject of interest (e.g., a mug shot). Therefore, how to address single-sample robust face recognition has been a challenging problem for researchers in related fields.

MM'13, October 21–25, 2013, Barcelona, Spain.
Copyright 2013 ACM 978-1-4503-2404-5/13/10 ...$15.00.
http://dx.doi.org/10.1145/2502081.2502158.

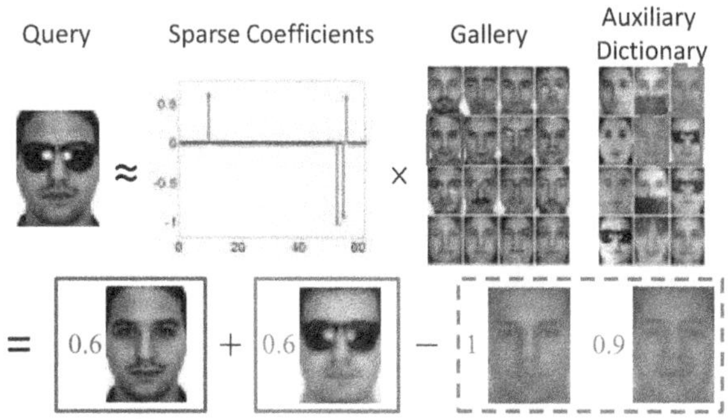

Figure 1: Illustration of our proposed method. Note that the gallery set contains only one training image per subject of interest, while the auxiliary dictionary to be learned utilizes external data for observing possible image variants (including occlusion).

For single-sample face recognition, Zhu *et al.* [12] proposed a multi-scale patch based collaborative representation (PCRC) approach. Since PCRC performs recognition based on patch-wise reconstruction error, it would be sensitive to corrupted face images (e.g., images with sunglasses). Recently, the use of *external* data (i.e., images collected from subjects *not* of interest) is considered as an alternative for solving single-sample face recognition problems. For example, Su *et al.* [9] proposed adaptive generic learning (AGL) for deriving a discriminant model using external data, while one training image per subject is available. Inspired by sparse representation based classification (SRC) [10], Deng *et al.* [4] presented extended SRC (ESRC), which considered external face data as an additional dictionary for modeling intra-class variations. Although both AGL and ESRC utilized external face data for modeling inter or intra-class variations, their direct use of external data might *not* be preferable, since such data might contain noisy, redundant, or undesirable information. Without proper selection or processing of external data, the direct use of such data does not necessarily improve the performance.

In this paper, we present a novel approach for solving single-sample face recognition. In order to model *intra*-class

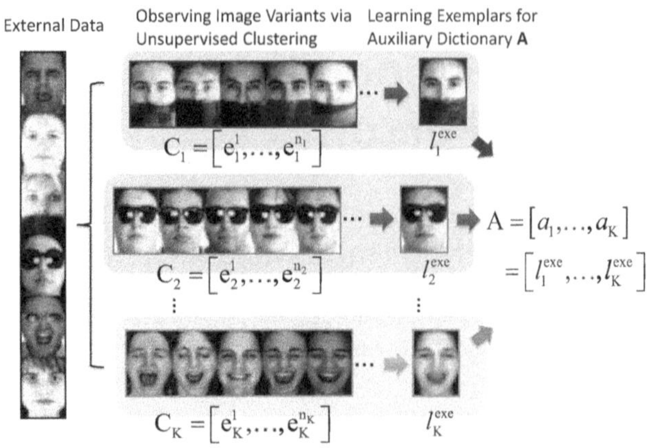

Figure 2: Learning of an exemplar-based auxiliary dictionary A from external face images for modeling intra-class variations.

variations, we propose the learning of an exemplar-based dictionary using external data. Based on the techniques of affinity propagation [5] and low-rank matrix decomposition [1], the derived dictionary is able to extract representative information from external data in terms of *image variants* instead of subject identities. Thus, each dictionary atom corresponds to a particular image variant like illumination, expression, or occlusion type. As illustrated in Fig. 1, together with gallery set images (only one per subject of interest), we apply the observed auxiliary dictionary for performing recognition via ESRC [4]. One of the advantages of our approach is that our dictionary size only depends on the number of types of image variants, *not* the size of external data. Our experiments will verify both the effectiveness and robustness of our method over state-of-the-art recognition approaches.

2. A BRIEF REVIEW OF SRC AND ESRC

Proposed by Wright *et al.* [10], sparse representation based classification (SRC) performs recognition by taking each test image $\mathbf{y}$ as a sparse linear combination of atoms in an overcomplete dictionary $\mathbf{D} = [\mathbf{D}_1, \mathbf{D}_2, \cdots, \mathbf{D}_k]$, where $\mathbf{D}_i$ contains the training images of class i. SRC calculates the sparse coefficient $\boldsymbol{\alpha}$ of $\mathbf{y}$ by solving:

$$\min_{\boldsymbol{\alpha}} \|\mathbf{y} - \mathbf{D}\boldsymbol{\alpha}\|_2^2 + \lambda\|\boldsymbol{\alpha}\|_1. \tag{1}$$

Once (1) is solved, the label j of $\mathbf{y}$ is determined by

$$j = \arg\min_i \|\mathbf{y} - \mathbf{D}\delta_i(\boldsymbol{\alpha})\|_2, \tag{2}$$

where $\delta_i(\boldsymbol{\alpha})$ is a vector whose nonzero entries are those associated with class i only. Thus, SRC performs recognition based on the minimum class-wise reconstruction error, which implies the query $\mathbf{y}$ approximately lies in the column subspace spanned by the training images of the associated class.

In practice, the use of SRC is limited due to its need to collect of a large amount of training data as the over-complete dictionary $\mathbf{D}$. To address this concern, Deng *et al.* [4] proposed Extended SRC (ESRC) by solving:

$$\min_{\boldsymbol{\alpha},\boldsymbol{\beta}} \left\|\mathbf{y} - [\mathbf{D},\ \mathbf{A}]\begin{bmatrix}\boldsymbol{\alpha}\\ \boldsymbol{\beta}\end{bmatrix}\right\|_2^2 + \lambda\left\|\begin{bmatrix}\boldsymbol{\alpha}\\ \boldsymbol{\beta}\end{bmatrix}\right\|_1, \tag{3}$$

where $\mathbf{A}$ is an auxiliary dictionary modeling the intra-class variants, and $\boldsymbol{\beta}$ is the associated sparse coefficient. Different from $\mathbf{D}$, the auxiliary dictionary $\mathbf{A}$ in [4] consists of images collected from external data (i.e., subjects *not* of interest). Similar to SRC, ESRC performs recognition by:

$$j = \arg\min_i \left\|\mathbf{y} - [\mathbf{D},\ \mathbf{A}]\begin{bmatrix}\delta_i(\boldsymbol{\alpha})\\ \boldsymbol{\beta}\end{bmatrix}\right\|_2. \tag{4}$$

Although modeling intra-class variants by utilizing external data has been shown to achieve improved performance for undersampled face recognition problems, applying all images from an external dataset might not be preferable. This is not only because that redundant or noisy information might be taken into account, the size of the auxiliary dictionary $\mathbf{A}$ will linearly increase with that of external data, which would make (4) very computationally expensive to solve.

3. AUXILIARY DICTIONARY LEARNING

3.1 Observing Image Variants

As depicted in Fig. 2, we propose to learn an exemplar-based dictionary from external face images. To model intra-class variations during recognition, each dictionary atom is expected to correspond to a particular type of image variant. As a result, our goal is to automatically identify different types of image variants from external data which contains possible variations (e.g., illumination, expression, or occlusion changes), so that we can extract representative information and derive the corresponding dictionary atoms.

We observe that face images with the same type of corruption/variation have similar distributions in terms of intensity gradients. Thus, we consider the use of Histogram of Oriented Gradients (HOG) [3] features for describing each image. Since it is *not* practical to assume the exact number of variant types to be known in advance, we need an *automatic* and *unsupervised* learning algorithm for solving this task. In our work, we advance affinity propagation (AP) [5], which is a unsupervised clustering technique and not requires the prior knowledge of the cluster numbers. To automatically identify different types of image variants, we solve the following problem which minimizes the net-similarity (NS) between different external face images:

$$\begin{aligned} NS \;=\; & \sum_{i=1}^{N}\sum_{j=1}^{N} c_{ij}s(\mathbf{e}_i, \mathbf{e}_j) \\ & -\gamma\sum_{i=1}^{N}(1 - c_{ii})(\sum_{j=1}^{N} c_{ij}) - \gamma\sum_{i=1}^{N}|(\sum_{j=1}^{N} c_{ij}) - 1|. \end{aligned} \tag{5}$$

In (5), $s(\mathbf{e}_i, \mathbf{e}_j) = exp(-\|HOG(\mathbf{e}_i) - HOG(\mathbf{e}_j)\|^2)$ measures the similarity between images $\mathbf{e}_i$ and $\mathbf{e}_j$ in terms of HOG features. The coefficient $c_{ij} = 1$ indicates that $\mathbf{e}_i$ is the cluster representative of $\mathbf{e}_j$ (i.e., $\mathbf{e}_j$ is assigned to cluster i). Thus, $c_{ii} = 1$ means that $\mathbf{e}_i$ is the representative and belongs to its own cluster i. The first term in (5) is to calculate the sum of similarity between images within each cluster, while the second term penalizes the case when images are assigned to an empty cluster (i.e. $c_{ii} = 0$ but with $\sum_{j=1}^{M} c_{ij} \geq 1$). The last term in (5) penalizes the cases when images are assigned to more than one cluster, or not belong to any of them. We set the parameter γ to $+\infty$ to strictly avoid the above problems.

It is necessary to verify the effectiveness and practicability of this unsupervised strategy for automatically dividing different image variants into distinct groups (instead of separating images of different subjects into different clusters).

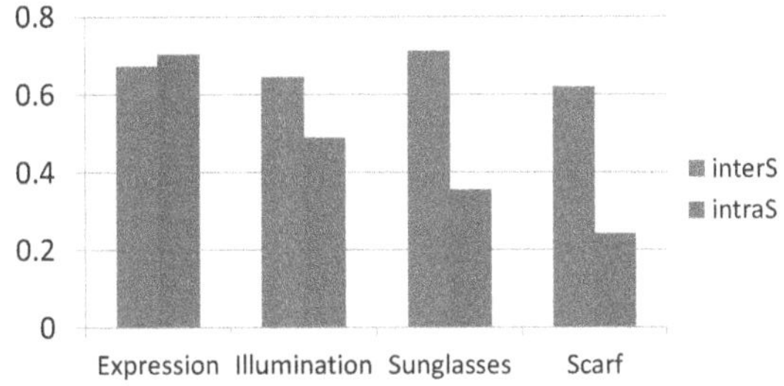

Figure 3: Average inter/intra-class similarity (*interS*/*intraS*) for the AR database using HOG features. The x-axis indicates four types of image variants, and the y-axis is the similarity value. Note that *intraS* measures the similarity between the neutral image and a particular image variant of the same subject, and *interS* is that between a face image and the most similar one of the same variation but from a different subject (chosen by Nearest Neighbor).

We statistically verified this observation on the images of the first session in the AR database [8], and the results are shown in Fig. 3. From this figure, it can be seen that images of the *same* variant type but from *different* subjects generally achieved *higher* similarities than those of different variations but from the same subject (i.e., *interS* > *intraS* in Fig. 3, except for expression changes in which the two values are comparable). This supports the use of our approach for identifying and separating face images into different groups in terms of their variant types instead of identities.

3.2 Learning Exemplars for Image Variants

After dividing external face images into different groups in terms of variant types, we need to extract representative information from each cluster, so that such information (and the derived auxiliary dictionary) can be utilized for modeling intra-class variations. To solve this task, we advance low-rank matrix decomposition (LR) [1] to learn exemplars for representing each cluster (and thus variant type).

As discussed in [1], LR seeks to decompose an input data matrix into a low-rank version and a matrix containing the associated sparse error. Since the resulting low-rank matrix can be considered as a compact and representative version of the original input, we advocate the use of LR for learning exemplars for face image variants in Fig. 2. In our work, we solve the following optimization problem:

$$\min_{\mathbf{L}_i, \mathbf{S}_i} \|\mathbf{L}_i\|_* + \lambda \|\mathbf{S}_i\|_1 \quad \text{s.t.} \quad \mathbf{C}_i = \mathbf{L}_i + \mathbf{S}_i. \qquad (6)$$

In (6), $\mathbf{C}_i = [\mathbf{e}_i^1, \ldots, \mathbf{e}_i^{n_i}]$ indicates the set of external face images grouped in cluster i (n_i is the number of images in it). The nuclear norm $\|\mathbf{L}_i\|_*$ (i.e., the sum of singular values) approximates the rank of $\mathbf{L}_i$, which makes the optimization problem of (6) convex and thus can be solved by techniques of augmented Lagrange multipliers (ALM) [1, 7]. As a result, we choose to decompose $\mathbf{C}_i$ into a low-rank matrix $L_i = [\mathbf{l}_i^1, \ldots, \mathbf{l}_i^{n_i}]$ and a sparse error matrix $\mathbf{S}_i = [\mathbf{s}_i^1, \ldots, \mathbf{l}_s^{n_i}]$. It is worth noting that, unlike [2] in which LR was applied to *remove* intra-class variations of each subject, our approach aims at extracting representative intra-class information of face images by disregarding their *inter-class* variations.

We now discuss how we learn the auxiliary dictionary by solving the above LR problems. Supposed that the jth image $\mathbf{e}_i^j$ is identified as the centroid of cluster i during the aforementioned unsupervised clustering process (see Sec. 3.1), we consider the corresponding low-rank component $\mathbf{l}_i^j$ as the exemplar $\mathbf{l}_i^{exe}$ for representing that particular type of image variant. Once all exemplars for all clusters (variant types) are obtained, we have the auxiliary dictionary $\mathbf{A} = [\mathbf{a}_1, \ldots, \mathbf{a}_K] = [\mathbf{l}_1^{exe}, \ldots, \mathbf{l}_K^{exe}]$.

The advantage of our proposed auxiliary dictionary learning strategy is two-fold. Firstly, we derive the dictionary $\mathbf{A}$ in an automatic and unsupervised way. Since $\mathbf{A}$ contains exemplars describing each type of image variants, it can be applied to model intra-class variations during recognition. Secondly, the size of $\mathbf{A}$ does not grow linearly with the amount of external data; otherwise it would significantly increase the computation time for SRC or ESRC. We also note that, when utilizing external data for learning the auxiliary dictionary, we do *not* require any label/identity information from such data. In other words, our method allows one subject from external data to provide some particular image variants (e.g., illumination changes), while another subject for other types of image variants (e.g., occlusion). This provides additional flexibility and practicability for the use of external data.

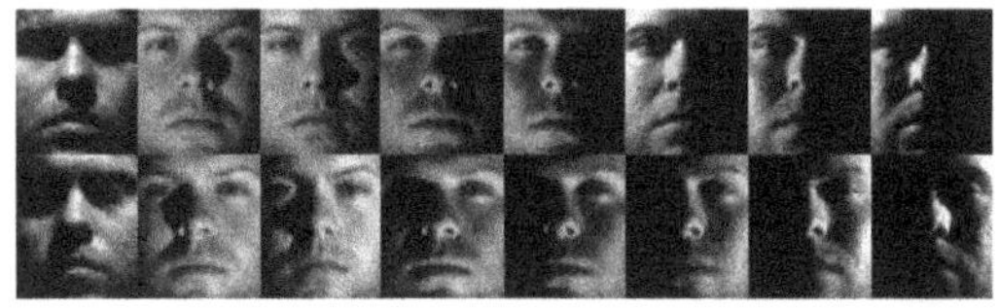

Figure 4: Example images of the Extended Yale database (only 16 out of 64 illuminations are shown).

Table 1: Recognition performance on the Extended Yale B dataset. * denotes that the auxiliary dictionary size of ESRC is the same as ours.

SRC [10]	RSC [11]	AGL [9]	ESRC* [4]	Ours
48.4	38.1	50.3	54.7	64.9

3.3 Performing Recognition

Once the auxiliary dictionary $\mathbf{A}$ is learned from external data, we perform recognition of queries $\mathbf{y}$ using ESRC (i.e., (3) and (4)). Recall that the gallery set $\mathbf{D}$ in (3) contains only one training image from each subject of interest. Thus, similar to SRC/ESRC, our recognition rule is also based on the minimum class-wise reconstruction error.

4. EXPERIMENTAL RESULTS

4.1 Extended Yale B Database

We first consider the Extended Yale B database [6] for our experiments. This database contains frontal-face images of 38 subjects, each with about 64 images taken under various illumination conditions. In our experiment, all images are converted into grayscale and cropped to 192×168 pixels. Examples of the images are shown in Fig. 4.

We randomly select 19 from the 38 people as the subjects of interest (i.e., to be recognized), and the rest as external data for learning the auxiliary dictionary. For the 19 subjects of interest, we select the neutral face (A+000 E+00) of each for training (as the gallery), and the remaining 63 images as query images for testing. For the 19 subjects *not* of interest), we randomly select 5 images out of the total 64 images for each subject as external data, and thus $\mathbf{E}$ con-

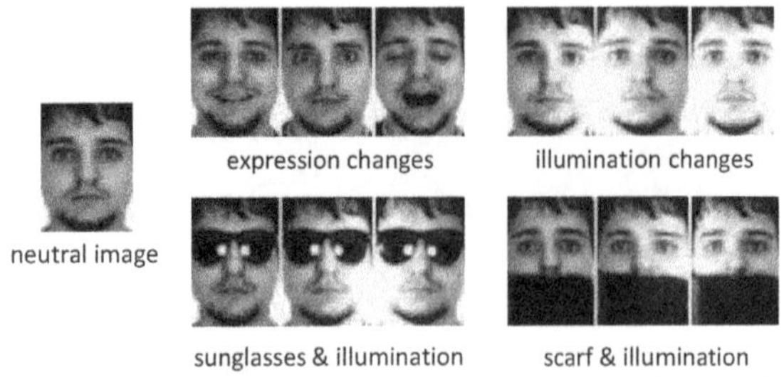

Figure 5: Example images of the AR database. Only the neural image of each subject is in the gallery set, and the rest are the queries to be recognized.

Table 2: Recognition results of the AR database for queries under different scenarios. * denote the use of the same auxiliary dictionary size.

	Expression	Illumination	Sunglasses	Scarf	Avg
SRC [10]	77.3	75.6	47.7	17.5	55.4
RSC [11]	**81.4**	32.7	59.3	34.3	53.1
AGL [9]	62.6	77.0	43.1	27.5	53.0
ESRC* [4]	77.0	82.7	60.2	25.8	62.1
Ours*	78.9	**89.1**	**71.9**	**36.9**	**69.6**

tains a total of $5 \times 19 = 85$ images. The parameter λ in (3) is set to 0.15, and we consider the default parameter choices for AP and LR as their original works do. We perform five random trials, and compare our method with SRC [10], Robust Sparse Coding (RSC) [11], AGL [9] and ESRC [4]. For AGL and ESRC, their gallery and external data selections are the same as ours. We perform five random trials, and list the average recognition rates of each in Table 1.

From Table 1, it can be seen that SRC and RSC were not able to perform recognition well for single-sample recognition without the use of external data. Compared to AGL and ESRC which applied the same size of the external/auxiliary data, our proposed method achieved the highest accuracy. This supports the use of our derived auxiliary dictionary for better modeling intra-class variations, and our proposed method for single-sample face recognition.

4.2 AR Database

The AR database [8] contains over 4,000 frontal images of 126 individuals taken under different variations, including illumination, expression, and facial occlusion. The AR images were taken in two separate sessions. For each session, thirteen images are available for each subject, see Fig. 5 for example. In our experiment, we choose a subset of AR consisting of 50 men and 50 women as [10] did, and all images are cropped to 165×120 pixels and converted to grayscale.

Among the 100 subjects, we randomly select 50 from them to be recognized (25 men and 25 women), and the remaining 50 as external data for auxiliary dictionary learning. For the subjects of interest, only the first *neutral* image is used for training, and the rest 25 images for testing (12 remaining from the first session and 13 from the second). To learn the auxiliary dictionary $\mathbf{A}$, we randomly select 2 images from each subject not of interest, and thus $\mathbf{E}$ contains a total of $2 \times 50 = 100$ images.

Similar to our experiments on the Extended Yale B dataset, we consider SRC, RSC, AGL, and ESRC for comparisons. We also perform five random trials (for external data selection) and compare the average recognition results of different approaches (see Table 2). From this table, we see that our approach outperformed others for most cases, except for the case of image variants with expression changes. This is consistent with our observation in Fig. 3, in which inter-class similarity for facial expression is actually lower than that for other types of facial variants. Although RSC is particularly designed for handle such expression variations [11]), it cannot be generalized well to other variant types such as illumination or occlusion variations (like ours does). From the above experiments, the robustness and effectiveness of our proposed method for single-image face recognition can be successfully verified.

5. CONCLUSION

We presented a novel ESRC-based approach for solving single-sample face recognition problems. In order to handle face images of different variations or occlusions, we learned an exemplar-based dictionary as the auxiliary dictionary. By observing external face data, this dictionary was able to automatically identify and thus model intra-class variations and corruptions. Together with the gallery set containing only one training image per subject of interest, our proposed method was shown to preserve inter-class variations, while intra-class variations can be well observed. Experimental results on two face databases confirmed the effectiveness of our method, which was shown to outperform state-of-the-art with or without using external face data.

Acknowledgement This work is supported in part by National Science Council of Taiwan via NSC100-2221-E-001-018-MY2.

6. REFERENCES

[1] E. Candès, X. Li, Y. Ma, and J. Wright. Robust principal component analysis? *Jour. ACM*, 58, 2011.
[2] C.-F. Chen, C.-P. Wei, and Y.-C. F. Wang. Low-rank matrix recovery with structural incoherence for robust face recognition. In *Proc. IEEE CVPR*, 2012.
[3] N. Dalal and B. Triggs. Histograms of oriented gradients for human detection.
[4] W. Deng, J. Hu, and J. Guo. Extended SRC: Undersampled face recognition via intraclass variant dictionary. *IEEE PAMI*, 2012.
[5] B. J. Frey and D. Dueck. Clustering by passing messages between data points. *Science*, 2007.
[6] A. S. Georghiades et al. From few to many: Illumination cone models for face recognition under variable lighting and pose. *IEEE PAMI*, 2001.
[7] Z. Lin et al. The augmented lagrange multiplier method for exact recovery of corrupted low-rank matrices. *UIUC Tech. Rep. UILU-ENG-09-2215*, 2010.
[8] A. M. Martinez and R. Benavente. The AR face database. *CVC Technical Report*, 1998.
[9] Y. Su, S. Shan, X. Chen, and W. Gao. Adaptive generic learning for face recognition from a single sample per person. In *Proc. IEEE CVPR*, 2010.
[10] J. Wright et al. Robust face recognition via sparse representation. *IEEE PAMI*, 2009.
[11] M. Yang et al. Robust sparse coding for face recognition. In *Proc. IEEE CVPR*, 2011.
[12] P. Zhu et al. Multi-scale patch based collaborative representation for face recognition with margin distribution optimization. In *Proc. ECCV*, 2012.

Weakly-supervised Multi-class Object Detection Using Multi-type 3D Features

Asako Kanezaki
Grad. School of Information Science and Technology
The University of Tokyo
kanezaki@isi.imi.i.u-tokyo.ac.jp

Yasuo Kuniyoshi
Grad. School of Information Science and Technology
The University of Tokyo
kuniyosh@isi.imi.i.u-tokyo.ac.jp

Tatsuya Harada
Grad. School of Information Science and Technology
The University of Tokyo
harada@mi.t.u-tokyo.ac.jp

ABSTRACT

We propose a weakly-supervised learning method for object detection using color and depth images of a real environment attached with object labels. The proposed method applies Multiple Instance Learning to find proper instances of the objects in training images. This method is novel in the sense that it learns multiple objects simultaneously in a way to balance the scores of each training sample across all object classes. Moreover, we combine 3D features considering different properties, that is, color texture, grayscale texture, and surface curvature, to improve the performance. We show that our method surpasses a conventional method using color and depth images. Furthermore, we evaluate its performance with our new dataset consisting of color and depth images with weak labels of 100 objects and various backgrounds.

Categories and Subject Descriptors

I.4.8 [**Image Processing and Computer Vision**]: Scene Analysis—*Object recognition, Range data, Sensor fusion*; I.2.6 [**Learning**]: Analogies—*Concept learning, Parameter learning*

Keywords

multi-class object detection, weakly-supervised learning, 3D features

1. INTRODUCTION

Object detection is significantly in demand for intelligent autonomous systems such as robots and smart phones. However, there remains a crucial problem on how to prepare training datasets such as bounding boxes of objects in images, which is a time-consuming job for us. To facilitate the training process, weakly-supervised learning of object detection without objects' bounding boxes is widely researched. In this approach, the object labels (i.e. names) instead of their bounding boxes are attached to each training image if there is at least one instance in the image, so that the system should estimate the corresponding instances of the objects. Multiple Instance Learning (MIL) [2] is effective to deal with this problem, which introduces a concept of "bag" containing multiple instances. A bag is positive if it contains at least one positive instance, while it is negative otherwise. In the scenario of weakly-supervised object detection, a region (or segment) in an image corresponds to an instance, whereas an image corresponds to a bag. There are a couple of state-of-the-art methods [9, 10] that approached the weakly-supervised object detection using MIL and Deformable Part Models (DPM) [3]. However, DPM is not "deformable" enough to detect objects in a messy daily living environment because it uses rotation-variant 2D features.

The most important aspects in tasks of weakly supervised learning of object detection via MIL are **how to extract instances as reasonable candidates of target objects in each image (bag)**, and **how to acquire features' robustness against viewpoint and illumination variance**. The former is difficult especially when the segmentation of image regions is difficult because of cluttered background, and the latter is difficult especially when the postures or the scales of objects are various in 2D images. To solve these problems, a method that utilized 3D information both in extracting instances and computing features from color and depth images is proposed [5]. This method achieves segments as reasonable object candidates via normal estimation of 3D points, and also realizes object detection in various postures in a cluttered environment using rotation-invariant and scale-invariant 3D features. However, it uses only color texture features, which cannot handle illumination changes. Besides, it learns each target object independently, which lacks proper balancing of the scores of each instance across all objects.

Our objective is to learn multi-class object detectors with high distinguishability from weak supervision. We propose a new MIL method that learns multi-class object detectors while balancing the scores of each instance across all object classes. Moreover, we combine several 3D features that represent color textures, grayscale textures and surface curvatures, showing that they give better results than respective single-type features. The additional contribution is that we provide a new dataset consisting of color and depth images with weak labels of 100 objects in various cluttered backgrounds.

MM'13, October 21–25, 2013, Barcelona, Spain.

http://dx.doi.org/10.1145/2502081.2502159.

2. METHOD

The proposed method performs over-segmentation via normal estimation, creates multiple instances by combining various numbers of the primitive segments, extracts multiple voxel features, and solves MIL to obtain multi-class object detectors. To extract instances, we used the method proposed in [5]. The details of the proposed method of learning multi-class object detectors and feature extraction are shown below.

2.1 Learning of multi-class object detectors

Our method learns linear classifiers for multi-class object detection in a MIL setup. We use Passive Aggressive (PA) [1], which is an online (thus efficient and scalable) learning algorithm to obtain multi-class classifiers. Here, we describe PA algorithm for the multi-class setting. Let N be the number of target classes and D be the feature dimension. Let us define the weight matrix as $W \in \boldsymbol{R}^{D\times N}$, the k-th column of W as $\boldsymbol{w}_k$, and the k-th element of $f(\boldsymbol{x})$ as $f_k(\boldsymbol{x})$. Now we optimize the function $f_k(\boldsymbol{x}_t) = \boldsymbol{w}_k \cdot \boldsymbol{x}_t$ that gives the score of the t-th sample $\boldsymbol{x}_t$ belonging to the k-th target object. First, we pick up the r-th class when we observe a training sample $< \boldsymbol{x}_t, y_t >$:

$$r = \underset{y \neq y_t}{\operatorname{argmax}}\, \boldsymbol{w}_y^{(t)} \cdot \boldsymbol{x}_t. \quad (1)$$

Then the hinge loss, which represents the classification error, becomes $\max(0, 1 - f_{y_t}(\boldsymbol{x}_t) + f_r(\boldsymbol{x}_t))$. Introducing a slack variable ζ, the model parameters are updated by the following equation (PA-I in [1]).

$$W^{(t+1)} = \underset{W}{\operatorname{argmin}}\, \frac{1}{2}\|W - W^{(t)}\|^2 + C\zeta, \quad (2)$$

$$\text{s.t.} \;\; \max(0, 1 - \boldsymbol{w}_{y_t} \cdot \boldsymbol{x_t} + \boldsymbol{w}_r \cdot \boldsymbol{x_t}) \leq \zeta, \zeta \geq 0, \quad (3)$$

while C is called "aggressiveness parameter", which controls the aggressiveness of fitting $\boldsymbol{w}$ to each training sample. Solving the Lagrange multiplier, we obtain the following update function.

$$\boldsymbol{w}_{y_t}^{(t+1)} = \boldsymbol{w}_{y_t}^{(t)} + \tau \boldsymbol{x}_t \;\; \text{and} \;\; \boldsymbol{w}_r^{(t+1)} = \boldsymbol{w}_r^{(t)} - \tau \boldsymbol{x}_t, \quad (4)$$

while τ is computed as follows.

$$\tau = \min\left\{C, \frac{1 - \boldsymbol{w}_{y_t}^{(t)} \cdot \boldsymbol{x_t} + \boldsymbol{w}_r^{(t)} \cdot \boldsymbol{x_t}}{2\|\boldsymbol{x}_t\|^2}\right\}. \quad (5)$$

To deal with weakly-supervised learning, the system should estimate which instance is positive as a target object. We alternate the estimation of positive instances and the update of model parameters. Here, we describe the processing "Phase 1" where we obtain the model parameters of each class independently by selecting positive instances randomly, and the processing "Phase 2" where we refine the model parameters of all the classes simultaneously with balancing samples' scores across the object classes. Although the PA solver itself is an existing technique, the design of overall processing in a MIL setup described below is novel.

Phase 1 – independent –

We setup samples for the k-th class as follows.

- label all the instances in the images which do not have k-th object label as "negative".
- pick up a single instance randomly out of all the images which have k-th object label, duplicate it γ times, and label them as "positive".

We set γ to one-tenth of the number of negative samples. Then we optimize model parameters by applying PA with $N = 2$. We repeat this cycle M times and adopt the best model with the minimum hinge loss.

Phase 2 – simultaneous –

Letting K be the number of target classes, we setup samples as follows.

- label all the instances in the images which do not have k-th object label as $k + K$.
- pick up a single instance with the highest score $f_k(\boldsymbol{x}_n)$ out of each image which has k-th object label and label them as k. However, if this instance has the label $k'(k' \neq k)$ and $f'_k(\boldsymbol{x}_n)$ is larger than $f_k(\boldsymbol{x}_n)$, we pick up another instance with the next highest score and label it as k.

Beginning with the model parameters obtained in "Phase 1", we optimize $2K$ model parameters $\boldsymbol{w}_k, b_k(k = 1, \ldots, 2K)$. Here, we define positive labels as $Y^+ = \{y^1, \ldots, y^K\}$ and negative labels as $Y^- = \{y'^1, \ldots, y'^K\}$. When an observed sample's label is $y_t \in Y^+$, we replace Equation (1) by the following one.

$$r = \underset{y \in \{y'_t \cup Y^+ \setminus y_t\}}{\operatorname{argmax}}\, \boldsymbol{w}_y^{(t)} \cdot \boldsymbol{x}_t. \quad (6)$$

On the other hand, if an observed sample's label is $y'_t \in Y^-$, we set $r = y_t$. In this way, the decision surface is optimized among the target classes if a positive sample is observed, and otherwise it is optimized among one target class and all the rest. The former works for achieving distinguishability and the latter works for achieving detectability.

2.2 3D features

We use multiple 3D voxel features of different types; Circular Color Cubic Higher-order Local Auto Correlation (C^3-HLAC) features [6] that consider color texture, Intensity Spin Image [7] that considers gray-scale texture, and Global Radius-based Surface Descriptor (GRSD [8]) that considers surface curvature. The details of how to extract respective features are described below.

C^3-HLAC

C^3-HLAC descriptor [6] is represented by color 3D textures. Let $\boldsymbol{x}$ be the position of a voxel and $r(\boldsymbol{x})$, $g(\boldsymbol{x})$ and $b(\boldsymbol{x})$ be its RGB values normalized between 0 and 1. By defining $r_1 \equiv sin\left(\frac{\pi}{2}r(\boldsymbol{x})\right)$, $g_1 \equiv sin\left(\frac{\pi}{2}g(\boldsymbol{x})\right)$, $b_1 \equiv sin\left(\frac{\pi}{2}b(\boldsymbol{x})\right)$, $r_2 \equiv cos\left(\frac{\pi}{2}r(\boldsymbol{x})\right)$, $g_2 \equiv cos\left(\frac{\pi}{2}g(\boldsymbol{x})\right)$, and $b_2 \equiv cos\left(\frac{\pi}{2}b(\boldsymbol{x})\right)$, a voxel status $\boldsymbol{f}(\boldsymbol{x}) \in \mathbb{N}^6$ is defined as $\boldsymbol{f}(\boldsymbol{x}) \equiv [r_1\, r_2\, g_1\, g_2\, b_1\, b_2]^T \in \mathbb{N}^6$. Note that $\boldsymbol{f}(\boldsymbol{x})$ becomes a zero vector when the voxel has no measure point inside. Similarly to [5], we use the redefined rotation-invariant C^3-HLAC descriptors. Letting the color property of a voxel obtained when $r(\boldsymbol{x})$, $g(\boldsymbol{x})$ and $b(\boldsymbol{x})$ are binarized in a preprocessing be $\boldsymbol{f'}(\boldsymbol{x})$, a rotation-invariant version of C^3-HLAC descriptor is calculated as presented below.

$$\boldsymbol{z}_1 = \boldsymbol{f}(\boldsymbol{x}), \boldsymbol{z}_2 = \boldsymbol{f}(\boldsymbol{x})\boldsymbol{f}(\boldsymbol{x})^T, \boldsymbol{z}_3 = \boldsymbol{f}(\boldsymbol{x})\boldsymbol{f}(\boldsymbol{x}+\boldsymbol{a})^T, \quad (7)$$

$$\boldsymbol{z}_4 = \boldsymbol{f'}(\boldsymbol{x}), \boldsymbol{z}_5 = \boldsymbol{f'}(\boldsymbol{x})\boldsymbol{f'}(\boldsymbol{x})^T, \boldsymbol{z}_6 = \boldsymbol{f'}(\boldsymbol{x})\boldsymbol{f'}(\boldsymbol{x}+\boldsymbol{a})^T. \quad (8)$$

Therein, $\boldsymbol{a}$ is a displacement vector for a neighboring voxel, in which at least one of the x, y, and z coordinates is one. Eventually, a C^3-HLAC descriptor is obtained as a 117-dimensional vector by concatenating all elements in Equation (7) and Equation (8).

GRSD

GRSD [8] is represented by surface curvature. This descriptor is calculated by counting transitions from a Radius-based Surface Descriptor (RSD) of a voxel to that of a neighboring voxel. The RSD consists of the following six surface types defined by the highest curvature r_{min} and the lowest curvature r_{max} among voxels within a sphere of a certain radius: "planes" (large r_{min}), "cylinders" (medium r_{min}, large r_{max}), "edges" (small r_{min} and r_{max}), "rims" (small r_{min}, medium to large r_{max}), "spheres" (similar r_{min} and r_{max}), and "free space". Distinguishing all pairs of these six surface types except for the pair of "free space" and "free space", GRSD is obtained as a 20 $(= 6 \cdot 7/2 - 1)$-dimensional histogram.

C^3-HLAC and GRSD are originally defined as global features, where a feature vector is obtained by summing up local descriptors in a whole point cloud.

Intensity Spin Image

The Intensity Spin Image descriptor [7] is represented by a grayscale texture. This descriptor is based on the idea of Spin Image [4]. Spin Image is a 2D histogram of the projection angles α and β of surrounding points to the tangent plane of a point. Intensity Spin Image is a 2D histogram of the distances between a point and its surrounding points within a certain distance and their intensity level. Letting the quantization level of the distance between a point and its surrounding point be L_1 and that of its intensity be L_2, the dimension of this descriptor becomes $L_1 \cdot L_2$. In this work, we set L_1 to four and L_2 to five. Therefore the dimensions become twenty. We set the maximum distance to 50 mm. The Intensity Spin Image is originally a 2D image descriptor and is extracted from affine normalized patches. However, we skip this process because we use 3D point clouds, which are fundamentally affine invariant. Similarly to C^3-HLAC and GRSD, we sum up the Intensity Spin Image descriptors in a whole point cloud of an instance to obtain a global feature vector. Although C^3-HLAC, Intensity Spin Image, and GRSD are 3D features of different types represented respectively by color textures, grayscale textures and surface curvatures, they are computed efficiently in a uniform manner that extracts local descriptors of 3D points and sums them up to obtain a global feature vector.

3. RESULTS

3.1 Comparison to a conventional method

We used a color and depth image dataset[1] [5] to evaluate our method. Mean Average Precision (MAP) values of all the twelve target objects with EM-DD [11], which is a conventional MIL method, and with the proposed method are shown in Table 1. We set the number of the initial instances M to 100 both for EM-DD and our method. The putative detection was considered correct if the intersection of its bounding box with the ground-truth bounding box was larger than 50% of their union, as in Pascal VOC[2]. The results with C^3-HLAC, GRSD, Intensity Spin Image, and their combination are shown. When we permit a single instance to be attached with multiple labels so as to evaluate the performance of each class independently ("inclusive"), our method was superior to EM-DD with C^3-HLAC but was inferior with other features. However, when we attach to each instance a single label with the top score among all the target objects ("exclusive"), the performance with the combination features was also superior with our method to EM-DD. Because our method balances the scores of each instance across all the target objects while EM-DD learns each object detector independently, our method is more proper in the "exclusive" case where the distinguishability is important. Note that C^3-HLAC and EM-DD were used in a conventional work [5], and that the MAP in the "exclusive" case with our method (with "Combined" features and "Ours" learning method) was nearly twice larger than that with C^3-HLAC and EM-DD.

Table 1: MAP values in the 1st experiment.

Features	inclusive		exclusive	
	EM-DD	Ours	EM-DD	Ours
C^3-HLAC	0.0979	**0.1146**	0.0679	**0.0886**
Intensity-SI	**0.0530**	0.0411	**0.0415**	0.0349
GRSD	**0.0615**	0.0140	**0.0519**	0.0090
Combined	**0.1395**	0.1373	0.0932	**0.1227**

Table 2: MAP values in the 2nd experiment.

Features	inclusive		exclusive	
	Phase 1	Phase 2	Phase 1	Phase 2
Combined	0.218	0.217	0.222	0.250

3.2 Evaluation on a new dataset

We provide a new dataset[3] consisting of color and depth images inside a laboratory room captured by a Kinect sensor. There are 1,398 pairs of color and depth images for training and 315 pairs of them for testing (Fig. 1). The conventional dataset [5] used in Section 3.1 has a fixed background respectively for training and testing, whereas our dataset includes various backgrounds all around the laboratory room. Moreover, there are 100 object labels in our dataset while there are only 12 in the conventional one [5]. We used the combination features of C^3-HLAC, GRSD and Intensity Spin Image. We set M to 300 in this experiment.

Three instances with the highest scores of each target object are shown in Fig. 2. The ground truth objects are shown in the top row and the first, second and third ranked instances are shown below. The segments of the objects with 14 lowest hinge loss are shown from the first column to the 14th, and those with 6 highest hinge loss are shown from the 15th column to the end. Whereas there were 60 out of 100 objects whose regions were correctly ranked as top when we used the object detectors learned in "Phase 1", there were 70 when we used the object detectors learned in "Phase 2". It implies that balancing the scores of each instance across all the target objects is important to find correct objects in a weakly-supervised learning. MAP values of all the 100

[1] http://www.isi.imi.i.u-tokyo.ac.jp/software/

[2] http://pascallin.ecs.soton.ac.uk/challenges/VOC/

[3] http://www.mi.t.u-tokyo.ac.jp/kanezaki/color_depth_dataset_100

Figure 1: Example Images of the new dataset used in the 2nd experiment.

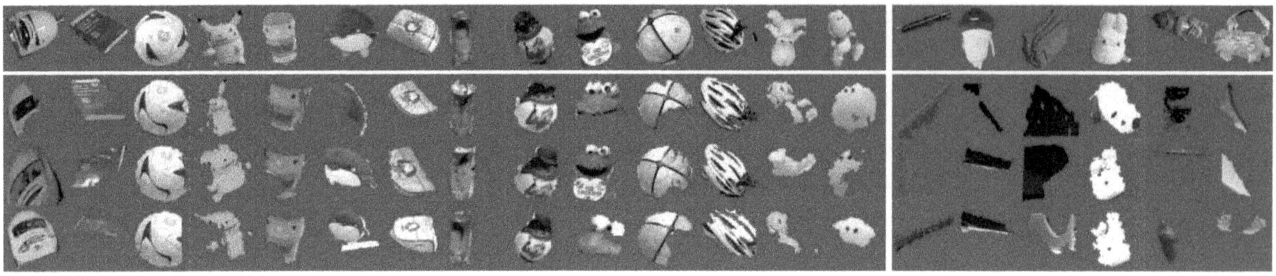

Figure 2: Obtained segments of the training dataset. Ground-truth segments are shown in the first row and the segments obtained with 1st, 2nd and 3rd ranks are shown in the rest rows. The segments of the objects with 14 lowest hinge loss are shown from the first column to the 14th, and those with 6 highest hinge loss are shown from the 15th column to the end.

target objects (with test data) are shown in Table 2. There is almost no difference between "Phase 1" and "Phase 2" in the "inclusive" case, however, the performance with "Phase 2" surpasses that of "Phase 1" in the "exclusive" case, where we attach to each instance a single label with the top score among all the target objects.

4. CONCLUSION

We proposed a weakly-supervised learning method that uses color and depth images attached with object labels to learn multi-class object detectors. Our method combines three different types of 3D features efficiently to achieve better performance. Moreover, this method is novel in that it learns multiple objects simultaneously in a way to balance the scores of each training sample across all the object classes. We showed that our method outperforms a conventional method using color and depth images with the dataset provided in its work. Moreover, we provided a new dataset with more object labels and various backgrounds, which we used to evaluate our method. We showed that our method is effective especially when we attach to each instance a single label with the top score among all the target objects, which is the case where the distinguishability is important.

5. REFERENCES

[1] K. Crammer, O. Dekel, J. Keshet, S. Shalev-Shwartz, and Y. Singer. Online passive-aggressive algorithms. *Machine Learning Research*, 7:551–585, 2006.

[2] T. G. Dietterich, R. H. Lathrop, and T. Lozano-Perez. Solving the multiple-instance problem with axis-parallel rectangles. *Artificial Intelligence*, 89, 1997.

[3] P. Felzenszwalb, R. Girshick, D. McAllester, and D. Ramanan. Object detection with discriminatively trained part based models. *Trans. on PAMI*, 32(9), 2010.

[4] A. E. Johnson and M. Hebert. Using spin images for efficient object recognition in cluttered 3D scenes. *Trans. on PAMI*, 21:433–449, 1999.

[5] A. Kanezaki, T. Harada, and Y. Kuniyoshi. Scale and rotation invariant color features for weakly-supervised object learning in 3D space. In *Proc. ICCV Workshop on 3D Representation and Recognition (3dRR-11)*, 2011.

[6] A. Kanezaki, T. Suzuki, T. Harada, and Y. Kuniyoshi. Fast object detection for robots in a cluttered indoor environment using integral 3D feature table. In *Proc. ICRA*, 2011.

[7] S. Lazebnik, C. Schmid, and J. Ponce. A sparse texture representation using local affine regions. *Trans. on PAMI*, 27:1265–1278, 2005.

[8] Z.-C. Marton, D. Pangercic, R. B. Rusu, A. Holzbach, and M. Beetz. Hierarchical object geometric categorization and appearance classification for mobile manipulation. In *Proc. Int. Conf. on Humanoid Robots*, 2010.

[9] M. Pandey and S. Lazebnik. Scene recognition and weakly supervised object localization with deformable part-based models. In *Proc. ICCV*, 2011.

[10] P. Siva and T. Xiang. Weakly supervised object detector learning with model drift detection. In *Proc. ICCV*, 2011.

[11] Q. Zhang and S. A. Goldman. EM-DD: An improved multiple-instance learning technique. In *Proc. NIPS*, 2001.

Querying for Video Events by Semantic Signatures from Few Examples

Masoud Mazloom, Amirhossein Habibian and Cees G. M. Snoek
ISLA, Informatics Institute, University of Amsterdam
Science Park 904, 1098 XH Amsterdam, The Netherlands
{m.mazloom, a.habibian, cgmsnoek}@uva.nl

ABSTRACT

We aim to query web video for complex events using only a handful of video query examples, where the standard approach learns a ranker from hundreds of examples. We consider a semantic signature representation, consisting of off-the-shelf concept detectors, to capture the variance in semantic appearance of events. Since it is unknown what similarity metric and query fusion to use in such an event retrieval setting, we perform three experiments on unconstrained web videos from the TRECVID event detection task. It reveals that: retrieval with semantic signatures using normalized correlation as similarity metric outperforms a low-level bag-of-words alternative, multiple queries are best combined using late fusion with an average operator, and event retrieval is preferred over event classification when less than eight positive video examples are available.

Categories and Subject Descriptors

H.3.3 [**Information Storage and Retrieval**]: Information Search and Retrieval

General Terms

Algorithms, Experimentation

Keywords

Video retrieval, multiple queries, fusion

1. INTRODUCTION

The goal of this paper is to retrieve complex events from web video using only a handful of video query examples, like the ones in Figure 1. So far, the common approach to event retrieval is to represent a video in terms of fused audiovisual features and to learn a ranker from hundreds of positives and negative labeled examples *e.g.*, [5, 9]. We differ from this supervised classification solution to event retrieval in three ways. 1) We focus on the more realistic scenario where only a few positive examples for an event are available. In contrast to [6, 7] deliberately ignoring the negative examples as these are not necessarily available at query time. 2) We prefer a high-level over a low-level video representation as events are often characterized by similarity in semantics rather than appearance. 3) We query directly by the example videos rather than a textual label.

MM'13, October 21–25, 2013, Barcelona, Spain.
Copyright 2013 ACM 978-1-4503-2404-5/13/10 ...$15.00.
http://dx.doi.org/10.1145/2502081.2502160 .

Figure 1: Each row shows a video query for the event *Attempting a board trick*. Due to the variance in both audiovisual and semantic appearance of events in video, a multiple query approach to retrieval, as we propose and evaluate, seems mandatory.

We draw inspiration from progress in query-by-image retrieval, where it is known to be advantageous to fuse multiple queries for retrieving concepts [10] or specific objects [1], but only for a low-level feature representation. In this paper we study the influence of combining multiple queries as well, but for the problem of retrieving complex events in video. In addition, we consider a *semantic signature* representation, consisting of off-the-shelf concept detectors [2, 12], which we deem more suited for capturing the variation in semantic appearance of events. We extend upon existing semantic image search approaches [11] by explicitly addressing fusion of multiple queries and pooling of the semantic representation for video. While approaches for video event classification using semantic representations have recently started to appear in the literature [3, 8], to the best of our knowledge this is the first work on query-by-video retrieval using semantic representations with multiple examples.

Since it is unknown what similarity metric and query fusion to use in such an event retrieval setting, as well as the influence of having only a handful of video query examples available, this paper conducts an experimental study to shed light on the matter.

2. SEMANTIC QUERY FUSION

2.1 Semantic Signatures

A video representation based on semantic signatures has the advantage of evaluating video similarity at a higher level of abstraction, and therefore potentially better semantic generalization than what is possible with a low level bag-of-words representation. To arrive at a semantic representation for video retrieval, we consider a lexicon consisting of n concept detectors that include *scenes, objects, people*, and *activities*. Thanks to efforts like TRECVID [12] and ImageNet [2] these detectors are commonly available these days, *e.g.*, [3, 8]. We compute concept detector scores per video frame, which are extracted once every s seconds. By concatenating and normalizing the detector outputs, each frame is represented by a concept score histogram of n elements. Finally the concept score histograms are aggregated into a video-level representation by average-pooling, which is known to be a stable choice for video classification [8]. We call the final histogram of concept detector scores a semantic signature.

2.2 Similarity Metrics

There are many well known methods for measuring the similarity distance between two histograms, see Table 1. However, it is not clear what metric is the most suited for the purpose of querying video by semantic signatures. In a semantic signature the presence of a concept is much more descriptive than absence of the concept. Hence, we expect that a similarity metric which only relies on the difference between elements while ignoring their values, such as the chi-square and histogram intersection, perform worse for retrieval. To illustrate, consider the cases where two videos contain a certain concept with the same probability. For the first case suppose this probability is 1 for both videos, and for the second case they are 0. From the chi-square point of view for both cases the similarity is identical. However, we know that for the second case the video content is different. A different semantic signature that results in the same similarity is problematic for fusing multiple queries. Since normalized correlation explicitly considers the value of the histogram elements, we expect this metric to be more suited. The same holds for metrics inspired by information theoretic divergence such as Kullback-Leibler and Jensen-Shannon.

2.3 Query Fusion

Since a single video query cannot cover all possible semantic variations of an event (see Figure 1), we consider a retrieval scenario where a limited set of video example queries is available. In such a multi query scenario, it is important to select the appropriate query fusion. We consider early and late query fusion. In early query fusion we simply combine the semantic signatures of each query into a single signature, which we call *signature pooling*. To arrive at a single signature, we consider both the average and max operator. In early query fusion, we query videos in the test set based on a single semantic signature, making it a very efficient query method. In contrast, for late query fusion, we search the test set based on each query individually making it slightly more demanding than early query fusion. For late query fusion we combine the retrieval results afterwards by *score pooling*. Again, we consider both the average and max operator. We anticipate that the average operator is preferred for both early and late query fusion, as it decreases the influence of noisy or irrelevant concept scores. Continuing the example from Figure 1, the average operator decreases the effect of the concepts *monkey* and *animal* which appear in the query at the bottom.

Table 1: Similarity metrics that we consider when querying for video events by a semantic signature containing n concept detector scores, where q and d are two semantic signatures for the query and a retrieved video, respectively.

Similarity Metric	Formula
Normalized Correlation	$\frac{\sum_{i=1}^{n} q_i * d_i}{\sqrt{\sum_{i=1}^{n} q_i^2} * \sqrt{\sum_{i=1}^{n} d_i^2}}$
Kullback-Leibler	$\sum_{i=1}^{n} q_i \log(\frac{q_i}{d_i})$
Histogram Intersection	$\frac{\sum_{i=1}^{n} min(q_i, d_i)}{min(\sum_{i=1}^{n} q_i, \sum_{i=1}^{n} d_i)}$
Chi-Square	$\frac{1}{2} \sum_{i=1}^{n} \frac{(q_i - d_i)^2}{(q_i + d_i)}$
Jensen-Shannon	$\frac{1}{2} \sum_{i=1}^{n} q_i \log(\frac{2q_i}{q_i + d_i}) + \frac{1}{2} \sum_{i=1}^{n} d_i \log(\frac{2d_i}{d_i + q_i})$

In order to establish the effectiveness of using query fusion with semantic signatures for video event retrieval, we perform three experiments on a large corpus of challenging real-world web video.

3. EXPERIMENTAL SETUP

3.1 Data Sets

Video data For the event retrieval experiments, we rely on the web video training corpus from the TRECVID 2012 Multimedia Event Detection task [12]. It comes with ground truth annotations at video level for 25 real-world events, including life events, instructional events, sport events, etc.. Following the protocol for event classification outlined in [3], we split the corpus into two partitions: consisting of 1,736 and 4,434 videos respectively. In this paper we use the first partition as the *query set* that consist of several queries for each of 25 event classes (and an additional set of 7,104 negatives which we use for comparison against event classification approaches). We report all results on the second partition, the independent *test set*.

Concept detectors For ease of comparison we adopt the publicly available concept detector scores for this dataset provided by [3]. It consists of a lexicon of 1,346 concept detectors. The 1,346 concept detectors are trained using the training data for 346 concepts from the TRECVID 2012 Semantic Indexing task [12] and for 1,000 objects from the ImageNet Large-Scale Visual Recognition Challenge 2011 [2]. The detectors are trained using a linear SVM atop a standard bag-of-words of densely sampled color SIFT with Fisher vector coding and spatial pyramids, for implementation details see [3]. The concept scores are computed for 1 frame every 2 seconds. We convert them into semantic signatures using the procedure outline in Section 2.1. We experimented with the length of the signature and observed only a small retrieval performance difference when increasing length from 500 to 1,346 concepts. For all the reported experiments we use the full, length as it provided the best retrieval result overall.

Table 2: Experiment 1: Single Query Baseline. The results are averaged over 25 events and repeated 500 times. Best MAP result in bold. We observe only a minimal variance for all events, therefore not shown.

		Similarity Metric				
Video representation	*Random*	*Normalized Correlation*	*Kullback-Leibler*	*Histogram Intersection*	*Chi-Square*	*Jensen-Shannon*
Semantic signature	0.011	**0.059**	0.054	0.033	0.030	0.053
Bag-of-words	0.011	0.046	0.040	0.032	0.024	0.038

Table 3: Experiment 2: Early vs Late Query Fusion. For the fusion we sample eight queries per iteration. The results are averaged over 25 events and repeated 500 times. Best MAP result in bold. We observe only a minimal variance for all events, therefore not shown.

			Early Query Fusion		Late Query Fusion	
Event category	**Available Queries**	**Single Query**	*AVG*	*MAX*	*AVG*	*MAX*
Attempting a board trick	98	0.062	0.123	0.058	**0.135**	0.117
Feeding an animal	95	0.023	0.056	0.052	**0.069**	0.030
Landing a fish	71	0.086	0.120	0.102	**0.128**	0.061
Wedding ceremony	69	0.078	0.232	0.089	**0.294**	0.037
Working on a woodworking project	79	0.026	**0.092**	0.086	0.087	0.037
Birthday party	121	0.055	0.151	**0.184**	0.159	0.054
Changing a vehicle tire	75	0.045	0.106	0.078	**0.118**	0.027
Flash mob gathering	115	0.175	0.254	0.224	**0.305**	0.115
Getting a vehicle unstuck	85	0.083	0.147	0.101	**0.159**	0.055
Grooming an animal	91	0.068	0.195	0.071	**0.214**	0.016
Making a sandwich	83	0.047	**0.141**	0.087	0.138	0.020
Parade	105	0.120	**0.221**	0.202	**0.221**	0.055
Parkour	75	0.082	**0.231**	0.121	0.219	0.037
Repairing an appliance	85	0.082	0.213	0.146	**0.221**	0.028
Working on a sewing project	86	0.046	0.094	0.052	**0.101**	0.042
Attempting a bike trick	43	0.057	0.108	0.101	**0.110**	0.046
Cleaning an appliance	43	0.024	0.069	0.070	**0.072**	0.051
Dog show	43	0.059	0.116	0.067	**0.130**	0.083
Giving directions to a location	43	0.022	0.102	0.010	**0.114**	0.006
Marriage proposal	43	0.012	0.019	0.009	**0.025**	0.005
Renovating a home	43	0.054	0.200	0.130	**0.207**	0.023
Rock climbing	43	0.042	0.071	**0.103**	0.065	0.019
Town hall meeting	43	0.036	0.060	**0.113**	0.055	0.076
Winning a race without a vehicle	43	0.065	0.083	0.074	0.085	**0.121**
Working on a metal crafts project	43	0.021	0.029	0.022	**0.030**	0.015
Mean average precision		0.059	0.129	0.095	**0.138**	0.047

3.2 Experiments

Experiment 1: ***Single query baseline*** In this experiment we compare semantic signatures with a standard bag-of-words using densely sampled SIFT descriptors with VLAD difference coding [4] using a 1024 words codebook. We consider all five similarity metrics from Table 1. We use all available queries once and report the average of their retrieval accuracy.

Experiment 2: ***Early vs Late Query Fusion*** To assess the effect of using multiple queries instead of using only one query, we compare the early and late query fusion schemes described in section 2.3. We perform the experiment using semantic signatures with the best similarity metric from experiment 1. We follow [1, 10, 11] and use eight queries per event, which we select randomly from all available queries. We compute the retrieval accuracy using early and late fusion. We repeat this process 500 times.

Experiment 3: ***Event Retrieval vs Event Classification*** In this experiment we compare event retrieval with event classification when only a limited number of positive examples are available. We vary the number of video queries (or positive examples) from 1 to 20 by randomly sampling from our pool of positive query examples. For event retrieval we use the best performing fusion scheme from experiment 2. For event classification we employ a linear Support Vector Machine on top of each semantic signature, similar to [3]. We consider the video query examples per event jointly as positive examples and the other videos from the query set as negative examples. We also report results using an exemplar-SVM [7] trained on each individual positive query and all available negative examples, and then fused over all queries using average pooling. We measure event retrieval and event classification performance on the test set. We repeat this process 50 times for both event retrieval and event classification with different number of positive examples, and a fixed number of negatives for the event classification scenario. Note that we do not rely on negative examples for the event retrieval scenario.

Evaluation criteria The retrieval performance is measured in terms of the well known average precision (AP), which combines precision and recall into a single metric [12]. We also report the average retrieval performance over all events as the mean average precision (MAP).

4. RESULTS

Experiment 1: ***Single query baseline*** We present the results of experiment 1 in Table 2. While the overall MAP using a single query is modest, but always much better than random, the video representation using semantic signatures outperforms bag-of-words for all metrics. As expected, the semantic signatures can generalize better than the bag-of-words. Table 2 also confirms that the normalized correlation metric and two information theory based metrics, are better than the histogram intersection and chi-square metrics for computing the similarity between events, as predicted in

Section 2.2. For the remaining experiments we consider the semantic signatures with normalized correlation.

Experiment 2: ***Early vs Late Query Fusion*** Table 3 presents the results of experiment 2. The results show considerable improvement in event retrieval performance when we use multiple queries instead of a single query (0.138 vs 0.059). For both fusion methods using the average operator is better than the maximum. We explain this by the fact that the average operator reduces the effect of noisy and irrelevant concepts that may occur accidentally in one or two event queries, as noted in Section 2.3. By contrast, the max operator is sensitive to irrelevant and noisy concepts scores with a high value. This results in a big drop in retrieval performance (from 0.138 to 0.047), even lower than the single query baseline. However, for some events such as *Rock climbing*, *Town hall meeting* and *Birthday party* early query fusion with the max operator results in the best retrieval performance. We attribute this to the presence of reliable relevant concepts in one of the queries. Indicating, that much is to be expected from adaptive semantic signatures that determine concept relevance at query time. The results of experiment 2 show that using multiple queries improves the performance of event video retrieval in comparison to a single query, especially for late query fusion. Moreover, we observe that in multiple query video retrieval the average operator is preferred for the fusion.

Experiment 3: ***Event Retrieval vs Event Classification*** We plot the result of experiment 3 in Figure 2. As expected the accuracy of both event retrieval and classification increases when more and more queries or positive event example are available. However, when we use only a limited number of queries, *i.e.*, from 1 to 8, we observe that the accuracy of event retrieval is higher than event classification. After increasing the number of queries, *i.e.*, from 8 to 20, we see the difference in accuracy increasing in favor of event classification. Using the available positive examples jointly is a better choice than bagging them individually with an exemplar-SVM. The exemplar-SVM needs up to 16 positive examples (and a bunch of negative examples) before it outperforms event retrieval. We conclude that when more than eight positive examples are available per event, as well as a set of negative examples, it pays off to learn a classifier. However, for more realistic event video retrieval scenarios where only a handful of positive examples are available, it is advantageous to rely on late query fusion retrieval with an average operator.

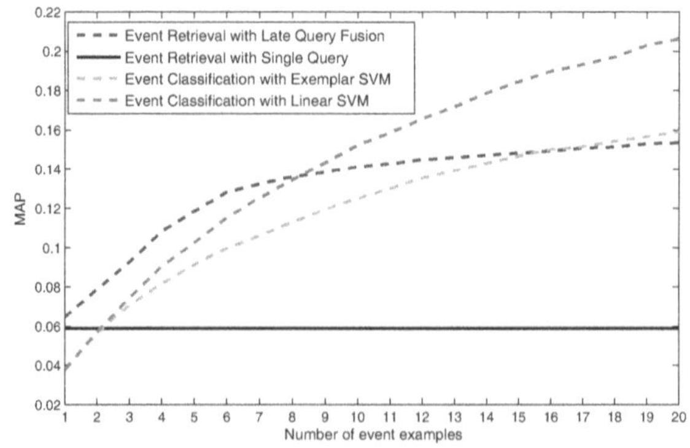

Figure 2: Experiment 3: Event Retrieval vs Event Classification. When only a handful of semantic signature queries are available per event, classification is outperformed by retrieval.

5. CONCLUSIONS

This paper studies the behavior of multiple video queries for event retrieval, by performing three experiments on an unconstrained web video collection. The result of experiment 1 provides an indication that querying for event video using semantic signatures generalizes better than a low-level bag-of-words alternative. In addition, we find that normalized correlation is a suitable similarity metric when considering retrieval using semantic signatures. The results of experiment 2 shows that video retrieval using multiple event queries in combination with late query fusion and an average operator outperforms event retrieval using only a single query. With only a handful of examples the results increase from 0.059 to 0.138. A considerable improvement. Finally, experiment 3 reveals that it is advantageous to rely on event retrieval rather than event classification, when the number of available video examples is less than eight.

Acknowledgments This research is supported by the STW STORY project, the Dutch national program COMMIT, and by the Intelligence Advanced Research Projects Activity (IARPA) via Department of Interior National Business Center contract number D11PC20067. The U.S. Government is authorized to reproduce and distribute reprints for Governmental purposes notwithstanding any copyright annotation thereon. Disclaimer: The views and conclusions contained herein are those of the authors and should not be interpreted as necessarily representing the official policies or endorsements, either expressed or implied, of IARPA, DoI/NBC, or the U.S. Government.

6. REFERENCES

[1] R. Arandjelovic and A. Zisserman. Multiple queries for large scale specific object retrieval. In *BMVC*, 2012.

[2] A. Berg, J. Deng, S. Satheesh, H. Su, and F.-F. Li. ImageNet large scale visual recognition challenge 2011. `http://www.image-net.org/challenges/LSVRC/2011`.

[3] A. Habibian, K. E. A. van de Sande, and C. G. M. Snoek. Recommendations for video event recognition using concept vocabularies. In *ICMR*, 2013.

[4] H. Jégou, F. Perronnin, M. Douze, J. Sánchez, P. Pérez, and C. Schmid. Aggregating local image descriptors into compact codes. *TPAMI*, 2012.

[5] Z.-Z. Lan, L. Bao, S.-I. Yu, W. Liu, and A. G. Hauptmann. Double fusion for multimedia event detection. In *MMM*, 2012.

[6] Z. Ma, Y. Yang, Y. Cai, N. Sebe, and A. G. Hauptmann. Knowledge adaptation for ad hoc multimedia event detection with few exemplars. In *ACM MM*, 2012.

[7] T. Malisiewicz, A. Gupta, and A. A. Efros. Ensemble of exemplar-svms for object detection and beyond. In *ICCV*, 2011.

[8] M. Merler, B. Huang, L. Xie, G. Hua, and A. Natsev. Semantic model vectors for complex video event recognition. *IEEE TMM*, 2012.

[9] P. Natarajan et al. Multimodal feature fusion for robust event detection in web videos. In *CVPR*, 2012.

[10] A. Natsev, M. R. Naphade, and J. Tesic. Learning the semantics of multimedia queries and concepts from a small number of examples. In *ACM MM*, 2005.

[11] N. Rasiwasia, P. J. Moreno, and N. Vasconcelos. Bridging the gap: Query by semantic example. *IEEE TMM*, 2007.

[12] A. F. Smeaton, P. Over, and W. Kraaij. Evaluation campaigns and TRECVid. In *ACM MIR*, 2006.

Towards Cover Group Thumbnailing

Peter Grosche
Saarland University
and MPI Informatik
Saarbrücken, Germany
pgrosche@mpi-inf.mpg.de

Meinard Müller
International Audio
Laboratories Erlangen
Erlangen, Germany
meinard.mueller@audiolabs-erlangen.de

Joan Serrà
Artificial Intelligence Research
Institute (IIIA-CSIC)
Bellaterra, Spain
jserra@iiia.csic.es

ABSTRACT

In this paper we investigate whether we can extract the commonalities shared by a group of cover songs or versions of the same musical piece. As a main contribution, we introduce the concept of cover group thumbnail, which is the most representative, essential subsequence for an entire group of versions. Opposed to previous approaches, we jointly consider all versions of a given song to compute a single cover group template, which then shows a high degree of robustness against version-specific aspects. To compute such a template, we introduce a modification of a recent audio thumbnailing technique. To evaluate the reliability of our conceptual contribution, we consider the task of template-based version identification, where we show comparable accuracies to existing systems.

Categories and Subject Descriptors

H.5.5 [**Sound and Music Computing**]: Methodologies and Techniques, Systems.

Keywords

Cover song, music retrieval, audio thumbnailing.

1. INTRODUCTION

Cover songs are alternative versions or performances of a previously recorded musical piece. They often differ from the original in several musical aspects such as timbre, tempo, song structure, tonality, arrangement, lyrics, or language of the vocals. The goal of cover song or version identification is to automatically detect all versions of the same piece of music within a pool of documents [4, 11]. Version identification is usually interpreted as a document-level retrieval task, where a single similarity measure is used to globally compare entire documents. However, successful methods perform this global comparison on a local basis, obtaining the final similarity measure by comparing parts (or subsequences) of the documents. The global similarity measure can then be derived from the best matching subsequence (e.g. [3, 6, 11]).

MM'13, October 21–25, 2013, Barcelona, Spain.
Copyright 2013 ACM 978-1-4503-2404-5/13/10 ...$15.00.
http://dx.doi.org/10.1145/2502081.2502161.

State-of-the-art approaches based on subsequence matching show a significant robustness to musical variations (see [11] for a review). However, requiring pairwise comparisons of the query and all subsequences of all available documents, they typically do not scale to large audio collections. One step towards better scalability is to employ indexing schemes to exhaustively compute similarities between subsequences [2, 3]. Another, possibly complementary strategy is to reduce the number of subsequences that need to be compared. This approach, which motivates the present paper, has been rather unexplored, with the notable exceptions of [6, 8].

In an ideal case, for a given song, a single subsequence that acts as a compact descriptor or *template* for the entire song would be sufficient to identify all other versions. In [6, 8], *music thumbnailing* approaches were employed to determine the most representative and repetitive segment of every single song. Typically, such a segment has many (approximate) repetitions covering large parts of the song [1, 7, 10]. The underlying assumption is that a segment which represents a song well might also capture aspects of the different versions. However, as thumbnails are extracted for each version individually, they often do not correspond to the same musical section in all versions. As a result, performing comparisons of entire songs only on the basis of the individually extracted templates might not reveal the desired similarities.

Here, our goal is to extract a single robust template that captures the essence of a group of cover songs. The idea is to compute a *cover group thumbnail*: a single segment that is the most representative and repetitive segment for an entire group of versions of a piece. Conceptually, our approach differs from previous approaches as we jointly consider all versions of a given song to compute a single thumbnail, whereas previous approaches consider individual songs to compute a thumbnail for each version separately [6, 8] or consider groups in a post-processing step [11, 12]. As shown in [12], considering entire groups of versions provides meaningful information which can enhance current systems.

As our main technical contribution, we introduce a modification of a recent audio thumbnailing technique [10], so that the following problem can be solved: Given a group of sequences (let say K sequences $Y_1, \ldots, Y_K$) and a reference sequence X, find a subsequence of X that simultaneously "explains" in each of the sequences $Y_1, \ldots, Y_K$ a suitable subsequence. The resulting subsequence of X is called *cover group thumbnail* and the resulting K subsequences are called *induced subsequences*. The hypothesis is that these induced subsequences are similar to the cover group thumbnail. To obtain a *cover group template* that captures aspects of all versions, we compute an average representation of the cover group thumbnail and all induced subsequences.

Cover group templates have two main advantages over individual song templates. First, based on a joint analysis of an entire group, they show a higher degree of robustness against some version-specific aspects. Second, a single template is sufficient to represent the entire group, which could potentially allow reducing the computational load in a retrieval scenario. In our experiments, we analyze to which extent an entire cover group can be characterized by a single segment and show that cover group thumbnails can be effectively used for template-based version identification.

2. COVER GROUP TEMPLATES

Audio features: For our approach, we employ chroma features capturing information that closely correlates to harmonic and melodic properties of the audio recording. Such features have become a widely used tool for processing and analyzing music data in general [1, 3, 9] and cover song identification in particular [3, 6, 11]. The 12-dimensional chroma vectors express how the short-time energy of the audio signal is distributed over the twelve chroma bands. Following [9], we decompose the audio signal into subbands that correspond to the semitones of the equal-tempered scale. Then, adding up the bands that belong to the same pitch class, we obtain a chroma representation. Finally, applying suitable quantization, smoothing, downsampling, and normalization operations results in enhanced chroma features referred to as CENS[1] [9]. In the following, we use a feature resolution of 1 Hz (one feature vector per second).

Similarity matrices: Let $X := (x_1, x_2, \ldots, x_N)$ and $Y := (y_1, y_2, \ldots, y_M)$ be two chroma sequences. Furthermore, let $\mathbf{s}$ be a similarity measure that allows for comparing two chroma features (we here use the cosine measure). Then, an $M \times N$ *similarity matrix* (SM) is obtained by comparing the elements of X and Y in a pairwise fashion: $\mathcal{S}(m,n) := \mathbf{s}(y_m, x_n)$ for $m \in [1:M]$ and $n \in [1:N]$. Furthermore, we apply a smoothing filter [9], which results in an emphasis of diagonal information in $\mathcal{S}$. For handling tonality differences across the versions, we adopt the concept of transposition-invariant similarity matrices [7]. We first compute the similarity between the sequence X and each of the twelve cyclically shifted versions of Y resulting in twelve similarity matrices. Then, the transposition-invariant SM $\mathcal{S}$ is obtained by taking the point-wise maximum over these matrices. Subsequently, we apply a thresholding operation with the goal to achieve that relevant paths lie in the positive part of $\mathcal{S}$, whereas all other cells receive a negative penalty $\delta \leq 0$. As proposed in [11], we use a relative threshold that identifies cells that belong both to the 30% of the cells having the highest value in each column and to the 30% having the highest value in each row (the remaining cells are set to $\delta = -1$). These experimentally found parameter values did not have a significant impact on the results.

In our scenario, we jointly consider similarity matrices for an entire group of K cover songs. Let Y_k denote the feature sequence of the version $k \in [1:K]$ and Y the concatenation of the Y_k. Furthermore, we fix a version $k_0 \in [1:K]$ to serve as reference and define $X = Y_{k_0}$. Note that any version $k_0 \in [1:K]$ could act as a reference. Let N denote the length of X, M_k the length of Y_k, and $M := \sum_{k\in[1:K]} M_k$ the length of Y. Then, we compute an $M \times N$ similarity matrix $\mathcal{S}$ for the sequence Y and the reference X.

[1]*Chroma Energy Normalized Statistics*, an implementation of these features is available online: `http://www.mpi-inf.mpg.de/resources/MIR/chromatoolbox/`.

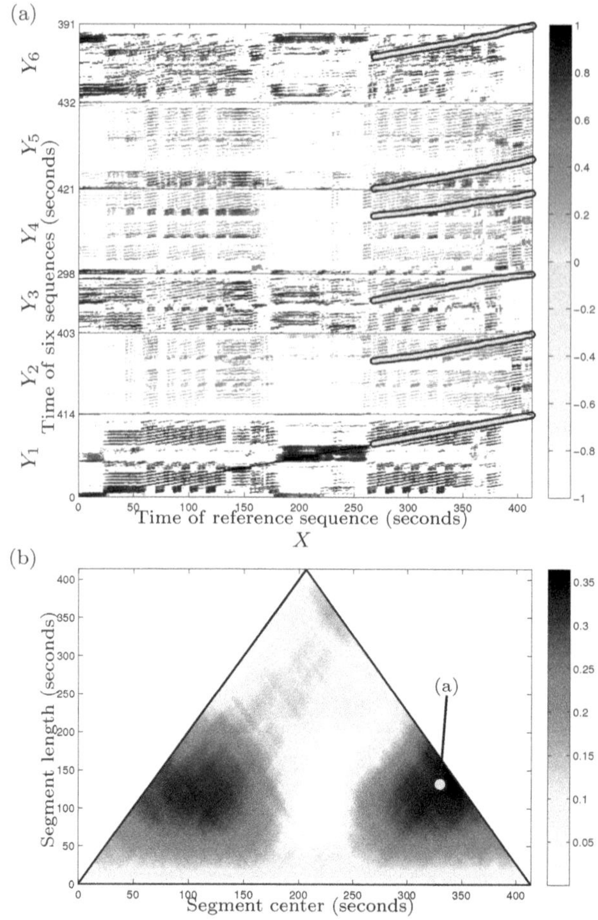

Figure 1: (a) Similarity matrix for a group of six versions of Kraftwerk's "Radioactivity" and optimal path family. Horizontal lines indicate boundaries between versions. (b) Fitness scape plot.

Fig. 1a shows $\mathcal{S}$ for a group of $K = 6$ versions of Kraftwerk's *Radioactivity*. In this example, $X = Y_1$ corresponds to the original version and the sequences Y_k, $k \in [2:6]$ are covers. Each path of cells of high similarity within $\mathcal{S}$ indicates the similarity between subsequences of X and Y given by the projections of the path onto the horizontal and vertical axis, respectively. In the case that two versions are very similar, one observes a long path. In the case of musical variations, however, the paths are often fragmented.

Cover group thumbnail: Let $\alpha = [s:t] \subseteq [1:N]$ denote a subsequence of X specified by its starting point s and end point t. In [10], a fitness measure is introduced that assigns to each α a fitness value $\varphi(\alpha) \in \mathbb{R}$ that simultaneously captures two aspects. It indicates (i) how well α explains other subsequences of X and (ii) how much of X is covered by these subsequences. The thumbnail of X is then defined to be the subsequence α^* with maximal fitness φ.

In the computation of the fitness measure, the main technical idea is to assign to α a so-called *optimal path family*

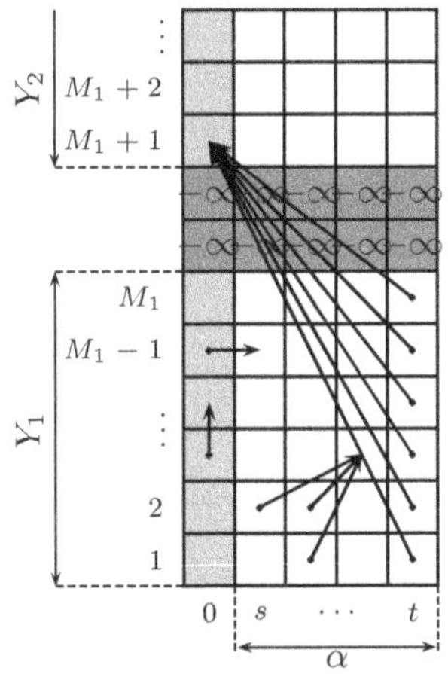

Figure 2: Illustration of the modifications of the thumbnailing algorithm for an excerpt of the similarity matrix $\mathcal{S}(m,n)$ for $n = [s:t]$ and $m = [1:M]$ corresponding to the subsequence $\alpha = [s:t]$.

that reveals the relations between α and all other similar subsequences. A path family over α is defined to be a set $\mathcal{P} := \{p_1, p_2, \ldots, p_I\}$ of size I, consisting of paths p_i over α, $i \in [1:I]$. Fig. 1a shows a path family consisting of $I = 6$ paths for the segment $\alpha = [269:414]$. Each path over α of length L is a sequence $p_i = ((m_1, n_1), \ldots, (m_L, n_L))$ of cells $(m_\ell, n_\ell) \in [1:M] \times [1:N]$, $\ell \in [1:L]$, satisfying $n_1 = s$ and $n_L = t$ as well as $(m_{\ell+1}, n_{\ell+1}) - (m_\ell, n_\ell) \in \Omega$, where Ω denotes a set of admissible step sizes. We use $\Omega = \{(1,2),(2,1),(1,1)\}$, as it has been shown to perform well for the task of version identification [9, 11]. Importantly, a path family induces an entire family of related subsequences α_i that are similar to α, given by the projection to the vertical axis $\pi(p_i) := [m_1 : m_L]$ of each path p_i.

Instead of analyzing songs individually, we here analyze a group of versions simultaneously. In particular, our goal is to extract for each segment α of the reference sequence X exactly one subsequence in each of the versions. To do so, we modify the original algorithm presented in [10] and use additional constraints to enforce that the number of paths equals the number of versions ($I = K$) and that $\alpha_i \subset Y_k$ for $i = k \in [1:K]$, i.e., there is exactly one α_i in each Y_k. Among all possible subsequences of Y_k, α_i corresponds to the one that is most similar to α.

In [10], a dynamic programming algorithm is introduced for computing optimal path families. Our technical modification is twofold (Fig. 2). First, to ensure that no path p_i induces a subsequence in more than one Y_k, we insert cells with a score of $-\infty$ between Y_k and Y_{k+1} for $k \in [1:K-1]$. As a result, a path which crosses the boundary between two versions gets a score of $-\infty$ (Note that, because of the step size condition $\Omega = \{(1,2),(2,1),(1,1)\}$, two entries with $-\infty$ are needed). Second, to ensure that there is a path p_i inducing a subsequence in each sequence Y_k, we add the condition that the extraction of a path is stopped at the end t of α and a new path is started in the next version Y_{k+1} (Fig. 2, arrows starting in the last column). As this is the only way to cross the $-\infty$ rows, the combination of both modifications ensure that the resulting path family $\mathcal{P}$ consist of exactly one path for each version Y_k.

Fig. 1b shows an example of fitness values $\varphi(\alpha) \in \mathbb{R}$ for all reference segments α in the form of a scape plot representation, where each point corresponds to one subsequence α represented by its center $c(\alpha) := (s+t)/2$ and its length $|\alpha| := t - s + 1$. The fitness $\varphi(\alpha)$ indicates how well α explains subsequences of Y and how much of Y is covered by all these subsequences. The subsequence $\alpha^* = [269:414]$ having maximal fitness φ is considered to be the *cover group thumbnail*, the subsequence that best explains and is most similar to the entire group. The optimal path family over α^* encodes the relation between α^* and the induced subsequences α_k^*, one in each of the versions, see Fig. 1a.

Template extraction: To obtain a cover group template for a given group and reference $X = Y_{k_0}$, we compute the thumbnail α^* and extract the chroma features of the induced subsequences α_k^*. The cover group template is then obtained by averaging all chroma sequences. Here, we exploit the multi-alignment between α^* and α_k^* given by the paths p_k to determine for each chroma vector x_n the corresponding vectors $y_{k,m}$ in all versions $k \in [1:K]$. Actually, this operation results in a temporal warping which compensates for temporal differences in the versions. Furthermore, we compensate for possible transpositions by employing a circular shift strategy [11]. The necessary cyclic shift index is determined by estimating the global similarity between X and the warped chroma sequences using the cosine measure. The shift index with maximum similarity is used to compensate for a transposition. The final cover group template $\mathcal{T}_{k_0}$ with respect to the reference k_0 is then obtained by point-wise averaging all K chroma sequences.

3. TEMPLATE-BASED RETRIEVAL

To quantify our assumption that cover group templates capture characteristic aspects of a group of versions, and to evaluate the reliability of cover group thumbnails, we consider the task of cover song identification. Given a cover group template, we investigate if it is possible to retrieve all versions of the group from a dataset. We use a dataset $\mathcal{D}$ obtained from [11] that consists of $G = 17$ groups, each containing $K = 6$ versions ($|\mathcal{D}| = G \times K = 102$).

Since our goal is to gauge the potential of cover group templates, in this proof-of-concept experiment we perform training and evaluation on the same dataset (notice however that we do not perform any exhaustive parameter tuning). For each group $\mathcal{G}_g \subset \mathcal{D}$ with $g \in [1:G]$, we compute K templates $\mathcal{T}_{g,k_0}$ by selecting, in turn, each song $k_0 \in [1:K]$ as reference. Then, we perform retrieval on the whole dataset employing a subsequence matching strategy. Specifically, we compare $\mathcal{T}_{g,k_0}$ locally with all chroma subsequences of the database using a DTW-based distance measure [9]. The final distance values for a song are obtained by minimizing the distances of all subsequences of that song.

Following standard practice [11], we express the retrieval accuracy in terms of *mean of average precision* (MAP). Given the group $\mathcal{G}_g$ of K versions that are relevant to the template $\mathcal{T}_{g,k_0}$, we obtain the precision ψ_{g,k_0} at rank $r \in [1:|\mathcal{D}|]$ as $\psi_{g,k_0} = \frac{1}{r}\sum_{i=1}^{r} \Gamma_{g,k_0}(i)$, where $\Gamma_{g,k_0}(r) \in \{0,1\}$ indicates whether the version at rank r is contained in $\mathcal{G}_g$. The average precision $\overline{\psi}_{g,k_0} \in [0,1]$ is then defined as $\overline{\psi}_{g,k_0} = \frac{1}{K}\sum_{r=1}^{|\mathcal{D}|} \psi_{g,k_0}\Gamma_{g,k_0}(r)$. Table 1 shows $\overline{\psi}_{g,k_0}$ values when using the version $k_0 \in [1:K]$ as reference (the higher, the better). MAP values $\overline{\psi}_g = 1/K \sum_{k_0=[1:K]} \overline{\psi}_{g,k_0}$,

g	$\overline{\psi}_{g,1}$	$\overline{\psi}_{g,2}$	$\overline{\psi}_{g,3}$	$\overline{\psi}_{g,4}$	$\overline{\psi}_{g,5}$	$\overline{\psi}_{g,6}$	$\overline{\psi}_{g}$	$\overline{\psi}_{g,k_0^*}$	$\overline{\psi}_{g}^{+}$	$\overline{\psi}_{g}^{-}$
1	0.41	0.45	0.12	0.57	0.15	0.19	0.31	0.45	0.57	0.12
2	0.90	0.88	0.93	1.00	0.97	0.86	0.92	0.90	1.00	0.86
3	0.47	0.78	0.39	0.42	0.24	0.55	0.47	0.78	0.78	0.24
4	1.00	1.00	1.00	1.00	1.00	0.74	0.96	1.00	1.00	0.74
5	0.93	0.62	0.75	0.80	0.78	0.34	0.70	0.80	0.93	0.34
6	0.64	0.07	0.81	0.81	0.67	0.67	0.61	0.67	0.81	0.07
7	1.00	1.00	1.00	1.00	1.00	1.00	1.00	1.00	1.00	1.00
8	0.59	0.59	0.68	0.51	0.54	0.35	0.54	0.68	0.68	0.35
9	0.94	0.69	0.59	0.67	0.71	0.64	0.71	0.71	0.94	0.59
10	0.88	0.97	0.59	0.78	0.77	0.77	0.79	0.88	0.97	0.59
11	0.97	0.90	1.00	0.88	1.00	0.94	0.95	1.00	1.00	0.88
12	0.74	0.61	0.65	0.69	0.73	0.79	0.70	0.73	0.79	0.61
13	0.61	0.67	0.58	0.37	0.74	0.20	0.53	0.74	0.74	0.20
14	0.42	0.70	0.67	0.65	0.79	0.86	0.68	0.79	0.86	0.42
15	0.86	1.00	1.00	0.86	0.87	1.00	0.93	1.00	1.00	0.86
16	1.00	1.00	1.00	1.00	1.00	1.00	1.00	1.00	1.00	1.00
17	1.00	1.00	1.00	0.89	1.00	1.00	0.98	1.00	1.00	0.89
ø	0.78	0.76	0.75	0.76	0.76	0.70	0.75	0.83	0.89	0.57

Table 1: MAPs for each of the 17 cover groups, consisting of 6 songs each (see text).

$\overline{\psi}_g^+ = \max_{k_0}(\overline{\psi}_{g,k_0})$ and $\overline{\psi}_g^- = \min_{k_0}(\overline{\psi}_{g,k_0})$ are also shown for each group $g \in [1:G]$. The values $\overline{\psi}_{g,k_0^*}$ are obtained by choosing for each group the reference $k_0^* \in [1:K]$ that has maximum fitness $k_0^* = \mathrm{argmax}_{k_0}(\varphi^*_{k_0})$.

The values $\overline{\psi}_g^+$ indicate the best possible results that can be achieved by our template-based approach. It turns out that the average over all groups $\overline{\psi}^+ = 0.89$ is similar to the results for the state-of-the-art subsequence matching algorithm reported in [11], which indicates the potential of a template-based approach. Note that instead of comparing all subsequences of all $|\mathcal{D}|$ documents with all subsequences of all $|\mathcal{D}|$ documents, one main advantage of our template-based approach is that we need only to compare G templates with the subsequences of $|\mathcal{D}|$ documents. Thus, as the number of comparisons and the complexity of the similarity measure is reduced, the template-based approach also facilitates efficient retrieval.

Importantly, we observed that the selection of a single template representing a group turned out to be a crucial step. For some groups (e.g., $g = 7, 11, 16, 17$) one obtains rather consistent results for all choices of a reference k_0. For other groups, however, the choice of a reference has a large influence on the retrieval results. For example, in the case of the group $g = 6$, the maximum average precision is $\overline{\psi}_{6,k_0} = 0.81$ when using the reference $k_0 = 4$. However, with $k_0 = 2$, one only obtains $\overline{\psi}_{6,k_0} = 0.07$. One strategy to select a proper reference is to use the reference $k_0^* \in [1:K]$ that has maximum fitness (this could also be a potential application of our approach to querying databases containing cover groups). For the group $g = 6$, k_0^* corresponds to $k_0 = 5$ which results in $\overline{\psi}_{6,k_0^*} = 0.67$. In average over all 17 groups, one obtains $\overline{\psi}_{k_0^*} = 0.83$, only a minor reduction in accuracy in comparison to the ideal case $\overline{\psi}^+ = 0.89$.

4. CONCLUSION

The modification of a recent thumbnailing approach allowed us to analyze all versions of the same piece simultaneously and to extract a cover group template that is invariant to version-specific aspects: the cover group thumbnail. We evaluated the reliability of our conceptual contribution under a cover song retrieval scenario, assuming that all versions of a song have a common, essential subsequence. First experiments showed that a template-based cover song identification system may have the potential of yielding similar results as state-of-the-art approaches and, as a by-product, reducing the number of necessary comparisons.

The selection of a reference version, however, turned out to have a large influence on the resulting templates, which weakens our assumption of a common subsequence for all versions (cf. [12]). Being based on chroma features, our approach can only capture harmonic similarities. In many groups, however, cover versions are characterized by similarities of the melody line, bass line, or rhythm pattern. A more robust cover group template extraction requires additional features which capture the many facets of similarities between cover versions (cf. [5]).

5. ACKNOWLEDGMENTS

This work was supported by the Cluster of Excellence on Multimodal Computing and Interaction at Saarland University, JAEDOC069/2010, FP7-ICT-2011-8-318770, and 2009-SGR-1434. The International Audio Laboratories Erlangen are a joint institution of the Friedrich-Alexander-Universität Erlangen-Nürnberg (FAU) and Fraunhofer IIS.

6. REFERENCES

[1] M. A. Bartsch and G. H. Wakefield. Audio thumbnailing of popular music using chroma-based representations. *IEEE Trans. on Multimedia*, 7(1):96–104, 2005.

[2] T. Bertin-Mahieux and D. Ellis. Large-scale cover song recognition using hashed chroma landmarks. In *Proc. of IEEE WASPAA*, pages 117–120, 2011.

[3] M. A. Casey, C. Rhodes, and M. Slaney. Analysis of minimum distances in high-dimensional musical spaces. *IEEE Trans. on Audio, Speech and Language Processing*, 16(5):1015–1028, 2008.

[4] D. Ellis and G. E. Poliner. Identifying 'cover songs' with chroma features and dynamic programming beat tracking. In *Proc. of IEEE ICASSP*, IV:1429–1432, 2007.

[5] R. Foucard, J.-L. Durrieu, M. Lagrange, and G. Richard. Multimodal similarity between musical streams for cover version detection. In *Proc. of IEEE ICASSP*, pages 5514–5517, 2010.

[6] E. Gómez, B. S. Ong, and P. Herrera. Automatic tonal analysis from music summaries for version identification. In *Proc. of the AES Convention*, 2006.

[7] M. Goto. A chorus section detection method for musical audio signals and its application to a music listening station. *IEEE Trans. on Audio, Speech and Language Processing*, 14(5):1783–1794, 2006.

[8] M. Marolt. A mid-level melody-based representation for calculating audio similarity. In *Proc. of ISMIR*, pages 280–285, 2006.

[9] M. Müller. *Information Retrieval for Music and Motion.* Springer Verlag, 2007.

[10] M. Müller, P. Grosche, and N. Jiang. A segment-based fitness measure for capturing repetitive structures of music recordings. In *Proc. of ISMIR*, pages 615–620, 2011.

[11] J. Serrà. *Identification of versions of the same musical composition by processing audio descriptions.* PhD thesis, Universitat Pompeu Fabra, Barcelona, Spain, 2011.

[12] J. Serrà, M. Zanin, P. Herrera, and X. Serra. Characterization and exploitation of community structure in cover song networks. *Pattern Recognition Letters* 33(9): 1032–1041, 2012.

Multi-feature Canonical Correlation Analysis for Face Photo-Sketch Image Retrieval

Dihong Gong[1], Zhifeng Li[1], Jianzhuang Liu[1,2,3], and Yu Qiao[1]

[1]Shenzhen Key Lab of Computer Vision and Pattern Recognition
Shenzhen Institutes of Advanced Technology, Chinese Academy of Sciences, China
[2]Media Lab, Huawei Technologies Co. Ltd., China
[3]Department of Information Engineering, The Chinese University of Hong Kong, China
{dh.gong, zhifeng.li, yu.qiao}@siat.ac.cn, liu.jianzhuang@huawei.com

ABSTRACT

Automatic face photo-sketch image retrieval has attracted great attention in recent years due to its important applications in real life. The major difficulty in automatic face photo-sketch image retrieval lies in the fact that there exists great discrepancy between the different image modalities (photo and sketch). In order to reduce such discrepancy and improve the performance of automatic face photo-sketch image retrieval, we propose a new framework called multi-feature canonical correlation analysis (MCCA) to effectively address this problem. The MCCA is an extension and improvement of the canonical correlation analysis (CCA) algorithm using multiple features combined with two different random sampling methods in feature space and sample space. In this framework, we first represent each photo or sketch using a patch-based local feature representation scheme, in which histograms of oriented gradients (HOG) and multi-scale local binary pattern (MLBP) serve as the local descriptors. Canonical correlation analysis (CCA) is then performed on a collection of random subspaces to construct an ensemble of classifiers for photo-sketch image retrieval. Extensive experiments on two public-domain face photo-sketch datasets (CUFS and CUFSF) clearly show that the proposed approach obtains a substantial improvement over the state-of-the-art.

Categories and Subject Descriptors

I.4.9 [**IMAGE PROCESSING AND COMPUTER VISION**]: Applications; I.5.4 [**PATTERN RECOGNITION**]: Applications

General Terms

Algorithms

Keywords

Image retrieval, face photo-sketch matching, canonical correlation analysis.

1. INTRODUCTION

Matching face sketch to face photo has been a challenging problem in the face recognition community. It refers to matching a given face sketch drawn by artist to a gallery of photos in the reference databases. It has important applications in law enforcement. Based on a drawn face sketch, the police can use it to automatically retrieve the face photos in police mug-shot databases to narrow down potential suspect quickly. The major challenge of face photo-sketch image retrieval is the great discrepancy between the photo and the corresponding sketch, which is conventionally referred to as modality gap. As illustrated by Figure 1, in the sketches, much texture information is missing, and the outlines are also distorted. Thus, it is expected that the matching performance cannot be good if we match a face sketch directly to a face photo.

Due to its important applications in the law enforcements, a variety of studies have been carried out on this topic, which can be summarized as the following three categories: 1) Convert images from one modality to the other by synthesizing a pseudo-image from the query image such that the matching process can be done within the same modality [1-3]. 2) Design an appropriate representation that is insensitive to the modalities of images. For example, Klare et al [4] used SIFT feature descriptors and multi-scale local binary patterns to represent both the sketch and photo images; Zhang et al [5] proposed a learning-based algorithm to capture discriminative local face structures and to effectively match photo and sketch. 3) Compare the heterogeneous images on a common subspace where the modality difference is believed to be minimized. Tenenbaum et al [6] applied the Bilinear Model (BLM) by Singular Value Decomposition (SVD) to develop a common content (associated to identity) space for a set of different styles (corresponding to modalities); In [7], Yi et al used the Canonical Correlation Analysis (CCA) technique to construct a common subspace where the correlations between infrared and optical images can be maximized; In [8-9], authors applied the CCA on cross-pose and 2D-3D face recognition; In [10], Sharma et al applied the Partial Least Squares (PLS) method to derive a linear subspace in which cross-modality images are highly correlated.

In this paper, we propose a new framework called multi-feature canonical correlation analysis (MCCA) to reduce the modality gap between the sketch and photo images. The key idea is to learn a series of canonical bases that map the features of both a sketch and a photo into a subspace where the correlation between their features is maximized. To improve the matching performance, we also incorporate two random sampling techniques (bagging [18] and random subspace [17]) with multiple features, histograms of oriented gradients (HOG) [12] and multi-scale local binary pattern (MLBP) [11], into our framework. Extensive experiments on two large photo-sketch databases clearly reveal that our framework can notably improve the matching performance over the state-of-the-art.

MM '13, October 21 - 25 2013, Barcelona, Spain
Copyright 2013 ACM 978-1-4503-2404-5/13/10 $15.00.
http://dx.doi.org/10.1145/2502081.2502162

The contributions of this paper are summarized as follows: (i) We propose a new framework called MCCA to effectively address the face photo-sketch image retrieval task. (ii) We observe a substantial performance improvement over published algorithms using our new approach on two public domain face photo sketch databases (CUFS [2] and CUFSF [5]).

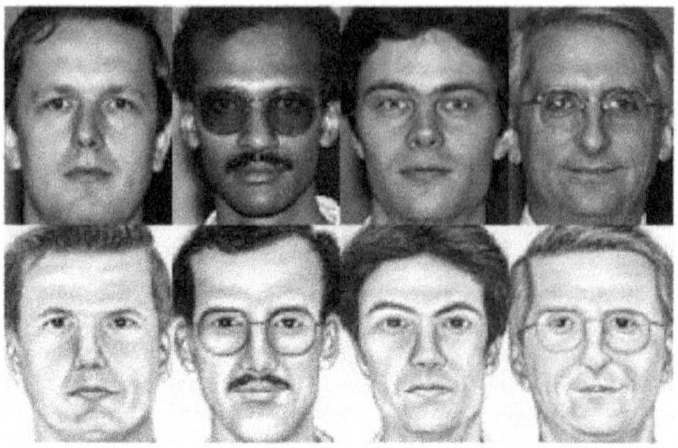

Figure 1. Examples of photos and corresponding sketches from CUHK Face Sketch FERET Database [5].

2. PROPOSED APPROACH

The proposed framework consists of two major components: a patch-based local feature representation and canonical correlation analysis (CCA) based feature classification. We will describe each component of the framework in the following subsections.

2.1 Local Feature Representation

Local facial features have been shown to be more effective than global facial features in representing face images at diverse scales and orientations [14]. Considering that the entire face image (which has high structural complexity) is difficult to be characterized by a single image descriptor, we use a patch-based local feature representation scheme in this paper. We first divide the whole face images into a set of overlapping patches with size 12x12 pixels (overlapping factor = 0.5) and then apply local image descriptors to each patch. The extracted features from these patches are concatenated together to form a long feature vector for further analysis.

Among the existing local feature descriptors, histograms of oriented gradients (HOG) [12] and multi-scale local binary pattern (MLBP) [11] are among the most successful ones. Hence, we will use both of them as feature description in our study. The HOG feature descriptor quantizes the gradient orientations into 8 directions with 45 degrees for each, and compute a histogram within the local patch such that each bin corresponds to the total gradient magnitude of that orientation. For the MLBP, we compute the MLBP descriptors with radii {1, 3, 5, 7} using u2 coding [11].

In our study, we will fuse the two extracted local features (HOG and MLBP) as feature representation for each face photo or face sketch.

2.2 Multi-feature Canonical Correlation Analysis

2.2.1 Canonical Correlation Analysis (CCA)

In statistics, the Canonical Correlation Analysis (CCA) is an effective technique to maximize the correlation between two random variables. Let us suppose that we have $d_1 \times N$ and $d_2 \times N$ data matrices $X = \{\vec{x}_1, \vec{x}_2, \ldots, \vec{x}_N\}$ and $Y = \{\vec{y}_1, \vec{y}_2, \ldots, \vec{y}_N\}$, consisting of N observations with dimension d_1 and d_2, respectively. Then the CCA seeks one pair of vectors $\vec{a} \in R^{d_1 \times 1}$ and $\vec{b} \in R^{d_2 \times 1}$ such that the correlation between random variables $\vec{a}^T X$ and $\vec{b}^T Y$ can be maximized. Formally,

$$\mathrm{argmax}_{\vec{a},\vec{b}} \{\mathrm{corr}(\vec{a}^T X, \vec{b}^T Y)\} \qquad (1)$$

Then the $u = \vec{a}^T X$ and $v = \vec{b}^T Y$ are the first pair of canonical variables. One can further seek another pair of vectors $\vec{a}'$ and $\vec{b}'$ maximizing the same correlation, subject to the constraint that they are to be uncorrelated with the first pair of canonical variables, which gives the second pair of canonical variables. This procedure may be continued up to $k = \min\{rank(X), rank(Y)\}$ times, yielding k pairs of mutually uncorrelated canonical variables $U = \{u_1, u_2, \ldots, u_k\}$ and $V = \{v_1, v_2, \ldots, v_k\}$, along with the corresponding projection vector pairs $A = \{\vec{a}_1, \vec{a}_2, \ldots, \vec{a}_k\}$ and $B = \{\vec{b}_1, \vec{b}_2, \ldots, \vec{b}_k\}$, which we will refer to as the k-correlation matrix.

2.2.2 Learning CCA bases

Let $\Sigma_{XX} = \mathrm{cov}(X, X)$ and $\Sigma_{YY} = \mathrm{cov}(Y, Y)$.

Optimizing (1) is equivalent to maximizing:

$$\rho = \frac{\vec{a}^T \Sigma_{XY} \vec{b}}{\sqrt{\vec{a}^T \Sigma_{XX} \vec{a}} \sqrt{\vec{b}^T \Sigma_{YY} \vec{b}}} \qquad (2)$$

According to [8], the optimal correlation defined in (2) can be obtained if $\vec{a}$ is the eigenvector with the maximum eigenvalue of the matrix:

$$\Sigma_{XX}^{-1} \Sigma_{XY} \Sigma_{YY}^{-1} \Sigma_{YX}$$

and $\vec{b}$ is the eigenvector with the maximum eigenvalue of the matrix:

$$\Sigma_{YY}^{-1} \Sigma_{YX} \Sigma_{XX}^{-1} \Sigma_{XY}$$

The subsequent pairs of the correlation vectors can be found by using the eigenvectors corresponding to the eigenvalues of decreasing magnitudes. The uncorrelated constraint of canonical variables is guaranteed by the orthogonality of the eigenvectors.

2.2.3 Multi-classifier Ensemble

CCA has been shown to be very effective in cross-modality matching problem [8]. However, if we directly use it for face photo-sketch image retrieval, we will encounter the following problems. First, the data size will be very large. In our study, there are two kinds of local features (HOG and MLBP) with each one spanning a high-dimensional space feature vector. So the fused HOG and MLBP feature is of high dimension (as high as 115200 in our experiments). Directly applying CCA on such a high-dimensional feature vector is too costly. Second, a more serious problem is the overfitting problem because of the large feature dimension, which would degrade the matching performance. To solve these problems, we apply two popular random sampling methods: random subspace [17] and bagging [18]. In the random subspace method, multiple classifiers are constructed by randomly sampling the feature space. The final matching score is the sum of matching scores from individual sub-classifiers. In the Bagging, multiple training subsets are generated by randomly sampling the training set. A classifier is then constructed from each training subset, and the results of these multiple classifiers are integrated. In order to better address the overfitting problem, we utilize both

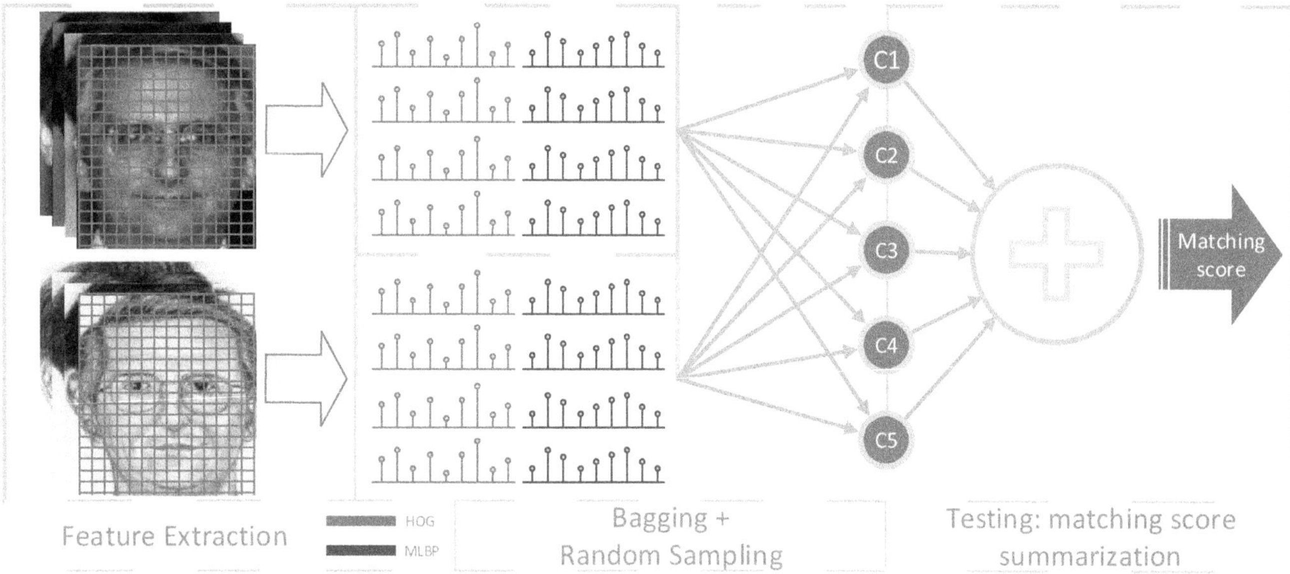

Figure 2. Illustration for the pipeline of the MCCA system. At the training stage, HOG and MLBP features of the face images are extracted and then concatenated to form a long feature. Secondly, for each of the classifier (we only show 5 classifiers in the figure), training samples are selected with replacement randomly and then sampled 5% of the components. Finally, the CCA is applied on each of the random training set to construct a sub-classifier. At the testing stage, features of the probe face are extracted and sampled using the same way as the training procedure, which are then fed into the sub-classifiers to compute the matching scores. The final matching score is the summarization of scores from all the sub-classifiers.

random subspace and bagging schemes. The detailed algorithm is as follows (illustrated in Figure 2).

Suppose N pairs of face training images are represented as $F_{HOG} = \{\vec{f}_H^1, \vec{f}_H^2, \ldots, \vec{f}_H^N\}$ and $F_{MLBP} = \{\vec{f}_M^1, \vec{f}_M^2, \ldots, \vec{f}_M^N\}$ for HOG and MLBP features respectively. Then the final feature descriptor is obtained by concatenating the two features into one for each face image: $F = \{\vec{f}^1, \vec{f}^2, \ldots, \vec{f}^N\}$. The following two random sampling techniques are then applied on the F:

1) Randomly sample N pairs of training face images from F with replacement, forming a new training set $F' = \{\vec{f}^{i1}, \vec{f}^{i2}, \ldots, \vec{f}^{iN}\}$ (there may be duplicated samples in F' since we are sampling with replacement).

2) Randomly sample p components for each of the features in F', forming the final training set $Ft = \{\vec{f}^{i1}_{[c1\ldots cp]}, \vec{f}^{i2}_{[c1\ldots cp]}, \ldots, \vec{f}^{iN}_{[c1\ldots cp]}\}$, where operator $[c1\ldots cp]$ means taking the corresponding components of that vector.

With the above random sampling methods, we can generate one training set at each run of the algorithm. For each of the generated training set, we first apply Principle Component Analysis (PCA) [15] to remove the redundant information, and then the CCA projection matrix is learned with the algorithm described in Section 2.2.2, which serves as a sub-classifier. In our experiments, 100 sub-classifiers are constructed and the matching score of each sub-classifier is the cosine distance between photo and sketch pairs computed in the CCA subspace. The final matching score is computed by summing the scores of all the sub-classifiers.

The MCCA algorithm is an improvement and extension of the CCA algorithm. From the experimental comparison in Section 3, we can see the significant performance improvement of our MCCA algorithm over the CCA algorithm.

3. EXPERIMENTS

In this section, we investigate the performance of our approach for the face photo-sketch image matching. Two public domain sketch-photo databases are used in our study. The first is the CUHK Face-Sketch FERET database (CUFSF) [5] which is the largest publicly available database for sketch-photo recognition. The dataset consists of 1194 pairs of sketch and photo images. In our study we use 300 pairs as training, and the rest 894 pairs as testing. Another is the CUFS database [2], which consists of 606 pairs of sketch and photo images. Following the configuration of training and testing split for CUFS in [2], we use 306 pairs as training and the rest 300 pairs as testing.

3.1 Comparison with subspace analysis methods in cross-modality face matching

Since the proposed MCCA approach is inherently a subspace analysis method, in this part we compare it against (i) PCA+LDA [16] (a popular subspace analysis method for face matching) and (ii) several newly developed subspace analysis methods for cross-modality face matching including PLS [10], LFDA [4], and CCA [8]. Here the CCA algorithm refers to applying CCA directly to the fused HOG and MLBP features, which is a regular practice in the literature. In this experiment, all the algorithms are using the same fused HOG and MLBP features for fair comparison. Also, all the algorithms are tuned to the best configurations according to their papers. The comparative results are illustrated in Figure 3. We illustrate the results of our approach for both the Bagging version (using both the random subspace and bagging techniques) and the one without bagging (using only the random subspace technique). It is very clear that the both of these two MCCA versions notably outperform the CCA algorithm, and the one with Bagging ensemble slightly outperforms the one without it. As discussed earlier, directly applying CCA to the fused HOG and MLBP feature may degrade the performance. The comparative results in Figure 3 clearly confirm this point. It is desirable to propose the MCCA approach to improve the photo-sketch matching performance. Moreover, it is very encouraging to see that the proposed MCCA approach obtains a significant performance improvement over the existing subspace analysis methods for face photo-sketch matching. This shows the effectiveness of the MCCA approach.

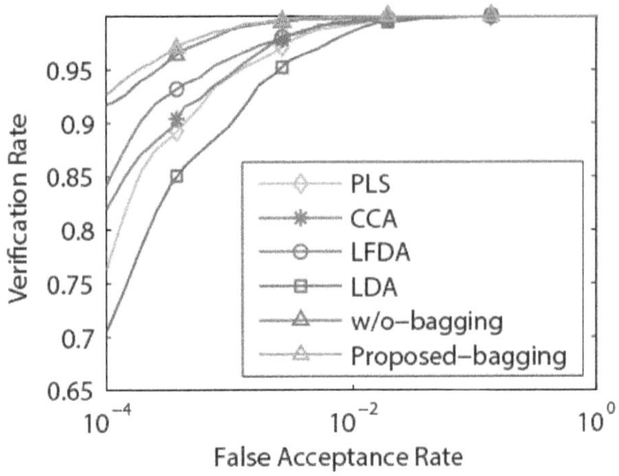

Figure 3. Comparison of verification accuracy on the CUFSF dataset [5].

3.2 Overall Benchmark Comparison

In addition to subspace analysis based methods, there are some other photo-sketch matching methods on the CUFS and CUFSF datasets. In this part, we compare our approach (with Bagging) to the state-of-the-art methods for photo-sketch matching on the CUFS and CUFSF datasets. The comparative results are reported in Table 1 and Table 2. From these results we can see that our approach also has superior performance over the state-of-the-art algorithms on the two datasets.

Table 1. Comparison of rank-1 identification accuracy on the CUFSF dataset [5].

CCA [8]	PLS [10]	LFDA [4]	CITE [5]	Ours
86.71%	85.55%	87.29%	89.54%	**92.17%**

Table 2. Comparison of rank-1 identification accuracy on the CUFS dataset [2].

MRF+RS-LDA [2]	LFDA [4]	CITE [5]	GS [19]	Ours
96.30%	99.47%	99.87%	99.91%	**100%**

4. CONCLUSIONS

In this paper, we have proposed a new algorithm called MCCA for matching face sketch to face photo. Extensive experiments are conducted on two public domain face photo-sketch datasets to demonstrate the effectiveness of MCCA over the state-of-the-art. In the future work, we will adapt our system to general heterogeneous face matching problems, such as infrared-optical recognition or matching faces of different poses.

5. ACKNOWLEDGMENTS

This work was supported by grants from Natural Science Foundation of China (61103164, 61002042, 61070148), Science, Industry, Trade, and Information Technology Commission of Shenzhen Municipality, China (JC201005270378A), and Guangdong Innovative Research Team Program (No. 201001D0104648280).

6. REFERENCES

[1] X. Tang and X. Wang, "Face Sketch Recognition", IEEE Transactions on Circuits Systems for Video Technology, 14(1), 50-57, 2004.

[2] X. Wang and X. Tang, "Face photo-sketch synthesis and recognition", IEEE Transactions on Pattern Analysis Machine Intelligence, 31(11), 1955-1967, 2009.

[3] Q. Liu, X. Tang, H. Jin, H Lu, S. Ma, "Nonlinear Approach for Face Sketch Synthesis and Recognition", Proceedings of CVPR, 1005-1010, 2005.

[4] B. Klare, Z. Li and A. K. Jain, "Matching forensic sketches to mugshot photos", IEEE Transactions on Pattern Analysis and Machine Intelligence, 2010.

[5] W. Zhang, X. Wang, and X. Tang, "Coupled Information-Theoretic Encoding for Face Photo-Sketch Recognition," Proceedings of CVPR, 2011.

[6] J. B. Tenenbaum, W. T. Freeman, "Separating style and content with bilinear models". Neural Computation 12 (6), 1247-1283, 2000.

[7] Dong Yi, Rong Liu, RuFeng Chu, Zhen Lei, and Stan Z. Li, "Face Matching Between Near Infrared and Visible Light Images," Advances in Biometrics: International Conference, pp. 523–530, 2007.

[8] Annan Li, Shiguang Shan, Xilin Chen1 and Wen Gao, "Maximizing Intra-individual Correlations for Face Recognition Across Pose Differences", Proceedings of CVPR, pp.605-611, 2009.

[9] W. Yang, D. Yi, Z. Lei, J. Sang, and S. Z. Li, "2D-3D Face Matching Using CCA". Proceedings of IEEE International Conference on Automatic Face and Gesture Recognition, 2008.

[10] Abhishek Sharma, David W Jacobs, "Bypassing Synthesis: PLS for Face Recognition with Pose, Low-Resolution and Sketch," Proceedings of CVPR, pp. 593 - 600, 2011.

[11] T. Mäenpää, M. Pietikäinen, "Multi-Scale Binary Patterns for Texture Analysis". Proceedings of the SCIA, Gothenberg, Sweden, pp. 885–892, 2003.

[12] Dalal, N.; Triggs, B, "Histograms of Oriented Gradients for Human Detection", Proceedings of CVPR, vol.1, pp.886-893, 2005.

[13] Johnson, Richard A.; Wichern, Dean W. (2007). "Applied Multivariate Statistical Analysis (Sixth ed.)". Prentice Hall. ISBN 0-13-187715-1, ISBN 978-0-13-187715-3.

[14] K. Mikolajczyk and C. Schmid, "A performance evaluation of local descriptors," IEEE Trans. Pattern Analysis and Machine Intelligence, vol. 27, no. 10, pp. 1615-1630, Oct. 2005.

[15] M. Turk and A. Pentland, "Face recognition using eigenfaces," IEEE International Conference Computer Vision and Pattern Recognition, pp. 586-591, 1991.

[16] P. Belhumeur, J. Hespanda, and D. Kiregeman, "Eigenfaces vs. fisherfaces: Recognition using class specific linear projection," IEEE Trans. on PAMI, Vol. 19, No. 7, pp. 711-720, July 1997.

[17] T. K. Ho, "The random subspace method for constructing decision forests," IEEE Transactions on Pattern Analysis and Machine Intelligence, vol. 20, no. 8, pp. 832-844, 1998.

[18] L. Breiman, "Bagging predictors," Machine Learning, vol. 24, no. 2, pp. 123-140, 1996.

[19] H. Galoogahi and T. Sim, "Face Photo Retrieval by Sketch Example," ACM MM 2012.

Hand and Foot Gesture Interaction for Handheld Devices

Zhihan Lv[†,‡] Muhammad Sikandar Lal Khan[‡] Shafiq Ur Réhman[†,‡*]

† Shenzhen Institutes of Advanced Technology(SIAT), Chinese Academy of Science, 518055, China.

‡ Immersive Interaction Lab(i2Lab),
Institutionen för Tillämpad Fysik och Elektronik, Umeå University, 90187 Umeå, Sweden.

ABSTRACT

In this paper we present hand and foot based immersive multimodal interaction approach for handheld devices. A smart phone based immersive football game is designed as a proof of concept. Our proposed method combines input modalities (i.e. hand & foot) and provides a coordinated output to both modalities along with audio and video. In this work, human foot gesture is detected and tracked using template matching method and Tracking-Learning-Detection (TLD) framework. We evaluated our system's usability through a user study in which we asked participants to evaluate proposed interaction method. Our preliminary evaluation demonstrates the efficiency and ease of use of proposed multimodal interaction approach.

Categories and Subject Descriptors

H.4 [**Information Systems Applications**]: Miscellaneous

Keywords

immersive multimodal interaction; smart phone games; foot gesture; HCI; mobile; vibrotactile.

1. INTRODUCTION

Recently there have been significant progress in multimodal human computer interaction(HCI) research due to advances in digital vision techniques and advanced sensor technologies. Modern HCI interfaces need not to rely on signal interaction modality (e.g. speech, touch and video only) or explicit input command from a single user [5]. The presence of computing power ranging from intelligent walls to hand held interfaces demand intuitive ways of interaction and human-centered design approaches. For effective human-machine communications researchers are considering different combinations of modality and multisensory approaches such as hand gesture [7], tooth clicks [11], eye blink [3] and foot based interaction [10] etc. Handheld devices (such as smart phones) are equipped with advance signal processing techniques and improved hardware, making real-time fusion of data and multimodal interaction possible.

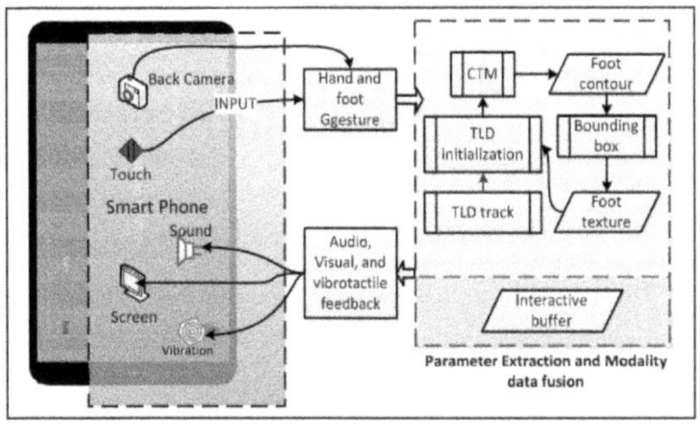

Figure 1: A block system diagram of hand and foot-gesture multimodal interaction for a smart phone.

We use feet along with hands in various everyday tasks (such as driving) and coordinated control mechanism of both modalities has been proven effectiveness in human computer interaction especially in virtual environments [12]. Considering handheld computing various foot gesture detection and tracking system have been proposed such as multitoe [1], kick [4], foot tapping [2] etc. Sangsuriyachot et al. [9] presented hand and foot gesture based interaction for tabletop environment. We believe that hand and foot gesture interaction can enhance immersive experience on handheld devices such as smart phone. To the best of our knowledge there has not been any study considering combination of hand and foot gesture for handheld devices.

In this study, we present a novel multimodal approach based on hand and foot interaction for smart phones (Fig. 1). The proof of concept is an immersive football game application on smart phone. For this game the user controls an augmented ball in virtual football field using hand and foot gestures on a smart phone screen. The foot gesture is detected and traced by smart phone camera sensor. The vibrotactile feedback is provided to user hands (through smart phone vibration) and to foot (using additive vibration sensor) along with visual and audio output. The primary contributions of this paper are

- An extended algorithm for foot detection and tracking for smart phone application without additive hardware.

*Corresponding author 'shafiq.urrehman@umu.se'

MM'13, October 21–25, 2013, Barcelona, Spain.
Copyright 2013 ACM 978-1-4503-2404-5/13/10 ...$15.00.
http://dx.doi.org/10.1145/2502081.2502163.

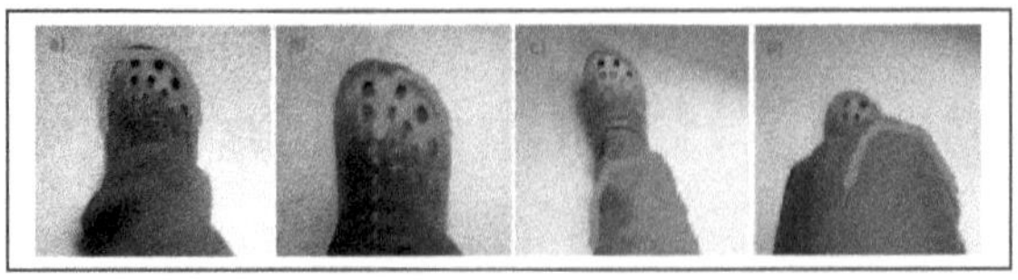

Figure 2: Example frames of unexpected detected contour due to sudden motion. a) Correct foot-contour detection; and false foot-contour because of (b) the pattern on the shoe (when zoom in), (c) the bottom of a trouser when stretch out leg; (d)the knee when the foot is obscured

- A novel multimodal hand and foot gesture interaction platform for hand held devices.

2. IMMERSIVE FOOTBALL - A PROOF OF CONCEPT

To study the physical capabilities of user and effectiveness of proposed hand-foot based immersive multimodal interaction for smart phones, we develop a multimodal interaction game based on hand and foot interaction.

2.1 Enhanced Foot Gesture Tracking

In this work, we have extended algorithm presented in [8] for robust foot gesture tracking in real time using Tracking-Learning-Detection (TLD) framework [6].

One limitation of previous algorithm [8] is observed in the *'shoe target test'*; i.e. a visual inspection to check how good the algorithm has localized the users' shoe in each and every video frame. The false detection is noticed due to sudden appearance of foot like shape contours on nonfoot areas of smart phone's camera view such as bottom of a trouser, the part prominent pattern on the shoe, and/or even the knee shape (while sitting) as shown in Fig. 2. The motion of the most similar contour isn't equivalent to the motion of the foot exactly. Furthermore, the applications which need more accurate localization of the foot, such as kicking dynamic football, a minor foot-contour detection error can lead to undesired outcomes. Whereas in previously presented applications, such as foot piano, the motion of the most similar contour is classified as equivalent to the motion of the foot-contour. But in the foot game, if the other parts of body besides foot become interactive in the football game, the player will loose the control of the football. Secondly, the computation complexity of the contour based template detection approach is $O(M \times N \times L)$, where M and N are the width and height of the image, L is the length of the template curve. Even if it is enough to detect the foot-contour in the image in most case, it is not fast enough for tracking specified object in each and every frame. In practice, although the camera screen image is resized into about one quarter as (320×240), but still maximum performance can not be achieved for current multimodal application scenario using previous algorithm [8].

Our algorithm uses dynamic programming to localize the foot-contour and employ tracking, learning and detection (TLD) framework to strengthen the tracking process. TLD algorithm combines elements from tracking, learning and detection in the 2D image space to make it a long-term tracker [6]. The TLD tracker uses a tracking strategy of the overlapping blocks, and tracks every block by Lucas-Kanade optical flow method. Hence it can only trace the user-specific foot texture image during tracking, but can't initialize by importing a generic foot model automatically. Even if the TLD always does the dynamic PN-learning process, the shoes with different appearance can't be detected by presetting only one shoe texture image initially and the shoes with totally different property such as different pattern or color can't be learned. Moreover, in TLD tracking algorithm, the off-line trained generic detector localizes object based on specific features and the online trained validator decides which object correspond to the object of interest. In case of the shoe, which may not have distinctive feature, the classification learning and training method such as cascade can't detect diverse shoes from a content-rich image. In view of this, the contour based template detection (CTD) approach is an indispensable step for identifying a variety of shoes in the beginning. CTD gives TLD the region of interest(ROI) for initialization. Our enhanced algorithm has following steps:

1 - Using CTD [8] detect and localize the user shoe, and create a bounding box BB $=\{$ top-left(x^{min}, y^{min}), bottom-right$(x^{max}, y^{max})\}$, where $x^{min}, y^{min}, x^{max}, y^{max}$ are the minimum and maximum values of the x and y in given frame;

2 - The bounding box is given to TLD algorithm as ROI; ROI$=\{(p^{11}, p^{12}, \cdots, p^{1M}), (p^{21}, p^{22}, \cdots, p^{2M}), \ldots, (p^{N1}, p^{N2}, \cdots, p^{NM})\}$; where p represent the density of every point of the bounding box;

3 - TLD algorithm tracks the ROI from the camera view with the PN-learning process, and provides the information to the application layer;

The enhanced algorithm (see algo. 1) successfully solves all of the unexpected detection results of foot/shoe look-likes. Our algorithm execution time is faster and is accurate even when the foot/shoe is moving fast and in image blur cases. It's worth mentioning that this method can detect almost all obscured foot and almost all kinds of the foot-gesture in the football game, as long as the correct foot texture is detected in the first frame. As in Fig. 3, 1st row is the result of the shoe with obvious feature and 2nd row is the result of the shoe with weak feature. To improve the efficiency of the proposed algorithm, the size of first frame is scaled down to 25% and then CTD is applied. From the second frame the image is scaled to 12.5% and then TLD tracking is employed. The 'shoe target test' results indicate increase in both efficiency and accuracy success rate of the tracking. We have performed extensive test to evaluate the robustness of the foot detection and tracking algorithm on our own collection of foot-gesture video data-set. Algorithm

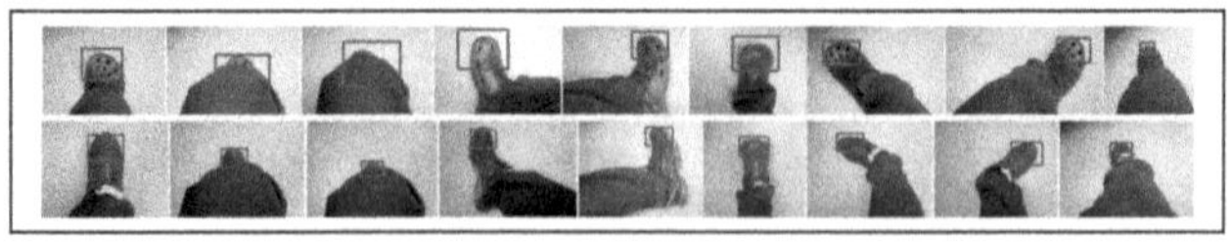

Figure 3: The tracking results for a variety of foot-gestures with either obvious (1st row) or weak features (2nd row).

results are very much improved as compared to previous studies. The proposed algorithm successfully located and tracked the foot-gesture in almost all videos even when a sudden appearance of other objects covers most of foot. The overall foot-gesture recognition rate of 99% for various foot gestures and the real-time processed time consuming is only 18% of the previous studies.

Algorithm 1: The TLD algorithm with CTD localization

Input: ROI_0 , which is the ROI of the first frame, $L_0 = \{R_0\}$, where R_0 is the content surrounded by ROI_0 in the first frame; L_0 is the online model in time $t = 0$.
Output: current localization ROI_t

initial localization $\leftarrow ROI_0$;
current localization $\leftarrow 0$;
while *active input feed from camera in time t* **do**
  Tracking
    -Forward-Backward tracking by running Lucas-Kanade
    -Compute median flow
  Detection R in online model L_{t1}
    -Variance Filter
    -Ensemble Classifier
    -Nearest Neighbor Classifier
  Learning
    -$P - N$ Experts
      -$Lt \leftarrow L_{t1} \cup$ *Positive samples from growing.*
      -$Lt \leftarrow L_{t1} \setminus$ *Negative samples from pruning.*
  Integrator
    -Validation
    -$R_t \leftarrow$ *the most confident evaluated result*
  $ROI_t \leftarrow$ *bounding box of* R_t

2.2 Multimodal Football Game

We develop a real-time multimodal football game smart phone application. It renders the game graphics and game status information using smart phone's screen, audio and vibration. Augmented reality image rendering technology is employed. The players interact with the game using both foot gestures and finger touch on screen, which triggers the interaction event and generate activity sequences for interactive buffers. The trajectory of the football is changed by interactive buffers. In our system, the players use foot to kick the ball on the smart phone screen, meanwhile, they guard the goal post area using hand-finger. The game rules are as following:

1. The player interacting-foot must be placed in mobile camera view for 5 sec. for detection and localization.
2. The football always bounces back and forth on the whole screen area till end of the game and the players try to keep the football (using touch and kicks) under his/her control while preventing it going to goal-post with hands-gesture(i.e. touch on the smart phone screen).
3. The player get 1 score if she/he touches (or kicks) the football once, and the game is over if the football enters into the highlighted goalpost.

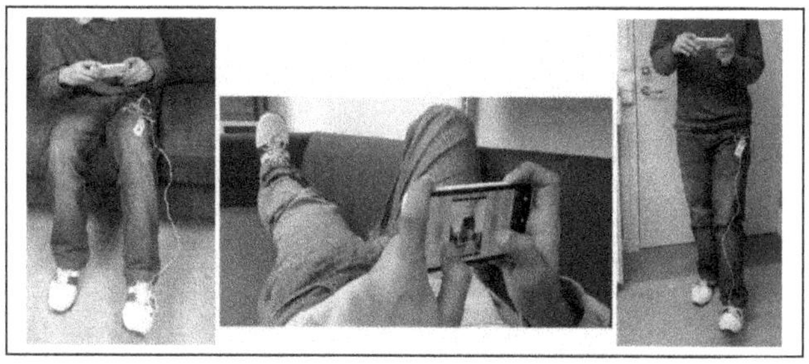

Figure 4: The players can play immersive football game application in a variety of postures; i.e., sitting, lying, and/or standing.

Questionnaire Items	Mean (M)	Standard Deviation (SD)
Playing the game was Interesting	2.14	0.69
Playing the game was Fun	3.05	0.89
Playing the game was Esay	3.15	1.02
Playing the game was Tiresome	3.31	1.15
Playing the game was Difficult	3.57	0.78

Table 1: Perceived suitability of immersive multimodal football using descriptive statistics before the game (fully agreed=5).

We also present the players with two types of vibrotactile rendering. Firstly, the football motion and collision with the player's finger is presented to user's hands through smart phone's built in vibration motors. Secondly, an additive vibrotactile rendering device is attached to the player's interacting foot; i.e., an extended vibration feedback to the foot kicking the ball. For this purpose an IOIO device is connected to the smart phone by USB cable; it is used for controlling a vibration motor attached to the interacting foot. The vibration feedback on foot renders a similar tactile sensation to the player, as if the player's foot is really kicking a football. The system not only merges the hand and foot interaction with the scene but also broadcasts information to the sight, auditory and vibrotactile directly. These modalities are integrated into a small smart phone, so the players can play immersive football game in variety gestures, for example standing, sitting, lying as shown in Figure 4.

3. PRELIMINARY USER STUDY AND RESULTS

There were 12 subjects aging from 25 to 35 in total involved in the preliminary user study. All the participants had smart phones and had prior experience with mobile sensors such as camera, vibration etc. The motivation of our user test had been clearly explained to all the participants. First, we introduced the purpose of our experiments to the participants and explained how to use the GUI and application scenarios. The game rules were also explained to the users. Each participant held the smart phone in both hands such that the camera's eye could view the user's lower leg. The users were asked to perform as they like i.e, sitting, standing and or lying. 90% of the participants preferred playing game while siting. In order to evaluate the popularizing and players mood values, we used PANAS ques-

Questionnaire Items	Mean (M)	Standard Deviation (SD)
Playing the game was Interesting	4.42	0.79
Playing the game was Fun	4.52	0.89
Playing the game was Esay	3.85	0.69
Playing the game was Tiresome	2.88	0.59
Playing the game was Difficult	2.77	0.95

Table 2: Suitability of immersive multimodal football using descriptive statistics after the game (fully agreed=5).

tionnaire [13] before and after the game. For PANAS questionnaire analysis we used paired sample t-test. A useful measure of user satisfaction can be made if the system evaluation measure is based on observations of user attitudes towards the system. Thus, it is possible to measure user attitudes using a questionnaire, e.g., "Is this application interesting? 1 very boring (negative) to 5 very interesting (positive)". The satisfaction levels of our experiments were measured by giving participants questionnaires.

There was significant increase in overall positive affect after playing multimodal football game app. on smart phone. After the game M=3.79 , SD= 0.85 as compared to before the game M= 2.56, SD= 0.69 with $t_{11} = -3.99$ and $p = 0.001$. However very slight change was observed in negative affect before and after the game; i.e., after M= 1.35, SD= 0.39 and before M= 1.57, SD= 0.49. The questionnaire showed that the designed multimodal football game was perceived easy and fun as shown in Table 1 and 2. It was also noted from the participants remarks that the game had positive affect on their alertness. It was also mentioned that the vibrotactile feedback on foot improved their experience and increased excitement. The technical implementation of the game also showed successful performance. The participants were able to perform all desired foot gestures.

In a real world football game, the players kick the football in various direction using different foot postures. The approach proposed in this paper can only get the 2D location of the foot on the ground plane. Although the approach can track foot-gesture with different 2D-postures, it can't get all of the exact 3D angle parameters. These issues can be solved using additive sensor devices and/or software algorithm modification. We do not have any measure to quantify the performance of the user; so cognitive workload questions can not be answered in this work.

4. CONCLUSIONS AND FUTURE WORK

In this study, we propose an immersive multimodal interaction game on smart phone, with focus on the detection and tracking of the foot-gesture and hands in real time. Based on the optimized interaction approach, we combine both foot and hand gestures as input and render game feedback to the users using vibrotactile patterns (both on hands and foot), sound and vision. Through the analysis of the user study results, it is found that the combination of multiple input and output is an intuitive method for novice users and combination of modalities can provide an enhanced immersive experience. It allows players to mobilize more body part for multitasking interaction. In future studies, we will consider hardware and software modification to extract the foot-gesture orientation (i.e., yaw, pith, roll) parameter. We believe that it's entirely possible that the multi-player competition for the football by the real foot interaction can be rendered on the smart phone in the near future. To evaluate the multi-dimensional tracking approach, we will consider a real-time 3D football-kicking application as the interactive framework.

Acknowledgments.

The authors are thankful to the Chinese Academy of Sciences Fellowship for Young Foreign Scientists (2012Y1GA0002) and National Natural Science Fund of China (61070147).

5. REFERENCES

[1] T. Augsten, K. Kaefer, R. Meusel, C. Fetzer, D. Kanitz, T. Stoff, T. Becker, C. Holz, and P. Baudisch. Multitoe: high-precision interaction with back-projected floors based on high-resolution multi-touch input. In *23rd Annual ACM Sym. UIST*, 2010.

[2] A. Crossan, S. Brewster, and A. Ng. Foot Tapping for Mobile Interaction. In *24th BCS Conf. HCI, UK*, 2010.

[3] K. Grauman, M. Betke, J. Gips, and G. R. Bradski. Communication Via Eye Blinks - Detection and Duration Analysis in Real Time. In *IEEE Conf. Comp. V. and P. Recognition*, 2001.

[4] T. Han, J. Alexander, A. Karnik, P. Irani, and S. Subramanian. Kick: Investigating the Use of Kick Gestures for Mobile Interactions. In *13th Int. Conf. HCI with Mobile Devices and Services*, 2011.

[5] A. Jaimes and N. Sebe. Multimodal Human computer Interaction: A survey. *Comp. V. and Im. Understanding*, 108:116–134, 2007.

[6] Z. Kalal, K. Mikolajczyk, and J. Matas. Tracking Learning Detection. *IEEE Trans. on Pattern A. and M. Int.(TPAMI)*, 6(1), 2010.

[7] P. Mistry and P. Maes. SixthSense: a wearable gestural interface. In *ACM SIGGRAPH ASIA 2009 Sketches*, 2009.

[8] S. Réhman, A. Khan, and H. Li. Interactive Feet for Mobile Immersive Interaction. In *ACM Int. Workshop MobiVis Workshop at MobileHCI*, 2012.

[9] N. Sangsuriyachot and M. Sugimoto. Novel Interaction Techniques based on a Combination of Hand and Foot Gestures in Tabletop Environments. In *10th Asia Pacific Conf. HCI*, 2012.

[10] J.-H. Seo, J.-Y. Yang, and D.-S. Kwon. Laser scanner based Foot Motion Detection for Intuitive Robot User Interface System. In *IEEE RO-MAN*, 2012.

[11] T. Simpson, M. Gauthier, and A. Prochazka. Evaluation of Tooth-Click triggering and Speech Recognition in Assistive Technology for Computer Access. *Neurorehabil Neural Repair*, 24:188–194, 2010.

[12] D. Valkov, F. Steinicke, G. Bruder, and K. Hinrichs. Traveling in 3D Virtual Environments with Foot Gestures and a Multi-Touch enabled WIM. In *Int. Conf. Virtual Reality*, 2010.

[13] D. Watson and L. A. Clark. Development and Validation of Brief Measures of Positive and Negative Affect: The PANAS scales. *J. Personality and Social Psychology*, 54(6):1063–1070, 1988.

AirTouch Panel: A Re-Anchorable Virtual Touch Panel

Shih-Yao Lin[δ,1], Chuen-Kai Shie[1], Shen-Chi Chen[2], Yi-Ping Hung[1,2]

[1]Graduate Institute of Networking and Multimedia, National Taiwan University, Taiwan, ROC

[2]Dept. of Computer Science and Information Engineering, National Taiwan University, Taiwan, ROC

{ [δ]d00944001, hung} @csie.ntu.edu.tw

Figure 1. ***AirTouch Panel*** **is a re-anchorable virtual touch interface, which can be positioned at any place with various orientations around users. Our** ***AirTouch Panel*** **provides a potential ability to remotely control the home appliances, such as TV**

ABSTRACT

To achieve maximum mobility, device-less approaches for home appliance remote control have received increasing attention in recent years. In this paper, we propose a screen-less virtual touch panel, called *AirTouch Panel*, which can be positioned at any place with various orientations around users. The proposed virtual touch panel provides a potential ability to remotely control the home appliances, such as television, air conditioner, and so on. The proposed system allows users to anchor the panel at the place with comfortable poses. If the users want to change panel's position or orientation, they only need to re-anchor it, and then the panel will be reset. In this paper, our main contribution is to design a re-anchorable virtual panel for digital home remote control. Most importantly, we explore the design of such imaginary interface through two user studies. In our user studies, we analyze task completion time, satisfaction rate, and the number of miss-clicks. We are interested in the feasibility issues, for example, proper click gesture, panel size and button size, etc. Moreover, based on the *AirTouch Panel,* we also developed an *intelligent TV* to demonstrate the usability for controlling home appliance.

Categories and Subject Descriptors

H.5.2 [Information interfaces and presentation]: User Interfaces. - Graphical user interfaces.

MM '13, October 21 - 25 2013, Barcelona, Spain

http://dx.doi.org/10.1145/2502081.2502164

Keywords

Remote control, gesture, computer vision, imaginary interface

1. INTRODUCTION

In the indoor environment, the user input of many home appliances, such as television, DVD players, air conditioner, and so on, are controlled remotely. People are used to adopting human-machine interface to control the functions of the machines.

Generally, the interfaces can be categorized into two branches: handheld devices and device-less. Keyboard, mouse and joystick can be the traditional art of the handheld devices for home appliance control. However, the aforementioned user interfaces are restricted and not intuitive. For example, while using the handheld device, the users have to distract between the content of the home appliances and the response of the handheld device. However, this distracting problem forces users to switch their attention between the device and the visual content of home appliances. Obviously, the hand-held controller decreases the actual effort for controlling the home appliances in both mental and physical aspects.

On the other hand, in order to achieve maximum mobility, device-less approaches for home appliance remote control have received increasing attention. In recent years, 3D mid-air gestures [2] have become the most common approaches for spatial interaction. However, the principal drawback of the 3D mid-air gestures is the fatigue problem. For a long time of raising hand operation, users are easy to feel fatigue. In 2010, Gustafson et al. [4] propose a revolutionary interface, namely imaginary interface, to allow users to perform spatial interaction using empty hands without visual feedback. The imaginary interface senses the user's hand gesture through a webcam attached on user's body. Based on [4], Gustafson et al. [5] propose an imaginary phone. Unlike the original imaginary interfaces, the imaginary phone utilizes the palm of the non-dominant hand as an interaction device. Users interact with the palm by mimicking the use of a physical screen-touch phone without visual feedback. Dezfuli et al.[6] propose a

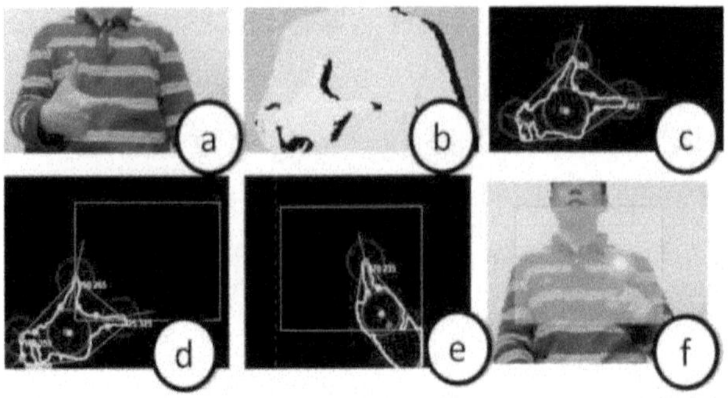

Figure 2. The manipulation of our *AirTouch Panel*: (a) the user raises his left hand and forms an L-shaped gesture to create an *AirTouch Panel* in 3D space; (b) the depth map; (c) finger position detection by convex hull algorithm. (d) recognizing the L-shape gesture; (d) A virtual panel is created; (e) track the tip of forefinger for cursor shift (f) user interacts with the virtual panel

palm-based imaginary surface for TV remote control, without visual feedback on the palm. Unlike Gustafson et al.'s imaginary interface need to wear a sensor, in this paper, we propose an *AirTouch Panel*, which is a device-less virtual interface. The proposed interface senses users' gesture through a RGB-D camera (e.g., Microsoft Kinect [1]) installed in an indoor environment. The main reason of adopting the RGB-D camera is that the depth information can be utilized to extend the feasibility of gesture operation. Therefore, our *AirTouch Panel* can recognize the 3D gestures through the depth information and allow users to freely anchor the panel in various orientation and location, see Figure 1. Besides, different to the imaginary interface, our system provides visual feedback through an optical display, which helps users to track the cursor. Most importantly, our system allows users to re-anchor the *AirTouch Panel*, which means users can freely change the panel's position or orientation.

In this paper, we focus on exploring an appropriate design for the proposed *AirTouch panel*. We emphasize three critical aspects that need to be considered: (1) task completion time, (2) satisfaction rate, and (3) miss-click number. With our user studies, we investigate the feasibility issues: What is the proper click gesture for *AirTouch Panel*? How to determine the appropriate panel size for individuals? Moreover, we also developed an *intelligent TV* based on our *AirTouch Panel* to demonstrate the usability for controlling home appliance. The primary contributions of this paper are as follows:

- We propose a new platform interface, *AirTouch Panel*, which allow users to re-anchor a virtual panel in various orientation and location so as to achieve maximum mobility.
- We provide a comprehensive user studies to investigate the issues to design an appropriate panel size and proper click gesture for *3D AirTouch panel*.
- In addition, based on the proposed *AirTouch Panel*, we also develop an intelligent TV with a hierarchical control mode framework.

2. Design and Implementation

Our system is developed by using a Kinect sensor and Candescent NUI [3]. The Candescent NUI is a set of libraries for detecting 3D hand and finger positions. Firstly, based on the functions of Candescent NUI, the fingers are extracted by using convex hull algorithm. Our system gains 3D positions and directions of the finger tips through depth information. In addition, the convex hull algorithm also provides other hand features, for example, the volume of the hand, the palm position, the number of fingers, each finger's base position and ID.

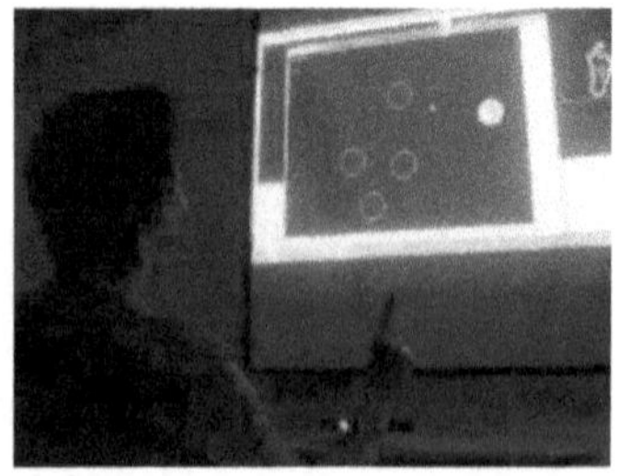

Figure 3. Experimental environment: users are asked for clicking the virtual buttons which are generated randomly

The manipulation procedure of our system is shown in Figure 2. Firstly, users freely anchor the origin and orientation of the *AirTouch Panel* through forming a specific gesture (L-shaped gesture) by their left hand, see Figure 2a. Our gesture recognition system extracts palm region through depth information (Fig. 2b), and then we evaluate the position and direction of each finger using Candescent NUI [3]. We detect the positions of index finger, thumb finger, and palm center for recognizing the key gesture, see Figure 2c. If the positions of index finger, thumb and palm center can be formed as an L-shaped, an *AirTouch Panel* will be generated. Figure 2d demonstrates the recognition result of finding the L-shaped posture which creates the *AirTouch Panel*. Then, users drop their left hand and raise their right hand to interact with the generated the *AirTouch Panel*, see Fig. 2e and Fig. 2f.

3. User Studies

In order to design the *AirTouch Panel*, we conducted two user studies. The main goal across these studies is to determine an appropriate click gesture, and to find a proper panel size.

The first study is investigated in what kind of the click gesture will be appropriate. We test three general gesture types and choose the most suitable one. In the test procedure, we randomly generate several virtual buttons and ask participants to perform "click" task using different click gestures. After the participants complete these tasks, we consider the task completion time, the number of miss-clicks, and the satisfaction rate to determine the appropriate click gesture type. The experimental environment is shown in Figure 3.

The second study investigated in finding appropriate panel size for individuals. We defined five various panel sizes, and similar to the first user study, the testing system randomly generates several virtual buttons and participants are asked for clicking them. We determine the proper panel by considering the task completion time, the number of miss-clicks, and users' satisfaction rate.

The experiment was run on our prototype imaginary touch panel. The resolution of optical display is 640*480 pixels. The resolution of the depth map captured by a Kinect sensor is 640*480. The distance between the Kinect sensor and participants is required to be in a range from 80 cm to 110 cm. Before beginning the experiment, all the participants were guided to gesticulate at the camera to generate the *AirTouch Panel*.

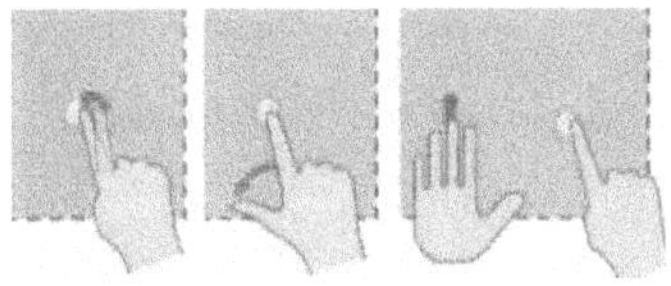

(a) (b) (c)

Figure 4. The three clicking gestures we defined in Study 1: (a) tapping click; (b) specific gesture click; (c) left hand click.

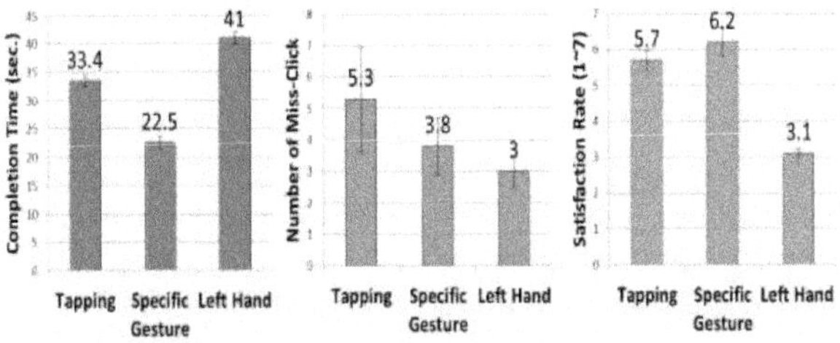

(a) (b) (c)

Figure 5. The evaluation result of click gesture in Study 1: (a) task completion time; (b) number of miss-clicks; (c) satisfaction rate.

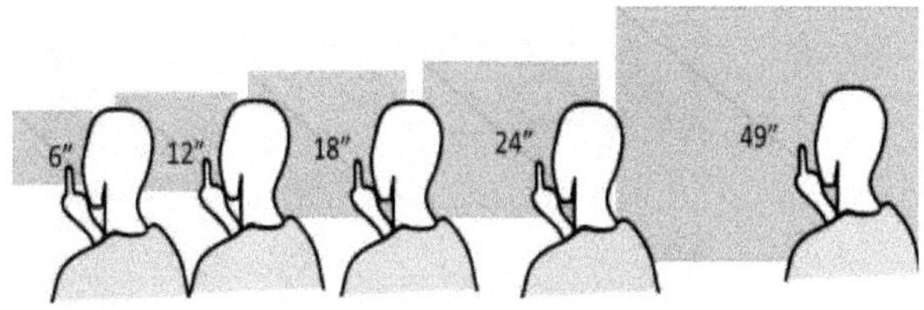

Figure 6. The different panel size defined in Study 2

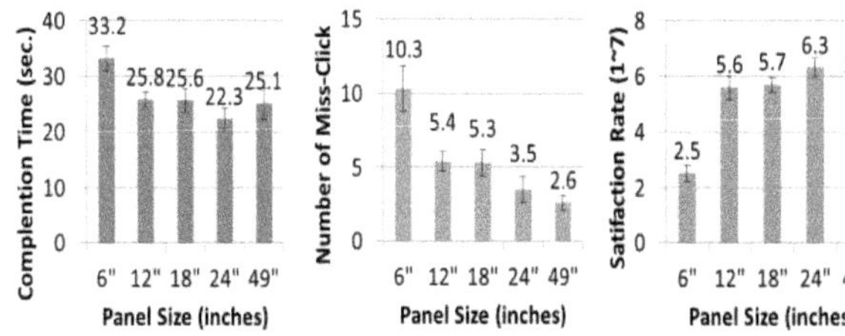

(a) (b) (c)

Figure 7. The evaluation result of different panel size in Study 2: (a) task completion time; (b) number of miss-clicks; (c) satisfaction rate.

3.1 User Study 1: Click Gesture

The goal of this study is to determine the proper click gesture for the *AirTouch Panel*. We compare three common click gestures [7] including "tapping", "specific gesture click", and "left hand click" in completing the task of virtual button click. Our testing system randomly generated 15 virtual buttons one by one. Participants are asked for clicking these buttons using aforementioned pointing gestures.

3.1.1 Task and Procedure

Participants performed a target clicking task. For each trail, participants can choose a comfortable posture, that is, participants are allowed to sit or stand. When the participants indicated they were ready, the gesture recognition system was turn on. All the participants form the 'L-shaped' gesture with their left hand for generating the *AirTouch panel*. The participants can determine the 3D orientation and location of the panel, and use their right index fingers as mouse cursors. They can shift the cursor to the virtual buttons, and then click them. The panel size in this experiment is 24 inches (500x375 mm) and the diameter of the virtual button is 125 mm

3.1.2 Participants

12 participants (4 female) between the age of 22 and 35 were recruited at our institution. (M=25.5, SD=1.3). All participants were right-handed. All of them had some experience with touchscreens and touch panels.

3.1.3 Click Gestures Design

As the right forefinger move to the target (virtual button), the "tapping" is performed through quickly tap on the panel, see Figure 4a. For "specific gesture click," we use "stretch thumb" for a click, see Figure 4b. For "left hand click," we use "left hand raising" to perform a click, see Figure 4c.

3.1.4 Hypothesis

We propose three hypotheses for this experiment: (Those in **bold** are confirmed)

[H1] The completion time with "Left hand click" is longer than with "tapping" and with "specific gesture" because users are required to raise their hands for click confirm.

[H2] "Left hand click" suffers fewer miss-clicks than the other click gestures because a click is accomplished by left hand, instead of right hand. The scheme of "Left hand click" prevent the false alarm caused by false finger detection.

[H3] Users prefer to use "tapping click" than others because it is more intuitive.

3.1.5 Results

Figure 5 shows the evaluation result of pointing gesture in Study 1. We perform repeated measure ANOVA and find that there are significant main effects for completion time ($p<0.001$) but not for number of miss-clicks ($p<0.05$).

H1: Figure 5a shows the task completion time among the three click gestures. The "left hand click" gesture takes the longest time to complete the task.

H2: Figure 5b demonstrates that the miss-click number with "left hand click" is fewer than others.

H3: Figure 5c shows the survey results in Study 1. Wilcoxon sign-rank test is performed. According to experimental results, we found out that users prefer to use "specific gesture click" ($p<0.05$).

3.1.6 Discussion

Even though the "Left hand click" suffers few miss-clicks than the others, the main drawback of "Left hand click" gesture is the fatigue problem. We found out that the numbers of average miss-clicks with "specific gesture click" and "Left hand click" are lower than "tapping click". In addition, we also found that the satisfaction rate with "specific gesture" click gains the highest satisfied rate, see Figure 5c. More importantly, the task completion time with "specific gesture" is shorter than the others. According to above experimental results, we choose the "specific gesture" to be click gesture in our system.

3.2 User Study 2: Panel Size

In this study, we compare five different panel sizes in completing the task of virtual button click. The size includes 6 inches, 12 inches, 18 inches, 24 inches, and 49 inches. Similar to Study 1, our testing system randomly generated 15 virtual buttons. Participants are asked for clicking them one by one, we then

(a) (b) (c)

Figure 8. The *AirTouch panel*–based *intelligent TV* : (a) manipulation environment of the *intelligent TV*; (b) interface of TV Control Mode: (c) interface of Channel Selection Mode

record the task completion time, number of miss-clicks, and users' satisfaction rate.

3.2.1 Task and Procedure

Same as the Study 1, Participants performed a target clicking task. For each trail, participants can choose comfortable posture before testing. As the participants indicated they were ready, the gesture recognition system would turn on. When the participants created the *AirTouch Panel*, the participants do not know the panel size, that is, they have to adapt to 5 different panel sizes, see Figure 6. The different panel sizes presented order. Based on the result of the first study, we adopt the "specific gesture" click gesture.

3.2.2 Participants

We recruited a new set of 12 participants (2 female) between the age of 22 and 30 years old (M=25.5, SD=1.3). All participants were right-handed. All of them had some experience with touchscreens and touch panels.

3.2.3 Hypothesis

We propose three hypotheses for this experiment: (Those bold are confirmed)

[H4] The task completion time with the largest panel (49") is shorter than with the other panels.

[H5] Panel with large panel size helps users to decrease miss-click rate because lager panel size helps user to perform click task.

[H6] Users prefer the largest size panel

3.2.4 Results

We perform repeated measure ANOVA and find that there are significant main effects for number of miss click ($p<0.05$). Figure 5 shows the evaluation result of panel size in Study 2.

[H4] Figure 7a shows the task completion time among these panels with five different sizes. The completion time of with 24" panel size takes the least time, but 49" panel size.

[H5] Figure 7b demonstrates that the panel with large panel size helps users to decrease miss-click rate.

[H6] Figure 7c shows the survey results in Study 2. Wilcoxon sign-rank test is performed. ($p<0.005$). The evaluation result shows that users prefer to use median panel size (24") instead of the largest panel size (49").

3.2.5 Discussion

The larger panel indeed helps users to decrease miss-click rate, but we found that the completion time with the panel size 24" is shorter than with biggest panel size 49." Besides, we found out that users prefer to use median panel size (24") instead of the largest panel size (49"). According to above studies, we adopt the panel size with 24" for our *AirTouch Panel.*

4. APPLICATIONS

Based on the *AirTouch Panel,* we developed an *intelligent TV* to demonstrate the usability for controlling home appliance. Figure 8a shows the manipulation environment of our *intelligent TV*. The detail manipulation framework is shown in Figure 9. While users want to change channel, they can turn on the TV Control Mode (Figure 8b) through generating an *AirTouch Panel*. In the TV Control Mode, users accomplish the channel surfing or sound volume setting by clicking the specific buttons, see Figure 9. In Channel Selection Mode (Figure 8c), users can browse the entire TV programs, and select a TV channel they are interested in.

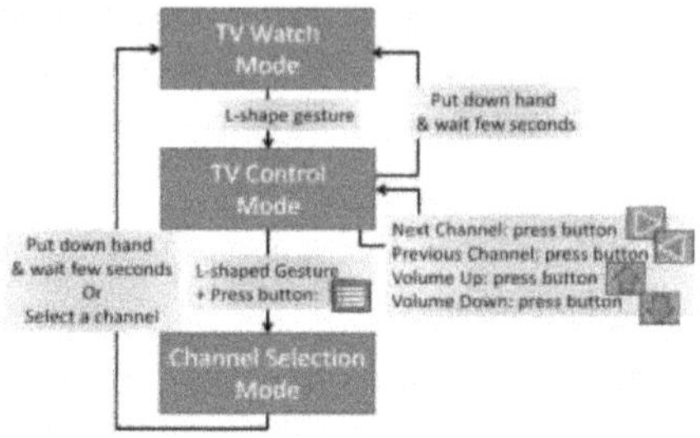

Figure 9. The manipulation framework of our *intelligent TV*

5. ACKNOWLEDGEMENT

This work was supported in part by the Excellent Research Projects of National Taiwan University, under grant 102R890857, and by National Science Council of Taiwan under NSC 101-2219-E-002-026.

6. CONCLUSION

In this paper, we propose a device-less virtual interface, called *AirTouch Panel*, which can be positioned at any place with various orientations around users. In addition, we provide a comprehensive user studies to investigate the issues to design an appropriate panel size, and proper click gesture for our *AirTouch panel.* Moreover, we also developed an intelligent TV to demonstrate the potential usability of our *AirTouch Panel.*

7. REFERENCES

[1] Microsoft Kinect: http://www.xbox.com/kinect

[2] Samsung: http://www.samsung.com/us/2012-smart-tv/

[3] Stefan Stegmueller, Candescent NUI

[4] Gustafson, S., Bierwirth, D., Baudisch, P., Imaginary interfaces: spatial interaction with empty hands and without visual feedback. In *Proc.* UIST'10, 3-12.

[5] Gustafson, S., Holz, C., Baudisch, P., Imaginary Phone: Learning Imaginary Interfaces by Transferring Spatial Memory from a Familiar Device. In *Proc.* UIST'11, 283-292.

[6] Dezfuli, N., Khalilbeigi, M., Huber, J., Müller, F., Mühlhäuser, M. Leveraging the Palm Surface as an Eyes-free TV Remote Control. In *Proc.* CHI EA'12, 27-34.

[7] Vogel, D., Balakrishnan, R, Distant freehand pointing and clicking on very large, high resolution displays. In *Proc.* UIST'05, 33-42.

Creation of Individual Photo Selections: Read Preferences from the Users' Eyes

Tina Walber
Chantal Neuhaus
Steffen Staab
University of Koblenz-Landau, Germany
{walber, neuhaus, staab}@uni-koblenz.de

Ansgar Scherp
University of Mannheim, Germany
ansgar@informatik.uni-mannheim.de

Ramesh Jain
University of California Irvine, USA
jain@ics.uci.edu

ABSTRACT

The automated selection of satisfying subsets from large collections of photos is a central challenge in multimedia research. Objective criteria like the depiction of persons or the photo quality are met by existing approaches. But it is difficult to know the users' personal interest, which plays an important role in the selection process. The expected spread of devices with eye tracking support in the near future allows us to measure this interest in a new way. In an experiment with 12 participants, we derive the most interesting photos of a collection for every person from gaze information recorded during the free viewing of the photos. We can show that the eye tracking information delivers valuable information about the users' preferences by comparing the results to a manual selection. The selection based on gaze information significantly outperforms baseline approaches and improves the results by up to 17%. For photo sets of personal interest this improvement is even up to 23%.

Categories and Subject Descriptors

H.5.2 [**User Interfaces**]: Input devices and strategies

General Terms

Human Factors

Keywords

Eye tracking, personalized photo selection, personal interest

1. INTRODUCTION

Existing solutions for creating photo selections are based on content-information such as histograms [1], make use of clustering based on photo meta data like capture time [1] or GPS coordinates [2]. These tools find their limitation in considering the user's interest. Savakis et al. [3] investigated humans selecting photos from a collection with the result that the selections are subjective and differ between the users. They also determine that it is hard to identify the attributes on which the decision is based, as it is part of a high-level human cognitive process. In order to provide an extension of photo selection algorithms, a new approach is needed that can cover personal preferences. In this work, we use gaze as measure for capturing individual user's interest.

Systems that can detect the eyes and can calculate the viewing direction from cameras integrated in common devices like Tablet PCs are already on the market (e. g., Natural User Interface Technology, OKAO Vision[1]). One of the market leaders in eye tracking systems offers with the Tobii Rex System[2] the first device for less than 1000 USD. Given the recent development in low-cost eye tracking hardware, we investigate the possibilities to create selections based on gaze information collected from users while viewing photos. Central to this approach is that the users are not burdened with additional tasks such as annotating the images. The manual selection of photos is often perceived as cumbersome, e. g., during the creation of slide shows or photo books. At the same time, users usually enjoy viewing photos.

Our approach benefits from this viewing and creates valuable information about the interest in certain photos from the recorded gaze information. The fixations in gaze paths show the areas of the highest visual perception and they are an indicator for the users' attention. Eye movements are influenced by different factors from low-level information like contrasts and colors to high-level factors like a given task. We investigate if the influence of "interest" is high enough to derive valuable information from the gaze paths about the users' preferences when viewing photos *without* a specific task, besides getting an overview of the photo collection. The attention while viewing the photos is used for creating personalized photo selections. Photos with the highest attention, i. e., those that are fixated longest, are assumed being most interesting to the user and should be part of a selection. We compare the gaze-based selections to selections based on related work. The analysis results on our data sets show that we achieve a significantly better selection of photos compared to a random baseline and a baseline based on [1]. We also compare the quality of the selection for sets

MM'13, October 21–25, 2013, Barcelona, Spain.
Copyright 2013 ACM 978-1-4503-2404-5/13/10 ...$15.00.
http://dx.doi.org/10.1145/2502081.2502165.

[1]http://www.omron.com
[2]http://www.tobii.com

of photos with a personal interest and sets that are less interesting. Personal interest in a photo collection significantly improves the results.

2. RELATED WORK

Approaches for the automatic creation of photo selections typically use low level image features and photo meta data. For example, Sinha et al. [2] present a framework for the generation of representative subsets of photos from large personal photo collections by using multidimensional content and context data like GPS coordinates or tags. Li et al. [1] create selective summaries based on time stamps and face features. Several approaches use eye tracking information to identify relevant images in search result lists and use this information as implicit user feedback to improve image search, e.g., [4, 5]. Kozma et al. [4] show that a comparison of the implicit gaze feedback with explicit user feedback by clicking on relevant images and a random baseline are promising. Pasupa et al. [6] apply a support vector machine algorithm using eye tracking information together with content-based features to rank images. Also Klami et al. [5] perform implicit user feedback on image search result lists by means of gaze information. They show that it is possible to use gaze information to detect image relevance in a controlled setup. Eye movements are strongly influenced by the task a human is performing as Yarbus [7] has already shown in 1967. In the existing work, concrete search tasks are given to the users. Images which are relevant concerning these tasks can be identified from the gaze information. In our approach, no concrete task for the viewing is given to the users. The subjects are asked to view the photos for getting an overview, but they were not told to concentrate, e. g., on the "best" photos. Thus, we do not measure how much a photo fits a given task but the personal interest of a user in a photo.

3. EXPERIMENT

We have conducted an experiment to compare our gaze-based approach for the creation of a selection S from a photo collection C to automatic approaches. After viewing the photos, a personal selection is created based on gaze information. These selections as well as baseline selections are compared to manually created selections, which serve as individual ground truth selection. 12 subjects (6 of them female) participated in our experiment. The age of the subjects ranged between 25 and 62 years (average: 34.4, SD: 13.4). Seven of them were graduate students, two post docs, the others were working in other professions.

Procedure.

In a first step, the subjects were asked to view all photos with the instruction to "get an overview". They were told that they would afterward, in a second step, create a selection of photos for their private photo collection. The instruction was to only view the photos, without time limit. While viewing the photos, the gaze paths were recorded by a Tobii X60 eye tracking device. Sets of 9 photos were presented in 3x3 photo grids. By clicking a button, the user advanced to the next set. The maximum height and width of the photos was set to 330 pixels. After having viewed all photos, the user created a manual selection S_m for every set by selecting exactly three photos from each set. The photos were selected in a ranked order (most important to third most important). No concrete instruction was given concerning the selection criteria. Thus, the subjects could apply their own (perhaps even not conscious) criteria. As motivation for the subjects, the manually created selection of photos was sent by email. Finally, the subjects completed a questionnaire.

Data set.

The experiment data set encloses two photo collections C_A and C_B taken during two different events A and B. Collection C_A consists of 164 photos, thus 18 sets of 9 photos. C_B has 126 photos (14 sets). The photos show events of two different research groups. The activities include team work situations, group meals, as well as leisure activities like bowling and hiking. The photos were taken by two resp. three different persons. Participants of the two events do not know each other, nobody participated in both events. The subjects in our experiment participated in event A or know participants of event A. Thus, the data set consists of photos that are of personal interest to the participants (C_A) and of photos of less interest, taken during event B. The sets were presented in chronological order but the photos in every set were displayed in random order. The first collection shown to the subjects is alternately C_A and C_B.

Gaze analysis.

The preprocessing of the raw eye tracking data for identifying fixations is performed with the fixation filter offered by Tobii Studio with its default thresholds. The obtained fixations are analyzed by the eye tracking measure *fixationDuration*. This measure calculates the sum of the durations of all fixations on a photo. The three photos with the highest results are selected as eye tracking selection S_e.

Baselines.

As the simplest possible baseline, we introduce a random baseline as used, e.g., by Kozma et al. [4]. It randomly selects three photos for every set. For the creation of the random selection S_r, the average over 10 random samples is built. Additionally, we implemented a baseline approach based on [1], which calculates a selection fully automatic based on three criteria:

- Many photos are taken within a short period of time during an important moment [1]. S_{bt} is built from photos taken from high concentrations in time.
- It is known that depicted persons play an important role in the selection of photos [1]. S_{bf} is built from photos best fulfilling three face conditions: a high number of depicted humans, a maximum area of the image is covered by human faces, and persons are depicted that frequently appear in the data set.
- Photo quality calculated by a sharpness score as presented by Xiao et al. [8]. The photos with the highest quality scores are selected for S_{bs}.

For each criterion a score is calculated for each photo. The scores are normalized for every set of 9 photos and lie between 0 and 1. The scores are summed up for each photo and the photos with the highest results build the baseline selection S_b. Clustering techniques as proposed by [1] delivered weak results on our data set and are

Figure 1: Sample photos including gaze path visualization (fixations displayed as circles) and three selections: manual S_m, eye tracking based S_e, and the baseline selection S_b.

therefore not included in the baseline. We also extend the baseline approach by information gained from gaze. For the selection S_{b+e}, *fixationDuration* values are added to S_b as an additional score.

Data analysis.

In the analysis of the data, we compare different selections in their capability to create selections similar to the manual selection S_m, which serves as "ground truth". For the evaluation, we calculate two measures for comparing selections S_x to the manual selection S_m. The first measure is precision P, which calculates the percentage of photos occurring in selection S_x as well as in S_m. The second one is the M measure, presented by Bar-Ilan et al. [9], which also considers the ranking of the photos in the selections. It is calculated as follows:

$$M' = \sum_{Z} \left| \frac{1}{S_m(i)} - \frac{1}{S_x(i)} \right| + \sum_{T_1} \left(\frac{1}{S_m(j)} - \frac{1}{k+1} \right) + \sum_{T_2} \left(\frac{1}{S_x(j)} - \frac{1}{k+1} \right)$$

where $Z = S_m \cap S_x$. T_1 and T_2 are the search result elements appearing only in one of the two selections: $T_1 = S_m \setminus S_x$, $T_2 = S_x \setminus S_m$. k is the number of investigated ranked result elements. Thus, $k = 3$ as the subjects selected the top three photos. Finally, the normalizing factor is the worst possible result, i. e., when the two lists do not share a single value. For $k = 3$ this factor is 3.12, thus $M = 1 - \frac{M'}{3.12}$.

4. RESULTS

Every set of nine photos was averagely viewed for 15.6 seconds (SD: 12.8). The shortest viewing time was 1.5 seconds and the longest 121.1 seconds. In average, 34 fixations were recorded per set (SD: 21.2). The highest number of fixations is 163. For one set, no fixation was recorded. Besides that the lowest number of fixations is 2.

Selections.

The results are evaluated by means of precision P and M measure as described in Section 3. The average results over all users and all sets can be found in Table 1. An example of a photo set with gaze path and three selections can be found in Figure 1.

Table 1: Precision P and M measure for eye tracking selection and different baseline selections

	S_r	S_e	S_b (S_{bt}, S_{bf}, S_{bs})	S_{b+e}
P	0.34	**0.42**	0.36 (0.36, 0.33, 0.33)	0.37
M	0.45	**0.53**	0.46 (0.45, 0.44, 0.44)	0.48

We can see that the best results are obtained by the gaze-based selection S_e. It improves the results compared to the baseline selection S_b by 17% for P and by 15% for M. The weak results for the baseline system show the difficulties of predicting the personal criteria for photo selections [3] by simple measures based on low-level features and meta information. The gaze-extended baseline approach S_{b+e} leads to a small improvement, compared to S_b. We have conducted a Friedman test with the average values per user to investigate the statistical significance of the results. We found that the differences between the selections S_r, S_e, and S_b are significant ($\alpha < .05$) for P ($\chi^2(2) = 11.167, p = .004$, $n = 12$) and M ($\chi^2(2) = 10.500, p = .005$, $n = 12$). Post-hoc analyses with pairwise Wilcoxon tests are conducted with a Bonferroni correction for the significance level (now: $\alpha < .017$). The eye tracking based selection S_e significantly outperforms S_r ($Z = -2,903, p = .004$) and S_b ($Z = -2,510, p = .012$) for the M measure as well as S_r ($Z = -2,667, p = .008$) for precision P. A comparison of precisions P for S_e and S_b does not show a significance ($Z = -2,275, p = .023$). Also no significance was determined comparing the results for S_r and S_b ($Z = -1,49, p = .136$). We did not find any correlations between the average viewing time on a set and the quality of the created selection.

The Infuence of Personal Interest.

We distinguish between photo sets of personal interest and of less personal interest, as described in the Section 3. The results of the questionnaire support our approach. 10 of the subjects rated the collection C_A, which contains photos taken during their own event, as more interesting than the other collection. A Wilcoxon signed-rank test shows a statistically significant difference between the answers concerning the interestingness over all users ($Z = -2.292, p = .022$). The average viewing time for C_A and C_B differs only slightly; photos of C_B were viewed longer (15.3 vs. 16.1 seconds).

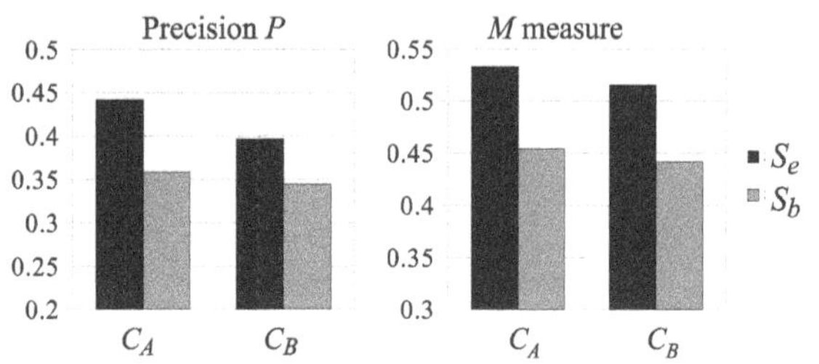

Figure 2: Results for interesting collection C_A and less interesting collection C_B.

P and M were calculated separately for C_A and C_B, the results can be found in Figure 2. The results are better for both measures when the subjects were viewing photos of personal interest. Compared to the baseline selection S_b an improvement of 23% for P and 17% for M can be stated. A Wilcoxon test showed a significant difference only for precision P ($Z = -2,353, p = .019$), but not for M ($Z = -1,098, p = .272$).

Analysis of Potential Bias.

Gaze paths could be subject to bias, e. g., from the starting position of a gaze path or from learned viewing patterns like a concentration on the center of the screen, where usually the content is displayed. Therefore, we investigated if such a bias occurs in our data. We can investigate a bias by analyzing the fixations depending on the positions of the images on the screen. In Figure 3 (a), the positions of the very first fixations on a photo set over all users are presented. One can see a clear concentration on the lower right corner and the center of the grid. The button for continuing with the next set is located in the right lower corner of the screen, which seems to have influence on the first fixation, as well a concentration on the center. In Figure 3 (b), the sum of all fixations over all users per image position in the grid is shown. We can see that the fixations are spread over the whole set quite evenly. We can also see a weak concentration in the center. However this concentration is small and does not play a role in our analysis as the photos were displayed in a random position.

5. CONCLUSION AND FUTURE WORK

In this work, we have shown that the usage of gaze information in the selection of photos delivers better results compared to random selection and baseline selections using low-level features and meta data. The results for a photo collection of personal interest are better compared to a collection of less personal interest.

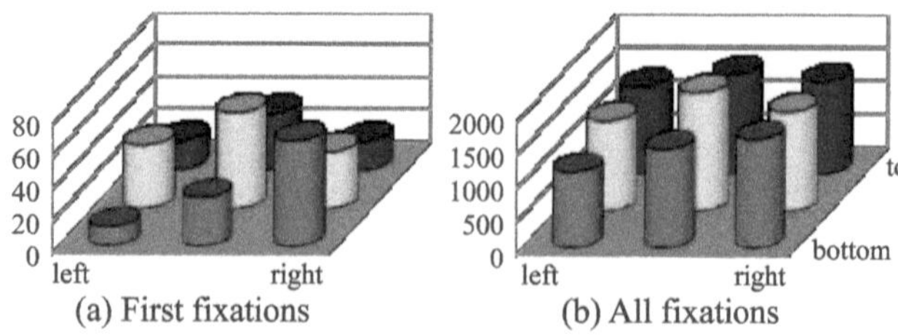

Figure 3: Number of fixations per image position for the first fixation of every user on every set (a) and all fixations (b).

In a next step, it has to be investigated if gaze information provided while viewing photos in less controlled environments, e. g., in a file system, delivers the same results. Additionally, the presented approach can be extended by the annotation of image regions describing the users' interest. This information can be used for authoring slide shows or photo books. The possibility to identify personal preferences from gaze information can also be adapted to other domains. One application could be the recommendation of products based on previous fixations on photos or objects in photos.

Acknowledgments

The research leading to this paper was partially supported by the EU project SocialSensor (FP7-287975). We thank all subjects for participating in our experiment.

6. REFERENCES

[1] J. Li, J.H. Lim, and Q. Tian. Automatic summarization for personal digital photos. In *Pacific Rim Conference on Multimedia*, volume 3, pages 1536–1540. IEEE, 2003.

[2] Pinaki Sinha, Sharad Mehrotra, and Ramesh Jain. Summarization of personal photologs using multidimensional content and context. *Multimedia Retrieval*, pages 1–8, 2011.

[3] A.E. Savakis, S.P. Etz, and A.C.P. Loui. Evaluation of image appeal in consumer photography. In *Electronic Imaging*, pages 111–120. International Society for Optics and Photonics, 2000.

[4] L. Kozma, A. Klami, and S. Kaski. GaZIR: gaze-based zooming interface for image retrieval. In *Multimodal interfaces*. ACM, 2009.

[5] A. Klami, C. Saunders, T.E. De Campos, and S. Kaski. Can relevance of images be inferred from eye movements? In *Multimedia information retrieval*, pages 134–140. ACM, 2008.

[6] K. Pasupa, C. Saunders, S. Szedmak, A. Klami, S. Kaski, and S. Gunn. Learning to rank images from eye movements. In *Workshops on Human-Computer Interaction*, 2009.

[7] A.L. Yarbus. *Eye movements and vision.* Plenum press, 1967.

[8] J. Xiao, X. Zhang, P. Cheatle, Y. Gao, and C.B. Atkins. Mixed-initiative photo collage authoring. In *ACM Multimedia*, pages 509–518. ACM, 2008.

[9] J. Bar-Ilan, M. Mat-Hassan, and M. Levene. Methods for comparing rankings of search engine results. *Computer Networks*, 50(10):1448–1463, 2006.

Strong Geometry Consistency for Large Scale Partial-Duplicate Image Search

Junqiang Wang
School of Computer Science,
Nanjing University of Science and Technology
Nanjing, P.R. China
free.wjq@gmail.com

Jinhui Tang
School of Computer Science,
Nanjing University of Science and Technology
Nanjing, P.R. China
jinhuitang@mail.njust.edu.cn

Yu-Gang Jiang
School of Computer Science,
Fudan University
Shanghai, China
ygj@fudan.edu.cn

ABSTRACT

The state-of-the-art partial-duplicate image search systems reply heavily on the match of local features like SIFT. Independently matching local features across two images ignores the overall geometry structure and therefore may incur many false matches. To reduce such matches, several geometry verification methods have been proposed. This paper introduces a new geometry verification method named as Strong Geometry Consistency (SGC), which uses the orientation, scale and location information of the local feature points to accurately and quickly remove the false matches. We also propose a simple scale weighting (SW) strategy, which gives feature points with larger scales greater weights, based on the intuition that a larger-scale feature point tends to be more robust for image search as it occupies a larger area of an image. Extensive experiments performed on three popular datasets show that SGC significantly outperforms state-of-the-art geometry verification methods, and SW can further boost the performance with marginal additional computation.

Categories and Subject Descriptors

H.3.1 [**Information Storage and Retrieval**]: Content Analysis and Indexing

Keywords

Image search, partial-duplicate images, geometry verification, scale weighting

1. INTRODUCTION

Given a query image and a large image dataset, the goal of this work is to accurately and efficiently identify partial-duplicate images, which may contain the same scenes or objects captured from different angles, or originally the same image altered manually in scale, contrast, etc. Figure 1 shows some example images. Automatic solutions for finding partial-duplicates have many potential applications like copyright violation detection, image annotation, web-scale image search, and so on.

Figure 1: Examples of partial-duplicate images.

In the past decade, the performance of large scale partial-duplicate image search has been significantly boosted by using local invariant features [5, 4, 6, 7] and the well-known Bag-of-Features (a.k.a. Bag-of-Visual-Words) representation [11, 8]. See a subset of representative works in [2, 9, 10, 18, 17, 14, 19, 15, 3, 12, 16, 13]. A typical step in many of these approaches is to match similar local features between each pair of images. Instead of exhaustively evaluating pairwise similarity of feature points, a more efficient way is to assume that feature points falling into the same visual word are matched, which has been widely used. Through evaluating the number of matched patches, the similarity (and the likelihood of having duplicate image regions) between two images can be estimated. A major limitation of pure local feature matching is that it ignores the spatial locations of the local features, which have been proved to be very useful in improving search accuracy [9].

One conventional approach to alleviate the problem is to use RANSAC [7], which is able to perform careful geometry verification of the matched local features, but is computationally slow. To more efficiently verify the consistency of the geometry structures of the matched features, weak geometry consistency (WGC) was proposed [2]. One assumption in WGC is that the matched features should have similar scale and rotation changes. Therefore it uses the peak values of scale and orientation changes histograms to measure

MM'13, October 21–25, 2013, Barcelona, Spain.

http://dx.doi.org/10.1145/2502081.2502166.

image similarity. An enhanced WGC (E-WGC) method was further proposed in [17], which holds that though the reverse transformation in scale and rotation, corresponding image regions will also share uniform or similar translation. The consistency of predicted translations is used as a measure of geometry consistency.

A different approach to tackle a similar problem, called Geometric Coding (GC), was proposed in [18]. GC encodes local feature points' spatial relationships, and iteratively removes matches that cause the largest inconsistency in geometry structure. Obviously, the computational complexity of GC is $O\left(n^2\right)$, which is much slower compared with WGC and E-WGC.

In this paper, we propose a new geometry verification measure called Strong Geometry Consistency (SGC), which is efficient to compute and robust to scale changes, rotation, slight 3D viewpoint changes, etc. The idea of SGC is motivated by WGC and E-WGC, with a key difference that SGC not only considers the magnitude of displacement but also fully uses translation in both x and y axes. In addition, SGC divides the matched features into several groups based on scale and orientation changes, which makes the evaluation of geometry structure consistency more strict and efficient. A simple scale weighting (SW) method is also proposed, which gives larger scale feature points greater weights, as features in larger scales cover larger image areas and are therefore expected to be more robust. In the following we first introduce our proposed SGC and SW and then verify their effectiveness using several benchmark datasets.

2. THE PROPOSED APPROACH

2.1 Strong Geometry Consistency

We start by briefly explaining the idea of WGC and E-WGC. Given two matched local feature points $p\left(x_p, y_p\right)$ and $q\left(x_q, y_q\right)$ where x and y represents the spatial coordinates of the two points, we can estimate the transformation from p to q as follows:

$$\begin{bmatrix} x_q \\ y_q \end{bmatrix} = s \times \begin{bmatrix} cos\theta & -sin\theta \\ sin\theta & cos\theta \end{bmatrix} \times \begin{bmatrix} x_p \\ y_p \end{bmatrix} + \begin{bmatrix} t_x \\ t_y \end{bmatrix} \quad (1)$$

where t_x, t_y indicate the translation in the horizontal and vertical directions respectively, s is a scaling parameter and θ is a rotation parameter. The two parameters can be approximated by [2]:

$$s = s_q/s_p, \theta = \theta_q - \theta_p \quad (2)$$

where s_p and s_q are the scales of the local feature points p and q respectively, indicated by the local feature detectors like the Differences of Gaussian (DoG) [5]. Similarly θ_p and θ_q are the dominant orientations of the two points, which can also be found in the outputs of the local feature detectors. The authors of [9] have found that using the simple transformation model in Eq. (1) is just slightly worse than the much more expensive RANSAC approach.

In WGC, s and θ for all the matched feature pairs are collected, which form two histograms. The peak values of the two histograms are used to directly measure or slightly adjust the values of image similarities, because the peak values can indicate the consistency of scale changes and rotation between the two set of matched features. E-WGC is directly motivated by WGC. Based on Eq. (1), we can easily derive the translation (t_x, t_y):

$$\begin{bmatrix} t_x \\ t_y \end{bmatrix} = \begin{bmatrix} x_q \\ y_q \end{bmatrix} - s \times \begin{bmatrix} cos\theta & -sin\theta \\ sin\theta & cos\theta \end{bmatrix} \times \begin{bmatrix} x_p \\ y_p \end{bmatrix} \quad (3)$$

In E-WGC, a histogram of the L-2 norm of the translation is used instead of the histograms of scale and orientation differences, and the peak L-2 norm of all the matched pairs is used to adjust the similarity of two images.

Reducing a two dimensional translation vector to a single L-2 norm value in E-WGC makes it easier to compute the peak values, but apparently also loses important information. In SGC, we consider the original 2-d vector. Specifically, we first divide the matched feature pairs into k groups softly, based on their rotation angles. Within each group, we first find the pair which has the most similarly translated pairs, its translation is defined as the dominant translation of the group, and then remove feature pairs which have a significantly different translation with the dominant translation. After that, we use the number of remaining pairs in the largest group to represent the similarity of two images:

$$Sim(i, j) = N_{max} \quad (4)$$

where N_{max} represents the cardinality of the largest group.

In addition to the benefit from directly using the 2-d translation vector instead of its L-2 norm, SGC is developed based on the assumption that there is a considerable portion of the image regions sharing similar scale changes, rotation and translation. In other words, the feature points with similar translation must have similar scale changes and rotation, while WGC and E-WGC do not explicitly consider this. This allows SGC to perform strict and accurate geometry consistency verification.

It is worth noting that in SGC the computational complexity of removing false feature pairs is $O\left(n^2\right)$, where n is the number of the matched feature pairs in each group. However, as feature pairs are divided into several much smaller groups by rotated angles, the speed is greatly improved since n becomes much smaller. We will experimentally evaluate the speed of SGC later.

Error Threshold of the Predicted Translation: While removing false matches in each feature pair group, we need a threshold of the predicted translation (t_x, t_y) to decide which pairs are false matches. Using a fixed threshold is a straightforward choice but is not very reliable as there can be many variations of duplicated image regions, which may lead to different levels of errors.

In this work, we propose a simple and efficient way to automatically and adaptively predict the most suitable threshold. To that end we need to make several error assumptions. First, the error of spatial locations of the detected feature points is (empirically) assumed to be within 5 pixels. Such an error exists because there may be a certain degree of offset in the detector outputs for the same interest region when image transformations exist. We also assume that the error of θ is within θ_{error} degrees. With these assumptions and Eq. (3), we can have the following error threshold of the translation:

$$\left\| \begin{bmatrix} t_{x_{error}} \\ t_{y_{error}} \end{bmatrix} \right\| \leq s \times \left\| \begin{bmatrix} cos\theta_{error} & -sin\theta_{error} \\ sin\theta_{error} & cos\theta_{error} \end{bmatrix} \times \begin{bmatrix} x_p + 5 \\ y_p + 5 \end{bmatrix} \right\| \quad (5)$$

With Eq. (5), we have a better way of threshold estimation, which allows more accurate filtering of false matches, as will be validated in the experiments.

2.2 Scale Weighting

A key assumption of scale weighting is that a feature point (a region more rigorously), like SIFT, in a larger scale tends to be more robust for matching, since it occupies a larger image region and contains more information. One example is that a leg of a table may be matched to many images with similar objects like chairs, but a larger object like the head of a movie star can be more rarely wrongly matched. With this intuition in mind, we give the feature points in larger scales greater weights during the process of ejecting false feature pairs, where the weight is computed as :

$$SW = (s_1 \times s_2)^n \quad (6)$$

we experiment with different n from 0 to 1 on the 1M image dataset. In the experiments we observe that the optimal value of n is around 0.75. However, we simply use 1 for n as it is only marginally worse than the optimal choice, but is much more efficient to compute Eq. (6).

3. EXPERIMENTS

In this section, we experimentally validate the effectiveness of our proposed approach and compare with several existing geometric verification methods. All the experiments are performed on a regular desktop computer with a single 2.53GHz Xeon CPU and 16GB RAM. Throughout the experiments we use DoG as the local detector and SIFT as the descriptor [5]. To generate initial local feature matches for geometry-based filtering, we adopt a codebook of 200k visual words.

3.1 Datasets and Evaluation Measure

We adopt three popular benchmark datasets:

The first one is Oxford5K, which was introduced in [9]. It contains 11 different landmarks in Oxford and 55 query images. Together with a large number of background images that do not contain any of the landmarks, this dataset has totally 5,062 high resolution images.

The second dataset, called Holiday, was originally used in [2], which consists mainly of personal holiday photos. The dataset has 500 image groups, each of which depicts a different scene. In total there are 1,491 images. Following existing works, the first image of each scene group is used as the query image and the correct search results should be the remaining images within the same group.

The third dataset used in our experiments was collected by the authors of [18], called GCdup. It contains 1,104 partial-duplicate images in 33 groups, all downloaded from the Web. 100 images are selected as the query images in our experiments.

To make the task more challenging and realistic, we further adopt the MIRflickr 1 million dataset [1] as distracters. By gradually adding images from this dataset to the above 3 datasets, we can better understand the robustness and scalability of different approaches.

For performance metric, we compute the widely adopted Average Precision (AP) for each query and use mean AP (mAP) to measure the overall performance of multiple queries.

3.2 Alternative Methods for Comparison

To show the effectiveness of SGC and SW, we conduct comprehensive comparative studies with the following approaches: (1) Standard BOF [8], using a codebook of 1 million visual words; (2) BOF+WGC [2], where initial search results of BOF are refined using orientation and scale of matched feature pairs as described earlier in Section 2; (3) BOF+E-WGC [17]; (4) Re-ranking based on RANSAC [9], which facilitates good affine-transformation verification. Because the computational cost of RANSAC is very high, we only re-rank the top 300 candidate images. (5) GC [18].

Table 1: Average time cost of various geometric verification methods on the Holiday dataset.

Method	Without HE	With HE
WGC	1.16s	0.34s
E-WGC	1.63s	0.45s
RANSAC	5.58s	1.49s
GC	3.87s	0.97s
SGC	1.72s	0.49s
SGC+SW	1.74s	0.50s

All these approaches are based on our own implementations, which may not be exactly the same with the original papers. However, several of the approaches have been evaluated on one or more of the three datasets in corresponding references. We have checked into those works and found our obtained results very similar.

3.3 Results and Discussion

Figure 2 gives the performance of all the approaches. Overall we can see that the proposed SGC significantly outperforms all the existing methods including BoF, WGC, E-WGC, RANSAC, and GC. BoF is the worst since it does not have any geometry verification capability and therefore involves lots of false matches. WGC and E-WGC perform similar in our experiments, which are all not as good as stronger verification algorithms RANSAC and GC. Interestingly, we find that the similar scale weighting strategy SW is very useful, leading to significant improvements over all the three datasets. On the GCdup dataset, using SW (SGC+SW) improves SGC alone by as high as 7%. This confirms the fact that feature points with larger scales are much more important for partial-duplicate image search.

To validate the effect of our adaptive error threshold estimation method in SGC, we also experiment with several fixed error thresholds on the GCdup dataset, and found the best fixed error threshold is around 80, with which the performance is still around 2 percent lower than that using our adaptive error threshold. During the computation of the adaptive threshold, we set the error of θ as 7 degrees for Holiday and GCdup, and 15 degrees for Oxford5K where 3D viewpoint changes are more popular. Although this parameter can lead to different final performance, the difference is fairly minor and does not affect the general conclusion observed from Figure 2.

Table 1 further summarizes the average time cost of all the geometric verification methods for one image query on the Holiday dataset with 1 million image distracters. As can be seen, our SGC has similar speed to E-WGC and is much faster than RANSAC and GC. The fact that it is faster than GC is mainly because it divides feature points into several small groups. Dividing feature points, as one of the core ideas in SGC, also leads to performance gain. Further adding SW does not incur too much extra computation.

4. CONCLUSION

We have proposed a new geometry verification method

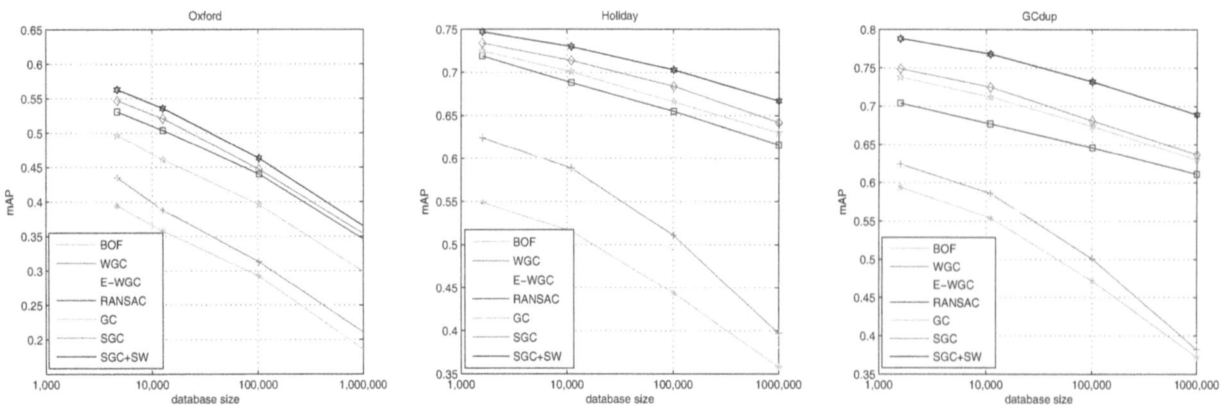

(a) Oxford5K (b) Holiday (c) GCdup

Figure 2: Performance (mAP) of various approaches on three datasets. The left end of each curve gives results on the original dataset without adding background images (distracters), while the other results are obtained on enlarged datasets with different numbers of distracters.

called SGC, which integrates the orientation, scale and location of the local feature points to quickly filter false matches from initial visual codebook based matching. On three popular datasets, we have shown that the proposed SGC significantly outperforms existing alternative solutions with minor additional computation. In addition, we also proposed a simple scale weighting strategy, which produces surprising good performance gains.

5. ACKNOWLEDGMENTS

This work was partially supported by the Natural Science Foundation of China (NSFC) under Grant 61103059, the National Basic Research Program of China (973 Program) under Grant 2012CB316304, the Program for New Century Excellent Talents in University under grant NCET-12-0632, The Natural Science Foundation of Jiangsu Province under Grant BK2012033 and BK2011700.

6. REFERENCES

[1] M. J. Huiskes, B. Thomee, , and M. Lew. New trends and ideas in visual concept detection. In *ACM MIR*, 2010.

[2] H. Jegou, M. Douze, and C. Schmid. Hamming embedding and weak geometric consistency for large scale image search. In *ECCV*, 2008.

[3] H. Jegou, H. Harzallah, and C. Schmid. A contextual dissimilarity measure for accurate and efficient image search. In *CVPR*, 2007.

[4] T. Lindeberg. Feature detection with automatic scale selection. *International Journal of Computer Vision*, 30(2):77–116, 1998.

[5] D. Lowe. Distinctive image features from scale-invariant key points. *International Journal of Computer Vision*, 60(2):91–110, 2004.

[6] J. Matas, O. Chum, M. Urban, and T. Pajdla. Robust wide baseline stereo from maximally stable extremal regions. In *BMVC*, 2002.

[7] K. Mikolajczyk and C. Schmid. Scale and affine invariant interest point detectors. *International Journal of Computer Vision*, 60(1):63–86, 2004.

[8] D. Nister and H. Stewenius. Scalable recognition with a vocabulary tree. In *CVPR*, pages 2161–2168, 2006.

[9] J. Philbin, O. Chum, M. Isard, J. Sivic, and A. Zisserman. Object retrieval with large vocabularies and fast spatial matching. In *CVPR*, 2007.

[10] J. Philbin, O. Chum, M. Isard, J. Sivic, and A. Zisserman. Lost in quantization: Improving particular object retrieval in large scale image databases. In *CVPR*, 2008.

[11] J. Sivic and A. Zisserman. Video google: A text retrieval approach to object matching in videos. In *ICCV*, 2003.

[12] J. Tang, R. Hong, S. Yan, G.-J. Qi and T.-S. Chua. Inferring semantic concepts from community contributed images and noisy tags. In *ACM Multimedia*, 2009.

[13] J. Tang, R. Hong, S. Yan, T.-S. Chua, G.-J. Qi and R. Jain. Image annotation by k nn-sparse graph-based label propagation over noisily tagged web images. *ACM TIST*, 2011.

[14] Z. Wu, Q. Ke, M. Isard, and J. Sun. Bundling features for large scale partial-duplicate web image search. In *CVPR*, 2009.

[15] W.Zhou, Y. Lu, H. Li, Y. Song, and Q. Tian. Spatial coding for large scale partial-duplicate web image search. In *ACM Multimedia*, 2010.

[16] D.-Q. Zhang and S.-F. Chang. Detecting image near-duplicate by stochastic attributed relational graph matching with learning. In *ACM Multimedia*, 2004.

[17] W. Zhao, X. Wu, and C.-W. Ngo. On the annotation of web videos by efficient near-duplicate search. *IEEE TMM*, 12(5):448–461, 2010.

[18] W. Zhou, H. Li, Y. Lu, and Q. Tian. Large scale image search with geometric coding. In *ACM Multimedia*, 2011.

[19] W. Zhou, H. Li, Y. Lu, and Q. Tian. Sift match verification by geometric coding for large-scale partial-duplicate web image search. *ACM TOMCCAP*, 9(1), 2013.

Segmental Multi-way Local Pooling for Video Recognition

Ilseo Kim
Kitware Inc.
ilseo.kim@kitware.com

Sangmin Oh
Kitware Inc.
sangmin.oh@kitware.com

Arash Vahdat
Simon Fraser University
avahdat@sfu.ca

Kevin Cannons
Simon Fraser University
kcannons@sfu.ca

A.G.Amitha Perera
Kitware Inc.
amitha.perera@kitware.com

Greg Mori
Simon Fraser University
mori@cs.sfu.ca

ABSTRACT

In this work, we address the problem of complex event detection on unconstrained videos. We introduce a novel multi-way feature pooling approach which leverages segment-level information. The approach is simple and widely applicable to diverse audio-visual features. Our approach uses a set of clusters discovered via unsupervised clustering of segment-level features. Depending on feature characteristics, not only scene-based clusters but also motion/audio-based clusters can be incorporated. Then, every video is represented with multiple descriptors, where each descriptor is designed to relate to one of the pre-built clusters. For classification, intersection kernel SVMs are used where the kernel is obtained by combining multiple kernels computed from corresponding per-cluster descriptor pairs. Evaluation on TRECVID '11 MED dataset shows a significant improvement by the proposed approach beyond the state-of-the-art.

Categories and Subject Descriptors

H.3 [**Information Storage and Retrieval**]: Content Analysis and Indexing; Information Search and Retrieval.

Keywords

Representation, Multimedia Event Recognition, TRECVID

1. INTRODUCTION

Detection of complex events on unconstrained real-world videos (e.g., YouTube) is a challenging problem. Most complex events (e.g., *birthday party* and *board trick)* exhibit large intra-class variations, and videos frequently consist of multiple segments exhibiting different and evolving contents that include not only a mixture of contents closely related to events but also temporal clutters such as title screens or irrelevant contents arbitrarily stitched-in by users.

Many reported successful retrieval systems (e.g., [3, 6]) for unconstrained videos share the common idea of constructing clip-level representations via global average-based pooling. For each feature type, a bag-of-words (BoW) descriptor (or variations) is built per video by pooling across the entire video. These globally pooled features work well, although the fact that these methods do not exploit detailed segment information leaves a room for further research, which started to be addressed by recent efforts such as [2, 10].

In this work[1], we present a multi-way local pooling (MLP) approach that leverages the detailed segment-level information and boosts the performance beyond the globally pooled descriptors. The overall scheme is illustrated in Fig.1. Our approach builds multiple descriptors per video, where each descriptor is designed to relate to one of the pre-built segment clusters. These clusters are constructed in an unsupervised manner and can be understood as rough themes interchangeably appearing as segments in videos. From an input video, a separate descriptor is built per cluster by accumulating features from segments which are *local* (or similar) to the represented cluster. The rationale behind the MLP strategy is partly inspired by the recently introduced theory of local pooling [1] which showed that pooling features similar in multi-dimensional input space separately improves the representational power and classification accuracy. In addition, we observe that the frequency of segment-to-cluster assignments provides a unique signature to indicate the importance of each cluster in describing a video sample. Accordingly, our approach intentionally avoids normalization on each descriptor, which is in contrast to [1, 2].

Consider the example video of *board trick* in Fig. 1, which consists of title screens at both ends and actual snowboarding segments in the middle. First, there are a set of segment clusters discovered by clustering segment-level features[2], which include clusters such as caption/titles, moving object on smooth background, and cube-shaped large objects[3]. It is worth noting that our framework is general and can be applied to various audio-visual features developed for multimedia videos. Accordingly, clusters with motion or audio patterns can be discovered as well, depending on the characteristics of the underlying features. For example, it can be seen in Fig. 1 that not only scene-based clusters but

MM'13, October 21–25, 2013, Barcelona, Spain.

ACM 978-1-4503-2404-5/13/10 ...$15.00.

[1]This work was supported by the Intelligence Advanced Research Projects Activity (IARPA) via Department of Interior National Business Center contract number D11PC20069. The U.S. Government is authorized to reproduce and distribute reprints for Governmental purposes notwithstanding any copyright thereon. Disclaimer: The views and conclusions contained herein are those of the authors and should not be interpreted as necessarily representing the official policies or endorsements, either expressed or implied, of IARPA, DOI/NBC, or the U.S. Government.

[2]For these results, (uncolored) HoG3D feature [4] is used.

[3]The clusters are manually named *a posteriori* after clustering.

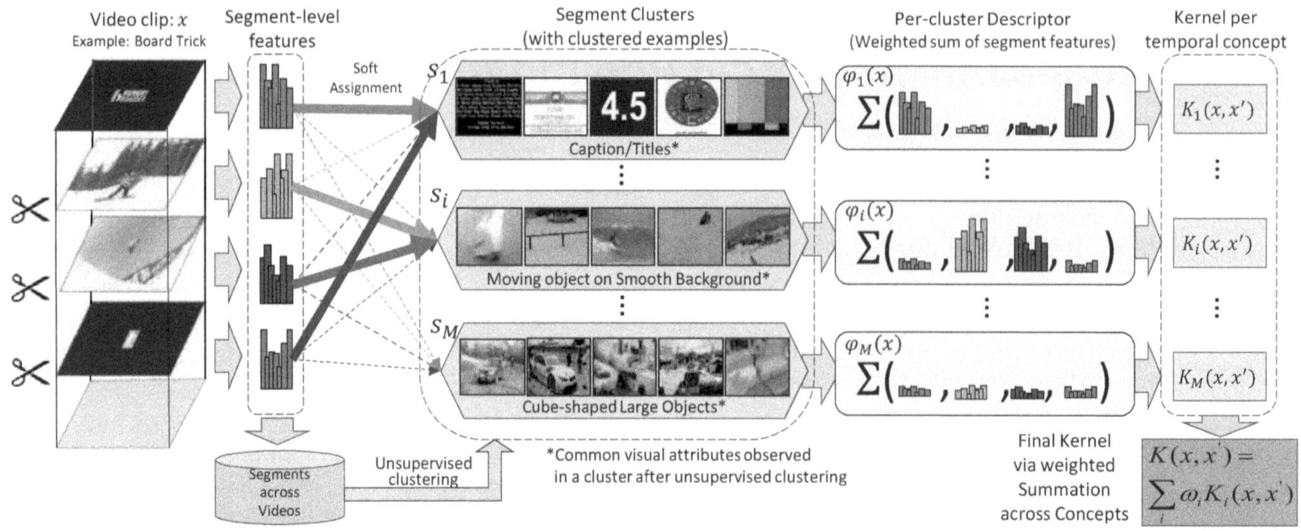

Figure 1: A video clip consists of multiple segments. Each segment-level feature is pooled multi-way into different descriptors based on their similarity and the corresponding segment clusters. Then, kernelization is separately applied per descriptor. The final kernel combines multiple kernels and provides improved discriminant power.

also motion-related clusters are discovered. Then, each per-cluster descriptor is built by pooling features from different parts of the input video using soft-assignment based on similarity between segments and clusters.

For classification, our work adopts the intersection kernel (IK) SVMs to build classifiers. In particular, the kernel between a pair of videos is computed by combining per-cluster kernels computed for every cluster. It is important to note that the per-cluster kernel values on a frequently assigned kernels tend to be high and vice versa, due to the captured frequency information. Accordingly, if certain clusters are poorly represented in exemplar videos, they will contribute towards kernel values in a limited way. In addition, our work explores an alternative strategy to combine kernels using multiple kernel learning (MKL) [11]. In essence, it is plausible that certain clusters are more discriminative even though they are rarely represented in exemplar videos, or vice versa. The use of MKL provides an opportunity to learn discriminative weights for kernel combination.

We have evaluated the proposed approach on the recently introduced challenging TRECVID '11 MED dataset [9]. The experimental results show that the proposed approach shows substantial improvement over the state-of-the-art.

2. RELATED WORK

The idea of multi-way pooling has been developed in [1], but it was only applied to low-level raw visual feature descriptors for image recognition. This work extends it to video recognition at higher-level granularity of segments. Recent work that characterizes videos at segment-level include [7], [10], and [2]. To represent complex activities, [7] identifies distinctive temporal segments (i.e., sub-actions) along with the temporal structure between them. Although the temporal structure allows certain flexibility, [7] is still most suitable to videos with fairly regularized structures (such as the Olympic dataset). In [10], a discriminative recursive hidden segmental Markov model is proposed to cope better with less regularized temporal structure in consumer videos. In the closely related work of [2], features from images in videos are pooled into different scene clusters, guided by the secondary GIST [8] feature. Although using a secondary feature might be necessary to incorporate extremely sparse feature types (e.g., sparse SIFT), it limits this method to be applicable to image-based features only, and exploring a unified feature pooling framework (without a secondary feature) for more general feature types is necessitated. In contrast, our method is simpler and more general because it is more widely applicable to diverse audio-visual features beyond image-based ones, and can utilize audio/temporal clusters. In contrast to [2], our approach also explores MKL variations to combine kernels across different clusters.

3. MULTI-WAY LOCAL POOLING

Our multi-way local pooling (MLP) method constructs multiple descriptors instead of a single descriptor given a feature type for a video clip, and then attempts to improve discriminant power using kernelization techniques. The key idea is to quantify and utilize similarities between two video samples with respect to (w.r.t.) various segment clusters, especially in unconstrained consumer video data, where it is difficult to apply conventional temporal models, e.g., HMMs.

The overall scheme is illustrated in Fig. 1. First, we divide a video clip into video segments and represent each segment with a given feature type. Then, every video segment is soft-assigned to segment clusters. These clusters are pre-constructed by unsupervised clustering from all segment-level feature descriptors in training data, and thus represent broad categories covering entire training corpus, e.g., caption/title, moving object on smooth background, or cube-shaped large object. A large assignment value of a video segment to an existing cluster indicates that they are highly correlated, and vice versa. Soft-assignment is important because it can substantially alleviate the arbitrary space partitioning built by unsupervised clustering of segments. Using this soft-assignment, every segment-level feature descriptor from a video is pooled into multiple different segment clusters with different weights, i.e., multiway-pooling. In other words, if we have M segment clusters, M video-level feature descriptors are constructed in a way that a highly correlated video segment to a corresponding segment cluster contributes more. In a sense, the newly constructed video-level feature descriptors can be considered to be projections of a video clip toward segment clusters. After multiple descriptors are constructed, kernelization is separately applied to measure similarity between different videos w.r.t. each corresponding segment cluster. Finally, multiple kernels are combined to a final kernel to provide improved discriminant power for video recognition. For brevity, the detailed derivations below are based on BoW features, although it can be generalized to other representations.

In detail, let $x = \{x^i | x^i \in R^D, 1 \leq i \leq n\}$ be a training video sample, where x^i is a D-dimensional BoW representation for the i-th segment, and n is the number of total segments in a video sample x. It is assumed that segment clusters are already available by collecting all of the video segments from the training corpus and clustering them in the D-dimensional feature space by an unsupervised k-means scheme. Then, our approach uses centroids of the clusters as segment clusters that compactly describe the segment types in the video. Let $S = \{s_j | s_j \in R^D, 1 \leq j \leq M\}$ be a set of M segment clusters, which are represented as D-dimensional vectors. Each D-dimensional feature descriptor $\varphi_j(x)$ of a video x w.r.t. the j-th segment cluster is formulated as a weighted-BoW representation computed across the entire video segments $\{x^1, x^2, \cdots, x^n\}$, with corresponding soft-assignment weights as

$$\varphi_j(x) = \frac{1}{n} \sum_{i=1}^{n} \omega_j(S, x^i) \cdot x^i, \tag{1}$$

where n is the number of video segments in a video sample x, and $\omega_j(\cdot)$ is a soft-weight assignment function between a corresponding segment cluster and a video segment. While the choice for the soft-weight assignment is flexible, we have adopted the following variant of the Gaussian function, which has shown superior performance across our experiments with diverse features:

$$\omega_j\left(S, x^i\right) = \exp\left[-\frac{\{d\left(s_j, x^i\right)\}^2}{\alpha}\right], \tag{2}$$

where α is a positive parameter that controls the sensitivity on the distance $d(\cdot)$ between a centroid and a sample point. For a distance measure, the negative geodesic distance (NGD) which provides an effective distance measure on BoW features [12] is used, defined as the following:

$$d\left(s_j, x^i\right) = -2 \arccos\left(\sum_{k=1}^{D} \sqrt{\frac{s_{j,k}}{|s_j|} \frac{x_k^i}{|x^i|}}\right). \tag{3}$$

For the kernel type, we select IK, which is a popular kernel type, along with the desirable property of not involving normalization during kernel computation. It is noted that the constructed BoW feature $\varphi_j(x)$ for a segment cluster s_j is not L_1-normalized. In this way, the IK $K_j(x, x')$ between two videos x and x' is determined by not only the similarity between the distribution of $\varphi_j(x)$ and $\varphi_j(x')$, but also $\|\varphi_j(x)\|$ and $\|\varphi_j(x')\|$, which reflect their assignment frequency and correlation to a segment cluster s_j. In other words, even if $\varphi_j(x)$ and $\varphi_j(x')$ show similar distributions, $K_j(x, x')$ might be small if one or both samples are loosely correlated to a segment cluster s_j, i.e., $\|\varphi_j(x)\|$ and/or $\|\varphi_j(x')\|$ are small. Then, a final kernel $K(x, x')$ is constructed as a linear combination of the multiple kernels constructed for multiple segment clusters. We applied both equal weights and those learned by MKL, and their results are reported in the following section.

4. EXPERIMENTAL RESULTS

We have applied the proposed framework on TRECVID '11 MED corpus [9], which is a challenging large-scale consumer video dataset. The dataset provides an excellent testbed for a real-world unconstrained video retrieval problem. It consists of 13K training and 32K test samples with 10 annotated test event classes. The number of positive and negative samples is highly imbalanced; e.g., there are only about 150 positive samples for each class in each of the training and test sets. For each event class, we trained SVMs in a one-vs-all manner across our experiments and report average precisions (APs) or mean AP (mAP) across all ten events as metrics. For training protocol, we followed the approach in a recent study [10] for fair comparison, across experiments.

The proposed approach is extensively compared with other strong baseline methods and/or state-of-the-arts for both visual and audio features. For the results in this paper, (visual) HoG3D [4] with 1,000 codewords and (audial) MFCCs with 1,024 codewords are used, respectively. For the length of video segments, we divided a clip uniformly into fixed 2-second-length segments, which we found to work well across feature types. The parameter α in Eq. 2 was set to be $\alpha = 0.3\pi^2$, and was found through cross validation.

Table 1: Retrieval results w.r.t. varying number of segment clusters on HoG3D, in mAP (%).

# of SCs	1	20	40	60	80	100
mAP	7.00	9.43	9.75	9.74	9.75	9.72

Our first result analyzes the sensitivity of the proposed framework against the number of segment clusters (SCs). Table 1 summarizes the mAP across all ten classes w.r.t. varying number of segment clusters on HoG3D. It is noted that using only one cluster is equivalent to using a conventional kernelized SVM (KSVM). It can be observed that significant improvement (relatively 39.3%) can be achieved as the number of clusters is increased to 40. Beyond 40, the performance stabilizes, showing the desirable property that the proposed approach is relatively immune to over-fitting even when large number of SCs are used, which can be credited to the proposed distance and soft-weighting schemes. Although the number of optimal segment clusters may differ by features types, event types, and datasets, we find that 30–50 SCs are generally sufficient to acquire the benefits of the proposed framework. For the remainder of the experimental results, 40 clusters have been used.

Our main experimental results on 32K test samples using visual HoG3D features are summarized in Table 2. The performance of Chance (i.e., random) is very low due to the imbalance between positive and negative samples. For MLP approaches, two variations using equal kernel weights (MLP-EQ) and those learned by generalized MKL [11] (MLP-MKL) are reported. The compared approaches used in our experiments include linear SVM (LSVM), KSVM, Niebles [7], Tang [10], and linear/kernelized SAP (LSAP/KSAP) [2]. It is noted that, for direct comparisons, we reproduced the results of Niebles and Tang from [10] by using the same quantized features and training/test protocol, and also re-implemented LSAP/KSAP using the same GIST [8] feature as a secondary image feature and parameters suggested by the authors [2]. In addition, we also evaluated a variant of KSAP (denoted as KSAP-H), in which scene clusters are constructed by using the same pooled feature (not a secondary image feature, suggested by [2]), i.e., HoG3D in this experiment. For KSVM,

Table 2: Comparison in AP(%) among the baseline systems including state-of-the-arts, and the proposed MLP frameworks. For each row, the best result is marked in bold. Overall, both MLP-EQ and MLP-MKL consistently outperformed baselines, showing notable improvement in mAP (illustrated in the right figure).

event ID	Chance	LSVM	Niebles	Tang	LSAP	KSVM	KSAP	KSAP-H	MLP-EQ	MLP-MKL
E006	0.54	1.97	2.25	4.38	3.95	6.08	4.24	4.73	6.34	**6.74**
E007	0.35	1.25	0.76	0.92	2.88	2.87	2.86	2.26	**3.01**	2.98
E008	0.42	6.48	8.30	15.29	17.31	20.75	22.33	22.99	**31.16**	30.87
E009	0.26	2.15	1.95	2.04	4.33	6.25	5.36	**7.61**	7.54	7.50
E010	0.25	0.81	0.74	0.74	1.31	1.43	1.14	1.34	2.11	**2.34**
E011	0.43	1.10	1.48	0.84	1.94	2.29	2.57	2.65	**4.07**	3.86
E012	0.58	5.83	2.65	4.03	7.43	8.44	7.08	8.7	10.63	**11.13**
E013	0.32	2.58	2.05	3.04	9.78	9.44	9.33	10.43	**15.57**	15.25
E014	0.27	1.18	4.39	10.88	5.25	10.00	9.79	11.89	14.81	**14.84**
E015	0.26	0.92	0.61	**5.48**	1.54	2.49	2.02	2.4	2.25	1.82
mAP	0.37	2.43	2.52	4.76	5.57	7.00	6.67	7.50	**9.75**	9.73

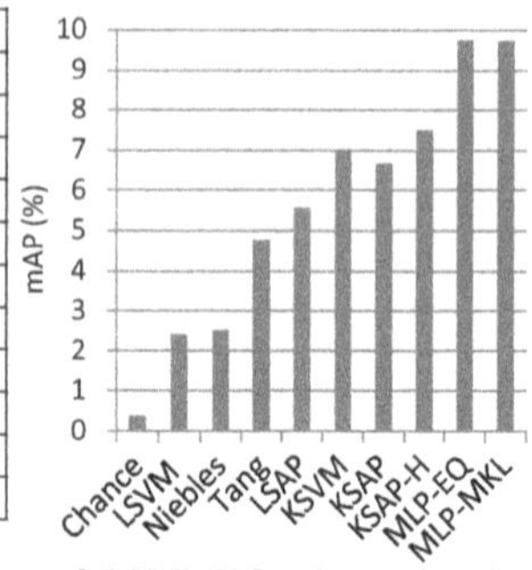

KSAP, and KSAP-H, we applied the same IK used in the proposed approach. Across all compared methods, the same HoG3D features have been used.

As shown in Table 2, the proposed approach consistently outperforms the compared systems for most event classes. In particular, the proposed MLP approaches show significant improvement of (relatively) 30% on average beyond KSAP-H, which is found to be the best baseline system. Such improvement was achieved by our soft-assignment scheme based on NGD distance and kernel combination without cluster-wise normalization. We also observed that KSAP-H outperforms KSAP. This implies that the use of a consistent feature in constructing SCs can improve the quality of SCs, when compared to the use of a secondary image feature, especially for densely extracted feature types (we note that our HoG3D feature is densely extracted, while features used in [2] are sparsely extracted). In addition, it can be observed that KSVM outperformed the other latest methods without kernelization (Niebles, Tang, and LSAP), which suggests that the use of kernelization is one of the critical techniques for successful event detection.

Table 3: Results in mAP(%) using MFCCs (MLP with audio features).

	Chance	LSVM	KSVM	MLP-EQ	MLP-MKL
mAP	0.36	1.25	5.98	6.83	**6.87**

In Table 3, we also compared the proposed framework using audio MFCC features against two baselines (LSVM and KSVM). Other baseline systems are not included because the non-image features can not be incorporated or they did not show better performance than KSVM. In this experiment, we excluded about 2% of test videos without audio, which makes the performance by Chance slightly different from Table 2. It is clear that our framework provides advantages in audio as well, showing on average 14.9% improvement (relative) over KSVM. These results show that the proposed framework is fairly general and can yield benefits across different feature modalities.

Among our methods, MLP-EQ and MLP-MKL showed comparable results across all of the event classes, with slight improvement by one or the other, depending on event classes. The surprising effectiveness of MLP-EQ can be attributed to the following reasons: (1) individual kernels constructed for corresponding segment clusters are already weighted by the assignment frequency, which seems to capture most discriminative information; and (2) when underlying features are constructed effectively with little redundancy, equally weighted kernels has been shown to have comparable performance to MKL [5]. These results suggest that, for time-sensitive applications, the use of MLP-EQ alone can be a good approach at the loss of minor accuracy for some classes.

5. CONCLUSION

We presented a novel multi-way feature pooling approach to address the problem of complex event detection on unconstrained videos, especially to capture relevant contents effectively from varying contents embedded within temporal structures. For this purpose, the proposed framework constructs multiple descriptors w.r.t. pre-constructed segment clusters. Our extensive experiments on the challenging TRECVID '11 MED dataset demonstrate the usefulness of the proposed framework, showing promising performance against strong baselines and the state-of-the-art.

6. REFERENCES

[1] Boureau, Y.-L., Roux, N. L., Bach, F., Ponce, J., and LeCun, Y. *Ask the locals: multi-way local pooling for image recognition. In* ICCV *(2011).*

[2] Cao, L., Mu, Y., Natsev, A., Chang, S.-F., Hua, G., and Smith, J. R. *Scene Aligned Pooling for Complex Video Recognition. In* ECCV *(2012).*

[3] Jiang, Y.-G., Ye, G., Chang, S.-F., Ellis, D., and Loui, A. *Consumer video understanding: A benchmark database and an evaluation of human and machine performance. In* ICMR *(2011).*

[4] Klasser, A., Marszalek, M., and Schmid, C. *A spatio-temporal descriptor based on 3d-gradients. In* BMVC *(2008).*

[5] Kloft, M., Brefeld, U., Sonnenburg, S., and Zien, A. *l_p-norm multiple kernel learning.* JMLR *(March 2011).*

[6] Natarajan, P., Wu, S., Vitaladevuni, S. N. P., Zhuang, X., Tsakalidis, S., Park, U., Prasad, R., and Natarajan, P. *Multimodal feature fusion for robust event detection in web videos. In* CVPR *(2012).*

[7] Niebles, J. C., Chen, C.-W., and Fei-Fei, L. *Modeling Temporal Structure of Decomposable Motion Segments for Activity Classification. In* ECCV *(2010).*

[8] Oliva, A., and Torralba, A. *Modeling the shape of the scene: a holistic representation of the spatial envelope.* IJCV 42, *3 (2001), 145–175.*

[9] Over, P., Awad, G., Fiscus, J., and Antonishek, B. *TRECVID 2011–Goals, Tasks, Data, Evaluation Mechanisms and Metrics.*

[10] Tang, K., Fei-Fei, L., and Koller, D. *Learning Latent Temporal Structure for Complex Event Detection. In* CVPR *(2012).*

[11] Varma, M., and Babu, B. R. *More generality in efficient multiple kernel learning. In* ICML *(2009).*

[12] Zhang, D., Chen, X., and Lee, W. S. *Text Classification with Kernels on the Multinomial Manifold. In* SIGIR *(2005).*

Efficient Video Quality Assessment Based on Spacetime Texture Representation

Peng Peng
Simon Fraser University
8888 University Drive
Burnaby, BC, Canada
pengp@sfu.ca

Kevin Cannons
Simon Fraser University
8888 University Drive
Burnaby, BC, Canada
kcannons@sfu.ca

Ze-Nian Li
Simon Fraser University
8888 University Drive
Burnaby, BC, Canada
li@cs.sfu.ca

ABSTRACT

Most existing video quality metrics measure temporal distortions based on optical-flow estimation, which typically has limited descriptive power of visual dynamics and low efficiency. This paper presents a unified and efficient framework to measure temporal distortions based on a spacetime texture representation of motion. We first propose an effective motion-tuning scheme to capture temporal distortions along motion trajectories by exploiting the distributive characteristic of the spacetime texture. Then we reuse the motion descriptors to build a self-information based spatiotemporal saliency model to guide the spatial pooling. At last, a comprehensive quality metric is developed by combining the temporal distortion measure with spatial distortion measure. Our method demonstrates high efficiency and excellent correlation with the human perception of video quality.

Categories and Subject Descriptors

I.4.9 [**Computing Methodologies**]: IMAGE PROCESSING AND COMPUTER VISION Applications

General Terms

Algorithms, Experimentation, Measurement

Keywords

Video quality assessment, spatiotemporal oriented energy (SOE), spacetime texture representation, visual attention

1. INTRODUCTION

Digital videos typically pass through several processing stages (e.g., lossy source encoding and transmission over error prone channels) that may result in impairment of quality before they reach the end users. Methods for evaluating video quality have received growing interest from content providers and network operators, as they play a crucial role in Quality-of-Service (QoS) monitoring, and perceptually optimal design and/or performance evaluation of video processing systems. Objective video quality assessment (VQA) methods are based on automated algorithms that attempt to predict video quality in a way consistent with the human perception. As a result, their performance is evaluated by how well the predicted quality correlates with the human-supplied subjective quality. Depending on the presence of a reference video, the VQA methods can be divided into three classes: full-reference, reduced-reference, and no-reference. In this study, we focus on the full-reference VQA algorithms.

Many factors affect the quality of digital videos. Distortions in video that arise primarily from the occurrence of motion are referred to as "temporal distortions" (e.g., ghosting, jerkiness, and mosquito effect), as opposed to the "spatial distortions" (e.g., blocking, ringing, and noise) [8]. Along with the progress of image quality assessment (IQA), there has been extensive research for measuring spatial distortions in videos. On the contrary, how to measure temporal distortions is much less studied.

In the context of video coding and quality assessment, motion has often been related to the notion of "optical flow", a motion vector at each spatiotemporal point with its length representing the magnitude of motion and its direction the direction of motion. It is no surprise that almost all existing VQA methods that explicitly incorporate motion estimation are based on the optical-flow representation. In early studies [12, 13], motion vectors are employed to estimate the weights for pooling the local quality measures into a single quality score. More recently, Moorthy et al. [6] proposed a motion compensated SSIM index for video quality assessment, in which the SSIM index [11] is performed on motion-compensated image blocks. Lately, Seshadrinathan and Bovik [8] propose the MOVIE index that captures the temporal distortions along motion trajectories by using Gabor filters tuned to the motion directions based on an optical flow method. It achieves the best quality prediction performance among a set of state-of-the-art VQA methods [9].

The optical-flow methods that attempt to precisely estimate motion vectors usually suffer from the high computational overhead caused by iterative optimization. A more critical issue is that the conventional optical-flow representation is inadequate in capturing general visual dynamics, such as pure temporal variations (e.g., campfire), and semi-transparency scene with more than one motion present at a single point (e.g., rising smoke) [3]. In this paper we introduce a recently proposed spacetime texture representation of motion [3] to the field of VQA. Besides its high efficiency,

MM'13, October 21–25, 2013, Barcelona, Spain.

ACM 978-1-4503-2404-5/13/10 ...$15.00.
http://dx.doi.org/10.1145/2502081.2502168.

it provides a distributed representation of motion and thus better descriptive power of general visual dynamics.

We first propose a local motion-tuned temporal distortion measure by exploiting the distributive characteristic of the spacetime-texture descriptors. The descriptors are then reused to build a spatiotemporal attention model for spatial pooling. In the end, the temporal distortion measure is combined with a simple spatial distortion measure to give a comprehensive evaluation of video quality. Our method achieves remarkable performance in both quality prediction and computational efficiency.

2. PROPOSED METHOD

2.1 Motion-tuned temporal distortion measure

To compute the spacetime texture representation [3], a video sequence is first filtered spatiotemporally using a bank of broadly tuned Gaussian third derivative filters, $G3_{\hat{\theta}}$, where $\hat{\theta}$ is a unit vector that captures the spatiotemporal direction of the filter symmetry axis. Each filter responds best to a stimulus moving in a specific direction in the spatiotemporal space. As in [3], the filter responses are point-wise rectified and summed over a spatiotemporal neighborhood (a spatiotemporal region Π) to yield a measurement of signal energy for this region at each orientation $\hat{\theta}$:

$$E_{\hat{\theta}}(x,y,t) = \sum_{(x,y,t)\in\Pi} (G3_{\hat{\theta}} * V)^2 \tag{1}$$

where $V = V(x,y,t)$ denotes the input spatiotemporal volume (i.e., the input video sequence), and the symbol "*" denotes convolution. The bandpass nature of the G_3 filters leads to the invariance of the energies to additive intensity variations. However, the local energy estimates still increase monotonically with contrast. In order to capture the temporal distortions irrespective of both the additive intensity variations and contrast change, a pixel-wise divisive normalization is performed. Specifically, the local energy measures are normalized by the summation of energy responses from all filters considered at each location.

Let $\hat{E}^r_{\hat{\theta}_k}(x,y,t)$ and $\hat{E}^d_{\hat{\theta}_k}(x,y,t)$ denote the normalized local energy measure along direction $\hat{\theta}_k$ in the reference video and distorted video, respectively. Now, we can obtain a local temporal distortion measure at each location (x,y,t) by calculating the similarity between the two corresponding energy distributions in the reference and distorted videos. In this paper, we use the efficient $\mathcal{L}_2$ distance:

$$TD(x,y,t) = [\sum_{k=1}^{K}(\hat{E}^r_{\hat{\theta}_k}(x,y,t) - \hat{E}^d_{\hat{\theta}_k}(x,y,t))^2]^{\frac{1}{2}}. \tag{2}$$

In this measure, each filter in the selected filter bank plays an equally important part. However, it has been shown that assigning biased weights to the filters according to the local motion pattern can better capture the temporal distortions [8]. Inspired by this, we propose a local motion-tuned temporal distortion measure. Following the method in [3], a distributed motion representation can be efficiently computed by "appearance marginalization" of the oriented energies in Eq. (1). The goal of this marginalization is to capture the purely dynamic properties of a scene, i.e., the motion-related properties independent from the spatial appearance. As a pattern with a specific velocity manifests itself as a plane through the origin in the frequency domain, the purely spatial orientation component in Eq. (1) can be discounted by summation across a set of spatiotemporal oriented energy measurements consistent with the corresponding frequency plane. Let a frequency plane be parameterized by its unit normal $\hat{n}_k$, and N the order of the Gaussian filters (here, $N = 3$). On each plane, $N+1$ equally spaced directions $\{\hat{\theta}_j, j = 1,\ldots,N+1\}$ are sampled for summation,

$$\tilde{E}_{\hat{n}_k} = \sum_{j=1}^{N+1} E_{\hat{\theta}_{k,j}}, k = 1,\ldots,K \tag{3}$$

with each $E_{\hat{\theta}_{k,j}}$ being the spatiotemporal energy given in Eq. (1). In this study, we selected 13 planes (i.e., $K = 13$) corresponding to the following motion directions: static (no motion), motion in eight directions (leftward, rightward, upward, downward and the four diagonals), and flicker in four directions (horizontal, vertical and two diagonals). We find that tuning the directions more finely did not lead to noticeably better performance but incurs greater computation. To attain insensitivity to contrast change, each $\tilde{E}_{\hat{n}_k}$ is normalized by their summation over all K directions. This results in a K-bin histogram $\{\hat{E}_{\hat{n}_k}, k = 1,\ldots,K\}$, which encapsulates a relative indication of the motion strength corresponding to each plane. Let $\hat{E}^r_{\hat{n}_k}(x,y,t)$ denote the histogram corresponding to a plane $\hat{n}_k$ at a spatiotemporal location (x,y,t) in the reference video. To obtain a motion-tuned temporal distortion measure, we integrate $\hat{E}^r_{\hat{n}_k}(x,y,t)$ into the temporal distortion measure in Eq. (2):

$$\begin{aligned} MT\text{-}TD(x,y,t) = [&\sum_{k=1}^{K}(\hat{E}^r_{\hat{n}_k}(x,y,t) \times \\ &\sum_{j=1}^{N+1}(\hat{E}^r_{\hat{\theta}_{k,j}}(x,y,t) - \hat{E}^d_{\hat{\theta}_{k,j}}(x,y,t))^2)]^{\frac{1}{2}}, \end{aligned} \tag{4}$$

where the $N+1$ filters $\{\hat{\theta}_{k,j}, j = 1,\ldots,N+1\}$ consistent with a certain frequency plane $\hat{n}_k$ are weighted by $\hat{E}^r_{\hat{n}_k}(x,y,t)$.

2.2 Attention-guided spatial pooling

In recent years, visual attention has received increasing interest in the area of visual quality assessment. While most attention-guided VQA methods employ attention models purely based on spatial cues (e.g., color, intensity and spatial orientation), some recent VQA methods take into consideration the motion-driven attention, in which the motion estimates are usually based on the optical-flow representation (e.g. [15]) or simply described by the adjacent frame difference (e.g., [5]). In this study, we reuse the local motion descriptors computed in Section 2.1 for visual attention modeling. Following the Attention by Information Maximization (AIM) principle proposed by Bruce and Tsotsos [2], a spatiotemporal saliency model is built based on the self-information of the local features, $\hat{E}_{\hat{n}_k}$ and $\tilde{E}_{\hat{n}_k}$. At each spatiotemporal location, we compute two self-information measures:

$$SI_M(x,y,t) = \sum_{k=1}^{K} -log(p(\hat{E}_{\hat{n}_k}(x,y,t))), \tag{5}$$

$$SI_{MC}(x,y,t) = \sum_{k=1}^{K} -log(p(\tilde{E}_{\hat{n}_k}(x,y,t))), \tag{6}$$

where $p(\hat{E}_{\hat{n}_k}(x,y,t))$ and $p(\tilde{E}_{\hat{n}_k}(x,y,t))$ are the probabilities of seeing certain values of the motion descriptors given their surround, which are estimated by histogram density estimation over all the pixels in the current frame. Note that, SI_M is based on a motion descriptor that is invariant to local luminance contrast. Hence it highlights the regions with motion patterns that are very different from their surround. On the other hand, SI_{MC} is based on a motion descriptor that is confounded by luminance contrast. As a result, it also highlights the regions of high luminance contrast. The overall saliency is a combination of SI_M and SI_{MC}. How to optimally combine saliency maps driven by multiple cues remains an open problem. A widely accepted principle is that salient motion plays a much more significant role than static features (including luminance contrast) in attracting visual attention [4]. Following this principle, we compute the combined saliency as

$$SI_{COM}(x,y,t) = \gamma \cdot SI_M(x,y,t) + (1-\gamma) \cdot SI_{MC}(x,y,t) \cdot SI_M(x,y,t), \tag{7}$$

where SI_M and SI_{MC} are normalized to the range of $[0,1]$, and γ is a free parameter in the range of $[0,1]$. In our implementation, we set $\gamma = 0.5$ empirically. With this combination scheme, if motion saliency exists, SI_M will dominate the overall saliency. Otherwise, if SI_M is largely smooth, SI_{MC} (in this case, primarily driven by luminance contrast) will play a significant role. In our implementation, we also take into account the center bias by combining the saliency map SI_{COM} with a center-bias map CB:

$$A(x,y,t) = SI_{COM}(x,y,t) \cdot CB(x,y), \tag{8}$$

where $CB(x,y) = 1 - d/D$ is a decreasing function of the distance d between the image center and the spatial position (x,y). D is the distance between the center and a corner. Based on this saliency model, an attention-guided motion-tuned temporal distortion measure at each frame t is computed as

$$AG\text{-}MT\text{-}TD(t) = \frac{\sum_{x,y} MT\text{-}TD(x,y,t) \cdot A(x,y,t)}{\sum_{x,y} A(x,y,t)}. \tag{9}$$

With this spatial pooling scheme, the temporal distortions in the highly attentional regions are heavily penalized.

2.3 Overall video quality prediction

It is clear that the human perception of video quality is affected by both temporal and spatial distortions. Therefore, we combine the proposed temporal distortion measure with a spatial distortion measure to give a comprehensive judgment of video quality:

$$D_{overall} = D_{AG\text{-}MT\text{-}TD} \cdot (1 - Q_{MS\text{-}SSIM}), \tag{10}$$

where $D_{AG\text{-}MT\text{-}TD}$ is a temporal distortion measure by temporally pooling the frame-level $AG\text{-}MT\text{-}TD(t)$ scores (see Eq. (9)), and $Q_{MS\text{-}SSIM}$ is a spatial quality measure by temporally pooling the frame-level MS-SSIM [14] scores. Note that a higher MS-SSIM score (always in the range of $[0,1]$) indicates high quality. The MS-SSIM index is selected because it has shown good effectiveness in measuring a variety of spatial distortions as well as high computational efficiency. For temporal pooling, we employ a method similar to the one used in [7] to penalize high temporal variations, which adjusts the mean value of the frame-level quality indices with an additive term that increases with the temporal variations of quality.

3. EXPERIMENTAL RESULTS

There are two commonly used public databases for VQA, namely, the VQEG FRTV Phase 1 database [1] and the LIVE video quality database [10]. The former was published in 2000, and the distortions in its test videos (e.g., MPEG-2 and H.263 compression) are considered to be outdated. The later was published in 2010, which was designed to be a replacement of the VQEG FRTV Phase 1 database. It contains videos compressed by H.264 and MPEG-2, as well as videos obtained by simulated transmission of H.264 compressed streams through error prone IP and wireless networks [10]. Consequently, most of the recent work uses the LIVE database for performance evaluation. We also follow this trend in this paper.

We employ two commonly used metrics, the Spearman's Rank Correlation Coefficient (SRCC) and the Pearson Linear Correlation Coefficient (PLCC), to measure the correlation between the algorithm-supplied and human-supplied quality scores – they measure the prediction monotonicity and prediction accuracy, respectively. The intermediate results are presented in Table 1, where the suffix "(tv)" indicates that the temporal variation of quality is taken into account in temporal pooling. Columns without the suffix use the mean of frame-level quality scores. By comparing the performance of the "TD", "MT-TD" and "AG-MT-TD" methods, we can see that both the motion-tuning scheme and the attention model play very beneficial roles in the proposed method. In addition, the "Proposed (tv)" method achieves considerable performance gain over "AG-MT-TD (tv)" and "MS-SSIM (tv)", which indicates that the two components compliment each other.

We have compared our method with a set of VQA algorithms studied in a recent survey paper [9] and two recent visual attention-guided VQA methods ("VA-You" [15] and "VA-Ma" [5]) in Table 2. In comparison, our method demonstrates remarkable quality-prediction performance. The optical flow-based MOVIE index [8] also achieves impressive results. It is worth mentioning that the MOVIE index does not incorporate a visual attention model and hence its performance may also be improved by exploring visual attention adequately.

We have also analyzed the computation time of our method. It shows that our method implemented in MATLAB took 178 seconds (26 seconds for the $D_{AG\text{-}MT\text{-}TD}$ component and 152 seconds for the $Q_{MS\text{-}SSIM}$ component) to evaluate a 10-second 25 fps 432×768 test video on a Linux machine with an Intel Core i2 CPU (2.33 GHz) and 8 GB memory. In our implementation, the $Q_{MS\text{-}SSIM}$ component was performed at five scales starting from the original scale to four gradually coarser scales, whereas the $D_{AG\text{-}MT\text{-}SD}$ component was performed at a coarse scale (144×256) for higher efficiency (if it was performed at the original scale, it would take about 254 seconds to run and give close prediction performance). Clearly, our method is highly efficient even when compared with the simple frame-by-frame MS-SSIM method. Under the same test condition, the MOVIE index took about 5.88 hours using the C++ code [8] provided by the authors, where a considerable portion of the running time (more than 55%) was purely devoted to the computation of optical flow.

Table 1: Intermediate results: SRCC and PLCC on the LIVE Video Quaity database

Metrics	TD	MT-TD	AG-MT-TD	AG-MT-TD (tv)	MS-SSIM	MS-SSIM (tv)	Proposed (tv)
SRCC	0.7011	0.7432	0.7736	0.7914	0.7367	0.7536	0.8215
PLCC	0.7116	0.7478	0.7777	0.7933	0.7441	0.7647	0.8274

Table 2: Comparative results: SRCC and PLCC on the LIVE Video Quality database.

Metrics	PSNR	SSIM	MS-SSIM	VSNR	SpeedSSIM	VQM	V-VIF	MOVIE	VA-You	VA-Ma	Proposed
SRCC	0.3684	0.5257	0.7367	0.6755	0.5849	0.7026	0.5710	**0.7890**	–	0.7484	**0.8215**
PLCC	0.4035	0.5444	0.7441	0.6896	0.5962	0.7236	0.5756	**0.8116**	0.776	0.7768	**0.8274**

4. CONCLUSION

In this paper, we present a unified and efficient framework for motion-tuned and attention-guided VQA based on a spacetime texture representation of motion. When evaluated on the LIVE video quality database, our method achieves excellent correlation with human perception of video quality. With the exciting success in this initial attempt, we believe spacetime texture can serve as an excellent alternative to the optical-flow methods in the field of VQA, especially in real-time and/or mobile device-based applications that require high computational efficiency. Despite this, spacetime texture as formulated is not a replacement of optical flow for all application domains, e.g., in cases that motion vectors need to (and can) be precisely estimated and that computation overhead is not a major concern. In the future, we will employ the reliable and efficient spacetime texture representation to conduct further analysis of the location (spatial and temporal), intensity and pattern of visual dynamics, which we believe will facilitate the modeling of visual attention and the measurement of several challenging temporal distortions, including stalling, frame freezing, and frame skipping.

5. REFERENCES

[1] VQEG FRTV Phase 1 Database. http://www.its.bldrdoc.gov/vqeg/projects/frtv-phase-i/frtv-phase-i.aspx.

[2] N. Bruce and J. Tsotsos. Saliency, attention, and visual search: An information theoretic approach. *Journal of Vision*, 9(3), 2009.

[3] K. Derpanis and R. Wildes. Spacetime texture representation and recognition based on a spatiotemporal orientation analysis. *IEEE Transactions on Pattern Analysis and Machine Intelligence*, 34(6):1193–1205, 2012.

[4] L. Itti and P. Baldi. A principled approach to detecting surprising events in video. In *IEEE Computer Society Conference on Computer Vision and Pattern Recognition (CVPR)*, volume 1, pages 631–637, 2005.

[5] L. Ma, S. Li, and K. N. Ngan. Motion trajectory based visual saliency for video quality assessment. In *IEEE International Conference on Image Processing (ICIP)*, pages 233–236. IEEE, 2011.

[6] A. Moorthy and A. Bovik. A motion compensated approach to video quality assessment. In *Conference Record of the Forty-Third Asilomar Conference on Signals, Systems and Computers*, pages 872–875. IEEE, 2009.

[7] A. Ninassi, O. Le Meur, P. Le Callet, and D. Barba. Considering temporal variations of spatial visual distortions in video quality assessment. *IEEE Journal of Selected Topics in Signal Processing*, 3(2):253–265, 2009.

[8] K. Seshadrinathan and A. Bovik. Motion tuned spatio-temporal quality assessment of natural videos. *IEEE Transactions on Image Processing*, 19(2):335–350, 2010. Code: http://live.ece.utexas.edu/research/quality/movie.html

[9] K. Seshadrinathan, R. Soundararajan, A. Bovik, and L. Cormack. Study of subjective and objective quality assessment of video. *IEEE Transactions on Image Processing*, 19(6):1427–1441, 2010.

[10] K. Seshadrinathan, R. Soundararajan, A. Bovik, and L. Cormack. A subjective study to evaluate video quality assessment algorithms. In *SPIE Proceedings Human Vision and Electronic Imaging*, volume 7527, 2010.

[11] Z. Wang, A. Bovik, H. Sheikh, and E. Simoncelli. Image quality assessment: From error visibility to structural similarity. *IEEE Transactions on Image Processing*, 13(4):600–612, 2004.

[12] Z. Wang, L. Lu, and A. Bovik. Video quality assessment based on structural distortion measurement. *Signal Processing: Image Communication*, 19(2):121–132, 2004.

[13] Z. Wang and Q. Li. Video quality assessment using a statistical model of human visual speed perception. *J. Opt. Soc. Amer. A*, 24(12):B61–B69, 2007.

[14] Z. Wang, E. Simoncelli, and A. Bovik. Multiscale structural similarity for image quality assessment. In *IEEE Conference Record of the Thirty-Seventh Asilomar Conference on Signals, Systems and Computers*, volume 2, pages 1398–1402, 2003.

[15] J. You, J. Korhonen, and A. Perkis. Attention modeling for video quality assessment: balancing global quality and local quality. In *IEEE International Conference on Multimedia and Expo (ICME)*, pages 914–919. IEEE, 2010.

Fitted Spectral Hashing

Yu Wang[1,2], Sheng Tang[1], Yalin Zhang[1,2], JinTao Li[1], DanYi Chen[3]
[1]Institute of Computing Technology, Chinese Academy of Sciences,Beijing 100190, China
[2]Graduate University of Chinese Academy of Sciences, Beijing 100190, China
[3]School of Information and Communication Engineering, Beijing University of Posts and Telecommunications, Beijing 100081, China
{wangyu, ts, zhangyalin, jtli}@ict.ac.cn, rainachen1216@163.com

ABSTRACT

Spectral hashing (SpH) is an efficient and simple binary hashing method, which assumes that data are sampled from a multidimensional uniform distribution. However, this assumption is too restrictive in practice. In this paper we propose an improved method, Fitted Spectral Hashing, to relax this distribution assumption. Our work is based on the fact that one-dimensional data of any distribution could be mapped to a uniform distribution without changing the local neighbor relations among data items. We have found that this mapping on each PCA direction has certain regular pattern, and could fit data well by S-Curve function, Sigmoid function. With more parameters Fourier function also fit data well. Thus with Sigmoid function and Fourier function, we propose two binary hashing methods. Experiments show that our methods are efficient and outperform state-of-the-art methods.

Categories and Subject Descriptors

H.3.3 [**Information Search and Retrieval**]: Retrieval models

General Terms

Algorithms, Experimentation

Keywords

Spectral hashing, Sigmoid function, Fourier function

1. INTRODUCTION

Similarity search is an essential problem in the field of machine learning, computer vision and information retrieval. However, with increasing amounts of data, similarity search faces following challenges: efficient storing millions of items in memory and quickly finding similar items to a query item. Recent work [1] shows that binary hashing methods are a powerful way to address those challenges:

- The highly compressed binary codes can be loaded into main memory efficiently;
- Searching similar items can be extremely fast with Hamming distances calculated by bit XOR operation: an ordinary PC today would be able to do millions of hamming distance computation in just a few milliseconds .

The basic idea of binary hashing methods is to formulate projections from items to binary codes, so as to approximately preserve a given similarity function of interest [2]. "Good" binary codes should meet the entropy maximizing criterion. According to the information theory [3], the maximal entropy of a source alphabet is attained by having a uniform probability distribution. If the entropy of binary codes over data set is small, it means that data are mapped to only a small number of codes, thus rendering the codes inefficient.

However, many state-of-the-art methods do not meet this criterion. One of the most well-known binary hashing methods is locality sensitive hashing method (E2LSH), which calculates binary codes by projecting data on random vectors with random thresholds, and as shown in [4] the hamming distance between binary codes will asymptotically approach the Euclidean distance between data items. The Kernelized version (KLSH) [5] widens the accessibility of E2LSH to generic normalized kernel functions. Rather than using random vectors, the authors have pursued machine learning approaches, e.g. the restricted Boltzmann method (RBM) [6] and Boosting [7], to accelerate the document and image retrieval.

When data are uniformly distributed in a hyper-rectangle, Spectral hashing (SpH) [8], derived from the spectral graph partitioning problem, meets the entropy maximizing criterion. Bits can be calculated efficiently by the eigenfunctions of the weighted Laplacian defined on R^1. This simple method outperforms above methods. However, the assumption of SpH is too restrictive in practice. Like SpH, Self-Taught Hashing (STH) [1] is also related to the spectral graph partitioning, but uses ration-cut to address the entropy maximizing criterion and applies support vector machine (SVM) to yield hash codes for out-of-sample objects. STH can work with any data distribution, while suffering with high computational cost. The binarized dimensionality reduction technique Latent Semantic Indexing (LSI) [9] and its improved version Laplacian Co-Hashing (LCH) [10] are efficient to get binary codes of documents. Via setting the threshold to the median value of left singular vectors of

MM'13, October 21–25, 2013, Barcelona, Spain.

http://dx.doi.org/10.1145/2502081.2502169.

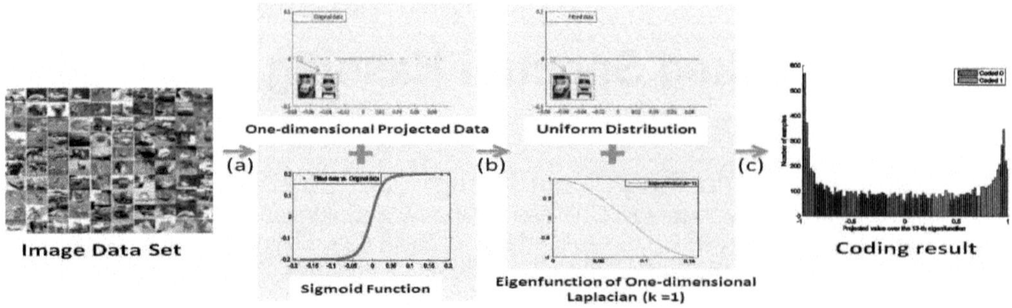

Figure 1: Illustration of using our method to generate one bit binary code for image data set, and the steps are: (a) Project data on one PCA direction; (b) Fit the projected data with Sigmoid function, in order to map one-dimensional data to a uniform distribution; (c) Use eigenfuction ($k = 1$) of one-dimensional Laplacian on uniform distribution to generate binary code.

the whole data matrix, they also meet the entropy maximizing criterion.

In order to relax the restrictive assumption of SpH on data distribution, we propose an improved version Fitted Spectral Hashing as shown in Figure 1. Our work is based on this obvious fact that any distribution of one-dimensional data could be mapped to a uniform distribution without changing the local neighbor relations among them. The main contributions are as follows:

1 We have found that this mapping has certain regular pattern on each PCA direction. It could be well fitted by S-Curve function, Sigmoid function. With more parameters, the Fourier function also fits data well.

2 We integrate Spectral hashing with fitting functions to approximately meet the entropy maximization criterion, and propose two binary hashing methods, Sigmoid Fitting Spectral Hashing (SFSpH) and Fourier Fitting Spectral Hashing (FFSpH).

2. SPECTRAL HASHING

In this section we briefly introduce the related binary hashing method, SpH. The SpH method is derived from the graph partitioning problem. Let $\{y_i\}_{i=1}^n$ be the list of binary codes for n data points $\{x_i\}_{i=1}^n$, and $W_{n\times n}$ be the similar matrix, where $W(i,j) = exp(-\parallel x_i - x_j \parallel^2 / \epsilon^2)$. The average Hamming distance between similar neighbors can be written: $\sum_{i,j} W(i,j) \parallel y_i - y_j \parallel^2$. With the assumption that data point x is sampled from a probability distribution $p(x)$, the SpH problem can be written as:

$$\min \int \parallel y(x_1) - y(x_2) \parallel^2 W(x_1,x_2)p(x_1)p(x_2)dx_1dx_2,$$
$$s.t. \int y(x)p(x)dx = 0, \int y(x)y(x)^T P(x)dx = I$$
$$y_i \in \{-1,1\}^k. \quad (1)$$

Relaxing the constraint that $y_i \in \{-1,1\}^k$ gives a spectral problem, whose solutions are eigenfunctions of the weighted Laplace-Beltrami operators defined on manifold [11]. When $p(x)$ is a separable and multidimensional uniform distribution $Pr(x) = \prod_i u_i(x_i)$, where $u_i(x_i)$ is a one-dimensional uniform distribution on $[a,b]$, the solutions are

$$\phi_k(x) = sin(\frac{\pi}{2} + \frac{k\pi}{b-a}x). \quad (2)$$

$$\lambda_k = 1 - e^{-\frac{\epsilon^2}{2}|\frac{k\pi}{b-a}|^2}. \quad (3)$$

The Eq.2 can be used to code data points $\{x_i\}_{i=1}^n$ directly. However, this simple algorithm has an obvious limitation: it assumes data points are generated from a multidimensional uniform distribution. When dealing with the actual data, we have found that the SpH algorithm can hardly meet the entropy maximizing criterion as shown in Figure 2(b).

3. PROPOSED APPROACH

The fitted SpH uses PCA to align the axes like SpH, but doesn't need the distribution assumption. It is based on this simple fact that any distribution of one-dimensional data could be mapped to a uniform distribution. Therefore, with a uniform distribution the fitted SpH algorithm can approximately meet the entropy maximizing criterion, and corresponding entropies[1] are shown in Figure 2(c) and Figure 2(d). However, there are two questions: (1) Does this mapping change local neighbor relations among data items? (2) Could this fitting model be efficiently computed for out-of-sample objects?

PROPOSITION 3.1. *Let $\{p_i\}_{i=1}^n$ be the projected values of $\{x_i\}_{i=1}^n$ on arbitrary PCA axis, $\{q_i\}_{i=1}^n$ be data, which obey uniform distribution, mapped from $\{p_i\}_{i=1}^n$. After this mapping, we claim that: (1) the entropy of binary coding $\{q_i\}_{i=1}^n$ can be maximized. (2) If the mapped function f is monotonically increasing function, the sequence of $\{p_i\}_{i=1}^n$ could be preserved by $\{q_i\}_{i=1}^n$. (3) The adjacency relationships among data items can be preserved after this mapping.*

PROOF. (1) q obey the uniform distribution on $[a,b]$, and are translated to $[0, b-a]$ without loss. Since $q \in (0, \frac{b-a}{2k})$, $\phi_k(q) > 0$; $q \in (\frac{b-a}{2k}, \frac{b-a}{k})$, $\phi_k(q) < 0$, half of q on uniform distribution could be coded as 1 or 0 by Eq.2 in the range $(0, \frac{b-a}{k})$. Because Eq.2 is a periodic function, the entropy of binary coding $\{q_i\}_{i=1}^n$ in every range $(0+(i-1)\times\frac{b-a}{k}, \frac{b-a}{k} + (i-1)\times\frac{b-a}{k}))$, $i = 1, ..., k$, can be maximized. (2) $f(p_i) = q_i$, when $\{p_i > p_z > \cdots > p_j\}$, because f is monotonically increasing function, then $\{q_i > q_z > \cdots > q_j\}$, the sequence of

[1]Let pr be the probability of one bit be 0, the entropy of pr is: $H(pr) = -prlog_2(pr) - (1-pr)log_2(1-pr)$

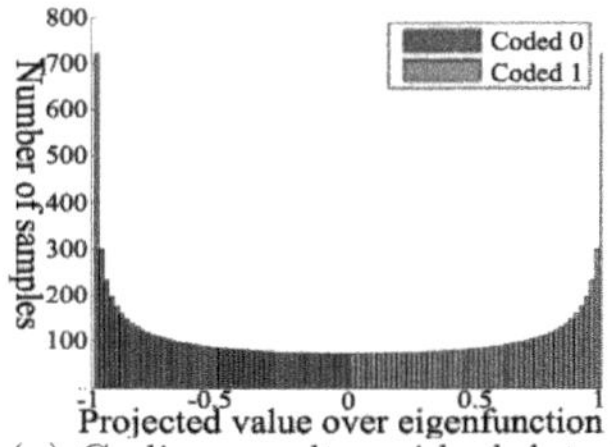

(a) Coding result on ideal data by SpH (Entropy: 1)

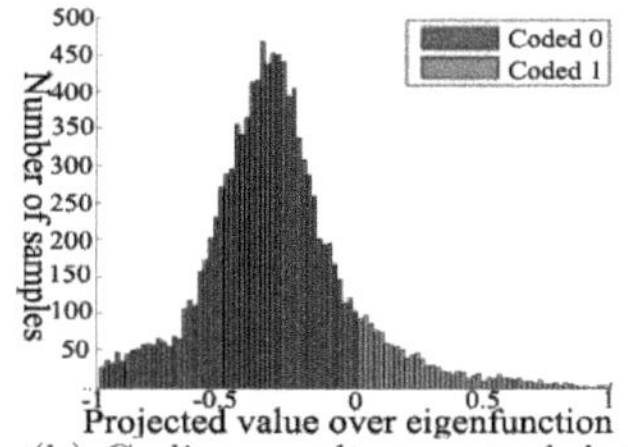

(b) Coding result on actual data by SpH (Entropy: 0.5574)

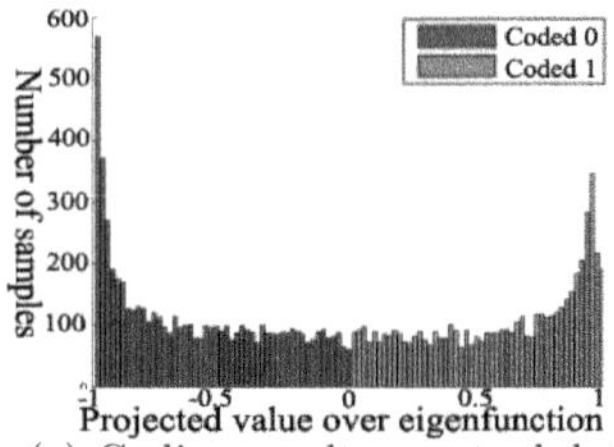

(c) Coding result on actual data by FFSpH (Entropy: 0.9935)

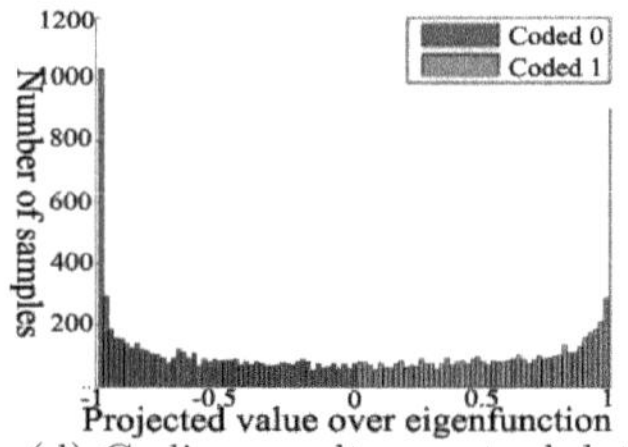

(d) Coding result on actual data by SFSpH (Entropy: 0.9909)

Figure 2: With ideal data(a), which obey uniform distribution, half of the training samples are coded as one or zero by SpH, while (b) is not balanced. (c) and (d) are approximately balanced.

Algorithm 1 Fitted Spectral Hashing

Input: Matrix $X \in R^{n \times m}$, the number of bits k
Output: Binary codes $Y \in R^{n \times k}$, Mode M
Compute eigenvectors and eigenvalues of X^*, $X^* = X' \times X$;
According to the order of eigenvalues, select k eigenvectors $\{V_1, V_2, \dots, V_k\}$ as the PCA axes and save them in M;
for i=1 to k **do**
  Compute projected value p with X and V_i
  Compute f_i using Eq.4 or Eq.5 with p
  Evaluate the k smallest eigenvalues $\{\lambda_1, \lambda_2, \dots, \lambda_k\}$ by Eq.3 with p
  Save f_i, $\{\lambda_1, \lambda_2, \dots, \lambda_k\}$ in M
end for
Select k eigenfunctions $\{\phi_1, \phi_2, \dots, \phi_k\}$ by Eq.2 according to the order of λ in M and save them in M
for j=1 to k **do**
  Find corresponding V_i according to λ_j
  Compute projected value p with X and V_i
  $q = f_i(p)$
  Threshold eigenfunctions $\phi_j(a)$ at zero to obtain binary codes $Y(:, j)$
end for

$\{p_i\}_{i=1}^n$ is preserved by $\{q_i\}_{i=1}^n$ (3) PCA axes are independent from each other, therefore the mapping on one PCA axis doesn't affect others. Because the adjacency relationships on each axis are preserved, the adjacency relationships among data items are preserved. □

For out-of-sample objects, we have found that this mapping could be well fitted by Sigmoid function:

$$f(x) = a_0 \times (1 + e^{(\frac{-(x-a_1)}{a_2})})^{-1} + a_3, \quad (4)$$

where a_0, a_1, a_2 and a_3 are 4 parameters of Sigmoid function. Obviously Eq.4 is monotonically increasing function. It has been observed in the literature [12] that the density projections of large high-dimensional data sets onto a random line generally follows a normal distribution, thus the Cumulative Distribution Function (CDF) function could be used as fitting function. Because Sigmoid function is the commonly used CDF of normal function, thus it can fit data well. For comparison, we also use the Fourier function which can approximate any function:

$$f^*(x) = a_0 + a_1 \times cos(x \times w) + b_1 \times sin(x \times w) + \dots$$
$$+ a_8 \times cos(8 \times x \times w) + b_8 \times sin(8 \times x \times w), \quad (5)$$

where $a_0, w, a_1, \dots, a_8, b_1, \dots, b_8$ are 18 parameters and more parameters ensure the low Sum of Squares due to Error (SSE) of Fourier function. Though with a little higher SSE, the computational cost of Sigmoid function is lower as showed in Experiments. There are many tools available to solve the fitting functions, and CFtool in Matlab is used in this paper.

In Algorithm 1, the cost of eigenvalue decomposition of matrix $X^* \in R^{m \times m}$ is lower than state-of-art methods dealing with $R^{n \times n}$ [1] [9] [10], where m is the dimensionality and n is the number of samples. This Algorithm first learns the fitting function on each selected PCA direction, and then uses Eq.2 to generate the binary codes for one-dimensional uniform data.

4. EXPERIMENTS

In this section, we evaluate the proposed methods and discuss their computational costs. We compare our methods with LSI [9], LCH [10] and STH [1], which are well known binary hash methods and meet the entropy maximization criterion. SpH is used as baseline.

4.1 Data Sets

We choose the well-known tiny image dataset CIFAR-10(60K) and real-world text dataset 20Newsgroups as our experiment data sets. CIFAR-10 contains 60K 32×32 color images of 10 classes and 6K images in each class. We extract 512-D GIST features for each image and use 80% images for training, 20% left for testing. The 20Newsgroups corpus contains 18846 documents distributed across 20 categories. The document dataset has been pre-processed by stopword removal, Poster stemming, and TF-IDF weighting. The time-based split leads to 11314 (60%) documents for training and 7532 (40%) documents for testing.

4.2 Results and Discussions

Retrieval performance: As shown in the Figure 3 the proposed methods give the best results on 20Newsgroup, and top-3 results on CIFAR-10. Our methods use fitting functions to approximately meet entropy maximization criterion and achieve average 60% improvement on 20Newsgroups and average 19% improvement on CIAFR-10 compared with SpH. Compared with other methods [9] [10] [1], the PCA directions, which represent the directions of maximum variance, ensure better retrieval performace.

Our methods, SFSpH and FFSpH, work almost the same on 20Newsgroups. With more parameters, the performance of FFSpH on CIFAR-10 is slightly better than SFSpH's.

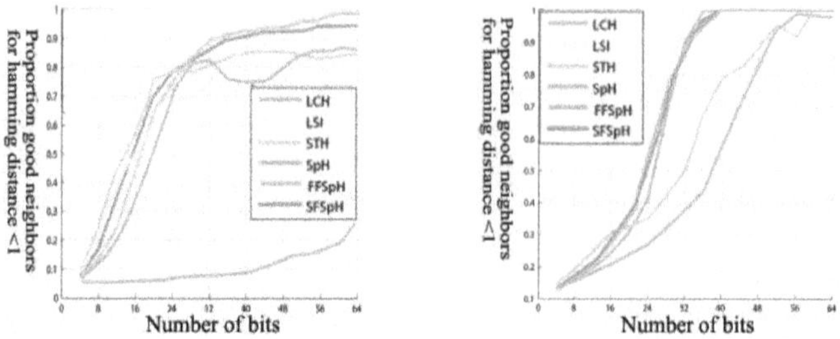

(a) 20Newsgroups (b) CIAFR-10

Figure 3: Comparisons with different methods:(a) Our methods give the best results on 20Newsgroups. (b) Our method give the top-three results on CIAFR-10.

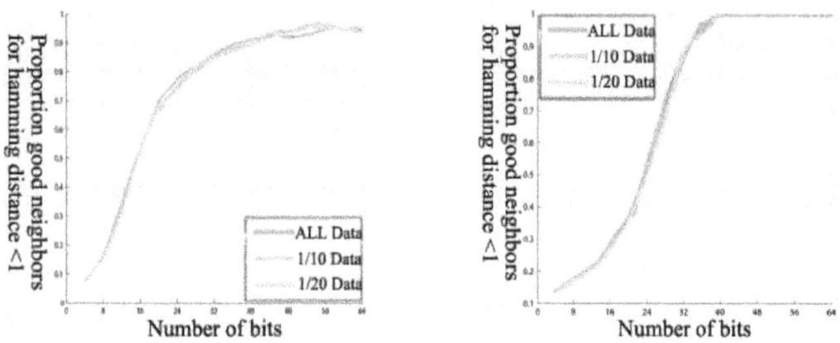

(a) 20Newsgroups (b) CIAFR-10

Figure 4: The performances of SFSpH under different sampling rates are almost as good as using all samples.

Thus we claim that Sigmoid function could fit data well with much less parameters.

Computational cost: As shown in Figure 5 the computational cost of SFSpH is much lower than other methods', only 60% of FFSpH's, 25.3% of LCH's, 25.2% of LSI's and 3% of STH's, while a litter higher than SpH's. Because SpH only needs to calculate the PCA directions, while our methods need extra fitting function computation.

The computational cost of fitting function is relevant with the number of parameters and the scale of samples. The Sigmoid function needs 4 parameters, while Fourier function needs 18 parameters. Therefore the cost of FFSpH is higher than that of SFSpH. Due to the simplicity of Sigmoid function, low sampling rate gives almost as good result as full sampling. The performance comparisons of SFSpH under different sampling rates are shown in Figure 4.

The LCH and LSI need the SVD (singular vectors decomposition) of whole data matrix $R^{n \times n}$ to compute projecting directions, thus the computational complexity is higher than proposed methods with matrix $R^{m \times m}$. The STH method has to construct the spectral graph with complexity of $O(mn^2)$, and compute the eigenvectors of similar matrix $R^{n \times n}$, then train k SVM models to generate binary codes, therefore its cost is the highest.

5. CONCLUSIONS

In this paper, we propose two fitted spectral hashing methods and prove their rationality. The hashing codes of our methods approximately meet the entropy maximizing criterion. Experiments show that these two fitted spectral hashing methods out-perform stat-of-the-art methods. Furthermore, due to the efficiency, we claim that our methods can be efficient to train large data sets with short code lengths.

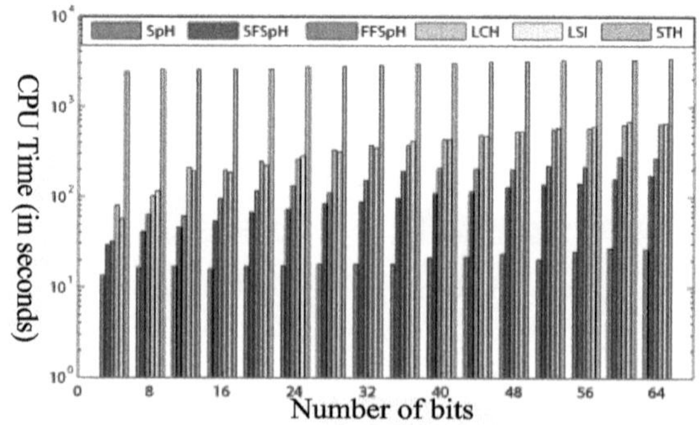

Figure 5: The CPU time comparisons of different methods. Compared with LCH, LSI and STH, which all meet the entropy maximization,the cost of our method is much lower. Though SpH has the lowest cost, it doesn't meet this criterion.

6. ACKNOWLEDGMENTS

This work was supported in part by the National Nature Science Foundation of China (61173054), and the National Key Technology Research and De-velopment Program of China(2012BAH39B02).

7. REFERENCES

[1] D. Zhang, J. Wang, D. Cai, J. Lu, Self-taught hashing for fast similarity search, In ACM SIGIR, 2010.
[2] R. Cipolla, S. Battiato, G. M. Farinella, Machine Learning for Computer Vision, Springer Berlin Heidelberg, 2013.
[3] C. E. Shannon, A mathematical theory of communication, Bell System Technical Journal, 1948.
[4] A. Andoni, P. Indyk, Near-optimal hashing algorithms for approximate nearest neighbor in high dimensions, In FOCS, 2006.
[5] B. Kulis, K. Grauman, Kernelized locality-sensitive hashing, In IEEE PAMI, 2012.
[6] R. Salakhutdinov, G. Hinton, Semantic hashing, In ACM SIGIR, 2007.
[7] A. Torralba, R. Fergus, Y. Weiss, Small codes and large image databases for recognition, In IEEE CVPR, 2008.
[8] Y. Weiss, A. Torralba, R. Fergus, Spectral hashing, Advances in Neural Information Processing Systems, 2009.
[9] S. Deerwester, S. T. Dumais, G. W. Furnas, T. K. Landauer, R. Harshman, Indexing by latent semantic analysis, Journal of the American Society of Information Science, 1990.
[10] D. Zhang, J. Wang, D. Cai, J. Lu, Laplacian co-hashing of terms and documents, In ECIR, 2010.
[11] B. Nadler, S. Lafon, R. R. Coifman, I. G. Kevrekidis, Diffusion maps, spectral clustering and reaction coordinates of dynamical systems, Arxiv, 2008.

Using Emotional Context from Article for Contextual Music Recommendation

Chih-Ming Chen[1], Ming-Feng Tsai[1], Jen-Yu Liu[2], Yi-Hsuan Yang[2]

[1]Department of Computer Science &
Program in Digital Content and Technology
National Chengchi University
Taipei 11605, Taiwan
{g10018, mftsai}@cs.nccu.edu.tw

[2]Research Center for Information
Technology Innovation
Academia Sinica
Taipei 11564, Taiwan
{ciaua, yang}@citi.sinica.edu.tw

ABSTRACT

This paper proposes a context-aware approach that recommends music to a user based on the user's emotional state predicted from the article the user writes. We analyze the association between user-generated text and music by using a real-world dataset with <user, text, music> tripartite information collected from the social blogging website LiveJournal. The audio information represents various perceptual dimensions of music listening, including danceability, loudness, mode, and tempo; the emotional text information consists of bag-of-words and three dimensional affective states within an article: valence, arousal and dominance. To combine these factors for music recommendation, a factorization machine-based approach is taken. Our evaluation shows that the emotional context information mined from user-generated articles does improve the quality of recommendation, comparing to either the collaborative filtering approach or the content-based approach.

Categories and Subject Descriptors

I.m [**Computing Methodologies**]: Miscellaneous

Keywords

Emotion-based music recommendation, Listening context

1. INTRODUCTION

Music usually carries people's emotions, and people sometimes express their feelings by writing articles while listening to music. In light of this obervation, we propose to employ the emotional context information manifested in user-generated articles to build a context-aware music recommendation system. Although emotion has been shown a useful cue for matching songs to documents according to the audio and text content [3], less work has been done on using emotional context features mined from user-generated articles to improve the quality of music recommendation.

MM'13, October 21–25, 2013, Barcelona, Spain.
Copyright 2013 ACM 978-1-4503-2404-5/13/10 ... $15.00.
http://dx.doi.org/10.1145/2502081.2502170.

There have been many studies on contextual recommendation. For example, Jiang *et al.* [8] developed a novel way to represent social networks with multiple relational domains and employed the hybrid random walk techniques to learn the pattern of users' preference. Kailong *et al.* [4] performed tweet recommendations by a collaborative ranking method that captures personal interests. In the KDDCup 2012 competition, Chen *et al.* [5] combined a variety of models by blending different features. Their result shows that adopting more diverse information helps cover more possible targets, suggesting that contextual information could be a good information source for recommendation. Many studies [7, 12, 15, 18] have tried to model the behavior of music listening via various contextual factors such as time, location and weather.

This paper attempts to model the relationship between user-generated text and the music listening behavior. To this end, we adopt factorization machine (FM) [13], an instance of matrix factorization (MF)-based algorithms, as our learning framework for incorporating large number of features extracted from heterogeneous sources, such as audio content features and contextual features extracted from text. The audio features are collected from the EchoNest website (`http://echonest.com/`), including the loudness, mode, and tempo, danceability of music. The text features include *term frequency* and *inverse document frequency*. In addition, the ANEW affective lexicon [2] is also used to generate affective features that characterize the user's emotion state from text. Text information has been shown useful for information filtering [10, 14, 16], but its application to music recommendation is relatively less studied.

The quality of the dataset is important for such a study. Instead of using a dataset collected in a controlled environment, we compile a dataset by crawling LiveJournal (`http://www.livejournal.com/`), a social blog website, as it contains rich contextual information that is entered by users spontaneously in their day-to-day lives [19]. The dataset contains 225,652 listening records from 19,596 users and 30,260 songs. From this dataset, we are able to know which song a user wants to listen to, given an article he or she writes in a real-world context.

We compare the performance of different learning algorithms and different features including CB ones and context-based ones. The result shows that, while the hybrid recommendation approach based on CF+CB performs better than the one using CF-based only, adding contextual emotion features from text further improves the recommendation quality remarkably. The mean average precision (mAP) reaches

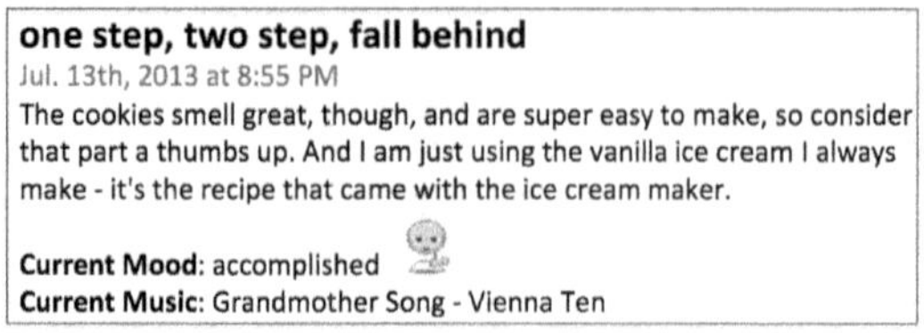

Figure 1: A sample post from LiveJournal.

0.5026, as opposed to 0.0578 for a random baseline, 0.3817 and 0.4708 for CF and CF+CB, respectively.

2. FACTORIZATION MACHINE

Factorization machine is a variant of MF-based methods [13]. Below we briefly describe the main idea of the technique. The FM is generally defined as:

$$\hat{y}(x) = w_0 + \sum_{i=1}^{n} w_i x_i + \sum_{i=1}^{n} \sum_{j=i+1}^{n} \hat{w}_{ij} x_i x_j \,, \qquad (1)$$

where w_0 learns the global bias, w_i learns each weight of features x_i, and $\hat{w}_{ij}$ models the interaction of each pair of features. Instead of using single parameter for each interaction, FM factorizes it as the dot product of two vectors:

$$\hat{w}_{ij} = \sum_{f=1}^{\kappa} v_{if} v_{jf} \,, \qquad (2)$$

where κ is the model complexity. This way allows high-quality parameters estimated by higher-order interactions under sparsity. Note that all features in FM are transferred into indicator variables, which can be incorporated with context information. Unlike the generic MF models, FM not only keeps the information on user-item matrix, but also incorporates the interactions between pairs via various features. With FM, it is possible of modeling contextual information and providing context-aware rating predictions by using factorized interaction parameters. Features can be easily embedded in FM, so our goals is to investigate the effect of different information, including content-based and context-based, on recommendation. For more details of FM, please refer to [13].

3. DATASET AND FEATURES

LiveJournal is a well-known blog website where users can write blogs, or online diaries. The users are able to listen to a song and label a mood tag that reflects his or her emotional state while writing an article, as exemplified in Figure 1. In our experiments, we consider only the users with more than 10 articles. The collected data contains 19,596 users, 225,652 articles, and 30,260 songs. For the experimental settings, we first split the users into two sets according to the following 80/20 rule: we keep the full listening history of the 80% users and the half of listening history for the remaining 20% users as the training data, and the missing half of the remaining 20% users as the test data. Given a set of user's articles and their listening history, we attempt to recommend the songs that the user will listen to.

There are six different features for experiments, including content-based features and context-based features. Below we describe these features in detail.

Table 1: Some examples of the ANEW lexicon

Description	Valence	Arousal	Dominance
dream	6.73	4.53	5.53
eat	7.47	5.69	5.60
good	7.47	5.43	6.41
hate	2.12	6.95	5.05

3.1 Content-based Feature

Content-based features generally refer to the characteristics of a recommended item. Considering the abundant information within music, we use 53 audio features to represent various perceptual dimensions of music, including danceability, loudness, mode, and tempo. They are extracted by using the EchoNest API (`http://developer.echonest.com/`), a commonly used audio feature extraction tool developed in the field of music information retrieval [17].

3.2 Context-based Feature

As for user-generated articles, two features are extracted to describe the user mood — mood tags (MOOD) and VAD. The former considers the mood tags labeled by users directly, whereas the latter tries to infer the emotional states of a user from his/her article, which is easier to obain than mood tags.

To this end, we also evaluate the case when we count the occurrence of terms in an article to characterize the content of the article. Considering that the high dimension of different words of the second feature may incur the so-called "curse of dimensionality" problem, the second feature can be considered as a result of dimension reduction of the word counts. Specifically, we convert the text of articles to an emotional word vector by using the lexicon of Affective Norms for English Words (ANEW) [2], which provides a set of normative emotional ratings for English words. The emotional words are rated by *valence* (or pleasantness; positive/negative affective states), *activation* (or arousal; energy and stimulation level) and *dominance* (or potency; a sense of control or freedom to act), the fundamental emotion dimensions found by psychologists [6]. Table 1 shows some words with their valence, arousal, and dominance ratings in the ANEW lexicon. By representing the affective content of an article in the 3-D space spanned by these emotion dimensions, we are able to obtain a compact yet informative representation of texts.

Specifically, we only leave the words which can be found in the ANEW lexicon. There are totally 2,476 emotional words in ANEW, and there are about 3% of articles discarded, because they have no ANEW words. Each emotional word is weighted by Term-Frequency Inverse-Document-Frequency (TFIDF) measure, which helps enhance the significance of terms with high weight and occurs rarely in the whole corpus.

$$tf(t,d) = \frac{f(w,d)}{\max\{f(w,d) : w \in d\}} \,, \qquad (3)$$

$$idf(t,d) = \log \frac{|D|}{|\{d \in D : t \in d\}|} \,, \qquad (4)$$

where D is the total number of articles. Each term in vector is scored by $tf(t,d) \times idf(t,d)$. After the TFIDF weighting, we can get the Valence, Arousal, and Dominance (VAD) values of an article by a weighted summation of the VAD

Table 2: **The feature sets considered in this work. *Cb* denotes the content-based feature that are extracted from songs, and *Cx* denotes the context-based feature that are extracted from user-generated articles**

Label	Attribute	#Unique Indices	Type
U	User ID	19,596	–
S	Song title	30,260	–
CB	Audio features	53	Cb
MOOD	Mood tag	132	Cx
TFIDF	Words of article	2,476	Cx
VAD	VAD of articles	3	Cx

values of the emotional words occur in the article. For example, for the sentence "*I had a dream last night, I was eating a marshmallow,*" the VAD values are 14.2, 10.22, and 11.13, respectively, according to Table 1. Note that in our experiments all the words are stemmed, and the values are normalized to a scale from 0 to 1. Table 2 summaries all the features used in this work along with their number of unique indices and notations.

4. EXPERIMENTAL RESULTS

In our experiments, two metrics are used for evaluating the recommendation performance: mAP and recall. Although mAP can take all retrieved items into account, we only focus on the top-k result. For each user, let $P(k)$ denotes the precision at cut-off k, in our experiments k is set to 10:

$$AP(u,o) = \frac{\sum_{p=1}^{k} P(k) \times r_{uo(p)}}{I(u)}, \quad (5)$$

where $o(p) = i$ means the item i is ranked at position p in the order list o, and r_{ui} means whether the user u has listened to song i or not$(1 = yes, 0 = no)$. The truncated mean average precision ($mAP@k$) is the mean of the average precision scores:

$$mAP@k = \frac{\sum_{u=1}^{U} AP(u,o)}{U}, \quad (6)$$

where U is the total number of target users. Recall, the fraction of listened songs that are recommended, are calculated as follows:

$$Recall = \frac{|\{Correct\ Songs\}| \cap |\{Returned\ Top\ k\ Songs\}|}{|\{Correct\ Songs\}|}. \quad (7)$$

High recall means that most of the listened songs have been recommended.

4.1 CF-based Recommendation

Our first evaluation focuses on the use of CF information only for music recommendation. We compare FM with the following three famous CF methods:

- **User-based CF** [1]: This method weights all users with respect to their similarity to each other, and selects a subset of users (who are highly similar to the target user) as neighbors. It predicts the rating of specific song based on the neighbors' ratings. Let $S(u)$ be the set of songs that are chosen by the user u. The similarity between user u and user v is calculated by

Table 3: **Evaluation result of CF-based algorithms**

Model	mAP@10	Recall
Randomize	0.0578	0.1656
User-based CF	0.3668	0.4748
Item-based CF	0.3093	0.5115
SVD++	0.3506	0.4844
FM	**0.3817**	**0.5216**

following formula:

$$s_{uv} = \frac{S(u) \cap S(v)}{|S(u)|^{\alpha}|S(v)|^{1-\alpha}}, \quad (8)$$

where $\alpha \in [0, 1]$ is a parameter to tune.

- **Item-based CF** [1]: This method is similar to the user-based CF method. It computes the similarity between songs and scores a song based on user's listening history. The song similarity is calculated as follows:

$$s_{ij} = \frac{U(i) \cap U(j)}{|U(i)|^{\alpha}|U(j)|^{1-\alpha}}, \quad (9)$$

where $U(i)$ the set of the users who have listened to the song i.

- **SVD++** [9]: This method is an extended version of SVD-based latent factor models by integrating implicit feedback into the model. In specific, the prediction formula can be the following:

$$r_{ui} = \mu + b_u + b_i + q_i^T \left(p_u + \frac{1}{\sqrt{|N(u)|}} \times \sum_{j \in N(u)} y_i \right), \quad (10)$$

where $N(u)$ is the set of implicit information, μ is the global mean rating, b_u is a scalar bias for user u, b_i is a scalar bias for item i, p_u is a feature vectors for user u, q_i is a feature vector for item i.

Table 3 lists the preliminary results of mAP@10 and recall. As the table shows, the performance of all the implemented methods, except for the random baseline, appears to be reasonable, achieving about 0.30 to 0.38 in terms of mAP. The item-based approach already gets a good recall in the task, but the FM model generate a more effective recommendation than it. Among the four methods, FM obtains the highest performance, which shows that FM can be a competitive framework for this task. We therefore focus on the use of FM hereafter.

4.2 FM with Content-based Recommendations

Next, we evaluate the performance of content-based recommendation. As the first two rows of Table 4 show, the hybrid CF+CB method (i.e., U + S + CB) outperforms the CF-based one (i.e., U + S) by a great margin. The CF-based approach usually suffers from the so-called "cold start" problem, which occurs when new items and new users are considered. As the experiments show, when the content-based features (i.e., audio information) are added, the quality of recommendation is improved from 0.3817 to 0.4708.

Table 4: Performance of factorization machine with different feature combinations

Features	mAP@10	Recall
U + S	0.3817	0.5216
U + S + CB	0.4708	0.6185
U + S + MOOD	0.4159	0.5628
U + S + TFIDF	0.4212	0.5643
U + S + VAD	0.4483	0.5905
U + S + CB + VAD	0.4901	0.6397
U + S + CB + MOOD + VAD	**0.5026**	**0.6540**

4.3 FM with Content-based and Context-based Recommendations

We evaluate the performance of context-based recommendation by using MOOD and VAD, both represent the users' mood. As shown in the third and fourth row of Table 4, the performance of adding the MOOD feature is improved from 0.3817 to 0.4159 in terms of mAP@10. This result shows that the contextual users' mood information indeed improves the performance of recommendation. With the another contextual VAD feature from user-generated context, the performance is even higher, with the mAP@10 attaining 0.4483. This result implies that the VAD feature provides more emotional information of the user context, which might not be easily captured by mood tags or words only.

Finally, we evaluate the hybrid model that combines the two contextual features and the content-based features (i.e., U + S + CB + MOOD + VAD). As the last row of Table 4 shows, this hybrid model greatly outperforms the content-based method, achieving 0.50 and 0.65 in terms of mAP@10 and recall, respectively. The performance differences between the hybrid model and the CF-based or content-based models are all significant under the two-tailed t-test (p-value< 0.001). On the other hand, we also provide an experimental result that without using the user-provided Mood tags (i.e., U + S+ CB + VAD). By comparing it to purely hybrid CF+CB method, we still see great performance improvement. In sum, the experimental results suggest that the contextual information mined from user-generated articles improves the quality of music recommendation.

5. CONCLUSIONS

In this paper, we have described a music-recommendation approach that combines the listening history and content-based audio information with the contextual emotion information mined from user-generated articles. By using the factorization machine technique, the propose system enhances the quality of music recommendation when evaluating on a real-world dataset. Instead of using simple word counts of the articles the users write as the context feature, we find it more informative to use affective contextual text information. For future work, we plan to use more sophisticated sentimental-analysis techniques, such as Sentimental Latent Dirichlet Association [11], to extract advanced contextual features for music recommendation. We also plan to use the grouping techniques of factorization machine to further improve its optimization process.

6. ACKNOWLEDGMENTS

This work was partially supported by the National Science Council of Taiwan via the grants NSC 100-2218-E-004-001, 101-2221-E-004-017, 102-2221-E-001-004-MY3, and a research grant from KKBOX.

7. REFERENCES

[1] F. Aiolli. A preliminary study of a recommender system for the million songs dataset challenge. In *Proc. ECAI*, 2012.

[2] M. Bradley and P. J. Lang. Affective norms for english words ANEW: Instruction manual and affective ratings. Technical report, The Center for Research in Psychophysiology, Univ. Florida, 1999.

[3] R. Cai et al. MusicSense: contextual music recommendation using emotional allocation modeling. In *Proc. ACM MM*, pages 553–556, 2007.

[4] K. Chen et al. Collaborative personalized tweet recommendation. In *Proc. ACM SIGIR*, pages 661–670, 2012.

[5] T. Chen et al. Combining factorization model and additive forest for collaborative followee recommendation. In *KDD CUP*, 2012.

[6] J. Fontaine et al. The world of emotions is not two-dimensional. *Psychological science*, 18(12):1050, 2007.

[7] M. Jiang, P. Cui, R. Liu, Q. Yang, F. Wang, W. Zhu, and S. Yang. Social contextual recommendation. In *Proc. ACM CIKM*, pages 45–54, 2012.

[8] M. Jiang et al. Social recommendation across multiple relational domains. In *Proc. ACM CIKM*, pages 1422–1431, 2012.

[9] Y. Koren. Collaborative filtering with temporal dynamics. In *Proc. ACM KDD*, pages 447–456, 2009.

[10] M. Levy and M. Sandler. A semantic space for music derived from social tags. In *Proc. ISMIR*, 2007.

[11] F. Li et al. Sentiment analysis with global topics and local dependency. In *Proc. AAAI*, 2010.

[12] H. Ma et al. Probabilistic factor models for web site recommendation. In *Proc. ACM SIGIR*, pages 265–274, 2011.

[13] S. Rendle. Factorization machines with libfm. *ACM Trans. Intelligent Systems and Technology*, 3(3):57:1–57:22, 2012.

[14] M. Schedl, T. Pohle, P. Knees, and G. Widmer. Exploring the music similarity space on the web. *ACM Trans. Information System*, 29(3):14:1–14:24, 2011.

[15] Y. Shi et al. TFMAP: optimizing MAP for top-n context-aware recommendation. In *Proc. ACM SIGIR*, pages 155–164, 2012.

[16] B. Sriram et al. Short text classification in twitter to improve information filtering. In *Proc. ACM SIGIR*, pages 841–842, 2010.

[17] D. Tingle et al. Exploring automatic music annotation with acoustically-objective tags. In *Proc. ACM MIR*, pages 55–62, 2010.

[18] J. Weston, C. Wang, et al. Latent collaborative retrieval. In *Proc. ICML*, pages 9–16, 2012.

[19] Y.-H. Yang and J.-Y. Liu. Quantitative study of music listening behavior in a social and affective context. *IEEE Trans. Multimedia*, 15(6), 2013.

Revisiting the VLAD image representation

Jonathan Delhumeau⋆, Philippe-Henri Gosselin⋆,∘, Hervé Jégou⋆ and Patrick Pérez•
⋆: INRIA Rennes •: Technicolor, Rennes ∘: ETIS, UCP/ENSEA/CNRS, Cergy

ABSTRACT

Recent works on image retrieval have proposed to index images by compact representations encoding powerful local descriptors, such as the closely related vector of aggregated local descriptors (VLAD) and Fisher vector (FV). By combining such a representation with a suitable coding technique, it is possible to encode an image in a few dozen bytes while achieving excellent retrieval results. This paper revisits some assumptions proposed in this context regarding the handling of "visual burstiness", and shows that ad-hoc choices are implicitly done which are not desirable. Focusing on VLAD without loss of generality, we propose to modify several steps of the original design. Albeit simple, these modifications significantly improve VLAD and make it compare favorably against the state of the art.

Categories and Subject Descriptors.
I.4.7.0 Image processing and computer vision

Keywords: image search, multimedia retrieval, VLAD

1. INTRODUCTION

Content-based image retrieval (CBIR) is a historical line of research in Multimedia. It receives a particular attention from this community because images are ubiquitous and a key modality in numerous applications. The problem usually consists in finding the images in a database that are most similar to a query image. In recent years, many solutions have improved the search quality. In particular, a sustained line of research has been initiated by the bag-of-words representation [18, 4] and shown effective to up to million-sized image sets [12]. It consists first in describing an image by a collection of local descriptors such as SIFTs [10], and then in aggregating these into a single vector that collects the statistics of so-called "visual words".

Recently, another step toward further more scalable CBIR was achieved with the VLAD [8, 9] and the Fisher vector [13, 14]. These image representations are also produced from local descriptors, yet they propose an alternative aggregation stage, which replaces bag-of-words histograms. They are both built as the concatenation of sub-vectors (SIFT-like in case of VLAD), one per visual-word. One of their main merits is that they can be reduced to very compact vectors by dimensionality reduction, while preserving high retrieval accuracy. This vector can then be compressed with binary codes [15] or product quantization (PQ) [7], both allowing the efficient search in the compressed domain, thereby reducing the memory requirement by orders of magnitude.

This paper shows that VLAD (likewise FV) makes undesirable assumptions that yield suboptimal results. This leads us to modify VLAD at two levels of the original design: The per-word aggregation step and the vector rotation prior to component-wise application of power law.

Firstly, the local descriptors of a given image do not contribute equally to the original VLAD representation. This is due to the encoding scheme, which accumulates residual vectors (vector difference between local descriptors and visual words) of arbitrary norms. It was argued [9] that this effect naturally down-weights the most common descriptors, which are closer to the centroids. In contrast, we show that it is not desirable: Enforcing equal norms for the residual vectors provides better results, which constitutes our first beneficial modification to VLAD.

Secondly, we consider the power-law normalization [14] that is applied to VLAD component-wise. The improvement provided by this post-processing in VLAD and FV is usually explained by its effect on the "visual bursts" [5], *i.e.*, the patterns that may massively recur in an image, like in repetitive structures, corrupting the comparison metric. However, power-law normalization is obviously not invariant by rotation and thus depends on the coordinate system in which VLAD's sub-vectors live. In [9], these blocks are rotated from natural SIFT coordinate system, which is arbitrary from the burstiness point of view, to a common pre-learned coordinate system. We propose a more elaborate way to optimize the basis so that it better captures the bursts on some components, thereby magnifying the positive effect of power-law normalization on accuracy.

This paper is organized as follows. Section 2 briefly reviews VLAD, while Section 3 presents our evaluation protocol. Section 4 describes our revisited VLAD, which is experimentally validated in Section 5 with comparisons to both original design and other state-of-art representations. Our experiments are performed on the popular Oxford5k [16] and INRIA Holidays benchmarks, as well as on an image set comprising 1 million images.

2. ORIGINAL VLAD PIPELINE

The vector of locally aggregated descriptors (VLAD) [8] is an encoding technique that produces a fixed-length vector representation $\boldsymbol{v}$ from a set $\mathcal{X} = \{\mathbf{x}_1, \ldots, \mathbf{x}_n\}$ of n local d-dimensional descriptors, *e.g.*, SIFTs, extracted from a given image. Similar to bag-of-word, a visual dictionary

MM'13, October 21–25, 2013, Barcelona, Spain.

http://dx.doi.org/10.1145/2502081.2502171.

$\mathcal{C} = \{\mu_1, \ldots, \mu_k\}$ is learned off-line. It is formally used as a quantization function assigning any input local descriptors to its closest centroid (visual word) as

$$q : \mathbb{R}^d \to \mathcal{C} \subset \mathbb{R}^d \quad (1)$$

$$\mathbf{x} \mapsto q(\mathbf{x}) = \arg\min_{\mu \in \mathcal{C}} \|\mathbf{x} - \mu\|^2, \quad (2)$$

where the norm operator $\|.\|$ refers to the L_2 norm.

Aggregation. The VLAD departs from bag-of-words on how this visual dictionary is used. For each quantization index $i \in [1, \ldots, k]$, a d-dimensional sub-vector $\boldsymbol{v}^i$ is obtained by accumulating the *residual vectors*, *i.e.*, the difference between the descriptor and the centroid it is assigned to:

$$\boldsymbol{v}^i = \sum_{\mathbf{x}:q(\mathbf{x})=\mu_i} \mathbf{x} - \mu_i. \quad (3)$$

The concatenation $\boldsymbol{v} = [\boldsymbol{v}^1 \ldots \boldsymbol{v}^k]$ is a D-dimensional vector, where $D = k \times d$.

Normalization. The VLAD is then obtained by applying two normalization stages. First, a component-wise non-linearity operation is applied: Each component v_j, $j = 1$ to D, is modified as $v_j := |v_j|^\alpha \times \text{sign}(v_j)$, where the quantity α is a parameter such that $\alpha \leq 1$. It's the "power-law normalization" [14], which is motivated in [9] by the presence of bursts in natural images [5]. The VLAD vector is finally L_2-normalized as $\boldsymbol{v} := \frac{\boldsymbol{v}}{\|\boldsymbol{v}\|}$.

SIFT processing. Prior to aggregation, it is optionally proposed in [8] to project all local descriptors of the image on the 64 first principal directions of a Principal Component Analysis (PCA) basis learned off-line.

Compact codes. The VLAD memory footprint is significantly reduced by performing a jointly optimized succession of dimension reduction [8, 9] and compression with product quantization [7]:

- The dimensionality of VLAD is reduced to $D' < D$ components by PCA, which is typically computed with the Gram dual method. See, for instance, [3] (paragraph 12.1.4).
- After a random rotation that balances the components of reduced vector, product quantization splits it into m sub-vectors, which are separately vector quantized with a k-means quantizer. This compression scheme allows the computation of distances between a query and a set of vectors in the compressed domain. It does not require the explicit decompression of the database vectors and is therefore very fast, see [7] for details.

The choice of D' and m is tuned thanks to an optimization procedure [7] that solely relies on a reconstruction criterion.

3. EVALUATION PROTOCOL

In order to evaluate our work, we adopt some datasets and corresponding evaluation protocols that are usually considered in this context.

Local descriptors. They have been extracted with the Hessian-affine detector [11] and described by SIFT [10]. We use the RootSIFT variant [1], in all our experiments. As for SIFT, RootSIFT descriptors are normalized w.r.t. L_2 norm. We also report some results with a dense detector. This choice is common in classification [14] but usually not considered for large-scale image retrieval.

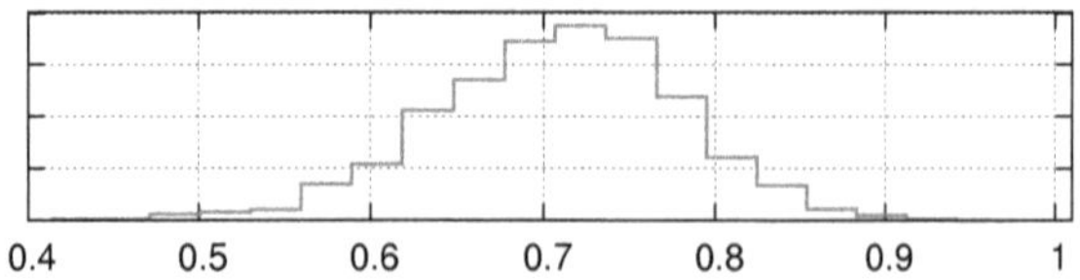

Figure 1: Norm's distribution of residual vectors in the VLAD of an image: because of the subtraction $\mathbf{x} - q(\mathbf{x})$, the contribution of individual descriptors in VLAD is uneven.

Oxford building datasets. *Oxford5k* dataset [16] consists of 5062 images of buildings and 55 query images corresponding to 11 distinct buildings in Oxford. The search quality is measured by the mean average precision (mAP) computed over the 55 queries. Images are annotated as either relevant, not relevant, or *junk*, which indicates that it is unclear whether a user would consider the image as relevant or not. These *junk* images are removed from the ranking before computing the mAP.

The *Oxford105k* dataset [16] is the combination of Oxford5k with a set of 100k negative images, in order to evaluate the search quality on a large scale.

The *Paris6k* dataset [17] consists of 6412 images collected from Flickr by searching for particular Paris landmarks. As standardly done in the literature, it is used for unsupervised learning of the parameters when evaluating the results on Oxford5k and Oxford105k.

INRIA Holidays and Flickr. INRIA Holidays [6] is a dataset comprising 1491 high resolution personal photos of different locations and objects, 500 of them being used as queries. The search quality is measured by mAP, with the query removed from the ranked list. To determine the parameters, we have used the independent dataset Flickr60K provided with Holidays. Large scale evaluation is performed by adding 1 million images collected from Flickr referred to as Flickr1M and used in [6] for large scale evaluation.

Parameters. For the power-law normalization, we will only consider two values: $\alpha = 1$ for no power-law normalization and $\alpha = 0.2$. This last choice is reasonable and often close to optimum for the regular VLAD. We fix it to ensure a fair comparison between the methods.

4. IMPROVING VLAD

This section introduces two complementary techniques that jointly improve the VLAD representation by re-visiting some choices which are implicitly done in the initial design.

4.1 Residual normalization (RN)

The standard VLAD method sums up all residuals to shape the final representation (Eq. 3). Although the SIFT descriptors are L_2-normalized, it is not the case of the residual vectors, whose norm varies significantly, as shown in Figure 1 for a representative image. As a result, the individual local descriptors contribute unequally to the VLAD representation. This fact was underlined by the authors of VLAD [9], who argue that it provides some sort of natural *inverse document frequency*, but without evaluating its actual merit. As we will demonstrate later in our experiments, this is not a desirable behavior. More specifically, we propose to normalize the residuals so that all descriptors

	PCA steps ↓	mAP on Holidays $\alpha = 1$	$\alpha = 0.2$
VLAD results with regular SIFT [9]			
VLAD	-	51.8	54.9
VLAD	C	51.8	54.0
VLAD	C,R	51.9	57.5
VLAD	C,R,D (64)	52.2	54.4
VLAD results with RootSIFT			
VLAD	-	53.9	57.3
VLAD	C,R	55.0	62.2
Impact of our method: RN and LCS			
VLAD+RN	C,R in LCS	54.3	63.1
VLAD+LCS	C,R in LCS	55.0	65.0
VLAD+LCS+RN	C,R in LCS	54.3	**65.8**

Table 1: From standard VLAD to its new version. (Top part): impact of (C)entering, (R)otation and (D)imensionality reduction by a factor 2 of regular SIFTs in original VLAD; (Middle part): impact of trading regular SIFT for RootSIFT; (Bottom part): impact of the two proposed modifications, RN and LCS. The dictionary size is $k = 64$ in all experiments.

contribute equally (at least at this stage) to the summation. This amounts to changing (3) as

$$\tilde{v}^i = \sum_{\mathbf{x}:q(\mathbf{x})=\boldsymbol{\mu}_i} \frac{\mathbf{x} - \boldsymbol{\mu}_i}{\|\mathbf{x} - \boldsymbol{\mu}_i\|}. \quad (4)$$

Note that the denominator is always greater than 0, because the SIFT descriptors lie on the unit sphere, while the centroids in $\mathcal{C}$ have norms strictly lower than 1.

Table 1 shows the interest of this modification. For the sake of comparison, we report the results both with regular SIFT (as results reported so far on VLAD and FV) and with RootSIFT, which already gives an improvement at no cost. Our discussion focuses on the relative improvement.

First, observe that the residual normalization (RN) tends to decrease the performance when $\alpha = 1$, *i.e.*, when no specific treatment is done to handle the bursts. Our interpretation is that descriptors coming into bursts are, on average, closer to their centroids, thus yielding lower normed residuals. However, one should not conclude that this implicit down-weighting of bursty patterns is beneficial: indeed, the power-law ($\alpha = 0.2$) appears as a better way to handle burstiness. When using it, RN consistently improves the results by almost 1 point of mAP at no cost. This suggests that all descriptors should equally contribute in the first place, while bursts are handled only by subsequent application of the power-law normalization. This is the first main modification we apply to original VLAD.

4.2 Local coordinate system (LCS)

Preliminary analysis of SIFT processing. It was shown that performing a PCA of SIFT descriptors improves Fisher and VLAD [9]. This processing actually encompasses three distinct operations: centering (C), rotation with PCA basis (R) and dimensionality reduction by a factor of 2 (D).

In present work, using RootSIFTs instead of such transformed SIFTs already yields a performance gain, achieving mAP=53.9 for $\alpha = 1$ and 57.3 for $\alpha = 0.2$ (Table 1). Nonetheless, in an attempt to get better insight into the original processing of regular SIFTs, we progressively incorporated the three above mentioned steps C, R and D (first part of Table 1) and made the following observations:

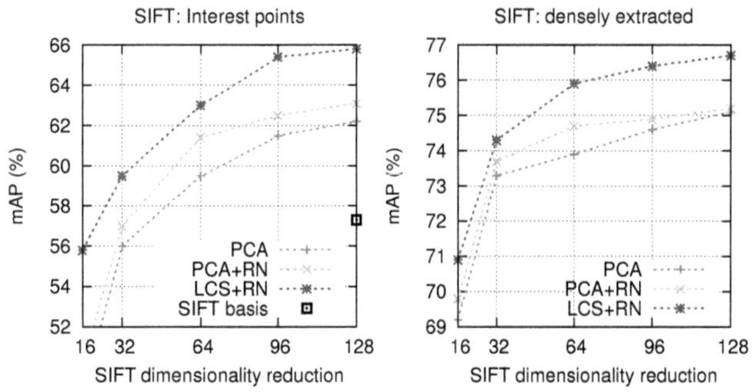

Figure 2: Performance on Holidays as a function of dimension reduction for RootSIFT descriptors (extracted from interest points or from a dense grid with 3 pixels shifts), using shared PCA (red), shared PCA and RN (green), LCS and RN (blue). Baseline is with no change on descriptors (black box). Parameters: $k = 64$ and $\alpha = 0.2$.

- For $\alpha = 1$, PCA rotation (R) has virtually no effect, which is to be expected: in the absence of power-law, this change of descriptor coordinate system has no impact on similarity measures between resulting VLADs.
- However, power-law normalization ($\alpha < 1$) introduces a subsequent non-linearity that makes final pipeline dependent on the basis. Using the basis obtained by PCA (on the Flickr60K dataset) gives a large improvement.
- Combined with power-law, dimension reduction (D) from 128 to 64 components decreases the performance (from mAP=63.1 to 61.4).

Therefore, it appears that it is not the dimensionality reduction that improves the results. On the contrary it is harmful, as also shown in Figure 2. The fundamental reason why PCA-based processing of local descriptors improves VLAD lies in its interplay with power-law normalization. In other terms, the impact of the power-law normalization (*e.g.*, for $\alpha = 0.2$) is magnified by a proper choice of the basis in which it is performed. This observation suggests to define a new and even better basis for building VLAD.

Proposed LCS. Our interpretation for PCA being a beneficial processing of SIFTs in conjunction with power-law normalization is that the first eigenvectors capture the main bursty patterns. However, this is so far a global operation applied to the whole descriptor space. It is therefore not likely to capture a large variety of bursty patterns. We argue that a better handling of burstiness should be achieved by adapting independently the coordinate system for each visual word. This is simply obtained by learning a "local" PCA per Voronoi cell of the partitioned feature space.

More precisely, for i-th visual word, $i = 1 \dots k$, we learn off-line (*e.g.*, on Flickr60K for Holidays) a rotation matrix $\mathbf{Q}_i$ from training descriptors mapped to this word. The k rotation matrices are then applied to the normalized residual vectors (or residual vectors if RN is not used) before their aggregation into VLAD. Equation 4 is thus replaced by

$$\tilde{v}^i = \sum_{\mathbf{x}:q(\mathbf{x})=\boldsymbol{\mu}_i} \mathbf{Q}_i \frac{\mathbf{x} - \boldsymbol{\mu}_i}{\|\mathbf{x} - \boldsymbol{\mu}_i\|}. \quad (5)$$

Table 1 and Figure 2 show that this new LCS method, when combined with power-law, significantly improves the results. Also, it is complementary with proposed RN vari-

Method	Size	Oxford5k	Oxford105k	Holidays
BoW [9]	20k	35.4	-	43.7
BoW [9]	200k	-	-	54.0
VLAD [9]	8192	37.8	-	55.6
Fisher [9]	8192	41.8	-	60.5
$VLAD_{Intra}$ [2]	8192	44.8	-	56.5
VLAD*	8192	50.0	44.5	62.2
LCS+RN	8192	**51.7**	**45.6**	**65.8**

Table 2: Comparison of proposed image representation with state of the art (mAP performance).

ant. The results are reported as a function of the dimensionality reduction in Figure 2 (blue curve), which clearly shows the improvement of our technique compared with original shared PCA (red curve) and with no PCA (black box).

5. COMPARISON TO STATE OF THE ART

The results presented in Table 1 and Figure 2 have shown the relative improvement provided by the residual normalization (RN) and by LCS on the INRIA Holidays benchmark. The relative gain is about +4% with respect to using only our SIFT processing (RootSIFT, (C) and (R)) and of +10% compared with the initial VLAD [9]. In this section, we provide a comparison with the state of the art and report our performance on other, larger datasets, namely the Oxford5k, Oxford105k and Holidays merged with 1 million images from Flickr. We use $k = 64$ in all experiments for the sake of consistency. We use the same SIFT descriptors as in [9] for a fair comparison.

Performance of the proposed methods - full vectors. Table 2 compares our technique with the results of the literature [9, 2], which includes different vector representations, in particular VLAD and FV, and a bag-of-words baseline. The improved VLAD obtained by our processing of SIFTs (RootSIFT, (C) and (R)) is referred to as VLAD* in order to demonstrate the own merits of the methods proposed in Section 4. As one can see from this table, the improvement provided by VLAD* is very large and further improved by LCS+RN, leading to outperform the best baseline by about 10% on Oxford5k and +5% on Holidays. We also compare our method to the intra-cell VLAD normalization recently proposed in [2] as a replacement for the power-law. In our experiments, this $VLAD_{Intra}$ variant is better than VLAD but not as good as the power-law when the input vectors are rotated by PCA. Our scheme significantly outperforms this choice in a similar setup. Note that we have not used multiple vocabularies in any of these comparisons.

Performance with projected and coded representations. Table 3 shows that the relative improvement of our technique is comparatively reduced when applying dimensionality reduction and using compact codes obtained by product quantization [7]. The gain remains very significant on the largest Holidays+Flickr1M dataset after dimensionality reduction, but not on Oxford105k. Overall, one should observe that compressing the data tends to reduce the gap between the different methods.

Dense. We also carried out experiments but with dense SIFT descriptors, reported in Fig. 2 (right). For better readability, we do not report in this case the result with no rotation of local descriptors (65.8%). As one can see, the same conclusions can be drawn when using dense or non-dense SIFT descriptors. One should note the very large improvement provided by dense descriptors.

Method	size	Oxf5k	Oxf105k	Hol.+Flickr1M
After final dimensionality reduction to D'=96/128 components				
VLAD [9]	D'=128	28.7		
FV [9]	D'=96	-	-	31.8
FV [9]	D'=128	30.1	-	-
VLAD*	D'=128	**32.5**	**26.6**	33.5
LCS+RN	D'=128	32.2	26.2	**39.2**
Encoded into compact codes with product quantization [7]				
FV [9]	16 bytes	-	-	28.7
VLAD*	16 bytes	28.9	**22.2**	29.9
LCS+RN	16 bytes	27.0	21.0	**32.3**

Table 3: Large scale comparison of compacted and encoded image representations (k =64).

6. CONCLUSION

This paper has analyzed the VLAD representation, and shows that it leads to sub-optimal results due to some undesirable properties: The descriptors do not contribute equally and the coordinate system used to apply the power-law normalization is arbitrary. We proposed two simple solutions to address these problems, at no cost. As a byproduct of our analysis, we have given some insight on the impact of the different steps of PCA on the accuracy.

Acknowledgments. J. Delhumeau supported by the Quaero project (Oseo/French Agency for Innovation), H. Jégou and P-H Gosselin supported by the FIRE-ID project (ANR-12-CORD-0016) and P. Pérez by the AXES project (FP7).

7. REFERENCES

[1] R. Arandjelovic and A. Zisserman. Three things everyone should know to improve object retrieval. In *CVPR*, Jun. 2012.
[2] R. Arandjelovic and A. Zisserman. All about VLAD. In *CVPR*, Jun. 2013.
[3] C. M. Bishop. *Pattern Recognition and Machine Learning*. Springer, 2007.
[4] G. Csurka, C. Dance, L. Fan, J. Willamowski, and C. Bray. Visual categorization with bags of keypoints. In *ECCV Workshop Statistical Learning in Computer Vision*, 2004.
[5] H. Jégou, M. Douze, and C. Schmid. On the burstiness of visual elements. In *CVPR*, Jun. 2009.
[6] H. Jégou, M. Douze, and C. Schmid. Improving bag-of-features for large scale image search. *IJCV*, 87(3):316–336, Feb. 2010.
[7] H. Jégou, M. Douze, and C. Schmid. Product quantization for nearest neighbor search. *Trans. PAMI*, 33(1):117–128, Jan. 2011.
[8] H. Jégou, M. Douze, C. Schmid, and P. Pérez. Aggregating local descriptors into a compact image representation. In *CVPR*, Jun. 2010.
[9] H. Jégou, F. Perronnin, M. Douze, J. Sánchez, P. Pérez, and C. Schmid. Aggregating local descriptors into compact codes. In *Trans. PAMI*, 34(9):1704–1714, Sep. 2012.
[10] D. Lowe. Distinctive image features from scale-invariant keypoints. *IJCV*, 60(2):91–110, Nov. 2004.
[11] K. Mikolajczyk and C. Schmid. Scale and affine invariant interest point detectors. *IJCV*, 60(1):63–86, Oct. 2004.
[12] D. Nistér and H. Stewénius. Scalable recognition with a vocabulary tree. In *CVPR*, Jun. 2006.
[13] F. Perronnin and C. R. Dance. Fisher kernels on visual vocabularies for image categorization. In *CVPR*, Jun. 2007.
[14] F. Perronnin, J.Sánchez, and T. Mensink. Improving the Fisher kernel for large-scale image classification. In *ECCV*, Sep. 2010.
[15] F. Perronnin, Y. Liu, J. Sanchez, and H. Poirier. Large-scale image retrieval with compressed Fisher vectors. In *CVPR*, Jun. 2010.
[16] J. Philbin, O. Chum, M. Isard, J. Sivic, and A. Zisserman. Object retrieval with large vocabularies and fast spatial matching. In *CVPR*, Jun. 2007.
[17] J. Philbin, O. Chum, M. Isard, J. Sivic, and A. Zisserman. Lost in quantization: Improving particular object retrieval in large scale image databases. In *CVPR*, Jun. 2008.
[18] J. Sivic and A. Zisserman. Video Google: A text retrieval approach to object matching in videos. In *ICCV*, Oct. 2003.

Human Behavior Sensing for Tag Relevance Assessment

Mohammad Soleymani
Dept. of Computing
Imperial College London, UK
m.soleymani@imperial.ac.uk

Sebastian Kaltwang
Dept. of Computing
Imperial College London, UK
sk2608@imperial.ac.uk

Maja Pantic
Dept. of Computing/ EEMCS
Imperial College London, UK/
Univ. Twente, Netherlands
m.pantic@imperial.ac.uk

ABSTRACT

Users react differently to non-relevant and relevant tags associated with content. These spontaneous reactions can be used for labeling large multimedia databases. We present a method to assess tag relevance to images using the non-verbal bodily responses, namely, electroencephalogram (EEG), facial expressions, and eye gaze. We conducted experiments in which 28 images were shown to 28 subjects once with correct and another time with incorrect tags. The goal of our system is to detect the responses to non-relevant tags and consequently filter them out. Therefore, we trained classifiers to detect the tag relevance from bodily responses. We evaluated the performance of our system using a subject independent approach. The precision at top 5% and top 10% detections were calculated and results of different modalities and different classifiers were compared. The results show that eye gaze outperforms the other modalities in tag relevance detection both overall and for top ranked results.

Categories and Subject Descriptors

H3.3 [**Information Search and Retrieval**]: Information filtering, Selection process

Keywords

implicit tagging, eye gaze, EEG, facial expressions

1. INTRODUCTION

We are witnessing a rapid growth in the number of images and videos captured by users. The proliferation of handheld devices with built-in cameras is the main contributor of this rapid growth. This rapidly growing content is in need of effective indexing to be browsable and reusable. Tags are any form of metadata that can be used to index multimedia content to facilitate its finding and re-finding. In contrast to classic tagging schemes where the users' direct input is mandatory, human-centered implicit tagging was proposed [9] to gather tags and annotations without any effort from users. The main idea behind this passive tagging strategy is to use users' spontaneous reactions to a given content to identify tags. The resulting tags are called "implicit" since there is no need for users' direct input, and reactions to multimedia are displayed spontaneously [9].

MM'13, October 21–25, 2013, Barcelona, Spain.
Copyright 2013 ACM 978-1-4503-2404-5/13/10 ...$15.00.
http://dx.doi.org/10.1145/2502081.2502172.

Implicit tagging has recently attracted attention of the research community [13]. Implicit tagging has been used for image annotation, video highlight detection, topical relevance detection and retrieval result re-ranking. The existing literature can be divided into two categories, one dealing with using emotional reactions to tag the content with the expressed emotion, e.g., laughter detection for hilarity [10], and the second group of studies using the spontaneous reactions for information retrieval or search results, e.g., eye gaze for relevance feedback [4].

Users respond differently to the expected (i.e. relevant) and mismatching (i.e. non-relevant) tags. Koelstra et al. [6] found significant differences between N400 Evoked Related Potential (ERP) in Electroencephalogram responses between relevant and non-relevant tags displayed on short videos. Facial expression and eye gaze were used to detect users' agreement or disagreement with the displayed tags on images [5, 12]. The results showed that not all the subjects in the experiment were expressing their agreement or disagreement on their faces and their eye gaze were more informative for agreement assessment. Eye gaze responses have been also used to detect interest for image annotation [3], relevance judgment [11], interactive video search [16], and search personalization [1].

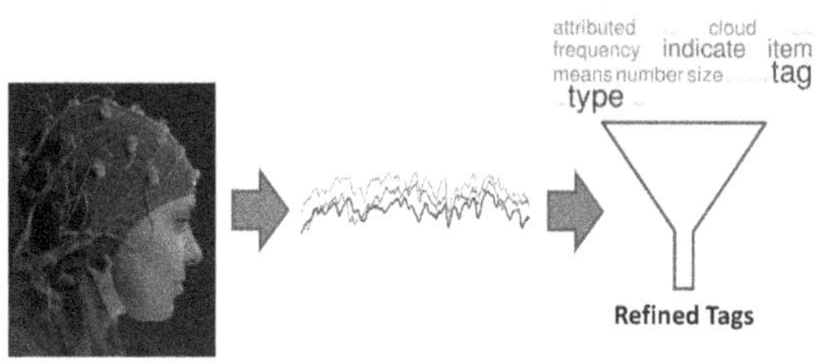

Figure 1: In our implicit tagging scenario, the information sensed from different sensors can be used to refine a set of tags assigned to images.

We propose a tag relevance assessment method to detect users' agreement with the displayed tag with a given content, i.e., images. Such a system can be used to filter out non-relevant tags from a noisy set of tags. Tags that are detected by an imperfect content based tagging system or user generated tags often contain non-relevant tags which are incorrectly assigned to content. In our proposed method, by sensing the non-verbal behavioral response of a user, our system will be able to better identify the non-relevant tags and discard them. We studied the performance of a multimodal approach using three different modalities: EEG, facial expressions and eye gaze. A schematic representation of our proposed method is shown in Figure 1.

2. APPARATUS AND DATA COLLECTION

The experimental data was collected from 28 healthy volunteers, comprising 12 male and 16 female between 19 to 40 years old. The subjects had normal or corrected to normal vision. The eye gaze response was collected at 60 Hz using a Tobii X120 Eye gaze tracker[1]. The experiment was controlled by the Tobii studio software. EEG signals were recorded from 32 active electrodes on 10-20 international system using a Biosemi Active II system. The frontal facial video was captured using an Allied Vision Stingray F-046B monochrome camera with the resolution of 780×580 pixels at 60 frames per second. The experiments were conducted in a room with controlled temperature and illumination. The synchronization method, hardware setup and the database details are given in [12]. MAHNOB-HCI is a publicly available database for multimedia implicit tagging[2].

During the experiment, 28 images depicting human actions (e.g. handshake) were subsequently shown on their own and accompanied by a word tag that is either relevant or non-relevant to the shown action. Images were downloaded from Flickr[3] and were cropped and resized to 1280×695 pixels to be displayed on a display size of $51.9 \times 32.45cm$ with a resolution of 1280×800 pixels. The space under and above the image was filled with black pixels. The tags were overlaid under the image (see Figure 2). For each image a correct and an incorrect tag was displayed in the total of 54 trials in random order. For each trial, the following procedure was taken. First, the untagged images were displayed for 5 seconds. This allowed the subject to get to know the content of the image. Second, the same image was displayed with a tag for 5 seconds. The subjects' behavior in this period contained their reaction to the displayed tag. Third, a question was displayed on the screen to ask whether the subject agreed with the suggested tag. Agreement or disagreement was expressed by pressing a green button for relevance or a red button for non-relevance feedback, respectively. The length of each trial was about 11 seconds. In this study, the trials in which the subjects' responses contradict the true tag relevance were discarded as confusing examples, e.g., a trial in which a subject agreed with a non-relevant tag was discarded.

3. DATA ANALYSIS

3.1 Analysis of Eye Gaze

A set of features is extracted from the different signals provided by the eye gaze tracker. These signals include gaze fixation, pupil dilation, scan path and eye gaze coordinates. Gaze fixations are the coordinates of the points on the display on which the eye gaze stayed fixed for a certain period of time. Each fixation is composed of its duration as well as the two-dimensional coordinates of the projection of the eye gaze on the screen. An example of an eye gaze pattern and fixation points on an image is shown in Figure 2. The scan path is the eye gaze trajectory in transition from one fixation to another. The image zone and the tag zone were defined on the screen based on the way the images were positioned on the display and the image size, which was constant. The features extracted from eye gaze are listed in Table 1.

Figure 2: Example image depicting a human action including a relevant tag ('Sit Down') as shown to the subjects. Part of the recorded eye gaze fixation and scan path of one subject is overlaid in red.

Table 1: List of 26 features extracted from eye gaze data for implicit tagging. The number of features extracted from each signal is indicated in brackets. Average (avg.) and standard deviation (std.) are abbreviated.

Signal	Extracted features
Pupil (2)	Avg. and std. of the dilation
Eye blink (2)	Avg. blink duration and blinking rate
Distance (1)	Range of viewer's distance to the screen
Scanpath (5)	Number of transitions between the tag zone and the image zone, avg. scan path length, std. of the scan path length, total length of the scan path
Saccades (2)	Avg. of standard deviations of eye gaze movements during each fixation period in horizontal and vertical axis
Fixation (6)	Avg. fixation duration in the tag zone, avg. fixation duration in the image zone, max. of the fixation duration in the tag zone, max. of the fixation duration in the image zone, number of fixations in the tag zone divided by the number of fixations in the image zone and number of fixations in the tag zone
Eye gaze (8)	Avg., std., skewness and kurtosis of horizontal and vertical gaze coordinates

3.2 Analysis of EEG

EEG signals were originally recorded with a 1024Hz sampling rate. The unwanted artifacts, trend and noise were reduced prior to extracting the features from EEG data by pre-processing the signals. Biosemi active electrodes record EEG signals referenced to common mode sense electrode (CMS) as a part of its feedback loop. In order to gain the

[1]http://www.tobii.com
[2]http://mahnob-db.eu/hci-tagging/
[3]http://www.flickr.com

full common-mode rejection ratio (CMRR) at 50Hz, EEG signals should be re-referenced to another reference. EEG signals were thus re-referenced to the average reference to maximize signal to noise ratio. EEG drift was removed by subtracting the moving averaged signal with a 5 seconds window. The noise reduction was done by applying a low-pass filter with the cut-off frequency of 10Hz, since the ERP responses are low frequency [7].

We expected the ERP responses to appear in 400ms to 600ms after showing the tag. Therefore, the EEG signals of the one second period after displaying overlaid tags under the images were downsampled 16 times and used as features. As a result, we had $32 \times 16 = 512$ features for every trial.

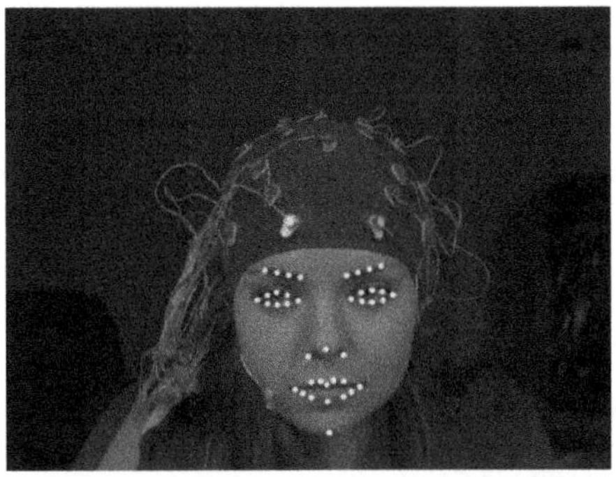

Figure 3: An example of the recorded camera view including tracked facial points.

3.3 Analysis of facial expressions

An active appearance model face tracker was employed to track 40 points [8] (see Figure 3). The facial points were extracted after registering the face to a normalized face and correcting the head pose. A reference point was generated by averaging the inner corners of eyes and points on the subjects' nose which assumed to be static. The distances of 33 point including eyebrows, eyes, lip and iris to the reference point were calculated and averaged to be used as features.

3.4 Classification

For this study, we conducted subject independent tag relevance detection. In this subject independent approach, we perform a leave-one-subject-out cross-validation, i.e. all trials of one subject are used for testing and all trials of the remaining subjects are used for training. This is repeated until each subject has been used for testing.

We used a Relevance Vector Machine (RVM) [15], a Support Vector Machine (SVM) [2] and Linear Discriminant Analysis (LDA) as classifiers. Both, the RVM and SVM are linear classifiers in the kernel space. The kernel space is defined by the training dataset and only a sparse subset is used for classification, the so called Relevance Vectors or Support Vectors. However, their optimization technique is different: the SVM formulates the problem within a max margin framework, i.e., the algorithm maximizes the margin around the hyperplane that discriminates between the classes. The RVM formulation is fully probabilistic, i.e., it defines a model fitting probability for the training data and a prior over the model parameters. The algorithm then proceeds by optimizing the posterior probability of the parameters given the data.

For RVM and SVM, we use a Gaussian radial basis function kernel with length scale parameter γ. Additionally, the SVM has the soft-margin cost parameter C. Both parameters are optimized within each cross-validation fold by a grid-search. We first calculate the mean value m of the pairwise kernel functions between all training data points and then start the grid-search within the interval $[m/2; 2m]$ for γ and $[1; 10]$ for C. The interval is searched with a logarithmic step size and it is extended if the optimal value is found at the border. The classifier is evaluated for each of the steps by a 2-fold cross-validation.

The LDA classifier is applied after reducing the dimensionality of features using a Principal Component Analysis and preserving 95% of the energy.

4. EXPERIMENTAL RESULTS

The goal of our proposed method is to filter out non-relevant tags. Therefore, we report the precision of the top 5% and 10% samples detected as non-relevant in Table 2. From the precision @5% and @10% SVM has a slight advantage for eye gaze and LDA for the other modalities. Facial expression analysis do not yield very convincing results. This can be due to the very subtle responses which were also highly varying between subjects. EEG signals have also a strong person specific component and ERP responses are not easily extractable from one trial. If we want to take advantage of EEG for such methods, the tag will have to be flashed for multiple times in order to get a sufficient level of signal to noise ratio. Eye gaze results are significantly better than the other modalities. Thus, after fusion of these modalities at decision level we could not achieve any better performance than the best single modality. Precision and recall curves of the best modality, eye gaze, is shown in Figure 4. The precision and recall results were calculated in each iteration of cross validation and then averaged to present the general performance of the system. Looking at the precision and recall curves, SVM performs the best to detect the top ranked non-relevant results and therefor is a good candidate for a filtering system that removes the top ranked non-relevant tags.

We examined the correlation between the labels and the different eye gaze features as indicators for their relevance. The fixation time in the tag zone was in average longer for non-relevant tags which means the participants spent more time looking at the labels. The vertical position of the eye gaze was more towards the bottom of the screen for non-relevant tags which is as a result of spending more time in the tag zone.

To compare our system to the previously published results, we calculated the classification rate and F1 scores. The best subject independent classification rate was obtained using only eye gaze whose classification rate is 59.5% with the average F1 score of 0.59. This is superior to the average subject dependent results reported in [5, 12, 14] and in the same line with the subject dependent results reported in [3] using eye gaze, the best F1 score reported was 0.6. It is worth noting that a subject independent approach is more useful in practice due to the higher chance of generalizing over a population.

5. CONCLUSIONS

We presented a method based for filtering non-relevant tags on images. We obtained promising results and our find-

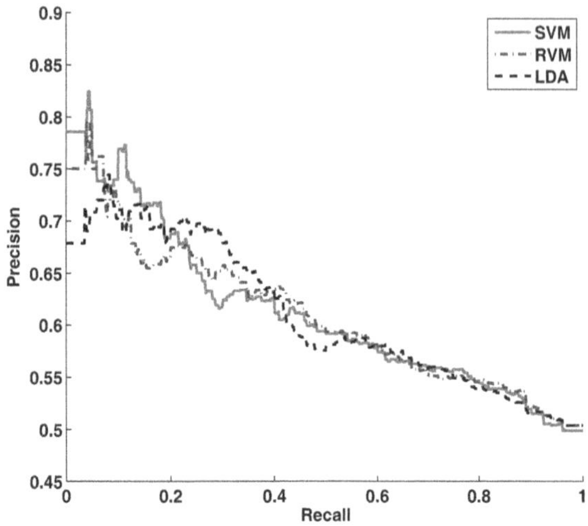

Figure 4: Recall and Precision curves. The RVM, SVM and LDA+PCA results on eye gaze are shown in different colors.

Table 2: The precision at top 5% and top 10% non-relevant detection for different modalities, namely, EEG, Eye Gaze (EG), Facial Expressions (FE) and different classifiers.

	RVM		SVM		LDA+PCA	
Metric	@5%	@10%	@5%	@10%	@5%	@10%
EEG	0.50	0.56	0.35	0.42	0.57	0.59
EG	0.73	0.70	**0.76**	**0.73**	0.74	0.73
FE	0.51	0.52	0.49	0.48	0.55	0.55

ings can pave the way for the future studies on this topic with possibly larger data collections. Although the overall detection rate is far from ideal, our system is able to detect more accurately the top ranked non-relevant results. This enables us to filter out non-relevant tags with a high confidence. We can repeat this with more than one subject to filter out more of the noisy and incorrect tags with higher confidence. Studying three different modalities, EEG, facial expressions and eye gaze, we found that eye gaze was the most informative and generalizable channel of information for such applications. Given the conclusions, the future studies can focus on collecting and analyzing larger datasets from the most informative modality, i.e., eye gaze.

6. ACKNOWLEDGMENT

The work of Soleymani is supported by the European Research Council under the FP7 Marie Curie Intra-European Fellowship: Emotional continuous tagging using spontaneous behavior (EmoTag). The work of Kaltwang is partially funded by EPSRC grant EP/H016988/1 (EmoPain). The work of Pantic is supported in part by ERC Starting Grant agreement no. ERC-2007-StG-203143 (MAHNOB). The authors want to thank B. Martinez and J. Orozco for the discussions and J. Doboš and J. Lichtenauer for their contributions to the data collection.

7. REFERENCES

[1] G. Buscher, L. van Elst, and A. Dengel. Segment-level display time as implicit feedback: a comparison to eye tracking. In *ACM SIGIR*, SIGIR '09, pages 67–74, 2009.

[2] C.-C. Chang and C.-J. Lin. LIBSVM: A library for support vector machines. *ACM Trans. on Intelligent Systems and Technology*, 2:1–27, 2011.

[3] S. Hajimirza, M. Proulx, and E. Izquierdo. Reading users' minds from their eyes: A method for implicit image annotation. *Multimedia, IEEE Trans.*, 14(3):805 –815, june 2012.

[4] D. Hardoon and K. Pasupa. Image ranking with implicit feedback from eye movements. In *Symp. on Eye-Tracking Research & Applications*, ETRA '10, pages 291–298. ACM, 2010.

[5] J. Jiao and M. Pantic. Implicit image tagging via facial information. In *Int'l Workshop on Social signal processing*, pages 59–64. ACM, 2010.

[6] S. Koelstra, C. Muhl, and I. Patras. EEG analysis for implicit tagging of video data. In *Int. Conf. on Affective Computing and Intelligent Interaction.*, pages 1–6. IEEE, 2009.

[7] F. Lotte and C. Guan. Learning from other subjects helps reducing brain-computer interface calibration time. In *ICASSP 2010*, pages 614–617. IEEE, 2010.

[8] J. Orozco, O. Rudovic, J. Gonzàlez, and M. Pantic. Hierarchical On-line Appearance-Based Tracking for 3D Head Pose, Eyebrows, Lips, Eyelids and Irises. *Image and Vision Computing*, 31(4):322–340, 2013.

[9] M. Pantic and A. Vinciarelli. Implicit human-centered tagging. *IEEE Signal Processing Magazine*, 26(6):173–180, November 2009.

[10] S. Petridis and M. Pantic. Is this joke really funny? judging the mirth by audiovisual laughter analysis. In *IEEE ICME*, pages 1444 –1447, 2009.

[11] J. Salojärvi, K. Puolamäki, and S. Kaski. Implicit relevance feedback from eye movements. In W. Duch et al., editors, *ICANN 2005*, volume 3696 of *Lecture Notes in Computer Science*, pages 513–518. Springer Berlin / Heidelberg, 2005.

[12] M. Soleymani, J. Lichtenauer, T. Pun, and M. Pantic. A multimodal database for affect recognition and implicit tagging. *IEEE Trans. Affective Computing*, 3:42–55, 2012.

[13] M. Soleymani and M. Pantic. Human-centered implicit tagging: Overview and perspectives. In *IEEE SMC*, pages 3304–3309, 2012.

[14] M. Soleymani and M. Pantic. Multimedia Implicit Tagging using EEG Signals. In *IEEE ICME*, 2013. in press.

[15] M. Tipping and A. C. Faul. Fast marginal likelihood maximisation for sparse Bayesian models. In *Proc. 9th Int'l Workshop on Artificial Intelligence and Statistics*, pages 1–13, 2003.

[16] S. Vrochidis, I. Patras, and I. Kompatsiaris. An eye-tracking-based approach to facilitate interactive video search. In *ACM Int. Conf. on Multimedia Retrieval*, ICMR '11, pages 43:1–43:8. ACM, 2011.

Robust Facial Expressions Recognition Using 3D Average Face and Ameliorated AdaBoost

Jinhui Chen
ianchen@me.cs.scitec.kobe-u.ac.jp

Yasuo Ariki
ariki@kobe-u.ac.jp

Tetsuya Takiguchi
takigu@kobe-u.ac.jp

Graduate School of System Informatics, Kobe University
1-1 Rokkodai, Nada, Kobe, Hyogo, 657-8501 Japan

ABSTRACT

One of the most crucial techniques associated with Computer Vision is technology that deals with facial recognition, especially, the automatic estimation of facial expressions. However, in real-time facial expression recognition, when a face turns sideways, the expressional feature extraction becomes difficult as the view of camera changes and recognition accuracy degrades significantly. Therefore, quite many conventional methods are proposed, which are based on static images or limited to situations in which the face is viewed from the front. In this paper, a method that uses Look-Up-Table (LUT) AdaBoost combining with the three-dimensional average face is proposed to solve the problem mentioned above. In order to evaluate the proposed method, the experiment compared with the conventional method was executed. These approaches show promising results and very good success rates. This paper covers several methods that can improve results by making the system more robust.

Categories and Subject Descriptors

I.3.5 [**Computational Geometry and Object Modeling**]: Curve, surface, solid, and object representations; I.5.4 [**Pattern Recognition**]: Applications—*Computer vision, Signal processing*

General Terms

Algorithms, Experimentation

Keywords

facial expressions recognition, 3D average face, AdaBoost

1. INTRODUCTION

One of the most crucial techniques associated with Computer Vision is technology that deals with facial recognition, especially, the automatic estimation of facial expressions. The need for this kind of technology in various different areas keeps pushing the research forward every year, and lots of achievements have been obtained due to its great potentials in real-life applications, such as human-computer interaction (HCI) [9], automatic recommendations analysis based on video contents [5] and cognitive and interactive abilities of robot. But lots of difficulties, there still exist, because of the variation and complexity of the facial expression across human population and even the same individual. So facial expressions recognition is an interesting research topic, and many researchers attach great importance to this field [6].

However many of the conventional methods above are focused on the single static picture, so that they are short of practical application. Under the condition of real-time recognition, when a face turns sideways, the expressional feature extraction becomes difficult or the view of a camera fixed in front of the user changes, and the recognition accuracy degrades significantly. Thus, many of the conventional approaches are limited to situations in which the face is viewed from the front.

Therefore, there is a great need to solve the problem that the face cannot be moved freely. Thus, in this paper, a method is proposed to estimate human emotions based on facial expression. We use a Look-Up-Table (LUT) for AdaBoost to be trained the multi-class features efficiently. Furthermore, we use three-dimensional average face, which is recovered from the original image based on Procrustes Analysis. With these approaches, we can solve the problem that many of the conventional facial expression recognition methods are limited to situations in which the face cannot be moved freely. In order to evaluate the proposed method, the experiment compared with conventional method was executed. The experimental results show that the proposed method provides better performance in comparison with the conventional approaches.

2. PROPOSED METHOD

In this section, the method to estimate facial expression is proposed. Fig. 1 shows a processing flow of the proposed method. First, the facial area is detected based on AdaBoost, using Haar-like features on the input images. Next, if the feature of facial expressions can be extracted, the facial expression on this facial area will be estimated by LUT AdaBoost; otherwise, we use 3D average face to estimate the facial expressions, and the average face model is reconstructed based on Procrustes Analysis [2] to obtain the shape of face including effective expressional features.

MM'13, October 21–25, 2013, Barcelona, Spain.
Copyright 2013 ACM 978-1-4503-2404-5/13/10 ...$15.00. .

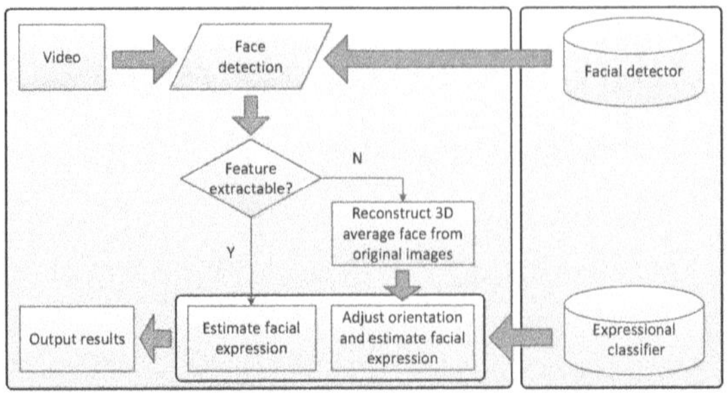

Figure 1: Processing flow of the proposed method

2.1 Average Face

Expressional features are extracted easily when the face is viewed from the front, but it is difficult to extract the feature points when the input video is lack of frontal facial frames. Therefore how to solve the problem is the gist of this subsection.

Procrustes analysis is a statistical tool for analyzing geometrical shapes. A shape (or equivalently a figure) P in R^P is represented by l landmarks. Two figures $P: l \times p$ and P': $l \times p'$ are said to have the same shape, if they are related by a special similarity transformation:

$$P' = \alpha P\Gamma + I_l \gamma^T \quad (1)$$

where the parameters of the similarity transformation are a rotation matrix Γ: $p \times p'$, $|\Gamma|$=1, a translation matrix γ: $p' \times l$, a positive scaling factor α, and I_l is a vector of ones. By using the generalized Procrustes analysis, it is possible to derive a consensus shape for a collection of figures [3], which is then used in registering new shapes into alignment with the collection by an Affine Transformation. In 3D model, the geometry of a face is defined as a shape vector $S_{3D} = (x_1, y_1, z_1, \cdots x_n, y_n, z_n) \in \mathbf{R}^3$, which contains the x, y, and z-coordinates of n vertices. And equation (1) is adjusted as follows

$$S = s_0 + \sum_{i=1}^{m} \beta_i s_i \quad (2)$$

where $\beta = (\beta_1, \beta_2, \cdots, \beta_m)^T$ is the shape parameter and m is the dimension of the shape parameter which was determined to represent the shape of 3D face model. Given the input face image indicated as $S_{2D} = (x_1, y_1, \cdots, x_n, y_n) \in \mathbf{R}^2$, the shape parameter β needs to be determined such that it minimizes the shape residual between the projected 3D facial shape generated by the shape parameter and the input 2D facial shape. The optimal shape and pose parameters (β, R_θ, T) are obtained from

$$E_r = \|P(R_\theta S_{3D} + T) - S_{2D}\|^2 \quad (3)$$

where S_{3D} is a $3 \times n$ matrix that is reshaped from the 3 $n \times 1$ model shape vector obtained using (1), P is a 2×3 orthographic projection matrix, T is a $3 \times n$ translation matrix consisting of n translation vectors $t = [t_x, t_y, t_z]^T$, and R_θ is a 3×3 rotation matrix where the yaw angle is θ. The average face creation is indicated as follows:

1. Initialization: set $\beta_0 = 0$ and $k = 1$.
2. Alignment: S_{2D} is aligned with the 2D shape obtained by projecting the frontal 3D shape (s_0) onto the $x - y$ plane.

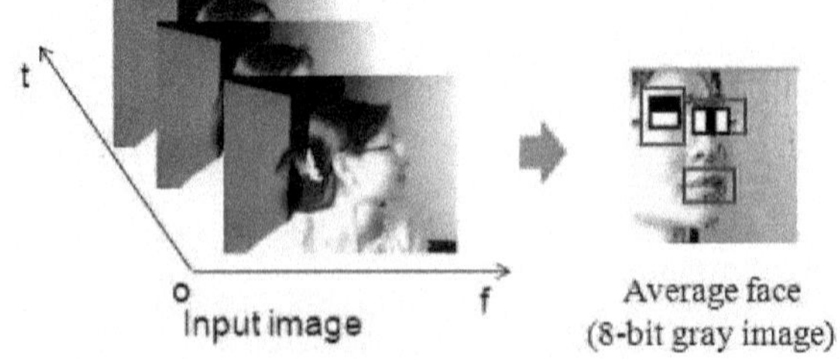

Figure 2: Example of average face creation

3. Update R_θ and T with the fixed shape parameter by $min \ \|P(R_\theta S_{3D} + T) - S_{2D}\|^2$, and reconstruct $(S_{3D})_k$ using the shape parameter β_k.
4. Verify whether $E_r \leq \varphi$ or $k > N$, if not, go to Step 3 and $k = k + 1$.
5. Reconstruct S_{3D} using the final shape parameters.

When E_r is below a threshold (e.g. in Ref. [3], Gower suggested setting φ =10^{-4}), or the landmarks are processed over, the reconstruction would be stopped, and the consensus shape would be output.

In theory, when images are consecutive, using the shapes of current image, it is possible to estimate the shapes of front image or next image by Procrustes analysis. Since our research is under condition of real-time, namely, images are consecutive, we can use an optimal image sample as a representation of short motion process when the face is moving freely, and we call it 3D Average Face (3DAF). However the cost of processing 3D model is quite expensive, the average model is projected into 8-bit gray image from which the emotion can be estimated by classifiers (see Fig. 2).

2.2 LUT AdaBoost

In order to make AdaBoost algorithm also be suitable for classifying multi-class objects, the theory of LUT is employed. By this method AdaBoost can estimate the facial expression in real-time. First of all we have to let it be able to classify the multi-class object, then treat training classifiers with high quality. The approaches will be indicated in this subsection.

2.2.1 *Multi-class AdaBoost*

AdaBoost is a learning algorithm that selects a small number of weak classifiers from a large weak classifier pool or hypothesis space to construct a strong classifier. The two-class AdaBoost algorithm has been successfully used in face detection, gender classification, etc. However, many problems such as expression recognition are multi-class in nature. Fortunately, based on a measure of Hamming loss, Schapire and Singer [7] have extended AdaBoost to a multi-class multi-label version. We denote the sample space by $\mathbf{X}$ and the label set by $\mathbf{Y}'$. A sample of a multi-class multi-label problem is a pair (x, Y) , where $x \in \mathbf{X}, Y \subseteq \mathbf{Y}'$. For $Y \subseteq \mathbf{Y}'$, define $Y[l]$ for $l \in \mathbf{Y}'$ as

$$Y[l] = \begin{cases} 1 & if \ \ l \in Y \\ -1 & if \ \ l \notin Y \end{cases} \quad (4)$$

Given: the sample set $S = \{(x_1, y_1), \cdots, (x_m, y_m)\}$, and the size of the final strong classifier $\mathbf{T}$.
Initialize:$D_t(i, l) = \frac{1}{mk}, i = 1, \cdots, m, l = 1 \cdots, k$, where $k = |\mathbf{Y}'|$. Let $t = 0, 1, 2, \cdots T_i$

1. Under the distribution D_t, select a weak classifier h_t:$\mathbf{X} \times \mathbf{Y}' \to [-1, 1]$ from the weak classifier pool to maximize the absolute value of

$$r_t = \sum_{i,l} D_t(i,l) Y_i(l) h_t(x_i, l) \tag{5}$$

2. Let

$$\alpha_t = \frac{1}{2} ln \left(\frac{1 + r_t}{1 - r_t} \right) \tag{6}$$

3. Update the distribution:

$$D_{t+1} = \frac{D_t(i,l) exp(-\alpha_t Y_i(l) h_t(x_i, l))}{Z_t} \tag{7}$$

where Z_t is a normalization factor,and D_{t+1} will be a distribution.

4. Output the final strong classifier:

$$H(x, l) = arg \ max \left(\sum_t \alpha_t h_t(x, l) \right) \tag{8}$$

and the confidence of H can be defined as

$$Conf_H(x) = \left| \frac{\sum_t \alpha_t h_t(x, H(x, l))}{\sum_t \alpha_t} \right| \tag{9}$$

2.2.2 LUT for Boosting Data Mapping

In order to train the emotional features by multi-class AdaBoost, weak classifier pool of simple features needs using to be configured. We construct a weak classifier based on the Haar-like feature, which is a kind of simple rectangle feature proposed by Viola and Jones [8], and we can calculated the value of it very fast through the integral image. For each Haar feature, one weak classifier is configured. In their paper, a threshold-type weak classifier, whose output is Boolean value, is used, that is, $h(x) = sign\,[f_{Haar}(x) - b]$ where f_{Haar} is the Haar feature and b is a threshold. The main disadvantage of this threshold model is that it is too simple to fit complex distributions, such as a multi-Gaussian model. For a multi-class, $\varpi_1 \cdots \varpi_k$, we use a real-valued 2D LUT type weak classifier, which is proposed by Y.Wang et al. [9]. It is indicated as follows:

1. Assuming f_{Haar} has been normalized to $[0, 1]$, the range is divided into n sub-ranges:

$$bin_j = [\frac{(j-1)}{n}, \frac{j}{n}], j = 1 \cdots, n \tag{10}$$

2. Define the weak classifier $h(x, l)$ as follows

$$if \ \ f_{Harr}(x) \in bin_j \ \ then \ \ h(x, l) = 2P_l^j - 1 \tag{11}$$

note

$$P^{(j)}{}_l = P\left(x \in \varpi_l | f_{Haar}(x) \in bin_j\right) \tag{12}$$

3. Given the characteristic function

$$B_n^{(j,l)}(u, y) = \begin{cases} 1 & u \in [(j-1)/n, j/n] \wedge y = l \\ 0 & otherwise \end{cases} \tag{13}$$

4. Finally, the LUT weak classifier can be formally expressed as:

$$h_{LUT}(x, y) = \sum_{j=1}^{n} \sum_{l=1}^{k} \left(2P_l^j - 1\right) B_n^{(j,l)}(f_{Haar}(x), y) \tag{14}$$

Based on the approaches above, it can be designed as a classifier to extract expressional features, and the expressional samples which are mainly extracted from eyes and mouth, are used to train the classifier.

3. EXPERIMENTS

Based on the theories indicated before, here we have to note that unless it is clearly specified we are dealing with faces under real-time condition. The performance of the system with profile faces is also evaluated in our research. We do not consider the use of both views: frontal and profile, but consider the condition of free facial movement.

3.1 Experimental Dataset

Training Database Set The database of JAFFE [4] is a set of 213 images of different expressions posed by 10 Japanese females. All the face samples were normalized to 64×64-pixel patches and processed by histogram equalization, no color information was used. However, the amount of JAFFE database has only 213 images, they are too less to train the classifier. In order to enhance the generalization performance of AdaBoost learning, we dealt with the images by some transformations (mirror reflection, rotate the images etc.), finally, we got 6816 face samples for training facial expression classifier.

Testing Database Set The testing set was obtained from soap opera and the surrounding persons with the total of 22. And they existed in 22 video clips individually, which were recorded by 25 fps with the length of 30 seconds.

Parameters Setting For training the expression classifier, the database was classified into 7 sets. We set $i = 7$. Parameters for total of 7-type classifiers were set as T_0=720, T_1=T_2=T_3=T_4=T_5=T_6= 1,400. It means that 720 weak classifiers were selected to construct the strong classifer of Natural. The amount of Anger, Disgust, Fear, Happy, Sadness, and Surprise were all set as 1,400.

3.2 Experimental Results

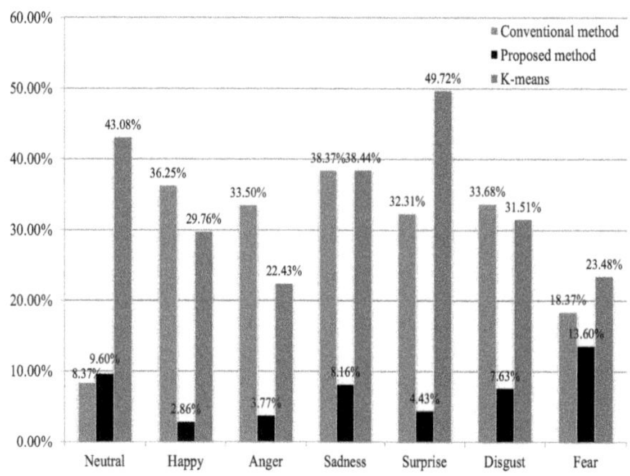

Figure 3: Experimental results

In order to evaluate the proposed method, we compared it among the conventional method which bases on LUT AdaBoost without 3DAF, and the method based on K-means [1] (k=13). Fig. 3 shows the error rate of experimental results in the facial expression estimation. The estimation maximum error rate of proposed method is 13.60%, and the best result is 2.86%. From this result, we can confirm the validity of proposed method. The conventional method keeps the error rate approximately 28.69%, and the method of K-means is about 34.06%. Table 1 shows the average processing time by PC with CPU Core i3-330M 2.13 GHZ and 2.0 GB memory per one image with the size of 640 × 480.

Table 1: Average processing time per one image.

Method	Proposed	Conventional	K-means
Time cost	19.36 ms	13.11 ms	31.70 ms

Moreover, in order to evaluate the efficiency of the weak classifier constructed by LUT AdaBoost, we compared the efficiency among conventional AdaBoost, Multi-class AdaBoost and LUT AdaBoost. The evaluation is executed through comparing the recognition rate in classifying the Multi-class probability events among the methods mentioned above.

Fig. 4 shows the processing time in training classifiers constructed by the methods mentioned above. The red line indicates the results of LUT AdaBoost, the blue is conventional AdaBoost and the green one shows the data of multi-class AdaBoost. We used the images of training set to test the processing time in training classifiers.

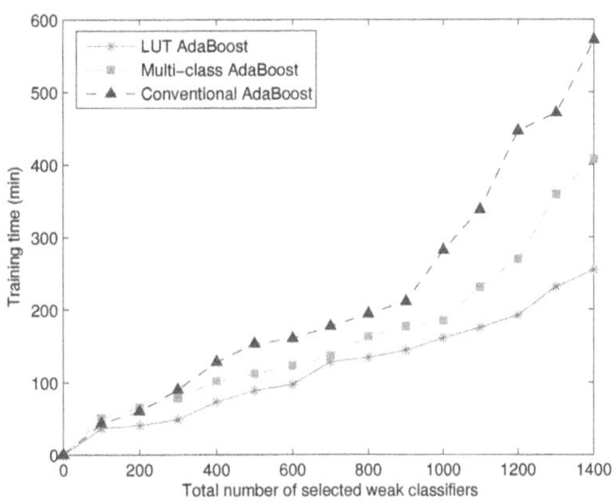

Figure 4: Processing time in training classifiers

In the experiments of classifying the Multi-class probability events, we took use of the JAFFE database to train classifiers. Each class trained by 30 images. We evaluated the efficiency of classifiers for 100 static images, which were obtained by Google Picture Searching Engine in advance. In Fig. 5, the recognition rates of conventional AdaBoost, Multi-class AdaBoost, and LUT AdaBoost are indicated by blue line, green one and the red, respectively. From the figure, we can find that LUT AdaBoost is an excellent method for classifying the multi-class probability events, especially for more than 3 classes. However we also recognized that it is not performing quit good in 2-class recognition, compared with the conventional AdaBoost.

4. CONCLUSIONS

In this paper, we proposed the method combining 3D average face and ameliorated AdaBoost to recognize facial expressions of face free moving. The experiments have shown

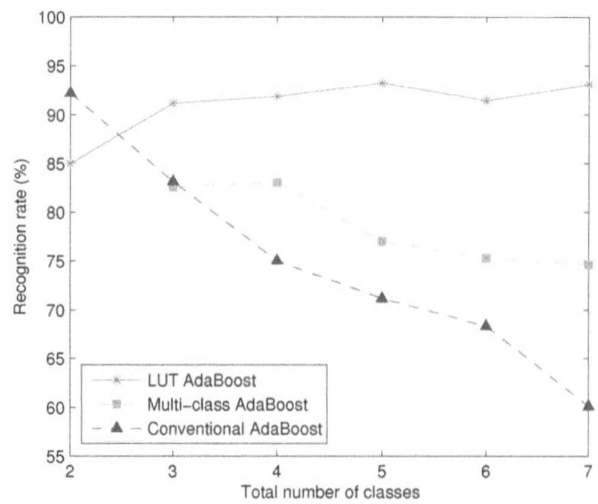

Figure 5: The recognition rate of classifiers

that our approaches obtained more effective classifiers and improved the exaction rate. As for future plan, considering a possible implementation in a real scenario, the research will be focussed on combining with speech recognition.

5. REFERENCES

[1] N. Alldrin, A. Smith, and D. Turnbull. Classifying facial expression with radial basis function networks, using gradient descent and k-means. *CSE253*, 2003.

[2] C. Goodall. Procrustes methods in the statistical analysis of shape. *Journal of the Royal Statistical Society. Series B (Methodological)*, pages 285–339, 1991.

[3] J. Gower. Generalized procrustes analysis. *Psychometrika*, 40(1):33–51, 1975.

[4] M. Kamachi, M. Lyons, and J. Gyoba. The japanese female facial expression (jaffe) database. *URL http://www. kasrl. org/jaffe. html*, 21, 1998.

[5] M. Miyahara, M. Aoki, T. Takiguchi, and Y. Ariki. Tagging video contents with positive/negative interest based on user's facial expression. In *Proceedings of the 14th international conference on Advances in multimedia modeling*, pages 210–219. Springer-Verlag, 2008.

[6] M. Pantic and L. Rothkrantz. Automatic analysis of facial expressions: The state of the art. *Pattern Analysis and Machine Intelligence, IEEE Transactions on*, 22(12):1424–1445, 2000.

[7] R. E. Schapire and Y. Singer. Improved boosting algorithms using confidence-rated predictions. *Machine learning*, 37(3):297–336, 1999.

[8] P. Viola and M. Jones. Rapid object detection using a boosted cascade of simple features. In *Computer Vision and Pattern Recognition, 2001. CVPR 2001. Proceedings of the 2001 IEEE Computer Society Conference on*, volume 1, pages I–511. IEEE, 2001.

[9] Y. Wang, H. Ai, B. Wu, and C. Huang. Real time facial expression recognition with adaboost. In *Pattern Recognition, 2004. ICPR 2004. Proceedings of the 17th International Conference on*, volume 3, pages 926–929. IEEE, 2004.

Visual Business Recognition - A Multimodal Approach

Amir Roshan Zamir, Afshin Dehghan, and Mubarak Shah*
Center for Research in Computer Vision, UCF, Orlando, FL 32816, USA
aroshan@cs.ucf.edu, adehghan@cs.ucf.edu, shah@eecs.ucf.edu
http://crcv.ucf.edu/projects/Business-Recognition/

ABSTRACT

In this paper we investigate a new problem called *visual business recognition*. Automatic identification of businesses in images is an interesting task with plenty of potential applications especially for mobile device users. We propose a multimodal approach which incorporates business directories, textual information, and web images in a unified framework. We assume the query image is associated with a coarse location tag and utilize business directories for extracting an over complete list of nearby businesses which may be visible in the image. We use the name of nearby businesses as search keywords in order to automatically collect a set of relevant images from the web and perform image matching between them and the query. Additionally, we employ a text processing method customized for business recognition which is assisted by nearby business names; we fuse the information acquired from image matching and text processing in a probabilistic framework to recognize the businesses. We tested the proposed algorithm on a challenging set of user-uploaded and street view images with promising results for this new application.

Categories and Subject Descriptors: I.4 [Image Processing and Computer Vision]: Applications

Keywords: Business Recognition; Storefront; Location Based Service; Business Review; Map; Scene Text; Multi-hypotheses; Yelp.

1. INTRODUCTION

A business recognition system can provide smartphone or wearable computer users with extensive information about a particular business of interest in an automatic and convenient fashion. Such system can be used for enhancing the user experience in surfing maps or location-aware image understanding as well.

The existing methods for providing a smartphone user with information about a specific business primarily use *non-visual sensors* such as embedded GPS, digital compass, and gyroscope [1, 2]. These approaches are often based on matching the sensor data to a reference set; e.g. matching the location received from the GPS-chip along with the compass direction to a geo-tagged business directory such as Yelp. Such methods do not benefit from image content and typically achieve limited success as they generally require very precise sensors and accurately tagged business

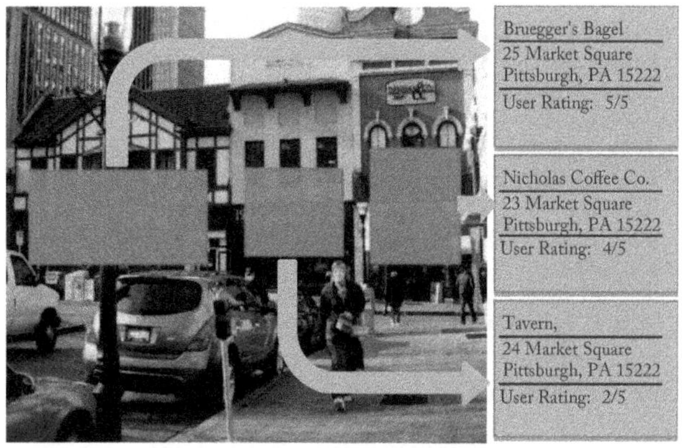

Figure 1: A business recognition system can automatically identify businesses in an image and provide additional relevant information such as reviews and similar nearby businesses.

datasets. Additionally, other potential approaches such as existing scene text processing methods [3, 5, 6] cannot sufficiently cope with the complex appearance of text in business signs and logos.

Therefore, we propose a method which utilizes multimedia information obtained from both visual content, such as storefront appearance and text, and non-visual information, such as GPS and business directories. We show that our method achieves a notable rate of success by employing a multimodal approach and is capable of finding multiple businesses in an image and their spatial location.

2. FRAMEWORK OVERVIEW

The block diagram of the proposed method is shown in fig. 2. The images captured using smartphones are usually associated with a coarse geo-tag which typically comes from the inbuilt GPS-chip, cell tower signal or WPS. We use this approximate location for generating a list of nearby businesses by querying business directories.

To utilize the textual information (subsection 2.1), we perform text detection on the query image; then, we apply a multi-hypotheses text recognition approach assisted by the business lexicon which yields a PDF specifying how well a detected word in the query image matches the nearby businesses. Since the business in the image may include several words, we combine the PDFs of matching businesses to each word through marginalization to have a single PDF representing the textual information in the whole query image.

In order to leverage the images on the web in business recognition, we use the list of nearby business names as search keywords and collect a set of images from the web for each one. The query image is expected to share some similarity with the web images of the business which is visible in it. Therefore, we match the query image to the collected web images in order to identify the similar ones (subsection 2.2). This process yields a PDF which represents how well the web images of each nearby business match the query image. Lastly, we combine the two PDFs acquired from text pro-

*The authors would like to thank Oliver Nina.

MM'13, October 21–25, 2013, Barcelona, Spain.
Copyright 2013 ACM 978-1-4503-2404-5/13/10 ...$15.00.
http://dx.doi.org/10.1145/2502081.2502174.

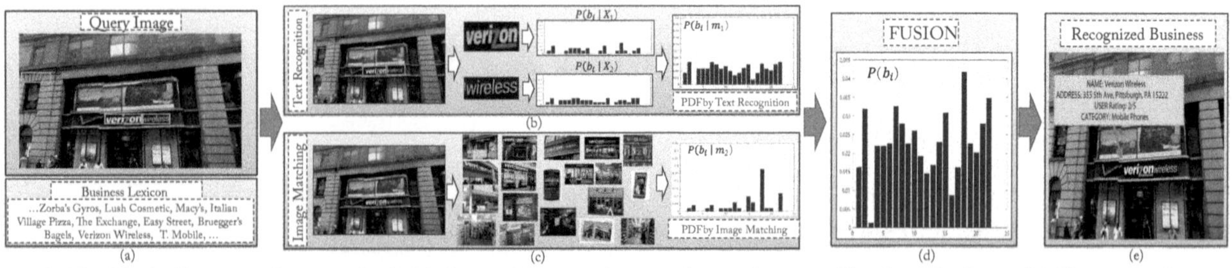

Figure 2: The block diagram of our method. (a) shows the query image, detected text and business lexicon. (b) illustrates the process of computing the PDFs of different words and marginalizing them into one PDF. (c) shows the query image, a subset of web images ordered based on how well they match the query, and the resulting PDF from image matching. (d) demonstrates the PDF obtained from the fusion process. (e) shows the business which achieves the highest probability after fusion, as the recognized business.

cessing and image matching in a probabilistic late fusion step to compute a PDF which utilizes both modalities (subsection 2.3).

Generating the Business Lexicon: We use the APIs of Yellow pages and Yelp to automatically retrieve and aggregate the nearby businesses within the distance of 150 meters to the approximate location. Regarding the inaccuracies in the business directories and the GPS-tag of the query, we set the radius to a large value to ensure the visible businesses in the query are among the retrieved results. $B = \{b_i | 1 \leq i \leq n_B\}$ represents the set of retrieved businesses where n_B denotes the number of nearby business. A business name may include more than one word, so $W = \{w_{i,j} | 1 \leq i \leq n_B, 1 \leq j \leq n_w(i)\}$ is the set of words in the name of all nearby businesses. $w_{i,j}$ represents the jth word of ith business's name, and $n_w(i)$ denotes the number of words the name of ith business includes.

2.1 Business Recognition Using Text

Business recognition using textual information is inherently similar to the problem of text recognition in natural scene. However, the goal of business recognition is to establish a relationship between the reference businesses and the text in the query image and not necessarily recognizing it. Such relationship can be probabilistic or fuzzy, while text recognition aims at recognizing the text deterministically. Additionally, scene text recognition does not address other problems specific to business recognition such as combining the information obtained from different query words in order to perform the recognition of a single business. We employ the text processing method described in the rest of this section which is specifically customized for the task of business recognition and addresses the aforementioned issues. Additionally, it makes representing the matching results in a probabilistic manner feasible, as such representation is required in our fusion process.

Multi-hypotheses Character Recognition: We use Stroke Width Transform (SWT) [8] as our text detection method which identifies the regions of the image which might contain a word and each character therein. We use Gabor features for performing text recognition [3] on each character patch. In our training step, we generate 62 synthetic character patches comprised of lower and upper case English alphabet along with single digit numbers using the font `Arial`. Additionally, we compute six variations for each character using four consecutive image dilation and two erosions as we observed that the business signs in natural scenes tend to significantly vary in the width of characters compared the standard fonts. we apply a bank of 108 Gabor filters comprised of $n = 6$ frequencies and $m = 18$ scales to each synthetic character. Each character is then divided into 9 sub patches using a 3 by 3 grid. The Gabor feature of each sub patch is defined as the mean of Gabor features of the pixels therein. Therefore, each character is represented by a 972 dimensional vector which is reduced to 50 dimensional using PCA. The feature vectors of all 62 characters and their erosion-dilation variations form our reference set of character features.

During the test step, the same 108 Gabor filters are applied to a character patch returned by text detection and the size of the feature vector is reduced to 50 using the mapping found by PCA during

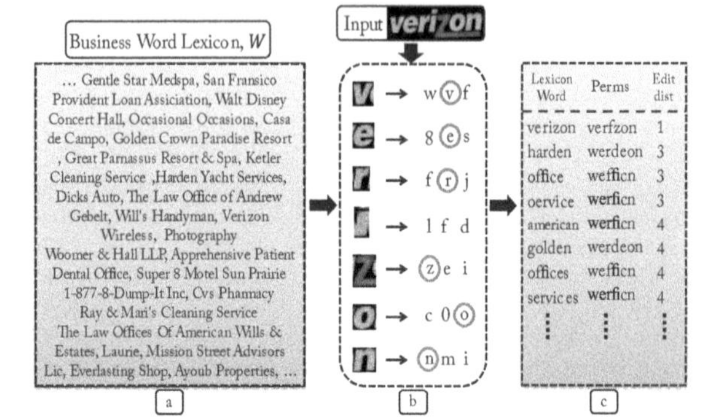

Figure 3: Illustration of the process of multi-hypotheses matching (eq. 1). (a): Business Lexicon. (b): the query word and nominated candidates for each query patch. The correct candidates are marked with red circles. (c): best matching permutations to each business word and their respective edit distance.

the training. Then we use a k-nearest neighbor classifier to find the most similar k reference characters to the query patch. In other words, instead of assigning one character to the query patch, we nominate k characters as the possible matches. We employ this approach as the right character may not necessarily be the first match, while it usually appears among the top few matches. This is shown for the sample query word "**verizon**" in fig. 3 (b).

We denote a feasible permutation of the candidates for a query word by $X = \{\chi_a^1, \chi_b^2, \chi_c^3, \ldots\}$, which means the ath candidate for the 1st query patch, the bth candidate for the 2nd query patch, and so on are selected. Hence, each query word possesses a large number of feasible permutations of its character candidates; eight feasible permutations for a sample query are shown in figure 3 (c).

Matching Character Permutations to Business Lexicon: We solve the following optimization problem to identify the best permutation which matches a particular business word in the lexicon:

$$\hat{X}_{i,j} = \underset{X}{\operatorname{argmin}} ||X - w_{i,j}||, \tag{1}$$

where $\hat{X}_{i,j}$ represents the permutation which best matches the business word $w_{i,j}$. $||.||$ represents Levenshtein distance between two strings. We solve eq. 1 once for every word in the business words lexicon W in order to find the best matching permutation to each. This process is illustrated in fig. 3 for a sample case. Eight permutations, their respective matching words in the business lexicon, and the edit distance between them are shown in (c).

Bear in mind that the name of one business may include more than one word. Thus, we solve the following equation to find the best matching business word to the query for each nearby business:

$$\zeta(b_i) = \min_j ||\hat{X}_{i,j} - w_{i,j}||, \tag{2}$$

where b_i represents the ith businesses among the nearby businesses B. $\zeta(b_i)$ is the Levenshtein distance between the query word and

Figure 4: Sample web images for two businesses. The red margin marks the positive examples. Green, yellow and blue markers denote the keywords "business name","business name+city"and"business name+storefront".

the best matching word in the name of business b_i. Therefore, ζ can be interpreted as a distance function which represents how well business b_i matches the query word.

We would like to have a PDF which specifies a probability for each of the nearby businesses matching the query word represented by X. Therefore, the distances function $\zeta(b_i)$ is converted to a PDF using the following equation:

$$p(b_i|X) = \frac{sig(\zeta(b_i))}{\sum_i sig(\zeta(b_i))}, \quad (3)$$

where $p(b_i|X)$ is the probability of the business b_i to match the given query word X. sig is the sigmoid function with the standard form $sig(x) = \frac{1}{1+e^{-\tau x}}$, where τ is a constant which we set to -0.5 in our experiments. Therefore, a large edit distance corresponds to a small probability and vice versa.

Utilizing multiple words for recognizing a Business: The probability distribution function $p(b_i|X)$ acquired from eq. 3 specifies how well the nearby businesses match one query word. However, the business sign in the query image may include more than one word. Therefore, we need to associate the query words pertaining to one business in order to utilize all of them for recognizing the respective business. Usually the words which belong to one business in the image are spatially close and have similar appearance features. For instance, the words "**verizon**" and "**wireless**" in figure 2 (a) have similar colors and are located next to each other. Therefore, for each bounding box acquired from the text detector, we form a feature vector by concatenating its RGB color histogram with (x, y) spatial location of its center. Then, we perform mean shift clustering on the feature vectors of all the bounding boxes to associate the words which belong to one business. The number of resulting clusters is the number of businesses in the query image, and the elements in each cluster are the bounding boxes associated together. A sample case is shown in figure 2 (b) where the bounding boxes shown in the same color are associated together.

To leverage the associated query words in business recognition, we combine the PDFs each one yields through marginalization:

$$p_t(b_i) = \sum_{j=1}^{\alpha} p(b_i|X_j)p(X_j), \quad (4)$$

where $p(b_i|X_j)$ is the PDF obtained from eq. 3 for the query word X_j, and α is the number of associated query words. $p(X_j)$ is the probability of looking at the jth query word for recognizing its respective business. We treat all the query words of one business sign equally by assigning equal chance to all: $p(X_j) = 1/\alpha$.

$p_t(b_i)$ in eq. 4 specifies the probability of each nearby business being visible in the query image based on the entire textual information in the query. In order to avoid confusing the PDFs obtained using text processing, image matching and fusion, we define $M = \{m_1, m_2\}$ as the set of approaches to business recognition which we employ. m_1 and m_2 represent text recognition and image matching respectively. Therefore, $p(b_i|m_1)$ represents the PDF obtained by employing text recognition which is equal to $p_t(b_i)$ of eq. 4. Fig. 2 (b) illustrates the described process for a sample query.

2.2 Business Recognition by Image Matching

Nowadays, for most of the businesses in urban area a number of images which show the storefront can be found on the web. Such images are typically uploaded by customers, business owners, or business directories for both franchise and non-franchise businesses.

In order to find the web images which pertain to a particular business, we generate four search keywords for each nearby business as: `"business name"`, `"business name+city"` and `"business name+storefront"`. We use the keywords to search for images on the web and download the retrieved ones using Ajax-based web image crawling. We save about 10 images per keywords which results in 40 images for each nearby business. We view the set of downloaded images as a reference dataset that each image therein is associated with a nearby business.

We employ bag of visual words (BoVW) model for matching the query image to the set of web images. We extract SIFT features from the web images and the query and compute their histogram of visual words using a vocabulary with 2000 words. The vocabulary is pre-computed on a set of 10000 random images. We employe tf-idf weighting scheme which reduces the contribution of less discriminative visual words [4]. We find the most similar web image of a business to the query using:

$$\psi(b_i) = \min_j |h_q - h_{i,j}|, \quad (5)$$

where h_q and $|.|$ represent the $BoVW$ histogram of the query, and L_2 distance respectively. $h_{i,j}$ represents the histogram of the jth web image of the ith business. Eq. 5 identifies the most similar image to the query for each nearby business. Therefore, the distance function $\psi(b_i)$ specifies how well the nearby business, b_i, matches the query based on the web images.

Using a method similar to the eq. 3 which was intended to convert edit distances to probability values, we convert the image matching distance function $\psi(b_i)$ to a PDF using, $p(b_i|m_2) = \frac{sig(\psi(b_i))}{\sum_i sig(\psi(b_i))}$, where $p(b_i|m_2)$ represents the probability of recognizing the business b_i in the query given the employed approach is image matching.

The procedure of downloading web images and computing their BoVW representation is relatively time consuming. However, since all the businesses in the broad area of interest, e.g. a city, are known, the web images can be downloaded and processed in an offline manner. That way, image matching between query and the web images of its nearby businesses can be done almost instantaneously.

2.3 Fusion of image matching and textual info

The purpose of the fusion step is to unify the information obtained from the two methods of text recognition and image matching to perform a more robust business recognition. Theoretically, the law of total probability is utilized for finding the probability of one event when it coincides with a random variable, so we employ it in fusing the PDFs acquired from text recognition and image matching. In our problem, the event is a nearby business, b_i, and the coinciding variable is m_i:

$$p(b_i) = p(b_i|m_1).P(m_1) + p(b_i|m_2).P(m_2) \quad (6)$$

where $P(m_1)$ and $P(m_2)$ are the probability of employing text recognition and image matching respectively. We define these two values using a training set of 50 query images. The training set consists of queries for which *only one* of the two methods worked successfully. We define $P(m_1)$ and $P(m_2)$ as:

$$P(m_1) = \frac{n_t}{n_t + n_i}, P(m_2) = \frac{n_i}{n_t + n_i} \quad (7)$$

where n_t is the number of images in the training set for which only text recognition identified the business. Similarly, n_i is the number

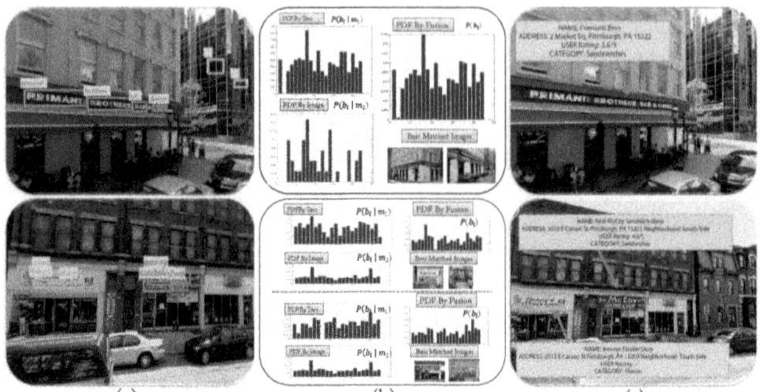

(a) (b) (c)

Figure 5: Business recognition results. (a): the query image, detected text and recognized words. (b): the PDFs found by text recognition, image matching and fusion along with the best matching web images. (c) the recognized businesses.

of images for which only image matching was successful. $n_t + n_i$ is the total number of images in the training set, i.e. 50.

The fusion process may not make a notable difference when both or none of the methods correctly recognize the business individually, regardless of the values of $p(b_i|m_1)$ and $p(b_i|m_2)$. However, when only one of the methods identifies the right business, proper values of $p(b_i|m_1)$ and $p(b_i|m_2)$ may results in successful overall recognition at the end. This is the reason our training set includes the query images for which only one of the methods worked. In other words, computing the values of $P(m_1)$ and $P(m_2)$ using the described method maximizes the chance of successful overall recognition for the cases where one of the methods fails.

If the word association method, explained in subsection 2.1, finds more than one business in the query, i.e. more than one cluster in mean-shift clustering, the text recognition and fusion process are repeated using the query words of each cluster in order to recognize multiple business. However, in case the best matching business in $p(b_i)$ has a low probability, typically < 0.10, we disregard it as it most likely corresponds to a false positive from the text detector.

3. EXPERIMENTS AND DISCUSSION

No dataset is currently available for evaluating the proposed framework as visual business recognition has not been studied to date. Therefore, we collected a data set of 1042 GPS-tagged images comprised of 642 user uploaded photos from Panoramio, Flickr and Picasa and 400 street view images for the cities of San Francisco, CA and Pittsburgh, PA. We manually filtered the images which do not show a business or have an incorrect GPS-tag. Each image may include up to four business. In case few businesses were retrieved by querying business directories for a particular query image, we added random businesses to make sure at least 20 businesses and 70 words existed in the lexicon to ensure each test is challenging enough. Fig. 5 shows sample business recognition results.[1]

Business recognition accuracy is defined as the number of correctly recognized businesses divided by the total number of businesses in the test set. We evaluated the proposed text processing and image matching methods on the test set individually to examine their performance in the single modal fashion; this resulted in the accuracy of 69% and 41% for text recognition and image matching respectively. However, when the two modalities were combined using the described fusion process, the accuracy increased to **75%** which signifies the effectiveness of our multimodal approach.

No other framework for visual business recognition has been proposed which we can use as a baseline. However, we compared the performance of our text processing method, which is customized for business recognition, with the state of the art scene text recognition algorithms in recognizing business *words*. The table in fig. 6 compares the performance of our approach to four baselines. The performance measure is the number of correctly recognized

[1] more results available at: `http://crcv.ucf.edu/projects/Business-Recognition/`

Method	Acc.
GNU-Ocrad OCR [8]	4%
Chen et al. [3]	7%
ABBYY OCR [6]	34%
Wang et al. [5]	42%
Proposed Method	**54%**

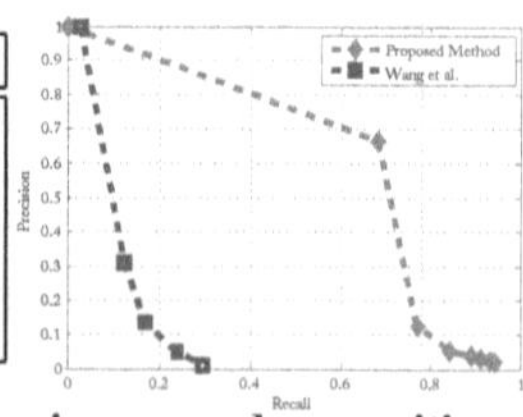

Figure 6: Left: Comparison of business-word recognition accuracies. Right: PR curve of our method vs. Wang et al.'s. [6]

words divided by the total number of words in our test images. Wang et al.'s [6] method which employs a pictorial structure for detection and recognition achieves the accuracy of 42% using the code of the authors with best parameters. Chen et al.'s [3] is another scene text recognition method for recognition of signs. Additionally, we compared our results with two OCR methods [7, 9] which have achieved notable success in document processing. In order to have a fair evaluation of text *recognition*, we manually adjusted the text detection results for our methods and the baselines, in case a word is completely missed in detection. For the baseline methods which do not need a separate text detection step [6, 7], we limited their search space to the adjusted text detection results to decrease their false positives. Fig. 6 (b) shows the precision-recall curves of our method (red) vs. Wang et al.'s [6] (blue).

Unlike the majority of existing scene text recognition methods [3, 6] which employ a heavy training process, e.g. by using a variety fonts and deformations, we used only one font and few deformations in our training. On the other hand, we leverage a more complex test step utilizing our multi-hypotheses character recognition approach. This is one of the reasons behind our superior performance in recognizing business words as they typically show a great deal of deformation and complexity which can not be effectively learnt in a training step. However, our multi hypotheses test step maximizes the use of business lexicon to alleviate this issue.

We observed that the majority of the failure cases of our method are due extreme deformation of characters and lack of a relevant image on the web for some businesses. Upon availability of an optimized parallel implementation of the framework, business recognition on a query can be done in no more than 3 seconds on average.

4. CONCLUSION

In this paper, we proposed a multimodal approach to a new application called *visual business recognition*. Our framework leverages textual information, web images and business directories and combines the results of each using a probabilistic late fusion process. We proposed a multi hypotheses approach to processing the text in images which is specifically customized for business recognition. The experiments showed the effectiveness of the proposed multimodal method for this new application.

5. REFERENCES

[1] Google Goggles, *https://sites.google.com/a/pressatgoogle.com/dec09searchevent/all-about-goggles*

[2] Nokia City Lens, *http://betalabs.nokia.com/trials/nokia-city-lens-for-windows-phone,http://tinyurl.com/nokia-city-lens*

[3] Chen et al., *Automatic detection and recognition of signs from natural scenes.* In: IEEE Trans. Image Processing, 2004.

[4] J. Philbin et al., *Object Retrieval with Large Vocabularies and Fast Spatial Matching.* In: CVPR, 2007.

[5] Amir Roshan Zamir, Alexander Darino, and Mubarak Shah, *Street view challenge: Identification of commercial entities in street view imagery.* In: ICMLA, 2011.

[6] K. Wang, B. Babenko and S. Belongie, *End-to-End Scene text recognition.* In: ICCV, 2011.

[7] ABBYY, *http://www.abbyy.com/.*

[8] B. Epshtein et al., *Detecting text in natural scenes with stroke width transform.* In: CVPR, 2011.

[9] GNU-Orcad, *http://www.gnu.org/s/ocrad/.*

3D View Synthesis with inter-view Consistency

David Wolinski
david.wolinski@inria.fr

Olivier Le Meur
olivier.le_meur@irisa.fr

Josselin Gautier
josselin.gautier@irisa.fr

University of Rennes 1 - IRISA
Campus de Beaulieu
35042 Rennes, France

ABSTRACT

In this paper, we propose a new pipeline to synthesize virtual views by extrapolation. It allows us to generate virtual views far away from each other, each presenting the exact same level of quality. This inter-view consistency is key to seamlessly navigate between viewpoints. Its computational cost is also lower than that of existing approaches. We compare the proposed approach with state-of-the-art methods and show the effectiveness of this new view synthesis pipeline.

Categories and Subject Descriptors

I.4.9 [**Image Processing and Computer Vision**]: Applications

Keywords

DIBR, FVV, 3DTV, view synthesis

1. INTRODUCTION

Virtual view synthesis consists in generating a new viewpoint from existing camera viewpoints. The most popular technique to synthesize virtual views is the Depth Image Based Rendering which relies on the depth information and allows to freely navigate in a scene. This application is called Free-Viewpoint Video (FVV) where virtual views are interpolated between two known ones [6] or extrapolated from one reference view. Unfortunately, DIBR methods suffer from several problems such as the recovery of disoccluded areas. Most of the time, an inpainting method is used to fill-in these areas. For instance, Daribo et Pesquet-Popescu [2] extended Criminisi's algorithm [1] by modifying the priority function and the patch matching criteria. Gautier et al. [3] also modified Criminisi's approach by taking into account a direction of filling, depending on the projection direction. Ma et al. [4] proposed a depth-guided inpainting using a new priority scheme and a background-foreground separation technique. Sun et al. [5] proposed a new framework using a joint optimization of inter-view texture similarity and geometry preservation. All these approaches provide new advances in view synthesis methods. However, they all overlook an important aspect which is the consistency between virtual views.

The goal of the presented work is to improve the quality of synthesized views in a context of FVV. Unlike for Zitnick et al. [6], virtual views are here extrapolated from one reference view (one texture image and its depth map).Traditionally, this is performed in the following order: (i) view projection which leads to cracks and disocclusions, (ii) crack filling which usually uses neighboring data and, finally, (iii) inpainting which aims to fill the disocclusions. We argue that the traditional pipeline, as illustrated in figure 1 (a) suffers from four main issues which essentially cripple the inpainting algorithms.

The first issue is foreground/background differentiation where inpainting algorithms are tempted to use foreground data when filling background disocclusions, leading to very disturbing "spillings". Moreover, as objects found in the scene don't always have the same edges on the texture and depth images, after projection, some foreground pixels can end up on the background and vice-versa. This "ghosting" further complicates the inpainting algorithm's job. Heuristics have been imagined, strengthening the inpainting algorithm but the problem, though minimized, largely persists.

The second issue is data corruption, which degrades the inpainting before it even started. This is caused by the inpainting algorithm using post projection, post crack-filling data.

The third issue concerns the lack of consistency between virtual views synthesized from the same reference view (as illustrated by the quality of local regions in figure 1 (a) right). For instance, a disocclusion that is visible in several virtual views is inpainted separately in each of these views. Since the point of view is not the same, this disocclusion is inpainted with differing data, producing different results which are immediately noticeable.

The fourth, last, issue lies with performance while synthesizing several views, when as mentioned, the inpainting step is done separately for each view. This not only introduces inconsistencies but is also redundant in that a disocclusion is inpainted once for each time it appears in a virtual view.

We aim to solve these issues, regardless of the inpainting algorithm that is used by essentially reversing the classical order of operations required to synthesize virtual views (figure 1 (b)). The overall idea is to inpaint the disoccluded areas before projection automatically removing any redundancy as each disocclusion is inpainted only once. This also

MM'13, October 21–25, 2013, Barcelona, Spain.
Copyright 2013 ACM 978-1-4503-2404-5/13/10 ...$15.00.
http://dx.doi.org/10.1145/2502081.2502175.

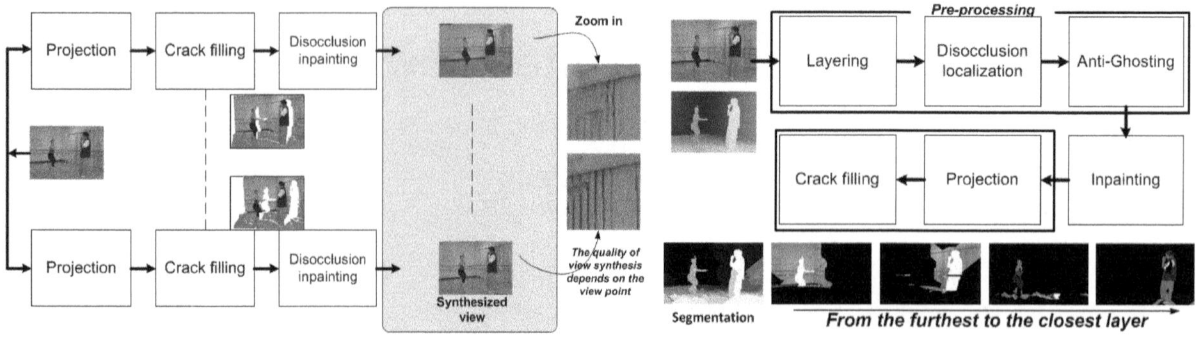

(a) Common method

(b) Proposed method

Figure 1: (a) Common method to synthesize a virtual view. First, the original view is projected. Second, disocclusions and cracks are inpainted. (b) Proposed method to synthesize virtual views - reversed order.

guarantees consistency between synthesized views. The data the inpainting algorithm uses is also free of any projection errors or cracks. Finally, we locate future disocclusions on the corresponding backgrounds separate from the foregrounds, allowing anti-ghosting and avoiding "spillings".

The paper is organized as follows. In section 2, the proposed pipeline is presented. Section 3 shows its performance and a comparison with state-of-the-art results. Conclusions are drawn in section 4.

2. PROPOSED METHOD

The proposed approach is composed of three main sequential operations (pre-processing, inpainting and projection) described in the following sections.

2.1 Pre-processing

First, the pre-processing projects the reference view into the extreme views in order to detect the largest possible disocclusions. With this information, we can then separate the various foregrounds and backgrounds into layers and apply any necessary anti-ghosting.

Depth-based segmentation: The first step is a depth-based segmentation which looks for pixels that are separated by a disocclusion and regroups pixels that remain connex after their projection into extreme virtual views (furthest from the reference view). The goal being to detect disocclusions, it is appropriate to use an edge-based segmentation of the depth map. Moreover, disocclusions should only appear between layers, meaning that the edges of our segmented depth map are the borders of the disocclusions. We thus define disocclusions as a loss of connexity between two pixels (p, p') after projection ($Proj$): $\forall p, p' \in Image,\ \{p, p'\} \in IEP\ iff$

$$p' \in neighbors(p)\ \wedge\ dist(Proj(p), Proj(p')) > \Delta$$

Two pixels which lose their connexity (edge-pixels) form an inter-exclusive pair (IEP): they are on each side of a future disocclusion and one of them is part of the corresponding foreground while the other is part of the corresponding background (see figure 2 (left)). Then, these edge-pixels are regrouped into regions which do not contain any inter-exclusive pairs (see figure 2 (middle)). All that remains to be done now is to assign all remaining pixels to one of these regions (see figure 2 (right)).

Layering: The depth-based segmentation leads to an over-segmented map. Indeed, some regions are separated by inter-exclusive pairs of pixels indicating that these regions

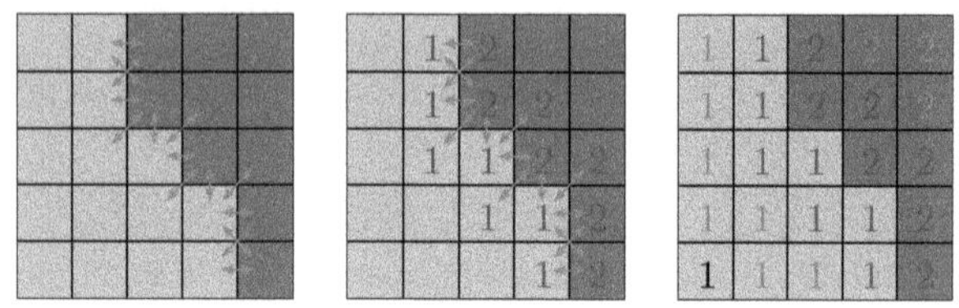

Figure 2: Left: double arrows represent inter-exclusive pixel pairs. Middle: labeled edge-pixels. Right: whole picture labeled, colors represent successive iterations of the region-growing algorithm.

belong to the foreground and background of a corresponding future disocclusion. However, this is not necessarily the case for all pairs of regions. The layering process aims to regroup into layers the regions that do not share any inter-exclusive pairs of pixels and that are close in terms of depth, that is, regions which do not create disocclusions amongst them. This is done by using an algorithm consisting of two nested loops as described in (Alg.1). As a result, the scene is not

Algorithm 1: Layering.

while *not layered regions exist* **do**
  layer := furthest not layered region
  foreach *not layered region, furthest to closest* **do**
    if $(\nexists\ p \in region,\ p' \in layer\ /\ \{p, p'\} \in IEP) \wedge$ $dist(depth(region), depth(layer)) < \alpha$ **then**
      add region to layer
    end
  end
end

over-segmented anymore and the resulting layers are ready for the remaining steps. Figure 1 (b) (bottom) illustrates some layers and segmentation.

Disocclusion localization between layers: As ensured by the way layers are constructed, disocclusions can only appear between layers and not inside any single layer. Thanks to this property, it is possible to easily locate the future disocclusions. To do this, we once again turn to the extreme projections. For every pair of layers L_1 and L_2, if these two layers share inter-exclusive pairs of pixels, it means that they share a common future disocclusion and that the further layer, say L_1, is the background while the closer layer,

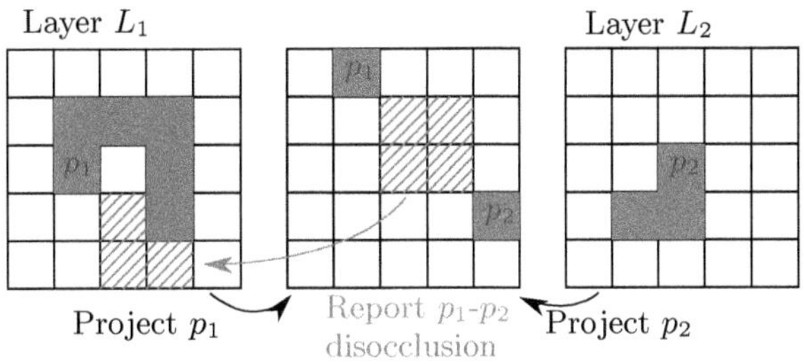

Figure 3: Left: further layer L_1. Right: closer layer L_2. Middle: pixels p_1 and p_2 projected. Red: discovered disocclusion reported on L_1.

say L_2, is the foreground. Now, considering each of these inter-exclusive pairs of pixels, let p_1 be the one belonging to layer L_1 (figure 3 (left)) and p_2 the one belonging to layer L_2 (figure 3 (right)). In the extreme projections, p_1 and p_2 lose connexity by a number of pixels greater than Δ (figure 3 (middle)). All corresponding pixels that are unknown on the L_1 layer (background layer) are then marked as disocclusion (reported pixels in red in figure 3 (left)). When this process is finished for all inter-exclusive pairs, all disocclusions have been found. More importantly, these disocclusions are now associated with the corresponding backgrounds which ensures background/foreground differentiation. This is a key point of the proposed approach and especially for the inpainting process (see section 2.2).

Anti-ghosting: The last phase of the pre-processing is the anti-ghosting which erodes known data around marked disocclusions. This way, any foreground data (according to the texture image) that can end up on the background (according to the depth-map) is erased and is not considered by the inpainting algorithm when filling the disocclusions.

2.2 Inpainting

The pre-processing allows us to decompose the scene into layers in which the disocclusions have been detected. Next, the disocclusions are inpainted using the algorithm (Alg.2).

In our case, we first inpaint the depth values by interpolating them and then inpaint the texture values using the algorithm presented in [3]. Note that we could have chosen another inpainting algorithm or improved it. However, this point is out of the scope of this paper.

Algorithm 2: Inpainting.

```
tmpImage := ∅
foreach layer furthest to closest do
    copy layer to tmpImage
    inpaint tmpImage
    copy inpainted pixels to layer
end
```

2.3 Projection and crack-filling

The last thing that remains to be done is to effectively synthesize the virtual views. The algorithm is shown in (Alg.3), where a view is assembled in "viewImage". Importantly, views are synthesized fast, without additional inpainting.

3. RESULTS

To evaluate the performance of the proposed approach, two multiview sequences, Ballet and Breakdancers, have

Algorithm 3: Projection and crack-filling.

```
foreach virtual view do
    viewImage := unknown pixels
    foreach layer closest to furthest do
        project layer
        remove cracks in layer
        foreach known pixel in layer do
            if pixel is unknown in viewImage then
                copy pixel to viewImage;
            end
        end
        remove cracks in viewImage;
    end
end
```

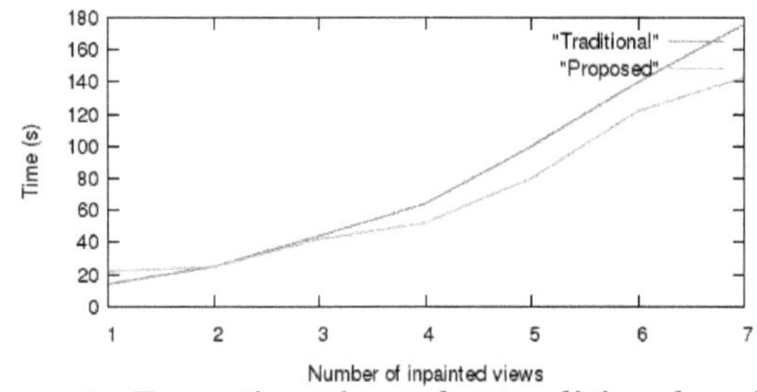

Figure 4: Execution times for traditional and proposed pipelines (for same settings).

been used [6]. They include 8 views (resolution is 1024×768) where the reference views are the views 5 and 3 respectively. The goal is to project these reference views into other camera viewpoints and to check if the visual quality between synthesized views is similar. We compare results with two state-of-the-art methods, Daribo [2] and Gautier [3]. As these two methods are based on depth maps, the used depth maps are the projected interpolated ones, as in the proposed approach. Figure 5 illustrates a comparison where the reference view is projected into 4 different viewpoints (we call $V_{i \to j}$, the projection of view i into j). The quality between synthesized views varies a lot for Daribo and Gautier's methods, whereas with the proposed approach, the quality is exactly the same ensuring a seamless transition between synthesized views. In other words, when a user wants to move his viewpoint, the quality level stays perfectly consistent. Also note that on Ballet, only the proposed approach correctly fills the hole between the man's arm and chest and correctly differentiates the woman from the wall. Figure 4 gives the running time of the proposed approach and a traditional one [3] in function of the number of synthesized views. When this number increases, the proposed approach clearly outperforms method [3]. Figure 6 illustrates the results of the proposed approach on the sequence BreakDancers. The quality is, again, the same on the different projected views. Note that a quantitative assessment is not provided due to both the ill-posed nature of the inpainting approach and the lack of space. More results on `http://people.irisa.fr/Olivier.Le_Meur/`.

4. CONCLUSION

We present a new pipeline to synthesize virtual views. In order to ensure inter-view consistency (in terms of quality), we propose to inpaint the disoccluded areas before projection. Results show the effectiveness of this approach both

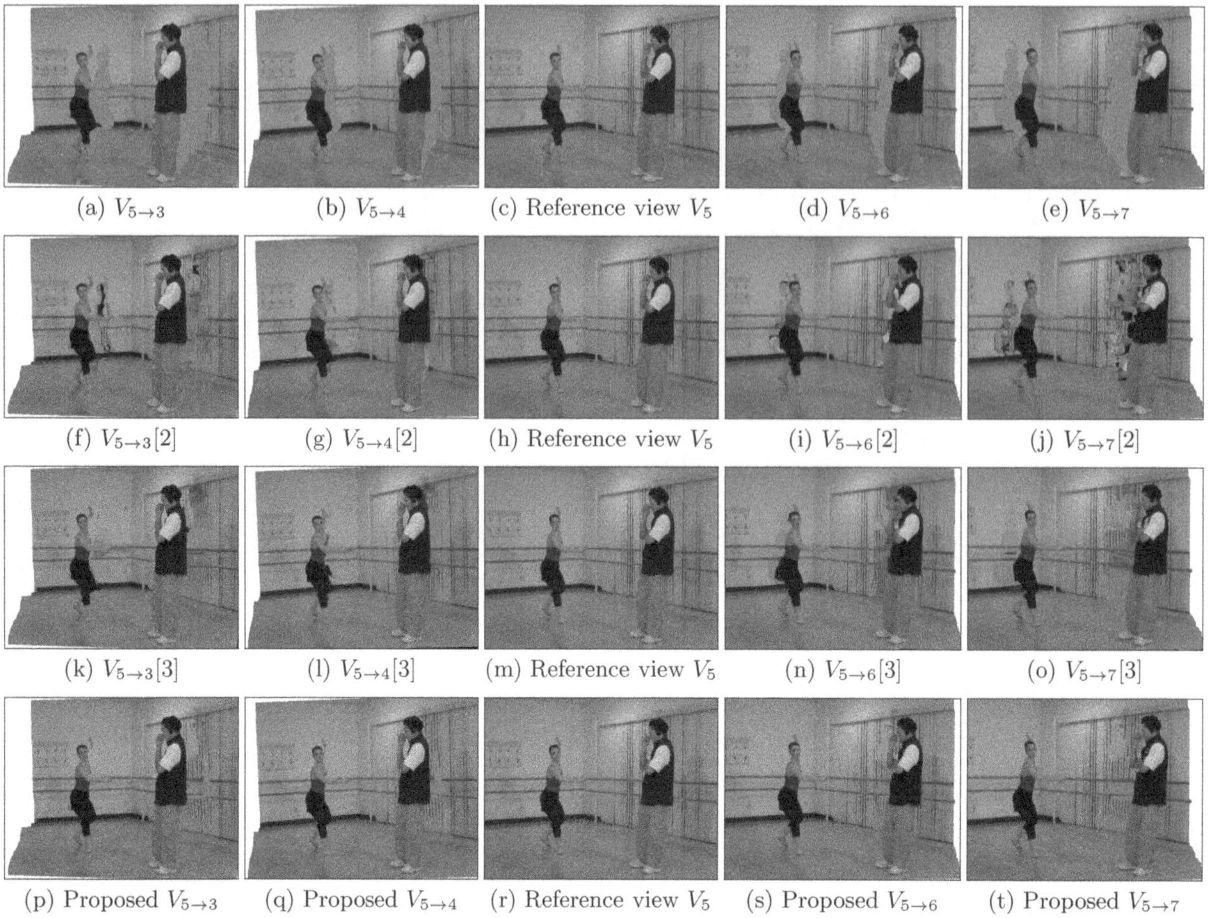

(a) $V_{5\to3}$ (b) $V_{5\to4}$ (c) Reference view V_5 (d) $V_{5\to6}$ (e) $V_{5\to7}$

(f) $V_{5\to3}$[2] (g) $V_{5\to4}$[2] (h) Reference view V_5 (i) $V_{5\to6}$[2] (j) $V_{5\to7}$[2]

(k) $V_{5\to3}$[3] (l) $V_{5\to4}$[3] (m) Reference view V_5 (n) $V_{5\to6}$[3] (o) $V_{5\to7}$[3]

(p) Proposed $V_{5\to3}$ (q) Proposed $V_{5\to4}$ (r) Reference view V_5 (s) Proposed $V_{5\to6}$ (t) Proposed $V_{5\to7}$

Figure 5: Virtual view synthesis on the sequence Ballet. (a) to (e): the view V_5 is projected into 4 viewpoints. Disoccluded areas are in red. (f) to (j): inpainting results of [2]; (k) to (o): inpainting results of [3]; (p) to (t): proposed approach. Note the quality of our results is superior and the same whatever the projection.

(a) Proposed $V_{3\to1}$ (b) Proposed $V_{3\to2}$ (c) Reference view V_3 (d) Proposed $V_{3\to4}$ (e) Proposed $V_{3\to5}$

Figure 6: Virtual view synthesis on the sequence BreakDancers.

in terms of running time and overall quality. A future study would be to consider more than one reference view. The temporal dimension is also an interesting avenue.

5. REFERENCES

[1] A. Criminisi, P. Pérez, and K. Toyama. Region filling and object removal by exemplar-based image inpainting. *IEEE trans. on Image Processing*, 13:1200–1212, 2004.

[2] I. Daribo and B. Pesquet-Popescu. Depth-aided image inpainting for novel view synthesis. In *Multimedia Signal Processing (MMSP)*, pages 167–170, 2010.

[3] J. Gautier, O. Le Meur, and C. Guillemot. Depth-based image completion for view synthesis. In *3DTV Conference*, 2011.

[4] L. Ma, L. Do, and P. de With. Depth-guided inpainting algorithm for free-viewpoint video. In *ICIP*, pages 1721–1724, 2012.

[5] W. Sun, C. A. Oscar, L. Xu, Y. Li, W. Hu, and Z. Yu. Extended criminisi's algorithm by modifying the priority function and the patch matching criteria. In *ACM Multimedia*, pages 733–736, 2012.

[6] C. Zitnick, S. Kang, M. Uyttendaele, S. Winder, and R. Szeliski. High-quality video view interpolation using a layered representation. In *ACM SIGGRAPH*, pages 600–608, 2004.

Improving event detection using related videos and Relevance Degree Support Vector Machines

Christos Tzelepis, Nikolaos Gkalelis, Vasileios Mezaris, Ioannis Kompatsiaris
Information Technologies Institute/CERTH
6th Km Charilaou-Thermi Road, Thermi 57001, Greece
{tzelepis, gkalelis, bmezaris, ikom}@iti.gr

ABSTRACT

In this paper, a new method that exploits *related* videos for the problem of event detection is proposed, where *related* videos are videos that are closely but not fully associated with the event of interest. In particular, the Weighted Margin SVM formulation is modified so that related class observations can be effectively incorporated in the optimization problem. The resulting Relevance Degree SVM is especially useful in problems where only a limited number of training observations is provided, e.g., for the EK10Ex subtask of TRECVID MED, where only ten positive and ten related samples are provided for the training of a complex event detector. Experimental results on the TRECVID MED 2011 dataset verify the effectiveness of the proposed method.

Categories and Subject Descriptors

H.3.1 [**Information Storage and Retrieval**]: Content Analysis and Indexing

General Terms

Algorithms, Experimentation, Theory

Keywords

Video event detection, Very few positive samples, Relevance Degree Support Vector Machines.

1. INTRODUCTION

High-level (or complex) event detection in video has recently received considerable attention in a wide range of applications such as video organization, annotation and retrieval [1]. This interest is motivated from recent studies in psychophysics indicating that high-level events play an essential role in structuring our memories and recalling our experiences [2]. That is, it is expected that an event-based organization of video content can significantly contribute to bridging the semantic gap between human and machine interpretations of multimedia.

MM'13, October 21–25, 2013, Barcelona, Spain.
Copyright 2013 ACM 978-1-4503-2404-5/13/10 ...$15.00.
http://dx.doi.org/10.1145/2502081.2502176.

There are numerous challenges associated with the detection of events in videos, related with the inherent complexity of events, the variability of videos of a given event that are captured with different video cameras, and other. To deal with these difficulties, usually a large-scale annotated dataset of training videos is used for capturing as much as possible of the variability in the appearance of each event. However, the creation of such a dataset is a tedious and expensive procedure, or sometimes not feasible, e.g., in cases of rare events. To this end, in this paper we investigate the problem of event detection where only a limited number of positive and related (i.e., videos that are closely related with the event, but do not meet the exact requirements for being a positive event instance [3]) event videos are provided. Specifically, the Weighted Margin SVMs (WMSVMs) presented in [4] are modified using an appropriate slack normalization function, so that event information in the related videos can be effectively exploited in the resulting Relevance Degree SVM (RDSVM) formulation.

The paper is organized as follows. In Section 2 related work is reviewed, and in Section 3 RDSVMs are described. Results of the application of RDSVMs to the TRECVID MED 2011 dataset are provided in Section 4, while conclusions are drawn and future work is discussed in Section 5.

2. RELATED WORK

Only a limited number of works have been reported that deal with the problem of event detection in video using a few training observations [3]. Most of them are in the context of the EK10Ex TRECVID MED subtask, where only 10 positive and 10 related videos are provided for each target event. For instance, in [5, 6] various low-level (e.g., SIFT, MoSIFT, etc), intermediate-level (e.g., semantic model vectors related to the TRECVID SIN task), and textual (OCR, ASR, etc) features are used to learn the events. In [7], an auxiliary set containing videos of several semantic concepts is exploited to leverage additional event information. However, differently from our method, none of these works takes full advantage of the related videos provided in the EK10Ex subtask; instead, related samples of each target event are either excluded from the training procedure, or are treated as purely positive or negative instances.

The exploitation of related videos can be achieved using a knowledge adaptation technique, such as WMSVMs [4], or maximum margin discriminant analysis [8]. Typically, these methods derive a weight for each positive observation in the training set and utilize this weight in their optimization criterion. To the best of our knowledge, the applicability of such techniques to video event detection problems such as that of the EK10Ex subtask has not been investigated.

3. SUPPORT VECTOR MACHINES WITH RELEVANCE DEGREES

Let $\mathcal{X} = \{(\mathbf{x}_i, y_i)|i = 1, ..., N\}$ be an annotated dataset of N observations, where $\mathbf{x}_i \in \Re^L$ is the feature vector representation of the i-th observation in the L-dimensional space with label $y_i \in \{0, \pm 1\}$ denoting that the i-th observation is a positive ($y_i = +1$), a negative ($y_i = -1$), or a related ($y_i = 0$) instance of the class. To allow the use of the RDSVM, the above problem is reformulated as $\mathcal{X} = \{(\mathbf{x}_i, y_i, u_i)|i = 1, ..., N\}$, where $y_i \in \{\pm 1\}$, and $u_i \in \{0, 1\}$ is the so-called relevance label denoting that the i-th observation is a true ($u_i = 0$) or a related ($u_i = 1$) instance of the class y_i.

For the exploitation of the related observations, the SVM formulation presented in [4] is utilized. In [4], each training sample $\mathbf{x}_i$ is associated with a confidence value v_i, and a monotonically increasing function $g(v_i)$ (called slack normalization function) is used to weight each slack variable ξ_i. In this way, the support vectors (SVs) that are associated with a higher confidence value have greater contribution to the computation of the separating hyperplane. Here, we modify this function so that only related class observations are associated with a confidence value $c_i \in (0, 1]$ (called hereafter relevance degree) indicating the degree of relevance of the i-th observation with the class it is related. That is, g is defined as follows:

$$g(u_i) = \begin{cases} 1 & \text{if } u_i = 0, \\ c_i & \text{if } u_i = 1. \end{cases} \quad (1)$$

We then wish to minimize

$$Q(\mathbf{w}, b, \boldsymbol{\xi}) = \frac{1}{2}\|\mathbf{w}\|^2 + C\sum_{i=1}^{N} g(u_i)\xi_i, \quad (2)$$

subject to the following constraints

$$y_i(\mathbf{w}^T\varphi(\mathbf{x}_i) + b) \geq 1 - \xi_i,\ i = 1...N, \quad (3)$$

where $\mathbf{w} \in \Re^L$, $\xi_i = \max(0, 1 - y_i\mathbf{w}^T\mathbf{x}_i)$, $b \in \Re$ and $C \in \Re_+$ are the weight vector, the slack variables, the bias and the penalty term, respectively. Moreover, φ denotes a mapping from the input space $\Re^L$ into a new, high-dimensional feature space $\mathcal{F}$ [9].

The corresponding primal Lagrangian is given from

$$L_P(\mathbf{w}, b, \xi, \boldsymbol{\alpha}, \boldsymbol{\beta}) = \frac{1}{2}\|\mathbf{w}\|^2 + C\sum_{i=1}^{N} g(u_i)\xi_i - \sum_{i=1}^{N} \alpha_i[y_i(\mathbf{w}^T\varphi(\mathbf{x}_i) + b) - 1 + \xi_i] - \sum_{i=1}^{N} \beta_i\xi_i, \quad (4)$$

where $\boldsymbol{\alpha} = [\alpha_1, ..., \alpha_N]^T$, $\boldsymbol{\beta} = [\beta_1, ..., \beta_N]^T$ are the corresponding non-negative Lagrange multipliers.

Using the Karush-Kuhn-Tucker (KKT) conditions [9] the dual formulation is retrieved:

$$L_D(\boldsymbol{\alpha}) = \sum_{i=1}^{N} \alpha_i - \frac{1}{2}\sum_{i,j=1}^{N} \alpha_i\alpha_j y_i y_j K_{i,j}, \quad (5)$$

subject to the constraints

$$\sum_{i=1}^{N} \alpha_i y_i = 0, \quad (6)$$

$$0 \leq \alpha_i \leq g(u_i)C,\ i = 1, ..., N, \quad (7)$$

where K_{ij} is a Mercer kernel such that $K_{ij} = \varphi(\mathbf{x}_i)^T\varphi(\mathbf{x}_j)$ [9]. This is a quadratic programming problem which can be solved using an appropriate optimization technique (e.g. see [4]).

An unlabelled test observation is then classified according to $y_t = \text{sgn}(\sum_{i \in S} \alpha_i y_i K_{it} + b)$, where S is the set of indices corresponding to the SVs, i.e., the training observations for which $\alpha_i \neq 0$ [9]. From the above equation we observe that the larger the α_i, the more significant is the contribution of the associated SV in the classification process. Therefore, using the above RDSVM formulation (2) and as shown by (7), the contribution of the related samples in the computation of the separating hyperplane can be regulated using appropriate relevance degrees c_i.

4. APPLICATION TO VIDEO EVENT DETECTION

4.1 Dataset description

The large-scale video dataset of the TRECVID MED 2011 task is used for the application of RDSVM in the problem of event detection. This dataset consists of 13113 development and 32037 test videos belonging to the "rest of the world" class, or to one out of 10 target event classes, namely: "Birthday party" (E006), "Changing a vehicle tire" (E007), "Flash mob gathering" (E008), "Getting a vehicle unstuck" (E009), "Grooming an animal" (E010), "Making a sandwich" (E011), "Parade" ("E012), "Parkour" (E013), "Repairing an appliance" (E014), "Working on a sewing project" (E015). Example keyframes for five of them are shown in Fig. 1.

4.2 Feature vector representation

A semantic model vector approach is used for the representation of each video, similarly to the approach described in [10]. In particular, each video signal is decoded and a 1×3 spatial pyramid decomposition scheme is applied to the keyframes. The dense sampling strategy along with the opponentSIFT interest point descriptor are then applied to derive a set of feature vectors in $\Re^{384}$ for each pyramid cell, as well as the entire frame, and the k-means algorithm is utilized to construct a Bag-of-Words (BoW) model of 1000 visual words for each cell. Concatenating the BoW models, each keyframe is represented with a BoW feature vector in $\Re^{4000}$.

Subsequently, a set of L pre-trained concept detectors, $\mathcal{G} = \{g_k : \Re^{4000} \mapsto [0, 1]|k = 1, ..., L\}$ is used to provide a model vector representation of the p-th keyframe of the i-th video $\mathbf{x}_{i,p} = [x_{i,p,1}, ..., x_{i,p,L}]^T$. That is, $x_{i,p,k}$ is the response of the concept detector g_k concerning the p-th keyframe of the i-th video, expressing the degree of confidence (DoC) that the k-th concept is depicted in the keyframe. In order to derive a model vector representation $\mathbf{x}_i$ of the i-th video, the model vectors at keyframe level are averaged, $\mathbf{x}_i = \sum_{p=1}^{T_i} \mathbf{x}_{i,p}$, where T_i is the length of the i-th video in keyframes.

(a) (b) (c) (d) (e)

Figure 1: Example keyframes for 5 of the target events: (a) birthday party, (b) changing a vehicle tire, (c) flash mob gathering, (d) getting a vehicle unstuck, (e) grooming an animal.

The above concept detectors have been designed using linear SVMs and the TRECVID SIN 2012 dataset [3], which contains annotated videos for $L = 346$ concepts.

4.3 Experimental setup

The training of each target event detector is performed using 10 positive, 10 related and 70 negative videos, selected from the development set (except for the events E007 and E015, where only 6 and 2 related videos are provided, respectively). That is, a setting similar to the EK10Ex one of the TRECVID MED 2012 task is used [3].

For evaluation purposes, the proposed approach is compared with three state of the art experimental scenarios of the literature:

1. **Scenario A (noRelatedSamples)**: Related videos are excluded from this experiment. That is, only 10 positive videos are used for learning each target event, as e.g. in [5].
2. **Scenario B (relatedAsPositive)**: Related videos are used as positive examples (i.e., $y_i = +1$ and $u_i = 0$), as e.g. in [11].
3. **Scenario C (relatedAsNegative)**: Related videos are used as negative examples of each target event (i.e., $y_i = -1$ and $u_i = 0$).

The proposed approach is used in two experimental settings, as follows:

1. **Scenario D (relatedAsWeightedPositive)**: Related videos are used as related positive examples (i.e., $y_i = +1$ and $u_i = 1$) in RDSVM.
2. **Scenario E (relatedAsWeightedNegative)**: Related videos are used as related negative examples (i.e., $y_i = -1$ and $u_i = 1$) in RDSVM.

In all above settings, two different approaches to treating the related samples are tested: i) all 10 related samples are used for training the SVM or RDSVM, ii) the median model vector of the 10 related samples is computed and only the 5 that are closer to that median are used for training.

The proposed RDSVM has been implemented using a modified version of LIBSVM [12]. The radial basis function (RBF) kernel ($K_{ij} = exp(- \parallel \mathbf{x}_i - \mathbf{x}_j \parallel^2 / 2\sigma^2)$, where $\sigma \in \Re_+$ is the scale parameter) has been used. Moreover, the relevance degrees for all related videos are set to the same constant value $c \in (0, 1]$, i.e., $c_i = c \, \forall \, i$. The optimization of the parameters (C, σ) for the scenarios A, B and C is performed using a grid search on a 10-fold cross-validation procedure, where at each fold the training set is split to 90% learning set

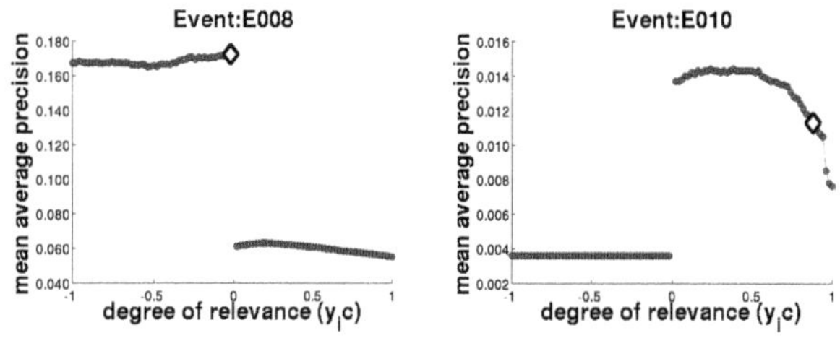

(a) E008 (b) E010

Figure 2: Selection of the relevance degrees for 2 target events using cross-validation.

and 10% validation set. For scenarios D and E, the (C, σ) values already selected for scenarios B and C, respectively, are used and the optimum value of c is selected again by cross-validation searching through the interval $(0, 1]$ with a step size equal to 0.02.

4.4 Results and discussion

Table 1 shows the performance of the proposed method, in terms of average precision (AP), for each experimental scenario and target event. Moreover, for each experimental scenario, the mean average precision (MAP) across all target events is shown in the last column. From these results we observe that the way the related videos should be treated (i.e., as positive or negative samples) depends on the particular event under consideration. It also depends heavily on the actual related samples that are employed. Overall, in terms of MAP, we see that scenarios D and E, which use RDSVM, outperform scenarios A-C, which represent the current state of the art. Moreover, when related samples are pruned using the median clustering, scenarios B-E consistently provide better results. In this case, overall, the best performance is achieved by scenario E.

In Fig. 2, we show the effect of the relevance degree c in the detection performance for two target events (E008 and E010) when related samples are pruned using median clustering as discussed above. In particular, for scenarios D and E we learn the events for different values of c in the range $(0, 1]$ with a step size equal to 0.02, and compute the corresponding MAP achieved in the evaluation set. For the sake of compactness, the results for both scenarios D and E concerning the same target event are depicted in the same diagram. This is achieved using the quantity $y_i c$ (instead of c) in the horizontal axis of the diagrams.

In conclusion, contrary to the most methods in the literature that use the related samples as either purely negative or positive (e.g. see [11]), the proposed method allows for

Table 1: Evaluation of event detection approaches on the TRECVID MED 2011 dataset.

Experimental Scenarios	Target Events *E006*	*E007*	*E008*	*E009*	*E010*	*E011*	*E012*	*E013*	*E014*	*E015*	*MAP*
Scenario A	0.0121	0.0076	0.0772	0.0190	0.0035	0.0137	0.0212	0.0615	0.1191	0.0083	0.0343
Full set of 10 randomly selected related samples											
Scenario B	0.0124	0.0317	0.0933	0.0205	0.0027	0.0080	0.0257	0.0551	0.0867	0.0082	0.0344
Scenario C	0.0210	0.0149	0.0613	**0.0299**	**0.0033**	**0.0101**	0.0159	0.0486	**0.1358**	0.0068	0.0348
Scenario D	0.0123	**0.0393**	**0.1197**	0.0205	0.0029	0.0080	**0.0264**	**0.0620**	0.0894	0.0059	**0.0386**
Scenario E	**0.0296**	0.0149	0.0658	**0.0299**	**0.0033**	0.0087	0.0201	0.0507	0.1357	**0.0089**	0.0368
Subset of 5 related samples using the median clustering method											
Scenario B	**0.0466**	0.0060	0.0551	0.0218	0.0076	**0.0098**	**0.0423**	0.0559	0.1249	0.0082	0.0378
Scenario C	0.0117	**0.0119**	0.1672	0.0377	0.0036	0.0085	0.0157	0.0881	0.0631	0.0068	0.0414
Scenario D	0.0447	0.0060	0.0573	0.0218	**0.0113**	**0.0098**	0.0422	0.0594	**0.1357**	0.0059	0.0394
Scenario E	0.0117	0.0118	**0.1721**	**0.0379**	0.0036	0.0092	0.0222	**0.0876**	0.0633	**0.0089**	**0.0428**
Selection D,E	0.0447	0.0118	0.1721	0.0379	0.0113	0.0098	0.0222	0.0876	0.0633	0.0059	0.0467

a more careful treatment of the related samples, which can provide a considerable performance improvement.

Finally, we should note that despite the limited number of positive training videos, for 7 out of 10 target events the best way of treating the related samples (i.e., as negative or positive) in RDSVM could be correctly decided automatically at the RDSVM training stage, by looking at the average of the AP values attained during cross-validation. For instance, in Fig. 2 the signed value of c that was selected in this way is shown using a diamond marker. The overall results of this automatic selection are shown in the last row of Table 1 (named "Selection D, E"), indicating that this process can lead to further improvement of the overall detection results in terms of MAP.

5. CONCLUSIONS AND FUTURE WORK

A method that effectivelly exploits related class observations for the detection of events in videos was proposed in this paper. The applicability of the method was verified using the TRECVID MED 2011 dataset, where similar to the EK10Ex subtask of MED 2012 only a limited number of positive videos were used during the training stage.

In the future, we plan to combine the proposed method with LSSVMs [13] so that relevance degrees can be exploited at the subclass level (i.e., using different values of c_i for different subclasses of the related samples).

6. ACKNOWLEDGMENT

This work was supported by the European Commission under contracts FP7-287911 LinkedTV, FP7-600826 ForgetIT and FP7-318101 MediaMixer.

7. REFERENCES

[1] Y.-G. Jiang, S. Bhattacharya, S.-F. Chang, and M. Shah, "High-level event recognition in unconstrained videos," *International Journal of Multimedia Information Retrieval*, pp. 1–29, 2012.

[2] N. R. Brown, "On the prevalence of event clusters in autobiographical memory," *Social Cognition*, vol. 23, no. 1, 2005.

[3] P. Over, G. Awad, M. Martial, J. Fiscus, G. Sanders, B. Shaw, W. Kraaij, and A. F. Smeaton, "TRECVID 2012 – an overview of the goals, tasks, data, evaluation mechanisms and metrics," in *Proc. of TRECVID 2012*. NIST, USA, 2012.

[4] X. Wu and R. Srihari, "Incorporating prior knowledge with weighted margin support vector machines," in *Proc. 10th ACM SIGKDD Int. Conf. on Knowledge discovery and data mining*. ACM, 2004, pp. 326–333.

[5] M. Akbacak, R.C. Bolles, J. B. Burns, M. Eliot, et al., "The 2012 SESAME multimedia event detection (MED) system," in *Proc. TRECVID 2012 Workshop*, Nov. 2012.

[6] H. Cheng, J. Liu, S. Ali, O. Javed, et al., "Sri-sarnoff AURORA system at TRECVID 2012 multimedia event detection and recounting," in *Proc. TRECVID 2012 Workshop*, Nov. 2012.

[7] Z. Ma, Y. Yang, Y. Cai, N. Sebe, and A. G Hauptmann, "Knowledge adaptation for Ad Hoc multimedia event detection with few exemplars," in *Proc. 20th ACM Int. Conf. on Multimedia*. ACM, 2012, pp. 469–478.

[8] W. Zheng, C. Zou, and L. Zhao, "Weighted maximum margin discriminant analysis with kernels," *Neurocomputing*, vol. 67, pp. 357–362, 2005.

[9] V. Vapnik, *Statistical learning theory*, New York: Willey, 1998.

[10] A. Moumtzidou, N. Gkalelis, P. Sidiropoulos, M. Dimopoulos, S. Nikolopoulos, S. Vrochidis, V. Mezaris, and I. Kompatsiaris, "ITI-CERTH participation to TRECVID 2012," in *Proc. TRECVID 2012 Workshop*. Nov. 2012, Gaithersburg, MD, USA.

[11] A. Moumtzidou, P. Sidiropoulos, S. Vrochidis, N. Gkalelis, S. Nikolopoulos, V. Mezaris, I. Kompatsiaris, and I. Patras, "ITI-CERTH participation to TRECVID 2011," in *Proc. TRECVID 2011 Workshop*, Dec. 2011.

[12] C.-C. Chang and C.-J. Lin, "LIBSVM: A library for support vector machines," *ACM Transactions on Intelligent Systems and Technology*, vol. 2, no. 3, pp. 27:1–27:27, May 2011.

[13] N. Gkalelis, V. Mezaris, I. Kompatsiaris, and T. Stathaki, "Linear subclass support vector machines," *IEEE Signal Process. Lett.*, vol. 19, no. 9, pp. 575–578, Sept. 2012.

Consistent Stereo Image Editing

Tao Yan[1,2], Shengfeng He[2], Rynson W.H. Lau[2] and Yun Xu[1]
[1]University of Science and Technology of China, China
[2]City University of Hong Kong, Hong Kong
yantao@mail.ustc.edu.cn, shengfeng_he@yahoo.com,
rynson.lau@cityu.edu.hk, xuyun@ustc.edu.cn

ABSTRACT

Stereo images and videos are very popular in recent years, and techniques for processing this media are attracting a lot of attention. In this paper, we extend the shift-map method for stereo image editing. Our method simultaneously processes the left and right images on pixel level using a global optimization algorithm. It enforces photo consistence between the two images and preserves 3D scene structures. It also addresses the occlusion and disocclusion problem, which may enable many stereo image editing functions, such as depth mapping, object depth adjustment and non-homogeneous image resizing. Our experiments show that the proposed method produces high quality results in various editing functions.

Categories and Subject Descriptors

I.4 [**IMAGE PROCESSING AND COMPUTER VISION**]: Enhancement

Keywords

Stereo Images Editing, Depth Mapping, Multi-label Optimization

1. INTRODUCTION

With the popularity of stereo (or 3D) videos, techniques for producing and editing of stereo media are attracting a lot of research attention in recent years. In general, a stereo image contains two regular 2D images, which are captured from the same scene at the same time but from slightly different locations. A naive solution for editing a stereo image is to separately process the left and right images and then recombine them to form the output stereo image. This will, however, introduce inconsistences between the left and right images. To address this problem, we may apply a global optimization algorithm to simultaneously process the left and right images to ensure consistence, e.g., [6] [11].

Most existing stereo editing works [3] [4] [6] [8] [7] [9] [11] are based on mesh warping, which treat the whole left or right image as a continuous plane by fitting a quad or triangle mesh to it and warp the shape of the mesh in a content-aware manner. Although this kind of methods are usually robust, they suffer from two major limitations. First, they cannot handle object boundaries well. Second, they cannot support editing functions that introduce new occlusion or disocclusion. As a result, some image editing functions such as depth mapping, object depth adjustment and non-homogeneous image resizing cannot be easily supported by mesh warping based methods. To address these limitations, we propose a novel framework for consistent stereo image editing in this paper. It is based on the shift-map method [10] and the multi-label optimization method [2]. The basic-idea of shift-map is that a pixel (x,y) in the output image can be obtained from a pixel $(x+t_x, y+t_y)$ of the input image. Hence, the output image can be computed as:

$$I'(x,y) = I(x+t_x, y+t_y) \quad (1)$$

where I is the input image. I' is the output image. A main objective of shift-map is to address the limitations of the mesh warping methods in regular 2D image editing.

The main contribution of this work is to extend the shift-map method for stereo image editing. The proposed method processes both the left and right images simultaneously to preserve photo consistence and minimize distortion in image editing. It is also able to handle occlusion and disocclusion, which are introduced by the editing operations, through a revised multi-label optimization algorithm. This allows the proposed method to support many different stereo editing functions, including depth mapping, object depth adjustment and non-homogeneous stereo image resizing.

The rest of this paper is organized as follows. Section 2 briefly summarizes related works on stereo image processing. Section 3 presents our consistent stereo image editing method. Section 4 discusses some experimental results and image editing functions.

2. RELATED WORK

Techniques for stereo image/video editing can be roughly classified into continuous methods and discrete methods. They are summarized as follows.

Continuous Methods: This type of methods is mainly based on mesh warping. Lang et al. [6] propose a disparity mapping method with four simple operators for adjusting the disparity range of stereo videos. However, their method does not consider the relative depths among objects in the stereo image and the relationship between depth perception and viewing parameters, such as display distance and size. They also do not consider 3D scene structure preservation. To overcome the display adaptation problem, Yan et al. [11] propose a depth mapping method that applies 3D image analysis techniques to remap the depth range of stereo videos according to the viewing parameters. Their method attempts to preserve 3D scene structures and enforce depth and temporal coherences through a global optimization algorithm.

There is some work on non-homogeneous stereo image resizing. Chang et al. [3] propose a mesh warping based method for resizing stereo images according to the change in viewing parame-

MM'13, October 21 - 25 2013, Barcelona, Spain

http://dx.doi.org/10.1145/2502081.2502177

ters. However, their method may introduce distortion to the shape of prominent objects. Lee et al. [7] fit a separate mesh to each depth layer of a stereo image, but they do not handle the disocclusion problem. In addition, they also rely on the user to segment the stereo image into different depth layers. There is also some work to develop specific stereo image editing techniques. Luo et al. [8] present a method for seamless stereo image cloning, which involves shape adjustment of the target object according to the depth and the color of the background stereo image. Tong et al. [4] propose a depth-consistent stereo image composition method, which allows interactive blending of a 2D image object on a stereo image. Niu et al. [9] extend the traditional 2D image warping technique for stereo images. Their objective is to preserve prominent objects and 3D scene structure.

Although warping based methods can produce visually pleasing results for many image processing functions, the main drawback is that they cannot handle object boundaries (or discontinuity) well. As a result, they cannot model scene occlusion and disocclusion.

Discrete Methods: Basha et al. [1] extend the seam carving method to non-homogeneous stereo image resizing. Their method simultaneously carves a pair of piece-wise continuous seams in both images, while minimizing distortion in appearance and depth. However, its performance is affected by the noise in the disparity map. In addition, as seam carving is based on dynamic programming, the result is not globally optimal. On the other hand, our method is a global optimization method and it is able to work with moderate quality disparity maps. Our method can also be applied to many stereo editing functions, in addition to non-homogeneous stereo image resizing.

The shift-map method [10] characterizes geometric rearrangement of a 2D image by a shift-map. It is a general tool for 2D image editing, such as resizing, composition and object removal. As it is not designed for handling stereo images, it does not consider consistence between the left and right images when applied to stereo images. It also cannot automatically handle occlusion and disocclusion introduced by image editing. In addition, it does not consider 3D structure correctness and preservation as it is just for 2D image editing. Our method extends the shift-map method to handle stereo images and addresses the above limitations.

3. OUR METHOD

We first denote the input stereo image pair as I_L (left image) and I_R (right image), their corresponding disparity maps as D_{LR} and D_{RL}, the output image pair as I'_L and I'_R, and their shift-maps as M_L and M_R, respectively. We formulate the stereo image editing problem as an energy minimization problem as follows:

$$E = E_{dc} + \omega_{sc} E_{sc} + \omega_{ph} E_{ph} + \omega_{pl} E_{pl} \quad (2)$$

where E_{dc} is the data cost for pixel rearrangement. E_{sc} is the smooth cost between neighboring pixels within the left or right image separately. E_{ph} is used to enforce photo consistence between the left and right images. E_{pl} is used to preserve 3D planes in the stereo image. $\omega_{sc} = 30$, $\omega_{ph} = 1$ and $\omega_{pl} = 10^4$ are weights used in our implementation. E_{dc} and E_{sc} are also used in [10] and are designed for 2D image editing. We modify them for stereo image editing. E_{ph} and E_{pl} are two new energy terms that we introduce to enforce photo consistence and feature preservation, respectively, in stereo image editing.

We apply the multi-label optimization method [2] to solve the above energy function. Each pixel in the output image is assigned a label, which is a vector indicating its location in the input image. The output stereo image can then be obtained according to the computed shift maps and the input stereo image.

3.1 Disparity Map Computation

In stereo image editing, we often need to determine the relationship between the left and right images. We compute the left to right D_{LR} and right to left D_{RL} disparity maps for the input stereo image pair using the method suggested by [2]. Since some disparity values, such as those in the occluded regions or near to the image boundary, may be incorrect, we perform a left-right consistence check on the computed disparity maps and delete those values that are inconsistent. We would like to emphasize here that the disparity maps needed in our method do not need to be very dense.

3.2 Data Cost

A lot of image editing functions involve pixel rearrangement. Energy term E_{dc} is used to model this data cost. To extend it to stereo images, we formulate this energy term as:

$$E_{dc} = \sum_{p \in I'_L \cup I'_R} w_s(w_I min(\|t_p - g(p)\|^2, \tau_L) + min(\|I(p+t_p) - \hat{I}(p)\|^2, \tau_I) + min(\|D(p+t_p) - \hat{D}(p)\|^2, \tau_D)) \quad (3)$$

where t_p is the label of pixel p in the output image. $g(p)$ is the target label of p, which is known in advance. w_S is the importance of pixel $p+t_p$ in the input image. The importance maps of a stereo image are computed by dividing the saliency of each pixel by its normalized disparity value. We then enhance the importance maps with user defined masks. $\hat{I}(p)$ and $\hat{D}(p)$ are the target color and disparity of p. In stereo image editing, it is possible that some pixels may move to the same location in the output image. Since only the nearest pixels should be visible, we use a depth buffer to determine the values of $\hat{I}(p)$ and $\hat{D}(p)$.

3.3 Smooth Cost

Energy term E_{sc} is used to enforce the smoothness of labels among neighboring pixels. Pritch et al. [10] only use color and image gradient information to compute the smooth cost of neighboring pixels. Since stereo images contain depth information, we extend the smooth cost to $\mathbf{V} = \langle I, \bigtriangledown I, D \rangle$, where I is the color information, $\bigtriangledown I$ is image gradient, D is the disparity value. We define our smooth penalty function as:

$$E_{sc} = \sum_{(p,q) \in N_L \cup N_R} min(\mathbf{w}_v^T(|\mathbf{V}_{p+t_p} - \mathbf{V}_{n'_q}| + |\mathbf{V}_{n'_p} - \mathbf{V}_{q+t_q}|), \tau_{sc}) \quad (4)$$

where N_L and N_R refer to neighboring pixel pairs in the left and right output images. Here, we only consider 4-connected pixel neighborhood. Consider two neighboring pixels, $p = (x_1, y_1)$ and $q = (x_2, y_2)$. t_p and t_q denote labels of p and q. $n'_p = (x_1 + t_{x_1} + 1, y_1 + t_{y_1},)$ and $n'_q = (x_2 + t_{x_2} - 1, y_2 + t_{y_2})$, if $x_1 < x_2$ and $y_1 = y_2$. $n'_p = (x_1 + t_{x_1}, y_1 + t_{y_1} + 1)$ and $n'_q = (x_2 + t_{x_2}, y_2 + t_{y_2} - 1)$, if $x_1 = x_2$ and $y_1 < y_2$.

We would like to point out here that the smooth cost defined in [10] is not suitable for us, as it does not satisfy the regularity constraint [5]: $E^{i,j}(0,0) + E^{i,j}(1,1) \leq E^{i,j}(0,1) + E^{i,j}(1,0)$. As such, the optimization step may not produce acceptable minimal energy values in stereo image editing. Obviously, our smooth cost is regular and metric [2] [5], and does not have this problem.

3.4 Photo Consistence

In a stereo image, each pair of matched pixels from the left and right images should have similar colors, and we use this matched pixel pair to estimate its depth. Energy term E_{ph} is used to ensure photo consistence between the left and right images through checking the color/depth consistence.

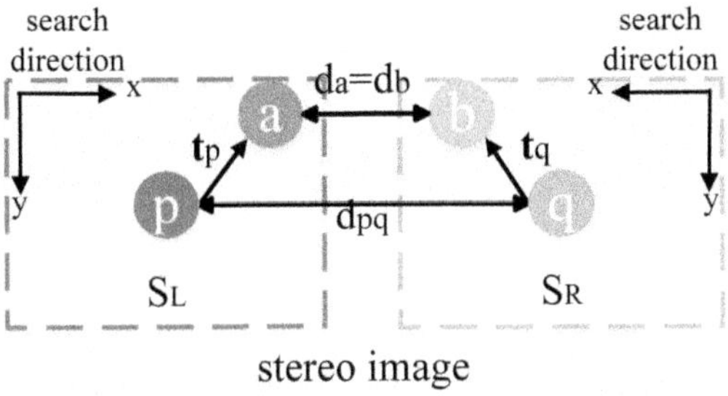

Figure 1: To find a candidate matched pixel pair in depth mapping. Pixel a is within search window S_L of p in the left image; pixel b is within search window S_R of q in the right image. If a and b are a corresponding pixel pair in the input images, $t_p = t_q$, and d_{pq} is within an acceptable disparity range, then p and q are considered as a candidate matched pixel pair in output images.

Our objective here is to produce a stereo output image that satisfies the photo consistence constraint. However, it is difficult to determine matched pixel pairs in the output stereo image before we obtain this output image. Here, we propose a strategy to dynamically determine matched pixel pairs for the output image in our global optimization step. We first select some candidate matched pixel pairs from the left image to the right image and some from the right image to the left image. We then put all these candidate matched pixel pairs into the global optimization process to determine the final matched pixel pairs.

As shown in Fig. 1, let p be a pixel in I'_L and q be a pixel in I'_R. We define the search windows for p and q as S_L and S_R. Search window S_L (or S_R) contains all pixels in the input image I_L (or I_R) that can be shifted to p (or q) in the output image I'_L (or I'_L). For different editing functions, the search directions (the order of labeling) of S_L and S_R may be different. For depth mapping, the search direction of S_L is from left to right and top to bottom, while that of S_R is from right to left and top to bottom. This is to satisfy the depth mapping constraint [11], and regularity and metric constraint.

We first consider how to determine the candidate matched pixel pairs from the left image to the right image. Let $a = I_L(x,y)$ be a pixel within S_L of p, where $x = x_p + t_{x_p}$ and $y = y_p + t_{y_p}$. Let $b = I_R(x + D_{LR}(x,y), y)$ be a pixel in S_R of q. If $D_{LR}(x,y) = D_{RL}(x + D_{LR}(x,y), y)$ and $|I_L(x,y) - I_R(x + D_{LR}(x,y), y)| < \phi$, then b is said to be the corresponding pixel of a. Now, if the distance $(2t_{x_p} + D_{LR}(x,y))$ between $p = (x_p, y_p)$ and $q = (x_p + 2t_{x_p} + D_{LR}(x,y), y_p)$ is within an acceptable disparity range, then we assume that p and q are a candidate matched pixel pair. (Here, an acceptable disparity range for pixels p and q in the output stereo image is defined as the range from $D_{LR}(a)$ to the user specified maximum disparity for a.) Finally, if there are no edges existed between p and q, we add an undirected edge between them.

We then consider how to determine the candidate matched pixel pairs from the right image to the left image. Let $b = I_R(x,y)$ be a pixel within S_R of q, where $x = x_q - t_{x_q}$ and $y = y_q + t_{y_q}$. Let $a = I_L(x - D_{RL}(x,y), y)$ be a pixel in S_L of p. Similarly, if $D_{RL}(x,y) = D_{LR}(x - D_{RL}(x,y), y)$ and $|I_R(x,y) - I_L(x - D_{RL}(x,y), y)| < \phi$, then a is said to be the corresponding pixel of b. Again, if the distance $(2t_{x_q} + D_{RL}(x,y))$ between $q = (x_q, y_q)$ and $p = (x_p - 2t_{x_q} - D_{RL}(x,y), y_q)$ is within an acceptable disparity range, then we assume that q and p are a candidate matched pixel pair. Finally, if there are no edges existed between p and q, we add an undirected edge between them. The penalty of undirected edge (p,q) is defined as:

$$\phi_{ph}(p,q,t_p,t_q) = \begin{cases} 0, & \text{if } t_p = t_q \\ K, & \text{else} \end{cases} \tag{5}$$

Figure 2: Depth mapping: (a) original stereo image; (b) our result.

where, $\phi = 30$ and $K = 10^2$ in our implementation. Obviously, this penalty definition is metric [2]. Thus, E_{ph} is defined as:

$$E_{ph} = \sum_{(p,q) \in M_{LR} \bigcup M_{RL}} \phi_{ph}(p,q,t_p,t_q) \tag{6}$$

where M_{LR} and M_{RL} are candidate matched pixel pairs from the left image to the right and the right image to the left, respectively.

3.5 3D Feature Preservation

In stereo image editing, 3D image features should be carefully preserved. Since edge preservation is already considered in our smooth cost function. We mainly consider plane preservation.

We use P_l and P_r to represent the same plane projected in the left and right images. Pixels within P_l should satisfy constraint $d = a_l x + b_l y + c_l$, and pixels within P_r should satisfy constraint $d = a_r x + b_r y + c_r$, where d is the disparity of (x,y). a_l, b_l, c_l and a_r, b_r, c_r are parameters of the plane equations, which can be determined by [11].

In our current implementation, we manually define a mask on the input left image to obtain a plane mask. The plane preservation mask for right image is then computed automatically. We use the method presented in [11] to compute the target coordinates $(\hat{x}_{i,l}, \hat{y}_i)$ and $(\hat{x}_{i,r}, \hat{y}_i)$ of each matched pixel pair $(x_{i,l}, y_i)$ and $(x_{i,r}, y_i)$ on P_l and P_r. We define the plane preservation penalty as:

$$E_{pl} = \sum_{(P_l,P_r)} \sum_i \{min(|t_{i,x,l} - (\hat{x}_{i,l} - x_{i,l})|, 1) + min(|t_{i,x,r} - (\hat{x}_{i,r} - x_{i,r})|, 1) + min(|t_{i,y} - (\hat{y}_i - y_i)|, 1)\} \tag{7}$$

4. RESULTS AND APPLICATIONS

We have implemented the proposed method in C and OpenCV. In our experiments, we used a 19*in* screen with a resolution of 1280×1024 and pixel density of $\beta = 0.293mm/pixel$. Other parameter setting include $w_l = 100$, $\tau_L = 10$, $\tau_l = 10^4$, $\tau_D = 2 \times 10^2$, $\mathbf{w}_v = \langle 1, 10, 1 \rangle$, and $\tau_{sc} = 10^4$. We ran the program (unoptimized) on a PC with an i5 3.1GHz CPU and 8GB RAM. The execution time is about 8 minutes for a stereo image of resolution 400×300.

In the following paragraphs, we discuss three popular image editing functions to show the effectiveness of the proposed method. Stereo images are shown as red(left)-cyan(right). More results can be found in the supplementary.

Depth Mapping: This is to modify the depth range of a stereo image. It is typically achieved by adjusting the content disparity of the stereo image. Our depth mapping function is based on linear depth mapping proposed by [11]. The relationship between disparity and depth perceived by the viewer can be described as:

$$Z = \frac{et}{e - s} \tag{8}$$

where e is the interaxial distance set as 65*mm*. t is the screen distance from the viewer and is set to 500*mm* in all our experiments. $s = d/\beta$ is the parallax of a matched pixel pair. d is the

(a) (b) (c)

Figure 3: Depth mapping: (a) original stereo image; (b) our result; (c) result from [11]. Target depth range set using $\eta_1 = 0$ and $\eta_2 = 1^o$.

disparity a matched pixel pair and β is the pixel density of the screen. Given the retinal disparity limits η_1 and η_2, the target depth range then becomes (Z'_{min}, Z'_{max}), where $Z'_{min} = et/(e-\eta_1 t)$ and $Z'_{max} = et/(e-\eta_2 t)$.

Fig. 2 shows that our method can enlarge the depth range of the original image in such a way that the small fish becomes nearer to the viewer, without destroying the background depth layer. Fig. 3 compares our method with [11]. The proposed method performs favorably against [11] in two aspects. First, our method can map an original depth range to a much larger depth range, while the editable depth range of [11] is limited by the mesh edge stretching constraint and other constraints. As an example, although both methods are set to the same target depth range in Fig. 3, we can see that the depth range of our result shown in the first and fourth rows of Fig. 3 is much larger than that of [11]; in the fourth row of Fig. 3, the depth distance between the car and the women on the right and the depth distance between the car and the distant men on the left are enlarged more obviously in our result than that of [11]. Second, our method preserves 3D scene structure better. As an example, our method can preserve the shape and the details of the buildings on the right of the images in the first and third rows of Fig. 3 better than [11]. In second row of Fig. 3, our method also preserves the lamppost and the fence on the bridge much better than [11]. In addition, the left and right images of each stereo result show that our method preserves 2D image features much better than [11] too.

Object Depth Adjustment: This is to change the depth of a selected/prominent 3D object. In Fig. 4, we move the man in the middle closer to the viewer. After the operation, our optimization step automatically fills the disoccluded pixels without obvious distortion.

Non-homogeneous Image Resizing: This is to change the aspect ratio of a stereo image non-homogeneously to adapt it to different displays. We compare our method with [1], which is a representative non-homogeneous method for resizing stereo images, as shown in Fig. 5. We can see that our method can preserve the plant and the flower pot much better than [1], and there is no perceptible distortion in our result.

(a) (b)

Figure 4: Object depth adjustment: (a) original stereo image; (b) our result.

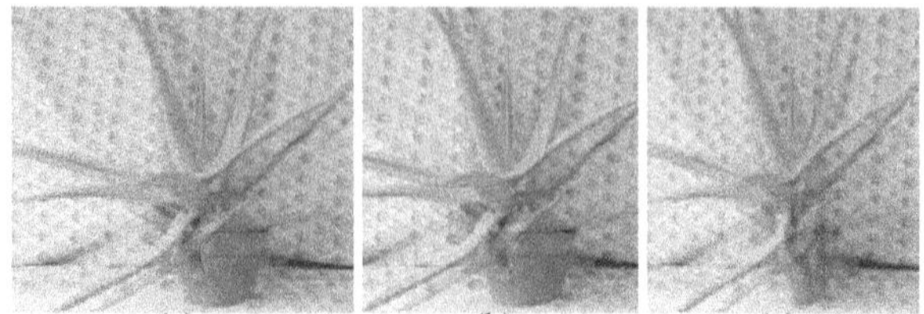

(a) (b) (c)

Figure 5: Non-homogenous stereo image resizing: (a) original stereo image; (b) our result; (c) result from geometrically consistent stereo seam carving [1].

5. CONCLUSION AND FUTURE WORK

In this paper, we extend the shift-map method for stereo image editing. The proposed method enforces photo consistence between the left and right images and preserves 3D scene structures well. It can also handle occlusion and disocclusion. We have demonstrated the application of the proposed method on depth mapping, object depth adjustment and non-homogenous image resizing.

The main limitation of the proposed method is the high computational cost, which depends on the size of the search window. We are currently working on a multi-resolution approach to address this problem. On the other hand, we are also exploring more stereo image editing functions based on our framework.

The work presented in this paper was partially supported by a SRG grant from City University of Hong Kong (Project Number: 7002768) and two National Natural Science Foundations of China (Project Numbers: 61033009 and 60970085).

6. REFERENCES

[1] T. Basha, Y. Moses, and S. Avidan. Geometrically consistent stereo seam carving. In *IEEE CVPR*, 2011.

[2] Y. Boykov, O. Veksler, and R. Zabih. Fast approximate energy minimization via graph cuts. *IEEE Trans. on PAMI*, 2001.

[3] C.-H. Chang, C.-K. Liang, and Y.-Y. Chuang. Content-aware display adaptation and interactive editing for stereoscopic images. *IEEE Trans. on Multimedia*, 2011.

[4] R. feng Tong, Y. Zhang, and K.-L. Cheng. Stereopasting: Interactive composition in stereoscopic images. *IEEE TVCG*, 2012.

[5] V. Kolmogorov and R. Zabin. What energy functions can be minimized via graph cuts? *IEEE Trans. on PAMI*, 2004.

[6] M. Lang, A. Hornung, O. Wang, S. Poulakos, A. Smolic, and M. Gross. Nonlinear disparity mapping for stereoscopic 3D. *ACM TOG*, 2010.

[7] K.-Y. Lee, C.-D. Chung, and Y.-Y. Chuang. Scene warping: Layer-based stereoscopic image resizing. In *IEEE CVPR*, 2012.

[8] S.-J. Luo, I.-C. Shen, B.-Y. Chen, W.-H. Cheng, and Y.-Y. Chuang. Perspective-aware warping for seamless stereoscopic image cloning. *ACM TOG*, 2012.

[9] Y. Niu, W.-C. Feng, and F. Liu. Enabling warping on stereoscopic images. *ACM TOG*, 2012.

[10] Y. Pritch, E. Kav-Venaki, and S. Peleg. Shift-map image editing. In *IEEE ICCV*, 2009.

[11] T. Yan, R. W. H. Lau, Y. Xu, and L. Huang. Depth mapping for stereoscopic videos. *IJCV*, 2013.

Superpixel Segmentation based Structural Scene Recognition

Shuhui Bu
Northwestern Polytechnical University
Xi'an, China
bushuhui@nwpu.edu.cn

Zhenbao Liu*
Northwestern Polytechnical University
Xi'an, China
liuzhenbao@nwpu.edu.cn

Junwei Han
Northwestern Polytechnical University
Xi'an, China
jhan@nwpu.edu.cn

Jun Wu
Northwestern Polytechnical University
Xi'an, China
junwu@nwpu.edu.cn

ABSTRACT

This paper presents a novel structural model based scene recognition method. In order to resolve regular grid image division methods which cause low content discriminability for scene recognition in previous methods, we partition an image into a pre-defined set of regions by superpixel segmentation. And then classification is modelled by introducing a structural model which has the capability of organizing unordered features of image patches. In the implementation, CENTRIST which is robust to scene recognition is used as original image feature, and bag-of-words representation is used to capture the local appearances of an image. In addition, we incorporate adjacent superpixel's differences as edge features. Our models are trained using structural SVM. Two state-of-the-art scene datasets are adopted to evaluate the proposed method. The experiment results show that the recognition accuracy is significantly improved by the proposed method.

Categories and Subject Descriptors

I.4.8 [**Image Processing and Computer Vision**]: Scene Analysis—*Object Recognition*; I.5.4 [**Pattern Recognition**]: Application—*Computer Vision*

General Terms

Algorithms, Experimentation, Performance.

Keywords

Scene recognition, Bag of words, Image segmentation, Superpixel, Structural SVM

MM'13, October 21–25, 2013, Barcelona, Spain.

http://dx.doi.org/10.1145/2502081.2502178.

1. INTRODUCTION

In recent decades, there has been growing interest in scene recognition. How to capture the intrinsic representation of a scene is the key to the success of scene recognition. Research from Oliva *et al.* [1] indicates that recognition of scenes could be accomplished by using global configurations, without detailed object information. They proposed Gist descriptor to represent such spatial structures. Nevertheless, its performance drops dramatically when applied for indoor environments. Lazebnik *et al.* [2] proposed a spatial pyramid matching (SPM) method for scene recognition. The method works by dividing the image into increasingly fine sub-blocks and building a bag of features representation from each sub-block. A major drawback of this method is their high dimensionality. Usually high accuracy is achieved when large numbers of visual words and sub-blocks are used to produce the image representation. Jia *et al.* [3] proposed a receptive field learning method for pooling image features which can overcome drawbacks of SPM. Russakovsky *et al.* [4] proposed object-centric spatial pooling approach for scene recognition which uses inferred location of objects to pool foreground and background features separately. Recently, Wu *et al.* [5] proposed the CENsus TRansform hISTogram (CENTRIST) descriptor which use the Census Transform to capture spatial relations between neighboring pixels. They showed that a spatial hierarchy of such descriptors combined with support vector machine (SVM) classifiers performs well on place recognition. Ehsan *et al.* [6] proposed histogram of oriented uniform patterns (HOUP) descriptor which has the capability invariant to rotations.

In this paper we present a novel framework for scene recognition. From the research results [5], the CENTRIST compared with SIFT has the advantage that it tend to group image regions with similar visual structure into the same code word. However, currently almost all works divide the image into a regular grid of sub-regions which decrease the discriminative power of visual words. Therefore, we propose to use superpixel segmentation method [7] to divide images into meaningful sub-regions and then extract the CENTRIST features of sub-regions as visual descriptors. Next, the original features are converted to bag of words (BoW) features for classification. In addition, differences

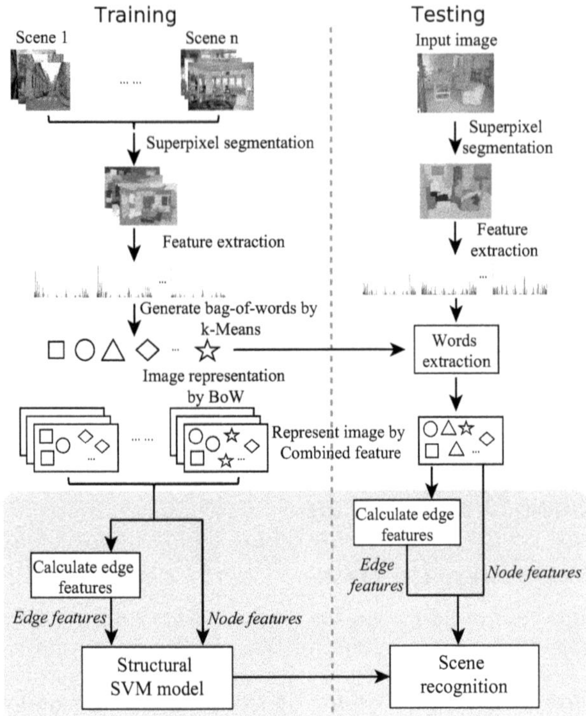

Figure 1: A schematically presentation of proposed framework. The left part represents the training process, and the right part is the test process.

between adjacent superpixels are also extracted as edge features which are adopted to construct a structural model. The structural model provides more semantic discriminability, therefore, they have better reorganization accuracy. We use UIUC dataset [2] to evaluate the proposed method, and it achieved the accuracy of 89.38%. In addition, we applied the proposed method to MIT 67-class scene dataset [8], and the average accuracy of scene reorganization is 48.3%.

2. STRUCTURAL MODEL BASED SCENE RECOGNITION

In this section, we first give a brief processing flow of the proposed method, and then details of each procedure are provided in subsections. Figure 1 shows processing flow of the proposed method for training and recognition. In the model training stage, the fist step is to segment the images into superpixels [7] which have more semantic discriminability. After that CENTRIST descriptor [5] of each superpixel is extracted, bag of features are generated for representing collection of semantic information of a scene. Finally, a structural model is constructed to obtain a discriminative classifier. In the recognition process, the superpixel segmentation and feature extraction are same as that in the training process. Bag of features are extracted using the trained data, and then structural SVM [9] is used to classify the scene category.

2.1 Superpixel Segmentation

In this study we divide the image into superpixels to represent meaningful image regions instead of regular grid based image partition. We have evaluated various superpixel segmentation methods, and found that entropy rate superpixel segmentation method [7] performs better than other methods, moreover it has a relatively fast processing speed.

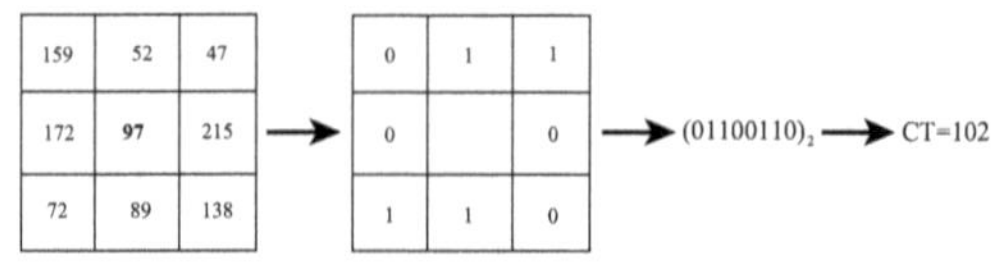

Figure 2: An example of census transform for a pixel which has intensity of 97.

2.2 Feature Extraction

In this study, we use CENRIST feature [5] for representing visual information of scenes, which has the following advantages: superior recognition performance on multiple standard data sets; no parameter to turn; extremely fast processing speed; easy to implement. The CENTRIST is one type of uniform pattern feature, and census transform (CT) [5] of each image pixel is calculated by subtracting the intensity at that pixel from each of its neighboring pixels and converting the results to a base-10 number which is illustrated in Fig. 2. After the CT value of each pixel is calculated, a histogram of CT values is obtained, and then PCA is adopted to reduce the dimension to $V = 42$. The compact descriptor is called as Pca Census Transform (PCT) descriptor.

In this study, the input image is segmented into meaningful S patches by superpixel method, and then each patch's feature is calculated by bag of words method. A bag of words model represents an image $\mathbf{x}$ by an unordered collection of visual words. In the model, a vocabulary $\mathbf{P} = \{\mathbf{p}_1, ..., \mathbf{p}_K\}$ with size K is a set of representative vectors in the descriptor space, obtained by means of unsupervised learning such as k-means. The second step is to quantize the descriptor space in order to obtain a compact representation in a vocabulary of visual words. For each image segment x_i with the descriptor $pct(x_i)$, we define the feature distribution $\theta(x_i) = (\theta_1(x_i), ..., \theta_K(x_i))^T$, a K dimensional vector, and each element is defined as

$$\theta_k(x_i) = ce^{-\frac{||pct(x_i)-\mathbf{p}_k||_2^2}{2\sigma^2}}, \quad (1)$$

where the constant c is selected in such a way that $||\theta_k(x_i)||_1 = 1$, and σ is set to be the maximum distance between any two visual words. In this work, the size of visual vocabulary is set to be K=200 in all of our experiments.

However only using the bag of features will lose the geometric layout of the scene. Thereby, in this study, we model the scene recognition using a model similar to graph matching with node and edge features. The first edge feature is histogram intersection [10], which has the definition of

$$\phi_{t1}(x_i, x_j) = \sum_{k=1}^{V} \min\{\theta_k(x_i), \theta_k(x_j)\}. \quad (2)$$

The second edge feature is the distance between corresponding visual words of adjacent superpixels x_i and x_j. It has the following definition

$$\phi_{t2}(x_i, x_j) = ||\mathbf{p}(x_i) - \mathbf{p}(x_j)||^2. \quad (3)$$

2.3 Structural Model for Scene Recognition

The discriminative approach such as SVM does not rely on explicit probabilistic models for the images in each class, as a consequence it has better performance. Given an image $\mathbf{x} = \{x_1, ..., x_S\}$ consisting of over-segmented image patches $\{x_i\}$, the purpose is to predict a category $\mathbf{y} = (y_1, ..., y_M)$ for the image. The scene category contains M binary values, with each $y_i \in \{0, 1\}$ indicating whether the image belongs to the category i. For an input image $\mathbf{x}$, the prediction $\mathbf{y}^*$ is computed as the argmax of a discriminant function $f_w(\mathbf{x}, \mathbf{y})$ that is parameterized by a vector of weight $\mathbf{w}$.

$$\mathbf{y}^* = \underset{\mathbf{y}}{\text{argmax}}\, f_w(\mathbf{x}, \mathbf{y}). \tag{4}$$

We model the features by an undirected graph $(\mathcal{V}, \mathcal{E})$, where vertices $\mathcal{V} = \{\theta(x_1), ..., \theta(x_S)\}$ and edges $\mathcal{E} \subseteq \mathcal{V} \times \mathcal{V}$, where S is the superpixel number of the image. This undirected graph is derived from the image by adding a vertex for each superpixel and adding an edge between vertices base on the spatial proximity of the corresponding superpixels. Given $(\mathcal{V}, \mathcal{E})$, the following discriminant function based on node features $\phi_n(x_i) = \theta(x_i)$ and edge features $\phi_t(x_i, x_j)$ is defined as

$$f_{\mathbf{w}}(\mathbf{x}, \mathbf{y}) = \sum_{i \in \mathcal{V}} \sum_{m=1}^{M} y_m [w_n^m \cdot \phi_n(i)] + \sum_{(i,j) \in \mathcal{E}} \sum_{m=1}^{M} y_m [w_t^{i,j} \cdot \phi_t(i, j)]. \tag{5}$$

To simplify the notation, note that Eq. (5) can be equivalently written as $\mathbf{w}^T \Phi(\mathbf{x}, \mathbf{y})$ by appropriately stacking the w_n^m and $w_t^{i,j}$ into $\mathbf{w}$ and the $y^m \phi_n(i)$ and $y^m \phi_t(i, j)$ into $\Phi(\mathbf{x}, \mathbf{y})$. Training can be formulated as the one slack formulation

$$\begin{aligned} min_{w,\xi} \quad & \frac{1}{2}\mathbf{w}^T\mathbf{w} + C\xi, \qquad (6) \\ s.t. \quad & \frac{1}{N}\sum_{i=1}^{N} [\Phi(\mathbf{x}_i, \mathbf{y}_i) - \Phi(\mathbf{x}_i, \overline{\mathbf{y}}_i)] \\ & \geq \frac{1}{N}\sum_{i=1}^{N} \Delta(\mathbf{y}_i, \overline{\mathbf{y}}_i) - \xi, \end{aligned}$$

where $\Delta(\mathbf{y}_i, \overline{\mathbf{y}}_i) = |\mathbf{y}_i - \overline{\mathbf{y}}_i|$ is the zero-one loss function quantifying the deviation between estimated and true scene category, C is a scaling constant, and N is the number of training images. This problem can be solved efficiently using the cutting-plane algorithm [9] for training the structural model.

Figure 3: Sample images of the UICU scene dataset.

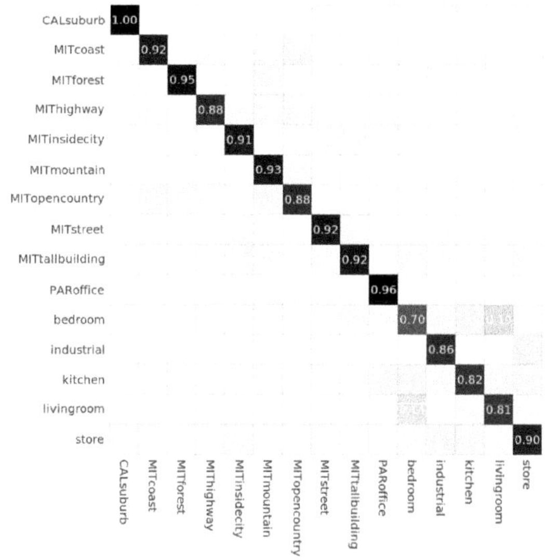

Figure 4: Confusion matrix from one run on UIUC 15-category scene dataset recognition.

3. EXPERIMENTS

To evaluate the proposed method, in the first experiment we use the public available UIUC dataset [2] which contains 4,485 images of 15 different categories. It includes both indoor scenes (office, bedroom, kitchen, living-rooming, store) and outdoor scenes (suburb, coast, forest, highway, inside-city, mountain, open-country, street, tall-building, industrial). Figure 3 shows some of the images from the dataset.

All processing in our experiments was performed in grayscale. The color information was discarded if it is available. In the experiment, the input images were segmented by entropy rate superpixel segmentation method [7] with segment number of $S = 30$. Then each segment's CENTRIST descriptor was calculated to define visual words. The visual vocabulary was created using k-means clustering on all segments of training images. The size of visual vocabulary was set to be K=200. The superpixel segmentation is most time-consuming step in the training, which need about 1 3 seconds. The classification time for a 400x300 image takes about 0.6 seconds.

Figure 4 presents the confusion matrix from one run on UIUC scene dataset, where row and column names are true and classified scene categories, respectively. From the figure, we observed that the highest recognition rate is 100% for 'CALsuburb'. The biggest confusion happens between 'bedroom' and 'livingroom', due to their similar global structure and spatial layout. Averaged recognition accuracy of stat-of-art methods are listed in Table I. Due to the Gist descriptor [6] has poor discriminative power for indoor environments, it output lowest accuracy. Spatial pyramid matching (SPM) method [2] incorporates spatial information, and consequently it outputs better results. The classification result which only uses CENTRIST [5] is 74.2%. Although it not good as SPM, it is still better than Gist. When use PCA to reduce the dimensionality of CENTRIST to 40 (which is called PACT), and uses a level 2 pyramid division [5], the accuracy improved to 83.8%. The proposed method outputs **89.38**% accuracy.

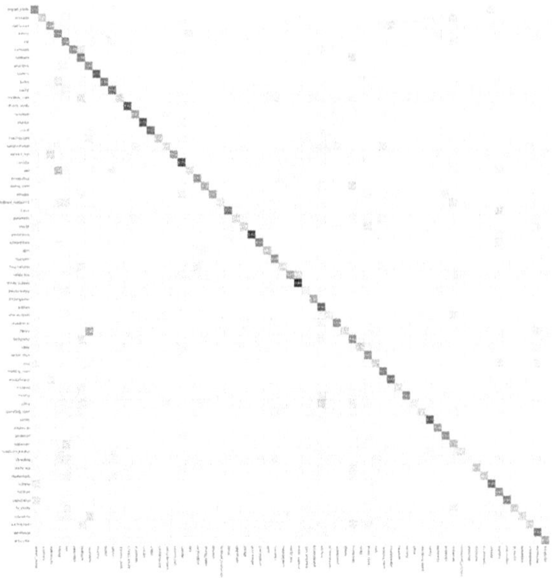

Figure 5: Confusion matrix from one run on MIT 67-class scene dataset.

Method	Accuracy
Gist [1]	65.8%
Spatial Pyramid Matching [2]	81.4 ± 0.50%
CENTRIST [5]	73.29 ± 0.96%
CENTRIST + PACT [5]	83.88 ± 0.76%
Proposed method	**89.38** ± 0.70%

Table 1: Performance comparison on 15 scenes dataset.

In the second experiment, we evaluated the proposed method on a challenging 67-class indoor scene recognition dataset [8]. There are 15,620 images in the dataset. The indoor scenes range from specific categories (e.g., dental office) to generic concepts (e.g., mall). In research [8], the global Gist feature achieved about 21% average recognition accuracy on this challenging dataset. When it was supplemented by local information (in the form of local prototypes based on image segmentation), the accuracy was improved to 25%. By using the PACT descriptor and RBF SVM [5], the average accuracy in five random split of train/test images is 36.9%. By our proposed method, the average accuracy also in five cross-validations improved to **48.3%**, which archives higher accuracy than other methods. Confusion matrix from one run is given in Fig. 5.

4. CONCLUSIONS

In this paper, we presented a novel scene recognition method. Our major contribution is that input image is first segmented into meaningful sub-regions for generating visual words which have higher discriminability. In addition, we constructed a structural model to train and learn scene categories, which incorporates spatial layout to represent the scene image. The UIUC scene dataset is used to evaluate our proposed method compared with other methods. From the results, we can conclude that proposed method has better performance. In addition, the proposed method was also evaluated on MIT 67-class scene dataset. We found that the proposed method has 48.3% average accuracy which is much higher than other methods. Although our proposed method has better performance, there also exist some limitations. First, compared with CENTRIST descriptor and SVM based scene recognition method, our method needs more computation time due to the superpixel segmentation. Second, currently we didn't consider temporal consistency. In the following work, we will improve the classification model which will has higher processing speed and modeling temporal consistency.

5. ACKNOWLEDGMENTS

We would like to thank the anonymous reviewers for their valuable feedback. This work is supported partly by grants from NSFC (61003137, 61202185), NWPU Basic Research Fund (JC201202, JC201220), Shaanxi Natural Science Fund (2012JQ8037), and Open Project Program of the State Key Lab of CAD&CG (A1306), Zhejiang University.

6. REFERENCES

[1] Aude Oliva and Antonio Torralba. Modeling the shape of the scene: A holistic representation of the spatial envelope. *International Journal of Computer Vision*, 42(3):145–175, 2001.

[2] Svetlana Lazebnik, Cordelia Schmid, and Jean Ponce. Beyond bags of features: Spatial pyramid matching for recognizing natural scene categories. In *Computer Vision and Pattern Recognition, 2006 IEEE Computer Society Conference on*, volume 2, pages 2169–2178. IEEE, 2006.

[3] Yangqing Jia, Chang Huang, and Trevor Darrell. Beyond spatial pyramids: Receptive field learning for pooled image features. In *Computer Vision and Pattern Recognition (CVPR), 2012 IEEE Conference on*, pages 3370–3377. IEEE, 2012.

[4] Olga Russakovsky, Yuanqing Lin, Kai Yu, and Li Fei-Fei. Object-centric spatial pooling for image classification. In *Computer Vision–ECCV 2012*, pages 1–15. Springer, 2012.

[5] Jianxin Wu and Jim M Rehg. Centrist: A visual descriptor for scene categorization. *Pattern Analysis and Machine Intelligence, IEEE Transactions on*, 33(8):1489–1501, 2011.

[6] Ehsan Fazl-Ersi and John K Tsotsos. Histogram of oriented uniform patterns for robust place recognition and categorization. *The International Journal of Robotics Research*, 31(4):468–483, 2012.

[7] Ming-Yu Liu, Oncel Tuzel, Srikumar Ramalingam, and Rama Chellappa. Entropy rate superpixel segmentation. In *Computer Vision and Pattern Recognition (CVPR), 2011 IEEE Conference on*, pages 2097–2104. IEEE, 2011.

[8] Ariadna Quattoni and Antonio Torralba. Recognizing indoor scenes. 2009.

[9] Thorsten Joachims, Thomas Finley, and Chun-Nam John Yu. Cutting-plane training of structural svms. *Machine Learning*, 77(1):27–59, 2009.

[10] Michael J Swain and Dana H Ballard. Color indexing. *International journal of computer vision*, 7(1):11–32, 1991.

Evaluation of Salient Point Methods

Song Wu Michael S. Lew
LIACS Media Lab, Leiden University
Niels Bohrweg 1, 2333 CA Leiden, The Netherlands
{wusong, mlew}@liacs.nl

ABSTRACT
Processing visual content in images and videos is a challenging task associated with the development of modern computer vision. Because salient point approaches can represent distinctive and affine invariant points in images, many approaches have been proposed over the past decade. Each method has particular advantages and limitations and may be appropriate in different contexts. In this paper we evaluate the performance of a wide set of salient point detectors and descriptors. We begin by comparing diverse salient point algorithms (SIFT, SURF, BRIEF, ORB, FREAK, BRISK, STAR, GFTT and FAST) with regard to repeatability, recall and precision and then move to accuracy and stability in real-time video tracking.

Categories and Subject Descriptors
Computing methodologies, computer vision

General Terms
Algorithms, Performance, Experimentation.

Keywords
Salient point methods, evaluation, video tracking

1. INTRODUCTION
Salient point detection and feature descriptors have become prevalent in diverse areas in computer vision and multimedia information retrieval [7,8,14,15]. A well known algorithm is the Scale Invariant Feature Transform (SIFT) by Lowe [1] which has been shown repeatedly to have good accuracy from the research literature. However, it has also been noted that the generated 128 dimensional descriptor may lead to relatively large descriptors and lower computational efficiency. A faster approach named SURF (Speeded Up Robust Feature) was developed by Bay et al [2].

In contrast to the real value descriptors (i.e. SIFT, SURF), binary string descriptors were developed with the aim to compute the feature descriptors more efficiently. The representative method of binary string descriptors is BRIEF [3], which is constructed by intensity comparison of pixel-pairs. Since BRIEF is not invariant to scale and orientation, a series of modified descriptors had been developed. Rublee et al [4] designed ORB (oriented FAST and Rotated BRIEF) as an alternative to SIFT and SURF. The ORB detector is an extension of FAST and the ORB descriptor is an improvement of the BRIEF descriptor. The drawback regarding scale invariance still exists. The BRISK (Binary Robust Invariant Scalable Keypoints) approach [5], which is a method for keypoint detection and description, performs much faster than the more well-established SIFT and SURF approaches. A recent new keypoint descriptor named FREAK (Fast Retina Keypoint) [6] was designed to enhance the performance of existing keypoints descriptor. It was formed by comparing image intensities over a retinal sampling pattern.

MM'13, October 21–25, 2013, Barcelona, Spain.

http://dx.doi.org/10.1145/2502081.2502179

The focus of this paper is to assess a wide set of older (i.e. SIFT) and more recent salient point approaches. The main contributions of this work are insights based on the precision-recall graphs from the main image transformations and also the comparison of the different approaches in video tracking. It should be noted that regarding objectivity, the authors did not submit any of their own algorithms for this evaluation.

1.1 Related Work
Schmid et al [7] used the measure of "repeatability rate" and "information content" to show the performance of different detectors. In addition, several works have been done on the evaluation of local descriptors by measuring the accuracy of matching and recognition [8]. Recall and precision are two widely used indicators to denote the performance under various affine translations. Accuracy and speed trade-offs [9] have been studied where different indexing structures were employed (such as approximate kd trees). Gauglitz et al. in [10] presented a comparison of different salient approaches on object tracking in video sequences. As far as we know, this is the only work which covers the newer descriptors such as BRIEF and FREAK regarding precision-recall and stability in the form of trajectory jitter noise.

2. DETECTORS AND DESCRIPTORS
SIFT and SURF are two of the most influential methods. However recent new binary string features have received significant attention. These are generated by comparing the intensity of pixel-pairs and use the Hamming distance (bitwise XOR followed by a bit count) for matching instead of Euclidean distance.

SIFT [1]: The implementation of SIFT begins by building the scale space which approximates the Laplacian-of-Gaussian function by the computationally efficient Difference-of-Gaussian function. It searches extrema over all scales and then eliminates the potential points which are sensitive to edge response. The orientation is assigned to each stable point according to the local image gradient direction. Furthermore, it accumulates the orientations of a 16x16 neighborhood sample points around the keypoint location into orientation histograms by summarizing the contents over 4x4 sub-regions. A 128 dimensional descriptor vector is finally generated for each feature point.

SURF [2]: The box-filters together with integral images are exploited to approximate the Hessian matrix which is used to measure the interest points. The scale space of SURF is established by up-scaling the size of the box-filter. The final salient points are assigned orientations which are calculated by summing the Haar-wavelet responses in a circular neighborhood of the salient point. In addition, the SURF descriptor is created by merging the values and absolute values of Haar-wavelet responses over a square region centered on and oriented along the salient point.

FAST detector [11]: A sample scheme of FAST corner detection is based on a circle (three pixels radius) of sixteen pixels around the candidate point, if a set of twelve contiguous pixels in the circle which are all brighter or all darker than the intensity of the point pixel value plus a threshold, the point will be classified as a corner point. Furthermore, a decision tree is generated by machine learning on training sets, and the rules of the FAST corner point classification are established to speed up the procedure.

STAR detector [12]: The STAR detector algorithm uses a simplified center-surround filter at all locations and all scales, and it detects the extrema in a local neighborhood. For each obtained extrema (based on the non-maximum suppression method, which is the same as SURF) the location of the potential points can be fixed. Furthermore, through computing the Harris measure for the potential points, those with strong edge response will be eliminated.

GFTT detector [13]: GFTT derived from an image motion model, is used as a method for feature selection, tracking and monitoring, and it performs well under image affine transformation. According to the proposed feature selection criteria, a candidate point is accepted if it is defined as a good feature which can be tracked well.

BRIEF descriptor [3]: BRIEF is a binary string feature descriptor. With regard to the located patches in an image, Gaussian smoothing is first introduced to reduce the effect of noise sensitivity so that it can achieve good performance in complex scenes. A small number of pixel-pairs are pre-selected randomly from a Gaussian distribution around the smoothed patch center and the BRIEF binary string descriptor is produced via the intensity comparison of pixel-pairs.

ORB [4]: ORB applies the FAST detector to find potential salient point locations on an image pyramid. It orders the detected points according to the Harris corner measure, and picks the top set of points as salient points. The direction of points is computed using intensity centroid. The ORB descriptor improves the BRIEF descriptor and compares the intensity of patch-pair to form the binary string vector. Then, the combination of learning and greedy search is further introduced to reduce correlation and minimize variance in the binary tests.

BRISK [5]: In the implementation of BRISK, salient points are detected using FAST within layers of the image pyramid as well as in continuous layers. BRISK presents a novel sampling pattern which consists of sample points equally distributed on concentric circles centered around the saline point, and it determines the orientation by computing local intensity gradients as well as generating a binary descriptor by comparing pairwise intensities.

FREAK descriptor [6]: The FREAK descriptor is inspired by the human retina system. FREAK samples pairs of pixels over a retinal sampling pattern and then compares their intensities. The direction is established by summing the local intensity gradients over selected pairs with symmetric receptive fields to the center of sampling pattern.

3. EXPERIMENTS

Our experiments use international public test sets in the domains of both image matching and video tracking and several evaluation measures from the research literature. The software is downloadable at http://press.liacs.nl/researchdownloads/. The experiment environment for the evaluation: AMD 64*2 Dual Core Processor (2.41GHz), and 3.2GB of RAM.

3.1 Detector Evaluation

The evaluation of different salient point detectors used the dataset provided by Mikolajczyk and Schmid [8, http://www.robots.ox.ac.uk/~vgg/research/affine/], which contains eight groups image samples with various transformations (rotation, viewpoint, scale, JPEG compression, illumination and image blur). Each group is consist of six texture or structured scene images, as well as the ground truth homography between the reference image and the transformed image.

One important evaluation measure from the research literature is repeatability [7, 8]. The repeatability score is calculated as the ratio between the number of correspondences and the minimum total number of m_1 and m_2 where m_1, m_2 denotes the number of points in reference and query images after projecting reference image points by homography and removing points outside common area.

$$\text{Repeatability}=C(m_1, m_2)/MIN(m_1, m_2)$$

$C(m_1,m_2)$ is the number of correspondences between m_1 and m_2. Overlap error is used to identify the correspondence. For a keypoint region in query image which is the nearest one to a projection keypoint region by using homograph in reference image, if the ratio between the intersection of two regions and the union of the two regions is larger than overlap error, it will be considered a correspondence. We compute the average repeatability scores on the whole dataset, thus, the detection performance of each method can be estimated in a comprehensive perspective. The trend of average repeatability under variant overlap error (in the range from 0.5 to 0.9) is shown in Figure 1.

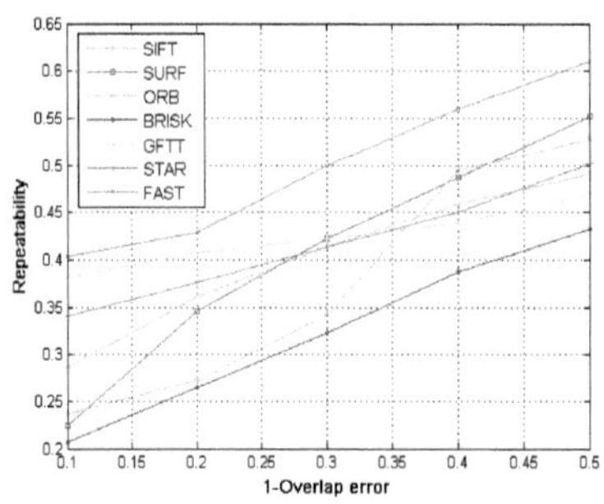

Figure 1. Comparison of various detectors using repeatability

Figure 1 illustrates that an increase in the repeatability scores is clearly indicated when overlap error becoming smaller. We also can notice that the FAST detector had the highest repeatability and the BRISK detector obtained the lowest score. All detectors can reach a stable and well performance when the value of overlap error is 0.5, the overlap error will be set at 0.5 to identify the correspondence in the following experiments.

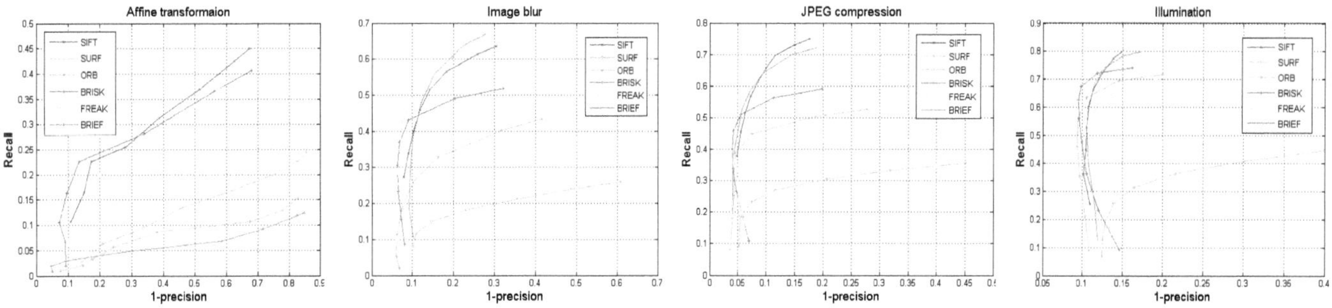

Figure 2. Comparison of various descriptors using recall vs 1-precision under different image degradation

Since different salient point detection mechanisms result in different time complexity, and different quantity of feature points can be extracted from the same image, time comparison should be compared statistically. We applied different types of detectors to various test images, in order to determine statistically significant results. The number of average detected points and the time cost of compared salient point methods are statistic in Table 1.

From the demonstration of Table 1, it reveals that the most efficient detector is FAST. FAST detected the largest number of salient points which is ten times than that obtained by other detectors. Moreover, the time cost is only 3.2(s) for the total 502924 points. The most time-consuming detector is SIFT which spends almost average 9(ms) on per point detection. The average time cost of SURF, BRISK, GFTT, and STAR is almost in the same order all with standard deviations less than 0.01.

Table 1. Comparison of average detection time

Method	Detection time(s)	Number of points	Per point time cost(ms)
SIFT	44.958	51788	8.68
SURF	62.929	148470	0.424
ORB	10.472	17336	0.604
BRISK	16.543	47236	0.35
GFTT	12.497	35000	0.357
STAR	9.69	29426	0.329
FAST	3.23	502924	0.0064

3.2 Descriptor Evaluation

The same dataset mentioned in the repeatability experiments is utilized in this part. Note that some of the salient point detectors from the previous section do not define descriptors and are not compared here. The evaluation starts by extracting salient point features from reference image and establishing KD-tree, or LSH index for them. Then, extract features from the query image and match them against the features of each reference image based on the approximate nearest neighbor method. In the procedure of matching descriptors in one pair-image, KD-tree index is established for SIFT, SURF descriptors and use Euclidean distance to realize the matching of real value descriptors.

In order to increase the matching accuracy, the Nearest Neighbor Distance Ratio (NNDR) is used as the matching strategy to find the similar descriptors in the image pairs. NNDR defines that two points will be considered a match if $||D_A-D_B||/||D_A-D_C||<threshold$, where D_B is the first and D_C is the second nearest neighbor to D_A. In addition we also computed recall and the 1-precision [8].

The noise is introduced by image degradation which results in the increase of distance between similar descriptors. Thus, we varied the value of *threshold* in the NNDR from 0.1 to 0.9 to obtain the curves about the tendency of average result of recall and 1-precision under each transformation, as shown in Figure 2. We can see that recall increases for an increasing threshold of NNDR. All descriptors perform better on image changes (blur, JPEG compression and illumination) than affine deformation. However, SIFT, BRISK and FREAK show good performance for all image degradations. Toward to the affine transformation, the curves obtained by different detectors could be classified as two groups: one is consist of SIFT, BRISK and FREAK and the other one contains SURF, ORB and BRIEF. The trend of the curves indicates that the descriptors created by SIFT, BRISK and FREAK are more robust and distinctive than SURF, ORB and BRIEF. This is mainly because that BRIEF descriptor conducted only by pixel-pair intensity comparison is not affine invariant, while ORB descriptor as an improved BRIEF is rotation invariant, resistant to noise, but not scale invariant.

For the curves in the graphs under changes of blur, JPEG compression and illumination, the rankings of all the descriptors are almost the same. SURF descriptor obtains the lowest recall and highest 1-precision, thus, SURF descriptor is more sensitive to those noises. In addition, SIFT, BRIEF, BRISK, ORB and FREAK descriptors illustrate close recall and 1-precision scores to each other, and it means all of them are robust to the influences of illumination.

The description time complexity of the compared salient point descriptor extraction methods is also statistic in the part. The average time spending on generation of per descriptor based on the dataset provided by Mikolajczyk and Schmid is shown in Table 2. It is clear that binary string descriptors are more efficient than real value descriptors. SIFT descriptor has the highest time consuming, followed by SURF. However, binary string descriptors perform nearly 250 and 30 times faster than SIFT and SURF, respectively. Binary string descriptors are more appropriate for the real-time applications.

Table 2. Comparison of average description time cost

Salient point method	Average extraction time(ms)
SURF+SIFT	7.5
SURF+SURF	0.96
SURF+ORB	0.022
SURF+BRISK	0.023
SURF+FREAK	0.045
SURF+BRIEF	0.023

In applications such as augmented reality, it is very important to not only measure detection accuracy but also to evaluate stability in the tracking. A concrete example is rendering a cube on a book or a hand. Low stability would be evident in visible vibration in the display of the 3D model and would not result in a positive experience for the viewer. We evaluate stability using a measure of trajectory jitter noise. It is computed as the change in the 3D trajectory which would be used for projecting the augmented reality. In the second experiment, the algorithms were evaluated with regard to jitter noise and accuracy. Moreover, the compared salient point algorithms are combined as follows: SIFT+SIFT, SURF+SURF, ORB+ORB, BRISK+BRISK, SURF+BRIEF and SURF+FREAK. Examples of the used video sequences are shown in Figure 3.

Our trajectory jitter experiments results are shown in Table 3. For a planar object image under affine transformation, it shows that SIFT, SURF, BRISK, and FREAK have better performance with lower variance. However, note there are no jitter results for BRIEF, because it failed to track the object.

Table 3. Comparison of jitter changes under affine changes

Method	Mean jitter	Max jitter	Variance jitter
SIFT+SIFT	0.1566	0.804	0.0113
SURF+SURF	0.3245	1.0541	0.0372
ORB+ORB	4.3226	21.0117	10.8559
BRISK+BRISK	0.5831	6.8654	0.6977
SURF+BRIEF	—	—	—
SURF+FREAK	0.472	1.9839	0.069

The Cambridge Hand Gesture Data set [16] contains different hand shapes and movements. We can see from Table 4 that SIFT had the best performance, while BRISK obtained the lowest score.

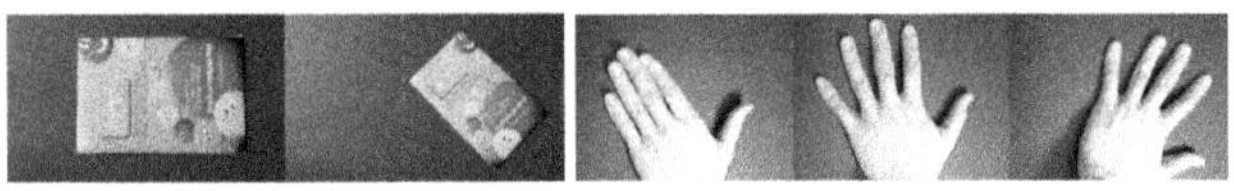

Figure. 3 Examples of planar object and hand data set

Table 4. Comparison on video hand detection accuracy

Salient point method	Average detection accuracy
SIFT+SIFT	68.7%
SURF+SURF	46.3%
ORB+ORB	58.5%
BRISK +BRISK	11.2%
SURF+FREAK	43.3%
SURF+BRIEF	36.9%

4. CONCLUSION

In this paper we presented a comparison of detectors and descriptors on diverse image distortions and also evaluated them on real-time video tracking. No single salient point algorithm was best in all evaluation aspects. The FAST detector had the highest repeatability score than other detectors, moreover and it had the least detection time cost per point. Regarding the criteria of recall-precision, our experiments showed that SIFT, BRISK, and FREAK are the best affine invariant descriptors, and the time complex showed the binary descriptors provide a very efficient description and matching. We also combined detector-descriptor methods for object tracking inside video frames. SIFT and FREAK outperformed the rest in terms of detection accuracy and trajectory jitter. In the future work, we will employ additional metrics and make a further overview on test sets such as the PASCAL and TRECVid benchmarks.

5. REFERENCES

[1] Lowe, D G. 2004. Distinctive Image Features from Scale-Invariant Keypoints. *International Journal of Computer Vision,* 60(2), 91-110.

[2] Bay, H., Ess, A., Tuytelaars, T., and Van Gool, L. 2008. Speeded-up robust features (SURF). *Computer Vision and Image Understanding*, 110(3), 346-359.

[3] Calonder, M., Lepetit, V., Strecha, C., and Fua, P. 2010. BRIEF: Binary Robust Independent Elementary Features. *European Conference on Computer vision*, 778–792.

[4] Rublee, E., Rabaud, V., Konolige, K., and Bradski, G. 2011. ORB: An Efficient Alternative to SIFT or SURF. *International Conference on Computer Vision*, 2564-2571.

[5] Leutenegger, S., Chli, M., and Siegwart, R. 2011. BRISK: Binary robust invariant scalable keypoints. *International Conference on Computer Vision*, 2548-2555.

[6] Alahi, A., Ortiz, R., and Vandergheynst, P. 2012. FREAK: Fast Retina Keypoint. *IEEE Conference on Computer Vision and Pattern Recognition.*

[7] Schmid, C., Mohr, R., and Bauckhage, C. 2000. Evaluation of interest point detectors. *International Journal Computer Vision*, 37(2), 151–172.

[8] Mikolajczyk, K., & Schmid, C. 2005. A performance evaluation of local descriptors. *IEEE Transactions on Pattern Analysis and Machine Intelligence*, 27(10), 1615–1630.

[9] Miksik, O., Mikolajczyk, K. 2012. Evaluation of Local Detectors and Descriptors for Fast Feature Matching. *International Conference on Pattern Recogntion*, 2681-2684.

[10] Gauglitz, S., Höllerer, T., and Turk, M. 2011. Evaluation of interest point detectors and feature descriptors for visual tracking. *International Journal of Computer Vision*, 335-360.

[11] Rosten, E., and Drummond, T. 2006. Machine learning for high-speed corner detection. *European Conference on Computer Vision*, 430-443.

[12] Agrawal, M., Konolige, K., Blas, M. 2008. Censure: Center Surround Extremas for Realtime Feature Detection and Matching. *European Conference on Computer Vision*, 102–115.

[13] Shi, J., and Tomasi, C. 1994. Good features to track. *IEEE Conference on Computer Vision and Pattern Recognition*, 593–600.

[14] Thomee, B., and Lew, M.S. 2012. Interactive search in image retrieval: a survey. *International Journal of Multimedia Information Retrieval*, 1(2), 71-86.

[15] Jiang, Y., Bhattacharya, S., Chang, S-F., and Shah, M. 2013. High-level event recognition in unconstrained videos. *International Journal of Multimedia Information Retrieval*, 2(2), 73-101.

[16] Kim, T-K., Wong, S-F., and Cipolla, R. 2007. Tensor Canonical Correlation Analysis for Action Classification, *IEEE Conference on Computer Vision and Pattern Recognition*, 1-8.

Cross-media Topic Mining on Wikipedia

Xikui Wang, Yang Liu, Donghui Wang, Fei Wu
College of Computer Science, Zhejiang University
Hangzhou, Zhejiang, China
{xkwang,liuy,dhwang,wufei}@zju.edu.cn

ABSTRACT

As a collaborative wiki-based encyclopedia, Wikipedia provides a huge amount of articles of various categories. In addition to their text corpus, Wikipedia also contains plenty of images which makes the articles more intuitive for readers to understand. To better organize these visual and textual data, one promising area of research is to jointly model the embedding topics across multi-modal data (i.e, *cross-media*) from Wikipedia. In this work, we propose to learn the projection matrices that map the data from heterogeneous feature spaces into a unified latent topic space. Different from previous approaches, by imposing the ℓ_1 regularizers to the projection matrices, only a small number of relevant visual/textual words are associated with each topic, which makes our model more interpretable and robust. Furthermore, the correlations of Wikipedia data in different modalities are explicitly considered in our model. The effectiveness of the proposed topic extraction algorithm is verified by several experiments conducted on real Wikipedia datasets.

Categories and Subject Descriptors

H.3.3 [**Information Search and Retrieval**]: Retrieval models

Keywords

Wikipedia, Cross Media, Topic Modeling, Sparsity

1. INTRODUCTION

As the world's largest collaboratively edited source of encyclopedia, Wikipedia contains 25 million articles covering various areas including social, nature, culture, art, *etc.*. By providing accurate and highly structured documents as well as related images and other multimedia resources, Wikipedia attracts millions of user to browse and contribute to these document entries. In Fig 1, we give one illustrative sample page that contains both text corpus and its related image captured from Wikipedia website.

MM'13, October 21–25, 2013, Barcelona, Spain.

ACM 978-1-4503-2404-5/13/10 ...$15.00.
http://dx.doi.org/10.1145/2502081.2502180.

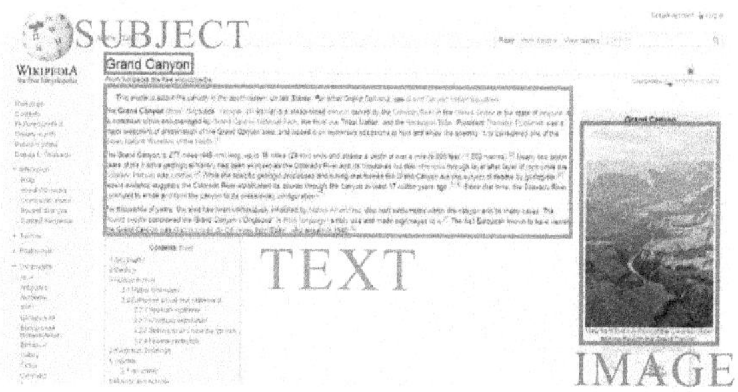

Figure 1: One sample page from Wikipedia.

Recently, quite a lot of studies have been focus on Wikipedia from many perspectives. In [8], Milne *et al.* used the Wikipedia data to identify significant terms in unstructured text. In [5], Wikipedia data was exploited to build a tag relationship graph for cross media search. Hu *et al.* utilized the semantics extracted from Wikipedia for text clustering in [4]. All of above works take advantages of Wikipedia data to facilitate their own applications and have made considerable improvements.

However, as an important characteristics of wikipedia, the relationships among the text corpus and multimedia resources, e.g. images, have not been given sufficient attention. With the topics extracted across textual and visual contents, we can find a more comprehensive and intuitive way for the readers to understand the digests and trends of Wikipedia. Furthermore, mining the cross media topics by means of the Wikipedia data also bridges the semantic gap between two heterogeneous modalities which can greatly facilitate some other multimedia applications, such as image classification and cross media retrieval.

Since images can be represented with bag-of-visual-words (BoVW) models based on SIFT descriptors, the literature of topic mining for textual data can be naturally extended to visual data. In [9], Rasiwasia *et al.* tried to jointly model the text and image components of multimedia documents which is most closely related to our approach. In their work, the correlations between the two different modalities are learned with Canonical Correlation Analysis (CCA) [3]. There are also some other algorithms that can be applied to capture the correlation between different modalities, such as kernel CCA [7], correspondence latent Dirichlet allocation (Corr-LDA) [1] and generalized multiview analysis (GMA) [10]. [12] and [11] also utilize correlations between different modalities to obtain better retrieval performance.

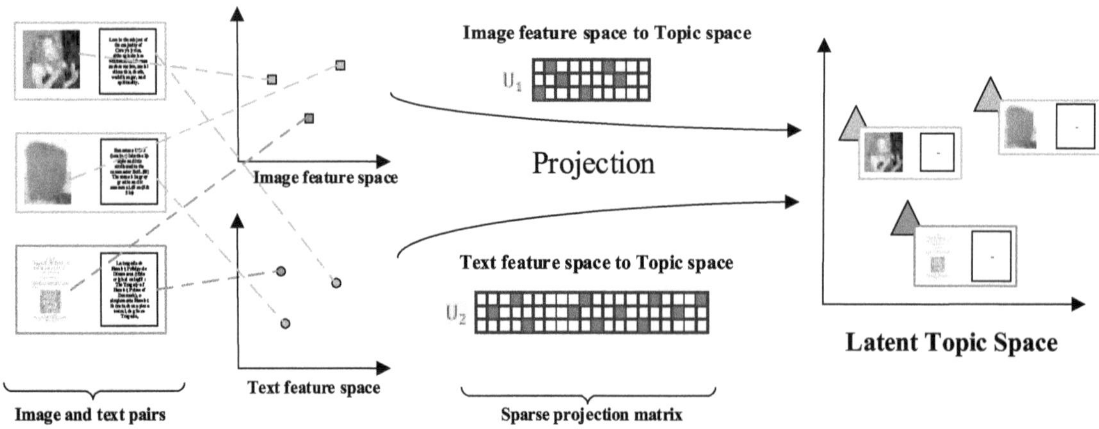

Figure 2: The illustration of the learning process. The sparse projection matrix $\mathbf{U}_1$ and $\mathbf{U}_2$ are respectively learned to map the image and text features from their original space to the latent topic space. The image and text features of one article have the same representation in the latent topic space.

In spite of the great success achieved by above algorithms, there are still some aspects on cross media topic modeling that can be further improved:

- How to find the most relevant visual word or text with respect to different topics.
- How to better utilize the correlation of data objects in different modalities.

In this work, we propose to learn the projection matrices that map both the images and texts into a latent topic space. Thus, both the images and their corresponding texts can be uniformly represented in terms of the extracted topics. Different from previous approaches, by imposing the ℓ_1 regularizers to the projection matrices, only a small number of relevant visual words or text are associated with each topic, which makes our model more interpretable and robust. Furthermore, the correlations of Wikipedia data in different modalities are explicitly considered in our model when learning the projections. We perform extensive experiments on the real Wikipedia datasets which demonstrates the effectiveness of our topic extraction algorithms.

The rest of this paper will be organized as follows. In Section 2, we present our approach in details. The experimental results and analysis are showed in Section 3. Finally, in Section 4, we conclude this paper and discuss the future work.

2. THE APPROACH

Suppose there exists l image-text pairs from Wikipedia where each pair corresponds to the same subject. Let $\mathbf{A} \in \mathbf{R}^{l \times m_1}$ represent the collection of images where m_1 is the dimensionality of their visual feature space. Correspondingly, matrix $\mathbf{B} \in \mathbf{R}^{l \times m_2}$ is used to represent the collection of texts where m_2 is the dimensionality of textual feature space.

Given the latent topic space with k unrelated variables as $\mathbf{X} = [\mathbf{x}_1, \mathbf{x}_2, \ldots, \mathbf{x}_k] \in \mathbf{R}^{l \times k}$, we aim to find two projection matrices $\mathbf{U}_1 \in \mathbf{R}^{k \times m_1}$ and $\mathbf{U}_2^{k \times m_2}$ that maps matrices $\mathbf{A}$ and $\mathbf{B}$ into the latent topic space $\mathbf{X}$. Ulteriorly, $\mathbf{U}_1$ and $\mathbf{U}_2$ also indicate the relevance between the topic and visual/textual words.

Algorithm 1 The Optimization Algorithm

Input: Image features $\mathbf{A} \in \mathbf{R}^{l \times m_1}$, text features $\mathbf{B} \in \mathbf{R}^{l \times m_2}$, latent topic space dimensionality k, and other training parameters: γ, λ_1, λ_2.

Initialization: $\mathbf{X} = \begin{pmatrix} \mathbf{I}_k \\ 0 \end{pmatrix}$

Iterate until convergence of X:

1. Compute $\mathbf{U}_1$, $\mathbf{U}_2$ through Eq. (4) by the lasso solver.
2. Concatenates the features and coefficients: $\widetilde{\mathbf{Y}} = [\mathbf{A}, \sqrt{\gamma}\mathbf{B}]$, $\widetilde{\mathbf{U}} = [\mathbf{U}_1, \sqrt{\gamma}\mathbf{U}_2]$.
3. Set $\mathbf{V} = \widetilde{\mathbf{Y}}\widetilde{\mathbf{U}}^T$.
4. Compute the SVD of $\mathbf{V} = [\mathbf{P}, \triangle, \mathbf{Q}]$ and let the $\mathbf{X} = \mathbf{PQ}$.

Output: Sparse projection matrix $\mathbf{U}_1$ and $\mathbf{U}_2$.

Assuming that the feature matrices $\mathbf{A}$ and $\mathbf{B}$ can be represented by the linear expansion with the latent variables $\mathbf{X}$, we have

$$\begin{aligned} \mathbf{A} &= \mathbf{X}\mathbf{U}_1 + \epsilon^1, \\ \mathbf{B} &= \mathbf{X}\mathbf{U}_2 + \epsilon^2. \end{aligned} \tag{1}$$

where ϵ^1 and ϵ^2 are two zero mean noise matrices.

Thus, we can write the objective function for solving $\mathbf{X}$, $\mathbf{U}_1$ and $\mathbf{U}_2$ as follows:

$$\begin{aligned} \min_{\mathbf{X}, \mathbf{U}_1, \mathbf{U}_2} & \|\mathbf{A} - \mathbf{X}\mathbf{U}_1\|_F^2 + \gamma\|\mathbf{B} - \mathbf{X}\mathbf{U}_2\|_F^2, \\ s.t. \quad & \mathbf{X}^T\mathbf{X} = \mathbf{I}, \end{aligned} \tag{2}$$

where γ is a trade-off parameter. The constraint $\mathbf{X}^T\mathbf{X} = \mathbf{I}$ is imposed to guarantee the uncorrelated property among latent variables.

After solving $\mathbf{U}_1$ and $\mathbf{U}_2$, for one unseen query image $\mathbf{a}_p$ or query text document $\mathbf{b}_q$, we can map $\mathbf{a}_p$ or $\mathbf{b}_q$ into the latent topic space as $\mathbf{a}_p\mathbf{U}_1^T$ or $\mathbf{b}_q\mathbf{U}_2^T$ respectively.

However, as discussed in Section 1, we hope the topic we learned is only relevant with a few visual words or text words that are closely related to the topics. For this purpose, we add the ℓ_1 norm regularize to the projection matrix $\mathbf{U}_1$ and $\mathbf{U}_2$ which induces the sparseness of the connection between topics and visual/textual words. Thus, we can rewrite the

Eq. (2) as follows:

$$\min_{\mathbf{X},\mathbf{U}_1,\mathbf{U}_2} =\|\mathbf{A}-\mathbf{X}\mathbf{U}_1\|_F^2+\gamma\|\mathbf{B}-\mathbf{X}\mathbf{U}_2\|_F^2 \\ +\lambda_1\|\mathbf{U}_1\|_1+\lambda_2\|\mathbf{U}_2\|_1 \\ s.t. \quad \mathbf{X}^T\mathbf{X}=\mathbf{I}, \tag{3}$$

where the λ_1 and λ_2 are the regularization parameters controlling the sparsity of $\mathbf{U}_1$ and $\mathbf{U}_2$ respectively.

The objective function in Eq. (3) has three variables to be optimized, i.e. $\mathbf{U}_1, \mathbf{U}_2$ and $\mathbf{X}$. Therefore, this objective function is difficult to be solved directly. However, it is convex with respect to each one variable when other two is fixed, thus we choose to alternatively solve this problem:

1. When X is fixed, the optimization of $\mathbf{U}_1$ and $\mathbf{U}_2$ are two individual lasso problem:

$$\min_{\mathbf{U}_1} \|\mathbf{A}-\mathbf{X}\mathbf{U}_1\|_F^2+\lambda_1\|\mathbf{U}_1\|_1; \\ \min_{\mathbf{U}_2} \|\mathbf{B}-\mathbf{X}\mathbf{U}_2\|_F^2+\lambda_2\|\mathbf{U}_2\|_1. \tag{4}$$

   This can be efficiently solved by the lasso solver [6].

2. When $\mathbf{U}_1$ and $\mathbf{U}_2$ are fixed, Eq. (3) can be rewritten as:

$$\min_{\mathbf{X}} \|[\mathbf{A},\sqrt{\gamma}\mathbf{B}]-\mathbf{X}[\mathbf{U}_1,\sqrt{\gamma}\mathbf{U}_2]\|_F^2 \quad s.t. \quad \mathbf{X}^T\mathbf{X}=\mathbf{I}. \tag{5}$$

   By introducing $\widetilde{\mathbf{Y}}=[\mathbf{A},\sqrt{\gamma}\mathbf{B}]$, $\widetilde{\mathbf{U}}=[\mathbf{U}_1,\sqrt{\gamma}\mathbf{U}_2]$, Eq. (5) can be further written as:

$$\min_{\mathbf{X}} \|\widetilde{\mathbf{Y}}-\mathbf{X}\widetilde{\mathbf{U}}\|_F^2 \qquad s.t. \quad \mathbf{X}^T\mathbf{X}=\mathbf{I}. \tag{6}$$

   Expanding the Eq. (6), we can obtain:

$$\|\widetilde{\mathbf{Y}}-\mathbf{X}\widetilde{\mathbf{U}}\|_F^2 \\ = tr((\widetilde{\mathbf{Y}}-\mathbf{X}\widetilde{\mathbf{U}})^T(\widetilde{\mathbf{Y}}-\mathbf{X}\widetilde{\mathbf{U}})) \\ = -2tr(\widetilde{\mathbf{U}}^T\mathbf{X}^T\widetilde{\mathbf{Y}})+tr(\widetilde{\mathbf{Y}}^T\widetilde{\mathbf{Y}})+tr(\mathbf{U}^T\mathbf{X}^T\mathbf{X}\mathbf{U}) \\ = -2tr(\widetilde{\mathbf{U}}^T\mathbf{X}^T\widetilde{\mathbf{Y}})+tr(\widetilde{\mathbf{Y}}^T\widetilde{\mathbf{Y}})+tr(\mathbf{U}^T\mathbf{U}).$$

   By the fact that $tr(\widetilde{\mathbf{U}}^T\mathbf{X}^T\widetilde{\mathbf{Y}}) \equiv tr(\mathbf{X}^T\widetilde{\mathbf{Y}}\widetilde{\mathbf{U}}^T)$, the objective function Eq. (6) can be written as:

$$\max_{\mathbf{X}} tr(\mathbf{X}^T\widetilde{\mathbf{Y}}\widetilde{\mathbf{U}}^T) \\ s.t. \quad \mathbf{X}^T\mathbf{X}=\mathbf{I}. \tag{7}$$

   As discussed in [2], given the singular value composition of $\mathbf{V}=\widetilde{\mathbf{Y}}\widetilde{\mathbf{U}}^T$ as $\mathbf{V}=\mathbf{P}\triangle\mathbf{Q}$, the optimal solution to Eq. (7) is $\mathbf{X}=\mathbf{P}\mathbf{Q}$.

After iteratively updating $\mathbf{X}$, $\mathbf{U}_1$ and $\mathbf{U}_2$ according to above steps, we can finally solve the objective function in Eq. (3). Due to the space limitation, the convergence of solution is omitted here. The projection scheme of the proposed method is shown in Fig. 2. The optimization procedure can be summarized in Algorithm 1.

3. EXPERIMENT

In this section, we conduct several experiments on real world Wikipedia data to show the effectiveness of the proposed method.

Table 1: The retrieval performance on different projection method.

		P@5	P@20	P@50	MAP
Text Query	Random	0.106	0.118	0.116	0.112
	CCA	0.127	0.122	0.119	0.121
	Ours	**0.147**	**0.145**	**0.136**	**0.142**
Image Query	Random	0.112	0.113	0.110	0.111
	CCA	0.123	0.115	0.111	0.116
	Ours	**0.161**	**0.157**	**0.140**	**0.153**

3.1 Experimental Setting

The Wikipedia dataset provided in [9] contains 2,866 image-text pairs. Each image is represented by a 1,000 dimensional bag-of-visual-words vector. Also, each text document is represented with a 5,000 dimensional vector generated by word frequency, rather than the LDA result used in [9].

The dataset is split into three subsets. The first subset is used for training the projection matrices $\mathbf{U}_1$ and $\mathbf{U}_2$. In the cross-media retrieval experiment, the other two subsets are used as base and retrieval sets while in the image classification experiment, they are used as training and testing set. The capacities of the three subsets are 1,436, 710 and 720 respectively.

3.2 Cross-media Retrieval

Two experiments on cross-media retrieval are conducted: image retrieval using text query; text retrieval using image query.

Firstly, both visual and textual features from the query and base set are projected into the 100 dimensional latent topic space. Then the similarity between text documents and images is measured by ℓ_2 distance on the projected topic space. We choose CCA and random projection for comparison. Precision at k (P@k, $k \in \{5, 20, 50\}$) and mean average precision (MAP) are used for performance evaluation.

The experiment results in Table 1 demonstrate the effectiveness of our approach. The superior performance of our method comes from two aspects: firstly, the connection between text and images are explicitly considered when learning the projections; secondly, the sparse constraints on the projection matrices ensures that each topic is only related to a few most relevant words.

3.3 Image Classification

In this subsection, we evaluate the image classification performance on the latent topic space obtained by our method.

The following methods are used for comparison: raw image feature, feature space projected by CCA and the feature space projected by random projection. We train the same linear classifiers on these subspaces for fair comparison. Area under the ROC (Receiver Operating Characteristics) curve (AUC) is used to measure the performance of classification.

The experiment result is summarized in Fig. 4. It can be seen that our method outperforms other compared methods on image classification in terms of AUC score. By integrating the text informative into the projection matrix, the latent topic space obtained from our method and CCA can be more effective for classification. Moreover, since the sparse mapping helps us get rid of much noise information, our method has better performance than CCA.

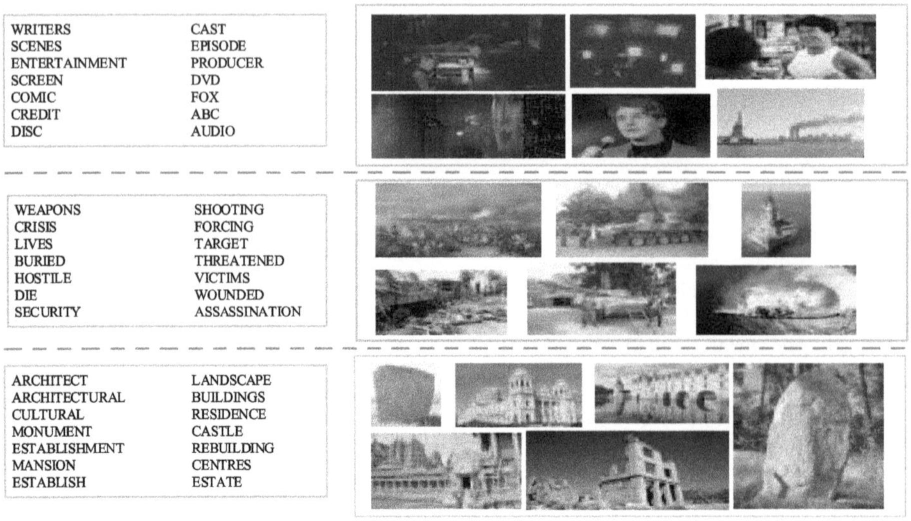

Figure 3: The topics learned by our proposed method.

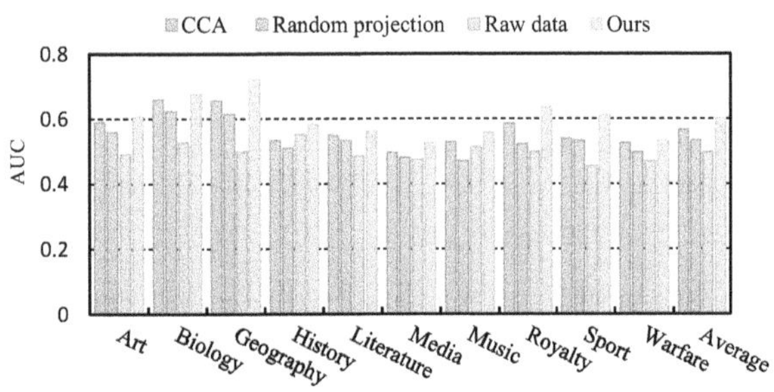

Figure 4: Image classification performance on each category.

3.4 Topic Illustration

One of the benefits of cross-media topic mining is that we can provide readers with a more comprehensive and intuitive way to understand the digests and trends of Wikipedia.

In this subsection, we show some of the topics we learned to demonstrate the effectiveness of our method in offering users with more informative topics. In Fig. 3, we show three topics with their most relevant words and images in our experiment based on the projection matrix $\mathbf{U}_1$ and $\mathbf{U}_2$.

4. CONCLUSIONS

In this work, we propose to learn the sparse projection matrices that map the image-text pairs in Wikipedia into a unified latent topic space. Different from traditional methods, our projection matrices only associate the most relevant features with each topic. The learned topic space not only gives a more intuitive way for readers to understand the Wikipedia content but also benefits some other multimedia applications, such as cross-media retrieval and image classification. Since the learned projections integrates much valuable information from the Wikipedia data, we can apply it to data from other sources for cross-domain applications in the future.

5. ACKNOWLEDGEMENT

Our work is supported in part by NSFC(61071218), 973 Program (2010CB327904), 863 program (2012AA012505) and the Fundamental Research Funds for the Central Universities and China Knowledge Centre for Engineering Science and Technology (CKCEST).

6. REFERENCES

[1] D. M. Blei and M. I. Jordan. Modeling annotated data. In *SIGIR*, pages 127–134, 2003.

[2] X. Chen, Y. Qi, B. Bai, Q. Lin, and J. G. Carbonell. Sparse latent semantic analysis. In *SDM*, 2011.

[3] H. Hotelling. Relations between two sets of variates. *Biometrika*, 28(3/4):321–377, 1936.

[4] J. Hu, L. Fang, Y. Cao, H. jun Zeng, H. Li, Q. Yang, and Z. Chen. Enhancing text clustering by leveraging Wikipedia semantics. In *SIGIR*, pages 179–186, 2008.

[5] C. Liu, B. C. Ooi, A. K. H. Tung, and D. Zhang. Crew: cross-modal resource searching by exploiting wikipedia. In *ACM MM*, pages 1669–1672, 2010.

[6] J. Mairal, F. Bach, J. Ponce, and G. Sapiro. Online learning for matrix factorization and sparse coding. *JMLR*, 11:19–60, 2010.

[7] T. Melzer, M. Reiter, and H. Bischof. Kernel canonical correlation analysis. In *ICANN*, pages 353–360, 2001.

[8] D. N. Milne and I. H. Witten. Learning to link with Wikipedia. In *CIKM*, pages 509–518, 2008.

[9] N. Rasiwasia, J. Costa Pereira, E. Coviello, G. Doyle, G. R. Lanckriet, R. Levy, and N. Vasconcelos. A new approach to cross-modal multimedia retrieval. In *ACM MM*, 2010.

[10] A. Sharma, A. Kumar, H. Daume, and D. W. Jacobs. Generalized multiview analysis: A discriminative latent space. In *CVPR*, pages 2160–2167. IEEE, 2012.

[11] F. Wu, H. Zhang, and Y. Zhuang. Learning semantic correlations for cross-media retrieval. In *ICIP*, 2006.

[12] Y. Yang, D. Xu, F. Nie, J. Luo, and Y. Zhuang. Ranking with local regression and global alignment for cross media retrieval. In *ACM MM*, 2009.

A Multigrid Approach for Bandwidth and Display Resolution Aware Streaming of 3D Deformations

Yuan Tian[†], Yin Yang[‡], Xiaohu Guo[†], Balakrishnan Prabhakaran[†]

[†]University of Texas at Dallas
800 W Campbell Road
Richardson, TX 75080 USA
{yxt114020,xguo,praba}@utdallas.edu

[‡]University of New Mexico
1 University Blvd NE
Albuquerque, NM 87131 USA
yyang@ece.unm.edu

ABSTRACT

In this paper, we propose a novel multimedia system adaptively streaming the animation according to display resolution and/or network bandwidth. A Multigrid-like technique is used in this framework to accelerate the converging rate of the optimization of the nonlinear deformation energy. The computation is performed from coarsest mesh at the top level to the finest mesh at the bottom level and then goes back to the top again. Such V-shape calculation provides great flexibility for the networked environment. Clients are able to receive the data streaming corresponding to its display resolution and network bandwidth. A more compact form of deformation data packaging is also used in this system such that a cube element only needs six parameters instead of 24 variables as used in regular mesh representation, which significantly reduces the network overhead for the streaming.

Categories and Subject Descriptors

I.3.2 [**COMPUTER GRAPHICS**]: Graphics Systems—*Distributed/network graphics*

Keywords

3D Streaming; Deformation; Multigrid

1. INTRODUCTION

Modern multimedia system involves more and more 3D geometries based computation, a large group of which is soft and deformable objects. This raises a new challenge of deformable model in the area of multimedia computing. The most critical ingredient of calculating 3D deformation of an object is to find an appropriate methodology to effectively evaluate the potential energy corresponding to the deformation. The deformed shape of the object can then be obtained as searching for the energy minimum. Large deformation normally requires energy defined nonlinearly w.r.t displacement. Therefore, a fast converging rate becomes a key fact in deformable model. Immediately followed by this challenge is another important issue regarding networking streaming. Since the deformation of mesh-based geometry normally requires large amount of information - each vertex on the mesh is subject to a certain displacement at each frame of the animation. Effectively reducing the data size and alleviating the network burden induced by the deformation streaming remain a technical challenge to many multimedia applications such as distributed virtual environments, remote education and online entertaining systems.

Contributions As shown in Fig. 1, we address these challenges with a novel multigrid computational framework and an adaptive streaming policy. The low resolution mesh guides the computation for finer mesh so that the computation at high resolution mesh gets converged much faster. The benefit of multigrid is not limited to the calculation. An adaptive streaming policy is naturally available and clients are able to choose data stream based on its display resolution and network connection as shown in Fig. 1. We also use a more condensed data representation of the deformed mesh. Each cube element requires only six parameters rather than 24 variables, which is only 25% data size. In addition, only the information of cube elements that will participate in the further computation of surface mesh displacement are streamed.

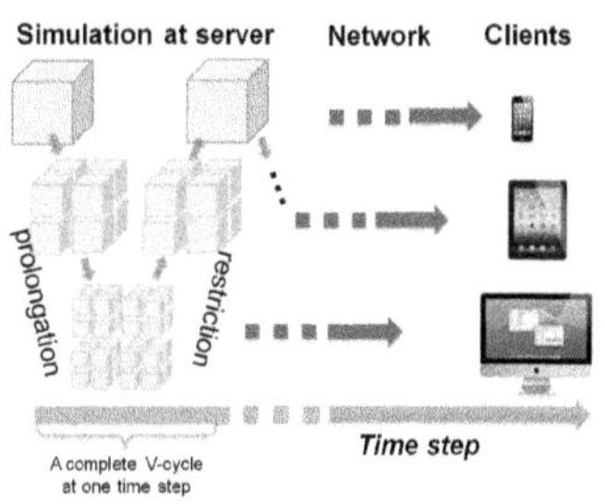

Figure 1: System overview.

2. RELATED WORK

3D deformation has been an open challenge in the community of computer graphics. The most commonly-adopted method is to use finite element method (FEM) to model the strain-stress relation of the material [7]. This method, however needs complicated pre-computation and matrix assembling. Therefore, it is rarely adopted for online multimedia system. On the other hand, some pseudo physics-based techniques are also very popular because of the simplicity and robustness [1, 6]. The computation is almost ready-to-go as soon as the mesh is loaded and such feature is more desired for real-time distributed multimedia system. 3D mesh com-

MM'13, October 21–25, 2013, Barcelona, Spain.

http://dx.doi.org/10.1145/2502081.2502181.

pression and transmission is also intensively studied such as single-rate compression [8], progressive meshing [2], subspace geometry representation [10], or to converge 3D geometry to 2D image sequences [5]. Different from previous methods handles surface mesh compression and transmission [10], our method transmits the hierarchical volumetric meshes adaptively instead of surface mesh to reduce network traffic, and the deformable model is handled by a semi physics-based multigrid optimization strategy [4] in our system.

3. MULTIGRID DEFORMATION

Deformation formulation For an arbitrary surface triangle mesh, we generate a voxel or cube mesh using squashing cube (SC) [3]. The deformation is computed with cube mesh and the corresponding shape of the surface mesh can be computed with barycentric interpolation. Similar to shape matching [6],the deformation energy of a cube is evaluated as the deviation between the deformed cube and the undeformed cube and the energy of the whole mesh is simply the summation over all the cubes. Since a rigid body motion does not bring any geometric shape change to the cube, computing the deformation of the element becomes a problem of finding its optimal rigid transformation. We arrange the rest positions of the eight nodes into a 3 by 8 matrix $\mathbf{P}$, such that each column of $\mathbf{P}$ represents the rest position of a cube node. Similarly, $\mathbf{Q} \in \mathbb{R}^{3\times8}$ stores the deformed position of the nodes and we need to find the optimal rotation and the translation corresponding to the rigid transformation of the cube such that:

$$E = \| \mathbf{RP} + \mathbf{T} - \mathbf{Q} \|^2, \text{ and } E \text{ is to be minimized,} \quad (1)$$

where $\mathbf{T} \in \mathbb{R}^{3\times8}$ is translation matrix and each column in $\mathbf{T}$ is the translation of the cube[1]. It can be computed as centroid shift of the cube caused by the deformation. $\mathbf{R} \in SO(3)$ represents the rotation. In order to calculate $\mathbf{R}$, we first relax the condition of rotation to a regular linear transformation $\mathbf{A}$, which can be computed as $\mathbf{A} = [(\mathbf{PP}^\top)^{-1}\mathbf{P}(\mathbf{Q}-\mathbf{T})^\top]^\top$. Then, we use the polar decomposition to extract the rigid rotation $\mathbf{R}$ of $\mathbf{A}$ such that $\mathbf{A} = \mathbf{RS}$, where $\mathbf{S}$ is a symmetric matrix corresponding to the stretching. Alg. 1 is the general algorithm for one shape matching iteration.

while *deformation energy is above threshold* **do**
  for *each cube element* **do**
    compute optimal translation $\mathbf{T}$;
    compute optimal transformation matrix $\mathbf{A}$;
    compute optimal rotation matrix $\mathbf{R}$;
  end
  for *each neighbor cube pair* **do**
    average displacement at interface nodes;
  end
end

Algorithm 1: shape matching iteration

Optimization with multigrid It is easy to understand that the shape matching (*i.e.*, finding the optimal rigid transformation for a deformed element) is actually searching for a *local minimum* of the energy at the corresponding element. We need to keep performing iterations until the iteration does not bring notable energy reduction and the system converges. Soft object with complex geometry typically requires a cube mesh of very high resolution and a large number of iteration is needed to get the system converged. In order to address this issue, we use a novel hierarchial computational method inspired by the idea of multigrid technique, a numerical algorithm accelerating the converging rate for such nonlinear optimization problem.

Multi-resolution meshing As the name implies, we create a multi-resolution cube mesh hierarchy correspondingly at the beginning of simulation. The coarsest mesh can be generated using SC. Each element is further divided into eight subcubes and the sub-cubes that do not have any influences to the surface mesh are simply discarded. Normally, the finest cube mesh is the one such that the resolution of the cube mesh somehow "matches" the resolution of the surface mesh.

Prolongation Iteration starts at the top-level mesh (*e.g.*, the one with lowest resolution) and captures the general sketch of the deformation. Such information is utilized so that the iteration at lower level mesh (*e.g.*, finer mesh) begins from well-estimated intermediate values and improves the local deformation details. The number of the iteration is also significantly reduced because of the inherited information from upper-level (UL) mesh. In order to obtain reasonable starting values for lower-level (LL) iteration, an estimation must be evaluated for each cube based on the result at UL mesh. This procedure is called *prolongation*. Each element in UL mesh has the information of rotation and translation. At the LL mesh, translation information is linear interpolated by blending the translation at neighboring UL elements. Similarly, rotation information is interpolated using spherical linear interpolation (Slerp) [9]. Both interpolations are weighted by the reciprocal of the squared distance. As shown in Fig. 2, the rotation at element $L1$ is computed as $\mathbf{q}_{L1} = Slerp(\mathbf{q}_{U1}, \mathbf{q}_{U2}, t)$, where $t = \frac{1}{d(L1,U1)^2}/(\frac{1}{d(L1,U1)^2} + \frac{1}{d(L1,U2)^2})$. $\mathbf{q}_{L1}, \mathbf{q}_{U1}$ and $\mathbf{q}_{U2}$ are the unit quaternions representing the rotation at element $L1, U1$ and $U2$. $d(L1, U1)$ and $d(L1, U2)$ are the Euclidean distances between centroids of element $L1$ and $U1$ as well as $L1$ and $L2$ in rest shape, respectively. Also,.

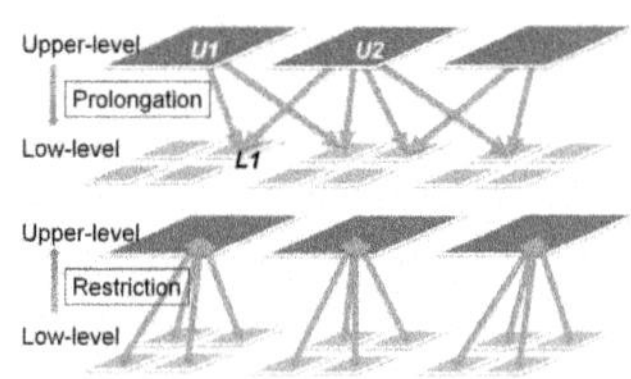

Figure 2: Prolongation and restriction.

Restriction Opposite to the prolongation, after the iteration at LL mesh is finished, the information needs to be uploaded to the UL mesh so that the UL mesh would have better starting values for next time step. This procedure is also referred as *restriction*. In restriction, the translation and the rotation of a UL element is computed as the average of values at corresponding LL elements. In each time step, the system begins with the top-level mesh and performs the prolongation downwards the LL mesh until the information reaches the bottom-level mesh. After the iteration at the bottom-level mesh is finished, the restriction is performed all the way back to the top to refine the result at UL meshes. The whole computation procedure is called *V-cycle*.

[1]All the columns in $\mathbf{T}$ are the same.

Dynamic simulation V-cycle is able to fast find the optimal deformation. However the result is "static" because all the computation is performed purely based on the displacement and we have no idea about the node velocity. In order to incorporate the dynamics into the system, we use a simplified Euler integration for each node to model the velocity ($\mathbf{v}$) and the displacement ($\mathbf{u}$):

$$\begin{aligned} \mathbf{v}(t+h) &= (1-\kappa)\mathbf{v}(t) + \alpha\frac{\mathbf{s}(t)-\mathbf{u}(t)}{h} + h\mathbf{f}_{ext}(t)/m \\ \mathbf{u}(t+h) &= \mathbf{u}(t) + h\mathbf{v}(t+h) \end{aligned} \quad (2)$$

where m is the mass of a node. The parameter κ is a scalar to simulate velocity damping. α is the spring constant that imitates the magnitude of the vibration of the object. $\mathbf{s} \in \mathbb{R}^{3\times 1}$ is the optimal rigid position of the node and h is the time interval between two V-cycles. $\mathbf{f}_{ext}$ is the external force applied at the node. After the velocity and displacement of the cube node are computed, the surface mesh is updated based on the pre-computed barycentric coordinate. The whole computation procedure is summarized in Alg. 2.

```
while simulation is active do
    for each level of mesh from top to bottom do
        if current level is not top then
            perform prolongation;
        end
        perform shape matching iteration (Alg. 1);
    end
    for each level of mesh from bottom to top do
        if current level is not bottom then
            perform restriction;
        end
        perform dynamic simulation using Eq. 2;
        update surface mesh;
    end
end
```

Algorithm 2: Dynamic simulation using V-cycle

4. ADAPTIVE STREAMING

High resolution mesh delivers more detailed geometry but consumes more hardware resource at the same time as the cost. Multigrid provides the flexible feasibility for the clients to choose to stream animations of different resolutions over the network. Naturally, the client with higher screen resolution is expecting for more geometry information of the simulation such that a LL deformation should be streamed. On the other hand, the user with small-screen-client such as a smart phone or other mobile devices is likely to obtain satisfactory experience with the streaming of only middle or low resolution deformation. Currently, our system is implemented with classic CS architecture. In this architecture as shown in Fig. 1, the server assumed with more hardware resource is in charge of the simulation task, that is performing the V-cycle iteration from the top to bottom and then back to top repeatedly at each time step. It is noteworthy that in a complete multigrid V-cycle, the static position of the cube meshes at each level is always computed. Accordingly, the clients that are interested in streaming of different resolution are able to choose to receive the data at different level of mesh in the V-cycle. Such multi-resolution streaming does not increase the computation load at the server.

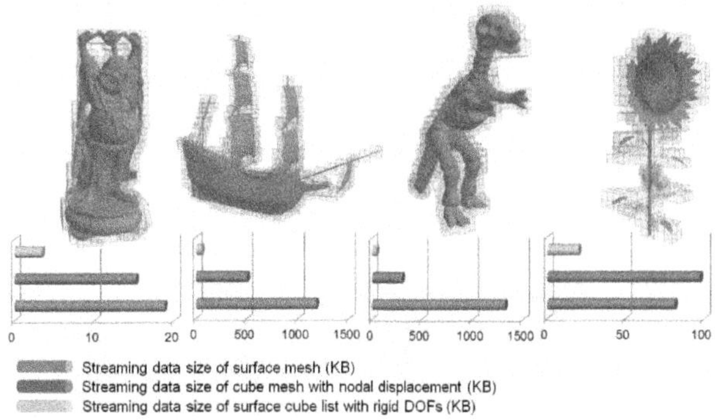

Figure 3: The size of stream data using different data representation.

Packetization In order to display the animation at the clients, the information of the deformed geometry of either a cube mesh or a surface mesh must be passed to the client and it is always preferred to transmit the data with smaller size to conserve the network bandwidth. The most intuitive choice would be directly sending the deformed geometry of the surface mesh to the client. Unfortunately, it requires calculating the deformation of surface mesh at different level using barycentric interpolation at the server side, which leads to extra computation load to the server. More importantly, with such streaming policy, the displacement of all the vertices on the surface mesh must be transmitted via the network. If we use *C++ double* type to store the displacements in x, y and z directions, the size of the streaming data could be as large as $\frac{num.\ of\ vertices \times 3 \times 8}{1024}\ KB$. Another choice would be to stream the cube mesh and the corresponding data size is $\frac{num.\ of\ cubes \times 8 \times 3 \times 8}{1024}\ KB$ as each cube has eight nodes. However, a much wiser choice is to only deliver the information of the cubes that are needed for surface barycentric interpolation. This corresponds to the outmost layer of cubes on the mesh. At the server side, a rigid rotation and translation is computed for each cube. Therefore, instead of transmitting the displacements at eight nodes on the cube, we only stream seven parameters corresponding to the rigid body motion of a cube which includes cube id, a 3 by 1 translation vector and a 3 by 1 rotation vector. As shown in Fig. 3, this streaming strategy reduces the data communication between server and client significantly. Clients, after receiving the data, update the surface mesh using barycentric interpolation. The corresponding barycentric coordinate for each surface nodes can be precomputed as soon as the surface mesh of proper resolution is set.

Adaptive streaming policy Our framework provides adequate freedom for the client to adjust the balance among information details, network bandwidth as well as the computation intensity. It is quite possible that streaming surface cubes still causes overloading for the narrow-band network connection, especially for many state-of-the-art mobile devices equipped with display screen of high resolution. In such scenario, the client could choose to receive the deformation streaming from UL mesh with much lower bitrate and locally do the LL iteration using its own CPU. This is like dividing the V-cycle into two parts, the server does the top part and passes to the client. Based on the computed results at UL meshes, the client can still finish the remain-

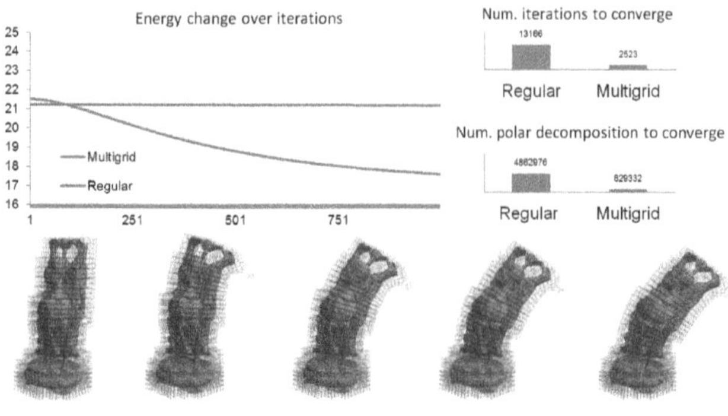

Figure 4: Multigrid technique greatly accelerates the converging rate: 13,166 iterations reduces to 2,523 iterations.

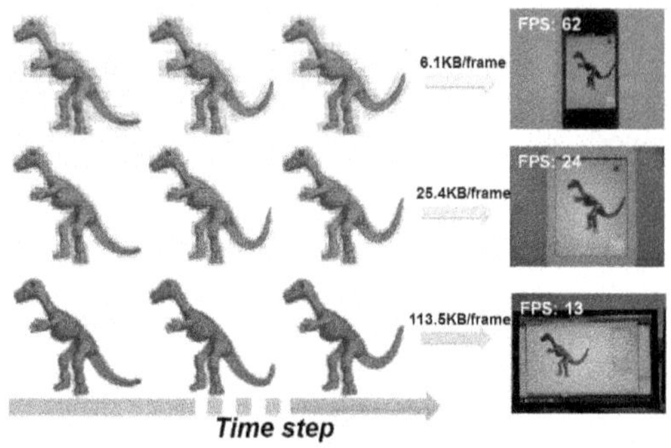

Figure 5: Adaptive streaming - different clients (an iPhone, an iPad as well as a desktop computer) choose different resolution of streaming.

ing cycle with just a few iterations. For the clients with low computation capability, adaptive streaming is also a good solution. The clients periodically check the current network condition and choose the best resolution accordingly to avoid local computation.

5. EXPERIMENTAL RESULTS

Deformation result Multigrid technique makes the converging rate much faster. As shown in Fig. 4, the buddha mode has 3,214 cube elements. With regular shape matching, the system needs 13,166 iterations[2] to get converged while with multigrid method, this number reduces to 2,523. Accordingly, the computation intensity at the server is also significantly reduced. The number of polar decompositions is reduced from 4,862,976 to 829,332.

Network streaming Fig. 5 shows the results of animation streaming with our system. The dinosaur model is simulated and manipulated by the user in real-time. Three levels of meshes with different resolutions are generated. The deformation is computed with multigrid V-cycle. Clients including an iPhone, an iPad as well as a desktop computer receive the animation streaming of different resolutions. The iPhone is with mobile network connection and chooses the streaming of lowest resolution. The iPad is connected with Wifi and receives the medium-size streaming. The computer is connected with local LAN and streaming with the data of highest resolution. Currently we use TCP as the primary streaming protocol as it guarantees the package ordering. *Please refer to the accompanying video for more results of the system.*

[2]The converging condition is set as 0.1% energy reduction per iteration such that each time step stops if an iteration brings the energy decrease less than 0.1% of previous iteration.

6. LIMITATION AND FUTURE WORK

Although our experiments demonstrate big potential of the proposed framework, there still exist some limitations in current version of the system. First of all, for congested network connections, additional mechanisms should be adopted to handle the delayed packages so that the user experiences at all clients are consistent. Second, If the cube mesh is dense, the streaming data could still be quite large. In the future, we are planning to explore the new compression algorithm to further reduce the data size for network streaming. Finally, we currently only implement our system with CS networking architecture and we are planning to transplant the system to other types of networking environments such as peer-to-peer architecture and to make the proposed system more practical for real-world applications.

Acknowledgments This material is based upon work supported by the National Science Foundation under Grant No. 1012975. Any opinions, findings, and conclusions or recommendations expressed in this material are those of the author(s) and do not necessarily reflect the views of the National Science Foundation.

7. REFERENCES

[1] M. Botsch, M. Pauly, M. Gross, and L. Kobbelt. Primo: coupled prisms for intuitive surface modeling. SGP '06, pages 11–20. Eurographics Association, 2006.

[2] A. Doran, S. Mondet, R. Grigoras, G. Morin, W. T. Ooi, and F. Boudon. A demonstration of mobitree: progressive 3d tree models streaming on mobile clients. In *Proceedings of the 17th ACM international conference on Multimedia*, MM '09, pages 955–956, 2009.

[3] D. L. James, J. Barbič, and C. D. Twigg. Squashing cubes: automating deformable model construction for graphics. In *ACM SIGGRAPH 2004 Sketches*, pages 38–. ACM.

[4] B. W. L., H. V. Emden, and M. S. F. *A Multigrid Tutorial, Second Edition.* Society for Industrial and Applied Mathematics, second edition, 2000.

[5] F. Lamberti and A. Sanna. A streaming-based solution for remote visualization of 3d graphics on mobile devices. *IEEE Transactions on Visualization and Computer Graphics*, 13(2):247–260, Mar. 2007.

[6] M. Müller, B. Heidelberger, M. Teschner, and M. Gross. Meshless deformations based on shape matching. SIGGRAPH '05, pages 471–478.

[7] A. Nealen, M. MÍźller, R. Keiser, E. Boxerman, and M. Carlson. Physically based deformable models in computer graphics. *Computer Graphics Forum*, 25(4):809–836, 2006.

[8] D. Shikhare, S. Bhakar, and S. Mudur. Compression of large 3d engineering models using automatic discovery of repeating geometric features. *Signal Processing*, 19(20):15, 2001.

[9] K. Shoemake. Animating rotation with quaternion curves. *SIGGRAPH 85*, 19:245–254, July 1985.

[10] Z. Tang, O. Ozbek, and X. Guo. Real-time 3d interaction with deformable model on mobile devices. MM '11, pages 1009–1012, 2011.

Error Recovered Hierarchical Classification

Shiai Zhu†, Xiao-Yong Wei‡, Chong-Wah Ngo†
†Dept of Computer Science, City University of Hong Kong, Kowloon, Hong Kong
‡College of Computer Science, Sichuan University, Chengdu, China
shiaizhu2@student.cityu.edu.hk, cswei@scu.edu.cn, cwngo@cs.cityu.edu.hk

ABSTRACT

Hierarchical classification (HC) is a popular and efficient way for detecting the semantic concepts from the images. However, the conventional HC, which always selects the branch with the highest classification response to go on, has the risk of propagating serious errors from higher levels of the hierarchy to the lower levels. We argue that the highest-response-first strategy is too arbitrary, because the candidate nodes are considered individually which ignores the semantic relationship among them. In this paper, we propose a novel method for HC, which is able to utilize the semantic relationship among candidate nodes and their children to recover the responses of unreliable classifiers of the candidate nodes, with the hope of providing the branch selection a more globally valid and semantically consistent view. The experimental results show that the proposed method outperforms the conventional HC methods and achieves a satisfactory balance between the accuracy and efficiency.

Categories and Subject Descriptors

H.3.1 [**Information Storage and Retrieval**]: Content Analysis and Indexing

Keywords

Concept Detection, Large-scale Hierarchy, Error Propagation

1. INTRODUCTION

Detecting semantic concept(s) from images is a multi-class classification problem, which has received intensive studies in the last decade. The complexity of the problem increases dramatically when the number of concepts exceeds a certain extent. To reduce the complexity, a practical way is to simplify the problem into a set of binary classification problems, where a binary classifier is trained for each concept, and during testing, all classifiers are applied to the target to which class label(s) are assigned by the classifier(s) with the highest response(s). While the *one (target)-vs-all (concepts)* simplification provides a much more feasible solution for multiple concept detection, nevertheless, it is still impractical when facing large-scale datasets (e.g., ImageNet [4] which includes 21,841 concepts with each of them associated with 1,000 images), because all classifiers have to be called at runtime for every image.

*Xiao-Yong Wei is the corresponding author.

MM'13, October 21–25, 2013, Barcelona, Spain.

http://dx.doi.org/10.1145/2502081.2502182.

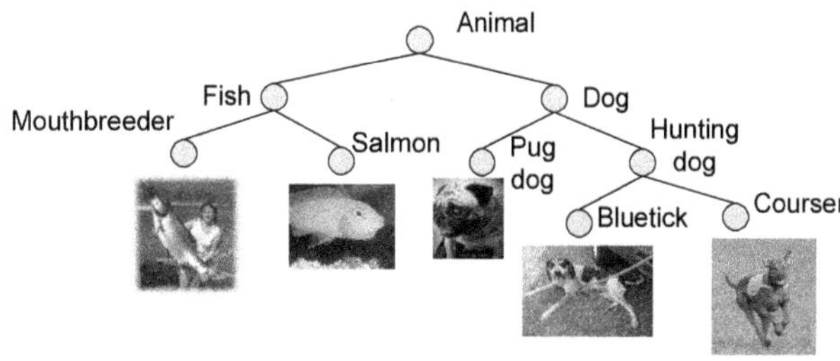

Figure 1: An example of image concept hierarchy.

To tackle the scalability issue, hierarchical classification is commonly adopted. Instead of applying all classifiers to a target image, hierarchical classification organizes concept classifiers into a hierarchy (e.g., Figure 1) according to the semantic relationship among concepts, and only selects a small set of classifiers for testing. The selection procedure usually starts from the root of the hierarchy and proceeds with a top-down manner that, for each node under investigation, hierarchical classification first applies the classifiers of the child nodes to the target, and then selects the child node with the highest response on its classifier as the next node to investigate. The procedure repeats recursively and results in a path from the root to a leaf node (e.g., Animal-Fish-Salmon), on the basis of which all the concept labels on the path will be assigned to the target image.

By reducing the number of classifiers to be visited, hierarchical classification significantly improves the efficiency of multiple concept detection, and thus has been widely employed (e.g, web categorization [3, 1] and gene function prediction [10]). However, as pointed out by Bennett et al [1], the improvement is paid at the price of scarifying effectiveness of the classification. More specifically, the top-down classification procedure will make the classification errors included at the higher levels of the hierarchy be propagated to the lower levels, and in turn significantly degrades the accuracy of those leaf nodes. A few methods have been proposed to address this problem. In [3], Xue et al. address the problem by selecting only a small number of nodes from the original hierarchy to construct a simplified hierarchy for classification. In this way, the chance of error propagation is reduced because the classification path from root to leaf node is significantly shorten. In [1], when building the set of negative instances for training each node, Bennett et al. also include the false positive instances which have been misclassified at its ancestor nodes, in the hope that those instances can be rejected by current classifier and the mis-classification errors will not be further propagated to the low level nodes.

Even those methods are able to improve the accuracy of hierarchical classification, we argue that the optimization schemes employed still have not addressed the core of the error propagation – the arbitrariness of the branch selection. In the top-down selection procedure, the classification will be led to a branch under the classifier with the highest response. This is arbitrary because it is well known that the performance of the visual concept detectors is still not satisfactory in a general sense, and therefore, it frequently happens that the high response is from an unreliable classifier. Selecting a branch under such node may seriously ruin the classification procedure follows. In addition, the highest-response-first strategy is lack of global perspective, in the way that the classification only focuses on the local responses of the nodes to be investigated, but never verifies if these responses are valid or globally consistent to the semantic relationship encapsulated in the hierarchy. With Figure 1 as an example, assuming that a target image includes a fish, the classification will be led to the branch under Dog if the classifier for Dog is unreliable and outputs higher response than that of Fish. When deciding next node to move on, the classifiers of the Pug Dog and Hunting Dog (if reliable enough) will output low responses. Globally speaking, this is conflicting to the semantic relationship in the hierarchy, in the sense that a parent node is with high response while all of its children nodes are with low responses. However, the procedure will never "doubt" the decision at the node Dog and continue to select between Pug Dog and Hunting Dog, resulting in further error propagation.

In this paper, we propose a novel branch selection scheme for hierarchical classification to address the core issue related to error propagation. Instead of arbitrarily selecting the node with the highest response, we introduce an error recovery scheme which first verifies the semantic consistency of the observation on a candidate node under investigation and those of its relatives (e.g., siblings, children and so on) in the hierarchy, and then adjusts the output of the node accordingly. The decision of which branch to go will be delayed when the verifications of all candidate nodes are finished. In other words, the proposed scheme makes the decision only when more observations are available and it is "confident" to do so. In the example mentioned above, the scheme is able to detect the inconsistency among the observation of Dog and those of its children nodes, and thus increase the chance of leading the classification to the correct branch (i.e., that under Fish in this example).

2. METHOD

In the proposed method, instead of considering only the candidate nodes, we also involve their children and siblings to form a committee for decision making. In practical, before deciding which branch to go, we adjust the response of each candidate node to be semantically consistent with those of other nodes in the committee, with the hope that the unreliable response of a candidate can be fixed if it is conflicting with those of its relatives in the hierarchy. Therefore, making decision on the adjusted response is with a more global view and can avoid the arbitrariness of the branch selection with the highest-response-first local strategy.

2.1 Problem Formulation

Given an instance x and a node c_t as the current node in a hierarchy, we denote the branch to go at next moment as a node c_{t+1}, so that

$$c_{t+1} = \arg\max_{c \in \mathcal{N}(c_t)} \hat{f}_c(x) \tag{1}$$

where $\mathcal{N}(c_t)$ is a set of child nodes of c_t, and $\hat{f}_c(x)$ is the adjusted response of c to x. Further denoting the original response of c as $f_c(x)$, we can formulate the highest-response-first local strategy by replacing $\hat{f}_c(x)$ with the original response $f_c(x)$. Moreover, our committee for decision making (denoted as $\mathcal{T}$) is a union of c_t's children (i.e., $\mathcal{N}(c_t)$) and its grandchildren (i.e., $\bigcup_{c \in \mathcal{N}(c_t)} \mathcal{N}(c)$). The problem to solve is then how to define the adjusting function $\hat{f}_c(x)$ with respect to both the semantical relationship and the observations of the nodes in the committee $\mathcal{T}$. Let us denote the semantical relationship among nodes as $\Phi_{\mathcal{T}}$ and compose the observations of the committee $\mathcal{T}$ into a vector $\mathbf{f}_{\mathcal{T}}(x) = [f_{c_1}, f_{c_2}, f_{c_3}, \cdots]$ where $c_1, c_2, c_3, \cdots \in \mathcal{T}$, the problem can be formulated as

$$\hat{f}_c(x) = P(c|\Phi_{\mathcal{T}}, \mathbf{f}_{\mathcal{T}}(x)). \tag{2}$$

2.2 Committee-based Response Adjustment

Once the hierarchy is known, there are a lot of priori can be utilized for modeling $\hat{f}_c(x)$. For example, by definition, the siblings in a hierarchy are semantically exclusive, so that the response for a candidate node should be approaching 1 if those of its siblings are all with responses close to 0. In addition, parent node represents a union of the instances of its child nodes, so that the response for a candidate node should be close to 0 if those of its child nodes are all with responses close to 0. In brief, confined by the semantic relationship $\Phi_{\mathcal{T}}$, the responses of nodes in a committee should always follow certain patterns. Therefore, we can use the observations of the committee $\mathcal{T}$ to predict that of a candidate node so as to implement the response adjustment.

Intuitively, this can be simply modeled by logistic regression, where we use the observations of the committee $\mathcal{T}$ as predictors for estimating a reasonable output for a target concept c. The semantic constraints $\Phi_{\mathcal{T}}$ is then modeled by a set of weights (i.e., a weight vector $\mathbf{w}_c = [w_1, w_2, \cdots]$) associated with the predictors. A weight given to a predictor reflects the ability of the predictor to estimate the output of the target concept. By further expanding the logistic regression to all the candidate nodes, we can learn their weights at the same time by multi-class regression (MLR), resulting a weight matrix $\mathbf{W}$. It is worth mentioning that learning the weights together not only brings convenience for the learning but also makes the inter-concept relationship among candidate nodes be modeled during the learning. By replacing the semantic relationship $\Phi_{\mathcal{T}}$ with $\mathbf{W}$, Eq. (2) can be implemented with MLR as

$$P(c|\mathbf{W}, \mathbf{f}_{\mathcal{T}}(x)) = \frac{\exp(\mathbf{w}_c^T \mathbf{f}_{\mathcal{T}}(x))}{\sum_{c_k \in \mathcal{N}(c_t)} \exp(\mathbf{w}_k^T \mathbf{f}_{\mathcal{T}}(x))}, \tag{3}$$

Table 1: Dataset statistics: number of leaf nodes (#Leaf) and internal nodes (#Int), depth of the hierarchy (#Dep), average number of instances of each concept for training (#Trn), validation (#Val) and testing (#Tst) respectively.

Dataset	#Leaf	#Int	#Dep	#Trn	#Val	#Tst
Caltech256	256	62	6	58	29	29
ILSRVC1K	1000	645	13	1261	50	150

where $\mathbf{w}_k$ is the weight vector for the corresponding candidate node $c_k \in \mathcal{N}(c_t)$.

Given a set of training instances $\mathbf{X} = \{x_1, x_2, \cdots\}$ with each of them associated with a class label $y_i \in \mathcal{N}(c_t)$, an optimal weight matrix $\mathbf{W}^*$ can be obtained by

$$\mathbf{W}^* = \arg\min_{\mathbf{W}} - \sum_{x_i \in \mathbf{X}}^{|\mathbf{X}|} \log P(\mathbf{y}_i | \mathbf{W}, \mathbf{f}_{\mathcal{T}}(x_i)) + \lambda \|\mathbf{W}\|^2, \quad (4)$$

where the second term is a regularizer used to control the model complexity, and λ is regularization parameter. Equ. 4 is referred to as L2-regularized MLR. This problem can be efficiently solved by Quasi-Newton method. In the experiment, we adopt the package released by Mark Schmidt*.

2.3 Verification and Recovery

Since the labels given to each instance always follow certain patterns which reflect the inter-concept semantic relationship in the hierarchy, the resulting weight matrix $\mathbf{W}^*$ in Equ. 4 is also embedded with those relationship which can be used to verify if a set of responses is consistent to those patterns, in the way that it results in larger response in Eq. (3) when it is consistent and smaller response otherwise. Note that, during learning, we put the candidate node itself in the committee, with the hope that the resulting weight can also reflect the classification reliability of the candidate node. According to the principle of MLR, if a candidate node is with an unreliable classifier, it will be assigned with a small weight to weaken its impact to the final results (i.e., the adjusted response Eq. (3)), and the predication for its label will mainly rely on the responses of other nodes in the committee. By contrast, if the node is a reliable classifier, it earns a large weight so its impacts will dominate those of others. This also explains why we put the candidate node itself in the committee. Therefore, the proposed method fulfills the semantic relationship verification and error recovery at the same time by MLR.

3. EXPERIMENTS

3.1 Settings

We use two image datasets for evaluation, Caltech256 [2] and ILSVRC1K [4]. Caltech256 consists of 256 labeled concepts for object annotation. In [2], a concept hierarchy is pre-defined using the 256 concepts as leaf nodes. ILSRVC1K is a subset of ImageNet, where the concepts are organized by WordNet. Starting from the 1,000 concepts in ILSRVC1K, a hierarchy is extracted from the ImageNet hierarchy. Table 1 lists the statistics. We follow the train/validation/test split in ILSRVC1K. For Caltech256, the instances of each concept are split to train/val/test by 50%-25%-25%.

*http://www.di.ens.fr/ mschmidt/Software/code.html

Table 2: Performance comparison of three hierarchical classification methods on Caltech256 and ILSRVC1K. Classification performance is measured by global accuracy (*Acc*), and testing efficiency is measured by average saved time cost (*MTC*).

Dataset		HC	SIB-HC	ER-HC
Caltech256	*Acc* (%)	26.7	27.0	30.5
	MTC (%)	91.5	91.1	67.1
ILSRVC1K	*Acc* (%)	9.4	9.6	11.2
	MTC (%)	98.1	98.3	88.7

Table 3: Performance comparison of three hierarchical classification methods on ILSRVC1K. Local classifiers are learnt on free-sampled web images.

	HC	SIB-HC	ER-HC
Acc (%)	4.3	5.1	5.6
MTC (%)	98.2	97.9	89.4

Each image is represented using Locality-constrained Linear Coding (LLC) with densely sampled SIFT features [6]. We employ a visual vocabulary of 4,000 visual words, and three level spatial partitions (1×1, 2×2 and 3×1). Consequently, the dimension of feature vector is 32,000. For each node c_i, a classifier $f_{c_i}(x)$ is learnt using linear SVM [7] on training set. In addition, a multi-class logistic regression model is learnt for each internal node on the validation set.

The testing instances are all from leaf nodes which are contextually exclusive. Thus we evaluate the classification performance using global accuracy among leaf nodes (*Acc*). An instance is correctly classified when the annotated leaf node hits the ground-truth. Similar to [5] where the efficiency of HC is measured using one-vs-all approach as baseline, we evaluate the efficiency using percentage of saved time cost compared to one-vs-all approach. Since we adopt linear SVM, the time cost is linear with the number of involved classifiers. Thus the saved time cost is defined as $TC = 1 - \frac{\#model}{\#concept}$, where $\#model$ and $\#concept$ denote the number of activated classifiers and the number of concepts in the hierarchy respectively. In this case, TC of one-vs-all approach is 0. We further define MTC as the average saved cost over all testing instances.

We use the standard hierarchical classification (HC) that employs the highest-response-first strategy as our baseline. Our proposed error recovered HC is referred to as ER-HC. To investigate the impact of different committees, we implement a simplified ER-HC by using only the candidate nodes to form the committee (i.e., only sibling relationship is considered). We denote this method as SIB-HC.

3.2 Performance on Benchmark Datasets

The results on two datasets are summarized in Table 2. For Caltech256, ER-HC improves the baseline by 14%, while by only taking the sibling relationship into account, SIB-HC only improves the baseline slightly by 1%. This result demonstrates the advantage of a larger committee which postpones the decision making until more observations are available and it is more confident to do so. In terms of efficiency, ER-HC sacrifices more computational cost than those of HC and SIB-HC, but the saved cost by 67.1% from the one-vs-all approach is still considered significant, an indication that ER-HC achieves a better balance between com-

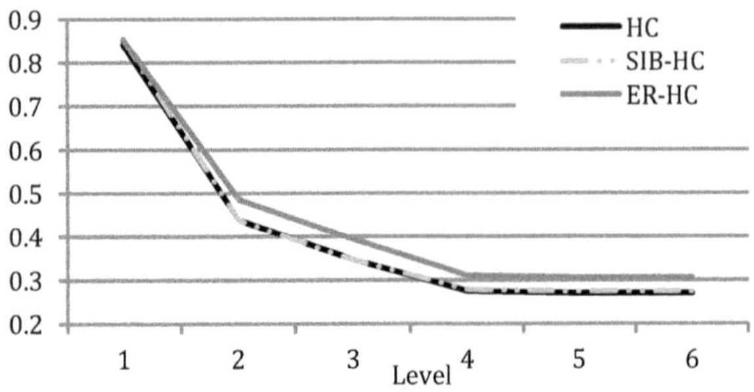

Figure 2: Accuracy on Caltech256 by level

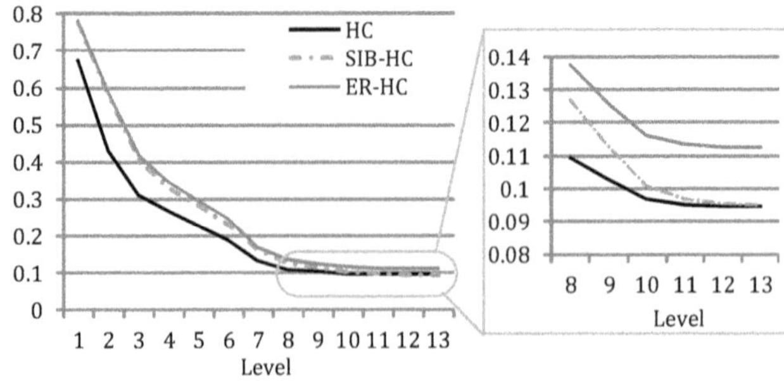

Figure 3: Left: accuracy on ILSRVC1K by level. Right: zoom-in from level 8 to level 13.

putational cost and accuracy. Similarly, for ILSRVC1K, ER-HC outperforms HC and SIB-HC by 19% and 16.6% in accuracy respectively, while remaining satisfactory in efficiency by saving 88.9% computational cost from the baseline. We can see that the advantage of ER-HC on ILSRVC1K is more obvious than that on Caltech256. This is due to the fact that the hierarchy of ILSRVC1K is in a larger scale which includes 1,327 more concepts than Caltech256. Therefore, the SVM models for nodes at higher levels of the ILSRVC1K hierarchy are with much more complex or vague decision boundaries than those in Caltech256, because more offspring concepts are attached to each high level node which bring the instances with more variances of visual appearances, and finally make the resulting classifier less reliable. In this case, the semantic relationship verification and error recovery embedded in MLR model of ER-HC are more necessary, because the error propagation is more serious.

To grasp more insights of the methods, we plot the accuracy of each method at each hierarchy level on the two datasets in Figure 2 and Figure 3 respectively. The error propagation becomes more serious with the increase level of depth, resulting in drop of accuracy. ER-HC has demonstrated consistent superiority over HC and SIB-HC, confirming its ability to address the issue of error propagation. Surprisingly, the performance of SIB-HC seems is better on ILSRVC1K than on Caltech256. This again confirms our analysis that the advantage of employing a committee for decision making over the arbitrary highest-response-first strategy will be more obvious when the classifiers of individual nodes are weaker.

3.3 Cross-dataset Evaluation

We also study the feasibility of applying the proposed approach on classifiers learnt from non-expert labeled examples. These classifiers are usually "weaker" classifiers and suffer from the problem of domain shift [9]. For this purpose, we adopt the approach in [8] to automatically crawl at most 1,000 positive training instances from Web for each leaf category. As a result, there are around 950,000 images being downloaded to train 1,645 classifiers. The results are shown in Table 3. The advantage of the proposed approach is more evidenced on classifiers that are learnt from these noisy training samples. Compared to that in Table 2, the accuracy of all methods degrades a lot. This is not surprising because free-sampled Web images are noisy and the domain-shift from training dataset to testing is more significant, which make most of the classifiers unreliable. However, ER-HC exhibits the best performance in accuracy with 27% improvement over baseline. The proposed approach thus has potential to be scalable to classifiers that are trained using non-expert labels, which is an important feature for large-scale multimedia applications as annotating training examples is a highly expensive process especially when thousands of classifiers are in demand.

4. CONCLUSION

We have presented the error recovered hierarchical classification approach, which utilizes the semantic relationship among concept nodes in a hierarchy for addressing the error propagation problem. The method has demonstrated significant and consistent performance improvements over conventional methods on Caltech256, ILSRVC1K, and free-sampled Web image dataset, while maintaining a satisfactory balance between efficiency and accuracy. Currently, we only consider the single label hierarchy where leaf nodes are contextually exclusive. Future work includes the extension of current work for multi-label hierarchical classification. We will also address the issue on reducing the error propagation, for example, by traversing the tree starting from reliable internal nodes, rather than from the root node.

5. ACKNOWLEDGMENTS

This work was supported in part by the National Natural Science Foundation of China under Grant 61272290, Grant 61228205 and Grant 61001148.

6. REFERENCES

[1] P. N. Bennett and N. Nguyen. Refined experts: Improving classification in large taxonomies. In *SIGIR*, 2009.

[2] G. Griffin et al. The caltech-256. *Caltech Technical Report*, 2007.

[3] G.-R. Xue et al. Deep classification in large-scale text hierarchies. In *SIGIR*, 2008.

[4] J. Deng et al. Imagenet: A large-scale hierarchical image database. In *CVPR*, 2009.

[5] J. Deng et al. Fast and balanced: Efficient label tree learning for large scale object recognition. In *NIPS*, 2011.

[6] J. Wang et al. Locality-constrained linear coding for image classification. In *CVPR*, 2010.

[7] R. E. Fan et al. Liblinear: A library for large linear classification. *Journal of Machine Learning Research*, 9:1871–1874, 2008.

[8] S. A. Zhu et al. Sampling and ontologically pooling web images for visual concept learning. *IEEE Trans. on MM*, 14(4):1068–1078, 2012.

[9] T. Yao et al. Predicting domain adaptivity: Redo or recycle? In *ACM MM*, 2012.

[10] Z. Barutcuoglu et al. Hierarchical multi-label prediction of gene function. *Bioinformatics*, 22(7):830–836, 2006.

Time Matters! Capturing Variation in Time in Video using Fisher Kernels

Ionuţ Mironică
LAPI, University Politehnica of Bucharest, Romania
imironica@imag.pub.ro

Jasper Uijlings
DISI, University of Trento, Italy
jrr@disi.unitn.it

Negar Rostamzadeh
DISI, University of Trento, Italy
rostamzadeh@disi.unitn.it

Bogdan Ionescu
LAPI, University Politehnica of Bucharest, Romania
bionescu@imag.pub.ro

Nicu Sebe
DISI, University of Trento, Italy
sebe@disi.unitn.it

ABSTRACT

In video global features are often used for reasons of computational efficiency, where each global feature captures information of a single video frame. But frames in video change over time, so an important question is: how can we meaningfully aggregate frame-based features in order to preserve the variation in time? In this paper we propose to use the Fisher Kernel to capture variation in time in video. While in this approach the temporal order is lost, it captures both subtle variation in time such as the ones caused by a moving bicycle and drastic variations in time such as the changing of shots in a documentary.

Our work should not be confused with a Bag of Local Visual Features approach, where one captures the visual variation of local features in both time and space indiscriminately. Instead, each feature measures a complete frame hence we capture variation in time only.

We show that our framework is highly general, reporting improvements using frame-based visual features, body-part features, and audio features on three diverse datasets: We obtain state-of-the-art results on the UCF50 human action dataset and improve the state-of-the-art on the MediaEval 2012 video-genre benchmark and on the ADL daily activity recognition dataset.

Categories and Subject Descriptors

I.4.8 [**Scene Analysis**]: Time-varying imagery

Keywords

Video Classification; Fisher kernels; Variation in Time

1. INTRODUCTION

In video retrieval, an important research problem is how to adequately capture temporal information. Until recently, most video retrieval systems relied mostly on single representative video frames where time is ignored for efficiency reasons [24]. Recent work simply accumulates features over a whole video sequence [4, 8, 22]. Such accumulation may capture more information, but also mixes information, disregarding appearance variation over time. For example, when a car approaches and then turns a corner, there are first straight movements followed by turning movements. It is important that both types of movement do not happen at the same time. We want to have a representation which keeps this distinction.

In this paper we propose a novel video representation method which aggregates frame-based features while retaining their variation in time. Specifically, we propose to use the Fisher representation [15] which was recently introduced for improving a Bag of Local Visual Features approach [2]. Bag of Local Visual Features captures the visual variation in space for images and in both space and time for video. The Fisher Kernel improves over the common k-means vocabulary by modelling the distribution of features within each visual word. In contrast to Local Visual Features, in this paper we apply the Fisher representation on frame-based features, effectively capturing variation *in time only* (as there is no variation in space). Like Bag of Local Visual Features, all ordering is lost but all variation is captured. Using the Fisher representation for modelling variation in time, (1) dissimilar frames will be represented by different mixture components (i.e. clusters), preventing blending of unrelated features while enabling them to co-exist in a single representation. This enables representing videos which consist of dissimilar parts (which may not even have a fixed temporal order) such as news broadcasts that switch between the news-anchor and on-site footage. Furthermore, (2) similar frames that fall in the same mixture component will be modelled with respect to the general distribution of that component, capturing subtle variations in time such as the different appearances of a person walking by.

We test our Fisher-based framework for modelling variation in time on a variety of video benchmarks: genre retrieval on the MediaEval benchmark [21], Human Action Recognition on the UCL50 dataset [17], and daily activity recognition on ADL [14]. Additionally, we employ a variety of frame-based features: global Histogram of Oriented Gradients (HoG) [3], global Histogram of Optical Flow (HoF) [17], global Colour Naming histogram (CN) [28], HoF-

MM'13, October 21–25, 2013, Barcelona, Spain.

ACM 978-1-4503-2404-5/13/10 ...$15.00.
http://dx.doi.org/10.1145/2502081.2502183.

based body-part histogram [18], and even on block-based audio features [13]. We show that the Fisher representation consistently and significantly outperforms simple accumulation. Additionally, by explicitly modelling the variation in time we obtain state-of-the-art results or better on all three datasets using a smaller array of simpler features.

To summarise, our main contributions are the following: (1) We introduce a Fisher-based representation for frame-based features in video that captures variation in time. (2) We demonstrate its generality in terms of applications by applying it to genre-recognition, sports-recognition, and daily activity recognition. (3) We demonstrate its generality in terms of features by using audio features, global visual features, and body-part features. (4) We achieve similar or better performance than the state-of-the-art using a smaller array of simpler features.

2. RELATED WORK

Recently, researchers have successfully captured local temporal information in video by using spatio-temporal features, visual features that are measured in the 3D volume spanned by the video frames. These features are extracted either at interest points which are stable in both space and time [4, 5, 8, 10, 27], or at stable trajectories [29]. The specific movement pattern captured by these features yields significant improvements over 2D features. However, these features are accumulated over an entire video sequence ignoring the visual variation at different parts of the video.

Some works include some form of variation in time by using a linear quantization of the video: the video is split into n sequences of an equal number of frames, where for each sequence all features are accumulated [1, 10, 19, 29]. Histograms of the individual sequences are concatenated, leading to good accuracy improvements. In [26] the authors use a linear quantization method for global features, where the features are averaged inside a sequence.

Few works focus directly on modelling the temporal order/variation between frames [24]. There is some work on using Hidden Markov Models [9, 16]. Other work uses temporal rules with high-level concepts [12, 25].

3. MODELLING VARIATION IN TIME

The Fisher Kernel [7] represents a signal as the gradient with respect to the probability density function that is a learned generative model of that signal. Recently, [15] introduced the Fisher Kernel as an improved visual vocabulary for Bag-of-Words. Its success shows that it meaningfully captures the visual variation of local descriptors.

In this paper we employ the Fisher Kernel to capture variation in time in video. We follow [15] and use a Gaussian Mixture Model with diagonal covariance matrices as generative distribution. Specifically, let μ_i and σ_i be the mean and standard deviation of the i-th Gaussian centroid, let $\gamma(i)$ be the soft assignment to the i-th Gaussian of the d-dimensional feature x_t captured at frame t. The gradient of the GMM with respect to μ_i and σ_i are calculated as [15]:

$$\mathcal{G}^x_{\mu,i} = \frac{1}{T\sqrt{\omega_i}} \sum_{t=1}^{T} \gamma(i) \frac{x_t - \mu_i}{\sigma_i} \tag{1}$$

$$\mathcal{G}^x_{\sigma,i} = \frac{1}{T\sqrt{2\omega_i}} \sum_{t=1}^{T} \gamma(i) \left[\frac{(x_t - \mu_i)^2}{{\sigma_i}^2} - 1 \right]. \tag{2}$$

The final Fisher vector is the concatenation of the $\mathcal{G}^x_{\mu,i}$ and $\mathcal{G}^x_{\sigma,i}$ for $i = 1...k$ and has a dimensionality of $2kd$.

Interpreting the formulas in terms of variation in time, Equation 1 averages *related* features over time, which are related as they fall in the same mixture component. Equation 2 models the variation of related features over the video sequence, capturing subtle visual changes (e.g. a car driving by). The different mixture components capture drastic variations in time such as a shot changes.

Important parameters or design choices are: (1) Applying PCA on initial features x_t, reducing dimensions of the final Fisher vector and potentially improving GMM clustering by decorrelation. (2) The number of GMM clusters. (3) Normalization of the Fisher vector. (4) Choice of classifier.

4. EXPERIMENTS

We demonstrate the advantages and generality of our framework on three different datasets using a variety of features. For brevity reasons we will mainly focus on the number of GMM clusters and only touch upon applying PCA. We normalise the Fisher vector by taking the square root followed by the $L2$-norm [15]. In contrast to [15], we use SVMs with RBF-kernels as these performed better than linear SVMs, even at an increased number of clusters for the latter. When combining different types of features we use weighted late fusion, learning weights on our optimization sets.

4.1 Genre Retrieval

We perform genre retrieval on the 2012 MediaEval Genre Tagging Task [21], consisting of 2000 hours in 14,838 videos, labelled according to 26 genres such as art, autos, and comedy. Performance is measured in terms of Mean Average Precision (MAP). We perform all parameter optimization on the training set which we split in two fixed, equally sized parts. We compare with the state-of-the-art using the official training set (5,288 videos) and test set (9,550 videos).

Baseline. We use the following features: (1) *Global Histogram of Oriented Gradients [3] (81 dimensions)* which calculates HoG over the whole frame using a 3x3 spatial division. (2) *Colour Naming histogram [28] (11 dimensions)* of the whole frame. (3) *Audio features [13] (98 dimensions)* which are general purpose audio descriptors extracted over a standard period of 1.28 seconds around the frame using [13]. Results of averaging features over the whole video are presented as the horizontal lines in Figure 1.

Optimizing the Fisher Representation. We ran experiments with PCA dimensionality reduction on the frame-based features, setting the number of cluster centres to 100. We found that for Colour Naming, applying PCA reduces performance. This is because the dimensions are decorrelated and non-redundant by design [28]. For HoG and Audio features the optimal reduction is to keep 80% of the dimensionality, where for HoG accuracy increased a full 5%. We choose these PCA settings for subsequent experiments.

Next, we determine the optimal number of clusters for each feature as shown in Figure 1. First of all, notice the big improvements of the Fisher representation over the baseline which simply averages the features: Even when using only a single (!) centroid, Colour Naming goes up from 0.18 MAP to 0.28 MAP, HoG goes up from 0.22 MAP to 0.38 MAP, and Audio goes up from 0.34 MAP to 0.45 MAP. The modelling of variation in time therefore significantly improves results. Increasing the number of clusters increases performance even

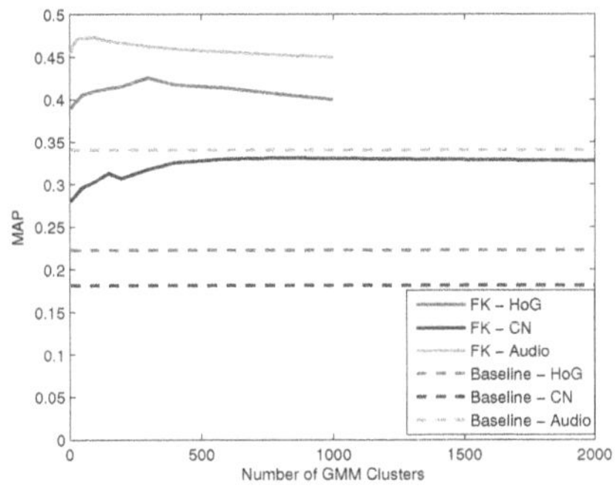

igure 1: Mean Average Precision (MAP) hile varying the number of cluster centres n the MediaEval 2012 training set.

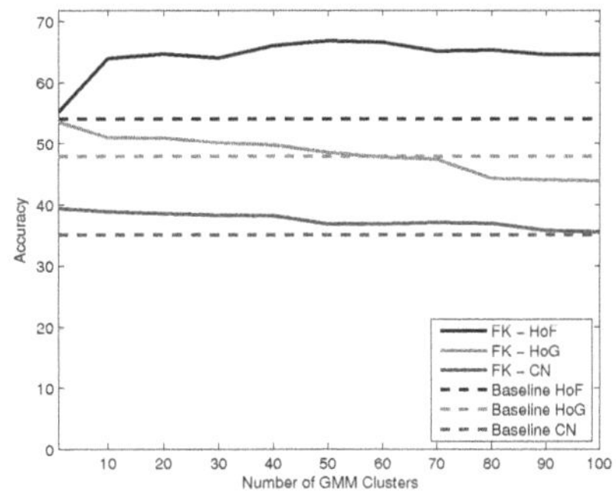

Figure 2: Classification accuracy on half of UCF50 sports while varying the number of cluster centres (8-fold cross-validation).

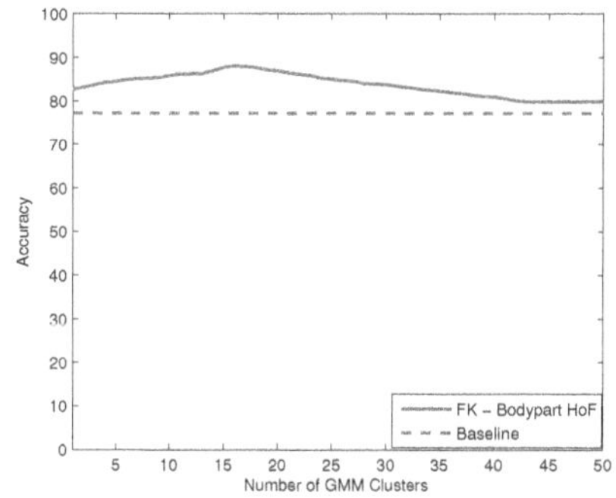

Figure 3: Classification accuracy on ADL daily activity recognition on half the dataset while varying the number of cluster centres.

further: Both Colour Naming and HoG increase an extra 0.05 MAP, reaching 0.33 MAP and 0.43 MAP at 800 clusters and 200 clusters respectively. Audio features increase to 0.47 MAP at 50 clusters. We will use this number of clusters in the next experiment. The final sizes of the Fisher vectors are reasonable at 17,600 for Colour Naming, 42,000 for HoG, and 9,000 for Audio features. Note that performance of both HoG and Audio features go down after the optimal points, likely due to the high dimensionality of the features (i.e. curse of dimensionality).

Comparison to State-of-the-Art. Results on MediaEval 2012 are shown in Table 1. For audio features our results are at 0.47 MAP much better than the best result of 0.19 reported at the MediaEval workshop [6]. For visual features only, at 0.46 MAP we perform significantly better than the best result of 0.35 MAP [23]. Remarkably, our combination of audio and visual features yields with 0.55 MAP a better performance than the use of text from automatic speech recognition and meta-data, which had the highest performance at MediaEval 2012 at 0.53 MAP.

To conclude, using the Fisher kernel to model variation in time significantly improves over a simple averaging of features, yielding much better results than the state-of-the-art on the MediaEval 2012 benchmark.

4.2 Human Action Recognition

We now evaluate our framework on the UCF50 Human Action Recognition dataset [17], which contains 6600 realistic videos from Youtube with large variations in camera motion, object appearance and pose, illumination conditions, scale, etc. It has 50 mutual exclusive categories such as biking, diving, drumming and fencing. Performance is evaluated in terms of classification accuracy. We perform all optimization on half of the dataset, using 8-fold cross-validation. We compare with the state-of-the-art using the standard leave-one-group-out cross-validation on the full dataset [17].

Baseline. We use the following features: (1) *Global Histogram of Oriented Gradients [3] (9, 36, 81, and 144 dimensions)* which calculates HoG over the whole frame using a 1x1, 2x2, 3x3, and 4x4 spatial division. (2) *Global Histogram of Optical Flow [17] (9, 36, 81, and 144 dimensions)* which measures the average velocity of non-stationary pixels over a region in 9 orientations. We use a 1x1, 2x2, 3x3, and 4x4 spatial division. (3) *Colour Naming Histogram [28] (11, 44, 99, and 176 dimensions)* using a 1x1, 2x2, 3x3, and 4x4 spatial division. In all experiments, we combine different spatial divisions for a single feature type using late fusion with equal weights. Results of averaging each feature over the whole video are shown as horizontal lines in Figure 2.

Optimizing the Fisher Representation. We first optimized the dimension reduction using PCA. We found that both the Colour Naming histogram and the Histogram of Optical Flow did not benefit. For HoG we found a good improvement by reducing dimensions to 90% (data not shown).

Next, in Figure 2 we evaluate the performance with respect to the number of GMM clusters, where we use the same number of clusters for all spatial divisions of a single feature type. For Colour Naming and HoG the use of a single cluster improves the baseline with 6% and 5% respectively. More clusters degrade performance as for this dataset the visual changes are subtle and do not require different mixture components. For HoF, using 50 clusters improves the baseline of 54% to 67%, a 13% improvement. Hence the optical flow changes drastically in time which is best captured in multiple clusters. Indeed, for example a baseball pitch has at least three distinct movement patterns: static (before the action), the pitch, and the batting. In the next experiment we use 1 cluster for CN and HoG, and 50 clusters for HoF.

Comparison to State-of-the-Art. We present the state-of-the-art in Table 2. As can be seen, we rank second with 74.7% accuracy after the 76.9% accuracy of Reddy et al. [17]. However, we use only global features whereas all other good performing methods use computationally more expensive Space-Time Interest Points (STIPs). Only the GIST3D entry of [8] does not use STIPs. They use global, frame-based features plus linear quantization. Our performance using the Fisher vector is a significant 9.4% higher.

We conclude that our framework yields similar performance as the state-of-the-art while using simpler features.

4.3 Daily Activities

We report results on daily activity recognition using the ADL dataset [14], consisting of ten human activities such as dialling a phone, peeling banana, and chopping banana. Each activity is performed three times by five people, totalling 150 videos. Performance is measured in accuracy. We do all optimization on half of the dataset and report final results on the full dataset. In both cases we use leave-one-person-out cross-validation [14].

Baseline. As human pose and body-part motion are important for distinguishing the different categories, we extract body-part features [18]. We use the state-of-the-art body-part detector of [31] and extract at every frame for all 18 body-parts a Histogram of Optical Flow in 8 orientations

Table 1: Comparison with State-of-the-Art (SoA) in terms of Mean Average Precision (MAP) on MediaEval 2012.

Feature type	Summary SoA method MediaEval 2012	MAP SoA	MAP ours
Audio	Block Based Audio Features and 5-NN [6]	0.192	0.475
Visual	Visual descriptors (Color, Texture, rgbSIFT) [23]	0.350	0.460
Audio & Visual	-	-	0.550
Metadata & Text ASR	BoW Text ASR & metadata [20]	0.523	-

Table 2: Comparison with State-of-the-art on UCF50 Human Action Recognition.

Method	Accuracy
Reddy et al. [17]	76.9%
This paper	**74.7%**
Solmaz et al. [26]	73.7%
Everts et al. [5]	72.9%
Kliper-Gross et al. [8]	72.6%
Solmaz et al. [26]: GIST3D	65.3%

Table 3: Comparison with state-of-the-art on the ADL Daily Activity Recognition dataset.

Method	Accuracy
This paper	**97.3%**
Wang et al. [30]	96.0%
Lin et al. [11]	95.0%
Messing et al. [14]	89.0%

(144 dimensions). The result of averaging this feature over the video is shown as the horizontal line in Figure 3.

Optimizing the Fisher Representation. We found no improvements by doing PCA on the bodypart HoF features.

Figure 3 shows accuracy with respect to the number of GMM clusters. Using only a single cluster yields a performance improvement from 77% to 82% accuracy. The best accuracy of 88% is obtained using 17 clusters. Note that the number of clusters is relatively low, likely due to the smaller dataset. At 17 clusters, the final feature has 4,896 dimensions. We use 17 clusters when testing on the full dataset.

Comparison to State-of-the-Art. We compare our work with others in Table 3. As can be seen, our approach yields the highest accuracy of 97.3%. This shows that the Fisher representation is also effective for modelling variation in time using local body-part features.

5. CONCLUSIONS

We propose to use the Fisher kernel to model variation in time for frame-based video features. While the temporal order is lost, the temporal variation is captured at two levels: similar features are grouped together while retaining variation, which enables capturing subtle variations over time such as a exhibited by a moving car. Dissimilar features are kept separate, preventing mixing features from unrelated parts of the video while keeping them in a single representation, which enables capturing different shots in a video.

We demonstrated that our framework is highly general: We showed significant improvements on a wide variety of features, ranging from global visual features, to body-part features, and to audio features. We also demonstrated that our method works on a wide variety of datasets: We obtained state-of-the-art performance on UCF50 using global features instead of the more complex STIPs used in other methods. We improved the state-of-the-art on ADL daily activity recognition. We significantly improved the state-of-the-art on the MediaEval 2012 genre classification task.

In future work we plan to model variation in time using Fisher kernels on more advanced features such as STIPs.

6. REFERENCES

[1] M. Bregonzio, S. Gong, and T. Xiang. Recognising action as clouds of space-time interest points. In *CVPR*, 2009.

[2] G. Csurka, C. R. Dance, L. Fan, J. Willamowski, and C. Bray. Visual Categorization with Bags of Keypoints. In *ECCV Workshop on Statistical Learning in CV*, 2004.

[3] N. Dalal and B. Triggs. Histograms of oriented gradients for human detection. In *CVPR*, 2005.

[4] P. Dollár, V. Rabaud, G. Cottrell, and S. Belongie. Behavior recognition via sparse spatio-temporal features. In *VS-PETS*, 2005.

[5] I. Everts, J. van Gemert, and T. Gevers. Evaluation of color stips for human action recognition. In *CVPR*, 2013.

[6] B. Ionescu, I. Mironica, K. Seyerlehner, P. Knees, J. Schluter, M. Schedl, H. Cucu, A. Buzo, and P. Lambert. ARF @ mediaeval 2012: Multimodal video classification. In *MediaEval workshop*, 2012.

[7] T. Jaakkola and D. Haussler. Exploiting generative models in discriminative classifiers. In *NIPS*, 1999.

[8] O. Kliper-Gross, Y. Gurovich, T. Hassner, and L. Wolf. Motion interchange patterns for action recognition in unconstrained videos. In *ECCV*, 2012.

[9] H. Kuehne, D. Gehrig, T. Schultz, and R. Stiefelhagen. On-line action recognition from sparse feature flow. In *VISAPP*, 2012.

[10] I. Laptev, M. Marszalek, C. Schmid, and B. Rozenfeld. Learning realistic human actions from movies. In *CVPR*, 2008.

[11] Z. Lin, Z. Jiang, and L. Davis. Recognizing actions by shape-motion prototype trees. In *ICCV*, 2009.

[12] K. Liu, M. Weng, C. Tseng, Y. Chuang, and M. Chen. Association and temporal rule mining for post-filtering of semantic concept detection in video. *IEEE TMM*, 2008.

[13] B. Mathieu, S. Essid, T. Fillon, J. Prado, and G. Richard. YAAFE, an easy to use and efficient audio feature extraction software. In *ISMIR*, 2010.

[14] R. Messing, C. Pal, and H. Kautz. Activity recognition using the velocity histories of tracked keypoints. In *ICCV*, 2009.

[15] F. Perronnin, J. Sanchez, and T. Mensink. Improving the Fisher Kernel for Large-Scale Image Classification. In *ECCV*, 2010.

[16] G.-J. Qi, X.-S. Hua, Y. Rui, J. Tang, T. Mei, M. Wang, and H.-J. Zhang. Correlative multilabel video annotation with temporal kernels. *ACM TOMCCAP*, 2008.

[17] K. Reddy and M. Shah. Recognizing 50 human action categories of web videos. In *MVAP*, 2012.

[18] M. Rohrbach, S. Amin, M. Andriluka, and B. Schiele. A database for fine grained activity detection of cooking activities. In *CVPR*, 2012.

[19] S. Sadanand and J. Corso. Action bank: A high-level representation of activity in video. In *CVPR*, 2012.

[20] S. Schmiedeke, P. Kelm, and T. Sikora. TUB @ MediaEval 2012 tagging task: Feature selection methods for bag-of-(visual)-words approaches. In *MediaEval Workshop*, 2012.

[21] S. Schmiedeke, C. Kofler, and I. Ferrané. Overview of MediaEval 2012 genre tagging task. In *MediaEval workshop*, 2012.

[22] C. Schuldt, I. Laptev, and B. Caputo. Recognizing human actions: A local svm approach. In *ICIP*, 2004.

[23] T. Semela, M. Tapaswi, H. Ekenel, and R. Stiefelhagen. Kit at mediaeval 2012 - content-based genre classification with visual cues. In *MediaEval workshop*, 2012.

[24] C. Snoek and M. Worring. Concept-based video retrieval. *Foundations and Trends in Information Retrieval*, 2009.

[25] C. G. Snoek and M. Worring. Multimedia event-based video indexing using time intervals. *IEEE TMM*, 2005.

[26] B. Solmaz, S. M. Assari, and S. Mubarak. Classifying web videos using a global video descriptor. *MVAP*, 2012.

[27] J. Stöttinger, A. Hanbury, N. Sebe, and T. Gevers. Sparse color interest points for image retrieval and object categorization. *TIP*, 2012.

[28] J. Van De Weijer, C. Schmid, J. Verbeek, and D. Larlus. Learning color names for real-world applications. *TIP*, 2009.

[29] H. Wang, A. Kläser, C. Schmid, and C.-L. Liu. Action recognition by dense trajectories. In *CVPR*, 2011.

[30] J. Wang, Z. Chen, and Y. Wu. Action recognition with multiscale spatio-temporal contexts. In *CVPR*, 2011.

[31] Y. Yang and D. Ramanan. Articulated pose estimation with flexible mixtures-of-parts. In *CVPR*, 2011.

A Multimodal Probabilistic Model for Gesture–based Control of Sound Synthesis

Jules Françoise
STMS Lab
IRCAM–CNRS–UPMC
1, Place Igor Stravinsky 75004
Paris, France
jules.francoise@ircam.fr

Norbert Schnell
STMS Lab
IRCAM–CNRS–UPMC
1, Place Igor Stravinsky 75004
Paris, France
norbert.schnell@ircam.fr

Frédéric Bevilacqua
STMS Lab
IRCAM–CNRS–UPMC
1, Place Igor Stravinsky 75004
Paris, France
frederic.bevilacqua@ircam.fr

ABSTRACT

In this paper, we propose a multimodal approach to create the *mapping* between gesture and sound in interactive music systems. Specifically, we propose to use a multimodal HMM to conjointly model the gesture and sound parameters. Our approach is compatible with a learning method that allows users to define the gesture–sound relationships interactively. We describe an implementation of this method for the control of physical modeling sound synthesis. Our model is promising to capture expressive gesture variations while guaranteeing a consistent relationship between gesture and sound.

Categories and Subject Descriptors

H.5.5 [**Information Interfaces And Presentation**]: Sound and Music Computing; J.5 [**Arts and Humanities**]: Music

Keywords

music, gesture, sound synthesis, music performance, HMM, multimodal

1. INTRODUCTION

Gestural interaction with audio and/or visual media has become ubiquitous. The development of gestural systems for sound control concerns not only musical applications, but also novel gaming applications [10], sonic interaction design to facilitate objects manipulation [11] or rehabilitation where interactive sound feedback could inform users on their movement performance.

In this paper, we focus on gesture–based control of sound synthesis targeting applications to music performance and movement sonification for rehabilitation. Specifically, we address current issues in designing the *relationship* (often called *mapping*) between gesture features and sound control parameters in such interactive systems (cf. figure 1).

MM'13, October 21–25, 2013, Barcelona, Spain.

ACM 978-1-4503-2404-5/13/10 ...$15.00.
http://dx.doi.org/10.1145/2502081.2502184.

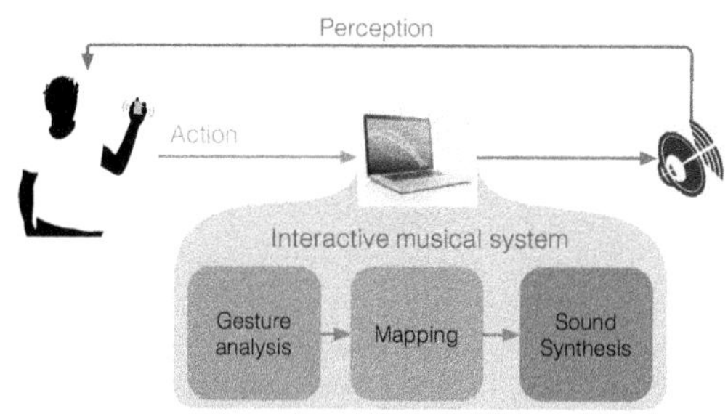

Figure 1: Overview of an interactive musical system. The *mapping* defines the coupling between actions and sound processing.

Our research follows recent approaches based on machine learning which aim at defining the mapping between gesture and sound from examples rather than by an analytical formulation. In this paper, we support a multimodal perspective on mapping by introducing a probabilistic model of the gesture–sound relationships. The system is based on a single multimodal Hidden Markov Model (HMM) representing both gesture and sound parameter morphologies. The model is trained by one or multiple gesture performances associated to sound templates. It captures the temporal structure of gesture and sound as well as the variations which occur between multiple performances.

Section 2 gives a short overview of existing research and issues related to gesture–sound mapping in musical instruments. Related works in other fields of multimedia are described in section 3. The multimodal HMM is described in section 4, with specific implementation details. Finally, section 5 presents an application of the model to gesture–based control of physical modeling sound synthesis.

2. GESTURE-SOUND RELATIONSHIPS IN DIGITAL MUSICAL INSTRUMENTS

Creating relationships between gesture and sound parameters has been recognized one of the crucial aspects of the design of digital musical instruments. Specific choices in this design influence the interaction possibilities, varying in terms of ease–of–use, expressivity, and learning possibilities. Most approaches require an analytical definition of the relationships between gesture and sound, for example using *explicit* parameter wiring or *implicit* models, e.g. dynamic systems.

Recent works support interaction–driven approaches that take advantage of machine learning to define the mapping by *demonstration*; i.e. from training examples provided interactively by the user. Notably, number of strategies exploit gesture recognition methods to link the identification of user-specific gestures to sound control [7, 5]. Fiebrink [4] recently proposed a *play-along* paradigm enabling users to edit the training examples by performing gestures while listening to sound examples.

We propose a similar approach, based on machine learning, allowing users to define the mapping by direct demonstration of their intended control strategy: the mapping is learned from examples of the relationships between gesture and sound. This implies several requirements. First, for the method to remain practical, the model should be trained with a limited number of examples. Second, gesture and sound parameters, as well as their relationship, evolve over time. A computational model must take into account these temporal variations. Finally, the model should be able to characterize the expressive variations between multiple performances of the same gesture.

Previous works already partially addressed these issues. Systems based on regression methods such as neural networks [4, 5], for example, generalize from multiple interpretations but are often limited to static relationships. Gesture recognition methods often model the temporal dynamics of gestures but are usually limited to classification, restricting mapping strategies to discrete interactions such as triggering [7, 5]. The *temporal mapping* method we recently proposed can learn the temporal relationship between a gesture and a sound using continuous gesture recognition and alignment [1]. Nevertheless, the method is limited to modeling the gesture only. Moreover, the model does not allow for characterizing expressive inter–performance variations. Our goal is to address such limitations by adopting a multimodal perspective on gesture–sound mapping through the introduction of a fully probabilistic multimodal model.

3. RELATED WORKS IN OTHER FIELDS OF MULTIMEDIA

Many recent systems for virtual character animation use speech–driven approaches, involving mapping from acoustic features to lip, face or body motion [2, 13, 3]. Similar issues are found in speaker conversion [14] or acoustic–articulatory inversion [8, 14], aiming at the retrieval of speech–producing movements from acoustic signals. Most of the current approaches are based on sequence models representing the output process in conjunction with the input modality. In particular, various extensions of HMMs were proved efficient for feature mapping, such as HMM remapping [2], the input-output HMM [6] and the multimodal HMM (sometimes called audio-visual HMM or HMM inversion) [8, 13, 3].

In spite of their similarity, our applications in gestural sound control contrast in critical points the applications we just mentioned. While the movements and sounds related to speech are generated by the same action and thus intrinsically related, the gesture–sound relationship can be arbitrarily defined by the user. Hereby, the choice might depend on the application, which limits the practicality of creating extensive databases. In many cases, the training examples should be provided by the user within a single workflow integrating training and performance. These aspects require adapting models and algorithms to an interactive learning paradigm, as argued by Fiebrink [5].

4. GESTURE–SOUND MAPPING WITH MULTIMODAL HMM

This section details the multimodal HMM and the specificities of our implementation, designed to fit the context of real-time music performance. In the remainder of this article, *gesture features* or *gesture observations* refer to the parameters extracted from a gesture capture system. Similarly, *sound features* or *sound observations* refer to the vector of control parameters of a sound synthesis model.

4.1 Multimodal HMM

The multimodal HMM is an extension of traditional HMM for handling multimodal data, allowing for the prediction of missing features. We assume that gesture and sound are generated by the same underlying Markov process by representing jointly their observation sequences. The Dynamic Bayesian Network representation of the model is presented in figure 2, where $\mathbf{q}_t$ is the hidden states at time t, $\mathbf{o}_t^g$ (resp. $\mathbf{o}_t^s$) is the gesture (resp. sound) observation vector.

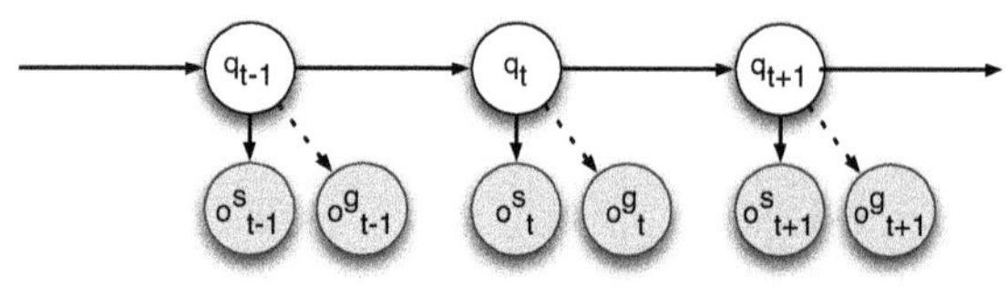

Figure 2: Graphical model of the Multimodal HMM.

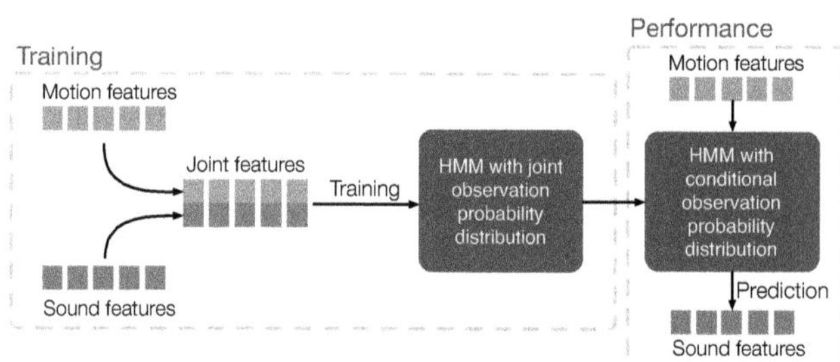

Figure 3: Gesture–sound mapping with the multimodal HMM.

For training, gesture and sound feature vectors are concatenated to form a multimodal sequence (cf. figure 3, left). The observation probability distribution at time t of a state j of the HMM with model parameters λ is defined as a joint multimodal Gaussian distribution:

$$P(\mathbf{o}_t^g, \mathbf{o}_t^s | q_t = j, \lambda) = \mathcal{N}\left([\mathbf{o}_t^g, \mathbf{o}_t^s]\,; \mu_j, \mathbf{\Sigma}_j\right)$$

where the mean of the distribution μ_j is the concatenation of the mean vectors for each modality, and $\mathbf{\Sigma}_j$ is a covariance matrix which can be decomposed in four sub-matrices representing unimodal and cross-modal covariances between gesture and sound parameters:

$$\mu_j = \left[\mu_j^g, \mu_j^s\right]$$
$$\mathbf{\Sigma}_j = \begin{bmatrix} \mathbf{\Sigma}_j^{gg} & \mathbf{\Sigma}_j^{gs} \\ \mathbf{\Sigma}_j^{sg} & \mathbf{\Sigma}_j^{ss} \end{bmatrix}$$

The HMM is trained using an Expectation-Maximization algorithm on the multimodal observations sequences [9].

For prediction, the joint observation distributions are converted to conditional distributions by marginalizing over the gesture observations at time t:

$$p(\mathbf{o}_t^s|\mathbf{o}_t^g, q_t = j, \lambda) = \mathcal{N}\left(\mathbf{o}_t^s; \hat{\mu}_j^s(\mathbf{o}_t^g), \hat{\boldsymbol{\Sigma}}_j^{ss}\right)$$

where the mean $\hat{\mu}_j^s(\mathbf{o}_t^g)$ and covariance $\hat{\boldsymbol{\Sigma}}_j^{ss}$ of the sound are re-estimated by combining the learned mean of the sound with a linear regression over the gesture features:

$$\hat{\mu}_j^s(\mathbf{o}_t^g) = \mu_j^s + \boldsymbol{\Sigma}_j^{sg}\left(\boldsymbol{\Sigma}_j^{gg}\right)^{-1}\left(\mathbf{o}_t^g - \mu_j^g\right)$$
$$\hat{\boldsymbol{\Sigma}}_j^{ss} = \boldsymbol{\Sigma}_j^{ss} - \boldsymbol{\Sigma}_j^{sg}\left(\boldsymbol{\Sigma}_j^{gg}\right)^{-1}\boldsymbol{\Sigma}_j^{gs}$$

Given a new gesture, the associated sequence of sound features is estimated by a real-time prediction algorithm presented in section 4.2.2 (figure 3, right).

4.2 Interactive learning and implementation specificities

4.2.1 Interactive learning workflow

An interactive learning situation places the user in constant interaction with the system. The workflow of a typical setup is an interaction loop divided in two steps:

1. *Training*: The user can edit the training set by demonstrating examples of gesture and sound *segments* (i.e. time profiles of parameters). The user can then adjust the parameters and train the model.
2. *Performance*: The user evaluates the results by interacting with the trained model, which synthesizes sonic feedback to his gestures in real-time.

This interaction paradigm enables the user to iteratively evaluate and adjust the model until it converges to his purposes. In this paper, we only consider "direct" evaluation of the results, i.e. user evaluation on subjective criteria during performance, as defined by Fiebrink [5].

4.2.2 Performance: real-time prediction of sound control parameters

Reactivity and low latency are strong requirements of a gesture–based music performance system: sound control parameters must be synthesized in real-time to provide instantaneous feedback to the user's gestures. This constraint prevents the use of either Viterbi estimation of the state sequence or an iterative estimation of the sound sequence based on the EM algorithm [13, 3]. Our implementation features a real-time prediction algorithm based on a causal estimation of state probabilities. At each incoming gesture observation $\mathbf{o}_t^g$, the sound feature vector $\mathbf{o}_t^s$ is estimated by maximum likelihood based on the state probabilities computed by a forward algorithm:

$$\mathbf{o}_t^s = \sum_{i=1}^{N} \alpha_t(i) \cdot \underset{\mathbf{o}_t^s}{\operatorname{argmax}}\left[p(\mathbf{o}_t^s|\mathbf{o}_t^g, q_t = i)\right]$$

where $\alpha_t(i) = P(\mathbf{o}_{1:t}^g, q_t = i|\lambda)$ is the probability of the partial gesture observation sequence $\mathbf{o}_{1:t}^g$ and state i at time t [9]. This causal estimation ensures a good reactivity of the system while guaranteeing the smoothness of the estimated sound feature sequence. Typically, 10ms latency is often considered sufficient to guarantee the consistency of the relationships between gesture and sound [12]. In our experiments with inertial sensors (see section 5), we reach a latency of approximately 5ms.

5. APPLICATION: GESTURE CONTROL OF PHYSICAL MODELING SOUND SYNTHESIS

5.1 Motivation

Physical modeling sound synthesis aims at simulating the acoustic behavior of physical objects. The gestural control of such sound physical models remains difficult since the captured gestural parameters are generally different from the physical input parameters of the sound synthesis algorithm. For example, sensing gestures using accelerometers might pose difficulties for controlling the physical model of a bowed string where force, velocity, and pressure are the expected input.

Our approach of defining gesture-sound relationship by an intermediate probabilistic model seems appropriate to tackle such an issue. We therefore propose a system for gesture–based control of physical models which relies on our interactive learning system. It allows users to craft gestural control strategies by demonstrating gestures associated with particular sounds designed with virtual physical instruments. Our goal is to provide a solution for quick prototyping and evaluation these control strategies using the multimodal HMM.

5.2 Application description

5.2.1 Modal synthesis

We use *Modalys*, a software dedicated to modal synthesis, i.e. that simulates the acoustic response of vibrating structures under an external excitation. Virtual instruments are built by combining *modal elements* – e.g. plates, strings, membranes – with various types of connections and excitators – e.g. bows, hammers, etc. Each model is governed by a set of physical parameters – e.g. speed, position and pressure of a bow. Specific sounds and playing modes can be created by designing time profiles combining these parameters.

5.2.2 Application Workflow

The workflow of the application fits in the interactive learning workflow described in section 4.2.1, and can be divided in a *training* phase and a *performance phase*, as illustrated in figure 4.

In the *training* phase, the user can draw time profiles of control parameters of the physical models to design particular sounds. Each of these *segments* can be visualized, modified, and played using a graphical editor. Then, the user can perform one or several demonstrations of the gesture he intents to associate with the sound example (figure 4a). In our experiments, gestures were captured using inertial sensors (3D accelerometers), and various synthesis models were used, such as a modified bowed string or a clarinet. Gesture and sound are recorded to a multimodal data container for storage, visualization and editing. Optionally, segments can be manually altered using the user interface.

During the *performance* phase, the user can gesturally control the sound synthesis. The system allows the explo-

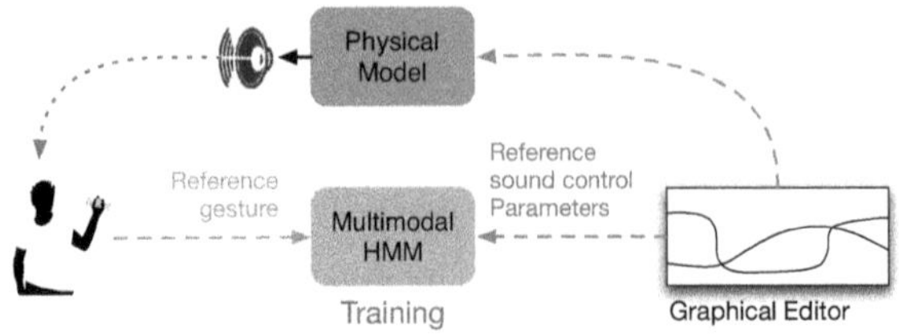

(a) *Training*: sounds are designed using a graphical editor, and reference gestures can be recorded while listening.

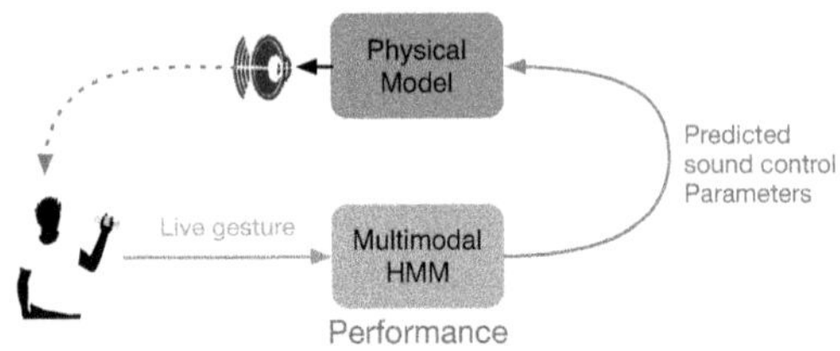

(b) *Performance*: the model is used to predict the sound parameters associated with a live gesture.

Figure 4: Application workflow.

ration of all the parameter variations that are defined by the training examples. Sound parameters are predicted in real-time to provide the user with instantaneous audio feedback (figure 4b). If needed, the user can switch back to *training* and adjust the training set or model parameters.

6. DISCUSSION AND CONCLUSION

A preliminary evaluation of the system, based on both qualitative observations and computational evaluation on synthetic signals, has been performed and shows promising results. In comparison with the template–based model introduced in [1], the multimodal HMM tolerates larger variation occurring between the performance and the training data. Precisely, an evaluation of the algorithm on synthetic data indicates a better ability of the multimodal HMM to capture gesture variations in relationship with sound variations. This is related to the fact that the gesture–sound relationships are encoded globally by the transition structure of the HMM, and locally by the covariance matrices at each state. The model seems therefore able to capture both the temporal dynamics of the mapping and its expressive variations on between several interpretations.

We plan to perform more detailed evaluations of the model. First, the model will be evaluated on a database of sound-related gestures in order to assess its ability to capture expressive variations between gesture performances, and to evaluate the benefits of the temporal modeling in comparison with static regression methods. Second, the model will be evaluated in the context of movement sonification for rehabilitation. The model will be used to generate informative audio feedback to physical gestures in order to enhance motor learning, for example by continuously sonifying the range of variations between the gesture of a patient with motor disabilities and a target movement.

7. ACKNOWLEDGMENTS

We acknowledge support from the French National Research Agency (ANR project Legos 11 BS02 012). We thank Thierry Artières for fruitful discussions.

8. REFERENCES

[1] F. Bevilacqua, N. Schnell, N. Rasamimanana, B. Zamborlin, and F. Guédy. Online Gesture Analysis and Control of Audio Processing. In *Musical Robots and Interactive Multimodal Systems*, pages 127–142. Springer, 2011.

[2] M. Brand. Voice puppetry. In *Proceedings of the 26th annual conference on Computer graphics and interactive techniques*, pages 21–28. 1999.

[3] K. Choi, Y. Luo, and J.-n. Hwang. Hidden Markov model inversion for audio-to-visual conversion in an MPEG-4 facial animation system. *The Journal of VLSI Signal Processing*, 29(1):51–61, 2001.

[4] R. Fiebrink, P. R. Cook, and D. Trueman. Play-along mapping of musical controllers. In *In Proceedings of the International Computer Music Conference*, 2009.

[5] R. Fiebrink, P. R. Cook, and D. Trueman. Human model evaluation in interactive supervised learning. In *Proceedings of the SIGCHI Conference on Human Factors in Computing Systems*, pages 147–156. 2011.

[6] S. Fu, R. Gutierrez-Osuna, A. Esposito, P. Kakumanu, and O. Garcia. Audio/visual mapping with cross-modal hidden Markov models. *Multimedia, IEEE Transactions on*, 7(2):243–252, Apr. 2005.

[7] N. Gillian and R. Knapp. A Machine Learning Toolbox For Musician Computer Interaction. In *proceedings ot the International Conference on New Interfaces for Musical Expression*, Oslo, Norway, 2011.

[8] G. Hofer. *Speech-driven animation using multi-modal hidden Markov models.* Phd dissertation, University of Edimburgh, 2009.

[9] L. R. Rabiner. A Tutorial on Hidden Markov Models and Selected Applications in Speech Recognition. *Proceedings of the IEEE*, 77(2):257–286, 1989.

[10] N. Rasamimanana, F. Bevilacqua, J. Bloit, N. Schnell, E. Fléty, A. Cera, U. Petrevski, and J.-L. Frechin. The urban musical game: using sport balls as musical interfaces. In *CHI '12 Extended Abstracts on Human Factors in Computing Systems*, pages 1027–1030. 2012.

[11] D. Rocchesso, S. Serafin, F. Behrendt, N. Bernardini, R. Bresin, G. Eckel, K. Franinovic, T. Hermann, S. Pauletto, P. Susini, and Y. Visell. Sonic interaction design: sound, information and experience. In *CHI '08 Extended Abstracts on Human Factors in Computing Systems*, pages 3969–3972. 2008.

[12] D. Wessel and M. Wright. Problems and Prospects for Intimate Musical Control of Computers. *Computer Music Journal*, 26(3):11–22, Sept. 2002.

[13] E. Yamamoto, S. Nakamura, and K. Shikano. Speech-to-lip movement synthesis based on the EM algorithm using audio-visual HMMs. In *Multimedia Signal Processing, 1998 IEEE Second Workshop on*, pages 2–5, 1998.

[14] H. Zen, Y. Nankaku, and K. Tokuda. Continuous Stochastic Feature Mapping Based on Trajectory HMMs. *Audio, Speech, and Language Processing, IEEE Transactions on*, 19(2):417–430, 2011.

Modeling Local Descriptors with Multivariate Gaussians for Object and Scene Recognition

Giuseppe Serra, Costantino Grana, Marco Manfredi, Rita Cucchiara
Dipartimento di Ingegneria "Enzo Ferrari", Università degli Studi di Modena e Reggio Emilia
Via Vignolese, 905/b, Modena MO 41125, Italy
{name.surname}@unimore.it

ABSTRACT

Common techniques represent images by quantizing local descriptors and summarizing their distribution in a histogram. In this paper we propose to employ a parametric description and compare its capabilities to histogram based approaches. We use the multivariate Gaussian distribution, applied over the SIFT descriptors, extracted with dense sampling on a spatial pyramid. Every distribution is converted to a high-dimensional descriptor, by concatenating the mean vector and the projection of the covariance matrix on the Euclidean space tangent to the Riemannian manifold. Experiments on Caltech-101 and ImageCLEF2011 are performed using the Stochastic Gradient Descent solver, which allows to deal with large scale datasets and high dimensional feature spaces.

Categories and Subject Descriptors

H.3.1 [**Information Systems Applications**]: Content Analysis and Indexing

Keywords

object recognition; image understanding; stochastic gradient descent; local features

1. INTRODUCTION

Image classification, including scene classification and object recognition, remains a major challenge to visual analysis that provides a solid basis for many applications related to multimedia. As summarized in [4], the typical object recognition pipeline is composed of three steps: the extraction of local image features (e.g. SIFT), encoding of the local features in an image descriptor (e.g. a histogram of the quantized local features), classification of the image descriptor (e.g. by a support vector machine).

While all elements are important, the encoding of the local features in global image statistics is definitely the step attracting most research efforts. The baseline method is to compute a histogram of visual word frequencies (quantized local features), commonly known as Bag of Words model [5]. Recent advances replace the hard quantization of the features with alternative encodings that retain more information about the original image features, such as soft quantization [7], local linear encoding [21], and Fisher encoding [4].

Historically many solutions started to describe local features with a short and compact descriptor, but later researchers realized that the summarization was too crude and reverted to enrich it with further information. Since the goal is to describe the descriptors distribution within an image (or windows on it), a reasonable solution has been to use histograms to provide a compact non parametric description. Instead, we propose to employ a parametric distribution and compare its capabilities to histogram based approaches.

A reasonable first choice is to assume that our data follows a Gaussian distribution, because it has useful mathematical properties, it was extensively used and studied, and its representation requires few parameters. The Gaussian distribution plays a crucial role in multivariate statistics in general, and in discrimination theory in particular [1].

A major aspect in statistical learning is to quantify the similarity/dissimilarity between two distributions. Many measures have been proposed in closed form expressions such as the Bhattacharyya divergence and the symmetric Kullback-Leibler (KL) divergence between two multivariate Gaussian densities [12]. By leveraging these dissimilarities, it is possible to build a non-linear kernel function, to run a learning task using the measured Gaussian parameters. Unfortunately this would require an enormous computational effort and would become soon prohibitive when moving to large scale problems with large feature vectors.

In this paper we propose to model the SIFT descriptors distribution as a multivariate Gaussian and to transform the mean/covariance couple in a high dimensional vector: we concatenate the mean vector and the projection of the covariance matrix on the Euclidean space tangent to the Riemannian manifold. With our representation, linear classification is now possible, opening the way to efficient and large scale image annotation. Differently from common techniques based on the Bag of Words model, our solution does not rely on the construction of a visual vocabulary, thus removing the dependence of the image descriptors on the specific dataset considered. We report results on two commonly used datasets (Caltech-101 and ImageCLEF2011), using both an off-the-shelf batch classifier and the Stochastic Gradient Descent on-line solver, which allows to deal with large scale datasets and high dimensional feature spaces.

MM'13, October 21–25, 2013, Barcelona, Spain.
Copyright 2013 ACM 978-1-4503-2404-5/13/10 ...$15.00.
http://dx.doi.org/10.1145/2502081.2502185.

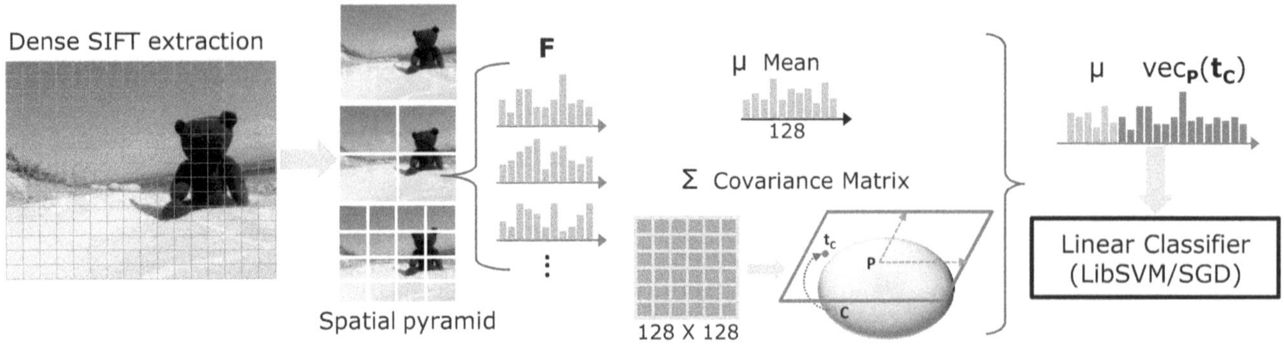

Figure 1: A schematization of the proposed approach. An image (or a window) is represented as a multivariate Gaussian distribution of the extracted local descriptors. The covariance matrix is projected on the tangent space and concatenated to the mean to obtain the final region descriptor.

2. MULTIVARIATE GAUSSIAN OF LOCAL DESCRIPTORS

The multivariate Gaussian distribution of a set of d-dimensional vectors F is given by

$$\mathcal{N}(\mathbf{f};\mu,\Sigma) = |2\pi\Sigma|^{-\frac{1}{2}} exp\{-\frac{1}{2}(\mathbf{f}-\mu)^T\Sigma^{-1}(\mathbf{f}-\mu)\}, \quad (1)$$

where $|\cdot|$ is the determinant, μ is the mean vector and Σ is the covariance matrix ($\mathbf{f},\mu \in \mathbb{R}^d$ and $\Sigma \in \mathbb{S}_{++}^{d\times d}$, with $\mathbb{S}_{++}^{d\times d}$ the space of real symmetric positive semi-definite matrices).

Let $F = \{\mathbf{f}_1 \dots \mathbf{f}_\mathbf{N}\}$ be a set of local features (e.g. SIFT descriptors, where $d = 128$) in an image (or a window) W, we suppose that they are normally distributed, and can thus be described with their distribution, that is by their mean and covariance. These can be estimated as:

$$\mu = \frac{1}{N}\sum_{i=1}^{N}\mathbf{f}_i, \quad (2)$$

$$\mathbf{\Sigma} = \frac{1}{N-1}\sum_{i=1}^{N}(\mathbf{f}_i-\mu)(\mathbf{f}_i-\mu)^T. \quad (3)$$

Although the covariance matrix is a very informative element of the distribution, which encode information about the variance of the features, it does not form a vector space. For example, the space is not closed under multiplication with negative scalars. Most of the common machine learning algorithms assume that the data points form a vector space, therefore a suitable transformation is required prior to their use. In particular we can observe that they are symmetric positive definite, and as such they can be formulated as a connected Riemannian manifold. In the following, matrices (points in the Riemannian manifold) will be denoted by bold uppercase letters, while vectors (points in the Euclidean space) by bold lowercase ones.

In [19] an approach to map from Riemannian manifolds to Euclidean spaces is described. The first step is the projection of the covariance matrices on an Euclidean space tangent to the Riemannian manifold, on a specific tangency matrix $\mathbf{P}$. The second step is the extraction of the orthonormal coordinates of the projected vector.

The projected vector of a covariance matrix $\mathbf{C}$ is given by:

$$\mathbf{t_C} = \log_\mathbf{P}(\mathbf{C}) = \mathbf{P}^{\frac{1}{2}}\log\left(\mathbf{P}^{-\frac{1}{2}}\mathbf{C}\mathbf{P}^{-\frac{1}{2}}\right)\mathbf{P}^{\frac{1}{2}} \quad (4)$$

where log is the ordinary matrix logarithm operator and $\log_\mathbf{P}$ is the manifold specific logarithm operator, dependent on the point $\mathbf{P}$ to which the projection hyperplane is tangent.

The orthonormal coordinates of the projected vector $\mathbf{t_C}$ in the tangent space at point $\mathbf{P}$ are then given by the vector operator:

$$\mathrm{vec}_\mathbf{P}(\mathbf{t_C}) = \mathrm{vec}_\mathbf{I}\left(\mathbf{P}^{-\frac{1}{2}}\mathbf{t_C}\mathbf{P}^{-\frac{1}{2}}\right) \quad (5)$$

where $\mathbf{I}$ is the identity matrix, while the vector operator at identity is defined as:

$$\mathrm{vec}_\mathbf{I}(\mathbf{C}) = \left[c_{1,1}\ \sqrt{2}c_{1,2}\ \sqrt{2}c_{1,3}\dots c_{2,2}\ \sqrt{2}c_{2,3}\dots c_{d,d}\right] \quad (6)$$

Substituting $\mathbf{t_C}$ from Eq. 4 in Eq. 5, the projection of $\mathbf{C}$ on the hyperplane tangent to $\mathbf{P}$ becomes

$$\mathbf{c} = \mathrm{vec}_\mathbf{I}\left(\log\left(\mathbf{P}^{-\frac{1}{2}}\mathbf{C}\mathbf{P}^{-\frac{1}{2}}\right)\right) \quad (7)$$

In this way, after selecting an appropriate projection origin, every covariance matrix of size $d \times d$ gets projected to a $(d^2+d)/2$-dimensional feature vector on an Euclidean space.

As observed in [16], the projection point $\mathbf{P}$ is arbitrary and, even if it could influence the performance (distortion) of the projection, from a computational point of view, the best choice is the identity matrix, which simply translates the mapping into a standard matrix logarithm, followed by unrolling.

Summarizing, the proposed approach is to extract some descriptors from an image and then collect them in a spatial pyramid (Fig. 1); each sub-region is described by the estimated parameters of a multivariate Gaussian distribution. The covariance matrix is projected on a Euclidean space and concatenated to the mean vector to obtain the final descriptor. If SIFT descriptors are used, the dimensionality becomes 128 + (128*128+128)/2 = 8384 per sub-region. Eventually, all the sub-region descriptors are fed to a linear classifier.

3. MOVING TO LARGE SCALE DATA

Although there exist many off-the-shelf SVM solvers, such as SVMlight, SVMperf or LibSVM/LIBLINEAR, they are not feasible for training large volumes of data. This is because most of them are batch methods, which require to go through all data to compute gradient in each iteration and often need many iterations to reach a reasonable solution. Even worse, most off-the-shelf batch type SVM solvers require to pre-load training data into memory, which is impossible when the size of the training data explodes. Indeed, LIBLINEAR released an extended version that explicitly considered the memory issue, but in a recent test [14] it was shown that the performance dropped considerably and even on 80GB of training data it could not provide useful results. Therefore, a better solution may be provided by the stochastic gradient descent (SGD) algorithm recently introduced for SVM classifiers training [3].

We have training data that consists of T feature-label pairs, denoted as $\{\mathbf{x}_t, y_t\}_{t=1}^{T}$, where $\mathbf{x}_t$ is a $s \times 1$ feature vector representing an image and $y_t \in \{-1, +1\}$ is the label of the image. Then, the cost function for binary SVM classification can be written as

$$L = \sum_{t=1}^{T} \frac{\lambda}{2} \|\mathbf{w}\|^2 + \max\left[0, 1 - y_t(\mathbf{w}^T \mathbf{x}_t + b)\right], \quad (8)$$

where $\mathbf{w}$ is $s \times 1$ SVM weight vector, λ (nonnegative scalar) is a regularization parameter, and b (scalar) is a bias term. In the SGD algorithm, training data are fed to the system one by one, and the update rule for $\mathbf{w}$ and b respectively are

$$\begin{aligned} \mathbf{w}_t &= (1 - \lambda\eta)\mathbf{w}_{t-1} + \eta y_t \mathbf{x}_t \\ b_t &= b_{t-1} + \eta y_t \end{aligned} \quad (9)$$

if margin $\Delta_t = y_t(\mathbf{w}^T \mathbf{x}_t + b)$ is less than 1; otherwise, $\mathbf{w}_t = (1 - \lambda\eta)\mathbf{w}_{t-1}$ and $b_t = b_{t-1}$. The parameter η is the step size. We set $\eta = (1 + \lambda t)^{-1}$, following the `vl_pegasos` implementation [20].

To parallelize SVMs training, we randomize the data on disk. We load the data in chunks which fit in memory, then train the different classifiers in parallel threads on further randomizations of the chunks, so that different epochs will get the chunks data with different orderings.

4. EXPERIMENTAL RESULTS

We tested the performance of our method on the Caltech-101 and ImageCLEF 2011. Caltech-101 is one of the most commonly used datasets for object recognition. It contains 9144 images from 101 object categories plus one background category. The number of images per category varies from 31 to 800. The images are with high shape variation, but objects are all centered and have no viewpoint diversity. ImageCLEF 2011 Annotation Task dataset is composed of a training set of 8000 images and the test set is 10,000 images large. The ImageCLEF photo corpus is a challenging concept detection dataset (multiple labels per image) due to its heterogeneity of classes. There are 99 concepts, which are concrete objects such as 'flowers', 'vehicles' as well as more abstractly defined classes like 'scary' or 'technical'.

For Caltech-101 we compute SIFT descriptors at multiple scales over a dense regular grid with a spacing of 4 pixels, using the function `vl_phow` provided by the `vl_feat` library [20]. For spatial pyramids we use 1×1, 2×2 and 4×4. We follow a common experimental setting: for training we randomly select 15 or 30 images; for testing we randomly select at most 50 images for each category, different from the training ones. We report the Mean Recognition Rate per class, the results are normalized based on the number of testing samples in that class. The reported results are the average over five independent runs.

Table 1: Comparison of accuracy percentage values with the state-of-the-art for Caltech-101.

	15 Training	30 Training
Our method	**71.62**	**79.68**
Grauman et al. [8]	50.00	58.20
Huang et al. [9]	66.88	74.25
Jia et al. [10]	-	75.30
Jiang et al. [11]	67.50	75.30
Lazebnik et al. [13]	56.40	64.60
Liu et al. [15]	-	74.21
Tuytelaars et al. [18]	69.20	75.20
Wang et al. [21]	65.43	73.40
Yang et al. [22]	67.00	73.20
Chatfield et al. [4]	-	77.78 *

* Note that Chatfield et al. tested on a slightly different setting (30 test images per class, in contrast to the standard 50)

For ImageCLEF 2011 we follow the same procedure to extract the SIFT descriptors, and the Mean Average Precision (MAP) is used to evaluate the performance.

Table 1 reports a comparison of the results our method with those of significant recent approaches obtained on the Caltech-101 dataset at two common number of training images per class (15 and 30). Our performance is definitely competitive with state-of-the art results, and is surpassed only by the Fisher Kernel results reported in Chatfield et al. [4]. Note that, differently from the common setting, they limit the number of testing images to only 30 images, so the results are not entirely comparable. Moreover our solution does not require to build a codebook, that must be trained on every specific dataset.

All the reported techniques use SIFT descriptors extracted with dense sampling. Usually the more features or kernels are taken into account, the more the results improve (e.g. in [6] a combination of 48 different kernels achieves 74.6% with only 15 training images).

The results reported for the Caltech-101 dataset were obtained with LibSVM, since the feature data could fit in memory and it is a well known and effective software package. We also trained the SVM classifiers using the SGD algorithm, starting from the public implementation provided by Leon Bottou[1], but the training time is largely higher and the results are slightly lower (74.23%).

Instead, with larger datasets such as ImageCLEF 2011, an on-line approach becomes the only viable choice, and its performance easily reach those of batch solvers. To select an appropriate regularization parameter λ, we randomly split the training set in two and run the SGD varying λ from 10^{-3} to 10^{-7} in power of 10 steps. Fig. 2 shows the MAP values at increasing number of training epochs (i.e. providing the algorithm all training samples in current split) for every λ value. While $\lambda = 10^{-3}$ leads to significantly worse results, all other values provide similar performance, with a slight improvement at $\lambda = 10^{-6}$, which we chose for our test. We then run the SGD algorithm on the whole 8000 training samples and tested on the testset, obtaining a MAP value of 0.332.

[1] http://leon.bottou.org/projects/sgd

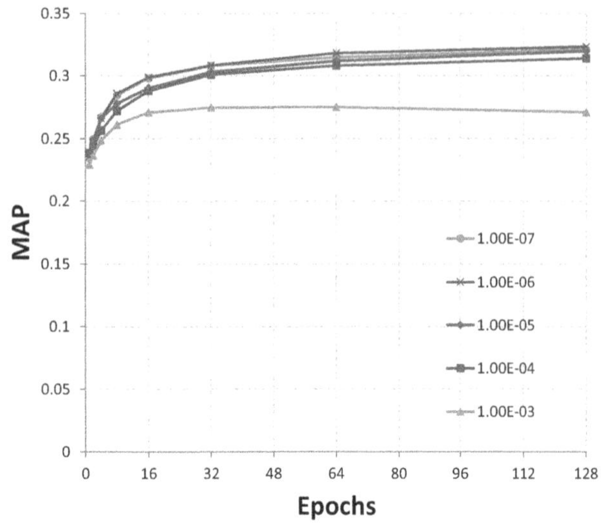

Figure 2: Cross validation results for choosing the parameter λ on the ImageCLEF2011 dataset.

The best run of the ImageCLEF workshop obtained a MAP of 0.388 using 4 different color SIFT variations, different sampling strategies and improvements and a Multiple Kernel Learning approach [2]. The feature and kernel computations required a cluster with 40 * 275 = 11,000 Core Units, which had (according to cpubenchmark.net) a speed rank of 134 in August 2011. Our tests were performed on a 2 * 6 cores machine, which clearly limits the affordable computational effort. A more comparable approach, from a computational requirements point of view, was followed in [17], which used 7 color SIFT variations with both Harris and Dense sampling, leading to 14 separate classifiers per concept, combined with late fusion (averaging). They obtained a MAP of 0.311, clearly showing that the summarization properties of our projected multivariate Gaussian descriptor, computed with only the basic gray-scale SIFT, are able to beat the description of the bag of visual words approach.

5. CONCLUSIONS

In this paper we proposed a new image representation based on the estimation of the multivariate Gaussian distribution of the SIFT descriptors, extracted with dense sampling on a spatial pyramid. Each distribution is converted to a high-dimensional descriptor, by concatenating the mean vector and the projection of the covariance matrix on the Euclidean space tangent to the Riemannian manifold. The reported results show promising performance, on par with state of the art approaches, without the need to build a codebook from training images.

6. REFERENCES

[1] S. Ali and S. Silvey. A general class of coefficients of divergence of one distribution from another. *J. of the Royal Stat. Soc. (B)*, 28(1):131–142, 1966.

[2] A. Binder, W. Samek, M. Kloft, C. Müller, K.-R. Müller, and M. Kawanabe. The Joint Submission of the TU Berlin and Fraunhofer FIRST (TUBFI) to the ImageCLEF2011 Photo Annotation Task. In *CLEF Workshop*, 2011.

[3] L. Bottou and O. Bousquet. The tradeoffs of large scale learning. In *Advances in Neural Information Processing Systems*, pages 161–168, 2008.

[4] K. Chatfield, V. Lempitsky, A. Vedaldi, and A. Zisserman. The devil is in the details: an evaluation of recent feature encoding methods. In *BMVC*, 2011.

[5] G. Csurka, C. R. Dance, L. Fan, J. Willamowski, and C. Bray. Visual categorization with bags of keypoints. In *ECCV Workshop Stat. Learn. Comput. Vision*, 2004.

[6] P. Gehler and S. Nowozin. On feature combination for multiclass object classication. In *ICCV*, 2009.

[7] J. C. Gemert, J.-M. Geusebroek, C. J. Veenman, and A. W. Smeulders. Kernel codebooks for scene categorization. In *ECCV*, 2008.

[8] K. Grauman and T. Darrell. The pyramid match kernel: Efficient learning with sets of features. *J. Mach. Learn. Res.*, 8:725–760, 2007.

[9] Y. Huang, K. Huang, C. Wang, and T. Tan. Exploring relations of visual codes for image classification. In *Proc. of CVPR*, 2011.

[10] Y. Jia, C. Huang, and T. Darrell. Beyond spatial pyramids: Receptive field learning for pooled image features. In *CVPR*, 2012.

[11] Z. Jiang, G. Zhang, and L. S. Davis. Submodular dictionary learning for sparse coding. In *CVPR*, 2012.

[12] T. Kailath. The divergence and Bhattacharyya distance measures in signal selection. *IEEE T. Commun. Techn.*, 15(1):52–60, 1967.

[13] S. Lazebnik, C. Schmid, and J. Ponce. Beyond bags of features: Spatial pyramid matching for recognizing natural scene categories. In *Proc. of CVPR*, 2006.

[14] Y. Lin, F. Lv, S. Zhu, M. Yang, T. Cour, and K. Yu. Large-scale image classification: Fast feature extraction and svm training. In *CVPR*, 2011.

[15] L. Liu, L. Wang, and X. Liu. In defense of soft-assignment coding. In *ICCV*, 2011.

[16] S. Martelli, D. Tosato, M. Farenzena, M. Cristani, and V. Murino. An FPGA-based Classification Architecture on Riemannian Manifolds. In *DEXA Workshops*, 2010.

[17] E. Spyromitros-Xioufis, K. Sechidis, G. Tsoumakas, and I. P. Vlahavas. MLKD's Participation at the CLEF 2011 Photo Annotation and Concept-Based Retrieval Tasks. In *CLEF Workshop*, 2011.

[18] T. Tuytelaars, M. Fritz, K. Saenko, and T. Darrell. The nbnn kernel. In *ICCV*, 2011.

[19] O. Tuzel, F. Porikli, and P. Meer. Pedestrian Detection via Classification on Riemannian Manifolds. *IEEE T. Pattern Anal.*, 30(10):1713–1727, 2008.

[20] A. Vedaldi and B. Fulkerson. VLFeat: An open and portable library of computer vision algorithms. http://www.vlfeat.org/, 2008.

[21] J. Wang, J. Yang, K. Yu, F. Lv, T. Huang, and Y. Gong. Locality-constrained linear coding for image classification. In *CVPR*, 2010.

[22] J. Yang, K. Yu, Y. Gong, and T. Huang. Linear spatial pyramid matching using sparse coding for image classification. In *CVPR*, 2009.

Anchor Concept Graph Distance for Web Image Re-ranking

Shi Qiu[1], Xiaogang Wang[2,3], and Xiaoou Tang[1,3]
[1]Department of Information Engineering, The Chinese University of Hong Kong
[2]Department of Electronic Engineering, The Chinese University of Hong Kong
[3]Shenzhen Institutes of Advanced Technology, Chinese Academy of Sciences, China
{qs010,xtang}@ie.cuhk.edu.hk, xgwang@ee.cuhk.edu.hk

ABSTRACT

Web image re-ranking aims to automatically refine the initial text-based image search results by employing visual information. A strong line of work in image re-ranking relies on building image graphs that requires computing distances between image pairs. In this paper, we present Anchor Concept Graph Distance (ACG Distance), a novel distance measure for image re-ranking. For a given textual query, an Anchor Concept Graph (ACG) is automatically learned from the initial text-based search results. The nodes of the ACG (*i.e.*, anchor concepts) and their correlations well model the semantic structure of the images to be re-ranked. Images are projected to the anchor concepts. The projection vectors undergo a diffusion process over the ACG, and then are used to compute the ACG distance. The ACG distance reduces the semantic gap and better represents distances between images. Experiments on the MSRA-MM and INRIA datasets show that the ACG distance consistently outperforms existing distance measures and significantly improves start-of-the-art methods in image re-ranking.

Categories and Subject Descriptors

H.3.3 [**Information Search and Retrieval**]: Retrieval models

Keywords

Web image search re-ranking; anchor concept graph; semantic gap

1. INTRODUCTION

The fast growing number of web images spurs the rapid development of image search engines, such as Google, Bing, and Flickr. Due to the success of text retrieval techniques in searching web pages and their efficiency, most web image search engines return images based on textual information including surrounding texts, titles, URLs, and user-given tags. However, text-based image search often suffers from noise in the textual information as well as the discrepancy between textual and visual contents, yielding unsatisfactory results. For example in Figure 1, when users search for the 'panda' animal, unexpected images of cars will also come out in the text-based search results. Researchers therefore employ visual information to re-rank the initial text-based search results. The aim is to boost images relevant to the textual query to top ranks, and lower down irrelevant ones without further user intervention.

A variety of methods have been proposed for web image search re-ranking. Topic models [1, 2] learn the latent topics among returned images and perform re-ranking based on the probability that each image belongs to the dominant topic. Such methods are effective in handling object-like queries, but may fail on general web images or when relevant images undergo significant variations because of their low discriminative power. Classification-based methods first train a discriminative model such as SVM [16] and boosting [15] which are further used to predict the relevance scores of returned images. The drawback of this type of methods is that they adopt pseudo-relevance feedback (PRF) to acquire training samples which are usually unreliable. There are also approaches [6] that train query-relative classifiers and do not involve PRF. However, they are shown to suffer from the overfitting problem [7].

Recently, graph-based methods have drawn increasing attention in image re-ranking [12, 4, 9, 7], as they are able to capture manifold structures underlying imagery data and provide a nice framework to integrate the initial text-based ranking information and visual consistency between images [17]. These methods mostly build on the assumption that the relevant images form a compact cluster in the search results. They typically involves (1) constructing a graph by computing distances of image pairs; (2) detecting confident samples (compact clusters) based on the graph; and (3) propagating the scores of confident samples over the graph. Therefore, the key to the success of graph-based methods lies in a proper distance measure between images, as it determines the structure of the graph which the rest of the methods build on. A good distance measure would close the semantic gap and reveal the manifold structure formed by images to be re-ranked. Despite of its importance in re-ranking algorithms, the choice of distance measure for graph construction is not well solved yet. Jing and Baluja [5] used the portion of matched SIFT features as the similarity between an image pair. It is effective only in ranking images of particular types of objects. Most methods [12, 9, 7] adopt distance between low-level features such as histograms of visual words or color moments. These features generally do not correlate well with the semantics of images, especially when the returned images are diverse in visual content.

In this paper, we propose the Anchor Concept Graph Distance (ACG Distance), an effective distance measure for graph construction in image re-ranking. A graphical illustration is shown in Figure 1. Instead of directly computing distances with low-level features, our proposed distance is computed using a semantic representation of the initial search results called Anchor Concept Graph (ACG). The ACG is automatically learned from the initial search results. Its nodes (called Anchor Concepts) are a set of concepts relevant

MM'13, October 21–25, 2013, Barcelona, Spain.
Copyright 2013 ACM 978-1-4503-2404-5/13/10 ...$15.00.
http://dx.doi.org/10.1145/2502081.2502186 .

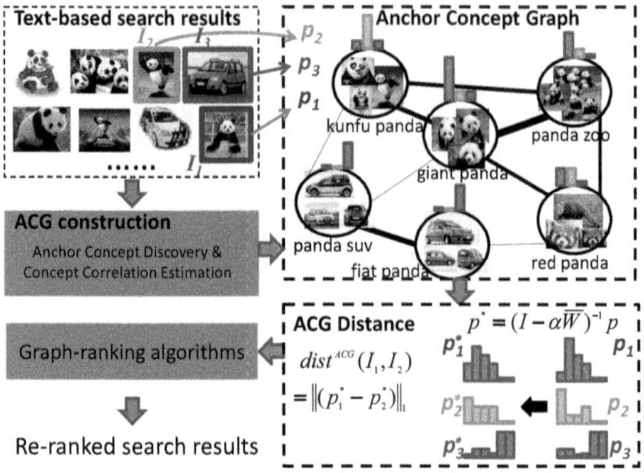

Figure 1: Illustration of the proposed ACG distance for web image search re-ranking. An anchor concept graph is learned from the initial text-based search results of a given query, *e.g.*, panda. Images are projected to the anchor concepts. Image distances are computed using the smoothed concept projections over the anchor concept graph.

to the returned search results. The correlation of these anchor concepts are represented by edges of the ACG. The visual features of images are then projected to the nodes of the ACG, forming a high-level representation that encodes the association of an image with the anchor concepts. The projection vector is further smoothed with a diffusion process which propagates information along the edges of the ACG and the distance between two smoothed projection vectors is defined as the ACG distance of two images. Since the ACG models the structure of initial search results at the semantic level, our ACG distance better reflects the semantic relevance of images and the image graphs constructed from it are more effective in image re-ranking. We demonstrate the effectiveness of our approach on two benchmark datasets and show that ACG distance leads to consistent and significant improvement of state-of-the-art image re-ranking methods.

2. ACG CONSTRUCTION

2.1 Anchor Concept Discovery

Given a textual query q, *e.g.*, "panda", in conjunction with the returned images $\mathcal{I}_q$ and their surrounding texts $\mathcal{T}_q$, a set of anchor concepts, such as "giant panda", "kungfu panda", and "panda suv", can be automatically discovered by employing both textual and visual information. These anchor concepts can more accurately model the visual and semantic content of the diverse images to be re-ranked. The anchor concepts are discovered through query expansions. The key idea is to identify expanded query keywords that occur frequently in visually similar images, as those keywords are more likely to correlate with the visual contents and thus can be viewed as descriptive concepts. The details are provided in Algorithm 1. The learned concepts are denoted as $\mathcal{C}_q = \{c_i\}_{i=1}^{M_q}$. In this paper, we set K, T, and M_q to 15, 3, and 25, respectively.

2.2 Estimating Concept Correlation

The anchor concepts are not isolated. Some anchor concepts are more semantically related, *e.g.*, "giant panda" and "kunfu panda", while some are less related, *e.g.*, "giant panda" and "panda suv". Such correlations are useful in determining image similarities as explained in Section 3.2. We adopt the Google Kernel to estimate correlations among anchor concepts. Google Kernel was first proposed by Sahami *et al.* [10] to measure the similarity of two short texts (typically a short text contains a number of keywords) at the semantic level. For a anchor concept c_i, a set of Google snippets $S(c_i)$ is obtained from the Google web search. A Goolge snippet is a short text summary generated by Google for each search result item with query c_i. We collect the snippets of the top N search result items, and they provide richer semantic context for the anchor concept c_i. We can more robustly determine the similarity between c_i and c_j by computing the textual similarity between $S(c_i)$ and $S(c_j)$ using the traditional term vector model and cosine similarity. We represent the learned correlations by a matrix W, where W_{ij} is the correlation value of c_i and c_j, and W_{ii} is set to 1.

Algorithm 1 Concept Discovery through Query Expansion

Require: Query q, image collection $\mathcal{I}_q$, surrounding texts $\mathcal{T}_q$.
Ensure: Learned concept set $\mathcal{C}_q = \{c_i\}_{i=1}^{M_q}$.

```
Initialization: C_q := ∅, r_I(w) := 0.
for all images I_k ∈ I_q do
    Find the top K visual neighbors, denote as N(I_k)
    Let W_{I_k} = {w^i_{I_k}}^T_{i=1} be the T most frequent words in the
    surrounding texts of N(I_k).
    for all wordS w^i_{I_k} ∈ W(I_k) do
        r_I(w^i_{I_k}) := r_I(w^i_{I_k}) + (T − i).
    end for
end for
Combine q and top M_q words with largest r_I(w) to form C_q.
```

3. RE-RANKING WITH ACG DISTANCE

3.1 Concept Projection

Once the ACG is built, we project images to be re-ranked to the M_q anchor concepts on the ACG, and obtain a high-level representation of images called concept projection. A concept projection of an image is a M_q dimensional vector that encodes its association with each of the anchor concepts. It reduces the semantic gap as it allows images with large difference in visual features to map to similar projection vectors. The projection is done using an multi-class SVM which requires an off-line training stage. Training samples for the anchor concepts are collected by a second round of querying to the search engine. The top N returned images are retained as positive samples for each anchor concept[1]. As the anchor concepts are much less ambiguous than the original queries, their search results are compact and compact enough to serve as training samples. The multi-class SVM is then learned with these training samples. When the training is finished, the learned model is applied to images to be re-ranked, and the probabilistic outputs of the SVM [14] are used as the concept projections.

3.2 ACG distance

The ACG distance for images is then calculated with the concept projection on the anchor concept graph. It is straightforward to define the L_1-distance between two concept projections as their distance. However, this distance is not optimal in that it treats each dimension of the concept projection independently, and the correlations between anchor concepts are ignored. Consider an extreme case that I_1 is an image ideally associated with the anchor concept of "giant panda" (thus its concept projection is a vector with an one in the dimension of "giant panda" and zeros elsewhere). I_2 and I_3 are images ideally associated with "kungfu panda" and

[1] N is fixed to 300 in our experiments. We observe the performance of our approach is not sensitive to the value of N.

Table 1: **Performance of different re-ranking methods on the MSRA-MM and the INRIA datasets. Values in the parentheses are the NDCG@k / MAP improvements over initial search results. M: results on the MSRA-MM dataset. I: results on the INRIA dataset.**

	Initial	IB[3]	Bayesian [12]	QRel [6]	RWalk [4]		KernelTopN [9]		KernelBVLS [9]	
					original	ACG	original	ACG	original	ACG
NDCG@10 (M)	0.582	0.594(0.012)	0.592(0.010)	–	0.597(0.015)	**0.621(0.039)**	0.598(0.016)	**0.647(0.065)**	0.645(0.063)	**0.657(0.075)**
NDCG@50 (M)	0.556	0.570(0.014)	0.565(0.009)	–	0.563(0.007)	**0.586(0.030)**	0.564(0.008)	**0.610(0.054)**	0.587(0.031)	**0.623(0.067)**
NDCG@100 (M)	0.536	0.554(0.018)	0.559(0.023)	–	0.550(0.014)	**0.580(0.044)**	0.560(0.024)	**0.607(0.071)**	0.580(0.044)	**0.617(0.081)**
MAP (I)	0.570	0.616(0.046)	0.658(0.088)	0.649(0.079)	0.637(0.067)	**0.650(0.080)**	0.661(0.091)	**0.674(0.104)**	0.674(0.104)	**0.689(0.119)**

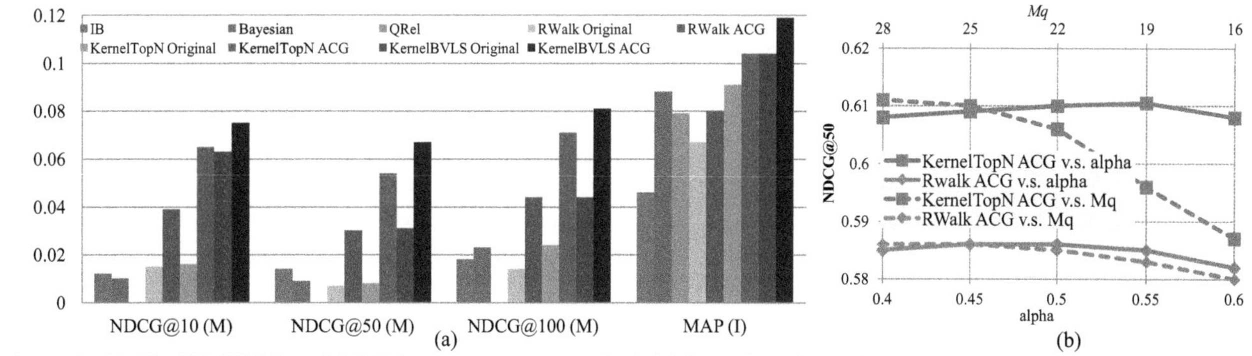

Figure 2: (a) The NDCG@k and MAP improvements over the initial text-based search results on the MSRA-MM and the INRIA datasets. M: results on the MSRA-MM dataset. I: results on the INRIA dataset (b) The performance on the MSRA-MM dataset when changing the value of parameters α and M_q.

"panda suv" respectively. When using L_1-distance, I_2 and I_3 have equal distance to I_1. However, it is clear to us that I_2 should be more similar to I_1 because they are both related to the panda animal while I_3 is related to vehicle. This limitation can be remedied by a smoothing operation on the concept projection before computing the L_1-distance. Concretely, we consider a diffusion process [17] on the ACG that gradually propagate association with one anchor concept (*e.g.* "giant panda") to other correlated concepts (*e.g.* "kungfu panda"). Let p_1 denote the concept projection of I_1, the smoothed concept projection is given by

$$p_1^* = \sum_{n=0}^{\infty} \alpha^n \bar{W}^n p_1 = (I - \alpha\bar{W})^{-1} p_1, \qquad (1)$$

where $\bar{W}$ is the column-normalized correlation matrix, *i.e.*, $\bar{W} = WD^{-1}$ and D is a diagonal matrix with $D_{ii} = \sum_{j=1}^{M_q} W_{ji}$. α $(0 < \alpha < 1)$ is a damping factor that controls the diffusion rate.

The ACG distance is calculated as $\|p_1^* - p_2^*\|_1$. After dropping constant terms, we have

$$dist^{ACG} = \|(I - \alpha\bar{W})^{-1}(p_1 - p_2)\|_1 \qquad (2)$$

The ACG distance can be used with any existing re-ranking methods that rely on pairwise image distances. As the semantic gap is reduced, the manifold structure underlying the returned images are better captured by the ACG distance. State-of-the-art methods can be significantly improved by the ACG distance as shown in the following section.

4. EXPERIMENTS

We conduct experiments on two benchmark datasets for web image re-ranking: INRIA [6] and MSRA-MM V1.0 [13], with 68 and 352 queries respectively. We report the mean average precision (MAP) [6] for the INRIA dataset, and NDCG@k [9] for MSRA-MM as its images are labelled with multiple relevance levels. In Section 4.1, we first combine the ACG distance with existing algorithms and show that the image re-ranking performance can be significantly improved. Several state-of-the-art re-ranking methods are also compared. Section 4.2 compares the ACG distance with other measures directly computed from low-level visual features and/or textual features. It shows that the ACG distance can better capture image semantics. The parameter α is fixed as 0.5 in both experiments. The sensitivity to α is investigated in Section 4.3.

4.1 Comparison with Existing Methods

We combine the ACG distance with state-of-the-art methods by replacing their graph construction component. We use the ACG distance to compute pairwise image distances, and keep the rest of the methods unchanged. We test on three re-ranking approaches: random walk (RWalk) [4], kernel-based re-ranking by taking top N images as confident samples (KernelTopN) [9], and kernel-based re-ranking by detecting confident samples based on bounded variable least square (KernelBVLS) [9]. The parameters involved in these methods are selected according to the original papers. We experiment on both INRIA and MSRA-MM and summarize the performance of the initial text-based search result, the three original approaches, and their counterparts with our ACG distance in Table 1. Three other methods, Information Bottleneck (IB) [3], Bayesian Visual Re-ranking (Bayesian) [12] and Query-relative Classifier (QRel) [6] are also included for comparison.

From Table 1, it is clear that our ACG distance consistently improves upon the state-of-the-art methods on both datasets. Figure 2 (a) shows the improvement of above methods over the initial search results. We can see that the ACG distance is very effective. On MSRA-MM, the NDCG@50 improvements over the initial search result are originally 0.007, 0.008, and 0.031 by using RWalk, KernelTopN and KernelBVLS, and the improvements are boosted to 0.030, 0.054, and 0.067 by using the ACG distance. Over 100% relative improvement are obtained. Some re-ranking results are shown in Figure 4.

4.2 Comparison of Different Distances

Next, we compare the ACG distance with other distance/similarity measures which are based on low-level visual features and/or textual features. Five different measures are used for graph construction in two re-ranking methods, RWalk [4] and KernelTopN [9]. The measures under comparison are (1) SpmSIFT: L_2-distance between spatial pyramids of the bag-of-words SIFT descriptors used

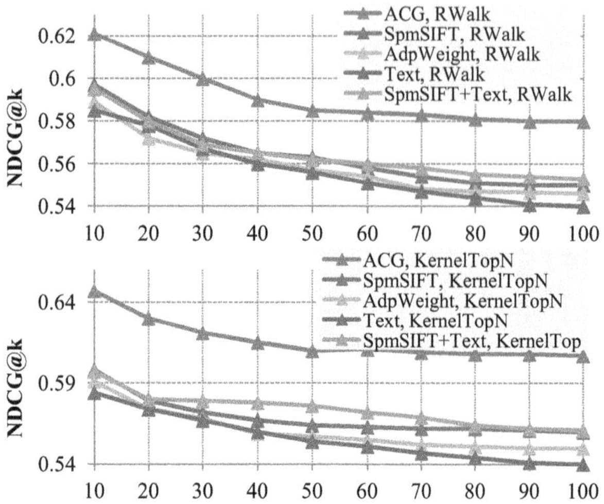

Figure 3: The Performance of four similarity/distance measures on the MSRA-MM dataset. Top: results using RWalk[4]. Bottom: results using KernelTopN [9].

in [9], (2) AdpWeight: distances of multiple visual features with adaptive weighting proposed in [11], (3) Text: cosine similarity between L_2-normalized word histograms extracted from the surrounding texts with tf-idf weighting [8], (4) SpmSIFT+Text, the weighted combination of SpmSIFT and Text, where the weight is optimally tuned, and (5) our ACG distance. The first three represent distance/similarity measures based on local visual feature, global visual feature, and textual feature respectively.

The re-ranking result is given in Figure 3. We can see that our ACG distance consistently outperforms the other measures. Moreover, it is observed that the performance gap increases with the ranking position, indicating that the graph constructed by our ACG distance works more robustly in propagating the relevance information along the semantic manifold. We therefore conclude that the ACG distance is more effective in reducing the semantic gap.

4.3 Parameter Sensitivity

We investigate how the free parameters α in Eqn. 2 and M_q, the number of anchor concepts, will affect the re-ranking performance. We change the value of α and M_q and use the corresponding versions of ACG distance to re-rank images. The NDCG@50 on MSRA-MM by two methods are reported in Figure 2 (b). It can be observed that the performance of ACG distance is robust against small changes in α, and that adding more concepts will always increase the performance. However, the performance gain diminishes quickly after M_q reaches around 25.

5. CONCLUSIONS

In this paper, we propose the ACG distance for web image search re-ranking. The proposed distance is computed over an Anchor Concept Graph which is automatically learned from the initial search results and well models the semantic structure of images to be re-ranked. Our ACG distance better computes image similarities by reducing the semantic gap. It is applicable to a variety of re-ranking approaches that rely on constructing graphs on images. We conduct experiments on two public benchmark datasets, and show that the proposed distance consistently outperforms commonly used distance/similarity measures, and significantly improves the start-of-the-arts methods in web image search re-ranking.

Figure 4: Top 10 re-ranked images for three queries in the MSRA-MM dataset. The green bar underneath each image indicates its groundtruth relevance level. (a) Initial text-based search. (b) KernelTopN [9] with original distance measure. (c) KernelTopN with ACG distance.

6. REFERENCES

[1] R. Fergus, L. Fei-Fei, P. Perona, and A. Zisserman. Learning object categories from google's image search. In *ICCV*, 2005.

[2] M. Fritz and B. Schiele. Decomposition, discovery and detection of visual categories using topic models. In *CVPR*, 2008.

[3] W. Hsu, L. Kennedy, and S.-F. Chang. Video search reranking via information bottleneck principle. In *ACM MM*, 2006.

[4] W. Hsu, L. Kennedy, and S.-F. Chang. Video search reranking through random walk over document-level context graph. In *ACM MM*, 2007.

[5] Y. Jing and S. Baluja. Visualrank: Applying pagerank to large-scale image search. *TPAMI*, 30:1877–1890, 2008.

[6] J. Krapac, M. Allan, J. Verbeek, and F. Jurie. Improving web image search results using query-relative classifiers. In *CVPR*, 2010.

[7] W. Liu, Y. Jiang, J. Luo, and S.-F. Chang. Noise resistant graph ranking for improved web image search. In *CVPR*, 2011.

[8] C. D. Manning, P. Raghavan, and H. Schütze. *Introduction to information retrieval*, volume 1. Cambridge University Press Cambridge, 2008.

[9] N. Morioka and J. Wang. Robust visual reranking via sparsity and ranking constraints. In *ACM MM*, 2011.

[10] M. Sahami and T. D. Heilman. A web-based kernel function for measuring the similarity of short text snippets. In *WWW*, 2006.

[11] X. Tang, K. Liu, J. Cui, F. Wen, and X. Wang. Intentsearch: Capturing user intention for one-click internet image search. *TPAMI*, 34:1342–1353, 2012.

[12] X. Tian, L. Yang, J. Wang, X. Wu, and X.-S. Hua. Bayesian visual reranking. *TMM*, 13:639–652, 2010.

[13] M. Wang, L. Yang, and X.-S. Hua. Msra-mm: Bridging research and industrial societies for multimedia information retrieval. Technical report, Microsoft Research Asia, 2009.

[14] T.-F. Wu, C.-J. Lin, and R. C. Weng. Probability estimates for multi-class classification by pairwise coupling. *JMLR*, 5:975–1005, 2004.

[15] R. Yan and A. Hauptmann. Co-retrieval: A boosted reranking approach for video retrieval. In *Proc. CIVR*. Springer, 2004.

[16] R. Yan, A. G. Hauptmann, and R. Jin. Multimedia search with pseudo-relevance feedback. In *Proc. CIVR*, 2003.

[17] D. Zhou, J. Weston, A. Gretton, O. Bousquet, and B. Schölkopf. Ranking on data manifolds. In *NIPS*, 2004.

Violence Detection in Hollywood Movies by the Fusion of Visual and Mid-level Audio Cues

Esra Acar, Frank Hopfgartner, Sahin Albayrak
DAI Laboratory, Technische Universität Berlin
Ernst-Reuter-Platz 7, TEL 14, 10587 Berlin, Germany
{name.surname}@tu-berlin.de

ABSTRACT

Detecting violent scenes in movies is an important video content understanding functionality e.g., for providing automated youth protection services. One key issue in designing algorithms for violence detection is the choice of discriminative features. In this paper, we employ mid-level audio features and compare their discriminative power against low-level audio and visual features. We fuse these mid-level audio cues with low-level visual ones at the decision level in order to further improve the performance of violence detection. We use Mel-Frequency Cepstral Coefficients (MFCC) as audio and average motion as visual features. In order to learn a violence model, we choose two-class support vector machines (SVMs). Our experimental results on detecting violent video shots in Hollywood movies show that mid-level audio features are more discriminative and provide more precise results than low-level ones. The detection performance is further enhanced by fusing the mid-level audio cues with low-level visual ones using an SVM-based decision fusion.

Categories and Subject Descriptors

I.2.10 [**Vision and Scene Understanding**]: Video analysis; H.3.1 [**Information Storage and Retrieval**]: Content Analysis and Indexing

Keywords

Bag-of-Audio-Words; Mel-Frequency Cepstral Coefficients; Motion; Decision Fusion; Support Vector Machine

1. INTRODUCTION

The advances in digital media management techniques have facilitated delivering digital videos to consumers. Therefore, accessing online movies through services such as Video-On-Demand has become extremely easy. As a result, parents are not always able to precisely monitor what their children watch. Children are, consequently, exposed to movies, documentaries, or reality shows which have not necessarily been checked by parents, and which might contain inappropriate content. One of these inappropriate contents is violence. Psychological studies have shown that violent content in movies has harmful effects, especially on children [5]. As a consequence, there is a need for automatically detecting violent scenes in videos, where the legal age ratings are not available. Although defining scenes as "violent" is subjective (i.e., person-dependent), in our work, we aim at sticking to the common definition of violence: "physical violence or accident resulting in human injury or pain" [7].

An important step in the task of movie violent content detection is the representation of movie segments. Many of the existing works (e.g., [6, 9]) proposed for violence detection represent videos using low-level representations, especially for the representation of audio signals. Making abstractions is better than directly using low-level features in order to bridge the gap between the features and high-level human perception of violence. However, high-level semantics are difficult to detect and state-of-the-art detectors are far from perfect. Therefore, using mid-level representations may help modeling video segments one step closer to human perception.

This paper aims at investigating the discriminative power of low-level and mid-level audio features to model violence in Hollywood movies. We also investigate how MFCC-based mid-level features perform when fused with average motion features for the detection of violent content and show that promising results are obtained by fusing these cues at the decision level.

The paper is organized as follows. Section 2 explores the recent developments and reviews methods which have been proposed to detect violence in movies. In Section 3, we introduce our method. We provide and discuss evaluation results on Hollywood movies in Section 4. Concluding remarks and future directions to expand our current approach are presented in Section 5.

2. RELATED WORK

Although video content analysis has been studied extensively in the literature, violence analysis of movies is restricted to a few studies. Due to paper length limitations, we only discuss some of the most representative ones which use both audio and visual cues.

Wang et al. [6] apply Multiple Instance Learning (MIL) (MI-SVM [4]) using color, textual and MFCC features. Video scenes are divided into video shots, where each scene is formulated as a bag and each shot as an instance inside the bag for MIL.

Giannakopoulos et al. [9] propose to use a multi-modal two-stage approach. In the first step, they perform audio and visual analysis of segments of one second duration. The classifications obtained in this first step are then used to train a k-NN classifier.

In [10], a three-stage method is proposed. In the first stage, they apply a semi-supervised cross-feature learning algorithm [14] on the extracted audio-visual features for the selection of candidate violent video shots. In the second stage, high-level audio events (e.g., screaming, gun shots, explosions) are detected via SVM training

MM'13 , Oct 21-25 2013, Barcelona, Spain

http://dx.doi.org/10.1145/2502081.2502187.

for each audio event. In the third stage, the outputs of the classifiers generated in the previous two stages are linearly weighted for final decision.

Lin et al. [12] train separate classifiers for audio and visual analysis and combine these classifiers by co-training. Probabilistic latent semantic analysis is applied in the audio classification part. In the visual classification part, the degree of violence of a video shot is determined by using motion intensity, the (non-)existence of flame, explosion and blood appearing in the video shot.

In order to provide a better description of audio signal, Rabiner et al. [13] propose to use discrete HMM through the use of Vector Quantization (VQ) in speech processing. In this work, we apply the VQ coding scheme on MFCCs for violence detection. Our approach differs from the aforementioned works in the following aspects: (1) we stick to a broad definition of "violence" [7], (2) we evaluate our approach on a diverse benchmarking dataset [2] (i.e., not a restricted dataset which contains only action movies), (3) we construct mid-level audio representations by a Bag-of-Audio-Words (BoAW) approach with the VQ coding scheme and show that these representations are more discriminative than low-level audio and visual ones, and (4) we further improve the performance by fusing mid-level audio representations with visual ones at the decision level by an SVM-based fusion and manage to be in the top 25% among submissions in the MediaEval Violent Scenes Detection (VSD) task [2] in terms of *average precision at 20*.

3. THE VIOLENCE DETECTION METHOD

In this section, we discuss the representation of video shots and the learning of a violence model which are the two main components of our method.

3.1 Video Representation

Sound effects and background music in movies are essential for stimulating people's perception. Therefore, the audio signals are important for the representation of videos. We represent the audio content at two different levels: low-level and mid-level. Both representations are based on MFCC features extracted from the audio signals of video shots as illustrated in Figure 1(a).

3.1.1 Low-level Audio Representation

Due to the variability in duration of the video shots annotated as violent or non-violent, each shot comprises a different number of MFCC feature vectors. Aiming at constructing audio representations having the same dimension, mean and standard deviation for each dimension of the MFCC feature vectors are computed. The resulting mean and standard deviation compose the low-level audio representations of shots.

3.1.2 Mid-level Audio Representation

In order to generate mid-level audio representations for video shots, we apply an abstraction process which uses MFCC-based BoAW. The first step in the BoAW scheme is to construct a dictionary of audio words. We follow an unsupervised way of constructing the audio dictionary. First, we cluster MFCC feature vectors extracted from shots with a k-means clustering, in which the centroid of each of the k clusters is treated as an audio word. For the dictionary construction, $400 \times k$ MFCC feature vectors are sampled from the training data (this figure has experimentally given satisfactory results). Once an audio vocabulary of size k ($k = 1000$ in this work) is built, each MFCC feature is assigned to the closest audio word in terms of Euclidean distance. Subsequently, a histogram is computed for each shot extracted from movies in the training dataset and the related shot is represented by a BoAW histogram representing the audio word occurrences.

3.1.3 Visual Representation

For the visual representation of video shots, the average motion which film-makers usually make use of in order to elicit some particular perception in the audience is adopted. Motion vectors are computed by block-based estimation and then average motion is deduced as the average magnitude of all motion vectors. This process is performed only around the keyframe of video shots (i.e., average motion values are computed between the keyframe and its preceding and succeeding frames, respectively).

3.2 Violence Detection Model

We train three two-class SVMs in order to learn violence models. One SVM model is constructed using low-level audio features, the second one using low-level visual features, and the third using mid-level audio features. As the last step, we fuse the predictions of the latter two SVM models using another two-class SVM for the final prediction as shown in Figure 1(b). In the learning step, the main issue is the problem of imbalanced data. In the training dataset, the number of non-violent video shots is much higher than the number of violent ones. This results in the learned boundary being too close to the violent instances. Consequently, the SVM tends to classify every sample as non-violent. Different strategies to "push" this decision boundary towards the non-violent samples exist. Although more sophisticated methods dealing with the imbalanced data issue have been proposed in the literature (see [11] for a comprehensive survey), we choose, in the current framework, to perform random undersampling to balance the number of violent and non-violent samples. This method proposed by Akbani et al. [3] appears to be particularly adapted to the application context of our work. In [3], different under- and oversampling strategies are compared. According to the results, SVM with the undersampling strategy provides the most significant performance gain over standard two-class SVMs. In addition, the efficiency of the training process is improved as a result of the reduced training data and, hence, is scalable to large datasets similar to the ones used in the context of our work.

4. PERFORMANCE EVALUATION

The experiments presented in this section aim at comparing the discriminative power of mid-level against low-level audio features. We also evaluate the performance of multi-modal (i.e., mid-level audio and low-level visual) SVM-based decision fusion. A direct comparison of our results with other works discussed in Section 2 is not straightforward due to the differences in the definition of "violence" in published works. However, we compare our method with the methods in the MediaEval VSD task which also stick to the same "violence" definition.

4.1 Dataset and Ground Truth

The MediaEval VSD dataset[1] consists of 32.708 video shots from 18 Hollywood movies of different genres (ranging from extremely violent movies to movies without violence), where each shot is labeled as violent or non-violent. The data set is divided into a training set consisting of 26.138 shots from 15 movies and a test set consisting of 6.570 shots from the remaining 3 movies. The movies of the training and test set were selected in such a manner that both training and test data contain movies of variable violence levels

[1] https://research.technicolor.com/rennes/vsd/

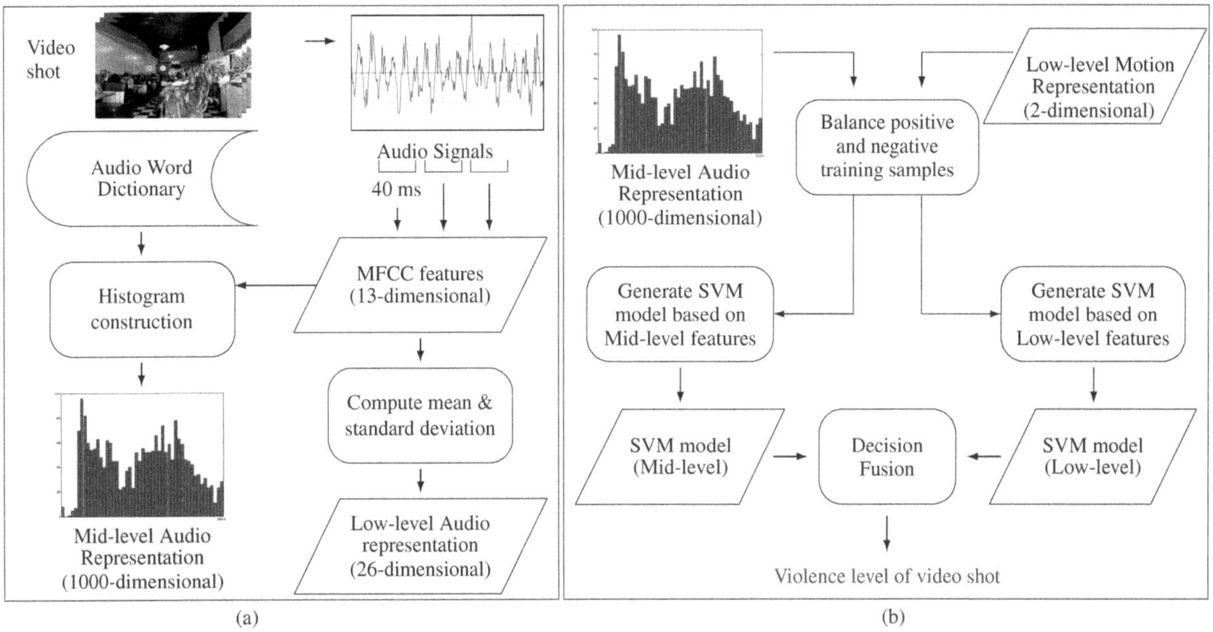

Figure 1: (a) The generation process of audio representations for video shots of movies. (b) The learning phase of the method.

(extreme to none). On average, around 11.5% of shots are annotated as violent in both datasets. Ground truth was generated by 9 human assessors, partly by developers, partly by possible users. Violent movie segments are annotated at the frame level. Automatically generated shot boundaries with their corresponding key frames are also provided for each movie. A detailed description of the dataset and the ground truth generation are given in [7] and [8], respectively.

4.2 Experimental Setup

We employed the MIR Toolbox v1.4[2] to extract the MFCC features (13-dimensional). Frame sizes of 40 ms without overlap are used to align with the 25-fps frames. Features are extracted as explained in Section 3. We trained the two-class SVMs with an RBF kernel using libsvm[3] as the SVM implementation. Training was performed using audio and visual features extracted at the video shot level. We trained one SVM using low-level audio, a second SVM using average motion and a third SVM using mid-level audio features. SVM parameters were optimized by 5-fold cross-validation on the training data.

4.3 Evaluation

Providing a ranked list of violent video shots to the user is more important for our use case. Thus, the evaluation metrics we used are *average precision at 20* and *100* which are also official metrics used in the MediaEval VSD task and *R-precision* which can be seen as an alternative to the *precision at k* in information retrieval.

4.4 Results and Discussions

Table 1 reports the *average precision at 100* values for a baseline method (i.e., random classification) provided by the organizers and for our methods based on mid-level audio and multi-modal (i.e., mid-level audio and low-level visual) SVM-based fusion. The results show that significant improvement is achieved with our approach compared to the baseline method in terms of *average precision at 100.*

Table 1: Average Precision at 100 for the Baseline and Our Methods

Movie	Baseline	Mid-level Audio	Multi-modal
Dead Poets Society	2.17%	15.6%	22.90%
Fight Club	13.27%	29.2%	28.34%
Independence Day	13.98%	72.2%	74.64%

Table 2 provides a comparison of our approach with the best run of participating teams (in terms of *average precision at 20*) in the MediaEval VSD task. The method where we only exploit the audio and disregard the visual modality of videos, manages to be in the top 35% of the submissions in the MediaEval VSD task. The method where we fuse audio cues with motion cues at the decision level, manages to be in the top 25% of the submissions. In addition, the *Mid-level Audio* method, among approaches making use of only one modality (unimodal, i.e., either audio or visual), ranks third among 16 other unimodal submissions in the MediaEval VSD task in terms of *average precision at 100.* The main differences between our approach and the best performing methods in the MediaEval are the fact that we achieve promising results even though we perform no post-processing on violence predictions such as temporal smoothing and the fact that our approach is independent from the concept annotations provided by the organizers, which reduces the need for training data.

Table 3 shows *average precision* (at 20 and 100) as well as *R-precision* for the low- and mid-level audio, low-level visual (i.e., average motion) and the SVM-based decision fusion methods. We observe that the mid-level audio representation provides more precise detections when compared to low-level audio or visual representation. We also note that the performance is further improved by fusing these mid-level audio cues with motion cues using SVM-based decision fusion.

[2] https://www.jyu.fi/hum/laitokset/musiikki/en/research/coe/materials/mirtoolbox
[3] http://www.csie.ntu.edu.tw/~cjlin/libsvm

Table 2: Average Precision (AP) at 20 for the Best Run of Teams in the MediaEval VSD Task and Our Methods (VQ: vector quantization, SIFT: Scale Invariant Features Transform, STIP: Spatial-Temporal Interest Points, VSD: Violent Scenes Detection) [1]

Team	Features	Modality	Method	APat20
Shanghai-Hongkong	Trajectory-based features, SIFT, STIP, MFCCs	audio-visual	SVM with chi-squared kernel + temporal smoothing	0.736
ARF	Color, texture, audio and concepts	audio-visual	Multi-layer perceptron	0.701
TEC	Color, motion, acoustic	audio-visual	Bayesian network with temporal integration post-processing	0.669
Multi-modal (ours)	Bag-of-Audio-Words (BoAW) with VQ, average motion	audio-visual	SVM with RBF kernel	**0.545**
TUM	Acoustic energy and spectral, color, texture, optical flow	audio-visual	SVM with linear kernel	0.504
Mid-level Audio (ours)	BoAW with VQ	audio	SVM with RBF kernel	**0.489**
NII	Visual concepts learned from color and texture	visual	SVM with RBF kernel (with chi-square distance)	0.401
LIG-MRIM	Color, texture, bag of SIFT and MFCCs	audio-visual	Fusion of SVMs and k-NNs with conceptual feedback	0.286
DYNI-LSIS	Multi-scale local binary pattern	visual	SVM with linear kernel	0.026

Table 3: Average Precision (AP) at k (k = 20 and 100) and R-precision (RP) on the Test Dataset

Method	APat20	RPat20	APat100	RPat100
Low-level Visual	0.317	0.253	0.244	0.188
Low-level Audio	0.403	0.323	0.353	0.318
Mid-level Audio	0.489	0.445	0.387	0.355
Multi-Modal	0.545	0.418	0.420	0.357

The evaluation results demonstrate that our method is able to suitably detect violent content such as disasters with explosions (e.g., a plane crash or a man hitting his head). On the other hand, the method wrongly classifies a video shot as violent when the shot contains disasters such as explosions (such explosions were, indeed, not annotated as "violent", since no one is injured) or exciting moments such as strong applauses. Shots which contain no excitement or action, e.g., containing normal speech or music in the background are also easily classified as non-violent. The most challenging violent shots are the ones which are "violent" according to the general definition of violence, but actually only contain actions such as self-injuries, or other moderate actions such as an actor pushing or hitting slightly another actor.

One significant point which can be inferred from the overall results is that the average precision variation of the proposed method is high for movies of varying violence levels (Table 1). Additionally, the method performs better when the violence level of a movie is higher (*Independence Day* is the one having the most violent shots in the test dataset - around 14.5% of all shots). The difference between the results obtained on *Fight Club* and *Independence Day* is most probably due to the nature of violent content present in these movies. The violent actions present in *Fight Club* are under-represented in the training dataset and, consequently, no related audio word(s) could be extracted for these actions (i.e., *Fight Club* has no proper representation in terms of audio words).

5. CONCLUSIONS AND FUTURE WORK

In this paper, we presented an approach for the detection of violent content in movies at video shot level. We showed that mid-level audio features (BoAW) provide a better performance than low-level audio and visual features. We also fused these mid-level audio cues with motion cues at the decision level for further improvement and achieved promising results in terms of average precision. Incited by the promising results obtained for this work, we currently investigate the construction of more sophisticated mid-level feature representations. Within this context, an interesting research question is whether augmenting the feature set by including mid-level motion features helps further improving classification. In addition, we plan to extend our approach to user-generated videos.

6. ACKNOWLEDGMENTS

We thank *Technicolor* (http://www.technicolor.com/) for providing the ground truth, video shot boundaries and the corresponding keyframes which have been used in this work.

7. REFERENCES

[1] MediaEval VSD task proceedings, 2012. http://ceur-ws.org/Vol-927/.

[2] VSD affect task, 2012. http://www.multimediaeval.org/mediaeval2012/.

[3] R. Akbani, S. Kwek, and N. Japkowicz. Applying support vector machines to imbalanced datasets. *ECML*, pages 39–50, 2004.

[4] S. Andrews, I. Tsochantaridis, and T. Hofmann. Support vector machines for multiple-instance learning. *Advances in neural information processing systems*, 15:561–568, 2002.

[5] B. Bushman and L. Huesmann. Short-term and long-term effects of violent media on aggression in children and adults. *Archives of Pediatrics & Adolescent Medicine*, 160(4):348, 2006.

[6] L.-H. Chen, H.-W. Hsu, L.-Y. Wang, and C.-W. Su. Horror video scene recognition via multiple-instance learning. In *ICASSP*, 2011.

[7] C. Demarty, C. Penet, G. Gravier, and M. Soleymani. The MediaEval 2012 Affect Task: Violent Scenes Detection in Hollywood Movies. In *MediaEval 2012 Workshop*, Pisa, Italy, October 4-5 2012.

[8] C.-H. Demarty, C. Penet, G. Gravier, and M. Soleymani. A benchmarking campaign for the multimodal detection of violent scenes in movies. In *ECCV*, 2012.

[9] T. Giannakopoulos, A. Makris, D. Kosmopoulos, S. Perantonis, and S. Theodoridis. Audio-visual fusion for detecting violent scenes in videos. *Artificial Intelligence: Theories, Models and Applications*, pages 91–100, 2010.

[10] Y. Gong, W. Wang, S. Jiang, Q. Huang, and W. Gao. Detecting violent scenes in movies by auditory and visual cues. *Advances in Multimedia Information Processing 2008*, pages 317–326, 2008.

[11] H. He and E. Garcia. Learning from imbalanced data. *Knowledge and Data Engineering, IEEE Transactions on*, 21(9):1263–1284, 2009.

[12] J. Lin and W. Wang. Weakly-supervised violence detection in movies with audio and video based co-training. *Advances in Multimedia Information Processing*, pages 930–935, 2009.

[13] L. Rabiner and B.-H. Juang. Fundamentals of speech recognition. *Signal Processing Series*, 1993.

[14] R. Yan and M. Naphade. Semi-supervised cross feature learning for semantic concept detection in videos. In *CVPR*, 2005.

A 3D Tele-Immersion Streaming Approach Using Skeleton-Based Prediction

Suraj Raghuraman, Karthik Venkatraman, Zhanyu Wang, Balakrishnan Prabhakaran, Xiaohu Guo
University of Texas at Dallas
{suraj, vkarthik, praba, xguo}@utdallas.edu

ABSTRACT
3D collaborative Tele-Immersive environments allow reconstruction of real world 3D scenes in the virtual world across multiple physical locations. This kind of reconstruction results in a lot of 3D data being transmitted over the internet in real time. The current systems allow for transmission at low frame rates due to the large volume of data and network bandwidth restrictions. In this paper we propose a prediction based approach that generates future frames by animating the live model based on few skeleton points. By doing so the magnitude of data transmitted is reduced to few hundred bytes. The prediction errors are corrected when an entire frame is received. This approach allows minimal amounts (few bytes) of data to be transmitted per frame, thus allowing for high frame rates and still maintain an acceptable visual quality of reconstruction at the receiver side.

Categories and Subject Descriptors
H.5.1 [**Multimedia Information Systems**]: *Artificial, augmented, and virtual realities*; I.3.5 [**Computational Geometry and Object Modeling**]: *Hierarchy and geometric transformations*

Keywords
3D reconstruction, Tele-immersion, segmentation, visualization

1. INTRODUCTION
3D Tele-Immersion (**3DTI**) allows users from remote sites to collaborate in a single virtual space using their 3D avatar. It also enables interaction with shared 3D objects in the virtual space in real time. 3DTI has potential applications in remote training, rehabilitation, entertainment [1] etc. It combines many aspects of computer vision for image acquisition, graphics for reconstruction and rendering, virtual reality for display and networking for high speed data transmission.

There are many challenges associated with providing such a system. A single frame of a person captured by a single camera has around 100,000 points of information resulting in a frame size of approximately 600 kBytes. A single site uses tens of such cameras for high visual quality. Sending such massive volumes of data across the Internet and still maintaining the quality of experience (QoE) is one of the major challenges in 3DTI systems. QoE consists of both the visual quality as well as the rendering rate, measured in frames per second (fps). These QoE requirements often involve tradeoffs, in that providing higher visual quality often results in lower fps and vice-versa. So, sending a detailed point cloud with a huge volume of data over the Internet results in excellent visual quality and accuracy, but it is also the biggest bottleneck that leads to the low frame rate, which ultimately results in an overall poor QoE.

Current methods to deal with this problem involve some form of compression of the data. Some methods use standard compression libraries directly on the color and depth data [2]. Some of the methods use a combination of standard compression libraries to compress the data before it is sent over the Internet [3]. [4] introduces a view-dependent real-time compression scheme geared towards use in mobile devices. [5] uses a reference stream to achieve inter stream compression. [6] uses a model based approach, where significant point (skeletal joints) are extracted from the point cloud frame and compression is achieved through motion estimation. All these compression schemes are able to achieve anywhere from 5-15 fps over the Internet.

Our approach uses the inherent redundancy in the data being transmitted by predicting and animating the point cloud at the receiver side based on few points of information received from human skeleton, rather than always compressing/decompressing data at the sender/receiver end. In the process we transmit only a few bytes of data every frame, which enables us to achieve good frame rates. The approach is motivated by three fundamental observations. Transmitting large amount of transient information over the Internet typically involves significant delay and jitter. However, it is possible to stream small pieces (less than 1KB) of human skeleton information at higher rate even on a slow internet connection. In computer graphics, 3D deformations are estimated by the impact of force or motion of a point corresponding to which all the other points around it get affected. By streaming only the locations of these key points and the relationships with its neighbors the entire scene can be reconstructed at the other end [7]. Also, the skeleton of any object in its most deformed state can be used to identify the points that influence the entire object [8]. By combining all these aspects in this paper a prediction based scheme is introduced that uses already transmitted point cloud as well as subsequent skeletal points to animate the point cloud at the receiver side. A small transmission of tens of points can be used to effectively predict the position of hundreds of thousands of points at the receiver side giving a frame rate equal to the rate at which data is captured.

MM '13, October 21 - 25 2013, Barcelona, Spain
Copyright 2013 ACM 978-1-4503-2404-5/13/10 $15.00.
http://dx.doi.org/10.1145/2502081.2502188

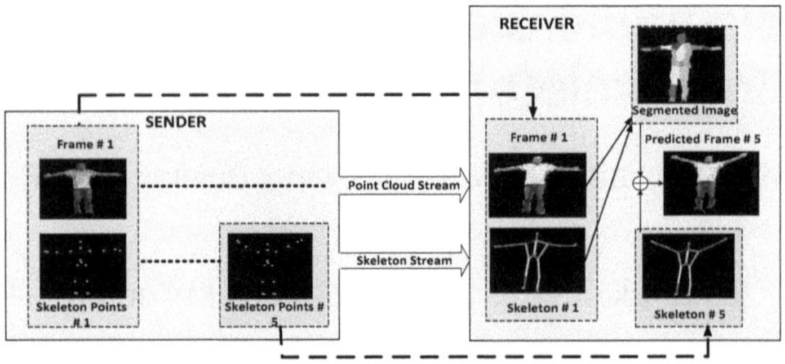

Figure 1. Overall sequence of processing for the approach (please refer to electronic version for better clarity)

Our contributions include a novel method for solving the excessive data streaming problem using a prediction based scheme. This scheme animates a live human 3D point cloud model based on human skeleton data that is streamed at higher rate (than the point cloud information). A fast segmentation and parallel prediction method is introduced to allow real time prediction of rigid body animation based on skeletal points.

2. OUR APPROACH

To achieve the reduction of the amount of data transmitted, our approach uses a multiple stage process as shown in Figure 1. In the first stage the skeletal points are identified from the point cloud at the transmitter side. These points along with the point cloud are transmitted to the receiver the first time. After this, the point clouds are sent only if the network bandwidth is sufficient to send it; otherwise the only data that is transmitted subsequently are the skeletal points. At the receiver side the point cloud is segmented based on the skeleton generated using the skeletal points. This segmentation is stored and used to predict the behavior of all the other points inside the region based on the movement of the skeletal points. Finally, transformation of the segmented region is estimated and applied in accordance with the skeletal point changes

2.1. Skeleton Identification

3DTI almost always involves transmitting the user point cloud; as a result in this paper we consider only human skeletons. So we use a human skeleton identification approach described in [9]. A computer vision based system is used to identify limbs of the person. Features are extracted from the depth image and a random decision forest algorithm is used to identify the various parts of body from these features.

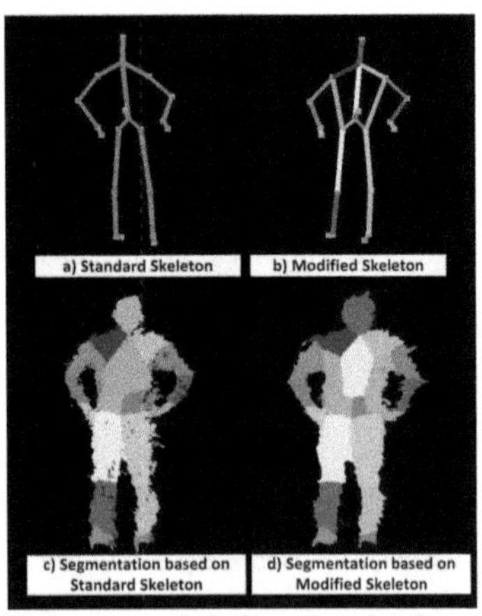

Figure 2. Skeletons and their point cloud segmentation

Once the broad level limbs have been identified a skeleton based on these limbs is fit to the overall model. The skeleton shown in Figure 2(a) is used. The estimated joint positions from this skeleton fitting are used in our approach.

The standard skeleton as shown in Figure 2(a) is sufficient for most representations of the human body, but it cannot track the rotation of the skeletal segment occurring about its axis. A few extra skeletal segments are added to allow for such motions to be tracked. Since only the point positions are transmitted, the extra information is generated at the receiver side from these points allowing for small packets. The modified skeleton uses more segments to represent the point cloud of a human as shown in Figure 2(b).

2.2. Segmentation

The entire point cloud is segmented into different Segmented Regions (SR) based on the distance between the point and the skeletal segment. Each skeletal segment has a control point $P_c = [x_c, y_c, z_c]^T$, which is typically a skeleton joint and a reference point $P_r = [x_r, y_r, z_r]^T$, which could be any point of the skeleton segment connecting two skeletal joints or any point inside the segmented region. To enable data reduction and ease of tracking, the control point of the next segment is used as the reference points where ever possible.

A Voronoi decomposition [10] based approach is used to segment the regions around the line segment (P_c, P_r) by estimating the distance between a point and the line. For a given point $P(x, y, z)$ and a line segment (P_c, P_r) the distance d is given by:

$$d = \begin{cases} ||P - P_r|| & if\ t \geq 1 \\ ||P_c - P|| & if\ t \leq 0 \\ \frac{||(P - P_c) \times (P - P_r)||}{||P_c - P_r||} & if\ 0 < t < 1 \end{cases} \quad (1)$$

$$t = \frac{(P - Pc)^T.\ (P_r - P_c)}{||P_r - c||^2}$$

Here t is the projection of point on the line segment. Using only the distance heuristic, the entire point cloud is segmented as shown in Figure 2(d). Using the skeleton with extra segments allows for better segmentation of the point cloud since the segmentation model is based on skeletal segments. It also allows us to capture deformation occurring due to rotation of points around the line as the axis, which normally cannot be captured by the line segment based representation.

2.3. Prediction

The segmented regions are treated as individual rigid bodies that can undergo transformations independent of each other. A local spherical space with the control point at origin is used to represent each point in the SR. A point in $P(x, y, z)$ is represented in the local spherical space as $P(r, \theta, \varphi)$ where

$$r = |P_c - P|$$
$$\theta = arcsin\frac{z-z_c}{r}$$
$$\varphi = arctan\frac{y-y_c}{x-x_c} \quad (2)$$

Refer Figure 3. Given a new value of control point P_{cn}, a new spherical value P_{rn} $(r, \theta_{rn}, \varphi_{rn})$ for P_r is estimated using P_{cn} as center. Since we assume a rigid body, the value of r is not going to change for any of the points. The new position of any point P in spherical space, P_n (r, θ_n, φ_n) is given by $(r, \theta + (\theta_{rn} - \theta_r), \varphi + (\varphi_{rn} - \varphi_r))$. This new point, represented in 3D space is P_n (x_n, y_n, z_n) where,

$$x_n = r\,cos\theta_n cos\varphi_n + x_{cn}$$
$$y_n = r\,cos\theta_n sin\varphi_n + y_{cn}$$
$$z_n = r\,sin\theta_n + z_{cn} \quad (3)$$

All the points in all the SRs are updated similarly using Equation 3. The prediction method relies on the relationship between the point and the control point of the segment. The transformation is applied based on the changes to the skeletal segment on which the reference point is situated. A direct mapping relationship allows for fast paralleled computations. This allows the prediction to run extremely fast on large number of points.

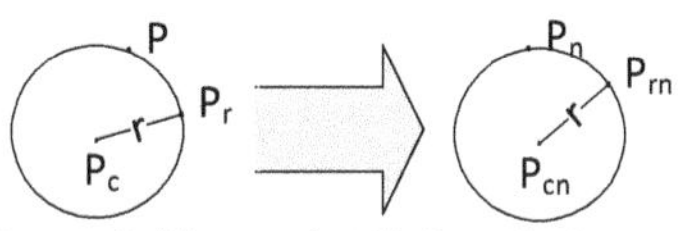

Figure 3. New point P_n in relation to P

3. IMPLEMENTATION

The architecture of the 3DTI system is as shown in Figure 4. Each site consists of a renderer, a gateway and a camera machine. For our experiments a single Kinect camera is used. The camera machine transmits the information to a central gateway. The Gateway acts as a channel between different sites and maintains the synchronization and flow of data. A modified version of the stop and wait protocol is used to transmit information across the network to the remote site. Every time a point cloud frame is sent out, the system waits for an acknowledgment (ACK) and then sends out only the most recent frame once the ACK is received. Deflate [11] is used for compressing the point cloud information and on average reduces the size of the data by 3-5 times. The skeleton points are transmitted as soon as they are generated.

The rendering machine combines the information coming in from the local sources and from remote sources through the gateway. It also performs the segmentation based on the skeleton and point cloud information it receives. The renderer maintains a skeletal buffer in order to match the point cloud with the skeleton it received in the past for proper segmentation. Every time a skeleton frame is received the renderer applies the prediction algorithm on the points associated with that skeleton based on the initial segmentation.

4. EXPERIMENTS AND RESULTS

A variety of experiments were performed to test the results of each stage and also to gauge the effectiveness of the approach in a real life situation. All the experiments used a single Kinect camera for acquisition of the point cloud data at a site. This reduced the size of the data and allowed for faster streaming rates of the acquired data over the network, facilitating better visual comparison and the same rendering view as the cameras for comparison of the results. Standard qualitative measures cannot be applied here directly since two consecutive frames from a static scene using a Kinect camera show significant differences. There is no direct one-to-one point level mapping that is possible between the frames without approximations. Consequently, comparing the predicted result for each point is also not possible. So the metric of Quality of Experience (QoE), in this case visual experience, was used to measure the performance of the approach as described in [12]. All the participants dressed normally and there were no special care taken to avoid loose clothes.

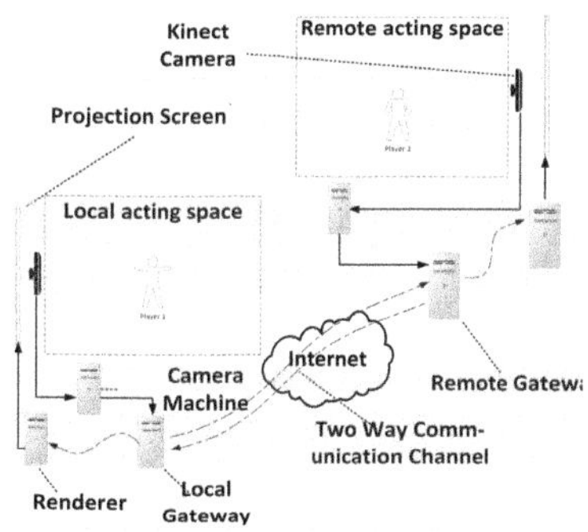

Figure 4. Architecture of the 3DTI system

To validate the **segmentation part** of the approach, poses extracted from six different actions/poses were used namely waving, punching, kicking, jumping jack, hands in pocket and folded hands. A visual validation scheme was used to gauge the correctness of the segmentation. All point cloud segment were colored as shown in Figure 2(d) and visually verified. It was noticed that the standard skeleton as shown in Figure 2(c) performed poorly in almost all the poses except when the hands were away from the body. The modified skeleton as shown in Figure 2(d) performed well in all cases except when the hands were very close to the body, especially in the case of folded hands as shown in Figure 5.

Point clouds generated at various frame rates (1 to 30fps) were used to validate the **effectiveness of the prediction** method. The same six actions were used. Numerous gaps were noticed when using the point cloud representation for rendering the data. The best way to see the effectiveness of the prediction algorithm and some shortcomings is in the demo video of the supplementary material. There is a direct correlation between the initial pose that is used to segment the points and the future predicted point clouds based on the activities performed. If the segmentation is perfect then the predicted point clouds are also very similar. If either the skeleton determination or the segmentation perform badly then the prediction results suffer too. Therefore it is important to select the right key poses that the predictions should be based on. In this paper no such determination is made and all predictions are based on the point cloud information that is made available.

A collaborative 3DTI system with two sites was setup to test the **overall effectiveness** of the solution in a real world scenario. This was measured by the visual experience of the user at the receiver end considering both the frame rates achieved and the visual quality of rendering. Both the sites used standard cable Internet with a 10 Mbps down and 1 Mbps up connection. The users at one end were asked to perform the same six actions as mentioned before. The user at the receiving end then looked at the results side by side in

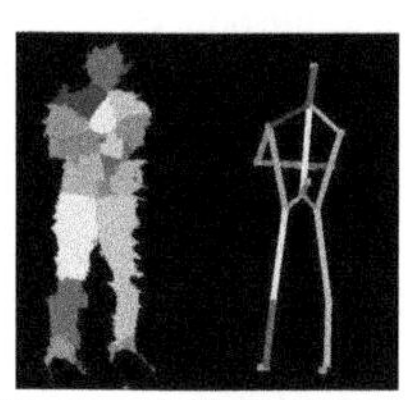

Figure 5. Point Cloud segmentation for a skeleton with folded hands

real time, one with our prediction method and the other using a standard compression method similar to [3], deciding which looked better. It was observed that in the case of visual quality the users did not prefer one method over the other. However, since the effective frame rates achieved by the prediction based method was much higher, the overall experience was far smoother and thus the users preferred this method overall. In the case of folded hands and few cases of hands in pocket activity, the visual quality of the prediction method suffered and the users preferred the overall experience of the standard method instead.

4.1. Improvement over current methods

Almost all of the related work discussed in Section 1 use a purely compression based method to reduce the amount of data to be sent over the network in order to achieve higher frame rates at the receiver end. A direct comparison with the existing methods is not possible because the data sets in use are different. However, based on the compression ratios of raw point cloud data achieved in their methods, we can estimate the effective frame rate (EFR) achieved at the receiver end using our data set. An uncompressed point cloud frame size in our data set is approximately 600 kBytes. Based on the compression ratios and the bandwidth available of ~128 kBytes per second, the table below gives the compressed frame size and an estimate of EFR at the receiver end for all the approaches.

Table 1. Comparison of effective frame rates.

Method	Compression Ratio	Compressed Frame size	EFR (fps)
[3]	5:1	~122 kBytes	~ 1-2
[5]	15:1	~ 40 kBytes	~ 3-4
[6]	50:1	~ 12 kBytes	~ 11-12
Prediction	5:1	~120 kBytes	~ 30

Even though our approach produces a compressed frame size similar to [3], we get an EFR of ~30 fps. We achieve this by affecting a render refresh with every skeletal frame received. Since the skeletal data is being received at 30 fps even with the limited bandwidth, we end up with an EFR of 30 fps at the receiver end. Visual quality remains fairly uncompromised as well according to the user studies. Together, the segmentation (< 15 millisecond) and prediction (< 3 millisecond) process do not add a significant overhead to the whole rendering process. As a result they are suitable for use in real time applications.

5. CONCLUSION AND FUTURE WORK

This paper introduces a novel method of improving the visual experience for the user of a 3DTI system by using a prediction based approach on received data by animating a live model based on variations in skeletal points being transmitted. A fast and robust method for segmentation and prediction is also introduced to allow for faster-than-real-time processing of large sets of points. It is shown that the solution works effectively in a real world physical training setup over a standard residential internet connection

Situations with occlusion need to be handled more effectively, for example, when hands are folded or in the pockets. Point clouds with potential for better segmentation need to be prioritized by reviewing the skeletal information before transmission.

6. ACKNOWLEDGEMENTS

This material is based upon work supported by the National Science Foundation under Grant No. 1012975. Any opinions, findings, and conclusions or recommendations expressed in this material are those of the author(s) and do not necessarily reflect the views of the National Science Foundation.

7. REFERENCES

[1] Z. Yang, B. Yu, W. Wu, and K. Nahrstedt, "Collaborative dancing in Tele-immersive environment," in in Proc. of ACM Multimedia (MM'06), 2006.

[2] A. Redert, M.O. de Beeck, C. Fehn, W. IJsselsteijn, M. Pollefeys, L. Van Gool, E. Ofek, I. Sexton, and P. Surman, "Advanced three-dimensional television system technologies," in 3D Data Processing Visualization and Transmission, 2002, pp. 313 – 319.

[3] Z. Yang, Y. Cui, Z. Anwar, R. Bocchino, N. Kiyanclar, K. Nahrstedt, R. H. Campbell, and W. Yurcik, "Realtime 3d video compression for tele-immersive environments," in in Proceedings of Multimedia Computing and Networking 2006, 2006.

[4] S. Shi, W. J. Jeon, K. Nahrstedt, and R. H. Campbell, "M-teeve: Real-time 3d video interaction and broadcasting framework for mobile devices," in ICST International Conference on Immersive Telecommunications (IMMERSCOM), Berkeley, CA, USA, 2009.

[5] S-U. Kum and K. Mayer-Patel, "Real-time multidepth stream compression," ACM Trans. Multimedia Comput. Commun. Appl., vol. 1, no. 2, pp. 128–150, May 2005.

[6] J-M. Lien, G. Kurillo, and R. Bajcsy, "Multi-camera tele-immersion system with real-time model driven data compression: A new model-based compression method for massive dynamic point data," Vis. Comput., vol. 26, no. 1, pp. 3–15, Nov. 2009.

[7] Z. Tang, G. Rong, X. Guo, and B. Prabhakaran, "Streaming 3D shape deformations in collaborative virtual environment," in Virtual Reality Conference (VR), 2010 IEEE, march 2010, pp. 183 –186.

[8] S. Yoshizawa, A.G. Belyaev, and H-P.Seidel, "Free-form skeleton-driven mesh deformations," in Proceedings of the eighth ACM symposium on Solid modeling and applications, New York, NY, USA, 2003, SM '03, pp. 247–253, ACM.

[9] J. Shotton, A. Fitzgibbon, M. Cook, T. Sharp, M. Finocchio, R. Moore, A. Kipman, and A. Blake, "Real-time human pose recognition in parts from single depth images," in Proceedings of the 2011 IEEE Conference on Computer Vision and Pattern Recognition, Washington, DC, USA, 2011, CVPR '11, pp. 1297–1304, IEEE Computer Society.

[10] F. Aurenhammer, "Voronoi diagrams - a survey of a fundamental geometric data structure," ACM Comput. Surv., vol. 23, no. 3, pp. 345–405, Sept. 1991.

[11] D. Salomon, Data Compression: The Complete Reference, Springer-Verlag, Berlin, Germany / Heidelberg, Germany / London, UK / etc., 2007.

[12] W. Wu, A. Arefin, G. Kurillo, P. Agarwal, K. Nahrstedt, and R. Bajcsy, "Color-plus-depth level-of-detail in 3d tele-immersive video: a psychophysical approach," in Proceedings of the 19th ACM international conference on Multimedia, New York, NY, USA, 2011, MM '11, pp. 13–22, ACM.

Fast Image/Video Collection Summarization with Local Clustering

Shuhei Tarashima, Go Irie, Ken Tsutsuguchi, Hiroyuki Arai and Yukinobu Taniguchi
NTT Corporation, Yokosuka, Kanagawa, Japan
{tarashima.shuhei,irie.go,tsutsuguchi.ken,arai.hiroyuki,taniguchi.yukinobu}@lab.ntt.co.jp

ABSTRACT

Image/video collection summarization is an emerging paradigm to provide an overview of contents stored in massive databases. Existing algorithms require at least $O(N)$ time to generate a summary, which cannot be applied to online scenarios. Assuming that contents are represented as a sparse graph, we propose a fast image/video collection summarization algorithm using local graph clustering. After a query node is specified, our algorithm first finds a small sub-graph near the query without looking at the whole graph, and then selects fewer number of nodes diverse to each other. Our algorithm thus provides a summary in nearly constant time in the number of contents. Experimental results demonstrate that our algorithm is more than 1500 times faster than a state-of-the-art method, with comparable summarization quality.

Categories and Subject Descriptors

H.3.1 [**Information Storage and Retrieval**]: Content Analysis and Indexing

Keywords

summarization, local clustering, image/video collection, graph, multimodal

1. INTRODUCTION

Overviewing a collection of images or videos is a key step to do content browsing and search, but it is becoming more and more difficult due to their explosive amount available online. Image/video collection summarization is an emerging paradigm to provide an overview of a collection stored in massive databases. Given a query, the problem is to find a subset of contents relevant to the query but as diverse as possible to each other in a constraint for resulting summary size (e.g., duration of a video summary or the number of images included in the summary).

A number of image/video collection summarization methods have been proposed in the literature. Yang et al. [13] have proposed a ranking method taking both relevance and diversity into account. Irie et al. [6] have improved Yang's approach, by optimizing the resulting summary so as to fit to small devices such as smartphones or tablets. Li et al. [9] have proposed multimodal summarization methods based on Maximal Marginal Relevance (MMR). Their methods are based on greedy optimization and extracts a set of relevant but less redundant video segments to each other. More recently, Hong et al. [4] have proposed a event-driven summarization method of video search results by mining and threading key shots in the contents.

Although the resulting summaries of these methods are sophisticated in terms of summarization quality, one crucial issue which has not been addressed before is time complexity of the algorithms, especially important against large-scale databases. Existing algorithms require at least $O(N)$ time to generate a summary. Suppose we have N images or videos in a database, time complexity of [13] [6] [4] each is $O(N^2)$ and that of [9] is $O(N)$. Although acceleration is possible by computing similarities between images/videos offline and having them in the storage, huge amount of storage size would be required because their spatial complexity is $O(N^2)$. Thus, existing methods may not be applicable to large-scale databases, especially for online scenarios.

Addressing this issue, our goal in this paper is to propose a fast image/video collection summarization algorithm. In our approach, we assume that the collection is represented by a sparse graph. After a query node is specified by a user, our algorithm first finds a small sub-graph near the query without looking at the whole graph based on a *local graph clustering* algorithm. Then our algorithm further reduces the nodes in the sub-graph by preserving the original structure of the sub-graph as much as possible, so as to satisfy the constraint of summary size. Therefore our algorithm takes nearly constant time in the number of contents N.

Each component of our algorithm is indeed not new. Our contributions in this paper are to provide a reasonable way to incorporate local graph clustering to solve collection summarization problem, and to demonstrate significant speed-up compared to existing methods (say 1500 times), with comparable summarization quality. To the best of our knowledge, this is the first work which introduces local graph clustering in multimedia summarization.

2. METHOD

We first define the problem focused on in this paper as a node selection problem over a graph. Suppose we have a collection of N images or videos, and the collection is repre-

MM'13, October 21–25, 2013, Barcelona, Spain.

http://dx.doi.org/10.1145/2502081.2502189 .

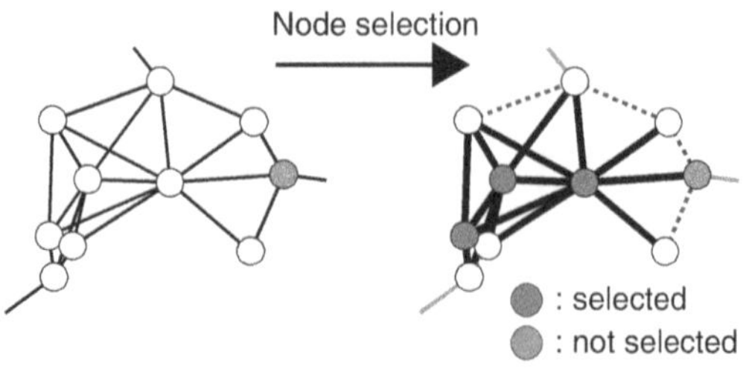

Figure 1: Node selection.

sented by an unweighted and undirected graph $G = \{E, V\}$ where each node $\{v_i \in V\}_{i=1}^{N}$ represents an element (image or video) of the collection, and each edge $\{e_{ij} \in E\}_{i=1,j=1}^{|E|}$ represents a relationship between nodes such as similarity or co-occurrence. Given a query $q \in V$ and the summary size constraint T, the task is to select a subset $\{V^* \in V \mid \text{size}(V^*) \leq T\}$ such that each node $v_i^* \in V^*$ is relevant to the query q but as diverse to each other as possible in the summary size constraint T.

To solve this problem efficiently, our assumption is that, relevant nodes to the query are also relevant to each other, hence they are densely connected by the edges in the graph. This means that relevant nodes form a cluster, i.e., nodes in the cluster are richly connected to each other but sparsely connected to the rest of them. Thus, what we have to do first is to find the cluster covering the query. Although such graph clustering problem is typically scale as $O(|E|N)$, we solve it with constant time in the size of the graph N by employing a local graph clustering algorithm. The detail is discussed in 2.1.

However, further selection is still required if the generated cluster does not satisfy a constraint of the summary size. We thus further reduce the nodes to form a summary satisfying the constraint. Our selection strategy is to preserve the structure of the cluster as much as possible. Based on the observation that edges in the cluster define the structure of the graph (cluster), we extract a subset of nodes so as to maximize the number of edges connected to the selected nodes as much as possible, as illustrated in Figure 1. We formulate this problem as maximum coverage optimization and solve it by a greedy-based algorithm. We discuss the detail in 2.2.

2.1 Cluster Generation by Local Clustering

After a query node q is specified, our algorithm finds a cluster by local graph clustering. Local clustering iteratively finds a sub-graph $G^S = \{E^S, V^S\} \in G$ until *conductance* $\Phi(V^S)$ gets smaller than c (c is manually specified) [12]. Conductance $\Phi(V^S)$ [11] is the ratio of the number of the external connections of a cluster to the number of total connections whithin the cluster, defined as follows:

$$\Phi(V^S) = \delta(V^S) / \sum_{v \in V^S} d(v) \tag{1}$$

where $d(v)$ is the degree of a node v and $\delta(V^S)$ is the number of edges leaving V^S. $\Phi(V^S)$ gets smaller if the number of edges within the cluster becomes larger or the number of edges from the cluster to the outside of the cluster becomes smaller. The key advantage of the conductance defined in

Algorithm 1 Cluster Generation by Local Clustering

input: graph $G = \{E, V\}$, query $q \in V$, $c \in [0, 1]$
output: sub-graph $G^S = \{E^S, V^S\} \in G$ with $\Phi(V^S) \leq c$.
$u \leftarrow q$, set $E^S = \emptyset$ and $V^S = q$
while $\Phi(V^S) > c$ **do**
  select v' with probability $p(v', u)$
  update $u \leftarrow v'$
  pick Z uniformly from the interval $[0, p(u, V^S)]$
  for $v \in \{v \mid e(v, V^S) \geq 1, v \in V\}$ **do**
    if $p(v, V^S) \geq Z$ **then**
      $V^S \leftarrow V^S \cup v$
      update E^S according to V^S
    end if
  end for
end while
return G^S

this way is that it can be computed without looking at the whole graph.

Local graph clustering is a framework and a series of methods to find a cluster (sub-graph) over a graph based on the conductance measure. Several variants of local clustering have been proposed so far [1, 12]. We employ EvoCut introduced by Andersen et al. [1], which is the fastest local clustering algorithm to the best of our knowledge. In EvoCut, assuming the Markov process of the sub-graph, the cluster grows by adding densely connected neighbor nodes to the cluster. Given the current subset of nodes $V' \in V$, The next subset $V'' \in V$ is defined as $V'' = \{v \mid p(v, V') \geq Z, v \in V\}$, where Z is uniformly sampled from the interval $[0, p(u, S)]$, $u \in V$ is a lazy random walk particle, and $p(v, S)$ is the transition probability from v to S defined as follows;

$$p(v, V') = \sum_{v' \in V'} p(v, v') = \frac{1}{2}\Big(\frac{e(v, V')}{d(v)} + \mathbf{1}(v \in V')\Big) \tag{2}$$

where $e(v, V')$ is the number of edges between v and V' and $\mathbf{1}(v \in V')$ is an indicator function that takes 1 if v is included in V' and otherwise 0.

The detail of the EvoCut algorithm is shown in Algorithm 1. If $\text{size}(V^S \setminus q)$, which means the summary size of V^S ignoring the query q, satisfies the summary size constraint T, $(V^S \setminus q)$ is the final summary of our algorithm. Otherwise, we proceed to the next node selection algorithm.

2.2 Node Selection by Edge Coverage Maximization

After finding the subset V^S, our algorithm further selects the fewer number of nodes from V^S to satisfy the summary size constraint T. Our strategy for node selection is to preserve the structure of the cluster as much as possible. Thus we pick up a subset of nodes, so as to be the number of edges connected to the selected nodes is maximized. To find such a subset of nodes $V^* \in V^S$, we formulate the problem as a kind of maximum coverage problem;

$$V^* = \underset{V^O \in V^S}{\arg\max} \, |\textstyle\bigcup_{v \in V^O} e(v)| \quad \text{s.t.} \quad \text{size}(V^O) \leq T \tag{3}$$

where $e(v)$ is a set of edges connected to a node v and $|\bigcup_{v \in V^O} e(v)|$ is the number of edges on V^S covered by the selected set of nodes V^O. This problem is known as Max-

Algorithm 2 Greedy Algorithm of Edge Coverage Maximization

input: cluster $G^S = \{E^S, V^S\}$,
  summary size constraint T, query $q \in V^S$
output: summary $V^* \in V^S$
1: $V^* \leftarrow \emptyset$
2: **while** size$(V^*) \leq T$ **do**
3: $\quad v_i^* \leftarrow \arg\max_{v \in V^S \setminus q} f(v), \quad f(v) = d(v)/\text{size}(v)$
4: $\quad V^* \leftarrow V^* \cup v_i^*$, delete v_i^* from V^S, update E^S
5: **end while**
6: **return** V^*

imum coverage problem with knapsack constraint (MCPK) which is NP hard. Notice that this problem is different from popular Knapsack problem, because each edge is shared by nodes at both ends. While several heuristic algorithms to solve this problem have been proposed, we employ a greedy based algorithm shown in Algorithm 2. In Algorithm 2, the node that has the highest ratio of the degree of the node to the size of the node size(v) is iteratively selected. This algorithm is guaranteed to be at least a $\frac{(e-1)}{e} \approx 0.632$-approximation to the optimum number of edges covered by the nodes in V^O [8]. Although the time complexity of this algorithm is $O(|V^S|)$, the following experiment (namely, Table 1) shows that the computation time of this algorithm is less than 10% of total computation time, which has a low impact for total computation time.

3. EXPERIMENTS

We conducted two experiments to evaluate our algorithm in terms of computation time and summary quality.

3.1 Datasets & Experiment Setup

3.1.1 Datasets

We use the following three popular image/video benchmark datasets publicly available:

- `CCV` [7]: `CCV`[1] is a video collection database containing 9317 Web videos of 20 semantic categories. Each video is represented by three feature types: 5000-dimensional SIFT bag-of-words (BoW), 5000-dimensional STIP BoW, and 4000-dimensional MFCC BoW (these features are also available at the site).

- `MIRFLICKR-25K` [5]: `MIRFLICKR-25K`[2] is an image collection database containing 25000 Flickr images of 23 image categories. We use 1000-dimensional SIFT BoW and 512-dimensional GIST to represent each image, both are publicly available[3].

- `NUS-WIDE` [2]: `NUS-WIDE`[4] is also an image collection database containing 269648 Flickr images of 81 concepts. We use 500-dimensional SIFT BoW available at the site.

[1] `http://www.ee.columbia.edu/ln/dvmm/CCV/`
[2] `http://press.liacs.nl/mirflickr/`
[3] `http://lear.inrialpes.fr/people/guillaumin/data.php`
[4] `http://lms.comp.nus.edu.sg/research/NUS-WIDE.htm`

Table 1: Computation time (msec) for generating a summary. In this case, the summary size constraints in each dataset are within 1000 second on `CCV`, 50 images on `MIRFLICKR-25K` and `NUS-WIDE`. Gain is defined as the ratio of the time cost of MMR to the total time cost of Proposed.

	Proposed		MMR	Gain
	EvoCut	MCPK		
`CCV`	0.89	0.09	1.65×10^3	1684
`MIRFLICKR-25K`	4.46	0.32	2.83×10^3	592
`NUS-WIDE`	5.07	0.35	3.59×10^3	662

All the three datasets above are multi-label datasets, i.e., each image can be assigned to multiple categories. To facilitate the evaluations, we removed images and videos that do not have any category, resulting that 6572 videos in `CCV` (about 150 hours), 24479 images in `MIRFLICKR-25K` and 209347 images in `NUS-WIDE` are used in our experiment. size(V^*) is defined as the total duration of the videos in the summary V^* for `CCV` and the total number of images in V^* for `MIRFLICKR-25K` and `NUS-WIDE`.

3.1.2 Graph Construction

To run our algorithm, we construct a graph for each dataset. We follow the standard way to construct a k-NN graph for each feature type (such as SIFT BoW, STIP BoW or MFCC BoW in `CCV` dataset), which is successfully applied to many multimedia applications such as [10]. We then fuse the resulting k-NN graphs to construct a multigraph which allows each node to have multiple edges. For simplicity, we use cosine similarity for k-NN graph construction and fix $k = 20$ for all the experiments.

Note that the time complexity of k-NN graph construction is generally $O(N^2)$. However, a number of sub-linear time algorithms have been proposed in the literature (e.g., [3]), which are indeed applicable to our case. Furthermore, graph construction can be performed offline in many real-world scenarios and is readily parallelized by using multiple CPUs.

3.1.3 Compared Method

We compare our algorithm to a recently proposed collection summarization method based on MMR principle [9]. We choose this method because this is based on greedy-based algorithm and is fast compared to the other existing collection summarization methods (provides $O(N)$ summary generation time, see Section 1). Specifically, MMR constructs a summary V^* by the following greedy-search iteration:

$$V_{t+1}^* = V_t^* \cup \arg\max_{v_i \in V \setminus V_t^*} \Big(\sum_m^M \lambda_m \text{sim}(v_i, q) - (1 - \lambda_m) \max_{v_j \in V_t} \text{sim}(v_i, v_j) \Big) \quad (4)$$

where M is the number of feature types and λ_m is the parameter between query relevance and information novelty. sim(v_i, v_j) represents cosine similarity between v_i and v_j. The first term sim(v_i, q) aims to measure the relevance level of a node v_i to the query q, and the second term sim(v_i, v_j) measures similarity between nodes in the candidate subset. In the following evaluation, we fix $\lambda_m = 0.5$ empirically. For

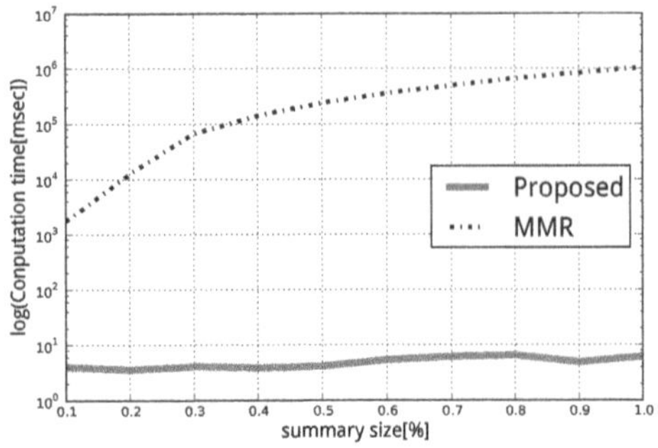

Figure 2: Computation time of each summary size

fair comparison, we compute the similarities between all the nodes offline in our experiments.

3.2 Computation Time Evaluation

Actual computation time to generate a summary is measured and shown in Table 1. The constraints of summary size T are set as $T = 1000$ (sec) on `CCV`, $T = 50$ (images) on `MIRFLICKR-25K` and `NUS-WIDE`. We set parameter $c = 0.7$ in our algorithm. Both methods are implemented on C++ compiled by GCC 4.7.2 with -O3 optimization and are run on a desktop computer with 3.7GHz CPU and 32GB RAM.

From the results, our algorithm is at most 1500 times faster than MMR-based summarization, and takes only 5.42 msec to generate a summary even on `NUS-WIDE` dataset. Moreover, the results on `MIRFLICKR-25K` (25K) and `NUS-WIDE` (210K) are almost the same. This suggests that our algorithm is quite scalable to the number of contents N, which is a strong advantage of our algorithm especially when it is applied to large-scale databases or used in online scenarios.

Figure 2 shows the computation time of different summary size (from 0.1% to 1.0%) on `MIRFLICKR-25K` dataset. Even when a summary size constraint get larger, the computation time of our algorithm is not so affected, while the MMR-based summarization gets longer computation time. This suggests that our algorithm is scalable not only to the number of contents, but also to a summary size.

3.3 Summary Quality Evaluation

We next evaluate the quality of summaries generated by each method. All the three datasets used in our experiments have manually annotated category labels, we therefore use these labels to evaluate relevance and diversity of the summaries. We judge a node in the final summary relevant if and only if the node and the query share at least one common class label. Relevance of a summary is defined as the ratio of the number of relevant nodes to the number of nodes in the summary. For diversity, we judge a node is diverse if it does NOT have completely the same labels with the query. Diversity of a summary is defined as the ratio of the number of diverse nodes to the number of nodes in the summary.

The results are shown in Figure 3. Both results suggest that the relevance and the diversity quality of the summaries generated by our algorithm are comparable to MMR.

From the results of these experiments above, our algorithm provides a summary of comparable summary quality to the state-of-the-art MMR-based method, even in significantly faster time.

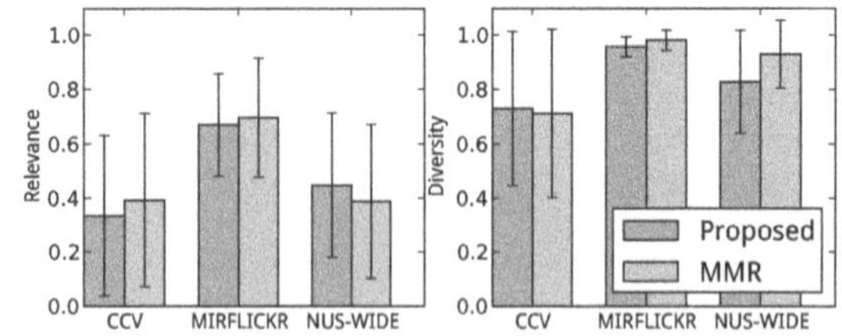

Figure 3: Relevance and divergence comparison. These results are obtained from the same constraints with Table 1.

4. CONCLUSIONS

We proposed a fast image/video collection summarization algorithm using local graph clustering. After the query node is specified, our algorithm has generated a summary without looking at the whole graph, which results in providing constant time summary generation both in graph size and summary size. Experimental results on three different image/video collection datasets demonstrated that our method was more than 1500 times faster than a state-of-the-art method, with comparable summary quality.

We have a plan to improve our algorithm by exploring more reasonable approaches for graph construction. Future direction includes the performance evaluation on larger databases like million-scale. Comparison to other state-of-the-art methods is also in our focus.

5. REFERENCES

[1] R. Andersen and Y. Peres. *Finding Sparse Cuts Locally Using Evolving Sets.* In *STOC*, pages 235–244, 2009.

[2] T.-S. Chua, J. Tang, R. Hong, H. Li, Z. Luo, and Y. Zheng. *NUS-WIDE: A Real-World Web Image Database from National University of Singapore.* In *CIVR*, Article No.48, 2009.

[3] W. Dong, M. Charikar, and K. Li. *Efficient K-Nearest Neighbor Graph Construction for Generic Similarity Measures.* In *WWW*, pages 577–586, 2011.

[4] R. Hong, J. Tang, H.-K. Tan, C.-W. Ngo, S. Yan, and T.-S. Chua. *Beyond Search: Event-Driven Summarization for Web Videos. TOMCCAP*, 7(4), 2011.

[5] M. J. Huiskes and M. S. Lew. *The MIR Flickr Retrieval Evaluation.* In *MIR*, pages 39–43, 2008.

[6] G. Irie, T. Satou, A. Kojima, T. Yamasaki, and K. Aizawa. *Image Collection Summarization for Search Result Overviewing on Mobile Devices.* In *IMMPD*, pages 21–26, 2011.

[7] Y. G. Jiang, G. Ye, S. F. Chang, D. Ellis, and A. C. Loui. *Consumer Video Understanding: A Benchmark Database and An Evaluation of Human and Machine Performance.* In *ICMR*, Article No.29, 2011.

[8] S. Khuller, A. Moss, and J. Noar. *The Budgeted Maximum Coverage Problem. Information Processing Letters*, 70(10):39–45, 1999.

[9] Y. Li and B. Merialdo. *Multi-Video Summarization Based on AV-MMR.* In *CBMI*, pages 1–6, 2010.

[10] D. Liu, G. Ye, C.-T. Chen, S. Yan, and S.-F. Chang. *Hybrid Social Media Network.* In *ACMMM*, 2012.

[11] S. Schaeffer. *Graph Clustering. Computer Science Review*, 1(1):27–64, 2007.

[12] D. A. Spielman and S.-H. Teng. *A Local Clustering Algorithm for Massive Graphs and its Application to Nearly-Linear Time Graph Partitioning.* In *CoRR*, *abs/0809.3232*, 2008.

[13] K. Yang, M. Wang, X.-S. Hua, and H.-J. Zhang. *Social Image Search with Diverse Relevance Ranking.* In *MMM*, pages 174–184, 2010.

Spot the Differences: From a Photograph Burst to the Single Best Picture

H. Emrah Tasli Jan C. van Gemert Theo Gevers

ISLA, Informatics Institute
University of Amsterdam

ABSTRACT

With the rise of the digital camera, people nowadays typically take several near-identical photos of the same scene to maximize the chances of a good shot. This paper proposes a user-friendly tool for exploring a personal photo gallery for selecting or even creating the best shot of a scene between its multiple alternatives. This functionality is realized through a graphical user interface where the best viewpoint can be selected from a generated panorama of the scene. Once the viewpoint is selected, the user is able to go explore possible alternatives coming from the other images. Using this tool, one can explore a photo gallery efficiently. Moreover, additional compositions from other images are also possible. With such additional compositions, one can go from a burst of photographs to the single best one. Even funny compositions of images, where you can duplicate a person in the same image, are possible with our proposed tool.

Categories and Subject Descriptors

H.4 [**Information Systems Applications**]: Miscellaneous; H.1.2 [**User/Machine Systems**]: Human factors, Human information processing; I.2.10 [**Vision and Scene Understanding**]: Image Analysis

Keywords

Organizing Personal Photo Albums

1. INTRODUCTION

The wide availability of digital cameras and the abundance of storage space has altered the way that photos are taken since the analog days. In the pre-digital era, a photo was preferably taken only once to reduce film development costs. This stands in contrast to modern days, where one photo of a scene is never enough. To not miss the possibility of a better shot, nowadays people take several, near-identical, photos of the same scene.

ACM Multimedia October 21 - 25 2013 Barcelona, Spain

http://dx.doi.org/10.1145/2502081.2502190.

These near-identical photos represent the same semantic event or scene and thus the final choice typically remains a single image. The single best image could be the one where everybody has their eyes open, has the best composition, or where there is less unwanted artifact such as motion blur or over-exposure. Several of these traits can be analyzed quickly on the camera itself, however the final selection process is often done at home, at a larger screen to appreciate small detailed aesthetic differences that can make or break a photograph.

Selecting the best image from multiple near-identical photographs is now typically done manually, by comparing all image pairs. Hence, after a quick scan to remove the obvious lesser quality images, a naive approach may require $N(N+1)/2$ operations to look at all image pairs, comparing minute differences to evaluate photo composition and image quality.

In this paper we present a system that helps the user in the photo selection process. We have two contributions. First, we help the user select the single best image by first aligning all images and visualizing the differences. Second, we allow the user to *create* completely new images by moving difference-regions from one photograph to another.

2. RELATED WORK

A related study in [4] proposes that people would like to make more than one photo of the same scene and hence, albums contain a considerable amount of near duplicate images. They propose to detect those near duplicates automatically. The study in [5] focuses on the activities of people with photos. They investigate the patterns of how people browse and search between photos. Another work on photo grouping [15] proposes a home photo management tool. An interface is also provided for easy browsing and searching. Another study [13] automatically groups photos from a single event into smaller selection of photos. The work in [14] focuses on a different aspect in organizing photos. They investigates the problem of matching images with different viewpoint, light and scale properties. The related work regarding selection of photos from a photo gallery mainly focuses on detecting similar or duplicate photos. In our proposed method, we also incorporate such a functionality but further extend it by providing an interface to actually create new compositions from the available images.

In order to merge different images, complete or remove some parts in a seamless fashion, we use the Poisson Image Editing Method [12]. This method requires a manually created foreground mask to merge the source and target image.

Other work addresses scene completion by using other images in an automatic manner [3]. The authors use manual selection of an image patch for automatic completion from a dataset of internet images. Training-set free inpainting methods focus on removing object patches; however they fill the removed region using the local information from the image itself [6, 17].

For the image alignment step we have used an affine transformation estimation between the images. This is a weak geometry transformation where plane models are well-preserved for viewpoint changes. For aligning images for harder constraints, we could also used more advanced methods as in [8, 9]. However computational complexity and performance of these methods makes them impractical in a responsive user interface.

3. PHOTO SELECTION

In order to create a interactive framework for selecting and/or creating a best composition of multiple shots of a scene, we developed a graphical user interface. In the design of the graphical interface, the main intention was to keep the interaction easy and intuitive.

In our photo selection tool, users start by selecting multiple photos of the same scene. Alternatively, the image folder can be input; and our system selects and groups the photos from the same scene. This is basically performed with a three channel color histogram comparison between the images in the folder and grouped by a similarity metric using a predefined threshold. In the image selection step, we have included an automatic image quality rating module. This module is useful for discarding the photos that are blurry or out of focus [7, 11]. One can also extend this functionality with more detailed aesthetic measures [1, 18]. However, some people might prefer to keep these shots on purpose. For such cases, image quality rating functionality can be manually deactivated.

3.1 Image Alignment

Once the images of the same scene are selected, they are aligned using an affine transformation between the images. To align two images, we have used the standard procedure as follows. 1) SIFT keypoints in the images [10] are found. 2) SIFT descriptor for each detected keypoint is computed. 3) The keypoints between two images are matched. 4) The affine transformation model is estimated using the standard RANSAC [2] procedure. The VLFeat implementation has been widely used in this part of the work [19].

3.2 Canvas Mode

When the images are aligned, images are shown in the "canvas" mode where one can see the panorama of different perspectives of individual shots from the same scene. This panorama is similar to a stitched image mosaic, with all original images visible. See Figure 1 for the canvas mode view. We believe that, this type of visualization is native when we want to select between multiple photos. We first go through the images and try to mark the individual differences; and select the one that best covers the salient regions in the scene (Buildings, statues, stationary or moving objects/people of interest).

Figure 1: Canvas visualization mode

Figure 2: Selecting between views using the slider.

3.3 Reference Viewpoint Selection

In the "canvas" visualization mode, user can interact with the GUI using a vertical sliding bar to switch between alternative viewpoints. At this point one can still observe which part of the whole canvas the selected single view corresponds to. Figure 2 shows the individual viewpoint selection for a three image setup. When one of the views is selected, others are visualized with a lower (60%) transparency value.

3.4 Spotting the Differences

The selection of the viewpoint defines the reference view; as seen in Figure 3(a). All the other views are aligned with respect to the reference view as in Figure 3(b). At this point, the differences between reference view and all the other images are computed. This step is performed by a window based histogram intersection. It satisfies the goal of detecting dissimilarity regions (blobs) between the reference and corresponding images. The dissimilarity is computed pixelwise,

$$D_{r,q}(p) = \sum_{q=1:N} min(h_i(p_r^W), h_i(p_q^W)), \quad (1)$$

where $D_{r,q}(p)$ corresponds to the dissimilarity of a pixel p between the reference r and other image q. $h_i(r)$ is the ith bin in an N bin histogram for a selected window size of W.

(a) Reference image (b) Image #2 aligned (c) Pixel dissimilarity (d) Detected blob (e) Merged output

Figure 3: The reference image (a) is selected in the "canvas" mode, other views are aligned with respect to the reference. Only one of the other views is shown here on (b). Estimated dissimilarity cost between reference (a) and source (b) is used to detect blobs. Detected blob is shown in a rectangle for user selection in (a). As an algorithmic output detected blob is visualized in (d) in red color. Blob shown in (d) is taken out from the source image(b) and painted on top of the reference image (a). The final output is shown on (e). Notice the missing flag on the boat at the bottom of the photo

The histogram intersection cost is computed for each pixel in the image.

The estimated pixel level dissimilarity (Figure 3(c)) is used to detect the regions where possible interesting differences between the aligned images are present. A multi-level thresholding on the dissimilarity image defines different blobs with varying sizes. The blobs that are defined in the highest threshold are selected as candidate regions and the final assignment is done using a watershed segmentation starting from these candidate region seeds. The detected blob is shown on the image in the red channel in Figure 3(d). Users can click inside this region to change between alternative paintings.

3.5 Painting the Photo

The detected dissimilarity blob on the image is used to modify the selected view with the detected region from the alternative view. When the blob is selected with the mouse, the corresponding patch from the alternative view is merged on the reference view. For a seamless modification on the reference image, the Poisson Image Editing tool [12] is used. The detected blob from the source image is painted on the target image. The resulting image is shown in Figure 3(e).

4. RESULTS

Our proposed tool offers user friendly interaction for selecting or creating images from a photo album. Visual results and ease of interaction supports this argument.

A careful look at the reference and painted images in Figure 3(a) and Figure 3(e), one can observe that the waves of the boat in the water are still present in the final painted image. This is a logical anomaly; however, not a visual show-stopper for such an application. Moreover, one can observe the disappearance of the flag of the bigger boat at the bottom of the final painted image. These artifacts are mostly due on the blob region segmentation and could be fixed with further user interaction [16].

As a proof of concept, Figure 4 shows possible modifications and capabilities of the proposed tool. Figure 4(a) shows the reference image selected in the canvas mode. Possible changes on top of the reference images are shown in Figure 4(b)-4(e). One can remove the foreground object like in Figure 4(b) as soon as the background is available in the other images. One can also add additional objects Figure 4(c) and Figure 4(d) (same in this case) from the other images.

Additional visual results are provided in a supplementary video. The graphical user interface, canvas mode, image selection using the slider, blob detection and image matting results can be seen in this video.

We have made a limited evaluation of our tool in terms of usability and output performance. More detailed analysis with regards to an evaluation metric might propose extensions for our future directions.

A main weakness of the proposed method is that possible misalignment of the images might cause erroneous blob regions. Such cases produce dissimilar area candidates; however this would cause no harm since user is supposed to select between dissimilar areas. In order to overcome such cases, we have tried more powerful image matching tools like [9] and [8]. However, these methods have been discarded due to performance issues. [9] can create major artifacts in aligned images and [8] requires very long (20 minutes for a 1200x900 resolution image) computation times; measured with a powerful Intel Xeon 3.4 GHz processor. Therefore the affine model is utilized for matching images in our photo gallery.

5. CONCLUSION

Our proposed method supplies an easy interface for detecting the differences in multiple images of the same scene. In contrast to previous methods, this tool enables not only the best image selection but also a composition of a new image using patches from different photos. With the canvas view module, an efficient viewpoint selection is followed by the dissimilar region identification. With the proposed composition capability, one can process commonly used bursts of photographs to create a single best image.

(a) Reference image

(b) Foreground removal

(c) Image duplication

(d) Image duplication

(e) Even more

Figure 4: (a) Reference image selected in the "canvas" mode (b) Foreground object can be removed from the image. (c)-(e) One can also add multiple objects from other images

6. REFERENCES

[1] R. Datta, D. Joshi, J. Li, and J. Z. Wang. Studying aesthetics in photographic images using a computational approach. In *ECCV*, 2006.

[2] M. A. Fischler and R. C. Bolles. Random sample consensus: a paradigm for model fitting with applications to image analysis and automated cartography. *Commun. ACM*, 1981.

[3] J. Hays and A. A. Efros. Scene completion using millions of photographs. *ACM Trans. Graph.*

[4] A. Jaimes, S. Chang, and A. C. Loui. Detection of non identical duplicate consumer photographs. In *Information Communications Signal Processing*, 2003.

[5] D. Kirk, A. Sellen, C. Rother, and K. Wood. Understanding photowork. In *SIGCHI conference on Human Factors in computing systems*, 2006.

[6] N. Komodakis and G. Tziritas. Image completion using efficient belief propagation via priority scheduling and dynamic pruning. *Transactions on Image Processing*, 2007.

[7] A. Levin. Blind motion deblurring using image statistics. In *NIPS*, 2006.

[8] W.-Y. Lin, L. Liu, Y. Matsushita, K.-L. Low, and S. Liu. Aligning images in the wild. In *Computer Vision and Pattern Recognition*, 2012.

[9] C. Liu, J. Yuen, A. Torralba, J. Sivic, and W. T. Freeman. Sift flow: Dense correspondence across different scenes. In *European Conference on Computer Vision, 2008.*

[10] D. Lowe. Object recognition from local scale-invariant features. *International Conference on Computer Vision*, 1999.

[11] Y. Luo and X. Tang. Photo and video quality evaluation: Focusing on the subject. In *ECCV*, 2008.

[12] P. Pérez, M. Gangnet, and A. Blake. Poisson image editing. In *ACM SIGGRAPH 2003 Papers*, 2003.

[13] K. Rodden. How do people organise their photographs. In *Proceedings of the BCS IRSG Colloquium*, 1999.

[14] F. Schaffalitzky and A. Zisserman. Multi-view matching for unordered image sets, or Şhow do i organize my holiday snaps?Ť. *ECCV*, 2002.

[15] Y. Sun, H. Zhang, L. Zhang, and M. Li. Myphotos: a system for home photo management and processing. In *Proceedings of the tenth ACM international conference on Multimedia*. ACM, 2002.

[16] H. E. Tasli and A. A. Alatan. Interactive object segmentation for mono and stereo applications : Geodesic prior induced graph cut energy minimization. *ICCV Workshop on Human Interaction on Computer Vision*, 2011.

[17] C. E. Toyama, A. Criminisi, P. Pérez, and K. Toyama. Object removal by exemplar-based inpainting. In *Computer Vision and Pattern Recognition*, 2003.

[18] J. C. van Gemert. Exploiting photographic style for category-level image classification by generalizing the spatial pyramid. In *International Conference on Multimedia Retrieval*, 2011.

[19] A. Vevaldi and B. Fulkerson. Vlfeat an open and portable library of computer vision algorithms. In *Proceedings of ACM International Conference on Multimedia*, 2010.

Semantic Pooling for Complex Event Detection

Qian Yu, Jingen Liu, Hui Cheng, Ajay Divakaran, Harpreet Sawhney
SRI International
201 Washington Rd, Princeton, NJ, 08648,USA
qian.yu@sri.com, jingen.liu@sri.com, hui.cheng@sri.com

ABSTRACT

Complex event detection is very challenging in open source such as You-Tube videos, which usually comprise very diverse visual contents involving various object, scene and action concepts. Not all of them, however, are relevant to the event. In other words, a video may contain a lot of "junk" information which is harmful for recognition. Hence, we propose a semantic pooling approach to tackle this issue. Unlike the conventional pooling over the entire video or specific spatial regions of a video, we employ a discriminative approach to acquire abstract semantic "regions" for pooling. For this purpose, we first associate low-level visual words with semantic concepts via their co-occurrence relationship. We then pool the low-level features separately according to their semantic information. The proposed semantic pooling strategy also provides a new mechanism for incorporating semantic concepts for low-level feature based event recognition. We evaluate our approach on TRECVID MED [1] dataset and the results show that semantic pooling consistently improves the performance compared with conventional pooling strategies.

Categories and Subject Descriptors

I.2.10 [**Artificial Intelligence**]: Vision and Scene Under standing Video analysis

General Terms

Algorithms

Keywords

Multimedia Event Representation, Complex Event Detection, Semantic Pooling

Figure 1: Semantic Pooling for Complex Event Detection. (a) shows a time-line of a video that contains "attempting a board trick" event. (b) shows a time-line of a video that contains "feeding an animal" event. In both examples, the important evidences are shown in red bounding boxes and the supporting evidences are shown in greed bounding boxes. As we can see, both important and supporting evidences are very sparse compared with other irrelevant content in the video. The important information will be buried in junk in averaging pooling. Also, some semantic concepts, such as "animal approach" may be irrelevant to on event (attempting a board trick) but can be very important to another event (feeding an animal).

1. INTRODUCTION

Detecting complex events from open source videos is receiving increasing attention from both multimedia and computer vision communities [10, 9, 2]. It is a quite challenging problem due to not only the unconstrained video capture process which results in all kinds of video quality issues such as occlusions, background clutter, camera motion, large view variations, and so on, but also the diversity and ambiguity of the visual contents of an event video. One event may consist of a variety of scene, object and action concepts. For example, event "Wedding Ceremony" consists of various concepts including actions such as "hugging" and "kissing", scenes such as "church" and "garden", and objects such as "cake" and "ring". These concepts, however, are not equally important for distinguishing one event from the other. When watching the open source videos of an event, we may notice that some concepts showing in a video might be totally irrelevant to this event, or even bring more ambiguities and noises for the detection. For example, Figure 1 (b) show the time-line of a video that contains an event "feeding an animal". However, the majority of the video is just irrelevant content while the important evidence (shown in red bounding box) and the supporting evidence (shown in greed bounding box) are scattered in the entire video, overall only a small portion of the entire video. Hence, in this work we aim at pooling according to the semantic relevance of the low-level words.

One recent popular strategy for visual recognition can be summarized by a standard processing pipeline as, (1) local feature extraction, (2) feature coding, (3) feature pooling, and (4) classification. Some commonly used local features include spatial interest points such as SIFT [8] and spatial-temporal interest points, such

MM'13, October 21–25, 2013, Barcelona, Spain.

http://dx.doi.org/10.1145/2502081.2502191.

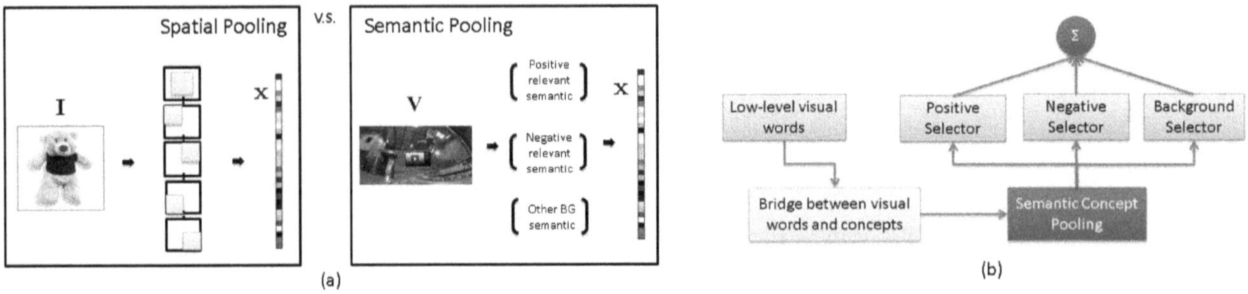

Figure 2: Analog between spatial pooling in image domain and semantic pooling in video domain. Due to various motions, spatial pooling is not appropriate for video event recognition. Instead, semantic pooling discovers abstract semantic regions (i.e., group of concepts) for pooling. (b)Overall framework of our approach

as STIP [5], and Dense Trajectory feature [12]. Feature coding approaches include vector quantization [6], LLC[13], and Fisher Vector [11]. Local feature extraction and feature coding techniques have been extensively studied in image recognition domain, and directly applicable to videos. Average pooling and max pooling are commonly used pooling strategies that have been directly applied to video content analysis. Another more effective strategy of pooling in image domain is to aggregate features in a spatial local region, such as spatial pyramid pooling and its variance. It usually cannot be not directly applicable to videos due to the variety of motion in videos. Figure 2 (a) shows an analog of spatial pooling and semantic pooling. All of these pooling technologies, however, solely focus on low-level features rather than semantic level. Hence, they are not able to tackle the aforementioned irrelevant concepts in an event video, as shown in Figure 1. More recently, [2] used unsupervised clustering of GIST features to guide feature (SIFT, colorHist, *etc.*) pooling at the image level. However, the unsupervised GIST clustering barely provides any semantic information.

Our approach is inspired by our observations and some common sense over the event videos. As shown in Figure 1(a) (b), if we could obtain some semantic information in the video, we can select a more meaningful spatial-temporal region to pool the local features than pooling over the entire video. Although it is difficult for the state-of-art approaches to reliably acquire perfect and detailed semantic information, coarse level semantic information is to some extent available with reasonable accuracy [14], such as person, animal and many action concepts. Rather than pooling local features over a spatial region (e.g., spatial pyramid), we have the pooling over *abstract* semantic "regions" including Positive Relevant Concepts, Negative Relevant Concepts, and Background Concepts. We first obtain semantic "regions" by a discriminative approach and then establish association between low-level visual words and concepts for the pooling purpose. The overall framework of this approach is shown in Figure 2 (b).

Our work is related to some resent works on concept based event representation for event recognition. Semantic concepts are introduced to bridge the semantic gap between high-level events and low-level visual feature. Fusing through early fusion and/or late fusion of low-level features and semantic features improve the overall performance on a smaller scale of evaluation such as MED10 [4]. However, on a bigger scale of evaluation such as MED11/12, the fusion of semantic and low-level feature can still give worse results [3]. It is still an open problem of how to fuse semantic information with low-level representation. Our work can also be regarded as the fusion of high-level information with low-level representation at the pooling stage.

The rest of this paper is organized as follows. In Section 2, we propose discriminative semantic relevance and present a way of bridging visual words and semantic concepts that is used in the semantic pooling. In Section 3, we show comparison between averaging pooling and semantic pooling followed by Section 4 where we summarize our approach and discuss future work.

2. SEMANTIC POOLING IN EVENT REPRESENTATION

2.1 Discriminative Semantic Relevance

In complex event detection, people recently propose to use semantic representation to account for the large variations in low-level features, and thus allow events to be expressed directly in terms of concepts, rather than low level features. Here, we also adopt representation of semantic concepts. But our goal is to figure out the relevance of such concepts to the complex event. For example, for an event "attempting board tricks", some concepts such as "person jumping", "spinning a board" and "person sliding a board" may be more relevant than others because they are positively correlated with the target event. People, however, often ignore the negatively correlated concepts, *i.e.* some concepts are more likely to occur with the negative videos. In fact, the negatively correlated concepts are also important in terms of discriminative power.

We use a data-driven approach to measure the discriminative relevance of semantic concepts to a complex event. First, we adopt "Bag of Concepts"(BoC) [7] by collecting the concept detection results from 185 discriminative concept detectors. The BoC feature measures the frequency of occurrence of each concept over the whole video clip. Then, based on the BoC event representation, we adopt the Support Vector Machines (SVMs) with Intersection Kernel to train event classifiers.

Given the BoC feature vector $\mathbf{x} \in R^n$, where n is the number of concepts, the SVM decision function $h(\mathbf{x})$ can be represented as follows.

$$h(\mathbf{x}) = \sum_{i=1}^{m} a_i K(\mathbf{x}, \mathbf{x}_i) \quad (1)$$

where $\mathbf{x}_i$ is one of m support vector, ie. $l = i, ..., m$, $K(\mathbf{x}, \mathbf{x}_i)$ is the kernel value between $\mathbf{x}$ and $\mathbf{x}_i$. a_i is the signed weight of $\mathbf{x}_l$. The intersection kernel function has the following form,

$$K(\mathbf{x}, \mathbf{x}_i) = \sum_{j=1}^{n} \min(\mathbf{x}^j, \mathbf{x}_i^j) \quad (2)$$

$\mathbf{x}^j$, $\mathbf{x}_i^j$ are the jth feature value of $\mathbf{x}$ and $\mathbf{x}_i$. Thus, the decision function can be rewritten as follows.

$$h(\mathbf{x}) = \sum_{j=1}^{n} \sum_{i=1}^{m} a_i \min(\mathbf{x}^j, \mathbf{x}_i^j) \quad (3)$$

Suppose $h_j(\mathbf{x}) = \sum_{i=1}^{m} a_i f(\mathbf{x}, \mathbf{x}_i^j)$ we can decompose the decision value of $h(\mathbf{x})$ as

$$h(\mathbf{x}) = \sum_{j=1}^{n} h_j(\mathbf{x}) \tag{4}$$

Now we decompose the global classifier Eq.1 in terms of contribution of each concept. Here $h_j(\mathbf{x})$ indeed tells how much jth concept contributes towards the final decision value. By sorting $h_j(\mathbf{x})$, we are able to list evidences according their relevance. For a positive sample, a bigger $h_j(\mathbf{x})$ indicates the concept is more positively correlated. For a negative sample, a smaller (more negative) $h_j(\mathbf{x})$ indicates the concept is more negatively important, *i.e.* more helpful in contributing to the negative decision.

2.2 Bridge Visual Words and Concepts

Now we are able to tell the discriminative semantic relevance of concepts according to $h_j(\mathbf{x})$ from a single video $\mathbf{x}$. By collecting this information over all positive samples and all negative samples in a validation dataset, we can have *weighted selectors* for positively correlated concepts and negatively contributed concepts. For positive one, we select the top 10 (~5% of 185) positively correlated concepts and build a histogram (the top histogram in Figure 3) while we select the top 10 negatively correlated concepts to build another histogram (the bottom histogram in Figure 3). Figure 3 shows some concepts (peaks in blue) appear very often in the top 10 positively contributed concepts and some concepts (peaks in red) appear very often in the top 10 negatively contributed concepts. Now, we can use these two histograms as our data-driven measurement of semantic relevance for most positively correlated concepts and the most negatively correlated concepts. These two histograms serve as two weighted selectors $\mathbf{S}^+$ and $\mathbf{S}^-$ that select the positive relevant information and negative relevant information. We also use a uniform histogram (but removes the peaks in $\mathbf{S}^+$ and $\mathbf{S}^-$) to represent the background concept selector $\mathbf{S}^0$.

In order to pool low-level features according to their semantic meaning, we need to establish the relationship between visual word and semantic concepts. Suppose we have n semantic concepts and m low-level visual words, as the semantic concepts are annotated as temporal windows within videos, we can establish a $n \times m$ matric $\mathbf{P}$ to capture the co-occurrence between the visual words and concepts. $\mathbf{P}_{ij}$ is the number ith low-level word that occurs in all temporal windows that are annotated as the jth concepts. Then, we normalize the sum of each column of $\mathbf{P}$ to be one. Thus, the jth column of $\mathbf{P}$ is the occurrence distribution of low-level words given jth concept. The $m \times n$ matrix $\mathbf{P}$ captures the conditional probability of the visual words and semantic concepts as follows.

$$p(w_i|c_j) = \frac{\text{Co-occurrence of } i\text{th visual words and } j \text{ concept}}{\text{Total visual words in } j\text{th concept}} \tag{5}$$

2.3 Semantic Pooling

Instead of pooling all low-level features into a single representation and mixing positive and negative evidence together, we aim to pool low-level features into different representation according to their semantic information. As we have shown in Section 2.1, we can differentiate concepts into positively correlated, negatively correlated and background concepts. Thus, we are able to use three Bag of Visual Word (BoW) representations to pool the low-level features and concatenate the three BoW as the final representation that is further used for training and testing. In this way, we avoid to mix low-level features that have too much variations (both positive and negative) into a single holistic representation.

The intuition of the semantic pooling is to pool the low-level words with different semantic relevance differently. In other words, when we construct the positively correlated BoW, we want to give more focus on pooling the low-level words that has positively correlated semantic meaning. The same procedure is applicable for negative and background concepts. It is achieved by applying three different weighted selectors $\mathbf{S}^+$, $\mathbf{S}^-$ and $\mathbf{S}^0$ on top of the co-occurrence matrix. Then, the weighted semantic concept selectors are transformed as the low-level words selectors while the semantic relevance is carried over. Suppose the original un-normalized low-level visual words is presented as $\mathbf{x}$, then semantic pooling procedure can be represented as follows.

$$\left[\frac{\mathbf{x}\cdot\mathbf{PS}^+}{||\mathbf{x}\cdot\mathbf{PS}^+||_1}, \frac{\mathbf{x}\cdot\mathbf{PS}^-}{||\mathbf{x}\cdot\mathbf{PS}^-||_1}, \frac{\mathbf{x}\cdot\mathbf{PS}^0}{||\mathbf{x}\cdot\mathbf{PS}^0||_1}\right] \tag{6}$$

It is worth noting that Eq.6 is NOT a fixed linear transformation for the entire original feature representation $\mathbf{x}$ due to the normalization factors. Thus, this is a not trivial weight factor that can be absorbed by SVM models.

3. EXPERIMENTS

3.1 Experiment Settings

We evaluate the semantic pooling approach on the TRECVID MED11 open source dataset [1]. This dataset contains high level semantic event categories, such as "making a sandwich", "parkour", "Change a vehicle tire", plus other unnamed negative events other than these events. There are two divisions of this dataset, Event Collection (EC), Development Transparent (DEVT). EC defines the positive samples for each event. The number of videos for each event ranges from around 110 to 170. DEVT dataset contains videos from event 1 to event 5 and other unnamed event videos. This is, so far, one of the largest complex event detection dataset where the event labels are available. We conducted the evaluation on this dataset: use EC as the training set and DEVT as the testing set. For all evaluation, we adopt binary SVM classifiers with Intersection Kernels. For training each binary event classifier, the videos that belong to this event are used as positive samples, the other videos in the training set are used as negative samples. For all the evaluation, we adopt the average precision as the metric. All the SVM training undergoes the cross-validation to determine the best parameter. In order to obtain the semantic information, we annotated about $6,000$ short video segments to develop 185 concept detectors. The complete list of concepts is included in the supplementary material of this paper.

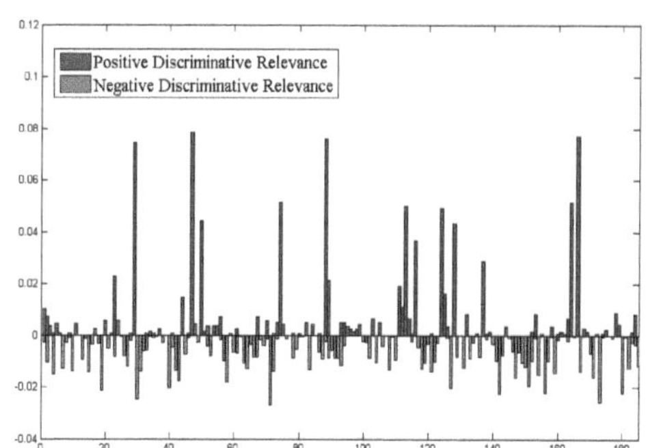

Figure 3: The most positively/negatively correlated concepts for positive and negative samples of Event 01.

Table 1: The top positive semantic selector and top negative semantic selector for the five event in DEVT.

Event	Positive Semantic Selector	Negative Semantic Selector
E001 Attempting a board trick	Standing on the board, spinning with the board, flipping the board and landing on it, jumping over obstacles, Landing with the board, grinding with the board	Polishing metal, standing on top of bike, Sewing, marking on metal, running next to dog, soaping rinsing an animal, group marching, taking a tire out, unscrewing screwing parts
E002 Feeding an animal	Animal grabs offered food and eats, animal eats food from a container, human holding food in front of an animal, Animal eating, Hands visible with animal, Person petting	Pulling pushing a vehicle, Putting fish in net bucket, blowing out candles on a cake, heating metal over a flame, Person cutting, Person sawing, Person turning wrench
E003 Landing a fish	putting fish in net bucket, reeling in, lurching of pole, removing fish from hook, Hands visible fishing, Person casting	Person sewing, Person sliding, Person drilling, slowing pace to a stop, standing on the board, falling, toasting bread, Person hammering
E004 Wedding Ceremony	Person kissing, Person kneeling, Person hugging, walking down the aisle, clapping, exchanging vows	passing a baton while running, gestures indicating directions, running, flipping the bike, Person casting, Person drilling, Person polishing
E005 Work on a wood work project	hammering metal, cutting and shaping wood, Person sawing, Person drilling, Person polishing, Person measuring	blowing out candles on a cake, jumping with the board, taking a tire out, Bike jumping, Hands visible fishing, Person painting

3.2 Results and Analysis

We compare with averaging pooling on four different types of features, STIP [5], SIFT[8], dense trajectory feature with HOG descriptor (DTF-HOG) and dense trajectory feature with motion boundary descriptor (DTF-MBH)[12]. In Table 2, we show the average precision of averaging pooling on each of the four features v.s. semantic pooling (**SP**) on each of the four features. As we can see, the semantic pooling version consistently improves the performance on all events and on all four features. Although direct comparison is hard due to many other factors, our performance in average precision on SIFT is better than the one (21.7%) in [2].

Table 2: Average Precision in % on MED11 DEVT Dataset.

Event	STIP / **SP-STIP**	SIFT / **SP-SIFT**	DTF-HOG / **SP-DTF-HOG**	DTH-MBH / **SP-DTF-MNH**
E01	28.54 / 33.00	22.88 / 26.71	43.46 / 47.10	51.39 / 53.06
E02	12.05 / 13.39	19.48 / 21.09	19.69 / 20.84	21.35 / 21.87
E03	26.31 / 29.45	27.96 / 30.11	47.30 / 49.26	41.12 / 45.08
E04	48.56 / 51.13	54.14 / 57.75	66.41 / 67.92	53.97 / 56.68
E05	27.34 / 29.66	25.09 / 27.36	31.02 / 33.22	33.56 / 36.10
mAP	28.56 / **31.33**	29.91 / **32.60**	41.58 / **43.67**	40.28 / **42.56**

We also evaluate individual positive, negative and background semantic pooled representation. We find that the individual representation performance is either worse or better than the original representation. The consistent improvement only happens when the all of these three representations are used together. We also conduct an interesting experiment by applying three random vectors in Eq.6 in many trials. It turns out that some of the random selectors also improve the results but on average the random selectors give poorer performance. This demonstrates that the improvement is not merely due to the increase of dimension of features.

We also analyze whether the positive semantic selectors and the negative semantic selector are meaningful.We list the positive and negative semantic selectors for the five events in Table 1. As we can see, the top positive semantic selectors are more or less positively correlated with the events while the top negative semantic selector are all negatively correlated with the events. We also notice that the positive selectors are quite sparse, *i.e.* only a few quite sharp peaks while the negative selectors do not have these property as we have seen in Figure 3 (other figures are included in the supplementary materials). We think this makes perfect sense because for positive samples, there are very few semantic concepts to tell it is positive while for negative samples, there are more semantic concepts to tell it is negative.

4. SUMMARY AND FUTURE WORK

In this paper, we proposed an approach to pool the low-level visual words according to their discriminative semantic relevance. By this way, we replaced the way of mixing all various low-level visual words into a single representation by pooling low-level feature according to their positive, negative and background semantic meanings. We adopted the co-occurrence matrix to bridge the semantic concepts and low-level words. Experiments show semantic pooling consistently improves the performance on all events and on all four types features in a large evaluation dataset MED11. In the future, we will investigate how to use the more detailed semantic concepts, including their spatio-temporal relationships.

5. ACKNOWLEDGMENTS

This work has been supported by the Intelligence Advanced Research Projects Activity (IARPA) via Department of Interior National Business Center contract number D11-PC20066. The U.S. Government is authorized to reproduce and distribute reprints for Governmental purposes notwithstanding any copyright annotation thereon. The views and conclusions contained herein are those of the authors and should not be interpreted as necessarily representing the official policies or endorsements, either expressed or implied, of IARPA, DOI/NBC, or the U.S. Government.

6. REFERENCES

[1] http://www-nlpir.nist.gov/projects/tv2011/tv2011.html, 2011.

[2] L. Cao, Y. Mu, N. Apostol, et al. Scene aligned pooling for complex video recognition. In *ECCV*, 2012.

[3] H. Cheng et al. Sri-sarnoff aurora system at trecvid 2012 - multimedia event detection and recounting. In *Trecvid Video Retrieval Evaluation Workshop*, CVPR2012.

[4] B. Huang, L. Xie, G. Hua, and A. Natsev. Semantic model vectors for complex video event recognition. *IEEE Transactions on Multimedia*, 2012.

[5] I. Laptev. On space-time interest points. *IJCV*, 64(2):107–123, 2005.

[6] S. Lazebnik, C. Schmid, and J. Ponce. Beyond bags of features: Spatial pyramid matching for recognizing natural scene categories. In *CVPR*, 2006.

[7] J. Liu, Q. Yu, O. Javed, et al. Video event recognition using concept attributes. In *IEEE (WACV)*, 2013.

[8] D. Lowe. Distinctive image features from scale-invariant keypoints. *IJCV*, 60(2):91–110, 2004.

[9] Z. Ma, F. Nie, Y. Yang, et al. Discriminating joint feature analysis for multimedia data understanding. *IEEE Transactions on Multimedia*, 2012.

[10] P. Natarajan, S. Wu, S. N. P. Vitaladevuni, et al. Multimodal feature fusion for robust event detection in web videos. In *CVPR*, 2012.

[11] F. Perronnin and C. Dance. Fisher kernels on visual vocabularies for image categorization. In *CVPR*, 2007.

[12] H. Wang, A. Klaser, C. Schmid, and C. Liu. Action recognition by dense trajectories. In *CVPR*, 2011.

[13] J. Wang, J. Yang, K. Yu, F. Lv, T. Huang, and Y. Gong. Learning locality-constrained linear coding for image classification. In *CVPR*, 2010.

[14] S. Wang, Y. Yang, Z. Ma, X. Li, C. Pang, and A. Hauptmann. Action recognition by exploring the data distribution and feature correlation. In *CVPR*, 2012.

SwarmVision: Autonomous Aesthetic Multi-Camera Interaction

George Legrady
UCSB Media Arts and Technology
Phelps Hall 3309
UC Santa Barbara, CA 93106
323-346-7619
legrady@mat.ucsb.edu

Danny Bazo
UCSB Media Arts and Technology
Phelps Hall 3309
UC Santa Barbara, CA 93106
805-455-1142
dannybazo@gmail.com

Marco Pinter
UCSB Media Arts and Technology
Phelps Hall 3309
UC Santa Barbara, CA 93106
805-452-1577
marco@marcopinter.com

ABSTRACT
A platform of exploratory networked robotic cameras was created, utilizing an aesthetic approach to experimentation. Initiated by research in autonomous swarm robotic camera behavior, SwarmVision is an installation consisting of multiple Pan-Tilt-Zoom cameras on rails positioned above spectators in an exhibition space, where each camera behaves autonomously based on its own rules of computer vision and control. Each of the cameras is programmed to detect visual information of interest based on a different algorithm, and each negotiates with the other two, influencing what subject matter to study in a collective way. The emergent behaviors of the system illustrate an ongoing process of scene reconstruction and video-based behavior generation.

Categories and Subject Descriptors
J.5 [**Computer Applications**]: Arts and Humanities: Media Arts

General Terms
Algorithms, Measurement, Documentation, Design, Experimentation, Human Factors.

Keywords
Human-centered computing, scene recognition, natural images, spatial layout, emergent behavior, aesthetic function, multi-robot interaction, computational photography.

1. INTRODUCTION
Through experimental testing, we examine the qualitative aspect of the machine-generated image's visual and semiotic structure. How do machine generated images differ from those made by humans? And what may be areas of relevance for machine vision study for utilitarian and other applications? Images generated by humans and machines cover the full breadth from simple to complex, from easily recognizable to undecipherable, from images that result from unintended disruptions, to studies of visual chaotic phenomena. There is a wide range of visual articulation possible, particularly when machines are designed to function on their own, as those cultural values not explicitly coded for are not the guiding or restraining factors in the creation of the image.

MM'13, October 21–25, 2013, Barcelona, Spain.

Image creation and its interpretation to a large extent involves cultural understanding [1]. It is a learned process following rules of visual ordering or structuring [2]. We have far to go to arrive at methods for translating processes in our understanding of images that are based on emotional, perceptual, cognitive factors at the level of affect and the aesthetic, and additionally where the symbolic, cultural, syntactic biases shape our reading of the image.

1.1 Motivation & Aesthetic Research
Research in computational photography is dedicated to advancing image-capture technology and extending the capabilities of digital cameras and systems. Our project's purpose is to suggest new directions through the study of such images, guided by an approach based in aesthetics and visual language, with the intent of discovering findings that may illuminate current research while inspiring further engineering development [3].

1.2 Related Work
A number of artistic precedents have explored machine-driven camera image-capture behavior driven by cultural or aesthetic interests. Michael Snow's 1971 pioneering film "La Region Centrale" [4] ceded aesthetic definition to the automated recording process of a programmed robot-arm mounted camera which explored its own reachable space. Our system similarly emphasizes a non-human approach to gaze driven by algorithmic processses. By contrast, Paul Garrin's and David Rokeby's 1998 "Border Patrol" [5] implemented early face recognition computer vision algorithms to create an aggressively invasive experience, ceaselessly capturing the presence of spectators, turning viewers into powerless targets. Seiko Mikami's "Desire of Codes" [6], uses a grid of multiple cameras to sense the presence of spectators present in the exhibition space, and displays the composited robotic images through a medium reminiscent of insectoid vision. Our system differs from these last two examples as its goal is to explore the gallery space the way a photographer might create compositions in search of visual saliency and therefore treats the presence of spectators, inanimate objects, and the wall surfaces of the exhibition space equally.. A key inspiration for the simulated 3D virtual representation in which the cameras' images are placed is Microsoft Photosynth's [7] positioning of online found photographs into a 3D defined point cloud. However, whereas technologies such as Photosynth aim to arrive at smooth melding of images, our project is engaged in illustrating the noisy intermediate moments present in the myriad layered images resulting from autonomous investigations occurring before their unification into a seamless whole.

1.3 Description

Three cameras mounted on motorized rails scan the room for visual information of interest as defined by computer vision algorithms. Even though each camera functions autonomously, they compare and address each other's results. When one of the cameras identifies subject matter of high saliency for its particular algorithm, the other cameras suspend their search and converge to examine the identified subject of interest from their different angles.

In the installation, four visualizations are featured on two screens/projections. The first screen features what each of the three cameras "see" - a depiction of what their vision algorithms are currently processing. Informational labels under each of the livefeed describe the incoming data and analysis giving a sense of each of the camera's performance. The second screen shows an overview in a 3D reconstruction of the gallery environment showing the location of the cameras, where they point, and the video they capture transformed into still images. Each camera continuously produces 10 still frames per second, and fills the 3D space with up to a hundred images per camera resulting in a volumetric form of layered stacked photographs that continuously change as images fade away. The images' sizes and locations are determined by the locations and poses of the cameras, as well as their focal planes and focus locations at a given moment. The 4th visualization features the sum of activities situating all generated images and the three camera locations within a reduced virtual 3D spatial reconstruction of the exhibition space.

In the exhibition setting, visual segments of spectators who enter the viewing space populate the images, leaving an imprint of their presence that is later erased as the images sequentially fade away. On the two screens, viewers can perceive both individual camera behaviors (microcosmic) and their relationships to each other (macrocosmic) through communication. Through these visualizations, the project explores the transformative condition of the photographic process as it transitions from a still image to one that is reified within physical space.

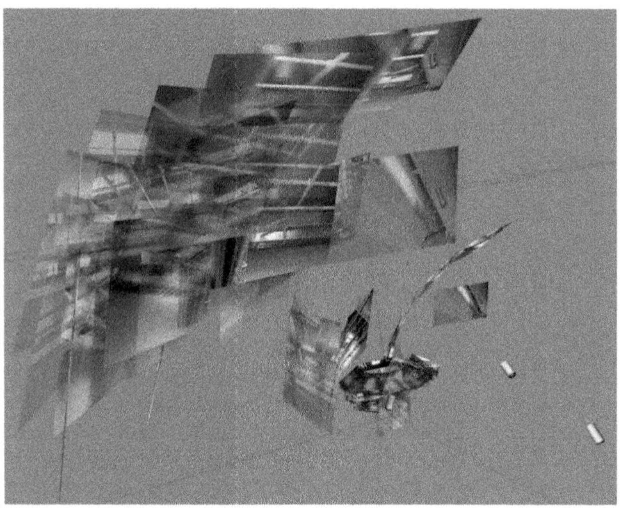

Figure 1. Image created by an autonomous swarm consisting of three robotic cameras. The cameras each seek out features of interest using separate computer vision algorithms, and together they generate a spatially reconstructed representation of their visual environment.

2. TECHNICAL DESCRIPTION

2.1 Hardware

2.1.1 PTZ Ethernet Cameras

SwarmVision's three cameras are commercial IP cameras of the type typically used for security applications. They have sufficient range of motion to cover approximately a hemisphere with their camera's view. Their video images are sent to the computer through ethernet as streaming videos, and control commands are sent from the computer via serial communication.

2.1.2 Motorized Rails

The custom-built, belt-driven rails are driven by a DC motor and have a range of motion of approximately six feet.

2.2 Software

2.2.1 Computer Vision

Each robot has a built-in computer vision algorithm based on either: a contrast-detecting Pyramid of Gaussians distance in pixel space, a straight-line-detecting Hough line filter, or a saturated-pixel-seeking algorithm. These three detectors were chosen for their variety and dissimilarity, and their relationship to the parallel, heterogeneous feature detectors operating in the visual systems of living creatures.

The computer vision algorithms each process incoming video frames and determine the locations of features of interest. The sub-region within the image with the largest concentration of detected features is found. The center of this sub-region is then designated the target gaze location and used in the camera control computations.

2.2.2 Control of Camera PTZ

For each robot, given a target location in its current video frame, along with its own position along the rail and pan/tilt/zoom state, a movement command is calculated such that the robot's gaze will center on the target gaze location. In this way, the robot will proceed to "seek out" features in the space.

Zoom control follows a maximization scheme as well. The robots adjust their zoom level between maximum wide-angle and maximum telephoto in increments. As they adjust their zoom level, the number of features found in the space is compared from moment to moment. The robots attempt to maximize this number, and move towards gradually achieving a zoom level that results in a large number of detected features.

2.2.3 Control of Rail Movement

Commands from the main computer drive the robots in the direction of their gaze. They dolly towards the subject of their attention in order to improve resolution of their image, if possible.

2.2.4 Communication Between Cameras

Over time, the robots converge on and explore the features of regions of high visual saliency in the environment together. This is enabled by a simple target acquisition and communication protocol. When a robot detects a local maximum in the saliency of its visual environment, it tells the other robots the location of its current gaze. All robots then converge on that location and proceed with their saliency-driven behavior.

2.2.5 Visualizations

Two visualizations display the information gathered by the robots. In the first visualization, a three-part screen shows the live stream from each robot's video camera. The three images have been processed by each robot's computer vision algorithm, and so each one highlights a different set of features in the visual environment.

The second visualization is a real-time, 3-D computer generated environment representing the installation space. Within this virtual environment, the robots' video streams are placed into space at a location determined by the robots' poses, focal planes, and zoom levels. The individual images making up the video streams are thus distributed throughout in the room, in their actual locations as "perceived" by the robots. The result is a constantly-evolving, fragmented visual database of the installation environment, incorporating the objects and people present.

3. DISCUSSION

3.1 Platform Development

The platform layout is flexible and has been tested in different configurations. Figure 4 illustrates one possible configuration, where all camera rails are horizontal and near the ceiling, looking down upon the subjects of the scene. Rails can also be positioned on the diagonal along a wall. Custom motor controls were developed to allow arbitrary angles and to compensate for the gravity on the camera. These varying configurations create visual interest for viewers in the space, and increase the potential angles of view for the system. The system has been accepted for installation at multiple international venues during summer and fall 2013. The ongoing research follows simultaneous tracks of engineering investigation and artistic exploration, with the guiding premise that artistic and aesthetic approaches to scene analysis can yield unexpected directions into computer vision and graphics research.

3.2 Engineering Approach

It was found that the key variables in creating and evaluating emergent behaviors of the system include:

- Types and variability of computer vision techniques in evaluating features of interest;
- Methods of control and communication between the camera agents; and
- Visualization of the resultant imaging on the screen/projection.

Early work with the platform led to exploration in the construction of a "reference image" by all three robot cameras. An image was input into the system, e.g. a drawing or a photograph, and the three cameras worked cooperatively to find subjects in the viewing field with features that matched those of the reference image, such that when the cameras' three live images were merged, there would be a clear match to the reference image. This early exploration was useful in providing an initial and defined set of goals for the robots, with a (qualitative) measure of evaluating success. This investigation was shelved for potential future refinement, but was important in informing the ongoing development of the system. It was determined that a more open-ended exploration by the robots could yield a higher chance of success in allowing interesting behaviors to emerge.

The visualization also evolved over the research period with the system. The current implementation displays a non-literal 3D reconstruction of the space, where the details and emphasis are based on the content of the subject versus simply the literal spatial layout of the room. Unexpected patterns emerge naturally in the three-dimensional representation. The ongoing work suggests that this type of content-influenced spatial visualization may provide, to humans studying the system, a more intuitive understanding of the scene analysis. This may suggest new approaches in the exploration of computer vision problems such as, for example:

- Human behavior analysis (through multi-camera communication),
- Conventional 3D scene reconstruction.

Finally, studying the impact on humans interacting in the space yielded unexpected results. Viewers watching the cameras became instantly aware that the robots were studying and analyzing the scene. Looking at the large lens of a camera, a viewer would know exactly where in the room a robot was "looking." Just as humans are drawn to look at an area of space indicated by the direction of gaze of another human, so were viewers drawn to look where the robots were watching. Viewers in the space also desired attention from the robots, and would often move in front of the camera eye, and experience satisfaction when having been designated a subject of interest. Further, during moments when the robot cameras appeared to be looking at each other, viewers experienced a sense of non-verbal communication between those autonomous agents.

3.3 Artistic Approach

Machine learning methods based on human approaches to compositional framing can be significantly enhanced by methods from the field of fine arts photography where the composition of an image generally involves the photographer's organization of forms, color and tonal contrasts, spatial subdivision of the rectangular frame, angle and point of view, and other such visual decisions that are combined to create an image that achieves complexity and coherence. A skilled photographer or visual artist mentally assembles or dissects complex images based on an understanding of the syntax of visual language. Acquired through repeated, disciplined, and conscious efforts in image creation, visual creators develop the means to analyze and identify how depth, spatial organization, form, color motion, texture, noise, uncertainty, etc (aesthetic primitives) function to articulate a visual experience, and once created, to analyze and evaluate how these elements form or fail to form an artistically coherent expression.

While much of this analysis often involves intuition, and functions at the implicit level (not unlike any expert performance such as playing tennis, chess, etc.), we argue that it is possible to identify systematic elements or rules of visual construction that are dependent on general cultural conventions. Artists arrange these elements in unconventional ways to continuously verify and expand the boundaries of the rules of visual language. These rules may serve to automate visual recognition increasing complexity in the performance of computer vision machine behavior.

While engineering research directs itself to enhancing signal quality, artistic practice tends to embrace noisy systems. For instance, whereas Photosynth will normalize and blend images towards seamlessness, our system is based on stacking images according to focus and zoom parameters, which results in a clustered form that requires and trains the viewer and the system to make sense of the mapped visual space. Through this process, we dwell into a perceptional and machine performance situation that sidesteps standard engineering work, but addresses a messy and realistic scenario that systems will generate. We initiate the process by giving the robots a set of rules such as search and capturing of frames for most salient regions. Our system then aims to center, constantly adjust zoom to maximize saliency, resulting in the dense layering of continuous images.

Public engagement offers rich opportunities for study. The robotic camera system will be installed in various exhibitions from engineering conferences to media arts festivals and fine arts museums to draw feedback from diverse knowledge domains. The project had its first public presentation at Siggraph 2013 and we noticed that spectators were engaged with both LED screen views, one showing the 3 camera behaviors and the other, a simulated 3D spatial overview, centered in the space as seen in the illustration. The audience's initial reactions many times were to wave at the cameras to see if that had any impact, eventually becoming aware that the system had an autonomous search mission other than one of human recognition. This led spectators to study camera behavior and feedback in detail, to infer what the system was seeking, and thereby to engage in reflection regarding the cultural and technological roles of autonomous machine vision systems.

Figure 3. Installation at Siggraph 2013, Anaheim, (July 2013), showing 3 cameras on hanging rails surrounding the study space and the two information screens showing camera behavior.

4. CONCLUSION & FUTURE WORK

The system of exploratory networked robotic cameras described here, guided by aesthetic techniques and rules of visual language, has begun to yield emergent image-making behaviors. We aim to inform scientific research in computer vision and computational photography through an aesthetics- and semiotics-based approach to camera systems engineering.

The camera agents utilized in the current research project have multiple degrees of freedom in orientation (via pan/tilt) but are limited to a single degree of spatial motion along a track. Continued research will incorporate wheel-based robots on the ground, adding an additional degree of freedom to spatial motion. Airborne drones suggest a promising direction, both in terms of features and affordability in number, despite limitations in maintaining certain orientations (pitch and roll) and overall imaging stability. Ground-based robots with vertically telescoping cameras, while expensive, allow multiple degrees of freedom in space and in orientation for highly stable imaging.

Ongoing research will investigate the integration of different types of agents with different abilities. For example, airborne drones may quickly search for potential areas of interest; then suggest, to the more stable wall-based and ground-based agents, that they position themselves appropriately and zoom in for more detailed examination. Integration of cameras with differing imaging systems will also be investigated, including thermal imaging, thus allowing investigation of a subject at both varying angles and varying spectral characteristics.

Throughout these explorations, a primary focus of ongoing research is the study of the emergent behaviors of the system. A formal approach to the characterization of emergent behaviors will be developed. This will involve the establishment of goals for the system that are subject to quantitative analysis. Additionally, the behavioral elements of the system will be designed flexibly to allow for rapid exploration of different variables. These include: the ability of the agents to act cooperatively versus antagonistically; the ability to exert control over one another in master/slave relationships; and the amount and type of information shared between agents. As the relationships are altered through ongoing iterations, the resultant emergent behaviors can be quantified for effectiveness. With the ability to automatically quantify the effectiveness of behavioral patterns, there is the possibility of applying genetic algorithms to the behavioral variables, thus allowing the system to autonomously explore and determine the most effective methods of communication and control for imaging tasks.

5. ACKNOWLEDGEMENTS

Special thanks to our colleagues Daniel Vaquero, Ahana Reddy, Yuan-Yi Fan for contributions of computer vision and image processing algorithms, literature review, and for the development of a stable controller for robotic diagonal movement. This project has been funded by the Robert W. Deutsch Foundation and National Science Foundation IIS # 1149001 grant.

6. REFERENCES

[1] N. Goodman, "Notation," in The Structure of Art, Indianapolis, IN, 1976.

[2] G. Peters, "Aesthetic Primitives – Information Visualization 2007 (IV '07)," in 11th Int. Conf., pp. 316-325, 2007.

[3] J. Elkins, "Interpreting non-art images," in The Domain of Images, Cornell University Press, 1999, pp. 31-51.

[4] http://www.medienkunstnetz.de/works/region-central/ Michael Snow, La Région Centrale

[5] http://www.davidrokeby.com/border_patrol.html

[6] http://www.virtualart.at/database/general/work/desire-of-codes.html Seio Mikami "Desire of Codes"

[7] Photosynth.net Mirosoft Photosynth Network

Segmenting Music through the Joint Estimation of Keys, Chords and Structural Boundaries

Johan Pauwels
STMS IRCAM-CNRS-UPMC
1, Place Stravinsky
75004 Paris, France
johan.pauwels@ircam.fr

Geoffroy Peeters
STMS IRCAM-CNRS-UPMC
1, Place Stravinsky
75004 Paris, France
geoffroy.peeters@ircam.fr

ABSTRACT

In this paper, we introduce a new approach to music structure segmentation that is based on the joint estimation of structural segments, keys and chords in one probabilistic framework. More precisely, the boundaries of a structure segment are determined by detecting key changes and by utilizing the difference in prior probability of chord transitions according to their position in a structural segment. In contrast to many of the recent approaches to structural segmentation, this system does not work with self-similarity matrices, although it has been designed to integrate this kind of approach into the framework at a later stage. However, just the current version of the system, using only the estimated harmony, is already producing encouraging results, especially with respect to the precise localization of the boundaries.

Categories and Subject Descriptors

I.5.4 [**Pattern recognition**]: Applications—*Signal processing, Waveform analysis*; J.5 [**Arts and humanities**]: Performing arts (e.g., dance, music)

Keywords

music information retrieval; structural segmentation; key and chord estimation

1. INTRODUCTION

Structural segmentation of music is the process in which an audio recording is divided into a number of non-overlapping sections that correspond to the macro-temporal organisation of the piece. These entities usually take the form of verses and choruses in popular music or of movements in classical music. The obtained sections can then be used for audio summarisation, synchronization or as an intermediate step in further content-based indexation.

Recent approaches in music structural segmentation have mostly focussed on processing so-called self-similarity matrices [1], obtained by comparing some low level acoustic feature, like MFCC's or chromas, to time-delayed copies of itself. An overview of these and other methods can be found in [8]. However, our proposed method takes a different approach. We present a framework for the joint estimation of structural boundaries, keys and chords that builds upon an existing system for key and chord estimation [9]. It is based on the premise that some chord combinations are more common around structural boundaries, especially when expressed as relative chords in a key, giving a musicologically richer representation that is made possible by the concurrent estimation of keys and chords. In that regard, it is more similar to previous work by Maddage [5] or by Lee [3], only do their systems work sequentially because the chord and key estimates are used as inputs to the structure estimation, whereas our model generates them concurrently.

In the remainder of this paper, we will first elaborate the assumption on which our system is based and provide a theoretical underpinning of its validity in Section 2. Afterwards, we will present our probabilistic framework that uses this information to concurrently estimate keys, chords and structural boundaries in Section 3. Its output will then be compared to a database of manual annotations in Section 4. Finally, some conclusions as well as possible directions for future work will be given in Section 5.

2. STRUCTURE DEPENDENT RELATIVE CHORD TRANSITION MODELS

The basic premise around which our approach is constructed, is that chord sequences have a different prior probability according to their position in a structural segment and more specifically, that the number of different chord combinations that occur around the structural boundaries is lower than those occurring in the middle of a segment. A supporting example for this assumption is that movements in music of the Classical period often end in a limited number of specific chord combination, the so-called *cadences*. In order to verify this statement in a more methodological way, we construct three different key-chord transition models depending on the position of the chords in a structural segment.

A key k is defined as the combination of a tonic t and a mode m ($m \in \{\text{major}, \text{(natural) minor}\}$). A chord c is defined as the combination of a root r and a type p ($p \in \{\text{maj}, \text{min}, \text{dim}, \text{aug}\}$). In the following we will consider pairs of keys and chords (k, c). We define a relative chord c' with respect to a key k by expressing the root r as the interval i between the tonic and the root $i = d(t, r)$.

MM'13, October 21–25, 2013, Barcelona, Spain.

ACM 978-1-4503-2404-5/13/10 ...$15.00.
http://dx.doi.org/10.1145/2502081.2502193.

Table 1: Perplexity of relative chord transition models per mode according to structural position

mode	intra	inter	final
major	6.10	4.10	2.88
minor	6.24	4.37	3.68

A key-chord pair can thus equivalently be written as a key-relative chord pair $(k, c) = (t, m, r, p) = (t, m, i, p) = (k, c')$. The latter representation is musicologically more informative and corresponds to the way scholars analyse harmony.

We then look at all successions of 2 consecutive chords in a corpus that is annotated with keys, chords and structural segments. It is annotated such that all positions are indicated where at least one of key, chord or structural segment changes. In order to study the harmonic movement like musicologists do, both chords are interpreted in the same key. Because of the forward motion in music, this will be the key annotated for the first chord. Finally, to take the circularity of pitch perception into account, we ignore the tonic of the key and only keep the mode. The resulting representation of local harmony then consist of a mode and a pair of relative chords $(m_{n-1}, c'_{n-1}, c'_n)$.

These pairs of relative chords in a mode are divided into three categories according to their position in a structural segment. Examples for each of them have been indicated in Figure 1. We define following classes: *final*, when the two chords are the last ones in a structural segment; *inter*, meaning that the chord change is straddling a segment boundary; and *intra*, for the remaining chord transitions. These classes We then construct transition models for each structural position classes by counting the relative number of occurrences in a corpus. We use the part of the Isophonics set [6] that has been used for the MIREX 2010 chord estimation competition. It consists of 217 full songs, mostly by the Beatles (180 songs), the remainder by Queen and Zweieck. There are genres other than pop music that are a better fit for our restricted harmony model of 48 chords and 24 keys, but this corpus is one of the few that contains audio aligned to annotations of all our three considered aspects.

We can then quantify the difference in chord distribution between the various models by calculating the model perplexity $PP(C'_1, C'_2|m)$ per mode m for each of them. C'_1 and C'_2 represent the collection of all relative chords that appear as first, respectively second, element in the sequence. The model perplexity is defined as the exponential of the entropy $H(C'_1, C'_2|m)$ expressed in nats:

$$PP(C'_1, C'_2|m) = \exp(H(C'_1, C'_2|m))$$
$$= \exp\left(-\sum_{c'_1} P(c'_1|m) \sum_{c'_2} P(c'_2|c'_1, m) \log P(c'_2|c'_1, m)\right)$$

This expresses the mean prior uncertainty of a bigram according to its position in the structural segmentation. A lower value means that the transition probability is concentrated into fewer combinations of two chords. As can be seen in Table 1, the values for the *intra*-model are indeed significantly higher than those for the *inter* and *final*-model, thereby confirming our hypothesis.

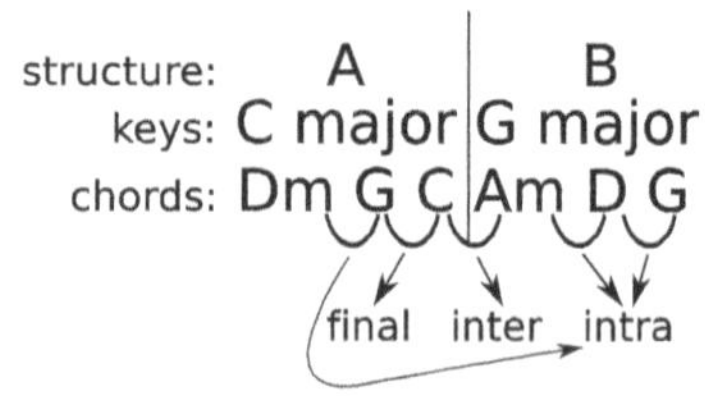

Figure 1: An example annotation with the three structural positions indicated

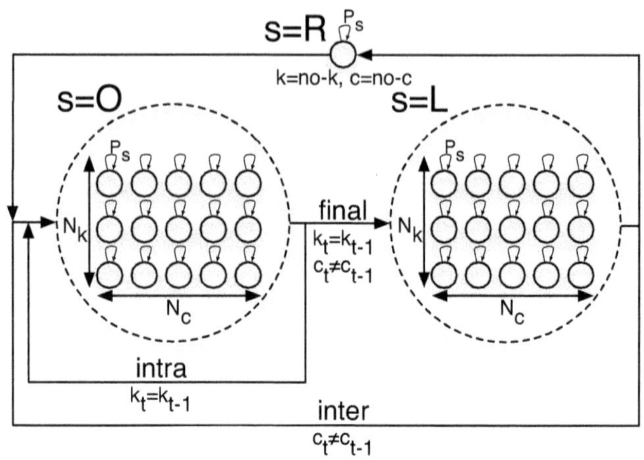

Figure 2: The state diagram

3. A PROBABILISTIC FRAMEWORK FOR THE JOINT ESTIMATION OF STRUCTURAL SEGMENTS, KEYS AND CHORDS

We will now describe a probabilistic framework in which the transition models as derived in the previous section will be used to determine a structural segmentation of a track, along with an estimation of the keys and chords. Our starting point is the system by Pauwels et al. [9] which concurrently estimates keys and chords, but does not estimate structural boundaries. It consists of an HMM in which each state represents a combination of a key and a chord. We extend it by letting each state q represent a structural position in addition to a key and a chord. A key k can take one of N_k values, a chord one of N_c values and the structural positions s can take one of two values: L which means that q is the last state of a structural segment or O which means that q is not the last state of a structural segment. In summary, $q = (k, c, s)$ with $k \in \{K_1, \ldots, K_{N_k}\}, c \in \{C_1, \ldots, C_{N_c}\}, s \in \{L, O\}$. Finally, we add a single state to handle the case when no chord is being played, notably at the beginning and end of a recording. In this state, the key will accordingly take a "no-key" value and the structural position will take a value of $s = R$. A simplified state diagram can be seen in Figure 2, in which states are grouped by their value of the structure variable. Only the transitions that change structure variable are drawn in order not to overload the picture, but the constraints on key and chord transitions are indicated next to the arrows. We are then looking for the state sequence $\hat{Q} = \{\hat{q}_1, \hat{q}_2, \ldots, \hat{q}_T\}$ that optimally explains the sequence of observations $X = \{x_1, x_2, \ldots, x_T\}$: $\hat{Q} = \arg\max P(Q|X)$. The resulting state sequence can then be split into separate sequences for keys, chords and structure states: $\hat{K}$, $\hat{C}$ and $\hat{S}$ respectively. The structural segmentation can be derived from the latter sequence simply by inserting a segment boundary for every transition from a state $s = L$ to one where $s = O$, or from or to $s = R$. Because the state variable q consists by definition of the combination of a chord, key and structure variable, these three optimal sequences will always be jointly decoded.

If we assume that the first order Markov property holds and that acoustic observations are independent from state to state, then we can rewrite the probability that needs to be maximized using Bayes' theorem to

$$\hat{S}, \hat{K}, \hat{C} = \arg\max \prod_{t=1}^{T} P\left(s_t, k_t, c_t | s_{t-1}, k_{t-1}, c_{t-1}\right) P\left(\mathbf{x_t} | s_t, k_t, c_t\right)$$

The transition probabilities $P(s_t, k_t, c_t | s_{t-1}, k_{t-1}, c_{t-1})$ are calculated by a prior musicological model that consists of a number of submodels. By introducing some musicologically motivated constraints to the transition probabilities, we want to enforce a number of relationships between the concepts of keys, chords and structural segments. These will ensure that our estimation always produces sensible results and have as an added benefit that this also speeds up the calculation. The first three constraints we impose are 1) a key change $k_t \neq k_{t-1}$ is only allowed to occur together with a chord change $c_t \neq c_{t-1}$, 2) there must be a change in chord or in key between segments, 3) a structural segment must contain at least two different chords (or a single no-chord). These three limitations can be easily enforced by ensuring that every state change implies a chord change. In other words, we let the chord level control the granularity of the key and structure estimations. This makes the state duration model effectively a chord duration model that we control by a single parameter P_s:

$$P\left(s_t, k_t, c_t | s_{t-1}, k_{t-1}, c_{t-1}\right) = \begin{cases} P_s & s_t = s_{t-1} \wedge k_t = k_{t-1} \\ 0 & s_t \neq s_{t-1} \vee k_t \neq k_{t-1} \end{cases}, \forall c_t = c_{t-1}$$

The remaining probabilities $P\left(s_t, k_t, c_t | s_{t-1}, k_{t-1}, c_{t-1}\right)$, $\forall c_t \neq c_{t-1}$ of the chord changing transitions are calculated by a combination of three submodels. We further apply Bayes' theorem repeatedly to arrive at a decomposition into three terms

$$\begin{aligned} &P\left(s_t, k_t, c_t | s_{t-1}, k_{t-1}, c_{t-1}\right) \\ &= P\left(c_t | s_t, s_{t-1}, k_{t-1}, c_{t-1}\right) P\left(k_t | s_t, s_{t-1}, k_{t-1}, c_t, c_{t-1}\right) \\ &\quad P\left(s_t | s_{t-1}, k_{t-1}, c_{t-1}\right) \end{aligned}$$

We can already recognize the structure-dependent relative chord transition models of the previous section in the first term $P\left(c_t | s_t, s_{t-1}, k_{t-1}, c_{t-1}\right)$. Our three categories of chord transitions – *inter*, *intra* and *final* – each correspond to a certain combination of the state variables. The *intra* model will be used when $s_{t-1} = O$ and $s_t = O$, *inter* when $s_{t-1} = L$ and $s_t = O$ and *final* when $s_{t-1} = O$ and $s_t = L$. Finally, from our definition of L it follows that when $s_{t-1} = L$ and $s_t = L$, only the self probability P_s should be allowed, to account for the fact that the last chord of a structural segment can – and most likely will – last more than one time step. The other probabilities are set to zero.

In the second term $P\left(k_t | s_t, s_{t-1}, k_{t-1}, c_t, c_{t-1}\right)$, we neglect the influence of the chords c_{t-1}, c_t in comparison to the other terms such that we end up with $P\left(k_t | s_t, s_{t-1}, k_{t-1}\right)$. We add the supplemental constraint that a key change can only occur between segments. This means that $s_{t-1} = O \vee s_t = L \Rightarrow P\left(k_t | s_t, s_{t-1}, k_{t-1}\right) = \delta_{k_t, k_{t-1}}$ with δ the Kronecker-delta. For the *inter* key transitions $P(k_t | s_t = O, s_{t-1} = L, k_{t-1})$, we reuse the model from [9], based on Lerdahl's theoretical distance [4] between keys.

The third term $P\left(s_t | s_{t-1}, k_{t-1}, c_{t-1}\right)$ will be used to control the ease of changing the structure variable s and thus to control the insertion of segment boundaries. We use a simple model that ignores the key and chord influence and consists of a single parameter ω that balances the probability of going to $s = O$ or $s = L$ after leaving $s = O$.

$$P\left(s_t | s_{t-1}\right) = \begin{cases} \omega & s_{t-1} = O \wedge s_t = O \\ 1 - \omega & s_{t-1} = O \wedge s_t = L \\ 1 & s_{t-1} = L \wedge s_t = O \\ 0 & s_{t-1} = L \wedge s_t = L \end{cases}$$

The result of adding the additional constraints is that the complete transition matrix will have a well-defined, sparse structure. The two upper quadrants consist of block diagonal matrices with N_k blocks of side N_c, the lower left quadrant is dense and the lower right quadrant is a diagonal matrix. In comparison to a system that only estimates keys and chords concurrently, the number of states gets doubled by repeating every key-chord state for $s = O$ and $s = L$. On the other hand, because of the sparsity of the transition matrix, the increase in the number of transitions stays limited. More specifically, the number of transitions is $(N_k N_c)^2 + 2N_k N_c^2 + N_k N_c + 1$, which corresponds in our configuration to an increase of 8% instead of the theoretically maximum of 400% that would be attained for a dense transition matrix. This sparsity will subsequently be used in the implementation of the Viterbi algorithm to limit the increase in computation time.

The features $\mathbf{x}$ that we use for the calculation of the acoustic probabilities $P(\mathbf{x_t} | s_t, k_t, c_t)$ are the Loudness Based Chromagrams as developed by Ni et al. [7]. These are 24-dimensional vectors that represent the loudness of each of the 12 pitch classes in both the treble and the bass spectrum. They are calculated with a step size of 23 ms and are afterwards averaged over interbeat segments as calculated by ircambeat [10].

We make the assumption that keys and chords can be independently tested for compliance with an observation and that the structure position is conditionally independent of the observations, such that $P\left(\mathbf{x_t} | s_t, k_t, c_t\right) = P\left(\mathbf{x_t} | c_t\right) P\left(\mathbf{x_t} | k_t\right)$. The key acoustic probability $P\left(\mathbf{x_t} | k_t\right)$ is then modelled as the cosine similarity between the observation vector x and Temperley's key templates [11]. These represent the stability of each of the 12 pitch classes relative to a given key. The chord acoustic probability $P\left(\mathbf{x_t} | c_t\right)$ is modelled by a multi-variate Gaussian with full covariance matrix. The models per chord are trained on the same data set from which the relative chord transition models have been derived.

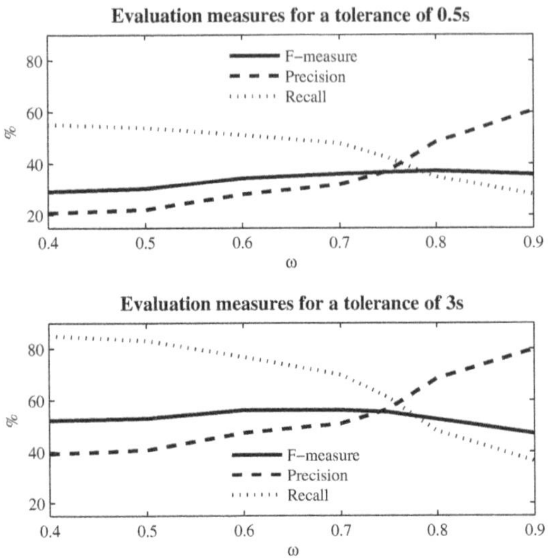

Figure 3: Evaluation measures for two tolerance settings

4. EXPERIMENTAL RESULTS

The performance of the generated structural boundaries will be evaluated by calculating a precision $\mathcal{P}(tol)$ and a recall $\mathcal{R}(tol)$ that is a function of a tolerance *tol*. The precision is defined as the number of estimated boundaries for which an annotated boundary falls within the window with length of *tol* centered around its estimated position. This number is expressed relatively to the total number of estimated boundaries. The recall on the other hand, is the relative number of annotated boundaries that have an estimated boundary within its tolerance window. Both measures are combined into an F-measure $\mathcal{F}(tol)$. These measures are calculated for every song of the previously mentioned data set and averaged.

We evaluate our output using two settings for the tolerance: 0.5 s and 3 s and the aforementioned Isophonics data set. The results in function of the structure change controlling parameter ω can be found in Figure 3. The movement in opposite directions of the precision and recall curves show that ω indeed is able to control the number of resulting structural segments. The optimal F-measures $\mathcal{F}(0.5s) = 36.04$ and $\mathcal{F}(3s) = 56.08$ are reached for $\omega = 0.7$.

Next, we will compare our results with a state-of-the-art segmentation algorithm by Kaiser & Peeters [2]. It calculates a novelty curve by taking the correlation between three types of kernels and the diagonal of an MFCC-based self-similarity matrix. Segment boundaries are then inserted at places where the novelty curve peaks. This system is a refinement of the one that ranked among the best segmentation algorithms during the MIREX 2012 contest. We obtained the output of their algorithm on the data set we use through personal correspondence with the authors.

From the results presented in Table 2, we can conclude that our approach is particularly strong in the fine localisation of the segment boundaries: we outperform Kaiser & Peeters' system for a tolerance of 0.5 s. However, increasing the tolerance to 3 s has a much larger beneficial effect on their performance than on ours. Consequently, their results for a tolerance of 3 s is significantly better, especially the

Table 2: A comparison between our proposed system and the state-of-the-art

	Kaiser & Peeters		Proposed ($\omega = 0.7$)	
tolerance	0.5s	3s	0.5s	3s
F-measure	32.94	64.53	36.04	56.08
precision	29.78	59.87	31.82	50.81
recall	39.28	73.50	47.91	69.85

precision. The latter is a consequence of the fact that our algorithm oversegments more than theirs (at least for the value of ω that gives the highest F-measure).

5. CONCLUSION AND FURTHER WORK

We presented a new approach to structural segmentation by means of a probabilistic framework that concurrently estimates keys, chords and structural boundaries. It is based on the assumption that key changes indicate structural boundaries and that there is lesser variety in chords around structural boundaries than in the middle of structural segments.

Currently, our system is still in its proof-of-concept phase. In the future, we will first perform additional experiments to test the scaling of our approach to different types of music. The final goal however, is to integrate our method with a self-similarity matrix (SSM) based approach, aspiring to construct a synergistic system. For instance, just a change in instrumentation won't be detected as a structure boundary in our current system, whereas SSM methods are pretty efficient at spotting those.

6. ACKNOWLEDGEMENTS

This work was partly supported by the Quaero Program funded by Oseo French agency.

7. REFERENCES

[1] J. Foote. Visualizing music and audio using self-similarity. In *Proc. of ACM Multimedia*, 1999.
[2] F. Kaiser and G. Peeters. Adaptive temporal modeling of audio features in the context of music structure segmentation. In *Proc. AMR workshop*, 2012.
[3] K. Lee. *A system for acoustic chord transcription and key extraction from audio using hidden Markov models trained on synthesized audio.* PhD thesis, Stanford University, 2008.
[4] F. Lerdahl. *Tonal pitch space.* Oxford University Press, New York, 2001.
[5] N. C. Maddage. Automatic structure detection for popular music. *IEEE MultiMedia*, 13(1), 2006.
[6] M. Mauch, C. Cannam, M. Davies, S. Dixon, C. Harte, S. Kolozali, D. Tidhar, and M. Sandler. OMRAS2 metadata project 2009. In *Proc. ISMIR*, 2009.
[7] Y. Ni, M. McVicar, R. Santos-Rodríguez, and T. De Bie. An end-to-end machine learning system for harmonic analysis of music. *IEEE Trans. Audio, Speech and Language Proc.*, 20(6), 2012.
[8] J. Paulus, M. Müller, and A. Klapuri. Audio-based music structure analysis. In *Proc. ISMIR*, 2010.
[9] J. Pauwels, J.-P. Martens, and M. Leman. Improving the key extraction accuracy of a simultaneous key and chord estimation system. In *Proc. AdMIRe*, 2011.
[10] G. Peeters. Simultaneous beat and downbeat-tracking using a probabilistic framework: theory and large-scale evaluation. *IEEE Trans. Audio, Speech and Language Proc.*, 19(6), 2011.
[11] D. Temperley. *The cognition of basic musical structures.* MIT Press, 1999.

3D Teleimmersive Activity Classification Based on Application-System Metadata

Aadhar Jain Ahsan Arefin Raoul Rivas Chien-nan Chen Klara Nahrstedt
University of Illinois at Urbana-Champaign
{jain37,marefin2,trivas,cchen116,klara}@illinois.edu

ABSTRACT

Being able to detect and recognize human activities is essential for 3D collaborative applications for efficient quality of service provisioning and device management. A broad range of research has been devoted to analyze media data to identify human activity, which requires the knowledge of data format, application-specific coding technique and computationally expensive image analysis. In this paper, we propose a human activity detection technique based on application generated metadata and related system metadata. Our approach does not depend on specific data format or coding technique. We evaluate our algorithm with different cyber-physical setups, and show that we can achieve very high accuracy (above 97%) by using a good learning model.

Categories and Subject Descriptors

H.4.3 [**Information Systems Applications**]: Communications Applications: Computer conferencing, teleconferencing, and videoconferencing; C.2.2 [**Multimedia Information Systems**]: Video

Keywords

3D Tele-immersion, Activity, Classification

1. INTRODUCTION

3D teleimmersion (3DTI) technology has expanded the horizon of telepresence conferencing applications by supporting full-body interaction of physical activities in virtual reality environments. Applications have been found in cyber-archeology, collaborative dancing, video conferencing, and online gaming (e.g., [6], [5], [11]).

In 3DTI, participants' 3D images are captured in real-time and exchanged among multiple participants to allow shared virtual collaborations. The system is characterized by the diversity and contingency of human activities[1]. This contingency of activities in 3DTI is critical as the nature of user-activity drives the type and the number of devices to be activated during 3DTI session run-time. Furthermore, the collaborative nature of 3DTI activities imposes different QoS requirements in terms of bandwidth, delay, jitter and skew across activities [1, 2]. For example, 3DTI conversation requires low skew and moderate video quality, while exer-gaming requires low delay and high video frame rate to ensure high interactivity. Therefore, detection and recognition of human activity is essential to provide efficient QoS provisioning and device management in 3DTI space. The primary goal of this paper is to identify *fine-grained* human activities (e.g., walking, sitting, running), which can be combined together to detect *coarse-grained* activities (e.g., video conferencing, exer-gaming).

A broad range of research has been devoted to analyze media data to identify human activity [7, 10], which requires the knowledge of application data format, data coding technique and computationally expensive image analysis. Here we propose a supervised learning-based *Activity Classification System (ACS)* that considers application generated metadata and related system metadata (*application-system* metadata) instead of application media data. A supervised learning algorithm trains our classification model for 3DTI setup without the knowledge of media data format or coding complexity. To our knowledge, our research is the very first attempt to use time-series application-system metadata in 3DTI activity detection.

Since we classify human activity based on time-series metadata, the classification process we propose here is fast (less than 4ms) and unobtrusive. However, the classification is influenced by several cyber-physical dimensions such as visual color and space volume of the physical contents (e.g., participants) which have impact on the application and system metadata (e.g., the reconstruction time and frame size). We quantify the extent of cyber-physical impacts on our activity classification model, and apply the experimental inferences to classify human activity in a real 3DTI setup efficiently. Using a real 3DTI setup, our solution achieves more than 97% accuracy in human activity classification.

2. SYSTEM MODEL

2.1 3DTI Application Model

3D teleimmersive system is a distributed platform that connects multiple remote participants into one virtual shared space for 3D collaborative activities. A large number of input and output devices (e.g., 3D cameras, microphones and displays) are connected at each participating location (called

MM'13, October 21–25, 2013, Barcelona, Spain.

http://dx.doi.org/10.1145/2502081.2502194 .

site) and they are accessed via a single entry point (site gateway). Though multiple parties are involved, we only focus on classifying fine-grained human activities independently at each site. Our algorithm can be easily used for multiple sites by running activity detection at each individual site.

2.2 Application-System Metadata Model

At each participating site, we monitor application-system metadata information corresponding to application I/O devices and underlying system resources. Application metadata includes camera frame rate, audio bit rate, 3D reconstruction time, rendering time, audio and video frame size. The system metadata includes CPU usage, memory usage and processing time of the participating hosts (such as camera node and gateway node). Each host generates a set of metadata values periodically at each epoch or interval (e.g., every 50ms). The combined set of application and system metadata will hereafter be referred to as 'metadata' in this paper. Metadata values are stored in a timestamp indexed database and are used for activity classification.

2.3 Activity Model

We attempt to achieve classification for fine-grained human activities including sitting, standing still and different walk movements performed by the 3DTI participants. We also analyze the impact of cyber-physical dimensions on the classification accuracy. As we mentioned before, this classification model can be extended to classify coarse-grained 3DTI activities by combining the contingency and extent of fine-grained activities.

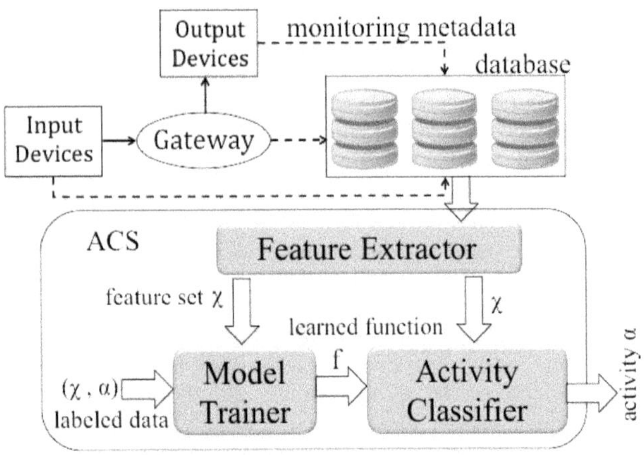

Figure 1: Architecture of activity classification system.

3. SYSTEM ARCHITECTURE

The system architecture of ACS is shown in Figure 1. It takes a supervised machine learning approach to classify human activity using application-system metadata. The time-series metadata values are stored in a local database attached to each site. ACS contains three components: 1) *Feature Extractor* that reads metadata from the database and extracts features to construct feature vectors interpretable by a machine learning model, 2) *Model Trainer* that uses these feature vectors and input activity labels to train a classification model, and 3) *Activity Classifier* that uses both the feature vectors and the model feeds to finally classify real-time human activity during 3DTI session run-time.

3.1 Feature Extraction

Feature extraction transforms recorded application and system metadata into a reduced representation of a set of features (also known as a feature vector). A feature vector is the smallest unit of training and testing. It consists of metadata corresponding to T consecutive time units. We consider three kinds of features extracted from the time-series metadata: 1) *absolute value*, 2) *time difference value*, which computes the variation of metadata value w.r.t. the previous time epoch, and 3) *device difference value*, which computes the variation of the metadata value generated from the correlated input devices (e.g., all local cameras) at the same time epoch. If there are N metadata parameters and x_i^t is the ith metadata value collected at time t, the feature vector (χ) contains: $\cup_{t=1}^{T} x_i^t$, $\forall_{1\leq i\leq N}$ (absolute values), $\cup_{t=2}^{T} x_i^t - x_i^{t-1}$, $\forall_{1\leq i\leq N}$ (time difference values), and $\cup_{t=1}^{T}(x_i^t - x_j^t)$ (device difference values), where i^{th} and j^{th} metadata values are generated from correlated devices and $1 \leq i, j \leq N$.

3.2 Model Training

Our objective is to train a classifier using a supervised machine-learning model to classify human activity based on 3DTI metadata. To this effect, we use the implementation of SVM [3] by Learning Based Java (LBJ) [9], which is a special purpose programming language based on Java for machine learning. Given labeled m samples containing feature vectors and associated labels $\{(\chi_1, \alpha_1), (\chi_2, \alpha_2), ..., (\chi_m, \alpha_m)\}$ where α_i is the class label for the sample feature vector χ_i, the SVM algorithm learns $f{:}\chi \rightarrow \{-1, +1\}$, where the function f maps samples χ to a class $\alpha \in \{+1, -1\}$ and is represented by $sgn(w^T\chi - \Theta)$ where $w \in R^n$ (weight vector) and $\theta \in R$ (constant threshold).

Since we consider multiple activities, for multi class classification, the LBJ library implementation of SVM employs the one vs. all strategy. This strategy learns independent binary classifiers for each class label α_i treating a sample (χ_i, α_i) as a positive training sample $(+1)$ only for class label α_i and negative (-1) for all other class labels.

3.3 Activity Classification

Once the model has been trained, it predicts the human activity given a feature vector. Having learnt independent classifiers (weight vectors w_j) for each class label α_j, the model performs the following calculation: $f(\chi)$=$argmax_j$ $w_j^T(\chi)$, where χ is the to-be-classified feature vector, w_j is the weight vector learnt for the jth activity class and $f(\chi)$ is the predicted class label.

4. EXPERIMENTS

Using ACS framework, we conduct a series of experiments to 1) study the impact of certain cyber physical parameters on our activity classification model, and 2) employ an efficiently trained model to classify activities.

4.1 Effect of Cyber Physical Parameters

We realize that human activity classification accuracy is influenced by certain cyber-physical dimensions. We consider two cyber-physical dimensions in our current study: 1) visual color of the cyber-physical content, and 2) volume of the cyber-physical content. Since backgrounds are usually subtracted, the visual color and physical texture of human body impact frame size metadata in mesh-based 3D

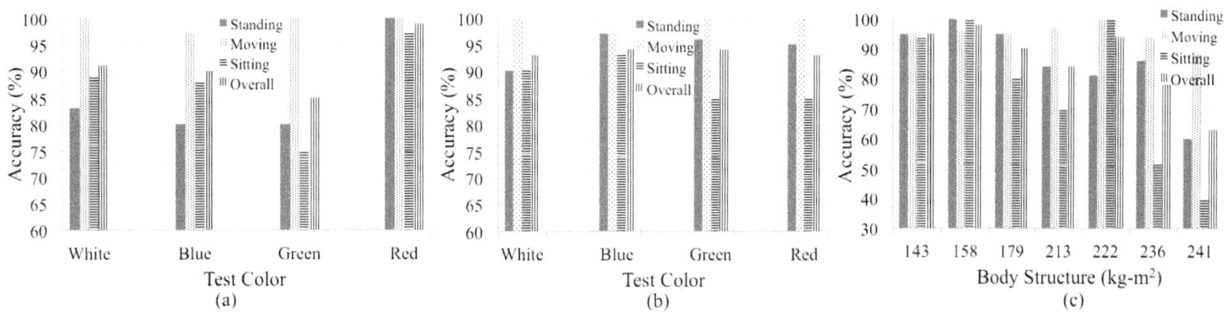

Figure 2: Activity classification accuracy with training model for (a) SC=red (phase-1), (b) SC values not included in the test (phase-2), and c) participant having BS=176 (phase-1).

reconstruction of fore-ground image. Likewise, the volume of the fore-ground content impacts frame size value of the constructed image. Change in frame size metadata changes 3D reconstruction time, data transmission time, network bandwidth and hence frame rate.

The visual color dimension is dependent upon physical lighting condition, shirt color as well as skin color of the participants. The volume dimension is dependent upon the participants' weights and heights. To quantify the impact of these two cyber-physical dimensions, we consider two metrics: 1) *Shirt Color (SC)*, and 2) *Body Structure (BS)*. We consider four different shirt colors: white, blue, green, and red. The body structure (BS) is derived from the height (H) and weight (W) of the participant as follows: $BS = H(m)^2 * W(kgs)$. Following the definition of *BMI (body mass index)*, we include the height parameter as squared in the BS computation formula.

4.1.1 Experimental Setup

We setup a 3DTI site with one gateway, two (upper and lower body) 3D bumblebee cameras (constructing mesh based 3D video streams via connected computers), one renderer and one database node. We run ACS on the local database machine and attempt to classify between a basic activity set $S = \{stand, sit, move\}$. For each activity session, 4 minutes of metadata is recorded. The data is collected under constant white lighting conditions. People involved in the experiments are given basic instructions on how to perform the respective activities, without any further information on how the application would classify their activity. Each classification unit is constructed with $T = 50$ and $N = 20$, which are the customizable parameters in 3.1.

To understand the impact of cyber-physical dimensions on human activity classification, we run experiments in two phases. In **phase-1**, we train the model on one random cyber-physical dimension value from the dimension spectrum (e.g., SC=blue) and record the classification accuracies given by the model on testing with other values (e.g., SC=red). In **phase-2**, we train the model on a more representative set (i.e., with multiple values) from the cyber-physical dimension spectrum, and record the classification accuracies on a random value (not included in the training).

4.1.2 Results and Discussion

Impact of Shirt Color (SC). To understand the impact of the SC dimension, we minimize the impact of content volume (i.e., BS) by recording application-system metadata for the same person under the same white light condition. We show the result for phase-1 in Figure 2(a). A high level of accuracy (> 85% overall) is achieved for activity classification where training is done based on activity (moving, standing and sitting) metadata collected only for SC=red. Changing the SC value (i.e., visual shirt color) of the participants shows limited impact on classification accuracy. We can conclude that the skin color of the participants and the lighting condition will not have high impact on activity classification accuracy either, since the learning is done based on the time-series patterns (which are similar across different SC values) of metadata.

In phase-2, the model is trained on data corresponding to all SC values except the SC value included in the test. The model achieves an average accuracy of about 94% as shown in Figure 2(b). This implies that when the ML algorithm is exposed to data corresponding to a wide range of SC values during training, the impact that the change in color has on the features helps it achieve higher accuracies for other values in the spectrum (even though the particular SC value is not seen during training).

Table 1: User data of body structure.

ID	Height (m)	Weight (kgs)	BS (kg-m^2)
1	1.73	59.0	176
2	1.70	54.5	158
3	1.80	65.7	213
4	1.75	72.5	222
5	1.77	77.0	241
6	1.66	65.0	179
7	1.62	54.5	143
8	1.77	75.0	236

Impact of Body Structure (BS). To study the effect of body structure, activity data is collected for 8 different people, all wearing a red shirt to minimize the impact of SC dimension. Table 1 shows the collected BS data for experiments' participants. The BS values range from 143 to 241. In phase-1, where the training of BS metadata is taken from the lower end of the spectrum (BS=176), we observe a general trend of dropping classification accuracies as we move towards the higher end of the spectrum (BS=236), with the overall (for all fine-grained activities) accuracy dropping as low as 65% (Figure 2(c)). This is because different cameras (upper and lower body cameras) get different spatial coverage of the participants (sometimes no inclusion of the participants' image) across the training and testing phase in ACS. This implies that BS shows high impact on the metadata and activity classification. This is especially true for the sitting activity, where the upper body and lower body camera captures different volume dimensions if we abruptly change BS value from the training to the testing phase. In this case, the classification accuracy falls to about 40%.

However, in phase-2, our classification model achieves an overall average accuracy of 97% whereby the training set included activity data corresponding to all BS values except the test BS value. This implies that if the machine learning model is trained with a representative set of data distributed uniformly over the whole BS spectrum, it is able to accurately classify activities for any data points throughout the spectrum.

4.2 Activity Classification

4.2.1 Experimental Setup

The experimental setup was the same as 4.1.1, with the exception that the model is trained to classify between a basic activity set S = {stand, sit, move00, move01, move10, move11}, where the definitions of the movement activities (moveXY) are given in Table 2.

Table 2: Movement Activity Definition

	Coverage = Low	Coverage = High
Speed = Low	move00	move01
Speed = High	move10	move11

The $Coverage \in \{Low, High\}$ refers to the spatial coverage of the participant in the physical space and the $Speed \in \{Low, High\}$ refers to the speed of movement and limb actions [1]. For each activity listed, 4 minutes of metadata was recorded for 5 people across the BS spectrum wearing the same color shirt (SC=RED), since earlier experiments in 4.1.2 have shown that body structure has a significant impact on activity classification accuracy.

4.2.2 Results and Discussion

The trained model is tested on random activity sessions' metadata, that is not seen during training. An (i, j) entry in the Table 3 denotes the percentage of activity samples corresponding to activity i that are classified as activity j. Based on the results, the following observations are made: 1) our model performs very well in classifying Stand and Sit, 2) classification between different movements is harder due to the minor variation in the impact of the different types of movement on metadata. However, we can still achieve 88% accuracy for move01 and 78% accuracy for move10, and 3) the major mis-classification occurs due to the variation in *Speed*; move00 is frequently mis-classified as move10, and move11 is frequently mis-classified as move01. In all cases, the *Coverage* dimension is classified correctly.

Table 3: Activity Classification Distribution (%)

	move00	*move01*	*move10*	*move11*	*stand*	*sit*
move00	47.50	0.00	32.50	0.00	17.50	2.50
move01	2.17	78.26	8.70	8.70	2.17	0.00
move10	7.14	0.00	88.10	4.76	0.00	0.00
move11	2.56	38.46	5.13	53.85	0.00	0.00
stand	0.00	0.00	4.17	0.00	95.83	0.00
sit	0.00	0.00	0.00	3.70	0.00	96.30

5. RELATED WORK

Niu et al in [7] attempted to detect human activity in a global 3D estimate by fusing estimates fro multiple 2D sensors and observing people trajectories. However, this approach was designed towards detecting questionable activities for video surveillance as opposed to identifying particular activities in our case. Many others have applied machine learning models for activity classification, e.g., employment of hierarchical maximum entropy markov model to classify human activity in unstructured environments from Kinect Sensor data [10], unsupervised learning to detect unusual activity in video [12], combining supervised and unsupervised learning to model human behavior from mobile sensor [8] and [4]. However, no approaches derive features and information from application-system metadata to classify human activity, which is agnostic to application logic.

6. CONCLUSION

We propose a system that addresses the activity classification problem in 3DTI systems from an unique perspective, using time-series application-system metadata. With a few exceptions, our system is able to achieve high accuracy for classifying a basic set of human activities in a running 3DTI session. The detection process is fast (4 ms). Moreover, the system provides a base for constructing a classification system for coarse-grained activity detection. Due to the decoupling of ACS from the application-specific media analyses, our solution is generalized and can be adopted as a middleware to many 3DTI setup.

7. REFERENCES

[1] A. Arefin, Z. Huang, R. Rivas, S. Shi, P. Xie, K. Nahrstedt, W. Wu, G. Kurillo, and R. Bajcsy. Classification and analysis of 3D tele-immersive activities. In *IEEE Multimedia*, 2013.

[2] A. Arefin, R. Rivas, and K. Nahrstedt. Prioritized evolutionary optimization in open session management for 3D tele-immersion. In *Proc. of MMSys*, 2013.

[3] B. Boser, I. M. Guyon, and V. N. Vapnik. A training algorithm for optimal margin classifiers. In *Proc. of COLT*, 1992.

[4] C. Chen and K. Grauman. Efficient activity detection with max-subgraph search. In *Proc. of CVPR*, 2012.

[5] G. Kurillo, M. Forte, and R. Bajcsy. Tele-immersive 3D collaborative environment for cyberarchaeology. In *Proc. of CVPR*, 2010.

[6] A. Maimone and H. Fuchs. Real-time volumetric 3D capture of room-sized scenes for telepresence. In *Proc. of 3DTV-CON*, 2012.

[7] W. Niu, J. Long, D. Han, and Y.-F. Wang. Human activity detection and recognition for video surveillance. In *Proc. of ICME*, 2004.

[8] D. Peebles, H. Lu, N. D. Lane, T. Choudhury, and A. T. Campbell. Community-guided learning: Exploiting mobile sensor users to model human behavior. In *Proc. of AAAI*, 2010.

[9] N. Rizzolo and D. Roth. Learning based java for rapid development of NLP systems. http://bit.ly/13J1kuq, 2010.

[10] J. Sung, C. Ponce, B. Selman, and A. Saxena. Human activity detection from RGDB images. In *Proc. of AAAI workshop on PAIR*, 2011.

[11] Z. Zhang, D. Chu, J. Qiu, and T. Moscibroda. Demo: Sword fight with smartphones. In *Proc. of SenSys*, 2011.

[12] H. Zhong, J. Shi, and M. Visontai. Detecting unusual activity in video. In *Proc. of CVPR*, 2004.

Object Co-segmentation Via Discriminative Low Rank Matrix Recovery

Yong Li[†],Jing Liu[†],Zechao Li[†‡],Yang Liu[†],Hanqing Lu[†]
[†]National Laboratory of Pattern Recognition, Institute of Automation, Chinese Academy of Sciences
[‡]School of Computer Science, Nanjing University of Science and Technology
{yong.li,jliu,liuyang6,luhq}@nlpr.ia.ac.cn, zechao.li@gmail.com

ABSTRACT

The goal of this paper is to simultaneously segment the object regions appearing in a set of images of the same object class, known as object co-segmentation. Different from typical methods, simply assuming that the regions common among images are the object regions, we additionally consider the disturbance from consistent backgrounds, and indicate not only common regions but salient ones among images to be the object regions. To this end, we propose a Discriminative Low Rank matrix Recovery (DLRR) algorithm to divide the over-completely segmented regions (i.e., super-pixels) of a given image set into object and non-object ones. In DLRR, a low-rank matrix recovery term is adopted to detect salient regions in an image, while a discriminative learning term is used to distinguish the object regions from all the super-pixels. An additional regularized term is imported to jointly measure the disagreement between the predicted saliency and the objectiveness probability corresponding to each super-pixel of the image set. For the unified learning problem by connecting the above three terms, we design an efficient optimization procedure based on block-coordinate descent. Extensive experiments are conducted on two public datasets, i.e., MSRC and iCoseg, and the comparisons with some state-of-the-arts demonstrate the effectiveness of our work.

Categories and Subject Descriptors

H.3.1 [**Information Storage and Retrieval**]: Content Analysis and Indexing; I.2.10 [**Artificial Intelligence**]: Vision and Scene Understanding

General Terms

Algorithms, Experimentation, Theory

Keywords

Object Co-segmentation, Low Rank Matrix Recovery, Discriminative Learning

Figure 1: Examples about the object region. The region inside red contour is the true object regions, while the one inside green contour is the non-object region although is salient.

1. INTRODUCTION

The object segmentation is a fundamental task in computer vision and multimedia, and it can benefit from many applications, e.g., object retrieval and image editing. Provided with some priors to indicate what or which the object regions are, some supervised or interactive object extraction approaches [9][6] can achieve good performance. However, they are hard to be extended to a large scale dataset due to expensive requirements on human interaction or manually labeled training data. Alexe et al. [1] proposed a general object detector, but it does not leverage the shared information among different images of the same or similar objects.

To alleviate such expensive requirements and leverage the shared information, recent researches focus on the task of object co-segmentation, which is to simultaneously segment the same or similar objects appearing in a set of images. A representative solution is to mine the similar object regions by a discriminative clustering framework [4], in which the clustering step is used to merge image pixels into two clusters while the discriminative learning step is to maximally distinguish the two clusters. Considering the diversity of background, Joulin et al. [5] proposed an improved multi-class co-segmentation method by combining spectral clustering and discriminative clustering. Besides, Mukherjee et al. [8] adopted a direct solution to make the possible object regions in images similar to each other. Most of previous approaches work on the assumption that the regions common among images are deemed as the object regions. However, the truth is not the case, in that the background regions may be consistent. For example, shown in Fig. 1, the 'grass' regions may be common within the 'baseball' images. How to

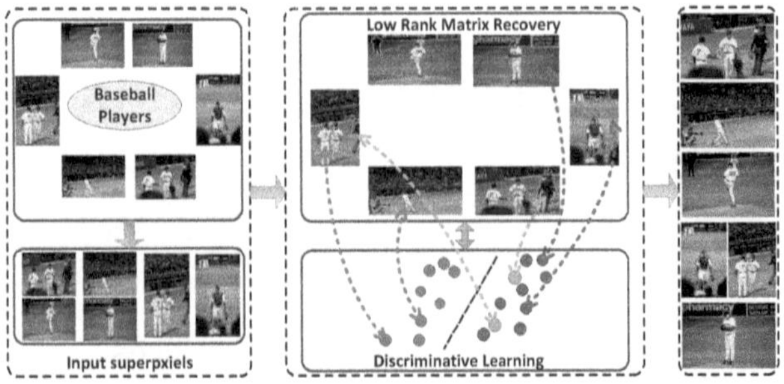

Figure 2: The flowchart of our method. In "discriminative learning" part, red points denote salient and common regions (i.e., object), green points denote salient but uncommon regions (i.e., non-object), and blue points denote non-object regions.

effectively resist the disturbance of such case, and further to precisely identify the true object regions become our focus in this paper.

To this end, we jointly exploit saliency detection and common region mining from a set of images to perform the task of object co-segmentation. That is, the object regions are assumed to be not only common among images but also salient in contrast with background regions. It can naturally eliminate the disturbance of those background regions consistent with each other. Just as shown in Fig. 1, we can easily catch the 'baseball player' regions as the true object regions because they are salient and simultaneously appear in these four images, while the common but non-salient regions (e.g., baseball field) and the salient but uncommon regions (e.g., baseball referee and billboard) are deemed as background.

For this purpose, we propose a unified learning framework, named as discriminative low rank matrix recovery (DLRR) for object co-segmentation, as shown in Fig. 2. Given a set of images of an object class, we first over-completely segment each image into super-pixels, and then employ the proposed DLRR to identify the salient and common regions in the image set. Inspired by the work in [7], we adopt the basic idea of low-rank matrix recovery to detect the salient regions of an image, i.e., decomposing the super-pixel-wise representation of each image into a low-rank matrix and a sparse matrix, and using the l_1-norm of each column in the sparse matrix to measure the saliency of the corresponding super-pixel. Besides, discriminative learning is incorporated on the image set to model the salient and common super-pixels. To promote the both terms each other, we import a regularized penalty to measure the disagreement between the predicted saliency and the discriminative output. By jointly considering the above three terms, a unified optimization problem is obtained, and a block-coordinate descent optimization algorithm is presented to solve the proposed problem. Extensive experiments on two publicly available benchmarks, i.e., MSRC and iCoseg, show the satisfied performance of our proposed method. Our main contributions are summarized as follows.

- To the best of our knowledge, we are first to consider the disturbance of consistent background regions for object co-segmentation.
- To overcome the disturbance, we propose to jointly perform saliency detection and common region mining among images to precisely identify the object regions.
- We propose a discriminative low-rank matrix recovery algorithm to solve the object co-segmentation problem, and an efficient optimizing process is also designed.

The rest of the paper is organized as follows. In Section 2, we elaborate our proposed model for object co-segmentation, and its optimization algorithm is presented in Section 3. The experimental evaluation is given in Section 4 followed with the conclusion in Section 5.

2. PROPOSED MODEL

Given a set of images τ with the same class label, image over-segmentation is performed by mean-shift clustering [3] to each image i based on extracted features including color, gabor feature and steerable pyramid feature, and N_i superpixels are obtained. For the j-th superpixel in the i-th image, we use the mean of the features in this superpixel as its feature representation $f_{ij} \in R^D$, then we get the feature representation of the i-th image $\mathbf{F}_i = [f_{i1}, f_{i2}, \cdots, f_{iN_i}]$. Let $y_i \in [0, 1]^{1\times N_i}$ denote the probability vector of superpixels to be foreground in the i-th image. The larger y_{ij} is, the more likely for the j-th superpixel in the i-th image to be target object.

2.1 Low Rank Matrix Recovery

For an image, the background usually lies in a low dimensional space, while the salient regions are usually unique and are quite different from the rest [10]. Therefore, low-rank matrix recovery method is adopted to detect image saliency. An image is represented as a low-rank matrix plus sparse noises in the feature space, where the low-rank matrix explains the non-salient regions (or background), and the sparse noises indicate the salient regions. That is, $\mathbf{F}_i = \mathbf{L}_i + \mathbf{S}_i$, where $\mathbf{L}_i$ is the low rank matrix corresponding to the background and $\mathbf{S}_i$ is the sparse noise matrix corresponding to the salient regions. Since the rank norm and l_0 norm lead to an NP-hard problem and it has been shown that the nuclear norm and the l_1 norm is the tight convex approximation for the rank and the l_0 norm [11]. Thus, we obtain the following convex surrogate:

$$\begin{aligned}(\mathbf{L}_i^*, \mathbf{S}_i^*) &= \arg\min(\|\mathbf{L}_i\|_* + \lambda\|\mathbf{S}_i\|_1)\\ s.t.\mathbf{F}_i &= \mathbf{L}_i + \mathbf{S}_i\end{aligned} \tag{1}$$

where $\|\cdot\|_*$ is the nuclear norm. The l_1-norm of each column S_{ij} in $\mathbf{S}_i$ can be used to measure the saliency of the corresponding superpixel [10]. The larger $\|S_{ij}\|_1$ is, the more likely for the j-th superpixel in the i-th image to be salient region.

However, not all the salient regions are meaningful, and some small regions with high-contrast and uniqueness may be considered as meaningless noise by human. Hence we consider some priors to handle the meaningless noise, which is integrated to the low rank recovery framework as follows.

$$\begin{aligned}(\mathbf{L}_i^*, \mathbf{S}_i^*) &= \arg\min(\|\mathbf{L}_i\|_* + \lambda\|\mathbf{S}_i\|_1)\\ s.t.\mathbf{F}_i\mathbf{P}_i &= \mathbf{L}_i + \mathbf{S}_i\end{aligned} \tag{2}$$

where $\mathbf{P}_i$ is a diagonal matrix corresponding to the high level prior such as color or location prior. Since objects near the image center are more attractive to people, a Gaussian distribution based on the distance to the image center is chosen as a high level prior to reduce small salient regions near the image edge in our experiments.

Algorithm 1: Object Co-segmentation by DLRR

Input: Feature Matrix $\mathbf{F}$, high level Prior $\mathbf{P}$ and the required parameters

Initialize: solve Equ.(2) by the method in [11]

1: **while** not converged do

2: $\alpha_i = \frac{1}{\max \|S_{ij}\|_1}$

3: $y_{ij} = \alpha_i \|S_{ij}\|_1$

4: **while** not converaged

5: $\theta^{t+1} = \theta^t - \alpha_{step1}\{[h(f_{ij}) - y_{ij}]f_{ij} + 2r\theta^t\}$

6: **end while**

7: **while** not converaged

8: $y^{t+1} = y^t - \alpha_{step2}[-\mu_1\theta^T\mathbf{F} + 2\mu_2(y^t - S)]$

9: **end while**

10: solve problem (6) in algorithm 2

11: **end while**

Output: foreground probability y

2.2 Discriminative Learning

The saliency detection is mainly evaluated from the view of a single image. However, it cannot exactly catch the object regions common among images. To this end, a logistic regression based discriminative learning is exploited to predict the probability of each superpixel to be the target object.The objective function is to minimize the following regularized function.

$$E_D = -\sum_{i=1}^{\tau}\sum_{j=1}^{N_i}[y_{ij}\log(h(f_{ij})) + (1-y_{ij})\log(1-h(f_{ij}))] + r\|\theta\|^2 \quad (3)$$

where θ is the model parameter to be learned. $h(f_{ij}) = \frac{1}{1+\exp(-\theta^T f_{ij}+b)}$ is the predictive result.

2.3 Proposed Formulation

As discussed in section 1, the ideal object regions as a result of co-segmentation are required to be both salient and common among a given set of images. Thus, we expect, the aforementioned two parts should be learned simultaneously and promote each other. We import a regularization penalty to measure the disagreement between their predicted results. Specifically, the l_1 norm of each column S_{ij} in $\mathbf{S}_i$ stands for the salient score of the j-th superpixel and y_{ij} in discriminative learning is the probability of the j-th superpixel to be target object. Consequently, the disagreement is measured by the following equation.

$$E_R = \sum_{i=1}^{\tau}\sum_{j=1}^{N_i}(y_{ij} - \alpha_i\|S_{ij}\|_1)^2 \quad (4)$$

where α_i is the normalized weight for the superpixel saliency in the i-th image. By jointly exploiting the above aspects, the proposed model is formulated as follows.

$$\min \sum_{i=1}^{\tau}(\|\mathbf{L}_i\|_* + \lambda\|\mathbf{S}_i\|_1) + \mu_1 E_D + \mu_2 E_R \quad s.t.\ \mathbf{F}_i\mathbf{P}_i = \mathbf{L}_i + \mathbf{S}_i, i \in \tau \quad (5)$$

where μ_1 and μ_2 are two non-negative trade-off parameters.

3. MODEL OPTIMIZATION

Considering the objective function is a difference of convex functions, a optimization procedure based on block-coordinate descent is designed and we summarize it in Algorithm 1, where $\mathbf{F} = [\mathbf{F}_1, \cdots, \mathbf{F}_\tau]$, $y = [y_1, \cdots, y_\tau]$, and $S = [\alpha_1\|S_{11}\|_1, \cdots, \alpha_\tau\|S_{\tau N_\tau}\|_1]$. Lines 4-6 is to learn model parameter θ in the discriminative algorithm. Lines 7-9 is to predict the probability to be target object based on saliency detection result and discriminative learning together. The low rank matrix recovery problem given the guidance information y can be solved by solving the following Augmented Lagrange Multiplier(ALM) problem.

$$(\mathbf{L}_i^*, \mathbf{S}_i^*) = \arg\min(\|\mathbf{L}_i\|_* + \lambda\|\mathbf{S}_i\|_1) + tr(\mathbf{Y}^T(\mathbf{F}_i\mathbf{P}_i - \mathbf{L}_i - \mathbf{S}_i)) + \frac{\beta}{2}\|\mathbf{F}_i\mathbf{P}_i - \mathbf{L}_i - \mathbf{S}_i\|_F^2 + \mu_2\sum_{j=1}^{N_i}(y_{ij} - \alpha_i\|S_{ij}\|_1)^2 \quad (6)$$

where $tr(\cdot)$ is the trace of a matrix, $\mathbf{Y}$ is the Lagrange multiplier and $\beta > 0$ is a penalty parameter. The inexact ALM method in [7] is used for efficiency and outlined in Algorithm 2, and $T_\varepsilon[\cdot]$ is the soft-thresholding (shrinkage) operator.

Algorithm 2: Solving problem (6) by inexact ALM

Input: matrix $\mathbf{F}_i$, $\mathbf{P}_i$, y_i; parameters λ, β, μ_2, α_i, D

Initialize: $\mathbf{Y}^0 = \mathbf{F}_i\mathbf{P}_i/J(\mathbf{F}_i\mathbf{P}_i)$; $\mathbf{S}^0 = \mathbf{0}$; $\beta^0 = 10^{-6}$; $\beta_{max} = 10^6$;$\rho = 1.5$; $k = 0$

while not converged do

$(\mathbf{U}, \Sigma, \mathbf{V}) = \text{svd}(\mathbf{F}_i\mathbf{P}_i - \mathbf{S}_i^k + (\beta^k)^{-1}\mathbf{Y}^k)$

$\mathbf{L}_i^{k+1} = \mathbf{U}T_{(\beta^k)^{-1}}[\Sigma]\mathbf{V}^T$

$\varepsilon = \frac{\lambda - 2\alpha_i\mu_2 y_n + 2\alpha_i^2\mu_2\sum_{t=1,\neq m}^{D}|S_i(t,n)|}{\beta + 2\alpha_i^2\mu_2}$

$\mathbf{x} = \frac{\beta}{\beta + 2\alpha_i^2\mu_2}(\mathbf{F}_i\mathbf{P}_i - \mathbf{L}_i^{k+1} + (\beta^k)^{-1}\mathbf{Y}^k)$

$S_i^{k+1}(m,n) = T_\varepsilon[x(m,n)]$

$\mathbf{Y}^{k+1} = \mathbf{Y}^k + \beta^k(\mathbf{F}_i\mathbf{P}_i - \mathbf{L}_i^{k+1} - \mathbf{S}_i^{k+1})$

$\beta^{k+1} = \min(\rho\beta^k, \beta_{max})$

$k \leftarrow k + 1$

end while

Output: $(\mathbf{L}_i^k, \mathbf{S}_i^k)$

4. EXPERIMENTS AND RESULTS

To validate the effectiveness of the proposed method, we conduct experiments on two publicly available benchmarks, i.e., MSRC-v2[1] and iCoseg [2]. And we compare the proposed DLRR with three state-of-the-art approaches [4][5][8], and two special cases of DLRR. The first special case is denoted as LRR, which directly uses the the saliency detection result based on low rank matrix recovery as the object probability. That is, μ_1 and μ_2 are both set to 0 in the proposed model (5). The second one is denoted as DIS, which is a two-step method. The low rank matrix recovery is first performed to get the image saliency $\|S_{ij}\|_1$, and then we learn the discriminative model with the fixed S_{ij}. The visual features used for over-segmentation include color features, gabor features, and steerable pyramid features, which are same to the work in [10]. The segmentation performance is measured by the *intersection-over-union* score and defined by $\frac{1}{|\tau|}\sum_{i\in\tau}\frac{R_i \cap GT_i}{R_i \cup GT_i}$, where R_i is the segmentation result of image i and GT_i is the ground truth. This evaluation metric is standard in PASCAL challenges.

MSRC-v2 consists of 14 classes of images, and each class contains 30 images, except that the 'cat' class contains 24 images. The comparison of different methods on the dataset is listed in Table 1, where we directly cite the results of [4] [5]

[1] http://research.microsoft.com/en-us/projects/ObjectClassRecognition/

Table 1: Results on MSRC Dataset

class	DLRR	LRR	DIS	[5]	[8]	[4]
Bike	48.8	45.3	**54.9**	43.3	42.8	42.3
Bird	44.4	45.0	32.3	**47.7**	-	33.2
Car	53.3	53.0	48.6	**59.7**	52.5	59.0
Cat	58.6	**59.4**	47.8	31.9	5.6	30.1
Chair	50.5	**52.1**	41.3	39.6	39.4	37.6
Cow	**63.8**	63.0	51.0	52.7	26.1	45.0
Dog	50.1	**51.3**	36.9	41.8	-	41.3
Face	52.1	52.7	44.2	**70.0**	40.8	66.2
Flower	**56.3**	54.2	53.3	51.9	-	50.9
House	51.1	49.3	45.4	51.0	**66.4**	50.5
Plane	**46.1**	43.8	44.2	21.6	33.4	21.7
Sheep	64.9	64.5	56.7	**66.3**	45.7	60.4
Sign	**62.4**	61.1	55.2	58.9	-	55.2
Tree	57.1	52.1	64.5	**67.0**	55.9	60.0
Avg.	**54.2**	53.3	48.3	50.2	40.9	46.7
Std	6.5	6.6	8.5	13.9	16.9	13.1

Table 2: Results on ICoseg Dataset

class	No.	DLRR	LRR	DIS	[5]	[4]
Baseball	25	**62.8**	55.2	55.8	13.6	31.4
Football	33	**39.3**	36.9	35.1	38.7	14.9
Monk	17	40.4	36.4	28.2	**73.8**	68.4
BrownBear	5	39.5	40.6	33.7	**57.5**	49.4
Ferrari	11	**54.5**	48.5	49.8	38.7	26.4
Skating	11	54.2	45.3	67.0	**72.7**	38.1
AlasBear	19	41.6	40.2	38.8	41.6	**46.1**
TajlMahal	5	**46.6**	45.4	41.1	37.1	38.4
Helicopter	12	62.4	**64.7**	50.8	33.3	61.0
Kite	18	45.8	43.9	37.3	22.1	**57.8**
Avg	16	**48.7**	45.7	43.8	42.9	43.2
Std	-	9.2	8.7	11.8	19.7	16.6

[8] reported in [5]. From the results in Table 1, DLRR outperforms all the compared methods in terms of the average performance, and specially achieves the best performance for 8 of 14 classes. In addition, our method is more robust than the others because of the minimum standard deviation. Compared with LRR, DLRR improves obviously for the classes with high coherence(e.g., sign, flower and tree). For DIS, using predicted saliency as the prior for discriminative learning in a progressive manner, it decreases the performance by a large margin compared with DLRR.

Table 2 gives a quantitative comparison with [4] [5] on the iCoseg dataset. Since we mainly focus on the segmentation of the common object regions from the background, then the class number in [5] is set to 2. We use the publicly versions of [5, 4] to get the co-segmentation results and prefer the regions with larger overlap with ground truth as the target object regions. From results in Table 2, we can find that DLRR achieves the best performance for 5 of 10 image classes, and the average segmentation score increases 12.7% relatively to [4]. Conclusions conducted above are further verified. DLRR outperforms the state-of-the-art methods for most classes and are more robust to class changes, and DLRR shares the advantages of LRR and DIS. Compared with LRR, DLRR improves obviously for the classes with high class coherence (e.g., baseball, skating and Tai Mahal).

Figure 3 presents some object co-segmentation results of the proposed method on the both datasets, in which the successful and unsuccessful examples are both shown.

Figure 3: Some object co-segmentation results.

The failed results may be due to the diversity of the object appearance.

5. CONCLUSIONS

In this paper, a novel discriminative low rank matrix recovery algorithm is proposed to perform object co-segmentation. Our method works on the assumption that object region should be not only common among images but salient one in an image. This is the first to be used in the task of object segmentation. We import the low rank matrix recovery term to measure the saliency of super-pixels so as to eliminate the disturbance from those consistent backgrounds, while a discriminative learning term is used to model the true object region simultaneously. Besides, a regularized penalty is employed to promote the both terms each other. A joint optimization algorithm is designed to solve the proposed formulation. Extensive experiments have shown the outperforming performance compared with some state-of-the-arts.

6. ACKNOWLEDGMENTS

This work was supported by 973 Program (2010CB327905) and National Natural Science Foundation of China (61272329, 61070104, and 60905008).

7. REFERENCES

[1] B. Alexe, T. Deselaers, and V. Ferrari. What is an object ? In *CVPR*, 2010.

[2] D. Batra, A. Kowdle, D. Parikh, J. Luo, and T. Chen. Interactively co-segmentating topically related images with intelligent scribble guidance. *IJCV*, 93(3):273–292, 2011.

[3] D. Comaniciu and P. Meer. Mean shift: a robust approach toward feature space analysis. *TPAMI*, 24(5):603–619, 2002.

[4] A. Joulin, F. Bach, and J. Ponce. Discriminative clustering for image co-segmentation. In *CVPR*, 2010.

[5] A. Joulin, F. Bach, and J. Ponce. Multi-class cosegmentation. In *CVPR*, 2012.

[6] D. Kuettel and V. Ferrari. Figure-ground segmentation by transferring window masks. In *CVPR*, 2012.

[7] Z. Lin, M. Chen, and Y. Ma. The augmented lagrange multiplier method for exact recovery of corrupted low-rank matrices. *UIUC Technical Report UILU-ENG-09-2214*, October 2010.

[8] L. Mukherjee, V. Singh, and J. Peng. Scale invariant cosegmentation for image groups. In *CVPR*, 2011.

[9] C. Rother, V. Kolmogorov, and A. Blake. "grabcut" - interactive foreground extraction using iterated graph cuts. *ACM Trans. Graph.*, 23(3):309–314, Aug 2004.

[10] X. Shen and Y. Wu. A unified approach to salient object detection via low rank matrix recovery. In *CVPR*, 2012.

[11] J. Wright, Y. Peng, and Y. Ma. Robust principal component analysis: Exact recovery of corrupted low-rank matrices via convex optimization. In *NIPS*, 2009.

πLDA: Document Clustering with Selective Structural Constraints

Siliang Tang, Hanqi Wang, Jian Shao, Fei Wu, Ming Chen, Yueting Zhuang
College of Computer Science, Zhejiang University
Hangzhou, Zhejiang, China
{siliang, hanqiw, jshao, wufei, mingchen, yzhuang}@zju.edu.cn

ABSTRACT

Segments, such as sentence boundaries in texts or annotated regions in images, can be considered as useful structural constraints (i.e., *priors*) for unsupervised topic modeling. However, some *segment units* (e.g., words in texts or visual words in images) inside a given segment may be irrelevant to the topic of this segment due to their characteristics. This paper proposes a model called πLDA, which introduces a latent variable π into LDA, a traditional topic model, to capture the characteristic of each segment unit. That is to say, the πLDA model is conducted to determine whether a segment unit is assigned (or *selected*) to the topic embedded in its corresponding segment. Compared with other approaches that assume all the segment units in one segment to share a common topic, our proposed πLDA has the *selective* ability to discover the discriminative segment units (e.g., informative words or visual words). Experimental results and interpretations of them are presented for demonstrating the promising performance of our method.

Categories and Subject Descriptors

H.3.3 [**Information Search and Retrieval**]: Clustering

Keywords

Topic Modeling; Selective Structural Constraints; Latent Dirichlet Allocation

1. INTRODUCTION

The increasing volume of unlabeled digital media data on the Internet gives rise to a great challenge of automatic document clustering. Therefore, many unsupervised probabilistic clustering models (also known as topic models), such as Latent Dirichlet Allocation (LDA) [1] and its extensions, have been developed for various problems from document summarization to new challenges like cross-collection modeling [4] and topic evolution analysis [8]. The original LDA model adopts the "Bag-of-Word" (BoW) representation, where documents are represented as an unordered collection of words, disregarding the linguistic structures between them. By assigning each word to a latent topic, LDA projects documents into a low dimensional topic space, where each topic is usually represented as a multinomial distribution over a fixed vocabulary. Such assumption has later been applied to image clustering [3] after extracting visual words from low level visual features. However, the BoW approach has been criticized for several reasons [7]. The most controversial deficiency of BoW is that it fails to utilize the intrinsic structural information of documents (such as paragraphs and sentences in texts, or object boundaries in images). Thus, some studies attempt to impose such inherent structural constraints directly to the LDA model. For example, the LDCC model [7] extended the original LDA by introducing an extra latent layer between topic proportions on documents and latent topic assignments to words, in which topics become distributions over the segments (i.e., chapters or paragraphs) in texts. Wang et al. [9] applied the similar idea to the task of document summarization, where the segments are the sentences in documents. On the other hand, for computer vision, some LDA variants also take the intrinsic structural priors in images into consideration. For example, in the Spatial-LTM model [2], all the image patches within a certain region are assigned with exactly one single topic to enforce the internal spatial constraints. The intuition behind those models is that documents are composed of meaningful single-topic segments, and all of the segment units in a segment are assumed to share exactly one single concept (topic). However, some segment units in a segment are probably noises and are irrelevant to the shared common topic. Therefore, they may even have an adverse effect on representing the topic of this segment. As a result, the selection of discriminative segment units for the shared common topic embedded in each segment is appealing. One hypothesis is that the key determining factor of whether a segment unit has the shared common topic within its corresponding segment relies on the characteristic of itself. Take sentence "Libya hosts its first film festival about human rights." for example, it is obvious that the most representative words to the topic of this sentence are the nouns, then the verbs, while the adjectives are less representative.

In order to select out the discriminative segment units from each segment to enhance the performance of topic modeling, this paper proposes a model called πLDA, which introduces a latent variable π into the original LDA to capture the characteristics of segment units. The πLDA model

MM'13, October 21–25, 2013, Barcelona, Spain.

http://dx.doi.org/10.1145/2502081.2502196.

Table 1: Notations in the πLDA Model

	Description
D	number of documents
K	number of topics
V	number of distinct words in vocabulary
T	number of distinct characteristics
L_d	number of segments in document d
s_{dl}	topic assignment of segment l in document d
N_{dl}	number of words in segment l of document d
w_{dli}	word i in segment l of document d
z_{dli}	topic assignment of word w_{dli}
π_{dli}	selector assignment of word w_{dli}
t_{dli}	characteristic of word w_{dli}
θ_d	distribution of topics specific to document d
ϕ_k	distribution of words specific to topic k
λ_t	distribution of selectors specific to characteristic t
α	hyper parameter of topic distributions $\boldsymbol{\theta}$
β	hyper parameter of word distributions $\boldsymbol{\phi}$
γ	hyper parameter of selector distributions $\boldsymbol{\lambda}$

can determine whether a segment unit is assigned (or *selected*) to the topic embedded in its corresponding segment. Compared with other approaches that assume all the segment units in a segment to share exactly one common topic, πLDA has the *selective* ability to discover the discriminative segment units (e.g., informative words or visual words). Clustering experiments on news articles and images demonstrate that our proposed πLDA can generate better topic clusters than related methods in terms of normalized mutual information (NMI) and clustering purity.

2. THE PROPOSED πLDA MODEL

In this section, we first describe the formulation of our model, and then give a detailed description about the parameter inference of πLDA.

2.1 The Generative Process of πLDA

Tabel 1 gives out the notations used in our model. Segments are taken as structural constraints in the πLDA model. Given a segment, πLDA tends to decide which segment unit can be selected to assign the shared common topic in this segment. The segments in texts are the sentences in each document, and the characteristics of segment units (words) are the part-of-speech tags they have. On the other hand, the segments in images are the annotated regions in each image, and the labels of objects that visual words belong to are regarded as characteristics. Assume w is a segment unit in segment s, and its characteristic is t, the πLDA model attempts to determine whether w has the shared common latent topic embedded in s by utilizing a binary selector π which is sampled from λ_t.

Denoting Dirichlet, Binomial and Multinomial distributions as "Dir", "Bino" and "Mult" separately, the whole generative process can be described as follows:

1. Draw word proportions $\phi_k \sim \text{Dir}(\beta)$ for each topic k
2. Draw selector proportions $\lambda_t \sim \text{Beta}(\gamma)$ for each characteristic t
3. For each document d:
   1) Draw topic proportions $\theta_d \sim \text{Dir}(\alpha)$
   2) For each segment l in document d:
      a) Sample topic assignment $s_{dl} \sim \text{Multi}(\theta_d)$
      b) Sample each topic assignment $z_{dli} \sim \text{Multi}(\theta_d)$
      c) Sample each selector $\pi_{dli} \sim \text{Bino}(\lambda_{t_{dli}})$
      d) Sample each word $w_{dli} \sim \text{Multi}(\phi_{s_{dl}})$ if $\pi_{dli} = 1$, otherwise $w_{dli} \sim \text{Multi}(\phi_{z_{dli}})$

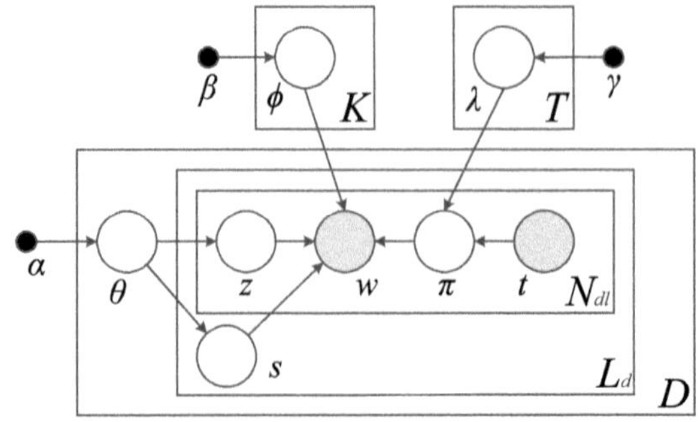

Figure 1: Graphical model representation of πLDA.

The graphical model representation of our proposed πLDA is shown in Figure 1. Plates from outer to inner represent the documents, the segments in each document, and the words in each segment respectively. Shaded nodes indicate observations, while the others represent latent variables. The black dots are the hyper parameters of our model.

2.2 Approximate Inference

Since exact inference of $\boldsymbol{\phi}$ in topic models is often intractable, some approximate methods are commonly conducted in parameter inference as substitutes, among which variational inference [1] and Gibbs sampling [5] are the most popular ones. In this paper, we utilize the collapsed Gibbs sampling method, in which all the proportions $\boldsymbol{\theta}$, $\boldsymbol{\phi}$ and $\boldsymbol{\lambda}$ are integrated out. We then iteratively sample the assignments of latent variables $\boldsymbol{z}$, $\boldsymbol{s}$, and $\boldsymbol{\pi}$.

Denoting $\{\boldsymbol{w}, \boldsymbol{z}, \boldsymbol{s}, \boldsymbol{\pi}, \boldsymbol{t}\}$ and $\{\alpha, \beta, \gamma\}$ as $\boldsymbol{\Phi}$ and Ψ respectively, the joint distribution of πLDA is written as:

$$\begin{aligned} p(\boldsymbol{\Phi}|\Psi) &= \int p(\boldsymbol{\Phi}, \boldsymbol{\theta}, \boldsymbol{\phi}, \boldsymbol{\lambda}|\Psi) \mathrm{d}\boldsymbol{\theta} \mathrm{d}\boldsymbol{\phi} \mathrm{d}\boldsymbol{\lambda} \\ &= p(\boldsymbol{t}) \times \prod_{d=1}^{D} \frac{\Gamma\left(\sum_{k=1}^{K} \alpha_k\right)}{\prod_{k=1}^{K} \Gamma(\alpha_k)} \frac{\prod_{k=1}^{K} \Gamma(\alpha_k + n_{dk} + l_{dk})}{\Gamma\left(\sum_{k=1}^{K} \alpha_k + n_{dk} + l_{dk}\right)} \\ &\quad \times \prod_{t=1}^{T} \frac{\Gamma(\gamma_0 + \gamma_1)}{\Gamma(\gamma_0)\Gamma(\gamma_1)} \frac{\Gamma(\gamma_0 + c_{t,0})\Gamma(\gamma_1 + c_{t,1})}{\Gamma(\gamma_0 + \gamma_1 + c_t)} \\ &\quad \times \prod_{k=1}^{K} \frac{\Gamma\left(\sum_{v=1}^{V} \beta_v\right)}{\prod_{v=1}^{V} \Gamma(\beta_v)} \frac{\prod_{v=1}^{V} \Gamma(\beta_v + n_{kv})}{\Gamma\left(\sum_{v=1}^{V} \beta_v + n_{kv}\right)} \end{aligned} \tag{1}$$

where n_{dk} denotes the number of words in document d whose corresponding topic is k, while l_{dk} is the number of segments with topic k in document d. We denote $c_{t\pi}$ as the number of selectors with characteristic t and value π, $\pi \in \{0, 1\}$, and $c_t = \sum_\pi c_{t\pi}$. n_{kv} denotes the frequency of word v generated from topic k, and $\Gamma(\cdot)$ is the Gamma function.

Then we move on to derive rules for updating Markov chain. First with other variables fixed, we sample a specific topic assignment z_{dli} as follows:

Table 2: Description of Datasets

Text Corpuses		
Name	NYT	CNN
Time period	2011.1.1-12.31	2012.1.1-12.31
Articles	2,856	3,516
Vocabulary size	9,056	9,267
Total Words	835,471	868,012
Total Segments	76,599	87,593
Categories	20	20
Image Datasets		
Name	MSRCv2	LabelMe
Images	591	2,121
Codebook Size	5,000	5,000
Total Words	223,508	3,574,567
Total Segments	1,435	8,192
Categories	20	15

$$\begin{aligned} p(z_{dli} = k|\mathbf{\Phi}_{-z_{dli}}, \Psi) &\propto \frac{p(\mathbf{\Phi}|\Psi)}{p(\mathbf{\Phi}_{-\{w_{dli}, z_{dli}, \pi_{dli}, t_{dli}\}}|\Psi)} \\ &\propto p(t_{dli}) \frac{\alpha_k + n_{dk}}{\sum_{k=1}^{K} \alpha_k + n_{dk}} \frac{\gamma_{\pi_{dli}} + c_{t_{dli}\pi_{dli}}}{\gamma_0 + \gamma_1 + c_{t_{dli}}} \frac{\beta_v + n_{kv}}{\sum_{v=1}^{V} \beta_v + n_{kv}} \\ &\propto (\alpha_k + n_{dk} + l_{dk}) \frac{\beta_v + n_{kv}}{\sum_{v=1}^{V} \beta_v + n_{kv}} \end{aligned} \quad (2)$$

We can make further simplification of Equation 2 that

$$p(z_{dli} = k|\pi_{dli} = 1, \mathbf{\Phi}_{-\{z_{dli}, \pi_{dli}\}}, \Psi) \propto \alpha_k + n_{dk} + l_{dk} \quad (3)$$

Note that if we set all $\pi_{dli} = 1$, our model is a simplified version of Unsupervised Spatial-LTM [2], which adopts the same method to enforce the internal spatial constraints, excluding appearance features since they cannot be obtained from textual data. We call it seg-LDA in this paper.

The rules for sampling $\boldsymbol{s}$ and $\boldsymbol{\pi}$ are obtained from similar derivations. To sample each segment topic s_{dl}, we have

$$\begin{aligned} &p(s_{dl} = k|\mathbf{\Phi}_{-s_{dl}}, \Psi) \\ &\propto (\alpha_k + n_{dk} + l_{dk}) \frac{\prod_{v=1}^{V} \prod_{x=1}^{R_v} (\beta_v + n_{kv} + x - 1)}{\prod_{y=1}^{R} (\sum_{v=1}^{V} (\beta_v + n_{kv}) + y - 1)} \end{aligned} \quad (4)$$

where R_v denotes the number of distinct word v in segment l whose corresponding selectors are 1, and $R = \sum_v R_v$. Finally, each selector π_{dli} can be sampled as follows:

$$p(\pi_{dli} = b|\mathbf{\Phi}_{-\pi_{dli}}, \Psi) \propto (\gamma_b + c_{t_{dli}b}) \frac{\beta_v + n_{kv}}{\sum_{v=1}^{V} (\beta_v + n_{kv})} \quad (5)$$

where $b \in \{0, 1\}$, $k = z_{dli}$ if $b = 0$, otherwise $k = s_{dl}$.

3. EXPERIMENTS

In this section, we describe the datasets for comparisons and illustrate experimental results.

3.1 Experimental Datasets

We collect two text corpus of news articles and two annotated image datesets for comparisons.

News articles are collected from CNN (Cable News Network) and NYT (The New York Times). They are divided into 20 categories according to their reported countries (such as Iran, Korea, the U.S., Libya and Russia). English stop words and words occurring fewer than 10 times are removed.

For experiments on images, the annotated images from MSRC v2[1] and LabelMe [6] are utilized. MSRC v2 is a well-annotated collection of images in 20 categories. In LabelME, we collect 15 sets of images that are well annotated and categorized, i.e., 7 sets are indoor scenes, 4 sets are outdoor scenes, 3 sets are animal images and the last one is portraits. It should be pointed out that each image is segmented into several regions (objects). We extracted visual words from SIFT features, and obtained 5000 visual words as the codebook on each dataset respectively.

More detailed description of our text corpus and image datasets can be found in Table 2.

Table 3: Clustering Performance Comparisons

Performance Comparisons on News Articles				
Method	NYT		CNN	
	NMI	Purity	NMI	Purity
LDA	0.370	0.265	0.598	0.491
seg-LDA	0.446	0.323	0.605	0.511
πLDA	**0.461**	**0.345**	**0.625**	**0.557**
Performance Comparisons on Images				
Method	MSRC v2		LabelMe	
	NMI	Purity	NMI	Purity
LDA	0.283	0.261	0.281	0.362
seg-LDA	0.301	0.276	0.285	0.363
πLDA	**0.312**	**0.290**	**0.294**	**0.381**

3.2 Quantitative Evaluation

The performance of clustering is evaluated by comparing the cluster label of each document with its category label provided by the ground truth. Two kinds of metrics, namely clustering purity and normalized mutual information (NMI), are utilized to evaluate the clustering performance. We have $\text{NMI}(K, C) = \frac{2 \sum_{k \in K} \sum_{c \in C} p(k,c) \log(\frac{p(k,c)}{p(k)p(c)})}{-\sum_{k \in K} p(k) \log_2 p(k) - \sum_{c \in C} p(c) \log_2 p(c)}$ and purity $= \frac{1}{D} \sum_{k \in K} \max_{c \in C} |D_k \bigcap D_c|$, where K is the number of topics over D documents, C is the number of categories, D_k denotes the set of documents that is assigned to topic k, and D_c is the set of documents in category c.

We compare the πLDA model with LDA and seg-LDA. As is mentioned above, the seg-LDA model assumes that all segment units in a segment share the same topic. For all the three models we set $\alpha = 0.01$, $\beta = 0.3$, and the parameter γ in πLDA is fixed to 0.2. The results are reported after Gibbs sampling is converged. The clustering results are shown in Table 3. It is observed that seg-LDA outperforms LDA to some extent, while our proposed πLDA has the best performance in terms of both NMI and purity metrics due to the selective structural constraints in it.

3.3 Qualitative Performance

Some qualitative results are shown in Table 4 and Figure 2, in which selected topics of the LDA model and our proposed πLDA are presented. These topics are represented by the words and images that have the highest probability in corresponding proportions of them. As shown in news articles, πLDA obtains more interpretable topics with less confusion, while LDA messes up with events in Korea and Iran,

[1] http://research.microsoft.com/projects/objectclassrecognition

Table 4: **Selected Topics Obtained by LDA and πLDA on Texts**

topic:*Korea*							
NYT				CNN			
LDA		πLDA		LDA		πLDA	
korea	0.020	korea	0.068	korea	0.070	korea	0.042
iran	0.020	north	0.048	north	0.052	north	0.032
north	0.016	south	0.035	south	0.032	south	0.023
south	0.011	kim	0.022	death	0.008	kim	0.019
nuclear	0.009	seoul	0.010	seoul	0.008	nuclear	0.011
topic:*Libya*							
NYT				CNN			
LDA		πLDA		LDA		πLDA	
libya	0.033	libya	0.040	libya	0.045	gadhafi	0.034
rebel	0.028	qadhafi	0.033	gadhafi	0.032	rebel	0.033
qadhafi	0.027	rebel	0.028	council	0.013	libya	0.028
colonel	0.018	colonel	0.022	tripoli	0.010	tripoli	0.023
tripoli	0.012	nato	0.012	city	0.010	nato	0.014

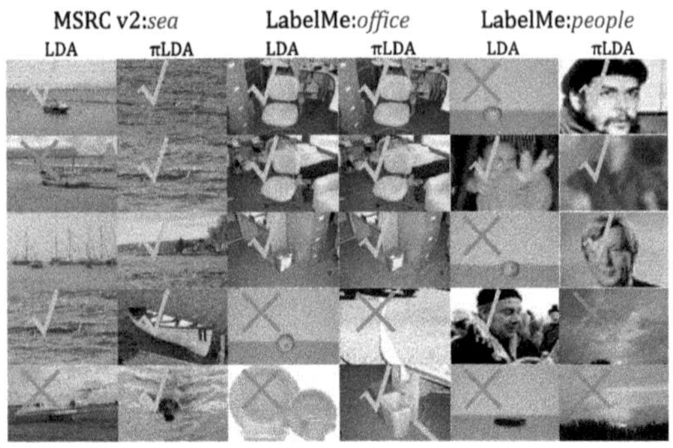

Figure 2: Most representative images in selected topics obtained by LDA and πLDA. Masks of correctness are gained from ground truth.

and does not reveal any relevant information about NATO in topic *Libya*. On the other hand, according to the ground truth of categories in image datasets, experimental results of images indicate that πLDA obtains more representative images and more reasonable clusters than LDA.

The latent variable λ is conducted to indicate the tendency of whether each segment unit is generated from the shared common topic in the segment it belongs to. In Figure 3, the proportions of segment units generated from the shared common topic in their corresponding segments are reported. As for texts, it is observed that most of nouns and verbs are selected to share the common topics in their corresponding sentences, while most of adjectives and adverbs are not selected. That is to say, given a topic embedded in a sentence, the nouns and verbs are more informative (therefore discriminative) than adjectives and adverbs in this sentence, which confirms our previous hypothesis that nouns and verbs are easier to convey the topic of their sentences. The same observation is also found on images that some objects are easier to convey the same concept of their regions.

4. CONCLUSION

In this paper, a model called πLDA is proposed, which introduces a latent variable into the original LDA model to enforce selective structural constraints. The proposed

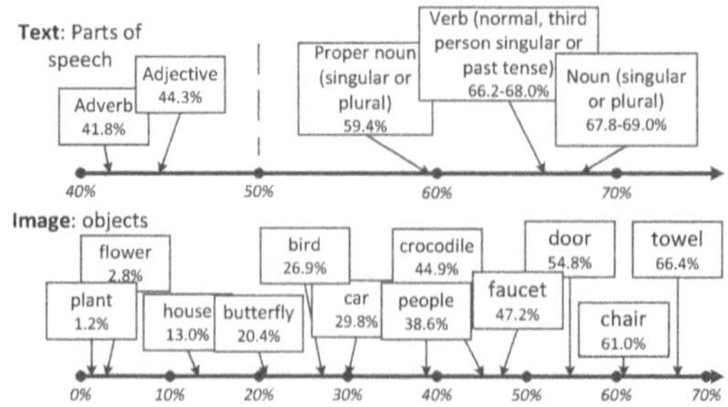

Figure 3: The proportions of words having the same part-of-speech selected to share the common topic in their corresponding segments

πLDA model can not only find meaningful topics, but also select out the informative segment units. Experimental results show that πLDA achieves better performance of clustering than related methods.

5. ACKNOWLEDGMENTS

This work was supported in part by National Basic Research Program of China(2010CB327904), NSFC(No. 6110 5074, 90920303), 863 program(2012AA012505), the Fundamental Research Funds for the Central Universities and Chinese Knowledge Center of Engineering Science and Technology (CKCEST).

6. REFERENCES

[1] D. M. Blei, A. Y. Ng, and M. I. Jordan. Latent dirichlet allocation. *Journal of Machine Learning Research*, 3:993–1022, 2003.

[2] L. Cao and L. Fei-Fei. Spatially coherent latent topic model for concurrent segmentation and classification of objects and scenes. In *11th International Conference on Computer Vision*, pages 1–8, 2007.

[3] P. K. Elango and K. Jayaraman. Clustering images using the latent dirichlet allocation model. Technical report, University of Wisconsin, 2005.

[4] H. Gao, S. Tang, Y. Zhang, D. Jiang, F. Wu, and Y. Zhuang. Supervised cross-collection topic modeling. In *Proceedings of the 20th ACM International Conference on Multimedia*, pages 957–960, 2012.

[5] T. L. Griffiths and M. Steyvers. Finding scientific topics. In *Proceedings of the National Academy of Sciences*, volume 101, pages 5228–5235, 2004.

[6] B. C. Russell, A. Torralba, K. P. Murphy, and W. T. Freeman. Labelme: a database and web-based tool for image annotation. *International Journal of Computer Vision*, 77(1-3):157–173, 2008.

[7] M. M. Shafiei and E. E. Milios. Latent dirichlet co-clustering. In *6th International Conference on Data Mining*, pages 542–551, 2006.

[8] S. Tang, Y. Zhang, H. Wang, M. Chen, F. Wu, and Y. Zhuang. The discovery of burst topic and its intermittent evolution in our real world. *China Communications*, 10(3):1–12, 2013.

[9] D. Wang, S. Zhu, T. Li, and Y. Gong. Multi-document summarization using sentence-based topic models. In *Proceedings of the ACL-IJCNLP 2009 Conference Short Papers*, pages 297–300, 2009.

Con-Text: Text Detection Using Background Connectivity for Fine-Grained Object Classification

Sezer Karaoglu, Jan C. van Gemert and Theo Gevers
Intelligent Systems Lab Amsterdam (ISLA), University of Amsterdam
Science Park 904 Amsterdam, The Netherlands

ABSTRACT

This paper focuses on fine-grained classification by detecting photographed text in images. We introduce a text detection method that does not try to detect all possible foreground text regions but instead aims to reconstruct the scene background to eliminate non-text regions. Object cues such as color, contrast, and objectiveness are used in corporation with a random forest classifier to detect background pixels in the scene. Results on two publicly available datasets ICDAR03 and a fine-grained *Building* subcategories of ImageNet shows the effectiveness of the proposed method.

Categories and Subject Descriptors

I.4.8 [**Scene Analysis**]: Object Recognition; I.5.4 [**Computer Vision**]: [Applications]

Keywords

Fine-grained classification; scene text recognition

1. INTRODUCTION

Automatic visual classification of very similar instances, a.k.a. fine-grained classification, is the problem of assigning images to classes where all instances differ only by minute details. Examples include flower types [8] or specific bird species [18]. In this paper, we propose to use recognized photographed texts images to aid in fine-grained classification. As an application, we focus on classification of *Buildings* into their sub-classes such as *Cafe*, *Tavern*, *Diner*, etc. This can be used to link images from Google Street View to textual business information as in the Yellow pages.

When text is present in natural scenes, the text is typically there to give semantic meaning beyond what is obvious from exclusively visual cues. For instance, in fig 1, the left and middle images share a very similar scene layout. However, if one wants to group these images based on the semantics of the scenes, the middle and the right images belong together because they share the same business name ("Starbucks").

MM'13, October 21–25, 2013, Barcelona, Spain.
Copyright 2013 ACM 978-1-4503-2404-5/13/10 ...$15.00.
http://dx.doi.org/10.1145/2502081.2502197.

Figure 1: An example of fine-grained *Building* classification. Visual cues would group (a)-(b) whereas scene text reveals that and groups (b)-(c).

Traditional optical character recognition (OCR) systems work well for controlled documents, however their performance deteriorates in recognizing natural scene text. The challenges in natural images include non-linear illumination, occlusion, motion blur and variations in text size, style and orientation. To overcome such issues, rather than trying to detect all variations in text appearance, we propose to detect the background in the image using a Random Forest (RF). Then, text regions are detected by eliminating the scene background.

This paper has two main contributions. First, instead of trying to detect text directly, we propose to learn the background of the scene to infer the location of text. Second, we propose a system which incorporates the additional semantics in the scene text to infer the image content. We give results of multimodal fusion of text and visual cues for fine-grained classification on sub-classes of the ImageNet *building* and *place of business* dataset. The proposed method improves significantly over a visual-only classification.

2. RELATED WORK

Existing text detection methods extract features either from connected components [3, 4, 7] or bounding boxes [16] to decide whether the region contains text or not. These methods try to verify geometric, structural and appearance properties of text based on some heuristics or learning scheme. Since these methods rely on training or simple rules designed for specific text styles, it is hard to maintain robustness to a-priori unknown text styles. In contrast, our proposed method does not focus on extracting text features but tries to detect background pixels to eliminate non-text regions.

Our approach is inspired by Wei et al. [17] who propose to use scene background regions for salient object detection. We also use the background, but now for text detection. In contrast to the strong boundary dependency of [17] we use a careful background seed selection step by training a *RF*.

Figure 2: (a) Original image and selected background seeds (blue dots) (b) reconstructed background and (c) background removed image regions.

Text information is fused with visual cues for better scene classification by Wang et al. [14]. The authors use Flickr images and their associated social tags in an object recognition problem. Others [19] propose to combine visual features extracted from the surroundings of text regions with features from the full image. In contrast to these two methods, we propose text recognition in the image and use the recognized text to directly aid scene classification. The approaches done by Karaoglu et al. [5] and Tsai et al. [10] are the most similar in spirit to ours. Both approaches propose to use scene text information in combination with visual features to improve visual recognition. While Karaoglu et al. [5] combines text and visual features for generic object recognition such as *Cars* and *Aeroplanes*, Tsai et al. [10] combines text and visual features for book spine recognition problem.

3. BACKGROUND DETECTION

Instead of detecting text regions directly, we propose to detect the scene background to eliminate non-text regions. Intuitively, removing background clutter will reduce false text detections.

Texts are typically designed to attract attention [3, 7, 9, 11, 15] they typically contrasts strongly against the background. Hence, strong intensity changes can be expected on text boundaries. This give us the opportunity to distinguish between text and the surroundings by using an intensity-level pixel connectivity measure. Our method starts from background seeds and grow these seeds until the background is reconstructed. Background pixels can then easily be eliminated by subtracting them from the original image. An illustration of seed growing is shown in fig 2a. Selected background seeds are represented by blue dots and some of the background pixels obtained based on connectivity to those seeds are represented by red lines.

Mathematical morphology is a well known tool for defining connectivity between pixels. Therefore, we make use of morphological operations to define connectivity in our background detection problem. Morphological reconstruction uses conditional dilation (δ) which can be defined as

$$\delta_S(\gamma|I) \triangleq (\gamma \oplus S) \cap I \ , \tag{1}$$

where S is the structuring element (3-by-3 square), γ is the binary image where background seeds are ones and I is the gray level input image. This operation is executed iteratively until the stability is sustained,

$$\rho_S^-(\gamma|I) \triangleq \bigcup_{n=1}^{\infty} \delta_S^n(\gamma|I) \ , \tag{2}$$

$$\text{repeat } \gamma_{n+1} = \delta_S(\gamma_n|I_n) \text{ until } \gamma_n = \gamma_{n+1} \ . \tag{3}$$

Figure 3: (a) Original image (b) color boosting (c) curvature and (d) objectness.

Careful selection of the seeds γ is essential for background reconstruction since the seeds will initialize the connectivity procedure. The proposed method selects the seeds based on learning scheme using color, contrast and objectiveness cues incorporation with *RF*.

3.1 Background Seed Selection

3.1.1 Color and Contrast

Color edges are useful to learn whether a region belongs to background or not. Color is homogeneous on most of the background scene such as on roads, sky, buildings and so on. Moreover, color edge responses correlate with high contrast texts. To exploit this, we use the color boosting algorithm proposed by Van de Weijer et al. [12] where the authors boost the color information in image gradients by replacing the gradient strength with information content carried by color. The response of the color boosting algorithm for each pixel is used as a feature in our RF, see fig 3b for an example. Moreover, we add RGB color values in addition to the color edge transition cues to help the classifier to distinguish unstructured regions such as sky, grass and trees.

In addition to color cues, we use the curvature (L) of colorless edges in the scene. Curvature is expressed by $L = \sqrt{I_{xx}^2 + I_{xy}^2 + I_{yy}^2}$, where I_{xx} and I_{yy} stand for the second-order derivatives of the intensity image $I(x, y)$ in the x and y dimensions, respectively. The response measured by curvature intensity for each pixel is used as a feature, see fig 3c for an example. Additionally, we extract two more features based on boundary priors which assumes that the border has a high likelihood to be background [5, 17]. We remove high responsive color boosting and curvature regions which are connected to the image border (equation 2).

3.1.2 Objectness

Generic object detection techniques have been widely used for text detection and recognition problem [6, 16]. In contrast, our goal here is not to detect text windows but to detect unstructured background context such as grass, bricks, fences and trees. The motivation to make use of object detectors is that they have low response on unstructured image regions and high response for structured image regions, as illustrated in fig 3d. We use a generic object detector called 'objectness' [1]. The score and coordinates of first 100 objectness windows are summed, normalized to the range [0,1] and mapped into image coordinates.

3.1.3 Learning with Random Forest

The described responses for color, contrast and objectness are extracted pixel-wise then smoothed and subsam-

Color [12]	Curvature (L)
(Boundary Prior + Color) [5]	(Boundary Prior + L) [5]
Objectness [1]	RGB values

Table 1: Features used for background detection.

Figure 4: Original (on top) and background removed (down) images using proposed algorithm.

pled (10x) to incorporate neighbor pixel information. For each pixel in the subsampled image we have six descriptive features for training a classifier to detect the background (see table 1). These features are used with a *RF* to classify background seeds. A *RF* is a combination of many un-pruned decision tree predictors [2]. In the training phase, each decision tree is constructed from randomly selected features at each split with bagging. When a new instance arrives to the forest for classification, the instance is put down each of the trees in the forest. Each tree gives a vote and the forest chooses the classification having the most votes.

We use 100 trees in the forest based on the out-of-bag error (*oob*) curve obtained for a small holdout set of the ICDAR03 dataset[1]. Each tree is constructed with three random features as suggested by Breiman [2] and is grown to the largest extent possible. The splitting of the nodes is made based on the GINI criterion [2]. The training for all experiments is done on the ICDAR03 training set where text bounding boxes are provided. We denote the pixels in the groundtruth text boxes positive and outside the boxes as negative.

4. EXPERIMENTS

To evaluate our system, the leading commercial OCR engine, ABBYY FineReader, is used for text recognition. After the background is detected and removed from the original image, ABBYY is fed with this output that retains the most likely text regions, see fig 4 for example outputs.

4.1 Character Recognition

The system takes roughly 5.2 seconds for objectness and 0.01 seconds for each color and curvature feature extraction processes to run on a 480×640 resolution image. The *RF* classification takes 0.01 seconds while conditional dilation to build connectivity takes 0.012 seconds.

The character recognition performance of the proposed method is evaluated on the publicly available ICDAR03 dataset. We present our results against ABBYY alone where ABBYY is directly fed with input image and with Karaoglu et al. [5] with their reported results in table 2. The results show that removing the background from the scene substantially increases the OCR performance. This is because traditional OCR systems only work well with controlled documents. We improve slightly (1%) over [5] which corresponds to an improvement of ± 100 characters.

Method	Cl. Rate (%)
ABBYY alone	37
Karaoglu et al [5]	62
Proposed Method	**63**

Table 2: Character recognition rates for different methods on ICDAR03.

We also evaluated how much of the true background is removed by using the ICDAR03 text localization ground truth. We counted the pixels which are correctly returned as a text region and the pixels which are not. Our proposed method removes 87% of the background regions. Since the dataset is not annotated with characters but with word bounding boxes only, we cannot give a precise estimation of the scene text amount that our method retains.

4.2 Fine Grained Classification

We use sub-classes of the ImageNet[2] *building* and *place of business* sets to evaluate fine-grained classification. The dataset consists of 28 categories with 24,255 images, see fig 5 for the category list. In the experiments, we use all images from these categories, i.e., many images do not necessarily contain photographed text. The number of images with text in the categories varies from 8% (*massage center*) to 30% (*bakery*).

We use average precision as the performance measure, and we repeat all experiments three times to obtain standard deviation scores to validate significance testing. We use a standard bag of visual words (BOW) approach with SIFT using 4000 words with 1×3 and 2×2 spatial pyramid as the visual classification baseline. We use the histogram intersection kernel in libsvm and use its built in cross-validation method to tune the C parameter. For text classification we use a bag-of-bigrams with the histogram intersection kernel. The two kernels are additive, and are thus fused by a simple addition. We compare results of visual-only, text-only and fused as our proposed method. The classification scores per category are given in fig 5.

The low accuracy of text cues over visual cues can be explained by the lack of photographed text in many images, as is the case for the *Massage Center* and *Bistro* classes. Moreover, this dataset is more realistic than existing text recognition datasets and therefore not all of the text in the scene is recognized. Nevertheless, text cues outperform visual cues for the *Discount House*, *Steak House*, *PawnShop*, *Cafe* and *Dry Cleaner* classes.

The images in *Discount House* and *Steak House* are visually not similar and are hard even for humans if there was no text information on them. The very low performance of the visual cues for *Discount House* cause it to be the only class where adding visual cues reduced the accuracy of the text-only score.

[1] `http://algoval.essex.ac.uk/icdar/`

[2] `http://image-net.org/`

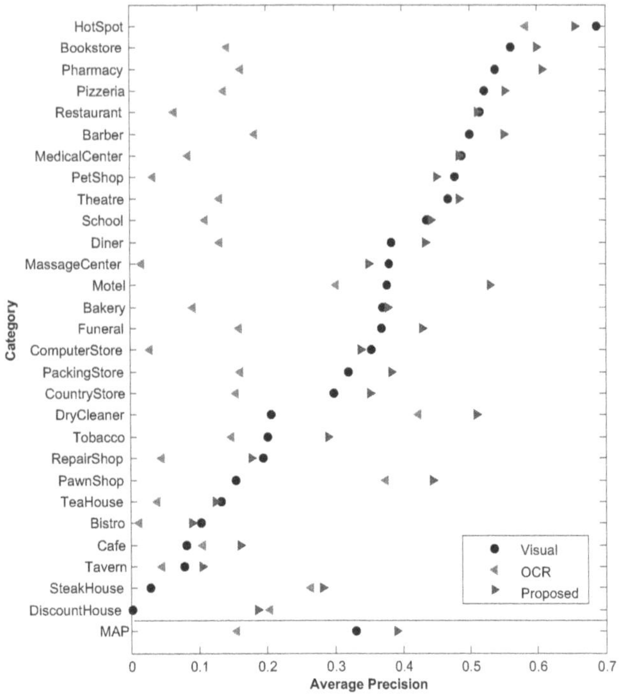

Figure 5: Fine-grained classification results for visual-only, text-only and proposed method. The visual MAP is 32.9 ± 1.7**, text is** 15.6 ± 0.4 **and proposed is** 39.0 ± 2.6**.**

Adding text information to visual cues significantly improved the accuracy of 19 out of the 28 classes. Note that the performance of each individual cue for classes *Cafe*, *Motel* and *Tobacco* are very close. However, the combination of visual and textual cues increases performance remarkably. This can be explained by reinforcing textual and visual cues where each modality brings new discriminative information. Moreover, when text is informative for a class (i.e. >0.1) combining visual and text cues always increases accuracy.

We show some example images in fig 6. The figure illustrates that the best cues can be learned per-category.

5. CONCLUSION

We have shown that background removal is a suitable approach for photographed text detection in natural scenes. Color, curvature and objectness prove valuable cues for background modeling.

We introduce a new fine-grained classification problem based on ImageNet subcategories and build a baseline for further research. We have shown that multimodal information fusion of visual and textual cues improves fine-grained classification on this dataset by 6%. For future work, we aim to build equivalence classes as proposed in [13] for text and non-text regions to exploit correspondences between text related visual features to help the system where OCR fails to recognize characters.

6. ACKNOWLEDGEMENT

This publication was supported by the Dutch national program COMMIT.

Figure 6: Result for *Discount House*.

7. REFERENCES

[1] B. Alexe, T. Deselaers, and V. Ferrari. Measuring the objectness of image windows. *TPAMI*, 34(11), 2012.

[2] L. Breiman. Random forests. *Machine Learning*, 45(1), 2001.

[3] B. Epshtein, E. Ofek, and Y. Wexler. Detecting text in natural scenes with stroke width transform. In *CVPR*, 2010.

[4] S. Karaoglu, B. Fernando, and A. Trémeau. A novel algorithm for text detection and localization in natural scene images. In *DICTA*, 2010.

[5] S. Karaoglu, J. van Gemert, and T. Gevers. Object reading: Text recognition for object recognition. In *ECCV Workshops (3)*, 2012.

[6] A. Mishra, K. Alahari, and C. V. Jawahar. Top-down and bottom-up cues for scene text recognition. In *CVPR*, 2012.

[7] L. Neumann and J. Matas. Real-time scene text localization and recognition. In *CVPR*, 2012.

[8] M.-E. Nilsback and A. Zisserman. A visual vocabulary for flower classification. In *CVPR*, 2006.

[9] A. Trémeau, B. Fernando, S. Karaoglu, and D. Muselet. Detecting text in natural scenes based on a reduction of photometric effects: Problem of text detection. In *CCIW*, 2011.

[10] S. S. Tsai, D. Chen, H. Chen, C.-H. Hsu, K.-H. Kim, J. P. Singh, and B. Girod. Combining image and text features: a hybrid approach to mobile book spine recognition. In *ACM Multimedia*, 2011.

[11] S. Uchida, Y. Shigeyoshi, Y. Kunishige, and Y. Feng. A keypoint-based approach toward scenery character detection. In *ICDAR*, 2011.

[12] J. van de Weijer, T. Gevers, and A. D. Bagdanov. Boosting color saliency in image feature detection. *TPAMI*, 2006.

[13] J. C. van Gemert. Exploiting photographic style for category-level image classification by generalizing the spatial pyramid. In *ICMR*, 2011.

[14] G. Wang, D. Hoiem, and D. A. Forsyth. Building text features for object image classification. In *CVPR*, 2009.

[15] H. C. Wang and M. Pomplun. The attraction of visual attention to texts in real-world scenes. In *CogSci*, 2011.

[16] K. Wang, B. Babenko, and S. Belongie. End-to-end scene text recognition. In *ICCV*, 2011.

[17] Y. Wei, F. Wen, W. Zhu, and J. Sun. Geodesic saliency using background priors. In *ECCV*, 2012.

[18] B. Yao, G. Bradski, and L. Fei-Fei. A codebook-free and annotation-free approach for fine-grained image categorization. In *CVPR*, 2012.

[19] Q. Zhu, M.-C. Yeh, and K.-T. Cheng. Multimodal fusion using learned text concepts for image categorization. In *ACM Multimedia*, 2006.

Relative Spatial Features for Image Memorability

Jongpil Kim*
jpkim@cs.rutgers.edu

Sejong Yoon*
sjyoon@cs.rutgers.edu

Vladimir Pavlovic
vladimir@cs.rutgers.edu

Department of Computer Science
Rutgers, The State University of New Jersey
Piscataway, NJ 08854-8136

ABSTRACT

Recent studies in image memorability showed that the memorability of an image is a measurable quantity and is closely correlated with semantic attributes. However, the intrinsic characteristics of memorability are not yet fully understood. It has been reported that in contrast to a popular belief unusualness or aesthetic beauty of the image may not be positively correlated with the image memorability. This counter-intuitive characteristic of memorability hinders a better understanding of image memorability and its applicability. In this paper, we investigate two new spatial features that are closely correlated with the image memorability yet intuitively explainable. We propose the Weighted Object Area (WOA) that jointly considers the location and size of objects and the Relative Area Rank (RAR) that captures the relative unusualness of the size of objects. We empirically demonstrate their useful correlation with the image memorability. Results show that both WOA and RAR can improve the memorability prediction. In addition, we provide evidence that the RAR can effectively capture object-centric unusualness of size.

Categories and Subject Descriptors

I.2.10 [**Artifical Intelligence**]: Vision and Scene Understanding—*modeling and recovery of physical attributes; representations, data structures, and transforms; perceptual reasoning*

Keywords

image memorability; feature extraction; relative correlation

1. INTRODUCTION

How memorable is an image? Some images are clearly more memorable than others. This is especially true for the images with known content, e.g. photos of a family or friends, attended events or visited places. However, studies show that some images are intrinsically more memorable than others without such subjectively recognizable content [2, 11]. According to recent studies, the latter case of memorability is measurable [9], closely correlated with semantic attributes [8] and even predictable [9, 10] to some extent. One key beneficiary of the image memorability prediction may be the advertisement industry, which can use the memorability score to quantitatively measure the effectiveness of prototype designs of advertisements for various consumer items. Moreover, predicting memorability may also affect a system's ability to understand scenes or improve object recognition.

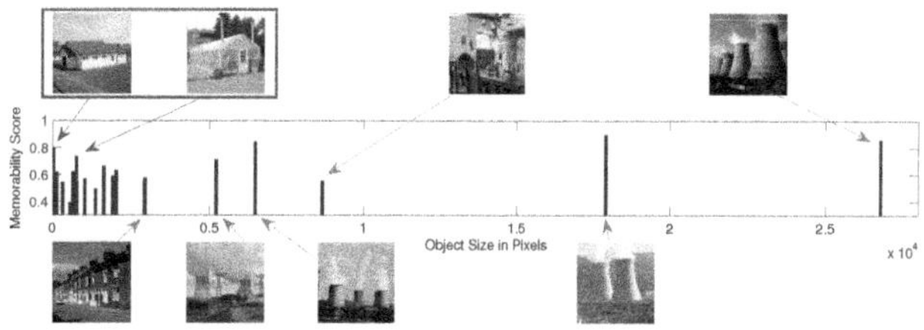

Figure 1: Image memorability score [9] against all 25 images containing the object *chimney*. Images with unusually sized, center-concentrated chimneys (1st, 2nd, 4th and 5th from the right) are more memorable than images with normally sized chimneys (6th from right). 3rd chimney is an indoor scene. Two outliers inside the blue box show that their high memorabilities are not directly related to the chimneys.

However, the natural characteristics of image memorability are not fully understood. Spatial and content-based attributes such as "people with visible faces" and "enclosed spatial structure" are reported to positively affect the memorability scores, while unusualness and aesthetic beauty of an image negatively correlate with the memorability scores [8]. The fact that the unusualness negatively correlates with the memorability score is especially counter-intuitive as we can easily find highly memorable images depicting unusual scenes, as depicted in Fig. 1. Qualitative analysis of these images seems to indicate that what correlates with image memorability is *not* the unusualness as a holistic attribute of an image *but* the unusualness of each object relative to its expected size and location within the image's semantic context. This hypothesis can be roughly supported by the fact that the image memorability is closely correlated with the spatial object size and semantics [9]. Nevertheless, a relationship between the relative unusualness of an object and the memorability has not been properly established.

The goal of this paper is to investigate relative size and location-based features both closely correlate with the image memorability and intuitively explainable for a better under-

*J. Kim and S. Yoon equally contributed to this work.

MM'13, October 21–25, 2013, Barcelona, Spain.

ACM 978-1-4503-2404-5/13/10 ...$15.00.
http://dx.doi.org/10.1145/2502081.2502198.

standing of the image memorability. We propose two spatial features in this paper: the Weighted Object Areas (WOA) and the Relative Area Rank (RAR). Exploiting the same experimental setting as in [9], we show that these basic spatial features are closely correlated with the image memorability. In addition, we provide evidence that RAR can effectively capture the object-centric unusualness defined as the object size realtive to the expected size of the object's class. We discuss possible extentions of the spatial features to the image memorability prediction in the concluding remark.

2. RELATIVE SPATIAL FEATURES

In this section, we introduce two relative spatial features for the image memorability measure, the Weighted Object Area and the Relative Area Rank. Both features are designed to encode spatial characteristics (size and position) of objects in an image as related to image memorability.

2.1 Weighted Object Areas

Size and location of an object in an image are two important factors to determine the object's importance [1]. Objects closer to the center and larger in size tend to be more important as they have higher probabilities of being mentioned by annotaters [1]. While the connection between the importance of objects in an image and the image memorability is unclear, object size and spatial location do have a strong correlation with the memorability [9]. Thus it is natural to presume that the two spatial characteristics of objects need to be treated jointly, with the location information being considered as relative to the center. However, previous studies on memorability used the location information of the object only by considering multiscale area coverage, i.e. we additionally consider the object's subareas covered in the quadrant. While this spatial pyramid encodes the location information, it only captures the existence with limited directional information. Moreover, it does not consider the relative displacement of the object from the center of the image.

Therefore, we introduce a new feature which jointly considers the size and location in an intuitive manner. The basic idea is simple: We give more weight to pixels around the center while reducing the weight of pixels closer to image boundaries. The bivariate Gaussian function over the image pixel locations natually conforms to the criteria. Formally, the weight for a pixel located at a pixel coordinate $\mathbf{x}$, $\mathbf{x} \in \mathbb{R}^2$ is defined as follows: $w(\mathbf{x}) \sim \mathcal{N}(\mathbf{x}; \boldsymbol{\mu}, \boldsymbol{\Sigma})$, where $\mathcal{N}(\cdot)$ is the bivariate Gaussian probability density function with the vector $\boldsymbol{\mu} \in \mathbb{R}^2$ and the matrix $\boldsymbol{\Sigma} \in \mathbb{R}^{2\times 2}$ as its mean and covariance, respectively. To give the largest weight at the center point, we set $\boldsymbol{\mu}$ to be the location of the image center. $\boldsymbol{\Sigma}$ is the covariance of the weight distribution and we do grid search and cross validation to find it. Then, for a given image Q, the weighted object area (WOA) histogram is calculated as follows:

$$\mathrm{WOA}(Q,k) = \sum_{\mathbf{x}\in \mathrm{OBJ}(Q,k)} w(\mathbf{x}), \qquad (1)$$

where k is an object index, and $\mathrm{OBJ}(Q,k)$ is the set of all pixels of object k in image Q. Clearly, when an object is larger or closer to the center of an image, the WOA for the object is higher. Moreover, the same sized objects may have different WOA values since the object closer to the center has a higher weight than objects closer to image boundaries.

2.2 Relative Area Rank

Earlier studies on image memorability demonstrated that natural scenes are less likely to be remembered [8, 9]. However, little has been known about the underlying reason of this unusual finding. One possible explanation of this phenomenon is that natural scene image components, such as skies, mountains, ground, trees, etc., in many cases do not vary in *relative image size*. Unlike other objects of varying sizes including the most memorable object, a person, the natural scene image components are expected to cover a certain portion of an image. Thus, putting it another way, the lack of unusualness of those natural scene components negatively affected the image memorability.

To verify our intuition, we need a way to capture the unusualness of each object size within an image compared to the object class' expected coverage. Note that considering the absolute size of each object and comparing the value with its own class' size distribution would make little sense since different images have different context and an object's coverage in an image may vary depending on the context. Therefore, we need a measure to capture this *relative coverage* of objects.

In image annotation literature, Hwang and Grauman [7] introduced the relative rank to capture the prominence of an object name by its order of annotation in the tag list. The relative rank is defined as the percentile of the rank for a tag in the given image, relative to all the ranks in the training images with the same tag. The higher the rank value, the more the tag climbs to the top of the list relative to where it typically occurs in any other list.

In this paper, we employ the relative rank to account for relative change of the object area from its expected area distribution. Similar to [7], we define the relative area rank of object k as the percentile of the rank for object k to all the ranks in the training images for that object label. Formally, the relative area rank is defined as follows. Let $S(Q,k)$ be the size of object k. Then, the relative area rank (RAR) of object k is

$$\mathrm{RAR}(Q,k) = \frac{\sum_{i\in T} I\left(S(Q_i,k) \leq S(Q,k)\right)}{|T|}, \qquad (2)$$

where T is the training data, $I(\cdot)$ is the indicator function and Q_i is the i-th image in the training data T. If the object k is not present in the image, we set the $\mathrm{RAR}(Q,k)$ to be 0. We next present empirical evidence to show that RAR is an effective feature to predict the memorability score. In this paper, we scale the size of all images to a same size in order to avoid the normalization issue due to image size difference.

3. EXPERIMENTAL SETTINGS AND RESULTS

In this section, we explain our experiment setting and demonstrate the utility of the proposed WOA and RAR features, as a proxy to predicting the image memorability.

3.1 Data and Experimental settings

We examine the correlation of the two proposed measures with the memorability score of the memorability dataset provided by [8] and [9]. The dataset has 2222 images randomly sampled from the SUN dataset [15]. As a pre-processing, all the images are cropped and scaled to 256×256 pixels. The memorability scores for the images are calculated us-

Figure 2: Upper panel: Top 2 images for which WOA and RAR reduce the prediction errors compared to `Object`, respectively. Bottom panel: Bottom 2 images for which the WOA and RAR increase the prediction errors compared to `Object`, respectively.

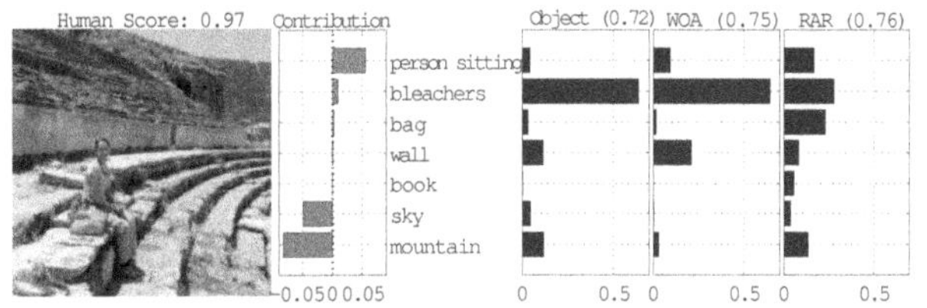

Figure 3: An example image where RAR gives the best prediction results. Three histograms on the right correspond to `Object` (left), WOA (center) and RAR (right) with numbers in parenthesis showing predicted memorability. Horizontal axis is the normalized size. Red plot on the left shows the averaged object-wise contribution to the memorability. Note that objects with large positive contribution gained more normalized area, leading to the better prediction.

ing Amazon Mechanical Turk with a "visual memory game". The game shows participants a sequence of images and asks them to press a space bar whenever they see a repeated image. After collecting the responses from the participants, the memorability score is calculated by the percentage of correct detections. To evaluate the proposed method, we follow the same process as [9]; we used the averaged Spearman's rank correlation (ρ) as the evaluation measure over 25 random split trials. This measure computes the correlation between the ranks of predicted and ground truth memorability scores.

3.2 Results

We compared the proposed features to previously used features, `Object`, `Scene` and `Attributes` which were used in [8, 9]. `Object` is a histogram of the labeled object areas over the spatial pyramid representation (i.e. labeled multi-scale object areas). In `Object`, each bin corresponds to one object. `Scene` is a scene category label assigned to the image. Because all images used in the experiments are in a subset of the SUN database, every image has a scene category label. `Attributes` is a collection of visual attributes, not only human-understandable but also highly informative for the memorability [5, 8]. `Attributes` data is built by Amazon Mechanical Turk workers. We trained a support vector regression (ϵ-SVR [3]) to predict the memorability as in [9]. Histogram intersection kernels are used for `Object`, `Scene` and the proposed features, and a Radial Basis Function (RBF) kernel for `Attributes`. We also evaluated combinations of the features using a kernel sum.

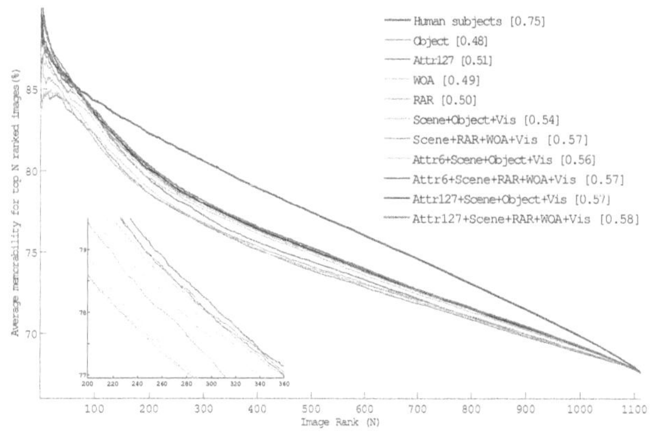

Figure 4: Comparision of prediction results averaged over 25 random splits. Images are sorted by predicted memorability scores and plotted against the cumulative ground truth memorability scores. Best viewed in color.

Table 1 shows the prediction results of the memorability for `Object`, `Scene`, `Attributes`, WOA and RAR. **`Human Subjects`** denotes the prediction results by people. The proposed features outperform `Object` and `Scene` used in [9]. Surprisingly, RAR is almost the same as the combination of `Object and Scene` by itself. Using all 127 attributes from `Attributes` shows the best performance. However, WOA/RAR are better than the top 6 best attributes proposed in [8]. Fig. 2 shows example images when WOA/RAR improved/degraded the prediction performance compared to `Object`.

We conducted further experiments using combinations of the considered features including additional global visual features. The visual features are Pixel histograms, GIST [13], SIFT [12], HOG2 $\times$ 2 [4, 6, 15] and SSIM [14]. We used the RBF kernel for GIST and the histogram intersection kernels for the other features as in [9]. Table 2 shows the results of predicting memorability using this large set of visual features, coupled with attributes. `VIS` denotes the combination of all the visual features using the kernel sum. We sought to substitute the `Object` with WOA in the best known combination of `Object`+`Scene`+`VIS` and `Attributes`. The result shows that WOA can constantly boost the available approach, from 0.56 to 0.57 and 0.57 to 0.58 correlation, for 6 and all 127 attributes, respectively. RAR showed little improvement in terms of the rank correlation but as shown in Bottom 20/100 rows of Table 2, RAR shows the larger improvement for the prediction of unmemorable images than Top 20/100 rows, i.e. it can classify unmemorable images. This confirms our intuition claimed in Section 2.2. Note that in the absense of attributes that requires the expensive high level human annotation, WOA and RAR have improved the prediction as from 0.50 to 0.52 without `VIS` and from 0.54 to 0.57 with `VIS`. Fig. 4 shows the comparison between `Object` and the proposed features pictorially.

Fig. 3 depicts another evidence in support of RAR. This image is the 3rd most memorable image in the dataset. However, using only the multiscaled area does not take the person in the image into account enough due to overwhelming size of *bleacher*. However, with RAR, the person's size is boosted due to the other object sizes being decreased, leading to improved overall memorability prediction.

Table 1: Results of memorability predictions on various features. Four rows with percentages show the average memorability scores (Recall that the memorability score is calculated by the percentage of correct detections). Top 20/100 row shows the average memorability score over the images of top 20/100 images with the highest predicted memorability scores. Bottom 20/100 row shows the average score over the bottom 20/100 images with the lowest predicted memorability scores. Thus, for Top 20 and Top 100, higher the better while for Bottom 20 and Bottom 100, lower the better. See [9] for details.

	[9]			[8]		Proposed		[9]
	Object	Scene	Object + Scene	Attributes (6)	Attributes (127)	WOA	RAR	Human Subjects
Top 20	84.4%	81.6%	84.5%	85.2%	87.6%	84.9%	85.5%	86.9%
Top 100	82.2%	77.3%	82.3%	82.5%	83.4%	82.2%	81.9%	84.3%
Bottom 100	56.2%	57.5%	55.3%	55.5%	55.3%	55.6%	55.6%	46.9%
Bottom 20	52.7%	56.2%	51.7%	55.6%	52.3%	51.2%	52.0%	39.6%
ρ	0.48	0.36	0.50	0.48	0.51	0.49	0.50	0.75

Table 2: Results of memorability predictions on combination of features. Attr127 used all 127 attributes from [8] while Attr6 used only 6 features suggested therein. Note that using features of [8], we can only obtain $\rho = 0.53$ even with the global visual features. Numbers at the bottom of each top and bottom box section show the improvements of average memorability score using our features over traditional feature `Object`. Note that Bottom shows larger improvements than Top for RAR.

	Without Attributes				Top Attributes (6)				All Attributes (127)			
	Object + Scene	WOA+RAR + Scene	Object + Scene + VIS	WOA+RAR + Scene + VIS	Object + Scene + VIS	WOA + Scene + VIS	RAR + Scene + VIS	WOA+RAR + Scene + VIS	Object + Scene + VIS	WOA + Scene + VIS	RAR + Scene + VIS	WOA+RAR + Scene + VIS
Top 20	84.5%	85.2%	86.1%	**86.5%**	87.0%	86.9%	**87.4%**	87.1%	87.5%	87.2%	**87.8%**	87.4%
Top 100	82.3%	82.7%	83.0%	**83.3%**	83.3%	83.5%	83.4%	**83.7%**	83.5%	83.6%	83.4%	**83.7%**
		+1.1%		+0.7%		+0.1%	+0.5%	+0.5%		-0.2%	+0.2%	+0.1%
Bottom 100	55.3%	54.6%	53.7%	**52.8%**	53.4%	53.2%	53.0%	**52.8%**	53.0%	53.0%	52.9%	**52.6%**
Bottom 20	51.7%	50.3%	49.4%	**48.5%**	49.4%	49.5%	**48.8%**	48.9%	49.6%	49.3%	**48.5%**	48.9%
		+2.1%		+1.8%		+0.1%	+1.0%	+1.1%		+0.3%	+1.2%	+1.1%
ρ	0.50	0.52	0.54	**0.57**	0.56	**0.57**	0.56	**0.57**	0.57	**0.58**	0.57	**0.58**

4. CONCLUSION

We introduced two relative spatial features to gain a better understanding of the image memorability. Weighted Object Area (WOA) jointly utilizes the object size and location. This contrasts to the traditional spatial pyramid based features that treat the two aspects independently. Thus WOA effectively replaces such features, e.g. `Object` in [8, 9]. Relative Area Rank (RAR) captures the relative changes of an object size compared to the other objects of same class in the training set, leading to effective encoding of the object-based unusualness. The proposed features can be easily calculated and do not require additional human labor. Experimental results show that, by replacing the classic simple area-based features, the proposed features can boost available image memorability prediction in combination with features from other domains, such as the image attributes. Moreover, the proposed features can improve the prediction without the attributes that normally require costly high level human annotations.

5. ACKNOWLEDGMENTS

This work was supported in part by the National Science Foundation under Grant No. IIS 0916812.

6. REFERENCES

[1] A. C. Berg, T. L. Berg, H. Daumé III, J. Dodge, A. Goyal, X. Han, A. Mensch, M. Mitchell, A. Sood, K. Stratos, and K. Yamaguchi. Understanding and Predicting Importance in Images. In *CVPR, IEEE Intl. Conf. on*, 2012.

[2] T. F. Brady, T. Konkle, G. A. Alvarez, and A. Oliva. Visual long-term memory has a massive storage capacity for object details. *PNAS*, 105(38):14325–14329, September 2008.

[3] C.-C. Chang and C.-J. Lin. LIBSVM: A library for support vector machines. *ACM Trans. on Intelligent Systems and Technology*, 2:27:1–27:27, 2011.

[4] N. Dalal and B. Triggs. Histograms of oriented gradients for human detection. In *CVPR, IEEE Intl. Conf. on*, volume 1, pages 886 –893 vol. 1, june 2005.

[5] S. Dhar, V. Ordonez, and T. L. Berg. High Level Describable Attributes for Predicting Aesthetics and Interestingness. In *CVPR, IEEE Intl. Conf. on*, 2010.

[6] P.F. Felzenszwalb, R.B. Girshick, D. McAllester, and D. Ramanan. Object Detection with Discriminatively Trained Part-Based Models. *IEEE Trans. Pattern Anal. Mach. Intell.*, 32(9):1627 –1645, sept. 2010.

[7] S. J. Hwang and K. Grauman. Reading between the Lines: Object Localization Using Implicit Cues from Image Tags. *IEEE Trans. Pattern Anal. Mach. Intell.*, 34(6):1145–1158, June 2012.

[8] P. Isola, D. Parikh, A. Torralba, and A. Oliva. Understanding the Intrinsic Memorability of Images. In *NIPS 24*, 2011.

[9] P. Isola, J. Xiao, A. Torralba, and A. Oliva. What makes an image memorable? In *CVPR, IEEE Intl. Conf. on*, 2011.

[10] A. Khosla, J. Xiao, A. Torralba, and A. Oliva. Memorability of Image Regions. In *NIPS 25*, 2012.

[11] T. Konkle, T. F. Brady, G. A. Alvarez, , and A. Oliva. Scene Memory Is More Detailed Than You Think: The Role of Categories in Visual Long-Term Memory. *Psychological Science*, 21(11):1551–1556, 2010.

[12] S. Lazebnik, C. Schmid, and J. Ponce. Beyond bags of features: Spatial pyramid matching for recognizing natural scene categories. In *CVPR, IEEE Intl. Conf. on*, volume 2, pages 2169 – 2178, 2006.

[13] A. Oliva and A. Torralba. Modeling the shape of the scene: A holistic representation of the spatial envelope. *Int. J. Comput. Vision*, 42(3):145–175, May 2001.

[14] E. Shechtman and M. Irani. Matching local self-similarities across images and videos. In *CVPR, IEEE Intl. Conf. on*, pages 1 –8, june 2007.

[15] J. Xiao, J. Hays, K. A. Ehinger, A. Oliva, and A. Torralba. SUN Database: Large-scale Scene Recognition from Abbey to Zoo. In *CVPR, IEEE Intl. Conf. on*, 2010.

Automatic Egyptian Hieroglyph Recognition by Retrieving Images as Texts

Morris Franken and Jan C. van Gemert
Intelligent Systems Lab Amsterdam (ISLA), University of Amsterdam
Science Park 904 Amsterdam, The Netherlands

ABSTRACT

In this paper we propose an approach for automatically recognizing ancient Egyptian hieroglyph from photographs. To this end we first manually annotated and segmented a large collection of nearly 4,000 hieroglyphs. In our automatic approach we localize and segment each individual hieroglyph, determine the reading order and subsequently evaluate 5 visual descriptors in 3 different matching schemes to evaluate visual hieroglyph recognition. In addition to visual-only cues, we use a corpus of Egyptian texts to learn language models that help re-rank the visual output.

Categories and Subject Descriptors

H.3 [**Information Storage and Retrieval**]: Information Search and Retrieval; I.4 [**Image Processing and Computer Vision**]: Features Measurement—*Feature representation, size and shape*

Keywords

Egyptian, Hieroglyphs, Automatic Recognition

1. INTRODUCTION

The ancient Egyptian hieroglyphs have always been a mysterious writing system as their meaning was completely lost in the 4th century AD. The discovery of the Rosetta stone in 1799 allowed researchers to investigate the hieroglyphs, but it wasn't until 1822 when Jean-François Champollion discovered that these hieroglyphs don't resemble a word for each symbol, but each hieroglyph resembles a sound and multiple hieroglyphs form a word. The ability to understand hieroglyphs has uncovered much of the history, customs and culture of Egypt's ancient past.

In this paper we present a system that is able to automatically recognize ancient Egyptian hieroglyphs from photographs. As illustrated in fig 4, a single photograph contains several, often overlapping, hieroglyphs without proper segmentation or a-priori reading order. Moreover, the passing of 4 millennia has introduced noise, and broken or destroyed the original symbols. These conditions present severe challenges to automatic hieroglyph recognition. Automatic hieroglyph recognition is useful for archaeology scholars, the interested amateur, cultural heritage preservation or as a smart-phone App for a tourist or museum visitor.

The paper has 3 contributions. First, we introduce a new hieroglyph dataset where we manually segmented and labeled 3993 hieroglyphs of 10 photographs from the pyramid of Unas. This pyramid is built in the fifth dynasty as a burial place for the Pharaoh *Unas* and is located just south of the city of Giza, see fig 1. We chose a single pyramid to avoid issues with different dialectic writing styles. Second, we show how to automatically locate, segment and recognize hieroglyphs based on visual information. The third contribution is a multimodal extension to the visual analysis with statistical language models from hieroglyph texts. In fig 2 we show a schematic of our approach.

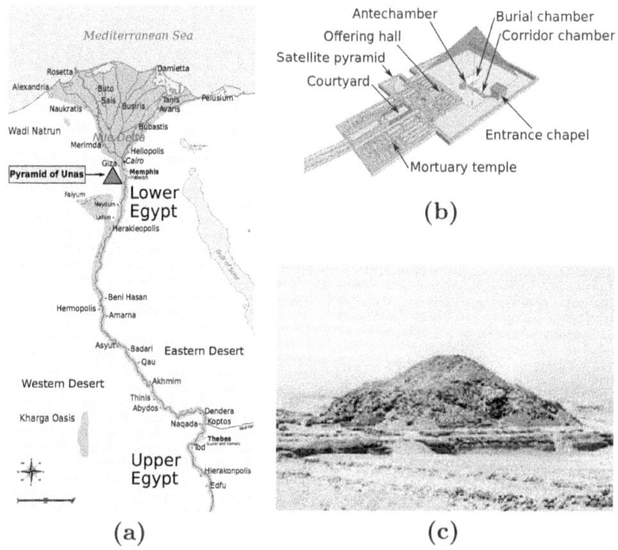

Figure 1: The pyramid of Unas. (a) Location at red triangle. (b) Schematic reconstruction. (c) Current state. *Images courtesy of Wikipedia, creative commons license.*

2. RELATED WORK

Multimedia tools have aided preservation, analysis and study of cultural, historical and artistic content. For ex-

MM'13, October 21–25, 2013, Barcelona, Spain.

http://dx.doi.org/10.1145/2502081.2502199 .

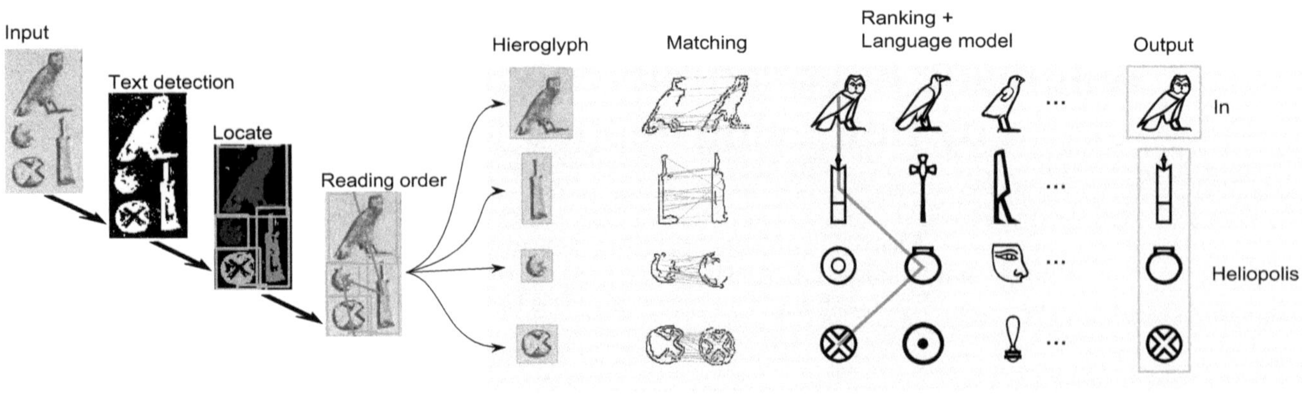

Figure 2: Pipeline for hieroglyph recognition. The 3rd output hieroglyph from the top is corrected by the language model in order to find the word 'Heliopolis' (birth-city of Unas).

ample, the digital Michelangelo project [12] created high quality 3D models of Michelangelo's sculptures and architecture. Furthermore, wavelet analysis of brush strokes in paintings can reveal artist identity [7], image composition has shown to aid category labeling [17] and photographs can be classified as memorable or not [6]. In this paper we follow in these footsteps, and propose a new dataset, and a multimodal (visual and textual) approach for automatic Egyptian hieroglyphs recognition.

Related work on automatic hieroglyph recognition focuses on Mesoamerican culture, and in particular on the ancient Maya hieroglyphs [5, 14, 15]. To this end, the HOOSC descriptor was developed [15], which is a combination of HOG [2] and the Shape-Context [1]. Such descriptors can be used for direct matching [14] or with a bag-of-words (BOW) approach [15]. Other work extracts detailed line segments for Maya hieroglyph matching [5]. In all these works the hieroglyphs are typically manually extracted and individually digitized. In contrast, our photographs consists of noisy plates, which each typically contain around 400 hieroglyphs (see fig 4). Moreover, the Maya culture used a considerable different type of hieroglyphs and we therefore evaluate the HOOSC and other descriptors on Egyptian hieroglyphs.

Current work on automatic scene text detection and recognition [4, 9, 10, 11] are typically hand-tuned to specific western or asian (e.g. Chinese or Hangul) characters which are quite different from Egyptian hieroglyphs. In our work, we will draw inspiration from text detection to localize the hieroglyphs and use generic image descriptors for the recognition.

3. HIEROGLYPH RECOGNITION

Our approach has a visual component where the reading order is determined, hieroglyphs are localized, pre-processed and visually matched. The top-N visual matches are subsequently input to a textual component that re-ranks the hieroglyphs according to a statistical language model trained on other texts. In fig 2 we show a schematic of our approach.

3.1 Localization and Pre-Processing

We localize hieroglyphs with a saliency-based text-detection algorithm [9] (software kindly provided by the authors). This algorithm does not make assumptions on the shape of the text, as done e.g. in [4]. The used algorithm creates a

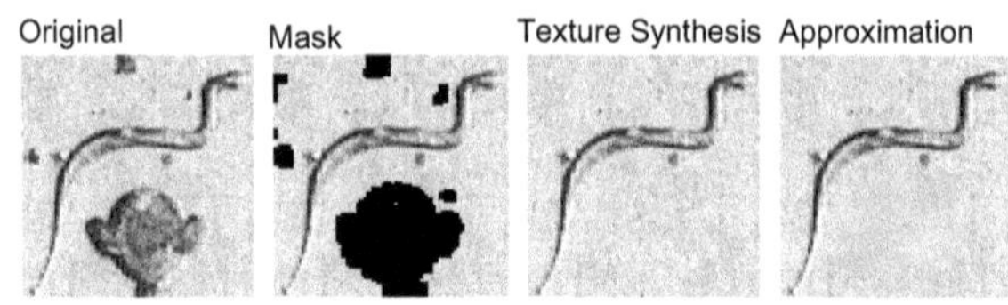

Figure 3: Removing unconnected hieroglyphs.

saliency map based on second order curvature statistics and subsequently uses conditional dilation from border-seeds to create a binary text/non-text mask. We group the noisy masks by connected components after a dilation. The output of the localization is an unordered list of bounding boxes (BBs) fitted around each glyph. We experimentally evaluate the localization performance in section 4.

From the unordered list the reading order is determined to facilitate textual language modeling. The reading order in Egyptian hieroglyphs is either from left to right, right to left or from top to bottom. The only indication of the correct reading order is that glyphs will face the beginning of a line, and top to bottom is indicated by columns separators. Multiple horizontal hieroglyphs in a column should be read as a single line. For the pyramid of Unas the reading order is top-down, from right to left. We sort the unorderd list accordingly to determine the sequence in which the hieroglyphs should be read.

The hieroglyphs BBs are often overlapping or they are in contact with a 'cartouche' (a frame around the name of a royalty). To generate individual hieroglyph images suitable for matching, we filled the overlapping parts with background texture by a non-parametric texture synthesis method [3]. This approach works well, however it is rather slow. We therefore implemented a faster approximation. For each pixel to generate we randomly sample from a search window around the closest filled-in pixel. If the sampled pixel is not part of the foreground mask it is kept, otherwise the process is repeated with a larger window size. After texture synthesis is complete, the final background is smoothed to reduce noise. Our approximation is in the order of 300 times faster, the results of both methods are shown in fig 3. As a final step the patches are extended to 50x75 while retaining their discriminative height/width ratio where the background is again texture synthesized if necessary.

3.2 Image Descriptors

We evaluate five image descriptors, two based on shape, one based on appearance, and the other two on a shape-appearance combination. The Shape-Context (SC) [1] is a shape descriptor originally designed for recognizing handwritten symbols and therefore interesting for hieroglyphs. The SC constructs a spatial log-polar histogram that counts the frequency of edge pixels. Similar to the SC, the Self-Similarity [16] (SS) descriptor was designed for shape matching. Where the SC counts edge pixels, the SS computes the pixel correlation between the central cell to the other cells in a log-polar shaped region. The SC and the SS are shape descriptors, but the hieroglyphs may also benefit from appearance matching. The Histogram of Oriented Gradients (HOG) [2] is a popular appearance descriptor that computes histograms of edge gradient orientations. A combination of shape and appearance can be achieved by merging the HOG and the SC. This combination is called the HOOSC [15] and was developed for Maya hieroglyph matching. The HOOSC replaces the edge pixels in the SC with a HOG. As the fifth descriptor we add a straightforward combination of the SS with HOG which we dub HOOSS. For this combination, the correlations in SS between pixels are replaced with similarities of HOGs. All similarities between K-dimensional descriptors i and j are computed with the χ^2-distance, $\chi^2(i,j) = \sum_1^K \frac{(i_k - j_k)^2}{i_k + j_k}$.

3.3 Visual Matching

To recognize a hieroglyph we compare it to labeled patches in the training set. To this end, we evaluate three common image patch matching schemes. The first method is simply using a single centered descriptor for a full patch. The second approach uses interest points with the popular bag-of-words framework as also used for Maya hieroglyphs [15]. The third approach has also been used for Maya glyphs [14] and uses pair-wise patch matching using interest points with spatial verification. This method starts with a variant of the Hungarian method [8] to assign each descriptor in one patch to a descriptor in the other patch. After obtaining matches, the final matching score s is obtained by fitting an affine transformation between the patches by using Ransac and is computed as $s = m * \sum_{(p_1,p_2)}^{P} \chi^2(p_1,p_2)/|P|^2$, where m is the number of matches, and (p_1,p_2) are matched pairs in the set of Ransac inliers P.

3.4 Language Modeling

The visual ranking is based on a single hieroglyph and does not take the neighboring hieroglyphs into account. The neighborhood can give valuable information since hieroglyphs often co-occur to form words and sentences. To take the context into account we employ language models of hieroglyph occurrences to improve the visual ranking. We compare two strategies: (1) a lexicon lookup and (2) N-grams which represent statistics of N-neighboring hieroglyphs.

The lexicon-based approach tries to match N consequative hieroglyphs to existing words in a dictionary. For each hieroglyph i, we look at the top K=10 results $(v_{i1}, v_{i2}, \ldots, v_{iK})$ of the visual ranking. We re-rank each hieroglyph i by word length $|w|$ and occurrence probability $P(w)$ as $(p(w) + \lambda_w) \cdot |w| \cdot \prod_{j=1}^{K}(v_{i1}/v_{ij})^2$, where w is any exact word match that is present in the Carthesian $N \times K$ space of possible words where N is equal to the largest word in the corpus. To reduce the influence of non-existing words we use a standard Laplace smoothing term λ_w, which we set to 1/20. In section 4 we give the details of the used corpus. We found the best non-linear weighting of visual scores (in this case v^2) on a small hold-out set.

...
he shall not write with his little finger. How beautiful is indeed the sight, how good indeed to see, so say they, so say the gods, (when) this god ascends to heaven, (when) Unas ascends to heaven while his power is over him
...

Figure 4: Part of a plate taken from the north wall of the antechamber (column 476) and its translation.

The N-gram approach uses the probability of hieroglyph sub-sequences of length N occurring in a row. We re-rank each hieroglyph i with $\prod_{i=1}^{N}\prod_{j=1}^{K}(v_{i1}/v_{ij})^3 \cdot (p(w) + \lambda_n)$, where w is a hieroglyph sequence of length $N = 3$. To reduce the influence of non-existing N-grams we use a Laplace smoothing term λ_n of 1/2000. Again, we found the best non-linear weighting of visual scores (v^3) on a hold-out set.

4. EXPERIMENTS

We evaluate all descriptors, matching techniques and language models on our new hieroglyph dataset.

4.1 Dataset

The dataset consist of two sets: one being photographs of hieroglyphic texts, the other being the textual corpus that is used for the language model. The visual set consists of 10 plate photographs with hieroglyphs [13], as illustrated in fig 4. These photographs contain 161 unique hieroglyphs with a total of 3993. We manually segmented all individual hieroglyphs with a bounding box and annotated them with their label. To record the label we use a form of transliteration which transforms the hieroglyphs into a character. Many transliteration variations exist among Egyptologists, which are rarely compatible with each other. In this research we chose to use the transliteration used by the open-source JSesh project[1] which also gave rise to the textual set of the database, containing 158 pyramid texts (with a total size of 640KB of text). This textual set is used to train the language models and does not contain any texts from the pyramid of Unas.

4.2 Implementation Details

To reduce differences between descriptors due to parameter setting we keep parameters as equal as possible over the five variants. For HOG we use 8 angle bins, and 4x4 spatial binning. The HOG inside HOOSC and HOOSS also use 8 angle bins. All log-polar histograms have 3 rings, and 8 segments. For the bag-of-words matching we found that a vocabulary size of 200 visual words works well. In the spatial matching we use 500 Ransac iterations. The interest

[1] `http://jsesh.qenherkhopeshef.org/`

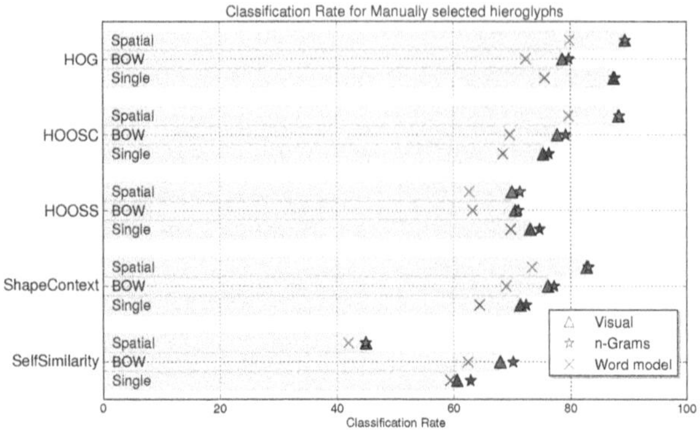

Figure 5: Results for manually cut-out hieroglyphs. The average score is $74 \pm 1\%$.

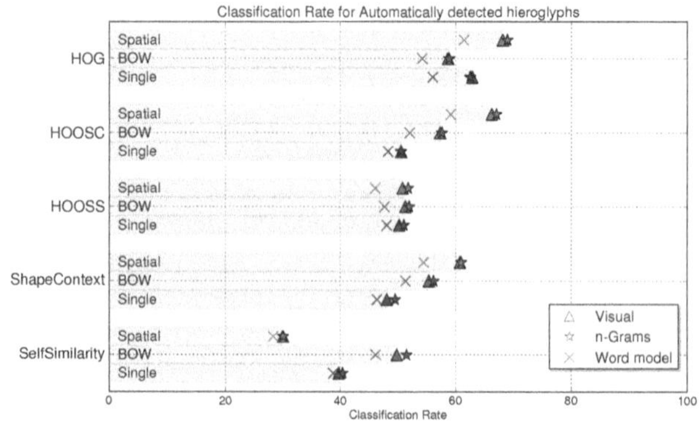

Figure 6: Results for automatically detected hieroglyphs. The average score is 53 ± 5.

points in the BOW and in the spatial matching are based on the contour [14, 15] of a Canny edge detector.

To simulate taking a single photograph, we use one plate for testing and the other plates for training. We repeat the experiment to obtain standard deviations.

4.3 Results

We give results for manually cut-out hieroglyphs recognition in fig 5 and for our automatic detection approach in fig 6. The automatic detection method finds 83% of all manually annotated hieroglyphs, and 85.5% of the detections are correct according to the Pascal VOC overlap criteria. The matching performance trend between the automatic and the manual annotated hieroglyphs is similar, although the single-descriptor HOG seems slightly more sensitive to localization errors.

From the 5 descriptors, the HOOSC and the HOG are the best performers. HOOSC is best on manually annotated hieroglyphs whereas HOG is more robust for automatically detected regions. This seems to indicate that flexibility in spatial structure is important, given the reduced performance of single descriptor HOG on the automatically detected glyphs.

Between the three matching schemes, the spatial-matching performs best. Only for the Self-Similarity the BOW is better. Generally the Self-Similarity does not perform as well on this dataset, which could be attributed to the lack of discriminative features such as color. The slightly better performance of the spatial matching scheme, however, is a factor of 8,000 times slower compared to a single descriptor and 1,000 times slower than the BOW.

Language modeling with a lexicon decreases results on average with 5%. This is due to a bias for smaller words and the lack of word-separators. The N-grams always improves results, albeit slightly, with on average 1%.

5. CONCLUSION

We presented a new Egyptian hieroglyph set with a thorough evaluation of five popular image descriptors, three common matching schemes and two types of language modeling.

6. REFERENCES

[1] S. Belongie, J. Malik, and J. Puzicha. Shape matching and object recognition using shape contexts. *TPAMI*, 24(4), 2002.

[2] N. Dalal and B. Triggs. Histograms of oriented gradients for human detection. In *CVPR*, 2005.

[3] A. Efros and T. Leung. Texture synthesis by non-parametric sampling. In *ICCV*, 1999.

[4] B. Epshtein, E. Ofek, and Y. Wexler. Detecting text in natural scenes with stroke width transform. In *CVPR*, pages 2963–2970, 2010.

[5] Y. Frauela, O. Quesadab, and E. Bribiescaa. Detection of a polymorphic mesoamerican symbol using a rule-based approach. *Pattern Recognition*, 39, 2006.

[6] P. Isola, J. Xiao, A. Torralba, and A. Oliva. What makes an image memorable? In *CVPR*, 2011.

[7] R. Johnson, E. Hendriks, J. Berezhnoy, E. Brevdo, S. Hughes, I. Daubechies, J. Li, E. Postma, and J. Wang. Image processing for artist identification. *Signal Processing Magazine, IEEE*, 25(4):37–48, 2008.

[8] R. Jonker and A. Volgenant. A shortest augmenting path algorithm for dense and sparse linear assignment problems. *Computing*, 38(4), 1987.

[9] S. Karaoglu, J. van Gemert, and T. Gevers. Object reading: Text recognition for object recognition. In *ECCV-IFCVCR Workshop*, 2012.

[10] S. Karaoglu, J. van Gemert, and T. Gevers. Con-text: Text detection using background connectivity for fine-grained object classification. In *ACM-MM*, 2013.

[11] F. Kimura, K. Takashina, S. Tsuruoka, and Y. Miyake. Modified quadratic discriminant functions and the application to chinese character recognition. *PAMI*, (1):149–153, 1987.

[12] M. Levoy et al. The digital Michelangelo project: 3D scanning of large statues. In *Computer graphics and interactive techniques*, 2000.

[13] A. Piankoff. *The Pyramid of Unas*. Princeton University Press, 1968.

[14] E. Roman-Rangel, C. Pallan, J.-M. Odobez, and D. Gatica-Perez. Retrieving ancient maya glyphs with shape context. In *ICCV Workshop*, 2009.

[15] E. Roman-Rangel, C. Pallan Gayol, J.-M. Odobez, and D. Gatica-Perez. Searching the past: an improved shape descriptor to retrieve maya hieroglyphs. In *ACM MM*, 2011.

[16] E. Shechtman and M. Irani. Matching local self-similarities across images and videos. In *CVPR*, 2007.

[17] J. van Gemert. Exploiting photographic style for category-level image classification by generalizing the spatial pyramid. In *ICMR*, 2011.

Query-Dependent Visual Dictionary Adaptation for Image Reranking

Jialong Wang
Xidian University
Xi'an, 710071 China
wangjialong@gmail.com

Cheng Deng
Xidian Univerisity
Xi'an, 710071 China
chdeng@mail.xidian.edu.cn

Wei Liu
IBM T. J. Watson Research Center, Yorktown Heights, NY, USA
weiliu@us.ibm.com

Rongrong Ji
Xiamen University
Xiamen, 361005 China
rrji@xmu.edu.cn

Xiangyu Chen
I2R, Astar
Singapore, 138632 Singapore
chenxy@i2r.a-star.edu.sg

Xinbo Gao
Xidian University
Xi'an, 710071 China
xbgao@mail.xidian.edu.cn

ABSTRACT

Although text-based image search engines are popular for ranking images of user's interest, the state-of-the-art ranking performance is still far from satisfactory. One major issue comes from the visual similarity metric used in the ranking operation, which depends solely on visual features. To tackle this issue, one feasible method is to incorporate semantic concepts, also known as image attributes, into image ranking. However, the optimal combination of visual features and image attributes remains unknown. In this paper, we propose a query-dependent image reranking approach by leveraging the higher level attribute detection among the top returned images to adapt the dictionary built over the visual features to a query-specific fashion. We start from offline learning transposition probabilities between visual codewords and attributes, then utilize the probabilities to online adapt the dictionary, and finally produce a query-dependent and semantics-induced metric for image ranking. Extensive evaluations on several benchmark image datasets demonstrate the effectiveness and efficiency of the proposed approach in comparison with state-of-the-arts.

Categories and Subject Descriptors

H.3.3 [**Information Search and Retrieval**]: Retrieval models

General Terms

Algorithms, Experimentation, Performance

Keywords

Image Reranking, Query Dependent, Dictionary Adaptation

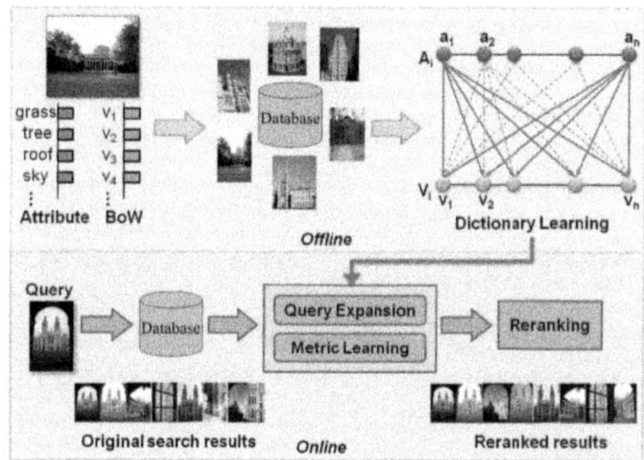

Figure 1: Framework of our proposed approach.

1. INTRODUCTION

Most popular web image search engines, such as Google and Microsoft Bing, are built under the "query by keyword" scenario, in which the related images are returned by using the associated textual information from web pages, including title, description, and surrounding caption of the related images [1]. However, text-based search schemes are known to be unsatisfying because textual information does not always describe image content accurately. Besides, mismatches between images and their associated text will inevitably introduce irrelevant images appearing in search results.

To boost the precision of text-based image search, image reranking [2], which is referred to as refining an initially ranked image list queried by an input keyword, has received increasing attention in recent years. By asking a user to select a query image that reflects the user's search intention, the initial ranking list is reordered by exploiting a similarity metric based on visual features to achieve better search performance. One basic assumption of image reranking is that visually similar images tend to be ranked together.

Although there have been many image reranking approaches from different perspectives, the major challenge of well capturing the user's search intention is still unsolved. In order to cope with this challenge, the recent efforts focus on "query expansion" which could correlate low-level visual features with high-level semantic meanings of images by absorbing more image cues. The existing query expansion in image reranking can be classified into two main categories:

visual expansion and *semantic expansion* [3]. The goal of visual expansion is to obtain multiple positive instances to learn a robust similarity metric which is expected to be specific to a particular query image. As a conventional means, relevance feedback is used to expand the positive instances [4], where a user is asked to label multiple relevant and irrelevant image instances. However, relevance feedback requires an extra burden of user's labeling. To reduce the user's burden, pseudo relevance feedback [5][6] is adopted to expand query images by taking top-ranked results as the positive instances and bottom-ranked results as the negative instances. These instances are further leveraged into training a classifier that outputs the ranking scores. Unfortunately, pseudo relevance feedback based methods are not guaranteed to work well due to the existence of false relevant images.

The idea of semantic expansion is to expand the original query image with additional query terms that are relevant to the query keyword [7]. Semantic expansion was initially proposed for document retrieval. The lexical-based methods leveraged the linguistic word relationships to expand query keywords, e.g., synonyms and hypernyms. The statistical approaches, such as term clustering [8] and Latent Semantic Indexing (LSA) [9], attempted to discover the term relationships based on term-document co-occurrence statistics. The other methods attempted to reduce the topic drift by seeking frequently co-occurred patterns with the same context instead of the entire document. However, the additional terms expanded by these methods do not always consist with the semantic concepts of the query images, which makes the ranking results unsatisfying.

In this paper, we propose a novel image reranking approach with query-dependent visual dictionary adaptation. Given an image retrieval list, we first construct a query-specific transposition probability dictionary between visual features and semantic concepts. Different from most of the existing methods, we represent semantic concepts as image attributes which can be obtained by using some off-the-shelf approaches, such as Classeme[1] and ObjectBank[2]. For a query image, its salient visual words and attributes can be acquired through performing encoding with the learned dictionary. On one hand, the semantic concepts of the query image are well expanded; on the other hand, the obtained semantic concepts are not only query-specific but also related to common-specific concepts belonging to the whole dataset. Hence, these obtained image cues can well reflect the user's search intention. To further preserve the similarities between the query image and the reranked top-K images visually and semantically, we then learn a similarity metric under which the query image and its related images are kept as close as possible in a new feature space, and meanwhile those irrelevant images are successfully filtered out.

The contributions of this work are summarized as follows:

(1) We construct a corpus-oriented dictionary which explicitly captures the latent consistency between visual features and semantic concepts. In our work, we use image attributes to represent semantic concepts. As far as we know, it is the first time to build such a co-occurring dictionary in the context of image reranking.

(2) We simultaneously accomplish visual expansion and semantic expansion for any query image with the learned co-occurring dictionary, which results in more flexible and accurate image reranking.

(3) We learn a similarity metric which yields a new feature space, where visual similarities and semantic correlations can be well preserved for any query image and its related top-K images. By doing so, the reranking performance can be further boosted.

[1]`http://www.cs.dartmouth.edu/~lorenzo/projects/classemes/`

[2]`http://vision.stanford.edu/projects/objectbank/`

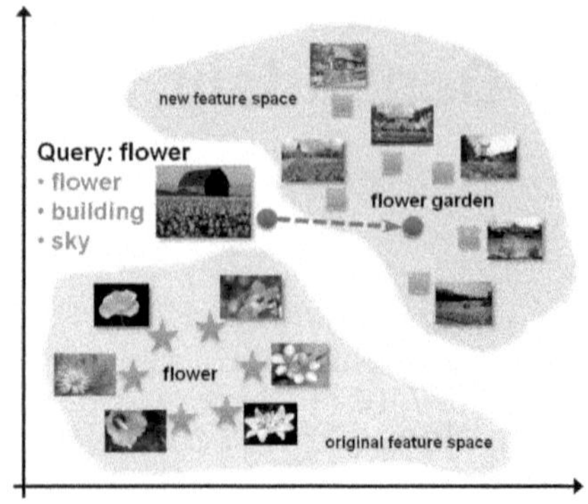

Figure 2: Similarity metric learning supervised by semantic expansion.

The rest of the paper is organized as: we propose our approach in Section 2; we describe the experiments including the experimental settings, the experimental results, and the discussions in Section 3; we conclude the paper in Section 4.

2. THE APPROACH

Figure 1 illustrates the proposed image reranking framework, which consists of offline transposition probability learning and online similarity metric learning. We detail both components respectively as below:

2.1 Formulation

Given a query image q, its retrieval set is denoted as $\mathcal{I}_q = \{I_1, \cdots, I_N\}$. For each image I_i in $\mathcal{I}_q$, we extract its visual vector $\mathbf{V}^{(i)} = [v_1^{(i)}, v_2^{(i)}, \cdots, v_m^{(i)}]$, and its attribute vector $\mathbf{A}^{(i)} = [a_1^{(i)}, a_2^{(i)}, \cdots, a_n^{(i)}]$.

In our work, Bag-of-Words (BoW) is used to describe visual feature, and Classeme is used to extract attribute vector to describe semantic concepts. We form visual dictionary $\mathbf{V}$ and semantic dictionary $\mathbf{A}$ on the retrieval set $\mathcal{I}_q$, respectively. Therefore, the transposition probability matrix $\tilde{\mathbf{W}}$ can be built based on the co-occurence of entries between $\mathbf{V}$ and $\mathbf{A}$. For the query image q, the visual and semantic query expansion correspond to the significant visual and semantic elements selected according to $\tilde{\mathbf{W}}$ respectively. This procedure can be formulated as

$$\tilde{\mathbf{V}}^{(q)} = f(\mathbf{V}^{(q)}, \tilde{\mathbf{W}}), \quad \tilde{\mathbf{A}}^{(q)} = g(\mathbf{A}^{(q)}, \tilde{\mathbf{W}}). \qquad (1)$$

Here, $f(\cdot)$ and $g(\cdot)$ are the selection functions respectively, which would be detailed later.

For image reranking, we hope the reordered top-K images are more related to the query image in terms of both visual and semantic similarity. To that effect, we propose to learn a similarity metric matrix $\mathbf{M}$ online, which is used to adapt the original visual features into a new subspace where semantics are preserved. Figure 2 shows an exemplar illustration of such a space, where an image close to the query images should be both visually and semantically relevant. In other word, we target at learning a semantic-induced manifold structure in the visual feature space to capture the essence of both metrics. This corresponds to minimizing both visual and semantic dissimilarities:

In terms of visual similarity, the accumulated distances between the top-K images and the query image should be minimized as

$$\min_{\mathbf{M}} \sum_{k=1}^{K} \|\mathbf{V}^{(k)}\mathbf{M} - \mathbf{V}^{(q)}\mathbf{M}\|_2^2. \tag{2}$$

In terms of semantic relevance, the accumulated distances of attribute vectors between the top-K images and the query image should be minimized. We have

$$\min_{\mathbf{M}} \sum_{k=1}^{K} \|\mathbf{V}^{(k)}\tilde{\mathbf{W}}\mathbf{M} - \mathbf{V}^{(q)}\tilde{\mathbf{W}}\mathbf{M}\|_2^2. \tag{3}$$

Jointing Equation 2 and Equation 3, we derive the overall objective function as

$$\begin{aligned}\mathcal{O} = \min_{\mathbf{M}} &\sum_{k=1}^{K} \|\mathbf{V}^{(k)}\mathbf{M} - \mathbf{V}^{(q)}\mathbf{M}\|_2^2 \\ &+ \sum_{k=1}^{K} \|\mathbf{V}^{(k)}\tilde{\mathbf{W}}\mathbf{M} - \mathbf{V}^{(q)}\tilde{\mathbf{W}}\mathbf{M}\|_2^2 + \lambda\|\mathbf{M}\|_1,\end{aligned} \tag{4}$$

where $\|\cdot\|_1$ is the ℓ_1-norm of a matrix, λ is a constant to control the sparsity degree. Here, the main role of the sparse matrix $\mathbf{M}$ lies in only selecting those significant elements. Thus, the expanded visual features and semantic concepts are not only query-dependent but also corpus-oriented.

Once obtaining the sparse metric matrix $\mathbf{M}$, we calculate the similarity in the new space, and use the similarity score as the reranking score to reorder the search results. The similarity between query q and image I_j is defined as

$$sim(q, I_j) = \frac{\sum_{i=1}^{d} \min(x_{qi}, x_{ji})}{\sum_{i=1}^{d} \max(x_{qi}, x_{ji})}. \tag{5}$$

2.2 Optimization

The smoothing nature of the first two terms in Equation 4 guarantees a convex and smoothing objective function. Therefore, a general Smoothing Proximal Gradient (SPG) approach is adopted in the optimization step. More specifically, we solve this ℓ_1-norm penalized sparse learning problem by the Fast Iterative Shrinkage-Thresholding Algorithm (FISTA) [10]. SPG has been proven to achieve $O(\frac{1}{\epsilon})$ convergence rate for a desired accuracy ϵ. The FISTA method is presented in Algorithm 1.

Algorithm 1: FISTA Algorithm.

Input: $\mathbf{V}^{(k)}$, $\tilde{\mathbf{W}}$, $\mathbf{M}_0$, λ.
Initialization: set $\theta_0 = 1$, $\mathbf{X}_0 = \mathbf{M}_0 = \mathbf{I}$.
for $t = 0, 1, 2, \ldots$ *until convergence of* $\mathbf{M}_t$ **do**
  Compute $\nabla\mathcal{O}(\mathbf{X}_t)$.
  Compute Lipschitz constant $L = \lambda_{max}(\nabla\mathcal{O}(\mathbf{X}_t))$, where λ_{max} is the largest eigenvalue.
  Perform the generalized gradient update step: $\mathbf{M}_{t+1} = \mathrm{argmin}_{\mathbf{M}} \frac{1}{2}\|\mathbf{M} - (\mathbf{X}_t - \frac{1}{L}\nabla\mathcal{H}(\mathbf{X}_t))\|_2^2 + \frac{\gamma}{L}\|\mathbf{M}\|_1$.
  Set $\theta_{t+1} = \frac{2}{t+3}$.
  Set $\mathbf{X}_{t+1} = \mathbf{M}_{t+1} + \frac{1-\theta_t}{\theta_t}\theta_{t+1}(\mathbf{M}_{t+1} - \mathbf{M}_t)$.
end
Output: $\mathbf{M} = \mathbf{M}^{t+1}$.

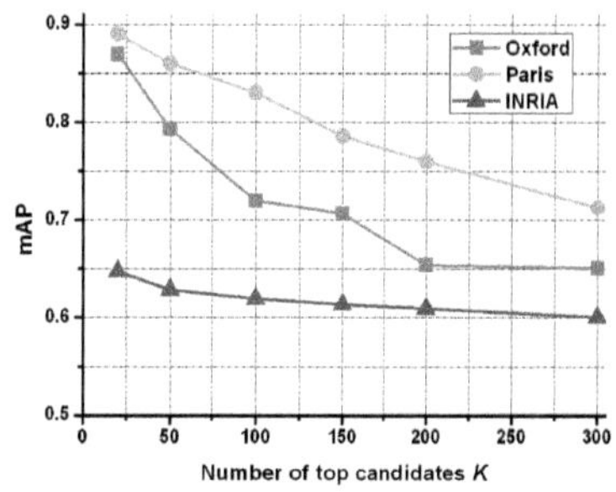

Figure 3: mAP under different number of candidates K for three datasets.

3. EXPERIMENTS

In this section, we first present the experimental settings, and then we illustrate and discuss the experimental results. Moreover, we will compare our approach with state-of-the-art reranking methods, such as noise resistant graph-based image reranking (NRGIR) [11], random walk-based image reranking (RWIR) [2], to demonstrate the effectiveness of our approach.

3.1 Experimental Settings

Datasets: Experiments are conducted on four popular datasets: Oxford Building[3], Paris[4], INRIA Holidays[5], and UKBench[6]. Oxford and Paris respectively contain 5,062 and 6,412 images, which are all provided with ground truth by manual annotation. INRIA includes 1,491 relevant images of 500 scenes or objects, where the first image is used as a query in each group. UKBench contains 10,200 images that always show the same object.

Feature: We use dense SIFT descriptor [12] computed from 16×16 sized image patches with a stepsize of 8 pixels using VLFeat library. Then, 1,024-dimensional visual words is constructed with 1M descriptors. We use 1×1, 2×2, 3×1 sub-regions to compute a BoW as the final image visual feature. Besides, we extract attribute vector for each image with Classeme.

Baseline: We design two baselines to show the improvement of the retrieval accuracy, which includes: (I) visual feature based reranking: we independently use BoW as visual feature to evaluate the similarity between images; (II) semantic feature based reranking: we independently use attribute as semantic feature to evaluate the image similarity.

Evaluation Metric: We use mean Averaged Precision (mAP) to evaluate the performance on the first three datasets, while the performance measure on the UKBench is the average number of correct returning in top-4 images, denoted as (Ave. Top Num.).

[3] `http://www.robots.ox.ac.uk/~vgg/data/oxbuildings/`
[4] `http://www.robots.ox.ac.uk/~vgg/data/parisbuildings/`
[5] `http://lear.inrialpes.fr/~jegou/data.php`
[6] `http://vis.uky.edu/~stewe/ukbench/`

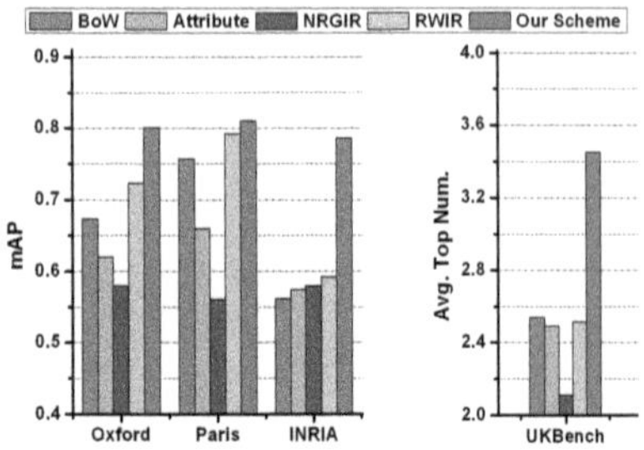

(a)

(b)

Figure 4: Comparison results and visual results on different dataset.

3.2 Results and Analysis

Parameter Tuning: In our method, the top-K dataset candidates for the query image I_q are considered to evaluate reranking performance. In the objective function learning, we set $\lambda = 0.05$.

We first evaluate the performance of our approach given different numbers of top dataset candidates K on baseline I. Figure 3 shows the performance on the first three datasets when we change K. When K becomes larger, the mAP values on Oxford decrease. With K increasing from 20 to 300, as shown in Figure 3, the mAP drops from 0.87 to 0.65.

A similar situation is also observed with all other datasets. We use the same setting (K from 20 to 300) in all these datasets. Specially, since the queries in UKBench only have three relevant images, K is set to 4. In the subsequent experiments, without specification, we fix $K = 200$ for all datasets but UKBench.

Comparison Results: Figure 4(a) illustrates the mAP of the baselines and some state-of-the-art methods on four datasets. As shown in Figure 4(a), the performances of all reranking methods are superior to the baseline I, i.e., direct reranking based on BoW visual feature. The mAP of our approach is about 0.14 and 1.01 higher than that of baseline I on the first three datasets and UKBench, respectively. Similarly, compared with NRGIR and RWIR, our approach obtains 0.23 and 0.1 improvements on the first three datasets, and 1.43 and nearly 1.0 improvements on UKBench, respectively. Figure 4(b) shows some visual results of our image reranking on datasets, in which three rows for each query are the results of NRGIR, RWIR, and our approach.

4. CONCLUSIONS

In this paper, we propose an image reranking approach using query-dependent visual dictionary adaptation. Through the offline visual-semantic co-occurring dictionary learning, we can not only effectively capture the query-specific relationship between low-level visual features and high-level semantic concepts but also wisely extend the query image's semantic space, thus capturing the user's search intention. Furthermore, we conduct similarity metric learning supervised by the attribute-based semantic concepts, which makes the query image and its relevant images closer in a new feature space. The experimental results show that our approach performs significantly better than the state-of-the-arts.

Although our approach achieves good performance, it is more suitable for constrained datasets but not for unconstrained web-scale image collections. The main drawback of our approach lies in that a limited number of semantic concepts cannot cover numerous images present on the Internet. Therefore, our future work will focus on gaining more diverse and accurate semantic concepts through mining more textual information from massive Internet images. We also plan to explore scalable similarity metric learning using robust large graphs [13] and accelerating the reranking operation using principled hashing methods like [14][15].

5. ACKNOWLEDGMENTS

We want to thank the helpful comments and suggestions from the anonymous reviewers. This research was supported partially by the National Natural Science Foundation of China (Nos. 61125204 and 61101250), the Program for New Century Excellent Talents in University (NCET-12-0917), the Program for New Scientific and Technological Star of Shaanxi Province (No. 2012KJXX-24).

6. REFERENCES

[1] X. Tian, L. Yang, J. Wang, Y. Yang, X. Wu, and X.-S. Hua. Bayesian video search reranking. In *Proc. ACM Multimedia*, 2008.

[2] W. Hsu, L. Kennedy, and S.-F. Chang. Reranking methods for visual search. *IEEE Multimedia*, 14(3):14–22, 2007.

[3] X. Tang, K. Liu, J. Cui, F. Wen, and X. Wang. Intentsearch: Capturing user intention for one-click internet image search. *IEEE Trans. PAMI*, 34(7):1342–1353, 2012.

[4] Y. Lu, H. Zhang, L. Wenyin, and C. Hu. Joint semantics and feautre based image retrieval using relevance feedback. *IEEE Trans. Multimedia*, 5(3):339–347, 2003.

[5] R. Yan, A. G. Hauptmann, and R. Jin. Negative pseudo-relevance feedback in content-based video retrieval. In *Proc. ACM Multimedia*, 2003.

[6] N. Morioka and J. Wang. Robust visual reranking via sparsity and ranking constraints. In *Proc. ACM Multimedia*, 2011.

[7] A. Natsev, A. Haubold, J. Tešić, L. Xie, and R. Yan. Semantic concept-based query expansion and re-ranking for multimedia retrieval. In *Proc. ACM Multimedia*, 2007.

[8] K. Sparck Jones. *Automatic Keyword Classification for Information Retrieval*. Archon Books, 1971.

[9] S. Deerwester, S. Dumais, G. Furnas, T. Landauer, and R. Harshman. Indexing by latent semantic analysis. *Journal of the American Society of Information Science*, 41(6):391–407, 1990.

[10] A. Beck and M. Teboulle. A fast iterative shrinkage-thresholding algorithm for linear inverse problems. *SIAM Journal on Imaging Sciences*, 2(1):183–202, 2009.

[11] W. Liu, Y.-G. Jiang, J. Luo, and S.-F. Chang. Noise resistant graph ranking for improved web image search. In *Proc. CVPR*, 2011.

[12] S. Lazebnik, C. Schmid, and J. Ponce. Beyond bags of features: Spatial pyramid matching for recognizing natural scene categories. In *Proc. CVPR*, 2006.

[13] W. Liu, J. He, and S.-F. Chang. Large graph construction for scalable semi-supervised learning. In *Proc. ICML*, 2010.

[14] W. Liu, J. Wang, S. Kumar, and S.-F. Chang. Hashing with graphs. In *Proc. ICML*, 2011.

[15] W. Liu, J. Wang, R. Ji, Y.-G. Jiang, and S.-F. Chang. Supervised hashing with kernels. In *Proc. CVPR*, 2012.

Correlated-Spaces Regression for Learning Continuous Emotion Dimensions

Mihalis A. Nicolaou
Department of Computing
Imperial College London, U.K.
mihalis@imperial.ac.uk

Stefanos Zafeiriou
Department of Computing
Imperial College London, U.K.
s.zafeiriou@imperial.ac.uk

Maja Pantic
Imperial College London, U.K.
U. of Twente, The Netherlands
m.pantic@imperial.ac.uk

ABSTRACT

Adopting continuous dimensional annotations for affective analysis has been gaining rising attention by researchers over the past years. Due to the idiosyncratic nature of this problem, many subproblems have been identified, spanning from the fusion of multiple continuous annotations to exploiting output-correlations amongst emotion dimensions. In this paper, we firstly empirically answer several important questions which have found partial or no answer at all so far in related literature. In more detail, we study the correlation of each emotion dimension (i) with respect to other emotion dimensions, (ii) to basic emotions (e.g., happiness, anger). As a measure for comparison, we use video and audio features. Interestingly enough, we find that (i) each emotion dimension is more correlated with other emotion dimensions rather than with face and audio features, and similarly (ii) that each basic emotion is more correlated with emotion dimensions than with audio and video features. Motivated by these findings, we present a novel regression algorithm (Correlated-Spaces Regression, CSR), inspired by Canonical Correlation Analysis (CCA) which learns output-correlations and performs supervised dimensionality reduction and multimodal fusion by (i) projecting features extracted from all modalities and labels onto a common space where their inter-correlation is maximised and (ii) learning mappings from the projected feature space onto the projected, uncorrelated label space.

Categories and Subject Descriptors

I.5.4 [**Computing Methodologies**]: Pattern Recognition Applications

Keywords

Continuous and dimensional emotion descriptions, valence, arousal, output-correlations, multi-modal fusion, component analysis, feature selection

MM'13, October 21–25, 2013, Barcelona, Spain.

http://dx.doi.org/10.1145/2502081.2502201.

1. INTRODUCTION

In recent years, the field of dimensional continuous emotion analysis has gained rising attention, and a significant number of works has been published on this topic [2, 3, 12, 10]. Introduced by Russel [11], this emotion description originated a radically different approach on describing emotional states. Instead of the traditional approach of discrete emotions (e.g., anger, joy), the emotional state of an individual is described by measurements on a set of latent dimensions. Most of the past-research has focused on the first two dimensions, valence and arousal, signifying respectively how negative/positive and active/inactive the subject's emotional state is. Claims from the field of psychology show that the dimensional descriptions of emotions are much more expressive than basic emotions, and better describe emotions expressed during our everyday lives, e.g., interest, boredom [2].

The contribution of our paper is twofold. Firstly we provide empirical answers to several important questions related to the correlations of emotion dimensions which so-far have found partial or no answer at all. Secondly, we present a regression algorithm which correlates both labels and multi-modal features by projecting them on a common space, eliciting an elegant framework for multi-modal fusion, dimensionality reduction and output-correlations learning. These contributions are discussed in detail in what follows.

Analysing emotion dimension correlations. The occurrence of inter-correlations amongst emotion dimensions such as valence and arousal has been well-supported by various research in psychology [5], and has recently been explored in affective computing in terms of valence and arousal [8]. Nevertheless, to the best of our knowledge, none of the previous work studies (i) correlation between emotion dimensions in isolation, (i.e. without including features), and (ii) the correlations of emotion dimensions to *basic emotions* such as joy and sadness. Furthermore, most works only employ valence and arousal without addressing dimensions such as power and expectation. We address all of these points in our paper. Firstly, by using a set $\mathbf{R}_s$ of 5 dimensions (Valence, Arousal, Power, Expectation and Intensity) [6], in our first experiment (Sec. 3.1), we essentially pose the problem of predicting dimension k given the rest. We also perform experiments using face/audio features for comparison. Interestingly enough, we show that the correlation of the $k-1$ other dimensions to dimension k is *higher* than the correlation of audio/face features to dimension k.

In our second experiment (Sec. 3.2), we attempt to answer an interesting question which has not been explored so far: *how correlated are emotion dimensions to basic emo-*

tions? Intuitively, the correlation should be high, since in theory there is a (rather abstract and relatively ambiguous) mapping from these dimensions to basic emotions (e.g., high valence, positive arousal can point to joy, excitement etc.). To verify this intuition empirically, we use a set of basic emotions $\mathbf{L}_s$ (e.g., anger, happiness). Using the set of dimensions $\mathbf{R}_s$, we evaluate how correlated the emotion dimensions are to basic emotions, in comparison to facial points and audio cues. Our findings are in line with the previous experiment: Emotion dimensions are positively correlated with the intensity of basic emotions, exhibiting higher correlations than face/audio features.

Exploiting emotion dimension correlations. An important contribution of our paper lies in the introduction of the Correlated-Spaces Regression (CSR), a principled, novel framework based on canonical correlation analysis, which elegantly combines multi-modal fusion, the learning of output-correlations and supervised dimensionality reduction. Our algorithm, heavily motivated by conclusions drawn from our empirical study, is shown to increase the accuracy of both single-cue and fused experiments and up to a point, "heal" the relatively weak correlation of face/audio features to the emotion dimensions[1].

2. DATA & FEATURE EXTRACTION

For evaluation, we employ the SEMAINE database [6], which contains a set of audio-visual recordings of subjects interacting with operators. Each operator assumes a certain personality, i.e. happy, gloomy, angry and pragmatic, with a goal of inducing spontaneous emotions during a naturalistic conversation. We use a portion of the database running approximately 85 minutes, which has been annotated for the emotion dimensions at hand by 5 raters, from which we use the averaged annotation[2]. For extracting facial expression features, we employ an Active Appearance Model (AAM) based tracker [9], designed for simultaneous tracking of 3D head pose, lips, eyebrows, eyelids and irises in video sequences. For each video frame, we obtain 113 2D-points, resulting in an 226 dimensional feature vector. To compensate for translation variations, we center the coordinate system to the fixed point of the face (average of inner eyes and nose), while for scaling we normalise by dividing with the inter-ocular distance. Regarding audio features, we utilise MFCC and MFCC-Delta coefficients along with prosody features (energy, RMS Energy and pitch). We used 13 cepstrum coefficients for each audio frame, essentially employing the typical set of features used for automatic affect recognition [14]. We obtain a feature vector with dimensionality $d = 29$, obtaining a frame-rate equivalent to 100-fps. To match the video fps, the audio features used are vertically concatenated for each pair of consecutive frames, thus obtaining 58 dimensional feature vectors. For feature-level fusion, the vectors are concatenated, resulting to 284 dimensions.

3. ANALYSIS OF EMOTION DIMENSIONS

In this section we present several experiments evaluating the correlations of emotion dimensions. For regression, we employ the Relevance Vector Machine (RVM [13]), which given the input-output pair $(\mathbf{x}_i, \mathbf{y}_i)$ models the function $\mathbf{y}_i = \mathbf{w}^T\phi(\mathbf{x}_i)+\epsilon_i, \epsilon_i \sim \mathcal{N}(0,\sigma^2)$ with $\phi(\mathbf{x}_i,\mathbf{x}_j) = \exp\left\{-\frac{||\mathbf{x}_i-\mathbf{x}_j||}{l}\right\}$ being the RBF kernel. Using the extracted features and annotations (Sec. 2) we perform cross-validation. For evaluation, we use the mean-squared error (MSE) to measure bias error and the correlation coefficient (COR) to measure the correlation deviation. We mostly refer to COR, since (i) it is most commonly used in related work [12], and (ii) the MSE bias errors are relatively very small.

[1]Regarding dimensionality reduction for regression, c.f. [4].

[2]For the basic emotion experiments, we use only the subset of this data which was annotated in terms of basic emotions.

3.1 Inter-Correlations and Multimedia

In this section we pose the problem of predicting an emotion dimension given a set of annotated dimensions. Let us assume we have a set of ρ annotations $\mathbf{R} = \{\mathbf{r}_1, \ldots, \mathbf{r}_\rho\}$ with $\mathbf{r}_i \in \mathbb{R}^{1\times T}$. In this experiment, we assume that $\mathbf{R}$ consists of dimensions valence, arousal, power, expectation and intensity, i.e. $\rho = 5$. Our problem can then be defined as

$$f : \mathbf{R}_{\setminus k} \to \hat{\mathbf{r}}_k, \forall k \in \{1, \ldots, \rho\} \tag{1}$$

where $\mathbf{R}_{\setminus k}$ denotes the entire set of annotations excluding dimension k and $\hat{\mathbf{r}}_k$ the estimated values of dimension k. The performance of the learnt functions is then compared against the performance obtained when using facial expressions and audio cues as features, in order to obtain a comparative measure of performance. By this experiment, we essentially ask the following question: *Which signal is most correlated with a specific emotion dimension k, the features extracted from audio/video cues or the annotations for the rest of the dimensions,* $\mathbf{R}_{\setminus k}$*?* Results are presented in Tab. 1 and Fig. 1. It is very interesting to observe that by using all the emotion dimensions except the one being tested provides better results for *all* dimensions at hand. This important observation empirically confirms that each and every emotion dimension has higher correlation with the rest of the dimensions than with the audio/face features. It is also interesting to observe that for the arousal and the intensity dimensions, the audio cues appear to perform better than the facial features in terms of correlation coefficient, a conclusion that confirms previous findings [7].

3.2 Correlations to Basic Emotions

Another question we address in this work refers to the correlations amongst the dimensional emotion descriptions, as perceived by Russel [11] and a set of emotions which are of discrete nature (e.g., basic emotions). Although emotion dimensions can be inherently more expressive in comparison to discrete emotions such as joy and sadness, no explicit mapping between the two descriptions has been established. One would of course assume that e.g., negative valence with negative arousal maps to sadness or boredom, nevertheless this is more of an abstract and relatively ambiguous correspondence. In this section we evaluate the correlations of emotion dimensions when learning to predict emotions such as anger, happiness, sadness, surprise etc. In more detail, given the set $\mathbf{R}$, as defined in Section 3.1 (consisting of dimensions valence, arousal, power, expectation and intensity) we aim to predict a specific emotion belonging in the set $\mathbf{L} = \{\mathbf{l}_1, \ldots, \mathbf{l}_\nu\}$, i.e.

$$f : \mathbf{R} \to \hat{\mathbf{L}}_k, \forall k \in \{1, \ldots, \nu\} \tag{2}$$

Results are presented in Tab, 2 and Fig. 1, where we also use face/audio features for comparison. The first conclusion is that the emotion dimensions (namely valence, arousal, power, expectation and intensity) are highly correlated with

Table 1: Results for predicting each emotion dimension, using the other four dimensions as features ($\mathbf{R}_s$), compared to using facial features (F), audio features (A) and the feature-level fusion of face and audio (F+A).

	Valence		Arousal		Power		Expectation		Intensity	
	MSE	COR	MSE	COR	MSE	COR	MSE	COR	MSE	COR
$\mathbf{R}_{s\setminus k}$	0.074	**0.28**	0.051	**0.47**	0.088	**0.28**	0.037	**0.15**	0.067	**0.30**
Face	0.088	0.14	0.061	0.41	0.131	0.06	0.024	0.02	0.066	0.17
Audio	0.072	0.14	0.050	0.44	0.082	0.05	0.018	0.01	0.042	0.26
F+A	0.880	0.16	0.055	0.44	0.080	0.06	0.020	0.02	0.058	0.20

Table 2: Predicting each basic emotion using the five emotion dimensions as features ($\mathbf{R}_{s\setminus k}$), compared to using facial features (F) and audio features (A).

COR	Anger	Happiness	Sadness	Contempt	Amusement
$\mathbf{R}_s$	**0.74**	**0.48**	**0.67**	**0.33**	**0.49**
F	0.06	0.11	0.13	0.05	0.06
A	0.02	0.10	0.10	0.11	0.02
MSE	**Anger**	**Happiness**	**Sadness**	**Contempt**	**Amusement**
$\mathbf{R}_s$	**0.07**	**0.10**	**0.06**	**0.02**	**0.07**
F	0.21	0.21	0.26	0.34	0.15
A	0.17	0.17	0.10	0.21	0.09

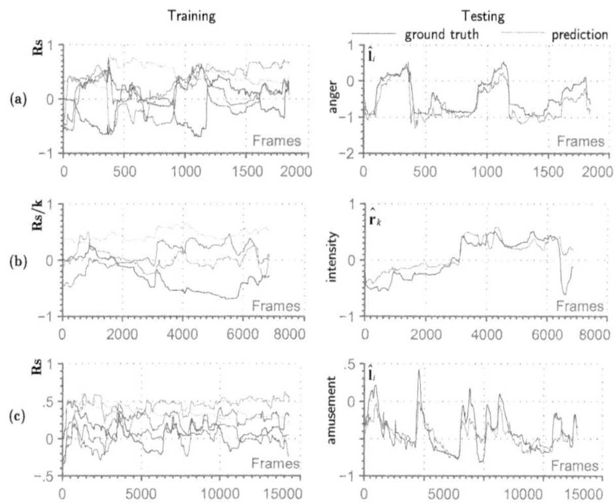

Figure 1: (a,c) Using emotion dimensions ($\mathbf{R}_s$) for predicting basic emotions, (b) using $k-1$ emotion dimensions ($\mathbf{R}_{s\setminus k}$) for predicting dimension k.

the discrete emotions we study. Similarly to the results regarding the previous experiment, the dimension to discrete-emotion correlation is quite higher compared to face or audio features. The most correlated discrete emotion to emotion dimensions appears to be anger.

4. CORRELATED-SPACES REGRESSION

Inspired by the results described in previous sections, we demonstrate a method which exploits output-correlations, while performing multi-modal fusion and dimensionality reduction. Note that the latter experiments also motivate the idea of dimensionality reduction on this problem: In the experiments in Sec. 3.1, $\mathbf{R}_{\setminus k}$ consists of 4-dimensional feature vectors and attains better performance than, i.e. the 226-dimensional facial expression vectors. We show how by exploiting feature-label, inter-feature and inter-label correlations we can significantly improve the results.

Let us assume that for a training sequence s, we have a set of annotations for emotion dimensions $\mathbf{R}_s$, containing the five dimensions used in Sec. 3.1, along with a given set of features, $\mathbf{F}_{j,s}, j=\{1,\ldots,\mu\}$ which can contain e.g., video or/and audio cues. Canonical Correlation Analysis (CCA) enables the discovery of projections of the features onto a space where they are maximally correlated. We reformulate the problem to match our context as follows

$$\underset{\mathbf{V}_{F_s},\mathbf{V}_R}{\arg\min} ||\mathbf{F}_s\mathbf{V}_{F_s} - \mathbf{R}_s\mathbf{V}_R||_2^F$$

$$s.t.\ \mathbf{F}_s\mathbf{V}_{F_s}\mathbf{V}_{F_s}^T\mathbf{F}_s^T = \mathbf{R}_s\mathbf{V}_R\mathbf{V}_R^T\mathbf{R}_s^T = \mathbf{I}$$

$$\mathbf{F}_s = [\mathbf{F}_{1,s},\ldots,\mathbf{F}_{j,s}],\ \mathbf{V}_{F_s}^T = [\mathbf{V}_{F_{1,s}}^T,\ldots,\mathbf{V}_{F_{\mu,s}}^T]^T, \quad (3)$$

where $\mathbf{I}$ is the identity matrix. Therefore, by applying CCA on *both* the labels and the features, we are in a sense employing supervision on the feature projections, i.e. performing supervised component analysis. This is due to the fact that the labels and features are projected into a common space where they maximally correlate. In fact, for problems where labels are discrete classes, it has been shown that applying CCA on both features and binary labels collapses to applying Linear Discriminant Analysis [1], where $\mathbf{F}_s\mathbf{V}_F$ are the discriminant projections. Furthermore, as an implication of the orthogonality constraints of the problem statement in Eq. 3, the projected label space will be uncorrelated, thus enabling regessors to learn output-correlations which exist in the label space. Finally, due to the block-matrix formulation we learn correlated features from *all* feature sets, i.e. we perform multi-modal supervised fusion. Our model is described in Alg. 1, and visually depicted in Fig. 2. During training, the projection vectors for the continuous label space $\mathbf{V}_R$ and the feature sets employed $\mathbf{F}_{1:\mu}$ are obtained.

Algorithm 1: Correlated-Spaces Regression

Data: Train=($\mathbf{R}_s, \mathbf{F}_{1,s}, \ldots, \mathbf{F}_{\mu,s}$)
Test=($\mathbf{F}_{1,t}, \ldots, \mathbf{F}_{\mu,t}$)
Result: $\hat{\mathbf{R}}_t$
train
Set $[\mathbf{V}_R, \overbrace{\mathbf{V}_{F_1},\ldots,\mathbf{V}_{F_\mu}}^{\mathbf{V}_{F_s}}]$ to the leading eigenvectors of
$$\begin{bmatrix} \mathbf{0} & \mathbf{F}_s\mathbf{R}_s^T \\ \mathbf{R}_s\mathbf{F}_s^T & \mathbf{0}\end{bmatrix}\begin{bmatrix}\mathbf{V}_{F_s} \\ \mathbf{V}_R\end{bmatrix} = \begin{bmatrix}\mathbf{F}_s\mathbf{F}_s^T & \mathbf{0} \\ \mathbf{0} & \mathbf{R}_s\mathbf{R}_s^T\end{bmatrix}\begin{bmatrix}\mathbf{V}_{F_s} \\ \mathbf{V}_R\end{bmatrix}\Lambda$$
(*Problem defined in Eq. 3*)
$\mathbf{F}_{i,s}^c = \mathbf{F}_{i,s}\mathbf{V}_{F_i}, \forall i \in \{1,\ldots,\mu\}$
$f : \mathbf{F}_{1:\mu,s}^c \rightarrow \mathbf{R}_s\mathbf{V}_R$
test
$\mathbf{F}_{i,t}^c = \mathbf{F}_{i,t}\mathbf{V}_{F_i}, \forall i \in \{1,\ldots,\mu\}$
$\hat{\mathbf{R}}_t^c \leftarrow f(\mathbf{F}_{1:\mu,t}^c)$
$\hat{\mathbf{R}}_t = \hat{\mathbf{R}}_t^c\mathbf{V}_R^{-1}$

Table 3: **Results for predicting each emotion dimension using Correlated-Spaces Regression (CSR) utilising facial features ($\mathbf{F}^{CSR}$), audio features ($\mathbf{A}^{CSR}$) and the fusion of face and audio ($\{\mathbf{F}+\mathbf{A}\}^{CSR}$) using CSR.**

	Valence		Arousal		Power		Expectation		Intensity	
	MSE	COR	MSE	COR	MSE	COR	MSE	COR	MSE	COR
$\mathbf{F}^{CSR}$	0.070	0.20	**0.046**	**0.46**	0.080	0.11	**0.020**	0.06	**0.044**	**0.29**
$\mathbf{A}^{CSR}$	0.070	0.15	0.510	0.45	0.075	**0.11**	0.022	0.02	0.040	**0.29**
$\{\mathbf{F},\mathbf{A}\}^{CSR}$	**0.056**	**0.21**	0.050	**0.46**	**0.063**	**0.12**	**0.020**	**0.07**	**0.044**	**0.29**

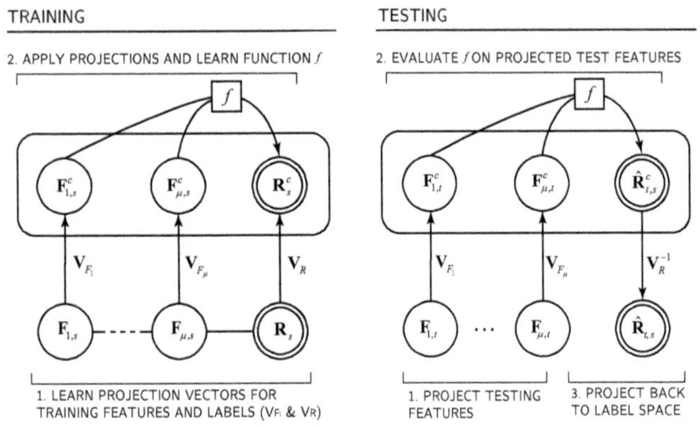

Figure 2: Correlated-Spaces Regression model, following Algorithm 1.

Using these projection matrices, the training features $\mathbf{F}_{1:\mu,s}$ and labels $\mathbf{R}_s$ are projected onto the space where they maximally correlate, obtaining the matrices $\mathbf{F}^c_{1:\mu,s}$ and $\mathbf{R}^c_s$. The regressor is subsequently optimised on this space

$$f : \mathbf{F}^c_{1:\mu,s} \rightarrow \mathbf{R}^c_s \tag{4}$$

For testing, we obtain a set of features $\mathbf{F}_{1:\mu,t}$, which we project as $\mathbf{F}^c_{i,t} = \mathbf{F}_{i,t}\mathbf{V}_{F_i}$. The learnt function f is evaluated on $\mathbf{F}^c_{i,t}$, obtaining the predictions $\hat{\mathbf{R}}^c_t$, which are then projected back to the annotation space. Results with our method are presented in Tab. 3. As can be clearly seen, our method performs much better than using simply the raw features or performing feature-level fusion, as seen in Tab. 1. In fact, it is interesting to observe that in some dimensions, our method achieves comparable correlation to using all the other annotations/labels as features ($\mathbf{R}_s$, Sec. 3.1). Essentially this means that the model manages to capture output-correlations and in addition propagate this information during dimensionality reduction onto the projected features.

5. CONCLUSIONS

In this work, we performed a thorough investigation on the inter-correlation of emotion dimensions and their correlation to basic emotions. We have shown that there are more dominant correlations within emotion dimensions rather than to face or audio features. Most importantly, we presented CSR, a CCA-based algorithm which learns output-correlations while performing multi-modal fusion and supervised dimensionality reduction. Our algorithm increases the accuracy both in terms of multi-modal fusion and single-cue regression, successfully learning output structure and maximising input-output correlations. Our algorithm can be straight-forwardly applied to any learning problem with a set of feature modalities and multi-dimensional output vectors.

6. ACKNOWLEDGEMENTS

This work has been funded by the European Community 7th Framework Programme [FP7/2007-2013] under grant agreement no. 288235 (FROG) and by the European Research Council under the ERC Starting Grant agreement no. ERC-2007-StG-203143 (MAHNOB).

7. REFERENCES

[1] F. R. Bach and M. I. Jordan. A Probabilistic Interpretation of Canonical Correlation Analysis.

[2] H. Gunes and B. Schuller. Categorical and dimensional affect analysis in continuous input: Current trends and future directions. *Image and Vision Computing*, 31(2):120 – 136, 2013.

[3] H. Gunes, B. Schuller, M. Pantic, and R. Cowie. Emotion representation, analysis and synthesis in continuous space: A survey. In *Proc. of IEEE FG'11-W*, Santa Barbara, CA, USA, March 2011.

[4] M. Kim and V. Pavlovic. Central subspace dimensionality reduction using covariance operators. *IEEE TPAMI*, 33(4):657–670, 2011.

[5] R. Lane et al. *Cognitive Neuroscience of Emotion.* Oxford University Press, 2000.

[6] G. McKeown et al. The semaine database: Annotated multimodal records of emotionally colored conversations between a person and a limited agent. *IEEE TAC*, 2012.

[7] M. A. Nicolaou et al. Continuous prediction of spontaneous affect from multiple cues and modalities in valence-arousal space. *IEEE TAC*, 2011.

[8] M. A. Nicolaou et al. Output-associative rvm regression for dimensional and continuous emotion prediction. In *Proceedings of IEEE FG'11*, pages 16–23, Santa Barbara, CA, USA, March 2011.

[9] J. Orozco et al. Hierarchical on-line appearance-based tracking for 3d head pose, eyebrows, lips, eyelids and irises. *Image and Vision Computing*, February 2013.

[10] G. A. Ramirez et al. Modeling latent discriminative dynamic of multi-dimensional affective signals. In *Proc. of ACII'11*, 2011.

[11] J. A. Russell. A circumplex model of affect. *Journal of Personality and Social Psychology*, 39, 1980.

[12] B. Schuller, M. Valstar, et al. Avec 2012: the continuous audio/visual emotion challenge - an introduction. In *ICMI*, pages 361–362, 2012.

[13] M. E. Tipping. Sparse bayesian learning and the relevance vector machine. *JMLR*, 1:211–244, 2001.

[14] Z. Zeng, M. Pantic, G. Roisman, and T. Huang. A survey of affect recognition methods: Audio, visual, and spontaneous expressions. *IEEE TPAMI*, 2009.

RealSense: Directional Interaction for Proximate Mobile Sharing Using Built-in Orientation Sensors

Chien-Pang Lin[1], Cheng-Yao Wang[2], Hou-Ren Chen[1], Wei-Chen Chu[1], Mike Y. Chen[1]
[1]Department of Computer Science and Information Engineering
[2]Graduate Institute of Networking and Multimedia
National Taiwan University
{r00922123,r00944052,r01922013,r01922002,mikechen}@csie.ntu.edu.tw

ABSTRACT
We present RealSense, a technology that enables users to easily share media files with proximate users by detecting the relative direction of each other only with built-in orientation sensors on smartphones. With premise that users are arranged as a circle and every user is facing the center of that circle, RealSense continuously collects the directional heading of each phone to calculate the virtual position of each user in real time during the sharing.
RealSense users can simply share photos to others by swiping and throwing the photo to another user's direction without remembering or searching the name and even the device id of a specific receiver. We evaluated the orientation sensor error and the minimal arc degree for selection, and compared RealSense with linear menu, pie menu and NFC. Our results show that the limitation that requires participants to face toward the circle center is rather acceptable and participants preferred RealSense than other sharing interactions especially they were unacquainted with each other.

Categories and Subject Descriptors
H.5.2. [**Information interfaces and presentation**]: User Interfaces – *Interaction styles, User-centered design, and Evaluation/methodology*

Keywords
Mobile devices, proximate, orientation sensor, relative direction, media sharing, interaction.

1. INTRODUCTION
With the population of mobile devices, more and more technologies and applications support interactions with approximate persons. BombPlus [13], a multi-player and multi-device game, uses NFC and orientation sensor to enhance social gaming experience for co-located players. Boring et al. presented an extension to the concept of Touch Projector to allow multiple users to interact collaboratively with media facades shown in live video on their mobile device [1].

MM'13, October 21-25 2013, Barcelona, Spain

http://dx.doi.org/10.1145/2502081.2502202

One usual interaction among co-located users is media sharing. A common scenario, for example, is that a group of friends or families get together and they would like to get copies of the photos and videos captured at the event. The possible Nearby Sharing Interactions can be classified into three types.

The first type is screen-based (virtual) interaction. Users might use Email or chat application, such as Line and WhatsApp, to select receivers from linear menu to transfer media files. However, when the sender tries to recognize the unfamiliar newly added names or indistinguishable device names on Linear Menu, the sharing becomes a troublesome task.

The second type, device-based (physical) interaction, shares media files by a physical gestures without remembering or searching names of receivers. Mobile apps such as Bump use smartphones' built-in accelerometer and GPS to detect users' locations and transfer files by bumping their phones. In addition, mobile phones with commodity hardware (e.g., NFC, accelerometers [2, 3] and RFID [4]) can transfer files with devices touched. However, this type of interaction provides only one-to-one sharing at a time and requests short distance between users.

The third type, combining virtual with physical interaction, provides context information such as locations or relative orientation with a screen interface, which supports more natural modes of interaction [5, 6, 7].

In this paper, we present RealSense, a technology that detects relative directions between devices only with built-in orientation sensors on smartphones. RealSense supports directional and spatial gestures, so user can simply share photos to others by swiping and throwing the photo to another user's direction. In order to examine the accuracy of RealSense, we recorded the orientation sensor errors of devices and figured out the minimal arc degree that enables correct selection.

We also conducted a 16-person user study to compare RealSense with other types of media sharing interactions, including linear menu, pie menu, and NFC. Our results show that the limitation that requires users to face the circle center is natural and acceptable, and that the accuracy of RealSense is considered satisfactory. In addition, RealSense is rated highest by participants regarding ease of use for both one-to-one and one-to-many sharing, and participants prefer RealSense to other sharing interactions especially when they are unacquainted.

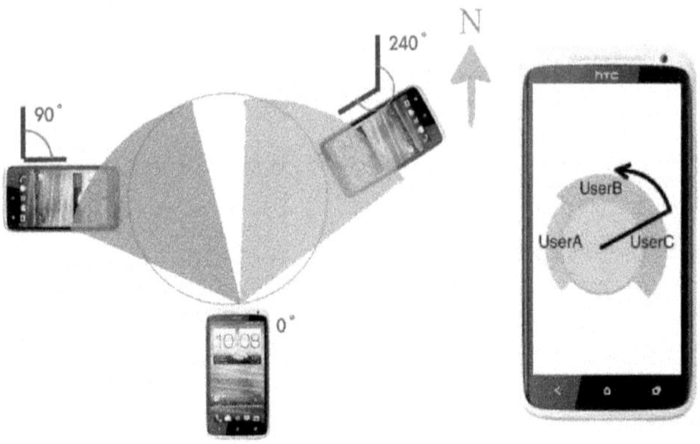

Figure 1. (a) RealSense calculates the virtual position of each mobile device. (b) A defined gesture for one-to-many sharing.

2. RELATED WORK

A variety of positioning methods are available to make computers or mobile devices aware of each other device's presence [5, 8]. In order to enhance positions accuracy, many solutions require a heavily instrumented space [9, 10]. Besides, there are some research focuses on determining the orientation relative to one another.

The Orienteer service [12] determines the relative orientation of proximate mobile devices by sampling images from each device's back camera stream and stitching together according to the overlapped features in both images. However, the distance between users is restricted under 1.5 meters with cameras pointing downwards, and the common image features are hardly to be distinguished in some scenarios, such as sitting around a table or placing mobile phones on it. Besides, using camera stream will drain the battery faster and have some privacy concerns.

Lucero et al. presented Pass-Them-Around that tries to capture the experience of users passing and sharing photos to each other while sitting around a table [11]. However, multi-antennae receivers and RF tags must be installed under the screens in order for the phones to locate each other.

3. SYSTEM DESIGN

3.1 Method and Implementation

RealSense developed on android 4.0 and constructed under a Wi-Fi hotspot client-server architecture, uses the built-in orientation sensors on smartphones to detect the relative directions of co-located users, working on the premise that users are arranged in a circle and everyone is facing the center.

RealSense continuously collects the directional heading (the angle between magnetic north) of each phone and broadcasts it to all the other devices through server. Then, the virtual position of each user can be calculated and updated in real-time.

Take Figure 1(a) for instance. If a device detects 0 degree, it is facing toward the north, and the other device which detects 90 degrees points to the east. Under the premise that all devices point to the center of the virtual circle, the 0-degree device lies to the south of the circle center and the 90-degree device to the west, which suggests that 90-degree device is on the left side of 0-degree device.

3.2 User Interface and Gesture Design

To display relative orientations of users, RealSense uses pie menu, a circular context menu where selection depends on direction, and distributes the selection region of the circle evenly to all users. In a 4-people scenario, for example, every user obtains a selection region of 90 degrees .For a user won't interact with himself/herself, he/she is not shown on the pie menu, replaced by a space.

Instead of showing the actual directions of devices on pie menu, RealSense arranges devices' relative orientations orderly and distributes them evenly around the circle. Therefore, the overlaps between nearby users can be avoided, and the relative directions still exist. Besides, RealSense supports one-to-many sharing by a defined gesture. After a user swipes out of the circle, he/she can select multiple adjoining targets continuously until releasing the finger. However, when the multiple targets are not located side by side on pie menu, several times of one-to-one gestures should be inevitable.

4. FACTORS OF ACCURACY

4.1 Devices' Orientation Sensor Errors

We examined the orientation sensor error of Galaxy Nexus, Galaxy S3, Nexus S, HTC One X, which were used in the later user studies. At the beginning, we put a compass at 8 locations in the room for user study, one at a time, and marked the direction of magnetic north on the desk. In each location, we firstly aligned each phone to the north mark, recording the angle measured by the device compass, and secondly, after waving the device in a figure 8 motion, we aligned it to the mark and recorded again. This procedure was repeated three times.

4.1.1. Result

According to the results, different devices have varied accuracy of orientation sensor, and the difference between the maximum and minimum angles among all devices is 16.5 degrees. Therefore, when users share files in a circle, and the included angle between 2 neighboring users and the circle center is less than 16.5 degrees, the relative orientation detected by RealSense might become inaccurate.

4.2 The Minimal Arc Degree for Selection

The goal of this experiment is to understand the accuracy of selection under different pie menu radii, and the minimal arc degree that enables correct selection. According to the minimal arc degree, we could figure out the maximum number of RealSense users at a time. 12 participants were recruited (9 male, 3 female, age 18-26) and all participants are familiar with using smart phones.

The experiment was constituted of two phases. The user held the phone with one hand and operated with his thumb in the first phase; in the second phase, the user operated with another hand.

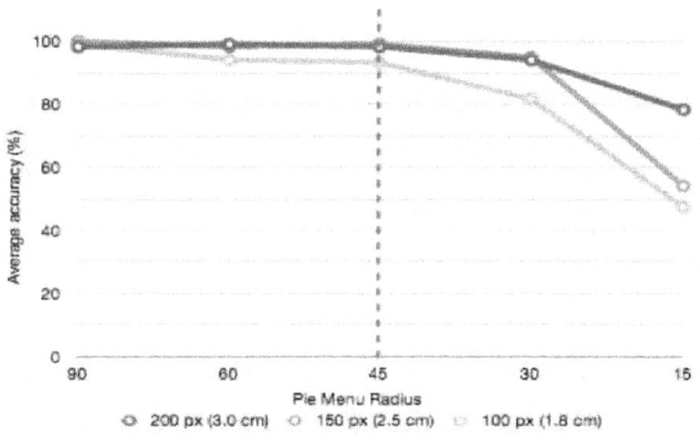

Figure 2. The average accuracy of selection in one-handed thumb interaction

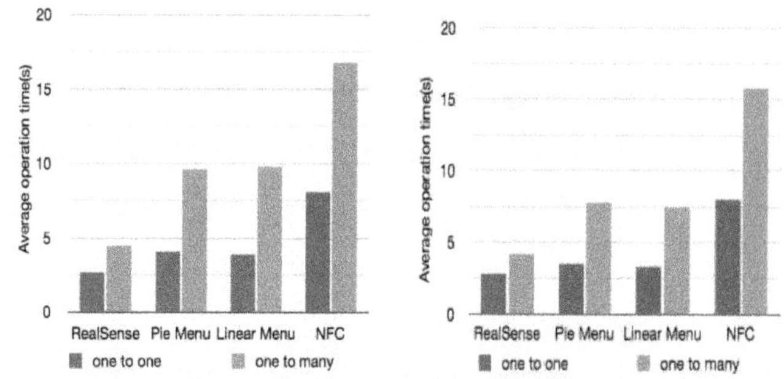

Figure 3. (a) The average operation time when participants were acquainted. (b) The average operation time when participants were unacquainted

Each phase was divided into three parts by the pie menu radius of 3.0, 2.5 and 1.6 cm. In each part, we tested 5 different arc degree, 90, 60, 45, 30, 15 degrees that represented the scenarios of group sharing by 4, 6, 8, 12, 24 persons. Each degree test contained 10 tasks, in which our program randomly designated an area on pie menu for participants to select the target with RealSense gesture, and the results if the selection worked were recorded.

4.2.1. Result

The accuracy of one-hand-operation decreases apparently in 30 and 15 degrees, and two-hand-operation has lower accuracy in 15 degrees, as shown in Figure 2. Therefore, we choose 45 degrees as the minimal arc degree to ensure the accuracy in both operations, and the corresponding optimal number of sharing users is under 8 persons.

In the testing of little circle (1.8cm radius), the accuracy in one-hand-operation with 45 arc degrees is only 93.33%. Besides, referring to the questionnaire results, 58% of users prefer middle circle (2.5cm radius) for one-hand operation, and 68% favor large circle (3.0cm radius) for two-hand operation. Consequently, we choose 2.75 cm, the average radius of 3.0 and 2.5, as the radius of RealSense's pie menu.

5. EVALUATION

We developed a mobile photo-sharing application to understand the user experience for various sharing interactions and to explore if the limitation that requires participants to face the circle center is acceptable. When using the application, 4 interaction types are provided: linear menu, where items are listed from top to bottom, pie menu, where items are placed at equal radial distances along the circumference, NFC, where device are brought into close proximity, and RealSense. After selecting an interaction type, the user can choose a photo and long-click it to share. The evaluation was conducted with 2 groups of 8 friends varied in gender (11 male, 5 female), age (between 18 and 23) and all participants are familiar with using smart phones.

The study consisted of two phases to represent the scenarios when participants were acquainted and unacquainted with each other. In each phase, we compared RealSense with other sharing interactions, including linear menu, pie menu and NFC, in one-to-one and one-to-many sharing.

5.1 Experiment Settings

The study focused on the operation time and user experience of selecting a receiver with various sharing interactions, before the testing, we connected all devices to the same Wi-Fi wireless network and grouped all devices under a Wi-Fi hotspot client-server architecture. In addition, all participants were arranged in a circle, facing the circle center.

5.2 First Phase

Firstly, participants were asked to enter their names in RealSense settings, so that the sender could easily identify the nearby receiver by names on the menu.

Secondly, we familiarized participants with the method randomly chosen from RealSense, Linear Menu, Pie Menu and NFC, and then randomly pointed at one user to designate him as the sender without mentioning his name or alphabetical id. Similarly, we randomly pointed at another user, also the receiver, and asked the sender to transfer a photo to him. The same process was repeated until every participant had both sent and received photos, and one-to-one experiment was completed.

For one-to-many testing, a user was selected randomly to transfer photos to another four random receivers by the same method. Also, the task was repeated until every participant had sent photos to multiple persons.

After finishing the testing for the first method, we continued the same procedures above with the rest three methods, completing the first phase.

5.3 Second Phase

After we selected a method randomly, our program assigned every participant an alphabetical id randomly, from A to H, to correspond to the premise that users were not acquainted with each other. The following procedures duplicated the first phase, finishing one-to-one and then one-to-many testing. The process was repeated until all the four methods had been operated.

After completing the two phases, we asked participants to fill out a questionnaire and held a five-minute interview.

5.3.1. Result

We define the operation time as the duration from long-clicking the selected photo to finishing choosing a receiver. As shown in Figure 3(a)(b), RealSense was the fastest interaction for both one-to-one and one-to-many sharing. Though NFC took the most operation time under the circumstances where the circled participants had to move close to each other before touching their phones, NFC has the advantage of quick and simplified connection, which is not the main concern in our study. According to the participants, the limitation that requires users to face the circle center is natural and acceptable. Though the accuracy of RealSense could be affected by orientation sensor error of devices, positions of users, and how the phone is held, the accuracy during

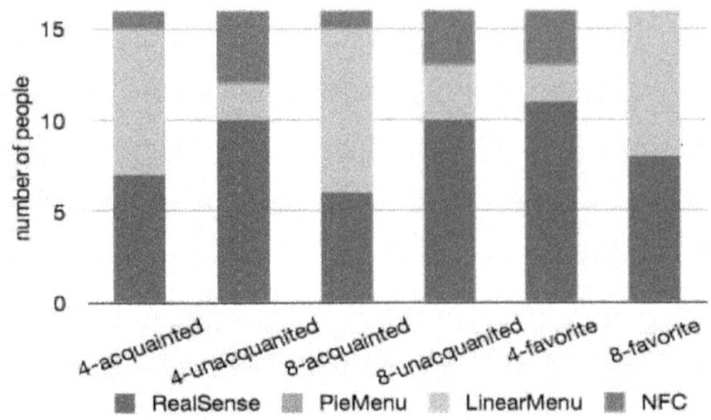

Figure 4. Users' preferred sharing interactions.

the experiment is satisfactory to participants and scores 5.21 in 7-likert scale.

RealSense was also rated highest by users in terms of ease of use for both one-to-one and one-to-many sharing (average 6.14 in one-to-one and 5.64 and in one-to-many). In addition, as shown in Figure 4, 64 percent of participants prefer RealSense to other sharing interactions when they are unacquainted with each other.

6. DISCUSSION

When sharing files, users will get around in a circle naturally, yet it's difficult to detect relative orientations correctly in some situations, such as the scenario when all users stay in a same row (e.g. Bar counter). Therefore, RealSense has to offer an explicit instruction to help users be arranged in a circle and face the center.

Besides, the device's built-in orientation sensor has a large deviation when it's activated at first, but after a figure 8 motion, the deviation becomes acceptable with the reduction to 5 to 10 degrees.

Although RealSense provides a gesture for multi-selection, users still have to operate several times of one-to-one gestures when the multiple targets are not adjacent on pie menu. In the future, we will try to combine the advantage of linear menu with RealSense. After selection procedure, user still can invalidate previous choices by clicking on them additionally.

7. CONCLUSION

In this paper, we present RealSense, a technology that enables users to easily share media files with proximate users by detecting the relative direction of each other only with built-in orientation sensors on smartphones. RealSense helps users interact with nearby users more instinctively without knowing device ids, which are perhaps unrecognizable, reducing the complexity of target selection in typical linear menu.

Although RealSense users have to face the center of the virtual circle formed by users, it's subconsciously achieved in face-to-face interaction. Moreover, the gestures in RealSense provide users with good efficiency of multiple-target selection. Although the accuracy declines with the number of users rising, RealSense still operates nicely in 8-person scenario.

We also have examined the orientation sensor errors of devices and the minimal arc degree, which ensures correct selection. According to our user study which compares RealSense with linear menu, pie menu, and NFC, users prefer RealSense because it is easy to use not only in one-to-one and one-to-many sharing but also under the scenario when they are unacquainted with each other.

8. REFERENCES

[1] Boring, S., et al. Multi-user interaction on media facades through live video on mobile devices. *Proc. of CHI*, ACM, (2011), 2712 - 2724.

[2] Holmquist, L.E., Mattern, F., Schiele, B., Alahuhta, P., Beigl, M. and Gellersen, H-W. Smart-Its friends: a technique for users to easily establish connections between artefacts. In *Proc. UbiComp 2001*, Springer- Verlag (2001), 116-122.

[3] Hinkley, K. Synchronous gestures for multiple persons and computers. In *Proc. UIST 2003*, ACM Press (2003), 149-158.

[4] Want, R., Fishkin, K.P., Gujar, A. and Harrison, B.L. Bridging physical and virtual worlds with electronic tags. In *Proc. CHI 1999*, ACM Press (1999), 370-377.

[5] Kortuem, G, Kray, C. and Gellersen, H. Sensing and visualizing spatial relations of mobile devices. In *Proc. UIST 2005*, ACM Press (2005), 93-102.

[6] R. Gostner, E. Rukzio, and H. Gellersen. Usage of spatial information for selection of co-located devices. In *Proc. of MobileHCI '08*, pages 427–430, 2008.

[7] Greenberg, S., Marquardt, N., Ballendat, T., Diaz- Marino, R. and Wang, M. Proxemic interactions: the new ubicomp? *Interactions 18*, 1 (January 2011), 42-50.

[8] Varshavsky, A. and Patel, S. Location in ubiquitous computing. In J. Krumm (Eds.), *Ubiquitous Computing Fundamentals*, Chapman & Hall (2009), 285-320.

[9] Ballendat, T. Visualization of and interaction with digital devices around large surfaces as a function of proximity. Master's Thesis, Dept. Insitut fur Informatik, Ludwig-Maximilians-University Munche, Munich, Germany, 2011.

[10] Marquardt, N., Diaz-Marino, R., Boring, S. and Greenbreg, S. The proximity toolkit: prototyping proxemic interactions in ubiquitous computing ecologies. In Proc. UIST 2011, ACM Press (2011), 315-326.

[11] Lucero, A., Holopainen, J. and Jokela, T. Passthem-around: collaborative use of mobile phones for photo sharing. In *Proc. CHI '11*, 1787-1796.

[12] Dearman, D., Guy, R. T., Truong, K. N., & Rd, P. M. Determining the Orientation of Proximate Mobile Devices using their Back Facing Camera. *Proc. of CHI*, ACM, (2012), 2231-2234

[13] Huang, C., Engineering, I., Lin, C., Tsai, M., & Hsu, F. BombPlus□: Using NFC and Orientation- Sensing to Enhance Social Gaming Experience for Co-located Players. *Proc. of CHI*, ACM, (2012), 1339-1344

Understanding and Classifying Image Tweets*

Tao Chen[1] Dongyuan Lu[1] Min-Yen Kan[1,2] Peng Cui[3]
[1]Web IR / NLP Group (WING), National University of Singapore
[2]NUS Interactive and Digital Media Institute
[3]Department of Computer Science and Technology, Tsinghua University
{taochen, ludy, kanmy}@comp.nus.edu.sg cuip@tsinghua.edu.cn

ABSTRACT

Social media platforms now allow users to share images alongside their textual posts. These *image tweets* make up a fast-growing percentage of tweets, but have not been studied in depth unlike their text-only counterparts.

We study a large corpus of image tweets in order to uncover what people post about and the correlation between the tweet's image and its text. We show that an important functional distinction is between visually-relevant and visually-irrelevant tweets, and that we can successfully build an automated classifier utilizing text, image and social context features to distinguish these two classes, obtaining a macro F_1 of 70.5%.

Categories and Subject Descriptors

H.3.3 [**Information Storage and Retrieval**]: Information Search and Retrieval

Keywords

image tweets; analysis; microblog; classification

1. INTRODUCTION

With improved bandwidth and camera phones, mainstream social media is no longer solely text but firmly multimedia. *Image tweets*, which we define as user-generated microblog posts that contain an embedded image, are now a staple of user-generated content.

While the ability to link images to microblog posts has existed for several years, the difficulty composing such posts made these type of posts a minority. Starting with China's Sina *Weibo* and later *Twitter* and third-party services such as *Instagram*, microblogging platforms now seamlessly include images into their posts.

There have been preliminary works that describe image tweets: as early as 2011, Yu *et al.* [10] reported that 56.43% of all microblog posts in Sina Weibo were image tweets. Zhao *et al.* [11] discovered that such image tweets were retweeted more often and survived longer than text-only posts. We may thus posit that users compose image tweets to attract and retain the interest of their readership.

While helpful, these findings only just start to answer the many questions about this new class of social communication. What types of images do users embed? Do the images distinctly differ from images on image- and photo-sharing websites (e.g., *Flickr*)? Do the textual contents of image tweets differ from posts that are text-only?

To answer these questions, we have collected a corpus of image tweets from Sina Weibo. Our contributions are in: 1) deconstructing the corpus to characterize such tweets' image and textual content and the correlation between the two; 2) collecting annotations for a subset of these image tweets in the corpus and; 3) building an automated classifier to distinguish two important subclasses of image tweets – *visual* and *non-visual* tweets.

2. WHAT ARE IMAGE TWEETS?

To answer these questions, we collected a corpus of tweets comprising of both image and text-only tweets. Over a period of 7 months in 2012, we sampled posts from the public timeline API of Weibo, accumulating a dataset of 57,595,852 tweets. To analyze the tweets in more depth, we further manually annotated a small ~5K subset of the corpus[1].

Image Characteristics. To date, the images in image tweets have been studied in only a few works. Ishiguro *et al.* [4] show that predicting the number of views of an image tweet using social curation evidence (i.e. favoriting and explicit listing) outperforms using image features. Wang *et al.* [9] designed a joint text and image topic model to detect the onset of new events from image tweets.

An idiosyncratic factor is that all embedded images in Weibo are processed by the Weibo uploader which imposes certain restrictions and post-processing: 1) only one image is allowed per post[2]; 2) images are scrubbed of their EXIF metadata; and 3) all images (excluding animated GIFs) are converted to JPEG.

*This research is supported by the National Natural Science Foundation of China, No. 61003097; International Science and Technology Cooperation Program of China, No. 2013DFG12870, and by the Singapore National Research Foundation under its International Research Centre @ Singapore Funding Initiative and administered by the IDM Programme Office.

MM'13, October 21–25, 2013, Barcelona, Spain.
Copyright 2013 ACM 978-1-4503-2404-5/13/10 ...$15.00.
http://dx.doi.org/10.1145/2502081.2502203 .

[1]Annotated corpus available at: `http://wing.comp.nus.edu.sg/downloads/imagetweets/`

[2]Note that since April 24 2013, Weibo has supported multiple images per post and displayed them in an album style.

In our corpus, 45.1% are image tweets, of which still images dominate: 97.5% image tweets contain a JPEG formatted picture while 2.5% contain an animated GIF. Figure 1 gives 18 examples which illustrate the variety of images in image tweets: there are photographs of varying quality (both candid and composed) and of varying topics, screenshots, cartoons, digital wallpaper and other forms of decorative images. Our manual inspection of our annotated corpus finds 69.5% of the images are natural photographs (including digitally edited ones), 13.2% are synthetic, and the remaining 17.4% are multi-photo collages. The collage form bypasses Weibo's one-photo-per-post limitation and are used for different narrative purposes: e.g., to compare objects, and tell stories through an image sequence.

With respect to posting habits, a survey of our annotators (who are users of Weibo) reveals that 85% self-reported that they used their camera phone as their photo-taking device, whereas 13.7% used a digital camera. This accords with our hypothesis that Weibo users care more about the photo content than quality, as most photos seem to be of low quality, which differs with Flickr [3].

Image-Tweets versus Text Posts. We attempt to uncover differences between image tweets and text-only ones by answering "when", "what" and "why". Plotting our tweets by posting hour (in Figure 2 (a)), we observe that image tweets are posted more frequently during the daytime. We posit that there are more tweet-worthy objects and events during the day, but we have yet to validate this.

For "what", we applied latent Dirichlet allocation (LDA; [1]) to a large, $\sim$1M subset of the whole dataset, to learn $k = 50$ latent topics, where k was tuned on a held-out set. Among these 50 topics, we observe that some exhibit an image- to non-image tweet ratio differing significantly from the average 45.1%. Figure 2 (b) lists sample topics with manually-assigned labels: advertisements and posts on fashion, travel and food are adorned with images, while posts about emotions and everyday routine are mostly text-only.

As to "why", many studies on text-only tweets have already been done. The motivation in posting can be summarized as either societal (daily chatter, conversations) or informational (sharing information, reporting news) in nature [5]. From the distribution of LDA topics, we see the preference of posting image tweets or text tweets is correlated with the content. For example, advertisement tweets tend to include a product image to make it more informative; whereas tweets about the everyday routine – tweets whose topics are about work or sleeping, for example – are prone to be text-only. This answers "why" from a collective standpoint, so next we drill down to investigate the relation of the image and text in individual tweets.

3. IMAGE AND TEXT RELATION

Though users can post an image without accompanying text, it is rare – 99.1% of our image tweets have corresponding text. We want to know why people post both image and text and the nature of their correlation.

Two previous studies have attempted to answer this for the general domain. Marsh and White [6] identified 49 relationships, grouping them into three major categories based on the closeness of the relationship. Martinec and Salway [7] studied text-image relations from two perspectives: status (in terms of relative importance) and logico-semantic (one expands or repeats the same meaning of another). While

Figure 1: 18 Example Images from Image Tweets.

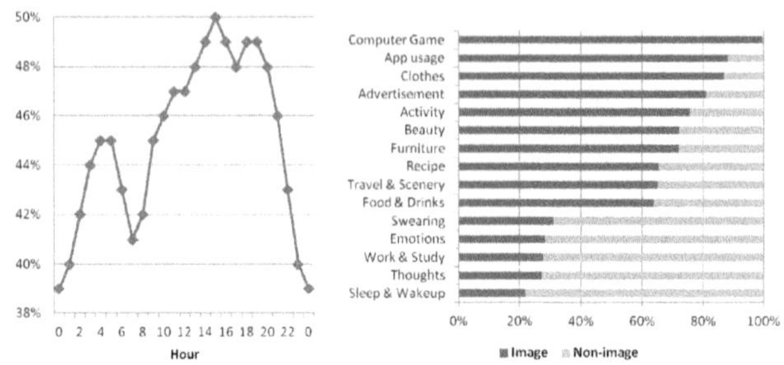

(a) (b)

Figure 2: (a) % of image tweets by hour. (b) % of image to non-image tweets in skewed topics.

insightful, these categorizations predate image tweets, and do not cater for the textual content found in social media. Furthermore, neither scheme has been operationalized into an automated classifier.

It seems natural to assume that the two mediums should complement each other – an embedded image should present visual highlights of the post, where the text gives contextual description: time, location, event or story. That is, the text and the image are visually related, and as such we deem both media to be of equal standing. We define *visually-relevant* image tweets (*visual* for short) as ones where at least one noun or verb corresponds to part of the image.

In our corpus analysis, we did observe this behavior, but interestingly, there was a surprisingly large proportion of *non-visual* image tweets, where the text and image have little or no visual correspondence. These are hard to detect by just looking at the images themselves: actually, in Figure 1, the left group of 9 images are from visual image tweets and the right group of 9 are non-visual image tweets. We find the distinction hinges jointly on text and image content together. Figure 3 shows two sample visual (top) and two sample non-visual (bottom) tweets. The motivations for posting images in a non-visual tweet vary. In the bottom row, the poster embedded an outdoor landscape which has no correspondence to the text, but which may entice readers to view the post.

We notice that a subset of non-visual image tweets that exhibit a consistent characteristic: that of *emotional* relevance. In such tweets, the text and the image share the same emotional state, as in the third example (anger, directed at mosquitoes). In such cases, the text is the primary medium; the image reinforces the emotional aspects of the text, similar to emoticon use. However, we notice that the distinction

Figure 3: Image tweets with their corresponding text, image and translation. The top two are examples of *visual* tweets, and the bottom two are *non-visual* ones.

between emotional and general non-visual tweets is difficult – our annotation efforts showed that it may be more a continuum than a binary distinction. As such we only consider the binary distinction between visual and non-visual categories, although we feel it is interesting.

The distinction between visual and non-visual has practical value. A text-based image search can utilize embedded images from visual tweets, but not non-visual tweets. E.g., the image in the first row of Figure 3 would be a suitable image result for the query "sago cream", but a search for "mosquitoes" should not retrieve the image in the third row. The classification may also help automated tagging methods filter out image-text pairs where the relevance assumption does not hold (i.e., non-visual tweets). Finally, as images in visual tweets hold semantic value, social media platforms may choose to prioritize images from visual tweets in loading or in assigning screen real estate for display.

4. VISUAL/NON-VISUAL CLASSIFICATION

We now turn to the task of making this distinction automatically via supervised classification. We first construct an annotated dataset via crowdsourcing, then describe the three classes of evidence we employ for machine learning.

Dataset Construction. To obtain gold standard annotations, we employed subjects from *Zhubajie*[3], as well as students at our university, to label a random subset of the image tweets. Subjects were native Chinese speakers and microblog users. We asked subjects to categorize the image-text relation as either visual or non-visual. Each image tweet was annotated by 3 different subjects, with the simple majority fixing the gold standard. In total, we collected annotations for 4,811 image tweets (also used in our manual analysis in Section 2) annotated by 72 different subjects. These broke down into 3,206 (66.6%) visual and 1,605 (33.4%) non-visual image tweets[4].

To utilize supervised machine learning, we employ multimedia features that leverage the text, image and social context of an image tweet.

Text Features. We preprocess the Chinese text by passing each tweet through a word segmenter, Part of Speech (POS) tagger, and a named entity recognizer (NER). We observed that vocabulary is a good indicator of image-text relation: e.g., tweets that mention a physical object and its color exhibit a visual bias. To make the resultant *word* feature more meaningful, we discard stop words and rare words unlikely to re-occur ($freq < 5$). The word features are binary; encoding just the presence (absence) of a word.

We incorporate the learned *topic* from LDA as another feature. We also encode *POS density* features (proportion of nouns, verbs, adjectives, adverbs and pronoun within a tweet), as well as the presence of different classes of *named entities*. These features are useful as visual tweets mention concrete objects, people's names (E.g, the second row in Figure 3), places and products. We also use four *microblog-specific* features that test for the presence of @mentions, #hashtags, geolocation coordinates and URLs.

Image Features. As images in the image tweets display a broad spectrum of types, we eschew object detection common in multimedia (TREC-MM) research. We employ *face* detection as an exception, recording the number of faces present, as instances of faces are often the poster herself, friends or family. For the same reason, we also included a composite co-occurrence feature that is activated only when a person's name and face is present. In our dataset, faces are detected in 22.2% of images.

Images with similar content tend to exhibit the same image-text relation. To capture this, we cluster the images by visual similarity. Following the bag-of-visual-words methodology, we first extract SIFT descriptors from the images as inputs, clustering them to form visual words by building a hierarchical visual vocabulary tree [8]. We then apply LDA to the corpus of images-as-documents' visual vocabulary, aiming to learn k hidden topics[5]. Subsequently, the *image topic* assignment is encoded as a single feature.

Context Features. From our earlier analysis, we know that the posting time affects the probability of a tweet being visual or not; for this reason, we include the hour of the *posting time* as a feature. As people share what they have just seen (visual tweet), we capture whether the *device* used to post the image tweets is mobile or not (e.g. desktops).

Social features round out our set. Weibo readers can post comments on the post. In our dataset, 46.3% of the image tweets have at least one comment, and 21.5% have been reposted; as opposed to 33.7% and 16.2% for text-only tweets. We use the number of *comments* and *retweets* normalized by the number of followers to the author's account as features. We also note that in visual tweets, the *author-replies* to the post herself (usually as a follow up to her reader's comments), so we encode that as another feature. Finally, we use the *follower ratio* (i.e., $\frac{\#followers}{\#followed}$) to differentiate ordinary users from celebrity and organizational accounts.

5. EXPERIMENT

We performed 10-fold cross validation experiments with the Naïve Bayes[6] implementation in Weka3 [2]. The three sets of features were linearly concatenated into a single vector. Due to the imbalanced distribution (66.6% of image

[3]`http://www.zhubajie.com`, a crowdsourcing website.

[4]To enable future work, we further asked subjects to distinguish emotional from other non-visual tweets. However, inter-annotator agreement was not as strong ($\kappa = 0.54$), so we do not discuss this further.

[5]k is tuned on a held-out set; $k = 35$ in our case.

[6]Experimenting with other learners (e.g., SVM, Logistic Regression) yielded worse results.

tweets are visual), simple accuracy is not an appropriate evaluation metric. Therefore, we report the macro-averaged F_1 score, as we feel both classes are equally valuable. The majority baseline (all visual) obtains a macro-F_1 score of 0.40.

To understand the impact of each feature class, we start with the best single feature (*words*, $F_1 = 64.8$) and measure the gain (loss) in F_1 when adding each feature in turn. The results are shown in Table 1. *POS density* turns out to be the second-most useful feature, increasing F_1 by 4.9. As a snapshot of content (e.g., noun) and function (e.g., pronoun) words distribution, this feature is effective in identifying non-visual tweets with heavy function words usage (e.g., pure exclamations). Other textual features – *topic*, *named entities* and *microblog-specific* – also lead to small performance increment. The addition of our two image features also make a marginal improvement over the baseline. However, not all the proposed context features are useful. The addition of *posting time*, *device*, and *follower ratio* improve the *word* baseline slightly, while the other three do not. Our final classifier (Row 14) that combines all features that improved the baseline, achieves an F_1 of 70.5.

Table 1: Experimental Results and Feature Analysis.

Class	Features	Macro-F_1 (%)
Text	(1): Words Only (Baseline)	64.8
	(2): (1) + Microblog-specific	65.2
	(3): (1) + Named Entities	65.3
	(4): (1) + Topic	66.6
	(5): (1) + POS Density	69.7
Image	(6): (1) + Topic	65.4
	(7): (1) + Face	65.7
Context	(8): (1) + Retweets	60.9 (–)
	(9): (1) + Comments	64.5 (–)
	(10): (1) + Replied by Author	64.7 (–)
	(11): (1) + Device	64.9
	(12): (1) + Follower Ratio	64.9
	(13): (1) + Posting Time	65.0
All	(14): (1–7 + 11–13)	70.5

We further analyzed the misclassified instances. While *words* are the most discriminative feature, microblog text is relatively short (tweets on Weibo are limited to 140 characters). The brevity of the text sparsifies the *word* feature, giving little information to the classifier. In an extreme case, e.g.,"吴氏 宗祠" (ancestral hall of the Wu family), where all the words are rare or out-of-vocabulary, word features are not helpful at all. This partly explains why the *words* only baseline plateaus at a F_1 of 64.8. The informal language used in microblogs – i.e., neologisms and misspellings – also poses a great challenge to standard natural language processing tools. We have observed many instances where misspellings are processed incorrectly by our word segmentation and named entity recognition tools. One such example is a mispelling of "阿狸" (a cartoon character) as "啊狸" in a visual tweet. The NER tool did not successfully tag this as a named entity. The propagation of this error downstream in our pipeline caused the eventual error.

Besides text features, the inaccuracy of face detection is another source of classification errors. We posit that this is due to the characteristics of images posted with visual tweets (e.g., low photo quality, photo collages). We also observe an inadequacy in our context features. We sampled the feeds and image tweets of some users and realise that users have different tweet posting behaviors. Some users are more inclined to post non-visual than visual tweets, and the inverse is true of others. This is not captured in our proposed context features and we believe that features which consider the behavioral characteristics of users will be very helpful.

6. CONCLUSION

The social Web 2.0 has embraced multimedia with the inclusion of facilities to embed images in microblog posts. We performed a multipronged analysis of these *image tweets* from visual, textual and social context perspectives. We discover that images from image tweets demonstrate a wider spectrum of image types as compared with image-sharing websites, and that the tweets differ from text-only ones in terms of their topical content and posting time.

We make an important distinction about image tweets – the *visually relevant* image tweet – where the focal point of the tweet is present in both the image and text, complementing each other. In contrast, non-visual tweets use the image as a way of adorning the text in a non-essential manner – i.e., to heighten interest in reading a post. We build an automated classifier leveraging features from text, image, and context evidence sources to achieve a macro F_1 of 70.5, an absolute improvement of 5.7% over a text only baseline. To encourage more investigation on these topics, we have made the annotated corpus available to the public to test and benchmark against.

We have further identified that non-visual tweets are often associated emotionally, and will classify such emotionally relevant image tweets in future work. We also plan to conduct similar study in other platforms (e.g., Twitter), and compare the findings with Weibo.

7. REFERENCES

[1] D. M. Blei, A. Y. Ng, M. I. Jordan, and J. Lafferty. Latent Dirichlet allocation. *Journal of Machine Learning Research*, 3:2003, 2003.

[2] M. Hall, E. Frank, G. Holmes, B. Pfahringer, P. Reutemann, and I. H. Witten. The weka data mining software: an update. *SIGKDD Explor. Newsl.*, 11(1):10–18, Nov. 2009.

[3] R. Herrema. Flickr, communities of practice and the boundaries of identity: a musician goes visual. *Visual Studies*, 26(2):135–141, 2011.

[4] K. Ishiguro, A. Kimura, and K. Takeuchi. Towards automatic image understanding and mining via social curation. In *ICDM*, 2012.

[5] A. Java, X. Song, T. Finin, and B. Tseng. Why we twitter: understanding microblogging usage and communities. In *WebKDD/SNA-KDD*, 2007.

[6] E. E. Marsh and M. D. White. A taxonomy of relationships between images and text. *Journal of Documentation*, 59:647–672, 2003.

[7] R. Martinec and A. Salway. A system for image–text relations in new (and old) media. *Visual Communication*, 4(3):337–371, 2005.

[8] D. Nister and H. Stewenius. Scalable recognition with a vocabulary tree. In *CVPR*, 2006.

[9] Z. Wang, P. Cui, L. Xie, H. Chen, W. Zhu, and S. Yang. Analyzing social media via event facets. In *MM*, 2012.

[10] L. Yu, S. Asur, and B. A. Huberman. What Trends in Chinese Social Media. In *SNA-KDD*, 2011.

[11] X. Zhao, F. Zhu, W. Qian, and A. Zhou. Impact of Multimedia in Sina Weibo: Popularity and Life Span. In *CSWS and CWSC*, 2012.

User Interest and Social Influence Based Emotion Prediction for Individuals

Yun Yang, Peng Cui, Wenwu Zhu, Shiqiang Yang
Tsinghua National Laboratory for Information Science and Technology
Department of Computer Science, Tsinghua University. Beijing, China
Beijing Key Laboratory of Networked Multimedia, Tsinghua University, China
yangyun11@mails.tsinghua.edu.cn, {cuip, wwzhu, yangshq}@tsinghua.edu.cn

ABSTRACT

Emotions are playing significant roles in daily life, making emotion prediction important. To date, most of state-of-the-art methods make emotion prediction for the masses which are invalid for individuals. In this paper, we propose a novel emotion prediction method for individuals based on user interest and social influence. To balance user interest and social influence, we further propose a simple yet efficient weight learning method in which the weights are obtained from users' behaviors. We perform experiments in real social media network, with 4,257 users and 2,152,037 microblogs. The experimental results demonstrate that our method outperforms traditional methods with significant performance gains.

Categories and Subject Descriptors

J.4 [**Computer Applications**]: Social and Behavioral Sciences

Keywords

Emotion prediction; Social influence; User interest; Social network

1. INTRODUCTION

Nowadays, emotions are playing important roles in daily life, ranging from market selling [4] to stock prediction [3]. What people feel may directly affect what decision they will make, which makes emotion prediction important.

Recent years have witnessed increasing research efforts on emotion prediction from text or image domain. For example, Picard's work [6] inferred sentence-level emotional affinity based on text. Takamura, Inui, and Okumura [8] expressed the impression of a word with the positive or negative emotion polarity value and applied the value to extract evaluation expressions. Not only from the text domain, affective image classification is also emerging from image perspective. One of the first affective image filtering system is K-DIME [2], which builds a retrieval system for users to retrieve affective images. Another work was done by Jana et al. [5], using the features inspired by psychology and art theory to classify affective images.

Previous works mainly focus on predicting the emotion for the masses. Since different people may have different emotions, it makes emotion prediction approach for the masses invalid for individuals. It's desired to develop emotion prediction methods for individuals.

The problem of emotion prediction for individuals is not trivial. So far, there are fewer works on emotion prediction for individuals. Emotions have long been viewed as passions produced on their own interest [7]. However. from social aspect, [11] has shown that how happy you're is influenced by your social links to people in social networks. More recently, Tang's work [10] quantitatively studies how an individual's emotion is influenced by his friends in social network.

It can be seen from the above that existing emotion prediction methods for individuals either focus on user interest or social influence. However, neither user interest or social influence alone can predict individual's emotion accurately. In this work, we propose a novel method jointly considering user interest and social influence in social network platform to predict user's emotion. We further propose a simple yet efficient weight learning method to balance the weights of user interest and social influence to figure out exactly what kind of roles they are playing in the final emotion prediction. Fig. 1 illustrates the conceptual framework of our proposed emotion prediction for individuals.

The contributions of our work can be summarized as follows:

- We present a novel emotion prediction method for individuals taking both user interest and social influence into account.
- We propose a simple yet efficient weight learning method to balance the user interest and social influence in which the weights are obtained from users' behaviors.

2. EMOTION PREDICTION FOR INDIVIDUALS

In this section, we first define some notions and problem setting, then elaborate emotion prediction by user interest and social influence separately. Finally we propose a simple weight learning method to combine these two factors together.

MM'13, October 21–25, 2013, Barcelona, Spain.
Copyright 2013 ACM 978-1-4503-2404-5/13/10 ...$15.00.
http://dx.doi.org/10.1145/2502081.2502204.

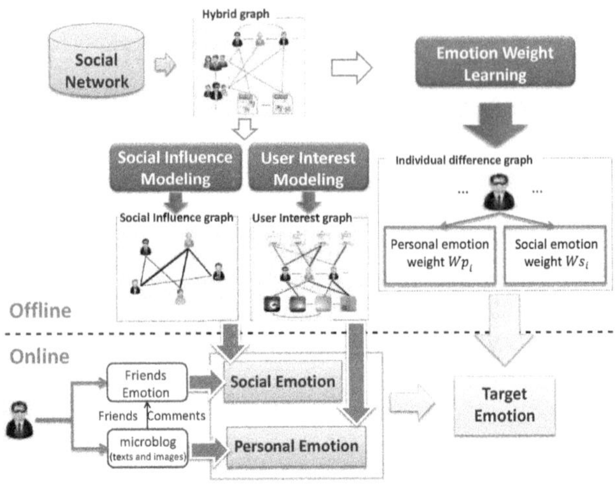

Figure 1: Conceptual framework of emotion prediction for individuals.

2.1 Problem Setup

The social network is a hybrid graph which can be represented as $G = (\{V, B\}, E)$, where V is the set of $|V| = N$ users, B is the microblog set posted or retweeted by users and $E \subset V \times V$ is the set of directed/undirected links between users. Given this, we can define the problem as follows:

Definition 1. **Personal emotion:** personal emotion is the subjective feeling when user seeing the microblog. It's the kind of emotion produced by user interest. We use $Ep_i^t(b)$ as the personal emotion for use v_i when seen microblog b at the time t.

Definition 2. **Social emotion:** social emotion is the emotion produced by the impact of other people's emotion (social influence). Here we use $Es_i^t(b)$ as the social emotion for user v_i when seeing friends' comments of microblog b at the time t.

Definition 3. **Target emotion:** a user v_i's target emotion is the final emotion user will make, it's a combination of personal emotion and social emotion, we use $y_i^t(b)$ as the target emotion for user v_i when seeing the microblog b at the time t, $y_i^t(b) \subset \mathcal{Y}$, where $\mathcal{Y}$ is the emotion space.

In this work the emotion space is covered by two categories: positive and negative, which is enough for most of applications. Thanks to [1], the dictionary has 23,419 Chinese regular words with positive or negative emotion polarity value with which we can get the groundtruth of users' emotions by their comments.

With all these definitions, we can represent our goal as follow:

Learning task: Given a dynamic continuous network G^t, the goal is to learn a prediction function f to infer the emotion of a user when seeing microblog b at the time t by taking both user interest and social influence into consideration. Mathematically, we have

$$G = f(\{V, B\}, E) = f(Ep_i^t(b), Es_i^t(b)) \rightarrow y_i^t(b) \quad (1)$$

where $y_i^t(b) \subset \mathcal{Y}$.

2.2 Personal Emotion Prediction

It is said that everyone has their own minds, different people may have different emotions even meeting the same situation or seeing the same thing. For example, someone may get excited when mentioned about "shopping", while some may feel exhausted. Not only in text, users also have interest in images, some like bright colors while some prefer delicate ones. Under the circumstances, we construct user interest model by taking text and image two domains into consideration.

2.2.1 *Emotion prediction from text*

Based on users' historical microblogs, we can get user interest in different topics and calculate the positive and negative probability of the words for each user, which is much like constructing a personalized dictionary other than [1] for the masses. In this way, we can get to know users well and make the emotion prediction more precise from text domain.

We use $p_{pos_i}(w)$ and $p_{neg_i}(w)$ to represent the positive and negative probability of word w for user v_i.

$$p_{pos_i}(w) = \frac{|\{b | b \in B_H(i), y_i(b) > 0, w \in b\}|}{|\{b | b \in B_H(i), w \in b\}|} \quad (2)$$

where $B_H(i)$ is the microblog set commented by user v_i in historical dataset. The $p_{neg_i}(w)$ is similar to $p_{pos_i}(w)$.

Therefore, the personal emotion from text domain for microblog b can be summarized as follow:

$$Ep_i(b) = \sum_{w \in b}(p_{pos_i}(w) - p_{neg_i}(w)) \quad (3)$$

where w is the word contained in the microblog b.

2.2.2 *Emotion prediction from image*

Nowadays, more than 60% microblogs are illustrated with images making microblogs more vivid and more expressive. In the meantime, images not only bring the physical scene content, but also have the ability to convey emotional information which makes people feel happy, or sad, etc. Generally, the visual features of an image include color, shape, composition and so on, while among all these features, color has been shown to play an important role in image affective analysis [9].

Here we use three basic kinds of color features to present images, brightness, colorfulness and hue, which are also used in most of the affective image classification or detection work [5]. We cluster positive and negative images separately for each user to find out the representatives in the two categories. When comes a new image, the distances between the image and representatives are measured to find out which category the image should belong to.

2.3 Social Emotion Prediction

With the popularity of social network, i.e. `Facebook, Twitter and Flicker`, more and more people are willing to share their own feelings towards hot events or their experiences in daily life, whether delivering positive or negative emotions, which makes it easier for people to know others' minds. More or less, users are getting increasingly easier to be influenced by others in social network.

However, different friends may have different extents of influences on the user based on how close they are or how much similarity they have in common. We use the emotion similarity when treated the same microblog to measure the social influence. $w(v_i, v_j)$ is defined as the influence of user v_j to user v_i. Here, user $v_j \in F(i)$ where $F(i)$ is the friend set of user v_i:

$$w(v_i, v_j) = \frac{|\{b|y_i(b) \cdot y_j(b) > 0, b \in B_H(i), b \in B_H(j)\}|}{|\{b|b \in B_H(i), b \in B_H(j)\}|} \tag{4}$$

where $B_H(i)$ is the microblog set commented by user v_i in historical dataset and $y_i(b)$ is the user v_i's emotion value for the commented microblog b.

We suppose when user v_i visits microblog b, he will also see all the comments made by his friends to microblog b within one day. Here, we only consider the emotion polarity made by their friends, whether positive or negative, rather than how strong the emotions are. In conclusion, we use the following equation to predict the social emotion for user v_i of microblog b.

$$Es_i^t(b) = \sum_{j \in F(i), t-1<t'<t} w(v_i, v_j) sign(y_j^{t'}(b)) \tag{5}$$

where t' can be anytime before t within one day.

2.4 Emotion Weight Learning

Different people have different characters. Some of them are independent and have their own minds, while some of them are more susceptible. We propose a simple weight learning method to measure the individual difference in the weights of personal emotion and social emotion for the target emotion.

We use Wp_i and Ws_i to represent the weights of personal emotion and social emotion for the target emotion of the user v_i. Through mining users' historical behavior, we find that prediction precisions of personal emotion and social emotion can very well measure the weights and more importantly, it is simple and make our method efficient.

$$Wp_i = \frac{|\{b|Ep_i(b) \cdot y_i(b) > 0, b \in B_H(i)\}|}{|\{b|b \in B_H(i)\}|} \tag{6}$$

$$Ws_i = \frac{|\{b|Es_i(b) \cdot y_i(b) > 0, b \in B_H(i)\}|}{|\{b|b \in B_H(i)\}|} \tag{7}$$

where $B_H(i)$ is the microblog set commented by user v_i from historical dataset.

In conclusion, we can summary our method as below:

$$Y^t = f(\{V, B\}, E) = f(Ep^t, Es^t) = Wp_i \cdot Ep_i^t + Ws_i \cdot Es_i^t \tag{8}$$

3. EXPERIMENTS

In this section, we first describe our experimental setup, and then present the performance of the proposed method and the comparison methods. Finally, we give our analysis and discussions based on the results.

3.1 Dataset

The dataset for our experiment is crawled from Tencent Weibo which is one of the biggest microblogging service with more than 780 million users in China. We collect all the microblogs between November 20th and November 30th of year 2011, as well as the relationship between the users. It turns out to have large number of users but only a few are active. For the efficiency and effectiveness of the experiments, we select 4,257 users who have more than 40 microblogs in 10 days and have strong relationship with others. 2,152,037 microblogs was produced within 10 days by these users.

On Tencent Weibo platform, users post microblogs with texts as well as images. Besides posting, users can also comment others' microblogs and retweet, which makes another new microblog authoring the reviewer. The original content will still exist in this new microblog, from which multimedia content can be analyzed. On the other hand, reviewer's comments can be an evidence showing his or her emotions when seeing the original microblog. We use traditional lexicon-based methods to find out the emotion polarity of the comments with a predefined Chinese words dictionary [1], which is the groundtruth for our experiments.

3.2 Evaluation Metric

We use *precision, recall* and *F1-Measure* as our metrics for positive and negative microblogs. The dataset is unbalanced, which needs to be mentioned. The number of microblogs conveying positive emotion is way much higher than the negative, which makes the proportion about 5:1. In this condition, predicting the negative emotion correctly will be more important than the positive ones. As the comprehensive metric, we need take the unbalanced situation into consideration. Therefore, we use the $F1_{avg}$ to measure the overall performance as a comprehensive metric.

$$F1_{avg} = \frac{F1_{pos} + F1_{neg}}{2}$$

3.3 Baseline Methods

Besides our proposed method which combines personal emotion and social emotion together with learned weight, we also implement the following baselines for comparison.

- General emotion prediction using images: the three basic kinds of color features [5], brightness, colorfulness and hue, was also used in this method. Different from our method, it's the prediction for the masses.

- General emotion prediction using texts: like Takamura et al. did in [8], the dictionary [1] was used to make predictions from original microblog as the emotion prediction result for users.

3.4 Evaluation

We first compare our method which combine personal emotion and social emotion together to the two baselines (based on images and texts) respectively. From Fig. 2 (a) and (b) we observe that our method achieve the best $F1$ performance in both positive and negative microblogs, which makes the comprehensive metric $F1_{avg}$ in our method huge success with 13% and 6.14% improvements compared to the other two baselines from (c).

Furthermore, we systematically study the effects of personal emotion and social emotion to our joint method. From Fig. 3 (a) and (b) we can observe that prediction from social emotion is better than the personal emotion for both positive and negative microblogs. That means most of the users have the same emotion (positive or negative) with others towards the same microblog. However, with the help of user interest, our method which combines the two factors together outperforms the social prediction. It indicates that there are particular some kinds of users who actually have their own minds and don't echo the sentiment of others.

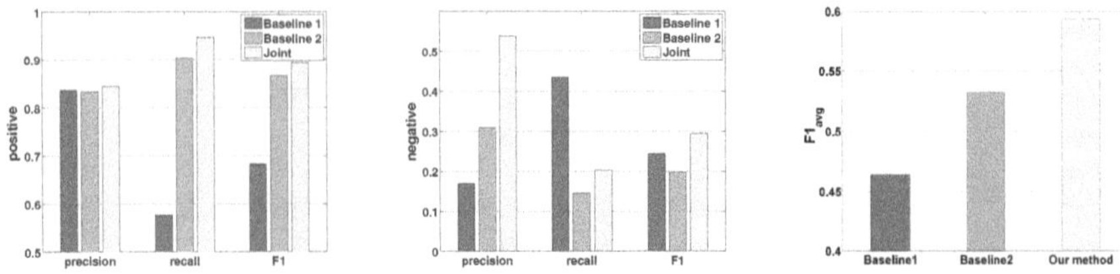

(a) (b) (c)

Figure 2: Comparison of our joint method based on personal emotion and social emotion with two baselines (based on image and text separately). (a) and (b) compare the three methods for positive and negative microblogs separately. (c) compares the three methods for all the microblogs using comprehensive measure $F1_{avg}$ which demonstrate our method outperform other two with 13% and 6% improvement.

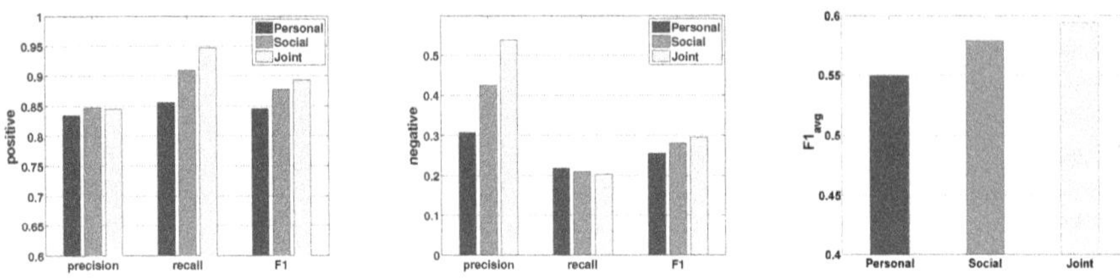

(a) (b) (c)

Figure 3: Comparison of our joint method with personal emotion prediction and social emotion prediction. From (a) and (b) we can observe social emotion prediction is more accurate than personal emotion prediction in both positive and negative microblogs. However, with the help of personal information, the joint method achieve the best performance from (c).

4. CONCLUSION AND FUTURE WORK

In this paper, we proposed a novel method taking both user interest in text and image domains and social influence among friends into consideration in social network for emotion prediction for individuals. A simple yet efficient weight learning method was proposed to balance the effects of the two factors to the target emotion. We conduct a set of comprehensive experiments to validate the effectiveness of our approach. From the experimental results, we can observe user interest and social influence play different roles in the target emotion, and our method which considers the both factors outperforms traditional emotion prediction methods with significant improvements.

5. ACKNOWLEDGMENTS

This work is supported by National Natural Science Foundation of China, No. 61003097, No. 60933013, and No. 61210008; International Science and Technology Cooperation Program of China, No. 2013DFG12870; National Program on Key Basic Research Project, No. 2011CB302206.

6. REFERENCES

[1] http://www.pudn.com/downloads462/sourcecode/math/detail1943885.html.

[2] N. Bianchi-Berthouze. K-dime: an affective image filtering system. *Multimedia, IEEE*, 10(3):103–106, 2003.

[3] J. Bollen, H. Mao, and X. Zeng. Twitter mood predicts the stock market. *Journal of Computational Science*, 2(1):1–8, 2011.

[4] K. A. Goyal and A. Sadasivam. A critical analysis of rational & emotional approaches in car selling. *International Journal of Business Research and Management (IJBRM)*, 1(2):59–63, 2010.

[5] J. Machajdik and A. Hanbury. Affective image classification using features inspired by psychology and art theory. In *Proceedings of the international conference on Multimedia*, pages 83–92. ACM, 2010.

[6] R. W. Picard. Affective computing: challenges. *International Journal of Human-Computer Studies*, 59(1):55–64, 2003.

[7] R. C. Solomon. *The passions: Emotions and the meaning of life.* Hackett Publishing, 1976.

[8] H. Takamura, T. Inui, and M. Okumura. Extracting semantic orientations of words using spin model. In *Proceedings of the 43rd Annual Meeting on Association for Computational Linguistics*, pages 133–140. Association for Computational Linguistics, 2005.

[9] J. Tanaka, D. Weiskopf, and P. Williams. The role of color in high-level vision. *Trends in cognitive sciences*, 5(5):211–215, 2001.

[10] J. Tang, Y. Zhang, J. Sun, J. Rao, W. Yu, Y. Chen, and A. Fong. Quantitative study of individual emotional states in social networks. *Affective Computing, IEEE Transactions on*, 3(2):132–144, 2012.

[11] J. Whitfield. The secret of happiness: grinning on the internet. *Nature*, 2008.

Bimodal Log-linear Regression for Fusion of Audio and Visual Features

Ognjen Rudovic
Dept. of Computing
Imperial College London
London, UK
o.rudovic@imperial.ac.uk

Stavros Petridis
Dept. Computing
Imperial College London
London, UK
sp104@imperial.ac.uk

Maja Pantic
Dept. Computing / EEMCS
Imperial College London /
Univ. Twente
London, UK / Enschede, NL
m.pantic@imperial.ac.uk

ABSTRACT

One of the most commonly used audiovisual fusion approaches is feature-level fusion where the audio and visual features are concatenated. Although this approach has been successfully used in several applications, it does not take into account interactions between the features, which can be a problem when one and/or both modalities have noisy features. In this paper, we investigate whether feature fusion based on explicit modelling of interactions between audio and visual features can enhance the performance of the classifier that performs feature fusion using simple concatenation of the audio-visual features. To this end, we propose a log-linear model, named Bimodal Log-linear regression, which accounts for interactions between the features of the two modalities. The performance of the target classifiers is measured in the task of laughter-vs-speech discrimination, since both laughter and speech are naturally audiovisual events. Our experiments on the MAHNOB laughter database suggest that feature fusion based on explicit modelling of interactions between the audio-visual features leads to an improvement of 3% over the standard feature concatenation approach, when log-linear model is used as the base classifier. Finally, the most and least influential features can be easily identified by observing their interactions.

Categories and Subject Descriptors

I.5.4 [**Computing Methodologies**]: Pattern Recognition—*Applications*; J.m [**Computer Applications**]: Miscellaneous

General Terms

Algorithms, Experimentation

Keywords

Bimodalss Log-Linear Regression-based Fusion, Audiovisual Fusion, Laughter Classification

MM'13, October 21–25, 2013, Barcelona, Spain.

http://dx.doi.org/10.1145/2502081.2502207 .

1. INTRODUCTION

Audiovisual fusion has attracted significant interest given its successful application in speech recognition, affect recognition and lately in laughter recognition [9]. The main contribution of the visual information is the addition of complementary and redundant information which cannot be corrupted by acoustic noise and therefore may improve the performance of a recognition system.

The most common types of audiovisual fusion are decision-level and feature-level fusion [10]. In decision-level fusion the audio and video modalities are processed independently and then the classifiers outputs are combined using various integration rules, e.g. a linear sum rule, or a second level classifier. As a consequence, the correlation between the audio and visual features is lost. In feature-level fusion the extracted audio and visual features are first combined, usually through concatenation, and then fed to a classifier. This increases the dimensionality of the problem but it provides additional information that can be relevant for a target task. In this paper, we limit our consideration to feature-level fusion.

The goal of this study is to investigate whether explicit modelling of interactions between audio and visual features can enhance performance of the traditional feature fusion approach where audio and visual features are simply concatenated. To this end, we propose a log-linear model, named Bimodal Log-linear regression, that modifies the parametrisation of the logistic regression model for binary outputs in order to account for interactions between audio and visual features. We should point out that other approaches which take into account the interactions between audio and visual features exist in the literature like [2, 5, 7]. However, the aim of this work is to compare the performance of the Bimodal Log-Linear Regression with the standard logistic regression.

The effectiveness of the proposed classifier is evaluated in the task of laughter-vs-speech discrimination, since both laughter and speech are naturally audiovisual events. Finally, the experimental evaluation is conducted using the recently released MAHNOB laughter database [8], which contains hundreds of examples of audiovisual speech and laughter episodes.

2. DATASET AND EXTRACTED FEATURES

For the purpose of this study we used the MAHNOB Laughter audiovisual dataset [1, 8]. In this dataset, laughter was elicited by showing amusing videos to subjects. In a

Table 1: Description of the MAHNOB dataset.

MAHNOB			
Type	No Episodes / No Subjects	Total Duration (sec)	Mean / Std (sec)
Laughter	554 / 22	863.7	1.56 / 2.2
Speech	845 / 22	2430.9	2.88 / 2.3

different set of sessions subjects were asked either to discuss with a friend or talk about a topic of their choice in English. In all cases, their reactions were recorded by a fixed camera (720 x 576, 25 fps), and two microphones, the camera microphone and a lapel microphone. Given that the subjects are watching a fixed screen, they are mostly in frontal pose and there is not significant head movement. In total, there are 22 subjects in total, 12 males and 10 females, with all but one being non-native speakers. In this study, we used the audio from the camera microphone (48 kHz) only, since it is noisier, and poses a more challenging generalisation problem. Finally, we use the annotations for speech and laughter provided with the database. The details of the dataset are summarised in Table 1.

Audio Features: In this study we use the most commonly used features in speech processing, the Mel Frequency Cepstral Coefficients (MFCCs). We use the first 6 coefficients, together with their deltas, which capture some local temporal characteristics. So in total there are 12 features which are computed every 10ms over a window of 40ms, i.e. the frame rate is 100 fps.

Visual Features: To capture face movements in an input video, we track 20 facial points using the particle filtering algorithm proposed in [6]. These points are the corners/extremities of the eyebrows (4 points), the eyes (8 points), the nose (3 points), the mouth (4 points) and the chin (1 point). The features are computed using the same Point Distribution Model (PDM) as in [9]. As suggested in [4], the facial expression movements are encoded by the projection of the tracking points coordinates to the N principal components (PCs) of the PDM which correspond to facial expressions. PCs 7-10 were found to correspond to facial expressions so our shape features are the projection of the 20 points to those 4 PCs. Further details of the feature extraction procedure can be found in [9, 4].

3. METHOD

In this section we present two different feature fusion methods for classification of speech and laughter. Throughout the paper, we assume a supervised setting: we are given a training set of N data triplets $D = \{(\mathbf{x}_i^A, \mathbf{x}_i^V, \mathbf{y}_i)\}_{i=1}^N$, which are i.i.d. samples from an underlying but unknown distribution $p_*(\mathbf{y}, \mathbf{x})$. Furthermore, $\mathbf{x}_i^A = (x_1^A ... x_{T_i}^A)^T$ and $\mathbf{x}_i^V = (x_1^V ... x_{T_i}^V)^T$ contain audio and visual features, respectively, per sample, and $\mathbf{y}_i = \{0, 1\}$ is the class label per sequence, with 0 denoting the speech class, and 1 the laughter class.

3.1 Logistic Regression

Logistic regression [3] is the simplest form of the log-linear models that deal with binary outputs. This model is appealing for the target task (i.e., classification of speech and laughter) because it is a discriminative model, so it directly models what we want, $p(y|x)$. Its predictor variables x can take any form since, in contrast to generative models, this model makes no assumption about the distribution of x. Therefore, x does not have to be normally distributed, linearly related or of equal variance within each group. Formally, logistic regression models the class-conditional probability given by

$$p(y = 1|x, \beta) = \frac{1}{1 + \exp(-s(x, \beta))} \tag{1}$$

and $p(y = 0|x, \beta) = 1 - p(y = 1|x, \beta)$, where the feature function $s(x, \beta)$ is defined as $s(x, \beta) = \beta_0 + \sum_{j=1}^d \beta_j x_j$. The parameter vector β has as its elements the intercept β_0 and the weights β_j, where we use j to index over the feature values x_1 to x_d of a single example of dimensionality d.

In the context of the target task, logistic regression can be used to perform feature fusion by concatenating audio and visual features per sample, i.e., $x = (x^A, x^V)$. Correspondingly, the score function of the logistic regression can be written as

$$\begin{aligned} s(x^A, x^V, \beta) &= \beta_0 + \textstyle\sum_{j=1}^{d_A} \beta_j^A x_j^A + \sum_{j=1}^{d_V} \beta_j^V x_j^V \\ &= \beta \cdot \left[1 \; x^A \; x^V\right]^T \end{aligned}, \tag{2}$$

where $\beta = \{\beta_0, \beta^A, \beta^V\}$, and d^A and d^V are the dimensions of the audio and visual features, respectively. With such feature function, the logistic regression is used to obtain the class-predictions per sample, which are then combined to obtain the class-probability for the whole sequence. This is explained in the following section.

3.2 Bimodal Log-linear Regression

Logistic regression [3] is limited in that its feature function treats audio and visual features independently. Thus, it ignores interactions between different audio and visual features that could be important for the classification task. To account for feature-interaction between the two modalities, we employ the log-linear model, which is an extension of logistic regression that allows modelling of arbitrary relationships among the input features. Specifically, we define the score function of the log-linear model as

$$s(x^A, x^V, \beta) = \beta_0 + \sum_{j=1}^{d_A} \beta_j^A x_j^A + \sum_{j=1}^{d_V} \beta_j^V x_j^V + \sum_{j=1}^{d_A} \sum_{k=1}^{d_V} \beta_{jk}^{AV} x_j^A x_k^V, \tag{3}$$

where β^{AV} measures the relevance of interactions between different audio and visual features for the classification task. Note that since we are interested in the fusion task we model only the first-order interactions between the features of two modalities, but not the features within these modalities. However, these and higher order interactions can be easily incorporated in the score function of the model. By plugging the score function in (3) into the conditional model in (1), we obtain a log-linear model for combining two modalities, and which we name Bimodal Log-linear Regression (BLR).

To better understand the BLR model, we re-write the score function in (3) using the matrix form

$$s(x^A, x^V, \beta) = \begin{bmatrix} 1 & x^A \end{bmatrix} \cdot \beta \cdot \begin{bmatrix} 1 \\ (x^V)^T \end{bmatrix}. \tag{4}$$

By comparing the score functions in (2) and (3), we see that the rank of the parameter vector β for logistic regression is 1, whereas for BLR is $r = min\{d_A, d_V\}$. Therefore, the former model performs linear classification in 1-D space, and

Table 2: The performance of the models evaluated on the MAHNOB dataset. L-F1 and S-F1 are obtained F-1 measures for Laughter and Speech, respectively, and CR is the classification rate, computed using all test subjects.

Model	L-F1[%]	S-F1[%]	CR[%]
A-LR	79.3	87.1	84.7
V-LR	82.5	88.6	85.9
AV-LR	87.2	91.1	89.4
AV-BLR	**90.5**	**94.3**	**92.7**
AV-NN[8]	86.5	92.2	90.1

the latter does so in the r-D space, in which the target classes may be better separated.

The training of the BLR model is accomplished by maximising the (balanced) conditional log-likelihood

$$\mathcal{L}(\beta) = \sum_{k=0}^{1} \frac{1}{N_k} \sum_{i=1}^{N_k} \sum_{j=1}^{T_i} \log p(y_i = k | x_{ij}^A, x_{ij}^V, \beta) - \lambda \left\| \beta \right\|_2^2, \tag{5}$$

where N_k is the number of sequences of the k-th class, and T_i is the number of frames in the i-th sequence. Parameter regularisation is attained using the Frobenious norm, which implicitly enforces low-rank representation of β. We also balance the data likelihood based on the number of samples from each class. This is important since the speech class usually dominates the laughter class in the number of training examples. The conditional log-likelihood in (5) is strictly convex, so we use gradient ascent with a fixed step γ to find the (globally) optimal parameters β as

$$\beta_{t+1} = \beta_t + \gamma \nabla \mathcal{L}(\beta_t), \tag{6}$$

where t is the number of iterations and $\gamma = 0.1$. In all our experiments, the algorithm converged in less than 10 iterations. Finally, inference of test sequences is performed using a two-step approach: first, we perform classification of the input features per frame based on the probability in (1), where the winning class is the class with $p > 0.5$. Then, we apply majority voting to obtain the sequence label.

4. EXPERIMENTS

We test the performance of the proposed BLR model in the task of laughter-vs-speech discrimination. In all our experiments, we applied a leave-one-subject-out cross-validation procedure. The regularisation term is obtained by running another cross validation among $\lambda = \{10^{-5}, 10^{-4}, ..., 1, 2\}$ on the training set. Both audio and visual features are z-normalized to zero mean and unity standard deviation. The means and standard deviations are computed on the training set only, and then applied to the test set. In addition, the audio and visual features are synchronised for audiovisual fusion, since they are extracted at different frame rates. This is achieved by upsampling the visual features by linear interpolation as in [9]. The generalisation performance is reported using F-1 measure (per class) and the classification rate (CR), computed on the predicted labels for sequences of all test subjects. We compare the BLR model, trained using audio-visual (AV) features, to logistic regression (LR) models trained using: (i) audio (A-LR), (ii) visual (V-LR), and (iii) concatenated audio-visual (AV-LR) features, as explained in Sec. 3.1. Table 2 shows comparative results of the

(a) Frame 984, 39.32-39.36 s (b) Frame 991, 39.60-39.64 s (c) Frame 998, 39.88-39.92 s (d) Frame1005 40.16-40.20 s

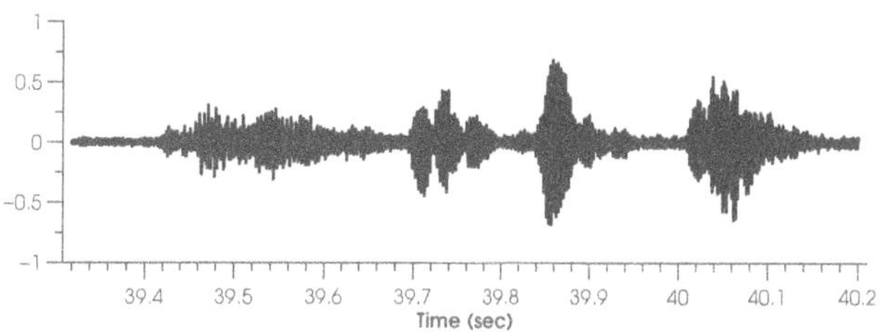

(e) Audio signal

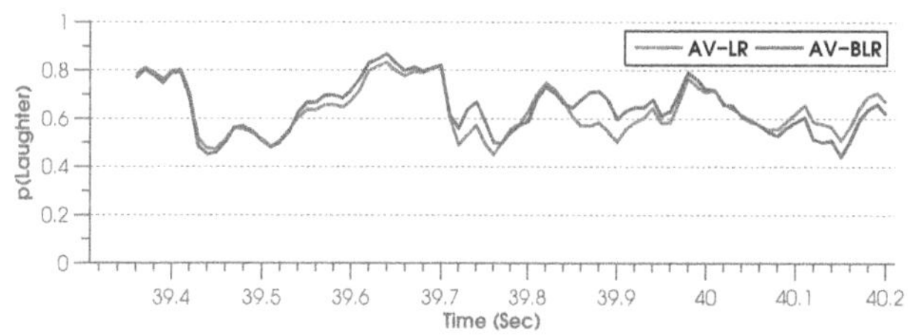

(f) Laughter probability for audiovisual fusion using logistic regression (LR) and bimodal logistic regression (BLR).

Figure 1: Example from subject S009, S009-001.

tested models. The models that rely on the single modality (A-LR and V-LR) are outperformed by the feature-fusion-based models. This is expected and the reader is referred to [8] for more insights about this. The proposed AV-BLR model attains better performance in terms of both F-1 measure and CR than the AV-LR model. We account this to modelling of the interactions between the two modalities in the BLR model. For the sake of comparison, we also include the baseline results for the MAHNOB dataset [8] obtained using a feedforward neural network for audio-visual feature fusion (AV-NN).

To better understand the effect of modelling the interactions between the audio and visual features in the AV-BLR model, in Fig.1 and 2 we contrast its classification per frame to that attained by the AV-LR model on two example sequences of Laughter. Note from Fig.1 that in the case of 'pronounced' laughter, both models achieve similar performance, with the AV-BLR model slightly outperforming the AV-LR model. This is expected since both audio and visual features vary sufficiently to discriminate between the target classes. However, note that in the case of 'soft' laughter (Fig.2), it is difficult to extract from the noisy audio signal the features that are typical for laughter. Although the probabilities of both models lie in close vicinity of the classification margin (p=0.5), the proposed AV-BLR model exploits the correlations between the two modalities, which, evidently, helps to extract useful information from the noisy audio features that are highly correlated with the visual features. This is especially the case in the second half of the sequence in Fig.2, where visual features provide more evidence of laughter, and hence, amplify the influence of the correlated audio features.

(a) Frame 706, 28.20-28.24 s (b) Frame 711, 28.40-28.44 s (c) Frame 716, 28.60-28.64 s (d) Frame 721, 28.80-28.84 s

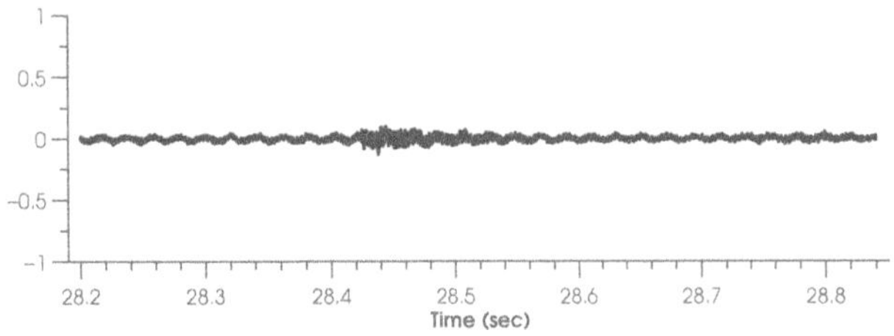

(e) Audio signal

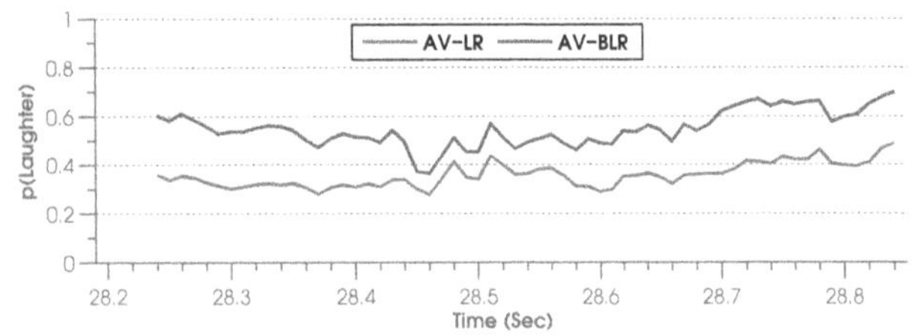

(f) Laughter probability for audiovisual fusion using logistic regression (LR) and bimodal logistic regression (BLR).

Figure 2: Example from subject S005, S005-008.

Finally, we inspect the parameters β of the AV-BLR model in order to see to what extent AV-BLR was able to learn interactions between the two modalities. To this end, we visualise β in Fig. 3. Note that the first visual feature has the highest influence on the score function in the AV-BLR model. The first visual feature corresponds to the 7th PC that captures mouth movements that are important for discriminating laughter vs. speech. Also, the first six MFCC features have much more influence than their deltas (features 8 to 13). Finally, note that the model has learned different weights for correlations between audio and visual features. For example, from Fig. 3, we can see that the first visual feature is negatively correlated with 1-3 MFCC features. These correlations make the whole classification process more robust to noise in the features of both modalities, as evidenced by the experiments presented before.

5. CONCLUSION

We have proposed a new log-linear model for bimodal feature fusion, named Bimodal Log-linear regression. In contrast to the standard feature-level fusion that is based on a simple feature concatenation, BLR explicitly models interactions between two modalities. Our experiments conducted on the MAHNOB dataset show that modelling those interactions improves the discriminative power of the log-linear classifier. In addition, the most influential features and their interactions can be easily identified by visualizing the fusion matrix of the BLR model.

6. ACKNOWLEDGMENTS

The research presented in this paper has been funded by the European Research Council under the ERC Starting Grant agreement no. ERC-2007-StG-203143 (MAHNOB). The work of Stavros Petridis is also supported in part by EPSRC grant EP/H016988/1: Pain rehabilitation: E/Motion-based automated coaching.

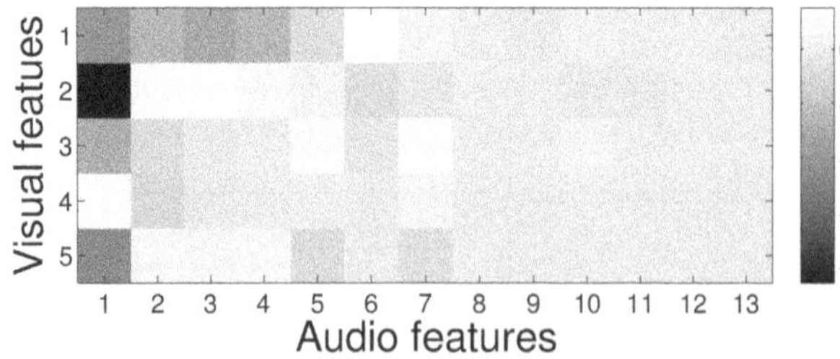

Figure 3: β parameters of AV-BLR. The element (1,1) corresponds to the intercept (β_0) of the model in (3). The rest of the elements in the first row and column are the weights of audio (β^A) and visual (β^V) features. The remaining elements are the weights of the interactions between the audio and visual features (β^{AV}). The (absolute) value of each element shows how strong the influence of the feature (feature pairs) on the score function in AV-BLR, and, thus, on its classification decision is.

7. REFERENCES

[1] http://mahnob-db.eu/laughter/.

[2] Z. Barzelay and Y. Schechner. Harmony in motion. In *IEEE CVPR*, pages 1–8, 2007.

[3] D. Cho and T. Bui. Multivariate statistical modeling for image denoising using wavelet transforms. *Signal Processing: Image Comm.*, 20(1):77–89, Jan. 2005.

[4] D. Gonzalez-Jimenez and J. L. Alba-Castro. Toward pose-invariant 2-d face recognition through point distribution models and facial symmetry. *IEEE Trans. Inform. Forensics and Security*, 2(3):413–429, 2007.

[5] W. Jiang and A. C. Loui. Audio-visual grouplet: temporal audio-visual interactions for general video concept classification. In *ACM MM*, pages 123–132, New York, NY, USA, 2011.

[6] I. Patras and M. Pantic. Particle filtering with factorized likelihoods for tracking facial features. In *FG*, pages 97–104, 2004.

[7] S. Petridis, S. Bilakhia, and M. Pantic. Comparison of prediction-based fusion and feature-level fusion across different learning models. In *ACM Multimedia 2012*, pages 813–816, Nara, Japan, November 2012.

[8] S. Petridis, B. Martinez, and M. Pantic. The MAHNOB laughter database. *Image and Vision Computing Journal*, 31(2):186–202, February 2013.

[9] S. Petridis and M. Pantic. Audiovisual discrimination between speech and laughter: Why and when visual information might help. *IEEE Transactions on Multimedia*, 13(2):216–234, April 2011.

[10] C. Snoek, M. Worring, and A. Smeulders. Early versus late fusion in semantic video analysis. In *ACM Multimedia*, pages 399–402, 2005.

Facilitating Fashion Camouflage Art

Ranran Feng
University of Texas at Dallas
800 W Campbell Road
Richardson, TX 75080 USA
(1) 972-883-4680
rrfeng@utdallas.edu

Balakrishnan Prabhakaran
University of Texas at Dallas
800 W Campbell Road
Richardson, TX 75080 USA
(1) 972-883-4680
bprabhakaran@utdallas.edu

ABSTRACT

Artists and fashion designers have recently been creating a new form of art – *Camouflage* Art – which can be used to prevent computer vision algorithms from detecting faces. This digital art technique combines makeup and hair styling, or other modifications such as facial painting to help avoid automatic face-detection. In this paper, we first study the camouflage interference and its effectiveness on several current state of art techniques in face detection/recognition; and then present a tool that can facilitate digital art design for such camouflage that can fool these computer vision algorithms. This tool can find the prominent or decisive features from facial images that constitute the face being recognized; and give suggestions for camouflage options (makeup, styling, paints) on particular facial features or facial parts. Testing of this tool shows that it can effectively aid the artists or designers in creating camouflage-thwarting designs. The evaluation on suggested camouflages applied on 40 celebrities across eight different face recognition systems (both non-commercial or commercial) shows that 82.5% ~ 100% of times the subject is unrecognizable using the suggested camouflage.

Categories and Subject Descriptors

I.4.9 [**Image Processing and Computer Vision**]: Applications.

General Terms

Algorithms, Measurement, Design, Experimentation, Security, Human Factors, Legal Aspects, Verification.

Keywords

Fashion Camouflage Art, Face Recognition.

1. INTRODUCTION

Recent technological advances, both in terms of hardware and software, as well as the increasing popularity of cameras and camera-enabled devices, have popularized face recognition from domains such as social networking to security checks. This in turn has led to controversary pertaining to privacy protection.

MM'13, October 21–25, 2013, Barcelona, Spain.

http://dx.doi.org/10.1145/2502081.2502121

To avoid being caught on camera, artists and designers have started exploring ways in which to thwart face detection, under the guise of high-fashion aesthetics (ambiguously deceptive fashion) [1] as shown in Figure 1. By utilizing makeup and hair styling, or other such aesthetic modifications, fashion/art design creates effective interference that renders the face unrecognizable[1] (and at times undetectable) to even advanced computer

Though this fashion-based camouflage art effectively breaks up the silhouette of the face, and covers certain facial features, it is difficult for the average person to expect to routinely camouflage their faces using the techniques shown in Figure 1. Unless a significantly larger number of people raise concerns about their privacy (at least enough to start wearing camouflage as shown in Figure 1), this camouflage art design is impractical for the following reasons: 1) the exaggerated design draws more attention to the wearers and makes them memorable (because they stick out more) as opposed to undetectable; 2) this design specifically aims to "trick" the Viola Jones face detection technique [2] and thus is not effective when other face detection/recognition techniques are used – for example, one commercial face recognition system [3] can successfully detect the faces in Figure 1 (b) and (c) as shown in Figure 2.

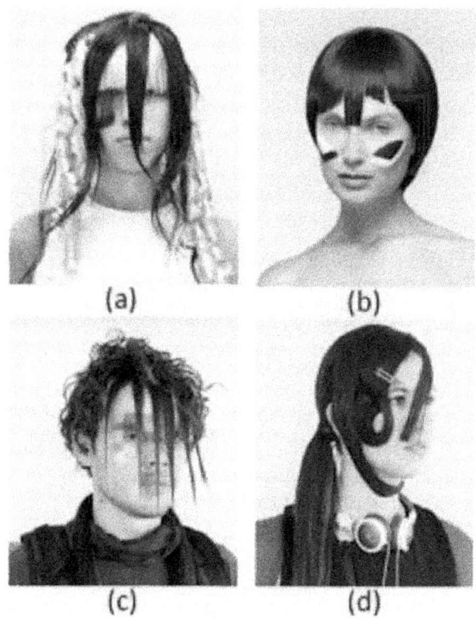

Figure 1. Fashion-based camouflage to avoid face detection [1].

[1] In this paper, "unrecognizable" refers both to the situation where the face is not recognized at all; or where the face is recognized incorrectly.

In fact, current advances in techniques are already able to tackle certain types of disguises, such as eyeglasses and masks, with respect to face detection and recognition [4][5]. However, we note that the ultimate goal of fashion-based camouflage is to protect privacy and thus, as long as the computer cannot recognize a subject's identity (i.e., even if a face is detected, as long as it is not recognized), the goal is achieved.

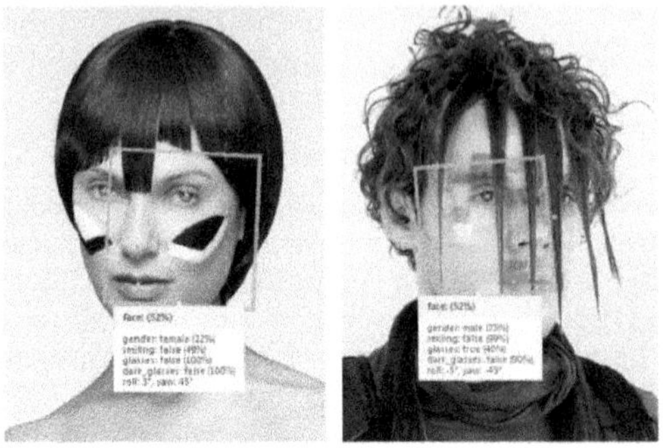

Figure 2. Camouflaged face can still be detected. Results from Sky Biometry Face Recognition [3].

As more artists and designers draw attention to this newly formed camouflage art, we want to have help these artists to have a more comprehensive understanding from computer vision perspective about how different types of camouflages interfere facial features and make the computer fail to recognize identity; and thus help them to create both effective and beautify designs on face. Apart from this, by analyzing effective camouflage inference on facial features that makes the face unrecognizable, we can pinpoint the weakness of current face recognition systems; and thus help researchers in face recognition to explore methods that can handle camouflage/disguises to improve accuracy - These are the main motivations for our study in this paper.

In this paper, we first define three types of fashion-based camouflage and give a comprehensive study of their various effects and interferences on different types of facial features; and then present a tool (developed by us) that can automatically locate the prominent or decisive features from facial images that allow the face to be recognized; and further provide effective camouflage suggestions to prevent the face from being recognized. To evaluate of the effectiveness of the camouflage suggestions, we collect 1200 facial images from 40 celebrities[2] and the results show that 82.5% ~ 100% of times the suggested camouflages can successfully make the subject unrecognizable by eight different face recognition systems.

The remainder of this paper is organized as follows: Section 2 provides an overview of work related to that which is presented herein, and Section 3 gives comprehensively study on camouflage types and interference on facial features. The facilitating tool that can automatically locate prominent facial features and give camouflage suggestions is then presented in Section 4. The evaluation on 40 celebrities camouflaged facial images against eight face recognition systems is given in Section 5. Finally a discussion on the conclusions and plans for future work appears in Section 6.

[2] All images of the 40 celebrities are publicly available on Internet, and collected only for research purpose. The dataset is available under appropriate terms and conditions. To request the dataset, please contact the authors.

2. RELATED WORKS

In the 1960s, researchers started to explore techniques in automatic face recognition from facial images, and over the course of the last several decades, it has become clear that the operational use of facial recognition on high-resolution frontal images taken in a controlled environment is feasible. This is ratified by the National Institute of Standards and Technology (NIST) Face Recognition Vender Test (FRVT) 2007 report [6]. In general, some face recognition algorithms extract facial features (geometric, holistic, or local) and find matches by comparing the features (e.g. [19][16]). Some other face recognition algorithms normalize a gallery of face images to generate compressed representation of face data and find matches by comparing face data (e.g. [15]).

As the utilization of face recognition applications on PCs and mobile devices has become more widespread, the concerns about privacy have arisen and people have started to be deceptive about their appearance, to hide from machines using camouflage. In general, there are two types of camouflage: concealment or deception. For example, army face paint is concealment camouflage; while the Dazzle pattern on ships during World War I is the deception type. As for human facial camouflage, there are several obvious approaches – for example, sunglasses are a known occlusion that some algorithms account for. There are also other functionally effective disguises, such as the use of a hood or facial mask; however these disguises make the wearer's intent to hide too obvious. As an alternative, the project called "CV Dazzle" in [1] pioneers the fashion camouflage art: exploring ways of using makeup and hairstyle or other modifications to transform a subject – the *deception type of camouflage*. As shown in Figure 1, the CV Dazzle project uses exaggerated hairstyle and high contrast patches on the cheeks to fool the Viola Jones Face Detector. However, as pointed out by DIS Magazine [7], the key to a good face-detection thwarting fashion-based camouflage should be inconspicuousness. To achieve an "inconspicuous" fashion camouflage, CV Dazzle is not yet practical.

Since ancient times, people have reported certain optical illusions caused by lighting conditions, shades, colors, etc. In modern times, artists or designers have adopted the concept of optical illusion in makeup to create different visual effects on a subject's face (change each facial parts and create different appearances) [8][9]. Examples in Figure 3 illustrate the visual illusion effects created using makeup products and fashion accessories [10]: the makeup instructor without any makeup (a) wears a regular makeup on a daily basis (b); however using advanced makeup she makes herself look similar to Angelina Jolie (c), Taylor Swift (d), and a Japanese Geisha (e) using makeup products and wigs. And she successfully disguised herself: a test on Google Face Search engine [11] and Baidu Face Search Engine [12] successfully recognized her in (a) and (b); while for (c) the top matching candidates returned are Angelina Jolie; and Taylor Swift is returned as first match for (d); while random match results (many different suggested matching subjects) are returned for (e). The deceptive camouflage in Figure 3 shows that one can successfully make oneself not just look different, but also look like a completely different person, by using colors, shades, and accessories (for occlusion).

It should be noted that more and more people choose plastic surgery to alter their appearances nowadays, given its increasing social acceptance and affordability. Though plastic surgery also

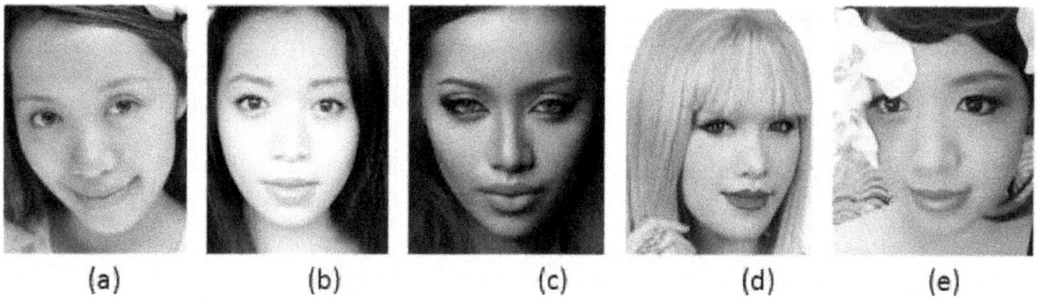

Figure 3. How makeup creates different visual effects on same subject.

functions as one type of camouflage that prevents a subject from being recognized, it is not the focus of this paper.

3. CAMOUFLAGE TYPES, INTERFERENCES, AND EFFECTIVENESS

From Figure 3, we can see clearly the illusive power of makeup and hairstyle. In order to understand why these illusion effects can fool algorithms and render the face "unrecognizable", in this section we first define three types of fashion camouflage; then study their camouflage interferences on different facial features; and explore the effectiveness of these camouflages.

3.1 Types of Fashion Camouflage

In nature, camouflage either makes animals/objects hard to see (crypsis), or disguises them as something else (mimesis). In this paper, we define 3 types of fashion camouflage on face; they are described as below.

3.1.1 Occlusion

Fashionable occlusion can be achieved by using stylish hair or accessories, e.g. forehead is occluded in Figure 3(c) using a wig; and upper cheek is occluded in Figure 3(d) by decorative flowers. Camouflage using occlusion covers certain facial features and thus makes the facial area incomplete or changes texture/pattern on facial parts. Different styles of hair in general are used to cover face shapes and forehead; while other decorative facial accessories such as body stickers, jewel/stud details, false eyelashes, and fake mustaches are used for to alter texture/color/pattern of certain facial parts (as shown in Figure 4).

Figure 4. Fashion Occlusion on face: (Left) Hair occlusion on face shape, forehead, and partial eye. (Right) Face sticker occlusion on eye.

3.1.2 Transformation

A stylish transformation enables the subject to alter the shape or color of facial parts, and thus look different from themselves, or even look like other subjects. Transformation look is mostly achieved using makeup products. Figure 3(c) is a good example of this transformation – the subject "transforms" her face to reassemble Angelina Jolie's face while no occlusions are used. Fundamentals to makeup-based transformation, is using different colors and shades to create false depth perception. Take Figure 3(c) as an example – it can be seen that the subject has an obvious nose hump compared with the look before (Figure 3(a)). This effect is achieved by using highlights in the middle of nose and darker shades around nose bridge. Similarly, any facial part such as eye shape, lip size, and cheekbone can be altered using transformative makeup technique.

3.1.3 Designer Face Paint

Face painting is the artistic application of cosmetic paint to a person's face. In ancient times, face painting has been used for hunting, religious reasons, and military reasons; while in modern times it has become common for people to decorate their faces, especially cheeks. As a form of art, face painting is in general used in special events such as performance and festivals. Figure 5 shows two examples of face painting effect (before and after).

Designer face paint is a special case which can have both occlusion and transformation effect on face. Take Figure 6 (b) for example, not only the forehead is occluded, but the eyes, eyebrows, and lips are transformed by face painting. Thus, in later sections we will only study the effect and interference of occlusion and transformation as face paint camouflage has both effects.

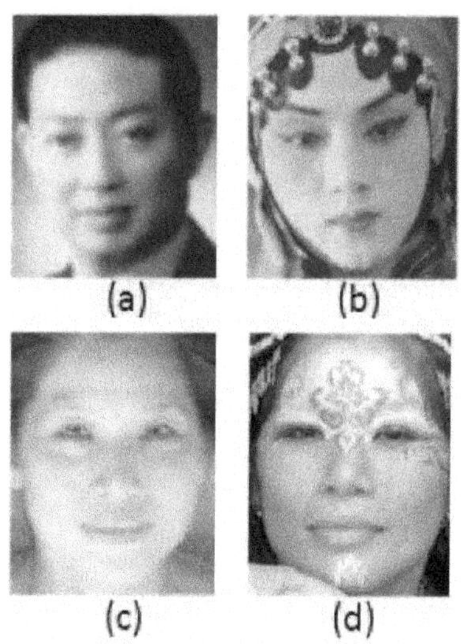

Figure 5. Effect of Face Painting: Peking Opera face painting before (a) and after (b). Casual face painting before (c) and after (d).

3.2 Camouflage Interference on Facial Feature

3.2.1 EigenFaces/FisherFaces

EigenFaces [14] is the most typical holistic representation in face recognition. It is based on lexicographic ordering of raw pixel values to yield one vector per image. And the dimensionality of the image vector corresponds directly to the size of the image in terms of pixels. Therefore, when the image is large, the high dimensional feature space slows or prohibits learning processing - the curse of dimensionality in the pattern recognition [13]. To deal with this, PCA (Principle Component Analysis) is employed in EigenFace and Linear Discriminant Analysis (LDA) is employed in FisherFace [15] to reduce the dimensionality. Theoretically, as performance increases with the dimension of the eigenspace, the Eigenface method does no better than correlation [16]. Thus, EigenFace is vulnerable to various illuminations, occlusions, expressions, etc.

As for FisherFace, though it outperforms EigenFaces with various illuminations and expressions, the performance drops rapidly when facial images are incomplete. This is because FisherFace tends to discount those portions of the face that are not significant for recognizing an individual, thus the reduced representation tends to mask the regions of the face that are highly variable (e.g. mouth area that is highly variable due to various expressions). The good (significant) features considered by FisherFace are stable ones such as face shape, nose, brows, and cheeks as they are relatively invariable across different illumination and expressions.

Now with a good understanding of how EigenFaces/FisherFace works, we can use corresponding fashion camouflages to exploit the weakpoints of the algorithms, thereby fooling them. From the discussion above, it is known that EgienFaces/FisherFace take a gallery of face images to generate compressed representation of face data during training; and find matches by comparing face data. In this scenario, occlusions on facial parts (face shape, cheek, nose) will achieve the goal of camouflage. Figure 6 show an example of using occlusions to make EigenFace and FisherFace incapable of recognizing Angelina Jolie.

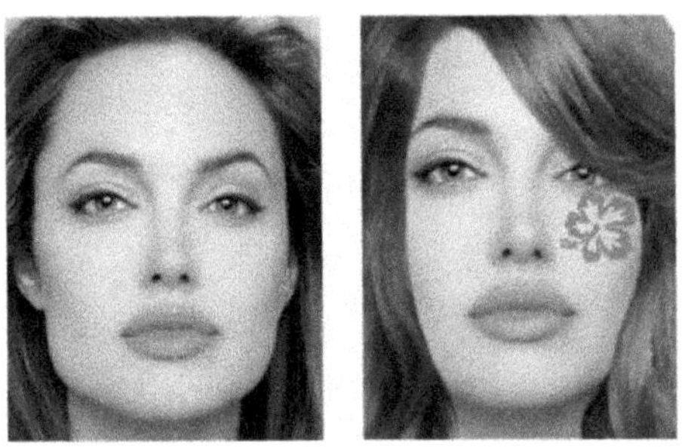

Figure 6. Facial Occlusions. (Left) Original Angelina Jolie facial image. (Right) Occlusion using hair and face sticker on the face on the left renders her unrecognizable.

3.2.2 Geometric Features

Early work using facial geometric features (e.g. ratios, distances) can be found in [17]. Later, researchers find more sophisticated features extraction techniques including vector of geometric features [18] (Figure 7(a)), Active Appearance Models [19] (Figure 7(b)), manually identified features [20] (Figure 7(c)), and Elastic Bunch Graphic Matching [21] (Figure 7(d)). Some techniques also combine geometric features together with other features (e.g. Gabor) to boost accuracy. Despite these variations of recognition techniques, the concept is basically to use distinct facial bio-geometrics on a subject face for recognition; and the accuracy of geometric feature-based method is highly dependent on the geometrical landmarks and geometrical constraints [22]. Moreover, no matter how the facial bio-geometric features are acquired (manually or located by algorithms), the key clue on getting the feature points are based on contour or gradient of the facial image; thus, whenever the facial parts are altered or occluded, the feature points and facial geometric features will be no longer accurate.

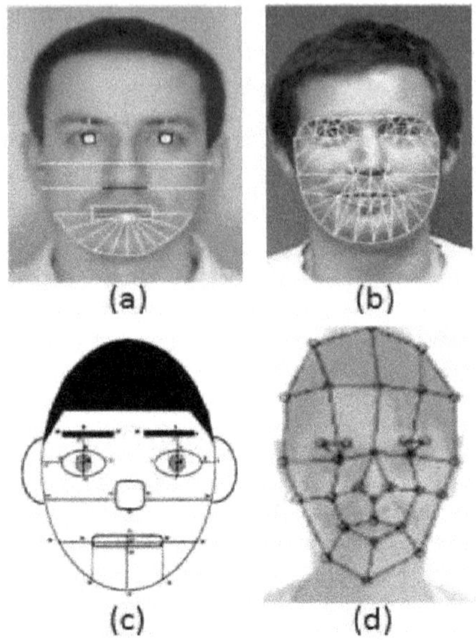

Figure 7. Various geometric features used in face recognition.

In this scenario, the goal of camouflage is to alter geometrics on face, such as face shape, eye shape, and lip size which can be achieved by Transformation camouflage. Figure 3 (b), (c) serves to illustrate this – the usage of makeup makes the geometric feature points on face different, and even inaccurate. As shown in the example in Figure 8 (a), the automatic fitted facial geometric landmarks fitting result (result is generated using Active Appearance Model [29]) gives a clear depiction of the subject's face; while on the transformed face (Figure 8 (b)) the fitting result is severely altered by the color shades created by makeup products.

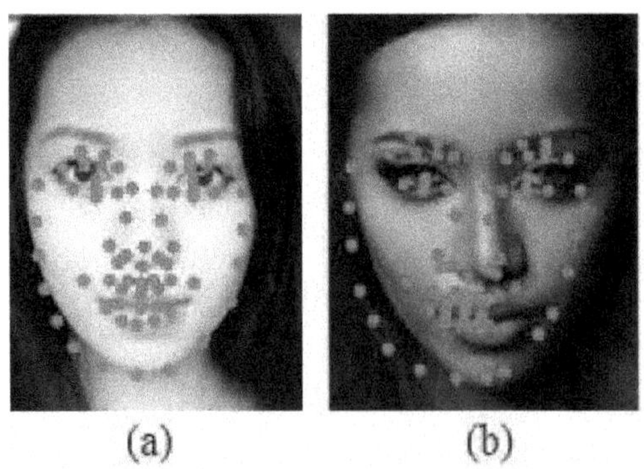

Figure 8. Example of transformation camouflage effects on Geometric Facial Features (results generated using Active Appearance Model [29]).

3.2.3 *Local Pattern/Features*

Unlike EigenFaces or geometric features that are extracted from the whole facial area, local patterns/features are extracted from a local area or patch from the facial image, e.g. eye area, or a 3*3 sized window area. The most popular local features used in face recognition systems are Local Binary Pattern [23] and Gabor Features [24]. In general, most of local areas from facial images are isolated using alignment first; and then patterns or features are extracted from each isolated local area; by combining all local features or patterns the final matching result will be given. Local feature based face recognition methods in general perform better because they are robust against local change on face while other parts of face remains unchanged.

In this scenario, the best way for fashion camouflage to trick local feature based algorithm is to alter two or more facial parts details – and this can be achieved using any type of camouflage: the occlusion, the transformation, or the designer facial paint. Figure 3(b)(c), Figure 5(a)(b) are good examples for altering local facial parts/features: it can be seen clearly that the face shape, the eye, the nose, and the lips are all different from the original look and this renders the subject unrecognizable. Moreover, as multiple facial local areas are altered by camouflage, the combined local features of face are no longer guaranteed to give correct face recognition results.

3.3 Camouflage Effectiveness

From the discussion in Section 3.2, we already know how to trick specific face recognition algorithms using certain types of camouflage. However, most existing face recognition systems (commercial or non-commercial) combine different features and techniques to achieve better accuracy. Take Figure 6 (Right) as an example, the occlusion camouflage is effective against EigenFace and FisherFace; however it is not effective against several other techniques such as biometric feature matching. Given an input face, we therefore, want to know how to maximize the camouflage effect across different face recognition algorithms - what position, what size, or which features to interfere with.

3.3.1 *Camouflage Positions*

In face recognition algorithms, no matter which features are extracted, contour (shape) information is one of the key factors. For example, as addressed in Section 3.2.1 the accuracy of FisherFace depends on whether a complete face shape is available; without contour information it will be very difficult to find facial geometric features or isolate each facial parts. Another example can be clearly seen in Figure 8 – the camouflage successfully confused the face recognition algorithm on extracting geometric facial features (the shape information). Thus, camouflages that can interfere with the contour or shape information would make the feature extraction more difficult and inaccurate for the algorithms. For example, by styling hair, one can successfully transform her face from square-face-looking into round-face-looking.

In this scenario, the positions of camouflage should be in general around the geometric facial contour regions - on the forehead that covers the upper face shape; around jawline and chin that covers the lower face shape; around the eyes that covers the eye contour; around the lip that covers the lip contour; or on the nose bridge that covers the nose contour. Figure 9 shows an illustration of all these effective camouflage areas on face.

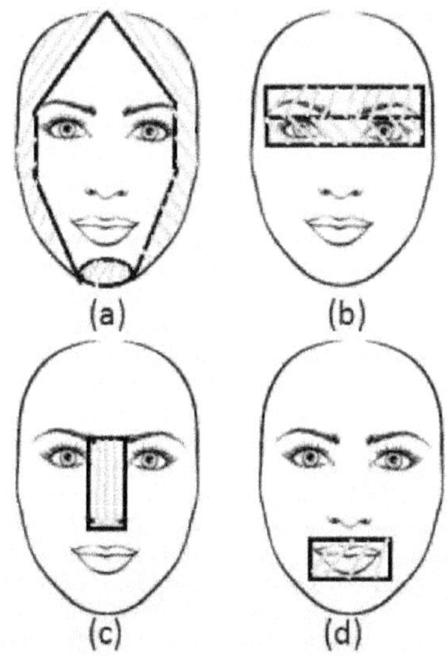

Figure 9. Effective camouflage positions: (a) face shape coverage; (b) eye/eyebrow coverage; (c) nose coverage; and (d) lip coverage.

3.3.2 *Camouflage Size*

The size of occlusion or painting could technically be as small as a dot, or as large as the whole face. When the size of occlusion or painting pattern increases, the result of camouflage in turn tends to get better. The example in Figure 10 demonstrates this: as the hair occlusion covers more facial area (the coverage percentages on face from (a) to (d) are ~15%, ~25%, ~35%, and ~50%), the return results (returned by Google [11] and Baidu [12]) of face search as less accurate. When the size of camouflage is as big as about half of the face (Figure 9(d)), no matching result is returned at all. This half-face-sized occlusion (Peek-A-Boo Bangs [25]) is a fashion style started since 1940s and it becomes a classic and beautiful style for any woman.

One thing to note here is that, the larger the camouflage is, the intention of occlusion is more obvious – this is not our goal. In this case the Peek-A-Boo Bangs is an exception since it is a well-accepted and applied style. In general, it is not desirable to have a more than 50% occlusion or painting on face on daily basis.

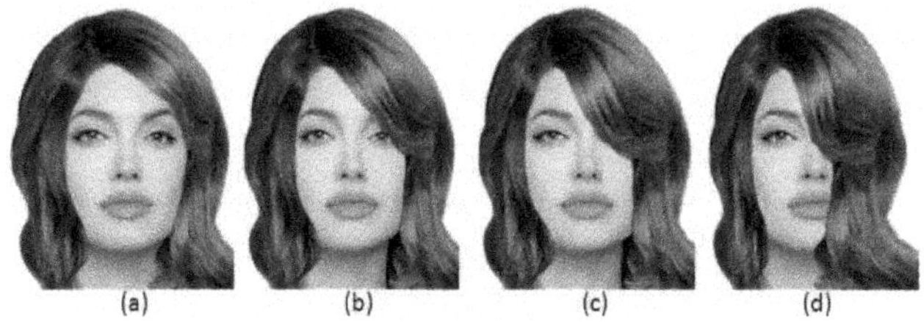

Figure 10. Effect of different sized camouflage.

3.3.3 *Prominent Facial Features for Camouflace*

Recall from Section 3.2, no matter what features are extracted, and what training method is used, the ultimate goal is to find the prominent features *PF* of one subject that can maximize the between-class difference and minimize within-class difference. This also works in cognitive science - people remember the most significant features of a face and recognize that feature to identify a subject. For example, Angelina Jolie is famous for her unique lips and face shape while Charlie Chaplin is famous for his hat and mustache. Thus, when we camouflage the prominent features *PF* on a subject's face the result is guaranteed to be effective. In this scenario, location of camouflage should be put on at/around the prominent facial parts. For example, in Figure 11 we show an example by camouflaging the lip area of Angelina Jolie (Figure 10(a)) by designer face painting (a black cat design [26]); and the top matched face returned (from Google and Baidu) for the camouflaged face (Figure 10(b)) is no longer Angelina Jolie. According to PicTriev [27], the similarity of Fig. 10(a) and Angelina Jolie is 80%; while the similarity drops to 23% for Fig. 10(b) when the lip is camouflaged.

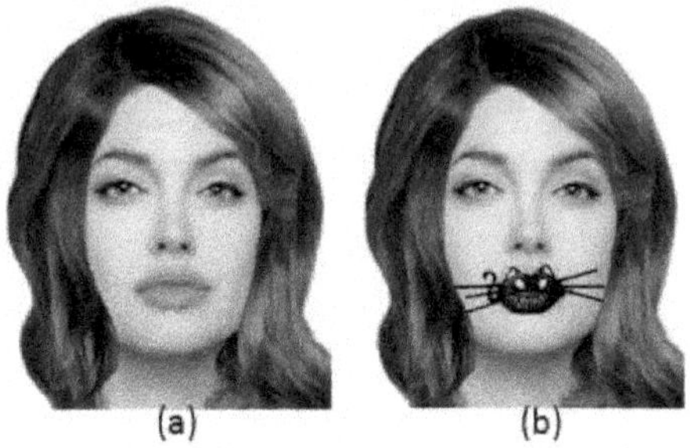

Figure 11. Example illustrating the camouflage of prominent facial features.

4. AUTO-CAMOUFLAGE SUGGESTIONS

From Section 3 we ascertain that the most effective camouflage is one that can camouflage the prominent features at the proper location with proper size. Based on this, we develop a tool that can facilitate camouflage art from a given input face by providing effective camouflage suggestions on prominent facial feature automatically.

4.1 Prominent Feature Extraction

In order to find the prominent features on face, we adopt the idea of automatic caricature generation by analyzing facial features [28], since the key characteristic of automatic caricature generation is to exaggerate the facial features that are not within the statistical normal range (e.g. Angelina Jolie's bigger-than-normal lips are always exaggerated in caricature).

In this paper, we divide the face area into 7 components: face shape, left eye, right eye, left eyebrow, right eyebrow, nose, and lip. And the Prominent Feature set ***PF*** is defined as any subset C' of the seven components C such that the geometric features of any face component C_i in C' is out of statistical normal range[3], where the geometric features extracted here are: (1) the ratio R_i of length to width of C_i, and (2) the size S_i of the C_i.

To find the prominent features that are out of normal range, it is necessary to perform quantitative analysis to obtain important statistics of the face components. Thus, we used 3755 facial images from the MUCT face dataset [30] for the measurement. Since the MUCT dataset has manually labeled landmarks (the illustration of the facial landmarks can be seen in Figure 12), thus the geometric features calculated from each face component C_i are presumably accurate. To compensate for the possible difference in imaging distance, we set the unit length to be the distance between the two inner eye corners. We also set the origin to be the midpoint between the two eyes. Aside from the normalized locations of the individual landmarks, the coordinates of the bounding box for each face component are also recorded.

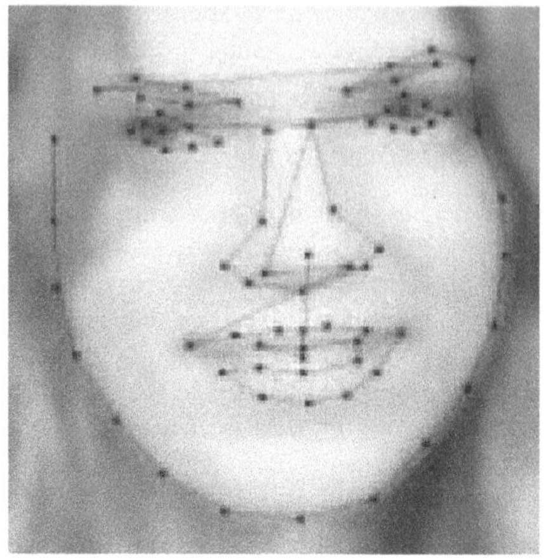

Figure 12. Illustration of 76 landmarks on face [30].

Table 1 lists some of the statistics of the resulting measurement. Note that these numbers were calculated using only middle 50% of the samples. This practice will limit the range of 'normal' samples and increase the chance of finding face components that are out of normal range.

With the statistic ranges set, for a given input face F, we first apply *Active Appearance Models* (AAM) [29] on the face to automatically get 76 landmarks on face (as shown in Figure 11). Then we calculate the geometric features of each component C_i, and if it is out of the statistical normal range, the component C_i is then put into the set of Prominent Features ***PF***.

Table 1. . Some statistics of face component measurement – the normal range of length to width ratio *R*.

Face Component	Normal Range
Face shape	1.1833 ~ 1.5179
Right eye	1.4921 ~ 1.7033
Left Eye	1.4921 ~ 1.7033
Right Eyebrow	3.9046 ~ 4.2738
Left Eyebrow	3.9046 ~ 4.2738
Nose	0.4478 ~ 0.5826
Lip	1.5731 ~ 2.1942

4.2 Camouflage Suggestions

Based on the discussion in Section 3, for each prominent facial feature (face component), we give the most effective camouflage types and suggestions. In some cases, certain type of camouflage can alter multiple components, e.g. a Bob hairstyle can cover face shape, eyebrows, and maybe partial eyes. In Figure 13 we give examples of each type of camouflages. Table 2 lists the effective camouflage type for each face component.

[3] In this paper, the *Statistical Normal Range* of facial geometric features is learned from quantitative analysis of 3755 subjects' facial geometric features and determined from the middle 50% of these samples.

It needs to be noted here that the intention of the work in this paper is to help the designers to create effective camouflage designs; not exact camouflage design patterns or options for the designers as designers have different tastes when creating a particular camouflage design. By understanding the fashion camouflage effect on face recognition algorithms and finding the prominent facial features ***PF*** of a subject's face *F*, we provide the tool to designers to give them a rough idea (e.g. what type of camouflage and where) about effective camouflage design for the subject and they can customize their own design based on it.

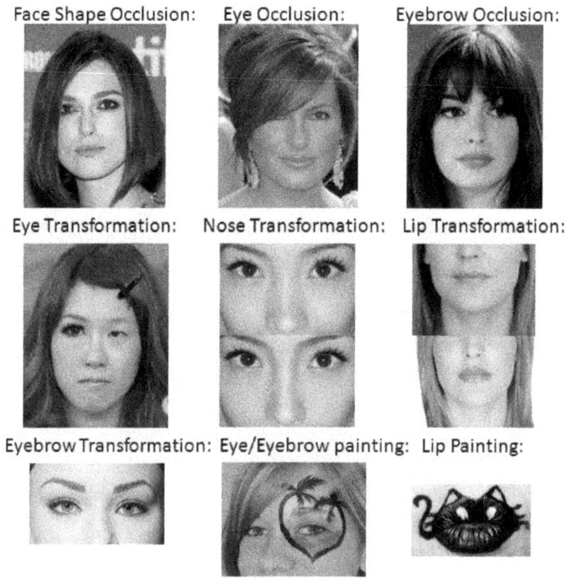

Figure 13. Examples of different types of camouflages on different face component.

Table 2. Effective camouflage types for each face component.

Face Component	Camouflage Type
Face shape	Hair Occlusion
Right eye	Occlusion, or Transformation, or Painting
Left Eye	Occlusion, or Transformation, or Painting
Right Eyebrow	Hair occlusion, or Transformation, or Painting
Left Eyebrow	Hair occlusion, or Transformation, or Painting
Nose	Transformation
Lip	Transformation, or Painting

5. EVALUATION AND APPLICATION

5.1 Evaluations

To evaluate the effectiveness of camouflage suggestions, we collected 1200 facial images of 40 celebrities with different styles, poses, illuminations, etc (Appendix A gives a full list of all these 40 celebrities). The reasons that we pick celebrity samples for evaluation are: (1) it is easy to collect a large number of samples of the same person with different conditions; (2) samples of celebrities have various fashion styles (hair, makeup), training on these samples will make the recognition robust against general facial changes; and thus if the camouflage suggestions are effective on celebrity samples, the suggestions will in general be effective on average people. All these collected sample images of celebrities are high-resolution images with normal illumination condition and they are all frontal or near-frontal facial images of the celebrities. Figure 14 givens one sample of Lucy Liu's frontal facial image and an example of camouflage suggestion for Lucy Liu.

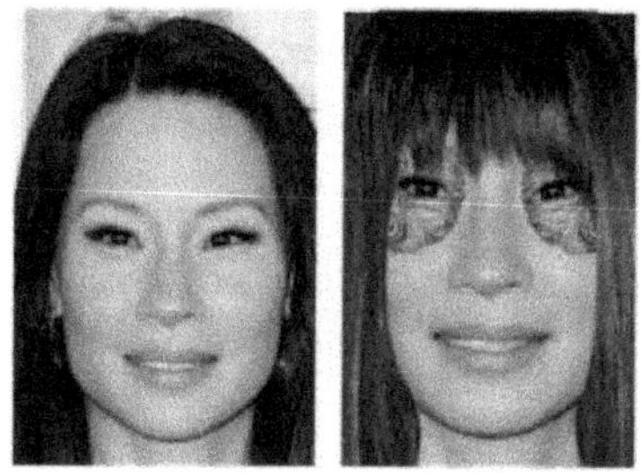

Figure 14. Camouflage Suggestion for Lucy Liu.

To evaluate the effectiveness of camouflage suggestions, we selected one default hair style (Figure 15(a)), two default eye paints (Figure 15(b)), one default lip paint (Figure 15(c)), one default color/shades for nose transformation (Figure 15(d)), and one face paint design for chin occlusion (Figure 15(e)). In this paper, we choose only these fixed camouflage designs and apply these camouflage effects on the subjects' face using digital image processing software (e.g. PhotoShop) for experiments and performance evaluation as we do not have fashion designers involved in the project yet (examples of camouflaged face generated in this paper can be seen in Appendix B). However, in the short future we will invite volunteers and beauty consultants to generate designers' camouflage facial images for future performance evaluation.

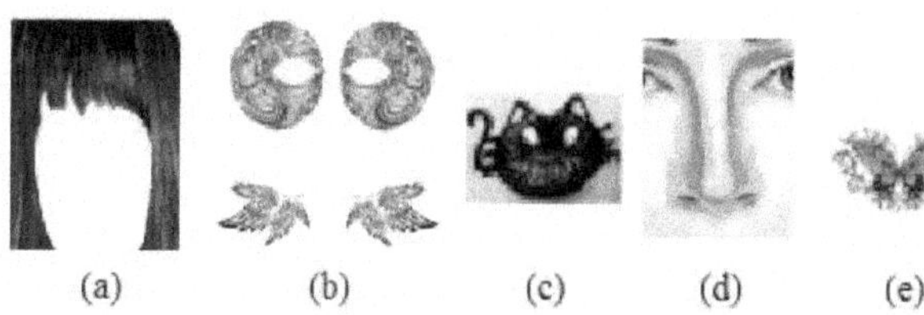

Figure 15. The default camouflage patterns used in the experiments in this paper.

For each input facial image, based on the suggestions, the default camouflage is applied to the face. We evaluated the suggestions on different face recognition systems: EigenFaces, FisherFace, Elastic Bunch Graphic Matching (EBGM), Local Binary Pattern (LBP), Gabor, Google+, PicTriev, and Baidu (the last three are commercial face recognition systems, and the last two do not require training). If the face recognition system still recognizes the celebrity, then the camouflage suggestion fails; otherwise the camouflage is successful. To evaluate the performance of suggested camouflage, we query the 40 camouflaged facial images generated according to the suggestions and collect the matching results. Successful Camouflage Rate (*SCR*) is used as evaluation metric that is calculated using Equation 1. Table 3 gives the evaluation results (the *SCR* over eight different face recognition systems).

$$SRC = \frac{number\ of\ unrecognized\ subjects}{number\ of\ all\ subjects} \times 100\%$$

Equation 1.

Table 3. Evaluation Result of camouflage suggestions.

Face recognition Systems	Successful Camouflage Rate (*SCR*)
EigenFace	100%
FisherFace	100%
EBGM	85%
LBP	90%
Gabor	87.5%
Google+	85%
PicTriev	82.5%
Baidu	90%

From Table 3, we can find that the camouflage suggestions work effectively (85% ~ 100%) on each single type of non-commercial face recognition algorithms.

As for the commercial face recognition systems (Google+, PicTriev, and Baidu), since these systems combines several face recognition algorithms to make the matching results more accurate, the camouflage suggestions are less effective compared with non-commercial algorithm overall. Further analysis on these three commercial face recognition system finds that: (1) PicTriev is a commercial website designed for celebrity matching which has better pre-knowledge (training) from a large set of celebrity sample images; thus the camouflage suggestions are least effective on PicTriev. (2) Unlike PicTriev, Baidu is a newly launched service which mainly serves in China, and thus has less pre-knowledge about western celebrities (the 40 celebrities selected are mostly American singers, pop star, etc) – therefore the suggested camouflage works as effective as LBP (the non-commercial face recognition algorithm). (3) As mentioned earlier, unlike the service provided by PicTriev and Baidu, Google+ requires manual training (Google+ service is similar to Facebook auto-tagging, the training is updated based on manual label each time), and thus the training on Goolge+ is the same as those non-commercial algorithms.

The overall effectiveness (***Successful Camouflage Rate***) of the suggested camouflage is satisfying over the celebrities sample set. As discussed before, if the camouflage suggestions are effective on celebrity samples, the camouflage suggestions will in general be effective on average people. (as the samples of celebrities have various styles (hair, makeup) which helps with robust training).

5.2 Applications

As mentioned before, the main motivations for our study in this paper is to facilitate artists or designers to efficiently create camouflage design that can make face unrecognizable for machines. For any input face, the tool will automatically find the prominent face components and then give suggestions about where to put the design and which type of the designs would be most effective. This study targets at helping artists or fashion designers to create an alternative facial appearance that is unrecognizable for a subject from computer vision perspectives; while we do not encourage criminal usage of this tool. Moreover, the camouflage design is supposed to be artistic, which is also presumably not suitable for any criminal usage.

On the other hand, as face recognition serves in various important application areas such as security check, the study in this paper also helps the researchers to pinpoint the weak points of current face recognition systems. And further by understanding the camouflage interferences and effects, the researchers in face recognition can find robust algorithms to identify faces while there are camouflages or disguises.

6. FUTURE WORK AND CONCLUSIONS

6.1 Future Work

As a pioneer, CV Dazzle started exploring fashion camouflage art for anti-face-recognition. Within the last several decades, researchers have put significant effort in making face recognition algorithms more and more accurate; while little or no work has been done on "hacking" these algorithms to fail them. Moreover, there is quite a few studies on tackling face recognition under fashion variations. In this paper, we define three types of fashion camouflage, and explore the camouflage effect on certain features in the purpose of privacy protection. However, we believe these to be only the tip of the iceberg, and future work should explore more on the characteristics of fashion camouflage effect on face recognition and further quantify the effect and study each type of camouflage's effect on different facial features. We also suggest exploring better methods on how to locate prominent facial features.

In this paper, all experimental images are simulated using image morphing algorithm or generated by image processing tool (e.g. PhotoShop); and the fashion touch up is based on the research done by Adam Harvey (author of CV Dazzle). In the short future, we will invite several fashion consultants and make up specialists and volunteers to get realistic facial images with fashion camouflage effect for studies and experiments.

6.2 Conclusions

In this paper, we define three types of fashion camouflages and explore their effects on certain facial features. Based on the comprehensive study of fashion camouflages, we develop a tool that can facilitate digital art design for fashion camouflage with the goal of anti-face-recognition. This tool can first find the prominent facial features from input facial image; and then give suggestions for camouflage options (makeup, styling, paints) on particular facial components from computer vision perspectives to artists. Evaluation of this tool shows that it can effectively aid the artists or designers in creating effective (thwarting) camouflage designs. The evaluation on suggested camouflages that applied on 40 celebrities across eight different face recognition systems (both non-commercial or commercial) shows that 82.5% ~ 100% of times the subject is unrecognizable using the suggested camouflage.

7. ACKNOWLEDGMENTS

The authors would like to thank Adam Harvey (the author of CV Dazzle) for encouragement and support.

This material is based upon work supported by National Science Foundation under Grant No. 1012975. Any opinions, findings, and conclusions or recommendations expressed in this material are those of the author(s) and do not necessarily reflect the views of National Science Foundation.

8. REFERENCES

[1] Harvey, A. 2010. CV Dazzle: Camouflage from Computer Vision. Available at: http://cvdazzle.com/

[2] Viola, P., and Jones, M. J. 2004. Robust Real-Time Face Detection. *Int. J. Comput. Vision*57, 2 (May 2004), 137-154.

[3] Sky Biometry. Available at: http://www.skybiometry.com/

[4] Ramanathan, N., Chowdhury, A., and Chellappa, R. 2004. Facial similarity across age, disguise, illumination and pose, in *Proceedings of International Conference on Image Processing*, 3, 1999-2002.

[5] Singh, R., Vatsa, M., and Noore A., 2009. Face recognition with disguise and single gallery images. *Image and Vision Computing*, 27, 3, 245-257.

[6] Phillips, J., Todd Scruggs, W., O'Toole, A.J., Flynn, P. J., Bowyer, K.W., Schott, C.L., and Sharpe, M. 2007. *FRVT 2006 and ICE 2006 Large-Scale Results*. NISTIR 7408.

[7] DIS Magazine, 2013. How to Hide from Machines. Available at: http://dismagazine.com/dystopia/evolved-life-styles/8115/anti-surveillance-how-to-hide-frommachines/

[8] Davis, G., and Hall, M. 2012. *The Makeup Artist Handbook: Techniques for Film, Television, Photography, and Theatre*. Taylor & Francis US.

[9] Luckiesh, M. 1922. *Visual Illusion: Their Causes, Characteristics and Applications*. D. Van Nostrand Company, New York.

[10] Phan, M. 2012. Michelle Phan Tutorials. Available at: http://michellephan.com/blog/cat/tutorials

[11] Google+/Google Picasa Face Recognition. 2012.

[12] Baidu Face Search. 2013. Available at: http://stu.baidu.com/

[13] Duda, R. O., Hart, P. E., and Stork, D. G. 2001. *Pattern Classification*, Wiley Interscience.

[14] Sirovich, L., Kirby, M. 1987. Low-dimensional procedure for the characterization of human faces. Journal of the Optical Society of America. 4 (3): 519–524.

[15] Belhumeur, P., Hespanha, J., and Kriegman, D. 1997. Eigenfaces vs. Fisherfaces: Recognition Using Class Specific Linear Projection, *IEEE Transactions on Pattern Analysis and Machine Intelligence*, 19(7):711—720.

[16] Brunelli, R., and Poggio, T. 1993. "Face Recognition: Features vs. Templates," *IEEE Trans. Pattern Analysis and Machine* Intelligence, 15(10): 1042-1053.

[17] Kanade, T. 1973. *Picture Processing System by Computer Complex and Recognition of Human Faces*. doctoral dissertation, Kyoto University.

[18] Brunelli, R., Poggio, T. 1993. Face recognition: features versus templates, IEEE Transactions on Pattern Analysis and Machine Intelligence, 15(10): 1042-1052.

[19] Edwards, G. J., Cootes, T. F., Taylor, C. J. 1998. Face Recognition using Acitive Appearance Models. *In Proceedings of 5th European Conference on Computer Vision* (ECCV '98), 2: 581-595.

[20] Cox, I.J., Ghosn, J., and Yianilos, P.N. 1996. Feature-based face recognition using mixture-distance. *IEEE Conference on Computer Vision and Pattern Recognition* (CVPR '96), 209-216.

[21] Wiskott, L., Fellous, J.-M., Kruger, N., and Von der Malsburg, C. 1997. Face recognition by elastic bunch graph matching. International Conference on Image Processing, 1:129-132.

[22] Craw, I., Tock, D., and Bennett, A. 1992. Finding Face Features. In *Proceedings of 2nd European Conference on Computer Vision* (ECCV '92), Springer-Verlag, London, UK, 92-96.

[23] Ahonen, T., Hadid, A., and Pietikainen, M. 2006. Face Description with Local Binary Patterns: Application to Face Recognition, *IEEE Transactions on Pattern Analysis and Machine Intelligence*, 28(12): 2037-2041.

[24] Liu, C., and Wechsler, H. 2003. Independent component analysis of Gabor features for face recognition, IEEE Transactions on Neural Networks, 14(4): 919-928.

[25] Anderson, I. 2008. *1940s Hairstyle Book by Anderson (Vintage Hairstyling)*. Bramcost Publications.

[26] Animal Painted on Lips. 2011. Available at: http://toxel.com/

[27] PicTriev. 2013. Available at: http://www.pictriev.com

[28] Chiang, P., Liao, W., Li, T. 2004. Automatic Caricature Generation by Analyzing Facial Features, in *Proceeding of 2004 Asia Conference on Computer Vision* (ACCV2004).

[29] Cootes, T.F., Edwards, G.J,; and Taylor, C.J., Active appearance models, *IEEE Transactions on Pattern Analysis and Machine Intelligence*, 23(6): 681-685.

[30] Milborrow, S., Morkel, J., and Nicolls, F. 2010. The MUCT Landmarked Face Database, *Pattern Recognition Association of South Africa.*

APPENDIX A: Full list of 40 celebrities used for evaluation.

Adele
Adriana Lima
Amy Adams
Angelina Jolie
Anne Hathaway
Audrey Hepburn
Beyonce
Britney Spears
Cameron Diaz
Claudia Schiffer
Eva Longoria
Gisele Bundchen
Halle Berry
Isabelle Adjani
J. K. Rowling
Jaclyn Smith
Jane Pauley
Janet Evanovich
Jennifer Aniston
Jennifer Lopez
Jessica Alba
Jody Watley
Julia Roberts
Kate Hudson
Katy Perry
Keira Knightley
Khrystyne Haje
Louise Erdrich
Lucy Liu
Margo Timmins
Megan Fox
Michelle Pfeiffer
Natalie Portman
Nicole Kidman
Nicollette Sheridan
Oprah Winfrey
Paulina Porizkova
Talisa Soto
Taylor Swift
Vivian Wu

APPENDIX B: Samples of camouflaged celebrity facial images.

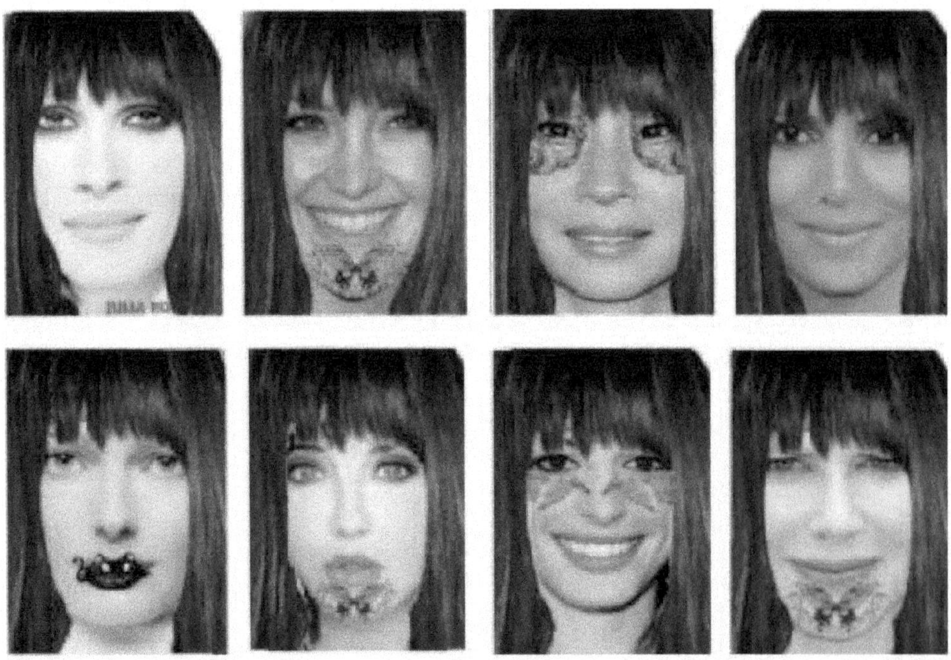

An Efficient Image Homomorphic Encryption Scheme with Small Ciphertext Expansion

Peijia Zheng, Jiwu Huang
School of Information Science and Technology
Sun Yat-Sen University
Guangzhou, 510006, China
peijiazh@gmail.com, isshjw@mail.sysu.edu.cn

ABSTRACT

The field of image processing in the encrypted domain has been given increasing attention for the extensive potential applications, for example, providing efficient and secure solutions for privacy-preserving applications in untrusted environment. One obstacle to the widespread use of these techniques is the ciphertext expansion of high orders of magnitude caused by the existing homomorphic encryptions. In this paper, we provide a way to tackle this issue for image processing in the encrypted domain. By using characteristics of image format, we develop an image encryption scheme to limit ciphertext expansion while preserving the homomorphic property. The proposed encryption scheme first encrypts image pixels with an existing probabilistic homomorphic cryptosystem, and then compresses the whole encrypted image in order to save storage space. Our scheme has a much smaller ciphertext expansion factor compared with the element-wise encryption scheme, while preserving the homomorphic property. It is not necessary to require additional interactive protocols when applying secure signal processing tools to the compressed encrypted image. We present a fast algorithm for the encryption and the compression of the proposed image encryption scheme, which speeds up the computation and makes our scheme much more efficient. The analysis on the security, ciphertext expansion ratio, and computational complexity are also conducted. Our experiments demonstrate the validity of the proposed algorithms. The proposed scheme is suitable to be employed as an image encryption method for the applications in secure image processing.

Categories and Subject Descriptors

K.6.5 [**Computing Milieux**]: Management of Computing and Information Systems—*Security and Protection*; H.4.m [**Information Systems**]: Information Systems Applications—*Miscellaneous*

MM'13, October 21–25, 2013, Barcelona, Spain.
Copyright 2013 ACM 978-1-4503-2404-5/13/10 ...$15.00.
http://dx.doi.org/10.1145/2502081.2502105.

General Terms

Algorithms, Security.

Keywords

image processing in the encrypted domain, ciphertext expansion reducing, homomorphic property, secure signal processing, efficient scheme, image encryption.

1. INTRODUCTION

Secure signal processing (SSP), also referred to as signal processing in the encrypted domain (s.p.e.d.), has attracted increasing attention in recent years [1] [2]. The main area of interest in this field is the manipulation of encryption data, in order to obtain the desired output in encrypted form. The development of techniques for secure signal processing promises extensive applications, especially the privacy-preserving applications in untrusted environment, such as privacy-preserving face recognition [3], privacy-preserving fingercode authentication [4], and privacy-preserving electrocardiogram (ECG) classification [5]. In order to prevent from illegal access and retrieval, cryptosystems are usually employed to encrypt the privacy-sensitive information. For example, in the application of privacy-preserving face recognition, we should encrypt both images captured from surveillance cameras in public places and facial templates stored in database of known suspects for privacy protection.

Cryptosystems play an important role in secure signal processing. Not all the existing cryptosystems are suitable to be used as encryption tools for s.p.e.d. applications. For most of the popular cryptosystems, such as Data Encryption Standard (DES), Advanced Encryption Standard (AES), and Blowfish Encryption, there are not available algebraic relations between the plaintext and the ciphertext spaces. Once the data are encrypted with those cryptosystems, it is impossible to manipulate the ciphertexts to change the value of the plaintexts. Fortunately, there are a special kind of cryptosystems, called the homomorphic cryptosystems, are able to keep certain algebraic structures from the plaintext space to the ciphertext space. With homomorphic cryptosystems, someone can perform the desired operations on the plaintexts by means of manipulating the corresponding ciphertexts.

The concept of homomorphic cryptosystem was first introduced as a privacy homomorphism by Rivest *et al.* [6], where privacy homomorphism is defined to have the property allowing ciphertexts to be operated without being decrypted into plaintexts in advance. The existing homomorphic cryptosystems are generally classified into two types, partially homomorphic cryptosystems and fully homomorphic cryptosystems. Partially homomorphic cryptosystems keep the relation of addition or multiplication between plaintexts and ciphertexts, such as the ElGamal cryptosystem [7], the Paillier cryptosystem [8], and the Damgård-Jurik cryptosystem [9]; while fully homomorphic cryptosystems permit to compute additions and multiplications homomorphically, and therefore allows the computation of any polynomials in the encrypted domain. For example, Gentry's fully homomorphic encryption scheme [10] works on binary values, and thus corresponds to the computation of any logical circuits. Another important concept is the probabilistic cryptosystem which is proposed by Goldwasser *et al.* [11]. With probabilistic cryptosystems, one can obtain different ciphertexts after different encryption procedures, no matter the input plaintexts are identical or not. There are cryptosystems satisfy the homomorphic and probabilistic properties, such as the Paillier cryptosystem [8] and the Damgård-Jurik cryptosystem [9].

There have been some reports on secure signal processing over the past few years. In [12] [13] [14] [15], some of the popular signal transforms have been implemented in the encrypted domain. A data encrypting method, which packs several samples as a single one, was proposed by Troncoso-Pastoriza *et al.* [16] and later generalized by Bianchi *et al.* [17]. The authors provide an effective approach to save storage space of the ciphertexts of samples, though the freedom of the packed samples is restricted by the packing method. In [3], Erkin *et al.* proposed a privacy-preserving face recognition system, which hides both the biometric data and the authentication result from the server. Sadeghi *et al.* [18] presented an efficient privacy-preserving face recognition scheme by using the garbled circuit technique. Barni *et al.* [5] proposed a system for the secure classification of electrocardiogram (ECG) signals with branching programs and neural networks. Some literature [4] has concentrated on the development of privacy-preserving fingercode authentication. Hsu *et al.* [19] proposed a privacy-preserving realization of image feature extraction in the encrypted domain.

However, applying the probabilistic homomorphic cryptosystems to SSP applications cause a problem, i.e., the storage space expansion of high orders of magnitude after encrypting plaintexts to ciphertexts [20]. For example, the ciphertext expansion of the Paillier cryptosystem has two orders of magnitude, and becomes more serous in image processing applications in the encrypted domain. The ciphertext expansion has become one of the main reasons to delay the widespread use of SSP techniques in practice. In this paper, we provide a new way to solve the problem of ciphertext expansion for the image processing applications in the encrypted domain. Since the image information is highly structured [21], it is reasonable to protect the image content by destroying the image structure. Based on this, we propose an image encryption scheme to achieve content protection. In order to reduce the storage space of ciphertexts, we represent ciphertexts of image pixels with small value indexes. Compared with the decompressed encrypted image, the compressed encrypted image has much smaller ciphertext expansion factor, which makes the proposed image encryption scheme useful for image processing applications in the encrypted domain. Furthermore, it is not necessary to design additional interactive protocols to apply the existing SSP tools to the compressed encrypted image. We prove that the compression procedure is theoretically secure and show that our encryption scheme can well protect the image content in security.

The remainder of this paper is organized as follows. Section 2 gives an introduction to the existing encryption methods in secure signal processing. In Section 3, we propose an image encryption scheme as well as its fast algorithm. We give detailed analyses on the security, ciphertext expansion, and computational cost in Section 4. Section 5 shows some experiments and investigates the perception security of the proposed encryption scheme. We conclude our paper in Section 6.

2. IMAGE ENCRYPTION METHOD IN SECURE SIGNAL PROCESSING

The image encryption method builds the foundation of image processing applications in the encrypted domain. In the field of s.p.e.d., data encryption schemes are required to have the homomorphic property. However, data encryption schemes are more preferred for practical SSP applications, if the following three properties are satisfied.

1. **Homomorphic.** The homomorphic property builds the foundation of most of the developed SSP tools.

2. **Non-Interactive.** An encryption scheme, which has the non-interactive property of sample-wise encryption scheme, will make the design of SSP applications based on it much more convenient and efficient.

3. **Tolerable Ciphertext Expansion.** Small ciphertext expansion will greatly reduce the overheads of storage, computation, and communication, which are considered to be very crucial in practice.

It is not an easy task to develop an image encryption scheme satisfying the above three properties. To the best of our knowledge, there exists no such image encryption scheme in the field of s.p.e.d.. There are some works which study the compression of the encrypted sequence, such as [22]. In the case of applying this technique in s.p.e.d., however, the whole computational cost will be more expensive than the homomorphic encryption procedure. There are two data encryption methods widely used in the field of s.p.e.d.. In the following, we provide a brief review of these two methods.

2.1 Element-Wise Encryption Scheme

In mathematics, a gray scale image is usually expressed by a matrix whose elements are integers ranging from 0 to 255. To encrypt a sequence, one way is to encrypt separately every element with certain cryptosystem and then place ciphertexts in sequence to form a sequence of ciphertext. This encryption method is sometime called element-wise encryption scheme or sample-wise encryption scheme. Concerning the security of the element-wise encryption scheme, if we work with a probabilistic cryptosystem, then all elements are securely mapped to distinct ciphertexts and therefore the security is automatically achieved. Furthermore, if the probabilistic cryptosystem employed has the homomorphic property, the element-wise scheme obviously satisfies the homomorphic property. Since all the encrypted elements remain independent, it is not necessary to design additional

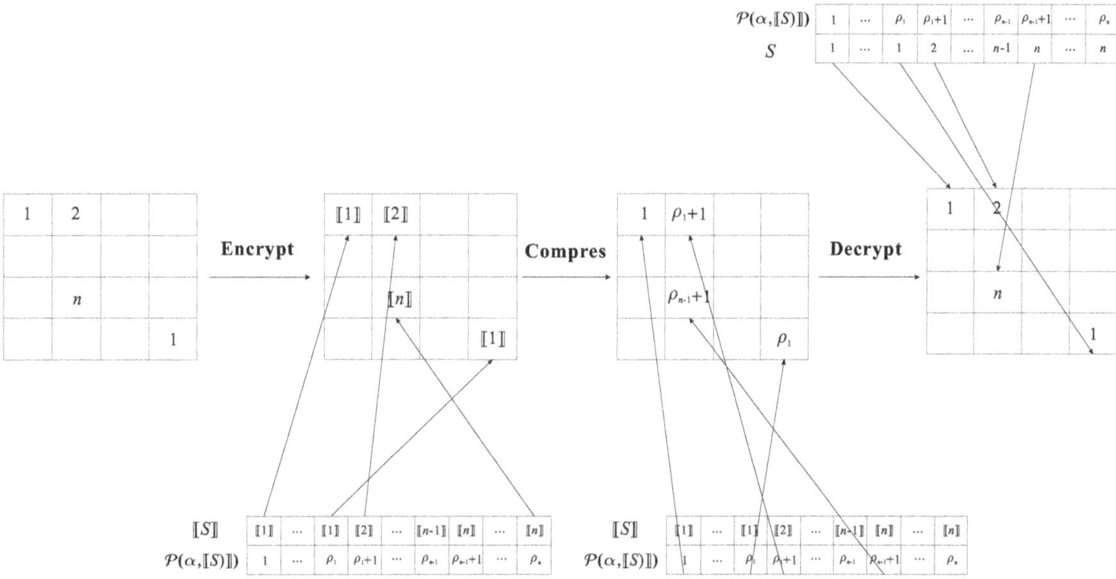

Figure 1: The framework of the proposed image encryption scheme. For simplicity, we do not draw the RandPermut procedure in this sketch.

interactive protocols to unpack encrypted signals for applying SSP tools. That is, the element-wise scheme satisfies the non-interactive property. Thanks to the homomorphic and the non-interactive properties, the element-wise encryption scheme is extensively used in the field of s.p.e.d..

However, the employment of a probabilistic homomorphic cryptosystem will make the element-wise encryption scheme cause serious ciphertext expansion, especially in the case of image processing in the encrypted domain. Let us consider the following example. A gray scale image is encrypted with the element-wise encryption scheme by using a Paillier cryptosystem whose modulus N is 1024 bits. Each pixel is an 8-bits-length integer, while the corresponding encrypted pixel is 2048 bits. Thus, the storage space of the encrypted image is expanded by 256 times, compared with the plaintext image. The huge ciphertext expansion induce heavy overhead of storage, computation, and communication, which limit the widely use of SSP tools in practice.

2.2 The Packing Method

Generally, the bit-length of samples of digital signals is always much shorter than the bit-length of the cryptosystem's modulus N. In order to make a better utilization of the bit-length of N, Troncoso-Pastoriza *et al.* [16] proposed a packing method, in which several elements are packed as a word and then the word is encrypted to obtain a ciphertext. Specifically, assume every element in the signal sequence can be expressed by a l-bits number. For any n samples $m_0, m_1, \ldots, m_{n-1}$, the encrypted packed ciphertext can be given as

$$[\![m_{\text{packed}}]\!] = \left[\!\!\left[\sum_{i=0}^{n-1} m_i \cdot 2^{\lambda i}\right]\!\!\right] \quad (1)$$

where $[\![\cdot]\!]$ is the encryption operator. λ denotes the bit-length allocated to each element in N. In order to prevent data confusion, $l \leq \lambda$ and $n\lambda \leq N$ are required. After performing processing on the encrypted packed ciphertext $[\![m_{\text{packed}}]\!]$, one should unpack the packed result to extract the desired result of the element m_i, $i = 0, 1, \ldots, n-1$. The unpacking procedure can be accomplished by using the `BITREP` protocol, which is proposed by Schoenmakers *et al.* [23]. Bianchi *et al.* [17] generalized the packing method by using any integer value B as the basis instead of some power of 2, in order to gain flexibility in the choice of the number of elements that can be packed into a single ciphertext. The packing procedure is then given as

$$[\![m_{\text{packed}}]\!] = \left[\!\!\left[\sum_{i=0}^{n'-1} m_i \cdot B^{i}\right]\!\!\right] \quad (2)$$

where $2^l \leq B$ and $n \log_2 B \leq N$. However, the design of efficient protocols which make the unpacking procedure applicable remains an open problem.

By exploiting a probabilistic homomorphic cryptosystem, the packing method satisfies the homomorphic property. The packing method can reduce the ciphertext expansion to make some SSP tools applicable in practice, and therefore satisfies the tolerable ciphertext expansion property.

However, since several elements are packed into a single ciphertext and manipulations are always applied to the packed ciphertext, all the packed elements undergo the same manipulations. It is therefore impossible to apply different manipulations to the packed elements, without interactive protocols. For example, it becomes a hard task to perform discrete Fourier transform (DFT) or discrete wavelet transform (DWT) on the whole image in the encrypted domain with the packing method. Thus, the packing method do not satisfies the non-interactive property. Furthermore, since the packed elements share the bit-length of the cryptosystem's modulus, the assigned data space for each element becomes smaller. For example, if n elements are packed into a single ciphertext with a Paillier cryptosystem, then the bit-length allocated to each element is only $\frac{N}{n}$ rather than N. Due to the characteristics of s.p.e.d., manipulations performed on encrypted signals will enlarge the value of plaintexts [12] [24]. Thus, the packing method limits the number of manipulations that can be correctly performed on encrypted signals, in order to avoid data overflow and underflow in the plaintext domain.

3. IMAGE ENCRYPTION SCHEME WITH SMALL CIPHERTEXT EXPANSION

In this section, we study the data characteristic of digital image and then propose an image encryption scheme which has the homomorphic property, non-interactive property, and small ciphertext expansion.

3.1 Proposed Algorithms

We summary two data characteristics of digital images. One characteristic is that digital images are highly structured [21] and partible. If we divide an image into non-overlapping blocks, then the image can be seen as a union of these blocks. The pixel values in the same block exhibit strong correlation in statistics. This characteristic is exploited extensively to develop industry standards and image applications. For example, the image coding standard JPEG [25], firstly splits the image into non-overlapping blocks and then encodes the discrete cosine transform (DCT) coefficients in every block. The other characteristic is that the number of pixels is much larger than the range of pixel values. For example, the pixel value of a gray scale image of 512×512 ranges from 0 to 255, while the number of pixels is 262144. According to the pigeonhole principle, at least one pixel value must appear no fewer than 1024 times. Thus, in the case that the image is encrypted with the element-wise encryption scheme, at least one pixel value must be encrypted to be 1024 different ciphertexts.

Based on the mentioned characteristics, we propose an image homomorphic encryption scheme to protect the contents of images and to preserve encrypted images in small storage space. In Fig. 1, we show the framework of the image encryption scheme, including the encryption, compression, and decryption. Firstly, we split the image into non-overlapping blocks and choose a sequence of ciphertexts encrypted componentwise with a probabilistic homomorphic encryption. We denote the sequence of ciphertexts by $[\![S]\!]$. Secondly, in each block, every pixel is encrypted with the element in $[\![S]\!]$, to make sure the encryption in each block is identical to the element-wise encryption scheme. A random permutation procedure is then employed to destroy the weak correlation between the blocks. Thus, the content of the image is well protected. Thirdly, since the number of the elements in $[\![S]\!]$ is less than the number of the pixels in the image, there are some encrypted pixels which have the same value. By exploiting a compression method, we express the ciphertexts of the same pixel value with the position of an element in $[\![S]\!]$ and therefore succeed in reducing the storage space of the encrypted image. In our scheme, all the pixels are encrypted with the probabilistic homomorphic encryption. Attackers cannot obtain the pixel values from their ciphertexts. The structural information expressed by the same pixel value among difference blocks is protected by the random permutation. It is difficult for attackers to recognize the image content from an encrypted image.

3.2 Encryption

Suppose the plaintext image is denoted by $I=\{I(x,y)\}$, $\forall x,y=0,1,\ldots,M-1$. Our image encryption scheme begins with the sequence of ciphertexts, whose plaintexts are in the interval from 0 to 255 and are encrypted with a probabilistic homomorphic cryptosystem, e.g., the Paillier cryptosystem. We use S to denote the sequence of the decryption of $[\![S]\!]$. If ρ_i denotes the number of the pixel value i in S, we have a vector

$$\boldsymbol{\rho}=(\rho_0,\rho_1,\cdots,\rho_{255}). \tag{3}$$

We make the distribution of S, i.e., the vector $\boldsymbol{\rho}$ similar to the histogram of I. There are many ways to achieve this goal. We provide one specific method in the following.

$$\rho_i=\left\lceil\frac{n_i}{Q}\right\rceil,\ i=0,1,\cdots,255 \tag{4}$$

where n_i denotes the number of the pixel value i in I, and Q is the scaling factor. The number of elements in $[\![S]\!]$ or S is equal to the L_1 norm of $\boldsymbol{\rho}$ - i.e., $\|\boldsymbol{\rho}\|_1\triangleq\rho$. We define ρ as the length of $[\![S]\!]$ or S.

We permute randomly the elements in $[\![S]\!]$ to obtain the out-of-order $[\![S]\!]$. The random permutation procedure leads to that the plaintexts of elements in $[\![S]\!]$ are independent to their positions, and therefore makes sure attackers cannot deduce the plaintext of the element in $[\![S]\!]$ from its position.

Thanks to the probabilistic property, different encryptions of the pixel value i yield different ciphertexts. Thus, there are not two elements in $[\![S]\!]$ which have the same values. We use $[\![S_\beta]\!]$ to denote the subsequence of $[\![S]\!]$, which consists of all the elements in $[\![S]\!]$ whose plaintexts are equal to β, i.e.,

$$[\![S_\beta]\!]=\{\alpha\in[\![S]\!]\,|\mathcal{D}[\alpha]=\beta\},\ \beta=0,1,\cdots,255 \tag{5}$$

where $\mathcal{D}[\cdot]$ is the decryption operator. The sequence of the decryption of $[\![S_\beta]\!]$ is denoted by S_β, i.e.,

$$S_\beta=\{\mathcal{D}[\alpha]\,|\alpha\in[\![S_\beta]\!]\},\ \beta=0,1,\cdots,255. \tag{6}$$

The image I is firstly split into non-overlapping blocks of $n\times n$. Thus there are totally $M_b=(M/n)^2$ blocks after the splitting. Let us denote these blocks by $\{X_1,X_2,\ldots,X_{M_b}\}$. The image encryption procedure is carried out block by block. In block X_j, the pixel value β is encrypted to be one element in $[\![S_\beta]\!]$. In order to make that every element in $[\![S_\beta]\!]$ is chosen with equal probability, the element in $[\![S_\beta]\!]$ will be chosen in sequence. Specifically, if the j-th element $\alpha_{\beta,j}$ in $[\![S_\beta]\!]$ has been chosen, we will choose the $(j+1)$-th element $\alpha_{\beta,j+1}$ in $[\![S_\beta]\!]$ when the pixel value β appears again in the image I. When all elements in $[\![S_\beta]\!]$ have been chosen, we randomly permute the elements in $[\![S_\beta]\!]$ before the element in $[\![S_\beta]\!]$ is chosen again. For convenience, we use RandPermut to denote the algorithm randomly permuting the elements in a sequence, and then the random permutation procedure can be given as

$$[\![S_\beta]\!]\leftarrow\mathsf{RandPermut}([\![S_\beta]\!]). \tag{7}$$

In this stage, the function of the random permutation procedure of $[\![S_\beta]\!]$ is to protect the image content by using disturbing, especially in the case that the image texture is consisting of the same pixel value. We show a simple example in Fig. 2.

Let us denote the number of the pixel value i in block X_j by $num(i,X_j)$. If $num(i,X_j)$ is not larger than the number of the corresponding pixel value i in S - i.e., $num(i,X_j)\leq\rho_i\ \forall i=0,1,\cdots,255$, then all the ciphertexts of block X_j are different from each other, no matter their plaintexts are the same or not. In other words, the encryption procedure of our

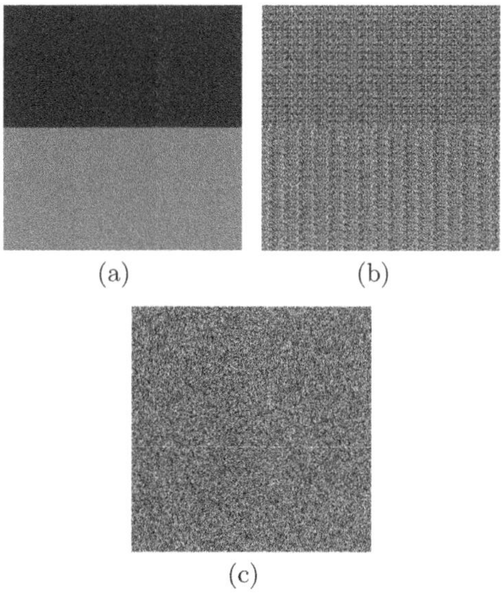

Figure 2: The function of RandPermut($[\![S_\beta]\!]$). (a) Original image; (b) Encryption without involving RandPermut; (c) Encryption with RandPermut.

image encryption scheme in block X_j achieves the same effect as the element-wise encryption scheme does. Thus, our image encryption scheme is effective to protect the contents of every block X_j, and the whole image I further. The image encryption scheme satisfies the homomorphic property, for the employment of a probabilistic homomorphic cryptosystem in the initialization of $[\![S]\!]$.

Note that, when ρ is large enough, our proposal is identical to the element-wise encryption scheme. However, when ρ is too small, the elements in $[\![S]\!]$ will appear too frequently and are unable to break the image structure. The image content is then unprotected. In the following, we will denote the ciphertext matrices of block X_j and the whole encrypted image of I by $[X_j]$ and $[I]$, respectively.

3.3 Compression

The storage space of the encrypted image $[I]$ is the same as the one with the element-wise encryption scheme. We propose a compression procedure to reduce the storage space of $[I]$. The practical applications require N to be at least 1024 bits to ensure the security. Some standards and applications even require N to be longer than 1024 bits. However, the size of $[\![S]\!]$ can be much smaller. For example, in order to make the encryption of block X_j has the same effect as the element-wise encryption scheme, let us consider the boundary condition $\rho_i = \max_j\{num(i, X_j)\}$ $\forall i = 0, 1, \cdots, 255$. Since every $num(i, X_j)$ is less than the number of elements in one block, we have

$$\rho_i = \max_j\{num(i, X_j)\} \le n^2, \tag{8}$$

$$\rho = \sum_{i=0}^{255} \rho_i \le 256n^2 \ll N^2. \tag{9}$$

Without loss of generality, we assume the size of $[\![S]\!]$ is less than the square of the size of the cryptosystem's modulus, i.e., $\rho < N^2$. For convenience, we introduce a two place function $\mathcal{P}(\cdot,\cdot)$, which outputs the position of the first variable in the second variable. Specifically, $\mathcal{P}(\alpha, [\![S]\!])$ denotes the position of α in sequence $[\![S]\!]$. For any $\alpha \in [I]$, there is one position of α in $[\![S]\!]$; and for any value k less than ρ, there is one ciphertext in $[\![S]\!]$ whose position is k. Thus, the encrypted image $[I]$ can be compressed as a matrix $\{\mathcal{P}(\alpha, [\![S]\!])\}_{\alpha\in[I]} \triangleq \mathcal{P}([I], [\![S]\!])$ and a sequence $[\![S]\!]$. We give a detailed storage space comparison between the decompressed encrypted image $[I]$ and the compressed encrypted image $\{\mathcal{P}([I], [\![S]\!]), [\![S]\!]\}$ in Section 4.2.

The compressed encrypted image $\{\mathcal{P}([I], [\![S]\!]), [\![S]\!]\}$ can be decompressed into $[I]$ by using a look-up table operation, as shown in Fig. 1. Specifically, given any element $\mathcal{P}(\alpha, [\![S]\!])$ in $\mathcal{P}([I], [\![S]\!])$ and the sequence $[\![S]\!]$, one can search the sequence $[\![S]\!]$ and obtain its $\mathcal{P}(\alpha, [\![S]\!])$-th element, which is explicitly equal to α. For convenience, let us denote the decompression function as $\mathcal{O}(\cdot,\cdot)$. The decompression procedure of the compressed encrypted image $\{\mathcal{P}([I], [\![S]\!]), [\![S]\!]\}$ is then given by $\mathcal{O}(\mathcal{P}([I], [\![S]\!]), [\![S]\!])$.

The encrypted image $[I]$ has the same effect as being encrypted the element-wise encryption scheme. Moreover, the uncompressed and the decompressed encrypted images are equivalent to be encrypted with the element-wise encryption, when ρ is large enough. In this sense, our encryption scheme is one variant of the element-wise encryption scheme. Therefore the same kind of image processing operations, which are allowed in the element-wise encryption scheme, are allowed to be performed on the encrypted images with our approach, e.g., encrypted domain DFT, DCT, and DWT. The proposed encryption scheme thus satisfies the non-interactive property, which is also held by the element-wise encryption scheme.

3.4 Decryption

Suppose a compressed encrypted image $\{\mathcal{P}([I], [\![S]\!]), [\![S]\!]\}$ has already been decompressed as $\mathcal{O}(\mathcal{P}([I], [\![S]\!]), [\![S]\!])$ - i.e., $[I]$. The existing SSP tools based on element-wise encryption scheme can then be directly applied to $[I]$. Let us denote the modified encrypted image by $[I']$. In order to decrypt the whole image $[I]$ or $[I']$, we just need to decrypt every ciphertext in $[I]$ or $[I']$ by using the decryption algorithm of the probabilistic homomorphic cryptosystem, without involving the ciphertext sequence $[\![S]\!]$ and the decrypted sequence S. The image decryption is not different from the image decryption of the element-wise encryption scheme. If the secret decryption of the employed probabilistic homomorphic cryptosystem is denoted by DK, then decryption key of our scheme is exactly DK.

In some applications, such as secure cloud storage and secure data transmission, the compressed encrypted image $\{\mathcal{P}([I], [\![S]\!]), [\![S]\!]\}$ may be the only result, for saving the storage space and the transmission bandwidth. In these cases, the image decryption can be accomplished straightly in the compressed encrypted domain. The decryption key of our scheme is the pair $(DK, [\![S]\!])$ or equivalently S. If $(DK, [\![S]\!])$ is used as the decryption key, the ciphertext sequence $[\![S]\!]$ will be previously decrypted with DK by using the decryption algorithm of the probabilistic homomorphic cryptosystem, in order to obtain S. The plaintext image I is then obtained by using the decompressing function $\mathcal{O}(\cdot,\cdot)$ with S, i.e., $I = \mathcal{O}(\mathcal{P}([I], [\![S]\!]), S)$.

3.5 Fast Algorithm of Image Encryption and Compression

The above algorithms of image encryption and compression are somewhat complicated. In the following, we propose a fast algorithm which unifies image encryption and compression. After splitting I into non-overlapping blocks $\{X_1, X_2, \ldots, X_{M_b}\}$, we use the positions of elements in S to encrypt the pixel values. Specifically, in block X_j, the pixel value β is 'compressed' to the position of one element in sequence S_β which is chosen in sequence, i.e., $\mathcal{P}(\beta, S)$. When all elements in S_β have been chosen, S_β will be rearranged before being chosen again, i.e.,

$$S_\beta \leftarrow \mathsf{RandPermut}\,(S_\beta)\,. \tag{10}$$

Let us denote the code stream of the plaintext image I by $\hat{I}$. We then encrypted S with a probabilistic homomorphic cryptosystem to obtain the ciphertext sequence $[\![S]\!]$. It is easy to show that $\{\hat{I}, [\![S]\!]\}$ is one variety of the compressed encrypted image $\{\mathcal{P}([I], [\![S]\!]), [\![S]\!]\}$. The image decryption algorithm can be applied directly to $\{\hat{I}, [\![S]\!]\}$. Since the 'compression' procedure is carried out before the encryption procedure, the fast algorithm greatly speeds up the proposed original image encryption scheme.

4. DISCUSSIONS

In this section, we give some discussions on the security, ciphertext expansion, and computational cost of the image encryption scheme.

4.1 Security

According to the image decryption algorithm, the plaintext image I is easily recovered from the code stream $\mathcal{P}([I], [\![S]\!])$ once $[\![S]\!]$ has been broken. Hence, the security of the proposed image encryption scheme mainly depends on the security of the ciphertext sequence $[\![S]\!]$, which relies on the underlying cryptosystem we used. If we work with the cryptosystem which has been proved to be semantically secure, e.g., the Paillier cryptosystem [7], the security of $[\![S]\!]$ is automatically achieved.

By using (4), we make every ciphertext in $[\![S]\!]$ occurs in the encrypted image with almost equal probability. Furthermore, different encryption procedures will yield different encrypted images, no matter the input plaintext images are identical or not. Thus, the encryption scheme can well protect the content of the plaintext image. We conduct a detailed experiment on the visual quality of encrypted images in Section 5.2.

As for the security of the image compression, we prove that there exist not probabilistic algorithms which can break $\mathcal{P}([I], [\![S]\!])$ in polynomial time. Assume for contradiction that there exists a probabilistic polynomial time algorithm $\mathscr{A}$ which directly obtains the plaintext image I from the code stream $\mathcal{P}([I], [\![S]\!])$. By using invert replacement, $\mathscr{A}$ is able to obtain the plaintext of every element in $[\![S]\!]$. Specifically, the plaintext of α in $[\![S]\!]$ is equal to the pixel value of I, which is encrypted to be the element $\mathcal{P}(\alpha, [\![S]\!])$ in $\mathcal{P}([I], [\![S]\!])$. Hence, $\mathscr{A}$ can break $[\![S]\!]$ to obtain S in polynomial time. The ciphertext sequence $[\![S]\!]$ with the semantically secure cryptosystem is then not secure, and thus we have a contradiction. Since the cryptosystem is secure, the compression procedure is of course secure. Therefore we have proven that the compression procedure in secure in theory.

Furthermore, the $\mathsf{RandPermut}$ function is not invertible by attackers in our image encryption scheme. If the cardinality of a set A is denoted by $\#(A)$, then the probability for attackers to invert A from $\mathsf{RandPermut}(A)$ is $\frac{1}{\#(A)}$. For a real image, this probability is almost equal to zero. In practice, we can use secure pseudo random permutation functions as the $\mathsf{RandPermut}$ function.

4.2 Ciphertext Expansion Factor

We define the ratio of the storage space between the compressed encrypted image $\{\mathcal{P}([I], [\![S]\!]), [\![S]\!]\}$ and the plaintext image I as the ciphertext expansion factor of our image encryption scheme, which is denoted by γ in the following. The value of γ depends on two parameters. One is the length of the ciphertext sequence $[\![S]\!]$, the other is the size of the plaintext image I. For convenience, let us consider the case that the Paillier cryptosystem is employed as the probabilistic homomorphic cryptosystem in our image encryption scheme. Suppose the modulus of the Paillier cryptosystem is 1024 bits, and the size of the considered image is of $M \times M$. The storage space required for the compressed encrypted image is

$$\nu_{\text{ComEnc}} = \rho \times 2048 + M^2 \times \log_2 \rho \;\; \text{(bits)}, \tag{11}$$

while the storage space of the plaintext image is

$$\nu_{\text{Plain}} = M^2 \times 8 \;\; \text{(bits)}. \tag{12}$$

Hence, under this situation, the ciphertext expansion factor of the proposed image encryption scheme is given as

$$\begin{aligned} \gamma = \frac{\nu_{\text{ComEnc}}}{\nu_{\text{Plain}}} &= \frac{\rho \times 2048 + M^2 \times \log_2 \rho}{M^2 \times 8} \\ &= \frac{256\rho}{M^2} + \frac{\log_2 \rho}{8}. \end{aligned} \tag{13}$$

As for the packing scheme, the number of samples which is packed together varies according to the requirement of applications. Thus, the number of the packed messages which will be encrypted is variable in different cases. Consider a scenario in which an encrypted gray scale image must undergo DFT task with 8-bit fixed-point implementation [12]. We compare the proposed image encryption scheme with the packing scheme in this scenario.

In order to provide comparison with other techniques for ciphertext expansion reducing, we show the curves of γ versus the size of I - i.e., M, for the element-wise encryption scheme, the packing method in the considered scenario, and the proposed encryption scheme with some values of ρ in Fig. 3(a).

4.3 Computational Cost

In order to make the security meet the piratical requirement, the probabilistic homomorphic cryptosystems usually use very large algebraic structures, e.g., the large-size modulus employed by the Paillier cryptosystem. For the fast algorithm of the image encryption scheme, the time cost in compressing the plaintext image I to the code stream $\hat{I}$ can then be negligible compared with the time cost in encrypting with the probabilistic homomorphic cryptosystem. Thus, the time cost in encrypting S dominates the entire computational cost, and the computational cost of the proposed image encryption scheme can be evaluated as the number of the operation of encryption with the probabilistic homomorphic cryptosystem.

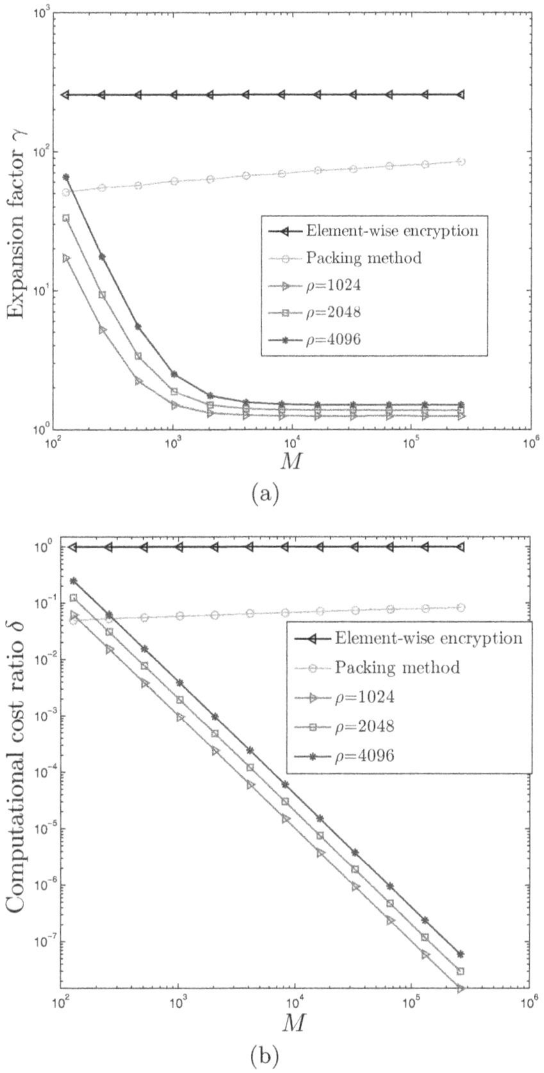

Figure 3: The performance comparison of the proposed encryption scheme, the element-wise encryption scheme, and the packing method in the considered scenario, with respect to the size of I - i.e., $M \times M$. (a) The ciphertext expansion factor γ; (b) The computational cost ratio δ.

In the following, we compare the computational costs between the proposed image encryption scheme and the element-wise encryption scheme. For an image I with the size $M \times M$, there are M^2 encryptions with the element-wise encryption scheme, while there are only ρ encryptions with the proposed image encryption scheme. The computational cost ratio of the proposed image encryption scheme to the element-wise scheme can be approximately given as

$$\delta = \frac{\rho}{M^2}. \tag{14}$$

The proposed image encryption scheme is much more efficient than the sample-wise scheme in practice, e.g., if $\rho = 4096$ and $M = 512$, then $\delta = 0.016$. Thus, the proposed image encryption scheme satisfies the tolerable ciphertext expansion property.

In our scheme, all the pixels are encrypted with the probabilistic homomorphic encryption. Although in a broader sense, δ can be also viewed as the percentage of pixels being encrypted. To provide comparison with other techniques for computational cost, we plot the curves of δ versus the size of I for the element-wise encryption scheme, the packing method in the considered scenario, and the proposed encryption scheme with some values of ρ in Fig. 3(b). From Fig. 3, it is observed the proposed encryption scheme outperforms the element-wise encryption scheme in term of ciphertext expansion reducing and computational cost.

5. EXPERIMENTAL RESULTS

In this section, we show the use of the proposed image encryption scheme and the visual quality of encrypted images.

5.1 Simulation Experiments

We test the proposed image encryption scheme on the public CVG-UGR gray level image database [26]. We show the results on 'Lena' image of $512 \times 512 \times 8$ bits first. Two large prime numbers p and q are chosen for the cryptosystem. The product of p and q is longer than 1024 bits, so the Paillier encryption is secure in practice.

Firstly, we choose a ciphertext sequence $[\![S]\!]$ with the length of 4096. We perform the fast encryption and compression algorithm on 'Lena' image to obtain the compressed encrypted image. The code stream image $\mathcal{P}([I], [\![S]\!])$ is shown in Fig. 4(a). We then preform the decompression function $\mathcal{O}(\cdot, \cdot)$ and obtain the decompressed encrypted image, which is shown in Fig. 4(b).

Secondly, we apply the image decryption algorithm to the decompressed encrypted image. We show the decrypted image in Fig. 4(c). Actually, the decrypted image is identical to the original 'Lena' image.

We also decrypt the compressed encrypted image directly and show it in Fig. 4(d). The mean squared error (MSE) of the two decrypted images in Fig. 4(c)–4(d) is 0.

Thirdly, we adopt $\rho = 16384$ as the length of the new ciphertext sequence $[\![S]\!]$, and carry out the experiments with this new parameter. After performing the fast encryption and compression algorithm, we obtain the compressed encrypted image, which is shown in Fig. 4(e). We then decompress the compressed encrypted image and show the decompressed encrypted image in Fig. 4(f). For comparison, we perform the element-wise encryption scheme on 'Lena' image and show the encrypted image in Fig. 4(g). Both the compressed encrypted and the decompressed encrypted images look as chaotic as the encrypted image with the element-wise encryption scheme. We decrypt the decompressed encrypted image and show it in Fig. 4(h). The decrypted image is identical to the original 'Lena' image. We then decrypt the compressed encrypted image, which come out to be identical to Fig. 4(h).

If the images encrypted with an encryption scheme are too chaotic to be understood, the employed image encryption scheme can be regarded as of high perception security [27]. According to the image encryption algorithm, $[\![S]\!]$ is encrypted with a probabilistic homomorphic cryptosystem and the image I is confused by a succession of random permutations - i.e., RandPermuts. Therefore it is difficult to break $[\![S]\!]$ and to recognize what the plaintext image is from the compressed encrypted image. We test the encryption and the compression algorithms on CVG-UGR gray level image

Figure 4: The experimental results on 'Lena' image: (a) Compressed encrypted image ($\rho = 4096$); (b) Decompressed encrypted image ($\rho = 4096$); (c) Decryption of the decompressed encrypted image ($\rho = 4096$); (d) Decryption of the compressed encrypted image ($\rho = 4096$); (e) Compressed encrypted image ($\rho = 16384$); (f) Decompressed encrypted image ($\rho = 16384$); (g) Encrypted image with element-wise encryption scheme; (h) Decryption of the decompressed encrypted image ($\rho = 16384$).

Figure 5: Four plaintext images and their corresponding compressed encrypted images, where $\rho = 16384$. The plaintext images are in the first row, and the compressed encrypted images are in the second row.

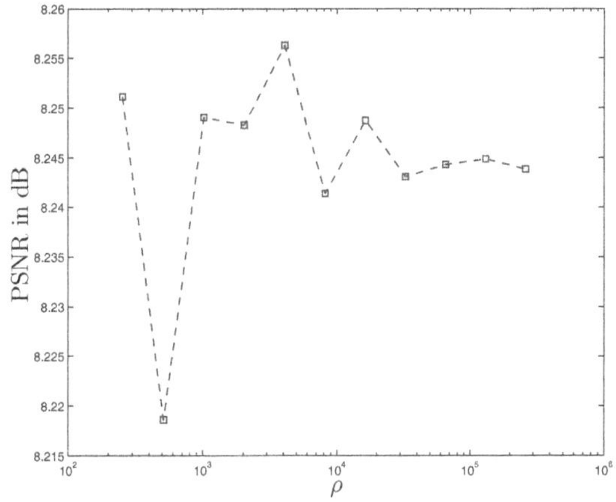

Figure 6: The average PSNR versus ρ on CVG-UGR gray level image database.

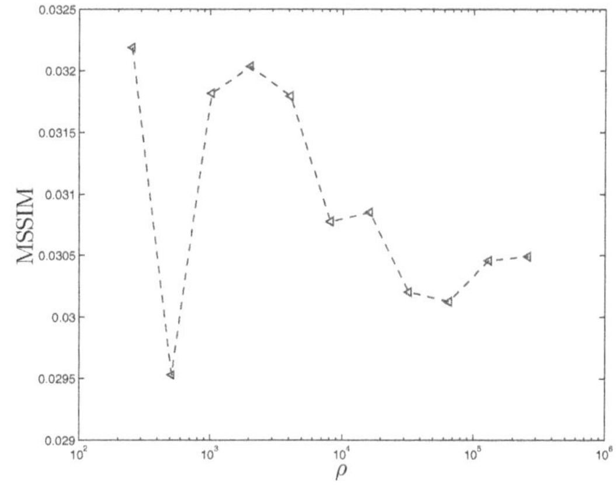

Figure 7: The average MSSIM versus ρ on CVG-UGR gray level image database.

database. In Fig.5, we show four of the images, which have different kinds of textures, e.g., complex texture (Fig. 4(a)), and smooth texture (Fig. 4(b)), and their compressed encrypted images. We observe that all the decompressed encrypted and the compressed encrypted images are chaotic enough, no matter what the image textures are. Therefore our image encryption scheme is high perception secure.

5.2 Visual Quality of Encrypted Images

One goal of image encryptions is to confuse the images and to prevent the image contents from being divulged. It is therefore reasonable to evaluate the chaos of encrypted images by using some image quality assessments. There are two popular image quality assessments. One is the peak signal-to-noise ratio (PSNR), and the other is the structural similarity (SSIM) index [21]. The PSNR can be defined as

$$\mathrm{PSNR}\left(I,\hat{I}\right) = 10\log_{10}\left(\frac{255^2}{\mathrm{MSE}\left(I,\hat{I}\right)}\right) \quad (15)$$

where MSE is the mean squared error, i.e.,

$$\mathrm{MSE}\left(I,\hat{I}\right) = \frac{1}{M^2}\sum_{x=1}^{M}\sum_{y=1}^{M}\left(I(x,y) - \hat{I}(x,y)\right)^2. \quad (16)$$

In practice, one usually uses the mean SSIM (MSSIM) index to evaluate the overall image quality, that is,

$$\mathrm{MSSIM}\left(I,\hat{I}\right) = \frac{1}{L}\sum_{l=1}^{L}\mathrm{SSIM}\left(\mathbf{x}_l,\mathbf{y}_l\right). \quad (17)$$

where $\mathbf{x}_l$ and $\mathbf{y}_l$ are the image contents at the l-th local windows of I and $\hat{I}$, respectively; and L is the number of local windows of the image. The MSSIM values lie in the interval from -1 to 1. When the MSSIM value is equal to 1, it means that the distorted image $\hat{I}$ is identical to the reference image I. The closer the MSSIM value to 0, the more difference between $\hat{I}$ and I there is. Low PSNR value also means less dependence between two images. In practice, the PSNR value of two independence images is roughly less than 10 dB.

Due to the variety of image texture, it is necessary to test the encryption scheme on different texture images. To investigate the visual quality of encrypted images, we study the relationships of PSNR versus ρ and MSSIM versus ρ, which may be helpful to evaluate overall performance of perceptual security. The value of ρ varies from 2^8 to 2^{18}, i.e., ρ = 256, 512, 1024, 2048, 4096, 8192, 16384, 32768, 65536, 131072, 262144. We employ the CVG-UGR gray level image database [26] in our experiment. There are totally 96 gray scale images of $512 \times 512 \times 8$ bits. Each image is split into non-overlapping blocks of 16×16, and thus there are 1024 blocks for each image. We encrypt the 96 images for each ρ and compute the average PSNRs and MSSIMs.

In Fig. 6, we show the curve of the average PSNR versus ρ. We observe that all the average PSNR values are smaller than 8.26 dB. Therefore there is less dependence between encrypted images and original images, and the image encryption scheme well protects the content of original images. In Fig. 7, we show the curve of the average MSSIM versus ρ. All the average MSSIM values are nearly equal to 0.0325, no matter what the value of ρ is. It means that all the encrypted images are almost independent of their corresponding plaintext image in statistics. Our experiments demonstrate that the proposed encryption scheme keeps the contents of plaintext images in high security.

6. CONCLUSIONS AND FUTURE WORKS

This paper proposes an image encryption scheme, which satisfies three properties, i.e., the homomorphic property, the non-interactive property, and the tolerable ciphertext expansion property. The main contributions are listed as follows:

1. We have described a technique to first encrypt the image and then compress the ciphertexts. Our scheme has a much smaller ciphertext expansion factor compared with the element-wise encryption scheme, while preserve the non-interactive property which the packing method loses.
2. We have presented a fast algorithm to speed up the encryption and the compression procedures. Compared with the element-wise encryption scheme, the fast algorithm makes our scheme much more efficient.
3. We have compared our image encryption scheme with the element-wise encryption scheme and the packing method, for ciphertext expansion and computational cost. We have analyzed the security and proved that the compression al-

gorithm is computational secure in polynomial time. The experiments demonstrate that our scheme achieves high perception security.

The proposed image encryption scheme can be used as a building block in the field of s.p.e.d.. It is suitable to be employed to design SSP applications, such as secure feature extraction, secure face detection and secure watermarking. The future works will be in two aspects. One is to address the concrete relationship between the value of ρ and the strength of the security of the proposed image encryption scheme. The other is to use our scheme in the existing develop SSP tools. It is interesting to adjust the initialization of $[\![S]\!]$ according to different requirements.

Acknowledgements

This work was supported by 973 Program (2011CB302204), National Science & Technology Pillar Program (2012BAK16B06), and NSFC (U1135001, 61272498).

The authors thank Prof. Fangguo Zhang for the helpful discussion.

7. REFERENCES

[1] Z. Erkin, A. Piva, S. Katzenbeisser, R. L. Lagendijk, J. Shokrollahi, G. Neven, and M. Barni. Protection and retrieval of encrypted multimedia content: when cryptography meets signal processing. *EURASIP J. Inf. Security*, pages 1–20, 2007.

[2] R. L. Lagendijk, Z. Erkin, and M. Barni. Encrypted signal processing for privacy protection: Conveying the utility of homomorphic encryption and multiparty computation. *IEEE Signal Process. Mag.*, 30(1):82–105, 2013.

[3] Z. Erkin, M. Franz, J. Guajardo, S. Katzenbeisser, I. Lagendijk, and T. Toft. Privacy-preserving face recognition. In *Privacy Enhancing Technologies*, pages 235–253. Springer, 2009.

[4] M. Barni, T. Bianchi, D. Catalano, M. D. Raimondo, R. D. Labati, and P. Failla. Privacy-preserving fingercode authentication. In *Proc. 12th ACM Workshop on Multimedia Security*, pages 231–240. ACM, 2010.

[5] M. Barni, P. Failla, R. Lazzeretti, A.R. Sadeghi, and T. Schneider. Privacy-preserving ECG classification with branching programs and neural networks. *IEEE Trans. Inf. Forensics Security*, (99):452–468, 2011.

[6] R.L. Rivest, L. Adleman, and M.L. Dertouzos. On data banks and privacy homomorphisms. *Foundations Secure Comput.*, pages 169–178, 1978.

[7] T. ElGamal. A public key cryptosystem and a signature scheme based on discrete logarithms. pages 10–18, 1985.

[8] P. Paillier. Public-key cryptosystems based on composite degree residuosity classes. In *Adv. Cryptology (EUROCRYPT'99)*, pages 223–238. Springer, 1999.

[9] I. Damgård and M. Jurik. A generalisation, a simplification and some applications of Paillier's probabilistic public-key system. In *Public Key Cryptography*, pages 119–136. Springer, 2001.

[10] C. Gentry. Fully homomorphic encryption using ideal lattices. In *Proc. 41st Annu. ACM Symp. Theory Comput. (STOC'09)*, pages 169–178, 2009.

[11] S. Goldwasser and S. Micali. Probabilistic encryption. *J. Comput. Syst. Sci.*, 28(2):270–299, 1984.

[12] T. Bianchi, A. Piva, and M. Barni. On the implementation of the discrete Fourier transform in the encrypted domain. *IEEE Trans. Inf. Forensics Security*, 4(1):86–97, 2009.

[13] T. Bianchi, A. Piva, and M. Barni. Encrypted domain DCT based on homomorphic cryptosystems. *EURASIP J. Inf. Security*, 2009:1, 2009.

[14] P. Zheng and J. Huang. Implementation of the discrete wavelet transform and multiresolution analysis in the encrypted domain. In *Proc. 19th ACM Int. Conf. Multimedia*, pages 413–422. ACM, 2011.

[15] P. Zheng and J. Huang. Walsh-Hadamard transform in the homomorphic encrypted domain and its application in image watermarking. In *14th Information Hiding Conf.*, pages 240–254, Berkeley, CA, 2012. Springer.

[16] J.R. Troncoso-Pastoriza, S. Katzenbeisser, M. Celik, and A. Lemma. A secure multidimensional point inclusion protocol. In *Proc. 9th ACM Workshop on Multimedia and Security*, pages 109–120. ACM, 2007.

[17] T. Bianchi, A. Piva, and M. Barni. Composite signal representation for fast and storage-efficient processing of encrypted signals. *IEEE Trans. Inf. Forensics Security*, 5(1):180–187, 2010.

[18] A.R. Sadeghi, T. Schneider, and I. Wehrenberg. Efficient privacy-preserving face recognition. In *Proc. 12th Int. Conf. Inf. Security Cryptology (ICISC'09)*, pages 229–244. Springer, 2010.

[19] C. Hsu, C. Lu, and S. Pei. Image feature extraction in encrypted domain with privacy-preserving SIFT. *IEEE Trans. Image Process.*, 21(11):4593–4607, 2012.

[20] W. Puech, Z. Erkin, M. Barni, S. Rane, and R. L. Lagendijk. Emerging cryptographic challenges in image and video processing. In *IEEE Int. Conf. Image Process. (ICIP'12)*, pages 2629–2632. IEEE, 2012.

[21] Z. Wang, A.C. Bovik, H.R. Sheikh, and E.P. Simoncelli. Image quality assessment: From error visibility to structural similarity. *IEEE Trans. Image Process.*, 13(4):600–612, 2004.

[22] Mark Johnson, Prakash Ishwar, Vinod Prabhakaran, Daniel Schonberg, and Kannan Ramchandran. On compressing encrypted data. *IEEE Trans. Signal Process.*, 52(10):2992–3006, 2004.

[23] B. Schoenmakers and P. Tuyls. Efficient binary conversion for Paillier encrypted values. *Adv. Cryptology (EUROCRYPT'06)*, pages 522–537, 2006.

[24] P. Zheng and J. Huang. Discrete wavelet transform and data expansion reduction in homomorphic encrypted domain. *IEEE Trans. Image Process.*, 22(6):2455–2468, 2013.

[25] W. K. Gregory. The JPEG still picture compression standard. *Commun. ACM*, 34(4):30–44, 1991.

[26] CVG UGR Image database. http://decsai.ugr.es/cvg/dbimagenes/.

[27] S. Lian, Z. Liu, R. Zhen, and H. Wang. Secure advanced video coding based on selective encryption algorithms. *IEEE Trans. Consum. Electron.*, 52(2):621–629, 2006.

Large-Scale Multimedia Content Analysis Using Scientific Workflows

Ricky J. Sethi
USC Information Sciences Institute
Marina del Rey, CA 90292
rickys@sethi.org

Yolanda Gil
USC Information Sciences Institute
Marina del Rey, CA 90292
gil@isi.edu

Hyunjoon Jo
USC Information Sciences Institute
Marina del Rey, CA 90292
hyunjoon@usc.edu

Andrew Philpot
USC Information Sciences Institute
Marina del Rey, CA 90292
philpot@isi.edu

ABSTRACT

Analyzing web content, particularly multimedia content, for security applications is of great interest. However, it often requires deep expertise in data analytics that is not always accessible to non-experts. Our approach is to use scientific workflows that capture expert-level methods to examine web content. We use workflows to analyze the image and text components of multimedia web posts separately, as well as by a multimodal fusion of both image and text data. In particular, we re-purpose workflow fragments to do the multimedia analysis and create additional components for the fusion of the image and text modalities. In this paper, we present preliminary work which focuses on a Human Trafficking Detection task to help deter human trafficking of minors by thus fusing image and text content from the web. We also examine how workflow fragments save time and effort in multimedia content analysis while bringing together multiple areas of machine learning and computer vision. We further export these workflow fragments using linked data as web objects.

Categories and Subject Descriptors

H.4 [**Information Systems Applications**]: Miscellaneous

Keywords

Social Media Analysis; Multimodal Information Fusion; Scientific Workflows; Human Trafficking Detection; Big Data

1. INTRODUCTION

Analyzing multimedia content on the web is of great interest but it often involves leveraging expertise in data analysis, as well as social media [1, 2]. This is especially apparent in detecting human trafficking on the web as trafficking of minors via the internet is a fast-growing security problem [3]. Traffickers of minors are increasingly using internet-based ads and social media to advertise their illicit wares. These ads consist of both text and image descriptions of people, some of whom are minors being trafficked.

In this paper, we present preliminary work which focuses on the task of Human Trafficking Detection (HTD). We present our initial work to help analyze posts on various sites on the internet, which add approximately 20GB of posts every day, in order to determine if the subjects of these posts are victims of human trafficking. The ultimate goal of the project is to create intelligence which may be used by law enforcement to detect and combat such trafficking of minors.

This complex task requires examination of both text and image information, as well as the fusion of these two distinct data domains. Our approach is based on scientific workflows, which capture end-to-end methods that combine fragments developed by different people with expertise in different aspects of the task. Workflows consolidate heterogeneous codebases and programs written in many different languages [4, 5, 6]. Such workflows, designed by domain experts in their own fields, may also be of great utility to scientists in other disciplines. The Wings workflow system, in particular, was developed to assist scientists in managing complex computations [7, 8] and it has been used in several large-scale distributed scientific applications. For this work, we re-purposed existing workflows [9, 10, 11] and developed new workflows for image processing and fusion of image and text analyses.

Contributions: We thus use semantic workflows which capture expert-grade text and image analytics. Using the Wings framework, we have started initial development of a prototype which examines both the text of the post, as well as the associated images, in order to make a determination of the age of the person represented in the ad. We are further extending this semantic workflows-based approach to support re-usability of workflow fragments and reproducibility of scientific research.

The main contribution of this paper is the re-use and re-purposing of workflow fragments to facilitate rapid development of applications and to bridge expertise across disci-

MM'13, October 21–25, 2013, Barcelona, Spain.

ACM 978-1-4503-2404-5/13/10 ...$15.00.
http://dx.doi.org/10.1145/2502081.2502082.

plines when analyzing multimedia web content. We introduce several workflow fragments for Text Analytics and Image Analysis, as well as for the fusion of these different data modalities. We also use linked data principles to export these workflow fragments as web objects for the research community. In particular, we show how a social media analysis task can be solved rapidly and extended to do a multimedia analysis, which involves both text and image analytics, by simply re-using the workflow fragments developed by us and by others.

The rest of this article is organized as follows: in Section 2, we provide some background on the initial development of the HTD project. Then, in Section 3, we discuss the Wings workflow system. In Section 4, we show several workflow fragments we created for Text and Image Analytics, as well as their fusion. Then, in Section 5, we show how the re-use of workflow fragments can extend this nascent social media analysis task. Next, in Section 6, we show the results of experiments and give details of our implementation. Finally, in Section 6.5, we highlight the time and work savings allowed by the re-use of workflows, followed by a discussion of future directions in Section 7.

2. HUMAN TRAFFICKING DETECTION

Human trafficking of minors for the purposes of illicit, commercial exploitation is a serious international crime. Increasingly, traffickers use Internet classified ads, bulletin boards, and social media to advertise the illicit services of the persons they offer [3]. A very common scenario is to have advertisements for trafficked persons, both adults and minors, injected into classified advertisement listings for licit and quasi-licit personal services. In order to attract clients online, such ads typically contain several of: phone numbers and/or other contact information; provider names (or pseudonyms); location(s) served; descriptions of provider race, physical characteristics, and purported age; suggested services and prices; and images. At the same time, providers try to avoid apprehension by law enforcement by omitting, falsifying, or obscuring information believed to be useful in apprehension, inclusion of deliberate features (or noise) believed to insulate against law enforcement action, and by changing details over time (e.g., multiple aliases) to defeat attempts to link separate ads together.

Accordingly, law enforcement efforts to combat human trafficking of minors seek to use the rich information source ads represent as a source of evidence. To do so effectively, one needs to:

1. Extract content from individual ads
2. Classify ad content as to whether the provider is trafficked into prostitution or engaged in some other activity and
3. Estimate provider true age (especially likelihood of underage participation). To assist in targeting apprehension, it is essential to
4. Determine the service modality the ad offers, whether "outcall" (provider travels to customer), "incall" (customer travels to provider), the setting, or agency referral, or other.
5. Records from individual ads so gathered must be linked together, a form of entity resolution [12], yielding a set of single-provider time profiles.

Information from third-party sites, such as missing child databases or recent nearby apprehension evidence, can be correlated with extracted information, when available, typically during this phase. These profiles are then cross-matched to suggest inter-provider relationships (e.g., co-advertised or shared phone) which, in turn, particularly when combined with provider mentions in certain discussion groups begins to populate a *social network*, whose members include providers, customers and procurers.

The TrafficBot project was initiated in late 2011 to address these information extraction needs for federal law enforcement. Initial efforts focused on identifying suitable classified ad listings, developing site-focused web crawlers, and developing site-specific extraction scripts. By mid-2012, the resulting archive, spanning 110 metropolitan markets (themselves composed of several hundred city-level crawl results), and had grown to nearly 500,000 harvested posts spanning an estimated 200,000 providers.

The current system with basic archive query capability supports some basic law enforcement goals. For example, users can filter ads from market M1 where reported age is less than 25 and where at least one reported phone number is tagged in market M2 (indicating likely provider movement).

Development of deeper data analytics, however, has lagged behind the collection results, especially since this task requires massive multimodal information fusion. For tasks such as age estimation and modality tagging, competing hypotheses include using supervised and unsupervised learning and clustering methods, across various proposed text, image, and network features. Moreover, various parameters and feature extraction schemes for each method need to be identified and tuned. The large search space, combined with an enormous and fast-growing data store, necessitates a systematic engineering approach.

The use of workflows offers notable advantages:

1. Support for natural modularization of the task space;
2. Ability to scale up via parallelization;
3. Access to a large and mature workflow fragment library to address many of the pending analytic needs;
4. Allowing incorporation of pre-existing data and existing code as fragments, as well as simple integration with an existing system; and
5. Ease of experimenting with workflows to set up various parameters and explore multiple scenarios quickly.

3. WINGS SEMANTIC WORKFLOWS

Our approach uses the Wings workflow system [13], which has three key features that make workflows accessible to users: a simple dataflow structure, an easy-to-use web interface, and an ability to export workflows and workflow fragments as web objects. This framework allows us to structure computer vision and machine learning tasks as computational workflow fragments described in high-level declarative notations and capable of processing large quantities of data that comes from multiple sources or files [6, 14]. Wings is open source, built upon open web standards from the World Wide Web Consortium (W3C), and is available at `http://www.wings-workflows.org/`.

A unique feature of Wings is that its workflow representations incorporate semantic constraints about datasets and workflow components. Wings reasons about dataset properties and component constraints to create and validate workflows and to generate metadata for new data products. Wings uses Pegasus as the execution engine for large-scale distributed workflow execution. Wings allows users to express high-level descriptions of their analysis goals, and assists them by automatically and systematically generating possible workflows that are consistent with that request. Users can be assisted in an interactive mode, where Wings generates suggestions and validates their inputs, or in an automatic mode, where Wings can elaborate their initial request and present the user with execution-ready workflows as options.

Using a semantic workflow system like Wings to assist with the design of such computational experiments allows for creating structured, systematic experiments that can be automated, thus allowing anyone to reproduce results, regardless of how parameters and thresholds are optimized for specific datasets. In addition, the Wings workflow system has an open modular design and can be easily integrated with other existing workflow systems and execution frameworks to extend them with semantic reasoning capabilities.

The Wings workflow framework thus has the ability to easily incorporate new algorithms and new data sources. In addition, the framework is self-adaptive in that it automatically selects methods and parameter values that are appropriate for the user's data and can analyze its current knowledge, detect missing information, attempt to induce it, and, when this is not possible, assess the value of seeking that missing information [15].

In fact, the Wings workflow system is pre-equipped with several expert-quality workflows that represent a powerful set of analytic methods [16]. It includes workflow fragments for general machine learning packages like Weka [17], document clustering packages like CLUTO, etc. We extend these repositories by creating workflow fragments based on popular computer vision [18, 19, 20, 21, 22] and machine learning packages like OpenCV [23], a standard computer vision library, and MALLET [24], a standard package for statistical processing and information extraction, as well as adding custom implementations of some state-of-the-art computer vision/machine learning models.

These packages have vastly heterogeneous implementations but the workflow fragments encapsulate the software with interfaces described by data types in the workflow system to make them reusable in different workflows. Wings ensures that only the right components are used in workflows by checking the semantic constraints of the input and output types for every component. The system ensures that only workflows with valid combinations of components are executed. The framework also includes several widely used datasets used for comparison purposes in the text analytics and computer vision community.

In addition, these workflow fragments can be exported in Wings by publishing them as web objects using Linked Data principles [25] and can be made available as part of a workflow library. These web objects, represented in RDF, allow direct access via unique URIs to workflow fragments or workflows, their components, and their associated datasets. Such web objects can then be imported into any workflow system that is compatible with the standard Open Provenance Model for workflow publication [25] so that other researchers can directly re-use or re-purpose any single workflow fragment or entire workflows.

4. WORKFLOW FRAGMENTS FOR MULTIMEDIA ANALYSIS

Workflows are usually composed of workflow fragments that are reused across workflows. Such predefined workflow fragments make complex analytics expertise readily available to new users. The components that make up workflow fragments can be written in heterogeneous languages: e.g., some components are in Java, others in matlab, and still others in C++ but the language of choice is irrelevant as the components are integrated into the workflows without reliance upon their individual implementation idiosyncrasies. This is possible because each individual program is converted into a workflow component via a short wrapper shell script (usually 3-5 lines of code) thus allowing any pre-existing program to be incorporated as a new component in a workflow or workflow fragment.

These previously defined workflow fragments can be executed independently from each other. This is helpful as some researchers might choose to focus on particular parts in order to optimize or improve their understanding of the behaviour in the individual steps. A good starting point for researchers in other disciplines, however, is to create end-to-end workflows that are formed by re-using and re-purposing workflow fragments. These end-to-end workflows would then incorporate and represent advanced expertise in that they would capture complex combinations of components that are known to work well in practice. Such re-usable workflow fragments are pre-defined by domain experts and available as part of workflow libraries. They can be executed with available datasets or adapted by adding or changing components.

Here, we detail some of the workflow fragments previously developed [9] for Text Analytics as seen in Figure 1 as well as workflow fragments we have developed for Image Analytics in Figure 2.

4.1 Text Pre-Processing and Feature Generation

Analytic tasks usually begin with some pre-processing steps to generate the features of a document. The workflow fragment for feature generation is shown in Figure 1(a). Morphological variations are removed from the dataset with a stemmer component. The Wings workflow system provides several choices, including a Porter Stemmer and a Lovins Stemmer. It further provides term weighting components that is used to transform the dataset into the vector space model format. Among them are term frequency-inverse document frequency, corpus frequency or document frequency for instance. The generated outcome can now be used with different other workflows and is independent of a particular implementation at this stage in the workflows.

4.2 Feature Selection

A very common step for many data analytics tasks such as classification and clustering is feature selection, as shown in Figure 1(b), whose main purpose is to reduce the training set by only using the most valuable features. This will reduce the necessary time for training the model and can improve the results of the classifier in some cases. The goodness of a feature in the dataset is measured with correlation scores

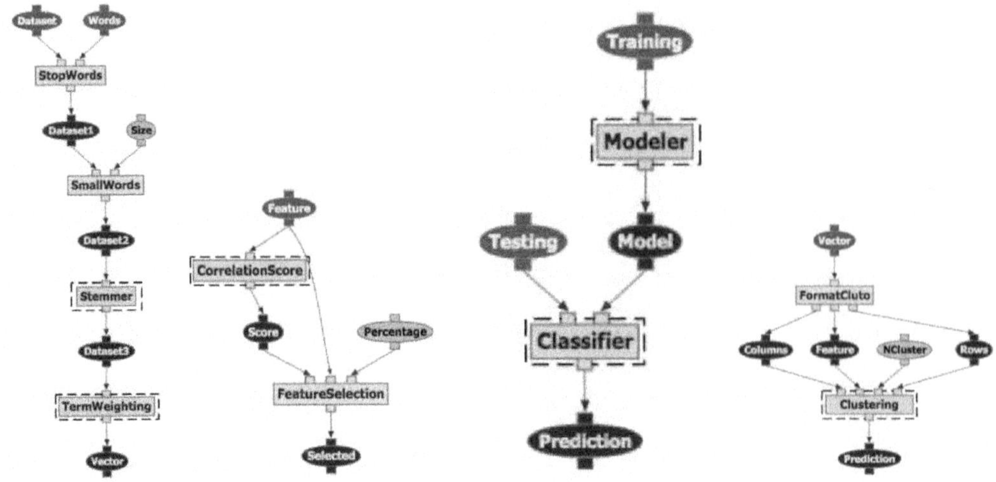

(a) Generation (b) Selection (c) Classification (d) Clustering

Figure 1: Workflow Fragments previously developed [9] for Text Analytics. Here we see workflow fragments for a) Feature Generation; b) Feature Selection; c) Training and Classification; and d) Clustering.

among the features. Typical implementations for this step are Chi Squared, Mutual Information or Information Gain that can be found in [26] and are all implemented in the framework. The resulting score is used in a feature selection step to retain the most valuable features in the training set. The percentage of selected features is typically changing for every dataset respectively classifier used in the computational experiment.

Another characteristic for this workflow fragment is that it uses heterogeneous implementations for the components. While the components for the computation of the correlation score take advantage of the capabilities of MATLAB to handle large matrices very elegant, the component for the feature selection uses an implementation written in Java.

4.3 Classification

The resulting training set after the feature selection can be used for the training of a model with the workflow fragment shown in in Figure 1(c). Both components in the workflow use the Weka machine learning framework. Thus, many different machine learning algorithms can be used to perform experiments with the dataset. Among them are very popular algorithms from the text analytic community like Support Vector Machines, Naive Bayes or k-Nearest Neighbor. The computed model can be stored in the data catalog and reused for later classifications. Since the training is usually a very time demanding task in the workflows, it is very desirable to reuse previously created models. Existing models are also easier to compare against each other, because the metadata information of the model carries provenance information from the components used and their configuration during the workflow execution. In the second step a classifier uses the trained model with the testing set to compute the predictions.

4.4 Clustering

In Figure 1(d), we see the workflow fragment for clustering. The Vector that results from the Feature Generation workflow fragment in Figure 1(d) can be used as input for clustering. It needs to be formatted into the suitable format for the clustering software. The result of this step is the Feature output with the transformed Vector. Next to this output there are additional intermediate files called Rows and Columns that contain the label names that are used to annotate the final result with the right names for the features and labels. The parameter for this component is used to specify the number of clusters to be applied on the data set.

4.5 Image Analysis

Here, we detail some of the Workflow Fragments we have developed for Image Analysis as seen in Figure 2. In particular, we created workflow fragments for a) Normalized Cuts Image Segmentation [27] which views image segmentation as the optimal partitioning of a graph by minimizing the cut with a modified cost function; b) Latent Dirichlet Allocation (MALLET) [24] for visual-word clustering and Support Vector Machines (libSVM) for visual-word classification [28, 29]; c) Statistics Evaluation (Confusion Matrices, Heatmaps, Precision Recall Curves, and Receiver Operating Characteristic Curves) [18, 19, 30]; and d) Topic Modelling (MALLET) [24] for video-word clustering. Visual-words and video-words are the image and video equivalent of text words used in textual bag-of-words models; in computer vision, they are created by partitioning an image or video into interest point cuboids or segments and then computing some features (for which it is possible to calculate a distance metric) for each interest point cuboid. The centers of each of these clusters are the visual words (codewords) in the visual vocabulary (codebook). The statistics evaluation workflow fragment allows for easy visualization of diverse summary and graphical statistical measures which are the outputs of that component (i.e., summary measures like Equal Error Rate, Mean Average Precision, etc., as well as the graphical outputs of Confusion Matrices, Heatmaps, Precision Recall Curves, and Receiver Operating Characteristic Curves).

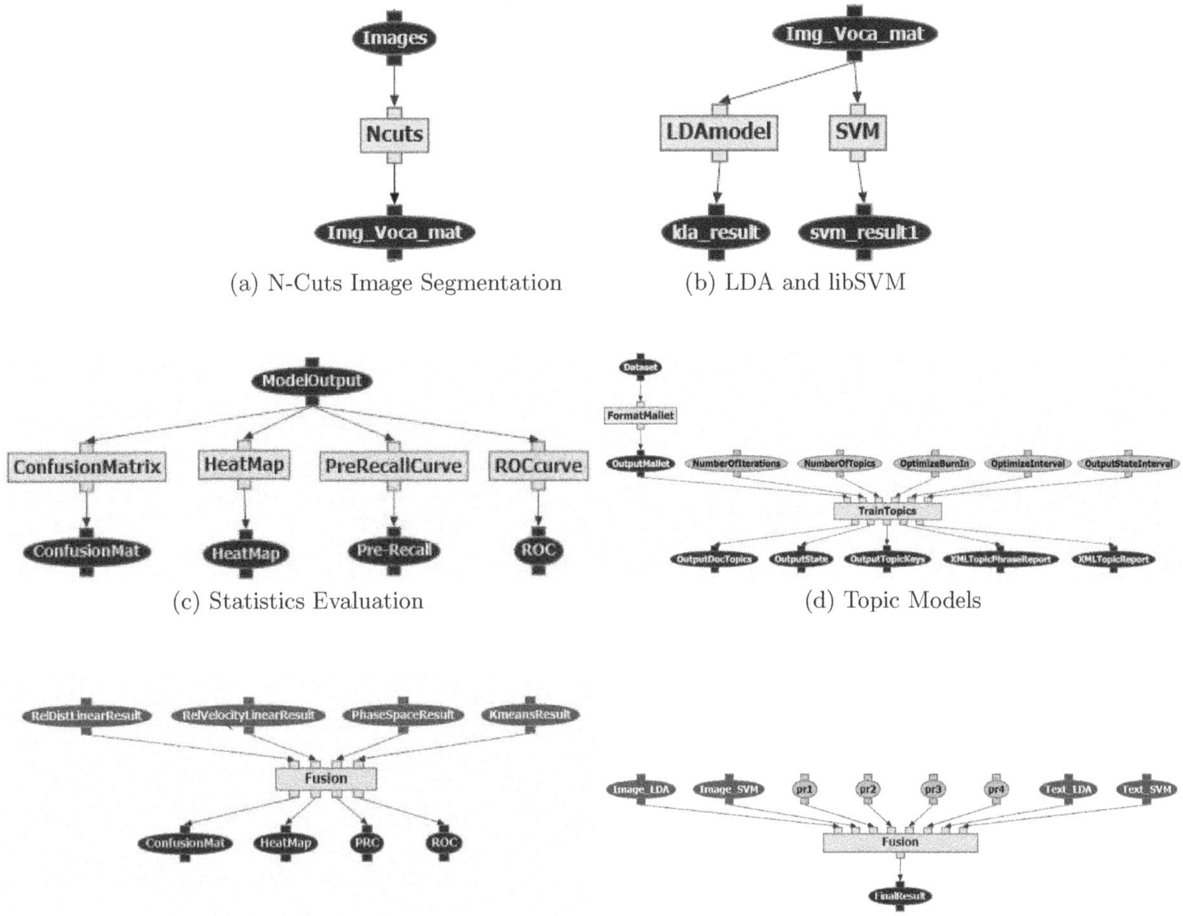

(a) N-Cuts Image Segmentation

(b) LDA and libSVM

(c) Statistics Evaluation

(d) Topic Models

(e) FUSION: weighted average of all other methods

(f) Alt. FUSION module with user-controlled weights

Figure 2: Workflow Fragments for Image Analysis. Here we see workflow fragments for a) N-Cuts Image Segmentation; b) Clustering and classification through Latent Dirichlet Allocation (mallet) and Support Vector Machines (libSVM); c) Statistics Evaluation (Confusion Matrices, Heatmaps, Precision Recall Curves, and Receiver Operating Characteristic Curves); d) Topic Modelling (mallet); e) FUSION: a weighted average of four input methods with normalized output scores; and f) Alternate FUSION module for the HTD.

5. EXTENDING HUMAN TRAFFICKING DETECTION VIA WORKFLOWS

The initial development of the project had progressed to creating a crawler, which downloads posts from various posting sites, and an extractor, which extracts the text and images and stores them in a database. However, there had been no substantial analysis of the posts in this nascent project. We extended the project to examine both the text of the post (using the Text Analytics workflow fragments we had already developed), as well as the associated images (using the Image Analysis workflow fragments we developed); a final determination about trafficking of the subject of the post was made by fusing the results of the Text and Image analysis via the Fusion workflow fragment we developed. The goal of this project is to use both the text and image content of posts to make a stronger determination of whether or not the subject of the post was trafficked. Thus, the re-use and re-purposing of workflow fragments allowed a multimedia analysis spanning data domains of text and image analysis, including the fusion of their results in the final determination.

Componentized	Crawler and Extractor Workflow Fragment
Re-Used	N-Cuts, Feature Generation, LDA, and SVM Workflow Fragments from Figures 1 [9] and 2 [11]
Re-Purposed	Fusion Workflow Fragment in Figure 2 [11]

Table 1: Workflow Fragment Componentization, Re-Use, and Re-Purposing.

We extended the nascent HTD project by re-using and re-purposing Image Analysis and Text Analytics workflow fragments. In particular, we componentized, re-used, and re-purposed the workflow fragments as shown in Table 1 for this social media analysis task.

We first componentized the previously developed crawler and extractor as workflow fragments using the Wings framework and then re-used/re-purposed our workflow fragments to create the final workflow for human trafficking detec-

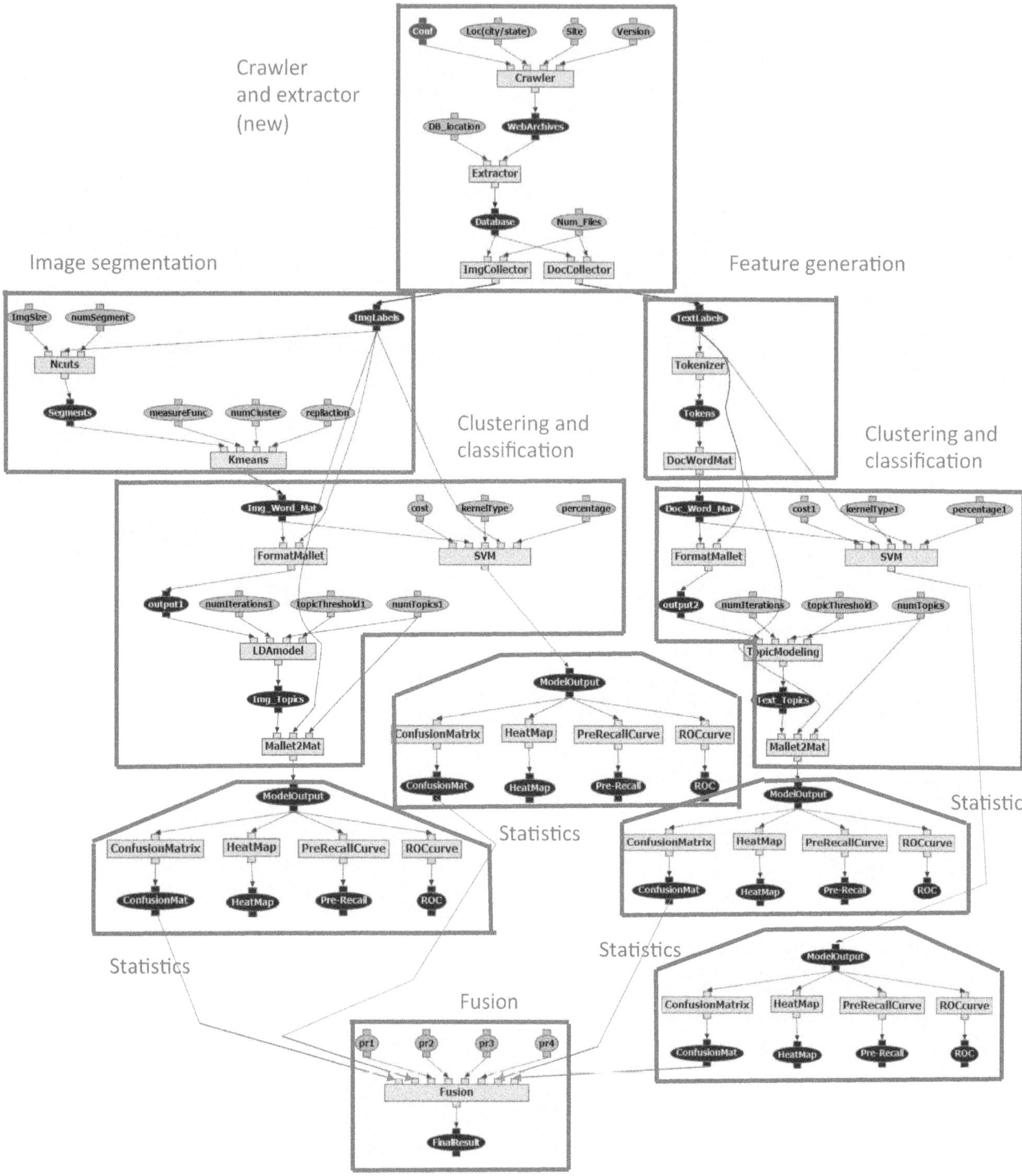

Figure 4: Detailed workflow for Fusion of Image and Text Analyses in the Multimedia Content Analysis workflow.

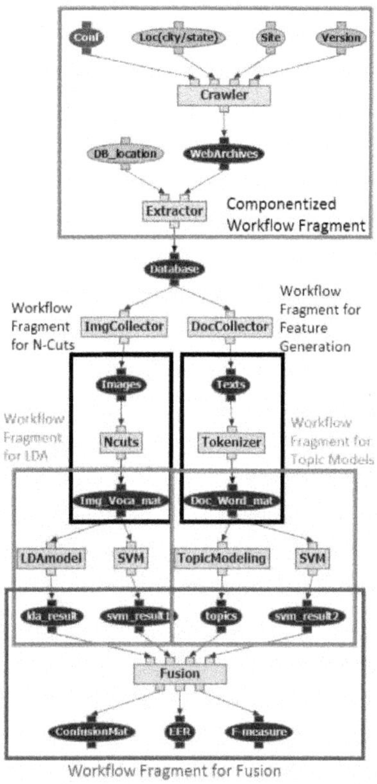

Figure 3: High level view of the workflow for Fusion of Image and Text Analyses in the Social Media Analysis workflow.

tion. The resulting workflow is shown in Figure 3 where the top black box labelled "Componentized Workflow Fragment" shows the original crawler and extractor incorporated as components in Wings. This is followed by:

- Re-Use: The next two black boxes labelled "Workflow Fragment for N-Cuts" and "Workflow Fragment for Feature Generation" show re-use of the Image Analysis workflow fragments from Figure 2 as well as the re-use of the Text Analytics workflow fragments from Figure 1, respectively. Here, the "Tokenizer" component represents the entire workflow fragment in Figure 1(a).

- Re-Use: The next two red boxes labelled "Workflow Fragment for LDA" and "Workflow Fragment for Topic Models" show the re-use of workflow fragments for unsupervised analysis using MALLET and supervised analysis using SVM in a bag-of-words model from both the Image Analysis workflow fragments in Figure 2 and the Text Analytics workflow fragments in Figure 1. Here, the "TopicModeling" component represents the entire workflow fragment in Figure 2(d).

- Re-Purpose: The final blue box labelled "Workflow Fragment for Fusion" shows the re-purposed Fusion workflow fragment from Figure 2 for fusing the results of the Text and Image Analysis and visualizing those results.

	F-Measure	Equal Error Rate
Image-LDA	0.500000	0.523810
Image-SVM	0.526316	0.400000
Text-TopicModel	0.600000	0.428571
Text-SVM	0.470588	0.300000
Fusion	0.506283	0.488095

Table 3: Cumulative Statistical Comparison of all 5 models.

The final, detailed workflow is shown in Figure 4, where all the workflow fragments in Figure 3 are expanded. For the image analysis, an N-cuts algorithm is used. The N-cuts component takes two parameters: the image size and the number of segments. The image size simply means resizing the input image for the process. How many segments an image should be divided into is a user choice, so it varies depending upon the application. For our experiments, 10 segments were used. For each segment, a color histogram is computed and this information is used as the input for the K-means algorithm in the next step. Thus, a visual vocabulary based on the color histogram of each segment is built up. The number of clusters determines how large a visual vocabulary is created. For the distance measure in K-means, we used the Euclidean distance method. The centroid of each cluster determines the visual vocabulary word. Using a Bag-of-Words model, we can create an image-word document for all the image inputs using these visual vocabularies. This matrix is fed into the LDA and SVM algorithms.

6. EXPERIMENTS AND RESULTS

In this set of experiments, the goal is to determine if the person represented in an ad is a minor or not. The workflow uses both the ad text, as well as the ad images, to make this determination. We present below the results of our experiments and discuss the benefits of using workflows.

6.1 Exploring Different Parameter Values

After extracting images and texts separately from the original posts, each data element is analyzed using unsupervised and supervised learning algorithms. One benefit of using workflows is the ability to easily experiment with different parameter settings, while the system tracks the provenance of the results of each run.

For the unsupervised case of the image analysis, the Mallet LDA in our design takes three parameters: number of iterations, number of topics, and the topic threshold. The important parameter is topic threshold. If the topic proportion is less than the threshold decimal value, then this topic will not be displayed in the result. The topic threshold is often used as an efficient filter when there are many topics existing in the document set. For our case, since we're only making the determination of whether or not the subject of a post is a minor, we only have a binomial case. Most of the percentages are close to 50%, either a little greater or a little less. Thus, setting topicThreshold to 0.1 ensures we get the topic in either case. After comparing the topic decision with the ground truth, the last step is to get the statistical result.

For the supervised learning case of the image analysis, we utilized an SVM. We did not want to set the cost control parameter for the SVM to be too large, which would cause

(a)

	Predicted	
	Negative	**Positive**
Negative	0.250000	0.225000
Positive	0.275000	0.250000

(b)

	Predicted	
	Negative	**Positive**
Negative	0.250000	0.250000
Positive	0.200000	0.300000

(c)

	Predicted	
	Negative	**Positive**
Negative	0.300000	0.175000
Positive	0.225000	0.300000

(d)

	Predicted	
	Negative	**Positive**
Negative	0.200000	0.300000
Positive	0.150000	0.350000

(e)

	Predicted	
	Negative	**Positive**
Negative	0.250000	0.237500
Positive	0.250000	0.262500

Table 2: Confusion Matrices for: (a) Image-LDA, (b) Image-SVM, (c) Text-TopicModeling, (d) Text-SVM, and (e) Fusion.

an overfitting to the data. In general, the boundary becomes smoother with smaller cost. We thus set the cost parameter for the SVM to 0.5 and chose the linear kernel (kernelType = 0). The percentage parameter determines how to divide training and testing set and we set it to the simplest case of 50%. At the end, the SVM component outputs a comparison between the ground truth and expected label for each image, and this result is fed into the statistical module, as well.

For the text analysis side, the same components are used. The difference is in the processing of the data prior to getting a document-word matrix. Using a tokenizer, a unique word list is created from all text inputs. Then, this list is used to build a document-word matrix. With the matrix, the rest of workflow is the same as in the image analysis case above.

6.2 Managing Multiple Code Versions

The first steps of the workflow include a crawler that downloads the data from the desired site. Given a location, consisting of both the city and state, and the URL of the site where these ads are posted, the crawler component gathers all the web posts on that site. Different scripts need to be written to crawl different types of sites. The crawler component includes a parameter that allows the user to select a different version of the crawler code based on the desired script version. Thus, a benefit of using this workflow framework is that the system can manage multiple versions of codes.

6.3 Analysis of a Labeled Dataset

We have tested the workflow with a sample set of data which consisted of 40 ads, 20 of which were labelled for training and 20 were used for testing. One of the main hindrances to creating a larger test dataset is the dearth of hand-labelled data by law enforcement experts. We are currently labelling a larger dataset to run the analysis with more in-depth results.

The workflow itself took approximately three minutes to run after the data was collected, extracted, and labelled. We show confusion matrices for the Image-LDA, Image-SVM, Text-TopicModeling, Text-SVM, and Fusion methods in Table 2. We further show cumulative statistical measures of Equal Error Rate and the F-Measure for each of the five methods in Table 3. Here, we see the Text-TopicModel and Text-SVM methods tend to outperform since the Fusion module is a simple average scheme. In future work, we intend to experiment with various fusion methodologies in addition to this simple boosting scheme, including utilizing more complex learner combination schemes in the fusion step as we increase the number of methods utilized in the overall workflow.

a) 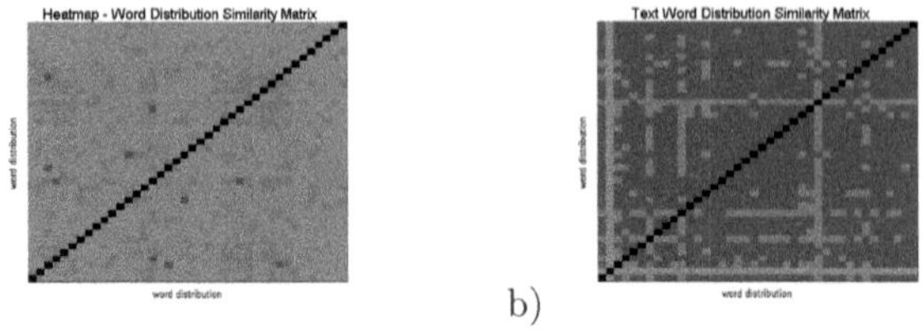 b)

Figure 5: Heatmaps to identify duplicate posts in the large sample dataset using a) image analysis and b) text analysis.

6.4 Analysis of an Unlabeled Dataset

In addition, we used the workflow to examine a larger dataset of 6,000 posts that have not been labelled to find duplicate posts within that dataset; duplicate posts would indicate the same trafficked minor is transferred to multiple cities or locations. Results for the duplicate posts are shown as heatmaps for the image analysis and text analysis components in Figure 5. To use the workflow with unlabeled data, we simply weighted down the supervised learning results.

6.5 Experimenting with Different Workflow Fragments

Adding in more modules into the workflow easily is one of the greatest advantages of using scientific workflows for rapid application development. We can incorporate the latest age estimation computer vision methods by componentizing them in exactly the same way as we componentized the crawler and extractor. In addition, we can easily vary the parameters to run multiple experimental configurations. This capability to experiment by including or excluding certain modules and adjusting parameters is exactly the kind of ability the final product will enable law enforcement agents to utilize. The ability to change configuration and include different methods is shown in [9], where high school interns utilized workflow fragments to experiment with a wide variety of experimental setups and customizations.

Workflows allow us to prototype faster, include or exclude multiple methods, parallelize for big data use, scale up in terms of data and processing, and allow experimenting with various setups and different parameter values. This ability to componentize existing programs and expand the functionality by using pre-existing workflow fragments also results in significant time and effort savings. Here, we show how easy

(a)

	Predicted	
	Negative	Positive
Negative	0.250000	0.237500
Positive	0.212500	0.300000
F-Measure	0.524226	
EER	0.413095	
Proportions	imgLDA = 1, imgSVM = 1,txtLDA = 1,txtSVM = 1	

(b)

	Predicted	
	Negative	Positive
Negative	0.241667	0.250000
Positive	0.200000	0.308333
F-Measure	0.515635	
EER	0.392063	
Proportions	imgLDA = 0.5, imgSVM = 1, txtLDA = 0.5, txtSVM = 1	

(c)

	Predicted	
	Negative	Positive
Negative	0.258333	0.225000
Positive	0.225000	0.291667
F-Measure	0.532817	
EER	0.434127	
Proportions	imgLDA = 1, imgSVM = 0.5, txtLDA = 1, txtSVM = 0.5	

(d)

	Predicted	
	Negative	Positive
Negative	0.250000	0.237500
Positive	0.204167	0.308333
F-Measure	0.527915	
EER	0.396825	
Proportions	imgLDA = 0.5, imgSVM = 0.5, txtLDA = 1, txtSVM = 1	

Table 4: Different weighting schemes for the Modified Fusion module from Figure 5 showing confusion matrices and summary statistics for four different runs of the modified Fusion module with the following schemes: (a) equally weighted supervised and unsupervised methods, (b) greater weighting on the supervised module, (c) greater weighting on the unsupervised module, and (d) greater weight on the text modules.

it is to vary the parameter values and do multiple runs to empirically determine the optimal fusion weighting. We first modified the Fusion component to allow the user to specify the weighting proportion for each input method, as shown in Figure 2 (f). We then experimented with varying the weights on the input modules by using equally weighted supervised and unsupervised methods (all modules are set to 1), greater weighting on the supervised module (LDA = 0.5, SVM = 1), greater weighting on the unsupervised module (LDA = 1, SVM = 0.5), and greater weight on the text modules (IMG = 0.5, TXT = 1). The results with confusion matrices and summary statistics for the four different runs of the modified Fusion module are shown in Table 4.

6.5.1 Analysis of Time/Work Savings

In this implementation, we incorporated the original crawler and extractor into Wings and then added on various Text Analysis and Image Analysis workflow fragments, including fusing their results and adding components to help visualize the results. This involved writing simple component wrapper scripts for both of the existing python scripts and setting up the mySQL database interface. The original development of the python version of the crawler/extractor had taken several months; this was quite involved as appropriate algorithms had to be researched, in addition to developing the code. The original crawler and extractor were componentized into Wings components, as shown in Figure 3.

This process took roughly two days as the original programs had to be made independent of the original development environment, account for supporting libraries, and had to interface with the external Database system that was distributed on the Web. Once this was done, the extension of the other components via workflow fragments for Image Analysis, Text Analysis, and their Fusion and visualization, took approximately one day, saving effort estimated to be on the order of 300 man-hours of work. This was estimated by the original developers using one postdoc and one graduate student working at a similar pace as in the development of the original prototype as they worked to identify appropriate algorithms for image and text analysis, implement them and incorporate them into their nascent crawler/extractor prototype, and then investigated a fusion methodology as well as the tools to visualize and analyze the results.

7. CONCLUSION

The multimodal information fusion of image and text data afforded by workflows helped to extend the Human Trafficking Detection (HTD) project in this preliminary work. In addition to extending the actual analysis, it also helped significantly reduce the time and work required in the development of those extensions. The benefits of workflows for large-scale multimedia content analysis, in fact, goes beyond the security applications shown in this paper and to the general analysis of the variety, volume, and velocity of big data, as well: workflows allow tracking of intermediate results, mapping to various execution resources, failure recovery, and full load management [8]. In future work, we intend to show how the ability to parallelize data processing by executing workflows in distributed resources would allow us to address the volume and velocity of big data that presents a great challenge in the HTD application as well as other multimodal information fusion problems.

8. ACKNOWLEDGMENT

We gratefully acknowledge support from the Defense Advanced Research Projects Agency with award FA8750-13-C-0016. This research was also partially supported by the National Science Foundation under Grant #1019343 to the Computing Research Association for the CIFellows Project. Thanks are due to our colleagues in federal law enforcement and the Los Angeles Metro Task Force on Human Trafficking.

9. REFERENCES

[1] S. C. Herring, "Web content analysis: Expanding the paradigm," in *International Handbook of Internet Research* (J. Hunsinger, L. Klastrup, and M. Allen, eds.), pp. 233–249, Springer Netherlands, 2010.

[2] C. Weare and W.-Y. Lin, "Content analysis of the world wide web: Opportunities and challenges," *Social Science Computer Review*, vol. 18, no. 3, pp. 272–292, 2000.

[3] M. Latonero, "Human trafficking online: The role of social networking sites and online classifieds," tech. rep., USC Annenberg School for Communication, 2011.

[4] T. M. Kurc, S. Hastings, V. S. Kumar, S. Langella, A. Sharma, T. Pan, S. Oster, D. Ervin, J. Permar, S. Narayanan, Y. Gil, E. Deelman, M. W. Hall, and J. H. Saltz, "High performance computing and grid computing for integrative biomedical research," *Journal of High Performance Computing Applications*, vol. 23, no. 3, pp. 252–264, 2009.

[5] A. Goderis, U. Sattler, P. Lord, and C. Goble, "Seven bottlenecks to workflow reuse and repurposing," in *The Semantic Web*, pp. 323–337, Springer Berlin / Heidelberg, 2005.

[6] Y. Gil, V. Ratnakar, E. Deelman, G. Mehta, and J. Kim, "Wings for pegasus: Creating large-scale scientific applications using semantic representations of computational workflows," in *AAAI*, pp. 1767–1774, 2007.

[7] Y. Gil, V. Ratnakar, J. Kim, P. A. Gonzalez-Calero, P. Groth, J. Moody, and E. Deelman, "Wings: Intelligent workflow-based design of computational experiments," *IEEE Intelligent Systems*, vol. 26, no. 1, 2011.

[8] Y. Gil, P. Szekely, S. Villamizar, T. Harmon, V. Ratnakar, S. Gupta, M. Muslea, F. Silva, and C. Knoblock, "Mind your metadata: Exploiting semantics for configuration, adaptation, and provenance in scientific workflows," in *Proceedings of the Tenth International Semantic Web Conference*, 2011.

[9] M. Hauder, Y. Gil, R. Sethi, Y. Liu, and H. Jo, "Making data analysis expertise broadly accessible through workflows," in *In Proceedings of the Sixth Workshop on Workflows in Support of Large-Scale Science (WORKS), held in conjunction with SC*, 2011.

[10] R. J. Sethi, H. Jo, and Y. Gil, "Re-using workflow fragments across multiple data domains," in *Supercomputing WORKS*, 2012.

[11] R. J. Sethi, H. Jo, and Y. Gil, "Structured analysis of the isi atomic pair actions dataset using workflows," *Pattern Recognition Letters*, vol. SI:SAHAR, 2013.

[12] I. Bhattacharya and L. Getoor, "Collective entity resolution in relational data," *ACM Trans. Knowl. Discov. Data*, vol. 1, Mar. 2007.

[13] J. Kim, Y. Gil, and M. Spraragen, "Principles for interactive acquisition and validation of workflows," *Journal of Experimental and Theoretical Artificial Intelligence*, 2009.

[14] I. J. Taylor, E. Deelman, D. B. Gannon, and M. Shields, *Workflows for e-Science: Scientific Workflows for Grids*. Springer-Verlag, 2006.

[15] Y. Gil, P. Szekely, S. Villamizar, T. C. Harmon, V. Ratnakar, S. Gupta, M. Muslea, F. Silva, and C. A. Knoblock, "Mind your metadata: exploiting semantics for configuration, adaptation, and provenance in scientific workflows," in *ISWC*, 2011.

[16] M. Hauder, Y. Gil, and Y. Liu, "A framework for efficient text analytics through automatic configuration and customization of scientific workflows," in *In Proceedings of the Seventh IEEE International Conference on e-Science*, (Stockholm, Sweden), 2011.

[17] I. H. Witten, E. Frank, L. Trigg, M. Hall, G. Holmes, and S. J. Cunningham, "Weka: Practical machine learning tools and techniques with java implementations," 1999.

[18] B. Song, R. J. Sethi, and A. K. Roy-Chowdhury, "Robust Wide Area Tracking in Single and Multiple Views," in *Visual Analysis of Humans* (T. B. Moeslund, L. Sigal, V. Krüger, and A. Hilton, eds.), pp. 1–18, Springer-Verlag, 2011.

[19] N. M. Nayak, R. J. Sethi, B. Song, and A. K. Roy-Chowdhury, "Motion Pattern Analysis for Event and Behavior Recognition," in *Visual Analysis of Humans* (T. B. Moeslund, L. Sigal, V. Krüger, and A. Hilton, eds.), pp. 289–309, Springer-Verlag, 2011.

[20] R. J. Sethi and A. K. Roy-Chowdhury, "Modeling and Recognition of Complex Multi-Person Interactions in Video," in *ACM MM MPVA*, pp. 0–3, 2010.

[21] R. J. Sethi, A. K. Roy-Chowdhury, and S. Ali, "Activity Recognition by Integrating the Physics of Motion with a Neuromorphic Model of Perception," in *WMVC*, WMVC, 2009.

[22] R. J. Sethi and A. K. Roy-Chowdhury, "Physics-based Activity Modelling in Phase Space," in *ICVGIP*, 2010.

[23] G. Bradski, "The OpenCV Library," *Dr. Dobb's Journal of Software Tools*, 2000.

[24] A. K. McCallum, "Mallet: A machine learning for language toolkit," 2002.

[25] D. Garijo and Y. Gil, "A new approach for publishing workflows: Abstractions, standards, and linked data," in *SC WORKS*, (Seattle, Washington), 2011.

[26] Y. Yang and J. O. Pedersen, "A comparative study on feature selection in text categorization," pp. 412–420, Morgan Kaufmann Publishers, 1997.

[27] P. Turaga, R. Chellappa, V. S. Subrahmanian, and O. Udrea, "Machine recognition of human activities: A survey," *CSVT*, 2008.

[28] J. Aggarwal and M. Ryoo, "Human activity analysis: A review," *ACM Computing Surveys*, 2012.

[29] M. Ryoo and J. Aggarwal, "Stochastic representation and recognition of high-level group activities," *CVPR*, 2009.

[30] J. Aggarwal and Q. Cai, "Human motion analysis: A review," *CVIU*, 1999.

Waisda? Video Labeling Game

Michiel Hildebrand
VU University Amsterdam
michiel.hildebrand@vu.nl

Maarten Brinkerink
Netherlands Institute for Sound and Vision

Riste Gligorov
VU University Amsterdam

Martijn van Steenbergen
Q42

Johan Huijkman
Q42

Johan Oomen
Netherlands Institute for Sound and Vision

ABSTRACT

The *Waisda?* video labeling game is a crowsourcing tool to collect user-generated metadata for video clips. It follows the paradigm of games-with-a-purpose, where two or more users play against each other by entering tags that describe the content of the video. Players score points by entering the same tags as one of the other players. As a result each video that is played in the game is annotated with tags that are anchored to a time point in the video. *Waisda?* has been deployed in two projects with videos from Dutch broadcasters. With the open source version of *Waisda?* crowdsourcing of video annotation becomes available for any online video collection.

Categories and Subject Descriptors

H.4 [**Information Systems Applications**]: Miscellaneous

Keywords

Video tagging; Crowdsourcing; GWAP; Waisda

1. INTRODUCTION

Waisda? is a Web application that provides a multiplayer video labeling game. It is based on the principles of the ESP image labeling game coined by Louis von Ahn [4], where two or more users compete with each other by entering tags. In *Waisda?* players score points by entering the same tag as one of the other players in a ten second interval. As a result each video that is played in the game is annotated with tags that are anchored to a time point in the video.

Waisda? was initiated by the Netherlands Institute for Sound and Vision and the VU University Amsterdam in the context of the Dutch project Images for the Future[1] and the European research project PrestoPRIME[2]. The software is developed by Q42, a Dutch internet development company.

[1]`http://imagesforthefuture.com/`
[2]`http://www.prestoprime.org/`

MM'13, October 21–25, 2013, Barcelona, Spain.
Copyright 2013 ACM 978-1-4503-2404-5/13/10 ...$15.00.
http://dx.doi.org/10.1145/2502081.2502221.

Waisda? was pioneered in two pilots using historic archive material as well as recent TV episodes from Dutch broadcasters. The two pilots together resulted in more than a million tags describing thousands of videos.

The open source version of *Waisda?* enables maintainers of an online video collection to start their own crowdsourcing initiative for time-based annotations. In particular, we believe that *Waisda?* is a valuable tool for cultural heritage institutions, as it provides a novel and engaging way for the public to access and interact with audiovisual material.

In this short paper we describe the gameplay and user interface of *Waisda?*, explain the software architecture, and discuss the lessons that we learned from the two pilot projects to provide guidelines for when and how to use *Waisda?*.

2. GAMEPLAY AND USER INTERFACE

The gameplay of *Waisda?* is straightforward: the player first selects a video from the *Homepage*, plays the *Game* by watching the video and entering tags, and finally studies the results in the *Game recap* to learn what he/she can improve in future games.

2.1 Homepage

Figure 1 shows the homepage of *Waisda?*, with six videos that the user can choose from. A player starts a game by selecting one of these videos. To give other players the opportunity to join the game, the player first enters the waiting room. In the waiting room the players can study the game instructions and after 20 seconds the game is automatically started. On the homepage the games that are waiting for players are shown at the bottom right. Players can quickly join a game by selecting one of the entries.

The homepage also contains the basic instructions that prepare the user for the game. To honor the top players, and motivate the other players, the homepage contains a leaderboard that displays the top players of the week. To engage the players with the purpose of the game a notification at the top of the page shows the total number of tags that were entered into the system, and the users contribution to this total. This part of the page also contains the links to register and login. Games can be played without registering, but only for registered players the score is maintained in the player's profile.

To explain the potential of the contributed tags, the page contains a tag cloud with the most popular tags. By selecting a tag the user can navigate the video collection. Finally, the bottom of the page has space reserved for logos and nav-

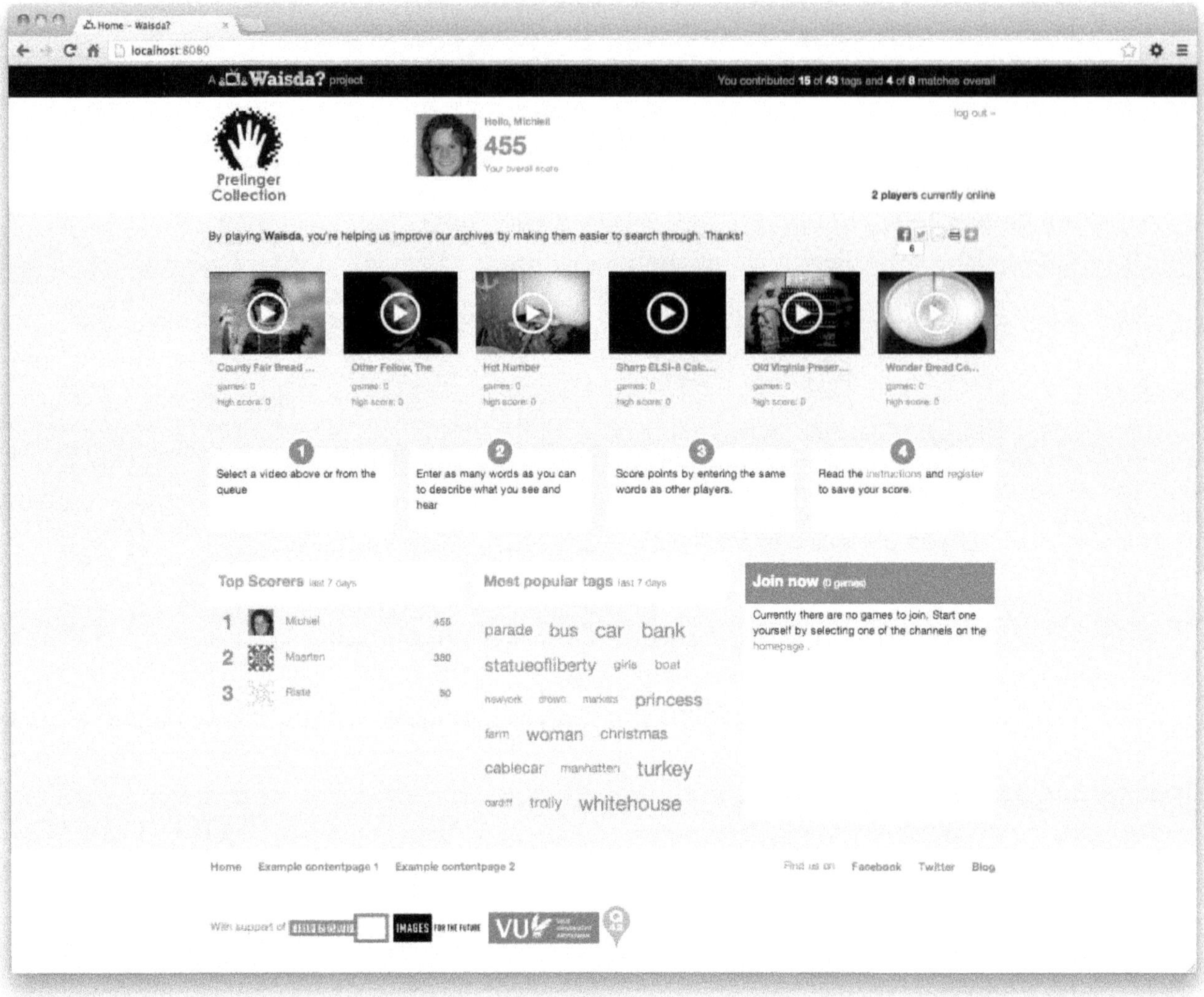

Figure 1: Screenshot of the *Waisda?* homepage with public domain video clips from the Prelinger Archives.

igation links to additional pages, such as an about page or a page with the terms of use.

2.2 Game

Figure 2 shows the game page of *Waisda?*. It contains a video player and below it a text-entry field. When the player enters the game page the video automatically starts playing, the text-entry field receives focus, and the player can start entering tags. The right side of the page contains the score board. It consists of the current score of the player, the current rank and a listing with all tags entered by the player. The tags are displayed with their score and an icon indicating the type of match and the tag type (person, location etc.).

Waisda? uses a scoring mechanism to motivate users to (keep) playing the game, and reward them for entering specific types of tags. The basic scoring mechanism is tag agreement, two players entering the same tag. From the perspective of the video collection tag agreement provides a mechanism to improve the quality, tags that are entered by more than one user are less likely to contain spelling errors and are more likely to provide a trustworthy description of the video. Tags are considered a match if they are syntactically the same after normalization and entered within a ten second interval of each other. The details of the normalization procedure are explained in the documentation. The matching procedure can be extended by importing tag similarity lists. For example, tags can be matched semantically by importing synonym lists, and specific tags (e.g. Labrador) can be matched with more generic tags (e.g. Dog) by importing word pairs derived from the hierarchical structures of linguistic or domain specific thesauri.

Waisda? also contains a mechanism to reward players for entering specific types of tags. For example, when tagging videos in the art domain the names of artists are important. By importing a dictionary with artist names *Waisda?* detects these tag types and rewards the players additional points.

As we can not expect that there are always sufficient users active at the same time, the scoring mechanism of *Waisda?*

Figure 2: Screenshot of the *Waisda?* game page with public domain video clip from Preligner Archives.

also motivates users to play alone. In this case a player scores points by matching with the tags that were entered for the same video in previous games. To ensure players not only tag in the most obvious ways, the scoring mechanism of *Waisda?* also motivates players to *pioneer* new tags. A player enters a pioneer tag when this tag is not entered for this video before, and afterwards it is matched with tags entered by other players (in the same or a later game).

2.3 Game recap

When the video ends the user is automatically redirected to the game recap. On this page the user can investigate his performance, learn about the details of the scoring mechanism and the behavior of other players. The game recap consists of two parts. The tag statistics give an overview of the number of tags entered by the player in different categories, including the number of matched tags, pioneer tags and specific types of tags. The tag details are listing of all the tags entered by the player. The listing is similar as the one provided in the game, but includes information about which player a tag was matched with.

3. IMPLEMENTATION

Waisda? is implemented using a typical open source Web application infrastructure. The backend is written in the Java programming language using the Spring framework. The views for the pages of the application are defined as Java Server Pages (JSP). The application is backed by a MySQL database. The code binds to the database using the Java Persistence API and Hibernate. The frontend uses HTML, JavaScript and CSS. jQuery and Twitter Bootstrap are used as the JavaScript and CSS libraries. The dynamic stylesheet language LESS is used to allow easy configuration of the presentation style.

The *Waisda?* source code and documentation is available from Github `http://github.com/beeldengeluid/waisda`. Installing and running *Waisda?* is handled by Maven and is initiated by the included *Makefile*. The *getting started* section of the documentation contains instructions to setup a deployment using videos from the Prelinger archive[3].

3.1 Backend

After installation the maintainer has to populate the database with videos and optionally with dictionaries and similarity lists. A *video* has a title, description, source URL, key frame URL, duration and video player type. There are currently two types of video players supported: the JWPlayer (HTML5 and Flash), and the NPO player (Silverlight) to play content from Dutch public broadcasting associations. Each video in the project specifies which of the two players it would like to use, in combination with the parameters required for the players. A *dictionary* is a set of word-type pairs. Dictionaries are used to reward additional points for specific types of tags. Examples are names of celebrities and names of geographical locations. A *similarity list* is a set of word-word pairs. Matching lists are used to extent the default syntactic tag matching with semantic similarity matching. Examples are synonym pairs or words that are hierarchically related (specific-generic).

[3]`http://archive.org/details/prelinger`

Videos, dictionaries and similarity lists can be added by directly modifying the MySQL database of *Waisda?*, or by importing a CSV file. Typically, dictionaries and similarity lists are generated from controlled vocabularies related to the video collection and/or open data sources, such as DBPedia[4] or WordNet[5].

Besides the video and dictionaries there are three types of entities that are internal to the software and should not be modified. A *player* is a user that registered in the system or played anonymously. Only for registered users the score is stored. A *game* is a session in which one or more players watch a video simultaneously and enter zero or more tags at specific timestamps relative to the video. Players can see the other participants names and their relative positions based on their session scores. A *tag entry* for a specific game is owned by a user and contains information on what tag was entered exactly, at what timestamp relative to the video it was entered and has a score based on whether the tag matches other users tags and/or words in dictionaries.

3.2 Frontend

The default interface of *Waisda?* is completely functional. In addition, basic branding and styling can be done by adding a logo and changing the color scheme. These changes can be made with little knowledge of the system and are described in detail in the documentation.

The documentation also describes how a maintainer can modify the advanced functionality of the system, such as the videos that are shown on the homepage, how tags are matched and which scores are given. It also describes how new pages can be added or how the page layout can be changed. Making such changes requires more advanced knowledge of HTML, CSS and Java Server Pages.

4. PILOTS AND LESSONS LEARNED

Waisda? was developed in two pilot projects. The first pilot was executed in 2009, in collaboration with the Dutch broadcaster KRO. More than 420,000 tags were collected for 612 videos, an average of almost 700 tags per video. Over 2,000 different players participated. This pilot used the full length videos of various TV shows, including the Dutch version of *Farmer Wants a Wife*. Based on interviews with *Waisda?* players [3], and analysis of the dataset [2] we observed that:

Waisda? is best suited for short video fragments (e.g. videos with a duration of a few minutes). In the first pilot full length videos were streamed, and when a player selected a channel he would join the video at the current playing time. There was no clear start or end of a game. Users indicated that they prefer to play multiple short games.

Users prefer to play against each other, but to achieve an active player community they should be continuously motivated. Visitor statistics showed that players were attracted by promotion activities, such as a banner on the Website of the TV show. Players were also motivated by short term goals, such as regular competitions where users are rewarded for entering the most tags in a week.

Power users (or super taggers) are responsible for the majority of the tags. Attracting and rewarding such super taggers is important.

[4]`http://dbpedia.org/`

[5]`http://wordnet.princeton.edu/`

Waisda? tags provide a user perspective on the videos that complement professional annotation. Comparison with the vocabulary used by professional cataloguers showed only small overlap, whereas most tags were found to be proper words.

Waisda? tags mainly provide general descriptions of What and Who is seen and heard in the video. Manual classification of a data sample showed that most tags describe the objects and concepts that occur in the video in a general way. Users also describe persons and locations, but to a lesser extent. The introduction of dictionaries in *Waisda?*, to detect the tag type and reward a higher score, is motivated by this finding.

The second pilot with Waisda? started in November 2011 and contained fragments from the television series *Man Bijt Hond*, a popular daily show that aired for the past 11 years. The series is well suited for *Waisda?* as each episode consists of 8 self-contained fragments of a few minutes. Over 750,000 tags were collected for over 5,000 videos. The data collected in this pilot was used to evaluate the usefulness of user-generated metadata for video fragment retrieval [1]. Using a subset of 197 video fragments and 50 realistic search queries the results that were retrieved with the *Waisda?* tags were compared with the results retrieved by existing metadata, such as captions, titles and descriptions and in-house tags created by the broadcaster.

Waisda? tags enables high recall fragment retrieval. The *Waisda?* tags from the second pilot outperform the in-house tags on average by 69% and captions by 39%.

Thus if any of the other metadata types are unavailable or costly to acquire, relying only on sufficient number of user tags for search could yield equal or even better results.

Acknowledgements

This research was partially supported by the PrestoPRIME project, funded by the European Commission under ICT FP7 (Seventh Framework Programme, Contract No. 231161)

5. REFERENCES

[1] R. Gligorov, M. Hildebrand, J. van Ossenbruggen, L. Aroyo, and G. Schreiber. An evaluation of labelling-game data for video retrieval. In *Advances in Information Retrieval - 35th European Conference on IR Research, ECIR 2013*, pages 50–61, Moscow, Russia, March 2013.

[2] R. Gligorov, M. Hildebrand, J. Van Ossenbruggen, G. Schreiber, and L. Aroyo. On the role of user-generated metadata in audio visual collections. In *Proceedings of the International Conference on Knowledge Capture (K-CAP)*, pages 145 151, Banff, Canada, June 2011.

[3] J. Oomen, L. Belice Baltussen, S. Limonard, A. van Ees, M. Brinkerink, L. Aroyo, J. Vervaart, K. Asaf, and R. Gligorov. Emerging practices in the cultural heritage domain - social tagging of audiovisual heritage. In *Proceedings of the WebSci10: Extending the Frontiers of Society On-Line*, Raleigh, US, April 2010.

[4] L. von Ahn and L. Dabbish. Labeling images with a computer game. In *CHI '04: Proceedings of the SIGCHI conference on Human factors in computing systems*, pages 319–326, New York, NY, USA, 2004. ACM.

GamingAnywhere: An Open-Source Cloud Gaming Testbed

Chun-Ying Huang[1], De-Yu Chen[2], Cheng-Hsin Hsu[3], and Kuan-Ta Chen[2]

[1]Department of Computer Science and Engineering, National Taiwan Ocean University

[2]Institute of Information Science, Academia Sinica

[3]Department of Computer Science, National Tsing Hua University

ABSTRACT

While cloud gaming opens new business opportunity, it also poses tremendous challenges as the Internet only provides best-effort service and gamers are hard to please. Although researchers have various ideas to improve cloud gaming systems, existing cloud gaming systems are closed and proprietary, and cannot be used to evaluate these ideas. We present GamingAnywhere, the first open-source cloud gaming system, which is extensible, portable, and configurable. GamingAnywhere may be used by: (i) researchers and engineers to implement and test their new ideas, (ii) service providers to develop cloud gaming services, and (iii) gamers to set up private cloud gaming systems. Details on GamingAnywhere are given in this paper. We firmly believe GamingAnywhere will stimulate future studies on cloud gaming and real-time interactive distributed systems.

Categories and Subject Descriptors: H.5 [Information Systems Applications]: Multimedia Information Systems

Keywords: Remote gaming; performance evaluation

1. MOTIVATION

Computer games have become very popular, e.g., gamers spent 24.75 billion USD on computer games, hardware, and accessories in 2011 [6]. Traditionally, computer games are delivered either in boxes or via Internet downloads. Gamers have to *install* the computer games on physical machines to play them. The installation process becomes extremely tedious because some games are complicated and the computer hardware and system software are fragmented. Take Blizzard's Starcraft II as an example, it may take more than an hour to install it on an Intel i5 PC, and another hour to apply the online patches. Furthermore, gamers may find their computers are not powerful enough to enable all the visual effects yet achieving high frame rates. Hence, gamers have to repeatedly upgrade their computers so as to play the latest computer games.

Cloud gaming is an alternative way to deliver high-quality gaming experience and opens new business opportunity [13].

MM'13, October 21–25, 2013, Barcelona, Spain.

Copyright 2013 ACM 978-1-4503-2404-5/13/10 ...$15.00.

http://dx.doi.org/10.1145/2502081.2502222.

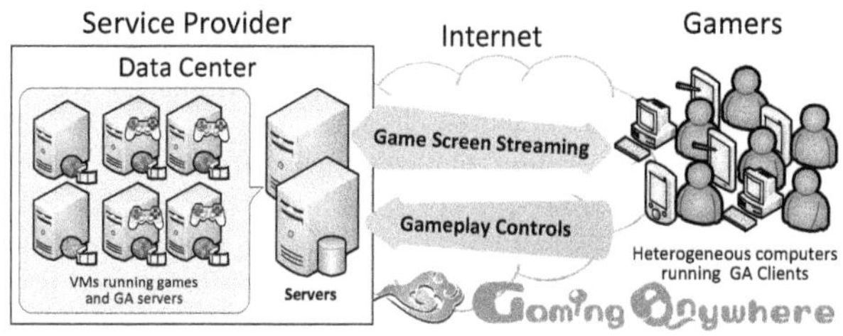

Figure 1: A cloud gaming service based on GamingAnywhere.

In a cloud gaming system, computer games run on powerful cloud servers, while gamers interact with the games via networked thin clients. The thin clients are light-weight and can be ported to resource-constrained platforms, such as mobile devices and TV set-top boxes. Figure 1 illustrates a sample cloud gaming service, in which game servers stream game screens to thin clients, and thin clients send gameplay controls, such as keystrokes and mouse movements, back to game servers. With cloud gaming, gamers can play the latest computer games anywhere and anytime, while game developers can optimize their games for a specific server configuration. The huge potential of cloud gaming has been recognized by the game industry: (i) a market report predicts that cloud gaming market will increase 9 times between 2011 and 2017 [4] and (ii) several cloud gaming startups were recently acquired by leading game developers [3, 5].

Although cloud gaming is a promising direction for the game industry, achieving good gaming experience without excessive hardware investment is a tough challenge. This is because gamers are hard to please, as they concurrently demand for high responsiveness and high video quality, but do not want to pay too much. Therefore, service providers have to not only design such systems to meet gamers' needs but also take efficiency, error resiliency, scalability, and resource allocation into considerations. This renders the design and implementation of cloud gaming systems extremely challenging. Indeed, while real-time video streaming seems to be a mature technology at the first glance, cloud gaming systems have to execute games, handle gamers' inputs, and perform screen rendering, capturing, encoding, packetizing, transmitting, decoding, and displaying in real time, and thus are much more difficult to optimize.

Fortunately, many system researchers have new ideas to improve cloud gaming experience for gamers, and reduce capital expenditure (CAPEX) and operational expenditure (OPEX) for service providers. However, all the existing

Table 1: Current supported platforms

Program	Windows	Linux	Mac OS X
Server	Windows 7+	Supported	No audio support
Client	Windows XP+	Supported	Supported

cloud gaming platforms [7, 12, 14] are closed and proprietary, which prevent the researchers from testing their ideas on real cloud gaming systems. Therefore, the new ideas were either only tested using simulators/emulators, or, worse, never evaluated and published. Without actual experiments, it is harder for new research ideas on improving cloud gaming (or real-time interactive distributed systems) to be transferred to the industry.

To better bridge the research community and the game/software industry, we initiate GamingAnywhere, which is the first open-source cloud gaming testbed. While in its infancy, we hope GamingAnywhere could gather enough attentions, and quickly grow into a community with critical mass, just like OpenFlow [11], which shares the same motivation with GamingAnywhere in a different research area.

The design philosophy of GamingAnywhere includes:

- *Extensibility*: GamingAnywhere adopts a modularized design. For example, platform-dependent components such as audio and video capturing and platform-independent components such as codecs and network protocols can be easily modified or replaced.
- *Portability*: Gamers may use devices with heterogeneous architectures to access GamingAnywhere, and thus it is important to port GamingAnywhere to as many platforms as possible. Table 1 summarizes the supported platforms as of July 2013. New platforms can be easily supported by replacing the platform-dependent components in GamingAnywhere.
- *Configurability*: System researchers may conduct experiments with diverse system parameters. A large number of built-in audio and video codecs are supported by GamingAnywhere. In addition, GamingAnywhere exposes all available configurations to gamers so that it is possible to try out the best combinations of parameters by simply editing a text-based configuration file for various usage scenarios.
- *Openness*: GamingAnywhere is publicly available at `http://gaminganywhere.org` [8]. Researchers are free to use and modify GamingAnywhere in academic research as long as the open-source license terms are followed.

2. TARGET USERS

GamingAnywhere is designed for three types of users. First, researchers and engineers may use GamingAnywhere to evaluate their new ideas without re-implementing the irrelevant software components. This will allow many new ideas to be tested in real testbeds and deployed in fields. Second, cloud gaming service providers may develop a cloud gaming front-end for gamers to choose the desired games, and integrate their front-end with GamingAnywhere. Compared to developing a brand new cloud gaming system from scratch, adopting GamingAnywhere largely reduces the time to market of new services. Third, gamers may set up GamingAnywhere on their powerful home PCs, and enjoy high-quality gaming experiences using thin clients via a LAN or the Internet. To reach wider audience, GamingAnywhere is written in C/C++ and it leverages several popular open-source libraries such as *ffmpeg* and *libSDL*. Detailed designs and implementations can be found in Huang et al. [10]. We also hope users contributing to this project by installing and playing with the system, providing comments and suggestions, sharing game configurations, and even submitting patches via the forum or public respositories.

3. DIRECTORY STRUCTURE

GamingAnywhere is released with two types of software packs: `all-in-one` and pre-compiled binary packs [8]. The `all-in-one` pack includes GamingAnywhere source codes, third-party library source code, pre-compiled binaries, while a pre-compiled binary pack such as the `bin.win32` pack includes only pre-compiled binaries for running the software on a certain platform. In any case, users can always build their own binaries that match their environments from scratch.

There are six subdirectories upon uncompressing the `all-in-one` pack; their descriptions are given below:

- `bin/`: Contains all the required run-time files, including the executables, shared objects, modules, fonts, and configuration files.
- `ga/`: Source codes of GamingAnywhere, which is divided into four parts: core, module, server, and client.
- `deps.posix/`: Dependencies for POSIX platforms, including libraries and headers. GamingAnywhere supports two POSIX platforms: Linux and Mac OS X. This subdirectory is empty by default, as the files in this subdirectory are supposed to be built from the sources in `deps.src`.
- `deps.win32/`: Dependencies for Win32 platform, including libraries and headers. This subdirectory is also empty by default, and the files in this subdirectory will be installed from the third-party packages in `deps.pkg.win32`.
- `deps.src/`: Source files of the dependent third-party packages. You will need these files to build dependencies, which is mandatory for POSIX platforms.
- `deps.pkg.win32/`: Pre-built dependencies for Win32 platform. You can install all the dependencies for Win32 by running `install.cmd` in this subdirectory. The dependencies are installed into the `deps.win32` subdirectory by default.

4. SETUP

GamingAnywhere can be installed by simply uncompressing the software packs, with or without the source code. If the `all-in-one` software pack is downloaded, the complete GamingAnywhere system can be compiled from scratch. One exception is the dependent Windows libraries: because building them can be tricky, we include the pre-built Win32 libraries in the software packs.

We briefly describe how to build GamingAnywhere binaries below. GamingAnywhere consists of three binaries: (i) `ga-client`, which is the thin client, (ii) `ga-server-periodic`, which periodically captures the desktop or a window as the game screen, and (iii) `ga-server-event-driven`, which directly hooks into the game executables to capture game screens.

POSIX. To build GamingAnywhere on POSIX platforms (i.e., Linux and Mac OS X), please make sure

Figure 2: A demonstration of GamingAnywhere system. There are four devices in the photo. One game server (the left-hand side laptop) and three game clients (a MacBook, an Android phone, and an iPad 2).

† LEGO Batman software is copyrighted by Traveller's Tales Games Publishing Ltd.

`g++`, `pkg-config`, `libX11`, `libXext`, `libXtst`, `libfreetype6`, and `libasound2` are installed. In addition, `libgl1-mesa`, `libglu1-mesa`, and `libpulse` are required on Linux. You must install both binaries and development files for the above packages. Next, the following instructions are recommended:

1. Edit the `env-setup` script and point `GADEPS` to the absolute path of `gaminganywhere/deps.posix/`.
2. Load environment variables from `env-setup` by using the `.` or `source` commands.
3. Build dependencies using `make` under `deps.src/`.
4. Build GamingAnywhere using `make all` under `ga/`.
5. Install GamingAnywhere using `make install` command under `ga/`. All the generated binaries will be copied into `bin/`.

Windows. To build GamingAnywhere on Microsoft Windows, please install Visual Studio (C++) 2010, Windows SDK, and DirectX SDK. Then, follow the instructions:

1. Install dependencies by running `install.cmd` under `deps.pkg.win32\`.
2. Install DirectX SDK into `C:\Microsoft DirectX SDK`. If you install it at a different location, please modify the SDK paths in `ga\module\vsource-desktop\NMakefile.d3d` and `ga\server\event-driven\NMakefile`.
3. Launch Visual C++ command line prompt.
4. Build GamingAnywhere by running `nmake /f NMakefile all` command under `ga\`.
5. Install GamingAnywhere by running `nmake /f NMakefile install` command under `ga\`. All the generated binaries will be copied into `bin\`.

5. EXECUTION

This section explains how to run GamingAnywhere servers and client. Before running the binaries, please check the following prerequisites. On POSIX, please add `deps.posix/lib` to the system-wide `ld.so` search path. Moreover, modify `bin/config/common/server-common.conf` to ensure that `display` is set to to an X-Window desktop with the XTEST extension enabled. The X-Window desktop can be a `VNC` or `Xvfb` desktop. On Windows, copy `deps.win32\bin\*.dll` to the same directory of GamingAnywhere binaries (i.e., `bin\`) or a directory in the system-wide DLL search path.

We give examples on how to run GamingAnywhere servers and client using DirectX SDK samples on Windows.

- **Run the periodic capture server.** To stream a game window to the client, launch the game first and then use the following command: `ga-server-periodic config\server.d3dex.conf`. The server configuration file sets either the `find-window-name` or `find-window-class` option to specify the title and the class name, respectively, of the game window to be streamed. Then, `ga-server-periodic` moves the specified window to the upper-left corner of the desktop, and starts capturing the images of the specified window periodically. Gamers should avoid moving the window manually as it may affect the mouse cursor functionality. If you do not know the window title or the class name, you can find the information for a window by using the `Spy++` tool and the `xwininfo` tool on Windows and Linux, respectively.
- **Run the event-driven server.** Rather than capturing a game's window periodically, GamingAnywhere provides another sample server which is able to capture the game window each time right after the game updates its screen. Please use the following command: `ga-server-event-driven config\server.d3dex.conf`. `ga-server-event-driven` launches the game executable specified by the `game-dir` and `game-exe` options in the configuration file; that is why each game has its own configuration file.
- **Run the client.** The GamingAnywhere thin client can be run by `ga-client config\client.abs.conf rtsp://192.168.1.1:8554/desktop`, where the server IP address is 192.168.1.1; by default GamingAnywhere uses TCP port 8554 for RTSP streams and TCP/UDP port 8555 for control messages. The `client.abs.conf` is a sample configuration which enables the absolute mouse cursor posi-

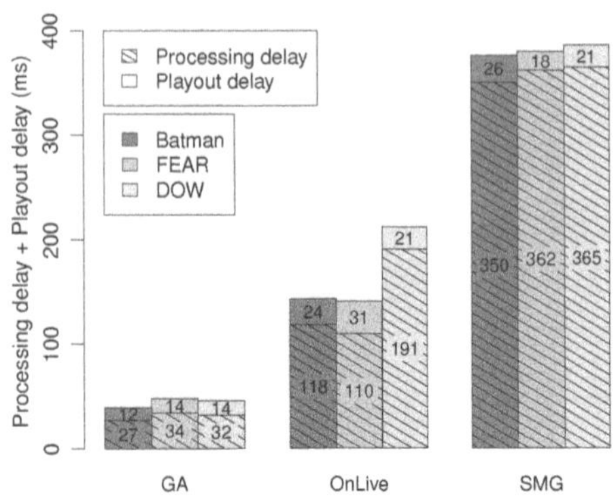

Figure 3: Response delays of GamingAnywhere, compared to two commercial systems, OnLive and StreamMyGame.

tioning. In contrast, `client.rel.conf` employs the relative mouse cursor positioning. The choice of either configuration files is game-dependent, as different games use different mechanisms for mouse position sensing and management.

6. DEMO

Figure 2 shows a GamingAnywhere testbed in our lab. In this figure, the laptop on the left-hand side runs the LEGO Batman game with GamingAnywhere event-driven server (i.e., `ga-server-event-driven`). The MacBook laptop on the right-hand side runs the GamingAnywhere client. Two additional clients also connect to the server at the same time. One client runs on an Android phone and another client runs on an iPad 2. Moreover, as GamingAnywhere server delivers audio and video frames using the standard RTSP/RTP protocol, any compatible RTSP/RTP players can be used to observe game plays.

We provide configuration files for several public-domain games [8], such as Armagetron Advanced, Assault Cube, and Neverball, so that gamers can quickly experience GamingAnywhere. Notice that the server configuration files are game-dependent, and therefore we provide a sample server configuration for each game. To get the server configuration working, please modify the `game-dir` and `game-exe` options in the configuration files to point to the game executables.

7. PERFORMANCE EVALUATION

Responsiveness is one of the most important factors affecting gaming experience [2, 9]. We define response delay to be the time difference between a user issuing a command and the in-game action appearing on the client. Cloud gaming systems have stringent response delay requirements, as gamers may demand for less than 100 ms response delay for certain games [2]. We adopt the measurement techniques proposed in [1] in order to compare the performance of GamingAnywhere against two commercial cloud gaming systems: OnLive [12] and StreamMyGame (SMG) [14].

The response delay consists of two components: (i) processing delay, which is the time required for the server to receive and process a gamer's command, and to encode and transmit the corresponding frame to the client and (ii) playout delay, which is the time required by the client to receive, decode, and render a frame on the display. We do not report network delay in our measurement studies as it is not controllable by the cloud gaming systems. Figure 3 summarizes the processing delay (at server) and the playout delay (at client) measured under 3 games and 3 cloud gaming systems. We note that the playout delay is small, $\leq$ 31 ms for all games and systems. Moreover, GamingAnywhere achieves much shorter processing delay ($\leq$ 34 ms), while OnLive and SMG suffer from up to 191 and 364 ms processing delay. Considering the 100 ms requirement suggested by Claypool and Claypool [2], GamingAnywhere works well when the network delay is < 50 ms, which is fairly achievable, e.g., a GamingAnywhere server running at Los Angeles can serve a client at as far as Oklahoma City. Due to the space limitations, detailed evaluation results on GamingAnywhere can also be found in Huang et al. [10].

8. CONCLUSION

In this paper, we have presented GamingAnywhere, the first open-source cloud gaming system. Different from closed and proprietary cloud gaming systems, GamingAnywhere allows researchers and engineers to quickly explore their new ideas on how to improve gamers' experience and increase service providers' revenue. Furthermore, GamingAnywhere is also designed to be extensible, portable, and configurable, and thus can be adopted in various usage scenarios, e.g., service providers may use GamingAnywhere to build up cloud gaming services, and gamers may use GamingAnywhere to set up private cloud gaming systems. We hope GamingAnywhere can become the cornerstone for multimedia research community to build and evaluate many cloud gaming and real-time interactive distributed systems in the future.

References

[1] K.-T. Chen, Y.-C. Chang, P.-H. Tseng, C.-Y. Huang, and C.-L. Lei. Measuring the latency of cloud gaming systems. In *Proc. of ACM Multimedia 2011*.

[2] M. Claypool and K. Claypool. Latency and player actions in online games. *Communications of the ACM*, 49(11):40–45, 2006.

[3] Cloud gaming adoption is accelerating ... and fast!, 2012. `http://www.nttcom.tv/2012/07/09/cloud-gaming-adoption-is-acceleratingand-fast/`.

[4] Distribution and monetization strategies to increase revenues from cloud gaming, 2012. `http://www.cgconfusa.com/report/documents/Content-5minCloudGamingReportHighlights.pdf`.

[5] Electronic Arts buys online gaming studio ESN, the developers behind battlefield's battlelog online social network, 2012. `http://techcrunch.com/2012/09/26/electronic-arts`.

[6] Entertainment Software Association: Industry Facts, 2013. `http://www.theesa.com/facts`.

[7] Gaikai web page, 2012. `http://www.gaikai.com/`.

[8] GamingAnywhere: An open source cloud gaming project, 2013. `http://gaminganywhere.org`.

[9] T. Henderson. *The Effects of Relative Delay in Networked Games*. PhD thesis, Department of Computer Science, University of London, 2003.

[10] C.-Y. Huang, C.-H. Hsu, Y.-C. Chang, and K.-T. Chen. GamingAnywhere: An open cloud gaming system. In *Proc. of ACM MMSys 2013*.

[11] N. McKeown, T. Anderson, H. Balakrishnan, G. Parulkar, L. Peterson, J. Rexford, S. Shenker, and J. Turner. OpenFlow: enabling innovation in campus networks. *SIGCOMM Comput. Commun. Rev.*, 38(2):69–74, Mar. 2008.

[12] OnLive web page, 2012. `http://www.onlive.com/`.

[13] P. Ross. Cloud computing's killer app: Gaming. *IEEE Spectrum*, 46(3):14, 2009.

[14] StreamMyGame web page, 2012. `http://streammygame.com/`.

The Social Signal Interpretation (SSI) Framework

Multimodal Signal Processing and Recognition in Real-Time

Johannes Wagner, Florian Lingenfelser, Tobias Baur,
Ionut Damian, Felix Kistler and Elisabeth André
Lab for Human Centered Multimedia, University of Augsburg
name@hcm-lab.de

ABSTRACT

Automatic detection and interpretation of social signals carried by voice, gestures, mimics, etc. will play a key-role for next-generation interfaces as it paves the way towards a more intuitive and natural human-computer interaction. The paper at hand introduces Social Signal Interpretation (SSI), a framework for real-time recognition of social signals. SSI supports a large range of sensor devices, filter and feature algorithms, as well as, machine learning and pattern recognition tools. It encourages developers to add new components using SSI's C++ API, but also addresses front end users by offering an XML interface to build pipelines with a text editor. SSI is freely available under GPL at `http://openssi.net`.

Categories and Subject Descriptors

I.5 [**PATTERN RECOGNITION**]: Applications—*Computer vision; Waveform analysis; Signal processing*

Keywords

Social Signal Processing, Real-time Pattern Recognition, Multimodal Fusion, Open Source Framework

1. INTRODUCTION

Today's computer interfaces are still based on explicit commands only. This of course differs greatly from natural human communication, which to a large extent is based on implicit interaction. A twinkle in one's eye, the wave of one's hand or the tone of one's voice sometimes tells more about a human's intentions than a hundred words. Moving towards more intuitive interaction is therefore an important aim of research on next-generation human-computer interfaces [7]. However, intuitive interaction requires the computer to perceive implicit user behaviour. Therefore, we have to equip machines with tools that are able to recognize and interpret diverse types of social signals carried by voice, gestures, mimics, etc.

ACM MM 2013 Oct 21–25, 2013, Barcelona, Spain
Copyright 2013 ACM 978-1-4503-2404-5/13/10 ...$15.00.
http://dx.doi.org/10.1145/2502081.2502223.

Challenges

Developing tools able to detect and react to user behaviour in real-time involves a number of challenges.

- *Synchronization and coherent treatment of signals*

Different kind of sensors have to be used to record the various signals that carry social cues. Microphones replace the human ear and capture the human voice and other sounds. Video and depth cameras replace human vision and allow spotting humans to analyze body and facial expressions. Motion sensors worn by the user measure body posture and motion at very high precision, while physiological sensors monitor physiological signals, such as heart rate or respiration. The signals delivered by these different types of sensors differ greatly in quantisation and sample rate, e. g. a video image consists of several thousand pixel values delivered at rates about 30 frames per second. An audio sample on the other hand can be represented by a single integer or floating point value, but should be sampled at a rate of at least 16kHz. In order to combine information generated by such varying sources raw signal streams need to be synchronized and handled in a coherent way.

- *High amount of variability, uncertainty and ambiguity*

Human communication does not follow the precise mechanisms of a machine, but is tainted with a high amount of variability, uncertainty and ambiguity. Hence, robust recognizers have to be built that use probabilistic models to recognize and interpret observed behaviour. Most often recognition can be broken down in three-steps: (a) *Data segmentation*, which is the process of detecting on- and offsets of actions, which carry relevant information about the user's intention and goals. (b) *Feature extraction*, which relates to the reduction of a raw sensor stream to a set of compact features – keeping only the essential information necessary to classify the observed behaviour. (c) *Classification*, which describes the mapping of observed feature vectors onto a set of discrete states or continuous values. To accomplish these tasks we need to collect large numbers of representative samples and train recognition models.

- *Fusing multimodal data*

To solve ambiguity in human interaction information extracted from diverse channels need to be combined. This can happen at various levels. Already at data level, e. g. when depth information is enhanced with color information. At feature level, when features of two ore more channels are put together to a single feature vector. Or decision level, when probabilities of different recognizers are combined. In the latter cases fused information should represent the same moment in time. If this is not possible due to temporal offsets (e. g. a gesture followed by a verbal instruction) fusion has to take place at event level. The preferred level depends on the type of information that is fused.

- *Real-time processing*

A natural and fluent interaction requires prompt reactions to observed behaviour. Therefore sensor information needs to be processed in pipelines on the fly, i. e. new sample values are constantly read by the sensors while feature extraction and recognition is applied simultaneously to buffered samples. The window length at which components operate should be variable as it depends on the type of signal and the level of processing. Usually, early processing steps are applied on possibly overlapping small windows of few milliseconds, while later processing takes place over segments of up to several seconds.

Existing Tools

There is a number of free and commercial software related to signal processing and machine learning. Some of them are specialized in a certain task, such as Weka[1], which offers a large collection of machine learning algorithms for data mining. Others are tailored to a certain modality, like Praat[2] for audio processing. Or Matlab[3], which offers a simplified scripting language for applying a large body of signal processing algorithms. Tools with support for live sensor input, on the other hand, are still rare. Examples of architectures for multimodal processing, are Pure Data[4], EyesWeb [1] or OpenInterface [9]. Here, developers can choose from a considerable large set of input, processing and output components, and patch them using a graphical programming environment to construct complex processing pipelines. However, they are not specially tuned for building machine learning pipelines and collecting training corpora. A toolkit developed for real-time affect recognition from speech is the openEAR toolkit with its feature extracting backend openSMILE [3]. It is, however, developed with a strong focus on audio processing.

Social Signal Interpretation (SSI)

The Social Signal Processing framework (SSI) complements existing tools by offering special support for the development of online recognition systems from multiple sensors. Mentioned problems are tackled in a number of ways:

- An architecture is established to handle diverse signals in a coherent way, no matter if it is a waveform, a heart beat signal, or a video image.
- Implementation details related to real-time processing such as buffering, synchronization, and threading are hidden from the developer.
- All tasks to assemble the machine learning pipeline, ranging from live sensor input and real-time signal processing to high-level feature extraction and online classification, are covered.
- Different strategies for fusing information gained from different modalities at various levels are available.

[1]http://www.cs.waikato.ac.nz/ml/weka/
[2]http://www.praat.org
[3]http://www.mathworks.com/products/matlab/
[4]http://puredata.info/

- Support for a large variety of sensors, as well as, filter and feature algorithms to process captured signals.

Two type of users are addressed: developers are provided a C++-API that encourages them to write new components and front end users can define recognition pipelines in XML from available components.

A previous version of SSI (v0.8) has been described in [13]. Apart from additional sensor devices and signal processing algorithms, a completely revised and way more powerful event handling (replacing the concept of a *Trigger*) makes the main contribution of the current version (v0.92).

2. ARCHITECTURE

SSI is implemented in C/C++ and optimized to run on multiple CPU cores. It has been developed with Visual Studio on Microsoft Windows. Since the integration of sensors is a highly platform dependent task other platforms are currently not supported. However, apart from sensor wrappers and the plugin interface large parts of the framework should be platform independent. External libraries, such as OpenCv, have been included to get rid of additional dependencies.

Data structures

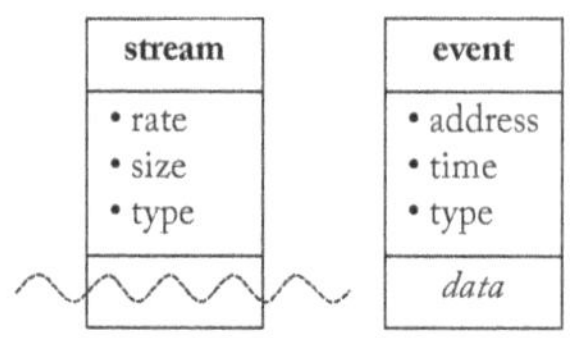

In order to keep the framework as generic as possible, data handling is broken down to two basic data structures: streams and events. Basically everything read from a sensor is transformed into a stream and handled as a continuous flow of samples at a fixed sample rate and size. Filter and feature algorithms can be applied to manipulate a stream. During such operations sample rate and size of a stream may change. To keep streams synchronized SSI constantly checks if the number of retrieved samples corresponds to the expected amount of samples according to the sample rate of the stream. If a mismatch is detected a stream is adjusted accordingly, i. e. samples are removed or added via interpolation.

The counterpart of streams are events. Events describe parts of streams that are relevant in some way, e. g. for classification. Events are usually generated from continuous streams by applying some kind of activity detection. Their length is variable and they may contain additional data, e. g. a feature set or a string.

Recognition

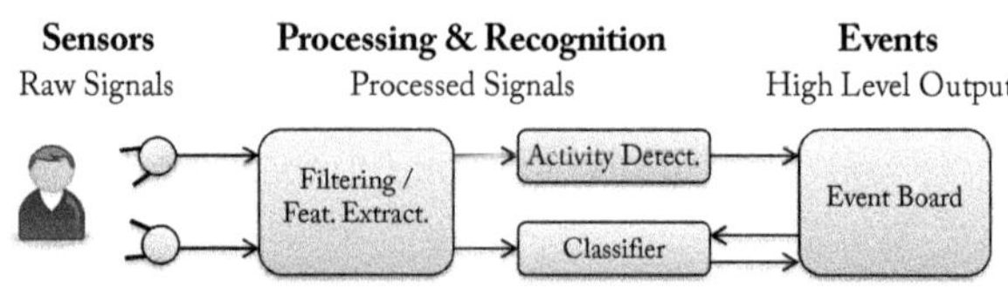

Figure 1: Scheme of a basic recognition pipeline.

A recognition pipeline is set up from several autonomic components. First, transformers can be applied to filter the raw signals and transform it to a compact set of features. Based on the pre-processed streams activity detection components are looking for parts in the signal relevant for recognition. If an on and offset is detected, an event is sent to the event board. Recognition components that have subscribed to the event are now informed. According to the segment they can request stream chunks and feed them to a classifier. Note that the architecture suits both, dynamic classification if streams of variable length are taken (e. g. HMMs), and statistical classification if streams are described by a set of statistical features (e. g. SVM). Finally, a new event containing the recognized class probabilities is generated and possibly received by other components, e. g. fusion algorithms.

Fusion

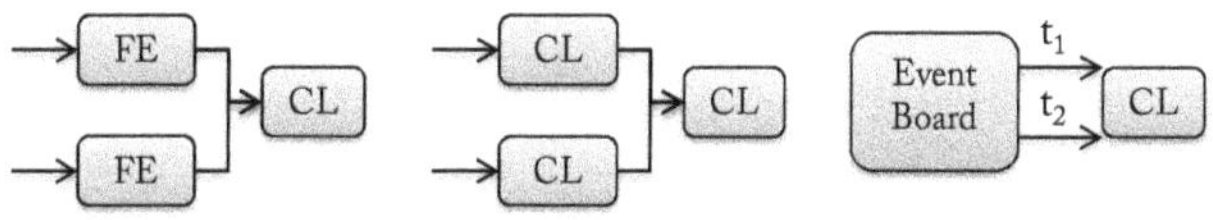

Figure 2: Ways of fusing information in SSI. (FE=feature extraction, CL=classifier)

Figure 2 shows ways of fusing information in SSI. Two or more feature extraction components can be plugged to the same recognition component, which combines features before recognition is applied. Likewise, outcome of two or more classifiers can be combined. Finally, fusion may be applied at event level. This allows combining information at different time scales.

3. AVAILABLE COMPONENTS

Currently, SSI supports streaming from multi-channel audio interfaces, web/dv cameras, Nintendo's Wii remote control, depth sensors such as Microsoft's Kinect, various physiological sensors (Nexus, ProComp, IOM, Alive Heart Monitor), mobile and stationed eye tracker (SMI), the Leap Motion, and a full body motion capture system by XSense. Raw and transformed streams can be stored, visualized and streamed via socket connections possibly using Open Sound Control, Yarp or ActiveMQ.

SSI involves a large set of transformer components, such as moving and sliding average filters, various normalization functions, dsp filters (Butterworth, Chebyshev), derivative, and integral filters, as well as, FFT and statistical features. Several open source libraries have been integrated, including OpenCV, ARToolKit, SHORE, Torch, or OpenSmile. Systems developed at our lab, such as FUBI [5] for Kinect based gesture or EmoVoice [12] for emotional speech recognition, are fully supported, too.

In order to accomplish the machine learning pipeline, classification models such as K-Nearest Neighbours, Naive Bayes, Linear Discriminant Analysis, Support Vector Machines or Hidden Markov Models are part of SSI. Fusion strategies range from weighted and unweighted voting schemes, algebraic combiners over specialist selection algorithms and constructed lookup tables to hybrid and meta level fusion. For feature selection, wrapper approaches such as Sequential Forward/Backward Search, as well as, filter approaches like Correlation-based Feature Selection are available [14].

4. EXAMPLE

Let us demonstrate SSI by means of a pipeline to detect gestures drawn with the mouse. This simple application is chosen to convey the main idea behind SSI, but could be easily extended to a more complex one, e. g. by replacing the mouse with a Kinect sensor to recognize free-hand gestures.

In an XML pipeline each component is represented by an XML element that includes information how it connects to other components. We start from the sensor and open a connection to each stream we would like to access (cursor coordinates and button state).

```
<sensor create="Mouse" mask="1">
  <provider channel="cursor" pin="p_cursor"/>
  <provider channel="button" pin="p_button" />
</sensor>
```

To each channel we assign a pin name that allows us to address the stream later on. By setting the option `mask=1` we tell the sensor to listen to the left mouse button. If it is pressed the stream will now switch from 0 to 1. We detect non-zero segments by plugging an instance of `ThresEventSender` that we connect to the button stream (`pin="p_button"`):

```
<consumer create="ThresEventSender" ...
  mindur="0.2" sname="mouse" ename="pressed">
  <input pin="p_button" frame="0.25s" />
</consumer>
```

As soon as the button is released an event is fired. The name of the event is set to `pressed` and the name of the sender to `mouse`. We also demand that an event is only sent if the segment has a duration of at least $0.2s$. Finally, we set the frame size to `0.25s`, i. e. the component will receive data in chunks of $0.25s$ length.

In order to smooth the cursor signal we include a Butterworth filter of order 5 and a cutoff frequency of $1Hz$:

```
<transformer create="Butfilt" order="5" low="1.0">
        <input pin="p_cursor" frame="0.1s"/>
        <output pin="p_cursor_low"/>
</transformer>
```

Next, the low-passed cursor stream is picked up by a classifier, but only when a button event was detected. Therefore – instead of using a frame size – we set `listen="pressed@mouse"`:

```
<consumer create="Classifier" ...
  trainer="numbers" sname="mouse" ename="gesture">
  <input pin="p_cursor_low" listen="pressed@mouse"/>
</consumer>
```

Via options we set the name of a pre-trained model (`numbers`) containing templates for numbers 0-9. The result of a classification generates a new event (`gesture@mouse`). Finally, we include an instance of `SignalPainter` to visualize current cursor position and an instance of `EventMonitor` to display mouse events during the last $2000ms$ (see Figure 3):

```
<consumer create="SignalPainter" size="10.0">
  <input pin="p_cursor" frame="1" />
</consumer>
<listener create="EventMonitor">
  <input listen="@mouse" span="20000" />
</listener>
```

Note that the frame size of the painter component is set to `1`, which forces the component to draw each sample.

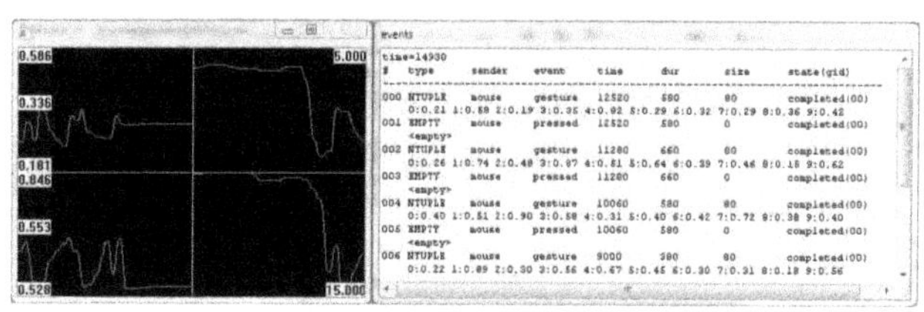

Figure 3: Output of example pipeline.

5. APPLICATION

SSI has been used by researchers around the world. Our EmoVoice component [12] (as part of SSI) was used in a various number of showcases in the European projects CALLAS and IRIS to analyse the expressivity in user speech. An example is the E-Tree [4], an Augmented Reality art installation of a virtual tree that grows, shrinks, changes colours, etc. by interpreting affective input from video, keywords and emotional voice tone.

SSI was also employed to construct the CALLAS expressivity corpus [2]. It consists of synchronized recordings from high-quality cameras and microphones, Nintendo's Wii remote controls and a data glove. Experiments have been conducted in three countries, namely Germany, Greece and Italy. In total, about 15 hours of interaction from more than 50 subjects was collected.

Within the AVLaughterCycle project, which aims at developing an audiovisual laughing machine, SSI has been used for recording and laughter detection in real-time [11]. The work is continued within the EU-funded ILHAIRE project. A first prototype of an interactive system that detects human laughs and responds appropriately is reported in [6].

TARDIS, another project under EU funding, aims to build a simulation platform for young people to improve their social skills. SSI is used for real-time detection of user's emotions and social attitudes through voice, body and facial expression recognition. A visualization tool called NoVA has been developed to visualize detected cues in graphs and heatmaps and give recommendations to the user.

The EU funded CEEDs project exploits the users' unconscious processes to optimize the presentation of large and complex databases. To this end, a sensor platform has been developed on top of SSI [15] and integrated into the eXperience Induction Machine (XIM), a multiuser mixed-reality space equipped with a number of sensors and effectors [10].

A research group at the Institute for Creative Technologies (ICT) from University of Southern California has developed a multimodal sensor fusion framework on top of SSI called MultiSense, which they use to investigate the capabilities of automatic non-verbal behavior descriptors to identify indicators of psychological disorders [8].

Outside an academic context, SSI was used at the Music Hack Day[5] 2013 in Barcelona to process physiological signals captured with the e-Health Sensor Platform for Arduino. During the hacking sessions participants were encouraged to use extracted user states to implement music related projects.

6. CONCLUSION

We introduced the Social Signal Interpretation (SSI) framework for real-time recognition of social signals. SSI supports a large set of sensor devices and allows users to set up recognition pipelines based on synchronized input from multiple modalities. A C++-API encourages developers to develop new components, while a simple XML interface is offered to front end users. SSI is freely available under GPL at `http://openssi.net`.

7. ACKNOWLEDGMENTS

The work described in this paper is funded by the European Union under research grant CEEDs (FP7-ICT-2009-5) and TARDIS (FP7-ICT-2011-7), and ILHAIRE, a Seventh Framework Programme (FP7/2007-2013) under grant agreement n°270780.

[5] `http://bcn.musichackday.org/2013/`

8. REFERENCES

[1] A. Camurri, P. Coletta, G. Varni, and S. Ghisio. Developing multimodal interactive systems with eyesweb xmi. In *Proc. NIME*, pages 305–308, New York, USA, 2007. ACM.

[2] G. Caridakis, J. Wagner, A. Raouzaiou, Z. Curto, E. André, and K. Karpouzis. A multimodal corpus for gesture expressivity analysis. In *Proc. LREC*, 2010.

[3] F. Eyben, M. Wöllmer, and B. Schuller. Opensmile: the munich versatile and fast open-source audio feature extractor. In *Proc. MM*, pages 1459–1462, New York, USA, 2010. ACM.

[4] S. W. Gilroy, M. Cavazza, R. Chaignon, S.-M. Mäkelä, M. Niranen, E. André, T. Vogt, J. Urbain, H. Seichter, M. Billinghurst, and M. Benayoun. An affective model of user experience for interactive art. In *Proc. ACE*, pages 107–110, New York, USA, 2008. ACM.

[5] F. Kistler, B. Endrass, I. Damian, C. Dang, and E. André. Natural interaction with culturally adaptive virtual characters. *JMUI*, pages 1–9.

[6] R. Niewiadomski, J. Hofmann, J. Urbain, T. Platt, J. Wagner, B. PIOT, H. Cakmak, S. Pammi, T. Baur, S. Dupont, M. Geist, F. Lingenfelser, G. McKeown, O. Pietquin, and W. Ruch. Laugh-aware virtual agent and its impact on user amusement . In *Proc. AAMAS*, Saint Paul, USA, May 2013.

[7] M. Pantic, A. Nijholt, A. Pentland, and T. S. Huang. Human-centred intelligent human-computer interaction (hci^2): how far are we from attaining it? *IJAACS*, 1(2):168–187, August 2008.

[8] S. Scherer, G. Stratou, M. Mahmoud, J. Boberg, J. Gratch, A. Rizzo, and L.-P. Morency. Automatic behavior descriptors for psychological disorder analysis. In *Proc. FG*, 2013.

[9] M. Serrano, L. Nigay, J.-Y. L. Lawson, A. Ramsay, R. Murray-Smith, and S. Denef. The openinterface framework: a tool for multimodal interaction. In *Proc. CHI*, pages 3501–3506, New York, USA, 2008. ACM.

[10] A. Spagnolli and L. Gamberini, editors. *Validating presence by relying on recollection: Human experience and performance in the mixed reality system XIM*, Padova, Italy, 16/10/2008 2008. CLEUP Cooperativa Libraria Universitaria Padova.

[11] J. Urbain, R. Niewiadomski, E. Bevacqua, T. Dutoit, A. Moinet, C. Pelachaud, B. Picart, J. Tilmanne, and J. Wagner. Avlaughtercycle. *JMUI*, 4:47–58, 2010.

[12] T. Vogt, E. André, and N. Bee. Emovoice - a framework for online recognitionof emotions from voice. In *Proc. PIT*, Kloster Irsee, Germany, June 2008. Springer.

[13] J. Wagner, F. Lingenfelser, and E. André. The social signal interpretation framework (ssi) for real time signal processing and recognition. In *Proc. of INTERSPEECH*, 2011.

[14] J. Wagner, F. Lingenfelser, E. André, and J. Kim. Exploring fusion methods for multimodal emotion recognition with missing data. *IEEE TAC*, 99, 2011.

[15] J. Wagner, F. Lingenfelser, E. André, D. Mazzei, A. Tognetti, A. Lanatà, D. D. Rossi, A. Betella, R. Zucca, P. Omedas, and P. F. Verschure. A sensing architecture for empathetic data systems. In *Proc. AH*, page 96–99, Stuttgart, Germany, 2013. ACM.

Recent Developments in openSMILE, the Munich Open-Source Multimedia Feature Extractor

Florian Eyben, Felix Weninger, Florian Gross, Björn Schuller
Machine Intelligence & Signal Processing Group, MMK
Technische Universität München
80290 Munich, Germany
eyben@tum.de

ABSTRACT

We present recent developments in the openSMILE feature extraction toolkit. Version 2.0 now unites feature extraction paradigms from speech, music, and general sound events with basic video features for multi-modal processing. Descriptors from audio and video can be processed jointly in a single framework allowing for time synchronization of parameters, on-line incremental processing as well as off-line and batch processing, and the extraction of statistical functionals (feature summaries), such as moments, peaks, regression parameters, etc. Postprocessing of the features includes statistical classifiers such as support vector machine models or file export for popular toolkits such as Weka or HTK. Available low-level descriptors include popular speech, music and video features including Mel-frequency and similar cepstral and spectral coefficients, Chroma, CENS, auditory model based loudness, voice quality, local binary pattern, color, and optical flow histograms. Besides, voice activity detection, pitch tracking and face detection are supported. openSMILE is implemented in C++, using standard open source libraries for on-line audio and video input. It is fast, runs on Unix and Windows platforms, and has a modular, component based architecture which makes extensions via plug-ins easy. openSMILE 2.0 is distributed under a research license and can be downloaded from http://opensmile.sourceforge.net/.

Categories and Subject Descriptors

H.5 [**Information Systems Applications**]: Sound and Music Computing

General Terms

Design, Performance

Keywords

audio features, video features, multimodal fusion, real-time processing

MM'13, October 21–25, 2013, Barcelona, Spain.

ACM 978-1-4503-2404-5/13/10 ...$15.00.
http://dx.doi.org/10.1145/2502081.2502224.

1. INTRODUCTION

Feature extraction is an essential part of many audio and multimedia retrieval tasks, including automatic speech recognition, speaker characterization (by traits such as age and gender, or states such as emotion or sleepiness), music information retrieval (such as genre or music mood recognition), or video information retrieval (such as tagging of web videos or violence detection in movies). openSMILE aims at uniting features from these worlds, allowing researchers from either domain to profit from state of the art speech, music and video feature extraction. openSMILE provides a simple, scriptable console application where modular feature extraction components can be freely configured and connected via a text-based configuration file. Besides flexibility, sharing of such configuration files among researchers is believed to foster reproducibility of results. A strong focus is put on fully supporting real-time, incremental processing, allowing the use of openSMILE as front-end for interactive applications such as dialogue systems (cf. the SEMAINE project[1] for a dialogue system prototype utilizing openSMILE). At the time of this writing, openSMILE has been used as official baseline for the series of INTERSPEECH challenges in the area of Computational Paralinguistics [7, 8] where it has been shown to deliver state-of-the-art results approaching very diverse recognition tasks with a unified feature extraction scheme. Furthermore, it has been used by researchers (other than the authors) in more than 50 accepted research papers[2].

SMILE is an acronym for *Speech and Multimedia Interpretation by Large-space Extraction.* The term *large-space extraction* refers to openSMILE's capability of 'chunking' of the features in various ways so as to provide either frame-wise features, summarization by statistical functionals over parts of the input or the whole input, or any combination thereof. This kind of systematic feature (over-)generation enables explorative analysis in a very wide range of audio(-visual) recognition tasks. Even though openSMILE originates from the audio processing domain – as such, it has been featured in the 2010 ACM MM Open Source Software Competition [4] – it has recently been extended with basic video features, and, more importantly, its design is principally modality independent. For instance, also physiological measurements such as heart rate or EEG signals can be analyzed, e.g. by means of statistics and short-time spectral analysis. An easy to use plugin interface moreover provides the ability to extend openSMILE with one's own components, thus virtually being

[1] `http://www.semaine-project.eu/`
[2] According to Google Scholar citations, May 2013

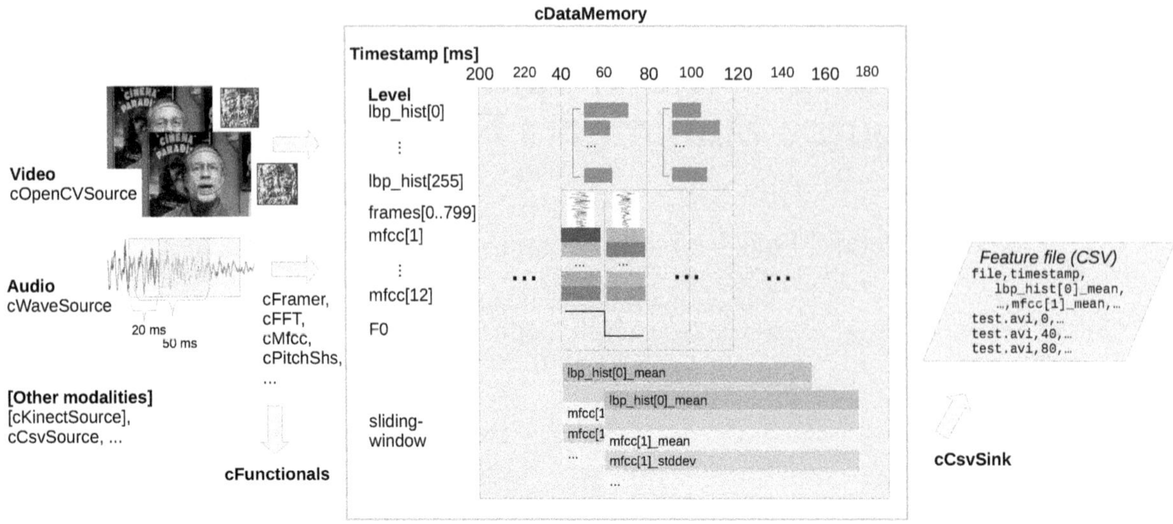

Figure 1: Exemplary audio-visual feature extraction process implemented using the openSMILE architecture. Audio and video frames are captured at 50/25 fps and stored along with timestamps in the data memory ring buffer. From the extracted low-level descriptors (LBP histogram, MFCCs 1–12 and pitch), the mean over 120 ms sliding windows is computed and written to a CSV file.

able to solve any feature extraction task and thereby using existing components as building blocks.

2. DESIGN AND FUNCTIONALITY

To meet our requirements, the following key design principles are implemented – a more detailed description can be found in the release documentation on the sourceforge project page[3]– : incremental ('on-line') processing from audio and video streams, as well as batch ('off-line') processing of audio, video and pre-extracted feature files; fast and lightweight algorithms implemented in C/C++ and tested against reference implementations; modular architecture allowing for arbitrary feature combination as well as integration of runtime plug-ins (e.g., for visualization or use in a dialogue system); scripting via configuration files to facilitate sharing and standardization of feature sets.

In the architecture of openSMILE, the *Data Memory* is the central link between all *Data Sources* (components which read data from external sources), *Data Processors* (components which copy and modify data), and *Data Sinks* (components which write data to external places such as files, or perform classification). Figure 1 visualizes an exemplary feature extraction process from audio and video. Audio, usually sampled at 16–44.1 kHz, is split into overlapping frames of 50 ms length at 20 ms frame rate (50 fps), and cepstral coefficients (MFCCs 1–12) and pitch (F0) are extracted. From the video, the local binary pattern (LBP) histogram is computed per video frame at 40 ms frame rate (25 fps) from faces detected from the frames converted to grey scale. The feature extraction process creates various *levels* of different size and frame rate in the data memory, as shown in detail in Figure 1. In particular, the framed audio is converted to 'row vectors' of size 16 kHz $\times$ 50 ms = 800 for subsequent processing, which are stored in the data memory for maximum flexibility: Any component can use the framed audio to apply its own processing steps. In contrast, the video source is implemented in a 'monolithic' fashion which does not involve storing the results of intermediate processing steps, such as conversion to grey scale, etc., for efficiency reasons. The frame-wise features such as MFCCs will subsequently be referred to as *low-level descriptors* (LLD).

In the example, statistical functionals (e.g., mean) are subsequently applied to the low-level descriptors over sliding windows of length 120 ms with 40 ms shift (in practice, one would usually use longer sliding windows). The data memory implements a first-in first-out (FIFO) ring-buffer architecture (hinted at by the timestamps displayed in Figure 1), where buffer sizes are determined automatically from the dependency graph of the components, by the amount of context that components need (e.g., computing the mean F0 over a sliding window of 120 ms as in the example requires at least $6 + 1 = 7$ audio frames to be buffered at a frame step of 20 ms). In addition, buffers of unbounded size are supported in case that a component requests the full input (e.g., for cepstral mean normalization). Details on the ring-buffer architecture can be found in [4] and on the project webpage. In addition, recently, a *multi-loop processing mode* has been introduced where components are able to reset the input pointer after reading the full input. In audio signal processing, this is useful, e.g., for de-noising and de-reverberation by spectral subtraction and long-term cepstral normalization. Finally, the computed sliding window means are written to a comma-separated values (CSV) file with header, along with timestamps referring to the start of the sliding window.

Let us conclude the discussion of functionality by summarizing the LLDs, functionals, and export functionalities (sinks) implemented in openSMILE. The LLD currently implemented are listed in Table 1. The Mel-frequency features, Mel-Spectrum and Mel-Frequency Cepstral Coefficients (MFCC), as well as the Perceptual Linear Predictive Coefficients (PLP) are extracted in full accordance with the popular Hidden-Markov Toolkit (HTK) [12]. Extraction of visual descriptors is currently provided by integration of OpenCV routines. Face detection and normalization by eye

[3]http://opensmile.sourceforge.net/

alignment is supported prior to feature extraction. From the LLD contours, delta regression (Δ) coefficients [12] can be computed, and contours can be smoothed. The functionals in Table 2 can be applied to the LLD and Δ LLD contours to summarize time series in fixed length vectors. Export to popular toolkit formats such as HTK and Weka's Attribute Relation File Format (ARFF) [11] is supported besides 'dumping' the features in binary or text format.

Feature Group	Description
Waveform	Zero-Crossings, Extremes, DC
Loudness	Energy, intensity, *auditory model loudness*
FFT spectrum	Phase, magnitude (lin., dB, dBA)
ACF, Cepstrum	Autocorrelation and Cepstrum
Mel/Bark spectr.	Bands 0-N_{mel}
Semitone spectr.	FFT based and filter based
Cepstral	Cepstral features, e.g. MFCC, PLP-CC
Pitch	F_0 via Autocorrelation and subharmonic summation, *smoothed by Viterbi algorithm*
Voice Quality	HNR, Jitter, Shimmer, Voice Prob.
LPC	LPC coeff., reflect. coeff., residual Line spectral pairs (LSP)
Auditory	Auditory spectra, *psychoacoustic sharpness*
Formants	Centre frequencies and bandwidths
Spectral	Energy in N user-defined bands, roll-off points, centroid, entropy, flux, and rel. pos. of max./min., *harmonicity*
Tonal	CHROMA, CENS, CHROMA-based features
Color	*HSV colorspace histogram*
Texture	*Local binary pattern histogram*
Motion	*Optical flow histogram*

Table 1: openSMILE's low-level descriptors. *Italics* denote new components in version 2.0.

Category	Description
Extremes	Extreme values, positions, and ranges
Means	Arithmetic, quadratic, geometric
Moments	Std. dev., variance, kurtosis, skewness
Percentiles	Percentiles and percentile ranges
Regression	Linear and quad. approximation coefficients, regression err., and centroid
Peaks	Number of peaks, mean/stddev peak distance, mean/stddev peak amplitude, etc. (*more robust peak picking algorithm in 2.0*)
Segments	Number of segments based on delta thresholding *or various fixed thresholds*, mean/stddev. segment length, etc.
Sample values	Values of the contour at configurable relative positions
Times/durations	Up- and down-level times, rise/fall times, duration
Onsets	Number of onsets, relative position of first/last on-/offset
DCT	Coefficients of the Discrete Cosine Transformation (DCT)
LPC	*Autoregressive coefficients*
Zero-Crossings	Zero-crossing rate, Mean-crossing rate

Table 2: Functionals (statistical, polynomial regression, and transformations) available in openSMILE. *Italics* denote new components in version 2.0.

Category	Description
Feature files	Binary float matrix, CSV, HTK [12], Weka ARFF [11]
Classifiers / Regressors	LibSVM [1], *recurrent neural networks* [5], VAD

Table 3: Sinks available in openSMILE.

3. CASE STUDIES AND BENCHMARKS

Let us now briefly discuss a few case studies in order to illustrate the usage potential of openSMILE's features in a wide range of multimedia recognition tasks.

3.1 Paralinguistic Information Extraction

openSMILE has been used as the feature extractor for the official baselines of the 2009–2013 INTERSPEECH Challenges on paralinguistic information extraction, including emotion, age, gender, interest, alcohol intoxication, sleepiness, personality, voice pathology, and non-linguistic vocalization recognition [7, 8]. Building on the 2009–2012 Challenges' features and the lessons learnt, a unified feature set, the ComParE (Computational Paralinguistics Evaluation) set has been designed, comprising 6 373 features by brute-force combination of audio LLDs with functionals and subsequent removal of zero-information features, such as the arithmetic mean of delta coefficients which is usually near zero. Details on the feature set can be found in [8, 9]. The general applicability of the ComParE feature set in paralinguistic information extraction, not limited to speech, has recently been demonstrated: By regression on the ComParE features and subsequent feature selection, emotion can be determined from speech (GEMEP corpus), music (NTWICM corpus) and sound (ESD corpus) with state-of-the-art accuracy on speech and sound, and with so far best results on music (cf. [9] and Table 4). Details on the corpora and regression using Weka's [11] SVR can be found in [9]. The ComParE configuration file is delivered with the current release candidate.

3.2 Speaker Characterization in Web Videos

Let us now turn to multimedia feature extraction by considering speaker characterization in web videos as in [10]. An audio-visual feature extraction scheme similar to the one described in [10] using a proprietary implementation of video feature extraction can now be realized by using openSMILE exclusively. The underlying idea is close to the 'toy' example from Figure 1, yet extracting over 1.5 k LLD-functional combinations from the audio (INTERSPEECH 2010 set, IS10, delivered as configuration file with the openSMILE distribution) and using sliding window lengths of 4 s. The configuration file for synchronized audio and video feature extraction is also delivered with the current release candidate. In the result (cf. Table 4), 96.4 % and 70.0 % recall are obtained for gender and ethnicity, which is notable given the real-life nature of the task. Details on the classification procedure using Weka's [11] SVM can be found in [10].

3.3 Violence Detection

Finally, let us exemplify the use of openSMILE in multimedia retrieval by the 2012 MediaEval campaign's violence detection task in retail versions of Hollywood movies. openSMILE is used to extract a set of spectral and loudness descriptors (delivered with the source code distribution) over sliding windows of 2 s length with 0.5 s shift. Furthermore, mean and standard deviation of the optical flow and color (hue-saturation-value) histograms are added from the video frames. Again, classification is done using Weka's [11] SVM.

Task	Modality/Features	Evaluation measure	
Emotion recognition [9]			Aro/Val
Speech	Audio/ComParE [8]	CC	.85/.50
Music	Audio/ComParE	CC	.67/.51
Sound	Audio/ComParE	CC	.59/.82
Speaker characterization in web videos [10]			
Gender	Video/LBP	UAR	78.2 %
	— +Audio/IS10 [7]	UAR	96.4 %
Ethnicity	Video/LBP	UAR	70.0 %
Violence detection in Hollywood movies [3]			
Violence	Audio/VSD_TUM [3]	MAP	48.4 %
Violence	Video/VSD_TUM [3]	MAP	32.0 %

Table 4: Task-based evaluation of openSMILE's feature extraction in 3 case studies (Sec. 3): Regression and classification of affect and speaker characteristics. CC: correlation coefficient, UAR: unweighted average recall, MAP: mean average precision.

4. CONCLUSION AND OUTLOOK

The development of the openSMILE open source feature extractor, introduced for explorative feature generation from audio, stays very active. The high flexibility of the basic architecture has allowed for the integration of a variety of new functions compared to the 2010 release. Recent developments include multi-modal feature extraction by the addition of basic video features using integration of OpenCV; improved audio descriptors including, e.g., psychoacoustic features, and a multi-loop mode opening up a wide range of possibilities for more complex multi-pass feature extraction procedures; and context-sensitive recurrent neural networks as a powerful classifier and regressor. During the eNTERFACE 2012 workshop a Microsoft Kinect input component was developed. It supports depth and color image, as well as source audio after beamforming. The code is in an experimental stage, and will be made available soon.

Future developments will likely include a joint front-end for audio and video input such as ffmpeg, as well as the implementation of various on-line audio enhancement algorithms such as beamforming, non-negative matrix factorization (cf., e.g., [2]) and independent component analysis (cf., e.g., [6]). Moreover, a TCP/IP network interface will be available to facilitate transparent real-time interaction with distributed third-party systems. So far, openSMILE has been mostly taken up by the research community in the area of computational paralinguistics, where it has become a quasi-standard reference toolkit. We hope that many significant contributions, also from other communities, will follow.

5. ACKNOWLEDGMENT

The development of openSMILE has received funding from the European Commission (grant nos. 211486 and 289021, SEMAINE and ASC-Inclusion). The authors would like to thank Christian Kirst for helpful contributions.

6. REFERENCES

[1] C.-C. Chang and C.-J. Lin. *LibSVM: a library for support vector machines*, 2001. `http://www.csie.ntu.edu.tw/~cjlin/libsvm`.

[2] Z. Duan, G. J. Mysore, and P. Smaragdis. Speech enhancement by online non-negative spectrogram decomposition in non-stationary noise environments. In *Proc. of Interspeech*, Portland, OR, USA, 2012.

[3] F. Eyben, F. Weninger, N. Lehment, G. Rigoll, and B. Schuller. Violent Scenes Detection with Large, Brute-forced Acoustic and Visual Feature Sets. In *Proceedings MediaEval 2012 Workshop*, Pisa, Italy, October 2012. 2 pages.

[4] F. Eyben, M. Wöllmer, and B. Schuller. openSMILE – The Munich Versatile and Fast Open-Source Audio Feature Extractor. In *Proc. of ACM MM*, pages 1459–1462, Florence, Italy, October 2010. ACM.

[5] A. Graves and J. Schmidhuber. Framewise phoneme classification with bidirectional LSTM and other neural network architectures. *Neural Networks*, 18(5-6):602–610, 2005.

[6] R. Maas, A. Schwarz, Y. Zheng, K. Reindl, S. Meier, A. Sehr, and W. Kellermann. A Two-Channel Acoustic Front-End for Robust Automatic Speech Recognition in Noisy and Reverberant Environments. In *Proc. of CHiME*, pages 41–46, 2011.

[7] B. Schuller. The Computational Paralinguistics Challenge. *IEEE Signal Processing Magazine*, 29(4):97–101, July 2012.

[8] B. Schuller, S. Steidl, A. Batliner, A. Vinciarelli, K. Scherer, F. Ringeval, M. Chetouani, et al. The INTERSPEECH 2013 Computational Paralinguistics Challenge: Social Signals, Conflict, Emotion, Autism. In *Proc. of INTERSPEECH*, Lyon, France, August 2013. ISCA. in press.

[9] F. Weninger, F. Eyben, B. W. Schuller, M. Mortillaro, and K. R. Scherer. On the Acoustics of Emotion in Audio: What Speech, Music and Sound have in Common. *Frontiers in Emotion Science*, 2013. DOI: 10.3389/fpsyg.2013.00292, in press.

[10] F. Weninger, C. Wagner, M. Wöllmer, B. Schuller, and L.-P. Morency. Speaker Trait Characterization in Web Videos: Uniting Speech, Language, and Facial Features. In *Proc. of ICASSP*, Vancouver, Canada, May 2013. IEEE. in press.

[11] I. H. Witten and E. Frank. *Data mining: Practical machine learning tools and techniques, 2nd Edition.* Morgan Kaufmann, San Francisco, 2nd edition, 2005.

[12] S. Young, G. Evermann, M. Gales, T. Hain, D. Kershaw, X. Liu, G. Moore, J. Odell, D. Ollason, D. Povey, V. Valtchev, and P. Woodland. *The HTK book (v3.4)*. Cambridge University Press, 2006.

ImproveMyCity - An Open Source Platform for Direct Citizen-government Communication

Ioannis Tsampoulatidis
Centre for Research and Technology Hellas - ITI
6th km Xarilaou - Thermi
Thessaloniki, Greece
itsam@iti.gr

Dimitrios Ververidis
Centre for Research and Technology Hellas - ITI
6th km Xarilaou - Thermi
Thessaloniki, Greece
ververid@iti.gr

Panagiotis Tsarchopoulos
Aristotle University of Thessaloniki - URENIO
P.O. Box 491
patsar@arch.auth.gr

Spiros Nikolopoulos
Centre for Research and Technology Hellas-ITI
6th km Xarilaou - Thermi
Thessaloniki, Greece
nikolopo@iti.gr

Ioannis Kompatsiaris
Centre for Research and Technology Hellas - ITI
6th km Xarilaou - Thermi
Thessaloniki, Greece
ikom@iti.gr

Nicos Komninos
Aristotle University of Thessaloniki - URENIO
P.O. Box 491
komninos@urenio.org

ABSTRACT

ImproveMyCity is an open source platform that enables residents to directly report to their public administration local issues about their neighborhood such as discarded trash bins, faulty street lights, broken tiles on sidewalks, illegal advertising boards, etc. The reported issues are automatically transmitted to the appropriate office in public administration so as to schedule their settlement. Reporting is feasible both through a web- and a smartphone-based front-end that adopt a map-based visualization, which makes reporting a user-friendly and intriguing process. The management and routing of incoming issues is performed through a back-end infrastructure that serves as an integrated management system with easy to use interfaces. Apart from reporting a new issue, both front-ends allow the citizens to add comments or vote on existing issues, which adds a social dimension on the collected content. Finally, the platform makes also provision for informing the citizens about the progress status of the reported issue and in this way facilitate the establishment of a two-way dialogue between the citizen and public administration.

Categories and Subject Descriptors

D.2.2 [**Software Engineering**]: Design Tools and Techniques; H.3.5 [**Information Systems**]: Information Storage and Retrieval; Online Information Services

Keywords

eParticipation, eGovernment, issue reporting, urban maintenance, open source

MM'13, October 21–25, 2013, Barcelona, Spain.

http://dx.doi.org/10.1145/2502081.2502225.

1. OVERVIEW

In modern societies there is a growing requirement for public administrations to directly communicate with their citizens, view the existing problems from their perspective and re-act to their needs. In meeting this requirement, modern technologies has turned into a particularly valuable instrument that, apart from being a rich source of information, is also an integral part of our daily activities. Based on the above and driven by the intriguing concept that every citizen can act as the living sensor of his city, we have developed the ImproveMyCity platform. Our platform provides, on the one hand, user-friendly interfaces for the citizens to directly report issues about their city such as potholes, illegal trash dumping, faulty street lights and broken tiles on sidewalks, and on the other hand the necessary back-end infrastructure and interfaces for public servants to keep track of the reported issues, schedule their settlement and provide feedback about the progress status. Although a number of systems for citizen-government communication are already present, none of them is offered as open source allowing the interested parties to build on top of an existing infrastructure, extent it with new functionalities, or even think of new paradigms to gain insights based on the collected information. This was our motive for developing ImproveMyCity, which is the first integrated solution for citizen-government communication that is made available as open source.

The ImproveMyCity platform is structured as a client-server application and is implemented as an extension of the Joomla framework. The platform consists of a web-based portal for allowing citizens to report issues from their desktop PC, a smartphone application for android devices that allows citizens to do the same process through their mobile phone and a back-end infrastructure for allowing the governmental agencies to easily handle the reported issues. The source code is available in GitHub both for the web-based front-end and the back-end infrastructure [2], as well as for the mobile front-end [5]. All source codes are provided with detailed user guides explaining how to download and install the applications and are licensed under the GNU Affero General Public License [1].

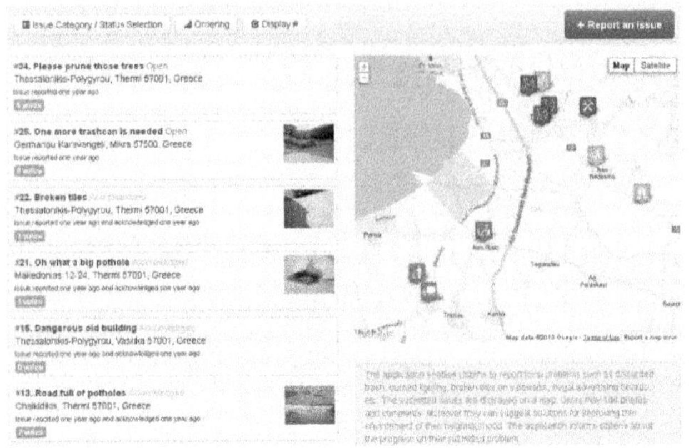

Figure 1: Map- and List-based view of the issues. The image is best viewed in color and with magnification.

2. DESCRIPTION

The ImproveMyCity platform consists of three main components: a) The web-based front-end for reporting issues through a desktop PC, b) The smartphone-based front-end for reporting issues through a mobile phone, and c) the back-end infrastructure and related interfaces for administering the incoming issues. Through these components the ImproveMyCity platform implements a variety of functionalities that are employed with the purpose to establish a two-way dialogue between the municipality and its citizens. In the following we describe the most important of these functionalities.

2.1 Web-based front-end

Both the web- and smartphone-based front-ends incorporate the functionalities described below. However, the smartphone-based front-end incorporates also a number of additional functionalities that are described in Section 2.2.

Map-based view of the issues: The reported issues are displayed on the city's map using a different icon for each issue category. The user can navigate himself using the standard map-based functionalities and acquire more information about a certain issue by clicking on the corresponding icon (see Figure 1).

List-based view of the issues: The reported issues can be also displayed in a list-based view. This view enables the interface to provide the user with the most important information about each issue such as: the title, the address, its progress status, the days passed from the submission date and the number of positive votes (see Figure 1).

Issue-based view: Upon clicking an icon or a list entry the issue-based view appears. This view presents in a separate page detailed information about the selected issue such as: title, category, address, name of the citizen who submitted the issue, the date of submission, a photo, description, user comments, location on the map, and the number of votes.

Filtering: Users can filter the issues that appear in both the map- and list-based view. The displayed issues can be filtered by: a) the issue category, b) the progress status, c) vote-based ranking, and d) submission-date ranking.

New issue reporting: The user can submit a new issue by: a) providing a short title, b) selecting the issue category among a predefined set of categories and sub-categories that have been determined by the municipality, c) determine the exact location of the problem by moving a marker on the city map (or provide a written address by hand), d) attach an image that describes the problem (this is optional), and f) provide the full description of the issue.

Commenting: Through the "Issue-based" view registered users can comment on issues submitted by other users, or answer to the comments made for their own issues by forming a discussion thread.

Voting: Through the "Issue-based" view registered users can provide a positive vote on issues they consider significant, allowing the municipality to prioritize the reported problems.

Feedback: The commenting functionality can be also used by the employees of the municipality to provide written feedback about the reported issues.

Progress status: The citizens are informed about the progress status of their requests by email, as well as through a progress status bar that appears in the "List-based" and "Issue-based" views. Initially the status of each issue is "Open". Once the municipality becomes aware of the issue and the citizen's report is forwarded to the appropriate department the status changes to "Acknowledged". Finally, the status becomes "Closed" when the issue is resolved.

2.2 Mobile-based front-end

The goal of the mobile-based front-end is to complement the web-based functionality by allowing citizens to report issues while they are on the move. The ImproveMyCity mobile application is fully interconnected with the web version, i.e. actions taken from the mobile application are visible through the web portal and vise-versa. It fully incorporates the functionalities described in Section 2.1, with the addition of a few extract features that are made possible due to the sensors embedded in all smartphones. More specifically, the additional functionalities include:

Automatic location extraction: Using the GPS sensor embedded on the phone and the reverse geocoding functionality offered by Google, the application is able to automatically extract the exact issue location, removing the need for the user to move the marker on the map or to type-in the address (see Figure 2).

Easy photo capturing: Using the built-in camera of the smartphone the application simplifies the process of attaching a photo to the problem description, which is particularly important for assessing the situation and planing the necessary actions for its settlement.

Offline use: The application makes provisions for storing the data locally on the phone and allowing its offline use.

Location-centered services: Knowing the citizen's GPS location when using the application, the mobile-based front-end incorporates functionalities like: i) download only the issues that lie within a specified radius around the phone's current position, so as to avoid unnecessary bandwidth consumption, ii) ignore issues that are reported outside the geographical boundaries of the municipality, so as to avoid junk entries.

2.3 Back-end infrastructure

After their submission, the reported issues should automatically become visible to the employees of the appropriate municipality department based on the issue category.

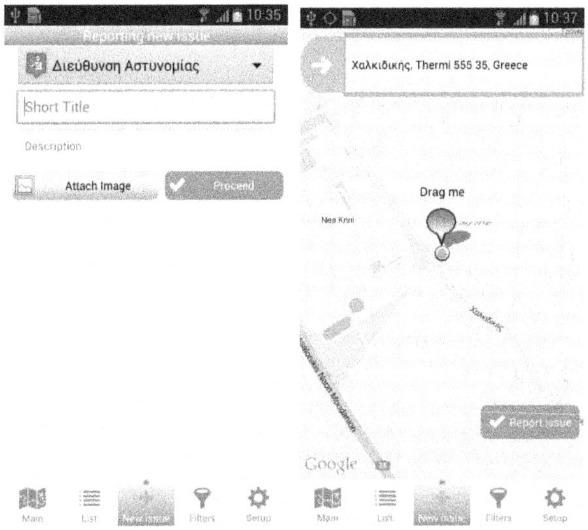

Figure 2: Automatic location extraction in reporting a new issue. The image is best viewed in color and with magnification.

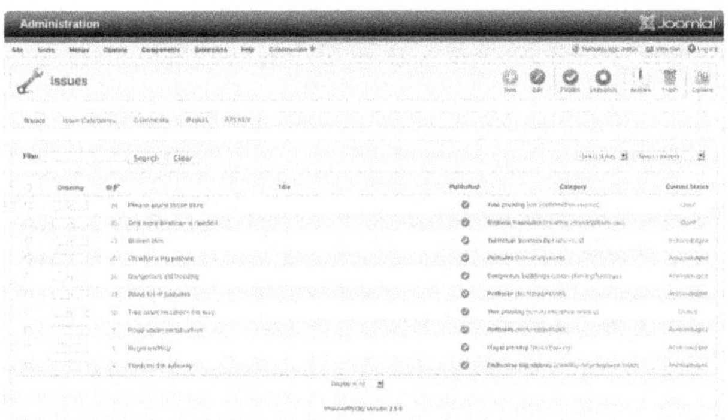

Figure 3: Integrated system for managing incoming issues. The image is best viewed in color and with magnification.

The departments depend on the internal organization of the municipality (e.g. technical service, municipal police, urban planning department, cleaning department, water supply & drainage department, etc.) and should be aligned with the categories presented to the user when submitting a new issue. The task of the designated employees is to initiate the established resolution process, reply to users' comments and change the progress status of the issues accordingly. To facilitate the above the ImproveMyCity platform has implemented the following set of functionalities:

Integrated issue management system: The submitted issues are managed through an integrated environment that is based on Joomla content management system (see Figure 3). This environment provides the necessary interfaces and rights management mechanisms, so as to make feasible the distribution of the management effort to the different departments of the municipality.

Web-based administration: The authorized employees manage the entries through a web form that presents all necessary pieces of information and applicable actions.

User comments management: The application provides a special page for displaying the submitted comments allowing the administrators and city officials to have an overview of the discussions about each issue.

Responsibility distribution: The back-end interface makes the necessary provision so that different municipality employees to be responsible for different categories. Moreover, the application allows the assignment of many accounts per category, so as to split the administration effort in more than one employees.

Easy customization: The back-end interface is fully customizable in terms of user rights, comments, number of categories, notifications on new issues and comments, etc.

Reporting: The application is able to produce reports with statistically aggregated information, so as to help the city officials in assessing the overall performance of the municipality.

3. INTENDED AUDIENCE

In its current form the ImproveMyCity platform mainly addresses the audience of: a) citizens (people who live, work or visit a municipality and who are willing to collaborate with public administration for improving their neighborhood), b) municipality's civil servants (who work in the municipality and who are searching for novel ways to offer better services with reduced cost), and c) city officials like the Mayor and city council members (whose job is to look for the best interest of the municipality and its citizens). Moreover, besides the main user groups there are also some other types of users such as journalists that publish local problems on the media that may also benefit from the establishment of such a platform. Given the above and due to its high degree of modularity and customization, the ImproveMyCity platform can be easily adopted by almost every municipality around the globe, independently of its size and location.

From a scientific perspective, ImproveMyCity encompasses textual descriptions, images, preference in the form of votes, GPS information, demographic data, etc. This content is likely to carry valuable pieces of knowledge such as popular topics, trends, public opinion, etc. In this respect the ImproveMyCity platform may very well serve as the enabling content platform for researchers working in the fields of topic detection, opinion mining and sentiment analysis.

Finally, although the developed platform has been built to facilitate the easy reporting, scheduling and settlement of non-emergent issues for urban maintenance, the workflow management rules and the established communication practices may as well be used to facilitate the optimization of many other processes. For instance, it can be used to optimize every process that requires the collection of information from distributed sensors, the routing of this information to the appropriate end-points, the triggering of certain actions based on the information received and the ability to push information back to the origin using a feedback mechanism. Examples of such processes may derive from the sectors of fleet management, roadside assistance companies, or any other business that relies on the distributed collection of local information through a human network.

4. SOFTWARE AND HARDWARE CONSIDERATIONS

In order to use the ImproveMyCity functionalities there is no need to connect with external sources of information except the Google Maps API that is used to provide geolocation data and the reverse geocoding service in the case of smartphones. The provided service is open for the citizens of the municipality who can create an account and start submitting issues. All services are available through the World Wide Web (WWW). There is no need for special network infrastructure. Users who use the service from their home computer should have a broadband internet access through an ADSL line. Users who use the service from a smartphone, should use a 3G or Wi-Fi broadband connection. The service doesn't require the deployment of any special hardware. The web-based services can be hosted on the same infrastructure that hosts the website of the municipality, or transferred in a dedicated server if the number of registered users becomes considerably high.

5. CUSTOMIZATION & LOCALIZATION

The ImproveMyCity platform has paid particular attention to make fully customizable all parameters needed to localize the platform for a certain city. In this respect all language-related menus, geo-positioning related parameters and layout options, are accessible through external files that can be easily edited. Similar is the case for the parameters that are needed to synchronize the mobile front-end with the back-end infrastructure.

Particular attention has been placed on language-based localization by initiating and maintaining a crowdsourcing project in Transifex[1]. This project has already resulted in the full translation of the ImproveMyCity language dependent information in nine languages, while there are many more languages that are still under way.

6. INSTALLATION PROCESS

Since the web-based front-end and the back-end infrastructure and interfaces are developed as standard Joomla components, their installation and running is a plain process. Indeed after a few simple steps described in [3], the ImproveMyCity back-end infrastructure and the web-based front-end are ready to be used and administered. Similarly, the mobile front-end requires a few extra steps described in [6], so as to connect with the server and get synchronized with the web-based front-end. If someone would like to change the features of ImproveMyCity, prior knowledge of the Joomla framework API is necessary. Similarly, for modifying the mobile part, knowledge of the Android development tool (ADT) and the Android SDK are necessary.

7. STATISTICS & DEPLOYMENT

The back-end infrastructure along with the web-based front end were made available as a Joomla extension component (available through the official Joomla Extension Directory (JED)) on July 2012. Since then, the ImproveMyCity component has been viewed more than 15000 times and downloaded more than 3800 times. The mobile-based front-end has become publicly available on GitHub on May 2013 and has already started to attract considerable attention from the established community. Both the Joomla extension component and the mobile-based front-end are supported by a Google Groups forum, as well as the "wiki page" and the "Issues tracker" functionality offered by Github, where all communications take place in English. The platform is open for any individual or consortium to use and contribute under the AGLP licence.

The ImproveMyCity platform was originally deployed in the Municipality of Thermi, Greece in April 2012 [4]. One year later more than 500 users have been registered and submitted 585 issues and 1350 comments. The mobile-based front-end has been officially launched by the municipality of Thermi-Greece on December 2012 and has since been installed in more than 190 devices.

[1]https://www.transifex.com/projects/p/improvemycity/

8. SUMMARY

Although the idea of engaging citizens into a two-way dialogue with their administration for improving their urban space has been around for some time, e.g. FixMyStreet[2], BuitenBeter[3], ImproveMyCity is the first integrated solution that is made available as open source and covers the full chain of information flow, ranging from the desktop user that reports issues from the leisure of his home and the mobile citizen that reports issues while on the move, all the way to the back-end management system for administering the incoming issues and the reports with aggregated statistics for performance assessment and future planning of resources.

Moreover, the ImproveMyCity platform is characterized by its simple installation process, its extensive customization options and its minimum requirements in terms of additional hardware or external software libraries. This makes it ideal for municipalities that are reluctant to invest any resources, until they are convinced about the benefits of citizen-government collaboration for urban maintenance and improvement.

9. ACKNOWLEDGMENTS

This work was supported by the project "PEOPLE: Pilot smart urban Ecosystems leveraging Open innovation for Promoting and enabLing future E- services" partly funded by the EC under contract no. 271027 and the EU 7th Framework Programme project Live+Gov under grant number IST-FP7-288815 (www.liveandgov.eu)

10. REFERENCES

[1] Free-Software-Foundation. Gnu affero general public license. https://www.gnu.org/licenses/agpl.html.

[2] icos urenio. Improvemycity - citizens requests, complaints & suggestions. https://github.com/icos-urenio/Improve-my-city.

[3] icos urenio. Improvemycity - citizens requests, complaints & suggestions - installation instructions. https://github.com/icos-urenio/Improve-my-city/wiki.

[4] icos urenio. Improvemycity - citizens requests, complaints & suggestions - municipality of thermi-greece. https://smartcity.thermi.gov.gr/improve/en/.

[5] MKLab-ITI. Improvemycity - application for android devices. https://github.com/MKLab-ITI/ImproveMyCity-Mobile.

[6] MKLab-ITI. Improvemycity - application for android devices - installation instructions. http://mklab-iti.github.io/ImproveMyCity-Mobile/.

[2]http://www.fixmystreet.com/

[3]http://www.buitenbeter.nl/

LIRE: Open Source Image Retrieval in Java

Mathias Lux
Klagenfurt University
Universitätsstr. 65-67
Klagenfurt, Austria
mlux@itec.uni-klu.ac.at

ABSTRACT

Content based image retrieval has been around for some time. There are lots of different test data sets, lots of published methods and techniques, and manifold retrieval challenges, where content based image retrieval is of interest. LIRE is a Java library, that provides a simple way to index and retrieve millions of images based on the images' contents. LIRE is robust and well tested and is not only recommended by the websites of ImageCLEF and MediaEval, but is also employed in industry. This paper gives an overview on LIRE, its use, capabilities and reports on retrieval and runtime performance.

Categories and Subject Descriptors

H.3.3 [**Information Storage and Retrieval**]: Information Search and Retrieval

Keywords

Image retrieval, image features, image search, image indexing

1. INTRODUCTION

How to search in large image data sets? While Google image search[1] is ready at hand and yields impressive results, software for doing the same in arbitrary applications and scenarios is rare. Search techniques based on meta data have been explored a lot. Retrieval is then based on time and date or GPS coordinates, i.e. from EXIF data embedded by the camera, or relies on user assigned keywords. However, there are scenarios, where automatically generated meta data is not sufficient and manual annotation is sparse. Then, content based image retrieval (CBIR) is one avenue to pursue.

In this paper I introduce LIRE[2] [15], short for *Lucene Image Retrieval*, a library for content based image retrieval. LIRE is based on *Lucene*, a well-known, robust and fast text search engine. It's also already well known in research, teaching and industry and has been applied to many different scenarios over the last years. Recently even a book on content based image retrieval with LIRE has been published [15] aimed at developers and students. Furthermore, LIRE is free, open source and known to work in Java VMs on Linux, Mac OS and Windows. LIRE aims to make life of software developers easier on a high level. Developers do not have to know specifics of content based image retrieval, but use the library to (i) index the images and (ii) search in the index. Parameter settings for features and indexing are hidden for users on the highest API level and are pre-tuned to yield reasonable performance. However, control on a lower level is possible and easily done. This document present LIRE in terms of general methods, usage and performance charts.

2. LIRE FEATURES

There are many different ways to implement a content based image search engine or integrate content based image retrieval capabilities into applications. The intuitive, but also most time-consuming way to do so, is to implement extraction, storage and retrieval of features oneself. However, a lot of time and effort can be saved if a library is used. Currently there are several libraries available, that allow for content based image retrieval. There is for instance the *Gnu Image Finding Tool* (GIFT)[3] developed by the University of Geneva, or *ImageTerrier* and *OpenIMAJ* [9]. Other libraries were developed with intentions different from providing content based image retrieval, i.e. libraries for computer vision or image processing. Nevertheless, those libraries can provide means for content based image retrieval. Examples are *OpenCV*[4] [3] or *scikit-image*[5].

Still, while there are several possibilities available, both open source and commercial, LIRE has two main features, that make it stick out of the crowd. First LIRE is extremely simple to use. With just a few lines of code an indexing routine with a selection of features is written, that makess optimal use of multi-core systems. Even more so LIRE provides an extensive offline GUI demo, which allows for visually testing different features on arbitrary data sets without programming knowledge. Second, LIRE is based on the well-known, well-supported and extremely efficient *Lucene* text search engine [10]. There is no need for an extra database or

[1]see `http://images.google.com/`
[2]see `https://code.google.com/p/lire/`
[3]see `http://www.gnu.org/software/gift/`
[4]see `http://opencv.willowgarage.com/wiki/`
[5]see `http://scikit-image.org/`

MM'13, October 21–25, 2013, Barcelona, Spain.

ACM 978-1-4503-2404-5/13/10...$15.00
http://dx.doi.org/10.1145/2502081.2502226 .

special file system and Lucene specific features, like memory mapped indexes, distributed indexes, multi-threaded access, etc. can be used with LIRE. LIRE can even be integrated in existing Lucene based search engines.

2.1 Image Features

A main contribution of LIRE is the extensive set of global image features supported out of the box. Most prominent global features include:

1. Color Histograms supporting different color spaces, like HSV and the Opponent color space [21], and quantization routines as well as different metrics for distance computation.
2. MPEG-7 descriptors Scalable Color, Color Layout and Edge Histogram, see [4].
3. The Tamura texture features coarseness, contrast and directionality, see [20]
4. Color and edge directivity descriptor, CEDD, see [5] and Fuzzy color and texture histogram, FCTH, see [6], which are joint histograms combining fuzzy color and edge histograms, as well as the JCD feature, which combines both descriptor to a joint histogram [7].
5. Auto color correlation feature defined by Huang et al. [11]
6. Pyramid Histogram of Oriented Gradients (PHOG) as defined by Bosch et al. [2].

For all global features in LIRE parameters have been set to default values, that led to good results on the SIMPLIcity data set [22] and the UCID data set [18].

For local features LIRE integrates the jopensurf[6] library implementing the Speeded Up Robust Features [1] and code from the JavaSIFT project[7] implementing the scale-invariant feature transform approach [14]. An included multi-threaded k-means implementation and indexing abstraction routines allow for using the *bag of visual words* search approach [19].

2.2 Indexing and Search

For each of the implemented image features LIRE defines an optimized, byte-array based descriptor. The CEDD feature for instance is defined as a 144 dimensional double vector. Still due to quantization it's possible to put two values into one byte. Moreover, trailing zero are omitted resulting in a descriptor size significantly smaller than $s144/2 = 77$ bytes. Tests on the data set associated with LIRE have shown that that omission of trailing zeros leads to a further reduction of 7.2% in size on average.

Locality Sensitve Hashing [8] has been implemented for LIRE in two different ways. (i) Random projections allows nearest neighbor search in euclidean spaces, while (ii) bit sampling [17] allows for approximation of search with the cosine coefficient.

[6]see `https://code.google.com/p/jopensurf/`

[7]see `http://fly.mpi-cbg.de/~saalfeld/Projects/javasift.html`

Table 1: Tests on the Wang SIMPLIcity data set [13]. Best value per column in bold face.

Feature	map	p@10	er
CEDD	0.513	0.706	0.193
Color Correlogram	0.498	**0.740**	**0.159**
Color Layout	0.439	0.612	0.303
Edge Histogram	0.333	0.500	0.401
FCTH	0.499	0.703	0.207
JCD	**0.520**	0.730	0.183
Joint Histogram	0.449	0.689	0.197
OpponentHistogram	0.450	0.635	0.270
PHOG	0.352	0.535	0.368
RGB Color Histogram	0.450	0.704	0.191
Scalable Color	0.305	0.470	0.464

3. USAGE

As already indicated indexing can be done utilizing available system resources in a few lines of code. Investigating runtime performance for the MIRFlickr [12] data set for extracting the global features Color Layout, Edge Histogram, JCD, Joint Histogram, Opponent Histogram, PHOG, and RGB Color Histogram and hashing the descriptors with LSH bit sampling shows that extraction takes about 44 ms per image on a current system[8]. Interpolating runtime the whole MIRFlickr data set can be indexed in under 13 hours. Approximate search using the hashes and re-ranking of the results returned by Lucene takes well below 100 ms running in a local Java VM. However, in the LIRE web demo[9] a search on 300,000 images from the MIRFlickr data set takes roughly 150 ms due to current configuration of the Java servlet container (the search is simply called within a Java servlet).

4. PERFORMANCE

The full source code of the evaluated features is available in the LIRE SVN, so results are reproducible. Test results for the Wang SIMPLIcity data [13] and the UCID data set [18] are given in Table 1 and Table 2. The benchmarking code is also part of LIRE and can be found in the classes *TestUCID* and *TestWANG*[10]. The tables give the performance in terms of mean average precision (map), precision at ten (p@10), and error rate (er). Note that the precision at ten is considerably lower with the UCID data set as the ground truth only features queries with very few – often only one – result. As can be seen easily for both test data sets CEDD, FCTH, JCD, and especially the Color Correlogram perform well. Still, all other features have their uses. Figure 1 for instance shows how well the PHOG feature can identify flower shapes. Figure 2 provides anecdotal evidence that the MPEG-7 Edge Histogram can be employed for finding logos having a similar overall structure.

5. DEMOS

Currently there are two different demos available for LIRE. One is the LireDemo GUI, which allows for indexing and

[8]an Intel Core i7, 16GB RAM, SSD, Windows 7, 64bit JVM running 8 threads

[9]see `http://demo-itec.uni-klu.ac.at/liredemo/`

[10]both to be found in *net.semanticmetadata.lire.benchmarking*, SVN rev. 88

Table 2: Tests on the UCID data set [18]. Best value per column in bold face.

Feature	map	p@10	er
CEDD	0.431	0.420	0.553
Color Correlogram	**0.586**	**0.480**	**0.370**
Color Layout	0.277	0.285	0.679
Edge Histogram	0.180	0.202	0.813
FCTH	0.447	0.415	0.531
JCD	0.470	0.435	0.508
Joint Histogram	0.348	0.313	0.603
Opponent Histogram	0.319	0.309	0.649
PHOG	0.238	0.238	0.714
RGB Color Histogram	0.403	0.358	0.550
Scalable Color	0.172	0.183	0.840

Figure 1: Results for a query-by-example search in the MIRFlickr data set [12] using the PHOG feature [2] taken from the LIRE web demo.

searching for arbitrary images, as seen in Figure 3. The second one, the LIRE web demo as shown in Figure 4, has been implemented recently and allows for searching in the first 300,000 images of the MIRFlickr data set based on selected features.

6. CONCLUSIONS

LIRE has been around for some time now. It started as a small side project and gradually became bigger and more important. It has been – and still is – employed in academia (i.e. as recommended library for imageCLEF [16]), in teaching, and industry (i.e. in the products of mediamid[11] or in the upcoming WIPO trademark search[12]).

LIRE provides a well balanced trade-off between (i) simplicity for the developer using the library and (ii) control over parameters at indexing and search time. With approximate nearest neighbor search based on locality sensitive hashing, retrieval times for data sets with more than 1.5 million images smaller than 70 ms have been observed.

LIRE is actively developed and available at `https://code.google.com/p/lire/`.

[11]see `http://www.mediamid.com/`

[12]see `http://www.wipo.int/`

Figure 2: Results for a query-by-example search in a trademark logo image data set using the MPEG-7 Edge Histogram feature.

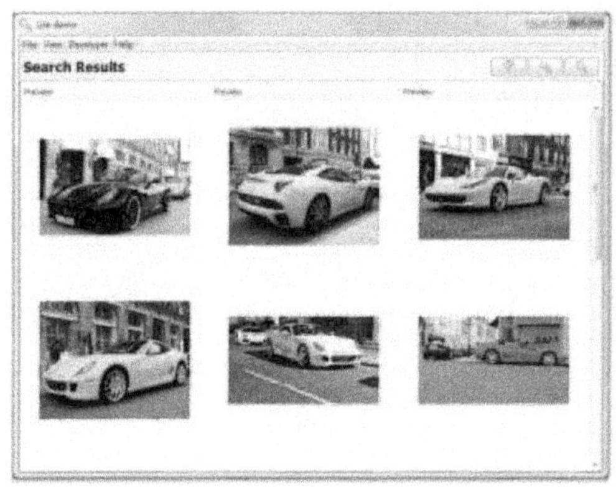

Figure 3: LireDemo user interface screen shot showing the first two rows of results.

Acknowledgments

I'd like to thank at least some of the numerous people having contributed code and ideas to Lire or having published their work as open source allowing integration into LIRE: Anna-Maria Pasterk, Arthur Li, Arthur Pitman, Bastian Hösch, Benjamin Sznajder, Christian Penz, Christine Keim, Christoph Kofler, Dan Hanley, Daniel Pötzinger, Fabrizio Falchi, Franz Graf, Giuseppe Amato, James Charters, Janine Lachner, Katharina Tomanec, Lukas Esterle, Manuel Oraze, Marian Kogler, Marko Keuschnig, Michael Riegler, Rodrigo Carvalho Rezende, Roman Divotkey, Roman Kern, Savvas Chatzichristofis and Sandeep Gupta.

This work was supported by Lakeside Labs GmbH, Klagenfurt, Austria and funding from the European Regional Development Fund and the Carinthian Economic Promotion Fund (KWF) under grant KWF-20214 22573 33955.

Figure 4: LIRE web demo user interface screen shot showing a query and the first row of results.

7. REFERENCES

[1] H. Bay, T. Tuytelaars, and L. Van Gool. Surf: Speeded up robust features. In *Computer Vision - ECCV 2006*, volume 3951 of *Lecture Notes in Computer Science*, pages 404–417. Springer, 2006.

[2] A. Bosch, A. Zisserman, and X. Munoz. Representing shape with a spatial pyramid kernel. In *Proceedings of the 6th ACM international conference on Image and video retrieval*, CIVR '07, pages 401–408, New York, NY, USA, 2007. ACM.

[3] G. Bradski and A. Kaehler. *Learning OpenCV: Computer vision with the OpenCV library*. O'Reilly Media, Incorporated, 2008.

[4] S.-F. Chang, T. Sikora, and A. Puri. Overview of the MPEG-7 standard. *IEEE Transactions on Circuits and Systems for Video Technology*, 11(6):688–695, June 2001.

[5] S. A. Chatzichristofis and Y. S. Boutalis. CEDD: Color and edge directivity descriptor. a compact descriptor for image indexing and retrieval. In A. Gasteratos, M. Vincze, and J. Tsotsos, editors, *Proceedings of the 6th International Conference on Computer Vision Systems, ICVS 2008*, volume 5008 of *LNCS*, pages 312–322, Santorini, Greece, May 2008. Springer.

[6] S. A. Chatzichristofis and Y. S. Boutalis. FCTH: Fuzzy color and texture histogram a low level feature for accurate image retrieval. In *Proceedings of the 9th International Workshop on Image Analysis for Multimedia Interactive Services, WIAMIS 2008*, pages 191–196, Klagenfurt, Austria, May 2008. IEEE.

[7] S. A. Chatzichristofis, Y. S. Boutalis, and M. Lux. Selection of the proper compact composite descriptor for improving content based image retrieval. In *The Sixth IASTED International Conference on Signal Processing, Pattern Recognition and Applications SPPRA 2009*, 2009.

[8] M. Datar, N. Immorlica, P. Indyk, and V. S. Mirrokni. Locality-sensitive hashing scheme based on p-stable distributions. In *Proceedings of the twentieth annual symposium on Computational geometry*, pages 253–262. ACM, 2004.

[9] J. S. Hare, S. Samangooei, and D. P. Dupplaw. OpenIMAJ and ImageTerrier: Java libraries and tools for scalable multimedia analysis and indexing of images. In *Proceedings of the 19th ACM international conference on Multimedia*, MM '11, pages 691–694, New York, NY, USA, 2011. ACM.

[10] E. Hatcher, O. Gospodnetic, and M. McCandless. Lucene in action, 2004.

[11] J. Huang, S. R. Kumar, M. Mitra, W.-J. Zhu, and R. Zabih. Image indexing using color correlograms. In *Proceedings of the 1997 Conference on Computer Vision and Pattern Recognition, CVPR '97*, volume 00, pages 762–768, San Juan, Puerto Rico, June 1997. IEEE.

[12] M. J. Huiskes and M. S. Lew. The mir flickr retrieval evaluation. In *Proceedings of the 1st ACM international conference on Multimedia information retrieval*, pages 39–43. ACM, 2008.

[13] J. Li and J. Z. Wang. Automatic linguistic indexing of pictures by a statistical modeling approach. *IEEE Trans. Pattern Anal. Mach. Intell.*, 25:1075–1088, September 2003.

[14] D. Lowe. Object recognition from local scale-invariant features. In *Computer Vision, 1999. The Proceedings of the Seventh IEEE International Conference on*, volume 2, pages 1150 –1157 vol.2, 1999.

[15] M. Lux and O. Marques. Visual information retrieval using java and lire. *Synthesis Lectures on Information Concepts, Retrieval, and Services*, 5(1):1–112, 2013.

[16] H. Müller, P. Clough, T. Deselaers, and B. Caputo, editors. *ImageCLEF*. Springer, 2010.

[17] S. Rüger. Multimedia information retrieval. *Synthesis Lectures on Information Concepts, Retrieval, and Services*, 1(1):1–171, 2009.

[18] G. Schaefer and M. Stich. Ucid: an uncompressed color image database. In *Electronic Imaging 2004*, pages 472–480. International Society for Optics and Photonics, 2003.

[19] J. Sivic and A. Zisserman. Video google: A text retrieval approach to object matching in videos. *Computer Vision, IEEE International Conference on*, 2:1470, 2003.

[20] H. Tamura, S. Mori, and T. Yamawaki. Textural features corresponding to visual perception. *IEEE Transactions on Systems, Man, and Cybernetics*, 8(6):460–472, June 1978.

[21] K. E. van de Sande, T. Gevers, and C. G. Snoek. Evaluating color descriptors for object and scene recognition. *Pattern Analysis and Machine Intelligence, IEEE Transactions on*, 32(9):1582–1596, 2010.

[22] J. Z. Wang, J. Li, and G. Wiederhold. Simplicity: Semantics-sensitive integrated matching for picture libraries. *Pattern Analysis and Machine Intelligence, IEEE Transactions on*, 23(9):947–963, 2001.

Golden Retriever - A Java Based Open Source Image Retrieval Engine

Lazaros T. Tsochatzidis, Chryssanthi Iakovidou, Savvas A. Chatzichristofis and Yiannis S. Boutalis
Democtitus University of Thrace
Department of Electrical and Computer Engineering
Xanthi, Greece
{lazatsoc,ciakovid,schatzic,ybout}@ee.duth.gr

SUBMITTED TO ACM MULTIMEDIA 2013 OPEN SOURCE SOFTWARE COMPETITION

ABSTRACT

Golden Retriever Image Retrieval Engine (GRire) is an open source light weight Java library developed for Content Based Image Retrieval (CBIR) tasks, employing the Bag of Visual Words (BOVW) model. It provides a complete framework for creating CBIR system including image analysis tools, classifiers, weighting schemes etc., for efficient indexing and retrieval procedures. Its eminent feature is its extensibility, achieved through the open source nature of the library as well as a user-friendly embedded plug-in system.

GRire is available on-line along with install and development documentation on `http://www.grire.net` and on its Google Code page `http://code.google.com/p/grire`. It is distributed either as a Java library or as a standalone Java application, both GPL licensed.

Categories and Subject Descriptors

H.3.3 [**Information Storage and Retrieval**]: Information Search and Retrieval

Keywords

Image Retrieval, Visual Words, Bag-of-Visual-Words, Open Source, Image Search, Image Indexing

1. INTRODUCTION

Content based image retrieval approaches can be mainly classified into two groups based on the types of low level visual features that they employ. The first group consist of methods that use global features while the second one is formed by approaches that employ local features. Additionally, CBIR systems can be separated into two general classes based on the type of the queries they handle. In applied research, CBIR systems are retrieving images with similar visual characteristics to the query image (e.g. if the query is a red image, the retrieved images are also red)[4]. To support these queries, mainly global features are employed. At the same time, many advanced systems are able to recognize the context of the query and to retrieve semantically similar images (e.g. if the query is a red luxurious car, the retrieved images are depicting a Ferrari). In this case, these queries are mainly supported by local features.

Recent CBIR approaches have strongly focused on the combination of global and local features. These approaches are employing the local features in order to produce a holistic, global representation of the image. An example of such approaches is the bag-of-visual-words (BOVW) approach. This BOVW representation is analogous to the bag-of-words representation, a well-known and widely used method in text retrieval, where a document is represented by a set of distinct keywords.

BOVW methods are fast becoming a widely used representation for CBIR, mainly for three reasons: their better retrieval effectiveness over global feature representations, the much better efficiency than local feature representations and the fact that they can be used both, by systems that attempt to identify the content of the query to retrieve images with semantically similar content and by systems designed to retrieve images with similar visual concept to the query.

Figure 1: Golden Retriever Logo.

This paper presents a new open source and extensible Java image retrieval library named Golder Retriever. The scope of the library is to provide solutions on how to integrate CBIR techniques in an easy way, on a wide range of applications. Additionally, GRire provides a testing platform for researchers that could be used to evaluate existing or new CBIR approaches.

Current version of the library is mainly focused on the BOVW approach, integrating a variety of local features, classifiers as well as methods from the field of information retrieval adjusted to meet the image retrieval perspective.

MM'13, October 21–25, 2013, Barcelona, Spain.

2. THE GRIRE PROJECT

The main objective of the project is to help developers create and evaluate their methods in any image database with minimum effort and without needing to concern about the details of the model itself. Furthermore, developers are welcome to integrate custom components, such as feature extractors and descriptors, into the GRire library. Thus, a whole BOVW system can be created and tested adopting the provided implemented weighting schemes and similarity models. Towards this direction, GRire combines an adaptable and easy-to-use plug-in system together with a powerful and efficient indexing and retrieving mechanism.

2.1 Project Structure

The GRire project can be operated in two ways; either as a Java library to be integrated into other applications or through an easily used graphical user interface called GRireFX. These two versions are distributed in the same file available for download, under the packages `org.grire` and `org.grirefx` respectively and they both provide the same functionality and extensibility. Essentially, the GRire library consists of two main parts: the core and the components.

2.2 The Core

The core of GRire implements the main work flow for the indexing and the retrieval procedures using a BOVW architecture. It consists of the classes required by the model and it is considered to be the 'fixed' part of the library. The classes of the core are organized into two different types hereby referred to as *Structures* and *Functions*. *Structures* are objects responsible for handling database's operations such as storing and fetching. On the other hand, *Functions* implement the procedures for generating the model, like indexing and retrieving. Furthermore, *Structures* are usually an 'extra layer' above the *GeneralStorer* which provides more basic structures described in sections 2.3 and 3.2.

2.2.1 Structures

ImagePool An image pool is a collection of images. It pairs a unique id with the absolute path of an image and stores it in a database. It provides all the required methods for adding and deleting an image from the pool.

PoolFeatures This structure is the collection of features extracted from an *ImagePool*.

Codebook The main component of the BOVW model. It is a lexicon of key-features selected from the *PoolFeatures* structure using various ways (clustering etc.).

Index This structure stores the representation (descriptor) of each image.

2.2.2 Functions

Importer This is a simple class that allows batch importing of image from multiple folders.

PoolFeatureExtractor It extracts features from all the images part of an *ImagePool* to generate a *PoolFeature* structure for storing them. These features are extracted using a *FeatureExctractor* component (kindly refer to section 2.3).

ClusteringCodebookFactory This class creates a new lexicon (codebook) by performing a *ClusteringAlgorithm* on the features provided. By default, the *ClusteringCodebookFactory* will create clusters using the 30% of the data but users have the ability to modify the percentage. The training set is stored temporary in the file system.

IndexFactory This function produces the index of the image representations (descriptors) using the *PoolFeatures* extracted earlier. The representation for each image is created according to the supplied *VisualWordDescriptor* component (details in section 2.3).

QueryPerformer This class performs the searching procedure for one or more queries, given as input, generating a TREC formatted file with the results for easy and accurate evaluation.

2.3 The Components

The BOVW model can be assembled by several different components that execute discrete steps of the architecture, thus making it highly customizable. The multiple possible component combinations provide a great variety of experimental setups of the model. Each component allows for independent enhancement attracting researchers/developers from varying scientific fields to explore and extend.

Type	Component Name
`GeneralStorer`	MapDB, See section 3.2
`FeatureExtractor`	SURF [3] SIFT [6] ORB [8] MSER [7] + FREAK [1] CEDD [5] (Bag of CEDDs[1])
`ClusteringAlgorithm`	K-Means SGONG [2]
`SimilarityMeasure`	Euclidean Distance Cosine Similarity
`WeightingScheme`	SMART [9]
`Stemmer`	Euclidean Stemmer

Table 1: A list of the currently implemented Components

These components are interfaces whose implementations are given as arguments to the core classes. A list of the components is shown below while Table 1 briefly presents the implemented components:

1. `GeneralStorer`. It manages the way data are written in the file system, providing simple structures such as maps and sorted maps.

2. `FeatureExtractor`. It is employed from the core for the extraction of local features from an image.

[1]The proposed library has the ability to adjust the information and the advantages derived from the Global low level Features (GF), into the BOVW model. GRire separates the images into a preset number of image blocks and calculates a global descriptor (e.g. CEDD) from each one. Based on this approach, every image is represented with multiple GFs. In the sequel, these global features are considered as visual words.

3. `ClusteringAlgorithm`. This component implements a clustering algorithm used for the creation of the codebook.

4. `SimilarityMeasure`. It is used for the comparison of the representation (descriptor).

5. `VisualWordDescriptor`. This component's task is to form the representation (descriptor) of an image using all the previously created structures.

6. `WeightingScheme`. The weighting scheme used during the retrieval process defines how the final representation (descriptor) of an image will be formed, just before it is compared with other representations.

7. `Stemmer`. Stemmers are the objects that define how a visual word derived from an image will be assigned to a word from the codebook.

2.4 Work-flow

Initially, the images are imported into an `ImagePool` object. Then, the `PoolFeatureExtractor` extracts the local features from the imported images, using a `FeatureExtractor` component and stores them in a `PoolFeatures` structure. In the sequel, the `IndexFactory` creates the representation (descriptor) for each image using a `VisualWordDescriptor` component, according to a `Codebook` structure. The results are stored it in the `Index`. The codebook was created by the `CluteringCodebookFactory` class in advance, using a `ClusteringAlgorithm` component on `PoolFeatures`. The system is now ready to perform any retrieval task using the `QueryPerformer` together with the `WeightingScheme` and `SimilarityMeasure` components.

3. TECHNICAL DETAILS

3.1 Extending GRire

GRire has been designed with particular attention to be highly customizable giving the opportunity to developers / researchers to implement their own methods and integrate them in the framework. This is achieved through the plug-in system which adopts the open source *jspf* [2]. Developers can easily create a plug-in without any constraints on the number of the needed parameters so as to implement one of the components described earlier. For the users' convenience a set of common parameters has been predefined to be recognizable by the framework. The plug-in interacts with GRire notifying it about the number and the type of the parameters and the program dynamically prompts the user for the right input method. Every plug-in has the following functionality:

- It implements only one component of GRire.
- It may require input parameters.
- It may require a setup process manually called by the user before it can be executed.
- Additional parameters for the aforementioned setup process may be also required.
- Default initialization values may be available for all or some of the parameters.

[2] `https://code.google.com/p/jspf/`

3.2 Storage

The GRire library employs the very powerful and promising *MapDB*[3] that supports fast and efficient storage and serialization of the data. This embedded database provides maps (Hash, Sorted and Multi-maps) as basic structures that are used to form all other more complex needed structures (Codebook etc.). *MapDB* offers its own serialization, compression and cache memory system while it is portable and allows processing of large amount of data, with minimum overhead in memory.

3.3 Compiling and Installation

It is decided that the components of GRire will be distributed separately from its core, grouped in plug-in packs. Every component may have its own dependencies, which may be external libraries or even programs. The *git* repository of the project includes the source code of the core along with the source code of every component pack that will be available as plug-in. A universal *ant* configuration file accompanies every module (core and packs) as well as every plug-in pack.

After obtaining the core *jar* file, the user can execute it to launch the GRireFX or import it as an external library to another Java application. The components can be used integrated with the following ways:

- If GRire operates as a Java library, then the plug-ins can be also imported to the application to be used like any other class.
- If GRire operates through its GUI then a text file named 'plugins' is required to be present in the same folder as the *jar* file. This text file contains the paths to the *jar* files of the plug-in packs.

4. GRIREFX

For users that do not wish to create their own application and just want to test their component of the BOVW model, the ideal solution is the graphical user interface of GRire. It is designed not to insert any limitation compared to the GRire library version, retaining its customizability by allowing enrichments in the form plug-in. In figure 2 there is a screen shot of GRireFX while the user is setting up a multi-query retrieval task. The results of the procedure is a TREC formated file.

As mentioned before, GRireFX automatically recognizes the number and the types of the parameters, as well as their default values (if they exist), and dynamically requests from the user the corresponding input. Figure 3 illustrates the dynamic tree of parameters that grows according to every component's needs while the user makes interacts with the interface.

5. PERFORMANCE

Indicative experiments have been performed to evaluate the performance of the GRire library. It is worth noting that, the proposed project is a framework for implementing and integrating various features with different computational costs and complexity, so the time needed for the indexing as well as for the retrieval procedure greatly varies and depends on the components that will be used (features,

[3] `https://github.com/jankotek/MapDB`

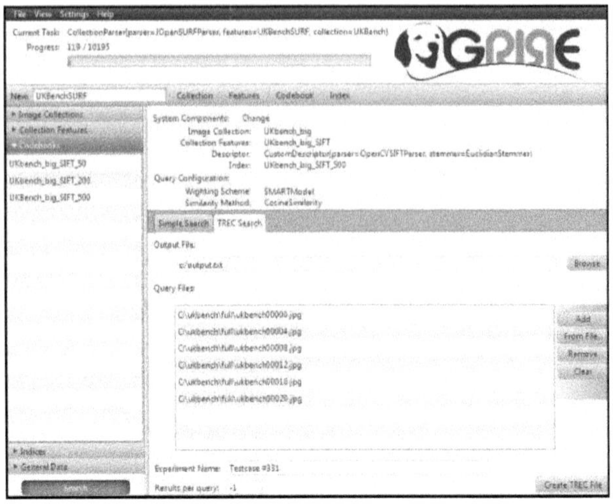

Figure 2: GRireFX performing a multi-query experiment.

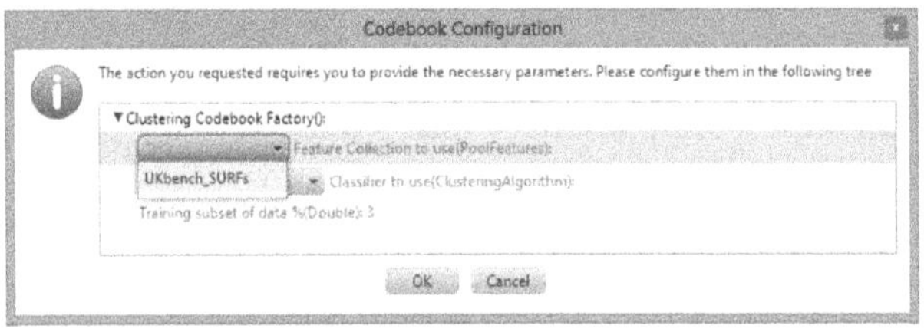

Figure 3: GRireFX dynamically adds leaves to the tree of parameters.

classifiers, codebook size, weighting scheme, database size, etc). Table 2 presents the time (in minutes) elapsed for two different experiments that have been performed.

	SURF	SIFT
Feature Extraction	109	163
Codebook Generation (K-Means)	73	158
Descriptor Calculation	20	26
Retrieval Procedure (100 queries)	<2	<2

Table 2: Results of the time needed for each process measured in minutes.

For the first experiment, the SURF(64) features were used as the local features, while for the second one, the SIFT(128) features were employed. In both cases, experiments conducted on the *UK-BENCH*[7] image dataset (10200 images), using a codebook of 1024 visual words. For the retrieval procedure, we executed a multi-query experiment (100 queries linear search) using the tf-idf weighting scheme and cosine similarity measure. Experiments carried out on a Core 2 Quad Q6600 CPU with 4GB of RAM system. The storage needs for the created databases reached a total of 2.89 GB and 5.48 GB respectively.

6. CONCLUSIONS

This paper presents a new framework for CBIR based on the BOVW approach, that can be used in a wide range of applications. The open source nature of the proposed library allows and encourages researches to extend GRire by implementing more components, methods and features. It's worth noting that apart from a powerful and fast indexing and retrieving mechanism, GRire additionally uses an extremely easy to use plug-in system. The GRire library is provided under GPL license and is available online along with install and development documentation on `http://www.grire.net` and on its Google Code page `http://code.google.com/p/grire`

7. ACKNOWLEDGMENTS

This research has been co-financed by the European Union (European Social Fund-ESF) and Greek national funds through the Operational Program "Education and Lifelong Learning" of the National Strategic Reference Framework (NSRF)- Research Funding Program: Heracleitus II. Investing in knowledge society through the European Social Fund.

8. REFERENCES

[1] Alexandre Alahi, Raphael Ortiz, and Pierre Vandergheynst. Freak: Fast retina keypoint. In *CVPR*, pages 510–517, 2012.

[2] Antonios Atsalakis and Nikos Papamarkos. Color reduction and estimation of the number of dominant colors by using a self-growing and self-organized neural gas. *Eng. Appl. of AI*, 19(7):769–786, 2006.

[3] Herbert Bay, Andreas Ess, Tinne Tuytelaars, and Luc J. Van Gool. Speeded-up robust features (surf). *Computer Vision and Image Understanding*, 110(3):346–359, 2008.

[4] S.A. Chatzichristofis, C. Iakovidou, Y. Boutalis, and O. Marques. Co.vi.wo.: Color visual words based on non-predefined size codebooks. *Cybernetics, IEEE Transactions on*, 43(1):192–205, 2013.

[5] Savvas A. Chatzichristofis and Yiannis S. Boutalis. Cedd: Color and edge directivity descriptor: A compact descriptor for image indexing and retrieval. In *ICVS*, pages 312–322, 2008.

[6] David G. Lowe. Distinctive image features from scale-invariant keypoints. *International Journal of Computer Vision*, 60(2):91–110, 2004.

[7] D. Nister and H. Stewenius. Scalable recognition with a vocabulary tree. In *CVPR*, volume 5, pages 2161–2168, 2006.

[8] Ethan Rublee, Vincent Rabaud, Kurt Konolige, and Gary Bradski. Orb: an efficient alternative to sift or surf. In *Computer Vision (ICCV), 2011 IEEE International Conference on*, pages 2564–2571. IEEE, 2011.

[9] G. Salton. *The SMART Retrieval System - Experiments in Automatic Document Processing.* Prentice-Hall, Inc., Upper Saddle River, NJ, USA, 1971.

Stage Framework - An HTML5 and CSS3 Framework for Digital Publishing

Rami Aamulehto
rami.aamulehto@icloud.com

Mikko Kuhna
mikko.kuhna@aalto.fi

Jussi Tarvainen
jussi.tarvainen@aalto.fi

Pirkko Oittinen
pirkko.oittinen@aalto.fi

Aalto University, Department of Media Technology, Espoo, Finland

ABSTRACT

In this paper we present Stage Framework, an HTML5 and CSS3 framework for digital book, magazine and newspaper publishing. The framework offers publishers the means and tools for publishing editorial content in the HTML5 format using a single web application. The approach is cross-platform and is based on open web standards. Stage Framework serves as an alternative for platform-specific native publications using pure HTML5 to deliver book, magazine and newspaper content while retaining the familiar gesture interaction of native applications. Available gesture actions include for example the page swipe and kinetic scrolling. The magazine browsing view relies entirely on CSS3 3D Transforms and Transitions, thus utilizing hardware acceleration in most devices and platforms. The web application also features a magazine stand which, can be used to offer issues of multiple publications. Developed as a part of master's thesis research, the framework has been published under the GPL and MIT licenses and is available to everyone via the framework website[1] and the GitHub repository[2].

Categories and Subject Descriptors

I.7.4 [**Document and Text Processing**]: Electronic Publishing

General Terms

Documentation, Performance, Design, Experimentation

Keywords

HTML5, CSS3, Digital Publishing, Tablet Magazine, Web Application, Browser Technology

[1]`http://stageframework.com`
[2]`http://github.com/ralatalo/stage`

MM'13, October 21–25, 2013, Barcelona, Spain.

ACM 978-1-4503-2404-5/13/10 ...$15.00.
http://dx.doi.org/10.1145/2502081.2502228.

1. INTRODUCTION

While browsers have been adopting the new HTML5 features, new implementation possibilities have emerged in digital publishing, especially for tablet and mobile platforms. These implementations can potentially match the performance of native applications and at the same time streamline the publishing process. The extended variation of devices and platforms has made it practically impossible to develop for each present and future device separately. Nevertheless, the content needs to adapt to these different devices. HTML5 can serve as a platform-independent content format while being presented in the most common execution environment in the world. Responsive design offers an approach to simplify content adaptation and lets publishers focus on the editorial content itself. Several native wrapper application frameworks for HTML5-based magazine content have been introduced, including Baker Ebook Framework[3] for iOS and Friar eBook Framework[4] for Android. However, few cross-platform web application frameworks have been available to date.

The field of research was focused primarily on tablet and mobile platforms, which have played a crucial role in the convergence of devices, media and technologies during the past years. This development has increased the significance of browser-based applications, content and services, which can flow across different devices and be accessed regardless of time, place and device. The typical performance difference between the web and native applications was addressed as a research problem in the context of the master's thesis research [1] in which Stage Framework was implemented. As a result, solutions that improve the web application performance were incorporated into the presented framework.

2. BACKGROUND

The HTML5 specification [2] and the larger technological context around it have introduced many enabling technologies that can effectively change the entire digital publishing environment. HTML5 and its related JavaScript APIs include technologies such as Application Cache, Canvas, Media Elements, Web Storage, Web Workers and WebGL while 3rd generation CSS offers Animations, Transforms, Transitions, Media Queries and Web Fonts. All these technologies together with Touch Events and SVG make the browser-based digital publishing a breeze. Publishers can achieve

[3]`http://bakerframework.com`
[4]`http://friarframework.com`

interactive and pixel perfect digital publications without relying on platform-specific development or proprietary distribution channels. The gap between native and web technologies is closing increasingly fast due to rapid advancements in both mobile hardware and browser technologies. The future device APIs will enable even more features to be reached using only pure web technologies.

During the past few years, several magazine web applications that utilize the new HTML5 and CSS3 technologies in creating the browsing experience or content have emerged. Implementations seen so far include for example The Financial Times[5] and Aside Magazine[6] while also many national newspapers and magazines such as Helsingin Sanomat[7] and Suomen Kuvalehti[8] (in Finland) have concretized their interest in these new publishing technologies.

In the presented framework, Application Cache is used to increase performance inside a single browsed issue as the content is delivered over the network. Web Storage is utilized for storing the user data such as last browsed page per issue. The web application user interface is responsive, relying on Media Queries. The browsing view is implemented using the CSS 3D Transform and Transition technologies, which are the most experimental parts of the framework. The content delivered using the framework is HTML5 formatted and can therefore utilize Canvas and Media Elements, offering interactive 3D graphics, video and audio. The visual appearance of publications can be enhanced with CSS Animations, Transforms, Transitions, Media Queries and Web Fonts. Media Queries serve as a base for the content adaptation and responsive design, whereas Animations, Transforms and Transitions can be used to create more detailed and immersive content such as animated infographics.

Important technology enabling the content adaptation and possibly progressive enhancement or graceful degradation is *feature detection* which can utilize a dedicated JavaScript library such as Modernizr[9]. Other libraries and frameworks used in the implementation of Stage Framework include jQuery[10], Swipe.js[11] and HTML5 Boilerplate[12].

3. FRAMEWORK

3.1 Web Application

The heart of Stage Framework is the web application, which was built using HTML5 Boilerplate. The web application has customizable resources for application icons and splash screens which can be fully utilized on the iOS platform, where the application can be added to the device home screen. The web application follows the single page application design paradigm and has a JavaScript frontend based on the jQuery library. All feature detection needed by the frontend is performed with Modernizr. The web application has two main views, the magazine stand and browsing view, which are introduced in the following subsections.

[5]http://app.ft.com
[6]http://asidemag.com
[7]http://hs.fi/paivanlehti
[8]http://digi.suomenkuvalehti.fi
[9]http://modernizr.com
[10]http://jquery.com
[11]http://swipejs.com
[12]http://html5boilerplate.com

Figure 1: The magazine stand presented on iOS.

3.1.1 Magazine Stand

The magazine stand view serves as the main view of the web application, listing the available publications and their issues using cover images. The responsive design of the stand adapts the layout depending on the browser viewport width using CSS Media Queries: on small screens, issues are presented in three columns, whereas larger screens show four columns. The cover images of each issue are provided in three different resolutions, one of which is chosen based on the viewport width and device pixel ratio. The latter is unofficial and not part of the Media Queries specification (yet is very well supported).

The magazine stand content is generated during the web application launch based on a single JSON file described more thoroughly in Section 4.2.2. The stand can contain issues of multiple publications, which are separated into their own sections. The order of the publications and issues is defined by the same JSON file containing all the stand data. An example of the stand view content is presented in Figure 1. Users can open the desired issue for browsing by tapping it. The browsing view contains a link back to the magazine stand.

3.1.2 Browsing View

The magazine browsing view renders the magazine content in real time based on the stand JSON file content, which also describes the HTML resources that represent the issue pages. As the user selects an issue from the magazine stand, placeholders are created for each page of the issue. However, the content is loaded only for the maximum of three consecutive pages as mobile browsers present serious constraints on how much content, such as images, can be loaded into the browser cache. The user can use swipe to browse between pages and scroll within a single page using kinetic scrolling. The view uses CSS Transitions to animate and snap to page boundaries when the user swipe ends. When the user is touching a page, either vertical or horizontal movement is registered and transformed into CSS 3D Transform. Vertical movement transforms a single page parent element while horizontal movement transforms all pages containing parent element. The browsing is based on the Swipe.js library which has been extended to support the kinetic scrolling and vertical page boundaries.

3.2 Publications

The framework requires a certain content formatting for its publications. The content of all publications and their issues are located in a folder named *content* under the web application root directory served from a remote web server. The stand JSON file **stand.json** is located in this folder. Each of the publications are separated into their own directory named by the publication identifier. Each publication directory contains the issues in their own folders named by issue identifier.

The issues are required to be HTML5 formatted, meaning each issue page is presented by a single HTML resource. The HTML resources can contain any type of content as long as they are complying with the HTML5 specification. For example video and audio elements can be placed in the issue content. The linked resources must be located under that specific issue directory, so for example external resources are not allowed. Issue content can be styled using CSS and responsive designs can be achieved using CSS Media Queries. Web Fonts can be included in the style sheets, giving publications more depth in the visual appearance.

The resources of publications and their issues are structured by the directory hierarchy described earlier. The data of this structure is represented in the **stand.json** file. The following is an example of a minimal stand JSON file describing one publication with a single issue consisting of two pages.

```
{
  "publisher": [
    "Aalto University"
  ],
  "content": [
    {
      "identifier": "aum",
      "title": "Aalto University Magazine",
      "issues": [
        {
          "identifier": "2013-06",
          "title": "AUM 06",
          "languages": [
            "en"
          ],
          "covers": {
            "high": "images/cover.jpg",
            "medium": "images/cover-2048.jpg",
            "small": "images/cover-1024.jpg"
          },
          "pages": [
            "p1.html", "p2.html"
          ]
        }
      ],
      "date": "2013-05-01"
    }
  ],
  "updated": "2013-05-01"
}
```

The publication issue content is injected into the web application using the LESS.js[13] library. LESS is needed to relocate the resources relative to the original HTML resources. Additionally, CSS styles assigned to *html* and *body* elements need to be replaced with corresponding *.html* and *.body* classes. As the page root element changes when the content is injected, the *rem* unit cannot be used in the page-specific style sheets. All the JavaScript resources included in the HTML resource of the original issue page are loaded when the user swipes or follows a link to the newly cached page.

[13]`http://lesscss.org`

3.3 Caching

3.3.1 Problem

Web applications are prone to constraints set by the browser they are executed in. This is especially the case with different mobile browsers. Web applications need to consider how much content the browser is caching at one time. Otherwise, both the browser and web application executed inside it may be terminated. For example, on iOS web applications are forced to remove any *href* and *src* attributes before unused elements are removed from the page DOM. Otherwise, these unused resources, such as images and videos, may remain in the browser cache and eventually crash the browser. The same type of problems may also be encountered with CSS backgrounds and background colors, especially if OpenGL enabled hardware accelerated features, such as CSS 3D Transforms, are used which may lead to unused texture caching. Avoiding content caching negatively affects the web application performance.

3.3.2 Solution

One solution to the caching problem was implemented in Stage Framework. The Dynamic Application Cache featured in the framework relies on the HTML5 Application Cache technology, which can be used to extend the limited browser caching capabilities. Application Cache technology can be made dynamic using a server-side database and unique identifiers for each client. The clients can request cached content in real time, making issue-specific performance tuning possible. It is also possible to use Application Cache to request full issue resources as per offline caching functionality. This however, requires the browser to have an adequate amount of Application Cache available, which ranges from 10 to over 100 megabytes in modern browsers. With rich magazine content, 100 megabytes is easily used.

4. PRACTICAL EXAMPLE

4.1 Aalto University Magazine

The most natural content for Stage Framework is magazine content, which can benefit from the feature-rich HTML5 format. One of the first applications of Stage Framework was the Aalto University Magazine tablet concept, which was implemented during the master's thesis and published as a native wrapper application for iOS using Baker Ebook Framework. The iOS version of the concept magazine is available from Apple App Store[14].

Aalto University Magazine, AUM, is a stakeholder magazine published by Aalto University Communications. The content of the tablet concept magazine was from the printed issue 03. The visual design of the concept magazine was done by an Aalto University student as coursework. One of the AUM concept specific JavaScript libraries was PhotoSwipe[15], which served as a picture gallery for the magazine. Users could activate the gallery by selecting a picture from the article. As the magazine was implemented using responsive design, the images were scaled according to the browser viewport width and device pixel ratio. However, the gallery had still always the original, full size images. Demo magazine content is illustrated in Figure 2. Apart from images the

[14]`http://itunes.apple.com/gb/app/aalto-university-magazine/id596682061`
[15]`http://www.photoswipe.com`

Figure 2: HTML5-based articles from AUM 03.

articles also included video and audio utilizing the extended expression power of HTML5.

4.2 Automated Publishing Process

With HTML5-based content, automated publishing dependent on the source format can be used. With Aalto University Magazine, a magazine content model[16] was used in which the magazine content was initially in the XML format. The XML described each article and its resources, such as images and videos. The resources were processed with a Ruby script to HTML5, accompanied with the stand JSON file in the case of Stage Framework. Haml and LESS templates were used as static publication-specific resources to generate the HTML5 using the issue-specific material. An image feature algorithm [3] was used to intelligently crop the images to fit the predefined article templates. Additionally, article theme colors were automatically selected from the publication color palette based on the algorithm's suggestion.

5. PERFORMANCE

As web application performance was considered to be one of the key research problems, extensive performance tests were executed for various devices and platforms focusing on the used HTML5 and CSS3 technologies. The results of these measurements have been published as a separate document [1]. According to the test results, iOS was the most mature platform considering the overall performance due to outstanding performance on GPU intensive tests when compared to the other platforms tested. The results also indicated that the software version and browser implementations played a crucial role in the performance. For example, the iPhone 4S and iPad 3 devices gained a substantial performance boost when updated to iOS 6.x from 5.x software version. When compared to the tested x86 architecture desktop devices, the mobile ARM devices have rapidly narrowed the performance gap with the latest device and software generations.

6. DISCUSSION

In addition to magazine publications, Stage Framework can be used to publish other publication types, including newspapers and books. The framework's web application does not set constraints on the visual appearance of publications. However, publishers need to consider the publication type when making design decisions, such as how the content is paged and how well the content adapts to different screen sizes, using for example CSS Media Queries. As a content format, HTML5 lets publishers freely decide the extent to which the new technologies are used, from basic visual expressions to the most intense brilliance onscreen.

The technologies used in the framework and its web application are rather new and pave the way for even advanced web applications. The software and related research attempts to encourage developers to use these previously immature technologies with confidence, thus affecting more than just digital publishers. The framework has a broad applicability considering there are no limitations for the published content. The responsive user interface with the single page application approach serves as a good starting point for a consolidated publishing platform. However, more work remains to be done to fully embrace for example the potential of desktop platforms.

The purpose of Stage Framework has been to identify and establish supporting technologies to deliver digital book, magazine and newspaper content using the web application approach. The traditional feature and performance gap between the web and native applications is closing as the tablet and mobile devices are reaching the desktop device performance levels. This media and device convergence serves as an environmental changer which raises the importance of HTML5 technology as a global content format which can flow across different devices. Performance and vast device variation are the key issues for digital magazine and newspaper publishers. Stage Framework attempts to present solutions to these problems.

7. ACKNOWLEDGMENTS

The framework was developed for a master's thesis conducted as a part of the Finnish national Next Media[17] program organized by the Strategic Centre for Science, Technology and Innovation, TIVIT, and funded by the Finnish Funding Agency for Technology and Innovation, TEKES.

8. REFERENCES

[1] Aamulehto, R. Performance Measurement Results - Digital Magazine and Newspaper Publishing with HTML5. Result document, 2013. Available at: `http://mediatech.aalto.fi/~ralatalo/PMR.pdf`. Referenced 18 April 2013.

[2] Berjon, R., Leithead, T., Navara, E. D., O'Connor, E., Pfeiffer, S. and Hickson, I. HTML 5.1 - A vocabulary and associated APIs for HTML and XHTML. Working Draft, W3C, 17 December 2012. Available at: `http://www.w3.org/TR/2012/WD-html51-20121217/`. Referenced 18 April 2013.

[3] Kuhna, M., Kivelä, I. M. and Oittinen, P. Semi-Automated Magazine Layout Using Content-based Image Features. In *Proceedings of the 20th ACM international conference on Multimedia*, MM '12, pages 379–388, New York, NY, USA, 2012. ACM. ISBN: 9781450310895, DOI: 10.1145/2393347.2393403.

[16] `http://mikkokuhna.com/researcher/model/`

[17] `http://www.nextmedia.fi`

ESSENTIA: an Open-Source Library for Sound and Music Analysis

Dmitry Bogdanov, Nicolas Wack, Emilia Gómez, Sankalp Gulati, Perfecto Herrera, Oscar Mayor, Gerard Roma, Justin Salamon, José Zapata, Xavier Serra
Music Technology Group, Universitat Pompeu Fabra
Roc Boronat, 138
08018 Barcelona, Spain
{name.surname}@upf.edu

ABSTRACT

We present Essentia 2.0, an open-source C++ library for audio analysis and audio-based music information retrieval released under the Affero GPL license. It contains an extensive collection of reusable algorithms which implement audio input/output functionality, standard digital signal processing blocks, statistical characterization of data, and a large set of spectral, temporal, tonal and high-level music descriptors. The library is also wrapped in Python and includes a number of predefined executable extractors for the available music descriptors, which facilitates its use for fast prototyping and allows setting up research experiments very rapidly. Furthermore, it includes a Vamp plugin to be used with Sonic Visualiser for visualization purposes. The library is cross-platform and currently supports Linux, Mac OS X, and Windows systems. Essentia is designed with a focus on the robustness of the provided music descriptors and is optimized in terms of the computational cost of the algorithms. The provided functionality, specifically the music descriptors included in-the-box and signal processing algorithms, is easily expandable and allows for both research experiments and development of large-scale industrial applications.

Categories and Subject Descriptors

H.5.5 [**Information Interfaces and Presentation**]: Sound and Music Computing; D.2.2 [**Software Engineering**]: Design Tools and Techniques—*Software libraries*; C.3 [**Special-Purpose and Application-Based Systems**]: [Signal processing systems]

General Terms

Algorithms, Design, Experimentation

Keywords

Open Source, Signal Processing, Audio Analysis, Music Information Retrieval, Sound and music computing

1. INTRODUCTION

There are many problems within the Music Information Research (MIR) discipline which are based on audio content and require reliable and versatile software tools for automated music analysis. Following the research necessities, different audio analysis tools tailored for MIR have been developed and used by academic researchers within the last fifteen years. These tools include the popular MIRtoolbox and MARSYAS, jAudio, jMIR, Aubio, LibXtract, yaafe,[1] openSMILE [5], Auditory Toolbox, and CLAM Music Annotator (the comparative overview of the majority of the available tools is presented in [9]). Furthermore, a number of Vamp plugins[2] were developed by different researchers for computation and visualization of music descriptors using hosts such as Sonic Visualiser software [4]. Apart from these software tools, there is the online service Echonest,[3] which provides a collection of audio features for any uploaded track via an API. This service, however, does not disclose the implementation details of the features offered to a user, which might be a significant limitation at least in the context of academic research.

The above-mentioned tools provide different limited sets of descriptors, and require different programming languages (Matlab, C++, Java) and software environments (standalone GUI-based or command-line applications, running within a Vamp host). The feature sets vary from tool to tool and one may have to combine different tools in order to obtain the desired expanded combination of features. The Matlab-based MIRtoolbox and C++ based MARSYAS provide the richest sets of spectral, time-domain, rhythmic, and tonal features. Tonal features are frequently missing in other existing tools (libXtract, jAudio/jMIR, yaafe) as well as rhythmic ones (openSMILE, libXtract). Even when such features are provided, they are incomplete and their implementation does not rely on the latest state of the art, which is the case for pitch detection and beat tracking. Furthermore no tools provide high-level description of music in terms of semantic categories such as genres or mood, out of the box, apart

[1] `http://sourceforge.net/projects/yaafe`
[2] `http://vamp-plugins.org/download.html`
[3] `http://developer.echonest.com`

from MIRtoolbox that includes emotion detection. Surely, all the above-mentioned tools are very important for the research community, nevertheless we believe there is a lack of generic robust tools which provide more comprehensive sets of state-of-the-art music descriptors and are optimized for faster computations on large collections.

2. ESSENTIA 2.0

We present Essentia 2.0, an extensive open-source library for audio analysis and audio-based music information retrieval released under the Affero GPL[4] license and well-suited for both research and industrial applications.[5] In its core, Essentia is comprised of a reusable collection of algorithms to extract features from audio. The available algorithms include audio file input/output functionality, standard digital signal processing (DSP) building blocks, filters, generic algorithms for statistical characterization, and spectral, temporal, tonal and high-level music descriptors. The library is written in C++, which provides considerable performance benefits. Importantly, it also includes Python bindings to facilitate the usage of the library for the users who are familiar with the matlab/python environment. Using Essentia's dedicated python modules, one can rapidly get familiar with the available algorithms and design research experiments, explore and analyze data on-the-fly. In addition, the majority of the MIR descriptors' algorithms are wrapped into a Vamp[6] plugin and can be used with the popular Sonic Visualiser software [4] for visualization of music descriptors.

The design of Essentia is focused on robustness, time and memory performance, and ease of extensibility. The algorithms are implemented keeping in mind the use-case of large-scale computations on large music collections. One may develop his own executable utility with a desired processing flow using Essentia as a C++ library. Alternatively a number of executable extractors are included with Essentia, covering a number of common use-cases for researchers, for example, computing all available music descriptors for an audio track, extracting only spectral, rhythmic, or tonal descriptors, computing predominant melody and beat positions, and returning the results in yaml/json data formats.

Essentia has been in development for over 6 years incorporating the work of more than 20 researchers and developers through its history. During these years it has been used for in-house research and development by Music Technology Group and a number of partners. Version 2.0 marks the first open-source release of the library, making it available to the wider public of researchers and developers. It contains the latest refactoring of the library, including performance optimization, simplified development API, and a number of new descriptors such as the state-of-the-art beat tracking and predominant melody detection algorithms. In addition, Essentia can be optionally complemented with Gaia,[7] a library released under the same license, which allows to apply similarity measures and classifications on the results of audio analysis, and generate classification models that Essentia can use to compute high-level description of music. Gaia is a C++ library with python bindings for working with points in high-dimensional spaces, where each point represents a song and each dimension represents an audio feature. It allows to create datasets of points, apply transformations (gaussianization, principal component analysis, relevant component analysis, classification with support vector machines), and compute custom distance functions. The functionality of Gaia can be used to implement search engines relying on item similarity of any kind (not limited to music similarity).

[4]`http://gnu.org/licenses/agpl.html`
[5]Commercial licensing is also offered.
[6]`http://vamp-plugins.org`
[7]`http://github.com/MTG/gaia`

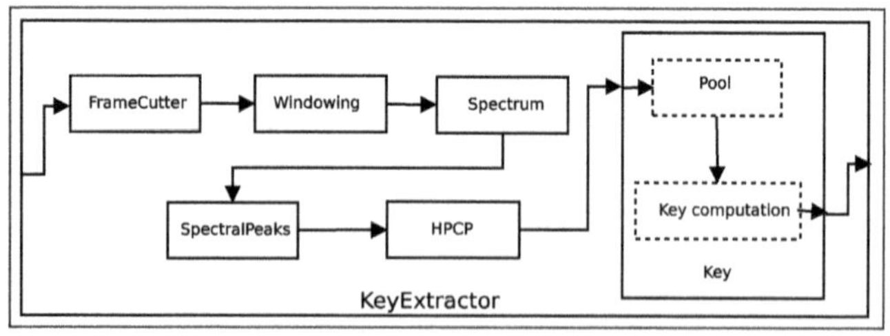

Figure 1: An example of the composite algorithm KeyExtractor combining the algorithms FrameCutter, Windowing, Spectrum, SpectralPeak, HPCP, and the Key algorithm composite itself.

3. OVERALL ARCHITECTURE

The main purpose of Essentia is to serve as a library of signal-processing blocks. As such, it is intended to provide as many algorithms as possible, while trying to be as little intrusive as possible. Each processing block is called an Algorithm, and it has three different types of attributes: inputs, outputs and parameters. Algorithms can be combined into more complex ones, which are also instances of the base Algorithm class and behave in the same way. An example of such a composite algorithm is presented in Figure 1. It shows a composite tonal key/scale extractor, which combines the algorithms for frame cutting, windowing, spectrum computation, spectral peaks detection, chroma features (HPCP) computation and finally the algorithm for key/scale estimation from the HPCP (itself a composite algorithm).

The algorithms can be used in two different modes: *standard* and *streaming*. The standard mode is imperative while the streaming mode is declarative. The standard mode requires to specify the inputs and outputs for each algorithm and call their processing function explicitly. If the user wants to run a network of connected algorithms, he/she will need to manually run each algorithm. The advantage of this mode is that it allows very rapid prototyping (especially when the python bindings are coupled with a scientific environment in python, such as ipython, numpy, and matplotlib).

The streaming mode, on the other hand, allows to define a network of connected algorithms, and then an internal scheduler takes care of passing data between the algorithms inputs and outputs and calling the algorithms in the appropriate order. The scheduler available in Essentia is optimized for analysis tasks, and does not take into account the latency of the network. For real-time applications, one could easily replace this scheduler with another one that favors latency over throughput. The advantage of this mode is that it results in simpler and safer code (as the user only needs to create algorithms and connect them, there is no room for him to make mistakes in the execution order of the algorithms), and in lower memory consumption in general, as the data is streamed through the network instead of being loaded entirely in memory (which is the usual case when working with the standard mode). Even though most of the algorithms are available for both the standard and streaming mode, the code that implements them is not duplicated as either the streaming version of an algorithm is deduced from its standard implementation, or vice versa.

4. ALGORITHMS

In this section we briefly review the most important algorithms included in the library. The interested reader is referred to the documentation for a complete up-to-date reference for all available algorithms.[8] Furthermore, [3] provides more details on the available algorithms and includes references to the related publications. A great part of the algorithms computes a variety of low-level, mid-level, and high-level descriptors useful for MIR. In addition there are tools for working with audio input/output and processing, and gathering data statistics.

4.1 Audio input/output and filtering

Essentia has a variety of audio loaders reusing the FFmpeg[9]/Libav[10] libraries to provide a very convenient way to load audio files from disk with the support of almost all existing audio formats. A special loader reads the metadata tags (ID3 tags) stored in the given file. Essentia can also write audio files to any format supported by FFmpeg/Libav, and may add beeps to the audio according to the given (onset) time positions. In addition, Essentia provides algorithms for basic processing of audio streams: it allows to apply replay gain, downmix, trim the audio to a given start/end time, frame cutting, windowing, resampling, FFT, autocorrelation computation, etc. A variety of audio filters are implemented in Essentia, including the generic IIR filtering, first and second order low/band/high/all-pass filtering and band rejection, DC component removal, moving average filter, and the filter approximating an equal-loudness curve.

4.2 MIR descriptors

The library contains a variety of algorithms which allow to compute:

- *low-level spectral descriptors* (the Bark/Mel/ERB band energies of a spectrum, the Mel-frequency and Gammatone feature cepstral coefficients cepstral coefficients, the spectral complexity, the spectral contrast feature, the inharmonicity and dissonance measures, etc);
- *time-domain descriptors* (the duration of the perceptually meaningful part of the signal above a certain energy level, Zero-crossing rate, different loudness estimation models, etc);
- *pitch and tonal descriptors* (the pitch salience function of a signal and the fundamental frequency of the predominant melody, the Harmonic Pitch-Class Profile of a spectrum also called chroma features, the tuning frequency, the key and the scale of a song, chords-related descriptors, etc);
- *rhythm descriptors* (the beats positions using the beat tracker based on the complex spectral difference feature and the multifeature beat tracker, the BPM histogram of a song, the novelty curve for the audio signal, and the BPM distribution and tempogram based on it, a number of onset detection functions, the rhythm transform, etc.);
- *SFX descriptors* characterizing signal envelope of short sounds;
- other *mid- and high-level descriptors* (the "danceability", the intensity, a number of classifier models including musical genre, ballroom music classification, moods, western/non-western music, live/studio recording, perceptual speed, male/female singer, dark/bright timbre, and speech/music classification, etc).

Table 1 summarizes the categories of MIR descriptors available in popular music analysis tools in comparison with Essentia. The latter provides the largest overall amount of features, according to a rough estimation, and includes a large number of high-level classifier-based features (genres, moods, etc.) in the box without a necessity of having the associated ground truth music collections. In contrast, MARSYAS and MIRToolbox (except for a single emotion-based classifier) lack pre-trained classifier models.

4.3 Extractors

A few useful extractors for commonly used MIR features have been written as algorithms. In addition, a number of executable extractors are included with the library as examples of its application. These standalone examples can be used straight away for batch computation of descriptors with no need to dive into the API of the library. They include a number of specific extractors (predominant melody, beat tracking, key, MFCCs, etc.) as well as generic extractors returning the majority of the available descriptors in yaml/json formats. For industrial applications, one may need to decide on the descriptors and type of processing required, and implement his own extractor.

5. APPLICATIONS

Essentia has served in a large number of research activities conducted at Music Technology Group since 2006. It has been used for music classification [13], and in particular for mood classification, semantic autotagging [12], music similarity and recommendation [2, 1], visualization and interaction with music [1, 7], sound indexing [10], musical instruments detection [6], cover detection [11], and acoustic analysis of stimuli for neuroimaging studies [8]. The systems based on Essentia/Gaia have been enrolled in the the Music Information Retrieval Evaluation eXchange (MIREX) campaigns for the tasks of music classification, music similarity, autotagging, and beat detection, and they have usually ranked among the best ones.

Essentia and Gaia have been used extensively in a number of research projects, including the CANTATA EU (music videos recommendation system), SALERO EU (search engine for sound effects), PHAROS EU (music search and recommendation), Buscamedia, PROSEMUS, DRIMS and CompMusic (automated low-level and high-level semantic description of music), and SIEMPRE EU (audio analysis for multimodal databases of music performances). Furthermore, previous versions of Essentia have been exploited for industrial applications including the non-commercial sound service Freesound[11] (large-scale indexing and content-based

[8] `http://essentia.upf.edu`
[9] `http://ffmpeg.org`
[10] `http://libav.org`
[11] `http://freesound.org`

Table 1: MIR descriptor categories available in the popular music analysis tools.

Tool	Environment	Spectral	Time-domain	Pitch	Tonality	Rhythm	High-level	Auditory
libXtract	C/Python/Java	+	+	−	+	−	−	−
jAudio/jMIR	Java	+	+	−	−	+	−	−
MARSYAS	C++/Ruby/Python/Java	+	+	+	−	+	+	+
MIRToolbox	Matlab	+	+	+	+	+	+	+
Aubio	C/C++/Python	+	−	+	−	+	−	−
yaafe	C++/Python/Matlab	+	+	−	−	+	−	−
openSMILE	C++	+	+	+	+	−	−	−
Essentia	C++/Python	+	+	+	+	+	+	−

search of sound recordings), industrial products by BMAT[12] and Stromatolite[13] (music recommendation), Yamaha's BODiBEAT (automatic playlist generation for runners), and Steinberg's LoopMash (audio-based sample matching for music production).

In addition to the off-line audio analysis we expect our library to be potential for real-time applications. However not all of the present algorithms can be used for such applications due to their computational complexity.

6. CONCLUSIONS

We have presented a cross-platform open-source library for audio analysis and audio-based music information research and development, Essentia 2.0. The library is versatile and may suit the needs of both researchers within MIR community and the industry. In our future work we will focus on expanding the library and the community of users, We plan to add new music descriptors, in particular, adding new semantic categories to the set of high-level classifier-based descriptors, and update the library for real-time applications. All active Essentia users are encouraged to contribute to the library. The detailed information about Essentia is located at the official web page.[14] It contains the complete documentation for the project and installation instructions for Debian/Ubuntu, Mac OS X and Windows. The source code is available at the Github repository.[15]

7. ACKNOWLEDGMENTS

The work on Essentia has been partially funded by the PHAROS (EU-IP, IST-2006-045035), CANTATA (ITEA 05010, FIT-350300-2006-33), Buscamedia (CEN-20091026), SIGMUS (TIN2012-36650), CompMusic (ERC 267583), and TECNIO (TECCIT12-1-0003) projects. We acknowledge all the developers who took part in working on this project and Alba Rosado for her help in coordination.

8. REFERENCES

[1] D. Bogdanov, M. Haro, F. Fuhrmann, A. Xambó, E. Gómez, and P. Herrera. Semantic audio content-based music recommendation and visualization based on user preference examples. *Inf. Process. & Management*, 49(1):13–33, 2013.

[2] D. Bogdanov, J. Serrà, N. Wack, P. Herrera, and X. Serra. Unifying low-level and high-level music similarity measures. *IEEE Trans. on Multimedia*, 13(4):687–701, 2011.

[3] D. Bogdanov, N. Wack, E. Gómez, S. Gulati, P. Herrera, O. Mayor, G. Roma, J. Salamon, J. Zapata, and X. Serra. ESSENTIA: an audio analysis library for music information retrieval. In *Int. Soc. for Music Inf. Retrieval Conf. (ISMIR'13)*, 2013.

[4] C. Cannam, C. Landone, and M. Sandler. Sonic visualiser: An open source application for viewing, analysing, and annotating music audio files. In *ACM Int. Conf. on Multimedia (MM'05)*, page 1467–1468, 2010.

[5] F. Eyben, M. Wöllmer, and B. Schuller. Opensmile: the munich versatile and fast open-source audio feature extractor. In *ACM Int. Conf. on Multimedia (MM'10)*, page 1459–1462, 2010.

[6] F. Fuhrmann, P. Herrera, and X. Serra. Detecting solo phrases in music using spectral and pitch-related descriptors. *Journal of New Music Research*, 38(4):343–356, 2009.

[7] C. F. Julià and S. Jordà. SongExplorer: a tabletop application for exploring large collections of songs. In *Int. Soc. for Music Inf. Retrieval Conf. (ISMIR'09)*, 2009.

[8] S. Koelsch, S. Skouras, T. Fritz, P. Herrera, C. Bonhage, M. Kuessner, and A. M. Jacobs. Neural correlates of music-evoked fear and joy: The roles of auditory cortex and superficial amygdala. *Neuroimage*. In press.

[9] K. R. Page, B. Fields, D. De Roure, T. Crawford, and J. S. Downie. Reuse, remix, repeat: the workflows of MIR. In *Int. Soc. for Music Inf. Retrieval Conf. (ISMIR'12)*, 2012.

[10] G. Roma, J. Janer, S. Kersten, M. Schirosa, P. Herrera, and X. Serra. Ecological acoustics perspective for content-based retrieval of environmental sounds. *EURASIP Journal on Audio, Speech, and Music Process.*, 2010.

[11] J. Serrà, E. Gómez, P. Herrera, and X. Serra. Chroma binary similarity and local alignment applied to cover song identification. *IEEE Trans. on Audio, Speech, and Language Process.*, 16(6):1138–1151, 2008.

[12] M. Sordo. *Semantic Annotation of Music Collections: A Computational Approach*. PhD thesis, UPF, Barcelona, Spain, 2012.

[13] N. Wack, C. Laurier, O. Meyers, R. Marxer, D. Bogdanov, J. Serra, E. Gomez, and P. Herrera. Music classification using high-level models. In *Music Inf. Retrieval Evaluation Exchange (MIREX'10)*, 2010.

[12] `http://bmat.com`
[13] `http://stromatolite.com`
[14] `http://essentia.upf.edu`
[15] `http://github.com/MTG/essentia`

SCReen Adjusted Panoramic Effect - SCRAPE

Carl Flynn
CASALA Research Centre
Dundalk Institute of Technology
Dundalk, Co. Louth
carl.flynn@casala.ie

David Monaghan
CLARITY: Centre for Sensor Web Technologies
Dublin City University
Dublin 9
david.monaghan@dcu.ie

Noel E. O'Connor
CLARITY: Centre for Sensor Web Technologies
Dublin City University
Dublin 9
noel.oconnor@dcu.ie

SUBMITTED to ACM MULTIMEDIA 2013 OPEN SOURCE SOFTWARE COMPETITION

ABSTRACT

A Cave Automatic Virtual Environment (CAVE) is an enclosed virtual reality room that uses multiple projectors to display images across its surfaces. It uses one or more computers to synchronise and combine the images and allows users to control virtual worlds using a host of interaction devices. Traditionally, a CAVE is used by a single user at any one time and by utilising some form of motion sensing, the user's head position can be tracked to allow for first virtual perception. The images are then displayed in stereographic 3D in order to complete the virtual reality effect.

Professional CAVE installations are expensive and can cost upwards of several hundred thousand euros. This tends to act as a significant barrier to their propagation, however, as the reduction in cost of high specification computers, projectors and graphics cards continues apace, it has sparked a renewed interest in CAVE environments and given rise to the realistic possibility of setting up low cost, amateur CAVEs. Unfortunately, one of the greatest disadvantages of CAVE systems is the lack of inexpensive, easy to use, specialised software. In this paper we present an open source and easy to use CAVE software toolkit called SCReen Adjusted Panoramic Effect or SCRAPE for short. We believe that SCRAPE is the first major piece in a longer-term vision that aims to bring easy to setup, easy to use, portable CAVE systems to all types of non-expert users.

Categories and Subject Descriptors

D.2 [**Software**]: Software Engineering; H.5.1 [**Multimedia Information Systems**]: [Artificial, augmented, and virtual realities]

General Terms

Design, Experimentation, Human Factors, Measurement

MM'13, October 21–25, 2013, Barcelona, Spain.
Copyright 2013 ACM 978-1-4503-2404-5/13/10 ...$15.00.
http://dx.doi.org/10.1145/2502081.2502230.

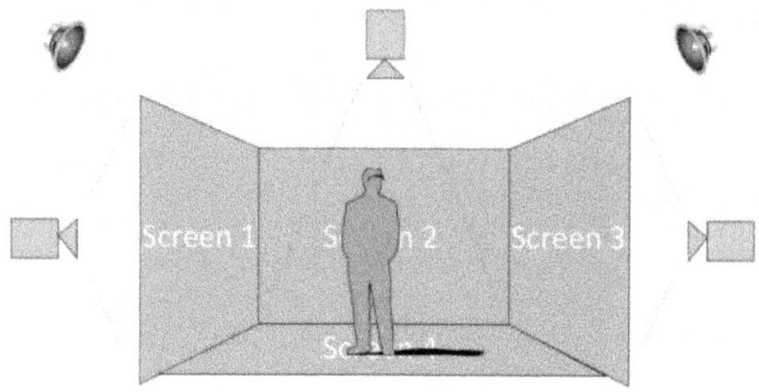

Figure 1: The standard layout for a CAVE

Keywords

CAVE; SCRAPE; Processing; Virtual Reality; 3D

1. INTRODUCTION

The standard setup for a CAVE [7, 6, 8] environment has not changed much since its inception and can be seen in figure 1. The archetypal CAVE is made up of four screens but anywhere between two and six screens is also possible. They typically consist of expensive hardware and software solutions and require extensive investment of time and expertise in order to develop useful interactive virtual environments. After assessing the many different CAVE software platforms available, it became clear that there was an opportunity to develop a simple application which would take the accessibility of one of the most interesting open source visual programming tools available today and adapt it to work in a CAVE.

The primary objective of the work described in this paper was to develop an application that could be easily configured to work in CAVEs of differing sizes, dimensions and screen numbers using a multitude of different inputs. We also put an added emphasis on the need for the software to be open source and freely available. The chosen software development platform is an open sourced tool called PDE (Processing Development Environment) or Processing for short [5]. Processing is released under the GNU GPL (General Public License) and its libraries are released under the GNU LGPL (Lesser General Public License). The technical project to adapt Processing to CAVE environments is called SCReen Adjusted Panoramic Effect or SCRAPE and is intended for use by anyone who works with a CAVE or similar virtual reality environment (see figure 2). SCRAPE is particularly suited to abstract data visualisations [9] but can be used for visualising a wide range of CAVE-based projects.

In this paper we describe the main motivations behind the development of SCRAPE. We present a technical description of the SCRAPE software platform, outline its configurations, reference key libraries and provide a brief summary of a standard SCRAPE setup.

2. MOTIVATION

The initial seed for SCRAPE was planted in 2010 when the primary author, based between the Centre for Affective Solutions for Ambient Living Awareness (CASALA) [1] and the Centre for Sensor Web Technologies (CLARITY) [2], started working with a CAVE installation. CASALA had recently purchased a CAVE for a six figure sum from well-known CAVE suppliers which provided everything from the physical CAVE structure to the 3D projectors, ceiling mirror, screens, workstations, IR trackers, IR emitters, glasses and interaction controller. They also installed the initial CAVE 3D and tracking software as well as an assortment of additional demo software installations and examples.

Using the supplied software one could take 3D models and quickly view and interact with them in the CAVE. It supported 6 degrees of freedom around 3D objects as well as head tracking to help with the sense of immersion but in reality it was little more than an extravagant stereo 3D model viewer. On discussing these limitations with the supplier, they suggested using an alternative software that would provide us with the levels of interactivity that we were looking for. However, this would have incurred a significant additional cost and the software required considerable expertise in low level 3D programming. Initial trials indicated that a lot of development time would be required to do even relatively simple 3D interactive worlds. Several other similar CAVE software packages were also investigated, however most had similar limitations in terms of accessibility or were simply too costly.

The high cost and inaccessibility of most CAVE software applications left us with a bad impression and initiated our thinking about the idea of creating a low cost CAVE and developing open source software that could cope with the particular requirements of a CAVE. At the same time we wanted to allow ordinary developers to code something that was both interactive and relatively easy to use.

The Processing open source programming language and data visualisation tool platform, created by Casey Reas and Benjamin Fry [5], holds as its tenets the fundamental concepts of being freely available and easy to use by non-experts. While Processing has some limitations, it is an excellent tool for developing 2D and 3D interactive visuals that can help in understanding and interpreting large quantities of data.

Over the nearly four years of using the CAVE we received a steady stream of enquiries from people from all over the world interested in setting up their own CAVE systems. In the majority of cases cost was an important factor and most were surprised when they discovered the price tag associated with both the hardware and the software. There was, however, a definite interest from people in setting up CAVEs for a wide range of different uses, such as data visualisation, product prototyping, training, exhibitions etc. Stemming from our familiarity with CAVE installations, the price tag

Figure 2: SCRAPE being used in a CAVE

associated with them did not seem to accurately reflect the technology and constructions involved. We were convinced that a four screen CAVE could be built for a few thousand euros rather than hundreds of thousands and even less for three screen and V-screen (i.e. two screens) builds. Jeffrey Jacobson, director of PublicVR, developed a set of modifications for the Unreal Tournament (UT) 2004 Game Engine many years ago which enabled the UT engine to display in a CAVE [4] . He also published an online article on how to build a low cost PC based CAVE with UT. Keeping examples such as this in mind, we were confident that it would be possible to build a reasonably comparable CAVE to our professional one for around €3000 but most importantly we wanted to provide a free software tool that even a relatively non-technical person could use.

Included amongst Processing's long list of library contributions lies one particularly interesting library called 'Most Pixels Ever' (MPE) [3]. MPE was created by Daniel Shiffman, an assistant arts professor at NYU and his library enables Processing sketches to run synchronously across multiple machines and across multiple screens in order to give the impression of one large screen. It works particularly well with 2D sketches displayed on a flat surface and was crucial in inspiring the initial idea for the development of SCRAPE.

For SCRAPE we have adapted MPE in conjunction with many other useful libraries in order to visualise seamless 3D sketches on screens placed at entirely different angles and positions to each other. SCRAPE is a setup that is flexible and can accommodate different screen numbers and sizes, different controllers and both stereo and non-stereo images. It was developed specifically to work well on both low budget homemade CAVE installations and six figure research CAVEs. Video demonstrations of SCRAPE in action can be viewed via a dedicated YouTube channel:
`http://www.youtube.com/user/cjflyn`

3. TECHNICAL DESCRIPTION

3.1 Overview of Software Components

SCRAPE works in a similar manner to all Processing sketches in that it uses the two key functions of Processing, setup() and draw(), in order to initialise and animate a 3D sketch. setup() handles all the initialisations for SCRAPE

Figure 3: Modified Processing Icon for the SCRAPE platform

and is only run once while draw() runs continuously and is used to animate the sketch. SCRAPE also contains multiple Processing sub classes which are displayed as tabs within the Processing IDE. Each sub class handles a specific aspect of the SCRAPE application such as the camera movements, the use of different controllers and the use of a stereo and a non-stereo sketch. The SCRAPE logo can be seen in figure 3.

The following is an explanation of the functionality of each class:

SCRAPE.pde This is the core of SCRAPE and defines its main configurations:

1. Imports key libraries
2. Configures main scene variables
3. Reads the mpe.ini configuration file settings and applies relevant functions
4. Sets up the Most Pixels Ever library which controls screen synchronisation and message broadcasting
5. Configures and applies the Obsessive Camera Direction library based on configurations set in the mpe.ini file

joypad.pde
This uses the proCONTROLL library to enable SCRAPE sketches to be easily configured to work with a multitude of different USB controllers. Each action of the controller is then broadcast out to all the other SCRAPE clients which then interpret that action via the 'navigation' code.

keyboard.pde
Some basic code that enables a SCRAPE scene to be controlled out of the box with the arrow keys and spacebar but can be expanded and modified as required. Similar to the 'joypad' code, each action of the keyboard is then broadcast out to all the other SCRAPE clients which then interpret that action via the 'navigation' code.

navigation.pde
This code listens for messages broadcast by other clients and translates those messages into actions within the SCRAPE scene. Actions are applied differently to different SCRAPE clients depending on which screen is set in the mpe.ini file for that particular client. Movements for the camera of a 'FRONT' screen will obviously be different to movements of a camera for a 'FLOOR' screen which point in different directions and sit on different axes.

nunchuckoo.pde
Nunchuckoo is a project in of itself but is incorporated into SCRAPE. The Nintendo Wii Nunchuck has proved to be an excellent controller for SCRAPE and this code allows you to easily connect and configure your Nunchuck and Arduino to SCRAPE. As with the 'joypad' and 'keyboard' code files, each action of the keyboard is then broadcast out to all the other SCRAPE clients which then interpret that action via the navigation code. More information on the Nunchuckoo project can be found at:
`https://github.com/c-flynn/Nunchuckoo`

scene.pde
Simply contains the non-stereographic scene code. This is the code that one would normally expect to find in a Processing draw() function

stereoScene.pde
This contains the same code one would expect to see in the 'scene' tab but also references the stereo library and splits the scene rendering per eye in order to be able to view SCRAPE in full stereo 3D in conjunction with active shutter glasses.

3.2 Configuration

One of the key goals in developing SCRAPE was to provide a system that could adapt dynamically to the requirements of different users with different CAVE specifications. In order to do this, SCRAPE uses a configuration file called mpe.ini. The mpe.ini file within SCRAPE is an extension of the original Most Pixels Ever configuration file and makes use of the previous MPE configurations but also adds a few CAVE specific elements such as screen selections, controller options and stereo activation. Using this file, SCRAPE is able to identify how many screens are being used, the position of each screen, the size of each screen etc. SCRAPE then takes this information and ensures that each camera is positioned according to the correct size, position and aspect ratio of each screen and that the images displayed on the screen appear and move seamlessly. This is a core function of what SCRAPE does and it is primarily handled on initialisation of SCRAPE in the SCRAPE.pde file within the setup() function.

3.3 Other Key Libraries

The key libraries used in order to enable SCRAPE to function correctly are:

Most Pixels Ever (MPE)
Controls the communication between the different sketch instances and synchronisation between screens
`https://github.com/shiffman/Most-Pixels-Ever/`

Obsessive Camera Direction (OCD)
Handles the multiple scene cameras required
`http://gdsstudios.com/processing/libraries/ocd/`

proCONTROLL
Allows users to connect a multitude of USB controllers in order to interact with SCRAPE
`http://creativecomputing.cc/p5libs/procontroll/`
stereo
Enables standard 3D sketches to be viewed in full stereoscopic 3D
`https://github.com/CreativeCodingLab/stereo/`

3.4 SCRAPE Setup

In this section we provide a brief summary of a standard SCRAPE setup. We assume that it is desired to install SCRAPE on a four wall CAVE which has one PC/workstation per screen and one master PC/workstation to control everything. Detailed instructions and open source code can be downloaded from:
`https://github.com/c-flynn/SCRAPE/`

1. Install the appropriate version of Processing onto each computer
2. Download SCRAPE from github onto each computer and copy the 'SCRAPE' folder into the Processing sketchbook folder
3. On the master computer copy the mpeServer.jar file from the SCRAPE folder and place in Processing's /lib directory. This file handles the communications between the different SCRAPE instances
4. Run the mpeServer.jar file on the master computer with the command: java -jar mpeServer.jar -framerate30 -screens5
5. Ensure all the other machines can talk to the master computer with telnet: telnet 192.168.1.x 9002
6. Modify the mpe.ini file for each instance of SCRAPE ensuring that the correct information and options are set for each; such as screen id (starting from 0 up), screen view (Front, left top etc.), screen size, stereo on/off etc.. The controller configurations should only be set and activated on the computer that a controller will be connected to
7. Run the sketch on each computer and once all 5 instances are running your SCRAPE sketch should be visible on all screens

4. CONCLUSIONS

We have presented an easy to use open source CAVE software creation toolkit called SCReen Adjusted Panoramic Effect or SCRAPE. With the ever increasing popularity of CAVE systems we believe that SCRAPE is one of the first major pieces in the overall CAVE jigsaw that will allow non-expert users, with modest budgets, to create and adapt stereoscopic virtual reality environments quickly and easily. The SCRAPE software platform can function in either professional or amateur based CAVE systems and is designed to adapt to multiple screen orientations and sizes using a multitude of inputs. SCRAPE is an ongoing project and continues to be developed as an open source platform for users of all levels to support the development of new and interesting 3D interactive CAVE virtual environments.

5. ACKNOWLEDGEMENTS

CASALA is funded under Enterprise Ireland's Applied Research Enhancement Program with support from EU structural funds. This work is supported by Science Foundation Ireland under grant 07/CE/I114. The research that lead to this paper was supported in part by the European Commission under the Contract FP7-ICT-287723 REVERIE.

6. REFERENCES

[1] Centre for Affective Solutions for Ambient Living Awareness. http://www.casala.ie/.
[2] CLARITY: Centre for Sensor Web Technologies. http://www.clarity-centre.org/.
[3] Daniel Shiffman's Most Pixels Ever. https://github.com/shiffman/Most-Pixels-Ever.
[4] Jeffrey Jacobson's Unreal Tournament. http://planetjeff.net/ut/CaveUT.html.
[5] Processing open source programming language. http://www.processing.org/.
[6] C. Cruz-Neira, D. J. Sandin, and T. A. DeFanti. Surround-screen projection-based virtual reality: the design and implementation of the CAVE. In *Proceedings of the 20th annual conference on Computer graphics and interactive techniques*, SIGGRAPH '93, pages 135–142, New York, NY, USA, 1993. ACM.
[7] C. Cruz-Neira, D. J. Sandin, T. A. DeFanti, R. V. Kenyon, and J. C. Hart. The CAVE: audio visual experience automatic virtual environment. *Commun. ACM*, 35:64–72, June 1992.
[8] A. Febretti, A. Nishimoto, T. Thigpen, J. Talandis, L. Long, J. Pirtle, T. Peterka, A. Verlo, M. Brown, D. Plepys, D. Sandin, L. Renambot, A. Johnson, and J. Leigh. CAVE2: a hybrid reality environment for immersive simulation and information analysis. In *Proceedings of IS&T/SPIE Electronic Imaging, The Engineering Reality of Virtual Reality 2013*, 2013.
[9] C. Flynn, H. Lee, and N. E. O'Connor. Visualising and interacting with a cave using real-world sensor data. In *iHCI 2011 - Irish Human Computer Interaction Conference*, Cork, Ireland, 2011.

Orcc: Multimedia Development Made Easy

Hervé Yviquel
University of Rennes 1
IRISA, Inria
Rennes, France
herve.yviquel@irisa.fr

Antoine Lorence,
INSA of Rennes, IETR
Rennes, France
antoine.lorence@insa-rennes.fr

Khaled Jerbi,
INSA of Rennes, IETR
Rennes, France
khaled.jerbi@insa-rennes.fr

Gildas Cocherel,
INSA of Rennes, IETR
Rennes, France
gildas.cocherel@insa-rennes.fr

Alexandre Sanchez,
INSA of Rennes, IETR
Rennes, France
alexandre.sanchez@insa-rennes.fr

Mickaël Raulet
INSA of Rennes, IETR
Rennes, France
mickael.raulet@insa-rennes.fr

ABSTRACT

In this paper, we present Orcc[1], an open-source development environment that aims at enhancing multimedia development by offering all the advantages of dataflow programming: flexibility, portability and scalability. To do so, Orcc embeds two rich eclipse-based editors that provide an easy writing of dataflow applications, a simulator that allows quick validation of the written code, and a multi-target compiler that is able to translate any dataflow program, written in the RVC-CAL language, into an equivalent description in both hardware and software languages. Orcc has already been used to successfully write tens of multimedia applications, such as a video decoder supporting the new High Efficiency Video Coding standard, that clearly demonstrates the ability of the environment to develop complex applications. Moreover, results show scalable performances on multi-core platforms and achieve real-time decoding frame-rate on HD sequences.

Categories and Subject Descriptors

12. [**Systems and Middleware**]: Tools; 5. [**Mobile & Multi-device**]: Miscellaneous

Keywords

Multimedia development, Dataflow programming, Integrated Development Environment (IDE), MPEG Reconfigurable Media Coding (RMC), High Efficiency Video Coding (HEVC)

1. INTRODUCTION

The growing demand and popularity of multimedia technologies has made multimedia application mainstream and is now used for a wide range of application domains. These multimedia applications have been achievable thanks to the advances in computing and communication technologies as well as algorithmic techniques. However, the deployment of these technologies is slowed down by the complex development process of these multimedia applications that involve time-consuming and error-prone tasks, and by the variety of the multimedia devices available on the market that have to support these multimedia applications.

In this paper, we present Orcc, an Integrated Development Environment that aims to make easier multimedia development by providing a set of modern tools based on dataflow programming. In fact, dataflow programming reduces the complexity of multimedia development by allowing a flexible development process, by describing the application in a portable manner, and by allowing scalable performances of the applications over multi-core platforms.

In the following, Section 2 gives an overview of dataflow programming. In Section 3, we provide a presentation of the main tools of Orcc and its implemented features. Finally, we give some results in Section 4.

2. DATAFLOW PROGRAMMING

A dataflow program is defined as a graph composed of a set of computational units interconnected by communication channels. In the dataflow approach, the communication corresponds to a stream of data composed of a list of tokens.

During the last twenty years, dataflow programming has been studied for the development of signal processing applications due to its consistency with the natural representation of the processing of digital signals, and particularly:

- The opportunity to use visual programming to describe the interconnection between its components. Such a graphical approach is very natural and makes it more understandable by programmers that can focus on *how things connect*.

- Its ability to express concurrency without complex synchronization mechanism. The internal representation of the application is a network of processing blocks that only communicate through the communication channels, making the blocks independent and side-effect free.

[1]Orcc is available at http://orcc.sf.net

MM'13, October 21–25, 2013, Barcelona, Spain.

http://dx.doi.org/10.1145/2502081.2502231.

However, most of the studies on dataflow programming focus on the statically schedulable dataflow Models of Computation because of the efficiency of synthesis techniques on such models. Unfortunately, they do not take into consideration the expressiveness and the practicality offered to the programmers by more general dataflow models, such as dynamic dataflow [10].

2.1 Enhancing multimedia development

In fact, dataflow programming can enhance the development of multimedia applications thanks to the following abilities:

- **Modularity:** The strong separation between the structural and behavioral modeling makes the application description very modular. For instance, a component can easily be replaced by another one while its interfaces (input and output ports) are strictly identical. Moreover, such descriptions are typically hierarchical, in that a component of the graph may represent another graph.
- **Parallelism:** A dataflow program states an abundance of parallelism thanks to the explicit exposition of the concurrency. In its structural view, the dataflow model presents three potential degrees of parallelism (task, data and pipeline) that can be applied to different granularities of description.
- **Portability:** The heterogeneity of multimedia devices makes portability an interesting properties of multimedia applications. High-level dataflow-based descriptions aim to be compiled in lower-level languages in order to bridge the gap between the existing programming models.

2.2 Innovative development framework

During the last twenty years, several new programming languages based on dataflow models were proposed by the scientific community to solve a large panel of problems, from parallel programming to signal processing, but only a few have been emerging enough to be involved in the development of *real world applications*. One of them, the CAL Actor Language (CAL) [5], is particularly interesting due to the practicality offered by the language specification and the expressiveness offered by its ability to describe data-dependent behavior specified by the dynamic dataflow Model of Computation [10].

Reconfigurable Media Coding (RMC) [3] is an innovative framework introduced by MPEG to overcome the lack of interoperability between the several video codecs deployed in the market. The framework is dedicated to the development of video coding tools in a modular and reusable fashion thanks to dataflow programming. The inclusion of a subset of CAL in the RMC framework enables the development of several video decoders along other applications using dataflow programming.

3. FULL DEVELOPMENT ENVIRONMENT

The development of multimedia applications, such as video codecs, is a time-consuming and error-prone task due to the complexity of the algorithm and the variety of the multimedia devices. The development of those applications is even getting harder since the emergence of parallel platforms, as a consequence of frequency wall, due to the difficulties to synchronize the different tasks, balance their loads, etc. Consequently, the need for efficient development methods and tools is becoming increasingly important to meet the time-to-market requirement:

1. **Assisted writing of the applications:** The development of applications is made easier thanks to an Integrated Development Environment.
2. **Fast validation of the code:** A fast functional verification is making possible by the integrated simulator.
3. **Develop once, run everywhere:** The embedded trans-compiler is able to generate both hardware and software code from a single description that can be executed on large panel of platform thanks to the availability of dedicated runtime libraries.

3.1 Rich eclipse-based editors

Orcc is delivered with an entire Eclipse-based Integrated Development Environment (IDE) presented in Figure 1, making easier the development of RVC-based applications thanks to graphical interfaces. This environment is composed of two dedicated editors to handle both hierarchical levels, actor and network, of dataflow programming:

First, an intuitive **graph editor** that enables fast and easy building of the actor network using visual programming. A few mouse clicks are sufficient to create a node and assign it to an existing component from the project, or to create an edge that represents the communication channels between two nodes. The editor also supports hierarchical representation, assigning a whole subnetwork to a graph node, and hierarchical navigation, opening a subnetwork with a simple click on a graph node.

Finally, a full-blown **RVC-CAL editor** with advanced features, such as syntax coloring, content assist and code validation for helping the development of the actors. Based on the Xtext framework [4], Orcc implements all features expected for a modern and efficient Domain-Specific Language editor. The development environment is able to parse the actors and build their intermediate representation on-the-fly, in a incremental fashion, allowing fast simulation and compilation.

3.2 Integrated simulator

Additionally to the editors, Orcc brings a complete Java-based simulator which allows developers to quickly test their applications without taking in consideration low-level details relative to the target platform. The simulator can be launched directly from eclipse to execute any RVC-CAL application. Indeed, the simulator simply interprets our intermediate representation of networks and actors, but it is however able to perform all basic interactions required to perform a functional validation, such as displaying text, images or videos to the screen.

3.3 Multi-target development tools

Orcc is delivered with a compiler and a runtime library that allows to write a single description of the application to target a variety of executing platforms such as General-Purpose Processors, FPGAs, embedded processors and so on.

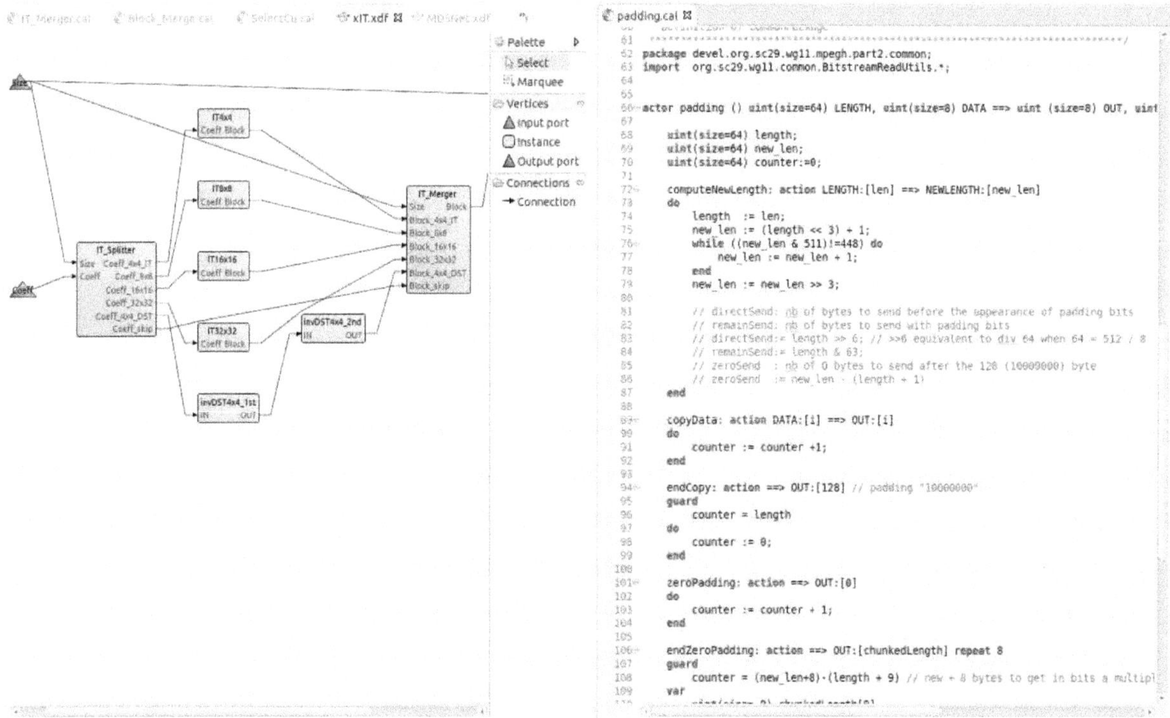

Figure 1: The Graph and RVC-CAL editors integrated into Eclipse IDE

Efficient dataflow trans-compiler.

The Orcc's compiler is able to translate a unique high-level dataflow program, written in RVC-CAL, into an equivalent description in both hardware and software languages for various platforms. A specific compiler back-end has been written to tackle each configuration case:

- Two **software** back-ends that generates C/C++ programs with multi-core abilities usable on most of the programmable processors [12]. A rapid prototyping can additionally be perform on static applications [9].
- Two **hardware** back-ends using well-known High-Level Synthesis tools to generate synthesizable HDL code for FPGA and ASIC implementations [1, 2].
- A back-end that targets **embedded multi-core platforms** [13]. The back-end is implemented as an entire co-design flow built upon the TCE toolset [7] that generates the software code as well as the hardware design that executes it.
- Two back-ends that produce **libraries of components** (in LLVM bitcode and Java), to implement the *Abstract Decoder Model* of the RMC framework [3]. The libraries of components are then used to perform adaptive execution based on virtual machine mechanism [8].

Each back-end is fully configurable using a set of parameters that affects the generated code. For example, the C back-end can use different scheduling strategies to execute a network of actors [14].

Additionally, some advanced analysis dedicated to dataflow applications can be performed during the compilation. A dynamic analysis, called actor classification [11], can detect predictable behavior within a network that may allow compile-time optimization such as static actors scheduling. Another analysis, based on model-checking techniques [6], can prune all unreachable execution paths to remove the unnecessary tests and accelerate the execution.

Cross-platform runtime library.

To allow developers creating full featured applications executable on any platform, Orcc defines a set of native functions callable from any CAL actor. Each one of these functions is implemented in a library exported at compile-time with the application, depending on the back-end used to produce source code. With these methods, developers are able to perform some basic I/O actions, such as opening and reading a file on disk, or initializing a window and sending raw data to display frames of a video sequence. All native functions available in Orcc library are implemented in the simulator as well.

4. RESULTS

This section presents the practicality of our development tool supported by the number of multimedia applications developed within it.

Library of applications.

Orcc is delivered with tens of open-source multimedia applications, developed by its community, that clearly demonstrate the ability of the environment to develop all kind of applications, from simple algorithm to complex system.

Additionally, these applications involve a large panel of domains in the multimedia including: **Video compression** with, for example, the descriptions of an MPEG-4 part 2

SP decoder, An MPEG-4 AVC decoder with 2 profiles, and an HEVC decoder; **Image compression** with the description of JPEG and JPEG2000 decoders; **File compression** (GZIP decoder); **Cryptography** (AES, DES, SHA); **Digital radio** (Zigbee protocol); **Digital filtering** (FIR and IIR filters); And so on.

Scalable performances of the applications.

We have experimented the 3 video decoders, including the one implementing the new High Efficiency Video Coding standard. The processor used during these experiments is an Intel Xeon W3530 composed of 4 homogeneous cores clocked at 2.8GHz. The processor is executing the compiled source code generating by the C back-end of Orcc. The experiments have been made from the following 720P sequences containing I/P/B frames: Old town cross (25fps and 6Mbps) for MPEG-4 Part 2; A Place at the Table (25fps and 6Mbps) for MPEG-4 AVC; Four People (60fps and 1Mbps) for MPEG HEVC.

Number of cores	1	2	4
MPEG-4 Part 2	30	54	93
MPEG AVC / H.264	4	7	12
MPEG HEVC / H.265	13	24	25

Table 1: Scalable video decoding frame rates (FPS) on a desktop multi-core processor

The results show that the RVC-CAL descriptions of the 3 video decoders can naturally take advantage of the multicore processor thanks to their explicit parallelism by offering scalable frame rates. Since the HEVC decoder is still under development, it does not yet fully take advantage of the parallel processing capabilities, even if its usage with 2 cores already allow to display a video sequence at real-time performance.

5. CONCLUSION

Orcc is a complete development environment, now used by industrials and research laboratories worldwide, that aims to make easier the development of multimedia applications. Based on dataflow programming that enables flexibility, scalability and portability, and especially on the RVC-CAL language that offers expressiveness and practicality, Orcc provides a set of tools that accelerates the development of multimedia applications in order to meet the requirement of the time-to-market.

6. ACKNOWLEDGMENTS

We would give special thanks to the Orcc community as a whole for actively participating in the development of the tools which offers solid basements to this work.

This work is done as part of COMPA, a French ANR project (ANR-11-INSE-0012), and 4EVER, a French national project with support from Europe (FEDER), French Ministry of Industry, and local authorities.

7. REFERENCES

[1] M. Abid, K. Jerbi, M. Raulet, O. Déforges, and M. Abid. System Level Synthesis Of Dataflow Programs: HEVC Decoder Case Study. In *ESLSyn*, 2013.

[2] E. Bezati, S. C. Brunet, M. Mattavelli, and J. W. Janneck. Synthesis and Optimization of High-Level Stream Programs. In *ESLSyn*, 2013.

[3] S. S. Bhattacharyya, J. Eker, J. W. Janneck, C. Lucarz, M. Mattavelli, and M. Raulet. Overview of the MPEG Reconfigurable Video Coding Framework. *Journal of Signal Processing Systems*, 63(2):251–263, July 2009.

[4] S. Efftinge, M. Eysholdt, J. Köhnlein, S. Zarnekow, W. Hasselbring, R. von Massow, and M. Hanus. Xbase: implementing domain-specific languages for Java. In *Proceedings of the 11th International Conference on Generative Programming and Component Engineering*, pages 112–121, 2012.

[5] J. Eker and J. W. Janneck. CAL language report: Specification of the CAL actor language. Technical report, University of California, Berkeley, Berkeley, 2003.

[6] J. Ersfolk, G. Roquier, F. Jokhio, J. Lilius, and M. Mattavelli. Scheduling of dynamic dataflow programs with model checking. In *Systems (SiPS), 2011*, pages 37–42, 2011.

[7] O. Esko, P. Jääskeläinen, P. Huerta, C. S. de La Lama, J. Takala, and J. I. Martinez. Customized Exposed Datapath Soft-Core Design Flow with Compiler Support. In *Proceedings of the 2010 International Conference on Field Programmable Logic and Applications*, pages 217–222, Washington, DC, USA, Aug. 2010. IEEE Computer Society.

[8] J. Gorin, H. Yviquel, F. Prêteux, and M. Raulet. Just-in-time adaptive decoder engine. *Proceedings of the 19th ACM international conference on Multimedia - MM '11*, page 711, 2011.

[9] J. Heulot, K. Desnos, M. Pelcat, H. Yviquel, J.-F. Nezan, M. Raulet, P.-L. Lagalaye, and J.-C. Le Lann. An experimental toolchain based on high-level dataflow models of computation for heterogeneous MPSoC. In *Design and Architectures for Signal and Image Processing (DASIP)*, pages 1–2, 2012.

[10] E. A. Lee and T. Parks. Dataflow process networks. *Proceedings of the IEEE*, 83(5):773–801, 1995.

[11] M. Wipliez and M. Raulet. Classification and transformation of dynamic dataflow programs. In *Design and Architectures for Signal and Image Processing (DASIP), 2010 Conference on*, 2010.

[12] M. Wipliez, G. Roquier, and J.-F. Nezan. Software Code Generation for the RVC-CAL Language. *Journal of Signal Processing Systems*, 63(2):203–213, June 2009.

[13] H. Yviquel, J. Boutellier, M. Raulet, and E. Casseau. Automated design of networks of Transport-Triggered Architecture processors using Dynamic Dataflow Programs. *Signal Processing Image Communication, Special issue on Reconfigurable Video Coding*, 2013.

[14] H. Yviquel, E. Casseau, M. Wipliez, and M. Raulet. Efficient multicore scheduling of dataflow process networks. In *IEEE Workshop on Signal Processing Systems (SiPS)*, pages 198–203, Washington, DC, USA, 2011. IEEE Computer Society.

Human vs Machine: Establishing a Human Baseline for Multimodal Location Estimation

Jaeyoung Choi[1], Howard Lei[1], Venkatesan Ekambaram[2], Pascal Kelm[3], Luke Gottlieb[1], Thomas Sikora[3], Kannan Ramchandran[2] and Gerald Friedland[1]

[1]International Computer Science Institute, Berkeley, CA, USA
[2]Department of Electrical Engineering and Computer Sciences, UC Berkeley, Berkeley, CA, USA
[3]Communication Systems Group, Technische Universität Berlin, Germany

[1]{jaeyoung,hlei,luke,fractor}@icsi.berkeley.edu
[2]{venkyne,kannanr}@eecs.berkeley.edu
[3]{kelm,sikora}@nue.tu-berlin.de

ABSTRACT

Over the recent years, the problem of video location estimation (i.e., estimating the longitude/latitude coordinates of a video without GPS information) has been approached with diverse methods and ideas in the research community and significant improvements have been made. So far, however, systems have only been compared against each other and no systematic study on human performance has been conducted. Based on a human-subject study with 11,900 experiments, this article presents a human baseline for location estimation for different combinations of modalities (audio, audio/video, audio/video/text). Furthermore, this article compares state-of-the-art location estimation systems with the human baseline. Although the overall performance of humans' multimodal video location estimation is better than current machine learning approaches, the difference is quite small: For 41 % of the test set, the machine's accuracy was superior to the humans. We present case studies and discuss why machines did better for some videos and not for others. Our analysis suggests new directions and priorities for future work on the improvement of location inference algorithms.

Categories and Subject Descriptors

H.3.3 [**Information Systems and Retrieval**]: Retrieval models

General Terms

EXPERIMENTATION, HUMAN FACTORS

Keywords

Location Estimation, Multimodal, Crowdsourcing

MM'13, October 21–25, 2013, Barcelona, Spain.

ACM 978-1-4503-2404-5/13/10 ...$15.00.
http://dx.doi.org/10.1145/2502081.2502123.

1. INTRODUCTION

With the widespread use of GPS-equipped handheld devices, location metadata (aka geo-tagging) has rapidly become an integral part of photos and videos shared over the Web. This trend has enabled location based multimedia organization, search and retrieval on many Internet services such as Google, Facebook, and Flickr. The main driving force behind these services is the creation of highly personalized user experiences, allowing for better recommendations and targeted advertisements.

Even with this trend, it has been estimated that only about 5 % of the existing multimedia content on the Internet is actually geo-tagged [8]. A significant amount of consumer-produced media content is still obtained using devices that do not have GPS functionality. Privacy concerns have motivated users to disable automatic geo-tagging of media. Furthermore, even GPS-enabled devices cannot provide accurate location information when the photo or video is captured in an indoor environment.

Nevertheless, the volume of high quality geo-tagged videos and photos on the Web represent a quantity of training data for machine learning on an unprecedented scale, giving rise to the idea of creating an automated task that would try to locate non-geo-tagged media from the web using models obtained through the geo-tagged subset. Put simply: Given a video and its associated textual metadata, can we infer the location where it was taken? This idea of "multimodal video location estimation", was proposed three years ago as a Brave New Idea in [8]. Since then, the "Placing Task" of the MediaEval evaluation [22] has evaluated the task on a global scale [19]. Therefore, the problem has been approached with diverse methods and ideas in the research community and significant improvements have been made. So far, however, approaches have only been compared against each other and there is little intuition on how humans would perform at this task. Some researchers even assume that the automated algorithms would probably always perform better on this task compared to humans. In this paper, we establish a human baseline for video location estimation and present a comparative analysis with automatic location inference systems. The baseline was created by asking qualified humans to perform a total of 9,000 video localizations. With the human baseline in our hand, we are able to analyze different cases of when machines perform better than humans, humans perform better than machines or when both fail.

Our paper is organized as follows. Section 2 provides a brief overview of the existing work in the field and positions our work in comparison to the available literature. Section 3 describes the task and the characteristics of the dataset that render the task difficult. Section 4 describes the experimental setup for establishing the human baseline using a crowdsourcing platform. Section 5 describes our technical approaches to utilizing audio, audio/visual, and audio/visual/textual metadata for automatic location inference. Section 6 provides a comparison of the performance of location estimation between machines and humans. In section 7, we present case studies and discuss why machines perform better for some videos and not for others. Section 8 concludes with a summary of the paper and future research directions based on our analysis.

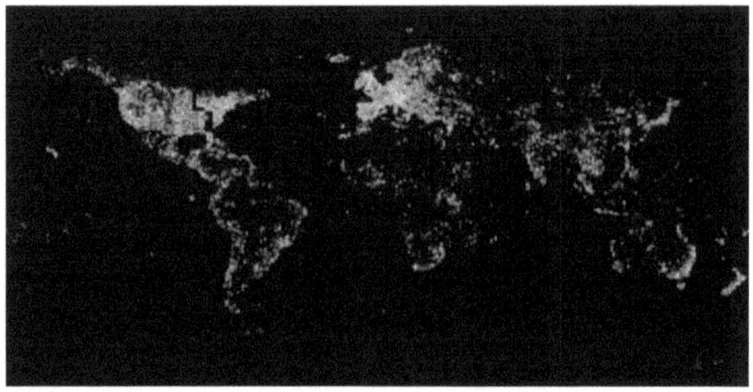

Figure 1: Distribution of the videos and images of the MediaEval 2010 Placing Task training dataset. Jet colormap was applied to show the density.

2. RELATED WORK

Initial approaches to location estimation started several years ago. In earlier articles [28, 33], the location estimation task is reduced to a retrieval problem on self-produced, location-tagged image databases. The idea is that if the image is the same then the location must be the same too. Hays and Efros [12] estimate a rough location of an image with several visual descriptors and represent the estimated image location as a probability distribution over earth's surface. A comprehensive overview of this early research work is presented in [21].

Previous work in the area of automatic geotagging of multimedia based on tags has mostly been carried out on Flickr images. In [26], the geo-locations associated with specific Flickr tags are predicted using spatial distributions of tag use. A tag which is strongly concentrated in a specific location has a semantic relationship with that location. User-contributed tags are exploited for geotagging by [29], who used tag distributions associated with locations as represented by grid cells on a map of the earth which is then used to infer the geographic locations of Flickr images.

Evaluations on multimodal location estimation on randomly selected consumer-produced videos were carried out in the 2010, 2011, and 2012 MediaEval Placing tasks [22]. One of the notable participants [18] used a combination of language models and similarity search to geo-tag the videos using their associated tags. Many participants in the Placing task try to utilize both visual and textual features for their location estimations. Friedland et al. [7] propose a hierarchical system that first uses spatial variance of tags to find initial estimates which are used as anchor points to set the search boundary for visual nearest neighbor search in the later stage. Kelm et al. [16] propose another hierarchical, multi-modal approach which first classifies a query video's location into possible regions and then applies a visual nearest neighbor method to find corresponding training images in those regions. Crandall et al. [6] propose a model that produces enhanced geographical annotation for web images using visual and tag features and an annotation lexicon. The approaches in [1] and [9] report on combining visual content with user tags as well.

Multimodal location estimation on videos that utilize audio was first attempted in [8] in which the authors matched videos containing audio from ambulance sirens in different cities, without the use of textual tags. Other works such as [5] reports the results of a location estimation system that incorporates all three modalities that are usable in video location estimation, i.e. textual, visual, and audio features.

All of the approaches described above have the common feature of processing each query video independently and estimating its geo-location based on textual, visual, and audio features using a geo-tagged training database. Clearly, the performance of these systems largely depends on the size and quality of the training database. However, data sparsity is one of the major issues that can adversely affect the performance of these systems. The work presented in [4] differs from the existing work in the literature in the respect that they *jointly* estimate the geo-locations of all of the input query images. Each query image added to the database enhances the quality of the database by acting as "virtual" training data and thereby boosts the performance of the algorithm. The system presented in this paper is an improvement over that work as the system presented here uses all three modalities (visual, audio, and textual features) whereas [4] only uses textual features collected from user-annotated metadata.

Crowdsourcing is currently used for a range of applications such as exploiting unsolicited user contributions, for spontaneous annotation of images for retrieval [27], etc. Systematic crowdsourcing platforms, such as Amazon Mechanical Turk have been used to mass-outsource artificial intelligence jobs [14]. Further, crowdsourcing has also been used for surveying and evaluating user interfaces [17], designs, and other technical approaches.

However, as the name coincidentally implies, platforms such as Mechanical Turk are often best used for mechanical tasks, i.e. tasks that only require simple intuition. Therefore, for a task like the one presented here, where there is a suspicion that humans might perform worse than machines and there is no clear intuition as to how to solve the task, one has to be very careful about how to approach it properly. Apart from [10], there is no previous work on using Mechanical Turk for geo-tagging videos, moreover there seems to be no previous work on how to use Mechanical Turk for a task that is not straightforward to solve.

So far, no human baseline exists for location estimation, and systems have only been compared against each other. At the same time, these systems differ quite dramatically. This paper establishes a human baseline and compares it against two state of the art systems from the literature to draw conclusions for future directions of this research. To ensure the quality of the human baseline, we rely on the qualification methodology described in [10] in combination with redundancy [15].

Figure 2: Several frames from the randomly selected videos that were used in the experiment. Most of them are very difficult to specifically geolocate.

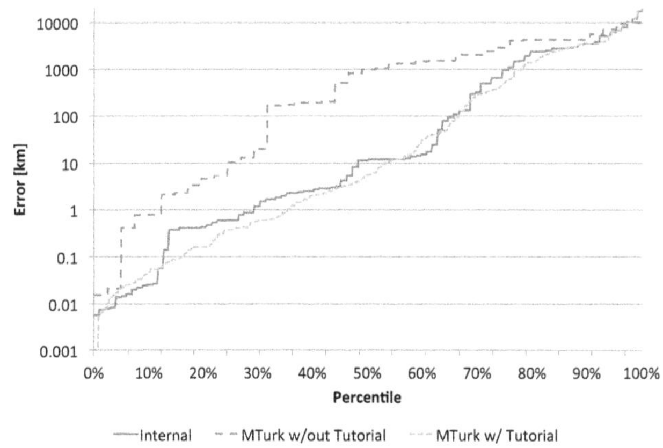

Figure 3: Comparison of performance results for Ideal10 set [10]. Error distance (y-axis) is in a log scale.

3. TASK AND DATASET

All experiments described in this article were performed using the dataset distributed for the Placing Task of the 2010 MediaEval benchmark[1]. The Placing Task is part of the MediaEval benchmarking initiative that requires participants to assign geographical coordinates (latitude and longitude) to each test video. Participants can make use of textual metadata, audio and visual features as well as external resources, depending on the test run.

The dataset consists of 3,185,258 photos and 10216 videos. All are Creative Commons-licensed and from Flickr[2]. The metadata for each video includes a user-annotated title, tags, and a description among others. The videos are not filtered or selected in any way to make the dataset more relevant to the task, and are therefore likely to be representative of videos selected at random [19]. Figure 1 shows the non-uniform distribution of Flickr videos and images due to geographical, economical, and political reasons.

Flickr requires that an uploaded video must be created by the uploader, and thus almost all videos on Flickr are home-video style. The relatively short lengths of each video should be noted, as the maximum length of a Flickr video was limited to 90 seconds when the dataset was collected. Moreover, about 70 % of videos in this data set have less than 50 seconds of playtime. Manual inspection of the randomly sampled 150 videos from the dataset shows that if given with only the audio and visual contents, 8% of the videos contained enough information for accurate guesses, and 10% with rough hints that would lead to city or country level estimations. The rest of the videos had very little cue for location estimation. Videos of indoor settings consist 36% of the videos and about half of them are private space such as one's house or in the backyard. 24% of the videos contained human speech in various languages including English, Spanish, Swedish, Japanese, etc. The metadata provided by the user often provided direct and sensible clues for location estimation. 98.8 % of videos in the training dataset were annotated by their uploaders with at least one title, tag, or description, which often included location information.

[1]http://multimediaeval.org/
[2]http://www.flickr.com

4. ESTABLISHING A HUMAN BASELINE

Collection of human baseline was performed in two steps. In the first step we qualified people, by filtering out incompetent or unmotivated workers and ensuring that the quality of submissions were high enough for the second stage. In the second stage, we collected the human baseline for 1000 videos. We used Amazon Mechanical Turk as the crowdsourcing platform.

4.1 Qualification

The task of location estimation is different from a standard Mechanical Turk task in that it is difficult for both humans and machines, whereas a standard Mechanical Turk task is usually easy for humans and difficult or impossible for machines. There are several notable challenges to finding skilled workers for this task: First, we must find what we term "honest operators" i.e., people who will seriously attempt to do the task and not just click quickly through it to collect the bounty. Second, we need to develop a meaningful qualification test set that is challenging enough to allow us to qualify people for the real task, but is also solvable by individuals regardless of their culture or location, although English language understanding was required for instructions. For example, in the process of selecting videos, there were videos of tourists in Machu Picchu, which our annotator immediately recognized, however there were no clues to reveal this location that would be usable to someone who had not heard or seen this location previously. These videos were ruled out for the qualification. In the end, ten videos, which we called 'Ideal10 set', were carefully chosen and presented to the workers. We created an in-depth tutorial which presented the workers with the basic tools and skills for approaching this challenging task. The workers are allowed to use any applicable resource from the Internet, including Google Maps and Streetview.

Our previous study show that, after the qualification process, workers on the crowdsourcing platform achieved almost equal level of accuracy as an internal expert volunteer

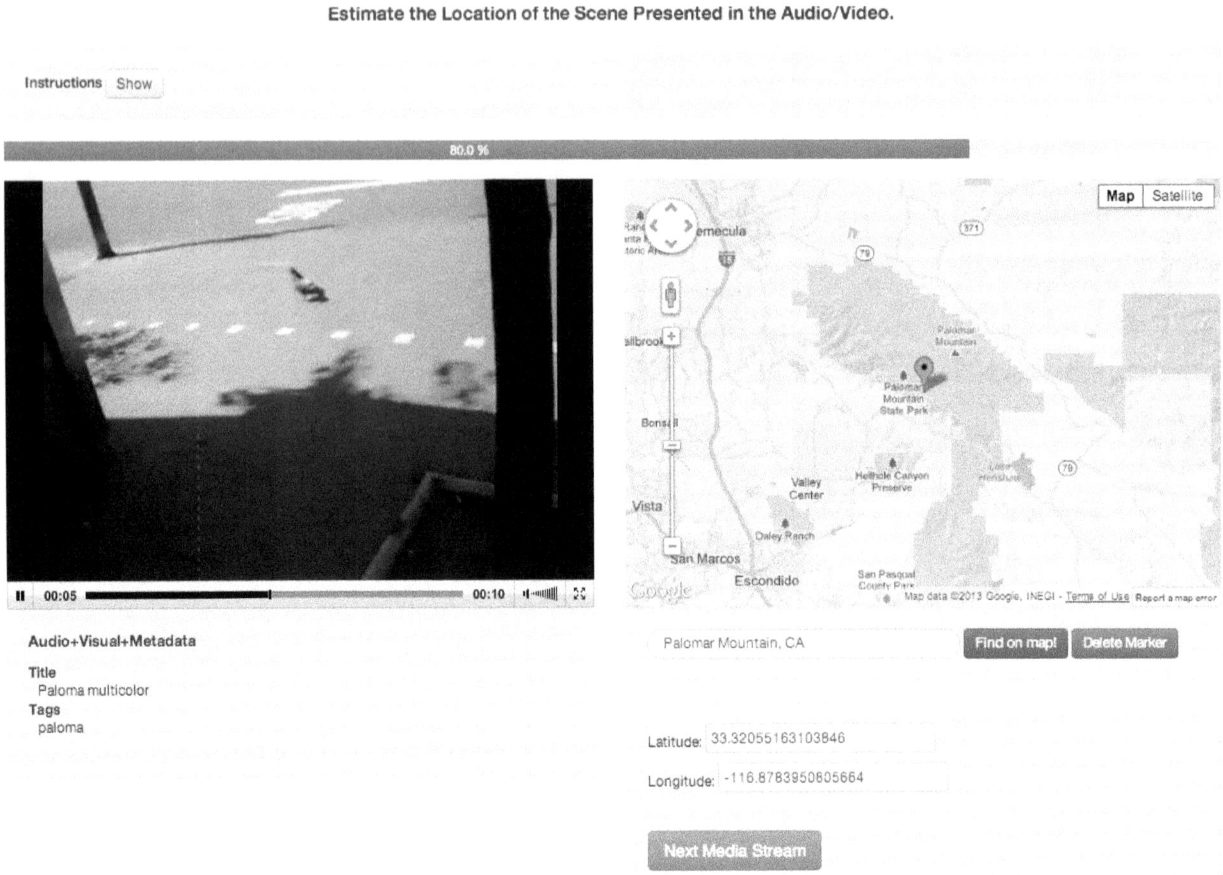

Figure 4: Screenshot of web interface used in the Amazon Mechanical Turk experiments described.

testers which was composed of highly-educated, well-trained and motivated researchers. In Figure 3, we have a comparison of the performance results for our internal testers, the initial test results of MTurkers, and their results with the tutorial. The internal tester and initial test results were derived by using the classification results from the first round for the videos in the Ideal10 set, as those videos are a subset of our larger annotation. We can see that while the internal testers still perform better than the Mechanical Turk workers, the addition of a tutorial greatly narrowed the performance margin. This led us to conclude that a worker who is adequately trained with a tutorial can be considered reasonably qualified.

However, to select only the highest quality workers, we applied a screening process to filter out not only bad but even workers who performed averagely well. Out of 290 workers on Mechanical Turk, who had participated in the qualification task, we qualified only 84 workers (29% acceptance rate), those who were able to achieve very high accuracy i.e., were able to put at least 8 of 10 qualification videos within a 5km radius of the ground truth location. We considered 5km margin of error as a city-level accuracy. When applied with the same evaluation criteria, internal volunteers showed similar acceptance rate of 34%. Additionally, time spent for each human video localization was recorded and often directly correlated with accuracy, giving us a further accuracy indicator for the actual localization test. After successful qualification, we paid USD 1.50 for each HIT (Human Intelligence Task), which consisted of 10 video localizations.

4.2 The Web Interface

Here, we describe our user interface which the Amazon Mechanical Turk workers used for the task. We went through several rounds of internal testing and feedback to enhance the usability of the tool.

Figure 4 shows the final version of this interface. The instructions on the top of the screen can be expanded and shrunk with a 'Show/Hide' button. It was shrunk by default to make the whole interface fit in a normal-sized window to minimize unnecessary scrolling of the screen. A progress bar was shown below the instructions box to let workers know where they are along the progress of a HIT. A video was played automatically once the page was loaded. All videos were re-uploaded to a private file server without the metadata so that simply following the link on the player would not reveal any additional information about the video. A Google Maps instance was placed to the right of the video. A marker would be dropped where the map was clicked, and it could be dragged around the map. The marker's position was automatically translated to the latitude and longitude and printed to the 'Latitude' and 'Longitude' boxes. A location search form was placed under the map to aid the search of the location. The form had an auto-completion feature which would help in cases where the worker did not know the exact spelling of the place, etc. At the end of the HIT, we asked participants to leave comments about the HIT. This enabled us to filter out submissions with incidents and other exceptions.

4.3 Collection of Human Intelligence

When we collected the human performance for a different set of modalities, we presented the media with least information to all i.e., first we gave audio then audio/visual, and lastly audio/visual and textual information (tags). For each HIT, a worker was given five videos with three different media combinations, thus the total of 15 media streams. For the same set of media streams, three identical HITs were generated redundantly for the comparison and to filter out the possible bad results. HITs were assigned with first-come first-served basis to the pool of 84 qualified workers. To distribute the HITs to as many as workers and as evenly as possible, we applied some throttle control to limit the number of HITs that an individual worker can accept. We started the reward for each HIT with USD 0.25 but, based on feedback, quickly increased it to USD 1.50, which resulted in a much faster collection result. Within 18 days, we were able to collect a total of 11,900 localizations (2900 from qualification, 9000 from localizing 1000 videos). Many workers have left comments that the task was challenging, especially for the cases when only the audio was given. At the same time, many of them reported the HIT to be fun and we believe that this motivated people to try to submit better results.

5. MACHINE-BASED LOCATION ESTIMATION

In this section, we describe the technical approach and our experimental setup for automatic location inference. We first describe the audio-based approach, then describe how visual feature was added to the modality, and finally, the method that uses all three modalities (audio, visual, and textual metadata).

5.1 Audio-based Location Estimation

We used the city identification system reported in [20] as our machine baseline for location estimation. We describe the main idea of the system as follows. The system involves training a total variability matrix T to model the variability (both city- and channel-related) of the acoustic features of all audio tracks, and using the matrix to obtain a low-dimensional vector characterizing the city of where each audio track was from. Specifically, for each audio file, a vector of first-order statistics M - of the acoustic feature vectors of the audio centered around the means of a GMM world model - is first obtained, and can be decomposed as follows:

$$M = m + T\omega \tag{1}$$

where m is the GMM world model mean vector, and ω are low-dimensional vectors, known as the identity vectors or i-vectors.

The system then performs Probabilistic Linear Discriminant Analysis (pLDA) [13] and Within-Class Covariance Normalization (WCCN) [11] on the i-vectors. pLDA linearly projects the i-vectors ω onto a set of dimensions to maximize the ratio of between-user scatter to within-user scatter of the i-vectors, producing a new set of vectors. WCCN then whitens the pLDA-projected vectors via a second linear projection, such that the resulting vectors have an identity covariance matrix. For our city identification system, 1,024 mixtures are used for the GMM world model, and a rank of 400 is used for the total variability matrix T, such that the i-vectors ω have 400 dimensions. pLDA projects the i-vectors onto a set of 200 dimensions. The cosine distance is used to obtain the city-similarity score of a pair of i-vectors ω between two audio tracks of user-uploaded videos [30]:

$$score(\omega_1, \omega_2) = \frac{(A^T\omega_1)^T W^{-1}(A^T\omega_2)}{\sqrt{(A^T\omega_1)^T W^{-1}(A^T\omega_1)}\sqrt{(A^T\omega_2)^T W^{-1}(A^T\omega_2)}} \tag{2}$$

where A and W are the LDA and WCCN projection matrices respectively, and ω_1 and ω_2 are i-vectors from the two audio tracks being compared against. The acoustic features consist of MFCC C0-C19+Δ+$\Delta\Delta$ coefficients of 60 dimensions, computed using 25 ms windows and 10 ms shifts, across 60 to 16,000 Hz.

Since we could not train the model to cover all regions of the earth due to the data sparsity, we clustered the distribution of videos into the 40 cities in the training dataset, and reduced the location estimation to a city-identification problem. We trained the system with models for each city using the collection of audio tracks extracted from each city. A video is defined to belong to a city when it is in a 50 km radius of the geographical city center. We then tested the audio tracks extracted from the test videos against the trained models and picked the city with the highest likelihood. For comparability, we converted the city labels to the (latitude, longitude) format with the geo-coordinates of the center of the city. Note, that this creates a slight disadvantage for the machine.

5.2 Visual Location Estimation

In order to utilize the visual content of the video for location estimation, we reduce location estimation to an image retrieval problem, assuming that similar images mean similar locations as in [12]. We used several visual descriptors extracted from sample frames of both query and training videos along with the images given as the Placing Task dataset and ran a k-nearest neighbor search on the training dataset to find the video frame or an image that is most similar. We used FCTH (Fuzzy Color and Texture Histogram) [3], CEDD (Color Edge Directivity Descriptor) [2], and Tamura [31] visual descriptors that were given as a part of the Placing Task dataset. In addition to these descriptors, we extracted Gist features [24] as it was shown to be very effective at scene recognition in [12]. Weighted linear combination of distances was used as the final distance between frames. The scaling of the weights was learned by using a small sample of the training dataset and normalizing the individual distance distributions so that each the standard deviation of each of them would be similar. We used L^2 norm to compare the combination of descriptors and used 1-nearest neighbor matching between the closest pre-extracted frame to the temporal mid-point of a query video and all photos and frames from the videos in the training dataset. In order to handle the large amounts of development data efficiently, we split the reference data set into chunks of 100,000 images, ran 1-NN in parallel on each subset to get intermediate results, and ran 1-NN once again on the intermediate results to get the final nearest neighbor. We used an approximate nearest neighbor library [23] for the experiment.

While videos with soundtrack were shown to the crowd, due to data sparsity, our comparison system did not use the acoustic modality and relied solely on the visual modality.

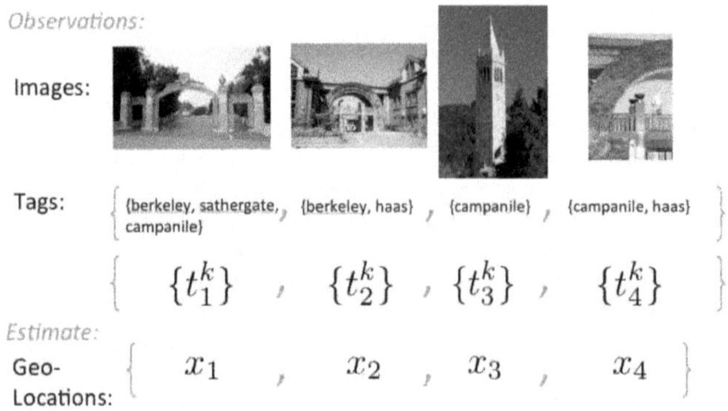

Figure 5: A theoretic viewpoint of the geo-tagging problem.

5.3 Multimodal Location Estimation

To integrate textual and visual data, we combined the visual search method with the system reported in [4]. Due to data sparsity, again, while the soundtrack was available to humans, the acoustic modality was not used. The approach based on graphical models is summarized as follows.

Graphical models provide an efficient representation of dependencies amongst different random variables and have been extensively studied in the statistical learning theory community [32]. The random variables in our setup are the geo-locations of the query videos that need to be estimated. We treat the textual tags as observed random variables that are probabilistically related to the geo-location of that video. Figure 5 illustrates the idea. The goal is to obtain the best estimate of the unobserved random variables (locations of the query videos) given all the observed variables. We use graphical models to characterize the dependencies amongst the different random variables and use efficient message-passing algorithms to obtain the desired estimates. In order to obtain a graphical model representation for our problem setup, we model the joint distribution of the query video locations given the observed data. We use a simplistic conditional dependency model for the random variables as described below. Each node in our graphical model corresponds to a query video and the associated random variable is the geo-location of that query video. Intuitively, if two images are nearby, then they should be connected by an edge since their locations are highly correlated. The problem is that we do not know the geo-locations a priori. However, given that textual tags are strongly correlated to the geo-locations, a common textual tag between two images is a good indication of the proximity of geo-locations. Hence, we will build the graphical model by having an edge between two nodes if and only if the two query videos have at least one common textual tag. Note that this textual tag need not appear in the training dataset.

Let x_i be the geo-location of the ith video and $\{t_i^k\}_{k=1}^{n_i}$ be the set of n_i tags associated with this video. Based on our model the joint probability distribution factorizes as follows:

$$p(x_1, ..., x_N | \{t_1^k\}, ..., \{t_N^k\}) \propto \prod_{i \in V} \psi(x_i | \{t_i^k\}) \prod_{(i,j) \in E} \psi(x_i, x_j | \{t_i^k\}, \{t_j^k\}).$$

We now need to model the node and edge potential functions. Given the training data, we fit a Gaussian Mixture Model (GMM) for the distribution of the location given a particular tag t, i.e., $p(x|t)$. The intuition is that tags usually correspond to one or more specific locations and the distribution is multi-modal (e.g., the tag "washington" can refer to the State of Washington or Washington D.C., among other locations). To estimate the parameters of the GMM, we use an algorithm based on Expectation Maximization that adaptively chooses the number of components for different tags using a likelihood criterion. Although distribution of the locations given multiple tags is not independent, for this experiment, we start with a naive assumption that different tags are conditionally independent. We take the node potential as follows, $\psi(x_i) \propto \prod_{k=1}^{n_i} p(x_i|t_i^k)$. For the potential functions, $\psi(x_i, x_j|\{t_i^k\}, \{t_j^k\})$, we use a very simple model. Intuitively, if the common tag between two query videos i and j occurs too frequently either in the test set or the training set, that tag is most likely a common word like "video" or "photo" which does not really encode any information about the geographic closeness of the two videos. In this case, we assume that the edge potential is zero (drop edge (i, j)) whenever the number of occurrences of the tag is above a threshold. When the occurrence of the common tag is less frequent, then it is most likely that the geographic locations are very close to each other and we model the potential function as an indicator function,

$$\psi(x_i, x_j | \{t_i^k\}, \{t_j^k\}) = \begin{cases} 1 & \text{if } x_i = x_j, \\ 0 & \text{otherwise.} \end{cases} \quad (3)$$

This model is a hard-threshold model and we can clearly use a soft-version wherein the weights on the edges for the potential functions are appropriately chosen.

Further, we propose the following simplification, which leads to analytically tractable expressions for the potential functions and message updates. Given that for many of the tags, the GMM will have one strong mixture component, the distribution $\psi(x_i)$, can be approximated by a Gaussian distribution with the mean $(\tilde{\mu}_i)$ and variance $(\tilde{\sigma}_i^2)$ given by,

$$(\tilde{\mu}_i, \tilde{\sigma}_i^2) = \left(\frac{\sum_{k=1}^{n_i} \frac{1}{\sigma_i^{k2}} \mu_i^k}{\sum_{k=1}^{n_i} \frac{1}{\sigma_i^{k2}}}, \frac{1}{\sum_{k=1}^{n_i} \frac{1}{\sigma_i^{k2}}} \right), \quad (4)$$

where μ_i^k and σ_i^{k2} are the mean and variance of the mixture component with the largest weight of the distribution $p(x_i|t_i^k)$. Under this assumption, the iterations of the sum-product algorithm take on the following simplistic form. Node i at iteration m, updates its location estimate $(\hat{\mu}_i(m))$ and variance $(\hat{\sigma}_i^2(m))$ as follows,

$$\hat{\mu}_i(m) = \frac{\frac{1}{\tilde{\sigma}_i^2}\tilde{\mu}_i + \sum_{j \in N(i)} \frac{1}{\hat{\sigma}_j^2(m-1)} \hat{\mu}_j(m-1)}{\frac{1}{\tilde{\sigma}_i^2} + \sum_{j \in N(i)} \frac{1}{\hat{\sigma}_j^2(m-1)}}, \quad (5)$$

$$\hat{\sigma}_i^2(m) = \frac{1}{\frac{1}{\tilde{\sigma}_i^2} + \sum_{j \in N(i)} \frac{1}{\hat{\sigma}_j^2(m-1)}}. \quad (6)$$

The location estimate for the ith query video $\hat{x}_i$ is taken to be $\hat{\mu}_i(m)$ at the end of m iterations, or when the algorithm

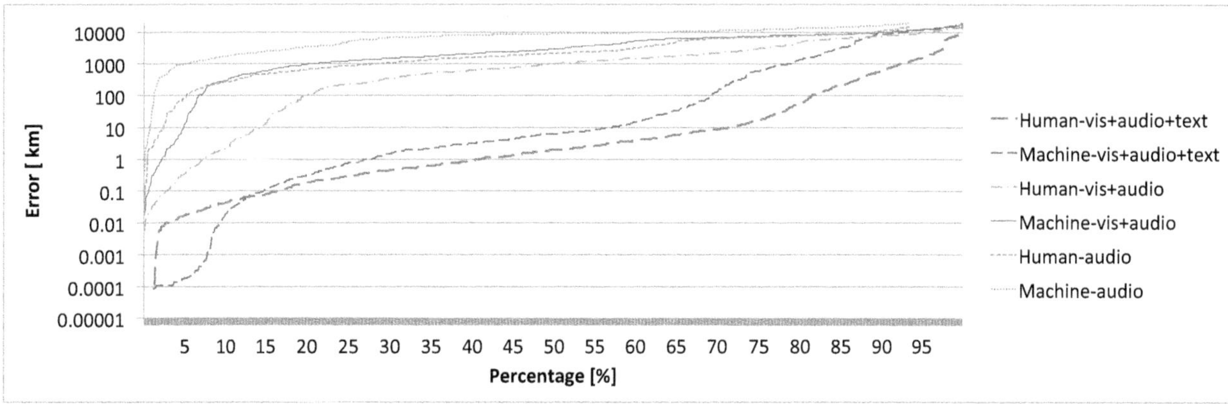

Figure 6: The human baseline of location estimation vs current stat-of-the-art algorithms on all modalities (audio, audio+visual, and audio+visual+text)

has converged. The variance $\hat{\sigma}_i^2(m)$ provides a confidence metric on the location estimate.

So far, only the textual features are used to estimate the location. We performed the same visual search described in section 5.2 around the location estimate $\hat{\mu}_i(m)$ with the search boundary set dynamically according to the variance $\hat{\sigma}_i^2(m)$. The intuition is that more we are certain about the location estimate from the graphical framework, we search a narrower range for similar images. Thus, if the variance is low, the search boundary would be set low as well, and vice versa. Since the visual search was limited to much smaller number of images and video frames dynamically adjusted from the confidence of the textual-based location estimate, the results were improved over searching naively across the whole training dataset or searching within the fixed range from the text-based location estimate.

All of the algorithms described above, except for the acoustic system that seems to be unique, achieve among the highest scores in the MediaEval 2012 evaluation and we therefore consider them a state-of-the-art machine baseline.

6. RESULTS

To evaluate the performance of both the online workers and the machine, the geodesic distance between the ground truth coordinates and those of the outputs from participants or the machine, respectively, are compared. To take into account the geographic nature of the evaluation, the Haversine [25] distance is used.

Figure 6 shows the performance of humans vs the machine given three different combinations of modalities: audio, audio+visual, and audio+visual+text. Human performance was measured by having 3 different qualified workers redundantly locate the same video. A total number of 1000 geotagged videos were presented in the 3 different forms (as discussed in section 4), resulting in a total number of 9000 experiments. The results of the qualification experiments are not included in this chart. To obtain a conservative baseline for this chart, the best answer out of the 3 was picked. For representing machine performance, we used the system as described in section 5 based on the combination of media tested.

Overall, humans are better at this task than machines. However, in the very accurate (below 50 m region) current algorithms outperform humans by about a 12 % margin (number of correctly located videos). The difference between the algorithm and human intelligence is quite low though, since overall only 59 % of the videos are located more accurately by the human than by the algorithm when all modalities are utilized. An unqualified worker base would most certainly have resulted in machine dominance of this task. As a control, choosing the second-best of the 3 results, resulted in the humans being less accurate than the algorithm in 60 % of the videos. Both the machine and humans do better once more modalities are available. Using only audio, the machine was better for only 16.4 % of the videos. In the visual case, the machine was only better in 25.5 % of the videos.

We will qualify the results in the following section.

7. DISCUSSION

In this section, we analyze the cases where humans were successful in inferring location while the machine failed and vice versa. We also investigate the videos where humans and computers have both failed to infer location. The threshold for determining the 'success' and 'failure' was set differently for each of the modalities given. We were more generous when only the audio was given, as it is much more difficult than the two other cases.

7.1 Machine vs. Human using only Audio

For audio only experiments, the threshold to be considered a successful estimate was set at 150km, and the failure threshold was set at 1000 km.

7.1.1 *When humans are better*

Out of 1000 audio-only test videos, there were 62 cases in which the audio provided enough information for humans to infer location while the machines failed. Close analysis of all of these audio tracks revealed that the cases where humans were better than machines can be categorized into the following three classes:

1. Humans were able to identify location based on the kind of language spoken or the distinctive accent or variation of the speakers in the video. With only this information at hand and no other clues, human annotators picked the capital city of the country or region where that language is mainly spoken or was originally from (Paris for French, Glasgow for Scottish accented English, London for British accented English,

Lisbon for Portuguese). We have no way to investigate whether the workers were able to use any additional information from understanding the contents of the speech.

2. Humans were able to pick up keywords from the speech that they were able to understand either entirely or at least in part providing a clue sufficient to estimate the location. For example, a Finnish singer saying, "Hello, Helsinki!" at the opening of a concert was the only understandable portion for people who don't speak Finnish, but this is a sufficient clue for estimating the location.

3. Humans were also able to infer location information from the context of the text spoken. In one video, the speech contained the keywords 'California', 'grapes', 'harvest', and 'wine' which could be inferred to be in the Napa Valley using a Google search or geographical knowledge.

On the machine side, the first category of videos could be localized with an audio-based language or dialect identification system. The second category of videos could be localized as if the textual metadata were given using the keywords extracted from the transcript of the speech obtained from passing the audio track to the automatic speech recognition system. The major challenge would be to deal with the noisy transcript from the 'wild' audio. The third kind of inference is the most difficult.

7.1.2 When machines are better

While humans were in general better at the task using only the soundtrack, there were 10 cases when machines did reasonably well (estimating location under 100km, which is the city-level boundary used for the audio-based approach) while all of the human annotators failed. One notable finding from the analysis was that three of these videos were from Prague, CZ. All three videos were from different users and contained different scenes and events, however, a close inspection of the audio revealed that three of the videos contained a musical noise in the background. Also, two of the training videos used to train the model for the city of Prague had music playing in the background. We believe that our city model from i-vector system picked up the common musical chords that are often played in the touristy locations in Prague.

The system also gave the highest score to Tokyo to a video that shows the Shinkansen train leaving from Tokyo station. Similarly with the above example, we believe that the i-vector system has learned the very specific sound of the Shinkansen train track.

These results are good news for automatic approaches: They show that machine learning approaches can exploit very specific sounds that are hard to spot for humans and use them for location matching.

7.1.3 When both fail

When a video is edited and the audio track is altered such as when its dubbed with background music, or if there's no audible speech, both humans and machines usually failed. However, human workers did tend to converge on certain locations for the audio tracks that can be inferred to be a stereotype of a broader category of locations such as "beach", "fireworks", or "farm". For example, for beaches, all three human annotators picked a beach in Los Angeles, CA when the audio track contains the sound of sea gull and the sound of breaking waves, whereas the ground truth was a beach in Liverpool, UK. Two of the annotators picked New York for the audio track that contained the sound of fireworks.

This scheme is actually applicable to machine learning as well. For example, the machine could be trained to classify the scene into a broader category to aid in the estimation of location. Classifying the scene of a beach at night could benefit from using audio as the visual features would not work well due to poor lighting conditions.

7.2 Machine vs. Human using Audio and Video

With the added visual feature, both machines and humans were able to get much better results than using audio alone. For these experiments, the threshold to be considered a successful estimation was set at 50 km, and the failure was set at 1000 km. We excluded cases where audio-only had already given a sufficient clue for humans to get below the 50 km error range as we could not independently evaluate the effectiveness of the visual feature. We also investigated cases where the audio and visual features complement each other whereas only one modality would have failed.

7.2.1 When humans are better

In 179 cases humans were better than machines. We could separate out about 4 classes.

1. The majority of cases where human workers perform extremely well (getting under 5 km or even 100 m error) belong to the class that contain textual information in the video. These can be in the form of captions added by the user, signs, or even messages written on buildings or machinery in the video. This category of videos could possibly be located with a video OCR system that extracts textual information.

2. When the visual and audio modalities complement each other but when used separately are less effective, humans are usually better. In other words, multimodal integration in machines is not yet successful. For example, one video showed a TV broadcast of an American Football game with the name of the team and the score shown on the screen. The uploader makes a cheering sound as the game ends and the all three human workers inferred that the the uploader is a resident of the winning team's region, which is true.

3. When the scene contains a famous landmark humans perform very well. However, our location estimation system was not specifically trained to recognize landmarks.

4. The atmosphere and context of the scene can be understood by the human workers. For instance, a video taken from a moving car shows the clothing style of the people on the street, the status of the road, and the shape of buildings. In one particular case, all three human workers inferred from this collected information that this could be a specific rural town in India, which was in fact was the right answer.

We did not find reasonable evidence that temporal information of the visual features impacted the location inference of human workers.

7.2.2 When machines are better

We found 81 cases where the machine was better than the humans using only visual features. Most of these cases consisted of specific tourist spots where the machine had many training videos of but the locations are not well known to a lot of people. For example, all three human workers failed to recognize the foggy Machu Picchu (mislabeled as pyramids in Mexico) or a mountain scene of Patagonia (mislabeled as Himalaya or Canadian Rockies).

7.2.3 *When both fail*

Most of the cases where both humans and machines failed was when videos were taken indoors such as the inside of a night club (poor lighting, poor audio), videos of babies in a house, and so on. Other cases were some generic scenes such as an unpopular mountain, outskirts of large cities with no landmarks or signs, etc.

7.3 Machine vs. Human using all Modalities

The threshold for success in this case is 5 km as the textual information is very effective at allowing inference of location for both humans and the machine. The threshold for failure is set at 1000 km. In 39 cases, the machine achieved less than 5 km error while all three qualified human annotators failed to estimate the location with an error of more than 1000 km. For the opposite case where the human does better than the machine, we found 162 cases.

7.3.1 *When humans are better*

In 162 cases, humans were successful at picking a correct location while the machines failed. Many of the errors were from the system failing to pick up a single keyword that represents the location within the list of tags.

1. We believe the critical advantage in some of these 162 cases was from the misspelling of a tag or that the tag was written in a foreign language (which was not included in the training). Human locators did not have a problems with the misspelled words.
2. The bias in the distribution of the training dataset results from the failure of the system to correctly process keywords if they were not seen in the training dataset. Although our system tries to address the problem of sparsity using the graphical framework, it is still bound by the quantity and quality of the data in both the training and test sets. The use of semantic computing-based approaches as done in [16] can be an effective solution in these cases.

7.3.2 *When machines are better*

1. Some of the videos contained multiple tags that were not helpful in inferring location but were repeatedly seen in other videos in the training dataset. For example, "iPhone, 3gs, or iphone3gs" does not have a specific meaning related to the location in one of the test videos. However, our system was able to pick up the repeated common appearance of these tags in the training data and was able to estimate the location under 0.5 km error. This is due to similar users using the same "language model" when tagging their videos. Keep in mind that test and training set had different sets of users.
2. Humans failed to pick up clues from combination of words when too many tags were given, whereas the machine was able to implicitly incorporate n-gram using the graphical framework.
3. Language barrier: In some cases the tags were written in a foreign language (not in the training dataset). Worker populations on Amazon Mechanical Turk are mostly English-based, thus the presence of non-English tags presents a language barrier. Some human workers managed to get over this by using translation services such as Google Translate.

7.3.3 *When both fail*

There were 26 cases where both the machine as well as all humans failed to get a location even with all possible sources of information present. This is expected because sometimes there are just no useful cues to estimate location. For example, a scene which is a closeup with no distinguishable sounds, and no textual description to indicate location. In the end, we were surprised though that only 2.5 % of all videos fell into this category (where the location was not estimated with under 1000 km accuracy by either the human or the machine). This indicates a high growth potential for future location estimation research.

8. CONCLUSION AND FUTURE WORK

In this article, we establish a human baseline for multimodal location estimation of random consumer-produced videos with textual descriptions. Even though algorithms work on low-level statistics, we show that humans outperform the algorithm sometimes and in other cases the algorithm outperforms humans. The difference between human performance and algorithmic performance is so close that we speculate that in a relatively short time, algorithms will become better than the human baseline. Surprisingly enough only about 2.5 % of the videos could not be located at all. This suggests a huge potential for future research in the field even though for some of the videos, the algorithm would already pass the "Turing test" as it was already better than humans for 41 % of the videos. The analysis of human vs machine errors suggests complementarity which implies future work might be very successful when concentrating on interactive systems. For example, for humans the acoustic modality works quite well when language and speech content can be picked up. Machines are better at picking up specific sounds that might be the fingerprint of a location. Similarly, in the visual domain, humans are very good at localization based on written text, signs, architecture, and vehicle styles while machines are very good at finding specific locations that appear often enough in the training data. Humans can remember or search for specific locations based on context, while machines can pick up patterns of tags or textual descriptions that indicate the location of a specific social group unknown to most humans. In summary, all three modalities (audio, video, and text) are very powerful at determining location both for humans and the machine even though recent researches mostly have concentrated on text-based systems with the aid of visual information. Future research on location estimation might gain improved results from including optical character recognition and sign interpretation as well as language identification and language-independent keyword spotting. The use of semantic information from Gazetteers and other knowledge bases will be very helpful for locations with limited training data.

9. ACKNOWLEDGMENTS

This research is supported in part by NSF EAGER grant IIS-1128599 and KFAS Doctoral Study Abroad Fellowship. Human subjects experiments are authorized under IRB approval CPHS 2011-06-3325.

10. REFERENCES

[1] L. Cao, J. Yu, J. Luo, and T. Huang. Enhancing semantic and geographic annotation of web images via logistic canonical correlation regression. In *Proceedings of the 17th ACM international conference on Multimedia*, MM '09, pages 125–134, New York, NY, USA, 2009. ACM.

[2] S. Chatzichristofis and Y. Boutalis. Cedd: Color and edge directivity descriptor: A compact descriptor for image indexing and retrieval. *Computer Vision Systems*, pages 312–322, 2008.

[3] S. Chatzichristofis and Y. Boutalis. Fcth: Fuzzy color and texture histogram-a low level feature for accurate image retrieval. In *Image Analysis for Multimedia Interactive Services, 2008. WIAMIS'08. Ninth International Workshop on*, pages 191–196. Ieee, 2008.

[4] J. Choi, G. Friedland, V. Ekambaram, and K. Ramchandran. Multimodal location estimation of consumer media: Dealing with sparse training data. In *2012 IEEE International Conference on Multimedia and Expo (ICME)*, pages 43–48. IEEE, 2012.

[5] J. Choi, H. Lei, and G. Friedland. The 2011 ICSI Video Location Estimation System. In *Proc. of MediaEval*, 2011.

[6] D. J. Crandall, L. Backstrom, D. Huttenlocher, and J. Kleinberg. Mapping the world's photos. In *Proc. of WWW '09*, pages 761–770, New York, NY, USA, 2009. ACM.

[7] G. Friedland, J. Choi, H. Lei, and A. Janin. Multimodal Location Estimation on Flickr Videos. In *Proc. of the 2011 ACM Workshop on Social Media*, pages 23–28, Scottsdale, Arizona, USA, 2011. ACM.

[8] G. Friedland, O. Vinyals, and T. Darrell. Multimodal Location Estimation. In *Proceedings of ACM Multimedia*, pages 1245–1251, 2010.

[9] A. Gallagher, D. Joshi, J. Yu, and J. Luo. Geo-location inference from image content and user tags. In *Proceedings of IEEE CVPR*. IEEE, 2009.

[10] L. Gottlieb, J. Choi, G. Friedland, P. Kelm, and T. Sikora. Pushing the Limits of Mechanical Turk: Qualifying the Crowd for Video Geo-Location. *Proceedings of the 2012 ACM Workshop on Crowdsourcing for Multimedia (CrowdMM)*, 2012.

[11] A. Hatch, S. Kajarekar, and A. Stolcke. Within-class covariance normalization for SVM-based speaker recognition. In *Proceedings of ISCA Interspeech*, volume 4, 2006.

[12] J. Hays and A. Efros. IM2GPS: estimating geographic information from a single image. In *IEEE CVPR 2008*, pages 1–8, 2008.

[13] S. Ioffe. Probabilistic linear discriminant analysis. *Computer Vision–ECCV 2006*, pages 531–542, 2006.

[14] P. G. Ipeirotis. Analyzing the amazon mechanical turk marketplace. *XRDS*, 17(2):16–21, Dec. 2010.

[15] D. Karger, S. Oh, and D. Shah. Budget-optimal crowdsourcing using low-rank matrix approximations. In *Communication, Control, and Computing (Allerton), 2011 49th Annual Allerton Conference on*, pages 284 –291, sept. 2011.

[16] P. Kelm, S. Schmiedeke, and T. Sikora. A hierarchical, multi-modal approach for placing videos on the map using millions of flickr photographs. In *Proc. of SBNMA '11*, pages 15–20, New York, NY, USA, 2011. ACM.

[17] A. Kittur, E. H. Chi, and B. Suh. Crowdsourcing user studies with mechanical turk. In *Proceedings of the twenty-sixth annual SIGCHI conference on Human factors in computing systems*, CHI '08, pages 453–456, New York, NY, USA, 2008. ACM.

[18] O. V. Laere, S. Schockaert, and B. Dhoedt. Ghent university at the 2011 placing task. In *Proc. of MediaEval*, 2011.

[19] M. Larson, M. Soleymani, P. Serdyukov, S. Rudinac, C. Wartena, V. Murdock, G. Friedland, R. Ordelman, and G. J. Jones. Automatic Tagging and Geo-Tagging in Video Collections and Communities. In *ACM International Conference on Multimedia Retrieval (ICMR 2011)*, pages 51:1–51:8, April 2011.

[20] H. Lei, J. Choi, and G. Friedland. City-Identification on Flickr Videos Using Acoustic Features. Technical report, ICSI Technical Report TR-11-001, 2011.

[21] J. Luo, D. Joshi, J. Yu, and A. Gallagher. Geotagging in multimedia and computer vision–a survey. *Multimedia Tools Appl.*, 51:187–211, Jan. 2011.

[22] Mediaeval web site. *http://www.multimediaeval.org*.

[23] D. M. Mount and S. Arya. ANN: A library for approximate nearest neighbor searching. In *CGC 2nd Annual Fall Workshop on Computational Geometry*, pages 153–, 1997.

[24] A. Oliva and A. Torralba. Building the gist of a scene: The role of global image features in recognition. *Progress in brain research*, 155:23–36, 2006.

[25] M. C. Palmer. Calculation of distance traveled by fishing vessels using gps positional data: A theoretical evaluation of the sources of error. *Fisheries Research*, 89(1):57–64, 2008.

[26] T. Rattenbury and M. Naaman. Methods for extracting place semantics from Flickr tags. *ACM Transactions on the Web (TWEB)*, 3(1), 2009.

[27] B. Russell, A. Torralba, K. Murphy, and W. Freeman. Labelme: A database and web-based tool for image annotation. *International Journal of Computer Vision*, 77:157–173, 2008. 10.1007/s11263-007-0090-8.

[28] G. Schindler, M. Brown, and R. Szeliski. City-scale location recognition. In *IEEE Conference on Computer Vision and Pattern Recognition, 2007. CVPR'07*, pages 1–7, 2007.

[29] P. Serdyukov, V. Murdock, and R. van Zwol. Placing Flickr photos on a map. In *ACM SIGIR*, pages 484–491, 2009.

[30] M. Soufifar, M. Kockmann, L. Burget, O. Plchot, O. Glembek, and T. Svendsen. iVector approach to phonotactic language recognition. In *Proc. of Interspeech*, pages 2913–2916, 2011.

[31] H. Tamura, S. Mori, and T. Yamawaki. Textural features corresponding to visual perception. *Systems, Man and Cybernetics, IEEE Transactions on*, 8(6):460–473, 1978.

[32] M. Wainwright and M. Jordan. Graphical models, exponential families, and variational inference. *Foundations and Trends® in Machine Learning*, 1:1–305, 2008.

[33] W. Zhang and J. Kosecka. Image based localization in urban environments. In *3D Data Processing, Visualization, and Transmission, 3rd Intl. Symposium on*, pages 33–40, 2006.

Cross-Media Semantic Representation via Bi-directional Learning to Rank

Fei Wu
College of Computer Science
Zhejiang University, China
wufei@cs.zju.edu.cn

Xinyan Lu
College of Computer Science
Zhejiang University, China
xinyanlu@zju.edu.cn

Zhongfei Zhang
Department of Information Science & Electronic Engineering
Zhejiang University, China
zhongfei@zju.edu.cn

Shuicheng Yan
ECE Department
National University of Singapore, Singapore
eleyans@nus.edu.sg

Yong Rui
Microsoft Research Asia, China
yongrui@microsoft.com

Yueting Zhuang
College of Computer Science
Zhejiang University, China
yzhuang@zju.edu.cn

ABSTRACT

In multimedia information retrieval, most classic approaches tend to represent different modalities of media in the same feature space. Existing approaches take either one-to-one paired data or uni-directional ranking examples (i.e., utilizing only text-query-image ranking examples or image-query-text ranking examples) as training examples, which do not make full use of bi-directional ranking examples (*bi-directional ranking* means that both text-query-image and image-query-text ranking examples are utilized in the training period) to achieve a better performance. In this paper, we consider learning a cross-media representation model from the perspective of optimizing a listwise ranking problem while taking advantage of bi-directional ranking examples. We propose a general cross-media ranking algorithm to optimize the bi-directional listwise ranking loss with a latent space embedding, which we call Bi-directional Cross-Media Semantic Representation Model (Bi-CMSRM). The latent space embedding is discriminatively learned by the structural large margin learning for optimization with certain ranking criteria (mean average precision in this paper) directly. We evaluate Bi-CMSRM on the Wikipedia and NUS-WIDE datasets and show that the utilization of the bi-directional ranking examples achieves a much better performance than only using the uni-directional ranking examples.

Categories and Subject Descriptors

H.3.3 [**Information Search and Retrieval**]: Retrieval Models

http://dx.doi.org/10.1145/2502081.2502097.

Keywords

Cross-Media Representation; Bi-directional Learning to Rank; Latent Space Embedding

1. INTRODUCTION

Nowadays, many real-world applications involve multi-modal data. Cross-media retrieval is imperative to many applications of practical interest, such as finding relevant textual documents of a tourist spot that best match a given image of the spot or finding a set of images that visually best illustrate a given text description [32, 29]. However, the *heterogeneity-gap* between multi-modal data has been widely understood as a fundamental barrier to successful cross-media retrieval. To reduce this gap, one way is to map the multi-modal data into a common feature space, with then the retrieval procedure conducted in the newly mapped space. For example, automatic annotation translates the images from the image space into the text space to support the image retrieval from text queries.

In recent years, there has been a great deal of research devoted to the development of algorithms for learning an optimal common representation of different modalities. These popular approaches map the data of multiple modalities into a common (or shared) space such that the distance between two similar objects is minimized, while the distance between two dissimilar objects is maximized. One kind of approaches exploits the symbiosis of multiple-modality data which are strictly one-to-one paired. Data with multi-modal symbiosis are pervasive to describe the rich literal and visual semantics, such as a web image with loosely related narrative text descriptions, and a news report with collateral text and images. Methods like Canonical Correlation Analysis (CCA) [12] and its extensions as well as the extensions of Latent Dirichlet Allocation (LDA) [5] fall into this category.

Different from the aforementioned category of approaches which do not maximize a criterion related to the ultimate retrieval performance, another direction of approaches is based on the techniques of learning to rank. These approaches (e.g., [10, 23, 2]) are supervised but do not enforce a strict assumption that the trained multi-modal data must be paired (e.g., one image is in pair-correspondence with its collateral text). They actually require some rankings of the data related to the queries for training, where the training examples can be easily obtained from the abundance of users' clickthrough data with little overhead [18, 9]. In this way, the learned representation for ranking multimodal data is generally optimized based on a ranking-based loss function (evaluation criterion) to preserve the order of the relevance instead of the purely absolute similarity (dis-similarity) values between multi-modal data. However, these approaches either project the images into the text space which cannot be applied to the text document retrieval from image queries, e.g., [10, 23], or they learn a common latent space for both text and imagery while only considering uni-directional ranking examples, e.g., [2]. All the above ranking-based methods optimize only one direction of the retrieval task (image-query-text or text-query-image); thus, when bi-directional training examples are available, two different models must be individually learned, each optimizing one direction of training examples. We argue that such approaches not only add unnecessary complexity and overhead, but more importantly lead to a worse performance than directly considering and optimizing bi-directional training examples.

We focus on the retrieval of cross-media data in this paper. Moreover, we aim to learn a latent space which can be applied to both image-query-text retrieval and text-query-image retrieval, assuming bi-directional ranking examples available for training. We also consider the learned space as a latent semantic space, in which two data objects with similar semantics are close to each other. The latent space is constrained to be a low-dimensional space since the intrinsic dimensionality of a semantic space is usually much lower than that of original feature space. We note that learning a latent semantic space is particularly appropriate for retrieval with long queries/documents, where a long search query (e.g., a whole document) is beneficial as users' intents can be described in detail [30].

This paper aims to bridge the gap between learning a latent space and the retrieval of cross-media data, especially taking bi-directional ranking examples into account, which can be seen as an extension of [22]. We consider the problem of learning a latent cross-media representation from the perspective of a listwise ranking problem in this paper. We propose a general cross-media ranking algorithm to optimize the listwise ranking loss while considering a latent space embedding and bi-directional ranking examples, called Bi-directional Cross-Media Semantic Representation Model (Bi-CMSRM). Bi-CMSRM employs the structural SVM [28] to support the optimization of various ranking evaluation measures (e.g., MAP [31] and NDCG [6]) under a unified algorithmic framework. Bi-CMSRM also incorporates a latent space embedding in the learning procedure in which the latent aspect space is induced to address the curse of dimensionality and to discover the correlations between different modalities. Moreover, Bi-CMSRM takes bi-directional ranking examples into account by which two directions of retrieval tasks are optimized simultaneously, yielding a better representation for multi-modal data.

It is worthwhile to highlight the main differences between the proposed method and the existing methods. The proposed method benefits from both the latent space embedding and the most recent advances in learning to rank techniques.

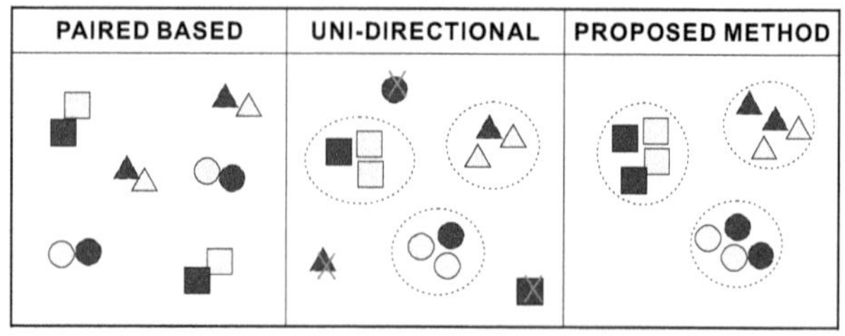

Figure 1: A simple demonstration of the latent spaces learned by different approaches. The same shape indicates relevant semantics. Colors represent modalities (i.e., text and imagery). The paired-based methods like CCA try to unite paired samples only. The uni-directional-ranking-based methods like PAMIR and SSI only capture the relationship between two modalities from one direction of retrieval but their generalization performances are limited since they do not capture the latent structure of the query modality, which is represented as blue queries with red cross in the figure. The proposed method Bi-CMSRM is trained with bi-directional training examples by which it can be applied to both directions of retrieval and the generalization performance is improved.

Moreover, the learned model considers the bi-directional ranking examples. As shown in Figure 1, the paired based methods like CCA try to unite paired samples only, which do not optimize the ultimate retrieval performance; the uni-directional-ranking based methods like PAMIR [10] and SSI [2] train asymmetric models, which cannot capture the latent structure of the query modality. To see this, assuming that we are given a corresponding image set related to a text query, the relevant images are pairwise close in semantics since they are all relevant to the same text query; thus, the latent structure of the image modality is explored. However, there is not much information about the semantics of the text query. When a new text query comes, it may not be mapped to the place near the semantics-similar text queries, and the generalization performance is limited. By this consideration, Bi-CMSRM is trained with bi-directional ranking examples such that not only both text and imagery are projected into the same semantic space such that a single learned model can be applied to both directions of retrieval, but also the performances of the two directions of retrieval are both improved.

We show experimental results on the retrieval performance of cross-media data obtained from two real-world datasets. The proposed Bi-CMSRM outperforms the existing cross-media retrieval approaches, especially in the case of the text modality with a lot of words. We also compare Bi-CMSRM with Uni-CMSRM which is trained only with uni-directional training examples, demonstrating that the utilization of bi-directional training examples does help achieve a better cross-media representation.

The rest of this paper is organized as follows. Section 2 discusses related work. In Section 3, we describe the method in detail and show its feasibility. We compare the proposed Bi-CMSRM with the existing cross-media retrieval approaches on two real-world datasets in Section 4. Conclusions are given at the end.

2. RELATED WORK

To perform cross-media retrieval, the typical method of bridging the semantic gap is through the automatic image annotation. The approaches of image annotation can be roughly classified into the generative models and the discriminative models. The generative models learn a joint distribution over image features and annotation tags. To annotate a new image, a learned generative model computes the conditional probability over tags given the visual features [4]. On the other hand, the discriminative models train a separate classifier from visual features for each tag. These classifiers are used to predict particular tags for test image samples [7].

As one of the most popular approaches to find a pair of linear transformations to maximize the correlations between two variables, Canonical Correlation Analysis (CCA) [15] and its extensions are applied in cross-media retrieval. For example, after the maximally correlated subspaces of text and image features are obtained by CCA, a logistic regression is employed to cross-media retrieval in [25]. As a supervised kernelizable extension of CCA, Generalized Multiview Analysis [27] is conducted to map data in different modality spaces to a single (non)linear subspace. Motivated by the fact that dictionary learning (DL) methods have the intrinsic power of capturing the heterogeneous features by generating different dictionaries for multi-modal data, multi-modal dictionary learning has been recently applied to cross-media retrieval [16, 24]. Following the seminal work of Blei *et al.* [5], LDA has been extended to learn the joint distribution of multi-modal data (e.g., text and imagery) such as Multi-modal Document Random Field [17]. LDA-based methods assume that the paired multi-modal data should share the same latent topic proportion.

The aforementioned approaches, either optimizing the similarity (distance) between pairs of samples or optimizing the likelihood of the topic models, do not optimize the ultimate retrieval performance directly. While bearing a resemblance to multi-modal representation learning which aims at preserving the similarity or the distance measure from multi-modal data, multi-modal ranking functions are generally optimized by an evaluation criterion or a loss function defined over the *permutation* space induced by the scoring function over the target documents.

Different from the classical *uni*-modal learning to rank techniques, to the best of our knowledge, Passive-Aggressive Model for Image Retrieval (PAMIR) is the first attempt to address the problem of ranking images by text queries directly [10]. PAMIR formulates the cross-media retrieval problem in a way similar to RankSVM and derives an efficient training procedure by adapting the Passive-Aggressive algorithm.

The authors of [23] studied metric learning as a problem of learning to rank. They presented a general metric learning algorithm MLR based on the structural SVM, to learn a metric such that the ranking of the data induced by the distance from a query can be optimized against various ranking measures. Different from Bi-CMSRM, both PAMIR and MLR optimize only uni-directional ranking examples and do not induce an intermediate latent space (e.g., the images are translated from the image space to the text space) such that the trained model is not applicable for the reverse direction of cross-media retrieval.

The text and imagery are usually represented as BoW and BoVW in a high-dimensional vector space respectively. However, the high-dimensional vector space representation suffers from its inability to cope with two classic problems, i.e., synonymy and polysemy. To capture the latent semantic associations of data and to address these problems, embedding words in a low-dimensional latent space to capture the semantics is a classic approach in text retrieval such as Latent Semantic Indexing (LSI) [8] and pLSA [14]. The idea of latent space embedding is also introduced into Supervised Semantic Indexing (SSI) originally proposed for cross-lingual retrieval [2]. SSI defines a set of linear low-rank models to take into account correlations between words (synonymy and polysemy). Related to SSI, Polynomial Semantic Indexing (PSI) [3] generalizes and extends the SSI approach to general polynomial models which could be used to capture the higher-order relationships among words. When SSI and PSI are applied to cross-media retrieval, they suffer from the uni-directional training examples despite inducing the latent space as mentioned before: first, the latent space is fully optimized for one direction of retrieval while the other direction is ignored; second, the generalization performance is limited. The Latent Semantic Cross-Modal Ranking algorithm [22], that optimizes for latent space embedding and direct ranking loss which we will build upon, still suffers from the above problem, i.e., only one direction of retrieval is optimized.

3. THE ALGORITHM OF BI-CMSRM

The proposed method Bi-CMSRM learns a general cross-media representation in the sense that it maps the two types of cross-media data into the same common space in which both directions of image-query-text retrieval and text-query-image retrieval can be applied. The training examples of Bi-CMSRM may cover the two directions of retrieval simultaneously, i.e., some examples are text queries with corresponding rankings of images while the other examples are image queries with corresponding rankings of text documents.

3.1 Notation

In this work, all vectors are assumed to be column vectors and a superscript T denotes the transpose of a matrix or vector. Denote m as the dimension of the text feature space (e.g., vocabulary size of bag-of-words (BoW)) and n as the dimension of the image feature space (e.g., vocabulary size of bag-of-visual-words (BoVW) quantized by clustering the low-level visual features such as SIFT [21]). We are given a training set of $N + M$ examples, with N text-query examples and M image-query examples. A query q here may be either an image p or a text document t. Similarly, the set of retrieved documents $\mathbf{d}$ can be either an image set $\mathbf{p}$ or a text document set $\mathbf{t}$. Each text-query example contains a text query $t_i \in \mathbb{R}^m$ $(i = 1, \dots, N)$, a set of corresponding retrieved images $\mathbf{p}_i$, as well as the true rankings over the image set $\mathbf{y}_i^* \in \mathcal{Y}$, where $\mathcal{Y}$ denotes the set of all possible permutations (rankings). Similarly, each image-query example contains an image query $p_j \in \mathbb{R}^n$ $(j = N+1, \dots, N+M)$, a set of corresponding retrieved text documents $\mathbf{t}_j$, as well as the true rankings over the text document set $\mathbf{y}_j^* \in \mathcal{Y}$. For simplicity, we omit the subscripts i and j denoting the order of a training example $(q,\mathbf{d},\mathbf{y})$ in the case where the formulation can be applied to every training example.

We denote a ranking as a matrix of pair orderings as is done in [31], $\mathcal{Y} \subset \{-1, 0, +1\}^{|\mathbf{d}| \times |\mathbf{d}|}$ where the operator $|\cdot|$ denotes the number of the elements in a set. For any $\mathbf{y} \in \mathcal{Y}$, $y_{ij} = +1$ if document d_i is ranked ahead of document d_j, and $y_{ij} = -1$ if d_j is ranked ahead of d_i, and $y_{ij} = 0$ if d_i and d_j have an equal rank. We consider only matrices corresponding to valid rankings, i.e., obeying antisymmetry and transitivity. In this paper, we assume that the true rankings are weak rankings with two rank values (*relevant* and *irrelevant*). For any query q, let $\mathbf{d}^+$ and $\mathbf{d}^-$ denote the set of relevant and irrelevant documents in $\mathbf{d}$, respectively. For example, the set of relevant text documents is denoted as $\mathbf{t}^+$ and the set of irrelevant documents as $\mathbf{t}^-$.

3.2 The Linear Mapping Functions

Motivated by the idea of latent space embedding, we would like to learn the linear mapping functions which map the text and imagery into a common latent space respectively, in which a text document and an image with similar semantics are close to each other.

Given a text $t \in \mathbb{R}^m$ and an image $p \in \mathbb{R}^n$, we consider a linear similarity function to measure the relevance between t and p:

$$f(t, p) = (Ut)^T Vp \qquad (1)$$

where $U \in \mathbb{R}^{k \times m}$ and $V \in \mathbb{R}^{k \times n}$. U refers to mapping the text t from the m-dimensional text space to the k-dimensional latent space by a liner mapping, and V refers to mapping the image p from the n-dimensional image space to the k-dimensional latent space. Therefore, the text and the image are mapped to a common k-dimensional latent *aspect* space, and then their similarity is measured by a dot product of the two vectors in the k-dimensional space, which is commonly used to measure the matching between textual vectors [1].

Intuitively, the linear model in Equation (1) helps deal with the problem of textual/visual *synonymy* and *polysemy* which particularly occur in both the text space and the image space. Note that Latent Semantic Indexing (LSI) [8] takes into account of the correlations between textual words (synonym and polysemy) in a single modality in an unsupervised manner, while the linear model in Equation (1) attempts to capture the correlation across two different modalities from a supervised manner. By constraining the form of Equation (1), the benefits are similar to LSI: U and V not only induce a k-dimensional latent aspect space but are also faster to compute and lead to much smaller storage by representing the imagery and text in the k dimensions than their original dimensions (k is chosen much smaller than m or n). Similar to [2], here U and V are different and there is no assumption that the text and the imagery should be embedded to the latent space in the same way. This is appealing to cross-media representation since the distributions of the text and the imagery are inherently different due to the heterogeneity-gap.

The rest is to learn U and V. We consider learning U and V from a supervised manner, especially from both directions of training examples, i.e., the ranking of images corresponding to a given text query and the ranking of text documents corresponding to a given image query. Note that the similarity function f can also be considered a ranking function: given a text query t and a set of images $\mathbf{q}$ in the other modality, the ranking prediction $\mathbf{y}$ is derived simply by sorting the documents in $\mathbf{q}$ by descending values of $f(t, p)$: $y_{ij} = 1$ if $f(t, p_i) > f(t, p_j)$ and $y_{ij} = -1$ otherwise. Thus, we aim to obtain the values of U and V by minimizing the following empirical ranking risk,

$$R^{\Delta}(f) = \frac{1}{N}\sum_{i=1}^{N} \Delta(\mathbf{y}_i^*, \mathbf{y}_i) + \frac{1}{M}\sum_{j=N+1}^{N+M} \Delta(\mathbf{y}_j^*, \mathbf{y}_j), \qquad (2)$$

where the non-negative loss function $\Delta : \mathcal{Y} \times \mathcal{Y} \to \mathbb{R}$ quantifies the penalty for making prediction $\mathbf{y}$ if the correct output is $\mathbf{y}^*$. The value of Δ is typically bounded in $[0, 1]$. For example, we define the loss function Δ with the average precision (AP, defined in Equation (15)) loss as follows:

$$\Delta_{ap}(\mathbf{y}^*, \mathbf{y}) = 1 - \text{AP}(\text{rank}(\mathbf{y}^*), \text{rank}(\mathbf{y})),$$

and then to minimize the empirical risk is to maximize the Mean Average Precision (MAP). Consequently, we can solve the problem of *learning to rank* to learn the cross-media representation which optimizes certain ranking criteria. Furthermore, note that one can optimize different ranking criteria by considering different ranking loss functions Δ.

3.3 The Formulation of Bi-CMSRM

In this section, we present the formulation of Bi-CMSRM in details. The proposed Bi-CMSRM is based on the structural SVM framework [28]. The motivation of Bi-CMSRM is to learn a cross-media ranking function $h : \mathcal{X} \to \mathcal{Y}$ between an input space $\mathcal{X}$ (a query q as well as all target retrieved documents $\mathbf{d}$) and an output space $\mathcal{Y}$ (rankings over the retrieved document set). Similar to the structural SVM, we derive a prediction by finding the ranking $\mathbf{y}$ that maximizes the following discriminant function h:

$$h(q, \mathbf{d}) = \text{argmax}_{\mathbf{y} \in \mathcal{Y}} F(q, \mathbf{d}, \mathbf{y}; U, V), \qquad (3)$$

where F is considered a compatibility function parameterized by U, V that measures how compatible the triple $(q, \mathbf{d}, \mathbf{y})$ is.

We first consider only one direction of the retrieval, i.e., ranking images from text queries. By adapting the most commonly used feature representation combined with *partial order* in [19] to the cross-media ranking, we define the compatible function as:

$$F(t, \mathbf{p}, \mathbf{y}) = \sum_{i \in \mathbf{p}^+} \sum_{j \in \mathbf{p}^-} y_{ij} \frac{(Ut)^T V(p_i - p_j)}{|\mathbf{p}^+| \cdot |\mathbf{p}^-|}, \qquad (4)$$

where for any $\mathbf{y} \in \mathcal{Y}$, $y_{ij} = +1$ if image p_i is preferred (more relevant to the text query t) to image p_j, and $y_{ij} = -1$ otherwise since we assume that the predicted rankings are complete (thus for the true ranking $\mathbf{y}^*$, y_{ij} are all $+1$). Note that the summation is over all the relevant/irrelevant document pairs since we assume that the true rankings are weak rankings and we only care about the relative ranking position between a relevant document and an irrelevant document.

One attractive property of F is that for the fixed U and V, the ranking $\mathbf{y}$ which maximizes function F (then the predicted ranking) is simply sorted by descending $f(t, p) = (Ut)^T Vp$. To see this, recall that F is a summation over all the relevant/irrelevant document pairs since we assume weak rankings with two rank values. Since F decomposes linearly over the pairwise representation, we maximize F by optimizing each y_{ij} individually: if $(Ut)^T Vp_i > (Ut)^T Vp_j$, y_{ij} is set to be 1, and $y_{ij} = -1$ otherwise. This is the same procedure as sorting documents by descending $f(t, p)$.

More details can be obtained from [19]. We note that this simple prediction rule establishes a connection between the compatibility function F and the aforementioned similarity function f.

Since U and V are independent of the summation in Equation (4), we rewrite F as a linear function of U^TV:

$$F(t, \mathbf{p}, \mathbf{y}) = < U^T V, \Psi(t, \mathbf{p}, \mathbf{y}) > \quad (5)$$

where

$$\Psi(t, \mathbf{p}, \mathbf{y}) = t \sum_{i \in \mathbf{p}^+} \sum_{j \in \mathbf{p}^-} y_{ij} \frac{p_i^T - p_j^T}{|\mathbf{p}^+| \cdot |\mathbf{p}^-|} \,. \quad (6)$$

Here the combined feature function $\Psi(t, \mathbf{p}, \mathbf{y})$ is a summation over the vector differences of all the relevant/irrelevant image pairs. By representing the scoring F as a Frobenius inner product of U^TV and Ψ, we see that it is straightforward to extend the idea of the structural SVM to learn the cross-media ranking function F.

For the purpose of learning to rank, the structural SVM takes a set of vector-valued features which characterize the relationship between the input query and a set of target documents as the input, and predicts a ranking $\mathbf{y} \in \mathcal{Y}$ of the target documents. The structural SVM is applied to maximize the margins between the true ranking $\mathbf{y}^*$ and all the other possible rankings $\mathbf{y}$. In this paper, Bi-CMSRM takes cross-media ranking into consideration, for $i = 1, \ldots, N$:

$$\forall \mathbf{y} \in \mathcal{Y} : \delta F(t_i, \mathbf{p}_i, \mathbf{y}) \geq \Delta(\mathbf{y}_i^*, \mathbf{y}) - \xi_{1,i} \quad (7)$$

where for compactness, we define

$$\delta F(t_i, \mathbf{p}_i, \mathbf{y}) = F(t_i, \mathbf{p}_i, \mathbf{y}_i^*) - F(t_i, \mathbf{p}_i, \mathbf{y}) \,.$$

Similarly, consider the other direction of the retrieval, i.e., ranking text documents from image queries. To apply structural SVM, the process is analogous. Define the compatible function:

$$F(p, \mathbf{t}, \mathbf{y}) = \sum_{i \in \mathbf{t}^+} \sum_{j \in \mathbf{t}^-} y_{ij} \frac{(Vp)^T U (t_i - t_j)}{|\mathbf{t}^+| \cdot |\mathbf{t}^-|} \,, \quad (8)$$

rewrite F as a linear function of V^TU:

$$F(p, \mathbf{t}, \mathbf{y}) = < V^T U, \Psi(p, \mathbf{t}, \mathbf{y}) > \quad (9)$$

where

$$\Psi(p, \mathbf{t}, \mathbf{y}) = p \sum_{i \in \mathbf{t}^+} \sum_{j \in \mathbf{t}^-} y_{ij} \frac{t_i^T - t_j^T}{|\mathbf{t}^+| \cdot |\mathbf{t}^-|} \quad (10)$$

and consider maximizing the margins for $j = N+1, \ldots, N+M$:

$$\forall \mathbf{y} \in \mathcal{Y} : \delta F(p_j, \mathbf{t}_j, \mathbf{y}) \geq \Delta(\mathbf{y}_j^*, \mathbf{y}) - \xi_{2,j} \quad (11)$$

where for compactness, we define

$$\delta F(p_j, \mathbf{t}_j, \mathbf{y}) = F(p_j, \mathbf{t}_j, \mathbf{y}_j^*) - F(p_j, \mathbf{t}_j, \mathbf{y}) \,.$$

Since we assume that the text and the imagery are embedded into a common latent space, respectively, Bi-CMSRM adapts the original structural SVM to learn the optimal U^* and V^* which maximize the margins between the true ranking and all the other possible rankings of the target documents for each query in the other modality. Hence, we replace the standard quadratic regularization $\frac{\lambda}{2}\|w\|_2^2$ with $\frac{\lambda}{2}\|U\|_F^2 + \frac{\lambda}{2}\|V\|_F^2$ where $\|\cdot\|_F$ denotes the Frobenius norm. Intuitively, this extension simplifies the model complexity, thereby promoting a better generalization performance.

The optimization problem is then presented as follows:

Optimization Problem 1.

$$\min_{U,V,\xi_1,\xi_2} \frac{\lambda}{2}\|U\|_F^2 + \frac{\lambda}{2}\|V\|_F^2 + \frac{1}{N}\sum_{i=1}^{N} \xi_{1,i} + \frac{1}{M}\sum_{j=N+1}^{N+M} \xi_{2,j}$$

$$\begin{aligned} s.t. \quad & \forall i \in \{1, \ldots, N\}, \forall \mathbf{y} \in \mathcal{Y} : \\ & \quad \delta F(t_i, \mathbf{p}_i, \mathbf{y}) \geq \Delta(\mathbf{y}_i^*, \mathbf{y}) - \xi_{1,i} \quad (12) \\ & \forall j \in \{N+1, \ldots, N+M\}, \forall \mathbf{y} \in \mathcal{Y} : \\ & \quad \delta F(p_j, \mathbf{t}_j, \mathbf{y}) \geq \Delta(\mathbf{y}_j^*, \mathbf{y}) - \xi_{2,j} \,. \quad (13) \end{aligned}$$

For each text-query example $(t, \mathbf{p}, \mathbf{y})$ and each image-query example $(p, \mathbf{t}, \mathbf{y})$ in the training set, a set of constraints (12) and (13) are added to the optimization problem. To see how these constraints indeed work, note that during the prediction, the model chooses the ranking $\bar{\mathbf{y}}$ which maximizes $F(q, \mathbf{d}, \mathbf{y})$ given the fixed U and V. If the predicted ranking is an incorrect ranking $\bar{\mathbf{y}}$, i.e., $F(q, \mathbf{d}, \bar{\mathbf{y}}) > F(q, \mathbf{d}, \mathbf{y}^*)$ where $\mathbf{y}^*$ is the true ranking, the corresponding slack variable ξ must be at least $\Delta(\mathbf{y}^*, \bar{\mathbf{y}})$ to satisfy the constraint. Considering all the triples $(t_i, \mathbf{p}_i, \mathbf{y}_i)$ for $i = 1, \ldots, N$ and $(p_j, \mathbf{t}_j, \mathbf{y}_j)$ for $j = N+1, \ldots, N+M$, the weighted sum of slacks (i.e., $\frac{1}{N}\sum_{i=1}^{N} \xi_{1,i} + \frac{1}{M}\sum_{j=N+1}^{N+M} \xi_{2,j}$) upper-bounds the empirical risk $R^{\Delta}(f)$ defined in Equation (2). This is stated formally in Proposition 1.

Proposition 1. *Denote by $\xi_1^*(U,V)$ and $\xi_2^*(U,V)$ the optimal solution of the slack variables in Optimization Problem 1 for the given parameters U and V. Then the weighted sum of slacks $\frac{1}{N}\sum_{i=1}^{N} \xi_{1,i}^* + \frac{1}{M}\sum_{j=N+1}^{N+M} \xi_{2,j}^*$ is an upper bound on the empirical risk $R^{\Delta}(f)$.*

Similar to SVM, to avoid overfitting, the objective function of Optimization Problem 1 to be minimized is a tradeoff between the model complexity and a hinge loss relaxation of Δ loss. A pre-chosen value of parameter λ controls this tradeoff and can be tuned to achieve a good performance via the validation procedure over a validation set. Similarly, a pre-chosen row number k of U and V representing the dimensionality of the latent semantic space is determined by the validation procedure.

Note that by exploring the latent semantics property, the optimization problem is not convex. The well-known *kernel trick* is difficult to be applied to Optimization Problem 1, while the kernel trick is considered one of the main benefits of the traditional support vector machine. Fortunately, a linear-SVM without using kernels has been shown to give competitive performances for textual document classification [13]. On the other hand, according to the cross-media retrieval approach PAMIR [10], a linear mapping of BoVW yields the highest performance of the other kernel mappings. As a result, with the multi-modal data under a certain feature representation, we argue that the model can indeed capture the linear structures of the multi-modal data to learn a cross-media semantic representation.

3.4 Algorithm and Implementation

Since $|\mathcal{Y}|$ is super-exponential in the size of the training set, our algorithm for learning U and V is adapted from the 1-slack margin-rescaling cutting-plane algorithm of Joachims *et al.* [20]. The algorithm alternates between two steps, one optimizing the model parameters (U and V in our case) and the other updating the constraints set with a new batch of rankings $(\hat{\mathbf{y}}_1, \ldots, \hat{\mathbf{y}}_N, \hat{\mathbf{y}}_{N+1}, \ldots, \hat{\mathbf{y}}_{N+M})$ that are violated the most by the current model, where $\hat{\mathbf{y}}_i$ $(i = 1, \ldots, N)$ is one ranking for one text-query example, and $\hat{\mathbf{y}}_j$ $(j = N+1, \ldots, N+M)$ is one ranking for one image-query example. Once reaching a stopping criterion based on the accuracy of the empirical risk, the algorithm terminates, where the new constraint batch's empirical risk is no more than that of the current set of constraints within a tolerance $\epsilon > 0$.

Algorithm 1 Bi-directional Cross-Media Semantic Representation Model (Bi-CMSRM).

Input: text-query examples $(t_i, \mathbf{p}_i, \mathbf{y}_i^*), i = 1, \ldots, N$, image-query examples $(p_j, \mathbf{t}_j, \mathbf{y}_j^*), j = N+1, \ldots, N+M$, trade-off control parameter $\lambda > 0$, accuracy tolerance threshold $\epsilon > 0$

Output: mapping parameters U and V, slack variables $\xi_1 \geq 0$ and $\xi_2 \geq 0$

1: $\mathcal{W}_1 \leftarrow \emptyset$, $\mathcal{W}_2 \leftarrow \emptyset$

2: **repeat**

3: Solve for the optimal U, V and slack ξ_1, ξ_2:

$$\min_{U,V,\xi_1,\xi_2} \frac{\lambda}{2}\|U\|_F^2 + \frac{\lambda}{2}\|V\|_F^2 + \xi_1 + \xi_2$$

$$\text{s.t.} \quad \forall(\mathbf{y}_1, \ldots, \mathbf{y}_N) \in \mathcal{W}_1 :$$

$$\frac{1}{N}\sum_{i=1}^{N} \delta F(t_i, \mathbf{p}_i, \mathbf{y}_i) \geq \frac{1}{N}\sum_{i=1}^{N} \Delta(\mathbf{y}_i^*, \mathbf{y}_i) - \xi_1$$

$$\forall(\mathbf{y}_{N+1}, \ldots, \mathbf{y}_{N+M}) \in \mathcal{W}_2 :$$

$$\frac{1}{M}\sum_{j=N+1}^{N+M} \delta F(p_j, \mathbf{t}_j, \mathbf{y}_j) \geq \frac{1}{M}\sum_{j=N+1}^{N+M} \Delta(\mathbf{y}_j^*, \mathbf{y}_j) - \xi_2$$

4: **for** $i = 1$ **to** N **do**

5: $\hat{\mathbf{y}}_i \leftarrow \operatorname{argmax}_{\mathbf{y} \in \mathcal{Y}} \Delta(\mathbf{y}_i^*, \mathbf{y}) + F(t_i, \mathbf{p}_i, \mathbf{y})$

6: **end for**

7: $\mathcal{W}_1 \leftarrow \mathcal{W}_1 \cup (\hat{\mathbf{y}}_1, \ldots, \hat{\mathbf{y}}_N)$

8: **for** $j = N+1$ **to** $N+M$ **do**

9: $\hat{\mathbf{y}}_j \leftarrow \operatorname{argmax}_{\mathbf{y} \in \mathcal{Y}} \Delta(\mathbf{y}_j^*, \mathbf{y}) + F(p_j, \mathbf{t}_j, \mathbf{y})$

10: **end for**

11: $\mathcal{W}_2 \leftarrow \mathcal{W}_2 \cup (\hat{\mathbf{y}}_{N+1}, \ldots, \hat{\mathbf{y}}_{N+M})$

12: **until**

$$\frac{1}{N}\sum_{i=1}^{N} \Delta(\mathbf{y}_i^*, \hat{\mathbf{y}}_i) - \frac{1}{N}\sum_{i=1}^{N} \delta F(t_i, \mathbf{p}_i, \hat{\mathbf{y}}_i) \leq \xi_1 + \epsilon$$

and

$$\frac{1}{M}\sum_{j=N+1}^{N+M} \Delta(\mathbf{y}_j^*, \hat{\mathbf{y}}_j) - \frac{1}{M}\sum_{j=N+1}^{N+M} \delta F(p_j, \mathbf{t}_i, \hat{\mathbf{y}}_i) \leq \xi_2 + \epsilon$$

13: **return** U, V, ξ_1, ξ_2;

The general optimization procedure of Bi-CMSRM is listed in Algorithm 1. To solve the optimization problem in Algorithm 1, there are two key issues to resolve. One is searching for the most violated constraints, the so-called *separation oracle*, in Step 5 and Step 9. For different loss functions $\Delta(\mathbf{y}^*, \mathbf{y})$, different methods are proposed to address this issue, for example, [19] for AUC loss (defined as $1 - \text{AUC}(\mathbf{y}^*, \mathbf{y})$) and [31] for MAP loss. Recalling that F can be written as a Frobenius inner product, their work [19, 31] can be easily applied to this algorithm with minor modifications in the implementation to reduce the computational complexity.

The other key issue is to solve the optimization problem in Step 3. Since the problem is not a convex problem, the parameters U and V are initialized with their previous (local) optimal values while in the beginning they are randomly initialized using a normal distribution with mean zero and standard deviation one. We have implemented a subgradient descent solver adapted from Pegasos algorithm [26] originally proposed for solving a traditional support vector machine. The Pegasos algorithm is a simple iterative algorithm which alternates between stochastic subgradient descent and projection steps, and is shown to be effective to solve the primal problem of SVM. In the problem, the subgradient descent is performed iteratively where each iteration picks the most violated ranking tuple $(\hat{\mathbf{y}}_1, \hat{\mathbf{y}}_2, \ldots, \hat{\mathbf{y}}_N)$ from the set $\mathcal{W}_1$ and $(\hat{\mathbf{y}}_{N+1}, \hat{\mathbf{y}}_{N+2}, \ldots, \hat{\mathbf{y}}_{N+M})$ from the set $\mathcal{W}_2$ simultaneously to minimize the slack variables.

On iteration t, the update for U is given by:

$$U_{t+\frac{1}{2}} \leftarrow (1 - \eta_t\lambda)U_t + \frac{\eta_t}{N}\sum_{i=1}^{N} V_t(\delta\Psi(t_i, \mathbf{p}_i, \hat{\mathbf{y}}_i))^T + \frac{\eta_t}{M}\sum_{j=N+1}^{N+M} V_t\delta\Psi(p_j, \mathbf{t}_j, \hat{\mathbf{y}}_j)$$

where $\delta\Psi(t_i, \mathbf{p}_i, \hat{\mathbf{y}}_i)$ is defined as $\Psi(t_i, \mathbf{p}_i, \mathbf{y}_i^*) - \Psi(t_i, \mathbf{p}_i, \hat{\mathbf{y}}_i)$, $\delta\Psi(p_j, \mathbf{t}_j, \hat{\mathbf{y}}_j)$ defined as $\Psi(p_j, \mathbf{t}_j, \mathbf{y}_j^*) - \Psi(p_j, \mathbf{t}_j, \hat{\mathbf{y}}_j)$, and η_t is the learning rate on iteration t which is adjustable. U_{t+1} is obtained by projecting $U_{t+\frac{1}{2}}$ onto the set for acceleration (see [26] and [11]):

$$B = \{U : \|U\|_F \leq 1/\sqrt{\lambda}\}. \tag{14}$$

The update for V can be derived similarly except for the most violated ranking tuple which is computed using the updated U_{t+1}. The update is calculated exactly as given by:

$$V_{t+\frac{1}{2}} \leftarrow (1 - \eta_t\lambda)V_t + \frac{\eta_t}{N}\sum_{i=1}^{N} U_{t+1}\delta\Psi(t_i, \mathbf{p}_i, \hat{\mathbf{y}}_i) + \frac{\eta_t}{M}\sum_{j=N+1}^{N+M} U_{t+1}(\delta\Psi(p_j, \mathbf{t}_j, \hat{\mathbf{y}}_j))^T$$

followed by the projection step (14).

Moreover, our problem is a bit different from [26]: the objective function is penalized by $\frac{\lambda}{2}(\|U\|_F^2 + \|V\|_F^2)$ to control the model perplexity. It should be noted that the optimal U and V must satisfy the condition $\|U\|_F = \|V\|_F$ since the prediction rule uses the product U^TV only. Thus after each subgradient descent, the updated U and V are forced to be multiplied by a constant respectively to ensure $\|U\|_F =$

Table 1: The statistics of the datasets used.

	Wikipedia	NUS-WIDE
BoVW vocabulary size	1,000	500
BoW vocabulary size	5,000	1,000
Avg. # of words/image	**117.5**	**7.73**
Documents Partition[a]	1,500/500 866	2,664/23,977 106,567
Queries Partition[a]	1,500/500 866	2,664/2,000 2,000

[a] Partitions are ordered by training/validation/test.

$\|V\|_F$ while keeping $\|U^T V\|_F$ fixed. Let $\alpha = \sqrt{\|U\|_F \|V\|_F}$,

$$U \leftarrow \alpha U / \|U\|_F ,$$
$$V \leftarrow \alpha V / \|V\|_F .$$

The experiments show that this strategy yields a much faster convergence rate. For fixing tolerance $\epsilon = 0.01$, the loop in Algorithm 1 usually terminates within 200 iterations.

4. EXPERIMENTS AND RESULTS

The main goal of the experiments is to evaluate the effectiveness of the proposed Bi-CMSRM approach. To show its competitive performance, Bi-CMSRM is compared with the other three state-of-the-art approaches (CCA, PAMIR and SSI) for cross-media retrieval. These comparative methods are elaborately chosen for fair comparisons. Comparing with the classical CCA method aims to test Bi-CMSRM's ability to learn a useful latent space; PAMIR has been shown to outperform PLSA and SVM [10]; however it is designed specifically for one direction of the retrieval; SSI introduces the similar parameterizations to that of Bi-CMSRM while it takes only uni-directional training examples as the input. We further highlight the advantages of considering the bi-directional ranking examples by comparing the proposed Bi-CMSRM with Uni-CMSRM (i.e., only the uni-directional ranking examples are available with only one direction of retrieval optimized).

4.1 Experimental Setup

4.1.1 Datasets

Two public real-world datasets are used in the comparative experiments. They are the largest available multi-modal datasets that are fully paired and labeled (tagged), to the best of our knowledge. Both datasets are bi-modal with the image and the associated text modalities. The statistics of the two datasets are summarized in Table 1.

The first dataset, Wikipedia feature articles[1], consists of 2,866 images, each with a short paragraph describing the image. The images are labeled with exactly one of the 10 different semantic classes, such as art and geography. In the originally provided dataset, the text comes with a 10 dimensional feature vector representing the probabilistic proportions over the 10 topics, which is derived from a LDA model [5]. We note that Bi-CMSRM and the comparative methods all resort to the raw low-level features rather than the high-level semantic features. For the training text, we extract 5,000-dimensional feature vectors using the bag of words (BoW) representation with the TF-IDF weighting scheme. For images, we first extract SIFT points from each image in the dataset. The randomly selected SIFT points are clustered by k-means to generate 1,000 centers as the visual dictionary. Then each image is quantized into a 1,000 dimensional histogram feature vector using the bag-of-visual-words (BoVW) model.

The second dataset, NUS-WIDE[2], contains 133,208 images with 1,000 tags and 81 concepts, which are pruned from the NUS dataset by keeping the images that have at least one tag and one concept. For the feature representation, we use the publicly available 1,000 dimensional text feature vector (namely tags) and 500 dimensional image feature vector based on SIFT BoVW kindly provided by the authors.

Another reason why we choose the two datasets is due to the large difference in the average number of the textual words per image and the dimensionality of the text space. In the Wiki dataset the textual descriptions are based on Wikipedia surrounding paragraphs which yield a 5,000 dimension text space with an average of 117.5 surrounding words per image. The NUS dataset, on the other hand, is based on user-provided tags which yield a 1,000 dimension text space and in average there are 7.73 words (tags) per image. A manual examination reveals that the synonymy and polysemy problem may occur more frequently in the Wiki dataset than in the NUS dataset. For this difference, first we want to examine our algorithm's ability to learn a latent semantic representation to address the problem of synonymy and polysemy for the Wiki dataset, and second we want to see whether our algorithm decays rapidly with the NUS dataset by learning a latent semantic representation.

4.1.2 Ranking Example Generation

Note that the two datasets are both presented by pairs of text and imagery where CCA can be trained by this setting. For the other three methods (PAMIR, SSI and Bi-CMSRM), the restriction of the paired correspondence between a text document and an image is not needed. On the contrary, the queries and the corresponding rankings over the documents are needed as training examples for the three methods. These training examples originate from both directions of text-query-image and image-query-text retrieval. For this purpose, we first define the relevance assessment. For the Wiki dataset, we define that a target document d is relevant to a query q if d and q belong to the same semantic class. Similarly, for the NUS dataset, a target document d is relevant if it shares at least one concept with query q. The query lists are generated as follows: for each text (image) query, we randomly select 40 images (text documents) in the other modality in the training set as candidates and then the selected target documents are automatically labeled as relevant or irrelevant to form a ranking example. For all the 2,866 generated ranking examples in the Wiki dataset, we randomly sample 1,500 to form the training set, of which 500 form the validation set. The rest are used to form the testing set. For the NUS dataset, 2,664 ranking examples are randomly selected to be the training examples and 2,000 to be validation examples (see Table 1).

4.1.3 Performance Evaluation

Note that the proposed Bi-CMSRM is different from the other comparative methods in the way that Bi-CMSRM requires bi-directional training examples. Thus for fairness,

[1] `http://www.svcl.ucsd.edu/projects/crossmodal/`

[2] `http://lms.comp.nus.edu.sg/research/NUS-WIDE.htm`

the retrieval performance evaluations are conducted with the following settings: the comparative methods PAMIR and SSI train two individual models optimized for the image-query-text and text-query-image retrieval tasks respectively, while Bi-CMSRM trains a unified model for both directions of retrieval.

For both datasets, performance evaluations are conducted using standard information retrieval metrics. We use *Mean Average Precision* (MAP) as the performance measures. Let $r^* = \text{rank}(\mathbf{y}^*)$ (true ranking with two rank value $+1$ and -1) and $r = \text{rank}(\mathbf{y})$ (predicted ranking with a total order). Given a query and a set of R retrieved target text documents or images, the *Average Precision* (AP) is defined as

$$\text{AP}(r^*, r) = \frac{1}{L}\sum_{j=1}^{R} Prec(j) \cdot Rel(j)\,, \qquad (15)$$

where L is the number of the relevant documents in the retrieved set, $Prec(j)$ is the percentage of the relevant text documents (images) in the top j text documents (images) in predicted ranking p and $Rel(j)$ is an indicator function equaling 1 if the item at rank j in predicted ranking p is relevant to the query, zero otherwise. We then average the AP values from all the queries in the query set to obtain the MAP score. The larger the MAP, the better the performance. In the experiments, R is the number of the retrieved text documents or images to be examined, where we set $R = 50$ for the top 50 retrieved text documents (images) or $R = all$ for all the documents (images). Recalling that our model can be optimized for various ranking measures, we implement the greedy algorithm for optimizing the average precision proposed in [31].

We report the performance results on both directions of ranking images from text queries (*text-query-image*) and ranking text documents from image queries (*image-query-text*). Besides, to give a pictorial demonstration of an algorithm's performance, the *Precision-Recall* curves are also reported for all the approaches.

4.1.4 Parameter Tuning

To achieve the best performance, all the comparative methods need manual parameter tuning. For the proposed method Bi-CMSRM, we tune the value of parameters k (the dimensionality of the latent space) and λ (the tradeoff between the model complexity and the empirical risk) of Optimization Problem 1 on the random sampled validation data. The respective range of k and λ are: $\{5, 10, 25, 50, 100, 200\}$ and $\{0.01, 0.1, 1, 10\}$. We choose those parameters which perform best for the validation data and then the values are fixed throughout the experiments.

For the other comparative methods, the procedures to tune the parameters are analogous except that the parameters needed to be tuned are different: the dimensionality of the latent space in CCA, the aggressiveness parameter in PAMIR, and the dimensionality of the latent space & the pre-chosen fixed learning rate in SSI.

4.2 Results on the Wiki Dataset

Table 2 reports the performance of Bi-CMSRM and the other comparative models on the test set of the Wiki dataset, showing that Bi-CMSRM outperforms all the comparative methods on both directions of the retrieval.

Table 2: The performance comparison in terms of MAP@R scores on the Wiki dataset. Each text document is represented as 5000-D BoW and each image is represented as 1000-D BoVW. Both directions of retrieval tasks are reported. The results shown in boldface are the best results.

Methods	Text Query		Image Query	
	R=50	R=all	R=50	R=all
CCA	0.2343	0.1433	0.2208	0.1451
PAMIR	0.3093	0.1734	0.1797	0.1779
SSI	0.2821	0.1664	0.2344	0.1759
Uni-CMSRM	0.3663	0.2021	0.2570	0.2229
Bi-CMSRM	**0.3981**	**0.2123**	**0.2599**	**0.2528**

First, this improvement is due to the latent semantic space. Recall that for the Wiki dataset, the text documents contain about 117 words in average and learning a latent semantic space is particularly appropriate for the cross-media retrieval with long queries/documents. To verify this, we see that the SSI also outperforms PAMIR in the image-query-text retrieval while PAMIR even controls the model complexity by optimizing an adapted cross-media RankSVM model. Further, both Uni-CMSRM and Bi-CMSRM outperform SSI due to the structural large margin that regularizes the model and optimizes MAP ranking loss directly. Second, though Uni-CMSRM outperforms other comparative methods except for Bi-CMSRM, the bi-directional training leads to a better performance of Bi-CMSRM than that of Uni-CMSRM.

The Precision-Recall curves on both directions are reported in Figure 2(a) and 2(b). The Precision-Recall curves further validate the superiority of Bi-CMSRM for the cross-media retrieval.

4.3 Results on the NUS Dataset

The improvement of Bi-CMSRM on the NUS dataset is not as significant as that on the Wiki dataset. The MAP scores of all the methods are shown in Table 3 and the Precision-Recall curves are reported in Figure 2(c) and Figure 2(d). For text-query-image retrieval, Bi-CMSRM outperforms the other comparative methods again, while for image-query-text retrieval, both PAMIR and Uni-CMSRM have a slightly better overall performance than Bi-CMSRM when $R = 50$ and $R = all$.

Recall that in the NUS-WIDE dataset, one image is associated with about seven annotated words in average. The latent space embedding does not help much for querying short text in the task of image-query-text retrieval. PAMIR and Bi-CMSRM both train a regularized model, and therefore, the performances of PAMIR and Bi-CMSRM are undoubtedly superior to that of SSI in the image-query-text retrieval. The reason why PAMIR and Uni-CMSRM even beat Bi-CMSRM in the case of image-query-text retrieval may be as follows. As mentioned above, the assumption of latent space embedding does not help much for querying short text. With adding another direction of ranking constraints, which still assumes a latent space embedding, the assumption is violated even more, resulting in a poorer generalization performance of Bi-CMSRM than that of Uni-CMSRM. We also note that though Bi-CMSRM does not achieve the best performance, the performance differences

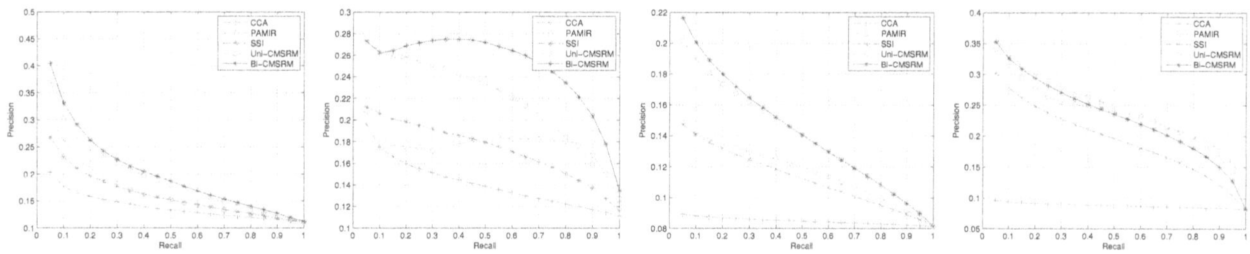

(a) Wiki Text-Query-Image (b) Wiki Image-Query-Text (c) NUS Text-Query-Image (d) NUS Image-Query-Text

Figure 2: Precision-Recall curves on the two datasets.

Table 3: The performance comparison in terms of MAP@R scores on the NUS dataset. Each text document is represented as 1000-D BoW and each image is represented as 500-D BoVW. Both directions of retrieval tasks are reported. The results shown in boldface are the best results.

Methods	Text Query		Image Query	
	R=50	R=all	R=50	R=all
CCA	0.1497	0.0851	0.1523	0.0883
PAMIR	0.2046	0.1184	**0.5003**	0.2410
SSI	0.2156	0.1140	0.4101	0.1992
Uni-CMSRM	0.2781	0.1424	0.4997	**0.2491**
Bi-CMSRM	**0.3224**	**0.1453**	0.4950	0.2380

among PAMIR, Uni-CMSRM and Bi-CMSRM are not significant.

5. CONCLUSIONS

In this paper, we have presented a new approach to solving the problem of learning a cross-media representation model for cross-media retrieval by casting the problem as a problem of learning to rank taking the bi-directional ranking examples into account. We have demonstrated the effectiveness of our proposed method Bi-CMSRM and shown significant improvements over the comparative methods on two datasets.

6. ACKNOWLEDGEMENTS

This work is supported in part by National Basic Research Program of China (2012CB316400), NSFC (No. 61070068, 90920303), 863 program(2012AA012505), the Fundamental Research Funds for the Central Universities and Chinese Knowledge Center of Engineering Science and Technology (CKCEST). ZZ is also supported in part by US NSF (IIS-0812114, CCF-1017828) and Zhejiang Provincial Engineering Center on Media Data Cloud Processing and Analysis.

7. REFERENCES

[1] R. Baeza-Yates and B. Ribeiro-Neto. *Modern Information Retrieval.* Addison-Wesley, 1999.

[2] B. Bai, J. Weston, D. Grangier, R. Collobert, K. Sadamasa, Y. Qi, O. Chapelle, and K. Weinberger. Learning to rank with (a lot of) word features. *Information Retrieval*, 13(3):291–314, 2010.

[3] B. Bai, J. Weston, D. Grangier, R. Collobert, K. Sadamasa, Y. Qi, C. Cortes, and M. Mohri. Polynomial semantic indexing. *Advances in Neural Information Processing Systems*, 22:64–72, 2009.

[4] K. Barnard, P. Duygulu, D. Forsyth, N. De Freitas, D. M. Blei, and M. I. Jordan. Matching words and pictures. *The Journal of Machine Learning Research*, 3:1107–1135, 2003.

[5] D. Blei, A. Ng, and M. Jordan. Latent dirichlet allocation. *the Journal of Machine Learning Research*, 3:993–1022, 2003.

[6] S. Chakrabarti, R. Khanna, U. Sawant, and C. Bhattacharyya. Structured learning for non-smooth ranking losses. In *Proceeding of the 14th ACM SIGKDD International Conference on Knowledge Discovery and Data Mining*, pages 88–96, 2008.

[7] Y. Chen and J. Z. Wang. Image categorization by learning and reasoning with regions. *The Journal of Machine Learning Research*, 5:913–939, 2004.

[8] S. Deerwester, S. Dumais, G. Furnas, T. Landauer, and R. Harshman. Indexing by latent semantic analysis. *Journal of the American Society for Information Science*, 41(6):391–407, 1990.

[9] J. Gao, W. Yuan, X. Li, K. Deng, and J. Nie. Smoothing clickthrough data for web search ranking. In *Proceedings of the 32nd International ACM SIGIR Conference on Research and Development in Information Retrieval*, pages 355–362, 2009.

[10] D. Grangier and S. Bengio. A discriminative kernel-based approach to rank images from text queries. *IEEE Transactions on Pattern Analysis and Machine Intelligence*, 30(8):1371–1384, 2008.

[11] N. Gupta et al. *Learning to reformulate long queries.* PhD thesis, Massachusetts Institute of Technology, 2010.

[12] D. Hardoon, S. Szedmak, and J. Shawe-Taylor. Canonical correlation analysis: An overview with application to learning methods. *Neural Computation*, 16(12):2639–2664, 2004.

[13] C. Ho and C. Lin. Large-scale linear support vector regression. Technical report, National Taiwan University, 2012.

[14] T. Hofmann. Probabilistic latent semantic indexing. In *Proceedings of the 22nd Annual International ACM SIGIR Conference on Research and Development in Information Retrieval*, pages 50–57, 1999.

[15] H. Hotelling. Relations between two sets of variates. *Biometrika*, 28(3/4):321–377, 1936.

[16] Y. Jia, M. Salzmann, and T. Darrell. Factorized latent spaces with structured sparsity. *Advances in Neural Information Processing Systems*, 23:982–990, 2010.

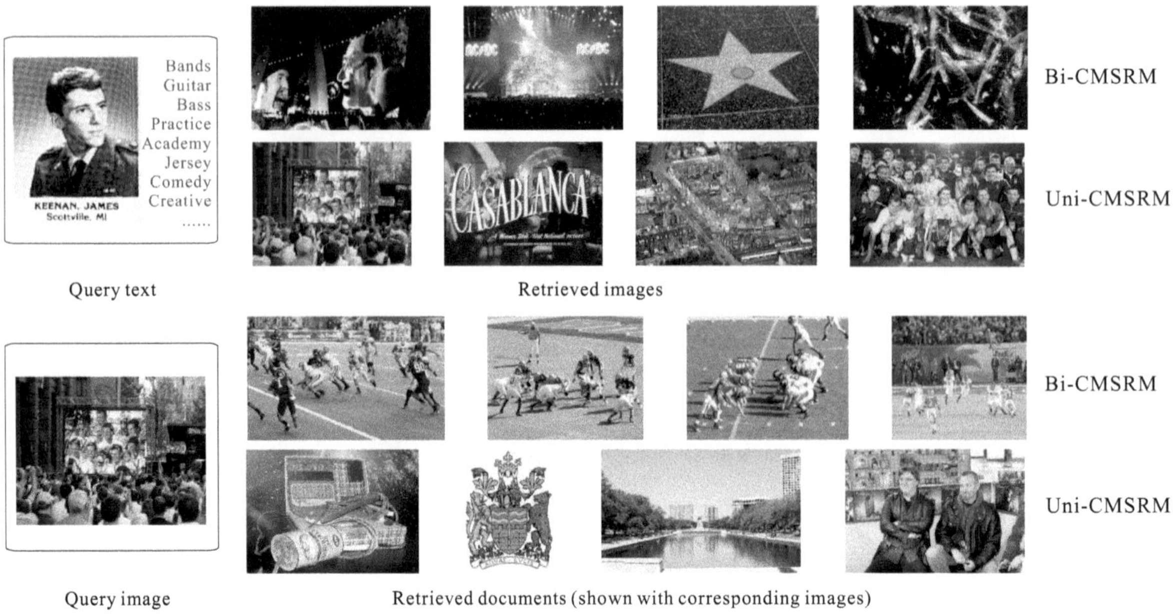

Figure 3: Exemplar retrieval comparison between the proposed Bi-CMSRM and Uni-CMSRM on the Wiki dataset. For text-query-image direction, the query text is shown with its corresponding image and selected words. For the image-query-text direction, the retrieved documents are shown with their corresponding images.

[17] Y. Jia, M. Salzmann, and T. Darrell. Learning cross-modality similarity for multinomial data. In *IEEE International Conference on Computer Vision*, pages 2407–2414, 2011.

[18] T. Joachims. Optimizing search engines using clickthrough data. In *Proceedings of the Eighth ACM SIGKDD International Conference on Knowledge Discovery and Data Mining*, pages 133–142, 2002.

[19] T. Joachims. A support vector method for multivariate performance measures. In *Proceedings of the 22nd International Conference on Machine Learning*, pages 377–384, 2005.

[20] T. Joachims, T. Finley, and C. Yu. Cutting-plane training of structural svms. *Machine Learning*, 77(1):27–59, 2009.

[21] D. Lowe. Distinctive image features from scale-invariant keypoints. *International Journal of Computer Vision*, 60(2):91–110, 2004.

[22] X. Lu, F. Wu, S. Tang, Z. Zhang, X. He, and Y. Zhuang. A low rank structural large margin method for cross-modal ranking. In *Proceedings of the 36th Annual International ACM SIGIR Conference on Research and Development in Information Retrieval*, pages 433–442, 2013.

[23] B. McFee and G. Lanckriet. Metric learning to rank. In *27th International Conference on Machine Learning, Haifa, Israel*. Citeseer, 2010.

[24] G. Monaci, P. Jost, P. Vandergheynst, B. Mailhe, S. Lesage, and R. Gribonval. Learning multimodal dictionaries. *IEEE Transactions on Image Processing*, 16(9):2272–2283, 2007.

[25] N. Rasiwasia, J. Costa Pereira, E. Coviello, G. Doyle, G. Lanckriet, R. Levy, and N. Vasconcelos. A new approach to cross-modal multimedia retrieval. In *Proceedings of the International Conference on Multimedia*, pages 251–260, 2010.

[26] S. Shalev-Shwartz, Y. Singer, and N. Srebro. Pegasos: Primal estimated sub-gradient solver for svm. In *Proceedings of the 24th International Conference on Machine Learning*, pages 807–814, 2007.

[27] A. Sharma, A. Kumar, H. Daume, and D. Jacobs. Generalized multiview analysis: A discriminative latent space. In *IEEE Conference on Computer Vision and Pattern Recognition*, pages 2160–2167, 2012.

[28] I. Tsochantaridis, T. Joachims, T. Hofmann, and Y. Altun. Large margin methods for structured and interdependent output variables. *Journal of Machine Learning Research*, 6(2):1453–1484, 2006.

[29] F. Wu, H. Zhang, and Y. Zhuang. Learning semantic correlations for cross-media retrieval. In *2006 IEEE International Conference on Image Processing*, pages 1465–1468, 2006.

[30] Y. Yang, N. Bansal, W. Dakka, P. Ipeirotis, N. Koudas, and D. Papadias. Query by document. In *Proceedings of the Second ACM International Conference on Web Search and Data Mining*, pages 34–43, 2009.

[31] Y. Yue, T. Finley, F. Radlinski, and T. Joachims. A support vector method for optimizing average precision. In *Proceedings of the 30th Annual International ACM SIGIR Conference on Research and Development in Information Retrieval*, pages 271–278, 2007.

[32] Y.-T. Zhuang, Y. Yang, and F. Wu. Mining semantic correlation of heterogeneous multimedia data for cross-media retrieval. *IEEE Transactions on Multimedia*, 10(2):221–229, 2008.

Listen, Look, and Gotcha: Instant Video Search with Mobile Phones by Layered Audio-Video Indexing*

Wu Liu [1,3], Tao Mei [2], Yongdong Zhang [1], Jintao Li [1], Shipeng Li [2]
[1] Institute of Computing Technology, Chinese Academy of Sciences, Beijing 100190, P. R. China
[2] Microsoft Research Asia, Beijing 100080, P. R. China
[3] University of Chinese Academy of Sciences, Beijing 100049, P. R. China
liuwu@live.cn; {tmei, spli}@microsoft.com; {zhyd, jtli}@ict.ac.cn

ABSTRACT

Mobile video is quickly becoming a mass consumer phenomenon. More and more people are using their smartphones to search and browse video content while on the move. In this paper, we have developed an innovative instant mobile video search system through which users can discover videos by simply pointing their phones at a screen to capture a very few seconds of what they are watching. The system is able to index large-scale video data using a new layered audio-video indexing approach in the cloud, as well as extract light-weight joint audio-video signatures in real time and perform progressive search on mobile devices. Unlike most existing mobile video search applications that simply send the original video query to the cloud, the proposed mobile system is one of the first attempts at instant and progressive video search leveraging the light-weight computing capacity of mobile devices. The system is characterized by four unique properties: 1) a joint audio-video signature to deal with the large aural and visual variances associated with the query video captured by the mobile phone, 2) layered audio-video indexing to holistically exploit the complementary nature of audio and video signals, 3) light-weight fingerprinting to comply with mobile processing capacity, and 4) a progressive query process to significantly reduce computational costs and improve the user experience—the search process can stop anytime once a confident result is achieved. We have collected 1,400 query videos captured by 25 mobile users from a dataset of 600 hours of video. The experiments show that our system outperforms state-of-the-art methods by achieving 90.79% precision when the query video is less than 10 seconds and 70.07% even when the query video is less than 5 seconds.

Categories and Subject Descriptors

H.3.3 [**Information Storage and Retrieval**]: Information Search and Retrieval—*Search process*; H.5.1 [**Information Interfaces and Presentation**]: Multimedia Information Systems—*Video*

General Terms

Algorithms, Performance, Design, Experimentation.

Keywords

Mobile Video Search, Audio-Video Signatures, Layered Audio-Video Indexing, Progressive Query Process, Instant Search.

* This work was performed at Microsoft Research Asia.

ACM MM '13, October 21-25, Barcelona, Catalunya, Spain.
Copyright 2013 ACM 978-1-4503-2404-5/13/10 ...$15.00.
http://dx.doi.org/10.1145/2502081.2502084.

(a) screenshot of mobile video search (b) instant search results

Figure 1: A snapshot of our proposed mobile video search system. (a) A user simply points his or her phone at a screen to capture a few seconds of what they are watching. While recording, the user can see instant search results on the right. (b) The search process can stop anytime once a confident search result is achieved. Thus, the user does not need to wait for a fixed time lag. The proposed system is characterized by its unique features such as layered audio-video indexing, as well as instant and progressive search.

1. INTRODUCTION

Mobile is reshaping the way video content is generated, searched, and consumed on today's Internet. The proliferation of increasingly capable mobile devices opens up exciting possibilities for mobile video applications. As a result, mobile video is quickly becoming a mass consumer phenomenon. Among many mobile video applications, mobile video search—searching similar or duplicate videos to identify a phone-captured query video—is emerging and becoming pervasive as: 1) while on the go, users always prefer mobile devices as their principal video search and browsing tools [4], and 2) the advanced built-in cameras have made video search very natural—mobile users can now discover videos by simply pointing their phones at a screen to capture a few seconds of what they are watching, as shown in Figure 1(a).

While extensive research has been made on mobile visual search (e.g., landmark recognition [9], product search [5], augmented reality [6], and so on), mobile video search is still in the early stages and remains a challenging research problem. Unlike traditional desktop video search, video search on mobile devices faces the following unique challenges: 1) *large aural-visual variance of query video*—due to the complex capture conditions, the query clip is naturally noisy with varying aural and visual qualities. Therefore, designing robust signatures that can deal with such significant variance is crucial for mobile video search. 2) *stringent memory and computation constraints*—as the CPU and memory of mobile devices are still not comparable with desktop computers, signatures with large memory costs or heavy computation are not suitable for mobile clients. 3) *network bandwidth limitations*—with low and unreliable bandwidth, signatures are expected to be as compact as possible to reduce network latency, and 4) *instant search experience*—because mobile users care more about their experience than in desktop search, the search process is expected to be instant and progressive; in other words, the captured query clip needed for search should be as short as possible, while the search results should be returned instantly or even progressively.

Many existing mobile applications have tried to provide video search functions. For example, IntoNow enables mobile phone users to record a 12-second audio clip as the query [7]. Although no algorithm details are available, it is likely that the search is accomplished by audio fingerprinting technology. However, as it heavily depends on audio information, it may not work well if the recording conditions are noisy or the recorded query video is silent. On the other hand, VideoSurf provides a video search service based on the visual information extracted from a 10-second recorded video clip [24]. Nevertheless, it needs users to choose the discriminative visual content for search. It is also worth noting that these applications fully rely on the computing power of the cloud by simply sending the original query video to a server, while neglecting the increasing computing capacity of mobile clients. As a result, users need to record a video clip of a fixed duration (e.g., 10 or 12 seconds). This paper investigates if we can leverage the computing capacities of advanced smartphones for extracting robust and compact audio-video signatures on the mobile client. In this way, instant and progressive video search can be achieved, where the duration of the query video is less than those in any existing systems and the search process can stop anytime once a confident result is achieved.

Although mobile visual search has attracted extensive attention in the research community [2, 4, 5, 8], few efforts have explored mobile video search. The most related research to video search on mobile devices is near-duplicate video search, which can be classified into three categories according to the type of data modality they rely on: audio-based [10, 25], video-based [18, 20], and fusion-based methods [21]. However, most existing approaches to duplicate video search predominantly focus on desktop scenarios where the query video is usually a subset of the original video without significant distortions. Moreover, the computational costs and compactness of descriptors are often neglected in those systems. Therefore, conventional approaches to duplicate video search have not taken the aforementioned mobile challenges into account, and thus are not suitable for mobile video search.

Motivated by the above observations, and aiming to address the aforementioned mobile challenges, we have developed an innovative instant mobile video search system through which users can discover videos by simply pointing their phones at a screen to capture a few seconds of what they are watching. In the cloud, the system is able to index large-scale video data using a novel Layered Audio-VidEo (LAVE) indexing scheme; while on the client, the system extracts light-weight joint audio-video signatures in real time and searches in a progressive way. Specifically, the LAVE scheme provides a new way to combine audio-video signatures through joint multi-layered audio-video indexing, which preserves each signature's individual structure in the similarity computation and considers their correlation in the combination stage. The joint audio-video signature is not only computationally cheap for mobile devices, but also mutually reinforces the discriminative power from individual modalities and thus is robust to the large variance (noise and distortion) in the query video. The learned hash function significantly reduces the bits to transfer from mobile to server. The design of the search process via a bipartite graph transformation and matching algorithm makes the video search progressive—the search can stop anytime once a confident result is achieved. The experiments show that our system can achieve 90.77% precision when the query video is less than 10 seconds and 70.07% when the query video is less than 5 seconds. Figure 1 shows a screenshot of the system.

In summary, this paper makes the following contributions:

- We have designed an innovative mobile video system that represents one of the first attempts towards instant and progressive video search, by leveraging the light-weight computing capacity of mobile devices. This is unlike most existing mobile video search systems.
- We propose a new layered audio-video indexing scheme to holistically exploit the complementary nature of audio and video signals for more robust video search.
- We propose a progressive query process to support varying lengths in the query video, where in most cases the length is much shorter than those in any existing mobile applications. This significantly reduces query time and thus improves users' search experience.

The rest of the paper is organized as follows. Section 2 reviews related work. Section 3 presents the proposed mobile video search system. Section 4 describes the experiments and evaluations, followed by the conclusion in Section 5.

2. RELATED WORK

We next review related research on near-duplicate video search and mobile visual search, which are closely related to the design of a mobile video search system.

2.1 Near-Duplicate Video Search

Although mobile video search is still in an early research stage, there has been intensive research on general near-duplicate video search. Depending on the query modality, existing approaches mainly fall into three categories: audio-based, video-based, and fusion-based approaches.

Extensive research has been conducted on using visual signatures to search near-duplicate videos. A widely adopted signature is global features [16, 18], where videos are represented by compact global signatures. For example, Shang *et al.* propose a compact spatiotemporal feature that leverages gray-level intensity distribution with respect to timeline to represent videos [18]. Similarly, Paisitkriangkrai *et al.* combine both spatial and temporal information into ordinal measures to construct compact and invariant global signatures [16]. Although these global representations achieve fast retrieval speeds in a large-scale video dataset, they usually become less effective in handing recorded query videos with serious distortions [28]. Compared with the global features, local descriptors are more distinctive and robust to these video distortions as they explore the local invariance (such as scale and orientation). Therefore, local descriptors are also employed to similar video search. However, due to the computational complexity, the efficiency becomes intractable. There are many approaches improving the speed of local descriptor matching. Bag-of-Words (BoW) is a popular scheme for near-duplicate video search [20]. Furthermore, Wu *et al.* construct a hierarchy structure to speed up the matching process [28]. However, local descriptor-based approaches still cannot be directly adopted on mobile devices without proper optimization due to the limited computing capability and memory of mobile devices.

On the other hand, audio plays an important role for near-duplicate video search [10, 25]. For example, Wang *et al.* propose a simple but effective landmark-based audio fingerprint to conduct similar audio search [25]. Furthermore, inspired by BoW, a bag of audio words (BoA) representation is proposed to characterize audio features for similar video search [10]. Compared with visual features, audio features are robust, computationally efficient, and compact, and therefore suitable to employ in mobile video search.

Recently, joint audio-visual near-duplicate video search has attracted attention as audio and video can complement each other. In particular, the TRECVID community has tried to explore the benefit of the audio-visual combination for large-scale video copy detection. The key problem of feature combination is the identification of the correlation between audio and video features. Early and late fusion strategies are widely used fusion methods [21]. However, both strategies have disadvantages—early fusion cannot well preserve the individual structural information of each individual feature while late fusion does not consider the correlation among features [21].

In summary, fusion of audio and visual features gives a neoteric avenue to near-duplicate video search. However, existing early or late fusion methods cannot sufficiently mine the advantage of audio-video signatures. In addition, although the existing near-duplicate video search methods can be used as references, few of them can be directly adapted in mobile video search to deal with unique mobile challenges.

2.2 Mobile Visual Search

Mobile visual search has attracted extensive attention due to its huge potential for numerous applications. Most research on this topic has predominantly focused on compact descriptor design on mobile devices. The most popular way to solve this problem is compressing descriptors through the technology of image coding. For example, the Compressed Histogram of Gradients (CHoG) encodes the raw features with 20x reduction by an entropy-based coding method on the mobile client [2]. On the server, the compressed descriptors are approximately decoded. Similarly, Ji *et al.* propose a multiple-channel coding scheme to extract compact visual descriptors [8]. In contrast, He *et al.* [5] and Tseng *et al.* [23] have suggested using the hashing function to compress the descriptors. Compared to the above schemes, the hash bits of the local features do not need to be decoded on the server, which can be directly viewed as a visual word index. In addition, it offers lower transmission costs, and cheaper memory and computation than other methods. However, there are few methods for mobile video search. Although Chen *et al.* design a dynamic query selection algorithm for mobile video retrieval [3], using only one keyframe can hardly handle the large variance of the query video captured in complex conditions. Furthermore, sending raw local features is also time and energy consuming. Wu *et al.* employ a similar video search in their mobile video question-answering system, which mainly address different challenges [27].

In summary, compared to the above methods, our proposed system aims to provide instant and progressive mobile video search. We have designed the search scheme to progressively transmit compact hash bits, which are derived from the joint and light-weight audio-video signature, to the cloud. The proposed LAVE indexing technique exploits the advantage of the audio-video signature for robust video search. Moreover, to improve users' search experience, a progressive query process via a bipartite graph based transformation and matching method has been developed.

3. INSTANT MOBILE VIDEO SEARCH

3.1 Overview

Figure 2 shows the architecture of the proposed mobile video search system, including the offline and online stages. In the offline stage, we first extract the audio-video descriptors for each video from a large-scale source video dataset. Then, these massive descriptors are indexed by a novel LAVE indexing method. The online query stage consists of the following steps: 1) Real time extraction of light-weight audio-video descriptors on mobile devices, while users are capturing query video clips. The signatures (including visual hash bits and audio fingerprint) are sent to the server at an interval of one second. 2) Once the server receives the one-second signature, the search for similar video keyframes is conducted through the LAVE index. 3) A fast and effective geometric verification-based visual re-ranking step is used to refine the search results. 4) A progressive query process via bipartite graph transformation and matching is performed to make the video search progressive. If there are no change in the instant search results for three consecutive seconds (i.e., a confident search result is regarded to have been achieved), then the search process can stop and the results will be returned to the users. In the next section, we describe each component in detail.

3.2 Joint Audio-Video Descriptor

In contrast to other media, the main advantage of video is that it contains both abundant audio and visual information. As the complementary nature of the audio and video signals, the joint audio-video descriptors are more robust

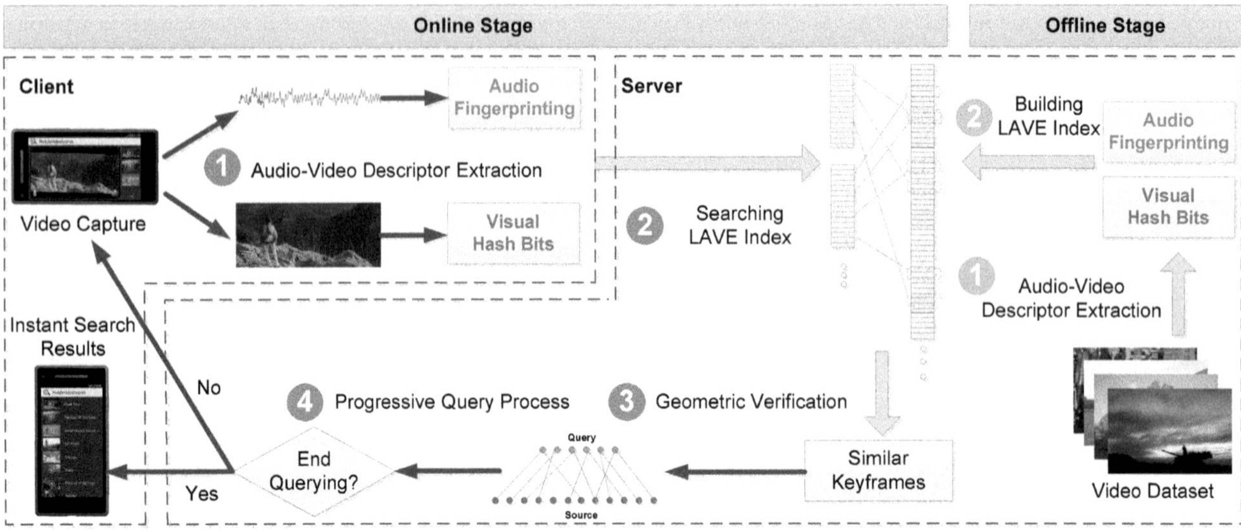

Figure 2: The overview of our proposed mobile video search system.

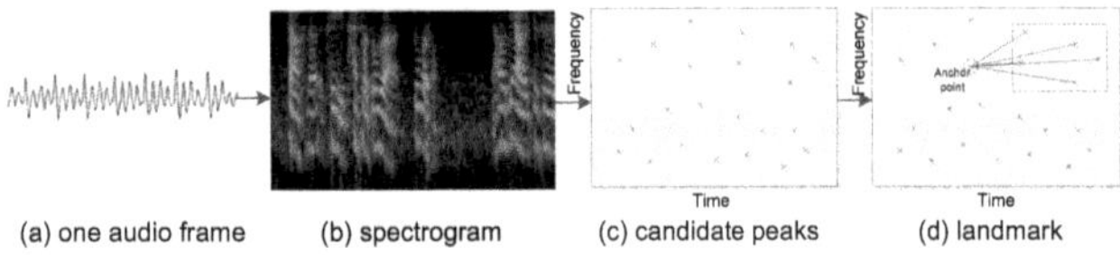

Figure 3: The extraction of landmark-based audio fingerprinting.

to the large variance of query videos, especially for complex mobile video capturing conditions (e.g., silent video or blurred video of low visual quality). Selecting effective audio-video descriptors is very important for a mobile video search system. There are three main principles for joint descriptor selection: 1) robust to the variance of the recorded query videos, 2) cheap to compute on mobile devices, and 3) easy to index for instant search. Consequently, we choose the Landmark-Based Audio Fingerprinting (LBAF)[25] and Speeded-Up Robust Features (SURF) [1] as follows.

3.2.1 *Audio Fingerprinting*

Among various audio features, LBAF is widely used in many near-duplicate video search methods. Its fast computation, efficient memory and invariant translation are also very suitable for mobile video search. In our system, we extract the LBAF as shown in Figure 3. First, the audio information is segmented into short and partly overlapping frames of length f_{m_l} and stride f_{m_d}. Second, for each frame, its spectrogram is calculated. Third, the candidate peaks are settled on the spectrogram of the frame according to three criteria: higher energy content than all its neighbors, higher amplitude than its neighbors, and a density criterion [25]. Fourth, anchor points are chosen from the peaks and each anchor has a fixed target zone. Each anchor point is sequentially paired with the candidate peak in its target. The pairs are called landmarks. Each landmark is represented as $l_i = \{t_i^a, f_i^a, \Delta t_i^a, \Delta f_i^a\}$, where $t_i^a$and f_i^a are the time offset and the frequency of the anchor point, and Δt_i^a and Δf_i^a are the time and frequency differences between the anchor point and the paired point in the target zone. Finally, we compress the fingerprint into $l_i = \{h_k^a, t_i^a\}$ where h_k^a is the hash value of the $f_i^a, \Delta t_i^a$ and Δf_i^a. Different l_i may have the same h_k^a.

In our experiments, we set $f_{m_l} = 256$ ms and $f_{m_d} = 32$ ms, and limit hash bits h_k^a to less than 25 bits. As there are also 15 bits for t_i^a, the length of l_i is 40 bits. For a one-second audio clip, we choose 100 landmarks in total. Hence, we only have to transmit 0.5 KB per second for audio fingerprinting.

3.2.2 *Visual Hash Bits*

According to our collected real-word mobile video query dataset (to be described in section 4.1), the recorded videos have great distortions, such as blurs, color change, reflection, and transformation. So the video descriptor in our system should be not only quickly extracted on the mobile device, but also robust to these distortions. According to previous research on mobile visual search [5, 8, 30], the SURF is a competent feature for achieving both high efficiency and robustness. Furthermore, accelerating SURF extraction methods on mobile devices could also be used [30].

However, directly sending raw SURF features is very time and energy consuming. Inspired by Bag of Hash Bits (BoHB) [5, 23], hashing methods are used to compress the local features to hash bits, such as its light computation and memory requirements. Here, Minimal Loss Hashing [14] or Spectral Hash [26] can be used to learn the hash function $h^v = sign(v^T x - t)$, where x is the SURF descriptor vector, v and t is the learned hash matrix and the threshold scalar, and h^v is the learned visual hash bits. According to [5] and [23], the binary code is limited to 80 bits. Finally, we use eight bits to save the angle value of the SURF descriptor, which will be used for geometric verification in the future. Therefore, for each SURF feature, we will compress it to $v_i = \{h_l^v, r_i^v\}$, which is only 88 bits in length.

On the other hand, because of the different camera resolutions on mobile devices, we will scale the query image to a small picture. There are two main advantages: First, it improves feature extraction speed on the mobile device. Second, it decreases the number of feature points that need to be transmitted. According to our experiments, the scaling has little influence on precision but seriously improves query speed. After the scaling, there are only 75 SURF points in one frame on average. In other words, the system only needs to transmit less than 1 KB of visual features to the server.

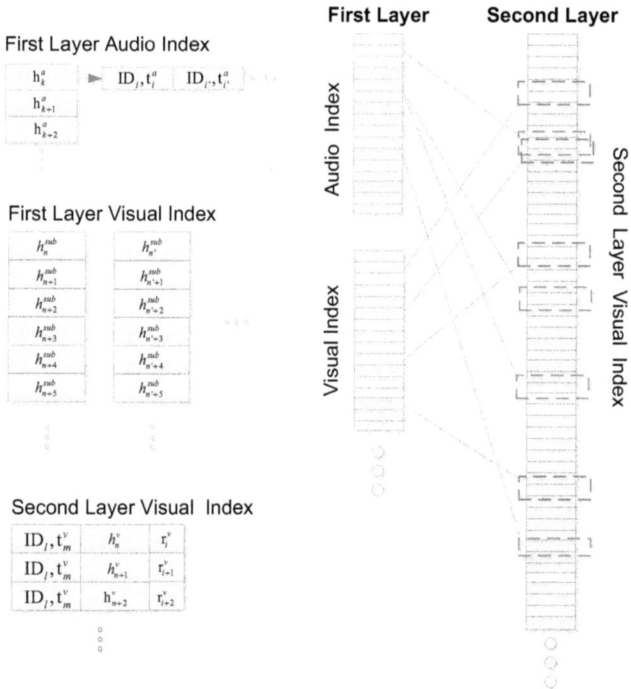

Figure 4: The illustration of layered audio-video indexing (LAVE).

In summary, after feature extraction, we obtain 100 audio feature points and 75 visual feature points. Through efficient compression, there are less than 2 KB of audio-visual signatures per second to be transmitted by the network.

3.3 LAVE Indexing

Even though the computing of the Hamming distance between binary audio and visual features is efficient, linear search for a big video dataset is still a bottleneck in real-time mobile video search. The most widely used binary feature indexing method is locality sensitive hashing (LSH). However, as it uses random selection, aim to achieve good search quality, it needs a large number of hash bits to build enough tables. As an improvement, Lv *et al.* propose the multi-probe method, which relies on looking through multiple buckets to reduce the number of hash tables [11]. Nevertheless, checking multiple buckets also costs a lot of time. Instead, Muja *et al.* propose the multiple hierarchical clustering trees indexing method [13]. Although the hierarchical decomposition of the search space can greatly reduce search time, it requires multiple trees to avoid the situation in which the closest neighbor to the query point lies across a boundary from the domain explored. As a result, the multiple tree structure increases the memory and query cost.

In our system, we propose LAVE indexing. As shown in Figure 4, there are two layers in the LAVE. The first layer is the index entry, containing a multi-index: audio indexing (red) and visual indexing (blue). The second layer is the visual hash bits, which are used for accurate feature matching and combination. There are two advantages to these structures: 1) effectively employing the hierarchical decomposition strategy to improve the visual points search speed, and 2) holistically exploiting the complementary nature of audio and video signals. The different indexing entries in the first layer preserve the individual structure of audio and video signatures. In the second layer, the combination of audio and video can be weighted by the hamming distance of visual hash bits.

3.3.1 Building LAVE Index

In contrast to the visual feature, the audio feature is highly compressed, only 25 bits for each point. Therefore, a linear search of the audio index can be quickly completed. We use the audio index as part of the first layer and each bucket in the audio index of the first layer is associated with the second layer by the video ID, audio time offset t^a and keyframe number t^v. Through the audio indexing, we can refine the number of visual points to be searched in the second layer, which obviously improves the search speed.

However, if the audio information is changed significantly or missed, it will be difficult to find the closet neighbor in the second layer. The multi-index idea in [15] is used to solve this problem. The hash bits from the second layer visual index are indexed by m different hash tables, which construct the visual index of the first layer. The hash bits h_n^{sub} of the visual index in the first layer are randomly selected from the hash bits in the second layer. For a received visual point, entries that fall close to the query in at least one such substring are considered neighbor candidates. The candidates are then checked for validity using the second layer index. In contrast to [15], we have $m+1$ multi-indexes: visual indexing and audio indexing. Finally, all the results are fused and the top N results are returned. With the help of the audio index, we can greatly reduce the number m for the hash table. In our experiments, even one hash table can still work very well.

3.3.2 Searching LAVE Index

The search process in the LAVE indexing is presented as follows. Let $P_a = \{l_1, l_2, \ldots, l_M\}$ be the received audio query points and $P_v = \{v_1, v_2, \ldots, v_L\}$ be the received visual query points. Through the search process, the top K visual points will be returned for each query visual point.

Step 1 For each audio point l_m in P_a, the nearest approximate neighbors will be acquired by a linear search in the audio index. Then the matching pairs are assigned to different candidate clusters $C = \{c_1, c_2, \ldots, c_N\}$. Two pairs are assigned to the same cluster if their nearest approximate neighbors come from the same video.

Step 2 All the clusters will be reordered by temporal verification. Here we define the temporal distance Δt to denote the time difference of the two LBAFs in the matching pairs. The histogram of Δt is computed for all pairs in c_n and the score of c_n equals h_n/M, where h_n is the maximum value of the histogram. This score is also used by the similar computation in Section 3.3. Then the top K' candidate clusters are chosen. All the buckets associated with the top K' candidate clusters in the second layer are regarded as a subset.

Step 3 For each v_l in P_v, the K nearest approximate neighbors are obtained as follows:

a. Top K approximate neighbors are determined by linear search in the subset of the second layer.

b. Use the multi-index indexing method to search other top K nearest neighbor points.

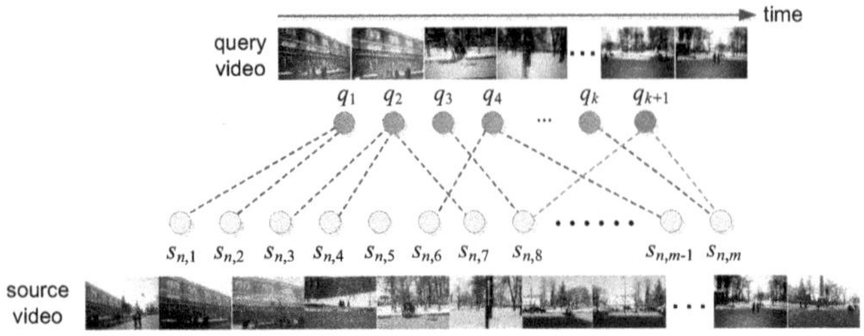

Figure 5: The examples of bipartite graph between video v_i and queries.

c. The $2K$ nearest neighbor points are reordered by similar distance. The top K nearest points are selected.

Step 4 Finally, the top K nearest visual points are returned as the search results.

In summary, according to the process, we combine the audio and video in two stages. The first stage is Step 1 – Step 3.a. In this stage, we use the higher compressed audio information as the crude filter and the more discriminative visual information as the fine filter, which obviously improves the final search speed. Furthermore, as the similarity is computed in separate layers, the combination stage also preserves the individual structure of each signature. The second stage is Step 3.b – Step 4. In contrast to the first combination stage, which heavily depends on audio search accuracy, the combination of audio and video can be weighted by the hamming distance of visual hash bits. The two combination stages holistically exploit the complementary nature of the audio and video signals for more robust mobile video search. Finally, as we have $m+1$ multi-index, i.e., m visual indexes and one audio index, the computational complexity of searching the LAVE index mainly depends on the multi-index indexing method used to search the nearest visual neighbor points, which can be found in [15].

3.3.3 Geometric Verification

With the top N points, the Hough Transfer method is used to get similar source keyframes of the query. Furthermore, a subsequent geometric verification (GV) considering the spatial consistency of local features is needed to reject the false-positive matches [17]. In order to reduce the time consumption of GV, we follow a fast and effective GV based re-ranking step [29] to find the most similar image. As the method only utilizes the orientation of descriptors, there is no need to transmit the location information of the local features by the network. First, the method hypothesizes two matched descriptors of duplicate images should have the same orientation difference. So for two duplicate images, the orientation distance $\Delta\theta_d$ between each matched local feature pair is calculated. Then all $\Delta\theta_d$ are quantized into C bins ($C = 10$ according to [29]). Furthermore, the histogram is scanned for a peak and the global orientation difference is set as the peak value. Finally, the geometric verification score is given by the number of the pairs in the peak, which is normalized by the number of total pairs.

3.4 Progressive Query Process

In contrast to existing mobile video search systems (i.e., search after achieving all the query data), our system provides a progressive query process. Along with the query advancing, the retrieval results can be dynamically calculated on the server after each second query has arrived. Search can stop anytime once a confident result is achieved. The progressive query process can significantly reduce the query cost and improve users' search experience.

Algorithm 1 *Progressive Query Process*

Input: a new query q_{k+1}.
Output: top K nearest videos

add q_{k+1} to Q
search q_{k+1}, get R_{k+1}
add R_{k+1} to R
for each $s_{n,m}$ in R_{k+1} **do**
  find the G_i contains $s_{n,m}$
  add $q_{k+1} \leftrightarrow s_{n,m}$ to E_i
end for
call $W = VideoSimilarScore(G)$
return top K nearest videos

Procedure *VideoSimilarScore(G)*

for each G_i in G **do**
  if $|E_i|$ is changed **then**
    calculate the MSM M_i
    if $|M_i| > \alpha$ **then**
      update $W_i = Sim(Q, V_i, W_i^a, W_i^v)$
    end if
  end if
end for
return W

In our system, the progressive query process is implemented via a bipartite graph transformation and matching algorithm. As shown in Figure 5, for each matched query and source video, we use a bipartite graph $G = \{N, E\}$ to represent the matching. In the bipartite graph, the green node $q_k \in Q$ denotes the received query at time k, the yellow node $s_{n,m} \in S$ denotes the *mth* keyframe in source video V_n. Let R_k denote all the returned similar keyframes $s_{n,m}$ of query q_k. There will be an edge $e_{k,m} \in E$ if $s_{n,m} \in R_k$. After each second search, we can update the bipartite graph G_i and then the similarity score of the matching can be progressively calculated through G_i.

The particulars of the progressive query process are shown in Algorithm 1. If one new query comes, a new node will be added. Then, the edges of the bipartite graph are updated according to the returned result. The red node and lines in Figure 4 show this process. For each bipartite graph, if its number of edges has no change, we will skip it. Otherwise, the similarity score of the matched video will be updated as follows: First of all, the Maximum Size Matching (MSM) M_i of G_i is calculated. If $|M_i| > \alpha$, the similar score W_i will be calculated by

$$\begin{aligned} W_i &= Sim(Q, V_i, W_i^a, W_i^v) \\ &= Sim_a(Q, V_i, W_i^a) + Sim_v(Q, V_i, W_i^v) + Sim_t(Q, V_i), \end{aligned} \quad (1)$$

where $Sim_a(Q, V_i, W_i^a)$ favors the audio content similarity, which can be computed as follows,

$$Sim_a(Q, V_i, W_i^a) = \frac{\sum w_{k,i}^a}{|Q|}, \quad (2)$$

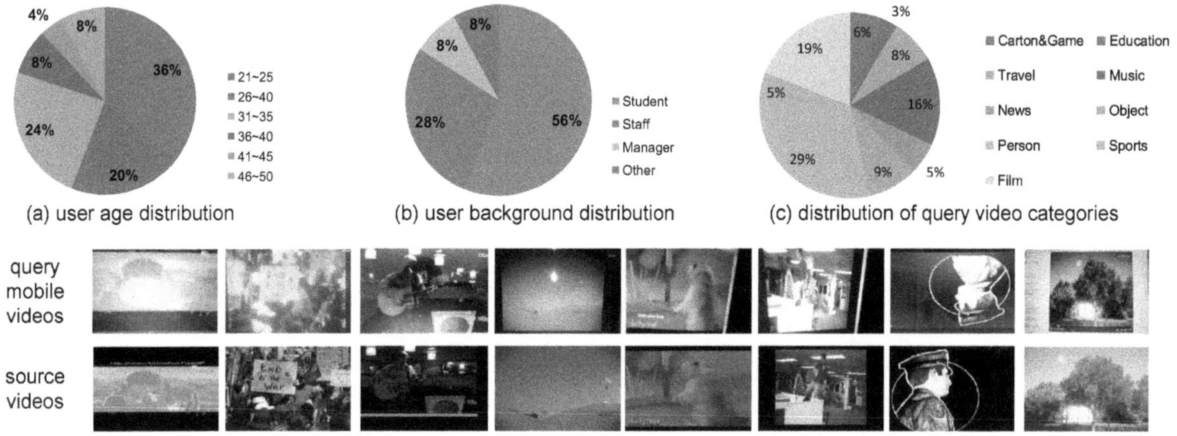

Figure 6: A dataset of real-world mobile video queries.

where $w^a_{k,i}$ is the audio similarity between query q_k and video V_i, $|Q|$ is the query length. $Sim_v(Q, V_i, W^v_i)$ indicates the visual similarity, given by

$$Sim_v(Q, V_i, W^v_i) = \frac{\sum w^v_{k,i}}{|Q|}, \tag{3}$$

where $w^v_{k,i}$ is the visual similarity between query q_k and video V_i. $Sim_t(Q, V_i)$ shows the temporal order similarity. This score guarantees that the matched video should have a similar temporal order. Given MSM M_i of G_k, its temporal matching number can be calculated by the Longest Common Subsequence (LCSS) mode [19]. The LCSS is a variation of the edit distance. We use it to denote the number of frame pairs of M_k matched along the temporal order.

$$LCSS(i,j) = \begin{cases} 0 & i = 0 \text{ or } j = 0 \\ LCSS(i-1, j-1) + 1 & e_{i,j} > 0 \\ max\{LCSS(i-1, j), LCSS(i, j-1)\} & e_{i,j} = 0 \end{cases} \tag{4}$$

Thus, $Sim_t(Q, V_i)$ can be obtained by

$$Sim_t(Q, V_i) = \frac{LCSS(|Q|, |V|)}{|Q|}. \tag{5}$$

Finally, after computing all the similarities between Q and V, the top K videos will be returned as the search results. The computational complexity of the progressive query process is $\mathcal{O}(|G| \times |N_i| \times |E_i|)$, where $|G|$ is the number of the bipartite graphs, $|N_i|$ and $|E_i|$ is the number of vertexes and edges in each bipartite graph, respectively. However, in actual similarity calculation process, as $|E_i|$ has no change in most bipartite graphs, the time consume is much less.

4. EXPERIMENTS

In this section, we first introduce the dataset and queries used for evaluation, and then show the evaluation of the system latency, and the retrieval accuracy. Finally, we conduct user studies to evaluate the usability of our proposed instant mobile video search system.

4.1 Real-World Mobile Video Query Dataset

To evaluate the performance of our instant mobile video search system, we use the video dataset in TRACVID 2011, which contains more than 19,200 videos, with a length of 600 total hours [22]. However, in past methods, the query videos are all generated by programs, which are different from real-world mobile video queries recorded by mobile users. Therefore, we asked 25 volunteers to record video clips from the source dataset as queries. In order to better imitate the possible habits of different mobile users, the choice of the volunteers favored diversity: there were eight females and 17 males. Their age distribution is shown in Figure 6(a) and their career distribution is shown in Figure 6(b). In addition, most of the volunteers had at least one year of experience using smart phones. All of them had watched videos on mobile devices, including eight users who frequently had done so. They recorded the videos according to their interests and used different mobile devices (iPhone 4S, HTC z710t, Samsung Galaxy S3, etc.). Finally, we obtained 1,400 query videos with an average length of 30 seconds [1]. Figure 6(c) shows the category distribution of the recorded query videos. Some keyframes of the queries can be seen in Figure 6(d). According to the examples, we found that the recording process produced serious image distortions, such as blurs, color changes, reflections and transformations. The recorded audio signals were also noisy or silent.

4.2 Evaluation of System Latency

Latency is very important for instant mobile video search. Basically, our system latency can be broken down into four components: video description extraction latency on the client, video description transmission latency with network, video retrieval latency on the server, and result transmission latency.

- **Video description extraction latency.** We tested the video description extraction time on two types of mobile devices. Device I is equipped with Android 4.1.1 OS, a Qualcomm APQ8064P processor with 1.5 GHz frequency, and a 2GB RAM+16GB ROM. Device II is equipped with Android 4.2.2 OS, a Texas Instruments OMAP 4460 processor with 1.2 GHz frequency, and a 1GB RAM+16GB ROM. Then, we separately extracted the video description from 100 query

[1] The query videos are released in "http://mcg.ict.ac.cn/mcg-mvq.html" as a benchmark for mobile video search in this community.

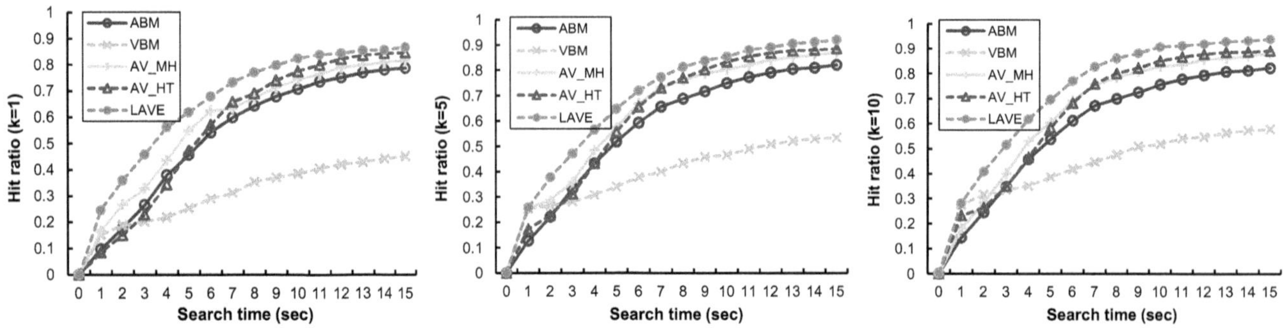

Figure 7: Comparison of search accuracy on the dataset of real-world mobile video queries (in terms of hit ratio).

videos on these two mobiles. For each one-second video steam, the average video description extraction time is listed in Table 1. In order to compare, we implemented the visual feature extraction method in [29], which compresses SURF features with a lossless coding method. It cost 398ms on Device I and 417 ms on Device II to extract the visual features, respectively.

- **Video description transmission latency.** With regards to query delivery, we prefer the query bit rate for quantitative computation, as the exact latency in time heavily depends on the type of network used. As introduced in Section 3.2, we hash the audio fingerprinting into 40 bits and totally choose 100 audio fingerprinting points in each second. Additionally, the visual signature is hashed into 88 bits and about 75 visual points are extracted in each second. So we only have to transmit less than 2 KB/s audio-visual signatures by the network. A typical 40 KB/s 3G network only requires 50 ms to transform the data [8].
- **Video retrieval latency.** To test video retrieval latency, we implemented our method on a server that had Intel(R) Xeon(R) CPU with 3.33 GHz frequency, and 48 GB of memory. Then, we retrieved the 1,400 recorded videos on the 600-hour video dataset. The average video retrieval latency for a one-second query includes 119 ms for the search in the LAVE index and 8 ms for the progressive query process.
- **Result transmission latency.** For the list to be complete, we should also add the video search results transmission latency. As we use an image thumbnail and title to represent each video (less than 3KB), we need to transmit 15KB data for the top 5 results to the client. The latency will depend on network setting. It approximately requires 375ms on a typical 40 KB/s 3G network [8].
- **The overall latency.** In our system, the above four components run in parallel. In order to test the whole system latency in the real network setting, we searched 100 different videos with Device I in a real Wi-Fi network and 3G network setting, respectively. The entire system latency was 626 ms with the Wi-Fi network and 781 ms with the 3G network.

4.3 Evaluation of Retrieval Accuracy

In order to evaluate our instant mobile video search system, we compared the following five methods on the collected real-world mobile query video dataset.

Table 1: Time (ms) for extracting video signatures for one-second query clip.

Video signatures	Device I	Device II
Audio fingerprint	120	130
Visual hash bits	389	405

(1) **Audio-Based Method (ABM).** The method only uses the audio fingerprinting as a video description and uses linear matching on the server.

(2) **Video-Based Method (VBM).** The method only uses the visual hash bits to describe the video and searches the signatures in the multi-index hash, which is also used in the LAVE.

(3) **AV_MH.** Similar to our method, this method also uses a linear index for audio signature and multi-index hashing for visual signature. The difference is that it combines the audio-video signatures using an average late fusion strategy.

(4) **AV_HT.** As opposed to AV_MH, this method utilizes randomized hierarchical tree indexing for visual signature retrieval. The indexing method is implemented in the Fast Library for Approximate Nearest Neighbors (FLANN) [12].

(5) **LAVE.** Our proposed mobile search approach.

The previous two methods are implemented as baselines for single signature methods. The last three approaches are designed to exploit the complementary nature of the audio and video signals. As the late fusion strategy is widely used by many methods, we use it as the baseline for feature combination methods. To measure the effectiveness of all the approaches, we used the hit ratio, which is defined as the number of correctly match the similar video in the top k results to the total search time. Because we will return the top 10 similar videos to the user, we separately computed the hit ratio when $k = 1$, $k = 5$, and $k = 10$.

4.3.1 *Results on the Entire Query Videos*

We first tested the five methods with all 1,400 query videos on the 600-hour video dataset. The hit ratio results of the different methods can be seen in Figure 7. From the results, we found that our method achieved the highest hit ratio among the five methods. Compared to the ABM and VBM, our methods can obviously improve the retrieval accuracy,

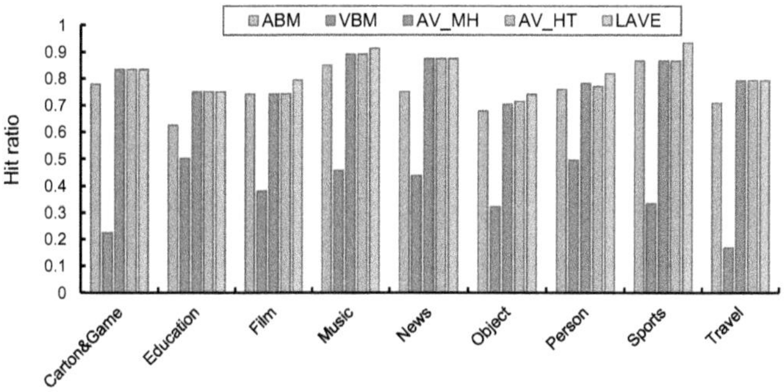

Figure 8: Comparison of search accuracy on different query categories (in terms of hit ratio).

which demonstrates that the complementary nature of the audio and video signals reinforce the discriminative power of individual modalities. As a result, our method is robust to the large variance in the recorded query videos. Among the methods combining the audio and video signatures, our method also achieves the highest accuracy. The reason is that the average late fusion strategy used by AV_MH and AV_HT does not consider the correlation among features in the combination stage. In contrast to late fusion, LAVE employs a multi-layer structure to indicate the similarity of audio features by the distance between the visual feature points. In the combination stage, the correlation among features is uniformly measured by the visual distance. So the combination stage of the LAVE scheme effectively chooses the more discriminative features for different queries.

As shown in the Figure 7, we also observe that the performance gain of retrieval accuracy tends to be large for the first ten seconds, while after that, the accuracy grows slowly. We can therefore choose 10 seconds as the longest query time. Our system can achieve 86.08% and 90.77% precision at eight and ten seconds, respectively.

4.3.2 Results on Different Query Categories

In order to further evaluate the effectiveness of our approach, we also tested the retrieval accuracy on nine different video categories. The query length was set to 10 seconds and the hit ratio was computed from the top five similar videos. As shown in Figure 8, the performance improvements of LAVE were consistent and stable, i.e., most query categories improved compared to the ABM and VBM. Compared to AV_MH and AV_HT, our method also achieved better results for some categories. For example, for the query category "sports," the AV_MH and AV_HT methods got the same hit ratio as the ABM. In other words, the late fusion provided no benefit to the final results. On the contrary, the hit ratio of LAVE was 7% higher than the baseline. The reason is that some sport videos have very similar audio signals. Although the visual signals can discriminate these videos, the average fusion of the audio and video similarity score decreases the information. On the other hand, LAVE indexing methods can easily discriminate these videos through the high weight on the video similarity score. The same situation also occurred in other categories (e.g., "film" and "person").

4.4 Subjective Evaluation of Usability

We randomly invited 12 users from the volunteers to use our proposed mobile video search system (LAVES). The subjects included three female and nine male company staff and college students, with ages ranging from 22 to 36. Other information about these subjects can be found in Section 4.1. As they have already participated in the recording task, after only three minutes of orientation and demonstration, all of them understood how to use the system very well. From the interview, we found that 10 subjects thought the instant video search process is very cool when they first saw it. It is worth noting that when they learned our system did not restrict users from recording either audio or video, all the subjects thought it was very convenient and said that they will try to use the system based only on audio or video manually. This indicates that the switch among single-modality-based and multi-modality-based solutions are preferred by users. After learning the system well, the subjects were asked to use the application to accomplish the following tasks.

- Task 1. Each subject selected 5~10 videos and tried to search for them using LAVES. As our system has not been released to the public yet, the subjects were unable to conduct the search outside the lab. Thus, the query videos were chosen from our video dataset described in Section 4.1. Also, the subjects could search for the video based on audio, video, or both.
- Task 2. In this task, we compared LAVES with popular mobile video search applications (i.e., IntoNow and VideoSurf). After learning how to use these applications, all subjects tried to use the three applications freely by themselves for 20 minutes. Then, a questionnaire was given to each subject to evaluate the usability, user friendliness, and user experience.

In Task 1, the subjects searched 120 videos in total, among which only 16 tasks failed to find similar videos from the top ten similar videos. In addition, all users thought the progressive search process reduced their query time and improved their search experience. According to our records, the average query time for all users was 8.5 seconds. For Task 2, the quantitative evaluation of user satisfaction scores with these mobile video search applications is listed in Table 2. This indicates the advantages of LAVES over the other two mobile video search applications. All the users thought our application was attractive and easy to use with a friendly user interface, and especially liked the lack of restrictions on the use of audio or video as a query input. 91.67% subjects were satisfied with the progressive search process and thought it was natural. They gave a 4.3/5.0 for its Effectiveness. Most of the subjects gave a positive response when

Table 2: A summary of the user study comparing three mobile video search applications: (a) IntoNow [7], (b) VideoSurf [24], and (c) LAVES (our method). 1~5 indicate the worst to the best level.

ID	Question	(a)	(b)	(c)
1	Attractiveness	3.4	3.8	4.2
2	Naturalness	3.8	3.6	4.3
3	Practicality	3.3	3.2	4.1
4	Easy to use	4.3	4.2	4.7
5	Efficiency	3.1	3	4.3
6	Effectiveness	2.8	3	4.3
7	Preference	3	3.2	4.2
8	Effectiveness of progressive search	—	—	4.4

they were asked whether they would install this application and recommend it to their friends. Moreover, the subjects provided comments, such as "add more fashionable videos," "add sharing search results function," and so on.

5. CONCLUSIONS

In this paper, we have investigated the possibility of instant video search on mobile devices, where a very short phone-captured video clip is used as the query to identify the captured video from a large-scale video database. We achieved this goal by designing an innovative mobile video search system that leverages the computing power of mobile clients to directly process video query mobile devices. Specifically, we process the video query to extract joint audio-video descriptors for robust video search (superior to a search via a single modality), and compose a compact signature with a new layered audio-video hashing algorithm. We design a novel progressive query process to instantly return search results to mobile users. As a result, the user search experience has been significantly improved with our proposed system due to the state-of-the-art search accuracy and the very short video query.

In the future, we will invite more subjects for field study evaluations to further evaluate the robustness of our system against video queries with large visual and aural distortions. Our future investigations will also include: 1) we will optimize the system in terms of more efficient descriptors, e.g., the speedup SURF optimized on specific mobile platform [30], and indexing schemes; 2) in addition to only search results, we are aiming to integrate social functions (such as recommendation of celebrities, TV programs, and information related to the captured videos) for social applications; 3) we are also aiming to collect real video data in a particular domain (e.g., TV program or movie) in the cloud.

6. ACKNOWLEDGEMENT

This work is partially supported by the National Key Technology Research and Development Program of China (No. 2012BAH39B02).

7. REFERENCES

[1] H. Bay, A. Ess, T. Tuytelaars, and L. J. V. Gool. Speeded-Up Robust Features (SURF). *Computer Vision and Image Understanding*, 110(3):346–359, 2008.

[2] V. Chandrasekhar, G. Takacs, D. M. Chen, S. S. Tsai, R. Grzeszczuk, and B. Girod. Chog: Compressed histogram of gradients a low bit-rate feature descriptor. In *CVPR*, pages 2504–2511, 2009.

[3] D. M. Chen, N.-M. Cheung, S. S. Tsai, V. Chandrasekhar, G. Takacs, R. Vedantham, R. Grzeszczuk, and B. Girod. Dynamic selection of a feature-rich query frame for mobile video retrieval. In *ICIP*, pages 1017–1020, 2010.

[4] B. Girod, V. Chandrasekhar, D. M. Chen, N.-M. Cheung, R. Grzeszczuk, Y. A. Reznik, G. Takacs, S. S. Tsai, and R. Vedantham. Mobile visual search. *IEEE Signal Process. Mag.*, 28(4):61–76, 2011.

[5] J. He, J. Feng, X. Liu, T. Cheng, T.-H. Lin, H. Chung, and S.-F. Chang. Mobile product search with bag of hash bits and boundary reranking. In *CVPR*, pages 3005–3012, 2012.

[6] J. Huber, J. Steimle, and M. Mühlhäuser. Mobile interaction techniques for interrelated videos. In *CHI Extended Abstracts*, pages 3535–3540, 2010.

[7] IntoNow. http://www.intonow.com/.

[8] R. Ji, L.-Y. Duan, J. Chen, H. Yao, Y. Rui, S.-F. Chang, and W. Gao. Towards low bit rate mobile visual search with multiple-channel coding. In *ACM Multimedia*, pages 573–582, 2011.

[9] H. Liu, T. Mei, J. Luo, H. Li, and S. Li. Finding perfect rendezvous on the go: accurate mobile visual localization and its applications to routing. In *ACM Multimedia*, pages 9–18, 2012.

[10] Y. Liu, W. Zhao, C.-W. Ngo, C. Xu, and H. Lu. Coherent bag-of audio words model for efficient large-scale video copy detection. In *CIVR*, pages 89–96, 2010.

[11] Q. Lv, W. Josephson, Z. Wang, M. Charikar, and K. Li. Multi-probe lsh: Efficient indexing for high-dimensional similarity search. In *VLDB*, pages 950–961, 2007.

[12] M. Muja and D. G. Lowe. Fast approximate nearest neighbors with automatic algorithm configuration. In *International Conference on Computer Vision Theory and Application*, pages 331–340, 2009.

[13] M. Muja and D. G. Lowe. Fast matching of binary features. In *Proceedings of International Conference on Computer and Robot Vision*, pages 404–410, 2012.

[14] M. Norouzi and D. J. Fleet. Minimal loss hashing for compact binary codes. In *ICML*, pages 353–360, 2011.

[15] M. Norouzi, A. Punjani, and D. J. Fleet. Fast search in hamming space with multi-index hashing. In *CVPR*, pages 3108–3115, 2012.

[16] S. Paisitkriangkrai, T. Mei, J. Zhang, and X.-S. Hua. Scalable clip-based near-duplicate video detection with ordinal measure. In *CIVR*, pages 121–128, 2010.

[17] J. Philbin, O. Chum, M. Isard, J. Sivic, and A. Zisserman. Object retrieval with large vocabularies and fast spatial matching. In *CVPR*, 2007.

[18] L. Shang, L. Yang, F. Wang, K.-P. Chan, and X.-S. Hua. Real-time large scale near-duplicate web video retrieval. In *ACM Multimedia*, pages 531–540, 2010.

[19] H. T. Shen, J. Shao, Z. Huang, and X. Zhou. Effective and efficient query processing for video subsequence identification. *IEEE Trans. Knowl. Data Eng.*, 21(3):321–334, 2009.

[20] J. Sivic and A. Zisserman. Video google: A text retrieval approach to object matching in videos. In *ICCV*, pages 1470–1477, 2003.

[21] C. Snoek, M. Worring, and A. W. M. Smeulders. Early versus late fusion in semantic video analysis. In *ACM Multimedia*, pages 399–402, 2005.

[22] TRECVID 2011. http://www-nlpir.nist.gov/projects/tv2011/.

[23] K.-Y. Tseng, Y.-L. Lin, Y.-H. Chen, and W. H. Hsu. Sketch-based image retrieval on mobile devices using compact hash bits. In *ACM Multimedia*, pages 913–916, 2012.

[24] VideoSurf. http://www.videosurf.com/mobile.

[25] A. Wang. An industrial strength audio search algorithm. In *ISMIR*, pages 7–13, 2003.

[26] Y. Weiss, A. Torralba, and R. Fergus. Spectral hashing. In *NIPS*, pages 1753–1760, 2008.

[27] G.-L. Wu, Y.-C. Su, T.-H. Chiu, L.-C. Hsieh, and W. H. Hsu. Scalable mobile video question-answering system with locally aggregated descriptors and random projection. In *ACM Multimedia*, pages 647–650, 2011.

[28] X. Wu, C.-W. Ngo, A. G. Hauptmann, and H.-K. Tan. Real-time near-duplicate elimination for web video search with content and context. *IEEE Transactions on Multimedia*, 11(2):196–207, 2009.

[29] Y. Wu, S. Lu, T. Mei, J. Zhang, and S. Li. Local visual words coding for low bit rate mobile visual search. In *ACM Multimedia*, pages 989–992, 2012.

[30] X. Yang and K.-T. T. Cheng. Accelerating surf detector on mobile devices. In *ACM Multimedia*, pages 569–578, 2012.

Parallel Field Alignment for Cross Media Retrieval

Xiangbo Mao
State Key Lab of CAD&CG
Zhejiang University
Hangzhou, China
mao.stingrey@gmail.com

Binbin Lin
The Biodesign Institute
Arizona State University
Tempe, US
binbin.lin@asu.edu

Deng Cai
State Key Lab of CAD&CG
Zhejiang University
Hangzhou, China
dengcai@gmail.com

Xiaofei He
State Key Lab of CAD&CG
Zhejiang University
Hangzhou, China
xiaofeihe@gmail.com

Jian Pei
School of Computing Science
Simon Fraser University
Burnaby, Canada
jpei@cs.sfu.ca

ABSTRACT

Cross media retrieval systems have received increasing interest in recent years. Due to the semantic gap between low-level features and high-level semantic concepts of multimedia data, many researchers have explored joint-model techniques in cross media retrieval systems. Previous joint-model approaches usually focus on two traditional ways to design cross media retrieval systems: (a) fusing features from different media data; (b) learning different models for different media data and fusing their outputs. However, the process of fusing features or outputs will lose both low- and high-level abstraction information of media data. Hence, both ways do not really reveal the semantic correlations among the heterogeneous multimedia data. In this paper, we introduce a novel method for the cross media retrieval task, named Parallel Field Alignment Retrieval (PFAR), which integrates a manifold alignment framework from the perspective of vector fields. Instead of fusing original features or outputs, we consider the cross media retrieval as a manifold alignment problem using parallel fields. The proposed manifold alignment algorithm can effectively preserve the metric of data manifolds, model heterogeneous media data and project their relationship into intermediate latent semantic spaces during the process of manifold alignment. After the alignment, the semantic correlations are also determined. In this way, the cross media retrieval task can be resolved by the determined semantic correlations. Comprehensive experimental results have demonstrated the effectiveness of our approach.

Categories and Subject Descriptors

H.3.1 [**Information Storage and Retrieval**]: Content Analysis; H.3.3 [**Information Search and Retrieval**]: Retrieval Models

MM'13, October 21–25, 2013, Barcelona, Spain.

ACM 978-1-4503-2404-5/13/10 ...$15.00.
http://dx.doi.org/10.1145/2502081.2502087.

Keywords

Cross media, manifold alignment, parallel field, text corpus and images, multimedia

1. INTRODUCTION

In recent years, multimedia contents including text, image, audio and video on the web have been growing rapidly. With the role switch between social media (Twitter, Facebook) and traditional media (newspapers, etc.), more and more multimedia contents are published on the web by people. However, the explosion of multimedia contents has not been matched by an equivalent increase in the sophistication of multimedia content retrieval technology [7, 24, 25]. Nowadays, the dominate search engines for multimedia retrieval, such as Google and Bing, are still text-based. To effectively leverage the massive explosion of multimedia content, a large number of approaches have been proposed in the areas such as information retrieval, multimedia retrieval and computer vision [2, 3, 5, 11, 16]. One of the well known challenges in the area of multimedia retrieval is the so called semantic gap, *i.e.*, low-level features are not sufficient to characterize high-level semantics of media data [34, 35]. Aiming at this point, many previous works [27] have been proposed to simultaneously utilize multiple types of information such as the original multimedia contents, surrounding texts (or labels), and links to improve the multimedia retrieval performance. However, these works do not consider the semantic correlation among different media types. Generally, they can be viewed as uni-media retrieval, in which the query example and the retrieved results are of the same media type [7].

It is common knowledge that an important requirement for further progress in these areas is the development of sophisticated joint models for multiple media types. In which the most significant is the development of models that support inference with respect to content that is rich in multiple media types [24]. Specifically, these models should utilize the full structure of document which has a body of text accompanied with images or videos. For example, wikipedia page or newspaper article usually contains several paragraphs of text and a number of related images for illustration. The performance of such models is referred as a cross media retrieval problem: the retrieval of all documents with the other media types in response to a media type query data. The task is crucial to many practical applications, such as finding images on the web that best illustrate a given text, finding the texts which are most related to a given image, or further, searching using a combination of different types of multimedia data and labelling media data automatically [24]. Figure 1 illustrates the following example, given an image of a horse, the cross media retrieval model should return all the contents related to the horse concept, *e.g.*, the sound of horse, the introduction text.

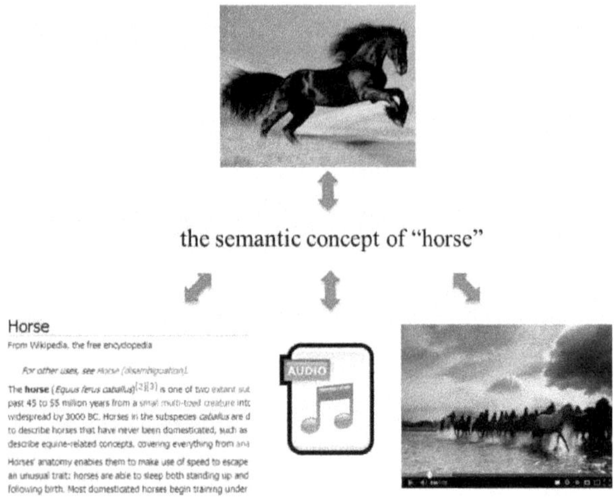

Figure 1: An example of cross media retrieval model.

To address the cross media retrieval problem, advances have been reported over the last decades [7, 26, 28]. These methods focus on two traditional ways to design cross media retrieval systems: (a) fusing features from different media data into a single vector [23, 33]; (b) learning different models for different media data and fusing their outputs [14, 32]. And most of these approaches require multiple-type queries, *e.g.*, queries composed of both image and text features. Hence, these methods are extensions of the classic uni-media retrieval systems.

The key challenge of cross media retrieval is to explore the semantic correlations among the heterogeneous media data. However, both of previous ways do not really reveal the semantic correlations. Semantic correlations can help us to better understand, organize and make use of the media data [34].

Recently, some developments bring new perspective to solve the cross media retrieval problem. Multimedia Correlation Space [34] and Correlation Semantic Space [24] introduce the idea of constructing a joint model to project original multimedia features to the semantic correlation space. And in the same period, manifold alignment methods [10, 29, 31] are proposed and shown that they are appropriate joint models for pair matching between heterogeneous data sources. However, most of existing manifold alignment methods use graph based regularizer *e.g.*, graph Laplacian, which focus on ensuring the first order smoothness of the mapping functions [21] in manifold alignment process. The first order smoothness of the mapping functions is not enough to reveal the underlying semantic correlations between heterogeneous types of multimedia data. In order to discover the latent semantic correlations, we would like to ensure the second order smoothness of the mapping functions in manifold alignment which preserve the geodesic distance of the manifolds. In some recent work, parallel fields [22] are found capable to keep the second order smoothness of the mapping functions [18].

Inspired by these developments in the cross media retrieval area, we propose a novel approach for cross media retrieval, called Parallel Field Alignment Retrieval (PFAR), which integrates a manifold alignment framework from the perspective of vector fields. Instead of fusing original features or outputs, we consider the cross media retrieval as a manifold alignment problem using parallel fields. The proposed manifold alignment algorithm can effectively preserve the metric of data manifolds, model heterogeneous media data and project their relationship into intermediate latent semantic spaces during the process of manifold alignment. After the alignment, the semantic correlations are also determined. In this way, the cross media retrieval task can be resolved by the determined semantic correlations. The empirical results from a real world data demonstrate the benefits of our approach over state-of-the-art cross media retrieval methods.

The rest of this paper is organized as follows. In Section 2, we introduce some basic background information about manifold alignment and parallel fields. In Section 3, we describe the proposed cross media retrieval algorithm (PFAR) in great detail. The experimental results of real world cross media data are presented in Section 4. Finally, Section 5 provides some concluding remarks.

2. BACKGROUND

As discussed in the previous section, our cross media retrieval approach involves manifold alignment and parallel fields techniques. In this section, we introduce some background on mainfold alignment and parallel fields.

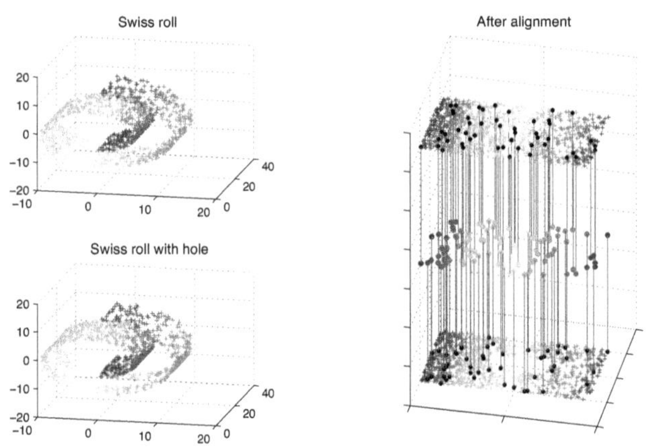

Figure 2: An example of manifold alignment. Two data manifold samples are shown in the left.The result of these two manifolds after alignment is shown in the right.

2.1 Manifold alignment

In many areas of machine learning and data mining, one is often confronted with very high dimensional data such as high definition videos and large vector-space documents. Learning problems involving these datasets are usually challenging. However, in many cases, there is a strong intuition that the high dimensional data may have a lower dimensional intrinsic representation. Manifold alignment is a class of machine learning algorithms which takes advantage of this assumption to produce projections between sets of data by aligning their underlying manifold representations [9, 30].

One of the pioneering work in manifold alignment is the paper of semi-supervised alignment [10]. Given certain labeled samples, semi-supervised alignment aims to find two maps which map two datasets to the new common space while satisfying the label constraint. Suppose $\mathbb{U}$ is the vertex space, there are l labeled vertices $\mathcal{V}_{label} = \{v_1, v_2, \ldots, v_l\}$, $\mathcal{V}_{label} \subset \mathbb{U}$, and $\mathcal{T}_{label} = \{t_1, t_2, \ldots, t_l\}$ ($t_i \in \mathbb{R}$), which is the vector of labeled target values. Similar to regression models, we would like to find a map defined on the vertices of the graph $f : \mathbb{U} \rightarrow \mathbb{R}$ which matches known target values for the labeled vertices. This can be solved by minimizing the following objective function:

$$E(f) = \sum_i \mu|f(v_i) - t_i| + f^T L f \qquad (1)$$

Here $v_i \in \mathcal{V}_{label}$, $t_i \in \mathcal{T}_{label}$, and L is the graph Laplacian matrix. The relative weighting of these terms is given by the coefficient μ. The symmetric graph Laplacian matrix $L = L^T$ provides the information of the data manifold structure. Given two datasets with corresponding labels, we can learn manifolds for each datasets according to Equation 1, and align these two manifold with the intrinsic coordinates of labels. An illustration of manifold alignment is shown in Figure 2.

2.2 Parallel field regularization

Given a manifold $\mathcal{M}$, a vector field is a mapping from the manifold to tangent spaces on the manifold [22]. We can think of a vector field on the manifold $\mathcal{M}$ in the same way as we think of the vector field in Euclidean space. For each point on the manifold, we assign an arrow on it, with a given magnitude and direction, chosen to be tangent to the manifold $\mathcal{M}$. A smooth vector field means that tangent vectors vary smoothly on the manifold. An example of vector fields is shown in Figure 3.

One kind of the most important vector fields are parallel fields. The definition of parallel fields on the manifold is given as follows.

Definition 1. (Parallel Fields [22]) A vector field X on the manifold $\mathcal{M}$ is a parallel field if

$$\nabla X \equiv 0,$$

where ∇ is the covariant derivative on $\mathcal{M}$.

The parallel field is closely related to the linear function on the manifold. Let V be a parallel field on the manifold. If it is also a gradient field for function f, $V = \nabla f$, then f must be a linear function on the manifold.

Parallel fields essentially captures the second order smoothness of functions on the manifold [18]. Some recent theoretical results [15] shows that penalizing the second order

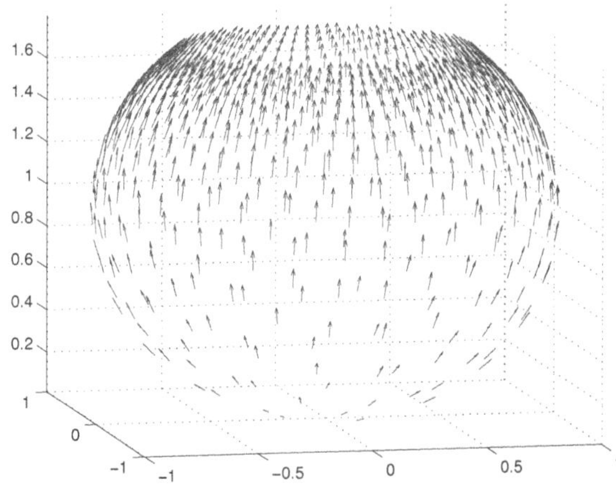

Figure 3: A vector field on punched sphere.

smoothness of functions helps achieve faster rates of convergence for semi-supervised regression problems. Moreover, parallel fields can also captures the metric structure of the manifold [17]. In other words, we can use parallel fields to preserve the distance on the manifold.

Next we briefly introduce Parallel Field Regularization (PFR). Let $\mathcal{M}$ be a d-dimensional manifold embedded in Euclidean space $\mathbb{R}^m$. Given l labeled data points $(x_i, y_i)_{i=1}^l$, $x_i \in \mathcal{M}$ and $y_i \in \mathbb{R}$, the goal of semi-supervised regression on the manifold is to learn a function $f : \mathcal{M} \rightarrow \mathbb{R}$. Specifically, PFR tries to learn the function f and it gradient field ∇f simultaneously via regularization. Formally, PFR aims to learn a function f and a vector field V by optimizing the following objective function:

$$E(f, V) = \frac{1}{l}\sum_{i=1}^{l} R_0(x_i, y_i, f) + \lambda_1 R_1(f, V) + \lambda_2 R_2(V), \quad (2)$$

where

$$R_1(f, V) = \int_{\mathcal{M}} \|\nabla f - V\|^2 \qquad (3)$$

and

$$R_2(V) = \int_{\mathcal{M}} \|\nabla V\|_F^2. \qquad (4)$$

The first term in Equation 2 is the loss function, and the second term enforces the vector field V to be close to the gradient field ∇f of f. ∇V in the third term measures the change of the vector field V. If ∇V vanishes, V must be a parallel field.

3. CROSS MEDIA RETRIEVAL

In this section, we present a novel approach to solve cross media retrieval problem.

3.1 The problem

Suppose we have a dataset $\mathcal{X} = \{X_1, \ldots, X_{|\mathcal{X}|}\}$ which contains documents of two different types of media data $\mathcal{A}$ and $\mathcal{B}$, *e.g.*, $\mathcal{A}$ is a collection of texts and $\mathcal{B}$ consists of images. Specifically, all X_i, $i \in (1, |\mathcal{X}|)$, in $\mathcal{X}$ can be quite diverse: from documents where a single text is complemented by one or more images to documents containing multiple images and texts. For simplicity, we consider the case where each document in $\mathcal{X}$ consists of two sample components, one is from $\mathcal{A}$ and the other one is from $\mathcal{B}$, *i.e.* $X_i = (\mathcal{A}_i, \mathcal{B}_i)$. All data points of $\mathcal{A}$ and $\mathcal{B}$ are of vector forms in feature spaces $\mathcal{R}^{\mathcal{A}}$ and $\mathcal{R}^{\mathcal{B}}$, respectively. Under this circumstances, each document establishes a one-to-one mapping between component from the $\mathcal{A}$ and component from $\mathcal{B}$ media data spaces.

We consider cross media retrieval problem based on the doument dataset $\mathcal{X}$. The fundamental concept of cross media retrieval is rather straightforward. Given a query $Q_{\mathcal{A}} \in \mathcal{R}^{\mathcal{A}}$ (or $Q_{\mathcal{B}} \in \mathcal{R}^{\mathcal{B}}$), the goal of cross media retrieval is to return the closest matches in the $\mathcal{B}$ (or $\mathcal{A}$) space $\mathcal{R}^{\mathcal{B}}$ (or $\mathcal{R}^{\mathcal{A}}$). Whenever the $\mathcal{A}$ and $\mathcal{B}$ media data spaces have a natural correspondence, the original cross media retrieval problem can reduce to a classical retrieval problem: finding an invertible mapping function f between $\mathcal{A}$ and $\mathcal{B}$:

$$f : \mathcal{R}^{\mathcal{A}} \rightarrow \mathcal{R}^{\mathcal{B}}. \tag{5}$$

Hence, if a query $Q_{\mathcal{A}} \in \mathcal{R}^{\mathcal{A}}$ is given, we would be able to find the nearest neighbor of $f(Q_{\mathcal{A}})$ in $\mathcal{R}^{\mathcal{B}}$. Similarly, given a query $Q_{\mathcal{B}} \in \mathcal{R}^{\mathcal{B}}$, it would be easy for us to find the nearest neighbor of $f^{-1}(Q_{\mathcal{B}})$ in $\mathcal{R}^{\mathcal{A}}$ [24].

However, since $\mathcal{A}$ and $\mathcal{B}$ are different types of media data, they tend to adopt different feature representations. Therefore, it is hard to reveal semantic correlations between $\mathcal{R}^{\mathcal{A}}$ and $\mathcal{R}^{\mathcal{B}}$, which means the semantic gap still exists. For example, suppose $\mathcal{A}$ is a dataset consists of texts and $\mathcal{B}$ is a dataset consists of images. And we adopt TF/IDF and Histogram of Oriented Gradients (HOG) [4] to be the feature representations for texts and images, respectively. Thus, it is hard for us to directly explore the semantic correlations between text and image data spaces.

In order to abridge the semantic gap between $\mathcal{R}^{\mathcal{A}}$ and $\mathcal{R}^{\mathcal{B}}$, it is possible to map these two representations into two intermediate spaces which have a natural correspondence [24] and semantic correlations [36]. Consider following mappings:

$$f_{\mathcal{A}} : \mathcal{R}^{\mathcal{A}} \rightarrow \mathcal{I}^{\mathcal{A}}, \tag{6}$$

and

$$f_{\mathcal{B}} : \mathcal{R}^{\mathcal{B}} \rightarrow \mathcal{I}^{\mathcal{B}}. \tag{7}$$

Here, $f_{\mathcal{A}}$ and $f_{\mathcal{B}}$ map original $\mathcal{R}^{\mathcal{A}}$ and $\mathcal{R}^{\mathcal{B}}$ media data spaces to a pair of intermediate spaces $\mathcal{I}^{\mathcal{A}}$ and $\mathcal{I}^{\mathcal{B}}$, respectively. Further, we would like to ensure that there is also an invertible mapping between $\mathcal{I}^{\mathcal{A}}$ and $\mathcal{I}^{\mathcal{B}}$:

$$f_{\mathcal{I}} : \mathcal{I}^{\mathcal{A}} \rightarrow \mathcal{I}^{\mathcal{B}}. \tag{8}$$

Now, if a query $Q_{\mathcal{A}} \in \mathcal{R}^{\mathcal{A}}$ is given, the cross media retrieval task becomes finding the nearest neighbor of $f_{\mathcal{B}}^{-1} \circ f_{\mathcal{I}} \circ f_{\mathcal{A}}(Q_{\mathcal{A}})$ in $\mathcal{R}^{\mathcal{B}}$. Similarly, the goal becomes finding the nearest neighbor of $f_{\mathcal{A}}^{-1} \circ f_{\mathcal{I}}^{-1} \circ f_{\mathcal{B}}(Q_{\mathcal{B}})$ in $\mathcal{R}^{\mathcal{A}}$ if a query $Q_{\mathcal{B}} \in \mathcal{R}^{\mathcal{B}}$ is given [24]. Under this circumstances, the original problem of cross media retrieval is equivalent to learn the intermediate spaces $\mathcal{I}^{\mathcal{A}}$ and $\mathcal{I}^{\mathcal{B}}$.

In our approach, we use manifold alignment with parallel fields to model disparate media $\mathcal{A}$ and $\mathcal{B}$ data and project their relationship into intermediate spaces, and the semantic correlations are determined during the process of manifold alignment. In this way, the cross media retrieval task can be resolved by the determined semantic correlation. We next show our proposed method, the parallel field alignment retrieval (PFAR), in detail.

3.2 Parallel field alignment retrieval

In order to learn intermediate spaces $\mathcal{I}^{\mathcal{A}}$ and $\mathcal{I}^{\mathcal{B}}$, An optimal correspondence between the representations in the original spaces $\mathcal{R}^{\mathcal{A}}$ and $\mathcal{R}^{\mathcal{B}}$ [24] is needed. One possible way is to apply the subspace learning framework which utilize some extremely well developed dimensionality reduction approaches, such as Principal Component Analysis (PCA) [13] or Latent Semantic Indexing (LSI) [6].

Our approach here utilizes manifold alignment algorithms [10, 30] to find mappings defined on the media data manifolds, and use these mappings to align the underlying media manifold representations in intermediate semantic spaces. In the sense of manifold alignment, the semantic correlations are learned after the alignment of the underlying media manifold representations. In addition, we would like to use parallel fields, which preserve the metric of the manifold to measure the disparate media data manifolds. Most of existing manifold alignment algorithms focus on ensuring the first order smoothness of the function. However, researchers have shown that the second order smoothness of the function is particularly important for preserving the metric. And the second order smoothness of the function is equivalent to the parallelism of the gradient field of the function [18]. Thus, we propose to learn two mapping functions and two vector fields simultaneously with two constraints in the process of manifold alignment. By designing the two constraints, we ensure each vector field to be close to the gradient field of each corresponding mapping function, and the vector fields should be as parallel as possible. In this way, the second order smoothness of the function is also ensured. The whole concept of our proposed parallel field alignment retrieval approach is shown in Figure 4.

We now consider aligning disparate media data manifolds, given some additional information of datasets, from the parallel field perspective. In our approach, the desired coordinates for labeled samples are provided. In detail, the coordinates of labels indicate the intrinsic information of paired data samples within the manifolds. With a small number of labeled examples, it is crucial to exploit manifold structures of datasets in manifold alignment [10]. Specifically, we first estimates the gradient field of the prediction function by a vector field, and then require the vector field to be as parallel as possible.

In the setting of parallel field alignment retrieval (PFAR), we denote the notations $A \subset \mathcal{R}^{\mathcal{A}}$ and $B \subset \mathcal{R}^{\mathcal{B}}$ as the datasets, and $\mathbf{s} = \{s_1, s_2, \ldots, s_l\}$ and $\mathbf{t} = \{t_1, t_2, \ldots, t_l\}$ are the vectors referred to the target paired information of the l "labeled" data samples for A and B respectively. Let f and g denote two mapping functions defined on the data manifolds that match known target labeled pairs. Following the above analysis, we try to integrate vector fields V_A and V_B on the manifold with two constraints to our alignment functions:

$$E(f, V_A) = \frac{1}{l_A} \sum_{i=1}^{l_A} (f(a_i) - s_i)^2 + \mu_{A,1} R_1(f, V_A) + \mu_{A,2} R_2(V_A) \tag{9}$$

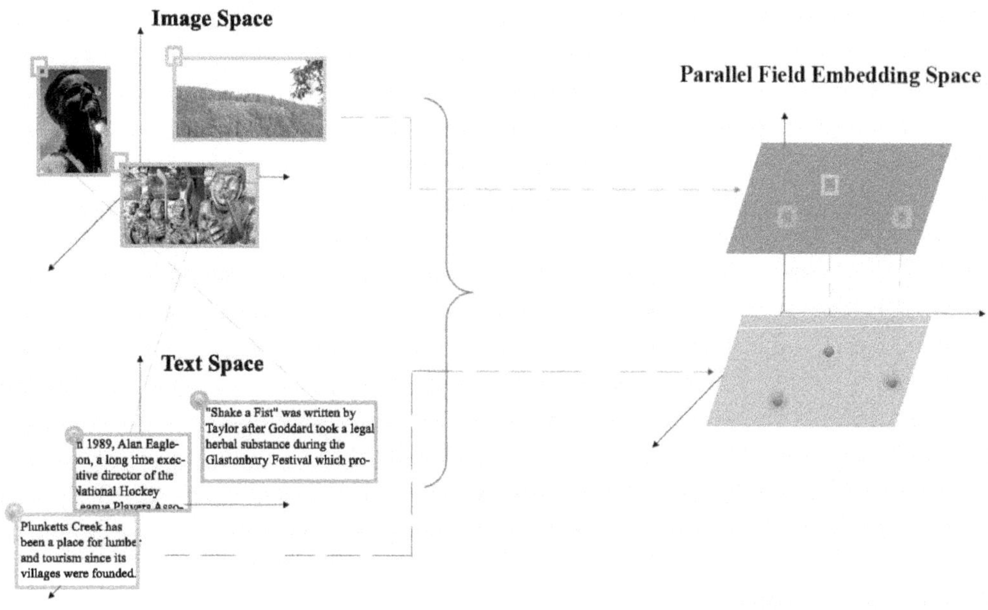

Figure 4: The PFAR concept illustration.

and

$$E(g, V_B) = \frac{1}{l_B}\sum_{i=1}^{l_B}(g(b_i) - t_i)^2 + \mu_{B,1}R_1(g, V_B) + \mu_{B,2}R_2(V_B), \tag{10}$$

where $a_i \in A$ and $b_i \in B$, R_1 and R_2 are regularizers defined in Equation 3 and 4, R_1 enforces vector fields V_A and V_B to be close to gradient fields ∇f and ∇g of mapping functions. As shown in Section 2, if R_2 vanishes, V_A and V_B must be parallel fields.

In order to explore how underlying data manifolds can be mapped into intermediate spaces and then aligned to each other through a common set of paired media data information in the process of PFAR, we should make sure that the vector field is close to the gradient field of the function and further the vector field should be as parallel as possible.

Next we show that how to discretize the continuous objective function. First of all, we give some notations:

- Let $T_{a_i}\mathcal{M}$ denote the d dimensional tangent space of a_i on the manifold $\mathcal{M}$.
- Let $T_i \in \mathbb{R}^{m\times d}$ denote the matrix whose columns constitute an orthonormal basis for $T_{a_i}\mathcal{M}$.
- Let V_{a_i} denote the value of the vector field V at data point a_i.

Following the above notations, define $P_i = T_i T_i^T$. It can be shown that P_i is the unique orthogonal projection from $\mathbb{R}^m$ onto the tangent space $T_{a_i}\mathcal{M}$ [8]. According to the definition of vector fields, each vector V_{a_i} should be on the tangent space $T_{a_i}\mathcal{M}$. Thus we can represent V_{a_i} by the coordinates of tangent spaces, *i.e.*, $V_{a_i} = T_i v_i$. Let $\mathbb{V}_A = (v_1^T, \ldots, v_n^T)^T \in \mathbb{R}^{dn}$ be a dn-dimension column vector which concatenates all the v_i's, $i \in (1, \ldots, n)$.

Then the regularizers R_1 and R_2 can be discretely reduced to:

$$R_1(f, \mathbb{V}_A) = \sum_i\sum_{j\sim i} w_{ij}\left((a_i - a_j)^T T_i v_i - f_j + f_i\right)^2 \tag{11}$$

and

$$R_2(\mathbb{V}_A) = \sum_i\sum_{j\sim i} w_{ij}\|P_i T_j v_j - T_i v_i\|^2, \tag{12}$$

where w_{ij}, weight parameters, which can be approximated by heat kernel weights $\exp(-\|a_i - a_j\|^2/\delta)$ or by 0 - 1 weights for simplicity.

Now, let $\mathbb{I}_A$ denote an $n\times n$ diagonal matrix where $\mathbb{I}_{Aii} = 1$ if a_i is labeled and $\mathbb{I}_{Aii} = 0$ otherwise. Then the discrete form of our parallel field alignment objective function $E(f, V_A)$ can be written as:

$$\begin{aligned} E(f, \mathbb{V}_A) = &\frac{1}{l_A}(f - \mathbf{s})^T \mathbb{I}_A (f - \mathbf{s}) \\ &+ \mu_{A,1}\sum_i\sum_{j\sim i} w_{ij}\left((a_i - a_j)^T T_i v_i - f_j + f_i\right)^2 \\ &+ \mu_{A,2}\sum_i\sum_{j\sim i} w_{ij}\|P_i T_j v_j - T_i v_i\|^2 \end{aligned}. \tag{13}$$

The optimal solution to this objective function is then obtained via solving the following linear systems:

$$\begin{pmatrix} \frac{1}{l_A}\mathbb{I}_A + 2\mu_{A,1}L_A & -\mu_{A,1}C_A^T \\ -\mu_{A,1}C_A & \mu_{A,1}G_A + \mu_{A,2}K_A \end{pmatrix}\begin{pmatrix} f \\ \mathbb{V}_A \end{pmatrix} = \begin{pmatrix} \frac{1}{l_A}\mathbf{s} \\ 0 \end{pmatrix}, \tag{14}$$

where L denotes the Laplacian matrix of the graph with weights w_{ij}, G_A is a $dn \times dn$ block diagonal matrix, and C_A is a $dn \times dn$ block matrix. Let us denote G_{Aii} and C_{Ai} as the i-th $d \times d$ diagonal block of G and the i-th $d \times n$ block of C respectively, and $z_{ij} \in \mathbb{R}^n$ is a selection vector of all zero elements except for the i-th element being -1 and the j-th element being 1. Then G_{Aii} and C_{Ai} are defined as

$$G_{Aii} = \sum_{j \sim i} w_{ij} T_i^T (a_j - a_i)(a_j - a_i)^T T_i \quad (15)$$

and

$$C_{Ai} = \sum_{j \sim i} w_{ij} T_i^T (a_j - a_i) z_{ij}^T, \quad (16)$$

K_A is a $dn \times dn$ sparse block matrix. If we use $K_{A_{ij}}$ to index each $d \times d$ block in A, $i, j \in (1, \dots, n)$, we have

$$K_{A_{ii}} = \sum_{j \sim i} w_{ij} (Q_{ij} Q_{ij}^T + I) \quad (17)$$

and

$$K_{A_{ij}} = \begin{cases} -2w_{ij} Q_{ij}, & \text{if } a_i \sim a_j \\ 0, & \text{otherwise} \end{cases} \quad (18)$$

where $Q_{ij} = T_i^T T_j$.

Similarly, the optimal solution for data set B is as follows:

$$\begin{pmatrix} \frac{1}{l_B}\mathbb{I}_B + 2\mu_{B,1} L_B & -\mu_{B,1} C_B^T \\ -\mu_{B,1} C_B & \mu_{B,1} G_B + \mu_{B,2} K_B \end{pmatrix} \begin{pmatrix} g \\ \mathbb{V}_B \end{pmatrix} = \begin{pmatrix} \frac{1}{l_B}\mathbf{t} \\ 0 \end{pmatrix}. \quad (19)$$

Given two datasets A and B with target paired values of labeled data samples, the solutions to f and g of Equation 14 and Equation 19 can be used to estimate coordinates of the other unlabeled data points in intermediate spaces, which further can be utilized to align their intrinsic data manifolds.

Given any query q from A, we use the mapping function f obtained in the training step to project the query q into the intermediate space. And the projected q is then semantic correlated aligned in the intermediate space. To find the best match samples in B, we can use the metric defined as: let $F = (f_1, \dots, f_r)^T$ and $G = (g_1, \dots, g_r)^T$ be the r dimensional representations of aligned manifolds of A and B. If the coordinates in F and G are aligned from known coordinates, the distance between $a_i \in A$ and $b_j \in B$ is then given by [10]:

$$d(a_i, b_j)^2 = \sum_k |F_{ik} - G_{jk}|^2, \quad (20)$$

then the best match $b_j \in B$ to $a \in A$ is given by:

$$\arg\min_j \, d(a, b_j). \quad (21)$$

The alignment framework is similar to some of the existing alignment methods [9, 10, 30]. However, most of the existing alignment approaches focus on preserving the pairwise similarity between data pairs. In this case, they may not preserve the relative order of the similarity measure. For example, suppose object A and object B are similar, object A and object C are also similar, however B is more similar to A than C. In existing alignment methods, they can find a space in which A, B, C are close, but they cannot tell whether B is closer to A than C or not. By using vector fields, we require the mapping function varies linearly along the geodesics on the manifolds and naturally the order can be preserved. This property is extremely important for multimedia retrieval problems.

4. EXPERIMENTS

In this section, we conduct some extensive experimental evaluation to demonstrate the effectiveness of our proposed *Parallel Field Alignment Retrieval* (PFAR) approach.

4.1 Dataset

The evaluation of a cross media retrieval system usually needs a document corpus with paired contents from disparate domains of multimedia source. In this experiment, we use the recently proposed Wikipedia dataset composed of text and image pairs[1] [24]. This real world dataset consists of a continually updated collection of Wikipedia's featured articles spread over 29 categories, since 2009. The articles are accompanied by one or more images from the Wikipedia Commons, supplying a pairing of the desired kind. Since some categories are very scarce, we will only consider the top 10 most categories in the experiment.

Each article was split into sections based on its section headings, and each image was assigned to the corresponding section in which it was placed by the author(s) of the Wikipedia page. Then this dataset was pruned to keep only sections that contained a single image and at least 70 words. The final corpus contains 2866 text-image pairs, each belongs to one of 10 semantic categories. And the corpus is random split into a training set with 2173 documents, and a test set with 693 documents [24]. The detail information of this corpus is summarized in Table 1.

Table 1: Experiment Dataset Summary [24]

Category	Training	Query	Total
Art & architecture	138	34	172
Biology	272	88	360
Geography & places	244	96	340
History	248	85	333
Literature & theatre	202	65	267
Media	178	58	236
Music	186	51	237
Royalty & nobility	144	41	185
Sport & recreation	214	71	285
Warfare	347	104	451
Summary	2173	693	2866

4.2 Data representation and evaluation

The data representation is similar to those of two previous works [20, 24]. In terms of image representations $\mathcal{R}^I$, we represented the image using the histogram over the popular scale-invariant feature transformation (SIFT) [19] with the codebook of 512 codewords. The text representation is derived from a Latent Dirichlet Allocation (LDA) [1] model with 10 topics (for training data, label information is derived based on the topics). Thus, in $\mathcal{R}^T$, text documents are represented by their topic assignment probability distributions among these 10 topics.

To test the proposed PFAR approach on real data, we conduct the retrieval task with two parts: text retrieval using an image query, and image retrieval using a text query. In the first part, each image in the test set is used as a query, and the goal is to rank all the texts in the test set based on their match to the query image. In the second, a text query

[1] http://www.svcl.ucsd.edu/projects/crossmodal

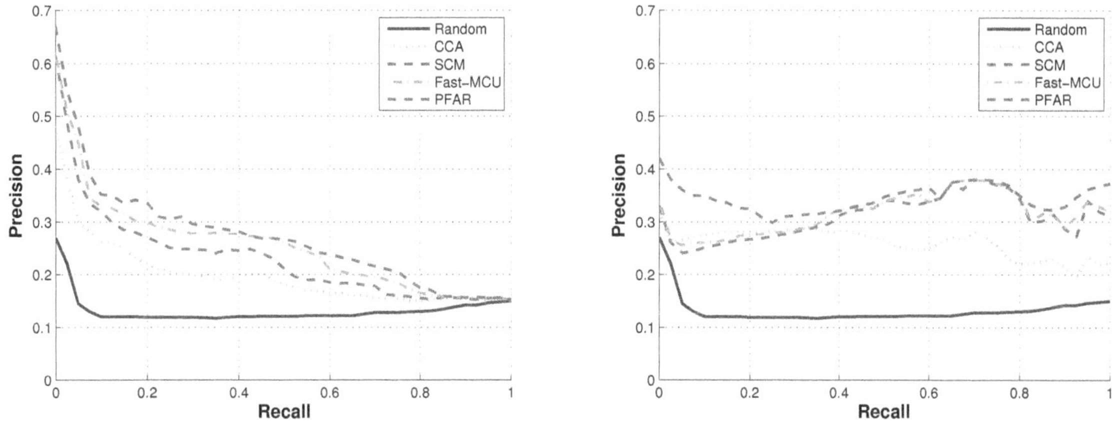

(a) PR curve of text query task

(b) PR curve of image query task

Figure 5: Precision recall curves: (a) text query and (b) image query

is used to rank the images. In both parts, the performance is measured using precision-recall (PR) curves and the mean average precision (MAP).

In the experiment, our approach learns the aligned intermediate spaces by incorporating the information of media data. We use $k = 8$ nearest neighbors method to construct the neighborhood for each media source in formulation of Equation 9, and we apply the 10-fold cross validation to select the parameters (*e.g.*, $\mu_{A,1}$ for R_1, $\mu_{A,2}$ for R_2). To demonstrate the performance of PFAR, we compare a number of state-of-the-art cross media retrieval approaches, CCA [12], Semantic Correlation Matching (SCM) [24], Fast version of Maximum Covariance Unfolding (Fast-MCU) [20] and Manifold Alignment (MA) [10] with PFAR.

In these retrieval approaches, given a test sample (image or text), it is first projected into the learned intermediate space. For CCA and SCM, this involves a linear transformation to the low dimensional subspace, while for Fast-MCU, the nearest neighbors of the test point among the training samples in the original space are used to obtain a mapping of the point as a weighted combination of these neighbors [20].

For PFAR, we use training datasets to learn the intermediate spaces during the parallel field alignment process and two manifolds are aligned at the same time. The same mapping is then applied to the projection of the neighbors in the learned intermediate space to compute the projection of the test point. To perform retrieval, all the test samples from both models, image and text, are projected on the aligned manifolds, respectively. For a given test point from one kind of media, we use the correlation distance shown in Equation 21 to compute its distance to all the other projected test points of the other medium, and then these distances are ranked. If a retrieved sample belongs to the same category as the query, it is considered to be correct.

4.3 Test of the cross media retrieval

The result of the retrieval task is shown in Table 2, which summarizes the MAP scores obtained for the 5 cross media retrieval approaches. This table contains scores for both image retrieval from a text query, and text retrieval from an image query, and the average. The performance of the random retrieval test is also shown to indicate the baseline chance level. From Table 2, it is clear that our proposed approach PFAR outperforms CCA, SCM and Fast-MCU in both image-to-text (image query) and text-to-image (text query) cross media retrieval tasks. PFRA leads non-trivial improvements over other approaches. In both parts, the average MAP of our approach is more than 2.5 times that of random method.

Table 2: Retrieval Performance (MAP Scores)

Experiments	Image Query	Text Query	Average
Random	0.118	0.118	0.118
CCA	0.246	0.196	0.221
SCM	0.274	0.225	0.250
Fast-MCU	0.287	0.224	0.256
MA	0.262	0.225	0.243
PFAR	**0.298**	**0.273**	**0.286**

To further analyze the performance of our proposed approach, we also presents the results of precision-recall (PR) curves for both image and text queries in Figure 5. According to the results of Figure 5, it is clear that our proposed approach PFAR, Fast-MCU, SCM, and CCA all gain improvements over random retrieval at all levels of recall. Compared the PR curves of PFAR with those of SCM and Fast-MCU, it shows that PFAR gets higher precision at all levels of recall for both text queries (on the left) and image queries (on the right). It shows that the PFAR approach is more effective to precisely find matches than the other approaches.

Figure 6 illustrates two examples of text queries and the top ranked images retrieved by PFAR to provide the visualization of cross media retrieval. These two examples are chosen from geography category and sport category, respectively. In each case, the query text is shown at the top, and the first image in the images row is the groundtruth image. As indicated in Figure 6, top four retrieved images are shown next to the groundtruth image. We can see that the retrieved images are quite semantic correlated to the query texts.

Figure 7 shows an example about topics distribution of retrieved texts by CCA, SCM, Fast-MCU, MA and our pro-

Second growth forests have since covered most of the clear-cut land. The beginnings of today's protected areas were established in the late nineteenth and early twentieth centuries: Pennsylvania's state legislature authorized the acquisition of abandoned clear-cut land in 1897, creating the state forest system. The Game Commission began acquiring property for State Game Lands in 1920, and established the Northcentral State Game Farm on Plunketts Creek in 1945 to raise wild turkey. It was converted to ringneck pheasant production in 1981, and, as of 2007, it is one of four Pennsylvania state game farms producing about 200,000 pheasants each year for release on land open to public hunting. The Northcentral State Game Farm is in the Plunketts Creek valley just south of Proctor, and a part of it is on the right bank of Loyalsock Creek downstream of the confluence. The Loyalsock State Game Farm is 13 miles (21 km) downstream on Loyalsock Creek, at the village of Loyalsockville. When a May 2007 fire destroyed a brooder house there just days before 18,000 pheasant chicks were due to hatch, the eggs were transferred to the nearby Northcentral State Game Farm without reduction in the production goal.

(a) Text query from geography category

On March 30, 1993, it was announced that Gil Stein, who at the time was the president of the National Hockey League, would be inducted into the Hall of Fame. There were immediate allegations that he had engineered his election through manipulation of the hall's board of directors. Due to these allegations, NHL commissioner Gary Bettman hired two independent lawyers, Arnold Burns and Yves Fortier, to lead an investigation. They concluded that Stein had "improperly manipulated the process" and "created the false appearance and illusion" that his nomination was the idea of Bruce McNall. They concluded that Stein pressured McNall to nominate him and had refused to withdraw his nomination when asked to do so by Bettman. There was a dispute over McNall's role and Stein was "categorical in stating that the idea was Mr. McNall's." They recommended that Stein's selection be overturned, but it was revealed Stein had decided to turn down the induction before their announcement.
In 1989, Alan Eagleson, a long time executive director of the National Hockey League Players Association, was inducted as a builder. He resigned nine years later from the Hall after pleading guilty to mail fraud and embezzling hundreds of thousands of dollars from the NHL Players Association pension funds."Honoured members: the Hockey Hall of Fame", p. 167 His resignation came six days before a vote was scheduled to determine if he should be expelled from the Hall. Originally, the Hall of Fame was not going to become involved in the issue, but was forced to act when dozens of inductees, including Bobby Orr, Ted Lindsay and Brad Park, campaigned for Eagleson's expulsion, even threatening to renounce their membership if he was not removed. He became the first member of a sports hall of fame in North America to resign.

(b) Text query from sport category

Figure 6: Two examples of text queries and the top images retrieved by PFAR. The query texts of (a) and (b) are chosen from geography category and sport category, respectively. In both (a) and (b), first image in bottom row is the groundtruth image, and others are top ranked retrieved images.

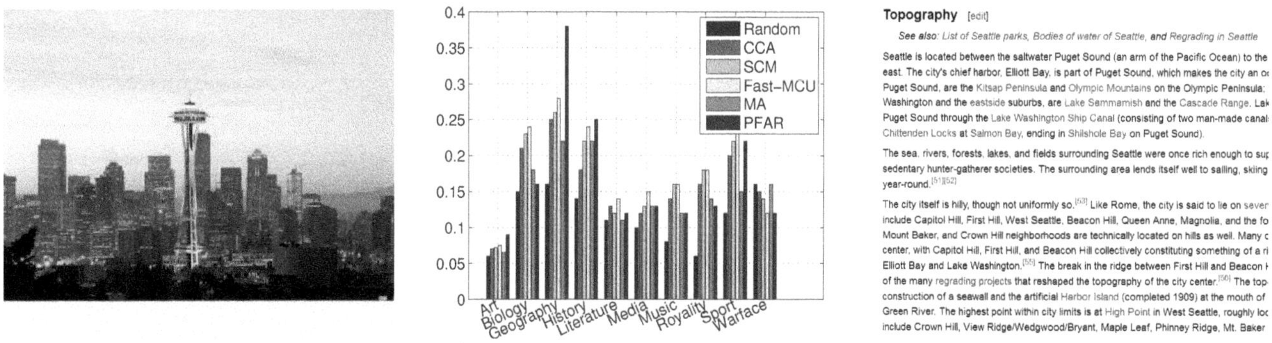

(a) Query image (b) Topics distribution of retrieved texts (c) The groundtruth text: Seattle from Wikipedia

Figure 7: A comparison example of cross media retrieval with given image query.

posed PFAR. Given a query image, we compared the topics distribution of all retrieved texts with respect to above methods. In Figure 7, the query image is taken from Seattle, the groudtruth text gives some description about the geography of Seattle. The result of PFAR can accurately give the topics distributions over other methods.

Actually, all methods tend to retrieve texts that are related specifically to the query image. However, PFAR is able to retrieve texts which are closer to the query image on the categorical level. This also indicates that the abstraction work with relative order infomation preserved by PFAR is especially important for exploratory tasks.

According to the experiment result analysis, PFAR can be viewed as one kind of semantic correlation spaces projection methods. In addition, the parallel field in the alignment process, which preserves the geodesic distance of media manifolds, also significantly contribute to the performance of the text and image cross media retrieval.

5. CONCLUSIONS

In this paper, we have proposed a novel approach for cross media retrieval, called Parallel Field Alignment Retrieval (PFAR), which integrates a manifold alignment framework from the perspective of vector fields. Our goal is to solve the fundamental problem in cross media retrieval area. Given a query $Q_{\mathcal{A}} \in \mathcal{R}^{\mathcal{A}}$ (or $Q_{\mathcal{B}} \in \mathcal{R}^{\mathcal{B}}$), the goal of cross media retrieval is to return the closest matches in the $\mathcal{B}$ (or $\mathcal{A}$) media space $\mathcal{R}^{\mathcal{B}}$ (or $\mathcal{R}^{\mathcal{A}}$).

Due to the semantic gap between low level features and high level semantic concepts of multimedia data, it is not easy for us to reveal the underlying semantic correlations among the heterogeneous multimedia data. Previous studies have shown that manifold alignment method is an appropriate model for pair matching between heterogeneous data sources. Hence, we consider the cross media retrieval as a manifold alignment problem and use parallel fields, which can effectively preserve the metric of media data manifolds, to model heterogeneous multimedia data and project their relationship into intermediate latent semantic spaces during the process of manifold alignment. And the most important factor is that the semantic correlations are also determined in the manifold alignment process.

Finally, the experimental results from a real world data illustrate the validity of our approach. In text and image cross media retrieval tasks, our approach attains significant in the retrieval performance over state-of-the-art cross media retrieval methods.

6. ACKNOWLEDGMENTS

This work is supported in part by National Basic Research Program of China (973 Program) under Grant 2012CB316400 and National Natural Science Foundation of China (Grant No: 61222207, 61125203, 61233011, 90920303), and by an NSERC Discovery Grant and a BCFRST NRAS Endowment Research Team Program project. All opinions, findings, conclusions and recommendations in this paper are those of the author and do not necessarily reflect the views of the funding agencies.

7. REFERENCES

[1] D. Blei, A. Ng, and M. Jordan. Latent dirichlet allocation. *The Journal of Machine Learning Research*, 3:993–1022, 2003.

[2] M. Casey, R. Veltkamp, M. Goto, M. Leman, C. Rhodes, and M. Slaney. Content-based music information retrieval: current directions and future challenges. *Proceedings of the IEEE*, 96(4):668–696, 2008.

[3] C. Cotsaces, N. Nikolaidis, and I. Pitas. Video shot detection and condensed representation. a review. *Signal Processing Magazine, IEEE*, 23(2):28–37, 2006.

[4] N. Dalal and B. Triggs. Histograms of oriented gradients for human detection. In *IEEE Conference on Computer Vision and Pattern Recognition*, volume 1, pages 886–893. IEEE, 2005.

[5] R. Datta, D. Joshi, J. Li, and J. Wang. Image retrieval: Ideas, influences, and trends of the new age. *ACM Computing Surveys*, 40(2):5:1–5:60, 2008.

[6] S. Deerwester, S. Dumais, G. Furnas, T. Landauer, and R. Harshman. Indexing by latent semantic analysis. *Journal of the American Society for Information Science*, 41(6):391–407, 1990.

[7] H. Escalante, C. Hérnadez, L. Sucar, and M. Montes. Late fusion of heterogeneous methods for multimedia image retrieval. In *Proceedings of the 1st ACM International Conference on Multimedia Information Retrieval*, pages 172–179. ACM, 2008.

[8] G. H. Golub and C. F. V. Loan. *Matrix Computations*. Johns Hopkins University Press, 1996.

[9] J. Ham, D. D. Lee, and L. K. Saul. Learning high dimensional correspondences from low dimensional manifolds. In *Workshop on the Continuum from Labeled to Unlabeled Data in Machine Learning and Data Mining*, pages 34–41, 2003.

[10] J. Ham, D. D. Lee, and L. K. Saul. Semisupervised alignment of manifolds. In *Proceedings of the Annual Conference on Uncertainty in Artificial Intelligence*, volume 10, pages 120–127, 2005.

[11] X. He, W. Ma, and H. Zhang. Learning an image manifold for retrieval. In *Proceedings of the 12th ACM International Conference on Multimedia*, pages 17–23. ACM, 2004.

[12] H. Hotelling. Relations between two sets of variates. *Biometrika*, 28(3/4):321–377, 1936.

[13] I. Jolliffe. *Principal component analysis*, volume 2. Wiley Online Library, 2002.

[14] T. Kliegr, K. Chandramouli, J. Nemrava, V. Svatek, and E. Izquierdo. Combining image captions and visual analysis for image concept classification. In *Proceedings of the 9th International Workshop on Multimedia Data Mining*, pages 8–17. ACM, 2008.

[15] J. Lafferty and L. Wasserman. Statistical analysis of semi-supervised regression. In *Advances in Neural Information Processing Systems 20*, pages 801–808, Cambridge, MA, 2008.

[16] M. Lestari Paramita, M. Sanderson, and P. Clough. Diversity in photo retrieval: overview of the imageclefphoto task 2009. pages 45–59. Springer, 2010.

[17] B. Lin, X. He, C. Zhang, and M. Ji. Parallel vector field embedding. *The Journal of Machine Learning Research*, 2013.

[18] B. Lin, C. Zhang, and X. He. Semi-supervised regression via parallel field regularization. In *Advances in Neural Information Processing Systems 24*, pages 433–441, Cambridge, MA, 2011.

[19] D. Lowe. Distinctive image features from scale-invariant keypoints. *International Journal of Computer Vision*, 60(2):91–110, 2004.

[20] V. Mahadevan, C.-W. Wong, T. T. Liu, N. Vasconcelos, and L. K. Saul. Maximum covariance unfolding: Manifold learning for bimodal data. In *Advances in Neural Information Processing Systems 24*, pages 918–926, 2011.

[21] B. Nadler, N. Srebro, and X. Zhou. Statistical analysis of semi-supervised learning: The limit of infinite unlabelled data. In *Advances in Neural Information Processing Systems 22*, pages 1330–1338, 2009.

[22] P. Petersen. *Riemannian Geometry*, volume 171. Springer, 2006.

[23] T. Pham, N. Maillot, J. Lim, and J. Chevallet. Latent semantic fusion model for image retrieval and annotation. In *Proceedings of the 16th ACM Conference on Information and Knowledge Management*, pages 439–444. ACM, 2007.

[24] N. Rasiwasia, J. Costa Pereira, E. Coviello, G. Doyle, G. Lanckriet, R. Levy, and N. Vasconcelos. A new approach to cross-modal multimedia retrieval. In *Proceedings of the 18th ACM International Conference on Multimedia*, pages 251–260. ACM, 2010.

[25] N. Rasiwasia, P. Moreno, and N. Vasconcelos. Bridging the gap: Query by semantic example. *IEEE Transactions on Multimedia*, 9(5):923–938, 2007.

[26] C. Snoek and M. Worring. Multimodal video indexing: A review of the state-of-the-art. *Multimedia Tools and Applications*, 25(1):5–35, 2005.

[27] C. Snoek, M. Worring, and A. Smeulders. Early versus late fusion in semantic video analysis. In *Proceedings of the 13th ACM International Conference on Multimedia*, pages 399–402. ACM, 2005.

[28] T. Tsikrika and J. Kludas. Overview of the wikipediamm task at imageclef 2008. pages 539–550. Springer, 2009.

[29] C. Wang and S. Mahadevan. Manifold alignment using procrustes analysis. In *Proceedings of the 25th International Conference on Machine Learning*, pages 1120–1127. ACM, 2008.

[30] C. Wang and S. Mahadevan. A general framework for manifold alignment. 2009.

[31] C. Wang and S. Mahadevan. Heterogeneous domain adaptation using manifold alignment. volume 2, pages 1541–1546. AAAI Press, 2011.

[32] G. Wang, D. Hoiem, and D. Forsyth. Building text features for object image classification. In *IEEE Conference on Computer Vision and Pattern Recognition*, pages 1367–1374. IEEE, 2009.

[33] T. Westerveld. Probabilistic multimedia retrieval. In *Proceedings of the 25th International ACM SIGIR Conference on Research and Development in Information Retrieval*, pages 437–438. ACM, 2002.

[34] Y. Yang, D. Xu, F. Nie, J. Luo, and Y. Zhuang. Ranking with local regression and global alignment for cross media retrieval. In *Proceedings of the 17th ACM International Conference on Multimedia*, pages 175–184. ACM, 2009.

[35] Y. Yang, Y. Zhuang, F. Wu, and Y. Pan. Harmonizing hierarchical manifolds for multimedia document semantics understanding and cross-media retrieval. *IEEE Transactions on Multimedia*, 10(3):437–446, 2008.

[36] Y. Zhuang, Y. Yang, and F. Wu. Mining semantic correlation of heterogeneous multimedia data for cross-media retrieval. *IEEE Transactions on Multimedia*, 10(2):221–229, 2008.

Analysis and Forecasting of Trending Topics in Online Media Streams

Tim Althoff Damian Borth Jörn Hees Andreas Dengel
German Research Center for Artificial Intelligence (DFKI)
D-67663 Kaiserslautern, Germany
althoff@stanford.edu, {damian.borth, joern.hees, andreas.dengel}@dfki.de

ABSTRACT

Among the vast information available on the web, social media streams capture what people currently pay attention to and how they feel about certain topics. Awareness of such trending topics plays a crucial role in multimedia systems such as trend aware recommendation and automatic vocabulary selection for video concept detection systems.

Correctly utilizing trending topics requires a better understanding of their various characteristics in different social media streams. To this end, we present the first comprehensive study across three major online and social media streams, Twitter, Google, and Wikipedia, covering thousands of trending topics during an observation period of an entire year. Our results indicate that depending on one's requirements one does not necessarily have to turn to Twitter for information about current events and that some media streams strongly emphasize content of specific categories. As our second key contribution, we further present a novel approach for the challenging task of forecasting the life cycle of trending topics in the very moment they emerge. Our fully automated approach is based on a nearest neighbor forecasting technique exploiting our assumption that semantically similar topics exhibit similar behavior.

We demonstrate on a large-scale dataset of Wikipedia page view statistics that forecasts by the proposed approach are about 9-48k views closer to the actual viewing statistics compared to baseline methods and achieve a mean average percentage error of 45-19 % for time periods of up to 14 days.

Categories and Subject Descriptors

H.3.3 [**Information Storage and Retrieval**]: Information Search and Retrieval —*Information filtering*

Keywords

Trending Topics, Social Media Analysis. Lifecycle Forecast, Twitter, Google, Wikipedia

MM'13, October 21–25, 2013, Barcelona, Spain.

ACM 978-1-4503-2404-5/13/10 ...$15.00.
http://dx.doi.org/10.1145/2502081.2502117.

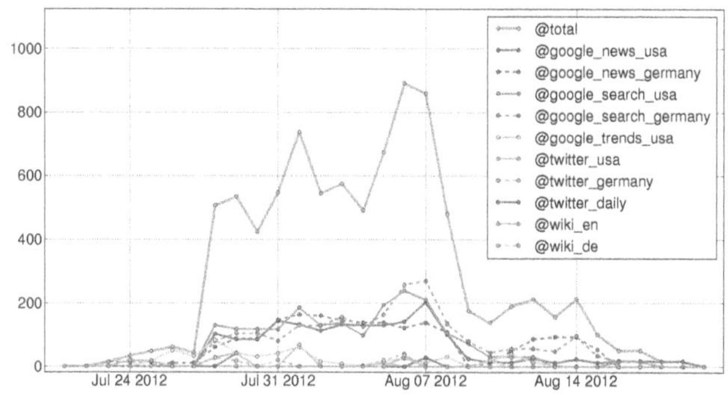

Figure 1: The trending topic "Olympics 2012" during summer 2012. The colored curves represent the contribution of the different online and social media streams.

1. INTRODUCTION

Currently, as multimedia content consumption is rapidly increasing on the internet we can consider ourselves as living in the zettabyte era[1]. To a large degree this vast amount of information is created, shared, and exchanged by the users themselves in social multimedia systems. These systems provide us with streams of information that capture how we are spending our time and what we are talking about. Over time, different topics arise in these media streams reflecting changing interests of groups of individuals. In this sense, social media streams mirror our society. These streams contain rich information and immediate feedback about to what people currently pay attention to and how they feel about certain topics.

Such *trending topics* [13] can be associated with a subject (i.e. a textual label) and experience sudden increases in user popularity ("trending"). They usually correspond to real world events such as sport events (Olympics 2012), product releases (iPhone 5), celebrity news (Steve Jobs' death), incidents (Sinking of the Costa Concordia), political movements (Occupy), and entertainment (Academy Awards). Awareness of trending topics plays a key role in building social multimedia systems satisfying users' information needs and enhancing the multimedia consumption experience [17].

Today, a large variety of social multimedia systems is available to users on the web such as Twitter, YouTube, Facebook, Flickr, Pinterest, Tumblr, Google News/Trends, and Wikipedia serving different kinds of needs such as information demand, social communication, as well as sharing

[1]Cisco, The Zettabyte Era. May 30, 2012.

and consumption of multimedia content. Because of this, many users turn to multiple of these online platforms, depending on their present individual needs, creating a heterogeneous multi-channel[2] environment within the social media landscape. While researchers have a general intuition about the nature of these channels (e.g. many current event detection systems are based on Twitter feeds [14, 22]), studies of the exact distribution of information across multiple channels have not been in the scope of the multimedia community until now. To the best of our knowledge, there does not exist a study on the behavior and lifecycle of trending topics across multiple media channels and on the correlations between topic categories and media channels over a one year observation period prior to this work. For example, the trending topic "olympics 2012" (the number one trend) manifests itself in multiple media channels which clearly exhibit different behavior (as illustrated in Figure 1).

A second and much more challenging task is *forecasting* the life cycle of a trending topic, i.e. forecasting the amount of user engagement towards it in the very moment they emerge. These forecasts enable us to anticipate changing information needs of users ahead of time and to allocate limited resources in trend aware multimedia systems such as recommender systems [9, 17] or video concept detection systems [5]). For example, such limited resources include time of content consumers and producers, screen estate and content recommendations on web pages [17], processing time for training models in video concept detection [5], and server load and replication capacity [21].

While obviously of great use, forecasting trending topics is a very challenging problem since the corresponding time series usually exhibit highly irregular behavior also known as structural breaks that can lead to large forecasting errors and unreliable models [7]. The complexity of this task will be illustrated in more detail in Sec. 4 (Figure 5).

We present a novel forecasting approach exploiting the assumption that semantically similar topics exhibit similar behavior in a nearest neighbor framework. Semantically similar topics are discovered by mining topics of similar type and category on DBPedia [3], a structured representation of the information on Wikipedia. We evaluate our fully automatic approach on a large-scale dataset of billions of views of several million articles on Wikipedia.

Summarizing, our contribution in this paper is three-fold. We present **(1)** the first comprehensive study of trending topics in three major social and online media channels with an observation period of one year, **(2)** a fully automatic forecasting technique for these trending topics based on a nearest neighbor approach exploiting semantic relationships between topics, and **(3)** an empirical evaluation of our forecasting model over real-world user behavior on a large-scale Wikipedia dataset.

The rest of this paper is organized as follows. In Sec. 2, we outline work related to trending topics in multimedia and social media based forecasting. The multi-channel analysis of trending topics is presented in Sec. 3. Our novel forecasting technique is described in Sec. 4 before evaluating the approach in Sec. 5. Sec. 6 concludes this paper with a short summary and an outline for future work.

[2]Note that we choose to use the term *channel* instead of *stream* as we believe it to fit the archive-alike properties of multimedia collections such as YouTube, Flickr, and Wikipedia better.

2. RELATED WORK

The overview over related work is divided into three parts. We first report work that analyzes or combines information from multiple media channels. Then, we focus on forecasting behavioral dynamics before finally presenting applications of trending topics to social multimedia systems.

Multi-Channel Analyses.

Detecting and tracking topics in news media has been studied since 1997 with the goal of understanding news in multiple languages and across multiple media channels (including television and radio sources) [2].

Ratkiewicz et al. [16] argue that online popularity of specific topics (e.g. "Barack Obama") cannot in general be characterized by the behavior of individual news-driven events (e.g. "Barack Obama inaugurated as U.S. President") since the former might subsume many different news stories. They further find bursts in Wikipedia traffic to be correlated with bursts of Google search volume.

Wikipedia article views have also been correlated with behavior on Twitter to analyze the effectiveness of creating new content for breaking news (e.g. Japan earthquake) or updating pages at the moment of news (e.g. Oscar winners) [22] and to filter spurious events on Twitter which indirectly resulted in the finding that Wikipedia lags behind Twitter by about two hours [14]. Adar et al. correlate several behavioral datasets such as general queries from an observation period of one month from MSN and AOL search logs with the general idea of understanding past behavior to predict future behavior [1].

The work of Yang and Leskovec [23] explores patterns of temporal variation in online media by clustering them to analyze the rise and fall of human attention with regard to certain phrases or memes. They report six distinct temporal patterns and find that weblogs trailed mainstream media by one or two hours for most of the considered phrases.

In contrast to the above, we explicitly focus our study on trending topics in online and social media channels over a long observation period. Similar to [8] using trending topics such as "oil spill" and "iPhone" to evaluate tweet selection, we utilize trending topics published by the media channels themselves and focus on multi-channel analysis and forecast. We further analyze the correlation between topic categories and media channels and propose a fully automatic approach of forecasting trending topics in terms of time series (as opposed to visualization tools [1] or predicting temporal clusters [23]).

Forecasting Behavioral Dynamics.

Much research has been devoted to predicting economic variables such as auto sales, unemployment claims [6] ("nowcasting"), or opening weekend box-office revenue for movies [10]. In the same way, popularity of online content has often been treated as a single variable (e.g. total number of views) instead of a time series. Either early popularity [19], or content-based features such as publisher, subjectivity, or occurrence of named entities [4] are used to forecast eventual popularity. More recent work treats popularity of queries and clicked URLs of search engines as time series and uses state space models adapted from physics for forecasting [15].

The only work on forecasting Wikipedia article popularity known to the authors of this paper restricts itself to the case of featured articles on the main page and accounts for daily cycles in viewing behavior [20]. However, trending topics lead to time series with unexpected shifts. These shifts are known as structural breaks in the field of econometrics and can lead to large forecasting errors and unreliable forecasting models [7]. A good example for such a structural break is Whitney Houston's death in February 2011 that caused 2000 times (!) more people to access her Wikipedia article than usual. Clements and Hendry find that structural breaks (also described as parameter non-constancy) are the main cause of large, unexpected forecast errors in practice. Pooling or combining forecasts from different models has often been found to outperform individual forecasts and to increase forecast robustness.

Forecasting trending topics is different in the sense that we require a fully automatic system and that often there is little historical information available (unlike for many economic variables of interest). For example, few people were aware of "Costa Concordia" before the ship sunk in January, 2012. Similarly, to make predictions about "54th Grammy Awards" one needs to understand the relationship of this event with previous ones such as previous instances of the Grammy Awards. We assume that semantically similar topics share characteristics and behavior and therefore could improve forecasting accuracy. This assumption has not yet been explored in previous work (e.g. [15]). In addition, our proposed approach can forecast popularity of arbitrary articles that exhibit very diverse viewing dynamics. This differs dramatically from the experimental conditions in [20] which are characterized by the authors as "nearly ideal".

Multimedia Applications.

One application using social media in our target domain of social multimedia systems has been explored in [12]. This work uses the Flickr photo upload volume of specific topics to inform autoregressive nowcasting models for monthly political election results and product sales (i.e. the model requires the Flickr upload volume at time t to produce a forecast for time t). Further, the Flickr queries relevant to the forecast subject of interest are chosen manually (e.g. using "Hillary" instead of "Clinton" to avoid images by Bill Clinton for the 2008 Democratic Party presidential primaries).

Another application that explicitly focuses on trending topics identified in different online and social media channels uses them to dynamically form and extend the concept vocabulary of video concept detection systems [5]. They further find trending topics to be strongly correlated with changes in upload volume on YouTube and demonstrate a visual classification of these trends.

SocialTransfer is another system that uses trending topics obtained from a stream of Twitter posts for social trend aware video recommendation [17]. Learning new associations between videos based on current trends is found to be important to improve the performance of multimedia applications, such as video recommendation in terms of topical relevance and popularity. The popularity of videos is also used in [21] to drive the allocation of replication capacity to serve social video contents. This work analyzes real-world video propagation patterns and finds that newly generated and shared videos are the ones that tend to attract the most attention (called temporal locality). They further formulate the challenge to estimate the videos' popularity for video service allocation for which they use the number of microblog posts that share or re-share the video. These insights are incorporated into the design of a propagation-based social-aware replication framework. Two other research prototypes that seek to enhance the multimedia consumption experience by extracting trending topics and events from user behavior on the Web are SocialSensor [9] and TrendMiner [18]. The first one emphasizes the real-time aspects of multimedia indexing and search over multiple social networks for the purpose of social recommendations and retrieval. TrendMiner focuses on real-time methods for cross-lingual mining and summarization of large-scale stream media and use cases in financial decision support and political and monitoring.

	Topic		Topic
1.	olympics 2012	11.	christmas
2.	champions league	12.	steve jobs
3.	iphone 5	13.	manhattan
4.	whitney houston	14.	academy awards
5.	mega millions numbers	15.	formula 1
6.	closer kate middleton	16.	justin bieber
7.	facebook	17.	joe paterno died
8.	costa concordia	18.	battlefield 3
9.	black friday deals	19.	muammar gaddafi dead
10.	superbowl	20.	ufc

Table 1: International Top 20 Trending Topics during Sep. 2011 – Sep. 2012. Please note that the US presidential election was in Nov. 2012.

3. MULTI-CHANNEL ANALYSIS

This section introduces the dataset used for the analysis of trending topics across media channels and presents an analysis of their temporal characteristics as well as insights into the relationship between channels and topic categories.

3.1 Trending Topics Dataset

To facilitate a comprehensive analysis of trending topics across multiple channels, we crawl the top trends from three major online media channels on a daily basis. With the intent to capture people's communication needs, search patterns, and information demand we choose to retrieve trends from Twitter, Google, and Wikipedia, respectively. We further cluster similar trends across time *and* channels to later be able to compare the different manifestations of a particular trend across multiple channels.

1. Raw Trending Topic Sources.

As motivated above, we use Google, Twitter and Wikipedia as a starting point by retrieving a ranked list of popular terms from 10 different sources on a daily basis: five Google channels (Search and News for USA and Germany as well as the Trends feed), three Twitter channels (daily trends for USA and Germany as well as the Daily Trends feed), and two Wikipedia channels (popular articles in the English or German language). For each of these feeds we retrieve 10-20 ranked topics (110 topics per day). In total the dataset covers the observation period Sep. 2011 – Sep. 2012 and contains roughly 40,000 potentially overlapping topics.

2. Unification and Clustering of Trends.

To connect multiple instances of the same trending topic across time and media channels we perform a unification and clustering of the individual topics obtained in the pre-

	#Topics	#Sequences
Total	200	516
Google	191 (95.5 %)	445 (86.2 %)
Twitter	118 (59.0 %)	232 (45.0 %)
Wikipedia	69 (34.5 %)	108 (20.9 %)
G & T	115 (57.5 %)	174 (33.7 %)
G & W	66 (33.0 %)	86 (16.7 %)
T & W	43 (21.5 %)	57 (11.0 %)
G & T & W	42 (21.0 %)	48 (9.3 %)

Table 2: Number of analyzed trend topics and sequences for Google (G), Twitter (T), and Wikipedia (W).

vious step. First, we map the individual topic strings to a corresponding Wikipedia URI by selecting the top-most Wikipedia result when performing a Google search for that topic (this approach was found to be more robust than more direct methods on Wikipedia [5]). Then we cluster two URIs together if their Levenshtein or edit distance is below a certain threshold (set to 0.35 × word length). This process can be thought of as a greedy version of a hierarchical agglomerative clustering using the Levenshtein distance. The method allows us to unify topics such as "super bowl time", "super bowl 2012", and "superbowl" into a single cluster. Overall this results in 2986 clusters or individual trends. A cluster is now represented by its most prominent member and will be referred to as a *trending topic* for the rest of this work.

3. Ranking Trending Topics.
To reason about the popularity of these trending topics we assign them trend scores based on the following method: For each each day and for each of our 10 feeds, we record the rank at which a topic appears. These ranks are combined using Borda count, obtaining a score for each day that is assigned to the topic's cluster (from the previous step). To measure the impact of a trending topic (cluster) over its overall lifetime, we define its global trend score by the sum of its daily scores over the observation period. The top trends with respect to this global trend score are shown in Table 1.

3.2 Lifetime Analysis

Some trending topics occur multiple times within our one year observation period. For example sport topics such as "Champions League" are discussed whenever important games are played. To allow for an analysis of when channels begin and stop featuring particular topics, we divide a trending topic into multiple sequences. For the Champions League example, we obtain one sequence per round of the tournament. Formally, topics are broken up into sequences such that their daily trend scores are non-zero for at least two out of any three adjacent dates, i.e. we compensate for "score gaps" of at most one day but form multiple sequences for gaps of two or more days. We perform an analysis of the lifetime of trending topics in the different channels for the top 200 trends (based on their global trend score) that were split into 516 sequences based on the described procedure. Table 2 summarizes the resulting number of topics and sequences for the different channels and their combinations. Note that we map the ten individual observed channels to their respective sources: Google, Twitter, and Wikipedia. The Google channel has the largest coverage of the trending topic sequences in our dataset (86.2 %). About 9.3 % of trending topic sequences occur in all three channels and between 11.0 % and 33.7 % occur in two channels.

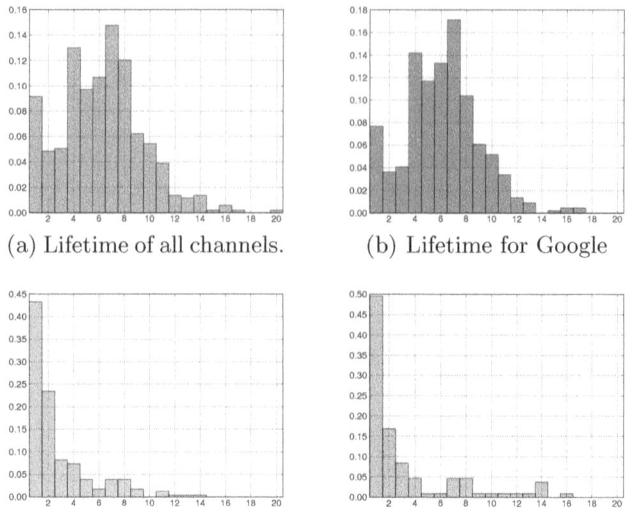

(a) Lifetime of all channels. (b) Lifetime for Google (c) Lifetime for Twitter (d) Lifetime for Wikipedia

Figure 2: Lifetime in days for top 200 trending topics.

We first deal with the question how long trending topics survive in general and whether there are differences in lifetime in the different media channels. In our case, lifetime is defined as the number of consecutive days with positive trend scores. Histograms of the lifetime of trending topics are shown in Figure 2. We observe that the trending topics in our dataset rarely survive for more than fourteen days with most trending topics having a lifetime of less than nine days. Since Google covers a large share of top trends, the distribution for the channel looks very similar to the overall distribution. The lifetime of topics on Twitter is much shorter complying with our expectations of the ephemerality of trends in this channel – about two thirds of the top trends only survive for one or two days. Interestingly, the distribution looks similar for Wikipedia. This raises the question when and why exactly people are turning to Wikipedia to satisfy their information needs.

For trending topics that occur in at least two of the three channels we record the day on which the trend starts, the day on which the trend peaks (defined by the trend score defined earlier), and the day on which the trend ends again. We then define the *delay* between two channels as the difference between the start/peak/end dates in channel X and the start/peak/end days in channel Y. Note that a positive delay means that the first channel X is slower, i.e. trends tend to start later in channel X than in channel Y. The mean delays for start, peak, and end are summarized in Table 3. Interestingly, there are only marginal differences in starting delays (first of the three numbers) between the three channels with Twitter and Wikipedia being slightly faster than Google. These results are not very surprising considering that Osborne et al. found Twitter to be around two hours faster than Wikipedia [14] – a difference almost impossible to observe in data of daily granularity. A much stronger effect is observed for peak and end delays (second and third number). Both Twitter and Wikipedia tend to peak more

	Twitter	Wikipedia
Google	-0.20 / 2.23 / 3.64	-0.41 / 2.35 / 4.16
Twitter	–	0.07 / 0.36 / 0.21
Google Trends	0.09 / 0.04 / 0.41	-0.42 / -0.32 / 1.25

Table 3: Mean delay in days between pairs of media channels (start/peak/end). Positive delay means that the "row channel" is slower than the "column channel".

than two days before Google. The picture is even clearer when looking at the end delays where Twitter and Wikipedia lead Google by three and four days respectively. Overall, these results add to the ephemerality of the Twitter and Wikipedia. However, through this analysis we found that some of the Google channels seem to be intentionally delayed or averaged, i.e. still displaying the top stories after several days. Since Google Trends is known not to be artificially delayed we added comparisons with this channel to Twitter and Wikipedia to our analysis. This channel peaks around the same time as Twitter and Wikipedia and trends tend to end around half a day after Twitter and more than one day after Wikipedia.

3.3 Topic Category Analysis across Channels

Considering trend aware multimedia applications it is critical to understand why people to turn to specific channels. To shed light on what kind of topics are the most popular in the individual channels we manually annotate the 200 top trends with categories. The categories are chosen by examining the main themes of trends we found in our dataset. Please refer to Table 4 for more information about the individual categories, their descriptions, and examples. Note that a trending topic might be assigned to multiple categories, i.e. the death of a popular music artist would be assigned to celebrity, entertainment, death, and artist to make an extreme example (similar to [1]). The engagement with respect to the different categories in a media channel is measured as follows: For each trend within the channel we assign its score to all of its categories. Finally, we normalize the scores for each channel, e.g. to account for the dominance of Google for the scores overall. The resulting distribution over categories is displayed in Figure 3.

We can observe that the channels tend to specialize in certain topic categories. For example, the most popular category in Google is sports. A large share of the scores further is assigned to celebrity and entertainment categories. Google also has the highest relative share (15 %) for politics. Twitter also features many trends in the celebrity and entertainment categories. Interestingly, it has the highest relative shares of trends related to products, companies and technology. One reason might be that many Twitter users are technology affine early adopters that like to share their thoughts on new products. Another interesting finding is that over 20 % of the scores on Twitter are assigned to the holidays category. We hypothesize that holiday related trends are big on Twitter as many people tag their posts and pictures with the same hashtags such as #christmas or #thanksgiving. Wikipedia clearly shows a specialization for categories that involve people and incidents such as disasters or the death of celebrities. Contrary to the intuition that Wikipedia is a slowly evolving channel which people use to read up on complicated topics, especially when also considering the temporal properties of the Wikipedia channel from the analysis above, we believe that many users use Wikipedia during these trends and events to learn about or remind themselves about related topics. For example, when Neil Armstrong died on August 25, 2012 many people viewed the corresponding Wikipedia article e.g. to learn about who he was (American astronaut), what he was famous for (first person on the moon), and how old he was when he died (82) (see Figure 4). Note that this trending topic also mistakenly subsumes the lifetime ban from sports competitions of Lance Armstrong on August 24, 2012.

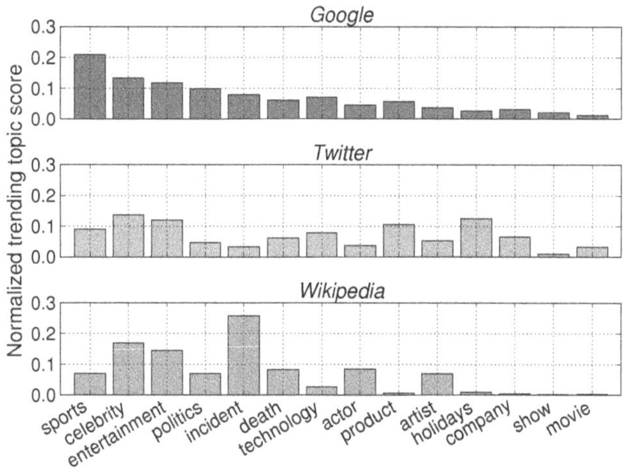

Figure 3: Normalized distribution of trending topic scores over trend categories in the individual channels. Note that channels tend to specialize in certain categories, e.g. Wikipedia for incidents.

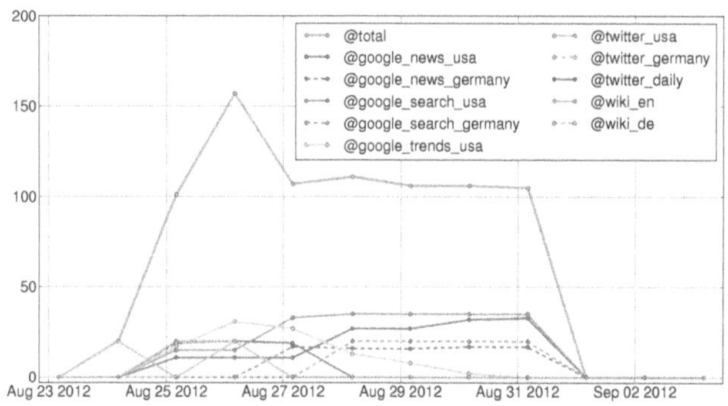

Figure 4: Neil Armstrong received much attention when he died on August 25, 2012. Note that the peak on Wikipedia (green) is at the beginning of the trending topic period whereas news coverage continued for a couple more days.

4. FORECASTING OF TRENDING TOPICS

As motivated in the introduction, anticipating changing information needs and shifts in user attention towards emerging trends is critical for trend aware multimedia systems. However, forecasting trending topics is a very challenging problem since the corresponding time series usually exhibit highly irregular behavior (structural breaks) when the topic becomes "trending". In the following, we will be using the multi-channel pipeline described in Sec. 3.1 as a robust trig-

Category	Description	#Seq	Examples
sports	sports events, clubs, athletes	52	olympics 2012, champions league, bayern muenchen
celebrity	person with prominent profile	49	steve jobs, kim kardashian, michael jackson, neil armstrong
entertainment	entertainers, movies, TV shows	39	grammys, emmys, heidi klum
politics	politicans, parties, political events, movements	32	paul ryan, occupy, christian wulff
incident	an individual occurrence or event	27	costa concordia, hurricane isaac, virginia tech shooting
death	death of a celebrity	22	whitney houston, joe paterno died, neil armstrong
technology	product or event related to technology	20	iphone 5, ces, nasa curiosity
actor	actor in TV show or movie	18	lindsay lohan, michael clarke duncan, bill cosby
product	product or product release	15	ipad, windows 8, diablo 3
artist	music artist	15	justin bieber, miley cyrus, beyonce baby
holidays	day(s) of special significance	11	halloween, thanksgiving, valentines day
company	commercial business	10	apple, chick fil a, megaupload
show	TV show	7	x factor, wetten dass, the voice
movie	a motion picture	6	dark knight rises, hunger games, the avengers

Table 4: List of categories of trending topics. Note that a trending topic might be assigned to multiple categories.

ger for trending topics but will perform time series forecasting utilizing historic time series data (see Sec. 5.1 for more details). In this section, we propose a novel forecasting approach that combines time series from multiple semantically similar topics.

A conceptual overview of our system is presented in Figure 5. On the very left you can see the trending topic for the Summer Olympics 2012 along with its Wikipedia page view statistics in 2012. The task to be solved is to forecast the number of page views for a period of 14 days (yellow area) from the day indicated by the red line. This forecast start is triggered by the emergence of a corresponding trending topic in our observed channels (see Sec. 3). Note that the time series exhibits complex behavior such as the smaller peak at the end of the forecasting period which most likely corresponds to the closing ceremony event on this day. Based on the finding that semantically similar events can exhibit very similar behavior, the first step is to automatically discover related topics such as previous Summer and Winter Olympics or FIFA/UEFA soccer championships (as illustrated by the second box). The second step in Figure 5 shows patterns of user engagement for Summer Olympics 2008, the Winter Olympics 2010, and the UEFA Euro championship 2012 that were found to match the historic behavior of the 2012 Olympics best. These patterns show certain commonalities such as a second peak for closing ceremonies or final matches. The identified sequences from the previous step are then combined to a forecast shown at the very right. In the following, these individual steps are explained in more detail.

Please note that we are neither able to nor do we attempt to predict incidents such as natural disasters or sudden deaths of celebrities in advance. However, even for unpredictable events like these, the patterns of user attention once this event has happened can be forecasted e.g. by taking previous instances of natural disasters or celebrity deaths into account.

4.1 Discovering Semantically Similar Topics

The basis for our forecasting approach is the hypothesis that semantically similar topics exhibit similar behavior. One example supporting this hypothesis is given in Figure 5 which clearly shows similar patterns of user engagement during the different sport events. For a given trending topic, we discover semantically related topics using DBPedia [3], a dataset containing structured information about several million named entities extracted from the Wikipedia project. Given category information (via `dcterms:subject`) and type (via `rdf:type`) from DBPedia, we build a set of (up to 200) semantically similar topics that share the most categories or types with a given trending topic. For example, the Wikipedia URI for "Olympics 2012" is assigned to the categories `Sports_festivals_in_London`, `Scheduled_sports_events`, `2012_Summer_Olympics`, and `2012_in_London`. Its types include `Event`, `SportsEvent`, `Olympics`, and `OlympicGames`, e.g. the 2012 Summer Paralympics share four categories with the Olympics 2012.

Formally, we use a topic set $\mathcal{T}_{sim}$ which includes all discovered similar topics. For later comparisons, we also define a topic set $\mathcal{T}_{self}$ that only includes the trending topic itself and $\mathcal{T}_{gen}$ which contains a wide variety of general topics (in our case the top 200 trending topics). In the following, we will use $\mathcal{T}$ as a placeholder for one of these topic sets. The elements will be referred to as similar topics or $\text{sim}_j \in \mathcal{T}$.

4.2 Nearest Neighbor Sequence Matching

Obviously not all time series corresponding to the discovered similar topics look the same. Therefore, we search within these time series for sequences that match historical behavior of our trending topic. For example, historical topics such as the 1896 Summer Olympics have gained very limited attention over the last years and are therefore unlikely to be representative for the large amount of engagement towards the 2012 Summer Olympics. To pick the right instances to inform our forecast, we compare a short history window of the trending topic to be forecasted, i.e. the viewing statistics for the last two months, to all partial sequences of the same length of similar topics in our topic set $\mathcal{T}$.

To capture this step in formal terms, let $S_{\text{topic}}[t] \in \mathbb{R}$ be the time series for the given topic at time $t \in \mathbb{N}$. Further define $S^{t_0}_{\text{topic}}[t] := S_{\text{topic}}[t_0 + t]$ as the shifted version of the time series (used for aligning multiple series below). In the following, we assume that we want to forecast S_{topic} with a horizon of h days starting at time $t_0 \in \mathbb{N}$.

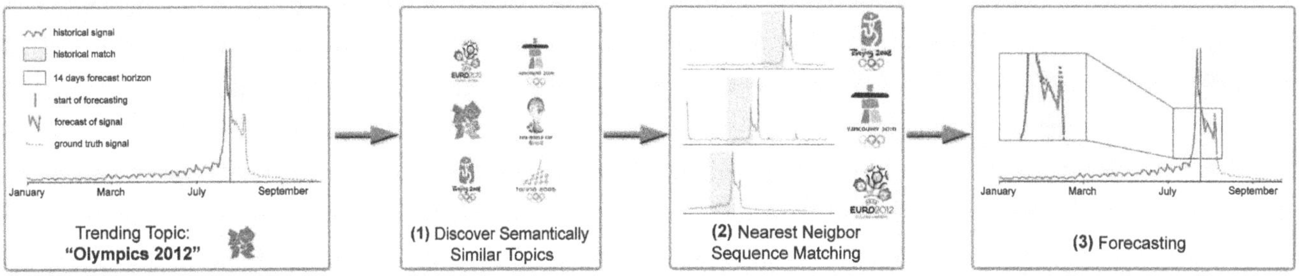

Figure 5: System overview of our proposed forecasting approach. For a given trending topic we first discover semantically similar topics which we search for patterns of similar behavior which are then used to produce a forecast.

Given a topic set $\mathcal{T}$ from the previous step, we define a sequence candidate set $C(t_0)$ that includes all possible shifted time series $S^t_{\text{sim}_j}$: $C(t_0) = \{S^t_{\text{sim}_j} | \forall \text{sim}_j \in \mathcal{T}, \forall t : t \leq t_0 - h\}$. The condition $t \leq t_0 - h$ ensures that we never use information more recent than $t_0 - h$, to allow for a forecast of h days, i.e. we do not utilize future information.

Given this candidate set, we now search for the k members $S^{t_i}_{\text{sim}_i}$ $(i = 1, \ldots, k)$ that are the best matches for our time series of interest $(S^{t_0}_{\text{topic}})$. Note that these nearest neighbors are already correctly aligned through shifting the time series S_{sim_i} by a corresponding t_i. Note that the same similar topic sim_i can occur multiple times (e.g. for repetitive signals).

Formally, the nearest neighbor set becomes $N^k(S^{t_0}_{\text{topic}}) = \{S^{t_1}_{\text{sim}_1}, \ldots, S^{t_k}_{\text{sim}_k}\}$ where the $S^{t_i}_{\text{sim}_i}$ are the k distinct elements that are smallest wrt. $d(S^{t_0}_{\text{topic}}, S^{t_i}_{\text{sim}_i})$ for all $S^{t_i}_{\text{sim}_i} \in C(t_0)$. Here, $d(\cdot,\cdot)$ is a distance metric between both time series which, in our case, only depends on a short history window of the time series. An interesting question is whether the metric should be scale invariant and in which form and to what degree. In Sec. 5, we compare three different distance metrics: (1) (squared) `euclidean` distance: $(d(x, y) = \sum_{i=1}^n (x_i - y_i)^2)$, (2) euclidean distance on normalized sequences $x'_i = (x_i - \mu)/\sigma$ (where μ, σ are mean and standard deviation estimated from the respective time series) referred to as `musigma`, and (3) a fully scale invariant metric (called `y_invariant`) that was proposed in [23] $(\min_\gamma d(x, \gamma \cdot y))$.

4.3 Forecasting

Even the best matching sequences identified in the previous step might not be a perfect fit for the time series to be forecasted. Therefore, we rescale the matching sequences such that they all match on the last observed value of $S^{t_0}_{\text{topic}}$. This ensures that the forecast will be a continuous extension of past behavior. Now, the forecast $\mathcal{F}$ becomes the median over scaled versions of the sequences from the previous step $(N^k(S^{t_0}_{\text{topic}}))$. We represent the days that we want to forecast by $\tau \in [0, \ldots, h-1]$ where again h is the forecasting horizon (usually $h = 14$). Our forecast can then be formally described as

$$\mathcal{F}(S^{t_0}_{\text{topic}})[\tau] = \underset{S^{t'}_{\text{topic}'} \in N^k(S^t_{\text{topic}})}{\text{median}} (\alpha(S^{t_0}_{\text{topic}}, S^{t'}_{\text{topic}'}) \cdot S^{t'}_{\text{topic}'}[\tau])$$

where $\alpha(S^{t_0}_{\text{topic}}, S^{t'}_{\text{topic}'}) = S^{t_0}_{\text{topic}}[-1](S^{t'}_{\text{topic}'}[-1])^{-1}$ adjusts the scale of nearest neighbor time series based on the last observed score. In practice, we limit α to a limited interval (e.g. $[0.33, 3.0]$) for robustness. We further evaluate our approach using the average instead of the median for forecasts. However, as presented in Sec. 5 the median proves to be more robust.

5. EVALUATION

In this section, first the Wikipedia page views dataset is described before presenting quantitative results for the forecasting approach proposed in the previous section.

5.1 Dataset Description

We evaluate our proposed forecasting approach on a large-scale dataset of page views on Wikipedia, an online collaborative encyclopedia that has become a mainstream information resource worldwide and is frequently used in academia [16, 22, 14, 20]. Reasons for this particular choice of social media channel were (a) the public availability of historical views data necessary to build forecasting models (hourly view statistics for the last five years), (b) the size of the dataset allowing a comprehensive analysis of our proposed method across a wide range of topics (over 5 million articles), and (c) previous results show that user behavior on Wikipedia (bursts in popularity of Wikipedia pages) is well correlated with external news events [16] and therefore support our proposed method's ability to generalize to different social media channels. Although we only provide results on Wikipedia our approach could be applied to any online and social media channel for which historic data is available.

The raw Wikipedia viewing statistics are published[3] by the Wikimedia foundation. We obtained hourly view statistics starting on January 1, 2008 (2.8 TB compressed in total). We aggregate these logs to daily viewing statistics where we drop URIs that have been viewed less then 25 times on that day. We believe that this does not introduce any bias since trending topics tend to accumulate volumes several orders of magnitude higher. For each day this results in approx. 2.5 million URIs attracting 870 million daily views. In total, the English and German Wikipedia features more than five million articles that can be used for forecasting. During data preparation we noticed that Wikipedia did not record view counts for a few short periods of time during the last five years for which we interpolate linearly.

Note that we use this dataset for forecasting of historical time series data (actual Wikipedia viewing statistics) while the multi-channel pipeline described in Sec. 3.1 serves as a robust trigger for trending topics.

[3] `http://dumps.wikimedia.org/other/pagecounts-raw/`

Trending Topic	Nearest Neighbor Topics
2012 Summer Olympics	**2008 Summer Olympics, UEFA Euro 2012, 2010 Winter Olympics** :: 2016 Summer Olympics, 2014 FIFA World Cup, 2006 Winter Olympics
Whitney Houston	**Ciara, Shakira, Celine Dion, Brittany Murphy, Ozzy Osbourne** :: Alicia Keys, Paul McCartney, Janet Jackson
Steve Jobs	**Mark Zuckerberg, Rupert Murdoch, Steve Jobs** :: Steve Wozniak, Bill Gates, Oprah Winfrey
Super Bowl XLVI	**Super Bowl, Super Bowl XLV, Super Bowl XLIV** :: Super Bowl XLIII, 2012 Pro Bowl, UFC 119
84th Academy Awards	**83rd Academy Awards, 82nd Academy Awards** :: List of Academy Awards ceremonies, 81st Academy Awards
Battlefield 3	**Mortal Kombat, FIFA 10, Call of Duty: Modern Warfare 2, Portal, Duke Nukem Forever** :: Call of Duty: Modern Warfare 3, Call of Duty 4: Modern Warfare, Pro Evolution Soccer 2011
Joe Paterno	**Terry Bradshaw, Joe Paterno, Jack Ruby, Paul Newman, Jerry Sandusky** :: Lane Kiffin, Donna Summer, Joe DiMaggio
54th Grammy Awards	**53rd Grammy Awards, 52nd Grammy Awards, 54th Grammy Awards** :: 51st Grammy Awards, 2012 Billboard Music Awards, 2012 MTV Europe Music Awards

Table 5: Selected trending topics along with their nearest neighbor topics using category and type information on DBPedia (step 1). The ones chosen by nearest neighbor sequence matching (step 2) are in bold print. In some cases the topic itself can be used for forecasting, e.g. if the time series contains repetitive patterns.

5.2 Experiments

We structure our experiments along the three main building blocks of our proposed approach to compare design choices for the individual methods independently (recall Fig. 5).

1. Discovering Semantically Similar Topics.

We evaluate the influence of discovering semantically similar topics in two ways. First, we present qualitative results by showing retrieved similar topics for a few trending topics. Second, we evaluate this part indirectly by comparing forecast performance (i.e. through the third step) of using semantically similar topics from DBPedia to using a general set of topics (the top 200 trending topics themselves).

Subsets of semantically similar topics for the top trends are shown in Table 5 (as generated by the approach described in Sec. 4.1). Note that we successfully identify similar events or previous instances for events like the Olympics, the Super Bowl, UFC events, or the Grammy Awards. We are also able to discover similar people like similar music artists, entrepreneurs, athletes, and even people that died from the same cause (such as lung cancer for Joe Paterno, Jack Ruby, and Paul Newman). On average, we retrieve 95 semantically similar topics per trending topic.

2. Nearest Neighbor Sequence Matching.

The main design choice when matching sequences from similar topics to a short history window of our time series is the choice of the distance metric. As introduced in Sec. 4.2 we compare `euclidean`, `musigma`, and `y_invariant`.

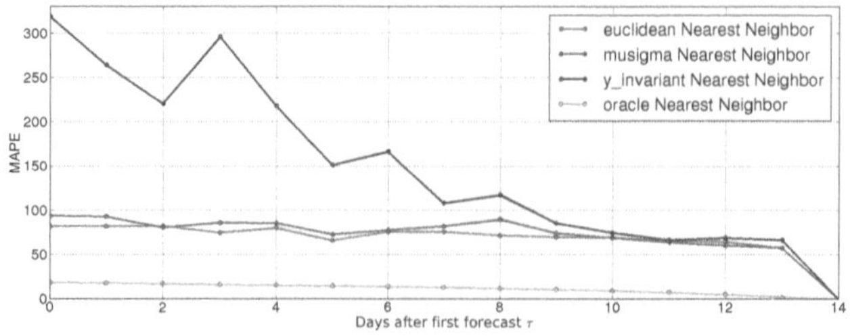

Figure 6: A comparison of Nearest Neighbor Distance Metrics. Euclidean distance performs at least as good as its more complex normalized counterparts.

Our experimental setup for this part as well as the forecasting looks as follows. We use the trending topics acquired in Sec. 3 as a trigger for forecasting, i.e. for each of the 516 sequences of the top 200 trending topics (see Table 2), we make a prediction for a horizon of 14 days, starting on the day they first emerge. We chose this window of 14 days since this represents the maximum lifetime for most trending topics (see Figure 2 (a)). Our method is evaluated by beginning with a forecast of 14 days, then a 13 day forecast after one day and so on (X axis in error plot).

To compare the distance metrics, we measure the quality of the (first) nearest neighbor returned by this metric by its similarity to the actual viewing statistics over the next 14 days (similar to the forecast setting but directly using the nearest neighbor as the forecast). The quality of this match is captured by an error metric. In this work, we use root mean squared error defined as $RMSE = \sqrt{\frac{1}{n}\sum_{t=1}^{n}(A_t - F_t)^2}$ where A_t is the actual value and F_t is the forecast value. As a relative error metric we choose mean absolute percentage error (MAPE) defined as $MAPE = \frac{100\,\%}{n}\sum_{t=1}^{n}|\frac{A_t - F_t}{A_t}|$. Note that unlike [15] we measure error on the actual view counts instead of normalizing by the total views for each day as we believe this glosses over large relative errors (i.e. even larger trends might only account for 10^{-5} of the daily views yielding very small error rates for virtually any forecast).

The results are depicted in Figure 6 and show the average MAPE error (lower is better) between the nearest neighbor and the actual viewing statistics (ground truth). We also show oracle performance by picking the best match for the ground truth from all sequence candidates. First, note that oracle performance is well above 0 % error as there might be no perfect match among the sequence candidates. Further, we observe that `y_invariant` can retrieve poor quality matches whereas the simple `euclidean` distance performs equally or better than the other two metrics. Apparently, the invariance of `musigma` and `y_invariant` does not help in this task. Therefore, we use the `euclidean` metric for all following experiments. Further note that the best matches have between 82 and 319 % error illustrating the high complexity of the task.

3. Forecast.

As introduced above we measure forecasting performance by forecasting the next 14 days for each of the 516 sequences of the top 200 trending topics at the point in time when they

	Method	RMSEs in 1000		
		$\tau = 0$	$\tau = 3$	$\tau = 7$
Baselines	naive	63.2	33.1	17.4
	linear trend	86.9	48.5	23.1
	average trend	49.3	25.9	19.9
	median trend	48.1	24.9	18.1
Self	average	46.0	23.7	18.0
	average_scaled	44.6	21.9	15.5
	median	46.1	23.8	17.7
	median_scaled	44.9	22.3	15.5
Gen	average	45.7	22.9	16.1
	average_scaled	45.7	22.5	14.1
	median	41.4	21.2	15.4
	median_scaled	40.1	19.5	12.8
Sim	average	41.4	18.8	14.0
	average_scaled	39.6	17.1	11.6
	median	42.1	19.9	14.0
	median_scaled	41.0	17.9	11.5

Table 6: RMSE forecasting error for our baselines as well as methods using only the trending topics itself (*Self*), a general set of topics (*Gen*), or similar topics (*Sim*).

first emerge. Our approach is compared to several baselines that use a short history window of the time series itself (similar to [15]): a *naive* forecast (tomorrow's behavior is the same as today's) and a *linear trend* based on the last 14 days. We further compare to the *average trend* and *median trend* in our trending topics dataset as a baseline that includes multiple time series. Note that this average and median trend are computed from μ/σ-normalized time series since the average/median of actual view counts are actually very far from most trending topics. To still be able to compute the error for actual view count prediction we then de-normalize the *average trend* and *median trend* baselines with the parameters of the time series to be predicted. Note that while we performed the following experiments for different numbers of neighbors (for the nearest-neighbor-based methods) we only report the results for $k = 3$ which performed best by a small margin.

The RMSE forecasting errors are summarized in Table 6 which reports the results for a number of instances of our proposed forecasting approach. *Self*, *Gen*, and *Sim* refer to the different topic sets $\mathcal{T}_{self}$, $\mathcal{T}_{gen}$, and $\mathcal{T}_{sim}$ from which the nearest neighbor sequences are chosen (as described in the last section). On average, the RMSE of our best method is about 9-48k views closer to the actual viewing statistics than the different baseline methods. Further, we observe that taking the median tends to perform about as good or better than taking the average, using scaled nearest neighbor is better than unscaled neighbors, and that using semantically similar topics (*Sim*) is better than using a general set of topics (*Gen*) which in turn is better than restricting oneself to a single time series (*Self*).

However, RMSE error has the disadvantage that it is dominated by the most popular trending topics with the largest view counts. Therefore, we choose the MAPE measure for the remaining analysis as this relative error metric is comparable across trending topics. Additionally, because MAPE errors can become disproportionally large (e.g. forecasting 1000 views when it is actually only 100 results in a 900 % relative error), we drop obvious outliers (5 %) and report the average error for the remaining sequences. We only show the results for the baselines and the best performing methods

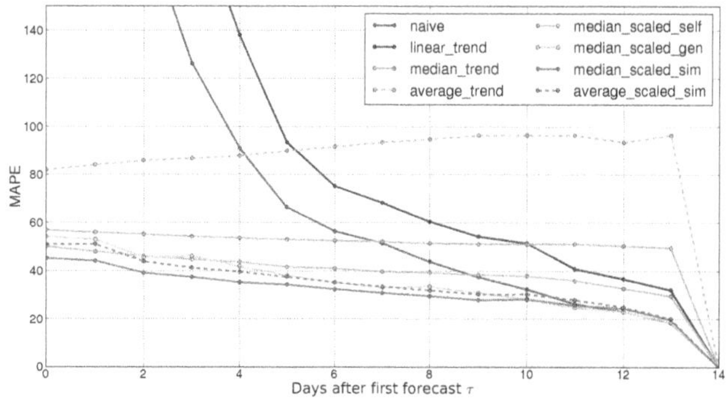

Figure 7: MAPE forecast error moving through a 14 day window, e.g. the error at 4 depicts the forecasting error of the following 10 days.

from Table 6 to be able to visually distinguish them in the error plot. Again, the methods are evaluated by beginning with a forecast of 14 days, then a 13 day forecast after one day etc. as illustrated by the X axis in Figure 7. We can observe that the proposed approach including median and scaling clearly outperforms all baselines as well as other instances of our framework. Our proposed method achieves a mean average percentage error (MAPE) of 45-19 %, a relative improvement over our baselines of 20-90 %.

We further performed a per-category analysis of the forecasting results (using the categories from Table 4). Summarizing, the forecasting performance across categories is similar. Product, company, artist and technology categories perform slightly better, and death, actor, sports, holidays and politics perform slightly worse. For all categories, the forecast quality improves with time (τ).

Example forecasts for two trending topics, "Battlefield 3" (computer game) and "The Hunger Games" (novel and movie), are given in Figure 8. Each column depicts multiple forecasts at different points in time (as indicated by the vertical red line). Our proposed method `median_scaled_sim` (*Sim*) is compared to its variants only using the trending topic itself (*Self*) or using a set of general topics (*Gen*). Note that in many cases, only using information from a single time series is not enough. Further, using semantically similar topics (*Sim*) leads to more accurate forecasts that e.g. are able to capture multiple peaks (such as in the Hunger Games example).

6. CONCLUSION

We present a comprehensive study of trending topics in three major social and online media streams with an observation period of one year. Our findings include that trends on Twitter and Wikipedia are more ephemeral than on Google, both rising and declining rapidly for newly emerging topics. Further, we find that the observed media channels tend to specialize in specific topic categories. The second key contribution is a fully automatic forecasting technique of trending topics exploiting semantic similarity between topics. Lastly, we evaluate our approach on a large-scale dataset of Wikipedia viewing statistics and show empirically that forecasts by the proposed approach are about 9-48k views closer to the actual viewing statistics than baseline methods and achieve a mean average percentage error

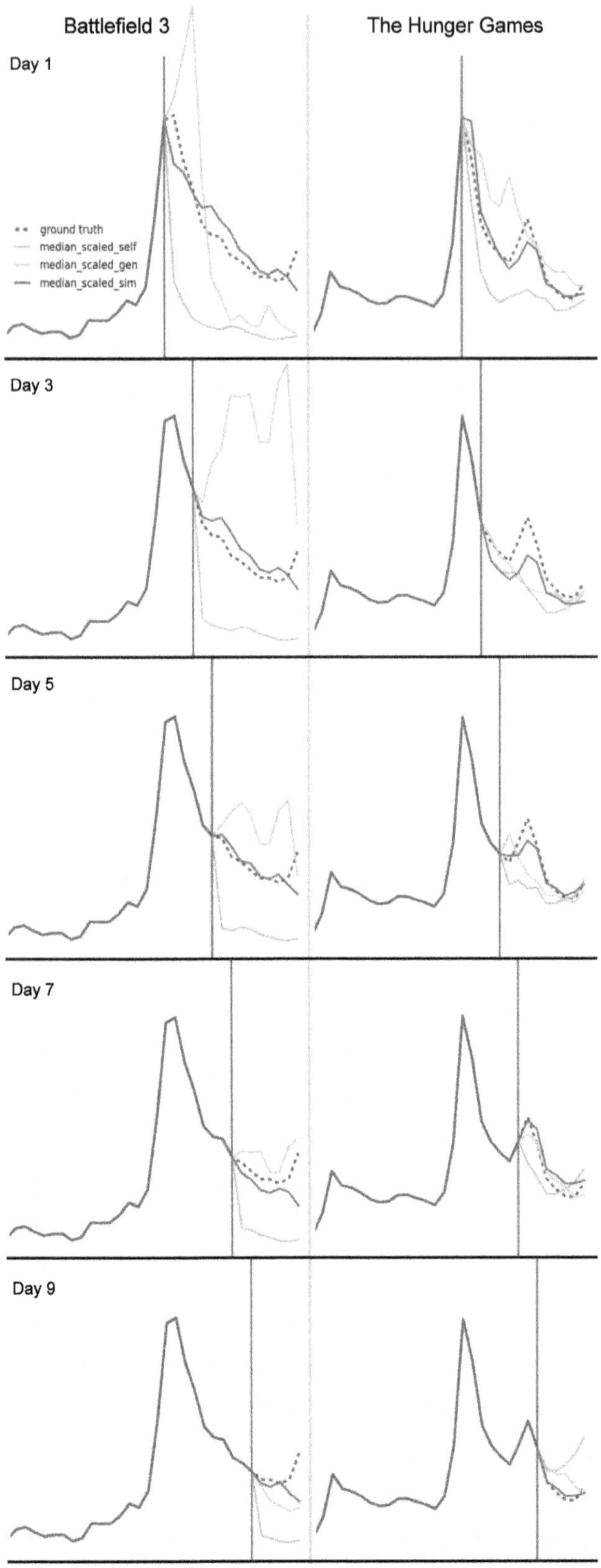

Figure 8: Visualization of trending topic forecasts for "Battlefield 3" and "The Hunger Games". Each column depicts multiple forecasts at different points in time (as indicated by the vertical red line).

of 45-19 % for time periods of up to 14 days, a relative improvement over baselines of 20-90 %.

As future work, the proposed model could be extended to explicitly detect and exploit seasonality as well as incorporate global changes in viewing statistics. In a more general ranking framework, the nearest neighbor sequence matching part could further be extended by e.g. the number of common semantic types and categories.

7. REFERENCES

[1] E. Adar et al. Why we search: visualizing and predicting user behavior. In *Proc. of WWW*, 2007.

[2] J. Allan. Introduction to topic detection and tracking. pp. 1–16. Springer, 2002.

[3] S. Auer et al. Dbpedia: A nucleus for a web of open data. *The Semantic Web*, pp 722–735, 2007.

[4] R. Bandari, S. Asur, and B. Huberman. The pulse of news in social media: Forecasting popularity. *Proc. of ICWSM*, 2012.

[5] D. Borth, A. Ulges, and T. M. Breuel. Dynamic vocabularies for web-based concept detection by trend discovery. In *Proc. of ACM MM*, pp. 977–980. ACM, 2012.

[6] H. Choi and H. Varian. Predicting the present with google trends. *Economic Record*, 88(s1):2–9, 2012.

[7] M. P. Clements and D. F. Hendry. Forecasting annual uk inflation using an econometric model over 1875–1991. *Frontiers of Economics and Globalization*, 3:3–39, 2009. Forecasting in the presence of structural breaks and model uncertainty.

[8] M. De Choudhury, S. Counts, and M. Czerwinski. Find me the right content! Diversity-based sampling of social media spaces for topic-centric search. In *Proc. of ICWSM*, 2011.

[9] S. Diplaris et al. Socialsensor: sensing user generated input for improved media discovery and experience. In *Proc. WWW companion*, pp. 243–246. ACM, 2012.

[10] S. Goel et al. Predicting consumer behavior with web search. *Proc. of NAS*, 107(41):17486–17490, 2010.

[11] R. J. Hyndman and Y. Khandakar. Automatic time series forecasting: The forecast package for r. *Journal of Statistical Software*, 27(3), 2008.

[12] X. Jin et al. The wisdom of social multimedia: using flickr for prediction and forecast. In *Proc. of ACM MM*, pp. 1235–1244. ACM, 2010.

[13] M. Naaman, H. Becker, and L. Gravano. Hip and trendy: Characterizing emerging trends on twitter. *Journal of ASIST*, 62(5):902–918, 2011.

[14] M. Osborne et al. Bieber no more: First story detection using twitter and wikipedia. In *SIGIR 2012 WS on Time-aware Information Access*, 2012.

[15] K. Radinsky et al. Modeling and predicting behavioral dynamics on the web. In *Proc. of WWW*, 2012.

[16] J. Ratkiewicz, A. Flammini, and F. Menczer. Traffic in social media I: paths through information networks. In *Proc. of SocialCom*, pp. 452–458. IEEE, 2010.

[17] S. D. Roy, T. Mei, W. Zeng, and S. Li. Socialtransfer: cross-domain transfer learning from social streams for media applications. In *Proc. of ACM MM*, 2012.

[18] S. Samangooei et al. Trendminer: An architecture for real time analysis of social media text. In *ICWSM*, 2012.

[19] G. Szabo and B. A. Huberman. Predicting the popularity of online content. *Comm. of the ACM*, 53(8):80–88, 2010.

[20] M. t. Thij, Y. Volkovich, D. Laniado, and A. Kaltenbrunner. Modeling and predicting page-view dynamics on Wikipedia. *arXiv*, 2012.

[21] Z. Wang et al. Propagation-based social-aware replication for social video contents. In *Proc. ACM MM*, 2012.

[22] S. Whiting and O. Alonso. Hashtags as milestones in time. In *SIGIR 2012 WS on Time-aware Info. Access*, 2012.

[23] J. Yang and J. Leskovec. Patterns of temporal variation in online media. In *Proc. of WSDM*, 2011.

Why Not, WINE?: Towards Answering Why-Not Questions in Social Image Search

Sourav S Bhowmick Aixin Sun Ba Quan Truong

School of Computer Engineering, Nanyang Technological University, Singapore

assourav|axsun|bqtruong@ntu.edu.sg

ABSTRACT

Despite considerable progress in recent years on *Tag-based Social Image Retrieval* (TAGIR), state-of-the-art TAGIR systems fail to provide a systematic framework for end users to ask why certain images are not in the result set of a given query and provide an explanation for such missing results. However, as humans, such *why-not* questions are natural when expected images are missing in the query results returned by a TAGIR system. Clearly, it would be very helpful to users if they could pose follow-up why-not questions to seek clarifications on missing images in query results. In this work, we take the first step to systematically answer the why-not questions posed by end-users on TAGIR systems. Our answer not only involves the reason why desired images are missing in the results but also suggestion on how the query can be altered so that the user can view these missing images in sufficient number. We present three explanation models, namely *result reordering*, *query relaxation*, and *query substitution*, that enable us to explain a variety of why-not questions. We present an algorithm called WINE (**W**hy-not quest**I**on a**N**swering **E**ngine) that exploits these models to answer why-not questions efficiently. Experiments on NUS-WIDE dataset demonstrate effectiveness as well as benefits of WINE.

Categories and Subject Descriptors

H.3.3 [**Information Storage and Retrieval**]: Information Search and Retrieval—*Information Filtering*; H.3.3 [**Information Storage and Retrieval**]: Information Search and Retrieval—*Search Process*

Keywords

Social Image, Flickr, Tag-based image search, Why-not questions, Explanation models

1. INTRODUCTION

The prevalence of digital photography devices (*e.g.,* digital cameras, mobile phones) and increasing popularity of social image sharing platforms and applications (*e.g.,* Flickr, Picasa, and Instagram) have made huge volume of images available online. Many of these

MM'13, October 21–25, 2013, Barcelona, Spain.

http://dx.doi.org/10.1145/2502081.2502098.

(a) Q(*Rome*) (b) Q(*Rome Colosseum*)

Figure 1: Search results of the two queries in Example 1.

online images are socially tagged by their uploaders or viewers and are searchable by tags, which are free-form keywords. Consequently, techniques to support *Tag-based Social Image Retrieval* (TAGIR) for finding relevant high-quality images using keyword queries have recently generated tremendous research and commercial interests. In simple words, given a keyword query (or search query) which expresses a user's information need, a TAGIR search engine returns a ranked list of images where the images annotated with the most *relevant* tags to the query are ranked higher.

Most existing efforts in TAGIR attempt to improve its search accuracy or diversify its search results so as to maximize the probability of satisfying users' search intents [15,16]. Despite the recent progress towards this goal, it is often challenging to generate high quality search results for a search query which can satisfy search intents of different users. This is because the search intents of users are not always precise and hence difficult to interpret accurately. Often, desired images may be unexpectedly missing in the search results. However, state-of-the-art TAGIR systems lack explanation capability for users to seek clarifications on the absence of expected images (*i.e.,* missing images) in the result set. Consider the following set of user problems[1]:

EXAMPLE 1. Ann is planning a trip to Rome to visit its famous landmarks. She issues a search query "`Rome`" on a tag-based social image search engine. The top-20 matches to her query retrieved by the search engine are depicted in Figure 1(a). Expectedly, many images of Rome's famous landmarks appear as top result matches, such as the *Spiral Stairs*, the *Gallery of Map*, and the *Sistine Chapel*. However, surprisingly, there are no images related to the *Colosseum*, a famous landmark of Ancient Rome, in the top-100 results. So why is it not in the result set? Note that expanding the query by adding the keyword `Colosseum` to it would garner images related to *Colosseum* (Figure 1(b)). However, Ann would

[1] All search results presented in our examples are obtained using a TAGIR system following the best performing configuration in [13] on NUS-WIDE data collection.

(a) Q(*lake*) (b) Q(*lake Hangzhou China*)

Figure 2: Search results related to Example 2.

lose images of other interesting landmarks, depriving her to get a bird eye view of different attractions of Rome. ∎

Example 2. Bob has returned from a trip to China. He really enjoyed the scenic *Xi Hu lake* in *Hangzhou* city of the *Zhejiang* province. However, Bob has forgotten its name. Hence, he posed the following query to retrieve images related to *Xi Hu lake*: "lake Hangzhou Zhejiang China". Surprisingly, no result is returned by the search engine! Why not? Note that searching for "lake" alone is ineffective as Bob primarily wants images of *Xi Hu lake* and not other lakes. In fact, the query "lake" returns more than 4000 images, many of these are irrelevant (Figure 2(a)). ∎

Example 3. Carlos, a young archaeologist researching on Mesoamerican culture, hopes to find images related to their pyramids. He submits the query "pyramid" which returns mostly images related to Egyptian and Louvre pyramids (Figure 3(a)). So why are Mesoamerican pyramids not in the result set? Perplexed, Carlos expands the query by adding the keyword "Mesoamerica", hoping to retrieve relevant images. However, only four images are now returned and among them, only two are really relevant to Mesoamerican pyramids (Figure 3(b)). Are there only two images of Mesoamerican pyramids in the image collection? Thinking that his modified query may be too strict, Carlos now removed the keyword "pyramid" from the query. However, only five additional results are returned now and none of these additional images are relevant (Figure 3(c)). So why not more images related to Mesoamerican pyramids can be retrieved? ∎

There is one common thread throughout these problems encountered above, despite the differences in search queries: the user would like to know why certain images are missing in the top-*m* result set of a given query (Examples 1 and 2) or not there in sufficient number (Example 3) and suggestion on how his/her query can be altered effectively to view these missing images in sufficient number. In this paper we refer to this problem as the Why Not? problem in TagIR (formally defined in Section 3). Note that in the above examples, one cannot expect the users to sift through the underlying social image dataset to seek for explanation when they encounter missing results.

At a first glance, it may seem that any large-scale social image search engine (*e.g.,* Flickr) may facilitate answering these original queries more effectively simply because they have very large collection of social images compared to the nus-wide data collection used in the aforementioned examples. For instance, the query in Example 2 returns several images related to *Xi Hu lake* when posed directly on Flickr[2]. Unfortunately, users' expectations are just too diverse to eliminate the Why Not? problem in Flickr (detailed in Section 7). For example, consider the query "pyramid" in Example 3 directly on Flickr. It only retrieves a single image related to Mesoamerican pyramid in its top-50 result set! In fact, even in large image collection provided by web search engines (*e.g.,* Google, Bing) where data associated with images are not as sparse as social images, the Why Not? problem is still encountered. For example,

[2]All results related to Flickr and Google Images are last accessed on July 14th, 2013.

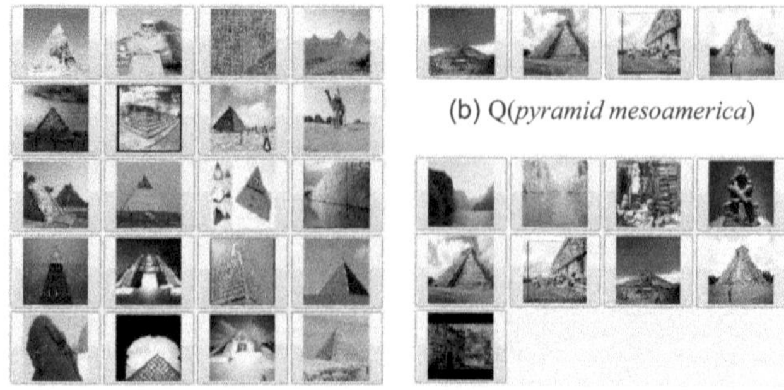

(a) Q(*pyramid*) (b) Q(*pyramid mesoamerica*) (c) Q(*mesoamerica*)

Figure 3: Search results of the three queries in Example 3.

suppose we issue the query "Manchester city" on *Google Images*. Interestingly, majority of top-50 images retrieved by it are about the *Manchester City Football Club*! For a user who is not a soccer fan, this result is unsatisfactory due to lack of images related to the city of Manchester.

Our initial investigation shed some light on the possible reasons for the Why Not? problem. First, the desired images may be ranked very low in the search results because the same keyword query may express very different search intents for different users. The top-ranked images may be considered relevant by some users but not by others. For instance, reconsider Example 1. The reason Ann could not see the images related to *Colosseum* is because they are ranked too low. The first Colosseum image is ranked 217-*th* in the result set and Ann is unlikely to explore more than 100 images to search for *Colosseum*.

Second, the set of tags associated with images may be noisy and *incomplete*. Note that tags are not from controlled vocabulary and are assigned by users with various different motivations. Consequently, not all keywords mentioned in the search query may appear as tags in relevant images. For instance, consider Example 2. A user may not annotate an image related to *Xi Hu lake* with the tag Zhejiang even if she tags it with Hangzhou. In fact, none of the images related to *Xi Hu lake* are tagged with Zhejiang in the underlying image collection! However, it is unrealistic to expect a user to be aware of this fact.

Third, the query formulated by the user may be too restrictive due to the user's limited understanding of the data collection. That is, there may be a mismatch between the tags that the user *expects* to be associated with her desired images and the *actual* tags that annotate these images in the data collection. In Example 3, Carlos failed to retrieve sufficient number of images annotated with the tag Mesoamerica because it is rarely used in tagging images in the image collection. However, Carlos is unlikely to have this knowledge or possess the skill to alter the query to retrieve his desired images.

Clearly, it would be very helpful to Ann, Bob, and Carlos if they could simply pose a follow-up why-not question to the TagIR engine to seek an explanation for desired missing images and suggestions on how to retrieve them. In this paper, we propose a novel framework called wine (**W**hy-not quest**I**on a**N**swering **E**ngine) to address this problem. We assume that a user specifies a why-not question in wine using a *why-not tag*. For instance, in Example 1, after receiving the results as in Figure 1(a), Ann may use a why-not tag Colosseum to seek some images related to *Colosseum* to appear in the result list. Similarly, in Example 2, Bob may issue a why-not tag lake to specify why he cannot view images related to lakes in *Hangzhou*. Our proposed framework *automatically* generates explanation to a why-not question and recommends *refined* query, if necessary, whose result may not only includes images related to the search query but also to the why-not question. *To the best of our knowledge, this is the first systematic effort to formulate and address the* WHY NOT? *problem in* TAGIR.

We propose three complimentary explanation models, namely *result reordering*, *query relaxation*, and *query substitution*, that are designed to address three different scenarios of the WHY NOT? problem (detailed in Sections 3.3 and 4-6). Going a step further, we also describe techniques that provide a user useful suggestions on how to alter her query in order to retrieve these desired images. A key feature of WINE is its portability as it is orthogonal to the result retrieval and ranking mechanism of the underlying search engine.

It may seem that the WHY NOT? problem can be addressed by leveraging existing search techniques such as query expansion, query suggestion, and search result clustering. Unfortunately, this is not the case. Specifically, these techniques assume that the search engine captures a user's information need in one way or another by analyzing either the underlying data including click-through data or by presenting the search results in a more organized manner. However, unlike a why-not question in the WHY NOT? problem, these techniques *do not* accept explicit feedback from a user when she is unsatisfied with the search results. Consequently, by modifying a query without such user input, a search engine may generate answers to a modified query that do not agree on the user's original search intent. For instance, in Example 1, if we add the why-not tag `Colosseum` to `"Rome"` (based on query expansion) then the search intent morphs from "famous landmarks of Rome including Colosseum" to "Colosseum in Rome". Consequently, as depicted in Figure 1(b), such query expansion leads to loss of images of interesting landmarks in *Rome* other than *Colosseum*. Notably a why-not question should not alter the original search intent. As another example, consider the query `"pyramid"` in Example 3. An existing query suggestion technique may recommend the tags `"Egypt"`, `"Louvre"`, `"Giza"`, `"Sphinx"`, etc., reflecting the commonly associated concepts to *pyramid*. Clearly, such suggestion not only modifies the search intent of Carlos, but also fails to address his why-not question. That is, without the explicit why-not tag `"Mesoamerica"`, state-of-the-art query suggestion models may fail to speculate that Carlos' interest is in *Mesoamerican pyramid*.

2. RELATED WORK

Tag-based Social Image Retrieval (TAGIR). The research efforts in TAGIR can be broadly categorized into three types, namely *indexing*, *scoring*, and *ranking*. *Indexing* an image in TAGIR involves two complementary tasks: (i) determining the set of tags best describing the image [3, 18], and (ii) quantifying how accurately each of these tags objectively describe the visual content of the image (also known as *tag relevance* [8]). *Scoring* aims to compute a *relevance score* between a keyword query and a tagged image. Relevance score computation typically considers the matching score between the keyword and the image tags and other factors derived from search logs and user click-through data [7, 12]. *Ranking* determines the order in which search results (*e.g.,* the top-ranked images) are presented to the searcher. The default image ranking is solely based on the relevance score [8]. More sophisticated methods may diversify the search results so as to satisfy the different possible search intents expressed by the same keyword query [15, 16].

It may seem that our proposed explanation models are closely associated with search results re-ranking [9] and query expansion/substitution [1, 17]. However, search results re-ranking techniques rely on *positive* user inputs (*e.g.,* a user selects relevant results from the initial search results) to improve user satisfaction [5, 9] whereas WINE allows a user to specify *explicit negative* feedback through a why-not tag instead of initial search results.

(a) $\alpha = 0.4$ (b) $\alpha = 0.9$

Figure 4: Reordered results for query (*Rome*) with why-not tag *Colosseum*.

Naturally, results re-ranking techniques cannot be effectively applied to address all why-not questions because there are very few positive results or even no results for users to provide any input.

Zha *et al.* [17] adopts the query suggestion model from IR into TAGIR. Consequently, the suggested tags in [17] are selected to be closely related to the query but distinct among each other. Furthermore, a few representative images are retrieved for each suggested tag to assist users in understanding the suggested tags. However, when there are very few results matching a user query, the co-occurrence based technique used in this scheme becomes unreliable. For instance, Example 2 demonstrates a case where the query is too selective so that adding new tags into the query fail to improve the result quality. Another example is the query `"Leningrad"` (Q_{26} in Section 7) which returns only five images. Consequently, in contrast to WINE, it fails to suggest the query `"saintpetersburg"` instead in order to retrieve more images. In addition, WINE provides clear explanation for reasons behind such suggestion.

Why-Not Questions in Databases. More germane to this work are recent efforts in the database community to provide automatic explanation to a why-not question [2, 6, 14]. To answer why-not questions (*i.e.,* why some expected data items are not shown in the result set) on relational databases, multiple answer models have been proposed, including: *database modification*, *manipulation identification*, and *query modification*. However, these approaches cannot be trivially extended to TAGIR setting due to fundamental differences in data model and query processing technique. Particularly, this is because: (i) the social image data in TAGIR is not represented using relational structure and (ii) there is no concept of query plan, which was exploited by these models, in the context of TAGIR.

3. THE WHY NOT? PROBLEM

We begin by introducing some terminology that is necessary to the understanding of the WHY NOT? problem. Then, we formally define the problem that we are addressing in this paper. Lastly, we introduce the explanation models and present the WINE algorithm.

3.1 Terminology

Given a social image collection $\mathcal{D}$ and the set of all tags $\mathcal{T}$ in $\mathcal{D}$, each image $d \in \mathcal{D}$ is user-annotated by a set of tags $T_d \subseteq \mathcal{T}$. The set of images annotated by tag t is denoted as $D(t)$. Given $T \subseteq \mathcal{T}$, we denote the set of images annotated by all tags in T as $D(T)$.

Given a search query Q with n query tags $t_1, \ldots, t_n$, let $R(Q, \mathcal{D})$ (or simply $R(Q)$ when the context is clear) denote the image search result list of Q on $\mathcal{D}$. For simplicity, we shall assume $t_i \in \mathcal{T}, \forall (i = 1, 2, \ldots, n)$. Each result image $d_r \in R(Q)$ is annotated by query tags $t_1, \ldots, t_n$ and is associated with a *relevance score*, denoted as $rel(d_r, Q)$. $R(Q)$ is assumed to be listed by descending order of the relevance scores. Recall that WINE is independent of the results ranking technique used to support TAGIR. Hence, we can use any state-of-the-art relevance score computation technique [7, 12, 13] for computing $rel(d_r, Q)$. By abusing the notation of lists, we denote the list of images in $R(Q)$ as the image set $D(Q)$. We use $R_m(Q)$ or $D_m(Q)$ interchangeably to denote the top-m images in $R(Q)$.

3.2 Problem Statement

A user asks a why-not question of the form "Why do (top-m) results of my query Q not contain sufficient number of images related to S." The predicate S is defined using a *why-not tag* t_w. So the aforementioned question is equivalent to the following form "Why do (top-m) results of my query Q not contain sufficient number of images related to tag t_w." For example, consider the query in Example 1. Here the query is "Rome" and the user Ann wishes to know why the top-100 results of her query do not contain any images related to *Colosseum*. Hence, t_w = "Colosseum".

Note that in this paper we focus on a single why-not tag. While more complex collection of why-not tags could be allowed in theory, our initial analysis of users suggested that such tag collection is often difficult to interpret as the semantics of the why-not question may become unclear (*e.g.*, view images with all why-not tags vs some why-not tags). It is even more challenging when the why-not tags themselves do not appear in the data collection[3].

When attempting to answer a why-not question during social image search, we have three known pieces from which to draw information: the query Q, the search results $R(Q)$ with their relevance scores, and the question t_w. An answer to a why-not question should exploit these information to return to the user potential reasons for the image(s) of interest is missing from the (top-m) results. Further, it should suggest solutions that will enable the user to retrieve and view these missing image(s) along with other relevant results. This leads to a formulation of the WHY NOT? problem.

DEFINITION 1. *Let Q be a search query on a social image database $\mathcal{D}$, and $R_m(Q)$ be the set of top-m ranked search results, where $0 < m \leq |R(Q)|$. Let t_w be the why-not question and α be a configurable parameter indicating the ratio of desired number of images related to t_w in $R_m(Q)$. Then the goal of the* **WHY NOT? *problem*** *is to find an answer $\mathbb{N}$ comprising (a) the reason for $\frac{|R(t_w) \cap R_m(Q)|}{|R_m(Q)|} < \alpha$, and (b) a suggestion, if executed, ensures any one of the followings: (i) $\frac{|R(t_w) \cap R_m(Q)|}{|R_m(Q)|} \geq \alpha$, or (ii) $\frac{|R(t_w) \cap R_m(Q')|}{|R_m(Q')|} \geq \alpha$, or (iii) $\frac{|R(t'_w) \cap R_m(Q')|}{|R_m(Q')|} \geq \alpha$, where Q' is a modification to Q based on the suggestion and t'_w is a closely related tag to t_w.*

3.3 Explanation Models

We propose the following three explanation models to tackle the WHY NOT? problem.

Result Reordering Model: Intuitively, in this explanation model we reorder the search results $R(Q)$ so that images related to the why-not tag t_w in $R(Q)$ appear in the top-m results. A key advantage of this approach is that it is simple, fast and is particularly well-suited when the relevant images are in $R(Q)$ but ranked too low (*e.g.*, Example 1). Sample output of promoting the why-not tag Colosseum in Example 1 is depicted in Figure 4(a).

Query Relaxation Model: In this model, we identify the set of *selective* tags in Q which are responsible for filtering majority of the relevant images related to t_w from $R(Q)$. These tags can then be removed from Q. Note that this model is suitable when the following two conditions are satisfied: (i) there are few images related to t_w in $R(Q)$; but (ii) there are a large number of images related to t_w in the image collection $\mathcal{D}$. Clearly, the former condition is reasonable since if there are enough images in $R(Q)$, result reordering is a simpler and more effective solution. The latter condition is intuitive because if there are too few relevant images in the image collection, it is impossible for large number of images related to t_w appearing in the result set. For example, consider Example 2. This model identifies that Zhejiang is a *selective* tag and advises Bob to remove it from the original query in order to view images related to *Xi Hu lake*. Figure 2(b) depicts the results containing images of *Xi Hu lake* for the relaxed query "lake Hangzhou China".

Query Substitution Model: This explanation model is suitable when there are too few relevant images annotated by t_w in $\mathcal{D}$ (as in Example 3). Consequently, it is impossible to either interpret which images are relevant to the why-not tag or deduce its relations with other tags using $\mathcal{D}$ alone. Therefore, we leverage an external data source (*Wikipedia*) to interpret the semantics of t_w and use this knowledge to infer some *closely related* tags to t_w in $\mathcal{D}$. These tags can then be used as a new query to retrieve the desired images. For instance, consider Example 3. The query "pyramid Mesoamerica" is modified to "pyramid Maya" after identifying maya to be most closely related to mesoamerica using Wikipedia. This new query generated 27 query results and many of which are images of Mesoamerican pyramid.

3.4 The WINE Algorithm

Algorithm 1 outlines the procedure for answering the why-not question using the aforementioned explanation models. It takes five inputs, namely, the original query Q, the why-not tag t_w, the number of displayed results m, a set of Wikipedia articles $\mathcal{W}$, and a user-configurable *desired image ratio* α. Note that α represents the fraction of images related to t_w that the user intends to see in her top-m results. Obviously, the why-not question is formulated by the user as α is too low for her satisfaction in the current result set. Hence, the goal of WINE is to explain to the user why there are insufficient images related to t_w in $R_m(Q)$ and provide her suggestion, if executed, will ensure that there are sufficient images related to t_w in $R_m(Q)$ *without* modifying the user's search intent in Q. Towards this goal, Algorithm 1 chooses among the three explanation models by comparing $\alpha \times m$ with two variables s_1 and s_2. Specifically, s_1 is the number of images in both $R(Q)$ and $R(t_w)$ and s_2 is the number of images in $R(t_w)$. Obviously, $s_1 \leq s_2$. We now describe the explanation model selection process.

If $s_1 > \alpha \times m$ (Line 4), then $R_m(Q)$ contains fewer than $\alpha \times m$ results related to tag t_w but $R(Q)$ contains many such images at lower ranks. This scenario is illustrated using a Venn diagram in Figure 5(a). The gray shaded circle represents the images in $R_m(Q)$ which are displayed to the user. The black shaded area represents images related to t_w that appear in $R(Q)$ but not in $R_m(Q)$. Observe that the intersection between $R_m(Q)$ and $R(t_w)$ is small but the intersection between $R(Q)$ and $R(t_w)$ is large enough. In this case, a simple but effective solution is to first notify the user that images related to t_w are lowly ranked (Line 5) and then invoke the *Result Reordering* model (REORDER method in Line 7) to reorder the results (elaborated in Section 4). Note that the reordering ensures that $\frac{|R_m(Q) \cap R(t_w)|}{|R_m(Q)|} \geq \alpha$. The effect of reordering is illustrated in Figure 5(b) where there are now more images with tag t_w in $R_m(Q)$ (the striped area). Notice that the size of $R_m(Q)$ remains unchanged (always equal to m).

If $s_1 \leq \alpha \times m$ but $s_2 > \alpha \times m$ and Q is a multi-tag query (Line 9), then the scenario indicates the followings. First, there are insufficient images in $R(Q)$ related to t_w so that, no matter how we reorder $R(Q)$, we cannot propel sufficient number of images related

[3]This issue can be addressed by building a *query interpretation module* on top of WINE to interpret the why-not question and allow WINE to evaluate multiple why-not tags using the proposed explanation models. However, this is orthogonal to the problem.

Algorithm 1: Algorithm WINE.

```
Input: A set of n query tags Q = {t_1, ..., t_n} with search result R(Q),
       why-not tag t_w with search result R(t_w), set of Wikipedia
       articles W, the number of displayed results m, the desired
       image ratio α
Output: A list of images R(Q_new) addressing the why-not question t_w
1  Set flag = false /* true if user accepts a suggestion */;
2  s_1 ← |R(Q) ∩ R(t_w)|;
3  s_2 ← |R(t_w)|;
4  if s_1 > m × α then
       // m × α < s_1 ≤ s_2
5      Send notification ℕ;
6      if flag = true then
7          R(Q_new) ← REORDER(R(Q), t_w, R(t_w), m, α);
8      return R(Q_new)
9  else if s_2 > m × α and Q is multi-tag query then
       // s_1 ≤ m × α < s_2
10     (ℕ, T') ← RELAX(Q, t_w);
11     if flag = true then
12         Q_new = Q\T';
13         Generate results R(Q_new);
14         return R(Q_new)
15 else
       // s_1 ≤ s_2 < m × α
16     (ℕ, t'_w) ← SUBSTITUTE(Q, t_w, β);
17     if flag = true then
18         Modify Q to Q_new based on t'_w;
19         Generate results R(Q_new);
20         return R(Q_new)
```

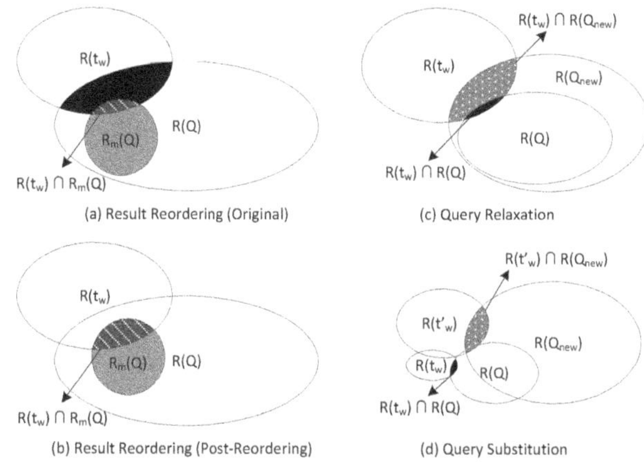

Figure 5: Venn diagram representation of the three models.

to t_w to the top-m results. Second, if $s_2 > \alpha \times m$, then there are sufficient number of images annotated with t_w in $\mathcal{D}$ which can be potentially retrieved using queries *other than* Q. Consequently, if Q is multi-tag, then it can be relaxed to Q_{new} to retrieve more results related to t_w. This situation is illustrated in Figure 5(c). Unlike in Figures 5(a)-(b), the intersection between $R(Q)$ and $R(t_w)$ is small (black area) but $R(t_w)$ remains large. So, it is reasonable to relax Q to a new query Q_{new} such that its intersection with $R(t_w)$ is larger. Such query relaxation process is invoked by the RELAX procedure (Line 10). Specifically, this procedure efficiently identifies the *selective* tags in Q and suggest to the user to remove them in order to retrieve result set $R(Q_{new}) \supseteq R(Q)$ which contains more images related to t_w. Hence, its output consists of a notification $\mathbb{N}$ that suggests the removal of a *selective tagset* T' from the query. If the user accepts this suggestion ($flag$ is set to `true`) then Q is modified to Q_{new} by removing these selective tag(s) and a new result set $R(Q_{new})$ is generated based on the modified query (Lines 11-13). We elaborate on the RELAX procedure in Section 5.

Lines 16-20 reflect the case when $s_2 \leq \alpha \times m$. In this case, $\mathcal{D}$ contains too few images tagged with t_w. Furthermore, Q simply cannot be relaxed (a tag cannot be removed from Q) as it is possible for Q to be single-tag query. Figure 5(d) illustrates such situation when $R(t_w)$ is too small. However, as tags are inherently noisy, it is possible to retrieve images related to t_w but annotated by *closely-related* tags. We use an external source $\mathcal{W}$ (a set of *Wikipedia* articles), to find the most *closely related* tags t'_w in $\mathcal{D}$ to t_w and Q such that it is associated with sufficiently large number of images in $\mathcal{D}$. The intuition behind this approach is that since t_w and t'_w are closely related, an image relevant to t'_w is likely to be relevant to t_w as well. These steps are encapsulated in the SUBSTITUTE procedure which returns a notification $\mathbb{N}$ that suggests closely related tag t'_w for refining Q (Line 16). Figure 5(d) depicts such situation where $R(t'_w) \cap R(Q_{new})$ is significantly larger than $R(t_w) \cap R(Q)$. If the user accepts the suggestion, then the algorithm substitutes the original query with Q_{new} and generates the new results $R(Q_{new})$ (Lines 17-19). Note that we ensure $|R(Q_{new})| \geq \alpha \times m$ to avoid retrieving too few results. We shall elaborate on this step in Section 6.

Notice that both the query relaxation and query substitution models aim to increase the size of $R(t_w) \cap R(Q)$ (the black area in Figure 5) while the main objective of our solution is to ensure that $R(t_w) \cap R_m(Q)$ (the shaded area in Figure 5) exceeds $\alpha \times m$. Therefore, for these models result reordering is applied (if necessary) when $R(Q_{new})$ is generated (Lines 13 and 19).

4. THE RESULT REORDERING MODEL

In short, the result reordering model reranks the original result images so that there are at least $\alpha \times m$ images relevant to the why-not tag appearing in the top-m results $R_m(Q)$. Given the query Q, each result image $d \in R(Q)$ is assigned a new score by *linearly combining* the relevance score $rel(d, t_w)$ of the why-not tag t_w and the original score $rel(d, Q)$ as follows.

$$rel_w(d, Q, t_w) = (1 - \theta) \times rel(d, Q) + \theta \times rel(d, t_w) \quad (1)$$

where $\theta = \frac{rel(d_0, Q)}{rel(d_0, Q) + rel(d_w, t_w)}$, d_0 is the $(1-\alpha)m$-th results in $R(Q) \backslash R(t_w)$ and d_w is the $\alpha \times m$-th result in $R(Q) \cap R(t_w)$. Note that we assume $rel(d, t_w) = 0$ when $d \notin R(t_w)$.

Informally, Equation 1 ensures that there are $\alpha \times m$ results with tag t_w in $R_m(Q)$ by ensuring that the $\alpha \times m$-th result in $R(Q) \cap R(t_w)$ appears at the m-th result in $R_m(Q)$ while maintaining the relative order among all results in $R(Q) \backslash R(t_w)$ and among all results in $R(Q) \cap R(t_w)$. The *desired image ratio* $0 \leq \alpha \leq 1$ indicates how many results in the top-m displayed results need to be replaced by images relevant to t_w. In other words, α indicates the user's level of dissatisfaction to the current result list $R(Q)$. Let us illustrate the intuition behind α with an example. Reconsider Example 1 and the why-not question "`Colosseum`". If we set α to a low value[4] (*e.g.*, $\alpha = 0.4$) then we can retrieve images related to `Colosseum` as well as other landmarks as top results (Figure 4(a)). On the other hand, if the value of α is high (*e.g.*, $\alpha = 0.9$) then more images related to `Colosseum` will be laid out as top results (Figure 4(b)). That is, appropriate value of α is driven by specific user's need.

Algorithm 2 outlines the procedure to realize the result reordering model. The key aspect here is that it is designed to avoid sorting $R(Q)$ again as it incurs a cost of $O(|R(Q)| \log(|R(Q)|))$ which can be

[4] In WINE a user does not need to specify any numeric value to set α. Rather she simply drags a slider in the GUI to specify different α values and interactively view the changes in the results (result reordering is very fast as we shall demonstrate in Section 7).

potentially expensive when $R(Q)$ is large. Observe that only the scores of images in $R(Q) \cap R(t_w)$ are modified. Thus, only these images need to be re-sorted. Also notice that $|R(Q) \cap R(t_w)|$ is usually small since users typically ask the why-not question when $|R(Q) \cap R(t_w)| \ll |R(Q)|$. Accordingly, after computing θ (Lines 1-3), we partition $R(Q)$ into two groups, namely L_1 and L_2, corresponding to $R(Q) \cap R(t_w)$ and $R(Q) \backslash R(t_w)$, respectively (Lines 5-10). Each image d in L_1 is assigned a new score $rel_w(d, Q, t_w)$ computed by Equation 1 (Line 7) and re-sorted based on this score (Line 11). Note that the relevance score of each image in L_2 is the same as that in the original query results. Lastly, these two sorted lists are merged into the final result list L (Line 12). The time complexity of Algorithm 2 is $O(|R(Q)| + |R(Q) \cap R(t_w)| \log(|R(Q) \cap R(t_w)|))$.

Algorithm 2: Algorithm Reorder.

Input: Result images $R(Q)$, why-not tag t_w with search results $R(t_w)$, α, the number of displayed results m
Output: A reordered list of result images L

1 $d_0 \leftarrow$ the $[(1-\alpha) \times m]$-th result in $R(Q) \backslash R(t_w)$;
2 $d_w \leftarrow$ the $[\alpha \times m]$-th result in $R(Q) \cap R(t_w)$;
3 $\theta \leftarrow \frac{rel(d_0, Q)}{rel(d_0, Q) + rel(d_w, t_w)}$;
4 Initialize two empty temporary list L_1 and L_2;
5 **for** *each result image* $d \in R(Q)$ **do**
6   **if** $d \in R(t_w)$ **then**
7         $rel_w(d, Q, t_w) = (1-\theta) \times rel(d, Q) + \theta \times rel(d, t_w)$;
8   Add d to L_1 with score $rel_w(d, Q, t_w)$;
9   **else**
10   Add d to L_2 with score $rel(d, Q)$;
11 Sort all images in L_1 by their assigned scores descendingly;
12 $L \leftarrow merge(L_1, L_2)$;
13 **return** L

5. THE QUERY RELAXATION MODEL

While result reordering model can efficiently display relevant images with the why-not tag t_w, it is ineffective when there are too few images with tag t_w in the result set. Notice that arbitrarily removing one or more query tags may not be effective as the query may become too generic leading to the retrieval of too many irrelevant results (*e.g.*, query "lake" in Example 2). Hence, a technique to effectively identify the "culprit" query tag(s) in a query for removal is desirable. The query relaxation model is proposed to address this issue. We begin by introducing the notion of *selective tagset* which we shall be exploiting subsequently.

5.1 Selective Tagset

We first introduce *relevance-aware cardinality* and *relevance-aware selectivity* to facilitate exposition. The *relevance-aware cardinality* of a set of query tags $T \subseteq Q$, denoted as $card(T)$, is the weighted sum of the relevance scores of all images annotated by all tags in T. The relevance score used here is the one associated with the why-not tag ($rel(d, t_w)$). Then, $card(T)$ is formally defined as:

$$card(T) = \sum_{d \in \mathcal{D}} rel(d, t_w) \tag{2}$$

Intuitively, a set of query tags T is *selective* when removing a single tag from T would generate *significantly larger* size of query results. Accordingly, given T, we define a child set of T as a $(|T|-1)$-subset of T[5]. We denote the set of all child sets of T as $children(T)$. Then, the *relevance-aware selectivity* of T, denoted as $select(T)$, is defined as follows.

$$select(T) = \frac{\frac{\sum_{T' \in children(T)} card(T')}{|children(T)|}}{card(T)} \tag{3}$$

Informally, a *selective tagset* of a multi-tag query Q is a set of tags $T_{max} \subset Q$ which has maximum relevance-aware selectivity among all possible tagsets in Q. If there are more than one set then the tie is broken arbitrarily. Formally,

Definition 2. *Let $Q = \{t_1, t_2, \ldots, t_n\}$ be a search query where $n \geq 2$. Let t_w be the why-not tag. Then $T_{max} \subset Q$ is a* ***selective tagset*** *iff $\nexists T' \subset Q$ such that $select(T') > select(T_{max})$ where $T' \neq T_{max}$.*

5.2 The RELAX Algorithm

We now discuss the algorithm to efficiently detect the selective tagset of a multi-tag query Q. Obviously, computing selectivity is straightforward when the cardinalities of all 2^n subsets of Q are known. The brute-force approach for this task requires traversing all images with tag t_w for each subset resulting in a time complexity of $O(2^n D(t_w))$. Clearly, this is inefficient. Hence, we propose an algorithm that scans $D(t_w)$ only once to detect the selective tagset.

[5]A k-subset of a set is a subset with exactly k elements.

Algorithm 3: Algorithm Relax.

Input: A set of query tags $Q = \{t_1, \ldots, t_n\}$ with search result $R(Q)$, why-not tag t_w with search result $R(t_w)$
Output: The most selective subset $T' \subset Q$, Notification $\mathbb{N}$

Initialize the cardinality of each subset of Q to 0;
for *each image* $d \in D(t_w)$ **do**
    $T \leftarrow Q \cap T_d$;
    Increase $card(T)$ by $rel(d, t_w)$;
for $i = 1 \rightarrow n$ **do**
    for *each subset* $T \subseteq Q$ **do**
        if $t_i \in T$ **then**
            $T' \leftarrow T \backslash \{t_i\}$;
            $card(T') \leftarrow card(T') + card(T)$;
for *each subset* $T \subseteq Q, T \neq \emptyset$ **do**
    $select(T) = \frac{\frac{\sum_{T' \in children(T)} card(T')}{|children(T)|}}{card(T)}$;
$T_{max} \leftarrow$ the subset T with maximum relevance-aware selectivity;
Generate notification $\mathbb{N}$ based on T_{max};
return $(\mathbb{N}, T_{max})$

Observe that based on Equation 2, an image d contributes its relevance score to the cardinality of a tagset T when $T \subseteq T_d$. Therefore, $T \subseteq Q \cap T_d$. Let $exactCard(T')$ be the sum of relevance scores $rel(d, t_w)$ of all images $d \in D(t_w)$ such that $Q \cap T_d = T'$. Then Equation 2 can be rewritten as:

$$card(T) = \sum_{T \subseteq T' \subseteq Q} exactCard(T') \tag{4}$$

That is, the contributing images to $card(T)$ are split into $2^{|Q|-|T|}$ groups, each corresponds to a superset T' of T. Notice that $(Q \cap T_d)$ is unique for all d. Therefore, $exactCard(T')$ can be computed for all sets $T' \subseteq Q$ in a single scan over $D(t_w)$.

Each subset T of $Q = \{t_1, \ldots, t_n\}$ can be encoded as an n-bit bitarray such that the i-th bit is 1 *iff* $t_i \in T$. Using bitarray encoding, a set is a superset of another set *iff* its bitarray supersedes the other set's bitarray[6]. Furthermore, the bitarrays can be arranged in an n-dimension hypercube such that two bitarrays are connected when they are different in only one bit. The sums are then computed using the Hypercube algorithm [11], a popular algorithm in parallel computing. In brief, given an n-dimension hypercube with 2^n nodes, each is labeled with an n-bit bitarray and assigned a value, the hypercube algorithm computes the sum of all values and stores

[6]Bitarray b_1 supersedes bitarray b_2 when $b_1 \wedge b_2 = b_2$

that sum at a node (assumed to be 00...0). The computation consists of n steps. At step i, the current sum of values at all nodes whose i-bit is 1 is added to the current sum of values of the corresponding nodes whose i-bit is 0. After n-steps, the total sum of all values in the hypercube is at node 00...0.

Not that although we do not employ parallel computation for finding the selective tagset, the Hypercube algorithm has a valuable property that can also be exploited for sequential computation. After n steps, the value at each node a is the sum of the original values at all nodes whose bitarrays supersede a's bitarray. Specifically, we can compute the cardinality of *all* subsets of Q using Equation 4 by a single n-step hypercube process having complexity $O(2^{n-1}n)$.

Algorithm 3 realizes the above intuitions to compute the selective tagset. Lines 1-4 compute the $exactCard(T)$ of each subset T of Q while Lines 5-9 add them into *card* following Equation 4 and the Hypercube algorithm. Lines 10-11 compute the selectivity score from the cardinality score following Equation 3. Line 12 simply finds the subset of Q with maximum relevance-aware selectivity. Based on this subset, the algorithm generates the explanation $\mathbb{N}$ for the user (Line 13). Notice that the relevance-aware selectivity of *all* query tag subsets is computed in the aforementioned steps. Consequently, we can easily extend our approach to notify the user with top-k most selective tagsets instead of the only most selective tagset and allow her to select the desired tagset for removal. The time complexity of the algorithm is $O(n \times 2^{n-1} + |D(t_w)|)$. Notice that in practice, n is usually small and $n \ll D(t_w)$.

6. THE QUERY SUBSTITUTION MODEL

The query relaxation model discussed in the preceding section is not effective when there are very few images (if any) associated with a why-not tag in the entire image collection. In this case, even the most relaxed query fails to retrieve sufficient number of desired results (Example 3). In this section, we present the query substitution model to tackle such scenario.

The lack of existence of sufficient images matching the why-not tag poses two intertwining challenges. Firstly, the user-specified why-not tag cannot be leveraged directly for generating explanation to the why-not question as it is unlikely that the user wishes to see a very small number of result images (if any) associated with this tag. Secondly, while the desired images are likely to be annotated by some closely related tag(s) to the why-not tag, it is difficult to find these related tags using traditional tag co-occurrence or tag relevance measures as both of these require sufficiently large number of matching images to be effective.

In order to address the aforementioned challenges, we resort to the external source *Wikipedia* to interpret the why-not tag. Specifically, we shall use it to measure the *strength* of relationship between tags to find a *closely related* tag t_c to the why-not tag. It is then used in lieu of the why-not tag to guide the why-not question answering process as well as modification of the query.

In particular, t_c must satisfy the following three conditions: (a) it must annotate sufficiently large number of images in the image collection; (b) it should be *closely related* to the why-not tag t_w; and (c) it should be *related* to the query keywords Q. The first condition is obvious. Otherwise t_c would offer little benefit compared to the why-not tag. The remaining conditions ensure necessary semantic relationship between t_c, t_w, and query tag(s). Notice that we use the phrase *closely related* for the second condition whereas *related* for the last. This is because t_c must be closest to the why-not tag. We now formally quantify the relatedness of a selected tag t_c.

DEFINITION 3. *Given a query $Q = \{t_1, \dots, t_n\}$, a why-not tag t_w, and a term t_c, the **tag relatedness** of t_c, denoted as $\Phi(t_c)$, is defined as follows:*

$$\Phi(t) = (1-\beta)\frac{\sum_{1\le i\le n} sim(t_c, t_i)}{n} + \beta * sim(t_c, t_w)$$

where $\beta \in [0,1]$ and sim denotes tag similarity of a pair of tags.

Clearly, in the above definition the key challenge is to compute *tag similarity* as we cannot simply compute it using tag co-occurrence or tag relevance measures.

Algorithm 4: Algorithm SUBSTITUTE.

Input: A set of n query tags $Q = \{t_1, \dots, t_n\}$ with search result $R(Q)$, why-not tag t_w with search result $R(t_w)$, a configurable parameter β
Output: The closely related tag t_c, Notification $\mathbb{N}$

Initialize $(n+1)$ sorted lists $s_0, s_1, \dots, s_n$, each stores the most similar tags to $t_w, t_1, \dots, t_n$, each neighbor tag also has large enough images in the image collection $\mathcal{D}$;
Initialize weights w_i with $w_0 = \beta$ and $w_i = \frac{1-\beta}{n}$ for $1 \le i \le n$;
Initialize a heap H with at most k tags, when it is full, the minimum is removed;
for *each* $i \in [0, n]$ **do**
  $t \leftarrow s_i.next()$ whose score is in $score_i(t)$;
  for *each* $j \in [0, n], j \neq i$ **do**
    $score_j(t) \leftarrow WLM(t, t_j)$;
  $score(t) = weightedSum(w_0, score_0(t), \dots, w_n, score_n(t))$;
  Add t to H;
  $thresDesc_i \leftarrow w_i \times (s_i.peekNext() - s_i.last())$;
$threshold \leftarrow weightedSum(w_0, s_0.last(), \dots, w_n, s_n.last())$;
while $threshold > H.min$ **do**
  $i \leftarrow arg\min_{i\in[0,n]} thresDesc_i$;
  $t \leftarrow s_i.next()$ whose score is in $score_i(t)$;
  for *each* $j \in [0, n], j \neq i$ **do**
    $score_j(t) \leftarrow WLM(t, t_j)$;
  $score(t) = weightedSum(w_0, score_0(t), \dots, w_n, score_n(t))$;
  Add t to H if $score(t) > H.min$;
  $thresDesc_i \leftarrow w_i \times (s_i.peekNext() - s_i.last())$;
  $threshold \leftarrow weightedSum(w_0, s_0.last(), \dots, w_n, s_n.last())$;
Related tag $t_c \leftarrow H.max$;
Generate notification $\mathbb{N}$ based on t_c;
return $(\mathbb{N}, t_c)$

6.1 Tag Similarity Computation

We compute tag similarity by adopting the *Wikipedia Link Measure* (WLM), an efficient and highly accurate technique to measure the similarity between two Wikipedia articles using hyperlinks [10]. Computing tag similarity using WLM consists of two steps as in [10], *disambiguation* and *article similarity*. The disambiguation process corresponds to the mapping process from each tag to each article. Specifically, this step exploits two heuristics: *dominant meanings* and *mutual disambiguation*. While a tag can have many meanings, it usually has only a few dominant meanings frequently used in most cases. For example, the tag `pyramid` probably refers to either the geometric shape pyramid or a building with that shape, but rarely refers to the arena at *Memphis*. *Mutual disambiguation* means that when two tags are used together, they are probably related to each other. For instance, in Example 3 since `pyramid` and `mesoamerica` are used together, `pyramid` probably refers to a building and not a geometric shape.

The *article similarity* $docSim(a_1, a_2)$ between two articles a and b is computed using WLM as:

$$docSim(a,b) = 1 - \frac{\log(max(|A|,|B|)) - \log(|A \cap B|)}{\log(|W|) - \log(min(|A|,|B|))}$$

where A and B are the sets of all articles that link to a and b, respectively, and W is the entire Wikipedia. The intuition behind the above formula is that two related articles tend to be referred to by lots of common articles. Finally, the tag similarity of a tag pair is computed as the article similarity of their disambiguated articles.

Let us illustrate the process using the tags `pyramid` and `mesoamerica`. In Wikipedia, `mesoamerica` only matches to a single article about *Mesoamerica* region whereas `pyramid` can match to multiple articles. Among them, only pyramid shape and pyramid building are dominant meanings. The article similarity between the *Mesoamerica* article and the two *pyramid* articles are then computed and compared. The larger one is the similarity between *Mesoamerica* and *pyramid* building. Thus, they are the disambiguated meanings of `mesoamerica` and `pyramid`, respectively. Hence, their similarity is the similarity score between the two tags.

6.2 The SUBSTITUTE Algorithm

We now discuss the algorithm to locate a tag with highest tag relatedness value efficiently and refine the query Q accordingly. Observe that the tag relatedness of t_c is effectively a linear combination of its similarities to all the query tags and the why-not tag which can be pre-computed and pre-sorted. Hence, we can cast our problem as the *combining fuzzy grade problem* which can be solved efficiently using the Threshold Algorithm (TA) [4].

Algorithm 4 outlines the procedure to identify a tag t_c with highest tag relatedness value. Specifically, we *extend* the TA as follows. Recall from Definition 3, the similarity to the why-not tag has largest impact on the overall score. Therefore, it is reasonable to proceed on the list storing the why-not tag's similarities faster instead of same speed as in TA. To this end, for each sorted list, we can estimate the threshold decrease when the next processed node is select from this list and choose the list with maximum threshold decrease. This optimization ensures the quickest termination.

Let us elaborate on Algorithm 4 now. Line 1 initializes $(n + 1)$ sorted lists containing the most similar tags to the why-not tag and the query tags. Each list is assumed to support three functions *next*() to proceed the list, *last*() to look at the last tag seen by sorted access and *peekNext*() to peek the next tag but does not proceed the list. Line 2 initializes the weights following Definition 3 which shall be used in the *weightedSum*() function to compute the weighted sum of all similarity scores. Line 3 initializes a min-heap H which automatically discards the minimum score tag when a tag with larger score is added. That is, H stores the top-k most related tags. Lines 4-10 simply process the first tag within each list similarly to the steps of TA. Note that processing the first tag of all lists is required to initialize the threshold (Line 11). Lines 13-20 are repeatedly executed until the *threshold* is smaller than the minimum value of H. Within each loop, the next processed tag is retrieved from the list with maximum threshold decrease (Line 13). Lines 14-20 are similar to Lines 5-11. Observe that since H stores top-k related tags, we can easily extend our approach to notify the user with top-k closely related tags instead of most closely related tag and allow her to select the desired tag for query modification.

The worst case time complexity of Algorithm 4 is basically the time complexity of TA which is $O(|\mathcal{T}|^{n/(n+1)}k^{1/n+1})$ where $\mathcal{T}$ is the set of all tags in the image collection $\mathcal{D}$ and n is the query size. Theoretically, in the worst-case, Algorithm 4 may iterate through all tags in $\mathcal{T}$. However, in practice, it is very unlikely. Since k is usually small, the top-k related tags to the why-not tags and the query tags are very likely to be very similar to either the why-not tag or the query tags. Consequently, Algorithm 4 usually terminates quickly and the execution time is very short. Additionally, for each tag (*i.e.,* keyphrase) in Wikipedia, we only need to sort and store a

Table 1: Sample queries for evaluating result reordering model

Id	Query [WHY NOT tag]	$\|R(Q)\|$	$\|R(t_w)\|$	$\|R(Q) \cap R(t_w)\|$	$F(Q, t_w)$
Q_1	Rome [colosseum]	909	20	18	7
Q_2	music [classical]	2213	119	27	6
Q_3	sea [fish]	9016	2279	556	6
Q_4	Paris [Louvre]	2338	2279	178	4
Q_5	Paris [arcdetriomphe]	2338	190	30	2
Q_6	Paris architecture [cathedral]	250	967	25	0
Q_7	sky clouds [bird]	8525	4031	132	1
Q_8	sky clouds [plane]	8525	2014	345	1
Q_9	newyork [statueofliberty]	3822	46	25	3
Q_{10}	sunset sunrise sky [horizon]	238	1195	43	40

small list of similar tags. This space optimization is crucial since there are more than three million articles in Wikipedia.

7. EXPERIMENTS

WINE is implemented in Java 1.7 using Lucene 3.0.3 as the underlying index engine[7]. All experiments are conducted on an Intel Xeon X5570 machine with 12GB memory. In our experiments, unless specified otherwise, we set the number of displayed images $m = 50$ and the desired image ratio $\alpha = 0.2$.

7.1 Experimental Setup

Dataset. Since off-the-shelf image search engines (*e.g.,* Flickr) typically disallow full access to their data and some statistics (*e.g.,* relevance scores) which are required by WINE, we cannot evaluate WINE directly on top of such search engines. Hence, we are confined to conduct experiments using the NUS-WIDE dataset containing 269,648 images from Flickr. All tags provided in the dataset are used in our experiments without filtering. The underlying TAGIR system used in our experiments follows the best performing configuration in [13] for multi-tag queries to facilitate evaluation of the query relaxation and query substitution models. For query substitution, we used the English Wikipedia dump released on 30 January, 2010[8] which contains 3.2 million articles and more than 266 million hyperlinks.

Query Set. We asked 14 volunteers (undergraduate students in computer science and business majors) each to evaluate a subset of more than 500 randomly chosen queries. A volunteer may issue a why-not tag if the results returned by a query do not completely satisfy his/her search intent. 114 queries received why-not tags from the volunteers. Note that some queries (*e.g.,* Q_7, Q_8) received multiple why-not tags resulting in 125 query why-not tag pairs. Then, for each query and why-not tag pair, we asked the volunteers to label which result images are relevant in the original *and* modified result set, taking into account both the original query and the issued why-not tag. Out of these 125 queries, 60, 36, and 29 queries invoked the result reordering, query relaxation, and query substitution models, respectively. Due to space limitation, here we chose to report 30 queries (10 queries per model) as described in Tables 1-3. These queries are chosen based on multiple factors. First of all, for these queries most volunteers demonstrated low satisfaction. Secondly, we ensure that the number of keywords in these queries vary from 1 to 4. Note that the average number of keywords in a search query is 2.2 [13]. Thirdly, we ensure that the number of images satisfying these queries vary significantly (*i.e.,* $R(Q)$ is varied from 0 to 9016). Last but not the least, majority of these queries fail to return sufficient number of result images annotated by the why-not tags even when they are posed directly on Flickr. Specifically, among the top-50 Flickr results [9], the number of images annotated

[7]The video of WINE is available at `http://youtu.be/A42i2geQZVk`.

[8]`http://download.wikimedia.org/enwiki/20100130/`.

[9]The setting used is the default setting of Flickr search available at `http://www.flickr.com/search/?q={query}`.

Table 2: Sample queries for evaluating the query relaxation model

Id	Query [WHY NOT tag]	$\lvert R(Q)\rvert$	$\lvert R(t_w)\rvert$	$\lvert R(Q) \cap R(t_w)\rvert$	Selective tag(s)	New query	$\lvert R(Q_{new})\rvert$	$\lvert R(Q_{new}) \cap R(t_w)\rvert$	$F(Q, t_w)$
Q_{11}	Apple Computer [iPhone]	152	196	4	computer	apple	1318	97	0
Q_{12}	Apple Computer [laptops]	152	37	8	computer	apple	1318	15	3
Q_{13}	Las Vegas Nevada [casino]	44	140	5	las nevada	vegas	224	54	24
Q_{14}	sea summer [surfing]	592	310	6	summer	sea	9016	81	1
Q_{15}	sea summer [tornado]	592	628	1	summer	sea	9016	13	0
Q_{16}	sea summer [carnival]	592	348	1	sea	summer	5055	76	4
Q_{17}	christmas night [santaclaus]	146	44	3	night	christmas	1400	31	1
Q_{18}	christmas night [firework]	146	48	1	christmas	night	8806	28	0
Q_{19}	sky cloud rain [rainbow]	92	1245	7	cloud	skyrain	384	33	2
Q_{20}	lake Hangzhou Zhejiang China [lake]	0	4336	0	zhejiang	lake hangzhou china	8	8	43

by the why-not tag t_w is reported in the last columns of Tables 1-3 ($F(Q, t_w)$). Observe that it is smaller than 10 ($\alpha < 0.2$) for all but four queries. *This demonstrates the need for why-not questions even in very large social image collection such as Flickr.*

Performance Metric. We conducted experiments to evaluate the *effectiveness* and *efficiency* of the three explanation models. The *effectiveness* is measured by *Precision@K* ($P@m$), which is the ratio of the relevant images among the top-m retrieved images for a query ($m = 50$ in our evaluation). To the best of our knowledge, this is the first work to answer why-not questions in TAGIR. Hence, there is a lack of benchmark dataset for the evaluation. The labels annotated by the volunteers are used as ground-truth labels.

7.2 Effectiveness of the Explanation Models

The sample queries and related features used for effectiveness study are reported in Tables 1-3. Notice that $|R(Q) \cap R(t_w)|$ and $|R(t_w)|$ for each query satisfies the condition necessary to invoke the corresponding model with $m = 50$ and $\alpha = 0.2$. The $P@50$ of all queries are reported in Figure 6 (for the time being, the reader is requested to ignore the bars related to Coo and PRF).

Result Reordering. Observe that the original results of Q_1-Q_{10} have relatively high $P@50$, reflecting the fact the user is generally capable of forming suitable queries for their needs. However, we also notice that their $P@50$ remains imperfect and for some queries' it is as low as 0.4. Such imperfection reflects the fact the some of users' expectations have not been met. For instance, in Q_3 for the query `sea`, the user expects some images related to fishes in the sea. But these images are missing in the original results. In summary, our results clearly show that the simple result reordering model can improve or at least maintain the $P@50$ for all sample queries and, for some queries, bring the precision close to perfect (Q_7, Q_8, Q_{10}).

Query Relaxation. Expectedly, we observe significant increase in result sizes ($|R(Q_{new})|$) for this model (Table 2) for Q_{11}-Q_{20}. By observing the changes in result sizes, it is clear that the query relaxation model successfully identifies and removes the selective tag(s) from the original query. For instance, for Q_{19}, a user expects to see `rainbow` when searching for rainy skies but rainbows usually only appear in clear rather than cloudy sky. Similarly, in Q_{13} and Q_{20}, `Vegas` and `Hangzhou` are common names for "`Las Vegas`" and "`Zhejiang`", respectively. Hence, the latter tags are not necessary. We also observe that query relaxation helps to rectify user's knowledge. For Q_{11}, although *Apple Computer* was a former name of *Apple Inc.*, it has dropped the word "Computer" when *iPhone* products were launched (as suggested by our solution). Figure 6 reports significant increase in $P@50$ values for most queries after query relaxation ($Q_{11} - Q_{20}$). Particularly, Q_{14}, Q_{17}, Q_{19} and Q_{20} reach near perfect value.

Query Substitution. Table 3 reports the top-3 most closely related tags based on Wikipedia and the suggested new queries. Note that in an interactive TAGIR system, a user can select one of these related tags for new query formulation. In our evaluation, we always choose the most closely related tag (top-1) for query substitution. For instance, the why-not tag "`mesoamerica`" in Q_{21} is replaced by "`maya`" to form a new query "`pyramid maya`". Note that a user may also use the query tag as why-not tag as in Q_{26} to reflect that images retrieved by tag "`leningrad`" are not what the user expects for "`leningrad`". Note that `Leningrad` is the former name of `Saint Petersburg` and, due to its recent popularity, there are significantly more images related to the modern `Saint Petersburg` than to the historical `Leningrad` in Flickr. Hence, using tag "`saintpetersburg`" will retrieve more relevant images.

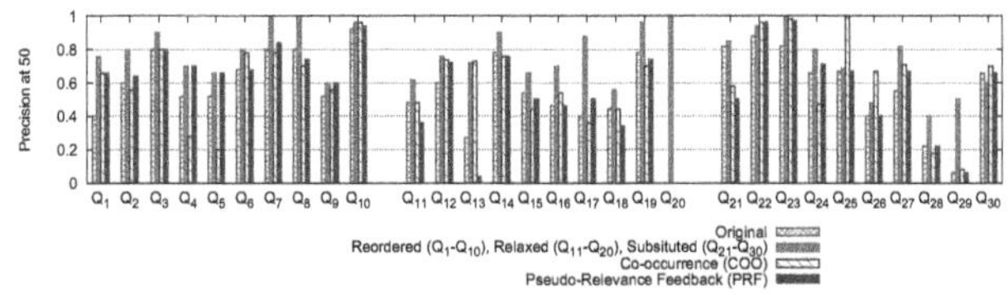

Figure 6: $P@50$ of WINE, COO, PRF against original. WINE: Reordered ($Q_1 - Q_{10}$), Relaxed ($Q_{11} - Q_{20}$), Subsituted ($Q_{21} - Q_{30}$)

The $P@50$ values of the original results and the results of the substituted queries are reported in Figure 6 (Q_{21}–Q_{30}). Among the 10 sample queries, six underwent significant increase in $P@50$ after query substitution, three do not have significant changes in $P@50$ (Q_{21}, Q_{22} and Q_{25}) while the remaining one suffers a slight drop in $P@50$ (Q_{30}) but the result qualities are not necessarily worst. Q_{30} highlights a situation where the image collection indeed has too few relevant data on `picasso`. Consequently, all suggested queries are not truly similar to `picasso`. Nevertheless, we notice that the drop in $P@50$ is small (6%).

7.3 Comparison with Query Expansion

Next, we compare WINE with two popular query expansion techniques based on *tag co-occurrence* and *pseudo-relevance feedback*, denoted as COO and PRF, respectively [1]. In brief, COO expands a query by finding the top-N tags which co-occurs with most query keywords, where tag co-occurrence is measured using Jaccard coefficient. PRF expands the query by analyzing the top-100 results from the original query and finding the top-N most significant tags in these images. The tag significance is measured as KL-divergence between their distribution in the top-ranked images and the whole collection. We set $N = 5$.

The $P@50$ of COO and PRF are reported in Figure 6 which clearly shows the superiority of WINE. For example, consider Q_{11} and Q_{12} which are identical queries (`apple computer`) except that the follow-up why-not questions are different (`iphone` versus `laptops`). Thus, COO and PRF detect same expanded tags for both Q_{11} and Q_{12} but their results on Q_{12} is clearly better than on Q_{11}. It is because, our dataset (NUS-WIDE) is built when iPhone is newly introduced but laptops and macbook have had a long history. Thus, both COO and PRF can only expand using tags `macbook` or `laptop` but not `phone` or `iphone`. Meanwhile, WINE can exploit the why-not tag and correctly modify the queries on both cases. Similarly,

Table 3: Sample queries for evaluating the query substitution model

Id	Query [Why Not tag]	$\lvert R(Q)\rvert$	$\lvert R(t_w)\rvert$	$\lvert R(Q) \cap R(t_w)\rvert$	Top-3 most related tag(s)	New query	$\lvert R(Q_{new})\rvert$	$F(Q, t_w)$
Q_{21}	pyramid [Mesoamerica]	605	9	4	maya teotihuacan aztec	pyramid maya	27	1
Q_{22}	skating [winters]	248	9	0	winter spring summer fall snow	winter skating	62	7
Q_{23}	Balkan [Serbian]	62	9	2	serbia montenegro bulgaria	balkan serbia	51	6
Q_{24}	pagoda lake [Zhejiang]	35	6	0	hangzhou jiangsu guangxi	hangzhou	20	4
Q_{25}	Lombardy lake [brescia]	3	8	0	lakegarda verona trento	lakegarda	13	10
Q_{26}	Leningrad [Leningrad]	5	5	5	saintpetersburg moscow kiev	saintpetersburg	21	9
Q_{27}	Persian city [Persepolis]	11	9	0	fars shiraz yazd iranian safavid	fars	22	4
Q_{28}	Japan [ninja]	3647	55	1	ninja katana samurai	ninja	55	0
Q_{29}	India [bangalore]	2938	0	0	bangalore karnataka chennai	bangalore india	85	1
Q_{30}	painting [picasso]	1294	74	0	cubism painter impressionism	cubism	595	0

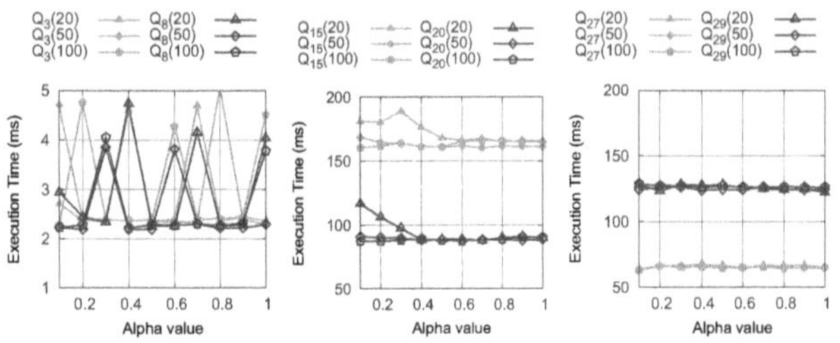

(a) Result Reordering(b) Query Relaxation(c) Query Substitution.

Figure 7: The impact of α and efficiency of WINE.

for Q_{21}, both Coo and PRF fail to speculate that the user's intent could be on `Mesoamerican pyramid` while for Q_6, both cannot recognize that `cathedral` architecture is a crucial part of `Paris architecture`. Furthermore, when the original results are irrelevant, PRF also suffers from query drift problem [1]. For example, PRF expands Q_{13} with tags `jet`, `flying`, and `flight`. Since WINE uses explicit user feedback (*i.e.,* the why-not tag), it does not suffer from these problems and offer better results. However, we also notice that, for queries where original results are fairly good (*e.g.,* Q_{10}, Q_{22}, Q_{23}), query expansion have comparable performance with WINE. For example, for Q_{10}, query `sky sunrise sunset` are expanded with tags `clouds`, `sun`, `blue`, and `sea` and images with both `sky` and `sea` tend to have a `horizon` (why-not tag).

7.4 Effect of α

In this experiment, we measure the effect of α and m on the efficiency of our proposed algorithms. We select two sample queries for each model and execute them using the corresponding model across different values of α and for $m \in \{20, 50, 100\}$. All queries are selected so that the conditions to execute their corresponding models are met. Figure 7 reports results of our experiment. We use $Q_i(j)$ to denote query Q_i for $m = j$. From the results, it is clear that our proposed algorithms are efficient across the whole spectrum of α and m and both these parameters do not greatly influence the query performance. It is worth noting that WINE *is efficient even if we consider very large image collection* as it is not very sensitive to the underlying dataset size. WINE focuses only on the top-m result images or the cases when the result size is too small. In both these scenarios, the number of images it needs to process is fractionally small compared to the underlying data.

8. CONCLUSIONS & FUTURE WORK

We have proposed a novel framework called WINE for explaining why-not questions on query results in a TAGIR system. WINE exploits three explanation models to automatically generate explanation for a user's why-not question as well provide suggestion for effective query modification to retrieve desired images. We empirically demonstrated that the techniques presented herein produce good quality response to user's why-not questions. Despite the proven effectiveness of WINE in handling a wide variety of why-not questions, it suffers from two limitations. First, WINE assumes that search results of a query are returned as a ranked list of images. While this is true for a broad spectrum of image search engines, more sophisticated search engines may organize the result images in form of clusters or summaries and directly return them to the user. It is interesting to explore how a user can pose why-not questions on them. Second, our query substitution model leverages Wikipedia to discover closely-related keywords of a why-not tag. Here we assume that such keywords indeed exists in Wikipedia. However, in certain cases (*e.g.,* images related to recent events) such closely-related tag may exists in the image collection but not in Wikipedia. We are currently exploring how WINE can be extended to address these limitations. Additionally, we intend to study the WHY NOT? problem in the context of social video search (*e.g.,* Youtube). In summary, the results of this paper are an important first step in this regard.

Acknowledgements: Aixin Sun and Ba Quan Truong were supported by Singapore MOE AcRF Tier-1 Grant RG13/10.

9. REFERENCES

[1] C. Carpineto, R. Giovanni. A Survey of Automatic Query Expansion in Information Retrieval, *ACM Comput. Surv.*, 44(1), 2012.
[2] A. Chapman and H. V. Jagadish. Why not?, *In ACM SIGMOD*, 2009.
[3] T.-S. Chua, et al. NUS-WIDE: a real-world web image database from National University of Singapore, *In ACM CIVR*, 2009.
[4] R. Fagin, A. Lotem, M. Naor. Optimal aggregation algorithms for middleware, *In PODS*, 2001.
[5] J. He, E. Meij, Maarten de Rijke. Result diversification based on query-specific cluster ranking, *JASIST*, 62(3), 2011.
[6] Z. He, E. Lo. Answering Why-not Questions on Top-k Queries, *In ICDE*, 2012.
[7] V. Jain, M. Varma. Learning to re-rank: query-dependent image re-ranking using click data, *In WWW*, 2011.
[8] X. Li, et al. Learning Social Tag Relevance by Neighbor Voting, *IEEE Trans. Multimedia*, 11(7), 2009.
[9] C. Liu, et al. Post-rank reordering: resolving preference misalignments between search engines and end users, *In CIKM*, 2009.
[10] D. Milne, I. A. Witten. An effective, low-cost measure of semantic relatedness obtained from Wikipedia links, *Proc. AAAI Workshop on Wikipedia and Artificial Intelligence*, 2008.
[11] David A. Padua. Encycl. of Parallel Computing, Springer, 2011.
[12] G. Smith, et al. Evaluating Implicit Judgments from Image Search Clickthrough Data, JASIST, 63(12), 2012.
[13] A. Sun, S. S. Bhowmick, et al. Tag-based social image retrieval: An empirical evaluation, *JASIST*, 62(12), 2011.
[14] Q.-T Tran, C.-Y Chan. How to ConQueR why-not questions, *In ACM SIGMOD*, 2010.
[15] R. H. van Leuken, et al. Visual diversification of image search results, *In WWW*, 2009.
[16] M. Wang et al. Towards a Relevant and Diverse Search of Social Images, *IEEE Trans. on Multimedia*, 12(8), 2010.
[17] Z.-J. Zha et al. Visual Query Suggestion, *In ACM MM*, 2009.
[18] G. Zhu, et al. Image tag refinement towards low-rank, content-tag prior and error sparsity, *In ACM MM*, 2010.

Automatic Generation of Social Media Snippets for Mobile Browsing

Wenyuan Yin [†], Tao Mei [‡], Chang Wen Chen [†]
[†] State University of New York at Buffalo, Buffalo, NY, USA
[‡] Microsoft Research Asia, Beijing, P. R. China
{wyin4, chencw}@buffalo.edu; tmei@microsoft.com

ABSTRACT

The ongoing revolution in media consumption from traditional PCs to the pervasiveness of mobile devices is driving the adoption of social media in our daily lives. More and more people are using their mobile devices to enjoy social media content while on the move. However, mobile display constraints create challenges for presenting and authoring the rich media content on screens with limited display size. This paper presents an innovative system to automatically generate magazine-like social media visual summaries, which is called "snippet," for efficient mobile browsing. The system excerpts the most salient and dominant elements, i.e., a major picture element and a set of textual elements, from the original media content, and composes these elements into a text overlaid image by maximizing information perception. In particular, we investigate a set of aesthetic rules and visual perception principles to optimize the layout of the extracted elements by considering display constraints. As a result, browsing the snippet on mobile devices is just like quickly glancing at a magazine. To the best of our knowledge, this paper represents one of the first attempts at automatic social media snippet generation by studying aesthetic rules and visual perception principles. We have conducted experiments and user studies with social posts from news entities. We demonstrated that the generated snippets are effective at representing media content in a visually appealing and compact way, leading to a better user experience when consuming social media content on mobile devices.

Categories and Subject Descriptors

H.5.1 [**Information Interfaces and Presentation**]: Multimedia Information Systems—*Evaluation/methodology*; I.4.7 [**Image Processing and Computer Vision**]: Feature Measurement—*Feature representation*

General Terms

Algorithms, Design, Experimentation, Human Factors.

Keywords

Social Media, Snippet Presentation, Multimedia Authoring, Mobile Browsing, Responsive Design.

MM'13, Oct. 21–25, Barcelona, Spain.
Copyright 2013 ACM 978-1-4503-2404-5/13/10 ...$15.00.
http://dx.doi.org/10.1145/2502081.2502116.

(a) (b) (c) (d)

Figure 1: Example of traditional social media posts on mobile devices and the snippet generated by the proposed system: (a) twitter post, (b) post details, (c) linked article of the post, and (d) proposed snippet.

1. INTRODUCTION

Social media networks, such as Facebook, Twitter, and Google+, has continued to revolutionize people's lives since the emergence of the first social media networks two decades ago. A huge number of people and organizations are actively sharing news, experiences, and opinions via social media. The overwhelming amount of information on social media networks and the distraction caused by the large number of irrelevant social posts makes it difficult and time-consuming to find relevant information, leading to an unintended consequence: information overload.

Meanwhile, the proliferation of mobile devices and rapid development of wireless networks enable people to use their mobile devices to explore the Internet anytime and anywhere. People are spending more time than ever accessing social media content via their mobile devices. The consumption of social media on mobile devices has become pervasive.

Although the pervasiveness of mobile devices and a variety of mobile social media applications have boosted the usage of social media, the limited display size of mobile devices remains an obstacle for mobile users to peruse social posts and efficiently find interesting information. This issue can be demonstrated, as in the example in Fig.1(a), in which there is a post from the Wall Street Journal on Twitter as circled, 'Ang Lee on his Oscar win and the elusive best-picture statue: on.wsj.com/ZDJ1FW.' However, it does not stand out from the surrounding posts for users who are interested in reading it. With a small screen, mobile users have to scan the posts one by one to discover interested posts, making it a time-consuming task on mobile devices. Moreover, mobile users occasionally browse social posts in between activities (e.g., when waiting for or taking buses). It is distracting for mobile users to read the posts to find their preferred content. Because of the above challenges, it is difficult for mobile users to discover interested information from the abundance of social media content.

In addition to the mobile display constraints, the limit in the number of characters in social posts restricts the amount of information and thus hinders mobile users from obtaining important information that interests them. For example, with the 140 character limit of each post in Twitter, a user often posts a short message with additional links, as with the highlighted instance shown in Fig. 1(a). If a viewer is interested in the post, he will have to click the post for details, such as what award Ang won, as shown in Fig. 1(b). The viewer then has to click the link to get the full article as shown in Fig. 1(c) for more information, e.g., for which movie Ang was awarded.

1.1 Challenges in Social Media Presentation

The challenges when browsing social media on mobile devices can be summarized as follows.

- First, social posts in traditional text summary form are unattractive and unappealing. Moreover, the text is difficult to perceive on the limited display. Therefore, interesting posts may not stand out from the surrounding posts.
- Second, it is not convenient for mobile users to laboriously read wordy sentences in the post and linked articles in traditional forms of social posts on mobile devices to obtain important information.
- Third, The limited display of mobile devices has not been sufficiently utilized to deliver key information to mobile users. The social media content should be well organized to efficiently provide useful information in the social post summary page and thus help users obtain desired information with a quick glance.

1.2 Motivation and Contributions

The multimodality of social media with prevalent images or video clips creates a good opportunity to help mobile users quickly understand social content. Images are superior at capturing attention [16, 17, 19]. The success of adoption of images in search results presentation provides great evidence that images can indeed help quicken understanding of webpage content and relevance judgment [15, 23]. This motivates us to generate social media snippets for mobile social media browsing by utilizing the images in social posts to help mobile users more quickly understand content. In addition, it is found that usability and aesthetics are highly correlated [2]. Moreover, the research in eye tracking [19, 22] and aesthetic study [1, 13] supply us solid theoretical foundations on how people browse and perceive media. Hence, we believe it is the proper time to build an automatic social media snippet generation system based on aesthetic rules and visual perception principles to help mobile users perceive social posts in an appealing way and thus obtain key information efficiently.

In this paper, we propose a system to automatically build attractive, appealing, and informative snippets in text-overlaid image styles for browsing social media on mobile devices. To discover key information in the posts and links, social media snippet elements, including dominant images and key phrases, are first extracted via a modified TextRank algorithm [18]. In this paper, we assume that a dominant image exists and its content is relevant to the social post, which is usually valid for social media posts. Addressing the missingness of the dominant image is beyond the scope of this paper and can be addressed in the future work by introducing external image as in [10]. Then, the extracted elements are systematically selected and composed to generate snippets based on aesthetic rules and visual perception principles, under the display constraints. Compared with existing systems such as Flipboard [7], which uses fixed patterns, the innovation of the proposed system is that we incorporate well studied aesthetic rules and perception principles to automatically generate attractive, appealing and informative social media snippet with text-overlaid image as shown in Fig.1(d) by formulating it as an optimization problem.

In summary, this paper makes the following contributions:

- First, we propose a system to automatically generate social media snippet to extract and present compact and dominant elements in multimodalities. The mobile users can perceive key information quickly on limited mobile displays.
- Second, we employ human visual perception principles and aesthetic rules to actively push important information to mobile users to expedite the discovery of interesting information.
- Last, we formulate the social media snippet generation process as a constrained energy minimization problem. In addition, we develop a multi-stage optimization procedure to tackle the search complexity, rather than attempt at an expensive and integrated optimization procedure.

The rest of this paper is organized as follows. Section 2 reviews related work. Section 3 presents our proposed social media snippet generation system. Section 4 describes experiments and user studies, followed by the conclusion in Section 5.

2. RELATED WORK

The research community has made some attempts at developing summarization and browsing systems. For example, a system called Eddi was developed to organize a user's Twitter feeds into coherently clustered trending topics and provide interactive topic-based browsing of social status streams in Twitter [3]. TwitterStand is a news processing system built upon tweets to capture late breaking news [21]. Another system deals with text-to-image summary, which automatically illustrates complex sentences as multimodal summaries that combine pictures, structure, and simplified compressed text [24]. Adding structured compressed text to pictures was shown to be more effective than either text or images alone. In [25], the authors developed a rich-media analysis system to sense and explore events from social media and allow magazine-style event visualization anchored on event facets. Although they visualize events in a magazine style, the visualization is based on some pre-designed templates and color schemes. Hence, user perception and aesthetic issues have not been systematically considered.

Some mobile applications, such as Flipboard [7], have been successfully developed to present social media in an appealing way in a magazine style to improve the viewing experience. When displaying a social post on smartphones, the post is fit into pre-defined templates where the title or summary is placed in a fixed position, scale, and color. Although it is more visually appealing than traditional social post presentations, without the consideration of content analysis and user visual perception, it still falls short in presenting maximum allowable information under mobile displays.

In a search scenario, instead of presenting search results in a traditional text snippet form, image excerpts [15] and visual snippets [23] are explored. It has been demonstrated that these webpage summarization forms with images can indeed help users more quickly and accurately understand the content for quick relevance judgment. In [15], properly selected pictures in webpages are added to search result pages to generate a webpage summary called "image excerpt" and it has been demonstrated that image excerpt can

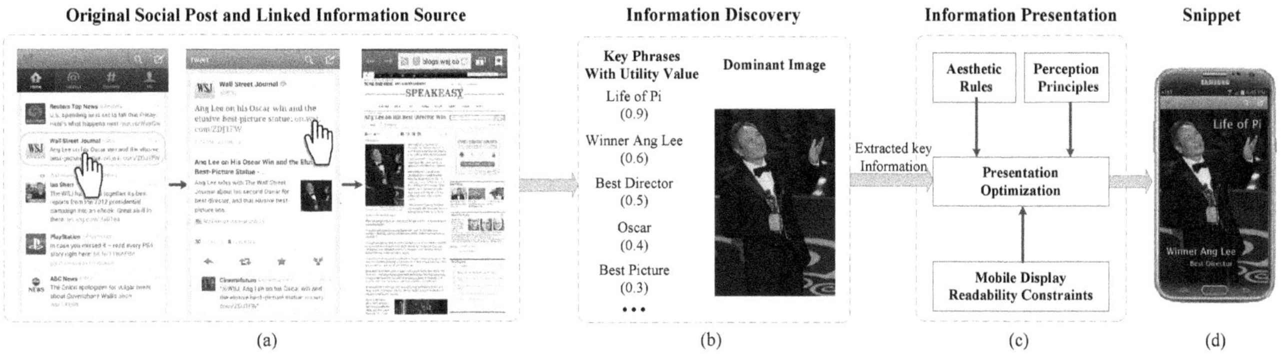

Figure 2: Social media snippet generation system overview. (a) original social post and linked information source (b) information discovery module (c) information presentation module (d) generated social media snippet.

significantly outperform traditional text snippets in terms of both search time and click numbers. Visual snippet is proposed to summarize webpages with title, image, and logo using a fixed template without consideration of how the pieces will be composed, (e.g., where to place the title on images to guarantee or enhance readability, visibility, and usability) [23]. Although these webpage summarization methods are designed for general search results presentation scenarios on desktop PCs, the successful usage of images in the summarization task in terms of visually attractiveness, ease of use, and quick understanding, demonstrate the effectiveness of images in summaries. Considering the text reading obstacle on small mobile devices, images will definitely benefit readability.

On the other hand, aesthetic studies in a variety of research areas, such as photographs [6], webpages [26], interfaces [1], and text-overlaid images [13], have drawn attention in recent decades due to their high correlation with usability. A great deal of research effort has been made to adopt the aesthetic rules in a wide range of applications, such as [12, 20]. To transform inherently dynamic social media into physical photo books to remember important moments, the authors utilize some known aesthetic principles such as the golden section and symmetry to generate appealing photo books automatically [20]. To automate magazine publishing for digital platforms, the authors develop a semi-automatic magazine layout system based on photography principles such as rule-of-space [12]. Both the aesthetic study and the successful adoption of aesthetic rules in various applications demonstrate the effectiveness of aesthetics on usability improvement.

In addition, studies on eye tracking for text-overlaid images in the advertising domain [19, 22] provide us theoretical and practical support on how people perceive text-overlaid images. In [22], the authors investigated how to improve return with various eye tracking studies such as how advertisements gain attention and how the composition of the advertisement elements influences the intended message delivery process. In [19], the authors studied how the advertisement elements (text, image, and brand) influence attention. The effect of the size of elements on attention is also studied. These studies on text-overlaid image perception and the intended message delivery process can be definitely adopted to improve information delivery for mobile users.

3. SOCIAL MEDIA SNIPPET SYSTEM

The proposed social media snippet generation system is composed of two modules: *information discovery* and *information presentation* as illustrated in Fig.2. First, information discovery is performed on the social posts to extract key phrases and dominant images as shown in Fig.2(b). Then, in the information presentation process the elements are systematically selected and composed

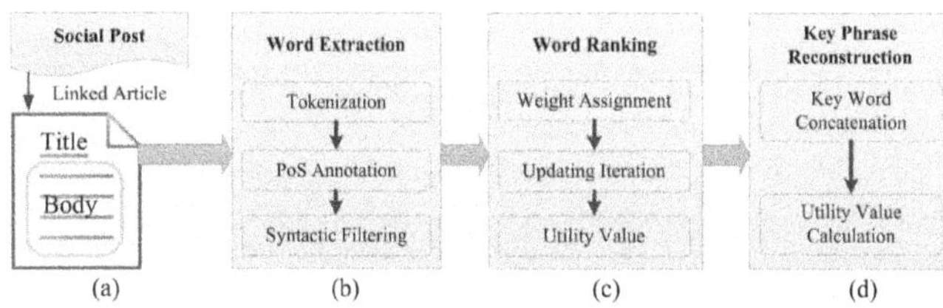

Figure 3: Key phrase extraction process: (a) original social post and linked article, (b) word extraction, (c) word ranking, and (d) key phrase reconstruction.

considering visual perception principles, aesthetic rules and mobile display constraints to guarantee readability and maximize usability as shown in Fig.2(c).

3.1 Information Discovery

To help mobile users obtain key information at a glance for quick content understanding, key phrases and dominant image are extracted from the social posts and linked articles in the information discovery process.

3.1.1 Dominant Image Extraction

Compared with pure text summary, images are more attractive, appealing, and informative from a phycological standpoint. Based on the study of search results presentation [15, 23], summaries with images can help users more quickly understand for faster relevance judgment. In our system, we focus on social posts in news categories with images. Based on our observations, the first image in the linked articles is usually dominant and utilized in the thumbnail as shown in Fig.1(b), so we extract the first image of the linked article as the dominant image for social media snippet generation. Learning approaches considering image position, content and surrounding texts can be adopted to refine the dominant image extraction in the future.

3.1.2 Key phrase extraction

Key phrases can express information concisely and accurately. Wordy sentences are difficult to view on mobile displays, while key phrases can stand out for mobile users who are interested in the post. Therefore, it is necessary to extract key phrases and determine their importance,i.e., utility values. We extract key phrases with a modified TextRank [18] approach. The key phrase extraction process is illustrated in Fig.3, which contains the following stages: word extraction, word ranking, and key phrase reconstruction.

Word Extraction. First, the social posts and linked articles are processed for key word extraction as in Fig.3(b). After tokenization and part of speech (PoS) annotation, we construct a graph by selecting nouns and adjectives as the vertices in the graph as in [18] and utilize the co-occurrence relationship controlled by the distance between words to generate the edges between vertices. Two vertices are connected if they co-occur within a window of $N_w (N_w = 2)$ words. The extracted text units and their relationships can be represented as an undirected graph $G = (V, E)$ with the set of vertices V and set of edges E.

Word Ranking. The word ranking process is illustrated in Fig.3(c). We follow a similar method to the one in [18] but take the higher importance of the post and the title of the linked article into consideration. We consider the superiority of the words in the post and title in terms of their confidence by weighting these vertices higher. The utility values of the vertices are decided by taking into account global information recursively from the entire graph by equation 1 until convergence. Here, we set the weights of vertices from the posts and titles as 1 and others as 0.2. Finally, the words from the posts and titles and important words highly related are ranked with high utility values. For a given vertex V_i, let $S(V_i)$ be the set of vertices that link to it. In contrast to the unweighted or the weighted edge graph in [18], we construct the graph with vertex weights. The confidence value of the vertex V_i is determined by its weight w_i. The utility value of a vertex V_i is defined as

$$U(V_i) = (1 - d) + d \times \sum_{V_j \in S(V_i)} \frac{w_i}{\sum_{V_k \in S(V_j)} w_k} U(V_j) \quad (1)$$

where d is the damping factor, which integrate the probability of jumping from a given vertex to another in the graph. We set d to 0.85 as in [18]. The top $\frac{1}{3}$ vertices are retained for post-processing.

Key Phrase Reconstruction. In this stage, multi-word key phrases are reconstructed from the retained key words. The workflow is shown in Fig.3(d). All the potential lexical units selected are marked in the text and the key words that are adjacent or connected with a preposition and a conjunction are concatenated together. For example, as shown in Fig.2(b), the selected words 'life' and 'pi' will be concatenated into key phrase 'life of pi,' since they are connected with a preposition. Finally, the utility values of key phrases are calculated by taking the sum of the utility values of the key words within them and normalized.

3.2 Information Presentation

Once the key phrases and dominant image are extracted from one social post and linked article, in the information presentation stage we aim to carefully select the elements and compose them into an appealing and attractive text-overlaid image to maximize the information perceived at a quick glance. This is conducted by adopting visual perception principles, aesthetic rules, and mobile display constraints.

3.2.1 Problem Formulation

Given a set of key phrases and a dominant image extracted from one social post and linked article, the aim is to generate a social media snippet in text-overlaid image form with the following properties:

- The presented region of the dominant image and the selected key phrases are representative of the social post and the linked article, summarizing its main messages to be delivered.
- The generated social media snippet should follow key aesthetic rules of text-overlaid images to make it appealing and attractive to enhance usability. As systematically investigated in text-overlaid image designs [13], visual balance shows a stronger relationship to aesthetic appeal in text-overlaid images than other factors such as symmetry. Hence, visual balance is considered in the social snippet generation process.
- Visual perception principles should be utilized so that the key phrases are placed in attractive regions that the user's eye tends to focus on.
- Visual perception principles should be utilized to highlight the most important key phrases. That is, the visual weights of the key phrases are consistent with their utility values in the social media snippets.
- Perception constraints on mobile displays are considered to guarantee readability.

The input of the problem is the original dominant image I_o and the extracted N_t key phrases $\Gamma = t_1, t_2, \cdots, t_{N_t}$ already sorted in descending order by their utility values. Hence, $u_1 \geq u_2 \geq \cdots \geq u_{N_t}$, where u_i is the utility value of the key phrase t_i. The key phrase t_i contains n_i characters. Given the string of t_i and the look-up table for the aspect ratio of the 26 characters, the aspect ratio of the key phrase t_i, r_i can be calculated. Here, we only consider one font style for the key phrase insertion. The image I is discretized into $h \times w$ grids. Each grid has $g \times g$ pixels and we set $g = 8$. The grid located at (x, y) is denoted as (x, y). Let (x_i, y_i) be the grid coordinates of the center, h_i and $\vec{c_i}$ be the height and HSV color vector of the key phrase t_i. The goal is to find the optimal set of key phrases $\Gamma' = t_1', t_2', \cdots, t_{N_{opt}}'$ and search for the optimal position, size, and color for each t_i' for all $i \in [1, N_{opt}]$.

Image Preprocessing. Image pre-processing is a prerequisite to avoid cropping or occluding important regions such as a face or salient objects. We perform saliency detection [8], face detection [14] and text detection [4] on the image. The pixel level importance map is computed by combining the face map, text map, and saliency map with a max operation. To deal with the aspect mismatch of the dominant image and the mobile display, the image is cropped to the maximum allowable size with the same aspect ratio of the mobile display by maximizing importance value. Then, the image I is discretized into $h \times w$ grids. The grid importance value $Imp(x, y)$ is obtained by the average importance values of the pixels within grid (x, y). To guarantee the non-intrusiveness of text insertion, the important regions have to be preserved. Hence, the importance map is binarized by a threshold. The binarized importance map is denoted as Imp', and the binarized importance value of grid (x, y) is $Imp(x, y)'$. Once the binarized importance map is obtained, each connected region is considered as a salient object for the following optimization process.

Energy Function. The presentation optimization problem is expressed as following. We aim to find the optimal set of key phrases $\Gamma' = t_1', t_2', \cdots, t_{N_{Opt}}'$ and their optimal position, size, and color that minimizes the energy $E(L)$. $L = L(i), i \in [1, N_t]$ completely specifies the text selection and insertion problem onto the image I. $L(i) = (a_i, (x_i, y_i), h_i, \vec{c_i})$ indicates the center coordinate (x_i, y_i), height h_i, and HSV color $\vec{c_i}$ of key phrase t_i. a_i is the indicator variable, taking the value 1 if the key phrase t_i is present in the social media snippet and 0 otherwise.

The energy of L comprises four terms as follows:

$$E(L) = E_r(L) + w_b E_b(L) + w_a E_a(L) + w_c E_c(L). \quad (2)$$

The representativeness term E_r evaluates how representative and informative the key phrases selected from the set of extracted key phrases Γ are. The visual balance term E_b measures how well the generated text overlaid image follows the dominant, visual balance aesthetic rule. The attention attractive term E_a measures how much users are inclined to focus on the key phrases in attractive regions. The consistency term E_c represents how consistent it is between the perception on the key phrases and their importance, i.e. utility values, to highlight the most important messages and hence improve information perception. w_b, w_a, and w_c are the weights of the energy term E_b, E_a, and E_c, respectively. Each of the energy terms and mobile display constraints will be described as follows in more details.

Representativeness. We consider that the utility values of the key phrases represent their representativeness in terms of information deliver. Hence, the representativeness term E_r is defined as follows:

$$E_r(L) = -\sum_{i=1}^{N_t} a_i u_i. \tag{3}$$

This energy term is a function of all indicator variables $a_1, \cdots, a_{N_t}$. It will favor the most representative key phrases and also encourage the use of as many key phrases as possible.

Visual Balance. Visual balance is a key aesthetic principle in interface design [1] and it has been proven to show a strong relationship with aesthetics in text-overlaid images in [13]. Hence, this aesthetic rule is considered to guarantee the aesthetics and usability of the generated social media snippets. As in [1, 13], visual balance is achieved when the center of gravity of all objects and text areas exactly located at the center of the text-overlaid image. In other words, the center of gravity of the selected key phrases should locate at its expected coordinate $\widehat{C_t}$, so that

$$\frac{\sum_{i=1}^{N_o} w_i C_o + \sum_{j=1}^{N_t} a_j w_j \widehat{C_t}}{\sum_{i=1}^{N_O} w_i + \sum_{j=1}^{N_t} a_j w_j} = C_m. \tag{4}$$

C_m is the center of the text-overlaid image. N_o is the number of objects within the image. C_o is the center of gravity of all objects, which can be obtained by

$$C_o = \frac{\sum_{i=1}^{N_o} w_i \cdot o_i}{\sum_{i=1}^{N_o} w_i}, \tag{5}$$

where o_i is the center of gravity of the ith object. The term w_i is the visual weight of the ith object and it is defined as the sum of the importance values of the grids occupied by the ith object Obj_i. w_j is the visual weight of the jth key phrase. We consider the two dominant factors of text visual weights in text overlaid images [13]. The visual weights of key phrases in the text-overlaid image depend on the area size of key phrases and their color contrast against the background color. The visual weight of the inserted key phrase is defined as the summation of the color contrast of all grids occupied by the jth key phrase as follows:

$$w_j = \sum_{x=x_j-\lfloor h_j/2 \rfloor}^{x_j+\lfloor h_j/2 \rfloor} \sum_{y=y_j-\lfloor \lceil h_j r_j \rceil/2 \rfloor}^{y_j+\lfloor \lceil h_j r_j - 1 \rceil/2 \rfloor} \triangle\, C(\vec{c_j}, \overrightarrow{c(x,y)}), \tag{6}$$

$\overrightarrow{c(x,y)}$ is the dominant color of grid (x, y) in the HSV space and the color contrast $\triangle\, C(\vec{c_x}, \vec{c_y})$ of two colors $\vec{c_x}$, $\vec{c_y}$ is defined in the HSV color space, as in [13].

From equation (4) we can obtain the expected coordinates of the center of gravity of the selected key phrases:

$$\vec{C_t} = \frac{(\sum_{i=1}^{N_o} w_i + \sum_{j=1}^{N_t} a_j wj) C_m - \sum_{i=1}^{N_o} w_i Co}{\sum_{j=1}^{N_t} a_j w_j}. \tag{7}$$

The maximum visual balance can be achieved by minimizing the distance between the expected center of gravity of selected key

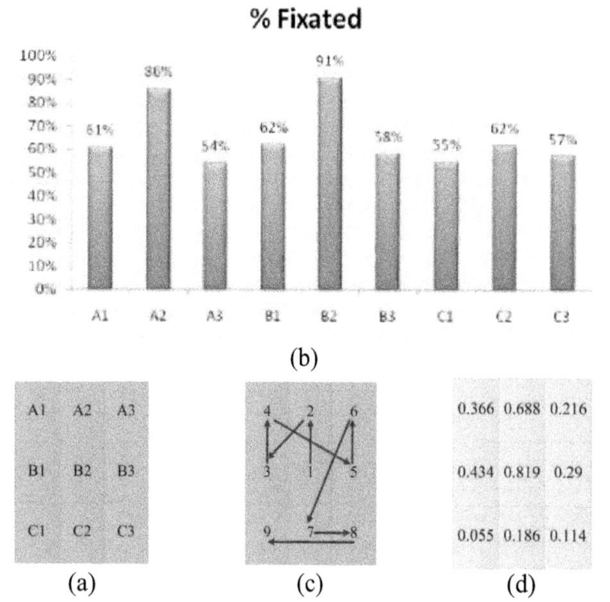

Figure 4: Eye tracking study results in [22] (a)nine areas (b)average fixation percentage (c)average scan path (d)fixation map.

phrases $\widehat{C_t}$ and the actual center of gravity C_t,

$$C_t = \frac{\sum_{j=1}^{N_t} a_j w_j \cdot o_j}{\sum_{j=1}^{N_t} a_j w_j}, \tag{8}$$

where o_j is the center of gravity of the jth key phrase. Since the text color is uniform, we consider $o_j = (x_j, y_j)$. Therefore, the term E_b is defined as the normalized distance between C_t and $\widehat{C_t}$ by

$$E_B(L) = \frac{d(C_t, \widehat{C_t})}{\sqrt{h^2 + w^2}}, \tag{9}$$

where $d(C_t, \widehat{C_t})$ is the distance between C_t and $\widehat{C_t}$. We have found that the term E_B depends on the position and visual weight of the selected key phrases, and the visual weights of the selected phrases further depend on their size and color contrast with the background color in the text location. Hence, this energy term is a function of all variables of L, i.e., $L(i) = (a_i, (x_i, y_i), h_i, \widehat{c_i}), \forall i \in [1, N_t]$.

Attractiveness. To measure attractiveness, we follow the eye tracking study results in [22], in which the average percentage of fixation and the average scan path on the divided nine equal areas of text-overlaid images are investigated. The areas are labeled as shown in Fig. 4(a). The average percentage for each area is demonstrated in Fig. 4(b), while the scan path using the average time for the first fixation is shown in Fig. 4(c) in which the numbers and arrows represent the average scan path from the first fixations to the last fixations with 1 to 9 respectively.

To adopt visual perception principle, we fuse the fixation percentage and fixation order to generate the fixation map as follows:

$$\begin{aligned} F(l) &= Fp(l) \cdot (1 - 0.1 \cdot Fo(l)) \\ where, l &= A_1, A_2, A_3, B_1, B_2, B_3, C_1, C_2, C_3. \end{aligned} \tag{10}$$

The areas fixated earlier are weighted higher. l is the index of the nine areas. $F(l)$ is the value on the fixation map of area l. $F_p(l)$ is the fixation percentage of area l as shown in Fig. 4(b) and $F_o(l)$ is the fixation order of area l as shown in Fig. 4(c). The generated fixation map is demonstrated in Fig. 4(d) with the fixation value indicated.

The goal of this energy term is to place the selected key phrases onto attractive regions and moreover, the more important key phrases should be inserted into more attractive areas that are fixated earlier for a longer period so that the key phrases are able to be viewed quickly for expediting information deliver. The energy term E_a is defined as follows:

$$\begin{aligned} E_a(L) &= 1 - \frac{\sum_{i=1}^{N_t} a_i u_i \frac{Att(x_i,y_i)-Min_{Att}}{Max_{Att}-Min_{Att}}}{\sum_{i=1}^{N_t} a_i u_i} \\ where,\ Min_{Att} &= \min_{1\le x\le h, 1\le y\le w} Att(x,y), \\ Max_{Att} &= \max_{1\le x\le h, 1\le y\le w} Att(x,y). \end{aligned} \quad (11)$$

$$Att(x,y) = F(l), \text{ if } (x,y) \in l, \quad (12)$$

where $Att(x,y)$ is the attractiveness value of position (x,y). By minimizing E_a, the attractiveness of the key phrases is maximized, while the utility value u_i is taken into account to insert more important key phrases into more attractive areas. The term $Max_{Att} - Min_{Att}$ is to make E_a range from 0 to 1. The term E_a is a function of the indicator variables $(a_1, \cdots, a_{N_t})$ and the positions of the key phrases $(x_1, y_1), \cdots, (x_{N_t}, y_{N_t})$.

Consistency. The more important phrases with higher utility values should be composed with larger visual weights. That is, the visual weights of the key phrases have to be proportional to their utility values. Hence, the energy term E_c is defined by

$$E_c(L) = \frac{\sum_{i=1}^{N_t} a_i |w_i - k u_i|}{hw}, \quad (13)$$

where k is the coefficient that will be discussed later. The energy term E_c is normalized by the total area of the image since the largest possible value of w_i is the area occupied by the key phrase t_i in the text-overlaid image. We have found that E_c depends on the visual weights of the key phrases, and thus depends on their size, color, and positions as described in equation 6. Hence, E_c is a function of all variables of L, i.e. $L(i) = (a_i, (x_i, y_i), h_i, \vec{c_i}), \forall i \in [1, N_t]$.

Constraints. The optimization of $E(L)$ is done under certain constraints, especially considering the small display and perception issues on mobile devices as listed below:

1. *Minimum font size.* To guarantee the readability of the key phrases on mobile displays, the font size has to be larger than a threshold T_s, which is three times the size of the grid.
2. *Maximum number of characters.* Considering the information perception on mobile displays, long sentences or too many words in the text-overlaid images will hinder the information capture of mobile users. The maximum number of characters is set to 39 according to the study in [11].
3. *Non-intrusiveness.* If the insertion of key phrases occludes salient objects or faces, the information perception on both the objects and the texts will be degraded and unappealing.
4. *Text area to image area ratio.* Too large a text area makes the text-overlaid image messy and unappealing. The principle in text-overlaid images, such as the cover pages of magazines that designers usually follow, indicated that the optimal text area to image area ratio is 1:4.
5. *Non-overlapping.* The key phrases inserted into the image I should not overlap with each other.
6. *Non-border crossing.* The key phrase insertion should not cross the border of image I.
7. *Color harmony.* The notion of color harmony has been studied by artists and scientists [9]. Eight color schemes have been discovered to quantify color harmony [5]. Due to the computation complexity, instead of searching through the whole color space using the color schemes, we carefully select from existing colors along with black and white for the key phrases coloring.
8. *Text size consistency constraint.* As discovered in [19], the attention to text elements in text-overlaid images is in proportion to their size.

In the following subsection, an optimization procedure is defined that searches efficiently in the allowed space to obtain the solution with low energy, but since the algorithm is approximate, it is not necessarily the global minimum.

3.2.2 Energy Minimization

The search space for optimization of the energy $E(L)$ defined in the previous subsection, is the entire space of L, i.e. $L(i) = (a_i, (x_i, y_i), h_i, \vec{c_i}), i \in [1, N_t]$, which results in a huge search space for the optimization. By analyzing the dependency characteristics of the energy terms, a heuristic but effective approach is developed in which the key phrase selection, and the position, size, and color of the key phrases are optimized in sequence. The optimization steps are described as follows.

Key phrase selection. The key phrase selection step in the sequence of optimizations, addresses the E_r term in the energy function equation 2. With the utility values and the number of characters of the N_t key phrases, the goal is to maximize the total utility values of the selected phrases under the maximum number of characters constraint, that is,

$$\max_{a_1,\cdots,a_{N_t}} \sum_{i=1}^{N_t} a_i u_i, s.t. \sum_{i=1}^{N_t} a_i n_i \le T_c. \quad (14)$$

The key phrase selection is converted to a 0-1 knapsack problem which can be solved efficiently by dynamic programming. Hence, the set of indicator variables $a_1, \cdots, a_{N_t}$ are solved in this step.

Position optimization. The energy term E_b and E_c both rely on the visual weights of the key phrases in the text-overlaid image, and their visual weights depends on their size and color contrast with their local surroundings as defined in equation (6). Therefore, the positions of the selected key phrases have to be solved first. Their positions are determined by the energy term E_b and E_a, and thus can be obtained by optimizing the term $w_b E_b(L) + w_a E_a(L)$ in the energy function (2). Here, we set $w_b = w_a = 0.5$. However, without determining the size and color of the selected key phrases, E_b is not able to be calculated. Considering the consistency energy term E_c, the term $w_b E_b(L) + w_a E_a(L)$ is optimized by assuming

$$w_i = k u_i, \forall i \in [1, N_t] \ s.t. \ a_i = 1. \quad (15)$$

In this way, the optimal positions of the selected key phrases $(x_i, y_i), \forall i \in [1, N_t] \ s.t. \ a_i = 1$ can be calculated under the non-intrusiveness, non-border crossing, and non-overlapping constraints with the assumption that $h_i = T_s, \forall i \in [1, N_t] \ s.t. \ a_i = 1$. At this step, taking the text area to image area ratio constraint, we set $k = \frac{0.2hw}{\sum_{i=1}^{N_t} a_i u_i}$, so that the selected phrases can split the optimal allowable text area according to their utility values. Note the maximum possible value of the visual weight of a key phrase is the area occupied by the key phrase in the text-overlaid image according to the definition of visual weight in equation 6, since the color contrast $\triangle C$ ranges from 0 to 1.

Size and color optimization. The size optimization together with the following color optimization step will minimize the energy term E_c. Since visual weights depends on the key phrase size and color contrast with local backgrounds, once the positions of the phrases are obtained from the position optimization, the visual weights can be directly achieved via size and color optimization. In this way, the size and color of each selected key phrase can be solved under the minimum font size, non-intrusiveness, color harmony, text area to image area ratio, and text size consistency constraints. It is possible that the initial solution would violate the non-overlapping or non-border crossing constraints. In that case, we iterate the position optimization as well as the size and color optimization several times, until all of the constraints are satisfied. Usually, the solution can be obtained within ten iterations.

3.2.3 Complexity Analysis

In this section we analyze the complexity of the proposed scheme. If we take the size of the key phrase set, the location, the size, and the color of the key phrases into consideration, the total search space of the proposed problem is $O(2^{N_t}) \cdot O((hw)^{N_t}) \cdot O(h^{N_t}) \cdot O(256^{3 \cdot N_t})$, which makes it almost unfeasible to carry out a brute-force search, even if the number of selected phrases is small. The proposed staged solution greatly reduces the complexity to $O(N_t^2) + O((hw)^{N_{Opt}}) + O(h^{N_{Opt}}) + O(C^{N_{Opt}})$, where C is the color space of image I. In real applications, N_{Opt} is usually no more than 3 and hence the search complexity is reduced significantly.

4. EXPERIMENTS

In order to evaluate the performance of the proposed social media snippet generation system, we performed experiments and user studies on a large social media dataset. Due to privacy concerns, we collected 1,000 news social posts on various topics, including economics, politics, fashion, sports, and science and technology from nine entities on Twitter, including ABC news, The New York Times, USA TODAY, ABC World News, Wall Street Journal, NBC News, The White House, FoxNews Science and Technology, and CNN. The linked articles were obtained together with the collected posts. Some of the posts contained no images in their linked articles for which related external images could be utilized in the social media snippet generation by semantic analysis. For now, our aim is to validate the effectiveness of the proposed social media snippet presentation form and the developed social media snippet generation approach, so those posts without images are excluded. The valid dataset contains the remaining 683 social posts with their linked articles.

4.1 Evaluation of Key Phrase Extraction

We randomly sampled 100 social posts with their linked articles from the valid dataset to label their key phrases. Since key phrase extraction is subjective, each social post along with the linked article was labeled by three people independently. For each post, each person was required to extract at least the ten most important key phrases from the post and the linked article. The key phrases voted by at least two people were considered the ground truth.

In order to evaluate the performance of key phrase extraction, we compared the developed approach with two other methods. The first one was an intuitive rule-based method, which scores the words in the graph vertices based on frequency. The second one was the key phrase extraction method proposed in [18], which computes the utility value using an unweighted graph with uniform vertices weights. All three methods process the social posts and linked articles with the same tokenization and syntactic filtering procedure to build the graph vertices, but they rank the vertices in different ways. As in [18], the number of selected key vertices T was set to a third of the total number of vertices in the graph. The three methods had the same number of key vertices selected and processed by the same key phrase reconstruction method as shown in Fig. 3. The precision, recall, and F-measure of the proposed key phrase extraction method along with the two comparison methods are presented in Table 1.

Table 1: The precision, recall, and F-measure of key phrase extraction with the frequency-based approach (frequency), the unweighted graph-based approach in [18] (unweighted), and the proposed weighted graph-based approach (proposed).

	Frequency	Unweighted [18]	Proposed
Precision	23%	37%	58%
Recall	35%	32%	34%
F-measure	28%	34%	43%

We found that by considering the superior confidence value of the words appearing in the post and titles, the precision of the developed weighted graph-based method was significantly improved compared with the frequency-based and unweighted graph-based approach. The recall was similar to the frequency-based and unweighted graph-based approach, since some key words were not connected with or far from the highly weighted vertices and thus could be discarded. However, in the social media snippet generation system, precision matters more than recall, because it is important to discover the most key phrases for the snippet generation, while the discovered phrases are not able to be shown all together due to mobile display constraints. In addition, the proposed approach achieved the highest F-measure compared with the other two methods.

4.2 Evaluation of Information Presentation

In order to evaluate whether the adoption of the aesthetic rules and visual perception principles is proper as well as to validate the proposed optimization process, we conducted a user study. We randomly selected 100 social posts along with their linked articles from the collected 683 posts. Once the data was ready, it was parsed to extract key phrases with their utility values and dominant images. Then, the extracted key phrases were selected by maximizing their total utility value under the number of characters constraint as illustrated in the key phrase selection process. We generated five snippets with the same required display aspect ratio in the following ways with the set of selected key phrases for comparison. All of the snippets were generated under the basic non-intrusiveness, non-overlapping, and non-border crossing constraints.

1. Snippet Set 1: We generated the snippets by randomly setting position, size, and color of the phrases.
2. Snippet Set 2: We generated the snippets by setting equal font height and the same color for the phrases while optimizing position based solely on the attractiveness term E_a.
3. Snippet Set 3: We generated the snippets by setting equal font height and the same color for the phrases while optimizing position based solely on the visual balance term E_b.
4. Snippet Set 4: We generated the snippets by setting equal font height and the same color for the key phrases while optimizing position based on the visual balance and attractiveness term $w_b E_b(L) + w_a E_a(L)$ with equal weights.
5. Snippet Set 5: We generated the snippets via optimization based on all aesthetic rules including visual balance and color

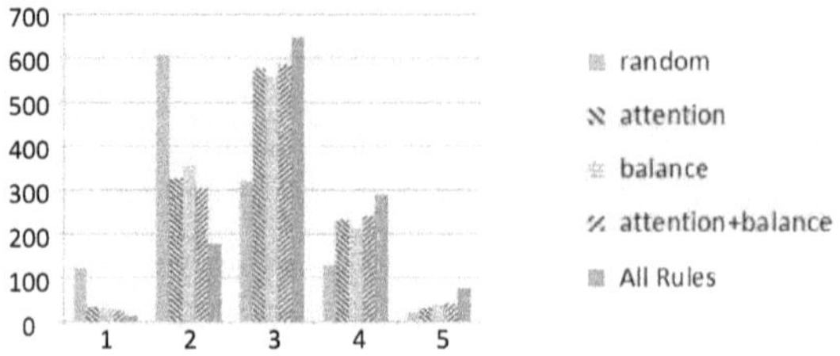

(a) Attractive Score

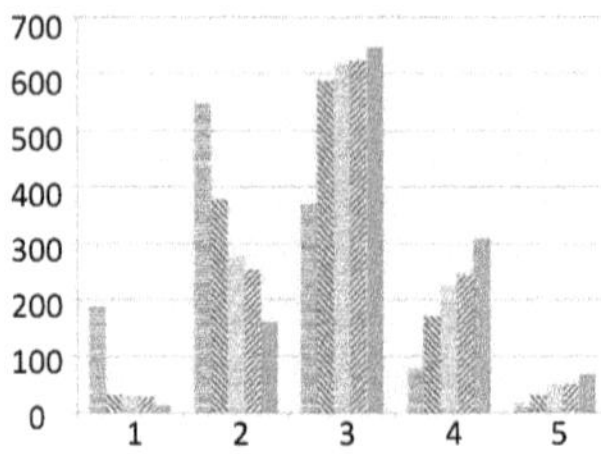

(b) Appealing Score

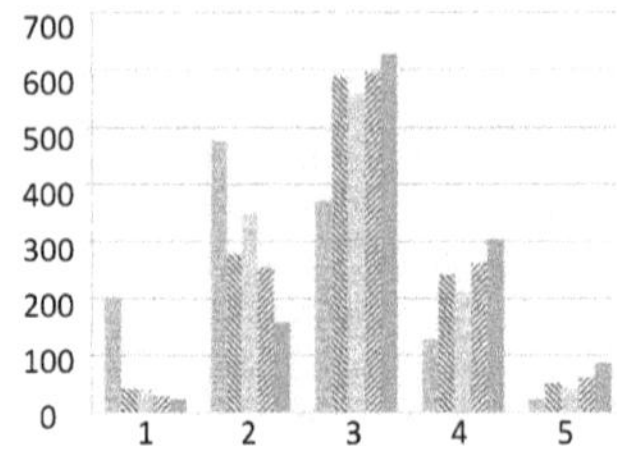

(c) Informative Score

Figure 5: The score distribution on the five sets of social media snippets based on different aesthetic and perception principles: (a) score distribution on attractiveness, (b) score distribution on appeal, and (c) score distribution on informativeness.

harmony as well as visual perception principles such as visual consistency and attractiveness as described in the energy minimization subsection in information presentation.

12 subjects with age ranging from 24 to 32 were invited, of which seven were females. To make the comparison fair, for each social post, the corresponding five social snippets were presented at the same time on the screen of a desktop PC with the same size of a smartphone model, i.e., 4.8 inch Samsung Galaxy S3. The original social posts and links were also presented. The subjects were allowed to click the linked webpage for more information. During the study, the order of the five snippets was shuffled so that the subjects were able to give fair rates. The subjects were asked to grade the five snippets for each social post according to the following aspects.

1. How attractive is the snippet, i.e., how good is the text on the image at drawing their attention?
2. How visually appealing is the snippet?
3. How informative is the snippet in terms of guiding user focus to the most important information?

The subjects were requested to rate the snippets with an integer from 1 (definitely no) to 5 (definitely yes). The score distribution of the 12 subjects on the five set of snippets were demonstrated in Figure 5. Some visual examples of the five generated social media snippets along with their average scores on the three questions are shown in Fig. 8.

Regarding the attractiveness in the Question 1, the randomly generated snippets had low rates, since the randomly selected position, size, and color for key phrases were sometimes unsuitable and hence made it difficult to find the texts. By placing the texts into regions that people tend to focus on via optimized attention attractiveness term E_a, the score of the snippet set 2 was higher than that of randomly generated ones on average. Comparing the score of set 2 and set 3, the number of rates at 1 and 5 were similar, and the number of rates at 3 and 4 of set 2 were larger than set 3 while the number of rates at 2 was smaller. Hence, the attractiveness of set 2 outperformed set 3 on average. With regards to the adoption of consistency perception rules, set 5 outperformed sets 2, 3, and 4.

Figure 7: Examples of (a) the original social posts, details and linked articles, (b) Flipboard results, and (c) generated social media snippets with the proposed system.

Hence, besides the introduction of the attention attractiveness perception rule, the visual weights consideration by optimizing text size and color improved the attractiveness further.

Regarding the appeal in the Question 2, a large portion of randomly generated snippets were rated with 2 and 3, due to the unsuitable color introduced for text insertion, while a small portion were rated 4 or 5 probably because the random solution happened to introduce the proper color at suitable positions, helping them to look appealing. The adoption of aesthetic rule visual balance made the appeal score of set 3 and 4 higher than set 1 and 2 on average. The harmonic color introduced in set 5 further improved the appeal score compared to set 3 and 4.

For the informative judgment in the Question 3, the randomly generated position, size, and color may have degraded the eye capturing process on important phrases, hence the score concentrated at 2 and 3. The position optimized by attention attractiveness term made the informative score of set 2 much higher than set 1. The proper size and color optimization on the consistency term made the important key phrase salient, and hence insured the score of set 5 was higher than set 2.

4.3 Evaluation of Social Media Snippet

To validate the effectiveness of the proposed social media snippet presentation form and the developed system, we compared the generated social media snippets by the proposed system with the traditional Twitter post presentation and the summarization form with Flipboard on smartphones.

Another randomly selected 100 social posts and their linked articles were processed through the information discovery and information presentation modules as described in Section 3. Another 12 subjects were invited to browse the original social post, the Flipboard results, and the generated social media snippets on a Samsung Galaxy S3 smartphone. For each post, the snippet, the Flipboard result, and the original social post were displayed by flipping the pages. The subjects were allowed to browse forward and backward for comparison. They were also allowed to access the linked webpages of the social post. The subjects were asked to rate the generated snippet, the Flipboard result, and the corresponding original post by answering the following questions:

1. How attractive is the social post presentation as a whole?
2. How visually appealing is the social post presentation?
3. How good is the information delivery for the social post presentation?
4. How good is the readability of the social post presentation?
5. What is your overall evaluation on the snippet?

The subjects were requested to rate with a satisfaction score with the scale of 1–5 (higher score indicating higher satisfaction). The

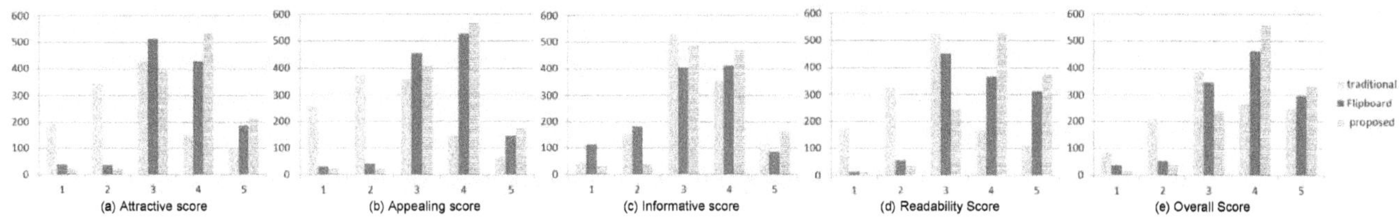

Figure 6: The score distribution of the social posts in the traditional form, Flipboard style, and the social media snippet.

score distributions of the 12 subjects on the 100 social posts in the traditional presentation form, Flipboard results, and the generated social media snippets are presented in Fig. 6. Some examples of the original social posts, the corresponding Flipboard results, and the generated social media snippets are shown in Fig. 7. We found that the social media snippets generated by the developed system significantly outperformed the traditional presentation form and Flipboard results in terms of attractiveness score, appeal score, and informative score. They were easier to read on mobile devices and preferred by mobile users.

5. CONCLUSION

To overcome the mobile social media browsing obstacles under mobile environment constraints, we have proposed a social media snippet generation system to summarize easy-to-be perceived important information for mobile users with optimized text-overlaid images. To generate the snippets, key information from social posts and embedded links as well as dominant images are extracted and systematically selected and organized. By taking visual perception principles, aesthetic rules, and mobile display constraints into consideration, we optimized the layout of the extracted elements. Extensive experiments and user studies show that the generated social media snippets indeed improve attractiveness, appealingness, and informativeness for mobile browsing and hence are much preferred by mobile users.

In the future, external images can be utilized to generate social media snippets for posts without images by analyzing post content and relationships among posts and other sources online. In addition, topic discovering can be adopted to generate social media snippet collages to facilitate mobile social media browsing in facets considering post timestamp, relationship and importance, as well as perception principles and aesthetic rules for collages. Moreover, social content and mobile user preference need to be analyzed to rank the social posts for better snippet generation based on perception rules.

6. REFERENCES

[1] M. Bauerly and Y. Liu. Computational modeling and experimental investigation of effects of compositional elements on interface and design aesthetics. *Int. J. Human-Computer Studies*, 64(8):670–682, Aug. 2006.

[2] T. Ben-Bassat, J. Meyer, and N. Tractinsky. Economic and subjective measures of the perceived value of aesthetics and usability. *ACM Trans. Computer-Human Interaction*, 13(2):210–234, June 2006.

[3] M. S. Bernstein, B. Suh, L. Hong, J. Chen, S. Kairam, and E. H. Chi. Eddi: interactive topic-based browsing of social status streams. In *Proceedings of ACM symposium on User interface software and technology*, pages 303–312, 2010.

[4] X. Chen and H. Zhang. Text area detection from video frames. In *Proceedings of IEEE Pacific Rim Conference on Multimedia*, pages 222–228, 2001.

[5] D. Cohen-Or, O. Sorkine, R. Gal, T. Leyvand, and Y.-Q. Xu. Color harmonization. *ACM Trans. Graph.*, 25(3):624–630, July 2006.

[6] R. Datta, D. Joshi, J. Li, and J. Z. Wang. Studying aesthetics in photographic images using a computational approach. In *Proceedings of European conference on Computer Vision*, pages 288–301, 2006.

[7] Flipboard. `http://www.flipboard.com`.

[8] X. Hou and L. Zhang. Saliency detection: A spectral residual approach. In *Computer Vision and Pattern Recognition*, pages 1–8, 2007.

[9] J. Itten. *The Art of Color: The Subjective Experience and Objective Rationale of Color.* A VNR book. Wiley, 1974.

[10] B. Jiao, L. Yang, J. Xu, and F. Wu. Visual summarization of web pages. In *Proceedings of ACM SIGIR conference on Research and development in information retrieval*, pages 499–506, 2010.

[11] S. Kaasten, S. Greenberg, and C. Edwards. How people recognize previously seen web pages from titles, urls and thumbnails. In *Proceedings of Human Computer Interaction*, pages 247–265, 2001.

[12] M. Kuhna, I.-M. Kivelä, and P. Oittinen. Semi-automated magazine layout using content-based image features. In *Proceedings of ACM Multimedia*, pages 379–388, 2012.

[13] C.-Y. Lai, P.-H. Chen, S.-W. Shih, Y. Liu, and J.-S. Hong. Computational models and experimental investigations of effects of balance and symmetry on the aesthetics of text-overlaid images. *International Journal of Human-Computer Studies*, 68(1-2):41 – 56, 2010.

[14] S. Z. Li, L. Zhu, Z. Zhang, A. Blake, H. Zhang, and H. Shum. Statistical learning of multi-view face detection. In *Proceedings of European Conference on Computer Vision*, pages 67–81, 2002.

[15] Z. Li, S. Shi, and L. Zhang. Improving relevance judgment of web search results with image excerpts. In *Proceedings of World Wide Web*, pages 21–30, 2008.

[16] T. Mei and X.-S. Hua. Contextual internet multimedia advertising. *Proceedings of the IEEE*, 98(8):1416–1433, 2010.

[17] T. Mei, X.-S. Hua, and S. Li. Contextual in-image advertising. In *Proceedings of ACM Multimedia*, pages 439–448, 2008.

[18] R. Mihalcea and P. Tarau. Textrank: Bringing order into text. In *Proceedings of Conference on Empirical Methods in Natural Language Processing*, pages 404–411, 2004.

[19] R. Pieters and M. Wedel. Attention capture and transfer in advertising: Brand, pictorial, and text-size effects. *Journal of Marketing*, 68(2):36–50, 2004.

[20] M. Rabbath, P. Sandhaus, and S. Boll. Automatic creation of photo books from stories in social media. *ACM Trans. Multimedia Comput. Commun. Appl.*, 7S(1):1–18, Nov. 2011.

[21] J. Sankaranarayanan, H. Samet, B. E. Teitler, M. D. Lieberman, and J. Sperling. Twitterstand: news in tweets. In *Proceedings of ACM SIGSPATIAL International Conference on Advances in Geographic Information Systems*, pages 42–51, 2009.

[22] M. Smit. Optimising advertising roi on print in a rapidly changing economic and media landscape - the contribution of eye tracking now and into the future. In *Proceedings of Southern African Marketing Research Association Conference*, 2012.

[23] J. Teevan, E. Cutrell, D. Fisher, S. M. Drucker, G. Ramos, P. André, and C. Hu. Visual snippets: summarizing web pages for search and revisitation. In *Proceedings of SIGCHI Conference on Human Factors in Computing Systems*, pages 2023–2032, 2009.

[24] N. UzZaman, J. P. Bigham, and J. F. Allen. Multimodal summarization of complex sentences. In *Proceedings of International Conference on Intelligent User Interfaces*, pages 43–52, 2011.

Figure 8: Visual examples of the original social media posts, details, and linked articles, as well as (e) the generated social media snippets with the proposed system and five other approaches, i.e., (a) random setting position, size and color of key phrases, (b) optimization based on solely attractiveness term, (c) optimization based on solely visual balance term, (d) optimization based on the attractiveness and visual balance.

[25] Z. Wang, P. Cui, L. Xie, H. Chen, W. Zhu, and S. Yang. Analyzing social media via event facets. In *Proceedings of ACM Multimedia*, pages 1359–1360, 2012.

[26] O. Wu, Y. Chen, B. Li, and W. Hu. Evaluating the visual quality of web pages using a computational aesthetic approach. In *Proceedings of ACM International Conference on Web Search and Data Mining*, pages 337–346, 2011.

Temporal Encoded F-formation System for Social Interaction Detection

Tian Gan
School of Computing
National University of Singapore
gantian@comp.nus.edu.sg

Yongkang Wong
Interactive & Digital Media Institute
National University of Singapore
yongkang.wong@nus.edu.sg

Daqing Zhang
Télécom SudParis, France
CNRS UMR 5157 SAMOVAR
daqing.zhang@it-sudparis.eu

Mohan S Kankanhalli
School of Computing
National University of Singapore
mohan@comp.nus.edu.sg

ABSTRACT

In the context of a social gathering, such as a cocktail party, the memorable moments are generally captured by professional photographers or by the participants. The latter case is often undesirable because many participants would rather enjoy the event instead of being occupied by the phototaking task. Motivated by this scenario, we propose the use of a set of cameras to automatically take photos. Instead of performing dense analysis on all cameras for photo capturing, we first detect the occurrence and location of social interactions via F-formation detection. In the sociology literature, F-formation is a concept used to define social interactions, where each detection only requires the spatial location and orientation of each participant. This information can be robustly obtained with additional Kinect depth sensors. In this paper, we propose an extended F-formation system for robust detection of interactions and interactants. The extended F-formation system employs a heat-map based feature representation for each individual, namely Interaction Space (IS), to model their location, orientation, and temporal information. Using the temporally encoded IS for each detected interactant, we propose a best-view camera selection framework to detect the corresponding best view camera for each detected social interaction. The extended F-formation system is evaluated with synthetic data on multiple scenarios. To demonstrate the effectiveness of the proposed system, we conducted a user study to compare our best view camera ranking with human's ranking using real-world data.

Categories and Subject Descriptors

I.2.10 [**Vision and Scene Understanding**]: Video analysis; I.4.8 [**Scene Analysis**]: Motion; I.5.4 [**Applications**]: Signal processing

http://dx.doi.org/10.1145/2502081.2502096.

Keywords

Social Interaction, Social Computing, F-formation, Video Analytics, Behaviour Modeling

1. INTRODUCTION

In social gatherings such as cocktail parties, conference receptions, etc., the interactions between the event participants are often captured with multiple cameras or smartphones. In many scenarios, the event participants play the role of the photographer, which forces them to become passive observers of the event. This goes against the primary purpose of socializing where the participants ought to enjoy the events. Furthermore, the participants may not capture all the important shots due to the fact that no one is able to observe the whole event [2]. Therefore, it would be desirable to have the photos taken by the professional photographer or by an automated photo-capture system. Hiring a professional photographer is generally expensive and hence not affordable for many types of informal social gatherings. With an automated photo-capture system, the cost can be negligible. Moreover, these approaches can be scaled to support closed-door events with privacy concerns, or a live streaming system that shows the latest photo on a public display, or to automatically annotate videos capturing a social event.

One potential solution for the automated photo-capture system is to configure a set of cameras to record the entire event. The recorded videos can be manually edited after the event, or analyzed using video post-processing [10, 18, 21]. Such works have been proposed for various applications in the literature, such as video summarization for video conferencing [13], lecture webcasting [10, 18], sport events [20], and video mash-up for live performance [21, 22]. However, these approaches require large storage capacity for the videos, as well as computationally expensive vision algorithms to analyze the footages. Therefore, these approaches cannot be scaled for large scale deployment. In addition, the aforementioned approaches can only be applied to specific predefined actions/tasks [10, 13, 18, 20, 21]. In practice, one cannot predict a priori where the interesting "events" will occur so it is difficult to zoom and take good photos by a priori setup.

In contrast to the aforementioned methods, another approach is to employ the F-formation concept for detecting the social interaction [1, 5, 12]. In the sociological literature,

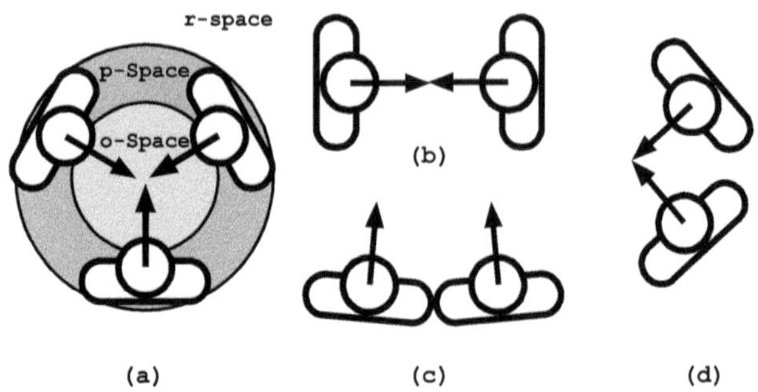

Figure 1: Example of various interaction arrangements in F-formation. (a) *Circular*, (b) *vis-a-vis*, (c) *side-by-side*, and (d) *L-arrangement*

F-formation is defined as a set of spatial patterns maintained during social interactions by two or more interactants, where the spatial and orientation relationship among multiple persons forms an interaction space [5, 9]. The F-formation is formalized into three social spaces: o-space, p-space, and r-space (see Figure 1). The o-space, also known as the joint transaction space, is the interaction space between the interactants. In practical systems, we can conclude that a social interaction is formed whenever an o-space is created [9]. The p-space and r-space are the area occupied by the interactants and the area that surrounds the interactants, respectively. Examples of various interaction patterns are shown in Figure 1.

The F-formation based approach has two main benefits. Firstly, a social interaction can be easily identified from the detection of o-space, which is derived from the orientations and spatial locations of the interactants. Secondly, the computational resources can be utilized only on the detected interaction regions. This also increases the likelihood of capturing photos that are more "interesting" without recourse to dense analysis on all video streams. However, most of the existing F-formation based approaches do not incorporate the temporal information. This gives negative classification result for some interaction arrangements. For example, two persons walking past each other would be immediately considered as a valid F-formation. This is intuitively against the idea of having a social interaction.

Recently, a heat map based approach is proposed to recognize the type of human group activity [4]. The heat map based approach models the human movement trajectory as a heat map with thermal diffusion. The resulting heat map is used to classify the query activity as one of the predefined activities (e.g., gather, follow, separate, etc.) with a surface fitting process [4]. We argue that the surface fitting approach is not suitable for the aforementioned social events. This is because the number of participants in social events is generally high, which results high intraclass variance for each type of group activity. Despite that, we acknowledge that heat map based approach is an effective method to incorporate the temporal information.

In this paper, we propose an extended F-formation system for robust interaction and interactant detection. The extended F-formation system employs a heat map based feature representation for each unique individual, namely Interaction Space (IS), to model their respective location, orientation, and temporal information. In our work, the individual's spatial location and orientation are retrieved

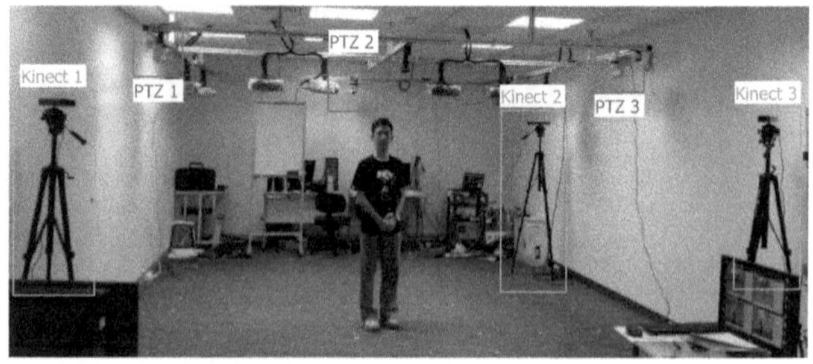

Figure 2: Snapshot of the experimental environment.

with the Kinect depth sensors. Given the IS of all individuals at the t-th frame, we detect the interaction centers (i.e., o-space) and the respective interactants, as well as the location of the best view camera. The proposed temporal-encoded IS based approach is evaluated on both the synthetic data and real-world experimental environment. For the real-world scenario, we configure a test environment with four Pan-Tilt-Zoom (PTZ) cameras and three Kinect depth sensors. The snapshot of the test environment is shown in Figure 2. To the best of our knowledge, this is the first time F-formation is used for automated social event photo-capture application.

The rest of this paper is organized as follows. The background and related works are discussed in Section 2. The details of proposed method are given in Section 3. Extensive evaluations on both the synthetic and real-world data are presented in Section 4. The main findings and possible future directions are covered in Section 5.

2. PREVIOUS WORK

In recent years, there is growing interest in the detection of social group behavior [1, 5, 7]. Social interaction detection requires modeling of two components: **(1)** individual activities, and **(2)** social relationships between individuals. The literature can be categorized into three approaches. The first category relies on the visual information and statistical models [15, 16, 19], however, its efficacy in real world application is questionable due to the uncontrolled nature of human behavior. The second category utilizes visual and audio data collected from various sensors, and performs multimodal processing to detect interaction [3]. The third category analyzes the social interactions using social behavioral cues [1, 5, 7, 24]. In [24], Vinciarelli *et al.* organized the social behavioral cues into five categories: (i) physical appearance, (ii) gesture and posture, (iii) face and eyes behavior, (iv) vocal behavior, and (v) space and environment. These cues have been recognized in Psychology literature as the most important factors in human judgments [24].

In this paper, we focus on the space and environment social behavioral cue for social interaction detection. A popular sociological concept to exploit this behavioral cue is the F-formation system [9]. This concept is commonly used in computer-supported cooperative work, where the interaction is established with an appropriate spatial relationship between participants. For example, Yamashita *et al.* [26] examined how changes in seating position across different sites affect the video-mediated communication by exploring the F-formation. While in [17], the F-formation knowledge is used to navigate the robot to join an interaction group using a socially adapted behavior with lower risk of collision

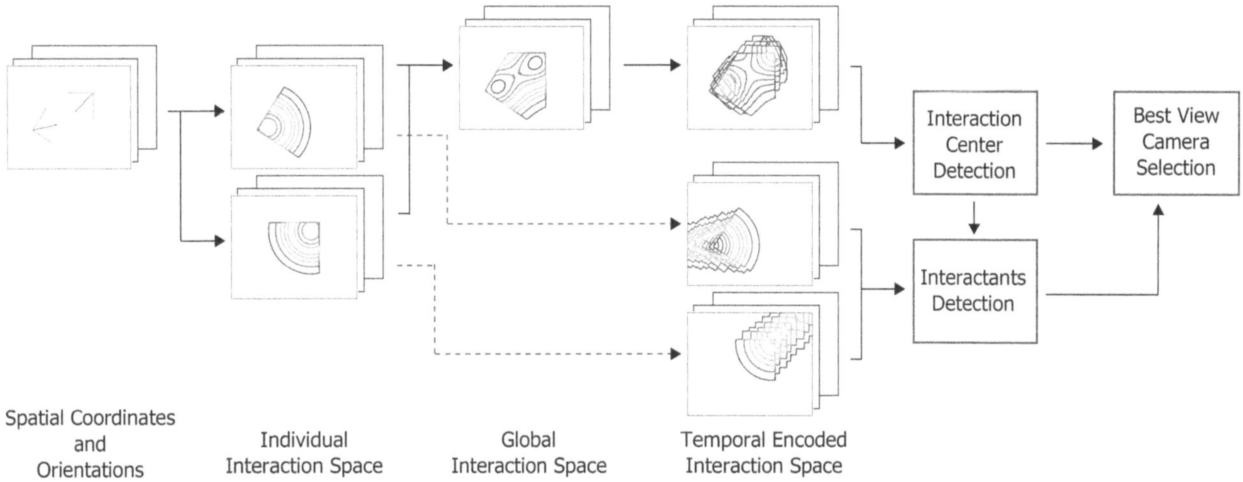

Figure 3: Conceptual diagram of the extended F-formation system. Given the spatial coordinates and orientations of all individuals, the individual Interaction Space (IS), global IS, and their respective temporal encoded IS are computed. The temporal encoded IS are used to detect the interaction center, their respective interactants, and the best view camera.

and disturbance. Despite being tangentially relevant to social interaction detection, it inspired us to make use of the F-formation to explore and analyze social interactions.

There are a number of methods to detect F-formation. Marquardt *et al.* [11] used the ubiquitous computing environment to sense the social proximity of people in the form of F-formation. Their goal is to motivate group interactions. Specifically, they define two persons to be in an F-formation if the following conditions are met: (1) they are not standing behind each other; (2) the angle between their orientation vectors is smaller than 180 degrees; (3) the distance between them is small enough. After the three conditions are met, the algorithm iterates over all pairs of people, calculates the distance and angle between them, and assigns an F-formation type (i.e., side-by-side, L-shaped, face-to-face, or none) based on tolerance thresholds. This work is intended to prove that small-group interaction can be sensed in the form of F-formation. Cristani *et al.* [5] designed an F-formation recognizer based on the Hough-voting strategy. First, they take a certain number of candidate sample interaction centers for each subject, then the candidate positions are voted by weighted samples. The interaction center is selected as the position which has the highest value. Their method incorporates the uncertainty by assuming the position and orientation of each subject as Gaussian random variables. However, this method detects the F-formation for each frame independently. Therefore, the temporal information, or the continuous group interactions, are not explored in this work. In [1], the social interaction is detected by taking temporal information into consideration. They determine whether two persons are interacting with each other when the following three conditions are satisfied: (1) the distance between the subjects are closer than 2 meters; (2) their Field of View (FoV) are overlapped; (3) their heads are positioned inside the reciprocal FoVs. Then they accumulate the existence of this relationship over a period of time. These conditions assume that each person should have at least one person to be related with, in terms of visual attention, within a single social group. However, the three simple rules define the interaction as the pairwise relationship. It cannot characterize many types of interaction spatial arrangements, such as "side-by-side" (refer to Figure 1(c)), in which each person need not to be in the reciprocal FoVs. This is a common scenario in social interaction, that is all people look towards a certain direction.

Different from F-formation based analysis, the heat map, a kind of graphical representation of data, has been employed to analyze some types of social interaction [23, 4]. It highlights the "hot" data regions in a visually pleasant way. The heat map can also be interpreted as a kind of knowledge accumulation. Heat map can be created with various types of information, by which rich information might be retained in the heat map for further analysis. For example, Singh *et al.* [23] aggregated social multimedia data spatiotemporally to derive semantic situation information. The result of the aggregated data is one kind of heat map. Chu *et al.* [4] proposed a heat-map based algorithm for group activity recognition. By using the heat map feature to represent activities, the temporal information can be modeled effectively. The recognition of group activity is based on this heat map feature with the surface fitting process [4].

3. EXTENDED F-FORMATION SYSTEM

We propose an extended F-formation system which uses a heat map based representation to encode the spatial location, orientation, and temporal information. In this work, we consider a video sequence of a social event, where the spatial coordinate and orientation for person k at t-th frame, $\boldsymbol{p}_k^t =< x_k^t, y_k^t, \theta_k^t >$, is first obtained from multiple Kinect depth sensors with Kinect for Windows SDK[1]. The t-th frame is represented as $\boldsymbol{P}^t = \{\boldsymbol{p}_1^t, \boldsymbol{p}_2^t, \ldots, \boldsymbol{p}_{|k|^t}^t\}$ where $|k|^t$ is the cardinality of t-th frame. The aim of this work is to identify all possible interaction centers, $\{\boldsymbol{I}_1^t, \boldsymbol{I}_2^t, \ldots, \boldsymbol{I}_i^t\}$, and their respective interactants $\boldsymbol{P}_{\boldsymbol{I}_i}^t \subset \boldsymbol{P}^t, t = 1, \ldots, n$.

We continue this section by first giving an overview of the proposed framework, followed by describing the heat map based F-formation detection algorithm. We then elaborate on the algorithm to detect the interactants for each F-formation and their respective best view camera.

[1]http://www.microsoft.com/en-us/kinectforwindows/

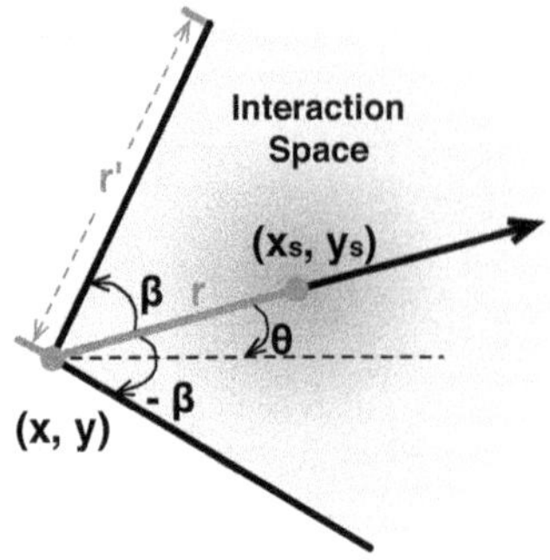

Figure 4: Graphical example of the *Interaction Space* **for person** p **at location** (x, y)**.**

3.1 Framework

A conceptual diagram of the proposed framework is shown in Figure 3. Given the spatial coordinates and orientations for each individual, we first compute the *individual Interaction Space* (iIS), where the *Interaction Space* (IS) is restricted by the individual's field of attention (see Figure 4). The IS is modeled as a heat map where the highest energy point is selected with prior knowledge obtained from sociology study [8]. For each time frame, a *global Interaction Space* (gIS) is computed by averaging the overlapped iIS. We then compute the temporal encoded IS for each individual and the global view (denoted as TiIS and TgIS, respectively). The computed TiIS and TgIS are used to detect the F-formation(s), interactants, and the respective best view camera(s).

3.2 F-formation Detection

3.2.1 Individual Interaction Space

Given person k at t-th frame, $\boldsymbol{p}_k^t = < x_k^t, y_k^t, \theta_k^t >$, we first represent its iIS as a heat map, where the point with the highest energy is called the individual's interaction center, denoted by $\boldsymbol{s}_k^t$. The spatial coordinate of $\boldsymbol{s}_k^t$ is defined as:

$$\boldsymbol{s}_k^t = (x_{k,s}^t, y_{k,s}^t) = (x_k^t + r\cos\theta_k^t,\ \ y_k^t + r\sin\theta_k^t) \quad (1)$$

where r and θ represent the distance from $\boldsymbol{p}_k^t$'s spatial location and its orientation, respectively. The $\boldsymbol{p}_k^t$'s iIS has the highest energy at $\boldsymbol{s}_k^t$ and diffuses towards the neighboring region. Furthermore, $\boldsymbol{p}_k^t$'s field of view is restricted between $[-\beta, \beta]$ degrees with respect to its orientation and a radius of r'. The field of view forms an active IS for each individual.

The value of iIS_k^t is assumed to have a Gaussian distribution, we apply the two-dimensional Gaussian function on $\boldsymbol{s}_k^t$ to compute iIS_k^t as follows:

$$\text{iIS}_k^t(x,y) = \begin{cases} \exp\left[-\left(\frac{(x-x_{k,s}^t)^2}{2\delta_x^2} + \frac{(y-y_{k,s}^t)^2}{2\delta_y^2}\right)\right] & \text{for } F_k^t(x,y)=1 \\ 0 & \text{otherwise} \end{cases} \quad (2)$$

where δ_x^2 and δ_y^2 are the variance on x-axis and y-axis, respectively. $\boldsymbol{F}_k^t$ represents the binary mask for $\boldsymbol{p}_k^t$'s field of view. A conceptual example is shown in Figure 4.

3.2.2 Global Interaction Space

Given the iIS for all individuals detected at t-th frame, $\text{iIS}^t = \left[\text{iIS}_1^t, \text{iIS}_2^t, \ldots, \text{iIS}_{|k|^t}^t\right]$, the gIS is computed to represent the common interaction space for all individuals. The gIS for pixel located at (x, y) is computed as

$$\text{gIS}^t(x,y) = \begin{cases} \frac{1}{||\text{iIS}^t(x,y)||_0} \sum_{k=1}^{|k|^t} \text{iIS}_k^t(x,y) & \text{if } ||\text{iIS}^t(x,y)||_0 \geq 2, \\ 0 & \text{otherwise} \end{cases} \quad (3)$$

where the notation $||\text{iIS}^t(x,y)||_0$ counts the number of nonzero entries of iIS^t at location (x, y). Example of iIS and gIS are shown in Figure 5.

3.2.3 Temporal encoded Interaction Space

To address the missing element of motion trajectory in the original F-formation system, the temporal information is encoded in both iIS and gIS using an energy decay based accumulation approach. In the following discussions, we elaborate on the temporal encoding algorithm with gIS, where the same method is applied to iIS. Consider the gIS at frame t_{cur}, the corresponding Temporal encoded gIS (TgIS) is modelled as

$$\text{TgIS}^{t_{cur}} = \int_0^{t_{cur}} \left(1 - e^{-K_t}\right) \cdot \text{gIS}^t \cdot e^{-K_t \cdot (t_{cur} - t)} dt \quad (4)$$

where the term $1 - e^{-K_t}$ is a scale factor to keep $\text{TgIS}^{t_{cur}}$ in the range of $[0, 1)$. The weight decay term $e^{-K_t \cdot (t_{cur} - t)}$ controls the contribution of gIS^t whereas the most recent frame has the highest weight. The constant K_t controls the rate of decay.

The example of IS and temporal encoded IS are shown in Figure 5. We demonstrate two unique scenarios here. In scenario 1, person 1 and person 2 initiate the first frame of the social interaction[2]. The gIS (top) shows an IS with high energy level. Based on the proposed interaction center detection algorithm (see Section 3.2.4), this will be classified as a valid F-formation. On the other hand, the energy level in TgIS (bottom) is much lower. In scenario 2, both person 1 and person 2 have maintained the social interaction for a period of time. Now, the energy level of TgIS has risen to a high level (similar to gIS). This is indeed a desired property. Consider a scenario where multiple persons are constantly walking pass each other, the original F-formation would give many false alarms.

In the preliminary experiment, we also observed that the temporal encoded iIS can stabilize the detection error (a side effect from hair style, clothing or accessories) from the Kinect depth sensors. In this case, the orientation of some individual gives the *shaking* effect over a period of time. Based on our observation, the temporal encoding can smooth the interaction space.

3.2.4 Interaction Centers Detection

The energy level in TgIS characterize the location of social interactions as several "hot spots". To locate these "hot spots", we first apply the Interaction threshold, T_i, to the heat map. Then, we apply a smoothing function $f(\cdot)$, e.g. the Gaussian filter, to the thresholded TgIS. This is because the temporal encoding step (i.e., Eq. 4) introduces a "staircase step" effect to the heat map. We note that this effect is largely influenced by the moving speed of each person and the selected frame rate.

Given the thresholded and smoothed TgIS, we locate all the local maxima in the heat map, which gives us a set of

[2]This scenario is the same as the *passing by* scenario

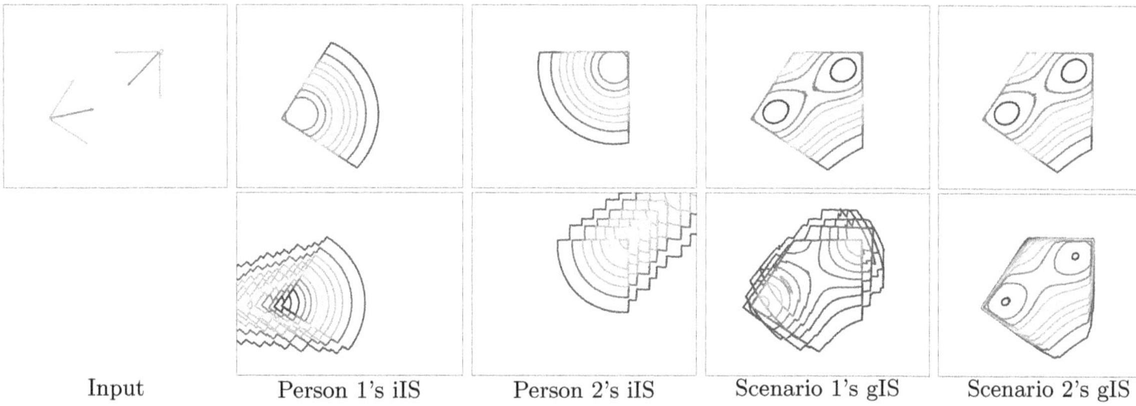

Figure 5: Example of individual Interaction Space (iIS) and global Interaction Space (gIS) in two scenarios. Top row: IS computed for each static frame; Bottom row: Temporal information is encoded for each IS. Red and blue indicate high and low energy level, respectively. Scenario 1 can represent the first frame when two persons form an interaction (similar to the *passing by* scenario). Scenario 2 represent a social interaction after a period of time.

Algorithm 1 Pseudo code for interaction centers detection

Input: Global Interaction Space gIS $\in \mathbb{R}^{M\times N}$, Interaction threshold $T_{\text{i}} \in [0,1]$, Interaction center radius r_{center}, and Smoothing function $f(\cdot)$.
Output: Interaction centers $\mathbb{I} = \{\boldsymbol{I}_1, \boldsymbol{I}_2, \ldots, \boldsymbol{I}_i\}$

for all $(x, y) \in$ gIS **do**
  if gIS$(x, y) < T_{\text{i}}$ **then**
    gIS$(x, y) \leftarrow 0$
  end if
end for
gIS$_{smooth} \leftarrow f$(gIS)
CandiCenters $\leftarrow$ *findLocalMaxima*(gIS$_{smooth}$)
while |CandiCenters| > 0 **do**
  Center$_{max} \leftarrow$ *findMaxCenters*(CandiCenters)
  mergeList $= \emptyset$
  for all $i = 1, 2, \ldots,$ |CandiCenters| **do**
    if *dist*(CandiCenters$_i$, Center$_{max}$) $\leq r_{\text{center}}$ **then**
      mergeList = mergeList $\cup$ {CandiCenters$_i$}
    end if
  end for
  newCenter = *merge*(mergeList)
  $\boldsymbol{I}_C = \boldsymbol{I}_C +$ {newCenter}
  CandiCenters = CandiCenters − mergeList
end while

candidate centers (denoted as `CandiCenters`). Then, we apply an iterative analysis to locate the interaction centers. In each loop, we first locate the candidate center with highest energy level, namely center$_{max}$. After that we create a `MergeList` which is the set of the candidates located within r_{center} from the center$_{max}$ and apply a merge function to them[3]. The output of the merge function is classified as an interaction center. We remove all members of `MergeList` from `CandiCenters` and repeat the loop until `CandiCenters` is empty. The pseudo code of the interaction center detection algorithm is shown in Algorithm 1.

[3]The merge function can be a choice of mean, max, medium, etc. We use the max function in this paper because it gave the best results in our preliminary tests.

3.3 Interactant Detection

The detection of interactant is performed by analyzing the contribution of each individual with respect to the interaction center. Given a detected interaction center I_i and a binary mask $\boldsymbol{M}_i^t$ for its o-space, we compute the contribution score S_c for person k at t-th frame via:

$$S_c^t(k,i) = \sum_{x,y} \left[TiIS_k^t(x,y) \times \boldsymbol{M}_i^t(x,y) \right] \tag{5}$$

The mask $\boldsymbol{M}_i^t$ has the value of 1 for a pixel within $2r_i$ radius from I_i. We consider a person as the interactant of I_i if and only if $S_c^t(k,i)$ is smaller than a predefined contribution threshold T_c. In other words, a person will be considered to be an interactant if the individual has stayed in the o-space for a period of time. We note that this is only valid for the TiIS. For the non-temporal encoded IS, each individual will be considered as an interactant when they enter the o-space.

3.4 Best View Camera Selection

We formulate the best view camera selection method as a ranking system. For each detected interaction space and the corresponding interactants, we compute the camera selection score for each camera and rank the camera based on the scores. As discussed in Section 1, the F-formation has three interaction spaces: o-space, p-space, and r-space. We define a *ring* region of camera ranking zone, A, on r-space, where the zone is equally divided in to N sub-zones.

The selection score for sub-zone n, $s(A_n)$, and interaction center I_i at t-th frame is computed as

$$s(A_n) = \frac{1}{|\boldsymbol{P}_{\boldsymbol{I}_i}^t|} \sum_{k \in \boldsymbol{P}_{\boldsymbol{I}_i}^t} \sum_{(x,y)\in A_n} TiIS_k^t(x,y) \tag{6}$$

where $|\boldsymbol{P}_{\boldsymbol{I}_i}^t|$ is the cardinality of the interactant set $\boldsymbol{P}_{\boldsymbol{I}_i}^t$.

For each camera, we assign the selection score of the sub-zone that is located between the camera and $\boldsymbol{I}_i^t$. Note that if the number of sub-zones of the camera ranking zone is small, the number of cameras assigned to each sub-zone would be higher. We argue that there is no rule of thumb for the selection of this value, the selection should be based on the target application and the number of available cameras, or be learnt for a particular application. A conceptual example are shown in Figure 6.

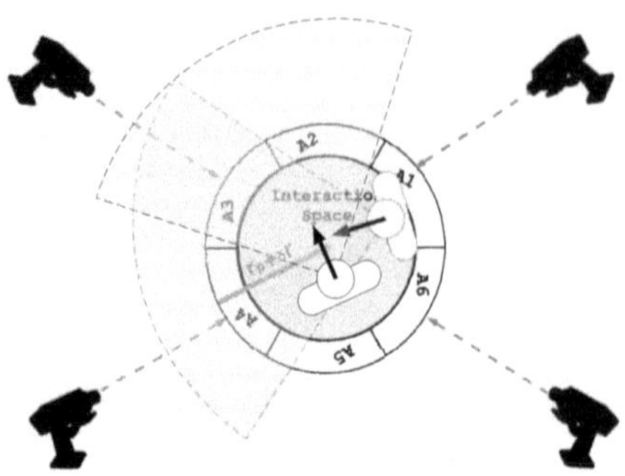

Figure 6: Conceptual diagram for the best view camera selection method. The interaction space covers both the o-space and p-space.

4. EXPERIMENTS

In this section, we examine the performance of the proposed extended F-formation system. We first evaluate the accuracy for both the interaction center detection and interactant detection. Then, the output of the best view camera selection algorithm is "visually inspected" on real-world recording and also evaluated with a user study.

Experiments were conducted on synthetic data and real-world video recording. For the synthetic data, we simulated 10 scenarios of social interaction with two variables (i.e., the number of unique individual and the concurrent interaction centers). Each scenario is denoted by a standard name scenario_#**people**_#**center**[4]. For each scenario, we randomly generate 5 sequences where each sequence consists of 600 frames with the frame rate of 5 fps. Each frame consists of the individual's ID, spatial location and orientation, as well as the spatial location of the interaction centers. The ground truth data consists of the number and location of each interaction centers, and its corresponding interactants. It was generated by the simulation script.

In order to collect video sequences from real-world environment, we set up a set of cameras, including three Kinect depth sensors and four PTZ cameras, in an indoor lab environment. The snapshot of the lab environment and the floor plan are shown Figure 2 and 7, respectively. All 7 cameras are calibrated to the ground plane. In addition, the Kinect depth sensor is used to extract the location and the orientation of all persons. Note that the extracted orientation information is more reliable if the person's orientation deviates within 30 degrees from the Kinect's principal axis. Therefore, we only consider the data that fall within this range. On some scenarios, where the Kinect depth sensor could not distinguish the frontal and back view, manual correction is applied. Furthermore, we manually correlate the label for each person across the seven cameras. For this work, we record three video sequences of four persons with eight unique group interactions.

4.1 Parameters Selection

In our application, we can define some of the parameters with the study from the sociological literature. Hall [8] introduced *proxemics* as a theory to study the interpersonal spatial relationships. The physical distance and the social distance between individuals can be correlated and categorized into four discrete zones: (1) intimate (0m - 0.45m), (2) personal (0.45m - 1.2m), (3) social (1.2m - 3.5m), and (4) public (> 3.5m). In this work, we set $r = 0.45$m as the distance between person's current location and his interaction center, $r' = 3.5$m as the maximum distance for this person's influence, $2\beta = 90$ degrees as the individual Interaction Space angle, and $\sigma_x^2 = \sigma_y^2 = 0.6$ to constrain the heat energy distribution. Based on the preliminary experiments, the remaining parameters are as follows: $K_t = 10$, $T_i = 0.65$, and $T_c = 0.22$.

[4]The simulated scenarios are scenario_2_1, scenario_3_1, scenario_4_1, scenario_4_2, scenario_5_1, scenario_5_2, scenario_10_1, scenario_10_2, scenario_10_3, and scenario_10_4.

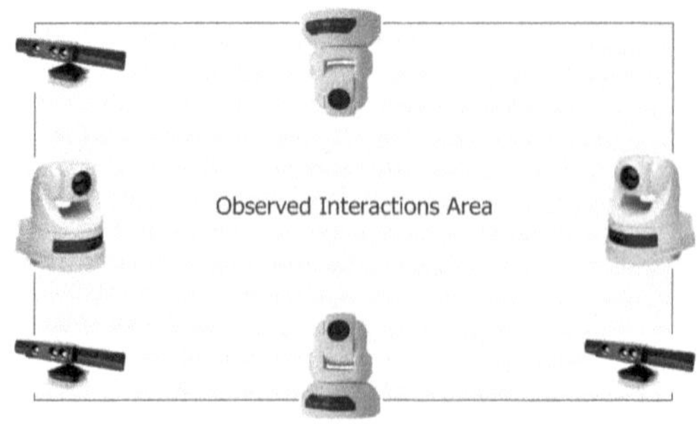

Figure 7: 2D view of the camera configurations.

Table 1: Experiment results for interaction center detection.

Method	Precision	Recall	F_1 score
Bazzani *et al.* [1]	0.745	0.631	0.674
Temporal encoded IS	0.798	0.770	0.783
IS	0.804	0.792	0.797

Table 2: Experiment results for interactant detection.

Method	Precision	Recall	F_1 score
Bazzani *et al.* [1]	0.687	0.690	0.688
Temporal encoded IS	0.823	0.849	0.836
IS	0.848	0.870	0.859

4.2 Interaction Detection Experiments

In this subsection, we evaluate the accuracy for detecting the interaction center and the respective interactants. We quantitatively report the results with the F-measure metric, which is

$$F_1 = 2 \cdot \frac{\text{precision} \cdot \text{recall}}{\text{precision} + \text{recall}} \quad (7)$$

where the precision and recall are defined as $\frac{tp}{tp+fp}$ and $\frac{tp}{tp+fn}$, respectively. The notations tp, fp, and fn are the total number of true positive, false positive, and false negative (in term of center/interactant detection), respectively.

We employ a similar evaluation metric as in [5] for the interaction center detection. The interaction center is considered correctly detected if the distance between the detected interaction center and the groundtruth data is smaller that r (2m in our experiments), and at least two-thirds of the participants of the ground truth are correctly identified. For the interactants detection, we evaluate the performance only when the interaction center is valid for frame t.

Two variants of our proposed method are evaluated. The first is the heat map based F-formation system without encoding the temporal information (denoted as IS), while the second is the temporal encoded F-formation system (denoted as Temporal encoded IS). We also compare our

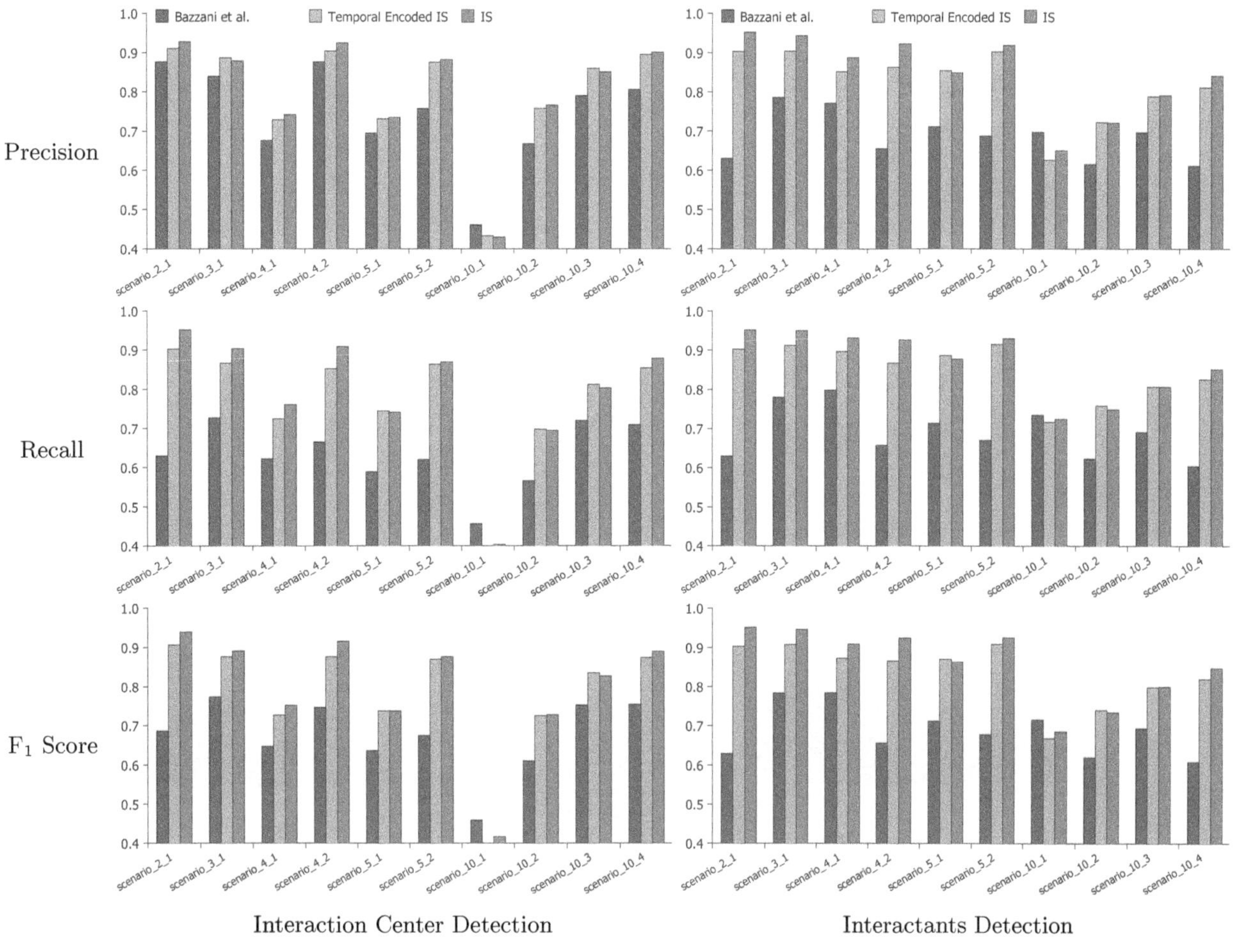

Figure 8: Accuracy of detecting the interaction center and interactants on synthetic data over all frame where the groundtruth is available. The accuracy is defined as the precision, recall, and $\mathbf{F_1}$ score.

method with Bazani *et al.*'s approach [1] (see Section 2 for more details). We denote their method as Bazani *et al.*.

The complete average precision, recall, and F_1 scores are shown in Figure 8. The left column shows the results for interaction center detection, and the right column indicates the performance of interactants detection. The average performance for all scenarios are shown in Table 1 and 2. As shown in the figure and tables, our approach outperforms Bazani *et al.* [1] with a noticeable margin. For the interaction center detection, the F_1 score of the Temporal encoded IS and IS outperformed Bazani *et al.* [1] by 16.2% and 18.2%, respectively. We observed that all the results for `scenario_10_1` are very low for all approaches. This is because the ratio between number of people and center is too high. The scenario is generally very crowded, therefore the algorithms which study the spatial relationship between the interactants are not suitable. Another observation is that the recall rate of the proposed method (for both variance) outperform Bazani *et al.* [1] with a significant margin. For `scenario_2_1`, the improvement is about 43.4% and 51.2% for Temporal encoded IS and IS, respectively.

For the interactants detection experiment, the difference in performance is even more obvious. In particular, we fix the number of people and increase the number of interaction centers (e.g., `scenario_4_1` and `scenario_4_2`). The difference of performance can be explained as follows. Our method models the interaction space as a common interaction area, and it can robustly handle group interaction with various spatial arrangements for a group of people. In contrast, Bazzani *et al.* [1] define the interaction as a pairwise relationship, where each person should be in the reciprocal visual field of view and the group is established based on this pairwise relationship. This method would fail to detect the common side-by-side interaction pattern (refer to Figure 1(c)), where each person is not within the reciprocal visual field of view of the corresponding interactant. This phenomenon is more obvious when the number of interaction centers increases. Under such a scenario, the distribution of the group is more sparse and the likelihood of the aforementioned problem is relatively higher.

During the comparison between the accuracy of IS and Temporal encoded IS, we find that the performance of Temporal encoded IS is generally worse than IS. This is contradictory to our expectation and we note that this is a problem of our ground truth data, where a frame is considered as having valid interaction center when two persons meet. The Temporal encoded IS can only identify an interaction center after a period of time (a side effect of the energy decay based accumulation approach). Despite that, we cannot determine a reasonable frame duration to form a mutual social interaction. Therefore, modifying the ground truth to accommodate this scenario is not reasonable. To establish

Figure 9: Experimental result with real-world video recording. Each column represents a unique social interaction. (a) The spatial locations and the orientations of the detected interactants, as well as the camera ranking zone; (b) Temporal encoded global Interaction Space; (c-f) The snapshots obtained from the top 4 ranked cameras with (c) having the highest rank.

Table 3: Simulated video sequence with no valid social interaction. Each sequence has 4 individuals and 1 interaction center. The mean precision is reported with 10 unique sequences.

Method	Precision
Temporal encoded IS	0.999
IS	0.800

our hypothesis, we generated 10 sets of simulated sequences with 4 individuals and 1 interaction center. Each sequence has a spatial dimension of 1000×1000 and 1000 frames in total. No interaction is allowed in these sequences and only precision is reported. The results are shown in Table 3. The results agree with our hypothesis where Temporal encoded IS gives a precision of 0.999 and IS gives 0.800.

4.3 Best View Camera Selection Experiments

In this subsection, we demonstrate an initial investigation of the effectiveness of the best view camera selection method. The snapshots of the top 4 ranked cameras in three unique social interactions are shown in Figure 9. Row (a) shows the interactants' spatial location and the respective orientation. The camera ranking zone is shown around the interactants. Row (b) are the TgIS. Row (c-f) are the snapshots obtained for each sequence where row (c) indicates the top rank image and row (f) to be the lowest rank. Each column shows a unique interaction. This preliminary experiment shows that the camera ranking zone with the highest selection score is indeed corresponding to TgIS. For the first and the third interactions, the top two ranked images also show more frontier view when compared to snapshots located in row (f).

To validate the efficacy of the best view camera rank, we conducted a user study to compare our camera ranking with human expectations. This study was conducted on fifty individuals (34 males and 16 females). The participants were asked to rank the camera views from eight detected social interactions. Each interaction consists of six views which were captured by different cameras at the same time. In order to compare our ranking with the users' camera view ranking, we calculate the average matching accuracy of our top-N rank with with k variation of users ranking. For each sequence, our top-N ranked cameras and users' top-K ranked cameras are considered as matched if one of the camera view was presented in both ranking. The results are presented with Cumulative Match Characteristic (CMC) curve.

As shown in Figure 10, the top-1 rank from our algorithm only agrees with 33% and 56% of users' top-1 and top-2 rank, respectively. We argue that the low accuracy for our top-1 rank is reasonable as the users' top-1 ranked camera are not consistent. When we consider the top-2 rank from our algorithm, the matching accuracy raised significantly to 65% for users' top-1 rank and 86% for users' top-2 rank. This indicates that our method generally agrees with users' expectation. Further investigation of the data shows that the performance is heavily biased by one specific detected social interaction. In this sequence, best view camera ranked by our algorithm contains a person who is partially cropped from the view (due to camera placement and interaction spatial location). Although the frontal face of all three persons were visible in this view, most user ranked this view as the *worst*. We acknowledge this problem in our algorithm and

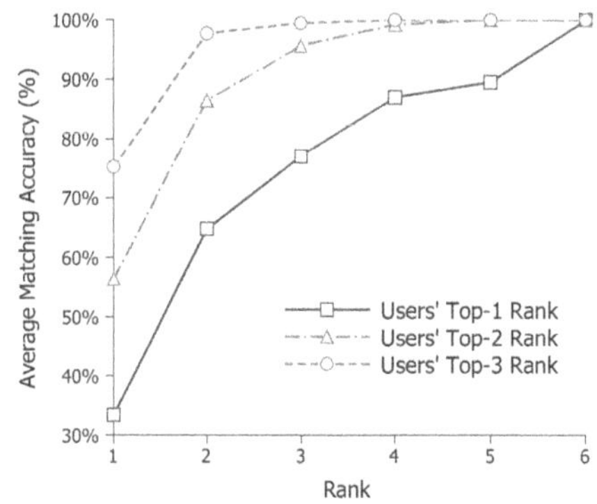

Figure 10: The Cumulative Match Characteristic (CMC) curve of our camera ranking with top-1 to top-3 users' ranking. The user study was conducted with 50 individuals on 8 unique detected social interactions.

highlight that this can be further addressed with automated PTZ camera control [14] to provide visually satisfying snapshots.

5. CONCLUSIONS AND FUTURE WORKS

In this paper, we proposed an extended F-formation system for robust interaction and interactant detection. Inspired by the heat map based method for human group activity recognition [4], we define the individual Interaction Space (iIS) and global Interaction Space (gIS) to model the objects' spatial locations and orientation. In order to address the problem of unintentional F-formation detection, such as two persons passing by or a person walking past a social interaction, we encoded the temporal information via an energy decay based accumulation function. The heat map based Interaction Space is used to detect the interaction center and the corresponding interactants. In addition, we further utilized it to detect the camera with high probability to capture good photos. We also propose a camera configuration for automated photo capturing application. In addition to the standard PTZ cameras, we added a number of Kinect depth sensors to obtain accurate spatial locations and the respective orientations.

We evaluate our proposed method with both the synthetic data and real-world video recording. Experiments on 10 unique scenarios show that the proposed method outperforms the rule based F-formation system in [1]. The results on interaction center detection in the Precision, Recall, and F_1 score show improvement of 7.1%, 22.0%, and 16.1%, respectively. The results on interactant detection are even more convincing. We evaluate the best view camera selection with the real-world video recording. The results on visual analytic and user study agree with our expectation.

For future work, we aim to apply machine learning techniques to model the prior knowledge with training data. In addition, we would like to explore the possibility of combining the proposed extended F-formation system with two components. First, we would like to apply automated PTZ camera control algorithm [14] to improve the image resolution, as well as to maximize the photo capturing range. Second, we would like to investigate the ability to perform automated photo capturing via key-frame selection [6, 25], or video summarization [10, 18, 27] to actively analyze the content of the video.

6. ACKNOWLEDGEMENT

This research was carried out at the NUS-ZJU Sensor-Enhanced Social Media (SeSaMe) Centre. It is supported by the Singapore National Research Foundation under its International Research Centre @ Singapore Funding Initiative and administered by the Interactive Digital Media Programme Office.

7. REFERENCES

[1] L. Bazzani, M. Cristani, D. Tosato, M. Farenzena, G. Paggetti, G. Menegaz, and V. Murino. Social interactions by visual focus of attention in a three-dimensional environment. *Expert Systems*, 30(2):115–127, 2013.

[2] M. Campanella and J. Hoonhout. Understanding behaviors and needs for home videos. In *British HCI Group Annual Conference on HCI*, pages 23–26, 2008.

[3] D. Chen, J. Yang, R. Malkin, and H. D. Wactlar. Detecting social interactions of the elderly in a nursing home environment. *ACM Transactions on Multimedia Computing, Communications and Applications*, 3(1), Feb. 2007.

[4] H. Chu, W. Lin, J. Wu, X. Zhou, Y. Chen, and H. Li. A new heat-map-based algorithm for human group activity recognition. In *Proceedings of ACM International Conference on Multimedia*, pages 1069–1072, 2012.

[5] M. Cristani, L. Bazzani, G. Paggetti, A. Fossati, D. Tosato, A. D. Bue, G. Menegaz, and V. Murino. Social interaction discovery by statistical analysis of F-formations. In *Proceedings of British Machine Vision Conference*, pages 1–12, 2011.

[6] F. Dufaux. Key frame selection to represent a video. In *Proceedings of IEEE International Conference on Image Processing*, pages 275–278, 2000.

[7] D. Gatica-Perez. Automatic nonverbal analysis of social interaction in small groups: A review. *Image Vision Computing*, 27(12):1775–1787, 2009.

[8] E. T. Hall. *The Hidden Dimension.* Doubleday, 1966.

[9] A. Kendon. *Conducting Interaction: Patterns of behavior in focused encounters*, volume 7. Cambridge University Press, 1990.

[10] F. Lampi, S. Kopf, M. Benz, and W. Effelsberg. An automatic cameraman in a lecture recording system. In *Proceedings of International Workshop on Educational Multimedia and Multimedia Education*, pages 11–18, 2007.

[11] N. Marquardt, T. Ballendat, S. Boring, S. Greenberg, and K. Hinckley. Gradual engagement: facilitating information exchange between digital devices as a function of proximity. In *ACM International Conference on Interactive Tabletops and Surfaces*, pages 31–40, 2012.

[12] N. Marquardt, K. Hinckley, and S. Greenberg. Cross-device interaction via micro-mobility and F-formations. In *ACM Symposium on User Interface Software and Technology*, pages 13–22, 2012.

[13] I. Mikic, K. S. Huang, and M. M. Trivedi. Activity monitoring and summarization for an intelligent meeting room. In *Workshop on Human Motion*, pages 107–112, 2000.

[14] P. Natarajan, T. N. Hoang, K. H. Low, and M. S. Kankanhalli. Decision-theoretic approach to maximizing observation of multiple targets in multi-camera surveillance. In *International Conference on Autonomous Agents and MultiAgent Systems*, pages 155–162, 2012.

[15] N. Oliver, B. Rosario, and A. Pentland. A bayesian computer vision system for modeling human interactions. *IEEE Transactions on Pattern Analysis and Machine Intelligence*, 22(8):831–843, 2000.

[16] S. Park and M. M. Trivedi. Multi-person interaction and activity analysis: a synergistic track- and body-level analysis framework. *Machine Vision and Applications*, 18(3-4):151–166, 2007.

[17] J. Rios-Martinez, A. Spalanzani, and C. Laugier. Understanding human interaction for probabilistic autonomous navigation using risk-rrt approach. In *IEEE/RSJ International Conference on Intelligent Robots and Systems*, pages 2014–2019, 2011.

[18] Y. Rui, A. Gupta, J. Grudin, and L. He. Automating lecture capture and broadcast: technology and videography. *Multimedia Systems*, 10(1):3–15, 2004.

[19] M. S. Ryoo and J. K. Aggarwal. Recognition of composite human activities through context-free grammar based representation. In *IEEE Computer Society Conference on Computer Vision and Pattern Recognition*, pages 1709–1718, 2006.

[20] D. A. Sadlier and N. E. O'Connor. Event detection in field sports video using audio-visual features and a support vector machine. *IEEE Transactions on Circuits System for Video Technology*, 15(10):1225–1233, 2005.

[21] M. K. Saini, R. Gadde, S. Yan, and W. T. Ooi. Movimash: online mobile video mashup. In *Proceedings of ACM International Conference on Multimedia*, pages 139–148, 2012.

[22] P. Shrestha, P. H. N. de With, H. Weda, M. Barbieri, and E. H. L. Aarts. Automatic mashup generation from multiple-camera concert recordings. In *Proceedings of ACM International Conference on Multimedia*, pages 541–550, 2010.

[23] V. K. Singh, G. Mingyan, and R. Jain. Social pixels: genesis and evaluation. In *Proceedings of ACM International Conference on Multimedia*, pages 481–490, 2010.

[24] A. Vinciarelli, M. Pantic, and H. Bourlard. Social signal processing: Survey of an emerging domain. *Image Vision Computing*, 27(12):1743–1759, 2009.

[25] Y. Wong, S. Chen, S. Mau, C. Sanderson, and B. C. Lovell. Patch-based probabilistic image quality assessment for face selection and improved video-based face recognition. In *IEEE Conference on Computer Vision and Pattern Recognition, Biometrics Workshop*, pages 74–81, 2011.

[26] N. Yamashita, K. Hirata, S. Aoyagi, H. Kuzuoka, and Y. Harada. Impact of seating positions on group video communication. In *Proceedings of ACM Conference on Computer Supported Cooperative Work*, pages 177–186, 2008.

[27] S.-P. Yong, J. D. Deng, and M. K. Purvis. Key-frame extraction of wildlife video based on semantic context modeling. In *International Joint Conference on Neural Networks*, pages 1–8, 2012.

Towards Efficient Sparse Coding for Scalable Image Annotation

Junshi Huang[1], Hairong Liu[2], Jialie Shen[3], Shuicheng Yan[1]
[1]Department of Electrical and Computer Engineering, National University of Singapore, Singapore
[2]School of Mechanical Engineering, Purdue University, USA
[3]School of Information Systems, Singapore Management University, Singapore
junshi.huang@nus.edu.sg, lhrbss@gmail.com, jlshen@smu.edu.sg, eleyans@nus.edu.sg

ABSTRACT

Nowadays, content-based retrieval methods are still the development trend of the traditional retrieval systems. Image labels, as one of the most popular approaches for the semantic representation of images, can fully capture the representative information of images. To achieve the high performance of retrieval systems, the precise annotation for images becomes inevitable. However, as the massive number of images in the Internet, one cannot annotate all the images without a scalable and flexible (i.e., training-free) annotation method. In this paper, we particularly investigate the problem of accelerating sparse coding based scalable image annotation, whose off-the-shelf solvers are generally inefficient on large-scale dataset. By leveraging the prior that most reconstruction coefficients should be zero, we develop a general and efficient framework to derive an accurate solution to the large-scale sparse coding problem through solving a series of much smaller-scale subproblems. In this framework, an active variable set, which expands and shrinks iteratively, is maintained, with each snapshot of the active variable set corresponding to a subproblem. Meanwhile, the convergence of our proposed framework to global optimum is theoretically provable. To further accelerate the proposed framework, a sub-linear time complexity hashing strategy, e.g. *Locality-Sensitive Hashing*, is seamlessly integrated into our framework. Extensive empirical experiments on NUS-WIDE and IMAGENET datasets demonstrate that the orders-of-magnitude acceleration is achieved by the proposed framework for large-scale image annotation, along with zero/negligible accuracy loss for the cases without/with hashing speed-up, compared to the expensive off-the-shelf solvers.

Categories and Subject Descriptors

H.3.3 [**Information Search and Retrieval**]: Retrieval models; I.2.6 [**Learning**]: Knowledge acquisition

MM'13, October 21–25, 2013, Barcelona, Spain.

http://dx.doi.org/10.1145/2502081.2502127.

Keywords

Hash-accelerated sparsity induced scalable optimization, Sparse coding, Large-scale image annotation

1. INTRODUCTION

With the integration of semantic information in image representation, content-based retrieval approach is still one of the most popular methods for image retrieval. Many efforts [16, 24, 25] have been devoted to improving the performance of retrieval methods. However, many retrieval methods cannot be performed unless the training process is completely operated. This becomes impracticable due to the massive number of images in the Internet. One possible way to improve the retrieval system is to focus on the semantic representation of images, and to this end, the automatic image annotation is thus inevitable.

In this paper, we aims to improve the retrieval system by proposing a scalable and flexible method for image annotation. Traditionally, the image annotation problem has been extensively studied for decades. The existing algorithms can be roughly divided into three categories, namely the classifier-based approaches, the probabilistic modeling-based approaches, and the graph-based approaches. The classifier-based approaches [4, 9, 10] are based on the foundation of discriminative classifiers, e.g. Support Vector Machine (SVM), and perform image annotation by encoding images as bags of localized features or other global features. The probabilistic modeling-based algorithms, e.g. [15, 32], attempt to infer the correlations or joint probabilities between images and annotation labels. Specifically, Feng et al. [15] proposed a multiple Bernoulli relevance model for image annotation. Wang et al. [32] used the probabilistic topic model to predict the labels of images. Besides, non-parametric graph-based algorithms [6, 21, 30], which construct informative graphs to propagate label information, are also widely explored. In particular, Tang et al. [30] proposed a graph-based semi-supervised sparse learning approach to harness both labeled and unlabeled data for image label propagation.

Due to the complex visual contents in images, calculating effective image signatures has become a long-standing challenge for image annotation task. Recently, the sparse coding-based image annotation, proposed by [33], shows that the semantic similarity between two images with overlapped labels can be well recovered in a reconstruction-based way. Chen et al. [7] adopted an exclusive LASSO model with overlapped groups for multi-labels image annotation. The success of [7, 33] inspired us to study image annotation problem based on sparse coding in this work. Moreover, motivated by the fact that these works [7, 33] mainly focus on the algorithmic effectiveness, yet are generally quite unsatisfactory in efficiency aspect, we particularly focus on accelerating the sparse optimization for large-scale datasets. Note that most recent sparse optimization methods [13, 19, 23], which are based on gradient descent, are only practical for small-scale or medium-scale sparse optimization problems. When handling large-scale settings, the computational burden of gradient computation becomes unbearable. In such case, even the first order methods might become inefficient, since the gradient with respect to all variables needs to be calculated at every iterative step.

Therefore, the key challenge of efficient optimization for large-scale sparse coding comes from the large number of variables to be optimized. Fortunately, the sparsity itself implies that most of variables should be zero when reaching the optimal solution. By leveraging such a strong prior, we can eliminate these zero variables and simplify the original problem into a much smaller-scale problem if these irrelevant variables can be identified. Though we can theoretically solve a large-scale image annotation problem by transforming it into a smaller one, it is still difficult and time-consuming to detect non-zero variables from a large set of variables corresponding to all the data. To address this issue, an effective and efficient approach is proposed by embedding a sub-linear time complexity method, e.g. locality-sensitive hashing (LSH) [2, 11, 18, 30], for efficiently seeking non-zero variables, with the theoretic convergence guaranteed. As the sparsity property and high efficiency of our solution, our framework is particularly suitable for the problem of large-scale image annotation.

To the best of our knowledge, it is worthy to highlight the main contributions of this work:

- Inspired by the success of sparse coding on image annotation problem, we propose a scalable and efficient framework which drives the optimal solution to the original large-scale image annotation problem by solving a series of simpler and much smaller-scale subproblems.

- In order to efficiently maintain the active variable set, which constructs a small-scale subproblem at each iterative step, the LSH method is seamlessly integrated into our framework to search the nearest neighbors of the intermediate residue vector in sub-linear complexity. The two strategies together bring orders-of-magnitude speed-up in sparse coding optimization, yet with almost negligible accuracy sacrifice in image annotation.

- As the size of the aforementioned active variable set is usually small and controllable, and the solution to each subproblem is usually a good initialization to the successive subproblem, the intermediate small-scale subproblems can be efficiently solved by applying any off-the-shelf sparse optimization methods.

The remainder of this paper is organized as following. Section 2 introduces the sparse coding and the theoretic foundation of LSH. In Section 3, we elaborate the proposed framework in terms of problem formulation and algorithm analysis. Experiments which extensively evaluate the proposed

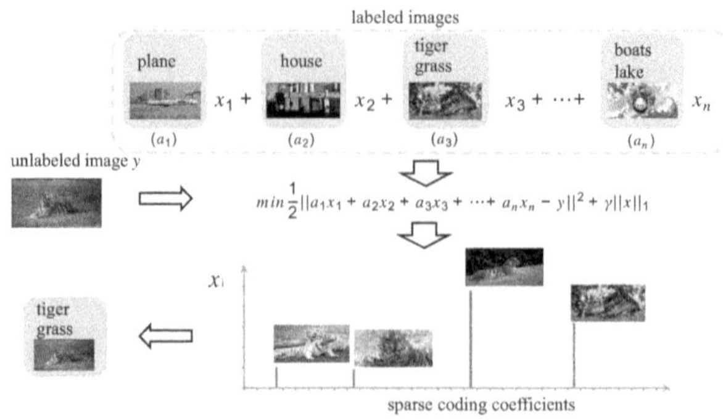

Figure 1: An illustration of sparse coding for scalable image annotation. Given an unlabeled testing image, its feature vector is sparsely reconstructed by a dictionary of labeled training images by solving a sparse coding problem. Then, the label(s) of this testing image are propagated from the labeled training images via the derived sparse reconstruction coefficients.

framework for image annotation problem are conducted in Section 4. Finally, conclusions and future works are listed in Section 5.

2. PRELIMINARIES

In this section, we will briefly introduce sparse coding and LSH, which together lay down the technical foundation of our proposed framework for accelerating image annotation.

2.1 Sparse Coding

Given a set of over-complete bases, sparse coding aims to find a succinct representations of stimuli. In the image annotation field, each stimulus, namely, unlabeled testing sample, can be approximately described as a weighted linear combination of a small subset of labeled training samples from the over-complete image set. Those training samples involved in the reconstruction usually well preserve the semantic information of the testing sample [6].

Concretely, given a set of n labeled training images $A = [a_1, \cdots, a_n]$, an unlabeled testing sample y usually can be reconstructed by using a sparse vector of weights $x \in \mathcal{R}^n$, i.e., $y = Ax$, if the set A is over complete. The sparse vector x, which is also known as reconstruction coefficient vector, is assumed to be zero for most of its components. The obtain x, it is generally to solve the following minimization problem

$$\min \parallel x \parallel_0 \quad \text{s.t. } y = Ax. \tag{1}$$

Unfortunately, problem (1) requires combinatorial search, and thus is usually intractable. Some greedy algorithms, such as the *matching pursuit* [27] and *orthogonal matching pursuit* [28], are proposed. Another approximate method, called *basis pursuit* [5], suggests using the l_1-norm to replace the l_0-norm, and converting the problem (1) into

$$\min_x \frac{1}{2} \parallel Ax - y \parallel_2^2 + \gamma \parallel x \parallel_1. \tag{2}$$

Problem (2), which is proved to give the same solution to problem (1) under certain assumptions, is convex and thus easier to be solved [12]. Figure 1 illustrates the idea of how to perform image annotation based on problem (2).

Many recent works [1, 14, 20, 26] focus on efficiently solving the problem (2). However, the proposed algorithms are based on direct iterative minimization, which is usually computationally expensive, especially when n is large. Therefore, reducing the computational complexity is valuable and essential, especially for large-scale problems.

2.2 Locality-Sensitive Hashing

This subsection briefly introduces LSH, which is a key module of our schema to improve the efficiency of large-scale sparse coding. Generally speaking, LSH is a approximate hashing method which aims to perform probabilistic dimension reduction on high-dimensional space [18]. It can search the approximate nearest neighbors in sub-linear time complexity. Particularly, LSH generates several randomized hash functions to guarantee that the collision probability of two samples is inversely proportional to their "distance", where the specific meaning of "distance" is task dependent. In other words, the larger the "distance" is, the smaller the collision probability is.

Formally, let $d = (\cdot, \cdot)$ be a distance function. For any $p \in S$, where S is the dataset to be indexed, denote $R(p, r)$ as the set of samples from S with distance to p less than r.

Definition 1. *Let h denotes a random choice of hash function from a family H. The family H is called (r_1, r_2, p_1, p_2)-sensitive for $d = (\cdot, \cdot)$ if for any $p, q \in S$*

- *If $p \in R(q, r_1)$, then $Pr[h_H(q) = h_H(p)] \geq p_1$,*
- *If $p \notin R(q, r_2)$, then $Pr[h_H(q) = h_H(p)] \leq p_2$.*

In order to utilize the family of functions, it must satisfy $p_1 > p_2$ and $r_1 < r_2$. For a B-bits LSH, it defines a bucket family $G = \{g : S \to U^b\}$ so that

$$g(p) = (h_1(p), h_2(p), \cdots, h_B(p)),$$

where $h_b \in H$, $1 \leq b \leq B$. Supposing M is the number of hash tables, LSH chooses K groups of functions $g_1, g_2, \cdots, g_K$ from G independently, uniformly and randomly. During the preprocessing stage, all the samples in dataset are mapped into the B hash tables which are indexed by

$$g_k(p) = (h_{k_1}(p), h_{k_2}(p), \cdots, h_{k_B}(p)),$$

with $k = 1, 2, \cdots, K$. To search a query p, LSH only needs to traverse the samples among the union of hash buckets indexed by p exhaustively.

Particularly, Datar et al. [11] proposed a novel LSH schema which works on samples in Euclidean space under l_2-norm without embedding. In this approach, the query can be retrieved in time $O(log(n))$. Furthermore, this hash method works more effectively if the data is extremely high-dimensional but sparse. In this paper, we utilize LSH to retrieve approximate nearest neighbors, so as to improve the overall efficiency of our framework on large-scale datasets.

3. OUR PROPOSED FRAMEWORK

In this section, we will elaborate our proposed framework for the problem of sparse coding based image annotation. First of all, we present some basic concepts and theoretic foundations. Then, a general framework, Sparsity Induced Scalable Optimization (SISO), is proposed to efficiently solve the sparse coding problem. Due to the seamless conversion between the expansion of active variable set and retrieval result of LSH, we integrate LSH into our framework, i.e., the Hash-accelerated SISO, to further improve the efficiency of our approach on large-scale dataset. Finally, the algorithmic convergence and computational complexity of Hash-accelerated SISO are carefully analyzed.

3.1 Problem Formulation and Analysis

Denote a set of n training images $A = [a_1, \cdots, a_n]$ where $a_i \in \mathcal{R}^m$ is the i-th sample of A. The corresponding label set of training samples is represented by matrix $L = [l_1, \cdots, l_n]$, where l_{ij} is set as 1 if a_i is annotated with the j-th label; otherwise 0. Given a testing sample $y \in \mathcal{R}^m$, we assume that y can be approximately reconstructed by A by the following way:

$$y \approx Ax = \sum_{i=1}^{n} a_i x_i, \tag{3}$$

where $x = [x_1, x_2, \cdots, x_n]^T$ is the reconstruction coefficients. Therefore, we can roughly predict the labels l_y of the testing sample y by

$$l_y = \sum_{i=1}^{n} l_i x_i. \tag{4}$$

Note that the number of images with similar label information may be huge on a large-scale image dataset, a "tiger" object in a testing sample, for example, can be semantically reconstructed by various training samples with "tiger" label. However, there are usually discrepancies between the "tiger" object in the training samples and the reconstructed testing sample. Meanwhile, those training samples, which are used to reconstruct the testing sample, may contain many irrelevant labels. For a good performance, we need to find certain training samples, which can not only precisely reconstruct the information of "tiger" object in the testing sample, but also contain as less irrelevant information as possible. On the other hand, as it is often the case that the dimension of features is typically smaller than the sample number in large-scale dataset, the problem (3) may be underdetermined, and the solution becomes ambiguous. Fortunately, the sparse coding, owing to its convexity property, can properly handle those problems, and thus demonstrates good performance in reconstructing label information of the testing sample. Particularly, the image annotation problem is reformulated as a LASSO problem [31] in problem (2).

Although the sparse coding is effective in image annotation problem, its inefficiency greatly discourages its applications in large-scale dataset. Before introducing our approach for speed-up, some definitions are firstly provided as followings.

Definition 2. *For the reconstruction coefficient vector $x \in \mathcal{R}^n$ in problem (1), the indices of all non-zero components of x, $\sigma(x) = \{i | x_i \neq 0, x_i \in x\}$, are called as its support.*

Definition 3. *Let $I = \{1, 2, \cdots, n\}$ denotes the index set for all samples in A, and P_I denotes the problem (2), which contains the whole set of samples as bases. Given any subset $C \subseteq I$, we define the subproblem P_C by instantiating the i-th reconstruction coefficient x_i as zero in problem P_I if $i \in I/C$.*

Definition 4. *Let $|C|$ denotes the cardinality of index set C. All the $|C|$ reconstruction coefficients in subproblem*

P_C, which are presented by a vector x_C, constitute the active variable set of P_C. Particularly, x_i is called an active variable if $x_i \in x_C$.

Obviously, C is the index set of active variable set x_C in subproblem P_C, and denote A_C as the corresponding bases in dictionary A. In order to transform x_C into a corresponding x, we can simply copy the values of x_C into x, and set the rest values of x as zero. On the other hand, we can directly discard the variable x_i if $i \in I/C$ and keep the rest to transform x into x_C.

Let $f(x) = \frac{1}{2}\| Ax - y \|_2^2 + \gamma\| x \|_1$, and according to the properties of convexity, the subproblem P_C inherits the convexity property of P_I:

THEORY 1. *In the problem P_I, if $f(x)$ is a convex function and the value field of x is a convex region, then for any subset $C \subseteq I$, the subproblem P_C is also convex.*

This theorem can be easily proved based on the definition of convexity and we omit the proof here.

THEORY 2. *If x^* is the optimal solution to the problem P_I, and let the index set C contains the support of x^*, i.e., $\sigma(x^*) \subseteq C$, then x_C^* is the solution to the subproblem P_C.*

Formally, Theorem 2 points out that if

$$x^* = \arg\min_{x} \frac{1}{2}\| Ax - y \|_2^2 + \gamma\| x \|_1, \tag{5}$$

i.e., x^* is the global optimal solution to the problem P_I. Then, for any index set C containing all the non-zero elements of x^*, namely, $\sigma(x^*) \subseteq C$, the following equation is always satisfied:

$$x_C^* = \arg\min_{x_C} \frac{1}{2}\| A_C x_C - y \|_2^2 + \gamma\| x_C \|_1. \tag{6}$$

As aforementioned, in the large-scale image annotation task, we need to solve the sparse coding problem (2). Since $|\sigma(x^*)| \ll n$ in this task, Theorem 2 indicates implicitly that we can solve the problem P_I quickly by solving a proper subproblem. So far, the key challenge lies on the determination of a proper subproblem P_C, or a proper index set C.

3.2 Sparsity Induced Scalable Optimization

Though it is difficult to construct a proper C directly, a proper strategy for solving the problem is to iterative deduction. Most existing sparse optimization methods are based on the gradient descent strategy. Specifically, starting from an initialization x_0, this strategy moves along a path $\{x(0), x(1), \cdots, x(t), x(t+1), \cdots, x^*\}$ with $f(x)$ monotonically decreased. Due to the sparse property of x^*, this process can be greatly accelerated if we can always move along a path with a small index set C. In other words, we can iteratively solve and update the much smaller subproblems P_C, until getting the optimal solution x^*. Based on this idea, we propose the SISO approach, which iterates between two phases, namely, *shrinkage phase* and *expansion phase.*

3.2.1 Shrinkage Phase

In the shrinkage phase, assuming the current active variable set is $x_{C(t)}$, we solve the subproblem $P_{C(t)}$ firstly if $x_{C(t)}$ is not the solution to $P_{C(t)}$. When solving the subproblem $P_{C(t)}$, the initialization is set as $x_{C(t)}$. In the optimization process of solving $P_{C(t)}$, x moves along a segment of path with $|\sigma(x_{C(t)})| \leq |C(t)|$, and $f(x)$ is monotonically decreasing. Obviously, some components in $x_{C(t)}$ may become zero, and thus the active variable set shrinks when setting $C(t) = \sigma(x_{C(t)})$, i.e., all zero components in the active variable set are discarded. Therefore, this phase is called shrinkage phase, whose time complexity is $O(|C(t)|)$.

3.2.2 Expansion Phase

In the expansion phase, $x_{C(t)}$ is already the solution to the subproblem $P_{C(t)}$. Then, we need to check whether $x(t)$, which is transformed from $x_{C(t)}$, is the solution of P_I or not. If yes, we can conclude that $x^* = x(t)$; Otherwise, some variables outside $C(t)$ should be activated and added into $C(t+1)$.

Denote the Lagrangian function of the subproblem P_C as

$$L_C(x_C) = \frac{1}{2}\| A_C x_C - y \|_2^2 + \gamma\| x_C \|_1. \tag{7}$$

Usually, $L_C(x_C)$ is non-differentiable, but has sub-differential $\frac{\partial}{\partial x_C} L_C(x_C)$, which is the set of all sub-gradients of $L_C(x_C)$. According to the generalized KKT condition [17], if x_C^* is the solution to P_C, then

$$0 \in \frac{\partial}{\partial x_i} L_C(x_C^*), \forall i \in C. \tag{8}$$

Formula (8) serves as a criterion to determine whether or not the solution x_C^* to the subproblem P_C can be transformed into the global optimal solution x^* to the problem P_I. If not, Formula (8) can also provide us a tool to guide the expansion of active variable set.

Note that if x^* is the solution to the problem P_I, according to the generalized KKT condition, we also have

$$0 \in \frac{\partial}{\partial x_i} L(x^*), \forall i \in I, \tag{9}$$

where $L(x)$ is the Lagrangian function of P_I.

Given a subproblem $P_{C(t)}$ and its derived solution $x_{C(t)}^*$, we have $\frac{\partial}{\partial x_i} L(x(t)) = \frac{\partial}{\partial x_i} L_{C(t)}(x_{C(t)}^*) = 0$ if $i \in C(t)$, where the vector $x(t)$ is transformed from $x_{C(t)}^*$. Therefore, we only need to consider the partial derivative of $L(x(t))$ with respect to x_i, where $i \notin C(t)$. Let $S = \{i | 0 \notin \frac{\partial}{\partial x_i} L(x(t))\}$ be the expansion set. According to the generalized KKT condition, if S is empty, then $x(t)$ is already the solution to P_I. Otherwise, we only need to add variables according to S into the active variable set $x_{C(t)}$ to generate $x_{C(t+1)}$, i.e., setting $C(t+1) = \sigma(x_{C(t)}^*) \cup S$.

Denote $z(x)$ the sub-gradient of $|x|$, we have

$$z(x) = \frac{\partial}{\partial x}|x| = \begin{cases} 1, & \text{if } x > 0 \\ z, & \text{if } x = 0 \\ -1, & \text{if } x < 0 \end{cases}, \tag{10}$$

where z is any value within the closed interval [-1,1].

Let $e(x) = \frac{1}{2}\| Ax - y \|_2^2$, then

$$\frac{\partial}{\partial x} L(x) = e'(x) + \gamma * z(x), \tag{11}$$

where $e'(x) = A^T(Ax - y)$, and the generalized KKT condition $0 \in \frac{\partial}{\partial x} L(x)$ can be expressed as

$$e_i'(x) = \begin{cases} -\gamma, & \text{if } i \in I, \text{and } x_i > 0 \\ -\gamma * z, & \text{if } i \in I, \text{and } x_i = 0 \\ \gamma, & \text{if } i \in I, \text{and } x_i < 0 \end{cases}, \tag{12}$$

where $e_i'(x) = a_i^T(Ax - y)$.

In the same way, if $x^*_{C(t)}$ is the solution to the subproblem $P_{C(t)}$, then $0 \in \frac{\partial}{\partial x^*_{C(t)}} L_{C(t)}(x^*_{C(t)})$, that is,

$$e_i'(x^*_{C(t)}) = \begin{cases} -\gamma, & \text{if } i \in C(t), \text{and } x_i > 0 \\ -\gamma * z, & \text{if } i \in C(t), \text{and } x_i = 0 \\ \gamma, & \text{if } i \in C(t), \text{and } x_i < 0 \end{cases}, \quad (13)$$

Since $|z| \leq 1$, we can summarize the index set of the expansion set as

$$S = \{i \mid |e_i'(x^*_{C(t)})| \geq \gamma\}. \quad (14)$$

Meanwhile, as

$$e_i'(x^*_{C(t)}) = \frac{\partial}{\partial x^*_i} e(x^*_{C(t)}) = a_i^T(A_{C(t)} x^*_{C(t)} - y), \quad (15)$$

where $a_i \in A_{C(t)}$. Thus, we can obtain that

$$S = \{i \mid |a_i^T(A_{C(t)} x^*_{C(t)} - y)| \geq \gamma\}. \quad (16)$$

Here, γ is a natural threshold to select the expansion set, and is empirically set as $\alpha \| A^T y \|_\infty$ in our experiments to make the solution sparse, where $\alpha = 0.002$.

Since $\sigma(x^*_{C(t)}) \subset C(t+1)$ and $0 \notin \frac{\partial}{\partial x_i} L(x(t))$ where $i \in C(t+1)/\sigma(x^*_{C(t)})$, the new subproblem $P_{C(t+1)}$ definitely can be further optimized such that $f(x(t+1)) < f(x(t))$, where the vectors $x(t+1)$ and $x(t)$ are derived from $x^*_{C(t+1)}$ and $x^*_{C(t)}$ respectively. Eventually, the function $f(x)$ will always arrive at the global optimum. If $f(x)$ does not converge, there must exist at least one sample x_i such that $0 \notin \frac{\partial}{\partial x_i} L(x(t))$, which conflicts with the convergent condition. To control the complexity, when $|S|$ is too large, we usually select k variables in S, corresponding to the top-k largest values of $|a_i^T(A_{C(t)} x^*_{C(t)} - y)|$, where k is set as 100-200 in our experiments.

In conclusion, we solve a subproblem containing a much smaller number of variables than original problem in the shrinkage phase. Usually, some active variables in the derived solution become inactive, and thus the active variable set shrinks. In the expansion phase, we expand the active variable set to form a new subproblem for the next shrinkage phase. Therefore, the iteration of these two phases leads to an efficient iterative procedure, and reaches the global optimal solution to the original problem eventually.

3.3 Hash Acceleration for SISO

Obviously, the expansion set casts an important role in our proposed approach. However, its computational complexity is heavily dependent on n, which is the number of bases and is extremely large in large-scale dataset. As aforementioned, with the current residue vector $r_C = y - A_C x_C$, the expansion set can be obtained by

$$\begin{aligned} S &= \{i \mid |a_i^T(A_C x^*_C - y)| \geq \gamma\} \\ &= \{i \mid |a_i^T(-r_C)| \geq \gamma\} \end{aligned}, \quad (17)$$

i.e.,

$$S = \{i \mid a_i^T r_C \geq \gamma \text{ or } a_i^T r_C \leq -\gamma\}. \quad (18)$$

Assuming each basis a_i is l_2-normalized as in general implementation, we can obtain

$$\begin{aligned} S = \{i \mid & -\frac{1}{2} \| a_i - \frac{r_C}{\| r_C \|} \|^2 + 1 \geq \frac{\gamma}{\| r_C \|} \\ \text{or } & \frac{1}{2} \| a_i - \frac{-r_C}{\| r_C \|} \|^2 - 1 \leq -\frac{\gamma}{\| r_C \|}\} \end{aligned}. \quad (19)$$

Let $d(p,q) = \| p - q \|$ be the l_2-distance between vector p and q, we have

$$\begin{aligned} S = \{i \mid & d(a_i, \frac{r_C}{\| r_C \|}) \leq \sqrt{2(1 - \frac{\gamma}{\| r_C \|}} \\ \text{or } & d(a_i, -\frac{r_C}{\| r_C \|}) \leq \sqrt{2(1 - \frac{\gamma}{\| r_C \|}}\} \end{aligned}. \quad (20)$$

To make the formula (20) valid, $\gamma \leq \| r_C \|$ must satisfy. If we use l_2-norm to measure similarity between training samples and the intermediate residue, the value of $\sqrt{2(1 - \frac{\gamma}{\| r_C \|})}$ is the threshold for finding expansion set. For the consideration of efficiency, one does not always want to find the exact similar training samples to the intermediate residue, but use the approximately similar samples instead. Based on this idea, to further enhance the efficiency of SISO, we utilize LSH to retrieve the approximate nearest neighbors of vector $\frac{r_C}{\| r_C \|}$ from A, as well as the approximate nearest neighbors of $-\frac{r_C}{\| r_C \|}$. Compared with Hash-based KNN, the LSH in our framework aims to search the approximate nearest neighbors of normalized residue r_C, instead of reconstructed sample y.

A proper type of hashing function in [11], with $O(log(n))$ computational complexity, is adopted in our experiments. Specifically, this hashing function can directly perform on samples in Euclidean space with l_p-norm, where $p \in (0, 2]$. Obviously, we can directly use the LSH with l_2-norm-based hash function for our implementation.

To be efficient, the size of expansion set should be small, and is usually set as 100 to 200 in our experiments. Overall, as $|C| \ll |I|$ and because of the limited number of iterations before convergence, the time for calculating the solution of subproblems can be ignored. Thus, the main computational complexity of our approach is on the part of searching approximate nearest neighbor.

Formally, let m be the dimension of features. The gradient strategy, which thoroughly goes through each training sample and calculates its sub-differential, requires $O(nm)$ time complexity. Comparatively, the hash-based approach, which can quickly obtain the approximate nearest neighbors by directly mapping the residue vector into similar buckets, is proved of the same time complexity with hashing search, i.e., $O(log(n))$ [11].

In conclusion, our proposed framework, i.e., Hash-accelerated SISO, is summarized in Algorithm 1. Since there is no restriction on the methods to solve the subproblem P_C, any appropriate off-the-shelf sparse optimization method can be applied. Meanwhile, the LSH can also be substituted by many other appropriate approximated nearest neighbors searching methods. Therefore, Algorithm 1 essentially provides a very general and effective framework to accelerate sparse optimization on large-scale problems. Note that in each round of shrinkage and expansion, the overall objective function value shall not be increased, and obviously be lower bounded

Algorithm 1 Hash-accelerated Sparsity Induced Scalable Optimization

Input: The large-scale sparse optimization problem P_I, including the training samples A, the initialization $x(0)$, and the parameter k.
Initialization: $C(0) = \sigma(x(0))$, transform $x(0)$ into $x_{C(0)}$, and normalize each basis in A;
Preprocessing: Create LSH tables and map all samples in A to the buckets;
while $x(t+1)$ is not the solution to P_I **do**
  Solve the sub-problem $P_{C(t)}$ with initialization of $x_{C(t)}$, and update $x_{C(t)}$ as the new solution;
  Set $C(t) = \sigma(x_{C(t)})$; {shrinkage}
  Calculate $r_{C(t)} = y - A_{C(t)}x_{C(t)}$;
  Construct the expansion set S according to the approximate nearest neighbours of $\frac{r_{C(t)}}{\| r_{C(t)} \|}$ and $-\frac{r_{C(t)}}{\| r_{C(t)} \|}$ by LSH;
  if S is empty **then**
    $x_{C(t+1)}$ is the solution to P_I, break;
  else
    Add S into $C(t+1)$ and update $x_{C(t+1)}$; {expansion}
  end if
end while
Output: The solution to P_I.

by zero. Thus, the algorithmic convergence can be naturally guaranteed.

4. EXPERIMENTS

This section presents a set of extensive experiments to evaluate the efficiency and effectiveness of Hash-accelerated SISO on large-scale dataset, including NUS-WIDE [8], its subset NUS-WIDE-LITE, and ImageNet [3]. The experiment results indicate that our proposed framework outperform most of competitors with less running time. Compared with LASSO and SISO, Hash-accelerated SISO proves of significant acceleration with negligible accuracy loss. All experiments are conducted on a PC equipped with Intel X5472 CPU of 3.00 GHz and 32.0 GB RAM.

4.1 Datasets

The first experiment are conducted on a large-scale real-world image dataset NUS-WIDE-LITE, whose images are randomly crawled from some popular image sharing websites, such as Flickr.com. The diversity and complexity of images in this dataset make it a good test-bed for large-scale image annotation problem [6, 8]. Meanwhile, the larger-scale image annotation experiments are conducted on the superset of NUS-WIDE-LITE, known as NUS-WIDE. To further highlight the efficiency of our proposed framework, we also conduct the experiments on ImageNet. For the experiments on ImageNet, we use the provided 1,000-D features (bag of visual words) to represent images and evaluate the efficiency of our framework on about 1.2 million training images and 50,000 testing images with 1,000 labels. For the evaluation of accuracy, we use the flat cost by predicting 5 labels per testing image.

NUS-WIDE-LITE consists of 55,615 images in total, within which 27,808 images are selected as the training set, and the rest of them are used as testing set. Each image is combined with a 81-D label vector to indicate its relationship to 81 distinct concepts. For the convenience, multiple types of local visual features for these images are provided, including 225-D blockwise color moments, 128-D wavelet texture, and 75-D edge direction histogram. To comprehensively demonstrate the performance of algorithms, we use variant percentages of labeled data. The percentage, which is denoted as $\tau \in (0, 1]$ in our experiments, ranges from 10% to 100% with a step of 10%.

NUS-WIDE contains 269,648 images. For each image, an 81-D label vector is maintained. Multiple types of local visual features, including 225-D blockwise color moments, 128-D wavelet texture, and 75-D edge direction histogram, are also provided in this dataset. The training image set consists of 161,789 images, and the rest of them are used for testing. Analogously, the same sampling strategy in the experiment of NUS-WIDE-LITE is adopted on this dataset.

ImageNet contains about 1.2 million training images with 1,000 object labels and one label per image. For each image, a 1,000-D bag of visual words through vector quantization, including vector quantized SIFT features, are provided. In the experiments, we randomly select several different numbers of training images from the training image set, ranging from 200,000 to 1.2 million with a step of 200,000. For different training set, we mainly evaluate the average running time of our framework on 50,000 testing images.

Table 1: The comparison algorithms

Name	Methods
KNN	k-Nearest Neighbors
SVM [10]	Support Vector Machine
RRML	Ridge Regression for Multi-Label Annotation
LNP [34]	Linear Neighborhood Propagation
EGSSC [29]	Entropic Graph Semi-Supervised Classification
LSMP [6]	Large-Scale Multi-label Propagation

4.2 Evaluation Criteria and Algorithms

In the experiments on NUS-WIDE-LITE and NUS-WIDE, we compare our approach with five state-of-the-art algorithms as reported in Table 1. Generally, those algorithms can be divided into three categories, namely classifier-based algorithms,reconstruction-based algorithms, and graph-based algorithms.

Classifier-based Algorithms: In this category, we select the traditional classification algorithm SVM [10] as the representative. In the experiments, SVM is implemented as multi-class classifier with RBF kernel by adopting One-vs-All approach. Particularly, we train several SVMs for each category by using different parameters C and γ, and select the optimal models for evaluation.

Reconstruction-based Algorithms: The main idea of the approaches in this category is to use training dataset as bases, and calculate the reconstruction coefficients for testing data on these bases. Then, the labels of testing data are calculated by multiplying the labels of training data and the reconstruction coefficients. As well-known approaches, KNN and RRML with different parameters are selected in this category. Note that sparse coding, e.g. LASSO, also belongs to this category. In the experiments, the implementation of LASSO is provided by the SLEP [22] package.

Table 2: The running time (unit: hour) of algorithms on NUS-WIDE-LITE dataset

Algorithm	Construction Time[1]	Prediction Time	Total Time	Ratio[2]
SVM	7.27	2.95	10.22	29.20
RRML	0.00	3.43	3.43	9.80
KNN	2.82	0.12	2.94	8.40
LNP	2.69	0.03	2.72	7.77
EGSSC	1.54	0.04	1.58	4.51
LSMP	0.68	0.03	0.72	2.06
Hash-accelerated SISO	0.01	0.34	0.35	1

1. Construction Time is the time for constructing graph or calculating the reconstruction coefficients.
2. $Ratio = \frac{Total\ Time\ of\ One\ Method}{Total\ Time\ of\ Hash\text{-}accelerated\ SISO}$

Graph-based Algorithms: Graph-based algorithms are extensively used for image annotation. In the experiments, three graph-based algorithms are selected as competitors. LNP [34], which is based on a linear-construction criterion, aims to propagate the supervision information by a local propagation and updating process. In our implementation, Local and Global Consistency (LGC) [36] is used as the inference algorithm of LNP. As an entropic graph-regularized semi-supervised classification method, EGSSC [29] is on the foundation of minimizing a Kullback-Leibler divergence over the graph created by k-NN Gaussian similarity. LSMP [6], which is also founded on the Kullback-Leibler divergence, uses hash strategies to accelerate the construction of l_1-graph.

The criteria used for comparing performance on NUS-WIDE-LITE and NUS-WIDE is the mean average precision (MAP) among all the labels. More importantly, the running time for model construction and label prediction among all algorithms are also compared. Particularly, the experiments on computational time and performance of LASSO and SISO are also conducted on NUS-WIDE-LITE and NUS-WIDE to highlight the significant acceleration of our framework. The experiment results indicate that Hash-accelerated SISO outperforms most other competitors in terms of MAP with least running time. Note that some competitors are not completely performed on NUS-WIDE due to the immense running time. For example, we only select 1000 testing samples from NUS-WIDE at random for the evaluation of LASSO.

As the huge size of ImageNet, we only conduct the full-scale experiment on ImageNet with Hash-accelerated SISO. For the LASSO and SISO, we only randomly select 1,000 unlabeled samples for testing. To evaluate the performance, we predict 5 labels for each testing image, and calculate the flat cost. Experiment results show that Hash-accelerated SISO can even achieve orders-of-magnitude acceleration when compared with LASSO and SISO.

Table 3: The running time (unit: hour) of LASSO, SISO and Hash-accelerated SISO on NUS-WIDE-LITE dataset

Algorithm	Total Time	Ratio[1]
LASSO	133.03	380.08
SISO	2.52	7.20
Hash-accelerated SISO	0.35	1

1. $Ratio = \frac{Total\ Time\ of\ One\ Method}{Total\ Time\ of\ Hash\text{-}accelerated\ SISO}$

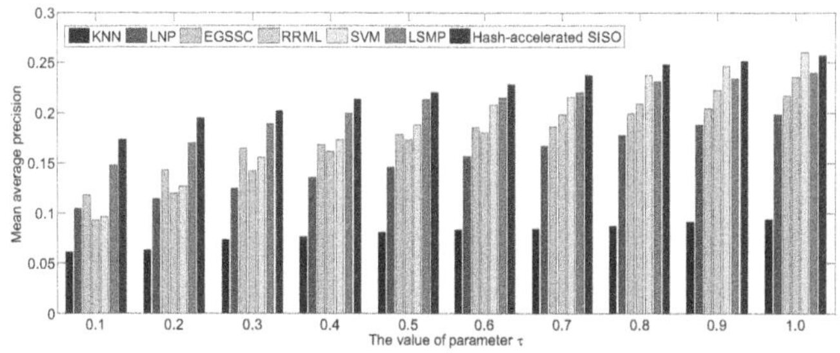

Figure 2: The MAPs of competitors and Hash-accelerated SISO on NUS-WIDE-LITE with various percentages of training dataset.

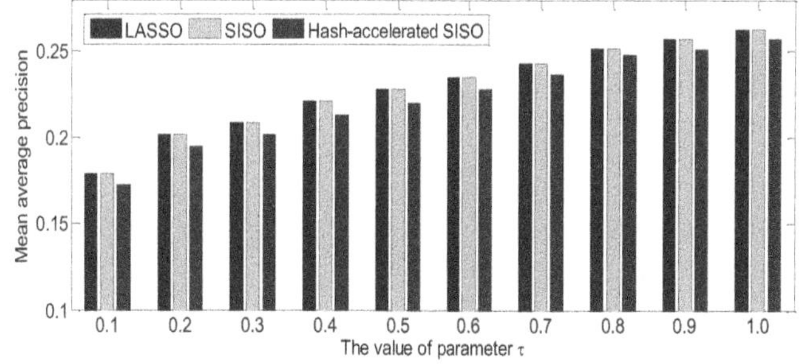

Figure 3: The MAPs of LASSO, SISO and Hash-accelerated SISO on NUS-WIDE-LITE with various percentages training dataset

4.3 Experiments on NUS-WIDE-LITE

In this experiment, we compare Hash-accelerated SISO with six state-of-the-art algorithms as reported in Table 2, including KNN, SVM, RRML, LNP, EGSSC and LSMP. Generally, we use various percentages, ranging from 10% to 100%, of labeled images as training data, and carefully tune the optimal parameters for each algorithm. Specifically 1) The number of nearest neighbors in KNN is set as 500 2) RBF kernel is adopted in SVM, and the searching ranges of its two parameters are $\gamma \in \{0.1, 0.2, ..., 1.0\}$ and $C \in \{0.5, 1, 2\}$. The optimal values of γ and C are set as 0.6 and 1 respectively. 3) The single parameter of RRML, denoted as k, is searched within $\{0.1, 0.2, ..., 1.0, 2.0, ..., 20.0\}$, and the optimal value of k is set as 8 in our experiments. 4) For LNP, LGC is selected as its inference algorithm. The fraction of useful label information that one image receives from its neighbors in LNP is denoted as α, and $\alpha \in \{0.8, 0.9, 0.95, 0.99\}$. The optimal value of α is 0.95. The number of nearest neighbors in LNP is searched among $K \in$

Table 4: The running time (unit: hour) of algorithms on NUS-WIDE dataset.

Algorithm	Construction Time[1]	Prediction Time	Total Time	Ratio[2]
SVM	153.1	15.5	168.6	26.76
KNN	143.6	0.7	144.3	22.90
LNP	56.4	0.9	57.3	9.09
EGSSC	35.4	1.4	36.8	5.84
LSMP	21.6	0.5	22.1	3.51
Hash-accelerated SISO	0.1	6.2	6.3	1

1. Construction Time is the time for constructing graph or calculating the reconstruction coefficients.
2. $Ratio = \frac{Total\ Time\ of\ One\ Method}{Total\ Time\ of\ Hash\text{-}accelerated\ SISO}$

$\{5, 10, 20, ..., 100\}$, and is set as 10. 5) In EGSSC, the values of its three parameters $\mu \in \{0.01, 0.02, 0.05, 0.1, 0.2, 0.5, 1\}$, $\nu \in \{0.01, 0.02, 0.05, 0.1, 0.2, 0.5, 1\}$, and $\beta \in \{1, 2, 3\}$ are set as 0.1, 1, and 2 respectively. To be specific, μ and ν are used for weighting the divergence term of Kullback-Leiber and Shannon entropy term respectively; β ensures the convergence of those two similar probability measures. 6) For LSMP, the two parameters, namely, $\mu \in \{1, 2, 5, 10\}$ and $\beta \in \{1, 2, 5, 10\}$, which are used to leverage the balance between terms, are set as 10 and 5 respectively. In our proposed framework, the threshold γ for expansion set is set as $\alpha \| A^T y \|_\infty$, where α is empirically set as 0.002. The maximal number of expansion set, denoted by k, is set as 100 in this experiment. The results of all algorithms are presented in Figure 2 and Table 2 in terms of MAP and running time respectively.

We have the following observations from Figure 2 and Table 2:

- As the number of training samples increases, the overall performances of all methods generally rise. Overall, the MAP of Hash-accelerated SISO outperforms KNN, LNP, EGSSC, RRML, SVM, and LSMP for most settings. Especially when $\tau < 0.6$, Hash-accelerated SISO maintains much higher MAP than LNP, EGSSC, and RRML.

- Table 2 shows that Hash-Accelerated SISO is faster than any other methods on NUS-WIDE-LITE. Particularly, compared with SVM, RRML, and LNP, our framework achieves much higher computational speed-up on NUS-WIDE-LITE dataset by several times. For example, SVM spends about 7.27 hours on training and about 2.95 hours on prediction. However, Hash-accelerated SISO only requires 0.35 hour for prediction with negligible construction time. It is almost orders-of-magnitude saving in terms of time.

- Note that the relatively low MAPs of other LASSO related algorithms, e.g. LSMP, result from the simplification in the LASSO step for efficiency consideration, To be specific, LSMP only considers a small number of nearest neighbors before performing LASSO, which causes the inaccuracy of initialization.

Additionally, we also compare the MAP and running time of LASSO, SISO and Hash-accelerated SISO for image annotation problem on NUS-WIDE-LITE with varying numbers of training samples. The results are reported in Figure 3 and Table 3. It is worthwhile to note that SISO has zero MAP loss, and achieves about 7 times of acceleration when compared with LASSO. The experiment result also shows that Hash-accelerated SISO is the most efficient approach, though LASSO and SISO do not require construction time (i.e., training-free). Compared with LASSO, Hash-accelerated SISO is much (more than 300 times) faster, with only less than 1% loss of MAP.

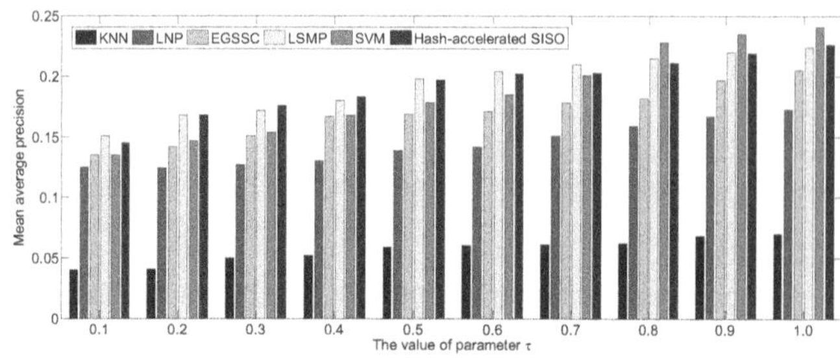

Figure 4: The MAPs of competitors and Hash-accelerated SISO on NUS-WIDE with various percentages training dataset.

4.4 Experiments on NUS-WIDE

In this experiment, we run five image annotation algorithms as competitors which are presented in Table 4, including KNN, SVM, LNP, EGSSC and LSMP. The experiment of RRML is omitted due to the lack of memory. The MAPs of each algorithm with various percentages of training data are presented in Figure 4. Simultaneously, the running time of each algorithm is reported in Table 4.

The parameters of these algorithms are set as following: 1) The number of nearest neighbors in KNN is 1000. 2) For SVM, RBF kernel are also adopted, and its two parameters γ and C are set as 0.8 and 2. 3) For LNP, the optimal fraction of label information is set as 0.99 in this experiment, and the number of nearest neighbors is 20. 4) EGSSC has three parameters, including μ, ν, and β which are set as 0.5, 1, and 1 respectively. 5) Two parameters of LSMP, μ and η, are set as 10 and 8 respectively. In our proposed algorithm, γ is just the same as the experiment on NUS-WIDE-LITE, and the maximal number of expansion set is set as 200 in this experiment.

From Figure 4 and Table 4, we may have the following observations:

- With the increasing number of training images, the MAP of each algorithm varies and monotonically increases. Generally, our proposed algorithm consistently performs better than most other methods. However, the MAP of SVM is higher than Hash-accelerated SISO

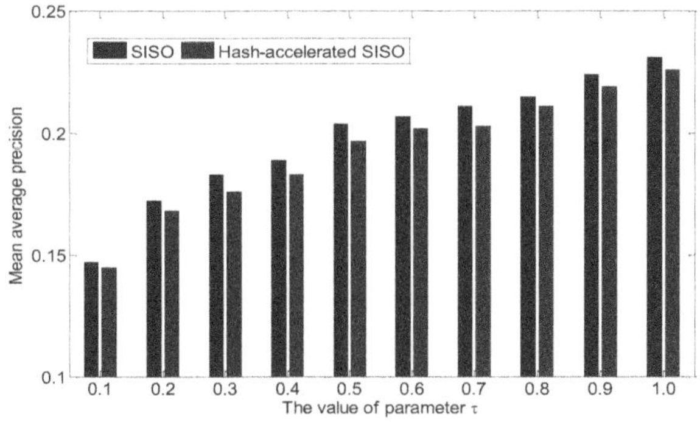

Figure 5: The MAPs of SISO and Hash-accelerated SISO on NUS-WIDE with various percentages training dataset

when $\tau > 0.7$. This situation may be caused by the inaccuracy of approximated nearest neighbors returned by LSH when the number of training samples increases.

- As we can see from Table 4, Hash-accelerated SISO requires nearly negligible time for constructing LSH on 161,789 training images, and spends only 6.2 hours on predicting the labels of 107,859 testing images. Compared with the competitors, our framework achieves significant speed-up by about 4-26 times. Note that our framework spends only 0.14 second on average on predicting the labels of each image when using the whole set of training samples. This is a huge improvement and indicates that Hash-accelerated SISO can provide significant improvement on handling large-scale dataset.

Additionally, we compare the MAP only between SISO and Hash-accelerated SISO on NUS-WIDE due to the unrealistic running time of image annotation by LASSO. The experiment result, which is presented in Figure 5, indicates that Hash-accelerated SISO can achieve comparable MAP when compared with SISO. Meanwhile, we should note that the MAP of SISO is higher than the corresponding MAP of SVM. For example, the MAP of SISO is 23.1% when $\tau = 1.0$; While the corresponding MAP of SVM is 23.0%.

Table 5: The average time (unit: second) of LASSO, SISO and Hash-accelerated SISO on NUS-WIDE dataset

Algorithm	Average Time	Ratio[1]
LASSO	124.05	886.07
SISO	1.78	12.71
Hash-accelerated SISO	0.14	1

1. $Ratio = \frac{Total\ Time\ of\ One\ Method}{Total\ Time\ of\ Hash\text{-}accelerated\ SISO}$

To estimate the prediction speed of LASSO, we run the LASSO on part of NUS-WIDE by randomly selecting 1000 testing samples from testing set, and using the whole training dataset of NUS-WIDE for reconstruction. The result is presented in Table 5 in terms of time cost. Experiment result shows that Hash-accelerated SISO performs much faster than SISO and LASSO. Especially when compared with LASSO, Hash-accelerated SISO significantly accelerates by more than 800 times.

4.5 Experiments on ImageNet

In this part, we only use Hash-accelerated SISO to run the experiment on the whole training dataset with original 1,000-D features. Due to the inefficiency of implementing other competitors, we mainly focus on the efficiency and speed-up achieved by Hash-accelerated SISO. For robustness, we randomly select various numbers of images, ranging from 200,000 to 1.2 million, from the training dataset of ImageNet for training. Meanwhile, 50,000 images are used as testing samples. We evaluate the performance of Hash-accelerated SISO on two aspects, i.e., flat cost and average time.

The parameters of Hash-accelerated SISO are set as following: $k = 200$, $\gamma = \alpha \| A^T y \|_\infty$, where $\alpha = 0.002$. As Table 6 demonstrates, the larger the number of training images is, the better the performance is. Specifically, when the number of training images is larger than 800,000, the performance of Hash-accelerated SISO is better than the baseline in [3], whose flat cost is 0.80. Note that many participants of ImageNet Large Scale Visual Recognition Challenge 2010 [3] achieve better performance than ours, which may owe to the additional features extracted by themselves. Importantly, the running time of our proposed framework increases slowly when the number of training images rises. Even when the number of training images reaches up to 600,000, the average time to predict the label of one image is only 1.24 second.

Table 6: The time (unit: hour) and flat cost of Hash-accelerated SISO on ImageNet dataset

Training Image Number	Total Time	Flat Cost
200,000	3.84	0.869
400,000	10.60	0.835
600,000	15.58	0.808
800,000	17.55	0.791
1,000,000	19.14	0.776
1,200,000	21.07	0.764

For comparison, we again randomly select 100 testing images and predict their labels by applying the LASSO and SISO over the whole training image dataset. Table 7 indicates that the average time of LASSO and SISO for prediction are about 3445.20 seconds and 45.82 seconds respectively. When compared with Hash-accelerated SISO, our proposed framework can significantly accelerate the speed of original LASSO and SISO by more than 2,000 and 30 times, respectively.

Table 7: The average time (unit: second) of LASSO, SISO and Hash-accelerated SISO on ImageNet dataset

Algorithm	Average Time	Ratio[1]
LASSO	3445.20	2266.58
SISO	45.82	30.14
Hash-accelerated SISO	1.52	1

1. $Ratio = \frac{Total\ Time\ of\ One\ Method}{Total\ Time\ of\ Hash\text{-}accelerated\ SISO}$

5. CONCLUSION AND FUTURE WORK

This paper aims to improve the retrieval system via the precise annotations of images. To effectively and efficiently annotate images, this paper turns to accelerate sparse coding optimization in the context of large-scale image annotation. Distinguished from the previous approaches, our proposed solution well utilizes the fact that the reconstruction coefficient vector is sparse in large-scale dataset, and solves the large-scale sparse coding problem by solving a series of much smaller-scale subproblems. The solution includes two phases, i.e., the shrinkage phase and the expansion phase. As the main computational burden is in the expansion phase, to further accelerate the optimization, we utilize the LSH technique to select new active variables more efficiently. Extensive experiments of large-scale image annotation problem show that the proposed solution is superior in both effectiveness and efficiency.

One of the promising future directions is to further evaluate the efficiency of our proposed solution on even larger-scale web multimedia dataset, and also evaluate whether other graph-based algorithms may benefit from the efficiently derived l_1-graph over the complete data by using the proposed solution instead of approximate l_1-graph over KNN as in [30]. It is also noted that LSH can only return the approximate nearest neighbors, thus it is valuable to investigate whether we can further improve the effectiveness of the proposed solution through incorporating other more advanced hashing approaches, e.g. spectral hashing [35].

6. ACKNOWLEDGMENTS

This research is partially supported by the Singapore National Research Foundation under its International Research Centre @Singapore Funding Initiative and administered by the IDM Programme Office.

7. REFERENCES

[1] M. Aharon, M. Elad, and A.M. Bruckstein. K-svd and its non-negative variant for dictionary design. In *SPIE*, 2005.

[2] A. Andoni and P. Indyk. Near-optimal hashing algorithms for approximate nearest neighbor in high dimensions. In *FOCS*, 2006.

[3] A. Berg, Deng J., and Li F.F. *ImageNet Large Scale Visual Recognition Challenge 2010 (ILSVRC2010)*. Stanford Vision Lab, 2010.

[4] G. Carneiro, A.B. Chan, P.J. Moreno, and N. Vasconcelos. Supervised learning of semantic classes for image annotation and retrieval. *TPAMI*, 29(3):394–410, 2007.

[5] S.S. Chen, D.L. Donoho, and M.A. Saunders. Atomic decomposition by basis pursuit. *SIAM review*, 43(1):129–159, 2001.

[6] X. Chen, Y. Mu, S. Yan, and T. Chua. Efficient large-scale image annotation by probabilistic collaborative multi-label propagation. In *MM*, 2010.

[7] X. Chen, X. Yuan, Q. Chen, S. Yan, and T. Chua. Multi-label visual classification with label exclusive context. In *ICCV*, 2011.

[8] T.S. Chua, J. Tang, R. Hong, H. Li, Z. Luo, and Y. Zheng. Nus-wide: A real-world web image database from national university of singapore. In *CIVR*, 2009.

[9] R. Collobert, F. Sinz, J. Weston, and L. Bottou. Large scale transductive svms. *JMLR*, 7:1687–1712, 2006.

[10] C. Cusano, G. Ciocca, and R. Schettini. Image annotation using svm. In *SPIE*. Citeseer, 2004.

[11] M. Datar, N. Immorlica, P. Indyk, and V.S. Mirrokni. Locality-sensitive hashing scheme based on p-stable distributions. In *SoCG*, 2004.

[12] D. Donoho and M. Elad. Optimally sparse representation in general (nonorthogonal) dictionaries via l1 minimization. In *Proc. Natl. Acad. Sci. USA*, 2003.

[13] J. Duchi, S. Shalev-Shwartz, Y. Singer, and T. Chandra. Efficient projections onto the l 1-ball for learning in high dimensions. In *ICML*, 2008.

[14] B. Efron, T. Hastie, I. Johnstone, and R. Tibshirani. Least angle regression. *The Annals of Statistics*, 32(2):407–499, 2004.

[15] S. Feng, R. Manmatha, and V. Lavrenko. Multiple bernoulli relevance models for image and video annotation. In *CVPR*, 2004.

[16] J.F. He, J.Y. Feng, X.L. Liu, T. Cheng, T.H. Lin, H. Chung, and S.F. Chang. Mobile product search with bag of hash bits and boundary reranking. In *CVPR*, 2012.

[17] J. Hiriart-Urruty and C. Lemaréchal. *Fundamentals of convex analysis*. Springer Verlag, 2001.

[18] P. Indyk and R. Motwani. Approximate nearest neighbors: towards removing the curse of dimensionality. In *STOC*, 1998.

[19] K. Koh, S. Kim, and S. Boyd. An interior-point method for large-scale l1-regularized logistic regression. *JMLR*, 8(8):1519–1555, 2007.

[20] H. Lee, A. Battle, R. Raina, and A.Y. Ng. Efficient sparse coding algorithms. In *NIPS*, 2007.

[21] D. Liu, X.S. Hua, L. Yang, M. Wang, and H.J. Zhang. Tag ranking. In *WWW*, 2009.

[22] J. Liu, S. Ji, and J. Ye. *SLEP: Sparse Learning with Efficient Projections*. Arizona State University, 2009.

[23] J. Liu and J. Ye. Efficient euclidean projections in linear time. In *ICML*, 2009.

[24] S. Liu, Z. Song, G.C. Liu, C.S. Xu, H.Q. Lu, and S.C. Yan. Street-to-shop: Cross-scenario clothing retrieval via parts alignment and auxiliary set. In *CVPR*, 2012.

[25] J. Lu, J. Zhou, J. Wang, T. Mei, X. Hua, and S. Li. Image search results refinement via outlier detection using deep contexts. In *CVPR*, 2012.

[26] J. Mairal, F. Bach, J. Ponce, G. Sapiro, and A. Zisserman. Discriminative learned dictionaries for local image analysis. In *CVPR*, 2008.

[27] S.G. Mallat and Z. Zhang. Matching pursuits with time-frequency dictionaries. *IEEE Tran. Signal Process.*, 41(12):3397–3415, 1993.

[28] Y.C. Pati, R. Rezaiifar, and PS Krishnaprasad. Orthogonal matching pursuit: Recursive function approximation with applications to wavelet decomposition. In *Asilomar Conference on Signals, Systems and Computers*, pages 40–44, 1993.

[29] A. Subramanya and J. Bilmes. Entropic graph regularization in non-parametric semi-supervised classification. In *NIPS*, 2009.

[30] J. Tang, S. Yan, R. Hong, G.J. Qi, and T.S. Chua. Inferring semantic concepts from community-contributed images and noisy tags. In *ACM MM*, 2009.

[31] R. Tibshirani. Regression shrinkage and selection via the lasso. *Journal of the Royal Statistical Society. Series B (Methodological)*, 58:267–288, 1996.

[32] C. Wang, D. Blei, and F.F. Li. Simultaneous image classification and annotation. In *CVPR*, 2009.

[33] C. Wang, S. Yan, L. Zhang, and H. Zhang. Multi-label sparse coding for automatic image annotation. In *CVPR*, 2009.

[34] F. Wang, C. Zhang, H.C. Shen, and J. Wang. Semi-supervised classification using linear neighborhood propagation. In *CVPR*, 2006.

[35] Y. Weiss, A. Torralba, and R. Fergus. Spectral hashing. In *NIPS*, 2008.

[36] D. Zhou, O. Bousquet, T.N. Lal, J. Weston, and B. Schölkopf. Learning with local and global consistency. In *NIPS*, 2004.

Learning with Limited and Noisy Tagging

Yingming Li[†], Zhongang Qi[†], Zhongfei (Mark) Zhang, and Ming Yang
Dept. of ISEE, Zhejiang University, China
{liymn, zhongangqi, zhongfei, cauchym}@zju.edu.cn

ABSTRACT

With the rapid development of social networks, tagging has become an important means responsible for such rapid development. A robust tagging method must have the capability to meet the two challenging requirements: limited labeled training samples and noisy labeled training samples. In this paper, we investigate this challenging problem of learning with limited and noisy tagging and propose a discriminative model, called SpSVM-MC, that exploits both labeled and unlabeled data through a semi-parametric regularization and takes advantage of the multi-label constraints into the optimization. While SpSVM-MC is a general method for learning with limited and noisy tagging, in the evaluations we focus on the specific application of noisy image tagging with limited labeled training samples on a benchmark dataset. Theoretical analysis and extensive evaluations in comparison with state-of-the-art literature demonstrate that SpSVM-MC outstands with a superior performance.

Categories and Subject Descriptors

H.3.3 [**Information Storage and Retrieval**]: Information Search and Retrieval—*Retrieval models*; H.2.8 [**Database Management**]: Database Applications—*Data mining, Image databases*

General Terms

Algorithms, experimentation

Keywords

Noisy image tagging, semi-parametric regularization, multi-label constraint, limited labels, discriminative method

1. INTRODUCTION

With the rapid development of social networks, recent years have witnessed fast booming photo sharing websites, such as Flickr and Picasa. These websites allow users to upload personal images and describe the image contents with tags. In particular, appropriate tags allow users to conveniently organize and access to those shared images. Thus, tagging is considered as an important means for the development of multimedia social networks. However, with the typically explosive amount of data to be tagged, it is very time-consuming and labor-intensive for manually labeling data. Consequently, machine learning techniques for image tagging have become an effective alternative attracting much attention in the literature. In order to reduce the manual effort, many semi-supervised learning or active learning methods have been developed. Two requirements are then immediately imposed for a robust image-tagging method.

First, since it is expensive to obtain labeled training samples, it is expected that a robust image tagging method need only a small portion of the labeled training samples. Second, even with the manual labeling of images, there is no guarantee that the provided labels are always correct as human may make mistakes, not even speaking that in many applications the labeled training samples are generated by machine from other sources such as the surrounding text in which case the given labels are very error-prone. On the other hand, even with manual labeling, it is always the case that given labels are not complete to describe everything in an image as human beings typically do not have the patience to give labels for all the details of an image. Both scenarios contribute to the typically *noisy* labeled training samples where noisy samples mean either samples are incomplete and/or samples are error-prone.

This paper is motivated to address both such requirements for developing a robust tagging method making use of the unlabeled data through a semi-parametric regularization. The geometric structure of the unlabeled data is encoded through a specific family of parametric functions. In particular, we consider the case where the un-

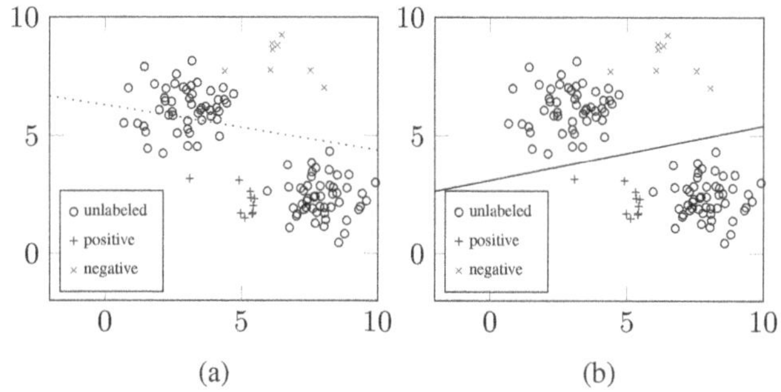

Figure 1: (a) The decision plane learned only from labeled data; (b) The decision plane learned by semi-parametric regularization with the labeled and unlabeled data.

[†]Contributed equally

MM'13, October 21–25, 2013, Barcelona, Spain.
Copyright 2013 ACM 978-1-4503-2404-5/13/10 ...$15.00.
http://dx.doi.org/10.1145/2502081.2502111.

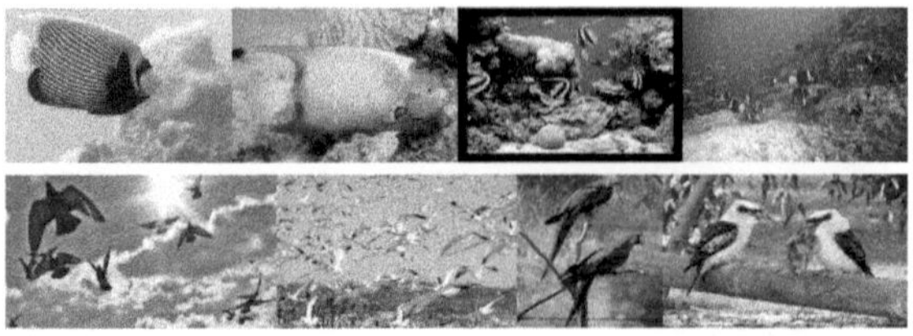

Figure 2: Exemplar images with multiple tags

labeled data are expected to determine the marginal distribution of the data if there is a small set of labeled data available along with a relatively large set of unlabeled data. Thus, we must consider the geometric structure of the marginal distribution of the whole data including the labeled data and the unlabeled data. An example is shown in Figure 1 for the binary classification problem. Moreover, in this paper we obtain these parametric functions by applying the Kernel Principal Component Analysis (KPCA) algorithm [15] to the whole data. Since in KPCA the kernel functions in the Reproducing Kernel Hilbert Space (RKHS) are used to extract important principal components, the geometric structure of the marginal distribution of the data can be obtained by the learned parametric functions. We extend the original RKHS to a discriminative method by these parametric functions learned from the whole data. Specifically, this extension is called semi-parametric regularized discriminative method.

Furthermore, we incorporate the information from the multi-label space into the semi-parametric regularized discriminative method to make it adaptive to the noisy data. In general the N-class classification problem can always be decomposed into N binary classification problems in the one-vs-all (OVA) mode. It is easy to understand that the more tags the data are given, the more information the tag space contains. However, the majority of the discriminative methods for the multi-label classification problem only consider the multi-label space as the classification target, and fail to make use of the information contained in the multi-label space effectively. Especially in the OVA mode, these classification methods only consider one tag at a time as the classification target and at the same time completely ignore the rest of the tags. In this paper, we explicitly consider all the given tags simultaneously as an additional feature which further helps improve the classification performance. We claim that when tags contain noise, taking advantage of all the given tags mitigates the influence of the noise compared with only considering one tag at a time as the classification target. In general, it is believed that most tags are correct, although there are many incorrect and missing tags. Thus, these tags can provide additional information to help improve the training accuracy even when instances may be incorrectly labeled in the OVA mode. Figure 2 shows exemplar images with multiple tags. The images in the first row in Figure 2, which are all tagged as *fish*, always have the accompanied tags of *water, coral,* and *ocean*, while the images in the second row in Figure 2, which are all tagged as *bird*, always have the accompanied tags of *sky, cloud, grass*, and *tree*. Obviously, these accompanied tags can be utilized as an additional feature to help better distinguish images tagged as *fish* from images tagged as *bird*.

In this paper we study the problem of learning with limited and noisy tagging not only exploiting the unlabeled data based on semi-parametric regularization but also denoising the noisy tagging by incorporating the multi-label space information. Even though there is recent literature to address the semi-supervised learning and noisy tagging separately, combining them as a single, overall problem and developing a synergistic solution to address them together in a single framework are still significant and challenging. We first propose a semi-parametric regularized discriminative method to encode the geometric structure of labeled and unlabeled data. Then we propose a distance measure to compute the distance between instances in the multi-label space. Consequently, a new framework is proposed to incorporate the information of the multi-label space into the semi-parametric regularized discriminative classification method, which we call Semi-parametric regularized Support Vector Machine with Multi-label Constraint (SpSVM-MC). While SpSVM-MC is a general method, we demonstrate through extensive evaluations in the application of image tagging using real data that the proposed method performs well in comparison with the peer methods in the literature as an effective and promising solution to the problem of learning with limited and noisy image tagging.

2. RELATED WORK

We begin by reviewing the literature on regularization, and then review the related work on denoising methods for classification.

Many machine learning algorithms including Support Vector Machine (SVM) and Regularized Least Square (RLS) can be interpreted as examples of regularization [14]. Research work [27] on sparse learning mainly exploits one norm as the regularization term. Semi-parametric regularization is also an attractive solution for many practical problems [13, 24, 2, 8]. Sun et al. [16] propose a manifold regularization based semi-supervised semi-parametric regression method. Bouboulis et al. [2] propose an image denoising method by employing a semi-parametric regularization.

Many existing semi-supervised learning methods exploit the regularization terms on the unlabeled data. Transductive SVM [20, 22] may be considered as SVM with an additional regularization term on the unlabeled data. Szummer and Jaakkola [17] propose an information regularization framework to minimize the mutual information on multiple overlapping regions covering the data space. Grandvalet and Bengio [7] use the entropy on the unlabeled data as a regularizer.

The noise among the data is categorized into two types: attribute noise and class noise [28]. In this paper, we focus on eliminating the bad effect raised by the class noise. There are a number of denoising methods for classification; they can be further classified into two categories: filtered preprocessing of the data and robust design of the algorithms. In the former category, filtered preprocessing is developed to remove the noise from the training set as much as possible [19, 29]. For the latter category, robust algorithms are designed to reduce the impact of the noise in the classification [9, 11, 18].

Most of the existing discriminative classification methods to the multi-label problem only consider one tag at a time as the classification target, and completely ignore the rest of the given tags at the same time. Boutell et al. [3] introduce several transformation methods that map the multi-label learning problem into the single-label classification problem. A more complicated situation beyond the multi-label learning problem is when an image is represented as a bag of instances, and belongs to a bag of classes[25]. Hence, the original annotation problem becomes a multi-instance and multi-label learning problem. Zhou and Zhang [25] solve this multi-instance and multi-label learning problem by mapping it into a single-instance and multi-label learning problem. The representative technique for this category of approaches is the classification technique SVM, which demonstrates a strong discrimination power [6, 12, 23]. Yang et al. [23] propose an asymmetrical support vector machine for region-based image annotation. There has been work on image tag refinement in the literature [21, 26, 10]. Wang et al.

[21] address the tag optimization problem given the tagging labels of images obtained by a classifier. Zhu et al. [26] propose a classification method to address the noisy tagging problem. Compared with the existing work, our work takes advantage of all the given multiple tags simultaneously not only as the classification target but also as an additional feature.

Among the existing work, the closest work to ours is the semi-parametric regularization method by Guo et al. [8]. We note that the difference from our work is significant. First, the two differ in theory. The essence of semi-parametric regularization lies in the strategy of regularized risk functional. While the regularized risk functional of [8] takes the same form as that in Chapter 4 of [14], we make a fundamental extension of the approach in [14] by adding a regularization constraint $\|h\|_{\Psi}^2$ to parametric functions in Eq. 6. Indeed, our semi-parametric regularization is a variation of the mixed semi-parametric regularization defined in [14]. Second, the two differ in the way of optimization. The new regularized risk functional makes our optimization problem different from the existing work and this plays a key role in the efficiency and accuracy of an algorithm.

3. LEARNING WITH LIMITED TAGGING

Since the labeled data are expensive to acquire, we utilize the information contained in the plentiful unlabeled data which better exploits the geometric structure of the data to solve the problem of learning with limited tagging. We begin with the brief review of the regularized risk functional. Then we propose a method which treats the information contained in the unlabeled data as the additional prior knowledge incorporated into the regularized risk functional to satisfy the first requirement that only a small portion of the labeled training samples are needed to learn a robust classifier.

3.1 Regularized Risk Functional

Suppose that there is a probability distribution F on $\mathcal{X} \times \mathcal{Y}$, $\mathcal{X} \subset \mathbb{R}^n$ according to which data are generated. We assume that the given data consist of l labeled data points $(\mathbf{x}_i, y_i)$, $1 \le i \le l$ which are generated according to F. In this paper, we assume the binary classification problem where the labels y_i, $1 \le i \le l$, are binary, i.e., $y_i = \pm 1$.

If we have no knowledge about the test patterns, we should minimize the expected error over all the possible training patterns. Hence we must minimize the expected loss called risk functional with respect to F and L

$$\mathcal{R}[f] = \int L(\mathbf{x}, y, f(\mathbf{x}))dF(\mathbf{x}, y) \tag{1}$$

where L is a loss function. A variety of loss functions have been considered in the literature. The simplest loss function is $0/1$ loss

$$L(\mathbf{x}_i, y_i, f(\mathbf{x}_i)) = \begin{cases} 0 & \text{if} \quad y_i = f(\mathbf{x}_i) \\ 1 & \text{if} \quad y_i \neq f(\mathbf{x}_i) \end{cases} \tag{2}$$

For the loss function Eq. 2, Eq. 1 determines the probability of a classification error for any decision function f. Unfortunately, in most applications the probability distribution F is unknown. All we have at our disposal is the actual training data $(\mathbf{x}_i, y_i)$, $1 \le i \le l$. What one usually does is to consider the empirical estimate of the risk functional [20], which is defined as

$$\mathcal{R}_{emp}[f] = \frac{1}{l} \sum_{i=1}^{l} L(\mathbf{x}_i, y_i, f(\mathbf{x}_i)) \tag{3}$$

Minimizing the empirical risk Eq. 3 may lead to numerical instabilities and a bad generalization performance [14]. A possible solution is to add a stabilization (regularization) term $\Omega[f]$ to the empirical risk functional. This leads to a better conditioning of the problem. Thus, we consider the following class of regularized risk functionals

$$\mathcal{R}_{reg}[f] = \mathcal{R}_{emp}[f] + \gamma\Omega[f]$$

where $\gamma > 0$ is the regularization parameter which specifies the tradeoff between the minimization of $R_{emp}[f]$ and the smoothness or simplicity enforced by a small $\Omega[f]$. When we equivalently think of the feature space as a reproducing kernel Hilbert space, $\Omega[f]$ is the norm of the RKHS representation of the feature space

$$\Omega[f] = \|f\|_K^2$$

where $\|\cdot\|_K$ is the norm in the RKHS $\mathcal{H}_K$ associated with the kernel K. In this case, we equivalently minimize

$$f^* = \arg\min_{f \in \mathcal{H}_K} \sum_{i=1}^{l} L(\mathbf{x}_i, y_i, f(\mathbf{x}_i)) + \gamma\|f\|_K^2 \tag{4}$$

The solution to Eq. 4 is determined by the loss function L and the kernel K. The following classic Representer Theorem [14] states that the solution to the minimization problem in Eq. 4 exists in $\mathcal{H}_K$ and gives the explicit form of a minimizer.

THEOREM 1. *Denote by $\Omega : [0, \infty) \to \mathbb{R}$ a strictly monotonically increasing function, by $\mathcal{X}$ a set, and by $\Lambda : (\mathcal{X} \times \mathbb{R}^2)^l \to \mathbb{R} \cup \{\infty\}$ an arbitrary loss function. Then each minimizer $f \in \mathcal{H}_K$ of the regularized risk*

$$\Lambda((\mathbf{x}_1, y_1, f(\mathbf{x}_1)), \ldots, (\mathbf{x}_l, y_l, f(\mathbf{x}_l))) + \Omega(\|f\|_K)$$

admits a representation of the form

$$f(\mathbf{x}) = \sum_{i=1}^{l} \alpha_i K(\mathbf{x}_i, \mathbf{x}) \tag{5}$$

with $\alpha_i \in \mathbb{R}$.

According to Theorem 1, we may use regularizers other than $\Omega(\|f\|_K) = \gamma\|f\|_K^2$ which is a strictly monotonic increasing function of $\|f\|_K$. This allows us in principle to design algorithms that are more closely aligned with the recommendations given by the bounds derived from the statistical learning theory. Moreover, given the loss function L and the kernel K, if we use the regularizer $\Omega(\|f\|_K) = \gamma\|f\|_K^2$, we could substitute Eq. 5 into Eq. 4 to obtain a minimization problem of the variables α_i, $1 \le i \le l$.

3.2 Semi-parametric Regularization Learning

In this section, we first propose a semi-parametric regularization approach by including a family of parametric functions. Then we demonstrate how to make use of the whole data including labeled and unlabeled data to obtain the parametric functions. Based on the semi-parametric regularization, we propose a novel semi-parametric regularized SVM to solve the problem of learning with limited tagging.

3.2.1 Semi-parametric Regularization

In the case that the training set only contains a small portion of the labeled samples, the plentiful unlabeled samples may contain some additional knowledge beyond the knowledge which the labeled ones contain. This additional knowledge can be taken advantage of to better exploit the geometric structure of the data. One method to utilize this additional knowledge is to introduce some parametric functions added into the regularized risk functional to refine the decision function.

Suppose that this additional prior knowledge is described as a family of parametric functions $\{\psi_p\}_{p=1}^M : \mathcal{X} \to \mathbb{R}$. These parametric functions may be incorporated into the regularized risk functional in Eq. 4 in different ways. In this paper we assume that $\text{span}\{\psi_p\} \triangleq \Psi \subset \mathcal{H}_K^\perp$ has the norm $\|\cdot\|_\Psi$, in which $\mathcal{H}_K^\perp$ is the complementary space of $\mathcal{H}_K$, and minimize the following regularized risk functional

$$\bar{f}^* = \arg\min_{\bar{f}} \sum_{i=1}^{l} L(\mathbf{x}_i, y_i, \bar{f}(\mathbf{x}_i)) + \gamma_1 \|f\|_K^2 + \gamma_2 \|h\|_\Psi^2 \quad (6)$$

where $\bar{f} \triangleq f + h$ with $f \in \mathcal{H}_K$ and $h \in \Psi$. Consequently, we extend the original RKHS $\mathcal{H}_K$ by including a family of parametric functions ψ_p. The following semiparametric representer theorem is an immediate extension of Theorem 1, that can be easily proven.

THEOREM 2. *Denote by $\Omega : [0,\infty) \times [0,\infty) \to \mathbb{R}$ a strictly monotonically increasing function, by $\mathcal{X}$ a set, and by $\Lambda : (\mathcal{X} \times \mathbb{R}^2)^l \to \mathbb{R} \cup \{\infty\}$ an arbitrary loss function. Let $\{\psi_p\}_{p=1}^M : \mathcal{X} \to \mathbb{R}$ be a set of M real valued functions with the property that the $l \times M$ matrix $(\psi_p(\mathbf{x}_i))_{ip}$ has rank M and span$\{\psi_p\} \triangleq \Psi \subset \mathcal{H}_K^\perp$ has the norm $\|\cdot\|_\Psi$. Then for any $\bar{f} \triangleq f + h$ with $f \in \mathcal{H}_K$ and $h \in \Psi$, minimizing the regularized risk*

$$\Lambda((\mathbf{x}_1, y_1, \bar{f}(\mathbf{x}_1)), \ldots, (\mathbf{x}_l, y_l, \bar{f}(\mathbf{x}_l))) + \Omega(\|f\|_K, \|h\|_\Psi)$$

admits a representation of the form

$$\bar{f}(\mathbf{x}) = \sum_{i=1}^{l} \alpha_i K(\mathbf{x}_i, \mathbf{x}) + \sum_{p=1}^{M} \beta_p \psi_p(\mathbf{x}) \quad (7)$$

with $\alpha_i, \beta_p \in \mathbb{R}$.

In Theorem 2, the parametric functions $\{\psi_p\}_{p=1}^M$ can be any functions. In this paper, the parametric function is learned from the whole data including the labeled and unlabeled data to incorporate the information contained in the unlabeled data. The details of the method to learn the parametric functions are discussed in Section 3.2.2. We denote by $\psi_p(\mathbf{x})$ the parametric function and by β_p the corresponding coefficient. Thus, the minimizer of Eq. 6 is

$$\bar{f}^*(\mathbf{x}) = \sum_{i=1}^{l} \alpha_i^* K(\mathbf{x}_i, \mathbf{x}) + \sum_{p=1}^{M} \beta_p^* \psi_p(\mathbf{x}) \quad (8)$$

where K is the kernel in the original RKHS $\mathcal{H}_K$.

3.2.2 Learning Parametric Functions

$\{\psi_p(\mathbf{x})\}_{p=1}^M$ is obtained by applying the KPCA algorithm [15] to the whole data set including l labeled data points $(\mathbf{x}_i, y_i)$, $1 \le i \le l$ and v unlabeled data points $\mathbf{x}_i$, $l+1 \le i \le l+v$. In other words, we consider the unlabeled data points as the additional prior knowledge to obtain the parametric functions, which make our approach different from a general semi-supervised learning algorithm. KPCA finds the principal axes in the feature space which carry more variance than any other directions by diagonalizing the covariance matrix

$$C = \frac{1}{l+v} \sum_{j=1}^{l+v} \phi(\mathbf{x}_j)\phi(\mathbf{x}_j)^T \quad (9)$$

where ϕ is a mapping function in the RKHS. To find the principal axes, we solve the eigenvalue problem, $C\mathbf{U} = \mathbf{U}\Xi$. Let Ξ denote the M largest eigenvalues and $\mathbf{U}$ the corresponding eigenvector space. Substituting Eq. 9 to this equation, we note that all solutions

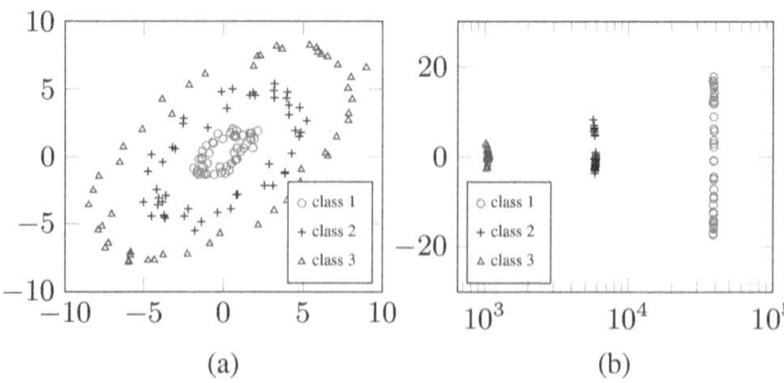

Figure 3: (a) Input points before kernel PCA; (b) Output after kernel PCA, with Gaussian kernel.

$\mathbf{U}$ lie in the span of $\phi(\mathbf{x}_1), \ldots, \phi(\mathbf{x}_{l+v})$. There exist coefficients $\theta_1, \ldots, \theta_{l+v}$ such that

$$\mathbf{U} = \sum_{i=1}^{l+v} \theta_i \phi(\mathbf{x}_i) \quad (10)$$

Given the data point $\mathbf{x}$, the projection onto the principal axes is given by $\phi(\mathbf{x})^T\mathbf{U}$. Consequently, we let $\psi(\mathbf{x}) = \phi(\mathbf{x})^T\mathbf{U}$. Fig. 3 shows an illustrative example for a classification problem in which we wish to use KPCA to identify three concentric clouds of points. As shown in this example, the first principal component is sufficient to distinguish the different groups. From this example, it is clear that the data points projected onto the most important principal axis still keep the original neighborhood relationship. In general, after projection on the principal axes, similar data points stay close and dissimilar data points are kept far away from each other. In the proposed model, we choose the top M largest eigenvalues and the corresponding eigenvectors from the results of KPCA to learn the parametric function for the training data.

3.2.3 Semi-parametric Regularized Support Vector Machine

Based on the semi-parametric regularization, a semi-parametric regularized SVM is proposed to solve the problem of learning with limited tagging. We first review the SVM approach to the binary classification problem which is the focus of this paper. In the binary classification problem, the classic SVM attempts to solve the following optimization problem on the labeled data.

$$\begin{aligned} &\min \frac{1}{2}\|\mathbf{w}\|^2 + C\sum_{i=1}^{l} \xi_i \\ &s.t.\ y_i(\langle \mathbf{w}, \phi(\mathbf{x}_i)\rangle + b) \ge 1 - \xi_i \\ &\xi_i \ge 0 \ \ i = 1, \ldots, l \end{aligned} \quad (11)$$

where ϕ is a nonlinear mapping function determined by the kernel and b is a regularized term.

Again, the solution is given by

$$f^*(\mathbf{x}) = \langle \mathbf{w}^*, \phi(\mathbf{x})\rangle + b^* = \sum_{i=1}^{l} \alpha_i^* K(\mathbf{x}_i, \mathbf{x}) + b^*$$

To solve Eq. 11 we introduce one Lagrange multiplier for each constraint in Eq. 11 using the Lagrange multipliers technique and obtain a quadratic dual problem of the Lagrange multipliers.

$$\min \frac{1}{2}\sum_{i,j=1}^{l} y_i y_j \mu_i \mu_j K(\mathbf{x}_i, \mathbf{x}_j) - \sum_{i=1}^{l} \mu_i$$
$$s.t. \sum_{i=1}^{l} \mu_i y_i = 0$$
$$0 \le \mu_i \le C,\ i = 1, \dots, l \tag{12}$$

where μ_i is the Lagrange multiplier.

We have $w^* = \sum_{i=1}^{l} \mu_i y_i \phi(\mathbf{x}_i)$ from the solution to Eq. 12. Note that the following conditions must be satisfied according to the Karush-Kuhn-Tucker theorem [20]:

$$\mu_i(y_i(\langle \mathbf{w}, \phi(\mathbf{x}_i)\rangle + b) + \xi_i - 1) = 0,\ i = 1, \dots, l \tag{13}$$

The optimal solution of b is determined by the above conditions.

Therefore, the solution is given by

$$f^*(\mathbf{x}) = \sum_{i=1}^{l} \alpha_i^* K(\mathbf{x}_i, \mathbf{x}) + b^*$$

where $\alpha_i^* = \mu_i y_i$.

The semi-parametric regularized SVM algorithm solves the optimization problem in Eq. 6:

$$\min \frac{1}{2}\|\mathbf{w}\|^2 + \frac{1}{2}\sum_{p=1}^{M} \beta_p^2 + C\sum_{i=1}^{l} \xi_i$$
$$s.t.\ y_i(\langle \mathbf{w}, \phi(\mathbf{x}_i)\rangle + b + \sum_{p=1}^{M} \beta_p \psi_p(\mathbf{x}_i)) \ge 1 - \xi_i$$
$$\xi_i \ge 0\ \ i = 1, \dots, l \tag{14}$$

4. LEARNING WITH LIMITED AND NOISY TAGGING

Since the noisy tagging exists in the training data in many real-world applications, we take advantage of the information contained in the multi-label space to satisfy the second requirement of utilizing the noisily tagged training data and at the same time mitigating the influence of the noise in the classification. In this section, we first propose a distance measure to compute the nearest neighbors for each instance in the multi-label space. Then we extend the semi-parametric risk functional by including the multi-label constraint. In particular, we propose a novel discriminative model called semi-parametric regularized SVM with multi-label constraint to solve the problem of learning with limited and noisy tagging.

4.1 A Distance Measure in the Multi-label Space

We denote a training dataset as $\mathcal{I}$. Each instance $I_i \in \mathcal{I}$ is labeled with various tags. The whole tag vocabulary for $\mathcal{I}$ forms the S-dimensional multi-label space $\mathcal{T}$. When one tag T_r ($1 \le r \le S$) is chosen as the classification target, the other tags can form the additional feature space of tags, denoted as $\mathcal{L}_r$. Obviously, the dimensionality of $\mathcal{L}_r$ is $S-1$. Let an S-dimensional vector $\mathbf{d}_i = (d_{i,1}, d_{i,2}, \dots, d_{i,S})'$ be the tag representation for I_i, where $d_{i,r} \in \{0,1\}, 1 \le r \le S$ represents the occurrence of the rth tag T_r for I_i. For each I_i and each T_r, we denote $y_{i,r}$ as the class label of I_i, where $y_{i,r} = 2 \cdot d_{i,r} - 1$. $I_i = (\mathbf{x}_i, \mathbf{d}_i)$, where $\mathbf{x}_i$ is the feature descriptor of I_i.

In general an N-class classification problem can always be decomposed into N binary classification problems in the OVA mode. From Eq. 14 we observe that in the OVA mode, the SVM-based methods only utilize one tag of the data at a time, and ignore the other tags the data contain at the same time.

In the OVA mode, when one tag T_r is chosen as the classification target, the other tags can form the additional feature space of the tags $\mathcal{L}_r$. It is a reasonable assumption that the similarity between the classification results of two instances is inversely proportional to the distance between the instances in $\mathcal{L}_r$. The closer the instances in $\mathcal{L}_r$ are, the higher the similarity in the classification is. We denote the feature vector of I_i in $\mathcal{L}_r$ as $\mathbf{t}_{i,r}$, where $\mathbf{t}_{i,r} = (d_{i,1}, \dots, d_{i,r-1}, d_{i,r+1}, \dots, d_{i,S})'$. However, measuring the distance for instances I_i and I_j in $\mathcal{L}_r$ by using $||\mathbf{t}_{i,r} - \mathbf{t}_{j,r}||_p$ directly is unreasonable in most cases, for it is based on the tag independence assumption, which is violated due to the potential existence of the relationships among the tags. Actually in the real-world scenarios, there may be various relationships among the tags, e.g., some tags may co-occur frequently, while other tags may never co-occur.

We discuss the relationship between T_r and T_k ($k \in \{1, \dots, r-1, r+1, \dots, S\}$) by examining the effect of $|d_{i,k} - d_{j,k}|$ ($\forall I_i,\ I_j \in \mathcal{I}$) on the distance between I_i and I_j in $\mathcal{L}_r$. When $|d_{i,k} - d_{j,k}| = 0$, the effect of $|d_{i,k} - d_{j,k}|$ on the distance between I_i and I_j in $\mathcal{L}_r$ is always zero; when $|d_{i,k} - d_{j,k}| = 1$, the effect of $|d_{i,k} - d_{j,k}|$ on the distance between I_i and I_j in $\mathcal{L}_r$ varies depending on the association degree between T_r and T_k. We describe the relationship between $|d_{i,k} - d_{j,k}| = 1$ and the value of $|d_{i,r} - d_{j,r}|$ as follows.

$$\begin{aligned}
&\forall I_i,\ I_j \in \mathcal{I}:\ |d_{i,k} - d_{j,k}| = 1 \Rightarrow |d_{i,r} - d_{j,r}| = 1,\\
&\text{when } \forall I_i \in \mathcal{I}:\ d_{i,k} = 0 \Rightarrow d_{i,r} = 0, \text{ and } d_{i,k} = 1 \Rightarrow d_{i,r} = 1\\
&\quad \text{or } \forall I_i \in \mathcal{I}:\ d_{i,k} = 0 \Rightarrow d_{i,r} = 1, \text{ and } d_{i,k} = 1 \Rightarrow d_{i,r} = 0\\
&\forall I_i,\ I_j \in \mathcal{I}:\ |d_{i,k} - d_{j,k}| = 1 \Rightarrow |d_{i,r} - d_{j,r}| = 0,\\
&\text{when } \forall I_i \in \mathcal{I}:\ d_{i,k} = 0 \Rightarrow d_{i,r} = 0, \text{ and } d_{i,k} = 1 \Rightarrow d_{i,r} = 0\\
&\quad \text{or } \forall I_i \in \mathcal{I}:\ d_{i,k} = 0 \Rightarrow d_{i,r} = 1, \text{ and } d_{i,k} = 1 \Rightarrow d_{i,r} = 1
\end{aligned} \tag{15}$$

We define $\mathcal{V}_r = \{I_i | d_{i,r} = 1\}$ ($I_i \in \mathcal{I}$ and $r \in \{1, 2, \dots, S\}$). Eq. 15 describes four special relationships between T_r and T_k. In reality, when T_r is distributed evenly in $\mathcal{V}_k$ and $\mathcal{I} - \mathcal{V}_k$, T_k is an undistinguished tag for T_r; when T_r is distributed unevenly in $\mathcal{V}_k$ and $\mathcal{I} - \mathcal{V}_k$, T_k is a distinguished tag for T_r. We show the conditional probabilities of $d_{i,r} = 0$ or 1 given $d_{i,k} = 0$ or 1 as follows, respectively.

$$\begin{aligned}
P_{00} &\triangleq P(d_{i,r} = 0 | d_{i,k} = 0) = \frac{|(\mathcal{I} - \mathcal{V}_r) \cap (\mathcal{I} - \mathcal{V}_k)|}{|\mathcal{I} - \mathcal{V}_k|}\\
P_{11} &\triangleq P(d_{i,r} = 1 | d_{i,k} = 1) = \frac{|\mathcal{V}_r \cap \mathcal{V}_k|}{|\mathcal{V}_k|}\\
P_{10} &\triangleq P(d_{i,r} = 1 | d_{i,k} = 0) = 1 - P_{00}\\
P_{01} &\triangleq P(d_{i,r} = 0 | d_{i,k} = 1) = 1 - P_{11}
\end{aligned} \tag{16}$$

From Eq. 15 to Eq. 16 we observe that, when the value of $P_{00} \cdot P_{11}$ or $P_{10} \cdot P_{01}$ is larger, the possibility that $|d_{i,k} - d_{j,k}| = 1$ leads to $|d_{i,r} - d_{j,r}| = 1$ is larger, and consequently the effect of $|d_{i,k} - d_{j,k}|$ on the distance between I_i and I_j in $\mathcal{L}_r$ is larger. When the value of $P_{00} \cdot P_{01}$ or $P_{10} \cdot P_{11}$ is larger, the possibility that $|d_{i,k} - d_{j,k}| = 1$ leads to $|d_{i,r} - d_{j,r}| = 0$ is larger, and consequently the effect of $|d_{i,k} - d_{j,k}|$ on the distance between I_i and I_j in $\mathcal{L}_r$ is smaller. We also note $P_{00} \cdot P_{11} + P_{10} \cdot P_{01} + P_{00} \cdot P_{01} + P_{10} \cdot P_{11} = 1$.

We denote the association degree vector for each tag T_r as $\mathbf{g}_r$, where $\mathbf{g}_r = (g_{r,1}, \dots, g_{r,r-1}, g_{r,r+1}, \dots, g_{r,S})'$, and the elements of $\mathbf{g}_r$ are the association degrees between tag T_r and the other tags. Hence, we define $g_{r,k}$ ($k \in \{1, \dots, r-1, r+1, \dots, S\}$) as follows:

$$g_{r,k} = P_{00} \cdot P_{11} + P_{10} \cdot P_{01} \tag{17}$$

Combining the feature vectors of the instances in $\mathcal{L}_r$ with the association degree vector for T_r, we obtain the distance between I_i and I_j in $\mathcal{L}_r$ as follows:

$$dis_r(I_i, I_j) = ||(\mathbf{t}_{i,r} - \mathbf{t}_{j,r}) \odot \mathbf{g}_r||_p \quad (18)$$

where $\odot$ indicates the Hadamard product between two vectors. The neighborhood of I_i in $\mathcal{L}_r$ (not including I_i itself) based on the distance measure in Eq. 18 is denoted as $\mathcal{N}_r(I_i)$. The size u of the neighborhood $\mathcal{N}_r(I_i)$ for each I_i is defined as the count of the nearest neighbors of I_i in $\mathcal{L}_r$. $\mathcal{N}_i^r \triangleq \{j | I_j \in \mathcal{N}_r(I_i)\}$.

4.2 Semi-parametric Regularization with Multi-label Constraints

The proposed method to take advantage of the information contained in the multi-label space is to introduce the multi-label constraints which minimize the difference between the classification results of each instance and its nearest neighbors in $\mathcal{L}_r$.

$$\forall_{i=1}^{l} \ and \ \forall j \in \mathcal{N}_i^r : \quad |\tilde{f}(\mathbf{x}_i) - \tilde{f}(\mathbf{x}_j)| \le \eta_{ij}, \ \ \eta_{ij} \ge 0 \quad (19)$$

Furthermore, we consider this constraint as a loss function defined as

$$\bar{L}(\tilde{f}(\mathbf{x}_i), \tilde{f}(\mathbf{x}_j)) = |\tilde{f}(\mathbf{x}_i) - \tilde{f}(\mathbf{x}_j)| \quad (20)$$

Combining these multi-label constraint with the semi-parametric regularized risk functional in Eq. 6, we have the following regularized risk functional

$$\tilde{f}^* = \arg\min_{\tilde{f}} \sum_{i=1}^{l} L(\mathbf{x}_i, y_i, \tilde{f}(\mathbf{x}_i)) + \sum_{i=1}^{l}\sum_{j\in\mathcal{N}_i^r} \bar{L}(\tilde{f}(\mathbf{x}_i), \tilde{f}(\mathbf{x}_j)) + \gamma_1 \|f\|_K^2 + \gamma_2 \|h\|_\Psi^2 \quad (21)$$

4.3 Semi-parametric Regularized SVM with Multi-label Constraints

In particular, in this paper we combine these multi-label constraints with the semi-parametric regularized SVM to solve the problem of learning with limited and noisy tagging. The optimization is as follows: where C and C^* are constants, and $C^* < C$.

$$\begin{aligned}
&\min_{\mathbf{w},\beta_k,b} \ \frac{1}{2}\|\mathbf{w}\|^2 + \frac{1}{2}\sum_{p=1}^{M}\beta_p^2 + C\sum_{i=1}^{l}\xi_i + \sum_{i=1}^{l}\sum_{j\in\mathcal{N}_i^r}\frac{C^*}{e^{dis_r(I_i,I_j)}}\cdot\eta_{ij}\\
&s.t. \ \forall_{i=1}^{l}: \ \ y_{i,r}\Big(\langle\mathbf{w},\phi(\mathbf{x}_i)\rangle + \sum_{p=1}^{M}\beta_p\psi_p(\mathbf{x}_i) + b\Big) \ge 1-\xi_i, \ \ \xi_i \ge 0\\
&\forall_{i=1}^{l} \ and \ \forall j \in \mathcal{N}_i^r : \ \ \eta_{ij} \ge 0,\\
&\Big|\langle\mathbf{w},\phi(\mathbf{x}_i)\rangle + \sum_{p=1}^{M}\beta_p\psi_p(\mathbf{x}_i) - \langle\mathbf{w},\phi(\mathbf{x}_j)\rangle - \sum_{p=1}^{M}\beta_p\psi_p(\mathbf{x}_j)\Big| \le \eta_{ij}
\end{aligned} \quad (22)$$

With the Lagrange multipliers, we have the target function

$$\begin{aligned}
\mathbf{L} = &\frac{1}{2}\|\mathbf{w}\|^2 + \frac{1}{2}\sum_{p=1}^{M}\beta_p^2 + C\sum_{i=1}^{l}\xi_i + \sum_{i=1}^{l}\sum_{j\in\mathcal{N}_i^r}\frac{C^*}{e^{dis_r(I_i,I_j)}}\cdot\eta_{ij}\\
&-\sum_{i=1}^{l}\mu_i\Big[y_{i,r}\Big(\langle\mathbf{w},\phi(\mathbf{x}_i)\rangle + \sum_{p=1}^{M}\beta_p\psi_p(\mathbf{x}_i) + b\Big) - 1 + \xi_i\Big]\\
&-\sum_{i=1}^{l}\tau_i\xi_i - \sum_{i=1}^{l}\sum_{j\in\mathcal{N}_i^r}\Big[\tau_{ij}\eta_{ij} + \lambda_{ij}^{+}\Big(\eta_{ij} - \langle\mathbf{w},\phi(\mathbf{x}_i)\rangle\\
&-\sum_{p=1}^{M}\beta_p\psi_p(\mathbf{x}_i) + \langle\mathbf{w},\phi(\mathbf{x}_j)\rangle + \sum_{p=1}^{M}\beta_p\psi_p(\mathbf{x}_j)\Big) + \lambda_{ij}^{-}\Big(\eta_{ij}\\
&+\langle\mathbf{w},\phi(\mathbf{x}_i)\rangle + \sum_{p=1}^{M}\beta_p\psi_p(\mathbf{x}_i) - \langle\mathbf{w},\phi(\mathbf{x}_j)\rangle - \sum_{p=1}^{M}\beta_p\psi_p(\mathbf{x}_j)\Big)\Big]
\end{aligned} \quad (23)$$

where μ_i, λ_{ij}^{+}, λ_{ij}^{-}, τ_i, and τ_{ij} are the Lagrange multipliers. We claim that if the KKT condition of Eq. 23 shown in Eq. 24 is satisfied, the solution to Eq. 22 is the same as that to its dual problem.

$$\begin{cases}
\nabla\mathbf{L} = 0\\
\forall_{i=1}^{l}: \ \tau_i\xi_i = 0,\\
\quad \mu_i\Big[y_{i,r}\Big(\langle\mathbf{w},\phi(\mathbf{x}_i)\rangle + \sum_{p=1}^{M}\beta_p\psi_p(\mathbf{x}_i) + b\Big) - 1 + \xi_i\Big] = 0,\\
\forall_{i=1}^{l} \ and \ \forall j \in \mathcal{N}_i^r: \ \tau_{ij}\eta_{ij} = 0,\\
\quad \lambda_{ij}^{+}\Big(\eta_{ij} - \langle\mathbf{w},\phi(\mathbf{x}_i)\rangle - \sum_{p=1}^{M}\beta_p\psi_p(\mathbf{x}_i)\\
\qquad + \langle\mathbf{w},\phi(\mathbf{x}_j)\rangle + \sum_{p=1}^{M}\beta_p\psi_p(\mathbf{x}_j)\Big) = 0,\\
\quad \lambda_{ij}^{-}\Big(\eta_{ij} + \langle\mathbf{w},\phi(\mathbf{x}_i)\rangle + \sum_{p=1}^{M}\beta_p\psi_p(\mathbf{x}_i)\\
\qquad - \langle\mathbf{w},\phi(\mathbf{x}_j)\rangle - \sum_{p=1}^{M}\beta_p\psi_p(\mathbf{x}_j)\Big) = 0.
\end{cases} \quad (24)$$

Let $\nu_{ij} = \lambda_{ij}^{+} - \lambda_{ij}^{-}$. From $\nabla\mathbf{L} = 0$, we have

$$\begin{cases}
\partial\mathbf{L}/\partial\mathbf{w} = 0 \Rightarrow\\
\quad \mathbf{w} = \sum_{i=1}^{l}\mu_i y_{i,r}\phi(\mathbf{x}_i) - \sum_{i=1}^{l}\sum_{j\in\mathcal{N}_i^r}\nu_{ij}\big(\phi(\mathbf{x}_i) - \phi(\mathbf{x}_j)\big),\\
\partial\mathbf{L}/\partial\beta_p = 0 \Rightarrow\\
\quad \forall_{p=1}^{M}: \ \ \beta_p = \sum_{i=1}^{l}\mu_i y_{i,r}\psi_p(\mathbf{x}_i)\\
\qquad - \sum_{i=1}^{l}\sum_{j\in\mathcal{N}_i^r}\nu_{ij}\big(\psi_p(\mathbf{x}_i) - \psi_p(\mathbf{x}_j)\big),\\
\partial\mathbf{L}/\partial b = 0 \Rightarrow \sum_{i=1}^{l}\mu_i y_{i,r} = 0,\\
\partial\mathbf{L}/\partial\xi_i = 0 \Rightarrow \forall_{i=1}^{l}: \ C - \mu_i - \tau_i = 0,\\
\partial\mathbf{L}/\partial\eta_{ij} = 0 \Rightarrow\\
\quad \forall_{i=1}^{l} \ and \ \forall j \in \mathcal{N}_i^r: \ \frac{C^*}{e^{dis_r(I_i,I_j)}} - \tau_{ij} - \lambda_{ij}^{+} - \lambda_{ij}^{-} = 0
\end{cases} \quad (25)$$

Substituting the results from Eq. 24 and Eq. 25 to Eq. 23, we obtain the dual problem of Eq. 22 as follows:

$$\begin{aligned}
\max \ &-\frac{1}{2}\sum_{i,q=1}^{l}\Big\{\Big[\mu_i y_{i,r}\phi(\mathbf{x}_i) - \sum_{j\in\mathcal{N}_i^r}\nu_{ij}\big(\phi(\mathbf{x}_i) - \phi(\mathbf{x}_j)\big)\Big]\\
&\cdot\Big[\mu_q y_{q,r}\phi(\mathbf{x}_q) - \sum_{h\in\mathcal{N}_q^r}\nu_{qh}\big(\phi(\mathbf{x}_q) - \phi(\mathbf{x}_h)\big)\Big]\Big\} + \sum_{i=1}^{l}\mu_i\\
&-\frac{1}{2}\sum_{p=1}^{M}\sum_{i,q=1}^{l}\Big\{\Big[\mu_i y_{i,r}\psi_p(\mathbf{x}_i) - \sum_{j\in\mathcal{N}_i^r}\nu_{ij}\big(\psi_p(\mathbf{x}_i) - \psi_p(\mathbf{x}_j)\big)\Big]\\
&\cdot\Big[\mu_q y_{q,r}\psi_p(\mathbf{x}_q) - \sum_{h\in\mathcal{N}_q^r}\nu_{qh}\big(\psi_p(\mathbf{x}_q) - \psi_p(\mathbf{x}_h)\big)\Big]\Big\}
\end{aligned}$$

$$s.t. \sum_{i=1}^{l} \mu_i y_{i,r} = 0; \qquad \forall_{i=1}^{l}: 0 \leq \mu_i \leq C; \tag{26}$$

$$\forall_{i=1}^{l}\, and\, \forall j \in \mathcal{N}_i^r: \lambda_{ij}^{+/-} \geq 0;\ \lambda_{ij}^{+} + \lambda_{ij}^{-} \leq \frac{C^*}{e^{dis_r(I_i, I_j)}}$$

Complexity Analysis. The computational complexity is similar to that of SVM. Specifically, the computational complexity of a typical SVM is $O(Q^3)$; the complexity of our method is $O(P^3)$, where Q and P are the sizes of support vectors for the two methods. $P \sim uQ$, where u is the size of the neighborhood in the paper. Practically, $u = 3$ is sufficient to secure a good performance.

5. EXPERIMENTS

5.1 Data and Parameter Setting

While SpSVM-MC is a general method for learning with limited and noisy tagging, we report the extensive evaluations in the specific application of noisy image tagging with limited labeled training samples. We compare our method with SVM, fuzzy SVM [9], SVM-HF [5], semi-supervised SVM (S^3VM) [1] and Guo (Semi-parametric regularization SVM) [8] using the noisily tagged training images combined with the plentiful untagged images to evaluate the performances of these methods.

The NUS-WIDE [4] image database is used in the experiments. It includes $269,648$ web images and 81 concepts which we treat as the ground truth tags. We choose the top 75 concepts whose numbers of positive examples are larger than 200 from the database to form the multi-label space $\mathcal{T}$. Hence, the dimensionality of the additional feature space of tags ($\mathcal{L}_r$) for each T_r is 74. For each concept, we randomly choose 150 positive examples and 150 negative examples as the training data. In the testing set, the numbers of the positive and negative examples are both 50. 10% examples are randomly selected from the training data to form the perfectly tagged training set, and the left 90% examples from the training data are used as the untagged training set. In the experiments, $s\%$ noise is added into both the positive and negative examples of the perfectly tagged training set to form the noisily tagged training set. We denote the 500-D bag of words feature based on SIFT descriptions as $\mathbf{V}1$, and denote the 1000-D bag of text words feature which describes the text information correlated to the images provided by the database as $\mathbf{V}2$. Two groups of comparative experiments are conducted to evaluate the performances of these methods, which use $\mathbf{V}1$ and $\mathbf{V}2$ as the feature of the data, respectively.

As we described before, the size u of the neighborhood $\mathcal{N}_r(I_i)$ for each I_i is the count of the nearest neighbors of I_i in $\mathcal{L}_r$. We define R as the ratio between the weight of the loss function for instances and the weight of the loss function for their nearest neighbors in the optimization. For SpSVM-MC, $R = C^*/C$. In the experiments, we choose the top M largest eigenvalues and the corresponding eigenvectors from the results of KPCA to learn the parametric function for the training data. $M = 0$ means that we learn no parametric function for the training data.

In addition, we design an experiment for SpSVM-MC with a different distribution on untagged training set. For this experiment, we reduce the numbers of negative samples on untagged training set to make sure that the proportion of positive and negative samples is 2:1. And we denote this experiment setup as SpSVM-MC(2:1).

5.2 Results and Discussions

For each tag T_r, let CT_r be the number of correctly predicted examples, GT_r be the number of the examples which actually have the tag as the ground truth, and PT_r be the number of all the predicted examples with the tag. Then the precision Pre_r, recall Rec_r, and $F1$ measure are defined as

$$Pre_r = \frac{CT_r}{PT_r}; \qquad Rec_r = \frac{CT_r}{GT_r};$$
$$F1_r = \frac{2Pre_r Rec_r}{Pre_r + Rec_r} = \frac{2CT_r}{PT_r + GT_r}$$

We evaluate the performances of the methods using the standard performance measures of Macro-$F1$ ($F1^a$) and Micro-$F1$ ($F1^i$). Macro-$F1$ averages the $F1$ measures on the predictions of different tags; Micro-$F1$ computes the $F1$ measure on the predictions of different labels as a whole.

$$F1^a = \frac{1}{S}\sum_{r=1}^{S} F1_r; \quad F1^i = \frac{2\sum_{r=1}^{S} CT_r}{\sum_{r=1}^{S} PT_r + \sum_{r=1}^{S} GT_r}$$

We randomly select 12 exemplar tags from the 75 concepts as the target tag T_r, and describe the top 10 tags (T_k) with the highest association degree $g_{r,k}$ for each T_r in Table 1. From Table 1 we observe that the most association tags (T_k) are different between different target tags (T_r). Some tags, e.g., *buildings* and *cityscape*, may co-occur frequently, while other tags, e.g., *sun* and *moon*, may never co-occur. All these relationships among the tags are utilized to determine the most distinguished tags for the given target tag. By using the distance measure we have proposed, the most distinguished tags are selected for each target tag T_r as the most important elements of the feature to measure the distances between instances in $\mathcal{L}_r$. This proposed distance measure is more reasonable and effective than directly using all the tags as the indiscriminate elements of the feature in finding the neighborhood of each instance in $\mathcal{L}_r$.

In Table 2, we summarize the $F1$ measure of the testing set when $M = 4$, $u = 3$, $R = 0.2$, and s is selected as 30, 25, 20, 15, 10, and 5 using feature $\mathbf{V}1$ and $\mathbf{V}2$ for SVM, fuzzy SVM, SVM-HF, S^3VM, Guo, SpSVM-MC, and SpSVM-MC(2:1), respectively. Note the impressive and robust performance of SpSVM-MC in comparison with those of the other methods with the rather limited labeled training samples (about 10%).

On the task of learning with limited and noisy image tagging, compared with our proposed method SpSVM-MC, SVM with the noisily tagged training set considers the training set as the perfectly tagged set and mistakenly takes the incorrect tags as perfect tags. Although fuzzy SVM considers the training set as noisily tagged dataset, it cannot take advantage of all the given multiple tags simultaneously as an additional feature as SpSVM-MC does. SVM-HF extends the original dataset with $|S|$ extra features containing the predictions of each binary classifier; then $|S|$ new binary classifiers are trained using the extended datasets. However, SVM-HF also considers the training set as the perfectly tagged set, and fails to make use of the original given multiple labels of each instance. Further, all the comparing methods, including SVM, fuzzy SVM, and SVM-HF, fail to take advantage of the information contained in the untagged data to improve the learning performance. S^3VM attempts to learn low-density separators by maximizing the margin over tagged and untagged examples, which utilizes the information contained in all the training data, including the tagged ones and the untagged ones. Guo makes use of the information contained in the untagged data through a semi-parametric regularization. However, S^3VM and Guo with the noisily tagged training set consider the training set as the perfectly tagged set and fail to take advantage of all the given multiple tags simultaneously as an additional feature as SpSVM-MC does. Consequently, from Table 2, we see that SpSVM-MC performs better than SVM, fuzzy SVM, SVM-HF, S^3VM and Guo on the task of learning with limited and noisy

Table 1: The top 10 tags (T_k) with the highest association degree $g_{r,k}$ for T_r.

Tag T_r	The top 10 tags (T_k) with the highest association degree $g_{r,k}$ for T_r
boats	harbor, reflection, lake, vehicle, ocean, water, town, sunset, beach, cityscape
buildings	cityscape, town, castle, house, nighttime, tower, street, window, harbor, temple
clouds	sunset, sun, rainbow, sky, valley, lake, mountain, beach, ocean, harbor
coral	fish, whales, swimmers, ocean, animal, water, beach, leaf, lake, flowers
flowers	plants, leaf, garden, grass, frost, coral, wedding, animal, sky, tree
horses	running, animal, grass, police, zebra, sand, cow, sports, frost, snow
military	plane, airport, police, vehicle, fire, road, clouds, harbor, sky, person
mountain	valley, glacier, rocks, snow, rainbow, lake, waterfall, reflection, clouds, house
reflection	harbor, lake, boats, water, bridge, sunset, cityscape, valley, nighttime, mountain
running	sports, horses, dog, zebra, elk, animal, beach, sand, grass, swimmers
sun	sunset, moon, ocean, lake, beach, reflection, harbor, tree, clouds, water
window	town, cars, vehicle, house, street, buildings, train, castle, police, airport

Table 2: The F1 measure for the testing set.

(a) The $F1^a \backslash F1^i$ for the testing set using **V**1 as the feature of the data.

	$F1^a \backslash F1^i$ *using feature* **V**1					
	$s=30$	$s=25$	$s=20$	$s=15$	$s=10$	$s=5$
SVM	0.5229\0.5631	0.5427\0.5810	0.5534\0.5856	0.5778\0.6050	0.6145\0.6345	0.6377\0.6504
Fuzzy SVM	0.5301\0.5734	0.5548\0.5915	0.5675\0.5892	0.5864\0.6193	0.6274\0.6408	0.6391\0.6535
SVM-HF	0.5254\0.5681	0.5463\0.5901	0.5697\0.5921	0.5813\0.6114	0.6230\0.6373	0.6385\0.6523
S^3VM	0.5460\0.5737	0.5610\0.5891	0.5712\0.5924	0.5979\0.6152	0.6304\0.6435	0.6429\0.6519
Guo	0.5260\0.5658	0.5480\0.5828	0.5579\0.5866	0.5815\0.6064	0.6146\0.6339	0.6353\0.6483
SpSVM-MC	**0.5641\0.5923**	**0.5743\0.6012**	**0.5822\0.6023**	**0.6179\0.6346**	**0.6379\0.6487**	**0.6456\0.6562**
SpSVM-MC(2:1)	**0.5633\0.5911**	**0.5636\0.5957**	**0.5844\0.6050**	**0.6215\0.6380**	**0.6416\0.6524**	**0.6500\0.6610**

(b) The $F1^a \backslash F1^i$ for the testing set using **V**2 as the feature of the data.

	$F1^a \backslash F1^i$ *using feature* **V**2					
	$s=30$	$s=25$	$s=20$	$s=15$	$s=10$	$s=5$
SVM	0.6438\0.6585	0.6789\0.6914	0.6872\0.7020	0.7180\0.7300	0.7703\0.7722	0.7953\0.7944
Fuzzy SVM	0.6521\0.6694	0.6863\0.6975	0.6932\0.7106	0.7260\0.7402	0.7799\0.7801	0.7970\0.7996
SVM-HF	0.6544\0.6663	0.6828\0.6948	0.6904\0.7041	0.7235\0.7340	0.7740\0.7751	0.7978\0.7968
S^3VM	0.6484\0.6640	0.6900\0.7027	0.7051\0.7173	0.7316\0.7404	0.7780\0.7797	0.8039\0.8035
Guo	0.6564\0.6696	0.6936\0.7051	0.7019\0.7136	0.7375\0.7456	0.7849\0.7852	0.8024\0.8011
SpSVM-MC	**0.6747\0.6931**	**0.7123\0.7295**	**0.7353\0.7492**	**0.7760\0.7784**	**0.7936\0.7945**	**0.8145\0.8116**
SpSVM-MC(2:1)	**0.6773\0.6966**	**0.7152\0.7315**	**0.7369\0.7504**	**0.7829\0.7840**	**0.7933\0.7940**	**0.8176\0.8139**

image annotation using either feature **V**1 or feature **V**2 when s is selected as 30, 25, 20, 15, 10, and 5, respectively. Further, based on the fact that SpSVM-MC(2:1) obtains the similar result as that of SpSVM-MC, it is shown that our method is capable of tackling with different kinds of distribution on untagged training set.

In general, Table 2 shows that the semi-parametric regularization which extends to the untagged data helps better exploit the geometric structure of the marginal distribution of the data, and taking advantage of all the given tags mitigates the influence of the noise compared with only considering one tag at a time as the classification target. Further, SpSVM-MC performs much better than the comparing methods when the noise ratio $s\%$ increases, which further verifies the robustness of SpSVM-MC.

We describe the $F1$ measure for the testing set as a function of M when $u=3$, $R=0.2$, and $s=20$ using feature **V**1 and feature **V**2 for SpSVM-MC in Figure 4(a) and Figure 5(a), respectively. From Figure 4(a) and Figure 5(a) we observe that the $F1$ measures for the testing set all increase when M increases, which shows that the semi-parametric regularization is helpful to further improve the performance of the classification by better exploiting the geometric structure of the marginal distribution of the data. The curves for the $F1$ measures of SpSVM-MC in Figure 4(a) and Figure 5(a) all exhibit their major elevation from $M=0$ to $M=4$, then level off when M continues to increase, indicating that there is no need to choose a much larger M since the top few largest eigenvalues and the corresponding eigenvectors can sufficiently capture the geometric structure of the data.

Figure 4(b) and Figure 5(b) show the $F1$ measure for the testing set as a function of u when $M=3$, $R=0.2$, and $s=20$ using feature **V**1 and feature **V**2 for SpSVM-MC, respectively. We observe from Figure 4(b) and Figure 5(b) that the $F1$ measures for the testing set all increase when the size of the neighborhood for each $\mathcal{N}_r(I_i)$ increases, which shows that it is helpful to use the nearest neighbors of each I_i in $\mathcal{L}_r$ to further improve the performance of the classification.

We describe the $F1$ measure for the testing set as a function of R when $M=3$, $u=3$, and $s=20$ using feature **V**1 and feature **V**2 for SpSVM-MC in Figure 4(c) and Figure 5(c), respectively. As we defined before, $R=C^*/C$ represents the ratio between the weight of the loss function for instances and the weight of the loss function for their nearest neighbors. When R increases, the effect of nearest neighbors from the multi-label space in the optimization

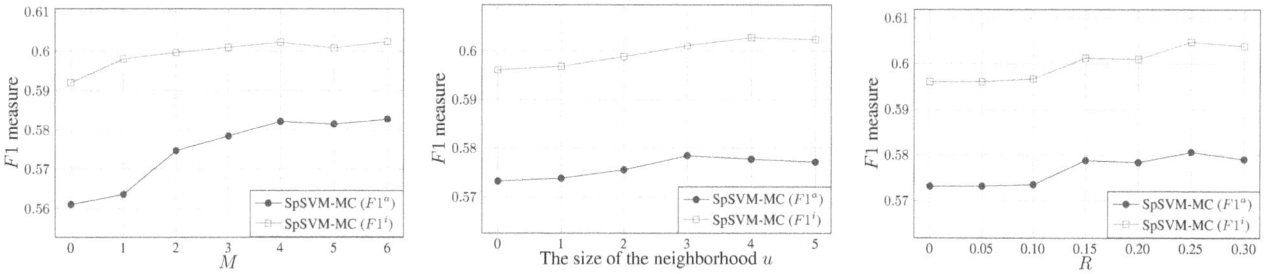

(a) $u = 3$, $R = 0.2$, and $s = 20$. (b) $M = 3$, $R = 0.2$, and $s = 20$. (c) $M = 3$, $u = 3$, and $s = 20$.

Figure 4: The F1 measure for the testing set as a function of M, u, and R using feature V1 for SpSVM-MC, respectively.

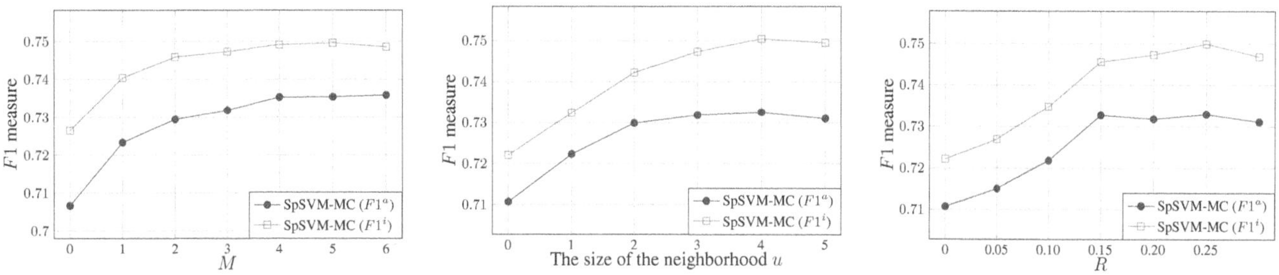

(a) $u = 3$, $R = 0.2$, and $s = 20$. (b) $M = 3$, $R = 0.2$, and $s = 20$. (c) $M = 3$, $u = 3$, and $s = 20$.

Figure 5: The F1 measure for the testing set as a function of M, u, and R using feature V2 for SpSVM-MC, respectively.

also increases. We observe from Figure 4(c) and Figure 5(c) that when R increases, the curves for the $F1$ measures of SpSVM-MC ascend, which also shows that it is helpful to use the nearest neighbors of each I_i in $\mathcal{L}_r$ to mitigate the influence of the noise in the classification.

After the training process, we use the trained model to reclassify the noisily tagged training set. Figure 6 describes the F1 measure of the 75 tags for the noisily tagged training set using feature $\mathbf{V}2$ for SVM and SpSVM-MC when $s = 20$, $M = 4$, $u = 3$, and $R = 0.2$. Figure 7 shows the F1 measure of the 75 tags for the testing set using feature $\mathbf{V}2$ for SVM and SpSVM-MC when $s = 20$, $M = 4$, $u = 3$, and $R = 0.2$. From Figure 6 and Figure 7 we observe that the performances of SpSVM-MC are better than those of SVM in most of the concepts not only for the testing set, but also for the noisily tagged training set, indicating that our proposed method is effective and promising to correct the incorrect tags originally given in the noisily tagged training set during the training process, and consequently to improve the performance of the classification.

6. CONCLUSION

Tagging has become an important means responsible for the rapid development of social networks. A robust tagging method must have the capability to meet the two challenging requirements: limited labeled training samples and noisy labeled training samples. We have studied the challenging problem of learning with limited and noisy tagging and have developed a powerful discriminative model, called SpSVM-MC, that exploits both labeled and unlabeled data through a semi-parametric regularization and takes advantage of the multi-label constraints into the optimization. While SpSVM-MC is a general method for learning with limited and noisy tagging, we have reported the extensive evaluations in the specific application of noisy image tagging with limited labeled training samples on a benchmark dataset. Theoretic analysis and extensive evaluations in comparison with state-of-the-art literature demonstrate that SpSVM-MC outstands with a superior performance.

Acknowledgments

We thank the area chair and reviewers for their constructive comments. This work is supported in part by the National Basic Research Program of China (2012CB316400), Zhejiang University — Alibaba Financial Joint lab, and Zhejiang Provincial Engineering Center on Media Data Cloud Processing and Analysis. ZZ is also supported in part by US NSF (IIS-0812114, CCF-1017828).

7. REFERENCES

[1] K. P. Bennett and A. Demiriz. Semi-supervised support vector machines. In *NIPS*, pages 368–374, 1998.

[2] P. Bouboulis, K. Slavakis, and S. Theodoridis. Adaptive kernel-based image denoising employing semi-parametric regularization. *IEEE Transactions on Image Processing*, 19(6):1465–1479, 2010.

[3] M. R. Boutell, J. Luo, X. Shen, and C. M. Brown. Learning multi-label scene classification. *Pattern Recognition*, 37(9):1757–1771, 2004.

[4] T. S. Chua, J. Tang, R. Hong, H. Li, Z. Luo, and Y. Zheng. Nus-wide: a real-world web image database from national university of singapore. In *Proceedings of the ACM International Conference on Image and Video Retrieval*, pages 1–9, 2009.

[5] S. Godbole and S. Sarawagi. Discriminative methods for multi-labeled classification. In *Proceedings of the 8th PAKDD*, 2004.

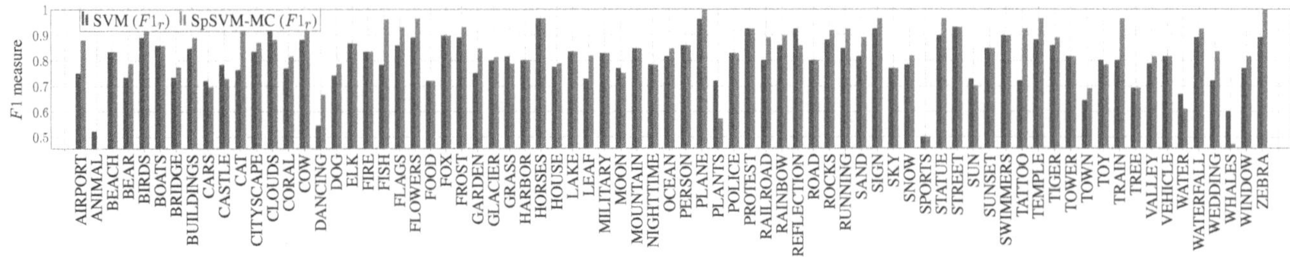

Figure 6: The F1 measure of the 75 tags for the noisy tagged training set using feature V2 for SVM and SpSVM-MC when s = 20, M = 4, u = 3, and R = 0.2.

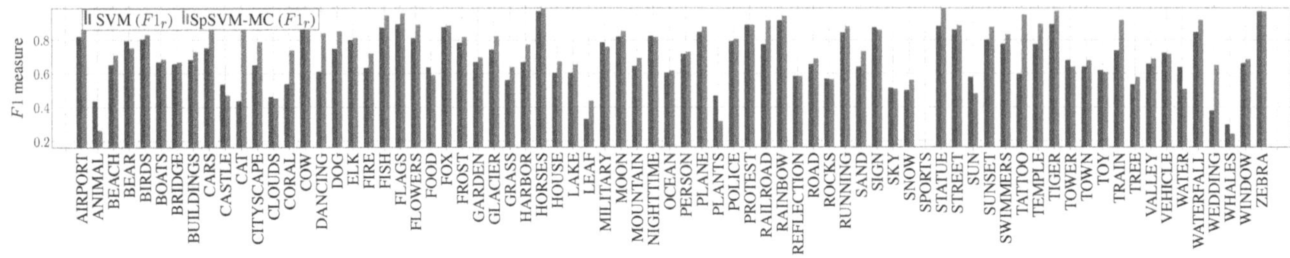

Figure 7: The F1 measure of the 75 tags for the testing set using feature V2 for SVM and SpSVM-MC when s = 20, M = 4, u = 3, and R = 0.2.

[6] K.-S. Goh, E. Chang, and K.-T. Cheng. SVM binary classifier ensembles for image classification. In *Proceedings of the tenth international conference on Information and knowledge management*, pages 395–402, 2001.

[7] Y. Grandvalet and Y. Bengio. Semi-supervised learning by entropy minimization. In *NIPS*, 2004.

[8] Z. Guo, Z. M. Zhang, E. P. Xing, and C. Faloutsos. Semi-supervised learning based on semiparametric regularization. In *SDM*, pages 132–142, 2008.

[9] C. F. Lin and S. de Wang. Training algorithms for fuzzy support vector machines with noisy data. *Pattern Recognition Letters*, 25:1647–1656, 2004.

[10] D. Liu, X.-S. Hua, M. Wang, and H.-J. Zhang. Image retagging. In *Proceedings of ACM MM*, pages 491–500, 2010.

[11] Y. Liu and Y. F. Zheng. Soft SVM and its application in video-object extraction. *IEEE Transactions on Signal Processing*, 55(7-1):3272–3282, 2007.

[12] X. Qi and Y. Han. Incorporating multiple SVMs for automatic image annotation. *Pattern Recognition*, 40:728–741, 2007.

[13] D. Ruppert, M. P. Wand, and R. J. Carroll. *Semiparametric Regression*. Cambridge University Press, Cambridge, UK, 2003.

[14] B. Schölkopf and A. J. Smola. *Learning with Kernels: Support Vector Machines, Regularization, Optimization, and Beyond*. The MIT Press, 2001.

[15] B. Schölkopf, A. J. Smola, and K.-R. Müller. Kernel principal component analysis. In *ICANN*, pages 583–588, 1997.

[16] Z. Sun, Z. Zhang, and H. Wang. Manifold regularization based semisupervised semiparametric regression. *Neurocomputing*, 73(10-12), 2010.

[17] M. Szummer and T. Jaakkola. Information regularization with partially labeled data. In *NIPS*, pages 1025–1032, 2002.

[18] J. Tang, R. Hong, S. Yan, T.-S. Chua, G.-J. Qi, and R. Jain. Image annotation by knn-sparse graph-based label propagation over noisily tagged web images. *ACM Transactions on Intelligent Systems and Technology*, 2:14:1–14:15, 2011.

[19] J. Van Hulse and T. M. Khoshgoftaar. Class noise detection using frequent itemsets. *Intelligent Data Analysis*, 10:487–507, 2006.

[20] V. N. Vapnik. *Statistical learning theory*. John Wiley and Sons, New York, 1998.

[21] C. Wang, F. Jing, L. Zhang, and H.-J. Zhang. Content-based image annotation refinement. In *Proceedings of CVPR*, pages 1–8, 2007.

[22] Z. Xu, R. Jin, J. Zhu, I. King, and M. R. Lyu. Efficient convex relaxation for transductive support vector machine. In *NIPS*, 2007.

[23] C. Yang, M. Dong, and J. Hua. Region-based image annotation using asymmetrical support vector machine-based multi-instance learning. In *Proceedings of CVPR*, 2006.

[24] Z. Zhang, G. Wu, and E. Y. Chang. Semiparametric regression using student t processes. *IEEE Transactions on Neural Networks*, 18(6):1572–1588, 2007.

[25] Z.-H. Zhou and M.-L. Zhang. Multi-instance multilabel learning with application to scene classification. In *Proceedings of NIPS*, pages 1609–1616, 2007.

[26] G. Zhu, S. Yan, and Y. Ma. Image tag refinement towards low-rank, content-tag prior and error sparsity. In *Proceedings of ACM MM*, pages 461–470, 2010.

[27] J. Zhu, S. Rosset, T. Hastie, and R. Tibshirani. 1-norm support vector machines. In *NIPS*, 2003.

[28] X. Zhu and X. Wu. Class noise vs. attribute noise: A quantitative study. *Artif. Intell. Rev.*, 22(3):177–210, 2004.

[29] X. Zhu, X. Wu, and Q. Chen. Eliminating class noise in large datasets. In *Proceeding of International Conference on Machine Learning*, pages 920–927, 2003.

Picture Tags and World Knowledge

Learning Tag Relations from Visual Semantic Sources

Lexing Xie, Xuming He
Australian National University, NICTA
Canberra, Australia

ABSTRACT

This paper studies the use of everyday words to describe images. The common saying has it that *a picture is worth a thousand words*, here we ask *which thousand*? The proliferation of tagged social multimedia data presents a challenge to understanding collective tag-use at large scale – one can ask if patterns from photo tags help understand tag-tag relations, and how it can be leveraged to improve visual search and recognition. We propose a new method to jointly analyze three distinct visual knowledge resources: Flickr, ImageNet/WordNet, and ConceptNet. This allows us to quantify the visual relevance of both tags learn their relationships. We propose a novel network estimation algorithm, Inverse Concept Rank, to infer incomplete tag relationships. We then design an algorithm for image annotation that takes into account both image and tag features. We analyze over 5 million photos with over 20,000 visual tags. The statistics from this collection leads to good results for image tagging, relationship estimation, and generalizing to unseen tags. This is a first step in analyzing picture tags and everyday semantic knowledge. Potential other applications include generating natural language descriptions of pictures, as well as validating and supplementing knowledge databases.

Categories and Subject Descriptors: H.2.8 [**Database applications**] Data Mining
Keywords knowledge graph; social media; folksonomy

1. INTRODUCTION

An image is worth a thousand words, but which thousand? A particularly interesting aspect of this question is how people use thousands of everyday words to describe photos and videos on the web. The sheer volume of visual data presents both a challenge and an opportunity. The challenge is in understanding collective photo tagging behavior. With users posting everything from family and social events, daily life, and amateur photography, has photo tags evolved into a language of its own? Do words in natural language and words used in photo tags differ (and how, if they do)? The opportunity that comes with this challenge is to leverage such understandings and design better systems to organize and search for pictures. Specifically, insights on visual tag vocabulary will help a number of applications: better visual search, improved picture annotation and tag suggestion, and enriching encyclopedic knowledge-bases with more visual content.

Online social tagging and automated photo annotation has been a very active research area for more than a decade, yet there are three gaps in the current approaches. The first gap is between the understanding of general tagging behavior[3, 9] and the practice of automated visual tagging [7]. This is in part because tagging behavior studies rely on semi-manual approach in classifying tags and surveying tagging practices, and there has not been sufficient data to connect the findings on tag types and tagging motivations to large amounts of visual data. The second gap is between visually recognizing a pre-defined list of words, and the real-world knowledge that express relationships among these words. Visual recognition systems has mostly relied on a particular relationship, such as co-ocurrence statistics [11, 36], pre-defined lexical hierarchical structure [13], data-driven graph structures [30]. With maturing resources to encode human knowledge and everyday relationships become available [5, 21], it is conceivable that this gap will be closing. The third gap is in addressing the long tail in visual recognition. The long-tail phenomenon, that there are a large number of items not occurring in the most popular part of the distribution, has been observed picture tags [9, 40] as well as many other problem domains such as recommender systems [24]. Visual recognition efforts tend to concentrate on the head of the distribution, acknowledging that recognizing rare tags is difficult. With reliable prior information about how tags relate to each other and models that effectively shares information across different tags, this gap can also be narrowed.

This work brings together several large-scale visual and semantic resources to analyze picture tags. We propose novel methods to connect the following resources: an annotated visual ontology ImageNet, online social tagging collections from Flickr, and the commonsense reasoning engine ConceptNet. Specifically, we jointly analyze ImageNet and Flickr photos to quantify how *visually relevant* a tag is, addressing the first gap. We then link photo tags with everyday knowledge from ConceptNet. Specifically, we propose Inverse Concept Rank (ICR), a novel network inference method from co-ocurrence statistics, for estimating latent relations between visual tags and constructing better tag space similarity, addressing the second gap. Lastly, we

MM'13, October 21–25, 2013, Barcelona, Spain.

ACM 978-1-4503-2404-5/13/10 ...$15.00.
http://dx.doi.org/10.1145/2502081.2502113.

propose a scalable approach for simultaneously learning and recommending many tags to photos. This approach uses the statistics from our analysis of visual and knowledge sources, and optimizes the MatchBox model, originally designed for large-scale recommender systems for long-tailed content, addressing the third gap. We report picture tag statistics on a collection of over 5 million photos, more than 20,000 words and 450K commonsense relations. Our tag recommendation approach is tested on an annotated Flickr dataset with more than 200K photos. The pilot evaluation yields over 70% precision among top-5 tags and 0.35 average precision scoring all tags. Our work analyzes data from openly available sources, and we will also make our data available at a companion website [2]. We see our method as taking the first steps towards closing three prominent gaps in social photo tags. Our method and results can lead to inquiries in several additional areas: to use tag relation for constructing sentences, to rank tags for their visual informativeness, and additional models to encode tag prior.

The main contributions of this work include:

- Novel joint analysis of three visual and semantic resources, connecting visual semantics to large-scale photo tagging behavior (Sec. 2).
- Inverse Concept Rank, a new model for estimating tag relationships from their co-occurrence statistics (Sec. 3).
- An approach for photo tag recommendation using both visual features, tag statistics, and semantic relationship (Sec. 4).
- Quantifying the visual relevance of both individual tags and tag relationships, mapping over 20,000 everyday words and their relations for the first time (Sec. 5).
- An evaluation on more than 200K photos, with promising results for photo annotation, generalizing to unseen tags, as well as relationship graph estimation (Sec. 6).

2. VISUAL AND SEMANTIC RESOURCES

We establish novel connection among three well-known visual semantic resources. This crucial connection enables us to analyze tens of thousands of photo tags and their visual and semantic relations for the first time.

The first resource is **Flickr photos and tags**. Being one of the most popular online photo sharing platforms, Flickr hosts billions of photos and makes their metadata available via its application programming interface (API). A fraction of photos are assigned one or more *tags*, a free-text string used (typically by the owner) to describe and organize the photo collection. This work also uses *owner* and photo content information on a relevant subset of Flickr photos.

The second resource is **ImageNet** [13][1], a research resource that annotates millions of pictures of nouns in the lexical database Wordnet [17]. ImageNet is organized along *synsets*, each synset is associated with a number of images, each image is deemed visually relevant to the corresponding meaning in Wordnet. There are about 14 Million annotated images in 21,841 synsets in total. These annotations were collected by crowd-sourcing, and verified by humans.

[1] http://image-net.org

Table 1: Summary of notations.

Notation	Meaning	Defined
$\mathbf{X}, \mathbf{x}_i$	Photo(s) and their features	Sec 4
$\mathbf{t}, t_i, \mathcal{T}$	tag/concept, tag vocabulary	Sec 2
$\mathbf{s}, \mathcal{S}$	ImageNet synset	Sec 2
ξ_{t_j}	Tag informative measure	Sec 2
B, b_{ij}	Flickr bigram count	Sec 2
$\mathbf{G}, g_{ij}$	Tag/concept relation graph	Sec 2
$\mathbf{W}, w_{ij}$	Row normalized version of G	Sec 2
$\mathbf{Z}, \mathbf{z}_i$	ICR stationary distribution	Sec 2
$\mathbf{e}, \mathbf{e}_i$	Vector constants	Sec 2
ν	ICR restart distribution	Sec 2
α	ICR teleportation probability	Sec 2
$\mathbf{R}, r_{ij}$	Labels, photo-tag association	Sec 4
$\mathbf{Y}, \mathbf{y}_j$	MatchBox: tag features	Sec 4
$\mathbf{U}, \mathbf{V}$	MatchBox: latent factors	Sec 4
λ	MatchBox: regularization weight	Sec 4
κ	MatchBox: # latent dimensions	Sec 4
m, n, p, q	MatchBox: data dimensions	Sec 4
$\mathcal{L}, \mathcal{U}$	MatchBox: labeled/unlabeled sets	Sec 4
J_R, J_M	Objective functions	Sec3&4
ε	Error term	Sec3&4
$h(\varepsilon)$	Loss function	Sec3&4
ρ, θ	Tag-pair polar coordinates	Sec 5
i, j, k, u, v	General index	–

The third resource, **ConceptNet** [21], is a semantic network based on Open Mind Common Sense[2]. Statements about everyday facts are collected online via a crowd-sourcing website, and are verified using a voting system. The statements are stored in a tuple format, with each tuple consist of a pair of concepts and a relation, such as a *zipper* is *Usedfor* a *jacket*. Note that these relationships are distinct from the ontological relationship encoded by WordNet. We choose ConceptNet over other large scale knowledge bases [5, 12] as such extensive coverage of everyday terms is not found in other language-focused sources such as Wikipedia. Here, ConceptNet is used to understand the relations between everyday words that are used to describe pictures.

We acquire and process data for each of these resource in three steps. Detailed data statistics are described in Section 5. (1) Obtain the original image URLs from ImageNet, keep images that are from Flickr. Only for these images we have both a visually describable concept (from ImageNet) together with rich metadata and user-supplied tags (from Flickr). We then download the photo and their metadata from Flickr, removing photo entries that are no longer available or do not have tags. We refer to this data as the ImageNet/Flickr collection. (2) Acquire ConceptNet, both version 4[3] and version 5[4]. We keep statements that are in English and has one of fourteen most common relations, i.e.*IsA, HasA, ConceptuallyRelatedTo, UsedFor, AtLocation, DefinedAs, InstanceOf, PartOf, HasProperty, CapableOf, SymbolOf, LocatedNear, ReceivesAction, MadeOf.* The other relations are either not directly recognizable in images (e.g. *HasSubevent*) or very rare (e.g. *HasPainCharacter*). The resulting data are in list-of-triplet format, e.g. *CapableOf,butterfly,fly.* (3) Normalize the different vocabularies from the three resources. We use the "2+2lemma" dictionary [1] that includes 80,431 words. This dictionary also includes a mapping to lemmatize each word to one of

[2] http://openmind.media.mit.edu

[3] http://csc.media.mit.edu/docs

[4] http://conceptnet5.media.mit.edu

32,606 "headwords". For example, *funnier, funnily, funniest* all map to *funny*.

We compute several counting statistics from these datasets to help characterize the relationships between photo tags of Flickr, visual synsets from ImageNet, and semantic relations from ConceptNet. Statistics on tens of thousands tags allow us to ask and start answering a few questions about the properties of photo tags and their relationships. Such as: If we were to use a thousand tags to distinguish visual content, which thousand should we use? Which tags are not about the picture content, but about the context that they were taken? Which tag-tag relationships are reflected in images, which aren't? Are there new relationships that we can discover from tag statistics, what would they be?

2.1 Tag statistics

The first statistic is called *visual informativeness*, derived from counts $\#(s_i, t_j)$ for tag t_j appearing in visual synset s_i. Specifically, this is counted as the number of distinct users that has issued tag t_j for any photo in s_i. Unique user count is an effective way of denoting photo tags when a user is uploading and tagging in batches [23, 28] – we found one synset contain 50 photos from the same user tagged with just *photo* and *canon*, for example. We estimate $p(s_i|t_j)$ by normalizing along each tag, i.e. $\#(s_i, t_j)/\sum_i \#(s_i, t_j)$. This visual word and tag association matrix is used to measure the visual distinctiveness of tags. For example, tags such as *pineapple* is distinctive and should only appear in a few synsets, i.e., $p(\mathbf{s}|pineapple)$ peak in synset related to *pineapple*; while *photo* and *canon* (camera brand) will be associated with many synsets, i.e. $p(\mathbf{s}|canon)$ would be flat. Conditioning on tag t_j changes the prior distribution $p(\mathbf{s})$ over visual words: the more the change, the more visually relevant t_j is. We call this quantity *visual informativeness*, and measure it with the KL-divergence [25] between the conditional probability of synsets given a tag $p(s|t_j)$ and their prior probability $p(s)$.

$$\xi_{t_j} = KL[p(\mathbf{s})||p(\mathbf{s}|t_j)] = \sum_i p(s_i) log \left[\frac{p(s_i)}{p(s_i|t_j)}\right] \quad (1)$$

2.2 Association between a pair of tags

We examine two different statistics of a pair of tags t_i and t_j. We first obtain the tag pair co-occurrence matrix $\mathbf{B}$, where count b_{ij} denotes the number of times that t_i and t_j are used to describe the same photo together in the ImageNet/Flickr collection. One natural question that arises is, does high/low co-occurrence in b_{ij} agree with high/low associations in ConceptNet?

To answer this question, we first need a measure of association for a part of concepts in ConceptNet. Denote a non-negative concept relationship graph $\mathbf{G} \in \mathcal{R}_+^{n \times n}$, where $g_{ij} > 0$ if concept i and j are related. In this paper, we obtain g_{ij} by counting the number of relations that exist between tag t_i and t_j.

We use a random walk model to describe the process of coming up with a series of tags for a picture, as this was shown to be close to human cognition in a seminal 2007 study by Griffth, Steyvers and Firl [20].

Starting from tag t_i, a user makes a transition to tag t_j (i.e. use as the next tag) with a probability proportional to g_{ij}; and return to the initial tag t_{i_1} with a fixed probability $1 - \alpha$ (i.e., finishing the tagging process for the current photo). Such a random walk process has been described as personalized PageRank (PPR) [26] or random walk with restart (RWR) [44] in the context of web search and graph mining. We note that the co-ocurrence of everyday image tags is not only driven by their conceptual relationship, but also driven by the physical colocation and other external factors. It is a simplifying assumption to capture these different types of relationships with one relationship graph, and initialize such a graph with ConceptNet and ImageNet. However, the different relations within ConceptNet, such as *Usedfor*, *LocatedNear* does account for a few different modes of co-occurences.

Given a relation graph $\mathbf{G}$, we generate a stochastic version $\mathbf{W}$ of the graph by normalizing along each row.

$$w_{ij} = \frac{g_{ij}}{\sum_k g_{ik}} \quad (2)$$

The RWR transition probability $\hat{\mathbf{W}}$ is computed from $\mathbf{W}$ as as a weighted combination between taking a step according to $\mathbf{W}$ and jumping back to initial distribution ν, with a *teleportation* constant $\alpha \in [0, 1]$, and $\mathbf{e}$ as an all-1 vector.

$$\hat{\mathbf{W}} = \alpha \mathbf{W} + (1 - \alpha)\mathbf{e}\nu^T \quad (3)$$

Denote vector z as the stationary probability distribution of Markov chain $\hat{\mathbf{W}}$, i.e, the personalized page rank vector. z satisfies:

$$\begin{aligned} \mathbf{z} = \hat{\mathbf{W}}^T\mathbf{z} &= [\alpha \mathbf{W}^T + (1 - \alpha)\nu\mathbf{e}^T]\mathbf{z} \\ &= \alpha \mathbf{W}^T\mathbf{z} + (1 - \alpha)\nu \end{aligned} \quad (4)$$

Note that the last step follows from normalization $\mathbf{e}^T\mathbf{z} = 1$. The initial distribution ν_i for starting from the note i is set as a vector with a 1 in the ith position and 0 elsewhere. Varying the starting node i will give a series of different stationary distribution z_i, forming a matrix $\mathbf{Z} = [\mathbf{z}_1^T; \ldots; \mathbf{z}_i^T; \ldots]$. We use $\mathbf{z}_{ij}$, the stationary probability of being at node j if started from node i, as the association between two concepts i and j under ConceptNet.

Detailed observations about ξ_t, as well as comparisons between $\mathbf{B}$ and $\mathbf{Z}$ are presented in Section 5, and learning algorithms that are motivated by such observations are in Sections 3 and 4.

3. INVERSE CONCEPT RANK

It would be desirable if concept-concept, or tag-tag relationships could explain the process for generating photo tags. As seen in Figure 3 and Section 5.2, however, that there are a number of mismatched cases between tag occurrence and concept relationships, this is in part due to incomplete relations in ConceptNet, noisy counts from both visual and non-visual tags, non-visual relations that do not manifest in photos, and person- and event- specific factors that are not explained by everyday semantic knowledge. In this section we propose a model to address the first two factors, by estimating latent relations, and unsmooth probability observations for better concept similarity.

3.1 An inverse random walk model

Section 2.2 described a random walk process of generating photo tags, and the resulting tag distribution can be computed by personalized PageRank. Here we are facing an inverse problem: if the stationary distributions of such a random walk is observed (via bigram statistics $\mathbf{B}$ and its normalization $\bar{\mathbf{Z}}$), but the underlying graph $\mathbf{G}$ is hidden or only partially known. The goal is to "recover" a graph $\mathbf{G}$

that generates $\bar{\mathbf{Z}}$. Hence we name this model Inverse Concept Rank (ICR).

Let observed stationary distribution be $\bar{\mathbf{Z}} = [\bar{\mathbf{z}}_1^T; \dots; \bar{\mathbf{z}}_n^T]$, where each $\bar{\mathbf{z}}_i$ is the personalized page rank vector starting from node i. The goal of the ICR model is to find an optimal relationship graph $\mathbf{G}$, from which an RWR process will generate $\mathbf{Z}$ that is close to $\bar{\mathbf{Z}}$. The objective function is define as follows:

$$\begin{aligned} \min_{\mathbf{G}} J_R &= \frac{\alpha_R}{2} tr(\mathbf{G}^T\mathbf{G}) + \sum_{i,j} h(|z_{ij} - \bar{z}_{ij}|) \quad (5)\\ & RWR(\mathbf{G}; \alpha) \to \mathbf{Z} \\ s.t. \quad & \mathbf{G} \geq \mathbf{G}_0 \end{aligned}$$

Here $RWR(\mathbf{G}; \alpha)$ is the RWR process on $\mathbf{G}$ with parameter α, as in Equations 2–4; $|z_{ij} - \bar{z}_{ij}|$ is an error term to be minimized; h is a monotonic loss function – common choices include L2, hinge loss, etc.; $\alpha_R tr(\mathbf{G}^T\mathbf{G})$ is a regularizer of the Frobenius norm of $\mathbf{G}$ weighted by hyper parameter α_R. This regularizer favors smaller graph weights. $\mathbf{G}_0$ is an initial graph with non-negative edge weights, the inequality constraints are element-wise on $\mathbf{G}$.

3.2 Optimizing Inverse Concept Rank

The ICR objective (5) has no closed-form solution, it is non-linear and non-convex with respect to graph entries g_{ij} due to the RWR process. Numeric solution such as quasi-Newton method can be used to minimize this objective. In particular, we use large-scale non-linear solver L-BFGS-B [32] with closed-form gradient computed as follows.

The partial derivative of J_R with respect to g_{ij}, $(i,j) \in \{1,\dots,n\}^2$ can be expressed in terms of z_{uv}, entries in the stationary distribution matrix and their associated error terms $\varepsilon_{uv} = z_{uv} - \bar{z}_{uv}$, with $(u,v) \in \{1,\dots,n\}^2$. Applying chain rule and matrix identities [35] to Equation (5) gives:

$$\frac{\partial J_R}{\partial g_{ij}} = \alpha_R g_{ij} + \sum_{u,v} \frac{\partial h(\varepsilon_{uv})}{\partial \varepsilon_{uv}} \sum_k \frac{\partial z_{uv}}{\partial w_{ik}} \frac{\partial w_{ik}}{\partial g_{ij}} \quad (6)$$

Each of the three terms in Equation (6) can be computed in closed form. $\frac{\partial h(\varepsilon)}{\partial \varepsilon}$ is easily computed for all common loss functions. For L2 loss $\frac{\partial h(\varepsilon)}{\partial \varepsilon} = 2\varepsilon$, for hinge loss we can use a sub-gradient, or a smoothed quadratic surrogate. $\frac{\partial w_{ik}}{\partial g_{ij}}$ is computed from the normalization equation (2):

$$\frac{\partial w_{ik}}{\partial g_{ij}} = \frac{\delta(k=j)}{\sum_l g_{il}} - \frac{g_{ik}}{(\sum_l g_{il})^2}$$

Here $\delta(k=j)$ is the indicator function, and the first term only appears when $k=j$.

The remaining term $\frac{\partial z_{uv}}{\partial w_{ik}}$ is the sensitivity of stationary distribution $\mathbf{z}$ with respect to the Markov matrix $\mathbf{W}$. Golub and Meyer [18] showed that for a irreducible Markov chain,

$$\frac{\partial \mathbf{z}}{\partial w_{ij}} = \alpha \mathbf{z} \mathbf{e}_i \mathbf{e}_j^T (\mathbf{I} - \hat{\mathbf{W}})^\sharp. \quad (7)$$

Here $\mathbf{A}^\sharp$ is the group inverse of $\mathbf{A}$, a unique matrix satisfying $\mathbf{A}\mathbf{A}^\sharp\mathbf{A} = \mathbf{A}$, $\mathbf{A}^\sharp\mathbf{A}\mathbf{A}^\sharp = \mathbf{A}^\sharp$, and $\mathbf{A}^\sharp\mathbf{A} = \mathbf{A}\mathbf{A}^\sharp$. $\mathbf{e}_i$ is a vector with 1 in the i-th position and the rest being zeros. The group inverse can be computed with QR decomposition. Let $(\mathbf{I} - \hat{\mathbf{W}}) = \hat{\mathbf{Q}}\hat{\mathbf{R}}$ be a QR factorization, $\hat{\mathbf{R}}$ must have the form

$$\mathbf{R} = \begin{bmatrix} \hat{\mathbf{U}} & -\hat{\mathbf{U}}\mathbf{e} \\ \mathbf{0} & 0 \end{bmatrix} \quad (8)$$

The group inverse is given by

$$(\mathbf{I} - \hat{\mathbf{W}})^\sharp = (\mathbf{I} - \mathbf{ez}) \begin{bmatrix} \hat{\mathbf{U}}^{-1} & 0 \\ \mathbf{0} & 0 \end{bmatrix} \mathbf{Q}^T (\mathbf{I} - \mathbf{ez}) \quad (9)$$

Note that we represent ConceptNet as a undirected graph, this necessarily make $\mathbf{G}$ irreducible, and satisfies the condition of Equation 7. Note that the computational complexity of each gradient step is cubic in graph size n, with QR decomposition taking $O(n^3)$ (but only need to be done once), and the summation in Equation 6 also taking $O(n^3)$. Quasi-Newton method finds a local minima in the J_R that is close to starting point $\mathbf{G}_0$. In practice, we run ICR within each synset, saving computational time and also retaining synset-specific relations.

Intuitively, graph $\mathbf{G}$ is parsimonious and will be free from noisy chain-cooccurrences observed in $\mathbf{B}$. For example, *hammerhead (shark), atlanta* is among the top tag-pairs in synset *n01494475*, but this is because *"shark isLocatedAt aquarium"*, and *"an aquarium isLocatedAt Atlanta"*, not because *"hammerhead LivesIn Atlanta"* – impossible for an inland city. Recovering the underlying graph $\mathbf{G}$ given observations $\bar{\mathbf{Z}}$ can have a number of applications. A direct use would be to interpret $\mathbf{G}$, such as finding and filling in missing entries in ConceptNet. Another type of application is to use $\mathbf{G}$ as an *un-smoothed* version of tag correlation, this can serve as feature for automatic or semi-automatic picture tagging. Observations and evaluations of the ICR model on Flickr data will be presented in Sections 5 and 6.

4. TAG RECOMMENDATION

One application of tag statistics (in Sections 2.1 and 5.1) is to serve as a similarity metric between different visual concepts. Tag similarity is a prior information that can help infer unknown picture tags that has too few or no training data, and to regularize individual tag predictors. We draw an analogy between photo tagging and collaborative recommendation problems that simultaneously infer the preferences to a large number of different items. Latent space models are effective choices for this purpose [24].

We denote each image as a feature vector $\mathbf{x}_i \in \mathbb{R}^n$, and each tag as t_j, $i = 1,\dots,n$, $j = 1,\dots,m$. Denote a tag matrix as $\mathbf{R} \in \mathbb{R}^{n \times m}$, each element $r_{ij} \in \{1,-1,0\}$ represent the label of a photo-tag pair $(\mathbf{x}_i, t_j)$. Here 1 means t_j describes $\mathbf{x}_i$, -1 means t_j does not describe $\mathbf{x}_i$, and 0 means unknown. Predicting unknown entries in R is akin to a recommendation problem [24], and one effective approach that takes into account item and tag features is the MatchBox model [41]. It approximates R with two latent factors: the photo factor $\mathbf{U} \in \mathbb{R}^{\kappa \times p}$ on the p-dimensional photo features and the tag factor $\mathbf{V} \in \mathbb{R}^{\kappa \times q}$ on the q-dimensional tag features. Denote the set of labeled photo-tag pairs as $\mathcal{L} = \{(i,j), \text{where } r_{ij} = \pm 1\}$ and unlabeled pairs are $\mathcal{U} = \{(i,j), \text{where } r_{ij} = 0\}$. This problem is expressed as a minimization problem for mean-square loss in R, regularized by the norms of latent factors $\mathbf{U}$ and $\mathbf{V}$,

$$J_M = \frac{1}{2} \sum_{(i,j)\in\mathcal{L}} (r_{ij} - \mathbf{x}_i^T \mathbf{U}^T \mathbf{V} \mathbf{y}_j)^2 + \frac{\lambda}{2}(tr(\mathbf{U}^T\mathbf{U})) + tr(\mathbf{V}^T\mathbf{V})) \quad (10)$$

Here $\mathbf{x}$ and $\mathbf{y}$ are features describing pictures and tags respectively, and λ and number of latent dimension κ are hyper-parameters. Note that objective function J is non-convex in $\mathbf{U}$ and $\mathbf{V}$, but is convex (quadratic) in either $\mathbf{U}$

or $\mathbf{V}$ if we hold the other fixed. We adopt an alternating gradient descent [24] approach to find a local minima in J. In short, we take derivatives of $\mathbf{U}$ and $\mathbf{V}$ in turn while holding the other constant. Then we apply gradient descent in a round-robin fashion until a local minima is reached for all parameters. This is implemented with an L-BFGS-B solver [32] with gradients defined as follows [35]:

$$\frac{\partial J_M}{\partial \mathbf{U}} = - \sum_{(i,j)\in\mathcal{L}} \varepsilon_{ij}\mathbf{V}\mathbf{y}_j\mathbf{x}_i^T + \lambda\mathbf{U} \quad (11)$$

$$\frac{\partial J_M}{\partial \mathbf{V}} = - \sum_{(i,j)\in\mathcal{L}} \varepsilon_{ij}\mathbf{U}\mathbf{x}_i\mathbf{y}_j^T + \lambda\mathbf{V}$$

Note that $\varepsilon_{ij} = r_{ij} - \mathbf{x}_i^T\mathbf{U}^T\mathbf{V}\mathbf{y}_j$ is a shorthand for the current error to predict r_{ij}. Also note that the computational cost of the objective function and its derivatives is linear in the number of labeled photo-tag pairs $|\mathcal{L}|$, linear in the number of labeled images n and tags m, linear in feature dimensions p and q, and quadratic in the (typically small) latent dimension κ, i.e. $O(|\mathcal{L}|mnpq\kappa^2)$. Compared to Wasabie [49], our bilinear model incorporates additional tag features. We currently use a square loss, on ε_{ij}, we observed that hinge loss performs comparably, and similarly, a ranking loss can also be incorporated.

4.1 Photo Matchbox applications

This latent-space model of photos and tags has many applications, this paper evaluates three: (A) "Collaborative" tagging. Minimizing equation (10), and then use $\hat{R} = \mathbf{x}^T\mathbf{U}^T\mathbf{V}\mathbf{y}$ to predict entries for the unlabeled set $\mathcal{U}$. (B) Multi-tag photo labeling. This applies the Matchbox model to a new photo x with no existing tags. The best labels $R_\mathbf{x}$ for x is obtained by directly applying the parameters without needing to re-optimize for U and V, i.e. $\hat{R}_\mathbf{x} = \mathbf{x}^T\mathbf{U}^T\mathbf{V}\mathbf{Y}$ with the label estimate $\hat{R}_x$ being a multiple linear combinations on feature x. (C) Inferring unknown tags. This is the dual of problem (B) above, where $\hat{R}_y = \mathbf{x}^T\mathbf{U}^T\mathbf{V}\mathbf{y}$ for an unknown tag with feature $\mathbf{y}$. Evaluations of these applications can be found in Section 6.2.

Note that there are different choices in supplying the photo and tag feature $\mathbf{X}$ and $\mathbf{Y}$. $\mathbf{X}$ can include low-level perceptual features [12], bag-of-local descriptors [45], or mid-level representations such as ObjectBank [27]. $\mathbf{Y}$ can include any feature that describe a tag, in this paper, we consider the synset-tag association matrix $\mathbf{T}$, top m rows sorted by *visual informativeness* ξ. We also consider graph structures from *un-smoothing* co-occurrence observations, as described in Section 3.

5. DATASET AND OBSERVATIONS

We acquire and process ImageNet and ConceptNet datasets as described in Section 2. Out of 14.2 million photos on ImageNet, 6.3 million are from Flickr, and 5,107,147 photos (or $\sim 35\%$) have one or more tags that can be found in the dictionary, as of March 2012. Out of all 21K+ synsets, 13,288 contain more than 5 tagged Flickr photos, and thus kept for analysis. We map both Flickr tags and ConceptNet terms using the *2+2lemma* dictionary [1]. We disregard the multi-word terms and any terms that did not match. We also prune words that appeared less than 5 times in the entire ImageNet/Flickr collection. This has left us a vocabulary of 20,366 words from Flickr tags, of which 7,796 also appears in ConceptNet.

5.1 Observation on tags

We compute the *visual informativeness* measure ξ (Eq. 1) from the co-ocurrence matrix of 13,288 synsets $\times$ 20,366 tags. These tags are visualized with its frequency $|t|$ vs *visual informativeness* ξ_t.

The middle overview graphs of Fig. 1 and the yellow background in Fig. 2 are scatter plots of all 20K+ tags, we can see that there is a wide range of *visual informativeness* value for tags of similar frequency. Fig. 1 (A) and (B) zoom in on the overall scatter plot, as indicated by the overview icons, showing the lower and upper envelope of the tag scatter, respectively. For Fig. 1, in particular, the light blue tags contain an annotated (partial) list of 194 food names (A), and 130 place names (B). These food and place names are collected from the top tags across a few dozen food- and travel-related Flickr groups, and then manually annotated by one of the authors. Overall, the upper and lower regions of the tagger scatter shows a clear trend of concrete, visual nouns (2A, 1B) versus abstract and non-visual tags (2B, 1A). This method for correlating a visual resource (ImageNet) with generic tagging resource (Flickr) can be used to re-rank tags in an image, or to decide which 1000 visual classifiers to train (first) for better usability and performance.

5.2 Observation on tag pairs

We obtain bigram statistics $\mathbf{B}$ and RWR probability $\mathbf{Z}$ on ConceptNet graph, as described in Section 2.2. There are 1,507,457 tag pairs that appeared in at least 5 images over the ImageNet/Flickr collection, a scatter plot of b versus z is in Fig 3 (left). There are three salient regions in this plot, quantified by transforming the $b - z$ plane to normalized polar coordinates. We first normalize the two quantities to be between 0 and 1: we take the log on bigram counts, and then divided by the log of the maximum bigram to obtain $\tilde{b}$; we divide z by the maximum of all z to obtain $\tilde{z}$. The polar coordinate of a point (b, z) is:

$$\rho = \sqrt{\tilde{b}^2 + \tilde{z}^2},\ \theta = arctan(\frac{\tilde{z}}{\tilde{b}}).$$

Intuitively, we notice three salient regions according to different values of θ, marked as I, II, and III on Fig 3 (left). Top tag-pairs of each region are shown on Fig 3 (right), obtained as the top 20 pairs by descending values of ρ, within the angles ranges specified according to θ. Region I ($\theta \sim 45° \pm 7.5°$) can be called *concurrence*, when we tend to observe high tag co-ocurrence with high associations in ConceptNet. Examples in Fig 3 (right) shows intuitively related tags that are also used to describe objects and scenes in photos, such as *sea* and *water*, *book* and *library*. Region II ($\theta \in [0° \pm 15°]$) can be called *new visual relations*, these tag-pairs frequently co-occur in photos but are not strongly associated in ConceptNet. The examples show intuitively related tags that are also used to describe pictures, such as *animal* and *nature*, *flower* and *spring*. Observations in these region can potentially be used to generate new statements for semantic networks including ConceptNet. Region III ($\theta \geq 68°$, the maximum θ is 72°) can be called *non-visual relations*, these tags are strongly associated in ConceptNet statements, but do not frequently appear together in photos. Examples show abstract words (e.g., *duty*, *domicile*) and as events *rent* and *house* that are difficult to depict in a single image.

The joint examination of commonsense and photo tag co-occurrence provides a number of interesting observations.

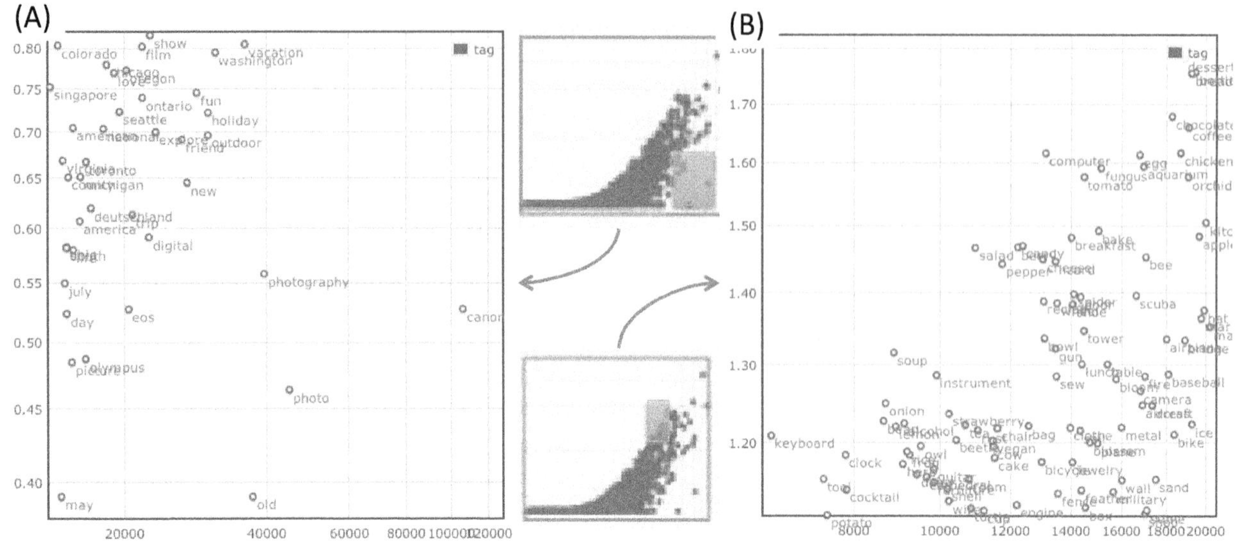

Figure 1: Zoomed-in view of the tag scatter in Fig 2. (A) An area with non-informative tags, containing abstract nouns, adjectives and place names; (B) An area with informative tags, mostly various object names. (For better readability, please view in color and with magnification).

They can be starting points for composing a sentence to describe photos, by providing a basis to include abstract and non-visual tags with visual ones. On the other hand, this analysis also exposes statistical biases in the data. Flickr bigrams are certainly biased by the sheer frequency of a tag, e.g. *blue* appeared many times in Figure 3, but other colors did not. The number of ConceptNet4 tuples (450K) is about an order of magnitude less than the Flickr bigrams (>5M total, 1.5M with counts >5). The example in regions II shows the prospect of better tag association from data. This is one of our motivations for the ICR model – leveraging Flickr as a source to infer the missing relationships in the ConceptNet graph.

6. EXPERIMENTS

We first evaluate the ICR algorithm alone for inferring concept relation graph, and then evaluate image tagging with a number of different tasks and tag features.

For ConceptNet, we keep two versions of the relation graph with 7,796 nodes: ConceptNet4 (CN4) has 450K total relations and 51,576 relations after tag and relation filtering (Sec 2); ConceptNet5 (CN5), released in 2012, has 69,120 relations on the same set of tags (or 1/3 new relations, "CN5-new" for short).

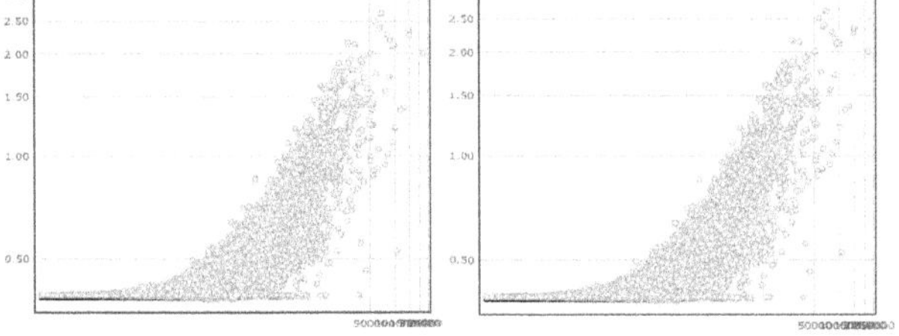

Figure 2: Scatter plot of log-frequency vs visual informativeness ξ for the ImageNet-Flickr collection. (A) Common food names against all tags; (B) Common place names against all tags;

We measure image tagging performance on the NUS-WIDE [43] dataset, containing 269K images collected from Flickr, annotated with 81 visual tags, split 60-40 into training/testing sets. This dataset is suitable for our evaluation, not only as it is from the same source as the ImageNet-Flickr collection, More importantly, it contains almost complete yes/no judgment including negatives, most other datasets including ImageNet only has positive examples, and provide no negative judgement on picture-tag tuple. We download photos directly from Flickr with the provided URL, and then extract an 177-dimensional ObjectBank feature from each image. ObjectBank [27] produces for each object a response map containing 2 views x 6 scales x 3 pyramid levels ($1+2^2+4^4=21$), and the responses for each object are aggregated by taking the maximum. This vector is used to populate X in MatchBox. We map the visual tags annotated by NUS-WIDE [12] to ImageNet synsets using dictionary lookup on all words in the synset. We removed a few that either has no matches (e.g. *sunset*) or matched synset does not have more than 50 photos. We also filtered a few tags that are too generic for ImageNet (e.g. people, the top of a wordnet tree with 2800+ synsets). We are left with 63 visual tags as targets for MatchBox annotation.

6.1 Inverse Concept Rank Evaluation

We use the ICR algorithm to learn the underlying concept graph, starting from CN4 and using bigram counts as observations $\bar{\mathbf{Z}}$. The evaluation target are relations in CN5-new, we note that these relations are incomplete (consistent with partial labeling in typical IR evaluations), but they are unknown to CN4 prior to model learning. We restrict ICR to work within each synset, since this preserves the particular relation context, and makes the algorithm execute fast – we note that ICR on different synsets can be trivially pararellized, and each synset typically take a few minutes on one CPU for ~100 related tags from 100s to

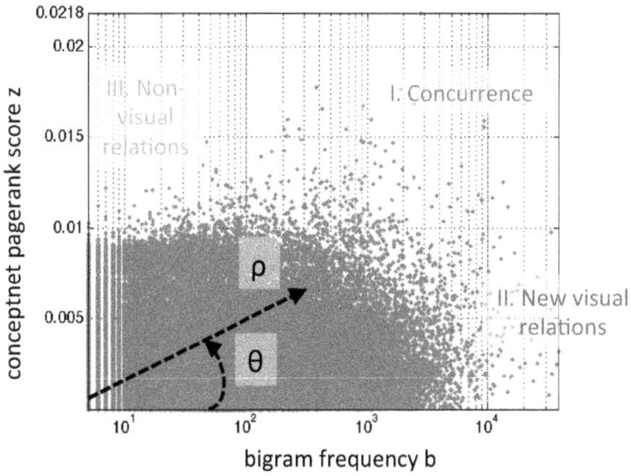

Region I		Region II		Region III	
ocean	water	animal	nature	toil	work
sea	water	flower	nature	house	rent
build	city	bird	nature	build	thing
tree	wood	nature	wildlife	employ	work
house	room	bird	wildlife	basement	build
office	work	flower	yellow	salary	work
drink	water	animal	wildlife	build	carpet
city	house	black	white	duty	work
build	construction	flower	pink	domicile	house
eat	food	green	red	pay	work
city	town	green	yellow	build	pen
build	home	flower	white	album	work
house	window	girl	woman	work	write
job	work	blue	red	build	you
door	house	flower	spring	act	work
build	office	garden	nature	construct	house
build	structure	flower	red	sing	work
fun	play	green	white	build	supermarket
book	library	flower	purple	alcohol	build
game	play	bug	insect	here	place

Figure 3: (Left) A scatter plot of Flickr bigram frequency b and ConceptNet pagerank z with three salient angular regions. (Right) Top 20 tag-pairs of each region by ρ. See description in Sec 5.2, best viewed in color.

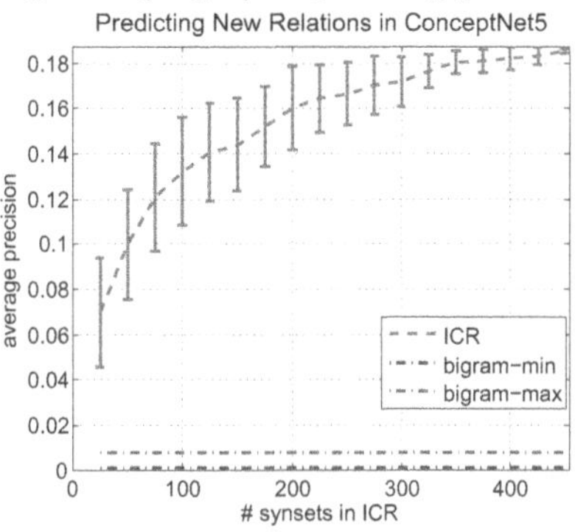

W1	Top10 -W2									
container	winery	alcohol	window	egg	head	lamp	table	oil	reflection	red
cross	animal	temple	chapel	pray	decoration	faith	band	crucifixion	red	white
cut	work	meat	tree	hole	rip	small	surgery	band	red	reflection
town	landmark	friend	rural	zoo	desert	field	bright	god	downtown	marina
army	national	weapon	jeep	infantry	big	glory	canon	pistol	museum	black
business	man	travel	suit	hotel	small	retail	reflection	portrait	town	design
corn	horse	cup	meal	fruit	carrot	soup	home	red	rural	holiday
guard	military	fence	weapon	sentry	work	canon	black	police	orange	brick
party	friend	night	play	fiesta	car	black	red	white	age	blue
rest	vacation	new	home	smile	body	perch	park	black	travel	nature

Relations in both ICR-400 and ICR-50   Relations in ICR-400 and not in ICR-50   Relations not in Concept5

Figure 4: Result of ICR on ILSVRC synsets. (Left) AP of new CN5 relations with varying number of input synsets. (Right) Example top relations from ICR. See descriptions in Sec 6.1, best viewed in color.

1000s photos. We use 1000 synsets from ILSVRC [1] in this evaluation, of which 462 synsets have sufficient data in the ImageNet/Flickr dataset. The graph $\mathbf{G}$ from different synsets are then dimension-aligned and aggregated by summing the weights. Hyper-parameters $\alpha = 0.5$, $\alpha_R = 10$, set with cross-validation.

Fig. 4(left) plots average precision of CN5-new relations after aggregating ICR on 25,50,..., 462 synsets. The error bars are generated with 10 random permutations with which the synsets are aggregated. We can see that ICR produces successively better predictions of CN5-new, and its predictions are significantly better than the best of using bigrams (the green baseline). Fig. 4(right) contains 10 example words (W1) and their respective top 10 related words ranked by ICR with 50 and 400 synsets (ICR-50 and ICR-400 for short). We can see that ICR-400 recovers many correct relations (red) in addition to those from ICR-50 (burgundy). We note that the learned relations can be: a) in ground-truth and reasonable (*army-weapon*), b) not in ground-truth but can be potential additions to ConceptNet (*rest-park*), c) specific to photography (*container-reflection*), and d) in ground-truth but no strong immediately connection *party-car*), due to noise in ConceptNet. Among the 333 words that have at least 10 relations in CN5-new and ICR-50, 52.5% and 76.9% have precision@10 $\geq$ 0.5 on ICR-50 and ICR-400, respectively.

6.2 Picture Tagging Evaluation

We use the wordnet-tag association matrix as tag feature $\mathbf{Y}$. We rank the tag-feature dimensions by the informative measure ξ_t, and take a subset of these dimensions from the top, i.e. with a threshold on the y-axis in Fig. 2. We optimize the objective function in Eq. 10. Positive entries of r_{ij} are kept, negative entries are subsampled up to 8x number of positive samples for each tag, the rest are treated as the unknown set $\mathcal{U}$. We use cross-validation to choose regularization weight λ, the number of latent dimensions κ, and the dimensionality of tag features q. Each of these parameters are shown to be performance-insensitive within a range, we also found hinge loss and square loss to perform similarly. We report results with square loss and the best configuration $\lambda = 100$, $\kappa = 5$ and $q = 150$. Training and testing on the entire NUS-WIDE dataset takes 2~3 hours on one CPU core. Details of model parameter tuning can be found in the supplemental material [2].

Fig. 5 compares MatchBox model to a number of baseline approachches. Fig. 5(A) reports *micro-* average precision where each (image, tag) pair $\hat{r}_{ij}$ is considered as a retrieval target; (B) reports macro AP (or mAP), mean average precision over different tags; (C) measures tag recommendation performance with precision @ 5 tags, for 1000 randomly selected test images with $\geq$5 tags. KNN and SVM are the visual-only results reported for NUS-WIDE [13], mAP of SVM classifier is shown to be below 0.06 and on par with

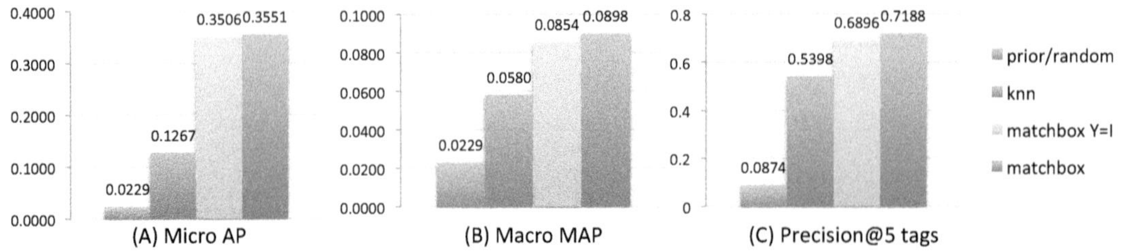

Figure 5: Image annotation results on NUS-WIDE dataset.

KNN. We can see that the bilinear matchbox model with tag features significantly outperforms the k-nearest neighbor (KNN) baseline and SVM reported earlier [43]. Matchbox with co-occurrence tag feature $\mathbf{Y}$ also outperforms the same bilinear model with identity features ($\mathbf{Y} = \mathbf{I}$) that do not share information across different tags.

6.2.1 *Tagging with unseen tags*

To evaluate the role of tag feature $\mathbf{Y}$ as a prior for tag-space similarity, we test the MatchBox model on new tags without training instances. This is similar to novel word recognition presented by Mitchell et al. [31], here we generalize using image features and tag usage, rather than using brain signals. Fig. 6 (A) reports annotation performance of the 20 most frequent tags without training data. We remove all positive instances of the tag from training set $\mathcal{L}$, and optimizes the same MatchBox objective. This model rely solely on $\mathbf{Y}$ to generalize across tags. We can see that the performance without training on the current tag are on average almost as good as those with training data, sometimes even better, such as *clouds* and *animal*. We also try to quantify the effects of tag features alone, and found that simple voting from the top-3 similar tags (T/1-voting) has comparable performance as those using feature similarities in $\mathbf{Y}$ (T/1). Fig. 6 (B) shows the top returned results for a number of free-text tags that are not in the NUS-WIDE labeled tag set. We can see that the top images of *travel* reflects two primary means of traveling: *cars* and *bicycle*; *blue* captures the color appearance of *water* and *sky*, and *architecture* is closet to learned tags *buildings, tower*, and *temple*. These results show that tag features indeed help generalize new, untrained tags in non-trivial ways.

6.2.2 *ICR for tagging*

We use the output of ICR for photo tagging. We start ICR on 93 synsets that directly map to, or mentions the NUS-WIDE tags in its name from CN5 to obtain a more complete graph estimate. We aggregate the set of resulting subgraphs $\hat{\mathbf{G}}^i$ over different synsets s_i by taking the max across elements indexed by the same tag-pair, generating $\hat{\mathbf{G}} = \{\hat{g}_{uv}\}$, where $\hat{g}_{uv} = \max_i\{\hat{g}^i_{uv}\}$. We then take elements of $\hat{\mathbf{G}}$ to the same row- and column-dimensions of the original tag feature $\mathbf{Y}$, denoted as $\hat{\mathbf{G}}_\mathbf{Y}$. We use the sum of $\mathbf{Y}$ and $\hat{\mathbf{G}}_\mathbf{Y}$ as the tag feature for MatchBox.

Figure 7 shows the mAP (macro average) for all 63 and the least frequent 43 tags. *cooc* is the original synset-tag co-occurrence feature (top bar in Fig. 5), *cn5* is using ConceptNet5 as-is for $\mathbf{G}_\mathbf{Y}$, and *icr5* uses $\hat{\mathbf{G}}_\mathbf{Y}$ after ICR. We can see that the adding *unsmoothed* tag relations from either *cn5* or *icr5* improves performance, and *icr5* further improves upon *cn5*. We also note that despite a small different mAP value, the improvement of *icr5* from *cooc* is statistically significant. Moreover, the relative improvement on the 43 rare tags (mAP-bottom43, 7.3%) is more than that across all tags (mAP-all, 3.6%). Further improvement can be expected when the target tag space is larger, and we leave this to future explorations.

7. RELATED WORK

A number of different research topics are related to our work, including understanding social tags, connecting words to pictures, picture tagging with multiple input modality and tag structure, multimedia knowledge sources, and network inference.

The recent rise of social tagging has elicited much research curiosity. Ames et al. [3] conduct surveys to understand motivation for user tagging on Flickr; Sigurbjornsson and Zwol [40] studies overall Flickr tag statistics; Bischoff et al. [9] classifies social tags into a few distinct categories, and Overellet al. [34] uses wikipedia for tag classification. A number of other work focus on the analyzing and recognizing specialized social tags, such as landmarks[23], events and places [39], or location names and proper nouns [48]. Weinberger and Slaney [48] propose a scalable approach to identify tags with ambiguous word senses, and suggest co-ocurring tags to disambiguate among its multiple meanings. All of these work provides useful insights and techniques for analyzing Flickr data, however none has profiled the use of everyday words as tags.

There are many methods for generating tags from visual and word input. Nearest-neighbor methods have been popular for large amounts of training data, photo tagging methods have relied on voting with photo metadata [40], or voting from neighbors in visual feature space and then aggregate their flickr tags [28]. Quelhas et al.[38] uses latent semantic analysis to extract visual scene patterns; Wang et al. [46] use bag-of-keypoints to illustrate a tag; Liu et al. [29], Tang et al. [43] and Qi et al. [37] design several algorithms for propagating picture tags from both visual content and noisy text. There has been competing approaches for learning multiple tags simultaneously, including full-connected graphical models [36], tree-structured graphical models derived from co-ocurrence data [11], pre-defined lexical hierarchies [14], co-ocurrence and colocations [30], Object Relation Network [10] for representing the most probable meaning of the objects and their relations in an image, and bilinear large-scale annotation model with approximate-rank loss called Wasabie [49]. A key differentiation of our work is two ways of representing prior knowledge, and a method to incorporate them as tag features for learning. Our proposed method is built upon recent developments in matrix factorization and social collaborative filtering [24, 41], while the particular application in image tagging is new.

Another related topic is to quantify the correspondence of visual elements and their descriptions. This include a "vi-

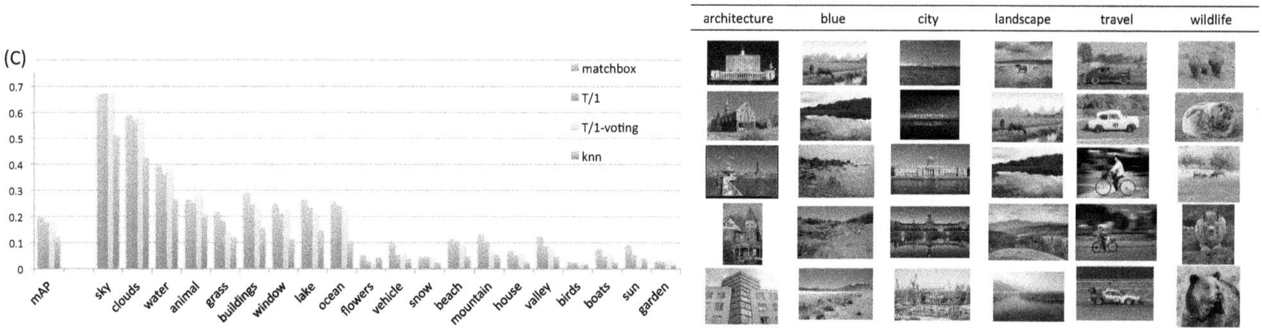

Figure 6: Annotation for unseen tags. (A) AP and mAP for the most frequent 20 NUS-WIDE tags with or without training instances (T/1), and nearest-neighbor voting in tag feature space (T/1-voting). (B) Top 5 returned images for freetext tags not in the NUS-WIDE set. See discussion in Sec 6.2.1.

sualness" measure via image region entropy [50], with both entropy and purity measures [22], determining representative web images [17], or a method to correlate visual and semantic similarities on ImageNet [15]. Recently the Stony Brook and UMD team worked on a complementary pair of problems: to predict the likelihood that a visual object is described in natural language from its properties (such as category, size and position) [8], and to detect which word(s) in a natural sentence has visual correspondence in the image that it is describing [16]. Compared to these interesting studies, our work quantifies the visual informativeness of a word by examining correlations in tagged collections alone, and do not rely on visual analysis on individual images.

Our work in mapping tag relations is inspired by research on representing real-world knowledge from web and multimedia sources. Several well-known visual ontologies have been manually designed by experts and covers a few dozen to a few hundred nodes [33]. Recently, ImageNet [13] uses images to illustrate a well-known language ontology WordNet [17], which contains tens of thousands of nodes, and has took over a decade to construct by a team of linguistic experts. Real-world knowledge databases has enlisted help from the general online crowd, YAGO and DBPedia [5, 42] are built upon Wikipedia, and ConceptNet [21] consist of crowd-sourced statements from a website over a number of years. This work can complement some of these large ontologies by providing statistical information about how words and word-to-word relations are grounded in images and used to describe images.

Inferring an underlying network from observed statistics is an interesting problem recently starting to receive more attention. The NetInf algorithm [19] estimates a directed network from observed diffusion traces, the supervised random walk [6] model learns a regressor on network parameters based on nodes reached by random walks. Our problem differs from the above as it estimates graph weights given aggregate stationary distribution statistics, not traces. This can be seen as the inverse of the well-known page-rank problem [26]. To the best of our knowledge, no solution to this problem exists.

8. CONCLUSIONS

We propose novel methods to analyze photo tags and tag relationships, using data from Flickr, ImageNet and ConceptNet. A novel network inference algorithm, ICR, is designed to estimate latent relationships from tag co-

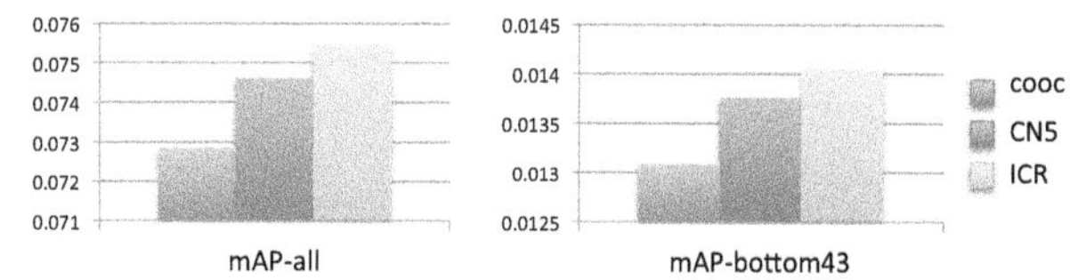

Figure 7: mAP for all and the least frequent 43 tags, with or without ConceptNet and ICR features. Note that the improvement from Co-occurence to ICR feature is statistically significant (p=0.008 from a paired t-test).

ocurrence. We obtain tag statistics on thousands of tags from millions of images. This allows us design an efficient tagging algorithm to simultaneously model many tags with image- and tag- features. The proposed tagging algorithm generalizes to unseen tags, and is further improved upon incorporating tag-relation features obtained via ICR. Core novel aspects of our work are in quantifying visual tag use and tag relations from social statistics, algorithms for network inference from aggregated occurrences, and using these insights for large-scale picture tagging.

The limitations of this work point to several directions for improvement and future work, such as: techniques to better incorporate multi-word terms and out-of-vocabulary words; advanced NLP techniques for learning word relations from free-form text; evaluation of latent concept relation suggestion, and predicting the type of relations.

Acknowledgments

This research was partially undertaken on the NCI National Facility in Canberra. NICTA is funded by the Australian Government through the Department of Broadband, Communications and the Digital Economy and the Australian Research Council.

9. REFERENCES

[1] ILSVRC, 2012.
http://www.image-net.org/challenges/LSVRC/2012 .

[2] Project webpage, 2013.
http://users.cecs.anu.edu.au/~xlx/proj/tagnet .

[3] M. Ames and M. Naaman. Why we tag: motivations for annotation in mobile and online media. CHI '07, pages 971–980, 2007.

[4] K. Atkinson. Official 12Dicts package.
http://wordlist.sourceforge.net , retrieved March 2012.

[5] S. Auer, C. Bizer, G. Kobilarov, J. Lehmann, R. Cyganiak, and Z. Ives. Dbpedia: A nucleus for a web of open data. *The Semantic Web*, pages 722–735, 2007.

[6] L. Backstrom and J. Leskovec. Supervised random walks: predicting and recommending links in social networks. WSDM '11, pages 635–644, 2011.

[7] K. Barnard, P. Duygulu, D. Forsyth, N. De Freitas, D. Blei, and M. Jordan. Matching words and pictures. *The Journal of Machine Learning Research*, 3:1107–1135, 2003.

[8] A. Berg, T. Berg, H. Daume, J. Dodge, A. Goyal, X. Han, A. Mensch, M. Mitchell, A. Sood, K. Stratos, et al. Understanding and predicting importance in images. In *CVPR*, pages 3562–3569. IEEE, 2012.

[9] K. Bischoff, C. S. Firan, W. Nejdl, and R. Paiu. Can all tags be used for search? CIKM '08, pages 193–202, 2008.

[10] N. Chen, Q.-Y. Zhou, and V. Prasanna. Understanding web images by object relation network. WWW '12, pages 291–300, 2012.

[11] M. Choi, A. Torralba, and A. Willsky. A tree-based context model for object recognition. *IEEE Trans. on Pattern Analysis and Machine Intelligence*, 34(2), 2012.

[12] T. Chua, J. Tang, R. Hong, H. Li, Z. Luo, and Y. Zheng. NUS-WIDE: A real-world web image database from national university of singapore. In *ACM CIVR*, 2009.

[13] J. Deng, W. Dong, R. Socher, L. Li, K. Li, and L. Fei-Fei. Imagenet: A large-scale hierarchical image database. In *IEEE CVPR*, pages 248–255. Ieee, 2009.

[14] J. Deng, S. Satheesh, A. Berg, and L. Fei-Fei. Fast and balanced: Efficient label tree learning for large scale object recognition. In *NIPS*, 2011.

[15] T. Deselaers and V. Ferrari. Visual and semantic similarity in imagenet. In *CVPR*, pages 1777–1784. IEEE, 2011.

[16] J. Dodge, A. Goyal, X. Han, A. Mensch, M. Mitchell, K. Stratos, K. Yamaguchi, Y. Choi, I. Hal Daumé, and A. Berg. Detecting visual text. In *North American Chapter of the Association for Computational Linguistics (NAACL)*, 2012.

[17] C. Fellbaum. Wordnet. *Theory and Applications of Ontology: Computer Applications*, pages 231–243, 2010.

[18] G. H. Golub and C. D. Meyer, Jr. Using the qr factorization and group inversion to compute, differentiate ,and estimate the sensitivity of stationary probabilities for markov chains. *SIAM J. Algebraic Discrete Methods*, 7(2):273–281, Apr. 1986.

[19] M. Gomez-Rodriguez, J. Leskovec, and A. Krause. Inferring networks of diffusion and influence. *ACM Trans. Knowl. Discov. Data*, 5(4):21:1–21:37, Feb. 2012.

[20] T. L. Griffiths, M. Steyvers, and A. Firl. Google and the mind predicting fluency with pagerank. *Psychological Science*, 18(12):1069–1076, 2007.

[21] C. Havasi, R. Speer, and J. Alonso. ConceptNet 3: a flexible, multilingual semantic network for common sense knowledge. In *Recent Advances in Natural Language Processing*, pages 27–29, 2007.

[22] J.-W. Jeong, X.-J. Wang, and D.-H. Lee. Towards measuring the visualness of a concept. CIKM '12, pages 2415–2418, 2012.

[23] L. Kennedy, M. Naaman, S. Ahern, R. Nair, and T. Rattenbury. How flickr helps us make sense of the world: context and content in community-contributed media collections. In *ACM Multimedia*, pages 631–640, 2007.

[24] Y. Koren, R. Bell, and C. Volinsky. Matrix factorization techniques for recommender systems. *Computer*, 42(8):30–37, 2009.

[25] S. Kullback and R. Leibler. On information and sufficiency. *The Annals of Mathematical Statistics*, 22(1):79–86, 1951.

[26] A. Langville and C. Meyer. *Google's PageRank and beyond: The science of search engine rankings*. Princeton University Press, 2009.

[27] L.-j. Li, H. Su, E. P. Xing, and L. Fei-fei. Object Bank : A High-Level Image Representation for Scene Classification & Semantic Feature Sparsification. In *NIPS*, pages 1–9, 2010.

[28] X. Li, C. G. M. Snoek, and M. Worring. Learning social tag relevance by neighbor voting. *IEEE Trans. Multi.*, 11(7):1310–1322, Nov. 2009.

[29] D. Liu, X.-S. Hua, L. Yang, M. Wang, and H.-J. Zhang. Tag ranking. WWW '09, pages 351–360, 2009.

[30] T. Malisiewicz and A. Efros. Beyond categories: The visual memex model for reasoning about object relationships. In *NIPS*, 2009.

[31] T. Mitchell, S. Shinkareva, A. Carlson, K. Chang, V. Malave, R. Mason, and M. Just. Predicting human brain activity associated with the meanings of nouns. *science*, 320(5880):1191–1195, 2008.

[32] J. Morales and J. Nocedal. Remark on "Algorithm 778: L-BFGS-B: Fortran subroutines for large-scale bound constrained optimization". *ACM Transactions on Mathematical Software (TOMS)*, 38(1):7, 2011.

[33] M. Naphade, J. Smith, J. Tesic, S. Chang, W. Hsu, L. Kennedy, A. Hauptmann, and J. Curtis. Large-scale concept ontology for multimedia. *Multimedia, IEEE*, 13(3):86–91, 2006.

[34] S. Overell, B. Sigurbjörnsson, and R. van Zwol. Classifying tags using open content resources. WSDM, 2009.

[35] K. B. Petersen and M. S. Pedersen. The matrix cookbook, oct 2008. Version 20081110.

[36] G. Qi, X. Hua, Y. Rui, J. Tang, T. Mei, and H. Zhang. Correlative multi-label video annotation. In *ACM Multimedia*, pages 17–26, 2007.

[37] G.-J. Qi, C. Aggarwal, and T. Huang. Towards semantic knowledge propagation from text corpus to web images. WWW '11, pages 297–306, 2011.

[38] P. Quelhas, F. Monay, J.-M. Odobez, D. Gatica-Perez, and T. Tuytelaars. A thousand words in a scene. *IEEE Transactions on Pattern Analysis and Machine Intelligence*, 29:1575–1589, 2007.

[39] T. Rattenbury, N. Good, and M. Naaman. Towards automatic extraction of event and place semantics from flickr tags. SIGIR, pages 103–110. ACM, 2007.

[40] B. Sigurbjörnsson and R. van Zwol. Flickr tag recommendation based on collective knowledge. WWW'08, pages 327–336. ACM, 2008.

[41] D. Stern, R. Herbrich, and T. Graepel. Matchbox: large scale online bayesian recommendations. In *Proc. World wide web*, pages 111–120. ACM, 2009.

[42] F. Suchanek, G. Kasneci, and G. Weikum. Yago: a core of semantic knowledge. In *World Wide Web*, pages 697–706. ACM, 2007.

[43] J. Tang, S. Yan, R. Hong, G.-J. Qi, and T.-S. Chua. Inferring semantic concepts from community-contributed images and noisy tags. In *ACM Multimedia*, pages 223–232, 2009.

[44] H. Tong, C. Faloutsos, and J. Pan. Fast random walk with restart and its applications. In *ICDM*. IEEE, 2006.

[45] K. Van De Sande, T. Gevers, and C. Snoek. Evaluating color descriptors for object and scene recognition. *Pattern Analysis and Machine Intelligence, IEEE Trans.*, 32(9):1582–1596, 2010.

[46] M. Wang, K. Yang, X.-S. Hua, and H.-J. Zhang. Visual tag dictionary: interpreting tags with visual words. In *Workshop on Web-scale multimedia corpus*, 2009.

[47] X.-J. Wang, Z. Xu, L. Zhang, C. Liu, and Y. Rui. Towards indexing representative images on the web. In *ACM Multimedia*, pages 1229–1238, 2012.

[48] K. Q. Weinberger, M. Slaney, and R. Van Zwol. Resolving tag ambiguity. In *ACM Multimedia*, pages 111–120, 2008.

[49] J. Weston, S. Bengio, and N. Usunier. Wsabie: Scaling up to large vocabulary image annotation. In *Proc. IJCAI*, pages 2764–2770. AAAI Press, 2011.

[50] K. Yanai and K. Barnard. Image region entropy: a measure of "visualness" of web images associated with one concept. In *Proc. ACM Multimedia*, pages 419–422, 2005.

Annotation for Free: Video Tagging by Mining User Search Behavior *

Ting Yao †, Tao Mei ‡, Chong-Wah Ngo †, Shipeng Li ‡
† City University of Hong Kong, Kowloon, Hong Kong
‡ Microsoft Research Asia, Beijing, P. R. China
tingyao.ustc@gmail.com; {tmei, shipeng.li}@microsoft.com; cscwngo@cityu.edu.hk

ABSTRACT

The problem of tagging is mostly considered from the perspectives of machine learning and data-driven philosophy. A fundamental issue that underlies the success of these approaches is the visual similarity, ranging from the nearest neighbor search to manifold learning, to identify similar instances of an example for tag completion. The need to searching for millions of visual examples in high-dimensional feature space, however, makes the task computationally expensive. Moreover, the results can suffer from robustness problem, when the underlying data, such as online videos, are rich of semantics and the similarity is difficult to be learnt from low-level features. This paper studies the exploration of user searching behavior through click-through data, which is largely available and freely accessible by search engines, for learning video relationship and applying the relationship for economic way of annotating online videos. We demonstrated that, by a simple approach using co-click statistics, promising results were obtained in contrast to feature-based similarity measurement.

Furthermore, considering the long tail effect that few videos dominate most clicks, a new method based on polynomial semantic indexing is proposed to learn a latent space for alleviating the sparsity problem of click-through data. The proposed approaches are then applied for three major tasks in tagging: tag assignment, ranking, and enrichment. On a bipartite graph constructed from click-through data with over 15 million queries and 20 million video URL clicks, we showed that annotation can be performed for free with competitive performance and minimum computing resource, representing a new and promising paradigm for video tagging in addition to machine learning and data-driven methodologies.

Categories and Subject Descriptors

I.2.10 [**Artificial Intelligence**]: Vision and Scene Understanding—*Video analysis*; H.3.3 [**Information Storage and Retrieval**]: Information Search and Retrieval—*Search process*

General Terms

Algorithms, Performance, Experimentation.

Keywords

Video Tagging, Tag Assignment, Tag Ranking, Tag Enrichment, Annotation, Video Search, Click-through Data.

*This work was performed when Ting Yao was visiting Microsoft Research Asia as a research intern.

MM'13, October 21–25, 2013, Barcelona, Spain.

http://dx.doi.org/10.1145/2502081.2502085.

1. INTRODUCTION

The advent of video sharing sites and rapid development of video technologies have led to the unprecedented Internet delivery of video content. Millions of users are searching, browsing, and sharing online videos as a source of information and entertainment daily. While the research on content-based video retrieval has been studied for decades, most commercial video search engines to date still heavily rely on user-provided tags for search. Therefore, tagging, or in another word, annotation, is the key not only to video search, but also to many applications such as video browsing and recommendation.

However, manually annotating video content is an intellectually expensive and time-consuming process. As a result, the tags provided by human subjects are often noisy, incomplete, subjective (biased), and sparse. This is particularly true for video, as video is a sequence of images with large content variance and complexity. Automatic annotation of videos with relevant and complete tags has attracted extensive research attentions in recent years.

The research on video annotation (tagging) has proceeded along two dimensions, i.e., model-based [8][14][23] and data driven [27][30] approaches. The model-based method always relies on pre-trained classifiers, while data driven approach aims to exploit video similarity for annotation. These approaches highly rely on computing the pair-wise video similarity in a high dimensional feature or semantic space. However, compared with the image, a video is typically associated with more complicated semantics. Furthermore, it is difficult to represent a video sequence using simple visual or aural features. As a result, the video similarity (or distance) computed in these spaces is usually not robust and computationally expensive, limiting the capacity of the existing approaches in scaling up to real data.

On the other hand, popular video search engines provide rich connection between users' search intent and video content. We are investigating in this paper if users' searching behavior can be exploited for measuring video similarity and

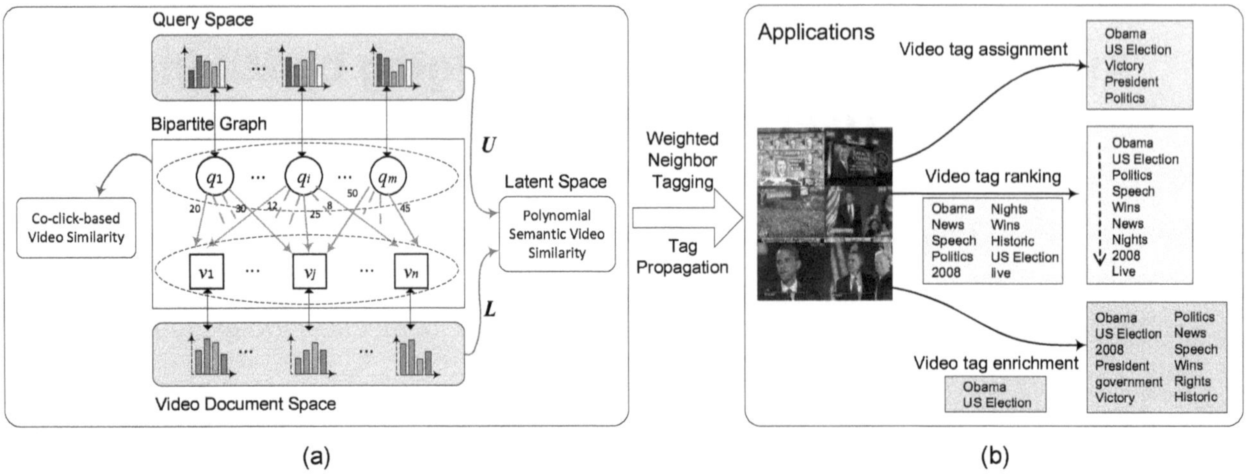

Figure 1: Unified video tagging framework. (a) Relationships mining between videos: the click-through bipartite enclosed in the rectangle is extracted from video search logs. Co-click-based video similarity captures video relationship only on the structure of the bipartite graph. Polynomial semantic video similarity combines video document features and click-through bipartite to learn two mappings. With this, video document features are projected into a latent space and then the dot product in the latent space is taken as the similarity function. (b) Based on the two proposed video tagging methods, i.e., weighted neighbor tagging and tag propagation, various applications on video tag analysis can be formulated within a unified framework. For better viewing, please see original color pdf file.

in turn resulting in scalable and efficient video tagging with million scale. This provides a new paradigm for video tagging by leveraging the "latent" and "crowdsourcing" human intelligence which is the underlying user click-through. As we all know that manual tagging of videos is expensive, but the search logs are not that expensive to obtain.

Using the implicit feedback from search engine users has been studied in the research, though not in the domain of web video. These efforts include web document search by query log analysis [6][15], query suggestion [17][19], query clustering [3][31], user behavior understanding [4][11][24] and image search [7][13]. Inspired by the successful use of click-through data in these domains, in this paper, we consider exploring and exploiting information from both click-through data and video document features to shed some light on video and video similarities measurement, and furthermore, demonstrating the utilization of searching behavior for three problems in video tagging. Figure 1 shows an overview of our proposed work. A bipartite graph between the user queries and videos is constructed by using the search logs of a video search engine. An edge between a query and a video is established, if the users who issue the query clicked and watched the video. The edges of the graph can capture some relations between query-query, query-video and video-video. For example, videos about "2008 US election" and "2012 US President Obama" are related to each other, since they are co-clicked with some queries such as "Obama", "election" and so on. Therefore, the basic idea of co-click is that two videos are similar if they are co-clicked by users with same queries, and thus leads to the intuition that the tags between them can be exchanged to enrich the descriptions. However, solely depending on click-through data overlooks the following challenges: on one hand, only click-through data is explored and exploited in the co-click method, thus the method can not be applied to videos with no clicks; on the other, users always looked at and clicked on the top search results for a query, which makes the click-through data with high sparsity. Therefore, in practice, the use of co-click method is challenging due to the high sparsity of click-through data.

To address the above issues, we leverage both the click-through data and the video document features to learn video similarities, which fully explores the relations between videos. Specifically, we use two mappings to project queries and video documents in a click-through bipartite into a same latent space. The two mappings are supposed to be different since the query distribution is very different to the video document distribution. We formalize the two mappings learning as an optimization problem, in which the objective is to minimize the margin ranking loss of the observed query-video pairs on the click-through bipartite. The dot product in the latent space is taken as the similarity function between video and video, and the tags of one video will be assigned to its similar videos as extra metadata. It is worth noticing that although we only utilize the video-video similarities for the video tagging problem, the learned query-query similarities and query-document similarities can be equivalently applied to any kind of related applications such as query suggestion and video search.

In summary, this paper makes the following contributions:

- We study the problem of video tagging by leveraging user click-through data. To the best of knowledge, this paper represents the first effort towards this target in the multimedia research community.
- We propose two video similarity measures, i.e., co-click-based and polynomial semantic video similarity. The former relies on the structure of click-through bipartite, while the later learns the similarity in a latent space based on the click-through data.
- The proposed approach can solve video tag assignment, tag ranking, and tag enrichment problems in a single framework. We evaluate the proposed video tagging approach on a large scale of user click-through data collected from a commercial video search engine.

The remaining sections are organized as follows. Section 2 describes the related work. Section 3 presents the video similarity measures including co-click-based and polynomial semantic methods, while Section 4 formulates the problem of video tagging over the discovered video-video similarities. In Section 5, we analyze the click-through data generated from large-scale query logs. Section 6 provides empirical evaluations, followed by the discussion and conclusions in Section 7.

2. RELATED WORK

We briefly group the related works into two categories: video annotation and search by using click data. The former draws upon research in automatically assigning tags (annotations) to a video sequence, and the later investigates Web search and mining by interpreting the click-through data.

2.1 Video Annotation (Tagging)

Video annotation has received intensive research attention since the early of year 2000 [28], and is probably the "hottest" topic with a large number of published papers in the area of multimedia. The research in this direction has proceeded along two different dimensions: model-based methods [8][14][23] and data driven approaches [27][30].

Model-based methods assume that a training set of videos along with keyword annotations is provided for developing concept classifiers. Cristianini *et al.* employed SVM with one-against-the-other strategy to learn a set of detectors, each of which independently models the presence/absence of a certain concept in [8]. Later in [14], Jiang *et al.* used a Context Based Concept Fusion-based learning method. Users are involved in their approach to annotate a few concepts for extra videos, and these manual annotations were then utilized to help infer and improve detections of other concepts. In [23], Qi *et al.* proposed correlative multilabel method to simultaneously model both the individual concepts and their correlations in a unifying formulation and the principle of least commitment was obeyed.

Different from model-based methods, data driven approaches construct video similarity for annotation. In [21], tag propagation technique is developed by crawling tags of similar videos for annotation by using text and visual features in a graph reinforcement framework. In [27], the overlapping or duplicated content of videos was exploited for measuring video similarity. With this, tags associated with similar videos were exchanged for generating new tag assignments. In another work by Wang [30], both distance between samples and the difference of their surrounding neighborhood sample distributions were taken into account for video similarity estimation.

2.2 Search by Using Click Data

Click-through data has been studied and analyzed widely with different Web mining techniques for improving search engines' efficacy and usability in recent years. The use of the click-through data for query clustering was suggested by Befferman and Berger [3], who proposed an agglomerative clustering technique to identify related queries and Web pages. Wen *et al.* [31] combined query content information and click-through information and applied a density-based method to cluster queries. The click-through data has been studied for query expansion in the past [9]. Mei *et al.* [20] proposed an approach to query suggestion by computing the hitting time on a click graph. Li *et al.* [18] presented the use of click graphs in improving query intent classifiers.

There are also several approaches that have tried to model the representation of queries or documents on the click-through bipartite. In [1], the authors introduced another vectorial representation for the queries without considering the content information. Queries were represented as points in a high dimensional space, where each dimension corresponds to a unique URL. The weight assigned to each dimension was equal to the click frequency. This is one of the traditional click frequency models. Poblete *et al.* [22] proposed the query-set document model by mining frequent query patterns to represent documents rather than the content information of the documents.

In addition, click-through data has also been used to learn the rank function [15]. Joachims *et al.* [16] observed the relationship between clicked links and the relevance of the target pages by an eye tracking experiment. Radlinski *et al.* [25] concluded that the click-through data is not reliable for obtaining absolute relevance judgements, and is also affected by the retrieval quality of the underlying system. For image search, click-through data has been found to be very reliable [7][13]. In [7], Craswell *et al.* built a query-image click graph and performed backward random walks to determine a probability distribution over images conditioned on the given query which can be used for ranking. Later in [13], Jain *et al.* reranked the image search results so as to promote images that are likely to be clicked to the top of the ranked list. In another work by Trevisiol *et al.* [29], an in-depth analysis of several ranking algorithms was performed on Flickr user log data to investigate the importance of many factors, including internal and external image popularity, the overall attentions, diversity, semantic categories and visual appearance. However, to the best of our knowledge, no work leveraging click data is proposed for video search domain.

3. LEARNING VIDEO RELATIONSHIP FROM CLICK-THROUGH

In this section, we first define the bipartite graph that naturally comes from user actions in the query log, followed by the co-click method to mine video similarity on the structure of the click-through bipartite graph. Then, a polynomial semantic video similarity algorithm is proposed to solve the issues of click-through data incompleteness and no-click data for new coming queries (videos) by combining the bipartite graph and video features.

3.1 Notation

Let $\mathscr{G} = (\mathcal{V}, \mathcal{E})$ denote a click-through bipartite as shown in the left part of Figure 2. $\mathcal{V} = Q \cup V$ is the set of vertices, which consists of a query set $Q = \{q_k\}_{k=1}^m \subset \mathbb{R}^D$ and a video set $V = \{v_k\}_{k=1}^n \subset \mathbb{R}^D$, and D is the feature dimension. $\mathcal{E}$ is the set of edges between query vertices and video vertices. In addition, there exists rich metadata on the vertices of the click-through bipartite and the metadata consists of queries (videos) content features.

3.2 Co-click-based Video Similarity

Given the click-through bipartite graph $\mathscr{G}$, we can define a co-click matrix from the structure of the bipartite graph. The element of the matrix stands for the number of queries

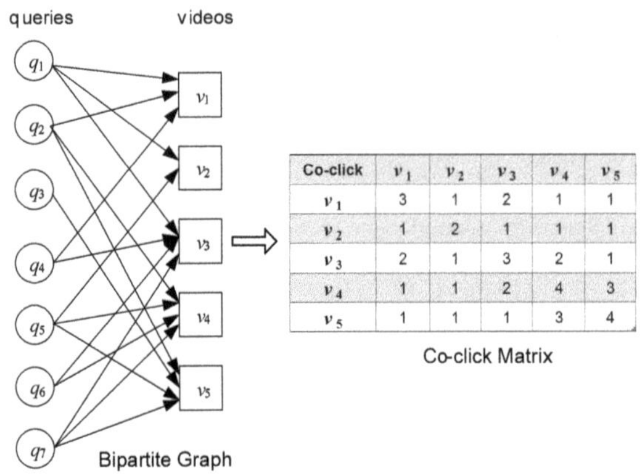

Figure 2: Co-click Method. A click-through bipartite with seven queries and five videos is illustrated and the co-click matrix on this bipartite is given accordingly.

with which the two video pages are both clicked. The co-click value of a video with itself is the number of clicks received by the video from all the queries. Figure 2 shows an example of one bipartite graph and its co-click matrix. For simplicity, we assume that each video is clicked by queries only once in Figure 2. Take v_1 as an example, the video is clicked by q_1, q_2 and q_4, thus the co-click number of v_1 with itself will be 3. Similarly, v_1 and v_2 are both clicked only by q_1, hence the co-click value of v_1 and v_2 is 1.

Next we describe how to measure the similarity of two videos based on the co-click matrix. The co-click number of a video v_i with itself is denoted as C_i, while the co-click value between v_i and v_j is denoted as C_{ij}. With these notations, the similarity $\omega(v_i, v_j)$ between two videos v_i and v_j based on the co-click relationship can be defined as

$$\omega(v_i, v_j) = \frac{C_{ij}}{\sqrt{C_i C_j}}. \qquad (1)$$

The rationale underlying this formula is that, if two videos are clicked by mostly the same queries, the two videos are likely to be similar to each other. The similarity is offset by the number of video clicks from all the queries, which moderates the similarity score in the case when some videos received more clicks than others. These videos are generally more common than others. With the normalization, the similarity measure is in the range of $[0, 1]$.

3.3 Polynomial Semantic Video Similarity

It is easy to demonstrate that co-click method could achieve promising performance if the click-through data is complete, i.e. each query is associated with all the related documents. But unfortunately, in real-world search, the key challenge in doing so arises from the fact that the click-through data is very sparse. For many of the queries, a handful of relevant videos had received a large number of clicks but the total number of clicked videos ranged typically from ten to a hundred. Generalizing co-click method to all the videos becomes very challenging in such scenarios. Deriving from the ideas of Polynomial Semantic Indexing (PSI) [2], and related methods such as Partial Least Squares (PLS) [26] and Latent Semantic Indexing (LSI) [10], we develop a polynomial semantic video similarity (PSVS) approach to model the relations in a click-through bipartite by projecting queries and videos into a latent space. With this, the video similarities can be calculated by the dot product of their mappings in the latent space.

Given a query q and a video v, we wish to learn two mappings, which can map query q from query space and video v from video document space into a common latent space. With this, the learned ranking function $f(q, v)$ that returns a score measuring the relevance of v given q can be better satisfied with the query-video click-through observations. Let us first consider the function $f(q, v)$ as

$$f(q, v) = \sum_{i,j=1}^{D} W_{ij} q_{(i)} v_{(j)} = q^T W v, \qquad (2)$$

where $q_{(i)}$ ($v_{(j)}$) stands for the ith (j^{th}) dimension of the feature vector and W is the learning matrix. As discussed in [2], the huge memory requirement and large amount number of parameters for W make the model training hardly be possible for realistic tasks. Thus, a low-rank approximation of W which will lead to capacity control, smaller memory and less computational cost is given by

$$\bar{W}_{ij} = (U^T L)_{ij} + I_{ij}. \qquad (3)$$

After plugging the approximation matrix into ranking function $f(q, v)$, we can derive that

$$f(q, v) = q^T (U^T L + I) v = \sum_{i=1}^{Y} (Uq)_{(i)} (Lv)_{(i)} + q^T v, \qquad (4)$$

where U and L are $Y \times D$ matrices and induce a Y-dimensional latent space.

The training of U and L could be many forms. From our click-through data, we can easily get a set of triplets $\mathcal{T}$, where each tuple (q, v^+, v^-) consists of the query q, a video v^+ with higher click and a lower clicked video v^-. Deriving from the idea of "learning to rank" [12][15], it aims to optimize U and L which makes $f(q, v^+) > f(q, v^-)$, i.e. video v^+ should be ranked higher than video v^-. The margin ranking loss [12] which has been used in several information retrieval methods [5][15] is employed and the optimization problem is defined as

$$\textit{minimize}: \sum_{(q,v^+,v^-) \in \mathcal{T}} \max(0, 1 - f(q, v^+) + f(q, v^-)). \qquad (5)$$

Algorithm 1 presents the learning procedure. We train this using stochastic gradient descent [5] for our model due to its efficiency and capability of applying to highly scalable problems. The algorithm of polynomial semantic video similarity has several characteristics in the following:

- Preference Relations: the proposed polynomial semantic video similarity advocates the training using preference relations, which are mined from user implicit feedback. Roughly speaking, if video A has significantly more clicks than video B when given a query q, then users should have a preference for A. These preferences are used as supervised signals for our training.

- Low Rank: the matrices U and L are $Y \times D$ dimensions, where $Y \ll D$. Thus, it will sharply reduce the memory and capacity cost, and speed up the training procedure. That makes the algorithm highly applicable and flexible when applied to the practical Web applications.

Algorithm 1 Polynomial Semantic Video Similarity

Input:
⋆ Click-through bipartite $\mathscr{G} = (\mathcal{V}, \mathcal{E})$.
⋆ Query feature q and video feature v.
Initialization:
⋆ Generate a set of triplets (q, v^+, v^-) as labeled data based on the click-through data.
⋆ Initialize the matrices U and L using a normal distribution with mean zero and standard deviation one.
⋆ Initialize the learning rate α.
For all the triplets:
Update the new matrices U and L:
$U = U + \alpha L(v^+ - v^-)q^T, \quad if \quad 1 - f(q, v^+) + f(q, v^-) > 0$
$L = L + \alpha Uq(v^+ - v^-)^T, \quad if \quad 1 - f(q, v^+) + f(q, v^-) > 0$
End
Output:
Similarity functions:
Video similarity: $\forall v, v', \quad \omega(v, v') = v^T L^T L v'$
Query similarity: $\forall q, q', \quad \omega(q, q') = q^T U^T U q'$

- Similarity Measurement: matrices U and L are the two mappings from query space and video document space into a Y-dimensional latent space. These two mappings are learned on the observations of query-video click-through bipartite. When obtaining the two mappings, the relations of query-query and video-video can be modeled by projecting them into the latent space. Although only video-video relations are used for the following video tagging problem, query-video and query-query relations can be equivalently used in their related applications.
- Incremental: the complexity of polynomial semantic video similarity algorithm is linear to the number of training triplets, which makes it easy to implement and update. When the new click-through data is coming, new query video preference triplets will be firstly generated and then used to update the two matrices U and L accordingly. Moreover, early stopping can be assessed with a validation set for further reducing the computational cost.

4. VIDEO TAGGING

After we get the relationships between videos, how to use them for automatic tagging? In this section, two video tagging approaches, i.e., weighted neighbor tagging and tag propagation, will be described. The weighted neighbor tagging method once only takes immediately neighbor video into account for automatic tag assignment, while the tag propagation approach further propagates the video relationships and considers all the related videos simultaneously.

4.1 Weighted Neighbor Tagging

Let $V_r = \{v_i : 1 \le i \le N\}$ be the video collection where each video has one or more relationships to others and let $Tag = \{t_1, \ldots, t_k, \ldots, t_M\}$ be the set of tags initially assigned to the videos in V_r. Let $I(t_k, v_i)$ be an indicator function, with $I(t_k, v_i) = 1$ if v_i was manually tagged with tag t_k, otherwise $I(t_k, v_i) = 0$. The tag relevance score $rel(t_k, v_i)$ of a tag t_k from neighbor videos is computed as

$$rel(t_k, v_i) = \sum_{\substack{v_i, v_j \in V_r \\ t_k \in Tag}} \omega(v_i, v_j) I(t_k, v_j). \tag{6}$$

In this way, we compute a weighted sum of influences of the related videos containing tags. Then we can automatically assign new tags for each video v_i. Basically, there are two major ways of utilizing the result. The simplest way is by sorting the tags according to their relevance scores and popping top k tags as the final result. An alternative way is by producing a threshold δ for tag relevancy. Tags whose relevance scores are above δ will be set as the new tags.

4.2 Tag Propagation

So far, we have just considered the direct relationships between videos. Next, all the relationships between videos are deployed holistically in a random walk framework to better compute the tag relevancy. It is worth noticing that the objective of tag propagation is not to assign relevance values for the videos, but it is an approach for computing relevance values of a tag t_k for a given video v_i.

Denote p_{ij} as the transition probability from video v_i to video v_j, and $I(t_k, v_i)$ and $TR(t_k, v_i)$ as the initial and updated relevance scores of a tag t_k to a video v_i, respectively. The tag propagation is formulated as following

$$\begin{pmatrix} TR(t_k, v_1) \\ TR(t_k, v_2) \\ \vdots \\ TR(t_k, v_N) \end{pmatrix} = \lambda \begin{pmatrix} p_{11} & \cdots & p_{1N} \\ p_{21} & \cdots & p_{2N} \\ \vdots & \ddots & \vdots \\ p_{N1} & \cdots & p_{NN} \end{pmatrix}^T \begin{pmatrix} TR(t_k, v_1) \\ TR(t_k, v_2) \\ \vdots \\ TR(t_k, v_N) \end{pmatrix} + (1 - \lambda) \begin{pmatrix} I(t_k, v_1) \\ I(t_k, v_2) \\ \vdots \\ I(t_k, v_N) \end{pmatrix}, \tag{7}$$

where the tradeoff parameter λ $(0 \le \lambda \le 1)$ weights the importance of the propagated and initial scores. Note that the first term in the equation represents information exchange from neighboring videos, while the second term is the original tag relevance score. The element p_{ij} is given by

$$p_{ij} = \frac{\omega_{ij}}{\sum_k \omega_{ik}}, \tag{8}$$

where ω_{ij} is the video similarity between video v_i and v_j, as discussed in Section 3.

The spirit of tag propagation is to give a higher relevance score for tag t_k to a video v_i if the video is in close proximity with other videos that are also highly relevant to the tag t_k. For each tag in the collection Tag, the above iterative propagation will be repeated. To the end, the refined relevance between tags and videos are produced and tags assigned to the video can be generated and ranked by their relevance scores.

4.3 Discussion

The proposed work can handle different practical scenarios in a unified framework. For a no-tag video, tagging can be carried out by crawling relevant tags from similar videos (tag assignment). For a video with only few tags, the coverage of tag list can be expanded by including additional tags from other similar videos not in the original tag list (tag enrichment). Finally, for videos with abundant tags, tags can be sorted according to their relevancy by getting clue from the appearance of the tags in similar videos (tag ranking). In all the tasks, tagging is for free as the click-through data, which plays the essential role in mining similar videos, are largely and freely available for access by search engines.

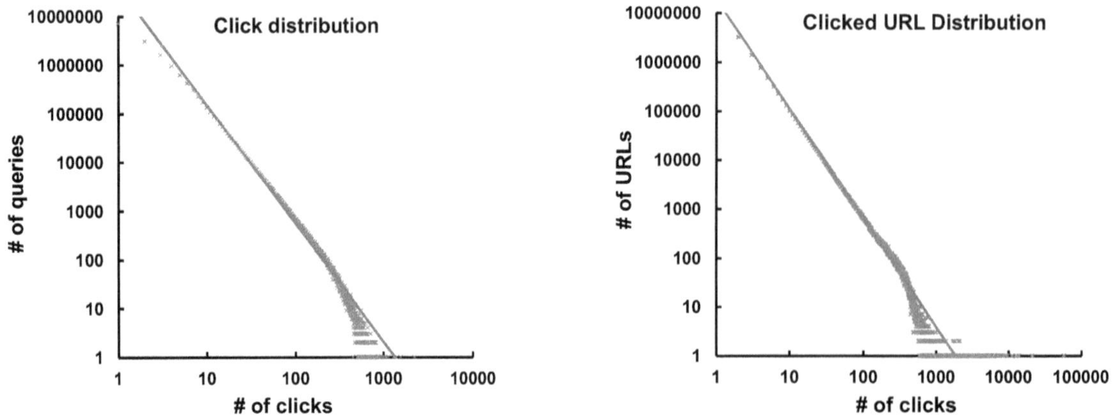

(a) Click Distribution (b) Clicked URL Distribution

Figure 3: Query click and clicked URL distribution for the click-through data. Red lines denote the fitting power law curves.

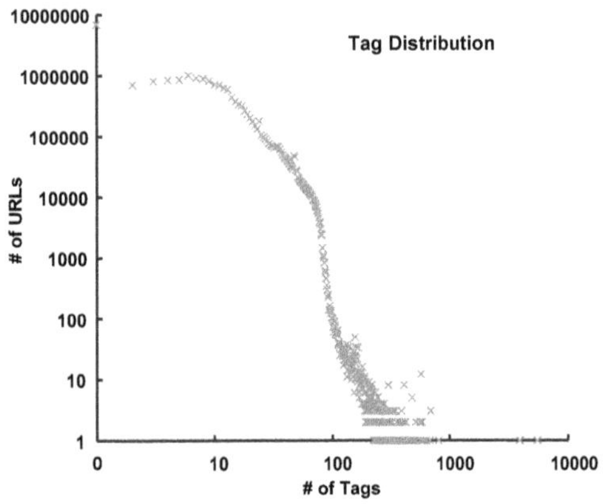

Figure 4: Tag distribution for the click-through data.

Table 1: Coefficients of Power laws of Click Distribution and Clicked URL Distribution, respectively.

Power laws: Ax^B	A	B
Click Distribution	41427273	-2.43
Clicked URL Distribution	19082457	-2.23

5. DATA ANALYSIS

We have collected one month query logs in November 2012 from a commercial video search engine. The query logs are represented as plain text files that contain a line for each HTTP request satisfied by the Web server. For each record, the following fields are used in our data collection:

$$< Query, ClickedURL, ClickCount, Title, Description, Tags >,$$

the *ClickedURL* and *ClickCount* represent the URL and number of clicks on this URL when user submit the *Query*, respectively. Note that *ClickCount* is cumulated over all identical queries. *Title*, *Description* and *Tags* denote the corresponding textual information associated with the clicked video.

For building the click-through bipartite, we used all the queries in the log with at least one click. There are 15,697,027 queries and 21,000,433 URLs on the bipartite graph. Figure 3 gives the main characteristics of the query and URL distribution. Figure 3(a) shows the query click distribution. Each point represents the number of queries (y axis) with a given number of clicks (x axis). The plot on Figure 3(b) shows the clicked URL distribution. Each point denotes the number of URLs with a given number of clicks. We can see that these two distributions clearly follow power laws. The observation is similar to [1], which also states that the user search behavior follows a power law. For details, the associated law is plotted in Figure 3, and the law coefficients are listed in Table 1. According to the statistics, each query has on average 4.08 clicked URLs and each URL was clicked by 3.12 times on average.

Figure 4 further shows the statistics of the video tags. Each point represents the number of videos with a given number of tags. Among all videos, more than 65% videos have 1 to 100 tags, followed by around 33% videos having no tags, and less than 0.1% videos having more than 100 tags.

6. EXPERIMENT

We conducted our experiments on the aforementioned click-through data and evaluated our approaches on video tag assignment, video tag ranking and video tag enrichment.

6.1 Experimental Settings

Compared Approaches: We compare the following approaches for performance evaluation:

- Initial tags. The original tag list associated with the video. We name this run as *Initial*. We simply treat the tag order in the original list, giving that the first tag is usually more representative than the second and so on.

- Cosine similarity. The video-video relationship is measured by the cosine similarity on the video features. Then two video tagging runs based on weighted neighbor tagging (WN) and tag propagation (TP) are performed, and named as $Cos + WN$ and $Cos + TP$ respectively.

- Partial least squares [26]. A typical method which aims to model the relations between two or more feature spaces by projecting them into a latent space. We employed the Partial Least Squares method on our

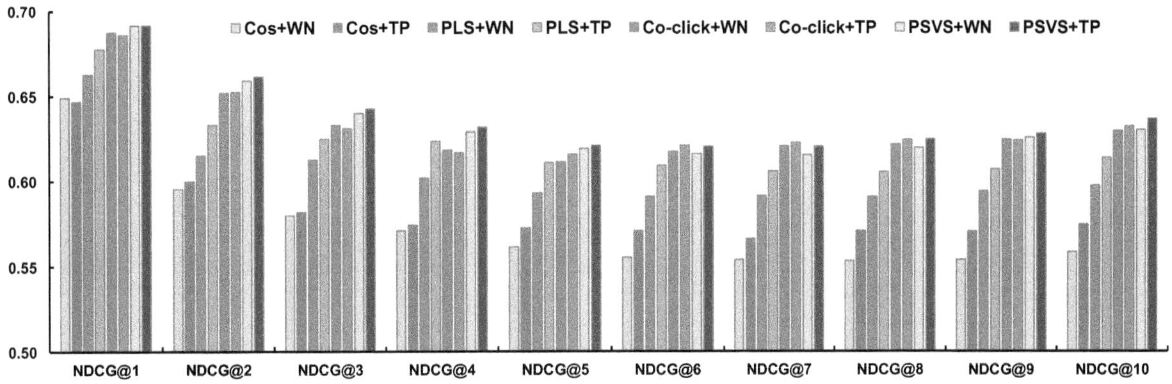

Figure 5: The NDCG of different approaches for video tag assignment.

click-through bipartite with query and video document features. We name the two runs as $PLS + WN$ and $PLS + TP$ by using the two video tagging methods, respectively.

- Co-click-based video similarity. We design two runs for co-click based video similarity described in Section 3.2: $Co\text{-}click + WN$ and $Co\text{-}click + TP$.
- Polynomial semantic video similarity. Similarly, two runs, i.e., $PSVS + WN$ and $PSVS + TP$, are experimented based on the polynomial semantic video similarity with the proposed two tagging approaches.

Parameter Setting: We take the word in queries and video URLs including title, description, and tags as features. Words are stemmed and stop words are removed. With word features, each query is represented by a $tf\text{-}idf$ vector in the query space, and each video is represented by a $tf\text{-}idf$ vector in the video document space. In our experiments, we use only the top 100,000 most frequent words. Moreover, we randomly select 2 million triplets as the training data for our polynomial semantic indexing. The learning rate α is fixed using a validation set of 0.5 million triplets and set as $\alpha = 0.06$ in the experiment. The dimension Y of latent space is empirically set to 200. For the tradeoff parameter λ in the tag propagation, we set $\lambda = 0.9$ for all the TP runs, making the similarities output by different approaches comparable.

Ground Truth: To facilitate the evaluation and comparison with other methods, we randomly selected 2,500 URLs as the test samples, in which 500 URLs without tags are evaluated for video tag assignment and the remaining 2,000 URLs with initial tags are tested in video tag ranking and enrichment tasks. For each URL, the top 20 tags in the ranked lists obtained by different approaches are all annotated during the final evaluation. We invited nine evaluators from different education backgrounds, including computer science, linguistics, physics, industry, business, and design. All evaluators are familiar with video sharing websites. Every URL-tag pair was annotated on a three point ordinal scale: 2-Highly Relevant; 1-Relevant; 0-Non-relevant. Note that obtaining just these annotations was very time-consuming. The evaluators are requested to watch the whole video before assigning labels. Whenever the relevancy judgments cannot be made by visual inspection alone, the evaluators have to read the text description and even refer to external sources (e.g., Web pages, Wikipedia) for understanding the background behind the video.

Evaluation Metrics: For the evaluation of video tag assignment and video tag ranking, we adopted Normalized Discounted Cumulative Gain ($NDCG$) which takes into account the measure of multi-level relevancy as the performance metric. Given a tag ranked list, the $NDCG$ score at the depth of d in the ranked list is defined by:

$$NDCG@d = Z_d \sum_{j=1}^{d} \frac{2^{r^j} - 1}{\log(1 + j)} \qquad (9)$$

where r^j represents the rating of a tag in the ground-truth, Z_d is a normalization constant such that $NDCG@d = 1$ for perfect ranking and 0 otherwise. In the evaluation of video tag enrichment, the metrics of Precision, Recall and F1-Measure are employed.

6.2 Evaluation of Video Tag Assignment

The problem of video tag assignment is to assign a set of tags to a given video for describing the video content. As described in section 6.1, 500 video URLs without tags are tested.

Figure 5 shows the $NDCG$ performances of eight runs. Note that the *Initial* run is excluded because the test video contains no tags. Overall, the results across different depths of $NDCG$ consistently indicate that using click-through data leads to a performance boost against cosine similarity, which relies on only video document features. Furthermore, $PSVS$ utilizing click-through data as relative relevance judgements also exhibits better performance than PLS, which uses the absolute click numbers for learning. The result basically indicates that click-through data does not convey absolute relevance judgements, but partial relative relevance judgements.

Comparing $PSVS$ to $Co\text{-}click$, performance improvement is observed especially in the top few ranked tags. Basically $PSVS$ has better capability in recalling relevant tags, for leveraging video document features to compensate the sparsity of click-through data. Compared to the weighted neighbor tagging, tag propagation can constantly lead to better performance gain. This somewhat reveals the weakness of linear fusion behind the weighted neighbor tagging, where the relationships between videos are considered individually. Tag propagation, in contrast, is benefited from the way of formulating the video tag assignment as a random

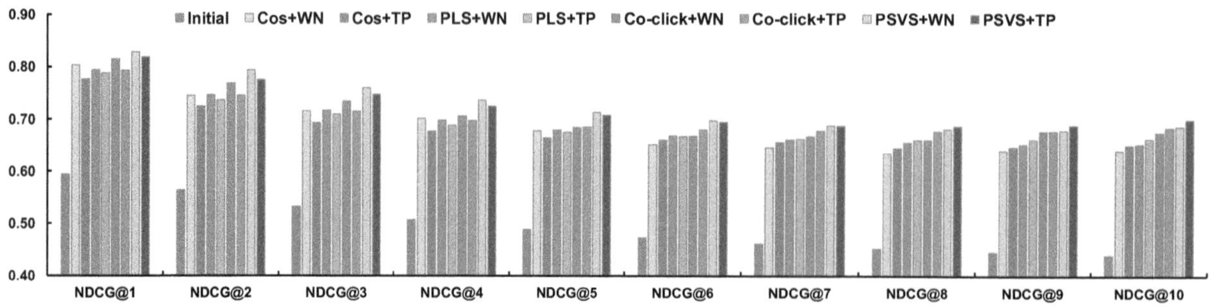

Figure 6: The NDCG of different approaches for video tag ranking.

Table 2: Quality comparison of the tags obtained by each method. Each measurement has been averaged over all evaluated URLs.

Method	Precision	Recall	F1-Measure
Initial	0.198	0.33	0.247
Cos+WN	0.376	0.72	0.453
Cos+TP	0.40	0.778	0.484
PLS[26]+WN	0.378	0.718	0.453
PLS[26]+TP	0.407	0.782	0.49
Co-click+WN	0.399	0.764	0.479
Co-click+TP	0.415	0.803	0.50
PSVS+WN	0.403	0.766	0.484
PSVS+TP	**0.419**	**0.808**	**0.504**

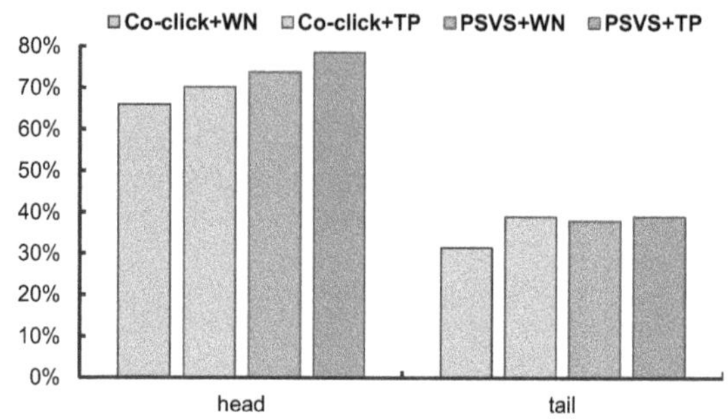

Figure 7: Performance improvement of test videos returned by head and tail queries, respectively. The performance are compared against the results w.r.t their tag ranking at NDCG@10.

walk over the whole video similarity graph. Figure 8(a) lists the tags generated by different methods on two exemplary videos. *PSVS* and *co−click* achieve better qualitative results than others, and quantitatively *PSVS+TP* recalls the most number of relevant tags than others.

6.3 Evaluation of Video Tag Ranking

In addition to tagging the no-tag videos, we also evaluated the performance of tag ranking on 2,000 videos with initial tags supplied by users. Based on the scores output by a run, the initial tags are ranked according to their relevancy to a video. Tag ranking is an important task that helps browsing of videos by prioritizing the tags to be displayed and indexed.

Figure 6 shows the performance of different runs. All the methods exhibit significantly better performance than the *Initial* run, clearly showing the advantages of exploiting video relationship for tag ranking. Particularly, by building the relationship based upon click-through data that underlies the latent human feedback, the similarities of videos are more objectively measured. This basically facilitates the evaluation of tag importance as evidenced by the good performance of *PSVS* and *Co−click* in comparison to others. Similar to the results of video tagging, *PSVS* shows the strongest performance followed by *Co−click*.

A different observation compared to evaluation of tag assignment, however, is that the runs based on weighted neighbor tagging exhibit better performance in ranking the top five tags than the runs based on tag propagation. One analysis shows that, when there are few tags that dominantly appear in the videos, the weighted neighbor tagging, which performs weighted voting of tags, is effective in boosting these tags into the top few positions. Tag propagation, on the other hand, somewhat diffuses the scores of these tags through random walk, but has a better ability in recalling more relevant tags not dominantly appear, and thus shows better performance when going deeper into the ranked list. Figure 8(b) shows the list of tags ranked by different approaches on two exemplary videos.

Furthermore, we split the test videos into two subsets, i.e., *head* and *tail*. The former is the video set returned by head queries, which have more than 100 clicks on different URLs, while the later represents the video set returned by tail queries, which have less than 100 clicks. Figure 7 shows the degree of improvement on two sets of videos. The result indicates that improvement can be generally expected, and larger degree of improvement is attained when the videos are returned by head queries.

6.4 Evaluation of Video Tag Enrichment

We adopted Precision, Recall and F1-measure as performance metric. The evaluation requires the full set of tags that are relevant to videos. However, practically such ground truth is difficult to obtain because there are rich of words that can potentially enrich the description of a video. Instead, we adopted the pooling strategy, which evaluates the top 20 tags pooled from different runs and generate the ground truth for measure the Recall.

Table 2 lists the performance of eight different runs. Compared to the initial tags assigned to videos, more new and relevant tags are introduced. As shown in the table, by using *PSVS + TP*, the newly brought in tags enhance the coverage of the initial tags, significantly raising the Recall from 0.33 to 0.808 while improving the Precision. Comparing all runs, *PSVS* again shows consistently better performance in both Precision and Recall.

Figure 8: Examples showing the tagging results by different methods (For better viewing, please see original color pdf file). For each row, the first block shows the keyframes of a test video, followed by each block showing the top 15 tags annotated by a method. The correct tags are highlighted by yellow color.

6.5 Complexity Analysis

The complexity of our proposed $PSVS$ learning is $O(|\mathcal{T}| \times Y \times D)$, where $|\mathcal{T}|$ represents the number of the training triplets. The training of 2 million triplets in our experiment can be finished within five days on one server. More importantly, the training complexity is linear to the number of triplets, which makes the update with incremental triplets very fast. For the video tagging, take 500 videos to perform video tag assignment for example, WN and TP take less than 2.5 and 13 seconds on a regular PC (Intel dual-core 3.33GHz CPU and 8 GB RAM) to complete the whole process, respectively. In other words, tagging one video only takes 5.0 and 26 milliseconds, respectively. Clearly, the speed is fast and provides almost instant response.

7. DISCUSSION AND CONCLUSION

We have presented an economy way of video tagging, by mining the video relationship through click-through data which can be viewed as the footprints of user searching behavior. Particularly, we propose two ways of exploiting the searching behavior, by co-click and polynomial semantic similarity, where the latter addresses the sparsity problem that generally exists in video click-through. Together with two tagging methods, we demonstrated in the experiments that the proposed approaches make improvement to three tagging tasks: assignment, ranking and enrichment, by leveraging the bipartite graph constructed from tens of millions of URL clicks. Basically, utilizing click-through, which is cheap to exploit and free for search engines, as a measure for characterizing video similarity, shows better performance than feature-based approach such as by using cosine similarity. By combining click-through and features for deriving a latent space and tackling the sparsity problem, further improvement was consistently observed in the experiments.

Our work can be enhanced by considering also partial visual near-duplicates, which frequently happen in Web videos. The visual features can be exploited together with click-through and document features for a more comprehensive manner of characterizing visual similarities. The cost, however, is the need for processing millions of videos, which is much more computationally expensive than processing the click-through data associated with videos.

8. ACKNOWLEDGMENTS

This work was supported in part by a grant from the RGC of the Hong Kong SAR under Grant CityU 119610, the National Natural Science Foundation of China under Grant 61272290, the Shenzhen Research Institute, City University of Hong Kong, and Microsoft Research Asia Windows Phone Academic Program FY12-RES-OPP-107.

9. REFERENCES

[1] R. A. Baeza-Yates and A. Tiberi. Extracting semantic relations from query logs. In *Proceedings of ACM Conference on Knowledge Discovery and Data Mining*, 2007.

[2] B. Bai, J. Weston, D. Grangier, R. Collobert, K. Sadamasa, Y. Qi, C. Cortes, and M. Mohri. Polynomial semantic indexing. In *Proceedings of Advances in Neural Information Processing Systems*, 2009.

[3] D. Beeferman and A. L. Berger. Agglomerative clustering of a search engine query log. In *Proceedings of ACM Conference on Knowledge Discovery and Data Mining*, 2000.

[4] M. Bilenko and R. W. White. Mining the search trails of surfing crowds: identifying relevant websites from user activity. In *Proceedings of International World Wide Web Conference*, 2008.

[5] C. Burges, T. Shaked, E. Renshaw, A. Lazier, M. Deeds, N. Hamilton, and G. Hullender. Learning to rank using gradient descent. In *Proceedings of International Conference on Machine Learning*, 2005.

[6] B. Carterette and R. Jones. Evaluating search engines by modeling the relationship between relevance and clicks. In *Proceedings of Advances in Neural Information Processing Systems*, 2007.

[7] N. Craswell and M. Szummer. Random walks on the click graph. In *Proceedings of ACM conference on Research and Development in Information Retrieval*, 2007.

[8] N. Cristianini and J. Shawe-Taylor. An introduction to support vector machines and other kernel-based learning methods. *Cambridge University Press*, 2000.

[9] H. Cui, J.-R. Wen, J.-Y. Nie, and W.-Y. Ma. Probabilistic query expansion using query logs. In *Proceedings of International World Wide Web Conference*, 2002.

[10] S. Deerwester, S. Dumais, G. Furnas, T. Landauer, and R. Harshman. Indexing by latent semantic analysis. *Journal of the American Society for Information Science*, 41(6):391–407, 1990.

[11] G. Dupret and B. Piwowarski. A user browsing model to predict search engine click data from past observations. In *Proceedings of ACM conference on Research and Development in Information Retrieval*, 2008.

[12] R. Herbrich, T. Graepel, and K. Obermayer. Advances in large margin classifiers, chapter large margin rank boundaries for ordinal regression. *MIT Press, Cambridge, MA*, 2000.

[13] V. Jain and M. Varma. Learning to re-rank: Query-dependent image re-ranking using click data. In *Proceedings of International World Wide Web Conference*, 2011.

[14] W. Jiang, S.-F. Chang, and A. C. Loui. Active concetx-based concept fusion with partial user labels. In *Proceedings of International Conference on Image Processing*, 2006.

[15] T. Joachims. Optimizing search engines using clickthrough data. In *Proceedings of ACM Conference on Knowledge Discovery and Data Mining*, 2002.

[16] T. Joachims, L. Granka, B. Pan, H. Hembrooke, F. Radlinski, and G. Gay. Evaluating the accuracy of implicit feedback from clicks and query reformulations in web search. *ACM Trans. on Information Systems*, 25(2), 2007.

[17] R. Jones, B. Rey, O. Madani, and W. Greiner. Generating query substitutions. In *Proceedings of International World Wide Web Conference*, 2006.

[18] X. Li, Y.-Y. Wang, and A. Acero. Learning query intent from regularized click graphs. In *Proceedings of ACM conference on Research and Development in Information Retrieval*, 2008.

[19] H. Ma, H. Yang, I. King, and M. R. Lyu. Learning latent semantic relations from clickthrough data for query suggestion. In *ACM Conference of Information and Knowledge Management*, 2008.

[20] Q. Mei, D. Zhou, and K. W. Church. Query suggestion using hitting time. In *ACM Conference of Information and Knowledge Management*, 2008.

[21] E. Moxley, T. Mei, and B. S. Manjunath. Video annotation through search and graph reinforcement mining. *IEEE Trans. on Multimedia*, 12(3):184–193, 2010.

[22] B. Poblete and R. A. Baeza-Yates. Query-sets: using implicit feedback and query patterns to organize web documents. In *Proceedings of International World Wide Web Conference*, 2008.

[23] G.-J. Qi, X.-S. Hua, Y. Rui, J. Tang, T. Mei, and H.-J. Zhang. Correlative multi-label video annotation. In *ACM International Conference on Multimedia*, 2007.

[24] F. Radlinski and T. Joachims. Active exploration for learning rankings from clickthrough data. In *Proceedings of ACM Conference on Knowledge Discovery and Data Mining*, 2007.

[25] F. Radlinski, M. Kurup, and T. Joachims. How does clickthrough data reflect retrieval quality? In *Proceedings of ACM Conference on Knowledge Discovery and Data Mining*, 2008.

[26] R. Rosipal and N. Krämer. Overview and recent advances in partial least squares. *Subspace, Latent Structure and Feature Selection*, pages 34–51, 2006.

[27] S. Siersdorfer, J. S. Pedro, and M. Sanderson. Automatic video tagging using content redundancy. In *Proceedings of ACM conference on Research and Development in Information Retrieval*, 2009.

[28] A. W. M. Smeulders, M. Worring, S. Santini, A. Gupta, and R. Jain. Content-based image retrieval at the end of the early years. *IEEE Trans. on Pattern Analysis and Machine Intelligence*, 2000.

[29] M. Trevisiol, L. Chiarandini, L. M. Aiello, and A. Jaimes. Image ranking based on user browsing behavior. In *Proceedings of ACM conference on Research and Development in Information Retrieval*, 2012.

[30] M. Wang, X.-S. Hua, J. Tang, and R. Hong. Beyond distance measurement: Constructing neighborhood similarity for video annotation. *IEEE Trans. on Multimedia*, 11(3):465–476, 2009.

[31] J.-R. Wen, J.-Y. Nie, and H. Zhang. Clustering user queries of a search engine. In *Proceedings of International World Wide Web Conference*, 2001.

Static Saliency vs. Dynamic Saliency: A Comparative Study

Tam V. Nguyen
National University of Singapore
tamnguyen@nus.edu.sg

Mengdi Xu*
National University of Singapore
g0900224@nus.edu.sg

Guangyu Gao
Beijing Institute of Technology
guangyu.ryan@gmail.com

Mohan Kankanhalli
National University of Singapore
mohan@comp.nus.edu.sg

Qi Tian
University of Texas at San Antonio
qitian@cs.utsa.edu

Shuicheng Yan
National University of Singapore
eleyans@nus.edu.sg

ABSTRACT

Recently visual saliency has attracted wide attention of researchers in the computer vision and multimedia field. However, most of the visual saliency-related research was conducted on still images for studying static saliency. In this paper, we give a comprehensive comparative study for the first time of dynamic saliency (video shots) and static saliency (key frames of the corresponding video shots), and two key observations are obtained: 1) video saliency is often different from, yet quite related with, image saliency, and 2) camera motions, such as tilting, panning or zooming, affect dynamic saliency significantly. Motivated by these observations, we propose a novel camera motion and image saliency aware model for dynamic saliency prediction. The extensive experiments on two static-vs-dynamic saliency datasets collected by us show that our proposed method outperforms the state-of-the-art methods for dynamic saliency prediction. Finally, we also introduce the application of dynamic saliency prediction for dynamic video captioning, assisting people with hearing impairments to better entertain videos with only off-screen voices, *e.g.*, documentary films, news videos and sports videos.

Categories and Subject Descriptors

H.4 [**Information Systems Applications**]: Miscellaneous

General Terms

Algorithms, Experimentation, Human Factors

Keywords

Static Saliency, Dynamic Saliency, Cinematography, Camera Motion

*indicates equal contribution

MM'13, October 21–25, 2013, Barcelona, Spain.
Copyright 2013 ACM 978-1-4503-2404-5/13/10 ...$15.00.
http://dx.doi.org/10.1145/2502081.2502128 .

1. INTRODUCTION

Visual saliency refers to the preferential attention on conspicuous or meaningful regions in a scene. Such visual attention scheme is naturally built into complex biological visual systems to rapidly detect potential prey, predators, or mates in a real world. The process of visual saliency has been the subject of numerous studies in psychology, neuroscience, computer vision and multimedia fields. Correspondingly, several computational models of saliency have been proposed in recent years [24, 9, 21, 32]. And many applications of automatic saliency detection have also been proposed such as image re-sizing [1], image automatic collage creation [30] and advertisement design [20]. Recently, other matters related to human attention such as depth information or attractiveness have also been explored [13, 22, 23].

Although visual saliency has attracted the attention of researchers in the computer vision and multimedia fields for quite a long time, most of the visual saliency-related research works are conducted on still images. Video saliency receives much less research attention, though it is becoming more and more important along with the rapidly increasing demand of intelligent video processing. Moreover, in the existing works of video saliency [15, 2, 31], camera motions such as tilting, panning or zooming are disregarded during the saliency estimation. However, these camera motions ubiquitously exist in videos and may have great impacts on the saliency distribution, as experimentally validated in this work. Motivated by these two considerations, in this work, we conduct comprehensive comparison between the static saliency in still images and dynamic saliency in videos. Inspired by the observations in the comparison, we propose to utilize the static saliency as *a prior* information to improve the performance of dynamic saliency estimation in videos. And we also investigate the role of camera motions in video saliency and integrate the estimated camera motion information into the saliency estimation procedure. Extensive experiments on two challenging benchmark datasets clearly show that our proposed saliency detection method outperforms the state-of-the-arts. Apart of proposing a novel method for saliency estimation, we introduce an interesting application of video saliency detection, *i.e.*, adaptive video subtitle insertion for assisting the patient with hearing impairment.

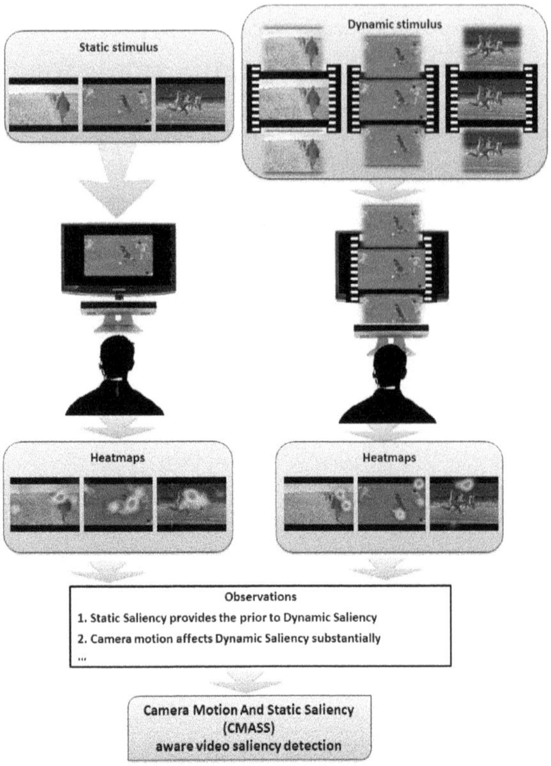

Figure 1: The comparative study of Static Saliency vs. Dynamic Saliency. We collect eye-tracking data on both static and dynamic viewing settings viewed by at least 10 observers. The CMASS framework is proposed to improve dynamic saliency detection.

To facilitate the comparative study of static saliency vs. dynamic saliency, we first collect two video datasets for dynamic saliency estimation, namely the Hollywood and the Camera Motion (CAMO). Each of the two datasets contains the videos with camera motions. Then, volunteers are invited to participate the eye fixation map collection for these videos. Afterwards, the raw fixation data are converted to human fixation maps, which are considered as the groundtruth for saliency estimation. As aforementioned, in this work, we consider both the prior information from static saliency and camera motions in the video saliency. And we present a novel learning framework, called Camera Motion And Static Saliency (CMASS), to integrate the valuable information into the video saliency estimation. In particular, we train two neural networks which takes the camera motion parameters and position as inputs and outputs the optimal weights for the static saliency map and dynamic saliency map. In this way, the two available saliency maps can be adaptively fused to produce an improved dynamic saliency map estimation.

The proposed framework is shown in Figure 1, which includes the static and dynamic saliency detection for the same video and the fusion of the two detected saliency maps. The major contributions of this work can be summarized as follows,

1. To the best of our knowledge, we comprehensively conduct the first comparative study on the static saliency vs. dynamic saliency detection.
2. This is the first work to investigate the effects of camera motions in the dynamic saliency detection.
3. Inspired by the observed relationship between static and dynamic saliency, we propose a novel learning framework, *i.e.*, the CMASS method, for automatically fusing these two kinds of saliency maps to improve the performance of dynamic saliency detection.
4. We introduce a new and useful application for the dynamic saliency detection, namely adaptive video subtitle insertion for assisting people with hearing impairment.

The rest of the paper is structured as follows. In Section 2, we discuss the related works. Then, we introduce our database construction and some observations in Section 3 and Section 4 respectively. The proposed CMASS method is introduced in Section 5. The experiments are presented in Section 6. The new application to insert the caption to the video is shown in Section 7. Finally, we give the conclusion in Section 8.

2. RELATED WORK

2.1 Learning to Predict Saliency

Through preliminary studies [3, 28], at early stages of free viewing, mainly bottom-up factors attract human attention (e.g., color, intensity, or orientation) and later on, top-down factors (e.g., humans, objects and interactions) guide eye movements. Some top-down factors in free-viewing are related to semantic factors. Elazary et al. suggested that interesting objects (annotations from LabelMe dataset [27]) direct human attention [7]. Einhauser et al. observed that objects are better predictors of fixations than bottom-up saliency [6]. Cerf et al. discovered that the meaningful objects such as faces and text attract human attention [4]. Judd et al., further showed that humans, faces, cars, text, and animals attract human gaze [11]. These interesting objects convey more information in a scene. During collecting NUSEF eye fixation dataset [26], Subramanian et al. found that fixations are focused on emotional and action stimuli.

Therefore, combining bottom-up and top-down factors may boost the existing models in order to better predict where human looks [12, 11, 25, 33]. The basic idea is that a weighted combination of features, where weights are learned from a large repository of eye movements over natural images, can enhance saliency detection compared with unadjusted combination of feature maps. [12], [11] and [25] used image patches, a vector of several features at each pixel, and scene gist, respectively for learning saliency. Zhao et al. learned optimal weights for saliency channel combination separately for each eye-tracking dataset [33].

2.2 Saliency Prediction Models for Static and Dynamic Scenes

Visual attention analysis in static scenes has been long studied, while there is not much work on the dynamic scenes. In reality, we absorb the rich visual information that constantly changes due to dynamics of the world. Due to the large amount of information, visual selection is performed on both current scene saliency as well as the accumulated knowledge from chronological events. In the early works, few researchers have extended the spatial attention from static images to video sequences where motion plays an important role. Cheng et al. has incorporated the motion information in the attention model [5]. The motion attention model analyzes the magnitudes of image pixel motion in horizontal and vertical directions. Bioman et al. proposed a spatiotemporal irregularity detection in videos [2]. In this work, instead of reading motion features, textures of 2D and 3D video patches are compared with the training database to detect the abnormal actions present in the video. Le Meur et al. proposed a spatiotemporal model for visual attention detection [14]. Affine parameters were analyzed to produce the motion saliency map.

Recently, several researchers have studied modeling temporal effects on bottom-up saliency. Some methods fuse static and dynamic saliency maps to produce the final visual saliency maps (e.g., Li et al. [15] and Marat et al.[17]). A spatio-temporal attention modeling approach for videos is presented by combining motion contrast derived from the homography between two images and spatial contrast calculated from color histograms. Zhai et al. introduced a dynamic fusion technique is applied to combine the temporal and spatial models in order to achieve the spatiotemporal attention model [31]. The dynamic weights of the two individual models are controlled by the pseudo-variance of the temporal saliency values.

3. FIXATION DATA COLLECTION

3.1 Data Collection

There are many datasets of still images (for studying static saliency) and videos (for studying dynamic saliency) [4, 11, 26]. However, none of the datasets can be used for studying the saliency for still images and videos simultaneously. Thus, in this work, we first construct two new datasets in order for studying these two kinds of saliency maps together.

3.1.1 Dataset Construction

To study the effects of camera motion in video saliency, we collect a new dataset named CAMO (Camera Motion) which consists of 120 videos of 6 different fundamental camera motions in cinematography: *dolly*, *zoom*, *trucking*, *tilt*, *pan*, and *pedestal motions*. Each video contains one single camera motion. Similar to the Hollywood dataset, we also randomly select one frame from each video for static saliency map collection. The information of each camera motions is listed as below.

- *Tilting*: the camera is stationary and rotates in a vertical plane.
- *Panning*: the camera is stationary and rotates in a horizontal plane.
- *Dolly*: the camera is mounted to the dolly and the camera operator and focus puller or camera assistant, usually ride on the dolly to operate the camera.
- *Trucking*: roughly synonymous with the dolly shot, but often defined more specifically as movement which stays a constant distance from the action, especially side-to-side movement.
- *Pedestal*: moving the camera position vertically with respect to the subject.

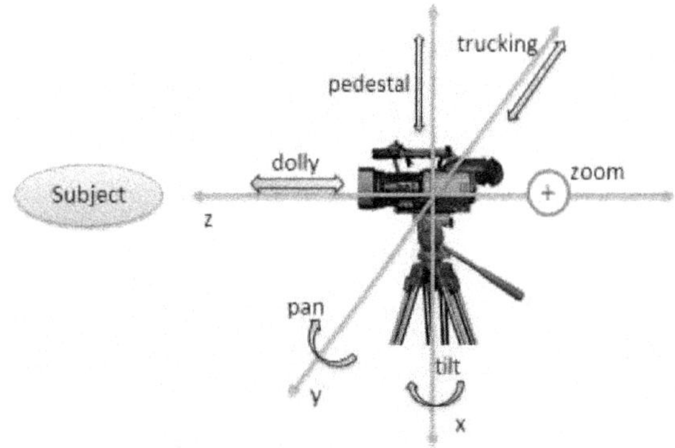

Figure 2: The fundamental camera motions in cinematography. Six basic types of motions are shown.

- *Zooming*: Technically this is not a camera move, but a change in the lens focal length with gives the illusion of moving the camera closer or further away.

Figure 2 illustrates six aforementioned camera motions. In the real world, many camera moves use a combination of these above mentioned techniques simultaneously. Therefore, we also collect another dataset named Hollywood. We select 500 random videos from Hollywood 2 dataset [18]. Hollywood 2 dataset consists of videos with natural human actions in diverse and realistic video settings. There exists one dataset collecting eye fixation on movies [19]. Therefore, we only collect fixation data on static images of that dataset. For each video, we extract one random frame which is not the shot boundary and stay close to the center frame of the video. The reason we select Hollywood 2 is that it contains realistic movies.

3.1.2 Human fixation data collection design

We invite 30 participants (students and staff members of a university), whose age ranged from 21 to 36 years old ($\mu = 26.9$, $\sigma = 3.1$), with normal or corrected-to-normal vision, to participate in the fixation map collection. All participants are naive to the purpose of this study and have no prior exposure to experiments on vision. The participants have been split equally into three groups. Each group view only one of three following categories freely: *Hollywood static images*, *CAMO static images* and *CAMO videos*.

We use a block based design and free viewing paradigm. The subject views one of four designed blocks. In order to record subject eye gaze data, we used an infra-red based remote eye-tracker from SensoMotoric Instruments Gmbh. The eye-tracker gives less than 1° error on successful calibration. The eye tracker was calibrated for each participant using a 9-point calibration and validation method. Then images were presented in random order for 6 seconds followed by a gray mask for 3 seconds.

Human fixation maps are constructed from the fixations of viewers to globally represent the spatial distribution of human fixations. Similar to [29], in order to produce a continuous fixation map of an image, we convolve a Gaussian filter across all corresponding viewers's fixation locations. Some examples of fixation maps of two new constructed datasets are shown in Figure 3, the brighter pixels on the fixation maps denote the higher salience values. These two datasets,

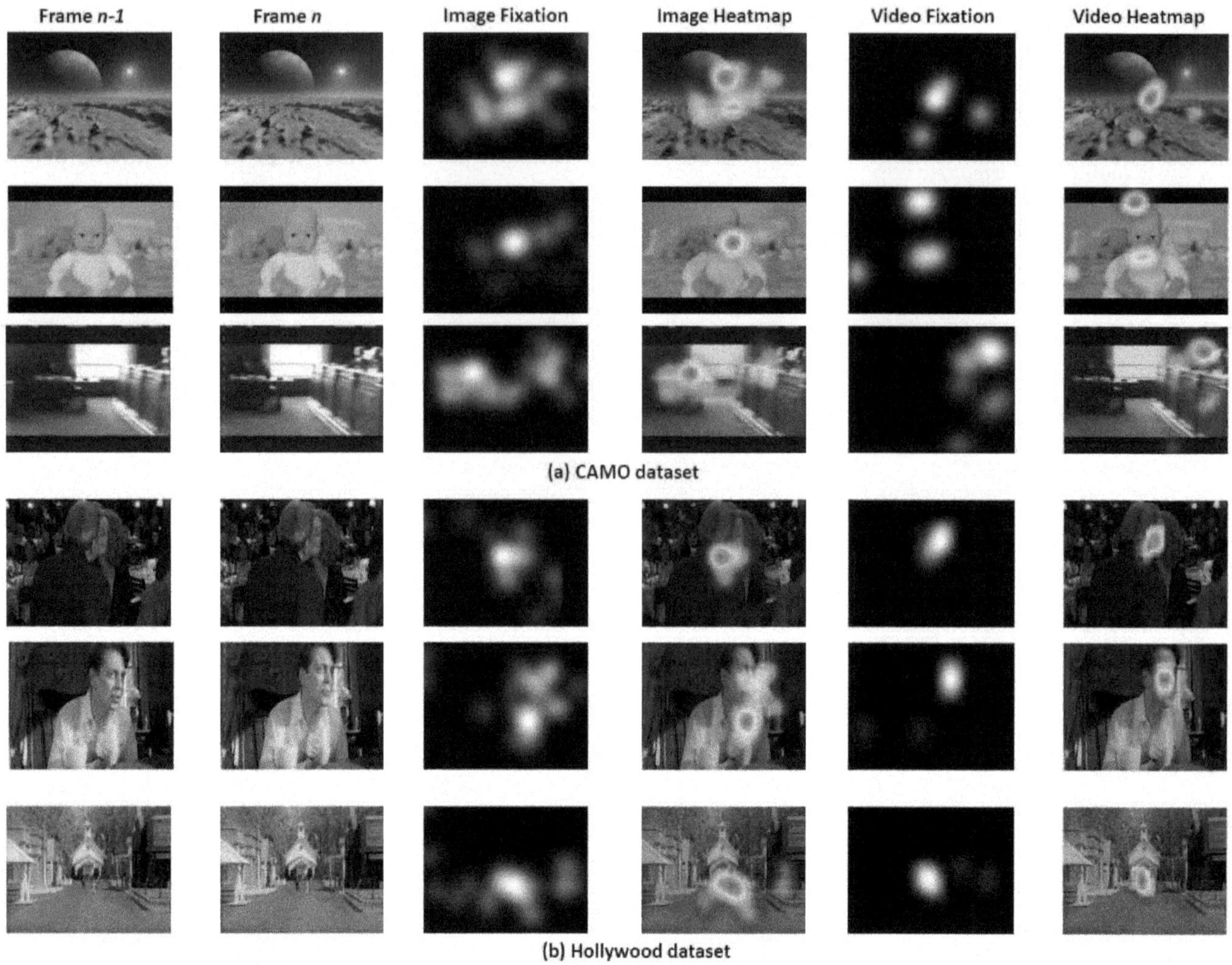

Figure 3: The exemplar images and their corresponding saliency maps and heat maps in CAMO and Hollywood datasets.

CAMO and Hollywood with the stimulus, fixation data and fixation maps shall be released for public usage.

4. OBSERVATIONS

4.1 Camera Motion Effects

Using the recorded eye tracker data, we mainly investigate whether spatial distributions of fixations are different in static and dynamic settings. The key observations are summarized as follows.

1. The fixations of each video form a subset of the ones of the corresponding image if there is only single person or object. This observation presents a close relationship between the static and dynamic saliency maps. We can use the static saliency map as a good prior to guide the dynamic saliency map estimation.
2. In some cases, for example, pedestal camera movement, the fixation lies on the anticipated direction, not on the objects. This observation shows the effect of camera motion on the dynamic saliency.
3. In the case that there are multiple persons or objects in the video, the fixations of the videos are not same as images. In other words, the fixations on videos and images focus on different people or objects.

Some examples of the camera motion effects mentioned in Observation 2 are shown in Figure 4. The details of discrepancies of each camera motions are summarized as follows.

- *Pan*: The fixations may be either on the object of interest (*e.g.*, face of a walking person) or in the anticipated direction of the motion.
- *Pedestal*: The subject often tends to fixate on the anticipated direction of motion.
- *Tilt*: In case of a tilt shot, the subject also tends to fixate on the anticipated direction of motion.
- *Trucking*: Fixations in video are either a subset of the fixations in static images or they are in the anticipated direction of motion.

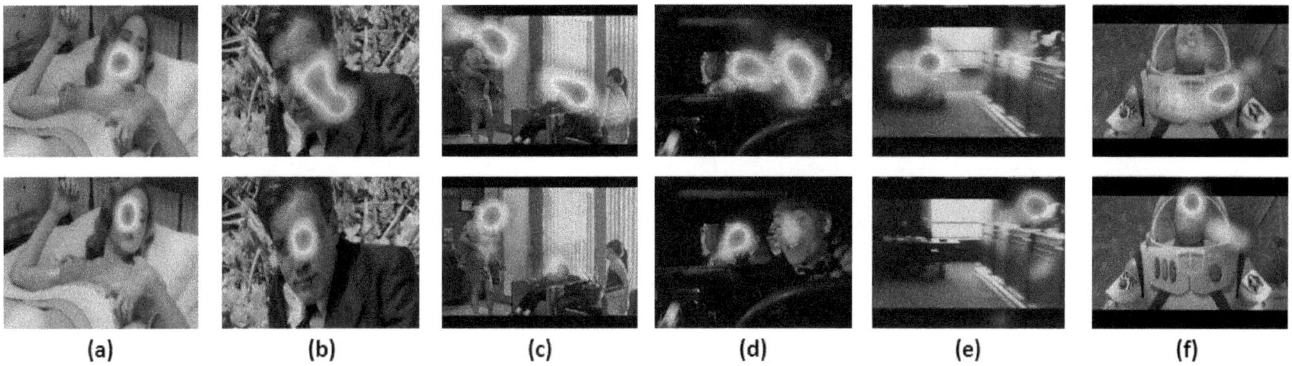

Figure 4: The observations of fixation data on the images (top row) and videos (bottom row). Note the difference of human fixations from column (c) to (f).

- *Dolly shot*: In the dolly shot, the cameraman is "moving closer" to the center or the object of focus. Therefore, the anticipated direction of motion can be considered to be the center or object of motion. While, the subject does fixate on the object of interest, it is not like the dolly shot which causes the subject to fixate more/less on the object of interest. Thus, in case of dolly, the movement of the camera does not cause the subject to fixate on the anticipated direction of motion as "Pan", "Pedestal", or "Tilt".
- *Zoom*: We notice that the fixations are either on the object of interest or the peripheral motion of the camera.

4.2 Central Bias Investigation

We compute the average fixation maps to investigate the central bias of the fixation maps. Due to different sizes of testing images, the average fixation maps have cross-like shape. As can be seen in Figure 5, the center bias remains strong in the average fixation map of original images in the static part of both datasets. This agrees with the finding in [11]. The average map for video part of CAMO dataset is not center-biased due to the strong effects of the camera motions. Meanwhile, the average fixation map of Hollywood video is not so strong as the static version. In summary, the central bias is not significantly observed in video fixation.

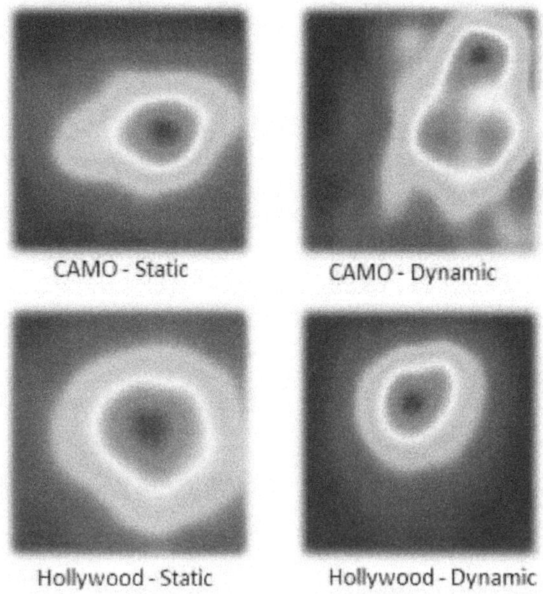

Figure 5: The average fixation static and dynamic maps from the two datasets. Warmer color indicates stronger fixation.

5. THE PROPOSED FRAMEWORK

In this section, we first explain the feature extraction applied on the given image or a certain frame in the video, followed by a novel framework which learns the mapping between image saliency and video saliency simultaneously.

5.1 Features

5.1.1 Static Features

To well describe the content of the images, we extract multiple static features and combine them together. The extracted features together describe both low-level appearance and high-level semantics. In particular, we use following low-level features: 13 local energy of the steerable pyramid filters in 4 orientations and 3 scales; 3 intensity, orientation, and color contrast channels (Red/Green and Blue/Yellow) as calculated by Itti and Koch's saliency method; 3 values of the red, green, and blue color channels as well as 3 features corresponding to probabilities of each of these color channels; 5 probabilities of above color channels as computed from 3D color histograms of the image filtered with a median filter at 6 different scales; 4 saliency maps of Torralba, SIM, SUN, and GBVS bottom-up saliency models. And we extract following high-level features: the horizontal line due to tendency of photographers to frame images and objects horizontally; person and car detectors implemented by Felzenszwalb's Deformable Part Model (DPM); face detector using the Viola and Jone's code.

5.1.2 Dynamic Features

In the temporal attention detection, saliency maps are often constructed by computing the motion contrast between image pixels. In this work, we generate dense saliency

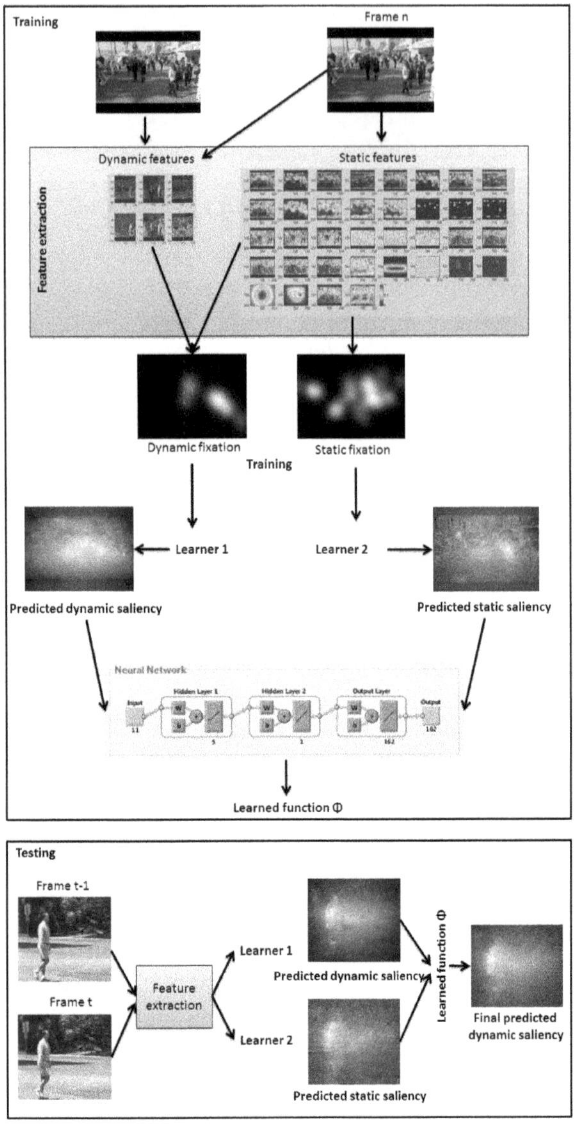

Figure 6: The learning framework. The upper panel shows the learning process, including the neural network parameters learning. The bottom panel shows the testing phase.

maps based on pixel-wise computations, mostly dense optical flow fields. Here, we first resize each image/video frame to 200×200 pixels and then extract a set of features as aforementioned for every pixel.

5.2 CMASS for Dynamic Saliency Detection

5.2.1 Learning to Predict Image/ Video Saliency

In this subsection, we provide a simple linear regression based saliency estimation method. In the training phase, each training sample contains features at one pixel along with a $+1$ (salient) or -1 (non-salient) label. Positive samples are taken from the top p percent salient pixels of the human fixation map (smoothed by convolving with a Gaussian filter with window size $\sigma = 0.1$) and negative samples are taken from the bottom q percent. We chose samples from the top 20% and bottom 40% in order to have samples that were strongly positive and strongly negative. Training feature vectors are normalized to have zero mean and unit standard deviation. Assuming a linear relationship between feature vector f and saliency map s, we solve the following optimization problem to obtain the linear model W:

$$\min \|FW - S\|^2 + \lambda \|W\|^2,$$

where F and S are matrices by column-wisely stacking the vectors f and s of the training data. W is obtained in a closed-form manner, $W = (F^T F + \lambda I)^{-1} F^T S$. For a testing image, features are first extracted and then the learned mapping was applied to generate a vector which is later resized to a 200×200 saliency map.

5.2.2 CMASS Video Saliency Prediction

Inspired by the observations given in Section 4, we propose a novel learning-based method, *i.e.*, Camera Motion And Static Saliency (CMAS), to improve the performance of dynamic saliency prediction by utilizing the information from camera motion and static saliency results. Each frame in the videos is divided regularly into patches with the size of 9×9 pixels. For the jth patch in the training samples, let p_i^j denote the saliency map vector obtained from the image and p_v^j denote the saliency map vector from the video. The groundtruth saliency map for the jth patch is denoted as p^j. The camera motion parameter is denoted as CM^j. The position of the patch in the image is denoted as (x^j, y^j). According to the Observation 1, the generated saliency map is a weighted combination of the static and dynamic saliency maps. According to the Observation 2, camera motion has great impact on the saliency map. For different patches, the camera motion and spatial position of the patches are different. Thus, the weights for their two kinds of saliency maps should be different. Based on these two considerations, in CMAS, we construct two neural networks to weight the static saliency map and dynamic saliency map in the final saliency estimation, respectively. The input to the neural network is the camera motion parameters and the position of the patches, and the output is the weight for the saliency map. The function of the neural networks are denoted as $\phi_i(CM^j, x^j, y^j)$ and $\phi_v(CM^j, x^j, y^j)$. And they are learned by minimizing the following loss function,

$$\mathcal{L}(\phi_i, \phi_v) = \sum_j \|\phi_i(CM^j, x^j, y^j) p_i^j + \phi_v(CM^j, x^j, y^j) p_v^j - p^j\|_2^2.$$

After learning the functions of the neural network ϕ_i and ϕ_v, we can directly obtain the saliency map for each new sample through

$$\tilde{p} = \phi_i(CM, x, y) p_i + \phi_v(CM, x, y) p_v,$$

where CM, x, y are the motion and position parameters for the input patch, and p_i and p_v are its two saliency maps.

However, directly training the neural network involves quite complicated optimization procedure, which damages the efficiency of the proposed method. In this work, we introduce two auxiliary variables w_i^j and w_v^j for ϕ_i^j and ϕ_v^j to simplify the optimization procedure. Then the loss function is formulated as:

$$\mathcal{L} = \sum_j \|w_i^j p_i^j + w_v^j p_v^j - p^j\|_2^2 + \lambda\{(\phi_i^j - w_i^j)^2 + (\phi_v^j - w_v^j)^2\}. \tag{1}$$

The above optimization problem can be solved by various methods. And the algorithm iteratively learns two phases

Algorithm 1 Solving Problem (1)

Input: Saliency map vectors p_i^j, p_v^j, p, parameters λ_0, $\rho = 1.5$.
Initialize: $t = 0$, $w_i^{j(t)} = 0.5$, $w_v^{j(t)} = 0.5$, $\lambda^{(t)} = \lambda_0$.
while not converged **do**

1. $t \leftarrow t + 1$

2. $f_i^{(t+1)} \leftarrow \phi_i(CM^j, x^j, y^j)$, $f_v^{(t)} \leftarrow \phi_v(CM^j, x^j, y^j)$

3. Update the auxiliary variables:

$$w_i^{j(t+1)} = (p_i^{jT} p_i^j + \lambda I)^{-1} \times \left(p_i^j p^{jT} - p_i^j p_v^{jT} w_v^j + \lambda(f_i^{(t)} + f_v^{(t)} - w_v^j)\right)$$

.

$$w_v^{j(t+1)} = (p_v^{jT} p_v^j + \lambda I)^{-1} \times \left(p_v^j p^{jT} - p_v^j p_i^{jT} w_v^j + \lambda(f_i^{(t)} + f_v^{(t)} - w_i^j)\right)$$

.

4. Train ϕ_i, ϕ_v.

5. Update parameters w_{ϕ_i} of ϕ_i, w_{ϕ_v} of ϕ_v.

6. $\lambda^{(t+1)} \leftarrow \rho\lambda^{(t)}$

end while
Output: The learned neural network ϕ_i and ϕ_v.

within the same objective function. The solver is used for efficiency and outlined in Algorithm 1. Step 1 of the algorithm has closed form solution. Step 2 is solved via the optimization of the neural network. To ensure that the auxiliary variables approximate the original variables, the trade-off parameter λ will be increased in each iteration.

For the camera motions, we extract homography matrix of 15 frames with the selected frame is the middle one. To avoid the motion of the human or object, we use the work of [8]. Then, 8 values of the homography matrix (except the last element on the diagonal line) represent the camera motions.

For the implementation, we utilize 2 hidden layers with Transfer functions are 'tansig', and 'purelin', respectively. Backpropagation network training function is Levenberg-Marquardt. Note that we initialize NN of this current step by using the weights of its previous step. λ is set as 0.1 which takes the role of controlling the convergence speed. 40 to 50 iterations are required for convergence.

6. EVALUATION

In this section, we describe the extensive experiments conducted on the new collected datasets for the better understanding about the performance of the proposed learning framework.

6.1 Learning to Predict Saliency

To quantitatively measure how well an individual saliency map predictors on a given frame, we compute the area under the receiver operating characteristic (ROC) curve (AUC) and linear correlation coefficient (CC) values. As the most popular measure in the community, ROC is used for the evaluation of a binary classifier system with a variable threshold (usually used to classify between two methods like saliency vs. random). Using this measure, the model is treated as a binary classifier on every pixel in the image; pixels with larger saliency values than a threshold are classified as fixated while the rest of the pixels are classified as non-fixated. Human fixations are then used as ground truth. By varying the threshold, the ROC curve is drawn as the false positive rate vs. true positive rate, and the area under this curve indicates how well the saliency map predicts actual human eye fixations. Meanwhile, CC measures the strength of a linear relationship between human fixation map and predicted saliency map.

Table 1: AUC and CC of saliency detection on the two datasets.

Dataset	AUC	CC
CAMO - images	0.74	0.52
CAMO - videos	0.64	0.20
Hollywood - images	0.71	0.45
Hollywood - videos	0.75	0.30

Table 1 shows the predicted results on our collected datasets, Hollywood and CAMO. We used static features to predict static saliency. Similarly, we used static features and dynamic features to predict dynamic saliency. The performance of dynamic saliency prediction is worse than the static saliency prediction based on static features only. That shows the need to improve the performance of dynamic saliency prediction.

6.2 Dynamic Saliency Evaluation

We compare the performance of CMASS framework with the following four baseline methods:

1. Video saliency prediction from visual features [11].

2. Video saliency prediction from visual and motion features.

3. Fixed mapping weight to fuse static saliency and video saliency.

4. Adaptive mapping weight to fuse static saliency and video saliency [31].

Their performance comparison in terms of AUC and CC are shown in Table 2. As can be seen in Table 2, the results of the dynamic saliency prediction method from static information only are the worst in all cases. Combining the visual and motion features improves the performance generally across the two dataset. Fixed mapping weight is learned from a simple linear regressor. And the performance is further improved incrementally. The adaptive weight method of Zhai *et al.* achieves better performance than the rest of baselines, improving the performance over fixed mapping weight by around 2 to 3 percentage. Our proposed CMASS achieves the best performance in terms of AUC and CC for both datasets, Hollywood and CAMO. Generally it outperforms the results from Zhai *et al.* by 4 to 6 percentages. This improvement is rather significant. It shows the advantages of our combined static saliency and camera motion in boosting the performance of dynamic saliency prediction.

Table 2: Performance of CMASS on video saliency prediction on CAMO and Hollywood datasets.

Method	Hollywood		CAMO	
	AUC	CC	AUC	CC
Judd *et al.* [11]	0.72	0.25	0.61	0.18
Visual and motion feat.	0.75	0.30	0.64	0.20
Fixed mapping weight	0.74	0.28	0.63	0.19
Zhai *et al.* [31]	0.76	0.31	0.64	0.22
CMASS	**0.80**	**0.37**	**0.69**	**0.28**

7. APPLICATION TO VIDEO CAPTIONING

Assisting the disabled persons by applying computer vision/multimedia techniques consistently attracts the attention from many researchers. Recently, a technique for assisting hearing impairment patients in watching videos [10] is developed, which automatically inserts the dialogue nearing the talking persons to help the patients understand who is talking and the content of the dialogue. However, there is often a need to insert the subtitle into the video without human appearance (*i.e.*, only narration appears in the video), such as documentary and introductory films. In this section, we introduce the new application which automatically insert the subtitle into such videos based on the video saliency map intelligently, in order to help the patients understand the content of the narration.

The basic criteria of the subtitle insertion are two-folds. Firstly, the selected position of the frame to insert the subtitle should have low saliency score. Otherwise, the inserted subtitle will overlap with the salient objects and worsen the watching experience of the audience. Second, the selected position should be near to the high saliency position. Thus the inserted subtitle will not distract the audience's attention.

The technique for the suitable position detection based on saliency map is introduced as follows. The predicted saliency map is first split into multiple blocks, each of which having the size of 10×10 pixels. Each small block i has the mean saliency value s_i. We transform the saliency map to the response map for the use of determining the position of inserted subtitles. The response value of a certain pixel k in block i is computed as below.

$$r_k = \alpha_1 \sum_{j \in \mathcal{N}(i)} |s_i - s_j| - \alpha_2 s_i, \qquad (2)$$

where $\mathcal{N}(i)$ represent the neighboring blocks of block i and s_i, s_j are the saliency values of the block i and block j respectively. r_k is the calculated response value for the kth pixel. The weights α_1, α_2 are empirically set as 0.5 and 0.5 throughout our implementation. The first term in the response calculation characterize the saliency contrast while the second term encourages to find the position with low saliency. The size of inserted text will be calculated based on its length. Then we perform the exhaustive search on the response map in order to find the most suitable position with the largest response value. Figure 7 and 10 illustrates the examples of inserting subtitle into the documentary video without human appearance.

To evaluate the quality of the inserted subtitle and whether the watching experience is improved, we conduct the user study on both the content comprehensive and user impression. There are 24 users participating in the study. Their ages vary from 22 to 30 years old. We prepare 5 video clips with embedded caption for the evaluation.

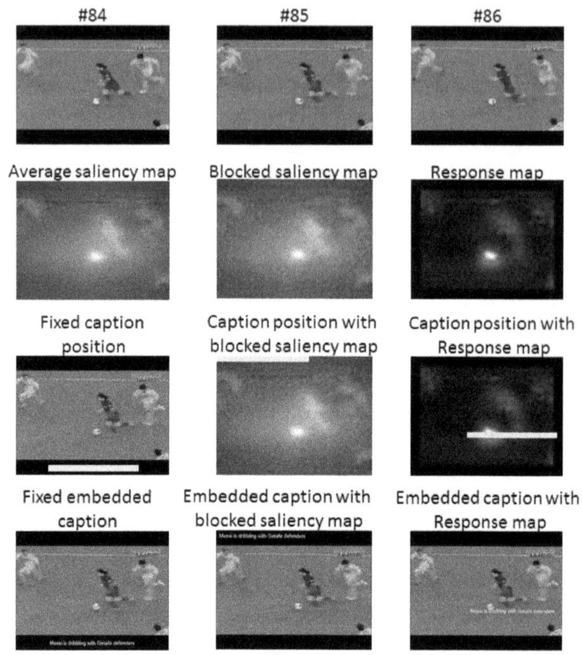

Figure 7: The usage of response map for inserting subtitles. The first row shows the frames of the video. The second row shows the saliency map from different saliency detection methods. The third row shows the found position for inserting the subtitles. And the last row shows the final results.

For the content comprehension study, we randomly divide all the participants into four groups (each group has 6 participants) to avoid the repeated playing of a video which will cause knowledge accumulation. Therefore, each group merely evaluates one of the four paradigms for each video clip. We have designed five questions related to caption content comprehension. These questions are carefully designed to broadly cover the content in the video clips. The participant watches the clips under the task-free setting. Their results are the converted percentage of the correct answers. We compare the proposed high-contrast (HC) driven method with the following three methods. The first one is that the position of the subtitle is fixed at the bottom of the frame. The second one is that the subtitles are inserted into the position with low saliency value, which is called low-saliency (LS) driven method. And the third one is also based on high-contrast but the saliency map is estimated from static saliency detection (Static). As shown in Figure 8, our method outperforms all of the other saliency detection methods for subtitle insertion. It demonstrates that the video saliency estimation method proposed in this work can find the most suitable position to insert the subtitle, where the subtitle is informative to the audience. In contrast, the image saliency based one performs worse since the inserted subtitle is not close enough to the salient regions. And the fixed caption performs worst as the audience cannot focus on the subtitle and video content at the same time.

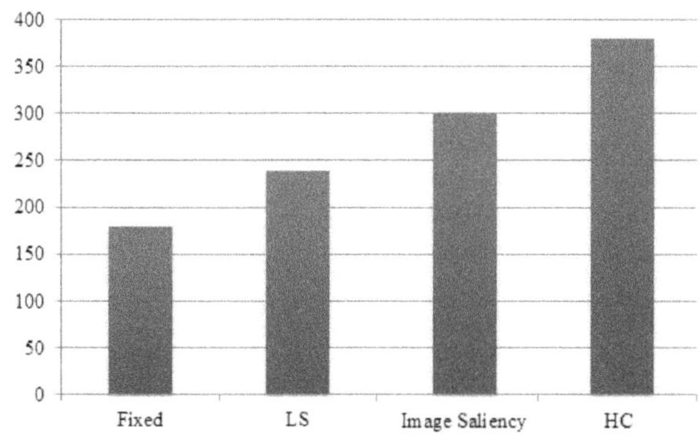

Figure 8: Results of evaluation of four methods in terms of the content comprehension. The compared methods include Fixed, Low Saliency Driven (LS), Static image saliency detection based and High Contrast Driven (HC). The vertical axis represents the sum of the scores obtained by each group of participants. Higher score indicates better performance.

We further compare the four subtitle insertion schemes, *i.e.*, fixed, LS, Image Saliency and HC, in terms of the user impression. We invite another 15 evaluators who are requested to indicate their satisfaction with respect to the following perspectives: 1) Enjoyment: How do you feel that the video is enjoyable? 2) Convenience: How do you feel the visual appearance of subtitle is convenient? 3) Preference: How do you prefer that captioning method? 4) Experience: How does the caption help you experience the video? For each sample, the participant rates each method on a 5-point scale from the best (5) to the worst (1)[16]. The video order is randomized. Figure 9 depicts the results of user impression evaluation. Generally, our method outperforms others in all aspects since it optimizes allocated position. Low saliency driven captioning yields relatively low score due to uncommon appearance in the video frames.

8. DISCUSSIONS AND FUTURE WORK

In this work, we have conducted a comparative study between the static saliency and dynamic saliency. To the best of our knowledge, this is the first research attempt to investigate this problem in depth. We first build the datasets of human fixation on both images and videos for the comparison purpose. Then we report several important observations of the relationship of static and dynamic saliency. Inspired by these observations, we propose the noval CMASS learning

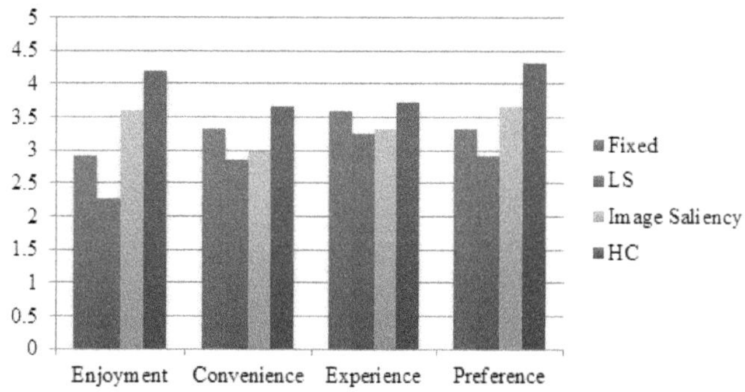

Figure 9: Results of evaluation on the user impression. Four methods are compared, namely Fixed, Low Saliency Driven (LS), Static image saliency detection based and High Contrast Driven (HC). The methods are compared in terms of four criteria, namely Enjoyment, Convenience, Experience and Preference. Each user has been asked to assign a score between 1 (most unsatisfactory) and 5 (most satisfactory) for each criterion.

framework to fuse static saliency into dynamic saliency estimation to improve the video saliency prediction. Extensive experimental evaluations on the constructed datasets well demonstrate the effectiveness of the proposed method for video saliency prediction. We also apply the video saliency prediction method to the application of helping patients with hearing impairment in watching videos with narration. Suggested future work includes extensive user studies as a means to explore the potential of our approach under different conditions and for different application domains.

9. ACKNOWLEDGEMENT

This work is partially supported by Singapore Ministry of Education under research Grant MOE2010-T2-1-087. This work is also partially funded by the Singapore A*STAR SERC grant, "Characterizing and Exploiting Human Visual Attention for Automated Image Understanding and Description". Dr. Qi Tian is supported by ARO grant W911BF-12-1-0057, NSF IIS 1052851, Faculty Research Awards by Google, FXPAL, and NEC Laboratories of America, and 2012 UTSA START-R Research Award respectively. This work is supported in part by NSFC 61128007. The authors would like to thank Jiashi Feng and Prerna Chikersal for valuable discussions.

10. REFERENCES

[1] S. Avidan and A. Shamir. Seam carving for content-aware image resizing. *TOG*, 2007.

[2] O. Boiman and M. Irani. Detecting irregularities in images and in video. *IJCV*, 2007.

[3] R. Carmi and L. Itti. Visual causes versus correlates of attentional selection in dynamic scenes. *Vision Research*, 2006.

[4] M. Cerf, J. Harel, W. Einhäuser, and C. Koch. Predicting human gaze using low-level saliency combined with face detection. In *NIPS*, 2007.

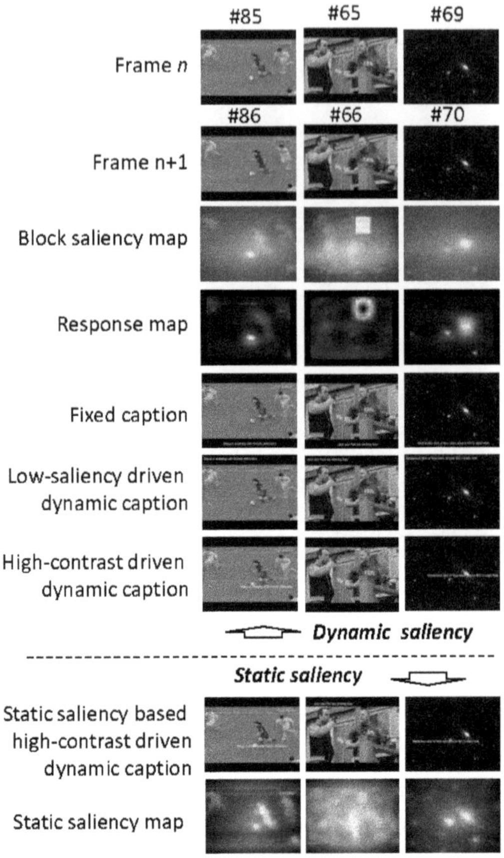

Figure 10: The examples of inserting subtitle into the documentary video. The original frames, the detected saliency maps, calculated response maps are shown from top to down. The top panel shows the result from the dynamic saliency detection. And the bottom panel shows the results from the static saliency detection.

[5] W. Cheng, W. Chu, J. Kuo, and J. Wu. Automatic video region-of-interest determination based on user attention model. In *ISCAS*, 2005.

[6] W. Einhauser, M. Spain, and P. Perona. Objects predict fixations better than early saliency. *Journal of Vision*, 2008.

[7] L. Elazary and L. Itti. A Bayesian model for efficient visual search and recognition. *Vision Research*, 2010.

[8] B. Ghanem, T. Zhang, and N. Ahuja. Robust video registration applied to field-sports video analysis. ICASSP, 2012.

[9] J. Harel, C. Koch, and P. Perona. Graph-based visual saliency. In *NIPS*, 2006.

[10] R. Hong, M. Wang, M. Xu, S. Yan, and T. Chua. Dynamic captioning: video accessibility enhancement for hearing impairment. In *ACM Multimedia*, 2010.

[11] T. Judd, K. A. Ehinger, F. Durand, and A. Torralba. Learning to predict where humans look. In *ICCV*, 2009.

[12] W. Kienzle, M. Franz, B. Scholkopf, and F. Wichmann. Center-surround patterns emerge as optimal predictors for human saccade targets. *Journal of Vision*, 2009.

[13] C. Lang, T. Nguyen, H. Katti, K. Yadati, M. Kankanhalli, and S. Yan. Depth matters: Influence of depth cues on visual saliency. In *ECCV*, 2012.

[14] O. Le Meur, P. Le Callet, and D. Barba. Predicting visual fixations on video based on low-level visual features. *Vision Research*, 2007.

[15] J. Li, Y. Tian, T. Huang, and W. Gao. Probabilistic multi-task learning for visual saliency estimation in video. *IJCV*, 2010.

[16] R. Likert. A technique for the measurement of attitudes. *Archives of Psychology*, 1932.

[17] S. Marat, M. Guironnet, and D. Pellerin. Video summarization using a visual attention model. *ESPC*, 2007.

[18] M. Marszalek, I. Laptev, and C. Schmid. Actions in context. In *CVPR*, 2009.

[19] S. Mathe and C. Sminchisescu. Dynamic eye movement datasets and learnt saliency models for visual action recognition. In *ECCV*, 2012.

[20] T. Mei, L. Li, X. Hua, and S. Li. Imagesense: Towards contextual image advertising. *TOMCCAP*, 2012.

[21] N. Murray, M. Vanrell, X. Otazu, and C. A. Párraga. Saliency estimation using a non-parametric low-level vision model. In *CVPR*, 2011.

[22] T. Nguyen, S. Liu, B. Ni, J. Tan, Y. Rui, and S. Yan. Sense beauty via face, dressing, and/or voice. In *ACM Multimedia*, 2012.

[23] T. Nguyen, S. Liu, B. Ni, J. Tan, Y. Rui, and S. Yan. Towards decrypting attractiveness via multi-modality cues. In *TOMCCAP*, 2013.

[24] A. Oliva and A. Torralba. Modeling the shape of the scene: A holistic representation of the spatial envelope. *IJCV*, 2001.

[25] R. Peters and L. Itti. Beyond bottom-up: Incorporating task-dependent influences into a computational model of spatial attention. In *CVPR*, 2007.

[26] S. Ramanathan, H. Katti, N. Sebe, M. Kankanhalli, and T. Chua. An eye fixation database for saliency detection in images. In *ECCV*, 2010.

[27] B. Russell, A. Torralba, K. Murphy, and W. Freeman. Labelme: A database and web-based tool for image annotation. *IJCV*, 2008.

[28] B. Tatler. The central fixation bias in scene viewing: Selecting anoptimal viewing position independently of motor biases and image feature distributions. *Journal of Vision*, 2007.

[29] B. Velichkovsky, M. Pomplun, J. Rieser, and H. Ritter. Eye-movement-based research paradigms. In *Visual Attention and Cognition*, 2009.

[30] J. Wang, L. Quan, J. Sun, X. Tang, and H. Shum. Picture collage. In *CVPR*, 2006.

[31] Y. Zhai and M. Shah. Visual attention detection in video sequences using spatiotemporal cues. In *ACM Multimedia*, 2006.

[32] L. Zhang, M. Tong, T. Marks, H. Shan, and G. Cottrell. Sun: A bayesian framework for saliency using natural statistics. *Journal of Vision*, 2008.

[33] Q. Zhao and C. Koch. Learning visual saliency by combining feature maps in a nonlinear manner using AdaBoost. *Journal of Vision*, 2012.

Building Holistic Descriptors for Scene Recognition: A Multi-objective Genetic Programming Approach

Li Liu
Department of Electronic and Electrical Engineering
University of Sheffield
Sheffield, S1 3JD
United Kingdom
elp11ll@sheffield.ac.uk

Ling Shao
Department of Electronic and Electrical Engineering
University of Sheffield
Sheffield, S1 3JD
United Kingdom
ling.shao@sheffield.ac.uk

Xuelong Li
State Key Laboratory of Transient Optics and Photonics, XIOPM
Chinese Academy of Sciences
Xi'an, 710119, China
xuelong_li@opt.ac.cn

ABSTRACT

Real-world scene recognition has been one of the most challenging research topics in computer vision, due to the tremendous intra-class variability and the wide range of scene categories. In this paper, we successfully apply an evolutionary methodology to automatically synthesize domain-adaptive holistic descriptors for the task of scene recognition, instead of using hand-tuned descriptors. We address this as an optimization problem by using multi-objective genetic programming (MOGP). Specifically, a set of primitive operators and filters are first randomly assembled in the MOGP framework as tree-based combinations, which are then evaluated by two objective fitness criteria *i.e.*, the classification error and the tree complexity. Finally, the best-so-far solution selected by MOGP is regarded as the (near-)optimal feature descriptor for scene recognition. We have evaluated our approach on three realistic scene datasets: MIT urban and nature, SUN and UIUC Sport. Experimental results consistently show that our MOGP-generated descriptors achieve significantly higher recognition accuracies compared with state-of-the-art hand-crafted and machine-learned features.

Categories and Subject Descriptors

I.4.8 [**Image Processing and Computer Vision**]: Scene Analysis; I.2 [**Artificial Intelligence**]: Learning; I.2 [**Artificial Intelligence**]: Problem Solving, Control Methods, and Search

General Terms

Design, Experimentation, Theory

Keywords

scene recognition, multi-objective genetic programming.

1. INTRODUCTION

Scene recognition has attracted much attention in robotics and computer vision, with a wide range of applications such as: image search and retrieval [10], path planning, scene reconstruction [6] and video surveillance [3]. Despite its popularity, how to precisely distinguish different scenes in real-world environments remains a challenging issue. The wide variety of scene categories, variations in lighting, different view angles and complex backgrounds all lead to obstacles in efficient learning and robust scene recognition. There are mainly two groups of methods in scene recognition: local feature-based and holistic feature-based.

For local feature-based methods, unsupervised techniques (*e.g.*, Harris corner detector [4] and Harris-Laplace detector [12]) are applied to detect interest points around which the most salient features (*e.g.*, SIFT, HOG) are extracted. Then bag-of-features is utilized to form a codebook and map obtained features in histogram representations which are fed to a classifier for scene classification. The local feature-based methods tend to be robust in challenging scenes, *e.g.*, indoor scenes, however, this kind of sparse representation is often not precise and informative because of the quantization error during codebook construction and the loss of structural relationships among local features. Because of this, holistic feature-based methods have regained popularity in recent scene recognition research.

Holistic feature-based algorithms represent scenes using visual information from the whole image [2] and have been utilized in a variety of applications. Commonly, texture, shape and color features are used for the holistic representation of a scene. The structure and orientation information of texture and shape can be successfully extracted by mimicking the biological mechanism of visual cortex for human perception. Color features have the advantage of being invariant with respect to scaling, rotation, perspective, and partial occlusion. A classical approach to compute the holistic features for scene recognition was developed by Siagian and Itti [19]. Their feature model, a multiview representation of spatial context and structure, is able to encode abundant orientation, intensity and color information for scene recognition. Although holistic visual features yield informative representations for scene recognition, they tend to be sensitive to small geometric and photometric distortions and shifting.

The schemes introduced above are all based on hand-crafted techniques which may achieve good performance on particular scene classes but would degrade for other classes. Therefore, in this paper, we propose to use multi-objective genetic programming (MOGP) [16] to automatically design holistic descriptors that are adaptive to scene domains and robust to shift, scaling and background cluttering for scene recognition. As an alternative to hand-crafted solutions, GP, a popular evolutionary method inspired by natural evolution, can be employed to solve problems without prior knowledge

MM'13, October 21–25, 2013, Barcelona, Spain.

ACM 978-1-4503-2404-5/13/10 ...$15.00.
http://dx.doi.org/10.1145/2502081.2502095.

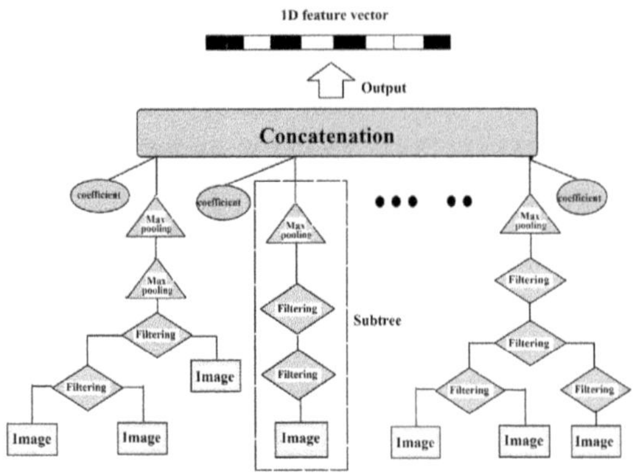

Figure 1: The grammatical structure of an individual.

and address a wide range of practical problems producing human-competitive results and even patentable inventions. We report, what we believe to be, the first application of MOGP for generating novel holistic feature descriptors for scene recognition.

Given a group of 2D primitive operators, MOGP evolves (hopefully) better-performing individuals in the next generation. Since the MOGP selection depends on two fitness objectives, we use the *Pareto front* [16] to represent a set of non-dominated 'rank-1' solutions which provides different trade-offs between the two objectives based on standard evaluation criteria. Furthermore, we apply these evolved solutions on the validation set to select the (near-)optimal one with the lowest independent test error as the final feature descriptor. To demonstrate generalizability, our approach has been tested on the MIT urban and nature scene dataset [14], the SUN scene dataset [23] and the UIUC Sport dataset [9] , respectively. For comparison, we show that the automatically generated holistic descriptors are superior to both hand-crafted and learned feature descriptors.

The remainder of the paper is organized as follows: In Section 2, related work is reviewed. The architecture of our methodology is detailed in Section 3. Experiments and results are described in Section 4. In Section 5, we conclude this paper.

2. RELATED WORK

Much of previous work has explored the use of low-level visual descriptors for scene recognition. As our paper is on holistic descriptors, we review mainly related works on holistic representations for scenes. Oliva and Torralba [14] used the shape of the scene, an underlying similar and stable spatial structure that presumably exists within scene images of the same class, to recognize scene categories. They proposed the Gist descriptor as a benchmark approach to represent such spatial structures through Discrete Fourier Transform (DFT) and achieve outstanding results for outdoor scene recognition. Song and Tao [20] performed scene classification adopting biologically inspired features (BIF), which simulate the human brain cortex by encoding orientation, intensity and color information of the scene and can tolerate shifting, translation, and scaling. Recently, Census transform histogram (Centrist) has been developed by Wu and Rehg [22]. This holistic representation captures the structural properties within an image and suppresses detailed textural information, and has strong generalizability for scene recognition (especially in indoor environments). Furthermore, the work in [23] computes the scene descriptor by adopting a bank of Gabor filters tuned to 8 orientations at 4 different scales. The square output of each filter is then averaged on a 4×4 grid. Beyond that, shape context [1], color histogram, and even texton histogram [11] have also been applied as holistic representations for high-level classifiaction. These hand-engineered features involve lots of testing and tuning of the parameters and are not scalable to different image domains.

Algorithm 1 Genetic Programming

Start
Initialization Randomly create an initial population of operation sequences from the
available primitives (terminal set & function set).
Repeat
(1) Evaluate the fitness of each individual.
(2) Choose individuals from the population with a particular probability biased in their fitness.
(3) Create a new generation of individuals applying genetic operations.
If An acceptable solution is found or the maximum number of generations
(defined by user) is exceeded.
Stop
Return The best solution is selected.
End

Recently, to facilitate automatic generation of features, deep learning algorithms such as the deep belief network (DBN) [5] and the convolutional neural network (CNN) [17, 7] have been applied to learn hierarchical features in images. The multi-layer architecture of these deep networks enables them to extract features at different levels (*i.e.*, edges, object parts, and objects). These methods aim to learn general-purpose features for any images. In this paper, we target to learn domain-adaptive feature descriptors particularly for scene recognition using multi-objective genetic programming. The components in our learned descriptors are automatically selected and assembled in the evolution rather than being pre-fixed. In deep learning, each new image has to go through the multi-layer architecture to obtain its final representation at the inference stage. In our approach, once the descriptor is built, it can be directly utilized on any new image similar as a hand-crafted descriptor. Another difference is that our MOGP programs use a tree-structure which can take multiple inputs and different branches of the tree can be composed of different detectors, which simultaneously fuses features from different color channels.

Genetic programming, as a powerful machine learning method, has been gradually adopted in computer vision. The general genetic programming algorithm is shown in Algorithm 1. In [15, 21], GP has been used for a variety of image analysis tasks such as segmentation, feature extraction and image retrieval. To control the *overfitting* caused by *bloat* [16] in evolutionary methods, multi-objective genetic programming (MOGP) has been applied to solve relevant problems [24, 13]. Inspired by these successful applications, we propose evolving holistic descriptors for scene recognition using MOGP.

3. SCENE DESCRIPTOR LEARNING

In this paper, we design a multi-tier feature extraction system by applying multi-objective genetic programming (MOGP) for scene recognition. A group of primitive 2D operators is adopted in our architecture to automatically evolve a single individual program that is able to extract meaningful features directly from the raw scene images. The proposed MOGP-based method is regarded as a generalized methodology for scene recognition rather than just as a spe-

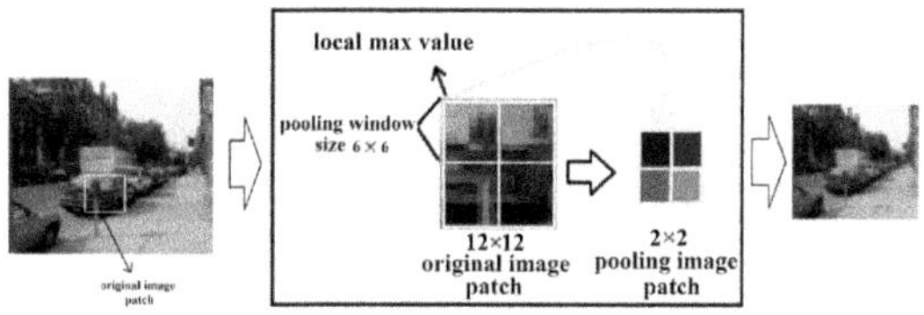

Figure 2: The illustration of the max-pooling mechanism.

cific one for a certain domain. This section describes the proposed program structure along with the required terminal set, function set and fitness function.

3.1 Program Structure Design

The program tree of an individual is broken down into four tiers: data input (bottom tier), filtering (middle tier 1), max-pooling (middle tier 2) and concatenation (top tier). The order of these tiers in our structure is always fixed, which is consistent with the physical structure of the human visual cortex [8]. Both data input and concatenation are one-level tiers, while the depth of the filtering and max-pooling tiers is dynamic and unrestricted according to the evolving procedure of MOGP. The proposed structure of an individual program is illustrated in Fig. 1.

The data input tier is located in the bottom of the whole structure and serves as the entry of the input 2D scene images which are all normalized into the same size by using bilinear interpolation. As a result, all the images are fed to the MOGP program with the identical size. The filtering tier is above the data input tier, and all the data are operated through the nodes in the filtering tier and the outputs of these nodes are still 2D images, which have the same size as the inputs. The third tier is max-pooling, where all of the data are processed by a max-pooling technique (see in Fig. 2), which is considered as a key mechanism for robust responses in the case of recognition in cluttered scenes or with multiple stimuli in the receptive field [18]. The top of our proposed structure is the concatenation tier, where all the data acquired from the adjacent tier are first 'flattened' from 2D images to 1D vectors which are then fed to the concatenation operators. It fuses the features computed from the below sub-trees of MOGP and constructs a more informative vector as the final extracted feature descriptor of the input image.

3.2 Terminal Set

Inspired by the human visual cognition system, we mimic the cortex of human brain to distinguish different scenes and objects based on the appearance features such as color, intensity and contrast. In this way, the terminal set for our proposed methodology is expected to be more specific than a general GP definition and highly depends on the nature of the task. Here, we consider extracting features from the color components (*i.e.*, Red, Green, and Blue) and intensity information (gray scale) of RGB-images and naturally fusing them into one representation. Additionally, the input of the bottom tier is image dependent, which means that each image I_i from the dataset set has a corresponding T_i defined by: $T_i = \{I_r$, I_g, I_b and $I_{gray}\}$.

Furthermore, to make the final feature fusion more flexible, we also define a group of double-precision number coefficients C in our terminal set for constructing a weighted linear concatenation of sub-MOGP-trees in the top tier. In the proposed architecture, the optimal weight coefficients for the sub-trees are randomly distributed and selected by MOGP. C is defined by: $C = coefficient \in (0, 5)$. Therefore, the complete terminal set is $T_i \cup C$. The data types used for the terminal of program nodes are listed in Table 1.

3.3 Function Set

A key concept of MOGP is the function set (*i.e.*, internal nodes of the tree) which is typically driven by the nature of the problem. The choice of functions is commonly based on the following principles:

(1)The set must contain functions which can extract meaningful information.

(2)To minimize the total running time of MOGP, all the operators in the function set should be relatively simple and efficient.

3.3.1 Functions for Filtering Tier

The filtering tier is the most significant part of our MOGP procedure, extracting the effective features from the input data. We construct the filtering tier by using 19 unary functions and 5 binary functions, shown in Table 2. All the filtering functions listed here operate on the images which are represented in the form of a pixel matrix.

In the proposed MOGP architecture, we adopt Gaussian filter series, Garbor filter series and some basic arithmetic functions. Since Gaussian and Gaussian derivative filters are widely used to successfully reduce the noise and smooth input images, we adopt them into our function set to achieve denoising and extract the meaningful contour information. 2D Laplacian filters are used for separating signals into different spectral sub-bands. Gabor filters are regarded as an effective method to obtain the orientation information. To simulate the biological mechanism of the human visual cortex, we follow Riesenhuber and Poggio's work [18] to define our GBO-θ_s (where θ_s=0, 45, 90 or 135) filters in two steps: first, convolving the input image with six different scale Gabor filters (7×7, 9×9, 11×11, 13×13, 15×15 and 17×17) in a certain orientation θ_s; second, using the max operation to pick the maximum value across all six convolved images within the filter scales in each orientation. Our multi-scale-max Gabor filter is defined below:

$$GBO\text{-}\theta_s = \max_{(x,y)}[I_{7\times7}(x, y, \theta_s), I_{9\times9}(x, y, \theta_s), \\ ..., I_{15\times15}(x, y, \theta_s), I_{17\times17}(x, y, \theta_s)] \quad (1)$$

where, GBO-θ_s is the output of a multi-scale-max Gabor filter. $I_{i\times i}(x, y, \theta_s)$ denotes the convolved images with the scale $i \times i$ and the orientation θ_s.

In addition, basic arithmetic functions are chosen to realize operations such as addition and subtraction of the internal nodes of the tree to make the whole evolution procedure more natural. Simultaneously, some binary arithmetic functions can stretch the MOGP tree by splits and make the individual programs more variable and diversified.

To ensure operator closure [16], we have only used functions which map one or two 2D images to a single 2D image with the identical size (*i.e.*, the input and the output of each function node have the same size). In this way, a MOGP tree can be an unrestricted composition of function nodes but still always produce a semantically legal tree.

3.3.2 Functions for Max-pooling Tier

The max-pooling function set is listed in Table 3. All the functions in this set are performed over local neighborhoods with windows varying from 2×2 to 10×10 with a step of 2 pixels. The max-like feature selection operation is a key mechanism for object recognition in the human brain cortex and provides a robust response in the case of recognition with clutter or multiple stimuli in the receptive field. This kind of mechanism achieves invariance to

Table 1: Statement of terminal nodes

Terminal	Type	Description
I_r	Image	Red component of the RGB-image
I_g	Image	Green component of the RGB-image
I_b	Image	Blue component of the RGB-image
I_{gray}	Image	Gray scale image calculated from the RGB-image
C	double	Returns a random double from 0 to 5

Table 2: Filtering tier functions

Operator Name	Input	Function Description
Gau1	1 Image	Gaussian filter with $\sigma = 1$
Gau2	1 Image	Gaussian filter with $\sigma = 2$
GauX	1 Image	The derivative along X axis of Gaussian filter
GauY	1 Image	The derivative along Y axis of Gaussian filter
LoG1	1 Image	Laplacian of Gaussian filter with $\sigma = 1$
LoG2	1 Image	Laplacian of Gaussian filter with $\sigma = 2$
Lap	1 Image	Laplacian filter
GBO-0	1 Image	Multi-scale-max Gabor filter with orientation of 0 degree
GBO-45	1 Image	Multi-scale-max Gabor filter with orientation of 45 degrees
GBO-90	1 Image	Multi-scale-max Gabor filter with orientation of 90 degrees
GBO-135	1 Image	Multi-scale-max Gabor filter with orientation of 135 degrees
Aver	1 Image	Averaging filter with 5×5 sampling window
Med	1 Image	Median filter with 5×5 sampling window
EHIS	1 Image	Histogram equalization
ABS	1 Image	Take the absolute value pixel by pixel
ADD	2 Images	Add two input images pixel by pixel
SUB	2 Images	Subtract two input images pixel by pixel
ABSsub	2 Images	Absolute subtraction of two input images pixel by pixel
MULTI	2 Images	Multiply two input images pixel by pixel
DIV	2 Images	Protected-division: divide two input images pixel by pixel and return 0 if divisor is 0
SQR	1 Image	Square the input image pixel by pixel
SQRT	1 Image	Square root of the input image pixel by pixel
LOG2	1 Image	Take the logarithm with 2 at the bottom of the input image
TIME-0.5	1 Image	Multiply 0.5 to the input image pixel by pixel

Table 3: Max-pooling tier functions

Operator Name	Input	Function Description
Maxpooling2	1 Image	Max-pooling with window size 2×2
Maxpooling4	1 Image	Max-pooling with window size 4×4
Maxpooling6	1 Image	Max-pooling with window size 6×2
Maxpooling8	1 Image	Max-pooling with window size 8×8
Maxpooling10	1 Image	Max-pooling with window size 10×10

image-plane transforms such as translation and scaling. One noteworthy point here is that the output of the max-pooling filters is inevitably shrunk in size relative to the input. To ensure the closure property mentioned above, we further resize each output calculated from max-pooling filters to an identical size as the input using linear interpolation.

3.3.3 Functions for Concatenation Tier

After the max-pooling tier, we have extracted the corresponding features from the original input images through the tree-based MOGP programs. By first converting the obtained 2D images to 1D vectors, we further concatenate these 1D feature vectors calculated from different sub-trees into a weighted linear concatenation vector with coefficients random selected from the terminal set. To make the weighted concatenation work for different numbers of sub-trees, in our architecture, we include four different concatenation functions. The relevant functions are illustrated in Table 4. Since the concatenation tier is the last tier in our program structure,

Table 4: Concatenation tier functions

Operator Name	Input	Function Description
Cat1	1 Image and 1 coefficient	'Flatten' 2D input image to 1D vector with coefficient
Cat2	2 Images and 2 coefficients	'Flatten' two 2D input images to 1D vectors and concatenate these into a long vector with coefficients
Cat3	3 Images and 3 coefficients	'Flatten' three 2D input images to 1D vectors and concatenate these into a long vector with coefficients
Cat4	4 Images and 4 coefficients	'Flatten' four 2D input images to 1D vectors and concatenate these into a long vector with coefficients

the output of this tier is the final feature descriptor extracted from the input image.

Note that, in our proposed MOGP architecture, not all functions in the function set have to be used in a given tree, and the same function can be also used more than once.

Each function in the function set is regarded as a tree node in evolved programs, which connect the outputs of lower level functions or inputs. Note that, in our proposed MOGP architecture, not all the functions listed in the function set have to be used in a given structure and the same function can be used more than once. The topology of our MOGP structure ihe function set are effective filters for feature extraction, *i.e.*, Gaussian filters, Gabor filters, Laplacian filters, s essentially unrestricted. Besides, functions in the function set are also highly related to our problem domain. For this work, we aim to construct novel discriminative feature descriptors for image classification. So, what we choose in t *etc.* We expect the whole learned architecture is consistent with the physical structure of the human visual cortex.

3.4 Fitness Function

The basis of evolutionary methods is to maximize the performance of individual solutions gauged by some appropriate fitness functions. In our approach, we apply MOGP to evolve the individual programs under two fitness objectives and finally the system selects the best-preformed individual as the optimal solution.

3.4.1 Two Defined Fitness Objectives

Classification error rate: To evaluate a candidate MOGP-evolved feature descriptor, we estimate its classification error rate E_r using a linear support-vector-machine (SVM) on the *learning set*. We apply a candidate descriptor to images in the learning set and adopt principle component analysis (PCA) keeping the 98% principal components to reduce the dimension. The reduced vectors are fed to the SVM for classification. To obtain a more reliable fitness evaluation, for each candidate MOGP tree, we estimate the classification error rate with the SVM by using 10-fold cross-validation. We divide the GP learning set randomly into ten equal parts and perform ten repetitions of training the SVM on 9/10-ths of the set and testing on the remaining tenth. The overall fitness of the candidate MOGP tree is measured as the average of the 10 SVM test-fold

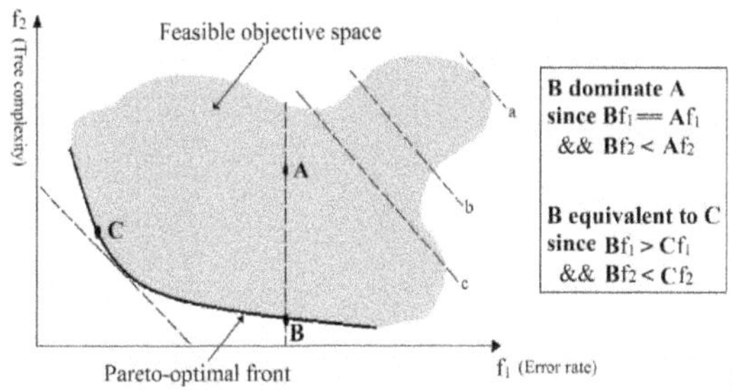

B

Figure 3: A simple illustration of *Error-Complexity* Pareto front. Point B significantly dominates Point A, but is equal to point C. In our approach, we consider both point B and point C as 'rank-1' on the Pareto-optimal front.

error rates. Note that, here we just adopt SVM as a classifier in the fitness function to evaluate the recognition rate of learned features. As an alternative way, other classifiers, such as K nearest neighbor (KNN), can be also used for fitness evaluation. The related fitness function is defined as follows:

$$E_r = (1 - (\sum_{i=1}^{n} (SVM[acu_i])/n)) \times 100\% \qquad (2)$$

where, $SVM[acu_i]$ denotes the classification accuracy of fold i by the SVM, n indicates the total number of folds executed with cross-validation. Here n is equal to 10.

Tree complexity measurement: We usually measure solutions' complexity by counting nodes of the tree structure. Unless inhibited from doing so, trees in GP have a tendency to grow without limit, which is termed *bloat*. As an undesirable phenomenon, *bloat* may cause poor generalizability, a manifestation of the well-known *overfitting* effect in machine learning. In addition, bloated trees are also time-consuming for evaluation, which slows the evolution and heavily influences the efficiency of program running, especially for on-line GP learning. According to [16], minimizing the tree node count in a multi-objective setting can effectively suppress tree *bloat*.

3.4.2 Tree Optimization

In our MOGP evolution, each individual is evaluated against these two fitness objectives, each of which is expected to be minimized simultaneously. In fact, what we can obtain is a set of solutions which are all listed as 'rank-1' according to the *Pareto front* shown in Fig. 3. Members on the *Pareto front* dominate the other candidates but are equivalent to each other. We further test the set of 'rank-1' solutions on an independent *evaluation set* to select the (near-)optimal one with the lowest test error (average classification error rate) by adopting the same 10-fold cross-validation procedure mentioned above. In this way, we obtain the best-preformed solution through MOGP as the final feature descriptor for scene classification.

4. EXPERIMENTS AND RESULTS

In this section, we describe the details of our MOGP implementation and the experimental results of our method.

4.1 MOGP Implementation

We evaluate our proposed method using Matlab 2011a (with the Genetic Programming toolbox GPLAB[1]) on a server with a 12-core

[1]http://gplab.sourceforge.net/download.html

Table 5: Parameter settings for genetic programming running

Population Size	400
Generation Size	70
Crossover Rate	90%
Mutation Rate	10%
Selection for Reproduction	'tournament'
Survival Method	'totalelitism'
Stop Condition	$E_r \leq 0.5\%$

Figure 4: Some scene examples of three datasets. Images in the top black-box are from the MIT urban and nature scene dataset, images in the middle black-box are from the UIUC-Sport dataset and images at the bottom black-box are from the SUN scene dataset.

processor and 54GB of RAM running the Linux operating system. The user-defined GP parameters are listed in Table 7.

For the MOGP evolution, we use 'tournament' as the selection method, which chooses each parent by randomly drawing a number of individuals from the population and selecting only the dominant one of them. In addition, we have adopted the 'totalelitism' scheme as the survival module in which all the individuals from both parents and children populations are ordered by the *Pareto front*, regardless of being parents or children. We also set the MOGP termination as $E_r \leq 0.5\%$, which means if the value calculated by the fitness function is equal to or lower than 0.5%, our MOGP running will be stopped and return the best-so-far individual to users.

4.2 Datasets

Our proposed method is systematically evaluated on three challenging scene datasets, *i.e.*, the MIT urban and nature scene dataset, the SUN scene dataset and the UIUC Sport event scene dataset. Some scene examples from these three datasets are shown in Fig. 4.

The **MIT urban and nature** scene dataset is composed of 2688 color images with eight categories including *'coast&beach'*, *'highway'*, *'open country'*, *'tall building'*, *'forest'*, *'street'*, *'mountain'* and *'city center'* . In the pre-processing stage, each image in this dataset is normalized to the size of 125 × 125 pixels by linear interpolation and then the first 100 images from each category are selected as the learning set, the following 50 images from each category form the evaluation set and the remaining images construct the independent testing set.

The **SUN** scene dataset is a more diverse dataset which contains 899 categories and 130,519 images. Considering the computa-

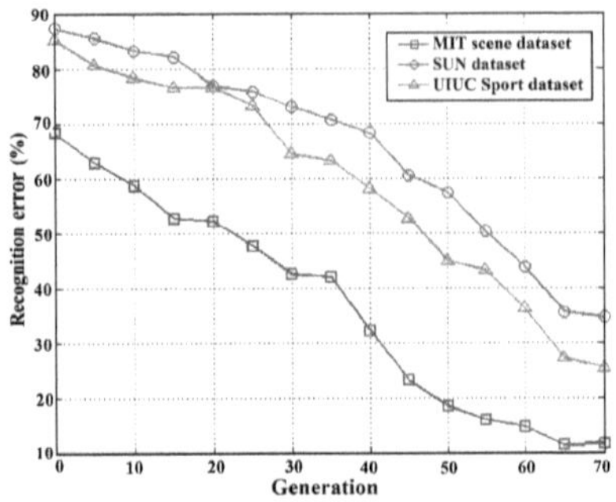

Figure 5: The evolution of the average 'rank-1' values on the error rate. The general trend of average error rates is decreasing during the MOGP evolving.

Cat2(Maxpooling4(Gau1(Aver(GBO-0(GauX(GBO-90(GauX(LoG1(Lap(SUB(DIV(ADD(GauY(LoG1(Aver(Gau2(Ir)))),SUB(Ig,Igray)),Aver(ADD(Ig,SUB(Ib,GauY(Igray))))),ABSsub(ABS(GBO-90(Gau1(Ig))),Ig)))))))))),1.83,GBO-90(GauX(LoG1(ABS(SUB(GauY(LoG1(ABS(Igray))),ABSsub(SQRT(Med(Ib)),Igray)))))),0.70)

Figure 6: The LISP format of the (near-)optical feature descriptor generated through MOGP on the MIT urban and natural scene dataset.

tional cost, in our experiments, we use 54 randomly-sampled categories with totally 8302 images to evaluate our MOGP algorithm for scene recognition and compare with other state-of-the-art techniques. Each image has been pre-processed into 100×100 pixels. Since the numbers of the scene images in different categories differ greatly, we randomly divide images of each category into three equal parts, which are used as our learning, evaluation and independent testing sets, respectively.

The **UIUC-Sport** dataset contains 8 sports event categories: rowing (250 images), badminton (200 images), polo (182 images), bocce (137 images), snowboarding (190 images), croquet (236 images), sailing (190 images), and rock climbing (194 images). In our experiment, each image has been resized to 100×100 pixels. For each scene class, 50 randomly selected images are used for MOGP learning, 40 are used for evaluation and the rest is used for independent testing.

4.3 Results

For the MIT urban and nature scene dataset, our approach automatically selects and fuses RGB color components and generates machine-learned descriptors for scene recognition. We select the best MOGP-evolved feature descriptor with a classification rate of 88.3% from a set of potential solutions using the evaluation set and finally achieve a classification accuracy of 88.5% on the independent testing set using 'ten-fold' cross-validation with the linear SVM classifier [2]. Fig. 6 shows the LISP format of the corresponding MOGP program. The detailed information of error rate and tree complexity during the genetic evolution can be seen in Fig. 5. Since MOGP can effectively restrain the *overfitting* and the number of samples in the testing set is much larger compared with the evaluation set, the (near-)optimal descriptor achieves an unexpectedly higher result in the testing set. On the other hand, this has somehow demonstrated the scalability of our approach for large-scale scene recognition.

[2]the cross-validation with the linear SVM classification has been used three times in our approach, the first one is to be adopted for fitness function on learning set; the second one is used to select the best preformed descriptor from evaluation set; the third one is here used for compute the final recognition rate on independent testing set.

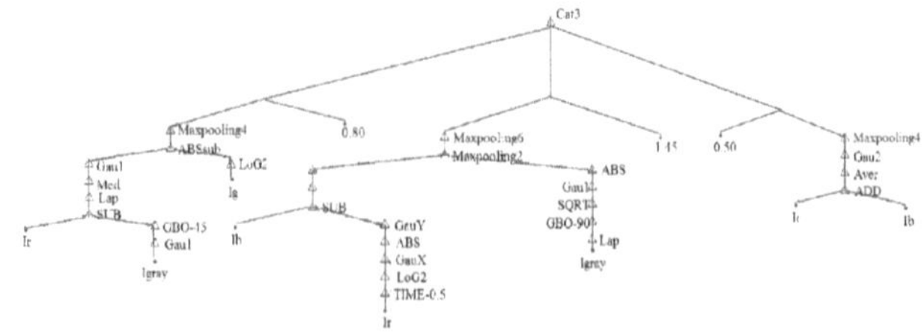

Figure 7: The tree-based (near-)optimal feature descriptor generated through MOGP on the SUN scene dataset.

The results we obtained on the SUN dataset are lower, since this real-world dataset has much more scene categories with complex backgrounds and large intra-class variations. Some categories are even hard to distinguish reliably by human eyes. Consequently, the best MOGP-evolved feature descriptor achieves classification accuracies of 67.1% on the evaluation set and 65.4% on the independent testing set under the same experimental setting. The corresponding MOGP program is visualized in Fig. 7, in which Gaussian, Laplacian and Gabor operators can be automatically selected by MOGP at the filtering layer to extract the orientation and intensity features, and several scales of pooling operators can get the most robust and distinctive responses to different data resolutions on the top layer. The whole learned architecture is indeed consistent with the physical structure of the human visual cortex.

To prove the generalizability of our method, we have also tested it on the UIUC Sport dataset whose background of each image is highly cluttered and diverse and sizes of instances from a same object are very different for a same scene category. It is a very challenging dataset for recognition. The results show that the optimally evolved MOGP program can achieve 77.2% on the evaluation set and 74.6% on the final independent test set by automatically fusing the R,G,B and gray scale components via genetic evolving. Fig. 8 illustrates the tree structure of the corresponding MOGP program. The error rate and tree complexity during the genetic evolution can also be seen in Fig. 5.

For comparison, we have also evaluated some prevalent hand-crafted holistic descriptors including flattened image, shape context [1], color histogram, Gabor bank [23], BIF [20], Texton histogram [11], Gist [14] and Centrist [22]. Most of these descriptors in comparison are designed for gray scale images. To fully exploit the color information in scene images, we compute these descriptors on both the gray scale and the color versions of the images. For color scene images in the datasets, we calculate features on R, G, B and grey scale components, respectively, and then concatenate them into a long vector as the final representation. As the BIF method already encodes color information, we directly extract the BIF features from color images instead of calculating on color components. Under the same setting, we first adopt PCA for dimension reduction and then apply the linear SVM with 'ten-fold' cross-validation on the independent testing set to compute the recognition accuracies. All the results on color images are shown in Table 6. Fig. 9 displays results of these hand-crafted descriptors on gray scale images. By comparing Table 6 and Fig. 9, we can conclude that the color version of each method performs better than its

Table 6: Comparison of scene classification accuracies (%) based on color images.

Method \ Accuracy	Method description	RGB fusion method	MIT urban and nature	SUN	UIUC-Sport
Proposed	MOGP-evolved holistic descriptors.	Tree structure fusion	**88.5**	**65.4**	**74.6**
Hand-crafted features					
Flattened image	Flatten the 2D raw image to a 1D vector.	Concatenation	22.3	14.7	16.3
Shape context	Apply *Canny* edge detector to obtain contour information and diagram log-polar histogram bins (5 bins for $log\ r$, 12 bins for θ) are used in computing the shape context.	Concatenation	49.2	17.6	20.1
Color histogram	Build joint histograms of color in RGB space and for each color component 4 bins (*e.g.*, $0-63$, $64-127$, $128-191$, and $192-255$) are used for a total of 64 dimensions.	Concatenation	27.6	16.1	17.7
Gabor bank	Gabor filtering with 4 orientations at 6 different scales and output of each filter is then averaged on a 4×4 grid to form a vector.	Concatenation	77.2	46.4	57.9
BIF	Biologically-inspired feature combining orientation, intensity and color information to represent images, see in [20].	Contained in method	82.1	58.3	62.7
Gist	Use a very low dimensional feature to represent the dominant spatial structure of a scene, see in [14].	Concatenation	78.0	56.8	65.3
Texton histogram	A 512 entries texton dictionary [11] is built by clustering responses to a bank of filters with 8 orientations, 2 scales and 2 elongations and then mapping all images into 512D histograms.	Concatenation	77.4	58.7	67.2
Centrist	Census transform histogram encoding the structural properties within an image and suppressing detailed textural information, see in [22].	Concatenation	84.0	62.3	64.2
Machine-learned features					
DBN	Train a hierarchical architecture (with neuron numbers in hidden layers 500-500-2000) using the deep brief network with backpropagation fine-tuning for feature extraction.	Learned	82.3	63.7	71.4
CNN	Train a 5-layer feature extraction mechanism using the convolutional neural network.	Learned	80.8	58.1	69.2

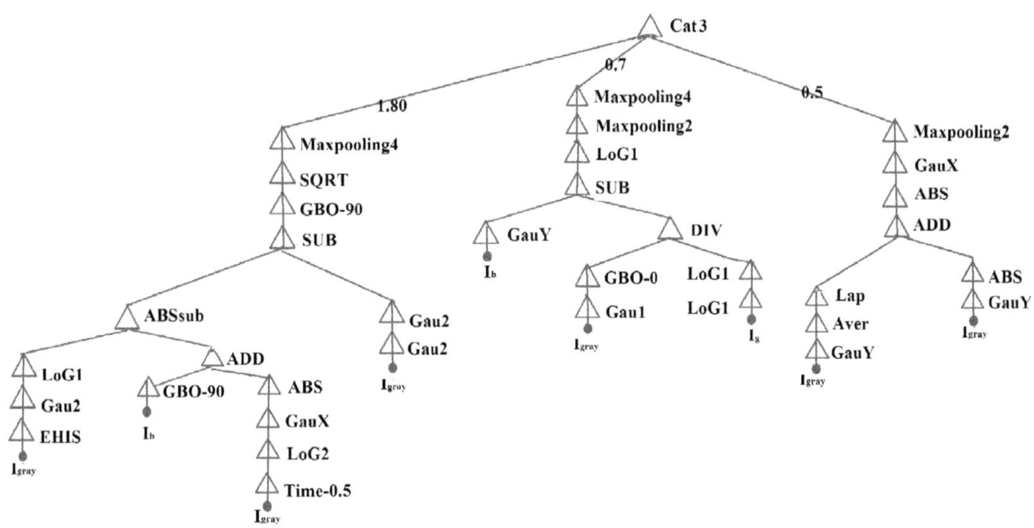

Figure 8: The tree-based (near-)optimal feature descriptor generated through MOGP on the UIUC Sport dataset.

gray scale version. In addition, we have also utilized two popular deep learning methods, *i.e.*, DBN [5] and CNN [17], to learn hierarchical architectures for feature extraction on the combined learning and evaluation sets. We then apply the learned architectures (and associated parameters) to extract features on the testing sets and a same 'ten-fold' cross-validation is used with the linear SVM to calculate the recognition accuracies. To make the comparison fair, all the images used as the inputs of the architectures are the combinations of the R, G, B and gray scale components of the original color images. From Table 6, it is obvious that our MOGP-learned descriptors significantly outperform the state-of-the-art hand-crafted and machine learned features on these three scene datasets. The superior performance is mainly accredited to the simultaneous description and fusion of color components automatically assembled by the proposed methodology. The implicit supervised nature of the descriptor learning mechanism also contributes to the discriminative power of the MOGP-built descriptors. Note that, in this paper, we only aim to prove that our MOGP-learned descriptors can outperform state-of-the-art hand-crafted and learned descriptors in a fair experimental setting rather than comparing with results from published recognition systems (which often use different settings, features, classifiers, etc.), because comparing with whole recognition systems under different settings is unfair and meaningless.

In addition, to illustrate time complexity of the feature learning process, we show the evolving time costs of MOGP and the single-objective GP in Table 7. It can be observed that our MOGP spends less time on evolving out a (near-)optimal feature descriptor than the single-objective GP. As many learning algorithms, the training of the descriptors is time-consuming, but it can be performed off-line. Once the optimal descriptor is obtained from the MOGP training phase, the classification phase will be very efficient, as the optimised descriptor can be just used as a handcrafted descriptor like SIFT. Of course, with the rapid development of silicon technologies, future computers will be much faster and even the training will become less a problem.

5. CONCLUSION

We have developed a domain-adaptive learning approach based on multi-objective genetic programming (MOGP) to generate (near-)optimal feature descriptors for scene recognition. Our method addresses scene description as an optimization problem, and allows a computer to automatically synthesize holistic descriptors from a pool of primitive operators, which are devised according to the general knowledge of feature extraction. Since our proposed MOGP approach can effectively fuse the RGB color components and extract discriminative features, it achieves outstanding results for high-level scene recognition tasks. We have systematically evaluated our method on the MIT urban and nature scene dataset, the SUN dataset and the UIUC Sport dataset achieving accuracies of 88.5%, 65.4% and 74.6%, respectively, with the obtained descriptors evolved by MOGP. In all three datasets, the MOGP-generated descriptors significantly outperform prevailing hand-designed and machine-learned features.

6. ACKNOWLEDGEMENTS

This work is partially supported by the University of Sheffield, the National Basic Research Program of China (973 Program) (Grant No.: 2012CB316400), and the National Natural Science Foundation of China (Grant No.: 61125106).

7. REFERENCES

[1] S. Belongie, J. Malik, and J. Puzicha. Shape matching and object recognition using shape contexts. *T-PAMI*, 24(4):509–522, 2002.

[2] M. Boutell, C. Brown, and J. Luo. Review of the state of the art in semantic scene classification. *Rochester, NY, USA, Tech. Rep*, 2002.

[3] R. Cucchiara. Multimedia surveillance systems. In *Proceedings of the third ACM international workshop on Video surveillance & sensor networks*, pages 3–10, 2005.

[4] C. Harris and M. Stephens. A combined corner and edge detector. In *Alvey vision conference*, volume 15, page 50, 1988.

[5] G. Hinton, S. Osindero, and Y. Teh. A fast learning algorithm for deep belief nets. *Neural computation*, 18(7):1527–1554, 2006.

[6] R. Ji, Y. Gao, B. Zhong, H. Yao, and Q. Tian. Mining flickr landmarks by modeling reconstruction sparsity. *ACM Transactions on Multimedia Computing, Communications, and Applications*, 7(1):31, 2011.

[7] Y. LeCun, K. Kavukcuoglu, and C. Farabet. Convolutional networks and applications in vision. In *IEEE International Symposium on Circuits and Systems*, pages 253–256, 2010.

[8] T. Lee and D. Mumford. Hierarchical bayesian inference in the visual cortex. *JOSA A*, 20(7):1434–1448, 2003.

[9] L.-J. Li and L. Fei-Fei. What, where and who? classifying events by scene and object recognition. In *ICCV*, pages 1–8, 2007.

[10] X. Li, L. Chen, L. Zhang, F. Lin, and W.-Y. Ma. Image annotation by large-scale content-based image retrieval. In *14th annual ACM international conference on Multimedia*, pages 607–610, 2006.

[11] D. Martin, C. Fowlkes, D. Tal, and J. Malik. A database of human segmented natural images and its application to evaluating segmentation algorithms and measuring ecological statistics. In *CVPR*, volume 2, pages 416–423, 2001.

[12] K. Mikolajczyk and C. Schmid. Scale & affine invariant interest point detectors. *IJCV*, 60(1):63–86, 2004.

[13] G. Olague and L. Trujillo. Interest point detection through multiobjective genetic programming. *Applied Soft Computing*, 2012.

[14] A. Oliva and A. Torralba. Modeling the shape of the scene: A holistic representation of the spatial envelope. *IJCV*, 42(3):145–175, 2001.

[15] R. Poli. Genetic programming for image analysis. In *the First Annual Conference on Genetic Programming*, pages 363–368, 1996.

[16] R. Poli, W. Langdon, and N. McPhee. *A field guide to genetic programming*. 2008.

[17] M. Ranzato, F. Huang, Y. Boureau, and Y. LeCun. Unsupervised learning of invariant feature hierarchies with applications to object recognition. In *CVPR*, pages 1–8, 2007.

[18] M. Riesenhuber, T. Poggio, et al. Hierarchical models of object recognition in cortex. *Nature neuroscience*, 2:1019–1025, 1999.

[19] C. Siagian and L. Itti. Rapid biologically-inspired scene classification using features shared with visual attention. *IEEE T-PAMI*, 29(2):300–312, 2007.

Table 7: **The time costs of feature learning and testing on the three datasets by applying the proposed MOGP method (Note that Matlab 2011a is used for coding)**

Datasets \ Time	(MOGP) Learning time	(Cross-validation) Testing time
MIT Urban and Nature	3.3h (1200 images)	141sec (1488 images)
SUN	6.9h (5534 images)	253sec (2768 images)
UIUC Sport	2.8h (720 images)	92sec (859 images)

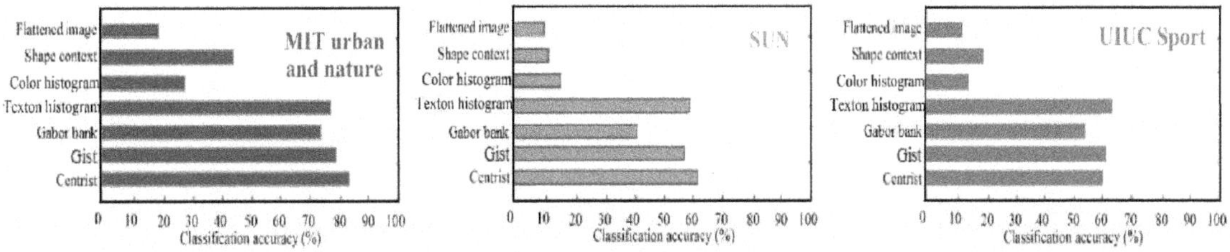

Figure 9: The results on three datasets of some state-of-the-art descriptors only using gray scale scene images.

[20] D. Song and D. Tao. Biologically inspired feature manifold for scene classification. *IEEE Transactions on Image Processing*, 19(1):174–184, 2010.

[21] L. Trujillo and G. Olague. Synthesis of interest point detectors through genetic programming. In *Proceedings of the 8th Annual Conference on Genetic and Evolutionary Computation*, pages 887–894, 2006.

[22] J. Wu and J. Rehg. Centrist: A visual descriptor for scene categorization. *T-PAMI*, 33(8):1489–1501, 2011.

[23] J. Xiao, J. Hays, K. Ehinger, A. Oliva, and A. Torralba. Sun database: Large-scale scene recognition from abbey to zoo. In *CVPR*, pages 3485–3492, 2010.

[24] Y. Zhang and P. Rockett. Feature extraction using multi-objective genetic programming. *Multi-objective machine learning*, pages 75–99, 2006.

Scale Based Region Growing For Scene Text Detection

Junhua Mao †, Houqiang Li †, Wengang Zhou ‡, Shuicheng Yan ♯, Qi Tian ‡
† Dept. of EEIS, University of Science and Technology of China, Hefei 230027, P. R. China
‡ Dept. of Computer Science, University of Texas at San Antonio, Texas, TX 78249
♯ Dept. of ECE, National University of Singapore, Singapore 117583
{mjhustc@mail., lihq@}ustc.edu.cn; zhwgeeis@gmail.com; eleyans@nus.edu.sg; qitian@cs.utsa.edu

ABSTRACT

Scene text is widely observed in our daily life and has many important multimedia applications. Unlike document text, scene text usually exhibits large variations in font and language, and suffers from low resolution, occlusions and complex background. In this paper, we present a novel scale-based region growing algorithm for scene text detection. We first distinguish SIFT features in text regions from those in background by exploring the inter- and intra-statistics of SIFT features. Then scene text regions in images are identified by scale-based region growing, which explores the geometric context of SIFT keypoints in local regions. Our algorithm is very effective to detect multilingual text in various fonts, sizes, and with complex background. In addition, it offers insights on efficiently deploying local features in numerous applications, such as visual search. We evaluate our algorithm on three datasets and achieve the state-of-the-art performance.

Figure 1: Examples of the detected text regions by our algorithm (highlighted by the red bounding box) in natural scene images from three databases. (a) The sample images from the ICDAR database [1]. (b) The sample images from the SWT database [2]. (c) The sample images from the MSRG database.

Categories and Subject Descriptors

I.4.8 [**Computing Methodologies**]: Image Processing and Computer Vision—*scene analysis*; I.4.9 [**Computing Methodologies**]: Image Processing and Computer Vision—*Applications*

General Terms

Algorithms, Experimentation, Performance.

Keywords

Scene Text, SIFT, Region Growing, Neural Network.

1. INTRODUCTION

With the increasing popularity of high-performance and low price digital camera devices and smart phones, explosive growth of photos/images are taken in daily life. In those images, it is widely observed that scene text frequently appears in the form of ads, graffiti, and signs. Lots of efforts have been made to understand the content of these images in multimedia community. As one of the critical yet challenging tasks, scene text detection serves as the basis for numerous multimedia applications, such as license plate detection [35], landmark recognition [26], and automatic navigation [28]. In augmented reality, signs and texts of foreign languages can be translated for visitors by their smart phones [12]. All these applications require a scene text detection algorithm with robustness and effectiveness.

Moreover, image search based on visual features is becoming popular and promising [27, 36]. However, the existing techniques often ignore the information of embedded text in images. If scene text can be robustly detected and recognized, the accuracy of search is expected to be further boosted.

The ignorance of scene texts in current search engine is mainly due to the dramatic decrease of accuracy of scene text detection algorithm compared to that of document texts. There are two main reasons. Firstly, the image condition varies extensively in natural scene image. Many tough conditions, such as blur, occlusion, intensive light, and low resolution, make it very difficult for scene text detection. Secondly, while document and caption text is structured and characterized by homogenous background, scene texts have little prior information of their structure and background. They often appear in different colors, sizes, fonts, spatial configurations and suffer from deformation when embedded on non-planar objects. In addition, current image retrieval systems adopt some popular features, such as SIFT and SURF [25, 34]. But many state-of-the-art text detection algorithms use features particularly designed for text [5, 9, 29], which needs additional computational cost in order to combine them with the image retrieval systems.

In this work, we propose a novel method to robustly locate the text within natural scene images based on the SIFT descriptors [16]. We define SIFT keypoints in the interior region of text patches as text keypoints. These keypoints often have high entropy of their orientation distribution and relatively low variance of their scales.

MM'13, October 21–25, 2013, Barcelona, Spain.

ACM 978-1-4503-2404-5/13/10 ...$15.00.
http://dx.doi.org/10.1145/2502081.2502108.

Based on these properties, we present an efficient algorithm to initially filter obvious non-text keypoints. In addition, extensive experimental study reveals that SIFT features on text keypoints possess very distinctive patterns. With these clues, a neural network classifier with accuracy higher than 80% is trained to select possible text keypoints. We also find an interesting phenomenon that SIFT keypoints from text regions often cluster together geometrically. To further explore the relationship of the geometrically neighboring text keypoints, we propose a simple but effective region growing algorithm. The algorithm can group homogenous keypoints together in a local region with different scales. The few misclassifications of the single keypoint can be rectified by the voting of all the keypoints in a grown region. Finally, regions recognized as text are fused and bounding boxes are drawn to highlight text regions.

Our method differs from previous methods in that it fully explores both the property of a single SIFT keypoint and the relationship of neighboring keypoints in a local region. Some previous text detection and recognition algorithms use isolated SIFT [4] or multiple kinds of local features [8] to detect the structure of a specific character in a certain type of language. Because isolated SIFT features are sensitive to noise, these methods could be only used in the document text analysis or the detection of scene text with clean background. We address this problem by using the information of the geometrically neighboring keypoints. Although our algorithm is particularly effective on language with complex structure (e.g., hieroglyphics), it is not limited to any specific language. The properties we used, such as the high entropy of the orientation distribution, the strong contrast between text pixels and background, and the low variance of color along the stroke, are shared by various kinds of language and handwriting texts. Unlike some algorithms, we do not need the assistance of any language-specific process, such as OCR filtering step [6]. So, our algorithm is not constrained to a specific language and has promising potential for multilingual multimedia tasks.

In contrast to other approaches that use features which are only effective on text, such as low variance of stroke width [9] and special wavelet or Laplacian coefficients [24, 30], we adopt a commonly used feature (SIFT). Therefore, our text detection results can provide important clues for numerous SIFT applications. For example, the algorithm can be combined with visual search systems without further computational load to extract feature descriptors. The SIFT information on text can also assist OCR engines and verify their recognition results.

The experimental results on three scene text databases reveal that, compared to some state of the art algorithms, our method is less sensitive for a specific training set. We evaluate the performance of our algorithm by training and testing in different datasets. When trained on one English and Roman numerals dataset and tested on a multilingual dataset, the f measure drops only by 6% at most. Therefore, some of the properties of SIFT descriptor are shared by different languages.

The main contributions of this paper are as follows:

- We select candidate SIFT keypoints through the unique properties of single text keypoints, such as the high entropy of their orientation distribution within a local region, relatively low variance of their scales, and their distinctive 128-D descriptors. Those properties are shared by multilingual texts.
- We present a novel scale-based region growing algorithm to explore the relationship of geometrically neighboring candidate keypoints.

The remainder of this chapter is organized as follows. Section 2 reviews related work on text detection. Section 3 introduces the properties of SIFT feature and the motivation for our algorithm. Section 4 discusses the proposed scene text detection algorithm in details. In Section 5, experiments are conducted and results are compared with the state-of-the-art methods in English, Latin and multilingual databases. Section 6 concludes the work.

2. RELATED WORK

Many text detection methods have been proposed recently. Comprehensive surveys are also made in [13, 15, 19]. In general, existing methods can be categorized into three groups: thresholding-based, texture-based and region-based.

Thresholding-based methods define a global or local threshold to separate text from background. Many thresholding algorithms, such as adaptive binarization techniques [15] and histogram-based thresholding [23] fall in this category. These methods are computationally efficient, but cannot well address complex background or variations of the text color and intensity level. Some methods, such as OTSU algorithm [13], perform well for automatically thresholding in 1-D data and can be used to automatically determine some parameters.

Texture-based methods treat text as a unique object that has distinguishable features from background. Popular features used include special horizontal and vertical frequencies [33], wavelet or Laplacian coefficients [24, 30], and features with low entropy [6, 7]. These methods still suffer from many limitations, including high computational complexity, inapplicability to slanted text, and waste of the information provided by the transformation.

Region-based methods use geometric constraints and information to choose text candidates and form bounding boxes based on region patches in images. Epshtein et al. [9] proposed a transform (SWT) to find regions with small variance of stroke width and generate letter candidates. The candidate letters are grouped into bounding boxes with geometric constraints. Their method claims to achieve the best result on ICDAR database. Chen et al. [5] modified the method using edge-enhanced Maximally Stable External Regions (MSER) to detect interested regions and found stroke width by distance transform. Neumann et al. [22] also presented an end-to-end method for text localization and recognition using MSER. Yao et al. [29] extended the standard SWT methods by adding two sets of features and a two level classification step. Their work is more effective on multi-orientation texts than previous SWT algorithms. In general, this group of methods can detect text in different scales and directions. However, it may be difficult for them to detect text characters with larger variance of stroke width and complex structures, such as hieroglyph.

There are some existing algorithms using SIFT to detect characters. Block et al. [4] extracted local features on some specific portions of a certain character to create their database. The features from a testing image are compared and matched with the images in the database to recognize the character. The algorithm relies only on isolated SIFT keypoints and ignore the valuable information provided by the neighborhood. So, their method is sensitive to background noises. Zheng et al. [32] extended this framework to recognize Chinese, Japanese and Korea characters. Because their task is character recognition instead of text detection, their dataset images are machine-generated and clean without any background, and their geometric verification is strict. It leads to possible false negatives on the task of detecting text with complex background. Some works adopt multiple kinds of local features and bag-of-visual-words representation [8]. But they focused on the recognition of single characters and their method requires manually segmented individual characters in an image.

Our method falls in the region-based category. We use scale-based region growing scheme to group keypoints in a local region. These regions can be robustly classified by the voting of all the keypoints belong to that region. Similar to conventional region-based method, we take advantage of geometric constraints to link cluster candidates into bounding boxes. We also borrow some insights from methods in the thresholding-based and texture-based groups. Our method takes advantage of the discriminative properties of SIFT keypoints on various kinds of characters which distinguish themselves from those of the background. In addition, thresholding-based methods are modified to automatically determine some parameters in our algorithm instead of their initial purpose to separate foreground pixels. Experimental results show that our method is not limited to specific characters and languages. Finally, we address the drawback of some region-based method in that the complexity of the structure and large variance of stroke width are beneficial properties and are well explored in our method.

3. MOTIVATION

Before discussing our approach, we would like to introduce the background of the classic SIFT feature briefly. SIFT feature is designed to capture the appearance of a local image patch centered at an interest point. The interest point can be detected with invariance detectors, such as DoG [16], Hessian Affine [20], etc, and is characterized with scale and orientation parameters. In the standard SIFT feature, around an interest point, the local patch with radius proportional to the characteristic scale is evenly partitioned into sub-patches along the direction of the characteristic orientation. Then, each sub-patch is described with an 8-D orientation histogram. Consequently, a 128-D SIFT descriptor is obtained by concatenating the orientation histograms over all 16 sub-patches. The merit of SIFT feature lies in its invariance in rotation and scale changes and robustness in illumination changes [20]. A standard SIFT feature contains the following components: location, scale, orientation, and 128-D descriptor vector.

Recent works have shown that SIFT descriptors combined with bag-of-visual-words algorithm have very good discriminative property in some specific characters, such as the digits in the license plate [35] and manually segmented English and Kannada characters [8]. We develop their methods. Our experimental study of SIFT feature shows that the keypoints on text regions process special properties in three ways, which are shared with multilingual characters, especially for the ones with complex structure.

Firstly, statistics properties of geometrically neighboring keypoints in a local text region are unique. For example, keypoints in text regions have high entropy of their orientation distribution and relatively low variance of their scales. We take advantage of these properties to select text sensitive keypoints. Experiments in Section 5 show that this selection step increases the accuracy of the trained classifier.

Secondly, the 128-D SIFT descriptors in text regions usually appear in different patterns from those in non-text regions. As illustrated in Figure 2, a trained classifier can successfully classify single text keypoints and non-text keypoints with an acceptable low misclassification rate. It can effectively filter keypoints on random background clutters (such as grasses and leaves), which are big challenges of text detection algorithms [29].

Thirdly, as shown in Figure 2, if we define the local region of a text keypoint as a circle whose radius is the scale of the keypoint, we can often find other text keypoints located in the region. When iteratively grouping the keypoints, a large region can be achieved. Keypoints in these regions tend to belong to the same group (text or non-text). We propose a novel region growing algorithm to utilize this property. The algorithm is easy to implement and can integrate with the single SIFT keypoint classifier to improve the performance.

Table 1: The notations and descriptions of the variables

Notations	Descriptions
$loc(p)$	The location of a keypoint p.
$s(p)$	The scale of a keypoint p.
$ori(p)$	The orientation of a keypoint p.
$R_l(p)$	The local region of a keypoint p.
$N(p)$	The neighborhood of a keypoint p.
$R_c(k)$	The region candidate k.
$Range(k)$	The range of the region candidate k.
F	The free keypoint set.
D_f	The initial free keypoint set.
$l(p)$	The label of a keypoints p.
$label(k)$	The label of a region candidate k.
$R_t(k^{'})$	The text region candidate $k^{'}$.

4. THE TEXT DETECTION ALGORITHM

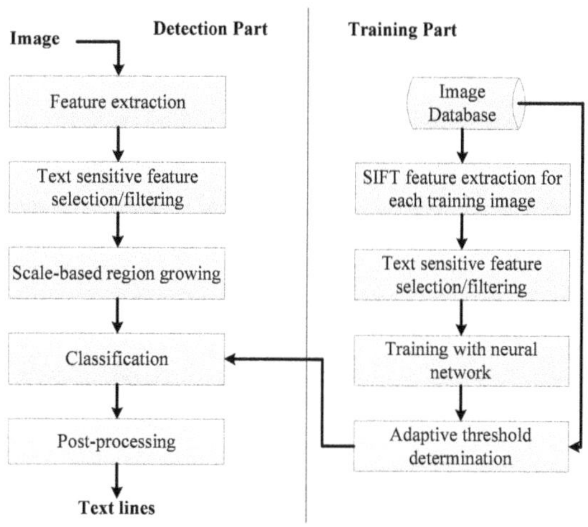

Figure 3: The flowchart of the text detection algorithm

The flowchart of our framework is shown on Figure 3. In Section 4.1, we discuss how to initially filter noisy SIFT features. In Section 4.2, a classifier is trained to label possible text keypoints. After that, in Section 4.3, a region-growing scheme is used to encapsulate those nearby sub-regions of interest and classify the regions according to their labels. Finally, in Section 4.4, a post-processing scheme is applied to determine bounding boxes for scene text in images. The notations and descriptions of the variables for our algorithm are summarized in Table 1.

4.1 Text Sensitive Feature Selection/Filtering

A large proportion of the keypoints actually serve as noise in the text detection process. By extensive experimental study of the statistic properties of keypoints in a local region, it is observed that there are two types of noisy SIFT features. The first type of noisy features is usually detected along straight edges with low entropy of their orientation distribution, while the second type exhibits very large or small scale. Those noises can be identified and removed by a fast filtering algorithm.

Figure 2: Illustration for the motivation of our algorithm. The images in the first row show all the SIFT keypoints after applying text sensitive feature section as described in Section 4 (Yellow rectangles represent some regions of interest (ROI)). The keypoint is represented as an arrow that starts with its location and points to its orientation with the length equal to its scale. We will adopt this representation format of keypoints in all the figures. A circle whose radius is equal to the scale of a keypoint is also drawn. The green and the red circles represent the keypoints that are classified as text keypoints and non-text keypoints respectively. The third row shows the ROI without the arrows and circles. The fourth row shows the ROI (zoom in). Note that text keypoints are often clustered together. If we carefully define a local region, the few misclassifications can be rectified by the voting of all the keypoints in that region. (Best viewed in color)

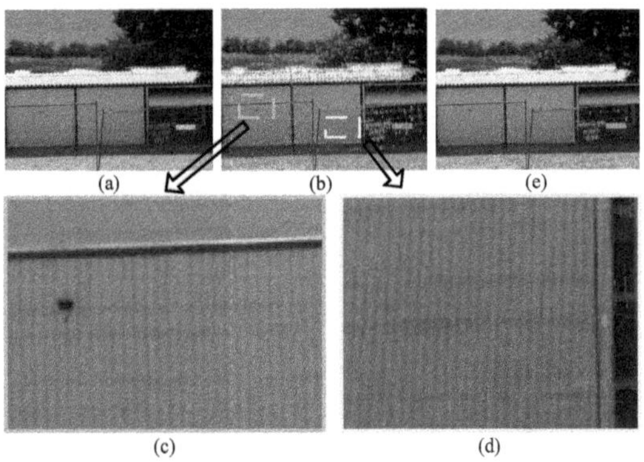

Figure 4: (a) The original sample image with size 1280×960. (b) The initial 5786 SIFT features. (c) The non-text paralleling keypoints along the long straight object (first type of noisy keypoints). (d) Useless keypoints with overly large scale (second type of noisy keypoints). (e) After applying the selection algorithm, 2202 keypoints remain. (Best viewed in color)

As shown in the green square of Figure 4(c), some non-text keypoints possess very distinctive property from text keypoints. They and their neighborhood have same or opposite directions to each other, thus possess low entropy of their orientation distribution. Such kind of SIFT keypoints is often observed along the long straight object. In contrast, high entropy often occurs for the orientation distribution of the neighborhood of a text keypoint. Experiment shows that, for text keypoints extracted from the three databases (described in Section 5.1), the entropy of the orientation distribution of their neighborhood is 0.9007 on average. For non-text keypoints, the entropy is 0.6489 on average, which is much lower than that of the text keypoints. Based on this observation, we filter the first kind of noisy keypoints using the following steps.

We denote the location of a keypoint p as $loc(p)$ and its scale as $s(p)$.We then define the local region $R_l(p)$ for a keypoint p as a circular region whose center is at $loc(p)$ and radius equals to $s(p)$.

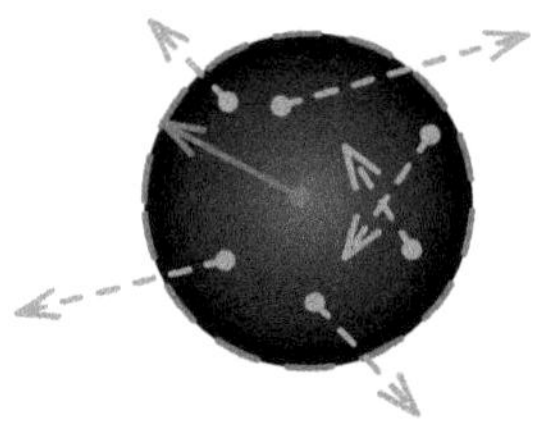

Figure 5: The sketch map for the local region of a keypoint. The solid line arrow represents a keypoint p. The dashed line arrows represent its neighborhood.

Figure 5 illustrates the local region of a keypoint. We also define the neighborhood keypoints of a keypoint p as all the keypoints locate in $loc(p)$, denoted as $N(p)$. For each keypoint p, we calculate the orientation entropy of all the keypoints in $N(p)$. If the entropy is larger than a threshold τ_1, the keypoint p will be pruned as the first kind of noisy keypoints.

It is intractable to calculate the entropy of the orientation distribution if we treat $ori(p)$ as a continuous random variable. Therefore, we quantize $ori(p)$ into m levels and treat $ori(p)$ as a discrete variable. In practice, a good performance can be achieved if m equals to 8 or larger. The threshold τ_1 could be learned easily in the training dataset by using OTSU algorithm [23]. This algorithm can automatically choose a threshold that maximizes the between-class variance. We will adopt the same algorithm to automatically determine the thresholds in this paper.

As shown in Figure 4(d), the keypoints in the yellow square are too large to be useful for the scene text detection. This kind of keypoints often represent the interaction between foreground and background objects. Since background changes in different images, these keypoints are not a trustworthy clue. So, we define the second type of noisy keypoints based on the proportion of the neighboring keypoints within a given scale interval. For each keypoint p, we calculate the number of keypoints in $N(p)$ whose scales are within the interval: $[r_{min} \cdot s(p) \;\; r_{max} \cdot s(p)]$. We denote the number as n_1. We also calculate the total number of keypoints in

$N(p)$, denoted as n_2. If $\frac{n_1}{n_2} < \tau_2$, the keypoint p will be pruned as the second type of noisy keypoints.

By testing and learning from training samples, the optimal numerical values of the variables are empirically selected as: $r_{min} = 0.67$, $r_{max} = 1.5$.

The experimental results show that about 70% of the SIFT keypoints on average can be pruned. Most of them are the noisy keypoints on non-text object. Some of the keypoints on the text regions are also eliminated. However, these keypoints are either the ones with overly large scale or the small scale ones among the long straight strokes of some characters. Both kinds of keypoints will disrupt the classifying process and are regarded as noise. Figure 4(e) shows the result of the noise filtering process.

4.2 Labeling of Single Feature

After coarsely filtering the two kinds of noisy keypoints, some non-text keypoints still remain. One method is to use the 128-D descriptor vector to discriminate such keypoints. We train a neural network to classify the single SIFT keypoint. The training process is described as follows.

The text keypoints and the non-text keypoints in the training database are treated as positive or negative training samples respectively. These keypoints are divided into 67% training samples and 33% testing samples.

A neural network with 128 dimensions input layers and 40 dimensions hidden layers are trained on the training dataset. The number of hidden layers is chosen to obtain the best training accuracy while avoiding huge computational cost. The trained neural network will label a testing keypoint as 1 (predicted as text keypoint) or -1 (predicted as non-text keypoint). We denote the label of a keypoints p as $l(p)$. Note that other machine learning algorithms, such as SVM, can also be applied.

4.3 Scale-based Region Growing

Due to the huge intra-class variations of characters, especially for text in multiple languages, it is difficult to distinguish each keypoint as text and non-text precisely because of potential noise in the background that is similar to text. Therefore, we propose a novel region growing algorithm to explore the context within the local region of a keypoint. After applying this algorithm, keypoints are grouped together to form several region candidates. The region candidates can be classified according to the labels of keypoints in the region.

4.3.1 Region Growing

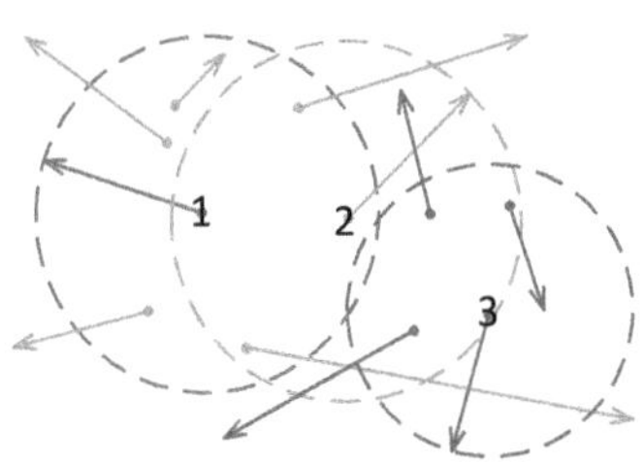

Figure 6: Region growing process. We start with keypoint 1 (the blue keypoint) as the seed point. Then, the keypoints in the local region of keypoint 1 (all the green keypoints) are included into the region. For each green keypoint (e.g., keypoint 2), all the keypoints within its local region are included (all the brown keypoints). We repeat such procedure for each newly included keypoint until no more new keypoints can be involved. (Best viewed in color)

Algorithm 1 Pseudo-code of the SIFT based region growing

Initialization:
  $k \leftarrow 0$; $F \leftarrow D_f$;
Iteration:
  while $F \neq \varnothing$ **do**
    $k \leftarrow k + 1$; $R_c(k) \leftarrow \varnothing$;
    $seed \leftarrow SelectSeed(F)$;
    $F \leftarrow F - seed$;
    AddKeypointToRegion($seed$,$R_c(k)$);
    while $\exists p \ : \ p \in F \wedge p \in Range(k)$ **do**
      AddKeypointToRegion(p,$R_c(k)$);
      $F \leftarrow F - p$;
    end while
  end while

It is easily observed that in a text region the keypoints are often densely clustered as shown in Figure 2. Inspired by the idea of region growing in image segmentation, an efficient scale-based region growing algorithm is developed to determine regions with such characteristics.

The proposed region growing process begins with randomly chosen keypoints as the seeds. We define the free keypoint set F as all the keypoints that have not been assigned to any region candidate. Initially, F is equal to the set of keypoints after the text sensitive filtering (denoted as D_f). The initial region candidates k (denoted as $R_c(k)$) only include the seed keypoints. We define the range of $R_c(k)$, denoted by $Range(k)$, as the sum of the local region of all the keypoints belong to that region candidate. The regions then gradually grow larger by including all the keypoints in F that fall in the range of the initial regions. This step is repeated until all the regions are stable. Finally, region candidates initialized by seeds of text keypoint will grow neatly to cover text regions while non-text seeds will grow to cover non-text regions. In other words, very few misconnections between non-text regions and text regions exist in this process as the experiment shows in Section 5.4. With the candidate regions, high accuracy can be achieved by rectify the incorrect classifications with correct ones in the same region. Some examples are shown in Figure 7.

The pseudo-code for the scale-based region growing process is shown in algorithm 1. The time complexity of this algorithm is $O(n)$ using the disjoint-set data structure, where n is the number of keypoints left after the text sensitive selection. The keypoint growing sequence as well as the initialization of the seeds has little influence on the final results.

4.3.2 Classification of the Region Candidates

After the above process, region candidates are obtained. Some of the region candidates are on the background, such as the leaves of plants. The next step is to classify them into text region candidates $R_t(k^{'})$ and non-text ones. We use the label of the region $label(k)$ calculated below to classify the region candidates.

$$label(k) = \frac{1}{N}\sum_{k=1}^{N} l(p), p \in R_c(k) \tag{1}$$

$$R_t = \bigcup_{k} \{R_c(k) | label(k) > \tau_3\} \tag{2}$$

N is the number of keypoints in $R_c(k)$. τ_3 is learned from the training dataset by OTSU algorithm. The region candidates whose labels are larger than τ_3 will be treated as text region candidates. As shown in our experiments (Section 5.4), the major part of most

(a) (b) (c) (d) (e)

Figure 7: Some examples of scale-based region growing and classification. The first row shows the results of the region growing. Note that the major part of the regions are either on texts or other objects. The second row shows the results of the classification (yellow rectangles represent some regions of interest (ROI)). The third row shows the ROI (zoom in). The fourth row shows the final results after applying post-possessing.

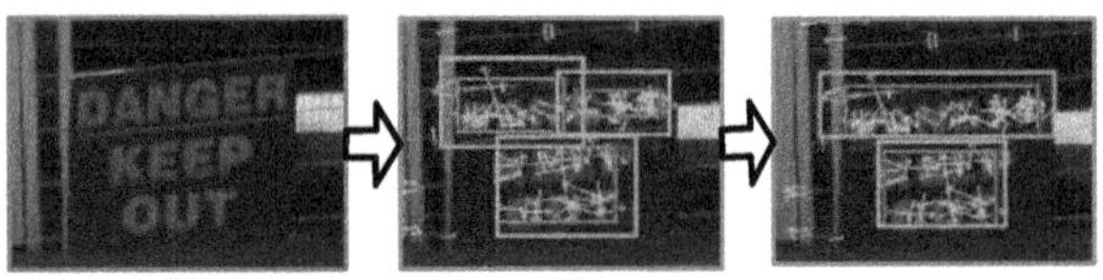

(a) (b) (c)

Figure 8: (a) Original image region. (b) The outer green rectangle indicates the impact rectangle of a text region candidate which will be used in the two-step text blocks formation. (c) The detected text blocks. (Best viewed in color)

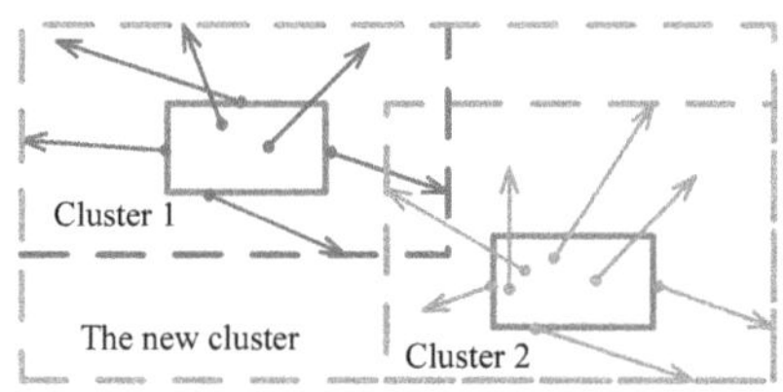

Figure 9: Merge region candidates with overlapped impact rectangles. Impact rectangle is the minimum rectangle that covers all the arrows of SIFT keypoints in the region candidate. (Best viewed in color)

grown regions are either within or outside the text regions. Therefore, the misclassification of a single keypoint by the neural network will be rectified by the voting of other keypoints in the same region candidate.

4.4 Post-processing

After obtaining text region candidates, the next process is to link them to form text blocks. The blocks which contain several text lines will be separated and adjusted to yield the final results.

4.4.1 Composition of Text Blocks

We form the bounding boxes embracing scene text by a two-step algorithm. Some scattered noisy cluster will also be eliminated by this step.

In step one, we define the impact rectangle of a region candidate as the minimum rectangle that covers all the arrows of SIFT keypoints as shown in Figure 8. The arrow of a SIFT keypoint starts with the location of the keypoints and points to its orientation with the length equal to its scale. Regions that have overlapped impact rectangles will be merged to form new text region candidates.

In step two, we group text region candidates to form the text block based on the following criteria:

- The grouped text region candidates appear in a linear form.
- The Possible Extending Distance (PDE) of a text region candidate is set as the width of the region.
- The distance for the centers of grouped neighboring region candidates must not exceed their minimum PDE.
- The grouping regions must have similar color histogram for their impact rectangles.

We use a scheme [14] which is originally developed for color quantization. This scheme extracts a 44-D color feature in HSV color space. It is adopted due to its simple procedure and good performance. We normalize the 44-D feature by their second order norm. The similarity of the color features for two cluster candidates are measured by their inner product.

In addition, we prune the scattered noisy keypoints by this step. A region candidate will be removed if it is too small (The area of the cluster is less than 100 pixels) and cannot be merged with other region candidates. Since small and isolated regions rarely appear in image as text, this step removes scatter noises effectively.

4.4.2 Division of the Text Blocks

As shown in Figure 8(c), for many natural scenes, several text lines are geometrically close to each other and the algorithm might group them as a single text block. Some background pixel lines are

Algorithm 2 Pseudo-code of text block division

Initialization:
  T=GetTextblock();
Process:
  $axis$=HoughTransform(T); S=Project(T, $axis$); v=Var(S);
  if $v < \tau_v$ **then**
    $T_1 = T$
  else
    τ_s=OTSU(S);
    $[B_1, B_2]$=BandDivision(S,T,τ_s);
    $[B_f, B_b]$=JudgeForeground(B_1,B_2);
    T_1=Getnoise(B_f,B_b);
  end if

also included in the text block. For example, the lower text block in Figure 8(c) contains two text lines and some background pixels. All these factors decrease the precision of the OCR algorithm or other text information applications. To solve this problem, we propose a fast text block division algorithm. The pseudo-code is shown in algorithm 2.

The vertical axis is determined by Hough transform for each text block. Grey level pixels are projected on the vertical axis to generate projection array S. To avoid the situation that the text block is actually a single text line, we use a threshold τ_v of the variance of S to determine whether a text block should be divided. As illustrated in Figure 10, the BandDivision() function separates the text block into two groups according to the adaptive threshold τ_s. Then we calculate the text SIFT keypoints in each group. The group with more text SIFT keypoints will be marked as the foreground group. In addition, the bands with very small height (fewer than 3 pixels) are also marked as foreground. We prune the background bands to form the initial bounding boxes.

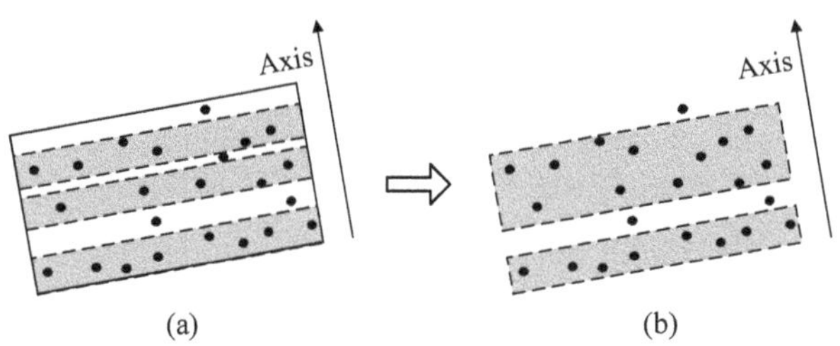

Figure 10: The sketch map of text block division. The points represent text SIFT keypoints in the text block. (a) Two groups that is represented by colored and blank bands respectively. (b) The result of text block division. The bands with very small height are marked as foreground.

4.4.3 *Adjustment of the Initial Bounding Boxes*

As shown in Figure 11, we need two steps to achieve the final result. Firstly, we adjust the size of the bounding boxes to the minimum rectangle that contains all the text keypoints in the initial bounding boxes. Secondly, we need to merge overly divided text blocks whose endpoints share the same horizontal or vertical coordinate. The final result is shown in Figure 11(c).

5. EXPERIMENTS

5.1 Experiment Databases

To compare with the state-of-the-art text detection algorithms, we evaluate our algorithm on two publicly available datasets and our new benchmark dataset of mixture language, such as English, Latin, Roman numerals and hieroglyphs. The description of these three datasets is presented below. Some sample images are shown in Figure 12.

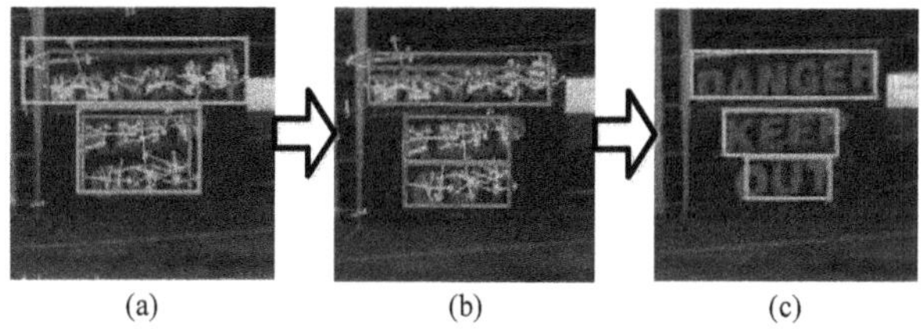

Figure 11: (a) Text blocks that contain more than one text line. (b) The result of the dividing algorithm. Note that unnecessary dividing occurs and the size of the text line square is not correct. (c) The result of the adjustment. (Best viewed in color)

ICDAR Database (ICDAR) This dataset [1] has been used in ICDAR 2003 and ICDAR 2005, which are the most popular text detection competitions. It contains 258 images for training and 251 images for testing. The images cover various text conditions, such as blur, curving, strong highlights, transparence, different viewing angles, non-planar, and so on. Text in the database is relatively large compared to the size of the image. Many images are taken from book covers, road signs, and trademarks with simple background and a few disruptive objects. Word separation is needed in this dataset.

SWT Dataset (SWT) This database [2] contains 307 color images with sizes ranging from 1024×368 to 1024×768. The scene in this database is more complex and the texts are smaller and more intensive compared to the database of ICDAR. Various plants and undistinguishable repeating patterns, such as windows and fences, are common in images of the dataset. Therefore this database is much more difficult and challenging than ICDAR.

Multilingual Database (MSRG) The two databases above contain text only in Latin and English. However, many characters in diversified languages have different properties from Latin and English character. For example, hieroglyphs possess com-

Figure 12: Examples of sample images and the detected text regions of our algorithm on the three databases. The images in the first, second, and third row are from the ICDAR, the SWT, and the MSRG database respectively.

plex structures and have dramatic variance of stroke width of some fonts. We construct the MSRG dataset, which contains a mixture of hieroglyphs, Latin, English and Roman numerals text in natural scene images. It includes 278 images of streetscapes, road signs, horizontal scrolls of painting or calligraphy, and so on, with various image conditions. The resolution of the images ranges from 922×692 to 1296×968. It is also more challenging than ICDAR database considering its complex background.

5.2 Evaluation Metric

To compare our work with the state-of-the-art algorithms, we choose the same evaluation metric of a benchmark reading competition, ICDAR 2003 [18]. In this system, the match m_p between two rectangles is defined as the area of intersection divided by the area of the minimum bounding box containing both rectangles. Therefore, m_p has the value one for identical rectangles and zero for rectangles that have no intersection. For each rectangle in the set of estimates (E), the closest match is found in the ground-truth set of targets (T), and vice versa. Hence, the best match $m(r, R)$ for a rectangle r in a set of Rectangle R is defined as:

$$m(r, R) = max\{m_p(r; r_0) | r_0 \in R\} \tag{3}$$

Then precision, recall and f measure are defined as:

$$precision = \frac{\sum_{r_e \in E} m(r_e, T)}{|E|} \tag{4}$$

$$recall = \frac{\sum_{r_t \in T} m(r_t, E)}{|T|} \tag{5}$$

$$f = \frac{2 \cdot precision \cdot recall}{precision + recall} \tag{6}$$

5.3 Training of Neural Network

5.3.1 *Training and Testing Samples*

Feature selection and noise filtering described in Section 4.1 are performed both on the training and testing samples. We label each keypoint as 1 (for possible text keypoints) and -1 (for possible non-text keypoints) depending on whether it is within the bounding box of the ground truth. Of the labeled keypoints, 67% are randomly sampled for training while the remaining samples are for testing. The accuracy is shown in Table 2.

Table 2: Accuracy for the three databases

	Num. of SIFTs	Non-text	Text	Accuracy
ICDAR	135,235	62.60%	37.40%	81.00%
SWT	193,198	82.70%	17.30%	87.90%
MSRG	138,912	80.20%	19.80%	86.46%

5.3.2 *Hidden Layer Number*

In order to obtain the optimal training accuracy, we test the hidden layer number n of the neural network. The results are shown in Figure 13 and Table 3, respectively. It can be observed that the training accuracy becomes stable when n increases to 40 and beyond, while the time cost keeps increasing. In our experiment, we choose 40 to be the number of hidden layers.

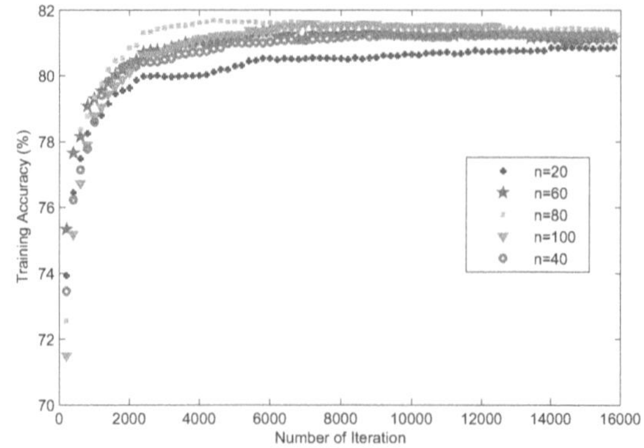

Figure 13: The performance of different hidden layer number

Table 3: Comparison of time per iteration

Hidden layer number	20	40	60	80	100
Time per iteration (seconds)	8	10.3	12.9	20.5	33

5.3.3 *Effectiveness of the Feature Selection*

In order to show the efficiency and necessity of our feature selection step, we train a neural network whose training samples do not undergo this step on SWT database. For this database, there are 1,481,816 initial SIFT keypoints in total. 90.8% of them are non-text keypoints. After applying the two-step pre-processing, 694,556 SIFT keypoints are kept while 88.2% of them are removed as non-text keypoints. We then carry out four tests which are described in Table 4. The results are shown in Table 5.

Here, t_p represents the number of true positives, t_n represents the true negative, f_p represents the false positive, and f_n represents the false negative. $precision' = \frac{t_p}{t_p+f_p}$. $recall' = \frac{t_p}{t_p+f_n}$. The standard f measure follows the same rule as Equation 6.

As shown in the four cases, the standard f measure reaches the highest when training samples and test samples both undergone the text sensitive filtering step. Therefore, the filtering step is effective to enhance the capability of neural network.

5.4 Statistics of Region Growing

To justify the effectiveness of our scale-based region growing algorithm, we count the Text Region Overlapping Ratio (TROR)

Table 4: Illustration of The Four Tests

	Training samples filtering	Testing samples filtering
T1	Yes	Yes
T2	Yes	No
T3	No	Yes
T4	No	No

Table 5: Performance comparison of the four tests

	T1	T2	T3	T4
Num. of SIFTs	694,556	1,481,816	694,556	1,481,816
t_p	5.40%	3.40%	7.70%	5.20%
f_p	2.60%	2.10%	12.40%	9.60%
t_n	85.60%	88.80%	75.80%	81.20%
f_n	6.30%	5.80%	4.10%	4.00%
$precision'$	67.50%	61.80%	38.30%	35.10%
$recall'$	46.20%	37.00%	65.30%	56.50%
f measure	0.548	0.463	0.483	0.433

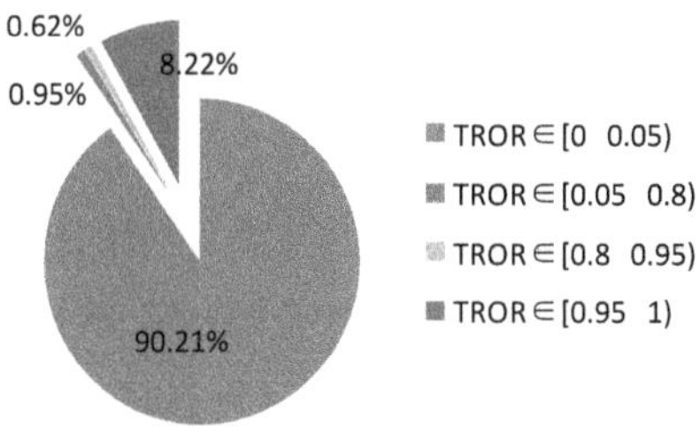

Figure 14: The pie chart of the TROR for all the grown regions generated from the three databases. Different colors represent grown regions with different value intervals of TROR. (Best viewed in color)

for every grown regions on the three databases mentioned above. The TROR for a grown region $R_c(k)$ is defined as the overlapped area of $R_c(k)$ with the ground truth of the text region divided by the total area of $R_c(k)$. Ideally, the region growing algorithm should only generate regions with the TROR equal to 0 or 1 (there is no misconnection between text region and non-text region).

The results are shown in Figure 14. 99.05% grown regions are the suitable regions we need. Among them, 90.22% regions have TROR less than 0.05 (they are grown on the non-text part of the testing images) and 8.22% ones have TROR larger than 0.95 (they are grown on the text part). Only 0.95% regions have TROR between 0.05 and 0.80. They are mostly regions grown on the interval between two nearby text line and can be handled by the post-processing steps.

Based on this experiment, the major part (> 95% area) of most grown regions are either within or outside the ground truth bounding boxes. This property is critical to enhance the performance of the text classifier using Equation 2.

5.5 Performance Comparison

5.5.1 Comparison on ICDAR Database

Though the algorithm in general does not include word separation part, to meet the demand of this database, we divide bounding boxes into isolated words using a simple algorithm similar to the division of text blocks. We adaptively use canny edge detection and the direct grey level projection depending on whether the background is simple or not (The background is treated as simple if its density of interest points is lower than a threshold). The results on this database from published paper are shown in Table 6. The lower half shows the algorithms proposed in ICDAR2003 and ICDAR2005. Becker [17] achieves the best performance in standard f measure of 0.62, but with a relatively large time cost for 14.4 seconds per image. The upper half shows the algorithms proposed after the competitions. Our algorithm gets the better recall rate than Epshtein [9] and Chen [5]. Because of our relatively simple word separation algorithm and the special evaluation metric (A bounding box containing two words can only achieve a precision and recall of 50%), our standard f measure is not very high. This problem can be solved by the text recognition step since the text lines can be separated into words more precisely in this step.

Our algorithm takes 1.65 seconds per image while Epshtein's algorithm takes 0.94 seconds per image [9]. After extracting the SIFT keypoints, our algorithm needs only 0.15 seconds on average. So the complexity of our overall detection algorithm is mainly driven by the SIFT extraction stage. Recently, there are some substitutions of SIFT, such as CARD [3], which is comparable to SIFT in discriminative property, but much more efficient and can be applied to real-time tasks. Such features may substitute SIFT feature used in our approach. Other fast features can also be adopted with a little modification of our algorithm. We will investigate this issue in our future work.

Table 6: Performance comparison in the database of ICDAR

Algorithm	Precision	Recall	f
Epshtein [9]	**0.73**	0.6	**0.66**
Chen [5]	**0.73**	0.6	**0.66**
Fabrizio [10]	0.46	0.39	0.43
Minetto [21]	0.63	0.61	0.61
Our algorithm	0.66	0.62	0.64
Chen [17]	0.6	0.6	0.6
Becker [17]	0.62	**0.67**	0.62

5.5.2 Comparison on SWT Database

As described in Section 5.1, the database is much more challenging than ICDAR. It requires to mark the whole text line without word separation. The results are shown in Table 7. Our algorithm outperforms other the state of the art algorithms on this database.

Table 7: Performance comparison in the database of SWT

Algorithm	Precision	Recall	f
Epshtein [9]	0.54	**0.42**	0.47
Chen [5]	0.45	0.39	0.42
Our algorithm	**0.58**	0.41	**0.48**

5.5.3 Comparison on MSRG Database

The above two subsections show the effectiveness of our algorithm in Latin, English and Roman numerals. These kinds of texts share some common properties, such as low variance of stroke width and a few letter categories. However, some kinds of language, such as hieroglyph characters, can probably exhibit large stroke width variances, complex structures and thousands of characters. To demonstrate the robustness of our algorithm, we test it on our multilingual database which contains texts of Latin, English, Roman numeral and hieroglyphs. Because there are no published results in this new dataset, we implement some of the state-of-the-art algorithms. As shown in Table 8, our algorithm achieves the best performance on this database.

All of the three databases contain mainly vertical and horizontal text, or tiled text within a certain degree. Our algorithm has the potential to handle seriously angled texts because both the SIFT features and the scale-based region growing algorithm are invariant to rotations. We will explore it in our future work.

Table 8: Performance comparison in the database of MSRG

Algorithm	Precision	Recall	f
Epshtein [9]	0.41	0.39	0.4
Chen [5]	0.4	0.37	0.38
Our algorithm	**0.54**	**0.55**	**0.54**

5.5.4 Training in Different Datasets

To further evaluate the robustness of our algorithm, we perform the cross-database experiment. We test the performance of our algorithm by the neural network trained on other datasets. When trained on ICDAR, the f measure drops 0.11 and 0.06 on SWT and

MSRG respectively. When trained on SWT, the f measure drops 0.04 and 0.04 on ICDAR and MSRG respectively. When trained on MSRG, the f measure drops 0.04 and 0.06 on ICDAR and SWT respectively.

The background of ICDAR is different from that of SWT and MSRG, so the performance drops most when trained on this dataset and tested on other ones. If the training set is MSRG or SWT, the performance drops at most by 6% when tested on other datasets. We consistently adopt the same parameter learned from experimental results. The result indicates that there are some common properties of the text keypoint in different databases, or even in different languages. These properties are well explored by our algorithm.

6. CONCLUSIONS

We present a novel approach for multilingual text detection from scene image in the wild. In this algorithm, we explore three types of unique properties of SIFT feature, including the often ignored statistical properties in a local region. Based on the properties, text regions in images are identified by the scale-based region growing algorithm. Without character recognition step as used in some previous work, our algorithm works well in Latin, English, Roman numeral and hieroglyph in scene images. The experimental results on three databases demonstrate the effectiveness and robustness of the proposed approach to detect various kinds of text in complex background.

The most time-consuming part of our algorithm is SIFT extraction. To address this issue, we will resort to other features (e.g., CARD [3]), faster extraction algorithms (e.g., a SIFT extractor with paralleling technology [31]), or fast approximated SIFT extractor [11] in our future work.

There are several possible extensions of this work. The discovered scene text information can be efficiently combined with the extracted SIFT features to provide more reliable context clue for visual search. In addition, SIFT features on text can be used as a valuable clue to improve the performance of OCR.

7. ACKNOWLEDGMENT

This work was supported in part to Prof. Houqiang Li by NSFC 61272316, in part to Dr. Qi Tian by ARO grant W911NF-12-1-0057, NSF IIS 1052851, Faculty Research Awards by Google, FXPAL, and NEC Laboratories of America, and 2012 UTSA START-R Research Award respectively, and in part by NSFC 61128007.

8. REFERENCES

[1] http://algoval.essex.ac.uk/icdar/.

[2] http://research.microsoft.com/enus/um/people/eyalofek/text_detection_database.zip.

[3] M. Ambai and Y. Yoshida. Card: Compact and real-time descriptors. In *Proc. ICCV*, pages 97–104, 2011.

[4] M. Block, M. R. Ortegón, A. Seibert, J. Kretzschmar, and R. Rojas. *SITT: A Simple Robust Scaleinvariant Text Feature Detector for Document Mosaicing*. Freie Univ., Fachbereich Mathematik und Informatik, 2007.

[5] H. Chen, S. S. Tsai, G. Schroth, D. M. Chen, R. Grzeszczuk, and B. Girod. Robust text detection in natural images with edge-enhanced maximally stable extremal regions. In *Proc. ICIP*, pages 2609–2612, 2011.

[6] X. Chen and A. L. Yuille. Detecting and reading text in natural scenes. In *Proc. CVPR*, volume 2, pages II–366, 2004.

[7] X. Chen and A. L. Yuille. A time-efficient cascade for real-time object detection: With applications for the visually impaired. In *Proc. CVPR*, pages 28–28, 2005.

[8] T. de Campos, B. R. Babu, and M. Varma. Character recognition in natural images. In *Proc. VISAPP*, 2009.

[9] B. Epshtein, E. Ofek, and Y. Wexler. Detecting text in natural scenes with stroke width transform. In *Proc. CVPR*, pages 2963–2970, 2010.

[10] J. Fabrizio, M. Cord, and B. Marcotegui. Text extraction from street level images. *CMRT*, 3, 2009.

[11] M. Grabner, H. Grabner, and H. Bischof. Fast approximated sift. In *Proc. ACCV*, pages 918–927. 2006.

[12] I. Haritaoglu. Scene text extraction and translation for handheld devices. In *Proc. CVPR*, volume 2, pages II–408, 2001.

[13] K. Jung, K. In Kim, and A. K Jain. Text information extraction in images and video: a survey. *Pattern recognition*, 37(5):977–997, 2004.

[14] M. Li. Texture moment for content-based image retrieval. In *Proc. ICME*, pages 508–511, 2007.

[15] J. Liang, D. Doermann, and H. Li. Camera-based analysis of text and documents: a survey. *IJDAR*, 7(2-3):84–104, 2005.

[16] D. G. Lowe. Distinctive image features from scale-invariant keypoints. *IJCV*, 60(2):91–110, 2004.

[17] S. M. Lucas. Icdar 2005 text locating competition results. In *Proc. ICDAR*, pages 80–84, 2005.

[18] S. M. Lucas, A. Panaretos, L. Sosa, A. Tang, S. Wong, and R. Young. Icdar 2003 robust reading competitions. In *Proc. ICDAR*, volume 2, pages 682–687, 2003.

[19] C. Mancas-Thillou and B. Gosselin. *Natural scene text understanding*. PhD thesis, PhD thesis, Faculté Polytechnique de Mons, Belgium, 2006.

[20] K. Mikolajczyk and C. Schmid. A performance evaluation of local descriptors. *TPAMI*, 27(10):1615–1630, 2005.

[21] R. Minetto, N. Thome, M. Cord, J. Fabrizio, and B. Marcotegui. Snoopertext: A multiresolution system for text detection in complex visual scenes. In *Proc. ICIP*, pages 3861–3864, 2010.

[22] L. Neumann and J. Matas. A method for text localization and recognition in real-world images. In *Proc. ACCV*, pages 770–783. 2010.

[23] N. Otsu. A threshold selection method from gray-level histograms. *Automatica*, 11(285-296):23–27, 1975.

[24] P. Shivakumara, T. Q. Phan, and C. L. Tan. A laplacian approach to multi-oriented text detection in video. *TPAMI*, 33(2):412–419, 2011.

[25] J. Sivic and A. Zisserman. Video google: A text retrieval approach to object matching in videos. In *Proc. CVPR*, pages 1470–1477, 2003.

[26] G. Takacs, V. Chandrasekhar, N. Gelfand, Y. Xiong, W.-C. Chen, T. Bismpigiannis, R. Grzeszczuk, K. Pulli, and B. Girod. Outdoors augmented reality on mobile phone using loxel-based visual feature organization. In *Proc. MIR*, pages 427–434, 2008.

[27] Q. Tian, S. Zhang, W. Zhou, R. Ji, B. Ni, and N. Sebe. Building descriptive and discriminative visual codebook for large-scale image applications. *Multimedia Tools and Applications*, 51(2):441–477, 2011.

[28] W. Wu, X. Chen, and J. Yang. Incremental detection of text on road signs from video with application to a driving assistant system. In *Proc. ACM MM*, pages 852–859, 2004.

[29] C. Yao, X. Bai, W. Liu, Y. Ma, and Z. Tu. Detecting texts of arbitrary orientations in natural images. In *Proc. CVPR*, pages 1083–1090, 2012.

[30] Q. Ye, Q. Huang, W. Gao, and D. Zhao. Fast and robust text detection in images and video frames. *Image and Vision Computing*, 23(6):565–576, 2005.

[31] Q. Zhang, Y. Chen, Y. Zhang, and Y. Xu. Sift implementation and optimization for multi-core systems. In *Proc. IPDPS*, pages 1–8, 2008.

[32] Q. Zheng, K. Chen, Y. Zhou, C. Gu, and H. Guan. Text localization and recognition in complex scenes using local features. In *Proc. ACCV*, pages 121–132. 2011.

[33] Y. Zhong, H. Zhang, and A. K. Jain. Automatic caption localization in compressed video. *TPAMI*, 22(4):385–392, 2000.

[34] W. Zhou, H. Li, Y. Lu, and Q. Tian. Large scale image search with geometric coding. In *Proc. ACM MM*, pages 1349–1352, 2011.

[35] W. Zhou, H. Li, Y. Lu, and Q. Tian. Principal visual word discovery for automatic license plate detection. *TIP*, 21(9):4269–4279, 2012.

[36] W. Zhou, Y. Lu, H. Li, and Q. Tian. Scalar quantization for large scale image search. In *Proc. ACM MM*, pages 169–178. ACM, 2012.

Visual Interestingness in Image Sequences

Helmut Grabner[1,2], Fabian Nater[1,2], Michel Druey[3], Luc Van Gool[1,4]

[1]Computer Vision Lab, ETH Zurich
{grabner, nater, vangool}@vision.ee.ethz.ch

[2]upicto GmbH
{grabner, nater}@upicto.com

[3]Cognitive Psychology Unit, University of Zurich
m.druey@psychologie.uzh.ch

[4]ESAT - PSI / IBBT, K.U. Leuven
luc.vangool@esat.kuleuven.be

ABSTRACT

Interestingness is said to be the power of attracting or holding one's attention (because something is unusual or exciting, etc.).[1] We, as humans, have the great capacity to direct our visual attention and judge the interestingness of a scene. Consider for example the image sequence in the figure on the right. The spider in front of the camera or the snow on the lens are examples of events that deviate from the context since they violate the expectations, and therefore are considered interesting. On the other hand, weather changes or a camera shift, do not raise human attention considerably, even though large regions of the image are influenced. In this work we firstly investigate what humans consider as "interesting" in image sequences. Secondly we propose a computer vision algorithm to automatically spot these interesting events. To this end, we integrate multiple cues inspired by cognitive concepts and discuss why and to what extent the automatic discovery of visual interestingness is possible.

Categories and Subject Descriptors

I.4 [**Image Processing and Computer Vision**]: Scene Analysis

Keywords

computer vision; image understanding; visual interestingness

[1]`http://www.thefreedictionary.com/Interestingness`, 2012/11/08.

MM'13, October 21–25, 2013, Barcelona, Spain.

ACM 978-1-4503-2404-5/13/10
http://dx.doi.org/10.1145/2502081.2502109 ...$15.00.

Figure 1: What makes an specific moment in an image sequence interesting and how can we computationally approach this question?

1. INTRODUCTION

What do we mean if we find something "interesting"? This frequently used expression is referred to in very broad, often highly subjective terms. Let us consider three examples to illustrate the concept. The scene in which the airplanes crash into the twin towers during the terrorist attack at 9/11, 2001 shockingly shows that such highly unexpected events strongly drawn our attention. At the moment when it happened, many of us were fixed to the TV-screens, with a mixture of disbelief, disgust and sympathy for the people in the towers. But up to this day, the images evoke great interest, even after seeing them many times and now knowing exactly what will happen. In contrast, the last minutes of a super-bowl final are extremely interesting and capture the attention of many people. This event gains its attraction from the fact that we don't know how the game will end; but loses much of its relevance to most as soon as the game is over. Finally, human interest is raised from very personal experiences. For example watching one's own child playing soccer is much more interesting for the parents than for outsiders.

These examples illustrate that interestingness highly depends on the context, but also on personal experiences and preferences, which makes it challenging to approach the concept in a principled manner (*cf.*, [23]). Nonetheless, there are scenes that raise widespread interest, whereas others are boring to a majority of people. Humans have a tremendous capacity to assess how interesting a scene or event is and this greatly helps us to navigate through our daily lives. In order to learn more about human visual perception, but also for commercial purposes (*e.g.*, the placement of advertisements), it is of great concern to understand what triggers human attention and interest.

In this work, we restrict ourselves to a particular category of visual input – image sequences recorded by a static video camera – in order to make the problem tractable. In particular, we aim to predict the parts in an image sequence that are considered interesting by many viewers. To this end, we propose to combine several cues to assess interestingness in a novel manner that leads to increased performances when compared to averaged human ratings. Finally, we interpret and discuss the ability of computational techniques to spot these interesting events automatically. The relatively constrained setting allows for the discovery of crucial properties of interestingness and will pave the way for further, more challenging scenarios.

2. RELATED WORK

Psychological Perspective. In the mid-50s, Berlyne was among the first to seriously consider interest as psychologically relevant for human learning. In his seminal work [1] he introduced four collative variables, which affect interest: *novelty*, *uncertainty*, *conflict* and *complexity*. More recent research empirically validates and refines this theory, *e.g.* Chen *et al.* [5] declare novelty, challenge, attentional demand, exploitation intention and instant enjoyment as sources for interestingness (see [23] for a survey and comprehensive discussion). These theories have one limitation however, as they cannot explain why people respond differently. This is due to the fact that they implicitly trace interest to events rather than to interpretations and appraisals of events. Summarizing, these classical theories have been applied successfully in order to answer the questions what and why some things are interesting to almost everybody. As this is the main focus of the paper at hand, we only take into account these theories.

(Visual) Cognitive Perspective. The concept of interestingness has mostly been studied through understanding which visual stimuli can attract human attention [27]. This is often done by recording gaze patterns of humans watching images or videos (*e.g.*, [8, 10]). Despite a number of unsolved issues, there is common agreement that capturing human attention involves two fundamental properties of human information processing (*cf.* [22]): First, stimulus-based or bottom-up processing and secondly, memory-based or top-down processing. The main bottom-up factors that contribute to the (covert as well as overt) spatial allocation of visual attention are saliency of an object and novelty of an event. The seminal work of Treisman and Gelade [26] introduced the feature-integration theory which has been picked up frequently. For instance, Itti and Koch [12] included three stimulus features (orientation, intensity, and color), and received considerable agreement of their model with human gaze measurements. Motion and abrupt onset are the other features sometimes viewed as relevant in bottom-up processing. Despite the evidence pointing to the crucial role of bottom-up cues, it is obvious that they alone are insufficient to guide visual attention. In fact, it has been repeatedly shown that top-down processes can bias or even override bottom-up visual processing, *e.g.* [8, 25]. Top-down processing means that individuals are willfully able to track and search for relevant information, while ignoring irrelevant visual stimuli. This processing is strongly affected by task instruction, individual attentional resources, prior knowledge, and personal motivation or goals.

Summarizing, it has been shown that saliency and novelty clearly trigger visual attention. However, we argue that this is not necessarily equivalent to interestingness. If a person scans an image or a video in order to understand what is happening, this does not mean that she or he really considers the observations as interesting.

Computational Perspective. Different approaches have been proposed for the automatic detection of visual concepts that relate to interestingness. Applications include event detection (*e.g.*, [15]), video summarization (*e.g.*, [18]) or content-based image retrieval (*e.g.*, [6]). For example, Johnson and Hogg [15] refer to statistical *outliers* as "possible incidents of interest" or Stauffer and Grimson [24] claim many of their detections to be of "most interest". Other related terms that are often used include *surprise*, *saliency*, *abnormality* or *novelty*. The related techniques can be categorized as follows.

Abnormality Detection. In many abnormality detection algorithms, a model of normality is trained from frequent observations. Outliers to these models must be novel concepts and are identified as abnormal events. Typically, such approaches work well for fixed cameras, modeling the entire scene (*e.g.*, [31, 2, 13]) or the behavior of objects within this scene (*e.g.*, [15, 24]). In practice however, it is often unclear to what extent such anomalies are also perceived as interesting by human observers.

Attention Modeling. A simple example shows that "novel" and "interesting" are not always identical. In the white snow paradox, a TV-screen presenting a white noise signal is completely unpredictable and always remains novel, but is unattractive to viewers. This was already noticed in the beginnings of cognitive psychology [1, 30] and calls for a direct modeling of visual concepts which attract human attention. For example, Itti and Baldi came up with a theory of Bayesian surprise [11] or Schmidhuber and co-workers [21, 20] define interestingness as allowing for learning new things: "Neither the arbitrary nor the fully predictable is truly surprising or interesting – only data with still unknown but learnable statistical regularities are".

Interestingness as Category. Machine learning methods are successfully used for many vision tasks, such as object detection or recognition (*e.g.* detecting faces). Recent works widen these techniques to more complex and less well-defined tasks, for example *emotions* [17], *human memorability* [9] or *aesthetics* [6]. Furthermore, Weinshall *et al.* [29] introduced a novel concept based on disagreement of specific and general classifiers. In all these approaches, a machine learning method is provided with various, low level or specifically designed features. To this end, labeled training data must be available, which is in practice hard to gather in sufficient quality and quantity. For example, Dhar *et al.* [6]

use per-image "interestingness" scores from the photo sharing site *flickr*[2]. Yet, we have some doubts about the more general usefulness of these scores since they are based on properties including number of clicks and comments or popularity of the photographer, that lack independent human ratings.

3. HUMAN CONSENSUS BASE-LINE

The evaluation of theories and computational techniques always requires a reliable ground truth to compare against. In the case of "interestingness" this is clearly a highly subjective judgment and no truly correct answer can be expected from a single person. Therefore, we rely on the assessment by multiple people and establish a human consensus that serves as base-line for further investigations. The entire sequences as well as the obtained ratings are available on the authors' web-page.

3.1 Dataset

We chose 20 sequences from publicly available webcams, see Tab. 1. These image sequences were recorded over a long period of time, capturing various – possibly interesting – situations. The sequences present typical webcam and surveillance scenes, such as panoramas (*Seq. 1,4,11,17*), highways (*Seq. 5,18*), public squares (*Seq. 3,6,8,15*), urban scenes (*Seq. 10,14,20*), and some particular scenarios (boat rental, *Seq. 2*; stork nest, *Seq. 7*; beach, *Seq. 9*; construction site, *Seq. 12*; the Panama Canal, *Seq. 13*; a port, *Seq. 16*; and the Tower Bridge, *Seq. 19*). Image resolutions range from 352 × 288 (PAL) up to 420 × 315. Images were recorded during several days and usually sampled at one frame per hour. We manually selected representative sub-sequences, *e.g.* excluding very dark night images. Each image sequence consisted of 159 color images, continuously displayed at approximately 1 fps.

3.2 User Study

Setup. 26 male and 20 female test persons, aged between 18 and 47 and having normal or corrected vision participated in the test. They were instructed to watch the image sequences, press a button if they considered something interesting, and they had to press the button again to release the interestingness tag. No further instruction was given and hence the participants were free to judge what they considered as interesting. Furthermore, they were asked to rate the overall interestingness of every sequence at the end of the experiment, once they had seen all image sequences. In order to recall the sequences, the beginning of each sequence was replayed briefly, and ratings were asked in 7 levels (1 = very boring, 7 = very interesting). Test persons completed the task unwatched and they could stop when they reached their personal time budget. Sequences and their ordering were chosen randomly. Each participant evaluated between 6 and 10 sequences and all sequences were viewed by at least 20 persons.

Human Consensus. Let $a_t^{(i)}$ be the individual binary interestingness annotations of person i for image I_t for a particular sequence. If the user considers the frame as interesting $a_t^{(i)} = 1$, and 0 otherwise. The human consen-

[2]`http://www.flickr.com/explore/interesting/`, 2012/11/12.

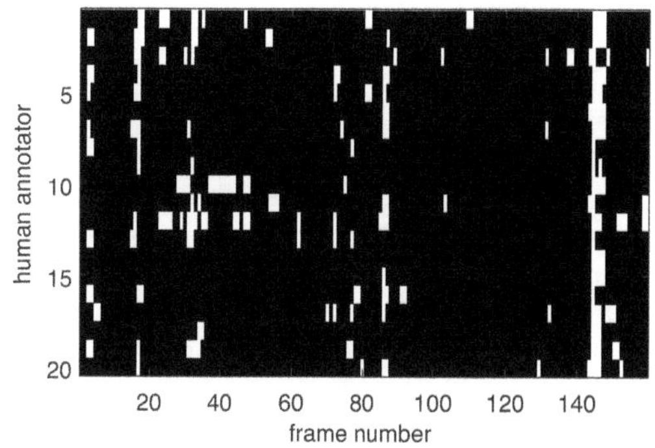

(a) human annotations $a_t^{(i)}$

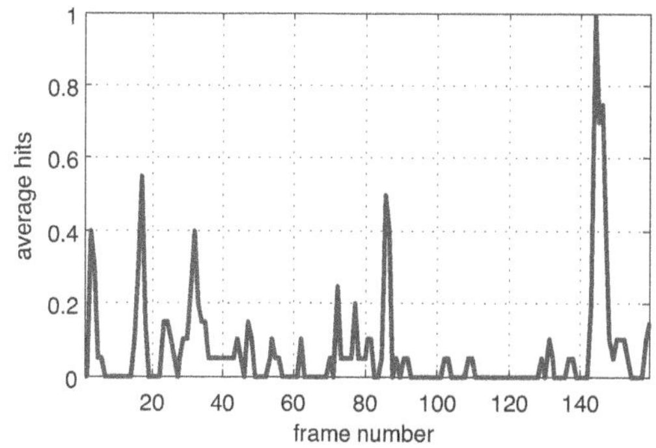

(b) human consensus s_t

(c) # 144 (d) # 17 (e) # 86

(f) # 32 (g) # 3 (h) # 72

(i) uninteresting (score = 0.00)

Figure 2: Example of user annotations (white = interesting) (a) and the obtained human consensus for *Seq. 1* (b). Interesting parts (c)-(h) include abnormal, unexpected events as well as "aesthetic" images. Images consistently considered as uninteresting (i) might have large variations at pixel level (*e.g.*, the sky region) but are semantically "normal".

Seq.	1	2	3	4	5	6	7
typical image							
most interesting image							
s_{max}	1.00	0.75	0.50	0.75	0.45	0.95	0.70
$s(\mu \pm \sigma)$	0.07 ± 0.14	0.14 ± 0.15	0.10 ± 0.11	0.12 ± 0.14	0.06 ± 0.08	0.21 ± 0.25	0.19 ± 0.14
$\#s > 0.50$	4	5	0	3	0	26	7
$\#s < 0.25$	146	123	136	129	152	100	113
α_{st}	0.90	0.82	0.73	0.79	0.74	0.93	0.82
$r(\mu \pm \sigma)$	2.5 ± 1.2	3.6 ± 1.0	2.5 ± 1.1	3.4 ± 1.5	1.9 ± 0.8	4.0 ± 1.3	4.7 ± 1.7
Seq.	8	9	10	11	12	13	14
typical image							
most interesting image						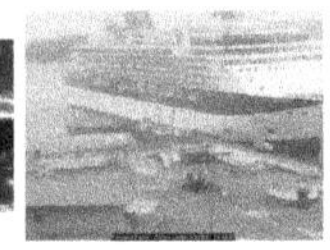	
s_{max}	0.80	0.70	0.95	0.70	0.70	0.80	0.80
$s(\mu \pm \sigma)$	0.05 ± 0.11	0.07 ± 0.13	0.08 ± 0.17	0.13 ± 0.14	0.09 ± 0.13	0.16 ± 0.18	0.11 ± 0.17
$\#s > 0.50$	2	4	8	2	3	7	7
$\#s < 0.25$	152	143	139	125	144	114	135
α_{st}	0.87	0.88	0.92	0.75	0.80	0.85	0.88
$r(\mu \pm \sigma)$	2.7 ± 1.1	2.5 ± 1.1	2.8 ± 1.1	4.0 ± 1.3	2.2 ± 1.2	3.6 ± 1.1	2.8 ± 1.3
Seq.	15	16	17	18	19	20	average
typical image	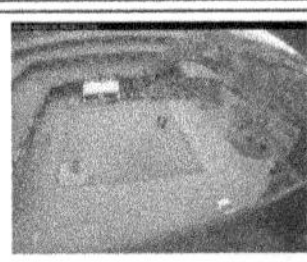						
most interesting image							
s_{max}	0.65	0.80	0.65	0.55	0.70	0.80	0.74
$s(\mu \pm \sigma)$	0.13 ± 0.18	0.13 ± 0.15	0.12 ± 0.14	0.06 ± 0.10	0.11 ± 0.14	0.09 ± 0.13	0.11
$\#s > 0.50$	11	6	5	1	4	3	5
$\#s < 0.25$	126	124	134	147	135	140	133
α_{st}	0.86	0.82	0.78	0.78	0.83	0.82	0.83
$r(\mu \pm \sigma)$	2.9 ± 1.0	3.2 ± 1.4	2.9 ± 1.6	1.9 ± 0.7	3.5 ± 1.6	3.6 ± 1.6	3.0

Table 1: Dataset and statistics of the obtained human consensus base-line. For each sequence are shown: a typical (uninteresting) image, the most interesting image with its corresponding score, mean and variance of the scores, the number of interesting and uninteresting events, and an overall interestingness rating.

sus interestingness score is defined as the per-frame average of the individual annotations for a particular sequence, *i.e.*, $s_t = \frac{1}{N}\sum_i a_t^{(i)}$, were N is the number of participants who annotated this sequence. Similarly, the overall interestingness rating r of a sequence is the average of the individuals' overall ratings. If many individuals consider a frame interesting (*i.e.*, $s_t > 0.5$), we call this an interesting event. Hence, the most interesting events in a sequence can be ranked with respect to their human consensus interestingness score, that is the agreement among individuals.

Example Sequence. A detailed example is given in Fig. 2, showing the raw user annotations (a), the average

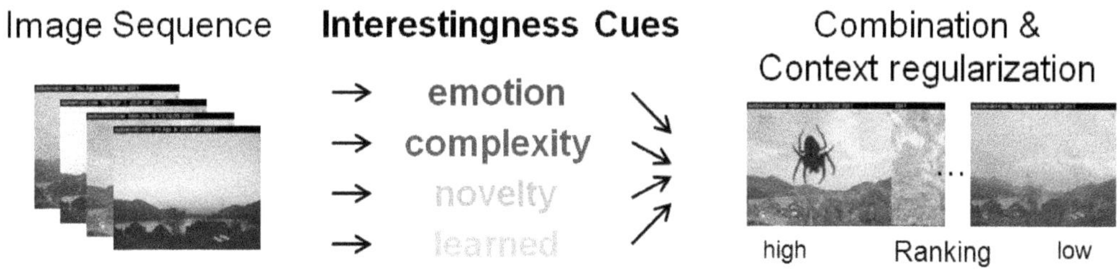

Figure 3: Given an image sequence, our aim is to automatically rank the images according to their interestingness. Psychological research suggests various cues that influence interestingness. In our approach, we use quite simple implementations for some of those cues and aggregate their outputs.

across persons – the established human consensus – (b) and examples of highly interesting (c)-(h) and uninteresting (i) frames. Interesting frames include surprising and unexpected events (the spider or snow on the lens) as well as aesthetic images (sunsets). Note that many other frames also might show large variations (especially in the sky region) but are consistently considered as uninteresting. Furthermore, at the very end of this sequence the camera settings were changed substantially (zoomed in). This change however, was mostly ignored by the viewers (Fig. 2 (i)). Hence, it seems that abstraction and semantic interpretation of what we expect is essential.

Dataset Overview. Tab. 1 summarizes results of the human responses. For each sequence are shown: a typical (uninteresting) image, the most interesting image with its corresponding human consensus interestingness score s_{max}, the number of interesting and uninteresting events, as well as the overall interestingness rating. Some events clearly appear interesting to many viewers, *e.g.* in *Seq. 6* many things are happening in the observed square (market, auto show, sports game, *etc.*). In each sequence however, there are frequent intervals that are consistently labeled as uninteresting.

3.3 Consistency

Per-frame Score. In order to quantify the consistency among the responses of test persons, we use standardized Cronbach's alpha. This widely used measure for the reliability of a psychometric test is defined as $\alpha_{st} = \frac{n\bar{r}}{1+(n-1)\bar{r}}$, where n is the number of persons and $\bar{r}$ the mean correlation between each of them.[3] As can be seen from Tab. 1, the measured consistency is generally high for most sequences (avg. $\bar{\alpha_{st}} = 0.83$, max. $\alpha_{st,max} = 0.93$). The responses of some sequences are less consistent (*e.g., Seq. 11*, $\alpha_{st} = 0.75$). This seems due to the influence of individual preferences such as special cloud formations or sunsets.

Overall Rating. We use Sperman's rank coefficient ρ to assess the consistency across the participants overall ratings of the viewed sequences. This measure reflects how well two variables can be explained by a monotonic relation, therefore we first rank the annotated scenes according to the participants' ratings. Overall we achieved a mean rank coefficient of $\bar{\rho} = 0.30$ across all participants ($\rho_{max} = 0.94$; $\rho_{min} = -0.83$). This rating consistency is relatively weak, compared to the consistent annotations of per-frame interestingness. Remarkably, we spotted a more significant correlation $\bar{\rho}_{\mu_s} = 0.41$ between the average interestingness score μ_s of a sequence with its' ranking. Hence, having reliable interestingness scores per frame would also allow for a rough overall ranking.

Summarizing, the human consensus base-line of per-frame scores provides a solid basis and can be used to (i) build computational models and (ii) evaluate them.

[3]Literature suggests, $\alpha_{st} > 0.7$: acceptable; $\alpha_{st} > 0.8$: good; and $\alpha_{st} > 0.9$: excellent.

4. COMPUTATIONAL MODEL FOR INTERESTINGNESS

In this section we describe our approach for automatically predicting interestingness. More formally, given an image sequence $\mathbf{I} = [I_1, \ldots, I_n]$ we are looking for a ranking R of $\mathbf{I}$ with respect to its interestingness. The overview is sketched in Fig. 3 and consists of mainly two stages: (i) exploring various cues which serve as indicator for interestingness and (ii) combining these individual cues.

4.1 Cues for Interestingness

As reviewed in Sec. 2, psychological theories give us some ideas of what affects human interest. We select three cues, that are emotion, complexity and novelty. However, coming up with robust algorithms for these concepts is very challenging from a computer vision perspective. Due to the success of statistical and machine learning methods, we apply a learning technique as a fourth cue. Given an image, the learned model aims to directly predict its interestingness.

Features. Previous works have successfully used global scene descriptors as features to represent the images in tasks like scene characterization [13, 25], abnormality detection [2] or the rating of image memorability [9]. In the same vein, the features we use are raw pixel values, color histograms, histograms of oriented gradients (HOG), the Gist of the scene, and image self-similarity.

In the sequel we describe our implementations for the four cues. All these methods require specific parameter settings and critically depend on the employed distance measure and feature type. For the ease of clarity we restrict ourselves to report a few successful feature-algorithm combinations and parameter settings.

Each algorithm is supposed to return a score $\hat{s}_i \in \mathbb{R}$ for image I_i with respect to the interestingness, considering the entire image sequence $\mathbf{I}$, *i.e.*, $\hat{s}_i > \hat{s}_j$ iff I_i is considered to be more interesting than I_j. Examples of high ranked images for the different cues are shown in Fig. 4.

Emotion. Emotions can be characterized using the space of *pleasure*, *arousal* and *dominance* (see *e.g.* [16]).

(b) emotion

(d) complexity

(f) novelty

(h) learning

Figure 4: Typical examples of high ranked images for the individual cues obtained by our implementation.

We make use of empirical findings [28] in order to predict an emotion score from raw pixel values. As interesting events excite us (either positively or negatively), we propose to relate it to the arousal. Hence, the interestingness score is calculated as average over all pixels $p \in I_i$ as $\hat{s_i}^{(emo)} = \sum_p -0.31 \text{ brightness}(p) + 0.60 \text{ saturation}(p)$.

Complexity. To capture the complexity of an image, we quantify the visual structure present in the image. As a simple method, we use the the file-size of the image when encoded as PNG-image, *i.e.*, $\hat{s}_i^{(com)} = \text{bytes}(\text{encodePNG}(I_i))$.

Novelty. In the spirit of [31, 2], we perform outlier detection in the image stream. To this end, we use the Local Outlier Factor [3] with a 10-distance neighborhood. The predicted interestingness score $\hat{s}_i^{(nov)} = \text{LOF}_{10}(I_i, \mathbf{I})$ corresponds to the degree of being an outlier. As similarity measure we use sum of absolute differences $(\sum_p ||I_i(p) - I_j(p)||)^{-1}$ of the RGB-pixels values p within the two respective images i, j.

Learning. Finally we aim for directly learning a model of interestingness. Similar to [6, 9, 17] we train a classifier H to predict the interestingness score $\hat{s}_i^{(lea)} = H(I_i)$ for an image I_i. To this end, we extract Gist features and employ a Support Vector Regression (ν-SVR) [4][4] with an RBF kernel. The classifier is trained using the labeled data from the established human consensus baseline from all sequences except the sequence under test.

4.2 Combination

Model learning. The scores obtained from the respective cues are first normalized with respect to their mean and variance. Secondly, they are mapped into the interval $[0, 1]$ using a sigmoid function $\hat{s}_N = \frac{1}{1+exp(-a\hat{s}+b)}$. These normalized scores for emotion, complexity, novelty and learning, can be seen as high-level features. For combining them we train a simple linear model

$$\hat{s} = \mathbf{w}^\mathsf{T}\hat{\mathbf{s}}_N, \text{ with } \hat{\mathbf{s}}_N = [\hat{s}_N^{(emo)}, \hat{s}_N^{(com)}, \hat{s}_N^{(nov)}, \hat{s}_N^{(lea)}]^\mathsf{T} \quad (1)$$

The parameter a and b as well as the weights $\mathbf{w}$ were obtained by least square minimization[5] and cross-validation using the labeled data from the established human consensus baseline.

Regularization. So far, interestingness scores are obtained for each image in the image sequence independently. However, given the fact that we analyze an image sequence we can impose regularization terms which take this additional context into account.

We make use of the following two assumption: (i) visually similar images and (ii) temporally neighboring images should also have a similar interestingness score (*cf.* [14, 19], respectively). Please note that this is not automatically satisfied when using discriminatively trained classifiers, outlier detection methods and classifier combination methods as used in our case.

Graph based model. We cast the problem as transductive semi-supervised learning problem. By using a graph-based

[4]LIBSVM version 3.11, `http://www.csie.ntu.edu.tw/~cjlin/libsvm/`, 2012/02/23

[5]We also trained a ν-SVR [4] on these high-level features, which lead to a similar performance.

approach [32] the individual images are represented as the nodes in the graph and the assumptions are encoded by the graph structure. More formally, let $\hat{\mathbf{s}} = [\hat{s}_1, \ldots, \hat{s}_n]$ be the vector of initial interestingness scores and let $\mathbf{W} = [w_{ij}]$ be the weight matrix encoding the graph structure, where w_{ij} are the weights connecting images i and j and are defined as follows:

(i) similar images (similar appearance). As weights w_{ij} we used the visual similarity of image i and j measured using sum of absolute differences on RGB pixel values, as described above. The weights are normalized by the maximum within the whole image sequence **I**.

(ii) temporal consistency. In order to take the temporal consistency into account we added a constant c to the normalized weights $w_{i,i+1}, i = 1, \ldots, n-1$ of temporal neighboring images. In all our experiments we fixed $c = 0.25$ and obtained a good trade-off of temporal regularization (smoothing) and specificity (*i.e.*, avoiding over-smoothing).

The combined interestingness score $\hat{\mathbf{s}}$ is used as prior knowledge and the deduced labels $\bar{\mathbf{s}} = [\bar{s}_1, \ldots, \bar{s}_n]$ are inferred according to the graph structure as

$$\bar{\mathbf{s}} = (\mathbf{1} - (1-\eta)\mathbf{D}^{-1}\mathbf{W})^{-1}\eta\hat{\mathbf{s}}, \quad (2)$$

where $\mathbf{D}$ is a diagonal matrix with $D_j = \sum_j w_{ij}$ and $\eta \in [0,1]$ the regularization factor.

Ranking. The overall ranking R is determined by sorting the scores $\bar{\mathbf{s}}$ in descending order.

5. EXPERIMENTAL RESULTS

We first define the evaluation metrics and then present and discuss the results.

5.1 Evaluation of an Image Sequence

Top 3 Score (Top3). This metric quantifies how well the top 3 ranked frames of an image sequence analyzed by a computer vision technique capture the human interestingness score. To this end, we define the fraction $Top3 := \frac{\sum_{k \in A^{Top3}} s_k}{\sum_{k \in S^{Top3}} s_k}$, where s_k is the human consensus score of frame k, A^{Top3} the set of the top 3 ranked samples determined by the algorithm, and S^{Top3} the set of top 3 ranked samples of the human consensus, respectively. $Top3 \in [0,1]$, where a higher value corresponds to a better performance of the algorithm.

In the same manner, other scores, *e.g.* *Top10* or *Bottom3*, can be defined. Yet, due to the low number of interesting events, we experienced a good characterization with *Top3*. Furthermore, *bottom* scores as well as global rankings (*e.g.*Spermans ρ) are inappropriate measures as the dataset is highly unbalanced (cf. Tab. 1).

Average Precision (AP). As we are mainly interested in robustly spotting interesting events, we also perform a recall-precision analysis, using the average precision value AP [7]. Interesting events are defined to have a consensus score above 0.5. On the other hand, non-interesting frames are those for which the score is below 0.25 (*cf.* Tab. 1). Images with a score in between are ignored for the evaluation, due to the fact that also humans do not agree well on them.

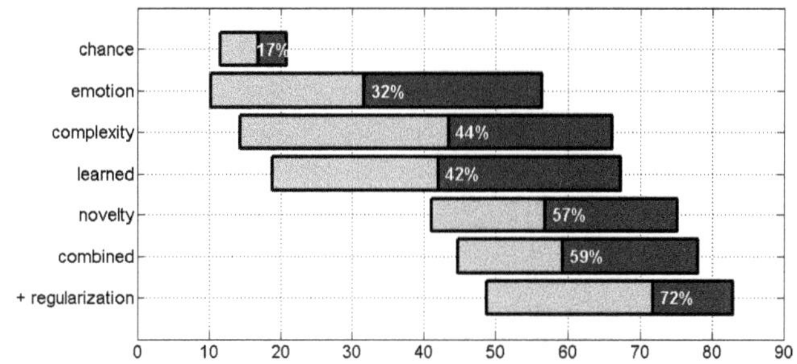

Figure 5: Boxplot of *Top3* performance (median values are printed) for the individual cues used and the proposed combinations with respect to the human consensus baseline. All individual cues are clearly above chance level, headed by novelty. However, not all novel images are necessarily interesting nor are all interesting images novel, thereby calling for a combination of these cues. This combination shows improved performance, especially when applying regularization.

5.2 Results and Discussions

Results per-sequence and overall statistics are presented in Tab. 2 and shown in Fig. 5.

Individual cues. The results for all individual cues are clearly above chance level, proving their usefulness for the task. The most dominant cue, however, is novelty. With respect to novelty detection, using low resolution (32×32 pixels) images already shows a good performance. We tried various other image resolutions, but sizes above 32×32 pixels yield marginal effects, whereas lower resolutions resulted in significantly decreased performance. Similar results were observed when using other features or other outlier detection methods[6]. On the one hand, this observations validates to some extent the assumptions used in many abnormality detection systems. On the other hand, the dominance of novelty might be also due to the current understanding and implementation of outlier detection methods. For the other cues unfortunately no satisfying implementations exists, which might be due to overly simple visual features and/or the limited amount of training data.

Combination. In many cases abnormal events are considered interesting. This is true for some large (unexpected) changes in the image sequence, as for instance the spider in *Seq. 1* or the crowd appearing in *Seq. 8*. On the other hand, abnormality detection can mislead the interestingness output, in particular in cases that are easily interpretable for humans. This occurs for large shadows, different weather conditions, camera failures or slightly shifted/zoomed camera views. Such cases call for the inclusion of other cues. Furhtermore, some very subtle but semantically meaningful changes make an image interesting, as for instance the appearing egg in *Seq. 7* or the crane in *Seq. 10*. In this respect, also the entire scene plays a role, as the two extreme

[6]We also experimented with *DB(p,D)*-Outliers, one-class Support Vector Machine and Meaningful Nearest Neighbors. Gaussian Mixture Models and Principle Component Analysis operating on pixel level do not perform that well, mainly due to the large data variance in the time-lapse image sequences.

cases of a very boring motorway in *Seq. 18* and the highly entertaining stork nest in *Seq. 7* show. Effectively handling such cases calls for a more semantic interpretation to filter out irrelevant information while sharpening the focus on relevant regions or objects. In the extreme case a complete understanding of the entire visual scene with all its objects and interactions might be necessary. However, our results show that the use of simple combination of even basic cues already yield affective results on average, for both *Top3* and *AP* measures (*Top3* med.: 0.72, *AP* med.: 0.36). In particular, integrating visual and temporal consistency turned out to have a significant effect. Some visual examples of success and failure cases are depicted in Fig. 6.

Relation to other works. To show the benefit of our method, we compare it to other related works. First, we have implemented a technique based on [20], where the interestingness score $\hat{s}_t = -\frac{\partial^2}{\partial t^2} l_C([I_1, \ldots, I_t])|_t$ is defined as the negative second derivative of an on-line compression capacity (l_C is the length of the resulting string when compressing the history of all images upon time t with a fixed compressor C). We therefore concatenate images one by one and use the file size of the resulting PNG image as compression measure. This technique exhibits inferior performance (*Top3* med.: 0.36, *AP* med.: 0.10). Our interpretation is that outliers and abnormal events are in many cases perceived as interesting by human observers, but such abnormalities are explicitly excluded here. Second, we also did not achieve good results using the theory of Bayesian surprise [11] (*Top3* med.: 0.17, *AP* med.: 0.07, which is around chance level). It appears that the goal there is a different one, *i.e.* detecting the most surprising regions in high frame-rate videos, whereas our goal is to label interesting frames in the context of (low frame-rate) image sequences.

6. CONCLUSION

We assessed the capacity of computational approaches to capture "interestingness" in image sequences. Therefore, we recorded moments of human interest and aggregated them to a consensus, which is used for training and evaluating our approach. Motivated by psychological findings, we proposed to use four different cues, and showed an effective way to combine them. The image sequences specifies a context in which humans judge events as interesting and therefore outlier detection techniques permit to capture a substantial fraction of interestingness already. While many abnormal events are consistently considered to be interesting, also a large portion of them are not, such as camera failures or different cloud formations. On the other hand, statistically well-explained, normal events might still be interesting, *e.g.* raising of the Tower Bridge. This calls for a combination of abnormality detection and methods relying on semantic image interpretation. We have demonstrated that – while still remaining far from a semantic interpretation – a number of basic cues and their straight forward combination already let us for a long way in mimicking human interest responses.

This said, this work is only a first attempt to quantify visual interestingness. In future work it will be important to add semantic cues and to exploit promising additional cues (*e.g.*examine the relationship between visual interestingness and other measures, such as memorability or image quality), widen the scope to more general settings, and taking the specific preferences of a particular observer into account.

7. ACKNOWLEDGMENTS

This research was supported by the Swiss CTI under project no. 15769.1, "Relevance feedback mechanisms for video surveillance".

8. REFERENCES

[1] D. Berlyne. *Conflict, arousal, and curiosity.* McGraw-Hill, 1960.

[2] M. Breitenstein, H. Grabner, and L. Van Gool. Hunting nessie: Real time abnormality detection from webcams. In *Proc. IEEE WS on Visual Surveillance*, 2009.

[3] M. Breunig, H. Kriegel, R. Ng, and J. Sander. Lof: Identifying density-based local outliers. In *Proc. ACM SIGMOD Int. Conf. on Management of Data*, 2000.

[4] C. Chang and C. Lin. LIBSVM : a library for support vector machines. *ACM Transactions on Intelligent Systems and Technology*, 2(27):1–27, 2011.

[5] A. Chen, P. Darst, and R. Pangrazi. An examination of situational interest and its sources. *British Journal of Educational Psychology*, 71:383–400, 2001.

[6] S. Dhar, V. Ordonez, and T. Berg. High level describable attributes for predicting aesthetics and interestingness. In *Proc. CVPR*, 2011.

[7] M. Everingham, L. Van Gool, C. Williams, J. Winn, and A. Zisserman. The pascal visual object classes (voc) challenge. *IJCV*, 88:303–338, 2010.

[8] J. Henderson. Human gaze control during real-world scene perception. *TRENDS in Cognitive Science*, 7(11):498–504, 2003.

[9] P. Isola, J. Xiao, A. Torralba, and A. Oliva. What makes an image memorable? In *Proc. CVPR*, 2011.

[10] L. Itti and P. Baldi. A principled approach to detecting surprising events in video. In *Proc. CVPR*, 2005.

[11] L. Itti and P. Baldi. Bayesian surprise attracts human attention. *Vision Research*, 49:1295–1306, 2009.

[12] L. Itti and C. Koch. Computational modeling of visual attention. *Nature Reviews Neuroscience*, 2(3):194–203, 2001.

[13] N. Jacobs, N. Roman, and R. Pless. Consistent temporal variations in many outdoor scenes. In *Proc. CVPR*, 2007.

[14] V. Jain and E. Learned-Miller. Online domain adaption of a pre-trained cascade of classifiers. In *Proc. CVPR*, 2011.

[15] N. Johnson and D. Hogg. Learning the distribution of object trajectories for event recognition. In *Proc. BMVC*, 1995.

[16] P. Lang, M. Bradley, and B. Cuthbert. International affective picture system (iaps): Affective ratings of pictures and instruction manual. Technical report, Technical Report A-8. University of Florida, 2008.

[17] J. Machajdik and A. Hanbury. Affective image classification using features inspired by psychology and art theory. In *Proc. ACM Multimedia*, 2010.

[18] A. Money and H. Agiu. Video summarisation: A conceptual framework and survey of the state of the art. *J. Visual Communication and Image Representation*, 19:121–143, 2008.

[19] F. Nater, H. Grabner, and L. Van Gool. Temporal relations in videos for unsupervised activity analysis. In *Proc. BMVC*, 2011.

[20] T. Schaul, L. Pape, T. Glasmachers, V. Graziano, and J. Schmidhuber. Coherence progress: A measure of interestingness based on fixed compressors. In *In Proc. Conf. on Artificial General Intelligence*, 2011.

[21] J. Schmidhuber. Driven by compression progress: A simple principle explains essential aspects of subjective beauty, novelty, surprise, interestingness, attention, curiosity, creativity, art, science, music, jokes. Technical report, TU-Munich, 2009.

sequence	chance	emotion	complexity	learned	novelty	combined	+ regular-ization
1	*0.09*	0.27	0.14	0.71	**0.88**	**0.88**	**0.88**
	0.04	0.10	0.15	0.64	0.83	**0.88**	0.84
2	*0.19*	0.10	0.10	0.03	0.41	**0.59**	**0.59**
	0.08	0.18	0.05	0.07	0.31	0.34	**0.36**
3	*0.23*	0.07	0.71	**1.00**	0.71	0.86	0.86
	NaN	NaN	NaN	NaN	NaN	NaN	NaN
4	*0.20*	**0.56**	0.10	0.46	0.18	0.13	0.26
	0.03	**0.18**	0.02	0.15	0.10	0.10	0.11
5	*0.14*	0.13	0.13	0.04	0.09	0.09	0.04
	NaN	NaN	NaN	NaN	NaN	NaN	NaN
6	*0.21*	0.36	0.68	0.68	0.79	**0.81**	0.74
	0.22	0.54	0.63	**0.80**	0.41	0.67	0.68
7	*0.28*	0.50	0.12	0.31	0.62	0.48	**0.76**
	0.12	0.25	0.09	0.05	0.26	0.23	**0.28**
8	*0.09*	**1.00**	**1.00**	0.21	0.74	0.62	**1.00**
	0.02	**1.00**	**1.00**	0.11	**1.00**	0.67	**1.00**
9	*0.13*	0.10	0.44	0.67	0.64	0.46	**0.72**
	0.04	0.04	0.11	0.15	**0.29**	0.27	0.15
10	*0.11*	0.06	0.45	0.06	0.60	0.60	**0.79**
	0.09	0.10	0.18	0.08	0.34	0.35	**0.36**
11	*0.21*	**0.66**	0.29	0.17	0.37	0.37	0.40
	0.06	0.04	0.02	0.03	**0.10**	0.05	0.04
12	*0.14*	**0.74**	0.44	0.36	0.54	0.38	0.72
	0.05	**0.68**	0.32	0.34	0.43	0.45	0.52
13	*0.20*	0.55	0.64	**0.71**	0.29	0.55	0.55
	0.11	0.28	**0.41**	0.35	0.14	0.25	0.17
14	*0.13*	0.57	0.43	0.61	**0.96**	**0.96**	0.87
	0.10	0.29	0.05	0.18	**0.90**	0.83	0.85
15	*0.23*	0.08	**0.92**	0.90	0.44	0.44	0.44
	0.12	0.14	**0.67**	0.57	0.10	0.22	0.22
16	*0.18*	0.10	0.14	0.50	0.76	0.76	**0.90**
	0.07	0.06	0.14	0.38	**0.93**	0.86	0.85
17	*0.19*	0.16	0.49	**0.62**	0.54	0.54	0.54
	0.07	0.05	0.24	**0.49**	0.31	0.39	0.36
18	*0.14*	0.28	**0.69**	0.38	0.41	**0.69**	0.41
	0.05	0.25	**0.50**	0.06	0.33	0.33	0.33
19	*0.16*	0.70	0.35	0.15	**0.80**	**0.80**	**0.80**
	0.11	0.28	**0.29**	0.03	0.28	0.28	0.27
20	*0.13*	0.40	0.40	0.38	0.48	**0.69**	**0.69**
	0.03	0.38	0.18	0.37	0.38	**0.59**	0.50
median	*0.17*	0.32	0.44	0.42	0.57	0.59	**0.72**
	0.07	0.22	0.18	0.16	0.32	0.35	**0.36**

Table 2: Results for automatically determining interestingness and spotting interesting events in image sequences (see also Fig 5). For each sequence, the first row shows the *Top3* score and the second row shows the *AP*. Best results are printed in bold face.

[22] W. Schneider and R. Shiffrin. Controlled and automatic human information processing: Detection, search, and attention. *Psychological Review*, 84:1–66, 1977.

[23] P. Silvia. *Exploring the psychology of interest.* Oxford University Press, 2006.

[24] C. Stauffer and W. Grimson. Learning patterns of activity using real-time tracking. *PAMI*, 22(8):747–757, 2000.

[25] A. Torralba, A. Oliva, M. Castelhano, and J. Henderson. Contextual guidance of eye movements and attention in real-world scenes: The role of global features on object search. *Psychological Review*, 113(4):766–786, 2006.

[26] A. Treisman and G. Gelade. A feature-integration theory of attention. *Cognitive Psychology*, 12:97–136, 1980.

[27] J. Tsotsos, L. Itti, and G. Rees. A brief and selective history of attention. In *Neurobiology of Attention.* Elsevier, 2005.

[28] P. Valdez and A. Mehrabian. Effects of color on emotions. *Journal of Experimental Psychology: General*, 123(4):394–409, 1994.

(a) **true positives** ($s_t > 0.5$, I_t within the top 5 of our ranking)

(b) **true negatives** ($s_t < 0.25$, I_t within the bottom half of our ranking)

(c) **false positives** ($s_t < 0.25$, I_t within the top 5 of our ranking)

(d) **false negatives** ($s_t > 0.5$, I_t within the bottom half of our ranking)

Figure 6: Typical examples of correctly (a,b) and incorrectly (c,d) classified images. False positives are often caused by dominant weather conditions or shadows, whereas false negatives mostly depict some very subtle and highly semantic concepts, such as the pigeons in the storks nest or raising of the Tower Bridge.

[29] D. Weinshall, A. Zweig, H. Hermansky, S. Kombrink, F. Ohl, J. Anemüller, J. Bach, L. Van Gool, F. Nater, T. Pajdla, M. Havlena, and M. Pavel. Beyond novelty detection: Incongruent events, when general and specific classifiers disagree. *PAMI*, 2012.

[30] W. Wundt. *Grundzüge der physiologischen Psychologie.* Engelmann, Leipzig, 1874.

[31] H. Zhong, J. Shi, and M. Visontai. Detecting unusual activity in video. In *Proc. CVPR*, 2004.

[32] X. Zhu, Z. Ghahramani, and J. Lafferty. Semi-supervised learning using gaussian fields and harmonic functions. In *Proc. ICML*, 2003.

Using Tagged Images of Low Visual Ambiguity to Boost the Learning Efficiency of Object Detectors

Elisavet Chatzilari
Centre for Research & Technology Hellas - Information Technologies Institute
Centre for Vision, Speech and Signal Processing, University of Surrey Guildford, UK
ehatzi@iti.gr

ABSTRACT

Motivated by the abundant availability of user-generated multimedia content, a data augmentation approach that enhances an initial manually labelled training set with regions from user tagged images is presented. Initially, object detection classifiers are trained using a small number of manually labelled regions as the training set. Then, a set of positive regions is automatically selected from a large number of loosely tagged images, pre-segmented by an automatic segmentation algorithm, to enhance the initial training set. In order to overcome the noisy nature of user tagged images and the lack of information about the pixel level annotations, the main contribution of this work is the introduction of the visual ambiguity term. Visual ambiguity is caused by the visual similarity of semantically dissimilar concepts with respect to the employed visual representation and analysis system (i.e. segmentation, feature space, classifier) and, in this work, is modelled so that the images where ambiguous concepts co-exist are penalized. Preliminary experimental results show that the employment of visual ambiguity guides the selection process away from the ambiguous images and, as a result, allows for better separation between the targeted true positive and the undesired negative regions.

Categories and Subject Descriptors

I.2.6 [**Artificial Intelligence**]: Learning; H.3.3 [**Information Storage and Retrieval**]: Information Search and Retrieval

General Terms

Experimentation

Keywords

user tagged images, multimedia data augmentation, social bootstrapping, visual ambiguity, semantic segmentation

1. INTRODUCTION

The majority of state-of-the-art methods for automatic object detection rely on the paradigm of pattern recognition through machine learning. Based on this paradigm, a model is parametrized to recognize all different attributes of a concepts' form and appearance, using a set of training examples. The efficient estimation of model parameters mainly depends on two factors, the quality and the quantity of the training examples. High quality is usually accomplished through manual annotation, which is a laborious and time consuming task. This has a direct impact on the second factor since it inevitably leads into a small number of training examples and limits the performance of the generated models. On the other hand, the excessive use of Web 2.0 applications has made available large amounts of user tagged images. Motivated by the above and inspired by semi supervised learning [1], the goal of this work is to combine the advantages of manually labelled data with the cost effectiveness of social networks.

However, the nature of these annotations (i.e., global level) and the noise existing in the associated information disqualifies them from being directly appropriate learning samples. Nevertheless, the tremendous volume of data that is currently hosted in social networks gives us the luxury to disregard a substantial number of candidate examples, provided we can devise a gauging mechanism that could filter out any ambiguous or noisy samples. Towards this goal, the main contribution of this work is to define, model and utilize visual ambiguity, which arises when two semantically different objects share similar visual stimuli under the employed representation system. In the proposed approach, visual ambiguity is modelled through a measure of image trustworthiness and is employed within an adapted self-training technique designed to combine the benefits of both manual annotations in terms of effectiveness, and social sites in terms of scalability. More specifically, for every concept, a set of regions is selected to enhance the initial training set based on three parameters; a) the visual similarity of the region with the examined concept as expressed by the initial object detection model, b) the textual information (tags) of the image the region belongs to and, c) the trustworthiness of the image the region belongs to, as defined by the ambiguity characterizing its content.

The rest of this paper is organized as follows. In Section 2 the related literature is reviewed. The proposed approach is explained in Section 3 while experimental results are shown in Section 4 and conclusions are drawn in Section 5.

MM'13, October 21–25, 2013, Barcelona, Spain.
ACM 978-1-4503-2404-5/13/10.
http://dx.doi.org/10.1145/2502081.2502208.

2. RELATED WORK

In an attempt to minimize the labelling effort, approaches that rely on active learning (i.e. selectively sampling and annotating examples based on their *informativeness* as they are expected to improve the model performance) have been recently presented [12], [7]. The authors of [12] introduce the concept of *live learning* and propose to replace the human oracle in the typical active learning method with a crowdsourcing service like the MTurk to provide the annotations of the selected informative samples. On the other hand, social networks and user contributed content are leading the recent research efforts, mainly because of their ability to offer more information than the mere image visual content, coupled with the potential to grow almost unlimitedly. In this direction, the authors of [7] propose a solution for actively sampling the most misclassified user tagged images to enrich the negative training set of a concept classifier. The authors claim that the tags of such images can reliably determine if an image does not include a concept, thus making social sites a reliable pool of negative examples. However, active learning without an expert oracle is feasible in these cases because they either rely on non-expert, but still manual annotations (MTurk) or are applied on image level classifiers, which removes the additional factor of localization. In contrast, the proposed approach utilizes loosely tagged images which are provided at no cost and operates on segmented regions instead of global images.

A few approaches have been proposed towards fully unsupervised object detection exploiting user tagged images ([3], [9]). In [3], a theoretical and experimental study is presented to validate the assumption that if the set of loosely tagged images is properly selected, the most frequently appearing visual object and user contributed tag will coincide. Utilizing this assumption, object detection models are build in an unsupervised manner. In a similar fashion, the authors of [9] propose a multiple instance learning algorithm that operates on one million flickr images. They incorporate the various ambiguities between classes by constructing an object correlation network that models the inter-object visual similarities and the co-occurrences of the classes. Visual ambiguity is also considered in [11], where soft assignment of visual words is proposed by considering the *visual word uncertainty* (i.e. an image feature may have more than one candidates in the visual word vocabulary) and the *visual word plausibility* (i.e. when there is no suitable visual word for the image feature).

A preliminary version of the proposed work was presented in [2], where the approach was inspired by the bootstrapping method. Additionally, in this case, the visual ambiguity between regions is also considered and modelled. This measure, unlike other works, is exploited directly in the classification scheme for discarding the misleading images that contain ambiguous concepts, as in these cases selecting the targeted region would be rather difficult.

3. APPROACH

The proposed approach for extracting training samples from unambiguous loosely tagged images is depicted in Fig. 1. Given a concept c_k, an initial classifier is trained on a set of regions that are labelled with this concept and additional regions representing this concept are chosen from a pool of user tagged images harvested from the web. In these images, there is no knowledge of the real objects depicted, or of the exact location of the objects within the image. To overcome this obstacle, the following process takes place. The loosely tagged images are automatically segmented into regions that roughly correspond to semantic objects and visual features

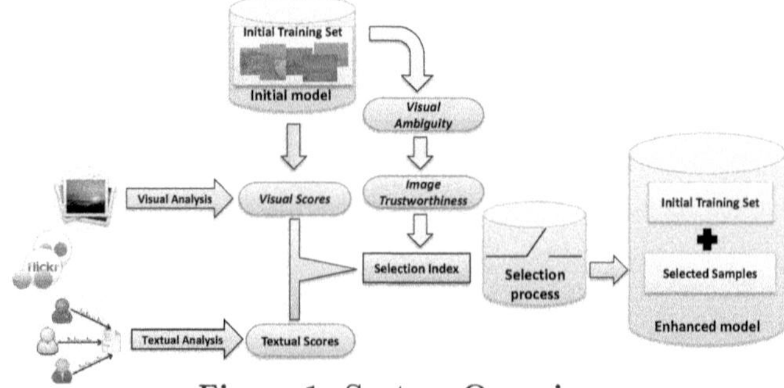

Figure 1: System Overview

are extracted to represent each region. Support Vector Machines (SVMs) are utilized to train initial classifiers using the visual features that were extracted by the labelled regions. Applying these classifiers to the unlabelled regions provides the visual scores. Next, the textual scores are extracted by the textual information that accompanies the loosely tagged images. Finally, visual ambiguity is modelled and transformed into image trustworthiness scores, which practically indicate how much a classifier is trusted to classify the regions that have been extracted from a specific image. In this way, regions are selected so that they represent the concept c_k while at the same time, the ambiguous content is identified and discarded. This luxury is provided by the exuberant amount of the available user contributed content.

Segmentation and feature extraction

In order to segment the images into regions the K-means with connectivity constraint (KMCC) segmentation algorithm [8] is employed. For the visual representation of the regions, a typical bag of visual words (BOW) approach is used. SIFT features [10] are extracted for every key-points detected by the Harris-Laplace and the dense detectors and they are subsequently encoded in a single vector using a vocabulary of 500 words and the soft assignment method [11].

Visual and Textual Scores Estimation

For every concept c_k, an object detection model (SVM_{c_k}) is trained using the one versus all approach. The distance of a region r_m^I, which belongs in image I, from the hyperplane of the SVM_{c_k} model will be referred to as visual score $VS_{c_k}(r_m^I)$ from now on. This score indicates the confidence of the model that the region r_m^I depicts the concept c_k.

In addition, in order to utilize the textual information provided with the user tagged images, the widely known lexical database WordNet [5] is utilized to measure the semantic relatedness between image tags and concepts. More specifically, for a loosely tagged image I with tags $Tag^I = \{tag_1^I, tag_2^I, ..., tag_{N_{tag}}^I\}$ the textual similarity score between its image tags and a concept $TSim(tag_j^I, c_k)$ is calculated using WordNet. For every concept c_k, its maximum similarity with the tags of image I is chosen to gauge the possibility $t_{c_k}^I$ that the concept c_k exists in the specific image resulting in a vector of textual scores for every image:

$$t_{c_k}^I = \max_j \{TSim(tag_j^I, c_k)\}$$

Visual Ambiguity and Image Trustworthiness

In order to model the visual ambiguity that arises between visually similar concepts the visual ambiguity scores are introduced and are estimated using the following process. For a concept c_k, given its model SVM_{c_k}, the visual scores of all the regions that have been used to train this model, are determined. In the ideal case the visual scores of all the regions depicting c_k should be much higher than the visual scores of all other regions. When regions that do not depict c_k are associated with high visual scores by SVM_{c_k}, the discriminative ability of SVM_{c_k} is low. This is considered as the visual ambiguity between c_k and the concept $c_l, l \neq k$, which is the actual concept depicted by the examined region. The visual ambiguity of c_k and c_l is selected to be the average of the visual scores that the regions belonging to the c_l class received:

$$VA_{c_k,c_l} = \begin{cases} \frac{1}{N_l}\sum_{i=1}^{N_l} VS_{c_k}(r_i^{c_l}) & \text{if } k \neq l \\ 0 & \text{if } k = l \end{cases} \quad (1)$$

where $r_i^{c_l}, i = 1 \ldots N_l$ are the regions that depict c_l. The visual ambiguity between two concepts c_k and c_l is high when the model that is trained to detect c_k produces high confidence scores for the $r_i^{c_l}$ regions, which practically means that our system tends to confuse the visual information that depicts c_k with the visual information that depicts c_l. For example, the visual ambiguity scores of the closely related couples of concepts *grass-plant* (0.824) and *grass-bush* (0,874) are higher than the visual ambiguity score of the couple *grass-fence* (0,638).

The visual ambiguity scores indicate how much a specific classifier is trusted to distinguish between two concepts when asked to classify a region. Having this knowledge for every couple of concepts, it could be applied on every image separately if the existent objects in the image were known. This information might not be available explicitly, but the possibility about the existence of an object within an image is available through the textual score of the image. If the textual score of a concept in the image is above a threshold th, we consider that the concept is present in the image. In order to express the trustworthiness of the classifier SVM_{c_k} to classify the regions of an image I, the dynamic visual ambiguity $VA_{c_k}^I$ of an image I with respect to a concept c_k, is calculated as a function of the static information **VA**:

$$\mathbf{VA^I_{c_k}} = \mathbf{T^I_{th}} * \mathbf{VA_{c_k}} \quad (2)$$

The difference between $\mathbf{VA^I_{c_k}}$ and $\mathbf{VA_{c_k}}$ is that $\mathbf{VA^I_{c_k}}$ is calculated for a specific image I and gauges how ambiguous is the specific image, whereas $\mathbf{VA_{c_k}}$ is static information, independent of the image that is based on the visual representation system. Finally, image trustworthiness is defined as the complement of the maximum visual ambiguity score exhibited among the existing concepts with respect to c_k. The trustworthiness score of an image I with respect to c_k gauges how much a classifier can be trusted to classify the regions of the image I with respect to the concept c_k:

$$Trust^I_{c_k} = 1 - \max_l(VA^I_{c_k,c_l}) \quad (3)$$

In the previous example for the concept *grass*, the classifier is trusted more to detect the grass regions within images that contain *fence*, than within images that contain *bush* ($VisualAmbiguity(grass, fence) = 0.638 <$ $VisualAmbiguity(grass, bush) = 0.874$).

Region relevance and selection of training samples

In order to combine the three aforementioned independent scores into a single region relevance score, the geometric mean is chosen over the more typical arithmetic mean due to its robustness when multiplying quantities with different normalizations.

$$RR_{c_k}(r^I_m) = VS_{c_k}(r^I_m) * t^I_{c_k} * Trust^I_{c_k} \quad (4)$$

The regions of the loosely tagged images are ranked according to their region relevance score, and finally the top N regions with the highest relevance scores are selected to enhance the initial training set.

4. PRELIMINARY RESULTS

Two datasets were used in the experimental study. The MIRFLICKR-1M dataset [6] consists of one million user tagged images harvested from flickr. This dataset consists the pool of tagged images, from where the training regions were selected to enhance the manually trained models. The second dataset, the SAIAPR TC-12 dataset [4], consists of 20000 images labelled at region detail and was split into 3 parts (70% train, 10% validation and 20% test). To acquire comparable measures over the experiments, the images of the SAIAPR TC-12 dataset were segmented and the ground truth label of each segment was taken to be the label of the hand-labelled region that overlapped with the segment by more than the 2/3 of the segment's area. The concepts that had less than 15 instances were removed to ensure statistical safety. The mean average precision (mAP) served as the metric for evaluating the proposed approach.

4.1 Sample Selection Performance

The objective of this experiment is to show the impact of employing the ambiguity and the image trustworthiness scores to the ranking of the regions. In order to be able to evaluate the selection process directly, the user tagged images should be annotated at region level. For this reason, the training set of the SAIAPR TC-12 dataset (14k images) was used by loosening the region labels to image tags-keywords. The initial models were trained using the validation set (2k images) and were applied to the regions of the training set of SAIAPR TC-12. The regions were ranked based on a) the visual scores (**V**), b) the geometric mean of the visual and textual scores (**VT**) and c) the proposed approach, i.e. applying Eq. 4 (**VTA**). In Fig. 2, the distribution of the region relevance scores, calculated as explained by each configuration (i.e. **V**, **VT** and **VTA**), is shown for the concept grass. The black solid line is the distribution of the positive examples, i.e. the targeted regions which we opt to select, and the red dashed line is the distribution of the negative examples. It is obvious, that without the auxiliary information the classifier performs poorly (Fig. 2(a)), since the two distributions overlap significantly. Moreover, we can see that the textual information has eliminated a large number of non-relevant regions (Fig. 2(b)), which was expected since in this case the tags are accurate. Finally the impact of visual ambiguity is clearly shown in Fig. 2(c), where part of the black distribution, i.e. true positives, now stands out receiving much higher region relevance scores compared to the rest. This effect would be ideal in the case of loosely tagged images since it makes more accurate the selection of the top N regions. Additionally, the mAP over all concepts is measured and written in the caption. The numerical results validate the aforementioned conclusions as well.

4.2 Retrained Models Performance

In this experiment the performance of the initial classifiers which were trained using the manually labelled regions is compared to the performance of the enhanced classifiers (i.e. the ones trained by the combination of the labelled and the selected regions). The initial classifiers were enriched by the top $1k$ regions ranked based on the configurations **V**, **VT** and **VTA**. The validation set of the SAIAPR TC-12

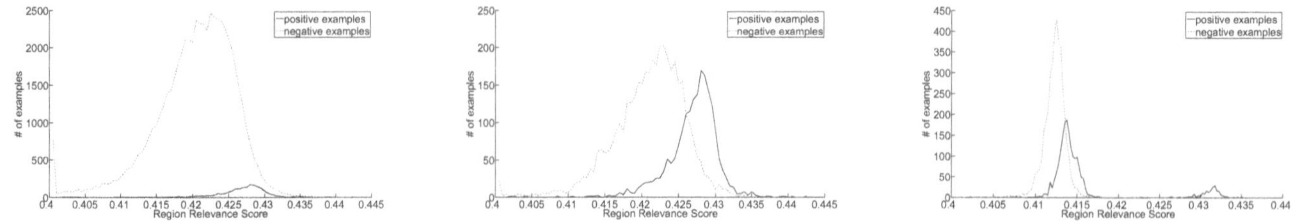

(a) **V** (4.56% mAP) (b) **VT** (58.78% mAP) (c) **VTA** (65.55% mAP)

Figure 2: The distribution of the *RR* scores (Eq. 4) based on the configuration a) V, b) VT and c) VTA.

dataset (2k images) is used for training the initial models and the test set (4k images) is used to evaluate the performance of all generated models. The mAP of the initial models is 5.9%, while adding regions ranked based on the **V** configuration degraded the models, to 4.9% mAP. Using the **VT** and **VTA** configurations, the enhanced models increased their performance to 6 and 6.3% respectively. These results comply with the conclusions reached in the previous section, showing the positive impact of ambiguity to the sample selection process. Examining each concept independently, the configuration incorporating visual ambiguity exhibits the highest performance in 26 out of the 62 examined concepts, compared to 19 for the **VT** configuration, 3 for the **V** configuration and 14 for the configuration based on the initial classifiers.

5. CONCLUSIONS AND FUTURE WORK

In this work we have presented a means to quantify and utilize the visual ambiguity that characterizes the image content, with a view to boost the efficiency of object detection classifiers. More specifically, we have relied on the self-training paradigm to validate the value of using visual ambiguity for the optimization of the sample selection process. Preliminary experimental results show that by using the proposed approach to cope with the existing ambiguities, the improvement in performance is higher than the one achieved using a typical self-training approach, where the sample selection process is based solely on the visual information of the initial models. An interesting observation that came our of our experimental study relates to the use of WordNet and the fact that this similarity metric does not take into account the context of the words to disambiguate their meaning. For example, the words palm and tree would always yield a very high similarity score regardless if the intended meaning for palm was the tree or the hand. In these cases our approach was heavily misled, making impossible the extraction of a reliable score for image trustworthiness. In our future work we plan to investigate ways for alleviating the negative effects of using WordNet and examine other context-based metrics. With respect to visual ambiguity we plan to investigate alternative, more sophisticated ways for fusing the available information from the various modalities towards a better selection strategy. Additionally, we are working on designing experimental set-ups for proving directly that the proposed method for quantifying visual ambiguity is a reasonable measure. Finally, the exploitation of a richer source for positive samples, like flickr groups, is within our future plans. Using better suited content rather than a canned dataset would allow for more iterations and for achieving better performance improvements.

Acknowledgements

This work was supported by the EU 7th Framework Programme under grant number IST-FP7-288815 in project Live+Gov (www.liveandgov.eu).

6. REFERENCES

[1] O. Chapelle, B. Schölkopf, and A. Zien, editors. *Semi-Supervised Learning*. MIT Press, Cambridge, MA, 2006.

[2] E. Chatzilari, S. Nikolopoulos, Y. Kompatsiaris, and J. Kittler. Multi-modal region selection approach for training object detectors. ICMR. ACM, 2012.

[3] E. Chatzilari, S. Nikolopoulos, I. Patras, and I. Kompatsiaris. Leveraging social media for scalable object detection. *Pattern Recognition*, 45(8):2962–2979, 2012.

[4] H. J. Escalante, C. A. Hernandez, J. A. Gonzalez, A. Lspez-Lspez, M. Montes, E. F. Morales, L. E. Sucar, L. Villase?or, and M. Grubinger. The segmented and annotated iapr tc-12 benchmark. *CVIU*, 2010.

[5] C. Fellbaum, editor. *WordNet An Electronic Lexical Database*. The MIT Press, Cambridge, MA ; London, May 1998.

[6] M. J. Huiskes, B. Thomee, and M. S. Lew. New trends and ideas in visual concept detection: The mir flickr retrieval evaluation initiative. In *MIR*. ACM, 2010.

[7] X. Li, C. G. M. Snoek, M. Worring, D. C. Koelma, and A. W. M. Smeulders. Bootstrapping visual categorization with relevant negatives. *IEEE Trans. on Multimedia*, In press, 2013.

[8] V. Mezaris, I. Kompatsiaris, and M. G. Strintzis. Still image segmentation tools for object-based multimedia applications. *IJPRAI*, 18(4):701–725, 2004.

[9] Y. Shen and J. Fan. Leveraging loosely-tagged images and inter-object correlations for tag recommendation. In *MM*, pages 5–14. ACM, 2010.

[10] K. E. A. van de Sande, T. Gevers, and C. G. M. Snoek. Evaluating color descriptors for object and scene recognition. *IEEE Trans. on Pattern Analysis and Machine Intelligence*, 32(9):1582–1596, 2010.

[11] J. C. van Gemert, C. J. Veenman, A. W. M. Smeulders, and J. M. Geusebroek. Visual word ambiguity. *IEEE Trans. on Pattern Analysis and Machine Intelligence*, 32(7):1271–1283, 2010.

[12] S. Vijayanarasimhan and K. Grauman. Large-scale live active learning: Training object detectors with crawled data and crowds. In *CVPR*, pages 1449 –1456, 2011.

Projective Identity and Procedural Rhetoric in Educational Multimedia: Towards the Enrichment of Programming Self-Concept and Growth Mindset with Fantasy Role-Play

Michael James Scott
Information Systems, Computing & Mathematics
Brunel University
Uxbridge, Middlesex, UB8 3PH
United Kingdom
michael.scott@brunel.ac.uk

ABSTRACT
There is a growing movement in the behavioral sciences towards exploring more situated, pragmatic and ontological accounts of human learning. Positive psychology shows that a reciprocal relationship may exist between self-concept and the development of expertise, while social psychology reveals that mindsets about the nature of personal traits can have profound impacts on practice behavior. Thus, nurturing psychological constructs through the learning environment may empower students, enabling them to learn more effectively. Educational multimedia is known to support learning in a range of contexts, but its role in facilitating such self-enrichment has seldom been explored. Consequently, it is not clear which designs can aid both self enhancement and skill development. This doctoral symposium paper proposes that an interplay between projective identity and procedural rhetoric, delivered in the form of a fantasy role-playing experience, could be one such practice. Early experiments in the area of introductory programming show promise, but raise questions about external validity, educationally relevant effect sizes and how multimedia elements within the tool could be utilized more effectively to enhance these effects.

Categories and Subject Descriptors
H.5.1 [**Information Interfaces and Presentation**]: Multimedia Information Systems; K.3.1 [**Computers and Education**]: Computer Uses in Education.

Keywords
Self-Concept, Projective Identity, Procedural Rhetoric, Implicit Beliefs, Self-Enhancement, Mindset, Programming, Multimedia, Fantasy, Role-Play, Education, Learning.

1. INTRODUCTION
Educational multimedia is widely used to support learning. Applications include: instructional videos; visualizations; training simulations; and serious games. Part of its popularity can be attributed to its availability, as learners in many parts of the world are able to access multimedia-enabled instruction due to the growing ubiquity of computer-based tools [24]. Furthermore, multimedia communication is often informed by the principles of cognitive science, so the delivery of learning material in such cases is optimized for human information processing [21, 23].

However, while retention and transfer of knowledge are highly desirable, direct instruction is not the only goal of education. At the tertiary level, in particular, there is a movement towards learner-centered paradigms which champion autonomy [2] and encourage self-regulation [41]. This has implications for practical disciplines, such as programming, where it is desirable for learners to immerse themselves in a regime of ongoing and reflexive deliberate practice. This is because ten years of such practice is often needed to obtain substantial expertise [10, 38].

Yet, despite this renewed emphasis, educators do not appear to have overcome some of the most pervasive challenges in introductory programming [13, 35]. Many novices do not appear to practice programming regularly, claiming they experience apprehension and discomfort when they attempt to do so [31]. Some authors describe this as *programming trauma* [17], and there is some neurological evidence which suggests such anxiety has a relationship with regions of the brain associated with visceral threat detection and pain [20]. Thus, negative experiences and their impact on avoidance behavior is an area of concern.

Scott and Ghinea [32] have reflected on several potential barriers that may influence programming avoidance. These being: the "radical novelty" of the learning material [8]; beliefs about the nature of programming aptitude [9, 39]; in addition to the relationship between self-concept and achievement [16, 22, 37]. They propose analytical and adaptable approaches to the design of learning environments, applying soft scaffolding, ongoing informative feedback, and a focus on self-enhancement alongside skill development, could help to overcome these barriers.

However, there are challenges in adopting these proposals. They do not trivially scale to large cohorts of students. Moreover, their realization is often left to teaching assistants who may not receive significant training on how to provide appropriate feedback, or in educational psychology more generally [3]. This is a significant disadvantage because appropriate feedback is pertinent to nurturing self-concept [27] and appropriate beliefs [6, 26].

The means through which these principles can be realized, nevertheless, do not rely solely on faculty alone. Educational multimedia and adaptive hypermedia systems can be used to support scalability. Therefore, suitable measurement, scaffolding and feedback for individual learners can be managed through virtual learning environments. This enables pedagogies that account for barriers to deliberate practice. So, what roles can educational multimedia have in facilitating self-enrichment?

MM'13, October 21–25, 2013, Barcelona, Spain.
ACM 978-1-4503-2404-5/13/10.
http://dx.doi.org/10.1145/2502081.2502209

2. BACKGROUND

One role that multimedia e-learning could support is the development of a strong learning identity. Pertinent to this, is the self-concept construct [16]. Recent work in this area suggests that a reciprocal relationship exists between self-concept and achievement, where it is defined as: individual self-perceptions about ability, situated within a sphere of activity, formed through experience with and interpretations of one's environment [16, 22]. Thus, a positive self-concept can facilitate achievement [37].

A practice that could reinforce self-concept is the use of a fantasy role-play within a dramatic narrative [34]. There has been some qualitative success in *Space Mission: Ice Moon*, enabling students to "think and act like scientists" [7] and among the creative learning environments, a similar approach can be seen in *GameStar Mechanic* [30]. Thus, it could be used to prepare less confident students for project-based learning, as in [29]—but conveying preparatory material in a way that avoids the pitfalls of just-in-time instruction, where the pace can create pressure.

Based on Gee's [12] notion of "projective identity", the role-play operates as an exploration of a virtual identity through embodied activity. It is argued that, as learners develop their identity while immersed in a role, it reinforces the real-world identity relating to that role. Thus, acting as a Lacanian mirror stage [18], learners project their beliefs onto their character and then witness a transformation as a consequence of the narrative. Subsequently, they reflect upon and potentially adopt the change.

While there is limited evidence, Yee and Bailenson [40] describe a somewhat similar phenomenon: the Proteus Effect. Under experimental conditions, they showed that manipulating the avatars of participants in a virtual environment had an impact on their attitudes and behavior. Furthermore some of these changes were maintained when measured a short time after the experiment, outside of the virtual environment. In another study, vicarious reinforcement was applied to avatars within a virtual world, changing their appearance in accordance with participants' behavior; which, in turn, reinforced positive habits [11]. This further supports the notion that transforming virtual characters can change attitudes that transfer to real-world contexts.

Another role that multimedia e-learning could support is changing beliefs about aptitude. According to this line of research, learners can have implicit beliefs about whether their personal traits are set (the fixed mindset) or malleable (the growth mindset). As a result, when learners encounter difficulties, those with a fixed mindset often assume maladaptive learning strategies. However, those with a growth mindset tend to remain resilient, applying a mastery-orientated approach [9, 26, 39].

There are few studies on this topic within the domain of computer science education. However, those that have been conducted suggest a domain-specific impact. There appears to be a distinct mindset for programming aptitude [33], and an intervention study targeting novice software developers only showed success when growth messages were reinforced with a programming crib-sheet [6]. In line with work that suggests feedback practice affects mindsets [26], feedback contextualization may also be needed.

Multimedia learning environments, however, can be designed to communicate immediate, situated and pervasive messages that promote the growth mindset. This can be achieved using a mechanism such as procedural rhetoric [4]. Unique to interactive media, this approach does not argue directly but rather allows a position to emerge through the dynamics of a system. For example, presenting a compiler as an apologetic character in need of assistance has helped novices to see compilation errors as challenges to be overcome [19]. Thereby, subtly emphasizing how skill improves as a consequence of effort.

3. PROPOSED APPROACH

This research investigates the impact of embedding a fantasy role-play within a multimedia learning tool. The proposed design leverages projective identity and procedural rhetoric, aiming to enhance programming self-concept and promote a growth mindset towards programming aptitude. The hypothesis is that such self-enrichment will encourage students to engage in deliberate practice. Central to this thesis is the notion that learners' beliefs about themselves influence their behavior [9, 32]. Thus, due to the strong nature of the emotions that arise while learning to program [17, 31], the work has been situated within the control-value appraisal theory of achievement emotion and motivation [28]. The focus is three section of a causal chain: the relationship between self-beliefs and value-control appraisals; how these appraisals influence emotions during programming tasks; and how these influence programming practice behavior. Thus, the framework, shown below in Figure 1, is proposed:

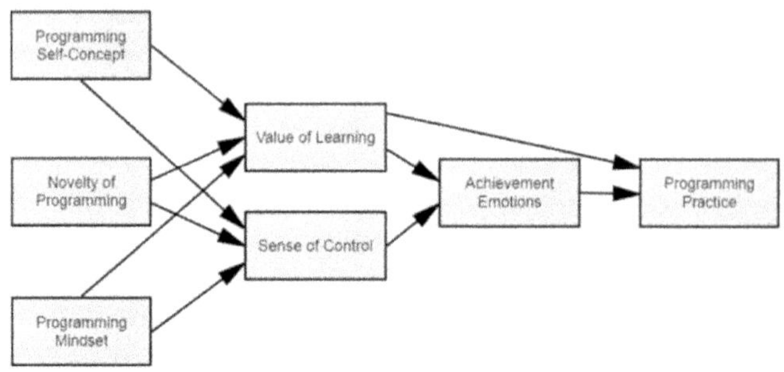

Figure 1. Proposed Conceptual Framework

Mindsets have an impact on students' sense of control over their learning, while self-concept reinforces the value of it. These beliefs, alongside students' familiarity with the learning material, form interactions affecting value-control appraisals. With such appraisals then influencing the emotions that students experience as they encounter challenge. For example, anxiety and frustration with low-control and high-value. This has an impact on practice behavior, which may be mitigated by high value. It is critical to first validate this framework to understand the potential impacts of the tool. Thus, the research is organized into two core branches.

The first branch of the project consists of three core elements: *psychometric scale construction*, to ensure that measurement is rigorous; and *correlational studies*, that analyze survey data to determine whether the hypothesized relationships exist. It is important to note that several relationships in the model may be reciprocal in nature [22]. This is based on evidence which suggests that, should educators enhance self-beliefs without also improving level of ability, then the gains in self-belief are likely to be short-lived [16]. Thus, the third core element will consist of *longitudinal studies*, using survey data to explore changes over time. This will situate the work in the wider context of learning to program, providing an indication of the educational relevance of detected effect sizes.

The second branch of the research will involve the development and evaluation of the proposed tool. This will consist of two core elements: *qualitative design research*, prototyping the design using a human-centered approach to ensure appropriateness and usability; and *experimental studies*, conducting experimental (pragmatic) trials to evaluate the effectiveness of tool.

4. WORK IN PROGRESS

Work has begun on psychometric scale development and an exploration of the correlations between the relevant psychological constructs. However, this has not been without challenge. In two initial surveys, reported in [33] and [34], response rates were low. While non-response bias was examined, concerns have been raised about representativeness. Thus, replication at other institutions, using random sampling strategies, are necessary to address these concerns about external validity. Nevertheless, the adaptation of several general self-belief constructs to the introductory programming context demonstrated adequate psychometric properties [34]. Furthermore, the notion of a programming-specific mindset construct was supported [33].

While these surveys were conducted, an initial prototype of the tool was developed, shown below in Figure 2. This implemented a simple 20 minute debugging exercise, intended to encourage students to improve their ability at identifying errors in existing Java code. A projective identity was embedded by enabling users to select an avatar and move around a virtual environment, assuming the role of a computer systems specialist on an advanced interstellar spaceship. In the role-play, the ship had become damaged, so repair robots had to be programmed to navigate the ship and repair various problems. Students were provided instruction before each task, receiving encouragement and advice by characters after submitting a solution. Upon success, they would then provided feedback based on the time taken and mistakes made.

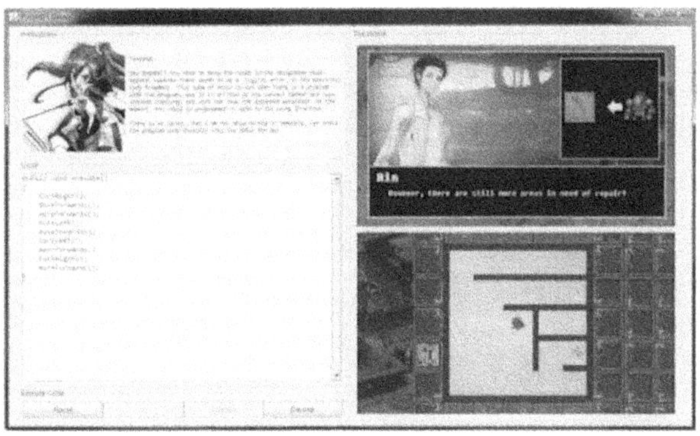

Figure 2. An Early Prototype of the Proposed Tool [34]

The prototype was intended to inform the design. However, as reported in [34], it was examined under experimental conditions to explore the feasibility of the study design. Inspired by several similar studies that focused on learning [14, 15, 25], a randomised trial using an *added value* approach [1] was adopted. A version tool including fantasy role-play (experimental) was compared to one without (control) using the pre-test post-test parallel group design. The sample consisted of 36 first and second year undergraduate students, several weeks into an introductory programming course. Typically, these students had little, or no, experience writing code prior to the start of this course.

An ANCOVA (Analysis of Covariance) revealed that the fantasy role-play version was more effective than the control case at enhancing self-concept ($F[1, 35] = 4.181$, $p < .05$, $\eta_p^2 = .112$). Nevertheless, the gain scores, illustrated below in Figure 3, reveal a modest increase in the experimental condition. This is challenging to place into context because a series of small effects may become educationally relevant over time. Thus, the power of the experiment should be increased. However, the result may also suggest further design considerations are needed. For example, what level of presence and embodiment (the sensation of being immersed in a virtual environment while inhabiting another self; see [5, 12, 25, 36]) is needed for the formation of a projective identity? Then, what multimedia features will facilitate that level? Does this lead to an acceptable trade-off with respect to extraneous content that violates the coherence principle [23]?

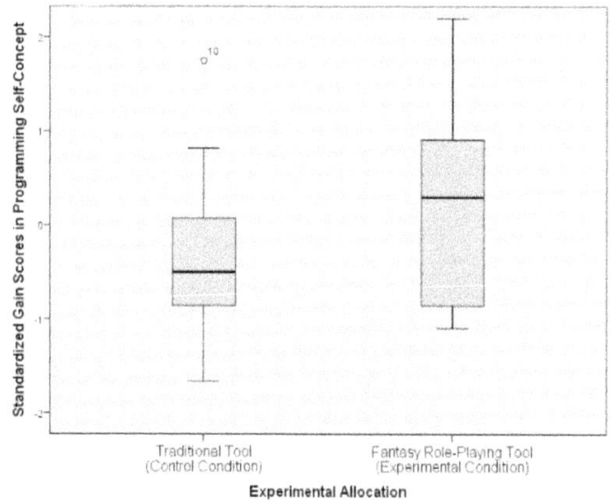

Figure 3. Distribution of Self-Concept Gain Scores [34]

5. EXPECTED CONTRIBUTION

It is anticipated that this research will be ongoing, but beyond the tool itself, three core contributions are expected:

- A validated psychometric scale that enables educators in tertiary institutions to measure programming aptitude mindset and programming self-concept;
- A model that explores the impact of programming self-concept and programming aptitude mindset on programming practice behavior;
- Experimental evidence that demonstrates the efficacy of educational multimedia, applying the notions of projective identity and procedural rhetoric, to enhance programming aptitude mindset and self-concept.

If it can shown that such self-enrichment effects exist, and they are educationally relevant, there could be significant implications for the design and use of multimedia to support affective goals in education. This will lead to further work exploring what media elements and arrangements provide effective support.

6. SUMMARY

It is hypothesized that high self-concept and a growth mindset enable desirable learning behaviors. Thus, this work explores how educational multimedia could facilitate an intervention. It is proposed that procedural rhetoric, using narrative and interactive characters to subtly persuade learners, and projective identity, shaping interactivity through the lens of a virtual character, can create self-enriching experiences that empower programming novices. Consequently, leading to higher achievement.

Initial results are promising, but have several limitations. Thus, results should be replicated to address concerns. Furthermore, the initial experiment was shown to have a small effect. It is unclear whether such a modest gain is educationally significant, as it could aggregate over time leading to long-term impact. Therefore, longitudinal study is necessary, once the research model has been evaluated. However, it also alludes that additional design considerations, such as the role of multimedia, are necessary.

7. ACKNOWLEDGMENTS

This work is being conducted under the supervision of Gheorghita Ghinea, with funding provided by Brunel University.

8. REFERENCES

[1] Adams, D., Mayers, R.E., MacNamara,A., Koenig,A. and Wainess, R. 2012. Narrative Games for Learning: Testing the Discovery and Narrative Hypotheses, *Journal of Educational Psychology*, 104, 1 (Feb '12), 235-249.

[2] Barr, R.B. and Tagg, J. 1995. A New Paradigm for Undergraduate Education, *Change*. 27, 6 (Nov. '95), 13-25.

[3] Beaubouef, T. & Mason, J. 2005. Why the High Attrition Rate for Computer Science Students: Some Thoughts and Observations. *ACM SIGCSE Bulletin*, 37, 2 (Jun. '05), 103-106.

[4] Bogost, I. 2008. The Rhetoric of Video Games. In *The Ecology of Games: Connecting Youth, Games, and Learning*. K. Salen, Ed. Cambridge: MIT Press, 117-139.

[5] Botvinick, M. and Cohen, J. 1998. Rubber Hands 'Feel' Touch That Eyes See. *Nature*, 391 (Feb. '98), 756.

[6] Cutts, Q., Cutts, E., Draper, S., O'Donnell, P. and Saffrey, P. 2010. Manipulating Mindset to Positively Influence Introductory Programming Performance. In *Proceedings of the 41st ACM Technical Symposium on Computer Science Education* (Milwaukee, WI, USA, Mar. 10-13, '10). SIGCSE '10. ACM, NY, 431-435.

[7] Daanen, H. and Grant, L. 2007. Space Mission: Ice Moon. In *Proceedings of the ACM SIGGRAPH Educators Conference* (San Diego, USA, 5-9 Aug., '07), SIGRAPH '07, ACM, NY, 19.

[8] Djikstra, E.W. 1989. A Debate on Teaching Computer Science: On the Cruelty of Really Teaching Computer Science. *Communications of the ACM*, 32, 12 (Dec. '89), 1398-1404.

[9] Dweck, C.S. and Master, A. 2008. Self-Theories Motivate Self-Regulated Learning. In *Motivation and Self-Regulated Learning: Theory, Research, and Applications*. D. Schunk & B. Zimmerman, Eds. NY: Routledge, 31-51.

[10] Ericsson, K.A., Krampe, R. & Tesch-Romer, C. 1993. The Role of Deliberate Practice in the Acquisition of Expert Performance. *Psychological Review*, 100, 3 (Jul. '93), 363-406.

[11] Fox, J. and Bailenson, J. 2009. Virtual Self-Modeling: The Effects of Vicarious Reinforcement and Identification on Exercise Behaviors, *Media Psychology*, 12, 1 (Mar. '09), 1-25.

[12] Gee, J.P. 2008. Video Games and Embodiment. *Games and Culture*, 3, 3 (Jul. '08), 253-263.

[13] Guzdial, M. From Science to Engineering: Exploring the Dual Nature of Computing Education Research. *Communications of the ACM*, 54, 2 (Feb. '11), 37-39.

[14] Habgood, M.P., Ainsworth, S.E., and Benford, S. 2005. Endogenous Fantasy and Learning in Digital Games. *Simulation and Gaming*. 36, 4 (Dec. '05), 483-498.

[15] Hainey, T., Connolly, T.M., Stansfield, M. and Boyle, E.A. 2011. Evaluation of a Game to Teach Requirements Collection and Analysis in Software Engineering at Tertiary Education Level, *Computers & Education*, 56, 1 (Jan '11), 21-35.

[16] Huang, C. 2011. Self-Concept and Academic Achievement: A Meta-Analysis of Longitudinal Relations. *Journal of School Psychology*. 49, 5 (Oct. '11), 505-528.

[17] Huggard, M. 2004. Programming Trauma: Can it be Avoided? In *Proceedings of the BCS Conference on Grand Challenges in Computing: Education* (Newcastle, UK, Mar. 29-31, '04). GCC '04. British Computer Society, Swindon, UK, 50-51.

[18] Lacan, J. 1953. Some Reflections on the Ego. *International Journal of Psychoanalysis*, 34, 1 (May '53), 11-17.

[19] Lee, M.J. and Ko, A.J. 2011. Personifying Programming Tool Feedback Improves Novice Programmers' Learning. In *Proceedings of the 7th International Workshop on Computing Education Research* (Providence, USA, Aug. 8-9, '11). ICER '11. ACM, NY, 109-116.

[20] Lyons, I.M. and Beilock, S.L. 2012. When Math Hurts: Math Anxiety Predicts Pain Network Activation in Anticipation of Doing Math, *PLoS One*, 7, 10 (Oct. '12), e48076.

[21] Mampadi, F., Chen, S.Y., Ghinea, G. and Chen, M.P. 2011. Design of Adaptive Hypermedia Learning Systems: A Cognitive Style Approach. *Computers & Education*, 56, 4 (May '11), 1003-1011.

[22] Marsh, H. & Martin, A. 2011. Academic Self-Concept and Academic Achievement: Relations and Causal Ordering. *British Journal of Educational Psychology*, 81, 1 (Mar. '11), 59-77.

[23] Mayer, R.E. 2008. Applying the Science of Learning: Evidence-Based Principles for the Design of Multimedia Instruction, *American Psychologist*, 63, 8 (Nov. '08), 760-769.

[24] Mitra, S. and Rana, V. 2001. Children and the Internet: Experiments with Minimally Invasive Education in India. *British Journal of Educational Technology*, 32, 2 (Mar. '01), 221-232.

[25] Moreno, R. and Mayer, R.E. 2002. Learning Science in Virtual Reality Multimedia Environments: Role of Methods and Media, Journal of Educational Psychology, 94, 3 (Sep. '02), 598-610.

[26] Mueller, C.M. and Dweck, C.S. 1998. Intelligence Praise Can Undermine Motivation and Performance, *Journal of Personality and Social Psychology*, 75, 1 (Jul. '98), 33-52.

[27] O'Mara, A.J., Marsh, H.W., Craven, R.G. and Debus, R.L. 2010. Do Self-Concept Interventions Make A Difference? A Synergistic Blend of Construct Validation and Meta-Analysis. *Educational Psychologist*, 41, 3 (Jun. '10), 181-206.

[28] Pekrun, R., Frenzel, A.C., Goetz, T. and Perry, R.P. 2007. The Control-Value Theory of Achievement Emotions: An Integrative Approach to Emotions in Education, *Emotion in Education*, P. Schutz and R. Pekrun, Eds. Amsterdam: Academic Press, 13-36.

[29] Repenning, A. 2012. Programming Goes Back to School. *Communications of the ACM*. 55, 5 (May '12), 38-40.

[30] Resnick, M. et al. 2009. Growing Up Programming: Democratizing the Creation of Dynamic, Interactive Media. In *Extended Abstracts from the SIGCHI Conference on Human Factors in Computing Systems* (Boston, USA, Apr. 4-9, '09). CHI '09. ACM, NY, 3293-3296.

[31] Rogerson, C. and Scott, E. 2010. The Fear Factor: How it Affects Students Learning to Program in a Tertiary Environment. *Information Technology Education*, 9, 1, 147-171.

[32] Scott, M.J. and Ghinea, G. 2013. Educating Programmers: A Reflection on Barriers to Deliberate Practice. In *Proceedings of the 2nd Annual HEA STEM Conference* (Birmingham, UK, Apr. 17-18, '13). Higher Education Academy, York, UK, 028P.

[33] Scott, M.J. and Ghinea, G. 2013. Implicit Theories of Programming Aptitude as a Barrier to Learning to Code: Are They Distinct from Intelligence? In *Proceedings of the 18th ACM Conference on Innovation and Technology in Computer Science Education* (Kent, UK, Jul. 1-3, '13). ITiCSE '13. ACM, NY, 347-347.

[34] Scott, M.J. and Ghinea, G. 2013. Integrating Fantasy Role-Play into the Programming Lab: Exploring the 'Projective Identity' Hypothesis. In *Proceedings of the 43rd ACM Technical Symposium on Computer Science Education* (Denver, USA, Mar. 6-9, '13). SIGCSE '13. ACM, NY, 119-122.

[35] Soloway, E., Bondar, J., and Ehrlich, K. 1983. Cognitive Strategies and Looping Constructs: An Empirical Study. *Communications of the ACM*, 26, 11 (Nov. '83), 853-860.

[36] Taylor, T.L. 2009. Living Digitally: Embodiment in Virtual Worlds. In *The Social Life of Avatars: Presence and Interaction in Shared Virtual Environments*. R. Schroeder Ed. London: Springer-Verlag, 40-62.

[37] Valentine, J.C., DuBois, D.L. and Cooper, H. 2004. The Relationship Between Self-Beliefs and Academic Achievement: A Meta-Analytic Review, *Educational Psychologist*, 39, 2 (June '04), 111-133.

[38] Winslow, L.E. 1996. Programming Pedagogy - A Psychological Overview. *ACM SIGCSE Bulletin*, 28, 3 (Sept. '96), 17-22.

[39] Yeager, D.S. and Dweck, C.S. 2012. Mindsets That Promote Resilience: When Students Believe That Personal Characteristics Can Be Developed. *Educational Psychologist*, 47, 4 (Oct. '12), 302-314.

[40] Yee, N. and Bailenson, J. 2007. The Proteus Effect: The Effect of Transformed Self-Representation on Behavior. *Human Communication Research*, 33, 3 (Jul. '07), 270-290.

[41] Zimmerman, B. 2002. Becoming a Self-Regulated Learner: An Overview. *Theory into Practice*, 41, 2 (Jun. '02), 64-70.

Recognition of Complex Events in Open-Source Web-Scale Videos: A Bottom up approach

Subhabrata Bhattacharya
Center for Research in Computer Vision
University of Central Florida
Orlando, FL
subh@cs.ucf.edu

ABSTRACT

Recognition of complex events in unconstrained Internet videos is a challenging research problem. In this symposium proposal, we present a systematic decomposition of complex events into hierarchical components and make an in-depth analysis of how existing research are being used to cater to various levels of this hierarchy. We also identify three key stages where we make novel contributions which are necessary to not only improve the overall recognition performance, but also develop richer understanding of these events. At the lowest level, our contributions include (a) compact covariance descriptors of appearance and motion features used in sparse coding framework to recognize realistic actions and gestures, and (b) a Lie-algebra based representation of dominant camera motion present in video shots which can be used as a complementary feature for video analysis. In the next level, we propose an (c) efficient maximum likelihood estimate based representation from low-level features computed from videos which demonstrates state of the art performance in large scale visual concept detection, and finally, we propose to (d) model temporal interactions between concepts detected in video shots through two new discriminative feature spaces derived from Linear dynamical systems which eventually boosts event recognition performance. In all cases, we conduct thorough experiments to demonstrate promising performance gains over some of the prominent approaches.

Category and Subject Descriptors: H.4 [Information Systems Applications] : Miscellaneous

Keywords: Complex Event recognition, Multimedia Event Detection, Covariance Matrices, Lie Algebra, Riemannian manifolds, Cinematographic Techniques, Shot classification, Video Descriptors, Maximum Likelihood Estimates, Linear Dynamical Systems, Block Hankel matrices

1. INTRODUCTION & MOTIVATION

Hundreds of hours of multimedia content are uploaded in video sharing portals everyday. Most of these videos are captured by amateur users with limited cinematographic knowledge, and are subject to camera motion, background clutter and frequent illumination changes. Usually these videos depict high-level social events - such as a music concert, birthday party or instructional events such as cooking a recipe or teaching a piano lesson. Thus, sifting through such enormous collections for a specific event is a crucial task and is often painstakingly frustrating given the technological maturity of current video browsing algorithms. Most algorithms, rely heavily on the generosity of the uploader to provide meaningful textual labels relevant to the uploaded video content. Since such textual labels are frequently noisy [10, 11], automatic analysis of such videos are gradually attracting a lot of researchers from computer vision and multimedia communities.

One task within the realm of automatic video content analysis is the recognition of complex events contained in the videos. The goal of complex event recognition is to automatically detect high-level events in a given video sequence. In addition to the obvious benefit of making video search and retrieval more efficient and rewarding experience for the user, tracking user interest based on the video content they watch, may (a) **promote effective advertisement** of certain products. Also, such rich automatic semantic description of videos can help broadcast agencies predict important statistics such as virality of views, geographical location of viewers etc. moments after videos are uploaded – thereby (b) **optimizing broadcast channel bandwidth**. Furthermore, it would enable human observers with (c) **semantically rich textual summary of a video** in a relatively short duration without substantial human intervention, for rapid analysis purposes.

MM'13, October 21–25, 2013, Barcelona, Spain.
Copyright 2013 ACM 978-1-4503-2404-5/13/10 ...$15.00.
http://www.sheridanprinting.com/acm/sigmm2/sigmm2.cfm?eid=5E5E01040653.

2. RECOGNITION OF COMPLEX EVENTS

High-level or complex events are long-term spatio-temporal object interactions that happen under certain scene settings. However, there are several technical challenges involved in understanding complex events from unconstrained videos. Some of them are listed in the following section.

2.1 Technical Challenges

Current approaches rely heavily on classifier-based methods employing directly computable low-level features from videos. Research strongly suggests the joint use of multiple features [6] such as static frame-based features, spatio-temporal features and acoustic features. Since these low-level features are designed with more controlled conditions in mind [2, 9], it is not clearly understood [3–5] if they are capable of capturing discriminative yet relevant information from diverse open-source videos.

Secondly, after features are computed, they are typically quantized into "video words" and each video is reduced to a histogram popularly known as bag-of-X representation (X being a feature modality). Classifiers are trained on these histograms with event labels to obtain models that can be used for testing videos with unknown labels. However, even with promising retrieval results [4, 5],

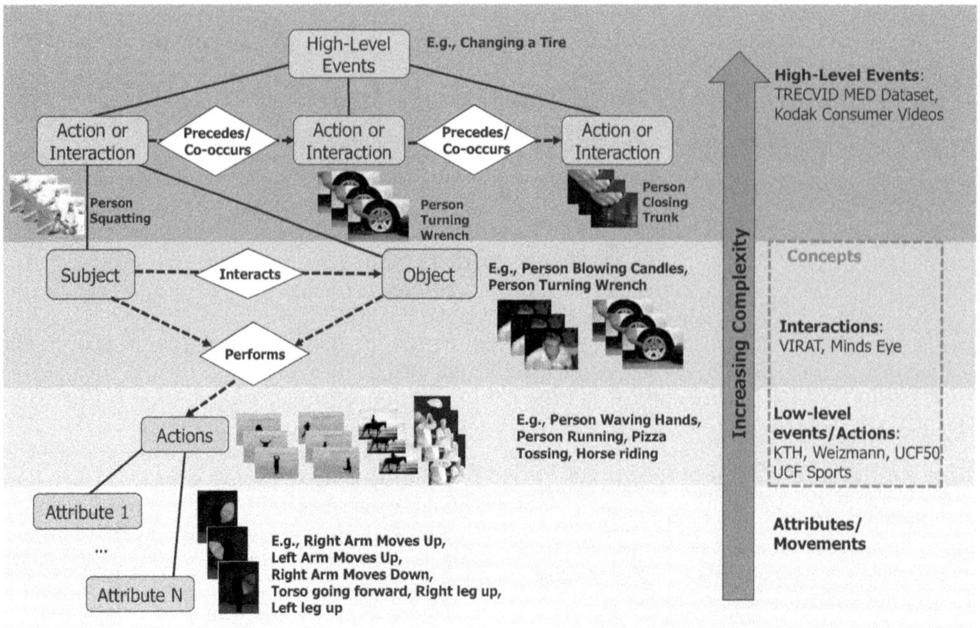

Figure 1: A hierarchical decomposition as proposed in [6] of complex events, with increased complexity from bottom to top. This bottom-up decomposition helps dividing the original problem of event recognition into tractable and simpler sub-problems with richer semantic understanding.

these methods suffer from the usual disadvantages of quantization used in converting raw features to discrete codewords. Alternatively, X can be replaced by mid-level concepts in the bag-of-X representation to obtain a semantically richer representation of a video [3–6]. A concept can be visualized as a spatial or spatio-temporal entity describing one of the following: (a) object (car, human etc.), (b) scene (forest, beach etc.), (c) action (jumping, running) and, (d) interaction (person riding a bike). Nevertheless these representations are semantically superior, they are unable to capture temporal order between concepts which may be useful for predicting the nature of events and drawing a textual summary of the same (motivation (c) in Section 1).

Thus, to solve this enormous problem, a systematic decomposition of an event is extremely necessary, which not only enables solving simpler and tractable problems but also facilitates developing a better semantic understanding of complex events. We propose the hierarchical decomposition in Fig. 1 appropriate in this context. Through the rest of this proposal, we propose how individual components of the hierarchy in Fig. 1 can be improved to improve the overall performance of recognition of complex events.

2.2 Design of Novel Features

Within the purview of this effort, we explore two complementary sources of information to design features that are fast to compute and also useful for realistic video analysis. Our first feature is computed from covariance of low-level appearance and motion cues obtained from all pixels in a short video clip (typically 20 frames) while the next feature encapsulates ambient camera motion present during the video capture process.

The **semi-global clip-level descriptor** is a concise representation of a temporal window/clip of subsequent frames from a video rather than localized spatio-temporal patches, which eliminates the use of specific detectors. The descriptor is based on covariance of complementary low-level motion (optical flow and their derivatives, vorticity, divergence etc.) and appearance cues (first and second order derivatives of pixel intensities etc.). Since covariance matrices capture joint statistics between individual low-level feature modalities, they automatically transform our random vector of samples into statistically uncorrelated random variables, leading to a compact representation of a video.

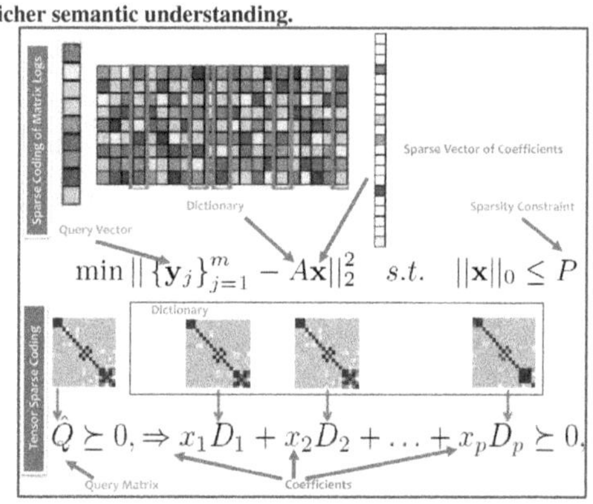

Figure 2: Two of our proposed sparse coding based classification techniques are illustrated here with the top one using matrix log descriptors as input, while the bottom one operating on covariance matrices directly.

Since these descriptors are computed on a dense temporal sampling basis, most of these can be expressed using only a few discriminative ones to form a dictionary, which can be randomly selected from a collection of labeled videos. This motivates us to resort to sparse coding based classification strategies (Fig. 2) instead of regular SVM classification strategies. Sparse coding on covariance matrices can be nicely formulated as a determinant maximization problem where each query covariance matrix is approximated using a linear combination of dictionary elements. Since vector addition and scalar multiplication of covariance matrices is not closed, additional modifications need to be performed in the original sparse coding formulation which expects a query to be expressed as linear combination of dictionary elements. A schematic illustration of these methods are provided in Fig. 2.

Using our techniques we achieve high recognition rates on the UCF50 [1], and HMDB51 [7]) datasets, which are considered benchmarks for action recognition in unconstrained scenarios. A summary of our results is provided in Tab. 1, where the bottom row

[1] http://server.cs.ucf.edu/~vision/data/UCF50.rar

Method	Desc.	Datasets KTH	UCF50	HMDB51
BoVW+SVM	HOG-HOF [8]	92.0%	48.0%	20.2%
BoVW+SVM	COV	81.3%	39.3%	18.4%
SVM	COV	82.4%	40.4%	18.6%
SVM	LCOV	86.2%	47.4%	21.03%
OMP	LCOV	88.2%	53.5%	24.09%
TSC	MAT	93.4%	57.8%	27.16%

Table 1: Comparison with the state-of-the-art methods: Last two rows show proposed methods against different representations and classification strategies.

shows two variants of our method, while the top four rows indicate conventional approaches with different feature representations.

Camera-motion is often an under-exploited cue when it comes to the analysis of videos of our concern. Complex events like "Attempting a board trick" and "Parkour" usually have a lot of jittery camera motion coupled with pan and tilt motions. Similarly, videos depicting events such as "Wedding Ceremony" and "Birthday Party" are mostly captured by stationary, tripod-mounted cameras with limited pan and some amount of zoom. The objective of this effort is to investigate an efficient set of methodologies, that can be leveraged to represent videos in terms of their ambient camera motion in large scale, without resorting to computationally prohibitive full-3D reconstruction techniques.

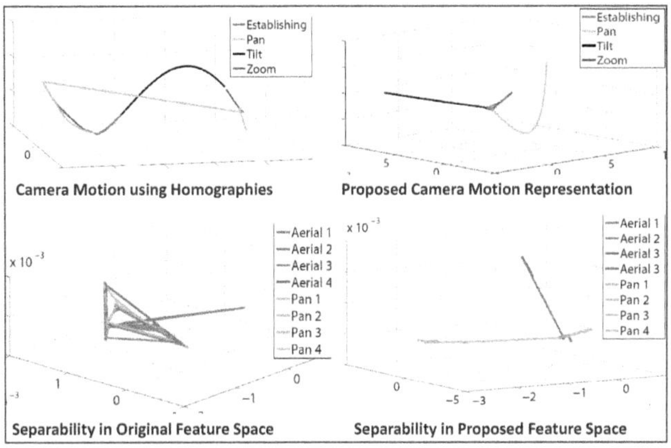

Figure 3: Discriminativity of our proposed representation of shots in contrast to pure frame-to-frame homographies. Figures on top show four classes of shots (Establishing, pan, tilt and zoom) in both feature space. Bottom figures show clear separability of "aerial" and "pan" shot classes in the proposed feature space.

We devise this novel representation on top of inter-frame homographies which serve as coarse indicators of the camera motion. Next, using Lie algebra of projective groups, we transform the homography matrices to an intermediate vector space that preserves the intrinsic geometric structure of the transformation (Fig. 3). Multiple time series are then constructed from these mappings. Features computed on these time series are used for discriminative classification of video shots. Our proposed camera motion based shot classification outperforms previously published algorithms and achieves comparable performance to an implementation that involves recovery of structure from motion on our dataset of eight shot categories. This encourages us to evaluate our method for complex event recognition in challenging datasets [3, 4], which demonstrates conclusive evidence towards its applicability in open-source video analysis (Fig. 4).

2.3 Intermediate representations

Designing intermediate representations on top raw features is very crucial for any recognition algorithm to handle outliers efficiently and reduce processing of large volumes of high dimensional data. We present an efficient alternative [1] to the traditional

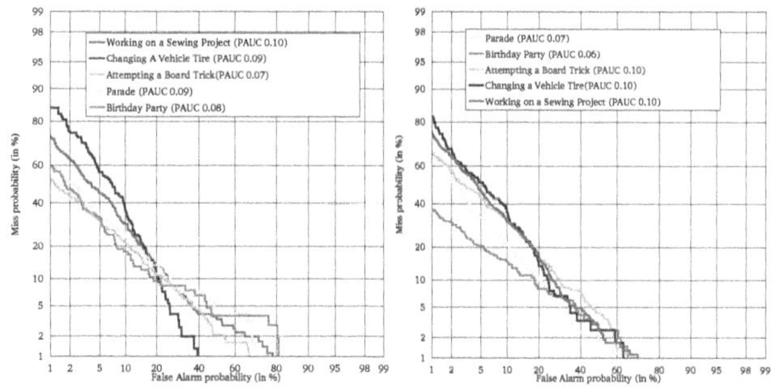

(a) (b)

Figure 4: Detection-Error Trade off (DET) curves for (a) 5 event classes best represented using our camera motion based features. (b) Curves for corresponding event classes obtained using Bag of SIFT features. .

vocabulary based on BoVW methods used for visual classification tasks. Our representation (Fig. 5) is both conceptually and computationally superior to the bag-of-visual words: (1) We iteratively generate a **Maximum Likelihood estimate** of an instance given a set of characteristic features in contrast to the BoVW methods (2) We randomly sample a set of characteristic features called **anchors** instead of employing computation intensive clustering algorithms used during the vocabulary generation step of BoVW methods. Since our proposed representation is based on MLE over a large set of supporting datapoints, we are able to capture more diversity in the data as opposed to conventional vector quantization based representations. This is indicated in Tab. 2.

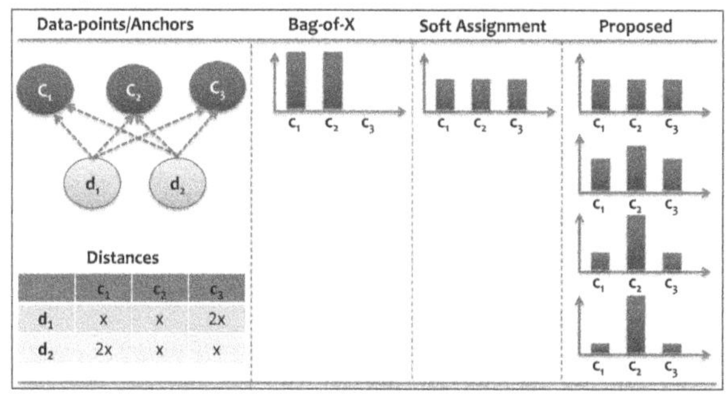

Figure 5: Toy example contrasting the proposed representation against traditional BoVW and soft-assignment BoVW. Note that the proposed representation is initially identical to soft BoW but diverges since it maximizes an instance-level likelihood score.

We integrate the above representation scheme to detect semantically accurate, human-understandable mid-level spatio-temporal concepts for modeling complex events. To this end, we introduce a benchmark dataset for spatio-temporal concepts, explicitly catering to the event recognition problem. This dataset consists of 62 mutually exclusive, concept categories over 10,000 annotated audio visual samples extracted from NIST's TRECVID MED 2011 event corpus that replicates complex events observed in common video footages. Detectors are trained on the proposed representation [1] specific to each concept category on different information modalities (motion, static, and audio). This approach achieved respectable target detection [4] in the annual NIST TRECVID Multimedia Event Detection 2011 competition.

2.4 Formulating complex event models

Just as low-level features and the associated intermediate representations are crucial for recognition, efficient complex event models can be created if temporal dynamics are effectively exploited. To this end we propose the use of Linear Dynamical systems to create complex events. We hypothesize that a video depicting a complex event, can be expressed as an ordered vector time-series,

	Representation			
	Bag-of-Features		Anchors	
Modality	Avg. PAUC	AP(%)	Avg. PAUC	AP(%)
Static [SIFT]	0.2203	22.01	0.1949	23.52
Static [GIST]	0.2718	18.21	0.2223	18.15
Motion [Dollar]	0.1948	16.22	0.1735	19.24
Motion [STIP]	0.1869	17.31	0.1878	19.42
Motion [MBH]	0.1721	19.21	0.1639	20.21
Audio [MFCC]	0.3121	11.13	0.2936	11.12
Fusion [SIFT+MBH]	0.1615	19.41	0.1524	21.02

Table 2: Spatio temporal concept detector performance evaluation summary: We summarize the performance of 62 concept detectors constructed from BoW (Baseline) and our proposed representation [1], across different feature modalities. Two different metrics – average area under DET curve (Avg. AUC), and average precision (AP) are used for evaluation. The lower the AUC measure (on a scale of 0 – 1) the more reliable the detector while for AP, the greater indicates better performance.

where each time-step is a vector containing confidences returned by a set of pre-trained spatio-temporal concept detectors [4]. Observing carefully, even for two visually similar events as shown in Fig. 6, we notice subtle differences in the concept evolution pattern for these two events – Repairing vs Cleaning an appliance.

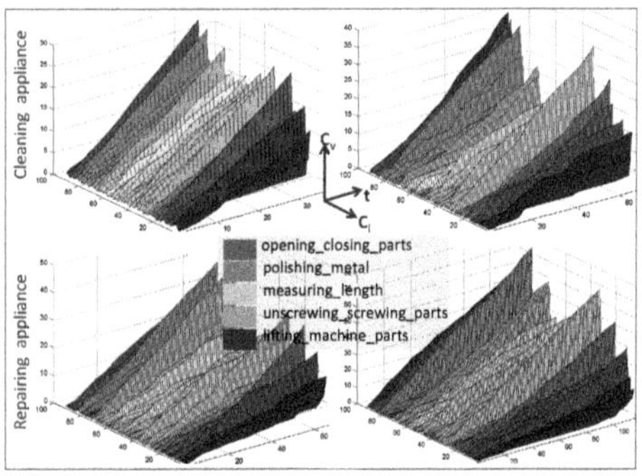

Figure 6: Temporal dynamics of spatio-temporal concepts within a pair of complex events. Each column illustrates cumulative distribution of concept detector responses from a video (color coded to enhance readability). Top 5 relevant concepts in both events are indicated as inset legend.

Hence, these evolving sequences can be modeled efficiently using linear dynamical systems (LDS). Now, direct estimation of LDS parameters – hidden state vector, state transition matrix etc. Conventional techniques use generative approaches – variants of discrete and continuous hidden markov models (HMM) to achieve this, however they are extremely sensitive to noise in training data. Since, concept detector responses are noisy, we propose to use alternative strategies that bypass this direct parameter estimation step. One technique is to construct a block-Hankel matrix for a vector time series which captures dependencies between each observation vector, within the context of the entire time-series. Eigenspaces of this matrix contains vital information which can be used to compute discriminative features to train any linear SVM classifier model, specific to a given event. Also, we can obtain meaningful statistics - such as periodicity, frequency, shift etc. and cluster the vector time-series into meaningful harmonic categories. Tab. 3 demonstrates the merits of our temporal models – Hankel Matrix based descriptors (HNK), Temporal Signatures (TS), and Late Fusion of HNK and TS based classifiers (FUSED), against some well known approaches – Discrete Cosine Transform based features computed from vector time-series (DCT), Discrete HMM (DHMM), and Continuous HMM (CHMM); from some preliminary experiments on TRECVID MED 2011 events collection dataset.

	Avg. Prec. from Method					
Event	DCT	DHMM	CHMM	HNK	TS	FUSED
E001	0.46	0.66	0.72	0.85	0.87	0.89
E002	0.44	0.64	0.71	0.89	0.91	0.91
E003	0.43	0.32	0.52	0.68	0.71	0.73
E004	0.39	0.39	0.39	0.61	0.59	0.59
E005	0.36	0.38	0.37	0.58	0.55	0.59
E006	0.34	0.38	0.51	0.87	0.87	0.85
E007	0.43	0.41	0.48	0.77	0.74	0.76
E008	0.67	0.69	0.71	0.88	0.89	0.87
E009	0.44	0.48	0.49	0.83	0.86	0.86
E010	0.38	0.48	0.51	0.74	0.75	0.75
E011	0.51	0.62	0.63	0.79	0.71	0.74
E012	0.37	0.73	0.68	0.78	0.76	0.78
E013	0.31	0.35	0.41	0.84	0.88	0.86
E014	0.34	0.46	0.48	0.68	0.68	0.67
E015	0.32	0.31	0.38	0.58	0.57	0.59
mAP	0.41	0.48	0.53	0.75	0.76	0.76

Table 3: Average Precision scores (MED11EC) Performance of our proposed temporal features with contemporary methods that model temporal interactions on all 15 events in the MED11EC dataset.

3. CONCLUSION

We presented a set of novel methodologies to perform semantic analysis of web videos. We introduced a principled decomposition of these videos into hierarchical components, highlighting our contributions in three key stages. As part of the first stage, we introduced two novel semi-global features which can be used to capture complementary information from videos. After that, we proposed an intermediate representation replacing the Bag-of-words model and demonstrated how this representation can be used to detect semantic concepts from videos. In the concluding section, we insinuated two discriminative feature spaces to model temporal interactions between detected concepts which can be efficiently integrated into existing classifiers for complex event recognition. In principle, the stages in the bottom-up approach suggested here, can be integrated in a common framework to perform semantic analysis of Internet videos.

4. REFERENCES

[1] S. Bhattacharya, R. Sukthankar, R. Jin, and M. Shah. A probabilistic representation for efficient large scale visual recognition tasks. In *IEEE CVPR*, pages 2593–2600, 2011.

[2] M. Blank, L. Gorelick, E. Shechtman, M. Irani, and R. Basri. Actions as space-time shapes. In *IEEE ICCV*, pages 1395–1402, 2005.

[3] H. Cheng, J. Liu, A. Hauptmann, S. Bhattacharya, M. Shah, and G. Friedland. SRI-Sarnoff AURORA System at TRECVID 2012: Multimedia Event Detection and Recounting. *NIST TRECVID and Workshop*, Dec. 2012.

[4] H. Cheng, H. S. Sawhney, A. Hauptmann, M. Shah, S. Bhattacharya, M. Witbrock, G. Friedland, R. Manmatha, and J. Allan. Team SRI-Sarnoff's AURORA System @ TRECVID 2011. *NIST TRECVID and Workshop*, Dec. 2011.

[5] Y. Jiang, X. Zeng, G. Ye, S. Bhattacharya, D. Ellis, M. Shah, and S. Chang. Columbia-UCF TRECVID 2010 multimedia event detection: Combining multiple modalities, contextual concepts, and temporal matching. *NIST TRECVID Workshop*, Dec. 2010.

[6] Y.-G. Jiang, S. Bhattacharya, S.-F. Chang, and M. Shah. High-level event recognition in unconstrained videos. *IJMIR*, November 2012.

[7] H. Kuehne, H. Jhuang, E. Garrote, T. Poggio, and T. Serre. HMDB: a large video database for human motion recognition. In *IEEE ICCV*, 2011.

[8] I. Laptev and T. Lindeberg. Space-time interest points. In *IEEE ICCV*, pages 432–439, 2003.

[9] C. Schuldt, I. Laptev, and B. Caputo. Recognizing human actions: A local SVM approach. In *IEEE ICPR*, pages 32–36, 2004.

[10] Y. Song, M. Zhao, J. Yagnik, and X. Wu. Taxonomic classification for web-based videos. In *IEEE CVPR*, pages 871–878, 2010.

[11] Z. Wang, M. Zhao, Y. Song, S. Kumar, and B. Li. YouTubeCat: Learning to categorize wild web videos. In *IEEE CVPR*, pages 879–886, 2010.

Motion Compensated Compressed Domain Watermarking*

Tanima Dutta
Department of Computer Science and Engineering
Indian Institute of Technology Guwahati, India
d.tanima@iitg.ac.in

ABSTRACT

The security has become an important issue in multimedia applications. The embedding of watermark bits in compressed domain is less computationally expensive as full decoding and re-encoding is not required. The motion coherency is an essential property to resist temporal frame averaging based attacks. The design of motion compensated embedding method in compressed domain is a challenging task. As far we know, no such embedding method is explored yet. In this paper, we propose a motion compensated compressed domain embedding method within a short video neighborhood that gives acceptable visual quality, embedding capacity, and robustness. The simulation results show the effectiveness of the proposed method.

Categories and Subject Descriptors

K.4.1 [**Computers and Society**]: Public Policy Issues; K.5.1 [**Legal Aspects of Computing**]: Software Protection—*Copyrights;Proprietary rights*

General Terms

Legal aspects, Security, Performance

Keywords

Video watermarking, compressed domain embedding, motion compensation, temporal frame averaging

1. INTRODUCTION

In several multimedia applications, security has become an important research topic. Video watermarking is a technique of hiding a secret signature into digital videos. Video watermarking methods must be robust *i.e.* subsequent processing of watermarked video should not weaken the detection of embedded data. The videos are mostly stored and transmitted in a compressed format that enhances the importance of compressed domain watermarking. Embedding watermarks in compressed domain is less computationally expensive as full decoding and re-encoding is not required for watermark embedding. Many video compression standards have emerged in the last few years. The aim of each standard is to provide more compressed data with better visual quality. H.264 is regarded as the most efficient compression standard used in a wide range of applications.

Many watermarking schemes for H.264 Advanced Video Codec (AVC) have been emerged in recent years. Noorkami and Mersereau have proposed a non-blind watermarking technique [9] to embed watermark in I-frames using the watson visual model, which is computationally expensive. The non-blind technique [9] is extended for P-frames [8] for better visual quality and embedded in all nonzero quantized residuals of P-frames. Full decoding re-encoding of the compressed video is required [9, 8] for watermark embedding. The location map is used to decrease synchronization error. Frame drop or alter attack is not handled in [9, 8].

Mansouri *et al.* have presented a blind compressed domain method to embed in I-frames of H.264/AVC videos [7]. The embedding method has changed the nonzero coefficients to zero value for hiding the watermark. Esen and Alantan [5] have designed a data hiding framework that selects the embedding region using the Forbidden Zone Data Hiding and exploits the error correction capability feature of Reed Solomon codes to make it robust. In [3], frame drop or alter attack is handled using the error correction capability feature of Reed Solomon codes.

1.1 Motivation

In [9, 7], the authors have embedded in I-frames. Embedding in I-frames degrade the visual quality significantly because embedding error in I-frame propagates in the remaining uncoded (not yet encoded) blocks of that I-frame due to intra prediction and P-frames and B-frames due to inter prediction in that Group of Pictures (GOP). In P-frames and B-frames, the embedding error propagates only in uncoded P-frames and B-frames in that GOP. So, embedding in such frames will provide better visual quality than I-frame embedding [8]. However, I-frames have the higher embedding capacity compared to P-frames and B-frames. In H.264/AVC compressed videos, one I-frame occurs in each GOP, the number of P-frames or B-frames are more than I-frames so embedding capacity of such frames can be exploited. To get more compressed video, the number of B-frames are kept more than P-frames in a GOP. However, embedding in such frames may be prone to frame drop or alter attack.

Frame drop or alter attack is quite common nowadays. It can be intentional or unintentional attack. Sometime due to

*(Produces the permission block, and copyright information).

MM'13, October 21–25, 2013, Barcelona, Spain.
ACM 978-1-4503-2404-5/13/10.
http://dx.doi.org/10.1145/2502081.2502211 .

less channel bandwidth or delay, some B-frames are dropped or attackers may drop some B-frames to make the exact extraction of watermark complicated. In addition, handling such attacks in compressed domain is a real complex task. In watermark estimation attack (WEA), the attacker removes the watermark completely from watermarked video. The watermark estimation attack is mainly performed using the temporal frame averaging. Nowadays, motion coherency is an desirable property to resist temporal frame averaging.

Pankajakshan *et al.* have designed a tool to check whether a video sequence contains any motion incoherent component using features extracted from frame prediction error [10]. In order to withstand temporal frame averaging along the motion axis, motion coherency has recently been identified as a desirable property for embedding watermarks within videos [10]. It is difficult to predict the impact of change in motion information in compressed video, so resistance from frame drop or alter attack and collusion attack is a challenging job. As far we know, no such compressed embedding method based on B-frames, where frame drop or alter attack is handled, is well explored yet. Moreover, none of them have handled watermark estimation attack [10] in compressed domain.

1.2 Our Contribution

The aim of this paper is to design an compressed domain embedding method that would provide acceptable visual quality and robustness. It would also be capable to withstand frame drop or alter attack and watermark estimation attack in compressed domain without using error correcting codes (unlike [5, 3]). In this paper, we propose a compressed domain embedding method, where the watermark is embedded in each motion compensated temporally averaged low pass frame obtained from B-frames of a GOP. Motion coherent 4×4 blocks are detected and trajectory of both motion and static blocks are determined. The low pass frame is extracted based on motion coherent blocks on B-frames of a GOP. High pass frames are also estimated. Watermark embedding is done using spread spectrum techniques on all nonzero quantized coefficients in low pass frames. B-frames are reconstructed from watermarked low pass frames and unwatermarked high pass frames. The complexity measure of the proposed method is elaborated. Simulation results show that embedding capacity, visual quality, and robustness against recompression error give acceptable results.

The rest of the paper is organized as follows. The proposed method is described in Section 2. Simulation results are given in Section 3. Finally, Section 4 concludes the paper.

2. PROPOSED METHOD

The goal of this paper is to design a motion compensated compressed domain watermarking for low bit compressed videos like H.264. Within a *short video neighborhood* (SVN), most video frames are visually coherent and no scene change is detected. The *motion compensated* blocks are those which have coherent motion within a SVN. A method for detection of motion compensated blocks is performed in compressed domain to avoid further decoding and re-encoding of video sequences. So the proposed method is computationally less expensive. To get more compressed low bit video, I-frame and B-frames are only coded to form a GOP.

The complete process of motion compensated compressed domain watermarking is performed in following steps. First, motion compensated blocks are detected in Section 2.1. Next, extraction of low pass frame based on motion compensated blocks and high pass frames in each GOP is performed in Section 2.2 and Section 2.3, respectively. Last, the embedding and extraction methods are proposed in Section 2.4.

2.1 Motion Compensated Block Detection

In this section, motion compensated blocks are detected within a SVN. The method of finding motion compensated blocks is given in the Procedure : Motion Compensated Block Detection. Unlike [4], motion coherent blocks are estimated for B-frames in this paper. Motion vectors of each non-overlapping blocks of B-frames are normalized to ensure that it point directly to the location in the immediate previous frame [6]. Since H.264/AVC supports multiple reference frames, therefore, normalization simplifies the referencing relationship. The normalized motion vectors are smoothened using 3×3 median filter. Motion vectors of intra-coded blocks in B-frames are zero so motion vectors of such blocks are estimated from neighboring blocks [13]. Accumulation operator [6] is used for all motion vectors to enhance coherent motion and suppress noisy motion. Accumulated motion vectors which have a magnitude of zero before accumulation are removed. Using spatial and temporal confidence measure [12] discontinuity in motion magnitude and direction is checked. The motion compensated blocks in the hall monitor and foreman video are depicted in Figure 1 and Figure 2, respectively.

(a) (b)

Figure 1: Red boxes indicate two motion compensated blocks in (a) 2nd frame and (b) 13th frame in 7th GOP and 9th GOP, respectively in the hall monitor video.

2.2 Extraction of Low Pass Frames

Embedding can be done in each low pass frame extracted using motion compensated temporal averaging (MC-TFA) [10] on B-frames in a GOP. MC-TFA is performed on B-frames in a GOP based on accumulated motion vectors of each block in B-frames obtained in Procedure : Motion Compensated Block Detection. All intra and inter predicted luminance blocks have accumulated motion vector. After detection of motion coherent blocks in B-frames, all blocks having zero (static) and nonzero (motion) motion vector have a motion trajectory. Based on this MC-TFA is performed over all B-frames in a GOP to extract a low pass frame. Motion compensated temporal averaging is estimated block wise. Assume N and L be the number of B-frames and the low pass frame extracted in a GOP based on MC-TFA, respectively. Therefore, the proposed low pass frame (L) can be obtained using [10] as follows:

$$L = \frac{\text{motion compensated temporal summation } (B_1 \ldots B_N)}{N} \quad (1)$$

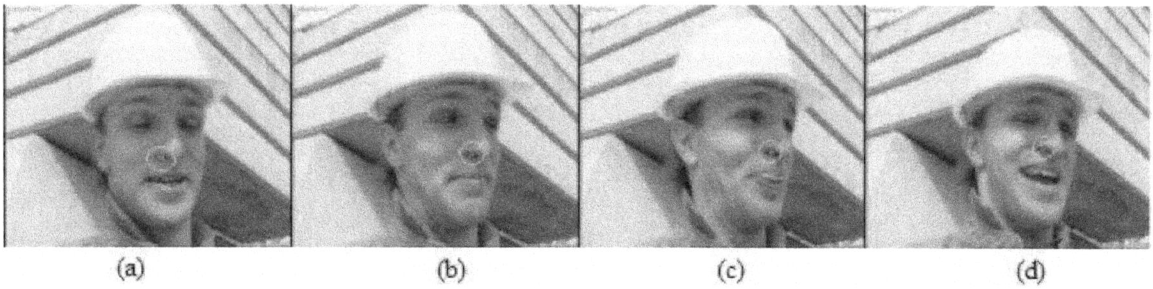

Figure 2: Red box shows a motion compensated block in (a) 2nd frame, (b) 5th frame, (c) 8th frame, and (d) 13th frame in 1st GOP in the foreman video.

```
Procedure : Motion Compensated Block Detection
Data: Unwatermarked Video
Result: Motion Compensated Blocks
foreach short video neighborhood (SVN) do      /* SVN not are accessed yet */
    foreach frame in a SVN do      /* frames not are accessed yet */
        Divide B-frames into non-overlapping blocks;
        Calculate motion vectors for all blocks in B-frames;
    foreach block in B-frames do      /* blocks are yet to access */
        Normalize each motion vectors [6] ;      /* Motion vector normalization */
        Smooth all normalized motion vectors by using a 3 × 3 median filter [2];      /* Median filtering */
        Estimate motion vector for intra-coded blocks from neighboring blocks [13] ;      /* Intra-coded blocks */
    Assign motion vector to I-frames by interpolating motion vectors of the nearest B-frame;      /* I-frame motion vector */
    foreach block within a SVN do      /* blocks are yet to access */
        Apply accumulation operator [6] to all motion vectors;      /* Accumulation process */
        Use spatial and temporal confidence measure [12];      /* Confidence measure */
```

where $B_1 \ldots B_N$ denotes the B-frames in a GOP in the order in which they are encoded.

2.3 Extraction of High Pass Frames

High pass frames ares extracted from motion compensated temporal difference between every two consecutive B-frames in a GOP. Motion compensated temporal difference is estimated block wise. The number of high pass frames extracted are $N-1$. Assume $H[k]$ denotes the motion compensated temporal difference between k^{th} B-frame and $k+1^{th}$ B-frame of a GOP, where $k \in N$. The kth B-frame and $k+1^{th}$ B-frame of a GOP are denoted by B_k and B_{k+1}, respectively. The proposed high pass frame can be extracted using [10] as follows:

$$H[k] = \text{motion compensated temporal difference } (B_k - B_{k+1}) \tag{2}$$

2.4 Watermark Embedding and Extraction

A bipolar invisible watermark sequence (0,1) is used for embedding. Embedding is done in all nonzero quantized residuals of intra and inter predicted blocks of motion compensated temporally averaged low pass frame using spread spectrum techniques [1]. Perturbing zero residuals will increase the video bit rate. The watermark embedding is performed as follows:

$$C^W = C(1+\alpha W), \qquad C \neq 0 \tag{3}$$

where α, C, and C^W denote the watermark strength, original coefficient, and watermarked coefficient. The value of α lies between 0 to 1. B-frames of a GOP are reconstructed from the watermarked motion compensated temporally averaged low pass frame L and high pass frames $H[1 \ldots N-1]$ of that GOP.

The watermark extraction is performed at the decoder after entropy decoding. The extraction procedure is exactly the reverse process of watermark embedding. The watermark is extracted as follows:

$$W^* = \frac{C^W - C}{\alpha}, \qquad C^W \neq 0, \;\; C \neq 0 \tag{4}$$

where W^*, C^W, and C denote extracted watermark, coefficient of the watermarked video, and original coefficient, respectively.

2.5 Watermark Similarity Measure

It is highly unlikely that the extracted watermark W^* will be identical to the original watermark W. Even the act of re-compressing the watermarked video for delivery will cause W^* to deviate from W. We measure the similarity of W^* and W by [1] as

$$sim(W, W^*) = \frac{W^* \times W}{\sqrt{W^* \times W}} \tag{5}$$

where $sim(W, W^*)$ denotes the similarity measure between W and W^* and $\times$ denotes an operator. With the increase in similarity measure, the robustness of the proposed method increases. In other words, $sim(W, W^*)$ measures the robustness of the proposed method.

3. EXPERIMENTAL RESULTS

The proposed method is implemented using H.264/AVC reference software JM 17.2 [11]. The proposed method is evaluated in foreman and hall monitor videos. The video sequence is in Quarter Common Intermediate format (QCIF) where frame resolution is 176×144. Frame Rate is 30 frames per second. The intra period is 16 and Quantization Parameter is 24 for both I-frame and B-frame. The fast full search in JM is employed and all intra and inter prediction sizes are enabled. Video sequences of 160 frames and payload=$\{200, 250, 300\}$ are taken. In our experiments, the value of $\alpha = \{0.1, 0.2\}$.

The number of coefficients available for embedding in the foreman video and the hall monitor video are depicted in

Figure 3. The Figure 3 illustrates that embedding capacity or number of coefficient available for embedding is acceptable.

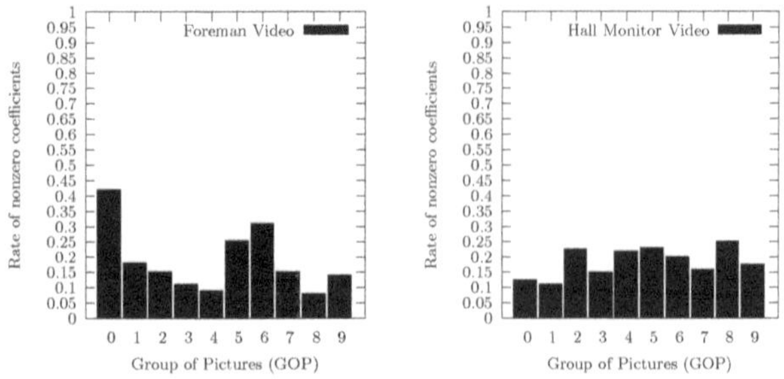

Figure 3: GOP wise embedding capacity in the foreman video (left) and hall monitor video (right).

The visual quality of the watermarked video is measured using Peak Signal-to-Noise Ratio (PSNR) for video sequences, such as, {Foreman and Hall Monitor}. The bit error rate is used for evaluating the robustness of the proposed scheme against image processing attacks.

It is clear from Figure 4 and Table 1 that with the increase in α, the PSNR decrease and robustness increases. However, the result shown in Figure 4 give acceptable visual quality. PSNR and robustness results at $\alpha = 0.1$ show better results than [7] and [8], while at $\alpha = 0.2$, the results are comparable. Similarly, Table 1 shows robustness against image processing attacks at $\alpha = 0.1, 0.2$.

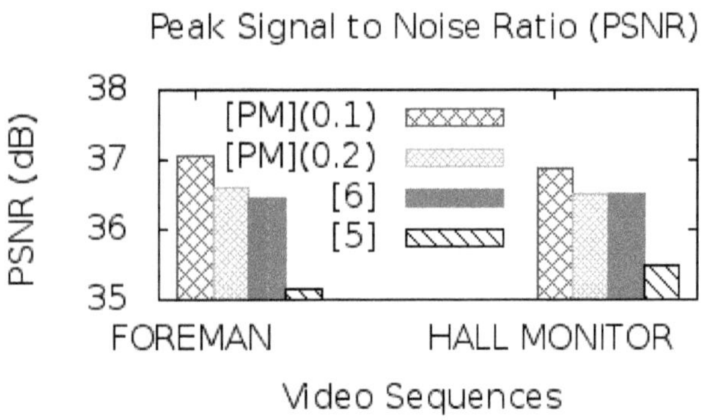

Figure 4: PSNR for (a) $\alpha = 0.1$ and (b) $\alpha = 0.2$.

Table 1: Robustness against three different attacks.

Videos	NoiseId	[7]	[8]	[PM](0.1)	[PM](0.2)
Foreman	(a)	72	65	75	78
	(b)	74	69	74	79
	(c)	71	67	73	76
Hall Monitor	(a)	70	66	73	75
	(b)	72	68	73	76
	(c)	73	69	75	78

Attacks	NoiseId
Salt and Pepper Noise	(a)
Circular Averaging Filter	(b)
Gaussian Filter	(c)

4. CONCLUSIONS

In this paper, a compressed domain watermarking method based on motion coherency is proposed for low bit compressed videos like H.264/AVC. Low pass frame and high frames are extracted for each short video neighborhood. The watermark is embedded in the low pass frame. Experimental results show the effectiveness of the proposed method. The proposed method can be further evaluated against watermark estimation attack and frame drop or alter attack in future.

5. ACKNOWLEDGMENTS

I would like to thank Tata Consultancy Services (TCS) for their support through the TCS Research Scholar Program for perusing my Ph.D. Degree.

6. REFERENCES

[1] I. Cox, J. Kilian, F. Leighton, and T. Shamoon. Secure spread spectrum watermarking for multimedia. *Image Processing, IEEE Transactions on*, 6(12):1673–1687, 1997.

[2] P. Dong, Y. Xia, L. Zhuo, and D. Feng. Real-time moving object segmentation and tracking for H.264/AVC surveillance videos. In *Proceedings of ICIP*, pages 2309–2312, 2011.

[3] T. Dutta, A. Sur, and S. Nandi. A Robust Compressed Domain Video Watermarking in P-frames with Controlled Bit Rate Increase. In *Proceedings of NCC*, pages 1–5, 2013.

[4] T. Dutta, A. Sur, and S. Nandi. MCRD: Motion Coherent Region Detection In H.264 Compressed Video. In *Proceedings of ICME*, 2013.

[5] E. Esen and A. Alatan. Robust Video Data Hiding Using Forbidden Zone Data Hiding and Selective Embedding. *IEEE Transactions on Circuits and Systems for Video Technology*, 21(8):1130–1138, 2011.

[6] Z. Liu, Y. Lu, and Z. Zhang. Real-time spatiotemporal segmentation of video objects in the H.264 compressed domain. *Journal of Visual Comunication and Image Representation*, 18(3):275–290, 2007.

[7] A. Mansouri, A. Aznaveh, F. Torkamani, and F. Kurugollu. A Low Complexity Video Watermarking in H.264 Compressed Domain. *IEEE Trans. on Information Forensics and Security*, 5(4):649–657, 2010.

[8] M. Noorkami and R. Mersereau. Digital Video Watermarking in P-Frames With Controlled Video Bit-Rate Increase. *IEEE Trans. on Information Forensics and Security*, 3(3):441–455, 2008.

[9] M. Noorkami and R. M. Mersereau. A Framework for Robust Watermarking of H.264-Encoded Video With Controllable Detection Performance. *IEEE Trans. on Information Forensics and Security*, 2(1):14–23, 2007.

[10] V. Pankajakshan, G. Doërr, and P. Bora. Detection of motion-incoherent components in video streams. *IEEE Trans. on Information Forensics and Security*, 4(1):49–58, 2009.

[11] K. Sahring. H.264 Reference Software Group, 2008.

[12] R. Wang, H. Zhang, and Y. Zhang. A confidence measure based moving object extraction system built for compressed domain. In *Proceedings of ISCAS*, volume 5, pages 21–24, 2000.

[13] T. Wiegand and G. Sullivan. *Advanced video coding for generic audiovisual services.* International Tellecommunication Union, 2003.

Social Interaction Detection Using A Multi-sensor Approach

Tian Gan
School of Computing
National University of Singapore
Singapore, 117417
gantian@comp.nus.edu.sg

ABSTRACT

In the context of a social gathering, such as a cocktail party, the memorable moments are often captured by professional photographers or the participants. The latter case is generally undesirable because many participants would rather enjoy the event instead of being occupied by the tedious photo capturing task. Motivated by this scenario, we propose an automated social event photo-capture framework for which, given the multiple sensor data streams and the information from the Web as input, will output the visually appealing photos of the social event. Our proposal consists of three components: (1) social attribute extraction from both the physical space and the cyberspace; (2) social attribute fusion; and (3) active camera control. Current work is presented and we conclude with expected contributions as well as future direction.

Categories and Subject Descriptors

I.2.10 [**Vision and Scene Understanding**]: Video analysis; I.4.8 [**Scene Analysis**]: Motion; I.5.4 [**Applications**]: Signal processing

Keywords

Social Interaction, Social Computing, F-formation, Video Analytics, Behavior Modeling

1. INTRODUCTION

In the events of social gathering, such as cocktail party, conference's poster session, etc., the interactions between the event participants are often captured with multiple cameras or smart phones. In many scenarios, the event participants play the role of the photographer, which turns them to become passive observers of the event. This is against the purpose of the social gathering where the participants should enjoy the events. Furthermore, the participants may not capture all the important views due to the fact that no one is willing to passively observe the whole event [2]. Therefore, it would be desirable to have the photos taken by a professional photographer or an automated photo-capture system. Hiring a professional photographer is generally expensive and hence not affordable for most types of social gatherings, such as a small birthday party. With an automated photo-capture system, the cost can be negligible. Moreover, these approaches can be scaled to support closed-door event with the privacy issues, or a live streaming system that shows the latest photo on a public display.

MM'13, October 21–25, 2013, Barcelona, Spain.
ACM 978-1-4503-2404-5/13/10.
http://dx.doi.org/10.1145/2502081.2502212.

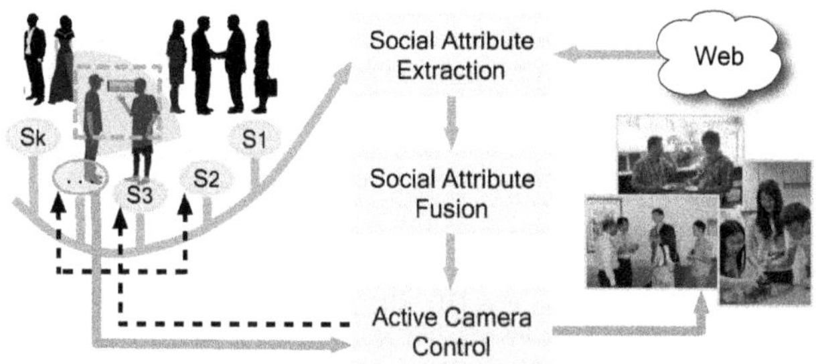

Figure 1: Overview of the proposed automated social event photo-capture framework.

Our proposed framework involves three components as illustrated in Figure 1. Firstly, we extract the social attributes from both the physical space and the cyberspace to characterize the social interaction. Secondly, we fuse these social attributes to identify and rank the interaction spaces. Finally, active camera control is applied for taking visually appealing photos.

The rest of the paper is organized as follows. The related works are discussed in Section 2. In Section 3 we describe the details of our proposed method. The progresse we have made so far is described in Section 4. We list our expected contributions in Section 5. Finally, the main findings and possible future directions are covered in Section 6.

2. RELATED WORK

In recent years, there is growing interest in the detection of social group behavior [1, 4, 6]. Social interaction detection requires modeling of two components: **(1)** individual activities, and **(2)** social relationships between individuals. The literature can be categorized into three approaches. The first category relies on the visual information and statistical models [14, 15, 17], however, its efficacy in real world application is questionable due to the uncontrolled nature of human behavior. The second category utilizes visual and audio data collected from various sensors, and performs multimodal processing to detect interaction [3]. The third category analyzes the social interactions using social behavioral cues [1, 4, 6, 18]. In [18], Vinciarelli *et al.* organized the social behavioral cues into five categories: (i) physical appearance, (ii) gesture and posture, (iii) face and eyes behavior, (iv) vocal behavior, and (v) space and environment. These cues have been recognized in Psychology literature as the most important factors in human judgments [18].

A popular sociological concept F-formation, which exploits the behavioral cue for analyzing social interaction, is more suitable for unconstrained social event scenario. In [1], the social interaction is detected with human spatial patterns. Specifically, they determine whether two persons are interacting with each other when several predefined conditions are satisfied based on human spatial information; and then they accumulate the existence of this relationship over a period of time for interaction detection. However, rule-based method cannot characterize many types of spatial interaction arrangements. For example, the common interaction pattern "side-by-side", in which each person need not to be in the reciprocal FoVs, does not satisfy one of the conditions in this method. Cristani *et al.* [4] designed an F-formation recognizer based on the Hough-voting strategy, which detects the F-formation for each frame independently. Therefore, the temporal information, or the continuous group interactions, is not explored in this work. Hung *et al.* [9] presented an F-formation detection method by formulating the problem in terms of identifying dominant sets. This graph-theoretic detection method is particularly designed for the crowded environment.

In order to obtain an aesthetically optimal view, visual saliency and aesthetic knowledge are commonly utilized for image re-targeting and photography. In [12], Mei *et al.* defined a set of domain-specific capture intention concepts, and built up a comprehensive scheme to track the capture intention of camcorder users. Ni *et al.* [13] developed a learning-based framework which discovers the underlying aesthetic photographic compositional structures, and utilizes these implicitly shared knowledge among the professional photographers for aesthetically optimal view recommendation. Zhang *et al.* [20] proposed graphlets to represent the aesthetic feature of photos and transfer the graphlets from the training aesthetic photos into the cropped photos based on a probabilistic model.

3. PROPOSED WORK

We propose an automated social event photo-capture framework. Our framework includes three major components (see Figure 1). Firstly, we extract the social attributes from both the physical space and the cyberspace. For example, the spatial location and orientation of people can be extracted from Kinect depth sensor, the human face can be extracted from the ordinary cameras, and the friendship relations can be extracted from the Web, etc. Secondly, we fuse these social attributes to identify and rank the interaction spaces of the social event. Thirdly, the PTZ cameras are controlled to actively shoot the interactions based on visual saliency with the aesthetic knowledge.

3.1 Social Attribute Extraction

Existing social interaction detection methods in the physical space are customized to their own applications by giving specific definitions for their desired camera views in advance [3, 6, 16, 17]. Considering the unconstrained nature of social interactions and the use of different types of sensors, it is desirable to detect the interactions with more generic descriptions, rather than the specific definition like "shaking hands". Also, the social relations and social structures investigated in sociology are on comparatively large temporal scales and spatial scales, which are not suited towards measuring social activities that "happen" on small temporal and spatial scales in the physical space [7].

Therefore, instead of defining every specific "social interaction", we propose to extract the social attribute from raw sensor data and the Web to characterize the social interaction. We plan to explore a social attribute based on the sociological concept F-formation [10]. F-formation is the spatial patterns maintained by the people who are interacting with each other. Specifically, we model the F-formation concept into a temporal-encoded heat map representation. The interaction centers and the people involved in the interaction are detected using the heat map. In addition, we plan to extract more social attributes such as human face, sensor metadata (i.e., location and time of social event), and friendship relations on the Web etc., to augment our social attributes formulation. Given the extracted social attributes, the interaction could be represented more comprehensive and be with less definition-specific constraints.

3.2 Social Attribute Fusion

Given the social attributes, which are the scattered information about the social event, it still remains unclear where and when the "interesting moment" would be. Current interaction detection methods mainly focus on detecting the existence of the interaction and interactants [1, 4, 9]. These information are not enough for social event photo capture. Also, the detected interactions would have different importance based on people's preference. For example, the birthday person is the main character for a birthday party event.

Therefore, we plan to perform information fusion on these social attributes. The results of the social interaction fusion are the information about the interaction spaces for the "interesting moment", i.e., location, time, interactants, priority, and the ranking of candidate cameras for capturing the desired views. Consequently, the social attribute fusion not only identifies the location and the respective interactants of the interaction space, but also provides richer information on how to shoot each interaction adapting to the situation.

3.3 Active Camera Control

The camera views obtained from the social attribute fusion did not consider the quality of the views such as occlusion, view angle, etc. In addition, showing the same social activity from various camera angles would add considerable interest and help emotionally draw viewers' attention.

Therefore we propose to control cameras to actively shoot the interaction space based on visual saliency with aesthetic knowledge. In comparison to process on the archived data in which the camera view might be poorly framed or even occluded [2, 3, 11], we plan to reposition the cameras to shoot the interaction space in a visually pleasant way. Specifically, visual saliency would be developed incorporating face [19], interaction area, view angle, occlusion status, and view varieties, etc., and the analysis of the visual saliency would be used as feedback to actively control the cameras to satisfy the human aesthetic preference.

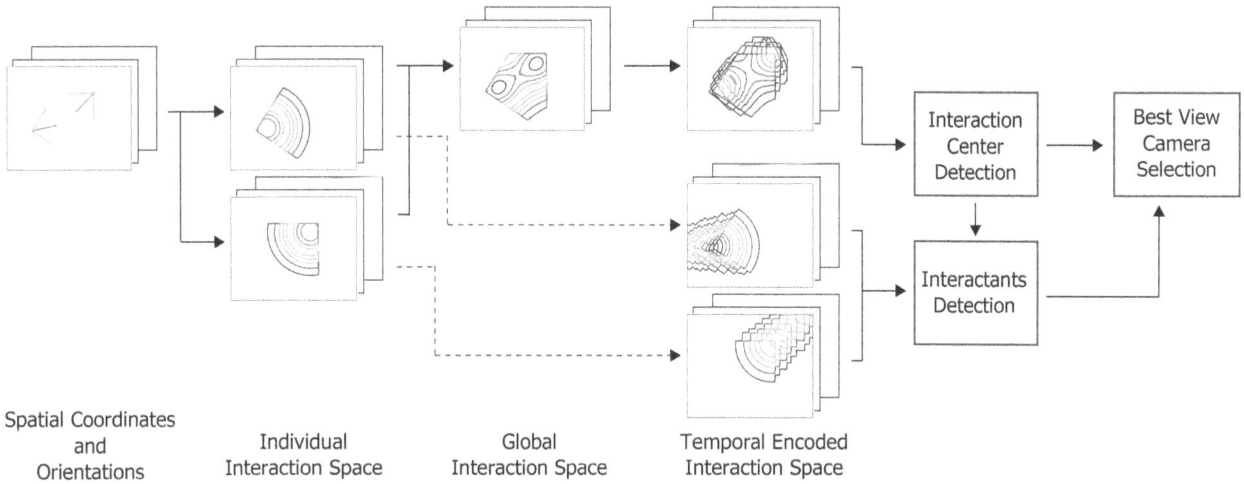

Figure 2: Conceptual diagram of the extended F-formation system. Given the spatial coordinates and orientations of all individuals, the individual Interaction Space (IS), global IS, and their respective temporal encoded IS are computed. The temporal encoded IS are used to detect the interaction center, their respective interactants, and best view cameras.

Table 1: Experiment results for interaction center detection.

Method	Precision	Recall	F_1 score
Bazzani *et al.* [1]	0.745	0.631	0.674
Temporal encoded IS	0.798	0.770	0.783
IS	0.804	0.792	0.797

Table 2: Experiment results for interactant detection.

Method	Precision	Recall	F_1 score
Bazzani *et al.* [1]	0.687	0.690	0.688
Temporal encoded IS	0.823	0.849	0.836
IS	0.848	0.870	0.859

4. RESEARCH PROGRESS

We have proposed a heat map based F-formation representation as the social attribute to model the social interaction, which has been accepted for publication at ACM MM 2013 [5]. Specifically, we model the F-formation with temporal information by creating a temporal-encoded heat map. The interaction centers, respective interactants, and the ranking of corresponding cameras are identified from the heat map.

The conceptual diagram of the proposed framework is shown in Figure 2. Given the spatial coordinates and orientations for each individual, we first compute the *individual Interaction Space* (iIS), where the *Interaction Space* (IS) is restricted by the individual's field of attention. The IS is modelled as a heat map where the highest energy point is selected with prior knowledge obtained from sociology study [8]. For each time frame, a *global Interaction Space* (gIS) is computed by averaging the overlapped iIS. We then compute the temporal encoded IS for each individual and the global view (denoted as TiIS and TgIS, respectively) with a temporal decayed accumulation method. The computed TiIS and TgIS are used to detect the F-formation(s), interactants, and the respective best view camera(s). The F-formation(s) are identified by extracting the "hot spots" from the heat map; and the related interactants are identified by considering the contribution of each person in terms of every "hot spot". For the ranking of corresponding cameras, we divide a ring region outside the interaction space into several camera ranking zones, and calculate a score based on the individual temporal-encoded heat map for each zone to rank the corresponding cameras.

To evaluate the work, we firstly conducted experiments evaluating the accuracy for interaction center detection and interactant detection on synthetic data, which were generated by the simulation script. There are in total 10 scenarios with two variables (the number of unique individual and the concurrent interaction centers) in the simulated data. Each scenario contains 5 sequences, and each sequence consists of 600 frames with the frame rate of 5 fps. Two variants of our proposed method were evaluated: the heat map based F-formation system without temporal information (denoted as IS), and the temporal encoded F-formation system (denoted as Temporal encoded IS). We also compared our method with Bazani *et al.*'s approach [1]. The average performance are shown in Table 1 and 2. As shown in the tables, our approach outperforms Bazani *et al.* [1] with a noticeable margin. In addition, the results in Table 1 and 2 show that the performance of Temporal encoded IS is generally worse than IS. This is because the Temporal encoded IS can only identifies an interaction center after a period of time (a side effect of the temporal encoded approach), however, in the ground truth a frame is considered as having valid interaction center immediately when two persons meet. Despite that, we cannot determine a reasonable frame duration to form a mutual social interaction. To establish our hypothesis, we generated 10 sets of simulated sequences with 4 individuals and 1 interaction center. No interaction is allowed in these sequences and only precision is reported. The results agree with our hypothesis where Temporal encoded IS gives a precision of 0.999 and IS gives 0.800.

Secondly, we conducted a user study to compare our camera ranking with human expectations. The result shows that the top-1 rank from our algorithm agrees with 33% and 56% of users' top-1 and top-2 rank. We argue that the low accuracy for our top-1 rank is reasonable as the users' top-1 ranked camera are not consistent. When consider the top-2 rank from our algorithm, the matching accuracy raised significantly to 65% and 86% for users' top-1 and top-2 rank.

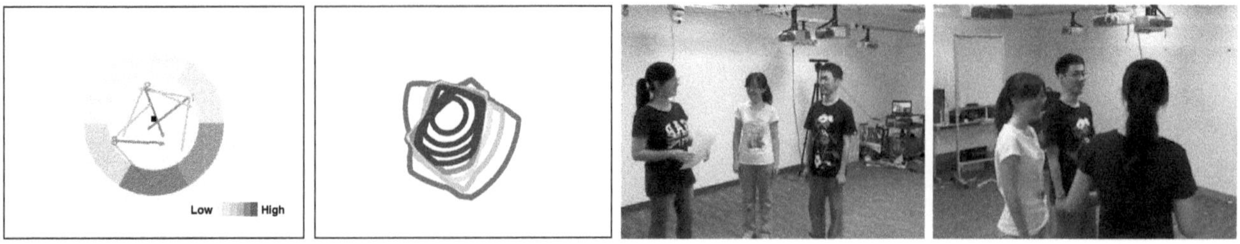

(a) (b) (c) (d)

Figure 3: Experimental result with real-world recording for one social interaction. (a) The spatial locations and the orientations of the detected interactants, as well as the camera ranking zone. (b) Temporal-encoded global Interaction Space. (c-d) The snapshot obtained from the camera with (c) having the higher rank.

This indicates that our method generally agrees with users' expectation. An example of the results from our experiment with real-world recording are shown in Figure 3.

5. EXPECTED CONTRIBUTIONS

The expected contributions are listed as follows:

1. A heat map based F-formation representation is proposed to characterize the social interaction. Also, additional social attributes like human face, sensor metadata (i.e., location and time of social event), and information on the Web (i.e., friendship), will be incorporated into a comprehensive set of social attributes.
2. Fusing the social attributes from both the physical space and cyberspace to identify and rank the space of the on-going social interaction and interactants, which provides richer information on how to shoot each interaction adapting to the situation.
3. Improving the quality of the camera views by sending saliency-based feedback to actively control the camera capture process.

6. CONCLUSION

We proposed an automated photo-capture framework for social event, which consists of three components: social attribute extraction, social attribute fusion, and active camera control for social event. Our initial work shows a heat map based F-formation detection method for extracting the social attributes with promising results. We would extend our work with more social attributes and more sophisticated information fusion algorithms. Finally the active camera control problem would be solved to complete the work.

7. ACKNOWLEDGEMENT

This research was carried out at the SeSaMe Centre. It is supported by the Singapore NRF under its IRC@SG Funding Initiative and administered by the IDMPO.

8. REFERENCES

[1] L. Bazzani, M. Cristani, D. Tosato, M. Farenzena, G. Paggetti, G. Menegaz, and V. Murino. Social interactions by visual focus of attention in a three-dimensional environment. *Expert Systems*, 30(2):115–127, 2013.

[2] M. Campanella and J. Hoonhout. Understanding behaviors and needs for home videos. In *British HCI Group Annual Conference on HCI*, pages 23–26, 2008.

[3] D. Chen, J. Yang, R. Malkin, and H. D. Wactlar. Detecting social interactions of the elderly in a nursing home environment. *ACM Transactions on Multimedia Computing, Communications and Applications*, 3(1), Feb. 2007.

[4] M. Cristani, L. Bazzani, G. Paggetti, A. Fossati, D. Tosato, A. D. Bue, G. Menegaz, and V. Murino. Social interaction discovery by statistical analysis of F-formations. In *Proceedings of British Machine Vision Conference*, pages 1–12, 2011.

[5] T. Gan, Y. Wong, D. Zhang, and M. Kankanhalli. Temporal Encoded F-formation System for Social Interaction Detection. In *Proceedings of ACM International Conference on Multimedia*, 2013.

[6] D. Gatica-Perez. Automatic nonverbal analysis of social interaction in small groups: A review. *Image Vision Computing*, 27(12):1775–1787, 2009.

[7] G. Groh, A. Lehmann, J. Reimers, M. R. Friess, and L. Schwarz. Detecting social situations from interaction geometry. In *Proceedings of the IEEE Second International Conference on Social Computing, SocialCom / IEEE International Conference on Privacy, Security, Risk and Trust, PASSAT*, pages 1–8. IEEE Computer Society, 2010.

[8] E. T. Hall. *The Hidden Dimension.* Doubleday, 1966.

[9] H. Hung and B. J. A. Kröse. Detecting F-formations as dominant sets. In *Proc of the International Conference on Multimodal Interfaces*, pages 231–238, 2011.

[10] A. Kendon. *Conducting Interaction: Patterns of behavior in focused encounters*, volume 7. Cambridge University Press, 1990.

[11] L. S. Kennedy and M. Naaman. Less talk, more rock: automated organization of community-contributed collections of concert videos. In *Proceedings of the 18th International Conference on World Wide Web*, pages 311–320, 2009.

[12] T. Mei, X.-S. Hua, H.-Q. Zhou, and S. Li. Modeling and mining of users' capture intention for home videos. *IEEE Transactions on Multimedia*, 9(1):66–77, 2007.

[13] B. Ni, M. Xu, B. Cheng, M. Wang, S. Yan, and Q. Tian. Learning to photograph: A compositional perspective. *IEEE Transactions on Multimedia*, 15(5):1138–1151, 2013.

[14] N. Oliver, B. Rosario, and A. Pentland. A bayesian computer vision system for modeling human interactions. *IEEE Transactions on Pattern Analysis and Machine Intelligence*, 22(8):831–843, 2000.

[15] S. Park and M. M. Trivedi. Multi-person interaction and activity analysis: a synergistic track- and body-level analysis framework. *Machine Vision and Applications*, 18(3-4):151–166, 2007.

[16] S. Park and M. M. Trivedi. Understanding human interactions with track and body synergies (tbs) captured from multiple views. *Computer Vision and Image Understanding*, 111(1):2–20, 2008.

[17] M. S. Ryoo and J. K. Aggarwal. Recognition of composite human activities through context-free grammar based representation. In *IEEE Computer Society Conference on Computer Vision and Pattern Recognition*, pages 1709–1718, 2006.

[18] A. Vinciarelli, M. Pantic, and H. Bourlard. Social signal processing: Survey of an emerging domain. *Image Vision Computing*, 27(12):1743–1759, 2009.

[19] Y. Wong, S. Chen, S. Mau, C. Sanderson, and B. C. Lovell. Patch-based probabilistic image quality assessment for face selection and improved video-based face recognition. In *IEEE Conference on Computer Vision and Pattern Recognition, Biometrics Workshop*, pages 74–81, 2011.

[20] L. Zhang, M. Song, Q. Zhao, X. Liu, J. Bu, and C. Chen. Probabilistic graphlet transfer for photo cropping. *IEEE Transactions on Image Processing*, 22(2):802–815, 2013.

Virtual Director Technology for Social Video Communication and Live Event Broadcast Production

Rene Kaiser
JOANNEUM RESEARCH
Institute for Information and Communication Technologies
Graz, Austria
rene.kaiser@joanneum.at

ABSTRACT

This thesis investigates several aspects of Virtual Director technology, i.e. software capable of intelligent real-time selection of live media streams. It addresses several research questions in this interdisciplinary field with respect to how a generic Virtual Director framework can be constructed, and how its behavior can be modeled and formalized to realize professional applications with many parallel users within real-time constraints. Prototypes have been built for the applications of group videoconferencing and live event broadcast. The engine executes cinematic principles aiming to enhance the user experience. In group videoconferencing, a Virtual Director aims to support communication goals by selecting from multiple available streams, i.e. automating cuts between shots according to the communication situation. In event broadcast, it enables personalization by framing, animating and cutting virtual camera views as cropping from a high-resolution panorama. While the technical approach and framework has been evaluated in lab experiments, further evaluation involving potential users and cinematic professionals is ongoing.

Categories and Subject Descriptors

C.2.4 [**Distributed Systems**]: Distributed applications; H.4 [**Information Systems Applications**]: Miscellaneous

Keywords

Virtual Director, live broadcast, video communication

1. VIRTUAL DIRECTOR TECHNOLOGY

The increase of services based on live video streams is very visible to users through a high rate of new multimedia applications with ever-improving audiovisual quality. New forms of content personalization can be enabled by intelligently cutting live AV sources. Since such personalization can not be executed by human operators on a large scale, intelligent *Virtual Director* software metaphorically aims to replace the work and knowledge of a live TV broadcast team. This concept is a key enabler for immersive experiences on top of that, and might enable future research advancements such as novel media formats and consumption paradigms.

This work explores the concept of Virtual Director systems and aims at research progress towards flexible re-usable software frameworks that can be adapted to a specific purpose by exchanging the production grammar, the Virtual Director's formalized behavior. This work reveals and addresses a set of research challenges regarding both the software framework and behavior definition aspects. Which technical approaches exist for implementing such software, what are their advantages and limitations? How could a generic Virtual Director framework be constructed that is capable of realizing professional large-scale applications, with a high number of parallel users, and tight real-time constraints? How can the execution of cinematographic principles in real-time media stream selection be automated? How can complex sets of Virtual Director behavior be modeled and formalized? How can it be designed such that it supports the users' aims best?

This paper discusses several aspects of this work on Virtual Director technology for the distinct domains of video communication and broadcast production. Before practical goals such as engineering a concrete Virtual Director behavior on an aesthetic level that meets user expectations can be taken on, underlying technical challenges need to be addressed. While this work builds to a certain extent on research using recorded multimedia content (for example [15]), it entirely focuses on applications using real-time live streams and their specific challenges, for example regarding delays in content transmission and user interaction. The requirements for a Virtual Director application in real-time scenarios are very challenging, and considerably different from remixing or abstracting recorded content. In this work, the audio-visual aesthetics and quality of automated cinematic principles are essential, unlike e.g. many surveillance applications based on different criteria and strictly professional users.

Even though the two domains of mediated communication and personalized event broadcast are significantly different, a common technical approach is sought. Each of these domains has specific requirements regarding the expected QoE delivered to the users, however, and each concrete production/setup requires a (domain-)specific set of Virtual Director behavior.

The focus so far was on understanding the concept's potential and limitations, and on developing a suitable tech-

MM'13, October 21–25, 2013, Barcelona, Spain.
ACM 978-1-4503-2404-5/13/10.
http://dx.doi.org/10.1145/2502081.2502213.

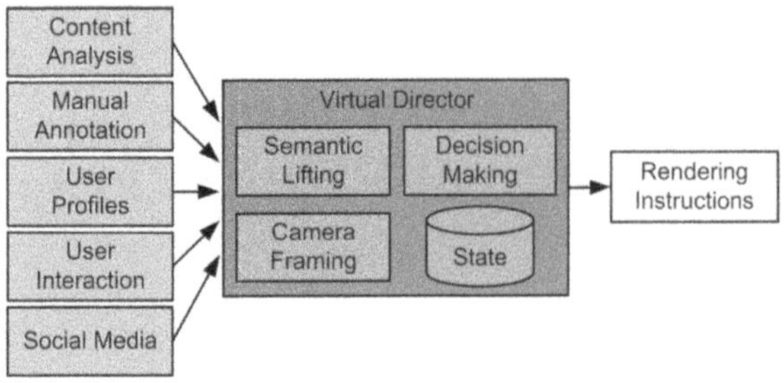

Figure 1: Generic workflow and sub-processes of a Virtual Director.

nical approach with the long-term research goal of creating a flexible Virtual Director software framework and behavior engineering methodology in mind. Software prototypes for both aforementioned application domains have been developed and applied. The prototypes execute dedicated Virtual Director behavior and are integrated with related system components in the realm of three larges research projects.

One of the thesis' core contribution is work on *semantic lifting*, i.e. on the semantic abstraction of low-level real-time information streams in order to inform the decision-making processes. In other words, this refers the understanding of the situation covered by the Virtual Director, i.e. the communication actions and patterns in one application domain, the actions going on in the scene in the other. Many approaches have been proposed for the detection of interesting events in video streams, e.g. a visual stream approach in [21]. An overview has been compiled recently in [7]. A Virtual Director's semantic lifting process however is typically operating at a very abstract level and has a slightly different aim, since it is triggering cinematic rules as a direct reaction.

Evaluation regarding both domains has been conducted via lab experiments and interviews, and initial results have been published as evaluation work is ongoing. While the Virtual Director concept is certainly bounded by practical limitations regarding the automation of human intuition, anticipation and creativity, several application domains are obvious candidates to exhibit added value to the users, most importantly through increased interaction possibilities and novel forms of personalization in the realm of live AV streams.

2. APPROACH AND ARCHITECTURE

Multiple technical approaches have been investigated in order to address the challenge of a flexible Virtual Director system that is both capable to reason with its information sources in real-time, and to take meaningful decisions based on them. One option is to represent the Virtual Director behavior in RDF/OWL, and to utilize Description Logics based reasoning and (Jena) rules. While the approach is well suited for static modeling of a production domain, experiments resulted in the conclusion that available reasoning frameworks are not fast and scalable enough for the requirements envisioned – see [9]. Ultimately, a rule-based approach was selected in combination with event processing technology [10], i.e. *Complex Event Processing* (CEP) [3] engines.

An abstract Virtual Director workflow is depicted in Figure 1. Such systems need to be informed about the content they cover in order to take meaningful decisions. This can be achieved through automatic content analysis (reported in [8]), manual annotation via dedicated user interfaces, or external sources such as the Internet.

A Virtual Director can be regarded as a software framework that executes a set of production grammar, its intended behavior. On a deeper level, the sub-processes deal with the distinct challenges of *understanding* the current situation, and of taking appropriate decisions based on that. While the concrete architecture depends on the intended personalization capabilities and user interaction requirements, three generic sub-processes of a Virtual Director are:

- **Semantic Lifting:** *Understanding* the scene or situation by semantically abstracting the low-level cue stream the Virtual Director is receiving through its sensors. Events and actions need to be detected that are on an abstraction level that allows to trigger Virtual Director behavior.
- **Camera Framing:** In order to achieve high QoE, cinematographic principles shall be applied. One key aspect is how to frame both static and moving shots. This is especially relevant if cropping from high-res cameras are utilized.
- **Decision Making:** Since the core added value of Virtual Director technology is grounded in the ability to personalize in real-time, efficient decision making is important. In contrast to a human production team, a Virtual Director can take a large amount of decision in parallel, enabling to take personalized decisions for every user or playout device.

The following Sections 3 and 4 discuss work in the two selected application domains in more detail.

3. GROUP VIDEOCONFERENCING

Enhancing social group communication through an *orchestrated* audiovisual link is a multifaceted and interdisciplinary research challenge. Within the European research projects TA2[1] and Vconect[2], Virtual Director prototypes have been built and evaluated [4, 18]. The so-called *Orchestration Engine* aims to support the communication goals of larger groups linked by an audio and video connection. As too many media streams are available (cp. [19]), this Virtual Director selects those most useful and enjoyable to the participants in order to support individual communication goals. Usefulness was measured by measuring the users' effectiveness in a task/game [6]. Experiments found that it does also influence the communication itself through its decisions. Support for validity of the concept has resulted from initial manual camera selection experiments [18].

The Virtual Director's role can be compared to human directors in live TV broadcast, calling the shots in a video conference in that case. Here, real-time constraints are even more crucial, since content delay affects bidirectional communication strongly. Social videoconferencing platforms for informal group communication vary in setup, using multiple microphones, loudspeakers, cameras and screens. Besides other social communication goals, one aim is to achieve a *telepresence* effect, i.e. to lose the feeling of communicating from distant locations.

[1]`http://www.ta2-project.eu/`
[2]`http://www.vconect-project.eu/`

Figure 2: Simultaneous virtual cameras as crops from high resolution panoramic video. The Production Scripting Engine frames shots based on its understanding of what is happening in the scene, as suggested by its semantic lifting sub-process.

Intelligent shot selection on that end aims to make sure the most relevant communication partners are visible large enough and at the right time. A high-quality full screen close-up shot for example allows to grasp also non-verbal communication cues well, which seems to be important especially for observing the communication partners reactions.

The domain is strongly related to business videoconferencing solutions such as Cisco's, but aims to support different communication processes and values (agenda-based, non-verbal communication less important). Videoconferencing has been looked into from many research angles. The use of multiple cameras to capture a person compared to current popular solutions like Skype and Google Hangouts has also been proposed by [20], but is available only in professional videoconferencing systems so far. While a lot of work has been reported with respect to eye gaze improvements and even 3D content capture (see [12]), this work is focusing on automatic shot selection.

One key advantage of being able to choose between multiple cameras that was investigated as part of this work is to select the most suitable camera view depending on the communication situation. While a frontal camera view might be most useful when speaking to someone directly, a dialogue between third parties is better shown from side angles. More detailed experiment results are reported in [18] and [10] and [6].

Regarding the semantic lifting sub-process, our current approach is to aim for understanding communication patterns, with turn taking events and patterns as the core concept to trigger camera selection decisions [5]. While both audio and video content analysis results are processed as real-time event streams, only the visual output is steered by the engine so far. To personalize dynamic content selection, static or dynamic information about the users may be exploited. From that end, we started analyzing communication behavior of users in social media, with the ultimate goal to predict conversation patterns such that they can be applied to camera selection in the video conferencing domain [16].

A future aim is to support dynamic communication topologies, intelligently mediated branching of side-conversations, which means that a sub-group from a communication session shall be able to create a separate communication space and come back to the main branch later. Another current focus is the integration of social videoconferencing with Social Network platforms, and the integration of the social group communication process with shared media consumption.

4. BROADCAST PRODUCTION

In a second application domain addressed by the FascinatE[3] project, a Virtual Director for live event broadcast [11] has been implemented, based on a scene-capture approach [13] using multiple microphones and a 180 degree panoramic camera, the OMNICAM [17]. See Figure 2 for an example frame with virtual cameras. The system automatically produces individual content streams for different playout devices and user preferences, i.e. mostly static or animated cropping from the high-resolution panoramic video. Viewers may watch different parts of the scene, based on their interests. This Virtual Director is informed by automatic content analysis (e.g. reported in [8]) and manual annotations. Manual input indicates the occurrence of high-level events not directly observable by content analysis, and manages virtual cameras.

For the prototype, called *Production Scripting Engine*, camera selection behavior was designed and implemented for the domains of soccer and dance performance, and different manual annotation strategies have been tried out to inform it. While high-level actions could be observed well by human operators in the soccer domain, the annotation of virtual camera candidates proved to be more useful in the dance domain, where few high-level concepts could be found that appeared to be intuitive enough to observe and annotate.

This work extends previous efforts by other researchers, many of which chose to work with sports content. Most work, however, is processing the media content in recorded form, not in real-time. Impressive results have been achieved within the APIDIS project (see e.g. [1]), though in different setups than this work. They utilized and registered multiple cameras in order to achieve stable player tracking for basketball matches, which is not possible to achieve when working with a limited set of camera angles, as conclusions and other issues occur. Daniyal and Cavallaro [2] also developed an algorithm for automated camera selection and used a Turing test to evaluate the quality of the output. Patrikakis et al. [14] aimed to create context-aware and personalized media in real-time streaming environments for broadcasting applications. Their approach is to allow users to create their own Virtual Director and to exploit the user profiles for camera selection decisions.

Evaluation confirmed that the quality of the visual decisions of the current prototype cannot compare with profes-

[3]`http://www.fascinate-project.eu/`

sional production teams and is lacking in perceived creativity, storytelling skills and intuition. Still, reasonable application areas exist. A Virtual Director provides the advantage of quicker reactions to low-level cues, and consistency in decision-making that is hypothesized to result in a more reliable experience. The main advantage of Virtual Director technology for live event broadcast, however, are the manifold possibilities to personalize camera selection to the benefit of the user. The concrete options depend on the production domain, and need to be made available to the users through an interface.

In initial user evaluations, we found that user expectations depend on the production domain. For some they are very high, as they are based on experience consuming professionally scripted and edited TV programmes. Still, both production professionals and unskilled users participating in evaluation interviews were able to ignore superficial deficiencies to understand and acknowledge the personalization opportunities enabled by such technology.

One option to circumvent some of the inherent quality limitations of the concept would be to go for director decision assisting instead of automatic decision making as a more short-term goal. While this approach makes sense in certain broadcasting applications, it could not be applied to the videoconferencing domain, where human professionals cannot be involved for economic reasons.

5. STATUS AND OUTLOOK

An efficient technical approach has been proposed that allows to build Virtual Director systems and to define their intended behavior. Virtual Director technology, however, remains a challenging research area.

This works' core aim is to advance towards the long-term goal of a generic software framework, a proper formalism and authoring tools for engineering Virtual Director behavior. Its goal is not to engineer a system with a perfect set of behavior for a certain application. Since the prototypes' practical limitations can not be disregarded in user evaluations, the evaluation of the concept is conducted with respect to several individual aspects as discussed above, rather than as direct comparison to e.g. a TV broadcast edited by a professional director. Quantitative results have been obtained evaluating both system performance and user goals.

While Virtual Director prototypes have been implemented successfully based on this approach, a key challenge of the approach is how to deal with competing and contradicting principles that need to be resolved dynamically for decision making [10]. Further future work is to put focus on steering audio playout, since so far mainly the visual domain had been addressed.

6. ACKNOWLEDGMENTS

The research leading to this paper has been supported by the European Commission under the contract FP7-287760, "Vconect - Video Communications for Networked Communities", and FP7-248138, "FascinatE – Format-Agnostic SCript-based INterAcTive Experience".

7. REFERENCES

[1] F. Chen, D. Delannay, and C. De Vleeschouwer. An autonomous framework to produce and distribute personalized team-sport video summaries: A basketball case study. *IEEE Transactions on Multimedia*, 13(6):1381–1394, 2011.

[2] F. Daniyal and A. Cavallaro. Multi-camera scheduling for video production. In *In Proceedings of the 9th European Conference on Visual Media Production*, pages 11–20, 2011.

[3] O. Etzion and P. Niblett. *Event Processing in Action*. Number ISBN: 9781935182214. Manning, 2010.

[4] M. Falelakis, M. Groen, M. Frantzis, R. Kaiser, and M. Ursu. Automatic orchestration of video streams to enhance group communication. In *SAM'12 Workshop at ACM MM*, pages 25–30. ACM, 2012.

[5] M. Falelakis, R. Kaiser, W. Weiss, and M. Ursu. Reasoning for video-mediated group communication. In *ICME*, 2011.

[6] M. Groen, M. Ursu, S. Michalakopoulos, M. Falelakis, and E. Gasparis. Improving video-mediated communication with orchestration. *Computers in Human Behavior*, 28(5):1575 – 1579, 2012.

[7] Y.-G. Jiang, S. Bhattacharya, S.-F. Chang, and M. Shah. High-level event recognition in unconstrained videos. *International Journal of Multimedia Information Retrieval*, pages 1–29, 2012.

[8] R. Kaiser, M. Thaler, A. Kriechbaum, H. Fassold, W. Bailer, and J. Rosner. Real-time person tracking in high-resolution panoramic video for automated broadcast production. In *CVMP*, pages 21–29, London, UK, 2011.

[9] R. Kaiser, C. Wagner, M. Hoeffernig, and H. Mayer. The interaction ontology model: supporting the virtual director orchestrating real-time group interaction. In *MMM'11*, pages 263–273, Berlin, Heidelberg, 2011. Springer-Verlag.

[10] R. Kaiser, W. Weiss, M. Falelakis, S. Michalakopoulos, and M. F. Ursu. A rule-based virtual director enhancing group communication. *ICME'12 Workshops*, pages 187–192, 2012.

[11] R. Kaiser, W. Weiss, and G. Kienast. The Fascinate Production Scripting Engine. In *MMM'12*, pages 682–692, Berlin, Heidelberg, 2012. Springer-Verlag.

[12] A. Maimone, J. Bidwell, K. Peng, and H. Fuchs. Enhanced personal autostereoscopic telepresence system using commodity depth cameras. *Computers & Graphics*, 36(7):791–807, 2012.

[13] O. A. Niamut, R. Kaiser, G. Kienast, A. Kochale, J. Spille, and O. Schreer. Towards a format-agnostic approach for production, delivery and rendering of immersive media. In *ACM MMSys'13*, Oslo, Norway, 2013.

[14] C. Patrikakis, N. Papaoulakis, P. Papageorgiou, A. Pnevmatikakis, P. Chippendale, M. Nunes, R. Cruz, S. Poslad, and Z. Wang. Personalized coverage of large athletic events. *IEEE MultiMedia*, 18(4):18–29, 2011.

[15] L. A. Rowe and V. Casalaina. Capturing conference presentations. *IEEE MultiMedia*, 13(4):76–84, 2006.

[16] J. Schantl, C. Wagner, R. Kaiser, and M. Strohmaier. The utility of social and topical factors in anticipating repliers in twitter conversations. In *WebSci*, 2013.

[17] O. Schreer, I. Feldmann, C. Weissig, P. Kauff, and R. Schäfer. Ultrahigh-resolution panoramic imaging for format-agnostic video production. *Proceedings of the IEEE*, 101(1):99–114, 2013.

[18] M. Ursu, M. Groen, M. Falelakis, M. Frantzis, V. Zsombori, and R. Kaiser. Orchestration: Tv-like mixing grammars applied to video-communication for social groups. In *ACM MM'13*, New York, NY, USA, 2013. ACM.

[19] M. Ursu, P. Torres, V. Zsombori, M. Franztis, and R. Kaiser. Socialising through orchestrated video communication. In *ACM MM'11*, pages 981–984, New York, NY, USA, 2011. ACM.

[20] P. N. Y. Wang and M. Kankanhalli. Multi-camera skype: Enhancing the quality of experience of video conferencing. In *PCM'11*, pages 193–202, 2011.

[21] B. Yu. *MyView: Customizable Automatic Visual Space Management for Multi-Stream Environment*. PhD thesis, University of Illinois at Urbana-Champaign, 2006.

Gesture–Sound Mapping by Demonstration in Interactive Music Systems

Jules Françoise
STMS Lab — IRCAM–CNRS–UPMC
1, Place Igor Stravinsky 75004 Paris, France
jules.francoise@ircam.fr
Advised by Frédéric Bevilacqua

ABSTRACT

In this paper we address the issue of mapping between gesture and sound in interactive music systems. Our approach, we call *mapping by demonstration*, aims at learning the mapping from examples provided by users while interacting with the system. We propose a general framework for modeling gesture–sound sequences based on a probabilistic, multimodal and hierarchical model. Two orthogonal modeling aspects are detailed and we describe planned research directions to improve and evaluate the proposed models.

Categories and Subject Descriptors

H.5.5 [**Information Interfaces And Presentation**]: Sound and Music Computing; J.5 [**Arts and Humanities**]: Music

Keywords

mapping, gesture, sound synthesis, music performance, HMM, multimodal, hierarchical modeling

1. INTRODUCTION

Gesture interaction with audio and/or visual media has become ubiquitous, requiring the development of intuitive software solutions for interaction design. In this paper, we focus on gesture–based interactive systems for sound and music performance. Today, the range of applications of such systems is widening, extending beyond the musical context to novel gaming applications [11], sonic interaction design to facilitate objects manipulation [12], or rehabilitation where interactive sound feedback could inform users on their movement performance.

In this paper we address current issues in the design of the relationship (often called *mapping*) between gesture features and sound control parameters in such interactive systems (cf. figure 1). Mapping has been recognized a crucial aspect of interactive music systems as it determines the degree of control accessible to a user interacting gesturally with sound

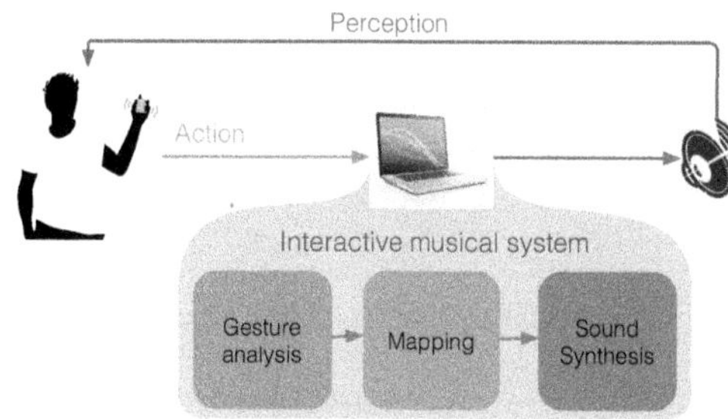

Figure 1: Overview of a gesture–based interactive music system. The *Mapping* relates gesture features to sound control parameters.

processes. Indeed, specific choices in the design of such mapping impact on the interaction possibilities, for example in terms of ease-of-use, expressivity, or metaphor.

This work investigates an approach we call *mapping by demonstration*[1], aiming to learn the mapping from examples provided interactively by the user, e.g. gestures performed while listening to sound examples. A typical situation involves a two-step interaction loop integrating *training* and *performance* (see Figure 2). During the *training* phase, a multimodal model of the mapping is trained on a set of user demonstrations. Once learned, the model can be used for *performance*: sound control sequences are predicted in real-time based on new gestures. This situation involves challenging research questions in terms of modeling, considering the complexity and diversity of possible mappings, and in terms of machine learning, regarding the need for efficient and interactive learning algorithms.

Section 2 details related work about mapping in music and multimedia. The research questions and specificities of our approach are detailed in section 3. Current research is summarized in section 4, and prospective work is described in section 5.

2. RELATED WORK

2.1 Gesture–Sound Mapping by Demonstration

This section details current approaches to mapping by demonstration. We identify three classes of approaches according to two properties of the learned mapping: the tem-

[1]This terminology is inspired by the field of robotics called *Programming by demonstration* [3].

MM'13, October 21-25, 2013, Barcelona, Spain
ACM 978-1-4503-2404-5/13/10.
http://dx.doi.org/10.1145/2502081.2502214.

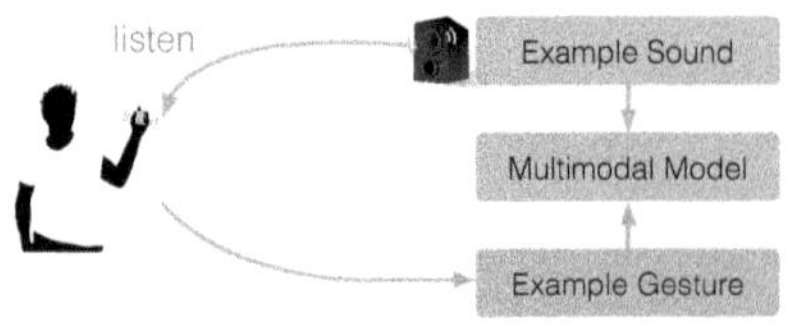

(a) *Training* phase.

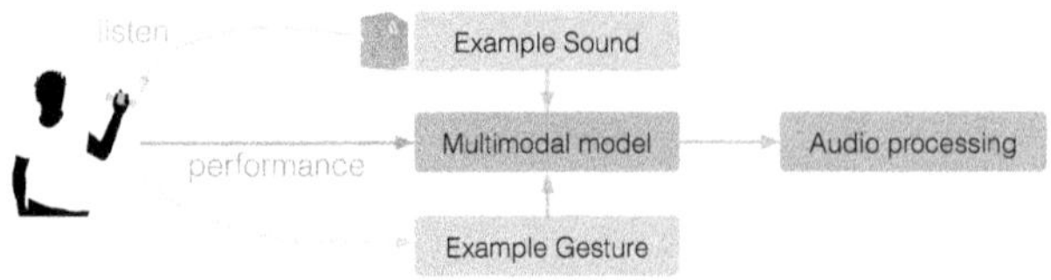

(b) *Performance* phase.

Figure 2: Workflow of a Mapping by Demonstration system.

poral aspect, and the discrete/continuous nature of interactions.

Various methods have been proposed to learn non-linear continuous mappings between gesture parameters and sound control parameters. Regression methods, in particular neural networks, have been extensively used for mapping by demonstration [10]. In particular, Fiebrink et al. proposed a *play-along* paradigm that allows to define a training set interactively by performing gestures associated with sound parameter sequences [5]. This class of methods, we call *Regression Mapping*, are often limited to static relationships between gesture and sound parameters.

Other approaches have investigated gesture recognition methods to consider the temporal aspect of the relationships between gesture and sound. We call this class of approaches *temporal mapping* and distinguish between discrete and continuous strategies. In *Discrete Temporal Mapping*, discrete gesture recognition is used to identify gestures carrying a particular meaning or metaphor, in order to trigger sound controls. Several gesture recognition techniques have been studied such as Hidden Markov Models (HMMs), Dynamic Time Warping (DTW) and Support Vector Machines (SVMs) [9]. *Continuous Temporal Mapping* refers to strategies using continuous–time models of gestures in relationship with sounds, therefore allowing to align gesture time profiles to sound morphologies [1]. The method is based on continuous gesture recognition — also called *gesture following* — using HMMs [2]. The method allows accurate control on the temporal dimension, but is limited by a one-shot learning procedure preventing the integration of expressive variations occurring in several interpretations of the same gesture.

If regression methods are powerful to learn non-linear parameter mappings from multiple demonstrations, they do not or poorly model the temporal relationships between gesture and sound. Discrete temporal mapping partially addresses this issue, but restricting gesture analysis to classification limits control strategies to simple triggering or selection. Finally, if continuous temporal mapping methods model accurately the temporal relationship between modalities, they poorly handle the variability occurring between several performances of the same gesture. Moreover, in this case gestures are modeled as continuous time profiles, limiting the integration of higher-level temporal representations related to musical sequences. Our goal is to address the limitations of current approaches by adopting a hierarchical and multimodal perspective on mapping inspired by recent work in other fields of multimedia.

2.2 Mapping in Other Fields of Multimedia

Many recent systems for virtual character animation use speech–driven approaches, involving mapping from acoustic features to lip, face or body motion [4]. Similar issues are found in acoustic–articulatory inversion [13], aiming at the retrieval of speech–producing movements from acoustic signals. Most of the current approaches are based on sequence models representing the output process in conjunction with the input modality. In particular, various extensions of HMMs were proved efficient for feature mapping [8].

In spite of their similarity, our applications in gestural sound control contrasts in critical points the applications we just mentioned. While speech-related movements and sounds are generated by the same action and thus intrinsically related, the gesture–sound relationships can be arbitrarily defined by the user. In many cases, the training examples should be provided by the user in a *mapping by demonstration* workflow integrating training and performance. These aspects require adapting models and algorithms to an interactive learning paradigm.

3. RESEARCH QUESTIONS AND PROPOSED APPROACH

We aim at overcoming the limitations of current approaches by the development of a general modeling framework for mapping integrating the following properties:

1. **temporal**: each example is a particular instance, intrinsically dynamic, of the underlying mapping. Therefore, learning from user demonstrations require modeling the temporal aspect of the mapping.

2. **expressive variations**: the model must be able to abstract not only the average time structure of gesture–sound segments but also the expressive variations arising between several interpretations of a same mapping.

3. **hierarchical**: in order to integrate high level representation of musical structures, the model must consider multiple time scales and build the mapping accordingly using hierarchical representations. Learned mappings must provide both accurate and high–level degrees of control.

Moreover, we stress the importance of the constraints related to the interactive learning situation required by a mapping by demonstration approach. The training examples are interactively demonstrated by the user. Therefore, the model must be trained from few examples. Moreover, during the *performance* phase, the prediction algorithm must work in real-time to ensure instantaneous feedback to the user's movements.

Our goal is to propose a fully probabilistic, multimodal and hierarchical sequence model of gesture–sound mappings addressing the above constraints. An overview of the general approach is represented on figure 3. Our approach takes advantage of multilevel segmentation of both gesture and sound to implement mapping strategies spanning over different time scales, from fine control to higher level strategies. In the next section we detail two contributions addressing orthogonal aspects of this framework. The former details a hierarchical approach to mapping, while the latter focuses on multimodal modeling.

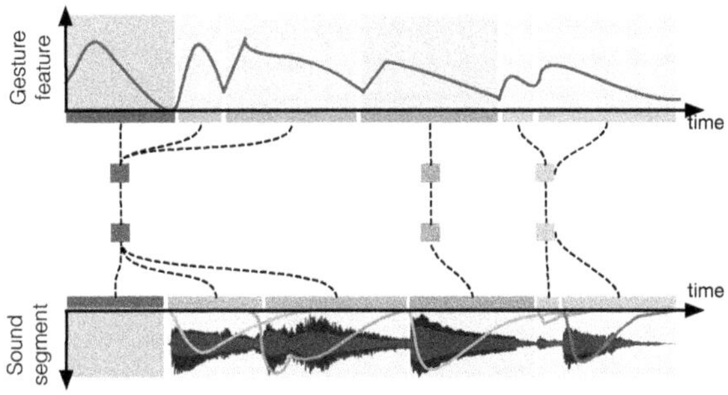

Figure 3: Overview of the general approach. The modeling framework is based on multilevel segmentations of gesture and sound to implement mapping strategies with different time granularity.

4. CONTRIBUTIONS

4.1 Hierarchical Approach to Mapping

This work follows recent developments in the Real-Time Musical Interactions team at Ircam regarding continuous temporal mapping. Our goal is to extend current systems for continuous gesture recognition [2] in order to integrate higher level representations of musical sequences. This work is described in [6] and addresses the issue (3) highlighted in section 3.

We propose the use of a Hierarchical HMM with two levels for real-time gesture segmentation and recognition. We adopt a template-based learning procedure allowing to build the model from a single example, as illustrated on figure 4. From a segmented example gesture, we build the model by associating each segment to a high level state, which generates a submodel encoding the time structure of the segment. The submodel is built by associating to each frame of the example a state in a left–right transition structure. The high–level transition structure can be authored by the user. Segmentation and recognition are then performed in real-time using a forward algorithm, estimating for each incoming observation the likeliest segment and the time alignment of the gesture to the reference.

The approach offers interesting possibilities for gesture-based control of sound synthesis. First, the recognition is improved because informed by the high level structure. Moreover, the possibilities of authoring the high level transition probabilities enable user to define sequence models or particular representations of gestures (see for example the PASR[2] representation we proposed in [6]). Finally, the segmental representation of sound-related gestures provides a means to define interactively some constraints on the sound synthesis for particular segments — e.g. imposing transient conservation on the attack phases of the sound.

[2]PASR is a representation of gestures as a sequence of 4 segments: Preparation-Attack-Sustain-Release

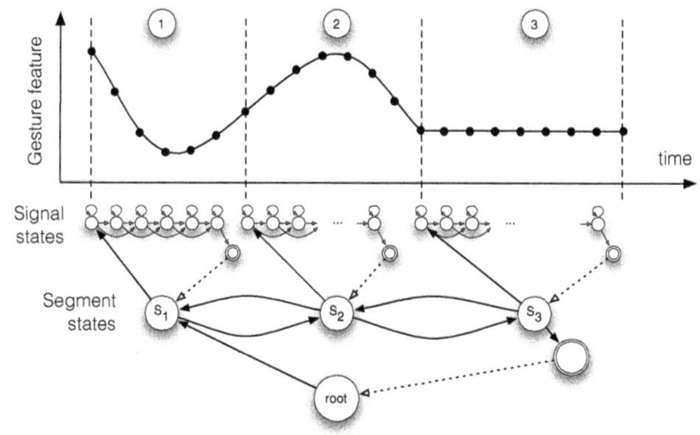

Figure 4: The two-level hierarchical HMM. The model is built from a single segmented example gesture.

4.2 Multimodal Modeling of Gesture–Sound Mapping

This section details another aspect of modeling addressing the constraints (1) and (2) highlighted in section 3. We support a multimodal perspective on mapping by introducing a probabilistic model able to learn gesture–sound mapping from several examples. The system is based on a multimodal HMM modeling the dependencies between gesture and sound. A more detailed description of the model with applications to gesture-based control of physical modeling sound synthesis can be found in [7].

The model assumes that gesture and sound are generated by the same underlying markov process. During training, gesture and sound feature vectors are concatenated to form multimodal sequences (figure 5, left). The observation probability distributions are therefore defined as joint multimodal Gaussian distributions with full covariance. The model is trained using an EM algorithm with pre-estimated parameters to ensure fast and efficient convergence. For prediction, the joint observation distributions are converted to conditional distributions. The sound observation sequence associated to a new gesture sequence can be predicted in real-time using a forward algorithm (figure 5, right).

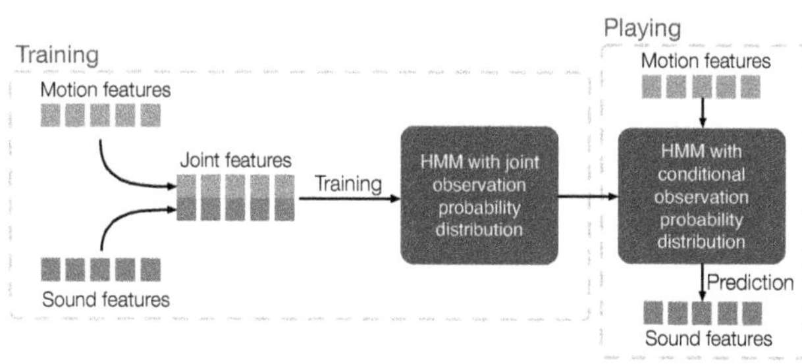

Figure 5: Mapping with the multimodal HMM.

A preliminary assessment of the system, based on informal observation and evaluation on synthetic signals, has been performed and shows promising results. In comparison with the template–based model introduced in [1], the multimodal HMM show a better ability to model the expressive gesture variations between different interpretations, guaranteeing a more coherent translation of gesture variations to sound variations.

5. PLANNED WORK

5.1 Modeling

We plan to address several issues of the proposed models. First, the convergence of the training procedure of the multimodal HMM might not be guaranteed in cases where the number of examples is critically limited. We are currently improving this limitation by examining various approaches for adding constraints in the training procedure. Moreover, the smoothness and consistency of the prediction could be improved by the integration of a trajectory model, as proposed by Zen [13]. Second, the two contributions presented in section 4 address orthogonal dimensions of the general approach we describe in section 3. The multimodal HMM precisely models the temporal and spatial relationships between gesture and sound at the segment level, while the hierarchical HMM provides higher–level control of musical sequences. We are currently working on a combination the two models to form a hierarchical multimodal model. Finally, in the current implementation, the high level structure of the hierarchical HMM can only be edited by the user. We plan to investigate online learning methods to adapt incrementally both the segment models and the transition parameters during the performance phase.

5.2 Evaluation

For now, the proposed models have not been extensively evaluated. One difficulty resides in the specificities of the context of music performance, for which there is no unique relationship between modalities but the design itself of this mapping is part of the creative process. We are planning two directions for the evaluation of the systems:

1. **Computational**: the models will be evaluated on a multimodal database implementing several specific mapping strategies. The models will be compared to state of the art methods regarding their ability to learn a mapping incrementally and to model temporal dynamics and expressive gesture variations.

2. **User Evaluation**: we plan to conduct two types of experiments. First, using a database similar to the one for computational evaluation, a qualitative assessment of the prediction of the algorithms will be performed by a panel of experts on subjective criteria. The second type of experiment will investigate user interaction with the machine learning models. Specifically, we plan to study how the user and the system can co-adapt and converge during the process of designing mapping strategies.

5.3 Applications

We plan to develop several concrete applications of the models in the contexts of music performance, sonic interaction design, and rehabilitation. In the framework of the ANR project *LEGOS*[3], we are investigating the benefits of auditory feedback for sensori-motor learning. In this case, the model will be used to learn mapping strategies for movement sonification, where the sound feedback would inform users on their movement performance.

[3] `http://legos.ircam.fr`

6. ACKNOWLEDGMENTS

We acknowledge support from the French National Research Agency (ANR project LEGOS 11 BS02 012).

7. REFERENCES

[1] F. Bevilacqua, N. Schnell, N. Rasamimanana, B. Zamborlin, and F. Guédy. Online Gesture Analysis and Control of Audio Processing. In *Musical Robots and Interactive Multimodal Systems*, pages 127–142. Springer, 2011.

[2] F. Bevilacqua, B. Zamborlin, A. Sypniewski, N. Schnell, F. Guédy, and N. Rasamimanana. Continuous realtime gesture following and recognition. *Gesture in Embodied Communication and Human-Computer Interaction*, pages 73–84, 2010.

[3] A. Billard, S. Calinon, R. Dillmann, and S. Schaal. Robot programming by demonstration. *Handbook of robotics*, 1, 2008.

[4] K. Choi, Y. Luo, and J.-n. Hwang. Hidden Markov model inversion for audio-to-visual conversion in an MPEG-4 facial animation system. *The Journal of VLSI Signal Processing*, 29(1):51–61, 2001.

[5] R. Fiebrink, P. R. Cook, and D. Trueman. Play-along mapping of musical controllers. In *In Proceedings of the International Computer Music Conference*, 2009.

[6] J. Françoise, B. Caramiaux, and F. Bevilacqua. A Hierarchical Approach for the Design of Gesture-to-Sound Mappings. In *Proceedings of the 9th Sound and Music Computing Conference*, pages 233–240, Copenhagen, Denmark, 2012.

[7] J. Françoise, N. Schnell, and F. Bevilacqua. A Multimodal Probabilistic Model for Gesture-based Control of Sound Synthesis. In *Proceedings of the 21st ACM international conference on Multimedia (MM'13)*, Barcelona, Spain, 2013.

[8] S. Fu, R. Gutierrez-Osuna, A. Esposito, P. Kakumanu, and O. Garcia. Audio/visual mapping with cross-modal hidden Markov models. *Multimedia, IEEE Transactions on*, 7(2):243–252, Apr. 2005.

[9] N. Gillian and R. Knapp. A Machine Learning Toolbox For Musician Computer Interaction. In *proceedings of the International Conference on New Interfaces for Musical Expression*, Oslo, Norway, 2011.

[10] P. Modler. Neural Networks for Mapping Hand Gestures to Sound Synthesis parameters. *Trends in Gestural Control of Music*, pages 301–314, 2000.

[11] N. Rasamimanana, F. Bevilacqua, J. Bloit, N. Schnell, E. Fléty, A. Cera, U. Petrevski, and J.-L. Frechin. The urban musical game: using sport balls as musical interfaces. In *CHI '12 Extended Abstracts on Human Factors in Computing Systems*, pages 1027–1030, Austin, Texas, USA, 2012.

[12] D. Rocchesso, S. Serafin, F. Behrendt, N. Bernardini, R. Bresin, G. Eckel, K. Franinovic, T. Hermann, S. Pauletto, P. Susini, and Y. Visell. Sonic interaction design: sound, information and experience. In *CHI '08 Extended Abstracts on Human Factors in Computing Systems*, pages 3969–3972, 2008.

[13] H. Zen, Y. Nankaku, and K. Tokuda. Continuous Stochastic Feature Mapping Based on Trajectory HMMs. *Audio, Speech, and Language Processing, IEEE Transactions on*, 19(2):417–430, 2011.

Learning Representations for Affective Video Understanding

Esra Acar
DAI Laboratory, Technische Universität Berlin
Ernst-Reuter-Platz 7, TEL 14, 10587 Berlin, Germany
esra.acar@tu-berlin.de

ABSTRACT

Among the ever growing available multimedia data, finding multimedia content which matches the current mood of users is a challenging problem. Choosing discriminative features for the representation of video segments is a key issue in designing video affective content analysis algorithms, where no dominant feature representation has emerged yet. Most existing affective content analysis methods either use low-level audio-visual features or generate hand-crafted higher level representations.

In this work, we propose to use deep learning methods, in particular, convolutional neural networks (CNNs), in order to learn mid-level representations from automatically extracted raw features. We exploit only the audio modality in the current framework and employ Mel-Frequency Cepstral Coefficients (MFCC) features in order to build higher level audio representations. We use the learned representations for the affective classification of music video clips. We choose multi-class support vector machines (SVMs) for classifying video clips into affective categories. Preliminary results on a subset of the DEAP dataset show that a significant improvement is obtained when we learn higher level representations instead of using low-level features directly for video affective content analysis. We plan to further extend this work and include visual modality as well. We will generate mid-level visual representations using CNNs and fuse these visual representations with mid-level audio representations both at feature- and decision-level for video affective content analysis.

Categories and Subject Descriptors

I.2.10 [**Vision and Scene Understanding**]: Video analysis; H.3.1 [**Information Storage and Retrieval**]: Content Analysis and Indexing

Keywords

Affect Analysis; Learning Feature Representations; Convolutional Neural Network; Support Vector Machine

MM'13, October 21–25, 2013, Barcelona, Spain.
ACM 978-1-4503-2404-5/13/10.
http://dx.doi.org/10.1145/2502081.2502215.

1. INTRODUCTION

Accessing online videos through services such as video on demand has become extremely easy thanks to equipments including DVB set top boxes (terrestrial, cable or satellite), Tablet PCs, high-speed Internet access or digital media-streaming devices. However, finding video content among the growing amount of multimedia which matches the current mood of users is still a challenge. One key issue in designing video affective content analysis algorithms is the representation of video content as in any pattern recognition task. The common way for video content representation is either using low-level audio-visual features or building hand-crafted higher level representations based on automatically extracted raw features. However, no dominant feature representation has emerged yet. In recent years, there is a growing interest for learning features directly from raw data in the field of audio or video content analysis. Within this context, deep learning methods such as CNNs and deep belief networks are shown to provide promising results (e.g., [12], [7]).

Inspired by the recent success of the deep learning methods in the field of audio-visual content analysis, we propose to learn feature representations directly from automatically extracted raw audio-visual features by deep learning for the issue of affective content analysis of videos. The aim of this research is to investigate the discriminative power of mid-level audio-visual representations which are learned from raw data by CNNs for modeling affective content of videos. Currently, we only exploit the audio modality of videos by employing MFCC features. The work will be extended by including visual modality of videos. Mid-level visual representations using CNNs will also be learned and will be fused with mid-level audio representations both at the feature- and decision-level for video affective content analysis.

The paper is organized as follows. Section 2 explores the recent developments and reviews methods which have been proposed for video affective content analysis with an emphasis on the feature representation of videos. In Section 3, we introduce our method for the affective classification of music video clips. We provide and discuss evaluation results on a subset of the DEAP dataset in Section 4. In Section 5, we present the future directions to expand our current approach. Finally, we present concluding remarks in Section 6.

2. RELATED WORK

Depending on the features employed for video representation, two different methods exist for affective content analysis, namely the methods based on low-level features and the ones based on mid-level or hierarchical features.

The most common type of affective content analysis approach is to employ low-level audio-visual features as video representations.

Soleymani et al. [13] address the affective representation of movie scenes based on the emotions that are actually felt by audience, where audio-visual features as well as physiological responses of participants are employed to estimate the arousal and valence degree of scenes. Canini et al. [2] aim at defining the emotional identity of a movie in a multidimensional space (along natural, temporal and energetic dimensions) based on audio-visual features in order to retrieve emotionally similar movies based on their emotional identities. In [4], a method for mood-based classification of TV Programs on a large-scale dataset is presented, where frame-basis audio-visual features are used as video representations. Srivastava et al. [14] address the recognition of emotions of characters present in movies. Low-level visual features based on facial feature points are employed for the facial expression recognition part of the work, whereas lexical analysis of dialogs is performed in order to provide complementary information for the final decision. Cui et al. [3] address affective content analysis of music videos, where they employ audio-visual features for the construction of arousal and valence models. Intended emotion tracking of movies is addressed by Malandrakis et al. [10], where audio-visual features are extracted for the affective representation of movies. In [15], a combined analysis of low-level audio- and visual representations based on early feature fusion is presented for the facial emotion recognition in videos. Yazdani et al. [18] present a method which employs audio-visual features as content representation for the affective analysis of music video clips.

The methods of the second category are based on mid-level or hierarchical representations of videos. These methods construct mid-level representations based on raw features and employ these mid-level representations for the affective content analysis of videos. The work presented in [16] combines both low-level audio-visual representations with higher-level video representations. In a first step, movies of different genres are clustered into different arousal intensities (i.e., high, medium, low) with fuzzy c-means [1] using low-level audio-visual features of video shots. In a second step, the results from the first step (i.e., higher level video representations) are employed along with low-level audio-visual features in order to perform emotional movie classification. Irie et al. [5] propose a latent topic driving model (LTDM) in order to address the issue of classifying movie scenes into affective categories at video shot level. For emotion modeling, the authors adopt Plutchik's eight basic emotions [11] and add a "neutral" category in order to reject movie scenes that arouse no emotion. Video shots are represented with a histogram of quantized audio-visual features and emotion topics are subsequently extracted via latent Dirichlet allocation. Emotions that a movie shot contains are determined based on the topics of the movie shot and predefined emotion transition weights based on the Plutchik's emotion theory. In an extended version of this work [6], Irie et al. propose to represent movie shots with so-called Bag-of-Affective Audio-visual Words and then apply the same LTDM architecture. Xu et al. [17] present a three-level affective content analysis framework, in which the purpose is to detect the affective content of videos (i.e., horror scenes for horror movies, laughable sections for sitcoms and emotional tagging of movies). They introduce mid-level representations which indicate dialog, audio emotional events (i.e., horror sound and laughter) and textual concepts (i.e., informative emotion keywords).

The abovementioned works represent videos with low- or mid-level hand-crafted features. However, there is a growing interest for learning features directly from extracted raw audio-visual features instead of representing audio or video data based on manually designed features. Schmidt et al. [12] address the feature representation issue for automatic detection of emotions in music by employing regression-based deep belief networks to learn features directly from magnitude spectra instead of handcrafting feature representations. By taking into account the dynamic nature of music, they also investigate combining multiple timescales of aggregated magnitude spectra as a basis for feature learning. These learned features are then evaluated in the context of multiple linear regression (MLR). Li et al. [9] propose to perform feature learning for music genre classification and use CNNs for the extraction of musical pattern features.

Our approach differs from the aforementioned works in the following aspects: (1) we learn feature representations from automatically extracted raw data by using a CNN and use the learned representations for the affective classification of music video clips by SVM, (2) we show that the learned mid-level audio representations are more discriminative and provide more precise results than low-level audio ones, and (3) we plan to further improve the classification performance by fusing the learned audio representations with mid-level visual representations which will also be learned through CNNs.

3. LEARNING REPRESENTATIONS

In this section, we present our current approach for the affective classification of music video clips. An overview of our solution is illustrated in Figure 1. Music video clips are first segmented into pieces, each piece lasting 5 seconds. We extract MFCC features for each piece. The resulting MFCC feature vectors of the segments are given as input to a CNN. The first layer (i.e., the input layer) of the CNN is a 125×13 map which contains the MFCC feature vectors from 125 frames of one music video segment. The CNN has three convolutional and two subsampling layers, one full connection and one output layer (this network size in terms of convolution and subsampling layers has experimentally given satisfactory results). After training the CNN with backpropagation algorithm, the output of the last convolutional layer is used as the mid-level audio representation of corresponding video segment. We apply convolutions with a kernel size of 4×4 in the first convolution layer. The kernel size of the second and the third convolution layers is 2×2. We apply 2×2 subsampling on each of the feature maps in all convolution layers. Hence, the MFCC feature vectors of one music video segment are converted into a 348 dimensional feature vector (which constitutes the mid-level audio representation) capturing the acoustic information in the audio signal of the music video segment. These mid-level audio representations are subsequently fed into a multi-class SVM in order to generate an affective video analysis model. In the test phase, mid-level audio representations are generated by using the trained CNN model for video segments of 5-second length based on MFCC feature vectors. The music video segments are subsequently classified by using the affective video analysis model. Final decisions for the classification of video segments are realized by a majority voting process as in [7].

4. PERFORMANCE EVALUATION

The experiments presented in this section aim at comparing the discriminative power of mid-level audio representations which are learned from raw data against low-level audio features.

4.1 Dataset and Groundtruth

We have used 38 music video clips from the DEAP dataset [8]. The dataset used in our experiments consists of 1.736 music video segments of 5-second length from 38 music video clips of different affective categories downloaded from YouTube. The data set is divided into a training set consisting of 1.202 segments from 28

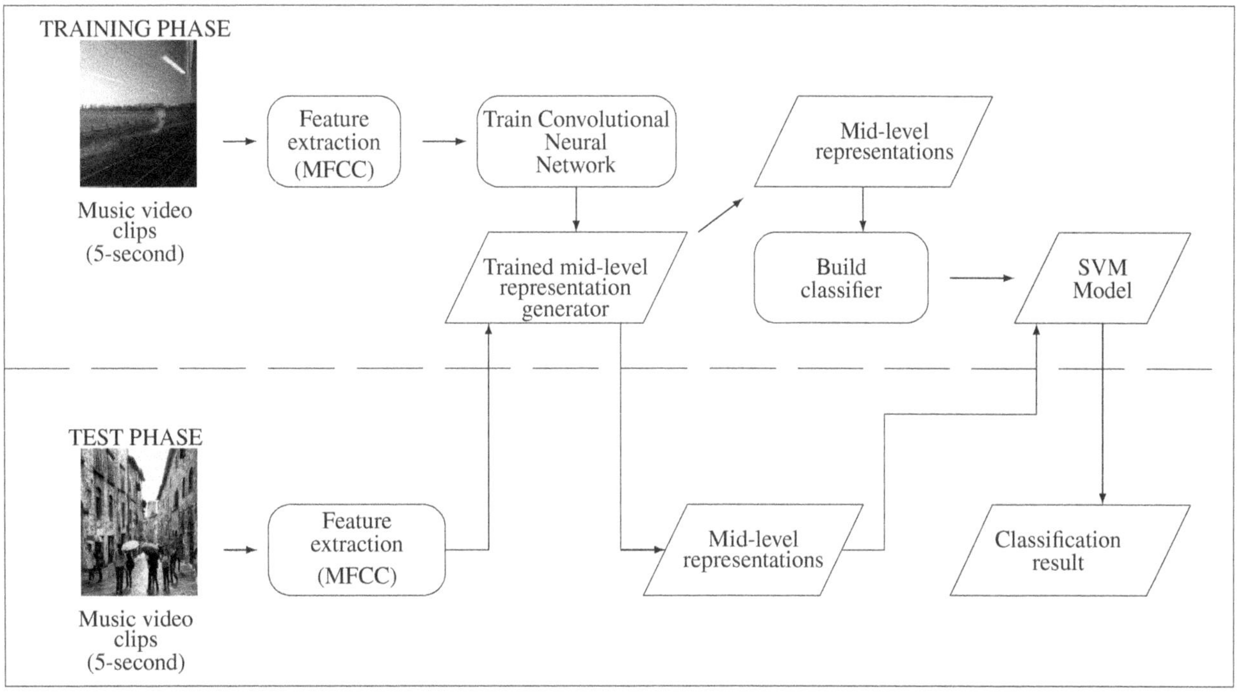

Figure 1: A high-level overview of our method for video affective analysis. Final classification decisions are realized by a majority voting process.

music video clips and a test set consisting of 534 segments from the remaining 10 music video clips.

Each clip is labeled according to the online ratings provided within the DEAP dataset. In order to assign only one label for each clip, we used a majority voting scheme on the online ratings for the related music video clip. The affective labels of music video clips are *elation*, *joy*, *interest*, *sadness*, *fear*, *disgust* and *anger*. In the training set, the *sadness* category contains 10 clips, the *joy* category 7, the *disgust* and *anger* categories 4, and the *elation*, *interest* and *fear* categories each contain 1 clip. In the test set, the *sadness* category contains 3 clips, the *joy* category 2, the *disgust*, *anger*, *elation*, *interest* and *fear* categories each contain 1 clip.

4.2 Experimental Setup

In order to extract the 13-dimensional MFCC features, we employed the MIR Toolbox v1.4[1]. Frame sizes of 40 ms without overlap are used to temporally match with the 25-fps video frames. Mean and standard deviation for each dimension of the MFCC feature vectors are computed, which compose the low-level audio representations of music video segments. We used the Deep Learning toolbox[2] in order to generate mid-level audio representations with a CNN.

We trained the multi-class SVMs with an RBF kernel using libsvm[3] as the SVM implementation. Training was performed using audio features extracted at the music video segment level. More specifically, we trained one SVM using the CNN-based mid-level audio features and a second SVM using the low-level audio features as input. The SVM parameters were optimized by 5-fold cross-validation on the training data. Our approach was evaluated using a training-test split.

[1] https://www.jyu.fi/hum/laitokset/musiikki/en/research/coe/materials/mirtoolbox

[2] https://github.com/rasmusbergpalm/DeepLearnToolbox/

[3] http://www.csie.ntu.edu.tw/~cjlin/libsvm/

4.3 Current Results and Discussions

Table 1 reports the classification accuracies of our method compared to the method which employs low-level audio features on the DEAP dataset. We achieved 50% classification accuracy with mid-level representations learned from raw data, while the classification accuracy is 30% for the method which uses low-level audio features. This demonstrates the potential of our approach for video affective content analysis.

Table 1: Classification accuracies on the DEAP dataset

Method	Accuracy (%)
Our method (mid-level audio)	50
The method (low-level audio)	30

In Figure 2, the confusion matrix of the classification results for the DEAP dataset is illustrated. The confusion matrix represents the performance of our method with the mid-level audio representations which are learned from MFCC feature vectors with a CNN model. As illustrated, the affect class pairs which are the most difficult to discriminate are *elation-joy* and *disgust-anger*. By integrating more features from different modalities such as visual and textual, we expect to better represent the affective content of video segments. There is also a tendency of our algorithm to classify video clips as *sadness*. We suspect that this is due to imbalanced data in the training set (i.e., there are more video clips labeled as *sadness*)

5. RESEARCH IN PROGRESS

In the current solution, we only employ audio features. We will augment this feature set with visual features. We plan to construct mid-level visual representations with CNNs and to fuse these representations with mid-level audio representations at the feature-

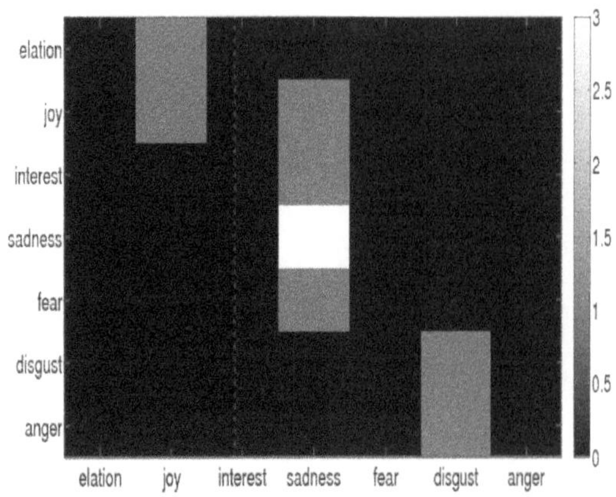

Figure 2: Confusion matrix on the DEAP dataset with mid-level audio representations learned from raw data (Mean accuracy: 50).

and decision-level. Exploring the architecture of the CNN (i.e., adjusting the number of convolution layers and kernel size) is another direction for future research. Comparing the performance of our method with methods which use hand-crafted mid-level feature representations such as the bag-of-words approaches is another track for future work. Currently, we obtained accuracy results for 38 music video clips selected from the DEAP dataset. Our final evaluation will include experiments on all video clips from the DEAP dataset (approximately 100 clips currently available on YouTube). We also plan to investigate the performance of our method on a movie dataset.

6. CONCLUSIONS

In this paper, we presented an approach for the affective classification of music video clips, where we learn higher level representations from raw audio features using CNNs. Preliminary results on a subset of the DEAP dataset support our belief that higher level representations which are learned using a CNN are more discriminative than low-level representations.

We currently exploit the audio modality only. We will extend this work by including features extracted from the visual modality. We will construct higher level representations using CNNs and fuse them with audio ones both at the feature- and decision-level in order to analyze the affective content of videos.

7. REFERENCES

[1] J. C. Bezdek. *Pattern recognition with fuzzy objective function algorithms.* Kluwer Academic Publishers, 1981.

[2] L. Canini, S. Benini, P. Migliorati, and R. Leonardi. Emotional identity of movies. In *Image Processing (ICIP), 2009 16th IEEE International Conference on*, pages 1821–1824. IEEE, 2009.

[3] Y. Cui, J. S. Jin, S. Zhang, S. Luo, and Q. Tian. Music video affective understanding using feature importance analysis. In *Proceedings of the ACM International Conference on Image and Video Retrieval*, pages 213–219. ACM, 2010.

[4] J. Eggink and D. Bland. A large scale experiment for mood-based classification of tv programmes. In *Multimedia and Expo (ICME), 2012 IEEE International Conference on*, pages 140–145. IEEE, 2012.

[5] G. Irie, K. Hidaka, T. Satou, A. Kojima, T. Yamasaki, and K. Aizawa. Latent topic driving model for movie affective scene classification. In *Proceedings of the 17th ACM international conference on Multimedia*, pages 565–568. ACM, 2009.

[6] G. Irie, T. Satou, A. Kojima, T. Yamasaki, and K. Aizawa. Affective audio-visual words and latent topic driving model for realizing movie affective scene classification. *Multimedia, IEEE Transactions on*, 12(6):523 –535, oct. 2010.

[7] S. Ji, W. Xu, M. Yang, and K. Yu. 3d convolutional neural networks for human action recognition. *IEEE Transactions on Pattern Analysis and Machine Intelligence*, pages 221–231, 2013.

[8] S. Koelstra, C. Muhl, M. Soleymani, J.-S. Lee, A. Yazdani, T. Ebrahimi, T. Pun, A. Nijholt, and I. Patras. Deap: A database for emotion analysis; using physiological signals. *Affective Computing, IEEE Transactions on*, 3(1):18–31, 2012.

[9] T. Li, A. B. Chan, and A. Chun. Automatic musical pattern feature extraction using convolutional neural network. In *Proc. Int. Conf. Data Mining and Applications*, 2010.

[10] N. Malandrakis, A. Potamianos, G. Evangelopoulos, and A. Zlatintsi. A supervised approach to movie emotion tracking. In *Acoustics, Speech and Signal Processing (ICASSP), 2011 IEEE International Conference on*, pages 2376–2379. IEEE, 2011.

[11] R. Plutchik. The nature of emotions human emotions have deep evolutionary roots, a fact that may explain their complexity and provide tools for clinical practice. *American Scientist*, 89(4):344–350, 2001.

[12] E. M. Schmidt, J. Scott, and Y. E. Kim. Feature learning in dynamic environments: Modeling the acoustic structure of musical emotion. In *International Society for Music Information Retrieval*, pages 325–330, 2012.

[13] M. Soleymani, G. Chanel, J. Kierkels, and T. Pun. Affective characterization of movie scenes based on multimedia content analysis and user's physiological emotional responses. In *Multimedia, 2008. ISM 2008. Tenth IEEE International Symposium on*, pages 228–235. IEEE, 2008.

[14] R. Srivastava, S. Yan, T. Sim, and S. Roy. Recognizing emotions of characters in movies. In *Acoustics, Speech and Signal Processing (ICASSP), 2012 IEEE International Conference on*, pages 993–996. IEEE, 2012.

[15] M. Wimmer, B. Schuller, D. Arsic, G. Rigoll, and B. Radig. Low-level fusion of audio and video feature for multi-modal emotion recognition. In *3rd International Conference on Computer Vision Theory and Applications. VISAPP*, volume 2, pages 145–151, 2008.

[16] M. Xu, J. S. Jin, S. Luo, and L. Duan. Hierarchical movie affective content analysis based on arousal and valence features. In *Proceedings of the 16th ACM international conference on Multimedia*, pages 677–680. ACM, 2008.

[17] M. Xu, J. Wang, X. He, J. S. Jin, S. Luo, and H. Lu. A three-level framework for affective content analysis and its case studies. *Multimedia Tools and Applications*, 2012.

[18] A. Yazdani, K. Kappeler, and T. Ebrahimi. Affective content analysis of music video clips. In *Proc. of the 1st Int. ACM workshop on Music information retrieval with user-centered and multimodal strategies*, pages 7–12. ACM, 2011.

Context-Aware Gesture Recognition in Classical Music Conducting

Álvaro Sarasúa
Sonology Department, Escola Superior de Música de Catalunya
Music Technology Group, Universitat Pompeu Fabra
Padilla 155, Barcelona, Spain
alvaro.sarasua@upf.edu

ABSTRACT

Body movement has received increasing attention in music technology research during the last years. Some new musical interfaces make use of gestures to control music in a meaningful and intuitive way. A typical approach is to use the orchestra conducting paradigm, in which the computer that generates the music would be a *virtual orchestra* conducted by the user. However, although conductors' gestures are complex and their meaning can vary depending on the musical context, this context-dependency is still to explore. We propose a method to study context-dependency of body and facial gestures of conductors in orchestral classical music based on temporal clustering of gestures into actions, followed by an analysis of the evolution of audio features after action occurrences. For this, multi-modal data (audio, video, motion capture) will be recorded in real live concerts and rehearsals situations using unobtrusive techniques.

Categories and Subject Descriptors

H.5.2 [**User Interfaces**]: Interaction styles, Theory and methods; H.5.5 [**Sound and Music Computing**]: Signal analysis, synthesis, and processing

General Terms

Algorithms, Theory

Keywords

gesture, classical music, conducting, music information retrieval

1. INTRODUCTION

Body movement plays a key role on the performance and perception of music. We can think of the movement musicians have to make in order to create sounds from their instruments, the way in which dancers move following what they hear or just the different movements (tapping, head-banging...) that we make when listening to music. The interest for these movements has increased in the last years in music technology research and we can find several studies dealing with music-related *gestures*. One of the reasons for this growing interest on musical gestures is that a multimodal analysis of music that includes not only sound or score but also gesture-related information can reveal information about co-expressive elements that are present in the communication process of music [5].

Our work studies body movement in the orchestral classical music scenario relating it to expressivity on the resulting music, with a special focus on conductors' gestures. To do so, we will carry experiments in real live concerts situations where we will record multimodal data (multitrack audio, video, motion). From these recordings, we will study correlation between conductors' gestures and expressivity-related audio features. Moreover, we will study how similar gestures can get different meanings depending on the musical context.

This work is done in the scope of the PHENICX project, which aims at creating a methodological and technical framework for live classical music concerts in such a way that they become enriched multimodal, multi-perspective, multilayer digital artifacts to be explored, (re)enjoyed and shared in different ways. The output of this particular work will be used for an application that allows impersonation of the conductor in a complex and meaningful way. Also, the study of relations between conductors' gestures and musical expressive parameters will be useful for live visualizations of conductor-ensemble interaction within the performance.

This paper is organized as follows. In Section 2, we review and discuss works related to this topic. In Section 3, the proposed methodology is explained. Finally, in Section 4 future work is briefly discussed.

2. RELATED WORKS

Different approaches have been considered in the study of musical gestures. For instance, there are cases in which the sound-producing gestures of a particular instrument are obtained and analyzed in detail in order to synthesize their sound in a realistic way. Maestre et al. [17] use bowing parameters of violin performances to achieve realistic sample-based synthesis. In [10], Guaus et al. present a system to track left-hand fingering in guitar and study expressivity. A similar approach is taken by García et al. in [9], with the recorder as a case study and using pressure sensors.

There are some other approaches, however, that study different music-related gestures which are not just those in-

MM'13, October 21–25, 2013, Barcelona, Spain.
ACM 978-1-4503-2404-5/13/10.
http://dx.doi.org/10.1145/2502081.2502216 .

volved in sound generation as the ones above. Jensenius [11] carried a comprehensive study of *music-related movements* including observations of *air instrument* performances, *free dance* to music and *sound-tracing*, showing that people are able to associate different movements with sound features regardless of their musical expertise. Dahl et al. [6] made experiments with participants rating perceived emotions from mute video performances and showed that some basic emotions (happiness, sadness and anger) can be communicated via movements only whereas some others are not (fear). A similar experiment was done by Luck et al. [16]: the kinematics of conductors' expressive gestures (represented by features extracted from motion capture data) were related to the perceived expression (achieved by continuous ratings made by participants). Their results suggest some correlation between gesture features and perceived expressivity (e.g. more expressive = vertically extended and accelerated hand movement). Similarly, Camurri et al. [4] showed that emotions can be perceived in dancing movement following features as *quantity of motion*.

Works closer to the Human-Computer Interaction (HCI) field have looked for meaningful ways of controlling music performed by a computer using gestures. A typical intuitive approach is to use the orchestra conducting paradigm, in which the computer would be a *virtual orchestra* that the user conducts using gestures captured by different kinds of devices. There have been several works in this direction [2, 3, 13, 19] that either use video or special batons to allow interaction with virtual orchestras by usually modifying tempo and dynamics. Fabiani [7] used the same conductor paradigm going a step beyond and creating mappings between gestural data and semantic descriptors to let the listener control how music is performed. However, this mapping, which uses the valence-arousal model of emotions introduced by Russell [23] by for example assigning quantity of motion to valence and position of the hands to arousal, remains simple compared to the tasks performed by a real conductor and allows limited music interaction when it comes to more creative applications. He uses the KTH rule system [8] (a computational model for expressive performance) in two different approaches: (1) synthesizing sound from MIDI information and (2) modifying tempo and dynamics of real audio.

The gestures of the conductor and their relation to the music have also been studied from a computational perspective. Luck [14] has done a series of works on computational analysis of conductors' temporal gestures by extracting features from audio and motion-capture recordings. The main focus of these works is the relation of the gestures to the beat and the musicians' synchronization. From the results, communication of the beat seems to be related to acceleration along the trajectory and synchronization is clearly influenced by the synchronizer's previous experience. However, conducting manuals [22, 21] tend to focus more on the expressive aspects of conducting rather than on just time-beating.

Regardless of how interactive systems commented so far map gestures to sound features, this mapping remains the same throughout all the interaction. However, as stated in cited manuals and in works such as Poggi's [20], the same gesture can have different meanings and effects depending on the moment. For example, the director can frown to express aggressiveness (thus asking to play loud) or disgust (giving feedback to the musicians about something (s)he does not like). For a system to be able to gather different meanings from a same gesture depending on the musical context, it should be able to analyze music at different time scales in a way that allows it to know what part of the piece or the phrase is playing at the moment. Also, it should be able to get real-time information about at least tempo, loudness and articulation, which account for about 90% of the communication of emotions in expressive music performance [12]. The analysis of expressiveness-related audio features has been broadly studied for computational models of expressive performance. Widmer offers a good overview on the topic in [24]. Furthermore, and again according to the manuals and Poggi's work, facial gestures carry an important amount of expressive information while computational approaches to classical music conducting have not addressed them in a comprehensive way.

3. METHODOLOGY

In this Section, we explain how we propose to study conducting gestures with context dependency. Concretely, we explain how the data will be acquired and stored, how we will extract meaningful features from it and how we will relate gestural and audio information in order to extract conclusions. An initial dataset from a concert has been created in June 2013 including almost 2 hours of data.

3.1 Recordings

Most works including motion capture data have been done in controlled scenarios instead of live concert situations. The main reason for this is that motion capture systems used so far are somehow intrusive as they use sensors on the body, special batons, etc. The appearance of depth-sense cameras (popularized by Microsoft's Kinect[1]) allow unobtrusive 3-D gesture capturing with an easy setup. We will perform recordings at rehearsals and concerts in the High School of Music of Catalonia (ESMUC). Thanks to having access to the concerts and rehearsals of ESMUC, we will be able to record performances from different conductors (including students). The recordings of every performance will include:

- Multi-track audio. The number of tracks will depend on the performed piece, but there will be at least one track per section and, in the case of the concerts, one track from every microphone used for PA (stereo pair and overheads).
- Multi-perspective video. Concerts and rehearsals will be recorded with several cameras. A dedicated camera on the conductor will be used to identify basic facial gestures.
- Conductor's motion capture. Microsoft's Kinect will be used to record conductor's body movement. This device tracks 20 joints (points in the body) at 30 frames per second.

All these data will be collected in RepoVizz[2][18], an online database and visualizer of multimodal recordings developed by the Music Technology Group. Figure 1 shows a screenshot of RepoVizz's visualizer with data of a string quartet performance. RepoVizz automatically extracts features of audio files using Essentia[3].

[1] http://www.xbox.com/kinect

[2] http://repovizz.upf.edu/

[3] http://www.mtg.upf.edu/technologies/essentia

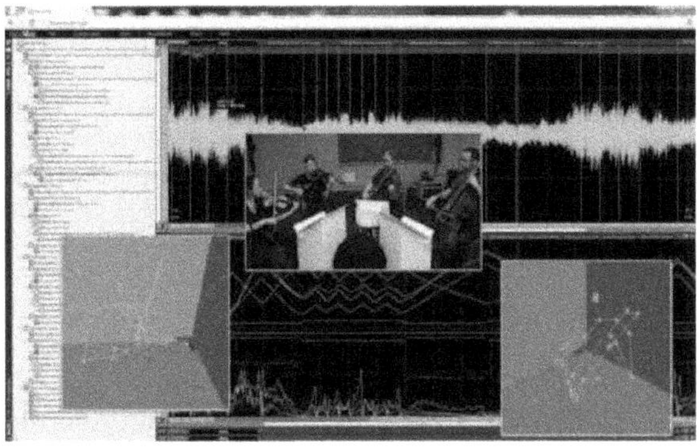

Figure 1: Screenshot of RepoVizz's visualizer, featuring some signals from computed audio descriptors, an audio file with annotations, video and motion capture display.

3.2 Gestures feature extraction

Previous work by Luck [15] on conductor's movement extracts features from gestures by deriving three-dimensional position, velocity and acceleration from markers at the body and the baton. Our motion capture data will allow to extract similar features from up to 9 points in the upper body (see Kinect's specifications).

From the conductor's video we will extract facial information using Kyle McDonald's MIT licensed libraries[4] for face tracking, including position of eyes, eye brows and mouth.

3.3 Gesture clustering

As explained in Section 1, one of our goals is to study how similar gestures can have different meanings depending on the musical context. The main problem here is to detect these "similar gestures" throughout an entire performance. Computational analysis of conductors' gestures so far do not consider *action units* as defined by Jensenius [11]: *goal-directed* movement excursions. In our approach, we will address this issue by looking for clusters of motion primitives from the conductor's gestures. Most common techniques for gesture clustering are based on Hidden Markov Models (HMMs) [1] and are suitable for real-time scenarios. Another approach we will consider for offline analysis is Hierarchical Aligned Cluster Analysis (HACA) [25], with which we can cluster time series of human motion in an unsupervised way. From time series of features explained in Section 3.2 we will look for points in time where similar gestures are being used.

3.4 Feature analysis

3.4.1 Relating gestures and audio

At this point, we will have two sets of data to relate audio with. On one hand, we will have direct gesture descriptors computed from the position of the body parts (upper body from Kinect and facial points from facial tracker). Cross-correlation between audio high level descriptors related to expressiveness and gestures descriptors will be computed and analysed in order to see how these gestures are actually influencing resulting audio. An analysis and correction of the lag (time difference between conductor's gestures and ensemble's response) similar to the one in [15] may be necessary. Figure 2 contains a block diagram that summarizes the overall process in this case. Features are extracted from audio and gestures and then correlated.

[4]https://github.com/kylemcdonald/ofxFaceTracker

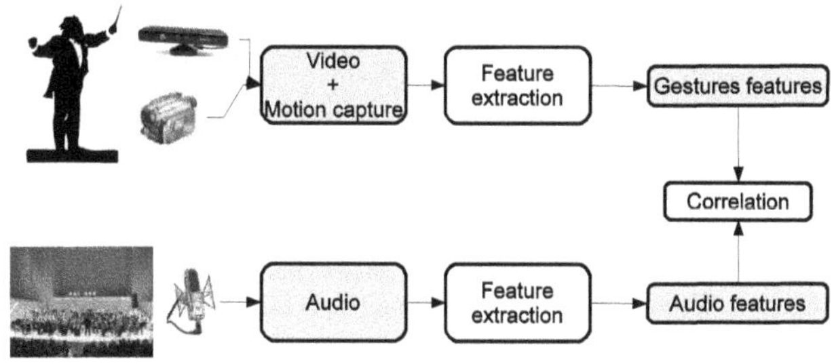

Figure 2: Block diagram of gestures-audio relation analysis. Features from audio and gestures are extracted and correlated.

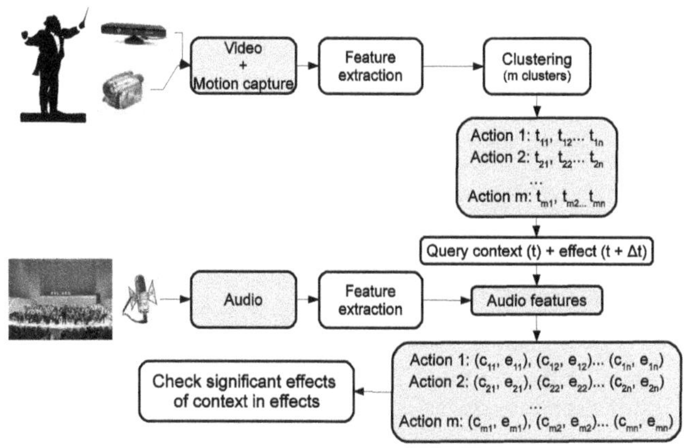

Figure 3: Block diagram of context-dependent analysis of gestures. Gestures are separated in m clusters corresponding to *actions*. Musical context and expressive change (effect) are represented by expressiveness-related audio features and their evolution in time after gesture occurrence.

3.4.2 Context-dependent analysis of gestures

On the other hand, we will have clusters of complex gestures and the different positions in time where they appear. Here, the approach will be slightly different and will include (a) identifying the context where the gesture occurs -part of the piece and features related to expressiveness-, (b) analysing the expressive changes in audio after the gesture and (c) studying similarity between context-effect pairs. We expect to find a significant effect of the context on the effect for a particular gesture, thus being able to define a set of rules of how an interactive system should react to that gesture depending on the context. The process now is more complex and implies more steps as showed in Figure 3. We start by extracting features from audio and gesture data. However, from the gesture data we build m clusters of *actions* that indicate the moments in time where different gestures occur. For a particular action and time t, the context will be defined by expressiveness-related audio features at the moment in which the gesture occurs. The effect will be defined by how these features evolve after some time Δt.

4. FUTURE WORK

The work so far has been focused on the definition of the presented framework and implementation of the gesture acquisition and storage software. In the near future, the plan is to work on the theoretical and practical definition of context for the orchestral music scenario. Also, using the initial dataset created this summer, experiments will be carried to evaluate different gesture feature extraction and clustering techniques that should, later, work in real-time scenarios. From the results of these experiments, changes in the acquisition procedure may be addressed in order to go towards a framework where gestures can be easily acquired, clustered and analyzed in relation to the resulting music.

5. ACKNOWLEDGMENTS

The research leading to these results has received funding from the European Union Seventh Framework Programme FP7 / 2007- 2013 through the PHENICX project under grant agreement n° 601166.

6. REFERENCES

[1] F. Bevilacqua, B. Zamborlin, A. Sypniewski, N. Schnell, F. Guédy, and N. Rasamimanana. Continuous realtime gesture following and recognition. In *Gesture in embodied communication and human-computer interaction*, pages 73–84. Springer, 2010.

[2] J. Borchers, E. Lee, W. Samminger, and M. Mühlhäuser. Personal orchestra: A real-time audio/video system for interactive conducting. *Multimedia Systems*, 9(5):458–465, 2004.

[3] B. Bruegge, C. Teschner, P. Lachenmaier, E. Fenzl, D. Schmidt, and S. Bierbaum. Pinocchio: conducting a virtual symphony orchestra. In *Proceedings of the international conference on Advances in computer entertainment technology*, pages 294–295. ACM, 2007.

[4] A. Camurri, I. Lagerlöf, and G. Volpe. Recognizing emotion from dance movement: comparison of spectator recognition and automated techniques. *International Journal of Human-Computer Studies*, 59(1):213–225, 2003.

[5] B. Caramiaux, F. Bevilacqua, and N. Schnell. Towards a gesture-sound cross-modal analysis. In *Gesture in Embodied Communication and Human-Computer Interaction*, pages 158–170. Springer, 2010.

[6] S. Dahl and A. Friberg. Expressiveness of musician's body movements in performances on marimba. In *Gesture-based communication in human-computer interaction*, pages 479–486. Springer, 2004.

[7] M. Fabiani. *Interactive computer-aided expressive music performance: Analysis, control, modification and synthesis*. PhD thesis, KTH, 2011.

[8] A. Friberg, R. Bresin, and J. Sundberg. Overview of the KTH rule system for musical performance. *Advances in Cognitive Psychology*, 2(2-3):145–161, 2006.

[9] F. García, L. Vinceslas, J. Tubau, and E. Maestre. Acquisition and study of blowing pressure profiles in recorder playing. In *Proceedings of the 2011 conference on New interfaces for musical expression*, 2011.

[10] E. Guaus, T. Ozaslan, E. Palacios, and J. L. Arcos. A left hand gesture caption system for guitar based on capacitive sensors. In *Proceedings of New interfaces for musical expression*, pages 238–243, 2010.

[11] A. R. Jensenius. *Action–Sound: Developing Methods and Tools to Study Music-Related Body Movement*. PhD thesis, University of Oslo, 2007.

[12] P. N. Juslin and P. Laukka. Communication of emotions in vocal expression and music performance: Different channels, same code? *Psychological bulletin*, 129(5):770, 2003.

[13] E. Lee, T. M. Nakra, and J. Borchers. You're the conductor: a realistic interactive conducting system for children. In *Proceedings of the 2004 conference on New interfaces for musical expression*, pages 68–73. National University of Singapore, 2004.

[14] G. Luck. Computational Analysis of Conductors' Temporal Gestures. *New Perspectives on Music and Gesture*, page 159, 2011.

[15] G. Luck and P. Toiviainen. Ensemble musicians' synchronization with conductors' gestures: An automated feature-extraction analysis. *Music Perception*, 24(2):189–200, 2006.

[16] G. Luck, P. Toiviainen, and M. R. Thompson. Perception of Expression in Conductors' Gestures: A Continuous Response Study. *Music Perception*, 28(1):47–57, 2010.

[17] E. Maestre, A. Pérez, and R. Ramirez. Gesture sampling for instrumental sound synthesis: violin bowing as a case study. In *International Computer Music Conference*, 2010.

[18] O. Mayor, J. Llop, and E. Maestre. RepoVizz: A multimodal on-line database and browsing tool for music performance research. In *Proceedings of the 12th International Society for Music Information Retrieval Conference*, 2011.

[19] L. Peng and D. Gerhard. A gestural interface for orchestral conducting education. In *Proceedings of 1st international conference on computer supported education (CSEDU), Lisboa, Portugal*, pages 406–409, 2009.

[20] I. Poggi. The lexicon of the conductor's face. *Advances in consciusness research*, 35:271–284, 2002.

[21] F. Prausnitz. *Score and podium: A complete guide to conducting*. WW Norton, 1983.

[22] M. Rudolf. *The grammar of conducting: a practical guide to baton technique and orchestral interpretation*. Schirmer Books, 1980.

[23] J. A. Russell. A circumplex model of affect. *Journal of personality and social psychology*, 39(6):1161–1178, 1980.

[24] G. Widmer and W. Goebl. Computational models of expressive music performance: The state of the art. *Journal of New Music Research*, 33(3):203–216, 2004.

[25] F. Zhou, F. De la Torre, and J. F. Cohn. Unsupervised discovery of facial events. *2010 IEEE Computer Society Conference on Computer Vision and Pattern Recognition*, pages 2574–2581, June 2010.

Bringing the Sport Stadium Atmosphere to Remote Fans

Pedro Centieiro
CITI, Faculdade de Ciências e Tecnologia, Universidade Nova de Lisboa
2829-516 Caparica, Portugal
+351 212948536
pcentieiro@gmail.com

ABSTRACT
While watching live sports broadcasts we do not feel so emotionally connected with the performers and the in-venue fans as if we were watching it live, where the event takes place. Moreover, both remote and in-venue fans do not share a social connection, resulting in defragmented social experiences. This work intends to establish a new paradigm that explores the use of mobile devices to enhance remote fans' interaction with a live event. This new paradigm will provide them with an emotional and social experience by bringing the stadium atmosphere, its immersion, and emotional levels, to remote supporters. As a result, remote fans will be more engaged in the broadcasted sports, and both, remote and in-venue, fans will all feel part of the same community.

Categories and Subject Descriptors
H.5.2 [**User Interfaces**]: Input devices and strategies, prototyping.

General Terms
Design, Experimentation, Human Factors.

Keywords
Sports fans, affective computing, persuasive technology, second screen, remote interaction, social experiences.

1. INTRODUCTION
The level of thrill and excitement felt during live sports is a unique experience. Experiencing a match in first hand, instead of watching it on TV, is a very different experience: the surrounding atmosphere involves us, performance happens in front of our eyes, in real time, and we can cheer, chant and support the performers along with the other thousands of fans at the venue. However, many fans do not have the possibility to go to the venue. When these fans watch a match on TV they feel less satisfaction and more loneliness, compared to when watching the match live [1].

To overcome these problems, we propose to develop mobile solutions that will bring the venue atmosphere, its immersion and emotional levels, to remote users. To accomplish this, we will explore the second screen concept, which has become widely popular in recent years [2]. We will also study how affective computing and persuasive technology principles can be applied through the mobile screen concept and establish new forms of bi-directional communication and interaction with mobile devices, to encourage remote fans to perform specific actions in order to enhance their experiences, so they can be involved as much as possible in the sport stadium experience. Moreover, by accessing the stadium media infrastructure (i.e. wall screens), it will be possible to show the support and encouragement coming from remote fans watching the match worldwide, to players and fans at the venue. This bi-directional approach requires the involvement of third parties, but it is something we are willing to explore.

This new interaction paradigm is based on identifying key moments during a match, and motivating remote fans to participate and take actions, such as applauding after a great play or hearing a heartbeat sound when a penalty kick is about to take place, to create a tension moment. Mobile devices and their built-in sensors can be used to detect users' actions, give them the corresponding feedback, and acknowledge their contribution.

Our research work has been focusing on soccer, although it is expected that most concepts can be applied to different sports, and even to events like concerts (similar to the work being researched in [3]). We chose soccer, because it is widely accepted as one of the world's most popular sports [4], it engages an incredible number of fans all over the world, and generates strong emotions. Thus, we saw it as a natural fit to study and apply our concepts.

2. RELATED WORK
In order to study what are the fans' motives for loving their team and attend matches, several instruments were proposed ([5], [6] and [7]). One popular instrument is the Sport Fan Motivation Scale (SFMS) [5], which is designed to identify the motivations of sports fans and to help sports decision makers, determine how to increase fans' involvement. SFMS comprises eight motivational factors, such as eustress, group affiliation and family. With the SFMS, Wann *et al* conducted a study [8] where sports fans reported affiliation as one of the top reasons for originally becoming a fan, their continuous support to the team, and ceased their support if they did not received the desired group affiliation.

Taking into account those motivational factors, Uhrich and Benkenstein [9] studied what is defined by Sport Stadium Experience, and presented the cause of the different stimuli that define this special atmosphere: organizers, spectators, game action, and stadium architecture. These factors end up resulting in amazing vibes, enthusiasm, strong emotions and general euphoria (as described by the fans enquired in the studies). The study conducted in [10] reveals that aspects of match attendance like cheering, singing and crowd size, might represent increased feelings of belongingness amongst supporters, since they see themselves as part of one voice, the 12th man, positively reinforcing their identity with the team. Moreover, the analysis of the crowd during live sports is of great importance to understand single and social behaviors between fans, and how they react to different events. Studies like the ones carried out in [11] and [12] present relevant insights on these matters, showing that fans prefer to be among a high density crowd, even if it means being in a

MM '13, Oct 21-25 2013, Barcelona, Spain
ACM 978-1-4503-2404-5/13/10.

small venue; and that factors like the spectators' excitement level can be inferred by observing the crowd activity. The more we understand about the stadium atmosphere, the better we are able to build applications that enhance the remote users' experience.

Affective computing studies how devices can recognize, interpret, and simulate human emotions. One of the goals of affective computing research is to give computers the ability to help communicate emotions, by receiving and sending emotional cues [13]. PANAS (Positive and Negative Affect Schedule) [14] is a paper-based questionnaire that assesses people's affective states. Another widely used tool for emotion assessment is Russell's Affect Grid [15]. This tool consists in a 10x10 table, where test subjects are required to check the grid position that best describes their current disposition. It is our objective to induce the emotions experienced by the in-venue fans, and verify if remote fans have similar emotions when interacting with the developed prototypes.

Persuasive technology is defined as the technology designed to change users' attitudes or behaviors through persuasion and social influence, but not through coercion [16]. Today, mobile devices have a great persuasion power to influence and motivate users [17], and this is something that we will take advantage of. Fogg [16] mentions three intrinsic motivators that involve interaction among people: competition, cooperation and recognition. These will play an important role in motivating users to perform certain actions by competing and cooperating with others, and by getting recognition when achieving milestones. Take for instance fantasy football, which is one of the most popular web games about sports in the world [18], and a good example how competition and recognition successfully work together. Thousands of friends create and join leagues, without any kind of reward, other than the simple satisfaction of beating their friends.

The use of a second screen provides functionalities to improve the viewer's experience. For instance, users can read additional event-related information, access social networks, and participate in interactive experiences synchronized with the live event's activity, such as polls or quizzes. However, the use of an extra screen results in a competition for the users' attention. This issue is studied by Holmes *et al* [19], where the authors suggest that adding a synchronized second screen application to the TV viewing experience has important impacts on the distribution of visual attention as indicated by point of gaze.

Another issue that needs to be taken into account is the synchronization between what is being watched, and the content displayed on the second screen. Both of these feeds have different sources (TV broadcast and the server handling the second screen application), and they need to be synchronized to provide a non-disruptive experience (i.e. the second device displaying content neither earlier nor later than the one presented on the TV). This problem can be solved by having either access to the TV feed like in Never.no[1] and SynchronizeTV[2] (allowing to synchronize the server and the broadcast) or by performing a fingerprinting process like the one performed by ConnecTV[3] (however this will not work in a live event where the application needs to react live to specific key moments). Since we cannot rely on having access to the TV feed, we plan to use a process similar to Kwarter[4], where a human operator is in charge of triggering the different key moments. Nevertheless, the synchronization problem between TV and the mobile devices can still remain. To this end, we intend to introduce a mechanism through which, users can adjust the delay they wish to have, in order to have the TV content synchronized with the application.

Although, there are second screen systems that provide users with extra information and game experiences (like Never.no[1] and Kwarter[4]), there is not a mobile concept that tries to explore the affective responses felt by remote sport fans, while watching their favorite teams. We think that in order for this concept to work, it is of great importance to persuade users to perform specific actions (like applauding or cheering), but without overwhelming them. The users' focus shall always be the broadcasted match, while the mobile application acts as a channel that seeks to enhance the users' emotions.

3. RESEARCH STATEMENT

The objective of this work is to create interesting experiences that induce remote spectators with affective responses similar to the ones felt at the stadium. To make that possible, we started by focusing on the sports fan motivation, in order to define what fans seek in a sports match. As previously mentioned in [1] and [8], group affiliation factors are among the top reasons for fans to get together to watch sports events. Fans are motivated to attend and watch sport events not only with their friends and family, but also with other (unknown) fans, which helps to increase social well-being. In other words, fans are motivated by social experiences. Thus, we outlined our investigation in two domains that will be interconnected through the development of this research work: user interactions and social experiences.

User Interactions

Different types of key moments (e.g. goal, free kick, chant) trigger different types of users' interactions and experiences. These can be divided in two kinds of interactions: passive and active.

Passive interactions do not require explicit user action. They are performed by the application in order to enhance user engagement in the event. For example, users can experience the match as if they were at the stands (by hearing or watching from a camera installed among the crowd), the TV volume can increase when our team scores, or the application can trigger moments of tension like playing a heartbeat sound before a penalty kick.

On the other hand, active interactions require users to interact with the application in order to mimic the actions happening in the stadium. This way, users are challenged to clap after a great play, scream after a goal or sing along a support chant. Of course that these interactions are more complex than the passive ones and thus, it is necessary to take different approaches to detect if users are performing them correctly (e.g. based on sound and motion).

All of these experiences will be designed as group-level challenges that motivate users to compete and cooperate to achieve recognition.

Social Experiences

It is our intention to create experiences not only for fans that are within a local community (sharing the same physical space), but also for fans that do not have that possibility. Therefore, these latter fans need to be connected through an online community. By having both these communities (local and online), we can deliver similar activities, yet different experiences, which increase sociability levels between individuals. Moreover, the existence of

[1] Never.no, http://never.no/tour-de-france-companion-app/.

[2] SynchronizeTV, http://www.synchronize.tv

[3] ConnecTV, http://www.connectv.com

[4] Kwarter, http://www.kwarter.com

extrinsic motivators (like achievements, badges or other digital rewards), together with the group-level intrinsic motivators previous mentioned, helps to further engage users in a social community. Besides that, it is crucial to integrate the application with the most popular social networks (like Facebook and Twitter) to support group promotion, sharing of results, social recommendation and influence, and rewarding.

Figure 1 gives an overview of our research work, showing how the user interactions and social experiences overlap to create the prototypes that we have planned.

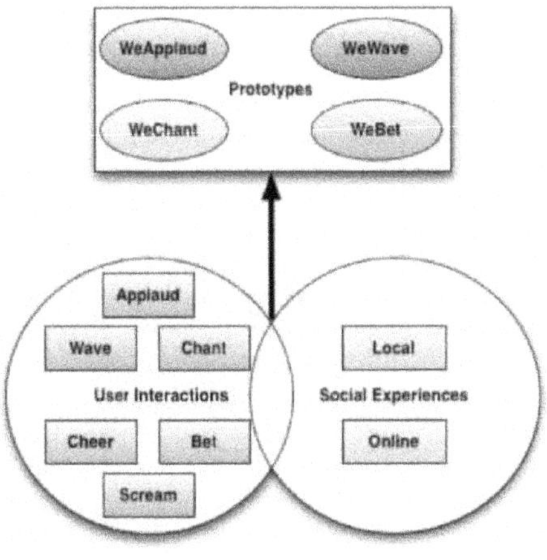

Figure 1. Research context overview.

3.1 Contributions

The final goal of this work is to bring the sport stadium experience to remote fans spread around the world. To achieve it, we aim to develop several prototypes that allow remote users to be involved in the sports stadium atmosphere, and provide them with new interaction mechanisms that enhance their experience during a broadcasted live sport event. We are not expecting that remote fans will be able to experience the exact stadium atmosphere as the ones in the stadium do, but we believe that it is possible to create an innovative and engaging user experience for worldwide fans that cannot attend the event. In summary, the contributions will focus on (1) the development of interactive methods that make the experience for remote users more similar to that of fans watching the match at the venue, and (2) the study of the implications of these new social experiences.

3.2 Prototypes

So far we have implemented two prototypes, WeApplaud [20] and WeBet [21], which are described next.

WeApplaud is a multiplayer mobile game that takes users, sharing the same physical location, to participate in the applauses happening in the stadium during a simulated match broadcast. Using a smartphone, each player must clap, synchronized with the audience in the match, to be awarded with points. The interaction is intuitive and non-intrusive, allowing users to clap like they do in real life. This way, users simply need to hold the mobile device on one hand, and then move it as if they would hit the palm of the other hand (Figure 1 (a)). This can be done by using either the front or back side of the device. Since a clap is only a clap if it hits something and generates a sound, we decided to use a combination of data from the smartphone's accelerometer and microphone. Therefore, when the mobile device detects a sound peak, it immediately checks if there was also a movement in a particular direction. If so, it is counted as a clap.

The goals of this prototype were to measure the users' receptivity for this new paradigm and to evaluate the entertainment concept created by WeApplaud (in order to ascertain if users would have fun with it), and the resulting user feedback was very positive. The user tests were conducted with 16 voluntary participants, with a mean age of 30.1. In these tests, each participant needed to choose to play for one of the two teams of supporters (red or blue team) that would compete head-to-head on a pre-recorded match. To create a real time competition between the two teams of supporters, both were challenged to applaud during the same key moments (i.e. goal, dangerous play), and supporting the same sports team, in order to promote group affiliation. Figure 2 (b) depicts two participants playing a game session of WeApplaud.

After each user test, participants were asked to rate statements in a questionnaire, using a five-point Likert-type scale, which ranged from strongly disagree (1) to strongly agree (5). Participants liked to use WeApplaud (43.75% rated 4; 56.25% rated 5), found it easy to learn (43.75% rated 4; 50% rated 5) and to use (31.25% rated 4; 56.25% rated 5). Most participants felt that claps were correctly detected by the application (56.25% rated 4; 25% rated 5) and the clapping interaction was natural (50% rated 4; 25% rated 5). Finally, users stated that the competition promoted by WeApplaud contributed to increase the level of entertainment during the broadcasted match (43.75% rated 4; 50% rated 5).

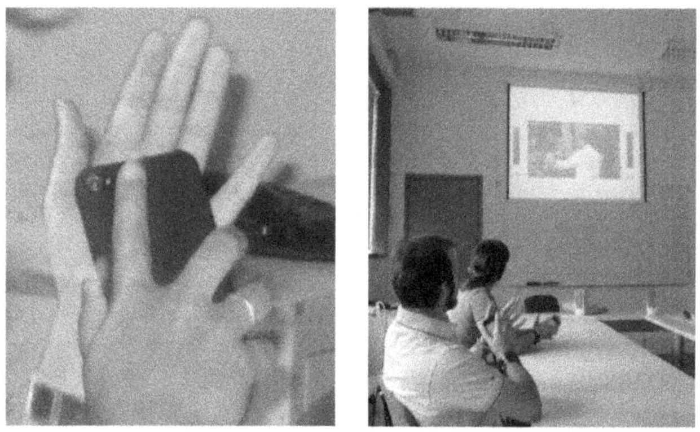

Figure 2. One participant performing the clapping action (a), while playing a WeApplaud game session (b).

WeBet is a mobile game that prompts users to bet if a goal is about to happen during a football match, without requiring their visual attention on the mobile device. To access the WeBet concept we developed a two-state interaction mechanism, resembling a jet fighter shooting button, relying on tactile and audible feedback to give users the perception of the application's state. To bet that a goal is about to happen, users can perform a gesture from outside to inside the screen and start pulling a special bet interface up as their fingers enter the bottom of the screen. As soon as the special interface is full screen, an upward sound is played and the phone starts vibrating repeatedly, in order to inform users that they can now place a bet by clicking anywhere on the screen. When a bet is placed, a sound is played, the phone stops vibrating, and the game will verify if there is a goal in the next 10 seconds. When the 10 seconds end, the outcome of the bet is presented. Figure 3 shows a user interacting with WeBet.

User tests were conducted with 16 voluntary participants, with a mean age of 28.5. Each participant played WeBet twice by watching two 5-minute highlight videos of two football matches. This allowed participants to better understand how WeBet worked and enabled us to analyze how the interaction evolved as users got more used to it. We also asked participants in the end of each user test, to answer a questionnaire by rating statements using a five-point Likert-type scale. Results showed that participants liked to use WeBet (18.75% rated 4; 81.25% rated 5), found it easy to learn (12.25% rated 4; 87.75% rated 5) and to use (18.75% rated 4; 75% rated 5). When asked if the vibration and sound helped to understand the application state, the answer was also positive (vibration: 31.25% rated 4; 62.5% rated 5; sound: 18.75% rated 4; 62.5% rated 5). Participants also rated the statement "watching a football match becomes more interesting using WeBet" and "I would use the concept on a real match" very positively (50% rated 4; 43.75% rated 5 and 43.75% rated 4; 50% rated 5, respectively).

Figure 3. Participant interacting with WeBet.

3.3 On-going and Future Research

Until now, we have produced a selection of emotional and social experiences we intend to bring to remote fans, which together with the different interaction mechanisms tailored to local and online social experiences, represent the backbone of our research.

Currently, we are improving the WeApplaud concept, so users can interact during a real TV broadcast of a live event. In addition, we also want to take the WeApplaud experience further, by adding new kinds of visual and audible effects. Regarding WeBet, we have just finished a comparison study to assess different interaction methods. In the near future, we aim to conduct remote user tests with WeApplaud and WeBet during real live event TV broadcasts, where users interact in real time from their homes, without being on the same shared place. We also plan to deploy these (and future) prototypes on public places (e.g. bars or cafes), where small communities of people meet to watch sports events.

Over the next year and a half, we will also introduce new prototypes that include passive interactions, as well as novel active interactions and social experiences, as described in section 3. An example of one of these new prototypes, takes users to do a geographical wave around the world. Users in different countries will need to get up and wave at specific times, giving the sensation that there is a worldwide wave going on.

4. ACKNOWLEDGMENTS

This work is funded by CITI/DI/FCT/UNL (PEst-OE/EEI/UI0527/2011) and by FCT/MEC in the scope of project DEAP (PTDC/AAC-AMB/104834/2008).

5. REFERENCES

[1] Wann, D. L., Martin, J., Grieve, F.G., and Gardner, L. 2008. Social Connections at Sporting Events: Attendance and its Positive Relationship with State Social Psychological Well-being. *North American Journal of Psychology*, 10, 2, 2008.

[2] Socialnomics. *TV Goes Social: The Rise of the Second Screen*. http://bit.ly/XX9D3o. Accessed 2013/04/02.

[3] Tarumi, H., Akazawa, K., Ono, M., Kagawa, E., Hayashi, T., and Yaegashi, R. 2012. Awareness support for remote music performance. In *Proc. ACE '12*. Springer-Verlag, 573-576.

[4] FIFA. *FIFA Research*. http://fifa.to/Zddqov. Accessed 2013/04/01.

[5] Wann D., Schrader M. and Wilson A. 1999. Sport Fan Motivation: Questionnaire Validation, Comparisons by Sport, and Relationship to Athletic Motivation. *Sport Behavior*, 22, 1, 114-139.

[6] Trail, G., Anderson, D. and Fink, J. 2000. A Theoretical Model of Sport Spectator Consumption Behavior. *Sport Management*, 1, 3, 154-180.

[7] Funk D., Filo K., Beaton A. and Pritchard M. 2009. Measuring the Motives of Sport Event Attendance: Bridging the Academic Practioner Divide to Understanding Behavior. *Sport Marketing Quarterly*, 18, 126-138.

[8] Wann, D. L., Tucker, K. B. and Schrader, M. P. 1996. An Exploratory Examination of the Factors Influencing the Origination, Continuation, and Cessation of Identification with Sports Teams. *Perceptual and Motor Skills*, 82, 3, 1996.

[9] Uhrich, S. and Benkenstein, M. 2010. Sport Stadium Atmosphere: Formative and Reflective Indicators for Operationalizing the Construct. *Sport Mgmt*, 24, 2, 2010.

[10] Charleston, S. 2006. English Supporter Views of Away Grounds in the English Premiere League. Unpublished data.

[11] Melnick, M. J. 1993. Searching for Sociability in the Stands: A Theory of Sports Spectating. Journal of Sports Management, 7, 1, 1993.

[12] D. Conigliaro, F. Setti, C. Bassetti, R. Ferrario, and M. Cristani. 2013. Watching Watchers: A Novel Challenge for Crowd Analysis. In *Int. Workshop on Social Behaviour Analysis, associated with ICIAP'13*. In press.

[13] Rosalind W. Picard. *Affective Computing*. The MIT Press, Cambridge, MA, 1997.

[14] Watson, D., Clark, L. and Tellegen, A. 1988. Development and Validation of Brief Measures of Positive and Negative Affect: The PANAS Scales. *Journal of Personality and Social Psychology*, 54, 6, 1988.

[15] Russell, J., Weiss, A. and Mendelsohn, G. 1989. Affect Grid: A Single-Item Scale of Pleasure and Arousal. *Journal of Personality and Social Psych*, 57, 3, 1989.

[16] Fogg, B. J. 2003. *Persuasive Technology: Using Computers to Change What We Think and Do*. Morgan Kaufmann, San Francisco, CA.

[17] Eckles, D. and Fogg, B. J. 2007. The Future of Persuasion is Mobile. In *Mobile Persuasion: 20 Perspectives on the Future of Behavior Change*. Stanford Captology Media, Stanford, CA, 5-11.

[18] HollywoodReporter. *Fantasy Football's $1 Billion-a-Year Business, 27 Million Players: 'It's a Sickness'*. http://bit.ly/15cnZOJ. Accessed 2013/07/22.

[19] Holmes, M. E., Josephson, S. and Carney, R. E. 2012. Visual Attention to Television Programs with a Second-Screen Application. In *Proc. ETRA '12*, ACM Press (2013),397-400.

[20] Centieiro, P., Romão, T., Dias, E. A. 2012. Applaud Having Fun: A Mobile Game to Cheer your Favourite Sports Team. In *Proc. ACE '12*. Springer-Verlag, 1-16.

[21] Centieiro, P., Romão, T., Dias, E. A. 2013. Enhancing Remote Live Sports Experiences through an Eyes-free Interaction. In *Proc. MobileHCI'13*. In press.

Automatic Melodic and Structural Analysis of Music Material for Enriched Concert Related Experiences

Juan J. Bosch
Universitat Pompeu Fabra,
Music Technology Group,
Roc Boronat 138, Barcelona
juan.bosch@upf.edu

ABSTRACT

This PhD thesis proposal deals with the automatic analysis of musical audio, focusing on the estimation of the predominant melodic lines, which are used as a basis for extracting musical themes, and (along with other features) for structure recognition. The main focus is set on classical western music in large ensemble settings, which poses interesting research challenges to current state-of-the art algorithms. We will study the limitations of current approaches in this genre, and elaborate specific descriptors and methods, combining audio based analysis with further sources of knowledge and modalities. The creation of appropriate datasets will also be a main aspect, in order to properly evaluate the developed approaches. This work will be used to enrich musical concert related experiences, from music consumers to editors.

Categories and Subject Descriptors

H.5.5 Sound and Music Computing (J.5): *Signal analysis, synthesis, and processing*

General Terms

Algorithms, Theory

Keywords

Multipitch estimation; melody extraction; musical voice; structure recognition; music segmentation; musical theme; classical music

1. INTRODUCTION

Music Information Research (MIR) is the field which covers all the research topics involved in the understanding and modeling of music and that use information processing methodologies [16]. Research on this area started in the 1960's, but has seen a major growth from the 2000's, reflected on the increasing number of participants in specialized conferences and evaluation forums in the field such as the Music Information Retrieval Evaluation eXchange (MIREX) [6]. Over the last decade, we have seen how the performance of the algorithms has been increasing, but most of the tasks seem to have reached an upper bound in their performance. Currently, most MIR algorithms are only focused in audio, but the incorporation of further modalities, such as text, score, video, tags, etc. will improve the understanding of musical data [16]. Music signal analysis has borrowed techniques from speech signal processing, but most approaches needed to consider the intrinsic characteristics of musical audio in the techniques and representations, in order to achieve better performance. Further improvements can be obtained by analyzing the characteristics of specific genres, providing tailored solutions. Knowledge coming from other disciplines, such as psychology and musicology is also necessary to approach music in a more integrated manner.

The goal of this PhD thesis is the extraction of predominant melodic lines and the analysis of structure in musical audio. We will deal with the following challenges:

- Multimodal audio analysis, e.g. with score or video
- Combination of a signal processing front-end with knowledge from music perception and musicology
- Consideration of genre-specific constraints

The main focus is set on classical music in large ensembles, which poses interesting research problems to music analysis algorithms. The complexity of three musical signals is visually depicted in the Figure 1, which shows the evolution of their spectrum along time.

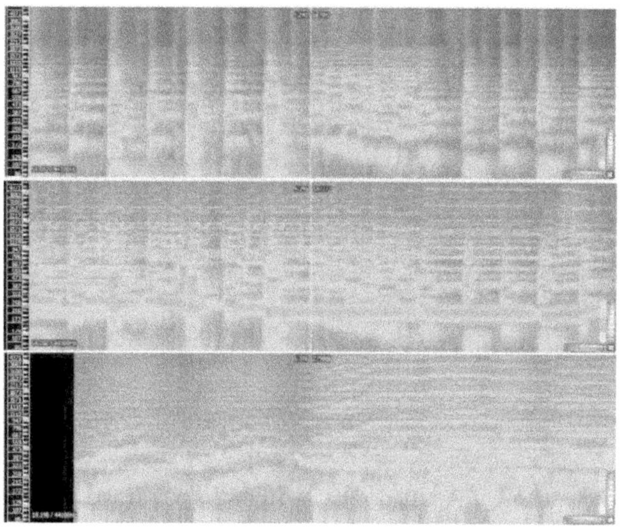

Figure 1: Difference in the spectrogram between a bassoon (top), and bassoon with the rest of a woodwind quintet playing the same piece (center). At the bottom, spectrogram from Smetana's "Ma Blast – Vltava": the first part (bottom-left) shows a section of the orchestra playing in unison. Other sections join (bottom-right) and start playing the main melody

Figure 1 (bottom) corresponds to the case of large ensembles, which in the last seconds presents a high spectral density, due to the high degree of polyphony and the large number of instruments. Additional research problems deal with the subtle

MM '13, Oct 21-25 2013, Barcelona, Spain
ACM 978-1-4503-2404-5/13/10.
http://dx.doi.org/10.1145/2502081.2502218

onsets and offsets, changes in tempo, the lack of a strong beat, complex tonality, and long-term musical structure, with non-obvious boundaries. On the other hand, some benefits of classical music are that the scores are more commonly available, and the musical works may have already fallen in the public domain.

This work is conducted in the scope of the PHENICX project [7], which aims to transform traditional live music concerts and enrich the experiences around them. The research conducted in this PhD thesis will be applied in several demonstrators, visualizing the extracted musical features such as structure, melodic lines, musical themes, etc., adapted to the user's musical knowledge. Concerts can also be experienced at home, where a more detailed analysis of the performance is considered. Additionally, editors which enrich the musical content would benefit of the application of this research, using automatic music analysis for an easier editing, segmentation and music summarization.

2. Scientific Background

This section will introduce the scientific background to be considered in this work. The main aspects are the estimation of multiple pitches, the use of music perception for the analysis of melodic streams and music structure analysis.

2.1 Multiple Pitch Estimation and Musical Stream Analysis

Multipitch estimation deals with the estimation of the fundamental frequencies of several simultaneous sounds. It is the first subtask towards automatic transcription, followed by: onset and offset estimation, instrument identification, and rhythm analysis. An overview of the transcription problem in presented in [10]. A related task is melody extraction, which deals with the estimation of only one pitch, commonly the most predominant. Salamon [14] mentions query-by-humming, karaoke and singer identification as applications of the research in this field, which is mostly focused on human voice.

Many multipitch and melody estimation algorithms start with a time-frequency transformation such as the short time Fourier transform, multi-resolution transforms, or perceptually motivated representations. Some of them use a pre-processing step (as spectral whitening or equal-loudness filters), or frequency refinement as a posterior step. The goal is to extract the (spectral) peaks, and compute the pitch salience, for instance using harmonic summation [9]. Most methods then use perceptual principles [3] or exploit additional musical knowledge such as timbre information, harmonicity (or inharmonicity), spectral smoothness, or synchronous evolution to separate partials, group salience peaks into streams or map them to a given pitched source. Figure 2 shows a salience function and pitch streams for the same orchestral piece as in Figure 1 (bottom), obtained with the MELODIA plugin[1], implementing the work by Salamon [14]. In the case of melody extraction, fundamental frequencies which belong to the melody line are identified by several approaches, e.g. Hidden Markov Models (HMM), dynamic programming, or ad-hoc rules. The last are currently obtaining the best results, especially when using features extracted from the pitch streams [14]. A further additional tracking step is commonly performed in order to correct some extraction errors. While estimating the pitch of a single semi-periodic sound (monopitch estimation) can be achieved with a high accuracy, multipitch estimation is still an unsolved task, especially when several instruments play notes with close harmonic relations.

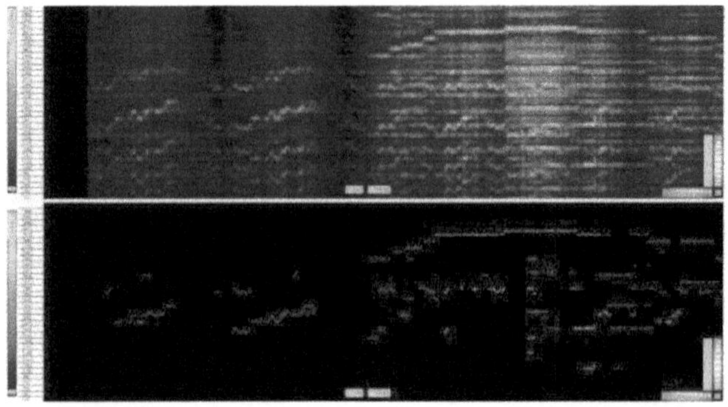

Figure 2: Salience function (top) and pitch streams (bottom) from Smetana's "Ma Blast – Vltava" computed with the MELODIA plugin[1] [14] for Sonic Visualiser[2].

The performance obtained in recent years in MIREX has kept almost constant, reaching 69% note accuracy for simple music material. Melody extraction algorithms have however been able to achieve better accuracies (up to 85% in MIREX-2011) [14].

Related work has also been conducted in the symbolic domain, in which several works deal with the separation of a polyphonic music score into musical voices. Commonly, they apply principles derived from auditory scene analysis [3] to group auditory stimuli into streams, as perceived by listeners. Huron [8] presents a review of them, and derives a set of rules to be considered for writing music with perceptibly different voices. Based on this work, Cambouropoulos [4] separated a musical score into voices, using the following principles: "Synchronous Note" (notes starting at the same time are likely to be merged into a voice), "Temporal Continuity" and "Pitch Proximity" (the closer in time and pitch, it is more likely that consecutive notes belong to the same voice). Chew [5] considers slightly different principles, with a different view of musical "voice", not allowing multiple notes in a single stream, as opposed to [4].

2.2 Structure Recognition

Music relies on temporal order, repetition, contrast, variation, and homogeneity of elements such as notes, melodies, chords, harmonies, rhythm, dynamics and timbre. In some periods of western classical music, musical themes have been the material forming the basis of a composition. Commonly, these are melodic elements repeated with some variations.

Structure recognition deals with the division of music into relevant temporal segments, and grouping into relevant clusters. The choice of the features for the automatic analysis restricts the kind of repetitions that can be found. Chroma, timbre, rhythm and dynamics have been mostly used so far, and some approaches use a combination of them. Paulus et al. [13] present a survey of state-of-the-art approaches, and classify them into repetition-based (identifying recurrent patterns), novelty-based (detecting transitions between contrasting parts), and homogeneity-based (finding regions with stationary properties). Serrà et al. [15] combine both homogeneity and repetition. Previous motif extraction approaches in the symbolic domain as [11] work by locating the repeating patterns, selecting those likely to be a theme, and deleting those included in a longer theme. In audio,

[1] http://mtg.upf.edu/technologies/melodia

[2] http://www.sonicvisualiser.org/

the problem is much harder, due to the presence of noise, musical interpretation and expressivity. Weiss [18] considers beat synchronous chromagrams as feature, and a variant of sparse convolutive non-negative matrix factorization. One of the difficulties of structure recognition is that repetitions do not usually take place in precisely the same manner, due to different instrumentation, tempo, dynamics, articulation, as well as melodic and harmonic variations. Muller et al. [12] presented a robust algorithm against such variations, with application to "thumbnailing", a subtask of structure recognition related to music summarization which deals with the determination of segments of audio which best represent the whole piece.

3. APPROACH

In the context of classical music in large ensembles, multipitch analysis becomes intractable with state-of-the-art methods, mainly due to the amount of instruments present and the shared harmonics between pitches. On the other hand, the extraction of a single melody could be too simplistic in certain pieces or styles as counterpoint, where the study of multiple melodic lines becomes necessary. In other orchestral pieces, several instruments contribute to the same melodic stream, which is a case not considered by melody extraction algorithms. The proposed approach considers these facts for the estimation of melodic lines and themes, which are then combined with other musical features for music structure analysis. As presented in the previous section, much research has been conducted in similar directions, but we expect this work to make the following contributions:

- Study the limitations of state-of-the-art multipitch estimation, melody extraction and structure recognition algorithms in orchestral music.
- Elaborate and evaluate appropriate descriptors and methods for genre-specific musical audio analysis, integrating audio based analysis with further sources of knowledge (musicology and psychology), and other modalities, as symbolic (score-based) analysis.
- Create custom and public corpora for the evaluation of the tasks with no appropriate ground truth available.

Figure 3 depicts the main components of the work developed in this PhD thesis, further detailed in the following subsections.

3.1 Multipitch oriented signal processing

Spectral peaks will be first extracted from the audio signal, followed by the creation of a salience function, in a similar manner as [14], but focusing on multipitch estimation instead of predominant melody extraction. We will study the most appropriate pre-processing techniques, time-frequency representations and salience functions.

3.2 Predominant melodic lines estimation

From the pitch salience, we will create pitch contours, following a similar approach to [14], using the principles from Huron [8]. The contours will then be characterized, and grouped into melodic line(s) allowing multiple pitches to contribute to a single auditory stream as in [4]. Three vertical aggregation principles will be considered: "Onset Synchrony", "Tonal Fusion", and "Pitch Co-modulation". The principle of "Tonal Fusion", states that concurrent tones are perceptually less independent if they are separated by intervals (in decreasing order: unisons, octaves, perfect fifths…) that promote tonal fusion.

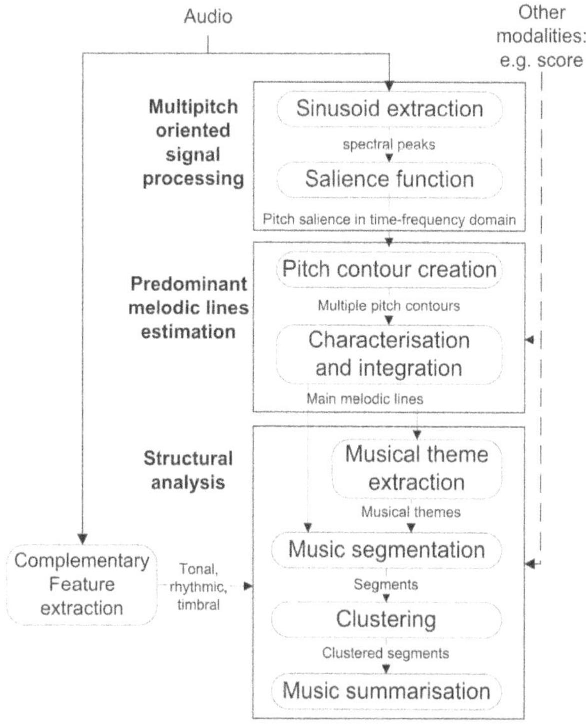

Figure 3: Schema of the main tasks of the PhD

The "Pitch Co-modulation" principle states that concurrent tones are perceptually less independent if their pitch motions are positively correlated. Further knowledge can be exploited, as the timbre, and information from other modalities as the score. Additionally, melodic stream analysis would benefit from the identification of melodic themes and vice versa, since notes within a theme should always belong to the same stream.

3.3 Structural analysis

The combination of timbral, rhythmic, tonal, dynamic, and other descriptors derived from the predominant melodic lines will be investigated for structural analysis. In classical music, an interesting aspect related to the repetition and variations of melodic elements is the identification of musical themes. Appropriate feature combinations and distance measures will be employed for the segmentation, focusing on the robustness against variations in tempo, instrumentation, dynamics, and possible errors in the estimation of melodic elements. The segments will then be clustered and used for creating summaries of the musical piece, considering genre specific characteristics, such as the longer lengths of classical music.

Regarding evaluation, an important corpus for structure recognition is the SALAMI dataset [17], with annotations of classical music from several periods (as well as pop, jazz and other genres). A recently proposed task in MIREX deals with the extraction of musical themes, and could be used for a public evaluation. However, it is currently mostly centered in the analysis of musical works in symbolic domain or from synthesized audio, but not from real recordings, which pose more difficulties for this task, so the creation of a custom dataset will be considered. The definition of musical structure and musical theme has some inherent degree of subjectivity, and the annotation process of the datasets will be carefully examined, or documented in case of a custom corpus.

4. WORK IN PROGRESS

Previous related published work deals with: score-informed melody extraction for predominant instrument source separation [2], and with instrument recognition in polytimbral mixtures [1]. Timber independent and score-informed predominant melody extraction is studied in [2], with application to lead instrument separation based on harmonic and pan-frequency masks. In this work, local and global misalignments between the score and the polyphonic audio mixture are considered. Global misalignments are considered to be due to differences in tempi, including variable tempi. Local misalignments are small misalignments in the onset and offset of the notes, understood as coming from human interpretation, the time envelope of the instrument (attack and decay) or mixing effects. Chroma based Dynamic Time Warping is proposed for the audio-score alignment, with a confidence measure on the score-derived information. The score-based lead instrument pitch tracking starts with a blind estimation of four pitch candidates for the melody. A two-step Viterbi algorithm is then employed to select either one of the candidate frequencies or none, adding probability to the estimated pitch candidates closer to the pitches derived from the score. The proposed solutions improved the estimation of the predominant melody and source separation. In [1] we studied the identification of predominant music instruments, and the benefits of dividing audio into streams, obtaining considerable performance improvement compared to the original instrument recognition algorithm, with several sound segregation algorithms.

Current work deals with the analysis of the problems of state-of-the-art methods for melody and multipitch estimation in large ensemble settings, and the design of a pitch salience function for multipitch estimation. A pitch tracking step will be implemented later, to follow the trajectories of the predominant melodic lines. The evaluation will be conducted against appropriate corpora, including a woodwind quintet, string quartets, and orchestral music recordings.

5. ACKNOWLEDGMENTS

This work is supported by the European Union Seventh Framework Programme FP7 / 2007-2013 through the PHENICX project (grant agreement no. 601166). It was also partially supported by "La Caixa" Fellowship Program.

6. REFERENCES

[1] Bosch, J.J. et al. 2012. A Comparison of Sound Segregation Techniques for Predominant Instrument Recognition in Musical Audio Signals. *Proc. ISMIR* (Porto, 2012), 559–564.

[2] Bosch, J.J. et al. 2012. Score-informed and timbre independent lead instrument separation in real-world scenarios. *Proc. EUSIPCO* (Bucharest, 2012), 2417–2421.

[3] Bregman, A.S. 1990. *Auditory Scene Analysis: The Perceptual Organization of Sound.* MIT Press.

[4] Cambouropoulos, E. 2008. Voice And Stream: Perceptual And Computational Modeling Of Voice Separation. *Music Perception.* 26, 1 (Sep. 2008), 75–94.

[5] Chew, E. and Wu, X. 2004. Separating voices in polyphonic music: A contig mapping approach. *Computer Music Modeling and Retrieval.* (2004), 1–20.

[6] Downie, J.S. 2008. The music information retrieval evaluation exchange (2005–2007): A window into music information retrieval research. *Acoustical Science and Technology.* 29, 4 (2008), 247–255.

[7] Gómez, E. et al. 2013. PHENICX: Performances as Highly Enriched aNd Interactive Concert Experiences. *Proc. of SMC Sound and Music Computing Conference* (Stockholm, 2013).

[8] Huron, D. 2001. Tone and Voice: A Derivation of the Rules of Voice-Leading from Perceptual Principles. *Music Perception.* 19, 1 (2001), 1–64.

[9] Klapuri, A. 2006. Multiple fundamental frequency estimation by summing harmonic amplitudes. *Proc. ISMIR* (2006), 216–221.

[10] Klapuri, A. et al. 2006. *Signal Processing Methods for Music Transcription.* Springer US.

[11] Meredith, D. et al. 2002. Algorithms for discovering repeated patterns in multidimensional representations of polyphonic music. *Journal of New Music Research.* 31, 4 (2002), 321–345.

[12] Müller, M. et al. 2013. A Robust Fitness Measure for Capturing Repetitions in Music Recordings With Applications to Audio Thumbnailing. *IEEE Transactions on Audio, Speech, and Language Processing.* 21, 3 (Mar. 2013), 531–543.

[13] Paulus, J. et al. 2010. State of the art report: Audio-based music structure analysis. *Proceedings of ISMIR 2010.* (2010), 625–636.

[14] Salamon, J. and Gómez, E. 2012. Melody extraction from polyphonic music signals using pitch contour characteristics. *IEEE Transactions on Audio, Speech, and Language Processing.* 20, 6 (2012), 1759–1770.

[15] Serrà, J. et al. 2012. Unsupervised detection of music boundaries by time series structure features. *Twenty-Sixth AAAI Conference on Artificial Intelligence* (2012).

[16] Serra, X. et al. 2013. *Roadmap for Music Information ReSearch.*

[17] Smith, J.B.L. et al. 2011. Design and creation of a large-scale database of structural annotations. *Proc. ISMIR* (2011).

[18] Weiss, R.J. and Bello, J.P. 2010. Identifying Repeated Patterns in Music Using Sparse Convolutive Non-Negative Matrix Factorization. *Proc. ISMIR* (Utrecht, Netherlands, 2010), 123–128.

Design, Development and Evaluation of an Adaptive and Standardized RTP/RTCP-based IDMS Solution

Mario Montagud
Universitat Politècnica de València (UPV), SPAIN
mamontor@posgrado.upv.es

ABSTRACT
Inter-Destination Media Synchronization (IDMS) is essential for enabling pleasant shared media experiences. The goal of my PhD thesis is to design, develop and evaluate an advanced RTP/RTCP-based IDMS solution fitting the requirements of the emerging distributed media consumption paradigm. In particular, standard compliant extensions to RTCP are being specified to allow for an accurate, adaptive and dynamic IDMS control when using RTP for streaming media. Moreover, the feasibility and suitability of several architectural schemes for exchanging the IDMS information, algorithms for allowing a dynamic IDMS monitoring and control, as well as adjustment techniques are being investigated. Objective and subjective testing are being conducted to validate the satisfactory performance of our IDMS solution and to provide insights about the users' tolerance on asynchrony levels in different IDMS scenarios.

Categories and Subject Descriptors
C.2.4 [**Computer-Communication Networks**]: Distributed Systems; H.5.1 [**Information Interfaces and Presentation**]: Multimedia Information Systems.

General Terms
Design, Human Factors, Performance, Standardization.

Keywords
IDMS, Media Synchronization, RTP/RTCP, Simulation.

1. INTRODUCTION & MOTIVATION
Traditional research on media synchronization (sync, hereafter) has been primarily focused on orchestrating the play out of incoming media streams locally at single devices. On one hand, *intra-stream sync* deals with the maintenance of the temporal relationships between the Media Units (MUs), e.g. video frames or audio samples, within a specific media stream. On the other hand, *inter-stream sync* refers to the preservation of the temporal dependences between MUs of independent, but correlated, media streams, being *lip-sync* the most representative example [1].

With the development of distributed multi-party media services, such as video-conferencing or Computer Supported Cooperative Work (CSCW), the need for a third type of media sync emerged: *Inter-Destination Media Sync* (IDMS) [2, 3], which involves the simultaneous synchronization of the media playout of a specific media stream across separated devices. The relevancy of IDMS is increasing in the emerging media consumption landscape. Nowadays, innovative forms of shared experiences are gaining momentum [4], allowing geographically distributed users to socially interact (e.g., using text, audio or video chat) within the context of simultaneous content consumption. Some examples are Social TV, networked games, 3D Tele-Immersion, synchronous e-learning, etc. However, realizing those shared interactive services faces a lot of challenges [5]. In particular, end-to-end (e2e) delay differences when streaming the same media content to a group of geographically distributed clients must be compensated for. Previous works have revealed that that e2e delay differences can range from a few milliseconds up to 8 s, depending on the technology in use [4, 6-8]. More specifically, the measurements in [7] showed that the e2e delays for the shortest and longest paths of an IPTV scenario can differ up to 6 s. These delay differences are significantly larger than acceptable limits in most of the IDMS use cases [4]. As an example, a controlled user study analyzed the effects of de-synchronization on the QoE in shared video watching scenario, in which users communicated each other (via text and voice chat) [9]. It was concluded that delay differences up to 1 s might not be perceptible by users, but differences over 2 s really become annoying for most of them. These results provide initial empirical evidence that actual e2e delay differences lead to high rates of user dissatisfaction. Moreover, Social TV is not, by far, the most restrictive IDMS use case, and other scenarios require stringent sync levels [4]. Consequently, this motivates the design, development and (objective and subjective) evaluation of an inter-operable, adaptive and accurate IDMS solution to compensate such e2e delay variability, thus enabling seamless and coherent shared media experiences. These are the *final goals* of my PhD thesis.

The design and specification of an IDMS solution comprises several aspects. A key issue is to choose or to specify suitable protocols to stream the media and to exchange timing information between the involved sync entities. Besides, different architectural schemes between the sync entities can be adopted. In addition, several monitoring and control algorithms, as well as adjustment techniques, need to be designed to achieve IDMS. Accordingly, *associated sub-goals* of my PhD thesis deal with the analysis of the feasibility and suitability of different alternatives for all the above components of the IDMS solution under development.

This paper provides an outline of the methodology, contributions and impact on the research community of my PhD thesis.

2. METHODOLOGY
In order to achieve the objectives of my PhD thesis I intend to use the methodology sketched in Fig. 1, which is briefly described in this Section.

MM'13, Oct 21-25 2013, Barcelona, Spain
ACM 978-1-4503-2404-5/13/10.
http://dx.doi.org/10.1145/2502081.2502219

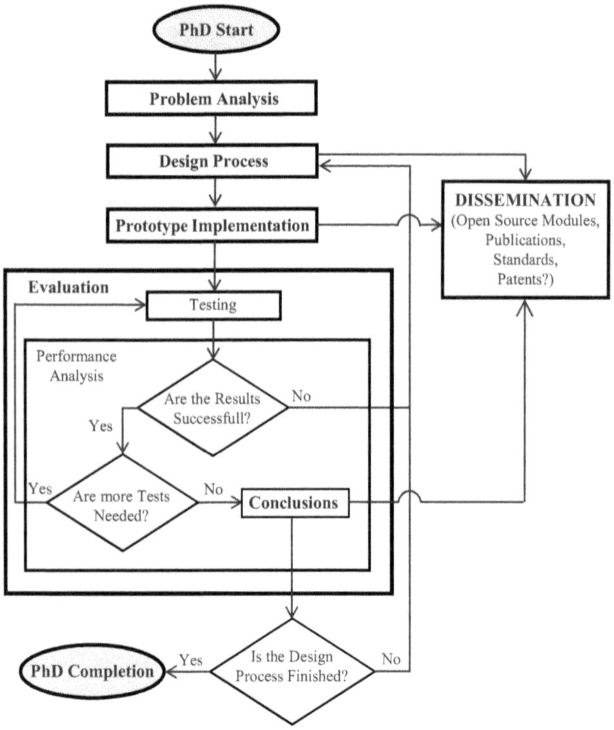

Figure 1. Workflow of the PhD thesis.

2.1 Problem Analysis

I started my research with a thorough review of the start-of-the-art and a compilation of use cases requiring IDMS [4]. This allowed me: i) to better understand the research problems and the associated challenges; ii) to identify the strengths and limitations of existing IDMS solutions; and iii) to derive the technical requirements that must be provided.

Several works have addressed this topic up to date (e.g., [2, 5, 10]). In [3], our research group presented a survey of existing IDMS solutions, which will be extended and updated in my PhD thesis. But apart from numerous papers, two recent PhD dissertations have addressed the IDMS problem. The PhD thesis by I. Vaishnavi [11] was focused on three relevant areas to provide coherence in shared media experiences in cross-domain scenarios: QoS, distributed media synchronization, and user mobility. In this research work, the *local-lag* algorithm [10], which was originally devised for networked games, was adapted to be used for shared video watching. The PhD thesis by Z. Huang [12] proposed a dissemination framework to meet the sync requirements (including IDMS) for multi-site tele-inmmersive systems involving time-correlated multi-sensory media streams.

2.1.1 Requirements for IDMS

Most of the existing IDMS solutions (surveyed in [3]) define new proprietary protocols that may increase the network load and make compatibility between (third-party) implementations more difficult. In addition, some of these IDMS solutions are only based on compensating the network delay variability, but do not take into account variable delays that are originated at the client side [4, 6, 7]. Some other solutions uniquely rely on syncing specific events (e.g., stream content or position updates), but do not support continuous monitoring and control processes.

My thesis acknowledges all the previous advances on IDMS, but mainly aims to design, develop and evaluate, both objectively and subjectively, a wider-applicable, inter-operable, adaptive and highly accurate IDMS solution, being capable of overcoming the above limitations while additionally fitting key requirements for IDMS, such as the following ones:

1. The IDMS solution must rely as much as possible on existing technologies (standard, if possible). This will assure interoperability when being deployed in large-scale scenarios, involving third-party infrastructure and communication devices.
2. Provisioning of timelines (and additional metadata, such as sequence numbers, payload type and source identifiers) in the media delivery units. This would enable a simpler reconstruction of the original media timing and allow for aligning timelines from different streams at the client side.
3. The IDMS solution must rely on wall-clock timing information. Additionally, the existence of mechanisms for negotiating the use of common global wall-clock sources between the involved sync entities is desired. This would allow a coherent framework for stamping, interpreting an aligning timelines in the media delivery chain.
4. Compensation of the e2e delay (i.e., from capture/retrieval at the server side to presentation at the client side) variability between distributed sync entities.
5. Need for a feedback control channel. This would enable a continuous monitoring and control of the IDMS process. This signaling channel, or an additional one, will also be very useful to negotiate key aspects for IDMS (e.g., group membership or clock sources).
6. Inherent rate adaption techniques (at the server-side, at the client-side, or both) to adjust the IDMS timing, allowing to dynamically maintain and restore the original synchronicity.
7. Support of the IDMS solution by both network and end-system entities. This would allow a future deployment of a highly scalable IDMS solution (e.g., for IPTV services) [8].

2.2 Design Process

The next step of my PhD thesis consists in the design of all components of the IDMS solution. This includes the protocol specification (fitting the above requirements), architectural schemes, monitoring and control algorithms, as well as adjustment techniques to achieve IDMS. More details about each of these sub-parts of the IDMS solution under design are in Section 3.

2.3 Prototype Implementation & Evaluation

According to the schedule of the design process, the prototype implementation and evaluation processes will not be performed at a single stage, but will be repeated for each individual component of the IDMS under design, as well as for the global IDMS solution at a later stage (see Fig. 1). In order to validate the performance of the IDMS solution, two main evaluation methodologies are being employed: simulation and user perception tests. Therefore, the first step consisted in selecting the most appropriate frameworks for deploying appropriate prototypes. Network Simulator 2 (NS-2) and GStreamer were chosen, respectively. The implementation in a simulation framework enables better flexibility for double checking assumptions and for identifying critical issues during the design and evaluation processes. The repeatability of the experimentation is more feasible than in real-world assessments. Moreover, it facilitates the assessment of the performance of our IDMS solution in heterogeneous network environments (under different and controllable conditions). Through simulation tests, the responsiveness, effectiveness and consistent behavior of all deployed control schemes, algorithms and adjustment techniques for IDMS can be assessed, by providing measurements about networking-related aspects, objective QoS statistics, as well as delay differences (asynchrony) between Sync Clients. In [13, 14], readers can find the obtained simulation results and conclusions up to date. However, even though considering the convenience of simulation tests, they cannot definitively validate the performance of our IDMS solution. This is because the user satisfaction (QoE) on the perceived shared media experience is the key aspect that will determine the benefits provided by our IDMS solution, and this cannot be obtained through simulation tests. Hence, the implementation of a prototype of a real media sharing application is also required, which is a key stage of my PhD thesis (work in progress). This will also allow me to carry out objective testing, but, most importantly, a subjective evaluation in real scenarios.

As a summary, the evaluation methodology I am employing in my PhD thesis, as well as the associated metrics under assessment, are sketched in Fig. 2. Based on the findings and conclusions from the complete evaluation process I will hopefully have gathered the necessary outputs to conclude my PhD thesis.

3. RESEARCH CONTRIBUTIONS

This section outlines the ongoing and expected research contributions of my PhD thesis.

3.1 Current Progress

3.1.1 Protocol Specification: RTP/RTCP for IDMS

Several standard protocols were analyzed for assessing their suitability for being extended for IDMS purposes [14]. But, definitely, RTP/RTCP were selected because of their compliance with most of the above-described requirements. Moreover, these protocols are extensively used in managed streaming services, they provide both intra- and inter-stream sync mechanisms, and their specification (RFC 3550) allows further extensions to them. After selecting RTP/RTCP for IDMS, the next step was to choose the most suited extension points to accomplish our requirements. RFC 5968 provides common guidelines for extending those protocols, while allowing for interoperability and protocol maintenance. Accordingly, a newly-defined RTCP XR block (RFC 3611) for IDMS, called IDMS report, was specified to enable Sync Clients to provide feedback about reception and/or presentation times for specific RTP packets. But apart from using RTCP for monitoring purposes, control of the timing of the Sync Clients is also needed. Therefore, an additional RTCP packet type for IDMS, called IDMS Settings packet, was specified to provide guidance on when to playout the media. Additionally, an SDP attribute was defined to signalize the use of these RTCP messages. The format of the RTCP messages and their exchange process to achieve IDMS can be found in [4, 14, 15].

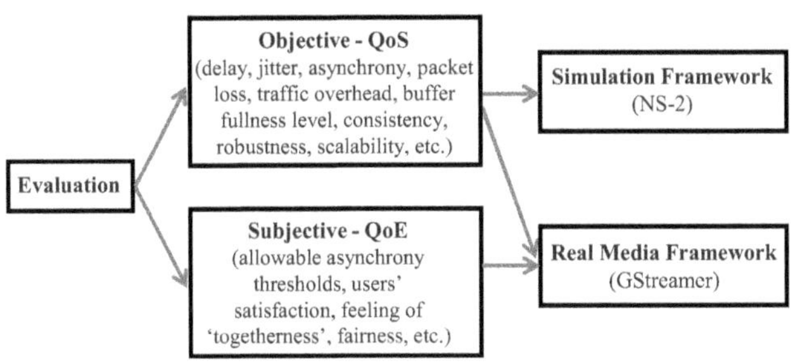

Figure 2. Evaluation Methodology.

I am actively involved in the standardization process of the protocol specification for IDMS within the IETF [15]. In my opinion, standardization will help the uptake of implementations, ensuring a more widespread use of IDMS in practice.

3.1.2 Group-based IDMS Control

One of the targeted goals of my thesis was to enable the co-existence of various logical groups of users in a shared media session, while allowing an independent control of their playout processes. The proposed RTCP messages and the SDP attribute for IDMS have taken into account this requirement [15]. Also, further control algorithms have been designed to achieve this capability, as proved in [13, 14].

3.1.3 Architectural Schemes for IDMS

Three main architectural schemes for IDMS can be distinguished [4]: two centralized schemes (Master/Slave or M/S Scheme and Synchronization Maestro Scheme or SMS) and a distributed one (Distributed Control Scheme or DCS). The involved sync entities and their communication process to achieve IDMS in each one of them is illustrated in Fig. 3. A qualitative comparison among these schemes, taking into account several key factors for IDMS, is provided in my PhD thesis [4] (summarized in Table 1). Each scheme has its own strengths and weaknesses, and is best suited for specific IDMS use cases. Subsequently, I also decided on their development in an extended version of our IDMS solution [14], which was initially based only on the use of SMS [13]. The consistent behavior and effectiveness of these control schemes for IDMS is validated in my PhD thesis [14]. Moreover, several techniques are being designed to enhance their responsiveness regarding specific features, such as coherence for DCS [14], as well as scalability and interactivity for SMS (see Section 3.2).

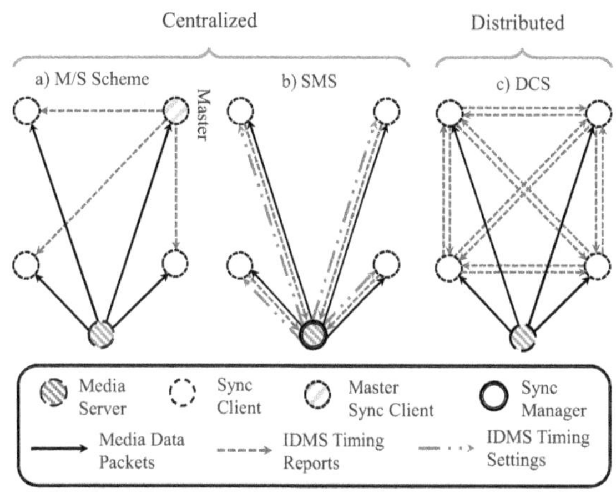

Figure 3. Architectural Schemes for IDMS.

Table 1. Qualitative Comparison Among IDMS Schemes

		Factors									
		Robustness	Scalability	Traffic Overhead	Interactivity	Consistency	Causality	Coherence	Flexibility	Fairness	Security
Scheme	DCS	1	2	3	2	3	3	2	2	1	3
	SMS	2	3	2	3	1	2	1	1	2	1
	M/S	3	1	1	1	2	1	3	3	3	2

1. Best Scheme, 2. Good Scheme, 3. Worst Scheme

3.1.4 Master Reference Selection Policies

Once the IDMS reports from all Sync Clients in a specific group have been gathered, a reference IDMS timing to synchronize with has to be selected. The feasibility and suitability (in terms of interactivity, efficiency, fairness, buffer fullness level, etc.) of different dynamic master reference selection policies, for each architectural scheme in use, are being explored (see e.g., [13, 14]).

3.1.5 Adjustment Techniques

After selecting the IDMS reference, the next step is to perform the required adjustments to synchronize. A compilation of server- and client-based techniques that can be used to prevent, maintain or restore sync between separated clients will be provided in my PhD thesis. From these, two reactive client-based techniques have been designed. The first one is based on aggressive playout adjustments (*skips & pauses*) whilst the second one makes use of smooth playout adjustments (Adaptive Media Playout or AMP). The performance of these techniques, for each one of the deployed IDMS schemes, is being assessed in my thesis (see e.g., [13, 14]).

3.2 Next Steps

This sub-section discusses the next steps to complete my PhD thesis, which are scheduled for the next 20 months.

3.2.1 Event-Driven RTCP Feedback Mechanisms

Novel event-driven RTCP reporting mechanisms will be designed for enhancing the performance of our IDMS solution in terms of interactivity, flexibility and accuracy when using SMS. In particular, these mechanisms will be targeted to allow the transmission of Early RTCP packets (RFC 4585) as a response to observed events of interest, while still adhering to the RTCP traffic bounds (RFC 3550). Three main advantages are expected to be provided: i) earlier correction of out-of-sync situations; ii) concurrent presentation of dynamic media-related events in a fine-grained synchronized way with the piece of content they refer to; and iii) delay reduction when joining IDMS-enabled sessions.

3.2.2 Optimized AMP Technique

Further research on AMP for IDMS will be targeted to meet two additional QoE-related goals. The first one is to find the best curve for minimizing abrupt changes in the playout rate. The second one is to meet a trade-off between a proper playout buffer occupancy in all Sync Clients and an overall IDMS control.

3.2.3 QoE Perception Tests

A key future step of my PhD thesis is to analyze the benefits on the QoE provided by our IDMS solution. To accomplish this, rigorous subjective testing in different media sharing scenarios will be carried out, complementing previous studies (e.g., [9, 11, 12]. These user perception studies will be targeted to answer the following research questions (one of the main contributions of my PhD thesis): i) which asynchrony levels are noticeable or annoying to users in different cases (as done by Prof. Steinmetz for inter-stream sync in [1]); ii) which architectural schemes and adjustment techniques are best suited for IDMS; and iii) the sync accuracy that can be achieved with our IDMS solution in real setups. A set of questionnaires will be employed and multiple interviews will be conducted to investigate the influence of several aspects on the perceived QoE. Statistical analysis will also be performed to confirm the validity of the experimentation.

3.2.4 Standardization

We plan to continue with our efforts for standardizing the proposed RTP/RTCP extensions for IDMS.

4. ACKNOWLEDGMENTS

This work was supported by UPV, under its R&D Support Program in PAID-01-10 and PAID-00-12 Projects. Moreover, I would like to thank my supervisor, Fernando Boronat (UPV), and Pablo Cesar (CWI) for their continuous support and very helpful advices.

5. REFERENCES

[1] Steinmetz, R., Human perception of jitter and media synchronization, *IEEE J. Sel. Areas Commun*, 14(1), 1996.

[2] Akyildiz F., Yen W., Multimedia group synchronization protocols for integrated services networks, IEEE J.Sel. A. Commun. 14, 1, 162-173, January 1996.

[3] Boronat, F., Lloret, J., García, M., Multimedia group and inter-stream synchronization techniques: A comparative study, Inf. Syst, 34(1), 108-131, March 2009.

[4] Montagud M., Boronat F., Stokking H., Brandenburg R. van, Inter-destination multimedia synchronization: schemes, use cases and standardization, *Multimedia Systems Journal*, 18(6), 459-482, November 2012.

[5] Vaishnavi I., Cesar P., Bulterman D., Friedrich O., Gunkel S., Geerts D., "From IPTV to synchronous shared experiences challenges in design: Distributed media synchronization", Signal Processing: Image Communication, Vol. 26, Issue 7, pp. 370-377, August 2011.

[6] ITU-T: G.1050 network model for evaluating multimedia transmission performance over internet protocol, 2007.

[7] van Deventer M.O., et al., Advanced Interactive Television Service Require Synchronization, *IWSSIP'08*. Bratislava.

[8] Stokking H., et al., IPTV inter-destination synchronization: A network-based approach, *ICIN'10*, Berlin, October 2010.

[9] Geerts, D., et alter., Are we in sync?: synchronization requirements for watching online video together, CHI 2011, New York (USA), May 2011.

[10] Mauve, M., et alter., Local-Lag and Timewarp: Providing Consistency for Replicated Continuous Applications, *IEEE Transactions on Multimedia*, 6(1), February 2004.

[11] Vaishnavi I., Coherence in Synchronous Shared Experiences, PhD Dissertation, Advisor: Dick Bulterman, Vrije Universiteit (Amsterdam), 2011.

[12] Huang Z., Synchronized distribution framework for high-quality multi-modal interactive teleimmersion, PhD Dissertation, Advisor: Klara Nahrstedt, University of Illinois at Urbana-Champaign, 2012.

[13] Montagud M. and Boronat F., Enhanced adaptive RTCP-based Inter-Destination Multimedia Synchronization approach for distributed applications, *Computer Networks Journal*, Volume 56, Issue 12, pp. 2912-2933, August 2012.

[14] Montagud M., Boronat F., Stokking H., Cesar P., Design, Development and Assessment of Control Schemes for IDMS in an Evolved and Standardized RTCP-based Solution, *Computer Networks*, Article in Review.

[15] Brandenburg R. van, Stokking H., van Deventer M.O., Boronat F., Montagud M., Gross K., RTCP for inter-destination media synchronization, draft-ietf-avtcore-idms-12, IETF AVTCORE Group, Internet Draft, July 2013.

Visual Object Analysis Using Regions and Interest Points

Carles Ventura
Technical University of Catalonia
Barcelona
carles.ventura@upc.edu

ABSTRACT

This dissertation research will explore region-based and interest points based image representations, two of the most-used image models for object detection, image classification, and visual search among other applications. We will analyze the relationship between both representations with the goal of proposing a new hybrid representation that takes advantage of the strengths and overcomes the weaknesses of both approaches. More specifically, we will focus on the gPb-owt-ucm segmentation algorithm and the SIFT local features since they are the most contrasted techniques in their respective fields. Furthermore, using an object retrieval benchmark, this dissertation research will analyze three basic questions: (*i*) the usefulness of an interest points hierarchy based on a contour strength signal, (*ii*) the influence of the context on both interest points location and description, and (*iii*) the analysis of regions as spatial support for bundling interest points.

Categories and Subject Descriptors

H.3.3 [**Information Storage and Retrieval**]: Information Search and Retrieval; I.4.6 [**Image Processing and Computer Vision**]: Segmentation; I.4.9 [**Image Processing and Computer Vision**]: Applications

General Terms

Algorithms, Design, Experimentation, Performance

Keywords

Image Representation, Hierarchical Segmentation, Interest Points, Object Retrieval

1. MOTIVATION

Object detection, image matching, query by example, etc. are some of the applications that in the recent years have kept image processing and computer vision fields active. This dissertation research will explore two of the most used image representations: region-based and interest-points based.

Region-based image representation considers an image as a set of groups of coherent pixels, called regions, obtained by a segmentation algorithm. This way, an object is described as a set of regions and their internal properties or descriptors, which are usually based on color, texture or shape information.

Interest-points image representation is one of the most popular approaches for state-of-the-art applications, such as image classification, object detection, object recognition, and object retrieval. Interest points are detected in regions where different edges intersect as well as along edges with high curvatures. They have a spatial neighborhood whose size depends on the scale at which have been detected and over which local descriptors are computed.

The main objective of this dissertation research will be to provide a new hybrid representation that takes advantage of the strengths and overcomes the weaknesses of both approaches. This dissertation research is structured in three main parts: (*i*) Section 2 analyzes how hierarchical region-based segmentation and interest points representation can benefit one from the other, (*ii*) Section 3 focuses on exploring the influence of the context on interest points location and description, and (*iii*) Section 4 analyzes the use of regions as spatial support for bundling interest points. Each of these three parts is divided into the following subsections: (*i*) Related work, (*ii*) Proposed approach, and (*iii*) Experiments. Finally, Section 5 shows some preliminary experiments carried out.

2. HIERARCHICAL SEGMENTATIONS AND INTEREST POINTS

2.1 Related work

2.1.1 The gPb-owt-ucm segmentation algorithm

Up to now, the gPb-owt-ucm [1] is the segmentation algorithm that offers the best performance on the Berkeley Segmentation Dataset [9]. It consists of 3 different blocks: (*i*) the gPb contour detector, (*ii*) the Oriented Watershed Transform (OWT), and (*iii*) the Ultrametric Contour Map (UCM).

The gPb contour detector couples multiscale local brightness, color and texture cues to a powerful globalization framework using spectral clustering. The local cues are computed by applying oriented gradient operators at every location in the image and at different scales.

MM'13, October 21–25, 2013, Barcelona, Spain.
ACM 978-1-4503-2404-5/13/10.
http://dx.doi.org/10.1145/2502081.2502220 .

The Oriented Watershed Transform constructs the set of initial regions from an oriented contour signal. First, region minimal of a non-oriented contour signal are taken as seed locations for homogeneous segments and standard watershed transform is applied. Then, consistency between the strength of the boundaries (watershed arcs) and the underlying oriented contour signal is enforced.

The Ultrametric Contour Map is the hierarchical region tree which results from an agglomerative clustering by iteratively merging the most similar regions, i.e. the two adjacent regions which are separated by the minimum weight contour.

2.1.2 *Interest points*

An image can be represented as a set of interest points distributed in the image plane. A desirable property of any interest point detector is scale invariance and affine invariance. The work in [14] presents an exhaustive survey and classification of interest points detectors.

One of the first well-known detectors is the Hessian detector [2]. The Hessian matrix is defined as the matrix containing the second-order image derivatives, which encode information about how the normal to the image surface changes spatially. The trace of this matrix, known as Laplacian, is used to detect interest points. The Harris detector [3] is also widely known and it is based on detecting corner points in the image. To do so, the structure tensor or second moment matrix is computed, which describes the main directions of the gradient of the image at the neighborhood of a given location. The determinant and the trace of this matrix was proposed as a measure of cornerness of the points of the image.

The authors in [5] proposed two simple methods for extracting interest points from the segmentation maps, which focus on the boundaries and centres of the gravity of the segments.

Apart from the interest point themselves, algorithms based on local features compute local descriptors. The most known and used local descriptor is the so-called Scale Invariant Feature Transform (SIFT) [6], which is invariant to affine transformations, partially invariant to illumination changes and robust to local geometric distortion.

2.2 Proposed approach

We propose to analyze if there exists any relationship between the gPb-owt-ucm segmentation algorithm and interest points. In such a case, we would like to study if one family could benefit from the other in both directions.

First, we consider how gPb-owt-ucm could benefit from interest points. In this direction, we propose to analyze whether the interest points scales could be used to adaptively select the appropriate scale at each location. This idea emerges from [1], in which the authors detected that high resolution images of complex scenes require more than a naive weighted average of signals across the scale range. This is because such an average blurs information, resulting in good performance for medius-scale contours, but poor detection of both fine-scale and large-scale contours.

Second, we consider how interest points could take advantage of gPb-owt-ucm. In this direction, we propose to analyze whether a hierarchy of interest points could improve object retrieval performance. This idea is based on the intuition that interest points located on strong contours could be more relevant than the ones located on smoother contours. In such case, we could benefit from $gPb(x, y, \theta)$, which has rich information about contours strength at different orientations, to establish a hierarchy among the interest points. More formally, we propose two ways of weighting a keypoint:

- Without considering the keypoint orientation:

$$W(k_i) = \max_{\theta} gPb(x(k_i), y(k_i), \theta) \qquad (1)$$

  where $W(k_i)$ is the weight assigned to the keypoint k_i, θ refers to the different orientations considered by gPb contour detector, and $x(k_i)$ and $y(k_i)$ are the location coordinates of the keypoint k_i. The weight is assigned taking the contour strength at the orientation which gives the maximum value.

- Considering the keypoint orientation:

$$W(k_i) = gPb(x(k_i), y(k_i), \theta(k_i)) \qquad (2)$$

  where $\theta(k_i)$ is the keypoint orientation. Therefore, the weight is assigned taking the contour strenght at the orientation given by the keypoint.

Furthermore, we also propose to analyze which would be the impact on object retrieval performance of replacing interest points by the junctions detected using the gPb contour detector [7].

2.3 Experiments

With regard to the evaluation of gPb-owt-ucm benefiting from interest points, we propose using the precision-recall framework on the Berkeley Segmentation Datasets (BSDS300 and BSDS500).

On the other hand, we propose to study the object retrieval performance by using only the interest points at an increasing depth in the hierarchy. We plan to use the TRECVID benchmark dataset provided for the Instance Search task [13].

3. USE OF CONTEXT IN OBJECT RETRIEVAL AND RECOGNITION

3.1 Related work

In object recognition and retrieval, there have been suggestions that a bounding box may be able to provide some degree of context and may actually be beneficial. However, one of the contributions of [16] is the evaluation of background features, which shows the pitfalls of training on datasets with uncluttered or highly correlated backgrounds.

In [8], it is confirmed that correct spatial support is important for object recognition. Thus, knowing the right spatial support leads to substantually better recognition performance for a large number of object categories, especially those that are not well approximated by a rectangle. Overall, the recognition performance using ground-truth segments is 15% better than using the bounding boxes.

In [11], the authors went further and proposed integrating segmentation into the BoF framework considering each region as a stand-alone image by masking and zero padding the original image. Then the signature of the region is computed as in regular BoF, but discarding any feature that falls entirely outside its boundary. As a consequence, masking greatly enhances the contrast of the region boundaries making features along the boundaries more shape-informative.

Furthermore, coarse spatial information is incorporated by clustering features in segments.

3.2 Proposed approach

Considering each region as a stand-alone image by masking and zero padding the original image as in [11], the local features computed in each region do not depend on the context. Therefore, if two images contain the same object but with different backgrounds and assuming that the object is rightly segmented, the local features for both objects will be the same. However, experimental results in [11] did not estimate which was the influence of masking the region for feature extraction.

Therefore, we propose to analyze which is the influence of the context in keypoint detection. We expect that for different instances of the same object in different contexts, the locations of the keypoints will be more unstable if the object is not masked. In addition to this, context is also expected to have an impact on the description of the detected keypoints. With this goal, some measures of stability will be used to objectively measure the context influence. Furthermore, since our final application will be object retrieval, we will also measure the impact of context in object retrieval benchmarks such as the Instance Search Task of Trecvid.

On the other hand, the idea of zero padding proposed in [11] seems not to be the best way to get rid of the context. They expected that the masking and zero padding process made features along boundaries more shape-informative. However, this claim depends clearly on the color of the object. In an extreme case, no local features should be detected in an object totally black, independently of the object shape. Therefore, we think that other strategies for background should be employed to keep the shape information.

3.3 Experiments

We plan to evaluate the impact of the context in object retrieval using the TRECVID benchmark dataset provided for the Instance Search task. The goal of this task is to retrieve the videos which contain a particular object. Some instances of the object as well as their masks are given as visual examples. The task is performed for a set of objects to be retrieved. The decision of evaluate the use of context in object retrieval has also been motivated by the fact that objects to be retrieved are instance of the same query object, whereas in object recognition datasets there exist a large intra-class variance, which would blur the real impact of the context.

For both query and target images we propose the following set ups:

- Feature detection. Whether regions are masked for keypoints detection or not.
- Feature description. Whether regions are masked for keypoints description or not.

Keypoint detection and description invariance to context will be evaluated on a benchmark based on [10].

4. BUNDLING INTEREST POINTS

4.1 Related work

Classic visual vocabularies are generated from single image local descriptors. However, these vocabularies are not able to capture the rich spatial contextual information among the local features. Basically, two differents ways of considering such spatial context can be distinguish: (*i*) algorithms that apply a post geometric verification step [12], and (*ii*) algorithms which consider combination of local features [15][17]. Since we want to analyze the benefits from using regions as spatial supports for bundling interest points, we briefly describe some previous works based on combination of local features. Generally, considering visual words in groups rather than single visual word could effectively capture the spatial configuration among them.

In [15], a scheme where local features were bundled into local groups was presented based on the ideas that (*i*) each group of bundled features becomes much more discriminative than a single feature, and (*ii*) within each group simple and robust geometric constraints can be efficiently enforced. More specifically, the ellipses resulting from MSER detection are enlarged to bundle SIFT features.

In [17], a maximum number of 3 local features in each local feature group are considered since if too many local features are combined, the repeatability of the combination will decrease. Each local feature group is formed by a centered local feature and one or two other local features within a circle of radius proportional to the scale of the centered local feature. The distance between two local feature groups take into account the spatial context of each local feature group, which is defined as the orientation and scale relationships between the local features inside the group.

Recently, a dense local detector that produces repeatable shape-preserving regions via a novel segmentation-driven sampling strategy was introduced in [4].

4.2 Proposed approach

Discriminative visual phrases were proposed in [18] to refer to the frequently co-occurring visual word pairs. If two visual words frequently co-occur within short spatial distance in images containing the same object but different backgrounds, spatially consistent visual words are more likely to be located on the object.

Assuming this, we propose to work with regions resulting from a robust contour detector, such as gPb, since they can provide a good suport for bundling local features, ensuring that local features being groupped belong to a support area with minimal boundary strength. Furthermore, any boundary strength threshold on the gPb-owt-ucm generates an image partition whose regions contain internal boundaries which are smoother than the given threshold. In contrast, previous works [17][15] do not consider contour information when bundling local features to the same group.

Once adopted regions as spatial supports for bundling local features, the question about how to describe the region from the set of local features arises. Therefore, we are planning to study if support regions are enough to encode the spatial context and, therefore, classic BoF could represent the region content, or geometric relationships between the local features within the same group should be also encoded.

4.3 Experiments

We propose to evaluate the performance for different set ups which consider: (*i*) combination of local features, and (*ii*) the representation form.

With regard to the combination of local features, we propose three different cases:

Figure 1: Matching individually SIFT descriptors

- Individual local features. This is the classic approach for both object retrieval and recognition.
- Bundling local features within the support region given by the interest point detector [17] [15].
- Bundling local features within gPb-owt-ucm regions from different hierarchical levels.

With regard to the representation form for a group of local features, the options can be mainly divided in two categories:

- No spatial information. In such case, region is consider to inherently convey enough spatial information. Classic BoF approach can be used to describe the region.
- With spatial information. Spatial coding techniques are used to enforce some geometric constraints when matching two group of local features.

5. WORK IN PROGRESS

We have carried out some preliminary experiments on using regions for bundling interest points. The images showed in Figure 1 belong to Pascal VOC 2012 Dataset. The goal of the experiment is to detect and localize the object (aeroplane) in the target image (right image of Figure 1) by using a visual example (left image of Figure 1). Keypoints and local descriptors have been obtained on each image by using the default implementation of SIFT descriptor available in OpenCV. Figure 1 shows the results of matching individually the keypoints and keeping the best matches. On the other hand, Figure 2 shows the results of region matching. For this, both query and target images have been first segmented by the gPb-owt algorithm which gives a finest partition. Then, SIFT features belonging to the each region are bundled and matched. For these preliminary experiments, the distance between two local feature groups G_1 and G_2 has been computed by averaging the distance values from each local feature of G_1 to its nearest feature of G_2.

6. ACKNOWLEDGMENTS

This dissertation research is partially founded by FPU-2010 Research Fellowship Program of the Spanish Ministry of Education.

7. REFERENCES

[1] P. Arbelaez, M. Maire, C. Fowlkes, and J. Malik. Contour detection and hierarchical image segmentation. *PAMI*, 2011.

[2] P. R. Beaudet. Rotationally invariant image operators. In *ICPR*, 1978.

Figure 2: Matching region-bundled SIFT descriptors

[3] C. Harris and M. Stephens. A combined corner and edge detector. In *Alvey vision conference*, 1988.

[4] J. Kim and K. Grauman. Boundary preserving dense local regions. In *CVPR*, 2011.

[5] P. Koniusz and K. Mikolajczyk. Segmentation based interest points and evaluation of unsupervised image segmentation methods. 2009.

[6] D. G. Lowe. Distinctive image features from scale-invariant keypoints. *IJCV*, 2004.

[7] M. Maire, P. Arbeláez, C. Fowlkes, and J. Malik. Using contours to detect and localize junctions in natural images. In *CVPR 2008*.

[8] T. Malisiewicz and A. A. Efros. Improving spatial support for objects via multiple segmentations. *BVMC*, 2007.

[9] D. Martin, C. Fowlkes, D. Tal, and J. Malik. A database of human segmented natural images and its application to evaluating segmentation algorithms and measuring ecological statistics. In *ICCV*, 2001.

[10] K. Mikolajczyk and C. Schmid. A performance evaluation of local descriptors. *PAMI 2005*.

[11] A. Rabinovich, A. Vedaldi, C. Galleguillos, E. Wiewiora, and S. Belongie. Objects in context. In *ICCV*, 2007.

[12] J. Sivic and A. Zisserman. Video google: Efficient visual search of videos. In *Toward Category-Level Object Recognition*. 2006.

[13] A. F. Smeaton, P. Over, and W. Kraaij. Evaluation campaigns and TRECVid. In *MIR '06*, 2006.

[14] T. Tuytelaars and K. Mikolajczyk. Local invariant feature detectors: a survey. *Foundations and Trends® in Computer Graphics and Vision*, 2008.

[15] Z. Wu, Q. Ke, M. Isard, and J. Sun. Bundling features for large scale partial-duplicate web image search. In *CVPR*, 2009.

[16] J. Zhang, M. Marszałek, S. Lazebnik, and C. Schmid. Local features and kernels for classification of texture and object categories: A comprehensive study. *IJCV*, 2007.

[17] S. Zhang, Q. Huang, G. Hua, S. Jiang, W. Gao, and Q. Tian. Building contextual visual vocabulary for large-scale image applications. In *ACM Multimedia*, 2010.

[18] S. Zhang, Q. Tian, G. Hua, Q. Huang, and S. Li. Descriptive visual words and visual phrases for image applications. In *ACM Multimedia*, 2009.

The ACM Multimedia 2013 Art Exhibition

Marc Cavazza
Teesside University
Borough Road
Middlesbrough, TS1 3BA, UK

m.o.cavazza@tees.ac.uk

Antonio Camurri
InfoMus Research Centre, DIBRIS
University of Genova
Viale Causa 13, 16145 Genoa, Italy

antonio.camurri@unige.it

ABSTRACT
The Art Exhibition of ACM Multimedia 2013 has attracted significant work from a variety of digital artists collaborating with research institutions. We have endeavored to select exhibits that achieved an interesting balance between technology and artistic intent. The techniques underpinning these artworks are relevant to several technical tracks of the conference, in particular those dealing with human-centered and interactive media. We briefly review how the various installations revisit current topics in Multimedia research, focusing more specifically on their approach to dynamic content generation, user experience, multimodality, and affective interfaces. Once again, the unique blend of technology and user experience does not limit itself to showcasing recent advances in interactive media, and should be of interest to all conference participants as well as the general public the exhibition space will be open to.

Categories and Subject Descriptors
J.5 [**Computer Applications**]: Arts and Humanities: Arts, fine and performing

General Terms
Design, Human Factors, Theory.

Keywords
Digital Arts, Interactive Art and Entertainment.

1. INTRODUCTION
This year (for its 10th edition), the Arts Exhibition offers a series of installations, each combining multimedia technology with artistic intent in its own specific way. The uniqueness of the ACM Multimedia Art Exhibition is that it avoids both extremes of just being another demonstration session for the conference, or conversely the simple digital remediation of artistic practice. We have imposed little constraints on the nature of the artworks, taking advantage of previous editions to provide realistic examples of what work would qualify for the exhibition. In particular, we have adopted an inclusive definition of Multimedia Art not demanding that traditional media content be at the heart of the installation, but allowing Multimodal interfaces supporting interaction and user experience.

We have endeavored to achieve a balance between novelty of concepts and techniques, and interest to an audience which encompasses not just conference attendees, but also the general public to which part of the exhibition will be open to. In a similar fashion, we have also considered, and selected, artworks that have been previously on display, so as to maximize interest and quality. As our conference track is designated as Arts, Culture and Entertainment, this is also reflected in the artworks on display: several of them including a cultural heritage element, for instance Chinese shadow puppetry. The exhibits are most often the result of collaborations between artists and technologists, with a good representation of research groups specializing in such joint creative activities. The proposers originate from several continents, with a notably strong participation from Far Eastern countries (Japan, Taiwan, Singapore, South Korea ...). Finally, the exhibition is hosted by the FAD (Foment de les Arts i del Disseny; Fostering Design and Arts) Museum in Barcelona[1].

2. MULTIMEDIA TECHNOLOGIES
Considering the technical tracks which constitute this edition of ACM Multimedia, we find artworks' underpinning technology and concepts to be predominantly indexed into the human-centered media aspects (e.g., multi-modal interfaces, mixed reality, interactive media). However, even within the limited scope of the installation, we benefit from a comprehensive coverage, spanning across video and sound processing, mobile systems, facial recognition, telepresence and Internet analytics.

Of those installations that are interactive, the majority is designed for single-user participation. This may reflect the necessity for a personal and reflective user experience, in particular when user experience is at the center of the installation (as in Faure's *SOMA*[2], Shen-Chi Chen et al.'s *Smile-Wall*...). This takes us away from the playful group interaction popularized by commercial entertainment systems. We should also notice the absence of computer graphics and game-based installations. Although this is consistent with the representation at the main conference, it contrasts with the popularity of computer games art in recent exhibitions. Only popular game-related I/O devices, such as the Kinect™ are part of several installations.

2.1 Current Topics in Multimedia Art
The Multimedia technologies and the design paradigms supporting the installations are a reflection of current research

MM'13, October 21–25, 2013, Barcelona, Spain.

[1] www.fad.cat

[2] We introduce artworks under the form < first_author_name's *Artwork title* >. Subsequent mentions of the artwork shall only make use of their title.

topics in Multimedia systems, in particular interactive and human-centered media. Two of the most represented areas are affective computing and gesture-based interfaces, including full-body interfaces.

Affective computing is well represented in this exhibition, yet the emphasis is on traditional emotional states experienced by users rather than aesthetic experience. An exception is the work of He-Lin Luo et al.'s *The Qi of calligraphy*. Based on the Chinese culture concept of Qi, *i.e.*, the essence and spirit of cursive writing of a calligrapher. The authors evoke through dance an interpretation of the emotional content in the 'qi' and 'rhythm' within Chinese calligraphy. The exploitation of concepts emerging from ancient cultures (another example is the Japanese concept of 'kansei') can be a relevant source of inspiration to scientific theories, in this case on affective computing.

In installations facing affective computing within traditional approaches, the emphasis has been on the overall concept rather than compliance with state-of-the-art emotional models. For instance, Maurice Benayoun's *Emotion Forecast* (Figure 1) can be described as performing visual analytics for emotions on the Internet. The system scans social networks for the use of emotional words focusing on 3,213 cities. This results in the equivalent of an 'emotional weather report' on a worldwide scale. To complete the weather metaphor, the system actually computes trends in the expression of such emotions so as to produce a proper emotional forecast. It uses a keyword-based approach, which is a selection of affective terms, constitutive of their own ontology of 48 emotions. This contrasts with traditional emotional language categorization, which attempts at indexing words into universal affective categories [1] or specific affective dimensions [2]. This lexical approach avoids the delicate issue of emotional modeling, while being consistent with the Internet search which stands at the heart of the system.

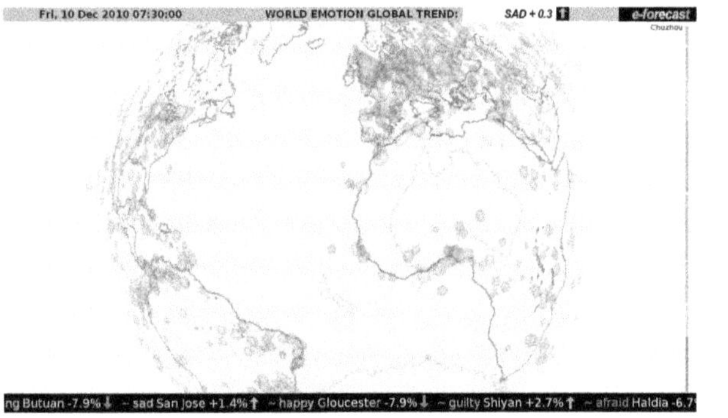

Figure 1. Benayoun's *Emotion Forecast* provides an emotional visual analytics of the Internet on a world scale.

Faure's *SOMA* proposes an artistic reinvention of neurofeedback through what is presented as a 'daydreaming machine' putting the artwork in touch with the non-rational component of the user's mind. The system displays recombined video images whose temporal parameters are matched to the user's physiological state captured through her Galvanic Skin resistance (GSR) signal. GSR is an extremely popular technique in affective interfaces whose main limitations are its partial correlation with arousal [3], and its response time, whose order of magnitude is in the hundreds of milliseconds, a limitation which has to be taken into account for interactive systems [4]. Beyond the metonymic connection between arousal and the motion content of the daydream's images, this installation includes mechanisms to smoothen signal transitions, which cope with the above issues within the design of the artwork itself.

Another work facing emotions is *Smile-Wall*, with a video wall of smiling faces captured from visitors and manipulated: from the affective computing perspective, this is an interesting work to reflect on emotion contagion and on the power of facial expression in conveying emotion, while in *Qi of calligraphy*, it is interesting to note the complementary role of the full-body movement (dance) to convey and evoke emotions.

2.2 Multimedia and Multimodal aspects: Content and Interaction Channels

Two major components are at play in digital artworks. The contents presented to the user, which are primarily a combination of images (video, symbols, abstract shapes) and sounds, constitute the Multimedia element. On the other hand, interaction channels combine different modalities that can themselves convey informational content, which we associate to the Multimodal aspect of the installation (how these two aspects interact is determined by interaction design in each installation).

Transforming video, for instance through collage techniques, is a means to produce interactive content and provide a backchannel for interaction. Several installations are based on this concept: in the absence of computer graphics and their natural support for procedural content generation, they make it possible for image and video content to become interactive. This is the case for *SOMA* as discussed above, but is also central to Sujin Lee's *3D Stroboscopy*. The concept behind this installation is to recreate multiple poses photographs that mimic those obtained through stroboscopy. User motion captured through a Kinect™ device is used to control the transformation of multiple photographic poses into a stroboscopic effect, reconstructing the time line of the user movements. The system acquires depth information through a Kinect™ and performs image warping (using Radial Basis Functions); finally, it outputs superimposed frames reproducing multiple exposure effects. The underlying software is developed using the OpenCV and OpenNI libraries.

Another installation making direct use of dynamic content generation is Anabela Costa's *Critical*. This installation features responsive patterns that evoke phase transitions between the various states of matter (liquid, gas). These are triggered by the perceived user interest detected through a sensing camera. The patterns are produced using the ArtiE-Fract software, a fractal generator based on evolutionary programming [5].

Content is also at the heart of those installations exploring cultural heritage, such as Zhenzhen Hu et al.'s *Feast of Shadow Puppetry*. Again, it is based on a deeply rooted cultural tradition, Chinese shadow puppetry: but in this case, the objective is not to consider it as a source of inspiration for scientific or artistic research; rather, it exploits digital art to preserve the precious traditional heritage Chinese shadow puppetry. It generates virtual Chinese shadow puppets using non-photorealistic rendering of user pictures, blending content creation with user participation. The personalized shadow puppets are subsequently animated using a scripting language based on bespoke animation primitives derived from motion sequences of traditional Chinese shadow puppets. It is interesting to note the importance of the concept of "shadow" from eastern cultures in scientific research: the Japanese concept of "Ba" has been a source of inspiration for an original approach for remote communication knows as 'Shadow Media' [6].

While the previous artwork is centered on content rather than interactivity, one prominent feature of this exhibition is the use of gestures and body motion to create or transform Multimedia content. Aside from *3D stereoscopy*, other installations implement a concept of performance in which full body motion mediates the production of new visual or aural content.

The Qi of Calligraphy features a complex interplay between users' body motion and the symbolic realm of Chinese characters. The vital energy (Qi) embedded in each stroke of a Chinese character is likened to the energy deployed by the user through dance movements. The game-like nature of this approach also lets the audience create calligraphy through body motion. This is a fairly sophisticated installation, comprizing a robotic arm composing Chinese calligraphy, and a full body interface. The arm is equipped with an LED light source, which is used as a virtual brush to compose calligraphy on a photosensitive surface. Users may follow the light movements, thus implicitly dancing to the tune of the brush strokes composing the Chinese character.

Keyaerts et al.'s *MashtaCycle* uses a rich code of performance gestures to retrieve various sound elements, again using full body interaction to drive media content. It is presented as a new kind of digital musical instrument, for its ability to retrieve sounds. The full body interface is used to explore the physical space, onto which audio features from the sound collection have been mapped using dimension reduction techniques. This creates an original technique for audio retrieval, one that can further evolve as the recognized gestures grow in complexity. Three concepts inspire the gestures in *MashtaCycle*: instinct, serenity and energy; these suggest another eastern influence, also claimed by the artist, and echoes some other installations in this exhibition.

In both cases, the combination of performance and content is somehow evocative of Pollock's legacy [7].

Finally, Pao and Larson's *Gestural Pen Animation* allows designers and artists to turn sketches on any regular paper into animated work, supporting new explorations of the creative process. The system aims at recreating the process of iterative modification of sketches to generate alternative designs by animating such sketches. The system is based on bespoke hardware in the form of a pen equipped with a wireless accelerometer. This hardware supports both stroke detection for sketching and the recognition of command gestures. The associated software reproduces the sketching process as an animated trajectory, while supporting multiple authors through separate colors for sketches.

3. PROVIDERS OF USER EXPERIENCE

Most installations are interactive and support user participation. However, the role of interaction differs widely according to the briefs and authors' intention. Some installations, such as *SOMA* and *Smile-Wall* are entirely centered on the user experience. Others use interactivity as a means to revisit the artistic experience, either from the process of exploring an existing artwork (*MixPerceptions*), or the creative process itself (*Gestural Pen Animation*).

Smile-Wall revisits communicational paradigms such as alignment [8]. This installation confronts the user to a wall of digital pictures representing an array of human faces, which can be displayed at various stages of smiling. The system is based on a markerless perceptual user interface that can detect face orientation, as well as recognizing whether the user is smiling, by tracking relevant Facial Animation Parameters (FAP) values. Using various morphing techniques, the installation responds to the user smiling by gradually transforming the expression of the various faces into smiling portraits. With a strong artistic intent, a technical implementation using state-of-the-art techniques and user evaluation data gathered from over 500 participants at previous exhibitions, *Smile-Wall* is certainly one of the most thorough digital artworks of this exhibition.

Critical also presents an interesting example on how to interact with a complex dynamic system, based on the metaphor of changing states of matter, conveying to the user the impact of her own interaction.

Kobayashi et al.'s *Tele Echo Tube* goes way beyond the telepresence paradigm that seems to underpins its implementation at first notice. Firstly, because of the allegoric stance taken by the authors, in reference to a cultural personalization of the echo phenomenon. Secondly, because of the interaction paradigms it introduces which targets the environment as a whole. The reference to Von Uexkull's 'Umwelt' is one shared with multiple works on computational semiotics, robotics and cognitive science, in particular on the issues of reactive systems and representations.

Dance and in general full-body movement are a natural, embodied approach that enables to experience, understand, and transfigure digital content, like in the dance interpreting the 'Qi' concept part of cursive Chinese calligraphy.

San Pedro et al.'s *MixPerceptions* (Figure 2) is of particular relevance/interest in that it adapts traditional artistic contents (paintings) to a Digital Experience. The experience proposed is that paintings containing colored blocks, apparently masking part of their content, would be revealed through interaction adopting a kind of mobile AR paradigm. We are here very far from the simple and often naïve remediation [9] of traditional art forms to the digital world. Nor are we simply using an installation to question artistic content or the spectator's experience; this work instead achieves a higher level of fusion by making the original artwork supporting the interactive experience without making it entirely dependent on it at first sight. This is further supported by the artistic genre of the paintings, which stems from the 'narrative figuration' movement [10], one naturally inclined towards a dynamic interpretation of visual contents.

Figure 2. San Pedro's *MixPerceptions* invites the visitor to explore apparently missing elements using mobile AR.

4. CONCLUSIONS

The Art Exhibition has been an integral part of the ACM Multimedia conference for several years, and we like to think of it not simply as an extension of the Arts, Culture and Entertainment track, but as bearing relevance to many other content-related or interaction-related conference tracks. The deployment of state-of-the-art Multimedia systems potentially interacting with a lay audience faces challenges, which are quite different from those of laboratory prototypes in terms of performance and robustness. This enterprise also participates to a reflective practice in questioning the usability of underlying models (e.g. emotional models, interaction paradigms ...). It is the privilege of artworks to dissociate their ability to elicit user experience from the academic rigor of their underpinning models. The interaction of science and art is a practice that in many occasions demonstrated a strong potential to boost cross-fertilization and to inspire scientific research, especially in the field of Multimedia and user interaction. We hope that this Art initiative at ACM Multimedia will contribute, once more, to shed light in this direction. The unique blend of technology and user experience does not limit itself to showcasing recent advances in interactive media, and should be of interest to all conference participants as well as the general public the exhibition space will be open to.

Welcome to the exhibition!

ACKNOWLEDGMENTS

Patricia Bueno of FAD and Mari Carmen Marcos of University Pompeu Fabra are thanked for their assistance in designing and organizing this exhibition. We acknowledge the support of the Conference sponsors. Figure 1: Copyright Maurice Benayoun. Figure 2: Copyright Jose San Pedro Waldemar. Presentation of artists' briefs have used their original submission material: however, any remaining misinterpretations are the authors' sole responsibility.

REFERENCES

[1] Strapparava, C. and Valitutti, A. 2004. WordNet-Affect: an Affective Extension of WordNet. In *Proceedings of the 4th International Conference on Language Resources and Evaluation* (Lisbon, May 2004), LREC 2004. 1083-1086.

[2] Russell, J. A. and Mehrabian, A. 1977. Evidence for a three factor theory of emotion. *Journal of Research in Personality*, 11, 273-294.

[3] Andreassi, J. 2006. *Psychophysiology: Human Behavior and Physiological Response*. Routledge, London.

[4] Gilroy, S.W., Porteous, J., Charles, F. and Cavazza, M. 2012. Exploring Passive User Interaction for Adaptive Narratives. In *Proceedings of the 17th International Conference on Intelligent User Interfaces* (Lisbon, Portugal, February 14-17) IUI'12. ACM, New York, NY, 119-128.

[5] Lutton, E. 2006. Evolution of fractal shapes for artists and designers. *International Journal of Artificial Intelligence Tools*, 15(4), 651–672.

[6] Miwa, Y and Ishibiki, C. 2004. Shadow communication: system for embodied interaction with remote partners. In *Proceedings of the 2004 ACM conference on Computer supported cooperative work* (CSCW '04). ACM, New York, NY, USA, 467-476.

[7] Fried, M. 1998. *Art and Objecthood: Essays and Reviews*. Chicago University Press, Chicago, IL.

[8] Giles, H., Coupland, N. & Coupland, J. 1991. Accommodation theory: Communication, context, and consequence. In: *Contexts of accommodation: Developments in applied sociolinguistics*, H. Giles, J. Coupland, & N. Coupland, Eds. Cambridge University Press, Cambridge.

[9] Bolter, J.D. and Grusin, R. 1999. *Remediation: Understanding New Media*. MIT Press, Cambridge, MA.

[10] Gassiot-Talbot, G. 1965. *La Figuration narrative*. Le Cercle d'Art, Paris (in French).

4th ACM/IEEE ARTEMIS 2013

International Workshop on Analysis and Retrieval of Tracked Events and Motion in Imagery Streams

Anastasios Doulamis
Technical University of Crete
Chania Crete, Greece
Polytecnhioupolis Campus
Tel: + 30 28210 37430
adoulam@cs.ntua.gr

Nikolaos Doulamis
National Technical
University of Athens, Greece
9, Heroon Polytechniou Street
Tel: + 30 210 772 2678
ndoulam@cs.ntua.gr

Marco Bertini
University of Florence
Media Integration and
Communication Center, Italy
+39 055 4796 468
bertini@dsi.unifi.it

Jordi Gonzalez
Universitat Autònoma de Barcelona, Spain
08193 - Bellaterra, Barcelona
Fax: +34 935811670
poal@cvc.uab.es

Thomas Moeslund
University of Aalborg,
Faculty of Engineering and Science
Sofiendalsvej 11, Aalborg, Denmark
Tel: 45 9940 8787
tbm@create.aau.dk

ABSTRACT

In this paper, we give a short summary of the papers proposed in ACMARTEMIS 2013 which is held in Barcelona Spain in conjunction with ACM Multimedia. The workshop handles the areas of features analysis both at low and high level for efficient events detection, retrieval of multimedia events and objects and video synchronization issues and also events and behavior recognition from visual data. All papers were classified into three session of a single track workshop. The first session named "Video Features and Scene Analysis" includes articles that handle low level and high level visual analysis appropriate for event detection. The second session entitled "Retrieval of Multimedia Objects/Events" applies schemes for media data retrieval and video synchronization. Finally the third session "Analysis of Visual Events" describes algorithms for detecting actions, behaviors and events in complex visual scenes.

Categories and Subject Descriptors

I.4.0 [**Image Processing and Computer Vision: General**]-*image processing software*; H.3.0 [**Information Storage and Retrieval: General**];

Keywords

Analysis of events, retrieval of actions, tracking, video analysis.

1. INTRODUCTION

Recently, it can be argued that the intelligence behind many pattern recognition and computer vision systems is mainly focused on two main approaches; (i) extraction of smart features able to efficiently represent the rich visual content and (ii) adoption of non-linear and adaptable (semi-supervised) learning strategies able to fill the gap between the extracted low level features and the high level concepts, humans use to perceive the content. The feature extraction is a data dimensionality reduction strategy that addresses the difficulty that learning complexity grows exponentially upon a linear increase in the dimensionality of data. It is also clear that extraction of representational features is a challenging and application-dependent process. Non-representative features significantly affect the recognition accuracy, especially for complex and dynamic environments even though they are processed by highly non-linear feature transformation models. Thus, the main goal of this workshop is to seek original articles in the area of multimedia research in the direction of detecting and recognizing high level concepts and their respective spatio-temporal and causal relations in order to identify semantic video activities.

The research topics covered in this workshop are very important for the multimedia community since automatic extraction of events in video data is still one of the main challenging and open research issues in the specific area. This is verified by the high success of all the previous ARTEMIS workshops held in Florence in 2010 in conjunction with ACM Multimedia, Barcelona in 2011 in conjunction with ICCV and in Florence again in 2012 in conjunction with ECCV. In these workshops, we need also to stress the success story of the relevant AREA 2008 workshop held in Vancouver Canada in conjunction with ACM Multimedia 2008.

The success of this workshop was so great that the Editor in Chief of the Multimedia Tools and Applications Journal (Springer) has asked twice the workshop organizers to prepare a special issue in this journal. The issue has been successfully completed with high quality papers and finally two volumes have been dedicated to this issue by the editor. The importance is also verified by other related events in high quality journals such as the recent special issues of the IEEE Transactions on Multimedia with title of "Semantic Image and Video Indexing in Broad Domains"

MM '13, Oct 21-25 2013, Barcelona, Spain
ACM 978-1-4503-2404-5/13/10.
http://dx.doi.org/10.1145/2502081.2503825

and the recent call for papers of the IEEE Transaction on Circuits & Systems for Video Technology with title of "Event Analysis in Videos [1], [2], [3].

2. Previous ARTEMIS Workshops

The goal of this proposal is to continuation the success story of ARTEMIS workshops launched from 2010 and then in conjunction with ACM Multimedia, IEEE International Conference of Computer Vision (ICCV) and European Conference of Computer Vision (ECCV). All these conferences organized as full day workshops in which 12-16 research papers were presented, carefully selected after a peer review process, and with an average success rate of about 50%. We should mention that three of the previous workshops were also related with journal papers publications at Computer Vision Image Understanding Journal and Multimedia Tools and Applications.

ARTEMIS 2010: In total, 27 papers from 17 different countries were submitted. To ensure the high quality, all submissions were refereed strictly by at least two experts in the related fields based on the criteria of originality, significance, quality and clarity. As a result, 14 papers (52%) were accepted. Out of these 14 papers, 9 were oral presentations (33%) and 5 were posters and 2 demos.

ARTEMIS 2011: In total, 24 papers from 9 different countries were submitted. All submissions were reviewed by three experts in related fields, and reviews were than assessed by the organizing chairs. As a result, 12 papers (50%) were accepted, all oral.

ARTEMIS 2012: In total, 32 papers from 10 different countries were submitted. All submissions were reviewed by three experts in related fields, and reviews were than assessed by the organizing chairs. As a result, 12 papers (50%) were accepted as oral and 4 as posters. They were presented as oral in 4 sessions. We should mention that ARTEMIS was the second most active ECCV workshop in terms of submissions.

3. SUMMARY OF ARTEMIS 2013 WORKSHOP

We have received works from all over the world. All papers were reviewed by at least three (3) Reviewers. However, most of the papers were reviewed by four or even five Reviewers. Only papers that are above the borderline were accepted for publication. We have organized the papers into three sessions according to the thematic areas covered.

3.1 Session I "Video Features and Scene Analysis"

The first session is dedicated to "Video Features and Scene Analysis" and includes algorithms, techniques and methods for video scene analysis. In particular, the first article deals with the application of a new algorithm that modifies optical flow on the use of textural features. Then, we introduce methods for hand gesture recognition on exploiting depth sensors from Kinect^{TM} cameras. The third paper describes a foreground detection method for traffic scenes within complex real-world urban environments. Finally, the fourth article of this session discusses the introduction of transfer learning for re-identifying persons from multiple cameras.

3.2 Session II "Retrieval of Multimedia Objects/Events"

The second session deals with "Retrieval of Multimedia Objects/Events". This session includes two papers. The first proposes a new non-parametric method for clustering image content with respect to the semantics. The clustering exploits visual features like the SIFT transform while cultural heritage objects are surveyed. The second and last paper of this session describes a methodology for synchronizing two video sources which capture the same scene from different views.

3.3 Session III "Analysis of Visual Events"

The third session describes events detection and abnormal behavior recognition from complex visual data. The title of this session is "Analysis of Visual Events". We start with an article which applies methods for abnormal behavior recognition from complex visual scenes. Then, we propose techniques for recognizing complex behaviors based on a human constrained descriptor and adaptable neural networks. The third article applies computer vision tools for maritime detection in outdoor environments of sea ports. Finally, the last nut not least paper of the workshop describes a methodology for cross-domain traffic scene understanding by the use of motion models.

4. ACKNOWLEDGMENTS

This event is supported by the European funded projects, *EXPERIMEDIA*, "Experiments in live social and networked MEDIA experiences", (http://www.experimedia.eu/), *4D-CH-World,* "Four Dimensional Cultural Heritage World", www.4d-ch-world.eu, and the Greek-Cypriot Collaborative project *POSEIDON* "Development of an Intelligent System for Coast Monitoring using Camera Arrays and Sensor Networks" (http://www.poseidonproject.eu/) and *e-Park*, "Exploitation of New Technological Trends in Management and Payment of Public Parkings," www.e-park.eu. In addition the Greek National Projects *Viopolis* (www.viopolis.gr) and *i-Promotion* support this event.

5. REFERENCES

[1] Shih-Fu Chang, Jiebo Luo, Steve Maybank, Dan Schonfeld, Dong Xu, "Event Analysis in Videos," *IEEE Trans. On Circuits and Systems for Video Technology*, Nov. 2008.

[2] A.D., Doulamis, L. Van Gool, M. Nixon, N.D. Doulamis, T.A. Varvarigou, "Guest Editorial: Analysis and retrieval of events/actions and workflows in video streams," Multimedia Tools and Applications 50 (1) , pp. 1-6, 2010.

[3] A. Doulamis, L. van Gool, M. Nixon, T. Varvarigou, Doulamis, "First ACM international workshop on analysis and retrieval of events, actions and workflows in video streams," Proceedings of the 2008 ACM International Conference on Multimedia, 2008.

Workshop Summary for the 3rd International Audio/Visual Emotion Challenge and Workshop (AVEC'13)

Michel Valstar
University of Nottingham
Mixed Reality Lab

Björn Schuller*
TU München
MISP Group, MMK

Jarek Krajewski
University of Wuppertal
Schumpeter School of
Business and Economics

Roddy Cowie
Queen's University
School of Psychology

Maja Pantic†
Imperial College London
Intelligent Behaviour
Understanding Group

ABSTRACT

The third Audio-Visual Emotion Challenge and workshop AVEC 2013 will be held in conjunction ACM Multimedia'13. Like the 2012 edition of AVEC, the workshop/challenge addresses the interpretation of social signals represented in both audio and video in terms of the high-level continuous dimensions arousal and valence, but importantly this year the data is that of a large number of clinically depressed patients and controls, with a sub-challenge in self-reported severity of depression estimation. Like both previous AVECs, the aim is to bring together the audio and video analysis communities.

Categories and Subject Descriptors

I [**Pattern Recognition**]: Applications

Keywords

Affective Computing, Social Signal Processing, Depression

1. INTRODUCTION

The third Audio-Visual Emotion Challenge and workshop (AVEC 2013) has been organised in conjunction with the 21st ACM International Conference on Multimedia, held in Barcelona, Spain, 21-25 October 2013 (ACM-MM'13). The goal of the challenge is to provide a common benchmark test set for individual multimodal information processing and to bring together the audio and video emotion recognition communities, to compare the relative merits of the two approaches to emotion and depression recognition under well-defined and strictly comparable conditions and establish to what extent fusion of the approaches is possible and beneficial. A second motivation is to advance the emotion recognition community beyond small sets of discrete emotions, into the recognition of multiple fully continuous affective dimensions. A third motivation is to build up a community of researchers working on automatic monitoring of objective cues of depression. The final motivation is the need to advance emotion recognition systems to be able to deal with naturalistic behaviour in large volumes of un-segmented, non-prototypical and non-preselected data as this is exactly the type of data that both multimedia retrieval, human-machine/human-robot communication interfaces, and automatic (home-based) depression monitoring systems will have to face in the real world.

*The author is further affiliated with Imperial College London, Department of Computing, London, U.K.

†The author is further affiliated with Twente University, EEMCS, Twente, The Netherlands.

AVEC'13 October 21 2013, Barcelona, Spain
ACM 978-1-4503-2404-5/13/10.
http://dx.doi.org/10.1145/2502081.2503826.

2. PARTICIPATION

The call for participation and papers attracted registrations of 27 teams from all over the world, resulting in 7 submissions. The programme committee accepted 4 papers in addition to the baseline paper, which was reviewed independently. Three papers used fully audio-visual techniques and one paper used only the audio modality. Three papers addressed the depression recognition challenge, and one the affect recognition challenge. We hope that these proceedings will serve as a valuable reference for researchers and developers in the area of audio-visual emotion recognition and depression analysis.

3. THE ROAD AHEAD

Audio-visual recognition of dimensional affect is far from a solved case, as the papers included in these proceedings clearly show. While the prediction accuracy of the arousal and valence dimensions was higher than those earlier reported in the AVEC 2012 challenge, this can be attributed probably as much to the more constrained context of the data as to technological development of the automatic emotion recognition systems. And while the dataset used for the AVEC series all contained displays of natural behaviour, they were all recorded under fairly strictly controlled conditions, which means that there's still a bigger challenge waiting for us, where researchers will be challenged to deal with both natural behaviour as well as natural environmental conditions.

Concerning the prediction of depression severity, it is clear that we have barely scratched the surface of this topic. The papers presented here provide a number of interesting different approaches to this problem, but even the best performing team only achieved moderately successful results, which are far from a level required to implement in a real-world application. Still, given the nature of the data and the seriousness of the problem it addresses, we believe the works presented here are an important step in the right direction, and it is clear that there are many avenues still to be considered.

Taking both the emotion and depression recognition into account, it is fair to say that it is highly likely that there will be more editions of the AVEC series.

Acknowledgments

The work of Michel Valstar is partly funded by the NIHR-HTC 'MindTech' and Horizon Digital Economy Research, RCUK grant EP/G065802/1. The work of Jarek Krajewski is partly funded by the German Research Foundation (KR3698/4-1). The challenge in general has been generously supported by the HUMAINE organisation and the EU network of excellence on Social Signal Processing SSP-Net (European Community's 7th Framework Programme [FP7/20072013] under grant agreement no. 231287). The authors further acknowledge funding from the European Commission(grant no. 289021, ASC-Inclusion).

Workshop Summary for the 5th International Workshop on Multimedia for Cooking and Eating Activities (CEA'13)

Kiyoharu Aizawa
The University of Tokyo
7-3-1 Hongo, Bunkyo-ku,
Tokyo 113-0033, Japan
aizawa@hal.t.u-tokyo.ac.jp

Yoko Yamakata
Kyoto University
Yoshida-honmachi, Sakyo-ku,
Kyoto 606-8501, Japan
yamakata@dl.kuis.kyoto-u.ac.jp

Takuya Funatomi
Kyoto University
Yoshida-honmachi, Sakyo-ku,
Kyoto 606-8501, Japan
funatomi@media.kyoto-u.ac.jp

ABSTRACT
This summary introduces the aim of the CEA'13 workshop and the list of papers presented in the workshop.

Categories and Subject Descriptors
H.4.m [**Information Systems Applications**]: Miscellaneous; H.5.m [**Information Interfaces and Presentation**]: Miscellaneous; I.m [**Computing Methodologies**]: Miscellaneous;

Keywords
Workshop, overview, cooking, eating

1. AIM OF THE WORKSHOP
Cooking is one of the most fundamental activities of humankind. It is not only connected with the joy of eating but also deeply affects various aspects of human life such as health, dietary, safety of food, culinary art, entertainment, human communication, and so on. Many people who cook at home require supports for cooking because it requires experience and knowledge. They may also need support for food-logging and menu planning for the health of their family. Needless to say, support for a good and enjoyable meal would improve the quality of life. Systematic cooking / eating supports for elderly or physically challenged people are also significantly important.

The call for papers attracted 21 submissions from France, Italy, Japan, Pakistan, Spain, Switzerland, Turkey, United Kingdom and United States. In this year, our workshop will have presentations about the recent technologies in the fields of Application for cooking and eating support, Menu planning, dietary management, and food-logging, Analysis and utilization on cooking recipe, Analysis of cooking video, Analysis of Web contents on cooking and eating activities, Cooking archiving and recognition, Learning contents creation for cooking, Recipe text / image / video retrieval and recommendation, Ubiquitous environment and interface in kitchen, and so on.

2. RELEVANT TOPICS
- Application for cooking and eating support
- Cooking archiving and recognition
- Learning contents creation for cooking
- Analysis of cooking video
- Recipe image / video retrieval
- Analysis and utilization on cooking recipe

MM'13, October 21–25, 2013, Barcelona, Spain.
ACM 978-1-4503-2404-5/13/10.

- Menu planning, dietary management, and food log
- Artificial agent for cooking/eating activity
- Sensing of taste / smell / texture
- Food communication (human-to-human / human-to-computer communication)
- Ubiquitous environment and interface in kitchen
- Intelligent home appliance
- Cooking navigation interface for the dementia and physically challenged person support
- Multimedia learning contents for dietary
- Multimedia information service for food safety and security
- Analysis of Web contents on cooking and eating activities

3. INVITED TALK
Dr. Amélie Cordier (LIRIS, CNRS, France)

"Cooking with computers, a winning recipe"

In our daily lives, cooking becomes more and more important. In many countries, you just have to switch television on to see the proliferation of cooking shows of all kinds: live cooking classes, cooking at home challenges, cooking contests (for everyone or for professionals), short recipes demos, etc. This witnesses two emergent phenomena: cooking gains a growing interest as a leisure, and people gain awareness of the role of food in our daily lives as well as the many reasons why should "eat well."

In academic research, this trend is also observed, and many funding are related to well-being, health, nutrition, and other issues related to food. In many research fields, cooking is present: smart cooking appliances, cooking robots, vision techniques to recognize ingredients, and so on. In the areas of Web and artificial intelligence, the challenges are also numerous. How to represent recipes? How to adapt recipes to meet the needs of users? How to take into account the social aspects of cooking? Can we create social recipes books?

In this presentation we will provide an overview of the challenges that cooking raises for computer science and information technology. We start by introducing the *Taaable* project, a website that makes use of case-based reasoning to adapt recipes. From that presentation, we draw a lessons learned while working on this project. Then we expand the scope of our study to other projects and initiatives combining computer and cooking. We adopt different points of view in that study, depending on the projects and their goals. We focus on the many issues addressed by these initiatives, such as representation of cooking recipes, suggestions, recommendations, dietary practices, personalization, social side, creativity, etc. Finally, we will review the prospects for research in this field and discuss current initiatives.

4. LIST OF PRESENTATIONS
4.1 Oral Session
Ahmet Iscen, Pinar Duygulu

"Knives are picked before slices are cut: Recognition through activity sequence analysis"

In this paper, we introduce a model to classify cooking activities using their visual and temporal coherence information. We fuse multiple feature descriptors for fine-grained activity recognition as we would need every single detail to catch even subtle differences between classes with low inter-class variances. Considering the observation that daily activities such as cooking are likely to be performed in sequential patterns of activities, we also model temporal coherence of activities. By combining both aspects, we show that we can improve the overall accuracy of cooking recognition tasks.

Hiromi Nakamura, Homei Miyashita
"Controlling saltiness without salt: Evaluation of taste change by applying and releasing cathodal current"
In this study, we evaluate the taste intensity of food when a saltiness enhancer is used, in order to verify the effectiveness of our system. In a previous study, we proposed a saltiness enhancer using a cathodal current, based on the knowledge of Hettinger et al. However, we have received feedback from subjects that other tastes (e.g., sourness, bitterness) are also enhanced. Therefore, we conducted the experimental tests that the comparing intensity of taste of fundamental tastes and metallic taste over three phases: (1) before the application of current, (2) during the application of current, and (3) after the current is released.

Trung Duc Nguyen, Diep Nguyen, Yasushi Kiyoki
"A regional food's features extraction algorithm and its application"
Automatically detecting food's taste is a non-trivial part. However, we realize that the taste of food can be extracted by directly analyzing recipes by the ingredients and the amount of them in the recipes. In this paper, we present a food analysis system to discover the taste of foods and to better understand the featured ingredients in each specific geographical region. The main features of this system are (1) to extract dominant ingredients and tastes in a region by analyzing the ingredients' frequency and its uniqueness, and (2) to transform user's existing materials or original recipe to a new recipe according to a targeted taste. To examine the feasibility and applicability of the algorithm, we have developed a web-based application with a recipe database collected from approximately 200 recipes in over 7 regions of Japan: Hokkaido-Tohoku, Kanto, Kansai, Shikoku, Chubu, Kyushu-Okinawa and Chugoku.

4.2 Short oral & Poster session

1. **Yasuhiro Hayashi, Keisuke Doman, Ichiro Ide, Daisuke Deguchi, Hiroshi Murase**, *"Automatic authoring of a domestic cooking video based on the description of cooking instructions"*
2. **Mutsuo Sano, Kenzaburo Miyawaki, Hiromi Mitsumori, Kimiko Ohtani, Syunichi Yonemura, Michiko Ohde**, *"Remote cognitive rehabilitation support system for menu and meal preparation"*
3. **Fumihiro Kato, Shoichi Hasegawa**, *"Interactive cooking simulator: Showing food ingredients appearance changes in frying pan cooking"*
4. **Sebastian Stein, Stephen Mckenna**, *"User-adaptive models for recognizing food preparation activities"*
5. **Marc Bolaños, Maite Garolera, Petia Radeva**, *"Active labeling application applied to food-related object recognition"*
6. **Ryuta Yasuoka, Atsushi Hashimoto, Takuya Funatomi, Michihiko Minoh**, *"Detecting start and end times of object-handlings on a table by fusion of camera and load sensors"*
7. **Alan Chamberlain, Chloe Griffiths**, *"Taste and place: Design, HCI, location and food"*
8. **Thierry Hamon, Natalia Grabar**, *"Extraction of ingredient names from recipes by combining linguistic annotations and CRF selection"*
9. **José H. Canós, Mª Carmen Penadés, Marcos R. S. Borges, Abel Gómez**, *"A product line approach to customized recipe generation"*
10. **Chang Xu, Ye He, Nitin Khanna, Albert Parra, Carol Boushey, Edward Delp**, *"Image-based food volume estimation"*

5. WORKSHOP ORGANIZERS

General chair:
Kiyoharu Aizawa (The Univ. of Tokyo, JP)
Organizing chair:
Yoko Yamakata (Kyoto Univ., JP)
Program chair:
Takuya Funatomi (Kyoto Univ., JP)
Publicity co-chairs:
Amélie Cordier (LIRIS, CNRS, FR)
Edward J. Delp (Purdue Univ., US)
Shinsuke Nakajima (Kyoto Sangyo Univ., JP)
Advisory co-chairs:
Mutsuo Sano (Osaka Inst. of Technology, JP)
Ichiro Ide (Nagoya Univ., JP)
Program committee:
Matthieu Cord (Univ. of Paris 6, FR)
Keisuke Doman (Chukyo Univ., JP)
Jill Freyne (CSIRO, AU)
Winston Hsu (National Taiwan Univ., TW)
Haley Hung (Delft Univ. of Technology, NL)
Masahiko Inami (Keio Univ., JP)
Tomoo Inoue (Univ. of Tsukuba, JP)
Kazuaki Kondo (Kyoto Univ., JP)
Hyowon Lee (Singapore Univ. of Tech. & Design / MIT, SG / US)
Qing Li (City Univ. of Hong Kong, HK)
Tao Mei (Microsoft Research Asia, CN)
Mirjam Minor (Univ. of Trier, DE)
Kenzaburo Miyawaki (Osaka Inst. of Technology, JP)
Frank Nack (Univ. of Amsterdam, NL)
Takuji Narumi (The Univ. of Tokyo, JP)
Satoshi Nishiguchi (Osaka Inst. of Technology, JP)
Kazushi Nishimoto (Japan Advanced Inst. of Science and Technology, JP)
Vincent Oria (New Jersey Inst. of Tech., US)
Man-Kwan Shan (National Chiao Tung Univ., TW)
Tomohide Shibata (Kyoto Univ., JP)
Charles Spence (Somerville College, Oxford, UK)
Mayumi Ueda (Univ. of Marketing and Distribution Sciences, JP)
Kimitoshi Yamazaki (Shinshu Univ., JP)
Shunichi Yonemura (Shibaura Inst. of Technology, JP)
Additional reviewers:
Xudong Mao (City Univ. of Hong Kong, HK)
Kazuaki Nakamura (Osaka Univ., JP)
Eric Schulte-Zurhausen (Goethe Univ. Frankfurt, DE)
Atsushi Hashimoto (Kyoto Univ., JP)

ACM Multimedia 2013 Workshop on Crowdsourcing for Multimedia

Kuan-Ta Chen
Academia Sinica
Taiwan
swc@iis.sinica.edu.tw

Wei-Ta Chu
National Chung Cheng University
Taiwan
wtchu@cs.ccu.edu.tw

Martha Larson
Delft University of Technology
Netherlands
m.a.larson@tudelft.nl

ABSTRACT
The topic "Crowdsourcing for Multimedia" encompasses the full range of techniques that combine human intelligence and a large number of individual contributors to advance the state of the art in multimedia research. The ACM Multimedia 2013 Workshop on Crowdsourcing for Multimedia (CrowdMM 2013) provided a forum for presenting new crowdsourcing techniques, exchanging innovative crowdsourcing ideas, and discussing crowdsourcing best practices for multimedia. The workshop program consisted of presented papers, a keynote speech and a panel discussion. A special feature of this year's workshop was the "Crowdsourcing for Multimedia Ideas Competition", the results of which were presented at the workshop.

Categories and Subject Descriptors
H.1.2 [Models and Principles]: User/Machine Systems – *Human factors*.

Keywords
Crowdsourcing, multimedia, human computation

INTRODUCTION
The power of crowds—leveraging a large number of human contributors and the capabilities of human computation—has enormous potential to address key challenges in the area of multimedia research. The term "crowdsourcing" was coined in 2006 [2], and the concept developed greatly in the subsequent years, as described, for example by [3]. Currently, applications of crowdsourcing in the area of multimedia range from the exploitation of unsolicited user contributions, such as using tags to aid understanding of the visual content of yet-unseen images, to utilizing crowdsourcing platforms and marketplaces to create test collections. Crowdsourcing platforms that have been successfully used for multimedia research include Amazon Mechanical Turk (http://www.mturk.com), CrowdFlower (http://crowdflower.com) and Microworkers (http://www.microworkers.com). These platforms make it possible to micro-outsource tasks such as semantic video annotation to a large population of workers. Further, crowdsourcing offers a time- and resource-efficient method for collecting large volumes of input for system design and evaluation, making it possible to optimize multimedia systems more rapidly and to address human factors more effectively.

At present, crowdsourcing remains notoriously difficult to exploit effectively in multimedia settings: the challenge arises from the fact that community of users or workers is a complex and dynamic system that is highly sensitive to changes in the form and the parameterization of their activities. For example, on a crowdsourcing platform, workers are known to react differently depending on the way in which a multimedia annotation task is presented or explained and on the manner in which they are incentivized (e.g., the compensation that is offered or the appeal of the task). Crowdsourcing workers are not always reliable. Separating reliable from unreliable workers requires an understanding of the factors that influence how crowdsourcing workers interpret tasks and also of the conditions under which they carry out their work. Additionally, insight into the factors that motivate workers to submit unserious work is also critical. In the coming years, a thorough understanding of crowdsourcing for multimedia is crucial in order to enable the field to effectively address these challenges.

The CrowdMM workshop was dedicated to novel contributions to multimedia research that make use of human intelligence, but also take advantage of human plurality. CrowdMM 2013 followed the successful CrowdMM 2012 workshop held at ACM Multimedia 2012 in Nara, Japan [1]. The workshop defined crowdsourcing in the broad sense, namely, as encompassing both unsolicited human contributions, e.g., tags assigned by users to images, and also solicited contributions, e.g., annotations gathered by making use of crowdsourcing platforms. CrowdMM put a special focus on soliciting contributions that propose solutions for the key challenges that face widespread adoption of crowdsourcing paradigms in the multimedia research community. These include: identification of optimal crowd members (e.g., user expertise, worker reliability), providing effective explanations (i.e., good task design), controlling noise and quality in the results, designing incentive structures that do not breed cheating, adversarial environments, gathering necessary background information about crowd members without violating privacy, and creating effective descriptions of tasks.

SIGNIFICANCE OF CROWDSOURCING
Crowdsourcing can be expected to exercise transformative impact on the field of multimedia in the coming years. While the use of human computation is not new (e.g., the term "computer" originally described a human worker), technological advances have created new opportunities to leverage human effort in concert with automated methods to address limitations of current

MM'13, October 21–25, 2013, Barcelona, Spain.
ACM 978-1-4503-2404-5/13/10
http://dx.doi.org/10.1145/2502081.2503828

automation or to enhance current capabilities. The further enhancement of human intelligence attainable when contributions from multiple individuals are combined ("Wisdom of the Crowd") has just begun to give indications of greater potential for the multimedia field. We expect that future multimedia computing innovations will increasingly explore judicious use of humans and human computation to complement and extend existing methodologies.

WORKSHOP TOPICS AND GOALS

CrowdMM 2013 encouraged the submission of work discussing theoretical, experimental, and/or methodological developments advancing state-of-the-art knowledge of crowdsourcing techniques for multimedia research. It also solicited work regarding novel applications using crowdsourcing to address both traditional and emerging challenges in multimedia research. Topics of interest include the use of crowds, the Wisdom of Crowds, and human computation in multimedia, in the following areas of research:

- **Creation:** content synthesis, authoring, editing, and collaboration, summarization and storytelling.
- **Evaluation:** evaluation of multimedia signal processing algorithms, multimedia analysis and retrieval algorithms, or multimedia systems and applications.
- **Retrieval:** analysis of user multimedia queries, evaluating multimedia search algorithms and interactive multimedia retrieval.
- **Annotation:** generating semantic annotations for multimedia content, collecting large-scale input on user affective reactions.
- **Human factors:** designing or evaluating user interfaces for multimedia systems, usability study, multi-modal environment, human recognition and perceptions.
- **Novel applications:** putting crowdsourcing to new users in the service of multimedia systems (e.g., human as an element in the loop of computation).
- **Effective learning:** learning from crowd-annotated or crowd-augmented datasets.
- **Quality assurance:** identification of high quality work and reliable workers.
- **Motivation:** economics and incentive structures.
- **Resources:** programming languages, tools and platforms providing enhanced support.
- **Challenges:** inherent biases, limitations and trade-offs of crowd-centered approaches.

CrowdMM 2013 benefited from a keynote by Daniel Gatica-Perez, who presented joint work carried out with Joan-Isaac Biel, in a presentation entitled, "When the crowd watches the crowd: understanding impressions in online conversational video." The talk presented a framework for understanding social impressions in online conversational video, which was applied to vlogging. The role that video crowdsourcing techniques can play in interpersonal perception research was examined, crowdsourcing techniques used to collect online impressions about vloggers were described, and associated challenges were discussed.

As with CrowdMM 2012, the high-level goals of the workshop were twofold. First, it provided a venue promoting multimedia research that both makes use of human intelligence and also of numerous human contributors. Second, through panel discussion and invited talks, the workshop encouraged the multimedia community to define best practices for the use of crowdsourcing in multimedia and to give form to new methodologies and new paradigms that will allow crowdsourcing to push forward the state of the art in multimedia research.

CROWDSOURCING FOR MULTIMEDIA IDEAS COMPETITION

In order to encourage the multimedia community to generate innovative ideas on ways in which crowdsourcing can be used, and encourage scientists to apply these ideas in practice, CrowdMM 2013 organized an ideas competition. The ideas submitted to the competition were judged using three criteria:

- The clarity and simplicity with which the idea is explained. (A clear and simple-to-understand task will run the most successfully on the crowdsourcing platform.)
- The relationship to the topics of the workshop.
- Innovation and contribution to the state of the art in crowdsourcing for multimedia.

In contrast to last year, the competition was larger in scale and also organized earlier than last year's competition, in order that the results could be presented at the workshop. At CrowdMM 2013, a total of 15 ideas were submitted. The result of the judgment of the submissions was that all ideas were sponsored by Microworkers, enabling them to be put into practice. The workshop provided the opportunity for the contestants to present their ideas in a dedicated poster session. The announcement of the winner of the best idea was scheduled as a highlight of the workshop.

ACKNOWLEDGEMENTS

The workshop organizers would like to thank Tobias Hossfeld of the University of Wuerzburg for organizing the "Crowdsourcing for Multimedia Ideas" competition. Also, we gratefully acknowledge the generous donation of crowdsourcing credit from Microworkers that made the competition possible. We would also like to extend a thank you to Daniel Gatica-Perez of Idiap Research Institute for his keynote speech. Finally, we would like to acknowledge the people who contributed their time and effort to support CrowdMM 2013, especially the communities associated with the projects Qualinet (http://www.qualinet.eu/) and CUbRIK (http://www.cubrikproject.eu/).

REFERENCES

[1] Chen, Kuan-Ta, Chu, Wei-Ta, Larson, Martha, and Ooi, Wei Tsang. 2012. ACM Multimedia 2012 Workshop on Crowdsourcing for Multimedia. In *Proceedings of the 20th ACM international conference on Multimedia* (MM '12). ACM, New York, NY, USA, 1505-1506.

[2] Howe, Jeff. 2006. The Rise of Crowdsourcing, *Wired*, June 2006.

[3] Quinn, Alexander J. and Bederson, Benjamin B. 2011. Human computation: a survey and taxonomy of a growing field. In *Proceedings of the 2011 annual conference on Human factors in computing systems* (CHI '11). ACM, New York, NY, USA, 1403-1412.

Second ACM Multimedia Workshop on Geotagging and Its Applications in Multimedia (GeoMM 2013)

Liangliang Cao
IBM Watson Research Center
New York, USA
liangliang.cao@us.ibm.com

Gerald Friedland
International Computer Science Institute
Berkeley, USA
fractor@icsi.berkeley.edu

Pascal Kelm
Technische Universitaet of Berlin
Berlin, Germany
Kelm@nue.tu-berlin.de

ABSTRACT

The Workshop on Geotagging and Its Applications in Multimedia (GeoMM 2013) focuses on new applications and methods of geotagging and in geo-location support systems. As the location based multimedia becomes more and more popular in the era of Web and mobile applications, the increase in the use of geotagging and improvements in geolocation support systems open up a new dimension for the description, organization and manipulation of multimedia data. This new dimension radically expands the usefulness of multimedia data both for daily users of the Internet and social networking sites as well as for experts in particular application scenarios. The workshop serves as a venue for the premier research in geotagging and multimedia, and continues to attract submissions from a diverse set of researchers, who address newly arising problems within this emerging field.

Categories and Subject Descriptors

H.2.4 [**Systems**]: Multimedia databases; I.2.10 [**Artificial Intelligence**]: Vision and Scene Understanding

General Terms

Algorithm, Application, Theory

Keywords

geotagging, geolocation, social media, location based service

1. BACKGROUND AND MOTIVATION

In recent years, the popularity of GPS sensors and open geographical databases has motivated a lot of research works on geotagging in the multimedia society. The goal of this workshop is to bring together cutting edge research in geotagging as well as novel applications related to geotagging. It will help facilitate in-depth discussions, share existing tools, and ultimately enhance the research efforts in this area.

MM'13, October 21–25, 2013, Barcelona, Spain.
ACM 978-1-4503-2404-5/13/10.
http://dx.doi.org/10.1145/2502081.2503829.

Given that ACM Multimedia is a leading forum on related problems, we believe such a workshop will present vision and insight from leading experts and practitioners on the developing directions of related research.

Geotagging is the process of adding geographical identification metadata to various media files such as photos, videos, websites, messages, and tweets. It is not limited to GPS sensor data but an extension of current multimedia files with a wide variety of location-specific information. Due to the geolocation functions of social media websites and the popularity of smart phones with GPS sensors, we have witnessed a huge amount of geotagged media in recently years. For example, Flickr now hosts 100+ million geotagged photos and Foursquare records 3 million geo-tagged checked-in per day. The large amount of geotagged data has opened doors to new commercial applications and attracted more and more research interests from the research community. In recent years, many researchers have carried out research studies on different aspects of geotagging, including photo annotation, 3D reconstruction, trajectory mining, tourism visualization, and so on. The research on geotagging also starts to gain significant support from the government funding agencies. For example, in 2011 IARPA announced a new program called "Finder" that aims to infer the geolocation for a given photo or video clip. In 2010, the MediaEval Multimedia Benchmark (www.multimediaeval.org) introduced a ŞPlacingŤ task dedicated to geo-tag prediction for videos. Many companies have provided services on geotagging applications, such as Google Map and Facebook Places.

The goal of this workshop is to bring together cutting-edge research in geotagging as well as novel applications related to geotagging. It will help facilitate in-depth discussions, share existing tools, and ultimately enhance the research efforts in this area. The workshop will serve as a forum for the presentation and synthesis of vision and insight from leading experts and practitioners on the developing directions of geotagging research related to multimedia.

2. TOPICS OF INTERESTS

In terms of author audience, this workshop focuses on three main themes: collection and estimation of geotags; application of geotagging; and visualization of geotagged information. More specifically, we solicited paper submissions with the following (but not limited to) research topics:

- Location estimation: inferring geolocation from visual and audio cues

- Mining unstructured web text (e.g., news, blogs) for location
- Knowledge discovery from open geographical databases and web photos
- Mining geotags from mobile devices and sensor network
- Photo and video annotation
- Business applications (e.g., geomarketing, targeted advertising, recommendation, etc.)
- Social networking
- Privacy and security issues
- 3D construction of world model
- Visualization of tourism, travel routes, and other spatial-temporal patterns

3. PROGRAM COMMITTEE

We are thankful to the members of our program committee:

- Jaeyoung Choi, International Computer Science Institute
- Noel Codella, IBM T.J. Watson Research Center
- Venkatesan Ekambaram, UC Berkeley
- Giulia Fanti, UC Berkeley
- Andrew Gallagher, Cornell University
- Claudia Hauff, Delft University of Technology
- Nathan Jacobs, University of Kentucky
- Rongrong Ji, Columbia University
- Shen Jialie, Singapore Management University
- Tao Mei, Microsoft Research Asia
- Michele Merler, IBM T.J Watson Research Center
- Yue Shi, Delft University of Technology
- Sebastian Schmiedeke, Technische Universitaet Berlin
- Steven Schockaert, Cardiff University
- Yang Wang, University of Manitoba
- Felix Yu, Columbia University
- Lei Zhang, Microsoft Research Asia

4. WORKSHOP ORGANIZERS

Liangliang Cao is a research scientist of the Multimedia Research Group at the IBM T. J. Watson Research Center. He also holds an adjunct faculty position at the Columbia University in the City of New York. He has published more than 40 peer-reviewed articles in the area of multimedia and computer vision. He and his colleagues won the First place in a number of visual recognition challenges including ImageNet Challenge2010, ImageCLEF medical classification challenge 2012 and 2013. He received many awards including IBM Outstanding Accomplishment(2012), the Best Paper Award in the First International Workshop on Big Data Mining (2012), IBM Watson Emerging Leader in Multimedia and Signal Processing (2010), Facebook Fellowship Finalist (2010), and UIUC Computational Science and Engineering Fellowship (2009-2010). He is an area chair of ACM Multimedia 2012 and IEEE WACV 2014. He is a guest editor of TOMCCAP, CVIU and IEEE Multimedia Magazine. He is a general chair of Greater New York Area Multimedia and Vision Meeting from 2012 to 2013.

Gerald Friedland is Director of Audio and Multimedia Research at the International Computer Science Institute, a private research lab affiliated with the University of California, Berkeley. He was program co-chair of the IEEE International Symposium on Multimedia 2008 and 2009. He co-founded the IEEE International Conference on Semantic Computing and is a proud founder and program director of the IEEE International Summer School on Semantic Computing at UC Berkeley. He is also a program co-chair of ICME 2012 and a program committee member of ACM Multimedia 2009, senior TPC member 2010, and Grand Challenge chair 2011. He has published more than 100 peer-reviewed articles in conferences, journals, and books. He is associate editor for ACM Transactions on Multimedia Computing, Communications, and Applications. He is the recipient of several research and industry recognitions, among them the European Academic Software Award and the Multimedia Entrepreneur Award by the German Federal Department of Economics. Most recently, he leads the team that won the ACM Multimedia Grand Challenge in 2009.

Pascal Kelm is a PhD student at the Communication Systems Group (Technische Universitaet of Berlin) and received his Dipl.-Ing. degree in electrical engineering from TU Berlin, in 2009. His research expertises include multimedia analysis and retrieval, machine learning and multimodal fusion techniques for automatic geotagging in social media. He has actively participated in several EU funded multimedia oriented research projects including Petamedia, OpenSEM, VideoSense and is organizing the Placing task in the MediaEval benchmarking initiative.

Fourth International Workshop on Human Behavior Understanding (HBU 2013)

Albert Ali Salah
Boğaziçi University
34342 Bebek
Istanbul, Turkey
salah@boun.edu.tr

Hayley Hung
Delft University of Technology
Mekelweg 4, 2628 CD
Delft, the Netherlands
H.Hung@tudelft.nl

Oya Aran
Idiap Research Institute
Rue Marconi 19, PO Box 592,
CH - 1920
Martigny, Switzerland
oya.aran@idiap.ch

Hatice Gunes
Queen Mary University of London
Mile End Road, E1 4NS
London, UK
hatice@eecs.qmul.ac.uk

ABSTRACT

With advances in pattern recognition and multimedia computing, it became possible to analyze human behavior via multimodal sensors, at different time-scales and at different levels of interaction and interpretation. This ability opens up enormous possibilities for multimedia and multimodal interaction, with a potential of endowing the computers with a capacity to attribute meaning to users' attitudes, preferences, personality, social relationships, etc., as well as to understand what people are doing, the activities they have been engaged in, their routines and lifestyles. This workshop gathers researchers dealing with the problem of modeling human behavior under its multiple facets with particular attention to interactions in arts, creativity, entertainment and edutainment.

Categories and Subject Descriptors

I.5.4 [**Computing Methodologies**]: Pattern Recognition-Applications; I.2.10 [**Computing Methodologies**]: Artificial IntelligenceVision and Scene Understanding; H.1.2 [**Information Systems**]: Models and Principles User/Machine Systems

Keywords

Human behavior understanding; computer analysis of human behavior

MM'13, October 21–25, 2013, Barcelona, Spain.
ACM 978-1-4503-2404-5/13/10.
http://dx.doi.org/10.1145/2502081.2503830.

1. INTRODUCTION

Re-defining the relationship between the computer and the interacting human, moving the computer from a passive observer role to a socially active participant role and enabling it to drive different kinds of interaction has implications across multiple domains, including arts, creativity, entertainment and edutainment. In these domains in particular, modes of interaction are highly variable and so observing, analyzing and interpreting behaviors systematically is a challenge.

The HBU workshop gathers researchers dealing with the problem of modeling human behavior under its multiple facets (expression of emotions, display of complex social and relational behaviors, performance of individual or joint actions, etc.), with particular attention to **interactions in arts, creativity, entertainment and edutainment**. Concrete examples are interactive art installations that sense and respond to their viewers in novel ways, persuasive and serious games, affect-sensing systems with educational goals, gesture-sensing tutoring systems, healthcare systems that improve the patients' physical or cognitive well-being, playful interaction settings that serve beneficial purposes, to name a few.

The HBU Workshops, previously organized as satellite to ICPR [1], AMI [2] and IROS [3] Conferences, have a unique aspect of fostering cross-pollination of different disciplines, bringing together researchers of multimedia, robotics, HCI, artificial intelligence, pattern recognition, interaction design, ambient intelligence, and psychology. The diversity of human behavior, the richness of multi-modal data that arises from its analysis, and the multitude of applications that demand rapid progress in this area ensure that the HBU Workshops provide a timely and relevant discussion and dissemination platform.

2. TOPICS

We have solicited papers whose topics would span one or more items from each of the following three topic dimensions:

1. **Human Behavior Analysis Systems**
    - Action and activity recognition
    - Affect analysis
    - Social signal processing
    - Face analysis
    - Gestures and haptic interaction
    - Voice and speech analysis
    - Learning and adaptation
    - Gaze, attention and saliency
2. **Theory and Methodology of Human Interactive Behaviors**
    - Theoretical frameworks of behavior analysis
    - Data collection, annotation, and benchmarking
    - User studies and human factors
    - Interaction design
3. **Interactive Applications**
    - Visual and digital arts
    - Games and entertainment
    - Healthcare and well-being
    - Education
    - Creativity
    - Robotics

3. FORMAT

The Workshop is organized as a one day, single track event with oral and poster presentations, and a panel discussion on the focus theme. Out of 50 submissions, 12 papers are selected for oral presentation, organized into tracks on "action and activity recognition", "social and affective signals" (two tracks), and "interactions in arts and entertainment". 8 papers are selected for poster presentation. A post workshop special issue is scheduled for publication with the journal *ACM Transactions on Interactive Intelligent Systems.*

4. KEYNOTES

The keynote speakers of the Workshop are Dr. Pushmeet Kohli (Microsoft Research Cambridge) and Dr. Antonio Camurri (Univ. of Genova, DIBRIS, Casa Paganini - InfoMus Research Centre). Dr. Kohli is an ACM Distinguished Speaker.

5. TECHNICAL PROGRAM COMMITTEE

We thank our technical program committee for their support:

- Elisabeth André, Univ. Augsburg, DE
- Nick Bryan-Kinns, Queen Mary Univ. London, UK
- Carlos Busso, Univ. of Texas at Dallas, USA
- Rafael E. Calvo, Univ. of Sydney, AU
- Antonio Camurri, Univ. of Genova, IT
- Jeffrey Cohn, Univ. Pittsburgh, USA
- Simon Colton, Imperial College London, UK
- Fernando de la Torre, CMU, USA
- Hamdi Dibeklioğlu, Delft Univ. of Technology, NL
- Thierry Dutoit, Univ. Mons, BE
- Abdulmotaleb El Saddik, Univ. of Ottawa, CA
- Gwenn Englebienne, Univ. of Amsterdam, NL
- Jordi Gonzalez, UAB-CVC Barcelona, ES
- Daniel Gonzalez-Jimenez, Gradiant, ES
- Stefan Göbel, TU Darmstadt, DE
- Zakia Hammal, CMU, USA
- Christian Jacquemin, LIMSI-CNRS, FR
- Alejandro Jaimes, Yahoo Barcelona, ES
- Dinesh Jayagopi, Idiap Research Intitute, CH
- Kostas Karpouzis, National Technical Univ. of Athens, GR
- Cem Keskin, Microsoft Research Cambridge, UK
- Ben Kröse, Univ. of Amsterdam, NL
- Dana Kulic, Univ. of Waterloo, CA
- Matei Mancas, Univ. of Mons, BE
- Louis-Philippe Morency, USC, USA
- Florian 'Floyd' Mueller, RMIT, AU
- Frank Nack, Univ. of Amsterdam, NL
- Hiroshi Okuno, Kyoto Univ., JP
- Isabella Poggi, Univ. Roma Tre, IT
- Thierry Pun, Univ. of Geneva, CH
- Francis Quek, Virginia Tech, USA
- Ben Schouten, Eindhoven Tech. Univ., NL
- Björn Schuller, Tech. Univ. Munich, DE
- Alan Smeaton, Dublin City Univ., IE
- Koray Tahiroğlu, Aalto Univ., FI
- Reiner Wichert, Fraunhofer IGD, DE
- Giorgios Yannakakis, Univ. of Malta, ML

We also thank the following external reviewers for their help: Enrique Aragones-Rúa, Sharon Chu, Wen-Sheng Chu, Raquel Dosil-Lago, Derya Özkan, Fumihide Tanaka, Esteban Vazquez-Fernandez, Kazuyoshi Yoshii.

6. ACKNOWLEDGMENTS

This workshop is supported by ACM Distinguished Speakers Program, Infomus-Casa Paganini, and Boğazici University project BAP-6531.

7. REFERENCES

[1] A. A. Salah, T. Gevers, N. Sebe, and A. Vinciarelli. *Human Behavior Understanding: First International Workshop, HBU 2010, Istanbul, Turkey, August 22, 2010, Proceedings*, volume LNCS 6219. Springer, 2010.

[2] A. A. Salah and B. Lepri. *Human Behavior Unterstanding: Second International Workshop, HBU 2011, Amsterdam, The Netherlands, November 16, 2011, Proceedings*, volume LNCS 7065. Springer, 2011.

[3] A. A. Salah, J. Ruiz-del Solar, Ç. Meriçli, and P.-Y. Oudeyer. *Human Behavior Understanding: Third International Workshop, HBU 2012, Vilamoura, Portugal, October 7, 2012. Proceedings*, volume LNCS 7559. Springer, 2012.

Immersive Media Experiences

(ImmersiveMe 2013 Workshop at ACM Multimedia)

Teresa Chambel
LaSIGE, Faculty of Sciences
University of Lisbon
Lisbon, Portugal
tc@di.fc.ul.pt

V. Michael Bove
MIT Media Lab
Cambridge, MA, USA
vmb@media.mit.edu

Sharon Strover
University of Texas at Austin
Austin, TX, USA
sharon.strover@austin.utexas.edu

Paula Viana
Polytechnic of Porto and INESC TEC
Porto, Portugal
paula.viana@inescporto.pt

Graham Thomas
BBC, UK
graham.thomas@bbc.co.uk

ABSTRACT

Immersive media has the potential for strong impact on users' emotions and their sense of presence and engagement. The main objective of this workshop is to bring together researchers, students, media producers, service providers and industry players in the area of emergent immersive media. The workshop will provide a platform for a deep discussion on ongoing work, recent achievements and experiences. It is expected not only to consolidate experiences but also to identify aspects where strong collaboration among all the interested players is needed and to point towards future working directions.

Categories and Subject Descriptors

H.5.1 [**Information Interfaces and Presentation**]: Multimedia Information Systems; I.2.10 [**Artificial Intelligence**]: Vision and Scene Understanding; H.3.3 [**Information Storage and Retrieval**]: Information Search and Retrieval

Keywords

Immersive media; multisensory interaction; user participation; personalization.

1. INTRODUCTION

Immersive media has the potential for strong impact on users' emotions and their sense of presence and engagement. Increasingly, technology is supporting their involvement by capturing, producing, sharing and accessing information based on their perspectives and experiences, over the Internet, in social media, and through video on demand services using iTV. We have been witnessing an increase in the amount of content and number of devices for capturing, viewing and sensing, many of them portable and offering tremendous opportunities for immersion, user participation and personalization. The integration of different media formats, including 3D content, panoramic displays, multiview, as well as the possibility of delivering and accessing content through different communication vehicles, promote the development of a new participatory paradigm and enable new perceptual user experiences that provide more realistic and immersive involvement.

Immersion may be influenced by sensory modalities, surround effect, and vividness through resolution, and it conveys the user's conscious feeling of being inside the virtual world and the sense of belonging. It has an impact on the users and may be augmented by personalized and context-aware environments and content. Given the complexity of emerging media environments, researchers have begun to grapple with the dynamics of contemporary media usage to face the challenges for the design and development of technology and applications that effectively support and realize this immersion potential.

This workshop takes place in the middle of a media revolution where users are expecting to take part in the action by interacting with and generating content and to experience immersive and personalized environments. Its goal is to bring together researchers and practitioners in this interdisciplinary and transversal emerging field and to foster discussion of ongoing work and future directions of related topics by providing a forum for focused exchanges on new ideas, developments, and results.

2. TOPICS OF INTEREST

The workshop covers a broad set of topics related to the concept of Immersive Media Experiences in terms of 1) the user's perceptual experience; 2) the consumer's participation; 3) context-aware service personalization; 4) new media formats, including 3D, multiview and panoramic video and interaction approaches; 5) the integration of technology to make media more realistic, and production more efficient. Papers presented at the workshop make contributions in one or more of the following areas:

- Perceptual Immersion and multisensory interaction (including smell, taste and touch)
- Audiovisual Immersion: 3D, panoramic, multiview, and holographic video, spatial and stereoscopic audio
- Immersive TV, film and cinema
- Multisensory telecommunication
- Participatory media experiences, including user generated content, collaborative scenarios and crowdsourcing

MM '13, Oct 21-25 2013, Barcelona, Spain
ACM 978-1-4503-2404-5/13/10.
http://dx.doi.org/10.1145/2502081.2503831

- Personalization and context-aware adaptation in immersive scenarios
- Enabling technologies and formats
- Immersive media applications
- Quality of experience in multiview environments
- Emotions and affective interaction for immersive media
- Social aspects in new media services
- Field trials and user studies of immersive media
- Design and evaluation of immersive media experiences

3. WORKSHOP CONTRIBUTIONS

This first edition of the workshop attracted high quality submissions from research labs around the world. Many of the papers presented at the workshop were motivated by real-life use cases and concrete application contexts, indicating practical relevance and applicability. These papers cover a broad number of relevant aspects that enable the creation of immersive experiences, including work in Perceptual Immersion aspects, Participatory and Collaborative approaches, Enabling Technologies, Applications and Field Trials in different areas. Authors describe work that deal with different formats of video and audio streams (360° video, 3D and multiview), the use of different senses to enhance media experiences, transmission and streaming approaches, experiments in fields that include performing arts, sports, and participatory and collaborative scenarios. All these visions brought an interesting Immersive Media Experience to the workshop.

4. WORKSHOP CHAIRS

Dr. Teresa Chambel is a professor at Faculty of Sciences, University of Lisbon (FCUL) in Portugal, and a senior researcher of the Human Computer Interaction and Multimedia group at the LaSIGE Lab. Her research interests include multimedia and hypermedia, with a special emphasis on video and hypervideo, human-computer interaction (HCI), creativity, immersion, visualization, accessibility, cognition and emotions, interactive TV, elearning, digital talking books and digital art. Along with her students, she received the best paper award at EuroiTV'2011.

Dr. V. Michael Bove, Jr. holds a Ph.D. in Media Technology, from MIT, where he is head of the Object-Based Media Group at the Media Lab, and co-directs the Center for Future Storytelling and the consumer electronics working group CE2.0. He has authored papers on digital TV systems, video processing HW/SW design, multimedia, scene modeling, visual display technologies, and optics. He holds patents relating to video recording, hardcopy, iTV, and medical imaging. He is co-author with the late Stephen A. Benton of the book Holographic Imaging (Wiley, 2008). He is on the Board of Editors of the SMPTE Journal, and served as associate editor of Optical Engineering. Bove is a fellow of SPIE and of the Institute for Innovation, Creativity, and Capital. He was a founder of and technical advisor to WatchPoint Media, Inc. and is technical advisor to OneLaptopPerChild.

Dr. Sharon Strover is the Philip G. Warner Regents Professor in Communication at the University of Texas where she teaches communications and telecommunications courses and directs the Telecommunications and Information Policy Institute. Her research investigates the relationship between economic outcomes, policy and investments in digital media programs; social media; the digital divide; rural broadband deployment; e-government; and market structure and policy issues for international audiovisual industries. She has worked with several government agencies on telecommunications policy matters. She recently stepped down from Chairing her Department, to work on a national broadband infrastructure program with the federal government in Washington, D.C.

Dr. Paula Viana is a Coordinator Professor at the Polytechnic of Porto and a Senior Researcher at INESC Porto, a research institute with more than 25 years of research results in the area of Telecommunications and Multimedia Services. She has authored papers in the areas of Digital TV, Multimedia Information Systems and Content Management. Her long collaboration with broadcasters and Industries enables an integrated vision of both future research topics as well as new applications for finished research. She has been serving as an expert for the European Commission on the evaluation of research proposals and on the assessment of project results.

Prof. Graham Thomas leads Immersive & Interactive Content Section at BBC R&D. Whilst the current work in his section spans both audio and video, his background is in image processing, computer vision and their application to 3D virtual graphics. He was involved in a number of projects that have gone on to commercial success, e.g. free-d camera tracking system, retro-reflective chroma-key cloth, and sports graphics systems. Prior to 3D graphics, he worked on video compression, PAL coding, and motion estimation based on phase correlation (in his PhD), commercialized in a standards converter, which won an Emmy award and a Queen's Award to Industry. Graham holds over 20 patents and is a Visiting Professor at the University of Surrey.

5. PROGRAMME COMMITTEE

Adrian Cheok (Keio University, Japan)
Anthon Nijholt (Twente University, The Netherland)
Artur Pimenta Alves (Univ of Porto and INESC TEC, Portugal)
David Geerts (CUO Social Spaces, iMinds-KU Leuven, Belgium)
Fabien Gouyon (INESC TEC, Portugal)
George Lekakos (Athens Univ. of Econ. and Business, Greece);
Hendrik Knoche (University of Aalborg, Denmark)
João Magalhães (New University of Lisbon, Portugal)
Kostantinos Chorianopoulos (Ionian University, Greece)
Maria da Graça Pimentel (Universidade de São Paulo, Brazil)
Marianna Obrist (Newcastle University, UK)
Nelson Zagalo (University of Minho, Portugal)
Nuno Correia (New University of Lisbon, Portugal)
Omar A. Niamut (TNO, Delft, The Netherlands)
Pablo Cesar (CWI, The Netherlands)
Patrick Vonderau (Media Studies, Stockholm Univ, Sweden)
Rene Kaiser (Joanneum Research, Graz, Austria)
Ryohei Nakatsu (National University of Singapore)
Teresa Andrade (University of Porto and INESC TEC, Portugal)
Teresa Romão (New University of Lisbon, Portugal)
Thibault Langlois (Lasige, Fac. Sciences, Univ. Lisbon, Portugal)
Wolfgang Vonolfen (Fraunhofer IAIS, Germany)

6. ACKNOWLEDGMENTS

This workshop was partially supported by: the Portuguese Foundation for Science and Technology through LaSIGE Multiannual Funding and the ImTV project FCT/UTA-Est/MAI/0010/2009; the North Portugal Regional Operational Programme (ON.2, O Novo Norte), under the National Strategic Reference Framework (NSRF), through the European Regional Development Fund (ERDF).

The Third ACM International Workshop on Interactive Multimedia on Mobile and Portable Devices (IMMPD'13)

Jiebo Luo
University of Rochester
Rochester, NY 14627, USA
jluo@cs.rochester.edu

Caifeng Shan
Philips Research
High Tech Campus 36
Eindhoven 5656 AE, The Netherlands
+31 40 2741601
caifeng.shan@philips.com

Ling Shao
The University of Sheffield
Mappin Street
Sheffield S1 3JD, United Kingdom
+44 114 222 5841
ling.shao@sheffield.ac.uk

Minoru Etoh
NTT DoCoMo
Yokosuka, Japan
etoh@nttdocomo.co.jp

ABSTRACT

With the mobile and portable devices become ubiquitous for people's daily life, how to design user interfaces of these products that enable natural, intuitive and fun interaction is one of the main challenges the multimedia community is facing. Following previous successful events, the third ACM International workshop on Interactive Multimedia on Mobile and Portable Devices (IMMPD'13) aims to bring together researchers from both academia and industry in domains including computer vision, audio and speech processing, machine learning, pattern recognition, communications, human-computer interaction, and media technology to share and discuss recent advances in interactive multimedia.

Categories and Subject Descriptors

F.1.2 **[Theory of Computation]**: Modes of Computation – *Interactive and reactive computation.* H.5.2 **[Information Systems]**: Information Interfaces and Presentation – *User Interfaces* I.1.2 **[Computing Technologies]**: Artificial Intelligence I.1.4 **[Computing Technologies]**: Image Processing and Computer Vision. I.1.5 **[Computing Technologies]**: Pattern Recognition

Keywords

Multimedia, Human-Computer Interaction, Consumer Electronics, Computer Vision, Pattern Recognition.

MM'13, October 21–25, 2013, Barcelona, Spain
ACM 978-1-4503-2404-5/13/10.
http://dx.doi.org/10.1145/2502081.2503832.

1. INTRODUCTION

With the development of silicon technologies, mobile and portable electronics devices, such as personal computers, mobile phones, digital cameras, and PDA, have become ubiquitous for people's daily life. These devices provide multimedia sources for entertainment, communication, and so on. How to design user interfaces of these products that enable natural, intuitive and fun interaction is one of the main challenges the multimedia community is facing.

Considering that mobile and portable devices are usually supplied with multiple sensors (e.g., camera and microphone), how to employ multimodal information for interaction has recently received much attention in both academia and industry. But interactive multimedia is still an under-explored field. Many challenges exist when moving to multimodal interaction: for example, how to annotate and search huge data acquired by using multiple sensors, especially in the unconstrained end-user environments? How to effectively extract and select representative multimedia features for human behavior recognition? How to select the fusion strategy of multimodal data for a given application? To address these challenges, we must adapt the existing approaches or find new solutions suitable for multimedia interaction on mobile and portable devices.

Multimedia interaction on mobile and portable devices is a hot topic, and records of recent ACM Multimedia conferences demonstrated this trend. Recent efforts have led to many exciting applications and products (prototypes). The major objectives of this workshop are: 1) collecting and seeking the recent advances in multimedia interaction; 2) exploiting potential challenges and possible advanced solutions in terms of theory and practice, and 3) illustrating the great value of multimedia interaction with successful real-world applications. The participants can also get in touch with a variety of recent techniques as well as the case studies of different tasks from multimedia interaction applications. This workshop can also serve to bridge laboratory research and industrial practice to a considerable degree.

This workshop builds upon the previous workshops and events organized by the workshop organizers: the second International Workshop on Interactive Multimedia on Mobile and Portable Devices (IMMPD'12), ACM Multimedia, 2012, the first International Workshop on Interactive Multimedia on Mobile and Portable Devices (IMMPD'11), ACM Multimedia 2011, and International Workshop on Interactive Multimedia for Consumer Electronics (IMCE'09), ACM Multimedia, 2009. The targeted audiences are mainly researchers, engineers as well as graduate students working on relevant areas.

2. TOPICS OF INTEREST

Topics related to interactive multimedia on mobile and portable devices include:

- Multimedia description and markup
- Multimedia representation and annotation
- Multimedia search and retrieval
- Presence and environment sensing
- Face detection, tracking, and recognition
- Hand detection, tracking, and recognition
- Emotion/mood recognition
- Gesture/action/activity recognition
- Audio-visual recognition and interaction
- Novel interaction (accelerometer, touch screen, haptics, voice, etc.)
- Multimodal data modeling and fusion
- Multimedia content adaptation
- Context-aware services
- Interaction with depth-sensing
- Social media computing and interaction

3. TECHNICAL PROGRAM

Based on review comments, seven papers are accepted for this workshop, covering different related topics. The accepted papers are from industry and academia, representing diverse geographic locations including USA, Europe, Japan, Singapore, Taiwan, and China.

The accepted papers are

- Optimized Speech Balloon Placement for Automatic Comics Generation, Wei-Ta Chu and Chia-Hsiang Yu (National Chung Cheng University, Taiwan)
- A Smart Watch-based Gesture Recognition System for Assisting People with Visual Impairments, Lorenzo Porzi, et al. (Fondazione Bruno Kessler, Italy)
- Convex object surface mapping for wide field of view video representation, Dan Mikami, et al. (NTT Lab, Japan)
- Sound Preferences of Deaf and Hard of Hearing People Playing an Audio-Based Computer Game, Rumi Hiraga and Kjetil Hansen (Tsukuba University of Technology, Japan)
- Hand Segmentation and Gesture Recognition in EGO-Vision, Giuseppe Serra, et al. (University of Modena and Reggio Emilia, Italy)
- Energy Efficient Multi-player Smartphone Gaming using 3D Spatial Subdivisioning and PVS Techniques, Anand Bhojan and Zeng Qiang (National University of Singapore, Singapore)
- Improved Binary Feature Matching through Fusion of Hamming Distance and Fragile Bit Weight, Dongye Zhuang (Chinese Academy of Sciences, China)

4. PROGRAM COMMITTEE

We would like to express our gratitude to the program committee, who worked very hard in reviewing papers and providing suggestions for their improvements. The Program Committee members and their affiliations are listed as follows.

- Marco Bertini, University of Florence, Italy
- Xavier Binefa, University of Barcelona, Spain
- Yun (Raymond) Fu, SUNY at Buffalo, USA
- Jordi Gonzalez, Universitat AutÒnoma de Barcelona, Spain
- Ling Guan, Ryerson University, Canada
- Richang Hong, Hefei University of Technology, China
- Gang Hua, Stevens Institute of Technology, USA
- Wolfgang Hurst, Utrecht University, The Netherlands
- Ichiro Ide, Nagoya University, Japan
- Xiaoyi Jiang, University of Munster, Germany
- Yu-Gang Jiang, Fudan University, China
- Michael Lew, Leiden University, The Netherlands
- Alexander C. Loui, Kodak Research Labs, USA
- Tao Mei, Microsoft Research Asia, China
- Anton Nijholt, University of Twente, The Netherlands
- Yoichi Sato, University of Tokyo, Japan
- Giuseppe Serra, University of Modena and Reggio Emilia, Italy
- Jialie Shen, Singapore Management University, Singapore
- Ning Xu, Dolby Laboratories, USA
- Hui Zhang, United International College, China

2nd International Workshop on Socially-Aware Multimedia (SAM'13)

Pablo Cesar
CWI: Centrum Wiskunde & Informatica
Science Park 123, 1098 XG
Amsterdam, Netherlands
p.s.cesar@cwi.nl

Matthew Cooper
FX Palo Alto Laboratory, Inc.
3174 Porter Drive, CA 94304
Palo Alto, USA
cooper@fxpal.com

David A. Shamma
Yahoo! Research
Santa Clara, CA, USA
aymans@acm.org

Doug Williams
BT Research & Technology
Adastral Park, IP5 3RE
Ipswich, UK
doug.williams@bt.com

ABSTRACT

Multimedia social communication is becoming commonplace. Television is becoming smart and social; media sharing applications are transforming the way we converse and recall events and videoconferencing is a common application on our computers, phones, tablets and even televisions. The confluence of computer-mediated interaction, social networking, and multimedia content are radically reshaping social communications, bringing new challenges and opportunities.

This workshop, in its second edition, provides an opportunity to explore socially-aware multimedia, in which the social dimension of mediated interactions between people are considered to be as important as the characteristics of the media content. Even though this social dimension is implicitly addressed in some current solutions, further research is needed to better understand what makes multimedia socially-aware.

Categories and Subject Descriptors

H.1.2 [**Models and Principles**]: User/Machine Systems – *Human factors*. H.5.1 [**Information Interfaces and Presentation**]: Multimedia Information Systems – *Audio, Video*.

General Terms

Algorithms, Design, Experimentation, Human Factors

Keywords

Social Interaction, social communication, social media, communication, Information retrieval, micro-blogging

MM '13, Oct 21-25 2013, Barcelona, Spain
ACM 978-1-4503-2404-5/13/10.
http://dx.doi.org/10.1145/2502081.2503833

1. INTRODUCTION

The goal of the workshop on socially-aware multimedia is to pave the way for future innovation by acting as a community-building event, where research challenges can be identified and classified. By doing so, the event will help enable innovative solutions for the challenges ahead.

Relevant insights can be found within a number of disciplines such as multimedia research, human-computer interaction, and sociology. In particular, multimedia research provides quantitative metrics regarding multimedia objects (e.g., precision and recall) and multimedia systems (e.g., delay, jitter). Human-Computer Interaction research incorporates both quantitative metrics and qualitative understanding regarding human perception (e.g., quality of experience); and sociology and communication science provide a better understanding about motivations and collective group behavior (e.g., conversational and interaction patterns, strength of interpersonal ties).

Nevertheless, we have yet to see a focus on how to measure, to formalize, and to consider social interactivity as a prime parameter for designing and developing multimedia systems and applications. For example, social media research is currently restricted to content curation, independent of the exchange of human conversations that happens around the media object. Acknowledging existing work, this workshop takes the field forward, by articulating the notion of socially aware-multimedia, focusing on the social interactions, on the shared activities, and on the group experiences.

2. CALL FOR PAPERS

The workshop on socially-aware multimedia provides a forum for researchers and practitioners to share novel and groundbreaking results. With special emphasis on innovative directions and on brave ideas, the final goal is to recognize an emergent inter-disciplinary area at the cross roads of multimedia research, social science, and human-computer interaction. In particular, we are interested in papers that focus on multimedia systems and applications, accounting for social interaction theories, metrics, and methodologies. We acknowledge the inter-disciplinary nature of the workshop, and encourage participation from different research disciplines such as multimedia information retrieval, systems, and applications.

Topics include, but are not limited to:

- Applications of socially-aware multimedia
- Interactive end-to-end systems
- Multimedia modeling (in particular for social interaction and shared experiences)
- Socially-Aware multimedia content analysis and understanding
- Collaborative authoring of videos and multimedia sharing
- Social interaction theories and metrics
- Field trials and user studies of socially-aware multimedia applications
- Qualitative and quantitative evaluation of social participation
- Micro-Blogging and multimedia information retrieval
- Multimedia-Enabled social networking

3. PROGRAM

The International Workshop on Socially-Aware Multimedia (https://sites.google.com/site/sociallyawaremultimedia2013/) will be held in conjunction with the ACM International Multimedia Conference. It will take place on October 21, 2013, in Barcelona, Catalunya, Spain. The most pertinent contributions have been selected for inclusion in the workshop's agenda.

The workshop is organized primarily as a forum for discussion and knowledge exchange. Hence, its format will not be restricted to paper presentations, but will include interactive sessions in which discussion and knowledge exchange are encouraged. The workshop will be structured as a working session, for encouraging interaction between the participants and for promoting discussions about the basis and principles behind socially-aware multimedia research.

As part of the program, there are two invited papers by **Dr. Munmun De Choudhury**, working at Microsoft Research, and **Dr. Lyndon Kennedy**, at Yahoo! Research.

The workshop includes as well two keynote speakers:

Dr. Dick C.A. Bulterman: Centrum Wiskunde & Informatica (CWI) / VU University and Vice Chair of ACM SIGWEB.

Dick is a senior researcher at CWI in Amsterdam, where he has led the Distributed and Interactive Systems group since 2004. He also holds the professorship of Distributed Multimedia Languages and Interfaces with the department of computer science at the Vrije Universiteit in Amsterdam, where he teaches and does research within the Computer Systems and Web and Media groups. His research interests include multimedia authoring and document processing. His recent research concerns socially-aware multimedia, interactive television, and media analysis. Together with his CWI colleagues, he has won a series of best paper and research awards within the multimedia community, and has managed a series of successful large-scale European Union projects. He was also the founder and first managing director of Oratrix Development BV. In October 2013, he will move to become President of the FX Palo Alto Laboratory in California.

Dr. Eric Gilbert: Assistant Professor in Georgia Tech's School of Interactive Computing

Eric joined the Tech faculty after finishing a Ph.D. in Computer Science at Illinois in 2010. His research lab is focused on building and studying social media. He has built a few computational systems to predict relationship strength and studied how emotions expressed on the web interact with stock prices. The research lab has recently received funding from DARPA and the NSF, and this year Google made Eric one of their faculty fellows. Most importantly: he really, really likes coffee.

4. ORGANISERS

The workshop is organized by:

Dr. Pablo Cesar is a researcher at the Distributed and Interactive Systems group at CWI (The National Research Institute for Mathematics and Computer Science in the Netherlands). He has (co)-authored over 50 articles about multimedia systems and infrastructures, social media sharing, interactive media, multimedia content modelling, and user interaction. He has given tutorials about multimedia systems in prestigious conferences such as ACM Multimedia, CHI, and the WWW conference. Webpage: http://homepages.cwi.nl/~garcia

Dr. Matthew Cooper is a senior research scientist in the multimedia analysis and visualization group at FX Palo Alto Laboratory (FXPAL). He has developed analysis techniques for indexing, retrieval, and management of digital music, text, photo, and video collections. He currently works on systems and interfaces for aggregation, annotation, and retrieval of web-distributed expository and presentation video. Webpage: http://www.fxpal.com/people/cooper/

Dr. David A. Shamma is a research scientist at Yahoo! Labs where he manages the HCI Research Group. He researches synchronous environments and connected experiences both online and in-the-world. Focusing on creative expression and sharing frameworks, he designs and prototypes systems for multimedia-mediated communication, as well as, develops targeted methods and metrics for understanding how people communicate online in small environments and at web scale. Webpage: http://labs.yahoo.com/author/shamma/

Dr. Doug Williams has been leading research into the way that broadband will change our lives for over ten years. He has led large projects looking at how television, the way we communicate and the way we play will change because of fast broadband speeds. He is currently working with BT strategy using his insights into the way behaviors and services are changing to better anticipate future demand for broadband capacity.

5. ACKNOWLEDGMENTS

We would like to thank the Technical Program Committee that helps shaping the program of the workshop.

Pablo Cesar and Doug Williams would like to thank the funding from the Vconect project; European Community's Seventh Framework Programme (FP7/2007-2013) under grant agreement no. ICT-2011-287760.

Summary Abstract for the 2nd ACM International Workshop on Multimedia Analysis for Ecological Data

Concetto Spampinato
Dep. of Electrical, Electronics and Computer Engineering
University of Catania
95125 Catania, Italy
cspampin@dieei.unict.it

Vasileios Mezaris
Centre for Research and Technology Hellas
Information Technologies Inst.
Thermi 57001, Greece
bmezaris@iti.gr

Jacco van Ossenbruggen
Centrum Wiskunde & Informatica
1098 XG Amsterdam, NL
Jacco.van.Ossenbruggen@cwi.nl

ABSTRACT

The 2nd ACM International Workshop on Multimedia Analysis for Ecological Data (MAED'13) is held as part of ACM Multimedia 2013. MAED'13, following the first workshop of the MAED series (MAED'12) that was held as part of ACM Multimedia 2012, is concerned with the processing, interpretation, and visualization of ecology-related multimedia content with the aim to support biologists in their investigations for analyzing and monitoring natural environments.

Categories and Subject Descriptors

H.1.0 [**Information Systems**]: Models and Principles

Keywords

Multimedia Content Analysis, Animal and Plant Identification, Ecological Multimedia Data Retrieval

1. MOTIVATION

With the recent progress in digital cameras and sensors, as well as in network bandwidth and information storage capacities, the production of multimedia data has become an easy task. This has resulted in a huge amount of multimedia available on the web, in broadcast data streams, or in personal and professional databases. This explosion of multimedia data has created the urgent need for efficient organization, browsing and retrieval tools. It has also generated new possibilities for exploiting multimedia data in diverse and specialized applications that can significantly gain from the analysis and understanding of such data. Whilst a large number of multimedia analysis and understanding techniques have been developed specifically for investigating events and behaviors in human-centered applications, such as sports and surveillance, relatively little attention has been paid to the understanding of ecology-related multimedia content. On the other hand, ecology is nowadays being considered an interdisciplinary, collaborative and data-intensive science and as such discovering, integrating and analyzing heterogeneous data are of key importance for researchers to address complex questions ranging from single particles to animals to the biosphere. This has led to the proliferation of ecology-related multimedia content in the last ten years: for instance, the EcoGrid project[1] has collected many Terabytes of data (videos, images and audio recordings) of monitoring forest animals as well as fish by the coral reefs in Taiwan. The wide range of cameras continuously capturing birds nests, but also variants filming wolves, badgers, foxes etc., and also the continuous collection of multimedia data for pollution monitoring, are other important examples. The automated analysis of such multimedia data poses new challenges, and the results of such analyses are of great interest to investigators such as biologists in their strive towards monitoring and analyzing the natural environment, promoting its preservation, and understanding the behavior and interactions of the living organisms (insects, animals, etc.) that are part of it.
The goal of the 2nd ACM International Workshop on Multimedia Analysis for Ecological Data[2] is to bring together the research community and to discuss the most recent progresses in multimedia data analysis in relation to the above challenges.

2. DESCRIPTION

The 2nd ACM International Workshop on Multimedia Analysis for Ecological Data aims at bringing together practitioners and researchers, both in multimedia and in ecology, to share ideas and experiences in designing and implementing novel multimedia analysis techniques and tools for ecological multimedia content. It specifically presents and reports on the most recent methods for the processing, interpretation, and visualization of multimedia data recorded for monitoring ecological systems, with particular attention to animal and plant identification and classification.
The workshop features two keynote talks, by Prof. Robert Fisher and Prof. Margrit Betke. It also includes seven papers, addressing the following topics:

- Animal detection and recognition. Zeppelzauer *et al.* in [6] present a method for the automated detection of elephant presence, motivated by the observation that the automated acoustic detection of elephants is an important factor in alleviating the human-elephant con-

[1]http://ecogrid.nchc.org.tw/
[2]http://maed2013.dieei.unict.it

MM'13, October 21–25, 2013, Barcelona, Spain.
ACM 978-1-4503-2404-5/13/10.
http://dx.doi.org/10.1145/2502081.2503834.

flict in Asia and Africa. They introduce a method for signal enhancement to improve the robustness of the detector in noisy situations, and evaluate it on a large dataset of wildlife recordings. Dusart *et al.* in [3], on the other hand, work with the visual modality, and present a framework for recognizing animals in videos by using any existing information that is included in the videos' subtitles.

- Fish and marine environment monitoring. Beauxis-Aussalet *et al.* in [2] present a system for fish population monitoring through the analysis of underwater videos. They describe the system's underlying video processing algorithms, and their connection to the user interface for on-demand data retrieval by biologists. They put special emphasis on the information needs of the biologists, and on the dynamic data extraction and retrieval mechanisms that can support them. Zhang *et al.* in [7] deal with the problem of monitoring and supporting the protection of sensitive marine ecosystems such as estuaries and coastal areas. Towards this goal, they demonstrate how an in-situ sensor network can be enhanced with the use of contextual image data, so as to detect turbidity spikes in water quality sensor measurements automatically and combine this with visual sensing to identify abnormal events.

- Benchmarking and user-appreciation of ecological multimedia technologies. Goeau *et al.* in [4] present a synthesis of the ImageCLEF 2013 plant identification task, a system-oriented testbed dedicated to the evaluation of image-based plant identification technologies. With 12 participating groups, the 2013 task confirmed the increasing interest of the multimedia community in ecology-related benchmarking challenges. In their paper, Goeau *et al.* present the resources and assessments of task, summarize the retrieval approaches employed by the participating groups, and provide an analysis of the main evaluation results. In [1], Beauxis-Aussalet *et al.* examine the issue of trust in automated video analysis. They argue that, in the application of monitoring underwater ecosystems, disclosing details about the video processing and provenance data allows biologists to compare the automated analysis results with their traditional statistical methods, thus increasing their trust in the automated results.

- Applications in biogeography. Mishima *et al.* in [5] present a social platform enabling field research on biodiversity using an iPhone application. The users of this application can easily collect field data with the phone's camera and the application's meta-data and tagging functions.

3. CONCLUDING REMARKS

The 2nd ACM International Workshop on Multimedia Analysis for Ecological Data brings together practitioners and researchers, both in multimedia and in ecology, to share ideas and experiences for the analysis of multimedia content for natural environment monitoring. We hope that the selected papers will serve as a valuable reference for the future research on this ground-breaking research area.

4. ACKNOWLEDGEMENTS

This workshop was partially funded by the EC under contract FP7-257024 Fish4Knowledge[3].

5. REFERENCES

[1] E. Beauxis-Aussalet, E. Arslanova, L. Hardman, and J. van Ossenbruggen. A case study of trust issues in scientific video collections. In *MAED 2013 @ ACM Multimedia 2013, Barcelona, Spain*, Oct. 2013.

[2] E. Beauxis-Aussalet, S. Palazzo, G. Nadarajan, E. Arslanova, and L. Hardman. A video processing and data retrieval framework for fish population monitoring. In *MAED 2013 @ ACM Multimedia 2013, Barcelona, Spain*, Oct. 2013.

[3] T. Dusart, A. Venkat, and M.-F. Moens. Cross-modal alignment for wildlife recognition. In *MAED 2013 @ ACM Multimedia 2013, Barcelona, Spain*, Oct. 2013.

[4] H. Goeau, A. Joly, P. Bonnet, V. Bakic, J.-F. Molino, D. Barthelemy, and N. Boujemaa. The imageclef plant identification task 2013. In *MAED 2013 @ ACM Multimedia 2013, Barcelona, Spain*, Oct. 2013.

[5] M. Mishima, T. Matsumoto, S. Takano, and O. Matsuda. A mobile platform for biogeography. In *MAED 2013 @ ACM Multimedia 2013, Barcelona, Spain*, Oct. 2013.

[6] M. Zeppelzauer, A. S. Stoeger, and C. Breiteneder. Acoustic detection of elephant presence in noisy environments. In *MAED 2013 @ ACM Multimedia 2013, Barcelona, Spain*, Oct. 2013.

[7] D. Zhang, E. O'Connnor, K. McGuinness, T. Sullivan, N. O'Connor, and F. Regan. Smart multi-modal marine monitoring via visual analysis and data fusion. In *MAED 2013 @ ACM Multimedia 2013, Barcelona, Spain*, Oct. 2013.

[3]www.fish4knowledge.eu

ACM MM MIIRH 2013: Workshop on Multimedia Indexing and Information Retrieval for Healthcare

Jenny Benois-Pineau
Univ. Bordeaux 1
Bordeaux, France
benois-p@labri.fr

Alexia Briassouli
Information Technologies Insitute
CERTH-ITI, Greece
abria@iti.gr

Alexander Hauptmann
Carnegie-Mellon Univ.
Pittsburg, USA
alex@cs.cmu.edu

ABSTRACT

Healthcare systems are depending on increasingly sophisticated and ubiquitous technology, while telehealth is rapidly gaining importance with the advent of low-cost and effective technological solutions in medicine. The increase in the worldwide elderly population and the burden this is inflicting upon the workforce, societies and economies are making remote care and independent living at home a necessity. MIIRH is the first workshop on multimedia analysis for remote care of and assisted living solutions which enable people that are incapacitated in some regard to continue living independently at home and remain active members of society. The topics addressed in MIIRH are extremely timely, as multitudes of cost-effective and high quality care solutions are already being developed and used, rendering the examination of new medical, healthcare paradigms an absolute necessity.

Categories and Subject Descriptors

J.3 [**Life and Medical Sciences**]: *Medical Information Systems.* H.3 [**Information Storage and Retrieval**]: *H3.1 Content Analysis and Indexing*

Keywords

Monitoring, Smart Homes, Multimedia Analysis/Indexing, Telehealth, Ambient Assisted Living, Feedback

1. INTRODUCTION

The worldwide increase in average life expectancy, the improvement of healthcare and the higher average age of the workforce is significantly affecting society, healthcare systems and world economies [1].

MM'13, October 21–25, 2013, Barcelona, Spain.
ACM 978-1-4503-2404-5/13/10.
http://dx.doi.org/10.1145/2502081.2503835

Multimodal data is playing an increasingly significant role in healthcare, with sophisticated technologies involved in monitoring and diagnosis [2], [3], [4], the advent of smart homes [5] enabling accurate and effective remote monitoring and care allowing elderly to live independently and remain active members of society. The processing of great quantities of multimodal data is now regarded as a necessary complement to physicians' diagnoses, with computers able to process vast amounts of multimodal data, statistics and the medical literature in an efficient manner, greatly supporting health professionals [6].

Multimodal data analysis, information retrieval and indexing is thus central to health professionals, people with medical conditions and society at large, as such solutions significantly decrease the cost of healthcare, while guaranteeing comprehensive and high quality care and enabling the prolongation of independent living at home, and the good health of the ageing workforce.

2. OBJECTIVES

MIIRH, held in conjunction with ACM MM 2013, will comprise the first Workshop on Multimedia Information Indexing and Retrieval for Healthcare and form a platform for the continued discussion of key research issues in multimedia for healthcare, remote monitoring and treatment.

Multimodal monitoring for health can take place at home, but should be discreet, unobtrusive and personalized. Theoretical, i.e. research-oriented and practical, application-specific issues related to the extraction of lifestyle, behavior and health information from multimodal data will be examined.

The setup of smart homes is also of interest, as the latter need to ensure accurate, reliable, discreet and cost-efficient measurements, involving, among others, privacy protection and appropriate sensor placement.

The interfaces and the effect of the feedback they provide both to the people being monitored and their carers are important issues addressed and presented in MIIRH, with related results from real applications.

Finally, personalization, unobtrusiveness, accuracy of analysis results, secure data storage, transmission, effective interfacing and communication and privacy concerns will be presented in MIIRH.

3. TOPICS OF INTEREST

The workshop will provide a forum for researchers to share information on their latest investigations on multimedia information retrieval and indexing for healthcare. In addition to paper presentations and posters, two invited talks will take place by well – known experts in the fields involved, namely Prof. Linda Shapiro and Prof. Jean – Francois Dartigues.

Topics in modeling and analyzing multimodal data related to healthcare include but not limited to:

- Multimedia indexing and retrieval for healthcare monitoring
- Machine learning and data mining for healthcare
- Recognition of activities of daily living
- Detection of abnormal behaviors/event detection for health monitoring and remote care
- Personalized data analysis, event detection, profile building from multimodal data
- Design of smart-homes for remote health monitoring
- Feedback solutions for remote healthcare
- Ethical and Legal Aspects of at home multimodal health monitoring

4. MIIRH PROGRAM

MIIRH will be a one day workshop, held on Oct. 22 2013 in conjunction with ACM MM 2013 in Barcelona, Spain. Presentations will be made from 9:00 am to 5:00 pm with breaks and 1-hour lunch.

MIIRH will feature two invited Keynote talks:

- Prof. Linda Shapiro: "Image Analysis for Biomedical and Healthcare Applications".
- Prof. Jean-Francois Dartigues: "Dementia and Dependency: a Major Challenge for the 21st century".

Authors of each accepted paper will have 20 min (including 5 min discussion) to present their work. Each paper can select to give a demo or poster at the break of the workshop.

5. ORGANIZERS

- Jenny Benois-Pineau (Univ. Bordeaux 1)
- Alexia Briassouli (CERTH -ITI)
- Alexander Hauptman (Carnegie-Mellon Univ.)

6. ACKNOWLEDGMENTS

ACM MM MIIRH 2013 is being organized with the support of the FP7/2007-2013 EU Project Dem@Care [7], under grant agreement 288199.

7. REFERENCES

[1] http://ec.europa.eu/health -eu/my_health/elderly/index_en.htm

[2] Ferdous S., Galatas G., Vyas K., Becker E., Fegaras L., Makedon F., *Multi person identification and localisation in pervasive assistive environments*, International Journal of Computer Science and Management Research, vol. 1, issue 4, Nov. 2012.

[3] Merletti R., Farina D., Hermens H., Freriks B., and Harlaar J., *European Recommendations for signal processing methods for surface electromyography*, European Recommendations for surface electromyography, 2nd edition, Chapter 3.

[4] Paradiso R, Loriga G, Taccini N, *A Wearable Health Care System based on Knitted Integrated Sensors*, IEEE Transaction Technology in Biomedicine, Vol. 9 (3), pp.337-345, 2005.

[5] Gentry T., *Smart homes for people with neurological disability: state of the art*, NeuroRehabilitation, Vol, 25, pp 209, 2009.

[6] Truong, T. B T; Frizon de Lamotte, F.; Diguet, J.-P., "Proactive remote healthcare based on multimedia and home automation services," *Automation Science and Engineering, 2009. CASE 2009. IEEE International Conference on* , vol., no., pp.385,390, 22-25 Aug. 2009 doi: 10.1109/COASE.2009.5234166.

[7] http://www.demcare.eu/

Summary Abstract for the 1st ACM International Workshop on Personal Data Meets Distributed Multimedia

Vivek K. Singh
The Media Lab,
Massachusetts Institute of Technology
singhv@mit.edu

Tat-Seng Chua
School of Computing,
National University of Singapore
chuats@comp.nus.edu.sg

Ramesh Jain
School of ICS,
University of California, Irvine
jain@ics.uci.edu

Alex (Sandy) Pentland
The Media Lab,
Massachusetts Institute of Technology
pentland@mit.edu

Abstract

Multimedia data are now created at a macro, public scale as well as individual personal scale. While distributed multimedia streams (e.g. images, microblogs, and sensor readings) have recently been combined to understand multiple spatio-temporal phenomena like epidemic spreads, seasonal patterns, and political situations; personal data (via mobile sensors, quantified-self technologies) are now being used to identify user behavior, intent, affect, social connections, health, gaze, and interest level in real time. An effective combination of the two types of data can revolutionize multiple applications ranging from healthcare, to mobility, to product recommendation, to content delivery. Building systems at this intersection can lead to better orchestrated media systems that may also improve users' social, emotional and physical well-being. For example, users trapped in risky hurricane situations can receive personalized evacuation instructions based on their health, mobility parameters, and distance to nearest shelter. This workshop bring together researchers interested in exploring novel techniques that combine multiple streams at different scales (macro and micro) to understand and react to each user's needs.

Categories and Subject Descriptors

H.5.1 [**Multimedia Information Systems**], D.3.3 [**Information Systems**]: World Wide Web – *Social Networks*

Keywords

Personal Data, Distributed Multimedia, Situation Recognition, Social Networks, Reality Mining, Sensor Networks.

1. INTRODUCTION

We are living in an age of abundance [1]. Humanity is more connected than ever before. With the growth trends in *social media*, *multimodal mobile sensing*, and *location driven sensing,* increasingly larger parts of human life are getting digitized and becoming available in the Cloud for sense making.

A primary purpose of data is to meet user needs based on the evolving situations [2]. An accurate understanding of the user's needs depends on a combination of the macro situation and the rich personal context [3]. While both threads have been studied separately in different context before, this workshop aims to bring together the researchers working in the two areas onto a common platform to develop synergistic techniques. Multimedia community has a long standing expertise in dealing with heterogeneous data and is the one of the only communities that has dealt with concept recognition across both space and across time. Multiple concepts in multi-scale data analysis, information fusion, real-time data indexing, spatio-temporal analysis, situation recognition, personalization, user persuasion, and recommendation algorithms related to the workshop are of interest to the Multimedia research community.

MM'13, October 21–25, 2013, Barcelona, Spain.
ACM 978-1-4503-2404-5/13/10.
http://dx.doi.org/10.1145/2502081.2503836

Table 1: Some potential applications at the intersection of personal data and distributed multimedia.

Category	Recommendation Task:	Personal Data	Macro Data
Food/Drink	Food/Drink	Preferences, eating history, hunger level, calorie count	Raw material provenance, Eco-friendliness, Restaurant reviews e.g. Yelp.
Mobility	Walking/ driving/ jogging route	Preferences, exhaustion, sensitivity to pollution, pollen etc.	Pollen count, pollution level, disease risk, traffic congestion
Health	Gym, physical activity, medicine, hospital	Heart rate, activity rate, mood, calories burnt.	Disease spread, medicine availability, appointment wait times.
Emergency response	Move to safe location, contact emergency service	Health, mobility, insurance, social ties	Hurricane, water, flood, snow, wind, disease impact, shelter/hospital availability
Lifestyle	Event or Place recommendation	Preferences, social ties, events (e.g., birthday)	Local trends, waiting time, weather, crime rate
Product recommendation	Advertisements, social coupons	Interests, behavioral preferences e.g. via gaze, bank balance, distance to travel	Local trends, global demand, online prices
Media personalization	Music, movies, lighting, ambient settings in home	Preferences, mood, body vitals, location	Countrywide popularity, local trends, social uploads, weather

It builds upon the recent trends on using multimedia approaches for rich personal sensing (e.g. [5, 6]), as well large-scale concept analysis (e.g. [4]). Based on a confluence of enabling technologies (mobile phones, internet-of-things), trends (media blogging e.g. Vine, Instagram, Twitter, novel sensors e.g. Fit-bit, Q-sensor, Google glasses, Apple iWatch), and research interest, this is an opportune time to organize this workshop for the first time. Table 1 presents a list of sample applications, which can benefit from this intersection of personal data and distributed multimedia data.

2. TOPICS OF INTEREST

Topics of interest for the workshop include, but are not limited to:

- Frameworks for information integration across macro and personal data
- Multi-scale data analysis
- Cross-modal information fusion
- Combining ego-networks with global network features
- Spatio-temporal data indexing
- Situation modeling and situation recognition
- Personalization based on sensor media
- Architectures for personal data management
- Privacy issues in combining personal and public data
- User persuasion through multimodal data presentation
- Social approaches for information integration
- Economic models of information utility
- Applications in different areas incl. mobility, advertisements, healthcare, media recommendations.

2. PROGRAM COMMITTEE

- Alan Smeaton, Dublin City University, Ireland
- Arjen de Vries, Centrum Wiskunde & Informatica (CWI), Netherland
- Dinesh Jayagopi, IDIAP, Switzerland
- Bruno Lepri, FBK and MIT, Italy
- Chidansh Bhatt, IDIAP, Switzerland
- Dhiraj Joshi, FXPAL, USA
- Eugene Agichtein, Emory University, Canada
- Hari Sundaram, Arizona State University, USA
- Harish Katti, Indian Institute of Science, India
- Huan Liu, Arizona State University, USA
- Huanbo Luan, National University of Singapore, Singapore
- Jiebo Luo, University of Rochester, USA
- Mingyan Gao, Google, USA
- Mohan Kankanhalli, National University of Singapore, Singapore
- Neal Lathia, University of Cambridge, UK
- Nicu Sebe,University of Trento, Italy
- Pradeep Atrey, University of Winnipeg, Canada
- Ramanathan Subramanian, ADSC/UIUC, Singapore
- Shuicheng Yan, National University of Singapore, Singapore
- Siripen Pongpaichet, UC Irvine, USA
- Steven Hoi, Nanyang Technological University, Singapore
- Sune Lehmann, Technical University of Denmark, Denmark
- Tao Mei, Microsoft Research Asia, China

3. REFERENCES

[1] Peter Diamandis, Coming Age of Abundance, TED Talk 2012.

[2] V. K. Singh, M. Gao and R. Jain, "Situation recognition: an evolving problem for heterogeneous dynamic big multimedia data." *Proceedings of the International Conference on Multimedia,* 2012 pp. 1209-1218.

[3] N. Eagle and A. Pentland, "Reality mining: sensing complex social systems," *Personal and Ubiquitous Computing,* vol. 10, pp. 255-268, 2006

[4] V. K. Singh, M. Gao and R. Jain, "Social pixels: Genesis and evaluation," in *Proceedings of the International Conference on Multimedia,* 2010, pp. 481-490.

[5] Wen Wu and Jie Yang, "Fast food recognition from videos of eating for calorie estimation" in *IEEE international conference on multimedia and expo 2009*, pp. 1210 - 1213.

[6] C. Peter, E. Ebert and H. Beikirch, "A wearable multi-sensor system for mobile acquisition of emotion-related physiological data," *Affective Computing and Intelligent Interaction,* pp. 691-698, 2005.

Semantic Technologies for Multimedia Content: Foundations and Applications

Ansgar Scherp
Data and Web Science
University of Mannheim, Germany
ansgar@informatik.uni-mannheim.de

ABSTRACT

Higher-level semantics for multimedia content is essential to answer questions like "Give me all presentations of German Physicists of the 20th century". The tutorial provides an introduction and overview to such semantics and the developments in multimedia metadata. It introduces current advancements for describing media on the web using Linked Open Data and other more expressive semantic technologies. The application of such technologies will be shown at concrete examples.

Categories and Subject Descriptors

H.2.4 [**Systems**]: Multimedia databases; H.5.1 [**Multimedia Information Systems**]

General Terms

Languages, Standardization

Keywords

Multimedia Metadata, Linked Open Data, Ontologies

1. INTRODUCTION

Multimedia content can be seen as collection of channels of information [1]. Some of these information channels are low-level and can be derived from the content itself (e. g., the color, shape, and texture). However, other channels encode higher-level semantics that cannot be derived from the multimedia content without external knowledge. Examples are the context in which some multimedia content like a photo has been taken or personal annotations that have been attached to the content by the creator.

In the context of this work, we will consider the higher-level semantics in multimedia as essential metadata information about the multimedia content that enables, e. g., to search along concepts like "Give me all presentations of German Physicists of the 20th century". In order to describe such higher-level semantics, the idea of Linked Open Data (LOD) has been suggested by Tim-Berners Lee some years ago.[1] LOD aims at publishing and interlinking semantic data from different origin and quality on the web using the Resource Description Framework (RDF)[2]. The LOD movement has gained tremendous popularity in recent years. It has been adopted by large industries like the search engine providers Google, Yahoo!, Bing, and Yandex in 2011. Around the same time, Facebook has started to support the movement with its social graph protocol. The New York Times publishes metadata about its articles as LOD. The BBC is an early adopter of the LOD technology and other media organizations like the Library of Congress, the Swedish National Library, and the German National Library are also publishing LOD.

Today, all formats for encoding multimedia content like the W3C standards HTML5, SVG, and SMIL as well as the proprietary Flash format by Adobe foresee the use of RDF in their specifications to describe the metadata of the multimedia content. Thus, overall LOD can be considered as next big movement in the modeling of multimedia metadata and description of higher-level semantics of multimedia content. The tutorial is inspired and motivated by the vivid and controversial panel discussion *"Disputatio" on the use of Ontologies in Multimedia* [2] at ACM Multimedia in Firenze, Italy in 2010.

2. BENEFITS AND IMPACTS

The tutorial gives both beginners and intermediate audiences an introduction and overview of the developments in multimedia metadata. It provides insights into the current advancements of using Linked Open Data and other more expressive semantic technologies. Overall, the benefits of the multimedia community from offering this tutorial on the foundations and applications of semantic technologies for multimedia content are:

- Step-by-step introduction into the LOD technology.
- Understanding the relevance of LOD for multimedia semantics and multimedia metadata.
- Obtain basic knowledge in features of RDF as well as get basic knowledge in more advanced features of formal ontologies.

[1]`http://www.w3.org/DesignIssues/LinkedData`, last accessed: April 2, 2013

[2]`http://www.w3.org/TR/REC-rdf-syntax/`, last accessed: April 2, 2013

MM'13, October 21–25, 2013, Barcelona, Spain.
ACM 978-1-4503-2404-5/13/10.
http://dx.doi.org/10.1145/2502081.2502165.

- Systematic overview of different existing works using LOD for multimedia metadata. The overview considers both industrial models, e.g., by Google and the other search engine providers and the New York Times, as well as current research works.

- Overview of today's applications and tools for modeling multimedia semantics and multimedia metadata using semantic technologies.

3. OUTLINE OF THE TUTORIAL

In the first part, the fundamentals of LOD will be introduced at the example of a fictitious media company in the UK[3]. Where relevant, current research questions and challenges in the context of the LOD movement are highlighted. In addition, different approaches for visualizing LOD and interacting with LOD will be provided. The introduction will be complemented by a brief look at more advanced features of RDF such as modeling class hierarchies, domain and range of properties, and lightweight inferencing techniques [3].

The second part of the lecture focuses on the use of LOD for describing the semantics of media content and multimedia content. To this end, different existing metadata models and metadata standards will be introduced and contrasted with the LOD movement. The use of LOD in the media sector will be demonstrated at examples such as the German National Library, the BBC, and the New York Times. Particular focus will be given on schema.org[4], a metadata vocabulary for web pages including media content developed by the three largest search engine providers in the world, namely Google, Microsoft, and Yahoo!. Since its release in June 2011, schema.org has been widely adopted by content providers on the web. In November 2011, the Russian search engine provider Yandex has also started supporting the schema.org vocabulary. In addition, we will see more advanced approaches for describing the semantics of multimedia content by means of formal ontologies. These have been adopted from well-known and standardized metadata models such as MPEG-7 [4] or derived as an abstraction from the existing solutions for multimedia metadata [5].

Finally, in the third block an overview of existing tools and approaches using LOD in the context of multimedia content will be given. One example is the semantic image retrieval system by Setchi et al. [6] in the car designer domain. It makes use of ontological concepts derived from the text that is found around the images. Another example is the semantic indexing and search in educational videos conducted in the MEMORAe project [7]. Example of a semantic cross-media search and retrieval system is the semantic search engine Squiggle for images and audio [8]. Regarding the context-driven creation and semantic enrichment of personalized multimedia content, we find authoring tools like in the domain of digital photo books [9]. Further applications make use of contextual information and semantic information for exploring social media from various distributed information sources [10] and on mobile phones [11].

4. SUMMARY

The use of high-level semantics in form of Linked Open Data and ontologies is an essential ingredient of current and future multimedia applications. Semantic technologies have made tremendous progress in the past years. Today, we witness the widespread adoption of such technologies by, e. g., search engine giants and large media companies. This tutorial aims at introducing into this next big movement of modeling multimedia metadata and higher-level semantics of multimedia content.

[3] `linkeddatabook.com/`, last accessed: June 20, 2013

[4] `http://schema.org`, last accessed: April 2, 2013

5. REFERENCES

[1] K. Seluk Candan and Maria Luisa Sapino. *Data Management for Multimedia Retrieval*. Cambridge University Press, New York, NY, USA, 2010.

[2] Simone Santini and Amarnath Gupta. "Disputatio" on the use of ontologies in multimedia. In *Multimedia*, pages 1723–1728, New York, NY, USA, 2010. ACM.

[3] Dean Allemang and James A. Hendler. *Semantic Web for the Working Ontologist - Effective Modeling in RDFS and OWL*. Morgan Kaufmann, 2011.

[4] Steffen Staab, Ansgar Scherp, Richard Arndt, Raphaël Troncy, Marcin Grzegorzek, Carsten Saathoff, Simon Schenk, and Lynda Hardman. Semantic multimedia. In *Reasoning Web, 4th International Summer School*, volume 5224 of *Lecture Notes in Computer Science*, pages 125–170. Springer, 2008.

[5] Carsten Saathoff and Ansgar Scherp. Unlocking the semantics of multimedia presentations in the web with the multimedia metadata ontology. In *World wide web*, pages 831–840, New York, NY, USA, 2010. ACM.

[6] Hiromitsu Hama, Thi Thi Zin, and Pyke Tin. Optimal crawling strategies for multimedia search engines. In *Intelligent Information Hiding and Multimedia Signal Processing*, pages 182–185. IEEE Computer Society, 2009.

[7] Ghalia Merzougui, Mahieddine Djoudi, and Amel Behaz. Conception and use of ontologies for indexing and searching by semantic contents of video courses. *CoRR*, abs/1201.5102, 2012.

[8] Irene Celino, Emanuele Della Valle, Dario Cerizza, and Andrea Turati. Squiggle: a semantic search engine for indexing and retrieval of multimedia content. In *Workshop on Semantic-Enhanced Multimedia Presentation Systems*, volume 228 of *CEUR Workshop Proceedings*. CEUR-WS.org, 2006.

[9] Susanne Boll, Philipp Sandhaus, Ansgar Scherp, and Utz Westermann. Semantics, content, and structure of many for the creation of personal photo albums. In *Multimedia*, pages 641–650, New York, NY, USA, 2007. ACM.

[10] Simon Schenk, Carsten Saathoff, Steffen Staab, and Ansgar Scherp. Semaplorer - interactive semantic exploration of data and media based on a federated cloud infrastructure. *J. Web Sem.*, 7(4):298–304, 2009.

[11] Alexander Kleinen, Ansgar Scherp, and Steffen Staab. Interactive faceted search and exploration of open social media data on a touchscreen mobile phone. *Multimedia Tools and Applications*, pages 1–22, 2013.

Towards Next Generation Multimedia Recommendation Systems

Jialie Shen
SMU, Singapore
jlshen@smu.edu.sg

Xian-Sheng Hua
Microsoft Research
xshua@microsoft.com

Emre Sargin
Google Research
msargin@google.com

ABSTRACT

Empowered by advances in information technology, such as social media network, digital library and mobile computing, there emerges an ever-increasing amounts of multimedia data. As the key technology to address the problem of information overload, multimedia recommendation system has been received a lot of attentions from both industry and academia. This course aims to 1) provide a series of detailed review of state-of-the-art in multimedia recommendation; 2) analyze key technical challenges in developing and evaluating next generation multimedia recommendation systems from different perspectives and 3) give some predictions about the road lies ahead of us.

Categories and Subject Descriptors

H.3.3 [**Information Search and Retrieval**]: Information Search and Retrieval

General Terms

Algorithms, Performance, Theory

Keywords

Multimedia, Next Generation Recommendation Systems

1. INTRODUCTION

Multimedia recommendation system is emerging as a promising technology to address the problem of information overload. However, multimedia recommendation can be a challenging research problem. The main reason is threefold. First, multimedia data often contains a lot of high-level semantic meanings. How to generate a concise and compact representation for such information is an important but unsolved problem. Second, in many real applications (e.g., video on demand), the scale of data is big and this requires huge amount of computing resources such as data processing and storage power. This issue becomes especially prominent with increasing prevalence of social multimedia and smart devices. Third, multimedia includes various kinds of content forms (e.g., audio, visual, text and others). In this case, it is infeasible to apply the traditional solutions developed for structured data (e.g., data from relational database) to achieve comprehensive analysis.

The signif cance of multimedia recommendation has led to intense research in various CS and IS disciplines [1, 2, 3, 4]. Meanwhile, various commercial online portals (e.g., YouTube, Flickr and Last.Fm) have applied the techniques to help the users to access accurate and comprehensive contents and services. This tutorial aims to 1) cover a wide range of both simple and advanced techniques in the domain of multimedia recommendation; 2) analyze key technical challenges and open issues in developing and evaluating next generation multimedia recommendation system from different perspectives and 3) give some predictions about the research problems and potential solutions. Multimedia recommendation is closely related to various aspects of multimedia computing. Thus, we expect the 3-hour class to attract a lot of attentions from multimedia community. Also from the seminar, we expect the attendees will gain (i) a good understanding of importance of recommendation system,(ii) knowledge about next generation multimedia recommendation development, and (iii) a comprehensive overview of existing tools and real systems.

MM'13, October 21–25, 2013, Barcelona, Spain.
ACM 978-1-4503-2404-5/13/10.

2. TUTORIAL OVERVIEW

The tutorial consists of four core sections. In the f rst section - introduction, the tutorial provide a comprehensive overview about the importance of multimedia recommendation and related work. We then present a detailed review of existing mobile and location based recommendation techniques. A few fundamental research issues are discussed and they include user mobility, location modeling, main business model and large scale system evaluation. After that, we introduce several techniques for social multimedia recommendation. We also discuss how to extract and integrate social contextual information to achieve accurate recommendation under different real environments. Finally, the tutorial is concluded with open discussions about future study, key research challenges and potential solutions.

3. REFERENCES

[1] G. Adomavicius and A. Tuzhilin. Toward the next generation of recommender systems: A survey of the state-of-the-art and possible extensions. *IEEE Trans. Knowl. Data Eng.*, 17(6):734–749, 2005.

[2] J. Davidson, B. Liebald, J. Liu, P. Nandy, T. V. Vleet, U. Gargi, S. Gupta, Y. He, M. Lambert, B. Livingston, and D. Sampath. The youtube video recommendation system. In *RecSys*, pages 293–296, 2010.

[3] F. Ricci, L. Rokach, B. Shapira, and P. B. Kantor. *Recommender Systems Handbook*. Springer, 2011.

[4] J. Shen, M. Wang, S. Yan, and P. Cui. Multimedia recommendation: technology and techniques. In *ACM SIGIR*, page 1131, 2013.

Crowdsourcing for Multimedia Research

Mohammad Soleymani
iBUG Group
Department of Computing
Imperial College London, UK
m.soleymani@imperial.ac.uk

Martha Larson
Multimedia Information Retrieval Lab
Delft Univeristy of Technology
Delft, The Netherlands
m.a.larson@tudelft.nl

ABSTRACT

Crowdsourcing techniques make use of intelligent contributions of large number of human crowdmembers. This tutorial introduces researchers to the applications of crowdsourcing to multimedia analysis with the aim of allowing them to understand the potentials and limitations of crowdsourcing tools and techniques. We emphasize the fact that crowdsourcing represents a further development along a preexisting continuum of techniques, and discuss the added advantages that new developments offer. We provide a basic overview of human computation, with an emphasis on example cases in which crowdsourcing has been applied to generate data sets, to improve automatic multimedia content analysis, and to elicit user needs or multimedia system requirements. Different techniques and considerations in using human computation methods to acquire high-quality data and annotations are discussed and demonstrated.

Categories and Subject Descriptors

H3.3 [**Information Search and Retrieval**]: Information filtering, Selection process

Keywords

crowdsourcing, multimedia annotation, user studies, testing

1. INTRODUCTION

Crowdsourcing refers to human computation techniques that exploit human intelligence and also take advantage of a large population of contributors. Crowdsourcing is frequently facilitated by crowdsourcing platforms where crowdmembers can find and carry out microtasks in exchange for a small payment. This tutorial is motivated by the enormous potential that crowdsourcing represents for the multimedia community. For example, in the area of multimedia content analysis, the main hurdle faced is bridging the semantic gap, i.e., the distance between pixel-based representations and human perceptions. Upon first consideration, exploiting human intelligence appears to be a silver-bullet solution for bridging the semantic gap. For this reason, there is an unprecendented amount of excitement and curiosity concerning crowdsourcing among multimedia researchers.

Upon further consideration, applying crowdsourcing to solve multimedia problems is riddled with challenges: Who are the crowd? What motivates them? How is it possible to guarantee the quality and consistency of crowd input? Crowdsourcing quickly reveals itself to be something far less than a panacea for all the challenges faced by multimedia researchers. There is a substantial chance that the enormous promise of crowdsourcing for multimedia will fail to be realized due to the feeling of disillusionment of the research community concerning crowdsourcing techniques.

In order for crowdsourcing to reach its full potential, it is necessary that researchers follow the middle way between euphoria and disappointment. This tutorial has been created to provide the multimedia researchers with the practical introduction to crowdsourcing for multimedia and the hands-on experience that will allow the multimedia community to make productive use of crowdsourcing methods informed by sensible best-practice guidelines, leading to steady and sustainable advancement of the state of the art.

2. CROWDSOURCING FOR MULTIMEDIA

The potential of crowdsourcing to drive forward the state of the art in multimedia, cross-cuts the entire research spectrum, from multimedia content analysis to multimedia system design and evaluation. Crowdsourcing was first brought to the attention of the multimedia research community by the early work exploiting Games With a Purpose in order to label large collections of images. Subsequently, large commercial crowdsourcing platforms (such as Amazon Mechanical Turk, Crowdflower and Microworkers) have established themselves as important tools for generating the ground truth necessary for training content analysis algorithms and also for system testing.

Although currently multimedia researchers are already deriving clear benefit by applying crowdsourcing techniques, the amount of work taking advantage of crowdsourcing remains relatively limited. Through our interactions with fellow researchers in the multimedia community, we have observed that there are four open questions for which clear and useful answers are not yet available to the community:

- How are the crowdsourcing techniques used for multimedia research related to conventional techniques that

MM'13, October 21–25, 2013, Barcelona, Spain.
ACM 978-1-4503-2404-5/13/10.
http://dx.doi.org/10.1145/2502081.2502234.

have been in widespread use in the field long before the term "crowdsourcing" was coined?

- What are the best practices that should be applied in order to achieve quality results with crowdsourcing systems?
- What are the limitations of crowdsourcing techniques for multimedia research and how can they be accommodated?
- How can we make sure that crowdsourcing is reaching its full potential for multimedia research? What lies in the future?

The tutorial aims to answer these questions and lay a solid and practical foundation that will allow researchers to confidently exploit and adapt crowdsourcing tools in order to benefit their own research.

3. LECTURE SESSIONS

The goal of this tutorial is to provide the participants with an introduction to crowdsourcing techniques for multimedia, including multimedia content analysis, multimedia task design and system evaluation. It familiarizes participants with the potential contribution of human computation to the field of multimedia with an emphasis on commercial crowdsourcing platforms. The tutorial includes Lecture Sessions on five different topics central to the application of crowdsourcing to multimedia analysis:

Introduction: A brief introduction to collective intelligence, human computation, and crowdsourcing will be given. We present basic terminology and concepts of crowdsourcing and discuss the history of crowdsourcing, mentioning how it is related to well-established, conventional techniques. Finally, we introduce types of tasks solvable by the crowd. These range from mechanical tasks, which have objective, verifiable responses (e.g., counting entities in images), and human judgment tasks, which have the goal of eliciting human judgements and opinions (e.g., reporting the emotional impact of a video).

Future of Crowdsourcing for Multimedia: We cover both the "bad news" and the "good news" about crowdsourcing. The "bad news" is that crowdsourcing is limited in terms of the types of tasks and the volumes of data that can be handled. We touch on the ethical and legal issues of crowdsourcing that are currently unresolved and are the source of uncertainty concerning the extent to which crowdsourcing can be sustainably exploited by multimedia researchers. The "good news" is that current research has only scratched the surface of the potential of crowdsourcing. The future of crowdsourcing is bright with a number of new opportunities appearing on the horizon, such as identifying and exploiting experts in the crowd, tighter linking of crowdsourcing and social computing, hybrid human/conventional computational approaches to multimedia challenges such as indexing and search and finally crowd participation in the design and definition of future multimedia challenges.

Quality Control: Quality control is a key challenge and a major concern for researchers planning to use crowdsourcing platform for their research. In this Lecture Session, different metrics and methods for assessing the reliability of crowdsourced annotation will be discussed. Aggregating crowdsourcing labels and further techniques for quality control, including exploiting consistency in the crowd and expertise to ensure high quality results, will be given.

Incentivization and Engagement: Crowdworkers' motivation plays an important role in the quality of the outcome as well as the completion rate of microtasks. Crowdworkers' incentivization is another topic which will be presented in this lecture. Maintaining user engagement; trust and designing engaging interaction methods are essential for microtask design, especially in the case of microtasks with no direct validation questions. Best practices including successful examples of exploiting microtask markets for mechanical and judgment tasks will be presented.

Crowdsourcing for Evaluation: Crowdsourcing contributes to evaluation in the field of multimedia along multiple dimensions. This Lecture Session covers each of these dimensions using examples from the literature that highlight best practices. The first dimension is data set development: by exploiting input from the crowd, it becomes possible to generate ground truth for multimedia data collections of unprecedented size. The second dimension is quality of experience: crowdsourcing platforms make it possible to recruit the large numbers and diverse populations of human subjects in large scale user studies that measure user satisfaction with multimedia systems. The third dimension is on-line testing: crowdsourcing platforms make it possible to carry out real-time testing of the performance (including accuracy, speed and stability) of online systems.

4. HANDS-ON SESSIONS

In order to achieve its learning objectives, which are fundamentally practical in nature, the tutorial includes Hands-on Sessions. These sessions are accelerated, highly condensed lab sessions that give tutorial participants a chance to directly experience the application of the concepts covered in the Lecture Sessions necessary to acquire basic crowdsourcing skills. During the Hands-on sessions, tutorial participants will gain experience with crowdsourcing from the perspective of the crowdworker and also practice designing their own microtasks. As a result of having participated in this tutorial, researchers will be equipped to apply crowdsourcing techniques to their own area of research, with confidence that they will attain useful, productive results.

5. TARGET AUDIENCE

The target audience includes any researcher who want to use the crowdsourcing techniques in his/her research, as well as researchers who are interested in moving from using crowdsourcing for "mechanical" objective tasks to discovering the opportunities for crowd judgments and evaluation tasks. Because of its practical nature, the tutorial is of use to researchers in every stage of their career and is of interest to both academic and industrial participants.

6. LITERATURE

The course material will consist of lecture slides and a set of conference and journal publications illustrating the ideas and paradigms discussed in the tutorial. References relevant to the tutorial will be made available on a online bibliography at `http://www.citeulike.org/group/17842`.

Massive-Scale Multimedia Semantic Modeling

John R. Smith
IBM T. J. Watson Research Center
Yorktown Heights
New York, USA
jsmith@us.ibm.com

Liangliang Cao
IBM T. J. Watson Research Center
Yorktown Heights
New York, USA
liangliang.cao@us.ibm.com

ABSTRACT

Visual data is exploding! 500 billion consumer photos are taken each year world-wide, 633 million photos taken per year in NYC alone. 120 new video-hours are uploaded on YouTube per minute. The explosion of digital multimedia data is creating a valuable open source for insights. However, the unconstrained nature of Şimage/video in the wildŤ makes it very challenging for automated computer-based analysis. Furthermore, the most interesting content in the multimedia files is often complex in nature reflecting a diversity of human behaviors, scenes, activities and events. To address these challenges, this tutorial will provide a unified overview of the two emerging techniques: Semantic modeling and Massive scale visual recognition, with a goal of both introducing people from different backgrounds to this exciting field and reviewing state of the art research in the new computational era.

Categories and Subject Descriptors

H.2.4 [**Systems**]: Multimedia databases; I.2.10 [**Artificial Intelligence**]: Vision and Scene Understanding—*Video analysis*; I.2.4 [**Knowledge Representation Formalisms and Methods**]: [Semantic networks]; I.2.6 [**Artificial Intelligence**]: Learning—*Concept learning*

Keywords

Multimedia information retrieval, video analysis, content-based search, machine learning, semantic modeling

1. INTRODUCTION

Across multiple generations of information technology that have dealt with structured and unstructured data, the explosion of multimedia data is creating the biggest wave of all. Huge volumes of multimedia - images, video and audio are being generated and consumed daily. Currently, multimedia makes up 60% of internet traffic, 70% of mobile phone traffic and 70% of all available unstructured data. To give specific examples, Web users are uploading 72 video-hours to YouTube per minute, and on an average day, social media users post 300 hundred million photos to Facebook. Consumers using mobile phones and digital cameras are taking 500 billion photos per year, or 78 per person on the planet [4]. Specialized domains are participating too. Medical institutions are acquiring one billion radiological images per year, and cities are installing hundreds of millions of video cameras worldwide for safety, security and law enforcement. Industries across life sciences, petroleum exploration, astronomy, insurance, retail and many others are faced with huge and growing volumes of multimedia data.

Multimedia is "big data" not just because there is a lot of it. Multimedia is big data because increasingly it is becoming a valuable source for insights and information. Multimedia data can tell us about things happening in the world, point out places, events or topics of interest, give clues about a person's preferences and even capture a rolling log of human history [4, 7]. However, the challenge with multimedia big data is that images, video and audio require much more sophisticated algorithms for content analysis than previous waves of structured and unstructured data. This is spurring on a tremendous amount of research on efficient and effective techniques for "bridging the semantic gap" to enable large-scale multimedia information extraction and retrieval [5, 2].

MM'13, October 21–25, 2013, Barcelona, Spain.
ACM 978-1-4503-2404-5/13/10.
http://dx.doi.org/10.1145/2502081.2502235.

2. TUTORIAL OVERVIEW

The instructors will share their knowledge in developing the leading industrial systems as well the winning experience in prestigious visual recognition competitions in the ImageNet Large Scale Visual Recognition Challenges, ImageCLEF recognition and TRECVID challenges. This tutorial will cover both the semantic and massive computing aspects:

- Semantic modeling: Many recent research works have recognized that detection of semantic concepts would significantly improve the effectiveness of image and video retrieval. One of the first large taxonomy is LSCOM [3], which defines more than 1,000 semantic concepts. The collection of ImageNet has collected more than 20K synsets. The efforts of building large scale semantic datasets have also motivated a lot of research on ontology design, web search and social media mining. Many research efforts have been paid on active learning and transfer learning to organize the large amount of unstructured data on the Web, of which the power will become more and more significant with the increasing amount of Web data.

- Massive scale visual recognition: Both the recent develop of computational resource (CPU, GPU, high performance computers) and the increasing amount of multimedia content have contributed to the success of massive scale visual recognition. In the past decade, we have witnessed many exciting techniques for massive visual recognition, including SIFT-like local features, sparse coding, hierarchical vocabulary tree search, supervector-based recognition, attribute learning, locality sensitive hashing, average stochastic gradient descent, and etc. These new techniques are being combined with the new parallel computing frameworks such as MapReduce and Stream computing.

In this talk we present a perspective across multiple industry problems, including safety and security, medical, Web, social and mobile media, and motivate the need for large-scale analysis and retrieval of multimedia data. We describe a multi-layer architecture that incorporates capabilities for audio-visual feature extraction, machine learning and semantic modeling and provides a powerful framework for learning and classifying contents of multimedia data. We discuss the role semantic Ontologies for representing audio-visual concepts and relationships, which are essential for training semantic classifiers [3]. We discuss the importance of using faceted classification schemes in particular for organizing multimedia semantic concepts in order to achieve effective learning and retrieval [6]. We also show how training and scoring of multimedia semantics can be implemented on big data distributed computing platforms to address both massive-scale analysis and low-latency processing [8]. We describe multiple efforts [1, 9] at IBM on image and video analysis and retrieval, including IBM Multimedia Analysis and Retrieval System (IMARS), and show recent results for semantic-based classification and retrieval. We conclude with future directions for improving analysis of multimedia through interactive and curriculum-based techniques for multimedia semantics-based learning and retrieval.

3. ABOUT THE PRESENTERS

John R. Smith is Senior Manager of the Intelligent Information Management Department at IBM T. J. Watson Research Center. He received his M. Phil and Ph.D. degrees in Electrical Engineering from Columbia University in 1994 and 1997, respectively. He currently leads R&D across multiple areas at IBM Research including multimedia, image/video analytics, biometrics, exploratory computer vision and machine learning. Dr. Smith is also principal investigator for the IBM Multimedia Analysis and Retrieval System (IMARS) project. Previously, Dr. Smith led IBM's participation in MPEG-7 / MPEG-21 standards and served as a Chair of the MPEG Multimedia Description Schemes Group and co-project Editor of MPEG-7 Standard. Dr. Smith is currently Editor-in-Chief of IEEE Multimedia and Fellow of IEEE.

Dr. Smith has given numerous tutorials at major conferences including ACM Multimedia, IEEE Intl. Conf. on Multimedia and Expo (ICME), World Wide Web (WWW), ACM Intl. Conference on Management of Data (SIGMOD), ACM International Conference on Conceptual Modeling (ER). Dr. Smith has published more than 100 papers at top conferences and journals. His papers have received more than 13,000 citations and have an h-index of 55 and i10-index of 164.

Liangliang Cao is a Research Staff Member in IBM T. J. Watson Research Center, and also an adjunct assistant professor at Columbia University. His research lies in the intersection of computer vision, new media and multimedia big data. His work has won three prestigious visual recognition competitions, include ImageCLEF Medical Image Classification (2012, 2013), ImageNet Large Scale Visual Recognition Challenge (2010), and TRECVID Airport Surveillance Competition (2008). He received many awards including the IBM Outstanding Accomplishment for multimedia group (2012), the Best Paper Award in the First International Workshop on Big Data Mining (2012), IBM Watson Emerging Leader in Multimedia and Signal Processing (2010), Facebook Fellowship Finalist (2010), and UIUC Computational Science and Engineering Fellowship (2009-2010).

Dr. Cao has authored more than 40 papers in top conferences and journals, including ACM Multimedia, ICCV, CVPR, ECCV, NIPS, WWW, TPAMI, and PIEEE. Dr. Cao is an area chair of ACM Multimedia 2012 and IEEE WACV 2014. He fulfills review duties for more than 15 journals and various conferences. He is a general chair of New York Area Multimedia and Vision Meeting in Greater in 2012 and 2013. He is a guest editor of ACM Transactions on Multimedia Computing, Communications and Applications (TOMCCAP), Computer Vision and Image Understanding (CVIU) Journal, and also IEEE MultiMedia.

4. REFERENCES

[1] L. Cao, L. Gong, J. R. Kender, N. C. Codella, and J. R. Smith. Learning by focusing: A new framework for concept recognition and feature selection. *Proc. of IEEE Conference on Multimedia and Expo*, 2013.

[2] A. Hanjalic, R. Lienhart, W.-Y. Ma, and J. R. Smith. The holy grail of multimedia information retrieval: So close or yet so far away? *Proc. IEEE*, 94(4):541–547, 2008.

[3] M. Naphade, J. R. Smith, J. Tesic, S.-F. Chang, W. Hsu, L. Kenendy, A. Hauptmann, and J. Curtis. Large-scale concept ontology for multimedia. *IEEE MultiMedia*, 13(3), July-September 2006.

[4] J. R. Smith. History made everyday. *IEEE MultiMedia*, 18(2), July-September 2011.

[5] J. R. Smith. Minding the gap. *IEEE MultiMedia*, 19(2):53–62, January-March 2012.

[6] J. R. Smith. Just the facets. *IEEE MultiMedia*, 20(1), January-March 2013.

[7] L. Xie, A. Natsev, J. R. Kender, M. Hill, and J. R. Smith. Visual memes in social media: Tracking real-world news in youtube videos. *Proc. of the 19th ACM Intl. Conf. on Multimedia*, pages 53–62, November 2011.

[8] R. Yan, M. O. Fleury, M. Merler, A. Natsev, and J. R. Smith. Large-scale multimedia semantic concept modeling using robust subspace bagging and map-reduce. *Proc. of the First ACM Workshop on Large-Scale Multimedia Retrieval*, 2009.

[9] F. Yu, L. Cao, R. S. Feris, J. R. Smith, and S.-F. Chang. Designing category-level attributes for discriminative visual recognition. *Proc. of IEEE Conference on Computer Vision and Pattern Recognition*, 2013.

Social Interactions over Geographic-Aware Multimedia Systems

Roger Zimmermann
School of Computing, Interactive & Digital Media Institute, National University of Singapore
Singapore 117417
rogerz@comp.nus.edu.sg

Yi Yu
School of Computing
National University of Singapore
Singapore 117417
yuy@comp.nus.edu.sg

ABSTRACT

User-centric Internet multimedia scenes challenge us to discover more interesting events and topics based on matching users' needs associated with personal preferences, geographic interests and social norms. Geotagged multimedia contents from online social sites, *e.g.*, Flickr and Twitter, provide large volumes of data about many given locations. Hence, location is one of the most important user-generated contexts and contains rich information about an individual's interests and behavior. Location-based social multimedia streams (*e.g.*, tweets, videos, images) can provide us with socially complementary information to predict users' needs.

By making use of geo-tagging, a cohesive set of social multimedia streams can be published to facilitate a more accurate analysis of user-centric big data information and further assess user tastes based on location activities. This tutorial delivers not only a better understanding of the basics of location-aware contextual descriptions and its relations to social multimedia scenes, but may also serve to highlight relationships that can be collaboratively applied to multimodal retrieval and recommendation technology.

Categories and Subject Descriptors

H.3.3 [**Information Storage and Retrieval**]: Information Search and Retrieval; I.4.8 [**Image Processing and Computer Vision**]: Scene Analysis—*Sensor Fusion*

Keywords

Geographic sensor information; location-based services; social interactions; mobile videos; location recommendations

1. BACKGROUND

Today the web is able to lively visualize modern life since we can upload our photos, audios, videos, views and blogs onto the Internet and share them with other people on various social media sites such as YouTube, Flickr, Foursquare, Twitter and Weibo. Images and videos are especially important because they are generated, tagged, and tweeted by users. With an overwhelming amount of social media content on the Internet, it is difficult to find what users are really interested in through navigating massive multimodal collections. For example, a search for "Merlion" may result in the return of thousands of social media items caused by diverse users' query intentions at different social websites.

In general many similar media content items appear on the Internet. To improve the quality of retrieval and recommendation systems, some extra information, such as geo-sensor information captured by mobile devices, can be considered to associate specific social media streams with locations and further predict what kind of topics over social interactions in multimedia streams are most important for users. This poses a number of interesting questions: (1) At a specific location, different media streams may have different views. How are they respectively influencing video popularity over social media streams? (2) Can these media streams be associated with each other to retrieve and recommend user-generated videos (UGV) based geo-sensor information? (3) Does geographic locality of users' behaviors and biases have an impact on the topics and events of video retrieval and recommendation? (4) What principles can be applied to incorporate social media streams into multimedia collection annotations according to geo-tagging information? These issues will be discussed in this tutorial.

2. MOTIVATION

Location-based services enable some social media streams to obtain users' places or coordinate information. Geo-location can represent several unique and semantic user contexts (*e.g.*, physical world, culture, behavior) that complement the performance of discovering and retrieving other social media by annotating geographic information. Basically, geographic metadata is utilized as an index to find relevant contents within area [4, 3]. Moreover, crowdsourcing (*e.g.*, leveraging the Foursquare API) as an affordable and effective tool can be used to annotate geographic metadata with meaningful categories [1, 5] to make them more informative for geographic-aware personalized location recommendations [1] and entertainment generation [5]. Although many researchers have investigated the association of additional visual features [2] to find relevant content, the performance of geographic multimedia retrieval and recommendation is still limited, especially for commercial big data sets on emerging social platforms.

We conjecture that geographic-aware social media streams provide a better unified set to predict the live needs of users. Interesting events and topics across various social multime-

MM'13, October 21–25, 2013, Barcelona, Spain.
ACM 978-1-4503-2404-5/13/10.
http://dx.doi.org/10.1145/2502081.2502236.

dia streams are varying at a specific location, which results in trends constantly changing (*e.g.*, images, videos, messages and tweets on social location services). Fortunately, geographic-based, aggregated social media streams are able to serve as a diverse, fresh and robust repository to predict the desired content for a particular user. It is appealing to model users' needs associated with personal preferences, geographic interests and social promotions by leveraging geographic-aware multimodal social media streams. In general we would like to consider various geographic-aware aggregated multimedia streams to address how and why three intuitive aspects (personal preference, geographic interest and social promotion) respectively or integrally influence a particular user's need findings. We investigate topics and methods for handling interesting user-generated video (UGV) discovery and multimodal retrieval and recommendations over geographic-aware social media streams.

3. OBJECTIVES

Inspired by the diversity of location-based, user-centric social multimedia data sources, this tutorial describes emerging users' needs and multimedia applications based on locations, reviews the state-of-the-art in social geo-tagged multimedia systems, surveys several intuitions of geo-aware social media streams, and shares some preliminary results obtained through crowdsourced annotations of a richer social multimedia dataset. We also will introduce different evaluation benchmarks and address some promising trends related to geographic-aware social multimedia recommendations. A more detailed outline is provided in the next section.

This tutorial is customized for intermediate-level audiences consisting of researchers who are quite familiar with indexing of geo-tagged images and videos or multimedia content analysis but are not familiar with social context analysis, and either intend to model the interactions among mobile people and multimedia events or wish to get involved into location-based topic discovery in multimedia systems. We hope to broaden the understanding of location-aware user-centric big data in multimedia systems beyond simple location-based contextual information. We plan to distribute materials including course slides, relevant links, online resources and source codes.

4. TUTORIAL OUTLINE

The tutorial is organized into four main modules. First, we introduce geo-tagging techniques as well as related features. We then discuss several issues of discovering the most important events and topics over multimedia streams. Next, we provide an extensive overview of location-based research trends in various multimedia scenarios covering a broad range of topics and methods. We also show demonstrations of location-based multimedia retrieval and recommendation systems.

Module One aims to give an understanding of the advantages and disadvantages of today's video tag annotations based on a rich set of meta-data obtained from GPS and compass sensors. Furthermore, participants will also be provided with an overview of geo-tagging techniques and they will learn how geo-tagging does differentiate itself from content-based or crowdsourcing-based video tagging. As a demonstration example, we introduce the recent development of the *GeoVid* georeferenced video smartphone app and its application (properties of viewable scene, geospatial video recording for Android and iOS, assigning tags to visible objects, association of tags with video segments).

Module Two aims to give an understanding of why we need to incorporate geographic-aware social media information (*e.g.*, mitigating cold-start for new individuals and data sparseness) to predict multimedia scenes desired by users and why we need to consider three aspects (personal preference, geographic interest and social promotion) to find the most interesting events and topics of videos. We also introduce recent geo-tagged multimedia applications and techniques (*e.g.*, land-use classification, geo-tagged image retrieval, preference-aware location recommendation). We further provide geo-tagged metadata to address how we are able to incorporate social media information to find the most interesting videos fitting a particular user's needs.

Module Three focuses on location-enabled social topics and interactions around multimedia contents and streams. We introduce a set of basic components (*e.g.*, personalized location, geographic-aware local interest, geo-category), topics (*e.g.*, social knowledge learning, personal preference mining, preference-based scoring, location rating, geographic distribution of social views), methods (*e.g.*, SVMhmm, iterative learning model, sparse additive generative model) and evaluation matrices (*e.g.*, recall, precision, mean reciprocal rank). We also provide some novel examples to address challenging issues, *e.g.*, how to link social media streams to multimedia contents over geographic information, and will share our studies with the participants.

Module Four guides the participants through various resources covering software tools, public datasets and crowdsourcing methods used in the research communities of multimedia, collaborative recommendations, topic tracking and social data mining & discovery. Various multimedia datasets have been collected and described as part of the ACM Multimedia Systems Dataset Track to help explore various application needs. We also demonstrate some typical location-based multimedia tasks according to different users' needs and different multimedia scenarios.

Acknowledgments

The work presented was in part supported by the Singapore National Research Foundation under its International Research Centre @ Singapore Funding Initiative and administered by the IDM Programme Office.

5. REFERENCES

[1] J. Bao, Y. Zheng, and M. F. Mokbel. Sensor Information Location-based and Preference-Aware Recommendation Using Sparse Geo-Social Networking Data. In *ACM SIGSPATIAL GIS*, pages 199–208, 2012.

[2] J. Kamahara, T. Nagamatsu, and N. Tanaka. Conjunctive Ranking Function using Geographic Distance and Image Distance for Geotagged Image Retrieval. In *ACM Geo Workshop*, pages 9–11, 2012.

[3] H. Ma, R. Zimmermann, and S. H. Kim. HUGVid: Handling, Indexing and Querying of Uncertain Geo-tagged Videos. In *ACM SIGSPATIAL GIS*, pages 319–328, 2012.

[4] Z. Shen, S. Arslan Ay, S. H. Kim, and R. Zimmermann. Automatic Tag Generation and Ranking for Sensor-rich Outdoor Videos. In *ACM Multimedia*, pages 93–102, 2011.

[5] Y. Yu, Z. Shen, and R. Zimmermann. Automatic Music Soundtrack Generation for Outdoor Videos from Contextual Sensor Information. In *ACM Multimedia*, pages 1377–1378, 2012.

Multimedia Information Retrieval: Music and Audio

Markus Schedl
Department of Computational Perception
Johannes Kepler University
Linz, Austria
markus.schedl@jku.at

Emilia Gómez
Music Technology Group
Universitat Pompeu Fabra
Barcelona, Spain
emilia.gomez@upf.edu

Masataka Goto
National Institute of Advanced Industrial Science and Technology (AIST)
Tsukuba, Ibaraki, Japan
m.goto@aist.go.jp

Keywords

multimodal music information retrieval, audio and music description, similarity, classification, personalization

Categories and Subject Descriptors

Information systems [**Information search and retrieval**]: Music information retrieval

Motivation

Music is an omnipresent topic in our daily lives, as almost everyone enjoys listening to his or her favorite tunes. Music information retrieval (MIR) is a research field that aims – among other things – at automatically extracting semantically meaningful information from various representations of music entities, such as a digital audio file, a band's web page, a song's lyrics, or a tweet about a microblogger's current listening activity.

A key approach in MIR is to describe music via computational features, which can be categorized into: *music content*, *music context*, and *user context*. The music content refers to features extracted from the audio signal, while information about musical entities not encoded in the signal (e.g., image of an artist or political background of a song) are referred to as music context. The user context, in contrast, includes environmental aspects as well as physical and mental activities of the music listener. MIR research has been seeing a paradigm shift over the last couple of years, as an increasing number of recent approaches and commercial technologies combine content-based techniques (focusing on the audio signal) with multimedia context data mined, e.g. from web sources and with user context information.

Goals and Structure

In this half-day tutorial we (i) explain standard and state-of-the-art techniques for music content-based feature extraction, (ii) report on the basics and the state-of-the-art in mining music-related information from the web and social media to infer context-based features, and (iii) demonstrate attractive applications based on MIR technologies (using both content- and context-based methods).

The main goal is to give a sound and comprehensive, nevertheless easy-to-understand, introduction to the scientific use of multimedia data sources in the music domain. The presented approaches are highly valuable for tasks such as automatic music video analysis and generation, music-synchronized computer graphics, automated music playlist generation, personalized web radio music recommendation systems, and intelligent user interfaces to music.

To reach this goal, we first summarize the ideas behind various computational music features and discuss advantages and disadvantages of each. We review state-of-the-art techniques for the automatic description of music signals in terms of timbre (instrumentation), pitch-content information (melody, harmony and tonality), and rhythm (tempo or meter). We then present how these descriptors are used to measure similarity between musical pieces (e.g. to retrieve covers or versions of the same song) and classify music according to semantic concepts such as artist, genre, or mood.

Hereafter, we focus on the contextual aspects of music which are accessible through web technology. To this end, we give an introduction to the field of web-based MIR and an overview of popular data sources (e.g., web pages, microblogs, social networks, user tags, lyrics). Then we present approaches to exploit these sources to construct similarity measures in order to automatically index and retrieve music.

Relevance for the Multimedia Community

The Multimedia and the MIR communities have not been too closely tied, so far. As the 2013 edition of ACM Multimedia will see for the first time a *Music and Audio* track, this might change soon, however.

Given that both communities frequently use similar concepts and techniques, we believe that a tutorial on MIR in the context of ACM Multimedia will be of benefit for both communities, increase mutual understanding, raise awareness of each others goals and challenges, and help each other to reach these goals. For instance, some aspects of MIR are closely related to image and video processing and analysis, in particular when it comes to tasks such as deriving semantic information from music video clips (either official ones or user-generated music videos) or analyzing the importance of album cover artwork for the perception and organization of music, both aspects that have been looked into in MIR research. In addition, the challenge of creating visualizations and intelligent browsing interfaces to music collections is obviously highly related to the Multimedia community.

MM'13, October 21–25, 2013, Barcelona, Spain.
ACM 978-1-4503-2404-5/13/10.

On the other hand, many tasks in the multimedia domain would benefit from incorporating audio and music analysis techniques more thoroughly, e.g., semantic analysis of video, video classification, synchronization of visual changes with musical beats, music video generation, or automatic slideshow generation. We are therefore sure that researchers in image and video processing could contribute to MIR and vice versa to realize mutual benefits.

In addition, the current boom of social media and user-generated multimedia content, which is also reflected in the frequent consideration of related scientific topics (e.g., Social Media Mining or Adaptive Multimedia Retrieval) in IR and multimedia conferences and journals, demands for a broader point of view on multimedia. The trend towards multimodal processing and retrieval of multimedia content requests audio- and music-related features of various kinds (considering, for instance, acoustic properties, textual data such as lyrics, image data such as album covers, and music video clips), in order to create holistic models.

Tutorial Outline

The tutorial lasts three hours; the presenters are researchers covering different subareas of MIR: content- and context-based music processing and retrieval, web- and social media-based MIR, similarity measurement, user interfaces including active music listening interfaces, and singing information processing.

The tutorial is accompanied by a comprehensive set of slides, including references to state-of-the-art methods. In addition, we provide links to existing software packages and toolboxes for music content- and music context-based feature extraction, similarity computation, knowledge discovery, and music visualization/exploration. As an example, we list here state-of-the-art technologies co-authored by the tutorial presenters:

- *CoMIRVA*[1], a framework providing a "Collection of Music Information Retrieval and Visualization Applications" [14, 13].
- *MELODIA*[2], a plugin for melody extraction from polyphonic music signals [11].
- *HPCP*[3], a plugin for chroma feature extraction from polyphonic music signals [2].
- *The Musical Avatar*[4], a system for generating an iconic representation of one's musical preferences [1].
- *The Mood Cloud*[9], a real-time music mood visualization tool.
- *Freesound*[5], a collaborative database of Creative Commons Licensed sounds with functionalities for user tagging and search by acoustic similarity.
- *NepTune*[6], a user interface to explore music by flying through artificial music landscapes [8, 12].
- *AGMIS*[7], a music information system automatically populated by mining the web for music-related information [15].
- *Music Tweet Map*[8], a visualization and exploration tool for music listening behavior inferred from microblogs [7].
- *SmartMusicKIOSK*[9], a music listening station with chorus-search function [3].
- *Songle*[10], a web service for active music listening improved by user contributions [6].
- *Musicream*[11], an integrated music-listening interface for active, flexible, and unexpected encounters with songs [4].
- *DanceReProducer*[12], an automatic mashup music video generation system by reusing dance video clips on the web [10].
- *VocaListener*[13] and *VocaWatcher*[14] for imitating a human singer by using signal processing [5].

[1]http://www.cp.jku.at/comirva

[2]http://mtg.upf.edu/technologies/melodia

[3]http://mtg.upf.edu/technologies/hpcp

[4]http://mtg.upf.edu/project/musicalavatar

[5]http://www.freesound.org

[6]http://www.cp.jku.at/projects/nepTune

[7]http://www.cp.jku.at/projects/agmis

[8]http://www.cp.jku.at/projects/MusicTweetMap

[9]http://staff.aist.go.jp/m.goto/SmartMusicKIOSK

[10]http://songle.jp

Acknowledgments

This research is supported by the Austrian Science Fund (FWF): P22856, P25655, and the EU FP7: 601166.

1. REFERENCES

[1] D. Bogdanov, M. Haro, F. Fuhrmann, A. Xambó, E. Gómez, and P. Herrera. Semantic Audio Content-based Music Recommendation and Visualization Based on User Preference Examples. *Information Processing & Management*, 49:13–33, January 2013.

[2] E. Gómez. *Tonal Description of Music Audio Signals.* PhD thesis, Universitat Pompeu Fabra, 2006.

[3] M. Goto. A chorus-section detection method for musical audio signals and its application to a music listening station. *IEEE Transactions on Audio, Speech, and Language Processing*, 14(5):1783–1794, 2006.

[4] M. Goto and T. Goto. Musicream: Integrated music-listening interface for active, flexible, and unexpected encounters with musical pieces. *IPSJ (Information Processing Society of Japan) Journal*, 50(12):2923–2936, 2009.

[5] M. Goto, T. Nakano, S. Kajita, Y. Matsusaka, S. Nakaoka, and K. Yokoi. VocaListener and VocaWatcher: Imitating a human singer by using signal processing. In *Proceedings of the 2012 IEEE International Conference on Acoustics, Speech, and Signal Processing (ICASSP)*, pages 5393–5396, 2012.

[6] M. Goto, K. Yoshii, H. Fujihara, M. Mauch, and T. Nakano. Songle: A web service for active music listening improved by user contributions. In *Proceedings of the 12th International Society for Music Information Retrieval Conference (ISMIR)*, pages 311–316, 2011.

[7] D. Hauger and M. Schedl. Exploring Geospatial Music Listening Patterns in Microblog Data. In *Proceedings of the 10th International Workshop on Adaptive Multimedia Retrieval (AMR)*, Copenhagen, Denmark, October 2012.

[8] P. Knees, M. Schedl, T. Pohle, and G. Widmer. Exploring Music Collections in Virtual Landscapes. *IEEE MultiMedia*, 14(3):46–54, July–September 2007.

[9] C. Laurier and P. Herrera. Mood cloud : A real-time music mood visualization tool. In *CMMR, Computer Music Modeling and Retrieval*, Copenhagen, 2008.

[10] T. Nakano, S. Murofushi, M. Goto, and S. Morishima. DanceReProducer: An automatic mashup music video generation system by reusing dance video clips on the web. In *Proceedings of the 8th Sound and Music Computing Conference (SMC)*, pages 183–189, 2011.

[11] J. Salamon and E. Gómez. Melody extraction from polyphonic music signals using pitch contour characteristics. *IEEE Transactions on Audio, Speech and Language Processing*, 20:1759–1770, 08/2012 2012.

[12] M. Schedl, C. Höglinger, and P. Knees. Large-Scale Music Exploration in Hierarchically Organized Landscapes Using Prototypicality Information. In *Proceedings of the ACM International Conference on Multimedia Retrieval (ICMR)*, Trento, Italy, April 2011.

[13] M. Schedl, P. Knees, K. Seyerlehner, and T. Pohle. The CoMIRVA Toolkit for Visualizing Music-Related Data. In *Proceedings of the 9th Eurographics/IEEE VGTC Symposium on Visualization (EuroVis)*, Norrköping, Sweden, May 2007.

[14] M. Schedl, P. Knees, and G. Widmer. Using CoMIRVA for Visualizing Similarities Between Music Artists. In *Proceedings of the 16th IEEE Visualization Conference (IEEE Vis)*, Minneapolis, MN, USA, October 2005.

[15] M. Schedl, G. Widmer, P. Knees, and T. Pohle. A Music Information System Automatically Generated via Web Content Mining Techniques. *Information Processing & Management*, 47, 2011.

[11]http://staff.aist.go.jp/m.goto/Musicream

[12]http://staff.aist.go.jp/t.nakano/DanceReProducer

[13]http://staff.aist.go.jp/t.nakano/VocaListener

[14]http://staff.aist.go.jp/t.nakano/VocaWatcher

Blending the Physical and the Virtual in Music Technology: From Interface Design to Multi-modal Signal Processing

George Tzanetakis
University of Victoria
Victoria, BC, Canada
gtzan@cs.uvic.ca

Sidney Fels
University of British Columbia
Vancouver, BC, Canada
ssfels@ece.ubc.ca

Michael Lyons
Ritsumeikan University
Kyoto, Japan
michael.lyons@gmail.com

ABSTRACT

Recent years have seen a significant increase of interest in rich multi-modal user interfaces going beyond conventional mouse/keyboard/screen interaction. The new interface technologies are broadly impacting music technology and culture. New musical interfaces use a variety of sensing (and actuating) modalities to receive and present information to users, and often require techniques from signal processing and machine learning in order to extract and fuse high level information from noisy, high dimensional signals over time. Hence they pose many interesting signal processing challenges while offering fascinating possibilities for new research. At the same time the richness of possibilities for new forms of musical interaction requires a new approach to the design of musical technologies and has implications for performance aesthetics and music pedagogy. This tutorial begins with a general and gentle introduction to the theory and practice of the design of new technologies for musical creation and performance. It continues with an overview of signal processing and machine learning methods which are needed for more advanced work in new musical interface design.

Categories and Subject Descriptors

H.5.5 [**Sound and Music Computing**]: Methodologies and techniques, Modeling, Signal analysis, synthesis, and processing systems

Keywords

New interfaces for musical expression, musical instrument design, human computer interaction, signal processing, machine learning, multimodal interaction, digital musical instruments

MM'13, October 21–25, 2013, Barcelona, Spain.
ACM 978-1-4503-2404-5/13/10.
http://dx.doi.org/10.1145/2502081.2502238.

1. INTRODUCTION

Traditional musical instruments offer some of the most fascinating technological artifacts ever created by human beings. The complexity and richness of control afforded by acoustic musical instruments, such as violin or piano, to professional musicians is impressive. Research in new interfaces for musical expression [2, 3, 1] has explored how such complex and delicate control can be combined with the ability to interact in real-time performance situations with computers. In some cases, research on musical interface technology has anticipated aspects of the development of rich multimodal interfaces in the field of augmented reality and has provided excellent examples of sensorially rich and temporally-detailed human-machine interaction. With this in mind, musical performance interfaces present intriguing working examples for gaining new insight into the field of multi-modal interaction.

From the viewpoint of music technology, advances in digital technologies have led to a situation where computers play a role in most music production and performance. Digital technologies offer unprecedented opportunities for the creation and manipulation of sound, however the flexibility of these new technologies implies a confusing array of choices for musical composers and performers. Some artists have faced this challenge by using computers directly to create music and leading to an explosion of new musical forms. However, most would agree that the computer is not a musical instrument, in the same sense as traditional instruments, and it is natural to ask "how to play the computer" using interface technology appropriate for human brains and bodies.

We are at the beginning of a new era in human computer interaction in which users will come to view the way we interacted with computers using keyboards and mice, as we view today punched cards and teletypes. The large diversity of affordable hardware in terms of sensors and actuators today, provides a fertile environment for creating rich multimodal interfaces. Frequently, their design and development requires interdisciplinary expertise combining concepts from digital signal processing (DSP) and human computer interaction (HCI).

There is an increasing interest in rich user interfaces that go beyond the traditional mouse/keyboard/screen interaction. In the past few years, their development has accelerated due to the wide availability of commodity sensors and actuators. For example, the Microsoft Kinect provides, at low cost, a structured light infrared depth camera, a regular color camera, and a microphone array. Moreover, smart phones contain a variety of additional sensors such as accelerometers that provide unique opportunities for control. Unlike traditional controllers such as a mouse that provide direct and simple sensor readings, these new rich interfaces provide high dimensional, noisy and complex sensor readings. Therefore sophisticated digital signal processing and machine learning techniques are required in order to develop effective human computer interactions using such interfaces [4]. At the same time they offer fascinating possibilities of blending physical and virtual worlds such as non-invasive full body control and augmented reality. Different algorithms and customizations are required for each specific application and possibly even for each user so there is a large design space for novel research and contributions.

The goal of this tutorial is to provide an overview of the field of new musical interface design and to give participants a brief but broad introduction to the major techniques needed to conduct research in the field: ranging from design and aesthetics of music technology to the digital signal processing and machine learning techniques required for advanced work in the field. Case studies will be taken from some of the recent work on new musical interfaces.

2. COURSE OUTLINE

2.1 Introduction and Tutorial Overview

The introductory module will give an outline and schedule of the tutorial and motivate the major questions to be addressed using a selection of case studies. Why does music technology represent an excellent application domain for the study of real-time multi-modal interaction? How can digital technologies be designed effectively for the requirements of real-time expressive performance? How have advances in sensor and actuator technologies changed the field of music technology research? What do advances in digital signal processing and machine learning techniques bring to the field?

2.2 A Practical Guide to Creating Multi-modal Musical Interfaces

This module offers a clear six step guide to prototyping a new musical interface. An overview of sensors and actuators as well as sound synthesis techniques is given. The issue of mapping between sensors, sound synthesis, and actuators is introduced. Finally the role of demonstration and performance on the research and development cycle will be described.

2.3 Design, Theory, and Aesthetics of Musical Interaction

This module makes contact with approaches drawn from the field of human-computer interaction that serve to guide the design of multi-modal real-time musical interfaces. A model of a multi-modal musical interface is described and some theoretical issues, such as feedback, mapping, transparency, control intimacy, and flow are introduced. Some aesthetic considerations relating to the design of real-time multi-modal interfaces are described. Finally some useful design heuristics (aka rules of thumb) applicable to the domain are introduced.

2.4 Case Studies I

The material from the first part of the course will be reviewed in the context of case studies from the published literature. These will be illustrated with video demonstrations.

2.5 Signal Conditioning & Feature Extraction

This module covers the basics of signal conditioning with topics such as denoising, dimensionality reduction, filtering, resampling, and dealing with missing samples with concrete examples using multi-modal sensor data. Topics to be introduced include: various types of time-frequency analysis (short time fourier transform (STFT), wavelets), basic image and video analysis, and modeling dynamics. The algorithms will be illustrated with specific examples using audio, video, and sensor data in the context of new interfaces for musical expression.

2.6 Dealing with Uncertainty and Time

In this module, techniques from machine learning and data mining such as supervised and unsupervised learning will be described. The algorithmic constraints of real time and causal implementations will also be covered. Techniques for time modeling such as Kalman Filters, Hidden Markov Models (HMM), and Dynamic Time Wrapping (DTW) will be described through specific examples from multi-modal interaction. Sensor fusion will also be discussed.

2.7 Case Studies II

Case studies to be presented include: a surrogate sensor methodology for training non-invasive signal acquisition using direct sensors through classification and regression, teaching a virtual violinist to bow using machine learning to automatically determine sound quality, self-tuning and self calibrating music robotic instruments, extending the performance possibilities of a vibraphone using the Microsoft Kinect controller, and the Soundplane, multi-touch, pressure sensitive new music interface that provides highly expressive control possibilities.

2.8 Conclusion

The conclusion will summarize the major points covered in the tutorial, provide suggestions for further study, as well as specific links to the published literature, conferences, and other resources in the related research community.

3. REFERENCES

[1] F. Bevilacqua, S. Fels, A. R. Jensenius, M. J. Lyons, N. Schnell, and A. Tanaka. Sig nime: music, technology, and human-computer interaction. In *Extended Abstracts CHI'13*, pages 2529–2532. ACM, 2013.

[2] S. Fels and M. Lyons. Creating new interfaces for musical expression: introduction to NIME. In *SIGGRAPH 2009 Courses*. ACM Press, 2009.

[3] I. Poupyrev, M. Lyons, S. Fels, and T. Blaine. New interfaces for musical expression. In *Extended Abstracts CHI'01*, pages 491–492. ACM Press, 2001.

[4] A. Tindale, A. Kapur, and G. Tzanetakis. Training surrogate sensors in musical gesture acquisition systems. *Multimedia, IEEE Transactions on*, 13(1):50–59, 2011.

Privacy Concerns of Sharing Multimedia in Social Networks

Gerald Friedland
International Computer Science Institute and University of California, Berkeley
1947 Center Street, Suite 600
Berkeley, CA 94704-1198
fractor@icsi.berkeley.edu

ABSTRACT
This article summarizes the corresponding 3-hour tutorial at ACM Multimedia 2013.

Categories and Subject Descriptors
H.1.2 [**User/Machine Systems**]:Human factors;

General Terms
Security

Keywords
Privacy; Societal Concerns; Multimedia Content Analysis

1. MOTIVATION
The growth of multimedia as demonstrated by social networking sites such as Facebook and YouTube combined with advances in multimedia retrieval (geo-tagging, web search, face recognition, speaker verification, location estimation, etc.) provides novel opportunities for the unethical use of multimedia. In small scale or in isolation multimedia analytics have always been a powerful but reasonably contained privacy threat. However, when linked together and used on an Internet scale, the threat can be enormous and pervasive. It is already well discussed that the multimedia community therefore has an obligation to understand and attempt to mitigate these risks. The press covers "horror stories" almost on a day-to-day basis often crating panic reactions that can even draw companies out of business for very little grounded reason. Other stories, however, have more depth and require our attention as technologists (some of which can be found on the proposer's own blog: http://cybercasing.blogspot.com).

Electrical engineering and computer science curricula usually include an abundance of material on how to improve retrieval based on the underlying multimedia content analysis but only rarely talk about the negative impacts of these technologies. Privacy research is often limited to steganography, encryption, and other well-known techniques and/or even moved out of scope as "ethical concerns not part of engineering". Therefore, even when acknowledged as a problem, many multimedia researchers lack the knowledge of how to react to society's concerns and mitigate some of the risk while working on developing better retrieval options. The reason often given is: "We'll deal with privacy and social issues later -- right now we need to focus on the development". The truth, however, is that, for example, if privacy and security had been a concern in the early stages of developing the Internet, many of todays' issues, such as spam and phishing email, would probably much less of a problem. At the same time, some of the solutions to security and privacy concerns are really simple and follow a limited set of basic principles, which, when already obeyed in the early stages of the development of a system can avoid large unresolvable issues later. Many of them are well known in the security and privacy communities but not so much in the multimedia community.

MM'13, October 21–25, 2013, Barcelona, Spain.
ACM 978-1-4503-2404-5/13/10.
http://dx.doi.org/10.1145/2502081.2502239

2. OBJECTIVES
The objective of the tutorial is to introduce interested multimedia students and researchers who are not specialized in security and privacy issues into the thinking of a security and privacy researcher. The tutorial will be a vivid class with many examples based on material developed for the CS10 course at the EECS department of UC Berkeley as well as from an NSF-sponsored project for teaching privacy to high-school students (http://teachingprivacy.icsi.berkeley.edu). The material has been selected from contemporary research from top-notch security and privacy conferences (see below). Using real-world examples and their consequences, the tutorial will focus on privacy and security threats induced by modern social networking practices in combination with multimedia retrieval. The tutorial's main thread of argument is that often small changes in interface and usability concepts can make a huge difference in how well privacy and security concerns are addressed. At the end of the tutorial, there will be a discussion.

3. OUTLINE
The following is a list of topics that the tutorial will cover:

Why privacy is a concern in multimedia research
- Privacy perception as a function of age, technical awareness, and cultural background
- Legal and ethical standpoint in the US
- Major privacy "invaders": Government, Industry, Research
- The state of the art in multimedia privacy
- Crimes potentially enabled by multimedia: cyberstalking, cybercasing, identity theft, and others

Examples
- Geotagging and it's implications for privacy
- Multimedia retrieval and it's implication for privacy
- Matching users across accounts with multimedia content analysis
- Facebook and LinkedIN vs Real World Social Networking

Mitigation Strategies

- Attacker model taxonomy
- Defense model taxonomy
- Quantifying the arms race
- 10 Principles for Social Media Privacy
- Concrete examples of using the strategies: Technical solutions that work

Conclusions

- Possible implications for research, education, industry
- Chances for startups, new research
- First steps everybody should do right now

Discussion

4. COURSE MATERIAL

The materials used for this tutorial will mostly be consisting of contemporary research articles from security and privacy conferences such as ACM MMSEC but also NSPW (New Security Paradigm Workshop), and Usenix Security dealing with Multimedia. The participants will also be handed the slides of the presentations. In addition, the attendees of the tutorial will have access to not yet published material at the teachingprivacy.com portal.

5. ABOUT THE PRESENTER

Dr. Gerald Friedland is the Director of Audio and Multimedia research at the International Computer Science Institute, a private lab affiliated with the University of California, Berkeley, where he is currently leading a group of multimedia researchers supported by NSF, IARPA, and industry grants. For the last two years, he has been heading an NSF-sponsored project on the privacy implications on multimedia content analysis, resulting in frequent press appearances, invited talks, and guest lectures about the topic.

More importantly, Gerald has presented and attended high class security and privacy conferences, working on building a bridge between the multimedia and privacy communities. Gerald has published more than 100 peer-reviewed articles in conferences, journals, and books and is currently authoring a new textbook on multimedia computing together with Dr. Ramesh Jain. Gerald co-founded the IEEE International Conference on Semantic Computing and is a proud founder and program director of the IEEE International Summer School on Semantic Computing at UC Berkeley. He is associate editor for ACM Transactions on Multimedia Computing, Communications, and Applications, is in the organization committee of ACM Multimedia 2011, 2012, and 2014. He is also serves as TPC Co-Chair of IEEE ICME 2012. He is the recipient of several research and industry recognitions, among them the European Academic Software Award and the Multimedia Entrepreneur Award by the German Federal Department of Economics. Most recently, he lead the team that won the ACM Multimedia Grand Challenge in 2009. Gerald received his doctorate (summa cum laude) and master's degree in computer science from Freie Universitaet Berlin, Germany, in 2002 and 2006, respectively.

Despite being mainly a researcher, Dr. Friedland is a passionate teacher. He held the ACM Workshop on Educational Multimedia and Multimedia Education at ACM Multimedia 2007, a subsequent panel on the same topic at ACM Multimedia 2008, gave a well-received tutorial at ACM Multimedia 2011 on acoustic processing for video analysis, and a previous version of this tutorial at ACM MM 2012. He is frequently participating in both undergraduate and graduate teaching activities at the EECS department of the University of California Berkeley. Part of the Tutorial will be based on material taught at UC Berkeley's CS10 class. Also, he has recently finished a new textbook "Introduction to Multimedia Computing" together with Dr. Ramesh Jain, to appear at Cambridge University Press by the end of 2013.

Author Index

www.ingramcontent.com/pod-product-compliance
Ingram Content Group UK Ltd.
Pitfield, Milton Keynes, MK11 3LW, UK
UKHW051418290926
15471UKWH00009B/1674

9 781450 326926